Footprint p[...]

Sleeping

LL	over US$200
L	US$151-200
AL	US$101-150
A	US$66-100
B	US$46-65
C	US$31-45
D	US$21-30
E	US$12-20
F	US$7-11
G	US$6 and under

Prices refer to the cost of double room in high season, including taxes.

Eating

¶¶¶	over US$12
¶¶	US$6-12
¶	US$5 and under

Prices refer to the cost of a two-course meal for one person, excluding drinks or service charge

Southeast Asia Handbook

Andrew Spooner, Paul Dixon,
Claire Boobbyer, Jock O'Tailan
and Steve Frankham

... these incredible [monastery] buildings [are]
unlike anything else I have seen, you are
taken aback, and you try to fit them into the
scheme of things, and then it makes you laugh
with delight to think that anything so fantastic
could exsist on this sombre earth. ...

Somerset Maugham, The Gentleman in the Parlour

Footprint story

It was 1921

Ireland had just been partitioned, the British miners were striking for more pay and the federation of British industry had an idea. Exports were booming in South America – how about a handbook for businessmen trading in that far away continent? The Anglo-South American Handbook was born that year, written by W Koebel, the most prolific writer on Latin America of his day.

1924

Two editions later the book was 'privatized' and in 1924, in the hands of Royal Mail, the steamship company for South America, it became The South American Handbook, subtitled 'South America in a nutshell'. This annual publication became the 'bible' for generations of travellers to South America and remains so to this day. In the early days travel was by sea and the Handbook gave all the details needed for the long voyage from Europe. What to wear for dinner; how to arrange a cricket match with the Cable & Wireless staff on the Cape Verde Islands and a full account of the journey from Liverpool up the Amazon to Manaus: 5898 miles without changing cabin!

1939

As the continent opened up, The South American Handbook reported the new Pan Am flying boat services, and the fortnightly airship service from Rio to Europe on the Graf Zeppelin. For reasons still unclear but with extraordinary determination, the annual editions continued through the Second World War.

1970s

Many more people discovered South America and the backpacking trail started to develop. All the while the Handbook was gathering fans, including literary vagabonds such as Paul Theroux and Graham Greene (who once sent some updates addressed to "The publishers of the best travel guide in the world, Bath, England").

1990s

During the 1990s the company set about developing a new travel guide series using this legendary title as the flagship. By 1997 there were over a dozen guides in the series and the Footprint imprint was launched.

2000s

The series grew quickly and there were soon Footprint travel guides covering more than 150 countries. In 2004, Footprint launched its first thematic guide: *Surfing Europe*, packed with colour photographs, maps and charts. This was followed by further thematic guides such as *Diving the World*, *Snowboarding the World*, *Body and Soul escapes*, *Travel with Kids* and *European City Breaks*.

2008

Today we continue the traditions of the last 87 years that has served legions of travellers so well. We believe that these help to make Footprint guides different. Our policy is to use authors who are genuine experts who write for independent travellers; people possessing a spirt of adventure, looking to get off the beaten track.

Ta Prohm, Angkor, Cambodia.

Put Southeast Asia through the prism of history and representation, a 1000 years of images, empire and, more recently, travel. Think of exotic and mysterious jungle-thronged temples, palm-fringed white beaches, redolent colours and enigmatic, gracious peoples; places to be discovered or to be returned to. Think of ultra-modern sci-fi cityscapes, burgeoning urban youth culture, the struggle for democracy and terrible wars. Then spend time immersing, absorbing and inhabiting Southeast Asia; a place that resonates with humanity yet dumbfounds and bewitches. If you're lucky enough to travel here, come with open eyes and minds, leave what you think Southeast Asia *should* be at home – only then will the real one emerge.

LAOS

East Sea
(South China Sea)

THAILAND

VIETNAM

CAMBODIA

BRUNEI

MALAYSIA

□ SINGAPORE

Indian
Ocean

INDONESIA

Contents

HEMIS.FR /SUPERSTOCK

Wat Xieng Thong, Laos.

Where to go

Southeast Asia is vast and the variety and scope of what's on offer is truly mind-boggling. This is a whistle-stop tour of the highlights.

Cambodia

Still emerging from the horrors of a lengthy civil war, Cambodia is becoming a firm favourite with travellers. The biggest draw are the temple complexes at Angkor Wat, near the town of Siem Reap. Vast, arcane and bewitching, the ruins of Angkor are an essential stop on any tour of Southeast Asia. Other highlights include the riverside charms of the cultured capital, Phnom Penh, the uncharted mass of forests of Ratanakiri and, in the south, the lazy resorts of Kep and Sihanoukville.

Indonesia

With 13,000 islands stretching over 5000 km, the Indonesian archipelago offers a hugely diverse spread of cultures and sights. Start in Java, where the massive volcanoes and groovy beaches are just a stone's throw ??from the capital, Jakarta. To the west is Sumatra, home to orang-utans, sweeping landscapes and the world's largest volcanic crater at Lake Toba. The east brings Bali, with luxurious resorts, excellent surf breaks, volcanoes and an ancient Hindu culture. Lombok offers tranquil beaches, and the Gili Islands with some of the world's best diving, while the fierce Komodo dragon resides on East Nusa Tenggara.

Laos

Landlocked and under-developed, Laos is still being discovered. The ancient royal capital of Luang Prabang makes an alluring starting point. Vang Vieng, tucked away among dramatic mountains to the south, is a backpacker hub while further east is the Plain of Jars. Luang Namtha to the north is an engaging patchwork of mountains and hill peoples. The sleepy capital, Vientiane, houses some interesting French colonial-era architecture and has good transport connections. In the far south is Pakse, a jumping-off point to Siphandon and the magical 4000 Islands.

Malaysia

In many ways Malaysia typifies this idiosyncratic region – it is a place of extreme contrasts where jungle and city, tradition and modernity mingle in extraordinary ways. There is glittering Kuala Lumpur with its thrusting skyscrapers and the colonial-era history of Penang and Melaka; developed beach resorts such as Langkawi and the

Opposite page left: Hoi An, Vietnam, **right:** Indonesian house. **Above:** Perhentian Islands, Malaysia.

languid hill stations of the interior; while the East Malaysian states of Sabah and Sarawak offer dense forests and mountains, home to multiple ethnicities, traditional longhouses and the endangered orang-utan.

Singapore
This tiny city-state is the most developed spot in Southeast Asia and makes for an excellent introduction to the region for novice travellers. Ethnically diverse, Singapore is famed for great food and cheap electronics. Changi Airport is also the best-connected transport hub.

Thailand
Start in the wild, sweaty human scrum of Bangkok. Head north into the cradle of Thai civilization and the ancient capitals of Sukhothai and Ayutthaya. To the west is Kanchanaburi and a vast, untamed forest that stretches up to northern Thailand, home to the walled city of Chiang Mai and the ethnically diverse hilltribes. East from Bangkok is a length of coast that includes riotous Pattaya and the lush islands of Koh Samet and Koh Chang.

The northeast, Isaan, delivers great food, the mighty Mekong river and intriguing Khmer ruins. Finally, the south, with the Gulf and Andaman coasts, offers the attractions of full-moon parties on Koh Phangan and the quintessential island getaway of Tarutao.

Vietnam
Begin in enterprising and engaging Ho Chi Minh City, a good base for a day trip to the Cu Chi Tunnels. To the south are the plains of the Mekong Delta. Head up the coast to the beaches of Nha Trang, before reaching the beautifully preserved town of Hoi An, and the last home of Vietnam's final imperial dynasty, Hué. In the north sits Hanoi, replete with ancient streets, pagodas and tasty street food, a gateway to Halong Bay and Sapa.

Brunei
If you have time, the Sultanate of Brunei can make for an interesting short break. Allow a day for the capital, Bandar Seri Begawan, then journey upriver to Tasek Merimbun (Brunei's largest lake) or Ulu Temburong National Park.

Itineraries

Two to three weeks

If time is short, use the regional hubs as entry and exit points and break the region down into more manageable chunks.

Arrive in Bangkok and spend a weekend in the Thai capital before heading south to the beaches or north for some trekking. Follow this up with a couple of days at Angkor in Cambodia and some time lazing by the Mekong in Luang Prabang, Laos. With a little more time take in Ho Chi Minh City and the nearby town of Dalat, a former French hill station, or make your way to Malaysia. Alternatively, start in Singapore before exploring Indonesia's Java and then head north to Langkawi Island or the Malaysian regions of Sabah and Sarawak.

Visiting Indonesia can easily take three or four weeks; with Jakarta, the beaches of Bali and Lombok, the volcanoes of Java, and some of the planet's most beautiful dive sites.

Six to eight weeks

With a longer visit, the enduring pleasures of Southeast Asia really begin to reveal. You can use Bangkok, Singapore, Jakarta and Bali as your focus for getting around. Take time to explore Thailand's ancient cities at Ayutthaya and Sukhothai or escape deep into the hills with an adventurous trek, before finishing up with a long, lazy retreat on the beaches of Koh Samui or Koh Phangan.

Steamy Bangkok's markets and temples make a perfect counterpoint to Phnom Penh's airy riverfront. Travel by boat up the Tonlé Sap from Cambodia's capital to the temples at Angkor, where from Siem Reap a short flight will deliver you to Hanoi, the hills of northern Vietnam or the Nha Trang beaches.

Visit Laos with time enough to fully absorb the atmosphere of Luang Prabang and its temples, and spend a few days in Vang Vieng visiting the caves or tubing down the river.

Vietnam can make a good entry point – spend a week travelling from Hanoi to Ho Chi Minh City before overlanding through Cambodia back to Bangkok, stopping at Phnom Penh, Angkor and the Thai islands pressed up against the Cambodian border.

Alternatively, take the train south from Bangkok and visit secluded Tarutao before crossing Thailand's southern border into Malaysia. From here either hop across to Borneo to trek in the jungle or visit the longhouses of Sarawak or continue south for some gadget shopping in Singapore before heading over to Sumatra and then on to Java.

Indonesia could easily take up all your time; climb up to Sumatra's Lake Toba and visit the Komodo dragons, jungles, beaches and remote peoples. It's even possible to begin in Bali and island-hop to Singapore, and Malaysia. Of course, you might find that perfect beach and decide to stay …

Three months

If travelling in Southeast Asia for three months or longer the options are endless. To make it even easier, all the countries in this part of Southeast Asia (except Vietnam) offer visas on arrival at the major points of entry.

Asy-Syakirin mosque and Petronas Towers, Kuala Lumpur.

Hindu God, Sri Srinivasa temple, Singapore.

Cai Rang floating market, Vietnam.

Arrive in Bangkok and you'll have a chance to get to grips with the pleasures of this vibrant Thai capital. Explore the lesser-visited beaches of the Gulf and Andaman coasts; learn to dive on Koh Tao; then look for whale sharks off the Similans. Thailand's interior and the lush cooling forests of the north and west would suit the more intrepid traveller. Visit Mae Hong Son and the backpacker haven of Pai, or follow the Mekong from Udon Thani to Nong Khai before crossing the Friendship Bridge into Vientiane, Laos. Travelling up from the Lao capital takes you to Luang Prabang and the hills around Luang Thami. Chase the Mekong back downstream to Pakse and the idyllic beaches of the 4000 Islands and then carry on until the Mekong reaches Cambodia, passing through Stung Treng, a great jump-off point for Ratanakiri and the distant hills of the northeast. Stop over in Phnom Penh before experiencing the somnambulant atmosphere of Kampot with its crumbling architecture. Nearby sits Kep, re-emerging as Cambodia's elite coastal resort town – but for beaches with all the trimmings head to Sihanoukville instead. Angkor should still be on your itinerary but this time take a boat trip to Battambang. Re-join the Mekong and it eventually reaches Vietnam and the Delta. From here, Ho Chi Minh City with its museums, bars, and frenetic atmosphere is a short distance away. Then jump on a northbound train and slowly tick off Vietnam's best spots. The Nha Trang beaches, atmospheric Hoi An and the history of Hué all merit attention before you reach Hanoi, the gateway to the northern hills.

Alternatively, start in northern Vietnam, head into Laos and then through Thailand before reaching the beaches of the south. Plough on to Malaysia, indulging in the luxury of Langkawi before getting a night view of Kuala Lumpur from the Petronas Towers. The hill stations of the Cameron Highlands, turtles of Rantau Abang and the beach at Kampong Cherating should whet the appetite for the wilds of Sarawak and Sabah. After Malaysia, Indonesia beckons, but first, pit-stop in Singapore to sample an array of cuisine in the absorbing street markets.

The more time you give Indonesia, the greater the rewards. Begin in Java, home to coastal resorts and the legendary volcano Krakatau. The capital, Jakarta, has great restaurants, museums and an appealing harbour area. Bali serves up a fabulous landscape, a mesmerizing culture and sacred crater lakes. Lombok offers gorgeous Senggigi and the Gilis, a group of islands to the north – the south, around Kuta, is more dramatic. Sumatra has great trekking and rafting opportunities, some of the finest national parks in the country and pristine beaches.

Southeast Asia highlights & itineraries

See colour maps in centre of book

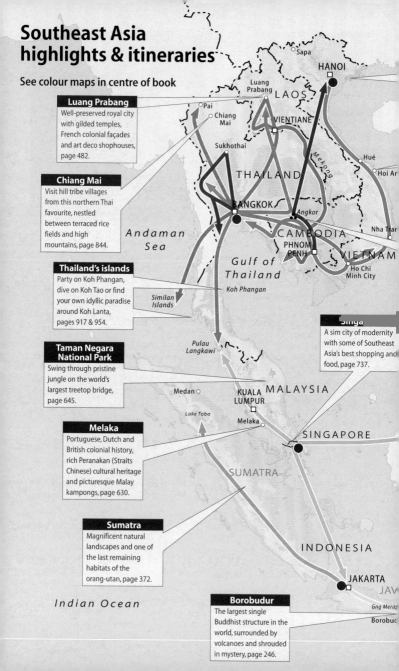

Luang Prabang
Well-preserved royal city with gilded temples, French colonial façades and art deco shophouses, page 482.

Chiang Mai
Visit hill tribe villages from this northern Thai favourite, nestled between terraced rice fields and high mountains, page 844.

Thailand's islands
Party on Koh Phangan, dive on Koh Tao or find your own idyllic paradise around Koh Lanta, pages 917 & 954.

Taman Negara National Park
Swing through pristine jungle on the world's largest treetop bridge, page 645.

Melaka
Portuguese, Dutch and British colonial history, rich Peranakan (Straits Chinese) cultural heritage and picturesque Malay kampongs, page 630.

Sumatra
Magnificent natural landscapes and one of the last remaining habitats of the orang-utan, page 372.

Singa
A sim city of modernity with some of Southeast Asia's best shopping and food, page 737.

Borobudur
The largest single Buddhist structure in the world, surrounded by volcanoes and shrouded in mystery, page 246.

Sapa

HANOI

Luang Prabang

LAOS

Pai

Chiang Mai

VIENTIANE

Sukhothai

Hué

Hoi An

THAILAND

Mekong

BANGKOK

Angkor

Nha Tra

Andaman Sea

CAMBODIA

PHNOM PENH

VIETNAM

Ho Chi Minh City

Gulf of Thailand

Koh Phangan

Similan Islands

Pulau Langkawi

Medan

Lake Toba

KUALA LUMPUR

MALAYSIA

Melaka

SINGAPORE

SUMATRA

Indian Ocean

INDONESIA

JAKARTA

JAV

Gng Merap

Borobu

Halong Bay
Magical limestone towers rise out of a sea dotted with sailing junks, page 1021.

Hoi An
A mercantile port town overflowing with traditional architecture, great shops and restaurants, page 1057.

East Sea
(South China Sea)

Angkor Wat
The best preserved of the ancient Khmer temples, and the spiritual and cultural heart of Cambodia, page 127.

Gunung Kinabalu
Feel on top of the world by climbing Borneo's highest peak, page 695.

Gng Kinabalu ▲
BANDAR SERI BEGAWAN
BRUNEI
SABAH

Longhouses in Sarawak
Head upriver to visit a traditional Iban, Bidayuh or Orang Ulu village, page 669.

MALAYSIA

SARAWAK

Bali
Excellent diving and surfing, traditional culture and a vibrant nightlife, page 273.

From Bangkok

2 - 3 weeks ●➜

6 - 8 weeks ●➜

3 months ●➜

From Hanoi

6 - 8 weeks ●➜

From Singapore

2 - 3 weeks ●➜

From Java

2 - 3 weeks ●➜

6 - 8 weeks ●➜

FLORES

BALI LOMBOK KOMODO

N

200 km
200 miles

Festivals

six of the best

Bon Om Tuk, Cambodia

During October/November (movable) is the Water Festival or Festival of the Reversing Current. This celebrates the movement of the waters out of the Tonlé Sap with boat races in Phnom Penh. Races extend over three days with more than 200 competitors but the highlight is the evening gala in Phnom Penh when a fleet of boats, studded with lights, row out under the full moon.

Independence Day, Indonesia

Held on 17th August, this is the most important national holiday, celebrated with processions, dancing and other merry-making. Although it is officially on the 17th, festivities continue for a whole month, towns are decorated with bunting and parades cause delays to bus travel; there seems to be no way of knowing when each town will hold its parades.

Pi Mai, Laos

Pi Mai is one of the most important annual festivals, particularly in Luang Prabang. The first month of Pi Mai (Lao New Year) is December but the three days of festivities

are delayed until April when days are longer than nights. By April it's also hotting up, so having hosepipes levelled at you and buckets of water dumped on you is more pleasurable. The festival also serves to invite the rains. Small stupas of sand, decorated with streamers, in wat compounds are symbolic requests for health and happiness over the next year. Similar festivals are celebrated in Thailand, Cambodia and Myanmar.

Thaipusam, Malaysia

Thaipusam (movable) is celebrated by many Hindus throughout Malaysia in honour of their deity Lord Subramanian (also known as Lord Muruga); he represents virtue, bravery, youth and power. Held during full moon in the Hindu month of Thai, it is a day of penance and

DAVID CHEREPUSCHAK/ALAMY

Right: Dolls of Pi Mai, Luang Prabang, Laos.
Bottom: Songkran, Thailand.

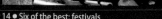

DARBY SAWCHUK/ALAMY

Left: Piercings on a devotee's back, Thaipusam procession, Singapore. **Right:** Ho Chi Minh City during Tet.

thanksgiving. Devotees pay homage to Lord Subramanian by piercing their bodies, cheeks and tongues with *vel* (sharp skewers) and hooks weighted with oranges, and carrying *kevadis* (steel structures). Although *kevadi* carrier can have up to 100 spears piercing his flesh he only loses a small amount of blood. Each participant tries to outdo the others in the severity of his torture. At some temples fire-walking is also part of this ceremony. The biggest gatherings are at Batu Caves just outside Kuala Lumpur, when thousands of pilgrims congregate in a carnival-like atmosphere; there are also festivals held in Melaka, Penang and Singapore.

Songkran, Thailand

This movable festival marks the beginning of the Buddhist New Year. The festival is particularly big in the north, much less so in the south and (understandably) the Muslim far south. It is a three- to five-day celebration with parades, dancing and folk entertainment. Traditionally, the first day represents the last chance for a 'spring clean'. Rubbish is burnt, in the belief that old and dirty things will cause misfortune in the coming year. The wat is the focal point of celebrations. Revered Buddha images are carried through the streets, accompanied by singers and dancers. The second day is the main water-throwing day. The water-throwing practice was originally an act of homage to ancestors and family elders. Gifts are given. This water-throwing continues for all three days. On the third day birds, fish and turtles are released, to gain merit and in remembrance of departed souls.

Tet, Vietnam

Vietnam's biggest annual festival celebrates the traditional new year and is held sometime between January and March (movable, 1st-7th day of the new lunar year). The word Tet is the shortened version of tet nguyen dan ('first morning of the new period'). Tet is the time to forgive and forget and to pay off debts. It is also everyone's birthday – everyone adds one year to their age at Tet. Enormous quantities of food are consumed and new clothes are bought. It is believed that before Tet the spirit of the hearth, Ong Tao, leaves on a journey to visit the palace of the Jade Emperor where he must report on family affairs. To ensure that Ong Tao sets off in good cheer, a ceremony is held before Tet, Le Tao Quan, and during his absence a shrine is constructed (Cay Neu) to keep evil spirits at bay until his return. On the afternoon before Tet, Tat Nien, a sacrifice is offered at the family altar to dead relatives who are invited back to join in the festivities.

Spas and therapies

Bon Ton Restaurant and Resort

For a laid-back escape in Malaysia away from the tourist hordes, head for Australian-owned Bon Ton Restaurant and Resort on Langkawi, a Malasian island boasting ancient virgin rainforest and serene blue waters. Just 10 minutes from the airport, Bon Ton is near the sea but overlooks tranquil wetland, full of birds, fish and otters. It has eight restored 100-year-old Malay villas facing a pool and surrounded by tall swaying palms. Intricate details have been preserved; silk throws and traditional textiles warm room interiors. Bon Ton can also arrange for an Indian ayurvedic masseur to visit.

Raffles Plaza

Hip sister to the famous Raffles Hotel, the Raffles Plaza in Singapore has a top-floor bar with views all the way to Malaysia. Enjoy luxurious treatments, plunge pools and a gym in the Amrita Spa, exclusive to Raffles guests. Singapore citizens are fast paced – Kiasu is a local word for a dynamic desire to get ahead – yet there's another sub-culture of locals and expats who embrace all things holistic, and you'll find a magic mix here of East and West.

Evason Hideaway and Spa

If you're jaded but flush with cash, hole up in a private villa at the Evason Hideaway and be eased back to humanity at its Six Senses Earth Spa. Hua Hin beach isn't as wondrous as most Thai beaches, but this is a serene and easy place to focus inwardly and be spoilt rotten by dedicated staff who take meditation and reiki courses as part of their training.

The Earth Spa is a collection of circular domed buildings made of mud mixed with rice husks and straw, surrounded by ponds and linked by wooden walkways. It offers exceptional sleep-inducing treatments with a holistic element, and a whole host of massages including jet lag recovery and *lomi lomi*. Spa Journeys are delicious facial and massage combos given by two therapists. Many treatments use ingredients grown on site, such as coconut, aloe vera, lemongrass and papaya.

Monte Vista Retreat Centre

With a warm, family feel and just nine simple wooden bungalows, this small healing centre in a peaceful spot overlooking the sea, offers a friendly, safe, supportive environment for individual development and exploration.

Although best known for its 'cleansing and self-healing' programmes, which consist mainly of fasting and colonic treatments, the centre also offers a huge variety of self-development programmes and activities, from daily yoga and meditation to reiki training. Shamanic Journey and Spiritual Initiation 'Life Flow' courses entail living and working as part of the Monte Vista community, individual counselling and daily tailor-made exercises designed to act as catalysts to aid personal change.

CAROLINE SYEGE

Opposite page: Float pool, Singapore. **Above:** Evason Hideaway & Spa, Thailand.

Programmes are designed specifically for each individual, and the caring team of holistic health practitioners offer 24-hour hands-on support for their guests. There are daily morning yoga sessions on a platform overlooking the sea, healthy home-made meals eaten together (for non-fasters), group sunset meditation and evening activities like story-telling, watching films or spontaneous dance sessions.

The Sanctuary

Set in a beautiful jungle environment atop a rugged beach on Koh Phangan, Thailand's wildest party island, The Sanctuary sells itself on a unique 'detox, retox' philosophy. Guests can opt to spend their time fasting on one- to seven-day cleansing programmes, or feasting on a variety of self-indulgent treats and lounging in the tropical surrounds.

The detox area offers a Wellness Centre with cleansing programmes focusing on fasting, relaxation and self-administered colonic irrigation, while the upbeat bar and restaurant retox space offers chill-out sounds, great food, beer, cocktails, fine wine and a distinctly bohemian beachside vibe. Both areas are blessed with stunning sea views and plenty of options for horizontal contemplation in the multiple hammocks and scattered floor cushions.

The selection of goodies on offer is varied. Yoga teachers provide daily classes in two separate halls built into a rock. Meditation classes are offered four days a week for free. A separate area houses a herbal sauna built into a rock, a plunge pool, and a therapy room offering exotic-sounding massages using natural local ingredients.

Tao Garden Health and Wellness Centre

This secluded retreat set among banana groves, papaya plantations and organic rice paddies on the outskirts of Chiang Mai, Thailand, was initially established as a training facility for the students of Taoist meditation and qigong master, Mantak Chia. A decade on and the garden retreat now provides a holistic hideaway for guests seeking spa treatments with a spiritual edge. Therapists from Chiva Som train here in the Thai abdominal massage, *chi nei tsang*.

The Tao healing system developed by Master Chia combines Taoism, Chinese, Thai and Ayurveda medicine with more technical facilities such as infra-red and ozone-based therapies. Guests have access to a variety of health specialists and doctors and can sample a huge range of massage techniques, therapies and treatments, including daily qigong, tao yin (Chinese yoga) and six healing sounds meditation.

When to go

Generally, you may want to avoid travelling during the monsoon season. However, the severity of the season is variable and while in some countries the monsoon will barely affect travelling, in others it will be impossible to get around. Many hotels offer out-of-season discounts, while prices shoot up in the dry season and during major festivals.

Cambodia is warm with cool evenings between November and April, although wind-blown dust invades everything. It heats up during April with rains from June to November. It is at its most lovely from June to July, although it can be difficult to travel during monsoon season. It is busy during Khmer New Year.

Although the whole of **Indonesia** is hot (at sea level) it encompasses several rainfall zones, meaning that the best tine to visit depends on where you are going. Travelling overland in the wet season in some areas can present problems: parts of Sumatra, Borneo and Nusa Tenggara can all be cut off after severe storms. However, the main highways are usually open all year round.

Laos is best visited November to April, when it is dry and not too hot. The highlands will be chilly but dry with blue skies. In the north, March through to the first rains in May can be hazy as smoke from burning off the forest hangs in the air. On the worst days this can cause eye itchiness, restricted views and sometimes cancelled flights. By June or July, it can become difficult to travel although this is when Loas is at its most beautiful. The height of the monsoon is September to November. It gets very busy during Pi Mai.

The best time to visit the east coast of **Malaysia** is between March and September. Trips along the coast and interior jungles are not advisable during the monsoon (November to February). It's impossible to take fishing boats to offshore islands as the sea can be very rough. Conversely, in the dry season, some rivers become un-navigable. Other parts of

A floating village in Cambodia.

Peninsular Malaysia can be visited year round. In Malaysian Borneo, March and June are the best times to visit. Recently the seasons in both Sabah and Sarawak have become less predictable with heavy rain at any time of year.

Travel to almost all of **Thailand** is possible at any time of year. The wet season runs from May to October in most parts of the country, although you'll still get sunshine and hotel rates will be lower. The best time to visit central, northern and northeastern regions is November to February; the west side of the peninsula between November and April; and the east coast May to October. In terms of festivals, it is worth considering Loi Krathong, Songkran, Chinese New Year, the King's Birthday, New Year's Day, the Surin Elephant Festival and the Isaan Rocket Festival.

Vietnam is best between November and April. In the south it is warm and in the north it is chilly but dry with clear skies. Upland areas can be very cold. Travel in the south and Mekong Delta can be difficult at the height of the monsoon (particularly September to November). Tet is not really a good time to visit as it's so busy.

Rainfall and climate charts

Phnom Penh

Month	Average temperature in °C max-min	Average rainfall in mm
Jan	31 - 21	07
Feb	32 - 22	10
Mar	34 - 23	40
Apr	35 - 24	77
May	34 - 24	134
Jun	33 - 24	155
Jul	32 - 24	171
Aug	32 - 26	160
Sep	31 - 25	224
Oct	30 - 24	257
Nov	30 - 23	127
Dec	30 - 22	45

Jakarta

Month	Average temperature in °C max-min	Average rainfall in mm
Jan	29 - 23	300
Feb	29 - 23	300
Mar	30 - 23	211
Apr	31 - 24	147
May	31 - 24	114
Jun	31 - 23	97
Jul	31 - 23	64
Aug	31 - 23	43
Sep	31 - 23	66
Oct	31 - 23	112
Nov	30 - 23	142
Dec	29 - 23	203

Vientiane

Month	Average temperature in °C max-min	Average rainfall in mm
Jan	28 - 14	05
Feb	30 - 17	15
Mar	33 - 19	38
Apr	34 - 23	99
May	32 - 23	267
Jun	32 - 24	302
Jul	31 - 24	267
Aug	31 - 24	292
Sep	31 - 24	302
Oct	31 - 21	109
Nov	29 - 18	15
Dec	28 - 16	03

Kuala Lumpur

Month	Average temperature in °C max-min	Average rainfall in mm
Jan	32 - 22	158
Feb	33 - 22	201
Mar	33 - 23	259
Apr	33 - 23	292
May	33 - 23	224
Jun	33 - 22	130
Jul	32 - 23	99
Aug	32 - 23	163
Sep	32 - 23	218
Oct	32 - 23	249
Nov	32 - 23	259
Dec	32 - 23	191

Kuching

Month	Average temperature in °C max-min	Average rainfall in mm
Jan	29 - 22	610
Feb	30 - 22	510
Mar	31 - 23	328
Apr	32 - 23	279
May	32 - 23	262
Jun	33 - 23	180
Jul	33 - 22	196
Aug	33 - 22	234
Sep	32 - 22	218
Oct	32 - 23	267
Nov	31 - 22	358
Dec	31 - 22	462

Singapore

Month	Average temperature in °C max-min	Average rainfall in mm
Jan	30 - 23	252
Feb	31 - 23	173
Mar	31 - 24	193
Apr	31 - 24	188
May	32 - 24	173
Jun	31 - 24	173
Jul	31 - 24	170
Aug	31 - 24	196
Sep	31 - 24	178
Oct	31 - 24	208
Nov	31 - 24	254
Dec	31 - 24	257

Bangkok

Month	Average temperature in °C max-min	Average rainfall in mm
Jan	32 - 20	08
Feb	33 - 22	20
Mar	34 - 24	36
Apr	35 - 25	58
May	34 - 25	198
Jun	33 - 24	160
Jul	32 - 24	160
Aug	32 - 24	175
Sep	32 - 24	305
Oct	31 - 24	206
Nov	31 - 22	66
Dec	31 - 20	05

Hanoi

Month	Average temperature in °C max-min	Average rainfall in mm
Jan	20 - 13	18
Feb	21 - 14	28
Mar	23 - 17	38
Apr	28 - 20	81
May	32 - 23	196
Jun	33 - 26	239
Jul	33 - 26	323
Aug	32 - 26	343
Sep	31 - 24	254
Oct	29 - 22	99
Nov	26 - 18	43
Dec	22 - 15	20

Ho Chi Minh City

Month	Average temperature in °C max-min	Average rainfall in mm
Jan	32 - 21	15
Feb	33 - 22	03
Mar	34 - 23	13
Apr	35 - 24	43
May	33 - 24	221
Jun	32 - 24	330
Jul	31 - 24	315
Aug	31 - 24	269
Sep	31 - 23	335
Oct	31 - 23	269
Nov	31 - 23	114
Dec	31 - 23	56

Voluntourism in Southeast Asia

Indonesia

With great social disparity and high levels of poverty, there is a need for volunteers. With such a diverse population with such different social concerns, there is also a need for protection of individuals and organizations. Below is a list of various volunteer projects available in Indonesia.

International Humanity Foundation, www.ihfonline.org/index.php. This group has educational centres and orphanages in Bali, Medan, Aceh, and Jakarta and looks for volunteers with talents or strong interests to help out at their centres. The work is a holistic type of volunteering with care giving, teaching and admininstration work allowing the volunteer plenty of scope for learning about development work and non-profit organizations. They also offer opportunities to those who can work a few hours a week from their home country doing some accounting, website work or writing sponsorship letters. The Aceh centre is an orphanage that educates children whose lives were ruined by the 2004 tsunami. After training, volunteers assist in teaching and care giving. Centres in Medan and Bali offer the chance to teach children maths, English and computer skills. The Jakarta centre looks for teachers and also

people who can do some building and maintenance work. There is a US$25-35 weekly fee, to cover food and lodging costs.

Go Make A Difference, www.go-mad.org. Run by volunteers based in Japan and affiliated with the JET scheme (English teachers in Japan), Go M.A.D help organize volunteer placements around the world. In Indonesia work is offered at The Seed of Hope Children's Home in Bali with 80 orphans and in need of care-giving adults who can also teach. Short and long term stays are possible and no fees are payable.

Habitat For Humanity, www.habitat.org.au. With estimates that Indonesia needs 735,000 new housing units a year and to repair 420,000 units annually, builders and funds are always needed in the archipelago. Around half of all new housing units are needed for people who simply can not afford them. Building and renovation projects combined with sightseeing can be arranged for groups and individuals. This group has recently achieved some notable goals including the completion of 1500 houses in tsunami ravaged Meulaboh (Aceh), 1000 houses in Jakarta for those whose were damaged or destroyed by recent flooding, and a further 1000 houses for those affected by the 2006 Bantul earthquake. Fees apply.

Peace Brigades International, www.peacebrigades.org, is a non-governmental organization that protects individuals from human rights violations and violence. This group's main work is to offer protective accompaniment, whereby a threatened individual or organization is accompanied by a member of the brigade whose presence can stop potential attacks. The PBI is a non-partisan group and does not take part in the work of the people they protect, but offers protection and moral support alone. In Indonesia there are four groups, based in Jayapura and Wamena (Papua), Aceh and Jakarta. Potential

TODD HACKWELDER/SHUTTERSTOCK

volunteers need to be well read on issues of human rights and justice. Workers receive a small stipend to cover cost of living.

Service Civil International, www.sciint.org. Long- and short-term work camps including renovations in Prambanan, environmental education in the Karimunjawa islands off Java, care giving to disabled children and elderly in Surabaya and mangrove conservation in Semarang. A fee of US$200 is levied for most projects.

Thailand

Projects range from conservation and teaching English to looking after elephants and generally need to be organized before you arrive. The application process almost always involves submitting a statement of intent, although generally no formal qualifications or experience are required. Volunteers need to be over 18 and pay fees upfront. Consult individual organizations about visas and lodgings – most include basic shared accommodation in the price but not travel to and from Thailand. The following international organizations run projects in Thailand: **British Trust for Conservation Volunteers**, Sedum House, Mallard Way, Potteric Carr, Doncaster, DN4 8DB, T01302-388888, www.btcv.org. Mangrove conservation and turtle monitoring from two weeks in duration. **Elephant Nature Park**, 209/2 Sridorn Chai Rd, Chiang Mai 50100, Thailand, T053-272855, www.thaifocus.com/elephant. Projects last for up to one month and involve administration and working with elephants. **Cross Cultural Solutions**, 2 Clinton Place, New Rochelle, NY 10801, USA, T1800 3804777 (US only), T191 4632 0022, www.crossculturalsolutions.org. Community work and research into local development. **Earthwatch**, 267 Banbury Rd, Oxford, OX2 7HT, T01865-318838, www.earthwatch.org. **Global Services Corps**, 300 Broadway, Suite 28, San Francisco, CA 94133-3312, USA, T415-788 3666, ext128, www.globalservicecorps.org. Volunteers must have an interest in international issues

Opposite: Food cart, Jakarta.
Above: Orang-utan.

KITCH BAIN/SHUTTERSTOCK

and sustainable development. **Involvement Volunteers**, PO Box 218, Port Melbourne, Vic 3207, Australia, T613-9646 5504, www.volunteering.org.au. Australian network with international reach, organic farming, teaching and community work. **VSO**, 317 Putney Bridge Rd, London, SW15 2PN, UK, T0208-780 7200, www.vso.org.uk. Worldwide voluntary organization.

Vietnam, Cambodia and Laos

Since the early 1990s there has been a phenomenal growth in 'ecotourism', which promotes and supports the conservation of natural environments and is also fair and equitable to local communities. While the authenticity of some ecotourism operators needs to be interpreted with care, there is clearly both a huge demand for this type of activity and also significant opportunities to support worthwhile conservation and social development initiatives by this means.

Sport and activities

Caving

ⓘ Climbing operators are listed in the relevant places throughout the book. **Green Discovery**, Vang Vieng, T023-511230, www.greendiscoverylaos.com.

Laos has some of the most extensive caves in the region. Some of the best can be found around Vang Vieng, where caving tourism has been developed. Another highlight is the amazing Kong Lor River Cave in the centre of the country. There are hundreds of caves around Vieng Xai but only a few open to tourists; for those interested in history these caves should be a first stop.

  Thailand has cave systems in many parts of the country, however, those that are open to the public are usually pretty sedate affairs. More adventurous cave expeditions are provided in Soppong in the north and a couple of other places.

  The Niah caves in **East Malaysia** include prehistoric cave paintings and one of the largest caverns in the world.

Above: Tham Kong Lor, Laos.
Below : Scuba diver and sea turtle, Indonesia.

Cycling and mountain biking

ⓘ Cycling operators are listed in the relevant places throughout the book. **Asian Trails**, www.asiantrails.com. **Exotissimo**, Hanoi, T04-828 2150, www.exotissimo.com. **Green Discovery**, T086-211484, www.greendiscoverylaos.com.

In **Cambodia** and **Laos**, cycling is offered by several tour agencies; Luang Namtha is a popular place to start, and Green Discovery run excellent trips. Many cyclists prefer to bring their own all-terrain or racing bikes but it's also possible to rent them.

  Large parts of **Vietnam** are flat so cycling is a popular activity, although the traffic on the roads can be hazardous. It's therefore recommended that any tour is planned off-road or on minor roads.

Diving

ⓘ See the centre colour section for full details.

With so much diving on the doorstep, there are more than enough operators in Southeast

Elephant trekking in Ayutthaya, Thailand.

Asia to meet the needs of everyone from a dedicated five-a-day diver to a never-tried-it-before rookie. In general, dive businesses are extremely professional and run by friendly and helpful staff. Many work closely with one of the international governing bodies (PADI, NAUI, CMAS, BSAC), however, facilities in far-flung areas may be limited. It's always worth asking around if you're unsure of what you are being offered. There are air evacuation services across the region but these can be limited and are extremely expensive. Likewise, hyperbaric chambers may be some distance away and can charge as much as US$800 per hour so good dive insurance is imperative. It is inexpensive and well worth it in case of a problem, real or perceived. Nowdays, many general travel insurance policies include diving but will also limit factors such as depth and stipulate that you must dive with a qualified guide. As always, there are a few simple rules to avoid getting the bends: don't dive too deep; don't ascend too quickly; use – and obey – your computer; always do a safety stop (three minutes at 5 m minimum); and drink plenty of water to avoid dehydration. Contact DAN (Divers' Alert Network) for more information, www.diversalertnetwork.org, DAN Europe, www.daneurope.org, or DAN South East Asia Pacific, www.danseap.org. You can join online. Every dive centre will have rental equipment but ensure you check this over carefully. Bringing your own will considerably reduce costs. Prior to departure, contact your airlines to see if you can come to some kind of arrangement for extra baggage allowance.

Elephant trekking

ⓘ Trekking operators are listed in the relevant places throughout the book.

There are several elephants camps in the north of **Thailand** where visitors can watch elephants perform tricks and go on a short saunter. In the northern region these include the Thai Elephant Conservation Centre outside Lampang, the Elephant Training Camp in the Mae Sa Valley outside Chiang Mai, and the Chiang Dao Elephant Training Centre near Chiang Dao, also not far from Chiang Mai. In the northeastern region there is the rather tacky Khao Yai Elephant Camp linked to the Khao Yai National Park and Ban Tha Klang, a village of traditional elephant tamers and trainers outside Surin. Slightly more adventurous elephant treks are sometimes

Longtail boats in turquoise waters, Koh Phi Phi, Thailand.

included in longer trekking programmes. Elephant trekking is also possible in Yok Don National Park, **Vietnam**, and around Vang Vieng and Tad Lo in **Laos**. T021-212251, www.trekkingcentrallaos.com.

Kayaking

ⓘ **Halong Bay Vang Vieng Buffalo Tours**, Hanoi, T04-828 0702; Ho Chi Minh City, T08-827 9169, www.buffalotours.com. **Exotissimo**, Hanoi, T04-828 2150; HCMC, T08-825 1723, www.exotissimo.com. **Green Discovery**, Vang Vieng, T023- 511 230, www.greendiscoverylaos.com. **Xplore-Asia**, www.xplore-asia.com. **Riverside tours**, www.riversidetourlaos.com.

Kayaking in **Vietnam** is centred around Halong Bay. This World Heritage Site, crammed with islands and grottoes, is a fantastic place to explore by kayak. Head to the Nam Song River at Vang Vieng for kayaking, rafting and tubing in Laos. There is also excellent kayaking around the Boloven Plateau.

Kayaking in **Thailand** has become popular over the last decade or so. Limestone areas of the south such as Phangnga Bay provide a pock-marked coast of cliffs, sea caverns and rocky islets. Specialist companies have now been joined by many other companies based in Phuket, Krabi, Ao Nang, Koh Tao and Phi Phi. Kayaks can also be hired on many commercial beaches by the hour.

Kitesurfing, windsurfing and wakeboarding

ⓘ Watersports operators are listed in the relevant places throughout the book.

Offered as an option in a few watersports centres, wakeboarding has its own specialist school in **Thailand**. Air Time, 99/9 Tambon Mae Nam Khu, Amphur Pluak Daeng, Dok Krai, Rayong, T08-6838 7841, www.air-time.net, runs wakeboard camps near Pattaya with dedicated English, French, German, Dutch and Thai-speaking coaches and the chance to try out monoboards, kneeboards, skyski and tubes. Thailand Kitesurfing School, Rawai, Muang Phuket, T076-288258, www.kitethailand.com, also runs courses. There are kitesurfing schools in Phuket and Hua Hin offering one- to three-day courses and instructor training.

Kitesurfing and windsurfing are found largely in Mui Ne, **Vietnam**, which offers just about perfect conditions throughout the year. The wind is normally brisk over many days and the combination of powerful wind and waves enables good kitesurfers to get airborne for several seconds at a time. Equipment can be rented at many places. Windsurfing is popular in Nha Trang where dive schools offer this and other watersports. Nha Trang Mui Ne Jibe's Beach Club, Mui Ne, T062-847405, www.windsurf-vietnam.com.

Spas and therapies

ⓘ See pages 16 and 17 for full details.

Spa resorts in **Vietnam** are the Ana Mandara in Nha Trang, the Evason Hideaway in Ninh Van Bay and the Evason Villas Dalat in the Central Highlands, www.sixsenses.com. There are other good hotels such as the Life Wellness Resorts and the Victoria Hotels that offer spa facilities. Hotels offering massage, treatments and therapies exist across the region and are good value for money.

There are also some wonderful spas in Luang Prabang, **Laos**; for extreme indulgence try the Spa at La Residence Phou Vao or for a cheaper luxury alternative the Spa Garden, T071-212325, spagardenlpb@hotmail.com.

In addition to **Thailand**'s growing spa industry, travellers can take advantage of opportunities for week-long fasting and alternative health programmes. Connect with your inner child, meditate on life or have a relaxing spot of self-administered colonic

irrigation on Koh Samui, the country's centre for alternative healing. Programmes range from three- to 21-day courses aimed at eliminating the body's toxins and rejuvenating body and mind through a range of wince-inducing techniques. These include fasting, colonic irrigation and reflexology alongside gentler methods of iridology, meditation, reiki, massage and yoga. Many Thai spas offer holistic therapy sessions, from massage to aromatherapy. Thai massage has become increasingly popular in the west and it is now possible to take courses of varying lengths and return home not just with cheap CDs but with a skill to impress your friends. The best-known centre for traditional Thai massage is Wat Pho in Bangkok. It offers 30-hour, 15-day courses. Chiang Mai also has a number of centres offering courses, some up to 11 days long. There's also a deluge of therapeutic massage places, some linked to guesthouses and hotels, where tourists can have their worries caressed away for a few bucks. Many masseuses are not trained.

Wat Mahathat is Bangkok's renowned meditation centre. Beyond Bangkok, Wat Suan Mokkh, outside Surat Thani, offers 10-day anapanasati meditation courses, T02-468 2857, while Wat Khao Tum on Koh Phangan supports a Vipassana Meditation

Cyclist in Hoi An, Vietnam.

Above: Surfer on Kuta beach, Bali. **Opposite:** Trekkers in the jungle, Thailand.

Centre offering 20-day courses and three-month retreats. There are centres elsewhere too, for example on Koh Tao.

Surfing

ⓘ Surf schools and organizations are listed in the relevant places throughout the book.

Kuta Beach in Bali, **Indonesia**, was the location upon which Bali's reputation as a surfer's paradise was based. Kuta is a beach break and these days the water is polluted with sewage: about 1 km out is a reef break, a left-hand barrel. However, there are other, better locations. Below is a very brief summary of conditions. Some of the best surfing in Bali is on the Bukit Peninsula. Uluwatu, about 2 km down a rough track, with a 'world famous' left break; the Peak is a high-tide break, Race Track a mid-tide, and Outside Corner a low-tide wave. If the current is too strong to reach the cave or onto the reef in front of the cave, make for the beach. Despite its reputation, waves can be crowded and over-rated. Padang Padang is close to Uluwatu and can be reached along a track or by car/motorbike. The very hollow left is dangerous because of the cliff; very dangerous below mid-tide. Down from Padang Padang is Bingin;

fast hollow left best at high to medium tides, at low tides it is dangerous and waves can 'suck dry' on the reef; often crowded. Next to Bingin is Dreamland, a very popular newcomer set on a dramatic beach with consistent year-round surf from a beach break. Nyang Nyang, accessible by track; both left and right. Suluban, not far from Jimbaran; international surf competitions are held here. Occasional bemos travel from Kuta to Uluwatu, although most surfers ride motorbikes or charter a taxi; tracks to surfing beaches are reasonably well-marked along the road. Other beaches include Canggu, near the village of Kerobokan, north on the Legian road (both left and right); and Medewi, about 75 km west of Denpasar, best above mid-tide. Boards can be hired; repair and other services are available. The surf is reasonable throughout the year, although it is definitely best between June and August. Between October and April there are good right-handers at Nusa Dua and Sanur, the latter only working for 20 days a year. Tubes Bar, Poppies Gang 2, Kuta, is good for information.

Try Grajagan Bay (known to surfers as G-Land) in the Alas Purwo National Park on the south coast of Java for a fine left break.

Surfing in Lombok and Sumbawa is not as good as Bali but both Gili Air and Desert Point off Bangko Bangko can be excellent. The south coast is more reliable: Kuta and Tanjung Aan, or further west, Selong Blanak and Blongas; going east, Awang Bay and Gumbang Bay. Modest surfing at Taliwang and Maluk on Sumbawa, better at Hu'u. Pulau Nias off is a well-established surfing location, and the Mentawai Islands have year-round surf .

Trekking

ⓘ Trekking operators are listed in the relevant places throughout the book. Trekking companies with websites include **The Ecotourist Center**, Umphang, www.umphanghill.com.

The main focus for trekking in **Vietnam** is Sapa but some trekking is also organized around Dalat. Some treks are straightforward and can be done without guides or support, whereas others require accommodation to be booked in advance and there may be a legal requirement to take a licensed guide. If staying with ethnic minorities this must be organized through a tour operator.

In **Laos**, Luang Namtha, Muang Sing and Phongsali all offer trekking in areas inhabited by a diverse range of ethnicities. There are also treks from Luang Prabang and Vang Vieng.

In **Thailand**, hundreds of thousands of tourists each year take a trek into the hills of the northern and western regions, partly to experience the (declining) natural wealth and partly to see and stay with one or more of the country's hilltribes. Treks are often combined with elephant rides and rafting and can stretch from single day outings to two-week trips. The main trekking centres are Chiang Mai, Chiang Rai, Mae Hong Son, Mae Sot, Mae Sariang, Pai, Soppong, Fang, Tha Ton, Chiang Saen, Sop Ruak, Mae Sai, Nan and Umphang.

There are numerous opportunities for trekking in **Malaysia**, especially in east Malaysia, in Sarawak and Sabah. Most national parks in this region offer hiking trails, but the best are in the Cameron Highlands, Endau Rompin National Park, Gunung Kinabalu National Park, Gunung Mulu National Park, Niah National Park, and Taman Negara National Park.

Climbing to the summit of Gunung Kinabalu in Sabah for sunrise is one of the most popular hikes. New and exciting multi-day hikes are opening up in more remote regions of Sabah and Sarawak, such as the spectacular route between waterfalls in the Maliau Basin Conservation Area.

Whitewater rafting

ⓘ Tour operators in Thailand include **K-Trekking**, 238/5, Chiangmai-hod Road, A Muang, Chiang Mai T053-431447, day tours from US$55; **New Frontier Adventure Co**, 53/54 Onnutch 17, Suan Luang, Bangkok, T02-391 1785, rafting and whitewater rafting; and **Sea Canoe Thailand**, Yaowarat Road, Phuket, T076-212172, www.seacanoe.net, full and half-day tours from Phuket, US$65 per day. Operators in Indonesia include **Sobek Expeditions**, T0361 287059, www.bali sobek.com; and **Bali Adventure Tours**.

Whitewater rafting in **Thailand** has become popular year-round activity. Among the best locations are Pai and the Mae Taeng and Mae Cham close to Chiang Mai. There is whitewater rafting in Sangkhlaburi in the western region and there are also opportunities on Phuket. June to November is a good time due to increased rainfall.

BEN HEYS/SHUTTERSTOCK

Above: Bali starling. **Opposite:** Akha women in traditional dress, Chiang Rai, Thailand.
Below: Komodo dragon in the wild, Indonesia.

Whitewater rafting is not an established activity in **Malaysia** although there are some good spots to take to the swirl. Fraser's Hill, Northern Peninsula; Kiulu river (grade II) and Padas river (grade III), Sabah.

In **Indonesia**, all rivers on Bali are grade II-III, but may rise in the wet season. Down the Ayung River near Ubud includes hotel pick-up, equipment, insurance and lunch, adults US$68, children US$45, organized by Sobek Expeditions.

Wildlife

ⓘ Wildlife tour operators are listed below and in the relevant places throughout the book.

In **Indonesia**, Bali Bird Walks, T0361-975009, is led by Victor Mason, ornithologist and resident of Bali for over 20 years, in the Ubud area. Bali Bird Park (Taman Burung), Jl Serma Cok Ngurah Gambir, Singapadu, Balubulan, T0361 299614, www.bali-bird-park.com, has around 250 species of birds including birds of paradise, the endangered Bali starling, and cassowaries. There is a rainforest walk-in aviary, restaurant, bar and souvenir shop, daily 0900-1730, adult US$12.50, child US$6.50. Bali Reptile Park (Rimpa Reptil), Jl Serma Cok Ngurah Gambir, Singapadu, Balubulan, next to the Bali Bird Park to the northeast of Denpasar, T0361-299344,

herpindo@denpasar.wasantara.net.id, daily 0900-1800, adult US$8, child US$4.50, has reptiles from Indonesia and the rest of the world, including Komodo dragons, king cobras, turtles and an 8-m reticulated python.

Thailand has an extensive network of national parks and protected areas. The more popular – such as Khao Yai and Phu Kradung in the northeast, Doi Inthanon in the north, and Khao Sok in the south – have trails, camping grounds, hides, accommodation, visitor centres and more. However, compared with other countries with a rich natural heritage, it is difficult not to feel that Thailand has not made the most of its potential. Trails are generally not well laid out and true nature lovers may find themselves disappointed rather than enthralled. However, the sheer luxuriance and abundance of the tropical forest, in addition to the unusual birds and insects, will probably make up for this.

Visiting the hilltribes of Thailand

There are many ways to see the hilltribes, ranging from an easy single-day visit to a strenuous week-long trek through the forest. If you do not want to live rough and trekking is not your thing, then opt for a half-day tour or day-trip by taxi, bus or hired motorbike. The major towns of the north all have hilltribe communities within easy reach and offer a hassle-free opportunity to get a taste of village life and see traditional costumes. On arrival you will probably be hounded by handicraft salespeople and be expected to pay for any photographs that you take, but you will at least leave satisfied in the knowledge that you have not contributed too much to the process of cultural erosion. For a more extended visit, tour operators offer two- or three-day excursions by bus, raft, boat and foot. The excursions are usually comfortable, highly organized, and do not venture far into the wilds of the north. They are easily booked through one of the many companies in Chiang Mai, Chiang Rai, Mae Hong Son and the other trekking towns of the region. Trekking into the hills is undoubtedly the best way to see the hilltribes. To keep the adventure alive (or perhaps, the myth of adventure), most companies now promote 'non-touristic' trekking, and guarantee a trek will not meet another trekking party. It is important to get a knowledgeable guide who speaks good English, as well as the language(s) of the tribe(s) that are to be visited. They are your link with the hilltribes: they will advise you what not to do and tell you about their customs, rituals, economy and religion, as well as ensuring your safety. Ask other tourists who have recently returned from treks about their experiences: a personal recommendation is hard to beat. Sometimes an even better alternative is to hire a private guide, although this is obviously more expensive. Finally, there is of course nothing to stop you setting off into the hills on your own, either on foot or by motorbike DIY trekking. This can be very rewarding, and is becoming increasingly popular, but it does have its risks: parts of the north are still fairly lawless. Take care preparing your trip and let someone know your schedule and itinerary. It is also easy to get lost, and, unless you go fully prepared with the appropriate books, maps and other information, it is unlikely that you will gain much of an insight into hilltribe life. Most hilltribe villages will offer a place to sleep - usually in the headman's house; expect to pay about ฿50. The advantage – from the hill peoples' perspective – is that the money goes directly to them rather than lining the pockets of an agent or trekking company. If you are intending to venture out on your own, it is a good idea to visit the Hilltribe Research Center at Chiang Mai University before you leave. Good maps of the hilltribe areas are available from DK Books, 234 Tha Phae Road, Chiang Mai.

How big is your footprint?

The benefits of international travel are self evident for both hosts and travellers: employment, understanding of different cultures and business or leisure opportunities. At the same time there is clearly a downside. Where visitor pressure is high and/or poorly regulated, there can be adverse impacts on society and the natural environment. Paradoxically, this is as true in undeveloped and pristine areas (where culture and the natural environment are less 'prepared' for even small numbers of visitors) as in major resorts.

The travel industry is growing rapidly and increasingly its impact is becoming apparent. These impacts can seem remote and unrelated to an individual trip or holiday (eg air travel is clearly implicated in global warming and damage to the ozone layer, resort location and construction can destroy natural habitats and restrict traditional rights and activities), but individual choice and awareness can make a difference in many instances and, collectively, travellers are having a significant effect in shaping a more responsible and sustainable industry.

Of course travel can have beneficial impacts and this is something to which every traveller can contribute. Many national parks are part funded by receipts from visitors. Similarly, travellers can promote patronage and protection of important archaeological sites and heritage through their interest and contributions via entrance and performance fees. They can also support small-scale enterprises by staying in locally run hotels and hostels, eating in local restaurants and by purchasing local goods, supplies and arts and crafts. In fact, since the early 1990s there has been a phenomenal growth in tourism that promotes and supports the conservation of natural environments and is also fair and equitable to local communities. This 'ecotourism' segment is probably the fastest-growing sector of the travel industry and provides a vast and growing range of destinations and activities. While the authenticity of some ecotourism operators' claims needs to be interpreted with care, there is clearly both a huge demand for this type of activity and also significant opportunities to support worthwhile conservation and social development initiatives.

Green Globe, T020-77304428, www.greenglobe21.com, and **Responsible Travel**, www.responsibletravel.com, offer advice for travellers on selecting destinations and sites focused on conservation and sustainable development. In addition, the **International Eco-Tourism Society**, www.ecotourism.org, **Tourism Concern**, T020-7753 3330, www.tourismconcern.org.uk, and **Planeta,** www.planeta.com, develop and promote ecotourism projects in destinations all over the world and their websites provide details for initiatives throughout Southeast Asia.

Travelling light

▸▸ The point of a holiday is, of course, to have a good time, but if it's relatively guilt-free as well, that's even better. Perfect ecotourism would ensure a good living for local inhabitants, while not detracting from their traditional lifestyles, encroaching on their customs or spoiling their environment. Perfect ecotourism probably doesn't exist, but everyone can play their part. Here are a few points worth bearing in mind:

▸▸ Think about where your money goes and be fair and realistic about how cheaply you travel. Try to put money into local people's hands; drink local beer or fruit juice rather than imported brands and stay in locally owned accommodation wherever possible.

▸▸ Haggle with humour and appropriately. Remember that you want a fair price, not the lowest one.

▸▸ Think about what happens to your rubbish. Take biodegradable products and a water filter to avoid using lots of plastic bottles. Be sensitive to limited resources such as water, fuel and electricity.

▸▸ Help preserve local wildlife and habitats by respecting rules and regulations, such as sticking to footpaths, not standing on coral and not buying products made from endangered plants or animals.

▸▸ Don't treat people as part of the landscape; they may not want their picture taken. Ask first and respect their wishes.

▸▸ Learn the local language and be mindful of local customs and norms. It can enhance your travel experience and you'll earn respect and be more readily welcomed by local people.

▸▸ And finally, use your guidebook as a starting point, not the only source of information. Talk to local people, then discover your own adventure.

Raflessia, the worlds biggest flower.

Southeast Asia on page and screen

Books to read

Much of the literature published from the 1960s onwards focuses on the region's struggles. Vietnam is the setting for Graham Greene's classic novel *The Quiet American* (1954), while Michael Herr's *Dispatches* (1977) focuses on journalists covering the Vietnam War. Norman Lewis's *A Dragon Apparent* (1951), is an essential travel account of his journey throughout Indo-China.

Cambodia has a slew of literature on the civil war – try David P Chandler's bio of Pol Pot, *Brother Number One* (1992) and François Ponchaud's, *Cambodia Year Zero* (1978). The USA's secret war in Laos is covered in Christopher Robbin's account of pilots in *The Ravens* (1989). In Thailand, Paul M Handley's controversial *The King Never Smiles* (2006), a biography of the present king, is banned. William Stevenson's more flattering account,

The Revolutionary King (2001) is not. Philip Cornwel-Smith's *Very Thai* (2007) gets to grip with difficult aspects of Thai popular culture.

Malaysia is the setting for Paul Theroux's series of short stories, *The Consul's File* (1979) and Redmond O'Hanlon's *Into the Heart of Borneo* (1984). Indonesia provides the backdrop for journalist Richard Lloyd Parry's *In the Time of Madness* (2007), set in the years 1996-1999 while Christopher Koch's novel, *The Year of Living Dangerously* (1983) is set in the 1960s.

Films to watch

Vietnam figures heavily in filmic representations of Southeast Asia, though a home-grown film industry is developing in Thailand and Indonesia. Oliver Stone's three films, *Platoon* (1986), *Born on the Fourth of July* (1989) and *Heaven and Earth* (1993) take on the Vietnam War as does Coppola's epic *Apocalypse Now* (1979) and the Oscar-winning documentary, *Hearts and Minds* (1974).

Cambodia is the backdrop for the Oscar-winning *Killing Fields* (1984), while the Matt Dillon-directed effort, *City of Ghosts* (2002), is set in the post-civil war period. Thailand produces its own films including the martial arts epic *Ong Bak* (2003) and the nutty cowboy film, *Tears of the Black Tiger* (2000). Indonesia has created the notable *Eliana, Eliana* (2002) about a

woman journeying to Jakarta and *Arisan* (2004), which featured Indonesia's first gay kiss. Christopher Koch's book, *The Year of Living Dangerously*, was also turned into a film of the same name (1983).

Contents

Footprint features

At a glance

◉ **Getting around** Bandar Seri Bagawan is served by bus and river taxi. Otherwise, it's best to hire a car.

◉ **Time required** 2 days for the capital, 1 week for the interior

☀ **Weather** Rainy season is officially Nov-Feb, but becoming less predictable.

✖ **When not to go** Roads may be impasable during the rainy season. Travel can be more difficult during Ramadan.

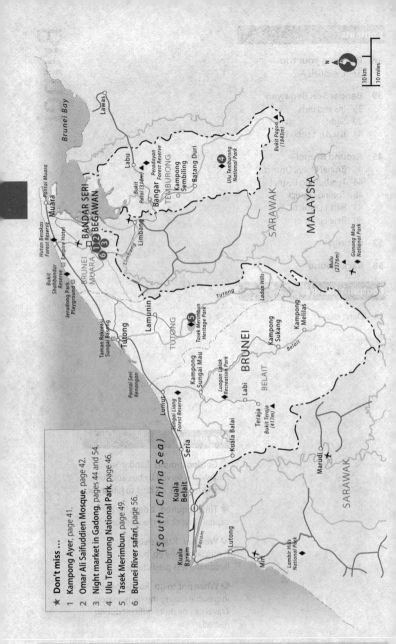

Don't miss ...

★

1 Kampong Ayer, page 41.

2 Omar Ali Saifuddien Mosque, page 42.

3 Night market in Gadong, pages 44 and 54.

4 Ulu Temburong National Park, page 46.

5 Tasek Merimbun, page 49.

6 Brunei River safari, page 56.

Brunei is a one-off; a tiny oil-rich sultanate on the north coast of Borneo, cornered and split in two by the Malaysian state of Sarawak. Fewer than 400,000 Bruneians are ruled over by one of the world's wealthiest men – the living link in a dynasty of sultans stretching back 600 years. At one time, Brunei was the driving seat of Borneo, but its territories were whittled away piece by piece, first by the Sulu kings, then by the British. Today Brunei is a peculiar mix of material wealth and Malay tradition. Affluence has numbed Sultan Bolkiah's subjects into submission to the political system – a monarchical autocracy, to all intents and purposes (albeit a benevolent one). Bruneians see no reason to complain: they pay no taxes and the purchase of cars and houses is heavily subsidized. Healthcare and education are free and trips to Mecca are a snip. Politics, it seems, is not their business. This climate of benign affluence, combined with the prohibition of alcohol and the complete lack of nightlife, makes Brunei's tagline – 'The Abode of Peace' – ring perfectly true.

Still, change is in the air. For the first time since independence, Brunei is turning its back on the introspection that has kept it largely hidden from the world. The Asian financial crisis of 1997 hit Brunei hard, almost halving GDP, and, with oil reserves expected to dry up by 2018, the economy needs to diversify. The sultan's latest plan is to transform his realm into an offshore tax haven. But Brunei holds another trump card for the future: ecotourism. One of the happy consequences of its dependence on oil is the amount of rainforest left intact. With three-quarters of its landmass covered by virgin rainforest, Brunei can claim the highest proportion of primary forest of any country in the world. Brunei is the easy way into Borneo, offering kampong culture, pristine jungle, endangered wildlife and all the creature comforts you could hope for. Just don't expect to rough it.

Planning your trip

Getting there

By air Bandar Seri Begawan airport (see page 39) has direct air links with most Southeast Asian capitals. **Royal Brunei Airlines** (www.bruneiair.com) is the only airline that flies direct from the UK; daily flights between **London Heathrow** and Bandar Seri Begawan take 16 hours, including a brief stop in Dubai for refuelling, and cost in the region of £450-650. **Royal Brunei** also flies direct to/from Australia and New Zealand, with three flights per week to and from **Sydney**, **Perth**, **Brisbane**, **Darwin** and **Auckland**. There are no direct flights to Borneo from the **USA** and **Canada**. A popular alternative is to fly to **Kuala Lumpur** (see page 593) or **Singapore** (see page 740) and then transfer flights for the remainder of the journey. Note that if you buy your ticket locally, it is much cheaper to fly from Malaysia to Brunei than vice versa because of the exchange rate. Departure tax from Brunei to Malaysia and Singapore is US$3.50 and US$8.50 to all other destinations.

By road The main overland route from Sarawak is by bus from Miri (see page 686) to Kuala Belait, in the far western corner of Brunei. It is also possible to travel overland from Limbang or Lawas to Bangar, in the Temburong district of Brunei, from where it is a short boat trip to Bandar Seri Begawan, although this is a relatively expensive option.

By boat There are daily express boats to Bandar Seri Begawan from Lawas and Limbang in northern Sarawak (see page 686), and from the duty-free island of Labuan in Sabah (see page 712), itself connected by boat to Kota Kinabalu.

Getting around

Thanks to subsidized vehicles and cheap petrol, most Bruneians drive and the public transport system is not comprehensive. Car hire is available at the airport and in Bandar (see page 57). Boats are used to get to the Ulu Temburong National Park, which is cut off from the rest of Brunei by the Limbang area of Sarawak. There are no internal flights within Brunei.

Sleeping → *For hotel price codes, see inside the front cover.*

Accommodation is expensive compared with neighbouring Sarawak and Sabah. Most of the hotels are functional, business-oriented places, and there are virtually no budget options, apart from the youth hostel (**Pusat Belia**, see page 52) in Bandar Seri Begawan and the indigenous longhouses, some of which offer homestay programmes. At the top end, Brunei boasts the impressive, six-star **Empire Hotel & Country Club** (see page 53), one of the world's flashiest hotels. Top-end hotels frequently offer excellent promotions.

Eating and drinking → *For restaurant price codes, see inside the front cover.*

The variety and quality of food is outstanding, with a medley of restaurants, market stalls and food courts offering a wide range of cuisines from Malay, Chinese and Indian, to Indonesian, Japanese and European. Because of Brunei's relative wealth, there is less streetfood than in other Southeast Asian countries. Nevertheless, the informal local restaurants and food courts are still the best places to sample good local cuisine – and at great prices. Brunei is a 'dry' country: sale of alcohol is banned, and consumption is prohibited for Muslims. Certain restaurants will allow non-Muslims to bring their own alcohol to drink with the meal. Bandar Seri Begawan itself is deserted after dark.

Festivals and events

Brunei is a Muslim country and during Ramadan travel can be more difficult and many restaurants close during daylight hours. A great time to visit is the week of the sultan's birthday celebrations in mid-July. The event is celebrated with parties and fireworks and this is the only time when the palace grounds are open to the public.

1 Jan New Year's Day (public holiday).
Jan/Feb Chinese New Year (public holiday), a 15-day lunar festival.
23 Feb Hari Kebangsaan Negara Brunei Darussalam/National Day (public holiday), processions and firework displays in BSB.
31 May Armed Forces Day (public holiday), celebrated by the Royal Brunei Armed Forces who parade their equipment around town.
15 Jul Sultan's Birthday (public holiday) is celebrated until the end of the 2nd week in Aug. There's a procession, with lanterns and fireworks and a traditional boat race in BSB.
25 Dec Christmas Day.

Shopping

Compared to Malaysia or Singapore, Brunei is not up to much when it comes to shopping; the range of goods on offer is limited and the prices much higher. That said, you'll have no trouble finding international branded and luxury items. There is no sales tax in Brunei.

Essentials A-Z

Accident and emergency
Ambulance T991; Police T993; Fire T995.

Customs and duty free
The duty-free allowance for those over 17 is 200 cigarettes or 250 g of tobacco, 60 ml of perfume and 250 ml eau de toilette. Non-Muslims are allowed 2 bottles of liquor and 12 cans of beer for personal consumption. All alcohol must be declared on arrival. Trafficking illegal drugs carries the death penalty.

Disabled travellers
Facilities for disabled travellers are better than in Malaysia, though they are still limited by Western standards. Contact **Brunei Tourism** (see page 39) for information. The top hotels have decent facilities for disabled travellers.

Electricity
220-240 volts, 50 cycle AC.

Embassies and consulates
Australia, 10 Beale Crescent, Deakin, Canberra, ACT 2606, T+61-(0)2-6285 4500.
Canada, 395 Laurier Av East, Ottawa, Ontario K1N 6R4, T+1-613-234 5656.

France, 7 rue de Presbourg, 75116 Paris, T+33-01-5364 6760.
Germany, Zentralverband des Deutschen Baugewerbes, 1st floor, Kronenstrasse 55-58, 10117 Berlin-Mitte, T+49-030-2060 7600.
Malaysia, 19 Menara Tan & Tan, Jl Tun Razak, 50400 Kuala Lumpur, T+60-03-2161 2800.
Singapore, 325 Tanglin Rd, Singapore 24795, T+65-733 9055.
UK, 19-20 Belgrave Sq, London SW1X 8PG, T+44-(0)207-581 0521, bhcl@brunei-high-commission.co.uk.

Gay and lesbian travellers
Brunei is not a good place to be gay – at least not officially: homosexual sex is illegal and punishable with jail sentences and fines. In reality, things are more easygoing, although it's best not to flaunt your sexuality. See www.utopia-asia.com for more information.

Internet
There are plenty of internet cafés and all the top-end and most of the mid-range hotels offer internet access. For those travelling with laptops, a dial-up internet service is provided by **BruNet**; visit www.brunet.bn to subscribe.

Language

The Malay language, Bahasa Melayu (see page 589) is the national language, although English is widely spoken and is taught in schools.

Media

There are 2 daily newspapers: the *Borneo Bulletin* (English) and the *Media Permata* (Malay), which cover local and international news. The most popular radio station is London's *Capital Radio*. *Capital Gold* is also broadcast live. The national television network transmits local programmes and Malaysian TV. Satellite TV is widespread in Brunei (even remote longhouses have dishes) and virtually all hotels provide a wide range of channels including CNN and the BBC.

Money ➜ *US$1 = B$1.37, £1 = 2.69 (Aug 2008).* The official currency is the Brunei dollar (B$), which is interchangeable with the Singapore dollar. Notes come in denominations of B$1, B$5, B$10, B$50, B$100, B$1000 and B$10,000. There are 1, 5, 10, 20 and 50 cent coins.

Exchange Banks charge a commission of B$10-15 for exchanging cash or traveller's cheques. Money changers often don't charge a set commission but their rates won't be as good. ATMs are widespread in Brunei and many accept debit cards (with Maestro), as well as credit cards. Depending on who you bank with, withdrawing money on your debit card is often free (there are plenty of HSBC ATMs around). Most hotels and many shops and establishments accept credit cards, too.

Cost of travelling Per capita, Brunei is one of the wealthiest countries in the developing world. This means that everything, from hotel rates to groceries and transport, is more expensive than in the rest of Borneo. Unless you hire a car, you may have to rely on taxis (the bus network is skimpy at best) and these are not cheap. By Western standards, however, Brunei is not particularly expensive. And, when it comes to local food at market stalls or in *kedai kopi* (traditional coffee shops), the prices are only marginally higher than those just across the border.

Opening hours

Businesses Mon-Fri 0900-1500, Sat 0900-1100 (banks).

Shopping malls daily 1000-2130.

Post offices Mon-Thu and Sat 0745-1630, Fri 0800-1100 and 1400-1600.

Post offices

Most hotels have postal services. The cost of a stamp for a postcard to Europe is around 50c.

Telephone ➜ *Country code +673.* Directory enquiries: T113. There are no area codes in Brunei. With a **Hallo Kad** phonecard (widely available) you can make international calls from any phone. You can also make international calls in many hotels. Coin phones take 10 and 20 cent pieces.

Time

8 hrs ahead of GMT.

Tourist information

www.aseansec.org Lots of government statistics, information and acronyms.

www.brunei.gov.bn The government of Brunei's official website.

www.jungle-drum.com An expat perspective on Brunei for visitors and people living there.

www.tourismbrunei.com Brunei's official tourism site.

Visas and immigration

All visitors must have valid passports, onward tickets and sufficient funds to support themselves. Visitors from the UK, Germany, New Zealand, Malaysia and Singapore do not need a visa for visits of up to 30 days. US nationals can stay for up to 3 months without visas. Visitors from Belgium, Denmark, France, Luxembourg, the Netherlands, Norway, Spain, Sweden, Switzerland, Japan, South Korea and Thailand do not need visas for visits of up to 14 days. Australian passport holders are issued visas on arrival at Brunei International Airport for stays of up to 14 days. Extend your visa is usually a formality; apply at the **Immigration Department**, Jl Menteri, Bandar Seri Begawan.

Bandar Seri Begawan

→ *Colour map 9, A/B4.*

Bandar Seri Begawan, more commonly referred to simply as Bandar ('sea port' in Malay), is the capital of Brunei and the only place of any real size. Even so, Bandar's population is barely 80,000 and, with most people living in the suburbs or among the stilted homes of the water village, downtown Bandar feels decidedly sleepy. This is no bad thing for the visitor; traffic and crowds are restricted to the suburbs, where most of the shops are located. The streets are clean and spacious, and the only persistent noise is the whirr of outboards, as water tambang (taxis) ferry people to and from the water village.

Bandar sits on a bend of the Sungai Brunei, with the stilted homes of Kampong Ayer (water village) reaching out across the river from the opposite bank. Back on dry land, the dominant feature is the impressive Omar Ali Saifuddien Mosque – though the primary point of reference nowadays seems to be the Yayasan Complex, a smart shopping mall whose two wings are aligned to provide a colonnaded vista of both the mosque and the river. ▸▸ *For listings, see pages 52-58.*

Ins and outs

Getting there
Brunei International Airport is 11 km south of Bandar Seri Begawan. Between 0630-1800, there are regular buses from the airport to the bus station on Jalan Cator, in downtown Bandar. Buses from Sarawak and other parts of Brunei also terminate here. A taxi from the airport costs about B$25, or B$30 after 1800. ▸▸ *See Transport, page 57.*

Getting around
Downtown Bandar is tiny and easy to negotiate on foot. Water taxis are the major form of public transport, with hundreds ferrying people to and from their stilted homes in Kampong Ayer. A short hop should cost no more than about B$2, while a 45-minute tour of the water village will cost about B$20 (less if you barter). The Brunei Museum, Malay Technology Museum and the suburb of Gadong are accessible on Central Line buses (daily 0630-1800), which pass through the bus station on Jalan Cator. Metered taxis cost B$3 for the first kilometre (B$4.50 2100-0600) and B$1 for every subsequent kilometre.

Tourist information
The helpful **Tourist Information Centre** ⓘ *General Post Office Building, corner of Jl Sultan and Jl Elizabeth Dua, T222 3734, Mon-Sat 0800-1200, 1400-1630*, has lists of hotels, car hire companies and tour operators. You can also pick up the *Explore Brunei* visitor guide, which has a fold-out map detailing the main bus routes. There is also the out-of-town **Brunei Tourism** ⓘ *Jl Menteri Besar, T238 2822, www.tourismbrunei.com.*

Sights

The main entry point to Bandar is via Jalan Tutong, which crosses the Sungai Kedayan tributary at Edinburgh Bridge, providing the first views of Kampong Ayer and the golden dome of the mosque. The road becomes Jalan Sultan, which cuts past a handful of museums and a small grid of shophouses, before hitting the waterfront. The city centre is bordered to the west by Sungai Kedayan, and, barely 500 m to the east, by the narrow Sungai Kianggeh tributary. Along its banks is the Tamu Kianggeh, an open-air market.

A number of the city's more interesting sights are located along the picturesque road that follows the course of the river east out of town. Jalan Residency runs past the Arts and Handicrafts Centre and the old British Residency itself, before becoming Jalan Kota Batu and bypassing the tombs of two sultans, the Brunei Museum and the Malay Technology Museum.

Bandar Seri Begawan

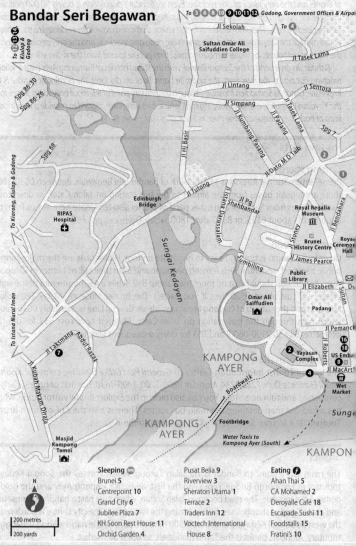

The suburbs of Kampong Kiarong and Gadong are several kilometres northwest of the centre. The former is a residential quarter, home to the enormous Kiarong Mosque, while Gadong is the main commercial centre, with department stores, restaurants and an excellent *pasar malam* (night market). North of town, near the airport, are the government offices and the impressive but ghostly quiet National Stadium.

Kampong Ayer

When people think of Bandar Seri Begawan, they think of Kampong Ayer, the stretch of stilted homes that extends for more than 3 km along the banks of Sungai Brunei. Officially, Kampong Ayer is not part of the municipality of Bandar – a reflection of the government's aim to rehouse the villagers on dry land. Not so long ago, however, Kampong Ayer was all there was of Bandar; it was the British who began to develop the town on land, starting with construction of the Residency in 1906 (see page 43).

The architecture of Kampong Ayer is perfectly suited to the tropical environment, making use of local materials and allowing for excellent ventilation. The oldest houses stand on mangrove and ironwood posts, with walls of woven nipa palm. The modern buildings stand on reinforced concrete piles, which allow for double-storey structures to be built. Many of the houses are painted in a profusion of colours, with pot plants and bougainvillea spilling from covered verandas. It may look primitive, but take a closer look and you notice the trappings of wealth: all houses have electricity and a piped water supply; many have satellite TV and internet.

Records of Kampong Ayer go back 14 centuries. In its 16th-century heyday, the 'village' had a population of 100,000 and was the centre of an empire stretching across most of Borneo, Mindanao and the Sulu archipelago. Though it still claims to be the world's largest water village, today's population is a mere 25,000 to 30,000. The village is separated into 42 units, each governed by a *tua kampong* (headman). These units are grouped into *mukims* (wards). The community is self-sufficient, with mosques, shops, schools and clinics – even fire stations and floating petrol stations.

Hua Hua **16**
I-Lotus **9**
Isma Jaya **17**
Le Taj **14**
Padian Foodcourt **2**
Pondok Sari Wangi **12**
Popular **7**

RMS Portview Seafood **4**
Seri Indah **8**
Teo Poi Hoon **13**
Zaika **2**

The future of Kampong Ayer looks somewhat uncertain. Many villagers have taken up the government's offer of free plots of land and subsidized housing and have moved on land. Meanwhile, the traditional cottage industries associated with each of the village units are giving way to new professions (today's young Bruneians aspire to become lawyers or computer programmers rather than blacksmiths or boat builders). Still, there are plenty of artisans left, and some will open their doors to passing visitors.

To visit Kampong Ayer, jump aboard any of the water taxis (*tambang*) by the pick-up point just south of the Yayasan Complex. The boatmen will compete raucously for your attention, then haggle with you over a price. The going rate is about B$20 for a 45-minute tour. Most boatmen are happy to pass by the Istana (the best views are from the river); you may want to combine the tour with a trip downriver to spot proboscis monkeys.

It is also possible to access part of the water village by foot: set off along the boardwalk that runs along west from the Yayasan Complex and you soon come to a bridge across the Kedayan tributary. From here there are good views across the maze of stilted homes as far as the copper-domed Masjid Kampong Tamoi, an elegant new mosque on the water's edge.

Omar Ali Saifuddien Mosque

ⓘ *Open daily 0800-2030; visiting hours for non-Muslims: Sat-Wed 0800-1200, 1400-1500 and 1700-1800; visitors must leave their shoes outside and dress conservatively.*

This mosque, built by and named after the 28th sultan (1950-1967), has become the symbol of Brunei, the nation's definitive monument. It is certainly one of Asia's finest-looking mosques, elegant and somehow modest, despite its great golden dome, its setting beside an artificial lake and its nightly illumination in unearthly green light.

Built in 1958 in classical Islamic style, the architecture is not overstated, although along with the sultan's hugely extravagant palace, the mosque was one of the first obvious signs of Brunei's oil wealth. When flakes of gold began falling from the central dome, due to contraction and expansion in the searing heat, the mosque quickly became something of a wonder to the villagers of Kampong Ayer (whose boardwalks run tight up to the edge of the mosque). Novelist Anthony Burgess' arrival as a teacher in Brunei coincided with the ceremonial opening of the mosque, and in his autobiography he recounts how this falling gold was "taken by the fisherfolk to be a gift from Allah".

The materials used to build and furnish the mosque came from right across the globe: carpets from Belgium and Arabia; chandeliers and stained glass from England; marble from Italy; granite from Shanghai; and, topping the central onion dome, a mosaic of more than three million pieces of gold-leafed Venetian glass. In the middle of the lake, which envelops the mosque on three sides, is a replica of a 16th-century *mahligai* (royal barge), used on special occasions and for Koran recital competitions.

Brunei Museumn

ⓘ *4 km east of downtown, Jl Kota Batu, Sat-Thu 0900-1700, Fri 0900-1130, 1430-1700, free. Eastern Line buses (Nos 11 and 39) run every 30 mins from the main bus terminal (or wait at the stop opposite the Arts and Handicraft Centre).*

Brunei's national museum holds a mixed bag of galleries, although it's certainly worth a visit. If you have limited time, head straight for the **Islamic Gallery**, an outstanding collection of artwork and artefacts from the sultan's personal collection. In pride of place on a marble pedestal in the centre of the gallery is a page of ornate calligraphy written by the sultan himself, in which he encourages his subjects to memorize the Koran. Around the pedestal, in rooms 1 and 2, are the real McCoy: Korans and beautifully preserved pieces of calligraphy dating from as early as the ninth century. Across one wall is a talismanic banner from 18th-century India, on which the whole Koran is transcribed in tiny script. Further rooms hold collections of pottery and ceramics from the Islamic world; gold and silver jewellery and coins dating back to AD 661; delicate perfume bottles alongside a collection of Indian and Ottoman sabres; and several oddities, such as a decorative wooden boot with compass, inlaid with mother-of-pearl.

Also on the ground floor is the mediocre **Natural History Gallery** and the obligatory **Petroleum Gallery**, which charts the discovery and extraction of Brunei's black gold. Upstairs, in Gallery 4, is the **Traditional Culture Gallery**, with examples of *keris* (ceremonial daggers), *bedok* (call-to-prayer drums), *gasing* (spinning tops), traditional dress, hand-crafted kites and board games such as *congkak* and *pasang*. Traditional customs are explained, too (after birth, a date is placed on the tongue of a newborn and the placenta is either hung from a tree, buried or floated downriver). Next door, the **Archaeology and History Gallery** (Gallery 5) provides a thorough introduction to the history of the region from Neolithic times.

A staircase leads down the hill from the back of the Brunei Museum to the **Malay Technology Museum**, where a series of dioramas explain the development of fishing techniques, boatmaking, stilt house construction, metalwork and *songkok* (hats worn by Muslim men) weaving. The top floor includes examples of indigenous dwellings (from the Murut, Kedayan and Dusun tribes), along with tools such as blowpipes and fishing traps.

Along the road between the museum and the centre of town, look out for the tombs of two of Brunei's greatest sultans. **Sultan Syarif Ali** (1426-1432) was the founder of Islamic rule in Brunei, while **Sultan Bolkiah** (1485-1524) presided over the 'golden age' of Brunei, conquering Sulu and the Philippines.

Bubongan Dua Belas
ⓘ *Jl Residency, 1 km east of the centre, Sat-Thu 0900-1630, Fri 0900-1130 and 1430-1630, free.*
Bubongan Dua Belas, which means Twelve Roofs, served as the British Residency until Brunei's Independence in 1984. It was built on the side of a hill overlooking Kampong Ayer in 1906 and is one of Brunei's oldest surviving buildings, with traditional wood shingle roofing and hardwood floors. The building now hosts a small Relationship Exhibition, celebrating the ties between Brunei and the UK. There are charts and maps of the Kampong Ayer area dating from the time of the first British contact in 1764. There is also a fascinating report on Brunei, penned by Acting Consul Stewart McArthur, which led to the appointment of the first British Resident in 1904. He describes the "strange and picturesque" ceremony of the *mengalai padi* harvest festival: "Everyone was feasting and I regret to say that, when I left, nearly everyone was overcome by *borak*, an extremely nauseous drink made locally from *padi* and of which I was forced to partake."

Arts and Handicraft Centre
ⓘ *Jl Residency, Sat-Thu 0745-1215 and 1330-1615, free.*
The Arts and Handicraft Centre was established as a means of preserving traditional skills, such as weaving, brass casting and *keris* making. The centre is focused more on workshops for young Bruneians than attracting tourists, though there is a handicraft shop selling hand-crafted jewellery, basketry, *keris* (ceremonial daggers), *songket* (traditional fabric woven with gold thread), *songkok* (hats worn by Muslim men) and other gifts.

Round the other side of the handicraft centre, past one of the most enormous strangler figs you're ever likely to see, is a small **art gallery** ⓘ *Sat-Thu 0830-1630, Fri 0830-1130 and 1400-1630,* with exhibits by local artists.

Royal Regalia Museum

ⓘ Jl Sultan, Sat-Thu 0900-1630, Fri 1430-1630, free.

Dedicated almost exclusively to the present sultan's life, this is the flashiest of all Brunei's museums, set in an extravagant domed building in the centre of town. Bring an extra top – the main galleries are air conditioned to fridge temperatures – and try not to take too much notice of the guards, who are armed to the hilt, each with truncheon, dagger and gun.

The museum's opening in 1992 coincided with the sultan's Silver Jubilee celebrations, and many of the exhibits relate to this event. The Royal Chariot – an enormous gold-winged thing that looks like a movie prop – is the largest exhibit, while the strangest is probably the creepy golden hand and forearm, used to support the chin of the sultan during the coronation. There are hundreds of photos, too, and a mass of ceremonial costumes, armoury and other regalia items. The **Constitutional Gallery** charts Brunei's recent history.

Next door is the **Brunei History Centre** ⓘ Sat-Thu 0745-1215 and 1330-1630, free, which serves as a centre of research for documenting the history and genealogy of the royal family. The centre is open to the public, but there's not much to see.

The enormous building across the road is the **Lapau Di Raja (Royal Ceremonial Hall)**, site of the 1968 coronation ceremony. The hall is closed to the public.

Parks and green spaces

For the best vantage point of Bandar and Kampong Ayer, head for the **Bukit Subok Recreational Park**, which rises steeply off Jalan Residency. The entrance to the park is just before Bubongan Dua Belas. A boardwalk loops through the forest between a series of viewing towers. The going is steep, but worth visiting during the middle part of the day.

The **Tasek Recreational Park** is a more sedate option, with a picnic area, small waterfall and reservoir. It is situated about 1 km north of the centre. To get there, head north along Jalan Tasek Lama and turn right opposite the Sultan Omar Ali Saifuddien College. From the park gates, it's another 500 m or so to the waterfall.

Bandar's suburbs ⬤❼ ▸▸ pp52-58.

The increasingly busy suburbs of Bandar lie a few kilometres to the northwest of the centre, across Edinburgh Bridge. **Gadong** is the commercial centre and primary suburb of Bandar Seri Begawan. It's not pretty on the eyes in the way that Bandar is (Gadong is a traffic-clogged grid of modern shophouses and department stores), but this is the modern-day heart and soul of the capital. It is where Bruneians come to shop and to eat, either in local restaurants and international franchises or at the food stalls of the excellent *pasar malam* (night market), which serves up (mainly) Malay food seven days a week. **Kiulap**, a little closer to the city centre, is really an extension of Gadong, with more shops and offices.

Just south of Kiulap is Kampong Kiarong, home to the striking **Kiarong Mosque** ⓘ Sat-Wed 0800-1200, 1400-1500, 1700-1800 and 2000-2130; sometimes closed to the public on Sat. Known officially as Masjid Jame'Asr Hassanal Bolkiah, the mosque was built in 1992 to commemorate the sultan's Silver Jubilee. Though it supplanted Masjid Omar Ali Saifuddien (see above) as Brunei's national mosque, there seem to be mixed opinions as to which is superior. The older mosque conforms more to classical convention and forms the focal point of Bandar itself. The Kiarong Mosque, meanwhile, is bigger and brasher, set in landscaped gardens and immense in size, with a quartet of intricate minarets and 29 gilded cupolas. Around 5 km north of the city centre are the government offices, scattered widely around a leafy grid of streets near Brunei International Airport.

Around Brunei

Bandar Seri Begawan makes the ideal base for forays deeper into Brunei. Most of the sights can be visited on day trips from the capital, either on guided tours or with a hire car. Of Brunei's four districts, Temburong is the least populated and, for many people, the most appealing, thanks to the Ulu Temburong National Park. Each of the remaining districts offers its own diversions, with the interior of Belait providing the most challenging itineraries. ►► *For listings, see pages 52-58.*

Brunei Muara District ●● ►► *pp52-58. Colour map 9, A/B4.*

Brunei Muara is the smallest of Brunei's four districts, with Bandar Seri Begawan at its heart. As well as several notable sights on the outskirts of Bandar, there are a few minor sights further afield, including sandy beaches, forest reserves and a theme park.

Istana Nurul Iman

Official residence of the sultan, the Istana Nurul Iman is situated several kilometres upriver from the capital, its twin gold cupolas clearly visible from the river. It is the largest residential palace in the world and must surely count as one of the most extravagant, too. Beneath the curving Minangkabau-style roofs lie a staggering 1778 rooms (including 257 toilets), which makes the Istana bigger than the Vatican and on a par with Versailles. The banquet hall seats 5000 and there's an underground car park to house the sultan's extensive collection of cars (which runs into three figures). Needless to say, the palace is not open to the public. For the best views, catch a water taxi from Bandar Seri Begawan. You'll pass by the royal jetty, where sultan's guests (including Queen Elizabeth II on her last visit) are welcomed.

Alternatively, make your way to the **Taman Persiaran Damuan**, a kilometre-long park which runs along the riverside just beyond the palace. Within the park are sculptures from each of the 10 ASEAN nations.

If you're lucky, and you visit the park at dusk, you may spot proboscis monkeys on **Pulau Ranggu**, the small island opposite the park. Proboscis monkeys, an endangered species endemic to Borneo. To guarantee sightings, take a proboscis tour by *tambang* along the Sungai Damuan tributary; it's one of the highlights of a trip to Brunei for any nature enthusiast. Look out for monkeys crossing the river (they swim doggy style, their bulbous noses raised above the water like snorkels). ►► *See Activities and tours, page 56.*

Jerudong Park Playground

ⓘ *Kampong Jerudong (along the Muara–Tutong highway northwest of Bandar Seri Begawan), Wed-Sat 1700-2400, Sat 1700-0200, Sun 1600-2400, B$15, B$5 children.*

This peculiar theme park opened in 1994 to coincide with the sultan's 48th birthday. By Western standards, it's nothing special, although there are plenty of rides, including a decent rollercoaster and an excellent log ride (expect to get wet). Today it has a slightly jaded feel and, thanks to Brunei's tiny population, it is probably the quietest theme park in the world – on some days you'll have the park more or less to yourself. Beware, many of the rides are often out of action (ask before handing over the entry fee).

Just along the coast from Jerudong Park is the extravagant **Empire Hotel & Country Club** (see page 53), which is worth a look for its towering, gold-adorned atrium; at 80 m it is said to be the tallest in the world. Both hotel and theme park were built by Prince Jefri, brother to the sultan and an endless source of scandal.

Muara and around

At Brunei's northeast tip is the port of Muara, a nondescript place with a single sleepy grid of shophouses and nothing much to draw visitors. There are several nearby beaches that are pleasant enough, if you can bear the heat. Pantai Muara is a 4-km stretch of sand north of Muara, with a kids' playground and picnic shelters among the casuarinas, while to the south, at the end of a road lined with mansions, is a sandy spit known as Pantai Serasa, home to a fleet of traditional fishing boats and the Serasa Watersports Complex.

There are two forest reserves worth visiting along the main Muara–Tutong highway, which runs beside Brunei's north-facing coastline. **Bukit Shahbandar Reserve** (just east of Kampong Jerudong) is a popular spot with joggers and cyclists, with narrow roads and trails running up and down seven hills. At the highest point, there's a wooden observation tower. The **Hutan Berakas Forest Reserve** (directly north of the airport) is wilder, with trails weaving through casuarina forests and *kerangas* (heath forest), the favoured habitat of carnivorous pitcher plants. There are paved trails here, a popular picnic area and a lovely long beach used by Bruneians for swimming.

Out in Brunei Bay itself is **Pulau Selirong**, an uninhabited island covered in mangrove forest. The island has recently been designated a forest reserve and 2 km of elevated walkways have been installed. Monitor lizards, crabs, mud skippers and wading birds can be viewed, along with the occasional mangrove snake and saltwater crocodile. Tours can be arranged with many of the Bandar-based tour operators (see page 56).

Temburong District ● ▸▸ *pp52-58. Colour map 9, B4.*

Temburong is the forested finger of land set adrift from the rest of Brunei by the Malaysian district of Limbang, which was snatched from Brunei's control in 1890 by Raja Brooke of Sarawak. The population of Temburong is barely 10,000, with Malays living alongside a scattered population of Iban, Murut and Kadazan tribespeople. The whole district has a village atmosphere; wherever you go in Temburong, it seems that everybody knows one another.

Speedboats for Temburong leave regularly from the jetty on Jalan Residency in Bandar Seri Begawan. They roar downriver, passing briefly into Brunei Bay, before weaving through the mangrove channels as far as Bangar, Temburong's main town. The journey itself is an adventure: look out for proboscis monkeys swimming across the narrow channels.

Bangar (not to be confused with Bandar) is a quiet place with a single row of shophouses and a sultry, sleepy air. There's a mosque, a few government offices, a resthouse and a few coffee shops for passing the time of day, otherwise there's no particular reason to linger. Most people carry straight on in the direction of the Ulu Temburong National Park, the principal attraction for visitors to the district.

Ulu Temburong National Park

① *Entry B$5. Obtain an entry permit in advance from the Forestry Department Ministry of Industry and Primary Resources, Bandar Seri Begawan BB3910, T238 1687, forestrybrunei@hotmail.com.*
The 50,000-ha Ulu Temburong National Park is the jewel in the crown of Brunei's eco-tourism push. It sits in the remote southern portion of Temburong, in the heart of the **Batu Apoi Forest Reserve**. The region has never been settled or logged, so there are no roads, and access to the park is by *temuai* (traditional longboat). Getting there is half the fun; the journey begins at Bandar Seri Begawan with a ride in a 'flying coffin', a wooden speedboat so called because of its shape (though, when you see the speed with which these things hurtle through the mangroves, you may suspect the name is fitting for other reasons). The

speedboat passes briefly into the Malaysian territory of Limbang, before turning into the mouth of the Temburong and speeding upriver as far as Bangar. A short car journey follows, passing a series of picturesque kampongs and longhouses, before the final leg by longboat from Batang Duri to the Park HQ, with towering dipterocarps climbing the river banks.

Despite being relatively unknown, Ulu Temburong compares favourably with the jungle reserves of neighbouring Malaysia. Work carried out at the **Belalong Rainforest Field Studies Centre** confirms that many new species have been found here; one scientist is reported to have identified more than 400 separate species of beetle on a single tree. The main attraction for visitors, however, is the towering canopy walkway, which stands 50 m tall and provides unbeatable views of the forest. The fact that few people visit is also part of the appeal – the park remains virtually unscathed by tourism, despite being easily accessible. There can't be many places in the world where you can leave the city mid-morning, have a picnic lunch deep in pristine rainforest and be back at your hotel by late afternoon. Most people use one of the Bandar-based tour operators (see page 56), who make all travel arrangements for you and provide guides and entry permits (with everything paid upfront).

If you prefer to visit independently, Bangar-bound speedboats leave from the jetty on Jalan Residency in Bandar Seri Begawan (every 30 minutes 0745-1600; 45 minutes journey time; B$6 one way). From the Bangar jetty, there are taxis to take visitors south along a sealed road to **Batang Duri**, a small settlement on the banks of Sungai Temburong. From here, visitors need to charter a longboat for the final leg of the journey upriver to the Park HQ (1½ hours, B$50-60 per boat). During the dry season (July and August) water levels can be low and passengers may have to get out and help push the boat.

At Park HQ, visitors need to sign a register and pay the entry fee before heading into the park proper. There's a small information centre with displays and a series of chalets and dormitories, linked by plankwalks. ►► *See Sleeping, page 53.*

Flora and fauna Borneo's rainforests are among the most biodiverse places on Earth and Ulu Temburong is no exception. More species of tree can be found in a single hectare here than in the entirety of North America. Animal life is abundant too, though hard to spot. Some of the more conspicuous creatures include flying lizards, Wallace's flying frog, pygmy squirrels, wild boar, mousedeer, gibbons (more often heard than seen), various species of hornbill (the biggest being the majestic rhinoceros hornbill, frequently seen gliding across the river) and of course myriad weird and wonderful insects, from the peculiar lantern beetle to the Rajah Brooke birdwing butterfly. The canopy walkway provides the opportunity to look directly down upon the jungle canopy, home to the greatest density of life. Notice the abundance of epiphytes, plants that survive at this height by clinging on to host trees. From the walkway, it is sometimes possible to see tiger orchids, one of the largest of their species.

Treks With 7 km of wooden walkways, few visitors stray off the main trail, though there is unlimited scope for serious trekking (either using Park HQ as a base, or camping in the forest). The terrain here is steep and rugged and not suited to those without a moderate level of fitness. Wherever you go, take plenty of water. Falling trees and landslides often lay waste to sections of the boardwalk, making it unlikely that the whole trail will be open at any one time.

The boardwalk begins at Park HQ and leads across Sungai Temburong via a footbridge to the foot of a towering hill, upon which stands the canopy walkway. The climb is steep and sweaty, with almost 1000 steps. Once you've conquered the hill, reaching the canopy walkway itself is no easy matter either; the walkway is suspended in sections between 50-m-tall aluminium towers built around a seemingly endless series of step ladders. The views from the top are truly magnificent, though vertigo sufferers will find it living hell. Standing on the walkway, above the jungle canopy, on top of a hill, you can see for many miles around, with the confluence of Sungai Temburong and Sungai Belalong at your feet. Gaze for long enough and you'll probably spot the black and white backs of hornbills as they glide from tree to tree along the riverbank.

From the walkway, the trail continues for several kilometres along a steeply descending boardwalk in the direction of a second suspension bridge. The boardwalk ends at Sungai Apan, a narrow stream. By following the course of the stream upriver, you soon come to a picturesque waterfall, with a plunge pool deep enough for swimming (outside dry season). A steep trail traverses the hillside with the aid of ropes to a second waterfall.

Most people make their way back to Park HQ by longboat from the confluence of Sungai Apan and Sungai Temburong (rather than retracing their steps along the boardwalk). You may cross tracks with local Iban, who fish this stretch of the river with traps and nets. They'll probably wave you over and offer you a swig of grog – rice wine, or more likely, Bacardi rum.

Those looking for the chance to explore largely uncharted rainforest may be interested in tackling the strenuous week-long trek to the summit of **Bukit Pagon** (1843 m), which is situated near the border with Sarawak in the southernmost corner of Temburong. Contact the tourist office, or one of the Bandar-based tour operators, for help with arrangements.

Elsewhere in Temburong

If time is very limited, you may consider skipping Ulu Temburong and heading instead for the **Peradayan Forest Reserve**, which is just 20 minutes east of Bangar by road (taxis cost around B$15 one-way). Within the reserve is a small forest recreation park with picnic tables and trails, one of which climbs to the summit of **Bukit Patoi** (310 m), passing caves along the way. The summit of the hill is a bare patch of stone, allowing wide views across the forest north to Brunei Bay and east to Sarawak. A tougher and less distinct trail continues from here to the summit of **Bukit Peradayan** (410 m).

Though the majority of Temburong's indigenous inhabitants have moved into detached homes, plenty still live in longhouses. In theory, unannounced visits are welcome but some have formal arrangements with tour operators for receiving guests. The largest is a 16-door Iban longhouse (home to 16 families) situated along the road to Batang Duri, at **Kampong Sembiling**. Guides will stop off here, allowing visitors to meet the inhabitants and try a glass of *tuak* (rice wine). If it's daytime, there won't be many people around, but you'll get a chance to see inside a modern Iban longhouse, complete with satellite TV and parking spaces for cars. Another longhouse offering homestays is the curiously named five-door **Amo C**, just north of **Batang Duri** itself. Overnight guests are set up with mattresses on the *ruai* (communal veranda) and guided treks along hunting trails can be arranged.

Tutong District ●○ ▸▸ pp52-58. Colour map 9, B4.

The central district of Tutong is wedged between Belait District to the west and Limbang (Malaysia) to the east, following the flood plain of Sungai Tutong. Recent growth in agriculture has seen the introduction of small-scale plantations in areas of Tutong, though most of the district is sparsely populated and covered by rainforest.

The coastal highway passes by the district capital, **Tutong**, a small and pleasant town on the banks of the river. There's nothing much for the visitor to do here, other than stop by the small wet market or the nearby *tamu* (the regional open-air market, held every Thursday afternoon through to Friday morning). The *tamu* draws Tutong's indigenous inhabitants

(Kedayan, Dusun and Iban tribespeople) who come down from the interior to sell their produce. It is mainly a food market, though there are handicrafts on sale, too. A kilometre to the north of Tutong is the **Taman Rekreasi Sungai Basong**, a small recreation park with a pond, a stream and picnic tables. Meanwhile, just west of town is **Pantai Seri Kenangan** (Unforgettable Beach), a largely forgettable spit of sand dividing Sungai Tutong from the sea. Still, the beach is kept clean and the sea here is calm. Every July a local festival is held on the beach, with Malay games such as top spinning and kite flying.

The road continues along the spit as far as **Kampong Kuala Tutong**, a sleepy place set among coconut palms. There's a small boatyard here called Marine Yard, where river trips can sometimes be organized. The arrangement is pretty informal, and you'll have to just turn up and hope there's someone around. The boat weaves upriver through mangrove-lined swampland, past Dusun and Malay kampongs. Look out for monkeys and estuarine crocodiles, which can sometimes be seen basking on the sandbanks. River tours along Sungai Tutong can be arranged through Ilufah Leisure Tours (see page 56).

Tasek Merimbun

Tasek Merimbun is a beautiful and remote spot rich in wildlife and popular as a weekend escape. The lake and its environs are home to Dusun tribespeople, who for many centuries took advantage of the abundance of fish and wildlife. Now that the lake has been set aside as a nature reserve only a handful of Dusun remain. The setting is magnificent: an S-shaped, peat-black body of water surrounded by dense jungle. In the centre of the lake is tiny island, accessible by boardwalk. The **Tasek Merimbun Heritage Park** encompasses the lake, plus wetlands, peat-swamp forest and lowland dipterocarp rainforest. The area is home to a great diversity of wildlife, including crocodile and clouded leopard (Borneo's biggest cat). The most important scientific discovery has been the white-collared fruit bat, which appears to be unique to Tasek Merimbun.

On the banks of the lake is a small visitor centre with a few fish tanks, plus chalets for accommodation. Local Dusun have kayaks for rent. Opposite the chalets is a 2-km botanical trail through the rainforest. Guides can be hired for longer treks in the area.

There is no public transport to Tasek Merimbun, Brunei's largest lake. If you've rented a car, head west from Bandar Seri Begawan on the old Tutong Road (rather than the coastal highway). At Mile 18, take the left fork for Lamunin. Beyond Kampong Lamunin itself, follow signs for Tasek Merimbun. The journey takes up to 1½ hours.

Belait District ● ›› pp52-58. Colour map 9, B3/4.

Belait wears two faces. On the one hand it is oil country, the driving force behind Brunei's economy and home to a large population of British and Dutch expats. On the other, it is the best example of 'old' Brunei – Brunei before oil.

When oil was first discovered at Seria in 1929, the whole region was largely uninhabited, the lowlands dominated by peat swamps, mangroves and rainforest, with indigenous Iban and Dusun tribespeople sticking largely to the valley of Sungai Belait. Though the coastal strip has developed beyond recognition, the interior remains largely unscathed.

Aside from Temburong, Belait District is the best place to explore Brunei's rainforest and visit indigenous longhouses. However, the tourism infrastructure remains underdeveloped so few people visit (apart from British Army recruits undergoing a round of brutal jungle training). The interior of Belait is earmarked as an important ecotourism destination for the future, and tour operators are beginning to put together itineraries into the region.

Seria

Seria is a surreal place. Once open swampland, Seria is now dominated by level fields full of lawn-mowing tractors, egrets and nodding donkeys – small land-based oil wells that nod back and forth as they pump oil to the surface. There is no real centre of town to speak of; row upon row of neat bungalows line the roads – home, presumably to Chinese and expat oil workers, whose wives ride about town in land cruisers. It is a strange, functional place with an odd mix of inhabitants that includes indigenous tribespeople and a garrison of Gurkhas.

The town straggles along the coastal strip between Seria and Kuala Belait, which serves as the centre of Brunei's oil production. On the edge of Seria is the **Billionth Barrel Monument**, commemorating the obscene productivity of Brunei's first oil field. For those who want to delve deeper into the history and technicalities of oil production, there is the **Oil & Gas Discovery Centre** (OGDC) ① *F20 Seria, T337 7200; Tue-Thu 0900-1700, Fri 1000-1200 and 1400-1800, Sat-Sun 1000-1800; B$5*, set in a building that resembles an oil drum. It's a fun place for kids, with a gyroscope, a bed of nails and a fish pond.

Kuala Belait

Though it all started at Seria, Kuala Belait (known locally as KB) is the district's principal town. It also serves as the border town with nearby Sarawak. Like Seria, Kuala Belait is a purely functional place which has developed over time to serve the needs of the oil workers. The centre of town comprises a large grid of streets with Chinese shophouses alongside multinational outlets such as the **Body Shop** and KFC.

Kuala Belait sits on the east bank of the Sungai Belait and it's possible to hire a boat upriver as far as Kuala Balai (see below). Boats leave from behind the market building on Jalan Pasar, at the southern end of Jalan McKerron (sometimes spelt Mackeron).

Belait interior

Kuala Balai

Before the oil boom, the main settlement in this part of Brunei was the riverine village of Kuala Balai, situated about an hour upriver from Kuala Belait. Between 1930 and 1980 the population slowly dwindled, until the village virtually ceased to exist. Today just a handful of permanent inhabitants remain.

The people from these parts are known as the Belait Malays and have a lot in common with the Melanau people of coastal Sarawak, including their Muslim faith, their traditional reliance on sago processing and their stilted longhouses. Despite the fact that Kuala Balai is now little more than a ghost town, it is possible to get a sense of how things once looked; the old longhouse, which deteriorated many years ago, has been rebuilt as part of a **Raleigh International** project. There are still one or two old sago processors around, though they use light machinery now, rather than trampling the sago scrapings underfoot, as was once the way. Just downriver from the longhouse is a small wooden box on stilts by the riverside. Inside are 20 human skulls, victims of headhunters from as long ago as the 17th century.

As elsewhere in Belait District, tourism hasn't yet taken off and few people visit the longhouse, but there are plans to market Kuala Balai more actively as a tourist destination.

Jalan Labi

The other route into the interior of Belait is via Jalan Labi, a decent road which turns south off the coastal highway at Kampong Lumut, near the border with Tutong District. A little way along the road is Brunei's oldest forest reserve, the **Sungai Liang Forest Reserve**, with ponds, picnic shelters and various well-maintained paths into the surrounding forest. One climbs a steep hill as far as a treehouse (closed for renovation at the time of writing). Close by is the **Forestry Department** building, set back from the road, with a small Palmetum leading up to the offices. There's a tiny forestry museum here, too – the **Muzium Perhutanan** ① *Mon-Thu and Sat 0800-1215 and 1330-1630*, with two rooms of displays that aren't worth going out of your way for.

The Labi road continues south through undulating rainforest as far as the village of Kampong Labi itself, passing another forest reserve along the way, the **Labi Hills Forest Reserve**. Within its boundaries is the 270-ha **Luagan Lalak Recreation Park**, covering an area of alluvial swampland, which floods to become a lake during the monsoon. The lake (or swamp, depending on the season) is accessible via a 200-m-long boardwalk.

Kampong Labi, some 40 km south of the coastal highway, is a small settlement that has served for years as a base for speculative (and unsuccessful) oil drilling in the surrounding hills. Tropical fruits, such as rambutan, durian, cempedak and jackfruit, are grown in the area. Beyond Labi, the road turns into a dirt track which serves as an access route to a number of Iban longhouses. The largest of these is the 12-door **Rumah Panjang Mendaram Besar**, home to 100 or so people. Like most of the longhouses in Brunei, this one has piped water and electricity, with the men commuting to the towns to work for either **Shell** or the government. A nearby trail leads to the **Wasai Mendaram**, a large waterfall with plunge pool for bathing.

At the end of the 12-km track is **Rumah Panjang Teraja**. The inhabitants of this six-door longhouse cultivate paddy, rear pigs and chickens, and grow their own fruit and vegetables. From the longhouse, a well-marked trail leads to the summit of Bukit Teraja, from where there are magnificent views as far as Gunung Mulu (see page 673) in Sarawak. Walking the trail to the summit takes about 1½ hours. Reported wildlife sightings along the way include orang-utans, Borneo bearded pigs, barking deer, macaques and hornbills.

Ulu Belait

Further longhouses can be found deep in the interior, along the upper reaches of Sungai Belait. These are accessible by longboat from Kampong Sungai Mau, which is situated halfway along the Jalan Labi. Of course, it is possible to begin the journey in Kuala Belait, passing Kuala Balai along the way, but this route takes many hours.

The journey upriver into Ulu Belait (Upriver Belait) depends very much on the level of the river; in the dry season its upper reaches are barely navigable. Kampong Sukang, some two hours from Kampong Sungai Mau by longboat, is a community of Dusun and Punan tribespeople, with two longhouses and a hamlet of family homes. The Punan are nomadic hunter-gatherers by tradition, though the inhabitants of Kampong Sukang were persuaded to settle here back in the 1970s. They now farm paddy rather than relying on the old staple diet of wild sago, but they still hunt in the traditional manner using blowpipes and poison darts.

If you're feeling even more intrepid, there is another hamlet of longhouses located at **Kampong Melilas**, located one to three hours – depending on the water level – upriver from Kampong Sukang. These are home to Iban people and, like the Labi longhouses, they are upgraded versions of the traditional longhouse, although this community supports a thriving cottage industry in traditional basketry and weaving. Beyond Kampong Melilas, there are hot springs and plenty of waterfalls; a guide can be arranged at the village.

Brunei listings

Sleeping

Bandar Seri Begawan *p39, map p40*
Large discounts are often available if you book in advance through hotel websites.
L Sheraton Utama, Jl Tasek Lama, T224 4272, www.sheraton.com. Bandar's best hotel, with 142 large comfortable rooms, each with internet, pool, 2 restaurants, health club with spa treatments and full business facilities. The centre of Bandar is within walking distance.
A Brunei, 95 Jl Pemancha, T224 2372, www.bruneihotel.com.bn. The most central of Bandar's hotels, next to the Tamu Sungai Kianggeh (market). The 63 rooms are spacious, with satellite TV, a/c and minibar. Restaurant and function room.
B Jubilee Plaza, Jubilee Plaza, Jl Kampong Kianggeh, T222 8070, jubilee@brunet.bn. Situated off a side road, 10 mins' walk from the waterfront, this is a functional place offering decent-sized (if plain) rooms with TV, minibar and en-suite bathrooms. Breakfast and airport transfers are included.
B Terrace, Jl Tasek Lama, 1 km from the waterfront, T224 3554, www.terracebrunei.com. 80 a/c, en suite rooms, with TV, kettle and safe. They're a touch worn, but nevertheless good value for money. There's a pleasant small outdoor pool, a restaurant and a karaoke lounge (which can get noisy), all with Wi-Fi.
C KH Soon Rest House, 140 Jl Pemancha, T222 2052, www.khsoon-resthouse.tripod.com. Airy functional hotel-style rooms a few mins' stroll from the Padang and Mosque. Clean, light and excellent value given the location. Loads of night time eating options nearby.

D Pusat Belia, Jl Sungai Kianggeh, T222 3936, jbsbelia@brunet.bn. Brunei's youth hostel, 5 mins' walk from the waterfront, with clean 4-bed dorms and a pool.

Bandar's suburbs *p44*
L The Centrepoint, Abdul Razak Complex, Gadong BE3519, T243 0430, www.arhbrunei.com. This 220-room hotel matches the **Sheraton** for luxury (and beats it for marble content), though it is situated several kilometres outside the city centre in the suburb of Gadong (Bandar's main shopping district). Special discounts can halve rates. Executive rooms come with kitchenettes. 24-hr business centre, but no pool or gym.
AL Orchid Garden Hotel, Lot 31954, Simpang 9, Kampong Anggerek Desa, Jl Berakas BB3713, T233 5544, www.orchidgardenbrunei.com. A 4-star hotel next to the National Stadium (between the airport and the government complex), a few kilometres from Bandar centre. Comfortable rooms with high-speed internet, 2 restaurants, a pool and spa. This is the closest hotel to the airport, so is handy for stopovers.
AL Riverview Hotel, Km 1, Jl Gadong, BS8670, T223 8238, rivview@brunet.bn. Set on its own near the suburb of Gadong, halfway between downtown Bandar and the airport. Rooms are big, if uninspiring. Pool, sauna and jacuzzi.
B Grand City, Lot 25115, Block G, Kampong Pengkalan Gadong, BE3719, T245 2188, grandcity@brunet.bn. A good mid-range option in the suburbs. Rooms have a/c, tea and coffee facilities, TV and phone. Price includes airport transfer.
B Traders Inn, halfway between the airport and the centre of BSB, in the new Beribi Commercial Area and just off Jl Gadong, T244 28208. Within easy walking distance of shops, banking and internet facilities of the Gadong. This superb hotel is good value, basic, comfortable. Wi-Fi in rooms.
C Voctech International House, Jl Pasar Baharu, Gadong BE1318, T244 7992, voctech@brunet.bn. A few kilometres from

Bandar centre. Spacious, clean, functional rooms, this is another good budget option, not least because it is within walking distance of the excellent *pasar malam* night market, where you can get great, cheap local food. All rooms have TV and fridge.

Brunei Muara District p45

LL Empire Hotel & Country Club, Jerudong BG3122, T241 8888, www.theempire hotel.com. Brunei's only beach resort and a monument to the extravagance of the sultan's brother, Prince Jefri. No expense was spared in the construction of this 6-star hotel, which centres around an 80-m-high, marble-pillared atrium. The 400-plus rooms all have large balconies and huge marble-clad bathrooms, with walk-in showers and vast bath tubs. The Presidential Suite covers more than 650 sq m and has its own lavish indoor pool, with attached sauna, steam room and jacuzzi. With the click of a button, a cinema screen descends from the ceiling above the pool. There are antiques aplenty and swathes of gold leaf. 18-hole Jack Nicklaus golf course, sports club, cinema and numerous pools, including a meandering 11,000-sq-m lagoon pool with fake, sandy beach (great for kids). Kids' club, 7 dining outlets, watersports including scuba diving, sailing, jet skiing, kayaking and parasailing. Free shuttle in and out of Bandar Seri Begawan, 4 times daily. Check for special discounts; low occupancy means rooms here are often excellent value.

Temburong District p46

B Ulu Temburong National Park, c/o Tourist Information Centre, General Post Office Building, corner of Jl Sultan and Jl Elizabeth Dua, Bandar Seri Begawan, T222 3734 (Mon-Sat 0800-1200 and 1400-1630). Virtually everyone visits Ulu Temburong on an organized tour, with accommodation pre-arranged for longer stays. If you want to arrange the trip yourself, there is plenty of basic (but clean and modern) chalet accommodation at Park HQ. Book in advance through the Bandar tourist office.

C Government Resthouse, Jl Batang Duri, Bangar, T522 1239. The only place to stay in Bangar, situated a short walk from the jetty along the road to Batang Duri. Simple, functional rooms, plus a few chalets for B$80.

D Longhouses. Visitors to Temburong District can stay at various longhouses, either informally or as part of an organized tour. Those most commonly visited are **Amo C** and the main longhouse at **Kampong Sembiling**, both along the Batang Duri road. Amo C longhouse has an informal homestay arrangement with guests: for a small amount of money (no more than B$10), they will feed you and set you up with mattresses on the *ruai* (common veranda). Hospitality is an important part of indigenous culture and, in theory, any longhouse will put you up for the night. In practice, this is only the case with the more traditional or remote longhouses. If you turn up at a longhouse unannounced, be sure to follow the correct etiquette. Always ask the permission of the headman, or Tuai Rumah, before heading inside. Remove shoes before entering a family room (*bilik*), or an area of the *ruai* laid with mats. More often than not, shoes are not worn at all in a longhouse and are left at the entrance to the *ruai*.

Tutong District p48

B Halim Plaza Hotel, Lot No 9003, Kampong Petani, Tutong TA1141, T426 0688, halim plazabrunei.com. Surprisingly attractive and good-value rooms set inside a small shopping centre in Tutong itself. Used mainly by Bruneians on business.

C Researchers' Quarter, Tasek Merimbun Heritage Park, c/o Director of Brunei Museum, T222 2713, bmdir@bunet.bn. If available, the Researchers' Quarter (a new wooden chalet) at Tasek Merimbun can be used by members of the public. Contact the Brunei Museum.

Belait District p49

AL Riviera Hotel, Lot 106, Jl Sungai, Kuala Belait KA2331, T333 5252. The best hotel in Kuala Belait, on the riverfront in the town centre. 30 rooms and suites, all modern in design and in great nick. All rooms feature tea- and coffee-making facilities, satellite TV, minibar, shower and bath. Frequent promotions make this hotel good value.

B Brunei Sentosa Hotel, 92-93 Jl McKerron, PO Box 252, Kuala Belait KA1131, T3334341, www.bruneisentosahotel.com. In the heart of town. A step down from the **Riviera**, but decent nonetheless, with added features such as in-room broadband access. Rooms are spacious, though some are a little dingy.

● Eating

The night market (*pasar malam*) in the suburb of **Gadong** is probably the best place to sample local fare. Every evening from 1700, hundreds of stalls turn out endless varieties of satay, curries, grilled meats and Malay coconut-based sweets. The same sort of food is available on a smaller scale at the **Tamu Kianggeh** (open-air market) in downtown Bandar.

Also worth trying are the foodstalls on the waterfront near the Temburong jetty for *nasi campur* and *teh tarik*. The **Padian Foodcourt** (1st floor, Yayasan Complex; daily 0900-2200) is great for cheap local food and drink, as well as Thai and Indonesian staples. There are also larger food courts in **Gadong**, including one on the top floor of The Mall, which serves the full range of Asian cuisines – try Malay *nasi lemak* and beef *rendang*.

You'll find yourself drinking vast amounts of fruit juice in Brunei (it's served in place of alcohol). Obviously, there is no bar scene here; the closest you get are the mocktail lounges in the top hotels. Still, if you have brought in your allowance of alcohol (and declared it at customs), top-end restaurants will often allow you to drink it with your meal.

Restaurants come and go with great frequency in Brunei. A selection of the current favourites is listed below.

Bandar Seri Begawan *p39, map p40*
Zaika, G24, Block C, Yayasan Complex, T223 0817. Daily 1130-1430, 1800-2000.

Excellent North Indian cuisine in pleasing wood-panelled surroundings (*zaika* means fine dining in Urdu). Try tandoori chicken or lamb (straight from an authentic oven) and Kashmiri *rogan josh*. Classical Indian lamps hang overhead, old Indian paintings adorn the walls, and gentle Indian music tinkles in the background. The menu is vast (12 pages).

Ahan Thai, ground floor, Jubilee Plaza, Jl Kampong Kianggeh, T223 9599. Daily 0700-2400. A fast turnover of Thai food with all the usual favourites, including *tom yam* soup, chicken with cashew nuts, and chilli squid.

De Royale Café, Jl Sultan, 2nd floor, Wisma Setia, T222 0257. Good coffees and cakes, plus spicy Thai meals, and free hotel/home delivery within the town centre.

Hua Hua, 48 Jl Sultan, T222 5396. Daily 0700-2100. An attractive-looking Chinese restaurant with a wide variety of well-priced dishes, including excellent dim sum; in the heart of town.

Mawar Coffee Garden, 95 Jl Pacancha, part of **Brunei Hotel**. Solid and pleasant city coffee shop with good juices and snacks.

RMS Portview Seafood, Jl MacArthur (opposite Yayasan Complex), T223 1466. Daily 1000-2300. Set right on the riverfront. Cheaper café downstairs (Malay, Chinese and Western) and a more formal restaurant upstairs serving Thai, Japanese and Chinese cuisine. Excellent steamboats.

CA Mohamed, Unit 202, Yayasan Complex, T2232999. Daily 0900-2200. Inexpensive Malay and Indian staples.

Isma Jaya, 27 Jl Sultan, T222 0229. Daily 0700-2100. A great place for Indian Muslim food, such as *roti canai*, as well as good biryani and curries.

Popular, Unit 5, ground floor, Norain Complex, T222 1375. Daily 0800-2200. Simple restaurant with plastic chairs serving North and South Indian cuisine: chicken masala, *roti kosong*, naan, dosa, chapati. All delicious.

Seri Indah, Jl MacArthur, T224 3567. A simple *mamak* (Indian Muslim) restaurant serving delicious *roti kosong* and *teh tarik*. Situated opposite the waterfront wet market.

Bandar's suburbs *p44*

Fratini's, No 1, Centrepoint Foodcourt, Abdul Razak Complex, Gadong, T245 1300. Daily 1000-2300. An Italian restaurant next door to the **Centrepoint Hotel**, with a big range of pizza and pasta dishes (gnocchi, too), along with steaks and seafood.

I-Lotus, 28 Spg 12-26, Perumahan Rakyat Jati, Rimba Gadong (just past Tungku Link), T242 2466. Daily 1030-1430 and 1800-2400. Serves a wide range of Chinese and Thai dishes, with frequent steamboat promotions. Specialities include coconut prawn curry and Nyonya steamed fish. Very good reputation.

Escapade Sushi, Unit 4-5, Block C, Abdul Raza Complex (opposite **Centrepoint Hotel**), Gadong, T244 3012. Sushi on a conveyor belt.

Pondok Sari Wangi, Unit 12-13, Abdul Razak Complex, Gadong, T244 5045. Daily 1000-2200. Popular Indonesian restaurant serving staples such as *crab masak* and *ikan bakar* (barbecued fish/seafood).

Teo Poi Hoon, 17-18 ground floor, Bang Hg Awang, Kiulap, T223 3938. Sat-Thu 0800-2200, Fri 0800-2300. Traditional Taiwanese and Cantonese cuisine, with specialities like *guisei* bean curd rice and *mamie* chicken. Very popular at lunchtime.

Le Taj, 2-3, 2nd floor, Seri Kiulap Complex, Kiulap, T223 8996. Daily 0800-2300. Full range of North Indian cuisine. Great lassis.

Brunei Muara District *p45*

Li Gong, Empire Hotel & Country Club, Jerudong BG3122, T241 8888 ext 7329. Tue-Thu and Sun 1830-2230, Fri-Sat 1100-1500 and 1830-2230. Excellent Chinese cuisine, set in a pavilion surrounded by koi ponds. The menu covers specialities from every province in China. There's an all-you-can-eat buffet on Wed and steamboat on Thu.

Spaghettini, Empire Hotel & Country Club, Jerudong BG3122, T241 8888, ext 7368. Daily 1830-2300, also Mon and Wed 1130-1430. Mimics an Italian trattoria, with its own authentic, wood-fired oven and dough-flinging chefs. Perched at the top of the towering atrium at the **Empire Hotel**.

☻ Festivals and events

Bandar Seri Begawan *p39, map p40*
Jan-Feb Chinese New Year. A 2-week celebration beginning with a family reunion dinner on New Year's Eve.
23 Feb National Day Celebrations. Celebration of Independence at the Hassanal Bolkiah National Stadium.
Mar-Apr The Prophet's Birthday. As well as religious functions, there's a procession through the streets of Bandar Seri Begawan.
31 May   Royal Brunei Armed Forces Day. Celebrates the creation of the Royal Brunei Armed Forces, with military parades.
15 Jul The Sultan's Birthday. One of the biggest events in the national calendar and the only time when the grounds of the Istana Nural Iman are open to the public. Royal address and an investiture ceremony.
Sep-Oct Ramadan. The holy month, when Muslims abstain from eating and drinking between dawn and dusk. During fasting hours it is considered ill-mannered to eat, drink or smoke openly in public. The end of Ramadan is marked by the **Hari Raya Puasa** celebration, when families gather for a feast.

☻ Entertainment

Bandar Seri Begawan *p39, map p40*
Brunei is a dry country and Bandar Seri Begawan is virtually deserted in the evening, except for the suburb of Gadong with its lively *pasar malam*. This is open until late and busy with Bruneians buying the local food on sale.

In the top hotels, you can sip mocktails in mock bars and listen to sedate local bands. The Jerudong theme park is about as lively as it gets when it comes to entertainment and even that is deadly quiet by Western standards.

Around Brunei *p45*
Stumble across a remote longhouse, and you enter another world. Guests are entertained with gusto and will usually be offered traditional rice wine (*tuak* in Iban), a drink so

ingrained in indigenous heritage that the sultan has exempted it from the ban on alcohol. But in the towns of Brunei, entertainment is something that happens – if at all – behind closed doors.

O Shopping

Bandar Seri Begawan *p39, map p40*
Brunei's main shopping district is centred on the suburb of **Gadong**, 4 km from the centre. The principal shopping malls here are **Gadong Centrepoint** and **The Mall**, both on the main thoroughfare. In **Bandar** itself, shopping is focused on the elegant **Yayasan Complex**, which has everything from small boutiques and restaurants to a supermarket and upmarket department store (**Hua Ho**).

Crafts
Traditional handicrafts include brassware, silverware, *keris* (ornate ceremonial daggers) and a type of *songket* known as *jong sarat* – a traditional cloth, hand woven with gold and silver thread. Bandar's **Arts and Handicraft Centre** (see page 43) sells all these, though the choice is limited. The major shopping malls have gift shops selling Southeast Asian crafts (again, prices are much higher than in Malaysia). The **Sheraton Utama** has upmarket gift and antiques shops.

There are sometimes handicrafts for sale at the **Tamu Kianggeh**, though this is predominantly a food market. **Kampong Ayer** is another place where it is possible to find crafts and antiques (at one time, the water village thrived as a centre for cottage industries, with silversmiths, brass casters, blacksmiths, boat builders and *songket* weavers). Ask the boatmen where to go.

Tutong District *p48*
For indigenous handicrafts that are better priced than those in Bandar Seri Begawan, you could try the weekly *tamu* (open-air market) in **Tutong**, which starts Thu afternoon and finishes late morning on Fri.

▲ Activities and tours

Around Brunei *p45*
Jungle trekking
The best place is the **Ulu Temburong National Park** (see page 46), but there are opportunities in each of Brunei's districts. The easiest (and often the cheapest) way of organizing a trip is through a tour operator, see below.

River trips
No trip to Brunei is complete without a *tambang* ride along the Brunei River (Sungai Brunei). These trips can combine tours of the water village, with a water safari in search of proboscis monkeys. Any of the tour operators listed below can arrange a river trip, though only **Mona Florafauna Tours** guarantees sightings of proboscis monkeys. Once the secret location has been reached, the boatman will cut the engine and paddle quietly into the mangroves to allow for a close encounter with the monkeys.

Tour operators
Independent travel in Brunei is more difficult than in Malaysia and it usually works out cheaper to go as part of an organized tour. Plus, it saves the hassle of applying for permits and organizing transport. Tourism in Brunei is still in its infancy so you're very unlikely to find yourself in a large tour group (you'll often have a guide to yourself; many of them are indigenous to the region and hugely knowledgeable). The major tour operators based in Brunei are listed below.
Century Travel Centre, first floor, Darussalam Complex, Jl Sultan, BSB, T222 1747, www.centurytravelcentre.com.
Freme Travel Services, Wisma Jaya, Jl Pemancha, BSB, T223 4277, www. freme.com. Recommended.
Ilufah Leisure Tours, 20A, Bangunan Awg. Hj Ahmad Awg. Hassan & Anak-Anak, Kiulap, Gadong, T223 3524, ilufah_tours@brunet.bn.
Intrepid Tours, PO Box 2234, T872 3702, www.bruneibay.net. Largely specializing in adventure and wildlife trips.

Mas Sugara Travel Services, 1st floor, Complex Warisan, Mata Simpang 322, Jl Gadong, T242 3963, www.massugara.com.

Mona Florafauna Tours, ground floor, Yayasan Complex, T223 0761, mft@brunet.bn. Recommended.

Pan Bright Travel Services, Haji Ahmad Laksamana Building, 38-39 Jl Sultan, T224 0980, www.panbright.com.

Scuba-Tech International, Empire Hotel & Country Club (see page 53), www.scubatechintl.com.

Sunshine Borneo Tours, No 2, Simpang 146, Jl Kiarong, T244 1791, www.exploreborneo.com.

Watersports

Your best bet is to contact **Scuba-Tech International**, based at the Empire Hotel & Country Club (see page 53). They can arrange parasailing, jet skiing, deep-sea fishing, sailing and scuba diving (there are a number of wreck sites off Brunei's coast and around Labuan).

⊖ Transport

Bandar Seri Begawan *p39, map p40*

Air

Royal Brunei Airlines, T221 2222, www.bruneiair.com. See also page 36.

Boat

Boats, of course, are the main form of transport around **Kampong Ayer**. Small, speedy *tambang* depart from the jetty behind the **Yayasan Complex** from dawn until late at night. A short journey across to the water village should cost no more than a couple of Brunei dollars. Regular speedboats leave from the **Jl Residency** jetty in Bandar Seri Begawan to **Bangar**, the main town in Temburong District (hourly 0630-1630; B$6). Speedboats also depart from the main jetty to East Malaysia: **Labuan**, **Lawas** and **Limbang** (see Malaysia, page 712). Access upriver to the interior of Brunei is by indigenous longboat. Journeys need to be pre-arranged (best to speak to a tour operator, see page 56).

Bus

Buses serve Bandar Seri Begawan and the Brunei Muara district fairly regularly during daylight hours. There are 6 bus routes: the Eastern, Western, Northern, Southern, Central and Circle Lines, each of which runs buses every 20 mins, 0630-1800. The handiest route is probably the Central Line, which links the main bus station in Bandar Seri Begawan (on Jl Cator) with **Gadong** and the Brunei Museum (B$1.50). Buses for **Muara** (B$3), **Tutong** (B$4), **Seria** (B$6) and **Kuala Belait** (B$7.50) leave less regularly from the **Jl Cator** bus station.

Car hire

The major car hire firms operate out of the airport or Bandar Seri Begawan, and there are plenty of cheaper local firms to choose from, too. Companies include: **AA Car Rental**, Unit 26, Simpang 69-44, Jl Kiarong, T242 7238, aacarrental@gmail.com; **Avis**, 16 Haji Daud Complex, Jl Gadong, T242 6345; **Hertz**, Lot Q33, West Berakas Link, T239 0300 (airport T245 2244), www.hertz.com; **Qawi Enterprise**, PO Box 1322, Gadong, T234 0380.

Taxi

Metered taxis ferry people about Bandar and its suburbs, with fares set at B$3 for the first kilometre (B$4.50 between 2100-0600) and B$1 for every subsequent kilometre. For longer journeys, it makes sense to hire a car. Taxis can be waved down. Otherwise call T222 2214 (**Bandar Seri Begawan**); T333 4581 (**Kuala Belait**); T322 2030 (**Seria**); T234 3671 (**airport**).

⊙ Directory

Bandar Seri Begawan *p39, map p40*

Banks Citibank NA, Jl Sultan, T223 3233; HSBC, Jl Sultan, T224 2305; **Malaysian Banking Berhad**, Jl Pemancha, T224 2494; **Overseas Union Bank**, RBA Plaza, Jl Sultan, T222 5477; **Standard Chartered Bank**, Jl Sultan, T224 2386. **Embassies and consulates** Australia, 4th floor, Teck Guan Plaza, Jl Sultan, T222 9435; ozcombrn@

brunet.bn; **Canada**, 5th floor, 1 Jl McArthur, T222 0043, hicomcda@brunet.bn; **Malaysia**, 27 Simpang 396, Lot 9075, Kampong Sungai Akar, Jl Kebangsaan, T234 5652, mwbrunei@brunet.bn; **New Zealand**, 36A Seri Lambak Complex, Jl Berakas, T233 1612; **Singapore**, 8 Simpang 74, Jl Subok, T226 2741, singa@brunet.bn; **UK**, Level 2, Block D, Yayasan Complex, T222 2231, brithc@brunet.bn; **USA**, 3rd floor, Teck Guan Plaza, Jl Sultan, T222 9670, amembbsb@brunet.bn.

Internet Deltech Communications, Unit 5, ground floor, Bangunan Hj Mohm Salleh, Simpang 103, Jl Gadong, daily 0900-2300,

B$5 per hr; **E-Mart Cyber Junction**, GP Properties Building, Jl Gadong, daily 0800-2300, B$3 per hr; **KASCO IT Centre**, ground floor, 5 Jl Ong Sum Ping; **LA Ling Cyber Café**, 2nd floor, Yayasan Complex, daily 0930-2130, B$3 per hr. **Laundry** Superkleen, 95 Jl Pemancha, T224 2372.

Medical services Jerudong Park Medical Centre, Jerudong, T261 1433. RIPAS Hospital, Jl Putera Al-Muhtadee Billah, T224 2424. **Post office** General Post Office Building, corner of Jl Sultan and Jl Elizabeth Dua, Mon-Thu and Sat 0745-1630, Fri 0800-1100 and 1400-1600.

Background

Brunei's early history is obscure, but although precise dates have been muddied by time, there is no doubt that the sultanate's early prosperity was rooted in trade. As far back as the seventh century, China was importing birds' nests from Brunei and Arab, Indian, Chinese and other Southeast Asian traders were regularly passing through. Links with Chinese merchants were strongest: they traded silk, metals, stoneware and porcelain for Brunei's jungle produce: bezoar stones, hornbill ivory, timber and birds' nests. Chinese coins dating from the eighth century have been unearthed at Kota Batu, 3 km from Bandar Seri Begawan. Large quantities of Chinese porcelain dating from the Tang, Sung and Ming dynasties have also been found. The sultanate was on the main trade route between China and the western reaches of the Malayan archipelago and by the 10th to the 13th centuries trade was booming. By the turn of the 15th century there was a sizeable Chinese population settled in Brunei.

It is thought that some time around 1370 Sultan Mohammad became first sultan. In the mid-1400s, Sultan Awang Alak ber Tabar married a Melakan princess and converted to Islam. Brunei already had trade links with Melaka and exported camphor, rice, gold and sago in exchange for Indian textiles. But it was not until an Arab, Sharif Ali, married Sultan Awang Alak's niece that Islam spread beyond the confines of the royal court. Sharif Ali – who is said to have descended from the Prophet Mohammad – became Sultan Berkat. He consolidated Islam, converted the townspeople, built mosques and set up a legal system based on Islamic Sharia law. Trade flourished and Brunei assumed the epithet Darussalam (the abode of peace).

The golden years

The coastal Melanaus quickly embraced the Muslim faith, but tribal groups in the interior were largely unaffected by the spread of Islam and retained their animist beliefs. As Islam spread along the coasts of north and west Borneo, the sultanate expanded its political and commercial sphere of influence. By the 16th century, communities all along the coasts of present-day Sabah and Sarawak were paying tribute to the sultan. The sultanate became the centre of a minor empire whose influence stretched beyond the coasts of Borneo to many surrounding islands, including the Sulu archipelago and Mindanao in the Philippines. Even Manila had to pay tribute to the sultan's court.

On 8 July 1521 Antonio Pigafetta, an Italian historian on Portuguese explorer Ferdinand Magellan's expedition, visited the Sultanate of Brunei and described it as a rich, hospitable and powerful kingdom with an established Islamic monarchy and strong regional influence. Pigafetta published his experiences in his book, *The First Voyage Around the World*. He writes about a sophisticated royal court and the lavishly decorated sultan's palace. Brunei Town was reported to be a large, wealthy city of 25,000 households. The townspeople lived in houses built on stilts over the water.

In 1526 the Portuguese set up a trading post in Brunei and from there conducted trade with the Moluccas – the famed Spice Islands – via Brunei. At the same time, more Chinese traders immigrated to Brunei to service the booming trade between Melaka and Macau and to trade with Pattani on the South Thai isthmus.

But relations with the Spaniards were not so warm; the King of Spain and the Sultan of Brunei had mutually exclusive interests in the Philippines. In the 1570s Spaniards attacked several important Muslim centres and in March 1578, the captain-general of the Philippines, Francesco de Sande, led a naval expedition to Brunei, demanding the sultan pay tribute to Spain and allow Roman Catholic missionaries to proselytize. The sultan would have none of it and a battle ensued off Muara, which the Spaniards won. They captured the city, but within days the victors were stopped in their tracks by a cholera epidemic and had to withdraw. In 1579 they returned and once again did battle off Muara, but this time they were defeated.

The sun sets on an empire

Portugal came under Spanish rule in 1580 and Brunei lost a valuable European ally: the sultanate was raided by the Spanish again in 1588 and 1645. But by then Brunei's golden age was history and the sultan's grip on his further-flung dependencies had begun to slip.

In the 1660s civil war erupted in Brunei due to feuding between princes and, together with additional external pressures of European expansionism, the once-mighty sultanate all but collapsed. Only a handful of foreign merchants dealt with the sultanate and Chinese traders passed it by. Balanini pirates from Sulu and Illanun pirates from Mindanao posed a constant threat to the sultan and any European traders or adventurers foolhardy enough to take them on. In return for protection from these sea-borne terrorists, the sultan offered the British East India Company a base on the island of Labuan in Brunei Bay in the late 1600s, although the trading post failed to take off.

For 150 years, Brunei languished in obscurity. By the early 1800s, Brunei's territory did not extend much beyond the town boundaries, although the Sarawak River and the west coastal strip of North Borneo officially remained under the sultan's sway.

James Brooke – the man who would be king

The collection of mini-river states that made up what was left of the sultanate were ruled by the *pangeran*, the lesser nobles of the Brunei court. In the 1830s Brunei chiefs had gone to the Sarawak valley to organize the mining and trade in the high-grade antimony ore, which had been discovered there in 1824. They recruited Dayaks as workers and founded Kuching. But, with the support of local Malay chiefs, the Dayaks rebelled against one of the Brunei noblemen, the corrupt, Pangeran Makota, one of the Rajah's 14 brothers. By all accounts, Makota was a nasty piece of work, known for his exquisite charm and diabolical cunning.

It was into this troubled riverine mini-state, in armed rebellion against Makota, that the English adventurer James Brooke sailed in 1839. Robert Payne, in *The White Rajahs of Sarawak*, describes Makota as a "princely racketeer" and "a man of satanic gifts, who practised crimes for pleasure". Makota confided to Brooke: "I was brought up to plunder the Dayaks, and it makes me laugh to think that I have fleeced a tribe down to its cooking pots." With Brooke's arrival, Makota realized his days were numbered.

In 1837, the Sultan of Brunei, Omar Ali Saiffuddin, had dispatched his uncle, Pengiran Muda Hashim, to contain the rebellion. He failed, and turned to Brooke for help. In return for his services, Brooke demanded to be made governor of Sarawak.

After he had been formally installed in his new role by Sultan Omar, Brooke set about building his own empire. In 1848 he said: "I am going in these revolutionary times to get up a league and covenant between all the good rivers of the coast, to the purpose that they will not pay revenue or obey the government of Brunei … " Brooke exploited rivalries between various aristocratic factions of Brunei's royal court, which climaxed in the murder of Pengiran Muda Hashim and his family.

No longer required in Sarawak, Hashim had returned to Brunei to become chief minister and heir apparent. He was murdered – along with 11 other princes and their families – by Sultan Omar. The sultan and his advisers had felt threatened by their presence, so they disposed of Hashim to prevent a coup. The massacre incensed Brooke. In June 1846 his British ally, Admiral Sir Thomas Cochrane, bombarded Brunei Town, set it ablaze and chased the sultan into the jungle.

Cochrane wanted to proclaim Brooke the sultan of Brunei, but decided, in the end, to offer Sultan Omar protection if he cleaned up his act and demonstrated his loyalty to Queen Victoria. After several weeks, the humiliated sultan emerged from the jungle and swore undying loyalty to the Queen. As penance, Sultan Omar formally ceded the island of Labuan to the British crown on 18 December 1846. The brow-beaten sultan pleaded proneness to sea sickness in an effort to avoid having to witness the hoisting of the Union Jack on Labuan Island. Although Brunei forfeited more territory in handing Labuan to the British, the sultan calculated that he would benefit from a direct relationship with Whitehall. It seemed that London was becoming almost as concerned as he was about Brooke's expansionist instincts. A Treaty of Friendship and Commerce was signed between Britain and Brunei in 1847 in which the sultan agreed not to cede any more territory to any power, except with the consent of the British government.

The sultan's shrinking shadow

The treaty did not stop Brooke. His mission, since arriving in Sarawak, had been the destruction of the pirates who specialized in terrorizing Borneo's coastal communities. Because he knew the Sultan of Brunei was powerless to contain them, he calculated that their liquidation would be his best bargaining chip with the sultan, and would enable him to prise yet more territory from the sultan's grasp. Over the years he engaged the dreaded Balanini and Illanun pirates from Sulu and Mindanao as well as the so-called Sea-Dayaks and Brunei Malays, who regularly attacked Chinese, Bugis and other Asian trading ships off the Borneo coast. As a result, Sultan Abdul Mumin of Brunei ceded to Brooke the Saribas and Skrang districts, which became the Second Division of Sarawak in 1853 and, eight years later, he handed over the region that was to become the Third Division of Sarawak.

But by now the sultan was as worried about territorial encroachment by the British as he was about the Brookes and, as a counterweight to both, granted a 10-year concession to much of what is modern-day Sabah to the American consul in Brunei, Charles Lee Moses. This 72,500 sq km tract of North Borneo later became British North Borneo and is now the East Malaysian state of Sabah.

With the emergence of British North Borneo, the British reneged on their agreement with the Sultan of Brunei again and the following year approved Brooke's annexation of the Baram river basin by Sarawak, which became its Fourth Division. The Sarawak frontier was advancing ever northwards.

In 1884 a rebellion broke out in Limbang and Rajah Charles Brooke refused to help the sultan restore order. Sultan Hashim Jalilul Alam Aqamaddin, who acceded to the throne in 1885, wrote to Queen Victoria complaining that the British had not kept their word. Sir Frederick Weld was dispatched to mediate; he sympathized with the sultan, and his visit resulted in the Protectorate Agreement of 1888 between Brunei and Britain, which gave London full control of the sultanate's external affairs. When Brooke annexed Limbang in 1890 and united it with the Trusan Valley to form the Fifth Division of Sarawak, while the Queen's men looked on, the sultan was reduced to a state of disbelief. His sultanate had now been completely surrounded by Brooke's Sarawak.

From sultanate to oilfield

In 1906 a British Resident was appointed to the sultan's court to advise on all aspects of government except traditional customs and religion. In his book *By God's Will*, Lord Chalfont suggests that the British government's enthusiastic recommitment to the sultanate through the treaty may have been motivated by Machiavellian desires. "More cynical observers have suggested that the new-found enthusiasm of the British government may not have been entirely unconnected with the discovery of oil ... around the turn of the century." Oil exploration started in 1899, although it was not until the discovery of the Seria oilfield in 1929 that it merited commercial exploitation. Historian Mary Turnbull notes the quirk of destiny that ensured the survival of the micro-sultanate: "It was ironic that the small area left unswallowed by Sarawak and North Borneo should prove to be the most richly endowed part of the old sultanate."

The Brunei oilfield fell to the Japanese on 18 December 1942. Allied bombing and Japanese sabotage prior to the sultanate's liberation caused considerable damage to oil and port installations and urban areas, necessitating a long period of reconstruction in the late 1940s and early 1950s. Australian forces landed at Muara Beach on 10 July 1945. A British Military Administration ruled the country for a year, before Sultan Sir Ahmad Tajuddin took over.

In 1948 the governor of Sarawak, which was by then a British crown colony, was appointed high commissioner for Brunei, but the sultanate remained what one commentator describes as "a constitutional anachronism". In September 1959 the UK resolved this by withdrawing the Resident and signing an agreement with the sultan giving Whitehall responsibility for Brunei's defence and foreign affairs.

Because of his post-war influence on the development of Brunei, Sultan Omar was variously referred to as the father and the architect of modern Brunei. He shaped his sultanate into the anti-communist, non-democratic state it is today and, being an Anglophile, held out against independence from Britain. By the early 1960s, Whitehall was enthusiastically promoting the idea of a North Borneo Federation, encompassing Sarawak, Brunei and British North Borneo. But Sultan Omar did not want anything to do with the neighbouring territories as he felt Brunei's interests were more in keeping with those of peninsular Malaysia. The proposed federation would have been heavily dependent on Brunei's oil wealth. Kuala Lumpur did not need much persuasion that Brunei's joining the Federation of Malaysia was an excellent idea.

Democrats versus autocrat

In Brunei's first general election in 1962, the left-wing Brunei People's Party (known by its Malay acronym, PRB) swept the polls. The party's election ticket had marked an end to the sultan's autocratic rule, the formation of a democratic government and immediate independence. Aware that there was a lot at stake, the sultan refused to let the PRB form a government. The sultan's emergency powers, under which he banned the PRB, which were passed in 1962, remain in force, enabling him to rule by decree.

On 8 December 1962, the PRB – backed by the communist North Kalimantan National Army, effectively its military wing – launched a revolt. The sultan's insistence on British military protection paid off as the disorganized rebellion was quickly put down with the help of a Gurkha infantry brigade and other British troops. Within four days the British troops had pushed the rebels into Limbang, where the hard core holed up. By 12 December the revolt had been crushed and the vast majority of the rebels disappeared into the interior, pursued by the 7th Gurkha Rifles and Kelabit tribesmen.

Early in 1963, negotiations over Brunei joining the Malaysian Federation ran into trouble, to the disappointment of the British. The Malaysian prime minister, the late Tunku Abdul Rahman, wanted the sultanate's oil and gas revenues to feed the federal treasury in Kuala Lumpur and made the mistake of making his intentions too obvious. The Tunku envisaged central government exercising absolute control over oil revenues – in the way it controls the oil wealth of Sabah and Sarawak today. Unhappy with this proposal and unwilling to become 'just another Malaysian sultan', Omar abandoned his intention to join the Federation.

Meanwhile, Indonesia's Sukarno was resolute in his objective of crushing the new Federation of Malaysia and launched his *Konfrontasi* between 1963 and 1966. Brunei offered itself as an operational base for the British army. But while Brunei supported Malaysia against Indonesia, relations between them became very strained following the declaration of the Federation in September 1963.

In 1975 Kuala Lumpur sponsored the visit of a PRB delegation to the UN, to propose a resolution calling on Brunei to hold elections, abolish restrictions on political parties and allow political exiles to return. In 1976 Bruneian government supporters protested against Malaysian 'interference' in Bruneian affairs. Nonetheless, the resolution was adopted by the UN in November 1977, receiving 117 votes in favour and none against. Britain abstained. Relations with Malaysia warmed after the death of Prime Minister Tun Abdul Razak in 1976, leaving the PRB weak and isolated. The party still operates in exile, although it is a spent force. Throughout the difficult years, the sultan had used his favourite sport to conduct what was dubbed 'polo diplomacy', fostering links with like-minded Malaysian royalty despite the tensions in official bilateral relations.

By 1967, Britain's Labour government was pushing Sultan Omar to introduce a democratic system of government. Instead, however, the sultan opted to abdicate in favour of his 21-year-old son, Hassanal Bolkiah. In November 1971, a new treaty was signed with Britain. London retained its responsibility for Brunei's external affairs, but its advisory role applied only to defence. The sultan was given full control of all internal matters. Under a separate agreement, a battalion of British Gurkhas was stationed in the sultanate. As Bruneians grew richer, the likelihood of another revolt receded.

Independence

Britain was keen to disentangle itself from the 1971 agreement: maintaining the protectorate relationship was expensive and left London open to criticism that it was maintaining an anachronistic colonial relationship. Brunei did not particularly relish the prospect of independence as, without British protection, it would be at the mercy of its more powerful neighbours. But in January 1979, having secured Malaysian and Indonesian assurances that they would respect its independence, the government signed another agreement with London, allowing for the sultanate to become independent from midnight on 31 December 1983 after 150 years of close involvement with Britain and 96 years as a protectorate.

Politics

In January 1984, Sultan Hassanal Bolkiah declared Brunei a 'democratic' monarchy. Three years later, he told his official biographer Lord Chalfont: "I do not believe that the time is ripe for elections and the revival of the legislature. What I would wish to see first is real evidence of an interest in politics by a responsible majority of the people … When I see some genuine interest among the citizenry, we may move towards elections." Independence changed little: absolute power is still vested in the sultan, who mostly relies on his close family for advice. Following Independence, the sultan took up the offices of prime minister, finance minister and minister of home affairs. In 1986, he relinquished the latter two, but appointed himself defence minister. He also took over responsibility for finance on the resignation of his brother, Prince Jefri.

In May 1985 the Brunei National Democratic Party (BNDP) was officially registered. Its aim was to introduce a parliamentary democracy under the sultan. But just before the Malays-only party came into being, the government announced that government employees would not be allowed to join any other political party. In one stroke, the BNDP's potential membership was halved. In early 1986, the Brunei United National Party – an offshoot of the BNDP – was formed. Unlike its parent, its manifesto was multi-racial. The sultan allowed these parties to exist until 27 January 1988 when he proscribed all political parties and imprisoned, without trial, two of the BNDP's leaders.

In the early 1990s, the sultan was reported to have become increasingly worried about internal security and about Brunei's image abroad. Eight long-term political detainees, in prison since the abortive 1962 coup, were released in 1990. The last political detainee, the former deputy leader of the Brunei People's Party (PRB), Zaini Ahmad, is said to have written to the sultan from prison following the releases. He apparently apologized for the 1962 revolt and called for the democratically elected Legislative Council – as outlined in the 1959 constitution – to be reconvened. To coincide with the sultan's 50th birthday in 1996, Zaini Ahmad was released from prison. The exiled PRB has been greatly weakened and increasingly isolated since Brunei's relations with Malaysia became more cordial following the sultanate's accession to the Association of Southeast Asian Nations (ASEAN) in 1984 and clearly the sultan and his adviser no longer feel threatened by the party.

Foreign relations

Brunei joined ASEAN on Independence in 1984. Prince Mohammed, the foreign affairs minister, is said to be one of the brightest, more thoughtful members of the royal family, but in foreign policy, Brunei is timid and goes quietly along with its ASEAN partners. Relations with Malaysia are greatly improved, but the sultanate's closest ties in the region, especially in fiscal and economic matters, are with Singapore. Their relationship was initially founded on their mutual distrust of the Malaysian Federation, which Brunei never joined and Singapore left two years after its inception in 1965. Singapore provides assistance in the training of Brunei's public servants and their currencies are linked.

As a member of ASEAN, on good terms with its neighbours, Brunei does not have many enemies to fear. But if its Scorpion tanks, Exocet rockets, Rapier ground-to-air missiles and helicopter gunships seem a little redundant, it is worth considering the experience of another oil-rich Islamic mini-state – Kuwait.

Modern Brunei

The last years of the 20th century saw Brunei's waning fortunes come to a head. By 2001, the country's per capita GDP was down almost 50% on what it had been at the time of Brunei's Independence. The troubles began with the Asian economic crisis of 1997 and were further compounded by falling oil prices and by the collapse of the country's biggest non-oil company, Amedeo Development Corporation, which had run up debts of US$3½ billion. Amedeo had been owned and run by the sultan's brother and finance minister, Prince Jefri, a man of excessive extravagance and little business acumen. The prince resigned from his position as finance minister, and a national scandal followed, with the sultan eventually suing his brother for siphoning billions of dollars from the Brunei Investment Agency, for which the prince had served as chairman. The brothers eventually settled out of court, but the publicity has had lasting consequences, damaging Brunei's credibility with foreign investors. Brunei's shaken economy has now stabilized, but the whole episode has served to highlight just how over-dependent Brunei is on oil (at present Brunei's economy relies almost exclusively on exports of oil and LNG – liquefied natural gas). As oil prices peak and trough, so do Brunei's fortunes. More worryingly, the nation's oil and gas reserves are expected to dry up in 2018 and 2033 respectively. This vulnerability has prompted the sultan to initiate reforms – both economic and political. Diversification of the economy has now become a priority and the sultan has curbed government spending while encouraging the growth of privatization.

One of his primary visions was to transform Brunei into an Offshore Financial Haven (in the vein of Bermuda or the Isle of Man) and the government has now achieved this. So-called Islamic Finance is also being targeted. In 2000, the BIFC (Brunei International Finance Centre) began trading successfully.

Ecotourism, meanwhile, is another of Brunei's trump cards for the future (more than 70% of the land mass remains cloaked in virgin rainforest). Still, many commentators point out that visitor figures are likely to remain low until the government eases laws on the prohibition of alcohol. Perhaps more significant has been the political fallout of Brunei's economic problems. The new-found desire to attract investors and tourists has forced the sultan to reconsider Brunei's international image. There has been a shift away from the Islamic conservatism of the 1990s – a fact underlined by the dismissal in 2005 of the education minister, a conservative Islamist whose introduction of a strict religious education had become increasingly unpopular. Prior to this, the first tentative move towards 21st-century democracy was instigated, with the appointment of a new legislative council. In September 2004, the country's parliament reopened for the first time since Independence. Though no political parties are allowed, a new 45-seat council was called for, with 15 elected members. To all intents and purposes, the sultan still retains authoritarian control over his kingdom – just as his ancestors have for 600 years. Nevertheless, the pending elections are being viewed as the first step towards a modern Brunei – a Brunei without oil, but with a new politics of consensus.

Cambodia

Contents

Footprint features

Border crossings

At a glance

⊕ **Getting around** The boats that ply the Tonlé Sap from Siem Reap to Phnom Penh tend to be less bumpy and more relaxed than the buses. The boat from Siem Reap to Battambang offers a slice of authentic Cambodia.

◉ **Time required** For the major sights 2 weeks is probably enough. To get beneath the surface you need a month.

◗ **Weather** The rainy season runs from May-Oct with the wettest period during the latter stages. Don't be too put off – visiting Angkor in the pouring rain can be spectacular and you're likely to have it to yourself. The dry season lasts from Nov to Apr.

✖ **When not to go** Apr-Jun can be unbearably hot and humid.

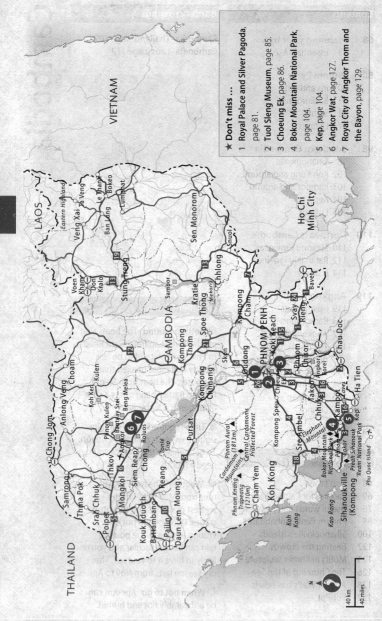

★ **Don't miss ...**

Impenetrable jungles; abandoned temples smothered in centuries of foliage; arching white-sand beaches fringed with swaying palms; exotic, smiling locals – in almost every respect Cambodia satisfies the hackneyed expectations of Southeast Asia. And, if you get off the beaten track, Cambodia also offers that increasingly elusive feeling of discovery; the feeling that you are entering into arcane and unknown worlds where few Westerners have been before. But this is a country that is still trying to make sense of itself after the horrors of the genocidal Khmer Rouge rule. While the UN-sponsored trial of the former leaders finally got underway in 2007, many of its minor officials still hold positions of influence and power in Cambodia and you don't have to spend long in the country to see the gulf between the indifferent rich and the absolute poor.

Yet, without doubt, ancient Cambodia produced one of the world's greatest civilizations at Angkor. This temple complex near Siem Reap is truly breathtaking. But don't just stop there; Angkor Wat is merely one temple at the heart of a thousand others.

Today's capital, Phnom Penh, with its charming riverside setting is rapidly shedding its laid-back dusty charm and becoming a dynamic city complete with Hummer-driving Khmer yuppies, chic bars serving cocktails, clubs with designer interiors and hangouts filled with the great and the gorgeous.

On the beaches to the south you can find relaxed resort towns on the coast, such as Kep. In the northeastern provinces, tracts of red earth cut through hills carpeted in jungle. Elephant rides are the order of the day around Sen Monorom, and at Ban Lung you won't be disappointed by the waterfalls, boat rides and the stunning, bottle-green waters of Yaek Lom Lake.

Planning your trip

Getting there

Air

International connections with Cambodia are poor – but improving – and most travellers will need to route themselves through **Bangkok**, as it is generally the cheapest regional hub and offers the best connections with **Phnom Penh** and **Siem Reap**. For international flights to Bangkok, see page 778. There are direct flights only from within the region. The most important entry point remains Phnom Penh but recently more international flights direct from Siem Reap have been launched. ▶▶ For airport tax, see page 77.

To/from Phnom Penh There are connections with Thailand (Bangkok), Malaysia (Kuala Lumpur), Singapore, Hong Kong, China (Guangzhou and Shanghai), Vietnam (Ho Chi Minh City), Taiwan (Taipei) and Laos (Vientiane and Pakse).

Boat

There are sailings from **Ho Chi Minh City** (Saigon) to Phnom Penh. Saigon tour cafés run minibuses to Chau Doc and on to the border which is crossed on foot. Change to a speed boat which will take you to **Neak Luong** in Cambodia. Disembark here and take a taxi/pick-up along Route 1 to Phnom Penh. From **Stung Treng** to the Laos border either charter a speed boat, which will take approximately 1½ hours, or board the slow ferry that leaves daily at around 0730 which will take approximately 3½ hours.

There are daily speedboat connections between Hat Lek in Thailand, and **Koh Kong** and Sre Ambel in Cambodia. From Koh Kong there are connections direct to **Sihanoukville**. The sea route, in open speedboats, is not recommended. The Sre Ambel connection is less reliable but it is quicker for visitors wishing to get to Phnom Penh. From Hat Lek or Trat there are buses to Pattaya, Bangkok and Bangkok's Don Muang airport. Check times before departing because Koh Kong is not the kind of place you want to hang around in for long. Cruise ships visit the international sea port of Sihanoukville.

To/from Siem Reap There are connections with Bangkok, Kuala Lumpur, Taipei, Singapore, Ho Chi Minh City (Vietnam), Hanoi (Vietnam), Luang Prabang (Laos) and Vientiane (Laos). The most popular international connection is with Bangkok.

Road

It is possible to enter Cambodia, overland, from Thailand, Vietnam and Laos. Travellers coming from Thailand usually cross at **Poipet** (they then face a long overland journey, on a particularly bad road, to Siem Reap) and this is the choice of those wishing to stretch their travel budget as far as it will go. There are now overland entries from Thailand through Pailin (very rough roads) and Koh Kong. The overland route from Vietnam via **Moc Bai** is the slow but cheap option for travellers coming from the east, and the border crossing at **Omsano** has enabled those coming from Vietnam to take the more scenic river route via Chau Doc. There is a new scenic border open via Kep between Cambodia and Vietnam (Ha Tien). There is also a crossing between Phnom Penh and Tinh Bien in Vietnam. The border crossing with Laos, close to the town at **Stung Treng**, is open but no visas are issued at the border.

Packing for Cambodia

In Phnom Penh it is possible to buy most toiletries and other personal items, although they are imported and therefore pricier than elsewhere in the region. Outside the capital the range of products is limited.

Dress in Cambodia is relatively casual. However, though formal attire may be the exception, dressing tidily is the norm.

You may want to pack antacid tablets for indigestion; antibiotics for diarrhoea (discuss with your doctor); antiseptic ointment (eg Cetrimide); anti-malarials (see page 74); mosquito repellents; travel sickness tablets; painkillers; condoms/contraceptives; tampons/sanitary towels; high-factor sun screen and a sun hat, and a blow-up pillow.

For longer trips involving jungle treks, take a clean needle pack, clean dental pack and water filtration devices. However, be wary of carring disposable needles as customs officials may find them suspicious. If you are a popular target for insect bites or develop bumps quite soon after being bitten, carry an Aspivenin kit. This syringe suction device is available is available from many chemists and provides quick relief.

Make sure your passport is valid for at least six months and take photocopies of essential documents, passport ID and visa pages, insurance policy details and student ID card. Spare passport photos are useful when applying for permits or in case of loss or theft.

Getting around

Air

At the moment the only domestic route within Cambodia which operates safely and with any frequency is between Phnom Penh and Siem Reap, with **Siem Reap Airways**, www.siemreapairways.com. The situation is developing though and you should check what routes are flying when you arrive in Cambodia. You should also take safety very seriously – a number of domestic flights have crashed in recent years. ►► *For domestic airport tax, see page 77.*

Boat

All the Mekong towns and settlements around the Tonlé Sap are accessible by boat. It is a very quick and relatively comfortable way of travel and much cheaper than flying. The route between Siem Reap and Phnom Penh is very popular while the route between Siem Reap and Battambang is one of the most scenic. For those on a budget it is the best way to go. With the new road opening, boats are no longer used as a main form of transport along the Mekong and in the northeast.

Rail

The UK Foreign Office continues to advise against rail travel in Cambodia, and with its ancient locomotives Cambodian state railways cannot be recommended. The railway is desperately slow, uncomfortable and unreliable. There are two lines out of Phnom Penh: one to Poipet on the Thai border which goes via Pursat, Battambang and Sisophon; the second, which runs south to Sihanoukville on the coast via Takeo, Kep and Kampot, is no longer operating at the moment. Check the situation when you arrive.

Road

Over the last few years the road system in Cambodia has dramatically improved. By the end of 2008 a trunk route of international standards, apart from a few bumpy stretches, from Stung Treng to Koh Kong will be fully open. Much of the rest of the network is pretty basic and journeys can sometimes be long and laborious. Also, to some parts, such as Ratanakiri, the road is a graded laterite track, unpaved and potholed. In the rainy season expect to be slowed down on many roads to a slithering muddy crawl. The Khmer-American Friendship Highway (Route 4), which runs from Phnom Penh to Sihanoukville, is entirely paved, as is the National Highway 6 between Siem Reap and Phnom Penh. The infamous National Highway 6 between Poipet and Phnom Penh via Siem Reap has also had extensive work, as has National Highway 1. The Japanese in particular have put considerable resources into road and bridge building.

Bus and shared taxi There are buses and shared taxis to most parts of the country. Shared taxis (generally Toyota Camrys) or pick-ups are usually the quickest and most reliable public transport option. The taxi operators charge a premium for better seats and you can buy yourself more space. It is not uncommon for a taxi to fit 10 people in it, including two sitting on the driver's seat. Fares for riding in the back of the truck are half that for riding in the cab. The Sihanoukville run has an excellent and cheap air-conditioned bus service.

Car hire and taxi A few travel agents and hotels may be able to organize self-drive car hire and most hotels have cars for hire with a driver (US$30-50 per day). There is a limited taxi service in Phnom Penh.

Moto The most popular and sensible option is the motorbike taxi, known as 'moto'. This costs around the same as renting your own machine and with luck you will get a driver who speaks a bit of English and who knows where he's going. Once you have found a good driver stick with him: handing out the odd drink, a packet of cigarettes or an extra dollar or two is a good investment. Outside Phnom Penh and Siem Reap, do not expect much English from your moto driver.

Motorbike and bicycle hire Motorbikes can be rented from between US$5 and US$8 per day and around US$1 for a bicycle. If riding either a motorbike or a bicycle be aware that the accident fatality rate is very high. This is partly because of the poor condition of many of the vehicles on the road; partly because of the poor roads; and partly because of the horrendously poor driving. If you do rent a motorbike ensure it has a working horn (imperative) and buy some rear-view mirrors so you can keep an eye on the traffic. Wear a helmet (even if using a motodop).

Sleeping → *For hotel price codes, see inside the front cover.*

Accommodation standards in Cambodia have greatly improved over the last couple of years. Phnom Penh now has a good network of genuine boutique hotels – arguably they are overpriced and sometimes management can be a bit Fawlty Towers but the bar has certainly been raised. Siem Reap, without doubt, has now become a destination for the upmarket international traveller. The range, depth and quality of accommodation here is of an excellent standard and is on a par with anywhere else in Asia. Even if you travel to some of the smaller, less visited towns, family-run Chinese style hotels should now provide hot water, a/c and cable TV even if they can't provide first class service. These places are often the best bargains in the country as many of the cheap backpacker places, while very, very cheap, are mostly hovels.

More expensive hotels have safety boxes in the rooms. In cheaper hotels it is not uncommon for things to be stolen from bedrooms. In Phnom Penh this poses a real dilemma for it is more dangerous to take valuables onto the night-time streets. Most hotels and guesthouses will accept valuables for safekeeping but do keep a close eye on your cash.

Eating and drinking → *For restaurant price codes, see inside the front cover.*

For a country that has suffered and starved in the way Cambodia has, eating for fun as opposed to eating for survival, has yet to catch on as a pastime. There are some good restaurants and things are improving but don't expect Cambodia to be a smaller version of Thailand, or its cuisine even to live up to the standards of Laos. Cambodian food shows clear links with the cuisines of neighbouring countries: Thailand, Vietnam, and to a lesser extent, Laos. The influence of the French colonial period is also in evidence, most clearly in the availability of good French bread. Chinese food is also available owing to strong business ties between Cambodia and China. True Khmer food is difficult to find and much that the Khmers would like to claim as indigenous food is actually of Thai, French or Vietnamese origin. Curries, soups, rice and noodle-based dishes, salads, fried vegetables and sliced meats all feature in Khmer cooking.

Phnom Penh and Siem Reap have the best restaurants with French, Japanese, Italian and Indian food being available. But those who want to sample a range of dishes and get a feel for Khmer cuisine should head for the nearest market where dishes will be cooked to order in a wok – known locally as a *chhnang khteak*.

International soft drink brands are widely available in Cambodia. Tea is drunk without sugar or milk. Coffee is also served black, or 'crème' with sweetened condensed milk. Bottled water is easy to find, as is local mineral water. Fruit smoothies – known locally as *tikalok* – are ubiquitous. Soda water with lemon, *soda kroch chhmar*, is a popular drink.

Local customs and laws

Cambodians are relaxed and easy-going people. Only crass behaviour, such as patting people on the head or invading their homes uninvited, will upset them.

Temples When visiting a temple, dress respectfully (keep bare flesh to a minimum) and take off your hat and shoes. A small donation is often appropriate. Put your legs to one side and try not to point the soles of your feet at anyone or the Buddha image. Females are not to touch monks or sit beside them on public transport.

Greeting Cambodians use their traditional greeting – the 'wai' – bowing with their hands held together. As a foreigner shaking hands is perfectly acceptable.

In private homes It is polite to take your shoes off on entering the house and a small present goes down well if you are invited for a meal.

General Displays of anger or exasperation are considered unacceptable and therefore reflect very badly on the individual. Accordingly, even in adversity, Khmers (like the Thais) will keep smiling. Displays of affection are also considered embarrassing and should be avoided in public areas. To beckon someone, use your hand with the palm facing downwards. Pointing is rude.

All visitors should **dress appropriately** and women should avoid wearing short skirts, midriff-baring and cleavage-exposing tops, as this may unwittingly attract undesirable attention and potentially offend some people.

Festivals and events

There are some 30 public holidays celebrated each year in Cambodia. Most are celebrated with public parades and special events to commemorate the particular holiday. The largest holidays also see many Khmers – although less than used to be the case – firing their guns, to the extent that red tracer fills the sky. Several interesting festivals enliven the Cambodian calendar which festival-goers would be disappointed to miss. The major festivals mark important events in the farming year, determined by seasonal changes in the weather, and are listed below.

1 Jan New Year (public holiday).

7 Jan Victory over Pol Pot (public holiday). Celebration of the fall of the Khmer Rouge.

Jan/Feb Chinese and Vietnamese New Year (movable); **Anniversary of the last sermon of Buddha** (movable).

8 Mar Women's Day (public holiday). Processions, floats and banners in main towns.

Apr Chaul Chhnam (movable). 3-day celebration, which involves the inevitable drenching, to welcome in the new year. A similar festival to Pimai in Laos and Songkran in Thailand.

13-15 Apr Bonn Chaul Chhnam (Cambodian New Year) (public holiday). A 3-day celebration to mark the turn of the year and to show gratitude to the departing demi-god and to welcome the new one. Homes are spring cleaned, householders visit temples and traditional games like *boh angkunh* and *chhoal chhoung* are played, and ritual festivities are performed.

17 Apr Independence Day (public holiday). Celebrates the fall of the Lon Nol government.

Apr/May Visak Bauchea (public holiday, movable). Anniversary of Buddha's birth, enlightenment and his Paranirvana (state of final bliss).

9 May Genocide Day (public holiday). To remember the atrocities of the Khmer Rouge. The main ceremony is held at Choeng Ek.

May Royal Ploughing Festival (public holiday, movable). As in Thailand, this marks the beginning of the rainy season and traditionally is meant to alert farmers to the fact that the job of rice cultivation is set to begin. Known as *bonn chroat preah nongkoal* in Khmer, the ceremony is held on a field close to Phnom Penh.

Jun Anniversary of the Founding of the Revolutionary Armed Forces of Kampuchea and **Anniversary of the Founding of the People's Revolutionary Party of Cambodia**. Founded in 1951, the main parades and celebrations are in Phnom Penh.

Jul Chol Vassa (movable). The start of the rainy season retreat – a Buddhist Lent – for meditation.

Sep End of Buddhist Lent (movable). In certain areas it is celebrated with boat races. **Prachum Ben** (public holiday). In remembrance of the dead, offerings are made to the ancestors.

Oct/Nov Water Festival, Bon Om Tuk (public holiday, movable) or **Festival of the Reversing Current**. To celebrate the movement of the waters out of the Tonlé Sap, boat races are held in Phnom Penh. The festival dates back to the 12th century when King Jayavarman VII and his navy defeated water-borne invaders. Most wats have ceremonial canoes, which are rowed by the monks to summon the Naga King. Boat races extend over 3 days with more then 200 competitors, but the highlight is the evening gala in Phnom Penh when a fleet of boats, studded with lights, row out under the full moon. The festival was only revived in 1990. In addition to celebrating the reversing of the flow of the Tonlé Sap River, this festival marks the onset of the fishing season.

30 Oct–1 Nov King Sihanouk's Birthday (public holiday). Public offices and museums close for about a week and a there is a firework display in Phnom Penh.

9 Nov Independence Day (public holiday). Marks Cambodia's independence from French colonial rule in 1953.

Dec Half marathon. A half marathon is held at Angkor Wat, surely one of the most spectacular places to work up a sweat.

Shopping

Phnom Penh's markets are highly diverting. Cambodian craftsmanship is excellent and whether you are in search of silverware, *kramas* – checked cotton scarves – hand-loomed sarongs or bronze buddhas you will find them all in abundance. A great favourite for its range and quality of antiques, jewellery and fabrics is the **Psar Tuol Tom Pong** (Russian Market). Silverware, gold and gems are available in the **Psar Thmei** (Central Market). *Matmii* – ikat – is also commonly found in Cambodia. It may have been an ancient import from Java and is made by tie-dyeing the threads before weaving. It can be bought throughout the country. Other local textile products to look out for are silk scarves bags and traditional wall-hangings. Colourful *kramas* can be found in local markets across the country and fine woven sarongs in cotton and silk are available in Phnom Penh and Siem Reap. Silk and other textiles products can be bought throughout the country. There has been a strong revival of pottery and ceramics in Cambodia in the last 30 years. Other crafts include bamboo work, wooden panels with carvings of the *Ramayana* and temple rubbings.

Essentials A-Z

Accident and emergency
Contact the relevant emergency service and your embassy. Make sure you obtain police/ medical records in order to file insurance claims. Ambulance T119 /724891, Fire T118, Police T117/112/012-999999.

Children
Powdered milk is available in provincial centres, although most brands have added sugar. Baby food can be bought in some towns and disposable nappies can be bought in Phnom Penh, but are often expensive.

Customs and duty free
A reasonable amount of tobacco products and spirits can be taken in without incurring customs duty – roughly 200 cigarettes or the equivalent quantity of tobacco, 1 bottle of liquor and perfume for personal use. Taking any Angkorian era images out of the country is strictly forbidden.

Disabled travellers
Cambodia is not an easy country for the disabled traveller: pavements are often uneven, there are potholes, pedestrian crossings are ignored, ramps are unheard of and lifts are few and far between. The Angkor complex can be a real struggle for disabled or frail persons. The stairs are very steep and semi-restoration of areas means that visitors will sometimes need to climb over piles of bricks. Hiring an aide to help you climb stairs and generally get around is a very good idea and can be hired for around US$5-10 a day.

While there are scores of hurdles that disabled people will have to negotiate, the Cambodians themselves are likely to go out of their way to be helpful. **RADAR**, 12 City Forum, 250 City Rd, London, EC1V 8AF, T0207-2503222, www.radar.org.uk. **SATH**, 347 Fifth Avenue, Suite 605, New York City, NY 10016, T0212-4477284, www.sath.org.

Drugs
Drug use is illegal in Cambodia but drugs are a big problem. Many places use marijuana in their cooking and the police seem to be quite ambivalent to dope smokers (unless they need to supplement their income with bribe money, in which case – watch out).

One of the biggest dangers for travellers who take drugs in Cambodia today is dying of an overdose. The backpacker areas near the lake in Phnom Penh and Sihanoukville are particularly notorious for heavy drug usage by Westerners, some of whom have actually died as a result of mistakenly overdosing on heroin. It is important to note that cocaine and ecstasy do not really exist in Cambodia, despite what you may be told. Avoid *yaa baa*, a particularly insidious amphetamine. It has serious side effects and can be lethal.

In a nutshell – don't buy illicit drugs in Cambodia, it is dangerous.

Electricity
Voltage 220. Sockets are usually round 2-pin.

Embassies and consulates
Australia, 5 Canterbury Cres, Deakin, ACT 2600, Australia, T+61-2-6273 1259.
Laos, Thadeua Rd, KM2 Vientiane, BP34 T+856-21-314950.
Thailand, 185 Rajdamri Rd, Lumpini Patumwan, Bangkok 10330, T+66-2-254 6630, recbkk@cscoms.com.
UK, 64 Brondesbury Park, Willesden Green, London NW6 7AT, T+44-(0)207 451 7850.
USA, 4530, 16th St NW, Washington DC 20011, T1-202 726 8042.

Vietnam, 41 Phung Khac Khoan, HCMC, T0848-829 2751, cambocg@hcm.vmn.vn; 71 Tran Hung Dao St, Hanoi, T+844-942 4789, arch@fpt.vn.

Gay and lesbian
Gay and lesbian travellers will have no problems in Cambodia. Men often hold other men's hands as do women, so this kind of affection is nothing short of commonplace. Any kind of passionate kissing or sexually orientated affection in public is taboo – both for straight and gay people. The gay scene is just starting to develop in Cambodia but there is definitely a scene in the making. **Linga Bar** in Siem Reap and the **Salt Lounge** in Phnom Penh are both gay bars and are excellent choices for a night out.

Health
See your doctor or travel clinic at least 6 weeks before your departure for general advice on travel risks, malaria and vaccinations. Make sure you have travel insurance, get a dental check (especially if you are going to be away for more than a month), know your own blood group and if you suffer a long-term condition such as diabetes or epilepsy make sure someone knows or that you have a Medic Alert bracelet/necklace with this information on it.

The following **vaccinations** are usually advised before travel: BCG, diphtheria, hepatitis A, polio, tetanus and typhoid. The following are sometimes advised: hepatitis B, Japanese B encephalitis and rabies. A yellow fever vaccination certificate is required if coming from areas with risk of transmission.

Health risks
Malaria exists in most of Cambodia, but the risk is minimal in the capital Phnom Penh. The choice of malaria prophylaxis will need to be something other than chloroquine for most people, since there is such a high level of resistance to it. Always check with your doctor or travel clinic for the most up-to-date advice.

Malaria can cause death within 24 hrs. It can start as something just resembling an attack of flu. You may feel tired, lethargic, headachy, feverish; or more seriously, develop fits, followed by coma and then death. Have a low index of suspicion because it is very easy to write off vague symptoms, which may actually be malaria. If you have a temperature, go to a doctor as soon as you can and ask for a malaria test. On your return home if you suffer any of these symptoms, get tested as soon as possible, even if any previous test proved negative, the test could save your life.

The most serious viral disease is dengue fever, which is hard to protect against as the mosquitoes bite throughout the day as well as at night. Bacterial diseases include tuberculosis (TB) and some causes of the more common traveller's diarrhoea. Each year there is the possibility that avian flu or SARS might rear their ugly heads. Check the news reports. If there is a problem in an area you are due to visit you may be advised to have an ordinary flu shot or to seek expert advice. There are high rates of HIV in the region, especially among sex workers.

Medical services

Medical services are listed in the Directory section of the relevant areas. Hospitals are not recommended anywhere in Cambodia (even at some of the clinics that profess to be 'international'). If you fall ill or are injured the best bet is to get yourself quickly to either Bumrungrad Hospital or Bangkok Nursing Home, both in **Bangkok**. Both hospitals are of an exceptional standard, even in international terms. For further details, see Thailand, page 815.

Useful websites

www.btha.org British Travel Health Association (UK). This is the official website of an organization of travel health professionals.
www.cdc.gov US Government site which gives excellent advice on travel health and details of disease outbreaks.

www.fitfortravel.scot.nhs.uk A-Z of vaccine/health advice for each country.
www.who.int The WHO Blue Book lists the diseases of the world.

Insurance

Always take out travel insurance before you set off and read the small print carefully. Check that the policy covers the activities you intend or may end up doing. Also check exactly what your medical cover includes, eg ambulance, helicopter rescue or emergency flights back home. Also check the payment protocol. You may have to cough up first before the insurance company reimburses you. It is always best to dig out all the receipts for expensive personal effects like jewellery or cameras. Take photos of these items and note down all serial numbers. You are advised to shop around. **STA Travel** and other reputable student travel organizations offer good-value policies. Young travellers from North America can try the **International Student Insurance Service** (**ISIS**), which is available through **STA Travel**, T01-800-7770112, www.sta-travel.com. Other recommended travel insurance companies in North America include: **Access America**, www.accessamerica.com; **Travel Guard**, www.noelgroup.com; **Travel Insurance Services**, www.travel insure.com; and **Travel Assistance International**, www.travel assistance.com. Older travellers should note that some companies will not cover people over 65 years old, or may charge higher premiums. The best policies for older travellers (UK) are offered by **Age Concern**, www.age concern org.uk.

Internet

Cambodia is surprisingly well-connected and most medium-sized to large towns have internet access. Not surprisingly, internet is a lot more expensive in smaller towns, up to a whopping US$5 per hr. In Phnom Penh internet rates are US$1-2 per hr and in Siem Reap should be US$1 per hr or under.

Useful words and phrases

Hello	*JOOm ree-up soo-a*	Where is the	*Noev ai nah?*
Goodbye	*Lee-a hai*	Is it far?	*Ch'ngai dtay?*
Thank you	*Or-gOOn*	Today	*T'ngai ni(h)*
How much is...?	*...T'lai bpon-mahn?*	Tomorrow	*Sa-aik*
That's expensive	*T'lai na(h)*	Yesterday	*M'seri mern*

Language

In Cambodia the national language is **Khmer**. It is not tonal and the script is derived from the southern Indian alphabet. French is spoken by the older generation who survived the Khmer Rouge era. English is the language of the younger generations. Away from Phnom Penh, Siem Reap and Sihanoukville it can be difficult to communicate with the local population unless your speak Khmer.

Media

Cambodia has a vigorous English-language press which fights bravely for editorial independence and freedom to criticize politicians. The principal English-language newspapers are the fortnightly *Phnom Penh Post*, which many regard as the best and the *Cambodia Daily*, published 5 times a week. There are also several tourist magazine guides.

Money → *US$1 = 4078, £1= 7976, €1 = 6316* (Aug 2008).
The **riel** is the official currency though US dollars are widely accepted and easily exchanged. In Phnom Penh and other towns most goods and services are priced in dollars and there is little need to buy riel. In remote rural areas prices are quoted in riel (except accommodation). Money can be exchanged in banks and hotels. US$ traveller's cheques are easiest to exchange – commission ranges from 1% to 3%. Cash advances on credit cards are available. Credit card facilities are limited but some banks, hotels and restaurants do accept them, mostly in the tourist centres.

ANZ Royal Bank has recently opened a number of ATMs throughout Phnom Penh. Machines are also now appearing in other towns and a full ATM network should be established in the next couple of years. Most machines give US$ only.

Cost of travelling

The budget traveller will find that a little goes a long way. Numerous guesthouses offer accommodation at around US$3-7 a night. Food-wise, the seriously strapped can easily manage to survive healthily on US$4-5 per day, so an overall daily budget (not allowing for excursions) of US$7-9 should be enough or the really cost-conscious. For the less frugally minded, a daily allowance of US$30 should see you relatively well-housed and fed, while at the upper end of the scale, there are, in Phnom Penh and Siem Reap, plenty of restaurants and hotels for those looking for Cambodian levels of luxury. A mid-range hotel (attached bathroom, hot water and a/c) will normally cost around US$25 per night and a good meal at a restaurant around US$5-10.

Opening hours

Banks Mon-Fri 0800-1600. Some close 1100-1300. Some major branches are open until 1100 on Sat.
Offices Mon-Fri 0730-1130, 1330-1630.
Restaurants, **cafés** and **bars** Daily from 0700-0800 although some open earlier. Bars are meant to close by 2400 by law.
Shops Daily from 0800-2000. Some, however, stay open for a further hour or 2, especially in tourist centres. Most markets open daily between 0530/0600-1700.

Police and the law

A vast array of offences are punishable in Cambodia, from minor traffic violations through to possession of drugs. If you are arrested or are having difficulty with the police contact your embassy immediately. As the police only earn approximately US$20 a month, corruption is a problem and contact should be avoided, unless absolutely necessary. Most services, including the provision of police reports, will require paying bribes. Law enforcement is very haphazard, at times completely subjective and justice can be hard to find. Some smaller crimes receive large penalties while perpetrators of greater crimes often get off scot-free.

Post
International service is unpredictable but it is reasonably priced and fairly reliable (at least from Phnom Penh). Only send mail from the GPO in any given town rather than sub POs or mail boxes. **Fedex** and **DHL** also offer services.

Safety
Cambodia is not as dangerous as some would have us believe. The country has really moved forward in protecting tourists and violent crime towards visitors is comparatively low. Safety on the night-time streets of Phnom Penh is a problem. Robberies and hold-ups are common. Many robbers are armed, so do not resist. As Phnom Penh has a limited taxi service, travel after dark poses a problem. Stick to moto drivers you know. Women are, obviously, particularly targeted by bag snatchers. Khmer New Year is known locally as the 'robbery season'. Theft is endemic at this time of year so be on red alert. A common trick around New Year is for robbers to throw water and talcum powder in the eyes of their victim and rob them. Leave your valuables in the hotel safe or hidden in your room.

Outside Phnom Penh safety is not as much of a problem. Visitors should be very cautious when walking in the countryside, however, as landmines and other unexploded ordnance is a ubiquitous hazard. Stick to well worn paths, especially around Siem Reap and when visiting remote temples. There is currently unrest on the border with Thailand around the Preah Vihear temple, check the situation before travelling.

Student travellers
Anyone in full-time education is entitled to an **International Student Identity Card** (www.isic.org). These are issued by student travel offices and travel agencies and offer special rates on all forms of transport and other concessions and services. They sometimes permit free admission to museums and sights, at other times a discount on admission.

Tax
Airport tax. In Cambodia the international departure tax is US$25, domestic tax is US$6.

Telephone → Country code +855.
Landline linkages are so poor in Cambodia that many people and businesses prefer to use mobile phones instead. The 3-digit prefix included in a 9-digit landline telephone number is the area (province) code. If dialling within a province, dial only the 6-digit number. International calls can be made from most guesthouses, hotels and phone booths but don't anticipate being able to make them outside Phnom Penh, Siem Reap and Sihanoukville. Use public **MPTC** or **Camintel** card phone boxes dotted around Phnom Penh to make international calls (cards are usually sold at shops near the booth). International calls are expensive, starting at US$4 per min in Phnom Penh, and more in the provinces. To make an overseas call from Cambodia, dial 007 or 001 + IDD country code + area code minus first 0 + subscriber number. Internet calls are without a doubt the cheapest way to call overseas.

Time
7 hrs ahead of GMT.

Tipping
Tipping is rare but appreciated. Salaries in restaurants and hotels are low and many staff hope to make up the difference in tips.

Tourist information

Government tourism services are minimal at best. The **Ministry of Tourism**, 3 Monivong Blvd, T023-426876, is not able to provide any useful information or services. The tourism office in Siem Reap is marginally better but will only provide services, such as guides, maps, etc, for a nominal fee. In all cases in Cambodia you are better off going through a private operator for information and price.

Useful websites

www.cambodia-online.com Useful starting point. Tends to be a bit out of date.
www.tourismcambodia.com Cambodia's National Tourism Authority. Good source of general and practical information on travel, visas, accommodation and so on.
www.travel.state.gov Useful information for travellers.
www.embassyofcambodia.org Remarkably good website set up by the Royal Cambodian Embassy in Washington DC. Informative and reasonably up to date.
www.cambodia.org The Cambodian Information Centre. Wealth of information.
www.khmer440.com The forum is very good for bouncing any specific Cambodia questions to the predominantly expat crowd.
www.gocambodia.com Useful range of practical information.

Tour operators

For regional tour operators, such as **Asian Trails**, www.asiantrails.info, refer to the Activities and tours listings in the guide.

In the UK

Adventure Company, Cross & Pillory House, Cross & Pillory Lane, Alton, Hampshire GU34 1HL, T0845-450 5316, www.adventurecompany.co.uk.
Audley Travel, New Mill, New Mill Lane, Whitney, Oxfordshire OX29 9SX, T01993-838100, www.audleytravel.com.
Explore, Nelson House, 55 Victoria Rd, Farnborough, Hants GU14 7PA, T0870-333 4002, www.explore.co.uk.

Guerba Adventure & Discovery Holidays, Wessex House, 40 Station Rd, Westbury, Wiltshire BA13 3JN, T01373-826611, www.guerba.co.uk.
Regent Holidays, Fromsgate House, Rupert St, Bristol BS1 2QJ, T0845-277 3317, www.regent-holidays.co.uk.
Silk Steps, Odyssey Lodge, Holy Well Rd, Edington, Bridgwater, Somerset TA7 9JH, T01278-722460, www.silksteps.co.uk.
Steppes Travel, 51 Castle St, Cirencester, Glos GL7 1QD, T01285-880980, www.steppestravel.co.uk.
Symbiosis Expedition Planning, Holly House, Whilton, Daventry, Northants, NN11 2NN, T0845-123 2844, www.symbiosis-travel.com.
Trans Indus, Northumberland House, 11 The Pavement, Popes Lane, London W5 4NG, T020-8566 2729, www.transindus.co.uk. Tailor-made holidays and group tours.
Travel Indochina, 2nd floor, Chester House, George St, Oxford 0X1 2AY, T01865-268940, www.travelindochina.co.uk. Small-group journeys and tailor-made holidays.
Travelmood, 214 Edgware Rd, London W2 1DH; 1 Brunswick Court, Leeds LS2 7QU; 16 Reform St, Dundee, DD1 1RG, T0800-2989815, www.travelmoodadventures.com.
Visit Asia (Tennyson Travel), 30-32 Fulham High St, London SW6 3LQ, T020-7736 4347, www.visitasia.co.uk. Specializes in tours throughout Asia.

In North America

Adventure Center, 1311 63rd St, Suite 200, Emeryville, CA, T+1-800 227 8747, www.adventurecenter.com.
Global Spectrum, 3907 Laro Court, Fairfax, VA 22031, T+1-800 -419 4446, www.globalspectrumtravel.com.
Hidden Treasure Tours, 509 Lincoln Blvd, Long Beach, NY 11561, T01-87-7761 7276 (USA toll free), www.hiddentreasuretours.com.
Journeys, 107 April Drive, Suite 3, Ann Arbor MI 46103, T+1-800-255 8735 (USA toll free), www.journeys-intl.com.
Myths & Mountains, 976 Tree Court, Incline Village, Nevada 89451, T1-800 670 6984,

www.mythsandmountains.com.
Organizes travel to all 3 countries.
Nine Dragons Travel & Tours, 1476 Orange
Grove Rd, Charleston, SC 29407, T+1-317-
281 3895, www.nine-dragons.com.

In Australia and New Zealand
Intrepid Travel, 360 Bourke St, Melbourne,
Victoria 3000, T+61-03-8602 0500,
www.intrepidtravel.com.au
Travel Indochina, Level 10, HCF House,
403 George St, Sydney, NSW 2000,
T+61-1300-138755 (toll free), www.travel
indochina.com.au. Small group journeys
and tailor-made holidays.

In Southeast Asia
Discovery Indochina, 3A Cua Bac St,
Hanoi, Vietnam, T(0084) 47-164132,
www.discoveryindochina.com. Private
and customized tours covering Cambodia
as well as Vietnam and Laos.

Visas and immigration
Visas on arrival
Visas for a 30-day stay are available on arrival
at Phnom Penh and Siem Reap airport.
Tourist visas cost US$20 and your passport
must be valid for at least 6 months from the
date of entry. You will need a passport photo.

Officially, visas are not available on the
Lao border. Many people have reported
successfully obtaining visas here but don't
rely on it. Travellers using the Lao border
should try to arrange visa paperwork in
advance in either Phnom Penh, Bangkok
or Vientiane. The **Cambodian Embassy** in
Bangkok, 185 Rajdamri Rd, T+66-2546630,
issues visas in 1 day if you apply in the
morning, as does the **Consulate General**
in HCMC, Vietnam, 41 Phung Khac Khoan,

T+84-88292751, and in Hanoi at 71 Tran
Hung Dao St, T+84-49424788. In both
Vietnam and Thailand, travel agencies are
normally willing to obtain visas for a small
fee. Cambodia has a few missions overseas
from which visas can be obtained.

Travellers leaving by land must ensure
that their Vietnam visa specifies Moc Bai or
Chau Doc as points of entry otherwise they
could be turned back. You can apply for
a Cambodian visa in HCMC and collect in
Hanoi and vice versa.

Visa extensions
Extensions can be obtained at the
Department for Foreigners on the road
to the Airport, T023-581558 (passport photo
required). Most travel agents arrange visa
extensions for around US$40 for 30 days.
Those overstaying their visas are fined US$5
per day, officials at land crossings often try to
squeeze out more.

Weights and measures
Metric.

Women
Women travelling alone are an unusual
sight in Cambodia and can expect a good
deal of curious attention. Sexual harassment
is not uncommon and many moto/tour
guides will try their luck with women but
generally it is more macho posturing than
anything serious. It is a good idea to dress
modestly and travel in the company of
others in remote areas and after dark,
especially in Phnom Penh. While women
travelling alone can generally face more
potential problems than men or couples,
these are far less pronounced in Cambodia
than in most countries.

Phnom Penh

→ *Colour map 6, B2.*

It is not hard to imagine Phnom Penh in its heyday, with wide, shady boulevards, beautiful French buildings and exquisite pagodas. They're still all here but are in a derelict, dust-blown, decaying state surrounded by growing volumes of cars, pick-up trucks and motorcyclists. It all leaves you wondering how a city like this works. But it does, somehow.

Phnom Penh is a city of contrasts: East and West, poor and rich, serenity and chaos. Although the city has a reputation as a frontier town, due to drugs, gun ownership and prostitution, a more cosmopolitan character is being forged out of the muck. Monks' saffron robes are once again lending a splash of colour to the capital's streets, following the reinstatement of Buddhism as the national religion in 1989, and stylish restaurants and bars line the riverside. However, the amputees on street corners are a constant reminder of Cambodia's tragic story. Perhaps the one constant in all the turmoil of the past century has been the monarchy – shifting, whimsical, pliant and, indeed, temporarily absent as it may have been. The splendid royal palace, visible to all, was a daily reminder of this ultimate authority whom even the Khmer Rouge had to treat with caution. The royal palace area, with its glittering spires, wats, stupas, national museum and broad green spaces, is perfectly situated alongside the river and is as pivotal to the city as the city is to the country. ➤➤ *For listings, see pages 87-97.*

Ins and outs

Getting there

Air Phnom Penh International airport lies approximately 10 km west of the city on Road No 4. There are flights to Phnom Penh from Bangkok, Ho Chi Minh City, Vientiane and Siem Reap. A taxi from the airport to town costs US$7 and a moto about US$3. The journey takes between 40 minutes and one hour although at peak times the roads are often gridlocked so be prepared for delays in the morning and late afternoon.

Boat and bus There is a river crossing with Laos at Voen Kham with the first town of note being Stung Treng, see page 112. It is also possible to get to Phnom Penh by boat and bus from Chau Doc in Vietnam and by road crossing at Moc Bai. ➤➤ *See Transport, page 1116.*

Getting around

Taxis are rare on the streets of Phnom Penh, particularly after dark. A fleet of *lomphata* (tuk-tuks) have sprung up that provide a good, cheaper alternative to cars. Nevertheless, hotels can arrange car hire around town and surrounding areas. Most visitors use the local *motodops* (motorbike taxis). There are cyclos too. Horizontal streets are evenly numbered and odd numbers are used for the vertical ones.

The royal quarter lies to the east of the town; north of here is what might be regarded as a colonial quarter with government ministries, banks, hotels and museums, many housed in French-era buildings. Chinatown, the commercial quarter, surrounds the central covered market, Psar Thmei. Sisowath Quay is where many visitors head as it has the highest concentration of restaurants and bars.

Tourist information

Ministry of Tourism ① *3 Monivong Blvd, T023-427130.*

Background

Phnom Penh lies at the confluence of the Sap, Mekong and Bassac rivers and quickly grew into an important commercial centre. Years of war have taken a heavy toll on the city's infrastructure and economy, as well as its inhabitants. Refugees first began to flood in from the countryside in the early 1950s during the First Indochina War and the population grew from 100,000 to 600,000 by the late 1960s. In the early 1970s there was another surge as people streamed in from the countryside again, this time to escape US bombing and guerrilla warfare. On the eve of the Khmer Rouge takeover in 1975, the capital had a population of two million, but soon became a ghost town. On Pol Pot's orders it was forcibly emptied and the townspeople frog-marched into the countryside to work as labourers. Only 45,000 inhabitants were left in the city in 1975 and a large number were soldiers. In 1979, after four years of virtual abandonment, Phnom Penh had a population of a few thousand. People began to drift back following the Vietnamese invasion (1978-1979) and as hopes for peace rose in 1991, the floodgates opened yet again: today the population is approaching one million.

Phnom Penh has undergone an economic revival since the Paris Peace Accord of 1991. Following the 1998 coup, however, there was an exodus of businesses and investors for whom this bloody and futile atrocity was the final straw. The relative stability since the coup has seen a partial revival of confidence but few are willing to risk their capital in long-term investments.

Sights

Royal Palace and Silver Pagoda
ⓘ *Entrance on Samdech Sothearos Blvd. Daily 0730-1100, 1430-1700. US$3, plus US$2 for camera or US$5 for video camera.*
The Royal Palace and Silver Pagoda were built mainly by the French in 1866, on the site of the old town. The **Throne Hall**, the main building facing the Victory Gate, was built in 1917 in Khmer style; it has a tiered roof and a 59-m tower, influenced by Angkor's Bayon Temple. The steps leading up to it are protected by multi-headed nagas. It is used for coronations and other official occasions: scenes from the *Ramayana* adorn the ceiling. Inside stand the sacred gong and French-style thrones only used by the sovereign. Above the thrones hangs Preah Maha Svetrachatr, a nine-tiered parasol, which symbolizes heaven. There are two chambers for the king and queen at the back of the hall, which are used only in the week before a coronation when the royal couple are barred from sleeping together. The other adjoining room is used to house the ashes of dead monarchs before they are placed in a royal stupa.

The **Royal Treasury** and the **Napoleon III Pavilion** (summer house), built in 1866, are to the south of the Throne Room. The latter was presented by Napoleon III to his Empress Eugenie as accommodation for the princess during the Suez Canal opening celebrations. She later had it dismantled and dispatched it to Phnom Penh as a gift to the king.

The **Silver Pagoda** is often called the Pagoda of the Emerald Buddha or Wat Preah Keo Morokat after the statue housed here. The wooden temple was originally built by King Norodom in 1892 to enshrine royal ashes and then rebuilt by Sihanouk in 1962. The pagoda's steps are Italian marble, and inside, its floor comprises of more than 5000 silver blocks which together weigh nearly six tonnes. All around are cabinets filled with presents from foreign dignitaries. The pagoda is remarkably intact, having been granted special

1 Phnom Penh

To French
Embassy
International   British
Mosque   Embassy   84
Calmette   30
Hospital

Boeng Kak Lake

US Embassy

Confederation de Russie Blvd

Psar Thmei
(Central
Market)

Kampuchea Krom Blvd

Charles de Gaulle Blvd

Wat Koh

Croix Rouge

Olympic
Stadium

Preah Sihanouk Blvd

Wat Moha
Montrei

Tuol Sleng
Museum

Thai

Mao Tse Tung Blvd

Wat Tuol
Tom Pong

To Psar Tuol Tom Pong
(Russian Market) & Rajana

To **5**, Boat Piers & Route 5, Japanese
Friendship Bridge & Route 6

➡ **Phnom Penh maps**
1 Phnom Penh, page 82
2 Sisowath Quay,
page 86

N

200 metres
200 yards

Tonlé Sap

Wat
Phnom

To Siem
Reap

Sisowath Quay

Wat Ounalom

National
Museum of
Cambodia

Samdech Sothearos Blvd

Norodom Blvd

Royal
Palace

Silver
Pagoda

Sisowath Quay

Vietnam
Airlines

Silk Air

Air France

Independence
Monument

Wat Lang Ka

Lao Airlines

Samdech Sothearos Blvd

Former US
Embassy

Lao
Embassy

Vietnamese
Embassy

To **13 17**, Route 1 & Vietnam

Bassac River

Sleeping
Anise 20 *D4*
Aram 28 *C5*
Billabong 1 *B3*
Boddhi Tree 2 *E3*
Café Freedom 4 *A3*
Cambodiana 30 *D5*
Capitol 5 *C3*
Diamond 6 *B3*
Flamingo 8 *C4*
Golden Gate 10 *D4*
Grandview Guesthouse
12 *A3*
Happy Guesthouse
14 *C3*
Hello Guesthouse 15 *C3*
Himawari 30 *C5*
Holiday Villa 16 *B3*
Imperial Garden Villa
11 *C5*
Juliana 19 *C2*
KIDS Guesthouse 7 *C4*
Lazy Fish Guesthouse &
Restaurant 21 *A3*
Le Royal 22 *A3*
L'Imprévu 13 *E4*
Narin Guesthouse 24 *D3*
New York 25 *C3*
Number 10 Lakeside
Guesthouse 27 *A3*
Palm Resort 17 *E4*
Pavilion 38 *C5*
Phnom Penh 29 *A3*
Regent Park 31 *C5*
Royal Phnom Penh 23 *E5*
Scandinavia 32 *D4*
Simon 2 Guesthouse
34 *A3*
Spring Guesthouse
35 *C3*
Sunway 36 *A3*
Walkabout 37 *C4*

Eating
Asia Europe Bakery 1 *D3*
Baan Thai 2 *D4*
Boeung Bopha 5 *A4*
Comme à la Maison 3 *D4*
Elsewhere 6 *D4*
Family 7 *A3*

Garden Centre Café 4 *D4*
Gasolina 8 *E4*
Jars of Clay 11 *E3*
Java 10 *D5*
Khmer Surin 12 *D4*
La Marmite 13 *B4*
Lazy Gecko 14 *A3*
Living Room 29 *D4*
Monsoon 35 *A4*
Mount Everest 15 *D4*
Origami 16 *C5*
Pancho Villa 18 *B4*
Peking Canteen 17 *B3*
Pyong Yang 19 *D3*
Rendezvous 20 *B4*
Riverhouse 20 *B4*
Sam Doo 21 *B3*
Shiva Shakti 22 *D4*
Tamarind 23 *C4*
Tell 25 *A3*
The Deli 36 *C4*
The Shop 24 *C4*
Topaz 28 *E4*

Bars & clubs
Cathouse 26 *B4*
Heart of Darkness &
Howie's 27 *B4*
Manhattan at Holiday
International
Hotel 30 *A3*
Peace Café 32 *E4*
Pontoon 40 *B4*
Q-Bar 41 *D4*
Sharkys 9 *B4*
Zepplin 34 *C3*

dispensation by the Khmer Rouge, although 60% of the Khmer treasures were stolen from here. In the centre of the pagoda is a magnificent 17th-century emerald Buddha statue made of Baccarat crystal. In front is a 90-kg golden Buddha studded with 9584 diamonds, dating from 1906. It was made from the jewellery of King Norodom and its vital statistics conform exactly to his – a tradition that can be traced back to the god-kings of Angkor.

National Museum of Cambodia
ⓘ *Entrance is on the corner of streets 13 and 178. Daily 0700-1130, 1400-1730. US$2, plus US$3 for camera or video; photographs only permitted in the garden. French- and English-speaking guides are available, mostly excellent.*

The National Museum of Cambodia was built in 1920 and contains a collection of Khmer art – notably sculpture – throughout the ages (although some periods are not represented). Galleries are arranged chronologically in a clockwise direction. Most of the exhibits date from the Angkor period but there are several examples from the pre-Angkor era (that is from the kingdoms of Funan, Chenla and Cham). The collection of Buddhas from the sixth and seventh centuries includes a statue of Krishna Bovardhana found at Angkor Borei showing the freedom and grace of early Khmer sculpture. The chief attraction is probably the pre-Angkorian statue of Harihara, found at Prasat Andat near Kompong Thom. There is a fragment from a beautiful bronze statue of Vishnu found in the West Baray at Angkor, as well as frescoes and engraved doors.

The riverside and Wat Ounalom
Sisowath Quay is Phnom Penh's Left Bank. A broad pavement runs along the side of the river and on the opposite side of the road a rather splendid assemblage of colonial buildings looks out over the broad expanse of waters. The erstwhile administrative buildings and merchants' houses today form an unbroken chain – almost a mile long – of bars and restaurants, with the odd guesthouse thrown in. While foreign tourist commerce fills the street, the quayside itself is dominated by local Khmer families who stroll and sit in the cool of the evening, served by an army of hawkers.

Phnom Penh's most important wat, **Wat Ounalom**, is north of the national museum, at the junction of Street 154 and Samdech Sothearos Boulevard, facing the Tonlé Sap. The first building on this site was a monastery, built in 1443 to house a hair of the Buddha. Before 1975, more than 500 monks lived at the wat but the Khmer Rouge murdered the Patriarch and did their best to demolish the capital's principal temple. Nonetheless it remains Cambodian Buddhism's headquarters. The complex has been restored since 1979 although its famous library was completely destroyed. The stupa behind the main sanctuary is the oldest part of the wat.

Central Market, Wat Phnom and Boeng Kak Lake
The stunning Central Market (Psar Thmei) is a perfect example of art-deco styling and one of Phnom Penh's most beautiful buildings. Inside a labyrinth of stalls and hawkers sell everything from jewellery through to curios. Those after a real bargain are better off heading to the Russian Market where items are much cheaper.

Wat Phnom stands on a small hill and is the temple from which the city takes its name. It was built by a wealthy Khmer lady called Penh in 1372. The sanctuary was rebuilt in 1434, 1890, 1894 and 1926. The main entrance is to the east; the steps are guarded by nagas and lions. The principal sanctuary is decorated inside with frescoes depicting scenes from

Phnom Penh's inhabitants

Of the original population of Phnom Penh thousands died during the Pol Pot era so the population of the city now seems rural in character. The population tends to vary from season to season: in the dry season people pour into the capital when there is little work in the countryside but go back to their farms in the wet season when the rice has to be planted.

Phnom Penh has long faced a housing shortage – two-thirds of its houses were damaged by the Khmer Rouge between 1975 and 1979 and the rate of migration into the city exceeds the rate of building. Apart from the sheer cost of building new ones and renovating the crumbling colonial mansions, there has been a severe shortage of skilled workers in Cambodia: under Pol Pot 20,000 engineers were killed and nearly all the country's architects.

Exacerbating the problem is the issue of land ownership as so many people were removed from their homes. These days there are many more qualified workers but sky-rocketing property prices coupled with the confusing issue of land title has created a situation where a great land grab is occuring with people being tossed out of their homes or having them bulldozed to make way for profitable developments.

Buddha's life and the *Ramayana*. At the front, on a pedestal, is a statue of the Buddha. There is a statue of Penh inside a small pavilion between the vihara and the stupa, with the latter containing the ashes of King Ponhea Yat (1405-1467). The surrounding park is tranquil and a nice escape from the madness of the city. Monkeys with attitude are in abundance but they tend to fight between themselves.

Boeng Kak Lake is the main area budget travellers stay in. The lakeside setting with the all important westerly aspect – eg sunsets – appeals strongly to the nocturnal instincts of guests. Some bars and restaurants open 24 hours a day. The lake is quite beautiful, but close to the guesthouses it becomes more like a floating rubbish tip.

Around Independence Monument

South of the Royal Palace, between Street 268 and Preah Sihanouk Boulevard, is the **Independence Monument**. It was built in 1958 to commemorate independence but has now assumed the role of a cenotaph. **Wat Lang Ka**, on the corner of Sihanouk and Norodom boulevards, was another beautiful pagoda that fell victim to Pol Pot's architectural holocaust. Like Wat Ounalom, it was restored in Khmer style on the direction of the Hanoi-backed government in the 1980s. It is a really soothing getaway from city madness and the monks here are particularly friendly. They hold a free meditation session every Monday and Thursday night at 1800; anyone is welcome to join in.

Tuol Sleng Museum ('Museum of Genocide')

ⓘ *Street 113, Tue-Sun 0800-1100, 1400-1700; public holidays 0800-1800. US$2; free film at 1000 and 1500.*

After 17 April 1975 the classrooms of Tuol Svay Prey High School became the Khmer Rouge main torture and interrogation centre, known as Security Prison 21 or S-21. More than 20,000 people were taken from S-21 to their executions at Choeung Ek extermination camp, see below. Countless others died under torture and were thrown into mass graves in the school grounds. Only seven prisoners survived because they were sculptors and could turn out countless busts of Pol Pot. One block of classrooms is given over to photographs of the victims.

Former US Embassy

The former US Embassy, now home to the Ministry of Fisheries, is at the intersection of Norodom and Mao Tse Tung boulevards. As the Khmer Rouge closed on the city from the north and the south in April 1975, US Ambassador John Gunther Dean pleaded with Secretary of State Henry Kissinger for an urgent airlift of embassy staff. But it was not until the very last minute (just after 1000 on 12 April 1975, with the Khmer Rouge firing mortars from across the Bassac River onto the football pitch near the compound that served as a landing zone) that the last US Marine helicopter left the city. Flight 462, a convoy of military transport helicopters, evacuated the 82 remaining Americans, 159 Cambodians and 35 other foreigners to a US aircraft carrier in the Gulf of Thailand. Their departure was overseen by 360 heavily armed marines. Despite letters to all senior government figures from the ambassador, offering them places on the helicopters, only one, Acting President Saukham Khoy, fled the country. The American airlift was a deathblow to Cambodian morale. Within five days, the Khmer Rouge had taken the city and within hours all senior officials of the former Lon Nol government were executed on the tennis courts of the embassy.

Choeung Ek

ⓘ *Southwest on Monireth Blvd, about 15 km from town. US$2. Return trip by moto US$2-5. A shared car (US$10) is more comfortable.*

In a peaceful setting, surrounded by orchards and rice fields, Choeung Ek was the execution ground for the torture victims of Tuol Sleng, the Khmer Rouge extermination centre, S-21 (see above). It is referred to by some as 'The killing fields'. Today a huge

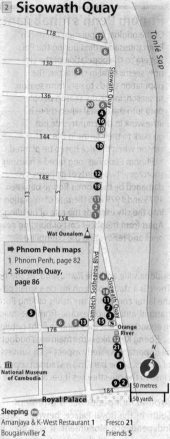

② Sisowath Quay

➡ **Phnom Penh maps**
1 Phnom Penh, page 82
2 Sisowath Quay, page 86

Wat Ounalom

National Museum of Cambodia

Royal Palace

50 metres
50 yards

Sleeping ⊜
Amanjaya & K-West Restaurant 1
Bougainvillier 2
Bright Lotus Guesthouse 3
California 2 4
Foreign Correspondents
  Club of Cambodia (FCCC) 12
Indochine 2 5
Paragon 6
Red Hibiscus 11
Renakse 12
River Star 8
Sunshine 10

Fresco 21
Friends 5
Frizz 11
Happy Herb Pizza 7
Khmer Borane 9
La Croisette 10
Metro 12
Pacharan 2
Pop Café 8
Rising Sun 13
Riverside 19
Veiyo 16

Eating ⊙
Bali 1
Cantina 4
Chiang Mai Riverside 4
Fortune Pho 15

Bars & clubs ⊙
Ginger Monkey 6
Memphis Pub 17
Pink Elephant Pub 18
Salt Lounge 20

glass tower stands on the site, filled with the cracked skulls of men, women and children exhumed from 129 mass graves in the area (which were not discovered until 1980). To date 8985 corpses have been exhumed from the site. Rather disturbingly, rags and crumbling bones still protrude from the mud.

⊙ Phnom Penh listings

Hotel and guesthouse prices
LL over US$200   L US$151-200   AL US$101-150
A US$66-100   B US$46-65   C US$31-45
D US$21-30   E US$12-20   F US$7-11
G US$6 and under

Restaurant prices
††† over US$12   †† US$6-12   † under US$6.

⊜ Sleeping

Phnom Penh p80, maps p82 and p86
Boeung Kak Lake has become somewhat of a Khaosan Rd, with most backpackers opting to stay there. Street 182 also offers a selection of cheaper alternatives. The majority of hotels organize airport pick-up and most of them for free.
LL Le Royal, St 92, Phnom Penh, T023-981 888, www.raffles-hotelleroyal.com. A wonderful colonial era hotel built in 1929 which has been superbly renovated by the Raffles Group. The renovation was done tastefully, incorporating many of the original features and something of the old atmosphere. The hotel has excellent bars, restaurants and a delightful tree-lined pool. 2 for 1 cocktails 1600-2000 daily at the Elephant Bar is a must.
L-AL Himawari, 313 Sisowath Quay, T023-214555, www.himawarihotel.com. With luxurious designer apartments/suites, the Himawari offers an upmarket spot on the river. The usual a/c, cable TV and en suite facilities enhance great river views. Good restaurants, gym and nice pool.
L-A Cambodiana, 313 Sisowath Quay, T023-426288, www.hotelcambodiana.com. Originally built for Prince (as he was then) Sihanouk's guests. This eyesore of a building has more than a few Communist touches and

it's not surprising that in a former life under the Lol Non regime, it was a military base. The place is redeemed by its vista, which overlooks the confluence of the Mekong, Tonlé Sap and Bassac rivers. 300 rooms, every one of which is equipped with an internet connection. Exceptional facilities.
L-A Phnom Penh Hotel, 54 Monivong Blvd, T023-724851, www.phnompenhhotel.com. This hotel comes most recommended from almost everyone in Cambodia's tourism industry. 407 well-appointed rooms with TV, a/c, internet. Health club, spa and an outdoor swimming pool. Exceptional value.
AL Amanjaya, corner St 154 and Sisowath Quay, T023-219579, www.amanjaya.com. Gorgeous rooms full of amenities, beautiful furniture and creative finishing touches. The balconies have some of the best views on the river. Service can be a little ragged – you'll be asked to pay in full when you check-in – but they get enough right to make this probably the nicest place by the river. Free Wi-Fi and awesome breakfast are both included in the room rate. Good location. Recommended.
AL-A Imperial Garden Villa and Hotel, 315 Sisowath Quay, T023-219991, www.imperialgarden-hotel.com. Another unsightly architectural development. The term 'garden', in this context, seems to refer to an area of concrete with the odd plant chucked in for good measure. The rooms (and suites) have a reasonably good view over the river, with wide screen TV, safe and all modern conveniences. Swimming pool, tennis, massage centre and restaurant.
AL-A Sunway, No 1 St 92, T023-430333, asunway@online.com.kh. Overlooking Wat Phnom, this is an adequate hotel in an excellent location. 140 ordinary though well-appointed rooms, including 12 spacious

suites, provide comfort complemented by facilities and amenities to cater for the international business and leisure traveller.

A Aram, St 244, T012-565509, www.boddhi tree.com. Nice little guesthouse tucked away in a small street near the palace. The stylish rooms are a bit small and overpriced.

A Bougainvillier Hotel, 277G Sisowath Quay, T023-220528, www.bougainvillierhotel.com. Lovely riverside boutique hotel, rooms decorated in a very edgy, modern Asian theme, with a/c, safe, cable TV and minibar. Good French restaurant.

A Foreign Correspondents Club of Cambodia (FCCC), 363 Sisowath Quay, T023-210142, www.fccccambodia.com. Known locally as the FCC. 3 decent sized rooms are available in this well-known Phnom Penh landmark.

A Juliana, No 16, St 152, T023-366070, www.julianacambodia.com.kh. A very attractive resort-style hotel with 91 rooms, and decent sized pool in a secluded garden which provides plenty of shade; several excellent restaurants.

A The Pavilion, 227 St 19, T023-222280, www.pavilion-cambodia.com. A popular and beautiful small, 10-room hotel set in an old French colonial villa. Each room is unique with a/c, en suite and TV. The restaurant also serves decent food. However, the management has a reputation for being prickly and a penchant for banning organisations and individuals. Children are completely banned (unless friends of the owner) – we've had several reports of the management abruptly and unceremoniously asking women with children to leave the restaurant.

A Royal Phnom Penh, Samdech Sotheraos Blvd, T023-982673, royalphnompenh@ bigpond.com.kh. On the Bassac River, a short drive south of the centre, this hotel is set in a large park. A tad run down but still sufficient. Swimming pool, spacious rooms.

A-D Diamond, 172-184 Monivong Blvd, T023-217221/2, diamondhotels@online. com.kh. Hotel in a good central location. A little overshadowed by some of the newer

and better hotels but the staff are exceptionally helpful and friendly. Rooms are clean with TV and bath.

A-D Holiday Villa, 89 Monivong Blvd, T023-990888, www.holidayvilla.com.my. A bit 1970s but well appointed, with bath, internet, TV, safe, IDD phone. Breakfast included.

A-D Regent Park, 58 Samdech Sotheraos Blvd, T023-427131, regentpark@online. com.kh. The well-designed lobby belies a collection of ordinary rooms and apartment-style suites. Still, it's reasonable value and in a good location. Thai and European restaurant. Price includes breakfast.

C-D Flamingo Hotel, No 30, St 172, T023-221640, reservation@flamingo.com.kh. Reasonably new hotel, bit garish from the outside but good facilities. Well-fitted rooms with all the amenities, including a bath. Free internet, a gym and a restaurant.

C-D Red Hibiscus, No 277c Sisowath Quay, T023-990691, www.redhibiscus.biz. Stylish rooms, some with river views, in an excellent location. A/c, en suite and with TV.

C-D Renakse, 40 Samdech Sotheraos Blvd, T023-215701, renakse-htl@camnet.com.kh. Splendid yellow French colonial building in large grounds immediately opposite the Royal Palace. This hotel has the feel of a bygone era. Rooms are decorated in a tasteful, modern Asian style.

C-D River Star Hotel, corner of Sisowath Quay and St 118, T023-990501, river_star_ hotel@yahoo.com. Decent hotel on the riverfront. The only thing extraordinary about the rooms is the view. All rooms have a/c, bathroom and seating area.

C-D Scandinavia Hotel, No 4, St 282, T023-214 498, nisse@online.com.kh. Well-appointed, clean rooms with a/c and TV. Rooftop restaurant/bar. Pool and sauna.

C-E Anise, 2c St 278, T023-222522, www.anisehotel.com. Excellent value in the heart of a busy area. All rooms are en suite with cable TV and a/c. Pay a little more and you'll get a room with a bath and private balcony. Included in the price is laundry, internet and breakfast. Recommended.

C-E Golden Gate Hotel, No 9 St 278 (just off St 51), T023-721161, goldengatehtls@hotmail.com. Very popular and comparatively good value for the facilities offered. Clean rooms with TV, fridge, hot water and a/c. Within walking distance to restaurants and bars. Visa/MasterCard.

C-E New York Hotel, 256 Monivong Blvd, T023-214116, www.newyorkhotel.com.kh. The rooms aren't going to set the world on fire but the facilities are good for the price – massage centre, sauna, restaurant and in-room safe.

C-E Palm Resort, on Route 1, 5 km out of Phnom Penh, T023-3086881. Beautiful bungalows surrounded by lush gardens and a very large swimming pool. A/c rooms with very clean bathrooms. Excellent French restaurant. Recommended.

C-F Paragon Hotel, 219b Sisowath Quay, T023-222607, info_paragonhotel@yahoo.com. The Paragon gets the simple things right – it's a well-run and friendly hotel. The best and priciest rooms have private balconies overlooking the river. The cheaper rooms at the back are dark but still some of the best value in this part of town. Colour TV, hot water and private shower or bath, a/c or fan. Recommended.

D-E Billabong, No 5, St 158, T023-223703, www.billabongcambodia.com. Reasonably new hotel with well-appointed rooms. Breakfast included. Swimming pool, poolside bar and deluxe rooms with balconies overlooking the pool. Internet.

D-F Bright Lotus Guesthouse, No 22 St 178 (near the museum), T023-990446, sammy_lotus@hotmail.com. Fan and a/c rooms with private bathroom and balconies. Restaurant.

D-F Hotel California 2, No 317 Sisowath Quay, T023-982182. One block up from the FCC, overlooking the Tonlé Sap. TV, a/c, attached hot water bathroom with bath. Bored-looking staff. Front rooms are single only but with splendid views of the river.

D-F Indochine 2 Hotel, No 28-30 St 130, T023-211525. Great location and good, clean, comfortable rooms.

D-F KIDS Guesthouse, No 17A, St 178, T012-410406, ryan@ryanhem.com. Rather a good find. Guesthouse of the Khmer Internet Development Service (KIDS) set in a small tropical garden, spotted with a couple of cabana-style internet kiosks. A couple of rooms are a decent size, quite clean and equipped with a huge fridge. Discount on internet use for guests. Welcoming, safe and free coffee.

D-F L'Imprévu, on Hwy 1, 6 km past the Monivong Bridge, T023-360405, imprecas@everyday.com.kh. French-run. Lovely bungalows with TV, fridge and hot water. Good pool and garden. Tennis court, petanque, snooker, table tennis and a gym.

D-G Sunshine, No 253 Sisowath Quay, T023-725684, F023-18256. With 50 rooms, a few with a glimpse of the river. Facilities, from a/c to fan, in accordance with price.

D-G Walkabout Hotel, corner of St 51 and St 174, T023-211715, www.walkabouthotel.com. A popular Australian-run bar, café and guesthouse. 23 rooms ranging from small with no windows and shared facilities to large rooms with own bathroom and a/c. Rooms and bathrooms are okay but lower-end rooms are a little gloomy and cell-like. 24-hr bar.

E-F Boddhi Tree, No 50, St 113, T016-865 445, www.boddhitree.com. A tranquil setting. Lovely old wooden building with guest rooms offering simple amenities, fan only, some rooms have private bathroom. Great gardens and fantastic food. Very reasonable prices.

E-F Spring Guesthouse, No 34, St 111 (next to the German Embassy), T023-222155, spring_guesthouse@yahoo.com. Newly established guesthouse in good location. Fan, cable, a/c and hot shower.

E-G Capitol, No 14, St 182, T023-364104, capitol@online.com.kh. As they say, 'a Phnom Penh institution'. What, in 1991, was a single guesthouse has expanded to 5 guesthouses all within a stone's throw. All aim at the budget traveller and offer travel services as well as a popular café and internet access. There are a number of other cheap guesthouses in close proximity, such as **Happy Guesthouse** (next door to Capitol Guesthouse) and **Hello Guesthouse** (No 24, 2 St 107) – all about the same ilk.

E-G Narin Guesthouse, No 20 St 111, off Sihanouk Blvd, T023-986131, touchnarin@ hotmail.com. In the western part of the city, not far from the Olympic stadium. Popular but has a bit of a seedy feel to it. Some with en suite bathroom, some with shared. Travel arrangements made.

G Café Freedom, lakeside, T012-807345, www.cafefreedom.org.uk. There are only 7 rooms so more often than not this place is booked out. Nice, relaxing atmosphere, except for the fierce guard dogs.

G Grandview Guesthouse, just off the lake, T023-430766. This place is streets ahead of local competition. Clean, basic rooms. A few extra bucks gets you a/c. Nice rooftop restaurant affording good sunset views, with large breakfast menu, pizza, Indian and Khmer food. Travel services and internet.

G Happy Guesthouse and Restaurant, No 11, St 93, lakeside, T023-877232. If your idea of good accommodation is staying in a cupboard, then this is the place for you. 40 basic rooms, most with shared facilities but a few with private bathroom. Restaurant, free pool and lovely veranda area.

G Lazy Fish Guesthouse and Restaurant, No 16 St 93, lakeside, T012-703368. Very basic guesthouse with shared bathroom facilities.

G No 10 Lakeside Guesthouse, No 10 St 93, Boeng Kak Lake, T012-454373. It is rather dingy and stuffy. Hammocks, pool tables and lockers.

G Simon 2 Guesthouse, the road in front of the lake. This place has the largest, cleanest rooms.

⊙ Eating

Phnom Penh *p80, maps p82 and p86*
Most places are relatively inexpensive – US$3-6 per head. There are several cheaper cafés along Monivong Blvd, around the lake,

Kampuchea Krom Blvd (St 128) in the city centre and along the river. Generally the food in Phnom Penh is good and the restaurants surprisingly refined. One of the most remarkable assemblages of restaurants is to be found on Hwy 6, several kilometres beyond the Japanese Friendship (or Chruoy Changvar) Bridge. Also around here is an area that the expats refer to as the 'hammock bar stretch'. A strip of restaurants and beer parlours with a multitude of hammocks which boast great sunset views. Excellent, cheap Khmer food and loads of cold beer, a must. To get there just look for the anchor beer signs on the side of the road.

TTT Bougainvillier Hotel, 277G Sisowath Quay, T023-220528. Upmarket French and Khmer food. Superb foie gras and you can even find truffles here. Fine dining by the river. Recommended.

TTT Comme à la Maison, No 13, St 57, T023-360801. Great French delicatessen-type restaurant-cum-café. Good pizzas and breakfast is exceptional.

TTT Elsewhere, No 175, St 51, T023-211348. An oasis in the middle of the city offering delectable modern Western cuisine. Seats are speckled across wonderful tropical gardens, all topped off by a well-lit pool. This place has everything right – the food, the setting, the music.

TTT Foreign Correspondents Club of Cambodia (FCCC), No 363 Sisowath Quay, T023-210142. A Phnom Penh institution that can't be missed. Superb colonial building, 2nd floor bar and restaurant that overlooks the Tonlé Sap. Extensive menu with an international flavour, fantastic pizzas and creative salads.

TTT K-West, Amanjaya Hotel, corner of St 154 and Sisowath Quay, T023-219579, open 0630-2200. Beautiful, spacious restaurant offering respite from the outside world. Khmer and European food plus extensive cocktail list. Surprisingly, the prices aren't that expensive considering how upmarket it is. Come early for the divine chocolate mousse – it sells out quickly. Free Wi-Fi. Recommended.

Origami, No 88 Sothearos Blvd, T012-968095. Best Japanese in town, fresh sushi and sashimi. Pricey – one local describes it as where "good things come in very small, expensive packages".

Pacharan, 389 Sisowath Quay, T023-224394, 1100-2300. Excellent Spanish tapas and main courses in a old colonial villa with views across the river and an open kitchen. Stylish Mediterranean feel to it. While the tapas are good value the prices of the main courses are about the highest in town. Part of the FCC empire. Recommended.

Red Hibiscus, 277c Sisowath Quay, T023-990691. Eclectic range of crocodile and ostrich steaks on sale at this riverside establishment – the cow steaks are not bad either.

Riverhouse, corner of St 110 and Sisowath Quay, T023-220180. Mediterranean/Thai restaurant in a lovely restored building overlooking the river. Brilliant food, particularly the steak, which is cooked to perfection. Upstairs is a comfortable lounge bar which also serves light meals.

Shiva Shakti, 70 Sihanouk Blvd, T012-813817, open until 2230, closed Mon. Facing the Independence Monument. Indian and Moghul specials, vegetarian and meat dishes. The option of pavement eating does not appeal by the side of this busy boulevard but the calm and aromatic atmosphere of the interior is enormously attractive. Quite expensive for Phnom Penh but a good range of excellent food. Selection of cigars.

Tell, No 13 St 90, T023-430650. Restaurant closes at 2300, bar at 2400. Swiss German specials including excellent raclette, fondue and wurst. Generous portions authentically prepared. Imported German beer. Owners maintain high standards in the kitchen and in the chalet-esque dining room. There's another branch in Siem Reap.

Topaz, 182 Norodom Blvd, T012-333276, 1100-1400, 1800-2300. Has set its sights on being the most upmarket place in town – a/c restaurant or outside dining, upstairs bar and cigar room. Recommended if you can afford it.

Baan Thai, No 2, St 306, T023-362991, 1130-1400, 1730-2200. Excellent Thai food and attentive service. Popular restaurant. Garden and old wooden Thai house setting with sit down cushions.

Bali, No 379 Sisowath Quay, T023-982211, 0700-2300. A wide range of very tempting Indonesian dishes on offer. Upstairs balcony facing the river.

Boddhi Tree, No 50, St 113, T016-865445, www.boddhitree.com. A delightful garden setting and perfect for lunch, a snack or a drink. Salads, sandwiches, barbecue chicken. Very good Khmer food.

Cantina, No 347 Sisowath Quay. Great Mexican restaurant and bar opened by long-time local identity, Hurley Scroggins III. Fantastic food made with the freshest of ingredients. The restaurant attracts an eclectic crowd and can be a source of great company.

The Deli, near corner of St 178 and Norodom Blvd. Great cakes, bread, salads and lunch at this sleek little diner. Sandwich fillings, for the price, are a bit light, though.

Gasolina, 56/58 St 57, T012-373009, 1100-late. Huge garden and decent French-inspired food await in this friendly, relaxed restaurant. The owner also arranges t'ai chi and capoeira classes. They normally have a BBQ at the weekends.

Khmer Borane, No 389 Sisowath Quay, T012-290092, open till 2300. Excellent Khmer restaurant just down from the FCC. Wide selection of very well prepared Khmer and Thai food. Try the Amok.

La Croisette, No 241 Sisowath Quay, T023-882221. Authentically French and good value hors d'oeuvres and steak. Good selection of wines.

La Marmite, No 80 St 108 (on the corner with Pasteur), T012-391746, closed Tue. Excellent value French food – some of the best in town. Extremely large portions.

Living Room, No 9 St 306, T023-726139, Tue-Thu 0700-1800, Fri-Sun 0700-2100. The Japanese owner has done a superlative job at this pleasant hangout spot. The food and coffee is spot-on and the set plates are great value but it's the laid back, calming vibe that is the clincher. There's a purpose-built kids play area downstairs. Free Wi-Fi if you spend over US$3. Highly recommended.

Metro, corner of Sisowath and St 148, 1000-0200. Huge, affordable tapas portions make this a great spot for lunch or dinner. Try the crème brûlée smothered in passion fruit. Free Wi-Fi. Recommended.

Monsoon, 17 St 104, T016-355867, 1800-0200. They serve a fine curry at this funky South Asian restaurant-cum-wine bar. The drinks list is also pretty good. Recommended.

Mount Everest, 98 Sihanouk Blvd, T023-213821, 1000-2300. Has served acclaimed Nepalese and Indian dishes for 5 years, attracting a loyal following. There's also a branch in Siem Reap.

Pancho Villa, No 2 St 108 (just off Sisowath Quay). Good Mexican food, breakfast and coffee. The bar claims to be able to make any cocktail. The Hawaiian-shirt-clad owners are good for a chat.

Pop Café, 371 Sisowath Quay, T012-562892, 1100-1430, 1800-2200. Almost perfect, small, Italian restaurant sited next door to the FCC. Owned and managed by Italian ex-pat Giorgio, the food has all the panache you'd expect from an Italian. The home-made lasagne is probably one of the best value meals in town. Recommended.

Pyong Yang Restaurant, 400 Monivong Blvd, T023-993765. This North Korean restaurant is an all-round experience not to be missed. The food is exceptional but you need to get there before 1900 to get a seat before their nightly show starts. All very bizarre: uniformed, clone-like waitresses double as singers in the nightly show, which later turns into open-mic karaoke.

Rendezvous, No 239 Sisowath Quay, T023-736622. Large comfortable chairs, great place for breakfast or a leisurely lunch and very popular for its 2 for 1 happy hour everyday from 1600-1800. Khmer owned.

Rising Sun, No 20, St 178 (just round the corner from the FCC). English restaurant

with possibly the best breakfast in town. Enormous roasts and excellent iced coffee.

Riverside, corner 148 and Sisowath Quay, T023-766743. Enjoy omelettes and burgers while dining inside or out.

Talking to a Stranger, No 21 St 294, T012-798530, Wed-Sun. Fantastic bar and restaurant with beer garden. Run by a friendly Australian couple, Derek and Wendy. High on atmosphere, brilliant photographic display, wide selection of innovative meals.

Tamarind, No 31 St 240, T012-830139. Stylish place specializing in French and Mediterranean, great kebabs and couscous. Bar and tapas. Atmospheric.

Veiyo (River Breeze), No 237 Sisowath Quay, T012-847419. Pizza and pasta, etc along with Thai and Khmer cuisine.

Boeung Bopha, Hwy 6 (over the Japanese Friendship Bridge), T012-928353, open until 2300. Large Khmer restaurant with huge menu which includes a number of Khmer dishes and buffet.

Chiang Mai Riverside, No 227 Sisowath Quay, T011-811456, open until 2200. Riverfront location for this small but successful Thai restaurant. Simple picture menus (always a turn-off but common in Cambodia where little English is spoken). Endorsed by the Thai government.

Family Restaurant, St 93, lakeside. Small, unassuming family-run, Vietnamese restaurant serving brilliant (and quite adventurous) food at ridiculously low prices. Great service, lovely owners.

Fortune Pho, St 178, just behind the FCC, 0800-2100. Great Vietnamese noodles in this small shop. Unfortunately the experience can sometimes be ruined by dreadful service.

Friends, No 215, St 13, T023-426748. Non profit restaurant run by street kids being trained in the hospitality industry. The food is delicious and cheap.

Frizz, 335 Sisowath Quay, T023-220953. Awesome Khmer food. Friendly service and great location. One of the best spots to eat local food on the riverside. Incredibly cheap as well. Recommended.

Happy Herb Pizza, No 345 Sisowath Quay, T023-332349. A Phnom Penh institution. Watch out for the 'happy' pizza full of hash – it has a nasty kick. Free pizza delivery.

Khmer Surin, No 9, St 57, T023-363050, closes at 2230. Set in an attractive building with some traditional Thai-style seating on cushions, this restaurant is a little way south of Sihanouk Blvd. Quiet.

Lazy Gecko, St 93, lakeside. Popular, chilled out restaurant/café/bar offering a good selection of sandwiches, burgers and salads in large portions. Good home-cooked Sun roast. Affable owner, Juan, is a good source of information. Selection of new and used books for sale. Good trivia night on Thu.

Peking Canteen, No 393, St 136, T011-909548, open till 2200. Hole in the wall Chinese restaurant famous for its cheap dumplings (which come either steamed or fried). Very busy at lunch time.

Sam Doo, 56 Kampuchea Krom Blvd, T023-218773, open until 0200. Late night Chinese food and the best and cheapest dim sum in town.

The Shop, No 39, St 240, T012-901964, 0900-1800. Deli and bakery serving sandwiches, juices, fruit teas, salads and lunches.

Cafés and bakeries

Asia Europe Bakery, No 95 Sihanouk Blvd, T012-893177. One of the few Western-style bakery/cafés in the city. Delicious pastries, cakes and excellent breakfast and lunch menu. Recommended.

Fresco, 365 Sisowath Quay, T023-217041. Just underneath the FCC and owned by the same people. They have a wide selection of sandwiches, cakes and pastries of mixed quality and high price.

Garden Centre Café, No 23, St 57, T023-363002. Popular place to go for lunch and breakfast, perhaps not surprisingly, the garden is nice too.

Jars of Clay, No 39 St 155 (beside the Russian Market). Fresh cakes and pastries.

Java, No 56 Sihanouk Blvd. Contenders for best coffee in town. Nice use of space –

open-air balcony and pleasant surroundings. Delightful food. Features art and photography exhibitions on a regular basis.

T&C Coffee World, numerous branches – 369 Preah Sihanouk Blvd; Sorya Shopping Centre; 335 Monivong Blvd. Vietnamese-run equivalent of **Starbucks**, but better. Surprisingly good food and very good coffee. Faultless service.

⦿ Bars and clubs

Phnom Penh *p80, maps p82 and p86*
The vast majority of bars in Phnom Penh attract prostitutes.

The Cathouse, corner of St 51 and St 118, open till 2400. Around since the UNTAC days of the early 1990s and one of the oldest running bars in the city. Not a bad place to have a beer.

Elephant Bar, Le Royal Hotel. Open until 2400. Stylish and elegant bar in Phnom Penh's top hotel, perfect for an evening gin. 2 for 1 happy hour every day with unending supply of nachos, which makes for a cheap night out in sophisticated surroundings. Probably the best drinks in town.

Elsewhere, No 175, St 51. Highly atmospheric, upmarket bar set in garden with illuminated pool. Great cocktails and wine. Very popular with the expats, who have been known to strip off for a dip. Livens up on the last Sat of every month for parties.

Foreign Correspondents Club of Cambodia (FCCC), 363 Sisowath Quay. Satellite TV, pool, *Bangkok Post* and *The Nation* both available for reading here, happy hour 1700-1900. Perfect location overlooking the river.

Ginger Monkey, No 29, St 178. Stylish, well decorated bar with faux Angkorian reliefs. Chilled out atmosphere. Quite popular with the younger expat crowd.

Heart of Darkness, No 26, St 51. Reasonable prices, friendly staff and open late. Has been Phnom Penh's most popular hangout for a number of years. Full of prostitutes, but your best bet for a night of dancing. There have been many violent 'incidents' here, so it is advisable to be on your best behaviour in the bar as they do not tolerate any provocation. An increasingly popular option is **Howie's Bar** next door.

Hotel California 2, 317 Sisowath Quay. Restaurant and bar, quite similar to the others on the riverfront. Staff not particularly helpful. US$0.75 pasties a major drawcard.

La Croisette has live music every Thu and Fri. See Eating.

Manhattan, in the rather dubious **Holiday International Hotel**, St 84, T023-427402. One of Phnom Penh's biggest discos. Security check and metal detectors at the door prevent you from bringing in small arms.

Memphis Pub, St 118 (off Sisowath Quay), open till 0200. Small bar off the river. Very loyal following from the NGO crowd. Live rock and blues music from Tue to Sat.

Metro, corner Sisowath and St 148, T023-217 517, 1000-0200. Serves fine grub and is home to a fabulous bar. Popular with rich Khmers and expansive ex-pats. Recommended.

Peace Café (Sontipheap), No 234, St 258. Chilled-out bar with cheap drinks and friendly owner.

Pink Elephant Pub, 343 Sisowath Quay. Predominantly male bar with English football, pool, beer and bar food.

Pontoon, on the river at end of St 108, T012-572880, weekdays 1200-2330, until late at weekends. Great little spot for a drink and dance. Hosts international DJs and serves good cocktails. Recommended.

Q-Bar, 96 Sothearos Blvd, T092-541821, 1600-0400. This bar has 'imported' (or stolen) most of its design from the famous **Bed Supper Club** in Bangkok. Expensive, Q-Bar attracts yuppie locals and wannabe foreigners.

The Rising Sun, No 20, St 178, T023-970719, closes at 2400. Just around the corner from the FCCC. An English pub whose emphasis is just as much on food as beer.

Riverside Bar, 273a Sisowath Quay. Great riverfront bar. Tasty food. Recommended.

Riverhouse Lounge, No 6, St 110 (Sisowath Quay), 1600-0200. Upmarket, cocktail bar and

club. Nice views of the river and airy open balcony space. Live music (Sun) and DJs (Sat).

Salt Lounge, No 217, St 136, T012-289905, www.thesaltlounge.com. Funky minimalist bar. Very atmospheric and stylish. Gay friendly.

Sharkys, No 126 St 130. "Beware pickpockets and loose women" it warns. Large, plenty of pool tables and food served until late. Quite a 'blokey' hangout.

Talking to a Stranger, see Eating. Great cocktails, relaxed atmosphere. Recommended.

Zepplin Bar aka Rock Bar, No 128, St 136 (just off Monivong beside the Central Market), open until late. Hole in the wall bar owned by a Taiwanese man named Joon who has more than 1000 records for customers to choose from. Cheap beer and spirits.

● Entertainment

Phnom Penh p80, maps p82 and p86
Pick up a copy of the Cambodia Daily and check out the back page which details up-and-coming events.

Dance

National Museum of Cambodia, St 70. Folk and national dances are performed by the National Dance group as well as shadow puppets and circus. Fri and Sat 1930, US$4.

Live music

Memphis Pub, St 118 (off Sisowath Quay), open till 0200. Small bar off the river, very loyal following from the NGO crowd. Live rock and blues music from Tue-Sat.

Riverhouse Lounge, No 6, St 110 (Sisowath Quay). Usually has a guest DJ on the weekends and live jazz on Tue and Sun.

○ Shopping

Phnom Penh p80, maps p82 and p86
Art galleries
Reyum Institute of Arts and Culture, No 4, St 178, T023-217149, www.reyum.org. This is

a great place to start for those interested in Cambodian modern art. Some absolutely world-class artists have been mentored and exhibit here.

Handicrafts

Many non-profit organizations have opened stores to help train or rehabilitate some of the country's under-privileged.
Disabled Handicrafts Promotion Association, No 317, St 63. Handicrafts and jewellery made by people with disabilities.
Le Rit's Nyemo, 131 Sisowath Quay. Non-profit shop with a wide range of silk products.
The National Centre for Disabled People, 3 Norodom, T023-210140. Great store with handicrafts such as pillow cases, tapestries and bags made by people with disabilities.
Orange River, 361 Sisowath Quay (under FCCC), T023-214594, has a selection of beautifully designed decorative items and a very good stock of fabrics and silks which will leave many wishing for more luggage allowance. Pricier than most other stores.
Rajana, No 170, St 450, next to the Russian Market. Traditional crafts, silk paintings, silver and jewellery.

Markets

Psar Thmei (Central Covered Market), just off Monivong Blvd, distinguished by its central art deco dome (built 1937), is mostly full of stalls selling silver and gold jewellery.
Tuol Tom Pong, between St 155 and St 163 to east and west, and St 440 and St 450 to north and south. Known to many as the Russian Market. Sells antiques (genuine articles and fakes) and jewellery as well as clothing, pirate CDs and computer software, videos, sarongs, fabrics and an immense variety of tobacco – an excellent place for buying souvenirs, especially silk. Most things at this market are about half the price of the Central Market.

Shopping centres

Sorya Shopping Centre, St 63, besides the Central Market. The only 'mall' in the country; a modern, 7-floor, a/c shopping centre.

Silverware and jewellery

Old silver boxes, belts, antique jewellery along Monivong Blvd (the main thoroughfare), Samdech Sothearos Blvd just north of St 184, has a good cluster of silver shops.

Supermarkets

Sharky Mart, No 124, St 130 (below **Sharkys Bar**), T023-990303. 24-hr convenience store.

▲▲ Activities and tours

Phnom Penh *p80, maps p82 and p86*
Cookery courses
Cambodia Cooking Class, No 14, St 285, T023-882314, www.cambodia-cooking-class.com.

Language classes
The Khmer School of Language, No 529, St 454, Tuol Tumpung 2, Chamcar Morn, T023-213047, www.camb comm.org.uk/ksl.

Tour operators
Asian Trails Ltd, No 22, St 294, Sangkat Boeng Keng Kong I, Khan Chamkarmorn, PO Box 621, T023-216555, www.asiantrails.info. Offers a broad selection of tours: Angkor, river cruises, remote tours, biking trips.
Capitol Tours, No 14AE0, St 182 (see **Capitol Guesthouse**), T023-217627, www.bigpond. com.kh/users/capitol. Cheap tours around Phnom Penh's main sites, tours around the country. Targeted at budget travellers.
Exotissimo Travel, 46 Norodom Blvd, T023-218948, www.exotissimo.com. Wide range of day trips and classic tours covering mainstream destinations: Angkor, Sihanouk-ville, etc. Also offers tailor-made trips.
PTM Tours, No 333B Monivong Blvd, T023-986363, www.ptm-travel.com. Reasonably priced package tours to Angkor and around Phnom Penh. Offers cheap hotel reservations.
RTR Tours, No 54E Charles de Gaulle Blvd, T023-210468, www.rtrtours.com.kh. Organizes tours plus other travel services, including ticketing. Friendly and helpful.

⊖ Transport

Phnom Penh *p80, maps p82 and p86*

Air

Royal Phnom Penh Airways has connections with **Siem Reap** and **Stung Treng**. **Bangkok/Siem Reap Airways** has connections with **Siem Reap**.

Airline offices Most airline offices are open 0800-1700, Sat 0800-1200. **Air France**, Samdeck Sothearos Blvd (Hong Kong Ctr), T023-2192200. **Bangkok/Siem Reap Airways**, No 61A, St 214, T023-426624, www.bangkokair.com. **Lao Airlines**, 58C Sihanouk Blvd, T023-216563. **President Airlines**, 13-14, 296 Mao Tse Toung Blvd, T023-993088/89. **Silk Air**, Himawari Hotel, 313 Sisowath Quay, T023-426808, www.silk air.com. **Thai**, 294 Mao Tse Tung Blvd, T023-890292. **Vietnam Airlines**, No 41, St 214, T023-363396/7, www.vietnamairlines.com.

Bicycle

Hire from guesthouses for about US$1 per day. Cycling is probably the best way to explore the city. It's mostly flat, so not too exhausting.

Boat

Ferries leave from wharves on the river north of the Japanese Friendship Bridge and from Sisowath Quay daily. There are supposed to be connections to **Siem Reap**, **Kratie** and **Stung Treng**. In recent times the Mekong service (Kratie, Stung Treng) hasn't been running as they can't get enough customers now the roads have been improved. Fast boat connections (5 hrs) with **Siem Reap**, US$25 1-way, **Kratie**, US$7.85, and **Stung Treng** US$15.70. In low season the trip to Siem Reap can take up to 6-7 hrs. Boats sometimes break down and promised express boats often turn out to be old chuggers but it costs less than flying. All boats leave early, 0700 or earlier. Most hotels will supply ferry tickets.

Bus

Most buses leave southwest of Psar Thmei (Central Market) by the Shell petrol station.

Capitol Tours, T023-217627, departs from its terminal, No 14, St 182. **GST**, T012-838910, departs from the southwest corner of the Central Market (corner of St 142). **Phnom Penh Public Transport Co** (formerly Ho Wah Genting Bus Company), T023-210359, departs from Charles de Gaulle Blvd, near the Central Market. To **Kratie**, 1 bus per day (US$4); **Capitol Tours** runs a bus to **Kampot**, 0800, US$2.50. There are also frequent departures from the Central Market (Psar Thmei) bus terminal. Around Khmer New Year and during the peak season you will need to book tickets the day before travel. **Phnom Penh Bus Co** to **Sihanoukville**, 5 times daily. **GST** buses leave 4 times daily, 4 hrs. To **Siem Reap**, see page 142.

Car

Chauffeur-driven cars are available at most hotels from US$25 per day upwards. Several travel agents will also hire cars. Prices increase if you're venturing out of town. **Car Rental**, T012-950950.

Cyclo

Plentiful but slow. Fares can be bargained down but are not that cheap – a short journey should be no more than 1000 riel. A few cyclo drivers speak English or French. They are most likely to be found loitering around the big hotels and can also be hired for the day (around US$5).

Moto

'Motodops' are 50-100cc motorbike taxis and the fastest way to get around Phnom Penh. Standard cost per journey is around US$0.50 for a short hop but expect to pay double after dark. If you find a good, English-speaking moto driver, hang on to him and he can be yours for US$8-10 per day.

Shared taxi

These are either Toyota pick-ups or saloons. For the pick-ups the fare depends upon whether you wish to sit inside or in the open; vehicles depart when the driver has enough fares. **Psar Chbam Pao**, just over Monivong Bridge on Route 1, for **Vietnam**. For **Sihanoukville** and **Siem Riep**, take a shared taxi from the Central Market (Psar Thmei). Leave early 0500-0600. Shared taxi to **Kampot** takes 2-3 hrs, US$4, leaving from Doeum Kor Market on Mao Tse Tung Blvd.

Taxi

There are only a few taxis in Phnom Penh as the risk of being held up at gunpoint is too high. It is possible to get a taxi into town from the airport and 1 or 2 taxi companies can be reached by telephone but expect to see no cabs cruising and no meter taxis. **Taxi Vantha**, T012-855000/ 023-982542, 24 hrs.

Phnom Penh hotels will organize private taxis to **Sihanoukville** for around US$25.

O Directory

Phnom Penh *p80, maps p82 and p86*
Banks ANZ Royal Bank, Russian Blvd, 20 Kramuon Sar (corner of street 67), has opened ATMs throughout Phnom Penh; near the Independence Monument; 265 Sisowath Quay. **Canadia Bank**, No 126 Charles de Gaulle Blvd, T023-214668; 265-269 Ang Duong St, T023-215286. Cash advances on credit cards. **Cambodia Commercial Bank**(CCB), No 130 Monivong Blvd (close to the Central Market), T023-426208. Cash advance on credit cards, TCs and currency exchange. **Union Commercial Bank** (UCB), No 61, St 130, T023-724931. Most banking services, charges

no commission on credit card cash advances. **Embassies and consulates** Australia, No 11, St 254, T023-213470, australia.embassy. cambodia@dfat.gov.au. **Canada**, No 11, St 254, T023-213470, pnmpn@ dfait-maeci.gc.ca. **France**, 1 Monivong Blvd, T023-430020, sctipcambodge@online.com.kh. **Laos**, 15-17 Mao Tse Tung Blvd, T023-983632. **Thailand**, 196 Norodom Blvd, T023-7263 0610, thaipnp@mfa.go.th. **UK**, No 29, St 75, T023-427124, britemb@online.com.kh. **USA**, No16, St 228, T023-216436, usembassy@ camnet.com.kh. (A new US Embassy was under construction near Wat Phnom at the time of publication). **Vietnam**, 436 Monivong Blvd, T023-362531, embvnpp@ camnet.com.kh. **Immigration** Opposite the international airport. Visa extensions, photograph required, 1-month US$30. **Internet** Cheap and ubiquitous. Rates can be as low as US$0.50 per hr although in many places they are higher. **Medical services** It is highly advisable to try and get to Bangkok if you are seriously ill or have injured yourself as Cambodia's medical services are not up to scratch. **Calmette Hospital**, 3 Monivong Blvd, T023-426948, is generally considered the best. 24-hr emergency. **Surya Medical Services**, No 39, St 294, T016-8450000, Mon-Fri 0700-2000, Sat-Sun 0700-1800. General medicine and tropical medicine. After hours emergency care available 24 hrs. **Pharmacy de la Gare**, 81 Monivong Blvd, T023-526855. **Post office** Main post office, St 13, possible to make international telephone calls from here.

Southern Cambodia

With the opening of the Vietnamese border near Kampot at Ha Tien, southern Cambodia is now firmly grasping its tourist potential as a staging post for overland travellers. Yet, in many ways it manages to encompass the worst and best of what tourism can offer to a developing country such as Cambodia. Take Sihanoukville, which not so long ago was a sleepy port offering idyllic beaches. Now, with human waste pouring directly into the sea from dozens of generic backpacker shanty bars and flophouses, this town could almost offer a textbook study in environmental catastrophe.

Travel down the coast to Kep and Kampot, and things couldn't be more different. An old French trading port overlooking the Prek Kamping Bay River and framed by the Elephant Mountains, low-key Kampot is filled with decrepit dusty charm. Just outside Kampot is Kep, the resort of choice for France's colonial elite, which is now slowly reasserting its position as a place for rest and recuperation. Don't go to Kep expecting wild nights or even a great beach, but perfect views, good seafood and serenity are on offer here.

Northwest from Sihanoukville is Koh Kong province, a vast, wild and untamed expanse of jungle that smothers the stunning Cardamom Mountain range in a thick green blanket. There's now a sealed road through here linking Sihanoukville with Thailand. With logging companies waiting in the wings, this area is now facing an uncertain future. ▸▸ *For listings, see pages 105-109.*

Sihanoukville ●❷❼❶▲●❸❶ ▸▸ *pp105-109. Colour map 5, B6.*

If Sihanoukville was being tended with care it would occupy a lovely site on a small peninsula whose knobbly head juts out into the Gulf of Thailand. The first rate beaches, clean waters, trees and invigorating breezes are slowly being replaced with human effluvia, piles of stinking rubbish and nasty flophouses. Cambodia's beaches could be comparable to those in Thailand but are slowly being horribly degraded. Most people head for beaches close to the town which, starting from the north, are Victory, Independence, Sokha, Ochheauteal and, a little further out, Otres. Sihanoukville's layout is unusual, with the 'town' itself, acting as a satellite to the roughly equidistant three beaches. The urban area is pretty scattered and has the distinct feel of a place developing on an ad hoc basis.

Ins and outs

From Phnom Penh there are regular departures in comfortable, well-maintained, air-conditioned coaches to Sihanoukville, costing US$3-4. Buses generally leave every half hour from 0700 until 1330. Taxis cost US$20-30. Without a proper bus linking Sihanoukville to Kampot and Kep, journey along the shoreline is not always the easiest though there are plentiful buses from Phnom Penh to these coastal jewels. Departing from Sihanoukville there are taxis to Kampot and Phnom Penh around 0700-0800, US$5-6. You can travel to Koh Kong via the brand new road (a whole series of bridges are due to open in late 2008) from Sihanoukville or Hat Lek, Thailand. ▸▸ *See Transport, page 108.*

Background

Sihanoukville, or Kompong Som as it is called during the periods the king is in exile or otherwise 'out of office', was founded in 1964 by Prince Sihanouk to be the nation's sole deep-water port. It is also the country's prime seaside resort. In its short history it has crammed in as much excitement as most seaside towns see in a century – but not of the sort that resorts tend to encourage. Sihanoukville was used as a strategic transit point for weapons used in fighting the USA, during the Vietnam War. In 1975, the US bombed the town when the Khmer Rouge seized the container ship *SS Mayaguez*.

Sihanoukville has now turned a corner, however, and with rapid development has firmly secured its place in Cambodia's 'tourism triangle', alongside Phnom Penh and Angkor Wat. Not much of this development is sustainable and incredibly bad taste, tacky and overpriced resorts already being built. While a liberal attitude towards the smoking of marijuana attracts a youthful crowd, no amount of intoxicants can cover up the fact that Sihanoukville is rapidly becoming an environmental stain on this already horribly scarred country. If it all becomes too much there is the coastal Preah Sihanouk 'Ream' National Park close by.

Sihanoukville

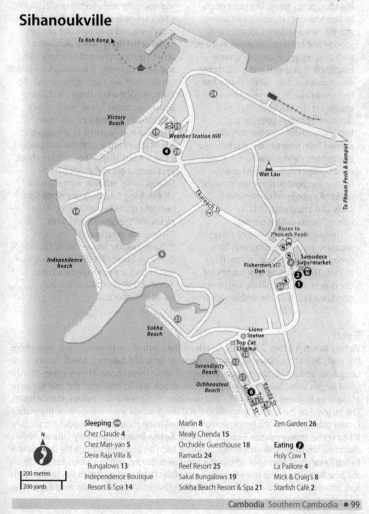

Sihanoukville's islands

More than 20 beautiful islands and pristine coral reefs lie off Sihanoukville's coastline. Most of the islands are uninhabited except Koh Russei (Bamboo Island), Koh Rong Salaam and a few others that contain small fishing villages.

Diving and snorkelling around the islands is pretty good. The coast offers an abundance of marine life including star fish, sea anemones, lobsters and sponge and brain coral. Larger creatures such as stingrays, angel fish, groupers, barracuda, moray eels and giant clams are ubiquitous. Baby whale sharks and reef sharks also roam the waters. More elusive are the black dolphins, pink dolphins, common dolphins and bottle-nosed dolphins but they are sighted from time to time. It is believed that further afield (closer to Koh Kong) are a family of dugongs (sea cows). No one has sighted these rare creatures except for one hotel owner who sadly saw a dugong head for sale in Sihanoukville's market.

The islands are divided into three separate groups: the Kampong Som Group, the Ream Group and the Royal Islands. The Kampong Som Islands are the closest to Sihanoukville and have quite good beaches. Here the visibility stretches up to 40 m. Koh Pos is the closest island to Sihanoukville, located just 800 m from Victory Beach. Most people prefer Koh Koang Kang also known as Koh Thas, which is 45 minutes from shore. This island has two beautiful beaches (with one named after Elvis) and the added attraction of shallow rocky reefs, teeming with wildlife, which are perfect for snorkelling. More rocky reefs and shallow water can be found at the Rong Islands. Koh Rong is about two hours west of Sihanoukville and has a stunning, 5-km-long sand beach (on the southwest side of the island). To the south of the Koh Rong is Koh Rong Salaam, a smaller island that is widely considered Cambodia's most beautiful. There are nine fantastic beaches spread across this island and on the east coast, a lovely heart-shaped bay. It takes about 2½ hours to get to Koh Rong from Sihanoukville. Koh Kok, a small island off Koh Rong Salaam, is one of the firm favourite dive sites, warranting it the nickname 'the garden' and takes 1¾ hours to get there.

During winter (November to February) the Ream Islands are the best group to visit as they are more sheltered than some of the other islands but they are a lot further out.

Sights

Victory Beach is a thin, 2-km-long beach on the north of the peninsula, just down from the port, and at its extremes offers reasonably secluded beaches. Beach hawkers are ubiquitous and outnumber tourists at a ratio of about three to one. The area does afford a good sunset view, however. **Independence Beach** was at one time the sole preserve of the once bombed and charred – and now beautifully restored – **Independence Hotel**. The location of the hotel is magnificent and the grounds are a reminder of the place's former grandeur. With the restoration of this sleek hotel complete, its re-opening will do a lot to revive Independence Beach's fortunes. **Sokha Beach** is arguably Sihanoukville's most beautiful beach. The shore laps around a 1-km arc and even though the large **Sokha Beach Resort** has taken up residence it is very rare to see more than a handful of people on the beach. It is stunning and relatively hassle-free. **Ochheauteal Beach** lies to the south and, bizarrely, is the most popular with hordes of backpackers. What was once a sparkling

The Ream Islands encompass those islands just off the Ream coast: Prek Mo Peam and Prek Toek Sap, which don't offer the clearest waters. The islands of Koh Khteah, Koh Tres, Koh Chraloh and Koh Ta Kiev are best for snorkelling. Giant mussels can be seen on the north side of Koh Ta Kiev island. Some 50 km out are the outer Ream Islands which, without a doubt, offer the best diving in the area. The coral in these islands though has started to deteriorate and is now developing a fair bit of algae. Kondor Reef, 75 km west of Sihanoukville, is a favorite diving spot. A Chinese junk filled with gold and other precious treasures is believed to have sunk hundreds of years ago on the reef and famous underwater treasure hunter, Michael Archer, has thoroughly searched the site but no one can confirm whether he struck gold.

Koh Tang, Koh Prins and Paulo Wai are seven hours away to the southwest. These islands are believed to have visibility that stretches for 40 m and are teeming with marine life, they are recommended as some of the best dive sites. It is believed that Koh Prins once had a modern shipwreck and sunken US helicopter but underwater scavengers looking for steel and US MIA guys have completely cleared the area.

Large schools of yellow fin tuna are known to inhabit the island's surrounding waters. Koh Tang is worth a visit but is quite far from the mainland so an overnight stay on board might be required. Many local dive experts believe Koh Tang represents the future of Cambodia's diving. The island became infamous in May 1975 when the US ship SS Mayaguez was seized by the Khmer Rouge just off here. The area surrounding Paulo Wai is not frequently explored, so most of the coral reefs are still in pristine condition.

Closer to Thailand lies Koh Sdach (King's Island), a stop off on the boat ride between Sihanoukville and Koh Kong. This undeveloped island is home to about 4000 people, mostly fishing families. The beaches are a bit rocky but there is some fabulous snorkelling. At the time of publication a guesthouse was being built on the island.

The Cambodian diving industry is still in its fledgling years; most of the islands and reefs are still in relatively pristine condition and the opportunities to explore unchartered waters limitless.

Some of the islands mentioned above now have guesthouses and hotels, see page 106 for details.

stretch of white sand has been reduced to an unending dustbin of rickety, badly planned budget bars, restaurants and accommodation. Much of this has been built directly on the beach, with concrete foundations poured into what could be a stunning waterfront. Coupled with this is a complete lack of proper sewerage and stinking waste pours straight into the sea. If all this isn't enough to put you off, then there is the unrelenting hassle you will get from hawkers and hordes of child vendors pursuing sales very aggressively. Watch your stuff as theft is also common here. The beach commonly referred to as **Serendipity Beach** is at the very north end of Ochheauteal and is basically Ochheauteal-like. This little strand has gained flavour with travellers due in part to being the first beach in Sihanoukville to offer a wide range of budget accommodation. At the time of publication, the many guesthouses and restaurants lining the shore of Serendipity and the extended Ochheauteal Beach area were at the centre of a land dispute with developers hankering to clear the budget accommodation to make way for large Thai-style resorts.

Preah Sihanouk 'Ream' National Park → *Colour map 5, B6.*
ⓘ *T012-875096, daily 0700-1715. Boat trip US$30 for 4 people. Nature trek with a guide (3-5 hrs), US$5 per person.*

This beautiful park is a short 30-minute drive from Sihanoukville, hugging the coastline of the Gulf of Thailand. It includes two islands and covers 21,000 ha of beach, mangrove swamp, offshore coral reef and the Prek Tuk Sap Estuary. Samba deer, endangered civet species, porcupines and pangolin are said to inhabit the park, as well as dolphins. To arrange a guided tour visit the park office or arrange one through a guesthouse in Sihanoukville.

Koh Kong and around ⬤❶❷❸ ➤➤ *pp105-109. Colour map 5, B6.*

Dusty Koh Kong is better known for its brothels, casinos and 'Wild West' atmosphere than for lying at the heart of a protected area with national park status (granted by Royal Decree in 1993). It is also often confused with its beautiful offshore namesake Koh Kong Island. The town is also reputed to have the highest incidence of HIV infection of anywhere in Cambodia and is a haven for members of the Thai mafia trying to keep their heads down and launder large sums of money through the casino. The place is only really used by travellers as a transit stop on the way to and from Thailand or two of the most scenic places in Cambodia – Koh Kong Island and the Cardamom Mountains.

Central Cardamoms Protected Forest → *Colour map 6, A1.*
ⓘ *The area remains relatively inaccessible but over the next few years it is anticipated that ecotourism operators will flock to the area. For now, it is best to make short trips into the park as the area is sparsely populated and heavily mined (so stay on clearly marked paths). Take a motorbike (with an experienced rider) or a boat. The latter option is more convenient in Koh Kong. There are usually several men with boats willing to take the trip down the Mohaundait Rapids, cutting through the jungled hills and wilderness of the Cardomoms. The cost of the trip is between US$25-30.*

In 2002, the government announced the creation of the **Central Cardamoms Protected Forest**, a 402,000-ha area in Cambodia's Central Cardamom Mountains. With two other wildlife sanctuaries bordering the park, the total land under protection is 990,000 ha – the largest, most pristine wilderness in mainland Southeast Asia. The extended national park reaches widely across the country, running through the provinces of Koh Kong, Pursat, Kompong Speu and Battambang. Considering that Cambodia has been severely deforested and seen its wildlife hunted to near-extinction, this park represents a good opportunity for the country to regenerate both flora and fauna. The Cardamoms are home to most of Cambodia's large mammals and half of the country's birds, reptiles and amphibians. The mountains have retained large populations of the region's most rare and endangered animals, such as the Indochinese tigers, Asian elephants and sun bears. Globally threatened species like the pileated gibbon and the critically endangered Siamese crocodile, which has its only known wild breeding population here, exist in the Cardamoms. Environmental surveyors have identified 30 large mammal species, 30 small mammal species, more than 500 bird species, 64 reptiles and 30 amphibians, that reside in the park. Conservationists are predicting they will discover other animals that have disappeared elsewhere in the region such as the Sumatran rhinoceros. With virgin jungles, waterfalls, rivers and rapids this area represents a huge untapped ecotourism potential. However, tourist services to the area are still quite limited.

Koh Kong Island → *Colour map 5, B6.*

ⓘ *The island is accessible by bridge from the mainland.*

The island (often called Koh Kong Krau) is arguably one of Cambodia's best islands. There are six white powdery beaches each stretching kilometre after kilometre, while a canopy of coconut trees shade the glassy- smooth aqua waters. It's a truly stunning part of the country and has been ear-marked by the government for further development, so go now, while it's still a little utopia. There are a few frisky dolphin pods that crop up from time to time. Their intermittent appearances usually take place in the morning and in the late afternoon. ⏭ *For the border with Thailand, see box, page 109.*

Kampot and around 🌙🍴🛍🛈 ⏭ *pp105-109. Colour map 6, B1.*

Kampot is a charming riverside town that was established in the early 1900s by the French. The town lies at the base of the Elephant Mountain Range, 5 km inland on the river Prek Thom and was for a long time the gateway to the beach resort at Kep (see page 104). On one side of the river are tree-lined streets, crumbling mustard yellow French shop fronts and a sleepy atmosphere, whilst on the other side you will find locals working in the surrounding salt pans. The town has the feel of another era – with a dabbling of Chinese architecture and overall French colonial influence – which, with a bit of restoration work, could easily be compared to UNESCO World Heritage Sites such as Hoi An in Vietnam and Luang Prabang in Laos. Life is very laid-back in Kampot and the town has become a regular expat retreat with Phnom Penh-ites ducking down here for a breath of fresh air and a cooler climate.

Kampot

To Bokor Mountain National Park (42 km) & Sihanoukville

Prek Thom

To Phnom Penh (Route 3) & Caves

Riverside Walk

Old Market

Canadia

Obelisk Roundabout

Acleda ⓢ

Taxis
Naga Statue

Statue of 3 Soldiers

To Kep (25 km) & Caves

N

200 metres
200 yards

Sleeping 🛏
Blissful Guesthouse 3
Bodhi Villa 6
Bokor Mountain Lodge 9
Borey Bokor 1 1

Little Garden Bar 5
Long Villa 13
Molieden 7

Eating 🍴
Epic Arts Café 2
Jasmine 3
Rusty Key Hole 4

Bokor Mountain National Park → *Colour map 6, B1.*

ⓘ 42 km (90 mins) from Kampot. US$5. Park rangers can speak some English and have a small display board on the flora and fauna in the park at their office. There are dorms (US$5) and double rooms (US$20) and a few basic dishes available. A moto and driver for the day will cost around US$15 or a car for around US$30.

Bokor Mountain National Park's plateau, at 1040 m, peers out from the southernmost end of the Elephant Mountains with a commanding view over the Gulf of Thailand and east to Vietnam. Bokor Hill (Phnom Bokor) is densely forested and in the remote and largely untouched woods scientists have discovered 30 species of plants unique to the area. Not for nothing are these called the Elephant Mountains and besides the Asian elephant there are tigers, leopards, wild cows, civets, pigs, gibbons and numerous bird species. At the peak of the mountain is **Bokor Hill Station**, where eerie, abandoned, moss-covered buildings sit in dense fog. The buildings were built by the French, who attracted by Bokor's relative coolness, established a 'station climatique' on the mountain in the 1920s. In 1970 Lon Nol shut it down and Bokor was quickly taken over by Communist guerrillas; it later became a strategic military base for the Khmer Rouge. In more recent years there was a lot of guerrilla activity in the hills, but the area is now safe, with the exception of the danger, ever-present in Cambodia, of landmines. The ruins are surprisingly well preserved but bear evidence of their tormented past. There is a double waterfall called **Popokvil Falls**, a 2-km walk from the station, which involves wading through a stream, though in the wet season this is nigh on impossible.

Kbal Romeas caves and temple → *Colour map 6, B1.*

Ten kilometres outside Kampot, on the roads to both Phnom Penh and to Kep, limestone peaks harbour interesting caves with stalactites and pools. It is here that you can find one of Cambodia's hidden treasures – an 11th-century temple slowly being enveloped by stalactites and hidden away in a cave in Phnom Chhnok, next to the village of Kbal Romeas. The temple, which is protected by three friendly monks, was discovered by Adhemer Leclere in 1866. Many motos and cars now do trips.

Kep ▣❷◐◓ ▶ *pp105-109. Colour map 6, B1.*

ⓘ Jul-Oct Kep is subject to the southeast monsoon, occasionally rendering the beach dangerous for swimming because of the debris brought in.

Tucked in on the edge of the South China Sea, Kep was established in 1908 by the French as a health station for their government officials and families. The ruins of their holiday villas stand along the beachfront and in the surrounding hills. They were largely destroyed during the civil war under Lon Nol and by the Khmer Rouge and were then further ransacked during the famine of the early 1980s when starving Cambodians raided the villas for valuables to exchange for food.

At the time of publication, Kep still hadn't hit the radar of many international tourists. It is very popular on weekends with holidaying Cambodians who have managed to keep this idyllic town one of the country's best kept secrets. Beautiful gardens and lush green landscape juxtaposed against the blue waters make it one of the most wonderfully relaxing places in the country. The town itself only has one major beach, a pebbly murky water pool which doesn't really compare with Sihanoukville beaches but they can be found at almost all of the 13 outlying islands where you can snorkel and dive although this is better around the islands off Sihanoukville; Kep is considerably more beautiful than

Sihanoukville and much more relaxing. It is famous for the freshly caught crab which is best eaten on the beach (US$1.50 per kilo) and the *tik tanaout jiu*, palm wine. From Kep it is possible to hire a boat to **Rabbit Island** (Koh Toensay). Expect to pay about US$10 to hire a boat for the day. There are four half-moon beaches on this island which have finer, whiter sand than Kep beach.

◉ Southern Cambodia listings

For Sleeping and Eating price codes,
see inside the front cover.

● Sleeping

Sihanoukville *p98, map p99*
L-AL The Independence Boutique Resort and Spa, Independence Beach, T034-934300. The most gorgeous hotel in town, beautifully restored to all its modernist glory. The rooms are minimalist, chic and complete with a/c, TV, bath and other luxuries. Great sea views from the hilltop perch, it's also set in some pleasing gardens with a pool. This is exactly the kind of thing Sihanoukville needs to pull itself out of its current malaise. You can also haggle the rates down when it is quiet. Highly recommended.
L-A Sokha Beach Resort and Spa, Street 2 Thnou, Sangkat 4, Sokha Beach, T034-935999, www.sokhahotels.com. A deluxe, 180-room beachfront resort and spa, set amid an expansive 15 ha of beachfront gardens and fronting a pristine white sandy beach. Guests have a choice between hotel suites or private bungalows dotted in the tropical gardens. The hotel has fantastic facilities including a landscaped pool, tennis court, archery range, children's club and in-house Filipino band at night. Rooms are impressive. The hotel has very low occupancy, so check if it can offer a discount as it's always running special deals.
AL-A Ramada Hotel and Resort, Port Hill, T034-393916. The most expensive accommodation in its part of town. All mod cons in this upmarket though faintly dull property. Pool and tennis courts.
C-D Chez Claude, between Sokha Beach and Independence Beach, T012-824870. A beautiful hillside spot with 9 bungalows

representing a cross-section of indigenous housing. The restaurant has fantastic views.
C-D Deva Raja Villa and Bungalows, Serendipity Beach, T012-1600374, www.devarajavilla.com. Stylish rooms, en suite facilities with nice baths, a/c. Good restaurant. Recommended.
C-D Reef Resort, Serendipity Beach, T012-315338, www.reefresort.com.kh. Well run, small hotel at the top of the hill near the garish golden lions roundabout. Rooms are a touch overpriced but there is a nice pool and breakfast included. Bar and restaurant. Probably the best mid-range place in town. Book ahead. Recommended.
D-F Chez Mari-yan, Sankat 3, Khan Mittapheap, T034-916468. Currently the best bungalow-style place to stay in this end of town. Offers a block of hotel rooms and simple wooden and concrete bungalows perched on stilts at the top of a hill affording nice sea views. Restaurant sports a short menu which features fish, squid and crab.
D-F Marlin Hotel, Ekareach St, T012-890373. This friendly hostel has been recently refurbished. Serves food and hosts a bar and there's Wi-Fi too. Good value a/c and fan rooms, but don't expect anything too fancy.
D-F Orchidée Guesthouse, Tola St, T034-933639, www.orchideeguesthouse.com. Well run, properly maintained, clean and well-aired rooms, with a/c and hot water. Restaurant with Khmer and Western seafood. Nice pool area, a 5-min walk to the Ochheauteal Beach.
E-G Mealy Chenda, on the crest of Weather Station Hill, T034-670818. Very popular hotel offering accommodation to suit a wide range of budgets from dorm rooms through to a/c double rooms. Sparkly clean with fantastic views from the restaurant.

G Sakal Bungalows, near the end of Weather Station Hill, T012-806155, 012806155@mobitel.com.kh. 10 simple but cheap bungalows. Restaurant and bar, cheap internet. Closest bungalows to Victory Beach.

G Zen Garden, just south of downtown area, T011-262376. Nice setting in an old wooden building in a relaxed back street. Rooms are very basic but very cheap. Good budget option. Also have dorms and serve food.

Sihanoukville Islands

D-G Jonty's Jungle Camp, Koh Ta Kiev Island, T092-502374, www.jontysjungle camp.com. Basic, hammock-style camping accommodation in this gorgeous island retreat. Don't come expecting any mod cons but you will be given a mosquito net. Price drops if you stay for more than one night. Great snorkelling nearby, idyllic if you like this sort of thing. Serve their own basic food. Price includes long-tail to and from the island.

E-F Koh Ru, Koh Russie Island, T012-388860. Run by the owner of **Bar Ru** this is a quaint collection of simple fan bungalows in a lovely beachside location. Totally relaxed and quiet, this is a decent spot to really get away from it all. Food and drink available.

Koh Kong and around p102

Many of the small guesthouses scattered around the town double as brothels.

E-G Bopha Koh Kong, 2 blocks east of the boat pier, T035-963073. Good, clean rooms with all amenities – a/c, cable, fridge. More expensive rooms have bath and hot water. Pretty good value. Also has a restaurant.

G Otto's, a block south of the boat pier, T012-924249, 012924249@mobitel.com.kh. Basic fan rooms in a nice wooden house. Shared bath, fan, mosquito net, rather random and kitsch decor. Old wooden structure, feels like a bungalow, bit dirty, good size though. The German owner also runs the best restaurant in town serving Western, Khmer and Thai food. Otto is a good source of tourist information. Books for sale/swap. Internet. Recommended.

Kampot and around p103, map p103

Kampot has a good range of accommodation.

C-D Bokor Mountain Lodge, 033-932314, www.bokorlodge.com. Old colonial property on the river front that has had several incarnations and was once even an HQ for the Khmer Rouge. It has bags of atmosphere and is probably the best spot in town for an icy sundowner. All rooms en suite with a/c, cable TV. Recommended.

D-E Little Garden Bar, T033-256901, www.littlegardenbar.com. Basic, clean rooms, fan and bathroom. Restaurant offering panoramic views of Mount Bokor.

D-F Borey Bokor Hotel 1, T012-820826. In an ostentatious style with all rooms offering a/c, fridge and comfy beds.

E-G Molieden, a block from the main bridge, T033-932798, chuy_seth@yahoo.com. A surprisingly good find, its hideous façade gives way to a very pleasant interior. Large, tastefully decorated modern art deco rooms with TV and fan. The rooftop restaurant also serves some of the best Western food in town. Very good value.

G Blissful Guesthouse, next to **Acleda Bank**. Converted colonial building with lovely surrounding gardens. Rooms are simple with mosquito net, fan and attached bath. High on atmosphere and very popular with locals and expats alike. Affable Khmer manager, Elvis, and owner, Angela, make this a very pleasant place to stay. Recommended.

G Bodhi Villa, 2 km northwest of town on Teuk Chhou Rd, T012-728884. Cheap and popular budget guesthouse in nice location just outside town, set on the riverbank. Owners seem well-intentioned, linking into local volunteer projects, though the hedonistic atmosphere and roaring speed boat which they've introduced to the peaceful river detracts from their efforts. Basic rooms, simple bungalows and US$1 a night dorm.

G Long Villa, T092-251418. Very friendly, well-run guesthouse. The unspectacular though functional rooms vary from en suite with a/c and TV through to fan with shared facilities. Recommended.

Bokor Mountain National Park *p104*
The park rangers run a simple guesthouse at the hill station – youth-hostel style. There are bunk beds (US$5) and doubles (US$20), with clean shared toilets and showers. Bring your own food: there is a large kitchen available for guests. Pack warm clothes and waterproofs.

Kep *p104*
Accommodation in Kep is better and cheaper than in the rest of the country.
L-AL Knai Bang Chatt, T012-349742, www.knaibangchatt.com. Set in a restored 20th-century modernist villa, this property seeks to recreate an elitist and colonial atmosphere. Some people will love the banality of exclusivity – others may judge that their money would be better spent elsewhere. Rooms come with all the usual luxury amenities.
A-D La Villa, T012-1702648, www.lavilla kep.com. An interesting old French villa forms the centre-piece of this brand-new bungalow operation set by the sea. The bungalows are well-appointed with verandas, a/c, en suite bathrooms, Wi-Fi and cable TV. There are plans to open a restaurant and art space in the villa. Recommended.
A-F Verandah Resort and Bungalows, next door to N4, further up Kep Mountain, T012-888619. Superb accommodation. Large wooden bungalows, each with a good-sized balcony, fan, mosquito net and nicely decorated mosaic bathroom. The more expensive of these include very romantic open-air beds. A few extra upmarket bungalows are about to be built (a/c and hot water). The restaurant offers the perfect vista of the ocean and surrounding countryside. Epicureans will love the variety of international cuisines including poutine of Quebec, smoked ham linguini, fish fillet with olive sauce (all under US$3). Recommended.
C-D The Beach House, T012-240090, www.thebeachhousekep.com. Arguably the nicest spot to stay in Kep. Great rooms, nearly all of which look out onto the mesmeric ocean – all have a/c, hot water, TV.

They have a small pool and soothing chill-out area. Unpretentious and good value. The staff can sometimes appear to be half-asleep but are very friendly when provoked. Recommended.

● Eating

Sihanoukville *p98, map p99*
₸₸₸ **Chez Mari-yan**, Victory Beach area. Has a good seafood restaurant with probably the nicest setting in Sihanoukville.
₸₸₸-₸₸ **La Paillote**, top of Weather Station Hill. This is the finest dining establishment in town and one of the best in the country. The service can't be surpassed and it is high on atmosphere. The chef from Madagascar greets the customers and the food is superb.
₸₸ **Holy Cow**, Ekareach St, on the way out of town. Ambient restaurant offering a selection of healthy, Western meals – pasta, salads, baked potatoes. The English owner is a long-term resident and very good source of local information. To his credit he has created a lovely atmosphere and provides impeccable working conditions for his staff.
₸₸ **Mick and Craig's**, Ochheauteal Beach. Thankfully, the menu here is a lot more creative than the venue's name. Sufficiently large meals with a bit of pizzazz – pizzas, burgers, hummus, etc. The restaurant also offers 'themed food nights', Sun roast, BBQ and 'all you can eat' nights.
₸₸ **Starfish Café**, behind **Samudera Super market**, T034-952011. Small café-cum-bakery in a very peaceful garden setting. Here you can eat great food, while knowing that you are supporting a good cause. The organization was originally established to help rehabilitate people with disabilities and has extended its services to cover a range of poverty-reducing schemes. A very positive place that oozes goodness in its food, environment and service – good Western breakfasts, cakes, sandwiches, salads and coffees. A non-profit massage business has also opened on premises.

Koh Kong and around *p102*

There are several places around town that sell Thai food – be warned, it tends to be a pale imitation of the real thing.

† - † Moto Bar, awesome Western breakfasts, one of the best in the country. Also serves other meals but it's at its best first thing.

† Otto's Restaurant, big menu with Western breakfasts, baguette sandwiches, schnitzels, seafood, soups, Khmer standards and lots of vegetarian options. Recommended.

Kampot and around *p103, map p103*

††† Molienden Restaurant, see Sleeping. On the roof of the guesthouse. Extensive selection of pastas, spaghetti, soup and Italian seafood dishes. Fantastic food. Recommended.

†† Bokor Mountain Lodge, see Sleeping. Great sandwiches made with the best ingredients – the fish and chicken amok is also divine. Recommended.

†† Jasmine, is a new riverside eatery set up by a Khmer woman (Jasmine) and her American photographer partner. They offer a slightly more up-market experience than many of the other places along the riverfront, Khmer and Western dishes. Recommended.

†† Rusty Key Hole Bar and Restaurant, River Rd, past **Bamboo Light**. Run by the very down to earth Mancunian, Christian, Rusty's is now something of a local legend. Western food served. Friendly and the best place to watch football in town. The BBQ seafood and ribs come highly recommended.

†† - † Little Garden Bar, T012-994161. This is an attractive and relaxed bar and restaurant on the riverfront offering delicious Khmer and Western food for reasonable prices. The rooftop bar is the place to be for spectacular sunsets over the Elephant Mountains.

† Epic Arts Cafe, is a brilliant little NGO-run establishment in the centre of Kampot. Set up as a project to employ local disabled people, they produce delicious cakes.

Kep *p104*

There are scores of seafood stalls on the beach, just before the tourist centre, that

specialize in cooking freshly caught crab. At the tourist office itself there is also a row of restaurants serving crab, shrimp and fish. Nearly every hotel or guesthouse serves food – see also Sleeping entries.

†† - † The Riel, is now Kep's only proper restaurant-cum-café-cum bar. Great friendly atmosphere and decent food should make this establishment a winner. Good rock 'n' roll stories from the owner as well.

⊙ Bars and clubs

Sihanoukville *p98, map p99*

Papagayo, Weather Station Hill. Pool tables, cheap cocktails, email, comfy cane lounges. The US$2 tapas is exceptionally good value.

▲ Activities and tours

Sihanoukville *p98, map p99*

Diving

Scuba Nation Diving Centre, Weather Station Hill, T012-604680, www.divecambodia.com. This company has the best reputation in the town and is the longest-established PADI dive centre. Prices vary depending on what you want. An Open Water Course is US$350, dive trips are US$70.

Fishing

The Fishermen's Den, 1 block back from Ekareach St, next to the **Small Hotel**. Runs daily fishing trips for US$25 per person. If you have caught something worth eating, the proprietor, Brian, will organize the restaurant to prepare a lovely meal from the catch.

⊖ Transport

Sihanoukville *p98, map p99*

Motos cost 2000 riel around town or 3000 from the centre to a beach. Taxis charge US$5 to a beach.

Border essentials: Cambodia–Thailand

Koh Kong

The border crossing is 12 km from Koh Kong, across the river (15-20 mins).
The border is open 0700-2000.

Transport The trip to the border at Cham Yem costs ฿60 by moto, ฿50 by shared taxi
and US$6 with own taxi. There are public minibuses on the Thai side to Trat (84 km,
1¼ hrs, until 1800, ฿150). You can find private taxis after 1800 but bidding will start
at ฿1000. From Trat buses run to Pattaya, Bangkok and Bangkok airport.

Buses to **Phnom Penh** leave from the
station on the corner of Ekareach and
Sopheakmong-kol St; **Phnom Penh Public
Transport Co** (5 times daily) and **GST**
(4 times daily). There are no longer security
risks on this route. To **Kampot** shared taxi,
around 10,000 riel per person, 4 hrs.

Koh Kong and around p102

Small minibuses/vans go to **Phnom Penh**
leaving Koh Kong Riverside Guesthouse,
0900, 5-6 hrs, ฿600. From Raksmei Bun
Thaim Guesthouse at 0830, 5-6 hrs, ฿500.
A shared taxi to **Sihanoukville**, 5-6 hrs,
leaves from market, US$10 person (6 per
car), US$60 own car, from 0600 onwards.

Kampot and around p103, map p103

Motos charge about 1000 riel for short trips
across town. They gather around the Sokimex
petrol station on the way into town.

There are 2 buses in both directions run
by the **Phnom Penh Sorya Transport Co.**
between Kampot and **Phnom Penh**. These
services also stop in **Kep**. There are presently
no regular bus services between Kampot
and **Sihanoukville**. However, a private
service has emerged run by the **G'Day Mate
Guesthouse** in Sihanoukville. However, at
the time of writing the timetable wasn't
being adhered to and the promised
twice-weekly service wasn't operating.

Vehicles leave from the truck station next
to the Total gas station for **Phnom Penh** at
0700 until 1400 for US$3.50, private taxi

US$20. Most guesthouses can arrange
transport and tickets. To **Sihanoukville**,
shared taxi, US$3, private US$18. To
Kep, US$8, return US$14-15.

Kep p104

Kep is 25 km (30-45 mins) from **Kampot**
on a good road. A large white horse statue
marks the turn-off to Kep. Buses now run
twice a day between Kep/Kampot and
Phnom Penh.

❶ Directory

Sihanoukville p98, map p99

Banks There are 4 banks in town (often
shut): **Acleda, UCB, Canadia** and the
Mekong Bank, all on Ekareach St. **UCB**
and **Canadia** do Visa/MasterCard cash
advances. Cash advances are also available
at **Samudera Supermarket**, in town, 5%
commission. **Lucky Web**, on Weather Station
Hill, charges 4% commission. **Internet**
All tourist areas in Sihanoukville have internet.
Prices vary from 3000-8000 riel per hr.

Kampot and around p103, map p103

Banks Canadia Bank, close to the Borey
Bokor 1 Hotel. Cash advances on Visa and
MasterCard (no commission). **Internet**
Cluster of cafés on the road between the
river and the central roundabout, US$1
per hr. International calls vary between
600-900 riel per min.

Northeast Cambodia

A wild and rugged landscape, consisting of the three provinces of Ratanakiri, Mondulkiri and Stung Treng, greets any visitor to Cambodia's remote northeast region. Vast forested swathes of sparsely inhabited terrain spread north and eastwards toward Vietnam and Laos and are home to several distinct ethnic groups. The thick jungles also provide sanctuary to the majority of Cambodia's few remaining tigers.

During the civil war, the Northeast was cut off from the rest of the country. Then came years of bad transport links, with only the most committed making the arduous run up from up Phnom Penh. Yet the Northeast, much like the rest of the country, is now developing. A brand new Chinese-built road, including an arcing road bridge over the river in Stung Treng, forms a strong link between Cambodia and Laos, cutting hours off the journey time.

Framing its western edge, and cutting it off from the rest of the country, is the Mekong River. It bifurcates, meanders and braids its way through the country and represents in its width a yawning chasm and watery superhighway that connects the region with Phnom Penh. Stung Treng and Kratie are located on this mighty river and despite the lack of any kind of riverboat service are still becoming excellent places to view the elusive Irrawaddy River Dolphin.

The dust-blown and wild frontier town of Ban Lung, the capital of Ratanakiri, is slowly emerging as a centre of trekking and adventure travel. ▸▸ *For listings, see pages 114-118.*

Mekong Provinces ⬤⬤⬤⬤⬤⬤⬤ ▸▸ *pp114-118.*

Kompong Cham, Kratie and Stung Treng make up the Mekong Provinces. Despite the Mekong River, its waterway and perpetual irrigation, these provinces are surprisingly economically unimportant and laid back. But with the new Chinese-built road now open and fully functioning – its easily one of the best in the country – the Northeast's provincial charms may soon be eradicated.

Kompong Cham and around → *Colour map 6, A2.*

Kompong Cham is the fourth largest town in Cambodia and is a town of some commercial prosperity owing to its thriving river port and also, it is said, as a result of preferential treatment received from local boy made good, the Prime Minister, Hun Sen. Town and province have a combined population of more than 1½ million people.

There is nothing in or around Kompong Cham to detain the visitor for long, most merely pass through, en route for Stung Treng and the northeast, but it is a pleasant enough town to rest awhile.

The small town of **Chhlong**, between Kompong Cham and Kratie, is one of Cambodia's best-kept secrets. The small town, nestled on the banks of the Mekong, 41 km from Kratie and 82 km from Kompong Cham, is one of the few places that survived the Khmer Rouge's ransacking and contains a multitude of French colonial buildings and traditional wooden Khmer houses. Of particular interest are the foundations of 120 antique houses and a 19th-century wooden Khmer house supported by 100 columns. Formerly a base for workers to surrounding rubber plantations, it is easy to feel nostalgic for a bygone era in Chhlong, with its wats and monasteries, an old school and charming market set in a colonial-style building. It takes four hours to get there get there by minibus, US$5; a whole boat, carrying 10 people, can be chartered for US$60.

Kratie → *Colour map 6, A3.*

Kratie (pronounced 'Kratcheay') is a port town on the Mekong roughly half way between Phnom Penh and Laos. It is a delightful place with a relaxed atmosphere and some good examples of shophouse architecture. In the dry season the deep blue Mekong peels back to reveal sandy beaches like those you might find at the Thai seaside. Sunset is a real highlight in Kratie, as the burning red sun descends slowly below the shore line.

Koh Trong Island, directly opposite Kratie town, has a lovely 8-km stretch of sandy dunes (in the dry season) where you can swim and relax. Aside from the beach, the island consists of small market farms and a simple, laid-back rural life – highly recommended for those who want to chill out. On the south side is a small Vietnamese floating village.

Kratie's main claim to some modicum of fame are the **Irrawaddy dolphins** that inhabit this portion of the Mekong (Kampi pool), 15 km north of the town on the road to Stung Treng. The best time to glimpse these rare and timid creatures is at sunrise or sunset when they are feeding. You can go by moto, US$3 return, then hire a longboat, US$2-3 per person per hour, at the official viewpoint (signposted on the left of the road).

Kampi Rapids ① *1000 riel* (also known as Kampi resort), 3 km north of Kampi Dolphin Pool, provides a refreshing and picturesque area to take a dip in the clear Mekong waters (during the dry season). A bridge leads down to a series of scenic thatched huts which provide shelter for the swimmers.

Twenty one kilometres further north of the Kampi pool is **Sambor**, a pre-Angkorian settlement, but today unfortunately not a single trace of this ancient heritage exists. The highpoint of a trip to Sambor is more in the getting there, as you pass through beautiful countryside, than in the temples themselves. Replacing the ancient ruins are two temples. The first and most impressive is the 100-column pagoda, rumoured to be the largest new pagoda in the country. It is a replica of the 100-column, wooden original, which was built in 1529. During the war, Pol Pot based himself out of the complex, killing hundreds of people and destroying the old pagoda. The new one was built in 1985 (perhaps the builders were slightly overzealous – it features 116 columns). Three hundred metres behind the gigantic pagoda sits a much smaller and arguably more interesting temple. The wat still contains many of its original features including a number of wooden pylons which date back 537 years.

Kratie

Stung Treng → *Colour map 4, C3.*

Yet another eponymous provincial capital on the Mekong, Stung Treng is just 40 km from Laos and a stopping off place on the overland route to Ratanakiri. The town has a frontier feel to it though it is now set to lose its wild and remote feel due to the building of the mammoth Chinese

Border essentials: Cambodia–Laos

Koh Chheuteal or Don Kralor

Lao immigration The border is open daily 0700-1700. You should aim to cross early in the day to avoid hassles and travelling at night. You will need to arrange visas beforehand in either Phnom Penh or Vientiane. Many tourists have encountered problems including inflated transportation costs and having to pay bribes, so try and be patient and keep smiling.

Transport A boat from Stung Treng to the Laos border (Koh Chheuteal) costs US$7 (per person or US$35 for the whole boat) and takes roughly 1 hr 10 mins. Boats depart quite regularly (depending on passengers), approximately every 2 hrs between 0700 and 1600. A departure tax of US$1-3 (depending on how greedy the customs officials are) will need to be paid at each side. Most hotels can organize tickets. Daily buses leave from Phnom Penh to Stung Treng but you wouldn't be able to make the trip from Phnom Penh across the border in a day. Phnom Penh Transport Company buses leave from Psar Thmei, Phnom Penh at 0700 and the journey takes 9-10 hrs, 40,000 riel.

Few people choose to stay in Stung Treng, as the town is short on charm. However, there is plenty of accommodation should you get stranded. Most tourists head to Kratie 3-4 hrs south of Stung Treng. To get to Kratie from Phnom Penh takes 6-7 hrs and both the Hour Lean Bus Company, T012-535387, and Phnom Penh Transport Company, T012-523400, both run buses to Kratie for US$4.50 at 0730, departing from Psar Thmei, Phnom Penh. Pick-ups and shared taxis also regularly connect Phnom Penh with Kratie.

road and a striking bridge that has created good links to Laos. Pigs, cows and the odd ox-cart still wander through the town's busy streets but there isn't a lot for tourists around Stung Treng. Some tour guides will organize a boat run to the Laos border to see riverine life and some waterfalls but you will need a Laos visa in order to do this. **Lbak Khone**, the 26 km rocky area that the Mekong rapids flow through en route to the Laos border, is one of the country's most stunning areas. Many tour operators will offer land transport to this area (as only the very, very brave would try by boat).

Ratanakiri Province 😀🕐🏍🏠⛰🚲🚐 ›› pp114-118.

Ratanakiri is like another planet compared to the rest of Cambodia – dusty, red roads curl through the landscape in summer, while in the rainy season the area becomes lush and green. Adventure enthusiasts won't be disappointed, with waterfalls to discover, ethnic minorities to meet, elephants to ride, river trips to take and the beautiful Yaek Lom volcanic lake to take a dip in.

Ban Lung and around → Colour map 4, C4.

Ban Lung has been the dusty provincial capital of Ratanakiri Province ever since the previous capital Lumphat was flattened by US bombers trying to 'destroy' the footpaths and tracks that made up the Ho Chi Minh Trail. There are no paved roads in or around the town, merely dirt tracks which in the dry season suffocate the town with their dust and in the wet season turn into rivers of mud. The town is situated on a plateau dotted with lakes and hills, many of great beauty, and serves as a base from which visitors can explore the surrounding countryside. At present you'll find basic guesthouse accommodation, and food and drink can be obtained in town.

Ins and outs Ban Lung is 13 hours from Phnom Penh. It is better to break your journey in Kratie and Stung Treng and take a pick-up/taxi from there. The chief mode of transport is the motorbike which comes with a driver, or not, as required (usually US$5 without driver and US$15 with, but you'll have to haggle). Bus services are sporadic. Cars with driver can be hired for US$40-50 a day.

Sights around Ban Lung The name Ratanakiri means 'jewel mountains' in Pali, and presumably comes from the wealth of gems in the hills, but it could just as easily refer to the beauty of the landscape. **Yaek Lom** ① *US$1 and a parking charge of 500 riel*, it is a perfectly circular volcanic lake about 5 km east of town and easily reached by motorbike. The crystalline lake is rimmed by protected forest dominated by giant emergents (dipterocarps and shoreas) soaring high into the sky. It takes about one hour to walk around the lake: in doing so you will find plenty of secluded bathing spots and, given the lack of water in town, it is not surprising that most locals and visitors bathe in the wonderfully clear and cool waters of the lake. There is a small 'museum' of ethnography and a couple of minority stilt houses to be seen.

There are three **waterfalls** ① *2000 riel each*, in close proximity to Ban Lung town. **Kachaang Waterfall** is 6 km away. The 12-m high waterfall flows year round and is surrounded by magnificent, pristine jungle and fresh mist rising from the fall. **Katien Waterfall** is a little oasis 7 km northwest of Ban Lung. Believed to have formed from volcanic lava hundreds of years ago, the 10-m plunging falls are sheltered from the outside world by a little rocky grotto. It is one of the better local falls to swim in as it is very secluded (most people will usually have the area to themselves), the water is completely clean. The best waterfall is arguably **Chaa Ong Falls**, with the 30-m falls plunging into a large pool. Those game enough can have a shower behind the crescent-shaped ledge. To get to the waterfalls, follow Highway 19 out of town and branch off 2 km out on the main road in the first village out of Ban Lung: Chaa Ong Falls are 9 km northwest at the intersection, turn right at the village and head for about 5 km to head to Katien Waterfall (follow the signs), the same road heads to Kachaang Waterfall.

The trip to **Ou'Sean Lair Waterfall**, 35 km from Ban Lung, is a wonderful day excursion offering a fantastic cross-section of what is essentially Ratanakiri's main attractions (without the riverside element). From Ban Lung, fields of wind-bent, spindly rubber trees provide a canopy over the road's rolling hills, a legacy left from the French in the 1960s. Punctuating the mottled natural vista is an equally diverse range of ethnic minority settlements. Tampeun and Kreung villages are dotted along the road and about half way (17 km from Ban Lung), in a lovely valley, is a tiny Cham village. The perfect end to the journey is the seven-tiered Ou'Sean Lair falls. The falls were reportedly 'discovered' by a Tampeun villager five years ago, who debated as to whether he should tell the Department of Tourism of their existence. In return for turning over the falls, they were named after him. The falls are most spectacular in the wet season but are still pretty alluring during the dry season.

For Sleeping and Eating price codes, see inside the front cover.

● Sleeping

Kompong Cham and around *p110*

E-F Mekong, on the river, T042-941536. A large hotel with 60 rooms, fan and a/c, fridge, TV and with bathrooms attached. Easily the best hotel in town and popular with the NGO community. Excellent views from the rooms.

E-F Rana, T012-696340. Set in a small village just outside Kampong Cham, this is a well-run and engaging homestay programme run by Kheang and her American husband, Don. Set up more for educational purposes than as a business you can get a real insight into rural life here. Rates include full-board but accommodation is basic. They offer free moto pick up from Kampong Cham if you book for 2 or more nights. Recommended.

Kratie *p111, map p111*

E-F Santepheap Hotel, on the river road, T072-971537. Rooms are adequate in this reasonable hotel. It has a quiet atmosphere and the clean and airy rooms come with attached bathrooms, fridge, fan or a/c.

E-G Oudom Sambath Hotel, 439 River Rd, T072-971502. Well-run place with a friendly English speaking Chinese-Khmer owner. The rooms are huge, with a/c, TV, hot water, etc. The more expensive rooms have large baths and regal looking furniture. The huge rooftop balcony has the best views of the Mekong in town – they have rooms up here as well but these fill quickly. Also has a decent and very cheap restaurant. Recommended.

G Star Guesthouse, beside the market, T072-971663. This has gained the reputation of being the friendliest guesthouse in town. It is very popular with travellers and its rooms are nicely appointed.

G You Hong Guesthouse, between the taxi rank and the market, T012-957003. Clean rooms with attached bathroom and fan. US$1

extra gets you cable TV. Friendly, helpful owners. The restaurant is often filled with drunk backpackers.

Stung Treng *p111*

D-G Ly Ly Guesthouse, opposite the market, T012-937859. Decent Chinese-style hotel with varying types of rooms – all come with private shower/toilet and cable TV. The ones at the back of the building have balconies and are the best value – you have the option of a/c or fan throughout. Friendly with some English spoken. Recommended.

D-G Stung Treng Hotel and Guest House, on main road near the river, T016-888335. Decent enough rooms in a good location – a reasonable 2nd option.

G Richies, on the River Rd, T012-686954. Very friendly English speaking Khmer owner, Richie, offers 2 small and basic rooms in this riverside guesthouse. Great food as well.

Ban Lung and around *p112*

A-D Terres Rouges Lodge, T/F075-974051, www.ratanakiri-lodge.com. Run by Frenchman Pierre Yves and his friendly Khmer wife Chenda, this hotel is housed in a large traditional wooden Khmer lodge overlooking the lake and offers cool, spacious and beautiful rooms, with the added bonus of a great CD collection in the comfortable sitting area. Pierre, like most other guesthouse and hotel owners in the area, runs a number of tour services, including elephant trekking and the use of a 4WD. This place mostly attracts small package-tour groups and is priced accordingly. You can haggle for a discount in the low-season.

D-F Lakeside Chenglock Hotel, beside Lake Konsaign, T012-957422. An improvement on its town counterpart. The rooms are very comfortable with the cheapest being roomy with fan and attached bathroom and, the more expensive bungalow-type rooms with attached hot water bathroom, a/c and view over the lake. Good value and recommended.

E-F Yaklom Hill Lodge, near Yaklom Lake, 6 km east of Ban Lung, T012-644240, www.yaklom.com. This rustic ecolodge is a bit out of town but offers guests the opportunity to experience first-hand the wonderful surrounding environs. Bungalows are interspersed in the natural surroundings, with good-sized balconies. Fan, mosquito net, attached bathroom, shower and thermos (for those that wish to have a warm traditional scoop shower out of the earthenware pots provided). Power is supplied via generator and solar panels. The friendly owner, Sampon, is planning on turning the lodge into a bird sanctuary – with 22 different species identified on the premises at the time of publication.

E-G Lake View Lodge, overlooking the lake, Old Governors House, T092-785259, www.lakeviewlodge-ratanakiri.com. Managed by the very switched-on Sophat – a Khmer former high school teacher – this is fast establishing itself as the budget traveller place of choice in Ban Lung. The rooms are nothing to get too excited about – from fan and coldwater through to a/c, TV and hot water – but the welcome is exceptional. Sophat will pick you up from the bus station in the middle of the night, provides internet access, decent food and trekking tours to outlying villages – there's even a small restaurant attached. Recommended.

🍴 Eating

Kompong Cham *p110*

🍴 **Ho An Restaurant**, Monivong St, T042-941234. Large, Chinese restaurant with a good selection of dishes. Friendly service.

🍴-🍴 **Mekong Daze**, on the riverfront. British owner Simon provides alcohol, cakes, fish and chips, and Khmer food from this new and friendly riverside establishment. He also has a free pool-table and you can watch the latest football on his TV. A good source of local info Simon can link you up with locals who rent boats and also local homestay programmes. Recommended.

Kratie *p111, map p111*

There are a number of food stalls set up along the river at night serving great fruit shakes. The market also sells simple dishes during the day.

🍴-🍴 **Red Sun Falling**, on the river road. Probably the best restaurant in town, it offers a variety of excellent Western dishes and a few Asian favourites. The full monty breakfast is fantastic. Good cocktails. The very friendly proprietor, Joe, also runs a very good bookshop on the premises. Closed Sun. Recommended.

🍴-🍴 **Star Guesthouse**, Street 10. A decent enough menu but sometimes the prices (almost US$1 for a squeeze of honey) and quality let the place down. Western food, and the home-made bread is excellent.

Stung Treng *p111*

🍴 **Richies**, on the river road near Sekong. One of the best places to eat in the region. Friendly Khmer owner, Richie, offers great Khmer and Western food. Highly recommended.

Ban Lung and around *p112*

🍴🍴-🍴 **Terres Rouges Lodge Restaurant** is considered the 'in' place to eat and is as fine dining as it gets in Ban Lung. Cambodian and French food. Good wine list/bar. The food is nothing exceptional, the service can be dodgy and they charge high corkage fees (US$10) should you decide to bring your own wine.

🍴 **American Restaurant**, on the crossroads opposite the petrol station – look for the badly painted sign. At first you think you've stumbled into someone's front room and then you find out you have! The humble surroundings, just 2 tables, belie the fact that the food is awesome and served by a very nice Khmer family – a true frontier town experience. The history of the name is that US MIA's were based here at some point. Highly recommended.

🍴 **Cyber Sophat**, near the market. Great little internet café run by the guys from **Lake View Lodge** offering all kinds of coffee, cakes and bus tickets. A beacon of modernity in the wilds of Ratanakiri.

Ratanak Hotel Restaurant. Quite a popular restaurant that serves a spectacular barbecue which you cook at your table. Cambodian food US$1-2.

Yaklom Hill Lodge offers a good selection of tasty and cheap Lao, Khmer and Thai-inspired meals with a few dishes to please the more Western-orientated palate.

Bars and clubs

Ban Lung and around p112
Since the local disco burnt down, the town has been lacking any vivid nightlife. There is only one bona fide bar – the **VP Bar**, opposite the Ratanak Hotel. A small, intimate setting.

Shopping

Kratie p111, map p111
The central market sells most things and there are a couple of pharmacies opposite. A good camera shop, Konica, is on the River Rd.

Ban Lung and around p112
Ban Lung market is large and set in a wasteland. During the day there is very little of interest for purchase although a few shops sell handicrafts but these have yet to develop and there are no local textiles, hence the eagerness with which kramas and T-shirts will be received. However from 0600-0700 the market is a hive of activity as nearby villagers come to sell their honey, nuts and other produce, and catch up on the morning gossip whilst eating their breakfast. From 1700-1800 the food market opens at the back; if you can face it, try their specialities.

Activities and tours

Stung Treng p111
Richies (see Eating). Can offer all manner of tours and boat rides to Laos, Irrawaddy Dolphin spotting and to local waterfalls.

Ban Lung and around p112
Lake View Lodge, T092-785259, offer a variety of tours and other adventures. They can also procure motos and dirt bikes of varying quality for rent.

Transport

Kompong Cham p110
Boat
Due to improved roads the boat service to and from Kompong Cham is non-existent. The boat service from Phnom Penh has also been curtailed.

Moto/tuk-tuk/taxi
Local transport is by moto, tuk-tuk or taxi. A moto for a day is between US$6-8 and between 500-1000 riel for short trips. Local tuk-tuk driver and guide Mr Vannat has an excellent reputation and is fluent in French and English, T012-995890. US$20 a day for a boat ride.

Shared taxi
The town is 120 km northeast of Phnom Penh via the well-surfaced Routes 5, 6 and 7. There are regular connections with **Phnom Penh** by shared taxi, US$1.85, 7000 riel. Several bus companies run services, US$2, 8000 riel, from Central Market, around 2 hrs, 8 buses a day. Pick-ups and shared taxis plough through to **Sen Monorom**, via **Snuol**, 2 hrs, US$3-4.

Kratie p111, map p111
Boat
The future of the express boat to and from Phnom Penh is uncertain but most believe the service won't resume.

Bus
Getting to Kratie is easy now the roads have improved. **Hour Lean Bus Company**, T012-535387, on Kratie's riverfront runs daily buses to **Phnom Penh** 0715, 7 hrs, US$4.50. **Phnom Penh Public Transport Co** also runs the trip to Phnom Penh for the same price –

the bus leaves at 0715 from the Central Market. The same bus company also charters buses to **Stung Treng** at around 1200. It is sometimes possible to hop on one of the buses coming from Phnom Penh to go to **Stung Treng** but seats can't be relied upon unless booked a few days in advance.

Motodop
Local transport by motodop US$1 per hr or US$6-7 per day.

Shared taxi
Shared taxis to **Stung Treng**, 3 hrs, US$4 per person. Shared taxis and pick-up to **Snuol** 0700, 2 hrs, US$2-3. Snuol is a good staging post for destinations such as **Sen Monorom** (further 3 hrs away). Via Snuol, 5-6 hrs, US$4-5.

Stung Treng p111
Boat
There are no longer any vessels plying the **Phnom Penh/Kratie** route and with the new road bridge opening in early 2008 the future of the boat from Stung Treng to the **Lao border** is now in doubt and services are very likely to cease in the near future. Ask at **Richies** for an update when you arrive in town. He can also arrange private boat transfer should you need it. Most hotels can organize tickets. Alternatively, you can go directly to the taxi/bus rank.

Bus
Buses to **Phnom Penh** leave from the bus stand (near the park but this office was declared 'temporary' at the time of writing) at 0700, 10 hrs, US$10. The same bus will stop at **Kratie**, US$5.

Shared taxi/pick-up
Pick-ups and shared taxis connect regularly with **Phnom Penh** via **Kratie** and with recent road construction the roads should be okay to travel along (a little bumpy). Shared taxis to **Phnom Penh** leave at 0600 from the taxi rank near the river, 7 hrs, US$15. To **Ban Lung** at 0700 from the taxi rank, 4-5 hrs, US$10.

Please note that all shared taxi services will not run unless the driver has a full car, so departure times and fares will vary depending on the number of passengers.

Ban Lung and around p112
Air
There is an airport in Ban Lung but the old plane that used to fly from Phnom Penh crashed near Bokor, taking several Korean tourists with it. There are no plans at the time of writing to begin flights again.

Motorbike/moto
Several guesthouses have motorbikes for hire, or can arrange hire, for around US$5 per day without driver and triple that with a driver. There are no garages/petrol stops outside the town of Ban Lung, though there are a few roadside places offering bottles of fuel of dubious quality, so it is advisable to set off with a full tank. **Lake View Lodge** can also arrange moto and dirt bike for US$5-10 per day.

Shared taxi/pick-up
If you are a glutton for punishment or just want another after-dinner story when you get home, it is possible to travel directly to **Phnom Penh** but be prepared to sit in a cramped pick-up/taxi for around 13 hrs. Taxi to **Kratie**, leaving the taxi stand at approximately 0800, 7 hrs, US$12-13. Taxi to **Stung Treng**, 0830, 2-3 hrs, US$5-7.

You can only get a moto to take you to **Lumphat** for around US$15 for the day trip. The road from Stung Treng is fairly well graded now and is constantly improving due to its use by logging companies. The trip to **Ban Lung** from Stung Treng takes about 3 hrs (if you get yourself in a nice new Camry), US$10. Unfortunately the same cannot be said of the road from Kratie to Stung Treng which barely deserves such an appellation. However, the road was being overhauled at the time of publication.

Tourists commonly ask about travelling between Ban Lung and **Sen Monorom**. At the time of publication this overland odyssey really wasn't an option, as the roads are almost impassable and difficult to navigate. Only experienced dirt bike riders with very good local knowledge should attempt this trip.

❻ Directory

Kompong Cham *p110*
Banks There are 2 banks in town – **Acleda** and **Canadia Bank**. Acleda, 0800-1600, will do Western Union transfers and Canadia will do advances on Visa and MasterCard. **Internet** ABC computers, in the centre of town, was the only internet shop operating at the time of writing, US$1 per hr, overseas phone calls. A new café was due to open on Pasteur St, opposite the Mekong Crossing.

Kratie *p111; map p111*
Banks There is an **Acleda Bank** half way down Street 11. It does not do advances on Visa or MasterCard but is a subsidiary for Western Union. **Internet** You Hong Guesthouse offer a good, cheap connection. Three Star Internet US$4 per hr. There is another internet café near Phnom Penh

Transport bus office but at the time of writing it was US$4 per hr.

Stung Treng *p111*
Banks There are no banks in town.
Internet Available at the computer shop opposite the market and the **Sekong Hotel**, US$4 per hr. **Telephone** There are telephone shops all over town.

Ban Lung and around *p112*
Banks Amazingly **ANZ** bank have opened an ATM near the airport. At the time of writing only locals could use it but foreign cards should be accepted by the time of publication. Beware of queues as the locals try to figure out how to use this new bit of technology. The **Mountain Guesthouse** and the **Ratanak Hotel** both change TCs but allow at least 3 days for your cheques to clear. **Internet** Cyber Sophat near the market claims the only broadband connection in the whole province. Otherwise expect slow dial-up download speeds. **CIC** near **Sovannikiri Hotel**. **Medical services** The hospital is on the road north towards O Chum. **Dr Vannara**, T012-970359, speaks very good English. **Post office** In the centre of town.

Angkor

The huge temple complex of Angkor, the ancient capital of the powerful Khmer Empire, is one of the archaeological treasures of Asia and the spiritual and cultural heart of Cambodia. Angkor Wat is arguably the greatest temple within the complex, both in terms of grandeur and sheer magnitude. After all, it is the biggest religious monument in the world, its outer walls clad with one of the longest continuous bas-relief ever created. The diverse architectural prowess and dexterity of thousands of artisans is testified by around 100 brilliant monuments in the area. Of these the Bayon, with its beaming smiles; Banteay Srei, which features the finest most intricate carvings; and the jungle temple of Ta Prohm are unmissable. Others prefer the more understated but equally brilliant temples of Neak Pean, Preah Khan and Pre Rup.

The petite town of Siem Reap sits nearby the Angkor complex, and is home to a gamut of world-class hotels, restaurants and bars. A hop, skip and a jump from the town is Southeast Asia's largest lake, the Tonlé Sap, with floating villages, teeming with riverine life. ▸▸ *For listings, see pages 135-142.*

Ins and outs

Getting there

Air The airport (REP), T063-963148, is 7 km from Siem Reap, the town closest to the Angkor ruins (see page 142), with flights from Phnom Penh, Ho Chi Minh City, Bangkok and Vientiane. A moto into town is US$1, by taxi US$7. Guesthouse owners often meet flights. Visas can be issued upon arrival US$20 (฿1000), photo required.

Boat From Phnom Penh, US$25, five to six hours. The trip is a good way to see the mighty Tonlé Sap Lake. It is a less appealing option in the dry season when low water levels necessitate transfers to small, shallow draft vessels. In case of extremely low water levels a bus or pick-up will need to be taken for part of the trip. The mudbank causeway between the lake and the outskirts of Siem Reap is hard to negotiate and some walking may be necessary (it's 12 km from Bindonville harbour to Siem Reap). Boats depart from the Phnom Penh Port on Sisowath Quay (end of 106 Street) 0700, departing Siem Reap 0700 from Chong Khneas on the Tonlé Sap Lake. ▸▸ *See Transport, page 142.*

Bus The air-conditioned buses are one of the most convenient and comfortable ways to go between Phnom Penh and Siem Reap, US$3.50-4, six hours. Almost every guesthouse or hotel sells the tickets although it is easy enough to pick-up from the bus stations/terminal. In peak periods, particularly Khmer New Year, it is important to purchase tickets a day or two prior to travel. A shared taxi from Phnom Penh will cost you US$10.

Getting around

Most of the temples within the Angkor complex (except the Roluos Group) are located in an area 8 km north of Siem Reap, with the area extending across a 25 km radius. The Roluos Group are 13 km east of Siem Reap and further away is Banteay Srei (32 km).

Cars with drivers and guides are available from larger hotels from around US$20 per day plus US$20 for a guide. The **Angkor Tour Guide Association** and most other travel agencies can also organize this. Expect to pay around US$7-8 per day for a **moto** unless the driver speaks good English in which case the price will be higher. This price will cover trips to the Roluos Group of temples but not to Banteay Srei. No need to add more than a dollar or two to the price for getting to Banteay Srei unless the driver is also a guide and can demonstrate to you that he is genuinely going to show you around. Tuk-tuks and their ilk have appeared on the scene in recent years and a trip to the temples on a motorbike drawn cart is quite a popular option for two people, US$10 a day (maximum of two people).

① Angkor, Siem Reap & Roluos

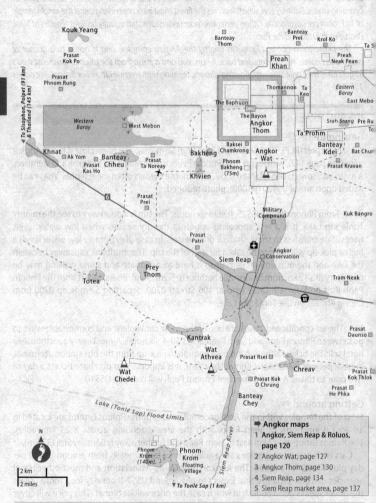

Kouk Yeang

Prasat
Kok Po

Prasat
Phnom Rung

To Sisophon, Poipet (91 km)
& Thailand (145 km)

Western
Baray

West Mebon

Khnat
Ak Yom
Prasat
Kas Ho
Banteay
Chheu
Prasat
Ta Noreay

Bakheng

Khvien

Prasat
Prei

6

Prasat
Patri

Prey
Thom

Totea

Siem Reap

Kantrak

Wat
Athvea
Prasat Rsei

Wat
Chedei

Banteay
Chey

Lake (Tonlé Sap) Flood Limits

Banteay
Thom

Banteay
Prei
Krol Ko

Preah
Khan

Preah
Neak Pean

Ta S

Thomannon
Ta
Keo

Eastern
Baray

East Mebo

The Baphuon
The Bayon
Angkor
Thom

Srah Srang
Pre Ru

Ta Prohm
To

Baksei
Chamkrong
Angkor
Wat

Banteay
Kdei
Bat Chur

Phnom
Bakheng
(75m)

Prasat Kravan

Military
Compound

Kuk Bangro

Angkor
Conservation

Tram Neak

Prasat
Daunso

Prasat
Chreav
Kok Thlok

Prasat Kuk
O Chrung

Prasat
He Phka

2 km
2 miles

Phnom
Krom
(140m)

Phnom
Krom
Floating
Village

Siem Reap River

To Tonlé Sap (1 km)

➡ Angkor maps
1 Angkor, Siem Reap & Roluos,
page 120
2 Angkor Wat, page 127
3 Angkor Thom, page 130
4 Siem Reap, page 134
5 Siem Reap market area, page 137

Bicycle hire, US$2-3 per day from most guesthouses, represents a nice option for those who feel reasonably familiar with the area. However, if you are on a limited schedule and only have a day or two at the temples you won't be able to cover an awful lot of the temples on a pedal bike as the searing temperatures and sprawling layout can take even the most advanced cyclists a considerable amount of time. Angkor Wat and Banteay Srei have official parking sites, 1000 riel (US$0.25) and at the other temples you can quite safely park and lock your bikes in front of a drink stall. For those wishing to see Angkor from a different perspective it is possible to charter a **helicopter**. **Elephants** are stationed near the Bayon or at the South Gate of Angkor Thom during the day. In the evenings, they are located at the bottom of Phnom Bakheng, taking tourists up to the summit for sunset. ▸▸ *See Activities and tours, page 141.*

To Banteay Srei (10 km) & Phnom Kulen

Wat Phnom Bok

Phnom Bok (212m)

Prasat To

Pradak

Banteay Samre

eak eang Prei Pasat

Pasat Komnap

Rolung River

Kuk Taleh

Prasat Pou Teng

Lolei

Prasat O Kaek   Preah Ko

Bakong   Roluos

Prahu   Prasat Prei Monti

Svay Pream

Prasat Totoeng O Thngai

Prasat Trapeang Phong

To Chau Srei Vibol Temple Complex (5km approx)

To Phnom Penh

Best time to visit
Angkor's peak season coincides with the dry season, November-February. Not only is this the driest time of year it is also the coolest (which can still be unbearably hot). The monsoon lasts from June to October or November. At this time it can get very muddy.

Tourist information
Guides can be invaluable when navigating the temples, with the majority being able to answer most questions about Angkor as well as providing additional information about Cambodian culture and history. Most hotels and travel agents will be able to point you in the direction of a good guide. The **Khmer Angkor Tour Guide Association** ① *on the road to Angkor, T063-964347*, has pretty well-trained guides. Most of the guides here are very well-briefed and some speak English better than others. The going rate is US$20-25 per day. If you do wish to buy an additional guidebook Dawn Rooney's *Angkor: An Introduction to the Temples* and *Ancient Angkor* by Michael Freeman and Claude Jacques are recommended.

Temple fees and hours One-day pass for US$23, two- or three-day pass US$43, four-to seven-day pass US$63. Most people will

Beating the crowds

These days avoiding traffic within the Angkor complex is difficult but still moderately achievable. As it stands, there is a pretty standard one-day tour itinerary that includes: Angkor Wat (sunrise), Angkor Thom, the Bayon, etc (morning), break for lunch, Ta Prohm (afternoon), Preah Khan (afternoon) and Phnom Bakheng (sunset). If you reverse the order, peak hour traffic at major temples is dramatically reduced. As many tour groups trip into Siem Reap for lunch this is an opportune time to catch a peaceful moment in the complex, just bring a packed lunch or eat at 1100 or 1400.

To avoid the masses at the draw-card attraction, Angkor Wat, try to walk around the temple, as opposed to through it. Sunset at Phnom Bakheng has turned into a circus fiasco, so aim for Angkor or the Bayon at this time as they are both relatively peaceful. Sunrise is still relatively peaceful at Angkor, grab yourself the prime position behind the left-hand pond (you need to depart Siem Reap no later than 0530), though there are other stunning early morning options, such as Srah Srang or Bakong. Bakheng gives a beautiful vista of Angkor in the early-mid morning.

be able to cover the majority of the temples within three days. If you buy your ticket after 1715 the day beforehand, you get a free sunset thrown in. For any ticket other than the one-day ticket you will need a passport photograph. The complex is open daily 0530-1830.

Safety Landmines were planted on some outlying paths to prevent Khmer Rouge guerrillas from infiltrating the temples; they have pretty much all been cleared by now, but it is safer to stick to well-used paths. Be wary of **snakes** in the dry season. The very poisonous Hanuman snake (lurid green) is fairly common in the area.

Photography A generalization, but somewhat true, is that black and white film tends to produce better-looking tourist pictures than those in colour. Plenty of hawkers have clicked onto this and sell Fuji SS fine-grain black and white film (US$2-3 a roll). The best colour shots usually include some kind of contrast against the temples, a saffron-clad monk or a child. Don't forget to ask if you want to include people in your shots. In general, the best time to photograph the great majority of temples is before 0900 and after 1630.

Itineraries

The temples are scattered over an area in excess of 160 sq km. A half-day would only allow enough time to visit the South Gate of Angkor Thom, Bayon and Angkor Wat. There are three so-called 'circuits'. The **Petit Circuit** takes in the main central temples including Angkor Wat, Bayon, Baphuon and the Terrace of the Elephants. The **Grand Circuit** takes a wider route, including smaller temples like Ta Prohm, East Mebon and Neak Pean. The **Roluos Group Circuit** ventures further afield still, taking in the temples near Roluos – Lolei, Preah Ko and Bakong. Here are some options for visiting Angkor's temples :

One day Angkor Wat (sunrise or sunset), South Gate of Angkor Thom, Angkor Thom Complex (Bayon, Elephant Terrace, Royal Palace) and Ta Prohm. This is a hefty schedule for one day; you'll need to arrive after 1615 and finish just after 1700 the following day.

Two days The same as above but with the inclusion of the rest of the Angkor Thom, Preah Khan, Srah Srang (sunrise) and at a push, Banteay Srei.

Three days **Day 1** Sunrise at Angkor Wat; morning South Gate of Angkor Thom, Angkor Thom complex (aside from Bayon); Ta Prohm; late afternoon-sunset at the Bayon. **Day 2** Sunrise Srah Srang; morning Banteay Kdei and Banteay Srei; late afternoon Preah Khan; sunset at Angkor Wat. **Day 3** Sunrise and morning Roluos; afternoon Ta Keo and sunset either at Bakheng or Angkor Wat. Those choosing to stay one or two days longer should try to work Banteay Samre, East Mebon, Neak Pean and Thomannon into their itinerary. A further two to three days warrants a trip to Prasat Kravan, Ta Som, Beng Melea and Kbal Spean.

Background

Khmer Empire

Under Jayavarman VII (1181-1218) the Angkor complex stretched more than 25 km east to west and nearly 10 km north to south, approximately the same size as Manhattan. For five centuries (ninth-13th), the court of Angkor held sway over a vast territory. At its height Khmer influence spanned half of Southeast Asia, from Burma to the southernmost tip of Indochina and from the borders of Yunnan to the Malay Peninsula. The only threat to this great empire was a river borne invasion in 1177, when the Cham used a Chinese navigator to pilot their war canoes up the Mekong. Scenes are depicted in bas-reliefs of the Bayon temple.

Jayavarman II (802-835) founded the Angkor Kingdom, then coined Hariharalaya to the north of the Tonlé Sap, in the Roluos region (Angkor), in 802. Later he moved the capital to Phnom Kulen, 40 km northeast of Angkor, where he built a Mountain Temple and Rong Shen shrine. After several years he moved the capital back to the Roluos region. Jayavarman III (835-877) continued his father's legacy and built a number of shrines at Hariharalaya. Many historians believe he was responsible for the initial construction of the impressive laterite pyramid, Bakong, considered the great precursor to Angkor Wat. Bakong, built to symbolize Mount Meru, was later embellished and developed by Indravarman. **Indravarman** (877-889) overthrew his predecessor violently and undertook a major renovation campaign in the capital Hariharalaya. The majority of what stands in the Roluos Group today is the work of Indravarman. A battle between Indravarman's sons destroyed the palace and the victor and new king Yasovarman I (889-900) moved the capital from Roluos and laid the foundations of Angkor itself. He dedicated the temple to his ancestors. His new capital at Angkor was called Yasodharapura, meaning 'glory-bearing city', and here he built 100 wooden ashramas, retreats (all of which have disintegrated today). Yasovarman selected Bakheng as the location for his temple-mountain and after flattening the mountain top, set about creating another Mount Meru. The temple he constructed was considered more complex than anything built beforehand, a five-storey pyramid with 108 shrines. A road was then built to link the former and present capitals of Roluos and Bakheng. Like the Kings before him, Yasovarman was obliged to construct a major waterworks and the construction of the reservoir – the East Baray (now completely dry) – was considered an incredible feat. After Yasovarman's death in 900 his son **Harshavarman** (900-923) assumed power for the next 23 years. During his brief reign, Harshavarman is believed to have built Baksei Chamkrong (northeast of Phnom Bakheng) and Prasat Kravan (the 'Cardamom Sanctuary'). His brother, Ishanarvarman II (923-928), resumed power upon his death but no great architectural feats were recorded in this time. In 928, **Jayavarman IV** moved the capital 65 km away to Koh Ker. Here he built the grand state temple Prasat Thom, an impressive seven-storey, sandstone pyramid. Following the death of Jayavarman things took a turn for the worst. Chaos ensued under Harshavarman's II weak leadership and over the next four years, no monuments were known to be erected. Jayavarman's IV nephew, **Rajendravarman** (944-968), took control of the situation and it's assumed he forcefully relocated the capital back to Angkor. Rather than moving back into the old capital Phnom Bakheng, he marked his own new territory, selecting an area south of the East Baray as his administrative centre. Here, in 961 he constructed the state temple, Pre Rup, and constructed the temple, East Mebon (953), in the middle of the baray. Srah Srang, Kutisvara and Bat Chum were also constructed, with the help of his chief architect, Kavindrarimathana. It was towards the end of his reign that he started construction on Banteay Srei, considered one of the finest examples of Angkorian craftsmanship in the country. Rajendravarman's son **Jayavarman V** (968-1001) became the new king in 968. The administrative centre was renamed Jayendranagari and yet again, relocated. More than compensating for the unfinished Ta Keo was Jayavarman's V continued work on Banteay Srei. Under his supervision the splendid temple was completed and dedicated to his father.

Aside from successfully extending the Khmer Empire's territory **King Suryavarman I** (1002-1049), made a significant contribution to Khmer architectural heritage. He presided over the creation of a new administrative centre – the Royal Palace (in Angkor Thom) – and the huge walls that surround it. The next in line was **Udayadityavarman II** (1050-1066), the son of Suryavarman I. The Baphuon temple-mountain was built during his relatively short appointment. After overthrowing his Great-Uncle Dharanindravarman, **Suryavarman II** (1112-1150), the greatest of Angkor's god-kings, came to power. His rule marked the highest point in Angkorian architecture and civilization. Not only was he victorious in conflict, having beaten the Cham whom couldn't be defeated by China, he was responsible for extending the borders of the Khmer Empire into Myanmar, Malaya and Siam. This aside, he was also considered one of the era's most brilliant creators. Suryavarman II was responsible for the construction of Angkor Wat, the current day symbol of Cambodia. Beng Melea, Banteay Samre and Thommanon are also thought to be the works of this genius. He has been immortalized in his own creation – in a bas-relief in the South Gallery of Angkor Wat the glorious King Suryavarman II sitting on top of an elephant. After a period of political turmoil, which included the sacking of Angkor, **Jayavarman VII** seized the throne in 1181 and set about rebuilding his fiefdom. He created a new administrative centre – the great city of Angkor Thom. The mid-point of Angkor Thom is marked by his brilliant Mahayana Buddhist state temple, the Bayon. It is said that the Bayon was completed in 21 years. Jayavarman took thousands of peasants from the rice fields to build it, which proved a fatal error, for rice yields decreased and the empire began its decline as resources were drained. The temple, which consists of sculptured faces of Avolokiteshvara (the Buddha of compassion and mercy) are often said to also encompass the face of their great creator, Jayavarman VIII. He was also responsible for restoring the Royal Palace, renovating Srah Srang and constructing the Elephant Terrace, the Terrace of the Leper King and the nearby baray (northeast of Angkor Thom), Jayatataka reservoir. At the centre of his reservoir he built Neak Pean. Jayavarman VII adopted Mahayana Buddhism; Buddhist principles replaced the Hindu pantheon, and were invoked as the basis of royal authority. This spread of Buddhism is thought to have caused some of the earlier Hindu temples to be neglected. The king paid tribute to his Buddhist roots through his monastic temples – Ta Prohm and Preah Khan.

Motifs in Khmer sculpture

Apsaras These are regarded as one of the greatest invention of the Khmers. The gorgeous temptresses – born, according to legend, 'during the churning of the Sea of Milk' – were Angkor's equivalent of pin-up girls and represented the ultimate ideal of feminine beauty. They lived in heaven where their sole raison d'être was to have eternal sex with Khmer heroes and holy men. The apsaras are carved in seductive poses with splendidly ornate jewellery and clothed in the latest Angkor fashion. Different facial features suggest the existence of several races at Angkor. Together with the five towers of Angkor Wat they have become the symbol of Khmer culture. The god-king himself possessed an apsara-like retinue of court dancers – impressive enough for Chinese envoy Chou Ta-kuan to write home about it in 1296.

Garuda Mythical creature – half-man, half-bird – was the vehicle of the Hindu god, Vishnu, and the sworn enemy of the nagas. It appeared relatively late in Khmer architecture.

Kala Jawless monster commanded by the gods to devour his own body – made its first appearance in lintels at Roluos. The monster represented devouring time and was an early import from Java.

Makara Mythical water-monster with a scaly body, eagles' talons and an elephantine trunk.

Naga Sacred snake. These play an important part in Hindu mythology and the Khmers drew on them for architectural inspiration. Possibly more than any other single symbol or motif, the naga is characteristic of Southeast Asia and decorates objects throughout the region. The naga is an aquatic serpent and is intimately associated with water (a key component of Khmer prosperity). In Hindu mythology, the naga coils beneath and supports Vishnu on the cosmic ocean. The snake also swallows the waters of life, these only being set free to reinvigorate the world after Indra ruptures the serpent with a bolt of lightning. Another version has Vishnu's servants pulling at the serpent to squeeze the waters of life from it (the so-called churning of the sea, see page 126).

Singha Lion in stylized form; often the guardians to temples.

The French at Angkor

Thai ascendency and eventual occupation of Angkor in 1431, led to the city's abandonment and the subsequent invasion of the jungle. Four centuries later, in 1860, Henri Mouhot – a French naturalist – stumbled across the forgotten city, its temple towers enmeshed in the forest canopy. Locals told him they were the work of a race of giant gods. Only the stone temples remained; all the wooden secular buildings had decomposed in the intervening centuries. In 1873 French archaeologist Louis Delaporte removed many of Angkor's finest statues for 'the cultural enrichment of France'. In 1898, the École Française d'Extrême Orient started clearing the jungle, restoring the temples, mapping the complex and making an inventory of the site. Delaporte was later to write the two-volume *Les Monuments du Cambodge*, the most comprehensive Angkorian inventory of its time, and his earlier sketches, plans and reconstructions, published in *Voyage au Cambodge* in 1880 are without parallel.

The Churning of the Sea

The Hindu legend, the *Churning of the Sea*, relates how the gods and demons resolved matters in the turbulent days when the world was being created. The elixir of immortality was one of 13 precious things lost in the churning of the cosmic sea. It took 1000 years before the gods and demons, in a joint dredging operation – aided by Sesha, the sea snake, and Vishnu – recovered them all.

The design of the temples of Angkor was based on this ancient legend. The moat represents the ocean and the gods use the top of Mount Meru – represented by the tower – as their churning stick. The cosmic serpent offered himself as a rope to enable the gods and demons to twirl the stick.

Paul Mus, a French archaeologist, suggests that the bridge with the naga balustrades which went over the moat from the world of men to the royal city was an image of the rainbow. Throughout Southeast Asia and India, the rainbow is alluded to as a multi-coloured serpent rearing its head in the sky.

Angkor temples → *Colour map 4, C1.*

The temples at Angkor were modelled on those of the kingdom of Chenla (a mountain kingdom centred on northern Cambodia and southern Laos), which in turn were modelled on Indian temples. They represent Mount Meru – the home of the gods of Indian cosmology. The central towers symbolize the peaks of Mount Meru, surrounded by a wall representing the earth and moats and basins representing the oceans. The devaraja, or god-king, was enshrined in the centre of the religious complex, which acted as the spiritual axis of the kingdom. The people believed their apotheosized king communicated directly with the gods.

The central tower sanctuaries housed the images of the Hindu gods to whom the temples were dedicated. Dead members of the royal and priestly families were accorded a status on a par with these gods. Libraries to store the sacred scriptures were also built within the ceremonial centre. The temples were mainly built to shelter the images of the gods – unlike Christian churches, Moslem mosques and some Buddhist pagodas, they were not intended to accommodate worshippers. Only priests, the servants of the god, were allowed into the interiors. The 'congregation' would mill around in open courtyards or wooden pavilions.

The first temples were of a very simple design, but with time they became more grandiose and doors and galleries were added. Most of Angkor's buildings are made from a soft sandstone which is easy to work. It was transported to the site from Phnom Kulen, about 30 km to the northeast. Laterite was used for foundations, core material, and enclosure walls, as it was widely available and could be easily cut into blocks. A common feature of Khmer temples was false doors and windows on the sides and backs of sanctuaries and other buildings. In most cases there was no need for well-lit rooms and corridors as hardly anyone ever went into them. That said, the galleries round the central towers in later temples, such as Angkor Wat, indicate that worshippers did use the temples for ceremonial circumambulation when they would contemplate the inspiring bas-reliefs from the important Hindu epic, *Ramayana* and *Mahabharata* (written between 400 BC and AD 200).

Despite the court's conversion to Mahayana Buddhism in the 12th century, the architectural ground-plans of temples did not alter much – even though they were based on Hindu cosmology. The idea of the god-king was simply grafted onto the new state religion and statues of the Buddha rather than the gods of the Hindu pantheon were used to represent the god-king (see Bayon, page 129). One particular image of the Buddha predominated at Angkor in which he wears an Angkor-style crown, with a conical top which is encrusted with jewellery.

Angkor Wat → Colour map 4, C1.

The awe-inspiring sight of Angkor Wat, first thing in the morning, is something you're not likely to forget. Angkor literally means 'city' or 'capital' and it is the biggest religious monument ever built and certainly one of the most spectacular. The temple complex covers 81 ha. Its five towers are emblazoned on the Cambodian flag and the 12th-century masterpiece is considered by art historians to be the prime example of classical Khmer art and architecture. It took more than 30 years to build and is dedicated to the Hindu god Vishnu, personified in earthly form by its builder, the god-king Suryavarman II, and is aligned east to west.

Angkor Wat differs from other temples, primarily because it is facing westward, symbolically the direction of death, leading many to originally believe it was a tomb. However, as Vishnu is associated with the west, it is now generally accepted that it served both as a temple and a mausoleum for the king. Like other Khmer temple-mountains, Angkor Wat is an architectural allegory, depicting in stone the epic tales of Hindu mythology. The central sanctuary of the temple complex represents the sacred Mount Meru, the

▣ Angkor Wat

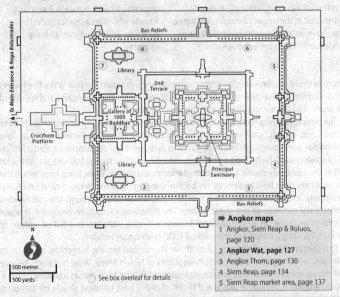

500 metres
500 yards

(✲ See box overleaf for details

Anti-clockwise round Angkor Wat's bas-reliefs

1 Western gallery The southern half represents a scene from the Mahabharata of a battle between the Pandavas (with pointed head dresses, attacking from the right) and the Kauravas. The two armies come from the two ends of the panel and meet in the middle. The south-west corner has been badly damaged – some say by the Khmer Rouge – but shows scenes from Vishnu's life.

2 Southern gallery The western half depicts Suryavarman II (builder of Angkor Wat) leading a procession. He is riding a royal elephant, giving orders to his army before leading them into battle against the Cham. The rank of the army officers is indicated by the number of umbrellas. The undisciplined, outlandishly dressed figures are the Thais.

3 Southern gallery The eastern half was restored in 1946 and depicts the punishments and rewards one can expect in the after life. The damned are depicted in the bottom row, while the blessed, depicted in the upper two rows, are borne along in palanquins surrounded by large numbers of bare breasted apsaras.

4 Eastern gallery The southern half is the best-known part of the bas-relief – the churning of the sea of milk by gods and demons to make ambrosia (the nectar of the gods which gives immortality). In the centre, Vishnu commands the operation. Below are sea animals and above, apsaras.

5 Eastern gallery The northern half is an unfinished representation of a war between the gods for the possession of the ambrosia. The gate in the centre was used by Khmer royalty and dignitaries for mounting and dismounting elephants.

6 Northern gallery Represents a war between gods and demons. Siva is shown in meditation with Ganesh, Brahma and Krishna. Most of the other scenes are from the Ramayana, notably the visit of Hanuman to Sita.

7 Western gallery The northern half has another scene from the Ramayana depicting a battle between Rama and Ravana who rides a chariot pulled by monsters and commands an army of giants.

centre of the Hindu universe, on whose summit the gods reside. Angkor Wat's five towers symbolize Meru's five peaks; the enclosing wall represents the mountains at the edge of the world and the surrounding moat, the ocean beyond.

The temple complex is enclosed by a square moat – more than 5 km in length and 190 m wide – and a high, galleried wall, which is covered in epic bas-reliefs and has four ceremonial tower gateways. The main gateway faces west and the temple is approached by a 475-m-long road, built along a causeway, which is lined with naga balustrades. At the far end of the causeway stands a **cruciform platform**, guarded by stone lions, from which the devaraja may have held audiences; his backdrop being the three-tiered central sanctuary. Commonly referred to as the Terrace of Honour, it is entered through the colonnaded processional gateway of the outer gallery. The transitional enclosure beyond it is again cruciform in shape. Its four quadrants formed galleries, once stocked full of statues of the Buddha. Only a handful of the original 1000-odd images remain.

The cluster of **central towers**, 12 m above the second terrace, is reached by 12 steep stairways, which represent the precipitous slopes of Mount Meru. Many historians believe that the upwards hike to this terrace was reserved for the high priests and king himself. Today, anyone is welcome but the difficult climb is best handled slowly by stepping sideways up the steep incline. The five lotus flower-shaped sandstone towers – the first appearance of these features in Khmer architecture – are believed to have once been covered in gold. The eight-storey towers are square, although they appear octagonal, and give the impression of a sprouting bud. The central tower is dominant, as is the Siva shrine and principal sanctuary, whose pinnacle rises more than 30 m above the third level and, 55m above ground level. This sanctuary would have contained an image of Siva in the likeness of King Suryavarman II, as it was his temple-mountain. But it is now a Buddhist shrine and contains statues of the Buddha.

More than 1000 sq m of bas-relief decorate the temple. Its greatest sculptural treasure is the 2-m-high **bas-reliefs**, around the walls of the outer gallery. It is the longest continuous bas-relief in the world. In some areas traces of the paint and gilt that once covered the carvings can still be seen. Most famous are the hundreds of figures of deities and apsaras in niches along the walls.

The royal city of Angkor Thom

Construction of Jayavarman VII's spacious walled capital, Angkor Thom (which means 'great city'), began at the end of the 12th century: he rebuilt the capital after it had been captured and destroyed by the Cham. Angkor Thom was colossal: the 100-m-wide moat surrounding the city, which was probably stocked with crocodiles as a protection against the enemy, extended more than 12 km. Inside the moat was an 8-m-high stone wall, buttressed on the inner side by a high mound of earth along the top of which ran a terrace for troops to man the ramparts.

Four great gateways in the city wall face north, south, east and west and lead to the city's geometric centre, the Bayon. The fifth, Victory Gate, leads from the royal palace (within the Royal Enclosure) to the East Baray. The height of the gates was determined by the headroom needed to accommodate an elephant and howdah, complete with parasols. The flanks of each gateway are decorated by three-headed stone elephants, and each gateway tower has four giant faces, which keep an eye on all four cardinal points. Five causeways traverse the moat, each bordered by sculptured balustrades of nagas gripped, on one side, by 54 stern-looking giant gods and on the other by 54 fierce-faced demons. The balustrade depicts the Hindu legend of the churning of the sea (see page 126).

The **South Gate** provides the most common access route to Angkor Thom, predominantly because it sits on the path between the two great Angkor complexes. The gate is a wonderful introduction to Angkor Thom, with well-restored statues of asuras (demons) and gods lining the bridge. The figures on the left, exhibiting serene expression, are the gods, while those on the right, with grimaced, fierce-looking heads, are the asuras.

The **Bayon** was Jayavarman VII's own temple-mountain, built right in the middle of Angkor Thom; its large faces have now become synonymous with the Angkor complex. It is believed to have been built between the late 12th century to early 13th century, around 100 years after Angkor Wat. The Bayon is a three-tiered, pyramid-temple with a 45-m-high tower, topped by four gigantic carved heads. These faces are believed to be the images of Jayavarman VII as a Bodhisattra, and face the four compass points. They are crowned with lotus flowers, symbol of enlightenment, and are surrounded by 51 smaller towers each with heads facing north, south, east and west. There are more than 2000 large faces carved throughout the structure. The first two of the three levels feature galleries of bas-relief (which should be viewed clockwise); a circular central sanctuary dominates the third level. The **bas-reliefs** which decorate the walls of the Bayon are much less imposing than those at Angkor Wat. The sculpture is carved deeper but is more naive and less sophisticated than the bas-reliefs at Angkor Wat. The relief on the outside depicts historical events; those on the inside were drawn from the epic world of gods and legends, representing the creatures who were supposed to haunt the subterranean depths of Mount Meru. In fact the reliefs on the outer wall illustrating historical scenes and derring-do with marauding Cham were carved in the early 13th century during the reign of Jayavarman; those on the inside which illuminate the Hindu cosmology were carved after the king's death when his successors turned from Mahayana Buddhism back to Hinduism. Two recurring themes in the bas-reliefs are the powerful king and the Hindu epics. Jayavarman is depicted in the throes of battle with the Cham – who are recognizable thanks to their unusual and distinctive headdress, which looks like an inverted lotus flower. The other bas-reliefs give a good insight into Khmer life at the time – the warrior elephants, ox carts, fishing with nets, cockfights and skewered fish drying on racks. Other vignettes show musicians, jugglers, hunters, chess players, palm-readers and scores of Angkor citizens enjoying drinking sessions. In the naval battle scenes, the water around the war-canoes is depicted by the presence of fish, crocodiles and floating corpses.

The **Royal Palace**, to the north of the Bayon, had already been laid out by Suryavarman I: the official palace was in the front with the domestic quarters behind, its gardens

3 Angkor Thom

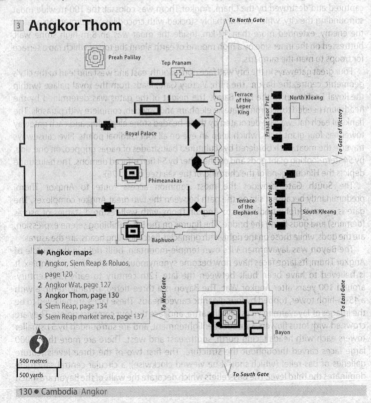

➡ **Angkor maps**
1 Angkor, Siem Reap & Roluos, page 120
2 Angkor Wat, page 127
3 Angkor Thom, page 130
4 Siem Reap, page 134
5 Siem Reap market area, page 137

500 metres
500 yards

surrounded by a laterite wall and moat. Suryavarman I also beautified the royal city with ornamental pools. Jayavarman VII simply improved his designs. In front of the Royal Palace, at the centre of Angkor Thom, Suryavarman I laid out the first Grand Plaza with the **Terrace of the Elephants** (also called the Royal Terrace). The 300-m-long wall derives its name from the large, life-like carvings of elephants in a hunting scene, adorning its walls. The 2.5-m wall also features elephants flanking the southern stairway. It is believed it was the foundations of the royal reception hall. Royalty once sat in gold-topped pavilions at the centre of the pavilion, and here there are rows of garudas (bird-men), their wings lifted as if in flight. They were intended to give the impression that the god-king's palace was floating in the heavens, like the imagined flying celestial palaces of the gods. At the northeast corner of the 'central square' is the 12th-century **Terrace of the Leper King**, which may have been a cremation platform for the aristocracy of Angkor. The 7-m-high double terrace has bands of bas-reliefs, one on top of the other, with intricately sculptured scenes of royal pageantry and seated apsaras as well as nagas and garudas which frequented the slopes of Mount Meru. Above is a strange statue of an earlier date, which probably depicts the god of death, Yama, and once held a staff in its right hand. The statue's naked, lichen-covered body gives the terrace its name – the lichen gives the uncanny impression of leprosy. The **Phimeanakas** (meaning Celestial or Flying Palace in Sanskrit) inside the Royal Palace was started by Rajendravarman and used by all the later kings. Lions guard all four stairways to the central tower. It is now ruined but was originally covered in gold.

South of the Royal Palace is the **Baphuon**, built by Udayadityavarman II. The temple was approached by a 200-m-long sandstone causeway, raised on pillars, which was probably constructed after the temple was built. **Preah Palilay**, just outside the north wall of the Royal Palace, was also built by Jayavarman VII.

Around Angkor Thom

Phnom Bakheng

ⓘ *Either climb the steep hill (slippery when wet), ride an elephant to the top of the hill (US$15) or walk up the gentle zig-zag path the elephants take.*

Yasovarman's temple-mountain stands at the top of a natural hill, Phnom Bakheng, 60 m high, affording good views of the plains of Angkor. A pyramid-temple dedicated to Siva, Bakheng was the home of the royal linga and Yasovarman's mausoleum after his death. It is composed of five towers built on a sandstone platform. There are 108 smaller towers scattered around the terraces. The main tower has been partially demolished and the others have completely disappeared. It was entered via a steep flight of steps which were guarded by squatting lions. The steps have deteriorated with the towers. Foliate scroll relief carving covers much of the main shrine – the first time this style was used. This strategically placed hill served as a camp for various combatants, including the Vietnamese, and suffered accordingly.

Ta Prohm

The temple of Ta Prohm, is the perfect lost-in-the-jungle experience. Unlike most of the other monuments at Angkor, it has been only minimally cleared of its undergrowth, fig trees and creepers. It is widely regarded as one of Angkor's most enchanting temples.

Ta Prohm was consecrated in 1186 – five years after Jayavarman VII seized power. It was built to house the divine image of the Queen Mother. The outer enclosures of Ta Prohm are somewhat obscured by foliage but reach well-beyond the temple's heart (1 km by 650 m).

The temple proper consists of a number of concentric galleries, featuring corner towers and the standard gopuras. Other buildings and enclosures were built on a more ad hoc basis.

Within the complex walls lived 12,640 citizens. It contained 39 sanctuaries or prasats, 566 stone dwellings and 288 brick dwellings. Ta Prohm literally translates to the 'Royal Monastery' and that is what it functioned as, home to 18 abbots and 2740 monks. By the 12th century, temples were no longer exclusively places of worship – they also had to accommodate monks, so roofed halls were increasingly built within the complexes.

The trees burgeoning their way through the complex are predominantly the silk-cotton tree and the aptly named strangler fig. Naturally, the roots of the trees have descended towards the soil, prying their way through the temples foundations in the process. As the vegetation has matured, growing stronger, it has forced its way further into the temples structure, damaging the man-built base and causing untold destruction.

Banteay Kdei, Srah Srang, Prasat Kravan and Pre Rup

The massive complex of **Banteay Kdei**, otherwise known as 'the citadel of cells', is 3 km east of Angkor Thom. Some archaeologists think it may be dedicated to Jayavarman VII's religious teacher. The temple has remained in much the same state it was discovered in – a crowded collection of ruined laterite towers and connecting galleries lying on a flat plan, surrounded by a galleried enclosure. It is presumed that the temple was a Buddhist monastery and in recent years hundreds of buried Buddha statues were excavated from the site. Like Ta Prohm it contains a Hall of Dancers (east side), an open roof building with four separate quarters. The second enclosure runs around the perimeters of the inner enclosure. The third inner enclosure contains a north and south library and central sanctuary. The central tower was never finished. And the square pillars in the middle of the courtyard still cannot be explained by scholars. There are few inscriptions here to indicate either its name or purpose, but it is almost certainly a Buddhist temple built in the 12th century, about the same time as Ta Prohm. The Lake (baray) next to Banteay Kdei is called **Srah Srang** – 'Royal Bath' – which was used for ritual bathing. The steps down to the water face the rising sun and are flanked with lions and nagas. This sandstone landing stage dates from the reign of Jayavarman VII but the Lake itself is thought to date back two centuries earlier. A 10th-century inscription reads 'this water is stored for the use of all creatures except dyke breakers', eg elephants. The baray (700 m by 300 m), has been filled with turquoise-blue waters for more than 1300 years. With a good view of Pre Rup across the lake, some archaeologists believe that this spot affords the best vista in the whole Angkor complex.

Prasat Kravan, built in 921, means 'Cardamom Sanctuary' and is unusual in that it is built of brick. By that time brick had been replaced by laterite and sandstone. It consists of five brick towers arranged in a line. The Hindu temple, surrounded by a moat, consists of five elevated brick towers, positioned in a North-South direction. Two of the five decorated brick towers contain bas-reliefs (the north and central towers). The central tower is probably the most impressive and contains a linga on a pedestal. The sanctuary's three walls all contain pictures of Vishnu.

Northeast of Srah Srang is **Pre Rup**, the State Temple of King Rajendravarman's capital. Built in 961, the temple-mountain representing Mount Meru is larger, higher and artistically superior than its predecessor, the East Mebon, which it closely resembles. Keeping with tradition of state capitals, Pre Rup marked the centre of the city, much of which doesn't exist today. The pyramid-structure, which is constructed of laterite with brick prasats, sits at the apex of an artificial, purpose-built mountain. The central pyramid-level consists of a three-tiered, sandstone platform, with five central towers sitting above. Its modern name, 'turning the body', derives from local legend and is named after a cremation ritual in which the outline of a body was traced in the cinders one way and then the other. The upper levels of the pyramid offer a brilliant, panoramic view of the countryside.

Preah Khan

The 12th-century complex of Preah Khan, one of the largest complexes within the Angkor area, was Jayavarman VII's first capital before Angkor Thom was completed. Preah Khan means 'sacred sword' and is believed to have derived from a decisive battle against the Cham, which created a 'lake of blood', but was invariably won by Jayavarman VII. It is similar in ground-plan to Ta Prohm (see page 131) but attention was paid to the approaches: its east and west entrance avenues leading to ornamental causeways are lined with carved-stone boundary posts. Evidence of 1000 teachers suggests that it was more than a mere Buddhist monastery but most likely a Buddhist university. Nonetheless an abundance of Brahmanic iconography is still present on site. Around the rectangular complex, is a large laterite wall, surrounded by large garudas wielding the naga (each more than 5 m in height), the theme continues across the length of the whole 3-km external enclosure, with the motif dotted every 50 m. Within these walls lies the surrounding moat.

Preah Neak Pean

To the east of Preah Khan is the Buddhist temple Preah Neak Pean built by Jayavarman VII. The temple of Neak Pean is also a fountain, built in the middle of a pool and representing the paradisiacal Himalayan mountain-lake, Anaavatapta, from Hindu mythology. It is a small sanctuary on an island in the baray of Preah Khan. Two nagas form the edge of the island, and their tails join at the back. The temple pools were an important part of the aesthetic experience of Preah Khan and Neak Pean – the ornate stone carving of both doubly visible by reflection.

Outlying temples

The Roluos Group → Colour map 6, A1.

The Roluos Group receives few visitors but is worth visiting if time permits. Jayavarman II built several capitals including one at Roluos, at that time called Hariharalaya. This was the site of his last city and remained the capital during the reigns of his three successors. The three remaining Hindu sanctuaries at Roluos are **Preah Ko, Bakong** and **Lolei**. They were finished in 879, 881 and 893 respectively by Indravarman I and his son Yashovarman I and are the best-preserved of the early temples. All three temples are built of brick, with sandstone doorways and niches. Sculptured figures which appear in the Roluos group are the crouching lion, the reclining bull (Nandi – Siva's mount) and the naga (snake).

Preah Ko, meaning 'sacred ox', was named after the three statues of Nandi (the mount of the Hindu god, Siva) which stand in front of the temple. Orientated east-west, there is a cluster of six brick towers arranged in two rows on a low brick platform, the steps up to which are guarded by crouching lions while Nandi, looking back, blocks the way. The front row of towers was devoted to Indravarman's male ancestors and the second row to the female. Indravarman's temple-mountain, **Bakong**, is a royal five-stepped pyramid-temple with a sandstone central tower built on a series of successively receding terraces with surrounding brick towers. Indravarman himself was buried in the temple. Bakong is the largest and most impressive temple in the Roluos Group by a long way. A bridge flanked by a naga balustrade leads over a dry moat to the temple. The central tower was built to replace the original one when the monument was restored in the 12th century and is probably larger than the original. The Bakong denotes the true beginning of classical Khmer architecture and contained the god-king's Siva linga. **Lolei** was built by Yashovarman I in the middle of Indravarman's baray. The brick towers were dedicated to the king's ancestors, but over the centuries they have largely disintegrated; of the four towers two have partly collapsed.

4 Siem Reap

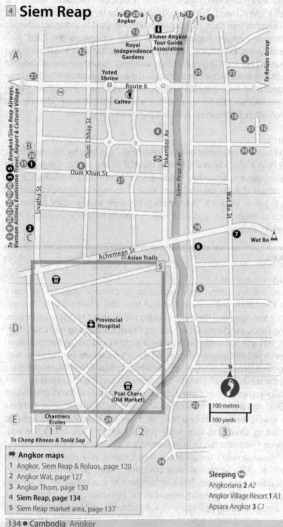

Bopha **5** *D3*
Borann **6** *A3*
Casa Angkor **8** *B1*
Earthwalkers **10** *C1*
Empress Angkor **11** *B1*
European Guesthouse **12** *B3*
FCC Angkor **4** *B2*
Golden Banana B&B **34** *E2*
Green Garden Home Guesthouse **35** *B1*
Home Sweet Home **14** *B3*
Jasmine Lodge **15** *B1*
La Residence D'Angkor **16** *C3*
La Villa Loti **17** *A2*
Le Meridien Angkor **7** *A2*
Mahogany Guesthouse **18** *B3*
Monoreach **19** *B1*
Neak Pean **20** *B1*
Paul Dubrule **9** *C1*
Passaggio **22** *E3*
Raffles Grand d'Angkor **13** *A2*
Rosy Guesthouse **25** *A3*
Secrets of Elephants Guesthouse **26** *B1*
Shinta Mani **27** *B2*
Sokha Angkor **21** *A1*
Sofitel Royal Angkor **28** *A2*
Sweet Dreams Guesthouse **31** *B3*
Ta Prohm **29** *E2*
Two Dragons Guesthouse **30** *B3*
Victoria Angkor **32** *A1*
Yaklom Angkor Lodge **33** *A3*

Eating ⑦
Abacus **1** *B1*
Barrio **2** *C1*
Madame Butterfly **5** *B1*
Moloppor **6** *C3*
Viroth's **7** *C3*
Pyongyang **3** *B1*

➡ **Angkor maps**
1 Angkor, Siem Reap & Roluos, page 120
2 Angkor Wat, page 127
3 Angkor Thom, page 130
4 Siem Reap, page 134
5 Siem Reap market area, page 137

Sleeping 🛏
Angkoriana **2** *A2*
Angkor Village Resort **1** *A3*
Apsara Angkor **3** *C1*

Banteay Srei → Colour map 4, C1.

Banteay Srei, 25 km from Ta Prohm along a decent road, was built by the Brahmin tutor to King Rajendravarman, Yajnavaraha, grandson of Harshavarman, and founded in 967. Banteay Srei translates to 'Citadel of Women', a title bestowed upon it in relatively recent years due to the intricate apsara carvings that adorn the interior. The temple is considered by many historians to be the highest achievement of art from the Angkor period. The explicit preservation of this temple reveals covered terraces, of which only the columns remain, which once lined both sides of the primary entrance. In keeping with tradition, a long causeway leads into the temple, across a moat, on the eastern side. The main walls, entry pavilions and libraries have been constructed from laterite and the carvings from pink sandstone. The layout was inspired by Prasat Thom at Koh Ker. Three beautifully carved tower-shrines stand side by side on a low terrace in the middle of a quadrangle, with a pair of libraries on either side enclosed by a wall. Two of the shrines, the southern one and the central one, were dedicated to Siva and the northern one to Vishnu; both had libraries close by, with carvings depicting appropriate legends. The whole temple is dedicated to Brahma. Having been built by a Brahmin priest, the temple was never intended for use by a king, which goes some way towards explaining its small size – you have to duck to get through the doorways to the sanctuary towers. Perhaps because of its modest scale Banteay Srei contains some of the finest examples of Khmer sculpture. Finely carved and rare pink sandstone replaces the plaster-coated carved-brick decoration, typical of earlier temples. All the buildings are covered in carvings: the jambs, the lintels, the balustered windows. Banteay Srei's ornamentation is exceptional – its roofs, pediments and lintels are magnificently carved with tongues of flame, serpents' tails, gods, demons and floral garlands.

Siem Reap ◎◐◑◒◓▲◉◖ → pp135-142. Colour map 6, A1

The nearest town to Angkor, Siem Reap is seldom considered as anything other than a service centre and it is true that without the temples, few people would ever find themselves here. The town has smartened itself up quite substantially in the past couple of years and, with the blossoming of hotels, restaurants and bars, it is now a pleasant place in its own right.

The Old Market area is the most touristy part of the town. Staying around here is recommended for independent travellers and those staying more than two or three days. A sprinkling of guesthouses are here but a much greater selection is offered just across the river, in the Wat Bo area.

◉ Angkor listings

*For Sleeping and Eating price codes,
see inside the front cover.*

● Sleeping

Siem Reap *p135, maps p134 and p137*
L-AL Hotel de la Paix, corner of Achemean and Sivatha, T063-966000, www.hoteldela paixangkor.com. Owned by the same

company that also runs Bangkok's famous **Bed Supper Club**, this is probably Siem Reap's best value luxury hotel. The rooms offer simple contemporary design with giant baths and plump bedding – all with a/c and cable TV. The pool is a maze of plinths and greenery and makes for a perfect spot to laze. Can feel a bit urban for Siem Reap but still a great hotel. Recommended.

L-AL Le Meridien Angkor, main road towards temples, T063-963900, www.lemeridien.com/angkor. From the outside this 5-star hotel resembles a futuristic prison camp – severe, angled architecture with small, dark slits for windows. Walk into the lobby and it is immediately transformed into space and light. Rooms are nicely designed and sized and all come with a/c, en suite and cable TV. Other facilities include spa, restaurants and pool. The garden is a lovely spot to take breakfast. Recommended.

L-AL Raffles Grand Hotel d'Angkor, 1 Charles de Gaulle Blvd, T063-963888, www.raffles.com. Certainly a magnificent period piece from the outside, Siem Reap's oldest (1930) hotel fails to generate ambience, the rooms are sterile and the design of the huge new wings is uninspired (unforgivable in Angkor). Coupled with this is a history of staff lock-outs and mass sackings that have caused the Raffles brand damage. However, it does have all the mod cons, including sauna, tennis, health and beauty spa, lap pool, gym, 8 restaurants and bars, nightly traditional performances, landscaped gardens, 24-hr valet service and in-house movie channels. Considering its astronomical rates guests have every right to feel disappointed.

L-AL Sokha Angkor, Sivatha St, T063-969 999, www.sokhahotels.com. One of the few Cambodian-owned 5-star hotels in the country, the rooms and services here are top notch, even if the decor is a little gaudy (if you can't afford to stay here, come and check out the incredibly over-the-top swimming pool, complete with faux temple structures and waterfalls). Also home to an excellent Japanese restaurant. Recommended.

L-AL Victoria Angkor Hotel, Route 6, T063-760428, www.victoriahotels-asia.com. Perfection. A beautiful hotel, with that 1930s east-meets-west style that exemplifies the French tradition of 'art de vivre'. The superb decor make you feel like you are staying in another era. Each room is beautifully decorated with local fabrics and fantastic furniture. Swimming pool, open-air salas,

jacuzzi and spa. It's the small touches and attention to detail that stands this hotel apart from the rest. Highly recommended.

AL Angkor Village Resort, T063-963561, www.angkorvillage.com. Opened in 2004, the resort contains 40 rooms set in Balinese-style surroundings. Traditional massage services, 2 restaurants, theatre shows and lovely pool. Elephant, boat and helicopter rides can be arranged. Recommended.

AL Apsara Angkor Hotel, Route 6 (between the airport and town), T063-964 999, www.apsaraangkor.com. Pretty standard hotel for the money they are asking. Well-appointed rooms with all amenities but they are rather kitsch. Facilities include gym, internet, swimming pool.

AL Empress Angkor, Airport Rd, opposite cultural village, T063-963999, www.empress angkor.com. One of the newest luxury hotels in town. The wooden interior is much nicer than you'd expect from the outside. 207 cosy guestrooms with all the usual inclusions, plus cable TV and balcony. Hotel facilities include restaurant (international and local cuisine), bar, massage, gym, swimming pool, jacuzzi spa and sauna. Visa/AMEX/MasterCard/JCB.

AL La Residence D'Angkor Hotel, River Rd, T063-963390, www.residence angkor.com. This is a hotel to aspire to. With its beautifully laid out rooms all lavishly furnished with marble and hardwoods, it is reassuringly expensive. Each room has a huge, free-form bath – which is the perfect end to a day touring the temples.

AL Monoreach Hotel, Airport Rd, T063-760182, www.monoreach.com. Newly established international hotel, with 110 rooms and suites. Has a real Chinese-hotel feel to it. The room amenities include a/c, cable TV, IDD, minibar, hot water, bath. On site is a swimming pool, gym and restaurant. Rooms on average are about US$70 a night but there are a few more expensive ones that have pushed this hotel up into this category.

AL Shinta Mani, junction of Oum Khun and 14th St, T063-761998, www.shintamani.com. This 18-room boutique, luxury hotel is wonderful in every way: the design, the amenities, the food and the service. The hotel also offers a beautiful pool, library and has mountain bikes available. Provides vocational training to underprivileged youth.

AL-A FCC Angkor, near the post office on Pokambor Av, T063-760280, www.fcc cambodia.com. The sister property of the famous FCC Phnom Penh this hotel is set in the grounds of a restored, modernist villa. Rooms offer contemporary luxury and plenty of space but be warned – there is a massive generator at one end of the complex running 24/7 so make sure you are housed well away

from here. Also tends to trade more on its reputation so service, food, etc can be ropey.

A Ta Prohm, T063-380117, www.angkor hotels.org/ta_prohm_hotel. 95 large rooms in a well-kept and long-established property overlooking the river. It is a touch overpriced but fair by Siem Reap standards. From the outside it can be difficult to tell whether the hotel is actually open but it is. Restaurant and tourist services.

A-D Angkoriana Hotel, 297 Phum Boeng Daun Pa, Khum (the main road to the temples), T063-760274, www.angkoriana hotel.com. Simply-furnished rooms with a/c,

5 Siem Reap market area

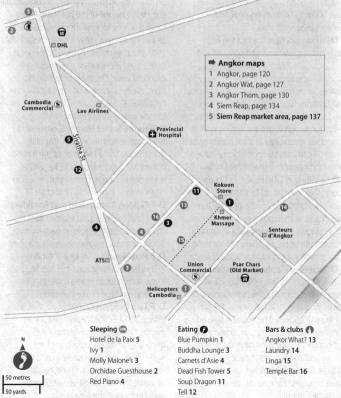

➡ **Angkor maps**
1 Angkor, page 120
2 Angkor Wat, page 127
3 Angkor Thom, page 130
4 Siem Reap, page 134
5 Siem Reap market area, page 137

DHL
Cambodia Commercial $
Lao Airlines
Sivatha St
Provincial Hospital
Kokoon Store
Khmer Massage
Senteurs d'Angkor
ATS
Union Commercial $
Psar Chars (Old Market)
Helicopters Cambodia

N
50 metres
50 yards

Sleeping
Hotel de la Paix **5**
Ivy **1**
Molly Malone's **3**
Orchidae Guesthouse **2**
Red Piano **4**

Eating
Blue Pumpkin **1**
Buddha Lounge **3**
Carnets d'Asie **4**
Dead Fish Tower **5**
Soup Dragon **11**
Tell **12**

Bars & clubs
Angkor What? **13**
Laundry **14**
Linga **15**
Temple Bar **16**

minibar, cable TV etc. Renovated restaurant serving Khmer and French cuisine. Pool.

A-D Casa Angkor, corner of Chhay St and Oum Khun St, T063-966234, www.casa angkorhotel.com. This is a good-looking, pleasant and well-managed 21-room hotel. 3 classes of room, all a decent size, well appointed and with cool wooden floors. Friendly reception and efficient staff. Restaurant, beer garden and reading room.

A-D Molly Malone's, Old Market area, T063-963533. Fantastic rooms with 4-poster beds and good clean bathrooms. Irish pub downstairs. Lovely owners. Recommended.

A-D Neak Pean, 53 Sivatha St, T063-924429, neakpean@camintel.com. 100 rooms, many in large wooden bungalows behind the main building. Swimming pool and garden. Large restaurant.

A-D Passaggio, near the Old Market, T063-760324, www.passaggio-hotel.com. 15 double and 2 family rooms, spacious, a/c, minibar and cable TV, internet, laundry service, bar and restaurant, outdoor terrace.

C-D Borann, T063-964740, borann@pig pond.com.kh. This is an attractive hotel in a delightful garden with a swimming pool. It is secluded and private. 5 small buildings each contain 4 comfortable rooms. Some have a/c, some fan only: price varies accordingly.

C-D La Villa Loti (also known as Coconut House), 105 River Rd, T012-888403, resinf@lavillaloti. com. Fantastic French-run guesthouse, with 8 rooms in a big, wooden house. Good for laying back in a deckchair, amongst the tropical gardens, after a tiring day at the temples. Internet, massage, bicycles.

C-D Secrets of Elephants Guesthouse, Hwy 6, Airport Rd, T063-964328, info@ angkortravel.com. Traditional wooden Khmer house, with just 8 rooms. French-run but English spoken. The house is beautifully furnished with antiques, silks, ornaments and hangings. All rooms have their own private bathroom but not necessarily en suite. Breakfast included and other meals prepared to order. Some rooms a/c, some fan only.

C-D Yaklom Angkor Lodge, Wat Bo St, T012-983510, www.yaklom.com. An attractive site with friendly, competent staff who speak good English. The 10 small, simple bungalows are built slightly too close together. Try to negotiate a discount. Breakfast and airport transfer included. **Sawasdee Thai restaurant**.

C-E Bopha, on the east side of the river, T063-964928, bopharesa@everyday.com.kh. Stunning hotel. Good rooms with all the amenities, decorated with local furniture and fabrics. Brilliant Thai-Khmer restaurant. Highly recommended.

C-E Paul Dubrule Hotel and Tourism School, airport road about 3km from town centre, T063-963672, www.ecolepauldubrule. org. Has to be one of the best bargains in town. You'll be looked after by wide-eyed trainees and there's only a skeleton staff after 1800, but the rooms, themed on the local hotels that help sponsor the project, are excellent value. There are only 4 to choose from, the most expensive representing the best deal. All are a/c, with TV, hot water and include breakfast. Recommended.

D-E Home Sweet Home, T063-963245, sweethome@camintel.com. Popular guesthouse and a favourite of the moto drivers (who get a kickback). Regardless, it is still quite good accommodation. Good clean rooms, some with TV and a/c.

D-F Golden Banana Bed and Breakfast, Wat Damnak Area (past **Martini Bar**), T012-885366, info@golden-banana.com. Good, clean rooms and decent restaurant.

D-F Red Piano, off Sivatha St (about 250 m from the restaurant), T063-963240, www.redpianocambodia.com. 15, clean a/c rooms with en suite bathroom.

D-F Two Dragons Guesthouse, Wat Bo Village, T012-868551. Really nice, clean rooms. Good little Thai restaurant. Gordon, the owner of this place, is one of the well-briefed guys in Siem Reap and runs www.talesofasia.com website. He can organize a whole range of unique and exciting tours in the area.

E-F Green Garden Home Guesthouse, down a small lane off Sivatha St, T012-890363. Price varies according to facilities required. A/c or fan, hot water or cold water, etc, cable TV. Garden not as great as their PR would suggest.

E-F Rosy Guesthouse, east side of river before **Noria**, T063-965059, www.rosy guesthouse. com. Good, clean rooms with bathroom. Very popular.

E-G Earthwalkers, just off the Airport Rd, T012-967901, mail@earthwalkers.no. Popular European-run budget guesthouse. Good gardens and pool table. Bit far out of town.

E-G European Guesthouse, T012-846803, john_oc@hotmail.com. 12 fan rooms in a lane off Wat Bo St occupied by 3 guesthouses.

E-G Ivy, across from the Old Market, T012-800860. Reasonable rooms above the restaurant and bar.

E-G Jasmine Lodge, Hwy 6, Airport Rd, T012-784980, jasminelodge@camnet.com.kh. Good budget accommodation with clean rooms and lots of travel services. Often gets booked out in advance so contact them first.

E-G Orchidae Guesthouse, T012-849716. A few houses down from the **Naga Guesthouse** and much better. Hammocks, restaurant and decent sized, clean rooms with shower or shared facilities. Recommended.

E-G Sweet Dreams Guesthouse, off Wat Bo St, T012-783013, homesweethome@everyday. com.kh. Clean and well kept rooms in this small guesthouse in a quiet cul-de-sac. A favourite of the motos who obviously get a commission for bringing you here. Restaurant.

G Mahogany Guesthouse, Wat Bo St, T063-963417/012-768944, proeun@bigpond. com.kh. Fan and now some a/c. An attractive and popular guesthouse, lovely wooden floor upstairs (try to avoid staying downstairs), coffee-making facilities and friendly guests.

● Eating

Angkor *p119, map p120*
Near the moat there are a number of cheap food and drink stalls, bookshops and posse

of hawkers selling film, souvenirs, etc. Outside the entrance to Angkor Wat is a larger selection of cafés and restaurants including the sister restaurant to **Blue Pumpkin**, serving good sandwiches and breakfasts, ideal for takeaway.

Siem Reap *p135, maps p134 and p137*
♥♥♥ Abacus, Oum Khun St, off Sivatha St, T012-644286. A little further out from the main Old Market area, this place is considered one of the best restaurants in town. Offering French and Cambodian, everything is fantastic here. The fish is superb, the steak is to die for. Recommended.

♥♥♥ Barrio, Sivatha St, away from the central area. Fantastic French and Khmer food. A favourite of the expats. Recommended.

♥♥♥ Carnets d'Asie, 333 Sivatha St, T016-746701. Primarily a French restaurant also offering some Khmer and Thai dishes. Outdoor and indoor seating. Set menu and à la carte. Good Australian beef. Can't beat this one for atmosphere.

♥♥♥ FCC, Pokamber Av, T063-760280. Sister to the Phnom Penh restaurant, this one is a bit more schmick. Good range of world-class food and drinks, nice surroundings, great armchairs, sophisticated.

♥♥♥ Madame Butterfly, Airport Rd. Fantastic French and Khmer food. Favourite with expats.

♥♥ The Blue Pumpkin, Old Market area, T063-963574. Western and Asian food and drinks. Sandwiches, ice cream, pitta, salads and pasta. Candidate for 'least likely eatery to find in Siem Reap' with its white minimalist decor reminiscent of the finest establishments in New York or London. Good breakfasts and cheap cocktails. Eat on the 2nd level. Branches at both the International and domestic terminals at the airport and across from Angkor. Recommended if you need a retreat for 30 mins.

♥♥ Bopha, on the east side of the river, slightly up from Passagio, T063-964928. Fantastic Thai-Khmer restaurant in lovely, tranquil garden setting. One of the absolute best in town. Highly recommended.

¶ **Buddha Lounge**, 184 Mondol St. Bar and restaurant offering mostly Western food.

¶ **Dead Fish Tower**, Sivatha Blvd, T063-963 060. Thai and Khmer restaurant in a fantastically eclectic modern Thai setting. Multiple platforms, quirky decorations, sculptures, apsara dance shows, small putting green and a crocodile farm all add to the atmosphere of this popular restaurant.

¶ **Ivy**, across from the Old Market, T012-800860. Cosy, airy restaurant and bar serving British-style meals, plus a few Khmer dishes. Good breakfasts and roasts. Very popular.

¶ **Molly Malone's**, T063-963533. Lovely Irish bar and restaurant offering classic dishes like Irish lamb stew, shepherd's pie, roasts, and fish and chips.

¶ **Pyongyang**, on the airport road about 1.5 km from the town centre. Excellent North Korean food is served in this twin restaurant of the eatery with the same name in Phnom Penh. This place is a true oddity and has to be seen to be believed. Hosted by a bevy of North Korean beauties who perform a dance routine every night at 2000, you'll find great *bulgolgi* (beef ribs), *kimchi* and other Korean specialties proffered here (including bear bile, by the way). Highly recommended.

¶ **Red Piano**, northwest of the Old Market, T063-964750. An institution in Siem Reap, based in a 100-year-old colonial building. Coffee, sandwiches, salad and pastas. Cocktail bar, offering a range of tipples, including one dedicated to Angelina Jolie (who frequented the establishment while working on Tomb Raider).

¶ **Soup Dragon**, T063-964933. Serves a variety of Khmer and Vietnamese dishes but its speciality is soups in earthenware pots cooked at the table. Breezy and clean, a light and colourful location. Upstairs bar, happy hour 1600-1930.

¶ **Tell**, 374 Sivatha St, T063-963289. Swiss, German, Austrian restaurant and bar. Branch of the long established Phnom Penh restaurant. Serves excellent fondue and raclette, imported beer and sausages. Reasonable prices and generous portions.

¶ **Viroth's Restaurant**, No 246 Wat Bo St, T016-951800. Upmarket place offering very good modern Khmer cuisine plus a few Western staples. Looks more expensive than it actually is and is good value.

¶ **Moloppor**, east of the river, near Bopha Hotel. Good cheap Japanese and pizzas.

¶ **Orchidae Guesthouse**, see Sleeping. Fantastic Asian meals.

¶ **Paul Dubrule Hotel and Tourism School**, airport road about 3km from town centre, T063-963672, www.ecolepauldubrule.org. Offers a pretty good set lunch. It can be hit and miss but the quality is often very high and they are always eager to keep their guests happy. Your money will also go to support an excellent vehicle for development: some of the school's graduates have gone on to be well-paid chefs at some of Asia's top hotels and restaurants.

🅞 Bars and clubs

Siem Reap *p135, maps p134 and p137*

Angkor What?, Bar St, T012-631136. Open early evening to early morning. Bar run by friendly staff, popular with travellers and young expats.

Dead Fish, bar and informal diner serving Thai food.

Easy Speaking, T012-865332. Good little bar with inside and outside seating.

Ivy, popular bar and restaurant opposite Old Market. 0700 until late. Pool table, all-day breakfast for US$4.

Laundry, near the Old Market, turn right off Bar St, T016-962026. Funky little bar open till late.

Linga, Laneway behind Bar St, T012-246912. Gay-friendly bar offering a wide selection of cocktails. Great whisky sour.

Red Piano, Bar St, Old Market Area, T012-854150. A comfortable bar/diner furnished with large wicker armchairs.

Temple Bar, Bar St. Popular drinking hole, dimly lit, good music.

⦿ Entertainment

Siem Reap *p135, maps p134 and p137*
Shadow puppetry
This is one of the finest performing arts of the region. The **Bayon Restaurant**, Wat Bo road, has regular shadow puppet shows in the evening. Local NGO, Krousar Thmey, often tour its shadow puppet show to Siem Reap. The show is performed by underprivileged children (who have also made the puppets) at **La Noria Restaurant** (Wed, 1930 but check as they can be a tad irregular). Donations accepted.

A popular Sat evening attraction is the one-man concert put on by **Dr Beat Richner** (Beatocello), founder of the Jayavarman VII hospital for children. Run entirely on voluntary donations the 3 hospitals in the foundation need US$9 million per year in order to treat Cambodian children free of charge. He performs at the hospital, on the road to Angkor, at 1915, 1 hr, free admission but donations gratefully accepted. An interesting and worthwhile experience.

⦿ Shopping

Siem Reap *p135, maps p134 and p137*
Outside Phnom Penh Siem Reap is about the only place whose markets are worth browsing in for genuinely interesting souvenirs. **Old Market (Psar Chars)** is not a large market but stallholders and keepers of the surrounding shops have developed quite a good understanding of what tickles the appetite of foreigners: Buddhist statues and icons, reproductions of Angkor figures, silks, cottons, kramas, sarongs, silverware, leather puppets and rice paper rubbings of Angkor bas-reliefs are unusual mementos.
Chantiers Écoles, down a short lane off Sivatha St, T/F063-964097. School for orphaned children which trains them in carving, sewing and weaving. Products are on sale under the name Les Artisans d'Angkor and raise 30% of the school's running costs.

Senteurs d'Angkor, opposite Old Market, T063-964801. Sells a good selection of handicrafts, carvings, silverware, silks, handmade paper, cards, scented oils, incense, pepper and spices.

▲ Activities and tours

Siem Reap *p135, maps p134 and p137*
Helicopter and balloon rides
Helicopters Cambodia, Old Market area, Siem Reap, T012-814500, helicopter.cam.s@ online.com.kh, run 8-min charter flights to Angkor Wat for US$204 per person (1-2 people) or US$68 (3-5 people) – great for gaining a perspective on the sheer scale of the complex. Provides a longer 14-min tour to some of the outlying temples, US$360 per person (1-2 people) or US$120 per person (3-5 people). For charter flights further afield, the company charges US$1400 per hr.

A cheaper (but not nearly as fun) alternative for a good aerial view is to organize a balloon ride above the temples. The tethered balloons float 200 m above Angkor Wat for about 10 mins, US$10 per trip. The balloon company is based about 1 km from the main gates from Angkor Wat, on the road from the airport to the temples.

Therapies
Khmer, Thai, reflexology and Japanese massage are readily available. Many masseuses will come to your hotel.
Frangipani, near old market, down the side street opposite Kokoon, T063-757120. Professional masseuse, offering aromatherapy, reflexology and other treatments.
Seeing Hands massage, T063-836487, by seeing impaired individuals, US$3 an hr. Highly recommended.

Tour operators
Asian Trails Ltd, No. 587, Hup Quan St, Mondol 1, Khum Svaydangkum, T063-964595, www.asiantrails.com. Many tours to Angkor and beyond. Also cruises and biking trips.

ATS, Sivatha St, T063-760041. All manner of local arrangements, boat tickets, minibus tickets, car hire. Visa service. Internet service.
Data Sight Travel, 430 Sivatha St, T063-963 081, info@datasighttravel.com. Very helpful travel agent. Organizes tours, ticketing and a whole range of tourist services. Ask for Lim.
Exotissimo Travel, No 300, Hwy 6, T063- 964323, www.exotissimo.com. Tours of Angkor and sites beyond.
Hidden Cambodia Adventure Tours, T012-934412, www.hiddencambodia.com. Specializing in dirt bike tours to some of Cambodia's remote areas and off-the-track temple locations. Recommended for the adventurers.
Journeys Within, on the outskirts of Siem Reap towards the temples, T063-964748, www.journeys-within.com. Specializes in private, customized tours, visiting temples and experiencing the everyday lives of Cambodians.
RTR Tours, No 331, Group 7, Modul 1 (in the Old Market Area) T063-964646, www.rtrtours.com.kh. Organizes tours plus other travel services, including ticketing. Friendly and helpful.
Terre Cambodge, on Frangipani premises, Old Market area, T012-843401, www.terre cambodge.com. Tours with a twist, including cruises on an old sampan. Particularly good for tours of the floating villages of the Tonlé Sap. Not cheap but worth it for the experience.

⊖ Transport

Siem Reap *p135, maps p134 and p137*
Air
Airline availability and flight schedules are particularly prone to sudden change, so ensure you check/book well in advance.
   Airline offices Bangkok Airways/ Siem Reap Airways, Hwy 6, T063-380191. 6 flights a day from Bangkok. **Helicopters Cambodia**, near Old Market, T012-814500. A New Zealand company offers chartered

flights around the temples. **Lao Airlines**, opposite provincial hospital, T/F063-963283, 3 flights a week to Vientiane via Pakse.
President Airlines, Sivatha St, T063-964338.
Vietnam Airlines, Hwy 6, T063-964488, www.vietnamairlines.com. Also general sales agent in town opposite provincial hospital, T063-964929.

Bicycle
Khemara, opposite the Old Market, T063-964512, rents bicycles for US$2 per day.

Bus
Neak Krorhorm Travel, GST, Mekong Express and **Capitol** go to and from Siem Reap. Most buses depart Phnom Penh bus station between 0630 and 0800 and the same from Siem Reap (departing near the Old Market). The best bus service is the Mekong Express, US$6, 5 hrs.

⊖ Directory

Siem Reap *p135, maps p134 and p137*
Banks Cambodia Commercial Bank, 130 Sivatha St. Currency and TC exchange. Advance on Visa, MasterCard, JCB, AMEX.
Mekong Bank, 43 Sivatha, Mon-Fri, Sat am, US dollar TCs cashed, 2% commission, cash advance on Visa and JCB cards only. **Union Commercial Bank**, north of Old Market, Mon-Fri and Sat am. Cash advance on MasterCard and Visa (no commission). Cash TCs. **Internet** Rates vary but should be around 3000 riel per hr. Most internet cafés now offer internet calls. **Medical services** The medical facilities are okay here but by no means of an international standard. In most cases it is probably best to fly to Bangkok. **Naga International Clinic**, Hwy 6 (airport road), T063-965 988. International medical services. 24-hr emergency care. **Post office** Pokamber Av, on the west side of Siem Reap river but can take up to a month for mail to be delivered, 0700-1700.

Background

Pre-history

Archaeological evidence suggests that the Mekong Delta and the lower reaches of the river – in modern-day Cambodia – have been inhabited since at least 4000 BC. But the wet and humid climate has destroyed most of the physical remains of the early civilizations. Excavated remains of a settlement at Samrong Sen on the Tonlé Sap show that houses were built from bamboo and wood and raised on stilts – exactly as they are today. Where these people came from is uncertain but anthropologists have suggested that there were two waves of migration; one from the Malay peninsula and Indonesia and a second from Tibet and China.

Rise of the Lunar and Solar dynasties

For thousands of years Indochina was isolated from the rest of the world and was virtually unaffected by the rise and fall of the early Chinese dynasties. India and China 'discovered' Southeast Asia in the first millennium AD and trade networks were quickly established. The Indian influence was particularly strong in the Mekong basin. The Khmers adopted and adapted Indian script as well as their ideas about astrology, religion (Buddhism and Hinduism) and royalty (the cult of the semi-divine ruler). Today, several other aspects of Cambodian culture are recognizably Indian in origin, including classical literature and dance. Religious architecture also followed Indian models. These Indian cultural influences which took root in Indochina gave rise to a legend to which Cambodia traces its historical origins. An Indian Brahmin called Kaundinya, travelling in the Mekong Delta area, married Soma, daughter of the Naga (the serpent deity), or Lord of the Soil. Their union, which founded the 'Lunar Dynasty' of Funan (a pre-Angkorian Kingdom), symbolized the fertility of the kingdom and occupies a central place in Khmer cosmology. The Naga, Soma's father, helpfully drank the floodwaters of the Mekong, enabling people to cultivate the land.

Funan

The kingdom of Funan – the forerunner of Kambuja – was established on the Mekong by tribal people from South China in the middle of the third century AD and became the earliest Hindu state in Southeast Asia. Funan was known for its elaborate irrigation canals which controlled the Mekong floodwaters, irrigated the paddy fields and prevented the incursion of seawater. By the fifth century Funan had extended its influence over most of present day Cambodia, as well as Indochina and parts of the Malay peninsula. Leadership was measured by success in battle and the ability to provide protection, and in recognition of this fact, rulers from the Funan period onward incorporated the suffix 'varman' (meaning protection) into their names. Records of a third century Chinese embassy give an idea of what it was like: "There are walled villages, places and dwellings. The men ... go about naked and barefoot. ... Taxes are paid in gold, silver and perfume. There are books and libraries and they can use the alphabet." Twentieth-century excavations suggest a seafaring people engaged in extensive trade with both India and China, and elsewhere.

The 'Solar Dynasty' of Chenla was a vassal kingdom of Funan, probably first based on the Mekong at the junction with the Mun tributary, but it rapidly grew in power, and was centred in the area of present day southern Laos. It was the immediate predecessor of

Kambuja and the great Khmer Empire. According to Khmer legend, the kingdom was the result of the marriage of Kambu, an ascetic, to a celestial nymph named Mera. The people of Chenla – the Kambuja, or the sons of Kambu – lent their name to the country. In AD 540 a Funan prince married a Chenla princess, uniting the Solar and Lunar dynasties. The prince sided with his wife and Funan was swallowed by Chenla. The first capital of this fusion was at **Sambor**. King Ishanavarman (616-635) established a new capital at Sambor Prei Kuk, 30 km from modern Kompong Thom, in the centre of the country (the monuments of which are some of the best preserved of this period). His successor, Jayavarman I, moved the capital to the region of Angkor Borei near Takeo.

Quarrels in the ruling family led to the break-up of the state later in the seventh century: it was divided into 'Land Chenla', a farming culture located north of the Tonlé Sap (maybe centred around Champassak in Laos), and 'Water Chenla', a trading culture based along the Mekong. Towards the end of the eighth century Water Chenla became a vassal of Java's powerful Sailendra Dynasty and members of Chenla's ruling family were taken back to the Sailendra court. This period, from the fall of Funan until the eighth century, is known as the pre-Angkorian period and is a somewhat hazy time in the history of Cambodia. The Khmers remained firmly under Javanese suzerainty until Jayavarman II (802-850) returned to the land of his ancestors around AD 800 to change the course of Cambodian history.

Angkor and the god-kings

Jayavarman II, the Khmer prince who had spent most of his life at the Sailendra court, claimed independence from Java and founded the Angkor Kingdom to the north of the Tonlé Sap in 802, at about the same time as Charlemagne became Holy Roman Emperor in Europe. They were men cast in the same mould, for both were empire builders. His far-reaching conquests at Wat Phou (Laos) and Sambhupura (Sambor) won him immediate political popularity on his return and he became king in 790. In 802 he declared himself a World Emperor and to consolidate and legitimize his position he arranged his for coronation by a Brahmin priest, declaring himself the first Khmer devaraja, or god-king, a tradition continued today. From then on, the reigning monarch was identified with Siva, the king of the Hindu gods. In the centuries that followed, successive devaraja strove to outdo their predecessors by building bigger and finer temples to house the royal linga, a phallic symbol which is the symbol of Siva and the devaraja. The god-kings commanded the absolute allegiance of their subjects, giving them control of a vast pool of labour which was used to build an advanced and prosperous agricultural civilization. For many years historians and archaeologists maintained that the key to this agricultural wealth lay in a sophisticated hydraulic – that is irrigated – system of agriculture which allowed the Khmers to produce up to three harvests a year. However, this view of Angkorian agriculture has come under increasing scrutiny in recent years and now there are many who believe that flood-retreat – rather than irrigated – agriculture was the key. Jayavarman II installed himself in successive capitals north of the Tonlé Sap, secure from attack by the Sailendras, and he ruled until 850, when he died on the banks of the Great Lake at the original capital, Hariharalaya, in the Roluos area (Angkor).

Jayavarman III (850-877) continued his father's traditions and ruled for the next 27 years. He expanded his father's empire at Hariharalaya and was the original founder of the laterite temple at Bakong. **Indravarman** (877-889), his successor, was the first of the great temple-builders of Angkor and somewhat overshadowed the work of Jayavarman III. His means to succession are somewhat ambiguous but it is generally agreed that he overthrew Jayavarman III violently. Unlike his predecessor, Indravarman was not the son of a king but more than likely the nephew of Jayavarman's II Queen. He expanded and renovated the capital, building Preah Ko Temple and developing Bakong. Indravarman is considered one of the key players in Khmer history. Referred to as the "lion among kings" and "prince endowed with all the merits", his architectural projects established precedents that were emulated by those that followed him. After Indravarman's death his sons fought for the King's title. The victor, at the end of the ninth century was **Yasovarman I (889-900)**. The battle is believed to have destroyed the palace, thus spurring a move to Angkor. He called his new capital Yasodharapura and copied the water system his father had devised at Roluos on an even larger scale, using the waters of the Tonlé Sap. After Yasovarman's death in 900 his son **Harshavarman (900-923)** took the throne, until he died 23 years later. Harshavarman was well regarded, one particular inscription saying that he "caused the joy of the universe". Upon his death, his brother **Ishanarvarman II**, assumed the regal status. In 928, **Jayavarman IV** set up a rival capital about 65 km from Angkor at Koh Ker and ruled for the next 20 years. After Jayavarman IV's death there was a period of upheaval as **Harsharvarman II** tried unsuccessfully to lead the empire. **Rajendravarman (944-968)**, Jayarvarman's nephew, managed to take control of the empire and moved the court back to Angkor, where the Khmer kings remained. He chose to build outside of the former capital Bakheng, opting instead for the region south of the East Baray. Many saw him as the saviour of Angkor with one inscription reading: "He restored the holy city of Yashodharapura, long deserted, and rendered it superb and charming." Rajendravarman orchestrated a campaign of solidarity – bringing together a number of provinces and claiming back territory, previously under Yasovarman I. From the restored capital he led a successful crusade against the Champa in what is now Vietnam. A devout Buddhist, he erected some of the first Buddhist temples in the precinct. Upon Rajendravarman's death, his son **Jayavarman V (968-1001)**, still only a child, took the royal reigns. Once again the administrative centre was moved, this time to the west, where Ta Keo was built. The capital was renamed Jayendranagari. Like his father, Jayavarman V was Buddhist but was extremely tolerant of other religions. At the start of his tenure he had a few clashes with local dissidents but things settled down and he enjoyed relative peace during his rule. The next king, **Udayadityavarman I**, lasted a few months before being ousted. For the next few years Suryavarman I and Jayaviravarman battled for the King's title.

The formidable warrior **King Suryavarman I (1002-1049)** won. He was a determined leader and made all of his officials swear a blood oath of allegiance. He undertook a series of military campaigns geared towards claiming Mon territory in central and southern Thailand and victoriously extended the Khmer empire into Lower Menam, as well as into Laos and established a Khmer capital in Louvo (modern day Lopburi in Thailand). Suryavarman holds the record for the greatest territorial expansion ever achieved in the Khmer Empire. The Royal Palace (Angkor Thom), the West Baray and the Phimeanakas pyramid temples were Suryavarman's main contributions to Angkor's architectural heritage (see page 131). He continued the royal Hindu cult but also tolerated Mahayana Buddhism.

On Suryavarman's death, the Khmer Kingdom began to fragment. His three successors had short, troubled reigns and the Champa kingdom captured, sacked and razed the capital. When the king's son, **Udayadityavarman II (1050-1066)**, assumed the throne, havoc ensued as citizens revolted against him and some of his royal appointments.

When Udayadityavarman II died, his younger brother, Harsharvarman III (1066-1080), last in the line of the dynasty, stepped in. During his reign, there were reports of discord and further defeat at the hands of the Cham.

In 1080 a new kingdom was founded by a northern provincial governor claiming aristocratic descent. He called himself **Jayavarman VI** (1080-1107) and is believed to have led a revolt against the former king. He never settled at Angkor, living instead in the northern part of the kingdom. He left monuments at Wat Phou in southern Laos and Phimai, in Thailand. There was an intermittent period where Jayavarman's IV brother, **Dharanindravarman** (1107-1112) took the throne but he was overthrown by his grand-nephew **Suryavarman II** (1113-1150), who soon became the greatest leader the Angkor Empire had ever seen. He worked prolifically on a broad range of projects and achieved some of most impressive architectural feats and political manoeuvres seen within the Angkorian period. He resumed diplomatic relations with China, the Middle Kingdom, and was held in the greatest regard by the then Chinese Emperor. He expanded the Khmer Empire as far as Lopburi, Siam, Pagan in Myanmar, parts of Laos and into the Malay peninsula. He attacked the Champa state relentlessly, particularly Dai Vet in Northern Vietnam, eventually defeating them in 1144-1145, and capturing and sacking the royal capital, Vijaya. He left an incredible, monumental legacy behind, being responsible for the construction of Angkor Wat, an architectural masterpiece that represented the height of the Khmer's artistic genius, Phnom Rung temple (Khorat) and Banteay Samre. A network of roads was built to connect regional capitals.

However, his success was not without its costs – his widespread construction put serious pressure on the general running of the kingdom and major reservoirs silted up during this time; there was also an intensified discord in the provinces and his persistent battling fuelled an ongoing duel between the Cham and Khmers that was to continue (and eventually be avenged) long after his death.

Suryavarman II deposed the King of Champa in 1145 but the Cham regained their independence in 1149 and the following year, Suryavarman died after a disastrous attempt to conquer Annam (northern Vietnam). The throne was usurped by **Tribhuvanadityavarman** in 1165, who died in 1177, when the Cham seized their chance of revenge and sacked Angkor in a surprise naval attack. This was the Khmer's worst recorded defeat – the city was completely annihilated. The 50-year-old **Jayavarman VII** – a cousin of Suryavarman – turned out to be their saviour. He battled the Cham for the next four years, driving them out of the Kingdom. In 1181 he was declared king and seriously hit back, attacking the Chams and seizing their capital, Vijaya. He expanded the Khmer Kingdom further than ever before; its suzerainty stretched from the Malay peninsula in the south to the borders of Burma in the west and the Annamite chain to the northeast.

Jayavarman's VII's first task was to plan a strong, spacious new capital – Angkor Thom; but while that work was being undertaken he set up a smaller, temporary seat of government where he and his court could live in the meantime – Preah Khan meaning 'Fortunate City of Victory' (see page 133). He also built 102 hospitals throughout his kingdom, as well as a network of roads, along which he constructed resthouses. But because they were built of wood, none of these secular structures survive; only the foundations of four larger ones have been unearthed at Angkor.

Angkor's decline

As was the case during Suryavarman II's reign, Jayavarman VII's extensive building campaign put a large amount of pressure on the kingdom's resources and rice was in short supply as labour was diverted into construction.

Jayavarman VII died in 1218 and the Kambujan Empire fell into progressive decline over the next two centuries. Territorially, it was eroded by the eastern migration of the Siamese. The Khmers were unable to prevent this gradual incursion but the diversion of labour to the military rice farming helped seal the fate of Angkor. Another reason for the decline was the introduction of Theravada Buddhism in the 13th century, which undermined the prestige of the king and the priests. There is even a view that climatic change disrupted the agricultural system and led to Kambuja's demise. After Jayavarman VII, no king seems to have been able to unify the kingdom by force of arms or personality – internal dissent increased while the king's extravagance continued to place a crippling burden on state funds. With its temples decaying and its once-magnificent agricultural system in ruins, Angkor became virtually uninhabitable. In 1431 the royal capital was finally abandoned to the Siamese, who drove the Khmers out and made Cambodia a vassal of the Thai Sukhothai Kingdom.

Explaining Angkor's decline

Why the Angkorian Empire should have declined has always fascinated scholars in the West – in the same way that the decline and fall of the Roman Empire has done. Numerous explanations have been offered, and still the debate remains unresolved. As Anthony Barnett argued in a paper in the New Left Review in 1990, perhaps the question should be "why did Angkor last so long? Inauspiciously sited, it was nonetheless a tropical imperium of 500 years' duration."

There are essentially five lines of argument in the 'Why did Angkor fall?' debate. First, it has been argued that the building programmes became simply so arduous and demanding of ordinary people that they voted with their feet and moved out, depriving Angkor of the population necessary to support a great empire. Second, some scholars present an environmental argument: the great irrigation works silted-up, undermining the empire's agricultural wealth. (This line of argument conflicts with recent work that maintains that Angkor's wealth was never based on hydraulic – or irrigated – agriculture.) Third, there are those who say that military defeat was the cause – but this only begs the question: why they were defeated in the first place? Fourth, historians with a rather wider view, have offered the opinion that the centres of economic activity in Southeast Asia moved from land-based to sea-based foci, and that Angkor was poorly located to adapt to this shift in patterns of trade, wealth and, hence, power. Lastly, some scholars argue that the religion which demanded such labour of Angkor's subjects became so corrupt that it ultimately corroded the empire from within.

After Angkor – running scared

The next 500 years or so, until the arrival of the French in 1863, was an undistinguished period in Cambodian history. In 1434 the royal Khmer court under Ponheayat moved to Phnom Penh, where a replica of the cosmic Mount Meru was built. There was a short-lived period of revival in the mid-15th century until the Siamese invaded and sacked the capital again in 1473. One of the sons of the captured King Suryavarman drummed up enough Khmer support to oust the invaders and there were no subsequent invasions during the 16th century. The capital was established at Lovek (between Phnom Penh and Tonlé Sap) and then moved back to the ruins at Angkor. But a Siamese invasion in 1593 sent the royal court fleeing to Laos; finally, in 1603, the Thais released a captured prince to rule over the Cambodian vassal state. There were at least 22 kings between 1603 and 1848.

Politically, the Cambodian court tried to steer a course between its powerful neighbours of Siam and Vietnam, seeking one's protection against the other. King **Chey Chetta II**

(1618-1628), for example, declared Cambodia's independence from Siam and in order to back up his actions he asked Vietnam for help. To cement the allegiance he was forced to marry a Vietnamese princess of the Nguyen Dynasty of Annam, and then obliged to pay tribute to Vietnam. His successors – hoping to rid themselves of Vietnamese domination – sought Siamese assistance and were then forced to pay for it by acknowledging Siam's suzerainty. Then in 1642, **King Chan** converted to Islam, and encouraged Malay and Javanese migrants to settle in Cambodia. Considering him guilty of apostasy, his cousins ousted him – with Vietnamese support. But 50 years later, the Cambodian **Ang Eng** was crowned in Bangkok. This see-saw pattern continued for years; only Siam's wars with Burma and Vietnam's internal disputes and long-running conflict with China prevented them from annexing the whole of Cambodia, although both took territorial advantage of the fragmented state.

By the early 1700s the kingdom was centred on Phnom Penh (there were periods when the king resided at Ondong). But when the Khmers lost their control over the Mekong Delta to the Vietnamese in the late 18th century, the capital's access to the sea was blocked. By 1750 the Khmer royal family had split into pro-Siamese and pro-Vietnamese factions. Between 1794-1811 and 1847-1863, Siamese influence was strongest; from 1835-1837 the Vietnamese dominated. In the 1840s, the Siamese and Vietnamese armies fought on Cambodian territory, devastating the country. This provoked French intervention – and cost Cambodia its independence, even if it had been nominal for several centuries anyway. On 17 April 1864 (the same day and month as the Khmer Rouge soldiers entered Phnom Penh in the twentieth century) King Norodom agreed to French protection as he believed they would provide military assistance against the Siamese. The king was to be disappointed: France honoured Siam's claim to the western provinces of Battambang, Siem Reap and Sisophon, which Bangkok had captured in the late 1600s. And in 1884, King Norodom was persuaded by the French governor of the colony of Cochin China to sign another treaty that turned Cambodia into a French colony, along with Laos and Vietnam in the Union Indochinoise. The establishment of Cambodia as a French protectorate probably saved the country from being split up between Siam and Vietnam.

French colonial period

The French did little to develop Cambodia, preferring instead to let the territory pay for itself. They only invested income generated from tax revenue to build a communications network and from a Cambodian perspective, the only benefit of colonial rule was that the French forestalled the total disintegration of the country, which would otherwise have been divided up between its warring neighbours. French cartographers also mapped Cambodia's borders for the first time and in so doing forced the Thais to surrender the northwestern provinces of Battambang and Siem Reap.

For nearly a century the French alternately supported two branches of the royal family, the Norodoms and the Sisowaths, crowning the 18-year-old schoolboy **Prince Norodom Sihanouk** in 1941. The previous year, the Nazis had invaded and occupied France and French territories in Indochina were in turn occupied by the Japanese – although Cambodia was still formally governed and administered by the French. It was at this stage that a group of pro-independence Cambodians realized just how weak the French control of their country actually was. In 1942 two monks were arrested and accused of preaching anti-French sermons; within two days this sparked demonstrations by more than 1000 monks in Phnom Penh, marking the beginning of Cambodian nationalism. In March 1945

Japanese forces ousted the colonial administration and persuaded King Norodom Sihanouk to proclaim independence. Following the Japanese surrender in August 1945, the French came back in force; Sihanouk tried to negotiate independence from France and they responded by abolishing the absolute monarchy in 1946 – although the king remained titular head of state. A new constitution was introduced allowing political activity and a National Assembly elected.

Independence and neutrality

By the early 1950s the French army had suffered several defeats in the war in Indochina. Sihanouk dissolved the National Assembly in mid-1952, which he was entitled to do under the constitution, and personally took charge of steering Cambodia towards independence from France. To publicize the cause, he travelled to Thailand, Japan and the United States, and said he would not return from self-imposed exile until his country was free. His audacity embarrassed the French into granting Cambodia independence on 9 November 1953 – and Sihanouk returned, triumphant.

The people of Cambodia did not want to return to absolute monarchy, and following his abdication in 1955, Sihanouk became a popular political leader. But political analysts believe that despite the apparent popularity of the former king's administration, different factions began to develop at this time, a process which was the root of the conflict in the years to come. During the 1960s, for example, there was a growing rift between the Khmer majority and other ethnic groups. Even in the countryside, differences became marked between the rice-growing lands and the more remote mountain areas where people practised shifting cultivation, supplementing their diet with lizards, snakes, roots and insects. As these problems intensified in the late 1960s and the economic situation deteriorated, the popular support base for the Khmer Rouge was put into place. With unchecked population growth, land ownership patterns became skewed, landlessness grew more widespread and food prices escalated.

Sihanouk managed to keep Cambodia out of the war that enveloped Laos and Vietnam during the late 1950s and 1960s by following a neutral policy – which helped attract millions of dollars of aid to Cambodia from both the West and the Eastern Bloc. But when a civil war broke out in South Vietnam in the early 1960s, Cambodia's survival – and Sihanouk's own survival – depended on its outcome. Sihanouk believed the rebels, the National Liberation Front (NLF) would win; and he openly courted and backed the NLF. It was an alliance which cost him dear. In 1965-1966 the tide began to turn in South Vietnam, due to US military and economic intervention. This forced NLF troops to take refuge inside Cambodia. When a peasant uprising in northwestern provinces in 1967 showed Sihanouk that he was sailing close to the wind his forces responded by suppressing the rebellion and massacring 10,000 peasants.

Slowly – and inevitably – he became the focus of resentment within Cambodia's political élite. He also incurred American wrath by allowing North Vietnamese forces to use Cambodian territory as an extension of the **Ho Chi Minh Trail**, ferrying arms and men into South Vietnam. This resulted in his former army Commander-in-Chief, **Marshal Lon Nol** masterminding Sihanouk's removal as Head of State while he was in Moscow in 1970. Lon Nol abolished the monarchy and proclaimed a republic. One of the most auspicious creatures in Khmer mythology is the white crocodile. It is said to appear 'above the surface' at important moments in history and is said to have been sighted near Phnom Penh just before Lon Nol took over.

Third Indochina War and the rise of the Khmer Rouge

On 30 April 1970, following the overthrow of Prince Norodom Sihanouk, US President Richard Nixon officially announced **Washington's military intervention in Cambodia** – although in reality it had been going on for some time. The invasion aimed to deny the Vietnamese Communists the use of Sihanoukville port through which 85% of their heavy arms were reaching South Vietnam. The US Air Force had been secretly bombing Cambodia using B-52s since March 1969. In 1973, facing defeat in Vietnam, the US Air Force B-52s began carpet bombing Communist-controlled areas to enable Lon Nol's inept regime to retain control of the besieged provincial cities.

Historian David P Chandler wrote: "When the campaign was stopped by the US Congress at the end of the year, the B-52s had dropped over half a million tons of bombs on a country with which the United States was not at war – more than twice the tonnage dropped on Japan during the Second World War.

The war in Cambodia was known as 'the sideshow' by journalists covering the war in Vietnam and by American policy-makers in London. Yet the intensity of US bombing in Cambodia was greater than it ever was in Vietnam; about 500,000 soldiers and civilians were killed over the four-year period. It also caused about two million refugees to flee from the countryside to the capital."

As Henry Kamm suggested, by the beginning of 1971 the people of Cambodia had to face the terrifying realisation that nowhere in the country was safe and all hope and confidence in Cambodia's future during the war was lost. A year after the coup d'etat the country was shattered: guerrilla forces had invaded Angkor, the country's primary oil refinery, Lol Non had suffered a stroke and had relocated to Hawaii for months of treatment, Lol Non's irregularly paid soldiers were pillaging stores at gunpoint and extreme corruption was endemic.

By the end of the war, the country had become totally dependent on US aid and much of the population survived on American rice rations. Confidence in the Lon Nol government collapsed as taxes rose and children were drafted into combat units. At the same time, the **Khmer Rouge** increased its military strength dramatically and began to make inroads into areas formerly controlled by government troops. Although officially the Khmer Rouge rebels represented the Beijing-based Royal Government of National Union of Cambodia (Grunc), which was headed by the exiled Prince Sihanouk, Grunc's de facto leaders were Pol Pot, Khieu Samphan (who, after Pol Pot's demise, became the public face of the Khmer Rouge), Ieng Sary (later foreign minister) and Son Sen (Chief of General Staff) – all Khmer Rouge men. By the time the American bombing stopped in 1973, the guerrillas dominated about 60% of Cambodian territory, while the government clung tenuously to towns and cities. Over the next two years the Khmer Rouge whittled away Phnom Penh's defence perimeter to the point that Lon Nol's government was sustained only by American airlifts into the capital.

Some commentators have suggested that the persistent heavy bombing of Cambodia, which forced the Communist guerrillas to live in terrible conditions, was partly responsible for the notorious savagery of the Khmer Rouge in later years. Not only were they brutalized by the conflict itself, but they became resentful of the fact that the city-dwellers had no inkling of how unpleasant their experiences really were. This, writes US political scientist Wayne Bert, "created the perception among the Khmer Rouge that the bulk of the population did not take part in the revolution, was therefore not enthusiastic about it and could not be trusted to support it. The final step in this logic was to punish or eliminate all in these categories who showed either real or imagined tendencies toward disloyalty". And that, as anyone who has watched *The Killing Fields* will know, is what happened.

'Pol Pot time': building year zero

On 1 April 1975 President Lon Nol fled Cambodia to escape the advancing Khmer Rouge. Just over two weeks later, on 17 April, the victorious Khmer Rouge entered Phnom Penh. The capital's population had been swollen by refugees from 600,000 to over two million. The ragged conquering troops were welcomed as heroes. None in the crowds that lined the streets appreciated the horrors that the victory would also bring. Cambodia was renamed Democratic Kampuchea (DK) and Pol Pot set to work establishing a radical Maoist-style agrarian society. These ideas had been first sketched out by his longstanding colleague Khieu Samphan, whose 1959 doctoral thesis – at the Sorbonne University in Paris – analysed the effects of Cambodia's colonial and neo-colonial domination. In order to secure true economic and political independence he argued that it was necessary to isolate Cambodia completely and to go back to a self-sufficient agricultural economy.

Within days of the occupation, the revolutionaries had forcibly evacuated many of the inhabitants of Phnom Penh to the countryside, telling citizens that the Americans were about to bomb the capital. A second major displacement was carried out at the end of the year, when hundreds of thousands of people from the area southeast of Phnom Penh were forced to move to the northwest.

Prior to the Khmer Rouge coming to power, the Cambodian word for revolution (*bambahbambor*) had a conventional meaning, 'uprising'. Under Pol Pot's regime, the word *pativattana* was used instead; it meant 'return to the past'. The Khmer Rouge did this by obliterating everything that did not subscribe to their vision of the past glories of ancient Khmer culture. Pol Pot wanted to return the country to '**Year Zero**' – he wanted to begin again. One of the many revolutionary slogans was "we will burn the old grass and new will grow"; money, modern technology, medicine, education and newspapers were outlawed. Khieu Samphan, who became the Khmer Rouge Head of State, following Prince Sihanouk's resignation in 1976, said at the time: "No, we have no machines. We do everything by mainly relying on the strength of our people. We work completely self-sufficiently. This shows the overwhelming heroism of our people. This also shows the great force of our people. Though bare-handed, they can do everything".

The Khmer Rouge, or *Angkar Loeu* ('The Higher Organization') as they touted themselves, maintained a strangle-hold on the country by dislocating families, disorientating people and sustaining a persistent fear through violence, torture and death. At the heart of their strategy was a plan to unfurl people's strongest bonds and loyalties: those that existed between family members. The term *kruosaa*, which traditionally means 'family' in Khmer, came to simply mean 'spouse' under the Khmer Rouge. In Angkar, family no longer existed. *Krusosaa niyum*, which loosely translated to 'familyism' (or pining for one's relatives) was a criminal offence punishable by death. Under heinous interrogation procedures people were intensively probed about their family members (sisters, brothers, grandparents and in-laws) and encouraged to inform on them. Those people who didn't turn over relatives considered adversaries (teachers, former soldiers, doctors, etc.) faced odious consequences, with the fate of the whole family (immediate and extended) in danger.

Memoirs from survivors detailed in the book *Children of Cambodia's Killing Fields* repeatedly refer to the Khmer Rouge dictum "to keep you is no benefit to destroy you is no loss." People were treated as nothing more than machines. Food was scarce under Pol

Pol Pot – the idealistic psychopath

Prince Norodom Sihanouk once referred to Pol Pot as "a more fortunate Hitler". Unlike his erstwhile fascist counterpart, the man whose troops were responsible for the deaths of perhaps two million fellow Cambodians has managed to get away with it. He died on 15 April 1998, either of a heart attack or, possibly, at his own hands or somebody else's.

Pol Pot's real name was Saloth Sar – he adopted his nom de guerre when he became Secretary-General of the Cambodian Communist Party in 1963. He was born in 1928 into a peasant family in Kompong Thom, central Cambodia, and is believed to have lived as a novice monk for nine months when he was a child. His services to the Democrat Party won him a scholarship to study electronics in Paris. But he became a Communist in France in 1949 and spent more time at meetings of Marxist revolutionary societies than in classes. In his 1986 book Sideshow, William Shawcross notes that at that time the French Communist Party, which was known for its dogmatic adherence to orthodox Marxism, "taught hatred of the bourgeoisie and uncritical admiration of Stalinism, including the collectivization of agriculture". Pol Pot finally lost his scholarship in 1953.

Returning to newly independent Cambodia, Pol Pot started working as a school teacher in Phnom Penh and continued his revolutionary activities in the underground Cambodian Communist Party (which, remarkably kept its existence a secret until 1977). In 1963, he fled the capital for the countryside, fearing a crackdown of the left by Sihanouk. There he rose to become Secretary-General of the Central Committee of the Communist Party of Kampuchea. He was trained in guerrilla warfare and he became a leader

Pot's inefficient system of collective farming and administration was based on fear, torture and summary execution. A veil of secrecy shrouded Cambodia and, until a few desperate refugees began to trickle over the border into Thailand, the outside world was largely ignorant of what was going on. The refugees' stories of atrocities were, at first, disbelieved. Jewish refugees who escaped from Nazi occupied Poland in the 1940s had encountered a similarly disbelieving reception simply because (like the Cambodians) what they had to say was, to most people, unbelievable. Some left wing academics initially viewed the revolution as an inspired and brave attempt to break the shackles of dependency and neo-colonial domination. Others, such as Noam Chomsky, dismissed the allegations as right wing press propaganda.

It was not until the Vietnamese 'liberation' of Phnom Penh in 1979 that the scale of the Khmer Rouge carnage emerged and the atrocities witnessed by the survivors became known. The stories turned the Khmer Rouge into international pariahs – but only until 1982 when, remarkably, their American and Chinese sympathizers secured them a voice at the United Nations. During the Khmer Rouge's 44-month reign of terror, it had hitherto been generally accepted that around a million people died. This is a horrendous figure when one considers that the population of the country in 1975 was around seven million. What is truly shocking is that the work undertaken by a team from Yale University indicates that this figure is far too low.

Although the Khmer Rouge era in Cambodia may have been a period of unprecedented economic, political and human turmoil, they still managed to keep meticulous records of what they were doing. In this regard the Khmer Rouge were rather like the Chinese during of the Khmer Rouge forces, advocating armed resistance to Sihanouk and his 'feudal entourage'. In 1975 when the Khmer Rouge marched into Phnom Penh, Pol Pot was forced out of the shadows to take the role of leader, 'Brother Number One'. Although he took the title of prime minister, he ruled as a dictator and set about reshaping Cambodia with his mentor, Khieu Samphan, the head of state. Yet, during the years he was in power, hardly any Cambodians – save those in the top echelons of the Khmer Rouge – had even heard of him.

The Vietnam-backed Hun Sen government, which took over the country after the overthrow of the Khmer Rouge in December 1978, calculated that by demonizing Pol Pot as the mastermind of the genocide, it would avert the possibility of the Khmer Rouge ever making a comeback. The Hun Sen regime showed no interest in analysing the complex factors which combined to bring Pol Pot to power. Within Cambodia, he has been portrayed simply as a tyrannical bogey-man. During the 1980s, 20 May was declared National Hate Day, when everyone reaffirmed their hatred of Pol Pot.

In a review of David Chandler's biography of Pol Pot (Brother Number One: A Political Biography of Pol Pot, Westview Press, 1992), Peter Carey – the co-director of the British-based Cambodia Trust – was struck by what he called "the sinister disjunction between the man's evident charisma ... and the monumental suffering wrought by his regime". Carey concludes: "one is left with the image of a man consumed by his own vision, a vision of empowerment and liberation that has little anchorage in Cambodian reality".

the Cultural Revolution, or the Nazis in Germany. Using Australian satellite data, the team was expecting to uncover around 200 mass graves; instead they found several thousand. The Khmer Rouge themselves have claimed that around 20,000 people died because of their 'mistakes'. The Vietnamese have traditionally put the figure at two to three million, although their estimates have generally been rejected as too high and politically motivated (being a means to justify their invasion of the country in 1978/1979 and subsequent occupation). The Documentation Center of Cambodia, involved in the heavy mapping project, said that 20,492 mass graves were uncovered containing the remains of 1,112,829 victims of execution. In addition, hundreds of thousands more died from famine and disease; frighteningly, the executions are believed to only account for about 30-40% of the total death toll.

How such a large slice of Cambodia's people died in so short a time (1975-1978) beggars belief. Some were shot, strangled or suffocated; many more starved; while others died from disease and overwork. The Khmer Rouge transformed Cambodia into what the British journalist, William Shawcross, described as: "a vast and sombre work camp where toil was unending, where respite and rewards were non-existent, where families were abolished and where murder was used as a tool of social discipline ... The manner of execution was often brutal. Babies were torn apart limb from limb, pregnant women were disembowelled. Men and women were buried up to their necks in sand and left to die slowly. A common form of execution was by axe handles to the back of the neck. That saved ammunition".

The Khmer Rouge revolution was primarily a class-based one, fed by years of growing resentment against the privileged elites. The revolution pitted the least-literate, poorest rural peasants (referred to as the 'old' people) against the educated, skilled and foreign-influenced urban population (the 'new' people). The 'new' people provided an endless flow of numbers for the regime's death lists. Through a series of terrible purges, the members of the former governing and mercantile classes were liquidated or sent to work as forced labourers. But Peter Carey, Oxford historian and Chairman of the Cambodia Trust, argues that not all Pol Pot's victims were townspeople and merchants. "Under the terms of the 1948 Genocide Convention, the Khmer Rouge stands accused of genocide," he wrote in a letter to a British newspaper in 1990. "Of 64,000 Buddhist monks, 62,000 perished; of 250,000 Islamic Chams, 100,000; of 200,000 Vietnamese still left in 1975, 100,000; of 20,000 Thai, 12,000; of 1800 Lao, 1000. Of 2000 Kola, not a trace remained." American political scientist Wayne Bert noted that: "The methods and behaviour compare to that of the Nazis and Stalinists, but in the percentage of the population killed by a revolutionary movement, the Khmer Rouge holds an unchallenged record."

It is still unclear the degree to which these 'genocidal' actions were controlled by those at the centre. Many of the killings took place at the discretion of local leaders, but there were some notably cruel leaders in the upper echelons of the Khmer Rouge and none can have been ignorant of what was going on. Ta Mok, who administered the region southwest of Phnom Penh, oversaw many mass executions for example. There is also evidence that the central government was directly involved in the running of the Tuol Sleng detention centre in which at least 20,000 people died. It has now been turned into a memorial to Pol Pot's holocaust (see page 85).

In addition to the legacy left by centres such as Tuol Sleng, there is the impact of the mass killings upon the Cambodian psyche. One of which is – to Western eyes – the startling openness with which Khmer people will, if asked, matter-of-factly relate their family history in detail: this usually involves telling how the Khmer Rouge era meant they lost one or several members of their family. Whereas death is talked about in hushed terms in Western society, Khmers have no such reservations, perhaps because it touched, and still touches, them all.

Vietnamese invasion

The first border clashes over offshore islands between Khmer Rouge forces and the Vietnamese army were reported just a month after the Khmer Rouge came to power. These erupted into a minor war in January 1977 when the Phnom Penh government accused Vietnam of seeking to incorporate Kampuchea into an Indochinese federation. Hanoi's determination to oust Pol Pot only really became apparent however, on Christmas Day 1978 when 120,000 Vietnamese troops invaded. By 7 January (the day of Phnom Penh's liberation) they had installed a puppet government which proclaimed the foundation of the People's Republic of Kampuchea (PRK): Heng Samrin, a former member of the Khmer Rouge, was appointed president. The Vietnamese compared their invasion to the liberation of Uganda from Idi Amin – but for the Western world it was unwelcome. The new government was accorded scant recognition abroad, while the toppled government of Democratic Kampuchea retained the country's seat at the United Nations.

The country's 'liberation' by Vietnam did not end the misery; in 1979 nearly half Cambodia's population was in transit, either searching for their former homes or fleeing across the Thai border into refugee camps. American political scientist Wayne Bert wrote: "The Vietnamese had long seen a special role for themselves in uniting and leading a greater Indochina Communist movement and the Cambodian Communists had seen with clarity that such a role for the Vietnamese could only be at the expense of their independence and prestige."

Under the Lon Nol and Khmer Rouge regimes, Vietnamese living in Cambodia were expelled or exterminated. Resentment had built up over the years in Hanoi – exacerbated by the apparent ingratitude of the Khmer Rouge for Vietnamese assistance in fighting Lon Nol's US-supported Khmer Republic in the early 1970s. As relations between the Khmer Rouge and the Vietnamese deteriorated, the Communist superpowers, China and the Soviet Union, polarized too – the former siding with the Khmer Rouge and the latter with Hanoi. The Vietnamese invasion had the full backing of Moscow, while the Chinese and Americans began their support for the anti-Vietnamese rebels.

Following the Vietnamese invasion, three main anti-Hanoi factions were formed. In June 1982 they banded together in an unholy and unlikely alliance of convenience to fight the PRK and called themselves the Coalition Government of Democratic Kampuchea (CGDK), which was immediately recognized by the United Nations. The Communist **Khmer Rouge**, whose field forces recovered to at least 18,000 by the late 1980s. Supplied with weapons by China, they were concentrated in the Cardamom Mountains in the southwest and were also in control of some of the refugee camps along the Thai border. The National United Front for an Independent Neutral Peaceful and Co-operative Cambodia (Funcinpec) – known by most people as the **Armée Nationale Sihanoukiste** (ANS) was headed by Prince Sihanouk although he spent most of his time exiled in Beijing. The group had fewer than 15,000 well-equipped troops – most of whom took orders from Khmer Rouge commanders. The anti-Communist **Khmer People's National Liberation Front** (KPNLF), headed by Son Sann, a former prime minister under Sihanouk. Its 5000 troops were reportedly ill-disciplined in comparison with the Khmer Rouge and the ANS.

The three CGDK factions were ranged against the 70,000 troops loyal to the government of President Heng Samrin and Prime Minister Hun Sen (previously a Khmer Rouge cadre). They were backed by Vietnamese forces until September 1989. Within the forces of the Phnom Penh government there were reported to be problems of discipline and desertion. But the rebel guerrilla coalition was itself seriously weakened by rivalries and hatred between the different factions: in reality, the idea of a 'coalition' was fiction. Throughout most of the 1980s the war followed the progress of the seasons: during the dry season the PRK forces with their tanks and heavy arms took the offensive but during the wet season this heavy equipment was ineffective and the guerrilla resistance made advances.

Road towards peace

In the late 1980s the Association of Southeast Asian Nations (ASEAN) – for which the Cambodian conflict had almost become a raison d'être – began steps to bring the warring factions together over the negotiating table. ASEAN countries were united primarily in wanting the Vietnamese out of Cambodia. While publicly deploring the Khmer Rouge record, ASEAN tacitly supported the guerrillas. Thailand, an ASEAN member-state, which has had a centuries-long suspicion of the Vietnamese, co-operated closely with China to ensure that the Khmer Rouge guerrillas over the border were well-supplied with weapons.

After Mikhail Gorbachev had come to power in the Soviet Union, Moscow's support for the Vietnamese presence in Cambodia gradually evaporated. Gorbachev began leaning on Vietnam as early as 1987, to withdraw its troops. Despite saying their presence in Cambodia was 'irreversible', Vietnam completed its withdrawal in September 1989, ending nearly 11 years of Hanoi's direct military involvement. The withdrawal led to an immediate upsurge in political and military activity, as forces of the exiled CGDK put increased pressure on the now weakened Phnom Penh regime to begin power-sharing negotiations (see page 156).

Modern Cambodia

In September 1989, under pressure at home and abroad, the Vietnamese withdrew from Cambodia. The immediate result of this withdrawal was an escalation of the civil war as the rebel factions tried to take advantage of the supposedly weakened Hun Sen regime in Phnom Penh. The government committed itself to liberalizing the economy and improving the infrastructure in order to undermine the political appeal of the rebels – particularly that of the Khmer Rouge. Peasant farmers were granted life tenancy to their land and collective farms were substituted with agricultural co-operatives. But because nepotism and bribery were rife in Phnom Penh, the popularity of the Hun Sen regime declined. The rebel position was further strengthened as the disparities between living standards in Phnom Penh and those in the rest of the country widened. In the capital, the government became alarmed; in a radio broadcast in 1991 it announced a crackdown on corruption claiming it was causing a "loss of confidence in our superb regime ... which is tantamount to paving the way for the return of the genocidal Pol Pot regime".

With the withdrawal of Vietnamese troops, the continuing civil war followed the familiar pattern of dry season government offensives, and consolidation of guerrilla positions during the monsoon rains. Much of the fighting focused on the potholed highways – particularly Highway 6 which connects the capital with Battambang – with the Khmer Rouge blowing up most of the bridges along the road. Their strategy involved cutting the roads in order to drain the government's limited resources. Other Khmer Rouge offensives were designed to serve their own economic ends – such as their capture of the gem-rich town of Pailin.

The Khmer Rouge ran extortion rackets throughout the country, even along the strategic Highway 4 which ferried military supplies, oil and consumer goods from the port of Kompong Som (Sihanoukville) to Phnom Penh. The State of Cambodia – or the government forces, known as SOC – was pressed to deploy troops to remote areas and allot scarce resources, settling refugees in more secure parts of the country. To add to their problems, Soviet and Eastern Bloc aid began to dry up.

Throughout 1991 the four warring factions were repeatedly brought to the negotiating table in an effort to hammer out a peace deal. Much of the argument centred on the word 'genocide'. The Prime Minister, Hun Sen, insisted that the wording of any agreement should explicitly condemn the former Khmer Rouge regime's 'genocidal acts'. But the Khmer Rouge refused to be party to any power-sharing deal which labelled them in such a way. Fighting intensified as hopes for a settlement increased – all sides wanted to consolidate their territory in advance of any agreement.

Rumours emerged that China was continuing to supply arms – including tanks, reportedly delivered through Thailand – to the Khmer Rouge. There were also accusations that the Phnom Penh government was using Vietnamese combat troops to stem Khmer Rouge advances – the first such reports since their official withdrawal in 1989. But finally, in June 1991, after several attempts, Sihanouk brokered a permanent ceasefire during a meeting of the Supreme National Council (SNC) in Pattaya, South Thailand. The SNC had been proposed by the United Nations Security Council in 1990 and formed in 1991, with an equal number of representatives from the Phnom Penh government and each of the resistance factions, with Sihanouk as its chairman. The following month he was elected chairman of the SNC, and resigned his presidency of the rebel coalition government in exile. Later in the year, the four factions agreed to reduce their armed guerrillas and militias by 70%. The remainder were to be placed under the supervision of the United Nations Transitional Authority in Cambodia (UNTAC), which supervised Cambodia's transition to multi-party democracy. Heng Samrin decided to drop his insistence that reference should be made to the former Khmer Rouge's 'genocidal regime'. It was also agreed that elections should be held in 1993 on the basis of proportional representation. Heng Samrin's Communist Party was promptly renamed the Cambodian People's Party, in an effort to persuade people that it sided with democracy and capitalism.

Paris Peace Accord

On 23 October 1991, the four warring Cambodian factions signed a peace agreement in Paris which officially ended 13 years of civil war and more than two decades of warfare. The accord was co-signed by 15 other members of the International Peace Conference on Cambodia. There was an air of unreality about the whole event, which brought bitter enemies face-to-face after months of protracted negotiations. There was, however, a notable lack of enthusiasm on the part of the four warring factions. Hun Sen said that the treaty was far from perfect because it failed to contain the word 'genocide' to remind Cambodians of the atrocities of the former Khmer Rouge regime and Western powers obviously agreed. But in the knowledge that it was a fragile agreement, everyone remained diplomatically quiet. US Secretary of State James Baker was quoted as saying "I don't think anyone can tell you there will for sure be lasting peace, but there is great hope."

Political analysts ascribed the successful conclusion to the months of negotiations to improved relations between China and Vietnam – there were reports that the two had held secret summits at which the Cambodia situation was discussed. China put pressure on Prince Norodom Sihanouk to take a leading role in the peace process, and Hanoi's new understanding with Beijing prompted Hun Sen's participation. The easing of tensions between China and Moscow – particularly following the Soviet Union's demise – also helped apply pressure on the different factions. Finally, the United States had shifted its position: in July 1990 it had announced that it would not support the presence of the Khmer Rouge at the UN and by September US officials were talking to Hun Sen.

On 14 November 1991, Prince Norodom Sihanouk returned to Phnom Penh to an ecstatic welcome, followed, a few days later, by Son Sen, a Khmer Rouge leader. On 27 November Khieu Samphan, who had represented the Khmer Rouge at all the peace negotiations, arrived on a flight from Bangkok. Within hours mayhem had broken out, and a lynch mob attacked him in his villa. Rumours circulated that Hun Sen had orchestrated the demonstration, and beating an undignified retreat down a ladder into a waiting armoured personnel carrier, the bloodied Khmer Rouge leader headed back to Pochentong Airport. The crowd had sent a clear signal that they, at least, were not happy to see him back. There were fears that this incident might derail the entire peace process – but in the event, the Khmer Rouge won a small public relations coup by playing the whole thing down. When the Supreme National Council (SNC) finally met in Phnom Penh at the end of December 1991, it was unanimously decided to rubberstamp the immediate deployment of UN troops to oversee the peace process in the run-up to a general election.

UN peace-keeping mission

Yasushi Akashi, a senior Japanese official in the United Nations, was assigned the daunting task of overseeing the biggest military and logistical operation in UN history. UNTAC comprised an international team of 22,000 peacekeepers – including 16,000 soldiers from 22 countries; 6000 officials; 3500 police and 1700 civilian employees and electoral volunteers. The first 'blue-beret' UN troops began arriving in November 1991, even before the SNC had agreed to the full complement of peacekeepers. The UN Advance Mission to Cambodia (UNAMIC) was followed four months later by the first of the main peacekeeping battalions. The odds were stacked against them. Shortly after his arrival, Akashi commented: "If one was a masochist one could not wish for more."

UNTAC's task

UNTAC's central mission was to supervise free elections in a country where most of the population had never voted and had little idea of how democracy was meant to work. The UN was also given the task of resettling 360,000 refugees from camps in Thailand and of demobilizing more than a quarter of a million soldiers and militiamen from the four main factions. In addition, it was to ensure that no further arms shipments reached these factions, whose remaining forces were to be confined to cantonments. In the run-up to the elections, UNTAC also took over the administration of the country, taking over the defence, foreign affairs, finance, public security and information portfolios as well as the task of trying to ensure respect for human rights.

Khmer Rouge pulls out

At the beginning of 1993 it became apparent that the Khmer Rouge had no intention of playing ball, despite its claim of a solid rural support base. The DK failed to register for the election before the expiry of the UN deadline and its forces stepped up attacks on UN personnel. In April 1993 Khieu Samphan and his entire entourage at the Khmer Rouge compound in Phnom Penh left the city. It was at this stage that UN officials finally began expressing their exasperation and anxiety over the Khmer Rouge's avowed intention to disrupt the polls. It was well known that the faction had procured fresh supplies of Chinese weapons through Thailand – although there is no evidence that these came from Beijing – as well as large arms caches all over the country.

By the time of the elections, the group was thought to be in control of between 10% and 15% of Cambodian territory. Khmer Rouge guerrillas launched attacks in April and May 1993. Having stoked racial antagonism, they started killing ethnic Vietnamese villagers and settlers, sending up to 20,000 of them fleeing into Vietnam. In one particularly vicious attack, 33 Vietnamese fishermen and their families were killed in a village on the Tonlé Sap. The Khmer Rouge also began ambushing and killing UN soldiers and electoral volunteers.

The UN remained determined that the elections should go ahead despite the Khmer Rouge threats and mounting political intimidation and violence between other factions, notably the Cambodian People's Party and Funcinpec. In the event, however, there were remarkably few violent incidents and the feared co-ordinated effort to disrupt the voting failed to materialize. Voters took no notice of Khmer Rouge calls to boycott the election and in fact, reports came in from several provinces of large numbers of Khmer Rouge guerrillas and villagers from areas under their control, turning up at polling stations and casting their ballots.

UN-supervised elections

The days following the election saw a political farce – Cambodian style – which, as Nate Thayer wrote in the *Far Eastern Economic Review* "might have been comic if the implications were not so depressing for the country's future". In just a handful of days, the Phnom Penh-based correspondent went on, Cambodia "witnessed an abortive secession, a failed attempt to establish a provisional government, a royal family feud and the manoeuvres of a prince [Sihanouk] obsessed with avenging his removal from power in a military coup more than 20 years [previously]". The elections gave Funcinpec 45% of the vote, the CPP 38% and the BLDP, 3%. The CPP immediately claimed the results fraudulent, while Prince Norodom Chakrapong – one of Sihanouk's sons – announced the secession of the country's six eastern provinces. Fortunately, both attempts to undermine the election dissolved. The CPP agreed to join Funcinpec in a power sharing agreement while, remarkably, the Khmer Rouge were able to present themselves as defenders of democracy in the face of the CPP's claims of vote-rigging. The new Cambodian constitution was ratified in September 1993, marking the end of UNTAC's involvement in the country. Under the new constitution, Cambodia was to be a pluralistic liberal-democratic country. Seventy-year-old Sihanouk was crowned King of Cambodia, reclaiming the throne he relinquished in 1955. His son Norodom Ranariddh was appointed First Prime Minister and Hun Sen, Second Prime Minister, a situation intended to promote national unity but which instead lead to internal bickering and dissent.

An uncivil society?

Almost from day one of Cambodia's rebirth as an independent state espousing the principles of democracy and the market, cracks began to appear in the rickety structure that underlay these grand ideals. Rampant corruption, infighting among the coalition partners, political intrigue, murder and intimidation all became features of the political landscape – and have remained so to this day. There are three bright spots in an otherwise pretty dismal political landscape. First of all, the Khmer Rouge – along with Pol Pot – is dead and buried. Second, while there have been coups, attempted coups, murder, torture and intimidation, the country does still have an operating political system with an opposition of sorts. And third, the trajectory of change since the last edition of this guide was published has been upwards. But, as the following account shows, politics in Cambodia makes Italy seem a model of stability and common sense.

From the elections of 1993 through to 1998, relations between the two key members of the ruling coalition, the CPP and Funcinpec, went from bad to quite appalling. At the end of 1995 Prince Norodom Sirivudh was arrested for plotting to kill Hun Sen and the prime minister ordered troops and tanks on to the streets of Phnom Penh. For a while the capital had the air of a city under siege. Sirivudh, secretary-general of Funcinpec and King Norodom Sihanouk's half brother, has been a vocal critic of corruption in the government, and a supporter of Sam Rainsy, the country's most outspoken opposition politician and the bane of Hun Sen's life. The National Assembly voted unanimously to suspend Sirivudh's immunity from prosecution. Few commentators really believed that Sirivudh had plotted to kill Hun Sen. In the end Hun Sen did not go through with a trial and Sirivudh went into self-imposed exile.

In 1996, relations between the CPP and Funcinpec reached another low. First Prime Minister Prince Norodom Ranariddh joined his two exiled brothers – princes Chakkrapong and Sirivudh – along with Sam Rainsy, in France. Hun Sen smelled a rat and when Ranariddh threatened in May to pull out of the coalition his worries seemed to be confirmed. Only pressure from the outside prevented a meltdown. Foreign donors said that continuing aid was contingent on political harmony, and ASEAN sent the Malaysian foreign minister to knock a few heads together. Some months later relations became chillier still following the drive-by killing of Hun Sen's brother-in-law as he left a restaurant in Phnom Penh.

Things, it seemed, couldn't get any worse – but they did. In February 1997 fighting between forces loyal to Ranariddh and Hun Sen broke out in Battambang. March saw a grenade attack on a demonstration led by opposition leader Sam Rainsy outside the National Assembly leaving 16 dead and 150 injured – including Rainsy himself who suffered minor injuries. In April, Hun Sen mounted what became known as the 'soft coup'. This followed a complicated series of defections from Ranariddh's Funcinpec party to the CPP which, after much to-ing and fro-ing overturned Funcinpec's small majority in the National Assembly. In May, Hun Sen's motorcade was attacked and a month later, on 16 June, fighting broke out between Hun Sen and Ranariddh's bodyguards leaving three dead. It was this gradual decline in relations between the two leaders and their parties which laid the foundations for the coup of 1997.

In July 1997 the stage was set for Cambodia to join ASEAN. This would have marked Cambodia's international rehabilitation. Then, just a month before the historic day, on 5-6 June, Hun Sen mounted a coup and ousted Norodom Ranariddh and his party, Funcinpec, from government. It took two days for Hun Sen and his forces to gain full control of the capital. Ranariddh escaped to Thailand while the United Nations Centre for Human Rights reported that 41 senior military officers and Ranariddh loyalists were hunted down in the days following the coup, tortured and executed. In August the National Assembly voted to withdraw Ranariddh's immunity from prosecution. Five months later, in January 1998, United Nations High Commissioner for Human Rights Mary Robinson visited Cambodia and pressed for an investigation into the deaths – a request that Hun Sen rejected as unwarranted interference. ASEAN, long used to claiming that the Association has no role interfering in domestic affairs, found it had no choice but to defer Cambodia's accession. The coup was widely condemned and on 17 September the UN decided to keep Cambodia's seat vacant in the General Assembly.

Following the coup of 1997 there was some speculation that Hun Sen would simply ignore the need to hold elections scheduled for 26 July. In addition, opposition parties threatened to boycott the elections even if they did occur, claiming that Hun Sen and his henchmen were intent on intimidation. But despite sporadic violence in the weeks and months leading up to the elections, all parties ended up participating. It seems that intense international pressure got to Hun Sen who appreciated that without the goodwill of foreign aid donors the country would simply collapse. Of the 4.9 million votes cast – constituting an impressive 90% of the electorate – Hun Sen's Cambodian People's Party won the largest share at just over 41%.

Hun Sen offered to bring Funcinpec and the SRP into a coalition government, but his advances were rejected. Instead Rainsy and Ranariddh encouraged a series of demonstrations and vigils outside the National Assembly – which quickly became known as 'Democracy Square', à la Tiananmen Square. At the beginning of September 1998, following a grenade attack on Hun Sen's residence and two weeks of uncharacteristic restraint on the part of the Second Prime Minister, government forces began a crack down on the demonstrators. A week later the three protagonists – Ranariddh, Sam Rainsy and Hun Sen – agreed to talks presided over by King Sihanouk in Siem Reap. These progressed astonishingly well considering the state of relations between the three men and two days later the 122-seat National Assembly opened at Angkor Wat on 24 September. In mid-November further talks between the CPP and Funcinpec led to the formation of a coalition government. Hun Sen became sole prime minister and Ranariddh chairman of the National Assembly. While the CPP and Funcinpec took control of 12 and 11 ministries respectively, with Defence and Interior shared, the CPP got the lion's share of the key portfolios. Sam Rainsy was left on the opposition benches. It was only after the political détente that followed the elections that Cambodia was given permission to occupy its UN seat in December 1998. At a summit meeting in Hanoi around the same time, ASEAN also announced that they had agreed on the admission of Cambodia to the grouping – which finally came through on 30 April 1999.

A return to some kind of normality
The year 1997 was the low point in Cambodia's stuttering return to a semblance of normality. The Asian economic crisis combined with the coup (see above) to rock the country back on its heels. On 3 February 2002 free, fair and only modestly violent local commune elections were held. The CPP won the vote by a landslide and although there is little doubt that Hun Sen's party used a bit of muscle here and there, foreign election observers decided that the result reflected the will of the 90% of the electorate who voted. The CPP, despite its iron grip on power, does recognize that democracy means it has to get out there and make a case. Around one third of the CPP's more unpopular commune chiefs were replaced prior to the election. Funcinpec did badly, unable to shake off the perception that it sold out its principles to join the coalition in 1998. The opposition Sam Rainsy Party did rather better, largely for the same reason: the electorate viewed it as standing up to the might of the CPP, highlighting corruption and abuses of power.

In July 2002 Hun Sen took on the rotating chairmanship of ASEAN and used a round of high-profile meetings to demonstrate to the region, and the wider world, just how far the country has come. Hun Sen, who hardly has an enviable record as a touchy-feely politician, used the chairmanship of ASEAN to polish his own as well as his country's credentials in the arena of international public opinion. But despite the PR some Cambodians are concerned that Hun Sen is becoming a little like Burma's Ne Win. Like Ne Win, Hun Sen seems to be obsessed with numbers. His lucky number is nine; in 2002 he brought the local elections forward by three weeks so that the digits in the date would add up to nine. In 2001 he closed down all Cambodia's karaoke bars. With over 20 years as prime minister there is no one to touch Hun Sen and he seems to revel in his strongman reputation. Judges bow to his superior knowledge of the judicial system; kings and princes acknowledged his unparalleled role in appointing the new king; many journalists are in thrall to his power. If even the most fundamental of rights are negotiable then it would seem that only Cambodia's dependence on foreign largesse constrains his wilder impulses.

Compared to its recent past, the last 10 years has been a period of relative stability for Cambodia. Political violence and infighting between parties continues to be a major problem – by international standards the elections were borderline unacceptable, although most of the major parties were reasonably satisfied with the results which saw Hun Sen's landslide victory. The 2003 election wasn't smooth-sailing either. Prior to the June 2003 election the alleged instructions given by representatives of the CPP to government controlled election monitoring organizations were: "If we win by the law, then we win. If we lose by the law, we still must win." Nonetheless a political deadlock arose, with the CPP winning a majority of votes but not the two-thirds required under the constitution to govern alone. The incumbent CPP-led administration assumed power and took on a caretaker role, pending the creation of a coalition which would satisfy the required number of National Assembly seats to form government. Without a functioning legislature, the course of vital legislation was stalled. After almost a year-long stalemate, the National Assembly approved a controversial addendum to the constitution, which allowed a new government to be formed by vote. The vote took place on July 15 2004, and the National Assembly approved a new coalition government, an amalgam of the CPP and FUNCINPEC, with Hun Sen at the helm as prime minister and Prince Norodom Ranariddh as president of the national assembly.

The government's democratic principles came under fire once again in February 2005, when opposition leader Sam Rainsy fled the country after losing his parliamentary immunity from prosecution. Rainsy is perceived as something of a threat due to his steadily gaining popularity with young urban dwellers, whose growing disenchantment with the current government he feeds off. On the one hand, his 'keep the bastards honest' style of politics has added a new dimension of accountability to Cambodian politics, but on the other, his nationalist, racist rantings, particularly his anti-Vietnamese sentiments, could be a very bad thing for the country. In May, 2005 Hun Sen said that Sam Rainsy would have to wait until the "next life" before he would guarantee his safety. However, having received a pardon in February 2006, he returned to the political fray soon thereafter.

The lingering death of the Khmer Rouge
What many outsiders found hard to understand was how the Khmer Rouge enjoyed such popular support among Cambodians – even after the massacres and torture.

The Khmer Rouge was not, of course, just a political force. Its political influence was backed up and reinforced by military muscle. And it has been the defeat of the Khmer Rouge as an effective fighting force which seems to have delivered the fatal blow to its political ambitions.

In mid-1994 the National Assembly outlawed the Khmer Rouge, offering a six month amnesty to rank and file guerrillas. By the time the six months was up in January 1995, 7000 Khmer Rouge had reportedly defected to the government, leaving at that time somewhere between 5000 and 6000 hardcore rebels still fighting. A split in this core group can be dated to 8 August 1996 when Khmer Rouge radio announced that former 'brother number two', Ieng Sary, had betrayed the revolution by embezzling money earned from mining and timber contracts, and branded him a traitor.

This was the first evidence available to Western commentators that a significant split in the Khmer Rouge had occurred. In retrospect, it seems that the split had been brewing for some years – ever since the UN-sponsored elections had revealed a division between 'conservatives' and 'moderates'. The latter, apparently, wished to co-operate with the UN, while the former group desired to boycott the elections. In 1996 the moderate faction, headed by Ieng Sary, finally broke away from the conservatives led by Pol Pot and hardman General Ta Mok. Hun Sen announced soon after the radio broadcast in August 1996 that two Khmer Rouge commanders, Ei Chhien and Sok Pheap had defected to the government. At the end of September Ieng Sary held a press conference to declare his defection. On 14 September King Norodom Sihanouk granted Ieng Sary a royal pardon.

The Cambodian government's conciliatory line towards Ieng Sary seemed perplexing given the man's past. Although he cast himself in the mould of 'misguided and ignorant revolutionary', there are few who doubt that he was fully cognisant of what the Khmer Rouge under Pol Pot were doing even if, as Michael Vickery argues, he was not Brother Number Two, just Brother Number Four or Five. Indeed he has admitted as much in the past.

Not only is he, as a man, thoroughly unpleasant – or so those who know him have said – but he was also a key figure in the leadership and was sentenced to death in absentia by the Phnom Penh government. Stephen Heder of London's School of Oriental & African Studies was quoted as saying after the September press conference: "It's totally implausible that Ieng Sary was unaware that people were being murdered [by the Khmer Rouge]". The split in the Khmer Rouge and the defection of Ieng Sary deprived the Khmer Rouge of 3000-5000 men – halving its fighting force – and also denied the group important revenues from key gem mining areas around Pailin and many of the richest forest concessions.

The disintegration of the Khmer Rouge continued in 1997 after a complicated deal involving Pol Pot, Khieu Samphan, Son Sen and Ta Mok, as well as members of Funcinpec, collapsed. In early June Khieu Samphan, the nominal leader of the Khmer Rouge, was thought to be on the verge of brokering an agreement with Funcinpec that would give Pol Pot and two of his henchmen immunity from prosecution. This would then provide the means by which Khieu Samphan might enter mainstream Cambodian politics. It seems that Hun Sen, horrified at the idea of an alliance between Khieu Samphan and Funcinpec, mounted the coup of June 1997 to prevent the deal coming to fruition. Pol Pot was also, apparently, less than satisfied with the terms of the agreement and pulled out – killing Son Sen in the process. But before Pol Pot could flee, Ta Mok captured his erstwhile leader on June 19th at the Khmer Rouge stronghold of Anlong Veng.

A little more than a month later the 'Trial of the Century' began in this jungle hideout. It was a show trial – more like a Cultural Revolution lynching. A crowd of a few hundred people were on hand. Pol Pot offered the usual Khmer Rouge defence: the revolution made mistakes, but its leaders were inexperienced. And, in any case, they saved Cambodia from annexation by Vietnam. (There is an argument purveyed by some academics that the Khmer Rouge was essentially involved in a programme of ethnic cleansing aimed at ridding Cambodia of all Vietnamese people and influences.) Show trial or not, few people had any sympathy for Pol Pot as he was sentenced by the Khmer Rouge 'people's' court to life imprisonment for the murder of Son Sen. A Khmer Rouge radio station broadcast that with Pol Pot's arrest and sentencing, a 'dark cloud' had been lifted from the Cambodian people.

Confirmation of this bizarre turn of events emerged in mid-October when journalist Nate Thayer of the *Far Eastern Economic Review* became the first journalist to interview Pol Pot since 1979. He reported that the former Khmer Rouge leader was "very ill and perhaps close to death". Even more incredibly than Ieng Sary's defence, Pol Pot denied that the genocide had ever occurred and told Nate Thayer that his 'conscience was clear'.

In March 1998 reports filtered out of the jungle near the Thai border that the Khmer Rouge was finally disintegrating in mutinous conflict. The end game was at hand. The government's amnesty encouraged the great bulk of the Khmer Rouge's remaining fighters to lay down their arms and in December 1998 the last remnants of the rebel army surrendered to government forces, leaving just a handful of men under hardman 'The Butcher' Ta Mok still at large. But even Ta Mok's days of freedom were numbered. In March 1999 he was captured near the Thai border and taken back to Phnom Penh.

The death of Pol Pot

On 15 April 1998 unconfirmed reports stated that Pol Pot – a man who ranks with Hitler, Stalin and Mao in his ability to kill – had died in a remote jungle hideout in the north of Cambodia. Given that Pol Pot's death had been announced several times before, the natural inclination among journalists and commentators was to treat these reports with scepticism. But it was already known that Pol Pot was weak and frail and his death was confirmed when journalists were invited to view his body the following day. Pol Pot was reported to have died from a heart attack. He was 73.

A new era?

The question of what to do with Ieng Sary was the start of a long debate over how Cambodia – and the international community – should deal with former members of the Khmer Rouge. The pragmatic, realist line is that if lasting peace is to come to Cambodia, then it may be necessary to allow some people to get away with – well – murder. As one Western diplomat pondered: "Do you owe fealty to the dead for the living?" This would seem to be Hun Sen's preferred position.

By late 1998, with the apparent end of the Khmer Rouge as a fighting force, the government seemed happy to welcome back the rank and file into mainstream Cambodian life while putting on trial key characters in the Khmer Rouge like Ta Mok, Khieu Samphan and Nuon Chea. While the government was considering what to do, former leaders of the Khmer Rouge were busy trying to rehabilitate their muddied reputations. After years of living pretty comfortable lives around the country, particularly in and around Pailin, by the end of 2007 the old guard of the Khmer Rouge were finally being brought to book. This turn of events was finally set in motion in March 2006 with the nomination of seven judges by the then Secretary General of the United Nations, Kofi Annan for the much anticipated Cambodia Tribunal. With Ta Mok dying in prison in early July 2006 the first charges were laid against the notorious head of the Tuol Sleng prison, Khang Khek Ieu – aka 'Comrade Duch'. Indicted on July 31st with crimes against humanity and after spending eight years behind bars, Duch is due to go on trial in September 2008. Yet it was with the arrests in late 2007 of Ieng Sary, Nuon Chea and Khieu Samphan that the tribunal finally began to flex its muscles. Each of these arrests made international news and it seems, almost 30 years after the Vietnam invasion ended the abhorrent Khmer Rouge regime, that Cambodia may finally be coming to terms with its horrific past.

However, with only the few living key Khmer Rouge figures standing trial most of the minor – and probably equally murderous – cadre are still in circulation. It could be argued that the Tribunal is purely a diversion that allows this coterie of killers and Hun Sen's nefarious past to remain hidden from scrutiny.

What is obvious is that as the Tribunal progressed, many of the old divisions that have riven Cambodian society for generations where taking hold again. In late 2007 Cambodia was officially and internationally recognised as one of the most corrupt countries in history. Spend five minutes in Phnom Penh and this air of corruption is staring you in the face – Toyota Land Cruisers, giant, black Lexus SUVs and Humvees plough through the streets without regard for anyone or anything. When these vehicles do crush or kill other road users, the driver's well-armed body guards hop out, pistols waving, and soon dissuade any eager witnesses. This kind of event is commonplace and the poorer locals know this. Speak to a moto or tuk-tuk driver and you'll soon sense the resentment, "We hate the corrupt and we'd be happy to see them die", is a frequent comment reminiscent of Cambodia's darker times. The establishment of a new, rich elite is not leading to the trickle down of wealth but the entrenchment of certain groups who have no regard at all for building a new society. Even the aid community is complicit in this – one senior worker made this damning off-the-record comment, "We view corruption as the only stabilising factor in Cambodian society. It is awful but what else is there?"

With elections planned for 2008 and no opposition to Hun Sen's rule to speak of, the international community and the Cambodian people can only expect more of the same.

Contents

Footprint features

Indonesia

At a glance

◎ **Getting around** Ferries connect islands. Buses and planes between major cities. Good trains on Java.

◉ **Time required** 2 weeks for the tourist highlights; 8 weeks to explore the country.

☼ **Weather** Average 30°C year-round. Wet Dec-Mar. Dry Apr-Oct.

✖ **When not to go** Some roads can be washed away during wet season.

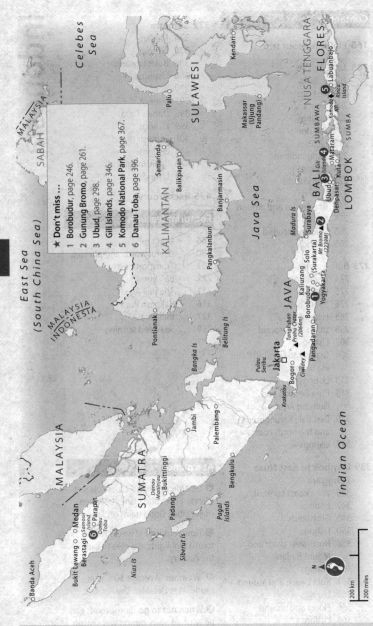

Celebes
Sea

MALAYSIA
SABAH

East Sea
(South China Sea)

MALAYSIA
INDONESIA

MALAYSIA

SUMATRA

Banda Aceh

Bukit Lawang   Medan
Berastagi   Samosir
Island
Danau
6   Parapat   Toba

Nias Is

Siberut Is

Pagai
Islands

Padang

Bengkulu

Danau
Maninjau
Bukittinggi

Jambi

Palembang

Pagai
Islands

Indian Ocean

N

200 km
200 miles

★ Don't miss ...
1 Borobudur, page 246.
2 Gunung Bromo, page 261.
3 Ubud, page 298.
4 Gili Islands, page 346.
5 Komodo National Park, page 367.
6 Danau Toba, page 396.

SULAWESI

Palu

Kendari

Makassar
(Ujung
Pandang)

Samarinda

Balikpapan

Banjarmasin

KALIMANTAN

Pangkalanbun

Pontianak

Bangka Is

Belitung Is

Pulau
Seribu

Krakatau

Jakarta

Bogor
Ciwidey

Tangkuban
Prahu Crater
(2064m)

Pangadaran

JAVA

Kaliurang
Borobudur
Yogyakarta
1

Solo
(Surakarta)

Madura Is

Surabaya

Gunung
Bromo ▲
(2233m)
2

Java Sea

BALI 3
Ubud
Denpasar
Kuta

Gili
Islands 4
Mataram

LOMBOK

SUMBAWA

NUSA TENGGARA

FLORES

Labuanbajo

Komodo 5
Mt.
Rinca
Island

SUMBA

Indonesia is one of those countries mothers wince at upon hearing that their child is planning to visit. Indeed, the last 10 years have seen this, the world's fourth most populous nation, in the headlines for all the wrong reasons. However, for a traveller the archipelago has always promised great adventure and has given the contemporary era swashbuckling tales of shipwrecks, headhunters, unheard of wealth and glorious birds of paradise. It has lured some of the great anthropologists, writers and scientists to delve deep into its myriad cultures and shady jungles for meaningful answers. Nowadays, there are still many adventures to be had: trekking through virgin rainforest, diving deep canyon walls while watching manta rays glide past, and raving in hip clubs with the beautiful elite. While parts of the country may seem empty of tourists, this provides a great opportunity to learn some *Bahasa*, mingle with the welcoming and extraordinarily resilient locals and have an experience that often feels more genuine than those on the well-worn tourist trails of mainland Southeast Asia.

With up to 17,000 islands (depending on the tide), and hundreds of different languages, Indonesia is the world's largest archipelago, one that was bound together by the Dutch and cemented as a nation by independence in 1945. While there are many who seek to find differences between the people in this unlikely nation, there are plenty of obvious links. Despite having the world's largest Muslim population, Indonesia is not an Islamic state although the religion is undoubtedly one of the most vital chains that binds the people. One of the great sensory memories of Southeast Asia is the scent of clove-laden *kretek* cigarettes, which permeates the entire country from the swankiest Jakarta restaurant to the bumpiest Sumatran bus. The enjoyment of these unique cigarettes is another of the unmistakeable bonds between the people of this huge country.

Planning your trip

Getting there

Air

The main international gateway into Indonesia is Jakarta's **Soekarno-Hatta International Airport**, with Bali and Medan (Sumatra) also popular. **Garuda**, the national flag carrier, flies between Jakarta, other Asian cities and Australia. Most of the major European carriers have reduced the number of flights to Jakarta; there are no direct flights from the UK to Indonesia, and most travellers transit via Europe, the Middle East or Southeast Asia. Most European carriers travel to Jakarta via Singapore. There are no direct flights from North America to Indonesia; most visitors travel with an Asian airline. See Singapore, page 740, and Bangkok, page 778, for further information. ▸▸ *For airport tax, see page 183.*

Boat

Batam is increasingly used as an international gateway, with arrivals mostly by sea, from Singapore (see page 741).

Road

There are three overland crossings into Indonesia. One is at Entikong, which links the East Malaysian city of Kuching in Sarawak with the capital of West Kalimantan, Pontianak. Another is at Motoain between Timor Leste and West Timor. The third is between Vanimo in Papua New Guinea and Sentani in Papua. There are no visa on arrival facilities available in any of these places: a visa must be obtained beforehand.

Getting around

Air → *Standards have improved drastically in the last year, after a spate of fatal accidents.*
This is the most convenient and comfortable way to travel around Indonesia. **Garuda** (www.garuda-indonesia.com) and **Merpati**, (www.merpati.co.id) service all the main provincial cities. Merpati tends to operate the short-hop services to smaller towns and cities, particularly in eastern Indonesia.

The other main domestic airlines are **Mandala**, (www.mandalaair.com) under new management and flying spanking new A320s, **Lion Air** (www.lionair.co.id), proud owner of a fleet of sparkling B737-900s, and **Indonesia Air Asia** (www.airasia.com). Other key players are **Batavia Air** (www.batavia-air.co.id) and **Sriwijaya** (www.sriwijayaair-online.com). All these airlines cover major destinations in Indonesia. Smallest of all are **DAS, SMAC** and **Deraya**, (www.deraya.co.id), which tend to service smaller towns in the outer islands, especially Kalimantan, Sumatra and Papua. In Nusa Tenggara, travellers often have to use Merpati, or one of the local outfits such as **Trans Nusa** (www.transnusa.co.id) and **Indonesia Air Transport** (www.iat.co.id). There are also non-commercial air services such as the **Missionary Aviation Fellowship** (MAF) and **Associated Missions Aviation** (AMA), which offer non-scheduled flights in Irian Jaya, Kalimantan and Sulawesi, to more out-of-the-way spots. **Note** These are not commercial airlines and can refuse passage.

By international standards, flights in Indonesia are cheap. It is also considerably cheaper buying tickets in Indonesia than it is purchasing them abroad. Airlines such as Lion Air, Mandala and Air Asia have an online booking system for use with Visa or

MasterCard. Garuda flights can be reserved online. Offices in larger towns will usually accept credit card payment, although smaller branch offices in out-of-the-way places will often only take cash payment. Some airlines give student reductions. During holiday periods, flights are booked up some time ahead. That said, there are often 'no shows' and it is always worth going to the airport even if the plane is said to be 'full'. It is essential to reconfirm tickets. ▶▶ *For details of domestic airport tax, see page 183.*

Bicycles
In some of the more popular tourist destinations, guesthouses and some tour companies hire out bicycles. These vary a great deal in quality – check the brakes before you set off! Expect to pay about 25,000Rp per day for a locally or Chinese-built mountain bike.

Boat
The national shipping company is **Pelayaran Nasional Indonesia** (PELNI). Its head office is at Jalan Gajah Mada 14, Jakarta, T021 63857747, (www.pelni.com). Many travel agents also sell PELNI tickets and, although they levy a small surcharge, may be far more convenient. PELNI operates an expanding fleet of modern passenger ships that ply fortnightly circuits throughout the archipelago. The ships are well run and well maintained, have an excellent safety record, and are a comfortable and leisurely way to travel. Each accommodates 500-2250 passengers in five classes, has central a/c, a bar, restaurant and cafeteria.

In addition to these ships, PELNI also operates a so-called 'pioneer' service – **Pelayaran Perintis** – serving smaller, more out-of-the-way ports. These ships have no cabins but take passengers 'deck' class. Like their more illustrious sister vessels, they are generally well run and safe, if not always comfortable. Finally, there are the mixed cargo boats and ships that go almost everywhere. Passage can be secured just by visiting the port and asking around. **Note** Safety equipment may not be up to standard, and the comfort level is minimal.

Bus
Road transport in Indonesia has improved greatly in recent years, and main roads on most of the islands are generally in reasonably good condition. The major exception is Irian Jaya, and to a lesser extent Kalimantan, where air transport is the only sensible way to get around. In many areas even main roads may be impassable during the rainy season and after severe storms.

Most Indonesians, as well as many visitors, get around by bus. The network is vast and although it is not always quick or comfortable, buses are the cheapest way to travel. Buses (and particularly non-a/c buses) are often overfilled and seats are designed for Indonesian, rather than western bodies. A/c buses are generally less cramped. 'VIP' (pronounced as it is spelt – 'vip') buses are more comfortable still. There are also *bis pariwisata* – tourist buses – which have more space and may stop-off at *objek wisata* (tourist sights) en route. There are a range of bus alternatives:

Bis ekonomi The bottom rung of the bus ladder. Slow, uncomfortable, often full, but dirt cheap. A great way to meet Indonesians and to interface with farm animals, but probably not recommended for long journeys.

Bis patas Express buses, non-a/c. Marginally more comfortable than *ekonomi*, and faster.

Bis malam (Over)night buses. Usually a/c (and cold), probably the fastest buses, tend to arrive at their destinations very early in the morning.

Bis pariwisata Tourist buses. More leg room, slightly cheaper than VIP buses but not as comfortable. Often minibuses rather than large coaches. Some stop off at sights en route.

Bis VIP 'Luxury' buses; a/c, more leg room, better service, usually driven with a little more care and attention.

The seats at the front of buses are the most comfortable, but also the most dangerous if there is a crash. Roads are often windy and rough, and buses are badly sprung (or totally un-sprung). Despite harrowingly fast speeds at times, do not expect to average much more than 40 kph (particularly on Flores) except on the best highways. Overnight buses are usually faster and recommended for longer journeys. However, a/c overnighters can be very cold and a sarong or blanket is useful. Their other disadvantages are that the scenery passes in the darkness and they invariably arrive at anti-social, inconvenient times of day (or night). Watch out for pickpockets.

Tickets can be obtained from bus company offices or through travel agents; shop around for the best fare – bargaining is possible. It is sensible to book a day or so ahead for longer journeys. During Ramadan and at Lebaran, all forms of public transport are packed. Estimated journey times are often wildly inaccurate. Connecting tickets, strangely, tend to work out more expensive than buying two single tickets.

Shuttle buses These are found in the main tourist areas on Java, Bali and Lombok. They operate almost exclusively for the benefit of foreigners connecting the most popular destinations, with a fixed daily timetable. They will pick up and drop off passengers at their hotels and take a great deal of the hassle out of ground travel, though you miss much of the local colour.

Car and motorbike hire

Cars can be hired for self-drive or with a driver. Generally, self-drive cars are only available at the more popular tourist destinations (for example, Bali and Lombok) and in the bigger cities (for example, Jakarta, Medan, Yogya and Surabaya).

Motorbike hire is available at many beach resorts and increasingly in other towns. It is illegal to ride without a helmet, although this can just be a construction worker's hard hat. Many machines are poorly maintained: check brakes and lights before paying.

Taxis

Taxis are metered in the major cities. Unmetered taxis can be shared for longer journeys. Drivers cannot usually change large bills. All registered taxis, minibuses and rental cars have yellow number plates; black number plates are for private vehicles, and red are for government-owned vehicles. Share taxis make particular sense for a party of four or five. Inter-city 'share taxis' are more expensive than buses, but are usually a quicker and cheaper alternative to going by air or private taxi. They are not available in all towns and only tend to run the busier routes, like Jakarta to Bandung. They depart when all five seats are taken.

Train

Passenger train services are limited to Java and certain areas of Sumatra, including a route in Lampung and South Sumatra, and in North Sumatra. Trains are usually slow and often delayed. Single track connects many major cities. First class is a/c with a dining car. There are two main trunk routes on Java: Jakarta-Cirebon-Semarang-Surabaya and Jakarta-Bandung-Yogyakarta-Solo (Surakarta)-Surabaya. The principal services are identified by name, for example, the **Bima** is the a/c night-express from Jakarta via Yogya and Solo, to Surabaya (14 hours); the **Mutiara Utara** is the northern route train to Surabaya via

Semarang; the **Senja Utama Solo** is the express train to Yogya and Solo; while the **Senja Utama Semarang** is the express train to Cirebon and Semarang. There are three classes: **Executive** is first class, with a/c, reclining seats and breakfast included. **Business** (*bisnis*) is fan-cooled, with pillows provided; and **Economy**, with rather run down, well-used coaches, broken fans and windows that may or may not open – this class is subject to overcrowding. All three classes can be booked. Reservations should be made well in advance; it is often easier through a travel agent in the town where you are staying.

Other forms of local road transport

Bajaj Small three-wheeled motor scooters similar to the Thai tuk-tuk. They are probably the cheapest form of 'taxi' after the becak, but are only available in big cities.

Becaks Becaks or bicycle rickshaws are one of the cheapest, and most important, forms of short-distance transport in Indonesia. Literally hundreds of thousands of poor people make a living driving becaks. However, they are now illegal in central Jakarta and often officially barred from main thoroughfares in other large cities. Bargain hard and agree a fare before boarding.

Bemos These are small buses or adapted pick-ups operating on fixed routes. They usually run fixed routes for fixed fares (it varies between towns, but around 2500Rp), but can also be chartered by the hour or day.

Bis kayu Trucks converted into buses with bench seats down each side.

Ojeks Motorcycle taxis. Ojek riders, often wearing coloured jackets, congregate at junctions, taking passengers pillion to their destination. Agree a price before boarding and bargain hard.

Oplets Larger versions of bemos carrying 10-12 passengers. They have a bewildering number of other names – daihatsu in Semarang, angkuta in Solo, microlets in Malang and Jakarta, while in rural areas they tend to be called colts. In larger cities, bemos/colts often follow fixed routes. They are sometimes colour coded, sometimes numbered, sometimes have their destinations marked on the front – and sometimes all three. For intra-city trips there is usually a fixed fare – it varies between towns, but around 2500Rp – although it is worth asking one of your fellow passengers what the *harga biasa* (normal price) is, or watch what is being handed to the driver or his sidekick by fellow passengers. In the countryside, routes can vary and so do fares; be prepared to bargain. Oplets can also be chartered by the hour or day (bargain hard).

Maps

Locally, maps may not be available beyond the larger cities, and often the quality is poor.

Nelles A good series of maps of the major islands and island groups.

Periplus Travel Maps Recent series of maps to the major islands including some to individual provinces. Good on tourist site information and often with good city insets.

Travel Treasure Maps Knaus Publications: arty map series concentrating on the major tourist destinations. Sometimes with inset city plans and hiking trails.

Regional maps Bartholomew *Southeast Asia* (1:5,800,000); Nelles *Southeast Asia* (1:4,000,000).

Other maps Tactical Pilotage Charts (TPC, US Airforce) (1:500,000); Operational Navigational Charts (ONC, US Airforce) (1:500,000). Both particularly good at showing relief features (useful for planning treks).

Sleeping → *For hotel price codes, see inside the front cover.*

Tourist and business centres usually have a good range of accommodation for all budgets. Bali, for example, has some of the finest hotels in the world – at a corresponding price – along with excellent mid- and lower-range accommodation. However, visitors venturing off the beaten track may find hotels restricted to dingy and over-priced establishments catering for local businessmen and officials. The best run and most competitively priced budget accommodation is found in popular tourist spots – like Bali and Yogya. It is almost always worth bargaining in Chinese hotels, and in mid- and upper-range establishments. This is particularly true for hotels in tourist destinations that attract a fair amount of local weekend business: the weekday room rate may be 50% less than the weekend rate. Cheaper places may not give discounts, although as a general rule it is worth negotiating. All hotels are required to display their room rates (for every category of room) on a *daftar harga*, or price list. This is invariably either in public view in the reception area or will be produced when you ask about room rates. Indonesians prefer to be on the ground floor, so rooms on higher floors are usually cheaper. In cheaper accommodation, the bed may consist only of a bottom sheet and pillow with no top sheet.

Terminology can be confusing: a *losmen* is a lower price range hotel (in parts of Sumatra and in some other areas, *losmen* are known as *penginapan*); a *wisma* is a guesthouse, but these can range in price from cheap to moderately expensive; finally, a *hotel* is a hotel, but can range from the cheap and squalid up to a Hilton.

There is a 'star' system in use in Indonesia and it can give a rough guide to the price of the establishment (although it is a rating of facilities not of quality). The '*melati*' (flower) system is for cheaper hotels; while the '*bintang*' (star) system is for higher rated, and therefore more expensive, hotels. As in most countries, five star (luxury) is top of the range.

Bathing and toilets

Baths and showers are not a feature of many cheaper *losmen*. Instead a *mandi* – a water tank and ladle – is used to wash. The tub is not climbed into; water is ladled from the tub and splashed over the head. The traditional Asian toilet is of the squat variety. (Toilets are called *kamar kecil* – the universal 'small room' – or *way say*, as in the initials 'WC'.) Toilet paper is not traditionally used; the faithful left hand and water suffice. In cheaper accommodation you are expected to bring your own towels, soap and toilet paper.

Eating and drinking → *For restaurant price codes, see inside the front cover.*

Food

The main staple across the archipelago is rice. Today, alternatives such as corn, sweet potatoes and sago, which are grown primarily in the dry islands of the East, are regarded as 'poor man's food', and rice is the preferred staple.

Indonesians will eat rice – or *nasi* (milled, cooked rice) – at least three times a day. Breakfast is often left-over rice, stir-fried and served up as *nasi goreng*. Mid-morning snacks are often sticky rice cakes or *pisang goreng* (fried bananas). Rice is the staple for lunch, served up with two or three meat and vegetable dishes and followed by fresh fruit. The main meal is supper, which is served quite early and again consists of rice, this time accompanied by as many as five or six other dishes. *Sate/satay* (grilled skewers of meat), *soto* (a nourishing soup) or *bakmi* (noodles, a dish of Chinese origin) may be served first.

In many towns (particularly in Java), *sate, soto* or *bakmi* vendors roam the streets with carts containing charcoal braziers, ringing a bell or hitting a block (the noise will signify what he or she is selling) in the early evenings. These carts are known as *kaki lima* (five legs). *Pedagang* (vendor) *kaki lima* (abbreviated to PK5 in newspaper reports) also refers to hawkers who peddle their wares from stalls and from baskets hung from shoulder poles.

Larger foodstalls tend to set up in the same place every evening in a central position in town. These *warungs*, as they are known, may be temporary structures or more permanent buildings, with simple tables and benches. In the larger cities, there may be an area of *warungs*, all under one roof. Often a particular street will become known as the best place to find particular dishes like *martabak* (savoury meat pancakes) or *gado gado* (vegetable salad served with peanut sauce). It is common to see some *warungs* being labelled *wartegs*. These are stalls selling dishes from Tegal, a town on Java's north coast. More formalized restaurants are known simply as *rumah makan*, literally 'eating houses', often shortened to just 'RM'. Another term for cheaper restaurants is 'Depot', which is often rather appropriate. A good place to look for cheap stall food is in and around the market or *pasar*; night markets or *pasar malam* are usually better for eating than day markets.

Feast days, such as Lebaran marking the end of Ramadan, are a cause for great celebration and traditional dishes are served. *Lontong* or *ketupat* are made at this time (they are both versions of boiled rice – simmered in a small container or bag, so that as it cooks, the rice is compressed to make a solid block). This may be accompanied by *sambal goreng daging* (fried beef in a coconut sauce) in Java or *rendang* (curried beef) in Sumatra. *Nasi kuning* (yellow rice) is traditionally served at a *selamatan* (a Javanese celebration marking a birth, the collection of the rice harvest or the completion of a new house).

In addition to rice, there are a number of other common ingredients used across the country. Coconut milk, ginger, chilli peppers and peanuts are used nationwide, while dried salted fish and soybeans are important sources of protein. In coastal areas, fish and seafood tend to be more important than meat. As Indonesia is more than 80% Muslim, pork is not widely eaten (except in Chinese restaurants) and in some areas, such as Bali, Christian Flores, and around Lake Toba in Sumatra, it is much more in evidence.

Regional cuisines

Although Indonesia is becoming more homogeneous as Javanese culture spreads to the Outer Islands, there are still distinctive regional cuisines. The food of **Java** embraces a number of regional forms, of which the most distinctive is **Sundanese**. *Lalap*, a Sundanese dish, consists of raw vegetables and is said to be the only Indonesian dish where vegetables are eaten uncooked. Characteristic ingredients of Javanese dishes are soybeans, beef, chicken and vegetables; characteristic flavours are an interplay of sweetness and spiciness. Probably the most famous regional cuisine, however, is **Padang** or **Minang** food, which has its origins in West Sumatra province. Padang food has 'colonized' the rest of the country and there are Padang restaurants in every town, no matter how small. Dishes tend to be hot and spicy, using quantities of chilli and turmeric, and include *rendang* (dry beef curry), *kalo ayam* (creamy chicken curry) and *dendeng balado* (fried seasoned sun-dried meat with a spicy coating). In **Eastern Indonesia**, seafood and fish are important elements in the diet, and fish grilled over an open brazier (*ikan panggang* or *ikan bakar*) and served with spices and rice is a delicious, common dish. The **Toraja** of Sulawesi eat large amounts of pork, and specialities include black rice (*nasi hitam*) and fish or chicken cooked in bamboo (*piong*). There are large numbers of Chinese people scattered across the archipelago and, like other countries of the region, **Chinese** restaurants are widespread.

Drink

Water must be boiled for at least five minutes before it is safe to drink. Hotels and most restaurants should boil the water they offer customers. Ask for *air minum* (drinking water), *air putih* or *air mendidih* (boiled water). You may have to try both *air putih* and *air mendidih* to get what you want; in some places, if you ask for *air mendidih* you will get boiling hot water rather than previously boiled water. On Bali, *air putih* usually means cold but previously boiled water. Many restaurants provide a big jug of boiled water on each table. In cheaper establishments it is probably best to play safe and ask for bottled water, although consider the environmental impact of this.

Over the last few years, '**mineral water**' – of which the most famous is *Aqua* ('aqua' has become the generic word for mineral water) – has become increasingly popular. It is now available in all but the smallest and most remote towns. Check the seal is intact before accepting a bottle. Bottled water is cheap: in 2008 a 1.5 litre bottle cost around 3000Rp.

Western **bottled and canned drinks** are widely available in Indonesia and are comparatively cheap. Alternatively, most restaurants will serve *air jeruk* – citrus **fruit juices** – with or without ice (*es*). The **coconut milk** is a good thirst quencher and a good source of potassium and glucose. Fresh fruit juices vary greatly in quality; some are little more than water, sugar and ice. Ice in many places is fine, but in cheaper restaurants and away from tourist areas many people recommend taking drinks without ice. Javanese, Sumatran, Sulawesi or Timorese *kopi* (coffee), fresh and strong, is an excellent morning pick-you-up. It is usually served *kopi manis* (sweet) and black; if you want to have it without sugar, ask for it *tidak pakai gula*. The same goes for other drinks habitually served with mountains of sugar (like fruit juices). *Susu* (milk) is available in tourist areas and large towns, but it may be sweetened condensed milk. *Teh* (tea), usually weak, is obtainable almost everywhere. Hot ginger tea is a refreshing alternative.

Although Indonesia is a predominantly Muslim country, alcohol is widely available. The two most popular **beers** – light lagers – are the locally brewed *Anker* and *Bintang* brands. Wine is becoming more popular, although you need to ask for a wine list, and choose from that before it is clandestinely brought out. A reasonable bottle can be had for around US$13. Imported **spirits** are comparatively expensive, however, a number of local brews including *brem* (rice wine), *arak* (rice whisky) and *tuak* (palm wine) are available.

Local customs and laws

As a rule, Indonesians are courteous and understanding. Visitors should be the same. Foreigners are often given the benefit of the doubt when norms are transgressed. However, it is best to have a grasp of at least the basics of accepted behaviour. There are also some areas – such as Aceh in North Sumatra – that are more fervently Muslim than other parts of the country. With such a diverse array of cultures and religions, accepted conduct varies. Generally, the more popular an area is (as a tourist destination) the more understanding local people are likely to be of tourist habits. But this is not to imply that anything goes. It is also true that familiarity can breed contempt, so even in places like Bali it is important to be sensitive to the essentials of local culture.

Calmness Like other countries of Southeast Asia, a calm attitude is highly admired, especially if things are going wrong. Keep calm and cool when bargaining, or waiting for a delayed bus or appointment.

Dress Indonesia is largely a Muslim country. Dress modestly and avoid shorts, short skirts and sleeveless dresses or shirts (except at the beach). Public nudity and topless bathing are not acceptable. Light clothing is suitable all year round, except at night in the mountains. Proper decorum should be observed when visiting places of worship; shorts are not permitted in mosques, shoulders and arms should be covered, and women must cover their heads. Formal dress for men normally consists of a batik shirt and trousers; suits are rarely worn. Local women usually wear a *kebaya*.

Face People should not be forced to lose face in public; especially in front of colleagues. Putting someone in a position of *malu* or social shame should be avoided.

Gifts If you are invited to somebody's home, it is customary to take a gift. This is not opened until after the visitor has left. Most small general stores have a range of pre-wrapped and boxed gifts, appropriate for a variety of occasions including weddings. These are usually items of china or glasses.

Heads, hands and feet The head is considered sacred and should never be touched (especially those of children). Handshaking is common among both men and women, but the use of the left hand to give or receive is taboo. When eating with fingers, use the right hand only. Pointing with your finger is impolite; use your thumb to point. Beckon buses (or any person) with a flapping motion of your right hand down by your side. When sitting with others, do not cross your legs; it is considered disrespectful. Do not point with your feet and keep them off tables. Shoes are often not worn in houses – remove them on entering.

Open affection Public displays of affection between men and women are considered objectionable. However, Indonesians of the same sex tend to be affectionate – holding hands, for example.

Punctuality **Jam karet** or 'rubber time' is a peculiarly Indonesian phenomenon. Patience and a cool head are very important; appointments are rarely at the time arranged.

Religion Indonesia is the largest Muslim country in the world. In Java, **Islam** is a synthesis of Islam, Buddhism, Hinduism and Animism – although the extent to which it is 'syncretic' is vigorously debated. Orthodox Islam is strongest in North Sumatra (Aceh), but is also present in parts of Sulawesi, Kalimantan and West Java.

Mosques are sacred houses of prayer; non-Muslims can enter a mosque, so long as they observe the appropriate customs: remove shoes before entering, dress appropriately, do not disturb the peace, and do not walk too close to or in front of somebody who is praying. During the fasting month of Ramadan, do not eat, drink or smoke in the presence of Muslims during daylight hours.

Bali has remained a **Hindu** island, and remnants of Hinduism are also evident in parts of Central and East Java. To enter a temple or *pura* on Bali, it is often necessary to wear a sash around the waist (at some temples a sarong is also required); these are available for hire at the more popular temples, or can be bought for about 5000Rp (15,000Rp for a sarong). Modest and tidy dress is also required when visiting Hindu temples; women should not enter wearing short dresses or with bare shoulders. Do not use flash-guns during ceremonies. Women menstruating are requested not to enter temples.

Christianity is a growing religion in Sulawesi and East Nusa Tenggara.

Indonesian festivals and events → *Muslim festivals are based on the lunar calendar*

January
Tahun Baru, New Year's Day (1st: public holiday). **New Year's Eve** is celebrated with street carnivals, shows, fireworks and all-night festivities. In Christian areas, festivities are more exuberant, with people visiting each other on New Year's Day and attending church services.

January/February
Imlek, Chinese New Year (movable, 26 Jan 2009, 14 Feb 2010, 3 Feb 2011). An official holiday; many Chinese shops and businesses close for at least 2 days. Within the Chinese community, younger people visit their relatives, children are given *hong bao* (lucky money), new clothes are bought and any unfinished business is cleared up.

March/April
Garebeg Maulad (or Maulud Nabi Muhammed, birthday of the Prophet Mohammad) (movable, 8 Mar 2009, 25 Feb 2010: public holiday), to commemorate Prophet Muhammad's birthday in AD 571. Processions and Koran recitals in most big towns. Celebrations begin a week before the actual day and last a month, with *selamatans* in homes, mosques and schools.
Wafat Isa Al-Masih, Good Friday (movable: public holiday, 10 Apr 2009, 2 Apr 2010, 22 Apr 2011). **Nyepi** (movable: public holiday, 26 Mar 2009, 16 Mar 2010, 4 Apr 2011).
Kartini Day (21 Apr). A ceremony held by women to mark the birthday of Raden Ajeng Kartini, born in 1879 and proclaimed as a pioneer of women's emancipation. The festival is rather like mother's day, in that women are supposed to be pampered by their husbands and children, although it is women's organizations like the Dharma Wanita who get most excited. Women dress in national dress.

May
Waisak Day (movable: public holiday). Marks the birth and death of the historic Buddha; at Candi Mendut outside Yogyakarta,

a procession of monks carrying flowers, candles, holy fire and images of the Buddha walk to Borobudur. **Kenaikan Isa Al-Masih** or Ascension Day (movable: public holiday).

July
Al Miraj (or Isra Miraj Nabi Muhammed) (movable, 18 Jul 2009, 9 Jul 2010). The ascension of the Prophet Mohammad when he is led through the 7 heavens by the archangel. He speaks with God and returns to earth the same night, with instructions that include the 5 daily prayers.

August
Independence Day (17th: public holiday). The most important national holiday, celebrated with processions, dancing and other merry-making. Although it is officially on the 17th, festivities continue for a whole month, towns are decorated with bunting and parades cause delays to bus travel, there seems to be no way of knowing when each town will hold its parades.
Awal Ramadan (movable, 22 Aug 2009, 10 Aug 2010). The 1st day of Ramadan, a month of fasting for all Muslims. Muslims abstain from all food and drink (and smoking) from sunrise to sundown – if they are very strict, Muslims do not even swallow their own saliva during daylight hours. It is strictly adhered to in more conservative areas like Aceh and West Sumatra, and many restaurants remain closed during daylight hours – making life tiresome for non-Muslims. Every evening for 30 days before breaking of fast, stalls selling traditional Malay cakes and delicacies are set up . The only people exempt from fasting are the elderly, those who are travelling, and women who are pregnant or menstruating.

September
Idul Fitri (Aidil Fitri) or **Lebaran** (movable, 19 Sep 2009, 8 Sep 2010: public holiday) is a 2-day celebration that marks the end of Ramadan, and is a period of prayer and

celebration. In order for Hari Raya to be declared, the new moon of Syawal has to be sighted; if it is not, fasting continues for another day. It is the most important time of the year for Muslim families to get together. Mass prayers are held in mosques and squares. This is not a good time to travel, public transport is booked up weeks in advance and hotels are often full.

October
Hari Pancasila (1st). This commemorates the Five Basic Principles of Pancasila.
Armed Forces Day (5th). The anniversary of the founding of the Indonesian Armed Forces, with military parades and demonstrations.

November
Idhul Adha (movable, 27 Nov 2009, 17 Nov 2010: public holiday). Celebrated by Muslims to mark the 10th day of Zulhijjah, the 12th month of the Islamic calendar when pilgrims celebrate their return from the Haj to Mecca. In the morning, prayers are offered and, later, families hold 'open house'. This is the 'festival of the sacrifice' and is the time when burial graves are cleaned, and an animal is sacrificed by those who can afford it to be distributed to the poor. This commemorates the willingness of Abraham to sacrifice his son. Indonesian men who have made the pilgrimage to Mecca wear a white skull-hat.

December
Muharram (movable, 17 Dec 2009, 5 Dec 2010: public holiday), Muslim New Year. Marks the 1st day of the Muslim calendar, and celebrating the Prophet Muhammad's journey from Mecca to Medina on the lunar equivalent of AD 16 Jul 622.
Christmas Day (25th: public holiday). Celebrated by Christians – the Bataks of Sumatra, the Toraja and Minahasans of Sulawesi and in some of the islands of Nusa Tenggara, and Irian Jaya.

Balinese festivals and events

Bali is the festival capital of Southeast Asia; there is a festival every day of the year. With 20,000 temples, each celebrating its anniversary or *odalan* every 210 days (according to the Balinese *wuku* calendar), it is easy to see why.

The tourist office supplies a booklet cataloging the year's festivals, while the *Bali News* lists current events. The Balinese calendar, in fact two calendars, is complex. The *wuku* calendar, which governs most festivals, is lunar and runs over 210 days. Locals do not object to tourists being present at most of their ceremonies, but they do ask that visitors dress appropriately, with sarong and sash, and behave discreetly.

Wuku Year Festivals (210-day calendar) **Day 1: Galungan**, the most important holiday of the Balinese year. It is a 10-day festival marking the Balinese New Year. It also commemorates the creation of the world by the Supreme God and symbolizes the victory of good over evil. Women make *banten* (offerings of sweets, fruits and flowers), while men make *lawar* (a food made of vegetables and meat). Both are thanksgiving offerings. *Penjors* are the long bamboo poles on the right-hand side of every house entrance, with offerings hanging from them as symbols of gratitude for the god's gift of life and prosperity. It is said that the offerings are hung on these tall poles – which it is a man's job to make – so that the gods can see them from their mountain abodes. *Barong* and other dances are traditionally held at this time.

Day 10: Kuningan, held 10 days after Galungan and marking the end of the holiday period. It is believed to be the day when the gods ascend back to Heaven, and is a time for honouring the souls of ancestors and saints. Temple compounds are decorated with flowers and offerings made.

Day 137: Saraswati, is for the Goddess of Learning and Knowledge, Batari Dewi Saraswati. All books are given to the Goddess to be blessed; no reading or writing is allowed.

Day 142: Pangerwesi, the word means 'iron fence', and the ceremony is dedicated to Shanghyang Pramesti Guru. It is particularly popular in the north.

Day 210: Penampahan Galungan, the day prior to Galungan when every Balinese prepares for the big day, slaughtering pigs and chickens and preparing offerings and food. It marks the end of the Wuku year.

Recurrent Wuku Festivals In addition to the above Wuku festivals, there are also a number of recurrent festival days which are regarded as propitious for making offerings. **Kadjeng-klion** is held every 15 days; **Tumpak**, every 35 days; **Budda-klion**, every 42 days; **Anggara-kasih**, every 35 days; and **Budda-wage**, every 35 days.

Saka Year Festivals (354 to 356-day calendar) **March: Pengerupuk** (movable), the last day of the Balinese year. Purification sacrifices and offerings are made, while priests chant mantras to exorcize the demons of the old year. At night, gongs and cymbals are struck, and torchlit processions with *ogoh-ogoh* (large monsters) parade through the streets in order to exorcize the spirits. The spectacle is best in Denpasar, where thousands gather in Puputan Square before the start of the march.

March-April: Nyepi (movable) celebrates the *saka*, solar New Year, which is held at the Spring equinox. In the recent past it was a day of silence when everything closed down and no activity was allowed. It is hoped that the evil spirits roused by the previous night's activities will find Bali to be a barren land and will leave the island. On the day before Nyepi long parades of traditionally dressed Balinese, carrying offerings and sacred objects, walk from their villages to nearby riverbanks and beaches to undertake ritual ablutions of purification and ask for their deity's blessing. As part of the *melasti* rites, the village gods in their *pratimas* (the small statue in which a god is invited to reside during a ceremony) are taken from the village temples and carried to the seashore for resanctification. Balinese believe that the sea will receive all evil and polluted elements, it is a place to cast off the evil words and deeds of the past year, and seek renewal and purification for the new Hindu year.

Note Visitors must stay within their hotel compounds from 0500 to 0500 the following day; the observance of Nyepi is very strict in this regard, you might choose to avoid being on the island during this time. Tourists are confined to their accommodation, which in a small guesthouse means you feel as if you have been placed under 'house arrest' – no swimming in the sea 10 m from your bungalow, no strolls or other forms of exercise. Anyone arriving at Denpasar airport on the eve of Nyepi should be aware that most taxi drivers go home at 1700. The few who continue to offer a taxi service up to midnight ask exorbitant rates and may be unlicensed. Travellers would be well advised to arrange transport in advance with their accommodation.

Shopping

Indonesia offers a wealth of distinctive handicrafts and other products. Best buys include textiles (batik and *ikat*), silverwork, woodcarving, Krisses, puppets, paintings and ceramics. Bali has the greatest choice of handicrafts. It is not necessarily the case that you will find the best buys in the area where a particular product is made; the larger cities, especially Jakarta, sell a wide range of handicrafts and antiques from across the archipelago at competitive prices.

Tips on buying

Early morning sales may well be cheaper, as salespeople often believe the first sale augurs well for the rest of the day. Except in the larger fixed-price stores, bargaining (with good humour) is expected; start at 50-60% lower than the asking price. Do not expect to achieve instant results; if you walk away from the shop, you will almost certainly be followed, with a lower offer. If the salesperson agrees to your price, you should feel obliged to purchase – it is considered very ill mannered to agree on a price and then not buy the article.

What to buy

Centres of batik-making are focused on Java. Yogyakarta and Solo (Surakarta) probably offer the widest choice, although Cirebon and Pekalongan (both on the north coast) offer their own distinctive styles. There is also a good range of batik in Jakarta. The traditional hand-drawn batiks (*batik tulis*) are more expensive than the modern printed batiks. *Ikat* is dyed and woven cloth found on the islands of Bali, Lombok and Nusa Tenggara, although it is not cheap and is sometimes of dubious quality. *Wayang* is a Javanese and Balinese art form and puppets are most widely available on these islands, particularly in Yogyakarta and Jakarta. Baskets of all shapes and sizes are made for practical use, out of rattan, bamboo, sisal, and nipah and lontar palm. The intricate baskets of Lombok are particularly attractive. Woodcarving ranges from the clearly tourist oriented (Bali), to fine classical pieces (Java), to 'primitive' (Irian Jaya). The greatest concentration of woodcarvers work in Bali, producing skilful modern and traditional designs.

A-Z Essentials

Customs and duty free

There are no restrictions on the import or export of foreign currency, either cash or TCs. Local currency between 5,000,000Rp and 10,000,000Rp must be declared at customs. Amounts more than this must be certified (enquire at branches of **BNI**).

The duty-free allowance is 2 litres of alcohol, 200 cigarettes or 50 cigars or 100 g of tobacco, along with a reasonable amount of perfume.

Prohibited items include narcotics, arms and ammunition, TV sets, radio/cassette recorders, pornographic objects or printed matter. In theory, approval should also be sought for carrying transceivers, movie film and video cassettes.

Disabled travellers

Indonesia has almost no infrastructure to enable disabled people to travel easily. Pavements are frequently very high, uneven and ridden with holes and missing slabs. Buildings are often reached via steps with no ramps. Public transport is frequently cramped and overcrowded. Some of the Western-owned hotels at the top end of the market do provide wheelchair access and facilities for disabled visitors. It would be best to contact a specialist travel agent or organization dealing with travellers with special needs. In the UK, contact **The Royal Association for Disability and Rehabilitation (RADAR)**, 12 City Forum, 250 City Rd, London EC1V 8AF, T020-72503222, www.radar.org.uk/radarwebsite. In North America, **Society for Accessible Travel and Hospitality (SATH)**, Suite 605, 347 5th Av, New York, NY 10016, T1-212-447 7284, www.sath.org.

Drugs

Penalties are harsh – expect a lengthy jail term at least – for trafficking even modest quantities. **Prisoners Abroad**, 83-93 Fonthill Rd, London N4 3JH, UK, T020-75616821, www.prisonersabroad.org.uk, is a charity dedicated to supporting UK nationals in

Useful words and phrases

Pronunciation is not difficult as there is a close relationship between the way the letter is written and the sound. Stress is usually on the second syllable.

You will be asked constantly 'Where are you going?' (*Wake mana?*) as it is a common form of Indonesian address. Try saying '*cuci mata*' ('washing my eye'), which means relaxing, or '*makan angin*' ('eating the air').

Yes/no	*Ya/tidak*
Thank you	*Terima kasih*
Excuse me, sorry!	*Ma'af*
Welcome	*Selamat datang*
Good morning	*Selamat pagi*
Good afternoon	*Selamat sore*
Good evening	*Selamat malam*
Where's the ...?	*... dimana?*
How much is ...?	*... berapa harganya?*
I (don't) understand	*Saya (tidak) mengerti*

prison abroad. If you or a friend find yourself in the unfortunate position of being in jail, or facing a jail term, then contact the charity.

Gay and lesbian travel

Indonesia is surprisingly tolerant of homosexuality given that it goes against the tenets of both traditional Muslim and Balinese religions. Homosexuality is legal; the age of consent is 16 years for men and women. Indonesian men are generally more affectionate in public, which allows foreign gay men to blend in more easily. Bali is the only island with an established gay area centred on Kuta, with some bars, restaurants and areas which are patronized by, but not exclusive to, gay people. Few Indonesian men make a living as 'rent boys'; however, as a foreigner you will be expected to pay for meals, transport and accommodation. For more information, see www.qrd.org/qrd/world/asia/indonesia/indonesian.lesbian.and.gay.network.

Health
Health risks

Mosquito repellent is essential. Malaria tablets are necessary for travel in some parts of the archipelago, but not necessary for Bali or Java. Some local residents swear by *Minyak Gosok Tawan* (lemon balm oil) or *Minyak Kayu Putih* (camphor oil) to keep mosquitoes at bay. **Tiger Balm** is also good for itchy bites. There are no strong mosquito repellents available outside

Jakarta. The locally produced **Autan** is not effective. Get advice from your doctor.

Vaccinations

None required unless visitors have been in a cholera, yellow fever or smallpox-infected area 6 days prior to arrival.

Internet

Email is very popular in Indonesia, and any town of any size has its internet café. Costs vary from 3000Rp-20,000Rp per hr.

Language

The national language is Bahasa Indonesia, which is written in Roman script. There are 250 regional languages and dialects, of which Sundanese (the language of West Java and Jakarta) is the most widespread. In Padang and elsewhere in West Sumatra, the population speak Minang, which is also similar to Bahasa. About 70% of the population can speak Bahasa. English is the most common foreign language, with some Dutch and Portuguese speakers.

Bahasa Indonesia is relatively easy to learn, a small number of useful words and phrases are listed in the box above. For visitors interested in studying Bahasa Indonesia in more depth, the Cornell course, though expensive, is recommended www.lrc.cornell.edu/asian/courses/summer/indonesian.

The best way to learn Indonesian is to study it intensively in Indonesia. In Jakarta

Transport costs

In May 2008, the Indonesian government raised fuel prices by 30% in order to counter the blows to the national budget caused by soaring oil prices. This has led to rising transportation and food costs and despite the subsidies promised to the nation's poor, has caused significant social unrest in many of the nation's larger cities. The research for parts of this book (Bali, Lombok, Flores) was done just before the price increase and readers should be aware that costs of food and transport have gone up, reflecting the 30% hikes in many cases.

and Bali, a variety of short and long courses (including homestay programmes in Bali) are available through **The Indonesia-Australia Language Foundation, (IALF)** T021 5213350, www.ialf.edu. In Yogyakarta, another centre where overseas students study Indonesian, courses are run by the **Realia Language School**, www.realia.com, T0274 583229, which is recommended. It is cheaper if a group learns together.

Media

The best English language newspaper is the *Jakarta Post*. The *Asian Wall Street Journal* and the *International Herald Tribune* can be purchased in Jakarta and some other major cities and tourist destinations; so too can the *Singapore Straits Times*.

Radio Republik Indonesia (*RRI*) broadcasts throughout the country. News and commentary in English is broadcast for about 1 hr a day. Shortwave radios will pick up *Voice of America*, the *BBC World Service* and *Australian Broadcasting*.

Televisi Republik Indonesia (*TVRI*) is the government-run channel. There are also private stations showing news and occasional English-language films and documentaries.

Money → *US$1 = 9143Rp (Aug 2008)*.

The unit of currency in Indonesia is the rupiah (Rp).1Rp equals 100 sen. Denominations are 100, 500, 1000, 5000, 10,000, 20,000, 50,000, 100,000. Coins are in 100Rp and 500Rp denominations. When taking US$ in cash, make sure the bills are new and crisp, as banks in Indonesia can be fussy about which bills they accept (Flores and Sumatra are particularly bad). Larger denomination US$ bills also tend to command a premium exchange rate. In more out of the way places it is worth making sure that you have a stock of smaller notes and coins – it can be hard to break larger bills.

Two of the better banks are **Bank Negara Indonesia (BNI)** and **Bank Central Asia (BCA)**. BNI is reliable and efficient and most of their branches will change US$ TCs. They also give one of the best rates and have offices across the archipelago. BCA is also very efficient, but does not have such a wide distribution of branches. Banks in larger towns and tourist centres have ATMs.

It is easiest to change cash or TCs in all major currencies in Bali, although all the tourist centres offer money-changing facilities at competitive rates. The very best rates are from the money changers in Kuta; larger denomination notes get a better rate.

Major credit cards (mainly Visa and Master-Card) are accepted in larger establishments, often subject to a 3% surcharge.

Credit card representatives Amex Bali Beach Hotel, Sanur, T0361 286060; **Diners Club** Jl Veteran 5, Denpasar, T0361 235584; **Visa and MasterCard** Jl Veteran 3, Denpasar, T0361 227138.

Cost of travelling

Visitors staying in 1st-class hotels and eating in hotel restaurants will probably spend upwards of US$110 a day. Tourists on a mid-range budget, staying in cheaper a/c accommodation and eating in local restaurants, will probably spend about US$33 a day. A backpacker, staying in fan-cooled guesthouses and eating cheaply, could live on US$16.50 a day. Because of the volatility of the domestic currency, coupled with rapid inflation, prices have been highly unstable. Or rather they have escalated in rupiah terms. There is every chance that the prices quoted here have increased, sometimes markedly. This is especially so at the moment; May 2008 saw oil prices increase in Indonesia by 30%.

Passports

All visitors to Indonesia must possess passports valid for at least 6 months from their date of arrival in Indonesia, and they should have proof of onward trave. It is not uncommon for immigration officers to ask to see a ticket out of the country. (A Batam–Singapore ferry ticket or cheap Medan–Penang air ticket will suffice). Many visitors find that immigration officials are happy with some indication that sufficient funds (for example a credit card) are available to purchase a return flight.

Post

The postal service is relatively reliable; though important mail should be registered. Every town and tourist centre has either a *kantor pos* (post office) or postal agent, where you can buy stamps, post letters and parcels; in many cases they also provide poste restante services.

Safety

Despite the recent media coverage of terrorist plots and attacks, riots and other disturbances in Indonesia, it remains a safe country and violence against foreigners is rare. Petty theft is a minor problem.

Avoid carrying large amounts of cash; TCs can be changed in most major towns. Pickpockets frequent the public transport systems. Keep a close watch on your bags going through security checkpoints at airports; some travellers have reported that their bags were stolen before they could retrieve them after having passed through the X-ray machine.

Beware of the confidence tricksters who are widespread in tourist areas. Sudden reports of unbeatable bargains or closing down sales are usual ploys.

Civil unrest The following areas of Indonesia have seen disturbances in recent years and visits are not recommended: Maluku (around Ambon), Central Sulawesi (around Palu). Both these places have been victims of sectarian violence. However, these incidents have been localized and almost never affected foreign visitors. Recent fuel price hikes have seen widespread civil unrest in major cities, especially in Java. These protests are not aimed towards foreigners.

Flying After a series of accidents the EU banned Indonesian airlines from entering its airspace over continuing concerns of poor maintenance and safety. The Indonesian government and airline companies have taken this very seriously and 2008 has seen brand new Boeings and Airbuses being rolled out by **Lion Air** and **Mandala**. Many European embassies still advise against domestic air travel. For the latest information, see www.fco.gov.uk/en/travelling-and-living-overseas/travel-advice-by-country/asia-oceania/indonesia1, and http://travel.state.gov/travel_warnings.html.

Student travellers

Anyone in full-time education is entitled to an **International Student Identity Card (ISIC)**. These are issued by student travel offices and travel agencies across the world, and offer special rates on all forms of transport and other concessions and services. www.isic.org.

Telephone → *Country code +62.*

Operator T101. International enquiries T102. Local enquiries T108. Long distance enquiries T106. Every town has its communication centres (**Warpostel**), where you can make local, interlocal (between other areas within Indonesia) and international calls and faxes. Most Warpostels open early in the morning and operate until around 2400. Interlocal calls are cheaper after 2100, so centres tend to be very busy then. International calls are cheap 2400-0800 and all Sat and Sun. Calls are expensive. Telephone cards (*Kartu telepon*) are sold in Warpostels, supermarkets and shops.

International calls can be made from card phones and from **Perumtel**, **Telekom** and **Wartel** offices, which are often open 24 hrs.

Mobile phones Known as handphones in Indonesia, use has sky rocketed and costs are unbelievably low. It usually costs around 10,000Rp to by a SIM card with a number. Top-up cards are sold at various denominations. If you buy a 10,000Rp or 20,000Rp card, the vendor will charge a few more thousand, in order to gain some profit. If you buy a 100,000Rp card, you will pay a few thousand less than 100,000Rp. This is standard practice throughout the country. Beware of vendors in Kuta, Bali who try and sell SIM cards at highly inflated prices. Popular companies include **Telkomsel**, **IM3** (the cheapest for international calls – ask vendor about necessary prefix) and **Pro XL**.

Tax

Expect to pay 11% tax in the more expensive restaurants, particularly in tourist areas of Bali and Lombok. Some cheaper restaurants serving foreigners may add 10% to the bill. **Airport tax** 75,000Rp-150,000Rp on international flights (Jakarta and Denpasar are both 150,000Rp), and anywhere between 5000Rp and 30,000Rp on domestic flights, depending on the airport.

Tipping

Tipping is not usual. A 10% service charge is added to bills at more expensive hotels. Porters expect to be tipped about 2000Rp a bag. In more expensive restaurants, where no service is charged, a tip of 5-10% may be appropriate. Taxi drivers (in larger towns) appreciate a small tip (1000Rp). *Parkirs* always expect payment for 'watching' your car; 1000Rp.

Tourist information

The Directorate General of Tourism is in Jakarta with sub-offices known as **Kanwil**

Depparposte throughout the country. Each of Indonesia's provinces also has its own tourist office, known as **Deparda** or **Dinas Pariwisata**.

Indonesia Government Tourist Offices Ministry of Culture and Tourism, www.budpar.go.id.

Directorate General of Tourism (DGT), Jl Kramat Raya 81, PO Box 409, Jakarta, T021-63103117, F021-63101146.

British Council, Wijoyo Centre, Jl Jend Sudirman 71, Jakarta, T021 2524115, www.britishcouncil.org/indonesia.htm.

Tour operators

Arc Journeys, arcjourney@aol.com, www.travelarc.com, small group or bespoke tours to Southeast Asia and elsewhere.

Dragoman, info@dragoman.co.uk, www.dragoman.co.uk, adventure and cultural tours and expeditions to Southeast Asia and beyond.

Exodus, www.exodus.co.uk, small-group walking and trekking holidays, adventure tours and more.

Explore Worldwide, www.explore.co.uk, small group adventure tours across the world, including Southeast Asia.

Footprint Adventures, www.footprint-adventures.co.uk, trekking and wildlife trips to Southeast Asia and wider.

Guerba, www.guerba.co.uk, adventure and discovery holidays.

The Imaginative Traveller, www.imaginative-traveller.com, adventure tours to the world, including Southeast Asia.

Silk Steps, www.silksteps.co.uk, specialized itineraries ranging from trekking, diving, cultural and wildlife trips to several destinations in Asia.

STA Travel, www.stratravel.com.

Teaching and Projects Abroad, www.teaching-abroad.co.uk, offers work and experiences while you travel.

Worldwide Adventures Abroad, www.adventures-abroad.com, adventure tours organized for/in small groups.

Visas and immigration

Visitors from several nations, including Malaysia, Philippines and Singapore are allowed a visa-free stay of 30 days in Indonesia. Visitors from nations including the following are able to get a non-renewable, non-extendable US$25 30-day visa on arrival (VOA): Australia, Canada, France, Germany, Holland, Ireland, Italy, New Zealand, Portugal, Spain, United Kingdom, and the USA. Check with your embassy. Pay at a booth at the port of entry. Visitors from these countries may also get a 7-day VOA for US$10. Visitors wishing to obtain a VOA must enter and leave Indonesia though certain ports of entry, including the following:

Sea ports Batam, Tanjung Uban, Belawan (Medan), Dumai, Jayapura, Tanjung Balaikarimun, Bintang Pura (Tanjung Pinang), and Kupang.

Airports Medan, Pekanbaru, Padang, Jakarta, Surabaya, Bali, Manado, Adisucipto in Yogyakarta, Adisumarmo in Solo, and Selaparang in Mataram, Lombok.

60-day visitor visas (**B211**) are available at Indonesian embassies and consulates around the world (a ticket out of the country, 2 photos and a completed visa form is necessary). Costs vary. They can be extended giving a total stay of 6 months (must be extended at an immigration office in Indonesia each month after the initial 60-day visa has expired; take it to the office 4 days before expiry). To extend the visa in Indonesia, a fee of US$27 is levied and a sponsor letter from a local person is needed. Many hotels and travel agencies in Bali offer a visa extension service for around US$98. To obtain a 60-day visitor visa in Singapore, a 1-way ticket from Batam to Singapore is adequate: purchase from the ferry centre at Harbourfront in Singapore. See page 741.

It is crucial to check this information before travelling as the visa situation in Indonesia is extremely volatile. Travellers who overstay their visa can expect a fine of US$20 a day. Long-term overstayers can expect a fine and jail sentence. See www.indonesianembassy.org.uk for more information.

Women travellers

Women travelling alone face greater difficulties than men or couples. Young Southeast Asian women rarely travel without a partner, so it is believed to be strange for a western woman to do so. Western women are often believed to be of easy virtue. To minimize the pestering that will occur, dress modestly – particularly in staunchly Muslim areas, and in more out-of-the-way spots where locals may be unfamiliar with tourists. Comments, sometimes derogatory, will be made however carefully you dress and act; simply ignore them. Older women travelling alone will not face such problems and will be treated with great respect. Toiletries such as tampons are available in Indonesia's main cities, but may not be elsewhere.

Working

A tourist visa does not give you the right to work. Those caught working illegally face large fines and a possible jail sentence. A **working permit** (**KITAS**) sponsored by a local company is needed. The number of language schools has mushroomed in recent years, offering a chance of long-term employment. There are also **National Plus** schools, where a lot of the subjects are taught in English. For jobs in these 2 types of school, it is usually necessary to have a degree and a teaching certificate of some kind (CELTA, TESOL). However, there are many people working as teachers without these. Salaries are always enough to lead a comfortable local lifestyle, but Indonesia is not a place to come to save up vast amount of cash as an English teacher. For those with PGCEs, opportunities for well-paid teaching jobs exist in the country's International school. See www.tefl.com, www.davesesl cafe.com or www.tes.co.uk for teaching jobs. If you have a specialist skill such as diving instructor, you might find work in that field. See: www.divehappy.com/category/ scuba-diving-jobs and www.traveltree.co.uk/jobs/scuba-diving-jobs_dive-employment-training.htm.

Java

→ *Colour map 10.*

Java is Indonesia's political, economic and cultural heartland. With 60% of the country's population, the capital Jakarta, and the great bulk of Indonesia's industrial muscle, Java is the critical piece in the Indonesian jigsaw. It was here that many of the early, pre-colonial empires and kingdoms were based – reflected in monuments like Borobudur and Prambanan, and in many smaller temples. Cities like Yogyakarta and Solo remain vibrant artistic and cultural centres, while Bogor and Bandung show more clearly the hand of the relatively short-lived Dutch presence. The latter, particularly, is renowned for its art deco architecture. Jakarta, as Indonesia's capital, has the most restaurants, the largest museums, and the widest array of shopping, but it is not a particularly enticing city.

The hand of humans has always had to contend with the forces of nature and nowhere is this clearer than in the battle against Java's volcanoes. From Krakatau off the west coast of Java to Gunung Bromo in East Java, a spine of active volcanoes runs through the island. While these volcanoes periodically bring destruction, they also provide the basis for a string of hill resorts and towns.

Finally, Java may not have coral reefs to rival those of Nusa Tenggara but it does have a number of beach resorts both popular with budget travellers and as weekend get-aways for hassled Jakartans.

Jakarta

→ *Phone code: 021. Colour map 10, A2.*

Jakarta is Indonesia's centre of commerce and communications, of manufacturing activity and consumption, of research and publishing. It has the highest per capita income and the greatest concentration of rupiah billionaires. Jakarta is not often rated very highly as a tourist attraction, but if visitors can tolerate the traffic, then it is possible to spend an enjoyable few days visiting the excellent museums, admiring the architectural heritage of the Dutch era, strolling through the old harbour or discovering some of the many antique, arts and crafts shops.

Today, Jakarta is a sprawling, cosmopolitan city, with a population of over 11,500,000 – making it the largest city in Indonesia. Growth has been extremely rapid. Jakarta, like Bangkok, is perceived by the poorer rural Indonesians as a city paved with gold, and they have flocked to the capital in their thousands.

The central area is dominated by office blocks, international hotels and wide, tree-lined roads. Off the main thoroughfares, the streets become smaller and more intimate, almost village-like. These are the densely inhabited kampongs where immigrants have tended to live – one-storey, tile-roofed houses crammed together and linked by a maze of narrow paths. Initially, kampongs developed their own identity, with people from particular language and ethnic groups, even from particular towns, congregating in the same place and maintaining their individual identities. Today those distinctions are less obvious, but the names of the kampongs are a reminder of their origins: Kampong Bali, Kampong Aceh (North Sumatra) and Kampong Makassar (Ujung Pandang), for example.

▸▸ *For listings see pages 194-204.*

Ins and outs

Getting there

Jakarta's Soekarno-Hatta Airport ① *T021 5505177*, where most visitors arrive, lies 25 km northwest of the city, and connects Jakarta with all other major cities and towns in the country, as well as regional and global destinations. State-owned **Garuda** and international airlines operate from Terminal 2. Domestic airlines use Terminal 1. Shuttle buses link the international and domestic terminals, but they stop early evening.

Facilities at the airport include car rental, currency exchange booths, ATMs, left-luggage facilities (outside the arrivals hall), hotel booking counter (although we have received complaints concerning the sending of visitors to sub-standard hotels for which the reservation office staff receive a commission), a taxi desk, tourist information desk (with maps), the **Transit Hotel**, the **Transit Restaurant**, fast food outlets, a 24-hour post office, long-distance calls, and fax facilities.

Metered taxis to the centre of town cost about 85,000Rp (plus toll fees of 10,500Rp). The unofficial taxi drivers who solicit for fares from unsuspecting tourists are usually a more expensive option than metered taxis – and also more risky. A good tip is to go up to the second floor where there is less hassle and many empty taxis. The airport authorities now hand out complaints cards for visitors to complete, setting out the toll charges and surcharges applicable. Allow at least an hour to reach the airport from the centre of town, more at peak times. **Damri** ① *T021 5501290*, runs air-conditioned buses from Terminal 2 F/E with Jakarta's Gambir railway station every half hour from 0500-1830 (one hour, 15,000Rp).

The **Gambir railway station** is also a major arrival point in Jakarta. There is a **Blue Bird** taxi rank just to the north of the station, which charges a 4500Rp surcharge. The journey to Jalan Jaksa costs around 20,000Rp (the centre for budget accommodation). Alternatively, those with little luggage will be able to manage the 10-minute walk. Air-conditioned Damri buses also run to Blok M, Jalan Bulungan, and Kemayoran (former domestic airport). There are also some buses running to Bogor, for those that want to avoid Jakarta. Many of the first-class hotels lay on transport. In addition, if travelling on **Merpati**, it is possible to check in at Gambir and then take advantage of their free airport shuttle. If you are travelling straight to Bogor, there is a frequent direct bus service from Terminal 2, recommended if you can't face Jakarta on Day 1.

Tourist information

The **Jakarta Tourist Office** ① *Jakarta Theatre Building, Jl MH Thamrin 9, T021 3142067, Mon-Fri 0900-1700, www.jakarta-tourism.go.id,* supplies maps and information on sights in the city and are the most helpful and friendly to be found in Jakarta.

Sights

Kota or Old Batavia

① *From the centre, take bus P16 or P17 to Terminal Bis Kota, or microlet M08 or M12 (among others), or a taxi.*

The city of Jakarta developed from the small area known as **Kota**, which stretches from the *Pasar Ikan* (Fish Market), to Jalan Jembatan Batu, just south of Kota train station. The area is about 8 km north of both Monas and many of the city's hotels and guesthouses. North of Pasar Ikan was the old harbour town of **Sunda Kelapa** ① *admission to harbour area 1500Rp,*

1 Jakarta

➡ Jakarta maps
1 Jakarta, page 187
2 Kota, page 188
3 Jakarta Centre, page 190

Eating 🍴
Anatolia 1
Cafe Amor 2
Gourmet Garage 3
Kinara 4
Loewy 5
Trattoria 6

Bars & clubs 🍸
Bugil's 7
CJs 8

Cork & Screw 9
Embassy 10
Fez 14
Red Square 11
Stadium 12
Vin + 13
Vino Embassy 14

800 metres
800 yards

daily 0800-1800, which thrived from the 12th century to 1527 and is still worth a visit today. *Sunda* refers to the region of West Java and *Kelapa* means coconut. Impressive Bugis or Makassar schooners dock here on their inter-island voyages and can be seen moored along the wharf. Gradually, they are being supplanted by modern freighters, but for the time being at least it is possible to see these graceful ships being loaded and unloaded by wiry barefoot men, who cross precariously between the wharf and the boats along narrow planks. Boatmen will offer visitors the chance to ride in a small boat around the harbour, which gives a fascinating glimpse into life on the water. A 30-minute trip should cost around 40,000Rp, but hard bargaining is required. It is also sometimes possible to arrange a passage on one of the boats to Kalimantan and elsewhere in the archipelago – ask around.

On the southern edge of Sunda Kelapa and close to the Lookout Tower (see below) is the original, and still functioning, **Pasar Ikan**. The market is an odd mixture of ship chandlers, tourist stalls and food outlets. Among the merchandise on sale are sea shells, toy *kijangs*, carvings and unfortunate stuffed animals. Close by at Jalan Pasar Ikan 1 is the **Bahari (Maritime) Museum** ⓘ *T021 6693406, Tue-Sun 0900-1500, 2000Rp*, which was one of the original Dutch warehouses used for storing spices, coffee and tea. Today it is home to an unimpressive maritime collection. However, upstairs is an interesting display of photographs dating from the late 19th and early 20th centuries, recording life on board the steamships that linked Batavia with Holland. The museum is worth a visit for the building rather than its contents. Other warehouses behind this museum were built between 1663 and 1669. The area around the Pasar Ikan is due to be developed further as a tourist attraction (this has been on the cards for some years now and has yet to manifest), recreating the atmosphere of the Dutch period by renovating and reconstructing the original buildings.

Overlooking the fetid **Kali Besar** (Big Canal), choked with rubbish and biologically dead, is the **Uitkijk** (Lookout Tower) ① *daily 0900-1700, 2000Rp*, built in 1839 on the walls of the Dutch fortress Bastion Culemborg (itself constructed in 1645). The tower was initially used to spy on (and signal to) incoming ships, and later as a meteorological post – a role it continued to fill until this century. From the top of the tower there are views north over the port of Sunda Kelapa and south to the city, over an area of poor housing and urban desolation.

Less than 1 km from the Bahari Museum and Sunda Kelapa, south along either Jalan Cangkeh or Jalan Kapak, is one of the last **Dutch-era drawbridges** across the Kali Besar. It was built over two centuries ago and is known as the Chicken Market Bridge, but it has been allowed to fall into disrepair. Continuing south for another 200 m or so, walking past old Dutch warehouses, godowns and other commercial buildings, is **Fatahillah Square**, or **Taman Fatahillah**. This was the heart of the old Dutch city and the site of public executions and punishments – hangings, death by impalement and public floggings. It was also a bustling market place. In the middle of the square is a small, domed building (rebuilt in 1972), the site of the old drinking fountain. The Dutch were unaware that the water from this fountain was infested, and it contributed to the city's high incidence of cholera and consequently high mortality rate. On the south side of the square is the **Fatahillah Museum**, on the site of the first City Hall built in 1620. A second hall was constructed in 1627 and today's building was completed in 1710. A fine example of Dutch architecture (reminiscent of the old city hall of Amsterdam), it became a military headquarters after independence and finally, in 1974, the **Museum of the History of Jakarta** ① *T021 6929101, Tue-Sun 0900-1500, 2000Rp*. It is a lovely building but, like so many Indonesian museums, the collection is poorly laid out. It contains Dutch furniture and VOC memorabilia. In the courtyard behind the museum, two *ondel-ondel* figures stand outside another room of rather down-at-heel exhibits. Below the main building are the prison cells.

➡ **Jakarta maps**
1 Jakarta, page 187
2 Kota, page 188
3 Jakarta Centre, page 190

Sleeping
Batavia 1

Eating
Café Batavia 1

The **Wayang Museum** ① *on the west side of the square at Jl Pintu Besar Utara 27, T021 6829560, Tue-Sun 0900-1500, 2000Rp,* was previously called the Museum of Old Batavia. All that remains of the original 1912 building is its façade. Until 1974 it housed the collection now in the Fatahillah Museum, and today contains a good collection of *wayang kulit* and *wayang golek* puppets. Well-made examples are sold here for US$22-77. Performances of *wayang kulit* or *wayang golek* are occasionally held here (enquire at tourist office). West from the Wayang Museum and over the Kali Besar (canal) is the **Toko Merah** or Red House. This was once the home of Governor-General Gustaaf van Imhoff. There are some other interesting 18th century Dutch buildings in the vicinity.

On the north side of Fatahillah Square is an old Portuguese bronze cannon called **Si Jagur**, brought to Batavia by the Dutch after the fall of Melaka in 1641. The design of a clenched fist is supposed to be a symbol of cohabitation and it is visited by childless women in the hope that they will be rendered fertile. On the east side of the square is the **Balai Seni Rupa** (Fine Arts Museum), formerly the Palace of Justice at Jalan Pos Kota 2. Built in the 1860s, it houses a poor exhibition of paintings by Indonesian artists. The building is shared with the **Museum Keramik** ① *T021 6907062, Tue-Sun 0900-1500, 2000Rp,* a collection of badly displayed ceramics. The most stylish place to eat and drink on the square is at the **Café Batavia** – itself something of an architectural gem in Indonesian terms. It was built in stages between 1805 and 1850 and is the second oldest building on the square (after the City Hall). Particularly fine is the renovated Grand Salon upstairs, made of Java teak. The café was opened at the end of 1993 and is frequented by foreigners and the Indonesian wealthy. There is a **tourist information office** next to the café and, next to this, a **clothes market,** which functions every day except Sunday.

East of Kota railway station on the corner of Jalan Jembatan Batu and Jalan Pangeran is the oldest church in Jakarta, **Gereja Sion** ① *admission by donation in the adjacent church office,* also known as the 'old Portuguese Church' or 'Gereja Portugis'. It was built for the so-called 'Black Portuguese', Eurasian slaves brought to Batavia by the Dutch from Portuguese settlements in India and Ceylon. These slaves were promised freedom, provided that they converted to the Dutch Reformed Church. The freed men and women became a social group known as *Mardijkers* (Liberated Ones). The church was built in 1693 and is a fine example of the Baroque style, with a handsome carved wooden pulpit and an elaborately carved organ. The four chandeliers are of yellow copper.

Central Jakarta

South of Fatahillah Square is **Glodok**, or **Chinatown**. This lies outside the original city walls and was the area where the Chinese settled after the massacre of 1740. Despite a national ban on the public display of Chinese characters that was only rescinded in August 1994, Glodok's warren of back streets still feels like a Chinatown: with shophouses, enterprise and activity, and temples tucked behind shop fronts. Midway between Fatahillah Square and Merdeka Square is the **National Archives** or **Arsip Nasional**. This building (which no longer holds the National Archives) was erected in 1760 as a country house for Reiner de Klerk, a wealthy resident who subsequently became governor-general. Since 1925, it has been owned by the state and now houses an interesting collection of Dutch furniture.

The enormous **Medan Merdeka** (Liberty Square) dominates the centre of Jakarta. It measures 1sq km and is one of the largest city squares in the world. In the centre of Medan Merdeka is the **National Monument (Monas)**, a 137-m-high pinnacle meant to represent a *lingga* and thus symbolize fertility and national independence. This massive obelisk was

3 Jakarta centre

➡ **Jakarta maps**
1 Jakarta, page 187
2 Kota, page 188
3 Jakarta Centre, page 190

Sleeping
Bloemsteen **6**
Borneo Hostel **7**
Borobudur **1**
Cemara **8**
Cipta **9**
Gondia International
 Guesthouse **3**
Karya Bahana **13**
Kresna Hostel **6**
Margot Homestay **15**
Nikko **12**
Rota International **11**
Sari Pan Pacific &
 Flanagan's Bar **5**
Sofyan Betawi **14**
Sofyan Cikini **2**
Tator **16**
Wisma Delima **17**
Yannie International
 Guesthouse **18**

Eating
Al Jazeerah **7**
Bakoel Koffie **5**
Bombay Blue **2**
Cafe au Cait **4**
Cafe Cartel **6**
Hanoi House **8**
Imperial Treasure La Mian
 Xiao Long Bao **23**
Jasa Bundo **9**
Kedai Tiga Nyonya **16**
KL Village Kopitiam **10**
Oh La La **6**
Pappa **11**
Penang Bistro **17**
Samarra **15**
Sate Khas Senayan **18**
Shanghai Blue **14**
Tony Roma's **13**
Warung Daun **3**
Y&Y **8**

Bars & clubs
Absolute Cafe **19**
Ali's **20**
BB's **21**
Memories Cafe **22**
Romance Cafe **12**

commissioned by President Sukarno in 1961 to celebrate Indonesia's independence from the Dutch. Construction entailed the bulldozing of a large squatter community to make way for the former President's monumental ambitions. It is known among residents of the city, rather irreverently, as Sukarno's Last Erection. Covered in Italian marble, it is topped by a bronze flame (representing the spirit of the revolutionaries), coated in 35 kg of gold leaf. Take the lift to the observation platform for magnificent views over the city. In the basement below the monument is a **museum** ① *T021 70649354, daily 0830-1700 (closed last Mon of the month), 7250Rp for the museum and trip to the top of the structure. For 2750Rp, visitors can access the museum and the lower part of the structure, ticket booth to the north of the monument. Avoid going at weekends when there are long queues and general mayhem, as tourists from all over the country descend on the site for a visit.* This houses dioramas depicting the history of Indonesia's independence. The entrance to the museum is north of the road immediately in front of the monument (access is through an underground tunnel), where there is a **statue of Diponegoro** (a Javanese hero) on horseback. He was held prisoner by the Dutch at the Batavia town hall, before being exiled to Manado in North Sulawesi.

On the west side of the square is the neoclassical **National Museum** ① *T021 3868172, Sun, Tue-Thu 0830-1430, Fri 0830-1130, Sat 0830-1330, 750Rp, guided English language tours available at 1030 on Tue and Thu. See the Jakarta Post for details as times and days vary, or call the Indonesian Heritage Society on T021 5725870.* Established in 1860 by the Batavian Fine Arts Society, it is an excellent museum and well worth a visit. Set around a courtyard, the collection consists of some fine stone sculpture (mostly of Hindu gods), a textile collection (recently skilfully reorganized), and a collection of mainly Chinese ceramics found in Indonesia. Next to the ceramics is a display of bronzeware, including some magnificent Dongson drums and krisses. The pre-history room is well laid out. Its collection includes the skull cap and thigh bone of Java Man, a rare example of *Homo erectus*. The ethnographic collection includes an excellent range of masks, puppets, household articles, musical instruments and some models of traditional buildings representing cultures from several of the main islands in the archipelago. There is also handicraft shop and a telecommunications centre here (visitors can send faxes, telexes and make long-distance phone calls), set up by a museum cooperative.

To the west of the National Museum is the rarely visited **Museum Taman Prasasti** or the **Ancient Inscription Museum** ① *Jl Tanah Abang, 1750Rp, Tue-Thu 0900-1500, Fri 0900-1300, Sat 0900-1400 (in theory – do not be surprised to find it closed).* This open-air museum occupies part of a former Christian cemetery, the Kebon Jahe Kober, where high-ranking Dutch officials were buried from the late 18th century onwards, including Mrs Olivia Marianne Raffles (Stamford Raffles' first wife). The curators have also felt the site appropriate for the display of traditional gravestones from Indonesia's 27 provinces.

On the north side of the square is the neo-classical Presidential Palace or **Istana Merdeka**, built in 1861 and set in immaculate gardens. Originally named **Koningsplein Paleis**. President Sukarno resided at the Istana Merdeka, but President Suharto moved to a more modest residence and the building is now only used for state occasions. Behind the palace is the older **State Palace** (Istana Negara), next to the Bina Graha (the presidential office building). This palace was built for a Dutchman at the end of the 18th century and was the official residence of Dutch Governors-General, before the Koningsplein Palace was built. To get to the State Palace, walk down Jalan Veteran 3 and turn west on Jalan Veteran.

In the northeast corner of Medan Merdeka is the impressive **Istiqlal Mosque**, finished in 1978 after more than 10 years' work. The interior is simple and is almost entirely constructed of marble. It is the principal place of worship for Jakarta's Muslims and reputedly the largest mosque in Southeast Asia, with room for more than 10,000 worshippers. Non-Muslims can visit the mosque when prayers are not in progress. Facing the mosque, in the northwest corner of Lapangan Banteng (see below), is the strange neo-Gothic **Catholic Cathedral**; its date of construction is unknown, but it was restored in 1901.

Due east of the mosque is **Lapangan Banteng**, (Buffalo Field), used by the Dutch military during the late 18th century. This area has some of Jakarta's best 19th-century colonial Dutch architecture. Daendels built a huge palace on this square in 1809; it is now the Department of Finance. Next door is the Supreme Court. In 1828, the Waterloo Memorial was erected in the centre of the Lapangan Banteng. Demolished by the Japanese during their wartime occupation, it has since been replaced by the **Irian Jaya Liberation Monument**. Positioned as it is in front of the Treasury, residents wryly joked that the figure's stance, with raised, open hands, was not one of freedom but represented the exclamation 'kosong', or 'empty' (referring to the Treasury).

From the south corner of Lapangan Banteng, Jalan Pejambon runs south past **Gedung Pancasila**, the building where Sukarno gave his famous proklamasi, outlining the five principles of Pancasila (see page 429). At the southern end of Jalan Pejambon, backing onto Merdeka Square, is the **Gereja Immanuel**, an attractive circular domed church, built by Dutch Protestants in the classical style in 1835.

West of the city centre

The **Textile Museum** ① Jl Satsuit Tuban 4, near the Tanah Abang Market (and railway station), T021 6907062, Tue-Thu 0900-1600, Fri 0900-1130, Sat 0900-1300, 2000Rp, take bus P16, is housed in an airy Dutch colonial house set back from the road. It contains a good range of Indonesian textiles, both batik and ikat.

South of the city centre

The **Adam Malik Museum** ① 29 Jl Diponegoro, west from the junction with Jl Surabaya, Tue-Sat 1000-1300, Sun 0930-1300, 2500Rp, get there by bus or taxi, houses a unique private collection. The quirky collection includes cameras, radios, walking sticks and watches, as well as Chinese ceramics, woodcarving from Irian Jaya, stone carvings from Java, ostentatious furniture, guns, krisses and some interesting Russian icons. The problem with this museum is its lack of discrimination. The interesting and the commonplace, the skilled and the inept, are all massed together.

The **Satriamandala Museum** ① Jl Gatot Subroto, opposite the Kastika Chandra Hotel, Tue-Sun 0900-1530, or Armed Forces Museum, was formerly the home of Dewi Sukarno, wife of the late President. Today it houses a display of armaments and a series of dioramas, showing steps towards Indonesia's independence.

A night-time drive, or perhaps even a walk down **Jalan Latuharhary** in Menteng, reveals a seedier – or at least an alternative – side of life in Jakarta. Transvestites, dressed up to the nines, and known as banci (meaning hermaphrodite or homosexual) or waria, hawk their wares. Foreign visitors may be astonished not only by their beauty, but also by the fact that this is countenanced in an otherwise relatively strict Muslim society. Transvestites have, in fact, a long and honourable tradition not just in Indonesia but throughout Southeast Asia.

The large, wholesale, **Pasar Cikini**, in the district of Menteng, is worth a visit to see the range of fruit, vegetables, fish and other fresh products trucked in from the surrounding countryside and the coast for sale in Jakarta. The second floor houses a gold market.

Around Jakarta

Taman Mini-Indonesia

ⓘ T021 8409214, www.tamanmini.com, park admission 9000Rp plus additional charges for major attractions, daily 0800-1700, 18 km and a rather arduous journey by public transport from the city centre – take a bus to Kampong Rambutan terminal and from there a bemo to the park (1-1½ hrs), or a taxi from town for about US$16.50.

This is a 120-ha 'cultural park', 10 km southeast of Jakarta (but closer to 20 km from the centre). Completed in 1975, there are 27 houses, each representing one of Indonesia's provinces and built in the traditional style of that region, although the building materials used are modern substitutes. Frustratingly, no translation of the descriptions is offered. All the houses are set around a lake with boats for hire. It is possible to drive around the park on weekdays or, alternatively, walk, take the mini train, cable car or horse and cart (small charges for these). The cable car takes passengers over the lake, upon which there is a replica of the whole archipelago. The **Keong Mas Theatre** ⓘ *daily 1100-1700, 20,000Rp* (so-called because its shape resembles a golden snail) presents superb not-to-be-missed films on Indonesia, projected on an enormous imax screen – check *Jakarta Post* for details of screenings). The **Museum Indonesia** ⓘ *0900-1500*, a Balinese-style building, houses a good collection of arts and crafts and costumes from across the archipelago. The **Museum Komodo** ⓘ *0800-1500* is, as the name suggests, built in the form of the *Varanus komodiensis*, better known as the Komodo dragon. It houses dioramas of Indonesian fauna and flora. There's also an aquarium, an insectarium, an orchid garden, aviaries and a swimming pool.

Pulau Seribu ⊖ ⟩⟩ pp194-204. Colour map 10, A1.

Pulau Seribu, or 'Thousand Islands', clearly named by the mathematically challenged, actually consists of 112 small islands. Just to the west of Jakarta, off Java's north coast, they are becoming increasingly popular as a tourist destination. The Dutch VOC had a presence on the islands from the 17th century, building forts, churches and shipyards.

Pulau Onrust is one of the closest islands to the mainland. It was used by the Dutch from the early 17th century and became an important ship repair centre; by 1775 as many as 2000 people were living on the island. But in the 1800s the British sacked and burnt the small settlement, so that today only ruins remain. **Pulau Bidadari** also has ruins of a fort and leper hospital built by the VOC. It lies 15 km from Ancol (45 minutes by speedboat). **Pulau Laki** is one of the inner islands situated 3 km offshore from Tanjung Kait west of Jakarta.

Venturing further north into the Java Sea, there are a succession of privately-owned resorts including **Pulau Ayer**, **Pulau Putri**, **Pulau Pelangi**, **Pulau Kotok** and **Pulau Panjang**, in that order. They have beautiful beaches and offer snorkelling, scuba-diving, jet skiing and windsurfing.

Krakatau ▲⊖ ⟩⟩ pp194-204. Colour map 10, A1.

Krakatau is the site of the largest volcanic eruption ever recorded. The explosion occurred on the morning of the 27 August 1883, had a force equivalent to 2000 Hiroshima bombs, and resulted in the death of 36,000 people. A tsunami (tidal wave) 40 m high, radiating outwards at speeds of reportedly over 500 kph, destroyed coastal towns and villages. The explosion was heard from Sri Lanka to Perth in Australia and the resulting waves led to a noticeable surge in the English Channel. The explosion was such that the 400-m-high cone was replaced by a marine trench 300 m deep.

Rupert Furneau writes in his book *Krakatoa* (1965): "At 10 o'clock plus two minutes, three-quarters of Krakatau Island, 11 square miles of its surface, an area not much less than Manhattan, a mass of rock and earth one and one-eighth cubic miles in extent, collapsed into a chasm beneath. Nineteen hours of continuous eruption had drained the magma from the chamber faster than it could be replenished from below. Their support removed, thousands of tons of roof rock crashed into the void below. Krakatau's three cones caved in. The sea bed reared and opened in upheaval. The sea rushed into the gaping hole. From the raging cauldron of seething rocks, frothing magma and hissing sea, spewed an immense quantity of water... From the volcano roared a mighty blast, Krakatau's death cry, the greatest volume of sound recorded in human history".

In 1927, further volcanic activity caused a new island to rise above the sea – Anak Krakatau (child of Krakatau). Today this island stands 200 m above sea-level and visitors may walk from the east side of the island upon the warm, devastated landscape through deep ash, to the main crater. It remains desolate and uninhabited, though the other surrounding islands have been extensively recolonized (a process carefully recorded by naturalists; the first visitor after the 1883 explosion noted a spider vainly spinning a web). Check that the volcano is safe to visit and take thick-soled walking shoes (Krakatau is still avowedly active: between 1927 and 1992 it erupted no less than 73 times). There is good snorkelling and diving in the water around the cliffs; the undersea thermal springs cause abundant marine plant growth and this attracts a wealth of sea creatures, big and small.

The sea crossing is calmest and the weather best from April to June and September to October. Between November and March there are strong currents and often rough seas.

Note Anak Krakatau is currently highly active and tourists are NOT permitted to climb the crater. This is due to spewing molten rocks and potentially fatal toxic gases. Tourists can land on Anak Krakatau for a wander, at their own risk. Check the latest information before heading out, as the volcano has been put on the highest alert several times already in 2008.

⊕ Jakarta listings

Hotel and guesthouse prices
LL over US$200 L US$151-200 AL US$101-150
A US$66-100 B US$46-65 C US$31-45
D US$21-30 E US$12-20 F US$7-11
G US$6 and under

Restaurant prices
♢♢♢ over US$12 ♢♢ US$6-12 ♢ under US$6

◐ Sleeping

Jakarta *p185, maps p187, p188 and p190*
Jalan Jaksa and around
This small street has been the backpackers' headquarters for years, with a large selection of budget lodgings, cheap Western eateries

and plenty of travel agents. Don't come here expecting Thailand's Khao San Rd, or the tourist quarter of Ho Chi Minh, this street is decidedly low key. Slightly more salubrious hotels are located in the streets around here.
B-C Hotel Cemara, Jl Cemara 1, T021 3908215, www.hotelcemara.com. For those that have travelled halfway around the world to get to Indonesia, this hotel is a fine place to get over the jetlag in comfort. Rooms are clean, and come with fridge and cable TV, and some have baths. Internet available in the room for 850Rp per min. Spa service available. Breakfast not included in the price. Recommended.
C-D Cipta Hotel, Jl Wahid Hasyim 53, T021 3904701, cipta1@cbn.net.id. Excellent service, although the mint walls and green carpet are

somewhat overbearing. Rooms are clean and spacious with cable TV and fridge. Wi-Fi is available in the lobby for 10,000Rp per hr. Tax and breakfast not included in the price.

C-D Rota International Hotel, Jl Wahid Hasyim 63, T021 3152858, www.rotatour-online.com. Plenty of choice, with a selection of clean a/c rooms (some are a bit dark, ask to see a selection) with TV and bath around a massive central courtyard.

D-E Hotel Karya Bahana, Jl Jaksa 32-34, T021 3140484, www.indo.com/hotels/karyabahana. Despite the somewhat seedy undertones, this place is not bad value, with clean a/c rooms with TV and bath. The big windows are a plus.

E Margot Homestay, Jl Jaksa 15C, T021 3913830, F021 31924641. Well-run place with a selection of a/c rooms with TV and decrepit furniture. There's a fair restaurant by the reception.

E-F Hotel Tator, Jl Jaksa 37, T021 31923940. Selection of a/c and fan rooms, which are a little faded but compare better than most of the other cheap Jaksa options.

F Borneo Hostel, Jl Kebon Sirih Barat 1, 37 (just off Jl Jaksa), T021 3140095. Hearty Christian vibes, but distinctly average lodgings with dirty walls and barred windows.

G Bloemsteen Hostel, Jl Kebon Sirih Timur 1, 175 (just of Jl Jaksa), T021 31923002. This has been the budget traveller's most popular choice for years now, and justifiably remains in pole position with small, spotless rooms and clean shared bathrooms. There is a pleasant balcony upstairs. It's often very busy, so booking ahead is wise. Recommended.

G Kresna Hostel, Jl Kebon Sirih Timur 175 (just off Jl Jaksa), T021 31925403. The few rooms here are in a family home. Rooms are spartan with a lightbulb hanging from the ceiling summing up the vibes. Squat toilet.

G Wisma Delima, Jl Jaksa 5, T021 31904157. This place used to be one of the most popular places on Jaksa, but it seems that literally no money has been invested here for a decade. Rooms are dirty, spartan and miserable. There are only 2 bathrooms (*mandi*) for the entire

hotel. Onwards bus tickets and overland tours can be booked from here.

Menteng and Cikini
There's a range of mid-priced accommodation scattered throughout this area.

B-C Hotel Sofyan Betawi, Jl Cut Meutia 9, T021 3905011, www.sofyanhotel.com. Popular with Indonesian business people, and has clean, comfortable rooms (some are a bit dark), with TV and bath. Broadband access is available.

B-C Hotel Sofyan Cikini, Jl Cikini Raya 79, T021 3140695, www.sofyanhotel.com. Prayer times are plastered all over this place, which is run with sharia principles and touts its high moral standards. The 110 smart rooms have TV, a/c and minibar (no booze).

E Gondia International Guesthouse, Jl Gondangdia Kecil 22, T021 3909221, www.geocities.com/gondia_hotel. Set down a small alley off Jl Gondangdia, this friendly place has decent, simple a/c rooms with TV and a small but pleasant garden.

E Yannie International Guesthouse, Jl Raden Saleh 35, T021 3140012. Yannie's is a little tricky to find, as there is no sign. Tell the taxi driver the address and he should be able to find it, also look for a large 'Y' sign. Popular with Arabs on a shoestring, this place has clean rooms with a/c and hot water.

Soekarno-Hatta Airport
A-B Jakarta Airport Hotel, Terminal 2 (above arrivals area), T021 5590008, www.jakartaairporthotel.com. Super location in the airport for those with a layover, or arriving late at night. Rooms are smart, and have a/c and cable TV. There is also a half-day (maximum 6 hrs stay) rate of US$50.

Elsewhere
LL-A Hotel Borobudur, Jl Lapangan Banteng Selatan, T021 3805555, www.hotelborobudur.com. This old dame is aging well, with friendly rather than stuffy service and a huge selection of rooms. The 693 rooms are set in rambling corridors

reminiscent of *The Shining*, seemingly identical and endless. Standard rooms are comfy, although a little aged. There is a raised seating area by the window with views over the hotel's extensive grounds.

L-A Hotel Nikko, Jl MH Thamrin 59, T021 2301122, www.nikkojakarta.com. Japanese minimalist style is in evidence aplenty here, in the gorgeous design and lack of staff. Rooms are clean, and super modern with good fabrics and plenty of space. Facilities include pool, fitness centre and plenty of restaurants, some with amazing views of the skyline. There is a shuttle bus from here to Plaza Indonesia (no more than 5 mins' walk), which gives some idea of the clientele.

AL-A Sari Pan Pacific, Jl MH Thamrin, T021 3902707, www.panpacific.com/jakarta. Busy business hotel, with intriguing façade. The carpeted a/c rooms are well decorated, although the beds look ancient, and have cable TV, bath and broadband access (US$15 for 24 hrs). Facilities include pool and fitness centre. Breakfast for 1 included in the price.

A-B The Batavia Hotel (formerly Omni Batavia), Jl Kali Besar Barat 44-46, T021 6904118, www.batavia-hotel.com. Stuck out on a limb down in Kota, this 4-star place is handy for a quick sightseeing trip around the old city, but not much else, and getting a cab from here takes some time. However, the price is not bad considering the good service, and clean rooms with cable TV and big, comfy beds. Pool, fitness centre.

🍴 Eating

Jakarta *p185, maps p187, p188 and p190*
Jakarta is the best place in Indonesia to eat, with a diverse collection of restaurants spread out all over the city and a growing middle class more willing to dip deeper into their pockets to fulfil gourmet fantasies.

Jalan Jaksa and around
₮₮₮-₮₮ Samarra, Jl Kebon Sirih 77, T021 3918690, 1100-2300. Gorgeous Arabic decor

lends a sense of opulence at this place serving Arab-Indonesian fusion food. The speciality of the house is *sate* served with numerous sauces. There is an excellent wine list and sheesha pipes are available. Belly dancers on Fri and Sat evenings. Recommended.

₮₮₮-₮₮ Shanghai Blue, Jl Kebon Sirih 79, T021 3918690, 1100-2300. Owned by the same group that runs Samarra next door, the decor here is similarly beautiful with modern, funky Chinese seating, 1920s portraits of Shanghainese ladies adorning the walls and sultry lighting. The fare is Betawi (local Jakarta)-Chinese fusion, with some interesting spins on the local cuisine. Marci, a renowned local singer, charms audiences on Wed and Fri nights.

₮₮-₮₮ Kedai Tiga Nyonya, Jl Wahid Hasyim 73, T021 8308360, 1100-2200. Peranakan (Straits Chinese) cuisine in a comfortable homely setting. This is a good place to try some *asam pedas* (hot and sour) dishes, or *soka* (soft crab).

₮₮-₮₮ Penang Bistro, Jl Kebon Sirih 59, T021 3190600, 1100-2200. Malaysian favourites served in sleek, clean a/c setting. Dishes include Hainan chicken rice, *roti canai* (Indian bread served with curry) and *kangkung belachan* (water spinach with prawn-based chilli sauce).

₮ The Cafe Cartel, Jakarta Theatre Building, Jl MH Thamrin 9, T021 3913875, Sun-Thu 1100-2400, Fri 1100-0100, Sat 1100-0300. Singaporean outfit serving up huge portions of ribs, burgers and naughty sticky deserts in a spotless environment.

₮ Tony Roma's, Jl Wahid Hasyim 49-51, T021 3842735, 1100-2300. North American favourites, specialising in ribs, with plenty of burgers and sandwiches all served on chequered table cloths.

₮ Jasa Bundo, Jl Jaksa 20, T0213905067, 1000-0100. Fair selection of *nasi Padang* dishes.

₮ KL Village Kopitiam, Jl Jaksa 21-23, T021 3148761, 0700-0100. Outdoor Malaysian eatery that has shaken up the scene on Jaksa with its delicious curries, *nasi lemak* (rice cooked in coconut milk with side dishes), and good-value set meals. Recommended.

¶ **Oh La La**, Jakarta Theatre Building, Jl MH Thamrin 9, T021 3160316, 24 hrs. Good selection of pastries, pies and cakes with an outdoor seating area, pleasant at night.

¶ **Pappa Restaurant**, Jl Jaksa 41, T021 31923452, 24 hrs. Cheap Western and Indonesian fare served round the clock to feed the hordes of drunken English teachers who need a burger and just 1 more beer before home.

¶ **Sate Khas Senayan**, Jl Kebon Sirih 31A, T021 31926238, 1000-2200. This is an excellent place to try *sate*. Set in a spotless clean environment, the restaurant serves up divine portions of chicken and beef *sate* along with good Javanese rice dishes, and some divine icy delights for dessert.

Kemang

Affectionately known as Little Bali, this area is a popular haunt for expats with money to burn on top-class dining. Traffic around here is notoriously nightmarish, and it can take almost 1 hr to get here from central and north Jakarta.

¶¶¶-¶¶ **Anatolia**, Jl Kemang Raya 110A, T021 7194617, 1100-2300. Sumptuous Ottoman decor, sheesha pipes and superb Turkish cuisine make this one of the city's most respected restaurants.

¶¶¶-¶¶ **Gourmet Garage**, Jl Kemang Raya, T021 7190875, 1000-2300. Smart collection of stalls including an oyster bar and a Japanese counter. There is a supermarket downstairs selling cheeses, meats, excellent bread and all the things homesick Westerners crave.

¶¶¶-¶¶ **Kinara**, Jl Kemang Raya 78B, T021 7192677. This place does Moghul architecture proud with its wonderful façade and interior. Tasty fare; the tandoori is well worth trying.

Elsewhere

¶¶¶-¶¶ **Al Jazeerah Restaurant**, Jl Raden Saleh 58, T021 3146108, 1000-2300. This street is packed full of authentic Arab eateries, and this is one of the best with dishes such as hummous, tabbouleh and plenty of kebabs on offer. No booze.

¶¶ **Bombay Blue**, Jl Cikini Raya 40, T021 3162865, 1200-2300. Slick decor and tasty Indian cuisine. Long menu featuring a good range of non-veg and vegetarian dishes.

¶¶ **Cafe Batavia**, Taman Fatahillah, T021 6915531, 0800-0100. While business here is no longer as brisk as it once was, this place still remains a classic venue, for a drink if nothing else. The bar is resonant with times past, with high ceilings, slowly whirring ceiling fans and 1920s class. Fare is Asian and Western.

¶¶ **Hanoi House**, Grand Indonesia, Jl MH Thamrin 1, T021 2350688, 1000-2200. Vietnamese classics served without MSG in a modern, clean setting. The beef tenderloin stew is impressive.

¶¶ **Imperial Treasure La Mian Xiao Long Bao**, Plaza Indonesia, T021 39835100. High-class Chinese dining with southern and eastern Chinese dishes in abundance.

¶¶ **Loewy**, Jl Lingkar Mega Kuningan E42 No 1, T021 25542378, 1100-0200. New Belgian restaurant with an excellent selection of wines and coffees. Notable dishes include steak, 3-cheese fondue and lamb shank. Recommended.

¶¶ **Trattoria**, Menara Karya Building, Jl HR Rasuna Said 1-2, Mega Kuningan, T021 57944727, 0900-2330. Excellent value authentic Italian cuisine, with good house wine and a rather tasty complimentary chocolate liqueur providing the icing on the cake. Recommended.

¶¶ **Y&Y**, Grand Indonesia, Jl MH Thamrin 1, T021 23580825, 1000-2200. While the a/c here leads visitors reaching for jumpers, the pizzas, pastas and sushi are good value and the Turkish delight ice cream is a fine way to aid digestion.

¶¶-¶ **Warung Daun**, Jl Cikini Raya 26, T021 3910909, 1100-1000. Popular with Indonesian ladies that lunch, the MSG-free fare, with organic vegetables, is a sure-fire winner. The cuisine is Sundanese and Javanese and features tasty *ikan gurame* (fried carp) and some splendid vegetable dishes.

Bakoel Koffie, Jl Cikini Raya 25, T021 31936608, 1000-2400. Spacious cafe with pleasant outdoor seating area and newspapers to browse. Plenty of coffees and cakes to indulge in.

Cafe Amor, Jl Kemang Raya 67, T021 7191333, 24 hrs. Long list of coffees, including some tasty ice blends, and a menu featuring good burgers, hot dogs and salads.

Cafe Au Lait, Jl Cikini Raya 17, T021 39835094, 0800-2400. European-style café, with high ceilings, free Wi-Fi access and a good range of coffee, cakes, sandwiches and simple pasta dishes. Occasional live music in the evenings.

There are also a large number of foodstalls, such as on **Jl HA Salim**, a great number of cheap regional restaurants; **Jl Mangga Besar**, with night-time *warungs*; **Jl Pecenongan** (also known as Jl used cars) with *warungs* at night, used-car workshops by day, particularly good seafood, recommended (BYOB); **Sarinah's Department Store** on Jl MH Thamrin (at the intersection with Jl KH Wahid Hasyim) has a food court in the basement, good range of cheap Indonesian dishes served in cleanish a/c restaurant, with English language menu; **Grand Indonesia mall**, excellent foodcourt in the basement; **Pasar Raya**, Blok M, has a variety of reliably good 'stalls' (not just Indonesian) in the basement; The top floor of **Sogo**, in the Plaza Indonesia, has similar stalls; and **Café Tenda Semanggi**, in the middle of the Central Business District, near Bengkel Night Park (taxi drivers know it), is an open air area that has been used for a cluster of upmarket food stalls, mainly Indonesian cuisine. A really happening place with great atmosphere. One of the nicest places to eat in Jakarta. Open 1800-0100.

Bars and clubs

Jakarta p185, maps p187, p188 and p190
If one were going to have just 1 night out in Indonesia, it would have to be in Jakarta, where the sun sets early and the night is long. There is an excellent choice of drinking venues to suit all and sundry. Nightlife is a very friendly affair, and many who go out on the tiles in Jakarta ending up slurping noodles at 0600 with a new group of friends and an impending hangover on the way.

Jalan Jaksa and around
Jl Jaksa has a reputation as being quite downmarket, and the bars conform to that stereotype, with plenty of hookers and local hangers-on. However, an evening out here can be great fun, slightly anarchic and is a great way to meet interesting characters.
Absolute Cafe, Jl Jaksa 5, T021 31909847, 1600-0400. A/c bar with pool tables, TVs screening football and cheap drinks.
Ali's, Jl Jaksa 25, T021 31900807, 1000-0300. Known as the African expat's bar of choice, this dark bar has TVs, plenty of nooks, crannies and a small dance floor.
D'Place, Sarinah Building, Jl MH Thamrin 11, T021 3107177. Small bar covered in rock memorabilia, with a good selection of drinks and plenty of weekend atmosphere.
Memories Cafe, Jl Jaksa 17, T021 3162548, 0900-0300. A Jaksa stalwart, this bar has seen it all. Bar girls flock here to join other drinkers in antics and occasional karaoke numbers.
Romance Cafe, Jl Jaksa 40, T021 3923969, 1000-0400. There's not much in the way of romance, but plenty of lonely men sipping cheap beer and watching the news on the huge TV. Nevertheless, it's not a bad place to escape the heat and rodents.

Elsewhere
BB's, near Menteng Plaza, Jl Hos Cokroaminoto, 1700-0200, T021 31931890. 3-storey complex housing a good bar on the 1st floor playing 90s classic rock, a forgettable middle floor and an excellent live music bar on the 3rd floor playing blues and reggae to a discerning audience. Recommended.
Bugil's, Taman Ria Senayan, Jl Gatot Subroto, T021 5747650. Expats flood to this friendly and fun bar for pitchers of beer, and special

offers such as free beer for bald people, or those wearing glasses (look in local media for details). Recommended.

CJs, Hotel Mulia, Jl Afrika Asia Senayan, T021 5747777, 1600-0300. Good live music at this raucous club popular with expats and bar-girls on the prowl.

Cork and Screw Wisma Kodel, Jl HR Rasuna Said Kav B-4, T021 52902030, 1100-0200. Currently one of the hottest spots in the city, withy excellent wine at good prices, and some fine food. Gets packed at weekends.

Embassy, Taman Ria Senayan, Jl Gatot Subroto, T021 5703704. Spacious playground for the rich and trendy to strut their stuff on the dancefloor to good house music.

Fez Bar, Jl Kemang Raya 78B, T021 7192677, 1600-0200. With decor inspired by the subcontinent, this classy bar is filled with the chosen few, and one too many here will leave a satisfying dent in the wallet.

Flanagan's, Sari Pan Pacific Hotel, Jl MH Thamrin, T021 3902707, 1000-0200. Irish bar with a/c so cold you'll be transported back home in a jiffy. Come here for the draught Guinness, Irish stews and excellent happy hour (30% off all drinks 1700-2000).

New Top Gun, Jl Falatehan 1, No 32-33, Blok M, T021 7395436, 1600-0300. Live music, pool tables, grinning expats and a busload of ladies of the night.

Red Square, Plaza Senayan Arcadia Unit X-210, Jl New Delhi, Pintu 9, T021 57901281. This highly successful lounge bar is currently the place to be seen, with sleek and ultra-modern interior featuring groovy lighting. Vodka-based drinks fly off the shelves. Recommended.

Stadium, Jl Hayam Wuruk 111, T021 6263323, Mon-Thu 2000-0600, Fri-Sun 24 hrs. One of Southeast Asia's most notorious clubs, attracting a loyal crowd of wide-eyed worshippers. This dark venue is a confusing maze, with numerous floors and plenty of sin, echoing with techno beats. Recommended.

Vin +, Jl Kemang Raya, Jl Kemang Raya 45, 1600-0200. Fashionable spot to sip wine, and people watch.

Vino Embassy, Jl Kemang Raya 67, T021 7191333, 1600-0200. Swish little bar, with dim lights and massive selection of wine.

⊛ Festivals and events

Jakarta *p185, maps p187, p188 and p190*
Ramadan There is an exodus from Jakarta during this time and services may be reduced. The upside is that there is no traffic.
Apr Anniversary of Taman Mini (20th), performances of traditional music and dance.
May Jakarta International Cultural Performance, a festival of music and dance from around Indonesia and also from other areas of Southeast Asia.
Jun Anniversary of Jakarta (22nd), commemorates the founding of Jakarta. Followed by the **Jakarta Fair**, lasting 1 month.
Aug Jalan Jaksa Street Fair, 7 days of entertainment, including dance and music.

⊛ Entertainment

Jakarta *p185, maps p187, p188 and p190*
For a schedule of events, look in the 'Where to Go' section of the *Jakarta Post* and the paper's website. The tourist office should also have an idea of what's going on in the city.

Cinemas
The Indonesian way is to provide subtitles rather than to dub, so soundtracks are generally in English. Films usually cost between 15,000Rp and 25,000Rp. Good cinemas can be found in the Jakarta Theatre Building (Jl MH Thamrin 9) and at the Grand Indonesia mall and eXMall.

Cultural shows
Erasmus Huis, Jl HR Rasuna Said S-3, T021 5241069, www.erasmushuis.co.id. Next to the Dutch embassy, cultural events, including interesting lectures are held here regularly.
Gedung Kesenian, Jl Gedung Kesenian 1, T021 3808282. This centre organizes *wayang*

orang performances, piano recitals, theatre and other cultural events, a modern art gallery is attached to the theatre, hotels should provide information on their program. **Taman Ismail Marzuki** (or TIM) just off Jl Cikini Raya, T021 31937325, www.taman ismailmarzuki.com. This complex is the focal point of cultural activities in the city with performances almost every night, the centre contains exhibition halls, 2 art galleries, theatres, cinema complex and a planetarium.

O Shopping

Jakarta *p185, maps p187, p188 and p190*
Fixed-priced stores are becoming more common in Jakarta, but bargaining is still the norm wherever there is no marked price. When buying antiques and handicrafts, bargain down to 30-40% of the original asking price, especially on Jl Surabaya. Shopping malls are a way of life in Jakarta, an escape from the traffic and smog, and new shopping malls are being constructed all the time. Some of the most convenient include **Grand Indonesia**, Jl MH Thamrin 1, with banks, designer clothes stores, bookshops and restaurants (recommended); **Plaza Indonesia**, Jl MH Thamrin Kav 28-30, with top brands, good dining options and beautiful people; **EX Mall**, Jl MH Thamrin Kav 28-30, favouring younger shoppers with high street brands, cinema and fast food joints; and **Plaza Senayan**, Jl Asia Afrika, 1000-2200. Suave and sophisticated and deliciously cool, with a cinema.
Batik **Ardiyanto**, Pasar Raya (3rd Flr), Jl Iskandarsyah 11/2. **Batik Keris**, Danar Hadi, Jl Raden Saleh 1A. **Batik Semar**, Jl Tomang Raya 54. **Government Batik Cooperative (GKBI)**, Jl Jend Sudirman 28. **Iwan Tirta**, Jl Panarukan 25 or Hotel Borobudur; 1 floor of Pasar Raya (Blok M), is devoted to batik. **Pasar Tanar Abang**, a market west of Merdeka Square, has good modern textiles, batik and *ikat* by the metre. **Srikandi**, Jl Melawai VI/6A. A batik factory at Jl Bendungan Hilir 2, in Senayan, is open to visitors.

Bookshops Jakarta is a good place to stock up on reading material, with bookshops in several malls. 2nd-hand books can be found along Jl Jaksa in **Margot Hotel** and **Memories Cafe** (after 1700).
Handicrafts **Sarinah Department Store** has 2 floors of handicrafts and batik from across Indonesia, Located on Jl MH Thamrin (at the Intersection with Jl KH Wahid Hasyim). This is a great place to stock up on gifts fork home, although if you are heading to other destinations in Java or Bali, it's best to wait, as prices in Sarinah are considerably higher.
Jewellery **Pasar Raya**, **Blok M. Sogo** (Plaza Indonesia), Jl Kemang Raya. For precious stones, try the **Indonesian Bazaar**, Hilton Hotel or **Pasar Uler**, northeast of town in Tanjung Priok. For 'cheap' jewellery, the prices are higher than in Yogya or Bali.
Supermarket There is a **Hero** supermarket beneath the Sarinah building on Jl MH Thamrin, which sells necessities. Most of the malls have supermarkets.

▲▲ Activities and tours

Jakarta *p185, maps p187, p188 and p190*
Language courses
IALF, Sentra Mulia, Jl Rasuna Said Kav X-6 No 8, T021 5213350, ialfjkt@ialf.edu, offer a variety of Bahasa Indonesia courses.

Tour operators
Most larger hotels have travel agents; this list is not comprehensive. Most will arrange city tours, out-of-town day tours and longer tours throughout Indonesia.

Many travel agents offer package tours to the islands. The price usually includes the boat trip to the island of choice and back to Jakarta, accommodation and food.

For agents and companies geared to the needs of those on a lower budget, Jl Jaksa is probably the best bet. Bus and train tickets are booked for destinations across the archipelago and other services provided.

Astrindo Tours and Travel, 45-47 Jl Kebon Sirih, T021 2305151. Professional outfit offering tailor-made tours.

Bayu Buana, Jl Kemang Raya 114, T021 71790662, www.bayubuanatravel.com. Branches all over the city, can arrange tickets, tours and help with visas.

Divalina Tour and Travel, Jl Jaksa 35, T021 3149330.

Graha Inata, Jl Jaksa 15A, T021 3143310. Can arrange tours to Krakatau and Pulau Seribu.

Gray Line Tours Jakarta, Panorama Tours, Jl Tanjung Selor 17, T021 6308105, www.panorama-tours.com. This American franchise offers tours around Jakarta, West Java and beyond, including a 2-day foray to Bali, Prices aren't cheap, but might suit those with minimal time to spare.

Indonesian Heritage Society, T021 5725870, may be offering city tours. These have been discontinued, but might start up again in the near future. There is a US$22 membership, worthwhile if you want to join several tours or are going to be based in the city.

Robertur Kencana, Jl Jaksa 20, T021 3142926. Gets the thumbs up from a lot of travellers.

Krakatau *p193*
Tour operators
Graha Inata (see above) offer all-inclusive trips to Krakatau. 1-day trips cost US$305, and 2-day, 1-night trips with a night in Carita cost US$430 per person. Before agreeing, check that the boat is twin-engine. This being Indonesia, all prices are negotiable, and large parties should be able to get a discount.

⊖ Transport

Jakarta *p185, maps p187, p188 and p190*
Air
Daily flights to most major cities in Indonesia. Fares are generally good value flying out of Jakarta. **Mandala** (mandalaair.com), **Lion Air** (www.lionair.co.id) and **Air Asia** (www.air asia.com) have online booking systems.

Bajaj
Bajaj, orange motorized 3-wheelers, Indian made, pronounced *bajai:* sometimes known as 'panzer' bajaj because of their tank-like behaviour. There have been rumours that the government would like to do away with bajajs, as they have been deemed 'anti-humane'. They are already barred from Jakarta's main thoroughfares. Nonetheless, they remain the cheapest way to get around other than by bus or on foot. Negotiate price furiously before boarding and expect to pay a minimum of 10,000Rp for a short journey.

Boat
Jakarta's port is **Tanjung Priok**, 15 km from the city centre. Take bus no 60 from Jl Pos or bus no P14 from Jl Kebon Sirih, off Jl Jaksa. Or take a taxi. Allow at least 1 hr. It is less than 1 km from the bus station at Tanjung Priok to the dock. The state-owned shipping company **PELNi** has its head office at Jl Gajah Mada 14, T021 6334342-45. Its ticket office is at Jl Angkasa 20, T021 4211921. A counter on the 2nd floor of the building is much less crowded for ticket purchase (entrance on right of building). 2 photocopies of passport are required (photocopying shop on left of building, as you face it). The PELNI ships **Kelud** (for North Sumatra, Riau), **Leuser** (Kalimantan, Java), **Dobonsolo** (Sulawesi, Kalimantan), **Bukit Raya** (Kalimantan, Riau) **Ciremai** (Sulawesi, Maluku, Papua) **Lambelo** (Sulawesi, Maluku, Riau), **Sirimau** (Sulawesi, Nusa Tenggara), and **Bukit Sigantung** (Nusa Tenggara, Maluku, Sulawesi, Papua), dock here. There are also more PELNI agents in town, which though they levy a small charge are often more convenient. The Jakarta Tourist Board, in the Jakarta Theatre Building, has approximate sailing schedules.

Bus
Local Most fares 2000Rp around town. Crowded, especially during rush hour, and beware of pickpockets. **Express buses** (marked 'P' for Patas) are smaller and less crowded, 3000Rp. Patas a/c express buses, 6000Rp.

Booking bus tickets: private bus companies have their offices at these terminals. Alternatively, purchase tickets from a travel agent. Getting bus tickets on Jl Jaksa has become increasingly difficult recently, but they can still be bought from Wisma Delima (see Sleeping). Another option is to ring the company and reserve a ticket, and pay for it on arrival at the terminal. Your hotel should be able to help you do this. Make sure you find out which terminal your bus from Jakarta departs from. Companies worth trying include: **Lorena**, Jl Hasyim Ashan 15C, T021 6341166, and **Kramat Jati**, Jl Sultan Iskandar Mudar 9B, T021 7290077.

The **Jakarta Transjarkarta** bus lines have taken a little away from the stress of city travelling, with clean a/c buses travelling along designated corridors that are for these buses only. There are 10 lines running at the moment, although more are in construction. Fares from point to point are 3500Rp, including any transits.

Corridor 1: Blok M–Jl Jend Sudirman–Jl MH Thamrin–Merderka Barat–Harmoni–Jl Gajah Mada–Stasiun Kota.

Corridor 3: Kalideres (bus terminal)–Daan Mogot–Tomang Raya–Harmoni.

Corridor 7: Kampong Rambutan (bus terminal) – Otto Iskandardinata – Letjend M.T Haryono.

Long distance There are 4 city bus terminals, all some distance from the city centre. **Kalideres Terminal**, on the west edge of the city, 15 km from the centre, serves the west coast, including **Merak** with a handful of connections on to **Sumatra** (most Sumatra buses depart from the Pulo Gadung terminal). Take **Transjakarta** busway corridor 3 buses to get here. **Kampong Rambutan**, about 15 km south of the city, serves **Bogor**, **Bandung** and other towns and cities in West Java. Take **Transjakarta** busway corridor 7 buses to get here. **Pulo Gadung Terminal**, 12 km east of the centre at the junction of Jl Bekasi Timur Raya and Jl Perintis Kemerdekaan, serves Central and East Java including the towns of **Cirebon** (5 hrs), **Yogya** (12 hrs), **Surabaya** (15 hrs) and **Malang** (18 hrs). Pulo Gadung is

also the main bus terminal for **Sumatra**, with buses going to all the major towns – even as far as Banda Aceh, some 3000 km north. **Bali** is served from Pulo Gadung. **Lebakbulus Terminal** has buses going to **Bandung** and **Bali**. This terminal is 10 km south of the city.

Fares from Jakarta include: **Denpasar** (24 hrs) US$37, **Surabaya** (18 hrs) US$23, **Probolinggo** (20 hrs) US$26, **Yogyakarta/Surakarta** (12-14 hrs) US$18 and **Padang** (32 hrs) US$36.

Car hire

Most international companies strongly recommend a driver and local expats believe it is pure madness to attempt tackling the streets of Jakarta oneself. Visitors do, though, and survive. Cars with driver can be hired by the day for about US$50. **Avis**, Jl Diponegoro 25, T3142900, F331845, also desks at Soekarno-Hatta Airport and the Borobudur Intercontinental Hotel. **Bluebird**, Jl Hos, Cokroaminoto T021 7944444. **National**, Kartika Plaza Hotel, Jl MH Thamrin 10, T021 333423/3143423. **Toyota Rentacar**, Jl Gaya Motor 111/3, Sunter 11, T021 6506565, F6512621. Considered to be the best in town, with new cars at a very competitive rate.

Minibus

Door to door services are offered by **4848** (Jl Prapatan 34, T021 3644488) and **Media Taxi** (Jl Johar 15, T021 3140343). Fares to **Bandung** are US$8 and to Yogya US$19. Bear it mind that it can take a hell of a long time to pick people up in a city of Jakarta's size, and then there is the traffic to contend with, making this a more stressful and less scenic option than the train ride.

Taxi

The most comfortable and convenient way to get around the city. There are numerous companies in Jakarta. **Blue Bird**, T021 79171234/7941234, www.bluebird group.com, is the only company worth using. They can be distinguished by the large Blue Bird Taxi sticker on the windscreen. Most drivers speak English and no smoking is allowed in the cabs. Drivers work reasonable shifts, unlike in other companies so there is less chance of them falling asleep at the wheel (although it happens).There are plenty of imitators who have taken to painting their taxis blue, and whose drivers will try to hustle as much as they can. Flag fall is 5000Rp and 2500Rp for each subsequent km (after the first). Blue Birds can be found outside most major hotels, shopping malls and condo complexes. Tipping is normal, so round up to the nearest 1000Rp if you wish.

Train

Jakarta has 6 railway stations, which are more central than the bus stations. The main station is **Gambir**, on the east side of Merdeka Square (Jl Merdeka Timur). There is an English-speaking information service that advises on timetables and costs, T021 6929194. Regular connections with **Bogor** (1 hr 20 mins) (economy class only, 2500Rp), or the non-stop a/c **Pakuan Express** trains from 0730-1640, (50 mins) 11,000Rp.

For **Bandung**, (2½ hrs) there are the useful **Parahiyangan** trains, departing nearly every hour from Gambir (*bisnis* 20,000Rp/*eksekutif* 30,000Rp). There are also 6 daily departures on the **Argo Gede**, a little more upmarket and costing 45,000Rp for an *eksekutif* seat.

For **Yogyakarta** (8 hrs) there is the **Taksaka**, 2 a day (*bisnis* US$14/*eksekutif* US$22). The *eksekutif*-only **Argo Lawu** departs at 2055 and calls in at **Yogya** before **Surakarta (Solo)** at 0430 (US$22 for either city). The **Argo Dwipangga** does the same trip departing at 0800 and arriving at **Solo** at1600 (US$24).

There are numerous trains to **Surabaya** (9 hrs) including the **Argo Anggrek**, 2 daily at 0920 (arrives at 1829) and 2045 (arrives at 0555) on *eksekutif* class for US$23.

There is 1 daily train to **Malang**, the **Gajayana** departing at 1730 and arriving the following morning at 0815, US$26.

Pulau Seribu *p193*

Air

There is an airstrip on Pulau Panjang. The trip takes 25 mins from Jakarta. Boat transfers to other islands.

Boat

A regular ferry service goes to **Onrust** and **Bidadari**, leaving Marina Jaya at Ancol at 0700 and returning from the islands at 1430. The journey takes 30 mins-1 hr. If you do not want to take the package option, then go to either Onrust or Bidadari and find a fisherman to take you out for the day to explore the outer islands. It should cost around US$55. Most of the resorts have their own boats, which pick up from Ancol in the mornings. People on day trips can also take these boats.

Krakatau *p193*

Boat

It may be possible to charter boats from Anyer, Carita and Labuan. Locals have gained a reputation for overcharging and then providing unseaworthy boats. (It is said that 2 Californian women spent 3 weeks drifting in the Sunda Strait, living on sea water and toothpaste, before being washed ashore near Bengkulu in West Sumatra.) A 2-engine speed boat suitable for 6-8 people should cost US$110-165. Bargain hard, and make sure you see the boat before handing over any cash. The boatsmen on the beach outside the Mutiara Carita Hotel in Labuan near Carita have a good range of vessels.

❶ Directory

Jakarta *p185, maps p187, p188 and p190*
Banks Most of the larger hotels will have money- changing facilities, and banks and money changers can be found throughout the city centre; eg, in shopping centres. Jl Jaksa also has many money changers, with competition keeping the rate good. Useful banks for visitors include **BNI** and **Lippo Bank** (both with ATMs accepting Visa and

MasterCard) on Jl Kebon Sirih. There are ATMs all over the city. Also a money changer with fair rates on the 1st floor of **Sarinah** department store. **Embassies and consulates** Austria, Jl Diponegoro 44, T021 338090, www.auambjak@rad.net.id. **Australia**, Jl HR Rasuna Said Kav C 15-16, T021 25505555, www.austembjak.or.id; **Belgium**, (in Deutsche Bank Building, 16th floor), Jl Imam Bonjol 80, T021 3162030, jakarta@diplobel.org. **Cambodia**, Jl Kintamani Raya C-15 no 33, T021 5741437. **Canada**, World Trade Centre, 6th floor, Jl Jend. Sudirman Kav.29, T021 25507800, www.dfait-maeci.gc.ca. **Denmark**, Menara Rajawali, 25th floor, Jl Mega Kuningan, T021 5761478, www.emb-denmark.or.id. **France**, Jl MH Thamrin 20, T021 3142807, www.amba france-id.org. **Germany**, Jl MH Thamrin 1, T021 3901750, www.german embjak.or.id. **Italy**, Jl Diponegoro 45, T021 337445, www.italambjkt.or.id. **Laos**, Jl Patra Kuningan XIV No 1A, T021 5229602. **Netherlands**, Jl HR Rasuna Said Kav S3, T021 5251515, www.netherlandsembassy.or.id. **New Zealand**, Gedung BRI II, 23rd floor, Jl Jend. Sudirman 44-46, T021 5709460, www.nz embassy.com. **Norway**, Menara Rajawali, 25th floor, Kawasan Mega Kuningan Lot 5.1, T021 5761523, www.norwayemb-indonesia.org **Philippines**, Jl Imam Bonjol 6-8, T021 3155118, phjkt@indo.net.id. **Singapore**, Jl HR Rasuna Said Block X, Kav 2, T021 5201489, www.mfa. gov.sg/jkt/main.html. **Spain**, Jl H Agus Salim 61, T021 3350771, embespid@mail.mae.es. **Sweden**, Menara Rajawali, 9th floor, Jl Mega Kuningan Lot 5.1, Kawasan Mega Kuningan, T021 25535900, www.swedenabroad.com/ jakarta. **Switzerland**, Jl HR Rasuna Said Block X, 3/2, T021 5256061, www.eda.admin.ch. **UK**, Jl MH Thamrin 75, T021 23565200, www.britain. or.id. **USA**, Jl Medan Merdeka Selatan 5, T021 34359000, www.usembassyjakarta.org. **Vietnam**, Jl Teuku Umar 25, T021 9100163. **Emergencies** 24-hr emergency ambulance service: T118. **Police:** Jl Jend Sudirman 45, T021 5234333. Tourist Police, Jakarta Theatre Building, Jl MH Thamrin 9, T021 566000. **Immigration Central Immigration**, Jl Terminal 2, Cengkareng (near the airport) T021 5507233. Kemayoran, Jl Merpati Kemayoran 3, T021 6541209. Also an office on Jl Rasuna Said, T021 5253004. These places will extend B211 visas, but get there at 0800 prompt. **Internet** A good Internet café is along Jl Jaksa, which provides free drinks for its users and travel services. Also **Top Internet** on Jl Wahid Hasyim 110, open 24 hrs, 10,000Rp per hr. **Medical services** Clinics: Global **Doctor**, Jl Kemang Raya 87, T021 7194565, 24 hr. English-speaking doctors at reasonable rates (US$19 for consultation plus treatment costs). Also **SOS Medika Klinik**, Jl Puri Sakti 10, T021 7505973, 24 hr. **Hospitals:** RS Jakarta, Jl Jend Sudirman Kav 49, T021 573 2241. RS MMC Kuningan, Jl HR Rasuna Said KC21, T021 5203435 (24-hr emergency room). **Pharmacy: Guardian Pharmacy**, Plaza Indonesia, Pondok Indah Mall or Blok M Plaza. There are a couple of pharmacies on Jl Wahid Hasyim. **Post office** Jl Pos Utara 2, Pasar Baru (or access from Jl Lapangan Banteng Poste Restante open Mon-Fri 0800-1600, Sat 0800-1300. **Telephone** Telkom, Jakarta Theatre Building, Jl M H Thamrin 81. (Open every day, 24 hrs. IDD and fax service available). Numerous **Warpostel** and other telephone offices dotted around. **Tourist information** PHKA Gedung Manggala Wanabakti Building, Jl Jend Gatot Subroto, Senayan, Block 1, 8th flr.

Bogor

→ *Phone code: 0251. Colour map 10, A2.*

Bogor is centred on the lush botanical gardens, with views over red-tiled roofs stacked one on top of the other and toppling down to the Ciliwung River, which runs through the middle of the town and gardens. The Ciliwung, which has cut a deep gorge, has also become a convenient place to discard rubbish, marring some of the views in the process. The town has a large Christian community and a surprising number of Western fast food outlets and department stores. These serve the population of wealthy Indonesians who live here and commute into Jakarta. A scattering of old colonial buildings is still to be found around town – for instance, set back from the road on Jalan Suryakencana.

The town lies 290 m above sea level in an upland valley, surrounded by Gunungs Salak, Pangrango and Gede. Average temperatures are a pleasant 26°C, significantly cooler than Jakarta, but rainfall is the highest in Java at 3000-4000 mm per year. The Dutch, quite literally sick to death of the heat, humidity and the swampy conditions of Jakarta, developed Bogor as a hill retreat. ►► *For listings, see pages 208-210.*

Ins and outs

Getting there

Bogor is just 60 km south of Jakarta and with a fast toll road is easily reached on a day trip from the capital. However, it is worth staying here for longer than just a few hours. Recent improvements in the Bogor–Jakarta link has made Bogor a thriving commuter town, and, increasingly, the first stop from the airport for tourists who only want to see Jakarta on day trips from Bogor (rather than the other way around). The bus station is south of the famous Botanical Gardens, a longish walk or short bemo ride from the town centre, and there are frequent connections with Jakarta's Kampong Rambutan terminal and Soekarno-Hatta International Airport. There are also buses onto Bandung via the Puncak Pass (three hours) and further afield to Yogya, Solo and Bali. The train station is close to the town centre and there are regular connections with Jakarta's Gambir station. ►► *See Transport, page 209.*

Getting around

Bogor is a small town and because it is much cooler here than Jakarta, walking is pleasant, but there are also plenty of public transport options including becaks, bajajs, taxis, colts and delmans (horse-drawn carts). Bogor's **tourist office** ⓘ *T0813 81172171, daily 0800-1700,* is easy to miss, in the bizarre Taman Topi complex on Jalan Kapten Muslihat. The staff are very helpful and have a good map as well as tips on the city. They arrange a number of interesting tours around West Java, and up to the summit of Gunung Salak.

Sights

Botanical gardens
ⓘ *Daily 0700-1700, 9500Rp.*

The superb botanical gardens (*Kebun Raya*) dominate the centre of the city, covering an immense 87 ha and housing 2735 plant species. The gardens are thought to have been established under the instructions of Sir Stamford Raffles. Certainly, Raffles was a keen botanist; however, it was the Dutch Governor-General Van der Capellen who commissioned the transformation of the gardens into arguably the finest in Asia. The botanist Professor Reinhardt, from Kew Gardens in England, undertook the major portion of the work in 1817. The gardens became world renowned for their research into the cash crops of the region (tea, rubber, coffee, tobacco and chinchona – from the bark of which quinine is derived). The giant water lily, as well as a variety of orchids, palms and bamboos, can be seen here today. It used to be possible to see the giant Rafflesia flower as well, but the specimen has now died.

Presidential Palace (Istana Bogor)

ⓘ *Those planning to visit the Istana Bogor must think ahead, only groups of 30 or more are admitted after permission has been secured through the Istana or the tourist office at least a week ahead of the planned visit, guests must be formally dressed and children under 10 are not admitted because of the value and fragility of the objects; if visitors can meet all these requirements they deserve a prize. In Jakarta, applications can be made through the Sekretariat Negara, on Jl Veteran 16.*

Deer graze in front of the imposing Presidential Palace or Istana Bogor, which lies within the botanical gardens, directly north of the main gates (there is also an entrance on Jalan Ir H Juanda). The palace was a particular favourite of President Sukarno and contains a large collection of his paintings, sculpture and ceramics (he had a passion for the female nude). Sukarno lived here under 'house arrest' from 1967 until his death in 1970. Today, it is used as a guesthouse for important visitors and high-level meetings.

Bogor

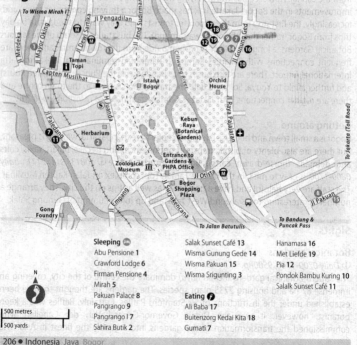

Sleeping 🛏
Abu Pensione **1**
Crawford Lodge **6**
Firman Pensione **4**
Mirah **5**
Pakuan Palace **8**
Pangrango **9**
Pangrango I **7**
Sahira Butik **2**

Salak Sunset Café **13**
Wisma Gunung Gede **14**
Wisma Pakuan **15**
Wisma Srigunting **3**

Eating 🍴
Ali Baba **17**
Buitenzorg Kedai Kita **18**
Gumati **7**

Hanamasa **16**
Met Liefde **19**
Pia **12**
Pondok Bambu Kuring **10**
Salalk Sunset Café **11**

Museums

The **Zoological Museum** ① *daily 0800-1600, 2000Rp,* is on the left of the entrance to the botanical gardens and was founded in 1894. It contains an extensive collection of stuffed, dried and otherwise preserved fauna (over 15,000 species), of which only a small proportion is on show at any one time. The museum also has a library. There is also a **Herbarium** ① *Mon-Thu 0800-1330 and Fri 0800-1000, 2000Rp,* associated with the botanical gardens, on Jalan Ir H Juanda, across the road from the west gate to the gardens. It is said to have a collection of 2,000,000 specimens, which seems suspiciously inflated.

Markets

Jalan Otista (also known as Otto Iskandardinata) is a road running along the south edge of the Botanical Gardens. The street is lined with stalls selling fruit, rabbits (not to eat), some batik, children's clothes and unnecessary plastic objects. The main **market area** is along Jalan Dewi Sartika, where stalls, hawkers, shoppers, colts and becaks struggle for space. A fascinating area to walk and watch, absorbing the atmosphere.

Gong foundry

① *Jl Pancasan 17, T0251 324132, near the river and southeast of the botanical gardens.*

The gong foundry is one of the few foundries left in Indonesia – on one side of the street is the foundry, and on the other the gong stands are carved from wood. Visitors can watch metalsmiths making gongs in the traditional manner – a process which takes between one and three days per gong. The factory is about a 35-minute walk southeast from the town centre. Walk south down Jalan Empang and then turn right onto Jalan Pahlawan. Next door to the foundry, in addition to selling gongs, **traditional puppets** of high quality are on offer – and at far lower prices than in Jakarta. About 200 m on from the gong foundry is a small **tofu factory**, a fascinating insight into the simple process of tofu making. Fresh tofu is sold to local villages. Enday Media, a *wayang golek* puppet maker has his home and factory ① *Kampong Sirnagalih 60, T0251 358808,* and offers *wayang* shows to groups. Visits can be arranged through the tourist office.

Jalan Batutulis

① *Admission by donation, daily 0800-1600, take an Angkutan (Green Colt) No 02.*

A **batutulis** (inscribed stone), dating from the 16th century and erected by one of the sons of a Pajajaran king, is housed in a small shrine 3 km south of town on Jalan Batutulis (which runs off Jalan Bondongon).

Around Bogor

Taman Safari

① *Daily 0900-1700, 70,000Rp (60,000Rp for children under 5). Take a bus heading for Cisarua and ask to be let off at the turning to the park, motorbike taxis ply the route from the main road to the park gates.*

Just before Cisarua, 2.5 km off the main road, is an open-air safari park. It also houses a mini zoo and offers amusement rides, elephant and horse riding, various animal shows throughout the day, a waterfall, swimming pool, restaurant and camping facilities. There is also a **weekend night safari** ① *1830-2100, adult 70,000Rp/children under 5, 60,000Rp.*

⊙ Bogor listings

*For Sleeping and Eating price codes,
see inside the front cover.*

⊜ Sleeping

Bogor *p205, map p206*
Given its proximity to Jakarta, Bogor is
unsurprisingly well endowed with good
mid-range and high-end hotels. There are
a few decent cheap hotels.
AL-A Sahira Butik Hotel, Jl Paledang 53,
T0251 322 413, www.sahirabutikhotel.com.
This new place has plenty of palatial
overtures, friendly staff and fair discounts
at weekends. The standard rooms are large
and have private balcony. Internet access
available. Pool. Recommended.
A Hotel Salak, Jl Ir H Juanda 8, T0251 350400.
www.hotelsalak.co.id. Top-notch hotel with
formal but comfortable rooms, all carpeted
and with in-house films and cable TV. Facilities
include spa, travel agent, pool and gym.
A-C Hotel Mirah, Jl Pangrongo 9A, T0251
348040. The rooms are a little overpriced, given
the competition in town. More expensive ones
come with cable TV and are nicely decorated.
Further down the price range, rooms are still
acceptable, although lose some of the mod
cons and become increasingly faded.
B-D Hotel Pangrango, Jl Pajaran 32, T0251
321482, www.hotel-pangrango.co.id. Popular
with Indonesian business folk, this 5-storey
beast has 97 rooms, including budget rooms,
which have an outside bathroom, TV and a/c
(centralized-no individual control). The a/c
standard rooms are spacious and have TV,
fridge and bath. Wi-Fi access in lobby
(expensive). Pool.
B-E Hotel Pangrango 1, Jl Pangrango 23,
T0251 328670, F0251 314060. Standard
rooms have dated furniture and garden
views. Mini rooms have fan, attached
bathroom but no natural light. There is a
small pool with sun loungers and expensive
Wi-Fi access in the lobby.

C Wisma Srigunting, Jl Pangrango 21A,
T0251 339660, F0251 333296. Offers 6 rooms
set in a spotless palatial family home covered
with photos. The rooms (all a/c) are massive
and have fridge and TV, and equally large
bathrooms. Recommended.
C-D Crawford Lodge, Jl Pangrango 2, T0251
322429, F0251 316978. Lashings of 1970s
style in this family home with extensive
garden and large pool. The 8 rooms are out
the back and are a little dark, but clean.
C-D Pakuan Palace Hotel, Jl Pakuan 5,
T0251 323062, hopakuan@indo.net.id. The
comfy standard rooms are not bad, with TV,
a/c and hot water. Spending a little more will
get international cable TV. Pool with outdoor
seating. Take angkot No. 6 to get here.
C-E Wisma Gunung Gede, Jl Raya Pajaran
36, T0251 324148. In a peaceful setting off the
main road, the rooms have TV, a/c and are
sparkling clean and have hot water. The
zebra-print blankets let the side down a bit.
D-E Wisma Pakuan, Jl Pakuan 12, T0251
319430, F0251 383918. Friendly, with helpful
staff and large clean a/c and fan rooms with TV
set around a pleasant garden. Recommended.
Take angkot No. 6 to get here.
E-F Abu Pensione, Jl Mayor Oking 15, T0251
322893. This place is the best budget bet in
town, with a wide variety of clean a/c and fan
rooms, some filled with the sound of the
gushing river below. The owner, Selfi,
is a great source of information and great
company, and offers tours around town
for a glimpse of local life. Recommended.
E-F Firman Pensione, Jl Paledang 48,
T0251 323246. The cheap downstairs
room are frankly grim, and need to be
improved drastically. They are cell-like,
dirty and have miserable shared toilets.
Things improve a little upstairs with
broad vistas over the red tiled roof tops
of the city, and a couple of tatty a/c rooms
with TV. The owner here is a good source
of info; she can arrange tours around the
town and beyond.

🍴 Eating

Bogor *p205, map p206*
Local specialities include *asinan Bogor*, sliced fruit in sweet water and *tuge gorehg*, fried beansprouts served with a spicy chilli sauce. Bogor, like many towns, has a profusion of Padang restaurants, but in this case they are almost all owned by one man and the food is virtually the same, so there is nothing to choose between them gastronomically.

The area around the **Giant** shopping centre on Jl Pajajaran has plenty of fast food options, further down the street towards Jl Otista, there are a few *nasi Padang* (**Trio** is very popular) and restaurants.

🍴 Hanamasa, Jl Gunung Gede 27A, T0251 324323, 1100-2200. Sparkling, large Japanese restaurant offering cook-yourself meals in *yakiniku* (grilled) and *shabu shabu* (steamed) styles. Popular.

🍴 Ali Baba, Jl Pangrango 13, T0251 348111, 1000-2200. This is the place to satisfy hummous cravings, with a fair menu of Middle Eastern standards.

🍴 Buitenzorg Kedai Kita, Jl Pangrango 21, T0251 324160, 0800-2300. Relaxed eatery with eclectic menu of pizza, steaks and delicious Sundanese and Javanese dishes. Locals flock here for the coffee from all over Sumatra, Timor and Sulawesi.

🍴 Gumati, Jl Paledang 26, T0251 324318, 1000-2300. Brilliant views and superb array of Sundanese food on display to choose from. There are a few concessions to Western tastes with steaks and some simple pastas. Recommended.

🍴 Met Liefde, Jl Pangrango 16, T0251 338909, 0900-2300 (2400 at weekends). Waitresses in Dutch outfits, plenty of clogs and a beautiful garden with outdoor seating. This is a fine spot for a bit of wining and dining for very reasonable prices. The menu is mainly Western, with plenty of Dutch desserts and a good range of juices. Live music at weekends. Recommended.

🍴 Pia, Jl Pangrango 10, T0251 324169, 0800-2200. Pies of every form to consume in a friendly outdoor setting, from chocolate to apple, the house special. There are also plenty of savoury offerings, with soups, salads and (strangely) spaghetti with apple sauce.

🍴 Pondok Bambu Kuring, Jl Pajajaran 43, T0251 323707, 0930-2130. Large restaurant with some *lesehan* (low tables) seating. Menu features a lot of good Indonesian seafood dishes with plenty of prawn and squid dishes and some tasty *ikan gurame*.

🍴 Salak Sunset Cafe, Jl Paledang 38, T0251 356045, 1100-2300. Fair Western and Indonesian dishes, with some good snacks including *pisang koreng keju coklat* (fried banana with cheese and chocolate), but the real reason to come here is for the amazing sunset views over the town, perfect for sharing with a friendly *Bintang*.

🛍 Shopping

Bogor *p205, map p206*
Batik Batik Semar, Jl Capten Muslihat 7.
Handicrafts Kenari Indah, Jl Pahlawan.
Pasar Bogor on Jl Suryakencana.
Market Kebon Kembang on Jl Dewi Sartika. **Wayang Golek**, Enday Media Kp Sirnagalih 60, T0251 358808.

🔺 Activities and tours

Bogor *p205, map p206*
Tour operators
Maghfiroh, Gedung Alumni IPB, Jl Pajajaran 54, T0251 393234, F0251 393231.
Vayatour, Jl Pajajaran 23, T0251 256861, www.vayatour.com. Also a branch of Natatour upstairs, which can book Air Asia flights.

🚍 Transport

Bogor *p205, map p206*
Bogor is 60 km south of Jakarta. A fast toll road makes the trip to Bogor rapid, though scenically unexciting.

Car hire

Car and driver are available for charter from **Abu Pensione**, Jl Mayor Oking 15.

Colt (angkutan/angkot)

Omnipresent green machines; seem to be more of them than there are passengers. Fixed fare of 2500Rp around town, destinations marked on the front. Blue angkots run to out-of-town destinations.

Bus

The station is just off Jl Raya Pajajaran, south from the Botanical gardens and opposite the intersection with the toll road from Jakarta. Frequent connections with Jakarta's **Kampong Rambutan** (7500Rp non a/c, 12,000Rp a/c). Bear in mind that Kampong Rambutan is still quite a distance to the centre of Jakarta, making the train trip a much more sensible option. Green bemos from here to the centre of town cost 2500Rp. Regular connections with Bandung, via the Puncak Pass, 3 hrs. For travel to Bandung, Deva Transport offer a door-to-door service. Phone and book, pay at the end of the journey (60,000Rp, 3 hrs) Jl Taman Yasmin Raya, T0251 7532582). For a/c buses to **Yogya**, **Solo** and **Bali**, it is best to go to use one of the well-established bus companies such as **Lorena** (Jl Raya Tajur 106, T0251 356666) and **Pahala Kencana** (Jl Sukasari 118, T0251 326482). Bookings can be made over the phone, or through one of their agents at the bus terminal. Routes include **Denpasar** (US$37, 27 hrs), **Yogya/Solo** (US$18 15 hrs) **Surabaya** (US$25, 19 hrs), **Padang** (US$36, 30 hrs), **Probolinggo** (US$27, 21 hrs). Also connections with Merak, Labuan and Pelabuhanratu. A very fast, efficient service runs from the Airport Bus Terminal on Jl Pajajaran to Soekarno-Hatta Airport. Every 30 mins from 0300-1900, 25,000Rp.

Taxi

Blue Bird, T0251 7156969.

Train

The station (a colonial building) is northwest of the Botanical Gardens on Jl Rajapermas, also known as Jl Stasiun. Regular connections every 30 mins or so with Jakarta's **Gambir** station. The uncomfortable economy trains take around 1hr 20mins and cost 2500Rp. Much better are the regular **Pakaun Express** a/c trains that take just under 1 hr and cost 11,000Rp. The first train leaves Bogor at 0540 and the final train out is at 1715. Trains leave from Jakarta's **Kota** station, but also stop at Gambir on their way through the capital, then stopping en route to Bogor. Note that there are no trains on to **Bandung**.

ⓘ Directory

Bogor p205, map p206
Banks A number on Jl Ir H Juanda and Jl Capten Muslihat, eg **BNI 46**, Jl Ir H Juanda 42 and **Central Asia**, Jl Ir H Juanda 24. ATMs can be found all over town.
Emergency Police: Jl Capten Muslihat 16. PHKA: Jl Ir H Juanda 9 (also for permits to visit national parks). **Immigration** Jl Jend A Yani 65, T0251 22870. **Internet** 5000Rp per hr, **Blue Corner**, Taman Topi, Jl Kapten Muslihat **Medical services** Hospital: RS PMI Bogor, Jl Pajajaran 80, T0251 393030, is run by the Palang Merah Indonesia (Indonesian Red Cross). There are a good selection of specialist doctors here.
Pharmacy: **Guardian,** inside Giant supermarket (2nd floor), Jl Pajajaran.
Post office Jl Ir H Juanda 3.
Telephone Wartels all over town.

Bandung

→ *Phone code: 022. Colour map 10, A2.*

Set in a huge volcanic basin at an altitude of 700 m and surrounded by mountains, Bandung has one of the most pleasant climates in Java, where the daytime temperature averages 22°C. The town centre is modern, unattractive and overcrowded, and some patience is needed in seeking out the town's main attraction: namely, its fine collection of art deco architecture, built between 1920 and 1940 when Bandung was the most sophisticated European town of the Dutch East Indies.

The third largest city in Indonesia, Bandung is also the capital of the province of West Java. The city has a population of over 2,000,000, with a further 3,000,000 living in the surrounding area, making this one of the most densely populated regions of Java. Such has been the growth of the city that in 1989 its administrative boundaries were extended, doubling the area of the city overnight. Bandung is regarded as the intellectual heart of Java, with over 50 universities and colleges situated in the area. ▶▶ *For listings, see pages 216-221.*

Ins and outs

Getting there

Bandung is 187 km southeast of Jakarta, 400 km west of Yogya. The airport is 4 km from town, but many more people arrive here by train or bus. The train station is in the centre of town and there are services travelling west to Jakarta and east to Surabaya. Less conveniently located are Bandung's two long-distance bus terminals. The Leuwi Panjang terminal is 5 km south of town and serves destinations to the west, including Jakarta and places in Sumatra. The Cicaheum terminal is on the edge of town to the east, and buses from here run to Yogya, Solo, Surabaya and Bali and to towns on Java's north coast including Cirebon and Semarang. Both bus terminals are linked to the centre of town by bemo. ▶▶ *See Transport, page 220.*

Getting around

This can be quite a struggle. Roads are often jammed and a rather complicated one-way system can be confusing to the uninitiated. However, because Bandung is 700 m above sea level, the climate is far cooler than lowland cities like Jakarta and Surabaya and walking is an option. Colts and town buses provide the main means of local transport. Taxis and car hire companies are also found here.

In their temporary office in the northern side of the Masjid Agung (take your shoes off before stepping onto the marble) on Jalan Asia Afrika, the staff of the **Bandung Visitor Information Centre** ① *T022 4206644, Mon-Sat 0900-1700 and Sun 0900-1400 (in theory)*, can tell you anything you want to know about Bandung and the surrounding area. The office organizes custom-made tours to suit each visitor's interests; eg, an architectural tour of the town, a pre-historic tour, a trip to the volcanoes, or a tour to Sundanese tribes and a Dragon village. They also organize transport on to Yogya, Pangandaran. Very helpful, particularly the English-speaking Ajid Suryana. There is also an office at the railway station.

Sights

If you want to photograph these buildings, bear in mind that several are occupied by the military and sensitivities are acute.

Colonial art deco

Bandung is recognized as one of three cities in the world with 'tropical art deco' architecture (the others being Miami, Florida and Napier, New Zealand). The Bandung Society for Heritage Conservation has a register of well over 600 category I and II monuments in Bandung. Of all the art deco architects the one most closely associated with Bandung was Wolff Schoemacher. He graduated with Ed Cuypers from the Delft Technical University in the Netherlands, and then moved to Bandung where he designed hundreds of buildings. In theory, any building over 50 years old is protected and the Mayor of Bandung is said to be appreciative of the need to preserve this heritage. But with the cowboy atmosphere that pervades many other towns and cities, the preservationists will need to be ever watchful.

The most impressive art deco building, lying in the centre of town, is the **Savoy Homann Hotel** on Jalan Asia Afrika, built in 1938 by AF Aalbers and still retaining period furniture and fittings. It has been meticulously renovated at a cost of US$2 million so that visitors can savour a hotel that numbers Charlie Chaplin, Ho Chi Minh and Zhou En-lai among its guests. From the exterior it has been likened to a radio; the interior to an ocean liner. Aalbers is said to have wanted to remind Dutch guests of the ships that brought them to the country. Opposite is the **Preanger Hotel**, built in 1889 but substantially redesigned by Wolff Schoemacher in 1928. The remaining art deco wing faces Jalan Asia Afrika. West on Jalan Asia Afrika is the **Gedung Merdeka** ① *Mon-Fri 0900-1500, permission needed for entrance, contact the tourist information office for details,* (also known as the Asia Afrika building). Originally built in 1895, it was completely renovated in 1926 by Wolff Schoemacher, Aalbers and Van Gallen Last, and today houses an exhibition of photographs of the first Non-Aligned Movement conference held here in 1955 (hence the name of the street).

Jalan Braga is often said to be Bandung's colonial heart. Sadly though, most of the original façades have been disfigured or entirely replaced. North of the railway line, also on Jalan Braga, is the **Bank of Indonesia** designed by Ed Cuypers in the 1920s. Either side are church buildings designed by Schoemacher.

North of the centre

The north suburbs of Bandung are the most attractive part of the city, leafy and green – this is University Land. **Gedung Sate** on Jalan Diponegoro was built in the 1920s and is one of Bandung's more imposing public buildings, with strong geometric lines and a formal garden. Within the building, but rather hidden away, is the **Museum Post and Philately** ① *Jl Cilaki 37, Mon-Fri 0900-1500, free.* Almost opposite is the **Geological Museum** ① *T022 7203205, Mon-Thu 0900-1530, Sat-Sun 0900-1330, adult 2000Rp, student 1500Rp,* at No 57 (reputed to be the largest in Southeast Asia). It houses skeletons of pre-historic elephants, rhinos, fossilized trees and a meteor weighing 156 kg that fell on Java in 1884. Most notably, it is home to the skull of 'Java Man'. Unfortunately, there's no information in English. Also north of the city centre on Jalan Taman Sari, the **Bandung Institute of Technology** or **ITB** was built by Maclaine Pont in 1918 and represents another good example of the architecture of the art deco era. Off Jalan Taman Sari, just before the

ITB travelling north, is the **Kebun Binatang** ① *daily 0800-1600, 10,000Rp, very crowded on Sun and holidays*, Bandung's **zoo** housing Komodo dragons among other beasts. It is set in beautiful surroundings and is well worth a visit. Not far south of the zoo is the rather bizarre '**Jean Street**' on Jalan Cihampelas. Shopkeepers vie for the most elaborate shopfront in an attempt to lure trade. It is a most surreal experience to wander amongst this collection of larger-than-life plaster Rambos, Superman leaping though a wall, and a huge Spiderman casting a web, helicopters, James Bonds and other figures and images, and worth a visit even if you are not intending to shop. There are not just jeans for sale here: all types of clothes, DVDs and merchandise for Bandung's large population of students and trendies. The streets are also lined with stalls selling fresh coconuts and

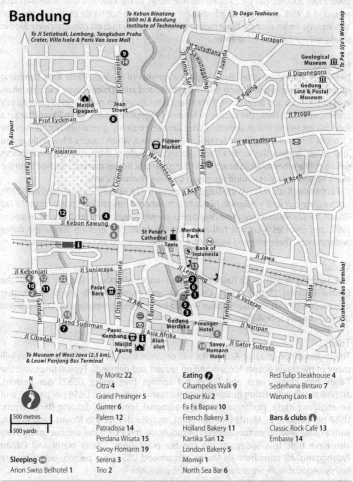

Bandung

To Kebun Binatang (800 m) & Bandung Institute of Technology

To Jl Setiabudi, Lembang, Tangkuban Prahu Crater, Villa Isola & Paris Van Java Mall

To Dago Teahouse

To Pak Ujo's Workshop

To Airport

Jl Cihampelas

Jean Street

Mesjid Cipaganti

Jl Prof Eyckman

Jl Pajajaran

Jl Pasir Kaliki

Jl Suladiana

Jl Sawunggaling

Taman Sari

Jl H. Juanda

Jl Surapati

Jl Agung

Geological Museum

Jl Diponegoro

Gedung Saté & Postal Museum

Jl Progo

Jl Cicendo

Jl Wartukencana

Flower Market

Jl Merdeka

Jl Martadinata

Jl Aceh

Jl Aceh

Jl Kebon Kawung

St Peter's Cathedral

Merdeka Park

Taxis

Bank of Indonesia

Jl Jawa

Jl Kebonjati

Jl Suniaraya

Jl Otto Iskandarinata

Jl Lembong

Jl Tamblong

Jl Veteran

Jl Sunda

To Cicaheum Bus Terminal

Pasar Baru

Jl ABC

Banceuy

Gedung Merdeka

Jl Naripan

Jl Gatot Subroto

Savoy Homann Hotel

Preanger Hotel

Jl Kebonjati

Gardujati

Jl Jend Sudirman

Jl Cibadak

Pasar Kembang

Masjid Agung

Jl Asia Afrika

Alun-alun

To Museum of West Java (2.5 km), & Leuwi Panjang Bus Terminal

N

500 metres
500 yards

Sleeping
Arion Swiss Belhotel 1

By Moritz 22
Citra 4
Grand Preanger 5
Gunter 6
Palem 12
Patradissa 14
Perdana Wisata 15
Savoy Homann 19
Serena 3
Trio 2

Eating ①
Cihampelas Walk 9
Dapur Ku 2
Fa Fa Bapau 10
French Bakery 3
Holland Bakery 11
Kartika Sari 12
London Bakery 5
Momiji 1
North Sea Bar 6

Red Tulip Steakhouse 4
Sederhana Bintaro 7
Warung Laos 8

Bars & clubs ①
Classic Rock Café 13
Embassy 14

durian ice cream – which emits the usual overwhelming smell. To get to the street, take an Angkutan kota running up Jalan Pasir Kaliki and then walk through Jalan Prof Eyckman (Jean Street itself is one-way running south). **Jalan Pasar Selatan** is a more recent imitation of the original, lined with stores selling denim.

South of the centre

South of town, the **Museum of West Java** ⓘ *Mon-Sat 0800-1600,1000Rp,* (Negeri Propinsi Jawa Barat), is on the corner of Jalan Otto Iskandarinata and the ring road. It houses artefacts tracing the development and history of West Java.

One of the minarets of the **Masjid Agung** ⓘ *Jl Jend Sudirman, Sat and Sun only 0900-1700, 2000Rp,* can be climbed for fine views of the city, and the mountains that surround it. Ajid, at the tourist information office (in the north side of the mosque) can also arrange for tours of the huge mosque, but remember to dress conservatively. Men in shorts will not be allowed to enter.

Markets

Like many Indonesian cities, Bandung has a number of markets. **Pasar Kota Kembang** runs along a narrow lane linking Jalan Asia-Afrika and Jalan Dalem Kaum, and specializes in clothes, shoes and accessories. **Pasar Baru** is in Chinatown and is a good place to buy textiles, including batik; the basement houses a vegetable market. **Jalan Pasar Utara** is a food market selling snacks and many West Javanese culinary specialities. Not far from the Ciroyom Terminal is the **Pasar Jatayu** on Jalan Arjuna, which houses a few antique and junk shops among the second-hand motorcycle outlets; there are also some places selling military memorabilia nearby. Bandung's largest **flower market**, supplied from the many upland nurseries around the city, is on Jalan Wastukencana.

Further north still (7 km) is the **Dago Teahouse** ⓘ *1500Rp daily, early morning until 2200, catch a Dago colt up Jl Ir H Juanda (the colts terminate at Terminal Dago, not far from the Tea House), the Tea House is behind the Pajajaran University housing complex.* It was renovated in 1991, and provides a cultural hall and open-air theatre for evening Sundanese dance performances. There are good views of the city from here and an excellent restaurant.

Walks

The Bandung tourist office has identified a number of walks in the city through the Central Business District (CBD), Chinatown and elsewhere. For maps and further information contact the tourist office – good background information on buildings and the city's history is available.

Tours

The tourist office on Jalan Asia Afrika will organize tours in and around town, as will many of the travel agents (depending on season and demand). Typical tours visit the Tangkuban Prahu crater and Ciater hot springs (five hours, US$27 per person), architecturally interesting buildings around town (three hours, US$8 per person) and an angklung music performance, plus traditional Sundanese dancing (three hours, US$8 per person). By Moritz (see Sleeping) organize day trips to Mount Papandayan, with a guide leading visitors all over the mountain and a bath in a sulphur spring.They also have trips to Ciwidey, to see the tea plantations, Cibuni crater and Danau Patenggang. All tours from By Moritz cost around US$38 per person, but prices are highly negotiable. ▸▸ *See Activities and tours, page 220.*

Around Bandung

Most visitors who venture out of the city travel north into the volcanic **Priangan Highlands** that surround Bandung, to see neat tea plantations, colossal craters and natural hot springs.

Villa Isola

ⓘ *Regular minibuses and colts ply this route out of Bandung. Either travel direct from the train station or via Terminal Ledeng at the northern edge of the city. This lies on the route north of Jalan Setiabudi, 6 km from the city centre, and is yet another fine art deco building, set on a hill overlooking the city.*

Lembang

Lembang, 16 km north of Bandung, is a popular resort town on an upland plateau with restaurants, hotels and pony-drawn carts. It is famous for its pleasant climate and abundance of fresh flowers and fruit. The town can be used as a base to explore the uplands and visit such places as the Tangkuban Prahu Crater and the Ciater Hot Springs (see below). Garden nurseries line the road into Lembang and the town also supports the internationally respected **Bosscha Observatory** ⓘ *visits must be prearranged, regular minibuses connect Lembang with Bandung's Terminal Ledeng, on Jl Dr Setiabudi on the northern edge of the city, to get to Terminal Ledeng, take a colt going up Jl Pasir Kaliki, there are also colts running direct to Lembang from the train station in the centre of town.*

Tangkuban Prahu Crater → Colour map 10, A2.

ⓘ *Daily 35,000Rp. Guides are available for off-path treks (inadvisable without a guide because of the emissions of sulphurous gases – get a guide from the tourist information centre (0700-1700) at the crater, there are plenty of charlatans, cost in the region of 75,000Rp), but unnecessary for the well-defined path to the Domas Crater. Bus or colt heading for Subang from either the Leuwi Panjang terminal or from the minibus stop opposite the train station – and ask to be dropped off at the entrance to the crater (about 25 km from the city), hitch or walk (3.5 km) from here, at the weekend there are colts that go all the way to the summit.*

Tangkuban Prahu Crater (the capsized boat crater) is one of the most popular tourist sights in the vicinity of Bandung and possibly the most accessible volcanic crater in Indonesia. The route up to the volcano from Lembang passes through rich agricultural land, with terraces of market garden crops clawing their way up the hillsides, chincona trees (the bark is used to produce quinine), teak and wild ginger. The entrance to the 'park' is 9 km from Lembang. The drive from the gate snakes through a forest of giant pines reminiscent of a set from *Jurassic Park*. Some 3 km from the gate is the lower car park (with restaurant and tourist stalls). From here road continues upwards for another 1 km to the rim of the impressive **Ratu Crater**. Alternatively, there is a footpath from the lower car park to the Ratu Crater (1.5 km), and another from there to the smaller **Domas Crater** (1 km). Another path links the Domas and Ratu Craters (1.2 km). It is also possible to walk all the way round the Ratu Crater. Though visited by numerous tour buses and inhabited by large numbers of souvenir sellers, the natural splendour of the volcano makes the trip worthwhile. Ratu rises to an altitude of 1830 m, and the crater drops precipitously from the rim. Bursts of steam and the smell of sulphur bear witness to the volcanic activity latent beneath the surface.

The curious shape of the summit of Tangkuban Prahu has given rise to the Sundanese *Legend of Prince Sangkuriang*, who unknowingly fell in love with his mother, Dayang Sumbi. She tried to prevent their marriage, insisting that her betrothed create a lake and canoe before sunrise on their wedding day. Sangkuriang seemed to be endowed with magical powers and he nearly achieved this impossible task when Dayang Sumbi called upon the gods to hasten the sun to rise, in order to prevent their forbidden union. Sangkuriang was so angry that he kicked his nearly finished canoe, which landed upside down on the horizon, thus creating this silhouette. The wildlife in the surrounding forest includes a small population of native gibbons. At the summit, hawkers sell anklungs to bemused tourists while tapping out *Auld Lang Syne* or *Happy Birthday*. They also vigorously proffer assorted lurid clothes, synthetic fur hats, bags and rucksacks, as well as wooden carvings, animals made of small seashells and herbal remedies such as *kayu naga*. This resembles green, hairy twiglets, and is reputedly good for rheumatism and backache. The twiglets are boiled in water and the resultant malodorous brew is drunk.

Ciater Hot Springs

ⓘ *T0260 471700, entrance 14,000Rp, 27,500Rp to bathe, daily 24 hrs, take a colt or bus towards Subang, ask to be let off at Air Panas Ciater; the hotel and springs are 150 m off the main road.*
Ciater Hot Springs are 6.5 km on from Tangkuban Prahu, the road following the mountain side and winding through tea plantations. There are brilliantly clear hot-water pools and waterfalls here situated on the side of a hill. Unfortunately, the complex is rather run down.

Ciwidey → *Colour map 10, A2*

ⓘ *Regular connections from the Kebon Kelapa terminal, 1½ hrs.*
Ciwidey is a small town about 14 km southwest of Bandung. It is much less touristy and more rural than Ciater – and well worth the effort of getting there. Continuing along the road, up the Ciwidey valley, the route climbs up past Cimanggu (at the 42 km marker) where there is a small park and hot pools fed from Gunung Patuha (2400 m). The hillsides here are planted with tea bushes. Among the largest estates are the Rancabali and Malabar estates.

Candi Cangkuang

ⓘ *Catch a bus from Bandung's Cicaheum terminal on Jl Jend A Yani, travelling east towards Tasikmalaya and Banjar; get off 2 km after Kadungura, in the village of Leles.*
Candi Cangkuang is an eighth-century Hindu monument and can be visited in a day from Bandung. The temple is 48 km from the city on the road to Garut.

◉ Bandung listings

For Sleeping and Eating price codes, see inside the front cover.

● Sleeping

Bandung *p211, map p213*
Bandung lacks the quality budget accommodation of other Javanese cities, and those in search of clean comfortable digs are advised to spend a little more money here. Many of the city's hotels are scattered conveniently near the train station around Jl Kebonjati and Jl Kebon Kawung. The cost of a room in mid-range and more expensive places increases by around 20% at weekends.
LL-B Arion Swiss Belhotel, Jl Otto Iskandarinata 16, T022 4240000, www.swiss-belhotel.com. Top-class lodgings with tastefully decorated rooms with cable TV, broadband access and all mod-cons. Spa, fitness centre and rooftop swimming pool.
LL-B Grand Preanger, Jl Asia Afrika 81, T022 4231631, www.preanger.aerowisata.com. A/c, restaurant (excellent food), pool, original art deco wing (1928), refurbished to a high

standard and offering the most interesting rooms, now with a 10-storey modern addition, central location, fitness centre, good facilities and well-run.

A Savoy Homann, Jl Asia Afrika 112, T022 4232244, www.savoyhomann-hotel.com. The wonderful art deco exterior of this hotel is immediately charming, proving that aging places of style can be maintained in this country. Rooms are spacious and stylish, and have internet access and cable TV. Discounts available. Recommended.

A-B Hotel Perdana Wisata, Jl Jend Sudirman 66-68, T022 4328238, F022 4232818. This is a well-managed 3-star hotel. Internet access available in rooms, which are clean, modern and some with pool views. Discounts available (20-30%).

B-D Hotel Trio, Jl Gardujati 55-61, T022 6031055, hoteltrio@bdg.centrin.net.id. Crowded with rooms, the Trio is popular with Chinese Indonesians and gets very busy at weekends. Rooms are all spotless and well maintained and come with TV and a/c. The more expensive rooms are huge and have a bath and fridge, with plenty of natural light. Pool. Discounts available (20-30%).

D Hotel Serena, Jl Marjuk 4-6, T022 4204317, F022 4260427. This is a good option for those wanting comfort, without being overly extravagant with the pennies. Clean, tiled rooms with a/c, hot water and cable TV are good value here. Recommended.

D-E Hotel Gunter, Jl Otto Iskandarinata 20, T022 4203763. Faded 1960s hotel with rooms surrounding an immaculate cat-filled garden. Rooms are tatty and have a fair number of spider webs, but bedding is clean. Fan and a/c rooms available, all with TV.

E Hotel Palem, Jl Belakang Pasar 119, T/F022 4232601. Exhaust fumes seem to creep up the stairs into this popular local place with fairly clean, but slightly decrepit fan and a/c rooms.

E Hotel Patradissa, Jl H Moch Iskat 9, T022 4206680. Sparkling reception area, festooned with family photos and ornate furniture. A/c and fan rooms are small and clean, but lack natural light.

F By Moritz, Jl Kebon Jati, Luxor Permai 35, T022 4205788, bymoritz_info@yahoo.com. Things have drastically improved in terms of cleanliness in recent times, although the place is very quiet. There is a maze-like assortment of very simple fan rooms, some with attached bathroom, and the cheaper rooms with common bathroom. The best rooms are the 2 on the roof, with small garden, pleasant seating area and views over the roofs to the south. The downstairs communal area has an assortment of books, TV, simple restaurant and a couple of guitars, occasionally utilised by the friendly staff for yet another rendition of Hotel California. Recommended.

F Hotel Citra, Jl Gadujati 93, T022 6005061. Cleanish rooms with TV and attched bathroom. Rooms are a little musty and none have windows. Breakfast not included.

⊕ Eating

Bandung p211, map p213
Local dishes including *gorengan*, a form of vegetable-based tempura, *bandrek* and *bajigur*, both drinks made of ginger and sweetened coconut milk respectively, *pecel lele* (fried eels with a piquant sauce) and *comro* made from cassava and tempe. There are also a large number of bakeries in Bandung, the best selection concentrated on Jl Braga.

♥♥ Momiji, Jl Braga 64, T022 4203786, 1100-2200. Calm and relaxing Japanese restaurant with an extensive menu of sushi, tempura, udon, tappanyaki and bento boxes. This place is particularly popular with European and East Asian expats at the weekend.

♥ Dapur Ku, Jl Lembong 12-18, T022 4206612, 1000-2200. Popular place to try Sundanese cooking, with set meals, or a huge buffet-style selection to choose from. The staff speak good English and can help with deciphering the menu.

♥ London Bakery, Jl Braga 37, T022 4207351, 0800-2200. Good selection of coffees, teas, sandwiches and pasta dishes (small portions), with the *Jakarta Post* to linger over. There is an outdoor seating area, although the exhaust fumes are choking.

♥ **Red Tulip Steakhouse**, Jl Kebon Kawung 2, T022 4207264, 0600-2300. The 10,000Rp breakfast sets at this cavernous place are a good deal, with enough carbs for a volcano trek. The menu features plenty of steaks, pastas and strange coloured juice drinks (the lemon juice is blue). Excellent service.

♥ **Sederhana Bintaro**, Jl Jendral Sudirman 111, T022 4207733, 0800-2200. Fans of *nasi Padang* won't want to miss this sparkling restaurant, with an extensive menu of spicy Sumatran favourites and some excellent value set meals. The *sirsak* juice from here is delicious. They can deliver to hotels for free. Recommended.

♥ **Warung Laos**, Jl Prof. Eyckman 2, T022 2030516, Mon, Tue 1800-2330, Wed-Sun 1100-2330. Excellent little place just off Jl Cihampelas with pleasant upstairs seating area serving good pizzas, pastas, juices and soups. Recommended.

Cihampelas Walk (see Shopping) has a number of good, clean places (mostly ♥) to eat at in a/c comfort. There are plenty of places to choose from including **Gokana Teppan** (T022 204111), which serves bargain priced Japanese set meals, and **Cing Wan** (T022 2061001), which has a menu of Thai and Chinese dishes. Another mall, **Paris Van Java**, has an excellent selection of eateries including Peranakan (Straits Chinese), Japanenese and Western cuisine. It is beautifully lit up at night and gets very busy. Well worth a visit.

Jl Gardajati has a selection of Chinese restaurants. **Mei Hwa** and **Red Top** (open for lunch and dinner) are worth investigating.

Bakeries

Fa Fa Bapau, Jl Gardajati 63, T022 607008. 0800-2100, head here for something a little different, has a fine selection of Chinese buns, filled with pork and spices, or sweet ones with bean paste.

French Bakery, Jl Braga 35, T022 4268188, 0800-2200. Cakes, bread and sandwiches.
Holland Bakery, Jl Gardajati, T022 4206225, 0600-0200. Decent selections of cakes, bread and some sandwiches.
Kartika Sari, Jl Haji Akbar 4, T022 4231355. Daily 0600-1900, an incredibly popular bakery and gets literally packed with customers at the weekend, who mostly come for their signature *pisang molan* (pastries filled with banana and cheese), which fly off the shelf.
La Patisserie, in the Grand Hotel Preanger (see Sleeping), 0800-2100, has some very naughty chocolate delights, cheesecake, and handy take away lasagnes and pizza.

Foodstalls

Probably the best are down a tiny alley off Jl Bungsu, near the Puri Nas Bakery (open 1730 onwards). Stalls are also on Jl Merdeka, Jl Martadinata, Jl Diponegoro (near the RRI building), Jl Cikapundung Barat and Jl Dalem Kaum, west of the Alun-alun Lor. Most are night stalls only. Of all the stalls, the one with the greatest local reputation is Pak Aceng's *Es campur* (mixed ice) cart which he sets up on Jl Kapatihan near the Damai shop. He has been selling here for over 25 years. 300 m west of the railway station is an excellent *martabak* (cheese, chocolate, banana) stall, in a notable art deco building.

🎵 Bars and clubs

Bandung *p211, map p213*
Bandung has a great array of bars, pubs and clubs, with good bands and atmosphere. Jl Braga is packed with bars (many of the somewhat seedy variety), and gets lively in the evenings. Bars worth checking out include **Escobar**, **North Sea Bar**, **Red 13** and **Violet Cafe**. Bars open in the afternoon and close around 0200.

Classic Rock Cafe, Jl Lembong 1, T022 4207982, 1200-0200. A fun venue covered with rock memorabilia, which has brilliant guitar door handles. Local musicians come to play classic covers and some Indonesian rock in the evenings to a lively crowd.
Embassy, Cihampelas Walks, T022 2061154, daily 2200-0600. Renowned club that plays trance and techno to a cool crowd, and attracts some of the nation's best DJs.

⦿ Entertainment

Bandung *p211, map p213*
The entertainment schedule is very changeable in Bandung. It is recommended that you check at the tourist information office before you head anywhere.

Adu domba (ram fights)
Most Sundays at **Ranca Buni**, near Ledeng, north of town on Jl Setiabudi. Get there by Lembung bus to Ledung terminal. Walk down Jl Sersan Bejuri then turn left; many helpful locals around, if you get lost.

Angklung (hand-held bamboo chimes)
Performances at **Pak Udjo's workshop**, Jl Padasuka 118 (8 km northeast of the town centre), 1530-1730. Take a Cicaheum colt and get off at the intersection with Jl Padasuka, near the Cicaheum bus station. Pak Udjo's workshop is a 7-min walk, on the right-hand side of the street.

Cinemas
Blitz Mulitplex, at Paris Van Java (see Shopping) shows all the latest English-language blockbusters, and has very comfy seats, all for 25,000Rp. Recommended.

Cultural shows
Dago Tea House, open stage Sat evenings, free (buy a drink). Sundanese dance and music performances.
Jl Naripan 7, dance rehearsals can be seen here most evenings.

Rumentiang Siang, Jl Barangsiang 1 (near Jl A Yani), T022 4233562. The schedule here is all over the place, but this is the place to go for performance of Jaipongan (Sundanese dance), epic *wayang golek* shows, *ketoprak* (traditional theatre).
STSI, (Institute of Fine Arts) Jl Buah Batu, T022 7314982. Performances and rehearsals of Sundanese dance, theatre and music here.

⦿ Shopping

Bandung *p211, map p213*
Art galleries Bandung is viewed as a centre for Indonesian arts and there are a number of galleries in town exhibiting work by promising young Indonesians. There are a few galleries along Jl Braga including **Barli**, Jl Prof Dr Sutami 91, T022 2011898, Mon-Sat 0900-1700. Collection of traditional and contemporary art, **Bunga Art Gallery** (Jl Braga 41, T022 7310960, daily 0900-1800), **Jalu Braga**, (Jl Braga 29, daily 0700-2200) and **Taman Budya Jawa Barat**, Jl Bukit Dago Selatan 53, T022 2505364, Mon-Sat 0900-2200. Sundanese art and occasional performances.
Batik Batik Abstrak, Jl Tirtasari 9, T081 56281358. Funky and super-modern batik designs.
Books There is a branch of **QB Books** on Jl Setiabudi to the north of town, daily 0900-2100. Good selection of English language books and a relaxed cafe with Wi-Fi access.
Ceramics There is a **Ceramics Research Institute** on Jl Jend A Yani near the Pasar Cicadas; examples can be purchased from **Bandung Gallery**, Jl Siliwangi 16, Kundhika, Jl Gunung Batu 178 and Uun Kusnadi, Jl Kenangan 9A.
Handicrafts Pa Aming, Jl M Ramdhan 4 and Pa Ruchiyat, Jl Pangarang Bawah IV No 78/17B (behind No 20 in the alleyway). Both are workshops where you can also buy and the latter is reputed to sell perhaps the finest worked examples. Pak Ruchiyat has over 35 years' experience; note that prices are fixed. Shops along Jl Braga sell puppets.

Cupumanik, Jl Haji Akbar, Mon-Sat 0900-1600. Collection of locally made masks, puppets and handicrafts. **Eddy Noor Gallery**, Jl Villa Bandung Indah, T022 7071135. Beautiful painted glass exhibition by a local artist.

Jewellery **Runa**, a husband-and-wife team, produce perhaps the best modern jewellery in Bandung. On sale at many major hotels.

Night market Jl Sudirman, cheap clothes and fruit, paraffin lamps add a mysterious romantic touch.

Shopping malls Chihampelas Walk, Jl Chihampelas 160, T022 2061122. Brand-name goods in a clean a/c environment. Good for taking a breather from manic Jeans St shopping.

Supermarket Carrefour (Braga Walk, daily 1000-2200) is a good place to stock up on necessities. You can also find a few decent cafes and fast food outlets here.

▲ Activities and tours

Bandung p211, map p213
Tour operators
Kangaroo Travel and Tours, Hotel Perdana Wisata, Jl Jebdral Sudirman 66-68, T022 4200334.
Nata Tours, Jl Kebon Kawung, T022 4260380, 24 hrs. Can book Air Asia flights.
Satriavi, Grand Hotel Preanger, Jl Asia Afrika 81, T022 4203657, www.aerowisata.co.id.

⊖ Transport

Bandung p211, map p213
Most roads in the centre of town are 1-way. This, coupled with the dense traffic, makes it quite a struggle getting around town. Bandung must have more orange-suited traffic wardens than any other town on Java, ready to direct traffic dangerously (and collect their 300Rp parkir). Colts (Angkutan kota): 3000Rp around town, up to 5000Rp for longer journeys. Station on Jl Kebonjati. Delmans are available for hire.

Air
Bandung's **airport** is 4 km from the city, T022 6041313. Fixed price transport to town by taxi, US$5.50. Flights have been cut down to a trickle. **Air Asia** (www.airasia.com) fly daily to **Kuala Lumpur**. Merpati and Sriwijaya have daily flights to **Denpasar**, **Mataram** and **Surabaya**.

Bus
Local City buses go north-south or east-west; west on Jl Asia Afrika, east on Jl Kebonjati (beware that Nos 9 and 11 stop at 2100) south on Jl Otto Iskandardinata, north on Jl Astanaanyar, 250Rp.

Long distance Bandung has 2 long-distance bus terminals: for destinations to the west is the **Leuwi Panjang** terminal, 5 km south of the city centre on Jl Soekarno-Hatta. (This has replaced the old Kebun Kelapa terminal). Serves destinations including to **Jakarta** (Kampong Rambutan terminal), **Bogor** and **Sumatra**. Terminal **Cicaheum** on Jl Jend A Yani serves destinations to the east and north, including **Yogya**, **Solo**, **Surabaya**, **Garut**, **Tasikmalaya**, **Cirebon** and **Semarang**. There are also direct buses to **Pangandaran**.

To avoid the hassle of going to the terminals, it is best to book bus tickets through **Pahala Kencana** (Jl Kebonjati, T022 4232911) and **Kramat Jati** (Jl Kebonjati (T022 420086). Both companies have buses departing from their offices to **Denpasar** (US$35, 24 hrs), **Probolinggo** (US$31, 19hrs), **Surabaya** (US$19, 19hrs) **Yogya** and **Solo** (US$11, 8-9 hrs). There are also some buses to **Lampung** and **Palembang** in Sumatra.

Minibus Phone to make a booking, or get the hotel staff to do it for you, and pay when you have reached your destination. **4848**, T022 4224848, has door-to-door services to **Jakarta** (US$9), **Cirebon** (US$6) and **Pangandaran** (US$7). **Deva Travel**, Jl Jend. A Ayani 810, T022 7200679, offers 2 daily door-to-door services to Bogor (US$7, 0400, 0900). **Kangaroo Travel** (see Tour operators), has 6 daily door-to-door trips to Jakarta's Soekarno-Hatta Airport, US$13.

Car hire
Mulia Car Rental, Batununggal Indah 39, T081 2015606, www.muliarental.com.

   Total Car Rental, Jl Jajaway Dago Atas 12A, T022 82520044, www.rental.total.or.id.

Taxi
Taxis in Bandung are notorious for rip-offs. The only company worth using is **Blue Bird**, T022 7561234.

Train
The station is in the centre of town behind the bemo station, on Jl Stasion Barat and has a helpful information line with English-speaking staff (T022 4266383). Regular connections with **Jakarta's** Jatinegara and Gambir stations. The best service is the **Argogede** with 6 daily departures to **Gambir** taking 2½ hrs (*bisnis* US$2/*eksekutif* US$5). The **Parahiyangan** leaves for **Jatinegara** 7 times daily (*bisnis* US$2/*eksekutif* US$4) and also takes around 2½ hrs. The **Lodaya** calls in at **Tasikmalaya**, Banjar (for **Pangandaran**), **Yogya** and **Solo** (*bisnis* US$10/*eksekutif* US$16.50). For **Surabaya**, hop on the daily

Argo Wilis (*eksekutif* US$22) and **Mutiara Selatan** (*bisnis* US$13).

❶ Directory

Bandung *p211, map p213*
Airline offices Garuda, Jl Asia Afrika 118, T022 4217747. **Merpati**, Jl Kebon Kawung 16, T022 42303180. **Sirwaijaya**, Jl Burangrang, T022 7334026. **Banks** There are banks all over Bandung. BNI, Jl Braga 23. **HSBC**, corner of Jl Tamblong and Jl Asia Africa. ATMs can be found along all commercial streets, particularly Jl Braga, Jl Cihampelas, Jl Jendral Sudirman and Jl Asia Afrika. **Money changers:** VIT Jl Cihampelas, in a small booth opposite Adventist Hospital. **Aneka Artha Mas**, Jl Naripan 43, T022 4241204. **Internet** One Byte, Jl Cihmapelas 74, T022 4263992, 5000Rp per hr, 24 hr. **Medical services** Chemist: Ratu Farma, Jl Kebon jati 106, T022 439892. **Hospital:** Adventist Hospital, Jl Cihampelas 161, T022 2034386. **Post office** Jl Asia Afrika 49, corner of Jl Asia Afrika and Jl Banceuy, Poste Restante available. **Telephone** Wartel, Jl Asia Afrika (opposite Savoy Homann Hotel), for international calls and fax.

Pangandaran

→ *Phone code: 0265. Colour map 10, B3.*

Pangandaran is situated on the neck of a narrow isthmus and offers the best beaches on the south coast of Java. Originally a fishing village, many of the local people now derive their livelihoods from tourism. At weekends, during peak season, the town is crowded with Indonesian tourists; out of season, on weekdays, it is like a ghost town and hotel and losmen prices can be bargained down. The high season is June to September, the low season October to March.

In 2006, Pangandaran was hit by a tsunami. The tidal wave, 3 m high, devastated the coastal strip, washing away numerous houses and businesses. Many locals have heartbreaking stories to tell and are trying hard to rebuild their lives, but there is still plenty of evidence of the disaster. Lia Natalia, owner of Lotus Wisata, whose business was washed away, is now happily rebuilt in a slightly different location and has an album of photos taken after the tsunami showing the immediate damage. Look for the Jalur Evakuasi (Evacuation Route) signs around town in the unlikely event of another disaster occurring. ▸▸ *For listings, see pages 224-226.*

Beaches

① *Admission to the isthmus is 2500Rp.*

The best beach is on the west side of the isthmus and is named **West Beach** (Pantai Barat). Swimming is not recommended as currents are vicious. Souvenir shops line the beach front and most accommodation is concentrated here. The east side of the isthmus (**East Beach** or Pantai Timur) is less developed; the water is often rough and swimming is poor, sometimes dangerous. Fishermen cast their nets from this shore and land their catches along the beach. Their colourful boats lining the shore are a lovely sight. The fish market is worth a visit in the mornings if you can stand the smell! The **PHKA tourist office** is on the borders of the park at the south end of the isthmus, near East Beach. Private tour companies and travel agents also often bill themselves as 'tourist information centres' to help attract business. Lia Natalia at **Lotus Wisata** speaks excellent English and is a good source of information.

The promontory of the isthmus is a park – the **Penanjung National Park** ① *0700-1730, only half of which is open to tourists, 5500Rp, guides 75,000Rp for a tour lasting 4 hrs and worth the money*. On both the east and west sides of the promontory are white sand beaches. It is possible to walk the 10 km around the shoreline of the peninsula, or hike through the jungle which is said to support small populations of buffalo, deer, tapirs, civet cats, porcupines and hornbills, although how they tolerate the herds of tourists is a mystery. The Rafflesia flower can apparently be seen here in season. The park also has some limestone caves.

Around Pangandaran

Batu Karas ① *get there by hired motorbike or take a bemo to Cijulang, then charter a motorbike the last 10 km to the beach from the main road*, is becomingly increasingly popular with Australian surfers.

Green Canyon ① *take a minibus from Pangandaran to Cijulang, and then an ojek from there, most hotels run tours to the canyon, which will also include a half-day visit to local farming and craft industries, alternatively visit the tourist information office for cheaper, good tours, starting at 100,000Rp per person, hire your own motorbike or bicycle for the day*, is a very popular day trip. Boat hire is regulated and costs 80,000Rp per *prahu* (which seat up to eight people). Travelling upriver, the foliage becomes denser and the rocks close in, until you find yourself entering a canyon. After 15-20 minutes, the boat's path is blocked by rocks. There is a large plunge pool here, swimming and rubber rings for hire. Best time to visit is during the week, as it gets crowded at weekends and holidays; a recommended trip.

Parigi Bay ① *regular buses run from Pangandaran bus station on Jl Merdeka, ask specifically for a beach, eg Batu Karas, the bus doesn't go all the way – only to the bridge over the Green River (9000Rp) ; from here you need to hire a motorbike or hitch a lift,* is west of Pangandaran, and offers better and quieter beaches than the isthmus, namely Batu Hiu, Batu Karas and Parigi, and good water for surfing.

A worthwhile alternative to the bus trip back to Banjar is the much more enjoyable ferry journey from Kalipucang to Cilacap (see Transport). Local trips around the peninsula, stopping to swim or snorkel can be bargained for with the local fishermen (around US$22). Trips to tiny white-sand islands (infrequently visited and uninhabited) off the peninsula cost about US$27 for a boat ride of about one hour, and then you can stay on the island as long as you wish. A trip to Nusakambangon is available from Pangandaran (US$27). The island, once forbidden to tourists because of a high-security prison located there, has unspoilt beaches and forests. The prison is no longer in use but worth a visit as part of the tour.

Pangandaran

Sleeping		
Adam's Homestay 1	Pangandaran Beach 6	Villa Angela 13
Komodo 2	Pantai Sari 7	
Laut Biru 3	Pondok Daun 8	**Eating**
Mini Tiga 4	Puri Alam 9	Chez Mama Cilacap 1
Nyuir Resort 5	Sandaan 10	Eka Bamboo Cafe 2
	Surya Pesona 11	Mungil 4

Only One Resto 5	
Pasar Ikan 3	
Relax 6	

Tour agencies organize jungle, boat (fishing, snorkelling), home industry, village and other tours. Tours include a six-hour trip to Green Canyon (US$11), Jungle Tour (US$8) and many more. All tours include appropriate entrance fee, guide and lunch on longer excursions. Most hotels offer tours, and they can also be booked at Lotus Wisata on Jalan Bulak Laut. Almost every hotel organizes trips to Yogya, Wonosobo and Bandung etc. ▸▸ *See activities and tours, page 225.*

It's also possible to charter a boat between Kalipucang (Pangandaran's 'port') and **Cilicap** through the Anakan Lagoon, an 'inland' sea. A recommended four-hour journey and a gentle form of transport, the boat sails down the mangrove-clothed Tanduy River, stopping off in various fishing villages, before crossing the Anakan Lagoon. The Tanduy River marks the border between West Java and Central Java; in West Java the local language is Sundanese; in Central Java, Javanese. The last village before the ferry turns into the lagoon – **Majingklak** – is the easternmost village in West Java. The large island bordering the south of the Lagoon, and protecting it from the Indian Ocean, is **Kampangan Island**. In 1912, the Dutch depopulated the island, resettling 3 fishing villages, with the intention of making it a prison. The lagoon is one of Indonesia's largest areas of wetland and has a varied water bird population. For keen birdwatchers it is possible to jump ship at one of the fishing villages, sleep in a homestay, and then charter a boat to explore the lagoon early the next morning, before continuing the journey to Cilacap (or vice versa). ▸▸ *See Transport, page 226.*

◉ Pangandaran listings

For Sleeping and Eating price codes,
see inside the front cover.

◉ Sleeping

Pangandaran *p222, map p223*
Accommodation is concentrated on the west side of the isthmus – there are around 100 hotels and *losmen*. Rates can be bargained down substantially during the low season (Oct-Mar) and week days. At Christmas and during Jul and Aug prices rise steeply, when Indonesian tourists flock here. Many hotels and guesthouses rent out family rooms– usually 2 double rooms and living area.
A-B Laut Biru, Jl Embah Jaga Lautan 17-18, T0265 639360, www.lautbiro.com. Handily located near a good stretch of beach and the entrance to the national park, this place has great facilities, comfortable rooms and good service. Pool. Substantial discounts available.
A-B Nyuir Resort Hotel, Jl Bulak Laut, T0265 639349, www.nyiurresorthotel.com. Rooms here are overpriced. However, the hotel has all the trimmings of a resort with a pleasant garden, pool and and restaurant.

B Surya Pesona, Jl Bulak Laut, T0265 639428, F0265 639289. Old-style resort with limited character. Pool. Discounts available.
C-E Sandaan, Jl Bulak Laut, T0265 639165, F0265 630017. Wide variety of rooms, all of which are clean, and improve dramatically as the price range is climbed. Standards have a/c and TV, but they face a brick wall. The more expensive deluxe rooms have a pleasant veranda and views of the pool.
D Adam's Homestay, Jl Bulak Laut, T0265 639396. Womderful gardens, with ponds and small streams aplenty. Rooms are huge, and have fridge, a/c and TV. Pool. Recommended.
D Pantai Sari, Jl Bulak Laut 80, T0265 639175. From the outside, this Saudi-owned place doesn't look like much, but money has recently poured in and the large rooms have been renovated with love, featuring flat screen TV, fridge, a/c and hot and cold water. Excellent value.
D Pondok Daun, Jl Bulak Laut 74, T0265 639788. Spacious clean rooms all with a/c, TV and outdoor bathroom, in a shady garden with small pool.

D Puri Alam, Jl Bulak Laut Depan Pasar Wisata, T0265 631699. The staff here don't speak English but are extraordinarily friendly and make every effort to ensure visitors feel at home. Good-value spacious new rooms, with TV, a/c and all the trimmings. Breakfast not included. Recommended.

E-F Komodo, Jl Bulak Laut, T0265 630753. Simple fan and a/c rooms, some of which are spacious. Very small pool.

E-F Villa Angela, Jl Bulak Laut, T0265 639641. Good value a/c and fan rooms popular with the surf fraternity.

F Mini Tiga, Jl Bulak Laut, T0265 639436, kalmaja@yahoo.fr. This homely hotel is a peaceful place to pull up a chair, read books, and drink all the free tea and coffee you can manage. Rooms are simple, but comfortable, and bathrooms have squat toilet and *mandi*.

F Pangandaran Beach Hotel, Jl Pantai Barat Pananjung 95, T0265 639062. Set in a fading colonial-style mansion, this place needs several licks of paint, but still has some of the cheapest a/c rooms in town.

🍴 Eating

Pangandaran *p222, map p223*
There are innumerable places to eat, many of which are geared to western tastes. Not surprisingly, seafood is the best bet.

🍴 Chez Mama Cilacap, Jl Kidang Pananjung, T0265 639098, 0730-2300. Excellent place for fresh seafood and breakfast. Also some Western standards. Recommended.

🍴 Eka Bamboo Cafe, Jl Bulak Laut, T081809740899, 0800-0100. Good place for a cheap breakfast, a late night beer or to sample some local cuisine including *nasi uduk*.

🍴 Mungil, Jl Bulak Laut, T081328098372, 0700-2300. Cupboard-like restaurant that attracts plenty of foreigners with fine views of the surf, steaks, pizza and seafood.

🍴 Only One Resto, Jl Bulak Laut, T0265 639969, 0700-2300. This comfortable and popular eatery has sea views, good fresh seafood, and tasty Indonesian cuisine.

🍴 Pasar Ikan, Jl Talanca, 0700-2000. Seafood fans will love this collection of clean restaurants serving up the catch of the day. There are huge prawns, shark, lobster and fish accompanied by huge portions of delicious *kangkung* (water spinach). One of the more popular places is **Sari Melati** (T0265 639735). Recommended.

🍴 Restaurant Relax, Jl Bulak Laut 74, T0265 630377, 0800-2300. Good variety of Western and Indonesian dishes, excellent juices and lassis and some rather tasty cakes in a homely European café-style setting.

🍸 Bars and clubs

Pangandaran *p222, map p223*
The Spot (at the **Surya Pesona**, see Sleeping), 2000-0100. Down a few bottles of *kratingdaeng* and dance with the local youth to the ear-bleeding techno. There are occasional *dangdut* nights here for those in search of something a little more laid-back.

🛍 Shopping

Pangandaran *p222, map p223*
Stalls on the beach and some shops on the central isthmus road, Jl Kidang Pananjung (for instance **Luta** at 107) – shell jewellery, shells, clothing, knick-knacks. There is a large **Pasar Wisata** (tourist market) 0800-2100, which is mournfully empty on weekdays, selling tourist goodies. There is also a supermarket on Jl Merdeka, open 0800-2200.

▲ Activities and tours

Pangandaran *p222, map p223*
Tour operators
Lotus Wisata, Jl Bulak Laut, T0265 639635, organizes local tours and transport to and from Pangandaran; recommended. There are plenty of unlicensed guides wandering the streets and hanging out in cafes looking for business.

⊖ Transport

Pangandaran *p222, map p223*
400 km from Jakarta, 129 km from Bandung,
66 km from Banjar and 312 km from Yogya.

Becak/bike/car/motorbike hire
Becaks and bicycle hire along the beach and
from guesthouses, around US$2 per day.
Lotus Wisata, Jl Bulak Laut 2, T0265 639635,
rents motorbikes for US$5.50 per day and
cars for US$38 for 24 hrs, or with driver
US$55 for 24 hrs.

Boat
A private boat journeys between **Kalipucan**
(15 km from Pangandaran; take a local bus)
and **Cilacap**, 4 hrs. Approaching Cilacap is LP
Nusa Kembangan, Indonesia's top security
prison. The boat docks at **Sleko**, outside
Cilacap. There is currently no public boat
service running; chartering a boat costs
US$33. See also page 224.

Bus
There are 2 stations on Jl Merdeka, north of
the hotels and guesthouses (outside the main
gates). Local bus connections tend to leave
from the station at the eastern end of Jl
Merdeka, not far from the main intersection
before the gate, while express buses leave
from the company terminal further west along
Jl Merdeka. Regular buses link Pangandaran
with **Banjar** (US$1), from where there are
frequent buses onward to **Jakarta** (7-10 hrs),
Bogor (via **Ciawi**), **Bandung** (6 hrs), **Yogya**
and **Solo**, and less frequent buses to **Wonogiri**
and **Madiun**. Jakarta–Banjar buses leave
Jakarta's Cililitan station every hour. There are
also some direct connections with **Jakarta** (8
hrs) and **Bandung**. More regular connections
with **Ciamis** (2½ hrs), **Kalipucang** and **Tasik
Malaya** (3 hrs). Travel agents in town sell
tickets for popular routes. For trips to Bandung,
head to the Budiman's office at the terminal
from where there are regular a/c buses (US$3,
6 hrs calling in at **Banjar**, **Ciamis**, **Cihaurbeti**
and **Tasik Malaya** on the way.

  Minibus An a/c door-to-door service
can be booked from **Lotus Wisata** (see
above) and most guesthouses in town.
2 departures to **Bandung** daily at 0600
and 1400, US$9. Also to **Jakarta Gambir**
station, US$16.50; and **Yogyakarta**
departing 0900, US$16.50.

Train
No direct trains link Pangandaran with
Jakarta, Yogya, Bandung or Solo. It is
necessary to change in **Banjar**, a small town
on the Bandung–Yogya road, and 66 km
from Pangandaran. There are a number of
cheap *losmen* over the railway bridge from
the rail and bus stations in Banjar, for those
who arrive too late to make a connection. The
train and bus stations are 500 m apart; becaks
wait to take travellers between them. Regular
connections with **Jakarta** (1 daily, Ekonomi
only, 10 hrs), **Bandung** (5 hrs), **Yogya** (*bisnis*
US$11, *eksekutif* US$18.50, 5 hrs) and
Surabaya to Banjar. Regular buses link Banjar
with Pangandaran.

❶ Directory

Pangandaran *p222, map p223*
Banks Bank Rakyat Indonesia, and BNI
both have branches on Jl Merdeka. There
is a BNI ATM on Jl Bulak Laut, opposite the
Relax Restaurant. **Lotus Wisata** will change
money. **Post office** Jl Kidang Pananjung
111 (Poste restante available here).
Telephone Telkom, Jl Kidang Penanjung,
has an international phone service.

Yogyakarta

→ Phone code: 0274. Colour map 10, B4.

Yogyakarta – usually shortened to Yogya and pronounced 'Jogja' – is probably the most popular tourist destination in Java. It is a convenient base from which to visit the greatest Buddhist monument in the world – Borobudur – and the equally impressive Hindu temples on the Prambanan Plain. The town itself also has a number of worthwhile attractions: the large walled area of the kraton, with the sultan's palace, the ruined water gardens or 'Taman Sari', and a colourful bird market. Yogya is arguably the cultural capital of Java, and certainly its many private colleges and university attest to its being the island's educational heart, which also accounts for the younger, relatively affluent individuals you will see in the city. For the tourist, it is also one of the best centres for shopping and offers a good range of tourist services, from excellent mid-range accommodation to well-run tour companies.

Yogya is situated at the foot of the volcano Gunung Merapi, which rises to a height of 2911 m, to the north of the city. This peak is viewed as life-giving, and is set in opposition to the sea, which is life-taking and situated to the south. The importance of orientation with relation to Gunung Merapi and the ocean is seen most clearly in the structure of the kraton, or sultan's palace (see below).

The May 2006 earthquake that virtually destroyed the town of Bantul (26 km to the south of Yogyakarta) and killed over 6000 people, badly affected many sights in the southern part of Yogyakarta. The quake killed 27 people in Yogyakarta and damaged the Taman Sari, the Kraton Kerata Museum and the Museum Perjuangan (which still remains closed). Yogyakarta recovered quickly and the tourist infrastructure, so important to the city's economy, is running as efficiently as ever. → For listings, see pages 236-245.

Ins and outs

Getting there

Yogyakarta may not be in the top league of Javanese towns by population, but because it is such an important destination for tourists it is well connected. **Adisucipto International Airport** ① *8 km east of town, T0274 486666*, there are flights from here to Malaysia, destinations in Java and further afield. The train station is centrally situated on Jalan Pasar Kembang, and there are regular services to Jakarta's Gambir station (565 km), and east to Surabaya (327 km). The night train is notorious for its nimble-fingered thieves. The Umbunharjo long-distance bus terminal is 4 km southeast of the city centre, at the intersection of Jalan Veteran and Jalan Kemerdekaan. Buses of all types from *ekonomi* to *super VIP* depart for most towns in Java. Agents for tourist buses and minibuses can be found throughout the hotel and *losmen* areas of town and particularly on Jalan Sosrowijayan. → See Transport, page 244.

Getting around

While Yogya is not a small town by any means, exploring the city on foot, or a combination of foot and becak, is not beyond the realms of possibility. Becaks can be chartered by the hour or by the trip. It is more attractive, perhaps, but also considerably more expensive, to take an *andong* (horse-drawn carriage). Town buses (pick up a route map from the tourist office), bemos and colts offer cheaper local transport options. Note that becak and bemo drivers have an unerring tendency to take their passengers on extended tours of shops and art galleries. Self-drive car and motorbike hire is also easy to come by in Yogya; this gives

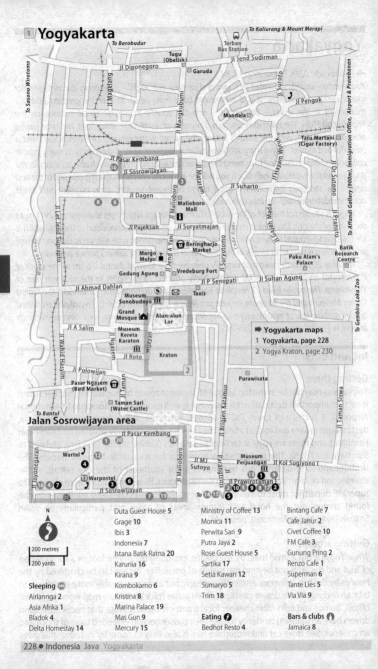

much greater flexibility when it comes to out of town excursions. Bikes are also available, and taxis for hire by the trip or charter by the hour, half-day or day.

Tourist Information office ① *Jl Malioboro 14, T0274 566000, Mon-Thu, Sat 0800-1900, Fri 0800-1800,* free maps of the town and environs, information on cultural events, bus routes, etc. One of the most helpful tourist offices in Indonesia. There is also a tourist office counter at the railway station and another at the airport.

Sights

Alun-alun Lor

Yogya's main street is Jalan Malioboro, which runs from north to south. At its south end, the street becomes Jalan Jend A Yani and then Jalan Trikora, which leads into the kraton and the grassed square known as the Alun-alun Lor. This square was the site of major events such as tiger and buffalo fights, which were staged here from 1769. A raised stand afforded the sultan and any visiting Dutch dignitaries a good view of the spectacle. The tiger was deemed to represent the foreigner and the buffalo, the Indonesian. Invariably, the buffalo would win the contest – often with some help – but the symbolism was lost on the Dutch. Nonetheless, the unperceptive Dutch still succeeded in dominating Yogya and Indonesia. There are two sacred *waringin* trees (*Ficus benjamina*) in the centre of the square. The *waringin* represents the sky and the square fence or *waringin kurung* surrounding the trees, the earth with its four quarters. At the same time, the tree is said to symbolize chaotic nature, and the fence human order.

At the northwest edge of the Alun-alun Lor is the **Museum Sonobudoyo** ① *Tue-Sun 0800-1400 except Fri 0800-1200, 5000Rp.* It was established in 1935 as a centre for Javanese culture, and the collection is housed, appropriately, within a traditional Javanese building. It contains a good selection of Indonesian art, largely Javanese, including a collection of *wayang* puppets, but also some Balinese woodcarvings. On the southwest side of the Alun-alun Lor is the **Grand Mosque**, built in Javanese style, with a wooden frame and a tiled roof.

The Kraton of Yogyakarta → *Numbers in brackets relate to key of plan on next page*

The **Kraton** of Yogyakarta was one of three such palaces that came into existence when the kingdom of Mataram was partitioned after the Treaty of Giyanti was signed with the VOC in 1755. It has been described as a city within a city; it not only houses the sultan's palace, but also a maze of shops, markets and private homes supporting many thousands of people. This section only deals with the inner palace; the kraton actually extends far further, 'beginning' 1 km north at the far end of Jalan Malioboro.

The kraton was started in 1756 by the first Sultan, Mangkubumi (who became Hamengkubuwono I in 1749), and finished almost 40 years later near the end of his reign. The teak wood used to construct the palace came from the sacred forest of Karangkasem on Gunung Kidul. It is largely made up of *pendopo* or open pavilions, enclosed within interconnecting rectangular courtyards. The entire complex is surrounded by high white washed walls. John Crawfurd, who was an assistant to Raffles and later to make his mark in both Siam and Burma, wrote of the kraton in 1811:

"The actual palace occupies the centre and is surrounded by the dwellings of the princes, and those of attendants and retainers. The principal approach is from the north, and through a square called the Alun-alun it is here that the prince shows himself to his subjects ..."

Facing the Alun-alun Lor is the **Pageleran** (1) ① *Sat-Thu 0830-1330, Fri 0830-1230, 3000Rp*, a large open *pendopo*, originally employed as a waiting place for government officials. Today, this pendopo is used for traditional dance and theatrical performances. There are a number of further pendopo surrounding this one, containing mediocre displays of regal clothing. The very first classes of the newly created Gajah Mada University were held under these shaded pavilions. To the south of the Pageleran, up some steps, is the **Siti Inggil** (2), meaning 'high ground'. This is the spot where new sultans are crowned. Behind the Siti Inggil is the **Bronjonolo Gate** (3), which is kept closed.

The entrance to the main body of the palace is further south, down Jalan Rotowijayan – on the west side of the Pageleran complex. The first courtyard is the shaded **Kemangdungan** or **Keben** (4), with two small pendopo, where the *abdi dalem* or palace servants gather. The 'black' sand that covers most of the ground around the pendopo and other buildings in the kraton is from the beaches of the south coast. In this way, it is ensured that the Queen of the South Seas, Nyi Loro Kidul, with whom the sultan is believed to have intimate relations, is present throughout the palace.

The **Srimanganti** (meaning 'to wait for the king') **Gate** (5) leads into a second, rather more impressive, courtyard with two pendopos facing each other; the **Srimanganti** (6) to

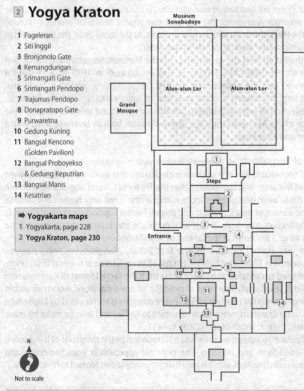

2 Yogya Kraton

1 Pageleran
2 Siti Inggil
3 Bronjonolo Gate
4 Kemangdungan
5 Srimangati Gate
6 Srimangati Pendopo
7 Trajumas Pendopo
8 Donapratopo Gate
9 Purwaretna
10 Gedung Kuning
11 Bangsal Kencono
   (Golden Pavilion)
12 Bangsal Proboyekso
   & Gedung Keputrian
13 Bangsal Manis
14 Kesatrian

➡ **Yogyakarta maps**
1 Yogyakarta, page 228
2 **Yogya Kraton, page 230**

Museum Sonobudoyo

Alun-alun Lor

Alun-alun Lor

Grand Mosque

Steps

Entrance

N

Not to scale

the right and the **Trajumas** (7) to the left. The former was used to receive important guests, while the latter probably served as a court of law. The Srimanganti now contains gongs and other instruments that make up a *gamelan* orchestra. The Trajumas houses palanquins, litters and chairs, as well as a cage in which the sultan's children played. It is said that the children were placed in here, aged eight months, and given a selection of objects – pens, money, books – to play with; whichever took their interest indicated their future careers.

The **Donapratopo Gate** (8), flanked by two *gupala* or *raksasa* statues to protect the palace from evil, leads into the heart of the palace where the sultan and his family had their private quarters. Notice the way that gateways never give direct access to courtyards; they were designed in this way to confuse spirits attempting to make their way into the complex.

Inside this gate, immediately on the right, is the sultan's office, the **Purwaretna** (9). Beyond it is the **Gedung Kuning** (10), an impressive yellow building which continues to be the sultan's private residence. Both are roped-off from the public.

The central and most impressive pavilion in the complex is the **Bangsal Kencono** (11) ① *T0274 373721, Sat-Thu 0830-1330, Sun 0830-1230, admission to complex 12,500Rp, camera 1000Rp extra, guides available with a donation, the palace can be partially closed on official ceremonial days,* or Golden Pavilion. The four teak pillars in the centre represent the four elements. On each is symbolized the three religions of Java: Hinduism (a red motif on the top of the columns), Buddhism (a golden design based on the lotus leaf) and Islam (black and gold letters of the Koran). Unfortunately, because the pavilion is roped off, it is difficult to see the pillars clearly. Behind the Golden Pavilion to the west is the **Bangsal Proboyekso** (12), which contains the armoury, and the **Gedung Keputrian** (12), the residence of the sultan's wives and children, both closed to the public. Immediately to the south of the Golden Pavilion is the **Bangsal Manis** (13), the dining room. **Kemakanan**, a pendopo to the south reached through a set of gates, is used for *wayang* performances at the end of Ramadan. To the east, through another gate (to the side of which is a large drum made from the wood of the jackfruit tree) there is another courtyard, the **Kesatrian** (14). The sultan's sons lived here. In the central pendopo of this courtyard there is another gamelan orchestra on display. Performances are held every Monday and Tuesday, 1000-1200 (the performance is included in the price of the entrance). At the east side of this courtyard is a collection of paintings, the best being by Raden Saleh, a 19th-century court painter who gained a reputation of sorts (and whose grave can be found in Bogor). The photographs of the sultans and their wives are more interesting. North of the Kesatrian is the **Gedung Kopo**, originally the hospital and now a museum housing gifts to the sultans. There are also a pair of rooms given over to memorabilia of Hamengkubuwono IX, who died in 1988.

Close to the palace, on Jalan Rotowijayan, is the **Museum Kereta Karaton** ① *Tue-Sun 0800-1600, 3000Rp plus 1000Rp for camera,* which houses the royal carriages.

Taman Sari

From the palace it is a five- to 10-minute walk to the Taman Sari. Walk south along Jalan Rotowijayan and turn left at the Dewi Srikandi Art Gallery. A number of batik painting galleries are down this road, which leads into Jalan Ngasem and then onto the **Pasar Ngasem** or bird market, an interesting place to wander. Song birds, and particularly turtle doves (Genus *Streptopelia*), are highly prized by the Javanese. It is sometimes said that wives take second place to a man's song bird and that they can cost as much as

US$15,000, although this seems hard to believe. Popular are the spotted-necked dove (*Streptopelia chinensis*), the Javan turtle dove (*Streptopelia bitorquata*) and the zebra dove (*Geopelia striata*). Handmade, split bamboo bird cages are a good buy.

By picking your way through the Pasar Ngasem it is possible to reach the **Taman Sari** ① *daily 0800-1530, 3000Rp*, which was known to the Dutch as the waterkasteel or 'Water Castle', as it is still called. This is a maze of underground passageways, ruins and pools, built as a pleasure garden by the first Sultan, Mangkubumi, in 1765, at the same time as the kraton. The *Babad Mangkubumi* gives a slightly later date – 1683 according to the Javanese calendar or AD 1757-1758. Surrounded by high walls, it was the sultan's hideaway. He constructed three bathing pools – for his children, his *putri* (girls) and himself. A tower allowed the sultan to watch his 'girls' bathing and to summon them to his company. In addition, there were a series of underwater corridors and even a partly underwater mosque. It is these labyrinths that have led some historians to speculate that it was also built as a retreat in times of war. By climbing the stairs over the entrance gate it is possible to look over the surrounding kampong: this was originally an artificial lake, with a large colonnaded pavilion in the middle. Unfortunately, the gardens were damaged during the British attack on Yogya in 1812 and restoration programmes have been rather unsympathetic. It is difficult to imagine the gardens as they were – as a place of contemplation. Most visitors enter the water gardens from Jalan Taman, through the east gate, which leads into the bathing pool area or Umbul Binangun. This small section is the most complete area of the gardens, having been reconstructed in 1971. The gardens fell into disrepair following the death of Hamengkubuwono III, a process which was accelerated by a devastating earthquake in 1865. Much of the garden has no water in it now, which is disappointing.

To the southeast of the kraton and Taman Sari on Jalan Kol Sugiyono is the small **Museum Perjuangan** ① *closed at the time of writing due to renovations, due to reopen in July 2008*, or the Struggle for Independence Museum. As the name suggests, this commemorates Indonesia's Declaration of Independence on 17 August 1945 and has a less than inspiring collection of historical artefacts relating to the episode. The museum suffered extensive damage during the earthquake of 2006.

Vredeburg Fort and around
① *Tue-Sun 0800-1600, 750Rp plus 3000Rp for camera.*

The Vredeburg Fort lies to the north of the kraton on the east side of Jalan Jend A Yani, near the intersection with Jalan P Senopati. It was built in 1765 by the Dutch as a military barracks. Restored in the late 1980s, the fort has lost what character it may have had, and today looks rather like an American shopping arcade (piped music adds to the effect). Now a museum, the fortress houses a series of dioramas depicting the history of Yogyakarta. Close by is the **March 1st Monument**, which commemorates the taking of Yogya from the Dutch in 1949 by a band of guerrillas led by (then) Colonel Suharto. The **Beringharjo Market** is set back from Jalan Jend A Yani on the same side of the street and just north of the Vredeburg Fort. A dimly lit mixed market, it is an interesting and colourful place to wander with fruit, vegetables, fish and meat, batik and household goods – all jumbled together and seemingly fighting for air. Locals warn that numerous pickpockets operate here. On the other side of Jalan Jend A Yani is **Margo Mulyo Church**, which dates from 1830.

Across the road from the fort is the **Gedung Agung**, built initially in 1823 and then rebuilt in 1869 after the devastating earthquake of 1865. It was the former home of the Dutch Resident in Yogya and is now a state guesthouse. Queen Elizabeth II of Great Britain, former Prime Minister Nehru of India and Queen Sirikit of Thailand have all stayed here. Between 1946 and 1949, President Sukarno lived in the Gedung Agung, while Yogya was the capital of an emerging independent Indonesia. South of the fort, on Jalan P Senopati, are three impressive **colonial buildings**, the General Post Office (1910), Bank Indonesia and the Bank Negara Indonesia (1923).

Jalan Malioboro and Jalan Mangkubumi

North from the Vredeburg Fort, Jalan Jend A Yani becomes Jalan Malioboro; this is the tourist heart of Yogya, with shops, restaurants and a smattering of hotels. The town has the largest student population in Indonesia, and in the evenings they congregate along Jalan Malioboro – no doubt for intellectual discussions, as well as eating and music – and stay there till 0400; this has become known as the 'Malioboro culture'. At its north extension, Malioboro becomes Jalan Mangkubumi.

To the west of Jalan Mangkubumi in Tegalrejo is **Sasono Wirotomo**, or the **Diponegoro Museum** ① *Tue-Sun 0900-1300 (new regulations state that foreign visitors need a special permit to enter the museum, granted only in Jakarta, ask at the tourist information office in Jakarta for further information)*, a house built on the site of Prince Diponegoro's residence, which was levelled by the Dutch in 1825. The museum contains the prince's memorabilia, including a collection of weapons. At the end of Jalan Malioboro is an **obelisk** or *tugu* which marks the north limit of the kraton. The original tugu was erected in 1755, but collapsed; the present structure dates from 1889. Aart van Beek, in his book *Life in the Javanese Kraton*, explains that this was "the focal point for the Sultan who would sit at an elevated place near the entrance of the palace and meditate by aligning his eyes with the *tugu* and the 3000-m-high Merapi volcano behind, in the distance".

East of the centre

To the east of the town centre, on Jalan Sultan Agung, is **Paku Alam's Palace** ① *Tue, Thu and Sun, 0930-1330, 7000Rp.* A small part of the palace in the East Wing is a museum. Further east still, on Jalan Kusumanegara, is the **Gembira Loka Zoo and Amusement Park** ① *daily 0800-1800, 4000Rp.* It contains a reasonable range of Indonesian animals, including the Komodo dragon, orang-utan, tiger and rhinoceros.

Kota Gede ① *admission by voluntary contribution, Fri 1300-1600 for the actual cemetery, but the other areas are open daily, get to the tombs and workshops by taxi or by town bus (bis kota) No 4 or 8 from Jl Jend Sudirman, No 11 from Umbunharjo terminal and No 14 from Jl Prawirotaman*, also known as Sar Gede, lies 5 km to the southeast of Yogya and was the capital of the 16th-century Mataram Kingdom. Nothing remains except for the **tombs** of the rulers of Mataram; in particular, Panembahan Senopati, the founder of the kingdom and his son Krapyak (the father of the famous Sultan Agung). Senopati's son-in-law, Ki Ageng Mangir, is also buried here, his tomb protruding into common ground as he was Senopati's foe. About 100 m from the cemetery is the Watu Gilang, a stone on which Senopati killed Ki Ageng Mangir by smashing his head against it. Walled gardens and ponds with fish and a yellow turtle, with claimed magical powers ('several hundred years old'), add to the atmosphere. Like the tombs of Imogiri, visitors must wear traditional Javanese dress which can be hired at the entrance (500Rp). Kota Gede is better known for its **silver workshops** which date back to the 17th-century rule of Sultan Agung. Both traditional silver and black (oxidized) silverwork can be purchased.

Taru Martani ① *Mon-Fri, 0730-1500, there are English-, Dutch- and German-speaking guides*, is a cigar factory on Jalan Kompil B Suprapto, on the east side of town, which visitors can visit to watch the process of cigar manufacture.

Education capital

The **ISI** (**Indonesian Art Institute**) is based in Yogyakarta, with faculties of Fine Art, Dance and Music, which partly explains why so much art can be found around town. (The town is the best place to see *wayang* performances and traditional dance.) In recent years it has become a popular town for Indonesian artists to base themselves. On the northern edge of the city is Indonesia's oldest, and one of its most prestigious, universities: **Gadjah Mada University** (UGM). It was 'founded' in December 1949, when Sultan Hamengkubuwono IX allowed students and their teachers to use the Siti Inggil within the kraton.

Around Yogyakarta ⊖ ⇥ *pp236-245.*

Hindu and Buddhist monuments, including the largest Buddhist monument in the world, Borobudur (see page 246), the magnificent Hindu temples at Prambanan (see page 250) and the small Hindu temples on the Dieng Plateau can also all be visited on day trips.

Tombs of the Mataram sultans

ⓘ *Admission by donation. Agung's tomb is only open Mon 1000-1300, Fri 1330-1630 and Sun 1000-1330, although it is possible to climb up to the site at any time. Get there by bus or colt, 1000Rp. (Buses continue on to Parangtritis from here – see below.) It is a 1 km walk east to the foot of the stairs from Imogiri town (ask for the makam or cemetery). The bus journey is lovely, along a peaceful country road past paddy fields.*

Imogiri, 17 km to the south of Yogya, is the site of the tombs of the Mataram sultans, as well as the rulers of the Surakarta Kingdom. Perhaps the greatest Mataram king, Sultan Agung (reigned 1613-46), is buried here. He built the cemetery in 1645, preparing a suitably magnificent site for his grave, on a hillside to the south of his court at Kartasura. It is said that he chose this site so that he had a view of the Queen of the South (the sea goddess Nyi Loro Kidul). To reach his tomb ⓘ *Sun and Mon 1000-1300 Fri 1300-1600, 1000Rp, directly in front at the top of the stairway,* and those of 23 other royal personages (Surakarta susuhunans to the left, Yogya sultans to the right), the visitor must stagger up 345 steps. Walk behind the tombs to the top of the hill for fine views of the surrounding countryside. Javanese dress, which can be hired at the site, is required to enter the mausoleums. The Yogyakartan equivalent of Chelsea pensioners, with turbans and krisses, make sure correct behaviour is observed at all times. A **traditional ceremony** to thank God for water involving the filling of four bronze water containers – known as *enceh* – is held in the Javanese month of Suro; the first month of the year (June). The containers are placed at the gates of the cemetery and are an expression of gratitude to God for the provision of water.

Parangtritis

ⓘ *Regular connections with Yogya's Umbunharjo bus terminal (10,000Rp), either via Kretek along the main road and over the Opak River, or via Imogiri and Celuk, the longer, rougher, trip via Imogiri passes through beautiful rural scenery.*

Parangtritis is a small seaside resort 28 km south of Yogya. It is accessible on a day excursion, although there are a number of places to stay.

Jatijajar caves

ⓘ *500Rp, 7 km west of Gombong, turn left; the caves are 13 km off the main road, there are minibuses from Kebumen (50 km) and from Gombong. Gombong is accessible from Yogya, Cilacap and Semarang, among other towns.*

Jatijajar caves are to be found in the side of a strange ridge of jagged hills, southwest of the small town of Gombong and 157 km west from Yogya. Outside the entrance is a large concrete dinosaur which acts as a spout for the underground spring (bathing pools here). Inside, there are stalactites and stalagmites, springs and theatrical statues of human beings and animals which apparently recount the history of the kingdom of Pahaharan.

Karang Bolong Beach, near to the Jatijajar Caves, is known as a site for collecting birds' nests for the soup of the same name.

Gunung Merapi → Colour map 10, B4.

① *It is imperative to take warm clothing – temperatures near the summit can reach zero – and energizing food. Tour operators often fail to stress the need for this kit.*

Gunung Merapi, whose name means 'giving fire', lies 30 km north of Yogya and is possibly the best known of all Java's many volcanoes. It rises to a height of nearly 3000 m and can be seen from the city. Because Merapi is still very active, it is closely watched by Indonesia's Directorate of Vulcanology who have an observatory here. Its first recorded eruption was in 1006 AD, when it killed the Hindu king Darmawangsa.

Climbing Gunung Merapi It has been closed since November 1994, when there was an eruption. However, assuming that it might be possible to climb Merapi some time in the future, here is how it used to be done. Most people start from the village of **Selo** (on the north slope), from where it is a four-hour trek up and three hours down. The trail is easy to follow but is steep and narrow in places (especially towards the top, where parts are quite gruelling); robust walking shoes are strongly advised – this is not suitable for the casual stroller. The spectacular views from the summit are best in the morning (0600-0800), which means a very early start, but it's well worth the effort. To see dramatic fireholes, take the path off to the left, about 25 m from the summit. The route passes a ravine before reaching the fireholes – a 10-minute walk. Guides at Selo charge about 50,000Rp and will offer their houses for overnight stays. Tours are not recommended, as the guides urge the group to walk fast, and walking in a group in volcanic cinder can be dusty.

A more challenging climb can be made from **Kinahrejo**, on the southern slope. The village, which has no accommodation, is an hour's walk from Kaliurang (see below), and is 9 km from the summit (a 10-hour walk).

Kaliurang ⊖🌐⊘▲⊕ ⤔ pp236-245. Phone code: 0293. Colour map 10, B4.

① *1000Rp admission fee payable at a booth upon entering Kaliurang.*

The mountain resort of **Kaliurang** is 28 km north of Yogya, on the southern slopes of Merapi at just under 1000 m. It is the only point from which you can climb part way up Gunung Merapi, good views of the lava avalanches. There are facilities at the **Hutan Wisata** (forest park) for tennis and swimming, and a waterfall ① *admission 500Rp*, near the bus station. Good walks include a 2.5-km trek to Plawangan Seismological Station, with views of the smoking giant (best in the morning, until about 0900-1000). The 'base stations' filled with warungs has an additional entrance charge of 500Rp per person. The Seismological Station and the road leading to it are periodically closed. If this is the case, there is an alternative 2 km walk from the bus station to a belvedere, which overlooks the lava flow resulting from Gunung Merapi's 1994 eruption. There are good views of the volcano on clear days.

Sights

Ullen Sentalu Museum (Museum of Javanese Art and Culture) ① *T0274 880158, www.ullensetalu.com, Tue-Sun 0900-1600, US$5 adult/US$2.50 student.* This brilliant museum is a wonderful place to learn more about Javanese culture, and the reasons for the differences between styles of Javanese batik. It is lovingly presented and well worth a look. **Direktorat Vulkanologi** (Pos Pengamatan Gunung Merapi) ① *Jl Cendana 15, T0274 895209, daily 24 hrs.* This is the observation centre for volcanic activity on Gunung Merapi, and the staff are happy for tourists to pop in an look at the seismograph and get information about the latest situation. There is a small exhibition with captions in Indonesian detailing recent eruptions, with some grim photographs showing just how dangerous this beautiful mountain can be. **Hutan Wisata** (Forest Park) ① *daily 0800-1600, 500Rp, next to the bus terminal,* this small forested park has a couple of decent strolls, allowing for some great views of Merapi.

◉ Yogyakarta listings

For Sleeping and Eating price codes,
see inside the front cover.

● Sleeping

Yogyakarta *p227, map p228*
Yogya's different accommodation categories tend to be grouped in particular areas of town. Most of the more expensive international-style hotels are to be found either on Jl Malioboro, in the centre of town, or on the road east to the airport (Jl Jend Sudirman). The former are in a convenient position if visitors wish to explore the city on foot from their hotels. Many of the middle-priced guesthouses are concentrated on Jl Prawirotaman, to the south of the kraton, about 2 km from the city centre (a becak ride away). These are smallish private villas converted into hotels, some with just a handful of rooms, some with small swimming pools. On Jl Prawirotaman, a gaggle of restaurants, shops and tour companies have grown up to service the needs of those staying here. Finally, there is the budget accommodation, which is concentrated on and around Jl Pasar Kembang and Jl Sosrowijayan, close to the train station. There are tour companies, travel agents, restaurants, car and motorcycle hire outfits, bus booking companies, and currency exchange offices here. Of course, there are also hotels and *losmen* outside these areas.

Jalan Marlioboro and Jalan Dagen
These centrally located hotels are more geared towards domestic tourists, and are more upmarket than those available in the Sosrowijayan area, but not as good value as those in the Prawirotaman area.
A-B Hotel Ibis, Jl Marlioboro, T0274 516974, admin@ibisyogya.com. Rooms at this 3-star chain hotel are spotless, comfortable and feature cable TV, minibar, and the more expensive come with bath. Hotel has spa, pool, fitness centre and restaurant.
D-E Hotel Kombokarno, Jl Dagen 39, T0274 515032. Clean a/c and fan rooms facing a central court yard with fish pond. More expensive rooms have TV (local channels only), a/c and hot water. Friendly staff.
D-E Hotel Kristina, Jl Dagen 71A, T/F0274 512076. Popular new place with a good selection of rooms. The standard singles are good value with TV, a/c and hot water.

Jalan Sosrowijyan area
This is prime backpacker territory, with plenty of cheap *losmen*. The area has seen better days, and with accommodation a long Jl Prawirotaman becoming markedly cheaper in recent years, this area has lost its edge. However, it is close to all the action on Jl Malioboro and within walking distance of the train station and the major sights.

B-C Grage Hotel, Jl Sosrowijyan 242, T0274 560125, www.gragegroup.com. Motel-style with limited atmosphere but spotless a/c rooms with cable TV and all the other trimmings one would expect at this price.

C Istana Batik Ratna, Jl Pasar Kembang, T0274 587012, www.dianagrouphotel.com. The slightly overpriced rooms here are clean and come with a/c, TV and Wi-Fi connection. Bathrooms are new, and the more expensive have baths. 10% discount in low season. Pool.

D-E Hotel Asia Afrika, Jl Pasar Kembang 21, T0274 514489, F0274 560139. The entrance to this hotel is stylish and new and leads on to nice gardens with a pool. The rooms haven't kept up pace with the development and are old, but clean.

D-F Bladok, Jl Sosrowijayan 76, T0274 560452, F0274 523832. Welcoming place with a good selection of rooms and a brilliant swimming pool with noisy waterfall, perfect for a back massage (they turn it off at 1700 for fear it will disturb guests). Cheaper rooms are small and have squat toilet, but the VIP rooms are huge, with a/c and TV. Breakfast not included. Recommended.

E-F Marina Palace Hotel, Jl Sosrowijayan 3-5, T0274 748659. Drab and charmless rooms. Bathroom with *mandi*.

E-F Monica Hotel, Jl Sosrowijayan, Gang 2 192, T0274 580598. Simple, clean rooms (the more expensive with TV and a/c), set around a pleasant courtyard with a fountain that functions occasionally.

F Hotel Trim, Jl Pasar Kembang, T0274 514113, F0274 560045. Simple rooms with tatty furniture and bars over the window for a true Midnight Express ambience. Pay a little more for hot water.

F-G Hotel Karunia, Jl Sosrowijayan 78, T/F0274 566057. Rooms here are clean and spacious with some artwork on the walls. Cheaper rooms have shared bathroom.

F-G Setia Kawan, Jl Sosrowijayan, Gang 2 127, T0274 552271, www.bedhots.com. Down a small alley off the gang, this popular place is covererd in contemporary artwork and has a gallery attached. There's no escape

from the art in the bedrooms too, with wonderfully painted walls. Light comes into some rooms through small windows in the ceiling. Rooms are small, but clean. Good homely atmosphere. Recommended.

G Hotel Indonesia, Jl Sosrowijayan 9, T0274 587659. Long-standing cheap lodgings, popular with shoestring Indonesian tourists, this hotel is looking a little tattered but has fairly spacious clean fan rooms set around a small garden.

Jalan Prawirotaman area

A good selection of superb value middle range accommodation is to be found on Jl Prawirotaman, south of the kraton, making this the best area to stay in. The hotels are the best of their kind in Yogya. The area's single obvious disadvantage is that it is not very central, but the street has numerous restaurants, shops, travel agents and cultural shows.

C-D Ministry Of Coffee, Jl Prawirotaman 1 15A, T0274 7473828, www.ministryof coffee.com. Tastefully decorated and comfortable, all the rooms here feature a/c, Wi-Fi and access to a library as well as all the tea and coffee you can manage. Each room has a private balcony. Reservations are advisable. Recommended.

D Kirana, Jl Prawirotaman 1 45, T0274 376600, F0274 372262. This place has undergone some loving renovations and is well decorated with Javanese furniture and antiques. Rooms are comfortable, have a/c and are sparkling clean. The rooms out the back near the small garden are peaceful, although have less light than those at the front of the property. TVs are available for an extra 40,000Rp a night. Discounts for long stays.

D-E Duta Guest House, Jl Prawirotaman 1 26, T0274 372064, www.dutagarden hotel.com. This well-run hotel has sparkling a/c and fan rooms, with TV (local channels only) and attached bathroom with bath. Pool and fitness centre. Recommended.

E Airlannga, Jl Prawirotaman 1 6-8, T0274 378044, www.geocities.com/airlangga_hotel. All the rooms here have a/c, TV, are clean, and have space for 3, though lack any real character. Rooms on the upper storeys have good views over the rooftops towards the east. The hotel has a pool and a pub.

E-F Delta Homestay, Jl Prawirotaman 2 597, T0274 747537, dutagardenhotel.com. Small, clean and basic fan and a/c rooms. Friendly staff. Pool.

E-F Perwita Sari Hotel, Jl Prawirotaman 1 31, T0274 377592, perwitasariguesthouse@ yahoo.com. Popular, with gregarious staff. The fan and a/c rooms are a bit dark, but clean. More expensive rooms have hot water. Pool.

E-F Rose Guest House, Jl Prawirotaman 1 122, T0274 377991. Sprawling place with plenty of spacious simple fan and a/c rooms, with old furniture. The suite rooms at the back come with a spacious communal veranda with views of Merapi, and a long balcony behind with views of the hills to the south. There is also a good-sized pool here.

F Mas Gun, Jl Prawirotaman 1 29, T0274 379804. Plain, clean fan rooms with cramped bathroom. Breakfast is not included and the car park is a bit of an eyesore.

F Mercury, Jl Prawirotaman 2 595, T0274 370846. Plenty of Javanese style at this popular hotel, which has a shady garden and an amazing restaurant with cushion seating. There is also a pool tucked away at the back. Rooms are a disappointment, spartan and lacking the jovial character of the exterior.

F Sartika, Jl Prawirotaman 1 44A, T0274 372669. Sleepy hotel with good-value rooms. The furniture is a little old, but the rooms are clean and feature TV and bathrooms with bath. Avoid rooms on the 1st floor, which are dim, in stark contract to the light and bright 2nd storey, which has good views over the rooftop and outdoor seating. The cheaper rooms have *mandi* only. Breakfast not included.

F Sumaryo, Jl Prawirotaman 1 22, T/F0274 377552. This quiet and shady place has friendly staff, an inviting pool and clean a/c and fan rooms with attached bathroom featuring *mandi* and shower.

G Putra Jaya, Jl Prawirotaman 1 10, T0274 375185. Firmly in shoestring budget territory,

the prices and rooms here seem to have stayed the same since 1998. Rooms are clean and adequate and feature bathroom with *mandi*. Breakfast is not included.

Kaliurang *p235*

There are over 100 places to choose from in Kaliurang, so availabity is never a problem. Many places are used to groups, and sell blocks of rooms, rather than single rooms. It is possible to get a single room at all the places listed here.

F Hotel Merapi, Jl Astamulya 57, T0274 895227. Plenty of choice here, although rooms are for the most part spartan and in need of some maintenance. Larger rooms have sofas and kitchens (with no fittings or equipment) and TV. The cheaper rooms are a little miserable, with squat toilet and *mandi*.

F Hotel Muria, Jl Astamulya, T0274 4464257. Spacious, clean rooms with TV. Bathrooms have hot water, squat toilet and *mandi*. Fair value for money.

F Wisma Brotosena, Jl Astamulya 279, T0274 895806, The owner doesn't speak much English and prefers group bookings, but will rent out individual rooms. Prices quoted are often exorbitant, so bargain (at least 50% cheaper than initial quote) to get a fair price at these simple rooms with hot-water bathroom.

F-G Vogel Hostel, Jl Astamulya 76, T0274 895208. There is plenty of charm at this laid-back hostel. The most backpacker savvy place in town, the rooms here are clean and simple. The bungalows at the foot of the garden are filled with bamboo furniture and have amazing views of Merapi early in the morning. Cheaper rooms in the main building have shared bathroom. There are plenty of magazines to browse, and good information about Merapi. Recommended.

F-G Wisma Joyo, Jl Astamulya 68, T0274 895359. Vast selection of rooms, with the more expensive having hot water. The cheapest rooms have squat toilet and *mandi*. Good deals are available for block bookings (2 or more rooms).

⊘ Eating

Yogyakarta *p227, map p228*
Central Javanese cooking uses a lot of sugar, tapped from the *aren* palm that produces 'red' sugar. Typical dishes include *tape* (a sweet dish made from fermented cassava) and *ketan* (sticky rice). Yogya specialities include *ayam goreng* (fried chicken) and *gudeg* (rice, jackfruit, chicken and an egg cooked in a spicy coconut sauce).

Jalan Sosrowijayan area
♈ Bedhot Resto, Jl Sosrowijayan, Gang 1 127, T0274 412452. Inviting atmosphere with plenty of artwork, world beats and a large menu of steaks and pastas with a good vegetarian selection. Recommended.
♈ Bintang Cafe, Jl Sosrowijayan 54, T0274 9127179, 0800-2400. Popular place serving good salads, milk shakes, pastas and Indonesian dishes.
♈ FM Cafe, Jl Sosrowijayan 10, T0274 7478270, 0600-0100. Good helpings of standard Western dishes and a few interesting Javanese options for the adventurous. Happy hour 1300-2000, when a large beer goes for 15,000Rp.
♈ Superman, Jl Sosrowijayan, Gang 1 71, T0274 513472, 0730-2300. Long-running travellers cafe that is looking a little undernourished these days. It's still a good place to fill up on kebabs, seafood and Indonesian and Chinese dishes.

Jalan Prawirotaman area
♈ Cafe Janur, Jl Prawirotaman 1 44, T081802653488, 1000-2300. Dutch-owned eatery with an amazing selection of antique posters covering the walls, enough to keep the eyes busy while a meal is prepared. The menu is huge with decent kebabs, steaks, Chinese food and fresh juices.
♈ Gunung Pring, Jl Prawirotaman 1 48, T0274 450328, 0800-2100. This place serves cheap Indonesian dishes, serving *nasi goreng* in every conceivable form. There is also decent seafood and some steak dishes.

♈ Renzo Cafe, Jl Prawirotaman 1 27, T081328772331, 0900-2300. The owner here is a great source of local information and has a very tourist-friendly menu, with sandwiches, kebabs, pastas and an all day happy hour.
♈ Tante Lies, Jl Parangritis, T0274 386719, 0900-2200. Essentially an overgrown *warung*, the best choices here are the east Javanese dishes, but there are some Western and Chinese choices.
♈ Via Via, Jl Prawirotaman 1 30, T0274 386557, www.viaviacafe.com, 0730-2300. This funky restaurant has walls festooned with contemporary art, branches in Senegal, Belgium and Argentina and fine music to accompany a meal. The menu features delicious salads, daily Indonesian specials, pastas and good ice cream. Part of the profits go to local charities. Live jazz every Fri evening. Recommended.
♈ Civet Coffee, Jl Prawirotaman 1 14, T0274 6639758, 0800-2300. This stylish lounge style coffee shop is the place to try *kopi luwak* one of the world's rarest coffees that comes from beans that have been digested and reclaimed from a civet (US$12 a cup). There is also a good selection of other Indonesian brews and plenty of juices and snack available. Wi-Fi.
♈ Ministry Of Coffee, Jl Prawirotaman 1 15A, T0274 7473828, www.ministryofcoffee.com, 0600-2300. A great place to pass time, with table games, free Wi-Fi access and plenty of delicious coffee. The spice espresso shake is delicious, and British travellers will be glad to get their hands on the roast beef and mustard salad. The selection of sweets is naughty, with excellent chocolate mousse. Recommended.

There is also a food court on the 3rd floor of the Matahari Mall (1000-2100) offering good portions of clean, cheap local cuisine.

Kaliurang *p235*
♈ Amboja, Jl Kaliurang Km 18.7, T0274 660 6904, Tue-Sun 1100-2100. Located 7 km down the road towards Yogya from Kaliurang, this place has its own organic herb garden and specializes in tasty Indonesian fare. The *ayam*

asam pedas (spicy sour chicken) is particularly good. There is also a range of herb- and spice-infused teas and coffees. Recommended.
† **Beukenhof** (part of the Ullen Sentalu Museum complex, T0274 895161, Tue-Sun 1300-2100). An absolute gem of a restaurant set in staggeringly attractive gardens with mysterious walls and plenty of leafy shade. The restaurant is set in a colonial villa with a great tropical veranda. European menu featuring classics such as *beouf bourgignon* and pastas, and some Dutch dishes such as *hutspot met klapstuk* (mashed potatoes with beef and sausage in red wine sauce). Locally made Javanese chocolate bars available. Recommended.

For cheap, simple travellers grub, try the restaurant at the **Vogel Hostel**. **Wisma Joyo** (see Sleeping) cooks up good Javanese fare.

◑ Bars and clubs

Yogyakarta *p227, map p228*
Cafe Janur (see Eating). Run by Arnold Schwarzenegger lookalike Wim, this place is popular with Dutch expats at the weekend and is a friendly place for a beer.

There are fun bars along Jl Parangritis, including **Made's**, **Rui's**, and the gay-friendly **Banana Cafe**.

Live music
Bintang Cafe, Jl Sosrowijayan 54, T0274 9127179, 0800-2400. Yogyakarta's musical cognoscenti descend on this place on Fri and Sat nights for live reggae and rock n' roll with occasional impromptu performances by well-known Indonesian bands.
Jamaica Bar, Jl Prawirotaman 30, T0274 383577, 1600-0000. Relaxed and stylish bar with a decent selection of drinks. Live reggae music, and some tribute bands play here from 2100 on Fri, Sat nights. Free Wi-Fi access.

Clubs
Boshe, Jl Magelang Km 6.5, T0274543477, Sun-Thu 1000-0300, Fri-Sat 1000-0330, cover charge 45,000Rp including 1 beer or soft drink. Indonesian bands and DJs play at this popular student hangout, that has a somewhat dubious massage centre downstairs. The atmosphere here is friendly, and unpretentious although you won't be allowed in wearing sandals.

✹ Festivals and events

Yogyakarta *p227, map p228*
Yogya is host to a number of colourful festivals.
End of Ramadan Grebeg Syawal (movable, Aug in 2009). A Muslim celebration, thanking Allah for the end of this month of fasting. The day before is *Lebaran Day*, when the festivities begin with children parading through the streets. The next day, the military do likewise around the town and then a tall tower of groceries is carried through the street and distributed to the people.
Apr/May Labuhan (movable – 26th day of 4th Javanese month Bakdomulud) (also held in Feb and Jul). Offerings made to the South Sea Goddess Nyi Loro Kidul. Especially colourful ceremony at Parangtritis, where offerings are floated on a bamboo palanquin and floated on the sea. Similar rituals are held on Mount Merapi and Mount Lawu.
Jun Tamplak Wajik (movable), ritual preparing of 'gunungan' or rice mounds in the kraton, to the accompaniment of gamelan and chanting to ward off evil spirits.
Grebeg Besar (movable), a ceremony to celebrate the Muslim offering feast of Idul Adha. At 2000, the 'gunungan' of decorated rice is brought from the inner court of the kraton to the Grand Mosque, where it is blessed and distributed to the people.
Jul Siraman Pusaka (movable, 1st month of the Javanese year), ritual cleansing, when the sultan's heirlooms are cleaned. The water used is said to have magical powers. **Anniversary of Bantul** (20th), celebrated with a procession in Paseban Square, Bantul, south Yogyakarta.
Aug Kraton Festival (movable), range of events including ancient ritual ceremonies,

cultural shows, craft stalls. **Turtle dove singing contest** (2nd week), a national contest for the Hamengkubuwono X trophy, held in the south Alun-alun from 0700. **Saparan Gamping** (movable), held in Ambarketawang Gamping village, 5 km west of Yogya. This ancient festival is held to ensure the safety of the village. Sacrifices are made of life-sized statues of a bride and groom, made of glutinous rice and filled with brown sugar syrup, symbolizing blood. **Sep** **Rebo Wekawan** (2nd), held at the crossing of the Opak and the Gajah Wong rivers, where Sultan Agung is alleged to have met the Goddess Nyi Loro Kidul. **Sekaten** (movable – the 5th day of the Javanese month Mulud), a week-long festival honouring the Prophet Mohammad's birthday. The festival starts with a midnight procession of the royal servants (*abdi dalem*), carrying 2 sets of gamelan instruments from the kraton to the Grand Mosque. They are placed in opposite ends of the building and played simultaneously. A fair is held before and during Sekatan in the Alun-alun Lor. **Tamplak Wajik** (5th day of Sekaten). Ritual preparation of 'gunungan' (see aboove), decorated with vegetables, eggs and cakes at the palace, to the accompaniment of a gamelan orchestra and chanting to ward off evil spirits. **Grebeg Mulud**, religious festival celebrating the birthday of Mohammad, and the climax of Sekatan. Held on the last day of the festival (12th day of Mulud), it features a parade of the palace guard in the early morning, from the Kemandungan (in the kraton) to the Alun-alun Lor.

⊕ Entertainment

Yogyakarta *p227, map p228*
Up-to-date information on shows can be obtained from the tourist office, travel agents or from hotels. There is a wide choice of performances and venues, with something happening somewhere every night.

Batik art galleries
Three batik painters from Yogya have achieved an international reputation – Affandi, Amri Yahya and Sapto Hudoyo. The **Affandi Gallery** is at Jl Adisucipto 167 (town bus 8) on the banks of the Gajah Wong River. It lies next to the home of the Indonesian expressionist painter Affandi (1907-1990). The gallery displays work by Affandi and his daughter Kartika. Open daily 0900-1600. The **Amri Gallery** is at Jl Gampingan 67 and **Sapto Hudoyo** has a studio on Jl Adisucipto, opposite the airport.

Batik lessons
At the **Batik Research Centre**, Jl Kusumanegara 2, plus a good exhibition; **Gapura Batik**, Jl Taman KP 3/177, T0274 377835 (phone to book), 3 or 5 day courses (near main entrance to Taman Sari); **Lucy Batik**, Jl Sosrowijayan Gang 1. **Via Via**, Jl Prawirotaman, run day courses.

Gamelan
Performances at the kraton, Mon and Wed 1030-1200.

Ketoprak
Traditional Javanese drama at the auditorium of **RRI Studio Nusantara 2**, Jl Gejayan 2030, twice a month (see tourist board for details).

Modern art gallery
Cemeti, Jl Ngadisuryan 7A (near the Taman Sari), has changing exhibits of good contemporary Indonesian and western artists. Open Tue-Sun 0900-1500.

Ramayana
Open-air performances at **Prambanan**, T0274 496408, held on 'moonlight nights' between May and Oct, starting at 1930 and year-round at the **Trimurti Covered Theatre**, 1930-2130. The story is told in four episodes over a period of four consecutive evenings coinciding with the climax during the full moon (outdoor Jan-Apr, Nov-Dec only, indoors year round). Tickets cost between 50,000-200,000Rp, less

at the Trimurti. Most agencies in town sell the tickets at face value but add on 40,000Rp for transport to and from Prambanan.

There are also regular performances at the **Purawisata Open Theatre** (THR), Jl Katamso, T0274 375705, daily 2000-2130. Admission 120,000Rp (it's worth it). Good buffet dinner served before the performance (220,000Rp for the ticket and the meal).

Wayang gedhog (classical masked dance)
Performances at the **Purawisata Open Theatre**, Jl Katamso, T0274 375705, every day starting at 2000 and finishing at 2130 (with dinner start at 1900, US$24 without dinner start at 2000, US$13).

Wayang golek
At the kraton on Wed 0930-1330, 12,500Rp.

Wayang kulit
Performances held at the **Museum Sonobudoyo**, Jl Trikora, daily 2000-2200, 20,000Rp; **Sasana Hinggil** (South Palace Square-Alun-alun Selatan), every 2nd Sat of the month, 2100-0500, 12,500Rp; **Gubug Wayang-44**, Kadipaten Kulon, Kp 1/44, is a *wayang kulit* puppet workshop run by Olot Pardjono, who makes puppets for the Museum Sonobudoyo. Ask at the museum for information on when his workshop is open and how to get there.

Wayang orang
At the kraton every Sun, 1000-1200. Javanese Poetry can be seen at the kraton on Fri between 1000-1200. Gamelan is performed at the kraton on Mon and Tue 1000-1200.

○ Shopping

Yogyakarta *p227, map p228*
Yogya offers an enormous variety of Indonesian handicrafts, usually cheaper than can be found in Jakarta. Avoid using a guide or becak driver to take you to a shop, as you will be charged more – their cut. There are hustlers everywhere in Yogya; do not be coerced into visiting an 'exhibition' – you will be led down alleyways and forced to purchase something you probably don't want. It is important to bargain hard. The main shopping street, Jl Malioboro, also attracts more than its fair share of 'tricksters', who maintain, for example, that their exhibition of batik paintings is from Jakarta and is in its last day, so prices are good – don't believe a word of it. The west side of Jl Malioboro is lined with stalls selling batik, *wayang*, *topeng* and woven bags. Best buys are modern batik designs, sarongs and leather goods. However, the quality of some items can be very poor – eg the batik shirts – which may be difficult to see at night.

Batik Yogya is a centre for both batik *tulis* and batik *cap* and it is widely available in lengths (which can be made up into garments) or as ready-made clothes. Many of the shops call themselves cooperatives and have a fixed price list, but it may still be possible to bargain. There are a number of shops along Jl Malioboro. Contemporary 'European' fashions can be found in a couple of shops on Jl Sosrowijayan Gang 1. Batik factories are on Jl Tirtodipuran, south of the kraton, where visitors can watch the cloth being produced. Batik paintings are on sale everywhere, with some of the cheapest available within the kraton walls. There are some more shops down Jl Prawirotaman and off Jl Malioboro. But perhaps the best known outlet is the **Ardiyanto Studio**, Jl Magelang Km 5.8, T0274 562777. The cloth may be expensive, but it is top quality. The Emperor of Japan and Hilary Clinton are reputed to be among the owner's clients. To get there, take any bus running towards Borobudur/Dieng, which pass the shop some 6 km out of the city. There is also an outlet shop, complete with prize photos of visiting signatories, in the mall of the Melia Purosani, Jl Suryotomo 31.

Bookshops **Periplus**, inside Marlioboro Mall, Jl Marlioboro, daily 0939-2100. with international newspapers, magazines, bestsellers and guidebooks. **Book Exchange Yogyakarta**, is a good place to swap books (added cost of around 20,000Rp per book). The best shops are in the Sosrowijayan area, notably **Mas** (Jl Sosrowijayan Gang 1, T081328420359, 0900-2200) and **Boomerang** Bookshop (Jl Sosrowijayan Gang 1, 0800-2100). There are a couple of 2nd-hand bookshops along Jl Prawirotaman, although the selection of titles is quite poor.

Handicrafts Government crafts centre, **Desa Kerajinan**, on Jl Adisucipto (Jl Solo), shops along Jl Prawirotaman, and stalls lining Jl Malioboro. The Marlioboro Mall has plenty of handicrafts at fixed prices.

Ikat Jadin Workshop, Jl Modang 70B.

Leatherware Bags, suitcases, sandals and belts. All made from buffalo, cow or goat. Jl Malioboro has a selection of roadside stalls, as well as several shops. Jl Bugisan also has many small good-value outlets.

Krisses **Kris Satria Gallery**, Rotowijyan 2/64, T0811286743, 0800-1800. Interesting selection of Kris (a type of dagger). There are a couple of other places on Jl Prawirotaman 2.

Pottery Earthenware is produced in a number of specialist villages around Yogya. Best known is Kasongan, 7 km south of the city, which produces pots, vases and assorted kitchen utensils. Get there by bus towards Bantul; the village is 700 m off the main road.

Silverware In Kota Gede, to the southeast of the city (most shops are to be found along Jl Kemesan), 2 major workshops – **MD Silver** (T0274 375063) and **Tom's Silver** (T0274 525416). Numerous shops on Jl Prawirotaman. Try making your own ring with **Via Via Tours**, Jl Prawirotaman, 40,000Rp with instruction, and take home your finished article.

Topeng masks Available from stalls along Jl Malioboro and near Taman Sari.

Wayang kulit and wayang golek Available from roadside stalls along Jl Malioboro. They come in varying qualities. Hard bargaining recommended. **Putro Wayang**, Kampek Ngadisuryan 1.172, T0274 386611, Sat-Thu 0900-1700, Fri 0900-1100, is a small puppet workshop where visitors can observe the creators at work. They have a small range of beautiful leather *wayang kulit* puppets, *wayang golek* puppets and masks.

▲▲ Activities and tours

For visitors without their own transport, one way to see the sights around Yogya is to join a tour. Although it is comparatively easy to get around by public transport, it can mean waiting around. Yogya has many companies offering tours to the sights in and around the city, mainly centred on Jl Prawirotaman.

There are city tours to the kraton, Taman Sari, batik factories, *wayang* performances and Kota Gede silver workshops.

Also out of town tours to Prambanan (US$7), Borobudur (US$5.50), the Dieng Plateau (US$22), Kaliurang, Parangtritis, Solo and Candi Sukuh, Gedung Songo, Gunung Bromo and Gunung Merapi. The cheapest companies charge around US$7 per day, depending on the distance, but make sure you get a seat to yourself rather than being forced to share it. Taxis can also be commissioned; from US$33 for a full day. Check various companies to select the vehicle, time of departure and cost (tours on non-a/c buses are considerably cheaper). Becak drivers will often take visitors for a tour of the city, and know of some good off the beaten track places. Prices start at US$8 for 5 hrs. Watch out for hidden entrance charges either for yourself or for parking your car.

Yogyakarta *p227, map p228*
Tour operators
There are a number of companies around Jl Sosrowijayan and Jl Pasar Kembang, as well as Jl Prawirotaman, who will organize onward travel by bis malam and train. Many of the hotels offer similar services.
Annas, Jl Prawirotaman 7, T0274 386556. Ticketing, car and motorbike rental.
Intras Tour, Jl Malioboro 131, T0274 561972, info@intrastour.com. Recommended by the tourist office for ticketing.

Kartika Trekking, Jl Sosrowijyan 8, T0274 562016. Bus, plane and train ticketing as well as tours around the region and beyond.
Via Via, (see Eating), offers excellent tours.
Vista Express, in Natour Garuda Hotel, Jl Malioboro, T0274 563074.
Yogya Rental, Jl Pasar Kembang 85-88, T0274 587648.

Kaliurang p235

Vogel's Hostel (see Sleeping), organizes sunrise walks up Merapi to see the lava flows. Walks are led by guides that have a great understanding of local fauna, and plenty of stories to keep walkers enthralled. Depart at 0400, return at 0900, US$8 per person (min 2 people) including breakfast.

⊖ Transport

Yogyakarta p227, map p228
Local
Becaks 7000-10,000Rp per trip. Bargaining hard is essential. Jl Prawirotaman to Jl Marlioboro and back should cost no more than 20,000Rp. Drivers are happy to wait for a few hrs. Beware of drivers who offer a very good price; they will almost certainly take you to batik or silverware shops.
Bicycle hire Along Jl Pasar Kembang or Gang 1 or 2, and hotels on Jl Prawirotaman for approximately 15,000Rp per day.
Bus Yoyga town buses (bis kota) travel 17 routes criss-crossing the town (3000Rp); the tourist office sometimes has bus maps available. Minibuses leave from the Terban station on Jl C Simanjuntak, northeast of the train station.
Car hire Self-drive from **Annas** Jl Prawirotaman 7, T0274 386556. Vehicles are in good condition and vary from US$27 to US$38 per day depending on the size of the car; **Yus** T085292820222, yoes_pnd@ yahoo.co.id, is a knowledgeable Yogya-based driver who drives tourists to Pangandaran and can offer tailor-made tours to most places in Java.

Motorbike hire Along Jl Pasar Kembang and at **Annas** (see above) 35,000-40,000Rp per day depending on bike size and condition. Check brakes, lights and horn before agreeing; bikes are sometimes poorly maintained.
Taxi The great majority of taxis in the city are now metered. Flagfall and 1st km, 5000Rp. Taxis/cars can be chartered for the day from **Annas** (see above), or for longer trips to Borobudur, Prambanan. Taxis can be ordered, call **Ria Taxi**, T0274 586166, or **Progo Taxi**, T0274 621055.

Long distance
Air **Adisucipto Airport** is 8 km east of town, along Jl Adisucipto (aka Jl Solo). Transport to town: minibuses from the Terban station on Jl Simanjuntak, travelling to Prambanan, pass the airport (10,000Rp), a taxi is 45,000Rp. (Taxi desk in arrivals hall.) Domestic departure tax is 30,000Rp; international is 100,000Rp.

Daily connections with **Kuala Lumpur** on **Air Asia** (www.airasia.com; book online) and 3 flights a week with **Malaysian Airlines**.

There are plenty of daily flights to **Jakarta** and **Denpasar** as well as as daily flights to **Makassar**, **Balikpapan**, **Matartam**, **Bandung** and **Surabaya**. **Merpati** fly to **Ambon** 4 times a week. Domestic airlines flying out of Yogyakarta include **Garuda**, **Mandala**, **Merpati** and **Lion Air**.

Airline offices **Garuda**, Hotel Inna, Jl Marlioboro, T0274 483706. **Mandala**, Jl Raya Solo Km 9, T0274 557736. **Merpati**, Jl AM Sangaiji, T0274 583478.
Bus Yogya is a transport hub and bus services are available to most places. As it is a popular tourist destination, there are also many a/c tourist buses and minibuses. Agents are concentrated in the hotel/losmen areas. The Umbunharjo bus station is 4 km southeast of the city centre, at the intersection of Jl Veteran and Jl Kemerdekaan. Fastest services are at night (bis malam). Check times at the bus station or at the tourist office on Jl Malioboro. Regular connections with **Jakarta** (9 hrs) and **Bandung** (6 hrs), as well as many other cities and towns. To get to **Solo** (1½-2 hrs), or north

to **Semarang** (3½ hrs), it is better to take a local bus, (hail on the main roads). A/c buses along Jl Sosrowijayan (board bus here too) or from Jl Mangkubumi to, for example, **Jakarta** 200,000Rp, **Bandung** 200,000Rp, **Surabaya** 120,000Rp, **Malang** 120,000Rp, **Probolinggo** 175,000Rp and **Denpasar** 220,000Rp.

Colt Offices on Jl Diponegoro, west of the Tugu Monument. **Rahayu**, Jl Diponegoro 9, T0274 561322 is a reputable company. Seats are bookable and pick-up from hotels can be arranged. Regular connections with **Solo** 20,000Rp, **Semarang** 36,000Rp, **Jakarta** 140,000Rp and **Surabaya** 80,000Rp.

Train Thieves are notorious on the overnight train between Jakarta and Surabaya via Yogya. The railway station is on Jl Pasar Kembang. Regular connections with **Jakarta**'s Gambir station as well as Jakarta Kota and Pasar Senen (10 hrs – the Gajayana night train leaves at 2352 and arrives at 0826) Costs depend on class of train, between US$19 (*eksekutif*) and US$12 (*bisnis*). Auseful connection is the **Fajar Utama Yogya**, which leaves at 0800 and pulls into Jakarta's Pasar Senen at 1658. 5 daily trains to **Bandung** (US$17/80,000Rp, 8 hrs), **Solo** (*bisnis* 7000Rp, 1 hr), 7 daily trains to **Surabaya** (100,000Rp/US$9, 7 hrs) and 1 daily train to **Malang** (*eksekutif* only, US$11). There's a hotel reservation desk at the railway station.

To Bali via Gunung Bromo A popular way to get to Bali includes a night in Cemoro Lawang, Gunung Bromo, before heading onto destinations in Bali including Lovina and Denpasar. A night's accommodation at the **Cafe Lava** is included. Prices start at US$30.50. Most travel agencies on Jl Sosrowijayan and Jl Prawirotaman sell this.

Gunung Merapi *p235*
Bus It is tricky getting to Selo on public transport. Take a bus from Yogya to Kartosuro

and then another bus to Boyolali, finally by minibus to Selo; leave Yogya in the morning, as afternoon buses are scarce.

Kaliurang *p235*
Bus There are regular buses from Yogya's **Giwangan** bus terminal and colts from **Condong Catur** bus terminal (8000Rp 1½ hrs).

❶ Directory

Yogyakarta *p227, map p228*
Banks There are many banks in Yogya, rates are good and most currencies and types of TC are entertained. Good rates are especially found along Jl Prawirotaman. **BNI**, near General Post Office, on Jl Senopati. Money changers next to the **Hotel Asia Afrika**, Jl Pasar Kembang 17 and on Jl Prawirotaman. ATMs on Jl Prawirorotaman and Jl Marlioboro, including inside Marlioboro Mall. **Embassies and consulates** France, Jl Sagan 3-1, T0274 566520. **Emergencies** Police Jl Utara, on city ring road, T0274 885494. **Tourist police** Tourist Information, Jl Malioboro, T0274 566000 for reporting robberies and seeking general information. **Immigration office** Jl Adisucipto Km 10, T0274 486165 (out of town on the road to the airport, close to Ambarrukmo Palace Hotel). **Internet** Queens Internet, Jl Pasar Kembang, T0274 547633, 24 hrs, 7000Rp per hr. **1+1=1**, Jl Parangritis, 24 hrs, 4000Rp per hr. **Medical services** Hospitals PKU Muhammadiyah, Jl KHKA Dahlan 14 T0274 512653. **24 On-Call Doctor**, T0274620091. **Post office** General Post Office, Jl Senopati 2. **Post Office** Jl Pasar Kembang 37 (for international phone calls and faxes).There are also small post offices by the ticket office at the kraton and along Jl Sosrowijayan. **Telephone** Jl Yos Sudarso 9. Open daily, 24 hrs. IDD international calls.

Borobudur and around

→ *Phone code: 0293. Colour map 10, B4.*

The travel business is all too ready to attach a superlative to the most mundane of sights. However, even travellers of a less world-weary age had little doubt, after they set their eyes on this feast of stone, that they were witnessing one of the wonders of the world. The German traveller Johan Scheltema in his 1912 book Monumental Java, wrote that he felt the "fructifying touch of heaven; when tranquil love descends in waves of contentment, unspeakable satisfaction". ▸▸ *For listings, see pages 254-255.*

Borobudur

Ins and outs
Best time to visit Early morning before the coaches arrive, although even by 0600 there can be many people here. Some visitors suggest sunset is the best time to be there as the view is not affected by mist (as it commonly is in the morning). Consider staying the night in Borobudur, to see the sun rise over the monument.

Tourist information
ⓘ *T0293 788266, www.borobudurpark.com, daily 0600-1700, ticket office closes at 1630, (tourists must leave the temple by 1720), US$11 adult/US$7 student, but the use of video/camera is free.*
Price does not include a guide, and although guides vary, some visitors have reported them to be useful and knowledgeable. The 50,000Rp fee for a guide is really worth it. In theory, visitors should wait for a group to accumulate and then be shown round by a guide. However, many people simply explore the candi on their own. There is an extra payment for those who wish to get into the temple at 0400, in time for the sunrise. This can be facilitated by the Manohara Hotel (see Sleeping). For guests of the hotel the additional fee is US$12.50, for non-guests it is US$27. Many consider this money well spent, as the temple is unusually quiet and watching the sun come up from here is quite magical.

Background
Borobudur was built when the Sailendra Dynasty of Central Java was at the height of its military and artistic powers. Construction of the monument is said to have taken about 75 years, spanning four or five periods from the end of the eighth century to the middle of the ninth century. Consisting of a nine-tiered 'mountain' rising to 34.5 m, Borobudur is decorated with 5 km of superbly executed reliefs – some 1500 in all – ornamented with 500 statues of the Buddha, and constructed of 1,600,000 andesite stones.

The choice of site on the densely populated and fertile valleys of the Progo and Elo rivers seems to have been partially dictated by the need for a massive labour force. Every farmer owed the kings of Sailendra a certain number of days labour each year – a labour tax – in return for the physical and spiritual protection of the ruler. Inscriptions from the ninth and tenth centuries indicate that there were several hundred villages in the vicinity of Borobudur. So, after the rice harvest, a massive labour force of farmers, slaves and others could be assembled to work on the monument. It is unlikely that they would have been resistant to working on the edifice – by so doing they would be accumulating merit and accelerating their progress towards nirvana.

Art historians have also made the point that the location of Borobudur, at the confluence of the Elo and Progo rivers, was probably meant to evoke, as Dumarçay says, "the most sacred confluence of all, that of the Ganga (Ganges) and the Yumna (Jumna)", in India. Finally, the monument is also close to a hill, just north of Magelang, called Tidar. Although hardly on the scale of the volcanoes that ring the Kedu Plain, this hill – known as the 'Nail of Java' – lies at the geographic centre of Java and has legendary significance. It is said that it was only after Java, which was floating on the sea, had been nailed to the centre of the earth that it became inhabitable.

The design

The temple is made of grey andesite (a volcanic rock), which was not quarried but taken from river beds. Huge boulders are washed down volcano slopes during flood surges, and these were cut to size and transported to the building site. The blocks were linked by double dovetail clamps; no mortar was used. It is thought that the sculpture was done in situ, after the building work had been completed, then covered in stucco and probably painted.

The large base platform was added at a later date and remains something of an enigma. It actually hides a panel of reliefs, known as the 'hidden foot'. Some authorities believe that this series of reliefs was always meant to be hidden, because they depict earthly desires (true of a similar series of panels at Angkor Wat in Cambodia). Other art historians maintain that this is simply too elaborate an explanation and that the base was added as a buttress. Inherent design faults meant that even during initial construction, subsidence was probably already setting in. In 1885 these subterranean panels were uncovered to be photographed, and then covered up again to ensure the stability of the monument.

The monument was planned so that the pilgrim would approach it from the east, along a path that started at Candi Mendut (see below). Architecturally, it is horizontal in conception, and in this sense contrasts with the strong verticality of Prambanan. However, architectural values were of less importance than the sculpture, and in a sense the monument was just an easel for the reliefs. Consideration had to be made for the movement of people, and the width of the galleries was dictated by the size of the panel, which had to be seen at a glance. It is evident that some of the reliefs were conceived as narrative 'padding', ensuring that continuity of story line was achieved. To 'read' the panels, start from the east stairway, keeping the monument on your right. This clockwise circumambulation is known as *pradaksina*. It means that while the balustrade or outer reliefs are read from left to right, those on the main inner wall are viewed from right to left. The reliefs were carved so that they are visually more effective when observed in this way.

The symbolism of Borobudur

Symbolically, Borobudur is an embodiment of three concepts: it is, at the same time, a *stupa*, a replica of the cosmic mountain *Gunung Meru*, and a *mandala* (an instrument to assist meditation). Archaeologists, intent on interpreting the meaning of the monument, have had to contend with the fact that the structure was built over a number of periods spanning three-quarters of a century. As a result, new ideas were superimposed on older ones. In other words, it meant different things, to different people, at different periods.

Nonetheless, it is agreed that Borobudur represents the Buddhist transition from reality, through 10 psychological states, towards the ultimate condition of *nirvana* – spiritual enlightenment. Ascending the stupa, the pilgrim passes through these states by ascending through 10 levels. The lowest levels (including the hidden layer, of which a portion is visible at the southeast corner) depict the Sphere of Desire (*Kamadhatu*), describing the cause and effect of good and evil. Above this, the five lower quadrangular galleries, with their multitude of reliefs (put end to end they would measure 2.5 km), represent the Sphere of Form (*Rupadhatu*). These are in stark contrast to the bare upper circular terraces with their half-hidden Buddhas within perforated stupas, representing the Sphere of Formlessness (*Arupadhatu*) – nothingness or nirvana.

The reliefs and the statues of the Buddha

The inner (or retaining) wall of the first gallery is 3½ m high and contains two series of reliefs, one above the other, each of 120 panels. The upper panels relate events in the historic Buddha's life – the *Lalitavistara* – from his birth to the sermon at Benares, while the lower depict his former lives, as told in the *Jataka* tales. The upper and lower reliefs on the balustrades (or outer wall) also relate Jataka stories as well as *Avadanas* – another Buddhist text, relating previous lives of the Bodhisattvas – in the northeast corner. After viewing this first series of reliefs, climb the east stairway – which was only used for ascending – to the next level. The retaining wall of the second gallery holds 128 panels in a single row 3 m high. This, along with the panels on the retaining walls and (some of the) balustrades of the third gallery, tells the story of Sudhana in search of the Highest Wisdom – one of the most important Buddhist texts, otherwise known as *Gandawyuha*. Finally, the retaining wall of the fourth terrace has 72 panels depicting the *Bhadratjari* – a conclusion to the story of Sudhana, during which he vows to follow in the footsteps of Bodhisattva Samantabhadra. In total there are 2700 panels – a prodigious artistic feat, not only in quantity, but also the consistently high quality of the carvings and their composition.

From these enclosed galleries, the monument opens out onto a series of unadorned circular terraces. On each are a number of small stupas (72 in all), diminishing in size upwards from the first to third terrace, pierced with lozenge-shaped openings, each containing a statue of the Buddha.

Including the Buddhas to be found in the niches opening outwards from the balustrades of the square terraces, there are a staggering 504 Buddha images. All are sculpted out of single blocks of stone. They are not representations of earthly beings who have reached nirvana, but transcendental saviours. The figures are strikingly simple, with a line delineating the edge of the robe, tightly-curled locks of hair, a top knot or *usnisa*, and an *urna* – the dot on the forehead. These last two features are distinctive bodily marks of the Buddha. On the square terraces, the symbolic gesture or mudra of the Buddha is different at each compass point: east-facing Buddhas are 'calling the earth to witness' or *bhumisparcamudra* (with right hand pointing down towards the earth); to the west, they are in an attitude of meditation or *dhyanamudra* (hands together in the lap, with palms facing upwards), to the south, they express charity or *varamudra* (right hand resting on the knee); and to the north, the Buddhas express dispelling fear or *abhayamudra* (with the right hand raised). On the upper circular terraces, all the Buddhas are in the same mudra. Each Buddha is slightly different, yet all retain a remarkable serenity.

The main central stupa on the summit contains two empty chambers. There has been some dispute as to whether they ever contained representations of the Buddha. Those who believe that they did not, argue that because this uppermost level denotes nirvana – nothingness – it would have been symbolically correct to have left them empty. For the pilgrim, these top levels were also designed to afford a chance to rest, before beginning the descent to the world of men. Any stairways except the east one could be used to descend.

The decline, fall and restoration of Borobudur

With the shift in power from central to east Java in the 10th century, Borobudur was abandoned and its ruin hastened by earthquakes. In 1814, Thomas Stamford Raffles appointed HC Cornelis to undertake investigations into the condition of the monument. Minor restoration was carried out intermittently over the next 80 years, but it was not until 1907 that a major reconstruction programme commenced. This was placed under the leadership of Theo Van Erp, and under his guidance much of the top of the monument was dismantled and then rebuilt. Unfortunately, within 15 years the monument was deteriorating once again, and the combined effects of the world depression in the 1930s, the Japanese occupation in the Second World War and then the trauma of independence, meant that it was not until the early 1970s that a team of international archaeologists were able to investigate the state of Borobudur once more. To their horror, they discovered that the condition of the foundations had deteriorated so much that the entire monument was in danger of caving in. In response, UNESCO began a 10-year restoration programme. This comprised dismantling all the square terraces – involving the removal of approximately 1,000,000 pieces of stone. These were then cleaned, while a new concrete foundation was built, incorporating new water channels. The work was finally completed in 1983 and the monument reopened by President Suharto.

Museum

ⓘ *Free with entrance ticket to Borobudur, daily 0600-1700.*

There is a museum close to the monument, which houses an exhibition showing the restoration process undertaken by UNESCO, and some pieces found on site during the excavation and restoration process.

Candis around Borobudur

Candi Pawon ⓘ *daily 0600-1700, 5000Rp, (admission fee includes admission to Candi Mendut, don't throw the ticket away)*, was probably built at the same time as Borobudur and is laid out with the same east-west orientation. It may have acted as an ante-room to Borobudur, catering to the worldly interests of pilgrims. Another theory is that it acted as a crematorium. Candi Pawon is also known as 'Candi Dapur', and both words mean kitchen. The unusually small windows may have been this size because they were designed as smoke outlets. The shrine was dedicated to Kuvera, the God of Fortune. The temple sits on a square base and has an empty chamber. The exterior has some fine reliefs of female figures within pillared frames – reminiscent of Indian carvings – while the roof bears tiers of stupas. Among the reliefs are *kalpataru* or wish-granting trees, their branches dripping with jewels, and surrounded by pots of money. Bearded dwarfs over the entrance pour out jewels from sacks. Insensitive and poor restoration at the beginning of the 20th century has made architectural interpretation rather difficult.

Candi Mendut ⓘ *Sun-Mon 0600-1700, 5000Rp, (admission fee includes admission to Candi Prawon, don't throw the ticket away)*, lies further east still and 3 km from Borobudur. It was built by King Indra in AD 800. It is believed the candi was linked to Borobudur by a paved walkway; pilgrims may have congregated at Mendut, rested or meditated at Pawon, and then proceeded to Borobudur. The building was rediscovered in 1836, when the site was being cleared for a coffee plantation. The main body of the building was restored by Van Erp at the beginning of this century, but the roof was left incomplete (it was probably a large stupa). The temple is raised on a high rectangular plinth and consists of a square cella containing three statues. The shrine is approached up a staircase, its balustrade decorated with reliefs depicting scenes from the *jataka* stories. The exterior is elaborately carved with a series of large relief panels of Bodhisattvas. One wall shows the **four-armed Tara** or **Cunda**, flanked by devotees, while another depicts **Hariti**, once a child-eating demon but here shown after her conversion to Buddhism, with children all around her. **Atavaka**, a flesh-eating ogre, is shown in this panel holding a child's hand and sitting on pots of gold. The standing male figure may be the **Bodhisattva Avalokitesvara**, whose consort is Cunda. There are also illustrations of classical Indian morality tales – look out for the fable of the tortoise and the two ducks on the left-hand side – and scenes from Buddhist literature. The interior is very impressive. There were originally seven huge stone icons in the niches; three remain. These three were carved from single blocks of stone, which may explain why they have survived. The central Buddha is seated in the unusual European fashion and is flanked by his two reincarnations (Avalokitesvara and Vajrapani). Notice how the feet of both the attendant statues are black from touching by devotees. The images are seated on elaborate thrones backed against the walls but conceived in the round (similar in style to cave paintings found in western Deccan, India).

There are no architectural remains of another, Sivaite, monument called **Candi Banon**, which was once situated near Candi Pawon. Five large sculptures recovered from the site, all examples of the Central Javanese Period, are in the National Museum in Jakarta.

Prambanan Plain and around ◉◉ ►► *pp254-255.*

① *Daily 0600-1800, admission to complex US$10 adult US$6 student. Guides will show you around, pointing out the various stories on the reliefs for 40,000Rp. Audiovisual show runs for 30 mins, most languages available, 2000Rp.*

The Prambanan Plain was the centre of the powerful 10th-century Mataram Kingdom that vanquished the Sailendra Dynasty – the builders of Borobudur. At the height of its influence, Mataram encompassed both central and east Java, together with Bali, Lombok, southwest Borneo and south Sulawesi. The magnificent temples that lie scattered over the Prambanan Plain – second only to Borobudur in size and artistic accomplishment – bear testament to the past glories of the kingdom. The village of Prambanan is little more than a way station, with a handful of *warungs*, a number of *losmen* and hotels, a market and a bus stop. There is a private **tourist information office** just east (towards Solo) of the bus stop.

Sights

There are six major candis on the Prambanan Plain, each with its own artistic character, and all well worth visiting. The account below describes the temples from east to west, travelling from Prambanan village towards Yogya. The Prambanan temple group were restored by the Indonesian Archaeological Service and now stand in a neat, landscaped and well-planned historical park.

Candi Prambanan or **Candi Lara Jonggrang** – Slender Maiden – as it is also known, stands on open ground and can be clearly seen from the road in Prambanan village. This is the principal temple on the Prambanan Plain, and the greatest Hindu monument in Java. In scale, it is similar to Borobudur, the central tower rising almost vertically, over 45 m. Built between 900 and 930 AD, Prambanan was the last great monument of the Central Javanese Period and – again like Borobudur – the architects were attempting to symbolically recreate the cosmic Gunung Meru.

Originally, there were 232 temples at this site. The plan was focused on a square court, with four gates and eight principal temples. The three largest candis are dedicated to Brahma (to the south), to Vishnu (to the north) and the central and tallest tower to Siva. They are sometimes known as Candi Siva, Candi Brahma and Candi Vishnu. Facing each is a smaller shrine, dedicated to each of these gods' 'mounts'.

Candi Siva was restored by the Dutch, after a 16th-century earthquake left much of the temple in ruins. It was conceived as a square cell, with portico projections on each face, the porticos being an integral part of the structure. The tower was constructed as six diminishing storeys, each ringed with small stupas, and the whole surmounted by a larger stupa. The tower stands on a plinth with four approach stairways, the largest to the east, each with gate towers imitating the main shrine and edged with similar shaped stupas. At the first level is an open gallery, with fine reliefs on the inside wall depicting the Javanese interpretation of the Hindu epic, the Ramayana. The story begins to the left of the east stairway and is read by walking clockwise – known as *pradaksina*. Look out for the *kalpataru* (wishing trees), with parrots above them and guardians in the shape of rabbits, monkeys and geese or *kinaras*. The story continues on the balustrade of Candi Brahma. Each stairway at Candi Siva leads up into four separate rooms. In the east room is a statue of Siva, to the south is the sage Agastya, behind him – to the west – is his son Ganesh, and to the north is his wife Durga. Durga is also sometimes known as Lara Jonggrang, or Slender Maiden, hence the alternative name for Prambanan – Candi Lara Jonggrang.

The name of this monument is linked to the legend of King Boko and his son Bandung Bondowoso. Bandung loved a princess, Lara Jonggrang, who rejected his advances until her father was defeated in battle by King Boko. To save her father's life, Princess Lara agreed to marry Prince Bandung, but only after he had built 1000 temples in a single night. Summoning an army of subterranean genies, Bandung was well on the way to meeting the target when Lara Jonggrang ordered her maids to begin pounding the day's rice. Thinking it was morning, the cocks crowed and the genies retreated back to their underground lair, leaving Bandung one short of his 1000 temples. In an understandable fit of pique he turned her to stone – and became the statue of Durga. For those leaving Yogya by air, there is a mural depicting the legend at Adisucipto Airport.

The two neighbouring candis dedicated to Vishnu and Brahma are smaller. They have only one room each and one staircase on the east side, but have equally fine reliefs running round the galleries. On **Candi Vishnu**, the reliefs tell the stories of Krishna, while those on the balustrade of **Candi Brahma** are a continuation of the Ramayana epic which begins on Candi Siva. On the exterior walls of all three shrines can be seen voluptuous *apsaris*. These heavenly nymphs try to seduce gods, ascetics and mortal men; they encourage ascetics to break their vows of chastity and are skilled in the arts.

Opposite these shrines are the ruins of **three smaller temples**, recently renovated. Each is dedicated to the mount of a Hindu god: facing Candi Siva is Nandi the bull – Siva's mount; facing Candi Vishnu is (probably) Garuda, the mythical bird; and facing Candi Brahma (probably), Hamsa the goose. The magnificent statue of Nandi is the only mount that still survives.

This inner court is contained within a gated outer court. Between the walls are 224 smaller shrines – all miniature versions of the main shrine – further enclosed by a courtyard.

Candis near Candi Prambanan

From Candi Prambanan, it is possible to walk north to the ruined **Candi Lumbung**, under restoration, as well as **Candi Bubrah**. Together with **Candi Sewu**, they form a loose complex.

Candi Sewu (meaning 'a thousand temples') lies 1 km to the north of Candi Prambanan and was constructed over three periods spanning the years AD 778-810. At first, the building was probably a simple square cella, surrounded by four smaller temples, unconnected to the main shrine. Later, they were incorporated into the current cruciform plan, and the surrounding four rows of 240 smaller shrines were also built. These smaller shrines are all square in plan, with a portico in front. The central temple probably contained a bronze statue of the Buddha. The candi has been renovated. The complex is guarded by *raksasa* guardians brandishing clubs, placed here to protect the temple from evil spirits.

Two kilometres to the northeast of Candi Prambanan is **Candi Plaosan**, probably built around AD 835, to celebrate the marriage of a princess of the Buddhist Sailendra Dynasty to a member of the court of the Hindu Sanjaya Dynasty. Candi Plaosan consists of two central sanctuaries surrounded by 116 stupas and 58 smaller shrines. The two central shrines were built on two levels with six cellas. Each of the lower cellas may have housed a central bronze Buddha image, flanked by two stone Bodhisattvas (similar to Candi Mendut, page 249). Again, the shrines are guarded by raksasa. The monument is currently being restored.

About 2 km to the south of Prambanan village is **Candi Sojiwan**, another Buddhist temple, undergoing restoration.

The ruins of the late ninth-century **Kraton Ratu Boko** occupy a superb position on a plateau, 200 m above the Prambanan Plain, and cover an area of over 15 ha. They are quite clearly signposted off the main road (south), 2 km. Because this was probably a palace (hence the use of the word kraton in its name), it is thought that the site was chosen for its strong natural defensive position. The hill may also have been spiritually important. Little is known of the palace; it may have been a religious or a secular royal site – or perhaps both. Some authorities have even suggested it was merely a resting centre for pilgrims visiting nearby Prambanan. Inscriptions found in the area celebrate the victory of a ruler, and may be related to the supremacy of the (Hindu) Sanjaya Dynasty over the Buddhist Sailendras.

For the visitor, it is difficult to make sense of the ruins – it is a large site, spread out over the hillside and needs some exploring. From the car park area, walk up some steps and then for about 1 km through rice fields. The dominant restored triple ceremonial porch on two levels gives an idea of how impressive the palace must have been. To the north of the porch are the foundations of two buildings, one of which may have been a temple – possibly a cremation temple. Turn south and then east to reach the major part of the site. Many of the ruins here were probably Hindu shrines, and the stone bases held wooden pillars, which supported large pendopo, or open-sided pavilions. Beyond the palace was a series of pools and above the whole complex a series of caves.

Getting there Take the road south before crossing the Opak River, towards Piyungan, for about 5 km. On the road, just over a bridge on the left-hand side, are steep stone stairs that climb 100 m to the summit of the plateau and to the kraton. Alternatively, it is possible to drive to the top; further on along the main road, a turning to the left leads to **Candi Banyunibo**, a small, attractive, restored Buddhist shrine dating from the ninth century. It is set in a well kept garden and surrounded by cultivated land. Just before the candi, a narrow winding road, negotiable by car and motorbike, leads up to the plateau and Ratu Boko.

Candis on the road west to Yogya

About 3 km west of Candi Prambanan and Prambanan village, on the north side of the main road towards Yogya, is **Candi Sari**. This square temple, built around 825, is one of the most unusual in the area, consisting of two storeys and with the appearance of a third.

With three cellas on each of the two levels and porticos almost like windows, it strongly resembles a house. Interestingly, reliefs at both Borobudur and Prambanan depict buildings of similar design – probably built of wood rather than stone. Some art historians think that the inspiration for the design is derived from engravings on bronze Dongson drums. These were introduced into Indonesia from north Vietnam and date from between the second and fifth century BC. There is an example of just such a drum in the National Museum in Jakarta. It is thought that both the lower and the upper level cellas of the candi were used for worship, the latter being reached by a wooden stairway. The exterior is decorated with particularly accomplished carvings of goddesses, Bodhisattvas playing musical instruments, the female Buddhist deity Tara, and male naga-kings. Like Candi Kalasan, the stupas on the roof bear some resemblance to those at Borobudur. Inside there are three shrines, which would originally have housed Buddha images. Nothing remains of the outer buildings or surrounding walls, but it would have been of similar design to Candi Plaosan. The candi was restored by the Dutch in 1929 and like Candi Kalasan is surrounded by trees and houses.

A short distance further west, and on the opposite side of the road from Candi Sari, is **Candi Kalasan** – situated just off the road in the midst of rice fields. The temple dates from AD 778, making it one of the oldest candis on Java. It is a Buddhist temple dedicated to the Goddess Tara and is thought to have been built either to honour the marriage of a princess of the Sailendra Dynasty, or as the sepulchre for a Sailendra prince's consort. The monument is strongly vertical and built in the form of a Greek cross – contrasting sharply with the squat and square Candi Sambisari. In fact, the plan of the temple was probably altered 12 years after construction. Of the elaborately carved kalamakaras on the porticos projecting from each face, only the south example remains intact. They would have originally been carved roughly in stone and then coated with two layers of stucco, the second of which remained pliable just long enough for artists to carve the intricate designs. The four largest of the external niches are empty. The style of the reliefs is similar to Southeast Indian work of the same period. The roof was originally surmounted by a high circular stupa, mounted on an octagonal drum. Above the porticos are smaller stupas, rather similar in design to those at Borobudur. The only remaining Buddha images are to be found in niches towards the top of the structure. The building contains a mixture of Buddhist and Hindu cosmology – once again evidence of Java's religious syncretism. The main cella almost certainly contained a large bronze figure, as the pedestal has been found to have traces of metallic oxide. The side shrines would also have had statues in them, probably figures of the Buddha.

Another 5 km southwest from Candi Kalasan, towards Yogya, is the turn-off for **Candi Sambisari**, 2 km north of the main road. If travelling from Yogya, turn left at the Km 12.5 marker – about 9.5 km out of town. Candi Sambisari, named after the nearby village, sits 6.5 m below ground level, surrounded by a 2-m-high volcanic tuff wall. It has only recently been excavated from under layers of volcanic ash, having been discovered by a farmer in the 1960s. It is believed to have been buried by an eruption of Gunung Merapi during the 14th century and as a result is well preserved. The candi was probably built in the early ninth century, and if so, is one of the last temples to be built during the Mataram period. A central square shrine still contains its linga, indicating that this was a Hindu temple dedicated to Siva. There are also smaller boundary lingams surrounding the temple. On the raised gallery, there are fine carvings of Durga (north), Ganesh (east) and Agastya (south). Pillar bases on the terrace indicate that the entire candi was once covered by a wooden pavilion.

*For Sleeping and Eating price codes,
see inside the front cover.*

◉ Sleeping

Borobudur *p246*

Most people visit Borobudur as a day trip
from Yogya. However, accommodation is
quite well established here and can get fully
booked over public holidays. Although large
international hotels are attracted to the area,
many budget hostels are in demand and,
as a result, the standard is generally poor.

LL Amanjiwo, 10 min-drive and 30 min-walk
from Borobudur, T0293 788333, www.aman
resorts.com. A gloriously opulent resort. The
hotel faces Borobudur and they arrange early
morning trips to the temple to see the sun rise;
magical. 35 gorgeous suites set around the
reception, each with a terraced area, shaded
day bed and private pool. Facilities include
restaurant, spa service, bar, library, art gallery
and tennis centre. They offer free rental of
good mountain bikes to explore the
countryside. Exceptional quality of service.

C Manohara Hotel, Borobudur Complex,
T0293 788131, www.yogyes.com/manohara.
Smart hotel set in well-manicured gardens,
fantastic position, a/c rooms in a peaceful
location are fairly good value. Guests do not
automatically get access to Borobudur before
the gates open at 0600 – this has an
additional fee. There are stunning views of
the sunrise and sunset over the temple. The
room price includes the temple entrance fee.

C-D Pondok Tingal Hostel, Jl Balaputradewa
32 (about 2 km from the temple towards
Yogya), T0293 788145. Traditional-style
wooden building set around courtyard, clean
smart rooms with bathroom and character,
dorm beds (**E**) also available, room rate
includes breakfast. There is a kris exhibition and
occasional evening *wayang* performances.

D-E Lotus Guesthouse, Jl Madeng Kamulan 2,
T0293 788281. This well-run establishment is a

popular choice for backpackers, with fair
rooms. The rooms are clean, but some have
bars over the windows. Cheaper rooms have
squat toilet and *mandi*. The owner is a great
source of local knowledge and can arrange
trips around the local area including rafting.

D-E Rajasa, Jl Badrawati 2, T0293 788276,
ariswara_sutomo@yahoo.com. On the road
to the Amanjiwa, this friendly hotel has
gorgeous views of verdant rice paddies, and
clean a/c and fan rooms with hot water.

Prambanan plain *p250*

There are a number of *losmen* in Prambanan
village. Few people stay here because the
candis are so easily accessible from either
Solo or Yogya, but it may be worth doing
so, to enjoy the sunrise and sunset.

B Prambanan Village, Taman Martani,
T0274 496435, F0274 496354. Very quiet
setting offering lovely views of sunset and
rise over Prambanan, separate cottages
with fully equipped rooms and al fresco
mandi. Pool, upstairs open restaurant
with views. Recommended.

D-F Hotel Prambanan Indah, Jl Candi Sewi 8,
T0274 497353. Simple hotel with a variety of
rooms, ranging from hotel type to dorm beds,
all share the same facilities including pool.

◉ Eating

Borobudur *p246*

There are 2 restaurants within the complex, a
number around the stall and car park area, and
in Borobudur village, although the quality at
most places is mediocre, and poor value.

⊪ Rajasa, Jl Pranudyawardini, 0700-2200
has a traveller-friendly menu of good curries,
seafood dishes and vegetarian options. If you
are staying at the their hotel (see Sleeping)
your meal will be delivered. Recommended.

⊪ Saraswati, Jl Pranudyawardini has a
reasonable restaurant with good set meals.

✳ Festivals and events

Borobudur p246
May **Waicak** (movable, usually during full moon), celebrates the birth and death of the historic Buddha. The procession starts at Candi Mendut and converges on Borobudur at about 0400, all the monks and nuns carry candles – an impressive sight.

▲ Activities and tours

Borobudur p246
Cycling
The tour guides in Borobudur offer 2-hr guided rides around the surrounding countryside for 50,000Rp per person (minimum 5 people). Ask at the ticket office for more information.

Elephant treks
Organized through the **Manahora Hotel** (see Sleeping). 2½-hr treks through the surrounding area. Contact the hotel for further information.

Whitewater rafting
Run by **Lotus Guesthouse** (see Sleeping). 9 km of Grade II-III rafting along the Progo river.

⊖ Transport

Borobudur p246
Bicycle hire Can be hired from some *losmen*/guesthouses (eg **Lotus Guesthouse**). An excellent way to visit candi Pawon and candi Mendut.

Bus Regular connections from Yogya's Umbunharjo terminal on Jl Kemerdekaan or from the street 10,000Rp, 2 hrs (ask at your hotel to find out where the bus stops). For those staying on Jl Prawirotaman, the best place is the corner of Jl Parangtritis and

Jl May Jend Sutoyo. The buses run along Jl Sugiyono, Jl Sutoyo and Jl Haryono (1½-2 hrs). Note that the last bus back to Yogya leaves at 1700. Leave at 0500 to arrive early and avoid crowds. From the bus station in Borobudur, it is a 500-m walk to the monument. Bis malam (night) and bis cepat (express) tickets can be booked from the office opposite the market in the village. Buses to **Yogya**, **Jakarta**, **Bogor** and **Merak**.

Taxi This may be the best option for 3-4 people travelling together – cheaper than a hotel tour and without time restrictions.

Prambanan plain p250
In order to see the outlying candis, it is best to have some form of transport. If on a tour, enquire which candis are to be visited, or hire a taxi, minibus or motorbike from Yogya. Horse-drawn carts and minibuses wait at the bus station; they can be persuaded to drive visitors around. For the main temple group, a road 'train' now takes visitors around the candis, although it is also possible to walk – hot and tiring in the middle of the day. Or, take a bus to Prambanan and work back, west or work east, ending at Prambanan.

Bus Regular connections with **Yogya's** Umbulharjo bus station, or by minibus from the main roads in Yogya (30 mins). Connections with **Solo** (1½ hrs).

ⓘ Directory

Borobudur p246
Banks Bank Rakyat Indonesia, near the entrance gate to Borobudur temple, inside the complex. There is a BNI ATM on Jl Medang Kamulan. **Post office** Jl Pramudyawardani 10. **Telephone** Wartel, Jl Pramudyawardani (opposite market).

Solo (Surakarta) and around

→ *Phone code: 0271. Colour map 10, B4.*

Situated between three of Java's highest volcanoes – Gunung Merapi (2911 m) and Gunung Merbabu (3142 m) to the west, and Gunung Lawu (3265 m) to the east – Surakarta, better known simply as 'Solo', is Central Java's second royal city. The kraton (palace) of the great ancient kingdom of Mataram was moved to Surakarta in the 1670s and the town remained the negara (capital) of the kingdom until 1755, when the VOC divided Mataram into three sultanates – two in Solo and one in Yogya. Although foreigners usually regard Yogya as Java's cultural heart, the Javanese often attach the sobriquet to Surakarta. Solo's motto is 'Berseri' – an acronym for Bersih, Sehat, Rapi, Indah (clean, healthy, neat, beautiful) – and the city has won several awards for being the cleanest in Indonesia.

Solo is more relaxed, smaller and less touristy than Yogya and has pleasant, wide, clean tree-lined streets. Solo has bicycle lanes (on the main east-west road – Jalan Slamet Riyadi) and they are almost as busy as the main roads. Reflecting the bicycle-friendly character of Solo, many tour companies run cycling tours of the city's places of interest. The city has gained a reputation as a good place to shop; not only is it a centre for the sale of batik – with a large market specializing in nothing else – there is also an 'antiques' market worth visiting. ►► *For listings, see pages 265-272.*

Ins and outs

Getting there
Solo's **Adisumarmo Airport** ① *T0271 780400*, is 10 km northwest of the city and there are connections with Singapore, Java and the outer islands. The **Balapan railway station**, just north of the city centre, has connections with Jakarta, Surabaya and points along the way including Yogya. The **Tirtonadi bus station** is 2 km north of the city centre, departures for many Javanese towns as well as destinations in Bali, Lombok and Sumatra. Book night and express bus tickets through hotels, *losmen* and at travel agencies. Local buses regularly leave Yogya for Solo (two hours). ►► *See Transport, page 270.*

Getting around
Cycling is the best way to explore Solo – the city is more bicycle-friendly than just about any other Javanese town. Angkutans and town buses run along set routes. Becaks are useful for short local trips or for charter (it is also worth taking a becak to explore the streets to find some of the interesting colonial houses) and there are also horse-drawn carts. Taxis are available for charter for out-of-town trips.

Tourist information
① *Jl Slamet Riyadi 275 (next to the Museum Radya Pustaka, T0271 711435, Mon-Sat 0800-1700.* Supply maps and cultural events information. Very helpful, good English spoken. Also tourist information at the bus station (very poor), the railway station and the airport.

Sights

Kraton Surakarta Hadiningrat
① *Mon-Thu 0900-1400, Sat and Sun 0900-1500, admission 8000Rp, 2000Rp for camera, all visitors are asked to wear a* samir *– a gold-and-red ribbon – as a mark of respect, guide obligatory (they are the* abdi dalem *– palace servants).*

The **Kraton Surakarta Hadiningrat**, better known as the **Kasunanan Palace**, is the senior of the city's two kratons and the more impressive. It lies south of the main east-west road, Jalan Slamet Riyadi. Like the kraton in Yogya, the Kasunanan Palace faces north onto a square – the Alun-alun Lor – and follows the same basic design, consisting of a series of courtyards containing open-sided pavilions or pendopos. On the west side of the Alun-alun is the **Grand Mosque**, built by Pangkubuwono III in 1750, though substantially embellished since then.

Entering the Kasunanan Palace, the first pendopo – the **Pagelaran** – is original, dating from 1745, and is used for public ceremonies. This is where visiting government officials would wait for an audience with the Susuhunan. From here, stairs lead up to the **Siti Inggil** (High Place), the area traditionally used for enthronements. Like Borobudur and Prambanan, the Siti Inggil represents the cosmic mountain Meru, but on a micro-scale. On the Siti Inggil is a large pendopo. The fore section of this pavilion was rebuilt in 1915,

Solo

Sleeping

Cendana **7**	
Dana **2**	
Istana Griya **8**	
Keprabon **17**	
Mama Homestay **9**	
Mawar Indria **5**	
Mawar Melati **11**	

Mulia Baru & Blonjo
Kue Cafe **15**
Nirwana **8**
Paradise **13**
Pension Lucie **14**
Sahid Kusuma **4**
Sahid Jaya Solo **10**
Westerners **16**
Wisata Indah **18**

Eating

Duta Minang **4**
Kusuma Sari **1**
Larasati **5**
O Solo Mio **7**
Ramayana **6**
Roda **3**
Tio Ciu 99 **8**
Warung Baru **2**

but the square section towards the rear (known as the **Bangsal Witana**), with its umbrella-shaped roof, is 250 years old.

Visitors are not permitted to enter the main palace compound through the large **Kemandungan Gates**. They must walk back out of the first compound, over a road, past the private entrance to the prince's quarters and an area used to store the royal carriages, through a second gate, to an entrance at the east of the main compound. Near the second gate is a school; this was originally a private school for the royal children but was opened to children of commoners at the time of independence. Walk through one courtyard to reach the large central courtyard, known as the **Plataran**. This shaded area, with its floor of black sand from the south coast, contains the main palace buildings. Much of the prince's private residence was destroyed in a disastrous fire in 1985, but has subsequently been restored. An electrical fault was the alleged cause of the fire, although local belief is that the Susuhunan neglected his duties and provoked the anger of the Goddess Nyi Loro Kidul. Restoration was followed by extensive ceremonies to appease the Goddess.

The three pendopo on the left are original and are used for gamelan performances. Behind them, along the walls of the courtyard, are palanquins once used for transporting princesses around the city. An octagonal tower, the **Panggung Songgobuwono**, survived the fire and was supposedly used by the Susuhunan to communicate with the Goddess Nyi Loro Kidul. Songgobuwono means 'Support of the Universe'.

The main pendopo, the **Sasana Sewaka**, is not original – it was restored in 1987 – although the Dutch iron pillars which support it, are. Strictly speaking, if members of the public are to have an audience with the sultan, they have to walk upon their knees across the pendopo: look out for the cleaners, who crouch to sweep the floor. It is used for four ceremonies a year and sacred dances are held here once a year. Behind this pendopo is the private residence of the prince, with the **kasatrian** (the sons' quarters) to the right and the **keputren** (the daughters' quarters) to the left. A concrete area to the left was the site of the Dining Hall, which burnt to the ground in the fire of 1985 and is awaiting restoration funds.

The guide leads visitors back to the first courtyard, where two sides of the square are a museum, containing an interesting collection of enthronement chairs, small bronze Hindu sculptures and three fine Dutch carriages which are 200-350 years old.

Pura Mangkune-garan
① *Mon-Sat 0900-1400, Sun 0900-1300, 10,000Rp, guide obligatory (about 1 hr), gamelan performances are held here.*

The less impressive kraton, Pura Mangkunegaran at the north end of Jalan Diponegoro, is still lived in by the princely family who built it. In 1757, the rebel prince Mas Said established a new royal house here, crowning himself Mangkunegoro I. But his power was never as great as the Susuhunan, and Mangkunegoro's deference to him is evident in the design of his palace, which faces south towards the Susuhunan's Kraton. Much of the original structure has been restored. Built in traditional style, the layout is like other kratons, centred around a pendopo.

This central pendopo is the **Pendopo Agung** ① *Mon-Sat 0900-1400, Sun 0900-1300*, built in 1810 and one of the largest and most majestic in Java. Note how the ceiling is painted with cosmic symbols. Behind the central pendopo is the **Paringgitan**, a large room that houses, among other things, a good collection of antique jewellery and coins of the Majapahit and Mataram periods. In a corridor behind this room are a number of topeng masks. Voyeurs can peer through the windows into the private rooms of the present prince. Next to the ticket office are three fine carriages from London and Holland.

Around Jalan Slamet Riyadi

The small **Museum Radya Pustaka** ① *Tue-Thu 0800-1400, Fri-Sat 0800-1300, 2000Rp,* is housed in an attractive building on the main road, Jalan Slamet Riyadi, next door to the tourist office. It contains a collection of *wayang kulit*, *topeng*, gamelan instruments, royal barge figureheads and some Hindu sculptures.

Next door to the museum is **Sriwedari** ① *daily 0800-2200, park entrance on a Sat is 1000Rp, Wayan orang performances Mon-Sat 2000-2200, 3000Rp,* an amusement park. It is also the home of one of the most famous Javanese classical dancing troupes, specializing in *wayang orang*. It is possible to go for a backstage visit to meet the artists and take photos (25,000Rp, ask at the tourist office).

Museum **Batik Danar Hadi**, ① *Jl Slamet Riyadi 261, T0271 714253, daily 0900-1530, 15,000Rp,* introduces visitors to the different methids of batik making including wax stamping and handwaxing, and it is possible to see workers producing batik There is also a great display of antique batik and batik from around Asia. Five-day batik courses are available here, but a minimum of 15 people is needed for the course to begin.

Markets

There are several markets in Solo worth visiting. The antiques market, **Pasar Triwindu**, is situated off Jalan Diponegoro, on the right-hand side, walking towards the Pura Mangkunegaran. This is the only authentic flea market in Central Java and is a wonderful place to browse through the piles of goods. There are some antiques to be found, but time is needed to search them out. Bargaining is essential. **Pasar Klewer**, situated just beyond the west gate of the Alun-alun Lor near the kraton, is a batik-lover's paradise. It is filled with cloth, mostly locally produced batik – a dazzling array of both *cap* and *tulis*. Prices are cheaper than the chain stores, but the market is very busy and first-time visitors may be bemused into paying more than they should. It's best to go in the mornings, as it starts to wind down after lunch. Again, bargain hard. At the east side of the Alun-alun are a small number of shops and stalls selling fossils, carvings, krisses, puppets and masks. Don't expect to find anything of real quality, though.

Candi Sukuh

① *Daily 0700-1700, 10,000Rp. Take a bus from Solo's Tirtonadi station on Jl Jend A Yani to Karangpandan (41 km). Or pick up a bus on Jl Ir Sutami travelling east to Karangpandan. From Karangpandan, it is 12 km to Candi Sukuh. Most minibuses travel as far as Ngolrok, from where there are motorbike taxis up on the steep road to the top. From Candi Sukuh there is a well-worn stone path to the mountain resort of Tawangmangu, an easy 1½-2 hrs' hike.* Candi Sukuh and Candi Ceto, two of the most unusual and stunningly positioned temples in Indonesia, lie to the east of Solo, on the west slopes of Gunung Lawu. Candi Sukuh stands at 910 m above sea-level, and was probably built between 1434 and 1449 by the last king of the Majapahit Kingdom, Suhita. This enigmatic candi is situated in an area that had long been sacred and dedicated to ancestor-worship. The style is unlike any other temple in Java and has a close resemblance to South American Maya pyramid temples (which led archaeologists to believe, wrongly, that it was of an earlier date). It is built of laterite on three terraces, facing west. A path between narrow stone gates leads up from one terrace to the next, and steep stairs through the body of the main 'pyramid' to a flat summit. Good views over terraced fields down to the plain below.

The first terrace is approached through a gate from the west, which would have been guarded by *dvarapalas* (temple guardians). The relief carvings on the gate are *candra* sangkala – the elements that make up the picture signify numbers which, in this instance, represent a date ('1359' is equivalent to AD 1437). On the path of the first terrace is a relief of a phallus and vulva: it is said that if a woman's clothes tear on passing this relief, it signifies excessive promiscuity and she must purify herself. The gate to the second terrace is guarded by two more dvarapalas. On the terrace are a number of carved stones, including a depiction of two blacksmiths, one standing – probably Ganesh – the other squatting, in front of which is a selection of the weapons they have forged. The third and most sacred terrace is approached through a third gate. There are a number of relief carvings scattered over the terrace. The figures of many are carved in *wayang* form with long arms, and the principal relief depicts the Sudamala story. This story is performed in places where bodies are cremated, in order to ward off curses or to expel evil spirits. Also on the third terrace are standing winged figures (Garuda), giant turtles representing the underworld (strangely similar to the turtle stelae of pagodas in North Vietnam), and carvings of Bima and Kalantaka. It is thought Bima was the most important god worshipped here. A Bima cult became popular among the Javanese élite in the 15th century.

The 'topless' pyramid itself has little decoration on it. It is thought that originally it must have been topped with a wooden structure. A carved phallus was found at the summit; it is now in the National Museum, Jakarta. Although Candi Sukuh is often called Java's 'erotic' temple, the erotic elements are not very prominent; a couple of oversized penises, little else.

Candi Ceto
① *Daily 0700-1700, 10,000Rp. From Karangpandan via Ngolrok there are minibuses to the village of Kadipekso; from Kadipekso it may be possible to hitch, or catch a motorcycle taxi, the final 2.5 km to the site. Alternatively walk; exhausting at this altitude. There are reportedly some direct bemos from Sukuh to Ceto, making this journey much easier. The easiest way to reach Ceto is to take a tour, see page 270.*

At 1500 m, Candi Ceto is considerably higher than Sukuh and lies 7 km to the north. Fewer people go here as it's harder to get to. It is possible to walk between the two candis (about four hours, no obvious trail, but worth it). It was built in 1470 and is the last temple to have been constructed during the Majapahit era. Candi Ceto shows close architectural affinities with the pura of Bali, where the Hindu traditions of Majapahit escaped the intrusion of Islam. Getting to the temple is an adventure in itself (although tours do run from Solo and Tawangmangu); the road passes tea estates, steeply terraced fields, and towards the end of the journey seems to climb almost vertically up the mountain – the road ends at the temple.

Candi Ceto is one of the most stunningly positioned temples in Southeast Asia. It has recently been restored and is set on 12 levels. Nine would originally have had narrow open gateways (like those at Sukuh), but only seven of these remain. Pairs of reconstructed wooden pavilions on stone platforms lie to each side of the pathway on the final series of terraces. There is some sculpture (occasionally phallic) and strange stone decorations are set into the ground – again, very reminiscent of Mayan reliefs. For best views visit the candi in the early morning; clouds roll in from mid-morning.

Candi Jabung
① *Minibuses running east towards Sitabundo will stop at Candi Jabung, the village or Jabung is small and the candi rather poorly signposted, it's situated 500 m off the main road, a pleasant walk through fruit groves.*

Candi Jabung lies 26 km east of Probolinggo, about 5 km on from the coastal town of Kraksaan, in the small village of Jabung. It was completed in 1354 and unusually is circular (although the inner cella is square). It was a Buddhist shrine, built as a funerary temple for a Majapahit princess. The finial is now ruined but was probably in the form of a stupa. The candi is built of brick and was renovated in 1987 – as too was a smaller candi 20 m to the west of the main structure. The candi is notable for its finely carved kala head. Visitors should sign the visitors' book.

Gunung Bromo ●❶❷❸▲◐ ⇢ pp265-272. Phone code: 0335. Colour map 10, B5.

→ Visit during the dry months from May-Nov. Avoid Indonesian public holidays.

This active volcano stands at 2329 m and is one of the most popular natural sights on Java, lying within the Bromo-Tengger-Semeru National Park. The park consists of a range of volcanic mountains, the highest of which (and Java's highest) is at 3676 m. Gunung Semeru is sometimes also called Gunung Mahameru, the mountain abode of the Hindu gods. Wildlife in the park includes wild pig, Timor deer, barking deer and leopard, as well as an abundance of flying squirrels. Perhaps the most distinctive tree is the cemara, which looks on first glance rather like the familiar conifer. It is, however, no relation and grows above 1400 m on the volcanic ash, where few other trees can establish themselves.

The **National Park Information Booth** ① Cemoro Lawang (near Bromo Permai I), is improving and is more frequently open. It has a range of photos and maps, and is a good place to gain some info before attempting Gunung Semeru. There are also information offices opposite Probolinggo bus terminal (not offices as such, but tour companies willing to offer free information with the hope they might also secure your business).

However, you are unlikely to see a lot of wildlife in the Bromo-Tengger Park, unless you manage to get off the beaten track and away from all the human and vehicular traffic. As in other national parks on Java, leopards, civets and monkeys inhabit the forested areas. The recent problems with forest fires have forced the monkeys down out of the hills, occasionally raiding the villages in search of food. Rangers attempt to prevent the local people from shooting them. Some visitors have been partial to taking edelweiss, which is strictly prohibited. However, the rangers have been cultivating some of the plants to sell.

The local inhabitants of this area are the Tenggerese people, believed to be descended from the refugees of the Majapahit Kingdom, who fled their lands in 928 following the eruption of Gunung Merapi. They embrace the Hindu religion and are the only group of Hindus left on Java today.

For many visitors to Indonesia, the trip to Bromo is their most memorable experience: seeing the sun bathe the crater in golden light, picking out the gulleys and ruts in the almost lunar landscape; sipping sweet Kopi manis after a 0330 start; and feeling the warmth of the sun on your face as the day begins. No wonder the Tenggerese view this area as holy, feeling a need to propitiate the gods. It is hard not to leave feeling the divine hand has helped to mould this inspired landscape.

That's the good experience. But like most good things, there are those who are disappointed. In particular, you may find yourself surrounded by literally hundreds of other tourists (especially July to August), chattering and listening to their radios. It is hard to feel the divine hand in such circumstances. The viewpoint at Gunung Pananjakan is also suffering from the curse of over-popularity: it has become a popular stop for package tours from Surabaya. The buses even travel to the crater floor, making this area even more crowded at sunrise and entrenching further unsightly vehicle marks across the sea of sand.

It is possible to visit the crater on a day trip from Probolinggo. The last minibus down the mountain from Cemoro Lawang leaves at 1500.

Reaching the crater

From Ngadisari via Probolinggo and Sukapura The easiest access to the park is from the north coast town of Probolinggo, via Sukapura and Ngadisari, and then to Cemoro Lawang on the edge of the caldera. The turning from Probolinggo is well signposted. The road starts in a dead straight line and begins to climb slowly through dense forested gulleys of dipherocarps. The road meanders, precariously at times, past fields of cabbage, onions and chillies. At some points a weave of lurid small trees and chopped branches line the road and divide the fields like trellising. The route becomes steeper and steeper and only first gear seems feasible in the overladen minibuses. After Sukapura, the road becomes yet more precipitous. The National Park begins at the village of Ngadisari. The road narrows through here and continues up to Cemoro Lawang, where the tourist sellers appear. The throng of ponies let you know you have reached the top.

On arrival in Ngadisari, it is important to obtain a ticket (25,0000Rp per person) from the **PHKA** boot ⓘ *T0335 541038, open 24 hrs*, in order to visit the crater's edge. This is the national park entrance fee and the money is used to protect and develop the area. The trip to the caldera is usually undertaken in the early morning, in order to watch the sun rise over the volcanoes. To reach the summit for dawn, an early start from Ngadisari is essential, leaving no later than 0330. It is easiest to travel to Cemoro Lawang (from Ngadisari) on one of the six-seater jeeps, organized by guesthouses in Ngadisari. It takes 20 minutes by road from Ngadisari to the outer crater at Cemoro Lawang, and is another 3 km walk from here to the edge of the crater. Either take a pony (it should cost about 50,000Rp per pony for a return trip) – a 30-minute ride – or walk for about one hour along a winding path marked by white concrete stakes, through a strange crater landscape of very fine grey sand, known as *Laut Pasir* (Sand Sea). Vegetables and other crops are grown in the sand, and it is surprising that it doesn't just get blown or washed away. It is also possible to walk the entire way, about 5.5 km, from Ngadisari (four to five hours). The final ascent is up 250 concrete steps to a precarious metre-wide ledge, with a vertical drop down into the crater. Aim to reach the summit for sunrise at about 0530. As this is their business, *Losmen*-owners will wake visitors up in good time to make the crater edge by sunrise, and are also used to arranging transport.

From Tosari via Pasuruan It is also possible to approach the summit from Tosari, on the north slopes of the mountain. (The turn-off for Tosari is about 5 km out of Pasaruan, on the road to Probolinggo.) Take a minibus from Pasuruan to Tosari (31 km). From Tosari, take an ojek the 3 km to **Wonokitri** (sometimes minibuses continue on to here). Both mountain villages have basic accommodation available. There is a **PHKA** office at Wonokitri, where it is necessary to pay the park entrance fee of 25,000Rp per person. Jeeps and ojeks are available here to take visitors all the way to the summit of Gunung Panajakan. For those who want to walk, it is 5 km from Wonokitri to Simpang Dingklik and then another 4 km up to the summit of Gunung Panajakan. From the summit, a path leads to Cemoro Lawang. Leave before 0400 to see the sunrise over the crater.

From Ngadas via Malang and Tumpang Visitors can also reach Bromo's summit from the west, via Malang, Tumpang and Ngadas. From Tumpang there are bemos to Gubugklakah, and from there it is a 12 km walk to Ngadas. From Ngadas it is a 2.5-km walk to the crater rim at Jemplang, and then another 12 km (three hours) across the crater floor to Bromo and Cemoro Lawang. At Jemplang it is also possible to branch off and climb Gunung Semeru (see below). This walk is much more of a trek and quite demanding – although easy enough for anyone with a reasonable level of fitness.

Equipment
Take warm clothing as it can be very cold before sunrise. A scarf to act as a mask to protect against the sulphurous vapour, and a torch to light the way, can also be useful. Avoid changing camera film at the summit; the thin dust can be harmful to the mechanism.

Trekking
There are several worthwhile treks in the Bromo-Tengger-Semeru National Park. Ask at your hotel/*losmen* for information and (in most cases) a map. It is possible to trek from **Cemoro Lawang** to **Ngadas**, or vice versa; from Ngadas, minibuses run down to Tumpang and from there to Malang. The trek takes four to six hours; guides are available, but the route is well marked. For the best view of Bromo, trek to **Gunung Penanjakan**, 6 km from Cemoro Lawang. This trek is well worth it if you are staying up in Cemera Lawang, as 6 km before sunrise is quite enough! The route is easy to follow but torches are a necessity, as is a degree of adventurous spirit. The trek takes about 1½ hours from Cemera, so it is best to leave before 0400 (ignore advice from hostels to leave by 0300, as that then entails a long, cold wait at the top). Take the road opposite the **Cemera Indah** and follow the winding track that turns to gravel and rock. There are white posts leading the way up but these are difficult to spot in the dark. The track is direct until you reach some steps leading up to the right; these steps can be hard to find, but the track comes to a halt and turns back on itself about 25 m after the steps up. At the top of the steps a large concrete shelter has been built. This is a great place to watch the sunrise as it is not busy, and only those who have made the effort to walk are up there. Jeeps can be hired for a sunrise trip taking in both Gunung Bromo and Gunung Penanjakan for US$33 for a group of six people, departing at 0400 and returning at 0830. Enquire at hotels. Alternatively, it is possible but not totally necessary to hire a guide for the walk up Gunung Penanjakan for US$11.

There is a **visitor centre** at Cemoro Lawang, not far from Café Lava. There is a range of photographs and maps; it's a good place to obtain information on Gunung Semeru, although it is rarely staffed.

Around Gunung Bromo ●❶ ₩ *pp265-272.*

Probolinggo → *Phone code: 0335. Colour map 10, B6.*
Probolinggo is a commercial town that doubles up as a Javanese holiday resort. The inhabitants are a mixture of Javanese and Madurese, and most foreign visitors only stop off here en route to Gunung Bromo. Probolinggo is noted for the grapes produced in the surrounding area, and in honour of the fruit the municipal authorities have created a giant bunch, out of concrete, on the main road into town from Pasaruan. It has earned Probolinggo a sobriquet *Kota Anggur* (Grape Town). More enjoyable still is the port, Pelabuhan Probolinggo, north from the town centre off Jalan KH Mansyur – about a 1½-km walk. Brightly-coloured boats from all over Indonesia dock, with their cargoes of mostly dry goods. The northern part of town, centred on Jalan Suroyo and the Alun-alun, is the administrative heart of Probolinggo; the portion further east on Jalan P Sudirman is the commercial heart, with the large **Pasar Barde** – a covered market. The **'tourist office'** faces the bus terminal. It is not a real tourist office, but an advice centre run by several tour companies. We have received complaints about the office and their business practices.

Gunung Semeru

Gunung Semeru, also known as Gunung Mahameru ('seat of the Gods'), is Java's highest Gunungain and lies 13 km (as the crow flies) to the south of Gunung Bromo. This route is only suitable for more experienced climbers/trekkers; a guide and appropriate equipment are also necessary.

Climbing Gunung Semeru Gunung Semeru can be reached from Cemoro Lawang or, more easily, from Malang. If you also wish to visit Gunung Bromo as well as climb Gunung Semeru, then it is possible to trek four hours across the sea of sand. Guided all-inclusive treks up the the summit of Gunung Semeru start at US$164 for the two-day/one-night trek, enquire at the Cemara Indah Hotel.

The approach from **Malang** starts with a 22-km bemo ride to **Tumpang**, from which it is a further 26 km (1½ hours) bemo ride to **Ngadas**, where *losmen* accommodation is available. A further 2.5 km from Ngadas is **Jemplang** village, which is the arrival point for trekkers coming across the sea of sand from Cemoro Lawang. **Ranu Pani** is 6 km further on, and this is where the PHPA post is located. For safety reasons, climbers must both check in and out at this post. It is possible to get a jeep as far as Ranu Pani, but any further and it's walking all the way to the summit (another 20 km).

Climbers usually spend one night at Ranu Pani, either camping or in **F Pak Tasrip's Family Homestay**, T0334 84887, where there is a small restaurant, baggage storage and camping equipment for hire. From Ranopani, the next stop is **Ranu Kumbolo**. It takes three to four hours to walk the relatively flat 10 km trail. Climbers may replenish their water supplies at the beautiful freshwater lake here (2400 m above sea-level). At Ranu Kumbolo, there is a camping area and resthouse with cooking facilities (free).

From Ranu Kumbolo, the climb continues to **Kalimati** (4.5 km), passing through savanna – a great area for bird spotting. There is a campsite at Kalimati and a fresh water supply at **Sumbermani** (30 minutes, following the edge of the forest). The next stop is **Arcopodo**, one hour away. This is a popular camping stop for the second night on the mountain. (Some of the soil is unstable.) The climb to the summit of Semeru has to be carefully timed, as toxic gas from the **Jonggring Saloko** crater is dangerously blown around later in the day. It is unsafe to be on the mountain after midday. The heat from the sun also makes the volcanic sand more difficult to walk on. This last climb should therefore commence between 0200 and 0300. From the summit, climbers, on a clear day, have a fantastic view down into the crater, which emits clouds of steam every 10-15 minutes. Climbers are advised only to attempt Gunung Semeru during the dry season, as sand avalanches and high winds can be a real danger during the wet season. The temperature at the summit ranges from 0-4°C, so come prepared with warm clothing. For more information, enquire at the PHKA office in Malang ① *Jl Raden Intan 6, T0341 491820*, or at the information centre at Cemoro Lawang.

An interesting walk is to **Widodaren Cave**, halfway up **Gunung Kursi**. It is rarely visited by tourists, but is a regular worshipping site for the local Hindu Tenggerese. There is a spring at the back of the *gua*, which may explain why local people view the site as sacred. To avoid hours of endlessly traversing the sand sea in search of the path leading up to Widodaren, ask for further directions from the park rangers in the visitor's centre or even get them to guide you. It is a 1½-hour walk from Cemoro Lawang.

Madakaripura waterfall

ⓘ *The turn off for the waterfall is on the main road up to Bromo from Probolinggo, just before Sukapura, hire an ojek or catch a bemo to Lumbang (1½ hrs drive) after which it is a further 15 mins ride to the waterfall.*

There are people on the approach to the 'air terju', who wait to lend visitors umbrellas to shield them from the water cascading down the narrow path through the hillside. Swimming is possible.

◉ Solo (Surakarta) and around listings

For Sleeping and Eating price codes, see inside the front cover.

◉ Sleeping

Solo *p256, map p257*
Solo has a good range of places to stay at all price levels.
LL-B Hotel Sahid Jaya Solo, Jl Gajah Mada 82, T0271 644144, sahidslo@indosat.net.id. The outfits worn by some of the staff here wouldn't look out of place at a *Star Wars* convention. This 5-star hotel has spotless rooms, that are well decorated featuring TV and mini bar. The hotel has a pool and fitness centre with numerous bars and restaurants. Discounts available.
A-B Hotel Sahid Kusuma, Jl Sugiyopranoto, T0271 646356, www.sahid.com. This hotel is filled with the sound of birdsong and makes for a quiet respite from the busy streets. The standard rooms are set in a dull block but are clean and spacious. The marginally more expensive cabana rooms have a pool view, TV, bath, mini bar and are good value. There is a pool, bar, fitness centre and spa. Efficient staff. Discounts available. Recommended.
A-C Hotel Dana, Jl Slamet Riyadi 286, T0271 711976, www.hoteldanasolo.com. The horrific concrete car park is in contrast with the tasteful Javanese reception. The cheaper rooms are dark and a little musty, but feature TV and a clean bathroom. More expensive rooms are brighter and well furnished. Friendly staff, sizeable discounts available.
D-E Hotel Wisata Indah, Jl Slamet Riyadi, T0271 646770. Spacious rooms lacking in

charm featuring a/c and TV. Ask for a room on the 2nd floor because the 1st-floor rooms face a car park.
E-F Hotel Keprabon, Jl Ahmad Dahlan 12, T0271 632811. There is art deco style aplenty here, evident in the chairs, façade and beautiful window shutters. Rooms have dirty walls, TV and the more expensive have a/c and hot water.
E-F Mawar Melati, Jl Imam Bonjol 54, T0271 636434, F0271 630566. The cheap fan rooms are a little grungy and have dark bathroom with squat toilet. Things improve drastically as you climb the price range, with spacious, clean a/c rooms with TV that are great value.
E-G Mawar Indria Hotel, Jl Monginsidi 125, T0271 632810, F0271 652389. Handy for the train station, the more expensive rooms have TV, old furniture and are clean. The cheapest rooms have a squat toilet.
E-G Hotel Mulia Baru, Jl Ahmad Dahlan 7, T0271 661884. The furniture is a little tatty and the rooms need a lick of paint, but they have plenty of natural light and TV. The cheapest rooms have shared bathroom.
F Istana Griya, Jl Ahmad Dahlan 22, T0271 632667, www.istanagriya.tripod.com. The most popular place in town for budget travellers, this hotel has a friendly atmosphere and offers lots of good local information. All rooms only have windows onto a dim corridor. Rooms are colourful, and have attached Western bathrooms. The more expensive rooms have cable TV and hot water. Free tea and coffee all day. Bike hire and internet access available.
F-G Paradise, Jl Empu Panuluh, T0271 652960. This rambling hotel oozes decrepit

charm, with antique lamps and old photos of Solo's past. Rooms are shady, and spacious and the a/c ones are surpisingly cheap and feature a bath. There's plenty of outdoor seating. Tax not included in the room price.

G Cendana, up an unnamed gang off Jl Gatot Subroto – look for the Toka Ada sign and turn left, T0813 11129295. Staff here seem a little flustered to see foreign guests, but these are the cheapest digs in town. Rooms are spartan and an attached bathroom costs an extra 5000Rp.

G Mama Homestay, Jl Cakra 35, T0271 652248. Set in a Javanese family compound with walls lined with old photos of family members, the 3 fan rooms here are fairly clean. Bathrooms are shared and have shower and *mandi*.

G Hotel Nirwana, Jl Ronggowarsito 59, T0271 632843. Simple fan rooms with bars over the window.

G Pension Lucie, Jl Ambon 12, T0271 653375. Like walking into a scene from an Irvine Welsh book, the rooms here have a mattress on the floor and that's it. Some rooms are even windowless. Dark shared bathroom. The owner speaks no English.

G The Westerners, Jl Empu Panuluh, T0271 633106. In a friendly family compound, this place has wholesome vibes. Simple fan rooms and attached Western bathrooms with cold-water shower.

Gunung Bromo *p261*
Ngadisari
D-F Yoschi's, Jl Wonokerto 1, 2 km before Ngadisari, T0335 541018, yoschi_bromo@ telkom.net. Restaurant and *losmen*, owner speaks good English. This is currently the best place to stay in Ngadisari, some rooms with hot water and showers, attractively furnished and designed with bamboo and *ikat*, the cottages are excellent value, restaurant serves good European and Indonesian dishes using local produce and the *losmen* is a good source of information. Highly recommended.

Sukapura
E-F Sangdimur Cottages, Desa Ngepung Sukapura, T0335 581193, F0335 422256. The location here is not good for an early morning ascent of the crater, but those who are lazing around the Bromo area and don't like the cold nights will enjoy the relative warmth. Rooms are large and some have lovely views. It's worth paying a bit more for the rooms with hot water. Tennis court and pool.

Tosari
B Bromo Cottages, T0343 571222. Restaurant, hot water, tennis courts, great views.

Cemoro Lawang
Hotels can be full during peak season (Jul-Aug). All hostels have their own restaurants. This is a good place to stay for early morning walks.

C-D Lava View Lodge, T0335 541009, www.globaladventureindonesia.com. Pleasant spacious rooms all come with TV, hot water and a large buffet breakfast. The rooms are in good shape and very clean.

C-F Hotel Bromo Permai, T0335 541021, www.bromo_permai_1.indonetwork.co.id. Usually packed with Indonesian tourists and very busy at weekends. The cheapies have shared bathroom and cold water and are poor value. As you go up the price range things improve with hot water, bath and TV. Prices increase at the weekend. Tax is not included in the price.

E-F Cafe Lava Hostel, T0335 541020, www.globaladventureindonesia.com. This well-run and friendly hotel has the best value rooms in town, with their superior doubles with TV, hot water and cosy beds trouncing all the other competition. As you slide down the price range, things get ordinary.

E-G Cemara Indah, T0335 541019, info@bromotrail.com. The most popular place for foreign visitors, the economy rooms are characterless ice boxes, but the standard rooms are fair value and have attached bathroom and hot water. It is possible to negotiate cheaper rates in low season.

G Losmen Setia Kawan, T0335 541006. Just down the road from the Cemara Indah, this place has small simple rooms in a family home with shared bathroom. The rooms certainly aren't the best in town, but will suffice for those who want to stay at the crater's edge during the busy high season.

Camping As the area is a national park, it is possible to camp (40,000Rp). The camping site is just before the **Lava View Lodge**, 20 m from the lip of the crater. Ask the National Park information booth, close to the Bromo Permai I, for more details and about renting equipment. All visitors who wish to camp must report to the **PHKA** post or the Forestry Department, T0852 32367281.

Around Gunung Bromo *p263*
Probolinggo
Most people get in and out of Probolinggo as quickly as possible, but there are a few fair options in town.
E-F Bromo Permai 2, Jl Panglima Sudirman 327, T/F0335 422256. This is the first port of call for most tourists needing a place to crash. Rooms are clean and spacious and some come with an attractive garden view. All the a/c and fan rooms have a Western bathroom. The staff here are friendly, and can help with booking train tickets out of town.
E-F Hotel Paramita, Jl Siaman 7, T0335 421535. Not far from the bus station and tucked just off the busy main street, follow the large signposts to find this hotel with clean and spacious a/c and fan rooms.
E-F Hotel Ratna, Jl Panglima Sudirman 16, T0335 412597. Decent clean and large a/c and fan rooms.

● Eating

Solo *p256, map p257*
Solo is renowned as a good place to eat and there is certainly no shortage of restaurants and warungs to choose from. Solo specialities include *nasi gudeg* (egg, beans, rice,

vegetables and coconut sauce), *nasi liwet* (rice cooked in coconut milk and served with a vegetable) and *timlo* (embellished chicken broth). The Yogyanese speciality *gudeg* is also popular here. Most places are closed by 2130.
♥ O Solo Mio, Jl Slamet Riyadi, T0271 664785, 1030-2300. Set in a beautifully painted restored shophouse, this authentic Italian restaurant is the best place in town for pizza, pasta and has carafes of Australian red and white wine. There is a monthly special menu, live acoustic music on Thu-Sun and free Wi-Fi access. Recommended.
♥ Duta Minang, Jl Slamet Riyadi 66, T0271 648449, 24 hrs. Great place to go for a fix of *nasi Padang*, with excellent *rendang* and plump *percedel* to satisfy a greedy appetite.
♥ Kusuma Sari, Jl Slamet Riyadi 111, T0271 656400, 1000-2100. Popular place with generous helpings of ice cream, and Western fare with a distinctively Indonesian slant.
♥ Larasati, Jl Slamet Riyadi 230, T0271 646600, 0800-1700. This delightful place serves up local treats such as *nasi asem asem* (beef in a sweet spicy sauce) and *nasi timlo* (soup with vegetables and Javanese sausage) as well as Indonesian favourites such as *nasi goreng* and *gado gado*. Recommended.
♥ Ramayana, Jl Imam Bonjol 49, T0271 646643, 0800-2100. Plenty of steaks, sizzling hot plates and Chinese and Indonesian favourites offered at this place which is popular with nearby office workers for lunch.
♥ Roda, Jl Slamet Riyadi (next to Radya Pustaka Museum), T0271 734111. Inexpensive and delicious freshly made *dim sum*, and good selection of Chinese cuisine in a friendly outdoor setting.
♥ Tio Ciu 99, Jl Slamet Riyadi 244, T0271 644361, 1000-2200. Good portions of Chinese favourites such as *Mapo tahu* (tofu in a spicy Sichuan pepper sauce), *sapi lada hitam* (beef in black pepper sauce) and *ayam kungpao* (chicken cooked with chilis and peanuts).
♥ Warung Baru, Jl Ahmad Dahlan, T0271 656369, 0700-2100. Friendly place with a huge menu of Western dishes, including some good sandwiches with home-made

brown bread. This is also a good, clean place to try Javanese dishes including *nasi liwet ayam* and *nasi gudeg*.

Cafes and bakeries
Blonjo Kue, Jl Ahmad Dahlan 7, T0271 634727, 24 hrs. This a/c coffee shop is a great place to escape the heat, choose from a long list of coffees and juices and indulge in cheesecake and their outrageous truffle cake. Recommended.
New Holland Bakery, Jl Slamet Riyadi 151, T0271 632452, recommended by many locals as the best bakery in the city.
Purimas, Jl Yosodipuro 51, T0271 719120, 0700-2100, bakery with good range of well priced Indonesian sweet breads and western-style baked goodies.

Foodstalls
There are many *warungs* and food carts to be found around Solo, which vary enormously in quality; 3rd floor of **Matahari** deptartment store at Singosaren Plaza offers a variety of Indonesian food. Fans of *bakso* should try the excellent street stall **Mas Tris**, Jl Honggowongso (south from the intersection with Jl Slamet Riyadi). There's a night market at Pujasari (Sriwedari Park), next to the Radya Pustaka Museum on Jl Slamet Riyadi, with Indonesian favourites like *sate* and *nasi ranies*, along with Chinese dishes and seafood like grilled fish and squid. Carts set up along the north side of Jl Slamet Riyadi in the afternoon and evening and sell delicious snacks (*jajan* in Javanese). On the south side of town, near Nonongan, *sate* stalls set up in the evenings. There are also stalls near the train station on Jl Monginsidi. Jl Tuangku Umar comes alive in the evenings and is a great place to try local Javanese favourites such as *nasi liwet* and *nasi gudeg*. Other street food to keep an eye open for include *intip* (fried rice crust with Javanese sugar or spices and shaped like a bowl), *srabi notosuman* (rice flour pancakes topped with sweet rice and chocolate or banana) and *wedang jahe* (warm drink made with ginger).

Gunung Bromo *p261*
Most people eat in hotel restaurants (all ¶, 0730-2130). Food in Bromo is nothing exciting. The **Cemara Indah** has a row of picnic benches on the lip of the crater with spectacular views to accompany their good range of Indonesian and Western dishes. **Cafe Lava Hostel** serves up pastas, fresh juices and good sandwiches in a homely setting. **Hotel Bromo Permai** has an extensive range of Indonsian and Chinese dishes. Other than the hotels, **Warung Sejati**, T0335 541117, 0600-2200, has a range of cheap Indonesian and Javanese dishes.

⊕ Bars and clubs

Solo *p256, map p257*
Most of the hotels have bars that get quite busy at the weekend and close around 0100. **Saraswati Bar**, Jl Slamet Riyadi 272, T0271 724555 has live music Mon-Sat evenings. You can sing karaoke at **Madunggondo Bar** in the Hotel Sahid Kusuma (see Sleeping).

Pounding house and plenty of dark corners until 0200 at **New Legenda Diskotik**, Komplek Pasar Gede Lantai 2, T0271 663924, and **Freedom Diskotik**, Komplek Balekambang. Small cover charges at both venues. Both packed at weekends.

⊛ Festivals and events

Solo *p256, map p257*
Mar/Apr 2-week fair held in the **Sriwedari Amusement Park**. On the 1st day there's a procession from the King's Palace to Sriwedari, with stalls selling handicrafts.
Jun/Jul Kirab Pusaka Kraton (movable), a traditional ceremony held by the 2 kratons to celebrate the Javanese New Year. A procession of heirlooms, led by a sacred albino buffalo (the *Kyai Slamet*), starts at the Pura Mangkunegaran at 1900 and ends at the Kasunanan Palace at 2400. The ceremony is 250 years old, from the time of Sultan Agung.

Sep Sekaten or **Gunungan** (movable), a 2-week long festival prior to Mohammad's birthday. The celebrations begin at midnight, with the procession of 2 sets of ancient and sacred gamelan instruments from the kraton to the Grand Mosque. A performance is given on these instruments and at the end of the 2 weeks they are taken back to the Kraton. A fair is held on the Alun-alun Lor in front of the mosque. The closing ceremony is known as *Grebeg Maulud*, when a rice mountain (*gunungan*) is cut up and distributed to the crowds. The people believe that a small amount of *gunungan* brings prosperity and happiness.

Gunung Bromo *p261*
Feb Karo (movable, according to Tenggerese calendar), held in Ngadisari and Wonokitri to commemorate the creation of Man by Sang Hyang Widi. Tenggerese men perform dances to celebrate the event.
Dec Kasodo (movable, according to Tenggerese calendar). This ceremony is linked to a legend that relates how a princess and her husband pleaded with the gods of the mountain to give them children. Their request was heeded on the condition that their youngest child was sacrificed to the mountain. The couple had 25 children, then finally conceded to the gods' wishes. When the child was thrown into the abyss she chided her parents for not offering her sooner and requested that on the night of the full moon in the month of Kasado, offerings be made to the mountain. The ceremony reaches a climax with a midnight pilgrimage to the crater. Ritual sacrifices of animals and offerings of fruit and vegetables are thrown in to appease the gods.

❸ Entertainment

Solo *p256, map p257*
Cinema
Multi-screen, the Studio 123 in the Matahari department store screens some English-language films.

Gamelan
At the **Pura Mangkunegaran** on Sat 1000-1200 and accompanied by dance on Wed at 0900. Admission – entrance fee to palace. Also at **Sahid Kasuma Hotel**, daily 1700-2000.

Ketoprak
Traditional folk drama performances at the **RRI** (Jl Abdul Rahmna Salleh, T0271 641178 every 4th Tue of the month, 2000-2400.

Wayang kulit
RRI, every 3rd Tue and 3rd Sat of the month, from 0900 to 0500 the next morning.

Wayang orang
At the **Sriwedari Amusement Park** on Jl Slamet Riyadi, Mon-Sat 2000-2300, 3000Rp. **Pura Mangkunegaran** dancing practice, Wed 1000 until finished, free. **STSI**, T0271 647658, has dancing and gamelan practice starting at 0900 daily except Fri and Sun, free.

❍ Shopping

Solo *p256, map p257*
Solo has much to offer the shopper, particularly batik and 'antique' curios.
Antiques Pasar Triwindu, off Jl Diponegoro (see sights). Much of the merchandise is poor quality bric-a-brac, but the odd genuine bargain turns up. Bargaining is essential. There is also a good jumble of an antique shop on Jl Urip Sumoharjo, south of Jl Pantisari – some good things are here for those with the time to search, includes batik stamps, old masks, carvings, Buddhas etc.
Batik Classical and modern designs, both *tulis* and *cap*, can be found at the Pasar Klewer, situated just beyond the west gate of the Alun-alun Lor, near the kraton. Prices are cheaper than the chain stores, but the market is very busy and bargaining is essential. It is best to go in the mornings, as the market starts to wind down after lunch. **Batik Danar Hadi**, Jl Slamet Riyadi 261, T0271 714326,

daily 0900-1530. **Batik Keris**, Jl Yos Sudarso
62, T0271 643292, Sun-Wed 0900-1900,
Thu-Sat 0900-2000. Both these shops are
great for browsing. Batik Keris has slightly the
edge on everyday wearability, and some of
their batik shirts are funky. All prices are fixed.
Handicrafts Bedoyo Srimpi, Jl Dr
Soepomo (opposite Batik Srimpi); **Pengrajin
Wayang Kulit Saimono**, Sogaten RT/02/RW
XV, Pajang Laweyan Surakarta; **Sriwedari
Amusement Park**, Jl Slamet Riyadi; **Usaha
Pelajar**, Jl Majapahit 6-10; **Solo Art**,
made-to-order tables, chairs, picture frames
and even doorstops, good prices, details
in Warung Baru Restaurant.
Krisses A fine example will cost thousands of
dollars. These traditional knives can be bought
at **Keris Fauzan**, Kampong Yosoroto RT 28/RW
82, Badran (Bpk Fauzan specializes in Keris
production and sale), and also from the stalls
at the eastern side of the Alun-alun Utara.
Markets Pasar Besar is on Jl Urip
Sumoharjo and is the main market in Solo,
excellent for fresh fruit and vegetables.
Supermarket In the basement of the
Matahari department store (Jl Gatot Subroto,
T0271 664711, 0930-2100).

▲ Activities and tours

Tour companies, *losmen* and hotels, as well
as independent guides, all run cycling tours
of Solo, trips to the kraton, batik and gamelan
factories, arak distillers, Prambanan, Sangiran,
Candi Sukuh, or to surrounding villages to
see rural life and crafts. Prices vary
considerably, but for city tours expect to
pay around 40,000 to 50,000Rp, and for
out-of-town tours around 75,000Rp,
depending on the distance covered.
Highly recommended is Patrick at the
Istana Griya and the guide from **Warung
Baru** (see Eating) also gets good reports.
Most tours are 0800-1400. Some *losmen*
and homestays will run batik classes, for
example the **Istana Griya**, 75,000Rp for
a 5-hr lesson including materials.

Solo p256, map p257
Tour operators
Mandira Tours, Jl Gadah Mada 77,
T0271 654558.
Miki Tours, Jl Yos Sudarso 17 T0271 665352.
Natratour, Jl Gadah Mada 86, T0271 634376,
natra@indo.net.id.
Pesona Dunia Tour, Jl Ronggowarsito 82,
T0271 651009.
Warung Baru, Jl Ahmad Dahlan 8, really a
restaurant, but this *warung* also runs highly
recommended bicycle tours.

Gunung Bromo p261
There is an interesting 2-hr guided tour at
the Gunung Bromo Volcanology Centre that
teaches visitors about the seismic activity
of Gunung Bromo. Tours can be booked at
Bromo Permai Hotel, 75,000Rp per person.

Around Gunung Bromo p263
Probolinggo
Tour operators Travel agents here are
notorious for charging inflated prices for bus
tickets. It seems that people are charged for a
return ticket to Bromo and then find that the
return vehicle fails to materialize. Avoid this is
by only getting buses at the terminal and
paying on the bus. The bus destinations are
clearly signposted above the bus lanes on the
roof. Queue here until the bus arrives or an
official (they have name badges) points you in
the correct direction. Ask for bags to be kept
with you at the back of the bus, rather than in
the luggage compartment. Normally space will
be made for you so you can watch your bag.

⊖ Transport

Solo p256, map p257
Angkutan Ply fixed routes around town.
The station is close to the intercity bus
terminal at Gilingan.

Air Solo's, Adisumarmo Airport, T0271
780400, is 10 km northwest of the city. Taxis
are available for the trip into town (50,000Rp);

there is no easy public transport. There are 2 daily flights to **Kuala Lumpur** with **Air Asia** (book online at www.airasia.com). **Silk Air** (www.silkair.com) have 3 expensive flights weekly direct to Singapore. If you want to get to Singapore cheaply it is better to fly from Jakarta. Domestic flights are only to **Jakarta**. If you want to fly elsewhere, you will have to fly from Yogya.

Becak For short trips around town, bargain hard.

Bicycle Solo is more bicycle-friendly than just about any other city on Java; bicycling is an excellent way to get around town. For hire from **Istana Griya**, **Warung Baru** and **Westerners** (see Sleeping). Daily rental is around 15,000Rp for a good mountain bike.

Bus The **Tirtonadi station**, T0271 635097, is on Jl Jend A Yani, 2 km north of the city centre. Most bus companies have their offices on Jl Sutan Syahrir or Jl Urip Sumoharjo. Regular *ekonomi* connections with most cities, including **Jakarta**, **Bogor**, **Bandung**, **Malang** (9 hrs), **Surabaya** (6 hrs), **Semarang** and **Denpasar**. Night buses and express buses can be booked through most tour companies and many hotels and *losmen*. They run to most places in Java, and also to **Lovina**, **Lombok/Mataram** and, in Sumatra, to **Padang**, **Medan** and **Bukittinggi**. Companies including **Java Baru**, Jl Dr Setiabudi 20, T0271 652967.

Minibus The Gilingan minibus terminal is near to the main Tirtonadi bus terminal; regular a/c door to door connections with **Yogya**, US$3, 1½ hrs; **Denpasar** US$19, 14 hrs; **Bandung** US$15; and **Jakarta**, US$16.50.Tickets can be booked at most guesthouses. For **Gunung Bromo**, minibuses run to **Probolinggo** (8 hrs, US$13).

Train Balapan station is on Jl Monginsidi, T0271 T63222. A/c connection with **Jakarta**, 8-12 hrs, 6 trains daily. The most useful connection is the overnight **Gajanya** departing at 2115 and arriving in Jakarta at

0618. The only a/c daytime connection with Jakarta is on the **Argolawu** departing 0800 and arriving at Gambir at 1518. If travelling to Jakarta, confirm which station your train is heading to, as trains travel to Gambir, Pasar Senin and Jakarta Kota. Gambir station is the most convenient for travellers. To **Surabaya**, 7 a/c trains daily, 7 hrs. To **Bandung** 5 daily a/c trains, 8 hrs. To **Malang** 1 daily a/c train departing at 0222 and arriving at 0750. To **Yogya** 9 a/c trains daily, 1 hr.

Around Gunung Bromo *p263*
Probolinggo
Night buses from Bali usually arrive just before sunrise. Travellers are often deposited bleary-eyed at a travel agency and subjected to the hard sell. Avoid this by hopping in a yellow bemo going to the bus terminal (2000Rp), where onward transport can be easily organized independently.

Bemo It is possible to charter a bemo cheaply, haggle for it. Bemos start running at sunrise.

Bus All the bus destinations are written up clearly at the terminal and it is best to deal directly with the bus companies, rather than the tourist office. The Bayuangga bus terminal is on the west side of town, about 5 km from the centre, on the road up to Bromo. Bemos whisk bus passengers into town (2000Rp). Regular connections with **Surabaya**, 20,000Rp, 2 hrs, **Malang** 3 hrs and **Banyuwangi** 4 hrs, 40,000Rp. Night buses to **Denpasar**, 8 hrs, at least 2 a day at 1200 and 1930, US$13, economy buses are every hr. A/c buses to **Singaraja**, Jakarta, US$23; **Denpasar**, **Yogya** and **Solo** US$9, are available at regular times. Many buses to Yogya and Solo go via **Surabaya**, check whether it's direct.

Minibus To **Cemoro Lawang**, 2 hrs, 15,000Rp, leave when full (15 people). The 1st bus is scheduled to leave at 0700, but there is often a long wait for it to fill up. The last bus to Cemoro Lawnag leaves at 1700. It is possible to charter a minibus for the trip for

75,000Rp per person, minimum of 2 people. Alternatively, hire an ojek for 50,000Rp, not much fun with a lot of luggage. If you arrive in Probolinggo later than 1600 for **Gunung Bromo**, the only option is to charter a minibus or hire an ojek (60,000Rp).

Train The train station is on the main square or Alun-alun, on Jl KH Mansyur, regular *eksekutif* and *bisnis* connections with **Surabaya** and **Banyuwangi**. There is a direct economy-class train to **Yogyakarta**.

ⓘ Directory

Solo *p256, map p257*
Banks Bank BCA, Jl Slamet Riyadi 7. Bank Rakyat Indonesia, Jl Slamet Riyadi 236. **Lippo Bank**, Jl Slamet Riyadi 136. Danamon, Jl Dr Rajiman 18. **Standard Chartered**, Jl Slamet Riyadi 136. **Golden Money Changer**, Jl Yos Sudarso 1. There are plenty of ATMs along Jl Slamet Riyadi. **Emergencies** Police Station Jl Adisucipto 52, T0271 714352.

Immigration Jl Laksda Adisucipto 8, T0271 712649. **Internet** Aloha in Sahid Kusuma Hotel (see Sleeping), 3000Rp per hr, **Y Online**, Jl Gajah Mada 132, 6000Rp per hr. **Istana Griya** (see Sleeping), 5000Rp per hr. **Medical services** Hospital Kasih Ibu, Jl Slamet Riyadi 404, T0271 744422, most doctors here speak English. **Post office** Jl Jend Sudirman 8, Jl Ronggo Warsite. **Telephone** Jl Mayor Kusmanto 1 (24 hrs). **Wartel** (telephone and fax) Jl Slamet Riyadi 275A (at intersection with Jl Prof Dr Sutomo).

Gunung Bromo *p261*
Banks Bank Rakyat Indonesia, Sukapura; Guesthouses at Ngadisari and Cemoro Lawang (poor rates). There is a BNI ATM in Cemoro Lawang that accepts Visa and MasterCard. **Post office** In Sukapura.

Around Gunung Bromo *p263*
Probolinggo
Banks Bank Central Asia, Jl Suroyo. Bank Rakyat Indonesia, Jl Suroyo. BNI, Jl Suroyo. **Post office** Jl Suroyo 33. **Telephone** Wartel, Jl Jend A Yani.

Bali

→ *Colour map 11.*

Bali is the original magical isle. From the earliest years after its bloody incorporation into the expanding territories of the Dutch East Indies in the early 20th century, Westerners have been entranced by the heady combination of fabulous landscape and mesmerizing culture. Streams cascade down impossibly green mountainsides from sacred crater lakes, while dance dramas are performed to please the gods. Artists and the artistically inclined settled, worked and died amidst the rice fields and temples, reluctant to leave their Garden of Eden.

The advent of cheap air travel has brought increasing numbers of visitors, interested more in the attractions of the beach than of the temple and theatre. Today, hundreds of thousands of people visit Bali, many scarcely aware of the world beyond the sun lounger and the cocktail shaker. But while Bali may have changed – and the notion that Bali is on the verge of being 'ruined' is a constant motif in writings about the island from the 1930s – the singular magic of the place has not been erased. As tourists continued to pour into the island the calm was shattered in October 2002 by bombings in Kuta blamed on Jemaah Islamiyah. Many people were killed, and for months afterwards tourists stayed away, savagely damaging the island's economy. Just as plane-loads of sun seekers were starting to return, a second wave of bombings hit Kuta and Jimbaran in 2005 further decimating the island's reputation and economy. It has been a rough decade for the Balinese tourism industry, and some places continue to be affected by low numbers of visitors. However, tourists are again returning in droves, particularly Asian tourists from Japan and China, and the future is looking bright.

Ins and outs

Getting there

Budget carriers flying into Bali include **Jet Star Asia** (www.jetstarasia.com) from Singapore, and **Air Asia** (www.airasia.com), who fly direct from Kuala Lumpur, Kuching and Kota Kinabalu (all Malaysia). Denpasar's airport, Ngurah Rai is very well connected with the rest of Indonesia with frequent flights throughout the country. The many flights to Mataram, Lombok, cost around US$38 and take only 25 minutes.

Getting around

The main form of the local transport is the bemo (a small van). Also, travel by bemo often requires several changes, especially in the south, and most trips are routed through Denpasar (see below), where there are five different bemo terminals in different parts of town, serving different directions. It can be almost as cheap and a lot quicker to charter a bemo or catch the tourist shuttle bus. It is also worth noting that bemo services are less frequent in the afternoons, and out of the tourist centres are almost non-existent after night-fall. **Note** Taxi/bemo drivers can be very pushy and find it hard to believe you may be happy to walk. Expect to be asked for double the correct fare, bemo drivers can sometimes be quite unpleasant in their attempts to overcharge you even when you know the correct fair, which you should ascertain in advance. Thefts on bemos are not as frequent as in past years but do still occur. Be wary of gangs pretending to run licensed bemos who pick up unsuspecting travellers, take them to a remote spot and steal their possessions and money. Always use registered bemos, which have yellow and black licence plates.

The different terminals are as follows (terminals serve other terminals as well as out of town destinations):

Ubung North of town on Jalan Cokroaminoto for trips to North and West Bali, including Gilimanuk and Singaraja, Mengwi, Tanah Lot, Bedugul, Negara and Java.

Tegal West of town, near the intersection of Jalan Imam Bonjol and Jalan G Wilis, for journeys to South Bali including Kuta, Legian, Sanur, Ngurah Rai Airport, Jimbaran, Nusa Dua and Uluwatu (in the morning).

Suci Near the intersection of Jalan Diponegoro and Jalan Hasanuddin for Benoa Port.

Batubulan 6 km northeast of town just before the village of Batubulan on the road to Gianyar, for buses running east to Gianyar, Semarapura, Padangbai, Candi Dasa, Amlapura and Tirtagangga, and north to Ubud, Tampaksiring, Bangli, Penelokan and Kintamani.

Kereneng At the east edge of town off Jalan Kamboja (Jalan Hayam Wuruk), has now been replaced as the station for central and East Bali by Batubulan; but bemos do still run from here to the other terminals.

Denpasar

→ *Phone code: 0361. Colour map 11, B1.*

Once the royal capital of the princely kingdom of Badung, there is little evidence now of Denpasar's past. Situated in the south of the island, about 5 km from the coast, Bali's capital has grown in the past 10-15 years from a sleepy village to a bustling city with choked streets buzzing with the sound of waspish motorbikes. Today, the town has a population of over 450,000 and is Bali's main trade and transport hub, with its central business area centred around Jalan Gajah Mada. Puputan Square pays homage to the tragic end of the Rajah and his court; it is named after the 'battle to the death' – or puputan – against a force of Dutch soldiers in 1906. ▸▸ *For listings, see pages 275-277.*

Ins and outs

Getting there

Denpasar's **Ngurah Rai International Airport** ① *24-hr airport information T0361 22238, flight information T0361 7571647, at the south end of the island, just south of Kuta,* is one of Indonesia's 'gateway' cities, with international connections with Australia, Hong Kong, Europe, Singapore, Japan North America, and Southeast Asia. It also has excellent domestic connections. International departure tax is US$16.50; domestic is US$3.30. A tourist office with a well-run hotel booking counter offers comprehensive details and prices of upmarket accommodation on Bali. Other facilities include money changers, ATMs, bars, restaurant, shops and taxi counter. Left baggage is US$2.20 per piece per day, with no limit on the time. The **Bali Satwika** is the airport restaurant, good value for such a place.

There are fixed-price taxis from the airport, currently at US$4.40; US$5 to Kuta 2 (in practice, anywhere past bemo corner is charged at the second rate); US$5.50 to Legian; US$19 to Ubud; US$31 to Padangbai and US$31 to Candi Dasa. Alternatively, catch a cab just after it has dropped someone off at the international departures area. This is a little cheeky, but the drivers use the meter and the cost of the drive to Kuta is around US$3. Some hardened souls walk all the way along the beach towards Tuban or Kuta.

Getting around

As Bali's capital, Denpasar is well connected with the rest of the island. No fewer than five terminals provide bemo services to various parts of the island and minibuses run between the different terminals. Metered taxis are also abundant in Denpasar. The **tourist office** ① *Jl Surapati 7, T0361 223602, www.pariwisata.denpasarkota.go.id, Mon-Thu 0730-1530, Fri 0730-1300,* is not utilized very often, which is a shame given the eagerness of the staff. The office provides a free map, calendar of events and Bali brochure.

Sights

Denpasar is not particularly attractive and the major tourist attraction is easily found in the centre of town and is a focus for local hawkers. The **Museum Bali** ① *T0361 222680, Mon-Thu 0800-1500, Fri 0800-1230, Sat 0800-1500, adult 2000Rp, child 1000Rp,* was established in 1931 and is situated on the east side of Puputan Square. The entrance is on Jalan Mayor Wismu. The museum, built in 1910, mirrors the architecture of Balinese temples and palaces, and is contained within a series of attractive courtyards with well-kept gardens. The impressive collection of pre-historic artefacts, sculpture, masks, textiles, weaponry and contemporary arts and crafts was assembled with the help of Walter Spies, the German artist who made Bali his home. Labelling could be better and there is no guide. Nonetheless, it gives an impression of the breadth of the island's culture.

Next door to the museum is the new **Pura Jaganatha**, a temple dedicated to the Supreme God *Sang Hyang Widi Wasa*. The statue of a turtle and two nagas signify the foundation of the world. The complex is dominated by the *Padma Sana* or lotus throne, upon which the gods sit. The central courtyard is surrounded by a moat filled with water-lilies and the most enormous carp.

From an archaeological perspective, **Pura Masopahit** is the most important temple in Denpasar. The main gateway to the pura faces the main street, but the entrance is down a side road off the west end of Jalan Tabanan. The temple is one of the oldest in Bali, probably dating from the introduction of Javanese civilization from Majapahit in the 15th century, after which it is named. It was badly damaged during the 1917 earthquake, but has since been partly restored. Note the fine reconstructed split gate, with its massive figures of a giant and a garuda.

The **Taman Werdi Budaya Art Centre** ① *Jl Nusa Indah, Tue-Sun 0800-1700, free,* was established in 1973 to promote Balinese visual and performing arts. It contains an open-air auditorium, along with three art galleries. Arts and crafts are also sold here. Activity peaks during the annual Bali Festival of Art, held from mid-June for a month.

◉ Denpasar listings

For Sleeping and Eating price codes, see inside the front cover.

◉ Sleeping

Denpasar *p274*
Most people head to the beach areas in southern Bali, which are closer to the airport. Accommodation in Denpasar is geared more towards the domestic market and can get busy during holidays.

C Inna Hotel Jl Veteran 3, T0361 225681, www.innabali.com. Built in the 1930s, this was the first hotel on Bali. Its glory has somewhat faded, but pockets of charm remain. Clean rooms, pool and a garden.

D Adinda Hotel, Jl Karma 8, T0361 249435. The superior rooms are huge, bright and have bath and TV. Standard rooms are a little pokey, and have tiny windows. Garden.

D Hotel Taman Suci, Jl Imam Bonjol 45, T0361 484445, www.tamansuci.com. Near Tegal bemo station, with spacious clean rooms, TV and mini bar. Deluxe rooms have bath.

F Wismasari, Jl May, Jend, Sutoyo 1, T0361 222437. Old-style *losmen*, with cleanish rooms set back from the road. Western toilet and *mandi*. Friendly owner.

⑦ Eating

Denpasar *p274*
Indonesian food dominates the scene. There is a collection of clean *warungs* outside the Inna Hotel selling Indonesian favourites.

♥ Aseupan, Jl Tukad Unda 7, Renon, T0361 7431501. Sundanese food served in clean, simple restaurant. Recommended.

♥ Mie 88, Jl Sumatra. Good range of juices and local food. Noodles are the speciality.

○ Shopping

Denpasar *p274*
Department stores Duta Plaza, Jl Dewi Sartika; **Tiara Dewata** and **Matahari** both have a wide range of goods. The former also has a public swimming pool.

Handicrafts The **Sanggraha Kriya Asta**, T0361 222942, 7 km east of the centre of town, is a government handicrafts shop, selling batik, jewellery, paintings and woodcarvings. The prices are set and quality is controlled. They organize free transport to the shop from your hotel if telephoned. There are also a number of handicraft shops on Jl Thamrin.

Markets The biggest market on Bali is the **Kumbasari Market**, off Jl Dr Wahidin, on the banks of the Badung River. It is a great place to browse, with a range of goods including textiles and handicrafts.

Textiles A large selection of textiles is to be found in the shops along Jl Sulawesi.

⊖ Transport

Denpasar *p274*
As Denpasar is the transport hub of the island, it's easy to get to most of the main towns, beaches and sights from here.

Air
There are plenty of airline offices at the domestic hall of the airport, including **Air Asia** (T08041333333, 0900-1700) **Garuda** (T08041807807, 0600-0130), **Mandala** (T0361 222751, 0600-2200) and **Merpati** (T0361 751011, 0600-1830).

Airline offices Mandala, Jl P Diponegoro 98 Kompl Pert Kerthawijaya Bl D/23, T0361-263388, **Garuda** Jl Sugianyar 5,T0361-254747, **Merpati**, Jl Melati 51, T0361-235358, **Batavia**, Jl Teuku Umar 208-210, T0361-254947.

Bemo
A few of the original, rickety and under-powered 3-wheeler bemos still travel between the main bemo terminals (4000Rp) criss-crossing town, although much more common these days are Japanese-built minibuses. It is also possible to charter these bemos for trips around town. From the terminals, of which there are several, bemos travel to all of Bali's main towns: the **Ubung terminal**, north of town on Jl Cokroaminoto for trips to **West Bali**, **North Bali** and **Java**; **Tegal terminal**, west of town, near the intersection of Jl Imam Bonjol and Jl G Wilis, for journeys to **South Bali**; **Suci terminal**, near the intersection of Jl Diponegoro and Jl Hasanuddin, for **Benoa Port**; **Kereneng terminal**, at the east edge of town off Jl Kamboja (Jl Hayam Wuruk), for destinations around town and for **Sanur**; and **Batubulan terminal**, east of town just before the village of Batubulan on the road to Gianyar, for buses running **east** and to **central Bali**. **Tegal**, the bemo terminal for Kuta, used to be a thriving place with crowded bemos leaving regularly. Nowadays, however, it is a shadow of its former self and you might find yourself

waiting around for a while before your bemo is ready to leave. Getting the correct fare can be a challenge. Try to ask one of the guys at the entrance to the station who record each departure. Fares from Tegal include **Kuta** 5000Rp, **Sanur** 5000Rp, **the airport** 8000Rp, **Jimbaran** 10,000Rp, and **Nusa Dua** 15,000Rp. Beware of pickpockets on bemos.

Due to terrible traffic congestion, bemos have been banned from Jl Legian and the road from Kuta to Seminyak is mercifully free of them. Bemos run from Bemo Corner, to Denpasar's Tegal terminal (5000Rp). Bemos for charter also hang around Bemo Corner. **Note** Many bemo drivers are reluctant to pick up Westerners, except for a highly inflated fare.

Bus
Minibuses run between the various terminals (4000Rp). There are also bus connections with **Java** from the **Ubung terminal**, just north of Denpasar on Jl Cokroaminoto.

Express and night bus offices are concentrated near the intersection of Jl Diponegoro and Jl Hasanuddin; for example, **Safari Dharma Raya**, Jl Diponegoro 110, T0361 231206. Journey time and fares for night and express buses: to **Jakarta**, 24 hrs, US$33; to **Solo**, 18 hrs, US$22; to **Yogyakarta**, 18 hrs, US$22.

Shuttles Various companies offer trips to destinations in Bali and beyond. **Perama** (see Tour operators) has the cheapest fares to **Sanur** (US$3), **Ubud** (US$5.50), **Lovina** (US$11) and **Padangbai** (US$7). It costs an extra US$1 for a hotel pick up.

Car hire
Arrange car hire through hotels, or one of the rental agencies in town, for approximately US$11 per day. There are also private cars (with drivers) that can be chartered by the hr or day, or for specific journeys. Bargain hard, expect to pay about US$19 per day (car plus driver). Drivers can be found around Bemo Corner and Jl Legian with their constant offers of transport.

Motorbike hire
Arrange hire through travel agents, hotels or from operations on the street, from 40,000Rp per day. **Artha Guna**, T0361 753431, arthaguna_rc@yahoo.co.id, has fair rates and is used by some hotels.

Ojek
Motorbike taxis, the fastest way around town, are identified by the riders' red jackets (4000Rp min).

Taxi
Numerous un-metered cars that can be chartered by the hr or day, or which can be hired for specific journeys. Bargain hard. Also some metered taxis. Like Kuta and Legian, the best company to use is the blue **Bali Taxi**, T0361 701111. **Praja Bali Taxi**, pale blue taxis, also operate with meters and make no extra charge for call-out service, T0361 289090.

South Bali

Most visitors to Bali stay in one of the resorts at the south end of the island. Most famous is Kuta, the original backpackers' haven, together with its northern extension, Legian; both of these are fairly noisy, crowded, downmarket resorts. Much nicer is Seminyak, further north, which is still relatively rural. To the south of Kuta is Tuban, a town with many hotels and restaurants. Further south still is Jimbaran, a large village, as yet unspoilt, with some of Bali's top resorts nearby. Sanur is on Bali's east coast and offers largely mid-range accommodation, though some newer budget places to stay have opened. Serangan, or Turtle Island, is a short distance offshore. Further off the east coast, in the Lombok Strait, are the two islands of Nusa Penida, with limited and very basic accommodation, and Nusa Lembongan, with a growing number of upmarket hotels; both are also accessible on a day trip. ▶▶ *For listings, see pages 285-297.*

Kuta and around ⊖❶❼⋂⬤⊕⛟⊖ ▶▶ *pp285-297. Colour map 11, B1.*

→ *Phone code: 0361.*

Kuta was the main port and arrival point for foreigners visiting south Bali for over 100 years, from early in the 18th century until first Benoa, and then the airport at Denpasar usurped its role. The town prospered as a hub of the slave trade in the 1830s, attracting an international cross-section of undesirables.

Miguel Covarrubias wrote in 1937 that Kuta and Sanur were "small settlements of fishermen who brave the malarial coasts". It was not until the 1960s that large numbers of Western travellers 'discovered' Kuta. Since then, it has grown into a highly developed beach resort with a mind-boggling array of hotels, restaurants and shops. While Sanur is no longer a backpackers' haven, there are still many cheap *losmen* in Kuta as well as a growing number of mid- to high-range accommodation. Central Kuta was decimated by the Bali bombings (see box, page 282), and the area acted as a barometer for the island's suffering, with many businesses forced out of action. Things now are returning to normal, and bars that were destroyed by the attacks, including **Paddies'**, are pulling in big crowds of pleasure-hungry punters once more.

Ins and outs

Traffic in Kuta frequently comes to a standstill, despite the one-way system. The main street, containing most of Kuta's shops, is Jalan Legian, which runs north-south (traffic travels one-way south). Jalan Pantai meets Jalan Legian at 'Bemo Corner' and is the main east-west road to the south end of the beach (with traffic going one-way west). The beach road is northbound only. There is also a government **Tourist Information Office** ⓘ *Jl Bakungsari, T0361 756176, daily 0800-1300, 1500-1800.*

The town

Many people dislike Kuta. Other than the beach, it is not an attractive place. However, it does offer a wide range of consumerist and hedonist treats and people often find themselves staying here longer than expected. Crowded beyond belief, with an infrastructure at breaking point, accommodation owners have taken to building multi-storey concrete blocks of rooms to let, often in what were once pretty Balinese gardens. In the rainy season the drainage system is hopelessly inadequate, and some areas of Kuta, noticeably Jalan Legian, become flooded easily.

Since the Bali bombings when business slowed down considerably in the area, tourists have increasingly complained of hassle from Javanese hawkers along Jalan Legian and Jalan Pantai Kuta who can get a little aggressive at times. There are also numerous women offering massage of a dubious nature on Jalan Legian. Pickpockets are less of a problem now than they have been, and children now swarm in packs selling friendship bracelets rather than rifling through your bag.

The beach

Kuta Beach is a fine beach; a broad expanse of golden sand where local officials have taken reasonable steps to limit the persistence of hawkers. It is because of its accessibility that it is popular with surfers, although better waves can be found elsewhere. It is an excellent spot for beginners and recreational surfers. Boards can be hired on the beach and there are usually locals who will offer insider's knowledge of surf conditions. Strong and irregular currents can make swimming hazardous so look out for the warning notices and coloured flags that indicate which areas are safe for swimming on any particular day: red flags represent danger; yellow and red flags represent safe areas for swimming. The currents change daily and there are teams of lifeguards keeping an eye on proceedings who won't hesitate to blow their whistle if they see people straying into dangerous waters. There are

Kuta

Kuta Bay

To Legian

Legian Clinic & Chemist

Jl Benesari

Jl R Pantai Kuta

Jl Legian

Clothes Shops

Poppies Gang II

Tubes

Memorial to Bali Bomb Victims

Jl Raya Kuta

Bars

Poppies Gang I

Perama

Jl Pantai Kuta

Bemo Corner

To Sanur

Wave Riders

Kuta Square

Shops

Jl Imam Bonjol

Matahari Department Store

Jl Tengalwangi

Jl Bungsari

Jl Buni Sari

Night Market

Supermarket

To Tuban

200 metres
200 yards

Sleeping
Barong 1
Dua Dara 2
Fat Yogi Cottages 3
Gemini Star 4
Kedin's 2 6

La Walon 7
Lima Satu 8
Mimpi Bungalows 9
Poppies I 10
Tanjung Bali Inn 12

Eating
Kori 1
Maccaroni 2
Made's Warung 3

Pepper Lunch 4
Poppies 5
TJ's 6
Un's Paradise 7
Urban Food Station 8
Warung 96 12
Warung Indonesia 10
Warung Pama 11

Bars & clubs
Bounty 10
Mbargo 11
Paddies 12
Sky Lounge 9

allegations that levels of contamination in the sea at Kuta are above internationally accepted safety levels, though many people swim in the sea with no apparent ill effects.

The sand is white to the south, but grey further north. The hawkers are less of a problem now they are forbidden to cross an invisible line that divides the beach. Sit on the half of the beach closest to the sea if you want to be safe from hassle. The beach faces west, so is popular at sunset, which can be truly spectacular. Religious ceremonies sometimes take place on the beach and are fascinating to watch.

Tuban → Phone code: 0361.

Although quieter and more up-market than Kuta, Tuban is still fairly built up. Lying just north of the airport and south of Kuta, the town is spread along busy Jalan Kartika Plaza, and one of its main attractions is the convenience of its close proximity to the airport. At the lower end of the market, Tuban represents poor value compared to the Kuta/Legian area. There is a string of upmarket hotels overlooking the bay beside a reasonable sandy beach, which cater mainly to tour groups. Tucked down side streets away from the beach are some budget places to stay, which would be convenient if you arrive late at night or have an early airport departure. There is limited access to the beach down a few public paths between the big hotels; the most useful path is on the extreme left, just inside the entrance to the Bali Dynasty Hotel. The large hotels have pools, sports and recreation facilities, and most also have organized cultural activities.

Tourist information ⓘ *Kuta Sidewalk Complex 1, Jl Kartika Plaza, T0361 764600, www. his-balifreak.com, 0900-2200.* A board displays all current domestic and international flight prices out of Bali and the operating airlines. It deals primarily with Japanese tourists. Internet access is available at 500Rp per minute.

Legian → Phone code: 0361

It is hard to say where Kuta ends and Legian begins, as the main shopping street, Jalan Legian, dominates both places. Like Kuta, Legian is a shopping haven. Legian is far more relaxed and less congested than Kuta and there are significantly fewer hawkers.

Seminyak → Phone code: 0361

This area to the north of Legian begins at Jalan Double Six and runs northwards into unspoilt ricefields. With a fabulous coastline, spectacular sunsets and views of the mountains of North Bali on a clear day, it is still relatively quiet compared to Kuta and Legian, but some long term residents are complaining that the place has lost its charm in recent years and are selling up. In August, Seminyak's villas are filled with European holidaymakers. There is good surfing, but be warned: the sea here can be lethal. There are strong undercurrents and riptides. Lifeguards patrol the beach, which is wide, sandy and much less crowded, with a few mostly mid- to upmarket hotels dotted along it. Jalan Pura Bagus Taruna is also known as Rum Jungle Road. Jalan Dhyana Pura is also known as Jalan Abimanyu.

Travelling north from Seminyak, you pass through **Petitenget** with its large temple made of white coral (covered in moss, so not looking white at all). Further north still, the village of **Batubelig** is in an undeveloped area, with a luxury hotel and a small guesthouse; again this is a surfing rather than swimming beach. Unless you are a keen walker, you will probably need to hire a car if staying in this area.

Legian & Seminyak

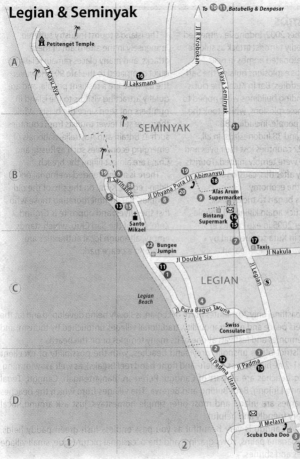

N

300 metres
300 yards

Sleeping 🛏
All Seasons **2** D2
Anantara **5** B1
Balisani Suites **10** A2
Bali Sorgowi **3** D3
Batubelig Beach
  Bungalows **11** A2
Dhyana Pura **15** B2
Green Room **8** B2
Inada Losmen **9** B2
Le Jardin **6** B2
Lokha **1** D3
Sarinande Beach Inn **19** B1
Sari Uma Cottages **38** B2

Sinar Bali **4** C2
Sun Island **7** C3

Eating 🍴
Gado Gado **13** B2
Indonational **10** D3
Lanai **11** C2
Lemongrass **14** B2
Pantarei **15** B3
Seaside **11** C2
Trattoria **16** A2
Warung Rima Masakan
  Manado **17** C3
Warung Yogya **12** D2

Zula Vegetarian
  Paradise **18** B2

Bars & clubs 🍸
Bush Telegraph Pub **19** B2
Dejavu **1** C2
Double Six **22** C2
Fabios **3** B3
Peanuts **23** D3
Q Bar **20** B2

Bali bombs

On 12 October 2002, Indonesia witnessed its most deadly terrorist attack as suicide bombers detonated bombs in near simultaneous explosions outside the **Sari Club** and **Paddies' Bar** in Kuta. The clubs and surrounding buildings were ripped to pieces by the explosions, which took the lives of 202 people, including 88 Australians and 38 Indonesians. In all, citizens of 22 countries lost their lives and many more were terribly injured. Tourists stayed away after this, causing serious damage to the economy.

As tourists began to trickle back, terrorists struck again killing 20 people on 1 October 2005 in explosions in a restaurant in Kuta square, and by beachside *warungs* in Jimbaran.

The island's tourist industry suffered immensely in the aftermath of these attacks, and many places remain relatively quiet compared to the late 90s. However, the Balinese are a resilient people, and are quietly attracting visitors to the island in numbers not seen since the blasts. While there are still fewer tourists from countries such as Britain and Australia, nationals of emerging economies such as Russia and China are almost filling the breach.

There is a well-tended memorial on Jalan Legian, Kuta, on the site of the old Paddies' Bar commemorating those who lost their lives, and opposite is Ground Zero, site of the Sari Club, which stands empty, although local authorities are planning a peace park.

Canggu

This area of coastline, only 20 minutes north of Legian, is slowly being developed and (at the moment) offers peace and rural tranquillity, traditional villages untouched by tourism, and frequent ceremonies and festivals at one of its many temples or on the beach.

Canggu district offers unspoilt, grey sand beaches, with the possibility of excellent surfing (easy 1-2 m-high waves off left- and right-hand reef breaks), as well as swimming. The following beaches are all part of Canggu: Pererean, Banjartengah, Canggu, Tegal Gundul, Padang Linjong, Batu Bulong and Berewa. The villages from which the beaches draw their names are inland and most offer simple homestays, just ask around, local people are very friendly and helpful.

The drive to Canggu is very beautiful as you pass endless lush green paddy fields, coconut and banana palms, cows grazing, and the occasional picturesque, small village full of temples and shrines.

Berewa beach

A very peaceful location (the drive from Kuta takes about 30-45 minutes; as yet there is no coast road) with an unspoilt beach backing onto ricefields, friendly local people and few tourists. There are a few unpretentious restaurants hoping to attract tourists from the local hotels; except during high season, these are usually only open for dinner. There are also a few small shops near the hotels. The main temple is 'Pura Dang Khayangan'; there has been a temple here since the 16th century. **Note** Swimming in the sea here can be dangerous.

▸ *Phone code: 0361.*

The first of Bali's international resorts, Sanur falls midway between the elegant, upmarket Nusa Dua and the frenetic, youthful Kuta and is situated 6 km from Denpasar. Attracting a more sedate, middle-aged clientele, many on package tours, Sanur's attractions are its white-sand beach, restaurants and shopping. This is also a centre for watersports with surfing, snorkelling by Serangan Island and diving. Noticeably more expensive than Kuta, hotels tend to be mid-range to upmarket, though there are some pretty, more reasonably priced small guesthouses and an increasing number of cheaper homestays. Nightlife here does not compare to that of Kuta, although there are outstanding restaurants and several clubs. The road parallel to the beach is lined with money changers, tourist shops (selling clothing and jewellery), tour companies, car rental outlets and shipping agents.

Sights

The **Le Mayeur Museum** ⓘ *Jl Hang Tuah, T0361 286201, adult 2000Rp, child 1000Rp, Mon-Thu 0800-1500, Fri 0800-1245, Sat 0800-1430*, is just to the north of the **Bali Beach Hotel** and is named after the famous Belgian artist Adrien Yean Le Mayeur, who arrived in Bali in 1932. He was immediately captivated by the culture and beauty of the island, made Sanur his home, married local beauty Ni Polok in 1935 and died in 1958. The museum contains his collection of local artefacts and some of Le Mayeur's work. The interior is dark and rather dilapidated, making the pieces difficult to view – a great shame because Le Mayeur's impressionistic works are full of tropical sunlight and colour. Le Mayeur's paintings were a great influence on a number of Balinese artists, including the highly regarded I Gusti Nyoman Nodya.

Temples made of coral are dotted along Sanur beach. The presence of primitive, pyramid-shaped structures at many of these temples suggests their origin dates back to pre-historic times. At the southern, south-facing end of Sanur beach is the **Pura Mertasari**, a small temple under a canopy of trees which is considered to harbour exceptionally powerful forces of black magic. The *odalan* festival of this temple falls at the most favoured time in the Balinese calendar, two weeks after the Spring equinox. An unusual ritual trance dance, the *baris cina* (Chinese dance), is performed on the night of the festival. The dancers wear old Dutch army helmets and bayonets and the evening can end with a dramatically violent dance movement. A nearby village, **Singhi**, is home to the Black Barong, the most powerful Barong in Bali, made from the black feathers of a sacred rare bird.

On a clear day there are fantastic views of several mountain ranges to the north, including Gunung Agung and Gunung Batur, especially beautiful at sunset and sunrise. There is a path running along the beach for the entire length of Sanur, though in places it is beginning to collapse. The beach varies in width along its length and disappears completely in some places; it is at its best in front of the the the **Tanjung Sari** and adjacent hotels, and at the southern end. At Batu Jimbar, where the ex-pat crowd have built their beautiful seaside villas, the beach disappears completely. There are several roads and tracks leading down to the beach from Jalan Danau Tamblingan along its length, including Jalan Pantai Karang, where the German consul is situated, and Jalan Segara Ayu.

🌙 *Kite flying is a popular activity, especially in August, when strong trade winds are blowing and competitions take place. Teams gather with huge kites that take several people to launch.*

Sanur

To Ubud & Batubulan

To Perama Office

Le Mayeur Museum

Buruan

SANUR

Gate

Jl Danau Buyan

Segara Agung Beach Market

Jl Segara Ayu

Segara

Jl Tegeh Agung

Jl Sindhu

SINDHU

Jl Danau Tamblingan

German Consulate

Jl Pantai Karang

Blue Season Bali

Supermarket

Legian Clinic 24 hrs

BATU JIMBAR

Jl Danau Tamblingan

Supermarket

Jl Duyung

Jl Ngurah Rai Bypass

Jl Danau Poso

Jl Sri Kesari

SEMAWANG

BLANJONG

Jl Mertasari

Jl Kesumasari

Bemo Terminal

Jl Mertasari

Pura Mertasari

N

Not to scale

Sleeping 🛏
Bumas **1**
Coco Homestay **2**
Gazebo Cottages **3**
La Taverna **5**
Lestari **6**
Luisa Homestay **2**
Little Pond Homestay **7**
Ratna Beach **8**
Swastika Bungalows **9**
Taman Agung Beach Inn **12**
Tanjung Sari **10**
Villa Dampati **11**
Yulia's **2**

Eating 🍴
Anjani **1**
Cafe Batujimbar **2**
Gateway of India **4**
Kalpataru **5**
Kopi Bali **6**
Manik Organik **7**
Sanur Rasa **8**
Smorga's **3**
Spirit **1**
Tambungan **9**
Tootsie **1**
Village Cucine Italiana **9**

Bars & clubs 🍸
Cat & Fiddle **13**
Lazer Sports Bar **14**

Serangan Island

Serangan Island is also known as Turtle Island and is, unsurprisingly, famous for its turtles. They are caught in the surrounding sea, raised in pens, and then slaughtered for their meat – which explains why they are becoming rarer by the year. The formerly common green turtle is now said to be virtually extinct in the area.

The beaches on the east coast of the island are best, with offshore coral providing good snorkelling. One of Bali's most important coastal temples is the **Pura Sakenan** in Sakenan village, at the north end of the island. Pura Sakenan's *odalan* or anniversary festival, held at Kuningan (the 210th day of the Balinese calendar), is thought by many to be one of the best on Bali.

Ins and outs

Boats can be chartered from Sanur or from Nusa Dua and Benoa. Usually visitors leave from a jetty just south of Kampong Mesigit and 2 km southwest of Sanur, from here there are regular public boats to Serangan Island. Unfortunately tourists are often forced to charter a boat for far more; share if possible and bargain furiously. It is easier, and often just as cheap, to go on a tour; it is also possible to wade out to the island at low tide.

◉ South Bali listings

For Sleeping and Eating price codes, see inside the front cover.

● Sleeping

Kuta *p278, map p279*

It's advisable to book accommodation during the peak periods of Jul/Aug and at Christmas and New Year, as hotels are often full. There are countless places to stay in Kuta. Taxi drivers are often reluctant to drive down Poppies Gangs I and II. Except when the area is flooded during the rainy season, Poppies Gang II is perfectly driveable, so it is worth trying to find a driver who will drop you by your chosen accommodation. Prices include 21% government tax and breakfast unless stated.

A Poppies I, Poppies Gang I, PO Box 3378, T0361 751059 www.poppiesbali.com. Running since 1973, tasteful Balinese-style a/c cottages set in beautifully landscaped gardens with pool. This well-run hotel is very popular so book in advance.

C Barong Hotel, Poppies Gang 2, T0361 751804, www.baronghotel.com. Located in the heart of the action on Poppies Gang 2, the a/c rooms here are clean and reasonably sized.

The draw is the large pool with swim-up bar and massage service. Popular with familes.

D Fat Yogi Cottages and Restaurant Poppies Gang 1, T0361 751665, www.indo. com/hotels/fat_yogi. Good selection of comfortable and spacious rooms some with a/c and hot water, pool. Yet staff are surly and the music from the restaurant is a bit loud.

D La Walon Hotel, Poppies Gang 1, T0361 757234, www.lawalonhotel.com. A spanking new exterior leads into an older wing with simple clean rooms with a/c and TV, or fan, with bathroom. Pool. Discounts available for stays of more than one week. Friendly staff.

D-E Gemini Star Hotel, Gang Ronta (off Poppies Gang 2), T0361 750558, aquarius hotel@yahoo.com. On the site of the old Jus Edith hotel, this new place has clean a/c and fan rooms with attached bathroom. Deluxe rooms include TV and mini-fridge.

D-E Tanjung Bali Inn, Poppies Gang 2, T0361 762990. Surrounding a mid-sized swimming pool are 3 big Balinese-style buildings. Clean, large a/c and a fan rooms with dimly lit balcony and private bathroom. Very popular.

E Lima Satu, just off Poppies Gang 1, T0361 754944, limasatu@dps.centrin.net.id. Simple, comfortable a/c and fan rooms with bathroom in a 3-storey building, hot water, pool, reasonable value.

E Mimpi Bungalows, Gang Sorga (just off Poppies Gang 1), T0361 751848, kumimpi@yahoo.com.sg. Simple a/c and fan rooms with hot water, some with newly renovated bathroom. Pool.

F Kedin's 2, Gang Sorga (off Poppies Gang 1), T0361 763554. Fan rooms with private cold-water bathroom lead onto private veranda. Pool. Warm and friendly staff, popular and relaxing hotel. Recommended.

F Ronta Bungalows, Gang Ronta (off Poppies Gang 2), T0361 754246. Very basic clean rooms with fan. Well located for shopping and bars. Deservedly popular, good value for money.

G Dua Dara, Jl Legian, Poppies Gang II, T0361 754031. Charmless simple fan rooms, private bathrooms with shower and Western toilet. New pool. Price includes breakfast, safety deposit boxes available.

Tuban p280

Tuban has plenty of expensive, and mid-range accommodation, but budget travellers will find a much better selection in Kuta. All rooms with private bathroom, Western-style toilet. Prices include government tax and breakfast unless otherwise stated.

AL Ramayana, Jl Bakung Sari, T0361 751864, www.ramayanahotel.com. Popular with Asian tourists, with well-furnished, spacious rooms, 2 pools, spa service, and private butler service. There is also a chapel for those wishing to tie the knot on the island. Balinese cooking and flower arranging classes available.

A Adhi Jaya, Jl Kartika Plaza, T0361 756884, www.adhijayahotel.com. This hotel has gone through extensive renovations, with the older standard rooms representing average value, compared to the spacious clean new deluxe rooms. Good pool and well-kept gardens. Each room has private veranda/balcony.

A Bali Rani, Jl Kartika Plaza, PO Box 1034, T0361 751369, www.baliranihotel.com.

Rooms set around a delightful lily pond. One of the better value hotels in this price range, with 104 comfortable rooms, each with a/c, satellite TV, minibar, balcony, free-form pool and children's pool, Thai Express restaurant and pool bar.

A-B Bali Garden, Jl Kartika Plaza, PO Box 1101, T0361 752725, F0361 752728. Low and dim corridors lead into musty rooms that open out onto a green, well tended garden. Rooms on the higher floors have sea view. 150 a/c rooms, 3 restaurants, 3 pools and extensive facilities.

E Bunut Gardens, Gang Puspa Ayu, Jl Kartika Plaza, T0361 752971. Average rooms (8 in all) in quiet location with plenty of greenery; fan, hot water, nice views from upstairs room. Also 4 rooms with shared *mandi*.

E Mustika Inn, Gang Puspa Ayu, Jl Kartika Plaza, T0361 753298. Bargain hard for a good price at this simple, budget place. Fairly clean, spacious rooms with fan, *mandi* and squat toilet. Pleasant views from upstairs rooms. No garden.

E Puspa Ayu Gang Puspa Ayu, Jl Kartika Plaza, T0361 756721. Incredibly lackadaisical staff rule the roost at these tired tiled cottages that need a thorough revamp and clean. Attached restaurant serves reasonable, cheap Western fare.

Legian p280, map p281

There is less budget accommodation available in Legian, but mid-range accommodation is good value here.

A The Lokha, Jl Padma Utara, T0361 767601, www.thelokhalegian.com. Boutique hotel, 49 spacious, stylish rooms, some with baths. 2 pools, café, massage and Wi-Fi.

C All Seasons, Jl Padma Utara, T0361 767688, F0361 768180, info@allseasonslegian.com. Excellent value popular and colourfully decorated hotel. 113 rooms surround a small garden and pool, with bar. Wi-Fi available.

D Bali Sorgowi Hotel, Jl Legian, T0361 755266, www.balisorgowi.com. Down a quiet alley on the Kuta/Legian border this place is much touted on the internet, comfortable pool-facing a/c rooms with TV and fridge.

D Sinar Bali Jl Padma Utara, T0361 751404, www.hotelsinarbali.com. Tucked away down an alley, this quiet hotel offers clean, comfortable a/c rooms with TV and bathroom. Good sized pool. Recommended.

Seminyak *p280, map p281*

Long a favoured haunt of ex-pats, some of the accommodation in Seminyak is in bungalows and houses available to rent monthly or long term. Look for signs along the streets, notices in the *Wartel* on Jl Dhyanapura or the real estate agents such as www.seminyakvillas.net and www.laksmanavillas.ne. For shorter stays there are only a handful of budget options, with most places in the mid to upper range.

LL Anantara, Jl Abimanyu, T0361 737773, www.bali.anantara.com. Newly built, with unsurpassed views of the beach, the 59 sea-view suites feature floor-to-ceiling windows, terrazzo tub and modern Balinese decor. 3 pools, including 1 infinity pool. 3 restaurants and a rooftop bar with DJs who spin chill out music as the sun sets. Private Wi-Fi access, and iPod dock in each suite.

LL Le Jardin, Jl Sarinande 7, T0361 730165, www.lejardinvilla.com. A short stroll from the beach, 11 2- to 3-bedroom walled villas each with small private pool, dining room, kitchenette and small garden. The surrounding walls makes each villa seem cramped. Well-furnished rooms and friendly staff. Also has gym, health spa and Wi-Fi.

LL Sun Island, Jl Raya Seminyak, T0361 733779, www.astonsunisland.com. 22 spacious and stylish villas opening onto a walked garden. Each has private plunge pool, kitchenette and bath tub. Private butler, chef service and in-room spa treatments available.

A Dhyana Pura, Jln Camplung Tanduk, T0361 730442, www.dhyanapura-beach-resort.com. In rambling large grounds, this hotel feels like a relic from a bygone era and could do with a spruce up. Rooms are simple and dark. Depends on European tour groups for much of its business The gardens back onto the beach. Considerably overpriced.

C-D The Green Room, Jl Abimanyu 63B, T0361 731412, www.thegreenroombali.com. Follow the signs down a small lane off the main street. Sociable and popular with young Europeans. Deluxe a/c rooms, simple comfortable fan rooms, pool, and a covered decking area with plenty of cushions.

C-D Sarinande Beach Inn, Jl Sarinande 15, T0361 730383, www.sarinandehotel.com. Cheerful, with friendly staff. Spotless comfortable rooms with mini bar, private terrace and private hot-water bathroom. Pool and restaurant serving Asian and Western cuisine. Often full, so reserve. Discounts available for stays of more than 14 days. Recommended.

D Sari Uma Cottages, Jl Sarinande 3, T0361 736476, F0361 730421, eddie_sariuma@yahoo.com.id. Set in pleasant gardens, this quiet place has 5 clean 2-bed cottages with a/c, kitchenette with TV and private bath. The owner prefers to rent by the month, but will negotiate daily rate.

F Inada Losmen, Jl Raya Seminyak, Gang Bima 9, T0361 732269, putuinada@hotmail.com. Very quiet rooms in a 2-storey building tucked down a quiet lane off the main street. The mellow vibes are enhanced by the sound of the owner's birds. Rooms are simple and clean, with bathroom. Good value for budget travellers.

Batubelig

AL Balisani Suites, Jl Batubelig, Kerobokan, T0361 730550, balisani@dps.mega.net.id. 126 rooms and suites in peaceful seaside location. Built in Balinese village style, attractively decorated. Swimming pool, 4 restaurants and bars. Free shuttle to Kuta and airport transfers.

A Intan Bali Village, PO Box 1089, Batubelig beach, T0361 752191, F0361 752475. A/c, several restaurants, 2 pools, extensive sports facilities, large central block with some bungalow accommodation. Caters almost exclusively to tour groups, with little to attract the independent traveller.

B Batubelig Beach Bungalows, Jl Batubelig 228, Kerobokan, T0361 30078. Well-built and attractively furnished thatched roof bungalows, with kitchen, large bedroom and bathroom, hot water, a/c, set in garden. Peaceful location 3 mins' walk to beach. Breakfast not included in rates. Longstay rates available. Sastika Restaurant on premises, very cheap and good value.

Canggu p282

The scenic countryside around Canggu is dotted with private villas, many of which are for rent. There are also many hotels being constructed and the sight of dumper trucks rattling along the rutted roads is common.

A Legong Keraton Beach Hotel, Jl Pantai Berawa, T0361 730280, www.legong keratonhotel.com Facing the sea, this spacious but somewhat characterless hotel has a/c rooms with TV and balcony. Sea-view rooms have bath. Hotel offers free daily shuttle service to Kuta. Restaurant, pool and open-air bistro serving Western food. Bike hire.

A Hotel Pisang Mas, Jl Tibu Peneng, Jl Pantai Berewa, T0361 7868349. Walled complex featuring 3 beautifully furnished 1-bedroom cottages built above a pool. There is a kitchen and outdoor dining area to seat 8. Would suit a group. Dogs barking incessantly outside are tiresome. The owner lives in Legian so needs to be contacted in advance.

C Villa Senyum, Jl Pemelisan Agung Jl Pantai Berewa, T0361 7464915, www.balilifestyle resort.com. Clean tasteful cottages with TV and attached bath with private balcony. Pool and restaurant. Very peaceful and fairly popular.

Sanur p283, map p284

Accommodation on Sanur is largely mid- to high-range, though recently a number of new and attractive budget guesthouses have opened along Jl Danau Tamblingan, which offer excellent value for money. Much of the guesthouse accommodation is overpriced and disappointing. Fan rooms are hard to come by. Prices are frequently geared to European tour groups who form the largest group of visitors; except during high season you should never have to pay more than 50% of the listed price,

and even then many places still seem overpriced. Unless otherwise stated, all accommodation includes private bathroom and Western toilet.

LL Villa Dampati, Jl Segara Ayu 8, T0361 288454, www.banyuning.com. 9 spacious 3-bedroom walled villas each with private garden and pool, internet access and a deep bathtub in immaculate bathroom.

LL-L Tanjung Sari, Jl Danau Tamblingan 41, T0361 288441, www.tandjungsarihotel.com. 26 bungalows set in atmospheric grounds, each crafted in traditional Balinese style and has different amenities such as bath, internet access and outdoor shower. Each bungalow is decorated differently – check first! Well-stocked library. Beach front bar and restaurant. Recommended for a splurge.

A Gazebo Cottages, Jl Danau Tamblingan 35, T0361 288212, www.baligazebo.com. 76 pleasant rooms in a range of styles. 3 smallish pools and large outdoor chess set, big, attractive Balinese-style gardens leading to beach. Peaceful, friendly, reasonable value.

A La Taverna, Jl Danau Tamblingan 29, PO Box 3040, T0361 288497, www.lataverna hotel.com. Discounts available, restaurant (recommended), pool. 34 well-decorated rooms with safety box, attractive gardens leading down to sea and a not particularly good beach. Deluxe rooms have private pool and kitchenette. Broadband. *Legong* dance every Fri evening at 2030 in the restaurant.

B-C Swastika Bungalows, Jl Danau Tamblingan 128, T0361 288693, swastika@ indosat.net.id. 81 rooms. Standard rooms have funky outdoor bathrooms and are cosy and filled with Balinese character. The new deluxe a/c rooms are huge, but have a lot less character. 2 pools, quiet location set back from road, 15 mins' walk from the beach, pleasant gardens, popular with families, central for shops and restaurants.

C Bumas Hotel, Jl Bumi Ayu 4, T0361 286306, www. bumashotels.com. Popular with German and Austrian tour groups, this hotel has spacious a/c rooms with bath, TV and veranda. Inviting pool.

C Ratna Beach Hotel, Jl Segara Ayu 10, T0361 288418, ratnahotel@telkom.net. This hotel has seen better days. Average bedrooms with small dark bathroom, pool, 4 mins' walk to the beach.

D Lestari Danau Tamblingan 188, T0361 288867. Small a/c rooms with TV set in quiet compound with pool. Bargain hard.

D Puri Made Hotel, Jl Danau Tamblingan 72, T0361 284219, F0361 288152. Pleasant clean rooms (15 in all) with a/c face a small pool and tidy garden. Lethargic owners. Slightly overpriced.

D Taman Agung Beach Inn Jl Danau Tamblingan 146, T0361 288549, taman agung@yahoo.com. Reasonably sized clean a/c rooms with TV and bath face a garden desperately needing more shade (unless you're an avid sun worshipper). Pool.

D-F Little Pond Homestay, Jl Danau Tamblingan 19, T0361 289902, www.ellora bali.com. Sparkling fan and a/c rooms with veranda, built around a small pool. A/c rooms have TV. The comfy fan rooms are great value. Free Wi-Fi. Recommended.

E Yulia's 1 Jl Danau Tamblingan 38 T0361 288089. The owner's prize-winning songbirds fill the shady gardens with tropical banter in this friendly and popular place with spacious fan and a/c rooms. Big fan rooms with private balcony on the 2nd floor of the building at the back are great value. Recommended.

F Coco Homestay, Jl Danau Tamblingan 42, T0361 287391. 8 simple small and clean rooms with friendly owner. This place needs redecoration, starting with the dull and dark bathrooms. Long-stay rates available.

F Luisa Homestay, Jl Danau Tamblingan 40, T0361 289673. 11 basic clean rooms. No garden. Friendly owner. About the cheapest place in Sanur.

⊘ Eating

Kuta p278, map p279

Most of the restaurants offer a range of food, including Indonesian and international

cuisines. There is also a line of cheap *warungs* selling Indonesian favourites such as *nasi goreng* and *soto ayam* in the middle of Gang Ronta, joining Poppies 1 and 2.

Poppies, Poppies Gang 1, T0361 751059, www.poppiesbali.com, open 0800-2300. In beautiful gardens, popular with couples. Food is a blend of Indonesian and Western with dishes such as half-moon swordfish and delectable steaks. Serves famed Toraja coffee from Sulawesi. Reservations recommended.

Kori, Poppies Gang 2, T0361 758605, www.korirestaurant.co.id, open 1200-2400. Soft jazz and trickling water features keep customers cool. Indonesian and Western fare is washed down with 2 for 1 on selected cocktails most nights.

Maccaroni, Jl Legian 52, T0361 754662, info@maccaroniclub.com, open 0900-0200. Sleekly designed for the hipper tourist, diners eat fusion food and Western and Asian favourites to mellow trip hop beats. Excellent value Asian set lunch before 1700.

Pepper Lunch, Kuta Suci Arcade 8-9, Jl Pantai Kuta, T0361 767219, open 1000-2300. Satisfy carnivorous cravings at this brightly lit Japanese-style steak house serving dishes such as shimoturi pepper steak. All meat is from Australia and New Zealand. The set meals represent good value. Wi-Fi .

TJ's, Poppies Lane 1, T0361 751093, open 0900-2330. Popular Mexican eatery serving large portions of fajitas and chimminchangas with an extensive tequila cocktail list. Service is good in this cheerfully decorated place.

Un's Paradise Restaurant, Un's Lane (off Jl Pantai Kuta), T0361 752607, open 1700-2400. A good place to sample some Balinese dishes such as *gulai babi* (pork stew), Balinese-style *sate*, and seafood such as the excellent potato-wrapped red snapper fillet. Also serves fair Western cuisine. Excellent service.

Made's Warung, Jl Pantai Kuta, T0361 75597, open 0900-2400. A bit quieter than it used to be, this Kuta institution has a mind-bogglingly long and rambling menu of Western and Indonesian fare. Homely ambience with friendly service.

¶ **Urban Food Station**, Jl Legian 61, open 24 hrs. Variety of well-filled sandwiches, juices and delicious salads in a fast-food setting in the heart of Kuta. Popular.

¶ **Warung 96**, Jl Benesari (off Poppies Gang 2), T0361 750557, open 1000-2400. Excellent pizzas served from a wood-fired oven are the highlight of this laid-back place popular with those fresh from the beach. Friendly service.

¶ **Warung Indonesia**, Gang Ronta (off Poppies Gang 2), T0361 739817, open 0900-2300. Extensive selection of delicious Indonesian food from across the archipelago, accompanied by fresh fruit juices and cool reggae after the sun goes down. Attracts a wonderfully diverse clientele. Recommended.

¶ **Warung Pama**, Gang Ronta (off Poppies Gang 2), T0361 752021, open 0800-2300. Spotlessly clean and popular place serving good, cheap Western food and some Indonesian classics such as *ayam panggang*.

The beach *p279, map p279*

There are plenty of places to choose from on Sindhu Beach.

¶¶ **Anjani**, Sindhu Beach Walk, T0361 289567, open 0900-2200. German and Thai dishes are the speciality at the beachside place with fine views over to Nusa Penida. Beach chairs and umbrellas for rent, 25,000Rp per day.

¶¶ **Spirit**, Sindhu Beach Walk, T0361 285908, open 0700-2300. Excellent-value seafood dishes coupled with Western and Asian favourites. Family favourite.

¶¶ **Tootsie**, Sindhu Beach Walk, T0361 286638, open 0700-2300. Menu that strides from mango dessert to *nasi goreng* and Balinese *cap cai* (vegetables) to pizza and pasta dishes. Mellow tunes and shady tables on the beach.

Tuban *p280*

¶¶ **Atmosphere Cafe**, Jl Kartika Plaza, T0361 769501, www.atmosphere.co.id, open 1100-2400. A great place for watching the sunset, with comfortable seating next to the beach. Fair food, including a few interesting Balinese dishes such as *bebek betutu* (roast duck) and pastas, burgers and salads.

¶¶ **Bluefin**, Kuta Side Walk 16, Jl Kartika Raya, T0361 764100, F0361 763200, open 1100-2330. Reasonably priced Japanese sushi, sashimi and other favourites in a cosy blue-lit setting. Good service and selection of wine and *sake*.

¶¶ **Fiori Ristorante**, Jl Kartika Plaza, T0361 750158, www.ifiorobali.com, open 100-0100. Italian pasta, salad, standard seafood and meat dishes including tasty *Ossobuco alla Milanese* in this brand new glassy restaurant, whose exterior and menu is somewhat at odds with the Whitney Houston records playing and the leopard-skin print cushions.

¶¶ **Thai Express**, Jl Kartika Plaza, T0361 751369, thaiexpress@baliranihotel.com, open 1100-2300. Superb Thai food including a large selection of salads, curries and lip-smackingly rich laksa from this well-priced eatery. Part of the Bali Rani Hotel complex. Recommended.

¶ **L'coffee** Jl Kartika Plaza 8, T0361 757940, open 1000-2200. Newly opened with friendly management and a good range of fresh coffee (starts from 12,000Rp a cup) in a pleasant, refreshing environment.

Legian *p280, map p281*

Warungs are scattered along the beach selling simple local fare and drinks.

¶¶ **Indonational**, Jl Padma Utara 17, T0361 759883, www.indonationalrestaurant.com, open 0900-2300. Popular Australian-owned restaurant that totes its high levels of hygiene. Offers good portions of Western grub in a family-friendly ambience.

¶¶ **Lanai**, Jl Pantai Arjuna 10, T0361 731305, open 0800-2300. Sea views and an eclectic menu that features sushi, sashimi and Mexican food. Decent kids' menu.

¶¶ **Seaside**, Jl Pantai Arjuna 14, T0361 737140, www.seasidebali.com, open 1100-2300. Stunning sunset views at this cool beachside eatery dishing up international cuisine. Daily special offers. Popular for sunset drinks accompanied by chilled-out tunes.

¶ **Warung Yogya**, Jl Padma Utara 79, T0361 750835, open 1000-2200. Tasty Javanese dishes in a friendly setting. Recommended.

Seminyak *p280 map p281*

Food is taken seriously in this part of the world, and a diverse selection of excellent cuisine can be found here. Restaurants are concentrated along Jl Abimanyu, Jl Raya Seminyak, and Jl Laksmana.

₩₩₩ Gado Gado, Jl Abimanyu, T0361 736966, open 0800-2300. Located on the beach, this eatery is popular for sundown drinks and good international fare. Some superb seafood dishes such as seared sea bream and grilled jumbo prawns. There is an extensive list of pasta dishes and salads. Good service.

₩₩ Lemongrass, Jl Raya Seminyak, T0361 7361549, lemongrass _thai@hotmail.com. An extensive menu of Thai dishes available including excellent curries and fish dishes. They guarantee not to add any MSG to your meal. Reasonable wine list.

₩₩ Pantarei, Jl Raya Seminyak 17 A, T0361 732567, adonis@indosat.net, open 1100-0100. Delicious Greek staples such as *dolmades* and *bourek* in this friendly and well-lit restaurant popular with couples and families.

₩₩ Trattoria, Jl Laksmana T0361 737082, open 1000-2400. Popular and friendly Italian restaurant with a menu that changes daily.

₩ Warung Rima Masakan Manado, Jl Raya Seminyak 2, T0361 735310, F0361 753111, open 0700-2300. Good Manado cuinine such as *ayam bakar rica rica* (grilled chicken with sweet chilli sauce) and passable Western cuisine. Friendly staff, but service is snail-like.

₩ Zula Vegetarian Paradise, Jl Abimanyu 5, T0361 731080, downtoearth@dps. centrin.net.id. Serves up healthy treats such as pumpkin and ginger soup, couscous with roasted vegetables and a range of antioxidant drinks. Also a grocery attached that sells healthy products and has a noticeboard detailing local events. Recommended.

There is also a small family-run *warung* selling inexpensive grilled seafood on the beach in front of the **Dhyana Pura Hotel**.

Sanur *p283, map p284*

Sanur has a glut of eateries ranging from fine dining to cheap and cheerful backpacker cafés. The more expensive places are attached to the beach-front hotels. However, good food doesn't need to cost the earth and is readily available on the beach and along Jl Danau Tamblingan. One reader has suggested that the turnover in all the restaurants on Jl Danau Tamblingan is low and, therefore, the food is not always fresh.

₩₩₩ The Village Cucine Italiana, Jl Danau Temblingan 47, T0361 285025, thevillage@santrian.com, open 1100-0000. Genuine Italian food in a trendy lounge environment. The dishes are classic Italian and cover the range from meat, pasta and seafood. Good range of antipasti. Free unlimited broadband access.

₩₩ Gateway of India, Jl Danau Tamblingan 103, T0361 281579 gatewayofindia@ dps.centrin.net.id, open 1100-2300. Serves up fair vegetarian and non-vegetarian Indian cuisine using a traditional clay oven. The thali (set meal) is good value.

₩₩ Kalpatharu, Jl Danau Tamblingan T0361 288457, open 0800-2300. Kids' menu, Western standards and some Balinese specials such as *bebek goreng* (roast duck). Prepares a decent *rijstaffel* at 95,000Rp for 2.

₩₩ Kopi Bali, Jl Danau Tamblingan 190, T0361 286242, open 0800-2300. You can find a good selection of Indonesian set meals and the classic Balinese suckling pig (needs to be ordered a day in advance). Happy hour 1800-2000, free transport in Sanur area, friendly staff.

₩₩ Tambingan, Jl Danau Tamblingan 47, T0361 281814, temblingan_sanur@ yahoo.com, open 1000-2300. Indonesian favourites and some decent Asian cuisine. Western food offered includes lobster and pastas in a pleasant outdoors setting. Good range of cocktails.

₩ Cafe Batujimbar, Jl Danau Tamblingan 75A T0361 287374, www.cafebatujimbar.com, open 0700-2230. Extremely popular, serving a crowd-pleasing mix of smoothies, toasted sandwiches and Indonesian favourites in a relaxed, modern setting. Recommended.

₩ Manik Organik, Jl Danau Tamblingan 85, T0361 8553380, manik.organik@gmail.com,

Australian owned, this organic cafe sells a delicious range of healthy sandwiches and juices as well as organic beauty products and offers life drawing classes on Sat for 70,000Rp.

Sanur Rasa, Jl Danau Tamblingan 53, T0361 281674. Friendly traditional Balinese *rumah makan* serving Balinese food such as *ikan bakar bumbu Bali* (grilled fish with Balinese spices) and fish *sate* paired with wonderfully fragrant condiments. Terrific value. Recommended.

Smorga's, Jl Pantai Karang 2 T0361 289361, open 0600-2100. Gourmet sandwiches with a range of fresh bread, coffees (start at 12,000Rp) and gelato. Has the *Jakarta Post* to linger over. Good value.

① Bars and clubs

Kuta *p278, map p279*
Kuta probably has the 'best' nightlife on Bali with venues for both the glamorous and the flip-flops crowd. Novel ideas are always being sought to pull in the tourist dollar, the latest of which is the cringeworthy 'sexy dancer show' that so many places now offer. Most of the bars are on Jl Legian. All these places are free for tourists, but locals often have to pay entry.

The Bounty, Jl LegianT0361 752529, open 2200-0600. Popular drinking hole bizarrely set on a recreated sailing ship. Gets sweaty and raucous as the night progresses.

Mbargo, Jl Legian, T0361 756280, open 1800-0400. This club has slightly more classy aspirations than its neighbours, with an interior that was once sleek but is now looking a little tired. Wear your bling as the DJs favour hip hop.

Paddies, Jl Legian, T0361 758555, open 1600-0300. Rebuilt after being destroyed in the 2002 bombings, and going from strength to strength. Clad in UV lights. Plays commercial music much loved by the drunken hordes. Happy hour buy-1-get-1-free 1930-2300.

Sky Lounge, Jl Legian 61, T0361 755423, open 24 hrs. Cocktails lovingly created at this popular new spot, which is growing famous

for its 14-day vodka-infused martini. Serves tapas during the day and early evening. Ladies drink for free 2200-2400 on Sun.

Legian *p280, map p281*
Dejavu, Jl Pantai Arjuna 7, T0361 732777, open 2100-0400. Stylish lounge bar facing the sea, popular with the glamorous set. 2-for-1 happy hour nightly 2100-2300.

Double Six Jl Arjuna, T0361 733067, info@doublesixclub.com, open 2200-0600, daily, free entrance Sun, Mon, Tues, 60,000Rp Wed, Thu, Fri, Sat (includes 1 drink). Top international and Indonesian DJs spin hard house at this trendy venue that starts to fill up after 0200.

Peanuts, Jl Legian, T0361 754149, open 1400-0400. Offers a pub crawl in vintage cars on Tue and Sat nights.

Seminyak *p280 map p281*
Bush Telegraph Pub, Jl Abimanyu, T0361 723963, open 1100-0200. Serves icy Aussie beers such as VB and Fosters and a range of grub from Australian steak to Asian staples.

Q Bar, Jl Abimanyu T0361 730923, open 1800-late. Popular gay bar with a golden stage area featuring live cabaret and nights such as 'Wet..Wet..Wednesday' and the imaginatively titled 'SaturGay Night Fever'.

Fabios, Jl Raya Seminyak 66, T0361 730562, floungebali@gmail.com. Stylish lounge bar with DJs spinning electro and funk into the wee hours to a glam crowd. Specializes in cocktails. Very popular and highly regarded.

Sanur *p283, map p284*
Not known for its wild night life; evenings are fairly sedate in Sanur. There are a few small bars scattered along Jl Danau Toba that could make for an amusing pub crawl.

Cat & Fiddle, Jl Cemara, T0361 282218, open 0730-0100. Live music, a good range of booze and good British food at this British-owned pub popular with expats. Recommended.

Lazer Sports Bar, Jl Danau Tamblingan 82, T0361 282840, open 0900 until the last customer staggers home. Keep up to date with English football in this relaxed bar with cool beers and live music on some nights.

⊕ Entertainment

Kuta *p278, map p279*
Kecak, *legong*, *Ramayana* dance and Balinese music; performances take place at many of the major hotels.

⊙ Shopping

Kuta *p278, map p279*
Kuta is one of the best places on Bali to shop for clothing; the quality is reasonable (sometimes good), and designs are close to the latest Western fashions, with a strong Australian bias for bright colours and bold designs. There is a good range of children's clothes shops. Silver jewellery is also a good buy (although some of it is of inferior quality). Kuta also has a vast selection of 'tourist' trinkets and curios. Quality is poor-to-average. The boys hawking watches, at an asking price of up to US$55, buy them in Surabaya for US$1.50 a kilo! Almost all the hawkers and stallholders are from Java. They are unskilled workers who live in cardboard boxes. This has led to a rise in petty crime, and has sorely tried the tolerance of the Balinese.
Batik PitheCanThropus, Jl Pantai Kuta, T0361 761880, pithecan@indosat.net.id, open 0900-2230. Sells everything and anything possible containing batik.
Bookshops Periplus has a small but great selection of books on Bali and Indonesia. Newspapers and the latest bestsellers are also available here. Also a 2nd-hand bookshop at the beach end of Poppies Gang 2 selling books in various languages.
Handicrafts Home Ide, Jl Legian, T0361 760014, homeide2006@yahoo.com, open 0800-2300. Locally made accessories for the home. **Jonathan Gallery**, Jl Legian 109, T0361 754209, legian109@hotmail.com, open 0800-2300. Well stocked with Balinese handicrafts including wood carvings, jewellery and *ikat*.

Uluwatu, Jl Legian, T0361 751933, www.uluwatu.co.id, open 0800-2200. This successful local venture has a number of outlets. It sells handmade Balinese lace paired with white cotton goods. Popular with Asian tourists.
Shopping mall Matahari, T0361 757588, open 0930-2200. A popular alternative for those fed up of haggling to pick up a wide selection of tourist trinkets at fixed prices.
Silver Ratna Silver, Jl Legian 72, T0361 750566, ratnasilver@dps.centrin.net.id, open 0900-1000, sells attractive contemporary silver jewellery made on Bali by a local artist. It has 3 branches on Bali. Other silver shops are along Jl Pantai Kuta and Jl Legian.
Supermarket In Matahari, selling fresh fruit and daily necessities.
Surfing clothes Surf Clothes Star Surf, Jl Legian, T0361 756251, open 0900-2230 and **Bali Barrel**, Jl Legian, T0361 767238, open 0900-2230, both huge stores selling trendy brand label surf wear at very reasonable prices.
  Numerous shops selling surfboards, DVDs and cheap clothing can be found along Poppies Gang 2.

Tuban *p280*
Discovery/Centro Shopping Centre, Jl Kartika Plaza, T0361 769629, Mon-Fri 1000-2200, weekends 1000-2230. Brand-name goods and tourist goodies.
Pasar Seni, Jl Kartika Plaza, daily. Open-air arts market selling the t-shirts and trinkets you can see everywhere else in Bali.
Plaza Bali, department store, duty-free shop (selection of perfumes and cosmetics, clothing and pricy liquor), restaurant, venue for Balinese dancing.

Legian *p280, map p281*
Hammocks Carga Jl Padma Utara, T0361 765275, hammockcross@ hotmail.com, open 0800-2200. Hammock specialist, friendly owner, expansive collection. Prices start at US$20 for a simple *ikat* hammock.

Handicrafts 'Antiques' and Indonesian fabrics at the north end of Jl Legian.

Swimwear and sportswear Several good shops on Jl Legian and side streets.

Seminyak *p280 map p281*

Jl Raya Seminyak is lined with interesting little boutiques, and shopping here is decidedly more upmarket than in Kuta. Locally made clothes and lifestyle stores dominate.

Clothes Neko, Jl Raya Seminyak, T0813 37387719, neko@telkom.net, open 0900-2100. Cotton clothes made by 2 Balinese ladies using natural tones. Welcoming staff and reasonable prices.

Paul Ropp, Jl Raya Seminyak, T0361 7342089, open 0900-2100. Bright cotton clothes made of fabric sourced in India and designed and made in Bali.

Sanur *p283, map p284*

Shopping in Sanur is a breeze, if you have just arrived from the tout-ridden pavements of Kuta. There is the usual tourist stuff, including a beachside market along Sidhu beach selling cheap T-shirts, sunglasses and hats, but also some art shops and galleries to peruse.

Antiques Gotta Antique Collection, Jl Danau Tamblingan, T0361 292188, open 0900-2200. Stocks a variety of antiques from around the archipelago, with a focus on carvings and *ikat* from Eastern Indonesia. Worth a browse.

Batik Puri Suar, Jl Danau Toba 9, T0361 285572, F0361 7939322, open 0900-2000. Sells a colourful selection of locally made Balinese batik and kebaya.

Supermarkets Hardy's Supermarket, Jl Danau Tamblingan 136, daily 0800-2230 has a cheap supermarket, an optician's and a **Periplus** bookshop, stocking paperbacks, guidebooks, trashy magazines and postcards.

The Pantry, Jl Danau Tamblingan 75, T0361 281008, the_pantry@indosat. net.id, open 0900-2100. Aimed mainly at resident expats, this grocery sells a range of Australian-produced goodies and has a good deli counter.

▲ Activities and tours

Major hotels often have tour companies that organize the usual range of tours: for example, to Lake Bratan (where water-skiing can be arranged); to Karangasem and Tenganan to visit a traditional Aga village; to Ubud; white-water rafting on the Agung River; to the temples of Tanah Lot and Mengwi; to the Bali Barat National Park; and to Besakih Temple.

Kuta *p278, map p279*

Diving Aquamarine Diving, Jl Raya Seminyak 56, T0361730107, www.aqua marinediving.com. Owned and run by an Englishwoman, Annabel Thomas, a PADI instructor. It offers a personal service, uses Balinese divemasters who speak English (and Japanese) and has well-maintained equipment. PADI courses up to divemaster can be provided in English, German, Spanish, French and Japanese. Dive safaris all over Bali are offered – check the website.

Body and soul Numerous masseurs – with little professional training – roam the beach and hassle tourists on Jl Legian; more skilled masseurs can be found at hotels or specialist clinics around Kuta. Jl Pantai Kuta has many aromatherapy and massage places such as: **Aroma Mimpi**, Jl Pantai Kuta, Kuta Suci Arcade 12, T0361 762891, open 0900-2400. Offers Balinese massage, body scrubs, facials and pedicures with treatments starting at around 50,000Rp for an hour.

Dupa Spa Jl Pantai Kuta 47, T0361 7953132, open 0900-2400. A 1-hr massage costs 85,000Rp.

Surfing Kuta is famous for its surfing, although the cognoscenti would now rather go elsewhere. Boards are available for rent on the beach at around 40,000Rp per hr. Body-boards can be rented for 25,000Rp per hr. The guys renting boards on the beach offer surf lessons at US$16.50 for 2 hrs. Bargain hard.

Big Kahuna, Jl Pantai Kuta, T361 765081, www.bigkahunasurfs chool.com. This school has similar packages and guarantees to get clients standing after 1 lesson or the next lesson is free. 2-hr lesson US$39.

Tubes, Poppies Gang 2, T0361 765726, open 1000-0200 is a popular meeting spot for surfers. The tide chart is posted outside and surfing trips to Java's G-land can be booked here (www.g-land.com).

Wave Riders, Jl Pantai 1, T0361 728299, reservations@waveridersbali.com. Offers lessons with professional instructors, and a package that includes insurance and hotel pick up. A half-day package costs US$44. Recommended.

Surf equipment and board repairs are available from **Mango Surf Station**, Poppies Gang 2, T0361 750627, open 1000-2200, and **Toke Surf Shop**, Poppies Gang 2, T0361 765726, open 1000-2200. They will provide information on currents, tides and latest surfing reports.

Tour operators Amanda Tours, Jl Benesari 7, T0361 754090. One of the many tour operators offering full-day multi-stop tours to places tuch as Kintamani, Tanah Lot and Lovina. They also offer car rental. Prices are negotiable.

Bali Adventure Tours, Jl Tunjung Mekar, T0361 721480, www.baliadventure tours.com. An organized company owned by long-term Australian resident, offers rafting or kayaking trips, mountain biking, elephant riding in Taro or trekking, US$36-63, including pick-up from hotel, lunch and insurance.

MBA, Poppies Gang 1, T0361 757349. www.mba-inlove.com. This company has branches all over Kuta, and offers domestic flight bookings, horse riding, river rafting and more. Enthusiastic service.

Perama, Jl Legian 39, T0361 751875, www.peramatour.com. Organize shuttle buses all over the island and tours further afield to destinations such as Flores and Lombok. Perama consistently manage to offer significantly cheaper fares than other operators and are developing something of a monopoly on the budget travel market. They give a 5000Rp discount to passengers who present a used **Perama** ticket for travel on shuttle buses on Bali.

Tuban *p280*
Bali Slingshot, Jl Kartika Plaza, T0361 758838, www.balislingshot.com, open 1100-late, US$22 per person. This Australian-owned ride involves being shot up into the air at ridiculous speeds, and advises tourists to 'make sure ya wear ya brown jocks'.

Waterbom Park, Jl Kartika Plaza, T0361 755676, www.waterbom.com. Adult US$12, child (under 12) US$11. Within walking distance of Tuban hotels, open daily 0900-1800, over 600 m of water slides. Other facilities include water volleyball, spa offering traditional massage etc, gardens, restaurant, lockers and towels for hire (children under 12 must be accompanied by an adult).

Tour operator Satriavi, Bali Rani Hotel, Jl Kartika Raya, T0361 7971560, fodps@ satriavi.co.id, open 0800-2000. Garuda and all other domestic and international air ticketing. Indonesia and Bali tour packages.

Legian *p280, map p281*
Body and soul Briella Spa and Salon, Jl Padma Utara, T0361 7987660, open 0900-2300. Offers a variety of treatments including massage, facials and reflexology in a pleasant environment. Has some good packages starting at US$13.50.

Bungee jumping AJ Hackett at Double Six Club, Jl Arjuna, T0361 752658, bali@ aj-hackett.com, open Mon-Fri 1200-2000, Sat and Sun 0130 until 0600. The 45-m leap of faith can be made towering above the raving masses at this popular nightspot. The price of US$59 includes a t-shirt, certificate and hotel pick-up.

Diving and surfing Scuba Duba Doo, Jl Legian 367, T0361 761798, www.divecente rbali.com. Dive centre and school that runs 4-day Open Water courses for US$375, and dive safaris to various locations around Bali including Nusa Penida and Menjangan Island.

Surfboards and bodyboards can be rented on the beach for 30,000Rp and 10,000Rp per hr, respectively.

Seminyak *p280 map p281*

Body and soul Putri Bali, Jl Raya Seminyak 13, T0361 736852, open 0900-2000. Javanese *mandi lulur* scrub treatment where the body is exfoliated using spices such as turmeric and ginger and then bathed in a milk moisturiser. Other local beauty treatments available here include Balinese *boreh* wrap and a coconut scrub technique imported from Sulawesi. 2-hr packages start at US$17.50.

Surfing Surfboards and bodyboards are available for rent on the beach. Bargain hard.

Canggu *p282*

Canggu Tua, T0361 7470644. A 2-hr ride including lunch costs US$50 and **Tarukan Equestrian Centre**, Jl Nelayan 29.

Sanur *p283, map p284*

Body and soul

Massages are available on the beach, or at the stylish and professional **Jamu Traditional Spa**, Jl Danau Tamblingan 41, T0361 286595, open 0900-2100. Numerous Indonesian beauty treatments are offered. Prices start at US$45 for a 1-hr balancing massage.

The **Bali Usada Meditation Center**, By Pass NgurahRai 23, T0361 289209, www.balimeditation.com, offers courses in meditation.

Cruises

Bali Hai, Benoa Harbour, T0361 720331, www.balihaicruises.com. Variety of packages to Nusa Lembongan from Benoa, which include hotel pick up from Sanur. Trips include the Reef Cruise on the company's purpose-built pontoon just off Lembongan. The Aristocrat Cruise is on a luxury catamaran and includes snorkelling, and use of the

facilities at a Lembongan beach club for the day (both US$85 adult/US$57 child).

Dance

The **Tandjung Sari Hotel** offers Balinese dance lessons for children Fri and Sun 1500-1700.

Diving

Blue Season Bali, Jl Danau Tamblingan 69, T0361 282574, www.baliocean.com. A 5-star IDC centre offering PADI scuba dive courses (US$260) and a variety of other courses such as Rescue Diver (US$350) and Night Diver (US$140). Also offers trips to Nusa Penida and Nusa Lembongan.

Mountain biking

Sobek, Jl Tirta Ening 9, T0361 287059, www.balisobek.com. Trips down the mountainside from Gunung Batur to Ubud with guide, buffet lunch and insurance cost US$68 adult and US$45 children (7-15).

Surfing

The reef here has one of the world's best right-hand breaks, but it is only on for about 28 days a year. It's best in the wet season Oct-Apr, and is possible with any tide depending on the size and direction of the swell. Beware of strong currents and riptides in high winds. To the north of Sanur, the right-hand break in front of the Grand Bali Beach Hotel is a fast 4-5 m with some good barrels, but is best on a mid- or high-tide and needs a large swell. Opposite the **Tanjung Sari Hotel** at high tide, there is the possibility of a long, fast wall. For the biggest waves, hire a jukung to take you out to the channel opposite the **Bali Hyatt**, very good right handers on an incoming tide.

Tour operators

Asian Trails, Jl By Pass Ngurah Rai 260, T0361 285771, www.asiantrails.info. Can arrange hotels, flights and tours.
Esapaces Voyages, Jl Tamblingan 47, T0361 285785, open Mon-Fri 1000-1700. French and English tours around Bali and further

including trips to Gunung Ijen and Gunung Bromo in East Java for US$160 and US$285 (min 2 people) respectively. Accommodation is included in the price.

Perama, Warung Pojok, Jl Hang Tuah 39, T0361 287594. Island-wide shuttle bus service.

Sobek, Jl Tirta Ening 9, T0361 287059. Arranges birdwatching and sporting activities.

Watersports
Equipment available from the bigger hotels or on the beach at Sindhu beach walk. Typical prices per person: jet ski US$25 per 15 mins; canoe US$5 per person per hr.

White Water Rafting Sobek, down grade III rapids on Telaga Wirta including professional guides, safety equipment and buffet lunch. Adult US$68, child (7-15) US$45.

⊖ Transport

Tuban *p280*
Airline office Transnusa Bandara Int'l Ngurah Rai, T0361-7877555.
Bicycles Available for hire along Gang Puspa Sari at 25,000Rp for 24 hrs.

Legian *p280, map p281*
Bemo To Tegal terminal in **Denpasar**, and from there, change to other terminals for next destination.
Car/motorbike hire Sudarsana, Jl Padma Utara, T0361 755916, open 0800-1800. Car rentals from US$16.50 per day (plus US$11 per day for a driver). Motorbikes US$5.50 per day.
Shuttle To most tourist destinations on the island; shop around for best price.
Taxi 28,000Rp to the airport. The best metered taxi company to use is the blue **Bali Taxi**, T0361 701111.

Canggu *p282*
To reach Canggu you will need your own transport. Follow the main road north from Legian until you pick up signs for Canggu. The beach signposted 'Canggu Beach' is in

fact Pererean Beach. To reach 'Canggu Beach' itself, turn left at the T-junction in Canggu village and keep going to the beach. If in doubt, ask for directions. The 25-min drive in a hired car or van should not cost more than 45,000Rp from the Kuta/Legian area.

Sanur *p283, map p284*
Air Sumanindo Graha Wisata, Jl Danau Tamblingan, T0261 288570, sumantravel@ dps.centrin.net.id, open 0800-1900. Domestic and international ticketing.
Bemo Short hops within Sanur cost 3000Rp. There are regular connections on green bemos with **Denpasar's** Kreneng terminal and on blue bemos with Tegal terminal (both 5000Rp); also regular connections with the Batubulan terminal, north of Sanur (5000Rp).
Bicycle hire Hire bikes along the beach for 20,000Rp a day.
Boat Perama have a daily service to Nusa Lembongan leaving at 1030 (1½ hours) from the jetty at the north of town for US$11. Public boat leaves at 0800 and costs US$4. Ticket booth at beach end of Jl Hang Tuah.
Lembongan Fast Cruises, Jl Hang Tuah, T0361 285522, sales@scoot cruise.com. 3 sailings per day (0930, 1330, 1600), 30-min trip. US$35/US$21 for adult return/1 way, US$29/17 child (12-16) return/1 way and US$23/US$15 child (5-11) return/1 way. Price includes pick-up and drop service.
Car/motorbike hire Places along Jl Danau Toba and Jl Danau Tamblingan. **A1 Rental** (Jl Danau Toba T0361 284287) offers cars staring at US$16.50 per day and motorbikes starting at US$4 per day.
Shuttles Perama (see Tour operators) have 4 daily to **Ubud** (US$4), 4 daily to **Kuta** (US$3), and 2 daily to **Padangbai** (US$7). They also run to other places on the island – enquire at office.
Taxi Most hotels will arrange airport transfer/pick-up and will charge the same as, or often more than, taxis for the service (25,000Rp). A metered trip from one end of Sanur to the other costs around 14,000Rp.

Ubud and around

→ *Phone code: 0361. Colour map 11, B1.*
Ubud is a rather dispersed community, spread over hills and valleys with deep forested ravines and terraced ricefields. For many tourists, Ubud has become the cultural heart of Bali, with its numerous artists' studios and galleries as well as a plentiful supply of shops selling clothes, jewellery and woodcarving. Unfortunately, the town has succumbed to tourism in the last few years, with a considerable amount of development.

During the rainy season Ubud gets more rain than the coastal resorts and can be very wet and much cooler. ▸▸ *For listings, see pages 303-307.*

Ins and outs

Getting there
Public bemos stop at the central market, at the point where Jalan Wanasa Wana (Monkey Forest Road) meets Jalan Raya, in the centre of Ubud. **Perama** ① *Jl Hanoman, T0361 96316,* which runs shuttle buses to the main tourist destinations, has a busy depot 15 minutes' walk away from the centre of town. They won't drop passengers off at accommodation. Arrivals are greeted with a small army of touts offering accommodation and transport. Public bemos run from Ubud to Batubalan for connections south including to Kuta and Sanur; Gianyur for connections east to Padangbai and Candi Dasa; and north to Singaraya and Louina and Kintaman. Perama also run regular shuttles to the airport.

The **Bina Wisata tourist office** ① *Jl Raya Ubud (opposite the Puri Saren), open 1000-2000,* is good for information on daily performances and walks in the Ubud area, but otherwise not very helpful.

Sights

Much of the charm and beauty of Ubud lies in the natural landscape. There are few official sights in the town itself – in contrast to the surrounding area (see page 300). The **Museum Puri Lukisan** ① *T0361 975136, 0900-1700, 30,000Rp, in the centre of Ubud,* contains examples of 20th century Balinese painting and carving (and that of Europeans who have lived here).

At **Antonio Blanco** ① *daily 0900-1700, 50,000Rp, walk west on the main road and over a ravine past Murnis Warung – the house is immediately on the left-hand side of the road at the end of the old suspension bridge,* a Western artist who settled in Ubud has turned his home into a gallery. The house is in a stunning position, perched on the side of a hill, but the collection is disappointing. Blanco – unlike Spies and Bonnet – has had no influence on the style of local artists.

The **Museum Neka** ① *daily 0900-1700, 20,000Rp, 1.5 km from town, up the hill past Blanco's house.* Six Balinese-style buildings contain a good collection of traditional and contemporary Balinese and Javanese painting, as well as work by foreign artists who have lived in or visited Bali. There is a good art bookshop here and a good restaurant with views over the ravine.

ARMA (Agung Rai Museum of Art) ① *Jl Pengosekan, T0361 976659, www.arma museum.com, daily 0900-1800, 25,000Rp,* has a fascinating permanent exhibition of paintings by Balinese, Indonesian and foreign artists who spent time in Bali. It is the only place on Bali that exhibits the delightful work of Walter Spies, as well as famed Javanese artist Raden Saleh. Classical *kamasan* (paintings on tree bark) are displayed here, alongside works by the Balinese masters and temporary exhibitions featuring local photographers and artists. The centre is also the venue to numerous cultural performances, and more interestingly to workshops on topics as diverse as Balinese dance, Hinduism in Bali, modernity in Bali and wood carving. Recommended.

The **Bali Botanic Gardens** ① *Jl Kutuh Kaja, T0361 7803904, www.botanicgarden bali.com, daily 0800-1800, 50,000Rp,* are 320-400 m above sea level and contain an

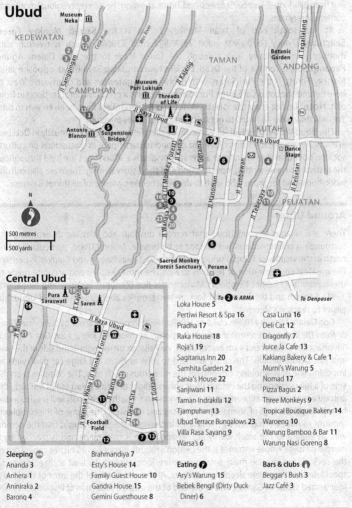

Ubud

Museum Neka

KEDEWATAN

Cerik River

Wos River

TAMAN

Botanic Garden

Jl Tegallalang

ANDONG

Jl Kajeng

Jl Sanggingan

Museum Puri Lukisan

Threads of Life

CAMPUHAN

Jl Raya Ubud

Antonio Blanco

Suspension Bridge

Jl Wanara Wana (Jl Monkey Forest)

Jl Karna

Jl Gotama

Jl Raya Ubud

KUTAH

Dance Stage

Jl Tembawan

Jl Hanoman

Jl Peliatan

Jl Tenesaya

PELIATAN

Sacred Monkey Forest Sanctuary Perama

N

500 metres
500 yards

Central Ubud

Pura Saraswati

Saren

Jl Kajeng

Jl Bisma

Jl Raya Ubud

Jl Wanara Wana (Jl Monkey Forest)

Jl Karna

Jl Gotama

Jl Dewi Sita

Football Field

To ② & ARMA · To Denpasar

Loka House 5
Pertiwi Resort & Spa 16
Pradha 17
Raka House 18
Roja's 19
Sagitarius Inn 20
Samhita Garden 21
Sania's House 22
Sanjiwani 11
Taman Indrakila 12
Tjampuhan 13
Ubud Terrace Bungalows 23
Villa Rasa Sayang 9
Warsa's 6

Casa Luna 16
Deli Cat 12
Dragonfly 4
Juice Ja Cafe 13
Kakiang Bakery & Cafe 1
Murni's Warung 5
Nomad 17
Pizza Bagus 2
Three Monkeys 9
Tropical Boutique Bakery 14
Waroeng 10
Warung Bamboo & Bar 11
Warung Nasi Goreng 8

Sleeping
Ananda 3
Anhera 1
Aniniraka 2
Baronq 4

Brahmandiya 7
Esty's House 14
Family Guest House 10
Gandra House 15
Gemini Guesthouse 8

Eating
Ary's Warung 15
Bebek Bengil (Dirty Duck Diner) 6

Bars & clubs
Beggar's Bush 3
Jazz Café 3

impressive collection of ferns, palms, bamboo and other tropical trees. The garden is crisscrossed with pathways in a ravine. The garden also houses Bali's first maze, an Islamic garden and three teak *joglos* (Javanese traditional house) where simple food is served. Also **Threads of Life** ① *Jl Kajeng 24, T0361 976581, www.threadsoflife.com, Mon-Sat 1000-1800*. A member of the Fairtrade Organisation, this textile centre provides an opportunity to learn about *ikat* and batik in Indonesia. There is a two-hour introduction course detailing the textiles and differences between hand-spun and commercial threads, essential if you are to purchase a pricey piece of *ikat*. The gallery has examples of *ikat* from Bali, Flores, Sumba, Sulawesi and Timor, showing the different regional motifs and contemporary uses.

At the south end of Jalan Monkey Forest is the **Sacred Monkey Forest Sanctuary** ① *daily 0830-1800, adult 15,000Rp, child 7500Rp*, which is overrun with monkeys. An attractive walk through the forest leads to the **Pura Dalem Agung Padangtegal**, a Temple of the Dead. Back in town on Jalan Raya Ubud, opposite Jalan Monkey Forest, is the **Puri Saren**, with richly carved gateways and courtyards. West of here behind the Lotus Café is the **Pura Saraswati**, with a pretty rectangular pond in front of it. **Note** Do not enter the forest with food – these monkeys have been known to bite. You will only have 48 hours to get to Jakarta for a rabies injection

The **Ubud Writers Festival** ① *www.ubudwritersfestival.com*, held annually in October, attracts literary notables from Asia and beyond to participate in discussions on culture, society, politics and religion from a literary perspective. Workshops are held throughout the festival on travel writing, novel writing and short story writing. There are also cultural workshops held for those who wish to deepen their knowledge of all things Balinese.

Around Ubud

There are villages beyond Ubud that remain unspoilt and it is worth exploring the surrounding countryside, either on foot or by bicycle. Around Ubud, particularly to the north in the vicinity of Tampaksiring, and to the east near Pejeng and Gianyar, is perhaps the greatest concentration of temples in Bali. The most detailed and accurate guide to these pura is AJ Bernet Kempers's *Monumental Bali* (Periplus: Berkeley and Singapore, 1991). **Sangeh** and the **Pura Bukit Sari** are two temples about 25 km west of Ubud, but easier to reach via Mengwi.

Goa Gajah ① *adult 4100Rp, children 2100Rp, dress: sarong, a short ride by bemo from Ubud or from the Batubulan terminal outside Denpasar; alternatively, join a tour*. Goa Gajah, or 'Elephant Cave', lies about 4 km east of Ubud, via Peliatan, on the right-hand side of the road and just before Bedulu. The caves are hard to miss as there is a large car park, with an imposing line of stallholders catering for the numerous coach trips. The complex is on the side of a hill overlooking the Petanu River, down a flight of steps. Hewn out of the rock, the entrance to the cave has been carved to resemble the mouth of a demon and is surrounded by additional carvings of animals, plants, rocks and monsters. The name of the complex is thought to have been given by the first visitors who mistakenly thought that the demon was an elephant. The small, dimly lit, T-shaped cave is man-made and is reached by a narrow passage whose entrance is the demon's mouth. It contains 15 niches carved out of the rock. Those on the main passageway are long enough to lead archaeologists to speculate that they were sleeping chambers. At the end of one of the arms of the 'T' is a four-armed statue of Ganesh, and at the end of the other, a collection of lingams.

The **bathing pools** next to the caves are more interesting. These were discovered in the mid-1950s by the Dutch archaeologist JC Krijgsman, who excavated the area in front of the cave on information provided by local people. He found stone steps and eventually uncovered two bathing pools (probably one for men and the other for women). Stone carvings of the legs of three figures were uncovered in each of the two pools. These seemed to have been cut from the rock at the same time that the pools were dug. Water spouts from the urns, held by the nymphs, into the two pools.

Stairs lead down from the cave and pool area to some meditation niches, with two small statues of the Buddha in an attitude of meditation. The remains of an enormous relief were also found in 1931, depicting several *stupas*. To get there, walk down from the cave and bathing pools, through fields, and over a bridge. The complex is thought to date from the 11th century.

Yeh Pulu ① *3100Rp, 350 m off the main Ubud-Gianyar road just south of the Tampaksiring turning, and is signposted to Bendung Bedaulu, bemos from Ubud will drop passengers at the turning; it is an easy walk from there to the site, dress: sarong and sash (for hire at site), it is probably possible to visit this site at any time, as there are no entrance gates.* Yeh Pulu is 2 km east of Goa Gajah, beautifully set amongst terraced ricefields, and a short walk along a paved path from the end of the road. This is a peaceful place, free from crowds and hawkers. It is also the location of the local bath house. Yeh Pulu is one of the oldest holy places in Bali, dating from the 14th or 15th century. Cut into the rock are 20 m of vigorous carvings depicting village life, intermingled with Hindu and Balinese gods: figures carrying poles, men on horseback, Krishna saluting, wild animals and vegetation. Originally these would have been plastered over – and perhaps painted – although almost all of the plaster has since weathered away. A small cell cut into the rock at the south end of the reliefs is thought to have been the abode of a hermit – who probably helped to maintain the carvings. Until 1937 when the site was renovated, water from the overhanging paddy fields washed over the carvings causing significant erosion. There is also a small bathing pool here. An old lady looks after the small shrine to Ganesh and ensures a donation is placed there.

On the road north from Bedulu, Gianyar Regency contains a number of important archaeological sites, the majority located near **Pejeng**, 4 km east of Ubud. This sacred area, inhabited since the Bronze age, contains over 40 temples as well as massive stone statues, carvings, sarcophagi, Buddhist sanctuaries, bathing sites and bronze artefacts. A number of artefacts have been removed to museums as far afield as Amsterdam, but many have remained *in situ*, beside rivers, in paddy fields or in nearby temples. Pejeng was once the centre of a great kingdom which flourished between the ninth and 14th centuries, before falling to the Majapahit. These days it is home to many Brahmin families.

The small, poorly labelled, **Purbakala Archaeological Museum**, consisting largely of a collection of sarcophagi, neolithic tools and Hindu relics, is 400 m north of Bedulu. About 200 m further north still is the **Pura Kebo Edan** ① *admission by donation, dress: sarong*, 'Mad Bull Temple', a rather ramshackle and ill-kept temple. Among the monumental weathered stone figures in the courtyard is a statue of Bima dancing on a corpse, its eyes open, protected under a wooden pavilion. The figure – sometimes known as the 'Pejeng Giant' – is renowned for its 'miraculous' penis, pierced with a peg or pin (used to stimulate women during intercourse, a feature of sexual relations across the region).

Pura Pusering Jagat (the 'Navel of the World' Temple) is 50 m off the main road, a short distance north from Kebo Edan. **Pura Panataran Sasih** ① *admission by donation, dress: sarong, bemo from Ubud or from the Batubulan terminal outside Denpasar*, lies another

250 m north in Pejeng and is thought to date from the ninth or 10th century. This temple was the original navel pura of the old Pejeng Kingdom. The entrance is flanked by a pair of fine stone elephants. Walk through impressive split gates to see the '**Moon of Pejeng**' (*sasih* means 'moon'). It is housed in a raised pavilion towards the back of the compound and is supposedly the largest bronze kettledrum in the world. In Balinese folklore, the drum is supposed to have been one of the wheels of the chariot that carries the moon across the night sky. The wheel fell to earth and was kept (still glowing with an inner fire) in the temple. It is said that one night a man climbed into the tower and urinated on the drum, extinguishing its inner fire, and paid for the desecration with his life. Visitors should on no account try to climb the tower for a better look at the drum. The drum is believed to date from the third century BC, although no-one is absolutely sure – certainly, it has been housed here for centuries. It may be a Dongson drum from Vietnam or it may be a later example produced elsewhere. The fine decoration on this incomparable piece of bronze work was first recorded – in a series of brilliantly accurate drawings – by the artist WOJ Nieuwenkamp in 1906 (although it was mentioned in a book by the blind chronicler GE Rumphius, published in 1705). A collection of 11th century stone carvings are also to be found here.

Gunung Kawi ① *4100Rp, dress: sash or sarong required. To get there catch a connection at Denpasar's Batubulan terminal or from Ubud to Tampaksiring. It is about a 3-km walk from here, passing Tirta Empul (see below), although bemos also make the journey to the temple site.* Gunung Kawi, the 'Mountain of the Poets', is one of the most impressive, and unusual, temples in Bali. A steep rock stairway with high sides leads down to the bottom of a humid, tree-filled, ravine. At the bottom lies the temple. The whole complex was literally hewn out of the rock during the 11th century, when it was thought to have been created as the burial temple for King Anak Wungsu and his wives, who probably threw themselves on his funeral pyre. You descend 315 steps to a massive rock archway, and from there to the nine tombs which face each other on either side of the Pakerisan River. These two rows of *candis*, four on the south side and five on the north, were cut out of the rock. It is believed that the five on the north bank of the river were for the King and his four wives, while the four on the south bank may have been for four concubines. They resemble temples and are the earliest traces of a style of architecture that became popular in Java in the following centuries. As such they may represent the precursor to the Balinese *meru*.

East of the five *candis*, on the far side of the river, is a cloister of various courtyards and rooms, also carved out of the rock. They were created for the Buddhist priests who lived here (visitors are asked to remove their shoes before entering). Still farther away, on the other side of the river, is the so-called 'tenth tomb'. The local people call this tomb 'the priest's house'. The tenth tomb is, in all likelihood, a monastery and consists of a courtyard encircled by niches. To get to the tenth tomb take the path across the paddy fields, that runs from the rock-hewn gateway that leads down into the gorge; it is about a 1 km walk. There is accommodation close by in Tampaksiring, which also has a number of good jewellery workshops.

Tirta Empul ① *2 km north of Tampaksiring, 1 km on from Mount Kawi, 4100Rp. To get there take a bemo from Denpasar's Batubulan terminal or Ubud towards Tampaksiring. The temple is 2 km north of the town centre; either walk or catch a bemo. From here it is a 1 km walk to Gunung Kawi (see above).* The temple is one of the holiest sights on Bali and is a popular pilgrimage stop, evident by the maze of trinket stalls. Tirta Empul is built on the site of a holy spring, which is said to have magical healing powers. In the past, *barong* masks were bathed here to infuse them with supernatural powers during the dance.

Originally constructed in AD 960, during the reign of Raja Candra Bayasingha, the temple is divided into three courtyards and has been extensively restored with little of the original structure remaining – just a few stone fragments. The outer courtyard contains two long pools fed by around 30 water spouts, each of which has a particular function – for example, there is one for spiritual purification. The holy springs bubble up in the inner courtyard. During the **Galungan** festival, sacred *barong* dance masks are brought here to be bathed in holy water.

◉ Ubud and around listings

For Sleeping and Eating price codes, see inside the front cover.

◉ Sleeping

Ubud *p298, map p299*
Ubud has a great choice of good value, clean and mostly high-quality accommodation, in often romantic and well-designed bungalows. Except in the more expensive hotels, breakfast is included in the rates. Cheaper accommodation often involves staying in a Balinese family compound. Discounts of up to 30% available at expensive places in the low season. Book ahead in peak seasons.
L Barong, Jl Monkey Forest, T0361 971758, www.barong-resort.com. A thatched reception filled with local antiques leads into a shady garden hosting 11 rooms. Tastefully decorated, in modern Balinese style, rooms have bathroom with sunken bath. Deluxe rooms with private pool. Spa and 2 pools. Discounts available.
A Pertiwi Resort and Spa, Jl Monkey Forest, T0361 975236, F0361 975559, pertiwi@ indosat.net.id. 50 rooms in 2-storey thatched cottages, popular with Asian tourists. Rooms have modern decor, although with decrepit doors. Bathrooms have baths. 2 restaurants, spa facility and pool. Some discounts available.
A Samhita Garden, Jl Bisma, T0361 975443, 0361 289348, santikg@indosat.net.id. Very clean a/c rooms facing attractive pool and well tended garden. Spacious bathrooms.
C-D Villa Rasa Sayang, Jl Monkey Forest. T0361 975491, vrs@telkom.net. Set in neat, trim gardens with pool, the 8 high-ceilinged rooms here are spacious with big windows. Some rooms with bath, fridge.

C Pradha, Jl Kajeng 1, T0361 975122, F0361 974291, www.pradhaubud.com. A/c rooms with bath set around a pool. Rooms a little musty, tired looking.
D-E Sagitarius Inn, spacious open gardens with an abundance of water features, simple cottages with clean rooms and veranda. Pool.
D-E Sania's House, Jl Karna 7, T0361 975535, sania_house@yahoo.com. Clean Balinese cottages on a quiet street. A/c and fan rooms with comfy bed and clean bathroom. Popular.
E Ubud Terrace Bungalows, Jl Monkey Forest, T0361 975690, ubud_terrace@ yahoo.com. Situated in a quiet, verdant grove, a/c and fan rooms with attractive decor including Balinese-style 4-poster bed. Hot water, upstairs rooms have good sunset views. Pool. Recommended.
F Esty's House, Jl Dewi Sita, T0361 980571. 6 excellent rooms with fan in quiet area, large and clean bathrooms. Recommended.
F Gandra House, Jl Karna 8, T0361 976529. Good value, simple clean fan rooms in friendly family compound with hot water and veranda.
F Loka House, Jl Monkey Forest, T0361 973326. Just behind the football pitch, this place has simple and fairly clean rooms on the 2nd floor of a family compound overlooking a field of cows. Good place for getting local vibes while being close to the action.
F Raka House, Jl Dewi Sita. Rooms in brand new 2-storey block are clean and functional. Friendly owner.
F Roja's, Jl Kajeng 1. Fairly clean fan rooms in attractive bungalows, well kept garden.
F Warsa's, Jl Monkey Forest, T0361 971548, www.baliya.com/warsabungalow. Good location slap bang in the heart of the action

on Jl Monkey Forest, a/c and fan rooms here are very simple and cleanish. Bathrooms feature hot water, shower and *mandi*.

G Brahmandiya, Jl Karna 11 (no phone). Very simple fan rooms with friendly owner who has limited English. Dirt cheap.

G Gemini Guesthouse, Jl Bisma Ubud, T0361 978280. Great value for these popular bungalows set in a quiet family compound. Fan rooms with hot water. Friendly owners.

West of Ubud Centre

The hotels to the west of Ubud offer breathtaking views and are often set among the rice paddies. However, they are a fair walk into town. Hotels are generally of high standard, and this is reflected in the prices.

LL Anhera Jl Raya Sanggingan 168, T0361 977843, www.anherahotelbali.com. 8 rooms each designed to reflect one of the major Indonesian islands, some more tasteful than others. Spacious and comfortable rooms, with CD player and mini bar. Obscenely large bathrooms feature a jacuzzi with beautiful views of the rice terraces. 2 pools. Restaurant and spa facilities. Big discounts available.

AL-A Tjampuhan, Jl Raya Campuhan, T0361 975368, www.tjampuhan-bali.com. Built in 1928 for the guests of the Royal Prince of Ubud, this charming hotel offers 67 well-decorated Balinese-style a/c and fan bungalows set on the side of a lush valley. The pool here is filled with spring water.

A Aniniraka, Jl Raya Sanggingan, T0361 975213, www.aniniraka.com. 11 rooms surrounded by bright green rice paddies. Each of the large rooms has a kitchenette, dining area, spacious sleeping area and bathroom with sunken bath. Other facilities include a sauna and pool. 20% discounts available.

A-B Ananda, Jl Raya Sanggingan, T0361 975376, www.anandaubud.com. Service is a bit slow, as the staff seem more interested in watching wrestling on the TV than serving clients. The huge grounds offer scope for privacy, but views are concealed by the abundant greenery. A/c and fan rooms in

2-storey thatched cottages are spacious, with high ceiling and private balcony.

E Taman Indrakila, Jl Raya Sanggingan, T0361 975017, www.bali_paradise/taman indrakila. The view across the Sungai Cerik valley is amazing, and is the main reason to stay here. 10 bungalows with Balinese-style 4-poster bed and balcony. Worn furniture, but reasonable value given the location.

East of Ubud Centre

The streets lying to the east of the village centre are leafy and quiet, and are lined with Balinese family compounds. Jl Tebesaya and Jl Jembawan have a lot of good-value guesthouse accommodation.

E Family Guest House, Jl Tebesaya 39, T0361 974054, family house@telkom.net. Spacious, well-decorated fan rooms with huge private balcony overlooking forest, good value. Bath. Breakfast includes home-made brown bread.

E Sanjiwani, Jl Tebesaya 41, T0361 973205, www.sanjiwani.com. Clean fan rooms with hot water in a friendly and peaceful family compound. Residents can use the kitchen.

❶ Eating

Ubud *p298, map p299*
Food in Ubud is good, particularly international food. Most restaurants serve a mixture of Balinese, Indonesian and international dishes.

♈♈♈ Ary's Warung, Jl Ubud Raya, T0361 975053, open 0900-2400. Classy eatery serving up Asian and fusion cuisine and cocktails in a modern lounge-style setting. The *sake* and soya grilled salmon is delicious.

♈♈ Bebek Bengil (Dirty Duck Diner), Jl Hanoman, T0361 975489, bebekbengil@ indo.net.id, open 0900-2200. This is the place to come for delicious Balinese duck dishes in a lovely setting that stretches out to the rice paddies behind. Popular.

♈♈ Casa Luna, Jl Raya Ubud, T0361 977409, www.casalunabali.com, open 0800-2300. Brunch here is scrumptious with a wide choice of Western favourites. The eggs

Benedict is superb. Throughout the day the kitchen produces excellent fare in a breezy setting with a nice view.

†† Dragonfly, Jl Dewi Sita, T0361 972973, dragonflyubud@yahoo.com, open 0800-2300. Innovative menu that features weekly specials and delicious dishes such as grilled gindara fish and a range of salads and Balinese dishes including *bebek betutu* (stuffed aromatic duck). Good selection of detox juices, lassis and Indonesian *jamu*. Live music most evenings. Recommended.

†† Murni's Warung, Jl Raya Campuhan, T0361 975233, www.murnis.com, open 0900-2200. Long menu of Western and Indonesian dishes. The Balinese food is worth trying, particularly the *tutu ayam* (chicken slow cooked in local spices for 8 hrs).

†† Nomad, Jl Ubud Raya 35, T0361 977169, nomad_crew@telkom.net, open 0900-2200. Super popular for its fantastic selection of fresh pasta dishes, soups, juices and salads. Good range of teas from around the world. Nice upbeat atmosphere.

†† Three Monkeys, Jl Monkey Forest, T0361 974830, open 0700-2300. Popular place with a great menu of fresh pastas, salads and some scrumptious desserts such as strawberry and mint salad with dark orange caramel praline sauce. Also Javanese chocolate bars on sale. The rice field out the back makes for a mellow place to pass the time.

†† Waroeng, Jl Monkey Forest, T0361 970928, open 0800-2300. Noodle bar with a variety of Asian noodle dishes including wonton, laksa and Indonesia's very own *soto ayam*. Slurp accompanied by a laid-back jazz and world soundtrack. Happy hour on cocktails 1700-1900. Free transport to Jazz Cafe.

†† Warung Bamboo and Bar, Jl Dewi Sita, T0361 975307, open 0900-2400. Offers a range of cheap international and Indonesian dishes, becomes a popular drinking hole in the evenings.

† Deli Cat, Jl Monkey Forest, by the football pitch, T0361 971284, open 0900-2400. Very good value, sells tasty sausages, cheese from around the world, chunky sandwiches, and

fish and meat main courses. The owner, from Iceland, has set the place up to be sociable, so expect interesting conversation while you get stuck into your bratwurst.

† Pizza Bagus, Jl Pengosekan, T0361 978520, www.pizzabagus.com, open 0830-2230. Popular Italian place serving the best pizza in Ubud, along with fine pasta and salads. They will deliver for any order over 20,000Rp. There is a deli attached that makes sandwiches and sells cheeses, hams and German chocolate biscuits. The weekly organic farmers market is held here on Sat 0930-1400. Recommended.

† Warung Nasi Goreng, Jl Hanoman, T0361 97716, open 0900-2200. Cosy place offering decent Indian and Thai food as well as brilliant dense home-made apple pie. Has good daily specials such as fish curry with naan and dhal for 35,000Rp. Recommended.

Cafes and bakeries

† Juice Ja Cafe, Jl Dewi Sita, T0361 971056, open 0730-2200. Laid-back organic café serving good range of fruit juices, salads and tasty bagels with delightful toppings such as kalamata olive cream cheese. The health cocktails here are very popular. There is also a noticeboard detailing interesting local events.

† Kakiang Bakery and Cafe, Jl Pengosekan, T0361 971551, open 0700-2100. Excellent and good-value set lunches include sandwich, soup, salad, fruit juice and 3 small slices of cake. Just enough to warrant an afternoon nap afterwards.

† Tropical Boutique Bakery, Jl Dewi Sita, T0361 7458667, www.tropical-bale.com, open 0800-2200. This East Timorese-owned café has a good selection of coffees accompanied by gourmet sandwiches, home-made cakes and biscuits and freshly baked bread.

◑ Bars and clubs

Ubud *p298, map p299*
Ubud isn't exactly a centre of hedonism and most places shut around 0100. However, there are a few spots for an evening drink.

Beggar's Bush, near Hotel Tjampuhan, west of town on Jl Raya Campuhan, T0361 975009. English pub (some food). Popular with the local expat community.

Jazz Café, Jl Sukma, T0361 976594, www.jazzcafebali.com, open daily except Mon until 0100. Atmospheric surroundings make this a relaxed place for a drink or meal (cheap), with enticing menu and good live music. 15% off food 1800-2000.

✪ Entertainment

Ubud *p298, map p299*

Artists' colonies Ubud has perhaps the greatest concentration of artists in Indonesia, exceeding even Yogya. Many will allow visitors to watch them at work in the hope that they will then buy their work. The **Pengosekan Community of Artists** is on Jl Bima.

Dance and cultural performances
Ubud has the most accessible cultural performances in Bali, with events every night at various locations scattered around town, and in villages around Ubud. Transport is usually included in the cost of the ticket if the venue is outside Ubud. Performances start around 1930 and last for 2 hrs, but this varies so check beforehand. Tickets cost between US$5.50 and US$16.50 and are available from Ubud Tourist Information on Jl Ubud Raya, or at the venue. Go to the tourist office to check performance and venue. Recommended dances are the *legong* dance, the *barong* dance and the *kecak* dance. The Puri Saren on Jl Raya Ubud is a convenient and charming venue.

Film screenings
Rendezvous Doux, Jl Raya Ubud (opposite the arts market), open 0900-2400. Nightly screenings of Bali-related documentaries.

◎ Shopping

Ubud *p298, map p299*
Art Ubud painters have a distinctive style, using bright colours and the depiction of natural and village scenes. There is a large selection of paintings in the town and galleries are concentrated along the east section of Jl Raya Ubud. It is possible to visit the artists in their homes; enquire at the galleries.
Macan Tidur, Jl Monkey Forest T0361 977121, info@macantidur.com. Has an excellent selection of stylishly presented ethnographica.
Nikini Art, Jl Monkey Forest, T0361 973354, open 0800-2200. Has a fascinating range of *ikat*, carvings and silver from Timor. **Tegun Folk Art Galeri**, Jl Hanoman 44, T0361 970581, www.tegun. com, daily 0800-2100. The overwhelming collection of eye-catching art and crafts from across the archipelago is well worth a browse. The owner is very friendly and has excellent English.
Books Adi Book Shop, Jl Hanoman, T0361 970920, open 1000-1900. Fair selection of used tomes available in various European languages. **Periplus**, Jl Monkey Forest, 0900-2200. Postcards, newspapers and a good selection of Indonesia-related books.
Textiles Kuno Kuno Textile Gallery, Jl Monkey Forest, T0361 973239, open 1000-1900. Has decent quality *ikat* and batik.
Woodcarving Concentrated on the Peliatan road out of town. The so-called 'duck man' of Ubud (Ngurah Umum) is to be found on the road to Goa Gajah, with a selection of wooden fruits and birds. Recommended shop near the **Bamboo restaurant**, off Jl Monkey Forest, facing the football field.

▲ Activities and tours

Ubud *p298, map p299*
Ubud has turned into something of an 'alternative' centre, and there is plenty to do here. Many people come to learn something, while others enjoy pottering about the countryside on 2 wheels.

Body and soul

Sedona Spa, Jl Raya Campuhan, T0361 975770, open 1000-2100. Treatments include Balinese *boreh* and Javanese *lulur* in friendly setting. Packages with massage, facial, hair treatment start at US$28. Includes hotel pick up.
The Yoga Barn, Jl Pengoseken, T0361 970992, balispirit.com. Classes start at US$10. This well-regarded centre offers an assortment of yoga, meditation and tai chi classes daily, in a relaxed and green setting.

Food activities

Casa Luna Cooking School, Jl Bisma, T0361 973282, www.casalunabali.com. Run by the owner of **Casa Luna** restaurant Janet de Neefe, this school offers the chance to explore the spices and kitchen myths of Bali. Each lesson concludes with a Balinese meal and notes. Different menu each day. Each lesson around 4 hrs. US$27 per person. Recommended.
Ibu Wayan, T0361 975447. Ibu Wayan and her daughter Wayan Metri provide Balinese cooking classes for groups and have a list of the food to be learned each day. The 2-hr lessons are followed by lunch or dinner. Morning or afternoon lessons US$38 per person. Phone ahead to reserve. Small groups.
Nomad's Organic Farm. Owner Nyoman throws open the gates of his organic farm in the village on Baturiti on Sun and Wed for an explanation of the different methods of organic farming and a lunch of salad made from vegetables chosen by the visitors.

Birdwatching

The Bali Bird Club sets off on walks around the Ubud countryside, on trails that differ according to the season. Birds that can be spotted include the Java Kingfisher, Bar-winged Prinia, the Black-Winged Starling and other birds endemic to Indonesia. The 3½-hr walks leave from the Beggar's Bush Pub at 0900 on Tue, Fri, Sat and Sun. The price of US$33 includes lunch and water along the trail.

Bike tours

Bike Baik, T0361 978052, www.balibike.com. Tours start with breakfast overlooking Gunung Batur and then cruise downhill to Ubud for 2½ hrs . Includes a walk around a coffee plantation, visit to a temple and lunch in a family compound. US$38 per person, including hotel pick up and drop.

Tour operators

Perama, Jl Hanoman, T0361 973316.
HIS Tourist Information, Jl Monkey Forest, T0361 972621, www.his-balifreak.com. Reliable agency for air tickets, both international and domestic. They also have a list of hotels.

Watersports

Bali Action Adventure, T0361 270744, www.baliraft.com. This Denpasar-based outfit has trips down the Telaga Waja with professionally trained guides. Adult US$65, child US$40. Also offers treks through the night to the summit of Gunung Agung for sunrise. US$95 per person.

⊖ Transport

Ubud *p298, map p299*

Bemos Leave from the Pasar Ubud in the centre of town, at the junction of Jl Monkey Forest and Jl Raya Ubud; regular connections with **Denpasar's** Batubulan terminal (Brown – 7000Rp), Gianyar (Green –7000Rp). 5 daily departures to **Kuta**/airport US$5.50, 5 departures to **Sanur** US$4, 1 daily to **Lovina** US$14, 3 departures to **Padangbai** US$5.50 and 1 daily further afield to **Mataram** from US$11 and the **Gili Islands** US$38. A ride to the airport in a taxi costs around US$14.
Bicycle hire Bicycles are the best way to get about (apart from walking); there are several hire places on Jl Monkey Forest, US$2 per day.
Car hire Hire shops on Jl Monkey Forest, US$11 per day plus insurance for Suzuki 'jeep'; US$15 per day for larger Toyota Kijang.
Motorbike hire Several outfits on Jl Monkey Forest, from US$5.50 per day.

Gianyar to Gunung Batur via Bangli

East of Ubud is the royal town of Gianyar; 15 km north of Gianyar, at the foot of Gunung Batur, is another former royal capital, Bangli, with its impressive Kehen Temple. A further 20 km leads up the slopes of Gunung Batur to the crater's edge – one of the most popular excursions in Bali. Along the rim of the caldera are the mountain towns of Penelokan and Kintamani, and the important temples of Batur and Tegen Koripan. From Penelokan, a road winds down into the caldera and along the west edge of Danau Batur. It is possible to trek from here up the active cone of Gunung Batur (1710 m), which thrusts up through a barren landscape of lava flows. North from Penulisan, the road twists and turns for 36 km down the north slopes of the volcano, reaching the narrow coastal strip at the town of Kubutambahan. ►► *For listings, see pages 313-314.*

Gianyar ⊕▲⊖ ►► *pp313-314. Colour map 11, B1.*

→ *Phone code: 0361.*

Gianyar is the former capital of the kingdom of Gianyar and in the centre, on Jalan Ngurah Rai, is the **Agung Gianyar Palace**, surrounded by attractive red brick walls. At the turn of the century, the Regency of Gianyar formed an alliance with the Dutch in order to protect itself from its warring neighbours. As a result, the royal palace was spared the ravages and destruction, culminating in *puputan*, that befell other royal palaces in south Bali during the Dutch invasion. The rulers of Gianyar were allowed a far greater degree of autonomy than other rajas; this allowed them to consolidate their wealth and importance, resulting in the regency's current prosperity and the preservation of the royal palace. It is not normally open to the public, but the owner, Ide Anak Agung Gede Agung, a former politician and the rajah of Gianyar, does let visitors look around his house if you ask him. The bemo station is five minutes' walk to the west of the palace, also on Jalan Ngurah Rai.

Traditionally regarded as Bali's weaving centre, there is only a limited amount of cloth on sale these days. There is accommodation at **Agung Gianyar Palace Guesthouse (B)**, within the palace walls.

Bangli ⊖⊘⊖ ►► *pp313-314. Colour map 11, B1.*

→ *Phone code: 0366.*

Bangli, the former capital of a mountain principality, is a peaceful, rather beautiful town, well maintained and spread out. Set in a rich farming area in the hills, there is much to enjoy about the surrounding scenery, especially the captivating views of the volcanic area to the north including Gunung Agung and Gunung Batur. Both the town itself and the countryside around afford many opportunities for pleasant walks. The area claims to have the best climate on Bali and the air is cooler than on the coast. Despite these attractions, Bangli is not on the main tourist routes and is all the more charming for that. There is a tourist office, however, **Bangli Government Tourism Office** ① *Jl Brigjen Ngurah Rai 24, T0366 91537, Mon-Sat 0700-1400.* Very friendly and helpful, but little English is spoken and they are not really geared up for foreigners. Free booklet and map.

Background

Balinese believe that Bangli is the haunt of *leyaks*, witches who practice black magic. In Bali, misfortune or illness is frequently attributed to *leyaks*, who often intervene on behalf of an enemy. In order to overcome this the Balinese visit a *balian*, a shaman or healer, who often has knowledge of the occult. As a result of the presence of leyak in the area, Bangli has a reputation for the quality of its *balian*, with supplicants arriving from all over the island, dressed in their ceremonial dress and bearing elaborate offerings. The people of Bangli are also the butt of jokes throughout Bali, as Bangli is the site of the island's only mental hospital, built by the Dutch.

Sights

There is a **market** every three days in the centre of town. Locally grown crops include cloves, coffee, tobacco, vanilla, citrus fruit, rice, cabbages, corn and sweet potatoes; some of which are exported. Bangli lies close to the dividing line between wet-rice and dry-rice cultivation.

Most people come to Bangli to visit the **Pura Kehen** ① *1000Rp per person plus 1000Rp for a car, on the back road to Besakih and Penelokan, outside there are stalls selling snacks and sarongs*, one of Bali's more impressive temples and one of the most beautiful, set on a wooded hillside about 2 km to the north of the town centre. The Pura was probably founded in the 13th century. There is some dispute over the true origin of the temple, because inscriptions within the compound have been dated to the ninth century. It is the second largest on Bali and the state temple of Bangli regency. Elephants flank the imposing entrance, leading up to three terraced courtyards, through finely carved and ornamented gateways decorated with myriad demons. The lower courtyard is dominated by a wonderful 400-year-old *waringin* tree (*Ficus benjamina*), with a monk's cell built high up in the branches. It is here that performances are held to honour the gods. The middle courtyard houses the offertory shrines, while the top courtyard contains an 11-tiered *meru* with a carved wood and stone base. The elaborate woodwork here is being beautifully restored and repainted by craftsmen. In the wall below, guides will point out the old Chinese plates cemented into it. Curiously, some of these depict rural England, with a watermill and mail coach drawn by four horses. Every three years in November (Rabu Kliwon Shinta in the Balinese calendar), at the time of the full moon (purnama), a major ceremony, Ngusabha, is held at the temple.

The **Sasana Budaya Arts Centre** stages performances of traditional and modern drama, music and dance, as well as art and cultural exhibitions. It is one of the largest cultural centres on Bali, located about 100 m from the Pura Kehen. Ask at the tourist office for information on performances. Bangli is particularly noted for its dance performances. Bangli also has one of the largest *gamelan* orchestras on Bali, captured from the ruler of Semarapura by the Dutch, who gave it to Bangli.

In the centre of town is the **royal palace**, which houses eight branches of the former royal family. Built about 150 years ago and largely restored by the present descendants, the most important section is the Puri Denpasar where the last ruler of Bangli lived until his death almost 40 years ago. The temple of the royal ancestors is situated on the northwest side, diagonally opposite the *Artha Sastra Inn*; important ceremonies are still held here.

There is an impressive **Bale Kulkul** in the centre of town, three storeys high and supported on columns made of coconut palm wood; it is about 100 years old. There are in fact two *kulkuls*, *kulkul lanang* which is male, and *kulkul wadon* which is female. In times past the *kulkul* was sounded to summon the people, or act as an alarm warning of impending danger. The people of Bangli consider these *kulkul* to be sacred, and they are used during important temple festivals.

At the other end of town, the **Pura Dalem Penjungekan** (temple of the dead) is also worth a visit. The stone reliefs vividly depict the fate of sinners as they suffer in hell; hanging suspended with flames licking at their feet, being castrated, at the mercy of knife-wielding demons, being impaled or having their heads split open. The carvings are based on the story of Bima on his journey to rescue the souls of his parents from hell. The destructive 'Rangda' features extensively. In the centre there is a new shrine depicting tales of Siwa, Durga and Ganesh. The temple is in a parkland setting with possibilities for walks.

Around Bangli

There are a number of pleasant places to visit, including **Bukit Demulih** ① *walk or take a bemo bound for Tampaksiring, get off after about 3 km, take the narrow, paved road south for 1 km to Demulih village*, at an altitude of about 300 m. The small, pretty village has some well-carved temples, and a *kulkul* tower by the *bale banjar*. From here the villagers will show you the track up the hill, at the top of which is a small temple; on the way you pass a sacred waterfall. If you walk along the ridge you will come to other temples and fine views over the whole of south Bali.

A pleasant walk east of Bangli leads to **Sibembunut**, and **Bukit Jati**, near Guliang about 2 km south of Bunutin, is another hill to climb for splendid views and scenic walks.

Sidan, just north of the main Gianyar to Semarapura road, 10 km south of Bangli, is notable for its **Pura Dalem** ① *1100Rp, car park opposite the temple, and a stage where dance performances sometimes take place*, which has some of the most vivid, spine-chilling depictions of the torture and punishment that awaits wrong-doers in hell. The carvings show people having their heads squashed, boiled or merely chopped off, and the wicked and evil widow Rangda dismembering and squashing babies.

Gunung Batur ○○ ►► *pp313-314. Colour map 11, B1.*

The spectacular landscape of Gunung Batur is one of the most visited inland areas on Bali. Despite the hawkers, bustle and general commercialization, it still makes a worthwhile trip. The huge crater – 20 km in diameter – contains within it Danau Batur and the active Gunung Batur (1710 m), with buckled lava flows on its slopes. The view at dawn from the summit is stunning. Although these days Gunung Batur is less destructive than Gunung Agung, it is the most active volcano on Bali having erupted 20 times during the past 200 years. **Danau Batur** in the centre of the caldera is considered sacred.

Trekking

A steep road winds down the crater side, and then through the lava boulders and along the west shore of Danau Batur. There are hot springs here and paths up the sides of Gunung Batur, through the area's extraordinary landscape. Treks begin either from **Purajati** or **Toya Bungkah** (there are four-, five- or six-hour treks), or around the lake (guides are available from the **Lake View Cottages** in Toya Bungkah). Aim to leave Toya Bungkah at about 0330. After reaching the summit it is possible to hike westwards along the caldera rim, though this hike is not for the faint-hearted as the ridge is extremely narrow in places with steep drops on both sides. The cinder track passes several of the currently most active craters, lava flows and fumaroles. In the north and east of the caldera the landscape is quite different. The rich volcanic soil, undisturbed by recent lava flows, supports productive agriculture. The vulcanology institute on the rim of the caldera monitors daily seismic activity.

The Bali Aga: the original Balinese

In pre-history, Bali was populated by animists whose descendants today are represented by the Bali Aga, 'Original Balinese'. The Aga are now restricted to a few relic communities in North and East Bali, particularly in the regency of Karangkasem. Most have been extensively assimilated into the Hindu-Balinese mainstream. Miguel Covarrubias visited the Aga village of Tenganan in the 1930s, a village which even then was extraordinary in the extent to which it was resisting the pressures of change. He wrote:

"The people of Tenganan are tall, slender and aristocratic in a rather ghostly, decadent way, with light skins and refined manners ... They are proud and look down even on the Hindu-Balinese nobility, who respect them and leave them alone. They live in a strange communistic ... system in which individual ownership of property is not recognized and in which even the plans and measurements of the houses are set and alike for everybody."

Even today, a distinction is still made between the Bali Aga and the Wong Majapahit. The latter arrived from Java following the fall of the Majapahit Kingdom at the end of the 15th century.

In former years, the Aga were probably cannibalistic. It has been said that Aga corpses used to be washed with water, which was allowed to drip onto a bundle of unhusked rice. This was then dried and threshed, cooked, moulded into the shape of a human being, and served to the relatives of the deceased. The eating of the rice figure is said to symbolize the ritual eating of the corpse, so imbibing its powers.

Trunyan

Boats can be hired from the village of **Kedisan** on the south shore of Danau Batur – be prepared for the unpleasant, hard-line sales people here – or from Toya Bungkah, to visit the traditional **Bali Aga** village (see box, above) of Trunyan and its cemetery close by at **Kuban**, on the east side of the lake.

The Bali Aga are the original inhabitants of Bali, pre-dating the arrival of the Majapahit; records show that the area has been inhabited since at least the eighth century. Trunyan's customs are different from Tenganan – but these differences can only be noted during festival time, which tend to be rather closed affairs. Despite its beautiful setting beside Danau Batur with Mount Abang rising dramatically in the background, a visit can be disappointing. Most people come to visit the cemetery to view the traditional way of disposing of corpses. Like the Parsees of India, corpses are left out to rot and be eaten by birds rather than being buried or cremated. It is claimed that the smell of rotting corpses is dissipated by the fragrance of the sacred banyan tree. The idea behind this custom is that the souls of the dead are carried up towards heaven by the birds; this flight to heaven propitiates the gods and results in improved prospects for the souls in their reincarnation in the next life. The corpses are laid out on enclosed bamboo rafts, but very likely all you will see is bones and skulls. The cemetery is only accessible by boat; make sure you pay at the end of your journey, otherwise the boatman may demand extra money for the return journey. The villagers are unfriendly and among the most aggressive on Bali; with a long tradition of begging for rice from other parts of the island as they were unable to grow their own, they now beg or demand money from tourists. **Note** Numerous visitors have written to us saying how unfriendly the villages of this area are. They report a distinct lack of hospitality, an oppressive and unpleasant air – even palpable hostility.

Penelokan and Kintamani

On the west rim of the crater are two villages, Penelokan and Kintamani. Large-scale restaurants here cater for the tour group hordes. The area is also overrun with hawkers selling batik and woodcarvings – some so vociferously as to scare the most hardened visitor. Penelokan is perched on the edge of the crater and its name means 'place to look'. About 5 km north of here, following the crater rim, is the rather drab town of Kintamani, which is a centre of orange and passionfruit cultivation. The town's superb position overlooking the crater makes up for its drabness. Ask locally for advice on the best walks in the area and for a guide for the more dangerous routes up to the crater rim.

Pura Batur

Just south of Kintamani is Pura Batur, spectacularly positioned on the side of the crater. This is the new temple built as a replacement for the original Pura Batur, which was engulfed by lava in 1926. Although the temple is new and therefore not of great historical significance, it is in fact the second most important temple in Bali after Pura Besakih. As Stephen Lansing explains in his book *Priests and Programmers* (1991), the Goddess of the Crater Lake is honoured here and symbolically the temple controls water for all the island's irrigation systems. Ultimately, therefore, it controls the livelihoods of the majority of the population. A nine-tiered meru honours the Goddess and unlike other temples it is open 24 hours a day. A virgin priestess still selects 24 boys as priests, who remain tied as servants of the temple for the rest of their lives.

Pura Tegeh Koripan
① *Daily, 5000Rp, catch a bemo running north and get off at Penulisan.*
Pura Tegeh Koripan is the last place on the crater rim, on the main road 200 m north of Penulisan. Steep stairs (333 in all) lead up to the temple, which stands at a height of over 1700 m above sea level next to a broadcasting mast. The temple contains a number of weathered statues, thought to be portraits of royalty. They are dated between 1011 and 1335. Artistically they are surprising because they seem to anticipate later Majapahit works. The whole place is run down at the moment, though there are some signs that repairs are being attempted.

Alternative routes from Ubud to Gunung Batur

If you have your own transport and are starting from Ubud, you can turn left at the end of Ubud's main street and take the back road heading north. This leads through an almost continuous ribbon of craft villages, mainly specializing in woodcarving, with pieces ranging in size from chains of monkeys to full size doors and 2 m high *Garudas*. There are good bargains to be found in this area off the main tourist track. Follow the road through **Petulu**, **Sapat** and **Tegalalong**, and continue northwards.

The road, its surface not too good in places, climbs steadily through rice paddies and then more open countryside where cows and goats graze, before eventually arriving at the crater rim – 500 m west of Penelokan.

The area around Gunung Batur is considered very sacred and comprises numerous temples, small pretty villages and countryside consisting of rice fields littered with volcanic debris. There are several rugged backroutes from Ubud through this region. One of the most interesting villages is **Sebatu**, northeast of Ubud near Pura Mount Kawi, reached via a small road leading east from the northern end of **Pujung Kelod**. This village has a number of temples and is renowned for the refined quality of its dance troupe, its gamelan orchestra and its wood carving. The dance troupe has revived several unusual traditional dances including the *telek* dance and makes regular appearances overseas. **Pura Gunung Kawi** is a water temple with well-maintained shrines and pavilions, a pool fed by an underground spring and open air public bathing.

From Gunung Batur to the north coast

From Penulisan, the main road runs down to the north coast, which it joins at **Kubutambahan**. It is a long descent as the road twists down the steep hillsides, and there are many hairpin bends.

If exploring the northeast coast, a very pleasant alternative is to take the minor road that turns directly north, just short of a small village called **Dusa**. The turning is not well signed – ask to make sure you are on the right road.

This is a steep descent but the road is well made and quiet. The road follows ridges down from the crater of Gunung Batur, with steep drops into ravines on either side. The route passes through clove plantations and small friendly villages, with stupendous views to the north over the sea. Behind, the tree-covered slopes lead back up to the crater.

The road eventually joins the coast road near Tegakula. Turn left, northwest, for Singaraja and Lovina, and right, southeast, for the road to Amlapura.

⊚ Gianyar to Gunung Batur via Bangli listings

For Sleeping and Eating price codes, see inside the front cover.

⊜ Sleeping

Bangli *p308*

F Artha Sastra Inn, Jl Merdeka 5, T0366 91179. 14 rooms. Located in the inner court of the royal palace with plenty of atmosphere, although don't expect anything too grand. This is the place to stay in Bangli. The more expensive rooms are very clean, simple, with private bathroom and Western toilet; cheaper rooms have shared *mandis* with squat toilets. Restaurant (♥). Recommended.

F Catur Aduyana Homestay, Jl Lettu Lila 2, T0366 91244. Clean and pleasant homestay located 1 km to the south of the town centre. 7 rooms: 3 with private *mandi*, squat toilet, 4 with shared *mandi*, squat toilet. Breakfast of tea/coffee and bread included. Friendly owner speaks no English.

G Losmen Dharma Putra a good, friendly, family-run *losmen*, price includes breakfast.

Gunung Batur *p310*
Toya Bungkah
D The Art Centre (or *Balai Seni*), Toya Bungkah. Quite old but still good.
G Under the Volcano, T08133860081. Clean rooms, friendly management, good restaurant.

Penelokan *p312*
B-D Lake View Homestay, basic but good views over the lake.
C-D Gunawan Losmen, clean, private bathroom, fantastic position.

Kintamani *p312*
C Puri Astina, large clean rooms.
Losmen Sasaka, stunning views over the crater and lake.
E Hotel Surya, T0366 51139. In a great position, new, comfortable rooms.

🍴 Eating

Bangli *p308*

There are *warungs* beside the bemo station in the centre of town, and a good night market opposite the **Artha Sastra Inn**, with the usual staple Indonesian/Balinese stall food including noodles, rice, *nasi campur, sate* etc. Near the **Catur Aduyana homestay**, opposite **Yunika**, is a clean Rumah Makan. Foodstalls near the Pura Kehan sell simple snacks.

🎭 Entertainment

Gianyar *p308*

At 1900 every Mon and Thu, a cultural show including dinner is staged at the **Agung Gianyar Palace**, T0361 93943/51654.

⛰ Activities and tours

Perama have a guided trek starting at 0300 from Pura Jati, on the edge of Danau Batur and reaching the peak in time for sunrise. US$65.50 per person, including transfers to Kuta, Ubud and Sanur. Or, you can arrange your own trek from Toya Bungka, using a local guide. It should cost around US$25 for a 4-5 hr trek to the summit and back. Bargain hard. The guides will find you, and ensure you don't climb alone. This can be annoying, and makes the prospect of the hassle-free Perama package look enticing.

Gianyar *p308*

Mountain biking Down into the volcano on the 'Batur Trail', organized by **Sobek Expeditions**, T0361 287059, www.bali sobek.com. Adult US$68, child US$45 including lunch. Pick-up from all the resorts.

🚌 Transport

Gianyar *p308*

Bemo 27 km from Denpasar. Regular connections with **Denpasar**'s Batubulan terminal.

Bus To **Semmarapura** (25 mins), **Padangbai** (50 mins) and **Candi Dasi** (1 hr 10 mins).

Bangli *p308*

Bemo Many (but not all) bemos are 'colour coded'. There are a plentiful supply of bemos running throughout the day, and most places are accessible by bemo if you are prepared to wait and do some walking. There are regular services between: **Denpasar**'s Batubulan terminal, many connect through to **Singaraja**; the market in **Gianyar** (these bemos are usually blue); and **Semarapura**. Blue bemos wait at the Bangli intersection on the main road between Gianyar and Semarapura at Peteluan; so it's easy to change bemos here. The road climbs steadily up to Bangli with good views to the south. Generally, orange bemos run from Bangli to **Kintamani**; to **Rendang** they are generally black or brown and white; bemos also run between to **Besakih** and to **Amlapura**, all fairly regularly from 0600-1700; fewer in the afternoon. The road from Bangli to Rendang is good but winding, with little traffic; it is also very pretty with deep ravines, streams and overhead viaducts made of bamboo and concrete.

Trunyan *p311*

Bemo From **Denpasar**'s Batubulan terminal to **Bangli** and then another to **Penelokan**. Some bemos drive down into the crater to Kedisan and Toya Bungkah.

Bus Regular coach services from Denpasar (2-3 hrs).

Pura Besakih and Gunung Agung

→ *Colour map 11, B1.*

The holiest and most important temple on Bali is Pura Besakih, situated on the slopes of Bali's sacred Gunung Agung. Twinned with Gunung Batur to the northwest, Agung is the highest mountain on the island, rising to 3140 m. It is easiest to approach Besakih by taking the road north from Semarapura, a distance of 22 km. However, there are also two east-west roads, linking the Semarapura route to Besakih with Bangli in the west and Amlapura in the east. Although little public transport uses these routes, they are among the most beautiful drives in Bali, through verdant terraced rice paddies.

Pura Besakih

Ins and outs
The site is open daily from 0800 and costs 7500Rp plus 1000Rp for a camera. There is another ticket office on the climb up the hill where you have to sign in and are invited to make a further donation (ignore the vast sums that are claimed to have been donated). Guides are available for around 15,000Rp. The best time to visit is early in the morning, before the tour groups arrive.

Getting there
Besakih is 22 km from Semarapura and 60 km from Denpasar, with regular minibuses services from both. From Denpasar catch a bemo from the Batubulan terminal to Semarapura, and then get a connection on to Besakih (via Rendang). However, bemos are irregular for this final leg of the journey and it makes more sense to charter a bemo for the entire trip, or rent a car or motorbike (chartering a bemo makes good sense in a group).

Pura Besakih is a complex of 22 puras that lie scattered over the south slopes of Gunung Agung, at an altitude of about 950 m. Of these, the central, largest and most important is the Pura Penataran Agung, the Mother Temple of Bali. It is here that every Balinese can come to worship – although in the past it was reserved for the royal families of Semarapura, Karangkasem and Bangli. The other 21 temples that sprawl across the slopes of Gunung Agung surrounding the Mother Temple are linked to particular clans. **Gunung Agung** last erupted in 1963, killing 2000 people. The area has been sacred for several centuries.

The **Pura Penataran Agung**, which most visitors refer to as Pura Besakih, is dedicated to Siva and is of great antiquity.

Temple layout
From the entrance gate, it is a 10-minute walk up to the temple. Although you can walk up and around the sides of the temple, the courtyards are only open to worshippers. It is the position of this pura that makes it special: there are views to the waters of the Lombok Strait.

Pura Besakih consists of three distinct sections (also see box, page 316). The entrance to the forecourt is through a *candi bentar* or split gate, immediately in front of which – unusually for Bali – is a *bale pegat*, which symbolizes the cutting of the material from the heavenly worlds. Also here is the *bale kulkul*, a pavilion for the wooden split gongs. At the far end of this first courtyard are two *bale mundar-mandir* or *bale ongkara*.

Entering the central courtyard, almost directly in front of the gateway, is the *bale pewerdayan*. This is the spot where the priests recite the sacred texts. On the left-hand wall is the *pegongan*, a pavilion where a gamelan orchestra plays during ceremonies. Along the

Balinese pura

In Bali there are more htan 20,000 *pura* (temples) – and most villages have at least three. The *pura puseh*, (navel temple), is the village-origin temple where the village ancestors are worshipped. The *pura dalem* (temple of the dead) is usually near the cremation ground. The *pura bale agung* is the temple of the great assembly hall and is used for meetings of the village. There are also irrigation temples, temples at particular geographical sites, and the six great temples or *sadkahyangan*.

There are nine directional temples, *kayangan jagat*, found at notable geographical sites around the island, particularly on mountains, on imposing outcrops overlooking the sea and beside lakes. These are among the most sacred temples on Bali and their strategic locations have been chosen to ensure that they safeguard the island. Besakih, high on the slopes of Bali's most sacred and highest mountain, Gunung Agung, is the pre-eminent of these directional temples and corresponds to the ninth directional point, (the centre). The others, of equal importance, guard the other eight directions. From the southwest they are: Pura Luhur Uluwatu, Pura Luhur Batukau on Mount Batukau, Pura Ulun Danu Batur high on edge of the crater of Mount Batur (this temple used to be beside the lake, but eruptions in 1917 and 1926 caused so much destruction that it was moved), Pura Ulun Danu Bratan beside Lake Bratan, Pura Pasar Agung near Selat on the slopes of Mount Agung, Pura Lempuyang on Mount Lempuyang near Tirtagangga, Pura Goa Lawah near Padangbai, Pura Masceti near Lebi, and the mother temple, Pura Besakih. Balinese visit the *kayangan jagat* nearest their home at the time of its *odalan*, anniversary festival, to seek protection and make offerings to the spirits.

Balinese pura are places where evil spirits are rendered harmless, but gods must be appeased and courted if they are to protect people, so offerings are brought. The temple buildings are less important than the ground, which is consecrated.

The temple complex consists of three courts (two in north Bali), each separated by walls: the front court, or *jaba*, the central court, or *jaba tengah*, and the inner court, or *jeroan*. The innermost court is the most sacred and is thought to represent heaven; the outermost, the underworld; and the central court, an intermediate place.

Note Macaques at temple sites should not be teased, fed, or purchased.

opposite (right-hand) side of the courtyard is the large *bale agung*, where meetings of the Besakih village are held. The small *panggungan* or altar, in front and at the near end of the *bale agung*, is used to present offerings. The similar *bale pepelik* at the far end is the altar used to present offerings to the Hindu trinity – Vishnu, Brahma and Siva. These gods descend and assemble in the larger *sanggar agung*, which lies in front of the *bale pepelik*.

From the central courtyard, a steep stone stairway leads to the upper section, which is arranged into four terraces. The first of these terraces in the inner courtyard is split into an east (right) and west (left) half. To the right are two large *merus*; the *meru* with the seven-tiered roof is dedicated to the locally venerated god Ratu Geng, while the 11-tiered *meru* is dedicated to Ratu Mas. The three-tiered *kehen meru* is used to store the temple treasures. On the left-hand side is a row of four *merus* and two stone altars. The tallest *meru*, with seven tiers, is dedicated to Ida Batara Tulus Sadewa. Up some steps, on the second terrace, is another 11-tiered *meru*, this one dedicated to Ratu Sunar ing Jagat or Lord Light of the World. There are also a number of *bale* here; the *bale* in a separate enclosure to the left

Balinese pura layout

The outer court or jaba

The entrance to the jaba is usually through a *candi bentar*, (split temple) gate – if the two halves of the gate are pushed together, closing the entranceway, they would form the shape of a complete *candi*.

Within the jaba are a number of structures. In one corner is the *bale kulkul* (*bale* pavilion, *kulkul* wooden gong), a pavilion in which hangs a large hollow, wooden, gong or drum. The kulkul is beaten during temple ceremonies and also in times of emergency or disaster – during an earthquake, for example. Also within the jaba, it is not uncommon to find a *jineng* – a small barn used to store rice produced from the temple's own fields (*laba pura*).

The central court or jaba tengah

The entrance leading to the central court is through the *candi kurung*. This is also in the form of a *candi*, but in this case a wooden doorway allows visitors to pass through. In a village pura, the centre of the jaba tengah will be dominated by an open pavilion with a roof of grass or reed. This is the *bale agung* or village conference hall. There is also often a *bale* for pilgrims who wish to stay overnight in the temple.

The inner court or jeroan

The entrance to the inner court is through a second, larger, *candi kurung* called the *paduraksa*. The entrance is usually guarded by a demon's head and rises up in the form of a pyramid. In larger temples, there may be three gateways. Along the back wall of the jeroan are the most sacred of the shrines. These may have multiple roofs – as many as 11. The greater the number of roofs, the more important the god. Also on the back wall, there is a stone pillar or *tugu*. It is at the tugu that offerings are left for the *taksu*, the god who's job it is to protect the temple and through whom the wishes of the gods are transmitted to the dancer during a trance dance. In the centre of the jeroan is the *parungan* or *pepelik* – the seat of all the gods, where they assemble during temple ceremonies. Finally, along the right-hand wall of the inner courtyard, are two *sanggahs* – Ngurah Gde and Ngurah Alit. These are the 'secretaries' of the gods; they ensure that temple offerings are properly prepared. (Condensed from: East Utrecht and B Hering (1986), *The temples of Bali*.)

is dedicated to Sira Empu, the patron god of blacksmiths. Up to the third terrace is a further 11-tiered *meru*, dedicated to Batara Wisesa. On the final terrace are two *gedongs* – covered buildings enclosed on all four sides – dedicated to the god of Gunung Agung.

At the back of the complex there is a path leading to three other major *puras*: **Gelap** (200 m), **Pengubengan** (2.5 km) and **Tirta** (2 km). There are over 20 temples on these terraced slopes, dedicated to every Hindu god in the pantheon.

Festivals

Seventy festivals are held around Pura Besakih each year, with every shrine having its own festival. The two most important festivals are occasional ceremonies: the **Panca Wali Krama** is held every 10 years, while the **Eka Dasa Rudra** is held only once every 100 years and lasts for two months. Two Eka Dasa Rudra festivals have been held this century. In March or April is the movable festival of **Nyepi** (on the full moon of 10th lunar month), the Balinese Saka new year, a month-long festival attended by thousands of people from all over Bali.

Gunung Agung

Gunung Agung is Bali's tallest and most sacred mountain, home of the Hindu gods and dwelling place of the ancestral spirits, it dominates the spiritual and physical life of the island. It is awe-inspiring, with its magnificent summit dominating the landscape over much of Bali. All directions on Bali are given in relation to this much revered mountain. Toward the mountain is called 'kaja', away from the mountain is 'kelod'. This is the site of the most important of the nine directional temples (see box, page 316). Water from its sacred springs is the holiest and most sought after for temple rites. According to local legend, the god Pasupati created the mountain by dividing Mount Mahmeru, centre of the Hindu universe, in two – making Gunung Agung and Gunung Batur.

Standing 3014 m high, at its summit is a crater about 500 m in width. In 1969, after lying dormant for more than 600 years, the volcano erupted causing massive destruction; over 1600 people died in the eruption, a further 500 in the aftermath and 9000 were made homeless. Even today the scars left by the destruction are visible in the shape of lava flows and ravines. Much was read into the fact that the eruption took place at the time of Bali's greatest religious festival, Eka Dasa Rudra. One theory is that the mountain erupted because the priests were pressured into holding the ceremony before due time, to coincide with an important tourism convention that was taking place on Bali.

Climbing Gunung Agung

Gunung Agung is a sacred mountain, so access is restricted during religious ceremonies, particularly in March and April. The arduous climb should only be attempted during the dry season, May to October; even then conditions on the summit can be quite different from the coast. There are several routes up Gunung Agung, but the two most popular depart from Besakih and Selat. You should be well prepared, the mountain is cold at night and you will need warm clothes, water, food, a good torch and decent footwear. You will also need a guide, and should aim to reach the summit before 0700 to witness the spectacular sunrise.

From Besakih The route takes you to the summit, providing the best views in all directions. The longer of the two ascents, this climb takes about six hours, with another four to five hours for the demanding descent. You start out in forest, but once you reach the open mountain it becomes extremely steep. The tourist office at Besakih hire guides (about US$60 per person, including temple offerings) and can arrange accommodation.

From Selat This route reaches a point about 100 m below the summit, which obscures all-round views. However, the climb only takes three to four hours; aim to set off by 0330. From Selat, take the road to Pura Pasar Agung, then climb through forest before reaching the bare mountain. Guides can be arranged in Muncan, Tirtagangga or Selat. A recommended guide is I Ketut Uriada ① T0812 3646426, a teacher who lives in Muncan; he can be contacted at his shop in that village. Costs start at about US$44, which includes temple contributions and registering with the local police. In Selat ask the police about guides, they should be able to advise. In Tirtagangga ask at your accommodation; rates here tend to be higher, US$45 per person, which should include transport. There is accommodation in Selat, or your guide may arrange cheaper lodgings at his home. **Perama** ① T0361 751875 in Kuta, T0361 973316 in Ubud, offer a one-night two-day trek up Gunung Agung including visits to Kamasan, Kertagosa and Sideman, where the climb begins at 0100. The four-hour trek arrives in time for sunrise on the summit. Transfers to Kuta, Ubud and Sanur are included in the price (US$110 per person).

East Bali, Karangasem and the north coast

→ *Colour map 10, B1.*

The greatest of the former principalities of Bali is Semarapura (formerly Klungkung), and its capital still has a number of sights that hint at its former glory. It is worth driving east of here into the Regency of Karangasem: to the ancient Bali Aga village of Tenganan, 3 km outside Candi Dasa, then inland and northeast to Amlapura (Karangkasem), with its royal palace, then 7 km north to the royal bathing pools of Tirtagangga. From here the road continues north, following the coast all the way to Singaraja (almost 100 km from Amlapura). The drive is very beautiful, passing black-sand beaches and coconut groves.

An area of great beauty dominated by Gunung Agung (3140 m), Bali's highest and most sacred volcano, Karangasem is one of the most traditional parts of Bali and one of the most rewarding areas to explore. During the 17th and 18th centuries, Karangasem was the most powerful kingdom on Bali. Its sphere of influence extended to western Lombok, and the cross-cultural exchanges that resulted endure to this day. During the 19th century, the regency cooperated with the Dutch, thus ensuring its continued prosperity.

The massive eruption of Gunung Agung in 1963 devastated much of the regency and traces of the lava flows can still be seen along the northeast coast, particularly north of Tulamben.

▶▶ *For listings, see pages 327-338.*

Ins and outs

Getting there

By bus Buses run most frequently in the morning starting early (from 0500 or 0600), and continue until about 1700, or later on major routes. The frequency of buses is continually improving. Buses from Denpasar (Batubulan terminal) run to **Semarapura** (1¼ hours), **Padangbai** (one hour 50 minutes) and **Candi Dasa** (two hours 10 minutes). There are also regular bus connections from Gianyar.

Several companies run tourist shuttle buses linking Padangbai, Candi Dasa, Tirtagangga and Tulemben with Ubud, Kuta, Sanur (and Nusa Lembongan by boat), Kintamani, Lovina, Bedugul and Air Sanih; Mataram, Bangsal, the Gili Islands, Kuta Lombok and Tetebatu on Lombok. One of the best is **Perama**, with offices in all the above places; allow three hours to get to Denpasar airport from Candi Dasa.

Note All times are approximate and can vary enormously depending on traffic conditions from Denpasar, particularly on the main road from Semarapura to Denpasar.

By boat From Padangbai there is a 24-hour ferry service (leaving every two hours) to Lembar port on Lombok (four to five hours). Small boats make the crossing to Nusa Penida very early every morning, taking about one hour 20 minutes. From Kusumba, small boats leave early every morning for Nusa Penida and Nusa Lembongan, one hour 15 minutes.

Getting around

While you can reach most of these villages by public bemo, it is better to hire a car. There are many scenic backroads that climb up into the hills, offering spectacular views when the weather is fine; be warned that some of these minor roads are in dreadful condition with numerous, huge potholes. The road leading up from Perasi through Timbrah and Bungaya to Bebandem is especially scenic and potholed. A much better road with outstanding views leads west from Amlapura to Rendang; en route you pass through an area famed for its salak fruit and in the vicinity of Muncan you will find beautiful rice terraces. From Rendang you can continue on up to Pura Besakih.

Semarapura and around ⊝⊕⊙⊙▲⊜ ➤➤ *pp327-338.*

➔ *Phone code: 0366.*

The **Puri Semarapura** was the symbolic heart of the kingdom of Semarapura. All that remains of this palace on Jalan Untung Surapati are the gardens and two buildings; the rest was destroyed in 1908 by the Dutch during their advance on the capital and the ensuing *puputan*. The **Kherta Ghosa** or Hall of Justice, built in the 18th century by Ida Dewa Agung Jambe, was formerly the supreme court of the kingdom of Semarapura. It is famous for its ceiling murals painted in traditional, *wayang* style, with illustrations of heaven (towards the top) and hell (on the lower panels). As a court, the paintings represent the punishment that awaits a criminal in the afterlife. The murals have been repainted several times this century. Miguel Covarrubias describes the nature of traditional justice in Bali in the following terms:

"A trial must be conducted with the greatest dignity and restraint. There are rules for the language employed, the behaviour of the participants, and the payment of trial expenses ... On the appointed day the plaintiff and the defendant must appear properly dressed, with their witnesses and their cases and declarations carefully written down ... When the case has been thoroughly stated, the witnesses have testified and the evidence has been produced, the judges study the statements and go into deliberation among themselves until they reach a decision. Besides the witnesses and the material evidence, special attention is paid to the physical reaction of the participants during the trial, such as nervousness, change of colour in the face, or hard breathing."

The Kherta Ghosa was transformed into a Western court by the Dutch in 1908, when they added the carved seats, as they found sitting on mats too uncomfortable. It is said – although the story sounds rather dubious – that one of the Rajahs of Semarapura used the Kherta Ghosa as a watch tower. He would look over the town and when his eyes alighted on a particularly attractive woman going to the temple to make offerings, he would order his guards to fetch her and add the unsuspecting maid to his collection of wives.

Adjoining the Kherta Ghosa is the **Bale Kambangg** (Floating Pavilion), originally built in the 18th century, but extensively restored since then. Like the Kherta Ghosa, the ceiling is painted with murals; these date from 1942.

Further along the same road, just past a school, is the attractive **Taman Gili** ① *5000Rp*, also built in the 18th century. This consists of a series of open courtyards with finely carved stonework, in the centre of which is a floating pavilion surrounded by a lotus-filled moat.

To the east of the main crossroads in the centre of town – behind the shop fronts – is a bustling **market**, held here every three days and considered by many to be the best market on Bali, and also a large monument commemorating the *puputan*.

Kamasan village

Four kilometres southeast of Semarapura is an important arts centre where artists still practise the classical *Wayang*-style of painting. Most of the artist families live in the banjar Sangging area of town. Artists from this village painted the original ceiling in the Kerta Gosa in Semarapura in the 18th century, as well as the recent restoration, using the muted natural colours (reds, blacks, blues, greens and ochres) typical of this school.

Diving Southeast Asia

Introduction

The waters surrounding Southeast Asia are the most biodiverse on the planet. This is due to the geological structure of the Pacific Ocean and the way that ocean currents are distributed around the planet. The science may not seem all that relevant to travelling divers, but it is worth knowing that if you dive in these intensely beautiful tropical waters you will be seeing some of the best that there is to see. There are an incredible number of fantastic dive destinations right across Asia, and there are many countries in this region where diving is a developing sport, but the countries to concentrate on are Indonesia, Malaysia and Thailand. Here, the dive experience is the most impressive and they have the best facilities. There are masses of dive operations looking to get you into the water: you can spend a moderate sum learning to dive in Koh Tao or the Gilis or max out your credit card by sailing into the unknown to Indonesian islands that are so remote they haven't even been named. But no matter where are, you will find colourful reefs, teeming with fish and animals and warm, clear water to immerse yourself in.

Beth and Shaun Tierney, authors of Footprint's Diving the World.

Above: Diver and fan corals at Tioman Island.
ii **Previous page**: Crystal-clear waters in Indonesia's Banda Sea.

The Indonesian archipelago consists of an estimated 17,000 islands stretching east to west over 5000 km. These sit ringed by five different seas and include around 18% of the world's coral reefs, so you can take it for granted that there's some pretty impressive diving here. The incredible variety of dive regions is only outdone by the number of dive sites at each. Dive styles vary region by region and sea by sea. The southern islands are affected by cooler, deep water upwellings from the Indian Ocean while some of the northern regions are more protected and characterized by nutrient-rich waters fed by ancient volcanic activity. Wherever you go, it is most important to know that this country is generally regarded as the world's most biodiverse marine environment. A recent survey in Irian Jaya found 950 species of fish, 450 corals and 600 molluscs. Try counting those in on a single tank! There are so many wonderful dive destinations in Indonesia that choosing between them can be a quite an effort. Geography doesn't help as, mostly, the diving is year round. There are plenty of professional dive operations in easy-to-get-to areas, such as Bali and Manado, while some of the more distant areas require a liveaboard and an adventurous spirit. Novices should head to Bali or the Gili Islands off Lombok where courses are good value and well run; advanced divers will love the drama and tougher conditions in Komodo or the isolation of Irian Jaya.

■ Bali

This tiny island is one of the world's most stunning with its combination of a balmy climate, unique culture and delightful people. However, Bali is also an incredible dive destination with fringing reefs that are simply too good to miss. The island's volcanic nature means rich nutrients support the many marine creatures that thrive in these conditions. There is a wide variety of diving styles too, with pretty reefs in the northwest's Menjangan Marine Park to shallow bays right around the coast. These may appear barren at first glance but are full to bursting with unusual marine creatures. And of course, there's the island's justifiably famous wreck dive, *The Liberty*, at Tulamben.

Above: Juvenile cuttlefish (left) and damselfish (right) on a fan.

≋ The wreck of *The Liberty*

The Liberty is part of diver folklore. Just 30 m from the shore at Tulamben is the broken hull of a Second World War US supply ship. Torpedoed in 1941 by a Japanese submarine, she lay beached for 20 years before Mount Agung erupted and pushed her down the sloping seabed where she broke up. Now, she is one of the best artificial reefs you will ever see. Divers come from all over the island to wander along the pebble-strewn beach then slide into the water. Visibility varies depending on the season and run-off from the nearby river mouth but, even when it's low, the dive is magnificent. As you fin towards the hull you pass the resident oriental sweetlips, then the wreck materializes from the blue. There are jacks swirling above, large Napoleon wrasse in amongst them and, on rare occasions, magnificent mola-mola. The structure is thick with corals, sponges, fans and crinoids all surrounded by lots of fish. Although you can't penetrate the structure you can see guns, toilets, boilers and the anchor chain. Right at the bottom are some gorgonians that are known to have pygmy seahorses on them. There are also leaffish, dragonets and more nudibranchs than you thought possible in one dive.

The bay to the side of the wreck is equally interesting. The black-sand slope drops gently to 15 metres or so before heading into deeper waters. There are small patches of coral, sponges and anemones plus plenty of detritus. Ornate ghost pipefish shelter in crinoids and even blue-ringed octopus can be caught prowling about. At the eastern end of the bay, the sand slope leads to a short wall that has basket sponges and gorgonians with longnose hawkfish in residence.

This page: *The Liberty* wreck at Tulamben. **Opposite page:** (clockwise) Asian reef dwellers include turtles; clownfish in their anemone hosts; imperial shrimps and gobies that live on whip corals.

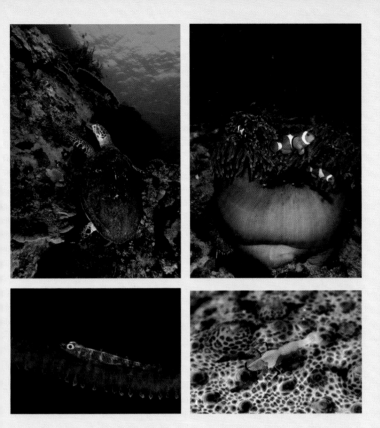

■ Lombok

A favoured haunt of the backpacking fraternity, Lombok's culture and style is quite different from her near neighbour. The main attraction for travellers and divers are the three coral islands just off her north coast. The Gilis (Air, Meno and Trewangan) have a casual lifestyle but Trewangan is the divers' haunt. It's a great place to take a course as conditions are generally easy going and although the reefs have suffered in the past, they are now protected. There are several turtle projects here so you will encounter these animals more often than almost anywhere else in Asia.

■ Komodo

The marine park encapsulating the tiny islands scattered around Komodo is a dream dive location. With few humans, but the world's highest population of Komodo dragons, this area is mostly visited by people who come to see what's under the waves. Dives here can be so thoroughly splendid they're hard to describe. In a single dive you might see 14 mobula rays in a squadron followed by the tiniest of pygmy seahorses on a deep pink fan coral. It is outstanding diving, but be aware that it's tough – currents are strong, deep water upwellings can be icy and either can wipe out a planned dive at a second's notice.

■ Manado

On the northern tip of Sulawesi, just off Manado city, is the first-rate Bunaken Marine Park. Established in 1991, this area has become very popular as dives are just a short hop from the coast. Bunaken, Siladen, Montehage and Nain islands are ringed by lush reefs with steep walls and prolific coral growth. Pelagics pass by, usually while you have your nose down admiring some small delightful, colourful creature. There is so much variety here, including a solitary wreck, that it's hard to see it all. Conditions are usually good but can be changeable with currents occasionally lifting to quite outrageous levels. They usually drop again as quickly as they appeared.

■ Lembeh Straights

About two hours from Manado, Lembeh is the ultimate muck diving destination, a term which refers to diving in areas that are notable for their dark-sand seabeds. This indicates a high level of local volcanic geography and extreme levels of nutrients in the water that support some unusual marine animals. The sea here is never crystal clear but that's part of its joy – getting down to the seabed and discovering just how many strange things are there. The area is best known for all things hairy – seahorses, frogfish and pipefish all seem to have grown protective coats of hair that allow them the best camouflage available.

Top: Curious octopus watching the divers. **Above**: Bluespotted ray.

🌊 Barracuda Point

Sipadan's most famous dive, this submerged point sits to the east of the island's boat jetty. The wall is sheer and the crusting corals, fans and sponges make it incredibly colourful. As you descend to 30 m there is a full quota of schooling small fish – butterflies, tangs and surgeons – but most outstanding is the enormous size and quantity of black coral bushes. Every one seems to have a longnose hawkfish in it, or be swarmed by lionfish, and interspersed with gigantic fans in many colours. Turtles swim along with divers to keep them company. Sometimes one will have a batfish hovering beneath his belly. At the top of the reef the corals are less impressive but whitetips rest peacefully on the sand. Grey reef sharks approach from behind, heading for the school of jacks that are just around the bend. Large turtles visit cleaning stations while Napoleon wrasse and giant tuna pass by in the blue. Although the dive starts along the wall and drifts towards them, the infamous barracuda school is usually spotted from the surface. There are hundreds in the ball, sitting right on the top of the reef. They move apart for a few moments then reconfigure into a perfect spiral – breathtaking.

■ Irian Jaya

The most isolated Indonesian region to come under diving scrutiny lies at the western end of New Guinea. It's as remote as anywhere can be, yet surprisingly easy to reach. The reefs here were surveyed a few years back and reported as having exceptional levels of diversity. Diving amongst clouds of fish so thick you can barely see through them is quite an experience. There are manta cleaning stations and Second World War plane wrecks have been located. Conditions vary but the diving is year round.

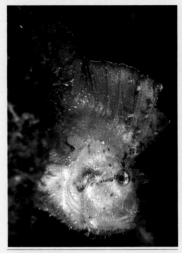

Leaf scorpion fish.

Ornate ghost pipefish.

Malaysia

With 11 states sitting on the Malaysian mainland between Thailand and Singapore plus another two states and a federal territory on the island of Borneo, this is a widespread and geographically diverse country. When it comes to diving, Borneo is the place with the reputation, the shores washed by the South China, Sulu and Celebes Seas. Being surrounded by open ocean currents makes for an incredibly diverse set of marine environments. Sabah – which translates as the 'Land below the Wind' – is ringed by a mass of marine reserves, idyllic islands and 75% of the country's reefs. The diving here is superlative and your only problem will be choosing between resorts. Sarawak, surprisingly, has little or no organized diving and although Labuan has some interesting wrecks, the unreliable conditions mean the territory is mostly bypassed. Peninsular Malaysia – which sits between the South China Sea and the Straits of Malacca – has plenty of diving but suffers in comparison to spectacular Sabah. The west coast is not regarded as much of a dive destination to those in the know. A history of heavy shipping, trade and industry has taken its toll on the marine environment. However, over on the east coast, a string of picturesque islands are favoured by Asian divers who live close by. Diving here is regarded as a 'stopover' or weekend destination for training, but if you are travelling overland, there are some ideal locations.

■ Layang Layang
North of Sabah, isolated Layang Layang is a tiny, man-made island built by the Royal Malaysian Navy to ensure their claim over the Spratley Islands. There is little more than an airstrip on the edge of a turquoise lagoon but around its edge is a large atoll with steep-sided walls dropping to unimaginable depths. Strong currents drag nutrients across the reefs, ensuring prolific hard coral growth. Turtles and reef sharks are common, and large schools of hammerheads arrive every April. Diving can be challenging so it is not a place for novices. The resort closes between September and February.

■ Lankayan

Nestled in the Sulu Sea, idyllic Lankayan is ringed by an iridescent white beach and covered in a labyrinth of unruly green jungle. The reefs are gentle slopes covered in hard corals. Visibility can be low due to proximity to the mainland and high plankton concentrations. However, diving here is about seeing the animals who thrive in these nutrient-rich conditions. There are plenty, including rare rhinopias and occasional whalesharks that come to feed, as well as several small shipwrecks. This is a year-round resort, conditions are mostly gentle and good shore diving also makes it ideal for new divers.

■ Sipadan, Mabul and Kapalai

The most famous of Borneo's dive destinations, Sipadan is an all out magnet for divers. The walls off the island drop to well over 600 m, which creates a spectacular marine environment. If you are looking for big stuff, then this is the place. Turtles are so

Top: Young whitetips at Layang Layang.
Above: Porcelain crab in the folds of an anemone.

prolific and curious that they follow divers around. Sharks are everywhere, whitetips snooze on sandy shelves and there are masses of barracudas. In a bid to become a World Heritage site, hotels here were closed in 2004. You can still dive, but only from nearby Mabul and Kapalai, two islands that are special places for spotting small creatures. The underwater topography around both is one of flat reef mounds that are a great haven for masses of weird and whacky critters. Diving is year-round and suitable for everyone.

■ Perhentian Islands

Inside the Terengganu Marine Park, the two Perhentian Islands are tiny, pretty and very 'Robinson Crusoe' in style. Dives tend to be around rocky outcrops with cracks and crevices to investigate. There's plenty of coral growth and all the typical fish species like angels, butterflies and jacks. In July and August bigger pelagics, even whalesharks, may make an appearance. Conditions are straightforward although the season is restricted to between May and October.

■ Redang Island

Just below Perhentian and also part of the marine park, Redang consists of a main island surrounded by a cluster of smaller ones. This was Malaysia's first marine park and has the best visibility as there are deeper drop-offs. Dive sites circle outcrops that have sandy terrain on the eastern side and rocky terrain on the west. This makes for quite a variety of sites with plenty of hard corals and fans. Conditions are much the same as those on the Perhentian Islands.

■ Tioman Island

Also a designated marine park, Tioman has two very distinct diver personalities. The water close to shore is very shallow and the flat reef dives are best suited to beginners. In fact, this can be a good place to take a course. However, where Tioman really comes into its own is on the dive sites that are a fair way offshore, where deeper waters are punctuated by gigantic boulders that have tumbled into groups and been colonized by corals and fish. The diving is far more challenging as the reefs are swept by stronger currents ensuring better and more prolific coral growth.

Above: Moray eel surrounded by hingebeak shrimp.
x **Opposite page:** Reef wall of fans, sponges and corals (top right); Schools of jacks (bottom).

Thailand's western coastline faces towards the Indian Ocean while the east borders the South China Sea. There are reef structures along both coasts but those in the western Andaman Sea are far more extensive, particularly around the beautiful Similan Islands. Colourful corals decorate huge granite boulders that form spectacular swim throughs. Pinnacles rise from the deep and submerged reefs offer protection in isolated regions. Serious divers will spend long periods sailing around the Similans and even heading much further north (to Burma). In contrast, the islands in the Gulf of Thailand sit in a very shallow sea. At less than 60 m, and with strong daily tides, these reefs are susceptible to heavy sedimentation and river run off. Reef diversity and coral numbers are lower but there is good diving to be had all the same. These charming islands are magnets for long-haul travellers and ideal learn-to-dive destinations. Deciding on which side of  Thailand to head to is straightforward once you realize the diving here is surprisingly weather dependant. May to October sees driving winds pushing across the Andaman Sea from the southwest. By November, calm seas return when the monsoon swaps over to the northeast. Over in the Gulf, the wind patterns have the opposite seasonal effect. Half the year you dive on the west, the other half on the east.

■ Phuket

Almost everywhere on this uptempo island has a dive centre, despite dive sites being a little way offshore. Ones closer to land tend to have lower visibility but are great places for less experienced divers. Those a little further away, between Phuket and the Phi Phi Islands are unexpectedly colourful. Shark Point, the King Cruiser and Ko Racha Noi are among the most popular but these dives do get currents.

❧ Richelieu Rock

Summing up the splendour that is Richelieu Rock in a paragraph or two is more than a challenge, it's nigh on impossible. This isolated, submerged hill in the Surin Islands is without doubt the dive site that has it all – from the tiniest of tiny critters to the ultimate in grace, size and beauty: the whaleshark. Entering over the top of the rock it's worth heading straight down to the base where there are masses of healthy, colourful soft corals and several enormous groupers. Back on the slopes there is a wealth of smaller creatures to admire: lionfish, seasnakes, cowries and trumpetfish, beautiful soft corals, angels and butterflies, seahorses, scorpionfish, white-eyed morays, clownfish, mantis shrimp, turtles, potato cod, reef sharks, barracuda, snappers and mantas. Every surface seems to house yet another fascinating resident. But at all times, divers keep an ear out for the sounds of manic tank banging. This is the signal that a whaleshark has been seen and you should make a mad dash towards the sound. When the conditions are right, you may be really lucky and see several in a day. Both adults and juveniles are attracted to the Rock and this is one of the few places in the world where you can still dive with them. Pay them the respect they deserve.

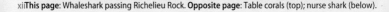

This page: Whaleshark passing Richelieu Rock. **Opposite page**: Table corals (top); nurse shark (below).

■ The Similans

There is no substitute for the Koh Similan National Marine Park, which attracts divers from the most experienced down to complete novices. Ringed by perfect beaches and amazing coral reefs, what makes the Similans so distinctive are their two completely different sides. To the east the islands have pure white sand and hard coral gardens that slope down to over 30 m. Colourful soft corals and sea fans are plentiful, the diving is easy and the pace is calm. The west, however, is much more dramatic, with currents that swirl around huge boulders, spectacular swim throughs and swarms of colourful fish. It's a bit like diving between flooded skyscrapers that have been reclaimed by the sea

■ Surin Islands

North of the Similans, Ko Bon, Tachai and Surin are enveloped by excellent reefs and prolific marine life. And as they're exposed to deep ocean currents, there are frequent pelagic sightings. All sorts of sharks, manta rays and schooling barracuda are regular visitors. Twenty kilometres north of Surin is the dive site that has it all – Richelieu Rock. This is the one do-not-miss dive in the country. On a single dive there may be minute harlequin shrimp and enormous whalesharks, curious turtles and elegant sea horses. You could spend a week here and still not see everything the Rock has to offer.

■ Ko Samui

This popular tourist island has an excellent dive infrastructure but the reefs around the island tend to be murky. However, the gentle, shelving beaches are popular spots for taking a dive course. Once training is underway, most centres take divers to the nearby Ang Thong National Marine Park where hidden lagoons and sheer limestone cliffs reflect the beauty of the underwater scenery. The diving is pleasant but not too challenging. This is also a good trip for snorkellers.

■ Ko Tao (Turtle Island) and Ko Nang Yuan

These neighbours are both an easy sail from Samui and have recently become the epicentre of diving in the Gulf of Thailand. The reason is simple. There's no need to travel for an hour or more to reach the best dive sites, these islands have good diving just seconds from the beach. It's an ideal area for beginners and there are many dive centres catering for them. However, you have to always remember that conditions in the Gulf are highly variable – even in peak season visibility can be as low as 3 m, but will clear to an incredible 40 m in an instant. The most famous dive is probably Sail Rock, a pinnacle that comes up from 30 m to the surface. The rock is often visited by schooling fish and larger animals but its highlight is entering a spectacular chimney that feels like swimming up a cathedral spire.

Keeping pace with a turtle.

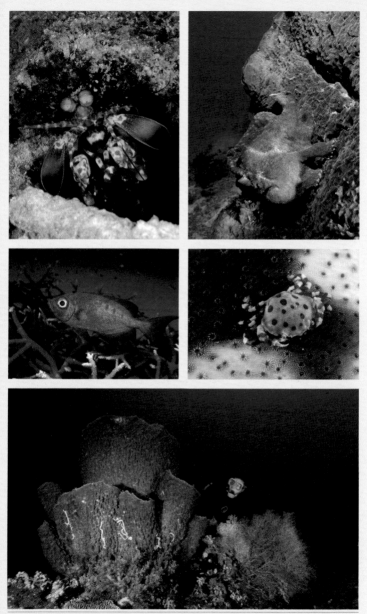

Clockwise from top left: More Asian reef dwellers include mantis shrimp, frogfish, swimming crab, the crescent-tail bigeye and enormous barrel sponges.

Goa Lawah

① *Take a bemo heading for Padangbai or Candi Dasa.*

Goa Lawah, or 'bat cave', is one of the state temples of Semarapura. There are tunnels here that are reputed to lead as far as Pura Besakih. As the name suggests, the temple is overrun by bats and corresponding smells.

Kusamba

Boats leave for **Nusa Penida** and **Nusa Lembongan** from the fishing village of Kusamba, 8 km southeast from Semarapura. On the beach are huts and shallow troughs used in salt production. The fishing fleet consists of hundreds of brightly painted outrigger craft with triangular sails, which operate in the Lombok Strait (similar to the *lis-alis* of Madura). They are fast and manoeuvrable, and can make way in even the lightest breezes.

Tirtagangga

① *5000Rp adult, 3000Rp child.*

Seven kilometres northwest of Semarapura is the site of the royal bathing pools of Tirtagangga. The pools are set on a beautiful position on the side of a hill, overlooking terraced rice fields. The complex is made up of various pools (some of which can be swum in; enquire at the entrance gate) fed by mountain springs, with water spouting from fountains and stone animals. It is popular with locals as well as foreign visitors, and is a peaceful spot to relax during the week, although those seeking tranquillity would be advised not to visit at weekends when the place is overrun with domestic tourists. There are a couple of places to stay, and a few restaurants.

Amed → *Phone code: 0363.*

For peace and quiet, this area on the east coast, north of Tirtagangga, has much to offer. The drive from Culik via Amed to Lipah Beach is quite spectacular, especially on the return journey, with Gunung Agung forming a magnificent backdrop to the coastal scenery. Numerous coves and headlands, with colourful fishing boats, complete the vista and offer endless possibilities for walks and picnics. The area became popular because of the good snorkelling and diving available here, the reef is just 10 m from the beach with some good coral and a variety of fish. Amed is developing slowly with new guesthouses, hotels, restaurants and dive centres opening every year, some with spectacular hillside locations and stunning views of Gunung Agung. At present much of the accommodation lies beyond Amed on the stretch from Jemeluk to Bunutan.

The area called Amed is in fact a 15 km stretch from Culik to Selang village, encompassing the villages of Amed, **Cemeluk** (also spelt Jemeluk), **Bunutan** and **Selang**. At present the first accommodation you come to is 5.7 km from Culik. If you go during the dry season you can watch the local men making salt; they also work year round as fishermen, setting off at 0500 and returning about 1000, and then going out again at 1500. It is possible to go out with them. As there is no irrigation system, farming is mainly done in the wet season when the men raise crops of peanuts, corn, pumpkin and beans, on the steeply sloping hillside inland from the road, to sell in the market at Amlapura. In dry spells, all the water needed for the crops is carried by the women up the steep slope, three times a day; a back-breaking chore. Most of the land is communally owned by the local Banjar.

Padangbai ⊙⊖⊙⊙⊙⊙ » pp327-338.

→ *Phone code: 0363.*

Padangbai has a beautiful setting, overlooking a crescent-shaped bay with golden sand beach, colourful *jukung* (fishing boats) and surrounded by verdant hills. This is the port for ferries to Lombok and boats to Nusa Penida, and is a hive of excitement when ferries arrive and depart. It is one of the best deep-water harbours in Bali, and many tankers ride at anchor in the approaches. There are beaches on either side of the town. Walking south from the pier and bus station, follow the road until you come to a tatty sign on the left indicating the rough, steep path that leads up and over the hill to **Pantai Cecil** (400 m). This is a beautiful, white-sand beach, the perfect setting for a quiet swim or evening stroll. There are two beachside *warungs*. Unfortunately, the once verdant hills behind the beach are being consumed by diggers in preparation for a massive development of luxury villas. The beach maintains its beauty, but the ambience is nowhere near as relaxed as it was, with the pounding of machinery drowning the area. The walk over the headland has good views of the town and hills beyond.

Padangbai to Candi Dasa

For many people Bali is at its best and most rewarding away from the tourist centres. Along the road leading from Padangbai to Candi Dasa there are several hotels and bungalow-style accommodation, which offer peace and quiet in secluded settings with beautiful sea views. Breakfast is included in the price except at the luxury hotels.

Padangbai

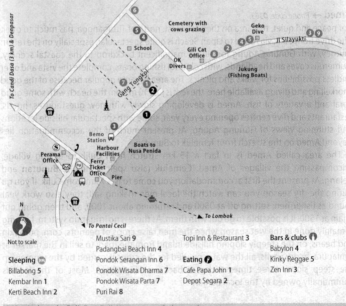

Not to scale

Sleeping
Billabong **5**
Kembar Inn **1**
Kerti Beach Inn **2**

Mustika Sari **9**
Padangbai Beach Inn **4**
Pondok Serangan Inn **6**
Pondok Wisata Dharma **7**
Pondok Wisata Parta **7**
Puri Rai **8**

Topi Inn & Restaurant **3**

Eating
Cafe Papa John **1**
Depot Segara **2**

Bars & clubs
Babylon **4**
Kinky Reggae **5**
Zen Inn **3**

Manggis and Balina Beach Balina Beach lies midway between Padangbai and Candi Dasa (approximately 4 km from the latter) adjacent to the village of Buitan, which runs this tourist development as a cooperative for the benefit of the villagers. It is a slightly scruffy black sand beach with a definite tourist feel to it. Sengkidu village and beach 2 km further east have more charm. Sometimes there are strong currents.

The village of **Buitan** has a public telephone, several small *warungs* and shops; the road to the beach and the accommodation is signposted. Perhaps the highlight of this village is the large advertisement promoting the advantages of artificial insemination in pig breeding. The village of **Manggis**, inland and to the west of Buitan, is known locally for its associations with black magic; it is said to be the haunt of *leyaks*, witches with supernatural powers. There is a road from here leading up to **Putung**, 6 km away, with spectacular views over the Lombok Strait.

At present there are two upmarket accommodations; the simpler, cheaper places seem to have disappeared.

Candi Dasa ⊕❶❷❸⓿▲⊕ ▶▶ pp327-338. Colour map 11, B1.

→ *Phone code: 0363.*

Candi Dasa is smaller, more intimate and offers better value for money than the main seaside resorts of Bali. It also provides an excellent base from which to explore the sights of East Bali.

The gold- and black-sand beach has been badly eroded. However, the lack of beach has saved Candi Dasa from overdevelopment. Even so, it is at its best off-season. There is no surf, so swimming is safe.

Candi Dasa gets its name from the **temple** on the hill overlooking the main road and the freshwater lagoon; the ancient relics in this temple indicate that there has been a village on this site since the 11th century.

Traditionally fishermen in these parts have gone out fishing each day from 0400 until 0800, and again from about 1430 until 1800. Although most people on Bali fear the sea as a place of evil spirits and a potential source of disaster, those who live near the sea and earn their living from it consider it a holy place and worship such sea gods as *Baruna*. The boats they use, jukung, are made from locally grown wood and bamboo, which is cut according to traditional practice. The day chosen for cutting down the tree must be deemed favourable by the gods to whom prayers and offerings are then made, and a sapling is planted to replace it. Carved from a single tree trunk without using nails and with bamboo outriders to give it stability, the finished boat will be gaily coloured with the characteristic large eyes that enable it to see where the fish lurk. The design has not changed for thousands of years; it is very stable due to the low centre of gravity created by the way the sail is fastened. These days there are fewer fish to catch and many fishermen take tourists out snorkelling on the reef. *Jukungs* cost about US$27 to hire for three to four hours.

In the rice field by the road to Tenganan are two ingenious **bird-scaring devices**, operated by a man sitting in a thatched hut. One is a metre-long bamboo pole with plastic bags and strips of bamboo; when the man pulls on the attached rope, the pole swings round, causing the bamboo strips to make a clacking noise and the plastic bags to flutter. The other consists of two four-metre-long bamboo poles that are hinged at one end, with flags and plastic bags attached; when the attached rope is pulled, the two poles swing round with flags and plastic bags waving.

Tenganan

ⓘ *Admission to village by donation, vehicles prohibited. It is possible to walk the 3 km from Candi Dasa; take the road heading north, 1 km to the west of Candi Dasa – it ends at the village. Alternatively, walk or catch a bemo heading west towards Semarapura, get off at the turning 1 km west of Candi Dasa and catch an ojek up to the village. Tours to Tenganan are also arranged by the bigger hotels and the tour agents on the main road. Bemos run past the turn-off for the village from Denpasar's Batubulan terminal.*

This village is reputed to be the oldest on Bali, and is a village of the Bali Aga, the island's original inhabitants before the Hindu invasion almost 1000 years ago (see box, page 311). The walled community consists of a number of longhouses, rice barns, shrines, pavilions and a large village meeting hall, all arranged in accordance with traditional beliefs. Membership of the village is exclusive and until recently visitors were actively discouraged. The inhabitants have to have been born here and marry within the village; anyone who violates the rules is banished to a neighbouring community. Despite the studied maintenance of a traditional way of life, the inhabitants of Tenganan have decided to embrace the tourist industry. It is in fact a very wealthy village, deriving income not only from tourism but also from a large area of communally owned and worked rice paddies and dryland fields.

Tenganan is one of the last villages to produce the unusual **double ikat** or *geringsing*, where both the warp and the weft are tie-dyed, and great skill is needed to align and then weave the two into the desired pattern. The cloth is woven on body-tension (back-strap) looms with a continuous warp; colours used are dark rust, brown and purple, although newer pieces suffer from fading due to the use of inferior dyes. Motifs are floral and geometric, and designs are constrained to about 20 traditional forms. It is said that one piece of cloth takes about five years to complete and only six families still understand the process. **Note** Much of the cloth for sale in the village does not originate from Tenganan.

About 13 km southwest of Candi Dasa is the temple and cave of **Goa Lawah** ⓘ *regular bemos run along the coast*. See page 321 for details.

Around Candi Dasa

The town and palace of **Amlapura** is within easy reach of Candi Dasa. **Three small islands with coral reefs** are to be found 30 minutes by boat from Candi Dasa. They make a good day trip for snorkelling or diving. Samuh village cooperative keeps goats on the largest of

Candi Dasa

To Tenganan (3km)

To Sengkidu & Balina Beach

Lenia Crafts   Asri   Candi Dasa Bookstore ❺

Jl Raya Candi Dasa

Perama Shuttle Bus Office

Amuk Bay

N

200 metres
200 yards

Sleeping 🛏
Agung Bungalows 10
Alam Asmara 2
Catra 6
Dasa Wana 1
Dewa Bharata 11

Genggong 12
Geringsering 7
Grand Natia Bungalows 15
Ida Beach Village 13
Ida's Homestay 14
Iguana Bungalows 5

Puri Oka 9
Seaside Cottages 4
Villa Sassoon 8
Watergarden 3

these islands, called **Nusa Kambing (goat island)** ⓘ *most hotels and losmen will arrange a boat for the day*. Every six months the goats are transported back to the mainland by boat. Quite a sight if you are lucky enough to witness it.

Sengkidu village → *Phone code: 0366.*

West of Candi Dasa (2 km) is an authentic Balinese village as yet unravaged by tourism. The pretty backstreets lead down to the sea and beach. If arriving by bemo, ask the driver to let you off in the centre of the village by the temple and sign for **Candi Beach Cottage**. Follow the signpost to the right of the temple; the track leads to the beach and accommodation, 400 m. Surrounded by coconut groves and tropical trees, Sengkidu offers an attractive alternative to Candi Dasa and is more pleasant and more interesting than Balina Beach. The village itself has a number of shops, fruit stalls and a temple where festivals are celebrated; foreigners are welcome to participate if they observe temple etiquette and wear the appropriate dress, otherwise they can watch.

Lovina ⬤🅿🄵🄰🅜🄾 ⤻ *pp327-338.*

→ *Phone code: 0362.*

Lovina, an 8 km stretch of grey sand, is the name given to an area that begins 7 km west of Singaraja and includes six villages. From east to west they are **Pemaron**, **Tukad Mungga**, **Anturan**, **Kalibukbuk**, **Kaliasem** and **Temukus**, all of which merge into one another. Lovina is one of the larger beach resorts on Bali and caters to all ages and price groups, from backpackers and a few remnant hippies to an increasingly upmarket and package tour oriented clientele. Kalibukbuk is the heart of Lovina, the busiest, most developed part, with the greatest number of tourist facilities and nightlife. Lying 1 km to the east of Kalibukbuk, **Banyualit** has a number of resort peaceful hotels scattered along the shoreline. There are also a couple of hotels slightly inland here, some of which are fair value.

Recent times have been hard on Lovina, with tourist arrivals a mere trickle of what they were a few years ago. Local residents blame the bomb attacks in Bali for the low numbers, and many lament the tough competition they face in gaining customers. For visitors, the upside of this situation is the great deals that can be had at empty hotels. Lovina has a relaxed pace of life and the inhabitants are friendly and welcoming, and is a great place to linger and make a local friend.

Eating 🅟
Candi Agung 3
Candi Dasa Cafe 1
Ganesha 2
Kubu Bali 5
Mr Grumpy 4
Raja's 6
Srijati 7
Toke 2

The beach

The beach itself is quite narrow in places and the grey/black sand is not the prettiest, but the waters are calm, so swimming is very safe and there is reasonable snorkelling on the reef just off-shore. The beach is interspersed with streams running into the sea, where some villagers wash in the evening. Several areas are the preserve of the local fishermen whose dogs can be menacing if you are out for a walk, particularly in the evening. You can usually scare them off by bending down to pick up a few stones, only the most persistent wait for you to actually throw the stone at them. Hawkers are not as bad as they used to be but can still be a nuisance, and it seems as if the entire resort is on commission for the much-touted dolphin trips.

The most popular outing is an early morning boat trip to see the **dolphins** cavorting off the coast; there are two schools of dolphin which regularly swim there. In the Kalibukbuk area the fishermen run a cooperative that fixes the number of people in each boat and the price, currently 50,000Rp; snorkelling is not included in the price. If you book through your hotel you will pay more for the convenience, but the price may include refreshments and the opportunity to go snorkelling afterwards. Boats set off at about 0600 and the tour usually lasts 1½ hours. Bear in mind that there is no shade on the boats. People have mixed reactions to the experience. If yours is the first boat to reach the dolphin area then you may be rewarded with 12 dolphins leaping and playing, but as other boats arrive the dolphins may be chased away. It is worth bearing in mind that at Lombok, and further east, dolphins can often be seen leaping out of the water alongside ferries and boats.

Around Lovina
About 5 km to the west of Lovina there are waterfalls at the village of **Labuhan Haji**, and a Buddhist monastery near the village of **Banjar Tegeha**, nearby which there are **hot springs** ⓘ *4100Rp adult, 2000Rp child. Drivers will offer to take tourists there and back again*

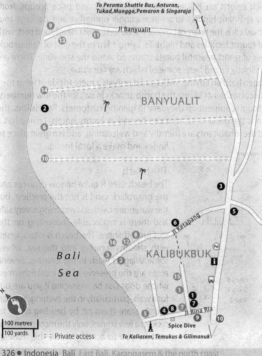

Lovina Beach

To Perama Shuttle Bus, Anturan,
Tukad, Mungga, Pemaron & Singaraja

Jl Banyualit

BANYUALIT

**Bali
Sea**

Jl Ketapang

KALIBUKBUK

Jl Bina Ria

Spice Dive
To Kaliasem, Temukus & Gilimanuk

100 metres
100 yards
= = Private access

Sleeping
Aneka 6
Angsoka 1
Astina 2
Banyualit Spa
  & Resort 9
Bayu Kartika Beach
  Resort 3
Elsa 15
Lovina Beach Resort 10
Nirwana Seaside
  Cottages 5
Pulestis Beach 7
Puri Bali Cottages 8
Ray Beach Inn 11
Rini 12
Suma 13
Sunari 14
Villa Jaya 16

Eating
Bakery Lovina 3
Bali Apik 1
Barcelona 6
Jasmine Kitchen 7
Kakatua 4
Khi Khi 5
Pappagallio 8
Spunky's 2

Bars & clubs
Jax 10
Poco Music 9

Bull races

Bull races, *sapi gerumbungan*, take place on Independence Day, 17 August, and on some other national holidays such as Singaraja Day, 31 March, check exact dates at the tourist office. The Balinese name for the races is derived from the huge wooden bells *gerumbungan*, which the bulls (*sapi* in Indonesian) wear around their necks during the races. These bull races are unique to Buleleng and originated as a religious ceremony to propitiate the gods before planting the new rice crop. The specially trained bulls, decorated with colourful ornaments and silk banners, and with equally well-dressed drivers, were originally raced over a flooded ricefield, usefully ploughing the field as they competed. Recently the event has been held on playing fields in the village of Kaliasem to the west of Kalibukbuk, primarily as a tourist attraction. However, in 1995 to commemorate the 50th anniversary of Indonesian Independence, the regional government decided to hold the event in its original form on a flooded ricefield in the village of Banjar, and planS to make this an annual event. The winner is not necessarily the fastest; the appearance of the bull and driver are an important consideration when the judge decides the overall winner.

---

for 100,000Rp, but this can easily be bargained down to 50,000Rp. Local expats have called into question the cleanliness of some of the pools. Make sure you bathe in one that has a fast flow of water running into it. To the south there are cool highland areas with **lakes** and **botanical gardens** in the area surrounding Bedugul and Gunung Batur; it can be very wet here except at the height of the dry season. To the east is **Singaraja**, the capital of the district, and beyond Singaraja there are interesting temples and other cultural sites, and the gamelan village of **Sawan**.

◉ East Bali, Karangasem and the north coast listings

For Sleeping and Eating price codes, see inside the front cover.

● Sleeping

Tirtagangga *p321*
B Tirta Ayu, (in the grounds of the water garden), T0363 22503, www.hotel tirtagangga.com. 4 comfortable a/c cottages with bathroom featuring sunken bath and shower with water spouting from a demonic head. Free access to the bathing pools in the water garden.
F-G Dhangin Taman Inn, T0363 22059. With a garden overlooking the water gardens, this place has whacky bright tiling and psychedelic ponds. Cleanish rooms, fair value.

Amed *p321*
All the accommodation is along the coastal road, and spread out sparsely over 11km. The greatest concentration of places to stay is from Jemeluk to Bunutan. Price codes here reflect their rates during high season. Many places double their rates during high season. Always negotiate accommodation costs, as often prices quoted are far too high. Most places have a restaurant but quality varies wildly.
L-AL Apa Kabar Villas, T0363 23492, www.apakabarvillas.com. Beautifully decorated cottages with spacious bathrooms that have a fish pond and bath, rooms here can accommodate up to 4 people. The hotel is next to the beach and has a pool, full spa service and a top-notch restaurant. Discounts available

A Anda Amed, T0363 23498, www.anda
amedresort.com. This hotel injects a bit of
glamour to Amed's lodging choices with
contemporary design, a sleek pool and a
Moorish terrace area.

B-C Puri Wisata Resort and Spa, T0363
23523, www.diveamed.com. Right down on
the beach, the a/c rooms here are big, and
some have private terrace looking out on the
sea. Some rooms are located in a block at the
back and have no view at all. There is a pool,
dive centre (see Activities and tours, page
336) and full spa service.

B-C Santai, T0363 23487, www.santai
bali.com. The 10 thatched a/c cottages,
with enough space to sleep 8, are tastefully
decorated and have a verdant outdoors
bathroom. This hotel has a pool, and is
right on the beach. You can rent bikes
for 50,000Rp per day.

B-C Wawa Wewe 2, T0363 23506,
wawawewevillas@yahoo.com. Right on the
beach, with a pool. Wide selection of rooms,
including a well-furnished family room with
space for 4 with sea view. Occasional
performances of local dances and *gamelan*
music. Book exchange. Restaurant (mid-range
to cheap) serving excellent local and Western
cuisine, with play area for children.

D Rising Star, T081936181368. New hotel
with only 4 rooms in a concrete block. All
rooms have a sea view, are clean and have
a/c and hot water. Pool.

E Aiona Kebun Obat (Health Garden),
Bunutan, Pos Keliling, Desa Bunutan, 80852
Abang, T0361 974865. 2 basic, bamboo
bungalows with private *mandi*, squat toilet, in
large overgrown gardens beside the sea. No
electricity. Offers traditional Balinese healing,
massage, meditation and sells locally made
health products. Vegetarian restaurant (¶-¶).

E Kusuma Jaya Indah, T0363 23488. Next
to the beach, this pleasant hotel has simple
a/c and fan rooms with outdoors bathroom
featuring shower and *mandi*. Some of the
rooms are a bit dark so ask to see a few. Pool.

E Prema Liong, T0363 23486, www.bali-
amed.com. The low-season prices for the 4

thatched cottages here are an absolute steal.
Cottages are set in a lush garden on the
hillside, and the sea can just about be seen
through the foliage. They have spacious
veranda with plenty of lounging potential.
Average restaurant. Recommended.

E Sunshine, T0363 23491, just opposite
Prema Liong on the seaward side of the road.
Plain rooms with fridge. Bathrooms have
baths (that need a good clean). Pool.

E Waeni's, T0363 23515, F0363 21044,
madesani@hotmail.com. Perched high on
a headland, these cottages have stunning
views of the sea and the surrounding hills;
Gunung Agung can be seen clearly in the
mornings, wrapped in cloud. The rooms are
comfortable and have a great outdoors
lounging area with bed and hammock.
Service is friendly and the restaurant serves
some great Balinese food. Recommended.

F Pupuan, T0363 23532. These cheapies are
clean, and have mosquito net and outdoors
bathroom. The veranda offers a sea view.
Good value.

Padangbai p322, map p322

The most attractive rooms are in town.
However, the best location is to the north
along the bay, where rooms and bungalows
are surrounded by gardens and coconut
groves and are quieter. You won't find the
luxury of Ubud and Seminyak available here,
but there is a lot of simple, good-value
accommodation available.

B Mustika Sari Hotel, Jl Silayukti, T0363
21540, F0363 21872. Padangbai's priciest
hotel seems to be suffering with plenty of
empty rooms and staff twiddling their fingers.
The hotel is set in pleasant gardens and
has a pool and massage service. Rooms are
large, clean and have a/c, TV, and bathroom
with a bath. Sizeable discounts available.

C-D Puri Rai, Jl Silayukti 7, T0363 41385,
F0363 41387, purirai_hotel@yahoo.com.
The 30 a/c and fan rooms here are spacious,
and clean with TV and fridge. Pool.

E-F Billabong, Jl Silayukti, T0363 41399.
The free breakfasts are good, and the simple

rattan-walled bungalows are acceptable, but not as good value as the standard bungalows, some of which have a sea view.

E-F Kembar Inn, Jl Segara 6, T0363 41364, F0363 41364. Precipitous stairs lead to the 2nd storey, which has a selection of spotless comfortable a/c and fan rooms. Some of the rooms are very dark, with windows leading onto the corridor outside, so ask to see a room with an exterior window. Friendly staff. Recommended.

E-F Kerti Beach Inn, Jl Silayukti, T0363 41391, kertibeachinn@yahoo.co.id. Fan rooms in *lumbung*-style 2-storey cottages are fairly large, and have a balcony and downstairs seating area. The other fan rooms are dark, but feature an outside bathroom.

E-F Pondok Serangan Inn, 2 Jl Silayukti, T0363 41425. Friendly, but quiet place with spacious fan and a/c rooms with hot water. The communal veranda on the 2nd floor has great view over the rooftops of the town and the boats in the bay. Recommended.

E-F Pondok Wisata Dharma, Jl Silaykuti, Gang Tongkol 6, T0363 41394, www.freewebs.com/dharmahomestay. Steep stairs lead to a common veranda and a selection of cheaper (darker, smaller) and more expensive clean fan and a/c rooms. Bathrooms have hot water.

E-F Pondok Wisata Parta, Jl Silaykuti, Gang Tongkol 7, T0363 41475. Next door to the Dharma, the rooms are of a similar standard, although the locks on the doors and windows could do with being replaced. You just about see the sea through a gap in the buildings in front.

F Padangbai Beach Inn, Jln Silayukti, T0363 41439, jelajah-bali@yahoo.com. The fan-cooled *lumbung* cottages have steep steps and plenty of gaps for the mosquitoes to get in and attack at night. However, the fan bungalows are spacious and clean.

F Topi Inn, Jl Silayukti 99, T0363 41424, www.topiinn.com. The 5 rooms here are average and quite dark, and with the smaller ones, guests have to use a communal bathroom. Nevertheless there is a great

common veranda with a hammock and cushions scattered around, and sea views, making this the most social place to stay in Padangbai. Breakfast is not included in the price. The larger rooms with attached bathrooms here are often full, so it might be worth reserving in advance.

Padangbai to Candi Dasa *p322*

LL Alila Manggis, Buitan, T0363 41011, www.alilahotels.com. Luxury hotel with 54 stylish rooms looking out onto a delightful coconut grove, and the ocean beyond. The hotel employs stunning use of lighting, which creates a soothing effect in the evenings. Cooking and diving courses offered. Pool. Good discounts available for online booking.

L Amankila (outside Candi Dasa near the village of Manggis), T0363 41333, www.amanresorts.com. One of the renowned Aman group of hotels, in an outstanding location spread out over the hillside with stunning sea views. Designed with simple elegance to create a calming and peaceful milieu, and with only 35 guest pavilions and 3 vast swimming pools on different levels of the hill, it is easy to imagine you are the only guest in residence.

C-D Matahari Beach Bungalows (formerly Sunrise Beach Bungalows), Buitan, Manggis, postal address: PO Box 287, Denpasar 80001, T0363 41008/41009. Signposted from the main road, follow a steep path down the hill for about 50 m. Beautiful secluded setting in a large coconut grove beside the sea, with a beach suitable for swimming though occasionally there is a current. 11 fairly attractive bungalows and rooms, very clean, some large family rooms, several of the cheapest rooms have a shared ceiling so your neighbours will probably hear your every movement; Ketut, the owner, speaks good English and is very helpful and knowledgeable about Bali.

D-E Ampel Bungalows, Manggis Beach, 6 km from Candi Dasa, just off the main road, T0363 41209. A peaceful, rural setting overlooking rice paddies and the sea.

4 simple, very clean bungalows, with private *mandi*, signposted from the main road shortly after the **Amankila Hotel**.

Candi Dasa *p323, map 325*

There are plenty of accommodation choices in Candi Dasa (almost too many it seems), although as the number of tourists visiting here has fallen, the upkeep of many of the places seems to have declined. Still, there are some good bargains to be had, and some stunning sea views. Most of the accommodation is on the seaward side of Jl Raya Candi Dasa. At the eastern end of Candi Dasa, where the main road bends to the left, a small road (Jl Banjar Samuh, there is no name sign but there are many signs indicating accommodations, including **Puri Oka** and **Genggong**) leads off on the right, lined with accommodation on the seaward side. Known as Samuh village, this slightly rural area is perhaps the most attractive place to stay. Expect power cuts if you visit during the rainy season unless yours is one of the many places with their own generator. Most include breakfast in their rates. Most hotels with swimming pools allow non-residents to use their pools for a small charge.

LL Villa Sassoon, Jl Puri Bagus, T0363 41511, www.villasassoon.com. Perfect for those seeking a little romance, the spacious, private villa compounds have 2 ensuite cottages and a further cottage with living room and kitchen area. The buildings face a central pool and outdoor lounging area. It's all very sleek and modern. Good discounts available for stays of more than 7 days.

L-A The Watergarden, Jl Raya Candi Dasa, T0363 41540, www.watergardenhotel.com. The beautiful, lush tropical gardens are filled with a variety of water features, and the private cottages have koi-filled lily ponds around the veranda. Rooms are spacious, spotless and quiet. There are good mountain views between the abundant foliage. This place is popular with foreign couples seeking a Balinese-style wedding. Pool, bar. Recommended. Discounts available.

A-B Alam Asmara, Jl Raya Candi Dasa, T0363 41929, www.alamasmara.com. Small fish-filled streams line the pathways in this new resort that offers elegant cottages with high ceilings and outdoor bathroom. Bedrooms have a safe and TV (no international channels). There is a resident dive master and a variety of diving courses are offered. Pool, access to the sea and full spa service. Discounts available.

B-C The Grand Natia Bungalows, Jl Raya Candi Dasa, T0363 42007, www.thefickeadventure.com. A path lined on both sides with koi-filled streams surrounds the 12 a/c cottages. The more expensive cottages have sea views from outside, but not from the bedrooms themselves. Cottages are tastefully decorated, and have a fridge. Pool.

B-D Catra, Jl Raya Candi Dasa, T0812 3660451. The pricing here is a little on the ambitious side, so bargaining is essential. The spacious a/c rooms have a kitchenette. There is a huge family suite with 2 bedrooms, a living area and enough space to sleep 5 that would be good value for a group. Pool.

B-E Puri Oka, Jl Puri Bagus, T/F 0363 41092. Large selection of rooms, some of which are vastly better value than the others. Cheap fan rooms are clean but have no hot water. Some of the a/c rooms need to be redecorated, but others, such as the sea view rooms feature TV, DVD player, outdoor bathroom and are tastefully decorated. The star is the spacious suite on the 2nd floor with plenty of light and a private terrace overlooking the sea. Pool.

C Dasa Wana, Jl Raya Candi Dasa, T0363 41444, F0361 462611. Variety of bungalows, with living room, kitchen and bathroom with bath. Some bungalows are much better furnished than others, so ask to see a selection. This place is not on the seaward side of the main road, but has great views of the mountains behind. Pool.

C Geringsering, Jl Raya Candi Dasa, T0363 41084. The 4 a/c rooms here are huge, 2 of which have lovely sea views and are filled with the sound of the surf. Rooms include mosquito net. Tax not included in the price.

C Ida Beach Village, Jl Puri Bagus, T0363 41118, F0363 41041. The 17 rooms here are each named after a local village. The red brick cottages look a bit wobbly from the outside, but have spacious interiors featuring bathrooms with bath. Some of the 2-storey cottages have a sea view. Pool.

C-D Dewa Bharata, Jl Raya Candi Dasa, T0363 41090, F0363 41091. The 20 fan and a/c rooms could do with a lick of paint, and the more expensive a/c rooms have a distinct masculine 1970s feel. A/c rooms feature TV and fridge. Fan rooms are a bit dark.

D Ida's Homestay, Jl Raya Candi Dasa, T0363 41096, jsidas@aol.com. An anomaly in Candi Dasa's accommodation choice in that it is set in a spacious palm grove, with the cottages being a minor feature of the property. Ida Ayu Srihati, the owner, has an extensive collection of Indonesian antiques that can be found littering the grounds; there's even an entire rice barn from Madura transplanted here. The gardens lead down to a small beach and a decking area overlooking the sea. There are 5 simple fan cottages, which are often full. Things are kept lo-fi, with a cow wandering the grove, chickens running free and hot water provided on demand rather than on tap. Book in advance. Recommended.

D-F Seaside Cottages, Jl Raya Candi Dasa, T0363 41629, www.balibeachfront-cottages.com. Set in pleasant tropical gardens leading down to the sea, with a good selection of bungalows. The small fan rooms have a single bed, but are clean and have attached bathroom. The larger bungalows have a/c and some have wonderful sea views. Tax and breakfast are not included in the price. Massage and salon services available.

E Iguana Bungalows, Jl Raya Candi Dasa, T0363 41973, iguana_cafe_bali@yahoo.com. The dense tropical garden contains a/c and fan bungalows that are clean, but look slightly worn, particularly the bathrooms. Some rooms have great sea views. Pool.

E-F Hotel Genggong, Jl Puri Bagus, T0363 41105. Set in extensive, slightly unkept grounds, the cheap fan rooms here are a bit tatty. The a/c rooms offer sea views and better value.

F Agung Bungalows, Jl Raya Candi Dasa, T/F0363 41535. Cheap, clean fan-only rattan-walled bungalows, some have excellent sea views (ask for the rooms at the front of the property). There's an enticing strip of beach here. Recommended.

Sengkidu village *p325*

A Candi Beach Cottage, reservations: PO Box 3308, Denpasar 80033, T0363 41234, F0363 41111. Luxury hotel set in large, scenic tropical gardens, in a quiet location beside sea with access to beach, offering everything you would expect from a hotel in this class, popular with tour groups.

C-D Pondok Bananas (Pisang), T0363 41065. Family-run, 4 spotless rooms/bungalows set in a large coconut grove beside the sea with access to beach, very peaceful and secluded.

D-E Puri Amarta (Amarta Beach Bungalows), T0363 41230. 10 bungalows set in large, attractive gardens beside the sea and beach, well-run and very popular, liable to be full even off-season, restaurant (†) beside sea.

E Dwi Utama, T0363 41053. 6 very clean rooms, with fan, private bathroom, beachside restaurant (cheap), access to good, small beach, well-tended, small garden, peaceful, good value.

E Nusa Indah Bungalows, Sengkidu, signposted and reached via a separate track to the left of the temple. Set in a peaceful location beside the sea, amid coconut groves and rice paddies, 7 clean, simple bungalows with fan, access to small, rocky beach, beachside restaurant (†).

Lovina *p325, map p324*

Mosquitoes can be a problem, not all bungalows provide nets. The central area of Kalibukbuk has the greatest concentration of accommodation, the widest choice of restaurants and nightlife, and most of the tourist facilities; however, it is becoming built up. Some of the side roads to the east in the Anturan area offer more attractive and peaceful surroundings. To the west of Kalibukbuk towards Temukus, the road runs close to the beach, so accommodation here can be noisy; there are some new, attractive places here with beachfront locations, though prices seem a bit high.

Kalibukbuk

D-E Puri Bali Cottages, Jl Ketapang, T0362 41485, www.puribalilovina.com. Selection of a/c and fan rooms in a nice garden. Rooms are large and have hot water, but are a little decrepit. Cheaper ones come with a mosquito net. Pool and basketball area for those who fancy shooting some hoops under the tropical sun.

D-E Rini, Jl Ketapang, T0362 41386, www.rinihotel.homepage.dk. In a large compound with a saltwater swimming pool, this hotel has an excellent selection of well-designed a/c and fan rooms, some of which are cavernous, with equally large balconies. The largest rooms are the upstairs fan rooms in the 2-storey buildings and have nice sunset views. Friendly staff. Recommended.

D-F Hotel Angsoka, Jl Bina Ria, T0362 41023, www.angsoka.com This hotel is extremely popular, and is a good place to meet other travellers. The rooms do not quite match the popularity though, as many are tired looking. Simple a/c and fan rooms with bath. Pool.

D-F Nirwana Seaside Cottages, Jl Bina Ria, T0362 41288, www.nirwanaseaside.com. Set in huge, pleasant gardens, this hotel has a range of a/c and fan rooms, some with sea view. The clean deluxe rooms, feature bath and a pleasant veranda, but the 2-storey bungalows with fan represent better value and come with a sea view. Pool.

E Villa Jaya, Jl Ketapang, T0362 7001238. 100 m down a path off Jl Ketapang. New hotel with cosy fan and a/c rooms overlooking the pool and views of the surrounding rice fields.

F-E Astina Seaside Cottages, Jl Ketapang, T0362 41187, selisakadek@hotmail.com.

Clean, simple a/c fan rooms with hot water and bath. Nice pool.

F-E Bayu Kartika Beach Resort, Jl Ketapang, T0362 41055, www.bayukartikaresort.com. Lots of space in this 2-hectare resort and featuring (so the owner claims) the largest pool in Lovina. Many rooms face the sea, but are a little faded. The more expensive rooms have an open air bathroom. Interestingly, there is a monitor lizard pond. Popular.

F Hotel Elsa, Jl Bina Ria, T0362 41448. A/c and fan rooms are clean, and have hot water. No garden or pool.

F Pulestis Beach Hotel, Jl Bina Ria, T0362 41035, jokoartawan@hotmail.com. You can't miss this hotel, with its extraordinarily garish Balinese façade, and equally bright rooms. The fan rooms are cleanish and comfortable and feature open air bathroom. Small pool.

Banyualit

This area is much quieter, but offers the usual range of facilities, including internet cafés, cheap restaurants and provision stores.

C-E Banyualit Spa and Resort, Jl Banyualit, T0362 41789, www.banyualit.com. Range of rooms set in a lush garden. A/c rooms are clean and have TV, but are a little cramped and dark. The fan rooms, with rattan walls are very simple and hugely overpriced. Full spa service with a host of friendly staff. Pool.

D Suma, Jl Banyualit, T0362 41566, www.sumahotel.com. The staff are vey welcoming at this hotel with clean and comfortable a/c and fan rooms. Pool and spa.

F Ray Beach Inn, Jl Banyualit, T0362 41088. Cheap, clean fan rooms and spa service.

Beachfront

LL-A Sunari, Jl Raya Lovina, T0362 41775, www.sunari.com (formerly Sol Lovina). A full range of facilities is available in this hotel including spa and gym. Rooms are spacious and the more expensive have private garden and a plunge pool. Business doesn't seem too brisk here. 50% discounts available.

B-C Aneka, Jl Raya Lovina, T0362 41121, www.aneka-lovina.com. This popular resort has 59 a/c rooms that are clean, well decorated and comfortable. Resort has a pool near the beach, fitness centre and offers Balinese dance lessons. Discounts available.

C-D Lovina Beach Resort, Jl Raya Lovina, T0362 41092, www.balilovinaresort.com (formerly Mas Lovina Beach). 20 *lumbung* (rice barn)-style cottages facing the sea. Some come with living room area downstairs with TV and DVD player. Rooms are clean and adequate if a little characterless. Pool. PADI diving courses offered.

ᴓ Eating

Tirtagangga *p321*
There are a few choices, mainly around the water garden.

ᵀᵀ Tirta Ayu Hotel, (see Sleeping) is the best restaurant here, with sublime views and serving good international cuisine.

ᵀ Gangga Cafe, T0363 22041, open 0700-2200. Cheap eatery near the entrance to the gardens, serves delicious home-made yoghurt, curries and Balinese food.

Amed *p321*
Many people choose to eat in the restaurants attached to their hotel. However, there are a handful of eateries along the road.

ᵀᵀ Pazzo, T08283685498, open 1000-2300. Pasta, pizza and the usual Western fare alongside a fair selection of Indonesia dishes. Pazzo doubles as a popular bar with a choice of wines and cocktails, live music, pool and Balinese dancing.

ᵀᵀ Wawa Wewe 1, T0363 23506, www.au.geocities.com/wawawewe1-2, open 0800-2200. 400 m down the road (away from Amed) from the hotel of the same name, this friendly restaurant has a good selection of international food and Balinese cuisine.

ᵀ Ari's Warung, T0852 37882015, open 0900-2100 and **Cafe C'est Bon**, T0852 348266778, open 0900-2200. Both these small places look a little forlorn with a distinct lack of custom. This is a shame as they are

both good places to try the catch of the day with tasty Balinese sauces. Both have sea views, and Ari's Warung offers free transport to and from the restaurant.

Padangbai *p322, map p322*
When you're a limp stone's throw to the sea, the seafood is going to be good, as is the case in Padangbai. It is quite common to see women walking around with large freshly caught yellow fin tuna thrown over their shoulder. Many of the hotels have restaurants, and there are numerous restaurants along the shoreline serving up the usual Indonesian and Western dishes. There are a lot of cheap *warungs* around the port and on Jl Pelabuhan Padangbai.

ᵀᵀ Topi Inn, see Sleeping, open 0730-2300. The best place to eat in Padangbai, with an extensive menu of fresh seafood, vegetarian dishes, great salads and delights such as a delicious cheese platter with olives. The staff are friendly and the restaurant is deservedly popular. You can refill your used water bottle here with fresh drinking water for 1000Rp.

ᵀ Cafe Papa John, Jl Segara, open 0700-2200. Good spot to watch the world go by and see boats pulling in to the bay. The delicious fish kebabs are served in a tangy spicy sauce.

ᵀ Depot Segara, Jl Segara, T0363 41443, open 0800-2200. Friendly staff and an acoustic guitar propped up the in the corner point to good times at this relaxed eatery offering a range of Balinese food and fresh seafood. The fish *sate* is super and freshly made each morning. There is also the usual range of sandwiches, burgers and good chilled lassis.

Candi Dasa *p323, map p325*
There are a variety of well-priced restaurants dotted along the main road with similar menus; seafood is the best bet. Most restaurants cater to perceived European tastes, which can be disappointing for anyone who likes Indonesian food. Many of the hotels have restaurants, often with sea views. The following are also recommended

though quality and ingredients can vary enormously from day to day; you might have a delicious meal one day, order the exact same dish the next day and be disappointed.

ᵀᵀ Candi Agung, Jl Raya Candi Dasa, T0363 41672. Shady and cool, lots of good seafood can be had here, along with a *rijstafel* for 2, also pizza and pasta. Long cocktail list.

ᵀᵀ Candi Dasa Cafe, Jl Raya Candi Dasa, T0363 41107, open 0800-2300. Clean and comfortable restaurant, Balinese fare and *rijstafel*. Delicious icy ginger ale.

ᵀᵀ Ganesha, Jl Raya Candi Dasa, T0813 38112898. Good-value set meals, plenty of fresh seafood, and suckling pig at this friendly good-value eatery, which has *legong* and mask dance performances nightly at 1930.

ᵀᵀ Kubu Bali, Jl Raya Candi Dasa, T0363 41532. Specializes in seafood with fish, crab, lobster and crab dishes cooked a variety of ways. Some standard international dishes.

ᵀᵀ Toke, Jl Raya Candi Dasa, T0363 41991, open 1100-2300. Known for its Indian cuisine, this is the place in Candi Dasa to get good mushroom masala, naan and aloo gobi. There's an extensive list of cocktails, and an excellent range of Western food. The kitchen here is open, so diners can watch their dinner being prepared. Recommended.

ᵀᵀ The Watergarden, Jl Raya Candi Dasa, T0363 41540, open 0700-2300. Excellent array of fresh seafood, including delicious *ikan pepes* and grilled *mahi mahi* glazed with soy sauce, available in this peaceful setting of lily ponds and fountains. Also international favourites and plenty of salads, as well as Dom Pérignon champagne for those in the mood to really push the boat out. Good service. Recommended.

ᵀ Mr Grumpy, Jl Raya Candi Dasa, T0363 41566, open 1000-2200. Football shirts cover the walls, and a huge TV takes centre stage here in this place offering light Western meals, all-day happy hour and pool table.

ᵀ Raja's, Jl Raya Candi Dasa, T0363 42034, open 0800-2200. This well-established roadside restaurant with pool table, and an extensive selection of DVDs, has a good

menu of set meals, including an Indian menu offering Goan curries and an interesting pork and banana curry. Happy hour 1700-1900.

ᵀ Srijati, Jl Raya Candi Dasa, open 0700-2100. Rustic and cheap venue to grab a lunch of *nasi goreng* or *opor ayam*. Also a fair number of authentic Balinese dishes.

Lovina p325, map p324

Lovina offers a great chance to tuck into some good, fresh seafood with excellent Balinese sauces, although there are plenty of places serving reasonable Western fare. There is also a line of *kaki-lima* and small *warungs* selling cheap *bakso*, *nasi goreng*, *roti bakar* and some Balinese street food on Jl Raya Lovina, near the traffic lights at the end of Jl Ketupang. It opens when the sun sets.

ᵀᵀ Bali Apik, Jl Bina Ria, T0362 41050, open 0800-2300. Slow staff, but a good range of vegetarian dishes and a good seafood menu that includes tasty tuna fish *sate*.

ᵀᵀ Barcelona, Jl Ketupang, T0362 41894, open 0900-2300. Popular family-run place, one of the better places to try Balinese food in Lovina. The *pepes babi guling* (grilled pork cooked in a banana leaf) and *sate pelecing* (fish sate with Balinese sauce) are excellent.

ᵀᵀ Jasmine Kitchen, Jl Bina Ria, T0362 41565, jasminekitchen@beeb.net, open 1130-2230. The cheery owner serves up good Thai favourites such as tom yum soup, steamed fish in a lime, lemongrass and coriander dressing and some delicious home-made cakes to the sound of the sitar in a relaxed setting. The daily specials are worth investigating.

ᵀᵀ Kakatua, Jl Bina Ria, T0362 41144, open 0800-2300. The water features make this restaurant a mellow place, serving Burmese fishballs, home-made cakes and baked fish.

ᵀᵀ Pappagallio, Jl Bina Ria, T0362 41163, open 1000-2300. The Italian menu and semi-slick interior shows this place has grand pretensions, which are always going to be difficult to fulfil. Nevertheless the pizzas here are pretty good.

¶ **Bakery Lovina**, Jl Raya Lovina, T0362 42225, open 0730-2130. This mini-market selling a range of cheeses, meats, wines and tinned Western food for the local expat community also makes excellent sandwiches, fresh bread and cakes.

¶ **Khi Khi**, Jl Raya Lovina, T0362 41548, open 1000-2200. Excellent value seafood sets that allow a choice of fish, Balinese *bumbu* (dressing for the fish) a Chinese-style sauce, and a large bowl of rice. The restaurant is simple and unfussy and has an open kitchen.

¶ **Spunky's**, on the beach near the Aneka Hotel, T0813 3736509, open 1300-2400. Owned by an Englishman, this is the place for homesick British tourists to get a long overdue helping of ham or sausage and egg. Also daily seafood specials. An unbeatable location – select one of the many cocktails on offer and watch the sun go down. Recommended.

Bars and clubs

Padangbai *p322, map p322*
Babylon Bar and Kinky Reggae Bar on Jl Silyakuti open in the afternoon and serve booze until late.
Zen Inn, Jl Segara, T0819 33092012, 0700-2300. Serves pies with mash and gravy, and rocks until almost 2400 with live music and a video screen in a comfortable and friendly pub-like setting.

Lovina *p325, map p324*
Many of the places on Jl Bina Ria offer all-day happy hour in an attempt to lure customers, but don't expect sophisticated nightlife.
Jax, Jl Raya Lovina, 1400-late. Decked out in Jamaican flags, with a TV playing recent football matches over the bar and live music you can join in with.
Poco Music Bar, Jl Bina Ria, T0362 41434, 1100-late. Live music every evening. Western bar food is served.

Entertainment

Candi Dasa *p323, map p325*
Balinese dance performances are staged nightly at various restaurants in town, though not quite up to Ubud quality.

Shopping

Semarapura and around *p320*
Textiles Although good examples are hard to find, Semarapura is the centre of the production of royal *songket* cloth, traditionally silk but today more often synthetic. The cloth is worn for ceremonial occasions and characteristically features floral designs, geometric patterns, *wayang* figures and animals. It takes 2 months to weave a good piece.

Padangbai *p322, map p322*
Books Wayan's Bookstore, Jl Penataran Agung, T081916153587, 0800-1800. On the way up to Pantai Cecil, Wayan's is down a small lane on the right hand side. He has a huge sign on the roof of his shop in red letters. This shop has the best selection of 2nd-hand books in Padangbai, and Wayan also offers rental and exchange services.

Candi Dasa *p323, map p325*
Books The best place is the **Candi Dasa Bookstore**, which has a reasonable selection of books on Bali and Indonesia as well as 2nd-hand books, magazines and newspapers. The lady who runs it speaks excellent English and is very friendly and helpful.
Crafts **Geringsing**, Jl Raya Candi Dasa, T0363 41084, open 0900-1800, on the main road, sells double *ikat* cloth from Tenganan and other Balinese arts and crafts. **Lenia**, Jl Raya Candi Dasa T0363 41759, open 1000-2000, a good place to see *ata* baskets, which are made from a locally grown vine much more durable than rattan. Water resistant, it is claimed these baskets can last for up to 100 years. There is also a small selection of Sumba blankets and other quality crafts.

Nusantara, Jl Raya Candi Dasa, open 0900-2100, is also a good place to pick up locally made handicrafts.

Groceries Asri, fixed-price store for film, food and medicine.

Tailor The lady who runs the Candi Dasa bookstore is also a tailor.

▲▲ Activities and tours

Amed *p321*

Diving and snorkelling The reef in Amed is very close to the beach, and the resorts are not far from the USAT Liberty wreck at Tulamben. Snorkelling gear can be hired from hotels or stalls along the road for between 20,000Rp and 30,000Rp per day.

ECO Dive Bali, T0363 23482, www.ecodive bali.com. Offers dives at Tulamben (US$70 for 2 dives), and in locations in Amed. They also run a variety of courses including the Open Water course for US$375.

Puri Wirata Dive Centre, T0363 23523. Slightly cheaper, offering 2 dives at Tulamben for US$55, 2 dives at the nearby Japanese wreck at US$50, and the Open Water course for US$360.

Body and soul Yoga and meditation sessions are available at **Aiona Kebun Obat** (see Sleeping), along with tarot card reading. **A Spa**, T0813 38238846, open 1000-1900. Lots on offer including an Indonesian massage US$18 for 1 hr, 90-min calming back treatment US$28. Roaming masseuses pop into hotels throughout the day clutching comments from satisfied customers looking for business. Bargain hard.

Padangbai *p322, map p322*

Diving and snorkelling Diving is a popular activity in Padangbai, with numerous operators along Jl Silayukti. Dives can be taken in waters around Padangbai, at nearby Gili Biaha with its shark cave, and further afield at the wreck of the USAT Liberty Bell at Tulamben. Marine life that can be seen

includes the giant tuna, napoleon wrasse, sea turtles and sharks. You can pick up a snorkel set along the seafront for 20,000Rp (though you'll have to bargain) and find reasonable snorkelling at the Blue Lagoon Beach over the headland at the east end of the town.

Geko Dive, Jl Silayukti, T0363 41516, www.gekodive.com. Slighty cheaper than OK Divers, this company offers PADI Open Water courses for US$300, Rescue Diver for US$300. They also run a Discover Scuba session for diving novces in their pool for US$65.

OK Divers, Jl Silayukti, T0363 41790, info@divingbali.cz. A popular Czech outfit that offers 2 dives for US$63, the PADI Open Water course for US$470, and Rescue Diver for US$470.

Workshops **Topi Inn** (see Sleeping) has workshops on a wide variety of topics including Balinese woodcarving, coconut tree climbing, batik and *ikat* weaving. You can also join discussions on Balinese Hinduism.

Candi Dasa *p323, map p325*

Diving and snorkelling Boat hire and snorkelling trips to Nusa Lembongan (US$33) can be organized through **Beli Made Tam**, T0818 551752, on the beach near the Puri Bali Hotel. He also offers snorkelling trips to White Sand Beach (3 hrs including equipment – US$27). You can rent snorkelling equipment from him for 20,000Rp for 2 hrs.

Sub Ocean Bali, Jl Raya Candi Dasa, T0363 41411, www.suboceanbali.com. 5-star PADI dive centre offering trips to Nusa Penida, Tulamben and Gili Mimpang. They also rent snorkelling equipment for US$8 per day.

Lovina *p325, map p324*

Boats and fishing Tours are organized by the larger hotels, tour and dive companies and *losmen* for 50,000Rp an hour per person. The wonderfully named **Captain Ketut Bonanza** (T081338221175) has excellent English and can regale customers with tales of tiger sharks and sea snakes.

Body and soul Araminth Spa,

Jl Ketapang, T0362 41901, open 0900-1900, www.arunaspa.com. Variety of treatments available including facials (US$9.20), ayurvedic massage (US$25) and Indonesian treatments such *as mandi lulur* and *mandi rempah* (spice bath). More of the same can be found at **Bali Samadhi Spa**, Jl Ketapang, T08133 8558260, www.balisamadhi.com, 0900-1800.

Cooking classes Putu's Home Cooking, T08122 8563705. Includes a trip to the local market and instruction in cooking 7 Balinese dishes followed by a local feast. Lesson lasts 4-5 hrs, US$16.50 per person.

Diving and snorkelling Average snorkelling just off the beach. Snorkel hire 20,000Rp for 1 hr or 60,000Rp an hour with a boat and captain; better marine life at Menjangan Island (with **Spice Dive**, see below). Equipment available from boat owners and dive shops, not all of equal quality. **Spice Dive**, Jl Bina Ria, T0362 41305, www.balispicedive.com. The waters around Lovina are not particularly special for diving, so this highly regarded dive centre offers a variety of diving courses and trips to nearby diving locations such as Pulau Menjangan and Tulamben as well as Zen Beach for muck diving. Introduction dives cost US$70, and a PADI Open Water course costs US$392. Rescue Diver, Divemaster and many other courses are also offered.

Trekking Trekking in the area around Sambangan village can be organized through **Putu Puspa**, T0815 58577404 and includes walks through rice fields, and waterfalls and visits to meditation caves for US$15 (short trek) to US$30 for a longer trek.

Watersports and swimming Most big hotels will let non-residents use the pool for between 10,000Rp and 20,000Rp if you look presentable.

Spunky's on the beach in Banyualit (see Eating) rents jet skis for US$77 per hr, surf bikes for US$11 per hr, canoes for US$5.50 per hr, and catamarans for US$22 per hr.

⊖ Transport

Semarapura and around *p320*
Bemo Regular connections with Denpasar's Batubulan terminal and points east – **Besakih**, **Amlapura**, **Candi Dasa**.
Boat Kusamba, from where there are boats to **Nusa Penida**.

Tirtagangga *p321*
Bemos Connect Tirtagangga with **Semarapura** and **Singaraja** (for connections with Lovina).
Shuttles 2 daily from **Padangbai** to Tirtagangga, US$14.

Amed *p321*
Bemo From **Semarapura** catch a bemo heading north to Culik (15,000Rp) and Singaraja. Change bemos at Culik; until 1200 there are a limited number of bright red bemos running along the coast east to Amed and Lipah, after 1200 you can catch an ojek or try and hitch a lift, otherwise it is a long walk.
Car 45 mins to Amed from Candi Dasa.

Padangbai *p322, map p322*
Bemo Padangbai is 2.5 km off the main coastal road; connections with **Denpasar's Batubulan terminal**, **Candi Dasa** and **Amlapura**. Blue bemos run to **Semarapura**, 15,000Rp, and orange bemos run to **Amlapura**, 15,000Rp.
Boat Ferries for Lembar on **Lombok** leave around the clock daily, every 1½ hrs, and take 4-5 hrs depending on the seas, 28,000Rp adult, 17,500Rp child. The busiest departure is 0800, which is fine if one of the 2 large ultra-modern ferries is doing that sailing; otherwise try to get on as early as possible to secure a decent seat. Boats also depart for **Nusa Penida**, tourist price

50,000Rp. To the **Gili Islands**, the fastest way is using **Gili Cat**. (Padangbai agent: Jl Silayukti, T0363 41441, www.gilicat.com). Their boats leave Padangbai daily at 0830 and sail to **Gili Tranwangan** in 1½ hrs. US$72 1-way, US$131 for a return. Equally direct, but taking longer is the Perama boat, which leaves Padangbai at 1330 and arrives on Gili Trawangan 4 hrs later, US$22. Aggressive porters at the ferry terminal can be a real pain. They try and grab your luggage, carry it on board and then charge an outrageous amount. If you need help to carry your belongings, negotiate a fair price beforehand. 5000Rp per piece should cover it.

Bus From the bus station you can catch long-distance buses, west to **Java** and east to **Sumbawa** and **Lombok**.

Shuttles (Perama office: Jl Pelabuhan Padangbai, T0363 41419). Daily connections to **Kuta** and **Ngurah Rai Airport**, 3 daily, US$6.50, **Ubud**, 3 daily, US$6.50, **Candi Dasa**, 3 daily, US$3 (sometimes the Perama shuttle to Candi Dasa does not run due to lack of customers and it will be necessary to jump on the orange bemo to Amlapura, US$1.20 or hire a bemo, US$4). To **Lovina**, 1 daily, US$16.50, **Senggigi**, 2 daily, US$6.50 and **Mataram**, 2 daily, US$6.50.

Candi Dasa p323, map p325

Bemo Regular connections with Denpasar's Batubulan terminal (2 hrs 10 mins), **Amlapura** and **Semarapura**.

Bicycle hire From Srijati (see Eating) for 20,000Rp a day.

Car/motorbike hire From hotels, *losmen* and from shops along the main road.

Shuttles Can be found at the western end of Jl Raya Candi Dasa, T0363 41114. To **Kuta** and **Ngurah Rai Airport**, 3 daily, US$6.50, **Ubud**, 3 daily, US$5.50, **Lovina**, 1 daily, US$16.50

via Ubud, **Padangbai**, 3 daily, US$3. Also to **Amed** 2 daily, US$14, 2 people min. It's just as easy to hire an ojek for the ride costing around US$8, including a stop in **Tirtagangga** (30 mins). If you want to go to Lombok, they will shuttle you first to the office in Padangbai.

Lovina p325, map p324

Bus From **Denpasar's** Ubung terminal, catch an express bus to Singaraja, 1½-2 hrs, from where there are regular buses to Lovina. There are also regular buses and minibuses from **Gilimanuk**, taking the north coast route, 1½ hrs (buses from Java will drop passengers off at Gilimanuk to catch a connection to Lovina – sometimes included in the cost of the ferry and bus ticket). Buses to Gilimanuk for the ferry to Java cost US$2. To **Java** jump on a Singaraja-Java bus as it passes along Jl Raya Lovina. Tickets need to be booked a day in advance and can be bought in several places in Kalibukbuk. To **Jakarta** is US$33, to **Yogyakarta** US$25, **Surabaya** 120,000Rp and **Probolinggo** (for Gunung Bromo) is US$13.

Car/motorbike/bicycle hire From several places around town for US$11/US$4/US$2 per day.

Shuttles Perama shuttles to **Kuta**, 1 daily, US$13.50, to **Ubud**, 1 daily, US$13.50, to **Padangbai**, 1 daily, US$16.50, and to **Candi Dasa**, 1 daily, US$16.50. Look around town for other shuttle bus prices, as Lovina is the one place Perama don't seem to have the monopoly. On arrival in Lovina, Perama take passengers to their office in Anturan for a lunch of *nasi goreng*, while touts hover around offering accommodation, After beating off the touts, you get back on the Perama bus and are taken to your hotel.

Lombok to East Nusa Tenggara

→ *Colour map 11.*

Lombok has been earmarked for tourist development for decades, on the pretext that it is in a position to emulate Bali's success. Whether the development plans will ever come to fruition is another matter and for the time being it remains a relatively quiet alternative to Bali, although considerably busier and more developed than the islands to the east. The number of visitors to Lombok is generally dependent on the numbers visiting Bali, and since the bombs, tourism in Lombok has very much taken a beating. While there are a number of first-class hotels along the beaches away from these tourist areas, Lombok is still 'traditional' and foreigners are a comparative novelty. It is also a poor island; the famines of the Dutch period and the 1960s remain very much in the collective consciousness.

Most visitors to Lombok stay on Senggigi Beach, on the west coast and just north of the capital Mataram, or on the Gilis, a small group of islands north of Senggigi. However, the south coast, around Kuta, with its beautiful sandy bays set between rocky outcrops, is more dramatic. There is now a surfaced road to Kuta and some good accommodation once you get there, including one international-class hotel (but be aware that plans are afoot to continue this tourist development). There are also a handful of towns inland with accommodation. While Lombok has gradually expanded over the years, with the exception of the Gili Islands, it has not yet taken off – which, of course, is why some people prefer it to Bali.

Ins and outs

Getting there

Carriers flying to Lombok include **Silk Air** (T0370 633987, www.silkair.com), flying from Singapore and **Merpati** (T0370-621111), flying from Kuala Lumpur, Malaysia. Internal carriers linking the Indonesian islands include **Lion Air** (T0370-663444, lionair.co.id), **Garuda** (T0370-646846, www.garuda_indonesia.com), **Merpati** and **Batavia Air** (T0370-648998, www.batavia-air.co.id).

Airport information **Selaparang Mataram Airport** lies north of Mataram and 20 minutes south of Senggigi Beach. It is possible to pick up a VOA (visa on arrival) at the airport. There is a money changer (for US dollars travellers cheques only and cash), information office and hotel booking counters. There are fixed-fare taxis from the airport to various destinations, bemos from the main road and a public bus to Bangsal (public bus towards Tanjung, ask to be dropped off at Pemenang. They are 500 m from the airport, to the left. When you reach the first crossroads, turn left and wait for your bus connection). A new airport is currently being built in central Lombok and should be ready in 2010.

Getting around

Lombok's main artery is the excellent road running east from Mataram to Labuhan Lombok. There is now a paved road to Lembar, Praya, Kuta and to Bangsal in the north. Most of Lombok's roads are paved, but the secondary roads are not well maintained and car travel can be slow and uncomfortable, plus there are hazards of potholes and random rocks.

Bemos and colts are the main forms of transport between towns and villages. They are a good cheap way to get around the island and, unlike Bali, frequent changes of bemo are not necessary to get from A to B.

Perama ① *66 Jl Pejanggik 66, Mataram, T0370 635928*, operate shuttle buses from Bali to Lombok.

Cidomos are a two-wheeled horse-drawn cart. In the west, cidomos are gradually being replaced by bemos, but in the less developed central and east they remain the main mode of local transport and are more elaborate, with brightly coloured carts and ponies decked out with pompoms and bells.

West coast Lombok

Most visitors to Lombok stay either at Senggigi beach or on the 'Gilis'. Senggigi Beach stretches over 8 km from Batulayar to Mangsit. The road from Mataram to Bangsal winds through impressive tropical forest in the foothills of Mount Rinjani. Travelling further north along the coast from Mangsit, the road reaches Bangsal, the 'port' for boats to the Gilis. Senggigi is the most developed tourist area on Lombok, with a range of hotels. It is easy to see why this area was chosen by investors and local entrepreneurs. The beaches here – and they extend over several kilometres – are picturesque and the backdrop of mountains and fabulous sunsets adds to the ambience.

The Gili Islands are becoming increasingly expensive and are no longer primarily geared to the backpacker market. There are no vehicles and there really isn't much more to do beyond sunbathing, swimming, snorkelling, walking and generally relaxing. ▸▸ *For listings, see pages 342-345.*

Senggigi ⬤🅟🅕🅖🅐🅜🅐🅑🅘 ▸▸ *pp342-345. Colour map 11, B2.*

→ *Phone code: 0370.*

Senggigi lies 12 km north of Mataram on the west coast. The beach overlooks the famous Lombok Strait the English naturalist Alfred Russel Wallace postulated divided the Asian and Australasian zoological realms. The sacred Mount Agung on Bali can usually be seen shimmering in the distance. While Senggigi village supports the main concentration of shops, bars, restaurants and tour companies, hotels and bungalows stretch along the coast and the road for several kilometres, from Batulayar Beach in the south, to Batubolong, Senggigi and Mangsit beaches to the north. Mangsit is quieter and less developed.

Many visitors express disappointment with Senggigi beach itself, which is rather tatty and not very attractive. The town's downfall as a destination has been meteoric. It never reached the status of Bali's main resorts and instead plunged dramatically in the wake of the Bali bombings: pavements are overgrown, rubbish lies strewn about, businesses are shutting at an alarming rate and hotels lie derelict. The increasingly easy connections with the Gili islands from Bali mean that fewer and fewer tourists ever make it to the mainland. Senggigi has many hotels catering largely for the package tour trade, and they are not always particularly well-managed, or maintained. Their rates are highly negotiable off season. Many of the best guesthouses on Lombok are Balinese owned, and as prices on Bali rise inexorably, they no longer seem as overpriced as they once did.

Further north, this area becomes more beautiful and peaceful, with unspoilt, windswept beaches and lovely views across the Lombok Strait to Mount Agung on Bali and superb sunsets. They are currently free of the hawkers that so mar a visit to Senggigi itself.

Sights

In the mornings between 0800 and 1100, hundreds of brightly coloured fishing boats return to the beach. The fishermen leave at 0500 and use traditional methods of fishing, eschewing nets for a length of string with 30 hooks; when the string feels heavy they know it is time to haul it in. If the wind is onshore they fish off Mangsit, if the wind is offshore they fish off Senggigi beach.

About 2 km south of Senggigi, on a headland, is the **Batubolong Temple**. Unremarkable artistically (particularly when compared with the temples of Bali), it is named after a rock with a hole in it (*Batu Bolong* or 'Hollow Rock') found here. Tourists come to watch the sun set over Bali – devotees, to watch it set over the sacred Mount Agung.

Each evening an informal **beach market** sets up on the beach in front of the Senggigi Beach Hotel; vendors lay out their wares (textiles, T-shirts, woodcarvings and 'antiques'); heavy bargaining is required – these people really know how to sell.

Tours: Lombok to Flores via Komodo by boat

Indonesian life is inextricably linked with the vast amount of water that surrounds the myriad islands, and it is definitely worth spending some time on a boat while you're in the country. There are a couple of companies that offer boat trips from Lombok to Labuanbajo, Flores via Komodo Island. The tours usually sail across the top of Sumbawa, stopping at Pulau Satonda for some snorkelling before continuing to Komodo and finally the port of Labuanbajo, Flores. Most trips last three days and two nights, and it is undoubtedly one of the most convenient ways of seeing the Komodo dragon, and for many, is the highlight of a trip to Indonesia. It is wonderful to fall asleep on deck to the sound of the sea and wake up with the sunrise, gliding past desolate islands and distant coastlines. However, these boats can get packed with tourists, and as the old adage goes, a boat gets smaller each day you spend on it. The seas in this area can be highly unpredictable, and sailing in a seaworthy vessel in crucial. It makes sense to research the trip you wish to undertake thoroughly, and if the boat is going to be packed with other tourists, will the trip be enjoyable? Perama offer three-day two-night trips starting at US$218 for a place on the deck, and US$284 for a cabin room. All meals are provided, though don't expect too much. (The first meal on board is usually quite lavish, but they go quickly downhill from there – stock up on crackers and snacks). The trip to Labuanbajo departs every six days. The return trip from Labuanbajo takes lasts two days and one night and sails via Rinca, another place to see Komodo dragons, and costs US$142 for deck and US$197 for a cabin. There are

Senggigi Beach

N

300 metres
300 yards

Sleeping 💤
Batu Bolong Cottages **6**
Beach Club **2**
Cafe Wayan **3**
Dharmarie **4**
Lina Cottages **12**
Mascot Beach Resort **15**
Ray **14**
Sanya Homestay **5**

Senggigi Beach **28**
Sunset Cottages **1**
Windy Beach Cottages **7**

Eating 🍴
Bumbu **8**
Cafe Alberto **6**
Gelateria **10**
Mario's **8**
Square **7**
Ye Jeon Korean **9**

Bars & clubs 🍸
Club 69 **1**
Gosip Discotique **1**
Papaya Cafe **11**

plenty of good snorkelling stops on the tour. Both trips can be combined for a five day four night epic, where both Komodo and Rinca are visited costing US$328 for deck class and US$437 for a cabin.

Bangsal ⊙ ►► pp342-345.

→ Phone code: 0370.

The coast road north from Senggigi is slow, steeply switchbacking over headlands and past some attractive beaches and a colony of monkeys. There is some surf on this part of the coast, mainly reef breaks, surfed by the locals on wooden boards.

Bangsal is just off the main road from Pemenang, and is little more than a tiny fishing village. However, as it is also the departure point for the Gilis, there are a couple of restaurants here that double up as tourist information centres, a ferry booking office, a money changer and a diving company. Vehicles stop around 300m short of the harbour, and it is necessary to walk or charter a cidomo (5000Rp) for the trip to the ticket office. The harbour area is a tatty little place, full of scam artists who will surround travellers and try numerous tricks to extract money. These guys are a real headache. Ignore them, and head to the ticket office to buy your ticket to the island of your choice. Boats leave when they are full, and there is an announcement telling passengers when their boat is ready to depart. Boats to Gili Trawangan fill up the quickest, followed by boats to Gili Air, which has a large local population. Boats to Gili Meno can take some time to fill up. The fare to Gili Trawangan is 8000Rp, Gili Meno 7500Rp and Gili Air 7000Rp.

⊙ West coast Lombok listings

For Sleeping and Eating price codes, see inside the front cover.

⊜ Sleeping

Senggigi *p340, map p341*
All the hotels and guesthouses are easily accessible by bemo from Mataram. The better hotels have generators for when the mains power fails, which it does quite often. Many of the cheaper hotels in Senggigi are poorly maintained, but the hotels in Batu Balong, 1 km from the centre are well-managed and popular and have access to a decent stretch of beach.
AL Senggigi Beach Hotel, Jl Pantai Senggigi, T0370 693210, www.senggigibeach. aerowisata.com. Set in 12 ha of gardens, with tennis courts, spa, a huge chess board, and numerous bars and restaurants. Rooms are in comfortable a/c cottages with cable TV. The more expensive bungalows have a sea view.

B-C Mascot Beach Resort, Jl Raya Senggigi, T0370 693365, mascot@telkom.net. Large selection of cottages in a large beachfront garden. More expensive ones have sea view. Rooms are simple and clean, and the more money you spend, the more space you get (and a bath thrown in). Discounts available.
C Sunset Cottages, Jl Raya Senggigi, T0370 692020, www.sunsethouse-lombok.com. 4 spacious rooms set in a block in a large garden, this place has effusive staff and access to the beach for splendid sunset views over the strait to Bali. The rooms are large, spotless and have cable TV, and a veranda with sea view. Recommended.
C Windy Beach Cottages, Mangsit, PO Box 1116, T0370 693191, F0370 693193. 14 attractive traditional-style thatched bungalows with fan, private bathroom with shower/bath, Western toilet, some with hot water. Set in large gardens amidst a coconut grove beside the sea, restaurant (†) offering

good Indonesian, Chinese and Western food. Well-managed. Recommended.

C-D The Beach Club, Jl Raya Senggigi, T0370 693637, thebeachclublombok@ hotmail.com. Well-furnished a/c rooms with semi-open bathroom and veranda overlooking the beach. Pool, popular bar, happy hour 1700-1900.

D Cafe Wayan, Jl Raya Senggigi, T0370 693098. This Balinese-owned place has 4 spacious rooms with bathroom with bath. The ambience is laid back and friendly.

D Dharmarie, Jl Raya Senggigi, T0370 693050, www.dharmarie.com. 18 rooms next to the seafront in extensive open grounds. Rooms are clean and have outdoor bathroom, although the furniture is looking tired.

E-D Batu Bolong Cottages, Jl Raya Senggigi, T0370 693198, www.lombok cottages.com. Well-managed hotel with a wide selection of cottages that straddle the busy road. Cheaper fan rooms have TV and are spacious and comfortable with a veranda facing the attractive garden. Somewhat tatty bathrooms. More expensive rooms have a/c, and are closer to the beach. One of Senggigi's better choices. Recommended.

F Lina Cottages, Jl Raya Senggigi, T0370 693157. Despite the restaurant with its excellent sea views, the a/c rooms here are spartan and tired.

F Ray Hotel, Jl Raya Senggigi, T0370 660559. These cheap lodgings with attached bathroom are not quite as charmless as those of Lina, and are cheaper. The floors are clean, although the walls are less so.

G Sanya Homestay, Jl Raya Senggigi, T0370 693447. A Senggigi favourite for budget backpackers, the rooms here are simple, and have bathroom with *mandi*. Ask for a room at the back, which face a bit of greenery. The staff are very friendly. You can refill your water bottle here for 2000Rp.

⊘ Eating

Senggigi *p340, map p341*
There are not many independent restaurants on Senggigi – most eating places are attached to hotels. Independent restaurants are struggling. Many places offer free transport.

† **Bumbu**, Jl Raya Senggigi, T0370 692236, 0900-2300. Friendly, offers fine Thai curries and salads, and has a great selection of Asian food, with some excellent deserts. Recommended.

† **Cafe Alberto**, Jl Raya Senggigi, T0370 693039, 0900-2400. Good Italian food served on the seafront. Pizzas, pastas and seafood dishes dominate the menu. The cocktail list is extensive, and the view makes this an ideal spot for a sunset drink. They have a van that cruises the streets in the evening offering to drive people to the restaurant.

† **Mario's**, Jl Raya Senggigi, T0370 692008, 0800-2300. A good selection of Western and Indonesian standards, a pool table, and large TV showing music and sports.

† **Square**, Senggigi Square Blk B-10, T0370 693688, www.squarelombok.com, 1100-2400. Sengiggi's concession to sophisticated dining, Square bills itself as a lounge restaurant, and has a decent wine list, good seafood and plenty of steaks to get your teeth into. They have a monthly cellar party, where for US$27 you can drink as much international wine and eat as much tapas as you can handle.

† **Ye Jeon Korean Restaurant**, Senggigi Plaza, T0370 693059, 0930-2100. This Korean-owned eatery serves authentic Korean favourites such as *bibimbap* and *bulgogi*. The set meals are good value and filling.

† **Café Wayang**, on main road in Senggigi, T0370693098. A branch of the one in Ubud, Bali, building has character (complete with family of mice in the rafters!), but slow service.

† **Gelateria**, Senggigi Plaza A1-04, 1000-1900. Perfect for a cheap lunch, offering lots of good Indonesian staples, including *bakso*, *nasi goreng*, and *mie goreng*. They also serve up a good coffee, and home-made gelato to the strains of modern Indonesian rock music.

☺ Entertainment

Senggigi *p340, map p341*
If you really want to party, it would be better to wait until you get to the hedonist pleasures of Gili Trawangan, however, there are a couple of options in Senggigi: **Papaya Cafe**, Jl Raya Senggigi, T0370 693616, 1000-0100. Papaya's has live music, serves pizza and steak and has a happy hour that strangely only lasts for 30 mins from 2130-2200, where you buy 1 drink, get 1 free.

There are a few late night options on Senggigi Square including **Gosip Discotique** (T0819 17341437, until 0400), which features 'super sexy dancers live', and the nearby **Club 69** (T0370 692211, 1300-0400), with private karaoke rooms and a disco.

○ Shopping

Senggigi *p340, map p341*
Senggigi Jaya on the main road has everything from food to T-shirts, film and gifts at reasonable prices. There are a few boutique/craft shops that are less prone to haggling than the old-school vendors.

▲ Activities and tours

Senggigi *p340, map p341*
Diving and snorkelling
Blue Coral, Jl Raya Senggigi, T0370 693441. Recommended.
Dream Divers, Jl Raya Senggigi, T0370 692047, www.dreamdivers.com. Dive trips to the Gilis and Nusa Penida and Tulamben in Bali, as well as trips to the waters of southern Lombok where hammerhead sharks can be seen. Each dive costs US$35.

Both also offer daily snorkelling trips to the Gilis with their dive boats for US$20.

Cycling
Lombok Biking, Jl Raya Senggigi, T0370 692164, 0830-1930. Seeing the countryside of Lombok on 2 wheels is highly recommended, and this outfit has a selection of 1/2 day trips to Lengsar, Pusuk Pass, and southern Lombok, as well as a surprise ride of the day. Costs vary between US$18-32 depending on length.

Trekking
Rinjani Trekking Club, Jl Raya Senggigi, T0370 693202, www.anaklombok.com. Senggigi is a good place to plan your ascent of Gunung Rinjani, and this place offers information and a variety of trips. Their 2-day trip to the summit costs US$197, the same as their 3-day trip. All costs include guide service, accommodation, transfers and food. Recommended.
Perama, Jl Raya Senggigi, T0370 693007. Offer all-inclusive treks to Rinjani's summit, departing from Senggigi at 0500. Treks cost between US$273 and US$328 depending on the number of nights. A minimum of 2 people is required.

Tour operators
Bidy Tour, Jl Raya Senggigi, T0370 693521. Full day fishing trips. International and domestic flight ticketing.
Perama, Jl Raya Senggigi, T0370 693007.

☺ Transport

Senggigi *p340, map p341*
Various forms of transport can be hired from travel agents along the main road.
Car hire US$13 per day.
Motorbike hire US$4.30 per day.
Taxi Blue Bird Taxi T0370 627000. Flag fall is 3850Rp.

Bemo
Bemos wait on Jl Salah Singkar in Ampenan to pick up fares for Senggigi beach and north to **Mangsit**. Regular bemos link **Ampenan** with **Mataram**, **Cakranegara** and the main **Cakra** bemo terminal between 0600 and 1800, 3000Rp. A bemo ride from 1 end of Senggigi to the other costs 1000Rp.

Perama have an office here (see Tour operators) and run a bus service geared to travellers. Shuttles include **Kuta Lombok** for US$14, **Padangbai**, 1 daily, US$33, **Kuta** and **Nguarah Rai Airport**, 1 daily, US$38, and **Ubud**, 1 daily, US$38.

Boat

Perama have a direct boat service to the Gilis, leaving at 0900 for US$11.
Dream Divers (see Activities and tours) are the Senggigi agent for Gili Cat, which has a fast ferry (1½ hrs) to Padangbai for US$66.

Bangsal *p342*

Bemo

Regular connections from Mataram or the Bertais terminal in Cakranegara; take a bemo heading for Tanjung or Bayan. Bemos stop at the junction at Pemenang, take a dokar the last 1 km to the coast. From Pelabuhan Lombok there are no direct bemos; either charter one (US$13) or catch a bemo to the Bertais Terminal in Cakranegara and then another travelling to Bayan/Tanjung. From the port of Lembar, it is easiest to club together with other passengers and charter a bemo to Bangsal.

Bus

Get your ticket on the islands for regular connections with Lembar with **Perama Tour**, who sell all-in bus/ferry tickets to most destinations in **Bali** (**Kuta**, **Sanur**, **Ubud**, **Lovina** and **Candi Dasa**).

⊙ Directory

Senggigi *p340, map p341*
Banks **Senggigi Beach Hotel** has a bank on site with exchange facilities for non-residents. Money changer at the **Pacific Supermarket**. ATMs can be found along Jl Raya Senggigi. There is a cluster of them by Senggigi Square. **Internet** **Millennium Internet**, Jl Raya Senggigi, 0800-0100, and **Superstar Internet**, Senggigi Plaza, Blk A2, 0800-2400. Both places charge 300Rp per min. Superstar has (marginally) better hardware. **Medical services** **Senggigi Medical Services**, at Senggigi Beach Hotel, T0370 693210, 24 hrs. Consultation US$27 plus tax and treatment costs. **Post office** Centre of town, along Jl Raya Senggigi, Mon-Thu 0730-1700, Fri-Sat 0730-1600. **Tourist police** Jl Raya Senggigi, T0370 632733.

Gili Islands

→ *Phone code: 0370. Colour map 11, B2.*
The three tropical island idylls that make up the Gili Islands lie off Lombok's northwest coast, 20-45 minutes by boat from Bangsal. They are now a well-established fixture on the southeast Asian trail. Known as the 'Gilis' or the 'Gili Islands' by many travellers, this only means 'the Islands' in Sasak. Most locals have accepted this Western corruption of their language and will understand where you want to go. Be extra careful swimming here as there are very strong currents between the islands. ►► *For listings, see pages 350-357.*

Ins and outs

With the development of Bali into an international tourist resort, many backpackers have moved east and the Gilis are the most popular of the various alternatives. This is already straining the islands' limited sewerage and water infrastructures, and a walk into the interior of Gili Trawangan will reveal large amounts of rubbish strewn about. During the peak months between June and August, Gili Trawangan becomes particularly crowded and it is advisable to book accommodation in advance.

The attraction of the Gilis resides in their golden sand beaches and the best snorkelling and diving off Lombok – for the amateur the experience is breathtaking. However, the coral does not compare with locations such as Flores and Alor: large sections are dead or damaged (because of dynamite fishing and the effects of El Nino, which raised the temperature of the water). Gili Meno and Gili Air are very quiet, and there is little to do except sunbathe, snorkel, swim, or dive. Gili Trawangan has the same attractions, but has also developed a reputation for its raucous nightlife, the most vibrant in Lombok, and it is the most popular of the islands, particularly with backpackers.

There is no police presence on any of the islands. In the event of anything untoward happening, contact the island's *kepala desa* – the village head (guesthouses or any of the dive centres should be able to point you in the right direction).

Getting there

Regular boats from Bangsal (see page 342) to the Gilis wait until about 20 people have congregated for the trip to the islands. Boats can also be chartered for the journey, 45 minutes to Gili Trawangan, 30 minutes to Gili Meno, 20 minutes to Gili Air. In the morning there is rarely a long wait, but in the afternoon people have had to wait several hours. An alternative is to buy a combined bus-and-boat ticket with one of the shuttle bus companies.

Perama have a boat that sails from a small harbour to the north of Senggigi at 0900, costing US$11. This avoids the port of Bangsal. Enquire at the Perama office in Senggigi. There are various alternatives. Within Lombok there are services from **Mataram** to the Gilis and from **Senggigi** to the Gilis. (From Senggigi, some of the dive centres operate boats throughout the day.) The most popular way to get to the Gilis from Bali is the Perama ferry from Padangbai, which takes four hours and calls in at all three islands. This costs US$33 and departs at 1330. The cheaper Perama alternative uses the slow ferry to Lembar, a shuttle bus to Bangsal and then a public boat to the Gili of your choice. This takes seven to eight hours, departs at 0900, and costs US$17.50. **Gili Cat** (www.gilicat.com) have a fast service from Gili Trawangan to Padangbai (Jalan Silayukti, T0363 41441, 1½ hours, US$72) departing at 1100.

Getting around

The islands are small and compact enough to walk around. Even Gili Trawangan, the largest of the three, is little more than 2 km from end to end. Gili Air and Gili Trawangan are great for cycling with good tracks running through the islands. Cidomo are the main form of transport used by locals for carrying goods around the islands. Some offer round-island trips costing around 50,000Rp, although costs are very negotiable.

There is a shuttle service between the islands, with tickets that can be bought at the ticket office at the harbour of each island. The shuttle leaves Gili Air at 0830, and arrives at Gili Meno at 0845, before continuing to Gili Trawangan. The shuttle then leaves Gili Trawangan at 0930, to Gili Meno where it continues to Gili Air at 0945. The shuttle runs again in the afternoon, departing Gili Air at 1500, Gili Meno at 1515, and Gili Trawangan at 1530. From Gili Meno the shuttle heads to Gili Air at 1600. Fares for shorter hops (neighbouring islands) are 18,000Rp, from Gili Air to Gili Trawangan and vice-versa, the fare is 21,000Rp.

Gili Trawangan ●❷❶❸▲❸❶ ›› *pp350-357.*

The largest of the three islands – and the furthest west from Bangsal – is Gili Trawangan (Dragon Island). It is the most interesting island because of its hill in the centre; there are several trails to the summit and excellent views over to Mount Rinjani on Lombok from the top. In the opposite direction, you can watch the sun set over Mount Agung on Bali.
Note Give the fly-covered cows a wide berth.

There is a coastal path around the island, which takes about 2½ hours to walk. Originally a penal colony, it now supports the greatest number of tourist bungalows. These are mostly concentrated along its east coast, as are a number of restaurants (serving good seafood) and bars. For lone travellers seeking company, this is the best island. But Gili Trawangan is in danger of ruining itself (like so many other tropical island idylls in the region). Indeed, for some it already has. The most developed area is becoming brash, loud and over-developed, but the island is large enough to offer peace and tranquillity as well. Gili Air and Gili Meno are quieter, though they too have their noisy areas of bars in high season.

The most luxurious accommodation is found in the developed south east area of the island behind the restaurants; locals already refer to it being like Kuta, although this is an exaggeration. Here you can find well-equipped modern air-conditioned bungalows with cable TV and personal chefs to cater to your whims; unfortunately you lose the peace and beauty associated with a small, relatively undeveloped island, as the accommodation is hidden behind the noisy restaurants away from the beach. To find a quiet tropical paradise, visitors have to accept more basic facilities at the outer edges of the developed areas, particularly the north and northeastern strip of coast, which remains accessible. Here guests can hear the waves lapping against the shore and the birds singing, watch truly inspirational sunrises and sunsets from the peace of their verandas and believe they are in paradise. Room rates triple at some of the more upmarket places in the high season. Even off-peak rooms can become scarce, so it is worth arriving on the island early. The cheapest accommodation can be found away from the beach, along the lanes in the village. Gili Trawangan offers the best choice of restaurants of the three Gilis, and many people consider that it has the best snorkelling. Snorkelling is good off the east shore, particularly at the point where the shelf drops away near *Horizontal* and at the north end of the beach.

Inland from the tourist strip is the original village where life goes on almost as usual, a world apart from the tourists and therefore interesting to stroll through. Further inland there are scattered farms among the coconut groves that dominate the interior, and some pleasant walks to be had.

Safety Given the conservative nature of Lombok, women should abstain from topless sunbathing. There have been plenty of reports of women being hassled by local men, and it is not wise to set off on long walks alone in the dark. Also, single women should keep an eye on their drinks in bars, to make sure nothing is slipped in. It is unlikely that this would happen, but not unheard of.

Gili Islands

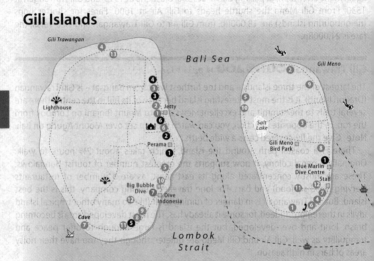

N

500 metres
500 yards

Gili Trawangan

Sleeping
Beach House 8
Beach Wind 1
Blue Beach Cottage 2
Coral Beach 2 13
Dream Village 3
Good Heart 3
Kelapa Kecil 2
Melati Bungalows 12
Nusa Tiga 4
Pesona Resort 5
Pondok Jessica 12
Pondok Maulana 12
Sama Sama Bungalows 6
Sunset Cottages 7
Tir Na Nog 9
Trawangan Cottages 12
Unique Bungalows 10
Villa Ombak 11
Warna Homestay 2

Eating
Blue Marlin & Dive School 1
Coco 2
Horizontal 3
Mozart 4
Scallywags 5
Wrap A Snapper 6

Bars & clubs
Rudy's 7

Gili Meno
Sleeping
Biru Meno 1

Blue Coral 2
Casablanca 3
Gazebo 4
Goodheart 5
Kontiki 6
Mallia's Child 7
Mimpi Manis 8
Pondok Meno 9
Sunset Gecko 10
Tao Kombo 11
Villa Nautilus 12

Eating
Rust Warung 1

Gili Meno » pp350-357.

Gili Meno (Snake Island), between Trawangan and Air, is the smallest of the islands, and also the quietest and least developed. The local residents are very friendly, and after half a day on the island most will know your name and where you stay. The disadvantage of staying on Gili Meno is that the hawker to tourist ratio is very high, so expect plenty of visits from trinket sellers (often the same ones repeatedly).

The snorkelling off Gili Meno – especially off the northeast coast – is considered by some to be better than Trawangan, with growths of rare blue coral. There is a path running round the island; a walk of 1-1½ hours. The salt lake in the northeast of the island provides a breeding ground for mosquitoes. Accommodation on Gili Meno tends to be more expensive than on the other two islands. Some of the guesthouse owners live on Lombok, and these bungalows are run by lads who are poorly paid and consequently have little motivation. However, the views from the many bungalows that face the sea are beautiful, especially towards the east and Mount Rinjani. Accommodation may be full as early as April, with the season running through to September.

Gili Meno Bird Park

ⓘ *T0361 287727, www.balipvbgroup.com, 0800-1700, 50,000Rp adult, 25,000Rp child, follow the signposted path near the harbour through the middle of the island, it's a 10-min walk.* The 2500-sq-m aviary contains over 300 species of birds, and offers interactive feeding times and guided tours. There are also komodo dragons, kangaroos and plenty of turtles. This makes for a nice break from the monotony of beaches for kids, and there is an interesting bar filled with Beatles memorabilia where mums and dads can take a break.

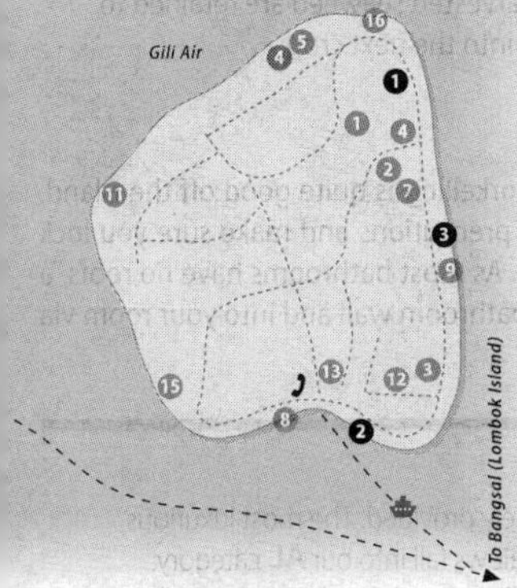

ili Air

leeping

bdi Fantastik **4**
oconut Cottages & Frangipani Restaurant **2**
ili Air **16**
ili Air Santay & Restaurant **7**
ili Indah **8**
ita Gili **9**
egend Bungalows & Bar **5**
ucky's **15**
Aatahari **11**
Mawar Cottages **12**
Resota **13**
Sejuk Cottages **1**
Sunrise **3**

Eating

Blue Marlin & Dive Centre **1**
Go Go Cafe **2**
Green Café **3**

Bars & clubs

Mirage **4**

Gili Air » pp350-357.

Gili Air (Turtle Island) is the easternmost island, lying closest to Bangsal. It has the largest local population, with a village of around 400 families in the centre of the island. The island takes about an hour to walk around. As the local population is Muslim, visitors should avoid topless sunbathing Despite the number of

Seaweed farming

Seaweed farming is being encouraged off Gili Air as an alternative to fishing, in order to protect the coral. Although laws against the use of dynamite fishing were passed in 1984, some fishermen still use it as well as stones to kill the fish, damaging the coral in the process. The waters round the island provide suitable conditions for seaweed farming: there is a good flow of water, but the reef protects the area from strong currents; the considerable depth of the Lombok Strait keeps sea temperatures from becoming too high and keeps salinity at a constant level. These are all prerequisites for the successful cultivation of seaweed. From the fishermens' viewpoint, seaweed farming has the attraction of being less hard work than fishing. The green Kotoni variety is grown and is exported for use.

The seaweed is farmed by fixing posts in the shallow seabed. Rope is attached to these posts, making a frame about 2 m sq. At roughly 30 cm intervals nodules of seaweed containing a seedhead are tied onto the rope using strips of shredded plastic bags. The seaweed must remain covered by water, so the ropes are held afloat just under the surface using plastic bottles, which are due to be replaced by more visually pleasing lengths of bamboo. After 40 days the seaweed is harvested and dried; 7 kg of wet seaweed producing 1 kg dry weight. This is then sold on Lombok for 800Rp a kilogram (or an equivalent value in rice and coffee), each family producing about 50 kg. Cuttings from the harvested seaweed are retained to grow into the next crop.

---

bungalows, it remains a peaceful place to stay. Snorkelling is quite good off the island. When leaving your accommodation take sensible precautions and make sure you lock both the door to the bathroom and the front door. As most bathrooms have no roofs, a favoured way for thieves to gain entry is over the bathroom wall and into your room via the bathroom door.

◉ Gili Islands listings

For Sleeping and Eating price codes, see inside the front cover.

● Sleeping

In the past few years, many foreigners have invested in the Gilis, resulting in a wide range of accommodation options. Many bungalows are being upgraded. Of the more basic ones there is often little difference – they tend to charge the same rates, and the huts are similar in design and size, attractively built out of local materials, in a local style, mostly raised on stilts. Mosquitoes can be a problem at certain times of year and mosquito nets are

routinely provided. The most luxurious bungalows fall into our **AL** category. Friendliness and the cleanliness of the *mandis* tends to be the deciding factor at the basic bungalows. The higher the price, the more likely tax and service charge will be extra, and the less likely breakfast will be included. During the peak months Jun-Aug it can be difficult to get a room, so arrive early in the day. Tips on where to stay from travellers are probably your best bet. The coastal strip on the easten side of each island is the most developed. Peace, solitude and outrageous sunsets can be found on the western side of each island. Unless otherwise stated, all bungalows have private bathrooms with shower. Fresh-water resources are scarce on the islands so water in the bathrooms can often be saline, as it is taken from wells. However, some places offer fresh-water showers. All prices quoted here are low season. Expect them to double during the high season.

Gili Trawangan *p347, map p348*

AL Villa Ombak, T0370 642336, www.hotelombak.com. Selection of 60 rooms, some in beautiful *lumbung*-style cottages set in well-tended gardens. The water here is saline, although they provide a jar of fresh water for guests to use to rinse off any residue after showering. These a/c rooms have large open bathroom, TV, and the more expensive *lumbung* cottages have a downstairs living area, and balcony with loungers. Full spa service, restaurant, pool and diving centre.

AL-D The Beach House, T0370 642352, www.beachhousegilit.com. This Australian-owned hotel is going from strength to strength, with its 17 rooms and 3 villas currently being added to. The cheaper a/c rooms are comfortable, and have private terrace and cable TV. However, it's the villas here that are a steal, offering privacy and featuring fresh water plunge pool, kitchenette, cable TV and space for 4 in tastefully decorated rooms. Consistently booked out well in advance, so reservations are essential. Fresh-water swimming pool. Recommended.

AL-D Tir Na Nog, T0370 639463, www.tirnanogbar.com. 10 comfortable and spacious a/c rooms with hot water set behind the popular bar. There is also a 2 bedroom villa available with small pool.

A Dream Village, T0370 6644373, www.dreamvillagetrawangan.com. The 5 large a/c bungalows have cable TV and fine sunrise views, but are a little overpriced. Reservations necessary.

B Kelapa Kecil, T0812 3756003, www.kelapa villas.com. Sleek and stylish but lacking island

grace, the 3 a/c rooms here are popular, and have great sea views. Small pool.

C Blue Beach Cottage, T0370 263846. Located next to Trawangan's finest stretch of beach, the stylish a/c bungalows here have massive bathrooms, high ceilings and mosquito nets. The staff are very friendly. Recommended.

C Good Heart, T0370 6630239, goodheart-trawangan@hotmail.com. No relation to the bungalows on Gili Meno, the comfortable a/c *lumbung* cottages are a stone's throw from the beach, with cool outdoor bathroom and good views from the private balcony. Rooms have cable TV, fridge and safety box. Recommended.

C-D Pesona Resort, T0370 6607233, www.pesonaresort.com. Owned by Indians and managed by an English lady, the bungalows are clean and comfortable, if a little overpriced. Rooms feature cable TV, DVD player and a big, modern bathroom. There is a pool ideal for enjoying the aroma of Indian food wafting on the tropical breezes.

D Sama Sama Bungalows, T0812 3763650, www.thesamasama.com. 4 a/c *lumbung* bungalows with high ceilings and tasteful decor. There is a bar in front playing live acoustic music, which the friendly owner insists is turned off at 0100.

D Unique Bungalows, T0818 05762803. No-one would dare deny that the day-glo exteriors of these bungalows are unique, and fortunately the interiors are a little more soothing on the eyes. The colourful private bungalows come with cable TV and access to a large DVD library. The bathrooms are poorly designed, but have a hairdryer. Private veranda with hammock. There are some cheaper standard rooms at the back, but these are dark and unattractive.

E Beach Wind, T0370 6619506. Cleanish fan and a/c rooms with mosquito net set in a somewhat noisy family compound featuring a table tennis table mobbed by youths. The fan rooms represent better value. Convenient for the harbour. Tax not included in the price.

E Coral Beach 2, T0370 639946. Well located at the quiet northern end of the island, and near good snorkelling, the rooms here are simple and quite clean. There is a restaurant attached serving good pizza and icy drinks.

E Warna Homestay, T0370 623859. 7 clean and comfortable rooms with plenty of light.

E-F Nusa Tiga, T0370 643249. Next to the Coral Beach 2, a fine spot for solitude, but the cheap fan rooms are worn and have prison-like bars over the windows. Friendly staff.

F Melati Bungalows, T0852 39521697. This laid-back place has 4 simple fan rooms with friendly staff.

F Pondok Jessica, T0819 17352908. This is the pick of the bunch amongst the cheapies in the village, with clean fan rooms in a beautiful green garden. Recommended.

F Pondok Maulana, T08175746118, www.pondokmaulana.bravehost.com. 4 spotless rooms, with large veranda. Popular.

F Sunset Cottages T0812 3785290. Simple bungalows with 2 beds, mosquito nets, hammocks on balconies and a large breakfast. Situated on the western side of the island, taking advantage of the splendid sunsets featuring Mount Agung on Bali as a breathtaking backdrop. Very peaceful. It's about a 40-min walk into 'town' for other restaurants and shopping, or take a cidomo (if you can find one).

F Trawangan Cottages, T0370 623582. Also in the village, lodgings here are popular and convenient for the bars along the main strip. Rooms are clean.

Gili Meno p349, map p348

B Villa Nautilus, T0370 642143, www.villanautilus.com. Beautifully designed private cottages facing the sea, with outside terrace, some with sea views. The room has a living area, and the large bed is on a raised platform, with good quality fabrics used for bedding and curtains.

B-D Gazebo, T0370 635795. Set in forest, with its own stretch of beach with loungers, the well-spaced-out cottages look dreary from the outside, yet internally are spacious,

well furnished and tastefully decorated with Indonesian artefacts. There is a small pool next the to the beach.

B-E Kontiki, T0370 632824. Used by tourists on Perama tours, near the beach, with large and clean rooms. The staff are a great source of local information and very friendly. Some rooms have fresh water shower and space to sleep 3 people.

C-E The Sunset Gecko, T0815 766418, www.thesunsetgecko.com. This Japanese-owned place blows all the Meno competition out of the water with its innovative eco-friendly ideals, unconventional communal washbasins, outdoor showers and toilets (very clean and secure) and comfortable accommodation in thatched bungalows. There is a 2-storey house with amazing views of Gili Trawangan and Gunung Agung from its terrace at sunset, that is often booked for weeks at a time. If you want the house, it is necessary to reserve in advance. Good snorkelling offshore. Recommended.

D Biru Meno, T08133 9758968, www.birumeno.com. At the southern end of the main beach strip, the 8 bungalows here are set in a very tranquil location and seem rather underused. Fan rooms have sea view.

D Mimpi Manis, T0817 9979579. Very spacious thatched bungalows with large balcony and hammock set in a large garden. Rooms come with a Bahasa Indonesia coursebook so guests can mingle with the locals better. Fresh water shower. Breakfast and tax are not included in the price.

D Tao Kombo, T0812 3722174, tao_kombo@yahoo.com. Away from the beach in a forest clearing, there is plenty of birdsong here. The *lumbung* bungalows are filled with light, and have high ceiling. The location is very peaceful, and the hotel offers lots of boardgames and a book exchange. Recommended.

D-G Casablanca, T0370 633847, lidybianca@mtr.wasantara.net.id. This Japanese-owned hotel has a curious mixture of rooms, from the cheap and low standard to the gargantuan super deluxe room with 4-poster bed and garden view. There is a small pool, and a delightful collection of flowers.

E Mallia's Child, T0370 622007, www.gili meno-mallias.com. These bungalows are right on the beach with excellent views over to Gili Air, Lombok and for the ambitious, of the sunrise. Rooms are clean, though a little small. Tax not included in the price.

F Blue Coral (No Telp). Seriously quiet, the 3 very simple bungalows here have wonderful views of the sea. The water is saline.

F Goodheart, T08133 6556976. Located on the western side of the island, the 5 2-storey *lumbung* cottages have precipitous stairs leading up to a simple bedroom. Access to the bathroom is through a trapdoor in the bedroom floor. A great beachside *berguga* (seating pavilion) to watch the sunset.

F Pondok Meno. Very simple bungalows with balcony facing the sea. Fresh-water shower.

Gili Air *p349, map p348*

To make the most of this 'paradise' island it's best to stay in one of the bungalows dotted around the coast within sound and sight of the sea. There's also accommodation inland from the point where the boats land on the south coast, but this does not offer sea views.

B-D Hotel Gili Air, T0370 634435, www.hotel giliair.com. Cheaper fan rooms look tired from the outside, but are cosy within. Overpriced. The more expensive a/c rooms are very clean, have TV, but strangely there is a blank wall where there should be a glorious sea view. The hotel has a small pool and a miserable-looking outdoor gym.

C-E Coconut Cottages, T0370 635365, www.coconuts-giliair.com. Owned by a friendly Glasgow native and her local husband, the 7 a/c and fan rooms here are great value, with well-designed comfortable interiors and huge bathrooms with power shower. The beds are king size, and there are reading lights. Recommended.

C-E Sejuk Cottages, T0370 636461, sejukcottages@hotmail.com. Down a path off the eastern side of the island, this new hotel has a good selection of bungalows. All are clean with spacious verandas. The more expensive feature TV and a/c.

C-E Sunrise, T0370 642370. Cottages, set in a garden so parched that walking through it makes you feel thirsty. Popular with a good selection of accommodation. The 2-storey *lumbung* have an outdoor lounge area downstairs and an outdoor bathroom.

D Hotel Gili Indah, T0370 637328. Comfortable fan and a/c rooms with sea views close to the harbour and handy for quiet walks on the island's west.

E Gili Air Santay, T0818 03758695, www.giliair-santay.com. Has a loyal following of regular Gili Air visitors, lured by the efficient Austrian management and simple yet comfortable bungalows. There are no locks on some of the bathroom doors.

E Lucky's, T0819 33160613, about a 15-min walk to the harbour. Out on the west side of the island, this friendly place doesn't get as much business as it ought to, given the marvellous sunset views and quiet vibes on offer. Fan and a/c rooms.

F Abdi Fantastik, T0370 622179. Simple bungalows with room for 3 people. All have sea view. Friendly staff. Good swimming and snorkelling offshore.

F Legend Bungalows, T0812 3787254. These bungalows have seen better days, but are located near the beach, just behind Legend Bar. Some bathrooms have squat toilets.

F Matahari. For serious seekers of isolation only, this simple place on the west coast is a great spot to leave the world behind, chat with local fishermen and watch clouds drift by. The owners can prepare decent Indonesian meals. It's a 25-min walk from the harbour along the western coastal path.

F Mawar Cottages, T0813 62253995. These guys will probably meet you off the boat and try to entice you to stay at their lodgings, which are set away from the beach in a quiet garden. This is definite backpacker territory

and an acoustic guitar looms ominously on the wall of the large communal area. All rooms with mosquito net and fan, although cheaper rooms feature squat toilet.
F Resota, T0859 36185928, marini_resota@ yahoo.co.uk. Clean thatched bungalows with fridge, spacious veranda with hammock set away from the beach. The cheapest room has a sea view.
G Gita Gili, T0813 39553395. The bungalows here are set in an unkempt garden close to the beach. Rooms are dark, with mosquito net. Bathrooms with shower and *mandi*.

⚬ Eating

The choice of food is best on Gili Trawangan. A number of restaurants serving excellent seafood, particularly fish; the specials board will tell you what is the fresh catch. In Gili Air there are also several small shops selling basic provisions and fruit.

Gili Trawangan *p347, map p348*
♔ The Beach House, T0370 642352, www.beachhousegilit.com, open 24 hrs. Popular beachfront eatery serving fish kebabs, pies and quiches, lovely home-made soups and some Indonesian dishes. Fresh seafood is laid out around 1800 and diners pick their choice.
♔ Blue Marlin, T0370 632424, open 0800-2300. Extremely popular place with good portions of Western food, fresh seafood and a decent vegetarian menu.
♔ Horizontal, T0878 63039727, open 0800-2300. An attempt at Seminyak style, which looks a little faded during daytime, but comes into its own as the sun sets. Good range of fare including pan-fried fillet of white snapper, Japanese tuna rolls, Thai curries and banoffee pie.
♔ Pesona, T0370 6607233, www.pesona resort.com, open 0800-2300. The owners are of Indian origin and you will find the best veg and non-veg Indian grub in the Gilis here. The *masala dosa* are worth a try. It doubles

up as a sheesha bar at night, where you can puff away on apple tobacco.
♔ Scallywags, T0370 631945, open 0800-2300. Beautifully designed restaurant, with some seating on the beach. The menu features delights such warm goat cheese salad, a changing daily Basque tapas dish and plenty of fresh seafood. Good wine selection. Recommended.
♔ Tir Na Nog, T0370 639463, www.tirnanogbar.com, open 0800-2300. Popular for pizza, steak-and-Guiness pie and a decent vegetarian selection.
♔ Wrap A Snapper, T0370 624217, open 0800-2200. Australian-owned, serving up fish n' chips, battered snacks and fish burgers, plus some healthy options! They deliver food to diners on the beach for 5000Rp.
♔ Coco, T081353535737, open 0700-1800. Ideal spot for a light lunch, this small and efficient café prepares baguettes with tasty fillings such as roasted vegetables and feta cheese. The small salad menu is quite dreamy, with offerings like spicy smoked marlin salad. Good coffee selection. Recommended.
♔ Mozart, T0819 17315862, open 0700-2300. Handy for the beach, the fare here is central European with goulashes, strudels and plenty of other indecipherable things on the German menu. They will translate for you.

There are plenty of cheap backpacker-oriented places along the beach. The food is a little average, so use your head and order local food for which they have the ingredients and know how to cook and you won't be disappointed. Places include **Sunrise Bungalows** and **Dayak Cafe**.

Gili Meno *p349, map p348*
The gourmet scene in Gili Meno is very quiet with eating mainly restricted to hotel restaurants, which can be highly variable in quality. Places close when the last patron leaves, which can be early.
♔ Villa Nautilus, T0370 642124, open 0700-2100. Good salads and pasta on offer and the service is very friendly. They do a

rather doughy wood-fired pizza smothered in cheese, if that's your thing.

†‡-† Good Heart, T0813 36556976, open 0700-2100. Fresh seafood including barracuda, tuna, snapper and some vegetarian dishes such as tofu curry. There is a good cocktail list.

†‡-† Rust Warung, T0370 642324, open 0700-2100. Dirt cheap sandwiches, soups and local favourites, but really comes alive at night when the local boys lay out the fresh fish for patrons to choose. There's a good atmosphere and many diners linger after they have finished to enjoy the cool breeze and a *Bintang*.

† Mallia's Child, T0370 622007, open 0700-2100. Cheap Indonesian fare, some reasonable Thai curries and a daily home-made soup.

† Sunset Gecko, T0815 766418, open 0700-2100. Local Sasak cuisine, some Western food and a delicious vegetarian red curry.

Gili Air *p349, map p348*
Many restaurants cater primarily to Western tastes and the 'Indonesian' food is often disappointingly bland. There have been some cases of food poisoning caused by eating fish that was not gutted prior to being stored.

†† Blue Marlin, T0370 634387. Hungry divers head here for good-quality Western food.

†† Frangipani (at Coconut Cottages), T0370 635365, open 0800-2200. Lots of tasty Indonesian, international and some Sasak cuisine served in a friendly, clean setting. Recommended.

†‡-† Gili Air Santay, T0818 03758695, open 0700-2200. Excellent array of Thai dishes and other Asian favourites served from a spotless kitchen. This laid back place is deservedly popular and social. Recommended.

† Go Go Cafe, T0817 5708337, open 0700-2400. Not far from the harbour, this breezy eatery dishes up fair Indonesian staples, pizza and pasta dishes. Slow service.

† Green Cafe, T0818 365954, open 0800-2300. This beachside place is a good place to

sample some Sasak cuisine, such as *urap urap* (vegetables in a coconut sauce). They also prepare fresh seafood dishes and have a lovely home-made yoghurt. Movies are often shown in the evenings.

Bars and clubs

Gili Trawangan *p347, map p348*
There is plenty of nocturnal action available, with local boys competing with foreigners for the attention of female visitors. Many places have a designated party night that goes on until the wee hours. Be careful of the magic mushroom milkshakes on sale in many places, they can be very strong and Lombok is a long way from home.

Horizontal, T0878 63039727, open 0700-0200. Cool lounge setting, plenty of drinks deals and chilled house music by the beach.

Rudy's Bar, T0370 642311, open 0800-0200. Popular with the backpacking set, this is the place to get feral, with plenty of reggae and house, happy hour 1500-2200.

Sama Sama, T0812 3763650, open 1900-0100. This friendly bar has chilled acoustic music in a mellow setting close to the beach.

Tir Na Nog, T0370 639463, open 0700-0200 except Wed 0700-sunrise. This Irish theme bar is cavernous, and caters for every whim, to the point where it almost becomes overwhelming. There is a darts board, table football, scattering of *beruga* with small TV and DVD player with an extensive film library, huge TV showing live football and a DJ spinning tunes nightly from 2100. They have a weekly party on Wed nights.

Gili Air *p349, map p348*
Most people are here to relax rather than get wild, so the beachfront restaurants double up as bars in the evening, and can be a great way to meet people. Gili Air Santay (see Eating) is recommended.

Legend Bar, T0812 3787254, open 0700-2300 except Wed 0700-sunrise. Harking back to mid-1990s Goa trance days, the walls of this small bar are festooned with fluorescent paintings of dolphins leaping from the sea and naughty-looking mushrooms. The Wed night party comes with a complete DJ line up until sunrise. Happy hour is 1700-1900. **Mirage Bar**, open 1000-2200. Next to **Legend Bar**, this quiet place has loungers, a good cocktail list and sublime sea views.

⏣ Entertainment

Gili Trawangan *p347, map p348*
Beautiful Life, open 1000-2400. On the busy southeastern coastal strip, this place offers movies in a darkened outdoor cinema, and personal movie booths on the beach side of the road where you can select a film from their library. You must buy some food or a drink to watch a film.

▲ Activities and tours

Gili Islands *p346, map p348*
Body and soul
Massage is available at many guesthouses and hotels on all 3 islands. Gili Trawangan has a few spa and massage places including **Villa Ombak**, T0370 642336, which has the most comprehensive spa and massage service.

Cycling
Gili Air and Gili Trawangan make superb places to get lost along island tracks, or follow the coastal paths for stunning views and peace and quiet. Bikes can be rented on Gili Air for 25,000Rp a day, and on Gili Trawangan for 35,000Rp a day.

Diving and snorkelling
While the diving here may not be quite as good as that in some other parts of Indonesia, it is ideal for less experienced divers as many of the dives are no deeper than 18 m and the waters are calm. Best diving conditions are late Apr through Aug. Good diving spots include Shark Point with white-and-

black tipped reef sharks, sea snakes and turtles; Meno wall, famed for turtles and nudibranches; and Air Slope, with its population of ghost pipe fish, frog fish and leaf scorpion fish. The dive centres on all 3 islands have formed an association to monitor control of diving on the islands, and protection of the reefs. Prices are the same at all schools, so as to maintain high standards and safety. Costs include PADI Open Water US$350, Advanced Open Water US$275, Discover Scuba US$60, and Divemaster US$650, with unlimited dives over a 1-month period. **Blue Marlin**, T0812 3766496, www.bluemarlindive.com, have dive schools on all 3 islands, and offer a free pool try-out for anyone interested in diving at their centres in Gili Trawangan and Gili Air. On Trawangan, **Big Bubble Dive**, T0370 625020, www.bigbubblediving.com, and **Dive Indonesia** (T0370 644174, www.dive indonesiaonline.com) have courses in numerous European languages, and are both highly regarded.

Snorkels and fins can be hired for 20,000Rp from many of the *losmen* or vendors along the beach. The snorkelling off Gili Trawangan is marginally the best; be careful off Gili Meno, as the tide is strong and the water is shallow, and it is easy to get swept onto the coral. Many agencies on all 3 islands offer snorkelling trips around all 3 islands in a glass-bottomed boat for 60,000Rp-70,000Rp. This trip is highly recommended.

Fishing
Night fishing can be organized from several places on Gili Air. Try **Abdi Fantastik** (see Sleeping). They have speargun fishing trips from 1800-2200 costing US$38 per person.

Kayaking
Kayaking Alberto, the owner of Dream Village, T0370 6644373, rents out sea kayaks for 35,000Rp per day.

Tour operators

Perama, T0370 638514, have their own office near the harbour on Gili Trawangan. On Gili Meno they can be found at the **Kontiki Hotel**, T0370 632824, and on Gili Air at the **Hotel Gili Indah**, T0370 637328.

⊝ Transport

Gili Islands *p346, map p348*
Don't purchase bus tickets to Senggigi or other Lombok destinations on the islands, they are more expensive. You can purchase a ticket on a shuttle bus to Sengiggi or Mataram at Bangsal for 40,000Rp. The shuttle bus touts will find you when you get off the boat. Be firm with your bargaining.

Boat

Public boats from the islands to **Bangsal** leave when full, except for Giili Meno, which has 2 sailings a day to Bangsal at 0800 and 1400 approximately, buy your ticket at the harbour. For onward connections to Bali, arrive at the ticket booth by 0730. At Bangsal you can also book through to Bali with 1 of the shuttle bus companies. The 'Island Hopping' boat makes 2 round trips a day connecting the islands.

To **Bali**, Perama have bus-boat ticket combination tickets. The direct Perama boat to **Padangbai** departs at 0700 and costs US$33. They have connections to other destinations in Bali. **Gili Cat**, www.gilicat.com, sails direct from Gili Trawangan to **Padangbai** in 1½ hrs for US$72 at 1100.

⊕ Directory

Gili Islands *p346, map p348*
Banks It is best to change money before leaving the mainland as rates are more expensive on the islands. There are money changers on all 3 islands. **Internet** On Gili Meno, there is a small place in the centre of the island opposite the Bird Park charging 500Rp per min. On Gili Trawangan there are numerous places with high-speed internet. **Tara**, 0800-2300, is near the harbour and charges 350Rp per min. On Gili Air there is internet access at the wartel next to **Coconut Cottages** for 400Rp per min. **Medical services** There is a small clinic on Gili Menoear the Bird Park. On Gili Trawangan there is a good clinic at Villa Ombak, T0370 642336. The doctor visits from the mainland on Tue, Thu and Sat. **Post office** There is a post box at the **Gili Indah Hotel** on Gili Air, where the boat docks. Letters *do* get through, but there are no stamps available on the island. **William's Bookshop** on Gili Trawangan is also a postal agent. Each of the islands has a **Wartel**. On Gili Air you can make phone calls at the wartel next to **Coconut Cottages**.

Northwest coast and Mount Rinjani

Following the coast north from Pemenang and Bangsal, the road passes the turn-off for Sir Beach (about 2 km north of Pemenang). This northwest coast is little touched by tourism and there are several 'traditional' villages where the more adventurous tour companies take visitors. The best-known of these is Bayan, at the foot of Mount Rinjani's northern slopes and about 50 km from Pemenang. Mount Rinjani, rising to 3726 m, dominates north Lombok. ▸▸ *For listings, see page 360.*

Northwest coast ◉ ▸▸ *p360.*

Siri beach
Siri beach is down a dirt track, to the left are coconut plantations, and reaches the deserted, long, narrow strip of soft, white sand on a headland looking across to Gili Air. Take all food and drink: there are no facilities here. This is worth a visit to get away from the crowds. To get there, take a bemo running north from Pemanang – the walk to the beach is about 2 km from the road.

Bayan
This is a traditional Sasak village and the birthplace of Lombok's unique Muslim 'schism' – *Islam Waktu Telu*. There is a mosque here that is believed to be 300 years old. The village is the jumping-off point for climbs up Mount Rinjani (see below). No accommodation.

Mount Rinjani ◉◉▲◉ ▸▸ *p360. Colour map 11, B2.*

Visitors who have made the effort invariably say that the highlight of their stay on Lombok was climbing Mount Rinjani. The views from the summit on a clear day are simply breathtaking. The ascent requires three days (although some keen climbers try to do it in two). Be warned that the summit is often wreathed in cloud, and views down to the blue-green lake within the caldera are also often obscured by a layer of cloud that lies trapped in the enormous crater.

Mount Rinjani is the second-highest mountain in Indonesia outside Irian Jaya – rising to an altitude of 3726 m. The volcano is still active but last erupted some time ago – in 1901, although in 1997 rumblings left dust raining for a week. The mountain, and a considerable area of land surrounding the mountain totalling some 400 sq km, has been gazetted as a national park.

The climb
There are two routes up Mount Rinjani. The easier and more convenient begins about 2 km to the west of the village of Bayan, on the way to Anyer. The track leads upwards from the road to the small settlement of **Batu Koq** and from there, 1 km on, to another village, **Senaru**. Tents, equipment and guides or porters can be hired in either of these two settlements (ask at the *losmen*); accommodation is available (see below). It is recommended that trekkers check in at the conservation office in Senaru before beginning the ascent. A guide is not essential as the trail is well marked from Senaru to the crater rim; however, suitable climbing gear is required (see below). From Senaru, the trek to the summit takes about two days, or 10 hours solid climbing. On the trek up, the

path passes through stands of teak and mahogany, then into pine forest and lichin. There are stunning views from the lip of the crater down to the beautiful blue-green and mineral rich lake, **Segara Anak** (Child of the Sea), below. A third day is needed to walk down into the caldera. The caldera is 8 km long by 5 km wide.

On the east side of the lake is **Mount Baru** (New Mountain), an active cone within a cone that rose out of the lake in 1942. It can be reached by boat and the climb to Mount Baru's summit, through a wasteland of volcanic debris, is rewarded with a view into this secondary crater. Along the base of the main crater are numerous hot springs – like **Goa Susu** (Milk Cave – so called because of its colour) – which are reputed to have spectacular healing powers: bathing in them is a good way to round off a tiring descent.

An alternative and more difficult route up the mountain – but some climbers who have done both claim this is the more interesting – is via **Sembalun Lawang, Sembalun Bumbung** or **Sapit** on the mountain's eastern slopes. This alternative route is less well marked. A guide is recommended to show climbers the route to the second rim. There is accommodation here (see below) and guides are also available, but there is a shortage of equipment for hire. There is food available to buy for the trek but the range is not as good as in Senaru. To get to Sembalun Bumbung, take a bus from Labuhan Lombok. The climb to the crater takes about nine hours. For ambitious climbers who intend to reach the true summit of Mount Rinjani – rather than just the caldera – this is the better of the two routes. **Note** In the past, some embassies in Jakarta have advises visitors not to climb Mount Rinjani because of fears of violent theft. However, no one going up, nor the guides, seemed concerned or particularly aware of any great problems. Nonetheless, check before beginning the climb.

Round trip taking in both sides of the mountain: because each side of Rinjani offers its own character, a recommended alternative is to climb up the eastern flank and down the western. To do this, go to Senaru to rent equipment and buy supplies (the choice is best here), return to Anyer or Bayan and take a bemo or ojek to Sembalun Lawang. (Start early, bemos to Sembalun Lawang are rare after 1600.) Hire a guide and porter in Sembalun Lawang and stay the night. The next day the guide can show the route to the second rim (six to seven hours); from here, the climb to the summit (three to four hours) and then down into the caldera (three hours), and from there up to the first rim and back down to Senaru (six to seven hours), is well marked and the guide is not needed.

Best time to climb From May to November, during the dry season, when it is less likely to be cloudy. Do not attempt the climb during the rainy season as the trail can be treacherous. The climb, though not technically difficult, is arduous and climbers should be in reasonable physical condition. **Recommended equipment**: water, sweater and coat, foam camping roll, sleeping bag, tough walking shoes, food/supplies, firewood (there is increasing evidence of climbers chopping down trees within this National Park in order to light a fire). *Please* take all your litter with you. **Note** Some climbers have complained of the poor quality of some of the equipment hired in Senaru; check it carefully. **Guides**: cost about US$11 per day and porters US$8 per day. A tent and/or sleeping bag hired for the guide would be greatly appreciated; it's cold on the mountain.

There is a US$16.50 admission fee to the Gununf Rinjani National Park, that needs to be paid at either the **Rinjani Trekking Club** ① *T0868 12104132*, in Senaru, or at the **Rinjani Information Centre** in Sembalun Lawang. You can also rent any necessary equipment at these places. Treks can be arranged in Senaru through the Rinjani Trekking Club, or through one of the local guides. Bahar at **Pondok Gunung Baru** ① *T0819 33128229*, is a knowledgable local guide with excellent English who offers all-inclusive two-day/one-night trips for US$98 per person, or three-day/two-nights for US$153. Treks can also be arranged in Senggigi with the reputable Rinjani Trekking Club (see Senggigi Activities and tours). Their prices are very reasonable and are all-inclusive. Alternatively you can book treks up Gunung Rinjani at any of the Perama offices. They have a variety of treks that depart from Senggigi. (See Senggigi Activities and tours).

◉ Northwest coast and Mount Rinjani listings

For Sleeping and Eating price codes, see inside the front cover.

● Sleeping

Mount Rinjani *p358*
It is possible to stay at Batu Koq and Senaru, as well as at Sembalun Lawang if making the climb from the east. Senaru has the best selection of (basic, all **E-G**) *losmen* and new ones seem to open almost every month.
Bale Bayan Guesthouse, T0817 5792943. Near the mountain, clean and friendly, the owner speaks reasonable English and German. Recommended.
Batu Koq Pondok Segara Anak, T0817 5754551. Has been recommended. Price includes breakfast and supper; some exquisite views.
Pondok Senaru, T0868 12104141. Clean, well run, big restaurant, ice-cold *mandi*.
Pondok Gunung Baru, T0819 33128229. 5 clean rooms. Good trekking information.
Rinjani Trekking Club, contact their Senggigi office, T0370 693860, and **Emy Homestay**. Both have simple acceptable lodging.

✪ Festivals and events

Mount Rinjani *p358*
Dec In the 2nd week of Dec, the **Pakelem**, offering feast is held on Segara Anak to ask for God's blessings.

▲ Activities and tours

Mount Rinjani *p358*
Tours
The most convenient way to climb Rinjani is by booking a place on a tour. Several tour operators in Senggigi (see Senggigi Activities and tours, page 344) and on the Gilis organize climbs (about US$180 all in). Tours are also available from *losmen* at various villages.

● Transport

Bayan *p358*
Bemo Connections with the Bertais terminal in Cakranegara. From Bayan bemos run up to Batu Koq. Bemos also run east from here along the very scenic coastal road to Labuan Lombok. From the looks of surprise it is clear that few *orang putih* make this (long) journey.

Mount Rinjani *p358*
Bemo For the more usual north route, take a bemo from the Bertais terminal to Bayan, and then a 2nd bemo from Bayan to Senaru. Alternatively, walk from Bayan. For the east route, take a bemo from Labuhan Lombok to Sembalun Bumbung.
Taxi A taxi from Bangsal to Senaru should cost about US$13.50.

Kuta beach and around

→ *Phone code: 0370.*
Kuta beach, also sometimes known as Putri Nyale beach, is situated among some of the most spectacular coastal scenery on Lombok; rocky outcrops and cliff faces give way to sheltered sandy bays, ideal for swimming and surfing. ➤➤ *For listings, see pages 363-365.*

Kuta beach ⬤⬤⬤⬤⬤⬤▲⬤ *pp363-365. Colour map 11, B2.*

Kuta itself has a stretch of sand on Lombok's south coast, in a bay with a little fishing village at its head. There is a substantial fishing fleet of sailing boats with brightly decorated dugout hulls and outriggers. There are no 'sights' other than the Sasak villages about 20 minutes' drive inland, beside the main Mataram to Kuta road.

The beach is the focal point of a strange annual festival, called the **Bau Nyale**, when thousands of seaworms come to the surface of the sea. Local people flock here to witness the event, and it is becoming quite a popular tourist attraction. See below for details.

Still a relatively quiet place to stay, there is a good road linking it to Mataram with regular shuttle bus connections.

At present the roads beyond Kuta are poor. The coast road continues east from Kuta past some magnificent, white sandy bays. After 2 km a potholed tarmac road turns off to Seger Beach, one of the beaches where the Nyale fish come ashore.

Further on again by 4 km, past low-lying swampy land, is the fine gold-sand beach at **Tanjung Aan**, set in a horseshoe-shaped bay; it is good for swimming, though there are stones and coral about 10 m out. Despite its distance from any development there are stalls, and hawkers materialize as soon as any foreigners appear. **Note** There is no shade on any of these beaches, just basic scrub. The track bends round to the south and ends at **Gerupak (Desert) Point**.

There are many **walks** in the area: climb the hill immediately to the west of Kuta for spectacular views over the south coast. The **Seger hills**, 2 km to the east, have numerous farm trails and a small cemetery; near Seger beach is a rocky promontory with more superb views, especially at sunset.

There are several good surfing beaches. The best are: **Are Guling**, **Mawi**, **Mawun** and **Selong Blanak**. **Gerupak (Desert Point)** is rated as one of the best surf spots in the world outside Hawaii. Kuta was originally 'discovered' by surfers.

Traditional villages that can be visited include: **Sade** and **Rembitan**, 9 km north of Kuta just off the main Mataram road, 20 minutes' drive.

Safety There is an 'honoured' tradition of inter-village theft in these parts. A thief from 1 village gained prestige by successfully stealing from other villages. We were warned to be very careful if out walking after dark. Take extra precautions to safeguard money and valuables. However, all over Lombok local neighbourhood watch-style groups have formed, HQ Praya, and will get your stolen goods back within the day! Hence crime has decreased considerably.

West of Kuta
There is now a sealed road running west of Kuta as far as Selong Blanak. Along the way there are several good beaches, all fairly deserted. The occasional bemo runs to Selong

Blanak from Praya. Twenty minutes' drive (10 km) west of Kuta is **Mawan Beach**. A perfect horseshoe shaped bay with a golden sand beach, a large tree and two bamboo shelters (called *garuga*) and several coconut palms offering some protection from the sun. Good for swimming, very protected though the sea bed slopes steeply near the shore. The road west climbs steeply out of Kuta, with spectacular views of the south coast, and mist covered hills in the rainy season. Further west near Selong Blanak are more good gold sand beaches at **Mawi** and **Rowok**. Mawi in particular offers good surfing. The road continues to the fishing village of **Selong Blanak**, with its wide, sandy bay and accommodation a little inland. Few travellers make the trip further west to **Pengantap**, **Sepi** and **Blongas**; the last of which has good surfing, snorkelling and diving, though be wary of sharks. From Sepi the poor road heads inland via Sekatong to the port of **Lembar**. All roads deteriorate west of Pengantap and should probably be avoided in the wet season. There are some bemos, though most people get here by private or chartered transport. The better accommodations offer free transport to Tanjung Aan Beach to the east and Mawan Beach to the west.

East of Kuta

Shortly before Tanjung Aan the road forks; taking the left fork, northeast, the road passes through Sereneng en route to Awang, 18 km from Kuta. The right fork goes to Gerupak about 9 km east of Kuta. From here there are boats across Gumbang Bay to Bumgang for about US$5.50. From Bumgang there is a path north which connects with the road to Awang. The villagers in this area make their living from fishing and seaweed farming and will hire out boats for about US$27 a day. A few bemos travel these routes and their numbers are slowly increasing, but the best way to see the area is with your own transport.

From Awang, boats can be chartered across the bay to Ekas for about US$13.50 return. **Ekas** has good surfing and snorkelling. There are spectacular views from the cliffs overlooking Awang Bay on both sides, particularly from Ekas. It is possible but

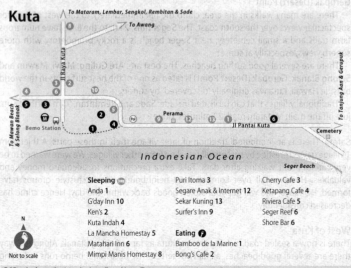

time-consuming to reach Ekas by public bemo: from Praya, catch a bemo bound for Tanjung Luar and Gubukdalem, get off just before Keruak at the turning south to Jerowaru and wait for a bemo going to Ekas, which is en route to Kaliantan in the southwest corner of the peninsula.

Tanjung Ringgit, on the southeastern tip of Lombok, is difficult to reach and for the most part the scenery is unexceptional. This place is shrouded in magic and mystery, with tales of spirits and demons living in the caves. (If a young woman goes there she will fall in love and never return.) It has connections with the Waktu Telu religion. To get here the choice is either an arduous overland journey ending in a rough dirt track, or chartering a boat from the fishing town of Tanjung Luar, approximately US$22.

◉ Kuta beach and around listings

For Sleeping and Eating price codes,
see inside the front cover.

◉ Sleeping

Kuta beach *p361, map p362*
Accommodation options have improved as Kuta's profile as a destination rises. The new airport in central Lombok, set to be completed in 2010, will make Kuta a much easier destination to reach, and should bring in greater investment. Many of the older established hotels here have struggled with maintenance and are slowly becoming faded. However, in recognition of this, their prices have dropped considerably, and it is possible to find some excellent value accommodation. Many of the popular budget surfer hotels are strung out along the beachside road.

C-D Ken's Hotel, Jl Raya Kuta, T0370 655057, www.southwind.tv. This new hotel caters mainly for Japanese surfers, and the owner is very knowledgeable about the area. The a/c rooms are large and clean, with TV and fridge. The more expensive suites are enormous and have 2 bathrooms. Service here is very efficient, and the kitchen serves up a couple of good Japanese dishes. There is a small but stylish pool and sunbathing area, with showers. Recommended.

C-F Matahari Inn, Jl Pantai Kuta, T0370 655000, F0370 654909. Beautiful gardens, with plenty of lush greenery and Buddha statues reclining and meditating on plinths. Faded rooms, the cheaper ones are musty, dark and charmless. Things improve as you go up the price range. Pool.

C-F Surfer's Inn, Jl Pantai Kuta, T0370 655582, www.lombok-surfersinn.com. Very popular with a nice pool and lounging area. Rooms are very simple and fairly large. They can arrange surfing lessons and take photos of surfers riding waves.

D-F Kuta Indah, Jl Pantai Kuta, T0370 653781, F0370 654628. This place was built with grand ideas in mind, but lack of custom has forced the owners to slash rates considerably. The a/c and fan rooms are good value, and the pool is extremely inviting.

E Puri Itoma, Jl Raya Kuta, T0370 655589. Also catering mainly to Japanese tourists, the a/c rooms here have hot shower and are fairly clean, although the staff seem genuinely bemused to see a tourist.

E-F Segare Anak, Jl Pantai Kuta, T0370 654846, www.kutalombok.com. The cheaper bungalows are wobbling on their stilts, but the slightly more expensive concrete rooms at the back are huge and clean and the bathrooms have a bath. Pool and badminton court.

F Anda, Jl Pantai Kuta, T0370 654836. Packed with chest-thumping surfers glued to the telly watching waves, this place definitely caters to a niche market, and is obviously succeeding. Rooms are bare and simple.

F G'day Inn, T0370 655342. Another popular place with the surf fraternity, 5 very simple rooms with bright bathrooms.

F Mimpi Manis Homestay, Desa Mong, T0818 369950, www.mimpimanis.com. It's a shame there aren't more lodgings like this in Indonesia, with extraordinarily friendly staff, good grub, a couple of choice volumes on the bookshelf, and a genuine homestay atmosphere. There are 2 rooms and a house on offer here, all of which are clean and come with TV and DVD player (there is a large library of films to choose from). It's 2 km inland, but the staff will drop you at the beach, and it is a cheap ojek ride back. Excellent value. Recommended.

F Sekar Kuning, Jl Pantai Kuta, T0370 654856. Clean rooms with fan and mosquito net.

G La Mancha Homestay, Jl Pantai Kuta, T0370 655186. 3 bungalows with concrete floor and mosquito net, a little dark. The bathroom has a squat toilet, shower and *mandi*.

☉ Eating

Kuta beach *p361, map p362*
Most places in Kuta have almost identical menus, and the town is no gourmet paradise. Nevertheless, it's easy to fill the belly for less than many places in Lombok, but cast your eyes over the cleanliness of a place before choosing to eat there. There are an awful lot of flies and rubbish around.

Most of the hotels offer food, although the kitchens usually close earlier than the restaurants. (♔♔♔) **Ken's Hotel** whips up a few Japanese dishes, as well as some Indonesian and international favourites; (♔) **Mimpi Manis** has a great *nasi campur*.

Be careful of the *warungs* on the beach, some tourists have reported cases of food poisoning after eating in them.

♔ **Bamboo De La Marine**, on a small road off Jl Pantai Kuta, T0878 63348095, open 0700-2200. Not far from the beach, this bright restaurant with its rather grandiose name has good vegetarian curry and seafood such as *ikan pepes*, as well as a few Sasak dishes.

♔ **Bong's Cafe**, Jl Pantai Kuta, T0819 16115552, open 0800-2300. Friendly place serving wood-fired pizza, sandwiches and lots of good Indonesian fare. Surf films shown nightly.

♔ **Cherry Cafe**, Jl Pantai Kuta, T0878 65168341, open 0800-2300. Lots of local options and a good salad menu at this friendly Balinese place.

♔ **Ketapang Cafe**, Jl Pantai Kuta, T0370 655194, open 0800-2100. This popular restaurant has a seaview and a menu favouring those starved of carbs, with good burgers, pizza and pasta dishes dominating.

♔ **Riviera Cafe**, Jl Pantai Kuta, T0819 2929210177, open 0730-2300. A large and diverse menu in a Spartan but friendly café near the Matahari Hotel. All the usual suspects are on offer here plus a few interesting local dishes such as *ayam taliwang* and *nasi begibung*. Happy hour 1800-2000.

♔ **Seger Reef**, Jl Pantai Kuta, T0370 655528, open 0800-2200. Lots of Indonesian food and pizza.

♔ **The Shore Bar**, next door to Seger Reef, open 0800-2400. A range of good fresh seafood.

☉ Bars and clubs

Kuta Beach *p361, map p362*
Nightlife is pretty thin on the ground. The **Shore Bar** (see Eating) is the place to be on Fri nights with live music, lots of surfers and local boys and even the occasional female. **Riviera Cafe** (see Eating) has live acoustic music on Wed and Fri evenings during the high season. Cultural shows are put on from time to time at the hotels.

☉ Festivals and events

Kuta beach *p361, map p362*
Feb/Mar (on the 19th day of the 10th month of the Sasak lunar calendar)
Nyale ceremony, thousands of mysterious sea worms called Nyale fish (*Eunice viridis*) 'hatch' on the reef and rise to the surface of the sea off Kuta. According to the legend of Putri Nyale, the episode is linked to the beautiful Princess Nyale, who drowned herself here after failing to choose between a bevy of eligible men. The

worms are supposed to represent her hair, and celebrations are held each year to mark her death. Traditionally, this was a time for young people to find a partner for marriage, and it is still an occasion when the usual strictures controlling contact between the sexes are eased. The worms are scooped from the sea and eaten.

O Shopping

Kuta beach *p361, map p362*
Local shops along the beachfront sell basics, including fruit, at reasonable prices. An endless stream of young children offer locally woven sarongs of variable quality, T-shirts and fruit. The pineapples here are delicious, as are the green bananas (to tell green bananas from unripe yellow bananas just squeeze; the ripe green bananas will feel soft). Kuta has its market on Sat.

▲ Activities and tours

Kuta beach *p361, map p362*
Cycling
There are a couple of bikes for rent at **Mimpi Manis** (see Sleeping) for 20,000Rp per day.

Fishing
Mimpi Manis (see Sleeping) offer the chance to go out with a local fisherman in his *perahu* to catch some fish and take it back to the hotel for a feast. Price is per boat rather than per person, and represents a good deal compared to fishing trips at many other places on Lombok (3 hrs, US$27, whole day US$65.50).

Surfing
Many people come to Kuta to surf. Boards, lessons, boat travel, repairs and nightly videos

of the biggest tubes and breaks in the world are shown at the **Kimen Surf Shop**, T0370 655064.

⊖ Transport

Kuta beach *p361, map p362*
Bemo
Public bemo to **Praya** from the bemo stop several times a day, about 6000Rp, 1 hr, from there you can catch a bemo to **Bertais**, 30 mins. Public bemos also connect Kuta with **Lahbuan Lombok** (for ferries to Sumbawa). Most people opt for the shuttle option (below), which is far less hassle.

Bemo services are increasing and more villages are coming on line, especially along the coast roads east and west of Kuta. Best to hire your own transport, though be aware that roads are bumpy. You can hire a car with driver, but self-drive is recommended here; the local drivers have limited skills for the most part. Mataram to Kuta is just over 1 hr, depending on traffic.

Motorbikes
Available to hire, often at very reasonable prices, eg 35,000Rp per day. Ask at your accommodation.

Ojek
It's easy to charter an ojek to **Senggigi** or **Mataram** for US$11 (1½ hrs) and stop to see the weaving village of Sukarara on the way. There are usually some fascinating local markets you can stop at along the way back, if you leave early enough. Ask your driver.

Shuttles
Daily **Perama** shuttles to Mataram and Senggigi leave at 0700 (US$13.50) for connections to Bali and the Gilis, the Perama office is in the **Segara Anak Hotel**.

Flores and around

→ *Colour map 11.*

Flores stretches over 350 km from east to west, but at most only 70 km from north to south. It is one of the most beautiful islands in the Lesser Sundas. Mountainous, with steep-sided valleys cut through by fast-flowing rivers, dense forests and open savanna landscapes, Flores embraces a wide range of ecological zones. One of the local names for the island is Nusa Nipa or 'Serpent Island', because of its shape. → *For listings, see pages 368-371.*

Ins and outs

Overland transport on Flores, 375 km in length, is neither quick nor comfortable. The Trans-Flores Highway is quite bearable, though travelling on it once is usually enough for most people. The road twists and turns through breathtaking scenery for more than 700 km. The Highway stretches from Labuanbajo in the east to Larantuka in the west. Buses are the main form of transport between centres. On minor roads, open trucks (known as *bis kayu*) with bench seats are still used. In towns like Ende and Maumere, bemos are the main form of local transport. Despite improvements in communications, overland travel is still exhausting. It is best to overnight in at least three towns on the journey across the island.

Labuanbajo ◯◯◯◯◯▲◯◯ → *pp368-371. Colour map 11, B4.*

→ *Phone code: 0385.*

Labuanbajo, or Bajo, is really just an overgrown fishing village. However, it marks the beginning of Eastern Indonesia, with Melanesian features and culture starting to dominate, and Christianity becoming the major religion (often blended with fascinating animist elements), with wonderful tropical churches and friendly nuns in the streets. The views of the harbour and surrounding islands are beautiful, making this one of Indonesia's most alluring harbour towns. There are some reasonable beaches, with excellent offshore snorkelling. It is also an excellent base from which to explore Komodo and Rinca, or to join a boat tour via the reserve and other islands on the way to Lombok (see below). The town is stretched out along one road that runs from the dock, along the seashore, and then south towards Ruteng. **Pramuka Hill**, behind the town, offers good views over the bay, especially at sunset.

Tourist information is available from the **PHKA information booth** ① *on the main street, opposite Gardena Hotel.* They can also provide information on Komodo and Rinca.

Around Labuanbajo

Waicicu Beach lies 15 minutes by boat north of town and offers good snorkelling and diving. One-day trips to the islands **Bidadari** and **Sabobo** can be arranged through hotels or tour operators (on main road), US$55 per boat for return boat ride. Good snorkelling in clear water and, potentially, the island to yourself.

Seraya Island Overnight stays on this island sleeping in bungalows on stilts can be arranged through Gardena Hotel (see Sleeping).

The principal reason people come to Komodo is to see the illustrious Komodo dragon. But there is more to the reserve than giant lizards – there is also good trekking, swimming and snorkelling. The park covers 59,000 ha, and is made up not just of Komodo Island, but also Rinca and a number of other surrounding islets. The highest peak on this rugged spot is Mount Satalibo (735 m).

Ins and outs

It is necessary to charter a boat from Labuanbajo (visit the Komodo Park offices in Labuanbajo for advice), or join a tour to get to the island. The rich and famous arrive direct by helicopter.

The national park

ⓘ *www.komodonationalpark.org. The island is a national park and visitors must register and buy an entrance ticket (US$15 plus US$4.50 valid for 3 days) on arrival at Loh Liang on Komodo, or Loh Buaya on Rinca. The park HQ at Loh Liang consists of an office, information centre, 4 bungalows, a souvenir shop, church and mosque, and a restaurant.*

After the luxuriant vegetation of Bali, Komodo can come as a bit of a shock – at least during the dry season. The islands of the Komodo archipelago are dry and rainfall is highly seasonal. For much of the year, therefore, the grasslands are burnt to dust and interspersed with drought-resistant savannah trees such as the distinctive lontar palm. In contrast the seas are highly productive, so there is good snorkelling, particularly off **Pantai Merah** and **Pulau Lasa** – a small island near Komodo village. The iridescent blue of the water, set against the dull brown of the islands, provides a striking backdrop. However, this image of Komodo as barren is transformed during the short wet season, when rainfall encourages rapid growth and the formerly parched landscape becomes green and lush.

Despite the other attractions of Komodo, it is still the **dragons** that steal the show. They are easily seen, with Timor deer (their chief natural prey) wandering among them. Other wildlife includes land crabs, wild pigs, black drongos, white-bellied sea eagles, and cockatoos, evidence that this is part of the Australasian faunal world. Monkeys are absent.

Walks

The most accessible viewing spot is the dry river bed at **Banu Nggulung**, 30 minutes' walk (2 km) from the accommodation at Loh Liang. Guides can take you there for a small fee, depending on the size of your group (30,000Rp per person). **Note** Visitors are only allowed to walk alone along marked trails. Those wishing to hike off the trails, and see the dragons in a more natural setting, must hire a guide. This is not just to generate income for the wardens; there have been fatalities. For around US$11 per person (but highly negotiable) a guide can take you to **Poreng Valley**, a 7-km walk from the PHKA office. There is a reasonably good chance of spotting a dragon and even if you don't, you will see plenty of other wildlife. There is a short 30-minute walk along the beach from Loh Liang bungalows to the stilt village of **Kampong Komodo**, which can be done without a guide. **Mount Ara** can be climbed in less than two hours (8.5 km to the summit)

Rinca Island 💬 ➤➤ *pp368-371.*

Ins and outs
Some boats travelling from Lombok to Flores stop off here. Ask about chartering a boat at the Princess office ① *Jl Kasimo 3, T0385 41744*. Rinca Island can also be reached from Komodo.

Wildlife
Rinca Island has a wider range of wildlife than Komodo, including wild horses, water buffaloes and dragons, and has the added advantage of fewer tourists. Only very simple food is available, so take your own snacks. It is more likely that you will go as part of an organized tour (arranged in Labuhanbajo or Lombok) and therefore you will be catered for. Rinca is fast gaining popularity over Komodo and recent visitors have been highly complimentary about trips there.

◉ Flores and around listings

For Sleeping and Eating price codes, see inside the front cover.

🛏 Sleeping

Labuanbajo *p366*
Accommodation in Labuanbajo is generally poor value for money, particularly when compared with Bali and Lombok.
C-D Golo Hilltop, T0385 41337, www.golo hilltop.com. Located up a dirt track to the north of the town, the views at sunset from here are amazing. The more expensive rooms are really comfortable, well decorated and have fan and a/c. Recommended.
C-D New Bajo Beach, Jl Pantai Pede, T0385 41069, F0385 41047. Set on a quiet beach 2.5 km from the centre of town, the rooms are large and clean and all have a/c. The cheaper rooms are tatty, the more expensive rooms have completely mismatched decor. The restaurant here is distinctly average so visitors trek to town for their meals.
E-F Chez Felix Hotel, T0385 41032. Set in spacious grounds on a hill above the town. The restaurant here has fine views. This is a peaceful place to stay, and all the rooms are tiled, clean and fairly spacious, although they face each other. The beds in the cheaper rooms are a little wobbly.

E-F Hotel Wisata, Jl Soekarno Hatta, T0385 41020. Indonesian-style hotel, with huge clean rooms, toilets that almost flush and friendly staff. The rooms face each other, so be prepared for some eyeballing.
F Gardena Jl Yos Sudarso, T0385 41258. Simple bungalows perched on the hillside overlooking the harbour, have great views but are in dire need of some maintenance. This is the most popular hotel in town, and is a nice retreat from the dusty main strip. Bathrooms have a mixture of squat and Western toilets (without seats or flush). Tourists have reported things going missing from their verandas and rooms. The hotel has a safety box. This place is often full.
F Losmen Matahari, T0385 41683. Cheap breezy place popular with Indonesians in transit. The rooms are small and boxy, and have squat toilet. This hotel is unique as it is built on stilts over the water, and the communal veranda is a great place to watch the goings on in the harbour.
F-G Bajo Beach Hotel, T0385 41008. This hotel takes the overspill from the Gardena. It's a rambling place with friendly, if somewhat eccentric staff. The simple tiled rooms have mosquito net, and bathroom with toilet (no flush), *mandi* and shower. They also rent snorkel equipment.

Seraya Island

E Seraya Island Bungalows, T0385 41258, www.serayaisland.com. 12 very simple bungalows on a lovely beach with superb snorkelling near by. Many visitors struggle to leave this place. There is a 2-night min stay, and transport there and back costs 40,000Rp. Contact the **Gardena Hotel** to book.

Sape

Sape is used as an overnight stop by travellers that have taken a leisurely trip across Sumbawa, and missed the early morning ferry connection to Flores (see page 371).
F Losmen Mutiara, right by the port entrance, T0374 71337. Clean simple rooms, more expensive with a/c. There are few places to eat nearby.

Komodo *p367*

It is very rare for people to stay the night on Komodo nowadays. If you wish to do so, contact the PHKA office in Labuanbajo before hand. The only accommodation on Komodo is in the **G PHKA bungalows** at Loh Liang, which has a capacity of about 40. They are simple but clean bungalows in a beautiful bay. Electricity from 1800 to 2200. Bedding consists of mattresses on the floor. During the peak season Jul-Sep, visitors must sleep in the dining room. Some rooms have their own *mandi* for no extra cost. The quality of the rooms is not great, but if you have the time, it is worth staying on the island. The cafeteria provides basic and rather overpriced food.

There is also a campground at Loh Liang.

Rinca Island *p368*

Most people visit Rinca on a day-trip rather than staying the night.
G PHKA bungalows, Loh Buaya. Basic accommodation, these stilted wooden cabins are the haunts of various rodent and insect populations, so be prepared.

❶ Eating

Labuanbajo *p366*
Most of the hotels have a restaurant, but quality varies enormously. There is a huge number of *nasi Padang* places in Labuanbajo. Poke your head behind the lace curtain to check the freshness first.

♥♥ The Lounge, T0385 41962, open 0800-2300. With a nice view and some breeze, this relaxing place has a small menu of Western food featuring fair burritos, feta salad and home-made ciabatta bread. Films are shown here occasionally and the staff are very friendly and keen to practice their English.
♥ Gardena, Jl Yos Sudarso, T0385 41258, open 0730-2200. The most popular travellers' hangout in town, with great views, huge fish hot plates and cheap salads. This is a very social spot, and a great place to meet other people in order to form a group for a trip to Komodo, or the island's interior. Recommended.
♥ Matahari, T0385 41008, open 0800-2200. Cheap pasta, seafood and soups with a wonderful view of the harbour.

❶ Bars and clubs

Labuanbajo *p366*
Paradise Bar, T0385 41533, flores@ indo.net.id, 24 hrs. Up a dirt track on the north side of the town, on the way to the Golo Hilltop, this is the place for connoisseurs of fine sunsets and cold beer. The views are truly beautiful. Sat night is when the bar comes alive, as locals and tourists head here in droves to listen to live acoustic and reggae music.

❶ Shopping

Labuanbajo *p366*
Between 0630 and 0900, multiple stalls set up along the main road selling vegetables. The usual shops can be found. There is a small

choice of sarongs and woven cloth; and a good shop for wooden carvings, including some rather gruesome masks. Hawkers linger at the entrance to the Gardena Hotel, with strings of pearls, and dragon carvings.

Komodo *p367*

There is a souvenir shop at Loh Liang and hawkers sell carved wooden dragons of various sizes, as well as other handicrafts.

▲ Activities and tours

Labuanbajo *p366*
Tour operators

There are a few tour operators offering boat trips as well as inland tours. Labuanbajo is the jumping-off point for journeys into the interior and there are companies offering breakneck 3-day tours of Flores. However, Flores is an island rich in natural beauty and cultural heritage and deserves more time to be spent on it. It is easy enough to organize independent travel around the island.
Princess, Jl Kasimo 3, T0385 41744. Have a boat for charter to Komodo and Rinca. They provide snorkelling equipment.
Lestari Jaya (at entrance to **Gardena Hotel**, T0852 39005498). Offer 4-day/3-night boat tours to Bangsal (Lombok), stopping at Komodo, Rinca and Pulau Moyo and Pulau Satonda (Sumbawa) en route, around US$110 per person. Food is included, but admission fee to the Komodo National Park isn't. Check out the boat before agreeing to a tour; some boats are overloaded. It also has a trip that takes in Bajawa, Moni and Kelimutu for US$246 (per group, 4 people max).
Perama, T0385 42016. Run a 2-day trip to Lombok via Rinca costing US$98.50 for a spot on the deck and US$153 for a cabin.

Komodo *p367*
Diving and snorkelling

The waters around Komodo are finally getting the recognition they deserve as having some of the finest diving spots in the world, and the local diving industry is growing by the year with more and more foreign investors opening up businesses. The waters around the national park are teeming with life, and with improved accessibility over recent years, are seeing increasing numbers of visitors, including liveaboards from as far away as Thailand. The reef is considered to be 99% pristine, with strong currents keeping the water temperature down and preventing the blanching effects of El Nino as seen around the Gili islands. Most companies operate day trips back and forth from Labuanbajo (see page 366) to the dives sites, rather than operating as liveaboards, although this option is available. It takes 1½-2 hrs to reach sites around Komodo. Typically a day trip with 2 dives costs around US$71. Packages are available for 3, 5, and 10 days. Highly recommended are **Reefseekers**, T0385 41433, www.reefseekers.net, whose British owners enthuse about marine life and offer 1½-hr briefings on the journey to the reef on the ecology of the reef relevant to the area being visited. They are building a top-notch resort of Pulau Bidadari, which should bring the diving even closer. Also recommended **Bajo Dive Club**, T0385 41503, www.komododiver.com, and **Dive Komodo**, T0385 41862, www.divekomodo.com. There is some great snorkelling off the nearby islands, and around Pantai Merah and Pulau Bidadari in the national park. You need to charter a boat to do this, which can cost between US$49 to US$77. Enquire at one of the agents around town.

⊖ Transport

Labuanbajo *p366*
Air

The airport is 2 km from town. Airport tax is 5000Rp. Flights are met by minivans, and private vehicles. It costs around 10,000Rp to get to the airport from the town. Between **Merpati** (on the way to the airport, T0385 41177), **Indonesia Air Transport** (Jl Kasimo, T0385 41088), and **Trans Nusa** (Jl Soekarno

Hatta, T0385 41800), there are daily connections to **Denpasar**. If you want to head to Lombok or Java you must transit in Bali. **Trans Nusa** offer onwards connections from Denpasar with **Mandala**, and plan to open up more routes from Labuanbajo to Kupang and Makassar in the near future. **Merpati** are notorious for cancellations. Flights get booked out in advance, so booking early is essential.

Road
Lestari Jaya, (see above), and **Manumadi**, JI Soekarno Hatta, T0385 41457, manumadi@ telkom.net, both have vehicles for hire to explore the surrounding countryside. Ojeks for travel around town cost 3000Rp during the day and 5000Rp after sunset.

There is no bus station; buses cruise the hotels and *losmen* picking up passengers. Connections with **Ruteng**, 4 hrs, and **Bajawa**, 10 hrs, 1 daily at 0600 – book at any of the tourist information offices in town. It is even possible to make the exhausting journey all the way to **Ende** on a bus that meets the ferry from Sape.

Lansung Indah, T0385 41106, has a small outlet in a mobile phone shop near the port entrance. They have bus – ferry combination tickets for **Bima**, **Mataram**, **Denpasar**, **Surabaya** and even **Jakarta**.

To Flores from Lombok via Sape, Sumbawa Many tourists opt to take an overnight bus from Lombok and across Sumbawa on the way to Flores. Typically, buses depart from Mataram, Lombok around 1500 and travel across Lombok and Sumbawa (with a 2-hr ferry crossing between) arriving in Bima around 0400. Most travellers book a through ticket (Mataram–Sape), and upon arrival in Bima are put on a small bus for the 2-hr ride to Sape. The Mataram–Sape bus ticket will need to be shown to the conductor on

this minibus, so don't throw the ticket away. The bus should arrive in time for the 0800 ferry to Labuanbajo, Flores. Some tourists find this heavy going and prefer to stay the night in Sape, or, if the bus breaks or is late, have to stay there. See page 369.

Sea
Daily ferries leave at 0800 for **Sape**, **Sumbawa**, 41,000Rp, 6-8 hrs. Buses meet the ferry from Sape and take passengers straight on to Ruteng. Boats travel frequently between Labuanbajo and Lombok, via Komodo on tours. The **Pelni vessel Tilongkabila** docks at Labuanbajo twice a month travelling alternately westwards to **Bima**, **Lembar** and **Benoa** (Bali) and northwards to **Sulawesi** with a handy connection to **Makassr**. The PELNI office, T0385 41106, is up a small dirt track past the football pitch. It is in a mechanic's workshop and not signposted.

⊙ Directory

Labuanbajo *p366*
Banks BNI, main road (150 m towards Ruteng from Bajo Beach Hotel), will change cash and TCs from major companies and have an ATM that accepts foreign cards. It is best to also bring some cash in case this breaks down, as the next ATM is a long way from here. **Internet** Pagi Swalayan, JI Soekarno Hatta, T0385 41877, 0800-2200. Above the Pagi Swalayan supermarket on the 3rd floor, this place is roasting but has a reasonable connection at 10,000Rp per hr. **Post office** In the centre of town. **Telephone** Telkom office, south of town, near the PHKA office. Several **Wartel** offices around town.

Sumatra

→ *Colour map 12.*

Although Sumatra does not have Java's historical and archaeological sights, it does offer magnificent natural landscapes. Perhaps most spectacular of all is the upland crater lake of Danau Toba. The forests, mountains, rivers and coasts all provide great trekking and rafting opportunities, some of the finest national parks in the country and pristine beaches.

There are also over a dozen ethnic groups on the island, who speak some 20 different dialects, including the peripatetic Minangkabau of West Sumatra, the Christian Bataks of North Sumatra, the Ferrant Muslims of Aceh and the tribal peoples of Nias and Mentawi.

As the world's fourth-largest island (nearly 475,000 sq km), Sumatra also acts as a 'safety valve' for Java's 'excess' population. About 60% of Indonesia's transmigrants – four million people – have been resettled on Sumatra, mostly in the south. Population densities here are less than one tenth of those on neighbouring Java, although some areas – such as Lampung province – are beginning to suffer the effects of overcrowding.

Sumatra is also crucial to the Indonesian economy. It was in North Sumatra that Indonesia's first commercial oil well was sunk in 1871, and over 60% of the country's total petroleum and gas production comes from the island and the seas that surround it.

Ins and outs

When to go

Sumatra's climate varies considerably across the island. North of the equator the rainy season extends from October to April, and south of the equator from October to January. Road travel during the dry season is quicker and easier, but overland travel in the wet season is fine on the (largely) all-weather Trans-Sumatran Highway. The most comfortable time to travel is during the onset of the rains (September-October), when temperatures have cooled but showers have not become torrential. Most tourists visit between June and October, so travelling out of those months is relatively quiet and hotel rates can often be bargained down.

Getting there

Air Most visitors arrive at Medan, in the north, near the west coast of Sumatra, which offers international connections with Kuala Lumpur and Penang, in Malaysia, and with Singapore. There are also flights from Singapore to Pekanbaru and Padang. There are domestic connections with Jakarta from all Sumatran provincial capitals.

Boat There is a twice weekly 'international' ferry linking Penang (Malaysia) with Belawan (Medan's port), 14 hours. Hydrofoils and high-speed catamarans also make the crossing five times a week, four to five hours. In addition to the popular Belawan–Penang route, there are also ferry connections from Belawan with Port Klang (Kuala Lumpur's port) and, via Penang, with Langkawi. For more details, see page 382. An alternative route into or out of Indonesia is to catch a regular high speed ferry from Singapore's World Trade Centre or Tanah Merah piers to Batam or Bintan islands in the Riau archipelago, 40 minutes. From there it is possible to catch a boat – fast or very slow – to Pekanbaru, up the Siak River on the Sumatran 'mainland'. There are also ferry connections between Melaka and Dumai, although this is not a very popular entry/exit point. The most important domestic entry/

exit point is Bakauheni on Sumatra's south tip; hourly ferries link Bakauheni with Merak, West Java. The **PELNI** ships Kelud and Sinabung call in on Medan on loops to Jakarta's Tanjung Priok via Balai Karimun and Batam respectively.

Getting around

Where to go Travelling in Sumatra can be a time-consuming business. Some key destinations – notably Danau Toba – have no airport and others – like Nias Island – have only intermittent air connections. Furthermore, distances can be great and with average road speeds of around 50 kph, even on the Trans-Sumatran 'highway', it can take a while to get from A to B. This means that anyone intending to sample Sumatra in anything more than the most cursory of ways will need to allocate at least 10 days. The classic 'route' is to travel between Medan and Padang (which both have airports with daily flights), via Berastagi, Danau Toba and Bukittinggi. This really requires a minimum of 10 days and preferably two weeks. However, there are opportunities for shorter stays, and people living in the region regularly come to Sumatra for a week or less. Residents of Singapore in their thousands, for example, take weekend breaks in the Riau islands. It would also be quite feasible to fly into Medan and make for Danau Toba for five days or to Padang and take the bus up to Bukittinggi for a similar length of time. But long-haul visitors, with jet lag to deal with and perhaps a new climate too, would probably find such a short visit exhausting and ultimately less than satisfying.

Air This is the most convenient and comfortable way to travel around Sumatra. **Garuda** and **Merpati** service all the main provincial cities. Merpati tends to operate the short-hop services to smaller towns and cities. The other main domestic airlines on Sumatra are **Mandala** and **Kartika**. Smallest of all are **DAS, SMAC** and **Deraya**, which tend to service smaller towns.

Train There is a limited rail network in South Sumatra. The only regular passenger service used by travellers links Bandar Lampung, Palembang and Lubuklinggau. In the north, there is a line running from Medan to Rantau Parapat, and from Medan to Tanjung Balai.

Bus Buses are the main mode of long-distance travel. Steady improvements to the 2500 km Trans-Sumatran 'Highway' (a misnomer – over large sections it is more like a village road, one and a half lanes wide), which runs down the entire island from Banda Aceh in the north to Bakauheni in the south, is making road travel much faster and more comfortable. It used to take 20 hours from Parapat to Bukittinggi, now it takes 10-14 hours depending on the vehicle. Roads off the Trans-Sumatran Highway are still generally poor, and in the rainy season delays of two days are not unknown while floodwaters subside. Travelling through the Bukit Barisan, or along the west coast, is still quite slow, with average speeds of 40-50 kph, as the road follows every turn of the mountain. There are a/c, VIP or express buses plying all the major routes. The most highly regarded private bus companies are *ALS* and *ANS*.

Because tourists tend to have a lower pain threshold than locals – and a lower tolerance threshold to delayed departures – tourist buses now ply the popular routes. In particular, the route from Padang, through Berastagi, Danau Toba and Sibolga, to Bukittinggi. These *bis parawisata* (tourist buses) are often eight-seat minibuses that leave at a set hour (roughly) and tend to arrive even more quickly than the *bis biasa* (ordinary bus) alternatives. Tourist services are safer; they often pick up and drop off at hotels in towns; and they may also include stops at designated tourist sights en route (the dreaded *objek wisata*). The main disadvantage (other than cost) is that they reduce contact between locals and tourists.

Medan

→ *Phone code: 061. Population: 2,000,000. Colour map 12, A1.*

Medan is big, hot, noisy, congested and dirty, with only a few havens of greenery – for example, Merdeka Square – and no obvious 'sights' to enthrall the visitor. However, while the architecture is not notable by international standards it is significant in the Indonesian context, and Medan does provide a vivid and vivacious introduction to Asia for those who are new to the region. In addition, and perhaps because foreign tourists are less in evidence, the local people are generally warm and welcoming. For those coming from other parts of Indonesia, Medan shows Indonesia in quite a different light, sharing plenty in common with Peninsular Malaysia. This is evident in the crumbling Chinese shophouses, with their five foot walkways, the smell of incense wafting out into the street. Visitors will also note presence of a permanent Indian population, not seen anywhere else in the archipelago, driving becaks (rickshaws), cooking fine curries and worshipping at garish southern Indian Hindu temples.
▶▶ *For listings, see pages 379-384.*

Ins and outs

Getting there

Medan is an international gateway and an easy one-hour hop by air from Singapore. There are also air connections with several Malaysian cities and all Indonesia's main centres. The airport is in the centre of town. Medan's port of Belawan provides ferry services to Penang in Malaysia and is also visited by several **PELNI** vessels that run fortnightly circuits through the Indonesian archipelago. Medan has two bus terminals. The Amplas terminal, 8.5 km south of the city centre, serves all destinations to the south. The Pinang Baris terminal, about 9 km to the northwest, serves destinations north of Medan. The train system is running, but services are limited. ▶▶ *See Transport, page 382.*

Getting around

Medan is a nightmare to get around, many of the main access roads are choked with traffic. The one-way system only seems to add to the frustration. However, becak drivers and taxis have become adept at chicken footing down side lanes and avoiding the main arteries. Going by rickshaw will provide your stomach with a nifty lead lining.

Tourist information

The **North Sumatran Tourist Office** (Dinas Pariwisata) ① *Jl Jend A Yani 107, T061 4528436, Mon-Fri 0800-1600*, has good maps and excellent city and regional guides. **Dinas Pariwisata** ① *Jl Brig Jend Katamso 43, daily 0900-1700, (no telephone)*, is another tourist office but this one is even less helpful and a quick peek into the visitor's book shows that around two tourists a month pop in. There is some material available but little English is spoken and it is often closed. Those who are interested in Medan's architectural heritage should try and get hold of *Tours through historical Medan and its surroundings*, by Dirk A Buiskool (1995). The pamphlet is sold in some hotel gift shops and is also available in the Dutch original.

Tours Tour companies have offices in most of the larger hotels and organize half-day city tours, and day tours to Berastagi and to the orang-utans at Bukit Lawang. Longer overnight tours to Danau Toba and to the Nias Islands are also offered by most tour agents.

Colonial buildings

The greatest concentration of colonial buildings is to be found along Jalan Balai Kota and its continuation, Jalan Jend A Yani, and around Merdeka Square. Few still perform their original functions as the headquarters of plantation companies, European clubs, and stately hotels. As Dirk A Buiskool explains in his pamphlet *Tours through historical Medan and its surroundings* (1995), from which much of the information below is taken, Medan underwent a building explosion during the first decade of the 20th century. The city's wealth and economic importance demanded many new buildings, and as these had to be constructed quickly there was a tendency towards standardization of design – producing what became known as 'normal architecture'.

Walking south from the northwest corner of the 'Esplanade', now **Merdeka Square** (Independence Square), the first building of note is the **Central Post Office** at Jalan Bukit Barisan 1. It was begun in 1909 and completed in 1911 and is refreshingly unchanged. Inside, the main circular hall beneath the domed roof still contains its original post office counters. On the other side of the road was Medan's most stately hotel, the **Dharma Deli**. Today, a new block so dominates the site that the original hostelry is all but invisible. The **Dharma Deli** was formerly the Hotel De Boer and began life in 1898 as a modest place with just seven rooms. However, as Medan's economic influence grew, so the Hotel De Boer also expanded and by 1930 it had 120 rooms. Among the innovations introduced at the hotel was the so-called 'mosquito-less room': rooms where the windows were entirely enclosed in wire gauze, allowing people to sleep without mosquito nets. Perhaps the most famous person to have stayed at the hotel was the spy, Mata Hari.

The **Padang** itself is notable for its huge, epiphyte-filled trees that skirt the square and provide relief from the sun. On the west side of the square are two more elegant buildings, side by side: the appropriately stolid Bank of Indonesia and the refined Balai Kota. The **Bank of Indonesia**, formerly the De Javasche Bank, was designed by Ed Cuypers in 1910 in Classical style. The **Balai Kota** was probably erected in 1908 and then modernized in 1923. The clock in the elegant tower was donated by Medan's most influential Chinese businessman – Tjong A Fie (see below). The new Balai Kota, or more fully the Kantor Wali Kotyamadya, is just over the river on Jalan Raden Saleh. The architect of this building has drawn on the original Balai Kota for inspiration, most obviously in the domed tower which imitates the original, barring the blank space where the clock should be.

The Chinese community

The strip of buildings running the length of Jalan Jend A Yani from Merdeka Square south to Jalan Pemuda are very different to the buildings on the Padang; the latter is representative of the colonial government and the economic interests that sustained and supported it. These, however, were largely owned by Medan's Chinese business community – they are small **Sino-Dutch shophouses** where families would at the same time run their businesses and live, sleep and eat. Although many are marred by modern façades, they are nonetheless notable for their use of both Dutch and Chinese architectural flourishes and for their variety. Most notable of all is the run-down and romantically decrepit **Tjong A Fie Mansion** at Jalan Jend A Yani 105. This quasi-colonial/ quasi-Chinese house, with its green-and-beige paint scheme and peacock-topped entrance arch, was built by a wealthy Chinese businessman, after which it is named. Like other Chinese who found their fortunes in Southeast Asia, Tjong A Fie arrived in Medan from Guangdong (Canton) in 1875 almost penniless – he reputedly had a few pieces of silver sewn behind his belt. In Medan he gained the trust of the Dutch authorities and the sultan, and became the supplier for many of the area's plantations. Before long he was a millionaire and Medan's 'Major' – the highest ranking member of the Chinese

Medan

Clock Tower (S)

Jl Jend Gatot Subroto

Pajak Petisar

University

To Pinang Baris Bus Terminal

Bank of Indonesia (S)

Bukit Barisan

Jl Bukit Barisan

Jl Kereta Api

Padang (Merdeka Square)

Balai Kota

Kantor Wali Kotyamadya

Jl Raden Saleh

Vihara Kong Ti Niong

Jl Balai Kota

Lapangan Benteng

Pasar Ikan Lama

Malahayati Hospital

Jl Pengadilan

Jl May Jend Sutoyo

Jl Ahmad Yani

8

16

Tjong A Fie Mansion

Pusat Makonan Erlangga

Jl Airlangga

Jl Listrik

Gleneagles

7

Jl Putri

Shri Mariamman (Candi Hindu)

16 17

Jl Teuku Umar

Jl Diponegoro

Jl H Zainul Arifin

Bukit Barisan (Military Musém)

Jl Palang Merah

Jl Mesjid

Jl Mangkubumi

Catholic Cathedral

Crispo Antiques

Babura River

6 5 (S)

15 (S)

Norwegian Consulate

Jl Imam Bonjol

1

Jl Suka Mulia

Jl Tengku Daud

Singapore Consulate

Jl Alumi

Mesjid Agung

Jl Cut Meutiah

Immanuel

Jl Badur

Jl S Parman

Jl Cik Ditiro

Jl R A Kartini

Jl Cut Nyak Dien

Jl Letjen Suprapto

Jl Medan

Vihara Gunung Timur

Jl Hang Tuah

Swedish, Finnish & Danish Consulate

Alliance Francaise

Malaysian Consulate

Jl Multatuli

Jl Jenderal Sudirman

Indian Consulate

Jl Imam Bonjol

Jl Samanhudi

Japanese Consulate

German Consulate

Russian Consulate

Jl Ir H Juanda

To Airport (400m)

N

200 metres

200 yards

Sleeping

Angel Homestay **2**
Belmondo **5**
Cahaya Baru **14**
Danau Toba International **1**
De Deli Darbar **16**

Dhaksina **3**
Garuda Citra **6**
Garuda Plaza **7**
Ibunda **8**
Inna Dharma Deli **4**
M&R **17**

Madani **9**
Merdeka Walk **18**
Novotel Soechi **10**
Residence **11**
Sri Deli **12**
Sumatra **13**

community. He was a great philanthropist, giving generously to good causes – a founder, for example, of the Colonial Institute (now the Tropical Institute) in Amsterdam.

Opposite the mansion is the side street Jalan Jend A Yani I, which has a little reminder of the early days of independence in the spelling of the road name: Djl Djenderal A Yani.

Walking north towards Merdeka Square a short distance is the **Tip Top Restaurant**, which began serving food and drinks in 1934 and continues to do so in a style redolent of the colonial period. Just across the railway line at the end of Jalan Jend A Yani V is the **Vihara Kong Ti Niong** – Medan's oldest Chinese pagoda.

Temples, Pogodas and Mosques

Another road with historical buildings is the garden-like Jalan Jend Sudirman (Polonia quarter), southwest of the town square. At the southwest edge of the city is the **Vihara Gunung Timur** ① *Jl Hang Tuah 16, photography is not allowed in the pagoda, remember to remove your shoes before entering the inner sanctuary*, just west of Jalan Cik Ditiro. This building, erected in the late 1970s, is the largest Chinese pagoda in Medan. Set in a peaceful area, the main entrance to the temple is flanked by guardian lions. Filled with lanterns, incense and demons, the temple is a rewarding retreat from the bustle of the city. The highly decorated roof is probably its most notable feature. Locally known as **Candi Hindu** (Hindu temple), the Shri Mariamman is at Jalan H Zainul Arifin 130. The complex serves Medan's large South Asian community and the brightly painted figures of gods and animals stand out a mile. The temple welcomes visitors. This part of town, reasonably enough, is the Indian quarter and the temple has been recently renovated and expanded. However, there has been a Hindu temple on the site from 1884. The **Immanuel Protestant Church**, built in 1921 in art deco style, can be found back towards the town centre at Jalan Diponegoro 25. Almost facing it on the other side of the road is the **Mesjid Agung**, with a towering new minaret.

The attractive **Mesjid Raya** or **Grand Mosque** ① *admission by donation*, with its fine black domes and turquoise tiles, can be found at the corner of Jalan Sisingamangaraja and Jalan Mesjid Raya. The mosque was built in 1906 in 'Moroccan' style by Sultan Makmun Al-Rasyid, and designed by the Dutch architect Dingemans. The marble came from Italy, the chandelier from Amsterdam, and the stained-glass from China. In the grounds is a small enclosed plot containing the tombs of the sultans of the Istana Maimun Palace (see below), and a fairy-tale style minaret. It is just a shame that the mosque is on such a busy and ugly road – which detracts from its beauty.

To the west of the mosque, set back from the road on Jalan Brig Jen. Katamso, is the **Istana Maimun** – also known as the **Istana Sultan Deli** ① *daily 0800-1700, 3000Rp*. This impressive building was designed by Captain Th van Erp, a Dutch architect working for the Royal Dutch Indies Army. It was constructed in 1888 as one element in a complex that included the Grand Mosque. The predominant colour is yellow – the colour of the royal house of Deli. It is eclectic architecturally, embracing Italian, Arab and Oriental styles. Inside are photographs of the various sultans and their wives, and a poor oil painting of the Sultan Deli himself who built the palace. The interior includes a few pieces of Dutch furniture and the sultan's throne. His descendants continue to live in one wing of the palace.

Museums and the zoo

The **Museum Sumatera Utara** ① *Jl HM Joni 51, T061 7716792, Tue-Sun 0830-1200, 1330-1700, 1000Rp*, some distance south of town off Jalan Sisingamangaraja, is an extensive building with an equally extensive – though of variable quality – collection of artefacts. Not surprisingly, it specializes in those of North Sumatran origin and upstairs has some fine wood and stone-carvings from the Nias Islands. Unfortunately it is ill-lit and poorly maintained, with little useful explanatory detail. The **Bukit Barisan Museum** ① *Jl H Zainul Arifin 8, T061 4536927, Mon-Fri 0800-1500, admission by donation*, also known as the Museum Perjuangan Abri or the Military Museum, displays a decaying selection of Sumatran tribal houses and arts and crafts, as well as military paraphernalia.

Markets

One of the greatest attractions of Medan is its markets, known locally as *pajak*. The huge **Pajak Pusat (Central Market)** – in fact an agglomeration of various markets selling just about everything – is located close to Jalan Dr Sutomo. It is renowned for its pickpockets. Safer is the **Pajak Petisar**, on Jalan Rasak Baru, just off Jalan Gatot Subroto. It is a fruit and vegetable market in the morning (0600), that later develops into a general market, selling clothes, food and general merchandise. The **Pasar (Pajak) Ikan Lama (Old Fish Market)** is a good place to buy cheap batik, other types of cloth and assorted garments. It is on Jalan Perniagaan, close to Jalan Jend A Yani. Visitors may see live fruit bats strung up for sale.

Around Medan

Binjai, **Berastagi** and the **Orang-Utan Rehabilitation Centre** at Bukit Lawang (see below) are all accessible as day trips from Medan. **Binjai**, 22 km west of Medan on Route 25, is famed for its fruit, especially its rambutans and durians. The best time to visit is when they are in season, July-August. It is possible to reach Berastagi and the Orang-Utan Rehabilitation Centre from here (about three hours). Bukit Lawang can be visited as a long day trip.

◉ Medan listings

*For Sleeping and Eating price codes,
see inside the front cover.*

● Sleeping

Medan *p374, map p376*

The rock-bottom budget digs in Medan are no
great shakes, but there are some good options
in the slightly more expensive categories.
There is a cluster of hotels on Jl S.M Raja
(Jl Sisingmangaraja), which is the best area
to have a wander and compare prices.

AL-B Novotel Soechi, Jl Cirebon 76, T061
4561234, www.novotelsoechipt.com. This
place is crawling with business people, and is
deservedly popular with its excellent service,
good facilities and spacious smart rooms
(some with pool views). Pool, fitness centre.
Free Wi-Fi in rooms. Excellent discounts
available. Recommended.

AL-C Danau Toba International, Jl Imam
Bonjol 17, T061 4157000, F061 4530553.
Sprawling hotel with long list of facilities,
including tennis courts and a large pool set
in a garden with plenty of outdoors seating.
The rooms are a tad antiquated, but
comfortable, and some have garden
views. Wi-Fi is available in the lobby.

A-C Hotel Inna Dharma Deli, Jl Balai Kota 2,
T061 4157744, www.innadharmadeli.com.
This hotel is filled with history, but areas are
looking a little rough round the edges
nowadays. The rooms are ultra clean,
spacious and have cable TV. Free Wi-Fi is
available for guests in the hotel café. Pool.

A-C Madani Hotel, Jl SM Raja 1, T061
7358000, www.madani-hotel.com. There
are plenty of Islamic vibes at this plush
new hotel, with corridors filled with Lebanese
music and cafés without beer. The staff are
friendly and the rooms are spotless and
clean with cable TV (most foreign language
channels are in Arabic). There is a 25%
discount available, making this place
excellent value. Recommended.

B-C Hotel Garuda Plaza, Jl SM Raja 18,
T061 7361111. Large hotel with friendly staff,
comfortable rooms (some with free Wi-Fi
access), cable TV and complimentary
newspapers. There is a pool out the back
with a pleasant lounging area.

C-D Dhaksina Hotel, Jl SM Raja 20, T061
7320000, F061 7340113. Garish hotel with fair
selection of clean a/c rooms, although many
have no windows. 10% discount available.

C-D Hotel Garuda Citra, Jl SM Raja 27,
T061 7367733, www.garudahotel.com.
New lobby area with free Wi-Fi access.
The a/c rooms are old and some are a
little musty. 10% discount available.

D Hotel Sumatra, Jl SM Raja 35, T061
7321551, F061 7321553. Big a/c rooms with
clean attached bathroom, TV and some with
balcony. Staff are friendly. Discounts available
for stays of 5 nights or more.

D-E Ibunda Hotel, Jl SM Raja 31-33, T061
7368787, www.ibundahotel.com. The pea-
green façade of the Ibunda is unmissable, and
the colour theme continues in the interior,
with its confusing staircases reminiscent of
an Escher painting. The rooms here are good
value, the more expensive ones are huge,
and the standard singles, though a little dark,
come with a/c and TV. Recommended.

D-F Hotel Sri Deli, Jl SM Raja 30, T061
7368387. Good selection of rooms, including
windowless economy rooms with *mandi*.
Things get better as prices rise, with cleanish
standard a/c rooms filled with light.

F-G Residence Hotel, Jl Tengah 1, T061
7600980. Dark cell-like rooms, with squat toilet
and not even a *mandi* to wash in (there is a
small red bucket with a scoop). A/c is available
in the most expensive category.

G Angel Homestay, Jl Mahkamah 26, T061
7461078, a_zelsy_travel@yahoo.com. The
cheapest place to crash in town, with a
collection of concrete cells with fans and
shared bathroom. The interior of this place is
so dark, a headlamp is needed to penetrate

the gloom. Staff can book ferry and bus tickets. Breakfast is not included, but there is free coffee and tea from 0700-1100.

G Hotel Zakia, Jl Sipiso Piso 10-12, T061 7322413. Staff are half conscious, but rooms here are not too bad for the price, with spartan fan rooms on the 2nd storey with veranda overlooking a small garden.

● Eating

Medan *p374, map p376*
Medan's large Chinese community means that the Chinese food here is excellent. There are many small eating houses in the street running off Jl Jend A Yani. The Indian area of town is centred on Jl Cik Ditiro and Jl H Zainal Arifin, close to Sri Mariamman temple.

♦♦♦ Belmondo, Jl Zainul Arifin 122, T061 4518846. Restaurant with sophisticated pretences popular with expats and locals at weekends. There is a good wine list, fusion food, seafood and a convivial atmosphere. Live jazz on Sat nights from 2000.

♦♦♦ De Deli Darbar, Jl Taruma 88, T06 415 6858, open 1100-2230. There is plenty of choice here, with a menu that features both southern Indian and frontier dishes. Curries are found in abundance, accompanied by some fine starters and a good selection of naan bread. Recommended.

♦♦♦ M&R, Jl Taruma 37, T06-453 6537, daily 1100-1500 and 1800-2100. Tidy eatery furnished in traditional Chinese style with caged song birds hanging from the ceiling, this is a fine place to sample nyonya (Straits Chinese fusion of Malay and Chinese flavours thought to have originated in Melaka, Malaysia) cuisine. The menu is heavy on seafood, with good crab dishes dominating.

♦♦-♦ Merdeka Walk, Jl Balai Kota (on the western side of Merdeka Square), daily 1200-2400. This is a smart collection of eateries including **Oh La La** (bakery serving filled croissants, lasagne and cakes), **Killiney Kopitiam** (Singaporean franchise offering kaya toast, half cooked eggs and plenty of coffee), as well as some smaller stalls serving Indonesian staples.

♦♦-♦ Sun Plaza, Jl Zainul Arifin 7, T061 4501500, daily 1000-2200. Shopping mall with plenty of places to eat in clean, air conditioned comfort. **Dome** and **De'Excelso** are cafés serving sandwiches, pastas, salads and a wide range of coffees and ice cream. **Ya Kun Kaya Toast** is a Singaporean outfit serving kaya toast (kaya is a rich jam made from coconut), thick coffee and half cooked eggs. There is also an excellent food court, and branches of **Bread Talk** and **Papa Ron's Pizza**.

♦ Cahaya Baru, Jl Teuku Cip Ditiro 12, T061 4530962, daily 1000-2200. Cheap vegetarian and non-vegetarian Indian cuisine in clean setting. Menu features biryanis, tasty thali and all the usual favourites at very sensible prices.

♦ Corner Café Raya, Jl Sipiso Piso 1, T061 7344485, open 24 hrs. English teachers pop in here for the city's coldest beer, and roast chicken and mashed potato with gravy served up in a friendly atmosphere.

♦ Imperial Cakery, Jl Zainul Arifin 116. T061 4516230, daily 1000-2200. Spotless bakery with good range of cakes, also serves simple pasta dishes and good sandwiches. The smoked salmon with scrambled egg on French brioche is a good way to start the day.

♦ RM Famili, Jl S.M Raja, T061 7368787, open 24 hrs. On the ground floor of the **Ibunda Hotel**, this clean rumah makan has some fine *nasi Padang* dishes, good Malay fare (the *ikan asam pedas* – spicy sour fish) and simple Indonesian favourites. The *sirsak* (soursop) juice here is delicious. Recommended.

♦ Rosvin, Jl Ahmad Yani 114, T061 77860446. Small eatery serving up a good range of spicy Acehnese and Malay dishes, including their signature *nasi lemak* (rice cooked in coconut milk with small side dishes).

♦ Simpang Tiga, Jl Ahmad Yani 83, T061 4536721. Glorious *nasi Padang* (spicy West Sumatran food) in full a/c comfort as well as a play area for kids.

♦ Tip Top, Jl Ahmad Yani 92, T061 4514442, daily 0800-2200. The venue of choice for the city's older Chinese-Indonesians for a morning coffee and a chat, the Tip Top has pleasant outdoor seating, plenty of ice cream, a touch of colonial decadence and distinctly average Indonesian and Chinese dishes.

⑩ Bars and clubs

Medan *p374, map p376*
Most local business people tend to drink in hotel bars and most of the hotels listed in the upper categories have bars. Most places close around 0200.

The **Hotel Danau Toba** International (see Sleeping) has 5 venues for boozing, including Dangdut International (with, unsurprisingly, live dangdut – Indonesian pop music heavily influenced by Bollywood and Arabic music), Rock Café and Tobasa Club with its different theme evenings including Ladies' Night on Thu and DJs at the weekend.

Zodiac at the **Novotel Soechi** (see Sleeping) has live music at weekends, and some good drinks promotions.

⑪ Entertainment

Medan *p374, map p376*
Cinema
There is a cinema on the 3rd floor of the Grand Palladium (see Shopping) showing all the latest blockbusters, and some Indonesian films (20,000Rp). For information on what is currently showing, phone T061 4514321.

⑫ Festivals and events

Medan *p374, map p376*
Idul Fitri (Islamic holy day), is a movable feast. Muslims descend on the Maimun Palace in traditional dress to mark the end of the fasting month of Ramadan – very colourful.
Mar-May **Medan Fair** is held each year at the Taman Ria Amusement Park on Jl Gatot Subroto. There are also permanent cultural exhibits at the park.

▲ Activities and tours

Medan *p374, map p376*
Tour operators
There are travel and tour companies all over town and most will provide a range of services from booking airline tickets through to providing tours and bus tickets. There is a concentration along Jl Katamso, south of the intersection with Jl Letjen Suprapto.
Amalia Amanda Tour and Travel, Jl Katamso 43, T061 4521666. Ferry tickets to Penang.
Erni Tour, Jl Katamso 43 J, T061 4564666. Ticketing and money changer.
Mutiara Tour and Travel, Jl Katamso 43 K, T061 4566700. Ferry tickets and flights to Malaysia.
Perdana Ekspres, Jl Katamso 35C, T061 4566222. Penang ferry tickets and PELNI agent.
Tobali Tour, Jl SM Raja 79, T061 7324472. Tourist buses to Danau Toba.
Trophy Tour, Jl Katamso 33, T061 4155777, www.trophytour.com. International and domestic ticketing. Very well established.

⑬ Shopping

Medan *p374, map p376*
Antiques Jl Jend A Yani is the main shopping area, with the largest concentration of 'antique' shops. Beware of fakes: old Batak artefacts are cunningly mass produced and there are few real antiques for sale these days.
Books There is a branch of **Gramedia** at the Sun Plaza (see below) with a small selection of English language books and magazines such as *Time* and *The Economist*.
Malls Sun Plaza, Jl Zainul Arifin 7, T061 4501500, daily 1000-2200, clothes shops, opticians, computer hardware and software and restaurants; **Grand Palladium**, Jl Kapten Mohlan Lubis 8, T061 4514939, daily 0900-2200, cinema, mobile phones, magazines, (a few English language titles) and a huge supermarket in the basement.
Supermarkets Kedai 24, Jl SM Raja, located near the hotels and has most daily

necessities, open 24 hrs. If you can't find what you need here, then head to the top floor of **Yuki Simpang Raya**, opposite the Mesjid Raya, which has a slightly more comprehensive selection.

Textiles Jl Jend A Yani III, which runs off Jl Jend A Yani, has a number of textile outlets. Browsing through the markets can be rewarding – either the massive Central Market or the Old Fish Market; the latter is the best place to buy batik (see 'Sights', above). Formal batik can be found at **Batik Danar Hadi**, Jl Zainul Arifin 117, T061 4574273, daily 0900-2100.

⊖ Transport

Medan *p374; map p376*
See also International connections below.
Local Becak, sudaco, mesin becak (motorized becak), bis damri, metered taxi, unmetered taxi and kijang – if it moves, it can be hired. The fare around town on an oplet (minibus) is 3000Rp. For a ride on a becak expect to pay a minimum of 5000Rp; with a bit of bargaining, taxis are often available for the same price as a becak; on a mesin becak, 5000Rp. Becaks can be chartered for about 25,000Rp per hr.

Air

Medan's **Polonia International Airport** is 3 km south of the town – effectively within the city. A taxi from the city centre to the airport costs 20,000Rp. Or take a bus from Pinang Baris terminal (in direction of Amplas terminal) and get off at traffic lights on Jl Juanda, the airport is 500 m on right (3000Rp). There is a fixed price taxi booth in the airport, on the right just before the exit. The fare to Jl SM Raja is a steep 35,000Rp.

Domestic Banda Aceh daily with **Sriwijaya**, **Garuda Indonesia** and **Kartika**; **Pekanbaru** daily with **Sriwijaya**; **Padang** daily with **Mandala**; **Batam** daily with **Lion Air** and **Sriwijaya**; **Padang** daily with **Mandala** and **Lion Air**; **Yogyakarta** daily

via **Padang** with **Mandala; Jakarta** daily with **Garuda**, **Air Asia**, **Lion Air** and **Sriwijaya**.

International Daily flights to **Singapore** with **Singapore Airlines** and 6 weekly flights on **Valuair** (www.valu air.com.sg) to **Kuala Lumpur**. Also daily direct flights to **Penang** with **Air Asia**, **Lion Air** and **Kartika Airlines**.

Boat

Medan's port, **Belawan**, is 26 km north of the city. Shuttle buses meet passengers from the ferry. The fare into town is 9000Rp. However, ferry companies provide transport to **Belawan** from their offices as part of the cost of the ticket to **Penang.** Town buses for Belawan leave from the intersection of Jl Balai Kota and Jl Guru Patimpus, near the TVRI offices. Oplets also travel to Belawan (the destination is displayed). The **PELNI** vessels Kelud and Sinabung call into Belawan on their way to Jakarta's Tanjung priok. Of most use to travellers is the Sinabung, which stops at **Batam** (30-min ferry ride from Singapore), before heading to **Java**. This vessel departs every Tue. Check the latest PELNI schedule at the booking agent at **Perdana Ekspres**, Jl Katamso 35C, T061 45662222.
Various companies run ferries:
Perdana Ekspres, Jl Katamso 35C, T061 4566222, and their partner **Amalia Amanda**, Jl Katamso 43, T061 4521666, have express boats to **Penang** sailing Tue, Wed, Thu, Sat, Sun at 1000. The journey takes 4-5 hrs. The one-way fare is US$48 plus US$3 seaport tax. The return fare is US$71 plus US$3 seaport tax. Transport to **Belawan** is provided free by the company, but the trip from Belawan to **Medan** is charged at 9000Rp. **Perdana Ekspres** have an office in Penang at Ground Floor PPC Building, Pesara King Edward, T04 2620802. Ferries leave Penang Tue, Wed, Thu, Sat, Sun at 0900. Fares are the same. It is possible to book a passage to **Langkawi**, Malaysia via Penang, but the onward ticket to Langkawi has to be picked up in Penang. **King's Star**, 24B Jl Pemuda,

T061 4521111, offer this service (as well as selling Batam – Singapore tickets). Penang to Langkawi tickets cost US$35 return and US$19 one way. Tickets can be picked up in Penang at **Langkawi Ferry Services**, Ground Floor PPC, Pesara King Edward, T04 2642088.

Bus

Medan has 2 main bus terminals: Amplas and Pinang Baris. **Amplas terminal** is on Jl Medan Tenggara VII, 8.5 km south of the city centre off Jl Sisingamangaraja, and serves all destinations south of Medan including **Bukittinggi, Parapat** and **Danau Toba** (25,000Rp, 6 hrs), **Jakarta, Bali, Jambi, Dumai, Pekanbaru, Palembang** and **Sibolga**. Get there by yellow oplet running south (Nos 24, 52 or 57), 3000Rp. Major bus companies like **ALS** have their offices on Jl Sisingamangaraja close to the terminal (at the 6.5 km marker). The most comfortable way of getting to Danau Toba is to take the tourist minibus service offered by **Tobali Tour**, Jl SM Raja 79C, T061 7324472, for 80,000Rp. They have a bus departing at 0900. Phone ahead to book a seat and ask to be picked up at your hotel.

The **Pinang Baris terminal** is on Jl Pinang Baris (off Jl Gatot Subroto, which becomes Jl Binjei), about 9 km northwest of the city centre, and serves **Banda Aceh** and other destinations north of Medan including **Bukit Lawang** (leaving every 30 mins, 3 hrs, 15,000Rp, – do not pay your fare to the touts who wait for tourists; pay the driver at the end of your journey); buses to **Berastagi,** 2 hrs, 7000Rp. Get to the terminal by orange or green microlet running along Jl Gatot Subroto. The best way of getting to Berastagi is to catch microlet number 41 from the front of Yuki Simpang Raya heading to **Padang Bulan**, 3000Rp. Tell the driver you want to get off at Simpang Pos, where the streets are lined with buses heading to Berastagi and **Kebonjahe,** 2 hrs, 7000Rp. **Jakarta,** US$38; **Yogyakarta,** US$40; **Padang** and **Bukittinggi,** 20-22 hrs, US$14 or a/c US$24.

Bus companies It makes sense to book a seat over the phone rather than traipsing all the way to the offices the day before departure. Your hotel should be able to help you. Pelangi, Jl Gajah Mada 56, T061 457011, **Pekanbaru, Palembang, Banda Aceh** and **Jakarta. PMTOH**, Jl Gajah Mada 57, T061 4152546, **Banda Aceh, Yogya, Solo, Jakarta. ANS**, Jl SM Raja 30, T061 786 0667, super Executive buses to **Jakarta, Bukittinggi, Padang** and **Bandung. ALS**, Jl SM Raja Km 6.5, T061 786685, **Dumai** (for ferries to **Batam** and for **Melaka**, Malaysia), **Jakarta, Banda Aceh, Yogya, Solo**.

Car hire

National Car Rental (Dharma Deli Hotel), (see Sleeping). Cars with driver can be rented from the **Sri Deli Hotel** (see Sleeping). **Taxis** can be rented by the day; ask at your hotel. Fares within Medan range from 10,000Rp to 25,000Rp (more if buying from the fixed price booth at the airport).

Taxi

Most of the taxi companies are located at Jl Sisingamangaraja 60-107.

Train

The station is on Jl Prof M Yamin. The schedule from the train station is a little erratic. There are a couple of daily departures to **Rantau Parapat** (4-5 hrs, 55,000Rp/ 75,000Rp). Check the latest schedule at the station.

❶ Directory

Medan p374, map p376
Banks If travelling from Penang to Medan via Belawan Port, it is advisable to change money in Georgetown (Penang) before departure – the exchange rate is much better than in Medan. There are numerous banks in Medan, all fairly internationally-minded. **Duta Bank** makes cash advances against Visa and MasterCard. The **Hong Kong Bank** has a

24-hr ATM. There are also a number of money changers on Jl Katamso. **Bank Central Asia**, Jl Bukit Barisan 3, will provide cash advances on Visa card). **Bank Dagang Negara**, Jl Jend A Yani 109. **Duta Bank**, Jl Sisingamangaraja (next to the Garuda Plaza Hotel). **Ekspor Impor (Bank Exim)**, Jl Balai Kota 8. **Bank Negara Indonesia**, Jl Jend A Yani 72. **Standard Chartered Bank**, Jl Imam Bonjol 17, T061 4538800. Money changers include: **King's Money Changer**, Jl Pemuda 24; and **PT Supra**, Jl Jend A Yani 101. **Embassies and consulates** Belgium, Jl Pattimura 459, T061 4527991; **Denmark**, Jl Hang Jebat 2, T061 4538028; **Germany**, Jl Let Jend Parman 217, T061 4537108; **Netherlands**, Jl Juanda, opposite Pardede Hotel, T061 4569853; **Norway**, Jl Zainul Arifin 55, T061 4510158; **Singapore**, Jl T Daud 3, T061 4513134; **Sweden**, Jl Hang Jebat 2, T061 4538028; **UK**, Jl Jend A Yani 2, T061 4518699; **USA**, Jl Imam Bonjol 13, T061 322200. **Immigration** Jl Binjai Km 6.2, T061 4512112. **Internet** Over the last couple of years, there has been a proliferation of internet cafés. **Novotel** Soechi Medan, Jl Cirebon 76A; **Pay@net**, Jl Ir H Juanda Baru 200. There is also a small email centre on the 1st floor of the **Deli Plaza** on Jl Guru Patimpus. There is a large email facility within the **Central Post Office**, Jl Bukit Barisan 1. **Medical services** Bunda Clinic (open 24 hrs), Jl Sisingamangaraja, T061 70321666; **Herna Hospital**, Jl Majapahit 118A, T061 4147715; **St Elizabeth's Hospital**, Jl Haji Misbah 7, T061 4144240; **Malahayati Hospital**, Jl Diponegoro, T061 4518766l; **Gleneagles Hospital**, Jl Listrik 6, T061 4566268, new and reputed to be the best in town. **Police** Jl Durian, T061 4520453. **Telephone** General Post Office, Jl Bukit Barisan 1 (on Merdeka Square). **Telephone offices:** Wartel, Jl Bukit Barisan 1 (at the Central Post Office) for overseas calls. There are additional Wartel offices all over town, including on Jl Sisingamangaraja (next to the Hotel Deli Raya and opposite the Mesjid Raya) and on Jl Irian Barat (just north of the intersection with Jl Let Jend MT Haryono). Telephone calls can also be placed from the Tip Top Café on Jl Jend A Yani.

Bukit Lawang

→ *Phone code: 061. Colour map 12, A1.*

Bukit Lawang, sometimes also named, probably for tourist consumption, 'Gateway to the Hills', is a small community on the edge of the Gunung Leuser Nature Reserve, an area of beautiful countryside. A few years ago Bukit Lawang was a thriving place with thousands of tourists coming to see the orang-utans. This is no longer true. The downturn in tourism in Indonesia has hit Sumatra hard. Things got worse for the town in November 2003 when a flash flood swept away much of the infrastructure and killed hundreds of residents. However, there is a real sense of resilience and community here, and the people are working hard to get the town firmly back on the tourist trail. Visitors will note the effort made to keep the area clean, with recycling and rubbish bins along all the paths in the village. ▶▶ *For listings, see pages 388-389.*

Ins and outs

Getting there

Direct buses leave from Medan's Pinang Baris terminal every 30 minutes (three hours, 15,000Rp). There is a choice of large, slightly cheaper (12,000Rp) and slower buses, or quicker and marginally more expensive (15,000Rp) minibuses. Tourist buses no longer run this route. From Berastagi catch a bus to Medan and get off at Pinang Baris; from here, catch a regular bus to Bukit Lawang. Taxis can be hired in Medan, the journey will take two hours. ▶▶ *See Transport, page 389.*

Tourist information

The **Visitor Information Centre** ⓘ *daily 0700-1500*, has free maps and can offer advice on hiking. It also sells a useful booklet on the park and its wildlife and flora (12,000Rp). You can get park permits here, including long-term research permits.

For free maps and a price list of guided tours, contact the guides association, **HPI** ⓘ *opposite the Visitorn Information Centre, T081 370730151, daily 0800-1500.*

Bukit Lawang

Sleeping 🛏
Bukit Lawang Eco Lodge 1
Bukit Lawang Indah
  Guesthouse 2
Garden Inn 3
Indra Inn 4

Jungle Inn 5
Jungle Tribe 6
Lizard Guesthouse 9
Sam's Guesthouse 8
Wisma Leuser Sibayak 7
Yusman 10

Eating 🍴
Rock Inn Cafe & Bar 1
Tony's 2

Not to scale

Orang-Utan Rehabilitation Centre

① *Regular buses and minibuses travel down Jl Gatot Subroto, which becomes Jl Binjei, leaving from the Central Market, 45 mins, 3000Rp. Locals come from Medan to frolic in the river, not to see the apes, so while the river may be busy, feeding time is comparatively quiet.*

Just outside the village is the famous centre established in 1973 – fast developing into one of Sumatra's most popular tourist destinations. The work of the centre is almost entirely supported now by revenue from tourism. The orang-utan (*Pongo pygmaeus*) is on the verge of extinction throughout its limited range across island Southeast Asia, and the centre has been established by the Worldwide Fund for Nature to rehabilitate domesticated orang-utans for life in the wild. The problem is that there is a ready black market for cuddly orang-utans and in Medan they sell for US$350. But when the young, friendly animals grow up into powerful, obstreperous adult apes, they are often abandoned and some of them end up at Bukit Lawang. In total, the Gunung Leuser National Park probably supports about 5000 apes; the carrying capacity of the park, though, is nearer 8000.

Getting there and entry to the park

The entrance to the reserve is a 30-minute walk from the village following the Bohorok River upstream, which then has to be crossed by boat; from there it is another 20 minutes or so up a steepish path to the feeding point. Visitors can see the apes during feeding times (0800-0900 and 1500-1600, you should aim to get there five minutes beforehand). The times do sometimes change, so check at the PHKA office in Bukit Lawang. Guides can be hired from the PHKA office for one-, two- or three-day treks of varying difficulty and visitors have reported seeing gibbons, monkeys and orang-utans. All visitors must obtain a permit from the PHKA office (one day: 20,000Rp, plus 50,000Rp for camera and 150,000Rp for video camera) before entering the park. Passport must be shown before a permit is issued (although this is not strictly enforced). Leave Bukit Lawang 45 minutes before feeding to leave time for the walk and river crossing. Afternoons are more crowded, especially at weekends; it is best to stay the night and watch a morning, weekday, feed if possible. Next door to the PHPA office is a **Visitor Information Centre** ① *daily 0700-1500, donation requested*, which shows films in English on Monday and Friday at 2000, and also has a study room, a display and a small collection of relevant literature.

Around Bukit Lawang

There are a number of caves in the vicinity of Bukit Lawang. For the **Bat Cave** ① *5000Rp*, take a torch and non-slip shoes; it is not an easy climb, a guide is recommended (10,000Rp). There is also a **rubber processing plant** close by – ask at the visitors centre for a handout and map.

Tubing

Floating down the Bohorok River on an inner tube has become a popular excursion. Tubes can be hired for 10,000Rp per day in the village for the 12 km (two to three hours) journey to the first bridge. There is public transport from the bridge back to Bukit Lawang. For US$55 you can trek upstream and return in the late afternoon by inner tube. Dry bags are provided for cameras and other valuables. Beware of whirlpools and allow for low branches; tourists have drowned in the past.

Hiking

Hiking is the best way to experience the forest and see the wildlife. The visitors centre has handouts and maps of hiking trails and guesthouses, and may also have jungle trek guides. Head to the Association of Indonesian Guides, HPI ① T081 370730151, daily 0800-1500, office near the visitor centre for a map, price list for treks and other information. Bukit Lawang has more than 130 guides, massively outnumbering the tourists and so there is some pressure to take one. The HPI office recommends getting a guide directly from their office as opposed to guesthouses or guides met on the bus from Medan. At the office they can match a guide to your interests and ensure the correct price. Note that all official guides carry an HPI identity card. Languages offered include English, German, Spanish, French and Dutch. Prices for all hikes are fixed by the HPI office. A three-hour hike costs US$24, one-day hike US$39 (plus US$16 to tube down the river back to Bukit Lawang after the trek), two days for US$87 (plus US$16 for tubing) and three days for US$118. All prices include guide, transportation, permit, food and tent.

It is possible to hike to **Berastagi** in three days at a cost of US$118. This trek is less popular because so much of the route has been deforested. Instead, those visitors wishing to trek through true jungle should opt for the five- to seven-day hike to **Kutacane** US$315. Most treks have a minimum lower limit of three to four people. Note that these are arduous treks requiring fitness and good hiking boots; check the credentials of guides carefully – many lack experience (your guide should be able to produce a legal licence and permit). During the rainy season (roughly August-December) there can be very heavy downpours: good waterproofs are essential.

Whitewater rafting

The HPI offer rafting trips on the nearby Wampu River, costing around US$70 per person per day. These are sometimes combined with a trek.

Tangkahan ● ›› pp388-389.

Tangkahan lies about 40 km north of Bukit Lawang, next to the Gunung Leuser National Park and there is only one resort here, the **Bamboo River Guesthouse** (see Sleeping, page 388). What is special about this place is its proximity to unspoilt lowland rainforest, and the absence of tourists. No trekking is promoted here, so bird and animal life is more active. It is possible to hike from here (guide strongly recommended), take a canoe trip down the Batang Serangan River, or visit some hot sulphur springs.

Getting there

Tangkahan is a five-hour chartered bus ride from Bukit Lawang, ask at the tourist office for more information. From Medan, catch a bus from the Pinang Baris terminal to Tangkahan (three hours). At the river crossing in Tangkahan, shout for the raft man.

Getting there

Tangkahan is a five-hour chartered bus ride from Bukit Lawang, ask at the tourist office for more information. From Medan, catch a bus from the Pinang Baris terminal to Tangkahan (three hours). At the river crossing in Tangkahan, shout for the raft man.

Bukit Lawang listings

For Sleeping and Eating price codes, see inside the front cover.

Sleeping

Bukit Lawang p385, map p385
The road ends at the bus stop, so reaching guesthouses further upstream means as much as a 25-min slog on foot. About 20 or so *losmen* line the Bohorok River up to the crossing-point for the reserve. Many guesthouses were badly damaged by the flood in 2003, and some were forced out of business. The slowdown in tourism means it is easy to find somewhere to sleep. The views and jungle atmosphere are best upriver, towards the park entrance.

A recent venture being organized through the Tourist Information Centre involves camping on the edge of the National Park, a 2-hr walk from the village past the Bat Cave. The campsite is on the edge of a river and is very secluded. A great way to escape the crowds and witness nature first-hand. Enquire at the HPI office. There are currently no tents available for rent.

C-F Jungle Inn, T081 375324015, emaila.rahman3775@yahoo.co.id. The most popular guesthouse in Bukit Lawang with an extraordinary selection of rooms. The cheapest rooms out the back have a balcony next to a small waterfall and gushing stream. There is one room with a rockface as a wall. The more expensive rooms are outrageously large and decadent (for Bukit Lawang) with 4-poster bed, thoughtful decoration and stunning jungle views. The staff here are very friendly, and the sunset sees guitars and bongos being taken from their hiding places for a Sumatran sing-along. Recommended.

D-E Bukit Lawang Eco Lodge, T081 26079983. Set in lovely gardens which produce some tasty vegetables for the evening meals, and with plenty of eco-friendly ideals, this hotel is one of the more popular places in the village. The rooms are clean, and comfortable, although don't have the views of some of the places further up the river. Recommended.

E Jungle Tribe, T081375126275. Only 1 room available, more planned. Spacious and new with balcony.

E-F Sam's Guesthouse, T081 370093597. The rooms that have been finished are pleasant, some with beautiful views over the river and comfortable beds with mosquito nets.

F Garden Inn, T081 396843235. Rickety wooden structures with perilous stairs and plenty of space. Rooms have balcony with sublime river views, and bathrooms with squat toilet. Recommended.

F Indra Inn, T081 397375818. Rattan-walled rooms, which are a little dark. However, there are fine jungle views from the veranda here.

F The Lizard Guesthouse. Friendly place right on the river with simple rattan-walled rooms. The café downstairs has a TV and massive selection of DVDs. The owner speaks superb English and is a good source of local information.

G Bukit Lawang Indah Guesthouse, T081 527615532. Has 38 clean and spacious concrete rooms with fan and squat toilet. This place has 24-hr electricity.

G Wisma Leuser Sibayak, T081 361010736. Has 20 tiled and charmless rooms set in a large orange block. Rooms upstairs have a balcony.

G Yusman, T081 3469835. Tatty concrete boxes with squat toilet and *mandi*. The rooms at the front are slightly better, with garden views and outdoors seating.

Tangkahan p387
F Bamboo River Guesthouse, on the Buluh River, Tangkahan, 40 km north of Bukit Lawang, no telephone, communication is by walkie-talkie. Opened in 1998 and owned by an English woman and a local senior guide. Has 10 rooms available and an evening meal costs around 25,000Rp.

🍴 Eating

Bukit Lawang *p385, map p385*
There are plenty of stalls near the bridges offering simple local fare. Most of the hotels have decent menus featuring simple Western and Indonesian cuisine (all ¶).

¶ **Green Hill café**, newly opened, with a pool table, simple snacks and plenty of cool Bintang in a breezy riverine setting.

¶ **Rock Inn Café and Bar**, daily 0900-2400. Built into a rockface, with a motorbike hanging from the wall, this local hang-out offers good curries, soups, tacos and spaghetti, and is a fun place for a swift beer.

¶ **Tony's Restaurant**, daily 0700-2300. Small bamboo eatery serving up fair pizzas. The friendly owner is proud of her fettuccine, which gets good reports from European visitors.

¶ **The Jungle Inn**, has fine potato and pumpkin curries and some good juices made with local honey.

¶ **Jungle Tribe**, has excellent macaroni cheese and pizzas, as well as an extensive list of cocktails for those wanting a jungle party.

⛰ Activities and tours

Bukit Lawang *p385, map p385*
Cruises
Boats can be hired from near the **Toba Hotel**. Trips around Samosir cost US$137, or a 1-hr ride around the lake can be had for US$44. These prices are highly ambitious and good bargaining should bring the price down significantly.

⊖ Transport

Bukit Lawang *p385, map p385*
Bus
There are no direct buses from Bukit Lawang to Berastagi. Instead head back to Pinang Baris and jump on a Berastagi bound bus (2 hrs, 7000Rp).

❶ Directory

Bukit Lawang *p385, map p385*
Banks *Losmen* and tour companies will change money, but rates are poor so it is best to bring sufficient cash. **Post office** Some stalls sell stamps at a small mark up. They will also post letters. **Telephone** Wartel office in the main 'village'.

Berastagi

→ *Phone code: 0628. Colour map 12, B1.*
Berastagi, is a hill resort town, lying 1400 m above sea level on the Karo Plateau among the traditional lands of the Karo Batak people. Though Berastagi may not be a one-horse town, it gives the impression of being a one-road town. There is also the distinct feel that it has become a way-station, a sort of trucking stop between other more important places.
▶▶ *For listings, see pages 393-395.*

Ins and outs

Getting there
Berastagi is 68 km from Medan and 147 km from Parapat. There are regular bus connections with Medan, two hours, 7000Rp. Getting from Parapat on a public bus is a little more complicated as it involves changes. The bus station is at the south end of the main road, Jalan Veteran. ▶▶ *See Transport, page 395.*

Getting around
Visitors can travel easily around town on foot, by hired bicycle and oplets. For the surrounding villages and towns cars can be hired, oplets service some routes. Dokars can also be used for short local journeys, in Berastagi these are known as *sados*.

Tourist information
Dinas Pariwisata ① *Jl Gundaling No 1, T0628 91084*. Staff here speak good English and are a useful source of local information. Prices for guided hikes up the nearby volcanoes are some of the cheapest in town from here. The **Sibayak Guesthouse** ① *Jl Veteran 119*, and the **Wisma Ginsata** ① *Jl Veteran 79*, are also excellent sources of information. The Sibayak keeps a particularly useful comments book.

Sights

The town does not have many specific sights of interest, but its position, surrounded by active volcanoes, is memorable. Unfortunately, Berastagi has a rather uncared-for feel, and it is somewhat featureless. Nonetheless, it is a good place to cool off after the heat and bustle of Medan, and go for a mountain hike. It is also a good base from which to explore the surrounding countryside.

For those without the time to visit the Batak villages outside Kabanjahe, there is a Batak village of sorts – **Peceren** ① *2000Rp for admission to village,* just outside town on the road to Medan, 100 m past the **Rose Garden Hotel**. It is rather run down and dirty, with a few Batak houses interspersed with modern houses; however, it is in some respects more authentic than those that have been preserved, showing how living communities are adapting to the changing world. Behind the market, opposite the monument, are a couple of ersatz **Batak houses** – another excuse to create an area of stalls. Just 200 m or so up Jalan Gundaling from here is a strange Buddhist temple – the **Vihara Buddha**. How the architect managed to arrive at this fusion of styles is not clear, but 'ungainly' would not be an unkind description. The general goods market behind the bus station is worth a wander.

Kabanjahe → Colour map 12, B1.

ⓘ 12 km south of Berastagi. Easily accessible by bus, regular departures from the bus station on Jl Veteran, 25 mins, 3000Rp.

Meaning 'Ginger garden', Kabanjahe lies on the main road and scores of buses and oplets make the journey. It is a local market town of some size and little charm, but it is worth visiting on Monday market day. Kabanjahe is an important communication town; from here it is possible to walk to traditional villages of the Karo Batak people (see below).

Lingga and Barusja → Colour map 12, B1.

ⓘ Catch a bus from the bus station on Jl Veteran to Kabanjahe, and from there a microlite or bemo onwards, in Kabanjahe they leave from the intersection of Jl Pala Bangun, Jl Veteran and Jl Bangsi Sembiring. To visit Lingga, an 'entrance fee' of 2000Rp must be paid at the tourist information centre in the main square (although visitors with a guide may not have to pay this).

Karo Batak villages are to be found dotted all over the hills around Berastagi. The more traditional villages are not accessible by road and must be reached on foot; to visit these communities it is recommended to hire a guide (ask at your hotel or the tourist centre). It can make sense to charter a bemo for the day – a lot more ground can be covered.

Two villages that can be visited with relative ease from Kabanjahe are **Lingga** and **Barusjahe**. Both can be reached by microlite from Kabanjahe. This ease of access has inevitably resulted in rather 'touristy' villages. **Lingga**, is about 4 km northwest of Kabanjahe and is a community of about 30 Batak houses, of which there are about a dozen traditional longhouses. Overpriced carvings for sale. Photographs of the local people will require payment. **Barusjah** is slightly more difficult to get to and as a result is marginally more 'traditional', but can still be reached by microlite from Kabanjahe. It is rather a dirty village with very few houses in the traditional style, but there are a few over two centuries old (and as a result are decaying badly). The soaring roofs are particularly impressive.

Dokan

ⓘ Catch a Simas bus at the bus terminal in Kabanjahe and ask to be set down at the Dokan turn (13 km from Kabanjahe), it is then a 3-km walk to the village, a donation is expected. Buses on to Sipisopiso are usually pretty crowded.

Berastagi

To Lingga
To Kabanjahe (12 km)

N

Not to scale

Sleeping 🛏️
Dien Karona 12
Ginsata & Wisma Ginsata 3
Kaliaga 15
Melati Bangkit Nan Jaya 14

Sibayak Losmen 5
Sibayak Internasional 9
Sibayak Multinational
Guesthouse 10
Wisma Sibayak 11
Wisma Sunrise 13

Eating 🍴
Eropa 1
Mexico Fried Chicken 4
Raymond Café 2

Dokan is a fine Karo Batak village that lies halfway between Kabanjahe and Sipisopiso, where villagers are less inclined to hassle.

Sipisopiso waterfalls

ⓘ *Catch a bemo to Pemangtangsiantar and ask to get off at Simpang Sitanggaling. The falls are a 30-min walk from here or a quick ojek ride away.*

There are waterfalls at Sipisopiso, (2000Rp) a one-hour drive southeast of Berastagi and 24 km from Kabanjahe. The falls cascade through a narrow gap in the cliffside and then fall 120 m to Danau Toba. It is possible to walk along a spur to a small gazebo for a good view of the falls, or to walk to the bottom and back takes about one hour. There are the usual array of souvenir stalls and *warungs* that congregate whenever an *objek wisata* gets to be on the standard tour itinerary. Inspite of the commercialism, the falls are a pretty spectacular sight. There is no accommodation here, but from Sipisopiso towards Parapat is **Siantar Hotel**, a nice place to stop for coffee and fried bananas. In its garden and restaurant you have a superb view of the lake, but despite its name you cannot sleep there, it is only a restaurant.

Mount Sibayak

Sibayak lies northwest of Berastagi at 2095 m and can be climbed in a day, but choose a fair weather day and leave early for the best views (and to avoid the rain). Take the trail from behind Gundaling Hill, ask at your hotel for directions before setting out. Guides can be easily found (again, ask at your hotel – they will charge 70,000-150,000Rp depending on the size of the party), a map of the route is available from the **Tourist Information Office** and information from either the **Ginsata** or **Sibayak** guesthouses. Wear good walking shoes and take a sweater as it can be chilly. It takes about two to three hours to reach the summit, along a logging road, or alternatively there is a jungle trek which is quicker if you take a bemo to Semangat Gunung, in the Daulu valley. Over the summit, the descent is down over 2000 steps to reach Hot Water and **Sulphur Springs** ⓘ *daily 0800-2300, 5000Rp.* The sulphur is collected by local people and is used as medicine and as a pesticide.

Mount Sinabung

Sinabung, which rises to 2454 m to the west of Berastagi, is another popular climb. There are now three routes up the volcano. The longest established is well marked, the other two are less obvious, but even so it is probably unwise to undertake it without a guide – heavy rain and mist can make it very dangerous. Seven people disappeared here in 1996/1997, when mist made it impossible for them to find the path. Maps are available from the **Sibayak guesthouses**.

To climb the mountain without a guide, catch a bus to Danau Lau Kawar (one hour, 6000Rp). The path from the village passes a restaurant; fork left just after the restaurant (do not continue along the main path). This path then passes a house and on the left you will see a small hut; you need to turn left again onto another path that passes the hut. The route then works its way through the forest for one hour and is relatively well marked with arrows and string. As the path leaves the forest it becomes very steep and enters a rock gully (also steep). The route passes an old campsite and then a cliff overhang decorated with graffiti. (This makes a good shelter in bad weather as hot steam issues through vents.) After around three to four hours in total, the path reaches the summit; paths skirt the crater lip but care is needed.

To climb the mountain take good hiking boots, a jumper, a change of clothes, and a water bottle. Tents can be hired from the **Sibayak guesthouses**. Leeches can be a problem.

Note The Tourist Information Service recommends that visitors take a guide with them on mountain hikes as the weather is very unpredictable and the thick jungle on the flanks of the mountains leads into the massive Gunung Leuser National Park where it is very easy to get lost. The Tourist Information Service and Ginsata have a list of recent tourist mishaps on the mountain, including details of an Austrian tourist who got lost on Sibayak in 2007, and was found nine days later unconscious in a garden in a small town. He claimed he was led further into the jungle by the ghosts of two German tourists, missing since 1997, a claim locals with their appreciation of anything connected to the supernatural seem to believe heartily.

Sidikalang → Colour map 12, B1.

This is a small, unremarkable town, 75 km southwest of Berastagi, which serves an important 'linking' function. From here it is possible to travel north, along the valley of the Alas River to Kutacane and the Gunung Leuser National Park, and from there to Takengon and the Gayo Highlands, and finally to Banda Aceh at the northern tip of Sumatra. Alternatively, it is possible to travel west to the coast and then north along the coast, again to Banda Aceh. The countryside around here is locally known for the quality of its coffee.

Tongging

Tongging is a small town on Danau Toba's northern shore. Like the much more popular Samosir Island, it is possible to swim in the lake and generally relax. The tourist infrastructure here is not nearly as developed though, although it is a good base to see the **Sipisopiso falls** (see page 392) and also a number of relatively untouristic Batak villages, including **Silalahi**. Tongging can also be used as an alternative route to Samosir – there are boats from Tongging to Samosir via Haranggaol every Monday at 0730.

◉ Berastagi listings

*For Sleeping and Eating price codes,
see inside the front cover.*

● Sleeping

Berastagi *p390, map p391*
Berastagi is not a particularly attractive town, but it does have a selection of some of the best *losmen* in Sumatra. Not only are the rooms clean and well maintained, but the owners go out of their way to provide travellers with information on the surrounding area. They arrange trips to traditional ceremonies, inform travellers on the best way to climb the mountains and on hikes, and are generally highly constructive. Breakfast is not usually included in the price.
AL-A Sibayak Internasional Hotel,
Jl Merdeka, T0628 91301, www.hotel sibayak.com. A 4-star hotel perched on a hillside overlooking the town. Rooms are clean,

with cable TV. There is a pool, tennis court, disco, putting green and free Wi-Fi access in the lounge area. 40% discount available.
D-E Dien Karona Hotel, Jl Pendidikan 148, T0628 91488. Indonesian-style hotel with chalets built around a car park. Rooms are in fair condition but could do with a lick of paint. Bathrooms have hot water and squat toilet.
E Hotel Melati Bangkit Nan Jaya,
Jl Pendidikan 82, T081 26465006. Relaxed place out of town, with pleasant rooms, some with TV. There is no restaurant, but they can prepare a simple evening meal on request. Bargain for a decent price.
E-F Hotel Kaliaga, Jln Gundaling 219, T0628 91116. Tiled rooms are a little run down and have TV and hot water showers.
F Sibayak Multinational Guesthouse,
Jl Pendidikan 93, T0628 91031, irnawati_pelawi@yahoo.co.id. Over 2 km out of town on the road leading towards Gunung

Sibayak, this place is set in sprawling gardens with excellent views and a quiet atmosphere. More expensive rooms are big with hot-water showers. The smaller, old-style rooms are passable, but have no hot water.

F Wisma Sibayak, Jl Udara 1, T0628 91104, bhirinxz@yahoo.com. What looks like a Malay doll's house from the outside, is home to the best budget accommodation in town, with excellent local information on offer, spotless rooms with or without attached bathroom (cold water), lots of communal space and friendly vibes. Recommended.

F-G Ginsata Hotel and Guesthouse, Jl Veteran 27, T0628 91441. The hotel is on the noisy main road and has clean rooms with cold water shower. The guesthouse (enquire at hotel office) around the corner is much quieter and has tidy simple rooms. The owner is an excellent source of local information. Recommended.

G Sibayak Losmen, Jl Veteran 119, T0628 91095. This *losmen* is reached by walking through a travel agent's office. One of the more homely options in town, the staff here are friendly and offer excellent information on tours. The rooms with attached bathroom (cold water, squat toilet) on the 2nd floor are clean, but some are windowless. The cheaper rooms on the top floor have shared bathroom and access to a lovely roof terrace. Hot-water showers are available for 5000Rp.

G Wisma Sunrise, Jl Kaliaga 5, T0628 92404. Simple, clean rooms with cold-water shower. This place has superb views over the town and down to the plains beyond. The owner works at the tourist office in town and can arrange tours to Danau Toba and Bukittinggi. There are no eating facilities here.

Sidikalang *p393*

A range of hotels and *losmen* is available.
G Hotel Merapi. Small, basic rooms, some are dirty so ask to see the rooms available before checking in, insects galore.

① Eating

Berastagi *p390, map p391*

There are a good number of restaurants along Jl Veteran – serving mainly Padang food. Fruits grown in the area include avocados and *marquisa* (passion fruit), the latter of which is made into a delicious drink.

Ⅰ Eropa, Jl Veteran 48G, T0628 91365, daily 0700-2100. Simple eatery with a long list of Chinese dishes and some Western dishes such as soups, pasta and steaks. This is a good place for those needing a dose of pork.

Ⅰ Losmen Sibayak. Serve decent Western and Indonesian fare.

Ⅰ Mexico Fried Chicken, Jl Veteran 18, T0628 93252, open 0800-2300. Fast food fans might want to pop in. The entrance has a sign with a Hispanic man wearing a panama hat with MFC emblazoned on it. Fried chicken set meals, burgers and coffee form the menu.

Ⅰ Raymond Café, Jl Trimurti, T081397428979, daily 0700-2300. Friendly and a good place to meet travellers, chat with locals and get a taste of the delicious local vegetables. The avocado salad with a lemon juice dressing is superb, as are the juices. Simple Western and Indonesian fare are good value here. Recommended.

Ⅰ Wisma Sibayak, serves decent Western and Indonesian fare.

Foodstalls There are many open-air *warungs* serving good, fresh food, using the temperate fruit and vegetables grown in the surrounding countryside. **Jl Veteran** has the best selection. The market near the monument just off Jl Veteran sells fresh produce.

▲ Activities and tours

Berastagi *p390, map p391*
Hiking
It is possible to hike through spectacular countryside, all the way to Bukit Lawang from Berastagi in 3 days. However, the government is anxious about visitors disturbing this culturally sensitive area and

trekkers should take the time and care to organize trips properly. Ask in town at the **Sibayak Guesthouse** or at the **Tourist Information Service**, Jl Gundaling 1, for trekking information. There are numerous guides offering treks to Bukit Lawang; this is a difficult and demanding trek requiring a degree of fitness and good walking boots. Most people trek this route in the other direction, from Bukit Lawang to Berastagi (see page 387). Many of the guides have little experience so check credentials carefully.

Tour operators
The best are those attached to the **Sibayak** and **Ginsata losmen**. They can arrange canoe or raft trips along the **Alas River** to the northwest of Berastagi. The journey passes through the **Gunung Leuser National Park** with traditional villages and tropical rainforest. An all-inclusive 3-day trip, about US$120. Or, take a jungle trek (with a guide) through the reserve; 3-day trek, about US$120. Other places worth visiting for tour information include: **CV Berastagi View**, Jl Veteran 4 (inside post office), T0628 92929, brastagiview@ yahoo.co.id. **Dinas Parawisata**, Tourist Information Service, Jl Gundaling 1, T0628 91084.

O Shopping

Berastagi p390, map p391
Antiques and handicrafts Sold in several shops along Jl Veteran. **Mamaken** at Jl Veteran 16, T0628 91256, daily 0800-2100, sell mostly Batak pieces.

⊖ Transport

Berastagi p390, map p391
Bus Getting to **Parapat,** for **Danau Toba**, on a public bus it is necessary to change twice, in **Kabanjahe**, 25 mins, 3000Rp, and **Pemangtangsiantar**, 3 hrs, 15,000Rp. Buses from Pemangtangsiantar to **Parapat**, 1 hr, 15,000Rp. Minibuses and oplets travel to

Kabanjahe continuously; from there, buses leave for **Pemangtangsiantar** every 30 mins between 0800 and 1500; from P Siantar to **Parapat**, every 30 mins. There are a couple of alternative and less used routes to **Toba** and **Samosir**. One is to catch a bus to **Haranggaol**, on the north side of Danau Toba. For **Bukit Lawang** catch a Pinang Baris bound bus, 2 hrs, 8000Rp, and connect with a Bukit Lawang bound bus, 3 hrs, 15,000Rp.

Sidikalang p393
Bus Regular connections with **Pangururan**, **Kutacane** and **Berastagi**.

Tongging
Boat A boat goes from Tongging to Haranggaol every Mon, 0730, which links with the 1500 boat from Haranggaol to Ambarita. **Bus** From Berastagi there are direct bus connections with **Tongging**, about 1 an hour in the afternoon, from Jl Kapiten Mumah Purba (10,000Rp). Alternatively, take a bus or bemo to **Kabanjahe** (3000Rp) and from there a minibus to **Simpang Situnggaling**, 1 hr (6000Rp). From here there are minibuses to **Tongging**, 1 hr (6000Rp). Leave enough time as buses only run through to about 1600 and there is a lot of hanging around.

⊙ Directory

Berastagi p390, map p391
Banks There are several banks and money changers in town, and they will change most TCs. **Bank Negara Indonesia**, Jl Veteran 53. **Putra Nusa Mandago Money Changer**, Jl Veteran 47. **PT Pura Buana International**, Jl Veteran. There are 2 authorized Lake Toba money changers, of which **Lagundri Tours**, Jl Veteran 55, gives the slightly better rate. **Medical services** Health centre, Jl Veteran 30. **Post office** Jl Veteran (by the monument at the top of the road). **Telephone** Wartel office for international telephone calls, Jl Veteran (by the Bank Negara Indonesia).

Danau Toba

→ Colour map 12, B1.

Danau Toba and the surrounding countryside is one of the most beautiful areas in Southeast Asia. The cool climate, pine-clothed mountain slopes, the lake and the sprinkling of church spires give the area an almost alpine flavour. After Medan or Padang, it is a welcome relief from the bustle, heat and humidity of the lowlands. The vast inland lake lies 160 km south of Medan and forms the core of Batakland in both a legendary and a geographical sense. The lake covers a total of 1707 sq km and is the largest inland body of water in Southeast Asia (87 km long and 31 km across at its widest point). Lodged in the centre of the lake is Samosir Island, one of Sumatra's most popular destinations.

Danau Toba was formed after a massive volcanic explosion 75,000 years ago, not dissimilar – although far more violent – to the one that vaporized Krakatoa in the late 19th century. The eruption of Toba is thought to have been the most powerful eruption in the last million years. The area is now volcanically dormant, the only indication of latent activity being the hot springs on the hill overlooking Pangururan (see page 405). The fact that Danau Toba's water is so warm for a lake at close to 1000 m leads one to assume that there must be some heat underwater too. ▶▶ *For listings, see pages 398-400.*

Ins and outs

Getting there

There is only one way to get to Danau Toba and that is by road. It is 147 km from Berastagi, 176 km from Medan and 509 km from Bukittinggi. The vast majority of visitors either approach from Medan (although some take the troublesome route from Berastagi), or from the south via Padangsidempuan (the road to Bukittinggi and Padang). Taking the Trans-Sumatran Highway from Medan via Tebingtinggi, is a fairly fast and direct route, taking about four hours on a good day. The main bus terminal is on Jalan Sisingamangaraja (Jalan SM Raja) – aka the Trans-Sumatran Highway – around 1 km from the centre of town. Some buses stop at bus agencies and others run from the ferry terminal to/from Samosir.

Getting around

Bemos can be hired for 2500Rp for trips around town. There are also various forms of water transport. Danau Toba's two main destinations are the town of Parapat on the mainland and the island of Samosir (see page 401). Buses drop passengers off in Parapat and from here there are regular passenger ferries to Samosir Island. A car ferry runs from Ajibata, just south of Parapat. ▶▶ *See Transport, pages 399 and 410.*

Parapat ●▲◐ ▶▶ *pp398-400. Colour map 12, B1.*

Parapat is a small resort on the east shores of Danau Toba frequented by the Medan wealthy, and increasing numbers of Asian tourists from beyond Indonesia. It was established by the Dutch in the 1930s, although today most Western visitors merely breeze through en route to Samosir Island (but must pay 1000Rp entrance for the privilege, although this is not strictly enforced). There are stunning views over the lake, but unfortunately there doesn't seem to have been any coherent attempt to plan the development of the town. This means that there are architectural monstrosities side-by-side with elegant villas.

Parapat gives off the air of a 1950s European beach resort, with its pedaloes, metal railings, light blue paint and low-rise villa accommodation. This would be a great selling point for nostalgists, but unfortunately all the most attractive hotels are being allowed to slide into ruin, unloved and under-invested. Instead money is being poured into new, large and rather insensitive places. Nowadays, most foreign visitors get out of Parapat as soon as possible and head to the more sedate and rural charms of Samosir.

Tourist information

The tourist office, **Pusat Informasi**, is on Jalan P Samosir, under the archway that welcomes visitors to the town. However, there is virtually no information available here and it is hard to know why it exists. More useful is the Periplus 'North Sumatra, Danau Toba and Medan' map, which has a good colour map of Danau Toba, Samosir Island and the surrounding area at a scale of 1:250,000.

Sights

There are few sights in Parapat. The best **beaches** are a little way out of town – but easily walkable – like those at Ajibata village, about 1 km south of Parapat. Saturday is market day when Bataks selling local handicrafts and 'antiques' converge on the town and particularly on the market area at **Pekan Tigaraja**, close to the ferry dock for Samosir. A smaller market is also held here on Tuesday and Thursday. The bright, rust-red roofed church above the town sits in well cared for gardens, with views over the lake. On Sunday, services have as many as eight to 10 hymns.

Parapat

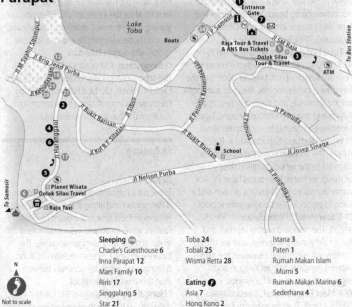

Sleeping	Toba 24	Istana 3
Charlie's Guesthouse 6	Tobali 25	Paten 1
Inna Parapat 12	Wisma Retta 28	Rumah Makan Islam
Mars Family 10		Murni 5
Riris 17	Eating	Rumah Makan Marina 6
Singgalang 5	Asia 7	Sederhana 4
Star 21	Hong Kong 2	

Samosir Island ① *regular ferries (see page 399); or charter a speedboat to visit the sights. US$11-US$16.50, with its Batak stone chairs and tables and* rumah adat, *is only a 30-minute boat trip from Parapat.* ▸▸ *For further information on Samosir Island, see page 401.*

◉ Danau Toba listings

For Sleeping and Eating price codes, see inside the front cover.

● Sleeping

Parapat *p396, map p397*
Most of the more expensive hotels are on the lakefront or up on the hillsides. Cheaper accommodation is concentrated along Jl Haranggaol. For those on a lower budget, the accommodation on Samosir Island is without doubt better and cheaper, see page 406.
A-C Hotel Inna Parapat, Jl Marihat 1, T0625 41012, F0625 7003012. With a distinct 1970s design, this 3-star hotel has a range of comfortable rooms with TV and bath. The rooms at the back are best, with beautiful views of the lake, and a balcony. There is a good swimming beach and jet skis for hire. Free Wi-Fi access in the lobby. Discounts available (30%). Recommended.
D Toba Hotel, Jl Pulo Samosir 8, T0625 41073, F0625 41086. Though the corridors here are virtually pitch black at noon and the furniture is rather ancient, the rooms are right on the shoreline, and there is access to a beach and relaxed outdoors seating. Upstairs rooms are comfortable, with better views.
D Wisma Retta, Jl Kebudayaan 4, T0625 41071. The modern concrete exterior is a contrast to the wood-panelled sleepy interior of this quiet hotel. The rooms have TV, hot water (*mandi* only). There is a garden and a soon to be back in action swimming pool.
D-E Star Hotel, Jl Kebudayaan 2, T0625 41655. The standard rooms are dark and have cold water and *mandi*, and are thus somewhat overpriced. However, the family room is gargantuan (can sleep 8) and represents a good deal for groups.
D-F Mars Family Hotel, Jl Kebudayaan 1, T0625 41459. The cheap rooms here are dark,

but clean. Paying a little more gets a spotless room, with lake views and TV. Peaceful and well-run hotel, recommended.
F Tobali Hotel, Jl Haranggaol 3, T0625 41156. Spacious rooms, the ones at the front having the most natural light, but also the most street noise. Cold-water *mandi* and toilet with no seat. Adequate to crash for a night.
F-G Riris, Jl Haranggaol 43, T0625 41392. The standard rooms are cleanish, have a tiny toilet and access to a decent veranda overlooking the busy streets below. The economy rooms are dark and grotty.
G Charlie's Guesthouse, Tigaraja, T0625 41277. The owner of this place is a popular Batak pop star, and speaks English with the peculiar cockney accent the locals develop here. Near the harbour for boats to Tuk Tuk, so is ideal for late night arrivals intending on leaving town the next morning. Homely and chaotic hotel with simple and comfortable rooms, although a little dark.
G Singgalang, Jl SM Raja 52, T0625 41260. Old-school cheap lodgings above a restaurant. Cleanish rooms, can be a little noisy. Will be handy when long-distance buses once again run from the bus station up the road.

❼ Eating

Danau Toba *p396*
There are 2 concentrations of restaurants: on Jl Haranggaol and along Jl Sisingamangaraja. Haranggaol restaurants are geared more to tourists, while locals and Indonesians tend to eat at those on Jl Sisingamangaraja. The Indonesian (and Chinese) restaurants along Jl Sisingamangaraja are generally better than those on Jl Haranggaol.
❡ Hong Kong, Jl Haranggaol 91, T0625 41395, daily 0800-2100. Clean place serving up good

portions of Chinese food and a smattering of Western fare. Recommended.

† **Istana**, Jl SM Raja 68, towards the bus terminal. Good *nasi Padang*. Recommended.

† **Paten**, Jl SM Raja (opposite the entrance gateway to Parapat). One of the better Chinese restaurants in this strip and well priced.

† **Restoran Asia**, Jl SM Raja 80-82, T0625 41450, daily 0700-2200. Chinese and Indonesian food, with excellent seafood and sweet-and-sour dishes. Also some fair steaks.

† **Rumah Makan Islam Murni**, Jl Harangaol 84, daily 0700-2200. Small but tasty selection of Malay cuisine. The *nasi soto* (chicken in rich coconut-based soup with potato patty served with rice) is excellent.

† **Rumah Makan Marina**, Jl Harangaol 48, daily 0800-2100. Simple Indonesian dishes, clean.

† **Sederhana**, Jl Harangaol 38. One of the best Padang restaurants in town, spicy *rendang* and good *kangkung*, clean and well-run.

● Entertainment

Danau Toba *p396*
Batak cultural shows are held on public holidays and during the **Danau Toba Festival** in Jun at the Open Air Stage on Jl Kebudayaan. The more expensive hotels (eg Inna Parapat) also sometimes organize cultural shows.

● Festivals and events

Danau Toba *p396*
Jun/Jul Danau Toba Festival (movable), held over a week. Hardly traditional, but there are various cultural performances and canoe races on the lake.

● Shopping

Danau Toba *p396*
Jl Sisingamangaraja and Jl Harangaol are the main shopping areas, and both have the same type of souvenir shops. **Batak Culture Art**

Shop, towards the bottom of Jl Harangaol, is better than most and sells some authentic Batak pieces. There's a market at **Pekan Tigaraja** near the ferry jetty, on Sat – a good place to buy batik and handicrafts. On other mornings there is a small food market.

▲ Activities and tours

Parapat *p396, map p397*
Rafting
Trips down the Asahan River (80 km from Parapat) for US$80 per person (minimum 2 people). Price includes all equipment, food and transportation. The trip lasts a day.

Swimming
There is a decent beach for swimming in front of the **Hotel Inna Parapat**.

Tour operators
Tour companies in Parapat have gained a rather poor reputation. Usually they are just used to book bus tickets and confirm flights, rather than arrange tours. Companies include:
Dolok Silau, Jl S Raja 56 and at the harbour near **Charlie's Guesthouse**, T0625 41467. ANS bus tickets to destinations in Sumatra and beyond. They can also arrange rafting trips down the Asahan River.
Planet Wisata, Jl Haranggaol 97, T0625 41037, F0625 41177. Bus and plane tickets. They can book Air Asia flights.
Raja Taxi, Tigaraja (opposite Charlie's Guesthouse). Minibuses to Medan.

Watersports
Hire water-scooters and pedal boats on the waterfront and from the **Hotel Inna Parapat**.

● Transport

Danau Toba *p396*
Boat
Parapat is the main port for Samosir Island, and ferries leave the town from the jetty in

the Tigaraja market at the bottom of Jl Haranggaol for Samosir every hour from 0730-1930, 30 mins, 7000Rp. Most ferries dock at Tuk Tuk on Samosir and they will drop off at the various hotel jetties, so state your destination. Some continue north to Ambarita, while others also dock at Tomok just south of the Tuk Tuk Peninsula. Most of the hotels and guesthouses have a ferry timetable posted. Check the schedule. For further details, see page 410. Note that arriving after dark makes it difficult to reach Samosir the same day. The only ferry operating after 1930 is the car ferry (see below). For those who arrive in Parapat after the last ferry has departed, and can't bear the thought of spending a night in town, it is possible to charter a boat for around US$44 (bargain hard).

Car ferry There is a car ferry from Ajibata, just south of town, to **Tomok**, every 3 hrs, 0830-2130, 4000Rp for foot passengers, 150,000Rp for a car.

Bus

There are no direct buses to **Berastagi** – it is necessary first to travel to **Pemangtangsiantar**, 1 hr, 15,000Rp, and then change to a **Kebonjahe** bus, 3 hrs, 15,000Rp, before finally getting on a bus bound for **Berastagi**, 25 mins, 3000Rp.

For **Medan**, minibuses pick passengers up off the ferry from Tuk Tuk and drive to the Amplas terminal, 5 hrs, 60,000Rp. More comfortable minibuses are available from **Raja Taxi** (see Tour operators) for 80,000Rp.

Economy buses to Medan depart from the terminal on Jl SM Raja, 6 hrs, 25,000Rp, and drop passengers at Medan's Amplas terminal. Because of a damaged road near Parapat, many long-distance buses to the south were no longer departing from Parapat in the first half of 2008. Buses were leaving from **Pematangsiantar**, around 30 km to the north. This added considerable hassle and time to long-distance bus trips out of the Toba area. It is expected that there will be sporadic disruption to this road throughout the year, and visitors should enquire at their guesthouse before leaving for Parapat or Pematangsiantar. All ticket agencies in Parapat and Tuk Tuk sell tickets, which include a shuttle to Pemangtangsiantar from Parapat. Destinations from Pemangtangsiantar include **Bukittingi**, 15 hrs, economy US$21, a/c executive US$31, **Padang**, 17 hrs, economy US$26, a/c executive US$32, **Sibolga**, 7 hrs, US$10, **Jakarta**, 50 hrs, economy US$55, a/c executive US$82. For masochists there are buses to **Yogyakarta** and **Denpasar**, which are more expensive than flights and take days.

Note that it is much more expensive getting tickets from travel agencies in Parapat and Tuk Tuk, than buying them directly from the bus station. **Andilo Nancy**, Parapat Bus Terminal, T0625 41548, sells ANS tickets for a/c buses to **Bukittinggi**, US$19. Avoid seats numbered 33, 34 and 35 as these are right at the back of the bus next to the toilet and do not recline.

⊙ Directory

Parapat *p396, map p397*
Banks Rates are poor in Prapat, but even worse on Samosir. It is best to arrive with sufficient cash for your stay, although that may present risks in itself. There is a series of places that will change money on Jl Haranggaol and in the market area. **Bank Rakyat Indonesia**, Jl Sisingamangaraja (almost opposite the bus terminal). **Pura Buana International**, Jl Haranggaol 75, money changer. **Medical services** Hospital, Jl P Samosir. **Police** Jl Sisingamangaraja (close to the inter-section with Jl P Samosir). **Post office** Jl Sisingamangaraja 90. **Telephone** Warpostel, Jl Haranggaol 74 (for fax and telephone), the most conveniently located of the telephone offices; **Warpostel** at Jl Sisingamangarja 72 (for fax and international telephone).

Samosir Island

→ Phone code: 0645. Colour map 12, B1.

With a large number of traditional Batak villages, fine examples of rumah adat or traditional houses, cemeteries, churches, enigmatic stone carvings, good swimming, hiking, cheap lodgings and few cars, it has proved a favourite destination for travellers. Surrounded by the lake and mist-cloaked mountains, which rise precipitously from the narrow 'coastal' strip on the eastern shore, it is one of the most naturally beautiful and romantic spots in Southeast Asia.

Accommodation is concentrated on the Tuk Tuk Peninsula, Tomok and Ambarita, although there are basic guesthouses scattered across the island. Rooms with a lake view are usually double the price of those without. Camping is also easy on Samosir. Food on the island is good and cheap, and there are a number of warungs in Tomok, Ambarita and on the Tuk Tuk Peninsula. Note that flight reservations cannot be confirmed on Samosir – it is necessary to visit Parapat. For listings, see pages 406-411.

Ins and outs

Getting there
There are regular passenger ferries to Samosir Island from Danau Toba. A car ferry runs from Ajibata, just south of Parapat. Passenger ferries drop passengers off at various points on the Tuk Tuk Peninsula, usually close to their chosen guesthouse or hotel. The crossing takes about 35 minutes. See Transport, pages 399 and 410.

Getting around
It is possible to hire motorbikes, but numerous guesthouses and tour companies have motorbikes for hire, in varying states of repair. Prices vary accordingly but range between 70,000Rp and 80,000Rp per day. A driving licence is not required. This is a recommended way to see the island, although accidents are all too frequent on the narrow roads. Note that although it is possible to drive across the island, there is no assistance available should you get a puncture – which means a long walk to the nearest motorbike repair outfit. Better still, hire a bicycle and slow the pace or embark on a hike or a walk.

A minibus service runs every 20 minutes in the morning between Tomok and Ambarita, and then on to Pangururan; the service runs less frequently in the afternoons. Note that the bus does not take the route that skirts around the lakeshore on the Tuk Tuk Peninsula – it cuts straight across the neck of the peninsula.

Sights

The various places of interest on Samosir are listed under the town entries below. However, there are two aspects of the island that are everywhere. First there are the tombs. These can be seen throughout the Batak area, but it is on Samosir where people find themselves, so to speak, face to face with them. Some are comparatively modest affairs: the tomb itself is topped with a restrained Batak house made of brick and stucco. Others are grandiose structures, with several storeys, pillars and ostentatious ornamentation. Still others seem to be tongue-in-cheek: the one surmounted with a Christmas tree, decorated with fairy lights just out of Ambarita on the road to Simanindo, is a case in point. All, though, show an imaginative fusion of Batak tradition and Christian symbolism. The need to construct these tombs must have been strong (the tradition is dying) – many took up valuable rice land.

The other aspect of Samosir are the **fish 'tanks'** known as *deke ramba*. These have been laboriously constructed on the lake edge, rocks carefully fashioned and then placed close enough together to allow the water in – while also keeping the fish in. Some appear to be very old, and most are still in use. Many have become ornamental, containing sometimes gargantuan *ikan mas*; others are still used to raise fish for the pot. The main fish raised are *ikan mas* (which are also eaten) and *mujahir*, which are native to Danau Toba. Fingerlings are caught in the lake and then raised in the tanks for about two years before being sold.

Tomok ❶❷❸ ▸▸ pp406-411. Colour map 12, B1.

Situated around 3 km south of the Tuk Tuk Peninsula, this was a traditional Batak village. People come here to see the museum, carved coffins and traditional Batak houses (see below), many on day trips from Parapat. This means that there are a host of souvenir stalls, drinks shops and *warungs*, but none that you would go out of your way to patronize. Tomok is also the docking point for the car ferry, which means that lorries roar through this rather sad place.

However, the town is not an entirely lost cause, as it contains some fine high-prowed **Batak houses** and **carved stone coffins, elephants** and **chairs**. Walking from the jetty inland, there is a path lined with souvenir stalls that winds up a small hill. Half way up – about 500 m – is the **Museum of King Soribunto Sidabutar** ① *admission by donation (about 2000Rp)*, housed in a traditional Batak house, containing a small number of Batak implements and photographs of the family.

Walking a little further up the hill, on from the mass of stalls and taking the path to the right, there is a carved stone coffin, the **King's Coffin**, protected by what remains of a large but dying *hariam* tree. The Sarcophagus contains the body of Raja Sidabutar, the chief of the first tribe to migrate to the area. The coffin is surrounded by stone elephants, figures, tables and chairs. Further up the main path, past the stalls, is another grave site with stone figures arranged in a circle. The **church services** at the town and elsewhere on Samosir are worthwhile for the enthusiasm of the congregations – choose between no fewer than three churches.

Tuk Tuk Peninsula ❺❻❼❽❾◍▲❻❶ ▸▸ pp406-411. Colour map 12, B1.

Tuk Tuk is the name given to the peninsula that juts out rather inelegantly from the main body of Samosir Island, about 4 km north of Tomok. It is really just a haven for tourists, with nothing of cultural interest. There is a continuous ribbon of hotels, guesthouses, restaurants, minimarts, curio shops and tour companies following the road that skirts the perimeter of the peninsula. This might sound pretty dire, but in fact the development is not as overbearing as it might be – the nature of the topography means that you don't get confronted with a vision of tourism hell. And in spite of the rapid development, Tuk Tuk is still a peaceful spot, with good swimming, sometimes great food and good-value accommodation. There are various places on Tuk Tuk that masquerade as **tourist information** centres, when they are actually tour companies and travel agents. Nonetheless, they can be a good source of information.

Ins and outs

If you decide to walk, it will take approximately one hour to get to Tuk Tuk and 1½ hours to reach Ambarita. Mountain bikes can be hired from many of the guesthouses and hotels for 25,000Rp per day and this is a recommended way to see the island; make sure you check over the bike carefully. Motorbikes can be hired for 70,000Rp-80,000Rp for a day.

1 Tuk Tuk Peninsula

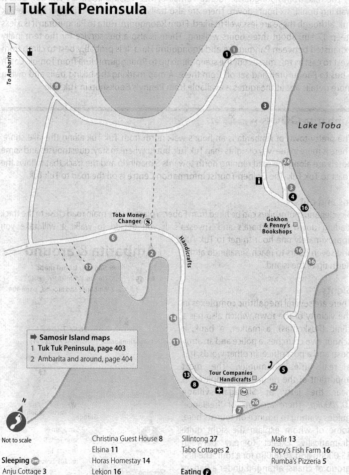

Samosir Island maps
1 Tuk Tuk Peninsula, page 403
2 Ambarita and around, page 404

Not to scale

N

Sleeping
Anju Cottage 3
Bagus Bay 6
Bamboo Guesthouse 1
Carolina Cottage 7
Christina Guest House 8
Elsina 11
Horas Homestay 14
Lekjon 16
Liberta Homestay 17
Samosir Cottages 24
Sibigo 26

Silintong 27
Tabo Cottages 2

Eating
Bamboo 1
Jenny's 4
Juwitas 8

Mafir 13
Popy's Fish Farm 16
Rumba's Pizzeria 5

Bars & clubs
Brando's Blues Bar 3

Hiking

Hiking across Samosir's central highlands is one of the most rewarding ways to see the island. The distance from east to west is only about 20 km as the crow flies, but the route is a steep and circuitous climb of 750 m, making the real walking distance about 45 km. It is just possible to walk the route in a day if hiking from west to east (eg from Pangururan to Tomok), but it is best to stay overnight at the interior village of Roonggurni Huta to recuperate from the climb. A number of homestays here charge about 20,000Rp for a bed.

The hike from Roonggurni Huta to Tomok or vice versa is about 29 km: 10 hours if walking uphill, six hours down. There are also trails to Ambarita and (longer still) to Tuk Tuk, although these are less well marked. From Roonggurni Huta to Pangururan it is a less steep 17 km, about three hours walking. There is also a bus service for the terminally exhausted between Pangururan and Roonggurni Huta. It is probably best to climb from west to east as this misses out the steep climb up to Roonggurni Huta from Tomok. Catch a bus to Pangururan and set off from there. A map marking the hiking trails and giving more details about the routes is available from **Penny's Bookshop** in Tuk Tuk.

Ambarita ◌◉◐◑ ⇒ *pp406-411.*

The pretty town of Ambarita is an hour's walk north from Tuk Tuk along the lake shore. There is more in the way of sights than Tuk Tuk, but nowhere to stay: guesthouses and some hotels are along the road running north towards Simanindo and the track that follows the coast to Tuk Tuk. The **Golden Tourist Information Centre** is on the road to Tuk Tuk.

Ins and outs

Bicycles and motorbikes can be hired from **Faber**, a place on the main road close to the track leading down to **Barbara's** and **Thyesza's**. If you decide to walk, it will take you approximately one hour to get to Tuk Tuk and seven hours to reach Simanindo at the north tip of the island.

Sights

There are several **megalithic complexes** in the vicinity of the town, which also has a clinic (Puskemas), a market, a bank, a school, two churches, a police and an army post, and a post office. In other words, it is a real little community. The most important of the megalithic complexes is near the jetty at **Siallagan village** ① *2000Rp.* There are lots of 'freelance' guides waiting to pounce on tourists here, some of whom explain the sight quite dramatically. Expect to pay between 15,000Rp and 20,000Rp for a tour. The first group of chairs, arranged under a hariam tree, are 300 years old and were used as the site for village councils, where disputes were settled and punishments decided.

2 **Ambarita & around**

⇒ **Samosir Island maps**
1 Tuk Tuk Peninsula, page 403
2 Ambarita and around, page 404

Lake Toba

Tuk Tuk Peninsula

Lumbanmadeli

Ambarita

Garoga

Partungkaon

Sanggam 6
Sapo Toba 9
Thyesza 1
Tuk Tuk Timbul 10

N
Not to scale

Sleeping ◌
Barbara Guest House 1
King's 2
Mas 4

Eating ❼
Joe's Vegetarian 5
No Name Pizzeria 1

The chief would sit in the armchair, while other village elders sat in the surrounding chairs. The person on trial would sit on the small chair closest to the table – having been incarcerated for seven days in the small cage close to the stone chairs. A medicine man would consult his diary to decide on the best day for any sentence to be meted out. A stone figure mysteriously occupies one of the seats. Guides hang around to recount the chairs' gruesome past with a certain amount of relish. The really gruesome part of the traditional legal system is associated with the second group of megaliths. The criminal sentenced to death would be blindfolded, tied hand and foot and bodily carried to the large stone block. He would then be sliced with a small knife and chilli, garlic and onions were reputedly rubbed into the wounds before a mallet – like a meat tenderizer – would be used to prepare the 'meat' for consumption (by pounding the man, already, no doubt, in a certain amount of pain). Having been sufficiently trussed and pummelled, the unfortunate would be carried to the block and his head cut off. The (strength-giving) blood was collected and drunk by the chief, while the meat was distributed to the villagers. The bones, finally, were collected up and thrown into the lake – which was unclean for a week and no activity occurred during this time. The chief's staff is carved with the faces of past chiefly generations. This gruesome tradition came to an end in 1816 when a German missionary (by the name of Nommensen – there's a university in Medan named after him) converted the population to Christianity. Facing the complex is a row of well preserved **Batak houses**.

Also here is the **tomb of Laga Siallagan** ① *turn right (coming from Tomok) off the main road in Ambarita, shortly after the post office walk past the football field and police post, and turn left to walk past tombs and ricefields to the complex, about 500 m in all, it is possible to approach from Tuk Tuk via the side road*, the first chief of Ambarita.

Simanindo ⊖ ›› *pp406-411.*

Sights

Simanindo is at the north tip of Samosir. The house of a former Batak chief, Raja Simalungun, has been restored and turned into an **Ethnological Museum (Huta Bolon)** ① *daily 1000-1700, 5000Rp*, containing a musty collection of Batak, Dutch and Chinese artefacts. The brief labels in English reveal little. There are souvenirs for sale in Batak houses.

Close by is a well-preserved **fortified Batak community** ① *shows are staged Mon-Sat 1030-1110, 1145-1239, and Sun 1145-1230, if a minimum of 5 tourists show up, 30,000Rp*, with fine examples of richly carved Batak houses. This is the best maintained of the various 'preserved' communities on Samosir. Visitors sit through a lengthy sequence of 12 dances, performed by a rather lacklustre crew – many of the dances seem more like loosening up exercises prior to a workout. Requisite audience participation number and the final dance gives an opportunity for guests to add a donation to their entrance fee.

Just offshore from Simanindo is the small 'honeymoon' island of **Tao**. There are secluded and rather expensive bungalows on the island for those who really do wish to be alone. Day trippers can visit Tao for a swim and a meal, it's a 10-minute boat ride.

Pangururan ⊖① ›› *pp406-. Colour map 12, B1.*

Pangururan, the capital of Samosir, is on the west coast, close to the point where the island is attached to the mainland by a small bridge. It is a dusty, ramshackle little town. There is no reason to stay here and most people visit the town on the way to the **hot**

springs on Mount Belirang. Pangururan is also probably the best place from which to set out to hike across the island to Tomok (see page 402).

Ins and outs

From Pangururan, a bus service operates to the interior village of Roonggurni Huta. An occasional service has begun operating in the south part of the island between Tomok and Nainggolan, and then on to Pangururan.

Mount Belirang hot springs

① *2.5 km or 1 hr from Pangururan if you walk, 1000Rp.*

The sulphurous gases and water have killed the vegetation on the hillside, leaving a white residue – the scar can be seen from a long way off on Samosir. Cross the stone bridge and turn right (north). They are about a third of the way up Mount Belirang (also known as Mount Pusuk Buhit). It is too hot to bathe at the point where they issue from the ground, but lower down there are pools where visitors can soak in the healing sulphurous waters. There are separate bathing pools for men and women and some warungs nearby for refreshments. Views of the lake are spoilt by uncontrolled, unattractive development, and even the spring site itself leaves rather a lot to be desired: plastic pipes and moulded concrete make it look, in places, more like a plumber's training site.

Haranggaol ◉◉ ▸▸ *pp406-411. Colour map 12, B1.*

This is a small, sleepy, rather run-down town on Danau Toba's northeastern shore. Few tourists visit the town, but there is an excellent **market** on Monday and Thursday – when there are early morning boat connections with Samosir from Ambarita and/or Simanindo – and good walks in the surrounding countryside. If visitors wish to experience the wonder of Toba, without the crowds at Parapat and on Samosir, then this is the place to come.

Ins and outs

Haranggaol lies off the main bus route, so it can take a time to reach the town. There are bus connections from Kabanjahe (easily accessible from Berastagi) to Seribudolok, and from there bemos run to Haranggaol. Getting to or from Parapat to Haranggaol is not easy; it involves three bus changes and it usually takes eight hours to cover the 50-odd kilometres. Taking the ferry is easier. ▸▸ *See Transport, page 410.*

◉ Samosir Island listings

For Sleeping and Eating price codes,
see inside the front cover.

● Sleeping

Tuk Tuk Peninsula *p402, map p403*
There are many places to stay in Tuk Tuk, from very simple affairs to large, comfortable hotels. Almost all accommodation is situated along the road (really just a lane) that skirts around the edge of the peninsula. To the north and

south there is a relatively steep drop into the lake, so the chalets seem to cling precariously to the hillside. To the east the land slopes more gently into the lake, so there is room for larger gardens and bigger guesthouses and hotels. Be sure to bargain for your accommodation, as stays of 3 or more nights often see prices dropping sharply.
B-D Silintong Hotel, T0625 451242, www.silintonghotel.bolgspot.com. Resort hotel mainly patronized by well-heeled

Indonesians. There is a faintly Mediterranean feel about the design here. Rooms are clean, and come with TV although are rather over-priced given the excellent accommodation available elsewhere. Breakfast is included.

B-G Tabo Cottages, T0625 451318, www.tabo-cottages.com. Those in the know stay here, in beautiful Batak cottages overlooking a large garden and the lake. The mid-priced rooms are clean and have hot water, and some have outdoor bathrooms. Economy rooms are good value, with cold water and lake views. Recommended.

D-G Samosir Cottages, T0625 41050, www.samosircottages.com. Sprawling and impersonal resort-style place that fills up with Indonesian tourists at weekends. Rooms are clean and the family room can sleep 4 and has cable TV, fridge and kitchen. Internet access available (expensive).

E-G Carolina Cottage, T0625 41520, carolina@indosat.net.id. By far the most popular place in Toba, with convenient access from Parapat, excellent swimming area with pontoon for diving, and well-manicured gardens. Selection of rooms in Batak houses, most with great lake views, the more expensive rooms have hot water and a breezy balcony. Recommended.

F Sibigo, down a small track next to **Carolina**, T0625 451017. Sleepy and quiet. Rooms are adequate and have beautiful views, but are sorely in need of a good clean.

F-G Anju Cottage, T0625 451265. Good selection of rooms, ranging from Batak houses to tiled concrete chalets in a breezy setting. There is decent swimming here and a diving board. Prices include breakfast.

G Bagus Bay, T0625 451287. Well-run and friendly place with a selection of spotless rooms in Batak houses, some with lake views. 4 new and attractive rooms in a concrete block set in a leafy garden. Extensive gardens with badminton and volleyball courts and children's play area. Good range of facilities including Internet café, 10,000Rp per hr, book exchange and satellite TV in the restaurant. Recommended.

G Bamboo Guesthouse, on the northeastern corner of the peninsula, T0625 451236. While rooms here are nothing special and are in need of some love, they are right on the waterfront and have magnificent sunset views.

G Christina Guest House, T0625 451027. On the road heading out towards Ambarita, rooms here are comfortable and fronted by an attractive lily pond with expansive views of the lake. The family house is superb value, with space for 5 people. There is a restaurant with cable TV. Internet café.

G Elsina, T0625 451067. Collection of Batak houses just above the shore line. Staff are somewhat surly.

G Horas Homestay, T081 396013643. Access to these rooms is via **Horas Chillout Café**, and down crumbling and overgrown steps that lead to the shoreline. Clean and quiet rooms. This place possesses a rural charm not found in most other Tuk Tuk lodgings.

G Lekjon, T0625 451259. Offers 22 rooms, some with hot water, set in a small garden facing the lake.

G Liberta Homestay, T0625 451035. Collection of Batak houses, some in a better state of repair than others, set in a lovely garden. This is a popular place, and gets busy at weekends. Locals bring along their guitars for musical evenings, and often like to challenge visitors to games of chess in the laid-back restaurant. Recommended.

Ambarita *p404, map p404*

The hotels and guesthouses listed here are scattered along the road towards Simanindo (over a distance of about 9 km from town) and the smaller road leading towards Tuk Tuk (over about 2 km). They are quieter than those in Tuk Tuk. They are also quite isolated, so staying here, if you want to try other restaurants and bars, means hiring a bicycle or motorcycle. This part of the island is also rather treeless near the lake shore, but has some good swimming. Guesthouse owners will often pick visitors up from Tomok or Tuk Tuk if they phone ahead. Otherwise, catch a minibus from Tomok heading towards

Simanindo (3000Rp) and tell the driver which hotel you wish to alight at. All the hotels mentioned here have restaurant attached.

C-D Sanggam, 5 km north of Ambarita, T0625 41344, F0625 41474. Holiday resort popular with Indonesians. Rooms are clean and have hot water but limited character. The villas are a better option, with space for 4.

D Sapo Toba, T0625 700009, F0625 41117. Collection of smart chalets built on a hillside overlooking the lake. All the rooms are identical and have hot water, TV, fridge and bathroom with bath. The reception is at the bottom of the hillside inside the restaurant on the left, just keep following those eternal steps down. Internet, 35,000Rp per hr.

F-G King's Hotel, T0625 41865. Rooms in a concrete block. Extensive but unremarkable garden by the lakeside. There are also a couple of Batak houses on the shoreline that are in a reasonable state.

F-G Thyesza, 4 km to the north of Ambarita, down a small track leading to the shoreline, T0625 41443, www.flowerofsamosir.com. Well-maintained place with 6 tidy tiled rooms in a flower covered concrete block slightly set back from the lake. Also a cheaper Batak house right on the shore. This part of the coast has excellent swimming and clear water. The open-air restaurant is good. Recommended.

F-G Tuk Tuk Timbul, about 1 km south of Ambarita towards Tuk Tuk, T0625 41374. Collection of smart cottages in a great isolated position off the road and down on the lake front on a small headland. The restaurant serves good food including home-baked bread. There is a large fish pond and good swimming.

G Barbara Guest House, T0625 41230. Down a small track and neighbouring **Thyesza**, accommodation is a little down at heel, but the friendly staff makes up for peeling paint. Some rooms have a lake view and hot water. Restaurant and good swimming.

G Mas, T0625 451051. Gorgeous views, a peaceful setting and a good selection of clean tiled rooms fronted by a small fish farm with swirling koi. This fine option for those

wishing to stay far enough outside of Tuk Tuk to escape the overtly touristy atmosphere, but close enough to have good dining options nearby. Tuk Tuk is a leisurely 30-min stroll away. Rooms are set in a concrete block, those downstairs have hot water. Recommended.

Haranggaol *p406*

E Haranggaol, situated in town rather than on the lake shore. The best place to stay. Some rooms have hot water. There's a large eating area, used to catering for tour groups.

E Segumba Cottages, 3 km out of town. Bali-style cottages situated in a beautiful, quiet position. Some rooms with *mandi*. Recommended.

● Eating

Tomok *p402*

There are several *warung* around the village, eg **Islam**. Nothing outstanding, but passable whether European, Chinese, Minang or standard Indonesian fare.

Tuk Tuk Peninsula *p402, map p403*

There are an increasing number of good restaurants on Tuk Tuk, many specialize in vegetarian travellers' food.

Bamboo, daily 0800-1000. Good spot for sunsets, cocktails and a range of simple Western food and Indonesian staples. The best option here is the beach barbecue when the owner grills fresh lake fish and serves them with a variety of lip-smacking sauces.

Jenny's, daily 0800-1000. Popular place with friendly staff in a colourful setting serving sandwiches and good salads and juices. There is often live Batak folk music here in the evenings.

Juwitas, T0625 451217, daily 0800-2200. Small wooden café with chatty owner serving decent vegetarian grub and some fine curries and lake fish dishes.

Mafir, T0625 41462, daily 0700-2200. Comfortable eatery with a range of decent

Indonesian dishes (the *rijstaffel* here is epic), fish curries and fresh lake fish.

♥ Popy's Fish Farm, T0625 451291, daily 0800-2200. Fresh fish cooked in every conceivable way in a breezy setting with booked lined walls. The menu also features some Chinese dishes and curries.

♥ Rumba's Pizzeria, there are 2 branches. On the southeastern side of the peninsula, T0625 451310, daily 0800-2300, reasonable create-your-own pizza with a variety of toppings; on the western side of the peninsula, T0625 451045, daily 1200-2100, considerably cheaper, with sunset views and good pizzas. Recommended.

Guesthouse restaurants

Some of the best dining is in Tuk Tuk's guesthouses. Generally serve food daily 0700-2200.

♥ Bagus Bay. Extensive menu with good pizza, vegetarian curry and a breakfast menu featuring baked beans with cheese on toast.

♥ Lekjon. This place uses locally made buffalo mozzarella on its pizzas and in some salads.

♥ Liberta Homestay. Mellow setting for a beer, healthy meal (lots of vegetarian offerings) and chat with some of the locals.

♥ Sibigo. Excellent fresh lake fish grilled and served with limes and local sauces. Also, for those missing chips, this place serves them with all manner of sauces including *sate* and *sambal*.

♥ Tabo Cottages. This is a haven for vegetarians with some lovely soups accompanied by fresh bread, good salads and aloe vera power drinks. Carnivores are not forgotten, with a few fish and chicken dishes on the menu. There is an excellent breakfast menu here, with a substantial buffet breakfast for 35,000Rp. At weekends the kitchen struggles to cope with demand and it can take some time for meals to materialize. Recommended.

Ambarita *p404, map p404*
There are a couple of coffee shops and *warungs* in town, but nothing that stands out. The best place to eat is at a nice little *warung*

next to the police post (turn off the main road and walk past the football field).

♥ Joe's Vegetarian Restaurant, Pindu Raya (a hamlet between Tuk Tuk and Ambarita). Best for its home-made cakes and coffee.

♥ No Name Pizzeria, 7 km or so north of town on the road to Simanindo just in front of the **King's Hotel**. Curiously, there is currently no pizza on offer depite the name, but the menu features simple western food and some standard Indonesian dishes. This place doubles up as a *tuak* (toddy) shop at night and can be a fun place to meet locals.

Guesthouse restaurants
Of the guesthouses on the strip between Ambarita and Simanindo, **Barbara's** and **Thyesza** (both ♥) are the most traveller savvy, and **Thyesza** cooks up some fine Batak dishes (including dog meat on request), simple Western fare and serves excellent fresh fruit juices including wonderfully refreshing local passion fruit juice.

🎵 Bars and clubs

Tuk Tuk Peninsula *p402, map p403*
Locals head to *tuak* (toddy) shops of an evening for a drink and chat. These can look fairly inconspicuous from the outside. Ask at your hotel which one is most accessible. Expect to pay 1500 to 2000Rp for a glass.
Brando's Blues Bar, T0625 451084, open 1800-0200. Reggae, Blues and a smattering of house music at this place, which has a small dance floor, some outdoors seating, a pool table and cheap, strong spirits to get the legs swaying to a different tune.

🎭 Entertainment

Tuk Tuk Peninsula *p402, map p403*
Traditional dance Batak folk song and dance performances every Wed and Sat, 2015 at **Bagus Bay** (see Sleeping). This is very popular and a fun way to spend an evening.

O Shopping

Tuk Tuk Peninsula *p402, map p403*
Books Gokhon Bookshop, offers a postal service; **Bagus Bay Bookshop**, for second-hand novels; **Penny's Bookshop**, has an excellent book lending section, maps and some DVDs to rent – for 8000Rp you can watch a DVD in the shop. There are a number of other places around the peninsula that sell second-hand books.
Crafts There are scores of craft and curio shops selling woodcarvings, medicine books, leather goods, Batak calendars, carved chess sets, wind chimes and so on. The chess sets are a good buy here but they vary enormously in quality and price, it's worth shopping around.

▲ Activities and tours

Samosir Island *p401*
Boat trips
There is a cruise around the north portion of the island every day of the week leaving from Tuk Tuk and Ambarita. It includes a visit to the hot springs on Mt Belirang.

Tours
There are no regular tours around the island at the moment, due to lack of tourists, but they can be arranged at one of the tour companies (if you can find anyone in). Most of the hotels will provide a map, and suggest a coherent day-trip itinerary taking in Tomok, Siallangan, Sangkal (weaving village), Simanindo, and over to the hot springs on near Pangguran. Many of the guys working in the hotels will offer to guide tourists for 50,000-100,000Rp.

Walking
This is one of the most enjoyable ways to see Samosir. Walking across the island takes 2 days, with an overnight stop at Roonggurni Huta in the highland interior. There are also other hiking trails across the island; ask at your hotel or *losmen*.

Tuk Tuk Peninsula *p402, map p403*
Cooking classes
Juwita's (see Eating). Visitors can choose from a list of Batak and Indonesian dishes and learn to cook them with the chatty owner in a 3-hr class, US$22.

Massage
Traditional massage available at guesthouses around the peninsula, about 50,000Rp per session. Ask at **Tabo Cottages** or **Bagus Bay**.

Tours operators
There are plenty of operators around the peninsular, browse for a good price. The companies listed here will book bus tickets and help arrange a tour of the island:
Anju Cottage, T0625 451265.
Bagus Bay Information, T0625 451287.

⊖ Transport

Samosir Island *p401*
Boat Most visitors get to Samosir by ferry from **Parapat**. The ferry leaves about every hour and takes 30 mins (7000Rp). Most ferries dock at Tuk Tuk on Samosir and they will drop off at the various hotel jetties, so state your destination. Some continue north to Ambarita, while others also dock at Tomok just south of the Tuk Tuk Peninsula. Most of the hotels and guesthouses have a ferry timetable posted. Check the schedule.

The 1st ferry from Parapat leaves at 0930, from Samosir at 0730. The last departs Parapat at 1730, Samosir at 1630. It is also possible to charter a 'special' boat, but this is expensive. The car ferry service from Ajibata, just south of Parapat (see map, page 397) to Tomok, runs every 3 hrs from 0700-2200, 4000Rp for foot passengers. A ferry also links Tuk Tuk and Ambarita with Haranggaol on Danau Toba's north shore, but this only runs on Mon – market day in Haranggaol. The ferry leaves Ambarita at 0700 and takes 2-3 hrs, largely because it stops to pick up market-goers all along the eastern shore. They leave Haranggaol for Samosir at 1300 and 1500; check in your hotel for the time of journeys in the other direction. To Haranggaol, there are buses to **Seribudolok**, then to **Kabanjahe** and finally to **Berastagi** and **Medan**. Ferries leave from Haranggaol for Tuk Tuk and Ambarita on Samosir every Mon and Thu at 1300 and 1500, 4 hrs.

Tomok *p402*
Boat There is a car ferry from Ajibata, just south of town, to **Tomok**, every 3 hrs from 0830-1730, last departure at 2100, 4000Rp for foot passengers, 150,000Rp for a car.
Bus In theory, every 20 mins to **Pangururan** and all stops along the route.

Tuk Tuk Peninsula *p402, map p403*
Boat Ferry connections with **Parapat** about every hour, 7000Rp.
Bus Walk to the main road to catch 1 of the buses running between **Tomok** and **Pangururan**, every 20 mins, 12,000Rp.

Ambarita *p404, map p404*
Bus Connections every 20 mins with **Tomok**, 3000Rp, and all stops to **Pangururan**.

Simanindo *p405*
Boat Ferries connect **Simanindo** with **Tigaras**, north of Parapat, leaving every 1½ hrs , 0630-1430. The ferry between **Ambarita** and **Haranggaol** also sometimes stops here.
Bus Regular connections with **Ambarita** and **Tuk Tuk**, and onwards to **Pangururan**.

Pangururan *p405*
Bus Buses leave Pangururan for **Medan**, **Sidikalang**, 0700 and 1600, and **Sibolga**, 0700-0900. Regular connections with **Simanindo**, **Ambarita**, **Tuk Tuk** and **Tomok**. Buses at 0500, 1200, 1700 to **Ronggurni Huta**.

Haranggaol *p406*
Boat A ferry connects Haranggaol with **Tuk Tuk** and **Ambarita** on Samosir Island on Mon and Thu. From Samosir there are many ferry boats making the crossing to **Parapat**.

❶ Directory

Samosir Island *p401*
Banks Rates of exchange on Samosir are poor, worse than in Parapat, although the larger hotels and some travel agents will change TCs and cash. There is also a money changer in Ambarita. **Telephone** International calls can be placed from many of the hotels and tour and travel agencies, this is usually advertised.

Tomok *p402*
Telephone Wartel office, on the northern edge of town on the main road, international calls and faxes.

Tuk Tuk Peninsula *p402, map p403*
Banks PT Andilo Nancy travel agent changes money at a better rate than other places. **Internet** Tabo Cottages, charges are high as the nearest server is Medan. **Medical services** Clinic (Puskesmas), on the southern side of the peninsula. **Post office** No post office but many places sell stamps and will post letters. **Telephone** Many guesthouses, hotels and tour companies offer IDD phone facilities and fax.

Ambarita *p404, map p404*
Banks Bank Rakyat Indonesia on Jl Raya (the main road). **Medical services** Clinic (Puskemas), in town. **Post office** Jl Raya 39, on the right-hand side from Tomok, shortly before the turning for the Siallangan megalithic complex.

Pangururan *p405*
Telephone Wartel office, part of Wisata Samosir, Jl Kejaksan.

Bukittinggi and around

→ *Phone code: 0752. Colour map 12, B2.*

Visitors to West Sumatra spend most of their time based in and around the highland settlement of Bukittinggi, its cultural heart. This is entirely understandable as it is one of the most attractive towns in Sumatra and has many places of interest in the immediate vicinity. The accommodation is good, the climate invigorating and the food excellent. The highly mobile Minang people who view this area as their ancestral home are fascinating, and the surrounding countryside is some of the most beautiful in Sumatra. There are peaceful highland lakes, like Maninjau and Singkarak, rivers for rafting and demanding mountain treks. But while Bukittinggi must be counted as West Sumatra's great draw, it is not a one-shot province. The coastal capital of Padang, the little visited but noteworthy Kerinci-Seblat National Park and the Mentawai Islands are also notable draws. ▶▶ For listings, see pages 419-424.

Ins and outs

Getting there
There is no airport at Bukittinggi; the nearest is at Padang, a two-hour bus journey away. Most people get to this popular destination by bus, and the journey overland from Medan via Danau Toba is pretty gruelling, just over 500 km or 15 hours' drive in total (if the bus doesn't break down, an all too frequent occurrence). But because it is such a popular destination, the range of buses and destinations is impressive for a town that is relatively small. ▶▶ *See Transport, page 423.*

Getting around
Bukittinggi itself is small and cool enough to negotiate on foot. One of the great attractions is the surrounding countryside, but trying to get around on public transport can be a bit of a drag so many visitors choose to charter a bemo, hire a motorbike or bicycle, or take a tour. Bemos cost about 2000Rp per trip, and bendis and oplets are good for longer journeys. Oplets can be found at the bus station at Aur Kuning, 3 km southeast of town. Motorbikes and mountain bikes can be hired from many guesthouses and tour companies; motorbike hire cost about 65,000Rp per day and mountain bikes 25,000Rp.

Visitors arriving at Aur Kuning may be encouraged to take a taxi to town; regular (red) oplets ply the route for a fraction of the price (2000Rp), or a bemo can be chartered for the trip to Jalan A Yani for 15,000Rp.

Sights

The geographic and functional centre of Bukittinggi is marked by a strange-looking **clock tower** at the south end of Jalan Jend A Yani, the town's main thoroughfare. The Jam Gadang, or 'Great Clock' as it is known, was built by the Dutch in 1827. It is a veritable Sumatran 'Big Ben' and has a Minangkabau-style roof perched uneasily on the top. The **central market** is close to the clock tower. Although there is a market every day of the week, market day is on Wednesday and Saturday (0800-1700) when hoards of Minangkabau men and women descend on Bukittinggi. The market – in fact there are two markets, the Upper Market (*Pasar Atas*) and Lower Market (*Pasar Bawah*) – covers an enormous area and sells virtually everything. Good for souvenirs, handicrafts, jewellery, fruit, spices and weird foods.

The north end of Jalan Jend A Yani runs between two hills that have recently been linked by a footbridge. On top of the hill to the west is **Fort de Kock**, built by the Dutch in 1825 as a defensive site during the Padri Wars. Very little of the fort remains apart from a few rusting cannons and a moat. The centre of the decaying fortifications is dominated by

Bukittinggi

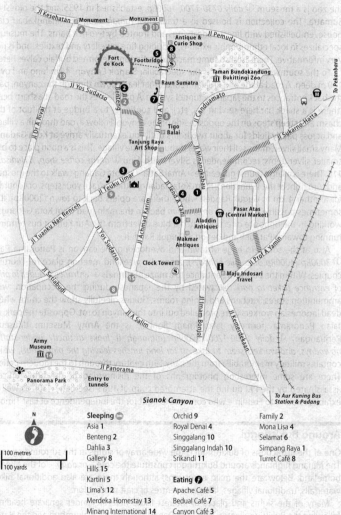

Jl Kesehatan — Monument — Monument
Jl Pemuda
Antique & Curio Shop
Fort de Kock — Footbridge
Taman Bundokandung Bukittinggi Zoo
Jl Yos Sudarso — Jl Benteng — Raun Sumatra
Jl Canduamato
To Pekanbaru
Jl Dr A Rivai
Jl Yos Sudarso
Tigo Balai
Tanjung Raya Art Shop
Jl Minangkabau
Jl Sukarno-Hatta
Jl Teuku Umar
Jl Jend A Yani
Jl Achmad Karim
Jl Tuanku Nan Renceh
Pasar Atas (Central Market)
Aladdin Antiques
Makmar Antiques
Clock Tower
Jl Setiabudi
Jl Imam Bonjol
Maju Indosari Travel
Jl Prof A Yamin
Jl A Salim
Jl Kemerdekaan
Army Museum
Jl Panorama
Panorama Park — Entry to tunnels
Sianok Canyon
To Aur Kuning Bus Station & Padang

N
100 metres
100 yards

Sleeping
Asia 1
Benteng 2
Dahlia 3
Gallery 8
Hills 15
Kartini 5
Lima's 12
Merdeka Homestay 13
Minang International 14
Orchid 9
Royal Denai 4
Singgalang 10
Singgalang Indah 10
Srikandi 11
Family 2
Mona Lisa 4
Selamat 6
Simpang Raya 1
Turret Café 8

Eating
Apache Café 5
Bedual Café 7
Canyon Café 3

a water tower. However, the views of the town and the surrounding countryside are worth the trip (although trees are beginning to obscure the view). To the east, and linked by a footbridge, on the other side of Jalan Jend A Yani, is Bukittinggi's high point, **Taman Bundokandung** – 'Kind-Hearted Mother Park'. The park contains both a museum and a zoo. The **Bukittinggi zoo** ⓘ *daily 0730-1700, fort and zoo: 5000Rp (8000Rp on public holidays)*, is hardly a lesson in how to keep animals in captivity, but it does have a reasonable collection of Sumatran wildlife, including orang-utans and gibbons. Within the zoo is a **museum** ⓘ *daily 0730-1700, 1000Rp*, established in 1935 and the oldest in Sumatra. The collection is housed in a traditional *rumah adat*, or Minangkabau clan house, embellished with fine woodcarvings and fronted by two rice barns. The museum specializes in local ethnographic exhibits, including fine jewellery and textiles, and is not very informative. There are also some macabre stuffed and deformed buffalo calves here.

To the southwest of the town is the spectacular **Sianok Canyon**, 4 km long and over 100 m deep. A road at the end of Jalan Teuku Umar leads down through the canyon, past the back entrances to the Japanese tunnel system. A path leaves the road at a sharp bend (there is a snack bar here serving tea, etc), and continues to a bridge at the foot of the chasm and steep steps on the opposite side of the canyon. Follow a road through a village and across paddy fields for about two hours until you eventually arrive at **Kota Gadang**. Many small silversmiths sell their wares throughout the village. This is a good place to buy smaller silver items; recommended is **Silversmith Aino** ⓘ *at the coffee shop, Jl Hadisash 115*. There is a large tourist gift centre – **Amai Satia** – in Kota Gadang (walk to the mosque and turn right at the T-junction). From Kota Gadang, either retrace your steps, or continue for another 4 km to Guguk Randeh where there are oplets back to town (2000Rp). It is sometimes possible to catch an *omprengan* back to the main road from Kota Gadang. If working in the opposite direction, catch a blue oplet from the Aur Kuning bus terminal running towards Parabek and get off at Guguk Randeh.

Also at the southern edge of town and overlooking the canyon is **Panorama Park** ⓘ *3000Rp (4000Rp on public holidays)*, a popular weekend meeting place for courting couples. Within the park is the entrance to a **maze of tunnels** ⓘ *entrance included in price of entrance ticket to park*, excavated by the Japanese during the Occupation, with ammunition stores, kitchens and dining rooms. Guides gleefully show the chute where dead Indonesian workers were propelled out into the canyon to rot. Opposite the park, on Jalan Panorama (formerly Jalan Imam Bonjol), is the **Army Museum** (Museum Perjuangan) ⓘ *daily 0800-1700, 2000Rp (although it looks distinctly under-staffed nowadays, and workers seem to take off for long lunches leaving the place shut)*, which contains military memorabilia from the early 19th century through to the modern period. There are some interesting photographs of the disinterring of the army officers assassinated by the PKI during the attempted coup of 1965 (see page 430), as well as exhibits relating to Fretilin – who continue to fight for the independence of East Timor.

Around Bukittinggi

One of the attractions of Bukittinggi is the wide array of sights in the surrounding area. The Minang highlands around Bukittinggi constitute the core – or *darek* – of the Minang homeland. Below are the main excursions, although there are also additional hikes, waterfalls, traditional villages, lakes and centres of craft production.

Many of the sights and places of interest listed here are under separate headings following the Bukittinggi entry. These are: **Danau Maninjau**, **Payakumbuh** and the **Harau**

Valley, **Batusangkar** and **Danau Singkarak**, and **Padang Panjang**. Seeing these sights, particularly if time is short, is easiest on a tour. Getting around the Minang area on public transport is time consuming (renting a motorbike for the day makes for greater mobility).

For treks in Nias or Siberut a guide is even more useful, given the difficulties of communication and getting around. A guide should, in theory, be able to offer some insights into the rich Minang culture. It is worth asking around and getting some first-hand assessments from travellers who have just returned from tours and who may be able to recommend a guide. If possible, find a guide and arrange a tour directly; the tour companies usually use the same guides and because they take a commission the rate rises. The guides working out of the **Orchid Hotel**, the **Canyon Café** have been recommended.

Local tours

There are a range of tours organized to Danau Maninjau, Batusangkar, Danau Singkarak and other sights around Bukittinggi. Tours tend to take one of three routes: the Minangkabau tour, featuring many different places that are representative of the Minangkabau culture, past and present (including Batusangkar, Pagaruyung and Danau Singkarak). Secondly, the Maninjau line (including Kota Gadang and Danau Maninjau), and finally, the Harau Valley line (including Mount Merapi and the Harau Valley). Most tour/travel agents organize these day-long tours for 75,000-150,000Rp; they are also arranged by many hotels and guesthouses.

Tours further afield

Many of the tour operators also organize tours further afield, for example, 10-day trips to the Mentawai Islands. Bukittinggi is an excellent place to arrange a tour to the islands off the West Sumatra coast, but bear in mind that it can take up to three days to get to Siberut Island, Mentawai. We have also had reports that letters of recommendation are photocopied and used by guides to whom they do not refer. Expect to pay around US$300 for an eight- to 10-day all-inclusive trip to the islands.

From Bukittinggi to Maninjau This trip is spectacular. After leaving the main Padang–Bukittinggi route at Kota Baru, the road twists through the terraced countryside to the town of Matur. Locals are said to call this stretch of road the Mercedes Bends, and the story is charming even if it might not be true. During the Dutch period there were two sugar cane processing plants at Matur and the Dutch manager of one owned the only car in the area: a Mercedes. When he drove to Bukittinggi local people would line the road to watch the strange machine wind its way to Kota Baru, earning this stretch of road the name the Mercedes Bends. On reaching the crater lip – an awesome spectacle – the road descends through 44 hairpin bends, each of which has been numbered (and sponsored by a cigarette company) by some bureaucratic mind, before arriving at the lake edge village of Maninjau.

A rewarding and spectacular hike from Bukittinggi, easily possible in a day for even the modestly energetic, is to walk to the crater edge at **Puncak Lawang** (Lawang Top) and then down the steep crater sides to the lake-side village of **Bayur**, before catching a bus back to Bukittinggi. To do this, take a pale blue oplet from Bukittinggi's Aur Kuning bus terminal to Lawang – sometimes called Pasar Lawang (Lawang Market) to distinguish it from Puncak Lawang (8000Rp). From Lawang walk the 4 km to Puncak Lawang at the lip of the crater and 1400 m up – a spectacular view – before taking the path down (a walk of around another two to three hours). The path can be narrow at times, and slippery when wet. Alternatively, catch a bus straight to Maninjau village on the lake shore, navigating

44 hairpin bends on the way down (one to two hours, 10,000Rp). The last bus leaves Maninjau village for Bukittinggi between 1600 and 1700, later on market days (Monday to Friday). Check there is no mist before departing.

Danau Singkarak → *Colour map 12, B2.*
① *Take a bus heading south towards Solok.*
The Minang area's other lake is Danau Singkarak. It is not as beautiful as Maninjau, but it is possible to come here on a circular journey via Batusangkar.

Batang Palupuh
① *A guide from the village will point the flower out for a small fee, catch a bus to Batang Palupuh on the Trans-Sumatran Hwy, or take an oplet and then walk to the reserve (30mins).*
This reserve, situated 12 km north of town, is for the monstrous *rafflesia* flower. Ask staff at your guesthouse when the flower will next be in bloom.

Pandai Sikat and other craft villages
① *Take a red oplet towards Padang Panjang from the Aur Kuning terminal, get off at Kota Baru and either walk the last 3 km or take an omprengan (a non-licensed bemo) from the intersection.*
One of a number of villages specializing in **traditional craft production**. It is situated 13 km south of town at the foot of Mount Singgalang, 3 km off the main road to Padang Panjang, and is a cloth and woodcarving centre. The carvings tend to use natural motifs (trees, animals, flowers, etc), as does the famous *songket* cloth that is produced here. About 1000 women weave richly patterned cloth. Note that the warp may be rayon, imported from Japan, and only the weft, cotton or silk. Other craft villages include **Desa Sunga**, 17 km south of town, which specializes in brasswork; and **Sungaipua**, on the slopes of Mount Merapi, which specializes in metalwork (knives, swords).

Mount Merapi
① *Catch a bus to Kota Baru from the Aur Kuning terminal (1st departure 0500), and then hike.*
This active volcano, southeast of town, stands at a height of 2891 m and last erupted in 1979. The difficult climb to the summit takes between four and six hours. Enquire at the Police Station in Kota Baru for more information. Register here before ascending and ask for directions; the route is indistinct in places. The best way to see the volcano is to hire a guide and climb up at night (costs US$27), arriving at the summit for sunrise and thus avoiding the heat of the day and the mist that envelopes the mountain by 1100. Wear warm clothes it is cold on the summit. The ground around the crater is loose and hikers should keep away from the lip. Many hotels and cafés can arrange tours and a good place to enquire is at the **Orchid Hotel** or **Canyon Café**. On Sat nights hoards of locals climb the volcano, following them is possible but not advisable as many do not know the way.

Mount Singgalang
① *Take an oplet to Kota Baru from the Aur Kuning terminal. From where you are dropped, turn right at the mosque and walk down to Kota Baru. In the centre of the village is a right-hand turn with the RTCI 4 km sign (referring to the radio installation situated 2 km above Pantai Sikat). Follow this track for 2 km to Pandai Sikat. The mountain path starts to the right of the RTCI installation behind a refreshment hut (often closed). For speed, it is possible to hire a motorbike to the RTCI site. Buses back to Bulettinggi run late, but it is advisable not to descend in darkness.*

Singgaland, which lies to the southwest of Bukittinggi, stands at a height of 2878 m and offers a less arduous climb than Mount Merapi. The trail starts at the village of Pandai Sikat, and the climb takes about four or five hours. It's a disappointing dirty footpath. Near the summit, the ground is scree, so good footwear is recommended. Start early, as mist often descends over the mountain later in the day. Tours are available from the **Canyon Café** and **Orchid Guesthouse** for US$27.

Payakumbuh → *Colour map 12, B2.*

① *Regular oplets from Bukittinggi, 1 hr, these run through Piladang.*

This key centre of Minang culture lies about 10 km east of Bukittinggi (see page 412). En route is the colourful local Friday market at **Piladang**, while on the other side of Payakumbuh is the **Harau Canyon** (see below).

Harau Canyon

① *Take one of the many buses from Bukittinggi to Payakumbuh. From there catch a white oplet – or a 'sago' as they are called locally – running towards Sarialamat to the turn-off for the Harau Valley (see the main entry for more details on the walk from there).*

The canyon lies around 44 km from Bukittinggi, off the road leading through Payakumbuh towards Pekanbaru.

Pariangan and other Minang villages

① *There are no direct buses from Bukittinggi, catch an oplet from Bukittinggi to Batusangkar, and then one heading towards Kota Baru – which passes through Parianagan. From Bukittinggi it is necessary to 1st catch an oplet to Batusangkar, and then a Solok-bound bus.*

Pariangan is a peaceful Minang village on the slopes of Mount Merapi. Balimbiang is about 10 km south of Batusangkar, and 1 km off the main road.

Danau Maninjau ⊖🏊🏔️🚲🏨 ‖ *pp-424. Colour map 12, B2.*

Danau Maninjau is one of the most beautiful and impressive natural sights in Sumatra, rivalling Danau Toba. It is a huge, flooded volcanic crater with steep 600 m-high walls. To the west and south the crater walls are largely forested, dropping straight into the lake and leaving scarcely any scope for cultivation and settlement. This part of the crater supports a fair amount of wildlife. To the east and north there is some flat land and this is where Maninjau's small settlements are to be found. Once a popular stop on a jaunt around Sumatra, Maninjau has suffered chronically in the downturn in tourism. Many hotels and restaurants have been forced out of business. If it's tourist-free isolation that a visitor craves, it can be found here in abundance.

Ins and outs

Regular buses service the route from Bukittinggi, taking 1½ hours. Bicycles and motorcycles can be hired from most guesthouses and provide an ideal means of getting around the lake and reaching surrounding villages. Bicycles cost about 25,000Rp per day and motorcycles 60,000Rp per day.

Sights

The lake offers reasonable swimming (although close to the shore it can be murky), fishing and waterskiing. In 1996, discharges of sulphur from hot underwater springs killed many of the fish that are raised here in cages along the shore. The springs explain why the water is surprisingly warm for a lake over 500 m above sea level.

Maninjau village lies on the east shore of the lake at the point where the road from Bukittinggi reaches the lake. It is a small but booming market and administrative centre. Most of the places to stay are in (and beyond) the northern extent of the village. Around 3 km north of Maninjau village is the small and charming hamlet of **Bayur**. This is quite simply a gem of a community. Most of the houses and other buildings are made of wood or are white stuccoed brick, and date from the Dutch period. On the northern edge of the village are several more guesthouses, some of the most peaceful in the area. Wandering around Bayur it is easy to imagine what villages were like before individualism and licence destroyed the bonds of community. This feels like a place, to paraphrase Jonathan Sacks, built on covenant, not on contract. Continuing further around the lake the road passes through Muko Muko and then onto Lubuk Basung, where the buses terminate. Most buses from Bukittinggi terminate in Lubuk Busung, a few kilometres past Bayur. Tourists who wish to stay in Bayur should inform the driver, and ask to alight at the desired guesthouse.

There are **hiking trails** through the surrounding countryside. Because the lake is some 500 m above sea level, it is cool even during the day and can be chilly at night.

Around Danau Maninjau

From Maninjau village, a worthwhile walk or bicycle ride is around the north edge of the lake to the village of **Muko Muko**, 16 km in all (buses also ply the route). Just before Muko Muko there are the **Alamada Hot springs** (rather small and insignificant), an excellent fish restaurant and a hydropower station. The total distance around the lake is about 50 km – 20 km on a good road; 30 km

Maninjau

To Muko Muko & Padang

Rice Fields

BAYUR

To Puncak Lawang

To Bukittinggi

Woodcarving Shop

Wartel

MANINJAU VILLAGE

Lake Maninjau

Kesuma Mekar Jaya

300 metres
300 yards

N

Sleeping
Abang **1**
Arlen's Paradise **13**
Batu C **2**
Beach Guesthouse **19**
Café 44 Homestay **5**
Febby Homestay **7**
Maranay Beach **10**
Lily's **3**

Pasir Panjang Permai **14**
Riak Danau **15**
Tan Dirih **18**

Eating
Bagoes **1**
Monica's **2**
Nabila/Sambalado **3**
Waterfront Zalino **4**

is a dirt track. Bicycles can be hired from many of the guesthouses and coffee shops (25,000Rp per day).

It is also possible to hike up to, or down from, **Lawang Top** (**Puncak Lawang**), on the crater lip. The trail to the crater edge begins in the middle of Bayur, 3 km north of Maninjau village.

◉ Bukittinggi and around listings

For Sleeping and Eating price codes,
see inside the front cover.

◉ Sleeping

Bukittinggi *p412, map p413*
Most of the travellers' hotels and guesthouses are concentrated along the north end of Jl Jend A Yani. Quieter, smaller and often cleaner homestays are located on the hills either side of Jl Jend A Yani. The downturn in tourism has meant that a lot of hotels have not been well maintained, and so tourists tend to congregate in the same few places.

Board and lodging in return for English conversation lessons is offered in the town of Batu Sangkar, 1 hr from Bukittinggi. Teaching duties are for 3 hrs a day. Contact Mr Edy at **Family International English School** (**FIES**), T0752 71099 or T081 26721599. The length of stay is negotiable.

A The Hills, Jl Laras Datuk Bandaro, T0752 35000, www.thehillsbukittinggi.com. This large hotel has a North African feel, with its arched entrance, fountains and huge atrium. Rooms are a bit of a shock, with bright mint green colour scheme and fairly old furniture. All rooms come with bath, hot water and TV. The deluxe rooms have views of the hills. Pool and full spa service available. No discounts, but a longer stay gets a room upgrade.

B-C Royal Denai Hotel, Jl Dr A Rivai 26, T0752 32920, www.royaldenaihotel.com. Sprawling 3-star hotel crowned with a traditional Minangkabau roof. The rooms are clean, some with pool view. The cheapest rooms are a bit tatty. Discounts available.

B-D Hotel Lima's, Jl Kesehatan 35, T0752 22641, F0752 32570. This place is popular with Indonesian tour groups and has a range of rooms in concrete blocks on a hillside. Superior rooms are carpeted and have hot water, bath, TV and a range of complimentary goodies. The cheaper rooms are fronted by a small garden, and have TV and hot water.

C-E The Gallery, Jl H Agus Salim 25, T0752 23515, F0752 31496. The deluxe rooms are nothing special, and have soft beds and average views. The economy rooms have a lovely sun terrace with marvellous views.

D Hotel Benteng, Jl Benteng 1, T0752 21115, www.bentenghotel.com. Perched on a hilltop next to the fort, the rooms have superb views and sizeable bathrooms with hot water. Discounts available.

D-F Hotel Asia, Jl Kesehatan 38, T0752 625277, F0752 625278. The large reception area is combined with a comfortable Chinese-inspired lobby, and makes for a nice spot for a morning tea. Deluxe rooms are spacious and have balcony with exceptional views over the town and to the mountains beyond. Cheaper rooms have shared bathroom but still have good views, some with access to a roof terrace. Recommended.

E Hotel Kartini, Jl Teuku Umar 6, T0752 22885. Homely hotel offering spotless rooms with TV and hot water. The more expensive rooms downstairs are next to the lobby and can be quite noisy. The rooms upstairs are quiet and very comfortable. Ask for the room at the front with a balcony. Recommended.

E Hotel Singgalang, Jl A Yani 130, T0752 628709. Rooms are clean but have no natural light. All have TV, the slightly more expensive ones have hot-water showers.

E Merdeka Homestay, Jl Dr A Rivai 20, T0752 23937. Large rooms with attached bathroom (cold water) in a villa near a busy intersection. Can be a little noisy.

E Minang International Hotel, Jl Panorama 20A, T075 2 21120. Soeharto stayed here in 1978, and it seems that little has changed since then. With violent green and purple carpets, kitsch furniture and peeling wallpaper, this place might appeal to a niche audience.

E-F Hotel Dahlia, Jl A Yani 106, T0752 627296, osrina@yahoo.com. This well-run hotel has hot -water rooms, but is quite low on atmosphere. The pricier rooms have access to a roof terrace with good views, but the cheaper rooms downstairs are dark. Breakfast is included.

F Hotel Singgalang Indah, Jl A Yani 130, T0752 21576. Cheaper rooms here have no natural light and bathrooms are shared. More expensive rooms have big windows, balcony, hot water and TV but are scruffy.

F-G Orchid Hotel, Jl Teuku Umar 11, T0752 32634. Currently the most popular cheap place in town, and deservedly so. Rooms are clean, the staff are courteous and helpful. Ask for a room on the side away from the mosque, if you don't want to be disturbed by the call to prayer. Recommended.

G Srikandi, Jl A Yani 117, T0752 22984. Cheerless service at this place with tidy but dark rooms, old sheets and cold-water bathroom with squat toilet and *mandi*.

Danau Maninjau *p417, map p418*

There are 2 concentrations of guesthouses, in Maninjau village and Bayur, both on the eastern shore. As these 2 communities are only 3 km apart, in effect the guesthouses and hotels merge into a single strand. As so often with places like Maninjau, the quality of the accommodation changes almost by the month. Because the guesthouses and hotels are close together, it is easy to wander around and check out the competition. Most places stand empty, and haven't been touched up for years. This is especially noticeable in the cheaper places.

D-E Pasir Panjang Permai, T0752 61111. Selection of a/c and non-a/c rooms in 2 concrete blocks. This hotel is geared towards Indonesian tour groups, and gets busy at weekends. More expensive rooms have TV, bath and good views from the balcony. Furniture is a little tatty. Discounts available.

E Tan Dirih, T0752 61461. Tidy, spotless rooms with TV and comfy beds. The large veranda has fine views, and there is free use of tubes here for a day of floating in the lake. You can eat here, but meals need to be ordered well in advance. Recommended.

F Beach Guesthouse, T0752 61082. Collection of cleanish rooms. The best thing is the lounging area next to the lake, perfect for an afternoon nap.

F Febby Homestay, T0752 61586. Prices are high given what's on offer. It's possible to get rooms down to at least half the initial quote. Rooms have grubby walls and squat toilet. Located next to a fish farm.

F-G Maransay Beach, halfway between Maninjau village and Bayur, T0752 61264. Large wooden hotel built out over the water, with a good restaurant and collection of simple rooms. The ones at the front have a decent amount of natural light. Some rooms have an outside bathroom. There is a small beach beside the hotel. Friendly staff.

G Abang, T0752 61073. Sleepy place with basic small rooms (some very dark). There's a good communal seating area over the water.

G Café 44 Homestay, T0752 61238. In a peaceful spot by the shoreline, rooms are in basic wooden chalets with shared bathroom. Rooms have a mattress on the floor and a mosquito net. It is possible to get simple meals.

G Riak Danau, T081 266512419. Average lodgings close to the village and down by the shore.

Bayur

There are fewer places to stay in Bayur than in Maninjau village, although north of the village is a group of 3 very peaceful guesthouses down a series of tracks that run from the road, through ricefields, to the lake, where there is a small beach. These guesthouses are the most peaceful; they are also some distance (3 km) from the main concentration of restaurants and coffee shops. Bemos into and out of Maninjau village stop at 1900, but the walk is beautiful and not far. Try not to arrive here at night, as negotiating the paths through the rice fields in the dark isn't much fun.

F Arlen's Paradise, T081 535204714. Clean bungalows with attached bathroom set in pleasant garden.

G Batu C, next to Lily's. If there is ever an overspill from Lily's, this place might get busy. Simple wooden chalets on the lake.

G Lily's, T081 374901435. This is the most popular guesthouse around the lake, although still very quiet. Rooms are very simple with shared bathroom. The front ones have excellent views. Staff are friendly and cook up some of the best *nasi goreng* with *tempe* in Sumatra. There is a stony swimming area and a small library of books. Recommended.

❼ Eating

Bukittinggi *p412, map p413*
Bukittinggi is renowned for the quality of its food. The upland climate means that temperate as well as tropical vegetables are available. The number of tourist-oriented cafés has decreased significantly over the last few years, but there are more than enough to cater for the small number of visitors. For some reason all serve the same range of dishes: steaks and omelettes, various toasts, milkshakes and salads, the more popular 1-dish Indonesian meals, jaffles, pancakes and so on. Fortunately there are also good local restaurants serving Minang/Padang and Chinese dishes, and many excellent foodstalls selling *sate*, *gulai* soup and other specialities.

¶ Apache Café, Jl A Yani 109, daily 0800-2300. Restaurant with rock-and-roll overtones, occasional live music and standard fare.

¶ Bedual Café, Jl A Yani 95, T0752 31533, daily 0800-2300. Chilled music and walls covered in eclectic art, this eatery has plenty of Indonesian and Western food including a roast chicken dinner for 2, a dream for those

arriving from the hinterlands. Internet is available for 5000Rp an hr. Recommended.

¶ Canyon Café, Jl Teuku Umar 8, T0752 21652, daily 0700-2300. Popular traveller's hang-out with a friendly atmosphere and staff offering good local information. The menu is packed with cheap Western food including a hearty set breakfast.

¶ Family, Jl Benteng 1, daily 0700-2100. Near the fort and with superb views over the town, the menu here offers good Indonesian food, the house special is *ikan baker* (grilled fish).

¶ La Mor Resto, Jl Dr A Rivai 18, T0752 33800, daily 0700-2100. This popular student hang-out has a long menu of Indonesian dishes such as *nasi goreng* and *soto ayam* and good cold juices.

¶ Mona Lisa, Jl A Yani 58, T0752 22644, daily 0900-2130. Over the years, this place has decreased in size but still serves up fair portions of Chinese food. The best thing on the menu here is the create-your-own tropical fruit salad.

¶ Selamat, Jl A Yani 19, T0752 22959, daily 0600-2100. One of the town's better *nasi Padang* places.

¶ Simpang Raya, Jl Minangkabau 77, T0752 21910, daily 0500-2100. With branches all over town, this chain churns out *nasi Padang* to hungry crowds all day. In the evening it is better to arrive earlier: the later it gets the more the selection diminishes.

¶ Turret Café, Jl A Yani 140, daily 0800-2300. Cosy and clean place with some outdoor seating. Internet access, 10,000Rp per hr.

Foodstalls
The best ones are all in and around the market area; *sate*, fruit, Padang dishes, etc.

Danau Maninjau *p417, map p418*
There are several good coffee shops geared to western tastes in Maninjau village, as well as the usual *warungs* and stalls, concentrated in the market area. Many of the guesthouses offer simple meals. **Maransy** and **Lily's** (both ¶) have the most comprehensive menus and

are worth trying. There are lots of roadside stalls serving *otak-otak* (minced fish with spices grilled in a banana leaf).

¶ Bagoes, T0752 61418, daily 0800-2200. Simple menu of Western and Asian food. Run by John who offers good local information. Internet available, 10,000Rp an hr.

¶ Monica Café, T0752 61879, daily 0800-2200. Quiet eatery with occasional movie screenings in the evenings. Pancakes, juices and comfy chairs. Internet available, 20,000Rp an hr.

¶ Nabila, daily 0800-2000. Local place serving fresh grilled lake fish and simple Indonesian standards.

¶ Sambalado, T0752 61020, daily 0700-2000. Big plates of *nasi Padang*.

¶ Waterfront Zalino, T0752 61740, daily 0800-2200. This clean place is a bit of an anomaly for the area, with well-tended lawns, spotless interior and a lovely pavilion over the water, ideal for a bit of romance. There is also a kids' pool, and lots of good local information available. The food is simple Western and Indonesian.

☻ Entertainment

Bukittinggi *p412, map p413*
Minangkabau dances Including *Pencak silat*, a traditional form of self-defence, can be seen performed at **Medan Nan Balindung**, Jl Khatib Suleiman 1, Fri-Wed 2030, 40,000Rp.
Minangkabau traditional arts Music, song, dance and *silat*: **Saayun Salankah**, Jl Lenggogeni 1A, Fri-Sat 2030, 40,000Rp.

▲ Activities and tours

Bukittinggi *p412, map p413*
Buffalo fights
Buffalo fights in the villages around Kota Baru, 10 km to the south of Bukittinggi, have been banned in West Sumatra, due to the gambling that goes on. Ask at your guesthouse.

Rafting
There used to be regular rafting trips down the Batang Anai River and the Sri Antokan rapids, which both flow from Danau Maninjau through the Ngarai Sianok Gorge to **Palupuh**, and along the Ombilin River that flows out of Danau Singkarak. However, due to a lack of numbers these have been suspended. Enquire at the **Orchid Hotel** if you are interested.

Rock climbing
In the late 1990s, Bukittinggi began to gain a reputation for the quality of its rock climbing and its rock climbers. Again, the downturn in tourism, and the fact that the local organizer of climbing trips moved to the USA has meant that trips are no longer offered. For independent climbers, it might be possible to get a guide from the **Canyon Café** or **Orchid Hotel** to show you the places. Climbers will need to bring their own equipment, and bear in mind the danger of attempting such climbs without local knowledge.

Baso is a limestone tower around 10 km due east of Bukittinggi, with a number of challenging routes (Australian grading) including Power Pancake (graded 5.12c), Bee Attack (5.11b), Priest (5.10b), Koorong Bana (5.12d) and Bastard (5.12c). The Harau Canyon (see page 417) offers around 24 routes including the technically demanding Liang Limbek (5.13a).

Swimming
The **Hills'** romantic Romanesque heated pool is open to non-residents, Mon-Fri 25,000Rp, Sat-Sun 30,000Rp, 2000Rp for children. If you have lunch at the hotel they will allow you to swim for free.

Tour operators
Tour companies are concentrated along Jl Jend A Yani. They can reconfirm flights and provide bus tickets, also organize local tours and tours further afield.
Maju Indosari Travel Bureau, Jl Muka Jam Gadang 17, T0752 21671.

Raun Sumatra, Jl A Yani 99, T0752 21133. Professional outfit.
Tigo Balai, Jl A Yani 100, T0752 627235.

Danau Maninjau *p417, map p418*
Tour operators
Kesuma Mekar Jaya, T0752 61300. Offers tours around the region, but they are more expensive than those on offer in Bukittinggi. Door-to-door minibuses can be organized from here, every 2 hrs to Padang, 60,000Rp. Money-changing service and flight ticketing.

O Shopping

Bukittinggi *p412, map p413*
Bukittinggi has a good selection of shops selling handicrafts, curios and antiques, and has a particular reputation for its silver and gold jewellery. The shops are concentrated on Jl Minangkabau (close to the Central Market) and along Jl Jend A Yani and Jl Teuku Umar. The most enjoyable way to shop is in the **Central Market** on Wed or Sat (see page 412). At other times it mainly sells products for local consumption – lots of clothes, fruit and vegetables, plastic trinkets, metal goods, fish, dried and otherwise, and so on.
Antiques and curios There is comparatively little for sale that originates from the area around Bukittinggi; most articles are from Nias and Mentawi, from the Batak areas around Danau Toba, and from further afield, like Kalimantan and Java. The art from Nias and Mentawi is easy to fake and it is likely that much on sale is neither old nor genuine – despite the appearance of authenticity that dust and grime may give. Shops include: **Aladdin**, Jl Jend A Yani 14; **Ganesha**, Jl Teuku Umar 2; **Makmar**, Jl Jend A Yani 10; **Tanjung Raya Art Shop**, Jl Jend A Yani 85.
Handicrafts There are the handicraft villages like Pandai Sikat, as well as a number of shops in town. Many of the antique shops are really jumped-up handicraft outlets. A place with better goods than most is **Sulaman Silungkang** on Jl Panorama.

Jewellery If interested in buying jewellery, it is worth visiting the Kota Gadang silversmithing village (see page 414), which specializes in producing silver filigree.

⊖ Transport

Bukittinggi *p412, map p413*
Air
Given the cheap price of flying in Indonesia, many people fly out of Padang Minangkabau International Airport to Medan or Jakarta rather than facing the Trans-Sumatran Hwy. Flights can be booked at all travel agencies in town, and **Raun Sumatra** and **Tigo Balai** (see Tour operators) have shuttle buses to the airport from Bukittinggi for 35,000Rp.

Bus
Local The station is at Aur Kuning, 3 km southeast of town. Buses to local destinations including **Batusangkar** (8000Rp), **Maninjau** (10,000Rp) and **Payakumbuh** (8000Rp) and **Padang** (15,000Rp) There are also buses to destinations further afield.
Long distance For **Parapat**, choose the bus company carefully as many people have been overcharged; ensure that you have a ticket with seat numbers. Note that the bus may not connect with the last ferry to Samosir (1830), which means a late-night arrival at Parapat and a limited choice of hotels. Also, ensure that your bus is travelling to Parapat, rather than **Pematangsiantar**, as there have been some problems with the roads around Toba recently. Tickets are also available from travel agents and guesthouses. The **Orchid Hotel** (see Sleeping) is a reliable place and has tickets for a/c express bus to Parapat for US$19 (including transfer to bus station).
ANS, T0752 22626, office at bus terminal and **ALS**, T0752 21214, bus terminal, have a/c buses to **Parapat**, 15 hrs, US$24; **Medan**, 20 hrs, US$24; **Jakarta**, 30 hrs, US$38; **Pekanbaru**, 6 hrs, US$6.50; **Bandung**, 36 hrs; US$41.

Taxi
Taxis can be hired, even as far as Medan.
Ask at one of the tour offices (see above).

Danau Maninjau p417, map p418
Air
To reach Padang Minangkabau International
Airport, there is a door-to-door minibus
service offered by **Raun Sumatra** and **Tigo
Balai** (see Tour Operators) in Bukittinggi for
35,000Rp. DAMRI buses meet each arriving
plane and shuttle passengers to **Padang** or
Bukittinggi for 15,000Rp.
   Domestic **Batam**, daily with **Mandala**;
Jakarta, daily with **Lion Air**, **Mandala**,
Sriwijaya and **Garuda**; **Medan**, daily with
Mandala. Tickets can be booked at travel
agencies in Bukittinggi and Padang.
   International **Singapore**, Tue, Thu, Sat,
Tiger Airways (www.tigerairways.com.sg),
this might be revised in the near future as
flights are very empty. **Kuala Lumpur**,
daily with **Air Asia** (www.airasia.com).

Bus
Regular buses from Bukittinggi to **Maninjau**
village, negotiating 44 bends down from the
crater lip to the lake, 1½ hrs, 10,000Rp. Buses
also continue on through Bayur to **Muko
Muko** on the northwest side of the lake.
Those wishing to get back to Bukittinggi
need to wait at the road near the entrance to
their hotel and flag down a bus from Lubuk
Basung to Bukittinggi via Maninjau village.
The last bus to Bukittinggi leaves around
1700. From Padang catch a bus to Bukittinggi
and ask to be let off at Kuto Tuo, the turn-off
for Maninjau, and wait there to catch a bus
down to the lake. There is a daily bus to
Pekanbaru, 7 hrs, 60,000Rp.

Oplets
Some oplets from Bukittinggi continue
anti-clockwise around the lake through Bayur
and Muko Muko to Lubuk Basung (3000Rp),
the end of the road, so to speak.

❶ Directory

Bukittinggi p412, map p413
Banks Banks close at 1100 on Sat. Many of
the tour and travel companies will change
money. **Bank Negara Indonesia**, Jl Jend A
Yani, run an efficient service and will change
most TCs. **Bank Rakyat Indonesia**, Jl Jend
A Yani 3 (near the clock tower). **PT Enzet
Corindo Perkasa**, Jl Minangkabau 51 (money
changer). **Internet** Harau Cliff Café has
3 internet terminals. **Medical services**
Dokter Achmad Mochtar Hospital, Jl Rivai
(opposite the Denai Hotel). **Post office**
Jl Kemerdekaan, on the south edge of town,
slow internet access; the 2 bookshops on
Jl Jend A Yani in the centre of town sell
stamps and have post boxes; **Branch Post
Office**, Clock Tower Square. **Telephone**
Wartel office, Jl Jend A Yani, for international
calls and faxes.

Danau Maninjau p417, map p418
Banks Bank Rakyat Indonesia, Jl SMP (a
short distance north of the bus stop in the
centre of town), will change US$, TCs and
cash. **Medical services** Clinic at the
southern end of Maninjau village. **Post
office** Jl Muara Pisang (facing the police
station and not far from the oplet stop).
Telephone Jl SMP (facing the oplet
stop in the centre of town), international
calls can be made from the office.

Background

Prehistory

After Thailand and East Malaysia, Indonesia – and particularly Java – has probably revealed more of Southeast Asia's prehistory than any other country in the region. Most significant was the discovery of **hominid fossils** in Central Java in 1890, when Eugene Dubois uncovered the bones of so-called 'Java Man' near the village of Trinil. He named his ape-man *Pithecanthropus erectus*, since changed to *Homo erectus erectus*. These, and other discoveries – particularly at Sangiran, also in Central Java and Mojokerto – indicate that Indonesia was inhabited by hominids as long as 1,800,000 years ago. Excavations in Central Java have also revealed other fossils of early Man – *Pithecanthropus soloensis* and *P modjokertensis*. Among the skulls of *P soloensis*, a number have been found to have had their cranial bases removed, leading scientists to postulate that the species practised anthropophagy – less politely known as cannibalism – which involved gouging the victim's brains out through the base. Alternatively, the surgery might have been part of a post mortem ritual.

Following the end of the last Ice Age 15,000 years ago, there began a movement of Mongoloid peoples from the Asian mainland, south and east, and into the Southeast Asian archipelago. As this occurred, the immigrants displaced the existing Austro-melanesian inhabitants, pushing them further east or into remote mountain areas.

The practice of **settled agriculture** seems to have filtered into the islands of Indonesia from mainland Southeast Asia about 2500 BC, along with these Mongoloid migrants. Settled life is associated with the production of primitive earthenware pottery, examples of which have been found in Java, Sulawesi and Flores. Later, **ancestor cults** evolved, echoes of which are to be seen in the megaliths of Sumatra, Java, Sulawesi, Bali, Sumbawa and Sumba. These cultures reached their height about 500 BC. Among the various discoveries has been evidence of the mutilation of corpses – presumably to prevent the deceased from returning to the world of the living. In some cases, ritual elements of these megalithic cultures still exist – for example, on the island of Sumba in Nusa Tenggara, among the inhabitants of Nias Island off West Sumatra, and among the Batak of North Sumatra.

The technology of **bronze casting** was also known to prehistoric Indonesians. Socketed axes have been discovered in Java, several islands of Nusa Tenggara (eg Roti) and in Sulawesi. But the finest bronze artefacts are the magnificent kettledrums of East Indonesia. It is thought these were made in Vietnam, not in Indonesia, and arrived in the archipelago when traders used them as barter goods. Later, locally made equivalents such as the *moko* of Alor were produced, but they never achieved the refinement of the originals.

Pre-colonial history

Unlike the states of mainland Southeast Asia, which did enjoy a certain geographical legitimacy prior to the colonial period, Indonesia was a fragmented assemblage of kingdoms, sultanates, principalities and villages. It is true that there was a far greater degree of communication and intercourse than many assume, so that no part of the archipelago can be treated in isolation, but nonetheless, it is still difficult to talk of 'Indonesian' history prior to the 19th century.

The great empires of the pre-colonial period did range beyond their centres of power, but none came close to controlling all the area now encompassed by the modern Indonesian state. Among these empires, the most powerful were the Srivijayan Kingdom based at Palembang in South Sumatra; and the great Javanese Dynasties of Sailendra, Majapahit and Mataram. There was also a string of less powerful, but nonetheless influential, kingdoms; for example, the Sultanate of Aceh in North Sumatra, the Gowa Kingdom of South Sulawesi, the trading sultanates of the Spice Islands of Maluku, and the Hindu kingdoms of Bali. The history of each of these powers is dealt with in the appropriate regional introduction.

Even after the European powers arrived in the archipelago, their influence was often superficial. They were concerned only with controlling the valuable spice trade, and were not inclined to feats of territorial expansion. To get around this lack of a common history, historians tend to talk instead in terms of common processes of change. The main ones affecting the archipelago were the 'Indianization' of the region from the 1st century AD and the introduction of Hinduism and Buddhism; the arrival of Islam in North Sumatra in the 13th century and then its spread east and south during the 15th century; and the contrast between inwardly-focused agricultural kingdoms and outwardly orientated trading states.

Colonial history

During the course of the 15th century, the two great European maritime powers of the time, Spain and Portugal, were exploring sea routes to the east. Two forces were driving this search: the desire for profits, and the drive to evangelize. At the time, even the wealthy in Europe had to exist on pickled and salted fish and meat during the winter months (fodder crops for winter feed were not grown until the 18th century). Spices to flavour what would otherwise be a very monotonous diet were greatly sought after and commanded a high price. This was not just a passing European fad. An Indian Hindu wrote that: "When the palate revolts against the insipidness of rice boiled with no other ingredients, we dream of fat, salt and spices".

Of the spices, cloves and nutmeg originated from just one location, the Moluccas (Maluku) – the Spice Islands of eastern Indonesia. Perhaps because of their value, spices and their places of origin were accorded mythical status in Europe. The 14th century French friar Catalani Jordanus claimed, for example, that the clove flowers of Java produced an odour so strong it killed "every man who cometh among them, unless he shut his mouth and nostrils".

It was in order to break the monopoly on the spice trade held by Venetian and Muslim Arab traders that the Portuguese began to extend their possessions eastwards. This finally culminated in the capture of the port of Melaka by the Portuguese seafarer Alfonso de Albuquerque in June 1511. The additional desire to spread the Word of God is clear in the speech that Albuquerque made before the battle with the Muslim sultan of Melaka, when he exhorted his men, stressing: "... the great service which we shall perform to our Lord in casting the Moors out of this country and of quenching the fire of the sect of Mohammet so that it may never burst out again hereafter".

From their base in Melaka, the Portuguese established trading relations with the Moluccas, and built a series of forts across the region: at Bantam (Banten), Flores, Ternate, Tidore, Timor and Ambon (Amboyna).

Many accounts of Indonesian history treat the arrival of the Portuguese Admiral Alfonso de Albuquerque off Malacca (Meleka) in 1511, and the dispatch of a small fleet to the Spice Islands, as a watershed in Indonesian history. As the historian MC Ricklefs argues, this view is untenable, writing that "... in the early years of the Europeans' presence, their influence was sharply limited in both area and depth".

The Portuguese only made a significant impact in the Spice Islands, leaving their mark in a number of Indonesian words of Portuguese origin – for example, *sabun* (soap), *meja* (table) and *Minggu* (Sun). They also introduced Christianity to East Indonesia and disrupted the islands' prime export – spices. But it was the Dutch, in the guise of the **Vereenigde Oost-Indische Compagnie** or **VOC** (the Dutch East India Company), who began the process of western intrusion. They established a toehold in Java – which the Portuguese had never done – a precursor to later territorial expansion. But this was a slow process and it was not until the early 20th century – barely a generation before the Japanese occupation – that the Dutch could legitimately claim they held administrative authority over the whole country.

The idea of Indonesia, 1900-1942

The beginning of the 20th century marks a turning point in Indonesian history. As Raden Kartini, a young educated Javanese woman, wrote in a letter dated 12 January 1900: "Oh, it is splendid just to live in this age; the transition of the old into the new!". It was in 1899 that the Dutch lawyer C Th van Deventer published a ground-breaking paper entitled *Een eereschuld* or 'A debt of honour'. This article argued that having exploited the East Indies for so long, and having extracted so much wealth from the colony, it was time for the Dutch government to restructure their policies and focus instead on improving conditions for Indonesians. In 1901, the Ethical Policy – as it became known – was officially embraced. Van Deventer was commissioned to propose ways to further such a policy and suggested a formulation of 'education, irrigation and emigration'. The Ethical Policy represented a remarkable change in perspective, but scholars point out that it was very much a creation of the European mind and made little sense in Indonesian terms.

The Indonesian economy was also changing in character. The diffusion of the cash economy through the islands and the growing importance of export crops like rubber and coffee, and minerals such as tin and oil, were transforming the country. Christianity, too, became a powerful force for change, particularly in the islands beyond Muslim Java. There was large-scale conversion in central and North Sulawesi, Flores, among the Batak of Sumatra, in Kalimantan, and Timor. In response to the inroads that Christianity was making in the Outer Islands, Islam in Java became more orthodox and reformist. The 'corrupt' *abangan*, who adhered to what has become known as the 'Javanese religion' – a mixture of Muslim, Hindu, Buddhist and animist beliefs – were gradually displaced by the stricter *santris*.

At about the same time, there was an influx of *trekkers*, or Dutch expatriates, who came to the East Indies with their wives and Dutch cultural perspectives, with the intention of going 'home' after completing their contracts. They overwhelmed the older group of *blijvers* or 'stayers', and there emerged a more racist European culture, one that denigrated *Indische* culture and extolled the life-style of the Dutch. The Chinese community, like the Dutch, was also divided into two groups: the older immigrants or *peranakan* who had assimilated into Indies culture, and the more recent *totok* arrivals who zealously maintained their culture, clinging to their Chinese roots.

So, the opening years of the 20th century presented a series of paradoxes. On the one hand, Dutch policy was more sensitive to the needs of the 'natives'; yet many Dutch were becoming less understanding of Indonesian culture and more bigoted. At the same time, while the Chinese and Dutch communities were drawing apart from the native Indonesians and into distinct communities based upon Chinese and European cultural norms, so the economy was becoming increasingly integrated and international. Perhaps inevitably, tensions arose, and these began to mould the social and political landscape of confrontation between the colonialists and the natives.

A number of political parties and pressure groups emerged from this maelstrom of forces. In 1912, a Eurasian – one of those who found himself ostracized from European-colonial culture – EFE Douwes Dekker founded the Indies Party. This was a revolutionary grouping with the slogan 'the Indies for those who make their home there'. In the same year, a batik merchant from Surakarta established the Sarekat Islam or 'Islamic Union', which quickly became a mass organization under the leadership of the charismatic orator HOS Cokroaminoto. Seven years later it had over 2,000,000 members. In 1914, a small group of *totok* Dutch immigrants founded the Indies Social-Democratic Association in Semarang. Finally, in 1920, the Perserikatan Komunis di India (PKI) or the Indies Communist Party was established.

In 1919, the Dutch colonial authorities decided to clamp down on all dissent. The flexibility that had characterized Dutch policy until then was abandoned in favour of an increasingly tough approach. But despite the rounding-up of large numbers of subversives, and the demise of the PKI and emasculation of the Sarekat Islam, it was at this time that the notion of 'Indonesia' first emerged. In July 1927, Sukarno founded the Partai Nasional Indonesia or PNI. In October 1928, a Congress of Indonesian Youth coined the phrase 'one nation – Indonesia, one people – Indonesian, one language – Indonesian'. At the same congress the Indonesian flag was designed and the Indonesian national anthem sung for the first time – *Indonesia Raya*. As John Smail writes in the book *In Search of Southeast Asia*:

"The idea of Indonesia spread so easily, once launched, that it seemed to later historians as if it had always existed, if not actually explicitly then inchoate in the hearts of the people. But it was, in fact, a new creation, the product of a great and difficult leap of the imagination. The idea of Indonesia required the denial of the political meaning of the societies into which the first Indonesians had been born".

In spite of Dutch attempts to stifle the nationalist spirit, it spread through Indonesian, and particularly Javanese, society. By 1942, when the Japanese occupied the country, the idea of Indonesia as an independent nation was firmly rooted.

The Japanese occupation, 1942-1945

Although the Japanese occupation lasted less than four years, it fundamentally altered the forces driving the country towards independence. Prior to 1942, the Dutch faced no real challenge to their authority; after 1945, it was only a question of time before independence. The stunning victory of the Japanese in the Dutch East Indies destroyed the image of colonial invincibility, undermined the prestige of the Dutch among many Indonesians, and – when the Dutch returned to power after 1945 – created an entirely new psychological relationship between rulers and ruled.

But the Japanese were not liberators. Their intention of creating a Greater East Asia Co-Prosperity Sphere did not include offering Indonesians independence. They wished to control Indonesia for their own interests. The Japanese did give a certain latitude to nationalist politicians in Java, but only as a means of mobilizing Indonesian support for their war effort. Sukarno and Muhammad Hatta were flown to Tokyo in November 1943 and decorated by Emperor Hirohito. For the Dutch and their allies, the war meant incarceration. There were 170,000 internees, including 60,000 women and children. About a quarter died in captivity.

One particularly sordid side of the occupation which has come to light in recent years is the role of 'comfort women'. This euphemism should be more accurately translated as 'sex slaves' – women who were forced to satisfy the needs of Japanese soldiers to aid the war effort. For years the Japanese government denied such comfort stations existed, but documents unearthed in Japan have indicated beyond doubt that they were very much part of the war infrastructure. Much of the attention has focused upon comfort women from Korea, China and the Philippines, but there were also stations in Indonesia. These women, so long cowed and humiliated into silence, are now talking about their experiences to force the Japanese government to accept responsibility. Dutch-Australian Jan Ruff is one of these brave women. A young girl living in Java before the war, she was interned in Camp Ambarawa with her mother and two sisters. In February 1944 she was taken, along with nine other girls, to a brothel in Semarang for the sexual pleasure of Japanese officers. In her testimony at a public meeting in Tokyo in December 1992 she recounted: "During that time [at the brothel] the Japanese had abused me and humiliated me. They had ruined my young life. They had stripped me of everything, my self-esteem, my dignity, my freedom, my possessions, my family." Belatedly, the Japanese government offered its 'sincere apologies and remorse' in August 1993, 48 years afterwards. The fact that the apology came on the last day of the Liberal Democratic Party's government detracted from the honesty of the remarks. Many still feel that Japanese leaders find it difficult to be sincere about events almost half a century old.

As the Japanese military lost ground in the Pacific to the advancing Americans, so their rule over Indonesia became increasingly harsh. Peasants were forcibly recruited as 'economic soldiers' to help the war effort – about 75,000 died – and the Japanese were even firmer in their suppression of dissent than the Dutch had been before them. But as the military situation deteriorated, the Japanese gradually came to realize the necessity of allowing nationalist sentiments greater rein. On 7 September 1944, Prime Minister Koiso promised independence, and in March 1945 the creation of an Investigating Committee for Preparatory Work for Indonesian Independence was announced. Among its members were Sukarno, Hatta and Muhammad Yamin. On 1 June, Sukarno mapped out his philosophy of Pancasila or Five Principles which were to become central tenets of independent Indonesia. On 15 August, after the second atomic bomb was dropped on Nagasaki, the Japanese unconditionally surrendered. Sukarno, Hatta and the other independence leaders now had to act quickly before the Allies helped the Dutch re-establish control. On 17 August 1945, Sukarno read out the Declaration of Independence, Indonesia's red and white flag was raised and a small group of onlookers sang the national anthem, Indonesia Raya.

Revolutionary struggle, 1945-1950

In September 1945, the first units of the British Army landed at Jakarta to re-impose Dutch rule. They arrived to find an Indonesian administration already in operation. Confrontation was inevitable. Young Indonesians responded by joining the revolutionary struggle, which became known as the Pemuda Movement (*pemuda* means youth). This reached its height between 1945 and mid-1946, and brought together young men and women of all classes, binding them together in a common cause. The older nationalists found themselves marginalized in this increasingly violent and fanatical response. Men like Sukarno and Hatta adopted a policy of *diplomasi* – negotiating with the Dutch. The supporters of the Pemuda Movement embraced *perjuangan* – the armed struggle. Not only the Dutch, but also minorities like the Chinese, Eurasians and Ambonese, suffered from atrocities at the hands of the Pemuda supporters. The climax of the Pemuda Movement came in November 1945 with the battle for Surabaya.

In 1947, the Dutch were militarily strong enough to regain control of Java, and East and South Sumatra. At the end of 1948, a second thrust of this 'Police Action' re-established control over much of the rest of the country. Ironically, these military successes played an important role in the final 'defeat' of the Dutch in Indonesia. They turned the United Nations against Holland, forcing the Dutch government to give way over negotiations. On 2 November the Hague Agreement was signed, paving the way for full political independence of all former territories of the Dutch East Indies (with the exception of West Irian) on 27 December 1949.

From independence to Guided Democracy to coup: 1950-1965

In 1950, Indonesia was an economic shambles and in political chaos. Initially, there was an attempt to create a political system based on the western European model of parliamentary democracy. By 1952 the futility of expecting a relatively painless progression to this democratic ideal was becoming obvious, despite the holding of a parliamentary general election in 1955 with a voter turnout of over 90%. Conflicts between Communists, radical Muslims, traditional Muslims, regional groups and minorities led to a series of coups, rebel governments and violent confrontations. Indonesia was unravelling and in the middle of 1959, President Sukarno cancelled the provisional constitution and introduced his period of Guided Democracy.

This period of relative political stability rested on an alliance between the army, the Communist PKI, and Sukarno himself. It was characterized by extreme economic nationalism, with assets controlled by Dutch, British and Indian companies and individuals being expropriated. The **Konfrontasi** with the Dutch over the 'recovery' of West Irian from 1960 to 1962, and with Malaysia over Borneo beginning in 1963, forced Sukarno to rely on Soviet arms shipments, and Indonesia moved increasingly into the Soviet sphere of influence. Cracks between the odd alliance of PKI and the army widened, and even Sukarno's popular support and force of character could not stop the dam from bursting. On 1 October 1965, six senior generals were assassinated by a group of middle-ranking officers, thus ending the period of Guided Democracy. MC Ricklefs writes: "... on that night the balance of hostile forces which underlay guided democracy came to an end. Many observers have seen tragedy in the period, especially in the tragedy of Sukarno, the man who outlived his time and used his popular support to maintain a regime of extravagant corruption and hypocrisy."

The coup was defeated by the quick-thinking of General Suharto whose forces overcame those of the coup's leaders. However, it undermined both Sukarno and the PKI as both were linked with the plot – the former by allowing the PKI to gain such influence, and the latter by allegedly master-minding the coup. Most Indonesians, although not all western academics, see the coup as a Communist plot hatched by the PKI with the support of Mao Zedong and the People's Republic of China. It led to massacres on a huge scale as bands of youths set about exterminating those who were thought to be PKI supporters. This was supported, implicitly, by the army and there were news reports of 'streams choked with bodies'. The reaction was most extreme in Java and Bali, but there were murders across the archipelago. The number killed is not certain; estimates vary from 100,000 to 1,000,000 and the true figure probably lies somewhere between the two (500,000 is widely quoted). In Bali alone some scholars believe that 80,000 people died – around 5% of the population. The difficulty is that the body count kept by the military is widely regarded as a gross under-estimate. Oei Tjoe Tat, a cabinet minister under Sukarno, was sent on a fact-finding mission to discover the scale of the massacres. He calculated that by January 1966 500,000 people had died. The military's figure at that time was 80,000. As it was an anti-Communist purge, and as China had been blamed for fermenting the coup, many of those killed were Chinese who were felt, by their mere ethnicity, to have leftist-inclinations and Communist sympathies. Few doubt that the majority were innocent traders and middlemen, whose economic success and ethnic origin made them scapegoats. Islamic clerics and members of youth groups seem to have been particularly instrumental in singling out people for extermination. While these uncontrolled massacres were occurring, power was transferred to General Suharto (although he was not elected president until 1968). This marked the shift from what has become known as the Old Order, to the New Order.

That the events of 1965 remain contentious is reflected in the government's attempts to re-write, and in places to erase, this small slice of history. In 1995, three decades after the events of 1965-1966, the authorities banned Oei Tjoe Tat's autobiography *Oei Tjoe Tat: assistant to President Sukarno*. It seems that the account of the anti-communist purge diverged too much from the official history. The fact that banned novelist and former political prisoner Pramoedya Ananta Toer had a hand in the book also cannot have endeared it to the authorities. By the time it was banned, however, around 15,000 copies had already been sold. Documents relating to the 1965-1996 upheaval are restricted, and instead the government produces its own sanitized version of events. This has it that the Communists were behind the attempted coup, that President Sukarno was misguided in allowing the Communists to gain so much power, and that only the quick-thinking and courageous military, with Suharto at the fore, thwarted the attempt and saved Indonesia from turmoil.

Political and economic developments under the New Order, 1965 to present

When Suharto took power in 1965 he had to deal with an economy in disarray. There was hyper-inflation, virtually no inward investment and declining productivity. To put the economy back on the rails, he turned to a group of US-trained economists who became known as the Berkeley Mafia. They recommended economic reform, the return of expropriated assets, and a more welcoming political and economic climate for foreign investment. In terms of international relations, Suharto abandoned the policy of support for China and the Soviet Union and moved towards the western fold. Diplomatic relations with China were severed (and only renewed in 1990), and the policy of confrontation against Malaysia brought to an end.

The 33 years from 1965 through to 1998 was one of political stability. Suharto stayed in power for over three decades, and he presided over a political system which in a number of respects had more in common with the Dutch era than with that of former President Sukarno. Suharto eschewed ideology as a motivating force, kept a tight control of administration, and attempted to justify his leadership by offering his people economic well-being. He was known – until the 1997-1998 economic crisis – as the 'Father of Development'.

Modern Indonesia

The last few years have seen a transformation in Indonesia's economic and political landscape. No commentator was sufficiently prescient to foresee these changes, and no one knows where, ultimately, they will lead. For the first time since the attempted coup of 1965, Indonesia is entering truly uncharted territory. The chronically pessimistic see Indonesia fragmenting and the economy continuing to bump along the bottom as political instability prevents investor confidence returning. Optimists see stability returning in a brighter post-East Timor/post Suharto era, and economic and investor confidence with it. With Aceh seemingly on the road to quasi or full independence, Irian Jaya clamouring for more autonomy, and resource-rich provinces like Riau and East Kalimantan demanding a larger slice of the pie, the central government in Jakarta is finding it almost impossible to keep people happy.

From 1965 through to 1998, Indonesia was under the control of a military-bureaucratic elite led by President Suharto. Power was exercised through Sekber Golkar, better known as just Golkar, the state's very own political party. In political terms at least, Indonesia was one of the world's most stable countries. It might not have been rich or powerful, but at least there was continuity of leadership. But in 1998 all that changed. Suharto was forced to resign after bitter riots in Jakarta brought on by the collapse of the Indonesian economy, but fuelled by decades of nepotism and corruption. What began as student protests escalated into communal violence and some 1200 people were killed. The critical Chinese community – central to the operation of the economy – fled the country (for the interim at least) and an already dire economic situation became catastrophic. Suharto's vice president, BJ Habibie, took over the helm, but with scarcely a great deal of enthusiasm from the general populace or from the military. Elections were held on 7 June 1999, the first free elections for 44 years, and they were contested by scores of parties. Megawati Sukarnoputri, former president Sukarno's daughter, won the largest share of the vote through her party PDI-Perjuangan (PDI-Struggle). Even with PDI-P's victory, however, some feared that BJ Habibie would call on the political muscle of Golkar to secure him victory in the presidential elections. But the tragedy of East Timor put paid to that and he had to face the humiliation, in October 1999, of a vote of censure and no confidence in the newly muscular and independent People's Consultative Assembly (Indonesia's parliament).

Politics in the post-Suharto era

On 7 June 1999, Indonesians enjoyed their first truly democratic elections since 1955. Despite dire predictions to the contrary, they were largely peaceful. About 112 million votes were cast – 90% of eligible voters – at 250,000 polling stations around the country. A total of 48 parties contested the poll, 45 of them new, and Megawati Sukarnoputri's Democratic Party of Struggle (PDI-P) won the largest share of the vote, attracting 34% of the total. In second place came Golkar with 22%. This was a surprise to some foreign observers, given the bad press Golkar had received, but reflected the party's links with the bureaucracy and a strong showing in the Outer Islands where 'reformasi' had less of an impact. The three other parties to attract significant numbers of votes were the National Awakening Party (12%), the National Mandate Party (7%) and the United Development Party (10%).

Indonesia's first taste of democracy since 1955 has led to profound changes in the character of both politics and politicians. In the past, MPs had no constituency as such and so were rarely bothered about the need to represent real people. They merely had to make sure they pleased the party bosses. Members of the new parliament, however, not only have responsibilities to their electorates, but are also likely to be much more outspoken. Because presidents will now have term limits (Suharto was in power for 32 years), this will confer greater power on parliament. As Dan Murphy said in mid-1999 and before the presidential elections, "the next president…will confront populist and legislative challenges like no one has faced since Megawati's father and Indonesia's first president, Sukarno, dispensed with democracy 40 years ago" (FEER, 19.8.99).

Under former President Suharto, **Golkar** was, in effect, the state's own party. All state employees were automatically members of Golkar, and during election campaigns the state controlled the activities of other parties. Not surprisingly, therefore, Golkar was able consistently to win over 60% of the votes cast in parliamentary elections, and controlled the Parliament (DPR) and the People's Consultative Assembly. Even before Suharto's resignation in 1998, there was the enduring sense that the tide of history was running against Golkar. The provinces where Golkar did least well were in the country's heartland – like Jakarta and East Java. It was here, in Java, that Indonesia's middle classes and 'new rich' were beginning to clamour for more of a say in how the country was run, and by whom. With Golkar's loss of the elections of 1999 to the PDI-P, the party has come to accept a new and less central role in the country. In the past all bureaucrats were automatically members of Golkar and were expected to support and represent Golkar. This is no longer the case.

But despite the fact that the PDI-P won the 1999 parliamentary elections, there were commentators who did not think that Megawati, the party's leader, would become president. Prior to the East Timor debacle, some feared that BJ Habibie would ally himself with one or two other parties and use Golkar to gain the presidency against the run of votes. That assumption was shattered when it became clear that the people of East Timor would vote for independence. But Habibie's mistake was not that he failed to control the army and the militias, but that he was foolish enough to offer the East Timorese a referendum on independence in the first place.

In October 1999 the People's Consultative Assembly voted for **Indonesia's new president** – and it was a cliffhanger. Indonesians could watch – another first for the country – democracy in progress as their representatives lodged their preferences. It was a close contest between Megawati Sukarnoputri, the people's favourite, and the respected **Abdurrahman Wahid**, an almost blind cleric and leader of the country's largest Muslim association, the Nahdlatul Ulama (NU), and a master of the politics of appeasement; a quality which in the President of such a diverse nation can stymie progress and blunt his effectiveness. As it turned out, Wahid won by 373 votes to 313 as he garnered the support of Golkar members and many of those linked to Muslim parties. Initially, Megawati's vociferous and easily agitated supporters rioted when they realized that their leader had been, as they saw it, robbed of her democratic entitlement. Wisely, Wahid asked Megawati to be his vice-president and she asked her supporters to calm down and return home. The election of Wahid and Megawati was, arguably, the best combination that could have been hoped for in the circumstances. It allied a moderate with a populist, and it kept army commander-in-chief General Wiranto out of the two leadership spots (although he was asked to join the cabinet). Wahid's cabinet, announced a few days after the election, showed a desire to calm tensions and promote pragmatic leadership. Significantly, he included two Chinese in his cabinet (one, the critical finance minister), as well as one politician from Aceh and another from West Papua – the two provinces with the greatest secessionist inclinations. On his election to the presidency, four critical questions faced Indonesia's new president. First, how to mend the economy; second, how to keep the country from disintegrating; third, how to promote reconciliation between the different racial and religious groups; and fourth, how to invent a role for the army appropriate for a democratic country entering the 21st century.

Indonesia has changed in other ways – although these changes could be reversed should the move towards democratization begin to falter. For a start, the judiciary and the press are increasingly independent. During the last few years of the Suharto era, hesitant steps towards greater press freedom were often followed by a crackdown on publications deemed to have crossed some ill-defined line in the sand. The independence of the judiciary was, if anything, an even more vexed issue. Political opponents of Suharto and his cronies could not expect a fair trial, and foreign businessmen found using the courts to extract payments from errant Indonesian businessmen and companies a waste of time. In 1997 a clerk at the Supreme Court was heard explaining to a litigant how Indonesia's legal system worked: "If you give us 50 million rupiah but your opponent gives us more, then the case will be won by your opponent" (quoted in *The Economist*, 2000). This approach to legal contests may have the advantage of simplicity, but it hardly instilled a great deal of confidence that a case would be judged on its merits.

In the six months following Suharto's resignation nearly 200 new publications were registered. The government under Habibie was rather more thick-skinned than its predecessor, and in June 1998 a law permitting the Information Ministry to ban any publication for criticizing the government was scrapped. This move towards greater press freedom in the post-Suharto era has meant a much more active, campaigning and, occasionally, sensationalist press – something that President Wahid has sometimes found rather harder to stomach than did Habibie.

The army in Indonesian politics

It has always been recognized that a critical ingredient – indeed a central element – in Indonesian political life is the army. For many years the army has been viewed as the only group in the country (beyond Golkar) with the necessary cohesion and unity of purpose to influence political events at a broad level. This wider role was enshrined in the constitutional principle of *dwifungsi*, or dual function, which gave the army the right to engage in politics and administration, as well as defend the nation from external aggressors and internal insurrection. (This was amply illustrated in the army response to events in East Timor.) According to political scientist Harold Crouch, around two-thirds of army personnel were, under this system, assigned to territorial rather than combat duties. As such they engaged in such things as "overseeing the activities of political parties and non-governmental organizations, intervening in land disputes, [and] dealing with striking workers or demonstrating students...". In the countryside the army was seen as a stabilizing force and the guarantor of ethnic and religious peace. The army has traditionally regarded itself as the protector of the nation, and more particularly the protector of ordinary Indonesians against potentially venal civilian politicians and their business associates. The key role that the military played in Indonesia's independence movement – after the civilian revolutionary government had capitulated to the returning Dutch after the end of the Second World War – gave it further credibility to speak not just for itself, but also for the country as a whole.

Like so much in Indonesia, these assumptions must be re-examined in the light of Suharto's fall from power, the army's response to the riots of 1998, its role in East Timor, and the democratic elections of 1999. In 1999 the army changed its name from Abri to TNI. This, though, does not detract from the fact that the army has lost credibility, particularly as a result of the way it has dealt with, some would say fermented, sectarian and secessionist conflicts from Jakarta to Aceh, East Timor and Maluku. Moreover, it has become clear that a new generation of officers is in charge. These men, importantly, cannot call on their revolutionary credentials to justify and legitimate their positions and their actions. Moreover, the great unifying message of the 1970s and 1980s – the need to fight communism – no longer carries much influence. (That said, the code ET is still attached to some people's ID cards, designating that they are former political prisoners, and in mid-1999 the Indonesian parliament debated a bill that would have banned the teaching of Marxist-Leninism outside universities.) However, while the army may have a smaller role to play in political and civilian affairs, the police are hardly ready to fill the void created by the retreating army. With just 200,000 poorly trained and paid officers, the police are barely able to keep the peace and in many cases stand idly by while civilian vigilantes mete out justice.

Disintegration?
It has long been said that Indonesia is one of the world's most unlikely countries, a patchwork of cultures and languages pieced together by little more than the industriousness of the Dutch. In early 1999 President BJ Habibie, as a sop to the international community, surprisingly offered the people of **East Timor** a referendum on independence. The UN was called in to supervise the vote on 30 August but, against UN advice and pleading, he refused even a small international peacekeeping force. The vote itself proceeded smoothly and with little intimidation. On 4 September the results of the vote were announced: 78.5% of a turnout of well over 90% chose independence. It seems, and this might seem incredible to anyone who has followed the East Timor story, that the Indonesian military were expecting to 'win' the vote and were piqued that the population were so patently ungrateful for all their hard work. So, with the announcement of the results, mayhem broke out. Militias, formed, encouraged, armed and orchestrated by the Indonesian military, murdered, raped and terrorized the population of the tiny province. Tens of thousands fled to the hills and into neighbouring West Timor. (On 13 September one UN official suggested that just 200,000 out of East Timor's 800,000 population were still living in their homes.) Dili was virtually razed to the ground. The UN compound was besieged. Only the most intense international pressure, and vociferously negative international press coverage, forced Habibie to allow the UN to authorize an Australian-led force to enter the province.

The reluctance of the military to allow East Timor's independence can be linked to two key factors. First, between the annexation of East Timor in 1975 and the referendum of 1999, the army lost perhaps as many as 20,000 men trying to quell the independence movement there. To give up was to admit that it was all a waste of time and blood. And second, and much more importantly, there was the fear that East Timor's independence might herald the break-up of Indonesia. Aceh and Irian Jaya were the most obvious provinces that could break away. Legally speaking, there is a clear difference between East Timor and anywhere else in Indonesia. East Timor's annexation by Indonesia was never recognized by the UN. (UN maps always indicated the territory as a separate country.) But the fear was that this nuance would be lost on people with desires for independence.

The 7500-strong Australian-led UN force landed in Dili in late September 1999 and control of the territory passed from the Indonesians to the UN. Alongside the Aussie troops, there were British Gurkhas, New Zealanders, and even contingents from the region, including Thai and Malaysian troops. (Asean came out of the crisis poorly, yet again showing an inability to act in a timely and forceful manner.) Even as UNIFET (the UN International Force for East Timor) strengthened its hold on Dili, the withdrawal of Indonesian troops destroyed the town they had called their own for nearly 25 years. As one soldier told *The Economist*: "We built this place up. Now we've torn it all down again" (02.10.99). During October, UNIFET extended its control east and west from Dili as far as the border with West Timor where the militias were holed up. Rumours of a militia build-up and possible major incursion did not materialize, although there were some firefights between UNIFET and militia gangs. At the end of October Xanana Gusmao, jailed for 20 years by Indonesia and the most likely person to become East Timor's first president, returned home. Before leaving Australia he said: "We will start from zero to reconstruct not only our country, but ourselves as human beings" (*The Economist*, 16.10.99).

A complication – and another reason why the Indonesian army were so reluctant to give up their hold on this dry and poverty-stricken land – was the decision taken by the UN on 27 September 1999 to investigate human rights abuses in the province. And they were right to be worried. When the UN and Indonesian reports were published at the beginning of 2000, six generals were mentioned by name, including General Wiranto (see below).

It was not just East Timor and Aceh that were wracked by violence. Indeed, the spread of unrest to other areas of the country seemed to bear out the army's fears: that taking the lid off more than three decades of top-down control would lead to an upsurge of violence right across the country. Conspiracy theories abounded as to which interested party was seeding this violence. Some believed that much of the unrest was being orchestrated by the military – anxious to prove that without their control the country would disintegrate. Influential individuals from the Suharto era might have been trying to destabilize the country in order to regain power. As criminologist Yohanes Sutoyo explained to Dini Djalal of the *Far Eastern Economic Review*: "The New Order [of former President Suharto] taught us that the only way to solve a problem is with violence", adding, "It is difficult to undo this" (FEER 13.07.2000). At the beginning of 2000, communal violence in the Spice Islands of Maluku escalated and by mid-year an estimated 3000 people had been killed. In Central Sulawesi, murderous groups were killing villagers. In central Kalimantan deadly clashes broke out between indigenous Dayaks and migrants from Madura Island, who came as part of the Suharto government's *transmigrasi* programme. Bali and Lombok were also the scenes of unprecedented violence at the beginning of 2000, some of it aimed at the Chinese community, many of whom are Christians. In Jakarta, and in some other cities on Java, vigilante groups have taken it upon themselves to mete out retribution on small time criminals. Reports of people stealing bicycles being lynched, beaten, doused with kerosene and set alight were common during 2000. The police, in such cases, stood by, powerless to intervene.

While disintegration, partial or otherwise, is a possibility, the government is in the process of introducing laws that will lead to far-reaching **decentralization** to try and head off those who would prefer even greater autonomy. But there are worries that this attempt to devolve power to the provinces will permit local power-brokers to dominate affairs and make corruption even worse. It will also mean that poor provinces such as East and West Nusa Tenggara will no longer be able to rely on cross-subsidization by richer provinces such as Riau and Aceh. Furthermore, it is far from clear that there are sufficient numbers of competent people in the provinces to handle such an increase in the power and role of local level government.

Gus Dur tried to put it back together

President Abdurrahman Wahid, better known as Gus (a term of respect) Dur (from his name), did not have an easy task when he assumed the presidency at the end of 1999.

Gus Dur was renowned for his cunning and wily ways – and his fondness for obtuseness. When he was leader of Nahdlatul Ulama (NU), the world's largest Muslim organization, he was one of President Suharto's very few critics. And he was also able to present himself as a moderate Muslim: one who would protect the interests of Indonesia's non-Muslim population while remaining a respected Muslim cleric, leader and thinker. In January 2000 he travelled to Saudi Arabia to court the Arab world and then flew to Davos in Switzerland for the World Economic Forum. Here he met with Prime Minister Barak of Israel and George Soros. He explained: "We need investments and, you know, the Jewish community everywhere are very active in the commercial side..." (FEER 10.02.2000). His critics said he undermined Indonesia's stability and economic recovery by his impulsiveness; he frequently made statements without consulting his cabinet (as happened when he said, while on an overseas trip, that General Wiranto should resign) and people also complained of his readiness to blame conspirators for the country's problems. His supporters believed he was a great master who disarmed his opponents by his seeming foolishness, before bringing them down. With few political cards to play, once many in his coalition government turned against him, his defenders believed that speaking out was his only weapon. Without the backing of a fully functioning bureaucracy, or the military power used by his predecessor, his force of personality and ability to bluff were the only tools at his disposal.

His greatest victory, or so it seemed at the time, was to sideline the army and emasculate its leadership as a political force. This also showed him at his wily best. Initially, Wahid included General Wiranto, the army's powerful chief of staff, in his cabinet, but not, significantly, as defence minister. Instead he appointed him as security minister. This helped to separate the General from his power base. Then the president said that he would sack anyone implicated in human rights abuses in East Timor. Reports commissioned by the Indonesian government and by the UN into just this issue were released on 31 January 2000. Moreover, both came to the same conclusion: that members of the Indonesian army had assisted the militias in East Timor to murder, rape and pillage. More to the point, the Indonesian report mentioned six generals by name, including General Wiranto. The president was abroad at the time but in an interview said he thought that Wiranto should resign. Instead the General pointedly turned up at a cabinet meeting. However, having initially said that the General could stay, he changed his mind once more and sacked the general from his post as security minister (although he remained an 'inactive' member of the cabinet). Cut off from the army and in a government post with no significance, General Wiranto was successfully trapped in a no man's land of Gus Dur's making.

But Wahid did not just get rid of Wiranto. He appointed a civilian as minister of defence and promoted officers in the navy and airforce to influential positions, thus downgrading the traditionally highly dominant army. This culminated in a major reshuffle at the end of February 2000. Furthermore, Wahid insisted that military men in the cabinet had to resign from their military posts before taking up their political appointments.

While Gus Dur sidelined the army, he didn't counted on the public taking up arms to deal with the problems of the nation (probably orcestrated from above – possibly by factions of the army). At the beginning of 2000, as Muslim-Christian violence in Maluku escalated, radical Muslims in Java began to prepare for a *jihad* (holy war) in this far-flung province. White-robed warriors in their thousands, some wielding swords, congregated in Jakarta to make their feelings clear – and then began to train for battle. Despite Gus Dur's attempts to stop them leaving for Maluku, they began to arrive in the region by the end of May 2000. As the year wore on it became increasingly clear that Wahid's victory over the generals was a pyrrhic one. Infuriated by the president's actions, the army began to undermine his leadership. In particular, a series of bombings in Jakarta would seem to involve the army, or groups in the army. By the end of 2000 the army seemed to be clawing back power.

During the course of 2000, many people who initially welcomed Wahid's accession to the presidency became increasingly disenchanted with his leadership – and with his methods. In an attempt to address this mounting criticism, he proposed far-reaching changes to the management of state affairs. In effect he proposed a more equal, four-way sharing of power between his marginalized Vice President Megawati Sukarnoputri, two new 'Coordinating' ministers, and himself. The two coordinating ministers were later announced as being Sulsilo Bambang Yudhoyono, a retired general, and Rizal Ramli. Significantly, neither of these two men had prior links with any political party. Under this system Wahid would become, in effect, Indonesia's face to the wider world: a sort of roving ambassador for the country. Wahid claimed in the speech that he was ceding 'duties and not authority', but the distinction was a fine one.

Wahid's proposed changes were tacit acceptance on his part that he had lost his way. It sometimes seemed, in the months leading up to the August 2000 meeting, that Wahid lacked the clarity of mind to address key issues, and especially those of an economic flavour. His woolly pronouncements and tendency to prevaricate exasperated many businessmen and foreign investors.

Towards the end of 2000, Indonesia continued to lurch from crisis to crisis, both economically and politically. President Abdurrahman Wahid became increasingly embattled as his problems mounted. In particular, he seemed to have lost control of the army and the police who were, apparently, ignoring or going against his orders. This extended from his order for the army and police to crack down on the militias in West Timor (following the murder of three UN personnel there); to his demand that Tommy Suharto, one of former President Suharto's sons, be arrested in connection with a spate of bombings in Jakarta (the police released him saying there was not sufficient evidence); to a ceasefire in the northern Sumatran province of Aceh, which the army also apparently chose to ignore. Some commentators wondered whether the army was once more out of control and it was even suggested that Wahid could be toppled by an army-inspired coup.

Domestic hangovers and international relations

Indonesia's acceptance into the international fold has been hampered for years by numerous small and large stumbling blocks. The 'occupation' of East Timor, government policy in Irian Jaya, corruption, the nature of the political system, the failure to respect labour rights, and the human and environmental impacts of the transmigration programme, to name just a few. Just when Indonesia is on the verge of expunging the stain on its credibility, one or more of these issues jumps out and progress is stymied.

There can be no doubt that the major stumbling block was East Timor. Even before the tragic events which followed the vote for independence in mid-1999, East Timor was a thorn in Indonesia's attempts to punch its weight. (For a country of over 200,000,000 people, the fourth most populous on earth, it has a remarkably low international profile.) Nationalist sentiment was stoked by the presence of UN forces in East Timor (widely seen to be Australian forces in East Timor), and Indonesia's failure to come to terms with its misguided imperialist spree raised the stakes still further. At the end of September 1999, US Secretary of Defence William Cohen warned that Indonesia could face 'political isolation' and 'economic consequences' if it did not control its military.

Large chinks began forming in the armour of Wahid's popular support. In 2001, as he pushed for further reconciliation with separatists in Papua and Aceh, martial law was imposed in Maluku as fighting between Christians and Muslims intensified. It was discovered that the government ordered the military to block all members of Laskar Jihad (an Islamist group made up of Muslims from across the archipelago) from travelling to Maluku to fight. Not only did the military fail to do this, it soon became clear that Laskar Jihad was being funded by the Indonesian military. Things got worse for Wahid when he became embroiled in two huge financial scandals involving large sums of money that went missing from the State Logistics Agency (the money – US$4 million – was found with Wahid's masseur) and from a donation given by the Sultan of Brunei.

After legalising the use of Chinese characters and making Chinese New Year a national holiday in January 2001, Wahid declared at a meeting of university rectors that if Indonesia fell into a state of anarchy, he would be forced to consider dissolving the DPR (House of Representatives), a remark that won him few friends. At a special convening of the DPR a memorandum was signed against Wahid. A second would force a Special Session in which the impeachment and removal of a president would be a legal action. The writing was on the wall for the President and in April as his NU (Nahdlatul Ulama – Wahid's Islamic group) offered to fight to the end in support of their president, it seemed as though the nation was again slipping into grave civil strife. A second memorandum against Wahid was written after he sacked two members of his own cabinet as dissidents. Wahid was growing desperate and demanded that Susilo Bambang Yudhyono (then Minister for Security) call a state of emergency, a request which was refused. The date of MPR (People's Consultative Assembly) session for the impeachment of Wahid was hurried forward and the Indonesian army rallied against the president, flooding Jakarta with troops and aiming their tanks at the presidential palace. The MPR declared the end of Wahid's term as president, which he initially refused to accept, before finally conceding and slipping off to the USA for medical reasons.

In July 2001 Megawati Soekarno-Putri took over the reigns of power. She was seen to take a very passive role, enjoying her status as a daughter of the cult figure and founding father of Indonesia, Soekarno. It was noted by critics that she seemed more interested in developing her hobbies of gardening and watching cartoons than intervening in government business. Three years after she had taken power, elections were called and although the economic situation had improved slightly, rates of poverty and unemployment remained high. It was during her reign that terrorists struck foreign targets Bali and Jakarta, prompting falling confidence from foreign investors and once again thrusting Indonesia into the international headlines for all the wrong reasons. Megawati lost the election to Susilo Bambang Yudhyono (SBY), and quietly left the palace.

Yudhyono was thrust into the deep end as two months after he had won the election Indonesia was devastated by the Boxing Day tsunami off Aceh. This blow was followed by the earthquake in Bantul, several more along the coast of West Sumatra, the eruption of Gunung Merapi and another deadly tsunami off Pangandaran. This series of natural disasters put an immense strain on the country and its leadership. This was only exaggerated by the 2005 suicide attacks in Bali. Yudhyono promised to track down the perpetrators with his forces managing to track down and kill Dr Azahari, one of the ringleaders of the attack, in Malang. However, the other key player in the attacks, Noordin M Top, remains at large. The plotters of the first Bali bomb attacks in 2001 still remain on death row in Indonesia, much to the dismay of many who would rather the Indonesian government showed a strong arm to the international community and execute them.

Twice in 2005, Yudhyono had to increase fuel prices, cutting subsidies and undermining much of the good work he had done to address the poverty issue. Fuel prices were again hiked up by 30% in 2008, causing large civil disturbances in cities across the nation.

There is no doubt that the new millennium, a time of reform in the post-Soeharto era, has been a troubled time for the country, with planes falling from the sky, the ever present threat of terrorism and growing Islamist sentiments, religious conflict, the string of deadly natural disasters and soaring oil and food prices making the people conspiring to make citizens more hungry than ever for stability. Indonesians devour newspapers hungrily and discuss politics eagerly, and their desire for change is strong. The question remains as to whether Yudhyono can sate their appetite. In January 2008 former president Soeharto died, and while he was a corrupt and nepotistic leader, many Indonesians are growing nostalgic for the stability he achieved, that no other leader has been given the time, or been able to achieve.

Contents

Laos

Footprint features

Border crossings

At a glance

⊖ **Getting around** Roads are improving. Major towns have daytime bus services. Songthaews and trucks cover more remote areas. Domestic flights available. Riverboats ply the Mekong.

◎ **Time required** 1-4 weeks

☼ **Weather** Nov-Mar is best, although it can be cool at higher elevations. Temperatures peak in Apr. Rainy season May-Sep/Oct.

⊗ **When not to go** Mar-May can be hot, humid and hazy. Outdoor activities such has hiking can be tricky in the wet season.

CHINA

VIETNAM

HANOI

Phongsali

Muang Khua
Muang
Ngoi Neua
Ban Lak Khamay
Muang
Sing
Ban Saphoun
Nong Khiaw &
Ban Saphoun
Xam Neua
Sao
Hintang
Vieng
Xai
Luang
Namtha
Udomxai

Pak Ou Caves
Houei Xai
Pak Beng
Luang
Prabang
Tran Ninh
Highlands
Muang
Kham
Mekong

Kuang Si Falls
Sayaboury
Phonsavanh
Plain
of Jars
Gulf of Tonkin

Vang Vieng
Nam Ngum
Reservoir

Phou Khao Khouay NPA
Paksan
Lac Sao
Annamite Range

VIENTIANE
Xieng Khuan
Friendship
Bridge
Tham Kong Lor
Kong Leng Lake
Tham Pa
That Sikhot
Thakhek

That Inheng
LAOS

Savannakhet

Dong Phu
Vieng NPA

Salavan
Tad Lo
Bolaven
Plateau
Sekong
THAILAND
Pakse
Paksong
Tad Fang & Tad Yeung
Champasak
Wat Phou
Xe Pian NPA
Attapeu

BANGKOK

Mekong

Don Khong

CAMBODIA

N

80 km
80 miles

★ Don't miss ...
1 That Luang, page 459.
2 Tubing in Vang Vieng, page 477.
3 Luang Prabang, page 482.
4 Minority villages around Muang
  Sing, page 500.
5 Plain of Jars, page 514.
6 Wat Phou, page 534.
7 Mekong Islands, page 540.

PHNOM PENH

Laos is fast becoming the darling of Southeast Asia, satisfying all the romantic images of perfumed frangipani trees, saffron-robed monks, rusty old bicycles and golden temples, all set amongst a rich tapestry of tropical river islands, ethnic minority villages, cascading waterfalls and vivid green rice paddies, and bound together by the mighty Mekong River, the country's lifeline. The vernacular architecture, which other countries have swept away in a maelstrom of redevelopment, survives in Laos. Simple wooden village homes, colonial-era brick-and-stucco shophouses and gently mouldering monasteries mark Laos out as different. Traditional customs are also firmly intact: incense wafts out of streetside wats, monks collect alms at daybreak and the clickety-clack of looms weaving richly coloured silk can be heard in most villages.

As compelling as these sights and sounds are, the lasting impression for most visitors is of the people and their overwhelming friendliness. Many believe the best thing about Laos is the constant chime of 'sabaidee' ringing out from schoolchildren, monks and other passers-by, extending an invitation to join their meal. This is a land that endures the terrible legacy of being the most bombed country per capita in the world, yet its people transform bomb casings into flower pots and bomb craters into fish ponds. Regardless of their history and their poverty, people here radiate a sunny, happy disposition.

Life is simple in Laos but the people share with their former French colonists an infectious *joie de vivre* that ensures that good food and great company are the pinnacle of enjoyment. If you're seeking a relaxed lifestyle and a warm welcome, you've come to the right place.

Planning your trip

Getting there

Air

The easiest and cheapest way to access the region is via **Bangkok**. Most major airlines have direct flights from Europe, North America and Australasia to these hubs. Laos is only accessible from within Asia. ▸▸ *For flights to Bangkok, see page 778.*

There are international flights to Vientiane from Cambodia (Phnom Penh and Siem Reap), China (Kunming), Taiwan (Taipei), Thailand (Bangkok) and Vietnam (Hanoi and Ho Chi Minh City). Most people visiting Laos from outside the region travel via Bangkok. There are also flights from Bangkok and Chiang Mai to Luang Prabang. A cheaper option for getting to Laos from Bangkok is to fly to **Udon Thani** (Thailand), about 50 km south of the border and travel overland via the Friendship Bridge. For full details, see page 462. An alternative route is to fly from Bangkok to **Chiang Rai** (Thailand), before travelling overland to **Chiang Khong** and crossing into northern Laos at **Houei Xai**. From Houei Xai there are flights to Vientiane and boats to Luang Prabang via Pak Beng. ▸▸ *For airport tax, see page 454.*

Road and river

Laos is a land-locked country and foreign visitors travelling overland between neighbouring countries are restricted to a handful of key crossing points. For much of its length, the Lao-Thai border is defined by the Mekong, with bridges and ferries to link the two countries. To the east, the Annamite mountain range forms a spine separating Laos from Vietnam, with a few cross-border buses running from Vientiane to Savannakhet. There is only one official border crossing between Laos and Cambodia in the south and between Laos and China in the north. Foreigners are not permitted to cross between Laos and Myanmar (Burma).

Getting around

Air

Lao Airlines runs domestic flights from Vientiane to Phonsavannh (Xieng Khouang), Houei Xai, Oudomxai and Pakse. Foreigners must pay in US dollars for all **Lao Airlines** flights. There are three types of plane: French-built *ATR-72s*, and Chinese-built *Y-7s* and *Y-12s*. The latter two are a risk. The most reliable, comfortable and newest machines – the *ATR-72s* – operate on the most popular routes (Vientiane-Bangkok, Vientiane-Luang Prabang, Vientiane-Pakse). Within Laos there is also a smaller, newer carrier, **Lao Air** (www.lao-air.com), which run flights to Xam Neua and Phongsali. ▸▸ *For domestic airport tax, see page 454.*

Boat

It is possible to take riverboats up and down the Mekong and its main tributaries. Boats stop at Luang Prabang, Pak Beng, Houei Xai, around Don Deth, Don Khong, and other smaller towns and villages. Apart from the main route, Houei Xai to Luang Prabang, there are often no scheduled services and departures may be limited during the dry season. Take food and drink and expect somewhat crowded conditions aboard. The most common riverboats are the *hua houa leim*, with no decks, the hold being enclosed by side panels and a flat roof (note that metal boats get very hot). Speedboats also chart some routes, but are very dangerous and never enjoyable. Prices vary according to size of boat and length of journey.

Packing for Laos

It is possible to buy most toiletries, photograpahic supplies and luxuries in Vientiane. Luang Prabang, Savannakhet and Pakse stock most basic items but outside these cities little is available beyond such items as soap, washing powder, batteries and shampoo. In terms of clothing, most people in Laos dress tidily and modestly but are relatively casual.

You may want to pack antacid tablets for indigestion; antibiotics for diarrhoea (discuss with your doctor); antiseptic ointment (eg Cetrimide); anti-malarials; mosquito repellents; travel sickness tablets; painkillers; contraceptives; tampons/sanitary towels; high-factor sun screen and a sun hat, and blow-up pillow.

Make sure your passport is valid for at least six months and take photocopies of essential documents (passport ID and visa pages, insurance details and student ID). Spare passport photos are useful when applying for permits.

Other useful items include a digital camera memory card; money belt; cotton or silk sheet sleeping bag; mosquito net; earplugs; padlock; sunglasses; penknife; torch; travel wash; umbrella; wet wipes.

Road

The roads are not good, but they are improving. Many have been repaired or upgraded in recent years, making journeys faster and infinitely more comfortable. Quite a few bus, truck, tuk-tuk, songthaew and taxi drivers understand basic English, French or Thai, although some (especially tuk-tuk drivers) aren't above forgetting the lowest price you thought you'd successfully negotiated before hopping aboard – it is best to take this sort of thing in good humour. Even so, in order to travel to a particular destination, it is a great advantage to have the name written out in Lao. Many people will not know road names, but they will know where all the sights of interest are – wats, markets, monuments, waterfalls, etc.

Bus/truck It is now possible to travel to most areas of the country by bus, truck or songthaew (converted pick-up truck) in the dry season, although road travel in the rainy season can be tricky if not impossible. VIP buses are very comfortable night buses, usually allowing a good sleep – but watch out for the karaoke. In the south of Laos a night bus plies the route from Pakse to Vientiane; book a double bed if you don't want to end up sleeping next to a stranger. Robberies have been reported on the night buses so keep your valuables secure.

On certain long routes, such as Vientiane/Luang Prabang to Xam Neua, big Langjian (Chinese) trucks are sometimes used. These trucks have been colourfully converted into buses with divided wooden seats and glassless windows. In more remote places (Xam Neua to Vieng Xai, for instance), ancient jeeps are common.

In the south of the country, Japanese-donated buses are used although you may see the occasional shiny Volvo bus. Breakdowns, though not frequent, aren't uncommon. For some connections you may need to wait a day. During the rainy season (June to December) expect journey times to be longer than those quoted; some roads may be closed altogether.

Car hire This costs anything from US$40-100 per day, depending on the vehicle, with first 150 km free, then US$10 every 100 km thereafter. The price includes a driver. For insurance purposes you will probably need an international driver's permit. Insurance is generally included with car hire but it's best to check the fine print. A general rule of thumb: if you are involved in a car crash, you, the foreigner, will be liable for costs as you have more money.

Motorbike and bicycle hire There are an increasing number of motorcycles available from guesthouses and other shops in major towns. 110cc bikes go for around US$4-10 a day, while 250cc Hondas are around US$20 per day. Bicycles are available in many towns and are a cheap way to see the sights. Many guesthouses rent bikes for US$1-2 per day.

Tuk-tuk The majority of motorized three-wheelers known as 'jumbos' or tuk-tuks are large motorbike taxis with two bench seats in the back. You'll find them in most cities and metropolitan areas; expect to pay around 10,000-15,000 kip for a short ride. They can also be hired by the hour or the day to reach destinations out of town.

In city centres make sure you have the correct money for your tuk-tuk as they are often conveniently short of change. Also opt to flag down a moving tuk-tuk rather than selecting one of the more expensive ones that shark around tourist destinations.

Sleeping → *For hotel price codes, see inside the front cover.*

Rooms in Laos are rarely luxurious and standards vary enormously. You can end up paying double what you would pay in Bangkok for similar facilities and service. However, the hotel industry is expanding rapidly. There is a reasonable choice of hotels of different standards and prices in Vientiane, Luang Prabang and Pakse and an expanding number of budget options in many towns on the fast-developing tourist trail. First-class hotels exist in Vientiane and Luang Prabang. The majority of guesthouses and hotels have fans and attached bathrooms, although more and more are providing air conditioning where there is a stable electricity supply, while others are installing their own generators to cater for the needs of the growing tourist trade. Smaller provincial towns, having previously had only a handful of hotels and guesthouses – some of them quaint French colonial villas – are now home to a growing number of rival concerns as tourism takes off. In rural villages, people's homes are enthusiastically transformed into bed and breakfasts on demand. While Vientiane may still have little budget accommodation, many towns in the north, such as Vang Vieng, Muang Ngoi, Muang Sing and Luang Namtha, have a large choice of very cheap, and in some cases very good accommodation, including dorm beds. In the southern provinces, upmarket and boutique accommodation has popped up in Pakse and Don Khong. There are several excellent ecolodges in the country, most notably the Boat Landing at Luang Namtha and the Kingfisher Ecolodge at Ban Kiet Ngong in the south. Many tour companies offer homestay in ethnic minority villages and camping as part of a package tour.

Eating and drinking → *For restaurant price codes, see inside the front cover.*

Lao food is similar to that of Thailand, although the Chinese influence is slightly less noticeable. Lao dishes are distinguished by the use of aromatic herbs and spices such as lemon grass, chillies, ginger and tamarind. The best place to try Lao food is often from roadside stalls or in the markets. The staple Lao foods are *kao niao* (glutinous rice), which is eaten with your hands and fermented fish or *pa dek* (distinguishable by its distinctive smell), often laced with liberal spoons of *nam pa*, fish sauce. Being a landlocked country, most of the fish is fresh from the Mekong. One of the delicacies that shouldn't be missed is *Mok Pa* steamed fish in banana leaf. Most of the dishes are variations on two themes: fish and bird. *Laap*, also meaning 'luck' in Lao, is a traditional ceremonial dish made from (traditionally) raw fish or meat crushed into a paste, marinated in lemon juice and mixed with chopped mint. It is called *laap sin* if it has a meat base and *laap paa* if it's fish based. Beware of *laap* in cheap street restaurants. It is sometimes concocted from raw offal and served cold and should be consumed with great caution. Overall though *laap* is cooked well for the falang palate.

Restaurant food is, on the whole, hygienically prepared, and as long as street stall snacks have been well cooked, they are usually fine and a good place to sample local specialities. Really classy restaurants are only found in Vientiane and Luang Prabang. Good French cuisine is available in both cities. A better bet in terms of value for money are the Lao restaurants.

Far more prevalent are lower-end Lao restaurants which can be found in every town. Right at the bottom end – in terms of price if not necessarily in terms of quality – are stalls that charge a US$1-2 for filled baguettes or simple single-dish meals.

Soft drinks are expensive as they are imported from Thailand. Bottled water is widely available and produced locally, so it is cheap (about 3000 kip for a litre). *Nam saa*, weak Chinese tea, is free. Imported beer can be found in hotels, restaurants and bars but is not particularly cheap. *Beer Lao* is a light lager (although the alcohol content is 5%). The local brew is rice wine (*lao-lao*) which is drunk from a clay jug with long straws.

Local customs and laws

Bargaining/haggling
While bargaining is common in Laos – in the market or in negotiating a trip on a *saamlor* or tuk-tuk, for example – it is not heavy-duty haggling. The Lao are extremely laid back and it is rare to be fleeced; don't bargain hard with them, it may force them to lose face and reduce prices well below their profit margin. For most things, you won't even really need to bargain. Approach bargaining with a sense of fun; a smile or joke always helps.

Clothing
Informal lightweight clothing is all that is needed, though a jumper is vital for the highlands in winter (November-March). An umbrella is useful during the rainy season (June-July). It's polite to dress modestly: sleeveless shirts, short shorts or skirts are not ideal. When visiting wats, shoulders should be covered and shoes removed. One of the reasons for the tight controls on tourism in Laos is because of the perceived corrosive effects that badly dressed tourists were having on Lao culture. 'Scruffy' travellers are still frowned upon and officials are getting fed up with people wandering around skimpily clad, particularly in Vang Vieng and Siphandon. If bathing in public, particularly in rural areas, women should wear a sarong.

Conduct
Wats Monks are revered, don't touch their robes. If talking to a monk your head should be lower than his. Avoid visiting a wat around 1100 as this is when the monks have their morning meal. It is considerate to ask the abbot's permission to enter the *sim* and shoes should be removed before entry. When sitting down feet should point away from the altar and the main image. Arms and legs should be fully covered when visiting wats. A small donation is often appropriate (kneel when putting it into the box).

Greeting Lao people are addressed by their name, not their family name, even when a title is used. The *nop* or *wai* – with palms together below your chin and head bowed, as if in prayer – remains the traditional form of greeting. Shaking hands, though, is very widespread – more so than in neighbouring Thailand. This can be put down to the influence of the French during the colonial period (whereas Thailand was never colonized). 'Sabaidee' (hello) is also a good way to greet. Avoid hugging and kissing to greet Lao people, as they tend to get embarrassed.

Eating etiquette In Laos, who eats when is important. At a meal, a guest should not begin eating until the host has invited him or her to do so. Nor should the guest continue eating after everyone else has finished. It is also customary for guests to leave a small amount of food on their plate; to do otherwise would imply that the guest was still hungry and that the host had not provided sufficient food for the meal. Sharing is a big thing at meal times, where plates of food are ordered and shared amongst everyone. Lao people often invite tourists to eat with them or share on buses, and it is a nice gesture if this is reciprocated (though Lao people tend to be shy so don't take any refusal as a rejection).

General Pointing with the index finger is considered rude. If you want to call someone over, gesture with your palm facing the ground and fingers waving towards you. In Lao your head is considered 'high' and feet are considered 'low'. So try to keep your feet low, don't point them at people or touch people with your feet. Don't pat children on the head (or touch people's heads in general), as it is considered the most sacred part of the body. If you visit a private home, remove your shoes. When seated on the floor, you should tuck your feet behind you.

Lao people have a passive nature. Yelling or boisterous people tend to freak them out and they go into panic mode. If a dispute arises, a smile and a few jokes will do the trick.

The Lao are proud people and begging is just not the done thing, so don't hand out money (or medicine) to local villagers. If you want to give a gift or a donation to someone, it is best to channel it through the village elder.

Festivals and events

The Lao celebrate New Year four times a year: international New Year in January, Chinese New Year in January/February, Lao New Year (Pi Mai) in April and Hmong New Year in December. The Lao Buddhist year follows the lunar calendar, so many festivals are movable.

Jan Boun Pha Vet (movable). To celebrate King Vessanthara's reincarnation as a Buddha. Sermons, processions, dance, theatre. Popular time for ordination.
1 Jan New Year's Day (public holiday). Celebrated by private *baci*.
6 Jan Pathet Lao Day (public holiday). Parades in main towns.
20 Jan Army Day (public holiday).
Jan/Feb Chinese New Year (movable). Many Chinese and Vietnamese businesses shut down for 3 days.
Feb Magha Puja (movable). Celebrates the end of Buddha's time in the monastery and the prediction of his death. Principally celebrated in Vientiane and at Wat Phou.
Apr Pi Mai (public holiday). The 1st month of the Lao New Year is Dec but festivities are delayed until Apr when days are longer than nights. By Apr it's also hotting up, so having hosepipes levelled at you and buckets of

water dumped on you is more pleasurable. The festival also serves to invite the rains. Pi Mai is one of the most important annual festivals, particularly in Luang Prabang (see page 493). There is usually a 3-day holiday. Similar festivals are celebrated in Thailand, Cambodia and Burma.
May Visakha Puja (movable). To celebrate the birth, enlightenment and death of Buddha, celebrated in local wats. **Boun Bang Fai** (movable). The 2-day rocket festival, is a Buddhist rain-making festival. Large bamboo rockets are built and decorated by monks and carried in procession before being blasted skywards. The higher a rocket goes, the bigger its builder's ego gets. Designers of failed rockets are thrown in the mud.
1 May Labour Day (public holiday). Parades in Vientiane.
Jun Khao Phansa (movable). The start of Buddhist Lent and a time of retreat and

fasting for monks. The festival starts with the full moon in Jun/Jul and ends with the full moon in Oct. It all ends with the *Kathin* ceremony in Oct when monks receive gifts.

1 Jun Children's Day (public holiday).

Aug Ho Khao Padap Dinh (movable). Celebration of the dead.

13 Aug Lao Issara (public holiday). Free Lao Day.

23 Aug Liberation Day (public holiday).

Sep Boun Ok Phansa (movable). The end of Buddhist Lent when the faithful take offerings to the temple. It is in the '9th month' in Luang Prabang and the '11th month' in Vientiane, and marks the end of the rainy season. Boat races take place on the Mekong River with crews of 50 or more men and women. On the night before the race small decorated rafts are set afloat on the river.

12 Oct Freedom from the French Day (public holiday). Only really celebrated in Vientiane.

Nov Boun That Luang (movable). Celebrated in all Laos' *thats*, although most enthusiastically and colourfully in Vientiane, see page 474. As well as religious rituals, most celebrations include local fairs, processions, beauty pageants and other festivities.

Dec Hmong New Year (movable).

2 Dec Independence Day (public holiday). Military parades, dancing and music.

Shopping

Popular souvenirs from Laos include handicrafts and textiles, sold almost everywhere. The market is usually a good starting point, as are some of the minority villagers. The smaller, less touristy towns will sell silk at the cheapest price (at about 40,000 kip a length). The best place to buy naturally dyed silk in Laos is in Xam Neua. This high quality silk often makes its way to Luang Prabang and Vientiane but usually at much greater cost. Most markets offer a wide selection of patterns and embroidery though amongst the best places to go are **Talaat Sao** (Vientiane Morning Market) or, behind it, the cheaper **Talaat Kudin**, which has a textile section in the covered area. If you wish to have something made, most tailors can whip up a simple *sinh* (Lao sarong) in a day but you might want to allow longer for adjustments or other items. **Ock Pop Tok** in Luang Prabang also has a fantastic reputation for producing top-shelf, naturally dyed silk. Vientiane and Luang Prabang offer the most sophisticated line in boutiques, where you can get all sorts of clothes from the utterly exquisite to the frankly bizarre. Those on a more frugal budget will find some tailors who can churn out a decent pair of trousers on Sisavangvong in Luang Prabang and around Nam Phou in Vientiane. If you get the right tailor, they can be much better than those found in Thailand both in terms of price and quality but you do need to be patient and allow time for multiple fittings. It is also a good idea to bring a pattern/picture of what you want.

Silverware, most of it is in the form of jewellery and small pots (though they may not be made of silver), is traditional in Laos. The finest silversmiths work out of Vientiane and Luang Prabang. Chunky antique ethnic-minority jewellery, bangles, pendants, belts and earrings are often sold in markets in the main towns, or antique shops in Vientiane, particularly congregating around Nam Phou. Xam Neua market also offers a good range of ethnic minority-style silver jewellery. Look for traditional necklaces that consist of wide silver bands, held together by a spirit lock (a padlock to lock in your scores of souls). Gold jewellery is the preference of the Lao Loum (lowland Laos) and its bright yellow colour is associated with Buddhist luck (often it is further dyed to enhance its orange goldness), this is best bought in Vientiane. Craftsmen in Laos are still producing **wood carvings** for temples and coffins. Designs are usually traditional, with a religious theme.

Essentials A-Z

Accident and emergency
Contact the relevant emergency service and your embassy. Obtain police/medical records in order to file insurance claims. If you need to report a crime visit your local police station, take a local who speaks English. Ambulance T195, Fire T190, Police T191.

Customs and duty free
Duty-free allowance is 500 cigarettes, 2 bottles of wine and a bottle of liquor. Laos has a strictly enforced ban on the export of antiquities and all Buddha images.

Disabled travellers
Pavements are often uneven, there are potholes and missing drain covers galore, pedestrian crossings are ignored, ramps are unheard of, lifts are few and far between and escalators are seen only in magazines, high end hotels and some shopping complexes. **RADAR**, 12 City Forum, 250 City Rd, London, EC1V 8AF, T0207-2503222, www.radar.org.uk. **SATH**, 347 Fifth Avenue, Suite 605, New York City, NY 10016, T0212-4477284, www.sath.org.

Drugs
Drug use is illegal and there are harsh penalties ranging from fines through to imprisonment or worse. Police have been known to levy heavy fines on people in Vang Vieng for eating so-called 'happy' foods, see page 465, or for being caught in possession of drugs. Note that 'happy' food can make some people extremely sick. Though opium has in theory been eradicated it is still for sale in northern areas and people have died from overdosing. *Yaa baa* is also available here and should be avoided at all costs.

Electricity
Voltage 220, 50 cycles in the main towns. 110 volts in rural areas; 2-pin sockets. Blackouts are common outside Vientiane and many smaller towns are not connected to the national grid and only have power in the evening.

Embassies and consulates
Australia, 1 Dalman Cres, O' Malley Canberra, ACT 2606, T+61-2-864595.
Cambodia, 15-17 Mao Tse Toung Bvd, Phnom Penh, T+855-23-982632.
France, 74 Av Raymond-Poincaré 75116 Paris, T+33-1-4553 0298.
Thailand, 502/1 Soi Ramkamhaeng 39, Thanon Pracha Uthit, Wangthonglang, Bangkok 10310, T+66-2-539 6667.
Vietnam, 22 Tran Binh Trong, Hanoi, T04-2854576; 181 Hai Ba Trung, Ho Chi Minh City, T+844-829 7667.

Gay and lesbian
Gay and lesbian travellers should have no problems in Laos. It does not have a hot gay scene per se and the Lao government is intent on avoiding the mushrooming of the gay and straight sex industry. Officially it is illegal for any foreigner to have a sexual relationship with a Lao person they aren't married to. Openly gay behaviour is contrary to local culture and custom and visitors, whether straight or gay, should not flaunt their sexuality. Any overt display of passion or even affection in public is taboo. In Vientiane there aren't any gay bars, although there are some bars and clubs where gays congregate. Luang Prabang has a few more options and is fast becoming one of Southeast Asia's most gay friendly destinations.

Health
See your doctor or travel clinic at least 6 weeks before departure for general advice on travel risks, malaria and vaccinations. Make sure you have travel insurance, get a dental check (especially if you are going to be away for more than a month), know your blood group and if you suffer a long-term condition such as diabetes or epilepsy make sure someone knows or that you have a Medic Alert bracelet/ necklace with this information on it. Note that medicine in developing countries, in particular anti-malarials, may be sub-standard or part of a trade in counterfeit drugs.

The following **vaccinations** are usually advised: BCG, diphtheria, hepatitis A, polio, tetanus and typhoid. The following are sometimes advised: hepatitis B, Japanese B encephalitis and rabies. A yellow fever vaccination certificate is required if coming from areas with risk of transmission.

Health risks

Malaria is prevalent but the risk is minimal in Vientiane. For most people, prophylaxis will need to be something other than chloroquine, since there is such a high level of resistance to it. Always check with your doctor or travel clinic for the most up-to-date advice. Malaria can cause death within 24 hrs. It can start as something resembling an attack of flu. You may feel tired, lethargic, headachy, feverish; or more seriously, develop fits, followed by coma and then death. If you have a temperature, go to a doctor as soon as you can and ask for a malaria test. On your return home if you suffer any of these symptoms, get tested as soon as possible, even if any previous test proved negative, the test could save your life.

The most serious viral disease is **dengue fever**, which is hard to protect against as the mosquitoes bite during the day as well as at night. Bacterial diseases include **tuberculosis** (TB) and traveller's **diarrhoea**. Each year there is the possibility that **avian flu** or **SARS** might rear their ugly heads. Check the news reports. If there is a problem in an area you are due to visit you may be advised to have an ordinary flu shot or to seek expert advice. There are high rates of **HIV** in the region, especially among sex workers. **Rabies** and **schistosomiasis** (bilharzia, a water-borne parasite) may be a problem.

Medical services

Medical services are listed in the Directory section of each town. Hospitals are few and far between and medical facilities are poor. Emergency treatment is available at the Mahosot Hospital and Clinique Setthathirath in Vientiane. The Australian embassy also has a clinic for Commonwealth citizens with minor ailments (see page 481); US$60 per consultation. Better facilities are available in Thailand; emergency evacuation to **Nong Khai** or **Udon Thani** (Thailand) can be arranged at short notice. For information on the hospitals in Thailand, see page 815.

Useful websites

www.btha.org British Travel Health Association (UK).
www.cdc.gov US Government site which gives excellent advice on travel health and details of disease outbreaks.
www.fitfortravel.scot.nhs.uk A-Z of vaccine/health advice for each country.
www.who.int The WHO Blue Book lists the diseases of the world.

Insurance

Always take out travel insurance before you set off and read the small print carefully. Check that the policy covers any activities you may end up doing. Also check exactly what your medical cover includes, eg ambulance, helicopter rescue or emergency flights back home. Also check the payment protocol. You may have to pay first before the insurance company reimburses you. It is always best to dig out all the receipts for expensive personal effects like jewellery or cameras. Take photos of these items and note down all serial numbers. **STA Travel** and other reputable student travel organizations offer good-value policies. Young travellers from North America can try the **International Student Insurance Service** (**ISIS**), which is available through **STA Travel**, T01-800-7770112, www.sta-travel. com. Other recommended companies in North America include: **Travel Guard**, www.noelgroup.com; **Access America**, www.accessamerica.com; **Travel Insurance Services**, www.travel insure.com; and **Travel Assistance International**, www.travel assistance.com. Older travellers should note that some companies will not cover people over 65 years old, or may charge higher premiums. The best policies for older travellers (UK) are offered by **Age Concern**, www.ageconcern.org.uk.

Useful words and phrases

Hello/goodbye	*Suh-bye-dee/lah-gohn*	Where is the	*Sa ta ni lot*
Thank you	*Kop jai*	Is it far?	*Kai baw?*
Yes/No	*Men/baw*	Today	*Muh-nee*
How much is...?	*Tow-dai?*	Tomorrow	*Muh-ouhn*
That's expensive	*Pheng-lie*	Yesterday	*Muh-van-nee*

Internet

Internet cafés have been popping up all over Laos. The connections are surprisingly good in major centres. Fast, cheap internet is available in Vientiane, Luang Prabang, Vang Vieng and Savannakhet for around 100-200 kip per min. Less reliable and more expensive internet can be found in Phonsavanh, Don Khone, Don Deth, Luang Namtha, Thakhek, Savannakhet and Udomxai. Many internet cafés also offer international phone services.

Language

Lao is the national language but there are many local dialects, not to mention the ubiquitous languages of the minority groups. Lao is closely related to Thai and, in a sense, is becoming more so as the years pass. Though there are important differences between the languages, they are mutually intelligible – just about. French is spoken, though only by government officials, hotel staff and many educated people over 40. However, most government officials and many shopkeepers have some command of English.

Media

The *Vientiane Times*, is published 5 times a week and provides interesting cultural and tourist-based features, as well as quirky stories translated from the local press and wire service. Television is becoming increasingly popular as more towns and villages get electricity. The national TV station broadcasts in Lao. In Vientiane, **CNN**, **BBC**, **ABC** and a range of other channels are broadcast. Thailand's **Channel 5** subtitles the news in English. The **Lao National Radio** broadcasts news in English. The **BBC World Service** can be picked up on shortwave.

Money → *US$1 = 8618, £1 = 16,831, €1 = 13,337 (Aug 2008).*

The kip is the official currency. The lowest commonly used note is the 500 kip and the highest, the recently introduced 50,000 kip tends to shadow the Thai baht but with a rather quaint 1 week delay. It is getting much easier to change currency and traveller's cheques. Banks are generally reluctant to give anything but kip in exchange for hard currency. US dollars and Thai baht can be used as cash in most shops, restaurants and hotels and the Chinese Yuan is starting to be more widely accepted in northern parts of Laos (closer to the Chinese border). A certain amount of cash (in US dollars or Thai baht) can also be useful in an emergency. Banks include the **Lao Development Bank** and **Le Banque pour Commerce Exterieur Lao (BCEL)**, which change most major international currencies (cash) and traveller's cheques denominated in US dollars and pounds sterling. Many of the BCEL branches offer cash advances on Visa/MasterCard. Note that some banks charge a hefty commission of US$2 per TC. While banks will change traveller's cheques and cash denominated in most major currencies into kip, some will only change US dollars into Thai baht, or into US dollars cash.

Thai baht are readily accepted in most towns but it is advisable to carry kip in rural areas (eg buses will usually only accept kip).

The BCEL has distributed several ATMs across the country but at the time of publication the majority of these were MasterCard only. Multi-card ATMS (only Visa and MasterCard) are only available in Vientiane but several more are planned in the future. At the time of writing, there were only a sprinkling of international multi-card ATMs in Vientiane (at the **BCEL** bank in Vientiane on Fa Gnum, near the Novotel and 500 m from Wat Simuang temple and across from the Lao Plaza Hotel), but will only dispense a maximum of 700,000 kip at a time. On weekends, the only other options for exchange or obtaining cash are the **BCEL** booth along the river.

Payment by credit card is becoming easier – although beyond the larger hotels and restaurants in Vientiane and Luang Prabang do not expect to be able to get by on plastic. American Express, Visa, Master Card/Access cards are accepted in a limited number of more upmarket establishments. Note that commission is charged by some places on credit card transactions. If they can route the payment through Thailand then a commission is not levied; but if this is not possible, then 3% is usually added.

Many BCEL banks will now advance cash on credit cards in Luang Prabang, Vientiane, Pakse, Phonsavanh, Savannakhet and Vang Vieng (not all cards are accepted at these banks, so it's better to check in advance).

Cost of travelling
The variety of available domestic flights means that the bruised bottoms, dust-soaked clothes and stiff limbs that go hand-in-hand with some of the longer bus/boat rides can be avoided by those with thicker wallets in Laos. As the roads improve and journey times diminish, buses have emerged as the preferred (most reasonably priced) transportation option. Budget accommodation costs US$3-10 with a mid-range hotel costing from US$20-30. Local food is very cheap and it is possible to eat well for under US$2. Most Western restaurants will charge between US$2-5.

Opening hours
Banks Mon-Fri 0830-1600 (some close 1500). **Bars/nightclubs** Usually close around 2200-2300 depending on how strictly the curfew is enforced. In smaller towns, most restaurants and bars will be closed by 2200.

Offices Mon-Fri 0900-1700; those that deal with tourists stay open later and many open at weekends. Government offices close at 1600.

Police and the law
If you are robbed insurers will require that you obtain a police report. The police may try to solicit a bribe for this service. Although not ideal, you will probably have to pay this fee to obtain your report. Laws aren't strictly enforced but when the authorities do prosecute people the penalties can be harsh, ranging from deportation through to prison sentences. If you are arrested seek embassy and consular support. People are routinely fined for drugs possession, having sexual relations with locals (when unmarried) and proselytizing. If you are arrested or encounter police, try to remain calm and friendly. Although drugs are available throughout the country, the police levy hefty fines and punishments if caught.

Post
The postal service is inexpensive and reliable but delays are common. As the National Tourism Authority assures: in Laos the stamps will stay on the envelope. Contents of outgoing parcels must be examined by an official before being sealed. Incoming mail should use the official title, Lao PDR. There is no mail to home addresses or guesthouses, so mail must be addresses to a PO Box. The post office in Vientiane has a poste restante service. EMS (Express Mail Service) is available from main post offices in larger towns. In general, post offices open 0800-1200, 1300-1600. In provincial areas, **Lao Telecom** is usually attached to the post office. **DHL, Fedex** and **TNT** have offices in Vientiane.

Safety
Crime rates are very low but it is advisable to take the usual precautions. Most areas of the country are now safe – very different from only a few years ago when foreign embassies advised tourists not to travel along certain roads and in certain areas (in particular Route 13 between Vientiane and Luang Prabang, and

Route 7 between Phonsavanh and Route 13). Today these risks have effectively disappeared. However, the government will sometimes make areas provisionally off-limits if they think there is a security risk – take heed!

There has been a reported increase in motorcycle drive-by thefts in Vientiane, but these and other similar crimes are still at a low level compared with most countries. If riding on a motorbike or bicycle, don't carry your bag strap over your shoulder – as you could get pulled off the bike if someone goes to snatch your bag. In the Siphandon and Vang Vieng areas, theft seems more common. Use a hotel security box if available.

Road accidents are on the increase. The hiring of motorbikes is becoming more popular and consequently there are more tourist injuries. Wear a helmet.

Be careful around waterways, as drowning is one of the primary causes of tourist deaths. During the rainy season (May-Sep) rivers have a tendency to flood and can have extremely strong currents. Make sure if you are kayaking, tubing, canoeing, travelling by fast-boat, etc, that proper safety gear, such as life jackets, is provided. 'Fast-boat' river travel can be dangerous due to the risk of hitting something in the river and capsizing.

Xieng Khouang Province, the Boloven Plateau, Xam Neua and areas along the Ho Chi Minh Trail are littered with bombies (small anti-personnel mines and bomblets from cluster bomb units). There are also numerous, large, unexploded bombs; in many villages they have been left lying around. They are very unstable so DO NOT TOUCH. Only walk on clearly marked or newly trodden paths.

Student travellers

Anyone in full-time education is entitled to an International Student Identity Card, www.isic.org. These are issued by student travel offices and travel agencies and offer special rates on all forms of transport and other concessions and services. They sometimes permit free admission to museums and sights, at other times a discount on the admission.

Tax

Airport tax

International departure tax is US$15, domestic tax is 5000 kip.

Telephone → Country code +856.

Public phones are available in Vientiane and other major cities. You can also go to **Lao Telecom** offices to call overseas. Call 178 in Vientiane for town codes. Most towns have at least one telephone box with IDD facility. The one drawback is that you must buy a phonecard. Because these are denominated in such small units, even the highest-value card will only get you a handful of mins talk time with Europe. Most calls are between US$0.80 and US$2 per min. All post offices, telecoms offices and many shops sell phone cards. Note: If ringing Laos from Thailand, dial 007 before the country code for Laos.

Mobile telephone coverage is now quite good. Pay-as-you-go sim cards are available for 30,000 kip to 50,000 kip. Coverage is available in most provincial capitals.

Many internet cafés have set up call facilities that charge US$0.20 per min and under to make a call. In Vientiane, Pakse, Luang Prabang and Vang Vieng most internet cafés are equipped with Skype, including headphones and web-cam, which costs a fraction of the price for international calls (as long as you have already set up an account).

International operator: 170. Operator: 16. The IDD for Laos is 00856. Directory enquiries: T16 (national), T171 (international).

Time

7 hrs ahead of GMT.

Tipping

Tipping is rare, even in hotels. However, it is a kind gesture to tip guides and, in some more expensive restaurants, a 10% tip is appreciated is service charge is not included on the bill. If someone offers you a lift, it is a courtesy to give them some money for fuel.

Tourist information

The **Laos National Tourism Authority**, Lane Xang, Vientiane, T021-212248, www.tourism laos.gov.la, provides maps and brochures. The provincial offices are usually excellent and as long as you are patient they will usually come through with the information you need. There are particularly good tourist offices in Thakhek, Vieng Xai, Savannakhet, Xam Neua and Luang Namtha. The authority has teamed up with local tour operators to provide a number of ecotourism opportunities, such as trekking and village homestays, www.ecotourismlaos.com.

Useful websites

www.travelfish.org
www.visit-laos.com
www.ecotourismlaos.com
www.laohotelgroup.org
www.laopdr.com
www.asean-tourism.com
www.muonglao.com
www.mekongcenter.com
www.visitmekong.com

Tour operators

For regional tour operators, such as **Asian Trails** (www.asiantrails.info), refer to the Activities and tours listings in the guide.

In the UK

Adventure Company, Cross & Pillory House, Cross & Pillory Lane, Alton GU34 1HL, T0845-450 5316, www.adventurecompany.co.uk.
Audley Travel, New Mill, New Mill Lane, Whitney, Oxfordshire OX29 9SX, T01993-838100, www.audleytravel.com.
Coromandel, Andrew Brock Travel Ltd, 29A Main St, Lyddington, Oakham, Rutland LE15 9LR, T01572-821330, www.coromandel abt.com. Tailored individual travel.
Guerba Adventure & Discovery Holidays, Wessex House, 40 Station Rd, Westbury, Wiltshire BA13 3JN, T01373-826611, www.guerba.co.uk.
Magic of the Orient, 14 Frederick Pl, Clifton, Bristol, BS8 1AS, T0117-3116050, www.magic oftheorient.com. Tailor-made holidays.

Regent Holidays, Fromsgate House, Rupert St, Bristol BS1 2QJ, T0845-277 3317, www.regent-holidays.co.uk.
Silk Steps, Odyssey Lodge, Holy Well Rd, Edington, Bridgwater, Somerset TA7 9JH, T01278-722460, www.silksteps.co.uk.
Steppes Travel, 51 Castle St, Cirencester, GL7 1QD, T01285-880980, www.steppes travel.co.uk.
Symbiosis Expedition Planning, Holly House, Whilton, Daventry, Northants, NN11 2NN, T0845-123 2844, www.symbiosis-travel.com.
Trans Indus, Northumberland House, 11 The Pavement, Popes Lane, London W5 4NG, T020-8566 2729, www.transindus.co.uk. Tailor-made holidays and group tours.
Travel Indochina Ltd, 2nd floor, Chester House, George St, Oxford 0X1 2AY, T01865-268940, www.travelindochina.co.uk. Small group journeys, tailor-made holidays.
Travelmood, 214 Edgware Rd, London W2 1DH; 1 Brunswick Court, Leeds LS2 7QU; 16 Reform St, Dundee, DD1 1RG, T0800-2989815, www.travelmoodadventures.com.
Visit Asia (Tennyson Travel), 30-32 Fulham High St, London SW6 3LQ, T020-7736 4347, www.visitasia.co.uk. Tours throughout Asia.

In North America

Adventure Center, 1311 63rd St, Suite 200, Emeryville, CA, T+1-800 227 8747, www.adventurecenter.com.
Global Spectrum, 3907 Laro Court, Fairfax, VA 22031, T+1-800 -419 4446, www.globalspectrumtravel.com.
Hidden Treasure Tours, 509 Lincoln Blvd, Long Beach, NY 11561, T01-87-7761 7276 (USA toll free), www.hiddentreasuretours.com.
Journeys, 107 April Drive, Suite 3, Ann Arbor MI 46103, T+1-800-255 8735 (USA toll free), www.journeys-intl.com.
Myths & Mountains, 976 Tree Court, Incline Village, Nevada 89451, T1-800 670 6984, www.mythsandmountains.com. Organizes travel to all 3 countries.
Nine Dragons Travel & Tours, 1476 Orange Grove Rd, Charleston, SC 29407, T+1-317-281 3895, www.nine-dragons.com.

In Australia and New Zealand

Intrepid Travel, 360 Bourke St, Melbourne, Victoria 3000, T+61-03-8602 0500, www.intrepidtravel.com.au

Travel Indochina, Level 10, HCF House, 403 George St, Sydney, NSW 2000, T+61-1300-138755 (toll free), www.travelindochina.com.au. Small group journeys and tailor-made holidays.

In Southeast Asia

Discovery Indochina, 3A Cua Bac St, Hanoi, Vietnam, T(0084) 47-164132, www.discovery indochina.com. Private and customized tours covering Cambodia, Vietnam and Laos.

Visas and immigration
Visa on arrival

A 30-day tourist visa can be obtained on arrival at: Vientiane's Wattay Airport; Luang Prabang International Airport; Pakse International Airport; the Friendship Bridge crossing near Nong Khai/Vientiane, Chiang Khong/Houei Xai crossing; Chongmek/Vang Tao (near Pakse) crossing; Nakhon Phanom/Thakhek crossing; and Mukdahan/ Savannakhet crossing. In China, Lao visas are available at the Mohan/Boten crossing. In Vietnam, they are available at: Lao Bao/Dansavanh in Savannakhet; Cau Treo/Nam Phao (Khammouane Province); and Nam Khan/Nam Can in Xieng Khouang Province.

At the time of publication, Lao visas were not available at the following borders: the Vietnam crossing Nam Xoi/Nameo; Na Phao/Cha Lo, Attapeu/Quy Nhon and the Cambodian crossing at Dom Kralor. For these crossings, visas will need to be organized in advance. You will need a passport photo or 2.

Visa prices are based on reciprocity with countries and cost US$30-42. 'Overtime fees' are often charged if you enter after 1600 or at a weekend. To get a visa you need to provide a passport photograph and the name of the first hotel you plan on staying

Visa extensions

Tourist visa extensions can be obtained from the Lao Immigration Office in the Ministry of the Interior opposite the Morning Market in Vientiane, T021-212529. They can be extended for up to a month at the cost of US$2 per day (although if you want to extend for a month it works out cheaper to cross the border); you will need 1 passport photo. It takes a day to process the extension and if you drop the paperwork off early in the morning it will often be ready by the afternoon. Travel agencies in Vientiane and other major centres can also handle this service for you for a fee (eg an additional US$1-2 per day). Visitors who overstay their visas are charged US$10 for each day beyond the date of expiration, they will be asked to pay this on departure from Laos.

Weights and measures
Metric.

Women travellers

While women travelling alone can generally face more potential problems than men or couples, these are far less pronounced in Laos than in most countries and it is rare for women to be harassed. Nonetheless, women should take care to dress modestly, especially in the smaller, more provincial towns.

If you are bathing in a waterfall or river, wear a sarong, as the locals are embarrassed or offended by the sight of bare flesh.

Working in Laos

Work is not easily available in Laos and is in great demand. Laos has one of the highest retention rates of foreign workers in the region, as once they get there they don't want to leave. There is a vibrant expat community, mostly of aid workers (with NGOs or bilateral/ multilateral agencies; see www.directoryof ngos.org) as well as the usual diplomatic corps. But, unlike Thailand, there is not great scope for people to teach English for a few months.

Jobs are advertised in the *Vientiane Times*. The *Vientiane Guide*, is available from bookshops in Vientiane and is a useful tool for those proposing to live in the country. It's a bit out of date but has handy tips.

Vientiane and around

→ Colour map 1, C5.

In 1563, King Setthathirat made the riverine city of Vientiane the capital of Laos. Or, to be more historically accurate, Wiang Chan, the 'City of the Moon', became the capital of Lane Xang. In those days it was a small fortified city on the banks of the Mekong with a palace and two wats, That Luang and Wat Phra Kaeo (built to house the Emerald Buddha).

Today Vientiane is, perhaps, the most charming of all Southeast Asia's capital cities. Cut off from the outside world and foreign investment for much of the modern period, its colonial heritage remains largely intact. While the last few years have brought greater bustle and activity, it is still a quiet city of tree-lined boulevards, where the image of the past is reflected in the present.

Snuggled in a curve of the Mekong, Vientiane is also the region's most modest capital. It is much more than a town, but it doesn't quite cut it as a conventional city. Here, colourless concrete Communist edifices sit alongside chicken farmers; outdoor aerobics fanatics are juxtaposed against locals making merit at the city's wats; and a couple of traffic lights command a dribble of chaotic cars, bikes, tuk-tuks and buses on the city's streets.

A short trip north of Vientiane is Vang Vieng, a favourite of adventure enthusiasts, with caving, kayaking, tubing, trekking and more on offer. ▶▶ For listings, see pages 467-481.

Vientiane ⊖⊕⊕⊕⊕⊛⊙▲⊖ ▶▶ pp467-481.

Vientiane's appeal lies in its largely preserved fusion of Southeast Asian and French colonial culture. Baguettes, plunged coffee and Bordeaux wines coexist with spring rolls, *pho* soup and papaya salad. Colourful tuk-tuks scuttle along tree-lined boulevards, past old Buddhist temples and cosmopolitan cafés. Hammer-and-sickle flags hang at ten-pin bowling discos, locals carry sacks of devalued currency and chickens wander the streets. But, as in the rest of Laos, the best thing about Vientiane, is its people. Stroll around some of the outlying *bans* (villages) and meet the wonderful characters who make this city what it is.

Close to the city is Xieng Khuan, popularly known as the Buddha Park, a bizarre collection of statues and monuments, while, to the north, Vang Vieng, the adventure capital of Laos, attracts backpackers with a multitude of outdoor activities.

Ins and outs

Getting there by air Most visitors arrive in Vientiane by air, the great bulk on one of the daily connections from Bangkok, with **Thai Air** or **Lao Airlines**, which also run international flights to/from Kunming, Phnom Penh and Siem Reap. **Vietnam Airlines** runs flights between Hanoi and Ho Chi Minh City. **Wattay International Airport** ① T021-212066, lies 6 km west of the town centre. Vientiane is the hub of Laos' domestic airline system and to travel from the north to the south or vice versa it is necessary to change planes here. Only taxis are allowed to pick up passengers at the airport (US$5 to the centre of town, 20 minutes) although tuk-tuks can drop off here. Tuk-tuks can be taken from the main road and sometimes lurk at the far side of the airport, near the exit (40,000 kip to the centre).

A cheaper alternative from Thailand is to fly from Bangkok to **Udon Thani** on a budget airline (www.nokair.co.th, www.airasia.com) and then continue by road to Vientiane via the Friendship Bridge, which lies just 25 km downstream from the capital (allow three hours). Shuttle buses from Udon Thani airport, ฿150, usually run to the border after every flight. There are several flights a day between Udon Thani and Bangkok.

Getting there by bus There are three public bus terminals in Vientiane. The **Southern bus station** is 9 km south of the city centre on Route 13. Most international buses bound for Vietnam depart from here as well as buses to southern and eastern Laos.

The **Northern bus station** is on Route T2, about 3 km northwest of the centre before the airport, T021-260255, and serves destinations in northern Laos. Most tuk-tuks will take you there from the city for 20,000 kip; ask for '*Bai Thay Song*'. There are English-speaking staff at the help desk.

The **Talaat Sao bus station** is across the road from the Morning Market, in front of Talaat Kudin, on the eastern edge of the city centre. This station serves destinations within Vientiane Province, buses to and from the Thai border and international buses to Nong Khai and Udon Thani in Thailand. It is also a good place to pick up a tuk-tuk.
▶ *See Transport, page 478.*

Getting around Vientiane is small and manageable and is one of the most laid-back capital cities in the world. The local catch phrase '*bopenyang*' (no worries) has permeated through every sector of the city, so much so that even the mangy street dogs look completely chilled out. The core of the city is negotiable on foot and even outlying hotels and places of interest are accessible by bicycle. Cycling remains the most flexible way to tour the city. It can be debilitatingly hot at certain times of year but there are no great hills to struggle up. If cycling doesn't appeal, a combination of foot and tuk-tuk or small 110-125cc scooters take the effort out of sightseeing.

Vientiane can be rather confusing for the first-time visitor as there are few street signs and most streets have two names, pre- and post-revolutionary but, because Vientiane is so small and compact, it doesn't take long to get to grips with the layout. The names of major streets or *thanon* usually correspond to the nearest wat, while traffic lights, wats, monuments and large hotels serve as directional landmarks. When giving directions to a tuk-tuk it is better to use these landmarks, as street names leave them a little bewildered.

Tourist information Lao **National Tourism Authority** ① *Lane Xang (towards Patuxai), T021-212251 for information, www.tourismlaos.gov.au*, can provide information regarding ecotourism operators and trekking opportunities. The **Tourist Police** ① *daily 0830-1200, 1300-1600*, are upstairs.

Background
Vientiane is an ancient city. There was probably a settlement here in the 10th century but knowledge of the city before the 16th century is sketchy. From the chronicles, scholars do know that King Setthathirat decided to relocate his capital here in the early 1560s. It seems that it took him four years to build the city, constructing a defensive wall (hence 'Wiang', meaning a walled or fortified city), along with Wat Phra Kaeo and a much enlarged That Luang. Vieng Chan remained intact until 1827 when it was ransacked by the Siamese; this is why many of its wats are of recent construction.

The city was abandoned for decades and erased from the maps of the region. It was only conjured back into existence by the French, who commenced reconstruction at the end of the 19th century. They built rambling colonial villas and wide tree-lined boulevards, befitting their new administrative capital, Vientiane. At the height of American influence in the 1960s, it was renowned for its opium dens and sex shows.

For the moment, the city retains its unique innocence: DJs are officially outlawed (although this is not enforced); there is a 2330 curfew; a certain percentage of music played at restaurants and bars every day is supposed to be Lao (overcome by banging out the Lao tune quota at 0800 in the morning) and women are urged to wear the national dress, the *sinh*. However, to describe the Lao government as autocratic is unfairly negative. Vientiane's citizens are proud of their cultural heritage and are usually very supportive of the government's attempts to promote it. The government has tried, by and large, to maintain the national identity and protect its citizens from harmful outside influences. This is already starting to change, as, with the government reshuffle in 2006 came a gradual loosening of the cultural stranglehold.

Sights

Most of the interesting buildings in Vientiane are of religious significance. All tour companies and many hotels and guesthouses will arrange city tours and excursions to surrounding sights but it is just as easy to arrange a tour independently with a local tuk-tuk driver; the best English speakers (and thus the most expensive tuk-tuks) can be found in the parking lot beside Nam Phou. Those at the Morning Market (Talaat Sao) are cheaper. Most tuk-tuk drivers pretend not to carry small change, so make sure you have the exact fare with you before taking a ride.

That Luang ⓘ *That Luang Rd, 3.5 km northeast of the city centre; daily 0800-1200, 1300-1600 (except 'special' holidays); 2000 kip. A booklet about the wat is on sale at the entrance.* That Luang is Vientiane's most important site and the holiest Buddhist monument in the country. The golden spire looks impressive at the top of the hill, overlooking the city.

According to legend, a stupa was first built here in the third century AD by emissaries of the Moghul Emperor Asoka. Excavations on the site, however, have only located the remains of an 11th- to 13th-century Khmer temple, making the earlier provenance doubtful in the extreme. The present monument, encompassing the previous buildings, was built in 1566 by King Setthathirat, whose statue stands outside. Plundered by the Thais and the Chinese Haw in the 18th century, it was restored by King (Chao) Anou at the beginning of the 19th century.

The reliquary is surrounded by a square cloister, with an entrance on each side, the most famous on the east. There is a small collection of statues in the cloisters, including one of the Khmer king Jayavarman VII. The cloisters are used as lodgings by monks who travel to Vientiane for religious reasons and especially for the annual **That Luang Festival** (see page). The base of the stupa is a mixture of styles, Khmer, Indian and Lao – and each side has a *hor vay* or small offering temple. This lowest level represents the material world, while the second tier is surrounded by a lotus wall and 30 smaller stupas, representing the 30 Buddhist perfections. Each of these originally contained smaller golden stupas but they were stolen by Chinese raiders in the 19th century. The 30-m-high spire dominates the skyline and resembles an elongated lotus bud, crowned by a stylized banana flower and parasol. It was designed so that pilgrims could climb up to the stupa via the walkways around each level. It is believed that originally over 450 kg of gold leaf was used on the spire.

Patuxai (Victory Monument) ⓘ *Junction of That Luang Rd and Lane Xang Av; Mon-Fri 0800-1100, 1400-1630 (officially, but these hours seem to be posted only for fun); 3000 kip.* At the end of That Luang is the Oriental answer to Paris's Arc de Triomphe and Vientiane's best-known landmark, the Victory Monument or Patuxai. It was built by the former regime in memory of those who died in the wars before the Communist takeover, but the cement ran out before its completion. Refusing to be beaten, the regime diverted hundreds of tonnes of cement, part of a US aid package to help with the construction of runways at Wattay Airport, to finish off the monument in 1969.

Wat Sisaket ① *Junction of Lane Xang Av and Setthathirat Rd; daily 0800-1200, 1400-1600; 5000 kip. No photographs in the sim.* Further down Lane Xang is the **Morning Market** or **Talaat Sao** (see page 475) and beyond, is one of Vientiane's two national museums, Wat Sisaket. Home of the head of the Buddhist community in Laos, **Phra Sangka Nagnok**, it is one of the most important buildings in the capital and houses over 7000 Buddha images.

Vientiane

Wat Sisaket was built in 1818 during the reign of King Anou. A traditional Lao monastery, it was the only temple that survived the Thai sacking of the town in 1827-1828, making it the oldest building in Vientiane.

The main sanctuary, or **sim**, with its sweeping roof, shares many stylistic similarities with Wat Phra Kaeo (see below): window surrounds, lotus-shaped pillars and carvings of deities held up by giants on the rear door. The sim contains 2052 Buddha statues (mainly terracotta, bronze and wood) in small niches in the top half of the wall. There is little left of the Thai-style *jataka* murals on the lower walls but the depth and colour of the originals can be seen from the few remaining pieces.

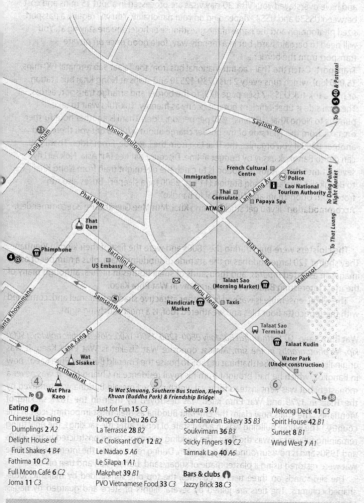

Eating 🍴

Chinese Liao-ning
Dumplings 2 *A2*
Delight House of
Fruit Shakes 4 *B4*
Fathima 10 *C2*
Full Moon Café 6 *C2*
Joma 11 *C3*

Just for Fun 15 *C3*
Khop Chai Deu 26 *C3*
La Terrasse 28 *B2*
Le Croissant d'Or 12 *B2*
Le Nadao 5 *A6*
Le Silapa 1 *A1*
Makphet 39 *B1*
PVO Vietnamese Food 33 *C3*

Sakura 3 *A1*
Scandinavian Bakery 35 *B3*
Soukvimarn 36 *B3*
Sticky Fingers 19 *C2*
Tamnak Lao 40 *A6*

Bars & clubs 🍸

Jazzy Brick 38 *C3*

Mekong Deck 41 *C3*
Spirit House 42 *B1*
Sunset 8 *B1*
Wind West 7 *A1*

Border essentials: Laos–Thailand

Friendship Bridge

The bridge is 20 km southeast of Vientiane. Shuttle minibuses take punters across the bridge every 20 mins for 5000 kip, stopping at the Thai and Lao immigration posts where an overtime fee is charged after 1630 and at weekends. The border is open daily 0600-2200. Allow up to 1½ hrs to get to the bridge and through formalities on the Lao side. The paperwork is pretty swift, unless you are leaving the country and have overstayed your visa. 30-day visas are processed in about 15 mins and cost between US$30 and US$42 depending on your nationality. You will require a passport-sized photograph and the name of the guesthouse or hotel you are staying at. You will need to bargain hard, but in a friendly way, for a good price on private transport from the border.

Transport Catch the Thai-Lao International bus from the Talaat Sao terminal (90 mins, 15,000 kip), which runs every 2 hrs 0730-12530 and stops at Nong Khai bus station, or hire a tuk-tuk US$5-7 (see page 479) to the border and arrange transport across. The Thai side is über-efficient but not nearly as friendly. Tuk-tuks wait to take punters to Nong Khai (10 mins), ฿50 per person; Udon Thani is another hour further on; taxis from the Thai side of the border charge about ฿700 to get you there; add another ฿300 if you organize the Thai taxi from the Lao side. From Udon Thani you can get to Bangkok easily by budget airline. Discount airlines (Air Asia, Nok Air) fly several times daily. Another option is to catch the overnight train from Nong Khai to Bangkok's Hualamphong Station (11 hrs, ฿800 for a sleeper). Buses also run from both Udon Thani and Nong Khai to Bangkok.

Accommodation If you get stuck in Nong Khai, Mut Mee Guesthouse is recommended.

The **cloisters** were built during the 1800s and were the first of their kind in Vientiane. They shelter 120 large Buddhas in the attitude of subduing Mara, plus a number of other images in assorted *mudras*, and thousands of small figures in niches, although many of the most interesting Buddha figures are now in Wat Phra Kaeo.

The whole ensemble is washed in a rather attractive shade of caramel and, combined with the terracotta floor tiles and weathered roof, is a most satisfying sight.

Wat Phra Kaeo ⓘ *Setthathirat Rd; daily 0800-1200, 1300-1600, closed public holidays; 5000 kip. No photographs in the sim.* Almost opposite Wat Sisaket is Wat Phra Kaeo. It was originally built by King Setthathirat in 1565 to house the Emerald Buddha (Phra Kaeo), now in Bangkok, which he had brought from his royal residence in Chiang Mai. It was never a monastery but was kept instead for royal worship. The Emerald Buddha was removed by the Thais in 1779 and Wat Phra Kaeo was destroyed by them in the 1827 sacking of Vientiane. (The Thais now claim the Emerald Buddha as their most important icon in the country.) The whole building was in a bad state of repair after the sackings, the only thing remaining fully intact was the floor. The building was expertly reconstructed in the 1940s and 1950s and is now surrounded by a garden. During renovations, the interior walls of the wat were restored using a plaster made of sugar, sand, buffalo skin and tree oil.

The sim stands on three tiers of galleries, the top one surrounded by majestic, lotus-shaped columns. The tiers are joined by several flights of steps and guarded by nagas.

Phou Khao Khouay National Protected Area

Phou Khao Khouay National Protected Area (pronounced poo cow kway) is one of Laos' premier national protected areas. The area extends across 2000 sq km and incorporates an attractive sandstone mountain range. It is crossed by three large rivers, smaller tributaries and two waterfalls at Tad Leuk and Tad Sae, which weave their way in to the Ang Nam Leuk reservoir, a stunning man-made dam and lake that sits on the outskirts of the park. Within the protected area is an array of wildlife, including wild elephants, gibbons, tigers, clouded leopards and Asiatic black bears.

Around the village of Ban Na the village's sugar cane plantations and river salt deposits attract a herd of wild elephants (around 30), which have, in the past, destroyed the villagers' homes and even killed a resident. This has limited the villagers' ability to undertake normal tasks, such as collecting bamboo, fearing that they may come across the wild elephants. To help compensate, the village, in conjunction with some NGOs, has constructed an elephant observation tower and has started running trekking tours to see these massive creatures in their natural habitat. The elephant tower is the primary attraction and it possible to stay over at the tower, 4 km from Ban Na, to try and catch a glimpse of the giant pachyderms who come to lap up salt from the nearby salt lick in the early evening hours. One-to three-day treks through the national park cross waterfalls, pass through pristine jungle and, with luck, offer the opportunity to hear or spot the odd wild elephant. It is too dangerous to get close. This is an important ecotour that contributes to the livelihood of the Ban Na villagers and helps conserve the elephant population. Advance notice is required so it's advisable to book with a tour operator in Vientiane. If you are travelling independently you will need to organize permits, trekking and accommodation with the village directly. To do this, contact Mr Bounthanam, T020-2208286. Visit www.trekkingcentrallaos.com and contact the National Tourism Authority in Vientiane or Green Discovery Tours (see page 476). Visitors will need to bring drinking water and snacks. Do not try to feed the elephants, they are dangerous.

Ban Hat Khai is home to 90 families from the Lao Loum and Lao Soung ethnic groups. It is also a starting point for organized treks through mountain landscapes, crossing the Nam Mang River and the Phay Xay cliffs. Most treks take in the Tad Sae Falls. Homestay accommodation is available.

Transport The park is northeast of Vientiane along Route 13 South. To get to Ban Na you need to stop at Tha Pabat Phonsanh, 80 km northeast of Vientiane; the village is a further 2 km from here. For Ban Hat Khai, 100 km northeast of Vientiane, continue on Route 13 to Thabok, where a songthaew or boat can take you the extra 7-8 km to the village. Buses to Paksan from the Talaat Sao bus station and That Luang market in Vientiane stop at Thabok.

The main, central (southern) door is an exquisite example of Lao wood sculpture with carved angels surrounded by flowers and birds; it is the only notable remnant of the original wat. (The central door at the northern end, with the larger carved angels supported by ogres, is new.) The sim now houses a superb assortment of Lao and Khmer art and some pieces of Burmese and Khmer influence, mostly collected from other wats in Vientiane. Although people regularly come and pray here the wat's main purpose is as a quasi-museum.

Lao National Museum ① *Samsenthai Rd, opposite the Cultural Centre Hall; daily 0800-1200, 1300-1600; 5000 kip.* Formerly called the Revolutionary Museum, in these post-revolutionary days it has been redesignated as the National Museum. The museum's collection has grown over the last few years and now includes a selection of historical artefacts from dinosaur bones and pre-Angkorian sculptures to a comprehensive photographic collection on Laos' modern history. The rhetoric of these modern collections has been toned down from the old days, when captions would refer to the 'running dog imperialists' (Americans). The museum features a dazzling array of personal effects from the revolutionary leader Kaysone, including his exercise machine and a spoon he once used. Downstairs there are ancient artefacts, including stone tools and poignant burial jars. Upstairs the museum features a range of artefacts and busts, as well as a small exhibition on various ethnic minorities. The final section of the museum comprises mostly photographs which trace, chronologically, the country's struggle against the 'brutal' French colonialists and American 'imperialists'.

Xieng Khuan ① *Route 2 (25 km south of Vientiane); daily 0800-1700, 5000 kip, camera 5000 kip.* Otherwise known as the **Garden of the Buddhas** or **Buddha Park**, Xieng Khuan is close to the border with Thailand. It has been described as a Laotian Tiger Balm Gardens, with reinforced concrete Buddhist and Hindu sculptures of Vishnu, Buddha, Siva and various other assorted deities and near-deities. There's also a bulbous-style building with three levels containing smaller sculptures of the same gods.

The garden was built in the late 1950s by a priest-monk-guru-sage-artist called Luang Pu Bunleua Sulihat, who studied under a Hindu *rishi* in Vietnam and then combined the Buddhist and Hindu philosophies in his own very peculiar view of the world. He left Laos because his anti-communist views were incompatible with the ideology of the Pathet Lao (or perhaps because he was just too weird) and settled across the Mekong near the Thai town of Nong Khai, where he proceeded to build an equally revolting and bizarre concrete theme park for religious schizophrenics, called Wat Khaek. With Luang Pu's forced departure from Laos his religious garden came under state control and it is now a public park.

To get there take the No 14 bus (one hour) from the Talaat Sao bus station, a tuk-tuk (100,000 kip), hire a private vehicle (US$15), or take a motorbike or bicycle because the road follows the river and is level the whole way. Vendors at the site sell drinks and snacks.

Vang Vieng ●❷❶▲❸❶ ▸▸ *pp467-481. Colour map 1, C5.*

The drive from Vientiane to Vang Vieng, on the much-improved Route 13, follows the valley of the Nam Ngum and then climbs steeply onto the plateau where Vang Vieng is located, 160 km north of Vientiane. The surrounding area is inhabited by the Hmong and Yao hill peoples and is particularly picturesque: craggy karst limestone scenery, riddled with caves, crystal-clear pools and waterfalls. In the early morning the views are reminiscent of a Chinese Sung Dynasty painting. The town itself is nestled in a valley on the bank of the Nam Song River, amid a misty jungle. It enjoys cooler weather and offers breathtaking views of the imposing mountains of Pha Tang and Phatto Nokham.

The town's laid-back feel has made it a popular haunt for the backpacker crowd, while the surrounding landscape has helped to establish Vang Vieng as Laos' premier outdoor activity destination, especially for rock climbing, caving and kayaking. Its popularity in many ways has also become its downfall: neon lights, pancake stands, 'happy' this and 'happy' that, and pirated *Friends* videos now pollute this former oasis. Nevertheless, the town and surrounding area is still full of wonderful things to do and see.

Tubing and kayaking in Vang Vieng

Vang Vieng has become synonymous with tubing down the Nam Song. Tubes can be picked up from the Old Market area where the tubing company has formed a cartel. Without stops the 3 km tubing trip from the **Organic Mulberry Farm** to town can take one to two hours, but most people do it in three to four hours, choosing to stop along the way at the many bars dotted along the river.

Many tour operators organize kayaking trips as well. Popular routes include kayaking down the Nam Song to incorporate the caves (especially Tham Nam – water cave), or the trip back to Vientiane via the drop-off point at Nam Lik. If you want to break the journey, there are several nice guesthouses at Nam Lik. For details, see Activities and tours, page 477.

Ins and outs **Safety** Laos is a very safe country for tourists but a disproportionate number of accidents and crimes seem to happen in Vang Vieng. **Theft** is routinely reported, ranging from robberies by packs of kids targeting tubers on the river to the opportunist theft of items from guests' rooms. Most guesthouses won't take responsibility for valuables left in rooms, so it is usually advisable to hand in valuables to the management. Otherwise, you will need to padlock your bag. Another major problem is the sale of illegal **drugs**. Police often go on sting operations and impose fines of up to US$600 for possession. Legal issues aside, many travellers have become seriously ill from indulging in the 'happy' supplements supplied by restaurants. ▸ *See Activities and tours, page 477.*

Caves ⓘ *Each cave has an entrance fee of 3000 -10,000 kip and many have stalls where you can buy drinks and snacks. You can buy hand-drawn maps from the town but all the caves are clearly signposted in English from the main road so these are not really necessary.* Vang Vieng is best known for its limestone caves, sheltered in the mountains flanking the town. Pretty much every guesthouse and tour operator offers tours to the caves (the best of these is **Green Discovery**) and, although some caves can be accessed independently, it is advisable to take a guide to a few as they are dark and difficult to navigate. Often children from surrounding villages will take tourists through the caves for a small fee. Don't forget to bring a torch, or even better a head-lamp, which can be picked up cheaply at the market both in Vang Vieng and Vientiane.

Of Vang Vieng's myriad caves, **Tham Chang** is the most renowned of all. Tham Chang penetrates right under a mountain and is fed by a natural spring perfect for an early morning dip. From the spring it is possible to swim into the cave for quite a distance (bring a waterproof torch, if possible). The cave is said to have been used as a refuge during the 19th century from Chinese Haw bandits and this explains its name: *chang* meaning 'loyal' or 'steadfast'. Entrance is via Vang Vieng resort south of town. For your US$1 or 10,000 kip entry fee you get into the caves and the lighting system will be turned on. Although the cave is not the most magnificent, it serves as a superb lookout point.

Another popular cavern is **Tham Poukham** ⓘ *7 km from Vang Vieng, 5000 kip.* The cave is often referred to as the cave of the Golden Crab and is highly auspicious. It's believed that if you catch a golden crab you will have a lifetime of fortune. To get there you need to cross the foot-bridge near the **Villa Nam Song**, and then follow the road for a further 6 km until you reach the village of Ban Nathong. From the village the cave is 1 km walk and a short climb up quite a steep hill. Mossy rocks lead the way into the main cavern area where a large bronze reclining Buddha is housed. Here there is an idyllic lagoon, with glassy green-blue waters, great for a swim.

Tham None ① *4 km north of Vang Vieng, 5000 kip*, is known locally as the 'Sleeping Cave' because 2000 villagers took refuge there during the war. The large cave is dotted with stalagmites and stalactites, including the 'magic stone of Vang Vieng', which reflects light. Lots of bats reside in the grotto.

Tham Xang ① *14 km north of Vang Vieng on the banks of the Nam Song, 2000 kip*, also known as the 'Elephant Cave', is named after the stalagmites and stalactites that

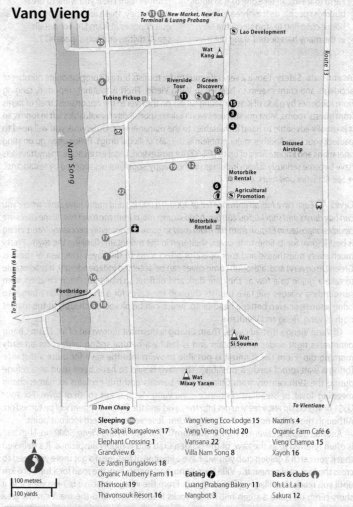

Vang Vieng

To ⑪ ⑬, New Market, New Bus Terminal & Luang Prabang

Ⓢ Lao Development

Route 13

Wat Kang ⚲

Riverside Tour   Green Discovery

⑳

⑥

Tubing Pickup   ⑪ Ⓢ Ⓢ ⑯

⑮
❸
❹

Disued Airstrip

✉

@

⑲ ⑫

Motorbike Rental

Nam Song

❻
Ⓢ Agricultural Promotion

⑳

Motorbike Rental

⑰

❶

⑯
Footbridge

❽ ⑱

To Tham Poukham (6 km)

Wat Si Souman ⚲

Wat Mixay Yaram ⚲

To Vientiane

◻ Tham Chang

N

100 metres
100 yards

have created an elephant formation (you may need to squint to see it). The cave also contains some Buddha images, including the Footprint of Buddha. Although the cave itself is relatively non-descript the bell used by monks is made of a former bomb. From this cave there is a signposted path that leads to **Tham Nam** (water cave) ① *15 km from town, 5000 kip*, a long spindly cave that is believed to stretch for at least 7 km. It takes about two hours to explore the cavern and at the entrance there is a crystal-clear pool. This is one of Vang Vieng's most interesting caves and in the wet season needs to be explored with an inner tube or by wading, while pulling yourself along a rope. It's not an easy task and should not be attempted alone. At times the cavern is an extremely tight fit and commando-type crawling is required; a hard helmet with lamp attached is necessary. However, this is an incredible caving experience. To get to these two caves follow Route 13 north and turn left at Km 14, follow this dirt road for 1 km until you reach the river. Boats charge 10,000 kip to cross the river to see Tham Xang; from there you can walk to Tham Nam.

● Vientiane and around listings

Hotel and guesthouse prices

LL over US$200 **L** US$151-200 **AL** US$101-150
A US$66-100 **B** US$46-65 **C** US$31-45
D US$21-30 **E** US$12-20 **F** US$7-11
G US$6 and under

Restaurant prices

††† over US$12 **††** US$6-12 **†** under US$6.

● Sleeping

Vientiane *p457, map p460*
There is very little quality accommodation in Vientiane under US$10 a night. There is a big difference in the quality of rooms between the US$10 and US$20-30 rooms, the extra US$10 is a worthwhile investment. Cheaper guesthouses will offer discounts in the wet season. Higher-end hotels offer better rates on the internet than the rate given if you walk in off the street. All guesthouses and boutique hotels, except for the most expensive, tend to get booked up so reserve in advance. As a rule, hotels over US$50 accept major credit cards.
LL Green Park Hotel, Khou Vieng Rd, T021-264297, www.greenparkvientiane.com. Designed in a modern East-meets-West style, this hotel is set alongside Vientiane's primary park. Beautiful rooms with all the mod cons, Wi-Fi and super-duper baths. Beautiful garden and excellent swimming pool. The only

drawback is that it is set a little further out from the city centre and river, but is still within walking distance. A fantastic luxury option.
LL-L Don Chan Palace Hotel, Piawat Village (off Fa Gnum Quay) T021-244288, www.don chanpalace.com. This 14-storey hotel is the largest in Vientiane and probably the ugliest. Once you can get past the ugly exterior, the 230 rooms and facilities are outstanding and afford the best views of the river and the city. There's a restaurant, private karaoke rooms, bar, poolside massage and gym.
LL-L Settha Palace Hotel, 6 Pang Kham Rd, T021-217581/2, www.sethapalace.com. The stunning **Settha Palace** was built in 1936 and opened as a hotel in 1999. Its French architecture, stunning colonial decor, period furniture and beautiful tropical gardens and pool sit more easily with the fundamental essence of Vientiane than the other top-level hotels. Often considered the best hotel in town. Recommended.
A-D Beau Rivage Mekong, Fa Ngum Rd, T021-243350, www.hbrm.com. One of the first Western-style boutique hotels in Vientiane, it is beautifully furnished, with fantastic baths. The pink exterior does not sit well with its surroundings but nonetheless this is a great hotel with superb Mekong river views. Its location, just out of the centre of town on the river, ensures peace and quiet

but it's still only a 5-min walk to the hustle and bustle. Includes breakfast.

A-D Lane Xang Hotel, Fa Ngum Rd, T021-214100, www.lanexanghotel.com. The original 'luxury' hotel in Vientiane, built by the French in the 1960s. It has an indefinable charm, despite the fact that some of its retro-hip Soviet fittings and furniture have been ripped out to make way for a more contemporary look. The a/c rooms are well equipped, with excellent bathrooms, making the hotel the best value in town. Opt for the deluxe room, with its own bar and velour bed fittings and indulge in a 1970s, porn-flick nostalgia trip. Other facilities include a dilapidated pool, nightclub and bar.

A-D Orchid Hotel, Chao Anou. T021-264 138, www.laoorchid.com. Beautiful spacious rooms with stunning modern furnishings, polished floorboards and large showers. Outstanding value for the price and very popular with business travellers. Very busy so advanced bookings essential. Includes breakfast and Wi-Fi. Visa and MasterCard accepted. Recommended.

A-E Hotel Day Inn, Pang Kham Rd, T021-222985, dayinn@laopdr.com. Run by a friendly Cambodian, this renovated villa is in a good position in a quiet part of town, just to the north of the main concentration of bars and restaurants. Attractive, airy, clean, large rooms, with a/c and excellent bathrooms. Bike hire.

A-E Intercity Hotel, 24-25 Fa Ngum Rd/ Chou Anou (next to Wat Chan), T021-242842, www.laointerhotel.com. This Singaporean-owned hotel is one of the oldest in Vientiane, it has been operating for over 30 years. Renovations have made it sparkle, and traditional shutters and silk hangings feature in every room. The a/c rooms are light and spacious, with slick bathrooms and fantastic balconies overlooking the Mekong.

C-D Chanthapanya, Nokeo Khoummane Rd, T021-244284, www.chanthapanyahotel.com. Fantastic modern Asian building. The rooms are new and very comfortable. Beautifully furnished with modern Lao wooden furniture, comfy beds, fridge, TV, hot water, phone and a/c. Includes breakfast.

C-E Le Parasol Blanc, behind National Assembly, close to Victory Gate (not very well marked), T021-216091. A very attractive leafy haven. Spacious a/c rooms, with wooden floors and sizeable bathrooms. Some look onto the garden, with sitting area in front, the most expensive are alongside the pool. Charming place, well run, mostly patronized by French visitors.

C-E Mali Namphu Guesthouse, 114 Pang Kham Rd (next door to Phonepaseuth Guesthouse), T021-215093, malinamp@ laotel.com. Difficult to spot as it looks like a small shopfront but the façade is deceiving, the foyer opens onto a beautifully manicured courtyard surrounded by quaint, terraced rooms. Clean, bright rooms are traditionally decorated with a modern twist and come with a/c, hot water, cable TV and a fantastic breakfast. The twin rooms are much nicer than the doubles. Friendly staff. Highly recommended.

C-E Vayakorn, 91 Nokeo Khoummane Rd, T021-241911. The rooms are clean, beautifully decorated with modern furniture and very comfortable. Hot water, a/c and TV. Sadly breakfast is no longer included with rooms but it is still excellent value. Great value, centrally located.

D-E Douang Deuane, Nokeo Khoummane Rd, T021-222301, www.bookings-asia.com/ la/hotels/douangdeane. From the exterior, this dilapidated building looks like a classic Communist edifice, but the a/c rooms have charm and character: parquet wood floors, art deco furniture, excellent bathrooms and satellite TV. Try and get a balcony room for lovely patchwork views of the roofs of the city. Although the room rates are no longer competitive, it is a good centrally located option-B if the others within this price-range are fully booked. Good-value motorbike rentals, 40,000 kip per day.

D-F Dragon Lodge, Samsenthai Rd, T021-250112, dragonlodge2002@yahoo.com. Somewhere between a guesthouse and a hotel. Fun, colourful downstairs restaurant area – good for a party; if you're looking for quiet this probably isn't the best choice. Nice, simply decorated rooms, with hot water, TV and a/c. 5-star service. Visa accepted.

E-F Thongbay Guesthouse, off Luang Prabang Rd, turn right before the **Novotel**, Ban Non Douang, T021-242292, www.thongbay-guesthouses.com. Lovely traditional Lao house set in a lush tropical garden. Rooms have traditional-style fittings, mosquito nets and fan or a/c. The guesthouse also runs cooking classes on request (US$10), which include buying ingredients at the local market. The only drawback of this place is the distance from the city centre. Perfect if you want to relax.

E-G Saysouly, 23 Manthathurath Rd, T021-218383. A variety of rooms, a bit on the musty side. Parquet floors, cheap US$5 single fan rooms with shared bathroom. The shared bathrooms are excellent with powerful showers. Extra for a/c. The more expensive US$10 rooms are quite good value.

E-G Soukchaleun Guesthouse, 121 Setthathirat Rd, T021-218723, soukchaleun_gh@yahoo.com. Quaint guesthouse with a variety of rooms ranging from US$5 with shared bathroom through to US$13 with a/c. Comfy, homely and very clean. The views are not scenic but the guesthouse is friendly and relatively good value.

E-G Syri II Guesthouse, Setthathirat Rd, T021-223178. This is probably one of the best options within the cheaper price range. 3-storey guesthouse with a variety of rooms including fan rooms with shared bathroom US$6 and private bathroom US$8. Clean and simply decorated with wooden furniture. Decorated with quirky curios from around Asia, with lounges and shared communal areas. Helpful staff. Recommended.

G Joe Guesthouse, 112 Fa Ngum Rd, T021-241936, joe_guesthouse@yahoo.com. Wonderful family-run guesthouse on the riverfront. Light, clean and airy. Good coffee shop downstairs. Fantastic service.

G Mixok Guesthouse, 188 Setthathirat Rd, T021-251606, bucnong@hotmail.com. The rooms are amongst the cheapest in town. Very basic and pokey, not for the claustrophobic, but they cost the same as hamburger and a Beer Lao. Shared bathroom with hot water. 11 rooms which are frequently booked out. Very friendly service and excellent location.

Vang Vieng *p464, map p466*

The town's popularity has ensured a uniformity among almost all places catering to budget tourists: most restaurants feature the same menu and there isn't much individuality in the cheaper guesthouses either. The majority are geared to the needs of travellers and offer a laundry service, guides and bicycles. However, in the last 2 years a couple of higher-end hotels have cropped up, providing more attractive options. Although the accommodation in the centre of town is usually cheaper, try and get a room with a view of the river, it's stunning.

A-D Vansana, by the river, T023-511598, vansana@laotel.com. Despite its soulless exterior this hotel boasts the best rooms and facilities in town. Large bedrooms fitted with all the mod cons have mountain and river views. Beautiful pool and bar by the river with deckchairs. Ask for a room with a view.

A-E Thavonsouk Resort, on the river, T021-511096, www.thavonsouk.com. Offers 5 different styles of accommodation across a sprawling riverfront premises. Bungalows range from US$18 to US$75. The US$35 bungalows are great value, with massive balconies fitted with sunbeds. There is a traditional Lao house, decorated with Lao furnishings, suitable for a family or big group, plus suites (TV, fridge, bath, a/c) and standard accommodation. Fantastic restaurant. Keep your eye out for local home-grown pop star, Aluna and her father Alom who run this family business.

C-D Elephant Crossing, on the Nam Song river, T023-511232, www.theelephant crossinghotel.com. A great mid-range option. Australian-owned riverfront hotel classically decorated. The big bath and sliding window between the bedroom and bathroom will be a big hit with romantics. All rooms have a view, fridge and a/c. Breakfast included.

C-D Villa Nam Song, reservation@ villanamsong.com, milestone at the gate. Quaint terracotta villas set in manicured gardens overlooking the Nam Song. Parquet floors, hot water. Restaurant attached. Although this is a beautiful hotel there is better value for money in town.

C-E Ban Sabai Bungalows, on the banks of the river, T021-511088. A stunning complex of individual bungalows in a spectacular location, with all the modern fittings. Hot water, a/c and breakfast included.

D-F Grandview, on the river, T023-511474, grandviewguesthouse@gmail.com. This newcomer offers spotless rooms with attached hot water bathroom. The cheaper rooms don't have a view. Option of paying US$4 extra for a/c. Excellent value. Highly recommended.

E-G Thavisouk, in the centre of town, T023-511340. Perfect budget option. No frills but very clean. Rooms with en suite bathrooms and hot water, US$3-4. While the accommodation is good value, their tours, tickets and other services aren't.

F-G Vang Vieng Orchid, on the river road, T023-5111172. Comfortable fan or a/c rooms. Hot water in the bathrooms and very comfortable rooms. Friendly owners. The rooms with the private balconies are well worth the few extra dollars for the phenomenal view.

G Le Jardin Bungalows, about 900 m from the centre of town along the river, T020-5474643. There are 3 sets of bungalows here: the best are superb; the worst, falling down and soulless, concrete blocks. It is far enough from town for the surrounding beauty to remain undisturbed but close enough for convenience. The views are remarkable and the restaurant is quite good too. The owners are lovely and don't suffer from the Vang Vieng jadedness quite often found in these cheaper bungalows.

Out of town

The places on the outskirts of town are great for those who wish to escape into a more natural landscape. The lack of facilities and transport in the area ensures tranquillity but also makes it quite difficult to get to town.

C-E Vang Vieng Eco-Lodge, 7 km north of town, T020-2247323, tatluang@laotel.com. Although this isn't an ecolodge it is still an exceptionally beautiful place to stay. Set on the banks of the river with stunning gardens and beautiful rock formations, it is a perfect place to get away from it all. The 10 chalet-style bungalows have been nicely decorated, with beautiful balconies, comfortable furnishings and big hot-water baths. The Management ensures a tuk-tuk is just a phone call away. Good Lao restaurant. Also arranges activities and offers a low season discount.

G Organic Mulberry Farm, 3 km north of town, T021-511220, www.laofarm.org. This mulberry farm has basic rooms with mosquito nets, dorm accommodation and full board. Cheaper rates in the low season. Hugely popular restaurant, serving great starfruit wine and famous mulberry pancakes. It is a very popular drop-off spot for tubers.

❼ Eating

Vientiane *p457, map p460*
The absolutely best place to get Lao food is from the open-air stalls that line the banks of the Mekong along **Fa Ngum**. The restaurants are ridiculously low in price and high in atmosphere, particularly at night with their flickering candles. From time to time the government kicks all the eateries off the patch but they usually return with a vengeance. The **Dong Palane Night Market**, on Dong Palane, and the night markets near the corner of **Chao Anou** and **Khoun Boulom Rd** are also good places to go for Lao stall food. There are various other congregations of stalls and vendors around town, most of which set up shop around 1730 and close down by 2100. Be sure to sample Lao ice cream with coconut sticky rice.

The **Chinese quarter** is around Chao Anou, Heng Boun and Khoun Boulom and is a lively spot in the evenings. There are a number of noodle shops here, all of which serve a palatable array of vermicelli, *muu daeng* (red pork), duck and chicken.

The **Korean-style barbeque**, *sindat*, is extremely popular, especially among the younger Lao, as it is a very social event and very cheap. It involves cooking finely sliced meat on a hot plate in the middle of the table, whilst forming a broth with vegetables around the sides of the tray. **Seendat** (see below) is a favourite amongst the older Lao.

♥♥♥-♥♥ Le Nadao, Ban Donmieng (on the right-hand side of the Patuxai roundabout). Daily 1100-1400, 1700-2230. This place is difficult to find but definitely worth every second spent searching the back streets of Vientiane in the dark. Sayavouth, who trained in Paris and New York, produces delectable French cuisine: soups, venison, lamb and puddings. The US$5 set lunch menu is one of the best lunches you will get in town. Fantastic.

♥♥♥-♥♥ Le Silapa, Sihom Rd, T021-219689. Mon-Sat 1130-1400, 1800-2200 (closed Sun and for a month in Jul). Anthony and Fred provide a fantastic French-inspired menu without blowing the budget. Innovative modern meals that would be just at home in the fine dining establishments of New York and London as they are here. Great set lunch menu. Part of the profits are donated to disadvantaged families, usually for expensive but life-saving surgical procedures.

♥♥♥-♥ Sakura, Luang Prabang Rd, Km 2/ Soi 3 (the soi runs along the side of the Novotel), T021-212274. Mon 1730-2200, Tue-Sun 1030-1400, 1730-2200. Regarded as the best Japanese food in town. Expensive for Vientiane but good value by international standards.

♥♥ Tamnak Lao Restaurant, That Luang Rd, T021-413562, open 1200-2200. It's well worth deviating from the main Nam Phou area for a bite to eat here. This restaurant and its sister branch in Luang Prabang have a reputation for delivering outstanding Lao and Thai food, usually prepared with a modern twist.

♥♥-♥ La Terrasse, 55/4 Nokeo Koummane Rd, T021-218550. Mon-Sat 1100-1400, 1800-2200. This is the best European restaurant in terms of variety and price. Large fail-safe menu offering French, European, Lao and Mexican food. Good desserts, especially the rich chocolate mousse, and a good selection of French wine. Fantastic service. Reasonable prices with an excellent 'plat du jour' each day. Great 1970s-style comfort food.

♥ Chinese Liao-ning Dumpling Restaurant, Chao Anou Rd, T021-240811. Daily 1100-2230. This restaurant is a firm favourite with the expats and it isn't hard to see why: fabulous steamed or fried dumplings and a wide range of vegetarian dishes. The place is spotlessly clean but the birds in cages outside are a bit off-putting. No one is ever disappointed by the meals here. Highly recommended.

♥ Fathima, Th Fa Gnum, T021-219097. Without a doubt the best-value Indian in town. Ultra-friendly service and a large menu with a range of excellent curries.

♥ Full Moon Café, François Ngin Rd, T021-243373. Daily 1000-2200. Delectable Asian fusion cuisine and Western favourites. Huge pillows, good lighting and great music make this place very relaxing. Fantastic chicken wrap and some pretty good Asian tapas. The Ladybug shake is a winner. Also a book exchange and music shop for ipods.

♥ Just for Fun, 57/2 Pang Kham Rd, opposite **Lao Airlines**. Good Lao food with vegetarian dishes, coffees, soft drinks and the largest selection of teas in Laos, if not Southeast Asia. The atmosphere is relaxed with a/c, newspapers and comfy chairs (also sells textiles and other handicrafts).

♥ Khop Chai Deu, Setthathirat Rd, on the corner of Nam Phou Rd. Daily 0800-2330. This lively place housed in a former colonial building is one of the city's most popular venues. Garden seating, good atmosphere at night with soft lantern lighting, and an eclectic menu of Indian, Italian, Korean and international dishes (many of which come from nearby restaurants). While the food is okay most come for the bustling atmosphere. The best value are the local Lao dishes though, which are made on site and toned down for the falang palate. Also serves draft or bottled beer at a pleasant a/c bar. Excellent lunch buffet. Live performances.

Makphet, Setthatihirat near Wat Inpeng, T021-260587, www.friends-international.org. Fantastic Lao non-profit restaurant that helps raise money for street kids. Run by the trainees, who are former street kids, and their teachers. Modern Lao cuisine with a twist. Selection of delectable drinks such as the iced hibiscus with lime juice. Beautifully decorated with modern furniture and painting by the kids. Also sells handicrafts and toys produced by the parents from vulnerable communities.

PVO Vietnamese Food, off Fa Gnum Quay. A firm favourite. Full menu of freshly prepared Vietnamese food but best known for baguettes, stuffed with your choice of pâté, salad, cheese, coleslaw, vegetables and ham. Bikes and motorbikes for rent too. Brilliant cheap food makes this a fantastic choice.

Seendat, Sihom Rd, T021-213855. Daily 1730-2200. This restaurant has been in existence for well over 20 years and is a favourite amongst the older Lao for its clean food (*sindat*) and good atmosphere. About US$1 per person more expensive than most other places but this is reflected in the quality.

Soukvimarn, T021-214441, open 1100-1400, 1800-2100. Heavily influenced by traditional southern Lao flavours. Well worth the experience as it offers the opportunity to tempt the taste buds with a wider variety of Lao cuisine than most other eateries offer.

Sticky Fingers, François Ngin Rd, T021-215972, Tue-Sun 1000-2300. Very popular small restaurant and bar serving Lao and international dishes, including fantastic salads, pasta, burgers, and everything from Middle Eastern through to modern Asian. Fantastic comfort food and the best breakfast in town. Great cocktails, lively atmosphere, nice setting. Deliveries available. **Stickies** should be the first pit-stop for every visitor

needing to get grounded quickly as, food aside, the expats who frequent the joint are full to the brim with local knowledge.

Floating restaurants

A couple of floating restaurants are docked on the Mekong. Off Fa Ngum Rd (just past the **Intercity Hotel**). At 1900 the restaurants cruise down the river for the sunset. The cruise is complimentary when you eat there. The food is cheap, so the cruises are exceptionally good value. 2 of the better ones are:

Champadeng, a bit further along from Lane Xang Av, T020-5526911. Daily 1000-2200, cruise at 1930. This is probably the most popular. Quite a good selection of Lao dishes. The food here is as good as you will find anywhere else and, when you get bored, you can pop down to the lower level and belt out a few tunes on the karaoke. When the river is too low the cruises won't run.

Lane Xang, T021-243397. Daily 1000-2230, cruise at 1900. It's a good idea to get in there early so you can watch the sunset, a lot of the cruise is actually in the dark.

Cafés, cake shops and juice bars

Pavement cafés are 10 a penny in Vientiane. You need not walk more than half a block for some hot coffee or a cold fruit shake.

Delight House of Fruit Shakes, Samsenthai Rd, opposite the **Asian Pavilion Hotel**, T021-212200. Daily 0700-2200. Wonderful selection of fresh shakes and fruit salads.

Joma, Setthathirat Rd, T021-215265, bakers @laopdr.com. Mon-Sat 0700-2100. A very modern, chic bakery with efficient service. Wi-Fi and arctic-style a/c. However, it is starting to get a bit pricey.

Le Croissant d'Or, top of Nokeo Khoummane Rd, T021-223740. Daily 0700-1800. French bakery, great for pastries.

Scandinavian Bakery, 71/1 Pang Kham Rd, Nam Phou Circle, T021-215199, scandinavian@laonet.net. Daily 0700-2000. Delicious pastries, bread, sandwiches and cakes. Great place for a leisurely coffee and pastries. Pricey for Laos but a necessary

European fix for many expats. The Nam Phou Circle outlet is much better value and has a wider selection of cakes and sandwiches.

Vang Vieng p464, map p466

There is a string of eating places on the main road through town. Generally, the cuisine available are hamburgers, pasta, sandwiches and basic Asian dishes. Most of the restaurants offer 'happy' upgrades – marijuana or mushrooms in your pizza, cake or lassi, or opium tea. Although many people choose the 'happy' offerings, some wind up very ill.

♥ Luang Prabang Bakery Restaurant, just off the main road, near BCEL. Excellent pastries, cakes and shakes, delicious breakfasts. Recommended but make sure you get a fresh batch.

♥ Nangbot, on the main road, T021-511018. This proper sit-down restaurant is one of the oldest tourist diners in town and serves a few traditional dishes, such as bamboo shoot soup and *laap* with sticky rice, alongside the usual Western fare.

♥ Nazim's, on the main road, T021-511214. The largest and most popular Indian restaurant in town. Good range of South Indian and biriyani dishes, plus a selection of vegetarian meals.

♥ Organic Farm Café, further down the main road. Small café offering over 15 tropical fruit shakes and a fantastic variety of food. Mulberry shakes and pancakes are a must and the harvest curry stew is delicious. Try the fresh spring rolls with pineapple dipping sauce. The food is highly recommended, the service could do with a little work. The sister branch is at the **Organic Mulberry Farm** (see Sleeping).

♥ Vieng Champa Restaurant, on the main road, T021-511037. Refreshingly, this family-run restaurant seems to have a greater selection of Lao food than most other places on the street. Most meals 15,000-20,000 kip.

♥ Xayoh, Luang Prabang Rd, T023-511088. Restaurant with branches in Vientiane and Luang Prabang. Good Western food in a comfy environment; pizza, soups and roast dinners.

Bars and clubs

Vientiane p457, map p460

There are a number of bar stalls, which set up in the evening along **Quai Fa Ngum** (the river road); a good place for a cold beer as sun sets. Most bars will close at 2300 in accordance with the local curfew laws; some places seem to be able to stay open past this time although that varies on a day-to-day basis. Government officials go through phases of shutting down places and restricting curfews.

Jazzy Brick, Setthathirat Rd, near Phimphone Market. Very sophisticated, modern den, where delectable cocktails are served with jazz cooing in the background. Garish shirts banned. Decorated with an eclectic range of quirky and kitsch artefacts. Very upmarket. Head here towards the end of the night.

Khop Chai Deu, Setthathirat Rd (near the corner with Nam Phou). Probably the most popular bar for tourists in Vientiane. Casual setting with a nightly band.

Mekong Deck, Fa Gnum. Fantastic location on the river. Huge modern, open-air deck. Limited drinks menu with beer, spirits and shakes but set to expand.

Spirit House, follow Fa Ngum Rd until it turns into a dirt track, past the Mekong River Commission, T021-243795. Beautiful wooden bar in a river location. Snacks and decent sushi. Watch the sunset in style. Wi-Fi.

Sticky Fingers, François Ngin Rd, opposite **Tai Pan Hotel**. Fantastic bar and restaurant run by 2 Australian women. Brilliant cocktails, especially the Tom Yum. Serves food.

Sunset Bar, end of Fa Ngum Rd. Although this run-down wooden construction isn't much to look at, it is a firm favourite with locals and tourists hoping to have a quiet ale and take in the magnificent sunset.

Wind West, by traffic lights, Luang Prabang Rd. Usually stays open after 2300. Seedier than others; many wild nights happen here.

Vang Vieng *p464, map p466*
The latest hotspot changes week to week.
Oh La La Bar, off the main street. Very
popular, open bar with pool table.
Sakura Bar, between the main road and the
river, near **Erawan Restaurant**. Big open bar
with loud, blaring and often live music.

🎭 Entertainment

Vientiane *p457, map p460*
Films and exhibitions Keep an eye in the
Vientiane Times for international performances
at the **Lao Cultural Centre** (the building that
looks like a big cake opposite the museum).
COPE Visitors' Centre, National Rehabilitation
Centre compound, Khou Vieng Rd, www.cope
laos.org, 0900-1600; 20,000 kip. At the time
of publication COPE (Co-operative Orthotic &
Prosthetic Enterprise) was setting up an
exhibition on unexploded ordnance (UXO)
and its effects on the people of Laos. The
exhibition includes a small movie room,
photography, UXO and a range of prosthetic
limbs (some crafted out of UXO). Helps raise
money for the work of COPE; production of
prosthetic limbs and rehabilitation of patients.
The French Cultural Centre, Lang Xang Rd,
T021-215764. Tue and Thu 1930, Sat 1530;
US$1. Screens the occasional French film and
also hosts the Southeast Asian film festival.
Often holds art exhibitions and concerts. Check
the *Vientiane Times* for up-to-date details.
**Lao International Trade Exhibition Centre
(ITEC)**, Ban Phonethane Neua, T021-416374.
Shows a range of international films.
T-Shop Lai, Th Inpeng (behind Wat Inpeng),
T021-223178, has an exhibition upstairs
devoted to Asian elephants.

Karaoke Almost the Lao national sport
and there's nothing like bonding with the
locals over a heavy-duty karaoke session.
Karaoke places are everywhere. The more
expensive, up-market **Don Chan Palace**
lets you hire your own room. **Champadeng
Cruise** has a good karaoke room below

deck, and no one can hear you howling
when you're on the river.

Traditional dance Lao National Theatre,
Manthaturath Rd, T021-242978. Lao dancing,
daily from 2030. Tickets, US$7. Performances
represent traditional dance of lowland Lao as
well as some minority groups. Performances
are less regular in the low season.

✡ Festivals and events

Vientiane *p457, map p460*
1st weekend in Apr Pi Mai (Lao New Year).
A 3-day festival and a huge water fight.
12 Oct Freedom of the French Day
Oct Boun Souang Heua (Water Festival)
A beautiful event on the night of the full
moon at the end of Buddhist Lent. Candles
are lit in all the homes and a candlelit
procession takes place around the city's wats
and through the streets. Then, thousands of
banana-leaf boats holding flowers, tapers
and candles are floated out onto the river.
The boats signify your bad luck floating away.
On the 2nd day, boat races take place, with
50 or so men in each boat; they power up
the river in perfect unison. Usually, a bunch
of foolhardy expats also tries to compete,
much to the amusement of the locals.
Nov (movable) **Boun That Luang** is
celebrated in all of Vientiane's *thats* but
most notably at That Luang (the national
shrine). Originally a ceremony in which
nobles swore allegiance to the king and
constitution, it amazingly survived the
Communist era. On the festival's most
important day, **Thak Baat**, thousands of
Lao people pour into the temple at 0600
and again at 1700 to pay homage. Monks
travel from across the country to collect
alms from the pilgrims. It is a really beautiful
ceremony, with monks chanting and
thousands of people praying. Women
who attend should invest in a traditional
sinh. A week-long carnival surrounds the
festival with fireworks, music and dancing.

O Shopping

Vientiane *p457, map p460*

Bookshops

Kosila Books, Nokeo Khoummane Rd, T021-241352. Small selection of 2nd-hand books.

Monument Books, T021-243708. The largest selection of new books in Vientiane, **Monument** stock a range of Southeast Asian speciality books as well as coffee-table books. Good place to pick up Lao-language children's books to distribute to villages on your travels.

Vientiane Book Centre, 54/1 Pang Kham St (next door to **Just for Fun**), T021-212031. A limited but interesting selection of used books in a multitude of languages.

Clothing and textiles

Couleur d'Asie, Nam Phou Circle. Modern-style Asian clothing. Pricey but high-quality fusion fashion.

Lao Textiles by Carol Cassidy, Nokeo Koummane Rd, T021-212123, Mon-Fri 0800-1200, 1400-1700, Sat 0800-1200. Silk fabrics, including *ikat* and traditional Lao designs, made by an American in a beautifully renovated colonial property. Dyeing, spinning, designing and weaving all done on site (and can be viewed). Expensive, but many of the weavings are real works of art; custom-made pieces available on request.

Mixay Boutique, Nokeo Khoummane, T021-25717943, contact@mixay.com. Exquisite Lao silk in rich colours. Clothing and fantastic photographs and artefacts.

Satri Laos, Setthathirat, T021-244387. If Vientiane had a Harrods this would be it. Upmarket boutique retailing everything from jewellery, shoes, clothes, furnishings and homewares. Beautiful stuff, although most is from China, Vietnam and Thailand.

Handicrafts and antiques

The main shops are along Setthathirat, Samsenthai and Pang Kham. The **Talaat Sao** (Morning Market) is also worth a browse, with artefacts, such as appliquéd panels, decorated hats and sashes, basketwork

both old and new, small and large wooden tobacco boxes, sticky-rice lidded baskets, axe pillows, embroidered cushions and a wide range of silver work.

CAMA crafts, Mixay Rd, T021-241217. NGO which sells handicrafts produced by the Hmong ethnic groups. Beautiful embroidery, mulberry tea and Lao silk.

T'Shop Lai Gallery, Wat Inpeng Soi. Funky studio exhibiting local sculptures and art. Artists can be seen at work every day except Sun. Media include coconut shells, wood and metal. Proceeds from sales are donated to Lao Youth projects. Upstairs there is an exhibition on Asian elephants.

Jewellery

Tamarind, Manthathurath, T020-5517031. Great innovative jewellery designs, nice pieces. Also stocks a range of beautiful clothes made in stunning silk and organza.

Markets

Vientiane has several excellent markets.

Talaat Sao (Morning Market), off Lane Xang Av. It's busiest in the mornings (from around 1000), but operates all day. There are money exchanges here (quite a good rate), and a good selection of foodstalls selling Western food, soft drinks and ice cream sundaes. It sells imported Thai goods, electrical appliances, watches, DVDs and CDs, stationery, cosmetics, a selection of handicrafts, an enormous choice of Lao fabrics, and upstairs there is a large clothing section, silverware, some gems and gold and a few handicraft stalls.

There is also the newer addition to the Morning Market – a modern shopping centre-style market. This is not as popular as it is much pricier and stocked with mostly Thai products sold in baht. On the second floor there is an reasonable food court, **Talat Khua-Din**.

There is an interesting produce section at the ramshackle market on the other side of the bus stop. This market offers many of the same handicrafts and silks as the morning market but is a lot cheaper.

▲▲ Activities and tours

Vientiane *p457, map p460*

Cookery classes
Thongbay Guesthouse (see Sleeping),
T021-242292. Cooking classes, covering all
of meal preparation, from purchasing the
ingredients to eating the meal.

Cycling
Bicycles are available for hire from several
places in town, see Transport, page 478.
A good outing is to cycle downstream along
the banks of the Mekong. Cycle south on
Tha Deua Rd until Km 5 (watch the traffic)
and then turn right down one of the tracks
(there are a number) towards the riverbank.
A path, suitable for bicycles, follows the
river beginning at about Km 4.5. There
are monasteries and drinks sellers en route
to maintain interest and energy.

Kickboxing
Soxai Boxing Stadium, 200 m past the old
circus in Baan Dong Paleb. Kickboxing is
usually held on the last Fri of every month
at 1700 (20,000 kip).

Massage, saunas and spas
The best massage in town is given by the blind
masseuses in a little street off Samsenthai Rd,
2 blocks down from Simuang Minimart (across
from Wat Simuang). There are 2 blind masseuse
businesses side-by-side and either one is
fantastic: **Traditional Clinic**, T020-5659177,
and **Porm Clinic**, T020-627 633 (no English
spoken). They are marked by blue signs off
both Khou Vieng and Samsenthai roads.
Mandarina, Pang Kham just off Nam Phou,
T021-218703. A range of upmarket treatments
between US$5-30. Massage, facials, body
scrubs, mini-saunas, oils and jacuzzi.
Papaya Spa, opposite Wat Xieng Veh,
T021-216550. Daily 0900-2000. Surrounded
by beautiful gardens. Massage, sauna, facials.
They also have a new branch that is more
accessible on Lane Xang Avenue just up
from the Morning Market.

Swimming and waterparks
Several hotels in town permit non-residents
to use their fitness facilities for a small fee,
including the Tai Pan Hotel (rather basic),
the **Lao Hotel Plaza**, the **Lane Xang Hotel**
and the luxurious **Settha Palace** (with a
hefty entrance price to boot). **The Australian
Embassy Recreation Club**, Km 3, Tha Deua
Rd, T021-314921, has a fantastic saltwater
pool with superb Mekong views. At the time
of publication a major water park was being
constructed in the park on Khou Vieng Rd,
just behind Talaat Kudin.

Thak Baat
Every morning at day-break (around 0530-
0600) monks flood out of the city's temples,
creating a swirl of orange on the streets,
as they collect alms from the city folk. It is
beautiful to see the misty, grey streets come
alive with the robe-clad monks. Foreigners
are more than welcome to participate, just
buy some sticky rice or other food from the
vendors and kneel beside others making merit.

Tour operators
To organize an ecotour, visit the **National
Tourism Authority** for general travel infor-
mation or specific recommendations. Most
agents will use 'eco' somewhere in their title
but this doesn't necessarily mean anything.
Asia Vehicle Rental, 354-356 Samsenthai Rd,
PO Box 4311, T021-217493, www.avr.laopdr.
com. Operate in all areas of Lao PDR and
cross-border into Thailand, Vietnam and China.
Asian Trails Ltd, PO Box 5422, Unit 10, Baan
Khounta Thong, Sikotthabong District,
T021-263936, www.asiantrails.info.
Southeast Asia specialists.
Diethelm Travel, Nam Phou Circle, T021-
213833, www.diethelm-travel.com.
Exotissimo, 6/44 Pang Kham Rd, T021-
241861, www.exotissimo.com. Tours
and travel services. Excellent but pricey.
Green Discovery Laos, Setthathirat Rd, next
to Kop Chai Deu T021-251564, www.green
discoverylaos.com. Specializes in ecotours
and adventure travel.

Weaving and dyeing courses
Houey Hong Vocational Training Centre, Ban Houey Hong, 20 mins north of Vientiane, T021-560006, hhwt@laotel.com. This small NGO runs training courses for under-privileged ethnic minorities. Tourists are welcome to join in the course for US$15 per day. To get there ask a songthaew to drop you off at Talaat Houey Hong, and follow the track 200 m west. Call the centre in advance.

Vang Vieng p464, map p466
Tour guides are available for hiking, rafting, visiting the caves and minority villages from most travel agents and guesthouses. Safety issues need to be considered when taking part in any adventure activity. There have been fatalities in Vang Vieng from boating, trekking and caving accidents. The river can flow very quickly during the wet season (Jul and Aug) and tourists have drowned here. Make sure you wear a life jacket during all water-borne activities and time your trip so you aren't travelling on the river after dark. A price war between tour operators has led to cost cutting, resulting in equipment that is not well maintained or does not exist at all. With all tour operators it is imperative you are given safety gear and that canoes, ropes, torches and other equipment are in a good state of repair. The more expensive, reputable companies are often the best option (see also Vientiane Tour operators, above). Reliable tour operators include:
Green Discovery, attached to **Xayoh Café**, T023-511440, www.greendiscoverylaos.com. By far the best tour operator in town. Caving, kayaking, hiking and rock climbing. Very professional and helpful. Recommended.
Riverside Tour T020-2254137, www.riverside tourlaos.com. Kayaking and adventure tours.

Kayaking and rafting
See also tour operators, above. Kayaking is a very popular activity around Vang Vieng and competition between operators is fierce. There are a wide variety of trips available, ranging from day trips (with a visit to the caves and surrounding villages), to kayaking all the way to Vientiane via the stop-off point at Nam Lik, US$15-25, about 6 hrs, including a 40-min drive at the start and finish. All valuables are kept in a car which meets kayakers at the end of their paddle. A few companies also offer 2-day rafting trips down the Nam Ngum River. The trip includes several grade IV and V rapids and usually an overnight camp. US$100 per person or less for groups of more than 3.

Be wary of intensive rafting or kayaking trips through risky areas during the wet season, as it can be very dangerous. Check equipment thoroughly before committing.

Rock climbing
Vang Vieng is the only really established rock climbing area in the country, with over 50 sites in the locality, ranging from grade 5 to 8A+. Almost all of these climbs had been 'bolted'. There are climbing sites suitable for beginners through to more experienced climbers. **Green Discovery** (see Tour operators, page 477) runs climbing courses almost every day in high season (US$20-45 per day, including equipment rental). The best climbing sites include: Sleeping Cave, Sleeping Wall and Tham Nam Them.

Trekking
Almost all guesthouses and agents in town offer hiking trips, usually incorporating a visit to caves and minority villages and, possibly, some kayaking or tubing. The best treks are offered through the major tour operators who will provide an English-speaking guide, all transport and lunch for US$10-15 per day.

Tubing
No trip to Vang Vieng is complete without tubing down the Nam Song. Floating slowly along the river is an ideal way to take in the stunning surroundings of limestone karsts, jungle and rice paddies. The drop-off point is 3 km from town near the **Organic Mulberry Farm**, where several bars and restaurants

have been set up along the river. Try and start early in the day as it's dangerous to tube after dark and the temperature of the water drops sharply. Women should take a sarong and avoid walking through town in a bikini, it is culturally unacceptable and highly offensive to the locals.

Tour operators and guesthouses offer tube rental, life jackets and drop-off for US$4. A US$7 fine is charged for lost tubes (people may offer to return the tubes for you; it is best to decline this offer). Dry bags can be rented for 10,000 kip. It is essential that you wear a life jacket as people have drowned on the river, particularly in the wet season (Jul and Aug) when the river swells and flows very quickly. Without stopping expect the journey to take 1-2 hrs. Most people stop along the way and make a day of it.

⊖ Transport

Vientiane *p457, map p460*
Air
Lao Airlines, 2 Pang Kham Rd (near Fa Ngum), T021-212054, www.laoairlines.com, also at Wattay Airport; T021-212051.
Lao Air office at Wattay Airport, T/F021-512027, laoair@laopdr.com. **Thai Airways**, Head Office, Luang Prabang Rd, not far past the Novotel, T021-222527/9, www.thai airways.com, Mon-Fri 0830-1200, 1300-1500, Sat 0830-1200; also on Pang Kham Rd, next to the bookshop and at Wattay Airport, 1st floor, Room 106, T021-512024, daily 0700-1200, 1300-1600. **Vietnam Airlines**, Lao Plaza Hotel, T021-217562, www.vietnamairlines.com.vn, Mon-Fri 0800-1200, 1330-1630, Sat 0800-1200.

Prices and schedules are constantly changing, so always check in advance.
Lao Airlines to **Bangkok** (80 mins) 3 flights daily; to **Luang Prabang** (40 mins) up to 3 flights daily; to **Pakse** (50 mins) daily. To **Oudomxay** and **Houei Xai** 4 flights a week; to **Siem Reap** 5 times a week, 3 times a week via Pakse; **Phnom Penh** (90 mins) twice a week via Pakse. **Kunming** 3 times a week

(2½ hrs); **Chiang Mai** daily. **Hanoi** daily. Lao Airlines schedules prone to change. **Lao Air** operates flights to **Xam Neua** twice a week (50 mins) and **Phongsaly** twice a week (60 mins). **Thai Airways** to **Bangkok** (70 mins), daily. **Vietnam Airlines**, to **Hanoi** (60 mins), daily; to **HCMC** (3 hrs), daily and **Phnom Penh** daily.

Bicycle and motorbike
Bike For those energetic enough in the hot season, bikes are the best way to get around town. Many hotels and guesthouses have bikes available for their guests, expect to pay about 10,000 kip per day. There are also many bike hire shops around town. Markets, post offices and government offices usually have 'bike parks' where it is advisable to leave your bike. A small minding fee is charged.
Motorbikes Available for hire from many guesthouses and shops. Expect to pay US$5-10 per day and leave your passport as security. Insurance is seldom available anywhere in Laos on motorbikes but most places will also hire out helmets, a necessity. **KT bikes**, Manthathurath St, T020-5816816 offers the best range of well-serviced Suzukis (US$7 per day) and dirt bikes (US$20 per day); discounts available for longer hire.

PVO, off Fa Ngum, also has a reliable selection of bicycles and motorbikes. Often a driving licence can be used in lieu of a motorbike licence if the police pull you over.

Bus
Vientiane has 3 main public bus terminals: **Southern**, **Northern** and **Talaat Sao** (Morning Market).

Southern bus station Route 13, 9 km south of the city centre. Public buses depart daily for destinations in southern Laos. At the time of writing bus prices were expected to increase by about 10,000 kip per trip. To **Thakhek**, 4 daily, 6 hrs, 40,000 kip. To **Savannakhet**, 7 daily (early morning), 8 hrs, 55,000 kip. To **Pakse**, 9 daily, 15 hrs, 85,000 kip; **Muang Khong**

1030, 110,000 kip; **Veun Kham** 1000, 110,000 kip. There are also overnight VIP buses to Pakse, 11 hrs, 110,000 kip, and a VIP service daily at 2030 by **Thongli** T021-242657, which takes about the same time but has beds, water, snacks, etc, 130,000 kip. Make sure you book a double if you don't want to be stuck with a strange bedfellow. **KVT**, T021-213043, also run VIP buses to Pakse at 2030. **Banag Saigon**, T021-720175, run buses to **Hanoi**, 1900, US$20; **Vinh**, 1900, US$16; **Thanh Hoa**, 1900, US$16; **Hué**, 1930, US$20; **Danang**, 1930, US$20. These services run on odd days so check in advance.

VIP buses are very comfortable, usually allowing for a good night's sleep during the trip, but watch out that they don't swap the normal VIP bus for a karaoke one! Robberies have been reported on the night buses so keep your valuables somewhere secure.

Northern bus station Route 2, towards the airport, 3.5 km from the centre of town, T021-260255.

Northbound buses are regular and have a/c. For the more popular routes, there are also VIP buses which will usually offer snacks and service. To **Luang Prabang** (384 km), standard buses 5 daily, 11 hrs, 90,000 kip; a/c buses daily at 0630, 0900, 1930, 10-11 hrs, 1000,000 kip; VIP buses daily at 0800, 9 hrs, 120,000 kip. To **Udomxai** (578 km), standard buses twice daily, 14-15 hrs, 110,000 kip; a/c buses daily at 1600, 120,000 kip. To

Luang Namtha (676 km), daily 0830, 19 hrs, 140,000 kip. To **Phongsali**, daily 0715, 26 hrs, 150,000 kip. To **Houei Xai**, Mon, Wed and Fri 1730, 30-35 hrs, 200,000 kip. To **Xam Neua**, 3 daily, 14-23 hrs (depending on whether it goes via Phonsavanh), 150,000 kip. To **Phonsavanh**, standard 4 daily, 10 hrs, 90,000 kip; a/c daily at 0730, 90,000 kip; VIP daily at 0800, 130,000 kip.

Talaat Sao bus station Across the road from Talaat Sao, in front of Talaat Kudin, on the eastern edge of the city centre. Destinations, distances and fares are listed on a board in English and Lao. Most departures are in the morning and can leave as early as 0400, so check departure times the night before. There is a useful map at the station, and bus times and fares are listed clearly in Lao and English. However, it's more than likely you will need a bit of direction at this bus station: staff at the ticket office only speak a little English so a better option is to chat to the friendly chaps in the planning office, who love a visit, T021-216506. The times listed below vary depending on the weather and the number of stops en route.

To the **Southern bus station**, every 30 mins, 0600-1800, 2000 kip. To the **Northern bus station**, catch the Nongping bus (8 daily) and ask to get off at '*Thay song*' (1500 kip). To **Wattay Airport**, every 30 mins, 0640-1800, 3000 kip. Buses to Vang Vieng 5 daily, 3½ hrs, 15,000 kip.

There are numerous buses criss-crossing the province; most aren't useful for tourists. To the **Friendship Bridge** (Lao side), every 30 mins, 0650-1710, 5000 kip. To **Nong Khai** (Thai side of the Friendship Bridge), 4 daily, 1 hr including immigration, 10,000 kip.

Taxi
These are mostly found at the Talaat Sao (Morning Market) or around the main hotels. Newer vehicles have meters but there are still some ageing jalopies. Flag fall is 8000 kip. A taxi from the Morning Market to the **airport**, US$5; to **Tha Deua** (for the Friendship Bridge and Thailand), US$10, although you can usually get the trip much cheaper but the taxis are so decrepit that you may as well take a tuk-tuk, US$6 (see below). For trips outside the city, around US$20 per day. **Lavi Taxi**, T021-350000. The only reliable call-up service in town but after 2000 you may not get an answer.

Tuk-tuk
Tuk-tuks usually congregate around **Nam Phou**, **Talaat Sao** and **Talaat Kudin**. Tuk-tuks can be chartered for longer out-of-town trips (maximum 25 km, US$10-15) or for short journeys of 2-3 km within the city (10,000 kip per person). There are also shared tuk-tuks, which run on regular routes along the city's main streets. Tuk-tuks are available around Nam Phou until 2330 but are quite difficult to hire after dark in other areas of town. The tuk-tuks that congregate on the city corners are generally part of a quasi cartel, it is thus much cheaper to travel on one that is passing through. To stop a vehicle, simply flag it down. A good, reliable driver is **Mr Souk**, T020-7712220, who speaks good English.

Vang Vieng p464, map p466
Bicycle and motorbike
There are many bicycles for rent along the road east up from the old market (10,000 kip per day). There are also a few motorbike rental places (US$5 per day), the best of these is opposite the **Organic Farm Café** in town.

Bus
Buses leave from the make-shift bus terminal on the east side of the airstrip, T021-511341. There are plans to relocate all buses to the terminal at the New Market, 2 km north of town. Check before going to either station. Mini-buses leave from most guesthouses to both Vientiane and Luang Prabang – this service is notoriously unreliable with passengers packed in like sardines and minivans often breaking down. Best to opt for the local bus. You can catch northbound buses headed from **Vientiane** to **Luang Prabang** hourly between 1200 and 2000, 8-10 hrs, 70,000 kip. The bus en route from Vientiane to **Phonsovan** passes through town at 0900, 85,000 kip. Public buses leave for **Vientiane** 5 times daily, 3½-4 hrs 25,000 kip; songthaews depart every hour.

Private transport and VIP buses
Tickets are usually sold by guesthouses and will include a tuk-tuk pick-up at your hotel to the bus. VIP buses leave for **Luang Prabang** at 1000, 6 hrs, US$10. The minivans leave at 0900. VIP Bus to **Vientiane** 1000 and 1300, 3 hrs, 55,000 kip (you are actually better off on the local bus for short stints like this). Minivan to Vientiane 0900, 3½ hrs, 70,000 kip (not recommended). Minibus to Luang Prabang 0900, 5 hrs, 105,000 kip. Every guesthouse and travel agent can book the VIP/minivans and they will pick up from your guesthouse. Seats get booked up really quickly and buses take at least 30 mins to make all their pick-ups, so expect long delays.

Tuk-tuk
A day trip to the caves should cost US$10 but there have been reports of some drivers offering trips to the caves for 10,000 kip per person and then demanding an outrageous fee for the return leg. Make sure all prices are set in stone before setting off.

❶ Directory

Vientiane p457, map p460

Banks At the time of writing there were only a handful of multicard Visa and MasterCard ATMs in the city. The **Banque Pour le Commerce Exterieur (BCEL)**, corner of Fa Ngum and Pang Kham roads, takes all the usual credit cards (maximum withdrawal 700,000 kip; much less on Sun). Other multicard ATMs can be found in front of the Novotel, the Lao Plaza Hotel and beside the petrol station near Wat Simuang. Other BCEL ATMs such as those on Setthathirat and near the Morning Market only take MasterCard. More ATMs are planned in the next few years. BCEL, 1 Pang Kham Rd, traditionally offers the lowest commission (1.5%) on changing US$ TCs into US$ cash; there is no commission on changing US$ into kip; also has an international ATM. **Joint Development Bank**, Lane Xane Ave, T021-213535, offers good rates on cash advances. ATM. **Embassies and consulates** Australia, Km3 Tha Deua Rd, T021-413602. **Britain**, contact the Australian Embassy. **Cambodia**, Tha Deua Rd, Km 3, T021-314952, visas daily 0730-1030; Cambodian visas US$20. **China**, Thanon Wat Nak Nyai T021-315105. Visas take 4-days. **France**, Setthathirat Rd, T021-215258. **Germany**, 26 Sok Paluang Rd, T021-312110/1. **Thailand**, Phon Kheng Rd, T021-900238 (consular section on That Luang arranges visas extensions), Mon-Fri 0830-1200. **USA**, That Dam Rd (off Samsenthai), T021-267000. **Vietnam**, That Luang Rd, T021-413400, visas 0800-1045, 1415-1615. One-month visa US$50, 3 days. Extra US$5 for the visa in 1 day. **Immigration** Immigration office, Phai Nam Rd (near Morning Market), Mon-Fri 0730-1200, 1400-1700. Visa extensions can be organized for US$2 per day. For visa information, see page 456. **Internet** Internet cafés have opened up all over the city, many on Setthathirat and Samsenthai roads. You shouldn't have to pay more than 100 kip per min. Most major internet cafés are fitted with Skype and headphones. **Apollo Internet**,

Setthathirat Rd, Mon-Fri 0830-2300, Sat and Sun 0900-2300. **Medical services** There are 2 pretty good pharmacies close to the Talaat Sao Bus Station. **Australian Clinic**, Australian Embassy, T021-413603, Mon-Fri, Fri 0800-1200, 1400-1700, for Commonwealth patients only (except in emergencies). US$60 to see the doctor. **Mahasot Hospital**, Fa Gnum, T021-214021, for minor ailments but for anything major it is advisable to cross the border to Nong Khai and visit **AEK Udon International Hospital**, T0066-42342555. For hospitals in Thailand, see page 815. In cases of extreme emergency where a medical evacuation is required, contact **Lao Westcoast Helicopters**, Hangar 703, Wattay Airport, T021-512023, which will charter helicopters to Udon Thani for US$1500-2000, subject to availability and government approval. **Police** Tourist Police Office, Lang Xang Av, T021-251128. **Post** Post Office, Khou Vieng Rd/Lane Xang Av (opposite market), T021-216425, local and international calls, good packing service. **DHL**, Nong No Rd, near the airport, T021-214868, or **TNT Express**, Thai Airways Building, Luang Prabang Rd, T021-261918. **Telephone** The international telephone office is on Setthathirat Rd, near Nam Phou Rd, 24 hrs.

Vang Vieng and around p464, map p466

Banks Agricultural Promotion Bank and the Lao Development Bank, on the main road, both exchange cash, 0830-1530. BCEL, T021-511480, exchanges cash, TCs and will also do cash advances on Visa and MasterCard, 0830-1530. MasterCard ATM. **Internet** There are a number of internet cafés along the main drag, all 300 kip per min; most offer international internet calls from 3000 kip per min. **Magnet** the best internet café; offers internet as well as music/movie transfer to ipod and cash advances from the EFTPOS facility for 3% commission. **Medical services** Vang Vieng Hospital, located on the road parallel to the river; it's terribly under-equipped. In most cases it is better to go to Vientiane. **Post office** Next to the former site of the old market, 0830-1600.

Luang Prabang and around

→ Colour map 1, C5.
Anchored at the junction of the Mekong and Nam Khan rivers, the former royal capital of Lane Xang is now a UNESCO World Heritage Site. It is home to a spellbinding array of gilded temples, weathered French colonial façades and art deco shophouses. In the 18th century there were more than 65 wats in the city. Yet for all its magnificent temples, this royal 'city' feels more like an easy-going provincial town: at daybreak, scores of monks in saffron robes amble silently out of the monasteries to collect offerings from the town's residents; in the early evening women cook, old men lounge in wicker chairs and young boys play takro in the streets. The famous Pak Ou Caves and the Kwang Si Falls are located near the town. ▶▶ *For listings, see pages 490-497.*

Ins and outs

Getting there Flying is still the easiest option with daily connections from Vientiane, plus flights from Bangkok and Chiang Mai to **Luang Prabang International Airport** (LPQ) ① *4 km northeast of town, T071-212172/3.* There is a standard US$2 charge for a tuk-tuk ride from the airport to the centre.

Route 13 is now safe, with no recent bandit attacks reported, and the road has been upgraded, shortening the journey from Vientiane to eight or nine hours. There are also overland connections with other destinations in northern Laos. Luang Prabang has two main bus stations: **Kiew Lot Sai Nuan** (northern bus station), located on the northeast side of Sisavangvong Bridge, for traffic to and from the north; and **Naluang** (southern bus station) for traffic to and from the south. Occasionally buses will pass through the opposite station to what you would expect, so be sure to double-check. The standard tuk-tuk fare to/from either bus station is 15,000 kip. If there are only a few passengers, it's late at night or you are travelling to/from an out-of-town hotel, expect to pay 20,000 kip. These prices tend to fluctuate with the international cost of petroleum. Another option is to travel by river: a firm favourite is the two-day trip between Luang Prabang and Houei Xai (close to the Thai border), via Pak Beng (see page 500). Less frequent are the boats to Muang Ngoi and Nong Khiaw, via Muang Khua. ▶▶ *See Transport, page 495.*

Getting around Luang Prabang is a small town and the best way to explore is either on foot or by bicycle. Bicycles can be hired from most guesthouses for US$1 per day. Strolling about this beautiful town is a real pleasure but there are also tuk-tuks and saamlors for hire.

Best time to visit The most popular time to visit is November and December but the best time to visit is from December to February. After this the weather is hotting up and the views are often shrouded in a haze, produced by shifting cultivators using fire to clear the forest for agriculture. This does not really clear until May or, sometimes, June. During the months of March and April, when visibility is at its worst, the smoke can cause soreness of the eyes, as well as preventing planes from landing.

Tourist information **Luang Prabang Tourist Information Centre** ① *Sisavangvong, T071-212487,* provides provincial information and offers a couple of good ecotourism treks (which support local communities), including one to Kwang Si and one in Chompet District. The Chompet trek receives quite good reviews and includes visits to hot springs, villages and the chance to watch a traditional performance from Hmong performers.

Background

According to legend, the site of Luang Prabang was chosen by two resident hermits and was originally known as Xieng Thong – 'Copper Tree City'. Details are sketchy regarding the earliest inhabitants of Luang Prabang but historians imply the ethnic Khmu and Lao Theung groups were the initial settlers. They named Luang Prabang, Muang Sawa, which literally translates as Java, hinting at some kind of cross-border support. By the end of the 13th century, Muang Sawa had developed into a regional hub.

A major turning point in the city's history came about in 1353, when the mighty Fa Ngum barrelled down the Nam Ou River, backed by a feisty Khmer army, and captured Muang Sawa. Here, the warrior king founded Lane Xang Hom Khao (Kingdom of a Million Elephants, White Parasol) and established a new Lao royal lineage, which was to last another 600 years. The name of the city refers to the holy Pra Bang, Laos' most sacred image of the Buddha, which was given to Fa Ngum by his father-in-law, the King of Cambodia.

The city had been significantly built up by the time King Visounarat came to power in 1512 and remained the capital until King Setthathirat, fearing a Burmese invasion, moved the capital to Vieng Chan (Vientiane) in 1563.

Luang Prabang didn't suffer as greatly as other provincial capitals during the Indochina wars, narrowly escaping a Viet Minh capture in 1953. During the Second Indochina War, however, the Pathet Lao cut short the royal lineage, forcing King Sisavang Vatthana to abdicate and sending him to a re-education camp in northeastern Laos where he, his wife and his son died from starvation. Despite the demise of the monarchy and years of revolutionary rhetoric on the city's tannoy system, Luang Prabang's dreamy streets have somehow retained the aura of old Lane Xang.

Sights

The sights are conveniently close together but, to begin with, it is worth climbing Phousi or taking a stroll along the river roads to get a better idea of the layout of the town. Most of Luang Prabang's important wats are dotted along the main road, Phothisarath.

Mount Phousi

ⓘ *The western steps lead up from Sisavangvong Rd, daily 0800-1800, 10,000 kip. If you want to watch the sun go down, get there early – don't expect to be the only person there.*

Directly opposite the Royal Palace is the start of the steep climb up Mount Phousi, the spiritual and geographical heart of the city and a popular place to come to watch the sunset over the Mekong, illuminating the hills to the east. Phousi is a gigantic rock with sheer forested sides, surmounted by a 25 m-tall *chedi*, **That Chomsi**. The *chedi* was constructed in 1804, restored in 1914 and is the designated starting point for the colourful Pi Mai (New Year) celebrations in April. Its shimmering gold-spired stupa rests on a rectangular base, ornamented by small metal Bodhi trees. Next to the stupa is a little sanctuary, from which the candlelit procession descends at New Year, accompanied by effigies of Nang Sang Kham, the guardian of the New Year, and Naga, protector of the city.

Royal Palace

ⓘ *Sisavangvong Rd, daily 0800-1100, 1330-1600; 20,000 kip. No shorts, strappy dresses or short-sleeved shirts. No photography.*

Also called the National Museum, the Royal Palace is right in the centre of the city on the main road and close enough to the Mekong to allow royal guests ready access by river.

Unlike its former occupants, the palace survived the 1975 revolution and was converted into a museum the following year.

It was built by the French for the Lao King Sisavang Vong in 1904 in an attempt to bind him and his family more tightly into the colonial system of government. Later work saw the planting of the avenue of palms and the filling in of one of two fish ponds. Local residents regarded the ponds as the 'eyes' of the capital, so the blinding of one eye was taken as inviting bad fortune by leaving the city unprotected. The subsequent civil war seemed to vindicate these fears. The palace is Khmer in style, cruciform in plan and mounted on a small platform of four tiers. The only indication of French involvement can be seen in the two French lilies represented in stucco on the entrance, beneath the symbols of Lao royalty. There are a few Lao motifs but, in many respects, the palace is more foreign than Lao: it was designed by a French architect, with steps made from Italian marble; built by masons from Vietnam; embellished by carpenters from Bangkok, and funded by the largesse of the colonial authorities.

1 Luang Prabang

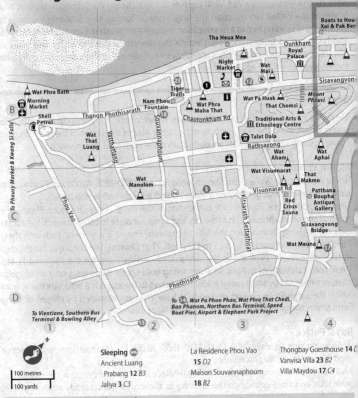

The small ornate pavilion of **Wat Ho Prabang** is located in the northeast corner of the palace compound, to the right of the entrance to the Royal Palace. The chapel contains four Khmer Buddhas, ivories mounted in gold, bronze drums used in religious ceremonies and about 30 smaller Buddha images from temples all over the city. The Pra Bang, see below, is due to be moved here.

The main **entrance hall** of the palace was used for royal religious ceremonies, when the Supreme Patriarch of Lao Buddhism would oversee proceedings from his gold-painted lotus throne. It now contains a collection of 15th- to 17th-century Buddha statues. The room to the immediate right of the entrance was the King's reception room, also called the **Ambassadors' Room**. It contains French-made busts of the last three Lao monarchs, a model of the royal hearse (which is kept in Wat Xieng Thong) and a mural by French artist Alex de Fontereau, depicting a day in the life of Luang Prabang in the 1930s.

In comparison to the state rooms, the royal family's **private apartments** are modestly decorated. They have been left virtually untouched since the day the family left for exile in Xam Neua Province. To the rear of the entrance hall, the **Coronation Room** was decorated between 1960 and 1970 for Crown Prince Sisavong Vatthana's coronation, an event which was interrupted because of the war. The walls are a brilliant red with Japanese glass mosaics embedded in a red lacquer base with gilded woodwork and depict scenes from Lao festivals.

To the left of the entrance hall is the reception room of the **King's Secretary**, and beyond it, the **Queen's reception room**, which together house an eccentric miscellany of state gifts from just about every country except the UK.

To the far right of the entrance to the palace is a room (viewed from the outside) in which sits the Pra Bang, or **Golden Buddha**, from which the city gets its name. The Buddha is in the attitude of Abhaya-Mudra or 'dispelling fear'. Some believe that the original image is kept in a bank vault, though most dispel this as rumour. It is 90% solid gold. Reputed to have originally come from Ceylon, and said to date from any time between the first and ninth centuries, the statue was moved to Cambodia in the 11th century, given to King Phaya Sirichanta, and was then taken to Lane Xang by King Fa Ngum, who had spent some time in the courts of Angkor and married into Khmer royalty. An alternative story has the Pra Bang following Fa Ngum to the city: it is said he

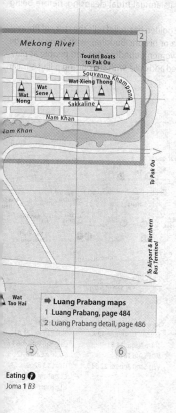

➡ **Luang Prabang maps**
1 Luang Prabang, page 484
2 Luang Prabang detail, page 486

Eating 🍴
Joma **1** *B3*

asked his father-in-law, the King of Angkor, to send a delegation of holy men to assist him in spreading the Theravada Buddhist faith in Lane Xang. The delegation arrived bringing with them the Pra Bang as a gift from the Cambodian King. The Pra Bang's arrival heralded the capital's change of name, from Xieng Thong to Nakhon Luang Prabang, 'The great city of the big Buddha'. In 1563 King Setthathirat took the statue to Lane Xang's new capital at Vientiane. Two centuries later in 1779 the Thais captured it but it was returned to Laos in 1839 and rediscovered in the palace chapel in 1975. The Pra Bang is revered in Laos as its arrival marked the beginnings of Buddhism in Lane Xang.

Wat Mai

ⓘ *Sisavangvong Rd, daily 0800-1700; 5000 kip.*

Next to the Royal Palace is Wat Mai. This royal temple, inaugurated in 1788, has a five-tiered roof and is one of the jewels of Luang Prabang. It took more than 70 years to complete. It was the home of the Buddhist leader in Laos, Phra Sangkharath, until he moved to That Luang in Vientiane. During Pi Mai (New Year), the Pra Bang is taken from the Royal Palace and installed at Wat Mai for its annual ritual cleansing, before being returned to the palace after three days.

The façade is particularly interesting: a large golden bas-relief tells the story of Phravet (one of the last reincarnations of the Gautama or historic Buddha), with several village scenes, including depictions of wild animals, women pounding rice and people at play. Inside, the interior is an exquisite amalgam of red and gold, with supporting pillars similar to those in Wat Xieng Thong.

2 Luang Prabang detail

Sleeping
Ammata Guesthouse **20** A3
Apsara **1** B4
Le Calao Inn **5** A4
Oui Guesthouse **21** B5
Pack Luck **7** A3
Sala Luang Prabang **9** A1

Sayo Guesthouse **11** A1
Silichit Guesthouse **12** A2
Three Nagas **14** B3
Villa Santi **16** B3
Villa Santi Annexe **22** B3

Eating
Blue Lagoon **21** A1
Café Ban Vat Sene **1** B3
Couleur Café **6** A2
Dao Fa **3** B2
L'Éléphant **7** A3
L'Étranger **8** B1

Wat Sene (Wat Saen)

Further up the promontory, Wat Sene was built in 1718 and was the first sim in Luang Prabang to be constructed in Thai style, with a yellow and red roof. The exterior may lack subtlety, but the interior is delicate and rather refined, painted red, with gold patterning on every conceivable surface. Sen means 100,000 and the wat was built with a local donation of 100,000 kip from someone who discovered 'treasure' in the Khan River.

Wat Xieng Thong

ⓘ *Xiengthong Rd, daily 0800-1700; 10,000 kip.*

Wat Xieng Thong Ratsavoraviharn, usually known as just Wat Xieng Thong, is set back from the road, at the top of a flight of steps leading down to the Mekong. It is arguably the finest example of a Lao monastery, with graceful, low-sweeping eaves, beautiful stone mosaics and intricate carvings. The wat has several striking chapels, including one that houses a rare bronze reclining Buddha and another sheltering a gilded wooden funeral chariot. Inside, resplendent gold-stencilled pillars support a ceiling with *dharma* wheels. The striking buildings in the tranquil compound are decorated in gold and post-box red, with imposing tiled roofs and mosaics, making this the most important and finest royal wat in Luang Prabang. It was built by King Setthathirat in 1559, and is one of the few buildings to have survived the successive Chinese raids that marked the end of the 19th century.

The **sim** is a perfect example of the Luang Prabang style. Locals believe the roof has been styled to resemble a bird, with wings stretched out to protect her young. The eight central wooden pillars have stencilled motifs in gold and the façade is finely decorated. The beautiful gold-leaf inlay is predominantly floral in design but a few images illustrate *Ramayana*-type themes and the interior frescoes depict *dharma* wheels and the enigmatic King Chantaphanit. At the rear of the sim is a mosaic representation of the thong copper 'Tree of Life' in glass inlay.

Behind the sim are two red *hor song phra* (side chapels): the one on the left is referred to as **La Chapelle Rouge** (the Red Chapel) and houses a rare Lao reclining Buddha in bronze, dating from the 16th century. The exterior mosaics which relate local tales, were added in 1957 to honour the 2500th anniversary of the Buddha's birth, death and enlightenment. The other *hor song phra*, to the right of the sim, houses a standing image of the Buddha which is paraded through the streets of the city each New Year and doused in water.

The **Chapel of the Funeral Chariot** is diagonally across from the sim and was built in 1962. The centrepiece is the grand 12-m-high gilded wooden hearse, with its seven-headed serpent, which was built for King Sisavang Vong, father of the last

➡ **Luang Prabang maps**
1 Luang Prabang, page 484
2 **Luang Prabang detail**, page 486

Morning Glory **23** *B3*
Tamarind **22** *A3*
Tamnak Lao **15** *B3*
View Khaem Khong **4** *A1*

Khily Wine Bar **24** *B5*
Khob Jai **19** *B1*
Lao Lao Garden **26** *B1*
Pack Luck **25** *B2*

Bars & clubs 🎵
Hive **18** *B1*

sovereign, and used to carry his urn to the stadium next to Wat That Luang where he was cremated in 1959. It was built on the chassis of a six-wheel truck by the sculptor, Thid Tan. On top of the carriage sit several sandalwood urns, none of which contain royal ashes. Originally the urns would have held the bodies of the deceased in a foetal position until cremation. The mosaics inside the chapel were never finished but the exterior is decorated with some almost erotic scenes from the *Ramakien* (the local version of the *Ramayana*), sculpted in enormous panels of teak wood and covered with gold leaf.

Wat Visunnarat (Wat Wisunarat) and That Makmo
① *Daily 0800-1700; 10,000 kip.*
This is better known as Wat Visoun and is on the south side of Mount Phousi. It is a replica of the original wooden building, constructed in 1513, which had been the oldest building in Luang Prabang, until it was destroyed by marauding Chinese tribes. The sim is virtually a museum of religious art, with numerous 'Calling to the Rain' Buddha statues: most are more than 400 years old and have been donated over the years by locals. Wat Visoun also contains the largest Buddha in the city and old stelae engraved with Pali scriptures (called *hiu chaluk*). The big stupa, commonly known as That Makmo ('melon stupa'), was built by Queen Visounalat in 1504. It is of Sinhalese influence with a smaller stupa at each corner, representing the four elements.

Wat Phra Maha That
Close to the **Hotel Phousi** on Phothisarath, this is a typical Luang Prabang wat, built in the 1500s and restored at the beginning of this century. The ornamentation of the doors and windows of the sim merit attention, with their graceful, golden figures from the Phra lak phra lam (the *Ramayana*). The pillars, ornamented with massive nagas, are also in traditional Luang Prabang style and reminiscent of certain styles adopted in Thailand.

Wat Manolom
South of Wat That Luang, Wat Manolom was built by the nobles of Luang Prabang to entomb the ashes of King Samsenthai (1373-1416) and is notable for its large armless bronze Buddha statue, one of the oldest Lao images of the Buddha, which dates back to 1372 and weighs two tonnes. Locals maintain that the arm was removed during a skirmish between Siamese and French forces during the latter part of the 19th century. While it is not artistically significant, the temple – or at least the site – is thought to be the oldest in the city, dating back, so it is said, to 1375 and the reign of Fa Ngum.

Wat Pa Phon Phao and Wat Phra That Chedi
① *3 km northeast of town, near Ban Phanom, daily 0800-1000, 1300-1630; donation expected.*
Outside town, Wat Pa Phon Phao is a forest meditation centre renowned for the teachings of its famous abbot, Ajahm Saisamut, one of the most popular monks in Lao history. More famous to tourists, though, is Wat Phra That Chedi, known as the Peace Pagoda. It looks as though it is made of pure gold from a distance but is rather disappointing close up. The wat was started in 1959 but was only completed in 1988; the names of donors are inscribed on pillars inside. It is modelled on the octagonal Shwedagon Pagoda in Yangon (Rangoon) and its inner walls are festooned with gaily painted frescoes of macabre allegories. Less grotesque paintings, extending right up to the fifth floor, document the life of the Buddha. On the second level, it is possible to duck through a tiny opening to admire the Blue Indra statues and the view of Luang Prabang.

Traditional Arts and Ethnology Centre

ⓘ *Ban Khamyong, T071-253364, www.taeclaos.org, Tue-Sun 0900-1800, 20,000 kip.*

A fantastic museum dedicated to the various ethnic groups in Laos. This non-profit centre has a permanent exhibition featuring fantastic photographs, religious artefacts, clothing, household objects and handicrafts. Within the exhibition there is a focus on the Hmong and their New Year celebrations; the Khmu and their baskets and art of backstrap looms; the Mien Yao embroidery and Lanten Taoist religious ceremonies, the Tai Dam bedding and Tai Lue culture. Truly this museum is a must-see in Luang Prabang – particularly for those that are venturing further north to go trekking. Attached to the centre is a handicraft shop that directly supports ethnic artisan communities. There's also a café and a small library.

Around Luang Prabang

Pak Ou caves → *Colour map 1, B5.*

ⓘ *US$1, free for children. Torches are available but candles make it possible to see reasonably well after your eyes have become accustomed to the dark. A boat trip from Luang Prabang is the best way to reach the caves. Rest houses, tables and a basic toilet are available.*

The Pak Ou Caves are perhaps the most popular excursion from Luang Prabang and are located 25 km upstream from the city, set in the side of a limestone cliff opposite the mouth of the Mekong's Nam Ou tributary (Pak Ou means 'Mouth of the Ou'). The two caves are studded with thousands of wood and gold Buddha images – 2500 in the lower cave and 1500 in the upper – and are one of the main venues for Pi Mai in April, when hundreds make the pilgrimage upriver from Luang Prabang.

The two sacred caves were supposedly discovered by King Setthathirat in the 16th century but it is likely that the caverns were associated with spirit (*phi*) worship before the arrival of Buddhism in Laos. For years the caves, which locals still believe to be the home of guardian spirits, were inhabited by monks.

Kwang Si Falls → *Colour map 1, C5.*

ⓘ *30 km south Luang Prabang; 20,000 kip, parking 2500 kip. Public toilets and changing rooms. Travel agents run tours or you can charter a tuk-tuk for about US$15 return. Slow boats take 1 hr down and 2 hrs back upriver, via Ban Muang Khai, where it is necessary to take a tuk-tuk for the last 6 km or so to the falls.*

These waterfalls are on a tributary of the Mekong. The trip to the falls is almost as scenic as the cascades themselves, passing through small Hmong and Khmu villages and vivid, green, terraced rice paddies. The falls are stunningly beautiful, misty cascades flowing over limestone formations, which eventually collect in several tiered, turquoise pools. Best of all, and despite appearances, it's still possible to take the left-hand path halfway up the falls and strike out through the pouring torrents and dripping caves to the heart of the waterfall. Note that swimming is only permitted in designated pools and, as the Lao swim fully clothed, you should wear modest swimwear and bring a sarong.

Hoykhua Waterfall (Tad Hoykhua)

ⓘ *14 km west of Luang Prabang in Ban Pakleung. To get to the falls cross the Mekong by boat at Tha Heua (boat station) in Luang Prabang to Xiang Men Village and then travel the rest by road.*

Beautiful two-tiered cascades that plummet 50 m, with a deep pool at the bottom. There are several Hmong and Khmu villages in the vicinity. There are three bungalows here at **Tad Hoykhua Guesthouse**, T020-557 0825.

For Sleeping and Eating price codes,
see inside the front cover.

● Sleeping

Luang Prabang *p482, maps p484 and p486*
Accommodation in Luang Prabang continues
to expand at the rate of knots. There were a
few new places in development at the time
of publication worth keeping an eye out for,
in particular a new hotel from the **Amman**
chain which will be in the old hospital and
will probably be completed in 2008.
LL La Residence Phou Vao, on a hill slightly
out of town, T071-2125303, www.residence
phouvao.com. Best hotel in town. Every little
detail in this plush hotel is perfect, from the
fragrance of frangipani, to the carefully lit pool.
Massive, beautiful rooms. In the low season
they drop their rates by about US$100.
**L-AL Three Nagas Boutique Hotel (Auberge
les 3 Nagas)**, Sakkaline Rd, T071-253888,
www.3nagas.com. Housed in a beautifully
restored building, with an annexe across the
road, this boutique hotel is a contender for
best room in town. Attention to detail is what
sets this hotel apart: from the 4-poster bed to
the large deep-set bath with hand-made
beauty products. Private balconies or rooms
lead onto a stunning courtyard. There's a lovely
sitting area in each room. Breakfast (included)
is served in the fantastic café downstairs.
Internet facilities for those with laptops.
A Ancient Luang Prabang, Sisavangvong Rd,
T071-212264, www.ancientluangprabang.com.
12 fantastically designed open-plan rooms
featuring a big modern bath (separate toilet).
The perfect romantic retreat for couples. At
US$65 these rooms represent good value.
Café downstairs with Wi-Fi and good coffees.
A Le Calao Inn, river road, T071-212100,
www.calaoinn.laopdr.com. This Portuguese/
French colonial (1902) building boasts
beautiful rooms in an incomparable position
overlooking the Mekong. Ensure you ask for
a room with water views.

A Maison Souvannaphoum, Phothisarath,
T071-212200, www.coloursofsangsana.com/
souvannaphoum. Formally Prince Souvanna's
residence, this place really is fit for royalty.
There are 4 spacious suites and 18 rooms, with
a/c, aromatherapy burners and special treats
left in the rooms. The service is top-notch.
A Pack Luck, opposite L'Éléphant, T071-253
373, packluck@hotmail.com. This boutique
hotel has 5 rooms that you couldn't swing
a cat in but are tastefully decorated and
have bathrooms with deep slate baths.
A Villa Maydou, set very close to the grounds
of Wat Meuna, T071-254601, www.villa
maydou.com. Slightly on the expensive side
but beautiful nonetheless. The hotel has a very
evocative Buddhist feel due to its location right
on the doorstep of Wat Meuna. The French-
owned hotel is set in restored government
buildings, originally built in 1925. Spacious, airy
a/c rooms simply decorated in a modern style.
A Villa Santi Hotel, Sisavangvong Rd, T071-
252157, www.villasantihotel.com. Almost an
institution in Luang Prabang, this is a restored
house from the early 20th century that served
as the private residence of the first King
Sisavong's wife and then Princess Manilai.
It's a charming place, full of character and
efficiently run but it is starting to get a bit run
down. There are 11 traditional rooms in the
old building, each of a different size, and
14 newer rooms, with baths and showers, in
a stylishly-built annexe. The daughter of the
official royal cook rustles up mouth watering
French cuisine in the **Princess Restaurant**
and there are attractive seating areas in
the garden, lobby or on the balcony.
A-D Sala Luang Prabang, 102/6 Ounkham
Rd, T071-252460, www.salaprabang.sala
lao.com. Very chic, renovated 100-year-old
building overlooking the Mekong. Rooms
have a minimalist, up-to-date edge with
a/c, modern bathrooms, and doors either
opening onto a small courtyard or river
balcony (more expensive). Bus, car and
bicycle hire available.

A-E The Apsara, Kingkitsarath, T071-212420, www.theapsara.com. Ivan Scholte, wine connoisseur and antique collector, has done a perfect job on this establishment. It oozes style. The beautiful rooms are themed by colour, with 4-poster beds, changing screen, big bath and lovely balcony. Very romantic with a modern twist. The rooms in 2nd building are equally magnificent and have large terrazzo showers. Room rate includes breakfast. Gets booked up in advance.

A-E Sayo Guesthouse, Sotikoumman Rd, T071-252614, sayo@laotel.com. A lovely hotel set in colonial mansion. The front rooms are beautifully and tastefully decorated and they boast a fantastic view over Wat Xieng Muang: you can watch the monks carving, painting and wood-working. The back rooms aren't as good value but are still recommended.

C-D Ammata Guesthouse, T071-212175, phetmanyp@yahoo.com.au. Very popular guesthouse with largish rooms decorated simply and stylishly. Hot water and en suite.

C-D Oui Guesthouse, at the end of the peninsula in Ban Khille on Sukkaserm, T071-252374, ouisguesthouse@gmail.com. Charming little guesthouse with sparkling new rooms with hot water, TV and fridge. Nicely decorated with local artefacts. Fantastic wine bar next door.

C-F Silichit Guesthouse, just off Ounkham Rd, T071-212758. Despite the dubious sounding name, this clean guesthouse is excellent value and well located. Comfortable rooms with fan, en suite bathroom and hot water. The very friendly owners speak English and French, and often invite guests to sit down for a family dinner or have a Beer Lao. As with most budget places, prices drop dramatically in the low season.

G Vanvisa Villa, T071-212925, vandara1@hotmail.com. Brightly coloured guesthouse down a quaint street. This is a little gem, with large, characterful and immaculate rooms and friendly owners. It's a bit run down but has a homely feel.

G Jaliya, Phamahapasaman Rd, T071-252 154. The ever-popular Jaliya has a range of bungalow-type rooms on offer, with varied facilities, from shared bathrooms and fan through to a/c and TV, so take a look around. Relaxing garden area with friendly pet deer. Bicycle and motorbike rental.

Hotels out of Luang Prabang

D-E Thongbay Guesthouse, Ban Vieng May, 3 km southeast of the centre of Luang Prabang, T071-253234, www.thongbbay-guesthouses.com. 12 modern bungalows, including 2 extra large family-sized ones. The rooms overlooking the river are the best. Bungalows have a fridge, 4-poster bed and hot water. Popular with tour groups so advanced booking is necessary. Recommended.

🍴 Eating

Luang Prabang *p482, maps p484 and p486* Note that, as Luang Prabang has a curfew; most places won't stay open past 2200.

The most famous local delicacy is *khai pehn*, dried river weed, mainly from the Nam Khan, which is mixed with sesame and eaten nationwide. One of the best local culinary experiences is to grab some Lao takeaway food from the night market that runs off **Sisavangvong Rd**, 1600-2200. There are also a number of cheap buffets where you can get a selection of local curries and dishes. If you don't want your food too hot ask for '*bo pet*'.

₮₮₮-₮₮ L'Éléphant, Ban Vat Nong, T071-252 482, contact@elephantrestau.com. About as fine as dining gets in Luang Prabang. Very upmarket and utterly delectable cuisine. Pan-fried fillet of snapper, with capers and basil-flavoured mash is delicious, as are the simmered scallops. Also a number of Lao dishes. There are 3 set menus and an extensive wine list.

₮₮-₮ The Apsara, see Sleeping. Beautifully decorated restaurant offering modern Lao/Thai cuisine. Try their delicious red curry cream soup with lentils and smoked duck or braised beef shin Chinese style. Great fish cakes. Good value.

♥♥–♥ Blue Lagoon, beside the Royal Palace, www.blue-lagoon-cafe.com, T071-253698. This restaurant offers a great selection of delicious hearty European meals – especially Swiss-inspired meals such as the *fondue chinoise*. Great steaks, pasta and ice creams. Indoor and outdoor seating in comfortable candlelit garden setting.

♥♥–♥ Couleur Café/Restaurant, Ban Vat Nong, T020-5621064. The French expats in town have nothing but praise for this place with its French and Lao meals and ambient setting. Good wine. This is the place for the carnivores as it has become renowned for its steaks.

♥ Dao Fa, Sisavangvong Rd, T071-215651, www.daofa-bistro.com. Great selection of teas and coffees, fab ice creams and tasty home-made pasta. The latter is the real draw and is recommended. Brightly decorated space with pavement seating.

♥ Morning Glory, Sakkaline Rd, 0800-1600. Small but cosy Thai restaurant. Intimate open-style kitchen serving up fantastic home-style meals – great juices, breakfasts and curries. Try the *Tom Kha Gai* and zesty juice.

♥ Tamarind, facing Wat Nong, T020-777 0484, www.tamarindlaos.com, Mon-Sat 1100-1800. Brilliant restaurant offering modern Lao cuisine; an utterly exceptional dining experience. Try the 5-bites (the Lao equivalent to tapas), the pumpkin soup is to die for and the tamarind juice is exceptional. Even better than their à la carte menu are the 'dining experiences' such as the traditional Lao Celebration meal 'Pun Pa', which includes succulent marinated fish and purple sticky rice dessert (60,000 kip per person, minimum 2 people), or the Adventurous Lao Gourmet degustation menu, which comes with explanations of what each dish is. They also do **market tours** with in-depth explanations of Lao delicacies (advance booking is essential) and can organize picnics.

♥ Tamnak Lao, Sisavangvong Rd, opposite **Villa Santi**, T071-252525. Brilliant restaurant, serving modern Lao cuisine, with a strong Thai influence. Very popular with tour groups. The freshest ingredients are used: try fish and coconut wrapped in banana leaf. Atmospheric surroundings and exceptional service. Best for dinner. Unmissable.

♥ View Khaem Khong, Ounkham Rd, T071-212726. The most popular of the dining establishments along the river. Good for a beer at sunset. Luang Prabang sausage and *laap*.

Cafés and bakeries
Café Ban Vat Sene, Sakkaline Rd. Great French food, more of a restaurant than a café, upmarket, great for breakfast.
Joma, Sisavangvong Rd, T071-252292. Delicious comfort foods. If you're planning a trek or boat trip get your picnic here.
L'Étranger, Kingkitsarath Rd, T020-54717036. This is a great little bookshop-cum-café. Outstanding breakfasts. Books rented here for 5000 kip per day. Movie shown daily at 1900.

① Bars and clubs

Luang Prabang *p482, maps p484 and p486*
L'Éléphant, **La Résidence Phou Vao** and **Apsara**, provide attractive settings for a drink. A sunset beer at the restaurants overlooking the river is divine. After everything closes between 2200 and 2300 most locals either head to the bowling alley for a beer (open until 0300) or have a bowl of soup and a cold beverage on Phou Vao Rd at one of the many *pho* noodle shops.
Dao Fa nightclub on the way to the Southern terminal. Extremely popular with locals, plays Asian dance music.
Hive Bar, Kingkitsarath Rd, next to **L'Étranger**. Luang Prabang's most happening bar-club is good for a dance, though it has become quieter now that the competition around it has started to grow.
Khily Wine Bar, tucked away next door to **Oui Guesthouse** at the end of the peninsula. A secret hotspot for locals. This intimate bar has a long bar stocked with an extensive selection of *lao-lao* and wine. Great for a quiet drink.
Khob Jai, Kingkitsarath Rd, opposite **Hive Bar** (sometimes known as **LPQ**). A dedicated gay bar but open to all and sundry.

Lao Lao Garden, Kingkitsarath Rd. A tiered landscaped terrace, with low lighting, that's become a favourite backpacker haunt with cheap, delicious cocktails.

Pack Luck, Sisavangvong Rd. For a more upmarket drink, this cosy wine bar has a great selection of tipples and well-selected wines. High on atmosphere, with comfy beanbags and modern art adorning its walls.

⚙ Entertainment

Luang Prabang p482, maps p484 and p486
Theatre and dance
Traditional dance performances are held Mon, Wed and Sat at 1800, at the **Royal Palace**; US$6-15.

⚙ Festivals and events

Luang Prabang p482, maps p484 and p486
Apr Pi Mai (Lao New Year; movable)
The time when the tutelary spirits of the old year are replaced by those of the new. It has special significance in Luang Prabang, with certain traditions celebrated in the city that are no longer observed in Vientiane. 11 days.
May Vien Thiene (movable). Candlelit festival.
Sep Boat races. Boats are raced by the people living in the vicinity of each wat.

O Shopping

Luang Prabang p482, maps p484 and p486
Ban Khilly Paper Gallery, Sakkaline St, T071-212611. A *sa* crafts centre (*sa* is a rough, leaf-effect paper). Sells scrolls, paper lanterns and cards and beautifully decorated and painted paper.
Caruso Gallery, Sisavangvong Rd (towards the **Three Nagas Boutique Hotel**) stunning but expensive wood furniture and artefacts.
Naga Creations, Sisavangvong Rd, T071-212775. A large collection of jewellery and trinkets, combining Lao silver with quality

semi-precious stones. Some truly innovative work by the jeweller **Fabrice**, including beautiful use of beetle wings (the same style that were once used to adorn royal clothing).
Ock Pop Tok, near L'Éléphant restaurant, T071-253219. Ock Pop Tok, which literally translates as 'East meets West', incorporates the best of both worlds in beautiful designs and fabrics. It specializes in naturally dyed silk, which is of a much better quality than synthetically dyed silk as it doesn't run. Clothes, household items, hangings and custom-made orders are also available (if ordered well in advance). Check out the **Fibre2Fabric** gallery next door to see the stories behind the fabulous creations.
Patthana Boupha Antique Gallery, Ban Visoun, T071-212262. This little gem can be found in a partitioned-off area in a fantastic colonial building. Antique silverware and jewellery, Buddhas, old photos and fine textiles. Less common are furniture and household items. Reasonable prices. Often closed, so ring beforehand.
Satri Lao Silk, Sisavangvong Rd, T071-219295. Beautiful silks and handicrafts for sale. Can sometimes be slightly over-priced, but definitely worth a look.

Markets
The **night market** sprawls down several blocks off Sisavangvong Rd (this market has been moving around the last few years but is expected to return to Sisavangvong Rd). Daily 1700-2230. Hundreds of villagers flock to the market to sell their handicrafts. The market shouldn't be missed and most visitors won't leave without a great souvenir or 2.
Phousy market, 1.5 km from the centre of town. This market is a real gem: aside from the usual fruit and vegetables, it is a fantastic place to pick up silk garments. Pre-made silk clothes are sold here for a fraction of the price in town. They just need the odd button sewn on or the hem taken up. Make sure that you are very detailed with instructions though and ensure the same colour thread is used in any alterations.

Talat Dala, housed in a market building in the middle of town on the corner of Setthathirat and Chao Sisophon roads, at the time of publication the market was being gloriously revamped to become a major market for artisans and jewellers to sell their wares.

Silver

There are several Lao silversmiths around the Nam Phou area (fountain), where you can watch the artisans ply their trade. **Thit Peng**, signposted almost opposite Wat That, is a workshop and small shop with jewellery and pots.

▲▲ Activities and tours

Luang Prabang p482, maps p484 and p486
Cookery classes

There are a number of classes offered in Luang Prabang. The cooking classes are ordered in preference.
Tamarind, facing Wat Nong, T020-777 0484, www.tamarindlaos.com. This successful restaurant has been running specialized custom-made classes for 1 or 2 people at a time. However, due to their immense popularity they will expand these courses to larger groups. Recommended.
Tamnak Lao, T071-252525, www.lao cookingcourse.com. US$25 per person for 1-day cooking class, including shopping at the markets.
Tum Tum Cheng, Sakkaline Rd, T071-253388, www.tumtumcheng.com. Mon-Sat. Popular cooking classes operating since 2001. 1 day, US$25; 2 day, US$45; 3 day, US$60. Advanced bookings are required.

Elephants tours and activities

Elephant Park Project, 25 km from Luang Prabang (can be organized through **Tiger Trails** office on Sisavangvong Rd, T071-252655, www.laos-adventures.com). Has been established in conjunction with Tiger Trails in Luang Prabang. In order to keep the old elephants active, the operators run a

number of activities. Tourists can participate in up to 25 activities at the elephant park. There are a few other similar elephant park projects but these are pale imitations which have compromised on quality.

Exhibitions and galleries

Fibre2Fabric, 71 Ban Vat Nong (next door to **Ock Pop Tok**), T071-254761, www.fibre2 fabric.org. A fantastic gallery exhibiting photography, weaving and explanations of local ethnic customs and cultures associated with textile production. Local weavers often on hand to explain the processes.
Kinnaly Gallery, Sakkaline Rd, T020-5557737. Photographic work and local art.
Kop Noi, Ban Aphay, www.kopnoi.com. This little shop has a rotating exhibition on the 2nd storey of their shop. They also exhibit a selection of photographs from renowned Lao photographer Sam Sisombat.

Sauna and massage

Aroma Spa, Sisavangvong Rd, T020-761 1255. Another mid-priced spa offering aromatherapy, facials, body scrubs, etc.
Khmu Spa, Sisavangvong Rd, T071-212092. A range of cheaply priced massages including the Khmu massage (gentler, lighter strokes), Lao massage (stretching, cracking and pressure points) and foot massage. Also has herbal sauna. Open until 2200.
Maison Souvannaphoum (see Sleeping). A spa with a range of luxurious and expensive treatments. For sheer indulgence.
Red Cross Sauna, opposite Wat Visunnarat, reservations T071-212303. Daily 0900-2100 (1700-2100 for sauna). Massage 30,000 kip per hr, traditional Lao herbal sauna 10,000 kip. Bring your own towel or sarong. Profits go to the Lao Red Cross.
Spa Garden, Ban Phonheauang, T071-212325, spagardenlpb@hotmail.com. More upmarket. Offers a wide selection of massage and beauty treatments including aromatherapy massage US$12 per hr, sports body massage, facial treatments, skin detox US$25 per hr. The best

value for money in luxury massage. Packages between US$5 and US$38.

The Spa at La Residence Phou Vao T071-212530, www.residencephouvao.com. Offers 3-hr massage courses, US$190 for 2 people. This includes a 1-hr massage for each person, the class, a handbook and oils.

Tour operators

All Laos Service, Sisavangvong Rd. Large successful travel agency organizing ticketing and travel services.

Green Discovery, T071-212093, www.green discovery.com. A range of rafting and kayaking trips that pass through grade I and II rapids. Cycling trips around Luang Prabang and surrounding countryside. Homestays, rafting, kayaking, trips to Pak Ou caves, etc.

Tiger Trail, Sisavangvong Rd, T071-252 655, www.tigertrail-laos.com. Adventure specialists: elephant treks, trekking, mountain biking tours, rafting, rock climbing, etc.

Weaving

Weaving Centre, 2 km out of town on the river (bookings at **Ban Vat Nong Gallery**, T071-253 219, info@ockpoptok.com). The team behind the fabulous creations at **Ock Pop Tok** have opened a weaving centre. ½-day dyeing classes introduce students to the world of silk dyes (US$35). A variety of 1- to 3-day weaving classes are offered at US$35 per day. Tailor-made courses are also available. Classes are run by professional weavers and their English-speaking assistants. At the time of publication a small café was to be opened on the site.

⊖ Transport

Luang Prabang *p482, maps p484 and p486*
Air
Luang Prabang International Airport (LPQ) about 4 km from town, T071-212172/3. **Lao Airlines**, Phamahapasaman Rd, T071-212172, has 3 daily connections with **Vientiane**, 40 mins, and a service to **Chiang Mai**, Pakse and Phonsavanh. They also run 3 flights a

week between **Bangkok** and Luang Prabang. These flights are notoriously prone to change so check schedule well in advance. **Bangkok Airways** runs daily flights to **Bangkok**. In the high season (from Nov onwards) **Siem Reap Airways** flies to **Siem Reap** via Pakse.

Early morning departures are often delayed during the rainy season, as dense cloud can sometimes make Luang Prabang airport inoperable until about 1100. Airline tickets are more often than not substantially cheaper from travel agents (see Tour operators, above) than from the actual airline. Confirm bookings a day in advance and arrive at the airport early, as flights have been known to depart as soon as they're full.

Bicycle
About US$1 per day from most guesthouses.

Boat
Tha Heua Mea Pier is the most popular departure point and has a blackboard listing all the destinations and prices available (daily 0730-1130 and 1300-1600). Prices are largely dependent on the price of gasoline. There is also a dock at **Ban Don** (15 mins north of town by tuk-tuk, US$1-2).

To Houei Xai/Pak Beng The 2-day boat trip down the Mekong between Houei Xai and Pak Beng has become a rite of passage for travellers in Southeast Asia. There are options to suit every budget. The **slow boat** to Houei Xai, leaves from the boat pier on Khem Khong Rd called the Tha Heua Mea pier, 2 days, with a break in Pak Beng after 6-7 hrs on the 1st day. It is US$11 for each leg of the trip and almost all travel agents sell tickets. It's often packed so bring some padding to sit on. Seats are usually basic wooden benches though you may luck out with one that has bus seats. The trip from Luang Prabang to Houei Xai (via Pak Beng overnight) is usually less busy than in the other direction. (If the boat to Pak Beng is full, you can charter your own for about US$200-300.) Tickets for the onward trip to Houei Xai, can be purchased in Pak

Beng. Take a good book and a grab some goodies from one of the bakeries to take on board. Most boats will have a vendor selling basic drinks. The boat usually leaves between 0800 and 0900 (changeable so check) but get there early to secure a good seat.

A mid-range option is the **Nagi**, a more comfortable, quicker boat. From Houei Xai the Nagi makes the trip to Luang Prabang in 1 day. The boat departs at 0830 and arrives at approximately 1730. Going upstream from Luang Prabang to Houei Xai the journey takes 2 days. Hot food and cold drinks are served on board. From Houei Xai to Luang Prabang – 1 day US$80; From Luang Prabang to Houei Xai (via Pak Beng) US$70 (not including accommodation in Pak Beng where you have to stay overnight).

The most luxurious way to make the trip is on the **Luangsay Cruise**, Sisavangvong Rd, T071-252553, www.asian-oasis.com, which makes the trip in 2 days and 1 night, stopping over at Pak Ou Caves en route and staying overnight at their luxurious lodge in Pak Beng. The boat is extra comfortable and has lounges, a stocked bar and lots of board games. Very popular in high season and will need to be booked 6 months in advance. In low season the boat runs from Houei Xai to Luang Prabang on Mon and Fri and in the opposite direction on Wed and Sat (US$243 twin/US$300 single). In the high season the boat runs from Houei Xai to Luang Prabang on Mon, Thu and Fri, and in the opposite direction Luang Prabang to Houei Xai on Tue, Wed and Sat (US$358 twin/US$422 single). In the low season it may be possible to get a standby rate if there is availability.

Speedboats (which are not recommended) depart from Ban Don to **Houei Xai** (on the Thai border; see page 500), US$30, around 6 hrs, with a short break in **Pak Beng**. Tickets available from most travel agents. The boats are noisy and dangerous (numerous fatalities have been reported from boats jack-knifing when hitting waves). Ear plugs are recommended and ensure boatmen provide a helmet and life jacket.

A few boats travel up the Nam Ou to **Nong Khiaw**. These are infrequent, especially when the river is low, 6 hrs to Nong Khiaw, 120,000 kip. The Nam Ou joins the Mekong near the Pak Ou Caves, so it is possible to combine a journey with a visit to the caves en route. The irregular travel dates to Nong Khiaw are posted on a board outside the boat pier or ask one of the travel agents on Sisavangvong Rd when the next departure is. It is possible to charter a boat for 1-6 people for US$150. Speedboats to Nong Khiaw sometimes leave from Ban Don, expect to pay 160,000 kip. These boats are hazardous, uncomfortable and not environmentally friendly.

Bus/truck

The northern bus terminal is for north-bound traffic and the southern for traffic to/from the south. Double-check which terminal your bus is using, unscheduled changes are possible.

From the northern terminal
To **Luang Namtha**, daily 0900 and 1730, 10 hrs, usually via **Udomxai**, 70,000 kip. The 1730 bus has usually come from Vientiane and is often full. An alternative option is to break the journey by catching the bus to **Udomxai**, daily 0900 and 1130, 5 hrs, 45,000 kip, and then continuing on to Luang Namtha in the afternoon. There are also daily departures (usually in the morning) to **Houei Xai** on the Thai/Lao border, 11-12 hrs, 100,000 kip. A VIP bus to Houei Xai passes through on Mon, Wed, Fri and Sun, 1000, 10 hrs, 160,000 kip There is a very long bus journey to **Xam Neua**, 1630, they say it takes 14 hrs but it can take up to 20 hrs, 100,000 kip. **Phongsali** 1600, 13-15 hrs, 100,000 kip. To Nong Khiaw, by songthaew, departures usually in the morning, 32,000 kip.

From the southern terminal There are up to 8 daily buses to **Vientiane**, though scheduled departures tend to decline in the low season, 10-11 hrs, 90,000 kip; most of these buses stop in **Vang Vieng**, 6 hrs, 75,000 kip. VIP buses to Vientiane depart

0800, 0900, 9 hrs, 115,000 kip; both these services stop in Vang Vieng, 100,000 kip. To **Phonsavanh**, daily 0830, 8-9 hrs, 85,000 kip. It should cost 10,000-15,000 kip to get to the centre of town from the station.

Saamlor and tuk-tuk

Lots around town which can be hired to see the sights or to go to nearby villages. A short stint across town should cost about 10,000 kip per person, but expect to pay 20,000 kip for anything more than 1 km. Most of the nearby excursions will cost US$5-10.

⊙ Directory

Luang Prabang p482, maps p484 and p486
Banks Lao Development Bank, 65 Sisavangvong Rd, Mon-Sat 0830-1200, 1330-1530, will change US$/Thai ฿/TCs into dollars or kip, but doesn't accept credit cards. **Banque pour le Commerce Exterieur Lao (BCEL)**, Sisavangvong Rd, Mon-Sat 0830-1200, 1330-1530; all transactions in kip, will exchange Thai ฿, US$, AU$, UK£, Euro and TCs, also offers

cash advances on Visa cards. Have an ATM but at the time of publication this was only for MasterCard. Many of the jewellery stalls in the old market, plus restaurant and tourist shop owners, will change US$ and Thai ฿. Many of the travel agencies will do credit card advances but charge 6-8% commission **Internet** There are a concentration of places on Sisavangvong Rd. **Medical services** The main hospital, on Setthathirat, T071-252049 is only useful for minor ailments. For anything major you're better off getting a flight to Bangkok. There are a few reasonably well-equipped pharmacies towards Villa Santi on Sisavangvong Rd. **Post and telephone** The post and telephone office is on the corner of Chau Fa Ngum and Setthathirat, Mon-Fri 0830-1730, Sat 0830-1200, express mail service, international telephone facilities. Hotels and some guesthouses allow international calls from reception (about US$5 a min). It is dramatically cheaper to make international calls from an internet cafés, which usually have Skype available.

Far north

The misty, mountain scenery of the far north conjures up classic Indochina imagery of striking rice terraces, golden, thatched huts and dense, tropical forests, all dissected by a cross-hatching of waterways. Here life is beautifully interwoven with the ebb and flow of the rivers. The mighty Mekong forges its way through picturesque towns, such as Pak Beng and Houei Xai, affording visitors a wonderful glimpse of riverine life, while, to the east, the Nam Ou attracts visitors to Nong Khiaw and, the latest traveller hot spot, Muang Ngoi Neua. The wonderful upland areas are home to around 40 different ethnic groups, including the Akha, Hmong, Khmu and Yao, and it's not surprising that the country's best trekking is also found here. ►► *For listings, see pages 504-512.*

Luang Namtha and around ●⊘▲●● ►► pp504-512. Colour map 1,B4.

This area has firmly established itself as a major player in Laos' ecotourism industry, primarily due to the **Nam Ha Ecotourism Project**, which was established in 1993 by NTA Lao and UNESCO to help preserve Luang Namtha's cultural and environmental heritage in the Nam Ha National Protected Area. The Nam Ha NPA is one of the largest protected areas in Laos and consists of mountainous areas dissected by several rivers. It is home to at least 38 species of large mammal, including the black-cheeked crested gibbon, tiger and clouded leopard, and over 300 bird species, including the stunning Blythe's kingfisher.

Udomxai → *Colour map 1, B5.*
Heading northwest from Luang Prabang, travellers will reach Udomxai, the capital of Udomxai Province. It's a hot and dusty town, with a truck-stop atmosphere that doesn't enamour it to tourists and unfortunately, the other bad elements that come with major transport thoroughfares seem to be raising their heads here too, such as prostitution and increased HIV/AIDS. However, the town does make a decent stop-off point at a convenient junction; it's one of the biggest settlements in northern Laos and has excellent facilities. One only has to look around at the presence of Chinese flags on shop fronts to get an inkling of the large presence of Chinese workers and businesses in town.

Luang Namtha → *Colour map 1, B4.*
Luang Namtha Province has witnessed the rise and decline of various Tai Kingdoms and now more than 35 ethnic groups reside in the province, making it the most

Luang Namtha

Sleeping
Boat Landing Guesthouse
 & Restaurant 12
Luang Namtha Guesthouse 7

Manychan Guesthouse 4
Vila Guesthouse 10
Zuela Guesthouse 5

Eating ⊘
Banana 3
Coffee House 6
KNT Internet 5
Panda 2
Yamuna 4

ethnically diverse in the country. Principal minorities include Tai Lu, Tai Dam, Lanten, Hmong and Khmu. The provincial capital was obliterated during the war and the concrete structures erected since 1975 have little charm but there are a number of friendly villages in the area. As with all other minority areas it is advisable to visit villages with a local guide or endorsed tourism organization.

The **Luang Namtha Museum** ① *near the Kaystone Monument, daily 0800-1130, 1330-1630; 5000 kip.* (was undergoing renovations at the time of publication). The museum houses a collection of indigenous clothing and artefacts, agricultural tools, weapons, textiles and a collection of Buddha images, drums and gongs.

In the centre of town is a **night market** with a range of food stalls. It is only in its infancy but the local authorities have aspirations to expand the market to include ethnic handicrafts, making it similar to the one in Luang Prabang.

Surrounding villages

Ban Nam Chang is a Lanten village, 3 km along a footpath outside town; **Ban Lak Khamay** is quite a large Akha village 27 km from Luang Namtha on the road to Muang Sing. The settlement features a traditional Akha entrance; if you pass through this entrance you must visit a house in the village, or you are considered an enemy. Otherwise you can simply pass to one side of the gate but don't touch it. Other features of interest in Akha villages are the swing, located at the highest point in the village and used in the annual swing festival (you must not touch the swing), and the meeting house, where unmarried couples go to court and where newly married couples live until they have their own house. **Ban Nam Dee** is a small bamboo papermaking Lanten village about 6 km northeast of town. The name of the village means 'good water' and not surprisingly, if you continue on 1 km from Ban Nam Dee there's a waterfall. The trip to the village is stunning, passing through verdant rice paddies dotted with huts. A motorbike rather than a bicycle will be necessary to navigate these villages and sights, as the road can be very rocky. Villagers usually charge 3000 kip for access to the waterfall.

The small Tai Lue village of **Ban Khone Kam** is also worth a visit. The villagers offer **homestays** here (30,000 kip per night, includes meals), for one or two nights. For trips between Luang Namtha and Houei Xai contact the **Luang Namtha Boat Station** ① *T086-211305*, or the environmentally friendly **Boat Landing Guesthouse** in Luang Namtha.

Ban Vieng Nua is a Tai Kolom village, 3 km from the centre of town, famous for its traditional house where groups can experience local dancing and a good luck baci ceremony (US$30 for the group). Contact the tourist information office to make a booking. Dinner can also be organized here at a cost of US$6 per head.

Nam Ha National Protected Area

Both Luang Namtha and Vieng Phouka are great bases from which to venture into the Nam Ha National Protected Area, one of a few remaining places on earth where the rare black-cheeked gibbon can be found. If you're lucky you can hear the wonderful singing of the gibbons in the morning. The 222,400 sq km conservation area encompasses more than 30 ethnic groups and 37 threatened mammal species. Organizations currently lead two- and three-day treks in the area for small groups of four to eight culturally sensitive travellers. Treks leave three to four times a week; check with the **Luang Namtha Guide Service Unit** or **Green Discovery** (see Tour operators, page 508) for departure days; an information session about the trek is given at the Guide's Office. The price will cover the cost of food, water, transportation, guides, lodging and the trekking permit. All the treks utilize local guides who have been trained to help generate income for their villages. Income for conservation purposes is also garnered from the fees for trekking permits into the area. ▶▶ *See Activities and tours, page 508.*

Tubing Several vendors on the main road offer inflated inner tubes for tubing on the Nam Ha River, though this is organized without the expertise in tubing and river awareness in other places in the country and is not always safe, particularly when the waters are high.

Muang Sing and around → *Colour map 1, B4.*
Many visitors consider this peaceful valley to be one of the highlights of the north. The only way to get to Muang Sing is by truck or pick-up from Luang Namtha. The road is asphalt but is sometimes broken and the terrain on this route is mountainous with dense forest. Muang Sing itself is situated on an upland plateau among misty, blue-green peaks. The town features some interesting old wooden and brick buildings and, unlike nearby Luang Namtha and several other towns in the north, it wasn't bombed close to oblivion during the struggle for Laos. Numerous hill peoples come to the market to trade, including Akha and Hmong tribespeople, along with Yunnanese, Tai Dam and Tai Lu.

Muang Sing Ethnic Museum ① *in the centre of town, Mon-Fri 0900-1200, 1300-1600; 5000 kip,* is a beautiful building housing a range of traditional tools, ethnic clothes, jewellery, instruments, religious artefacts and household items. The building was once the royal residence of the Jao Fa (Prince), Phanya Sekong.

The population of the district is said to have trebled between 1992 and 1996, due to the resettlement of many minorities, either from refugee camps in Thailand or from highland areas of Laos and, as a result, it is one of the better places in northern Laos to visit ethnic villages. The town is predominantly Tai Lu but the district is 50% Akha, with a further 10% Tai Nua. The main activity for visitors is to hire bicycles and visit the villages that surround the town; several guesthouses have maps of the surrounding area and trekking is becoming increasingly popular. However, do not undertake treks independently as it undermines the government's attempts to make tourism sustainable and minimize the impact on local villages. ▶▶ *See Activities and tours, page 508.*

From Muang Sing, trek uphill past **Phoutat Guesthouse** for 7 km up an 886-m hill to reach **That Xieng Tung**, the most sacred site in the area. The stupa was built in 1256 and is believed to contain Buddha's Adam's apple. It attracts lots of pilgrims in November for the annual full moon festival. There is a small pond near the stupa, which is also believed to be very auspicious: if it dries up it is considered very bad luck for Muang Sing. It is said that the pond once dried up and the whole village had no rice and starved. Most tourism operators will run to treks up to the stupa and will also stop at **Nam Keo** waterfall, a large cascade with a 10-m drop that trickles down into a little brook.

Along the Mekong ○●①▲△△ ▶▶ *pp504-512. Colour map 1, B/C4 .*
The slow boat along the Mekong between Houei Xai and Luang Prabang is a favourite option for visitors travelling to and from the Thai border. It's a charming trip through lovely scenery.

Houei Xai → *Colour map 1, B4.*
Located southwest of Luang Namtha on the banks of the Mekong, Houei Xai is a popular crossing point to and from Thailand. Few people spend more than one night in the town.

Boats run between here and Luang Prabang, two days' journey downstream, via Pak Beng. Most passengers arrive close to the centre at the passenger ferry pier. The vehicle ferry pier is 750 m further north (upstream). Although the petite, picturesque town is growing rapidly as links with Thailand intensify, it is still small and easy enough to get around on foot.

Wat Chom Kha Out Manirath, in the centre of town, is worth a visit for its views. The monastery was built at the end of the 19th century but, because it is comparatively well endowed, there has been a fair amount of re-building and renovation since then. There is also a large former French fort here called **Fort Carnot**, now used by the Lao army.

Most visitors who do stick around in Houei Xai do so to visit the **Gibbon Experience** ① *T084-212021, experience@gibbonx.org, US$150 (price includes tree house accommodation, transport, food, access to Bokeo Nature Reserve and well-trained guides).* This is a three-day trip into Bokeo Nature Reserve, where a number of tree houses have been built high up in the jungle canopy and linked by interconnected zip-lines. Staying in the trees and waking to the sound of singing gibbons is a truly awe-inspiring experience, as is zip-lining above the jungle canopy, through the mist. In the morning well-trained guides take visitors hiking to see if they can spot the elusive gibbons as well as other plant and animal species. Others to look out for are the giant squirrel, one of the largest rodents in the world, and the Asiatic black bear, whose numbers are in decline as they are hunted for their bile and gall bladders. First and foremost this is a very well-run conservation project. The **Gibbon Experience** was started to help reduce poaching, logging, slash-and-burn farming and the destruction of primary forest by working with villagers to transform the local economy by making a non-destructive living from their unique environment. Already the project has started to pay dividends: the forest conservation and canopy visits generate as much income year on year as the local logging company could do only once.

Pak Beng → *Colour map 1, C4.*

This long thin strip of a village is perched halfway up a hill, with fine views over the Mekong. Its importance lies in its location at the confluence of the Mekong and the Nam Beng. There is not much to do here but it's a good place to stop en route between Houei Xai and Luang Prabang (or vice versa). The village is worth a visit for its traditional atmosphere and the friendliness of the locals, including various minorities. Just downstream from the port is a good spot for swimming in the dry season, but be careful as the current is strong. There are also a couple of monasteries in town. The locals are now organizing guided treks to nearby villages; check with the guesthouses.

Northeast of Luang Prabang ⬤⬤▲⬤⬤ ➤ *pp504-512. Colour map 1, B5/B6.*

In recent years the settlements of Nong Khiaw and Muang Ngoi Neua in the north of Luang Prabang Province have become firm favourites with the backpacker set. In fact, idyllic Muang Ngoi Neua is often heralded as the new Vang Vieng, surrounded by stunning scenery and the fantastic ebb of life on the river. It is far more pleasant to travel between Luang Prabang and Nong Khiaw/Ban Saphoun, just south of Muang Ngoi Neua, by long boat, than by bus. The Nam Ou passes mountains, teak plantations, dry rice fields and a movable waterwheel mounted on a boat, which moves from village to village and is used for milling. But with the improvements that have been made to Route 13, road travel has now become the preferred option for many – partly because it is cheaper, and partly because it is quicker. Route 13 north runs parallel with the river for most of the journey to Nam Bak. There is trekking around Muang Khua further north upriver.

Phongsali

High up in the mountains at an altitude of about 1628 m, this northern provincial capital provides beautiful views and an invigorating climate. It is especially stunning from January to March, when wildflowers bloom in the surrounding hills. The town can be cold at any time of the year, so take some warm clothes. Mornings tend to be foggy and it can also be very wet. There is an end of an earth feel in the areas surrounding the main centre, with dense pristine jungle surrounded by mountains.

Phongsali was one of the first areas to be liberated by the Pathet Lao in the late 1940s. The old post office (just in front of the new one), is the sole physical reminder of French rule. The town's architecture is a strange mix of Chinese post-revolutionary concrete blocks, Lao wood-and-brick houses, with tin roofs, and bamboo or mud huts, with straw roofs. The town itself is home to about 20,000 people, mostly Lao, Phou Noi and Chinese,

while the wider district is a mixture of ethnicities, with around 28 minorities inhabiting the area.

It is not possible to hire bikes, tuk-tuks or even ponies here so walking is the only way to explore the fantastic landscapes of this region. Many paths lead out of town over the hills; the walking is easy and the panoramas are spectacular. Climb the 413 steps to the top of Mount Phoufa for humbling views of the surrounding hills. The **Provincial Tourism Office**, on the way to Phou Fa Hotel (now simply a restaurant), T088-210098, Monday-Friday 0730-1130, 1330-1630, can arrange guided ecotreks, including village homestays, for up to five nights. The rates depend on the number of people. Some people trek north from Phongsali to Uthai, staying in Akha villages en route. Uthai is probably as remote and unspoilt as it gets.

Sleeping Viphahone Hotel, next to the post office, T088-210111. A three-storey building with restaurant and 24 very

Nong Khiaw and Ban Saphoun → *Colour map 1, B6.*

Nong Khiaw lies 22 km northeast of Nam Bak and is a delightful, remote little village on the banks of the Nam Ou, surrounded by limestone peaks and flanked by mountains, the largest aptly named Princess Mountain. It is one of Laos' prettiest destinations. There are, in fact, two settlements here: Ban Saphoun on the east bank of the Nam Ou and Nong Khiaw on the west. Of the two, Ban Saphoun offers the best views and has the best riverside accommodation. Confusingly, the combined village is sometimes called one name, sometimes the other and sometimes Muang Ngoi, which is actually another town to the north (see below) and the name of the district.

One reason why the area has become a popular stopping place for travellers is because of its pivotal position on the Nam Ou, affording river travel from Luang Prabang to the north. It is also on the route between Udomxai and Xam Neau, which is one of the most spectacular in Laos, passing through remote villages. Despite its convenience as a staging post, this village is a destination in its own right. It is a beautiful spot, the sort of place where time stands still, journals are written, books read and stress is a deeply foreign concept. It is possible to swim in the river (women should wear sarongs) or walk around the town or up the cliffs. If you go to the boat landing it is also possible to organize a fishing trip with one of the local fishermen for very little money. You might need someone to translate for you. The bridge across the Nam Ou offers fine views and photo opportunities. There are caves in the area and the Than Mok waterfall.

clean, large and airy twin and double rooms, with hot-water bathrooms, some with Western flush toilets. **Sengsaly Guesthouse**, up the hill and around the bend from the market, T088-210165. Worn but comfortable rooms, with squat toilets and scoop showers.

Eating Yu Houa Guesthouse, across the road from the market. Has a short Lao and Chinese section on an English menu; cheap and good. The Phongsali Hotel is also a good bet and has a larger variety of dishes, including a few Thai, Chinese and Lao.

Transport You can travel from Muang Khua to Phongsali either by truck or by boat. Trucks also depart from Pak Nam Noi (near Muang Khua); buy lunch from the market before departure. The ride is long and difficult when the pick-up is full, but it's a great experience and the scenery near Phongsali is utterly breathtaking. Alternatively, catch a boat from Muang Khua to Hat Xa, 20 km or so to the northeast of Phongsali, five to six hours,

100,000 kip. In the low season there may not be any scheduled boats so it might be necessary to gather a few extra tourists and charter a boat, US$80-100. Depending on the season, the river is quite shallow in places, with a fair amount of white water. It can be cold and wet so wear waterproofs and take a blanket. Note that you may find your-selves stuck in Hat Xa, as there are no onward buses to Phongsali after mid-afternoon. Alternative routes to Phongsali are by bus to/from Udomxai, nine to 10 hours, 60,000 kip, or by plane to/from Vientiane, twice a week with Lao Airlines, T088-210794, although flights can be cancelled at short notice. More often than not they do not run and at the time of publication they had been discontinued. Another, newer option, is to fly with Lao Air, T021-512 027, laoair@laopdr.com, which has two scheduled flights a week US$75, one way/US$150 return.

Tham Pha Thok cave ⓘ *2.5 km southeast of the bridge; 5000 kip*, was a Pathet Lao regional base during the civil war. It was divided into sections – the hospital section, a police section and a military section. Old remnants exist like campfires and ruined beds but other than that there is little evidence of it being the PT headquarters until you see the bomb crater at the front. To get there you walk through beautiful rice paddies. There is a second cave about 300 m further down on the left, **Tham Pha Kwong**, which was the Pathet Lao's former banking cave. The cave is a tight squeeze and is easier to access with help from a local guide. It splits into two caves, one of which was the financial office and the other the accountant's office. A further 2 km along the road, at Ban Nokien is the **Than Mok** waterfall.

Muang Ngoi Neua → *Colour map 1, B6.*

The town of Muang Ngoi Neua lies 40 km (one hour) north of Nong Khiaw, along the Nam Ou. This small town surrounded by ethnic villages has become very popular with backpackers over the last few years. The town is a small slice of utopia, set on a peninsula at the foot of Mount Phaboom, shaded by coconut trees, with the languid river breeze wafting through the town's small paths. Most commonly known as Muang Ngoi, the settlement has had to embellish its name to distinguish it from Nong Khiaw, which is also often referred to as Muang Ngoi (see above). It's the perfect place to go for a trek to surrounding villages, or bask the day away swinging in your hammock. A market is held every 10 days and villagers come to sell produce and handicrafts. There are also caves and waterfalls in the area.

Muang Khua → Colour map 1, B5.

Muang Khua is nestled into the banks of the Nam Ou, close to the mouth of the Nam Phak, in the south of Phongsali Province. Hardly a destination in itself, it's usually just a stopover between Nong Khiaw and Phongsali. It only has electricity from 1900 to 2200 nightly. The Akha, Khmu and Tai Dam are the main hilltribes in the area. The nearest villages are 20 km out of town and you will need a guide if you want to visit them. Trekking around Muang Khua is fantastic and still a very authentic experience, as this region remains largely unexplored by backpackers. The friendly villages are very welcoming to foreigners, as they don't see as many here as in somewhere like Muang Sing. For these very reasons, it is very important to tread lightly and adopt the most culturally sensitive principles: don't hand out sweets and always ask before taking a photograph. Treks usually run for one to three days and involve a homestay at a villager's house (usually the Village Chief). ▶▶ See Activities and tours, page 508.

⊙ Far north listings

For Sleeping and Eating price codes, see inside the front cover.

● Sleeping

Udomxai *p498*

E-F Surinphone, T081-212789, srphone@lao tel.com. Clean and modern rooms with a/c rooms with TV, comfortable beds and hot-water bathrooms with bath. All in all a good choice. Very friendly.

F-G Litthavixay Guesthouse, about 100 m before the turning onto the airport road, T081-212175. This place has the best rooms in town, large singles, doubles and triples and all very clean. Rooms with lots of facilities including en suite hot-water shower. Best value internet in town. Has a small but good selection of foreign breakfast dishes.

Luang Namtha *p498, map p498*

B Boat Landing Guesthouse & Restaurant, T086-312398. Further out of town than most other guesthouses, this place is located right on the river. Time stands still here. It's an eco-resort that has got everything just right: pristine surroundings, environmentally friendly rooms, helpful service and a brilliant restaurant serving traditional northern Lao cuisine. There's a great restaurant attached serving local indigenous dishes. Recommended.

G Luang Namtha Guesthouse, 2 blocks west of the main centre, T086-312087. Run by 2 friendly Hmong brothers, one speaks English. The house is an impressive building for Luang Namtha, with a grand staircase. All rooms are clean and furnished, with en suite hot-water bathrooms and balconies. Satellite TV in the more expensive rooms.

G Manychan Guesthouse, on the main road in the centre of town, opposite the smaller bus station, T086-312209. One of the most popular places in town, probably due to the location and the restaurant. Decent, clean rooms with fan and hot-water bathrooms. Bikes can be hired next door for 15,000 kip per day. The staff are very friendly.

G Vila Guesthouse, on the south of the town, T086-312425. A 2-storey building with 11 of the cleanest rooms in town. Lounge and sparkling en suite bathrooms with hot water.

G Zuela Guesthouse, T086-312183. Fantastic value guesthouse in a beautiful, modern, wooden building with immaculate fan rooms. Extremely comfortable beds, en suite hot-water bathrooms and linen provided. This family-run guesthouse is truly a league apart from other budget options in town. Restaurant attached. Highly recommended.

Muang Sing *p500*

E-F Phoulou 2, at the southern end of town, T086-212348. Has great double bungalows and provides towels and bottled water. The lack of scenery is its only downfall.

E-F Phoutat Guesthouse/Black Stupa, 6 km out of Muang Sing on the main road towards Luang Namtha, T020-5686555. This place changes its name about every 6 months but remains the best accommodation in the vicinity. 10 wooden bungalows on the side of a hill, overlooking the town, mountains and rice paddies. Hot water, fan and Western toilet. There is also a decent restaurant on site, which affords views extending all the way to China. Very good value. Recommended.

E-G Adima Guesthouse, near Ban Oudomsin, north of Muang Sing towards the Chinese border, T020-2249008. A little hard to get to but the location is scenic. Peaceful bungalows constructed in traditional Yao and Akha style, plus a lovely open-air restaurant. Minority villages are on the doorstep. Footprint does not endorse DIY treks using the guesthouse map, which are having a negative effect on local villages. If you wish to trek please visit the local tourism office or **Exotissimo**, see page 508, to organize a bonafide eco-trek. To get there, take a tuk-tuk (20,000 kip) or hire a bike. Alternatively, the owner runs in and out of town about 3 times a day (depending on bus arrival times) and will pick you up from the bus station for a small fee.

G Taileu Guesthouse, above the restaurant on the main road, T030-1212375. There are 8 very basic rattan rooms with bamboo style 4-poster beds (the rickety backpacker version not some romantic type), squat toilets and temperamental hot water via solar power. The owners are lovely.

Houei Xai *p500*

E-F Arimid Guesthouse, northwest end of the town, T084-211040. The owners speak excellent French and a little English. Comfortable, rattan-style bungalows with en suite bathrooms, hot water, nice garden area and great balconies. Some with a/c. Mme Chitaly will cook tasty food and serve it to you at your bungalow. Close to the slow boat terminal.

E-F Taveensinh Guesthouse, northwest end of the town, T084-211502. The best value rooms in town with fan, TV and hot-water bathrooms. Great communal balconies overlooking the river.

G BAP Guesthouse, on the main Sekhong Rd, T084-211083. One of the oldest guesthouses in town consisting of a labyrinth of additions and add-ons as their business has grown over the years. A range of rooms, though the newer tiled ones with hot-water bathroom are the best. The female proprietor here is hard as nails but has loads of charisma and a wily sense of humour.

G Thanormsub Guesthouse, on the main Sekhong Rd, T084-211095. Clean double rooms with hot water, fan and satin curtains to boot. Nice, helpful staff.

Pak Beng *p501*

During peak season, when the slow boat arrives from Luang Prabang, about 60 people descend on Pak Beng at the same time. As the town doesn't have an endless supply of great budget guesthouses, it is advisable to get someone you trust to mind your bags, while you make a mad dash to get the best room in town.

A-D Pakbeng Lodge. A wooden and concrete construction, built in Lao style, this stunning guesthouse sits perched on a hillside above the Mekong and includes 20 rooms with fan, toilet and hot water. Good restaurant and wonderful views.

C-D Luangsay Lodge, about 1 km from the centre of town, T081-212296, www.mekongcruises.com. This is the most beautiful accommodation available in Pak Beng. A wooden pathway curves through luscious tropical gardens to wooden bungalows with fantastic balconies and large windows overlooking the river and the mountains. Hot-water bathrooms and romantic rooms make this a winner. Great restaurant. Book in advance.

C-D Phetsoxkai Hotel, T081-212299. Large, Lao-owned hotel that looks grand but doesn't live up to expectation. Nonetheless, the

28 rooms are beautifully decorated, though on the smallish side, hot-water bathroom, DVD player. Restaurant with Western, Lao and Thai cuisine. Very friendly owners.

E-G Salika, T081-212 306. This is an elegant structure on the steep cliff overlooking the river. Big, clean rooms with en suite toilet and shower (mostly cold). There is a great restaurant, serving reasonably priced meals (see Eating). Fantastic service.

G Donevilisack Guesthouse, T081-212315. The popular **Donevilasack** offers a reasonable choice of rooms. In the older, wooden building are basic budget rooms with fan, mosquito net and shared hot-water showers. More expensive rooms are in the newer concrete building and have private bathrooms.

Nong Khiaw and Ban Saphoun p502

C-E Nong Khiau, turn-off right beside the bridge in Ban Saphoun, T071-254770, www.nongkhiau.com. Stunning modern bungalows and restaurant. Beautifully decorated rooms with 4-poster beds, mosquito nets and hot-water bathrooms. For those looking for something upmarket this exquisite place fits the bill perfectly. The restaurant has a great selection of wines and access to the internet. Book in advance as it is a favourite with tour groups. Recommended.

G Phanoy Guesthouse, Bakery and Bookshop, 50 m past the bridge, Ban Saphoun, T071-253919. Guesthouse has 7 basic but clean and comfortable thatched bungalows with mosquito nets and squat toilets. Inside bathroom. Fantastic verandas overlooking the river. Some bungalows (50,000 kip) have hot water. Very nice family-owned business with a great atmosphere. The best of the cheaper options.

G Sunset Guesthouse, down a lane about 100 m past the bridge, Ban Saphoun, T071-253933. Right on the bank of the river – you couldn't ask for a more picturesque setting from which to watch the sunset. The charming, sprawling bamboo structure looks out onto tables and sun umbrellas liberally arranged over the various levels of decking

that serve as a popular restaurant in the evenings. Western toilet and hot-water shower outside. 8 rooms with hard mattresses. A bit dirty. Slow internet.

Muang Ngoi Neua p503

The accommodation in town is dirt cheap and of the same standard: bungalows with extremely welcoming hammocks on their balconies. Most offer a laundry service for around 10,000 kip per kg and all have electricity 1800-2200. Rats are a problem here, but mosquito nets keep them at bay.

G Lattanavongsa, concrete building, relatively comfortable rooms with en suite bathroom.

G Ning Ning Guesthouse, beside the boat landing. Has a great restaurant.

G Phet Davanh Guesthouse, on the main road, near the boat landing. Concrete rooms, restaurant, cleaner than the other alternatives.

Muang Khua p504

E-F Sernnali Hotel, in the middle of town, near the top of the hill, T081-212445. By far the most luxurious lodging in town. 18 rooms with large double and twin beds, hot-water scoop showers and Western-style toilets, immaculately clean. Balconies overlook the Nam Ou. Chinese, Vietnamese and Lao food served in the restaurant.

G Nam Ou Guesthouse & Restaurant, follow the signs at the top of the hill, T081-210844. Looking out across the river where the boats land, this guesthouse is the pick of the ultra-budget bunch in Muang Khua. Singles, twins and doubles, some with hot-water en suites, and 3 newer rooms with river views. Great food (see Eating, below). A popular spot. Go for an upstairs room.

☉ Eating

Udomxai p498

† **Sinphet Guesthouse & Restaurant**, opposite **Linda Guesthouse**. One of the best options in town. English menu, delicious iced coffee with ovaltine, great Chinese and Lao

food. Try the curry chicken, *kua-mii* or yellow noodles with chicken.

Litthavixay Guesthouse, can whip up some good dishes, including Western-style pancakes and breakfasts.

Luang Namtha *p498, map p498*

The night-market, though small, offers an interesting array of local cuisine with ubiquitous street food stands.

¶¶-¶ Boat Landing Guesthouse & Restaurant (see Sleeping), T086-312398. The best place to eat in town, with exceptionally innovative cuisine. Serves a range of northern Lao dishes made from local produce, thereby supporting nearby villages. Highly recommended.

¶ Banana Restaurant, main road, towards the **KNT Internet**, T020-5718026. This restaurant is gaining favour with the locals and tourists alike for its good fruit shakes and Lao food. Also serves a few Western dishes.

¶ Coffee House, off the main road around the corner from **Green Discovery**, T030-525 7842. This fantastic little hole-in-the-wall Thai restaurant with a range of delicious meals all under 10,000 kip. The meals are served on brown rice imported from Thailand and include Massaman curry, Tom Yum soup and a variety of other Thai staples. Fantastic espresso coffee and cappuccinos. Mr Nithat, the owner's husband, is good for a chat. Recommended.

¶ Panda Restaurant, T086-211304. Housed in a stilted building overlooking rice paddies. Cheap and tasty food. The curries are out-standing. The friendly owner speaks English.

¶ Yamuna Restaurant, on the main road, T020-5405698. Delicious Indian restaurant with vegetarian, non-vegetarian and halal dishes. Extensive, predominantly south Indian menu.

Cafés

For those with a sweet tooth, **KNT Internet** sells some fabulous home-made cakes.

Muang Sing *p500*

¶ Sengdeuane Guesthouse & Restaurant. A quieter option with an English menu, which

is mostly just for show. Nice garden setting and an ancient karaoke machine. Korean BBQ only (*sindat*). Open from 1700. Popular with the locals.

¶ Taileu Guesthouse & Restaurant (see Sleeping), T081-212375. The most popular place to eat due to its indigenous Tai Leu menu. Unique and tasty meals, including baked aubergine with pork, soy mash and fish soup. One of the few places in the country where you can sample northern cuisine. Try their local piña colada with *lao-lao*, their *sa lo* (Muang Sing's answer to a hamburger) or one of the famous *jeow* (chilli jam) dishes. The banana flower soup is fantastic. Stand-out option in town and an eating experience you won't find elsewhere in Laos. Noi, the owner, is very friendly. Highly recommended.

¶ Viengphone, next door to the **Viengxai Restaurant**, T081-212368. This place has an English menu offering the usual fare. Excellent fried mushrooms, although the service is a bit *bopenyang*.

¶ Viengxai Restaurant. Very good food, with some of the best chips in Laos. English menu, friendly service, reasonable prices. Good selection of shakes. Clean.

Houei Xai *p500*

¶¶-¶ Riverside, just off the main road, near the **Houay Xai Guesthouse**, T084-211064. Huge waterfront restaurant on large platform. Perfect position for taking in the sunset. Great shakes. Extensive menu that's a mixture of Lao and Thai food. The curries are quite nice. Usually there is live music, some of it decidedly off-key, played here.

¶ Deen Restaurant, on the main road, T020-5901871. Indian restaurant with an extensive menu of dishes, including a good selection of halal and vegetarian. Sparkly clean. The owner is very accommodating.

¶ Khemkhong Restaurant, across from the immigration stand. Good option for those who want a drink after the cross-border journey. Lao and Thai food.

¶ Nutpop, on the main road, T084-211037. The fluorescent lights and garish beer signs don't give a good impression. However, this is quite a pleasant little garden restaurant, set in an atmospheric lamp-lit building, with good Lao food including fried mushrooms and curry. The fish here is excellent.

Pak Beng p501

¶ **Kopchaideu Restaurant**, overlooking the Mekong. This restaurant has a large selection of Indian dishes with a few Lao favourites thrown in. Great shakes and fantastic service.
¶ **Salika** (see Sleeping). Atmospheric restaurant with wonderful river views and an amazingly varied menu. Interminably slow service.

Nong Khiaw and Ban Saphoun p502

Most of the guesthouses have cafés attached. For some fine dining the restaurant at the **Riverside** is absolutely fantastic, with an extensive wine menu. For those on a budget the **Phanoy Guesthouse** and **Bakery Bookshop** does reasonably good food. Ask for dishes to be served with *jeow*, which is delicious. Good selection of cakes.

Muang Ngoi Neua p503

¶-¶ **Sainamgoi Restaurant & Bar**, centre of town. Tasty Lao food in a pleasant atmosphere, with good background music. The bar, the only one in town, is in the next room.
¶ **Nang Phone Keo Restaurant**, next to **Banana Guesthouse**. All the usual Lao food, plus some extras. Try the 'Falang Roll' for breakfast (a combination of peanut butter, sticky rice and vegetables).
¶ **Sengdala Restaurant & Bakery**, on the main road, with a bomb casing out front. Very good, cheap Lao food, terrific pancakes and freshly baked baguettes.

Muang Khua p504

The **Nam Ou Guesthouse & Restaurant** (see Sleeping) is up the mud slope from the beach. An incomparable location for a morning coffee overlooking the river; it has an English menu and friendly staff.

▲ Activities and tours

Luang Namtha p498, map p498
Tour operators
Green Discovery, T086-211484, offers 1- to 7-day kayaking/rafting, cycling and trekking excursions into the Nam Ha NPA.
Luang Namtha Guide Service Unit, T086-211534. Information on treks into Nam Ha NPA.

Muang Sing p500
Trekking Trekking has become a delicate issue around Muang Sing as uncontrolled tourism was beginning to have a detrimental effect on some of the surrounding minority villages. Some sensible procedures and protocols have been put in place to ensure low impact tourism which still benefits the villages concerned. **Exotissimo**, www.exotissimo.com. In cahoots with **GTZ**, a German aid agency, have launched more expensive but enjoyable treks such as the **Akha Experience**, which include tasty meals prepared by local Akha people. Closed on weekends.

The **tourism office and trekking centre**, in the centre of town, T020-2393534, can organize pretty good treks for 1, 2 or 3 days including accommodation and food. The guides are supposedly from local villages and can speak the native tongue, Akha or Tai Leu. Most treks cost around US$25 per day and have received glowing reports from tourists, particularly the **Laosee Trek**. Trek prices are reduced with larger numbers. The tourism office, next door to **Exotissimo**, is open Mon-Fri 0800-1130, 1330-1700. Treks organized during the working week.

Muang Ngoi Neua p503
Trekking, hiking, fishing, kayaking, trips to the waterfalls and boat trips can be organized through most of the guesthouses for US$10 per day. Tubing for US$2 per day.
Lao Youth Travel, www.laoyouthtravel.com, daily 0730-1800. Half-day, day, overnight or 2-night treks. Also kayaking trips.

⊖ Transport

Udomxai p498
Air

There are flights to **Vientiane**, Tue, Thu and Sat from Udomxai. **Lao Airlines** has an office at the airport, T081-312047.

Bus/truck/songthaew

Udomxai is the epicentre of northern travel. If arriving into Udomxai to catch a connecting bus, it's better to leave earlier in the day as transport tends to peter out in the afternoon. These prices are subject to change.

The bus station is 1 km east of the town centre. Departures east to **Nong Khiaw**, 3 hrs, trucks are fairly frequent, most departing in the morning. If you get stuck on the way to Nong Khiaw it is possible to stay overnight in **Pak Mong** where there are numerous rustic guesthouses. The bus to **Nong Khiaw** leaves at 0900. **Pak Mong**, 1400 and 1600, 2 hrs, 22,000 kip. To **Luang Prabang**, 0800, 1100 and 1400, 5 hrs, direct, 48,000 kip. Direct bus to **Vientiane**, 1530 and 1800, 15 hrs, 100,000 kip. Vientiane **VIP** bus, 1600 and 1800, 121,000 kip (also runs via **Luang Prabang**). **Xam Neua**, Tue-Sat 1230, 100,000 kip. **Luang Namtha**, 0800, 1130 and 1500, 4 hrs, 32,000 kip. **Boten** (the Chinese border) 0800, 28,000 kip. It is possible for some nationalities to obtain Chinese visas at the border, check eligibility in advance (at the time of publication UK citizens could, but US citizens could not).

There are services north on Route 4 to **Phongsali**, 0800, 9 hrs, 60,000 kip; this trip is long so bring something soft to sit on and try to get a seat with a view.

There are an abundance of songthaews waiting to make smaller trips to destinations like **Pak Mong** and **Nong Khiaw**, if you miss one of the earlier buses it is worthwhile bargaining with the drivers, as if they can get enough money or passengers they will make the extra trip.

Luang Namtha p498, map p498
Air

The airport is 7 km south of town – 15,000 kip by tuk-tuk. At the time of publication there were no domestic flights to or from Luang Namtha as the airport was being upgraded to an international airport. **Lao Airlines**, T086-312180, has an office south of town on the main road. When flights do reopen it is imperative to book in advance.

Bicycle/motorbike

Bicycles for hire from next door to the **Manychan Guesthouse**, opposite post office, for 15,000 kip a day. Motorbikes for hire for US$5 a day from **Zuela guesthouse**.

Boat

Call T020-5686051 for information. Slow boats are the best and most scenic travel option but their reliability will depend on the tide and in the dry season (Mar-May) they often won't run as the water level is too low. There isn't really a regular boat service from Luang Namtha, so you will have to either charter a whole boat and split the cost or hitch a ride on a boat making the trip already. If you manage to organize a boat it should cost around US$150 to **Houei Xai**. It is cheaper to go from Luang Namtha to Houei Xai than vice versa. The **Boat Landing Guesthouse** is a good source of information about boats; if arrangements are made for you, a courtesy tip is appreciated.

Bus/truck/songthaew

The main bus station and its ticket office, T086-312164, daily 0700-1600, are about 100 m north of the Morning Market. This bus station is set to be abolished to make way for a new Malaysian Hotel. A new bus station is planned on the corner near **Panda Restaurant** on the main road.

To **Muang Sing**, daily 0800, 1100 and 1400, 1½ hrs, 20,000 kip, additional pick-ups may depart throughout the day, depending on demand. To **Udomxai**, daily 0830, 1200 and 1430, 4-6 hrs, 32,000 kip, additional services will leave in the early afternoon if there is demand, otherwise jump on a bus to Luang Prabang.

To **Houei Xai**, 0900 and 1330, 55,000 kip. To **Luang Prabang**, daily 0930, 10 hrs, 70,000 kip. To **Vientiane**, 20 hrs, 140,000 kip. To get to **Nong Khiaw**, 60,000 kip you need to go via Udomxai (leave early).

To **Boten** (Chinese border) daily 0800, 1100 and 1400, 1½ hrs, 25,000 kip. Many travellers have reported obtaining a visa here; however, it is less risky to organize a visa in advance in Vientiane. Tourist visas are US$70-150 depending on nationality. US citizens are unable to obtain visas at this crossing. Check with the Chinese embassy beforehand.

Muang Sing *p500*
Bicycle
Available for rent from some guesthouses and bicycle hire shops on the main street for 10,000 kip per day. The Muang Sing tourism office also hires bikes for 20,000 kip per day.

Boat
It is sometimes possible to charter boats from **Xieng Kok** downstream on the Mekong to **Houei Xai**, 3-4 hrs. This is expensive – around US$150-200.

Bus/truck
The bus station is across from the main market. To **Luang Namtha**, by bus or pick-up, 5 daily, 2 hrs, 20,000 kip. To charter a songthaew or tuk-tuk to Luang Namtha costs at least 200,000 kip. Songthaews also leave for **Xieng Kok**, 4 hrs, 30,000 kip.

Houei Xai *p500*
Lao National Tourism State Bokeo, on the main street up from immigration, T084-211 555, can give advice on the sale of boat, bus, pick-up and other tickets. Numerous travel agencies congregate around the immigration centre offering bus and boat ticket sales. See page 495 for information on boat travel between Houei Xai and Luang Prabang.

Air
Houei Xai airport is located 5 km south of town and has flights to **Vientiane**, Tue and Thu. US$85 one way; US$162 return. Book in advance as it is a small plane and tends to fill up quickly.

Boat
The **BAP Guesthouse** in Houei Xai is a good place to find out about boat services.

The 2-day trip to Luang Prabang has become part of the Southeast Asian rite of passage. The slow boat to **Pak Beng** is raved about by many travellers. However, in peak season the boat can be packed and the wooden chairs or ground extremely uncomfortable. Bring something soft to sit on, a good book and a packed lunch. The boat leaves from a jetty 1.5 km north of town, daily 0930-1000, 6-7 hrs, US$11 or US$22 for the 2-day trip (usually you buy the ongoing ticket at Pak Beng). If you can get enough people together it is possible to charter a boat, US$600. The trip, done in reverse, usually has fewer passengers.

For those looking for a luxury option there is the **Luangsay Cruise**, T071-252553, www.asian-oasis.com, which undertakes a 2-day/1-night cruise down the river in extreme comfort with cushioned deck-chairs, a bar and games on board. Guests stay at the beautiful **Luangsay Lodge** in Pak Beng.

For a mid-range option, **Phoudoi Travel**, on the main road in Houei Xai, sells tickets for US$60 on a boat direct to Luang Prabang that is roomier than the standard boat yet not as cosy as the Luangsay. The *Nagi*, for US$80, does the trip in 1 day in comfort.

Speedboats are a noisy, nerve-wracking, dangerous alternative; they leave from the jetty south of town, to **Pak Beng**, 3 hrs, US$15 and to **Luang Prabang**, US$29. There have been reports of unscrupulous boatmen claiming there are no slow boats in the dry season to encourage travellers to take their fast boats. This is usually untrue.

Bus/truck/songthaew

The bus station is located at the Morning Market, 7 km out of central Houei Xai, a tuk-tuk to the centre costs 20,000 kip. Trucks, buses and minivans run to **Luang Namtha**, 0930 and 1130, 7 hrs, 170 km, 65,000 kip; to **Udomxai**, 0930 and 1130, 7 hrs, 120,000 kip; to **Luang Prabang**, Fri 1130, 11 hrs, 140,000 kip; to **Vientiane**, 1130, 20 hrs, 200,000 kip.

Pak Beng p501
Boat

The times and prices for boats are always changing so check beforehand. The slow boat to **Houei Xai** leaves 0800-0900 from the port and takes all day, US$11. The slow boat to **Luang Prabang** leaves around the same time. Get in early to get a good seat. Speedboats to Luang Prabang (2-3 hrs) and Houei Xai leave in the morning, when full.

Bus/truck/songthaew

Buses and songthaews leave about 2 km from town in the morning for the route to **Udomxai**, 6-7 hrs, 40,000 kip. Direct songthaews to **Udomxai** are few, so an alternative is to take one to **Muang Houn** to catch the more frequent service from there.

Nong Khiaw and Ban Saphoun p502
Boat

Boat services have become irregular following road improvements, although you may find a service to **Muang Noi Neua**, 1 hr, 20,000 kip, from the boat landing. These boats won't run unless there are enough passengers. Likewise, boats to Luang Prabang only run if there are enough people, so you might find yourself waiting a couple of days. Some vessels also head upriver to **Muang Khua**, 5 hrs, 100,000 kip. The river trips from Nong Khiaw are spectacular. It is possible to charter boats to both of these destinations.

Bus/truck

Buses en route from surrounding destinations stop in Nong Khiaw briefly. As they usually arrive from Vientiane or Luang Prabang, the

timetables are unreliable. Basic timetables are offered but buses can be early or late, so check details on the day. It is often a matter of waiting at the bus station and catching the bus on its way through. Plonking yourself in a restaurant on the main road usually suffices but you will need to flag down the bus. Regular connections to **Luang Prabang**, 0830 and 1100, 3-4 hrs, 32,000 kip. Also several departures daily to **Nam Bak**, 30 mins, 10,000 kip and on to **Udomxai** 1130, 4 hrs, 31,000 kip. Alternatively, there are more regular songthaews to **Pak Mong**, 1 hr, 20,000 kip, where there is a small noodle shop-cum-bus station on the west side of the bridge, and from there travel on to Udomxai/Vientiane.

Travelling east on Route 1, there are buses to **Vieng Thong**, 2 hrs, 25,000 kip, and a village 10 km from **Nam Nouan**, where you can change and head south on Route 6 to **Phonsavanh** and the **Plain of Jars**. There are direct buses north to **Xam Neua** and the village near Nam Nouan, which can be caught from the toll gate on the Ban Saphoun side of the river when it comes through from Vientiane at around 2000-2200, 100,000 kip; it's usually quite crowded. If you miss a bus to/from Nong Khiaw you can always head to **Pak Mong** which is a junction town sitting at the crossroads to Luang Prabang, Nong Khiaw and Udomxai. Aim to get here earlier in the day to catch through traffic otherwise you may have to stay overnight. (If you do, try the **Pak Mong Guesthouse Restaurant**, T020-5795860, or any of the other 6 places to stay in town.)

Muang Ngoi Neua p503
Boat

From the landing at the northern end of town, slow boats travel north along the beautiful river tract to **Muang Khua**, 5 hrs, US$10, or charter your own for US$50 per boat. Slow boats also go south (irregularly) to **Nong Khiaw**, 1 hr, 20,000 kip, and **Luang Prabang**, 8 hrs, US$100 per boat. Departure times vary and whether they depart at all depends on whether there are enough passengers. For more information and tickets, consult the booth at the landing.

Muang Khua p504
Boat
Road travel is now more popular but irregular boats still travel south to **Muang Ngoi/Nong Khiaw**, 4-5 hrs, 100,000 kip, if there is enough demand. Also north to **Phongsali** via Hat Xa, 100,000 kip. Boats can be charted to Phongsali for around US$110. A jeep or truck transports travellers on from Hat Xa to Phongsali, 20 km, 2 hrs along a very bad road, 50,000 kip. Alternatively, charter a jeep, US$15.

Songthaew/truck
To get to **Phongsali**, take a songthaew to **Pak Nam Noi**, 0800, 1 hr, 30,000 kip, then the songthaew or bus that passes through from Udomxai at around 1000, 50,000 kip.

To **Udomxai**, pick-ups and buses leave 0700-0800 from the bus station alongside the market, 4 hrs, US$5 and **Luang Prabang**, 8 hrs, US$7.

❶ Directory

Udomxai p498
Banks Lao Development Bank, Udomxai, just off the road on the way to Phongsali, changes US$, Thai ฿ and Chinese ¥. The BCEL Bank, on the main road, offers the same services. No credit card advances. **Internet** Litthavixay Guesthouse, at the bus station; on the main road at **Samlaan Cycling**; and around the corner from there at the English school 100-200 kip per min. Quite often the whole town's internet is down.

Luang Namtha p498, map p498
Banks Mon-Fri only. **Lao Development Bank**, changes TCs and Thai ฿ to kip, also exchanges TCs but charges a sizeable commission. The **BCEL** changes US$ and Thai ฿ and does cash advances on Visa.

The BCEL has an ATM but it only accepts MasterCard. **Internet** KNT Computers, 200 kip per min. **Telephone** You can make international calls from **Lao Telecom**.

Muang Sing p500
Banks The small **Lao Development Bank** opposite the market will exchange Thai ฿, US$ and Chinese ¥.

Houei Xai p500
Banks Mon-Fri only. **Lao Development Bank**, next to the immigration office, changes TCs, US$ cash and ฿. **Immigration** At the boat terminal, daily 0800-1800, a small overtime fee is charged Sat and Sun and after 1600. Quite possibly the most friendly immigration post in the country.
Internet Small internet shop on the main street, 15,000 kip per hr.

Pak Beng p501
Bank There is no bank in Pak Beng, but most of the guesthouses and restaurants will exchange Thai ฿ and US$ cash at a hefty commission. **Internet** Available at the ferry office for a whopping 500 kip per min. High-speed internet is also available past the Pak Beng Market, 500 kip per min.

Nong Khiaw and Ban Saphoun p502
Internet Sunset Guesthouse and Riverside Guesthouse, 300 kip per min.

Muang Khua p504
Bank Lao Development Bank, near the truck stop, Mon-Fri 0800-1130, 1300-1630, can change US$, Thai ฿ and Chinese ¥ at bad rates. Won't change TCs or do cash advances on credit cards, so make sure you have plenty of cash before you come here.
Electricity Daily 1830-2200. **Telephone** International calls can be made from the **Telecom office**, a small unmarked hut with a huge satellite, halfway up the road, behind the bank.

Plain of Jars and the northeast

Apart from the historic Plain of Jars, Xieng Khouang Province is best known for the pounding it took during the war. Many of the sights are battered monuments to the plateau's violent recent history. Given the cost of the return trip and the fact that the jars themselves aren't that spectacular, some consider the destination oversold. However, for those interested in modern history, it's the most fascinating area of Laos and helps one to gain an insight into the resilient nature of the Lao people. The countryside, particularly towards the Vietnam frontier, is beautiful – among the country's best – and the jars, too, are interesting by dint of their very oddness: as if a band of carousing giants had been suddenly interrupted, casting the jars across the plain in their hurry to leave. ▶▶ *For listings, see pages 519-521.*

Background

Xieng Khouang Province has had a murky, blood-tinted, war-ravaged history. The area was the most bombed province in the most bombed country, per capita, in the world as it became a very important strategic zone that both the US and Vietnamese wanted to retain control of. The town of Phonsavanh has long been an important transit point between China to the north, Vietnam to the east and Thailand to the south and this status made the town a target for neighbouring countries. What's more, the plateau of the Plain of Jars is one of the flatter areas in northern Laos, rendering it a natural battleground for the numerous conflicts that ensued from the 19th century to 1975. While the enigmatic Plain of Jars is here, this region will also hold immense appeal for those interested in the modern history of the country.

Once the French departed from Laos, massive conflicts were waged in 1945 and 1946 between the Free Lao Movement and the Viet Minh. The Pathet Lao and Viet Minh joined forces and, by 1964, had a number of bases dotted around the Plain of Jars. From then on, chaos ensued, as Xieng Khouang got caught in the middle of the war between the Royalist-American and Pathet Lao-Vietnamese. The extensive US bombing of this area was to ensure it did not fall under the Communist control of the Pathet Laos. The Vietnamese were trying to ensure that the US did not gain control of the area from which they could launch attacks on North Vietnam.

During the 'Secret War' (1964-1974) against the North Vietnamese Army and the Pathet Lao, tens of thousands of cluster bomb units (CBUs) were dumped by the US military on Xieng Khouang Province. Other bombs, such as the anti-personnel plastic 'pineapple' bomblets were also used but by and large cluster bombs compromised the majority dropped. The CBU was a carrier bomb, which held 670 sub-munitions the size of a lemon. As the CBU was dropped each of these smaller bombs was released. Even though they were the size of a tennis ball, they contained 300 metal ball-bearings which were propelled hundreds of metres. As 30% of the original bombs did not explode these cluster bombs continue to kill and maim today. The Plain of Jars was also hit by B-52s returning from abortive bombing runs to Hanoi, who jettisoned their bomb loads before heading back to the US air base at Udon Thani in northeast Thailand. Suffice it to say that, with over 580,944 sorties flown (one-and-a-half times the number flow in Vietnam), whole towns were obliterated and the area's geography was permanently altered. Today, as the Lao Airlines Y-12 turbo-prop begins its descent towards the plateau, the meaning of the term 'carpet bombing' becomes clear. On the final approach to the town of Phonsavanh, the plane banks low over the cratered paddy fields, affording a

T-28 fighter-bomber pilot's view of his target, which in places has been pummelled into little more than a moonscape. Some of the craters are 15 m across and 7 m deep. Testament to the Lao people's resilience, symbolically, many of these craters have been turned into tranquil fish ponds; the bombs transformed into fences and the CBU carriers serving as planter pots. Because the war was 'secret', there are few records of what was dropped and where and, even when the unexploded ordnance (UXO) have been uncovered, their workings are often a mystery – the Americans used Laos as a testing ground for new ordnance so blueprints are unavailable. The UK-based **Mines Advisory Group (MAG)** ① *on the main road in the centre of town, daily 0800-1200, 1300-2000 (except the 12th and 18th of every month)*, is currently engaged in clearing the land of Unexploded Ordnance (UXO). They have an exhibition of bombs, photographs and information on the bombing campaign and ongoing plight of Laos with UXO. Usually there are staff on hand to explain exactly how the bombs were used. All T-shirts sold here help fund the UXO clearance of the area and are a very worthwhile souvenir.

Xieng Khouang remains one of the poorest provinces in an already wretchedly poor country. The whole province has a population of only around 250,000, a mix of different ethnic groups, predominantly Hmong, Lao and a handful of Khmu.

Plain of Jars and Phonsavanh ⊖❶❷❸▲❶❸ ›› *pp519-521. Colour map 1, C6.*

The undulating plateau of the Plain of Jars (also known as Plaine de Jarres or **Thong Hai Hin**) stretches for about 50 km east to west, at an altitude of 1000 m. In total there are 136 archaeological sites in this area, containing thousands of jars, discs and deliberately placed stones, but only three are open to tourists. Note that the plateau can be cold from December to March. **Phonsavanh** is the main town of the province today – old Xieng Khouang having been flattened – and its small airstrip is a crucial transport link in this

Phonsavanh

Sleeping ⊖	Orchid **15**	Phonexay **5**
Auberge de la	Nice Guesthouse **8**	Sangah **6**
Plaine Des Jarres **1**	Vansana **14**	Simmaly **7**
Dok Khoun **3**		
Khou Kham	**Eating ❷**	**Bars & clubs ❶**
Guesthouse **10**	Craters **2**	Maliyona Pub **8**
Maly **6**	Nisha Indian **3**	

N
Not to scale

mountainous region. It's the only base from which to explore the Plain of Jars, so it has a fair number of hotels and guesthouses. Note that travel agents and airlines tend to refer to Phonsavanh as Xieng Khouang, while the nearby town of 'old' Xieng Khouang is usually referred to as Muang Khoune.

Ins and outs

Getting there Phonsavanh Airport (aka Xieng Khouang airport) is 4 km west of Phonsavanh. A tuk-tuk to town costs 20,000 kip per person. The most direct route by road from Luang Prabang to Xieng Khouang is to take Route 13 south to Muang Phou Khoun and then Route 7 east. An alternative, scenic, albeit convoluted, route is via Nong Khiaw (see page 502), from where there are pick-ups to Pak Xeng and Phonsavanh via Vieng Thong on Route 1 or Nam Nouan.

The bus station is 4 km west of Phonsavanh on Route 7, although many buses still pass by the old bus station near the dry market; a tuk-tuk to/from the centre costs 10,000 kip.

Getting around Public transport is limited and sporadic. Provincial laws have occasionally banned tuk-tuks and motorbikes from ferrying customers around the area. These regulations have been relaxed recently but don't be surprised if they are brought into force again. It should be possible to drive from Phonsavanh to the Plain of Jars, see Site one and return to town in two hours. Expect to pay in the region of US$30 for an English-speaking guide and vehicle for four people, or US$60 for seven people and a minivan. A tuk-tuk to Site one costs approximately US$7 per person. Alternatively, hotels, guesthouses and tour companies in Phonsavanh run set tours to the Plain of Jars, Muang Khoune (Xieng Khouang) and Hmong villages northeast of Phonsavanh. If you arrive by air, the chances are you'll be inundated with official and unofficial would-be guides as soon as you step off the plane. Note that it is not possible to walk from the airport to Site one, as there is a military base in between. It is recommended that you hire a guide, for at least a day, to get an insight into the history of the area. The cost of admission to each site is 7000 kip. ▸▸ *See Activities and tours and Transport, page 520.*

Background

Most of the jars are between 1 m and 2.5 m high, around 1 m in diameter and weigh about the same as three small cars. The largest are about 3 m tall. The jars have long presented an archaeological conundrum, leaving generations of theorists nonplussed by how they got there and what they were used for. Local legend relates that King Khoon Chuong and his troops from Southern China threw a stupendous party after their victory over the wicked Chao Angka and had the jars made to brew outrageous quantities of *lao-lao*. However, attractive as this alcoholic thesis is, it is more likely that the jars are in fact 2000-year-old stone funeral urns. The larger jars are believed to have been for the local aristocracy and the smaller jars for their minions. Tools, bronze ornaments, ceramics and other objects have been found in the jars, indicating that a civilized society was responsible for making them but no one has a clue which one, as the artefacts seem to bear no relation to those left behind by other ancient Indochinese civilizations. Some of the jars were once covered with round lids and there is one jar, in the group facing the entrance to the cave, which is decorated with a rough carving of a dancing figure.

Vieng Xai (Viengsay) and the Pathet Lao caves

Tourists are often put off visiting Hua Phan Province by the long bus haul to get here but, considering the road passes through gorgeous mountain scenery, the trip is well worth it. The main roads in are the paved Route 6, from Phonsavanh and the south, and Route 1, from Vieng Thong and the west. Xam Neua (Sam Neua) is the main provincial town and the tourist office here can organize a car with driver to Vieng Xai caves. Summer is pleasant but temperatures plummet at night so you should bring a jumper. Mosquitoes are monstrous here; precautions against malaria are advised. Xam Neua is one of the most intriguing provincial capitals in Laos and is buzzing with a colourful outdoor food market and the eclectic dry market.

The village of Vieng Xai lies 31 km east of Xam Neua and the trip is possibly one of the country's most picturesque journeys, passing terraces of rice, pagodas, copper- and charcoal-coloured karst formations, dense jungle and friendly villages dotted among the mountains' curves. The limestone landscape is riddled with natural caves that proved crucial in the success of the Communists (Pathet Lao) in the 1960s and 1970s. From 1964 onwards, Pathet Lao operations were directed from cave systems at Vieng Xai, which provided an effective refuge from furious bombing attacks. The village of Vieng Xai grew from 4 small villages consisting of less than 10 families to a thriving hidden city concealing over 20,000 people in the 100 plus caves in the area. The Pathet Lao leadership renamed the area Vieng Xai, meaning 'City of Victory' and it became the administrative and military hub of the revolutionary struggle. The village itself was built in 1973, when the bombing finally stopped and the short-lived Provisional Government of National Union was negotiated. Today the former capital of the liberated zone is an unlikely sight: surrounded by rice fields at the dead end of a potholed road, it features street lighting, power lines, sealed and kerbed streets and substantial public buildings – all in varying stages of decay. Nonetheless it is truly one of the most beautiful towns in Laos, dotted with fruit trees, hibiscus and man-made lakes, and flanked by amazing karst formations.

Seven caves, formerly occupied by senior Pathet Lao leaders (Prince Souphanouvong, Kaysone Phomvihan, Nouhak Phounsavanh, Khamtai Siphandon and Phoumi Vongvichit), and open to visitors and all are within walking distance of the village; tickets are sold at the Viengxay Caves Visitor Centre, T064-314321, viengxaycavesvisitor centre@yahoo.com, daily 0800-1200, 1300-1630; guided tours are conducted at 0900 and 1300, 30,000 kip with guide. Tours are usually conducted on bikes which can be rented from the office.

The sites

More than 300 jars survive, mainly scattered on one slope at so-called 'Site one' or **Thong Hai Hin**, 10 km southwest of Phonsavanh. This site the largest jar. A path, cleared by MAG, winds through the site, with a warning not to walk away from delineated areas as UXO are still around. There are 250 jars at the site, each of which weighs about a tonne, although the biggest, called **Hai Cheaum**, is over 2 m tall and weighs over 6 tonnes.

True jar lovers should visit Site two, known as **Hai Hin Phu Salatao** (literally 'Salato Hill Stone Jar Site') and Site three called **Hai Hin Laat Khai**. Site two is 25 km south of

If you want to take the tour outside the designated times you must pay an additional fee. You will need to start early in the morning to see all the caves. If you plan on coming across from Xam Neua it is advisable to stay overnight.

The caves have been fitted with electric bulbs but you may find a torch useful. Each cave burrows deep into the mountainside and features 60 cm-thick concrete walls, encompassing living quarters, meeting rooms, offices, dining and storage areas.

Sleeping Most visitors to the caves stay in Xam Neua and take a day trip, but there is accommodation in Vieng Xai. **Kheamxam Guesthouse**, Xam Neua, T064-312111. Offers a wide range of fairly well appointed rooms with attached hot-water bathrooms, some with a/c. **Naxay Guesthouse** (there are two with this name), opposite the Vieng Xai Cave Visitor Centre, T064-314330. Offers five new bungalows with hot water, comfortable beds and a Western toilet. Recommended. **Naxay Guesthouse**, Vieng Xai, T064-314336. Very rustic accommodation with shared bathrooms. Beds as hard as rocks. **Shuliyo**, about 100 m from songthaew station, Xam Neua. Comfortable, modern rooms with hot-water.

Eating There is a very pleasant restaurant beside the main lake in Vieng Xai – the fish here is a winner. In Xam Neua, the colourful fresh food market offers a wonderful selection of local dishes.

Kittavanh Restaurant, opposite the Nam Xam river near the end of the market, offers great Lao food, particularly feu, with a good English menu on a whiteboard. **Dan Xam Muang**, a block back from the river, near the bridge, T064-314126, is another good option. The fried fish is excellent as is the *feu*, *laap* and French fries. Good service.

Transport Regular songthaews from Xam Neua to Vieng Xai, 60-90 minutes, 20,000 kip, although there are virtually no services after 1500 in either direction. If you get stuck you can charter a vehicle for a whole day for US$30-40, 50 minutes.

Xam Neua bus station is about 2 km from the centre of town and costs 5000 kip in a songthaew. Buses depart from Xam Neua to Vieng Xai 5 times daily in the morning, 20,000 kip; to Nameo (the Vietnam border) at 0630, 25,000 kip; Nam Nouan 0700, four hours, 27,000kip; Vieng Thong, 0720, 40,000 kip; Phonsavanh, 0800, 10 hours, 70,000 kip; Luang Prabang, 0800, 16 hours, 100,000 kip; Vientiane 0800 and 1230, 24 hours, 150,000 kip; Udomxai Saturday 0900, 100,000 kip; Thanh Hoa (Vietnam) Saturday 0800, 100,000 kip. The Luang Prabang bus goes via Nong Khiaw, 12 hours, 70,000 kip.

Lao Air runs flights to Xam Neua, Saturday and Monday, US$62 one way. Xam Neua airport is 2 km from the centre of town.

Phonsavanh and features 90 jars spread across two hills. The jars are set in a rather beautiful location, affording scenic views. A further 10 km south of Site two, Site three is the most atmospheric of all the sites, set in verdant green rolling hills, Swiss-cheesed with bomb craters. To get there you have to walk through some rice paddies and cross the small bamboo bridge. There are more than 130 jars at this site, which are generally smaller and more damaged than at the other sites. There's also a very small, basic restaurant, serving *feu* (noodle soup).

Tham Piu

ⓘ *The cave is to the west of the Muang Kham-Xam Neua Rd, just after the 183 km post, entry 5000 kip. A rough track leads down to an irrigation dam, built in 1981. To get there from Phonsavanh you can either go the easy way and hire a vehicle US$30-40, or go the hard way, by public transport. For the latter, take the bus to Nong Haet, and request to stop at the Tham Phiu turn-off. From here walk towards the towering limestone cliff and follow the small trails for the last kilometre. It is best to do this with a guide as UXOs still litter the area.*

This cave is more of a memorial than a tourist site but will be of interest to those fascinated by the war. More evidence of the dirty war can be seen here. The intensity of the US bombing campaign under the command of the late General Curtis Le May was such that entire villages were forced to take refuge in caves. If discovered, fighter bombers were called in to destroy them. In Tam Phiu, a cave overlooking the fertile valley near Muang Kham, 365 villagers from near-by Ban Na Meun built a two-storey bomb shelter and concealed its entrance with a high stone wall. They lived there for a year, working in their rice fields at night and taking cover during the day from the relentless bombing raids which killed thousands in the area. On the morning of 8 March 1968 two T-28 fighter-bombers took off from Udon Thani air base in neighbouring Thailand and located the cave mouth which had been exposed on previous sorties. It is likely that the US forces suspected that the cave contained a Pathet Lao hospital complex. Indeed, experts are at odds whether this was a legitimate target or an example of collateral damage. There are a few people still alive whose families died in the cave, and they certainly see it as innocent civilians being targeted. The first rocket destroyed the wall, the second, fired as the planes swept across the valley, carried the full length of the chamber before exploding. There were no survivors and 11 families were completely wiped out; in total 374 people died, many reportedly women and children. Local rescuers claim they were unable to enter the cave for three days, but eventually the dead were buried in a bomb crater on the hillside next to the cave mouth. You will need a torch to explore the cave but there isn't much inside, just eerily black walls. The interior of the cave was completely dug up by the rescue parties and relatives and today there is nothing but rubble inside. It makes for a poignant lesson in military history and locally it is considered a war memorial. Further up the cliff is another cave, **Tham Phiu Song**, which fortunately didn't suffer the same fate. Before the stairway to the caves there is a little memorial centre which displays photographs from the war and is usually attended by a relative of the victims. A poignant sculpture of a soldier carrying a dead child marks the site, free of the victory and glory of most other war monuments. Many bomb craters around the site have been turned into fish ponds now bearing beautiful lotus.

Sao Hintang

ⓘ *About 130 km north of Phonsavanh and 56.5 km southwest of Xam Neua on Route 6. Tours can be organized from Phonsavanh through Mr Sousath of Maly Hotel (see Sleeping, page 519).*

At the billboard-sized sign at the turn-off in Ban Liang Sat, turn up the dirt road heading east. This road is quite rough in places so you'll need a 4WD car or an all-terrain motorbike in order to get there. About 3 km up the road is a sign for the Kechintang Trail, a 90-minute walking trail that takes you to some of the sites. The first is visible from the road after a further 3 km, with Site two located another 3 km after that.

There are hundreds of ancient upright stone pillars, menhirs and discs, gathered in Stonehenge-type patterns over a 10-km area, surrounded by jungle. This enigmatic site is as mysterious as the Plain of Jars: no one is quite sure who, or even which ethnic group,

Border essentials: Laos–Vietnam

To Vietnam via Nam Xoi

It is possible to cross over to Vietnam from here at the Nam Xoi (Laos)/Nameo (Vietnam) border crossing if you have a Lao/Vietnam visa. The border is open 0730-1130, 1330-1700. It may be necessary to pay a processing or overtime fee at weekend and after 1630.

Sleeping There are 2 basic guesthouses in Nameo; Phucloc Nha Tru and Minhchien which both offer rudimentary facilities for US$3-5.

Transport The trip is 2 hrs from Vieng Xai and songthaews leave at 0640 from the main road between Xam Neua and Nameo, 1 km from the centre of Vieng Xai; 20,000 kip. It is also possible to travel from Xam Neua to the border by songthaew from the station at 0630 and 0715, 3-4 hrs, 30,000 kip or to charter a songthaew for about US$50. There have been several complaints about tourist operators on the Vietnamese side of this border charging a fortune for transport. A motorbike taxi to Quan Son should cost around US$10. If you get really stuck on the Vietnam side contact Mr Pham Xuan Hop in Nameo, T0084-9-923 7425 who may be able to organize minivan rental, US$50 to Quan Son.

---

is responsible for erecting the stones and they have become steeped in legend. It is believed that the two sites are somehow linked, as they are fashioned from the same stone and share some archaeological similarities. ▶▶ *See Activities and tours, page 520.*

◉ Plain of Jars and the northeast listings

For Sleeping and Eating price codes, see inside the front cover.

◯ Sleeping

Phonsavanh *p514, map p514*
None of the streets in Phonsavanh are named – or at least the names aren't used.
A-D Auberge de la Plaine des Jarres (aka Phu Pha Daeng Hotel), 1 km from the centre, T/F021-312044. In a spectacular position on a hill overlooking the town are 16 stone and wood chalets (occasional hot water). Clean and comfortable. Restaurant serves good food. More expensive Oct-May.
A-D Vansana, on a hill 1 km out of town, T061-213170. Big, modern rooms with telephone, TV and minibar. Opt for the rooms upstairs, with bath and balcony. Restaurant offers Lao and foreign cuisine. Excellent value, especially the VIP room for US$50. Highly recommended.

C-F Maly Hotel, down the road from local government offices, T061-312031. Rooms have hot water and are furnished with a hotchpotch of local artefacts, including a small (defused!) cluster bomb. More expensive rooms on the upper floors have satellite TV, internet for those who have laptops. Mr Sousath Phetrasy runs tours.
D-F Orchid, just off the main road in the centre of town, T061-312403. You can't miss this big green-blue building. Not quite hotel standard but close enough for it to be good value. TV, hot water, comfy beds and bath. Free breakfast and airport pick-up (ring in advance).
G Dok Khoun, Route 7, T061-312189. Tiled rooms with desk. So clean that the smell of ammonia could knock you out. The bathroom is in what looks like a cupboard.
G Khou Kham Guesthouse, on the main road through town. A Hmong-owned hotel. Large rooms with hot water, but the beds

are a bit like sleeping on a rock face. Mai and Khou, the friendly owners, speak English.
G Nice Guesthouse, on the main road, T020-5616246, naibthoj@hotmail.com. Clean decent sized rooms with hot water and comfy beds. Reasonable value.
G Sabaidee, a block back from the main road, sabaidee2000@hotmail.com. Clean rooms with hot-water bathroom. Very low, hobbit-like doors. Central location, family atmosphere.

🍴 Eating

Phonsavanh *p514, map p514*
🍴🍴 Maly Hotel, see Sleeping. Fantastic food.
🍴🍴-🍴 Craters, main street, T020-7805775. Modern, Western restaurant offering burgers, pizza and sandwiches. Good music, attentive service. Delectable but pricey cocktails.
🍴 Nisha Indian, on the main road. North and south Indian food.
🍴 Phonexay, on the main road, towards the Tourism Office. Excellent fruit shakes and good Asian dishes. Exceptionally friendly.
🍴 Sangah, main street. Thai, Lao, Vietnamese and Western dishes. Huge portions.
🍴 Simmaly, main street, T061-211013. Fantastic *feu* soup. Great service and immensely popular. Recommended.

🍸 Bars and clubs

Phonsavanh *p514, map p514*
Maliyona Pub, on the main road. This graffiti-decorated bar sticks out like a sore thumb. Ear-blastingly loud hip-hop and Thai music. Rather devoid of customers.

⊛ Festivals and events

Phonsavanh *p514, map p514*
Dec National Day on the 2 Dec is celebrated with horse-drawn drag-cart racing. Also in Dec is **Hmong New Year** (movable), which is celebrated in a big way in this area.

▲ Activities and tours

Phonsavanh *p514, map p514*
There are no shortage of tour operators in Phonsavanh and most guesthouses can now arrange tours and transport. A full-day tour for 4 people should cost up to US$50-60, although you may have to bargain for it. Most travel agencies are located within a block of each other on the main road.
Indochina Travel, on the main road, T061-31 2409. Expensive but well-regarded minivan tours (cheaper if you can organize a group).
Lao Youth Travel, on Route 7, T020-576 1233, www.laoyouthtravel.com. Offers a wide range of tours to the jars and post conflict sites.
The most knowledgeable tour guide is the owner of the **Maly Hotel**. Sousath Phetrasy spent his teenage years in a cave at Xam Neua (see page 516) during the war.

⊖ Transport

Phonsavanh *p514, map p514*
Air
Lao Airlines runs flights to **Vientiane**, 30 mins, every day except Tue and Thu. In peak season it is often possible to fly via **Luang Prabang**.

Bus
To **Luang Prabang**, daily 0800 (both local and VIP bus), 265 km on a sealed road, 90,000 kip. To **Vientiane**, daily 0700, 0930 and 1600, 9-10 hrs, 90,000 kip, also a VIP bus daily at 0730, 100,000 kip. To **Vang Vieng**, daily 0720, 75,000 kip, and a VIP bus 0730, 100,000 kip. To **Muang Kham**, 3 hrs, 30,000 kip. Also north to **Nam Nouan** 0900, 4 hrs, 35,000 kip (change here for transport west to **Nong Khiaw**). **Xam Neua**, daily 0800 and 1600, 70,000 kip, a 10-hr haul through beautiful scenery with some very windy roads towards the end (you may want to take something for motion sickness).
Buses travel to **Vinh** (Vietnam) on Tue, Thu and Sat, 0630, 12 hrs, US$12. If you want to cross the border here you will need to

organize a visa in advance, as there is no consulate in Phonsavanh and no agencies to send your passport to Vientiane.

Nam Noaun is a staging post that travellers bound for **Xam Neua** or **Nong Khiaw** will invariably find themselves stopping at. The through traffic for Xam Neua is relatively frequent and most buses/songthaews from Phonsavanh stop on the way through. Getting a connecting bus to Nong Khiaw is a little more complicated as Nam Noun sits 7 km south of the junction between Routes 1 and 6, the junction village is called **Ban Sam Nyay**. You can get to the junction by songthaew or by asking a local for a lift on a motorbike. Most buses to/from Nong Khiaw stop at the village and not Nam Nouan. It is a pleasant Khmu village but there is very little there in the way of amenities. If you are coming from Nong Khiaw you will probably arrive disorientated and dishevelled at some ungodly hour. Locals may try to charge you an extortionate rate to get a pick-up to Nam Nouan, if that is the case grab a lift with someone on a motorbike (US$5-6).

Car

A full car with driver to the **Plain of Jars** will cost US$20 (US$5 each) to Site one, or US$30-40 to all 3 sites. To hire a songthaew to go to **Tham Phiu** is US$30-40 for the day, a minivan costs US$60.

ⓘ Directory

Phonsavanh *p514, map p514*

Banks Lao Development Bank, Mon-Fri 0800-1200, 1330-1600, near Lao Airlines Office, 2 blocks back from the dry market. Changes cash and TCs. No advances on Visa. **Indochine Travel** has an exchange booth with Visa advance, the only place in town, but they charge 6.9% commission. Moneygram service. **Hairdressers** There are several hairdressers dotted around town that will give a good head massage and hairwash for 10,000 kip. **Internet** At the photo shop, 200 kip per min, and across from the songthaew station in town. Slow internet access. **Medical services** Lao-Mongolian Hospital, T061-312166. Sufficient for minor ailments. **Pharmacies** are ubiquitous in town. **Post office and telephone** The post office is opposite the dry market and has IDD telephone boxes outside. **Shopping** West of the town centre is the Chinese Market, which stocks ethnic clothes and jewellery.

Central provinces

The central provinces of Laos, sandwiched between the Mekong (and Thailand) to the west and the Annamite Mountains (and Vietnam) to the east, are the least visited in the country which is a shame as the scenery here is stunning, with dramatic limestone karsts, enormous caves, beautiful rivers and forests. In particular, the upland areas to the east, off Route 8 and Route 12, in Khammouane and Bolikhamxai Province, are a veritable treasure trove of attractions, mottled with scores of caves, lagoons, rivers and rock formations. Visitors will require some determination in these parts, as the infrastructure is still being developed but a lot of new roads are planned to coincide with the near-finished Nam Theun II Dam. The Mekong towns of Thakhek and Savannakhet are elegant and relaxed and are the main transport hubs in the region. If you are short on time, Thakhek is the best stopover point for the central provinces and Pakse is the optimum place to base yourself to explore the southern provinces. ▸▸ *For listings, see pages 528-531.*

Thakhek and around ☺🄾🄵☺ ▸▸ *pp528-531. Colour map 4, A2.*

Located on the Mekong, at the junction of Routes 13 and 12, Thakhek is a quiet town, surrounded by beautiful countryside. It is the capital of Khammouane Province and was founded in 1911-1912, under the French. Apart from Luang Prabang, Thakhek is probably the most outwardly French-looking town in Laos, with fading pastel villas clustered around a simple fountain area. It has a fine collection of colonial-era shophouses, a breezy riverside position and a relaxed ambience. One of Laos' holiest sites, That Sikhot, the stunning caves of the region and beautiful Mahaxai can all be visited from here. This town is the most popular stopover point in the central provinces, attracting a range of tourists with its vast array of caves, rivers, lakes and other attractions. Despite encompassing some of the most beautiful scenery in Laos: imposing jagged mountains, bottle green rivers, lakes and caves, the region is still not considered a primary tourist destination. Tourism infrastructure is still quite limited but a trip to this area will prove the highlight of most visitors' holidays to Laos.

Ins and outs

Getting there There are two bus terminals: the main terminal is about 5 km from town and offers inter-provincial and international buses, and the small songthaew station, near Soksombook market which services local regions.

Getting around Thakhek is small enough to negotiate on foot or by bicycle. A number of places organize motorbike hire, such as the **Thakhek Travel Lodge** and the Tourism Information Centre, which acts as an agent for motorcycle dealers. ▸▸ *See Transport, page 530.*

Tourist information **Tourism Information Centre** ⓘ *Vientiane Rd, in a chalet-like building beside a derelict Ferris wheel, T052-212512.* The staff are particularly helpful and are champing at the bit to take tourists out on their ecotours and hikes. This is a good stop-off place for advice. Proceeds from the tours are given to poor, local communities. The office is full of brochures and glossy displays of the surrounding sites.

That Sikhot → *Colour map 4, A2.*

ⓘ *6 km south of Thakhek, daily 0800-1800; 2000 kip. Tuk-tuk 10,000 kip.*

That Sikhot or **Sikhotaboun** is one of Laos' holiest sites. It overlooks the Mekong and the journey downstream from Thakhek, along a quiet road, reveals bucolic Laos at its best. The *that* is thought to have been built by Chao Anou at the beginning of the 15th century and houses the relics of Chao Sikhot, a local hero, who founded the old town of Thakhek.

According to local legend, Sikhot was bestowed with Herculean strength after eating some rice he had stirred with dirty – but as it turned out magic – sticks. At that time, the King of Vientiane was having a problem with elephants killing villagers and taking over the country (hard to believe now but Laos was once called Land of a Million Elephants). The King offered anyone who could save the region half his Kingdom and his daughter's hand in marriage. Due to his new-found strength, Sikhot was able to take on the pachyderms and secure most of the surrounding area as well as Vientiane, whereupon he married the King of Vientiane's daughter. The King was unhappy about handing over his kingdom and daughter to this man, and plotted with his daughter to regain control. Sikhot foolishly revealed to his new wife that he could only be killed through his anus, so the King of Vientiane placed an archer at the bottom of Sikhot's pit latrine and when the unfortunate Oriental Hercules came to relieve himself, he was killed by an arrow.

That Sikhot consists of a large gold stupa raised 29 m on a plinth, with a viharn upstream built in 1970 by the last King of Laos. A major annual festival is held here in July and during February.

Kong Leng Lake → *Colour map 4, A2.*

ⓘ *33 km northeast of Thakhek.*

This site is usually incorporated into hikes as there isn't direct road access to the lake. Steeped in legend, locals believe an underground Kingdom lies beneath the surface of the 100-m-deep lake. As a result, you must request permission to swim here from the local village authority and you can only swim in the designated swimming zone. Fishing is not permitted. The beautiful green waters of the lake morph into different shades season to season due to the dissolved calcium from the surrounding limestone crops. It is very difficult to get to on your own and the track is sometimes completely inaccessible except on foot. The Tourism Information Centre organizes excellent treks to the lake.

Tham Pha (Buddha Cave) → *Colour map 4, A2.*

ⓘ *Ban Na Khangxang, off Route 12, 18 km from Thakhek; 2000 kip. A songthaew will cost US$15, use of boat 5000 kip. Women will need to hire a sinh (sarong) at the entrance, 2000 kip.*

A farmer hunting for bats accidentally stumbled across the Buddha Cave (also known Tham Pa Fa, or Turtle Cave) in April 2004. On climbing up to the cave's mouth, he found 229 bronze Buddha statues, believed to be more than 450 years old, and ancient palm leaf scripts. These Buddhas were part of the royal collection believed to have been hidden here when the Thais ransacked Vientiane. Since its discovery, the cave has become widely celebrated, attracting pilgrims from as far away as Thailand, particularly around Pi Mai (Lao New Year). A wooden ladder and eyesore concrete steps have now been built to access the cave, but it is quite difficult to get to as the dirt road from Thakhek is in poor condition. It is recommended that you organize a guide through the **Thakhek Tourism Information Centre** to escort you. In the wet season, it is necessary to catch a boat. The journey itself is half the fun as the cave is surrounded by some truly stunning karst formations sprawling across the landscape like giant dinosaur teeth.

Tham Kong Lor (Kong Lor cave)

ⓘ *Entrance fee at cave 5000 kip.*

Tham Kong Lor cave can only be described as sensational. The Nam Hinboun River has tunnelled through the mountain, creating a giant rocky cavern, 6 km long, 90 m wide and 100 m high, which opens out into the blinding bright light at Ban Natan on the other side. The cave is apparently named after the drum makers who were believed to make their instruments here. Although very rare, it is also home to the largest living cave-dwelling spiders in the world, though it took conservationists decades to spot them so it is unlikely you will have a run in with the massive arachnid.

It is almost impossible to do the nine- to 10-hour return trip from Ban Na Hin to Kong Lor in a day, as boatmen won't travel in the dark. The first stage of the journey is by songthaew or tractor from Ban Na Hin to Ban Napur. From Ban Napur catch a boat along the Nam Hinboun to either Ban Phonyang, where **Sala Hin Boun** is located (see Sleeping, page 529), or to Ban Kong Lor, the closest village to the caves, where you can find a homestay for 50,000 kip, including food. Beyond Ban Phonyang the river route to Tham Kong Lor is gorgeous, with small fish skipping out of the water, languid buffalo bathing, kids

Route 12 and the 'Loop' → *Colour map 4, A1 and A2.*

ⓘ *Contact Thakhek Travel Lodge (see Sleeping, page 528) for details of the 'Loop' route and for motorbike hire.*

The impressive karst landscape of the Mahaxai area is visible to the northeast of town and can be explored on a popular motorbike tour from Thakhek, known as the **Loop**, which runs from Thakhek along Route 12 to Mahaxai, then north to Lak Sao, west along Route 8 to Ban Na Hin and then south back to Thakhek on Route 13, taking in caves and other beautiful scenery along the way. The circuit should take approximately three days but allow four to five, particularly if you want to sidetrack to Tham Kong Lor and the other caves.

The 'Loop' is mostly for motorcyclists, who pick up a bike in Thakhek and travel by road. For those with more patience the trip can be undertaken on public transport. The whole loop covers an area over 400 km (without the side-trips). This includes 50 km from Thakhek to the Shell Station before the turn-off to Mahaxai; 45 km between the shell Station and Nakai; 70 km between Nakai and Lak Xao; 66 km between Lak Xao and Ban Na Hin; 60 km between Ban Na Hin and Ban Lao and then 100 km between Ban Lao and Thakhek. The trip between Ban Lao and Ban Na Hin offers some spectacular views.

If on a motorbike pack light: include a waterproof jacket, a torch, a few snacks, a long-sleeved shirt, sunglasses, sun block, closed-toe shoes, a *sinh* or sarong (to use as a towel, to stop dust and – for women – to bathe along the way), a phrase book and a good map. It is a bumpy, exhausting but enjoyable ride. Few of the sites are particularly well signposted in English so you will need to ask around. Most sites charge a parking fee for motorbikes.

Note that this whole region is very susceptible to change due to the Nam Theun II dam, a US$1.45 billion hydropower project, and other developments in the area. It is imperative that you check for up-to-date information before travelling. Check on the status of the roads at the Tourism Information Centre and check the logbook at the **Thakhek Lodge**. This trip is difficult in the wet season and will probably only be possible for skilled riders on larger dirt bikes. In the dry season it's very dusty.

The caves along Route 12 can also be visited on day trips from Thakhek, although some are difficult to find without a guide and access may be limited in the wet season. Many of taking a dip and ducks floating by – all surrounded by a Lord of the Rings fantasyland of breath-taking cliffs and rocky outcrops. At the start of the cave, you will have to scramble over some boulders while the boatmen carry the canoe over the rapids, so wear comfortable shoes with a good grip. A torch or, better a head-lamp (2000 kip at Thakhek market), is also recommended. About two-thirds of the way through the cave is an impressive collection of stalagmites and stalactites. It is possible to continue from Ban Natan, on the other side of Kong Lor, into the awesome Hinboun gorge. This is roughly 14 km long and, for much of the distance, vertical cliffs over 300 m high rise directly from the water on both sides.

Don't expect the three- to four-hour boat trip to be cheap – it is around US$25 each way (if you are lucky). These prices will come down once the roads have improved and the boat drivers don't have a monopoly on transport. A new road, scheduled to be completed in 2008, is in the works and will take visitors the 50 km from Ban Na Hin (also known as Ban Khoun Kham) to Ban Kong Lor.

the sights have no English signposts but locals will be more than obliging to confirm you are going in the right direction if you ask. Turn south off Route 12 at Km 7 to reach **Tham Xang** (Tham Pha Ban Tham), an important Buddhist shrine that contains some statues and a box of religious scripts. It is considered auspicious due to the 'elephant head' that has formed from calcium deposits and in the Lao New Year the locals sprinkle water on it. At Km 13, turn north on a track for 2 km to **Tha Falang** (Vang Santiphap – Peace Pool), a lovely emerald billabong on the Nam Don River, surrounded by pristine wilderness and breathtaking cliffs. It's a nice place to spend the afternoon or break your journey. In the wet season it may be necessary to catch a boat from the Xieng Liab Bridge to get here. Turn south off Route 12 at Km 14 and follow the track south to reach **Tham Xiang Liab**, a reasonably large cave at the foot of a 300-m-high limestone cliff, with a small swimming hole (in the dry season) at the far end. It is not easy to access the interior of the cavern on your own and, in the wet season, it can only be navigated by boat, as it usually floods. This cave, called 'sneaking around cave' derived its name from a legend of an old hermit who used to meditate in the cave with his beautiful daughter. A novice monk fell in love with the hermit's daughter and the two lovebirds planned their trysts sneakily around this cave and Tham Nan Aen. When the hermit found out he flew into a rage and did away with the novice monk; the daughter was banished to the cave for the rest of her life.

At Km 17, beyond the narrow pass, turn to the north and follow the path for 400 m to reach **Tham Sa Pha In**, a cave with a small Lake and a couple of interesting Buddhist shrines. Swimming in the lake is strictly prohibited as the auspicious waters are believed to have magical powers. South of Route 12, at Km 18, a path leads 700 m to the entrance of **Tham Nan Aen** ① *5000 kip*. This is the giant of the local caverns at 1.5 km long and over 100 m high. It has multiple chambers and the entrances are illuminated by fluorescent lighting; it also contains a small underground freshwater pool.

Mahaxai → *Colour map 4, A2.*
Mahaxai is a beautiful small town 50 km east of Thakhek off Route 12. The sunset here is quite extraordinary but even more beautiful is the surrounding scenery of exquisite

valleys and imposing limestone bluffs. A visit to Mahaxai should be combined with a visit to one or more of the spectacular caves along Route 12 and some river excursions to see the Xe Bang Fai gorges or run the rapids further downstream.

Close to Ban Na, 25 km northeast of Thakhek is **Nam Don Resurgence**. This beautiful lagoon is difficult to find without a local guide as it's located within a cave. It is shaded by a sheer 300 m cliff and filters off into an underground waterway network.

Savannakhet ⓜⓕⓐⓢⓖ ⤻ pp528-531. Colour map 4, B2.

Situated on the banks of the Mekong at the start of Route 9 to Danang in Vietnam, Savannakhet – or Savan as it is usually known – is an important river port and gateway to the south. The city has a sizeable Chinese population and attracts merchants from both Vietnam and Thailand, while the ubiquitous colonial houses and fading shopfronts are an ever-present reminder of earlier French influence. Savannakhet Province has several natural attractions, although the majority are a fair hike from the provincial capital. For those short on time in Laos, Pakse makes a better stopover than Savannakhet.

Ins and outs

Getting there and around It is possible to cross into Vietnam by taking Route 9 east over the Annamite Mountains via Xepon. The border is at Dansavanh (Laos) and Lao Bao (Vietnam) (see page 1055), 236 km east of Savannakhet, with bus connections direct from Savannakhet to Danang, Dong Ha and Hué. It is possible to cross the border into Mukdahan via the new Friendship Bridge or by one of the more infrequent ferries. The government bus terminal is near the Savan Xai market has connections with Vientiane, Thakhek, Pakse and Lao Bao; a tuk-tuk to the centre should cost about 10,000 kip. Just west of the bus station is the songthaew terminal, where vehicles depart to provincial destinations. Tuk-tuks, locally known as *Sakaylab*, criss-cross town. ⤻ *See Transport, page 531.*

Tourist information The **Provincial Tourism Office** ⓘ *T052-214203*, is one of the best in the country and runs excellent ecotours and treks to Dong Natad and Dong Phu Vieng National Protected Areas, which should be organized in advance. Can also arrange guides and drivers for other trips. ⤻ *See Activities and tours, page 530.*

Sights

Savan's colonial heritage can be seen throughout the town centre. Perhaps the most attractive area is the square east of the Immigration office between Khanthabouli and Phetsalath roads. **Wat Sounantha** has a three-dimensional raised relief on the front of the *sim*, showing the Buddha in the *mudra* of bestowing peace, separating two warring armies. **Wat Sayaphum** on the Mekong is rather more attractive and has several early 20th-century monastery buildings. It is both the largest and oldest monastery in town, although it was only built at the end of the 19th century. Evidence of Savan's diverse population is reflected in the **Chua Dieu Giac**, a Mahayana Buddhist pagoda that serves the town's Vietnamese population. The **Dinosaur Museum** ⓘ *Khanthabouli Rd, Mon-Fri 0800-1200, 1400-1600; 5000 kip*, houses a collection of four different dinosaur and early mammalian remains, and even some fragments of a meteorite that fell to earth over 100 million years ago.

For those unable to get to the Ho Chi Minh Trail, there is some rusting war scrap in the grounds of the **Provincial Museum** ⓘ *Khanthabouli Rd, Mon-Fri 0800-1130, 1300-1600; 5000 kip*, and a tank just to the north. The museum offers plenty of propaganda-style displays but little that is terribly enlightening unless you are interested in the former revolutionary leader Kaysone Phomvihane. If it looks closed just go across to the School of Medicine and knock on the curator's quarters, housed in the wooden building.

Savannakhet

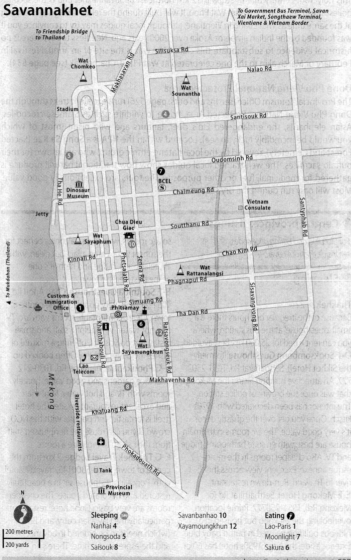

To Government Bus Terminal, Savan
Xai Market, Songthaew Terminal,
Vientiane & Vietnam Border

To Friendship Bridge
to Thailand

Wat Chomkeo

Stadium

Silisuksa Rd

Makhasavan Rd

Wat
Sounantha

Nalao Rd

Santisouk Rd

Oudomsinh Rd

Dinosaur
Museum

Tha He Rd

Jetty

BCEL

Chaimeung Rd

Vietnam
Consulate

Santyphab Rd

Chua Dieu
Giac

Wat
Sayaphum

Soutthanu Rd

Chao Kim Rd

Kinnali Rd

Phetsalath Rd

Senna Rd

Wat
Rattanalangsi

Phagnaput Rd

Simuang Rd

Tha Dan Rd

Siavangvong Rd

Mekong (Thailand)

Customs &
Immigration
Office

Phitsamay

Wat
Sayamungkhun

Ratsavongseuk Rd

Khanthabouli Rd

Lao
Telecom

Makhavenha Rd

Mekong

Khaluang Rd

Riverside restaurants

Phokadouath Rd

Tank

N

Provincial
Museum

200 metres

200 yards

That Inheng → *Colour map 4, B2.*

ⓘ *Any of the regular tuk-tuks which will make the trip for 80,000 kip return or take a shared songthaew to Xeno and ask to hop off at That Inheng. They will usually take you all the way there but if they drop you at the turning it is only a 3-km walk. Alternatively hire a bicycle in town and cycle.*

This holy 16th-century *that* or stupa is 12 km northeast of Savannakhet and is the second-holiest site in Southern Laos after Wat Phou. It was built during the reign of King Sikhottabong at the same time as That Luang in Vientiane, although local guides may try to convince you it was founded by the Indian emperor Asoka over 2000 years ago. Needless to say, there is no historical evidence to substantiate this claim. The wat is the site of an annual festival in February or March akin to the one celebrated at Wat Phou, Champasak (see page 534).

Dong Phu Vieng National Protected Area

The Provincial Tourism Office (see Ins and outs, page 526) runs excellent treks through the Dong Phu Vieng National Protected Area, home to wildlife such as Siamese crocodiles, Asian elephants, the endangered Eld's deer, langurs and wild bison (most of which you would be incredibly lucky to see). Located within the NPA is a **Song Sa Kae** (Sacred Forest and Cemetery), revered by the local Katang ethnic group, who are known for their buffalo sacrifices. The well-trained local guides show how traditional natural produce is gathered for medicinal, fuel or other purposes. The tours are exceptionally good value. Most will only run during the dry season.

◉ Central provinces listings

For Sleeping and Eating price codes, see inside the front cover.

● Sleeping

Thakhek *p522*

Because of the irregular bus hours there is a small 'guesthouse' at the bus station, where you can rent a bed for 25,000 kip. Best avoided.
D-F Sooksomboon Guesthouse (formerly the *Sikhot Hotel*), Setthathirat Rd, T051-250 777. An attractive building facing the Mekong that was once the provincial police station. The interior has been decorated with 1970s kitsch. Once you get over the ghastly decor it's very good value. The a/c rooms in the main house are best, with en suite bathrooms, fridge and TV. Also cheaper rooms in the motel-esque annexe. Excellent view across the river to Thailand. Run-down restaurant.
E-F Mekong Hotel, Setthathirat Rd (or Mekong Rd), T051-250777. Prime location overlooking the Mekong but housed in a hideous building painted in putrid baby blue. Exterior aside, the large 1950s hotel has 60 or

so a/c rooms, with wide balconies perfect for the sunset vista. Large, plain but clean, with TV, telephone, fridge and bath. It's one of the best deals in town.
E-F Southida Guesthouse, Chao Anou Rd, T051-212568. Very popular, in the centre of town. Clean, comfortable rooms with a/c, TV and hot water. Very helpful staff and small restaurant downstairs, offering a mixture of dishes including sashimi. Often booked up.
E-G Phoukanna, Vientiane Rd, T030-212 092. Nice gardens and good value, homely rooms with TV and hot water. Mini-mart and excellent restaurant on site. The hotel itself is fantastic, and popular with the NGO crowd, if you can rouse the nonplussed staff from their sleep to organize a room.
E-G Thakhek Travel Lodge, 2 km from the centre of town, T030-5300145, travell@laotel. com. Popular guesthouse set in a beautifully restored and decorated house. The cheaper rooms are very basic. Good hotel restaurant particularly the Hawaiian curry, and BBQ (which needs to be ordered in advance), and the espresso machine. There's an

excellent logbook for those intending to travel independently around the 'Loop'. Motorcycle hire, US$15 per day. Recommended for those planning adventure travel around the area. Ring in advance if you're arriving on one of the midnight buses.

G Khammuan International (formerly the **Chaleunxay Hotel**), Kouvoravong Rd, T052-212171. Military owned hotel that has a soulless penitentiary feel. Smallish rooms without windows but some have a/c and the en suite bathrooms have hot-water showers. Cheaper single rooms with powerful ceiling fans. Although the rooms are quite good value, you wouldn't put your mother up here as it may well double as a brothel.

Towards Tham Kong Lor

There are 2 guesthouses on Route 13 in **Ban Lao**, just past the Route 8 intersection, which are passable. Homestays are available in **Ban Kong Lor** and **Ban Natan**, US$5 per person including breakfast.

C-E Sala Hin Boun, Ban Phonyang, 10 km from Kong Lor cave, T020-5614016, www.sala lao.com. The best option. It enjoys a scenic location on the riverbank amongst karst rock formations and has 10 well-equipped and very pleasant rooms in 2 bungalows. Mr Kham, the manager, will arrange for a boat to pick you up in Napua for US$25, with advance notice. A tour to Kong Lor for 2-3 people is US$30 with picnic lunch. Discounts in low season.
E-G Sala Kong Lor Lodge, 6 km from Kong Lor cave, T051-214315. Lodge with 4 small huts with twin beds and a couple of rooms. There is also a campsite for US$2 per night.

Mahaxai *p525*

G Mahaxai Guesthouse. 10 large, clean and airy rooms with en suite showers. Upstairs rooms are brighter. Attractive balcony overlooking the river.

Savannakhet *p526, map p527*

C-E Nanhai, Santisouk Rd, T041-212371. This 7-storey hotel is considered one of the better places in town. The 42 rooms, karaoke bars and dining hall are a prime example of a mainland Chinese hotel. Rooms have a/c, TV, fridge, telephones and en suite bathroom but they smell musty and the single rooms are tiny. The pool has no water. Decent restaurant.
E-F Nongsoda, Tha He Rd, T041-212522. Oodles of white lace draped all over the house. Clean rooms with a/c and en suite bathrooms with wonderfully hot water. During the low season the hotel drops its room rate. Motorbike hire.
E-G Savanbanhao, Senna Rd, T041-212202, sbtour@laotel.com. Made up of 4 colonial-styles houses set around a quiet concrete courtyard. Most expensive rooms have en suite hot-water showers. Some a/c. **Savanbanhao Tourism Co** is attached (see Activities and tours, page 530). Good for getting in and out of Savannakhet quickly.
G Saisouk, Makhavenha Rd, T041-212207. Good-sized twin and double rooms, spotlessly clean, some a/c, communal bathrooms. Very friendly staff, reasonable English. Laundry service. Very friendly and homely.
G Xayamoungkhun (English sign just reads 'Guest House'), 85 Ratsavongseuk Rd, T041-212426. An excellent little hotel in an airy colonial-era villa. Centrally positioned. Range of very clean rooms available, the more expensive have hot water, a/c and a fridge. Very friendly owners. Second-hand books and magazines available. Recommended.

Eating

Thakhek *p522*

There is the usual array of noodle stalls – try the one in the town 'square' with good fruit shakes. Warmed baguettes are also sold in the square in the morning. The best place to eat is at one of the riverside restaurants on either side of fountain square, where you can watch the sunset, knock back a Beer Lao and tuck into tasty BBQ foods. Otherwise, most restaurants are attached to hotels.
† Kaysone Restaurant, in the centre of town, T051-212563. Looks like someone's backyard,

once inside you discover a sprawling restaurant. Very popular with the locals. *Sindat*, Korean BBQ and an à la carte menu. The ice cream is fantastic. There's karaoke on site.

¶ Phoukanna, see Sleeping. The best option, with good service and an array of Western and Lao dishes.

¶ Southida Guesthouse, see Sleeping. Good value, does a reasonable Western breakfast and has an eclectic menu including sashimi.

¶ Sukiyaki, on Vientiane Rd, T020-5751533. A pokey but exceptionally friendly restaurant where a buffet of food is on offer that you can BBQ yourself at the table.

¶ Thakhek Travel Lodge, see Sleeping. Recommended for their BBQs.

Savannakhet p526, map p527
Several restaurants on the riverside serve good food and beer. The market also sells good, fresh food, including Mekong river fish.

¶ Lao-Paris, Simung St. A crumbling building with 4 tables on the grey veranda and a dingy inside. Tasty falang fare and Lao/Vietnamese dishes, opens at 0800 and serves a good breakfast. Cheap but not haute cuisine.

¶ Moonlight Restaurant, Ratsavongseuk Rd, T030-5315718. Cosy café serving a range of reasonable Western dishes. Very popular with travellers and locals.

¶ Sakura, Sayamungkhun Rd, near the church, T041-212882. Very atmospheric. Good sukiyaki fondue and basic Asian fare, but it's the atmosphere that makes it special.

▲ Activities and tours

Savannakhet p526, map p527
Savanbanhao Tourism Co, Savanbanhao Hotel, see Sleeping, T041-212944, Mon-Sat 0800-1200, 1330-1630. Tours and trips to most sights in the area, bus tickets to Vietnam.
Savannakhet Provincial Tourism Authority, T041-214203. The tourism authority runs

excellent ecotours and treks to the national parks in the area. There are 14 keen, English-speaking guides who take tourists out to see the local culture and sights. 1- to 3-day treks have been established, with proceeds filtering down to local communities.

🚍 Transport

Thakhek p522
Bus/truck
Local The **local bus station** at Talaat Lak Sarm services towns and villages within the province. From here songthaews depart hourly between 0700 and 1400 to Mahaxai, 50 km, 2-3 hrs, 20,000 kip; Nakai, 2-4 hrs, 30,000 kip; Na Phao (Vietnam Border), 6-7 hrs, 40,000 kip; Na Hin 45,000 kip. There is also a songthaew to Kong Lor village at 0730, 75,000 kip but this only runs when the road conditions are good (not in the wet season).

Long-distance Thakhek's **main bus station** is 4 km northeast of town. It has a mini-market open throughout the night. Frequent daily connections northbound to **Vientiane**, 346 km, 6-7 hrs, 40,000 kip; the VIP bus also dashes through town at 1300, 60,000-80,000 kip. Southbound buses to **Savannakhet**, every hr, daily 1100-2200, 2½ hrs, 20,000 kip; to **Pakse**, every hr until 2400, 6-7 hrs; also to **Sekong**, 1030, 1530 and 2300, 60,000 kip; to **Don Khong**, 1600, 15 hrs, 60,000 kip. To get to **Dong Ha** (Vietnam), Sat 0800, 80,000 kip. Buses to Hué daily 0800, 80,000 kip; Danang Mon-Fri 2000, 160,000 kip and Hanoi Sat 2000, 18 hrs, 160,000 kip. It costs 20,000- 30,000 kip to get a tuk-tuk from the station to a guesthouse in town. Call guesthousesif you're arriving late.

Motorbike
Can be rented from **Thakhek Travel Lodge**, US$15 per day; and from the rental shop, on the left-hand side, near the traffic lights, US$8 per day (ask for Mr Na). Provincial Tourism Office can also organize motorbike rental.

Mahaxai p525

Songthaews leave from the station in the morning. The last bus to Thakhek is at 1500.

Savannakhet p526, map p527

Bus/truck

From the bus station on the northern edge of town, frequent northbound buses depart daily to **Vientiane**, 8-9 hrs, 55,000 kip. Most of the Vientiane-bound buses also stop at **Thakhek**, 2½-3 hrs, 25,000 kip. There are scheduled buses to **Thakhek** 4 times daily.

Southbound buses to **Pakse**, 6 times daily, 6-7 hrs, 30,000 kip; buses from Vientiane to Pakse will also pick up passengers here. To **Don Khon**, 0700, 9-10 hrs, 50,000 kip.

To Vietnam Eastbound buses depart daily to **Xepon** and **Lao Bao** (Vietnam border, see page 1055), 0630, 0930 and 1200, 5-6 hrs, 30,000 kip. A bus also departs daily 2200 for destinations within Vietnam, including **Hué**, 13 hrs, 110,000 kip; **Danang**, 15 hrs, 140,000 kip, and **Hanoi**, 22 hrs, 200,000 kip; there are additional services Sat 0700 and 1800, and Sun 0700. Luxury Vietnam-bound buses can also be arranged through the **Savanbanhao Hotel**, see Sleeping, US$12.

To Thailand Buses are expected to start running across the Friendship Bridge at the Mukdahan border. In the meantime, ferries leave the pier 6 times daily, 30 mins, 15,000 kip.

Car/bicycle/motorbike

Car and driver can be hired from the **Savanbanhao Hotel**. They rent motorbikes for US$10 per day. **Lao-Paris Restaurant**, rents bicycles for US$1, motorbikes for US$10.

Tuk-tuk

10,000 kip per person for a local journey.

❶ Directory

Thakhek p522

Banks Banque pour le Commerce Extérieur Lao (BCEL), Vientiane Rd, just across from the post office, T051-212686, will change cash and TCs and does cash advances on Visa. **Lao Development Bank**, Kouvoravong Rd (eastern end), exchanges cash but doesn't do cash advances. There is also an exchange counter at the immigration pier. **Internet** Thakhek Travel Lodge and stationary shop in the main street in town, 300 kip per min. **Post office** Kouvoravong Rd (at cross-roads with Nongbuakham Rd); international calls.

Savannakhet p526, map p527

Banks Lao Development Bank, Oudomsinh Rd, will change most major currencies. **Banque pour le Commerce Exterieur Lao (BCEL)**, Chalmeung Rd, will exchange currency. There are exchange counters around the market, any currency accepted, and at the pier (bad rate). **Customs and immigration** Lao customs and immigration, Tha He Rd, at the passenger pier, for exit to Thailand and Lao visas, daily 0830-1200, 1300-1600, overtime fees payable Sat and Sun. **Embassies and consulates** Vietnam Consulate, Sisavangvong Rd, T041-212737, Mon-Fri 0730-1100, 1400-1630. Provides Vietnamese visas in 3 days on presentation of 2 photos and US$50. **Thai Consulate**, Kouvoravong Rd, open 0830-1200 for applications, 1400-1500 for visa collection. Visas are issued on the same day if dropped off in the morning. **Internet** Phitsamay, Chaluanmeung Rd, is quite a decent internet café and shop in a convenient location. SPS Furniture Shop, Khanthabouli Rd, 100 kip per minute. Skype wasn't available at the time of publication. **Medical services** Savannakhet Hospital, Khanthabuli Rd, T041-212051. **Police** A block back from the river, near the Tourist Office, T041-212 069. **Post office** Khanthabouli Rd, daily 0800-2200. **Telephone** Lao Telecom Office, next door to the post office, for domestic and international calls. There are also plenty of call boxes around town (including 1 next to the immigration office at the river).

Far south

The far south is studded with wonderful attractions: from pristine jungle scenery to the cooler Boloven Plateau and the rambling ruins of Wat Phou, once an important regional powerbase. The true gems of the south, however, are the Siphandon (4000 islands), lush green islets that offer the perfect setting for those wanting to kick back for a few days. This region, near the border with Cambodia, is an idyllic picture-perfect ending to any trip in Laos. The three main islands offer something for all tourists: the larger Don Khong is great for exploring the island, take in the stunning vista and traditional Lao rural life; Don Deth is a backpacker haven and is good for those who want to while away the days in a hammock with a good book; Don Khone is better for tourist sites such as the Li Phi falls or old colonial ruins. There are roaring waterfalls nearby and pakha, or freshwater dolphins, can sometimes be spotted here between December and May. ▸▸ *For listings, see pages 544-555.*

Pakse

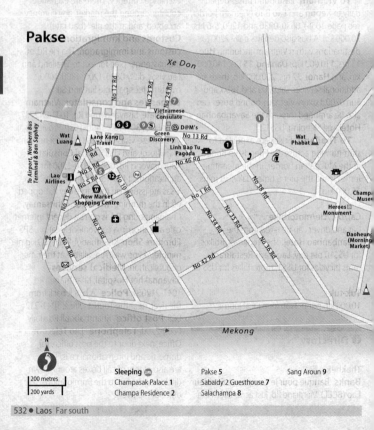

Sleeping	Pakse 5	Sang Aroun 9
Champasak Palace 1	Sabaidy 2 Guesthouse 7	
Champa Residence 2	Salachampa 8	

Pakse is the largest town in the south and is strategically located at the junction of the Mekong and Xe Don rivers. It is a busy commercial town, built by the French early in the 20th century as an administrative centre for the south. The town has seen better days but the tatty colonial buildings lend an air of old-world charm. Pakse is a major staging post for destinations further afield such as the old royal capital of Champasak, famed for its pre-Angkor, seventh-century Khmer ruins of Wat Phou. Close to Pakse are ecotourism projects where elephant treks, bird watching and homestays are possible.

The Cambodian recovery is more possible is the most phenomenally an colonial buildings an Laos. The daughter law residues and sense and tourists is tor open to some

Ins and outs

Getting there Pakse is Southern Laos' transport hub. The airport is 2 km northwest of town; tuk-tuks will make the journey for around 20,000 kip. International flights from Bangkok and Siem Reap, as well as domestic flights to/from Vientiane, run several times a week. There are three official bus terminals in Pakse: the Northern terminal (Km 7 on Route 13 north, T031-251508) is for buses to and from the north; the Southern terminal (Km 8 south on Route 13, T031-212981) is for buses to and from the south; and the VIP bus terminal is for northbound VIP buses. VIP buses to Ubon in Thailand are available from the evening market for ฿200. Tuk-tuks wait to transport passengers from terminals to the town centre; you shouldn't have to pay more than 7000 kip if there are multiple passengers but they will wait until the vehicle is full. ›› See Transport, page 552.

the ferry to Champasak 5,000 kip, person and to until 2000. Public boats don't exist make da ki VIP. You can also charter a boat from Pakse to pay about US$50-60 for this one hour. To Wat Muang Kao 4 km downstream from from Champasak. This is a public boats 10,000 for the ferry for 2000 kip.

foundation Champasak, District Visitor Information Centre ① Wat Phou Work opposite services tourbuses to Wat Phou and tours to the Bolaven Plateau every day or at least most day

Getting around Tuk-tuks and saamlors are the main means of local transport and can be chartered for half a day for about US$5. The main tuk-tuk 'terminal' is at the Daoheung market. Cars, motorbikes and bicycles are available for hire from some hotels and tour companies. The town's roads are numbered as if they were highways: No 1 Road through to No 46 road.

Tourist information Champasak Provincial Department of Tourism ① No 11 Rd, T031-212021, erratic hours but try Mon-Fri 0800-1200, 1400-1600. They have some fantastic ecotours on offer to unique destinations (some are offered in conjunction with local travel agents, such as Green Discovery (see Activities and tours, page 551). Mr Phouvanh, head of the information office, is very nice and knowledgeable.

VIP Terminal

Evening Market

Tuk-tuks

Stadium
No 13 Rd

To Southern Bus Terminal

Eating 🍴
Delta Coffee **1**
Jasmine **3**

Nazim's **6**
Xuan Mai **12**

The agricultural town of Champasak, which stretches along the right bank of the Mekong for 4 km, is the nearest town to Wat Phou and with enough comfortable accommodation, is a good base from which to explore the site and the surrounding area. It is about 40 km south of Pakse. The sleepy town is quaint and charming and a fantastic place to spend the night, though the trip can be done in a day. The town itself is dotted with simply stunning colonial buildings. Of these, the former residence of Champasak hereditary Prince Boun Oun and former leader of the right wing opposition, who fled the country in 1975 after the Communist takeover, is quite possibly the most magnificent colonial building in Laos. His daughter-in-law now resides there and although it is not open to tourists it is certainly worth a look from the outside. Champasak is known for its wood handicrafts, and vases, and other carved ornaments are available for sale near the jetty.

Ins and outs

Getting there Most songthaews run from Pakse's Southern bus terminal on Route 13 to Ban Lak Sarm Sip (which translates as 'village 30 km'), where they take a right turn to Ban Muang (2-3km). Here, people sell tickets for the ferry to Champasak (5000 kip; person and motorbike 8000 kip). The ferry runs from 0600 until 2000. Public boats from Pakse make the journey to Champasak in two hours (60,000 kip). You can also charter a boat from Pakse, which makes sense for a larger group; expect to pay about US$50-60 for boat hire for 15 to 20 people. The boat will probably dock at Ban Wat Muang Kao, 4 km downstream from Champasak; take a bus or tuk-tuk from here. From Champasak there is a public bus to Pakse at 0630, 0730 and 0800, two hours (with a wait for the ferry), 15,000 kip.

Tourist information Champasak District Visitor Information Centre ⓘ *Mon-Fri 0800-1600, T020-2206215.* Can arrange boats to Don Daeng, guides to Wat Phou and tours to surrounding sites. Guides charge US$10 per day or US$5 for a half day.

Wat Phou → *Colour map 4, C3.*

ⓘ *The site is officially open 0800-1630 but the staff are happy to let you in if you get there for sunrise, even as early as 0530, and you won't get thrown out until 1800. The admission fee of US$3 or around 30,000 kip goes towards restoration (entry to the Exhibition Centre is included). There is also the Wat Phu Exhibition Centre at the entrance; a surprisingly good museum with an array of*

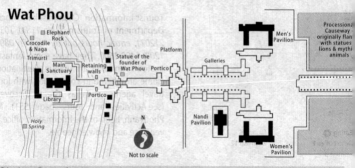

Wat Phou

Not to scale

artefacts such as the garuda and nandi bull. The centre closes at 1600. From the Champasak dock, you can catch a tuk-tuk to Wat Phou, 8-9 km, around 80,000 kip return. Most people prefer to hire a bicycle US$2 from one of the guesthouses in Champasak town and cycle to the ruins.

The archaeological site of Wat Phou is at the foot of the Phou Pasak, 8 km southwest of Champasak. With its teetering, weathered masonry, it conforms exactly to the Western ideal of the lost city. The mountain behind Wat Phou is called **Linga Parvata**, as the Hindu Khmers thought it resembled a linga – albeit a strangely proportioned one. Although the original Hindu temple complex was built in the fifth and sixth centuries, most of remains today is believed to have been built in the 10th to 11th centuries.

Wat Phou was a work in progress and was constructed and renovated over a period spanning several hundred years. Most of the ruins date back to the fifth and sixth centuries, making them at least 200 years older than Angkor Wat. At that time, the Champasak area was the centre of power on the lower Mekong. The Hindu temple only became a Buddhist shrine in later centuries.

Archaeologists and historians believe most of the building at Wat Phou was the work of the Khmer king, Suryavarman II (1131-1150), who was also responsible for starting work on Angkor Wat in Cambodia. The temple remained important for Khmer kings even after they had moved their capital to Angkor. They continued to appoint priests to serve at Wat Phou and sent money to maintain the temple until the last days of the Angkor Empire.

Exploring the site   The king and dignitaries would originally have sat on the platform above the 'tanks' or *baray* and presided over official ceremonies or watched aquatic games. In 1959 a palace was built on the platform so the king had somewhere to stay during the annual Wat Phou Festival (see page 551). A long avenue leads from the platform to the pavilions. This **processional causeway** was probably built by Khmer King Jayavarman VI (1080-1107) and may have been the inspiration for a similar causeway at Angkor Wat.

The sandstone **pavilions**, on either side of the processional causeway, were added after the main temple and are thought to date from the 12th century. Although crumbling, with great slabs of laterite and collapsed lintels lying aesthetically around, both pavilions are remarkably intact. The pavilions were probably used for segregated worship by pilgrims, one for women (left) and the other for men (right). The porticoes of the two huge buildings face each other. The roofs were thought originally to have been poorly constructed with thin stone slabs on a wooden beam-frame and later replaced by Khmer tiles. Only the outer walls now remain but there is enough still standing to fire the imagination: the detailed

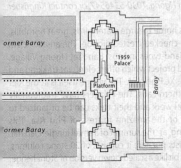

carving around the window frames and porticoes is well-preserved. The laterite used to build the complex was brought from **Ou Mong**, also called Tomo Temple, another smaller Khmer temple complex a few kilometres downriver, but the carving is in sandstone. The interiors were without permanent partitions, although it is thought that rush matting was used instead, and furniture was limited – reliefs only depict low stools and couches. At the rear of the women's pavilion are the remains of a brick construction, believed to have been the queen's quarters.

Above the pavilions is a small temple, the **Nandi Pavilion**, with entrances on two sides. It is dedicated to Nandi, the bull (Siva's vehicle), and is a common feature in Hindu temple complexes. There are three chambers, each of which would originally have contained statues – these have been stolen. As the hill begins to rise above the Nandi temple, the remains of six brick temples follow the contours, with three on each side of the pathway. All six are completely ruined and their function is unclear. At the bottom of the steps is a portico and statue of the founder of Wat Phou, Pranga Khommatha.

The **main sanctuary**, 90 m up the hillside and orientated east-west, was originally dedicated to Siva. The rear section (behind the Buddha statue) is part of the original sixth-century brick building. Sacred spring water was channelled through the hole in the back wall of this section and used to wash the sacred linga. The water was then thrown out, down a chute in the right wall, where it was collected in a receptacle. Pilgrims would then wash in the holy water. The front of the temple was constructed later, probably in the eighth to ninth century, and has some fantastic carvings: apsaras, dancing Vishnu, Indra on a three-headed elephant and, above the portico of the left entrance, a carving of Siva, the destroyer, tearing a woman in two.

The Hindu temple was converted into a Buddhist shrine, either in the 13th century during the reign of the Khmer king Jayavarman VII or when the Lao conquered the area in the 14th century. A large Buddha statue now presides over its interior.

Don Daeng Island

① *An ecotour is the way to get here; contact the Provincial Tourism Office in Pakse or the Tourism Office in Champasak. A trip by boat from Champasak will cost around US$1.*

This idyllic river island sits right across from Champasak. It stretches for 8 km and is the perfect place for those wishing to see quintessential village life, with basket weaving, fishing and rice farming, and without the cars and hustle and bustle. There is a path around the island that can be traversed on foot or by bicycle. A crumbling ancient brick stupa, built in the same century as Wat Phu, is in the centre of the island and there are a few ancient remnants in **Sisak Village** from the construction. The local inhabitants of **Pouylao Village** are known for their knife-making prowess. There is a lovely sandy beach on the Champasak side of the island, perfect for a dip. The island has only recently opened up to tourism, so it is important to tread lightly.

Xe Pian National Protected Area → *Colour map 4, C3.*

① *The provincial authorities are trying to promote ecotourism in this area. To organize an elephant trek go to the Visitor Centre in Ban Kiet Ngong, T030-5346547, or contact Kingfisher Ecolodge (see page 545).*

The Xe Pian National Protected Area (NPA) is home to large water birds, great hornbills, sun bears, Asiatic black bears and the yellow-cheeked crested gibbon. The area is rich in bird-life and is one of the most threatened land-types in Laos. Ban Kiet Ngong Village, 1½ hours from Pakse, has a community-based project which offers elephant trekking and homestay accommodation on the edge of the Xe Pian NPA. The village itself is at the Kiet Ngong Wetland, the largest wetland in Southern Laos. The villagers have traditionally been dependent on elephants for agricultural work and their treks can be organized to either the Xe Pian National Protected Area or the amazing fortress of **Phu Asa**. This ancient fortress is located 2 km from Kiet Ngong, at the summit of a small jungle-clad hill. It is an enigmatic site that has left archaeologists puzzled; it consists of 20 stone columns, 2 m-high, arranged in a semi-circle – they look a bit like a scaled-down version of Stonehenge.

Tahoy festival

There are several Tahoy settlements around the Boloven Plateau although the Tahoy population in Laos is only about 30,000. The village of Ban Paleng, not far from Tha Teng on Route 16, is a fascinating place to visit, especially in March (in accordance with the full-moon), when the animist Tahoy celebrate their annual three-day sacrificial festival. The village is built in a circle around the kuan (the house of sacrifice). A water buffalo is donated by each family in the village. The buffalo has its throat cut and the blood is collected and drunk. The raw meat is divided among the families and surrounding villages are invited to come and feast on it. The head of each family throws a slab of meat into the lak khai – a basket hanging from a pole in front of the kuan – so that the spirits can partake too. The sacrifice is performed by the village shaman, then dancers throw spears at the buffalo until it dies. The villagers moved from the Vietnam border area to escape the war, but Ban Paleng was bombed repeatedly: the village is still littered with shells and unexploded bombs.

To reach the village from Pakse, follow Route 13 until you get to the Km 48 junction with Route 18 at Thang Beng Village (the Xe Pian National Protected Area office is here). Follow route 18 east for 7 km, turn right at the signpost for the last 1.5 km to Ban Kiet Ngong.

There are several other ecotourism two- to three-day trekking/homestay ecotours offered in the area, contact the Provincial Tourism Information Office in Pakse or the Kingfisher Ecolodge.

Boloven Plateau ▲◉ ▶ pp544-555. Colour map 4, B3.

The French identified the Boloven Plateau, in the northeast of Champasak Province, as a prime location for settlement by hardy French farming stock. It is named after the Laven minority group that reside in the area. The soils are rich and the upland position affords some relief from the summer heat of the lowlands. However, their grand colonial plans came to nought and, although some French families came to live here, they were few in number and all left between the 1950s and 1970s as conditions in the area deteriorated. Today the plateau is inhabited by a colourful mix of ethnic groups, such as the Laven, Alak, Tahoy and Suay, many of whom were displaced during the war. The premier attraction in the area is the number of roaring falls plunging off the plateau; Tad Lo and Tad Fan are particularly popular tourist destinations, while the grand Tad Yeung makes a perfect picnic destination. The plateau also affords excellent rafting and kayaking trips.

Ins and outs

Tourist infrastructure is limited. Trips to **Tad Fan** and other attractions can be organized in Pakse through **Sabaidy 2** (see pages 545 and 551), and **Green Discovery Laos** (see page 551). Alternatively, the best base on the plateau is **Tad Lo** (see page 538), which can be reached by a bus or songthaew from Pakse, alighting at Ban Houa Set (2½ hours from Pakse). There is a blue sign here indicating the way to Tad Lo – a 1.5-km walk along a dirt track and through the village of Ban Saen Wang. You can usually get a tuk-tuk from Ban Houa Set to Tad Lo for around 10,000 kip. Before you set off, pop in to Tim's Guesthouse & Restaurant (see Sleeping, page 546) for a quick chat to Tim's English-speaking husband). A great source of free and friendly information, he is the foremost authority on all there is to do in the area and is unbelievably helpful. He seems to be able to arrange tours and excursions with less hassle and more local involvement than anyone else. He'll also give you a map that you can copy, www.tadlo.laopdr.com. ▶▶ *See Activities and tours, page 551, and Transport, page 554.*

Paksong (Pakxong) and around → *Colour map 4, B3.*

The main town on the Boloven Plateau is Paksong, a small town 50 km east of Pakse renowned for its large produce market. It was originally a French agricultural centre, popular during the colonial era for its cooler temperatures. The town occupies a very scenic spot, however, the harsh weather in the rainy season changes rapidly making it difficult to plan trips around the area.

On the way to Paksong, just past Km 38, is **Tad Fan**, a dramatic 120-m-high waterfall, which is believed to be one of the tallest cascades in the country. The fall splits into two powerful streams roaring over the edge of the cliff and plummeting into the pool below, with mist and vapour shrouding views from above. One of the best viewing spots for the falls is the **Tad Fan Resort**'s restaurant (see Sleeping, page 546), which offers an unobscured view of the magnificent site.

Tad Yeung and around

Around 2 km from Tad Fan and 40 km from Pakse is Tad Yeung. The falls are about 1 km from the main road. Set amongst beautiful coffee plantations and sprinkled with wooden picnic huts, these falls are possibly the best on offer on the plateau as they offer both height and accessibility. Packing a picnic in Pakse and bringing it along for an afternoon trip is recommended. The cascades plummet 50 m to a pool at the bottom, where it's possible to swim in the dry season. During the wet season the waterways create numerous little channels and islands around the cascades. Behind the main falls sits a cave, however it's best to get someone to guide you here. There is a slippery walkway from the top of the falls to the bottom, where you can swim. The falls can be reached by taking a local bus from the Southern Bus station in Pakse to a village Km 40 (ask to go to **Lak See Sip**). The turn-off is on the right from Pakse (and on the left from Paksong). There is a sign on the main road which indicates **Sihom Sabaidy Guesthouse**, follow this road about 700 m to the falls. These falls are a great option if you are trying to avoid the backpacker hordes.

Just 17 km from Paksong are the twin falls of **Tad Mone** and **Tad Meelook**. Once a popular picnic spot for locals, the area is now almost deserted and the swimming holes at the base of the falls are an idyllic place for a dip.

Some 35 km northwest of Pakse is **Pasuam Waterfall** and **Utayan Bajiang Champasak** ① *T031-251294, 5000 kip*, a strange ethnic theme park popular with Thai tourists. The large compound features small cascades, a model ethnic village, gardens and trails. There are bungalows, a tree house and rooms available for ฿1000. To get here from Pakse follow Route 13 towards Paksong and follow the left fork at 21 km and turn off at 30-km.

Tad Lo and around ◉❶❀▲◉ ▶▶ *pp544-555. Colour maps 4, B3.*

Tad Lo is a popular 'resort' on the edge of the Boloven Plateau, nestled alongside three rolling cascades. There are several places to stay in this idyllic retreat, good hiking, an exhilarating river to frolic in (especially in the wet season) and elephant trekking. In the vicinity of Tad Lo there are also several villages, which can be visited in the company of a local villager. All the guesthouses in Tad Lo can arrange guided treks to Ban Khian and Tad Soung.

The **Xe Xet** (or Houai Set) flows past Tad Lo, crashing over two sets of cascades nearby: **Tad Hang**, the lower series, is overlooked by the **Tad Lo Lodge** and **Saise Guesthouse**, while **Tad Lo**, the upper, is a short hike away.

Mekong islands

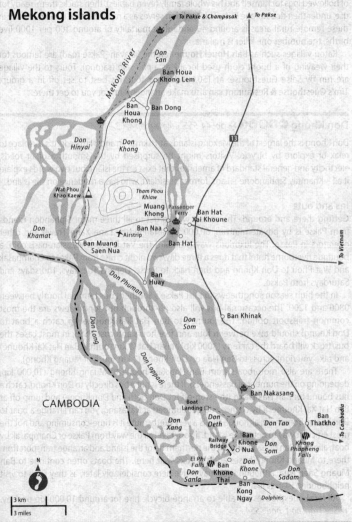

A new Community Guides office has been established with a number of trained guides offering treks around the Tad Lo area and to nearby Ngai villages. Elephant treks can also be arranged from here for US$5 per elephant for a 90-minute trek through the jungle and river.

There are two Alak villages, **Ban Khian** and **Tad Soung**, close to Tad Lo. Tad Soung is approximately 10 km away from the main resort area and are the most panoramic falls in the vicinity. The Alak are an Austro-Indonesian ethno-linguistic group. Most fascinating is the Alak's seeming obsession with death. The head of each household carves coffins out of hollowed logs for himself and his whole family (even babies), then stacks them, ready for use, under their rice storage huts. This tradition serves as a reminder that life expectancy in these remote rural areas is around 40 and infant mortality of around 100 per 1000 live births; the number one killer is malaria.

Katou villages such as **Ban Houei Houne** (on the Salavan–Pakse road) are famous for their weaving of a bright cloth used locally as a *pha sinh* (sarong). Tours to the village are run by **Saise Guesthouse**: at 150,000 kip per tour, it's best to set off in a group. **Tim's Guesthouse & Restaurant** can also make arrangements for you to get there.

Don Khong ◐❼✳◖◗ ▶▶ pp544-555. Colour map 4, C3.

Don Khong is the largest of the Mekong islands at 16 km long and 8 km wide. It's the place to relax or explore by bicycle. Visitors might be surprised by the smooth asphalt roads, electricity and general standard of amenities that exist on the island but two words explain it all – Khamtay Siphandone – Laos' former president, who has a residence on the island.

Ins and outs

Getting there and around The easiest way to get to all three major Siphandon islands from Pakse is by private minivan, 60,000 kip arranged by **Lane Xang Travel** and other operators in Pakse. The luxurious way is aboard the Vat Phou, www.asian-oasis.com, a boutique riverborne hotel that does a three day/two night cruise from Pakse to Champasak and Wat Phou to Don Khong and then back to Pakse. Departs Tuesdays, Thursdays and Saturdays from Pakse.

In the high season songthaews depart Pakse's Southern bus terminal hourly between 0800 and 1200. The occasional bus will also ply through but songthaews are the most common transport option. The journey to **Ban Hat Xai Khoune** (to catch a boat to Don Khong) should take between four and five hours and cost US$3; in most cases the bus/truck will board the car ferry (3000 kip) at **Ban Hat** (1 km south of Ban Hat Xai Khoune) and take you right across to **Ban Naa** on Don Khong (1 km south of Muang Khong).

There are also motorboats from Ban Hat Xai Khoune to Muang Khong (10,000 kip, depending on the number of passengers). If there is not a bus directly to Don Khong, catch a bus bound for **Ban Nakasang** (the stop-off for Don Deth and Don Khone) and jump off at Ban Hat Xai Khoune. If by chance you get dumped at Nakasang, you can arrange a boat to Don Khong from there; although this is a very pretty route it is time-consuming and not the most efficient way to get to the island. If you travel all the way from Pakse or Champasak by boat, alight at Ban Houa Khong on the northern tip of the island and arrange transport from there to Muang Khong (buses and tuk-tuks wait here). The boats often continue to **Ban Muang Saen Nua**, although they may arrive here considerably later, as they tend to visit neighbouring islands first.

All local guesthouses are able to arrange bicycle hire for around 10,000 kip per day.
▶▶ *See Transport, page 554.*

Around the island

Don Khong's 'capital' is **Muang Khong**, a small former French settlement. Pigs and chickens scrabble for food under the houses and just 50 m inland the houses give way to paddy fields. There are two wats in the town. **Wat Kan Khong**, also known as Wat Phuang Kaew, is visible from the jetty: a large gold Buddha in the *mudra* of subduing Mara garishly overlooks the Mekong. Much more attractive is **Wat Chom Thong** at the upstream extremity of the village, which may date from the early 19th century but which was much extended during the colonial period. The unusual Khmer-influenced sim may be gently decaying but it is doing so with style. The wat compound, with its carefully tended plants and elegant buildings, is very peaceful. The naga heads on the roof of the main sim are craftily designed to channel water, which issues from their mouths.

Most people come to Muang Khong as a base for visiting the **Li Phi** and **Khong Phapheng Falls** (see page 543) in the far south. However, these trips, alongside the dolphin-watching trips are much easier to arrange from Don Deth or Don Khone. This island is a destination in itself and offers a great insight into Lao rural life without all the hustle and bustle found in more built-up areas. To a certain extent, save electricity, a sprinkling of cars and a couple of internet terminals, time stands still in Dong Khong.

The island itself is worth exploring by bicycle and deserves more time than most visitors give it. It is flat – except in the interior where there are approximately 99 hills – the roads are quiet, so there is less risk of being mown down by a timber truck, and the villages and countryside offer a glimpse of traditional Laos. Most people take the southern 'loop' around the island, via **Ban Muang Saen Nua**, a distance of about 25 km (two to three hours by bike). The villages along the section of road south of **Ban Muang Saen Nua** are picturesque with buffalos grazing and farmers tending to their rice crops. Unlike other parts of Laos the residents here are fiercely protective of their forests and logging incurs very severe penalties.

About 6 km north of Ban Muang Saen Nua is a hilltop wat, which is arguably Don Khong's main claim to national fame. **Wat Phou Khao Kaew** (Glass Hill Monastery) is built on the spot where an entrance leads down to the underground lair of the nagas, known as **Muang Nak**. This underground town lies beneath the waters of the Mekong, with several tunnels leading to the surface – another is at That Luang in Vientiane. Lao legend has it that the nagas will come to the surface to protect the Lao whenever the country is in danger.

Tham Phou Khiaw is tucked away among the forests of the **Green Mountain** in the centre of the island. It's a small cave, containing earthenware pots. Buddha images and other relics and offerings litter the site. Every Lao New Year (April) townsfolk climb up to the cave to bathe the images. Although it's only 15 minutes' walk from the road, finding the cave is not particularly straightforward except during Lao New Year when it is possible to follow the crowds. Head 1.5 m north from Muang Khong on the road until you come to a banana plantation, with a couple of wooden houses. Take the pathway just before the houses through the banana plantation and at the top, just to the left, is a small gateway through the fence and a fairly well-defined path. Head up and along this path and, after 300 m or so, there is a rocky clearing. The path continues from the top right corner of the clearing for a further 200 m to a rocky mound that rolls up and to the left. Walk across the mound for about 20 m, until it levels out, and then head back to the forest. Keeping the rock immediately to your right, continue round and after 40 m there are two upturned tree trunks marking the entrance to the cave.

On the northern tip of the island is a sandy beach. Note that swimming is generally not advised due to parasites in the water and potentially strong currents. There is a rumour that Laos' former president, Khamtay Siphandone, will be building a resort here in the next few years. In nearby **Wat Houa Khong**, approximately 13 km north of Muang Khong, is the former President's modest abode set in traditional Lao style.

Don Deth, Don Khone and around ○○○▲○○○ ›› pp544-555. Colour map 4, C3.

The islands of Don Khone and Don Deth are the pot of gold at the end of the rainbow for most travellers who head to the southern tip of Laos, and it's not hard to see why. The bamboo huts that stretch along the banks of these two staggeringly beautiful islands are filled with contented travellers in no rush to move on. Don Deth is more of a backpacker haven, not dissimilar to the Koh Phangans and Vang Viengs of the region, meanwhile Don Khone has been able to retain a more authentically Lao charm. Travelling by boat in this area is very picturesque: the islands are covered in coconut palms, flame trees, stands of bamboo, kapok trees and hardwoods; the river is riddled with eddies and rapids. In the distance, a few kilometres to the south, are the Khong Hai Mountains, which dominate the skyline and delineate the border between Laos and Cambodia.

In the area are the Li Phi (or Somphamit) Falls and Khong Phapheng Falls – the latter are the largest in Southeast Asia and reputedly the widest in the world.

The French envisaged Don Deth and Don Khone as strategic transit points in their grandiose masterplan to create a major Mekong highway from China. In the late 19th century, ports were built at the southern end of Don Khone and at the northern end of Don Deth and a narrow-gauge railway line was constructed across Don Khone in 1897 as an important bypass around the rapids for French cargo boats sailing upriver from Phnom Penh. In 1920, the French built a bridge across to Don Deth and extended the railway line to Don Deth port. This 5-km stretch of railway has the unique distinction of being the only line the French ever built in Laos. On the southern side of the island lie the rusted corpses of the old locomotive and boiler car. Before pulling into Ban Khone Nua, the main settlement on Don Khone, Don Deth's original 'port' is on the right, with what remains of its steel rail jetty.

Ins and outs

A number of companies run tours to this area, especially from Pakse. To get to Don Deth or Don Khone independently from Pakse the bus/songthaew will need to drop you off at **Ban Nakasang**. This is not the most pleasant of Lao towns and several travellers have complained about being ripped off here. However, it has a thriving market, where most of the islanders stock up on goods, so it's worth having a look around before you head off, particularly if you need to pick up necessities like torches, batteries and film. It's a 500-m walk from the bus stop down to the dock. The 'ticket office' is located in a little restaurant to the right-hand side of the dock. However, you can ask anyone that's jumping across to the islands for a lift, at a dramatically reduced rate. The boats take about 15 to 20 minutes to make the easy trip to the islands and cost around US$3 per person. Prices will be higher (US$5-6) if you are travelling solo. A boat between Don Deth and Don Khone costs 30,000 kip; alternatively you can walk between the two islands, paying the 9000 kip charge to cross the bridge (also used as ticket to see Li Phi Falls). Both islands can easily be navigated on foot or bicycles can be rented from guesthouses for US$1 per day. ›› *See Activities and tours, page 551, and Transport, page 555.*

Don Deth → *Colour map 4, C3.*

The riverbank here is peppered with cheap-as-chips bamboo huts and restaurants geared to accommodate the growing wave of backpacker travellers that flood south to stop and

Don Deth & Don Khone

Sleeping
Auberge Sala Don
  Khone **11**
Boun Guesthouse **13**
Deng Guesthouse **18**
Lamphone Bungalows **25**
Mama Leuah **9**

Mama Mon & Papa **20**
Mama Tan On **4**
Miss Noy's **2**
Mr B's **3**
Mr Tho's **27**
Pan's Guesthouse **26**
Salaphae **10**
Santiphab Guesthouse **5**
Sompamit Guesthouse **12**
Souksan Guesthouse
  & Restaurant **1**
Xaymountry Residence **15**

Eating
Pool Room **5**

recoup in this idyllic setting. A good book, hammock and icy beverage is the order of the day here, but those with a bit more energy should explore the truly stunning surroundings. It's a great location for watching the sunrises and sunsets, for walking through shady palms and frangipani trees and for swimming off the beaches, which attract the hordes in the dry season. Away from the picturesque waterfront, the centre of the island comprises rice paddies and farms; you should take care not to harm crops when exploring the island.

The national tourism authorities have been coordinating with locals to ensure that the beautiful island doesn't become 'Vang Vieng-ified', so you'll find no *Friends* DVDs here, although 'happy' shakes have started appearing. The island has no electricity (except for a generator supply 1800-2200), no cars (except for the odd truck) and few other modern conveniences. Internet has amazingly made its way to the island, however, and it's possible to get mobile phone coverage. There has been talk for years about electricity coming to the island but for now it seems unlikely. Most guesthouses run tours to the falls/dolphins. A few entrepreneurial types are starting to promote adventure tourism here. Kayaking and rafting trips can be organized through **Xplore-asia/Lang Xang Travel** ① *near the main port, US$20 (minimum 4 people), T031-212893, www.xplore-asia.com.* Several guesthouses also have tubes for rent for 5000 kip. It is definitely inadvisable to go tubing in the wet season and probably not a good idea all year round. Swimming, visiting the falls and other activities all need to be undertaken with the utmost caution here. The river's current is probably the strongest in all of Laos and several tourists have drowned here.

Don Khone → *Colour map 4, C3.*

From the railway bridge, follow the south-west path through **Ban Khone Thai** and then wind through the paddy fields for 1.7 km (20 minutes' walk) to **Li Phi Falls** ① *9000 kip paid at the bridge.* Also known as Somphamitor or Khone Yai Falls, these are a succession of rapids, crashing through a narrow gorge. In the wet season, when the rice is green, the area is beautiful; in the dry season, it is scorching. From the main vantage point on a jagged, rocky outcrop, the falls aren't that impressive, as a large stretch of them are obscured. 'Phi' means ghost, a reference, it is believed, to the bodies that floated down the river from the north during the war. It's best to visit Li Phi around June or July, when all the fishermen are putting out their bamboo fish traps. These are dangerous waterfalls, do not swim here.

The Mekong, south of Don Khone, is one of the few places in the world where it is possible to see freshwater dolphins. They can be spotted in the late afternoon from December to May, from the French pier at the end of the island, not far from the village of **Ban Hang Khon**. The walk across Don Khone from the railway bridge is some 4 km and bicycles can be hired. It is more likely, however, to catch a glimpse of the dolphins if you're in a boat (US$5), as they reside in deep water pools. In 1996 there were thought to be 30 dolphins, after which numbers seemed to decline and, according to local data, there were fears that only four or five were left, although a new calf has recently been spotted. The Laos-Cambodia border transects the dolphin pool and the Lao boatmen have to pay US$1 to the Cambodian authorities in order to access the waters in which the dolphins live. Cambodia gets a bit tetchy about these 'border incursions' and may, on the odd occasion, deny access. ►► *See Activities and tours, page 551.*

Khong Phapheng Falls → *Colour map 4, C3.*
① *Near Ban Thatkho, US$1. Guesthouses organize trips for around 60,000 kip per person (minimum 5 passengers), usually be booked in conjunction with a trip to see the dolphins.*
About 36 km south of Ban Hat Xai Khoune at Ban Thatkho, a road branches off Route 13 towards Khong Phapheng Falls, which roar around the eastern shore of the Mekong for 13 km. One fork of the road leads to a vantage point, where a large wooden structure, built up on stilts, overlooks the cascades for a fantastic head-on view of the falls. When you see the huge volume of white water boiling and surging over the jagged rocks below, it is hard to imagine that there is another 10 km width of river running through the other channels. A path leads down from the viewpoint to the edge of the water, be very careful here. Unsurprisingly, the river is impassable at this juncture. Another road leads down to the bank, 200 m away, just above the lip of the falls; at this deceptively tranquil spot, the river is gathering momentum before it plunges over the edge. Boatmen will do a trip to both the falls and the dolphins for US$10, however, sometimes police will not allow it You can also visit the falls by catching a songthaew from Ban Nakasang, US$10 return.

◉ Far south listings

For Sleeping and Eating price codes, see inside the front cover.

◉ Sleeping

Pakse *p533, map p532*
A-D Champasak Palace, No 13 Rd, T031-212 263, champasak_palace_hotel@yahoo.com. This is a massive hotel, conceived as a palace

for a minor prince. There are some large rooms and 40 more modern, less elaborate rooms, which were added in 2000. Recent renovations have resulted in a loss of the original character but some classic touches remain. The restaurant is one of the most atmospheric place to eat in town, set on a big veranda. The friendly staff speak a smattering of English, there's a good terrace and the facilities are the best in town and include a massage centre. It's in a great position above the Xe Don and there are stunning views from the higher levels.

C-E Champa Residence (Residence du Champa), No 13 Rd, east of town near the stadium and museum, T031-212120, champare@laotel.com. Modern-style rooms, with a/c, minibar, hot water and satellite TV. Very clean, with some character. Visa accepted and tours arranged. Includes breakfast.

C-F Pakse Hotel, No 5 Rd (facing the new market), T031-212131, www.hotelpakse.com. This is one of the nicest places to stay in town with 65 rooms. The French owner, Mr Jérôme, has integrated local handicraft decorations and tasteful furnishings into this slick hotel. Good rooftop restaurant with a perfect view over the city and river, the dimly lit eatery oozes ambience. Breakfast included. Wi-Fi.

D-E Sang Aroun, Route 13, T031-252111. The most modern hotel in town, 58 rooms with cable TV and a/c. The more expensive rooms have baths. Modern but lacks character.

D-F Salachampa, No 10 Rd, T031-212273. The most characterful place in town. Choose a room in the main 1920s building: huge with large en suite bathrooms with warm-water showers; the upstairs rooms with balconies are best. There are quaintly rustic rooms in a 'new' extension. Recommended for those looking for a touch of colonial elegance and friendly service. Exceptional value for money.

G Sabaidy 2 Guesthouse, No 24 Rd, T031-212992, www.sabaidy2laos.com. A range of rooms on offer, from dorms to rooms with private bathrooms and hot water. Quite basic but the service is exceptional. The proprietor, Mr Vong offers tours, information and visa extensions. Very popular, you may need to book in advance. Basic food available. Motorbike rental.

Champasak p534

E-F Souchitra, along the river, T031-212366. A collection of cabins. Rooms with fridge, a/c and hot water, many are decorated with posters. The rooms in the newer annexe are better.

E-G Anouxa Guesthouse, 1 km north of the roundabout, T031-213272. A wide range of accommodation, from wooden bungalows to concrete rooms with hot water and either a/c (pay extra) or fan. The concrete villas are the best, with a serene river vista from the balconies. The restaurant is probably one of the best in town, overlooking the river and a shady cabana. The only drawback is that it is a little way out of town. Bikes for hire.

E-G Vong Pasued Guesthouse, 450 m south of the roundabout, T020-2712402. The grimy, dingy shop-front façade is deceiving, as out the back, beside the river, are a range of rooms to suit all budgets. A firm favourite with backpackers. The US$5 rooms by the river are great value; clean with hot water. The more basic US$3 rooms (mosquito nets, thin walls and cold water) in an old longhouse are a bit run down. Good restaurant, perfect for meeting fellow travellers.

G Khamphouy Guesthouse, west of Dokchampa. Family-run place. Bright but basic rooms in the main house with shared facilities and 1 cottage with 2 rooms and an en suite shower. Clean, comfortable, friendly and relaxed. Bikes for hire.

Don Daeng Island p536

A La Folie Lodge, T030-5347603, www.la folie-laos.com. 24 rooms housed in wooden bungalows, each with its own balcony. The lodge has a swimming pool surrounded by landscaped tropical gardens. Restaurant with good wine and cocktail selection.

G Homestays are offered in a community-lodge in Ban Hua Don Daeng for US$2. The wooden lodge has 2 common rooms, sleeping 5 people and has shared bathrooms and a dining area.

Xe Pian National Protected Area p536

C-E Kingfisher Ecolodge, 700 m east of Kiet Ngong, T030-5345016, www.kingfishereco lodge.com. Bonafide ecolodge. In the main lodge, wooden and thatched rooms with shared bathroom. More expensive are the glass-fronted bungalows. The restaurant, on the 2nd floor of the lodge affords stunning views over the Pha Pho wetlands.

G Boun Home Guesthouse, Ban Kiet Ngong, T030-5346293. Very basic guesthouse with wooden rooms and shared facilities.

Paksong and around *p538*

C-E Tad Fan Resort, T020-5531400, www. tadfane.com. Perched on the opposite side of the ravine from the falls is a series of wooden bungalows with nicely decorated rooms and en suite bathrooms (hot showers). The 2nd floor of the excellent open- air restaurant offers the best view of the falls and serves a wide variety of Lao, Thai and Western food. Great service. Treks to the top of falls and the Dan-Sin-Xay Plain can be arranged.

G Borlaven Guesthouse, Route 23 about 2 km north of the market, beyond Paksong town, T030-5758086. The new brick and wood building has a cabin feel and is surrounded by coffee trees, cornfields and a flower garden. The simple rooms are bright and clean with en suite bathrooms but no hot water. Very friendly owner speaks English.

Tad Yeung *p538*

G Sihom Sabaidy Guesthouse, at the time of writing Mr Vong from **Sabaidy 2** in Pakse was opening the new **Sihom Sabaidy Guesthouse** here. It is the only operational guesthouse in the vicinity of these falls. There are 8 basic rooms with shared hot-water bathrooms. There is an adjoining restaurant offering basic Lao meals, noodles, eggs and coffee. The guesthouse is set on a coffee plantation and tours are available to the waterfall as well as to nearby orchid areas and tours to see how coffee is made.

Tad Lo and around *p538*

C-G Saise Guesthouse (aka **Sayse Guesthouse**), T034-211886. The guesthouse, comprises 2 sections: the lower part sits near the restaurant at the foot of Tad Hang and consists of rooms and bungalows, all with hot water and fans. The more attractive and peaceful option is the so-called **Green House**

(the roof's a giveaway) above the falls. This is a wooden chalet with 6 huge rooms, 4 with en suite shower and toilet, and 2 of those with balconies overlooking the river. The beautiful garden restaurant offers Lao and Thai food. Breakfast is included with most rooms.

D-E Tad Lo Lodge, T034-211889, souriyavincent@yahoo.com. Reception on the east side of the falls with chalet-style accommodation (13 rooms) built right on top of the waterfalls on the opposite side; it's a bit of a hike from one to the other. Rates include breakfast and hot water. It's an attractive location during the wet season and the accommodation is comfortable; cane rocking chairs on the balconies overlook the cascades on the left bank. Good restaurant serving plenty of Lao and Thai food.

G Tim's Guesthouse & Restaurant, down the bridge road, T020-5648820, soulideth@ gmail.com. Twin and double wooden bungalows with hot water, fans and lock boxes. Soulideth is full of local information and advice. Also offers internet access (expensive at 1000 kip per min), international calls, room service, a laundry service, book exchange and a substantial music collection. Runs a good range of services, including bike rentals and just about anything else you could ask for.

Don Khong *p540*

Most of the guesthouses in Dong Khong have undergone name changes in recent years due to a change in legislation that requires any guesthouse with 14 or more rooms to be called a hotel and pay double the tax.

C-D Senesothxeune Hotel, Muang Khong, T031-5280577, www.ssxhotel.com. Tastefully designed, modern interpretation of colonial Lao architecture. Each room is fitted with mod cons like a/c, TV, hot water and minibar. Superior rooms have fantastic baths. For those willing to splurge, upgrade to the suite that comes with spa and living area for US$70. The hotel has a modern internet café and a restaurant. This relatively new hotel is the island's best accommodation by a long shot and is run by Mr Senesavath and his wife, both former mathematics professors from Don Dok University in Vientiane. Both speak English and French. Recommended.

C-D Villa Muong Khong Hotel Guesthouse, T031-2130111, www.khongislandtravel.com. This hotel is part chalet, part mock Tudor, part Lao and part Thai – all amalgamated together by someone with a fetish for wagon wheels and concrete. Despite the architecture, this guesthouse is in a perfect location and offers affordable rooms. It is popular with tour groups. The rooms are large but a little spartan. All the mod cons. Internet available.

C-E Auberge Sala Done Khong, Muang Khong, T031-212077, www.salalao.com. This traditional wooden house, the former holiday home of the previous regime's foreign minister, was once the best place to stay on Don Khong but although the exterior is still stunning the rooms just aren't worth the price. There are 12 tastefully decorated, large rooms with a/c and en suite hot-water bathrooms; the best are in the main building on the 1st floor where there is a balcony overlooking the Mekong. Starting to get a little bit run-down, but clean and professionally run. Tours and massages arranged, bicycles for hire, good food and very relaxing. Slightly cheaper rate in the low season.

C-G Mekong Hotel, Muang Khong, T031-213668. Simple, spotless rooms with fans, some overlooking the Mekong. Some rooms have a/c and hot-water showers (US$20). There are also cheaper rooms with shared facilities (equally clean) in a wooden building.

C-G Souksan Hotel, northern end of Muang Khong near Wat Chom Thong, T031-212071. Well-designed a/c rooms with en suite bathrooms and hot water, set around a concrete garden. US$5 fan rooms represent exceptional value. If you want a/c the price is hiked to US$30. They also run one of the most up-market guesthouses on Don Deth.

D-G KhangKong Villa Guesthouse, back from the main road, central Muang Khong, T031-213539. Fantastic traditional Lao wooden building. Spacious, clean rooms, with or without a/c.

E-G Pon Hotel and Restaurant, Muang Khong, T031-214037. The large, spotless rooms are very good value, with hot-water showers, mosquito nets and comfortable beds (US$6). For US$10 you get a/c. Mr Pon, who speaks French and English, is perhaps the most helpful of all accommodation proprietors on the island and can offer an endless supply of tourist information and travel arrangements. Motorbike rental, US$10 or ½-day, US$5 and bicycles, US$1 per day. He can also arrange trips to the Cambodian border, to Don Deth and Don Khone and back to Pakse. Mr Pon is a regular Mr Fix-it and should be your first point of contact. Massage can be organized in your room for 50,000 kip. Recommended.

Don Deth p542, map p543

Many people tend to make their choice of accommodation based on word-of-mouth recommendations from other travellers. Accommodation normally consists of spartan, threadbare bungalows with bed, mosquito net, hammock and shared squat toilets (unless otherwise stated). Always opt for a bungalow with a window, as the huts can get very hot. The wooden bungalows don't provide as much ventilation as the rattan equivalents but tend to attract fewer insects. Note that there may be a small price hike in the near future to ensure that tourism benefits all of the islands inhabitants, including the farmers. Costs are likely to double once the island gets electricity.

The accommodation runs across the both sides of the island, known as the **Sunset Side** and the **Sunrise Side**. There is a large conglomeration of accommodation towards the northern tip, which is a good option for those wishing to socialize and hop between the various establishments' restaurants/bars; this is also the most common drop-off point. As a general rule, if you want peace and quiet, head for the bungalows towards the mid-point along each coast; ask the boat drivers to drop you off directly at the bungalows as it can be a difficult hike with bags. There is very little difference between most lodgings on Don Deth, so if you're looking for inspirational accommodation pop across to Don Khone.

Sunset Side

E-G Souksan Guesthouse and Restaurant, Houa Deth at the northern tip of the island, at the pinnacle of the Sunset and Sunrise sides, T031-212071. There are 20 or so twin and double rooms with shared shower and toilets, not to mention a legendary Chinese restaurant. There are also a couple of concrete bungalows that are slightly more expensive. This place unfairly get a bad rap by those looking for ultra-budget accommodation, however if you're looking for something a little more comfortable this is the island's only option. This is the hands-down winner on the island and more than worth the extra few bucks. That being said, Don Khone offers better accommodation at a more reasonable price.
G Miss Noy's, very close to the island tip and a small hike from the main drop-off point, this place offers an excellent view of the sunset. Restaurant is in a prime position with a good variety of dishes. The service here is exceptional. The owners are about to open several, clean concrete bungalows which should be very comfortable and one of the island's more promising offerings.
G Mr B's, near the northern tip. The bungalows and grounds themselves are a bit lacklustre and the chickens pecking around in the backyard don't make for the most pleasing surroundings. However, the river views and the helpful staff make this an outstanding option.

Sunrise Side

F Mama Leuah, on the south side of the former French concrete port towards the centre of the island. Several bungalows that have seen better days. Shared squat toilet.
G Deng Guesthouse, next to **Mr Oudomsouk's**. Wooden bungalows on stilts. Very popular with those who want to laze in a hammock overlooking the water.

G Lamphone Bungalows, mid-way down the island. 3 rattan bungalows, basic but lovely. The restaurant here is good and an added bonus is the resident Australian baker who cooks up a mean focaccia, and chocolate and banana doughnuts.
G Mama Mon and Papa, on the northern peninsula. Typical thatched bamboo bungalows with mosquito nets and shared facilities. Nice shady position. The restaurant has battery-powered lights for the night-time blackout and serves exceptional lentil curry.
G Mama Tan On, T020-5835699. This place changes its name every year but the atmosphere remains unchanged. One of the first bungalows on the island. If you are having trouble finding it, try asking for some of its previous incarnations **Mama Rasta** or **Mama Tanon Rasta**. There is a beautiful view from the balcony and the effervescent Mama is good value. Small library. The place is somewhat rundown, with rattan huts and communal facilities but it is a popular place to hang out in hammocks.
G Mr Tho's, T020-6567502. Wooden stilt bungalows, good hammocks and views of Don Khone. The staff are friendly. Rooms have been given unusual names, such as 'sticky rice bungalow' and 'bamboo bungalow'. Restaurant attached.
G Santiphab Guesthouse, far end of the island, facing Don Khone. 7 basic rattan bungalows right beside the bridge, most have the quintessential hammock. Idyllic setting, flanked by the Mekong on one side and rice paddies on the other. Good for those who want seclusion but also quick access to Don Khone. Very cheap restaurant serves tasty fare with buckets of atmosphere. Very little English spoken. A friendly, timeless place.

Don Khone *p543, map p543*

Although Don Deth attracts the vast majority of tourists, Don Khone holds its own by offering some very pleasant accommodation alternatives and close proximity to most of the attractions. In general, Don Khone evokes a much friendlier atmosphere.

C-E Salaphae, along from **Auberge Sala Don Khone**, T030-5256390, www.salalao.com. This is the most unique accommodation in the whole Siphandon area. 3 raft-houses (and 6 rooms) are managed by ex-lawyer Lesotho. Rooms have been decorated simply, with all the minor touches that can make accommodation outstanding. Hot-water bathrooms, a wonderful deck overlooking the river and a fantastic restaurant. Starting to get a little run down but still a fantastic option. The proprietor also plans to create a deluxe campsite and bungalows on another nearby island, Khon Pasoi which is 1.5 km from Don Khong. When these are completed they will be a great option for those tourists truly wanting to get away from it all. Check website for details.

C-F Auberge Sala Don Khone, Ban Khone Nua, T020-5633718, www.salalao.com. A former French hospital built in 1927, this is one of the nicest places to stay on the island. 2 traditional Luang Prabang-style houses have also been built in the grounds, with 6 rooms, all with en suite hot-water shower and toilet, some with a/c. The restaurant, across from the guesthouse, is one of the best places to dine on any of the 3 islands. It offers an unobscured waterfront view, comfy deckchairs and a good selection of food that offers a welcome change from the menus found in every other establishment. Generator 1800-2200. Reduced rate in low season. Organizes tours and boat trips. The manager is very informative and speaks excellent English.

D-E Pan's Guesthouse, opposite **Xaymountry**, T030-5346939. A relative newcomer to Don Khone, these wooden bungalows are exceptionally good value for money. 6 simple and very clean riverside bungalows with hot water, fan and comfy mattresses. The proprietor runs a small generator which means the fans in stay on into the early hours. The owner, Mr Pan, is one of the most helpful hosts in Siphandon. Highly recommended for those on a limited budget.

G Boun Guesthouse, next door to **Auberge Sala Don Khone**. Mr Boun has built a couple of basic thatched bungalows with shared facilities, and a few newer wooden bungalows complete with en suite bathrooms.

G Sompamit Guesthouse, across from **Boun Guesthouse**, on the riverside, T020-5733145. Threadbare rattan thatched bungalows with mosquito nets and shared cold-water bathroom facilities. Also a couple of basic rooms with en suite bathrooms.

G Xaymountry Residence, towards the bridge, T020-5735755. This splendid old wooden villa does not live up to the potential grandeur of its exterior. Clean en suite bathrooms, some shared. No river views but a magnificent old building.

● Eating

Pakse p533, map p532

There are a couple of fantastic *sindat* (barbeque) places near the Da Heung market that are extremely popular with the locals.

If the weather is fine, the **Pakse Hotel** has a fantastic rooftop restaurant offering a range of Lao dishes plus pretty good pizza. It has an excellent selection of coffees.

Ψ Delta Coffee, Route 13, opposite the **Champasak Palace Hotel**, T020-5345895. This place is a real find for those craving some Western comfort food. The extensive menu is varied and offers everything from pizza and lasagne to Thai noodles. The coffee is brilliant and the staff are very friendly.

Ψ Jasmine Restaurant, No 13 Rd, T031-251 002. This small place has outdoor seating and is a firm favourite with travellers. Offering the standard Indian fare and a few Malaysian dishes, it's reasonable value.

Ψ Nazim's Restaurant, nearly next door to the **Jasmine**. A similar selection of Indian/Malaysian dishes, the service is a little slower.

Ψ Xuan Mai, near **Pakse Hotel**, T031-213245. Vietnamese restaurant with outdoor kitchen and eating area. Good shakes and fresh spring rolls. Can be a bit hit and miss.

Champasak p534

Most restaurants are located in the guesthouses; all are cheap (¶).

¶ **Anouxa Guesthouse**, see Sleeping. Has a small but delectable menu and lovely restaurant set over the river; opt for a fish dish. They also have a selection of wines.

¶ **Vong Paseud Guesthouse**, see Sleeping. Has a cheap and extensive menu ranging from backpacker favourites like pancakes through to *tom yum* soup.

Xe Pian National Protected Area p536

Eating in Ban Kiet Ngong is very basic and you will have to rely on the local food. *Feu* and noodle soup can be made on the spot.

¶ **The Kingfisher Ecolodge**, see Sleeping. A fantastic restaurant serving a range of Western and Lao dishes. Also stocks wine.

Paksong and around p538

¶ **Borravan Plateau**, Route 23 about 1 km from the market towards Tha Teng. Standard selection of Lao dishes in an indoor setting, safe from the weather. Unfortunately there is no menu and no English spoken – so opt for something easy like *feu* or *laap*. The owner is very friendly.

Tad Lo p538

¶ **Tad Lo Lodge**, see Sleeping. A variety of Thai, Lao and Western dishes on offer.

¶ **Tim's Guesthouse**, see Sleeping. A popular restaurant serving good hearty breakfasts and some generic Western dishes.

Don Khong p541

The majority of restaurants only serve fish and chicken. In the low season most restaurants will only be able to fulfil about half of the menu options. Special dishes such as a roast or *hor mok* will also need to be ordered at least a few hours, if not a day, in advance to ensure the proprietors have the required produce in stock. Although many other towns and areas also make such a claim, Don Khong is renowned for the quality of its *lao-lao* (rice liquor). Local fish with coconut

milk cooked in banana leaves, *mok pa*, is truly a divine local speciality and makes a trip to the islands worthwhile in itself.

¶¶–¶ **Souksan Chinese Restaurant**, Muang Khong. Attractive place on the Mekong with a stunning view of the river. Funnily enough there is an absence of Chinese food but there are other more generic Asian options, including good local fish and tasty honeyed chicken. In recent years a number of Western specialities have been added to the menu, including the US$5 roast (beef, chicken or pork with potatoes and gravy), which needs to be ordered a day in advance.

¶ **Mekong Restaurant**, attached to the **Mekong Hotel**. This restaurant is pleasantly positioned near the bank of the Mekong and provides legendary fare at seriously low prices. Good *feu*.

¶ **Pon's Restaurant**, see Sleeping. Good atmosphere and excellent food, try the fish soup. Also the *mok pa* here is excellent, order in advance. Very popular.

Don Deth p542, map p543

Most people choose to eat at their guesthouses; they all have pretty much the same menu.

¶¶–¶ **Mr B's**, see Sleeping. Italian bruschetta, rice pudding and a selection of burgers including chicken and pumpkin. Good cocktails.

¶¶–¶ **The Pool Room and Restaurant**, near the main port. Has a pool table and fantastic Indian and Malay food. Good service.

¶ **Miss Noy's**, see Sleeping. A large menu with some good Western offerings, a change from the rest of the places on the island.

¶ **Souksan Guesthouse and Restaurant**, see Sleeping. Excellent Chinese-inspired dishes in addition to well-cooked fish. The restaurant is in a prime location to take in sunset and the chef will cook up a roast for US$5 with advanced notice.

Don Khone p543, map p543

¶¶ **Auberge Sala Don Khone**, see Sleeping. There's a beautiful view from the restaurant and some fine options on the menu, such as tuna and orange salad, and steak salad. The service here is 5-star. Some of the more complicated options will need to be booked in advance.

†† Salaphae, see Sleeping. The best choice on the island, with a selection of scrumptious and creative dishes.

† Pan's Restaurant, see Sleeping. Across from the guesthouse, this is a fantastic, cheap option serving up brilliant home-made meals. The fish here is outstanding.

❋ Festivals and events

Wat Phou p534
Feb (movable) **Wat Phou Festival** lasts for 3 days around the full moon of the 3rd lunar month. Pilgrims come from far and wide to leave offerings at the temple. In the evening there are competitions – football, boat racing, bullfighting and cockfighting, Thai boxing, singing contests and the like.

Tad Lo p538
Mar Buffalo ceremony. This traditional Tahoy ceremony (see box, page 537) takes place in a nearby village on the 1st full moon in Mar and is dedicated to the warrior spirit, whom the local tribesmen ask for protection. Villagers are happy for tourists to come and watch (5000 kip per person). The spectacle kicks off at about 2000, with dancing; the buffalo is sacrificed the next morning at 0500. Throughout the day, the entire village shares the meat of the sacrificed animal, as well as leaving some choice pieces for the spirits of the dead warriors in the Ceremony House. **Tim's Guesthouse** (see Sleeping) is the best place to go for information about this event.

Don Khong p540
Dec A 5-day **Boat Racing** festival on the river opposite Muang Khong. It coincides with National Day on 2 Dec and is accompanied by a great deal of celebration, eating and drinking.

○ Shopping

Don Deth p542, map p543
There isn't much to buy here. A small grocery store across from the port has a few essential items and snacks but is not well stocked. If you're in desperate need of any items, make a quick trip to Ban Nakasang and pick up things from the market there. Most guesthouses go to Ban Nakasang on an almost daily basis and will usually buy things for you if you pay them 5000 kip or so.

▲ Activities and tours

Pakse p533, map p532
Tour operators
Most of the hotels in town arrange day tours to Wat Phou and Tad Lo; of these the best is the **Pakse Hotel**. There are a number of tour agencies in town.
Green Discovery, on the main road, T031-252908, www.greendiscoverylaos.com. Offers a range of adventure tours and eco-tourism treks around Champasak Province including Ban Kiet Ngong, rafting, kayaking and cycling trips. Highly recommended.
Lane Xang Travel, opposite **Jasmine Restaurant**, T020-2255176 (also known as **Xplore Asia**), www.xplore-asia.com. Offers a variety of tours and useful tour services (including a minivan service to Siphandon).
Sabaidy 2, see Sleeping, T031-212992. Mr Vong and crew offer a wide range of tours around a variety of top-notch provincial sites, very good value and recommended for visitors who are only around for 1-2 days (US$15 per person, 4 people min).

Xe Pian National Protected Area p536
There are several 2- to 3-day trekking and homestay trips offered in the area. These include elephant treks across the **Xe Pian** forests, wetlands and rocky outcrops; treks from Kiet Ngong Village to the top of **Phu Asa**; and birdwatching trips. There is also a 2-day canoe/trekking trip called the **Ta Ong**

Trail with guides trained in wildlife and the medicinal uses of plants. These tours are designed to ensure that local communities reap the rewards of tourism in a sustainable fashion and are highly recommended. The **Kingfisher Lodge** (see Sleeping), T030-534 5016, can arrange for you to train how to be a bona fide elephant rider with a traditional *mahout* (elephant keeper). Alternatively, contact the Provincial Tourism Office in Pakse, T031-212021.

Elephant treks
Elephant treks to the **Phu Asa** take about 2 hrs, US$13; the elephant baskets can carry 2 people. If you wish to travel independently to this area, you need to allow enough time for the elephants to be organized by the *mahouts* (elephant keepers) once you arrive. Contact **Boun Hom Guesthouse**, T030-534 6293 in advance. Although only minimal English is spoken in the village, most locals will understand the purpose of your visit.

Boloven Plateau *p537*
To organize kayaking and rafting trips to the Boloven Plateau contact **Green Discovery** in Pakse, see above.

Tad Lo *p538*
Elephant treks
This is an excellent way to see the area as there are few roads on the plateau and elephants can go where jeeps cannot. Contact any of the guesthouses for information (50,000 kip per person; 2 people per elephant).

Don Deth *p542, map p543*
Almost every guesthouse on the island can arrange tours, transport and tickets. The best way to book yourself onto a tour is through the new 'whiteboard' system. Whiteboards have been placed around the island (the most popular one is at the northern end, near the port); simply write your name down next to the tour or trip you wish to take.

Dolphin watching, boats from **Don Deth** leave when they have enough passengers

and charge about US$6 per person; put your name on the noticeboard the day before. Rates are highly subject to change as they are based on petrol prices and the individual boatman more than anything else. The best bet is to gather a group of 4 or 5 people together and then approach a boatman.

Khammunysai Bungalows organizes fishing trips, though most tour operators would be able to organize a day out fishing if you asked. All tour operators offer trips to **Khon Phapeng**, 70,0000 kip each, minimum 4 people.

For boat trips further afield, see Transport, page 555.

Don Khone *p543, map p543*
From Don Khone, it is possible to hire a boat for the day, to visit the islands and go fishing or dolphin watching. Boats depart from Kong Ngay, US$10, see Transport, page 555.

Swimming
There is a sandy beach on **Don Khone** where many travellers like to swim. In the wet season this can be dangerous as there is a nasty undercurrent and tourists have drowned, so be careful. Also bear in mind the risk of schistosomiasis.

❸ Transport

Pakse *p533, map p532*
Air
To Vientiane, Siem Reap and Phnom Penh, check with **Lao Airlines** for the latest information; it has offices at the airport and by the river in town, T031-212252. **Bangkok Airways** also runs flights direct to/from Bangkok a couple of times a week, US$140-one way.

Boat
Boats are much more irregular now that the roads have improved. Boats to Champasak are on again–off again. Ask around to see what the latest status is. If you have enough

people and money it is possible to charter a boat to Don Khong or Champasak, contact **Mr Boun My**, T020-5631008.

Bus/songthaew
You can charter a tuk-tuk to the airport, northern bus station or southern bus station for about 30,000 kip. To get to the VIP bus station, 2 km from the town centre, at *talaat lak song* costs about 10,000 kip.

Northern terminal 7 km north of town on Route 13. Local buses leave hourly 0800-1500 to **Savannakhet**, 5-6 hrs, 30,000 kip; to **Thakhek**, 8-9 hrs, 60,000 kip; to **Lak Sao**, 8-9 hrs, 75,000 kip; to **Vientiane**, 16-18 hrs, 85,000 kip. Local buses can be painfully slow due to the number of stops they make. For those heading to Vientiane it makes more sense to pay a couple of extra dollars and get on the much quicker and more comfortable VIP bus at the VIP station.

Southern terminal 8 km south of town of Route 13. There are Regular connections with **Champasak**; stay on the bus if you are travelling to **Wat Phou** (see page 534). Ask for Ban Lak Sarm Sip (translates as 'village 30 km'), here there is a signpost and you turn right and travel 4 km towards Ban Muang (5 km). In the village there are people selling tickets for the ferry. Local buses coming through from Vientiane provide the main means of transport to other destinations down south, so can be slightly off kilter. Buses depart for **Salavan**, 4 daily, 2-3 hrs, 20,000 kip. This is a good alternative for those wishing to head to **Tad Lo** 20,000 kip, just make sure that the bus is taking Route 20 (not Route 23) and that the driver understands you want to get off at the junction. Songthaews to the Bolaven Plateau; **Paksong**, 5 morning departures, 20,000 kip; **Tad Fan**, 5 morning departures, 1 hr, 15,000 kip; **Tha Theng**, 5 morning departures, 20,000 kip; A songthaew leaves for Ban Kiet Ngong at 1300, 2-3 hrs, 20,000 kip.

Buses/songthaews leave for Siphandon between 1000 and 1400 (Muang Khong) 3-4 hrs, 35,000 kip; for Ban Nakasang (the closest port to Don Deth/Don Khone) several departures between 0730 and 1400, 3-4 hrs, 30,000 kip. Several of the buses to Ban Nakasang also stop at Ban Hat Xai Khoune (the stop-off for Don Khong). Make sure that you let the bus/songthaew driver know that you are going to Ban Nakasang or Ban Hat Xai Khoune rather than saying the name of the islands.

A more comfortable alternative to Siphandon is to take the minivan service to **Don Deth/Don Khong** offered by **Lane Xang Travel**, 2 hrs, 60,000 kip. This is highly recommended as, once you have paid all the fees involved with local transport, it costs about the same. It is also a shorter trip.

VIP bus terminal Near the football stadium and Talaat Lak Song, T031-212228, just off Route 13. VIP buses to Ubon (Thailand) leave at 0800 and 01730, 200฿; VIP seat buses leave for Vientiane at 2000 arriving at 0600 (stopping in Thakhek en route), 150,000 kip. A VIP sleeping bus with comfy beds, duvet, cake and films leaves at 0830 arriving in Vientiane at 0600 (stopping en route to Thakhek), 150,000 kip. The beds are double, so unless you book 2 spaces you might end up sleeping next to a stranger. If you're tall ask for a bed towards the back of the bus. Make sure you secure your belongings on any of the overnight buses, as some passengers have sticky fingers.

Dao Heung market, the morning market, has regular songthaews for Champasak in the morning, 15,000 kip.

Motorbike/bicycle
Sabaidy 2, see Sleeping. Rents motorbikes with insurance for US$8 for the 1st day and US$7 for consecutive days. The **Lankham Hotel**, off Rd 13, rents bicycles for US$1 per day, standard small bikes US$8 and larger dirt bikes US$20 per day.

Tuk-tuk/saamlor
A tuk-tuk to the northern bus station should cost 30,000 kip. Shared tuk-tuks to local

villages leave from the Daoheung market and from the stop on No 11 Rd near the jetty. Tuk-tuks can also be chartered by the hour.

Champasak *p534*
A shared local songthaew to **Ban Thong Kop**, the village opposite Wat Phou costs around 10,000 kip; direct to **Wat Phou** is US$5-10 return (chartered).

Paksong and around *p538*
Regular connections to **Pakse**, 0630-1600, 1½ hrs, 15,000 kip.

Tad Lo *p538*
There are buses from Ban Houa Set (1.5 km north of Tad Lo) to **Pakse**, 5 daily, 20,000 kip. You may be able to catch the daily service to **Vientiane** on its way north, 0930 and 1430, 85,000 kip, don't expect it to be on time.

Don Khong *p540*
Boat
See also Ins and outs, page 540. **Pon's Hotel** (reliable and recommended) can arrange boats to **Don Deth** or **Don Khone**. There are also several boatmen on the riverfront who are more than happy to take people for the right price. Fares tend to fluctuate according to international fuel prices but the going rate at the time of publication was US$15-20 for up to 10 people, one way. Expect to pay 40,000 kip per person. Most leave around 0800-0830.

Chartering a boat to or from Pakse costs around US$100-140 (max 20 people) and will take about 8 hrs but is seldom done.

Bus or truck
A bus to **Pakse** departs from the intersection near Wat Kan Khong daily at around 0800 but it's worth asking the guesthouse owners for the most recent transport information; for earlier departures to **Pakse**, cross to **Ban Hat Xai Khoune** and try for transport south. Songthaews and buses head to Pakse on the hour from 0600-0900, 3-4 hrs, US$4.

Public buses for Don Khong leave from Pakse's Southern bus terminal to Ban Hat Xai Khoune. When you are at the bus terminal the bus drivers will get confused if you tell them that you want to go to **Siphandon/ Don Deth/Don Khong/ Don Khone**. You must explicitly tell them which village you are alighting at – to Ban Hat Xai Khoune (if you are bound for Don Khong) and Ban Nakasang (if you are bound for Don Deth or Don Khone). Buses depart for Ban Hat Xai Khoune hourly from 0600-0900, 3-4 hrs, 40,000 kip.

There is a minibus service from Pakse (recommended) which picks you up directly from your hotel and drops you off at either Ban Nakasang or Ban Hat Xai Khoune, 2 hrs, 60,000 kip. This actually works out to be much more cost-effective and saves time, most guesthouses in Pakse can arrange it. The return minivan service can be organized by Mr Pon for 70,000 kip, and includes the ferry ride and a hotel drop off in Pakse (2 hrs).

Don Deth, Don Khone and around *p542, map p543*
Ban Nakasang
Boat To **Don Deth** and **Don Khone**, 15-20 mins, 30,000 kip per person. To **Don Khong**, 2 hrs, US$15-20 (divided between passengers).

Bus/songthaew Decent buses depart from Ban Nakasang's market hourly between 0600-1000, north-bound for **Pakse**, 40,000 kip; some continue onwards to **Vientiane**; get off at **Ban Hat Xai Khoune** for the crossing to **Don Khong**, US$1. Most guesthouses can organize a trip to Dom Kralor (on the Cambodian border). Cambodian visas are available on the border but Lao visas weren't at the time of publication. Most guesthouses will sell tickets on a minivan to Stung Treng, the largest town on the other side of the Cambodian border, 2 hrs, 130,000 kip. Tickets can be organized to Kratie or Phnom Penh.

Buses to **Dom Kralow** (for the Cambodia border; see page 112) depart in the morning, 13 km, US$1; alternatively, you can charter a songthaew for US$5, or hire a motorbike.

To **Khong Phapheng**, take a tuk-tuk or motorcycle taxi for around US$6-7 return.

Don Deth and Don Khone
Guesthouses organize boat trips around the area; rates are susceptible to change: to **Ban Nakasang**, 30,000 kip per person; to **Khong Phapheng Falls**, 60,000 kip, min 5 people.

There are 2 ways to get to **Don Khong**, from Ban Nakasang, either by boat, 2 hrs, US$15, or by bus (see above); motorbike tax is also make the trip for US$3. Although it's slower and more expensive, the boat trip is one of the loveliest in Laos. Boat trip around the sites and islands costs US$15-20, per day.

ⓘ Directory

Pakse *p533, map p532*
Banks BCEL Bank, No 11 Rd (beside the river), changes US$ and most currencies, and offers a better commission rate on cash exchange than other banks, also Visa/MasterCard cash advances at 3% commission, Mon-Fri 0830-1530, they have a MasterCard only ATM; **Lao Development Bank**, No 13 Rd, T031-212168, cash and TCs exchanged; there is a branch of the **Lao Viet Bank** on the main road but it only changes TCs and cash, open Mon-Fri 0830-1530. **Embassies and consulates** Vietnam, No 24 Rd, Mon-Fri 0800-1300, 1400-1630, visas for Vietnam cost US$50 and take 3 days, so you are better off organizing your Vietnamese visa in Vientiane. **Internet** Expect to pay around 200 kip per min but discounts kick in usually after 1 hr: **D@M's Internet & Email Service**, No 13 Rd; **Medical services** There is a huge hospital between No 1 Rd and No 46 Rd, T031-212 018, but neither their English skills nor medical service will suffice for complex cases; in case of emergencies go across to Ubon in

Thailand; there is a pretty good pharmacy at the hospital which stocks most medications. **Police** T031-212145. **Post office** No 8 Rd, overseas telephone calls can also be made from here. **Telephone** Telecommunications office for fax and overseas calls on No 1 Rd, near No 13 Rd; all internet cafés have Skype.

Don Khong (Muang Khong) *p540*
Banks There is a basic **Lao Agriculture Promotion** bank in town; hours are erratic and it accepts only US$ or Thai ฿; guesthouses will also exchange cash at rates slightly poorer than market rate; a photocopy of your passport may be required. **Internet** Alpha Internet offers internet and Skype at 1000 kip per min; also burn CDs, hire canoes and do laundry. **Post and telephone** The post office is opposite the jetty; international dialling available.

Don Deth *p542, map p543*
Banks There are no banks on the island; a foreign exchange service near the port will change most major currencies; Mr B of **Mr B's** guesthouse will organize the cashing of TCs, but the commission here is quite hefty, so you are better off organizing your cash from Pakse. **Immigration** The **Riverside Restaurant** can organize Cambodian visas in 3 working days for US$55 or 5 working days for US$45. **Internet** There is a small internet café across from the port junction, 1000 kip per min; calls can also be made, min 10 mins. **Telephone** Most guesthouses will let you make calls from their mobiles, which can be incredibly expensive, up to US$4 a min.

Don Khone *p543, map p543*
Electricity No mains electricity but many places run generators daily 1800-2200. **Post and telephone** Guesthouses may allow you to make international calls from their mobile phones, for up to US$4 per min.

Background

Scholars of Lao history, before they even begin, need to decide whether they are writing a history of Laos; a history of the Lao ethnic group; or histories of the various kingdoms and principalities that have, through time, been encompassed by the present boundaries of the Lao People's Democratic Republic. Historians have tended to confront this problem in different ways without, often, acknowledging on what basis their 'history' is built. It is common to see 1365, the date of the foundation of the kingdom of Lane Xang, as marking the beginning of Lao history. But, as Martin Stuart-Fox points out, prior to Lane Xang the principality of Muang Swa, occupying the same geographical space, was headed by a Lao. The following account provides a brief overview of the histories of those peoples who have occupied what is now the territory of the Lao PDR.

Archaeological and historical evidence indicates that most Lao originally migrated south from China. This was followed by an influx of ideas and culture from the Indian subcontinent via Myanmar (Burma), Thailand and Cambodia – something which is reflected in the state religion, Theravada Buddhism.

Being surrounded by large, powerful neighbours, Laos has been repeatedly invaded over the centuries by the Thais (or Siamese) and the Vietnamese – who both thought of Laos as their buffer zone and backyard. They too have both left their mark on Lao culture. In recent history, Laos has been influenced by the French during the colonial era, the Japanese during the Second World War, the Americans during the Indochinese wars and, between 1975 and the early 1990s, by Marxism-Leninism.

It is also worth noting, in introduction, that historians and regimes have axes to grind. The French were anxious to justify their annexation of Laos and so used dubious Vietnamese documents to provide a thin legal gloss to their actions. Western historians, lumbered with the baggage of Western historiography, ignored indigenous histories. And the Lao People's Revolutionary Party uses history for its own ends too. The official three volume *History of Laos* is currently being written by Party-approved history hacks. The third volume (chronologically speaking) was published in 1989 and, working back in time, the first and second thereafter. As Martin Stuart-Fox remarks in his *A History of Laos*, "the Communist regime is as anxious as was the previous Royal Lao government [pre-1975] to establish that Laos has a long and glorious past and that a continuity exists between the past and the present Lao state". In other words, Laos has not one history, but many.

First kingdom of Laos

Myth, archaeology and history all point to a number of early feudal Lao kingdoms in what is now South China and North Vietnam. External pressures from the Mongols under Kublai Khan and the Han Chinese forced the Tai tribes to migrate south into what had been part of the Khmer Empire. The mountains to the north and east served as a cultural barrier to Vietnam and China, leaving the Lao exposed to influences from India and the West. There are no documentary records of early Lao history (the first date in the Lao chronicles to which historians attach any real veracity is 1271), although it seems probable that parts of present-day Laos were annexed by Lannathai (Chiang Mai) in the 11th century and by the Khmer Empire during the 12th century. But neither of these states held sway over the entire area of Laos. Xieng Khouang, for example, was probably never under Khmer domination. This was followed by strong Siamese influence over the cities of Luang Prabang and Vientiane under the Siamese Sukhothai Dynasty. Laos (the country) in effect did not exist, although the Laos (the people) certainly did.

The downfall of the kingdom of Sukhothai in 1345 and its submission to the new Siamese Dynasty at Ayutthaya (founded in 1349) was the catalyst for the foundation of what is commonly regarded as the first truly independent Lao Kingdom – although there were smaller semi-independent Lao *muang* (city states) existing prior to that date.

Fa Ngum and Lane Xang

The kingdom of Lane Xang (Lan Chang) emerged in 1353 under Fa Ngum, a Lao prince who had grown up in the Khmer court of Angkor. There is more written about Fa Ngum than about the following two centuries of Lao history. It is also safe to say that his life is more fiction than fact. Fa Ngum was reputedly born with 33 teeth and was banished to Angkor after his father, Prince Yakfah, was convicted of having an incestuous affair with a wife of King Suvarna Kamphong. In 1353 Fa Ngum led an army to Luang Prabang and confronted his grandfather, King Suvarna Kamphong. Unable to defeat his grandson on the battlefield, the aged king is said to have hanged himself and Fa Ngum was invited to take the throne. Three years later, in 1356, Fa Ngum marched on Vientiane – which he took with ease – and then on Vienkam, which proved more of a challenge. He is credited with piecing together Lang Xang – the Land of a Million Elephants – the golden age to which all histories of Laos refer to justify the existence (and greatness) of Laos.

In some accounts Lang Xang is portrayed as stretching from China to Cambodia and from the Khorat Plateau in present-day Northeast Thailand to the Annamite mountains in the east. But it would be entirely wrong to envisage the kingdom controlling all these regions. Lane Xang probably only had total control over a comparatively small area of present-day Laos and parts of Northeast Thailand; the bulk of this grand empire would have been contested with other surrounding kingdoms. In addition, the smaller *muang* and principalities would themselves have played competing powers off, one against another, in an attempt to maximize their own autonomy. It is this 'messiness' which led scholars of Southeast Asian history to suggest that territories as such did not exist, but rather zones of variable control. The historian OW Wolters coined the term *mandala* for "a particular and often unstable political situation in a vaguely defined geographical area without fixed boundaries and where smaller centres tended to look in all directions for security. *Mandalas* would expand and contract in concertina-like fashion. Each one contained several tributary rulers, some of whom would repudiate their vassal status when the opportunity arose and try to build up their own network of vassals".

Legend relates that Fa Ngum was a descendant of Khoum Borom, "a king who came out of the sky from South China". He is said to have succeeded to the throne of Nanchao in 729, aged 31, and died 20 years later, although this historical record is, as they say, exceedingly thin. Khoum Borom is credited with giving birth to the Lao people by slicing open a gourd in Muong Taeng (Dien Bien Phu, Vietnam) and his seven sons established the great Tai kingdoms. He returned to his country with a detachment of Khmer soldiers and united several scattered Lao fiefdoms. In those days, conquered lands were usually razed and the people taken as slaves to build up the population of the conquering group. (This largely explains why today there are far more Lao in northeastern Thailand than in Laos – they were forcibly settled there after King Anou was defeated by King Rama III of Siam in 1827 – see page 560.) The kings of Lane Xang were less philistine, demanding only subordination and allegiance as one part of a larger *mandala*.

Luang Prabang became the capital of the kingdom of Lane Xang. The unruly highland tribes of the northeast did not come under the kingdom's control at that time. Fa Ngum made Theravada Buddhism the official religion. He married the Cambodian king's daughter, Princess Keo Kaengkanya, and was given the Pra Bang (a golden statue, the most revered religious symbol of Laos), by the Khmer court.

It is common to read of Lane Xang as the first kingdom of Laos; as encompassing the territory of present-day Laos; and as marking the introduction of Theravada Buddhism to the country. On all counts this portrait is, if not false, then deeply flawed. As noted above, there were Lao states that predated Lane Xang; Lane Xang never controlled Laos as it currently exists; and Buddhism had made an impact on the Lao people before 1365. Fa Ngum did not create a kingdom; rather he brought together various pre-existing *muang* (city states) into a powerful *mandala*. As Martin Stuart-Fox writes, "From this derives his [Fa Ngum's] historical claim to hero status as the founder of the Lao Kingdom." But, as Stuart-Fox goes on to explain, there was no central authority and rulers of individual *muang* were permitted considerable autonomy.

After Fa Ngum's wife died in 1368, he became so debauched, it is said, that he was deposed in favour of his son, Samsenthai (1373-1416), who was barely 18 when he acceded the throne. He was named after the 1376 census, which concluded that he ruled over 300,000 Tais living in Laos; *samsen* means, literally, 300,000. He set up a new administrative system based on the existing *muang*, nominating governors to each that lasted until it was abolished by the Communist government in 1975. Samsenthai's death was followed by a period of unrest. Under King Chaiyachakkapat-Phaenphaeo (1441-1478), the kingdom came under increasing threat from the Vietnamese. How the Vietnamese came to be peeved with the Lao is another story which smacks of fable more than fact. King Chaiyachakkapat's eldest son, the Prince of Chienglaw, secured a holy white elephant. The emperor of Vietnam, learning of this momentous discovery, asked to be sent some of the beast's hairs. Disliking the Vietnamese, the Prince dispatched a box of its excrement instead, whereupon the Emperor formed an army of an improbably large 550,000 men. The Prince's army numbered 200,000 and 2000 elephants. The massive Vietnamese army finally prevailed and entered and sacked Luang Prabang. But shortly thereafter they were driven out by Chaiyachakkapat-Phaenphaeo's son, King Suvarna Banlang (1478-1485). Peace was only fully restored under King Visunarat (1500-1520).

Increasing prominence and Burmese incursions

Under King Pothisarath (1520-1548) Vientiane became prominent as a trading and religious centre. He married a Lanna (Chiang Mai) princess, Queen Yotkamtip, and when the Siamese King Ketklao was put to death in 1545, Pothisarath's son claimed the throne at Lanna. He returned to Lane Xang when his father died in 1548. Asserting his right as successor to the throne, he was crowned Setthathirat in 1548 and ruled until 1571 – the last of the great kings of Lane Xang.

At the same time, the Burmese were expanding East and in 1556 Lanna fell into their hands. Setthathirat gave up his claim to that throne, to a Siamese prince, who ruled under Burmese authority. (He also took the Phra Kaeo – Thailand's famous 'Emerald' Buddha and its most sacred and revered image – with him to Luang Prabang and then to Vientiane. The Phra Kaeo stayed in Vientiane until 1778 when the Thai general Phya Chakri 'repatriated' it to Thailand.) In 1563 Setthathirat pronounced Vieng Chan (Vientiane) the principal capital of Lane Xang. Seven years later, the Burmese King Bayinnaung launched an unsuccessful attack on Vieng Chan itself.

Setthathirat is revered as one of the great Lao kings, having protected the country from foreign domination. He built Wat Phra Kaeo (see page 462) in Vientiane, in which he placed the famous Emerald Buddha brought from Lanna. Setthathirat mysteriously disappeared during a campaign in the southern province of Attapeu in 1574, which threw the kingdom into crisis. Vientiane fell to invading Burmese the following year and remained under Burmese control for seven years. Finally the anarchic kingdoms of Luang Prabang and Vientiane were reunified under Nokeo Koumane (1591-96) and Thammikarath (1596-1622).

Disputed territory

From the time of the formation of the kingdom of Lane Xang to the arrival of the French, the history of Laos was dominated by the struggle to retain the lands it had conquered. Following King Setthathirat's death, a series of kings came to the throne in quick succession. King Souligna Vongsa, crowned in 1633, brought long awaited peace to Laos. The 61 years he was on the throne are regarded as Lane Xang's golden age. Under him, the kingdom's influence spread to Yunnan in South China, the Burmese Shan States, Issan in Northeast Thailand and areas of Vietnam and Cambodia.

Souligna Vongsa was even on friendly terms with the Vietnamese: he married Emperor Le Thanh Ton's daughter and he and the Emperor agreed the borders between the two countries. The frontier was settled in a deterministic – but nonetheless amicable – fashion: those living in houses built on stilts with verandas were considered Lao subjects and those living in houses without piles and verandas owed allegiance to Vietnam.

During his reign foreigners first visited the country, but other than a handful of adventurers, Laos remained on the outer periphery of European concerns and influence.

The three kingdoms

After Souligna Vongsa died in 1694, leaving no heir, dynastic quarrels and feudal rivalries once again erupted, undermining the kingdom's cohesion. In 1700 Lane Xang split into three: Luang Prabang under Souligna's grandson, Vientiane under Souligna's nephew and the new kingdom of Champasak was founded in the south 'panhandle'. This weakened the country and allowed the Siamese and Vietnamese to encroach. *Muang*, which previously owed clear allegiance to Lane Xang, began to look towards Vietnam or Siam. Isan muang in present day Northeast Thailand, for example, paid tribute to Bangkok; while Xieng Khouang did the same to Hanoi and, later, to Hué. The three main kingdoms that emerged with the disintegration of Lane Xang leant in different directions: Luang Prabang had close links with China, Vientiane with Vietnam's Hanoi/Hué and Champassak with Siam.

By the mid-1760s Burmese influence once again held sway in Vientiane and Luang Prabang and before the turn of the decade, they sacked Ayutthaya, the capital of Siam. Somehow the Siamese managed to pull themselves together and only two years later in 1778 successfully rampaged through Vientiane. The two sacred Buddhas, the Phra Bang and the Phra Kaeo (Emerald Buddha), were taken as booty back to Bangkok. The Emerald Buddha was never returned and now sits in Bangkok's Wat Phra Kaeo (see page 462).

King Anou (an abbreviation of Anurutha), was placed on the Vientiane throne by the Siamese. With the death of King Rama II of Siam, King Anou saw his chance of rebellion, asked Vietnam for assistance, formed an army and marched on Bangkok in 1827.

In mounting this brave – some would say foolhardy – assault, Anou was apparently trying to emulate the great Fa Ngum. Unfortunately, he got no further than the Northeast Thai town of Korat where his forces suffered a defeat and were driven back. Nonetheless, Anou's rebellion is considered one of the most daring and ruthless rebellions in Siamese history and he was lauded as a war hero back home.

King Anou's brief stab at regional power was to result in catastrophe for Laos – and tragedy for King Anou. The first US arms shipment to Siam allowed the Siamese to sack Vientiane, a task to which they had grown accustomed over the years. (This marks America's first intervention in Southeast Asia.) Lao artisans were frogmarched to Bangkok and many of the inhabitants were resettled in Northeast Siam. Rama III had Chao Anou locked in a cage where he was taunted and abused by the population of Bangkok. He died soon afterwards, at the age of 62. One of his supporters is said to have taken pity on the king and brought him poison, other explanations simply say that he wished himself dead or that he choked. Whatever the cause, the disconsolate Anou, before he died, put a curse on Siam's monarchy, promising that the next time a Thai king set foot on Lao soil, he would die. To this day no Thai king has crossed the Mekong River. When the agreement for the supply of hydroelectric power was signed with Thailand in the 1970s, the Thai king opened the Nam Ngum Dam from a sandbank in the middle of the Mekong.

Disintegration of the kingdom

Over the next 50 years, Anou's Kingdom was destroyed. By the time the French arrived in the late 19th century, the virtually unoccupied city was subsumed into the Siamese sphere of influence. Luang Prabang also became a Siamese vassal state, while Xieng Khouang province was invaded by Chinese rebels – to the chagrin of the Vietnamese, who had always considered the Hmong mountain kingdom (they called it Tran Ninh), to be their exclusive source of slaves. The Chinese had designs on Luang Prabang too and in order to quash their expansionist instincts, Bangkok dispatched an army there in 1885 to pacify the region and ensure the north remained firmly within the Siamese sphere of influence. This period was one of confusion and rapidly shifting allegiances.

The history of Laos during this period becomes, essentially, the history of only a small part of the current territory of the country: namely, the history of Luang Prabang. And because Luang Prabang was a suzerain state of Bangkok, the history of that kingdom is, in turn, sometimes relegated to a mere footnote in the history of Siam.

The French and independence

Following King Anou's death, Laos became the centre of Southeast Asian rivalry between Britain, expanding east from Burma and France, pushing west through Vietnam. In 1868, following the French annexation of South Vietnam and the formation of a protectorate in Cambodia, an expedition set out to explore the Mekong trade route to China. Once central and north Vietnam had come under the influence of the Quai d'Orsay in Paris, the French became increasingly curious about Vietnamese claims to chunks of Laos. Unlike the Siamese, the French – like the British – were concerned with demarcating borders and establishing explicit areas of sovereignty. This seemed extraordinary to most Southeast Asians at the time who could not see the point of mapping space when land was so abundant. However, it did not take long for the Siamese king to realize the importance of maintaining his claim to Siamese territories if the French in the east and the British in the south (Malaya) and west (Burma) were not to squeeze Siam to nothing.

However, King Chulalongkorn was not in a position to confront the French militarily and instead he had to play a clever diplomatic game if his kingdom was to survive. The French, for their part, were anxious to continue to press westwards from Vietnam into the Lao lands over which Siam held suzerainty. Martin Stuart-Fox argues that there were four main reasons underlying France's desire to expand West: the lingering hope that the Mekong might still offer a 'back door' into China; the consolidation of Vietnam against attack; the 'rounding out' of their Indochina possessions; and a means of further pressuring Bangkok. In 1886, the French received reluctant Siamese permission to post a vice consul to Luang Prabang and a year later he persuaded the Thais to leave. However, even greater humiliation was to come in 1893 when the French, through crude gunboat diplomacy – the so-called Paknam incident – forced King Chulalongkorn to give up all claim to Laos on the flimsiest of historical pretexts. Despite attempts by Prince Devawongse to manufacture a compromise, the French forced Siam to cede Laos to France and, what's more, to pay compensation. It is said that after this humiliation, King Chulalongkorn retired from public life, broken in spirit and health. So the French colonial era in Laos began.

What is notable about this spat between France and Siam is that Laos – the country over which they were fighting – scarcely figures. As was to happen again in Laos' history, the country was caught between two competing powers who used Laos as a stage on which to fight a wider and to them, more important, conflict.

Union of Indochina
In 1893 France occupied the left bank of the Mekong and forced Thailand to recognize the river as the boundary. The French Union of Indochina denied Laos the area which is now Isan, northeast Thailand, and this was the start of 50 years of colonial rule. Laos became a protectorate with a *résident-superieur* in Vientiane and a vice-consul in Luang Prabang. However, Laos could hardly be construed as a 'country' during the colonial period. "Laos existed again", writes Martin Stuart-Fox, "but not yet as a political entity in its own right, for no independent centre of Lao political power existed. Laos was but a territorial entity within French Indochina." The French were not interested in establishing an identifiable Lao state; they saw Laos as a part and a subservient part at that, of Vietnam, serving as a resource-rich appendage. Though they had grand plans for the development of Laos, these were only expressed airily and none of them came to anything. "The French were never sure what to do with Laos", Stuart-Fox writes. Unlike Cambodia to the south, the French did not perceive Laos to have any historical unity or coherence and therefore it could be hacked about and developed or otherwise, according to their whim.

In 1904 the Franco-British convention delimited respective zones of influence. Only a few hundred French civil servants were ever in Vientiane at any one time and their attitude to colonial administration – described as 'benign neglect' – was as relaxed as the people they governed. To the displeasure of the Lao, France brought in Vietnamese to run the civil service (in the way the British used Indian bureaucrats in Burma). But for the most part, the French colonial period was a 50-year siesta for Laos. The king was allowed to stay in Luang Prabang, but had little say in administration. Trade and commerce was left to the omni-present Chinese and the Vietnamese. A small, French-educated Lao élite did grow up and by the 1940s they had become the core of a typically laid-back Lao nationalist movement.

Japanese coup
Towards the end of the Second World War, Japan ousted the French administration in Laos in a coup in March 1945. The eventual surrender of the Japanese in August that year

gave impetus to the Lao independence movement. Prince Phetsarath, hereditary viceroy and premier of the Luang Prabang Kingdom, took over the leadership of the Lao Issara, the Free Laos Movement (originally a resistance movement against the Japanese). They prevented the French from seizing power again and declared Lao independence on 1 September 1945. Two weeks later, the north and south provinces were reunified and in October, Phetsarath formed a Lao Issara government headed by Prince Phaya Khammao.

France refused to recognize the new state and crushed the Lao resistance. King Sisavang Vong, unimpressed by Prince Phetsarath's move, sided with the French, who had their colony handed back by British forces. He was crowned the constitutional monarch of the new protectorate in 1946. The rebel government took refuge in Bangkok. Historians believe the Issara movement was aided in their resistance to the French by the Viet Minh – Hanoi's Communists.

Independence

In response to nationalist pressures, France was obliged to grant Laos ever greater self government and, eventually, formal independence within the framework of the newly reconstructed French Union in July 1949. Meanwhile, in Bangkok, the Issara movement had formed a government-in-exile, headed by Phetsarath and his half-brothers: Prince Souvanna Phouma (see box, page 564) and Prince Souphanouvong. Both were refined, French-educated men. The Issara's military wing was led by Souphanouvong who, even at that stage, was known for his Communist sympathies. This was due to a temporary alliance between the Issara and the Viet Minh, who had the common cause of ridding their respective countries of the French. Within just a few months the so-called Red Prince had been ousted by his half-brothers and joined the Viet Minh where he is said to have been the moving force behind the declaration of the Democratic Republic of Laos by the newly-formed Lao National Assembly. The Lao People's Democratic Republic emerged – albeit in name only – somewhere inside Vietnam, in August 1949. Soon afterwards, the Pathet Lao (the Lao Nation) was born. The Issara movement quickly folded and Souvanna Phouma went back to Vientiane and joined the newly formed Royal Lao Government.

By 1953, Prince Souphanouvong had managed to move his Pathet Lao headquarters inside Laos and with the French losing their grip on the north provinces, the weary colonizers granted the country full independence. France signed a treaty of friendship and association with the new royalist government and made the country a French protectorate.

The rise of Communism

French defeat

While all this was going on, King Sisavang Vong sat tight in Luang Prabang instead of moving to Vientiane. But within a few months of independence, the ancient royal capital was under threat from the Communist Viet Minh and Pathet Lao. Honouring the terms of the new treaty, French commander General Henri Navarre determined in late 1953 to take the pressure off Luang Prabang by confronting the Viet Minh who controlled the strategic approach to the city at Dien Bien Phu. The French suffered a stunning defeat which presaged their withdrawal from Indochina. The subsequent occupation of two north Lao provinces by the Vietnam-backed Pathet Lao forces, meant the kingdom's days as a Western buffer state were numbered. The Vietnamese, not unlike their previous neighbours, did not respect Laos as a state, but as a extension of their own territory to be utilized for their own strategic purposes during the ensuing war.

With the Geneva Accord in July 1954, following the fall of Dien Bien Phu in May, Ho Chi Minh's government gained control of all territory north of the 17th parallel in neighbouring Vietnam. The Accord guaranteed Laos' freedom and neutrality, but with the Communists on the threshold, the US was not prepared to be a passive spectator: the demise of the French sparked an increasing US involvement. In an operation that was to mirror the much more famous war with Vietnam to the East, Washington soon found itself supplying and paying the salaries of 50,000 royalist troops and their corrupt officers. Clandestine military assistance grew, undercover special forces were mobilized and the CIA began meddling in Lao politics. In 1960 a consignment of weapons was dispatched by the CIA to a major in the Royal Lao Army called Vang Pao – or VP, as he became known – who was destined to become the leader of the Hmong.

US involvement: the domino effect

Laos had become the dreaded first domino, which, using the scheme of US President Dwight D Eisenhower's famous analogy, would trigger the rapid spread of Communism if ever it fell. The time-trapped little kingdom became the focus of superpower brinkmanship. At a press conference in March 1961, President Kennedy is said to have been too abashed to announce to the American people that US forces might soon become embroiled in conflict in a far-away flashpoint that went by the inglorious name of 'Louse'. For three decades Americans have unwittingly mispronounced the country's name as Kennedy decided, euphemistically, to label it 'Lay-os' throughout his national television broadcast.

Coalitions, coups and counter-coups

The US-backed Royal Lao Government of independent Laos – even though it was headed by the neutralist, Prince Souvanna Phouma – ruled over a divided country from 1951 to 1954. The US played havoc with Laos' domestic politics, running anti-Communist campaigns, backing the royalist army and lending support to political figures on the right (even if they lacked experience or political qualifications). The Communist Pathet Lao, headed by Prince Souphanouvong and overseen and sponsored by North Vietnam's Lao Dong party since 1949, emerged as the only strong opposition. By the mid-1950s, Kaysone Phomvihane, later prime minister of the Lao PDR, began to make a name for himself in the Indochinese Communist Party. Indeed the close association between Laos and Vietnam went deeper than just ideology. Kaysone's father was Vietnamese, while Prince Souphanouvong and Nouhak Phounsavanh both married Vietnamese women.

Government of National Union

Elections were held in Vientiane in July 1955 but were boycotted by the Pathet Lao. Souvanna Phouma became prime minister in March 1956. He aimed to try to negotiate the integration of his half-brother's Pathet Lao provinces into a unified administration and coax the Communists into a coalition government. In 1957 the disputed provinces were returned to royal government control under the first coalition government. This coalition government, much to US discontent, contained two Pathet Lao ministers including Souphanouvong and Phoumi Vongvichit. This was one of Souvanna Phouma's achievements in trying to combine the two sides to ensure neutrality, although it was only short-lived. In May 1958 elections were held. This time the Communists' Lao Patriotic Front (Neo Lao Hak Xat) clinched thirteen of the 21 seats in the Government of National Union. The Red Prince, Souphanouvong and one of his aides were included in the cabinet and former Pathet Lao members were elected deputies of the National Assembly.

Prince Souvanna Phouma

Prince Souvanna Phouma was Laos' greatest statesman. He was prime minister on no less than eight occasions for a total of 20 years between 1951 and 1975. He dominated mainstream politics from independence until the victory of the Pathet Lao in 1975. But he was never able to preserve the integrity of Laos in the face of much stronger external forces. "Souvanna stands as a tragic figure in modern Lao history," Martin Stuart-Fox writes, a "stubborn symbol of an alternative, neutral, 'middle way'."

In 1950 Souvanna became a co-founder of the Progressive Party and in the elections of 1951 he headed his first government which negotiated and secured full independence from France.

Souvanna made two key errors of judgement during these early years. First, he ignored the need for nation building in Laos. And, second, he underestimated the threat that the Communists posed to the country. With regard to the first of these misjudgements, he seemed to believe – and it is perhaps no accident that he trained as an engineer and architect – that Laos just needed to be administered efficiently to become a modern state. He appeared either to reject, or to ignore the idea that the government first had to try and inculcate a sense of Lao nationhood. The second misjudgement was his

long-held belief that the Pathet Lao was a nationalist and not a Communist organization. He let the Pathet Lao grow in strength and this, in turn, brought the US into Lao affairs.

By the time the US began to intervene in Lao affairs in the late 1950s, the country already seemed to be heading for catastrophe. But in his struggle to maintain some semblance of independence for his tiny country, he ignored the degree to which Laos was being sucked into the quagmire of Indochina. As Martin Stuart-Fox writes: "He [Souvanna] knew he was being used, and that he had no power to protect his country from the war that increasingly engulfed it. But he was too proud meekly to submit to US demands – even as Laos was subjected to the heaviest bombing in the history of warfare. At least a form of independence had to be maintained."

When the Pathet Lao entered Vientiane in victory in 1975, Souvanna did not flee into exile. He remained to help in the transfer of power. The Pathet Lao, of course, gave him a title and then largely ignored him as they pursued their Communist manifesto.

From Martin Stuart-Fox's *Buddhist Kingdom, Marxist State: the Making of Modern Laos* (White Lotus, 1996).

Almost immediately problems which had been beneath the surface emerged to plague the government. The rightists and their US supporters were shaken by the result and the much-vaunted coalition lasted just two months. Driven by Cold War prerogatives, the US could not abide by any government that contained Communist members and withdrew their aid, which the country had become much dependent upon. Between 1955 and 1958 the US had given four times more aid to Laos than the French had done in the prior eight years and it had become the backbone of the Lao economy. If Laos was not so dependent on this aid, it is quite plausible that the coalition government may have survived. The National Union fell apart in July 1958 and Souvanna Phouma was forced out of power. Pathet Lao leaders were jailed and the rightwing Phoui Sananikone came to power. With anti-Communists in control, Pathet Lao forces withdrew to the Plain of Jars in Xieng Khouang province. A three-way civil war ensued, between the rightists (backed by the US), the Communists (backed by North Vietnam) and the neutralists (led by Souvanna Phouma, who wanted to maintain independence).

Civil war

CIA-backed strongman General Phoumi Nosavan thought Phoui's politics rather tame and with a nod from Washington he stepped into the breach in January 1959, eventually overthrowing Phoui in a coup in December and placing Prince Boun Oum in power. Pathet Lao leaders were imprisoned without trial.

Within a year, the rightist regime was overthrown by a neutralist *coup d'état* led by General Kong Lae and Prince Souvanna Phouma was recalled from exile in Cambodia to become prime minister of the first National Union. Souvanna Phouma incurred American wrath by inviting a Soviet ambassador to Vientiane in October. With US support, Nosavan staged yet another armed rebellion in December and sparked a new civil war. In the 1960 general elections, provincial authorities were threatened with military action if they did not support the rightwing groups and were rigged to ensure no Pathet Lao cadres could obtain a seat in office. By this stage, the Pathet Lao had consolidated considerable forces in the region surrounding the Plain of Jars and, with support from the Vietnamese, had been able to expand their territorial control in the north. This represented a major crisis to the incoming Kennedy administration that Stuart Martin-Fox describes as "second only to Cuba".

Zurich talks and the Geneva Accord

The new prime minister, the old one and his Marxist half-brother finally sat down to talks in Zurich in June 1961, but any hope of an agreement was overshadowed by escalating tensions between the superpowers. In 1962, an international agreement on Laos was hammered out in Geneva by 14 participating nations and accords were signed, once again guaranteeing Lao neutrality. By implication, the accords denied the Viet Minh access to the Ho Chi Minh Trail. But aware of the reality of constant North Vietnamese infiltration through Laos into South Vietnam, the head of the American mission concluded that the agreement was "a good bad deal".

Another coalition government of National Union was formed under the determined neutralist Prince Souvanna Phouma (as prime minister), with Prince Souphanouvong for the Pathet Lao and Prince Boun Oum representing the right. A number of political assassinations derailed the process of reconciliation. Moreover, antagonisms between the left and the right, both backed financially by their respective allies, made it impossible for the unfunded neutralists to balance the two sided into any form of neutrality. It was no surprise when the coalition government collapsed within a few months and fighting resumed. This time the international community just shrugged and watched Laos sink back into civil war. Unbeknown to the outside world, the conflict was rapidly degenerating into a war between the CIA and North Vietnamese jungle guerrillas.

Secret war

The war that wasn't

In the aftermath of the Geneva agreement, the North Vietnamese, rather than reducing their forces in Laos, continued to increase their manpower on the ground. With the Viet Minh denying the existence of the Ho Chi Minh Trail, while at the same time enlarging it, Kennedy dispatched an undercover force of CIA men, green berets and US-trained Thai mercenaries to command 9000 Lao soldiers. By 1963, these American forces had grown to 30,000 men. Historian Roger Warner believes that by 1965 "word spread among a select circle of congressmen and senators about this exotic program run by Lone Star rednecks and Asian hillbillies that was better and cheaper than anything the Pentagon was doing in South Vietnam." To the north, the US also supplied Vang Pao's force of Hmong guerrillas, dubbed 'Mobile Strike Forces'. With the cooperation of Prince Souvanna Phouma, the CIA's commercial airline, Air America, ferried men and equipment into Laos from Thailand (and opium out, it is believed). Caught between Cold War antagonisms it was impossible to maintain a modicum of neutrality as even the most staunch neutralist, Souvanna Phouma, began to become entangled. As Robbins argues, by the early 1960s, Sovanna Phouma – trying to reinforce the middle way – had given permission "for every clandestine manoeuvre the United States made to match the North Vietnamese. In turn Souvanna demanded that his complicity in such arrangements be kept secret, lest his position in the country become untenable." Owing to the clandestine nature of the military intervention in Laos, the rest of the world – believing that the Geneva settlement had solved the foreign interventionist problem – was oblivious as to what was happening on the ground. Right up until 1970, Washington never admitted to any activity in Laos beyond 'armed reconnaissance' flights over northern provinces.

Meanwhile the North Vietnamese were fulfilling their two major strategic priorities in the country: continued use of the Ho Chi Minh trail (by this stage the majority of North Vietnamese munitions and personnel for the Viet Cong was being shuffled along the trail) and ensuring that the Plain of Jars did not fall under the control of the right, where the US could launch attacks on North Vietnam. This latter goal amounted to supporting the Pathet Lao in their aim to hold onto as much territory as possible in the north. The Pathet Lao, in turn, were dependent on the North Vietnamese for supplies – both material and manpower. With both the US bankrolling the Royalist right and the Vietnamese puppeteering the Pathet Lao, within the country any pretence of maintaining a balance in the face of Cold War hostilities was shattered for neutralists like Souvanna Phouma.

Souvanna Phouma appropriately referred to it as 'the forgotten war' and it is often termed now the 'non-attributable war'. The willingness on the part of the Americans to dump millions of tonnes of ordnance on a country which was ostensibly neutral may have been made easier by the fact that some people in the administration did not believe Laos to be a country at all. Bernard Fall wrote that Laos at the time was "neither a geographical nor an ethnic or social entity, but merely a political convenience", while a Rand Corporation report written in 1970 described Laos as "hardly a country except in the legal sense". More colourfully, Secretary of State Dean Rusk described it as a "wart on the hog of Vietnam". Perhaps those in Washington could feel a touch better about bombing the hell out of a country which, in their view, occupied a sort of political never never land – or which they could liken to an unfortunate skin complaint.

Not everyone agrees with this view that Laos never existed until the French wished it into existence. Scholar of Laos Arthur Dommen, for example, traces a true and coherent Lao identity back to Fa Ngum and his creation of the kingdom of Lane Xang in 1353, writing that is "a state in the true sense of the term, delineated by borders clearly defined and consecrated by treaty" for 350 years. He goes on:

"Lao historians see a positive proof of the existence of a distinct Lao race (sua sat Lao), a Lao nation (sat Lao), a Lao country (muong Lao) and a Lao state (pathet Lao). In view of these facts, we may safely reject the notion, fashionable among apologists for a colonial enterprise of a later day, that Laos was a creation of French colonial policy and administration".

American bombing of the North Vietnamese Army's supply lines through Laos to South Vietnam along the Ho Chi Minh Trail in East Laos started in 1964 and fuelled the conflict between the Royalist Vientiane government and the Pathet Lao. The neutralists had been forced into alliance with the Royalists to avoid defeat in Xieng Kouang province. US bombers crossed Laos on bombing runs to Hanoi from air bases in Thailand and gradually the war in Laos escalated.

America's side of the secret war was conducted from a one-room shack at the US base in Udon Thani, 'across the fence' in Thailand. This was the CIA's Air America operations room and in the same compound was stationed the 4802 Joint Liaison Detachment – or the CIA logistics office. In Vientiane, US pilots supporting Hmong General Vang Pao's rag-tag army, were given a new identity as rangers for the US Agency for International Development; they reported directly to the air attaché at the US embassy. In his book *The Ravens* (1987), Christopher Robbins writes that they "were military men, but flew into battle in civilian clothes – denim cut-offs, T-shirts, cowboy hats and dark glasses ... Their job was to fly as the winged artillery of some fearsome warlord, who led an army of stone age mercenaries in the pay of the CIA and they operated out of a secret city hidden in the mountains of a jungle kingdom ..."

The most notorious of the CIA's unsavoury operatives was Anthony Posepny – known as Tony Poe, on whom the character of Kurtz, the crazy colonel played by Marlon Brando in the film *Apocalypse Now*, was based. Originally, Poe had worked as Vang Pao's case officer; he then moved to North Laos and operated for years, on his own, in Burmese and Chinese border territories, offering his tribal recruits one US dollar for each set of Communist ears they brought back. Many of the spies and pilots of this secret war have re-emerged in recent years in covert and illegal arms-smuggling rackets to Libya, Iran and the Nicaraguan Contras.

By contrast, the Royalist forces were reluctant warriors: despite the fact that civil war was a deeply ingrained tradition in Laos, the Lao themselves would go to great lengths to avoid fighting each other. One foreign journalist, reporting from Luang Prabang in the latter stages of the war, related how Royalist and Pathet Lao troops, encamped on opposite banks of the Nam Ou, agreed an informal ceasefire over Pi Mai (Lao New Year), to jointly celebrate the king's annual visit to the sacred Pak Ou Caves (see page 489). Most Lao did not want to fight. Correspondents who covered the war noted that without the constant goading of their respective US and North Vietnamese masters, many Lao soldiers would have happily gone home. Prior to the war, one military strategist described the Lao forces as one of the worst armies ever seen, adding that they made the [poorly regarded] "South Vietnamese Army look like Storm Troopers". "The troops lack the basic will to fight. They do not take initiative. A typical characteristic of the Laotian Army is to leave an escape route. US technicians attached to the various training institutions have not been able to overcome Lao apathy". (Ratnam, P, *Laos and the Superpowers*, 1980).

Air Force planes were often used to carry passengers for money – or to smuggle opium out of the Golden Triangle. In the field, soldiers of the Royal Lao Army regularly fled when faced with a frontal assault by the Vietnam People's Army (NVA). The officer corps was uncommitted, lazy and corrupt; many ran opium-smuggling rackets and saw the war as a ticket to get rich quick. In the south, the Americans considered Royal Lao Air Force pilots unreliable because they were loath to bomb their own people and cultural heritage.

The air war

The clandestine bombing of the Ho Chi Minh Trail caused many civilian casualties and displaced much of the population in Laos' eastern provinces. By 1973, when the bombing stopped, the US had dropped over two million tonnes of bombs on Laos – equivalent to 700 kg of explosives for every man, woman and child in the country. It is reported that up to 70% of all B-52 strikes in Indochina were targeted at Laos. To pulverize the country to this degree 580,994 bombing sorties were flown. The bombing intensified during the Nixon administration: up to 1969 less than 500,000 tonnes of bombs had been dropped on Laos; from then on nearly that amount was dropped each year. In the 1960s and early 1970s, more bombs rained on Laos than were dropped during the Second World War – the equivalent of a plane load of bombs every eight minutes around the clock for nine years. This campaign cost American taxpayers more than US$2 million a day but the cost to Laos was incalculable. The activist Fred Branfman, quoted by Roger Warner in *Shooting at the Moon*, wrote: "Nine years of bombing, two million tons of bombs, whole rural societies wiped off the map, hundreds of thousands of peasants treated like herds of animals in a Clockwork Orange fantasy of an aerial African Hunting safari."

The war was not restricted to bombing missions – once potential Pathet Lao strongholds had been identified, fighters, using rockets, were sent to attempt to destroy them. Such was the intensity of the bombing campaign that villagers in Pathet Lao-controlled areas are said to have turned to planting and harvesting their rice at night. Few of those living in Xieng Khouang province, the Boloven Plateau or along the Ho Chi Minh Trail had any idea of who was bombing them or why. The consequences were often tragic, as in the case of Tham Piu Cave (see page 518).

After the war, the collection and sale of war debris turned into a valuable scrap metal industry for tribes' people in Xieng Khouang province and along the Ho Chi Minh Trail. Bomb casings, aircraft fuel tanks and other bits and pieces that were not sold to Thailand have been put to every conceivable use in rural Laos. They are used as cattle troughs, fence posts, flower pots, stilts for houses, water carriers, temple bells, knives and ploughs.

But the bombing campaign has also left a more deadly legacy of unexploded bombs and anti-personnel mines. Today, over 30 years after the air war, over 500,000 tonnes of deadly unexploded ordnance (UXO) is believed to still be scattered throughout nine of Laos' 13 provinces. Most casualties are caused by cluster bombs, or 'bombis' as they have become known. Cluster bombs are carried in large canisters called Cluster Bomb Units (CBUs), which open in mid-air, releasing around 670 tennis ball-sized bomblets. Upon detonation, the bombie propels around 200,000 pieces of shrapnel over an area the size of several football fields. This UXO contamination inhibits long-term development, especially in Xieng Khouang Province, turning Laos' fertile fields, which are critical for agricultural production, into killing zones.

The land war

Within Laos, the war largely focused on the strategic Plain of Jars in Xieng Khouang province and was co-ordinated from the town of Long Tien (the secret city), tucked into the limestone hills to the southwest of the plain. Known as the most secret spot on earth, it was not marked on maps and was populated by the CIA, the Ravens (the air controllers who flew spotter planes and called in air strikes) and the Hmong.

The Pathet Lao were headquartered in caves in Xam Neua province, to the north of the plain. Their base was equipped with a hotel cave (for visiting dignitaries), a hospital cave, embassy caves and even a theatre cave.

The Plain of Jars (colloquially known as the PDJ, after the French Plaine de Jarres), was the scene of some of the heaviest fighting and changed hands countless times, the Royalist and Hmong forces occupying it during the wet season, the Pathet Lao in the dry. During this period in the conflict the town of Long Tien, known as one of the country's 'alternate' bases to keep nosy journalists away (the word 'alternate' was meant to indicate that it was unimportant), grew to such an extent that it became Laos' second city. James Parker in his book *Codename Mule* claims that the air base was so busy that at its peak it was handling more daily flights than Chicago's O'Hare airport. Others claim that it was the busiest airport in the world. There was also fighting around Luang Prabang and the Boloven Plateau to the south.

The end of the war

Although the origins of the war in Laos were distinct from those which fuelled the conflict in Vietnam, the two wars had effectively merged by the early 1970s and it became inevitable that the fate of the Americans to the east would determine the outcome of the secret war on the other side of the Annamite Range. By 1970 it was no longer possible for the US administration to shroud the war in secrecy: a flood of refugees had arrived in Vientiane in an effort to escape the conflict.

During the dying days of the US-backed regime in Vientiane, CIA agents and Ravens lived in quarters south of the capital, known as KM-6 – because it was 6 km from town. Another compound in downtown Vientiane was known as 'Silver City' and reputedly also sometimes housed CIA agents. On the departure of the Americans and the arrival of the new regime in 1975, the Communists' secret police made Silver City their new home. Today, Lao people still call military intelligence officers 'Silvers' – and from time to time during the early 1990s, as Laos was opening up to tourism, Silvers were assigned as tour guides.

A ceasefire was agreed in February 1973, a month after Washington and Hanoi struck a similar deal in Paris. Power was transferred in April 1974 to yet another coalition government set up in Vientiane under the premiership of the ever-ready Souvanna Phouma. The neutralist prince once again had a Communist deputy and foreign affairs minister. The Red Prince, Souphanouvong, headed the Joint National Political Council. Foreign troops were given two months to leave the country. The North Vietnamese were allowed to remain along the Ho Chi Minh Trail, for although US forces had withdrawn from South Vietnam, the war there was not over.

The Communists' final victories over Saigon (and Phnom Penh) in April 1975 were a catalyst for the Pathet Lao who advanced on the capital. Grant Evans in a *Short History of Laos* says that the most intriguing element of the Communist takeover of Laos was the slow pace in which it was executed. It is widely hailed as the 'bloodless' takeover. Due to the country's mixed loyalties the Pathet Lao government undertook a gradual process of eroding away existing loyalties to the Royalist government. As the end drew near and the Pathet Lao began to advance out of the mountains and towards the more populated areas of the Mekong valley – the heartland of the Royalist government – province after province fell with scarcely a shot being fired. The mere arrival of a small contingent of Pathet Lao soldiers was sufficient to secure victory – even though these soldiers arrived at Wattay Airport on Chinese transport planes to be greeted by representatives of the Royal Lao government. It is even possible that they were not even armed.

Administration of Vientiane by the People's Revolutionary Committee was secured on 18 August. The atmosphere was very different from that which accompanied the Communist's occupation of Saigon in Vietnam the same year. In Vientiane peaceful crowds of several hundred thousand turned out to hear speeches by Pathet Lao cadres. The King remained unharmed in his palace and while a coffin representing 'dead American imperialism' was ceremonially burned this was done in a 'carnival' atmosphere. Vientiane was declared 'officially liberated' on 23 August 1975. The coalition government was dismissed and Souvanna Phouma resigned for the last time. All communications with the outside world were cut.

While August 1975 represents a watershed in the history of Laos, scholars are left with something of a problem: explaining why the Pathet Lao prevailed. According to Martin Stuart-Fox, the Lao revolutionary movement "had not mobilized an exploited peasantry with promises of land reform, for most of the country was underpopulated and peasant families generally owned sufficient land for their subsistence needs. The appeal of the Pathet Lao to their lowland Lao compatriots was in terms of nationalism and independence and the preservation of Lao culture from the corrosive American influence; but no urban uprising occurred until the very last minute when effective government had virtually ceased to exist … The small Lao intelligentsia, though critical of the Royal Lao government, did not desert it entirely and their recruitment to the Pathet Lao was minimal. Neither the monarchy, still less Buddhism, lost legitimacy." He concludes that it was external factors, and in particular the intervention of outside powers, which led to the victory of the Pathet Lao. Without the Vietnamese and Americans, the Pathet Lao would not have won. For the great mass of Laos' population before 1975, Communism meant nothing. This was not a mass uprising but a victory secured by a small ideologically committed elite and forged in the furnace of the war in Indochina.

As the Pathet Lao seized power, rightist ministers, ranking civil servants, doctors, much of the intelligentsia and around 30,000 Hmong escaped into Thailand, fearing they would face persecution from the Pathet Lao. Although the initial exodus was large, the majority of refugees fled in the next few years up until 1980 as the Lao government introduced new reforms aimed at wiping out decadence and reforming the economic system.

The refugee camps

By the late 1980s, a total of 340,000 people – 10% of the population and mostly middle class – had fled the country. At least half of the refugees were Hmong, the US's key allies during the war, who feared reprisals and persecution. From 1988, refugees who had made it across the border began to head back across the Mekong from camps in Thailand and to asylum in the US and France. More than 2000 refugees were also repatriated from Yunnan Province in China. For those prepared to return from exile overseas, the government offered to give them back confiscated property so long as they stayed for at least six months and become Lao citizens once again.

Nonetheless, many lived for years in squalid refugee camps, although the better connected and those with skills to sell secured US, Australian and French passports. For Laos, a large proportion of its human capital drained westwards, creating a vacuum of skilled personnel that would hamper – and still does – efforts at reconstruction and development. But while many people fled across the Mekong, a significant number who had aligned themselves with the Royalists decided to stay and help build a new Laos.

Laos under communism

The People's Democratic Republic of Laos was proclaimed in December 1975 with Prince Souphanouvong as president and Kaysone Phomvihane as secretary-general of the Lao

People's Revolutionary Party (a post he had held since its formation in 1955). The king's abdication was accepted and the ancient Lao monarchy was abolished, together with King Samsenthai's 600-year-old system of village autonomy. But instead of executing their vanquished foes, the LPRP installed Souvanna and the ex-king, Savang Vatthana, as 'special advisers' to the politburo. On Souvanna's death in 1984, he was accorded a full state funeral. The king did not fare so well: he later died ignominiously while in detention after his alleged involvement in a counter-revolutionary plot (see below).

Surprisingly, the first actions of the new revolutionary government was not to build a new revolutionary economy and society, but to stamp out unsavoury behaviour. Dress and hairstyles, dancing and singing, even the food that was served at family celebrations, was all subject to rigorous official scrutiny by so-called 'Investigation Cadres'. If the person(s) concerned were found not to match up to the Party's scrupulous standards of good taste they were bundled off to re-education camps.

Relations with Thailand, which in the immediate wake of the revolution remained cordial, deteriorated in late 1976. A military coup in Bangkok led to rumours that the Thai military, backed by the CIA, was supporting Hmong and other right-wing Lao rebels. The regime feared that Thailand would be used as a spring-board for a royalist coup attempt by exiled reactionaries. This prompted the arrest of King Savang Vatthana, together with his family and Crown Prince Vongsavang, who were all dispatched to a Seminar re-education camp in Sam Neua province. They were never heard of again. In December 1989 Kaysone Phomvihane admitted in Paris, for the first time, that the king had died of malaria in 1984 and that the queen had also died "of natural causes" – no mention was made of Vongsavang. The Lao people have still to be officially informed of his demise.

Re-education camps

Between 30,000 and 40,000 reactionaries who had been unable to flee the country were interned in remote, disease-ridden camps for 're-education'. These camps referred to as Samanaya took their name from the Western word, seminar. The reluctant scholars were forced into slave labour in squalid jungle conditions and subjected to incessant political propaganda for anything from a few months up to 15 years. Historian Grant Evans suggests that many internees were duped into believing that the government wanted complete reconciliation and so went away for re-education willingly. Evans says the purpose of the camps was to "break the will of members of the old regime and instil in them fear of the new regime." Old men, released back into society after more than 15 years of re-education were cowed and subdued, although some were prepared to talk in paranoid whispers about their grim experiences in Xam Neua.

By 1978, the re-education policy was starting to wind down, although, in 1986, Amnesty International released a report on the forgotten inhabitants of the re-education camps, claiming that 6000-7000 were still being held. By that time incarceration behind barbed wire had ended and the internees were 'arbitrarily restricted' rather than imprisoned. They were assigned to road construction teams and other public works projects. Nonetheless, conditions for these victims of the war in Indochina suffered from malnutrition, disease and many died prematurely in captivity. It is unclear how many died, but at least 15,000 have been freed. Officials of the old regime, ex-government ministers and former Royalist air force and army officers, together with thousands of others unlucky enough to have been on the wrong side, were released from the camps, largely during the mid to late 1980s. Most of the surviving political prisoners have now been re-integrated into society. Some work in the tourism industry and one, a former colonel in the Royal Lao Army, jointly owns the Asian

Pavilion Hotel (formerly the Vieng Vilai) on Samsenthai Road in downtown Vientiane. After years of being force-fed Communist propaganda he now enjoys full government support as an ardent capitalist entrepreneur. The Lao are a gentle people and it is hard not to leave the country without that view being reinforced. Even the Lao People's Revolutionary Party seems quaintly inept and it is hard to equate it with its more brutal and sinister sister parties in Vietnam, Cambodia, China or the former Soviet Union. Yet five students who meekly called for greater political freedom in 1999 were whisked off by the police and have not been heard of since.

Reflecting on 10 years of 'reconstruction'

It is worth ending this short account of the country's history by noting the brevity of Laos' experiment with full-blown Communism. Just 10 years after the Pathet Lao took control of Vientiane, the leadership were on the brink of far-reaching economic reforms. By the mid-1980s it was widely acknowledged that Marxism-Leninism had failed the country and its people. The population were still dreadfully poor; the ideology of Communism had failed to entice more than a handful into serious and enthusiastic support for the party and its ways; and graft and nepotism were on the rise.

Modern Laos

Politics

President Kaysone Phomvihane died in November 1992, aged 71. (His right-hand man, Prince Souphanouvong died just over two years later, on 9 January 1995.) As one obituary put it, Kaysone was older than he seemed, both historically and ideologically. He had been chairman of the LPRP since the mid-1950s and had been a protégé and comrade of Ho Chi Minh, who led the Vietnamese struggle for independence from the French. After leading the Lao Resistance Government – or Pathet Lao – from caves in Xam Neua province in the north, Kaysone assumed the premiership on the abolition of the monarchy in 1975. But under his leadership – and following the example of his mentors in Hanoi – Kaysone became the driving force behind the market-orientated reforms. The year before he died, he gave up the post of prime minister for that of president.

His death didn't change things much, as other members of the old guard stepped into the breach. Nouhak Phounsavanh – a sprightly 78-year-old former truck driver and hardline Communist – succeeded him as president. Nouhak didn't last terribly long in the position and in February 1998 he was replaced by 75-year-old General Khamtai Siphandon – the outgoing prime minister and head of the LPRP. Khamtai represents the last of the revolutionary Pathet Lao leaders who fought the Royalists and the Americans. In April 2006, Siphandon, the last of the old guard from the caves in Vieng Xai, was replaced as president by Choummaly Sayasone.

Recent years

With the introduction of the New Economic Mechanism in 1986 so there were hopes, in some quarters at least, that economic liberalization would be matched by political *glasnost*. So far, however, the monolithic Party shows few signs of equating capitalism with democracy. While the Lao brand of Communism has always been seen as relatively tame, it remains a far cry from political pluralism.

In 2007, the politburo still largely controlled the country and, for now, sweeping changes are unlikely. Most of the country's leaders are well into their 60s and were educated in Communist countries like Russia and Vietnam. However, the younger Lao people (particularly those that have studied abroad in Japan, Australia, UK or the US) are starting to embrace new political and economic ideas. The government takes inspiration from Vietnam's success and is more likely to follow the lead of its neighbour rather than adopting any Western model of government.

Foreign relations

Laos is rapidly becoming a keystone in mainland Southeast Asia and sees its future in linking in with its more powerful and richer neighbours. To this end Laos joined the Association of Southeast Asian Nations (ASEAN) on 23 July 1997, becoming the group's second Communist member (Vietnam joined in July 1995). By joining, Vientiane hoped to be in a better position to trade off the interests of the various powers in the region, thereby giving it greater room for manoeuvre. It was also hoped that tiny Laos would be able to develop on the economic coat tails of Southeast Asia's fast-growing economic 'tigers' – a hope rudely dashed by the region's economic crisis which began with the collapse of the Thai baht on 3 July 1997.

Laos is the only landlocked country in Southeast Asia and Vientiane is keen to pursue a cooperative 'equilibrium policy' with its neighbours. There is a widely held view that Laos is best served by having multiple friends in international circles. It has often been referred to as a 'buffer' state, which exists to ensure that none of the surrounding countries have to border each other. The leadership in Vientiane is in the tricky situation of having to play off China's military might, Thailand's commercial aggressiveness and Vietnam's population pressures, while keeping everyone happy. The answer, in many people's minds, is to promote a policy of interdependence in mainland Southeast Asia.

Relations with Thailand

From the 1980s the government took steps to improve its foreign relations – and Thailand has been the main beneficiary. Historically, Thailand has always been the main route for international access to landlocked Laos. Survival instincts told the Vientiane regime that reopening its front door was of paramount importance. The border disputes with Thailand have now been settled and the bloody clashes of 1987 and 1988 are history. Thailand is Laos' largest investor and the success of the market reforms depend more on Thailand than any other country. Economic pragmatism, then, has forced the leadership in Vientiane to cosy up to Bangkok. This does not mean that relations are warm. Indeed, Vientiane is irredeemably suspicious of Thai intentions, a suspicion born of a history of conflict.

The sleeping giant awakens: relations with China

In 1988 China and Laos normalized relations and this was followed by a defence co-operation agreement signed in 1993. Recently, Beijing has taken a particular interest in developing Laos' infrastructure, more out of self-interest than altruism. As China continues to develop at a breakneck speed, its interest in Laos' natural resources is expected to escalate substantially. China is now Laos' second largest trading partner and foreign investor. Over the last few years the economic giant has secured a deal to build numerous roads in Laos pro bono, in exchange for logging the areas around the roads. In 2005, it seemed China had logged well beyond the limits that were initially agreed upon.

Laos' ever-tightening relationship with China could jeopardize ties with the country's closest ally, Vietnam, which shares a 1300-km-long border with Laos and historically has had poor relations with China.

Relations with Vietnam

The Lao government has a special relationship with Vietnam, as it was Hanoi that helped the LPRP achieve power. Vietnam is also one of Laos' biggest trading partners. However, as Laos has turned to the West, Japan and Thailand for economic help, the government has become more critical of its closest Communist ally, Vietnam. Following Vietnam's invasion of Cambodia in December 1978, thousands of Vietnamese moved into northern Laos as permanent colonizers and by 1978 there were an estimated 40,000 Vietnamese regulars in Laos but, in 1987, 50,000 Vietnamese troops withdrew. In 1990 a Vientiane census found 15,000 Vietnamese living illegally in the capital, most of whom were promptly deported. With the death of President Kaysone Phomvihane in November 1992, another historical link with Vietnam was cut. As the old men of the Lao Communist Party, who owed so much to the Vietnamese, die off, so their replacements are looking elsewhere for investment and political support. They do not have such deep fraternal links with their brothers in Hanoi and are keen to diversify their international relations.

Relations with the USA

Laos is the only country in Indochina to have maintained relations with the US since 1975, despite the fact that, thirty years since the illegal bombing campaign of Laos subsided, the US has neither offered a substantial sum of money for reparations. Washington even expected the Lao government to allocate funds to help locate the bodies of US pilots shot down in the war. At a meeting between the Foreign Affairs Minister, General Phoune Sipaseuth, and the US Secretary of State, James Baker, in October 1990, Vientiane pledged to co-operate with the US over the narcotics trade and to step up the search for the 530 American MIAs still listed as missing in the Lao jungle. In mid-1993, tri-lateral talks between Laos, Vietnam and the US allowed for greater cooperation in the search for MIAs, many of whom are thought to have been airmen, shot down over the Ho Chi Minh Trail. In October 1992, America's diplomatic presence in Laos was upgraded to ambassadorial status from chargé d'affaires and, at the end of 1997, a high-level US mission to Laos promised greater support in the country's bomb-defusing work. However, until 2004, Laos remained one of the few countries to be denied normal trade relations with the US, the others being North Korea, Cuba and Myanmar (Burma).

Relations between the two countries have improved. This is somewhat driven by the US desire to counterbalance growing Chinese influence in the region. Most mainland Southeast Asian countries are reaping the rewards by simultaneously playing off the two superpowers and securing as much aid and trade as possible from both.

Relations with other countries

Fortunately Laos is unwilling to put all its eggs in one basket. Japan is now Laos' biggest aid donor and Vientiane has also courted other Western countries, particularly Sweden (a long-time ally), France, Germany and Australia, who have donated significant sums of aid. These days Washington and Tokyo offer more in the way of hope for the embattled regime than Moscow: in 1991, 100 Soviet economic and technical advisers were pulled out of the dilapidated flats they occupied on the outskirts of Vientiane; their withdrawal from the country signalled the end of the era of Soviet aid. While Russia gave Vientiane some leeway before it had to pay back its rouble debt, the country's former lifeline with Moscow has become of scant importance to Laos' economic future.

Contents

Footprint features

Border crossings

Malaysia–Thailand, *pages 628, 660*
Malaysia–Singapore, *page 642*
Sawarak–Brunei, *page 686*

At a glance

⊖ **Getting around** Efficient network of buses, trains and taxis. Cheap internal flights. Some places in Borneo only accessible by boat or plane.

◎ **Time required** 1-3 weeks, more if heading to Malaysian Borneo.

☼ **Weather** Dry season is Apr-Oct, monsoon Nov-Mar.

✘ **When not to go** School holidays.

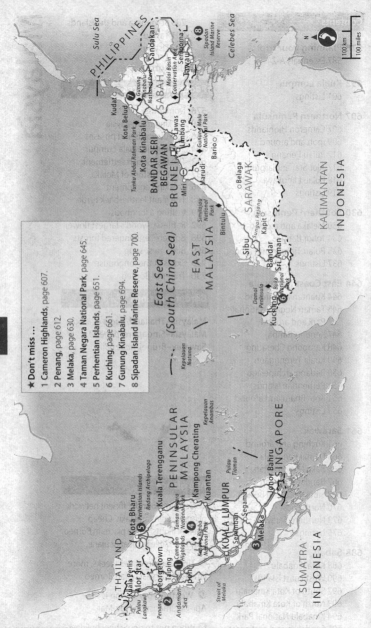

★ Don't miss ...
1 Cameron Highlands, page 607.
2 Penang, page 612.
3 Melaka, page 630.
4 Taman Negara National Park, page 645.
5 Perhentian Islands, page 651.
6 Kuching, page 661.
7 Gunung Kinabalu, page 694.
8 Sipadan Island Marine Reserve, page 700.

The 'Malay Archipelago' is a term intimately associated with the mystery of the East. It conjures up images of sultans and headhunters; munificent jungles brimming with exotic wildlife and clippers cutting through the warm waters of the South China Sea. Of course, today's Malay archipelago is another world: the jungles are contained in national parks or have been ploughed up into rubber and palm oil plantations; the cities of Singapore and Kuala Lumpur are modern metropolises of glass; and container ships, not clippers, now plough through the Strait of Melaka.

Even so, Malaysia retains its cross-cultural stamp with the sharp spices of its Indian markets, its flamboyant red Buddhist temples and the prayer call of the muezzin echoes from a multitude of mosques across the country. Sandwiched between Singapore to the south and Thailand to the north, the Peninsula states support the great bulk of the country's population. And, just as Malaysia itself is a country of two halves, so the Peninsula too can be broadly divided into a vibrant western side and a bucolic east separated by the Barisan Titiwangsa, the Peninsula's jungled spine. Malaysian Borneo – the states of Sabah and Sarawak – dovetails more closely with the romantic vision of 'Malaya'. The countryside remains dominated by tribal groups, collectively known as Dayaks, and much of it is still forested.

Planning your trip

Getting there

Air

The majority of visitors arrive at one of two international airports: Kuala Lumpur (KL), see page 593, or Singapore (page 740). Those headed to Borneo can also fly to Brunei (page 39). Some international flights go direct to Penang, Langkawi, Kota Kinabalu (KK) and Kuching. Smaller airlines also run services between Singapore and island resorts such as Langkawi and Pulau Tioman. ▸▸ *For airport tax, see page 591.*

From Europe Malaysia Airlines (MAS, www.malaysiaairlines.com) offers direct services from London Heathrow to Kuala Lumpur (12½ hours). MAS also operates non-stop services from Amsterdam, Frankfurt, Paris, Rome and Zurich. KLM (www.klm.com) flies from Amsterdam non-stop. From other cities a change of plane is usually necessary en route.

From the USA and Canada MAS flies from LA and New York. Approximate flying time from Los Angeles International Airport (LAX) is 20 hours.

From Australasia MAS offers direct flights from Sydney, Melbourne, Adelaide, Brisbane, Darwin and Perth (flight times range between five and nine hours). It also offers flights from Sydney and Perth to Kuching (Sarawak) and from Auckland to KL.

From Southeast Asia There are flights to KL from all regional capitals. **Air Asia** (www.air asia.com) has flights connecting KL with Jakarta and Bangkok, and Bangkok with Penang. **Bangkok Airways** (www.bangkokair.com) flies between KL and Koh Samui. Many airlines fly from Hong Kong, Manila and Tokyo. Flights between Singapore and Malaysia cost the same amount in US dollars whether bought in Malaysia or Singapore, so it saves money buying a return ticket in Malaysia.

Discount flight agents

UK and Ireland
STA Travel, www.statravel.co.uk. Branches across the UK. Specialists in low-cost student/youth flights, student IDs and insurance.
Trailfinders, 194 Kensington High St, London, T020-7938 3939. www.trailfinders.com.

North America
Air Brokers International, 323 Geary St, Suite 411, San Francisco, T1-800-883 3273, www.airbrokers.com. Consolidator and specialist on RTW and Circle Pacific tickets.
Discount Airfares Worldwide On-Line, www.etn.nl/discount.htm. A hub of consolidator and discount agent links.

STA Travel, 5900 Wilshire Blvd, Suite 2110, Los Angeles, T1-800-777 0112, www.sta-travel.com. Branches across the USA.
Travel CUTS, 187 College St, Toronto, T416-979 2406, www.travelcuts.com. Specialist in student fares, IDs and travel services. Lots of branches.
Travelocity, www.travelocity.com. An online consolidator.

Australia and New Zealand
Flight Centres, www.flightcentre.com.au. Branches in Sydney, Auckland and other places.
STA Travel, www.statravel.com.au. Good deals on flights, insurance and hotels.
Travel.com.au, 80 Clarence St, Sydney, T02-929 01500, www.travel.com.au.

Packing for Malaysia

Almost everything is available in towns and cities – often at a lower price than in Western countries. Laundry services are cheap and quick, so there is no need to bring loads of supplies. It's a good idea to carry photocopies of important documents and spare passport photos.

Malaysia is a Muslim country so women in particular should dress appropriately in certain areas; see Local customs and laws, page 585. Take a sweater if visiting the Cameron Highlands or other upland areas as it can get chilly in the evenings. The air-conditioning on buses and trains can also be very cold. For jungle treks, a waterproof is advisable, as are canvas jungle boots, which dry faster than leather. If climbing Gunung Kinabalu, you will need a warm jacket, hat and gloves; these can be hired at Park HQ.

Those intending to stay in budget accommodation should take a cotton sheet sleeping bag, padlock and student card. There are camping grounds in Borneo and Peninsular Malaysia. The usual equipment is necessary including a tent, stove, cooking utensils and sleeping bag.

Iodine drops – for purifying water, sterilizing jungle cuts and scratches and loosening leeches – are difficult to come by in Malaysia but easily obtained at home in camping and outdoor shops.

Rail

Keretapi Tanah Melayu (KTM), www.ktmb.com.my, runs express trains daily between Singapore and the major cities on the west coast of Malaysia. There is a daily express train from Bangkok (Thailand) to Butterworth. This connects with the KL service, and from KL onwards to Singapore. Another railway line runs from Gemas, halfway between KL and Johor Bahru (JB), to Kota Bharu on the northeast coast.

The most luxurious way to travel by train to Malaysia is aboard the **Eastern & Oriental Express (E&O)**, www.easternorientalexpress.com. This air-conditioned train carries just 132 passengers and includes a salon car, dining car, bar and observation deck, and runs from Singapore to Bangkok and back. Elegant carriages, fine wines and food designed for European rather than Asian tastes make this not just a mode of transport but an experience. The journey takes two days with stops in KL, Butterworth, Hua Hin and the River Kwai.

Road

It is possible to travel to Malaysia overland by bus or shared taxi from Thailand and **Singapore**. Direct buses and taxis are much easier than the local alternatives which terminate at the borders. Singapore is six hours by taxi from KL (via JB) and about seven hours by bus (see page 642). Taxi fares are approximately double bus fares.

There are direct buses and taxis from **Thailand** to most major towns in northern Malaysia and six border crossing points. For those using the north-south highway – which is most people – the crossing point is at Bukit Kayu Hitam (see page 628), which links up with the Thai city of Hat Yai. On the western side of the Peninsula there are also crossings at Wang Kelian and Padang Besar. The Wang Kelian crossing to Satun in Thailand, is convenient if you are driving; it is quiet and usually pretty quick. The Padang Besar (see page 628) crossing is easy on foot and makes sense if travelling to Pulau Langkawi. In Perak the crossing is at Pengkalan Hulu, and in Kelantan, on the eastern side of the Peninsula there are two more crossing points: Pengkalan Kubar, and from Kota Bahru to Rantau Panjang/Sungai Golok (see page 660). The more popular of these is the Rantau Panjang crossing; few people cross at Pengkalan Kubar. **Note** The southern Thai provinces suffer from serious separatist violence. Bombings and shootings occur daily, with fatalities. Check the situation if you intend to cross the border. Local buses and taxis terminate at the border crossing points, but there are regular onward connections on each side.

It is also possible to cross overland from **Brunei** to the East Malaysian state of Sarawak. The main crossing points with Sarawak are from Kuala Belait to Kuala Baram (see page 686), from where there are regular buses to Kuching, and Kuala Lurah to Limbang.

Sea

Most passenger ships and cruise liners run between Port Klang, west of KL, Georgetown (Penang), Kuantan, Kuching and KK. **Feri Malaysia** connects these Malaysian ports and **Singapore**. Deluxe cabins are available. Schedules change annually; contact **Tourism Malaysia** for bookings, see page 595.

From **Sumatra**, ferries run regularly from Dumai to Melaka, and from Medan to Georgetown (Penang). Passenger boats connect Langkawi Island with Satun in southern **Thailand**. Small boats run between Johor state and **Singapore**'s Changi Point. In Malaysian Borneo, there is a regular ferry service between **Brunei** and Pulau Labuan in Sabah. There is also a regular ferry service between Sandakan in Sabah and Zamboanga in the southern **Philippines**.

Getting around

Transport around the East Malaysian states of Sabah and Sarawak is not as easy as it is on the Peninsula since there are fewer roads and some are in a poor state of repair. There are excellent coastal and upriver express boat services in Sarawak and the national airline, **Malaysian Airlines (MAS)**, and **Air Asia** have an extensive network in both states; flying is by far the easiest way to travel around Sabah and Sarawak, with frequent and inexpensive flights between the main towns. Speed ferries skirt the island of Borneo, passing immigration points either en route or at the departure and arrival points. The cheapest (and slowest) means of travelling here is by bus. Remember that Sarawak and Sabah have their own immigration rules (independent to those of Malaysia), with visitors receiving a one-month entry stamp, which needs to be renewed in Kuching for longer stays. ▶▶ *See Visas and immigration, page 592.*

Air

Non-Malaysian passport holders are eligible for the **Discover Malaysia Pass**, if they fly into (or out of) the country on **Malaysia Airlines (MAS)**, www.malaysiaairlines.com. The basic pass is US$199 for travel for up to three flights within the country. The pass must be purchased at a MAS office within 14 days of arrival in Malaysia and must be used within 28 days. It offers significant savings on domestic air travel and offers an extensive network. Bear in mind that holders can only cross between Peninsular Malaysia and East Malaysia (Sabah/Sarawak) once; ie a return journey. Local MAS offices are listed in the Transport section of each town. Head office: Bangunan MAS, Jalan Sultan Ismail, 50250, KL, T1300-883000 (within Malaysia, 24 hours), T+60-3-7843 3000 (24 hours).

The budget airline Air Asia, www.airasia.com, flies to Alor Star, Bintulu, JB, KL, KK, Kuala Terengganu, Kuching, Labuan, Langkawi, Miri, Penang, Sandakan, Sibu and Tawau. Domestic flights from KL leave from the international airport, KLIA, see page 593. Flights get very booked up on public holidays. ▶▶ *For airport tax, see page 591.*

Boat

On the Peninsula, there are regular scheduled ferry services between the main islands – Pangkor, Penang and Langkawi – and the mainland. There are passenger and car ferries between Butterworth and Georgetown, Penang, every 20 minutes. For other offshore islands, mostly off the east coast, fishing boats, and sometimes regular boats, leave from the nearest fishing port. Pulau Tioman is accessed from Mersing.

Local water transport comes into its own in Sarawak, where lack of roads makes coastal and river transport the only viable means of travel. On larger rivers in Sarawak, such as the Rajang and the Baram, there are specially adapted express boats. If there is no regular boat, it is nearly always possible to charter a local longboat although this can be expensive. In the dry season the upper reaches of many rivers are unnavigable except by smaller boats. In times of heavy rain, logs and branch debris can make rivers unsafe. There is still some river transport on the Peninsula's east coast.

Rail

The KTM train (see Getting there, page 579) is an economical and comfortable way to travel round the Peninsula. However, trains are much slower than buses and often arrive at awkward times in the middle of the night.

There are two main lines. One runs up the west coast from Singapore, through KL, Ipoh and Butterworth, connecting with Thai railways at Padang Besar. The other line branches off from the west coast line at Gemas (halfway between KL and Singapore) and heads northeast to Kota Bahru. The express service (Ekspres Rakyat or Ekspres Sinaran) only stops at major towns; the regular service stops at every station but is slightly cheaper. All overnight trains have sleeping berths and all classes have air conditioning (very cold). Reservations can be made for both classes. First and second class carriages are equipped with videos.

Rail passes for five, 10 and 35 days are available to all foreign visitors, except those from Singapore. Passes are available from railway stations in Singapore, KL, JB, Butterworth, Padang Besar, Rantau Panjang, Wakaf Bahru (Kota Bahru). A 15-day pass costs US$70; a 10-day pass US$55, and a five-day pass US$35. There are concessions for children, family groups, disabled travellers and senior citizens. If travelling overnight, standard berth charges are RM50-70 for deluxe; and RM11-14 for second class.

In Malaysian Borneo, in Sabah, there is a railway line, running from KK to Tenom, via Beaufort (see page 693). It passes through the stunning Padas River Gorge (see page 712).

Road

Bus Peninsular Malaysia has an excellent bus system with a network of public express buses and several privately run services. Air-conditioned express buses connect the major towns; seats can be reserved and prices are reasonable. The air conditioning is often very cold. Prices vary between companies. Note that buses are less frequent on the east coast.

Recommended companies are **Pluskiner**, T03-2274 0499, www.plusliner.com, and **Transnasional**, T03-4047 7878, www.nadi.com.my/transportation_routes_express2.asp. Although these may cost a few ringgit more, it's usually money well spent. In larger towns there may be a number of bus stops; some companies operate directly from their own offices rather than the bus station.

Buses in East Malaysia are more unreliable because of the poorer road conditions. With heavy rain, the highway connecting KK with Sandakan is sometimes blocked by mudslides. Recently the governments of Sabah and Sarawak have started to invest extensively in road infrastructure; in some places road surfacing has outpaced public transport.

Car and motorbike Car hire companies are listed in the transport listings of individual towns. Visitors can hire a car provided they are have an international driving licence, are aged 23-65 and have had a licence for at least a year. Car hire costs RM100-RM250 per day. Cheaper weekly and monthly rates and special deals are available.

Driving is on the left; give way to drivers on the right. However, local drivers often don't obey traffic lights or road signs and hardly ever give way so you will need to have your wits about you. Within towns the speed limit is 50 kph; the wearing of seat belts is compulsory for front seat passengers and the driver. Road maps are on sale at most petrol stations; Petronas produces an excellent atlas, *Touring Malaysia by Road*. Most roads are kept in good repair. However, during the monsoon season, heavy rains may make some east coast travel difficult and the west coast roads can be congested.

In Sarawak the road network is limited: air or water transport are sometimes the only option. In Sabah, 4WDs are readily available, but expensive. On some islands, such as Penang, Langkawi and Pangkor, motorbikes are available for hire, starting around RM25 per day. If bringing your own car into the country, no carnet or deposit is required.

Cycling Bicycles are available for hire from some guesthouses and hire shops, especially on islands such as Pangkor, Penang, Langkawi and Tioman, but also in some towns and hill resorts. Compared with motorbikes, bike hire can seem expensive – RM10-20 per day and substantially more by the hour. Prices vary a good deal depending on the type of bike.

Touring, hybrid or mountain bikes are fine for most roads and tracks in Malaysia. Mountain bikes have made a big impact in the country, so accessories and spares are widely available. Less common are components made of unusual materials – titanium and composites. Cycling clubs are springing up across the country. Unlike Indonesia and Thailand, a foreigner on a bike is not such an object of interest. Cars and buses rarely give way to a bicycle so be very wary; avoid major roads and major towns. Cheaper buses usually carry bicycles, but air-conditioned tour buses may refuse. Many international airlines take bicycles for no extra cost, provided they are not boxed. Take the pedals off and deflate the tyres.

Useful items include: pollution mask if travelling to large cities; puncture repair kit; spare inner tubes; spare tyre; pump; a good map of the area; bungee cords; and a water filter.

Hitchhiking It is easy for foreigners to hitch; look reasonably presentable and it shouldn't be long before someone will stop. Hitching is not advisable for lone women.

Taxi There are two types of taxi in Malaysia: local and 'out-station' (long-distance). The latter, usually Mercedes or Peugeot, connect all major towns and cities. They operate on a shared-cost basis – as soon as there are four passengers, the taxis set off. It is possible to charter the whole taxi for the price of four single fares. Taxi stands are usually next door to major bus stations. If shared, taxi fares usually cost about twice as much as bus fares, but they are much faster. For groups travelling together taking a taxi makes good sense. It is easier to find other passengers in the morning than later in the day.

Local taxi fares in Malaysia are fairly cheap, but it is rare to find a taxi with a meter (except in KL); you will need to bargain. On the east coast, air-conditioned taxis cost more.

Trishaws In KL it has long been too dangerous for trishaws, apart from around Chinatown and suburban areas. In towns such as Melaka, Georgetown and Kota Bharu, as well as in many other smaller towns, trishaws are still available but they have largely become an expensive way to travel for well-heeled tourists.

Maps

Maps are widely available in Malaysia. Good country maps include Nelles *Malaysia* (1:1,500,000) and Nelles *West Malaysia* (1:650,000). The Malaysian tourist board produces a good map of Kuala Lumpur and a series of state maps, although these are much poorer in quality. The Sabah and Sarawak tourist boards also publish reasonable maps.

In the UK, the best selection is available from Stanfords ① *12-14 Long Acre, London WC2E 9LP, T020-7836 1321, www.stanfords.co.uk.* Also useful is McCarta ① *15 Highbury Place, London N15 1QP, T020-7354 1616.*

Sleeping → For hotel price codes, see inside the front cover.

Malaysia offers a good selection of international-standard hotels as well as guesthouses and hostels. Room rates are subject to 5-10% tax. Many major international chains have hotels, such as Hilton, Holiday Inn and Hyatt. The number of four- and five-star hotel rooms has multiplied and this, combined with a weak ringgit and depressed economy, has helped to keep prices stable. Even the most expensive hotels are good value for visitors.

In tourist resorts, many hotels have different tariffs for weekdays, weekends and holiday periods. Room rates can vary substantially between these periods. In popular holiday destinations like the Cameron Highlands, accommodation can become scarce during the school holidays (April, August and December). Book ahead if travelling during these months.

There are youth hostels in KL, Georgetown (Penang), Cameron Highlands, Kuantan, Kota Bahru, Kota Kinabalu and Pulau Pangkor. On the east coast of Peninsular Malaysia and in Malaysian Borneo, it is often possible to stay with families in Malay kampongs (villages) as part of the homestay programme (contact the local tourist office for information). The most popular place to do this is at Kampong Cherating (see page 648) or Marang (see page 650).

Along many of Malaysia's beaches and on the islands there are simple *atap*-roofed A-frame bungalows and wooden chalets. Towns and cities on the tourist trail also often have guesthouses with dorms for the seriously shallow of pocket.

Accommodation in Borneo does not offer such good value for money as hotels on the Peninsula but there are some bargains. For accommodation in national parks it is necessary to book in advance. In Sarawak and Sabah it is possible to stay in longhouses, where rates are at the discretion of the visitor (see page 669).

Eating and drinking → For restaurant price codes, see inside the front cover.

Cuisine

Malaysians love their food, and the dishes of the three main communities – Malay, Chinese and Indian – comprise a hugely varied national menu. Every state has its own **Malay** dishes. The staple diet is rice and curry, which is rich and creamy due to the use of coconut milk. Herbs and spices include chillis, ginger, turmeric, coriander, lemongrass, anise, cloves, cumin, caraway and cinnamon. Favourite dishes include satay, *nasi campur* (curry rice buffet with meat, fish, vegetables and fruit), *nasi goreng* (rice with meat and vegetables fried with garlic, onions and sambal), and *nasi lemak* (a breakfast dish of rice cooked in coconut milk and served with prawn sambal, *ikan bilis*, a hard boiled egg, peanuts and cucumber).

The former Straits Settlements of Penang and Melaka have an amalgamation of Chinese and Malay cuisine called **Nyonya** (also known as Straits Chinese). Nyonya food is spicier than Chinese food and, unlike Malay, it uses pork. In Penang the dishes have adopted flavours from neighbouring Thailand, whereas Melaka's Nyonya food has Indonesian overtones. Emphasis is placed on presentation and the fine-chopping of ingredients.

Cantonese and Hainanese cooking are the most prevalent **Chinese** cuisines in Malaysia. Some of the more common dishes are Hainanese chicken rice (rice cooked in chicken stock and served with steamed or roast chicken), *char kway teow* (Teochew-style fried noodles, with eggs, cockles and chilli paste), or *luak* (Hokkien oyster omelette), *dim sum* (steamed dumplings and patties) and *yong tow foo* (beancurd and vegetables stuffed with fish). Steamboat, the Chinese answer to fondue, consists of thinly sliced pieces of raw meat, fish, prawns, cuttlefish, fishballs and vegetables tossed into a bubbling cauldron in the centre of the table. They are then dunked into hot chilli and soy sauces and the resulting soup provides a flavoursome broth to wash it all down.

With a large ethnic **Indian** population, vegetarian food is usually available, especially on the Peninsula. North Indian dishes tend to be subtly spiced, use more meat (no beef) and are served with bread. Southern dishes use fiery spices, emphasize vegetables and are served with rice. Pancakes include roti, dosai and chapati. Malaysia's famous mamak-men are Indian Muslims who are highly skilled in everything from *teh tarik* (see Drink) to rotis.

In the East Malaysian states of Sabah and Sarawak, there are various **tribal specialities**, such as *jaruk* (wild boar fermented in a bamboo tube, served with sticky rice and jungle ferns). The Kadazans form the largest ethnic group in Sabah. Their food tends to use mango and can be on the sour side.

In recent years a profusion of restaurants, representing other Asian and European cuisines, have set up, mainly in the big cities. **New Asia (fusion)** is a blending of cuisines and ingredients from East and West.

Eating out
Malaysia has everything from street stalls to swanky international restaurants. The cheapest, and often the best, places to eat are in **hawker centres** and roadside stalls (usually close to night markets), where you can eat well for RM3-4. Stalls generally serve Malay, Indian or Chinese dishes. **Kedai kopi** (coffee shops) can be found on almost every street; a meal costs from RM5. Usually run by Chinese or Indian families, they open at around 0900 and close in the early evening, many are 24 hours. Some open at dawn to serve dim sum to commuters on the way to work.

Restaurants geared to travellers tend to be concentrated in beach resorts and serve backpacker staples such as banana pancakes, fudge cake, smoothies and jaffles. Hotel restaurants regularly lay on buffet spreads, which are good value at RM20-30.

Drink
Soft drinks, mineral water and freshly squeezed fruit juices are readily available. Anchor and Tiger beer are widely sold, except in the more strict Islamic states of the east coast such as Kelantan, and are cheapest at the hawker stalls (RM5-7 per bottle). A beer costs RM8-15 per bottle in coffee shops. Malaysian-brewed Guinness is popular; the Chinese believe it has medicinal qualities. Malaysian tea is grown in the Cameron Highlands and is very good. One of the most interesting cultural refinements of the Indian Muslim community is the Mamak-man, who is famed for *teh tarik* (pulled tea), which is thrown dramatically from one cup to another with no spillages. The idea is to cool it down, but it has become an art form. Most of the coffee comes from Indonesia, although some is locally produced. Malaysians like strong coffee and unless you specify *kurang manis* (less sugar), *tak mahu manis* (no sugar) or *kopi kosong* (black, no sugar), it will come with lashings of condensed milk.

Festivals and events

The timing of Islamic festivals is calculated on the basis of local sightings of various phases of the moon. Dates are approximations and can vary by a day or two. Muslim festivals move forward by around nine or 10 days each year. Chinese, Indian (Hindu) and some Christian holidays are also movable. Sultans' and governors' birthday celebrations are marked with processions and festivities. State holidays can disrupt travel, particularly in east coast states where they run for several days. Each state also has its own public holidays when shops and banks close. Schools in Malaysia have five breaks throughout the year. Dates vary from state to state but generally fall in the months of January (one week), March (two weeks), May (three weeks), August (one week) and October (four weeks). To check dates for all festivals visit www.tourism.gov.my. Popular festivals include:

Jan-Feb Thaipusam celebrated by Hindus during the full moon. Devotees pay homage to Lord Muraga by piercing their bodies, cheeks and tongues with *vel* (skewers) and hooks weighted with oranges, and carrying *kevadis* (steel structures bearing the image of the Lord). Thousands of pilgrims gather at Batu Caves near KL (see page 600).

Jan-Feb Chinese New Year, a 15-day lunar festival that sees Chinatown streets crowded with shoppers buying oranges to signify luck. Lion, unicorn or dragon dances welcome in the New Year and thousands of firecrackers are ignited to ward off evil spirits.

31 May–1 Jun Gawai Dayak. Sarawak's major festival marks the end of the rice harvest. Vast quantities of food and *tuak* are consumed. Urbanites return to their rural roots for a binge.

Jun The **Dragon Boat Festival** honours the ancient Chinese poet hero, Qu Yuan who drowned himself in a protest against corruption. His death is commemorated with dragon boat races and the eating of dumplings; the biggest celebrations are in Penang.

Aug Mooncake or **Lantern Festival**. Marking the overthrow of the Mongol Dynasty in China, this is celebrated with the eating of mooncakes and the lighting of festive lanterns.

Aug Festival of the Hungry Ghosts. Souls in purgatory return to earth to feast. Food is offered to the spirits. Altars are set up in the streets and candles with faces are burned.

Oct Festival of the Nine Emperor Gods This marks the return of the emperor god spirits to earth. Mediums go into a trance and are carried on chairs comprised of sharp blades or spikes. A strip of yellow cotton is worn on the right wrist as a sign of devotion. Ceremonies may end with a firewalking ritual.

Oct-Nov Deepavali, the Hindu festival of lights commemorates the victory of good over evil and the triumphant return of Rama. Hindu homes are brightly decorated for the occasion.

Oct-Nov Awal Ramadan, the first day of Ramadan. Muslims must abstain from all food and drink (as well as smoking) from sunrise to sundown. Every evening stalls sell traditional Malay cakes and delicacies.

Local customs and laws

Conduct As elsewhere in Southeast Asia, 'losing face' brings shame. Using a loud voice or wild gesticulations will be taken to signify anger and, hence, 'loss of face'. Similarly, the person you shout at will also feel loss of face, especially in public. In Muslim company it is impolite to touch others with the left hand. Men shake hands but men don't usually shake a woman's hand, except in Kuala Lumpur. Using the index finger to point is insulting; the thumb or whole hand should be used to wave down a taxi. Before entering a private home, remove your shoes; it is usual to take a small gift for the host, not opened until after the visitor has left.

Useful words and phrases

Yes/no	Ia/tidak	I'm fine	Baik
Thank you	Terimah kasih	Excuse me/sorry	Ma'af saya
You're welcome	Sama-sama	Where's the...?	Dimana...
Good morning	Selamat pagi	How much is this...?	Ini berapa?
Good afternoon	Selamat petang	My name is...	Nama saya...
How are you?	Apa kabar?	What is your name?	Apa nama anda?

Dress Malaysians dress for the heat. Clothes are light, cool and casual but tidy, especially in cities; tourists in vests, shorts and flip-flops look out of place in KL. Exclusive restaurants may require formal wear. Although many Malaysian business people have adopted the Western jacket and tie, the batik shirt, or *baju*, is the traditional formal wear for men, while women wear the graceful *sarung kebaya*.

Dress codes are important to observe from the point of view of Islamic sensitivities, particularly on the Peninsula's east coast. Topless sunbathing is completely taboo, and in some places (such as Marang or Kelantan) bikinis will cause great offence. In Muslim areas, women should keep shoulders covered and wear below-knee skirts or trousers. A wedding ring may help ward off the attentions of amorous admirers. Malaysia's cross-cultural differences are most apparent on the streets: many Chinese girls think nothing of wearing brief mini-skirts and shorts, while their Malay counterparts are clad from head to toe.

Prohibitions Malaysia is well known around the world for its stringent laws against drugs and there is a mandatory death sentence upon conviction for anyone in possession of 15 g or more of heroin or morphine, 200 g of cannabis or hashish or 40 g of cocaine. Those caught with more than 10 g of heroin or 100 g of cannabis are deemed to be traffickers and face lengthy jail sentences and flogging with a rotan cane.

While alcohol is not illegal in any part of Malaysia, be aware of Muslim sensibilities, particularly in the East Coast states of Kelantan and Terengganu.

Religion Remove shoes before entering mosques and Hindu/Buddhist temples; in mosques, women should cover their heads, shoulders and legs and men should wear long trousers.

Shopping

Most big towns now have modern shopping complexes as well as shops and markets. Department stores are fixed price, but nearly everywhere else it is possible to bargain. At least 30% can be knocked off the asking price; your first offer should be roughly half the first quote.

What to buy

The islands of Langkawi, Tioman and Labuan have duty-free shopping; the range of goods is poor, however. Electronic, computer and camera equipment are cheaper in Singapore. Kuala Lumpur and most state capitals have a Chinatown which usually has a few curio shops and a *pasar malam* (night market). Indian quarters, which are invariably labelled 'Little India', are found in bigger towns and are the best places to buy sarongs, longis, dotis and saris (mostly imported from India) as well as other textiles. Malay handicrafts are usually only found in markets or government craft centres.

Handicrafts

The Malaysian arts and crafts industry has suffered as craftspeople head to the cities in search of more lucrative jobs. The growth of tourism in recent years has helped to reinvigorate it, particularly in traditional handicraft-producing areas, such as the east coast states of Terengganu and Kelantan. The **Malay Arts and Crafts Society** set up Karyaneka centres to market Malaysian arts and crafts in KL and state capitals. Typical handicrafts that can be found on the Peninsula include woodcarvings, batik, *songket* (cloth woven with gold and silver thread), pewterware, silverware, kites, tops and *wayang kulit* (shadow puppets).

The traditional handicraft industry is still flourishing in Sarawak, and Kuching is full of antique shops selling tribal pieces collected from upriver. Those going upriver themselves can often find items being sold in towns and even longhouses en route. Typical handicrafts include woodcarvings, *pua kumbu* (rust-coloured tie-dye blankets), beadwork and basketry.

Essentials A-Z

Accident and emergency
Ambulance, police or fire, T999.

Children
Malaysia (particularly the Peninsula) is one of the easiest and safest places in Asia to travel with children. Food hygiene is good, bottled water is sold everywhere, public transport is cheap (including taxis) and most museums and other attractions provide good discounts for children. A/c rooms are available virtually everywhere. Powdered milk and baby food and other baby/child items, including disposable nappies, are widely sold and high chairs are available in most restaurants. Malaysians love children and they will receive lots of attention, especially in remote areas. You will also receive the best service, and help from officials and the public when in difficulty.

A checklist might include: baby wipes; child paracetamol; disinfectant; first aid kit; immersion element for boiling water; oral rehydration salts (such as Dioralyte); sarong or backpack for carrying child; Sudocreme (or similar); high-factor sunblock; sunhat; thermometer.

Customs and duty free
200 cigarettes, 50 cigars or 250 g of tobacco and 1 litre of liquor or wine. Cameras, watches, pens, lighters, cosmetics, perfumes and portable music players are duty free in Malaysia. Visitors bringing in dutiable goods such as electronic equipment may have to pay a refundable deposit for temporary importation. It is advisable to carry receipts to avoid this.

Export permits are required for animals and plants, gold, platinum, precious stones and jewellery (except reasonable personal effects) amongst other items. To export antiques a permit must be acquired from Director General of Museums, Muzium Negara, Kuala Lumpur; see page 597.

Disabled travellers
Disabled travellers are not well catered for. Pavements are treacherous for wheelchairs, crossing roads is a hazard, and public transport is not well adapted for those with disabilities. For those who can afford to stay in the more expensive hotels, the assistance of hotel staff makes life a great deal easier, and there are also lifts and other amenities. Those staying in budget accommodation will find that local people are helpful. Useful contacts include: the **Royal Association for Disability and Rehabilitation** (RADAR), 12 City Forum, 250 City Rd, London, EC1V 8AF, T020-7250 3222, www.radar.org.uk, and the **Society for Accessible Travel and Hospitality** (SATH), Suite 605, 347 5th Av, New York, NY 10016, T1-212-447 7284, www.sath.org.

Electricity
220-240 volts, 50 cycle AC. Some hotels supply adaptors.

Embassies and consulates

Australia, Malaysian High Commission, 7 Perth Av, Yarralumla, Canberra, ACT 2600, T+61-(0)2-6273 1543.

Brunei, Malaysian High Commission, 61 Simpang 336, Jl Kebangsaan BA 1211 kg. Sungai Akar, Bandar Seri Begawan BS8675, T+673-238 1095.

Canada, Malaysian High Commission, 60 Boteler St, Ottawa, Ontario, T+1-613-241 5182.

New Zealand, Malaysian High Commission, 10 Washington Av, Brooklyn, Wellington, T+64-04-385 2439.

UK, Malaysian High Commission, 45 Belgrave Sq, London, T+44-(0)20-7235 8033.

USA, Malaysian Embassy, 3516 International Court, NW, Washington, T+1-202-572 9700.

Gay and lesbian travellers

Malaysia – officially at least – is not particularly accepting of what might be regarded as alternative lifestyles and homosexuality remains a crime. Gay or lesbian sexual activity can be punished with flogging and male transvestism with imprisonment. Police may arrest and harass any gay person (Muslim or non-Muslim) in a public place, so discretion is advised. (Bear in mind, that even Malaysia's former deputy prime minister, Anwar Ibrahim, was charged with sodomy in 1999.) However, there is a buzzing gay scene in KL and, to a lesser extent, in Johor Bahru, Melaka, Penang, Kota Kinabalu and Kuching. Useful websites include www.fridae.com, www.utopia-asia.com/tipsmala.htm and www.geocities.com/swkgayscene.

Health
Before you go

Visit your GP or travel clinic at least 6 weeks before your departure for advice on travel risks such as malaria. Recommended **vaccinations** include diphtheria, tetanus, poliomyelitis, hepatitis A and B, and typhoid. A yellow fever certificate is required if coming from an infected area. Make sure you have travel insurance, get a dental check (especially if you are going to be away for more than a month),

know your blood group and if you suffer a condition such as diabetes or epilepsy make sure you wear a Medic Alert bracelet/necklace.

Medical care in Malaysia is good, especially in Kuala Lumpur. Most problems can be adequately dealt with. Medical services are listed in the Directory section of each town.

Health risks

The following covers some of the more common risks to travellers in Malaysia, but is by no means comprehensive.

Altitude sickness can occur from 3000 m upwards and is more likely to affect those who ascend rapidly or over-exert themselves. Symptoms include headache, lassitude, insomnia, dizziness, loss of appetite, nausea and vomiting. If symptoms are mild, the treatment is rest and painkillers (not aspirin-based). If symptoms are severe or prolonged descend to a lower altitude immediately. Avoid alcohol, cigarettes and heavy food.

Bites and stings are rare but if you are bitten by a snake, spider or scorpion, stay as calm as possible, try to identify the culprit and seek medical advice without delay.

Dengue fever is spread by mosquitoes that bite during the day. Symptoms are similar to malaria and include fever, intense joint pain and a rash. There are no effective vaccines or antiviral drugs. Rest, plenty of fluids and paracetamol is the best treatment. Travellers rarely develop the more severe form of the disease, which can be fatal.

Diarrhoea is common but if symptoms persist beyond 2 weeks medical attention should be sought. Also seek medical help if there is blood in the stools and/or fever. Keep well hydrated (rehydration sachets are invaluable) and eat bland foods. Bacterial diarrhoea is the most common; your GP may prescribe antibiotics for you to take with you.

To minimize the chances of diarrhoea be careful with water (see below) and food, particularly salads, meat and unpasteurized dairy products. Where possible, watch food being prepared fresh. There is a simple adage that says wash it, peel it, boil it or forget it.

The main risk of **HIV** and other **STDs** is from unprotected sex; always use a condom. HIV is widespread, as are chlamydia, herpes, syphilis and gonorrhoea.

Malaria is present in Malaysia, so talk to your doctor about prophylaxis before you go. Symptoms include lethargy, headaches and fever (similar to flu) but can cause death within 24 hrs if left untreated. If symptoms occur seek medical help immediately, even after returning home. The best action is to avoid being bitten: wear long light coloured clothes, particularly at dusk, and use effective insect repellent. Use a mosquito net at night.

Rabies is a problem in Malaysia so be aware of the dangers of the bite from any animal. If bitten clean the wound and treat with an iodine-based disinfectant or alcohol. Always seek urgent medical attention even if you have been previously vaccinated.

Typhoid is spread by the insanitary preparation of food. A number vaccines are available, including one taken orally. Typhim Vi is expensive but causes few side effects.

Water should be treated with iodine and filtered. Avoid tap water and ice in drinks. Check seals on bottled water are unbroken.

Useful websites

www.fco.gov.uk Foreign and Commonwealth Office.
www.fitfortravel.scot.nhs.uk Has a useful A-Z of vaccine and travel health advice requirements for each country.
www.nathnac.org National Travel Health Network and Centre.
www.who.int World Health Organization.

Internet

Malaysia has fully embraced the age of technology. Internet cafés have sprung up even in remote corners. Most places charge RM3-5 per hr, some hotels charge up to RM10 per hr. Internet cafés geared to tourists tend to be more expensive than those serving the local market, where teenage boys spend hours playing online games. Upmarket hotels and coffee shops routinely offer free Wi-Fi.

Language

The national language is **Bahasa Melayu** (normally shortened to Bahasa). It is very similar to Bahasa Indonesia. All communities, Malay, Chinese and Indian, as well as tribal groups in Sabah and Sarawak, speak Malay. Nearly everyone in Malaysia speaks some English, except in remote areas. Chinese is also spoken, mainly Hokkien but also Cantonese, Hakka and Mandarin. The Indian languages of Tamil and Punjabi are spoken too.

Language courses are available in KL (ask at the Tourism Malaysia office, see page 595) and other big cities. A recommended teach-yourself book is *Everyday Malay* by Thomas G Oey (Periplus Language Books, 1995), which is widely available. A Malay/English dictionary or phrase book is also useful.

The basic grammar is very simple, with no tenses, genders or articles. Stress is usually placed on the second syllable of a word. The **a** is pronounced as *ah* in an open syllable, or as in *but* for a closed syllable; **e** is pronounced as in *open* or *bed*; **i** is pronounced as in *feel*; **o** is pronounced as in *all*; **u** is pronounced as in *foot*. The letter **c** is pronounced *ch* as in *change* or *chat*. The **r** is rolled. For useful phrases, see box page 586.

Media

The daily English-language **newspapers** are *The New Straits Times*, *Business Times*, *The Star* (best for local news), and *The Malay Mail* (basically a gossip mag). The main Sunday papers are *The New Sunday Times*, *The Sunday Mail* and *The Sunday Star*. *The Sun* is a free English-language daily found in train stations and shopping centres but is packed with ads. The English-language dailies are government-owned. *Aliran Monthly* analyses current affairs from a non-government perspective. *The Rocket* is the Democratic Action Party's opposition newspaper. International editions of foreign newspapers and magazines can be found at news stands and book stalls. In East Malaysia the English-language newspapers are the *Sabah Daily News* and the *Sarawak Tribune*. See also www.aliran.com.

There are 6 government **radio** stations in various languages including English. In KL you can tune into the Federal Capital's radio station; there are a number of local stations. The *BBC World Service* can be picked up on FM in southern Johor, from the Singapore transmitter. Elsewhere it can be received on shortwave. The main frequencies are (in kHz): 11750, 9740, 6195 and 3915.

RTM1 and RTM2 are operated by Radio **Television Malaysia**, the government-run station. Some American and British series are shown. Singaporean programmes can be received as far north as Melaka. Satellite and Cable TV is widely available. Many hotels carry the ASTRO service which offers HBO, STAR movies, ESPN, CNN, BBC, Discovery and MTV as well as a host of Chinese channels.

Money → *US$1=RM3.3; £1 = RM6.4 (Aug 2008)*.
The unit of currency is the Malaysian dollar or ringgit (RM), which is divided into 100 cents or sen. Bank notes come in denominations of RM1, 5, 10, 20, 50, 100, 500 and 1000. Coins are issued in 1, 5, 10, 20 and 50 sen.
Cost of travelling Malaysia is good value for overseas visitors. If you stay in the bottom-end guesthouses, eat at hawker centres and use public transport, you can get by on US$15-20 (RM60-80) per day. Cheaper guesthouses charge US$5-10 (RM20-40) a night for 2 people. Dorms are available in big towns, US$3 (RM10-20). It is usually possible to find a simple a/c room for US$10-20 (RM40-80). A tourist-class hotel, with a/c, room service, restaurant and swimming pool costs US$26-40 (RM100-150). International-class hotels charge US$80-130 (RM300-500). Eating out is also cheap: a good curry can cost as little as US$0.50-1 (RM2-4). Overland travel is a bargain; the bus network is extremely good and fares are very good value.
Exchange Most of the bigger hotels, restaurants and shops in Sarawak and Sabah accept international credit cards, including American Express, BankAmericard, Diners, MasterCard and Visa. The latter 2 are the most widely accepted. Cash advances can be issued

against credit cards in most banks, although some banks limit the amount that can be drawn. A passport is usually required for over-the-counter transactions. It is also possible to draw cash from ATMs, using a credit or debit card. **Maybank** will accept Visa and MasterCard at its ATMs; cards with the Cirrus mark will also be accepted at most ATMs. TCs can be exchanged at banks and money changers and in some big hotels (often guests only). Money changers often offer the best rates, but shop around. Major currencies are widely accepted, but US dollars are probably best.

Opening hours
Most government offices (including some tourist offices and post offices) are closed on the 1st and 3rd Sat of each month. In Terengganu and Kelantan states, weekend days are Thu-Fri, as many of the local Muslim residents visit the mosques for prayers on Fri.

Post
Malaysia's postal service is cheap and reliable, although incoming and outgoing parcels should be registered. To send postcards overseas costs RM1.50; letters cost RM1.50 (up to 10 g) or RM1.50 (up to 20 g). Post office opening hours are Mon-Sat 0830-1700. Fax services are available in most state capitals. Poste restante is available at post offices in major cities; make sure your family name is capitalized and underlined. Most post offices provide a packing service for RM5. You can also buy **Air Asia** tickets at post offices.

Safety
Normal precautions should be taken with passports and valuables; many hotels have safes. Pickpocketing and bag snatching are problems in KL, JB and Penang. Women travelling alone need have few worries – although take the usual precautions like not walking alone in deserted places at night.

Student travellers
Anyone in full-time education is entitled to an **International Student Identity Card (ISIC)**,

www.isic.org. These are issued by student travel offices and travel agencies across the world and offer special rates on all forms of transport and other concessions and services. Students can benefit from discounts on some entrance charges and special deals on transport. But there is no institutionalized system of discounts for students.

Tax
Airport departure tax RM10 for domestic flights, RM45 for international, but these are usually included in the ticket price.
GST Sales tax is generally 10%.

Telephone → *Country code +60.*
IDD code 00. Operator T101. Directory enquiries T102/103. International operator T108.

TM **italk** gives excellent rates for international calls, around RM10 for 1 hr. However, you can't call from all public phones in Malaysia – find a phone before you buy a card. Buying a local mobile and SIM card is cheap and easy. **Celcom** and **DiGi** are the main providers. You can use mobiles with **italk** cards, but you need to pay local call rates in addition to the **italk** card itself, but it's still good value.

Time
Official time is 8 hrs ahead of GMT.

Tipping
Tipping is unusual. A service charge of 10% is automatically added to restaurant and hotel bills, plus a 5% government tax (indicated by the + and ++ signs). For personal services, such as porters, a modest tip is appropriate.

Tour operators
In the UK
Audley Travel, New Mill, New Mill Lane, Whitney, OX29 9SX, T01993-838000, www.audleytravel.com.
Discovery Initiatives Ltd, The Travel House, 51 Castle St, Cirencester, GL7 1QD, T01285-643333, www.discoveryinitiatives.co.uk.

Eastern Oriental Express, 20 Upper Ground, London SE1 9PF, T020-7921 4000, www.orient-expresstrains.com.
Exodus, Grange Mills, Weir Rd, London, SW12 0NE, T020-8675 5550, www.exodus.co.uk.
Explore Worldwide, Nelson House, 55 Victoria Rd, Farnborough, Hants GU14 7PH. T0870-333 4001, www.explore.co.uk.
Kuoni Travel, Kuoni House, Dorking, Surrey, T01306-747002, www.kuoni.co.uk.
Magic of the Orient, 14 Frederick Place, Clifton, Bristol, BS8 1AS, T0117-311 6050, www.magicoftheorient.com.
Realworld-travel, Lower Farm, Happisburgh, Norwich, NR12 0QQ, T0709-23322, www.4real.co.uk.
Regaldive, 58 Lancaster Way, Ely, CB6 3NW, T0870-220 1777, www.regal-diving.co.uk.
Silk Steps, Compass House, Rowdens Rd, Wells, Somerset, BA5 1TU, T01749-685162, www.silksteps.co.uk.
Travel Mood, 214 Edgware Rd, London W2 1DH; 1 Brunswick Ct, Bridge St, Leeds, LS2 7QU; 16 Reform St, Dundee, DD1 1RG, T0207-087 8400, www.travelmood.com.
Trekforce Expeditions, Way to Wooler Farm, Wooler, Northumberland, NE71 6AQ, T0845-241 3085, www.trekforce.org.uk.
Trips Worldwide, 14 Frederick Place, Clifton, Bristol BS8 1AS, T0117-311 4400, www.tripsworldwide.co.uk.

In North America
Asian Pacific Adventures, T+1-800-825 1680, www.asianpacificadventures.com.

In Australia
Intrepid Travel, 11 Spring St, Fitzroy, Victoria, T+61-1300-360887, www.intrepidtravel.com.au.

Tourist information
The main **Tourism Malaysia** is in KL; see page 595. It has a tourist information bureau in most large towns; it is very efficient and can advise on itineraries, help with bookings for travel and cultural events and provide information on hotels, restaurants and air, road, rail, sea and

river transport timetables and prices. If there is no **Tourism Malaysia** office in a town, travel agents are usually helpful and well informed.

The **Malaysia Tourism Centre** is another tourist information bureau (see page 595). Regional tourism offices in state capitals are all reasonably efficient.

For what's on listings, the best sources are the online magazine www.visionkl.com.my, *Night & Day*, published weekly, and the What's On section of the *Malay Mail*.

Useful websites

www.aseansec.org Government statistics, acronyms and information.
headlines.yahoo.com/full_coverage/world/malaysia Excellent for current affairs.
www.journeymalaysia.com Covers the majority of Malaysia's tourist sites in an entertaining and factual way. Also books tours.
www.sabahtourism.com Well-designed but hard-to-navigate site about Sabah by the state's tourism board.
www.sabahtravelguide.com Great travel site with links to the official tourist board. Interactive maps, tour agents, up-to-date descriptions of destinations, travel advice.
www.sarawaktourism.com Heaps of information on the state.
www.tourismmalaysia.gov.my Tourism Malaysia's website.
www.virtualtourist.com A good website with content by other travellers. Put in your destination and find information on hotels, restaurants, things to see and avoid.

Visas and immigration

No visa is required for a stay of up to 3 months in Malaysia (provided you are not going to work) for citizens of the UK, the US, Australia, New Zealand, Canada, Ireland and most other European countries. If you intend to stay longer, 2-month extensions are usually easy to get at immigration offices in KL, Penang or JB. Note that Israeli passport holders are not allowed to enter Malaysia.

Visitor passes for Peninsular Malaysia are not automatically valid for entry into Sabah

and Sarawak, as the Bornean states maintain their own control over immigration (even Malaysian visitors from the Peninsula require a travel permit). On entry into these states visitors will have to go through immigration and receive a new stamp in their passport, usually valid for 1 month. Apply to the immigration offices in Kota Kinabalu and Kuching for a 1-month extension; 2 extensions are usually granted. There are certain areas of East Malaysia where entry permits are necessary; for example, Bario and the Kelabit Highlands in Sarawak. These can be obtained from the residents' offices (details provided in the relevant towns).

Weights and measures

Metric, although road distances are marked in both kilometres and miles.

Women travellers

Women, if not accompanied by men, usually attract unwarranted attention, especially in more Islamic areas, like the east coast. Most male attention is bravado and there have been few serious incidents. However women should be sensitive to the fact that Malaysia is a predominantly Muslim country. See Dress, page 586. When travelling it is best to keep to public transport and to travel during the day. Hitching is not advisable for women travelling on their own.

Working in Malaysia

For jobs in Malaysia and tips on working there, see www.escapeartist.com/as/pac.htm. The government runs an incentive programme for foreigners to move or retire to the country called 'Malaysia: My Second Home'. This scheme offers a renewable 5-year multiple-entry visa called a Social Visit Pass. The catch is you need RM150,000 banked in Malaysia and a minimum RM7000 monthly income. Apply at Malaysian embassies or **Tourism Malaysia** offices. The **Ministry of Human Resources (MOHR)** provides information on labour law and practice in Malaysia, details of which can be found on www.mohr.gov.my.

Kuala Lumpur

→ *Colour map 8, D2.*

In the space of a century, Kuala Lumpur grew from a trading post and tin-mining shanty town into a colonial capital of 1.5 million people. Today it is a modern, cosmopolitan business hub and centre of government. The economic boom that started in the late 1980s has caused a building bonanza to rival Singapore's. In downtown Kuala Lumpur, old and new are juxtaposed. The jungled backdrop of the Supreme Court's copper-topped clocktower has been replaced by scores of stylish, high-rise office blocks, dominated by the soaring, angular-roofed Maybank headquarters. The Victorian, Moorish and Moghul-style buildings, the art deco central market, and the Chinese shophouses stand in marked contrast to these impressive skyscrapers. The Petronas Twin Towers offer the most impressive addition to the modern skyline and are part of the Kuala Lumpur City Centre (KLCC) development. ▶▶ *For listings, see pages 601-606.*

Ins and outs

Getting there

Airport information Kuala Lumpur (KL) is well linked to the rest of Malaysia and to the wider world. **Kuala Lumpur International Airport (KLIA)** ① *Sepang, 72 km south, T03-8776 2000, www.klia.com.my*, provides a slick point of entry. Glitzy and high-tech, it has all the usual facilities including restaurants, shops and banks. The **Tourism Malaysia** desk has pamphlets and a useful map.

Some domestic air connections (including to Sabah and Sarawak) pass through Sepang, although the **Low Cost Carrier Terminal (LCCT)** ① *20 km south of KLIA, www.lcct.com.my*, is used by most budget airlines. Shuttle buses connect KLIA and the LCCT (20 minutes) for RM1.50. Always check your ticket to confirm which terminal you're flying from.

The LCCT terminal is dominated by the hugely successful **Air Asia** ① *T03-8775 4000, www.airasia.com*, which is the region's main low-cost carrier, with flights as far afield as Manila and southern China. Internet bookings provide the best deals. Tickets booked a few weeks in advance are the cheapest and most travellers moving onto Malaysian Borneo find this is the most convenient option. Travel passes are available, see page 580.

Airport departure tax is RM10 for domestic flights and RM45 for international, but this is usually included in the ticket price. ▶▶ *See Transport, page 605.*

Transport from the airport From KLIA, the **KLIA Ekspres Coach Service** ① *T03-6203 3064, www.kliaekspres.com*, provides an efficient service into the city centre to Hentian Duta (near the Tun Razak Hockey Stadium). From the KLIA arrivals hall, go one floor down to where the coaches depart; follow the clearly marked signs. Coaches run every 30 minutes, 0500-2230 (one hour, RM25 one way). The coach goes to Hentian Duta bus station where passengers transfer to a shuttle bus (RM1) for a connection to major hotels.

The **KLIA Ekspres** ① *T03-2267 8000, www.kliaekspres.com*, runs an air-rail service every 20 minutes, 0500-2400 between the airport and **KL Central** train station. From here you can take a taxi to your hotel. The journey takes 30 minutes and costs RM35 one way. Travellers using the KLIA Ekspres can check their luggage in at KL Central for outgoing flights.

Alternatively, the **KLIA Transit** ① *www.kliaekspres.com*, takes 35 minutes to make the same journey, and costs RM35. The train stops at three stations and runs 0550-0100. If your plane arrives outside these hours, take a taxi into KL or hire a car (see below).

24 hours in Kuala Lumpur

Begin the day by heading to the **Petronas Twin Towers**. Queue for a free ticket to the **skybridge** (closed Mondays) to survey the city from above. Head back to earth, pick up a copy of the *New Straits Times* and enjoying a leisurely coffee before making a foray for the classic Malay breakfast: *nasi lemak* – rice cooked in coconut milk served with prawn sambal, *ikan bilis* (like anchovies), hard boiled egg and peanuts.

Head over to Chinatown and discover the two facets of Malaysia's cultural heritage: the **Sri Mahamariamman Temple** and the **Chan See Shu Yuen Temple**. For cultural balance make your way to the **Masjid Negara** (National Mosque), stopping en route at the art deco **Central Market** to browse for handicrafts.

At midday enjoy a dim sum buffet lunch, which you can work off with a walk in the 90-ha **Lake Gardens** before looking around the **Islamic Arts Museum** near its southern tip.

Shake off the past and witness Malaysia's tryst with modernity. Start the evening with a cold beer at the **Coliseum Café** before heading back to Chinatown around 1930 when the copy-watch sellers and all kinds of other hawkers emerge from their workload.

For dinner, sample another slice of this culinary melting pot in the unique Nyonya cuisine of the Straits Malays.

While KL doesn't have the liveliest nightlife, there is still a reasonably hot stock of bars and clubs on Jl Pinang and Jl P Ramlee, and less touristy options in **Bangsar Baru** west of the city centre and near the university of Malaya. If your stomach grumbles after midnight, 24-hour mamak canteens are plentiful in Bangsar.

For a taxi expect to pay RM60-80 (RM86.10 after midnight). Taxis operate on a coupon system; collect one from the taxi counter at the exit in arrivals (near Door 3). Touts charge more than double the official rate; bargain hard. Many hotels provide a pick-up service, but make sure they are aware of your arrival details; there is a hotel pick-up office just outside the terminal exit. Major car rental companies have desks in arrivals, open 24 hours.

From the LCCT terminal the **Skybus** ⓘ *www.skybus.com.my*, runs to KL Central Station. The journey takes just over one hour and costs RM9. If arriving on **Air Asia** at the LCCT, the official taxi charge to KL city centre is RM60. Buy a coupon from the arrivals hall to avoid arguments. ▸▸ *For information on getting to the airport from the city, see page 605.*

Getting around

Kuala Lumpur is not the easiest city to navigate, with its sights spread thinly over a wide area. Pedestrians have not been high on the list of priorities for Malaysian urban planners, with many roads, especially outside the city centre, built without pavements, making walking both hazardous and difficult. The heavy pollution and the hot, humid climate add to the problem and, with the exception of the area around Central Market, Chinatown and Dayabumi, distances between sights are too great to cover comfortably on foot. Kuala Lumpur's bus system is labyrinthine and congested streets mean that travelling by taxi can make for a tedious wait in a traffic jam. Try to insist that taxi drivers use their meters, although don't be surprised if they refuse. The two **Light Rail Transit** (LRT), the Monorail and the **KMT Komuter** rail lines, are undoubtedly the least hassle and provide a great elevated and air-conditioned view of the city. The **Malaysian Tourism Centre**, see page 595, gives free, detailed pocket-sized maps of KL, with bus stops, monorail and LRT systems. See also www.kiat.net/malaysia/KL/transit.html.

Worth considering if short of time is the **KL Hop-on Hop-off City Tour** ① T03-2691 1382, www.myhoponhopoff.com, daily 0830-2030, RM38, a hi-tech variant on the London tour bus theme. Tickets are for 24 hours and can be bought at hotels, travel agents and on the bus itself which stops at 22 clearly marked points around town. A recorded commentary is available in eight languages as the bus trundles around a circuit that includes KLCC, the Golden Triangle, Petaling Street (Chinatown), KL Central Station, the National Mosque and the Palace of Culture.

Orientation

The **colonial core** is around the Padang and down Jalan Raja and Jalan Tun Perak. East of the Padang (the cricket pitch in front of the old Selangor Club, next to Merdeka Square), straight over the bridge on Lebuh Pasar Besar, is the main commercial area, occupied by banks and finance companies. To the southeast of Merdeka Square is KL's vibrant **Chinatown**. If you get disorientated in the winding streets around Little India and Chinatown a good point of reference is the angular Maybank Building situated in Jalan Pudu, very close to both Puduraya Bus Terminal and Jalan Sultan. The streets to the north of the Padang are central shopping streets with modern department stores and shops.

To find a distinctively Malay area, it is necessary to venture further out, along Jalan Raja Muda Musa to **Kampong Baru**, to the northeast. To the south of Kampong Baru, on the opposite side of the Klang River, is **Jalan Ampang**, once KL's millionaires' row, where tin magnates, or *towkays*, and sultans first built their homes. The road is now mainly occupied by embassies and high commissions. To the southeast of Jalan Ampang is KL's so-called **Golden Triangle**, to which the modern central business district has migrated.

Tourist information

Malaysian Tourism Centre (MTC) ① 109 Jl Ampang, T03-2163 3664, daily 0700-2400, is housed in an opulent mansion formerly belonging to a Malaysian planter and tin miner. It provides information on all 13 states, as well as money-changing facilities, an express bus ticket counter, tour reservations, Malay restaurant, cultural shows every Tuesday, Thursday, Saturday and Sunday at 1500 (RM5), demonstrations of traditional handicrafts and a souvenir shop. There is a visitor centre on Level 3 of the airport's main terminal building.

Other useful contacts are: **Tourism Malaysia** ① Level 2, Putra World Trade Centre, 45 Jl Tun Ismail, T03-2615 8188, www.tourismmalaysia.gov.my, Mon-Fri 0900-1800; **KL Tourist Police** ① T03-2149 6593, and the **Wildlife and National Parks Department** ① Km 10, Jl Cheras, T03-9075 2872, www.wildlife.gov.my.

Many companies offer half-day city tours, which include visits to Chinatown, the National Museum, railway station, Masjid Negara (National Mosque), the Padang area and Masjid Jamek – most of which cost about RM30. City night tours take in Chinatown, the Sri Mahmariamman Temple and a cultural show (RM60). Other tours visit sights close to the city such as Batu Caves, a batik factory and the Selangor Pewter Complex (RM30), as well as day-trips further afield.

Best time to visit

The weather in KL is hot and humid all year round with temperatures rarely straying far below 20°C or much above 30°C. There is no rainy season per se, although you can get rainstorms throughout the year. Try to be here for one of the festivals (see page 585), particularly the Thaipusam Festival, one of the most colourful and shocking. For up-to-date weather reports, check www.kjc.gov.my.

Sights

Kuala Lumpur is a sprawling city. The big shopping malls, hip restaurants and bars are clustered around The Golden Triangle and the KLCC. Here too are the Petronas Towers, once the tallest in the world, and the KL Tower, another mighty spike on the landscape. The ethnic neighbourhoods lie southwest of here – there's Chinatown, a web of bustling streets filled with temples, funeral stores, restaurants and shophouses, and Little India, packed with shops selling Bollywood CDs, saris and spices. Also here is the colonial core where the remnants of the British empire ring Merdeka Square. You can escape from the hustle a few streets southwest of here in the Lake Gardens, which house the fine Islamic Arts Museum and a bird and orchid park.

Colonial core and Little India

Behind the Masjid Jamek mosque, from the corner of Jalan Tuanku Abdul Rahman and Jalan Raja Laut, are the colonial-built public buildings, distinguished by their grand Moorish architecture. The **Sultan Abdul Samad Building**, with its distinctive clocktower and bulbous copper domes, houses the Supreme Court.

The Sultan Abdul Samad Building faces on to the Padang on the opposite side of the road, next to **Merdeka Square**. The old Selangor Club cricket pitch is the venue for Independence Day celebrations. The centrepiece of Merdeka Square is the tallest flagpole in the world (100 m high) and the huge Malaysian flag that flies from the top can be seen across half the city, particularly at night when it is floodlit.

South of the Masjid Jamek mosque, on Jalan Raya, is the 35-storey, marble **Dayabumi Complex**, one of KL's most striking landmarks. It was designed by local architect Datuk Nik Mohamed and introduces contemporary Islamic architecture to the skyscraper era.

On the opposite bank to the Dayabumi Complex is the **Central Market** ① *www.central market.com.my*, a former wet market built in 1928 in art deco style, tempered with local baroque trimmings. In the early 1980s it was revamped to become a focus for KL's artistic community and a handicraft centre. It is a warren of boutiques, handicraft and souvenir stalls, some with their wares laid out on the wet market's original marble slabs.

Northwest of the old railway station is the **Masjid Negara** (National Mosque) ① *Sat-Thu 0900-1800, Fri 1445-1800; Muslims can visit the mosque 0630-2200; women must use a separate entrance*, the modern spiritual centre of KL's Malay population and the symbol of Islam for the whole country. Completed in 1965, it occupies a 5-ha site at the end of Jalan Hishamuddin. Close to the National Mosque is the **Islamic Arts Museum Malaysia** ① *Jl Lembah Perdana, T03-2274 2020, www.iamm.org.my, daily 1000-1800, RM12*, which provides a fascinating collection of textiles and metalware from diverse areas such as Iran, India, South Asia and China. It's a wonderful oasis in the midst of the city.

Little India's streets – Jalan Masjid India and nearby lanes – resonate to the sounds of Bollywood CDs and hawker cries. There are stalls and stores selling garish gold, saris, fabrics, great *kurta* (pyjama smocks), traditional medicines, flowers and spices. It is also a good place to eat cheap Indian snacks and sip on sweet lassis. Although the streets are fairly scruffy, the smells and colours make up for its lack of gloss.

At the muddy confluence of the Klang and Gombak rivers where KL's founders stepped ashore stands the **Masjid Jamek** ① *entrance on Jalan Tun Perak, daily 0900-1100, 1400-1600*, formerly the National Mosque. Built in 1909 by English architect, AB Hubbock, the mosque has a walled courtyard (*sahn*) and a three-domed prayer hall. It is striking with its striped white and salmon-coloured brickwork and domed minarets, cupolas and arches.

Chinatown

Southeast of the Central Market, Chinatown is bounded by Jalan Tun HS Lee (Jalan Bandar), Jalan Petaling and Jalan Sultan. A mixture of crumbling shophouses, coffee shops and restaurants, this quarter wakes up during late afternoon, when its streets become the centre of frenetic trading and haggling. Jalan Petaling and parts of Jalan Sultan are transformed into an open-air night market, *pasar malam*, and food stalls selling Chinese, Indian and Malay delicacies, and all manner of impromptu boutiques line the streets.

The extravagantly decorated **Sri Mahamariamman Temple** is south of Jalan Hang Lekir, tucked away on Jalan Tun HS Lee (Jalan Bandar). Incorporating gold, precious stones and Spanish and Italian tiles, it was founded in 1873 by Tamils from South India who had come to Malaya as contract labourers to work in the rubber plantations or on the roads and railways. It has a silver chariot dedicated to Lord Murugan (Subramaniam), which is taken in procession to the Batu Caves during the Thaipusam Festival (see page 585).

The elaborate Chinese **Chan See Shu Yuen Temple**, at the southern end of Jalan Petaling, was built in 1906 and has a typical open courtyard and symmetrical pavilions. Paintings, woodcarvings and ceramic sculptures decorate the façade. Ornate clan houses (*kongsis*) can be seen nearby; a typical one is nearby the **Chan Kongsi** on Jalan Maharajalela.

Lake Gardens and around

① *Bus 21C or 48C from Kotaraya Plaza, or bus 18 or 21A from Chow Kit; alight at old train station.*
Near the southern tip of the Lake Gardens, is the **Muzium Negara** ① *T03-2282 6255, www.museum.gov.my, daily 0900-1800, RM2*, with its Minangkabau-style roof and two large murals of Italian glass mosaic on either side of the main entrance. They depict the main historical episodes and cultural activities of Malaysia. The museum provides an excellent introduction to Malaysia's history, geography, natural history and culture.

Close to the museum is the south entrance to the 90-ha **Lake Gardens**. Pedal boats can be hired at the weekend. The gardens also house a hibiscus garden, orchid garden and sculpture garden; as well as children's playgrounds, picnic areas, restaurants and cafés, and a small deer park. At the north end of the Lake Gardens is the **National Monument**. This 15-m memorial provides a good view of Parliament House.

The showpiece of the Lake Gardens is the **Bird Park** ① *daily 0900-1830, RM22*. The world's largest covered bird park, it houses more than 2000 birds from 200 species, ranging from ducks to hornbills.

The **Butterfly Park** ① *daily 0900-1800, RM10*, is a miniature jungle, which is home to almost 8000 butterflies from 150 species. There are also small mammals, amphibians and reptiles and rare tropical insects in the park.

Kuala Lumpur City Centre (KLCC)

This area has been the focus of extraordinary redevelopment and is known as the **Kuala Lumpur City Centre (KLCC)** ① *www.klcc.com.my*, a 'city within a city'. The complex is one of the largest real estate developments in the world, covering a 40-ha site and including the Petronas Towers. The city's offices, hotels and shopping complexes are mostly concentrated in the Golden Triangle, see below, on the east side of the city.

The **Petronas Twin Towers** were designed by American architect Cesar Pelli and the surrounding park by the Brazilian landscape artist Roberto Marx Burle. The **Sky Bridge** ① *T03-2331 8080, Tue-Sun 0900-1700*, links the two towers on the 41st floor. Visitors must queue for a first-come first-served ticket that gives free access to the bridge and some stunning views. Only a limited number of people are allowed up every day, so it is advisable

Kuala Lumpur

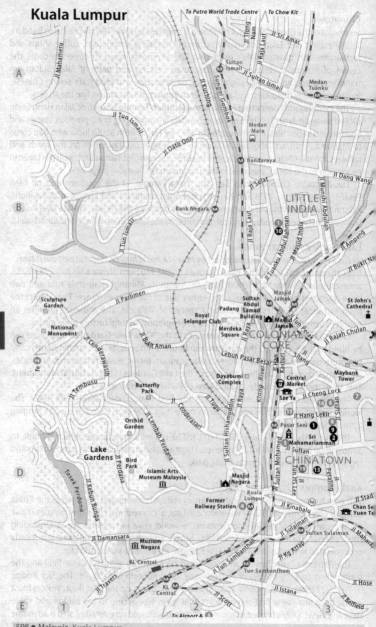

To Putra World Trade Centre · To Chow Kit

Jl Mahameru

Jl Tiong Nam · Jl Raja Laut · Jl Sri Amar

Sultan Ismail · Jl Sultan Ismail

Medan Tuanku

Jl Tun Ismail

Medan Mara

Jl Kuching

Jl Dato Onn

Sungai Gombak

Bandaraya

Jl Selat

Jl Dang Wangi

Jl Munshi Abdullah

LITTLE INDIA

Abdul Rahman

Bank Negara

Jl Raja Laut

Jl Tuanku Abdul Rahman

Jl Ampang

Jl Bukit Nanas

Jl Parlimen

Sculpture Garden

National Monument

Jl Cenderawasih

Jl Bukit Aman

Jl Tembusu

Jl Tugu

Jl Cenderasari

Jl Lembah Perdana

Jl Perdana

Butterfly Park

Orchid Garden

Bird Park

Lake Gardens

Tasek Perdana

Jl Kebun Bunga

Islamic Arts Museum Malaysia

Royal Selangor Club

Padang

Merdeka Square

Sultan Abdul Samad Building

Masjid Jamek

Masjid Jamek

Jl Tun Perak

St John's Cathedral

COLONIAL CORE

Jl Rajah Chulan

Lebuh Pasar Besar

Kasturi

Silang

Klang River

Dayabumi Complex

Central Market

Sze Ya

Jl Cheng Lock

Maybank Tower

Jl Hang Lekir

Jl Tun HS Lee

Pasar Seni

Sri Mahamariamman

Jl Sultan

CHINATOWN

Jl Petaling

Masjid Negara

Kuala Lumpur

Jl Kinabalu

Chan See Yuen Temple

Jl Damansara

Muzium Negara

Former Railway Station

Jl Sultan Hishamuddin

Jl Raya

Jl Mohamed

Jl Sulaiman

Sultan Sulaiman

Jl Maharaj

Jl Travers

KL Central

Jl Tun Sambanthan

Tun Sambantham

Jl Kg Attap

Jl Istana

Jl Hose

Jl Belfield

KL Central

Jl Scott

To Airport &

A B C D E

1 2 3

KAMPONG BARU

Jl Raja Muda

Kampong Baru Sunday Market

Jl Sungai Baharu

Australian High Commission

Jl Yap Kwan Seng

Jl Mayang

Jl Ampang

KLCC

Kampong Baru

Jl Ampang

Jl Lumba Kuda

Petronas Twin Towers

Discovery Centre

Dang Wangi

Bukit Nanas

Jl Sultan Ismail

Kampong Baru

Jl P. Ramlee

Jl Pinang

KUALA LUMPUR CITY CENTRE (KLCC)

To 8

KL Tower

Jl Puncak

Jl Perak

Jl Kia Peng

Jl Stonor

To 12

Bukit Nanas Forest Reserve

Jl Tengah

Rajah Chulan

Rumah Penghulu Abu Seman

Jl Raja Chulan

Jl Nagasari

Jl Conlay

Karyaneka Handicraft Centre

Jl Ceylon

Jl Berangan

Cangat Bukit Bintang

GOLDEN TRIANGLE

Jl Bukit Bintang

Bukit Bintang

Jl Inai

Jl Kamuning

Puduraya

Jl Pudu

Tinkat Tong Shin

Jl Sultan Ismail

HW Grenier

Jl Imbi

Plaza Rakyat

Jl Gallaway

Jl Eberwein

Jl Imbi

Times Square Shopping Complex

Jl Horley

Jl Kampong Barat

nku Abdul hman Park

Jl Hang Jebat

Jl Pudu

Changkat Tambi Dollah

Hang Tuah

N

500 metres

500 yards

Sleeping
AnCasa **7** C3
Backpackers Travellers
  Inn **6** D3
Carcosa Seri Negara **2** C1

Coliseum **1** B3
Crown Princess **17** A6
Equatorial **14** B5
Federal **9** C5
Fortuna **12** C5
Heritage Station **4** D2
Puduraya **11** C4
Putra Bintang **10** C5
Red Dragon Backpackers **8** C3
Regent **13** C5
Saujana Hotel & Country
  Club **3** F2

Shangri-La **15** B5
Starlight **5** D3
StayOrange **16** C3
Traders **18** B5
Wheelers Guest House **19** D3

Eating
Bombay Palace **8** B6
Ciao **12** B6
Coliseum Café **10** B3
Eden Village **5** C6
Formosa Vegetarian **2** D3

Gourmet Food Court **1** D3
King's Café **9** D3
Madam Kwan **11** B5
Marco Polo **14** C5
Old China Café **13** D3
Seri Melayu **6** C6
Teppanyaki **4** C5 & D5
Top Hat **7** B6
Zura Traditional **3** C5

Bars & clubs
Reggae **19** D3

to get there before 0900, especially on weekends. The **Discovery Centre** ① *Level 4, Suria KLCC Petrosains, T03-2331 8181, RM12,* has rides and hands-on computer games glorifying the petroleum industry but is a great place for children.

Menara KL and the Bukit Nanas Forest Reserve

① *T03-2020 5448 for reservations, www.menarakl.com.my. Daily 0900-2200. RM15. There is no public transport, so take a taxi or walk from one of the nearby roads.*

Near the intersection of Jalan Ampang and Jalan Sultan Ismail atop Bukit Nanas stands the **Menara KL** (KL Tower). This 421-m-high tower is the fourth tallest in the world (the viewing platform stands at 276 m). The tower is the brainchild of former prime minister Dr Mahathir Mohammed. At ground level are several shops, fast-food restaurants and a mini amphitheatre. Above the viewing platform is the **Seri Angkasa** revolving restaurant.

Combine a visit to the tower with a walk in the **Bukit Nanas Forest Reserve** ① *free,* a beautiful 11-ha area of woodland in the city centre with marked trails. KL is perhaps the only city with a patch of rainforest at its heart. Butterflies, monkeys and birds live in the forest.

Golden Triangle

The **Rumah Penghulu Abu Seman** ① *Jl Stonor, T03-2162 7459, Mon-Fri 1000-1600,* otherwise known as the **Heritage Centre of the Badan Warisan Malaysia,** is in a mock-Tudor building off Jalan Conloy, on the northern edge of the Golden Triangle. In the garden is a reconstructed headman's house made of timber displaying detailed carvings and furnished in the style of a 1930s house. Just to the east of the Heritage Centre is the **Komplex Budaya Kraf,** a handicraft centre offering you the chance to watch artists at work.

One of the newest shopping plazas in the Golden Triangle is **Times Square** on Jalan Imbi, with a rollercoaster, Imax cinema, shops, hotel and restaurants.

The **Karyaneka Handicraft Centre** ① *Jl Conlay, daily 0900-1800, take a minibus or Intrakota No 40 from Jl Tuanku Abdul Rahman,* to the east of the city centre, is popular with tour groups. There is a small museum illustrating batik, weaving and pottery. Craft demonstrations are held from 1000 to 1800, and there are crafts on sale.

Around Kuala Lumpur

The most popular day trip is the **Batu Caves** ① *13 km north, open until 2100, RM1, taxi (30 mins) or bus No 11 or 11D (1 hr) from Central Market,* which is a fun day out. This series of caverns is reached by a sweat-inducing flight of steps with colourful Hindu paraphernalia. Set high in a massive limestone outcrop, the caves were 'discovered' by American naturalist William Hornaby in the 1880s. In 1891 Hindu priests set up a shrine in the main cave dedicated to Lord Muraga and it has now become the biggest Indian pilgrimage centre in Malaysia during the Thaipusam Festival (see page 585), when 800,000 Hindus congregate.

Kuala Selangor Nature Park ① *T03-3289 2294, www.mns.org.my, RM4, buses from KL's Puduraya bus terminal to Kuala Selangor, then taxi 8 km to Kampong Kuantan, boat trips from Kampong Kuantan cost RM10 each or RM40 to charter,* consists of 250 ha of coastal mangrove swamp and wetland. It has several observation hides, 156 bird species (including bee eaters, kingfishers and sea eagles) and leaf monkeys. It is also one of the best places to see Malaysia's famous **synchronized fireflies** – the only fireflies in Southeast Asia that coordinate their flashing; they are best observed on a moonless night, from about one hour after sunset. There are various trails, a mangrove walk and a visitor centre (daily 0900-1800). It's possible to stay overnight at the centre; accommodation includes A-frame huts, chalets and dorms and should be booked in advance.

● Kuala Lumpur listings

Hotel and guesthouse prices
LL over US$200 **L** US$151-200 **AL** US$101-150
A US$66-100 **B** US$46-65 **C** US$31-45
D US$21-30 **E** US$12-20 **F** US$7-11
G US$6 and under
Restaurant prices
₸₸₸ over US$12 ₸₸ US$6-12 ₸ under US$6.

● Sleeping

Most top hotels are between Jl Sultan Ismail and Jl P Ramlee, in KL's Golden Triangle. South of Jl Raja Chulan, in the Bukit Bintang area, there is another concentration of big hotels. Many reduce their room rates Mon-Fri.

There are also lots of cheap hotels in the Golden Triangle and along Jl Bukit Bintang. Chinatown is home to rock-bottom budget places, some of which are rather run-down, others are tailor-made backpacker hostels.

Many of the cheaper hotels are around Jl Tuanku Abdul Rahman, Jl Masjid India and Jl Raja Laut, all of which are within easy walking distance of the colonial core of KL (although these tend to be quite sleazy and run down), northeast of the Padang.

Colonial core and Little India *p596, map p599*
E Coliseum, 100 Jl Tuanku Abdul Rahman, T03-2692 6270. For those on a budget who want a taste of the 1920s. Large, simple rooms with fans or a/c, shared bathrooms. Rooms facing the main street are very noisy. Famous bar and restaurant (see page 603), friendly.

Chinatown *p597, map p599*
A-B AnCasa, Jl Cheng Lock, next to Puduraya bus station, T03-2026 6060. Well-furnished, clean a/c rooms with TV, internet, minibar and safe. Restaurant and bar. Breakfast included. Walking tours of KL available. Recommended.
C-D Puduraya, 4th floor, Puduraya bus station, Jl Pudu, T03-2072 1000. Convenient for the bus station, a/c, restaurant, health club, breakfast included. Clean, spacious rooms, some with spectacular views over the city.

C-G Heritage Station, Banguanan Stesen Keretapi, Jl Sultan Hishamuddin, T03-2272 1688, www.heritagehotelmalaysia.com. Part of the magnificent Moorish-style railway station. It has retained some of its colonial splendour, but the rooms are furnished in a contemporary style. Cranky lifts, saggy floors and lukewarm food, but unbeatable for atmosphere and location. Also backpacker dorms in a/c rooms with their own bathroom.
E Red Dragon Backpackers, 83 Jl Sultan, T03-2070 6000. Converted from the old Rex cinema. Big complex of nondescript a/c doubles and dorms, with shared bathrooms, many with no windows. Backpacker-friendly lounge and chill-out point downstairs, with a big screen TV. Book exchange and beer.
E Starlight, 90-92 Jl Hang Kasturi, T03-2078 9811. A/c, spacious rooms with (basic) en suite facilities. Excellent staff. Well situated for Central Market, Chinatown, bus stations, shops and sights. Located opposite the Klang bus station, it can be noisy. Recommended.
E StayOrange, 16 Jl Petaling, T03-2070 2208, www.stayorange.com. Great location in the hub of Chinatown's street market. Spotless rooms with a/c, TV and Wi-Fi. Despite the vibrant paintwork, the rooms seem fairly clinical. Cheaper 2 bed bunk rooms available.
E-F Backpackers Travellers Inn, 2nd floor, 60 Jl Sultan (opposite **Furama Hotel**), T03-2078 2473, www.backpackerskl.com. Centrally located in Chinatown next to excellent stalls and restaurants, popular and professionally run. Rooms are small but generally clean, ranging from non-a/c dorms to a/c rooms with attached showers. Internet, left luggage, book exchange, video, TV and laundry. Cheap and pleasant rooftop bar, good-value tours. Recommended.
E-F Wheelers Guest House, 131-133 (1st floor), Bangunan Siew Yuen, Jl Tun HS Lee, T03-2070 1386, www.wheelers_kl@ yahoo.com. Similar to **Backpackers Travellers Inn** but with a funkier rooftop bar. Good value, very clean. Fan and a/c rooms available, along with a/c dorms for RM12. Good, friendly choice.

Lake Gardens and around *p597, map p599*
LL Carcosa Seri Negara, Taman Tasek Perdana, T03-2282 1888, www.ghmhotels.com. Former residence of the British High Commissioner built in 1896 and now a high-class hotel where important dignitaries, presidents and prime ministers are pampered on state visits. Set in a secluded wooded hillside overlooking the Lake Gardens. A/c, restaurant, pool.

KLCC p597, map p599
LL-AL Crown Princess, City Sq Centre, Jl Tun Razak, T03-2162 5522, www.crown princess.com.my. 500 spacious rooms with panoramic views, opulent decor, a/c, 10th floor pool and restaurant, good for high tea buffet. **Taj Indian** restaurant, lobby lounge with baby grand piano and cafés. Business centre, adjacent shopping centre with 168 shops.
L-AL Shangri-La, 11 Jl Sultan Ismail, T03-2032 2388, www.shangri-la.com. With its grand marble lobby and 720 rooms, the 'Shang' remains KL's ritziest hotel. It plays host to political leaders and assorted royalty for dinner. The best feature is its ground floor **Gourmet Corner** deli, which stocks a great variety of European food. A/c, small, rather old-fashioned pool, health club, sauna, jacuzzi, tennis.
L-AL Traders, KLCC, T03-2332 9888, www.tradershotel.com. Good value, stylish business hotel with pricey but excellent **Skybar** on the roof facing the Petronas Towers; see Bars and clubs, page 604. The cocktails are small, but you pay for the view of the Towers and KLCC, which is fabulous. There's a beautiful if shallow pool, some small jacuzzi-like ponds to cool off in, a gym and a spa. Very popular, so book in advance.
L-B Equatorial, Jl Sultan Ismail, T03-2161 7777, www.equatorial.com. One of KL's earlier international hotels. Its 1960s-style coffee shop has become one of the best in town, open 24 hrs. With an international news agency in the basement. A/c, restaurant (excellent Cantonese), pool. Rooms at the back get less traffic noise.

Golden Triangle *p600, map p599*
LL Regent, 160 Jl Bukit Bintang, T03-2141 8000, www.regenthotels.com. The ultimate hotel in KL. All suites have butler service and rooms and bathrooms are lavishly appointed, while the enormous lobby is designed around a pool of cascading water. A/c, Western, Cantonese and Japanese restaurants, beautiful pool, gym with Roman baths, health club.
LL-AL Federal, 35 Jl Bukit Bintang, T03-2148 9166, www.federalhotel.com.my. When it opened in the 1960s this hotel was the pride of KL: its **Mandarin Palace** restaurant was once rated as the most elegant in the Far East and is still good. A/c, Indian restaurant, revolving restaurant, ice cream bar, cafés, bowling, shopping arcade, business centre, pool.
A-B Fortuna, 87 Jl Berangan, T03-2141 9111, www.fortunakl.com. Tucked away just off Bukit Bintang. Slightly quieter than most and good value for money. A/c, health centre, coffee house with live music. Recommended.
E-F Putra Bintang, 72 Jl Bukit Bintag, T03-2141 9228. Gleaming new, popular and efficient. Very clean, basic rooms with a/c, attached shower. 24-hr internet. Book ahead.

Around Kuala Lumpur *p600*
L-AL Saujana Hotel & Country Club, 2 km off Sultan Abdul Aziz Shah Airport Highway, Petaling Jaya, T03-7846 1234, www.the saujanahotel.com. Low-rise hotel set in landscaped gardens. Free airport shuttle, bars and restaurants, pool and fitness centre.

❶ Eating

Many of KL's big hotels in the **Jl Sultan Ismail/Bukit Bintang** areas serve excellent-value buffet lunches. **Cangkat Bukit Bintang** and **Tingkat Tong Shin** streets, west of Jl Bukit Bintang are the latest trendy eating areas.

Food stalls
The best area is **Chow Kit**. On Jl Raja Muda Abdul Aziz there is a food court with great Indian and Afghan food. Jl Haji Hussien has a

collection of superb food stalls. Walk up Jl Haji Hussien and turn right. The food court on the top floor of **The Mall** is run down but has an attractive ambience. The Indian, Malay and Chinese choices are all good, but the majority close by 2000. It's cheap too -- tandoori chicken, naan, dhal and a drink cost just RM8. Jl Raja Alang and Jl Raja Bot stalls, off Jl Tuanku Abdul Rahman, are mostly Malay. **Kampong Baru** and **Kampong Datok Keramat** are Malay communities. On the riverfront behind Jl Mesjid India are good Indian and Malay night stalls. Jl Masjid India, **Little India**, has many good Indian and Malay foodstalls. **Sunday Market**, Kampong Baru (main market actually takes place on Sat night), has many Malay hawker stalls. For lovers of Chinese and Malay food, noodle bars and deep fried delights, you'll find the Chinatown markets on Jl Sultan, Jl Tun HS Lee and Petaling St very rewarding.

Colonial core and Little India *p596, map p599*
♥♥ **Coliseum Café**, 100 Jl Tuanku Abdul Rahman (Batu Rd). Famed for its sizzling lamb and beef steaks, Hainanese (Chinese) food and Western-style (mild) curries. During the Communist Emergency, planters were said to come here for gin and curry, handing their guns in to be kept behind the bar.
♥♥ **Sangeetha Vegetarian**, 65 Lebuh Ampang, T03-2032 3333. Good vegetarian Indian food, huge portions – tasty, clean and reliable, with a variety of desserts.

Chinatown *p597, map p599*
♥♥ **Kings Café**, 60 Jl Sultan, T/F03-2057 2877. Expensive European-style café. Popular with tourists and wealthy locals, serving excellent pastries, cakes and good coffee. Decent lunch promotions. A good place to take an a/c breather from the frenetic Chinatown markets.
♥♥ **Old China Café**, 11 Jl Balai Polis, T03-2072 5915, www.oldchina.com.my. Good, interesting food, noodles, olde worlde colonial style. Fine choice for a romantic evening out.

♥ **Formosa Vegetarian**, 48 Jl Sultan. Huge menu of fake meats and fish, beancurds and other creative veggie dishes.
♥ **Gourmet Food Court**, Jl Petaling, opposite The Swiss Inn. A great vegetarian counter with a dozen choices of tasty vegetables and beancurd to pile on rice. Best cheap breakfast in Chinatown.

Lake Gardens and around *p597, map p599*
♥♥♥ **Carcosa Seri Negara**, see Sleeping, page 602. Served in a sumptuous, colonial setting, English-style high tea (recommended), expensive Italian lunches and dinners are also served in the Mahsuri dining hall on fine china plates with solid silver cutlery.

KLCC *p597, map p599*
♥♥♥ **Ciao**, 428 Jl Tun Razak, T03-9285 4827. Tue-Sun 1200-1430, 1900-2230. Authentic, tasty Italian food served in a beautifully renovated bungalow.
♥♥ **Bangles**, 270 Jl Ampang, T03-4532 4100. Reckoned to be among the best North Indian tandoori restaurants in KL. It's often necessary to book in the evenings.
♥♥ **Bombay Palace**, 388 Jl Tun Razak, next to the US Embassy, T03-2145 4241. Good-quality North Indian food in tasteful surroundings with staff in traditional Indian uniform. Menu includes vegetarian section. Winners of the Malaysian Tourism Award for several years.
♥♥ **Madam Kwan**, on level 4, T03-2026 2297. This local favourite serves traditional Malay dishes in an upmarket atmosphere. Well known for its *nasi padang* and curry laksa.
♥♥ **Seri Melayu**, 1 Jl Conlay, T03-2145 1833. Open 1100-1500, 1900-2300. One of the best Malay restaurants in town in a traditional Minangkabau-style building. Beautifully designed interior. Don't be put off by cultural shows or big groups – the food is superb and amazingly varied; it's very popular with locals too. Individual dishes are expensive, the buffet is the best bet (more than 50 dishes), with promotions featuring cuisine from different states each month. Those arriving in shorts will be given a sarong to wear.

Top Hat, 7 Jl Kia Peng, T03-2241 3611. Good Eastern Nyonya set menu, some Western dishes. Set in a 1930s colonial bungalow, just south of KLCC.

Golden Triangle p600, map p599

Lai Ching Yuen, Regent Hotel, Jl Bukit Bintang, T03-2141 8000. Set in a mock Chinese pavilion, has won several awards, popular with Chinese gourmets, luxury table settings, revolving solid granite table centres.

Zipangu, Shangri-La Hotel, 11 Jl Sultan Ismail, T03-2032 2388. Regular winner of best restaurant, with a small Japanese garden. Limited menu but highly regarded.

Eden Village, 260 Jl Raja Chulan. Wide-ranging menu, but probably best known for seafood. Resembles a glitzy Minangkabau palace with a garden behind. Cultural Malay, Chinese and Indian dances every night.

Marco Polo, Wisma Lim Foo Yong, 86 Jl Raja Chulan, T03-2142 5595. Open 1200-1500, 1900-2300. Extensive menu, barbecue roast suckling pig recommended, 1970s-style decor, very busy at lunchtimes.

Zura Traditional, 19 Tingkat Tong Shin (just behind Jl Bukit Bintang), T03-2148 6466. Arty eatery serving traditional Peranakan cuisine. The spicy coconut fish is recommended.

Lodge Coffee Shop, Jl Sultan Ismail. Good value for money, particularly local dishes – *nasi goreng*, curries and buffets. Recommended.

Teppanyaki, 2nd floor, Sungai Wang Plaza, Jl Bukit Bintang and Lot 10, Jl Sultan Ismail, basement. Excellent Japanese fast food, set meal for RM10.

Teahouses

Try out the Chinese teahouse opposite the **Sungai Wang Hotel** on Jl Bukit Bintang.

🍷 Bars and clubs

Kuala Lumpur p593, map p599

Kuala Lumpur has a vibrant bar scene. Several streets have emerged over the past 5 years or so as hip scenes to be seen in. The **Golden Triangle** is a good place to find bars and clubs especially in the main bar and club street, Jl P Ramlee, but a few bars have begun setting up pumps in **Cangkat Bukit Bintang**, and this area is set to grow more popular. **Bangsar** and **Desi Sri Hartamas** are 2 areas just outside the centre of KL that have developed into popular nightlife spots. Bars, restaurants, coffee shops and *mamaks* stand side by side in a network of streets in both these areas. Most venues stay open until the early hours of the morning.

See the Metro section in *The Star* (Malaysia's most widely read English-language daily) for what's on. Also check out freebie magazines such as *Juice* (available in bars and clubs) or *KL lifestyle*, *KLUE* and *KL Vision* (usually free in hotels; if not, they are available in newsagents for about RM5).

Night-time on the streets around Chinatown is pretty busy and there are plenty of bars offering cheap beer. **Reggae Bar**, 158 Jl Tun HS Lee, below **Backpackers Travellers Lodge**, Chinatown. Offers the standard mix of Bob Marley music, cheap drinks and reasonable food. Occasional big screen football matches. **Skybar**, Traders Hotel, see Sleeping, page 602, KLCC. For a much more classy night-time experience, try this bar, for fabulous views of the Petronas Towers. **Zouk**, 113 Jl Ampang. Perhaps KL's longest-running fashionable nightclub. A glowing domed exterior with changing hue encapsulates the groovy interior. Occasional gay parties. International DJs such as Tiesto and has a great chill-out bar, **Velvet Underground**. Recommended.

🎭 Entertainment

Kuala Lumpur p593, map p599
Cultural shows

Central Market, T03-2274 6542. Weekends at 1945, performances of Chinese Opera, Bangsawan (Malay Traditional Theatre) and Nadagam (Indian Traditional Theatre).

Temple of Fine Arts, 116 Jl Berhala, Brickfields, T03-2274 3709, www.templeoffinearts.org. This organization, set up in Malaysia to preserve and promote Indian culture, stages cultural shows every month with dinner, music and dancing. The temple organizes an annual Festival of Arts, which involves a week of traditional and modern Indian dance. It also runs classes in classical and folk dancing.

O Shopping

Kuala Lumpur *p593, map p599*
Many of the handicrafts are imported from Indonesia. The areas to look for Chinese arts and handicrafts are along Jl Tuanku Abdul Rahman and in the centre of **Bangsar**. Jl Masjid India, running parallel with Jl Tuanku Abdul Rahman, is a treasure trove of all things Indian, from saris to sandalwood oil, bangles to brass incense burners. For clothes, shoes, bags and textiles try Jl Sultan and Jl Tun HS Lee, close to Klang bus station. In Petaling St, **Chinatown**, you can barter for Chinese lanterns, paintings and incense holders.
Batik Corner, Lot L1.13, Weld Shopping Centre, 76 Jl Raja Chulan. Excellent selection of sarong lengths and ready-mades in batiks from all over Malaysia and Indonesia.
Central Market, Jl Hang Kasturi. A purpose-built area with 2 floors of boutiques and craft stalls including pewter, jewellery, jade, wood and ceramics. Stalls of note include one that sells all kinds of moulds and cutters for baking, a wonderful spice stall, another one for nuts and for dried fruits. Downstairs are hand-painted silk batik scarves and sarongs.
Evolution, G24, City point, Dayabumi Complex, Jl Sultan Hishamuddin, T03-291 3711. Fashionable range of ready-mades and other batik gift ideas by designer Peter Hoe.
Faeroes, Weld Shopping Centre, Jl Raja Chulan (also at 42B Jl Nirvana, just off Jl Tun Ismail). Exclusive and original batiks. Recommended.
Jl Melayu is an interesting area for browsing, with its Indian shops filled with silk saris and brass pots and Malay outlets specializing in Islamic paraphernalia such as *songkok* (velvet Malay hats) and prayer rugs as well as herbal medicines and oils.
Jl Tuanku Abdul Rahman, Batu Rd. This was KL's best shopping street for decades and is transformed weekly into a pedestrian mall and night market every Sat 1700-2200.
Kampong Baru Sunday Market (Pasar Mange), off Jl Raja Muda Musa (a large Malay enclave at the north end of KL). This open-air market comes alive on Sat nights, when a variety of stalls selling batik sarongs, bamboo birdcages and traditional handicrafts compete with dozens of food stalls. However, the Pasar Mange has largely been superseded by Central Market as a place to buy handicrafts.
Pertama Shopping Complex, Jl Abdul Tunku Abdul Rahman. In the Chow Kit area near the Bandaraya LRT station. A great place for bargain hunters, with a wide range of products from souvenirs to fashion, photographic/electronic goods. KL's original department store.
Suria KLCC. This vast shopping complex is great for a Western splurge, with most designer brands you'd expect; however, don't expect prices to be much lower than in Europe or North America. One good find in the complex is **Kinokuniya Book Store** on Level 4. The shop boasts one the best ranges of English language books in Southeast Asia. On level 1, **Royal Selangor Pewter** has been recommended for its luxury gifts.

▲ Activities and tours

Kuala Lumpur *p593, map p599*
Asian Trails, Sdn Bhd 11-2-B Jl Manau, off Jl Kg Attap 50460, T03-2274 9488, www.asiantrails.info.

⊖ Transport

Kuala Lumpur *p593, map p599*
Air KL's international airport is at Sepang; see page 593, for airport information and details of transport to the city.

For a taxi from the city to KL Airport (1 hr) expect to pay RM70-90 when you buy a coupon. Hotels can arrange a good fare in the RM60 range. Make sure the taxi fare includes the motorway toll for either direction. Taxis to LCCT for **Air Asia** flights charge similar prices. **Skybus** services to LCCT leave from KL Central; however, taking a shared taxi is probably the easiest and most painless way. **Bus** The network is run by **RapidKL**, T03-7625 6999, www.rapidkl.com.my. See their website for details of fares, routes and timetables.

Car hire Companies have desks at the airport terminal. Arrange a hotel pick-up service in advance or at the office outside the terminal.

Taxi KL is one of the cheaper cities in Southeast Asia for taxis and there are stands all over town, but you can hail a taxi pretty much anywhere you like. Most are a/c and metered, but it is a challenge sometimes to get the driver to use the meter: RM2 for the first kilometre and RM0.10 for every 200 m thereafter. Extra charges apply 2400-0600 (50% surcharge), for each extra passenger in excess of 2, as well as RM1 for luggage in the boot. Waiting charges are RM2 for the first 2 mins and RM0.10 for every subsequent 45 seconds. During rush hours, shift change (around 1500) or if it's raining, it can be very difficult to persuade taxis to travel to the centre of town; negotiate a price (locals claim that waving a RM10 bill helps) or jump in and feign ignorance. For a 24-hr taxi service try the following: **Comfort**, T03-8024 2727; **KL Taxi**, T03-9221 4241; **Teletaxi**, T03-9221 1011.

Train Within the city there are 5 rail systems: 2 **LRT** lines, the Putra (pink) and Star (yellow and light green); 2 **KTM Komuter** lines (blue and red), and the new **monorail** (light blue). Trains leave every 5-15 mins, and tickets cost upwards of RM1.20. Going from one line to the other often means coming out of the station and crossing a road. All lines except the **Star LRT** go through KL Central. The trains are a great way to see the city as they mostly run on elevated rails, 10 m above street level. LRT lines are run by **RapidKL**.

For details of fares, routes and timetables, call T03-7625 6999 or visit www.rapidkl.com.my. **KTMB** operates commuter lines, T03-2267 1200, www.ktmb.com.my. For monorail information, see www.monorail.my.com.

❸ Directory

Kuala Lumpur *p593, map p599*
Banks Money changers are in all the big shopping centres and along the main shopping streets and give better rates than banks. Most branches of the leading Malaysian and foreign banks have foreign exchange desks, although some (for example, **Bank Bumiputra**) impose limits on charge card cash advances. There are ATMs everywhere for Cirrus, Visa, MasterCard, Maestro or Plus cards. **American Express**, 18th floor, The Weld (near KL Tower), Jl Raja Chulan, T03-2050 0000. **Embassies and consulates** Australia, 6 Jl Yap Kwan Seng, T03-2146 5555. **Canada**, 7th floor, Plaza MBS, 172 Jl Ampang, T03-2162 2362. **France**, 192 Jl Ampang, T03-2162 0671. **Germany**, 3 Jl U Thant, T03-2148 0073. **Netherlands**, 4 Jl Mesra (off Jl Damai), T03-2161 0148. **New Zealand**, 191 Jl Ampang, T03-2078 2533. **UK**, 185 Jl Ampang, T03-2148 2122. **USA**, 376 Jl Tun Razak, T03-2168 5000. **Emergencies** Fire: T994. **Police/ambulance**: T999. **Internet** Internet cafés are everywhere, many open 24 hrs. There are dozens along Jl Bukit Bintang and a few around Chinatown. Expect to pay upwards of RM3 per hr. If you're travelling with a laptop, buy a drink at an upmarket hotel bar or café – like **Starbucks** – and you'll usually get free Wi-Fi. **Medical services** Casualty wards are open 24 hrs. **Gleneagles Hospital**, 282-286 Jl Ampang, T03-4257 1300, www.gimc.com.my. **Pantai Medical Centre**, T03-2296 0888, www.pantai.com.my. **Pudu Specialist Centre**, Jl Baba, T03-2142 9146. **Tung Shin Hospital**, 102 Jl Pudu, T03-2072 1655.

Northern Peninsula

North of KL are the temperate hill resorts and tea plantations of the Cameron Highlands, reminiscent of the English countryside and a popular weekend retreat. The former tin-rush town of Ipoh offers Straits Chinese architecture and some superb food. It is off the beaten track for many tourists, so makes a welcome break from the travel network. Offshore there is the 25-km-long island of Penang with its fine capital Georgetown packed with Chinese shophouses, temples and clan houses, and an array of beachside hotels. Less developed are the islands of Pulau Pangkor to the south and Pulau Langkawi to the north. The latter is closer to Thailand than to mainland Malaysia and offers world-class resorts, fine beaches and jungle adventures. ➤➤ *For listings, see pages 619-629.*

Cameron Highlands ● ● ● ● ● ● ➤➤ *pp619-629. Colour map 8, C2.*

The biggest and best known of Malaysia's hill stations lies on a jungle-clad 1500-m-high plateau. The hills and forests provide excellent opportunities for walking, and the fertile conditions make it an important farming area. There are three main townships: **Ringlet**, famous for its tea plantations, **Tanah Rata**, the main town with shops, hotels and restaurants, and **Brinchang**, with its temples, rose gardens and strawberry farms. In recent years, the highlands have lost some of their charm with the development of golf courses and luxury tourist resorts, but visitors still flock here to escape the heat and enjoy the peaceful surroundings. The weather is reassuringly British – unpredictable, often wet and decidedly cool – but when the sun blazes out of an azure-blue sky, the Camerons are hard to beat.

Ins and outs

Getting there and around Buses run from KL's Puduraya terminal and Georgetown direct to the Cameron Highlands. Alternatively catch a bus or train to Tapah, from where local buses run every two hours to Tanan Rata and Brinchang. A new highway now links Ipoh to the Cameron Highlands and runs to Gua Musang for connections to the east coast. Getting around is easiest if you have your own car, however there are local buses and taxis.

Best time to visit Due to their altitude, the highland resorts are a good escape from the heat of the plains all year round. However, it might be worth avoiding it during school and public holidays when it gets very crowded. It gets chilly at night, so bring warm clothes.

Tourist information There is no official tourist office but information can be obtained from backpacker guesthouses and the tour agencies in Tanah Rata. **Golden Highlands Adventure Holidays** ① *T05-490 1880, www.gohighadventure.com*, has an office in the bus station and offers tours of the area including forest treks and visits to tea plantations, strawberry, rose and bee farms. **Tourism Pahang** publishes a free guide. Also see www.cameronhighlands.com.

Ringlet

Ringlet, the first township on the road to the Cameron Highlands is not the most attractive place, with 1960s apartment blocks, a cluster of hawker stalls in the town centre and a well-used temple. The main reason for coming here is to visit the **BOH (Best of Highlands) tea plantations** ① *8 km northeast of town, www.boh.com.my, free guided tours every hour*, where you can see the tea being picked and packed. After Ringlet, the road follows a wide river to a lake, connected to a hydroelectric dam. From here a road leads up to the plantation.

Tanah Rata

Tanah Rata is the biggest of the three Cameronian towns and is a good base for walking. It is a friendly place, with a resort atmosphere rather like an English seaside town. There are souvenir shops selling Asli crafts, ranging from blowpipes to woodcarvings. **Gan Seow Hooi**, seowhooigan@hotmail.com, will let customers sample the local high-grade leaf tea. It is worth a visit for the traditional tea ceremony as well as the tea itself. The shop also stocks traditional Chinese clay teapots and other handicrafts.

Cameron Highlands

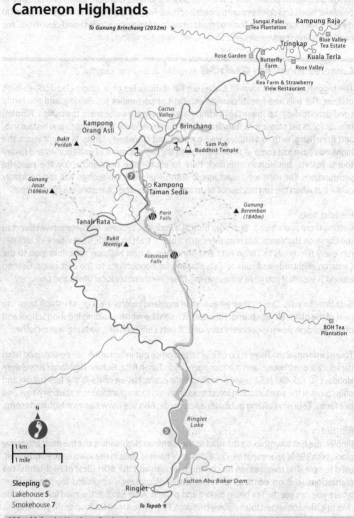

Sungai Palas Tea Plantation
Kampung Raja
Blue Valley Tea Estate
Tringkap
Kuala Terla
Rose Garden
Butterfly Farm
Rose Valley
Kea Farm & Strawberry View Restaurant
To Gunung Brinchang (2032m)
Cactus Valley
Kampong Orang Asli
Brinchang
Bukit Perdah
Sam Poh Buddhist Temple
Gunung Jasar (1696m)
Kampong Taman Sedia
Gunung Beremban (1840m)
Parit Falls
Tanah Rata
Bukit Mentigi
Robinson Falls
BOH Tea Plantation
Ringlet Lake
Sultan Abu Bakar Dam
Ringlet
To Tapah

N
1 km
1 mile

Sleeping
Lakehouse 5
Smokehouse 7

Footprint Mini Atlas
Southeast Asia

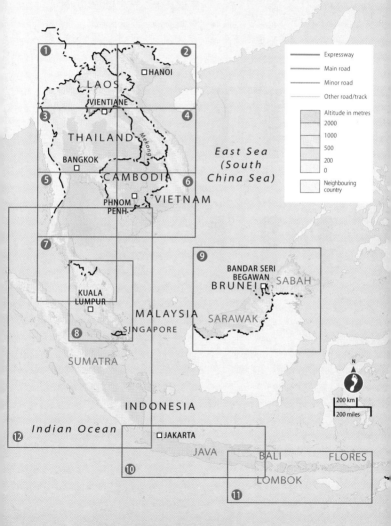

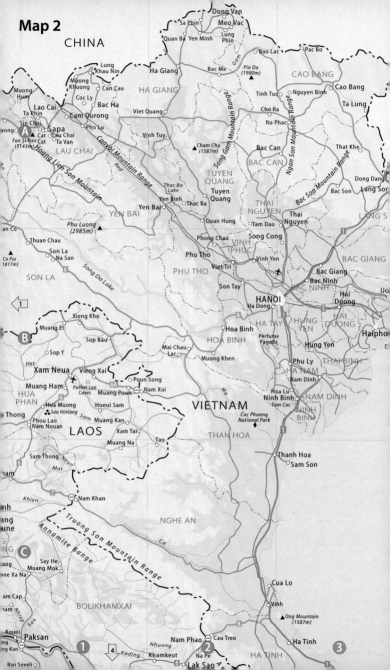

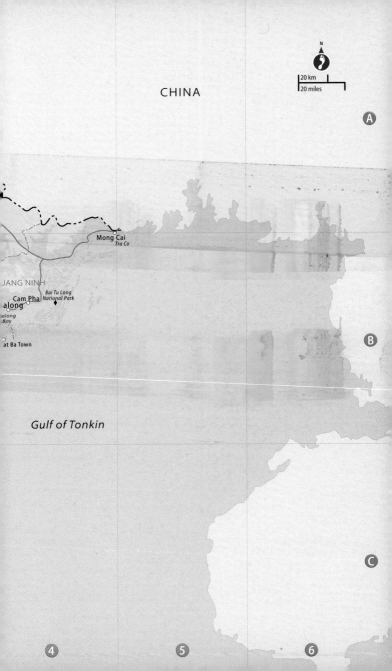

CHINA

N

20 km
20 miles

A

Mong Cai
Tra Co

JANG NINH

Cam Pha
along   Bai Tu Long
National Park
along
Bay

at Ba Town

B

Gulf of Tonkin

C

4   5   6

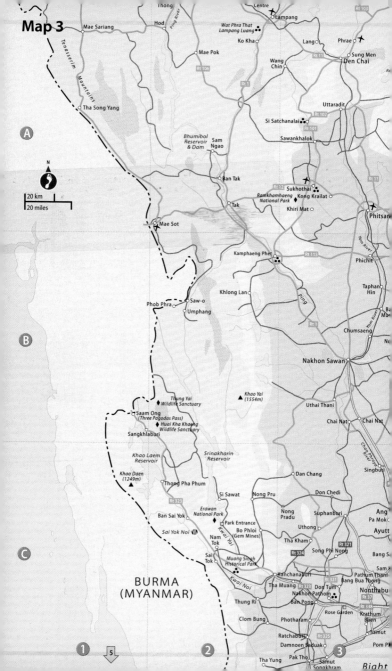

Map 3

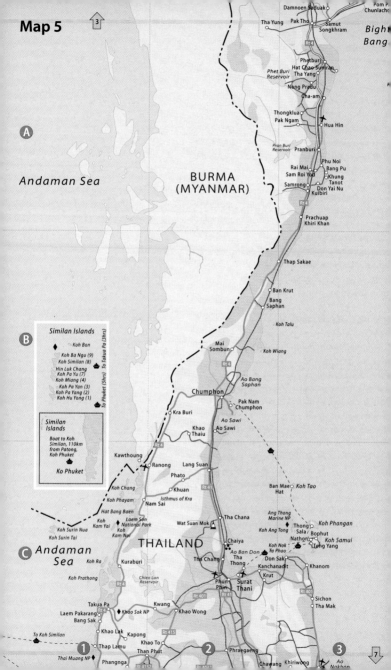

Map 5

↑ 3

Andaman Sea

BURMA (MYANMAR)

Damnoen Saduak
Pom P
Chulache

Tha Yung   Pak Tho   Samut
                        Songkhram

Bigh
Bang

Phetburi
Hat Chao Sumran
Phet Buri   Tha Yang
Reservoir
Nung Pradu
Cha-am

Thongklua
Pak Ngam   Hua Hin

Pran Buri
Reservoir   Pranburi

Phu Noi
Rai Mai   Bang Pu
Sam Roi Yot   Khung
                Tanot
Samrong   Don Yai Nu
Kuiburi

Prachuap
Khiri Khan

Thap Sakae

Ban Krut
Bang
Saphan

Koh Talu

Mai
Sombun   Koh Wiang

Ao Bang
Saphan

Chumphon

Pak Nam
Chumphon

Kra Buri

Khao
Thaiu   Ao Sawi
             Ao Sawi

Similan Islands

♦ Koh Bon
♦ Koh Ba Ngu (9)
  Koh Similan (8)
Hin Luk Chang
  Koh Pa Yu (7)
  Koh Miang (4)
  Koh Pa Yan (3)
  Koh Pa Yang (2)
  Koh Hu Yong (1)

Similan Islands

Boat to Koh
Similan, 110km
from Patong,
Koh Phuket

♦ Ko Phuket

To Phuket (5hrs) To Takua Pa (3hrs)

Kawthoung

Ranong   Lang Suan

Phato

Khuan   Ban Mae   Koh Tao
Isthmus of Kra   Hat

Nam Sai

Koh Chang

Koh Phayam

Hat Bang Baen   Tha Chana   Ang Thong   Koh Phangan
                                    Marine NP
Koh Surin Nua   Laem Son   Wat Suan Mok   Thong   Koh Samui
Koh Surin Tai   National Park Koh Kam Yai   Koh Ang Tong   Sala   Bophut
                 Koh Kam Noi   Chaiya   Nathon   Tong Yang
THAILAND   Koh Nok
                              Ao Ban Don   Ta Phao
Koh Ra   Tha
                              Thong   Don Sak
Andaman   Kuraburi   Tha Chang   Kanchanadit   Khanom
Sea
Koh Prathong   Phun   Krut
             Chieo Lan   Phin   Surat
             Reservoir   Thani   Sichon
                                               Tha Mak
Takua Pa   Kwang   Rt 401
Laem Pakarang ♦ Khao Sok NP
Bang Sak   Khao Wong
           Khao Lak   Kapong
           Thap Lamu Khao To
♦ Thai Muang NP   Than Phut
To Koh Similan   Phangnga   Phraegaeng
                    Chawang   Khiriwong   Ao
                                          Nakhon

1   2   3   7

Rt 4

Rt 41

Rt 401

Rt 415

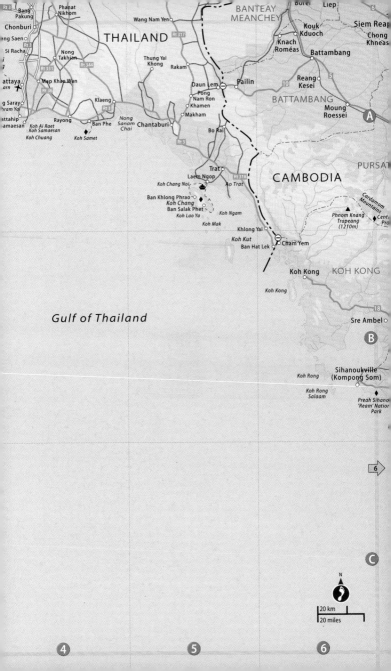

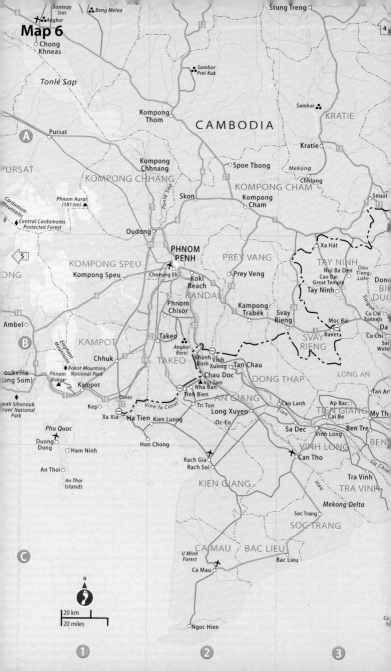

Map 7

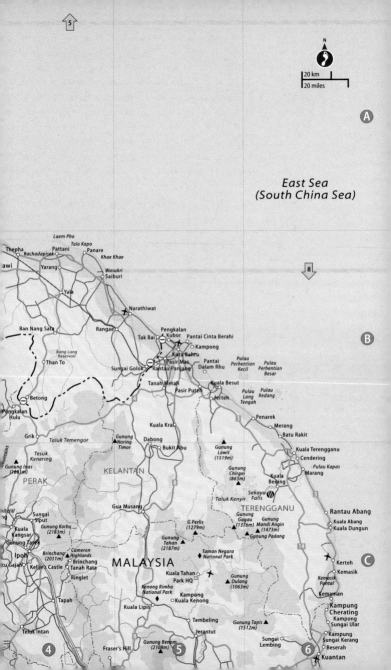

Map 8

N

40 km
40 miles

7

Andaman Sea

East Sea
(South China Sea)

THAILAND

MALAYSIA

KEDAH

PERLIS

PENANG

PERAK

KELANTAN

TERENGGANU

Boat from Koh Tarutao
Koh Rawi Koh
Koh Adang Koh
Butong Koh Tanga
Koh Lipe Koh Tarang

Pulau Langkawi

Kuah

Satun

Khlong Ngae

Pedang Besar

Sadao

Bukit Kayu Hitam

Kangar

Kuala Perlis

Kaju Uttam

Alor Star

Kuala Kedah

Citra

Gunung Jerai

Bujang Valley

Sungai Petani

Batu Ferringhi

Georgetown

Butterworth

Bukit Mertajam

Batu Muang

Pasir Puteh

Batu Pinan

Kubah Gajah

Bukit Mertajam

Taiping

Maxwell Hill

Bukit Larut

Kuala Sepatang

Na Thawi

Wasukri Saiburi

Yarang

Khoe Khae

Narathiwat

Rangae

Ban Nang Sata

Than To

Bang Lang Reservoir

Betong

Pengkalan Hulu

Grik

Teluk Temengor

Gunung Mas

Tesuk Kenering

Sungai Kenering

Kuala Kangsar

Gunung Bubu

Gunung Korbu (2183m)

Cameron Highlands (2031m)

Brinchang

Tanah Rata

Ringlet

Tapah

Teluk Batik

Lumut

Pulau Pangkor

Bukit Pangkor

Pulau Pangkor Laut

Ipoh

Batu Gajah

Kellie's Castle

Sungai Siput

Gunung Tahan (2187m)

Gua Musang

Gunung Noring Timor

Dabong

Kuala Krai

Bukit Abu

Tanah Merah

Sungai Golok

Rantau Panjang

Pasir Mas

Kota Bahru

Pengkalan Kubor

Tak Bai

Pantai Cinta Berahi

Kampung

Dalam Rhu

Pantai

Pulau Perhentian Besar

Pulau Perhentian Kecil

Pulau Lang Tengah

Pulau Redang

Jerteh

Kuala Besut

Penarek

Merang

Batu Rakit

Kuala Terengganu

Cendering

Pulau Kapos

Pulau Marang

Rantau Abang

Kuala Dungun

Kerteh

Kemasik

Kemboli Pahtai

Kemaman

Kampong Cherating

Kampong Sungai Ular

Kampong Sungai Kerang

Sungai Lembing

Gunung Tapis (1512m)

Gunung Dulang (1065m)

Sekayu Falls

Gunung Gagau (1376m)

Gunung Mandi Angin (1462m)

Gunung Padang

Gunung Lawit (1519m)

Gunung Chingai (1863m)

Taluk Kenyir

G Perlis (1279m)

Taman Negara National Park

Kampong Kuala Tahan Park HQ

Kenong Rimba National Park

Kampong Kuala Kenong

Kuala Lipis

Tembeling

Jerantut

Kuala Lipis

Gunung Berlam

A

B

C

Map 9

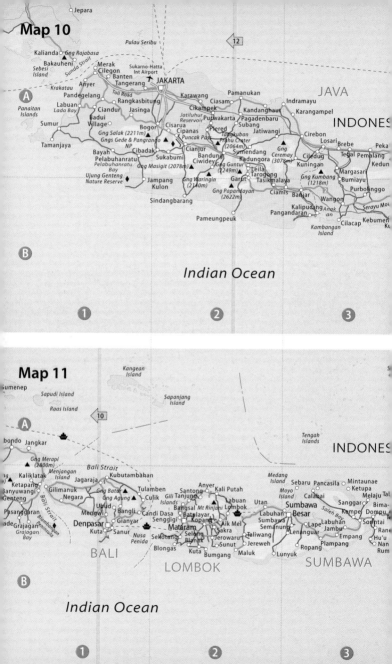

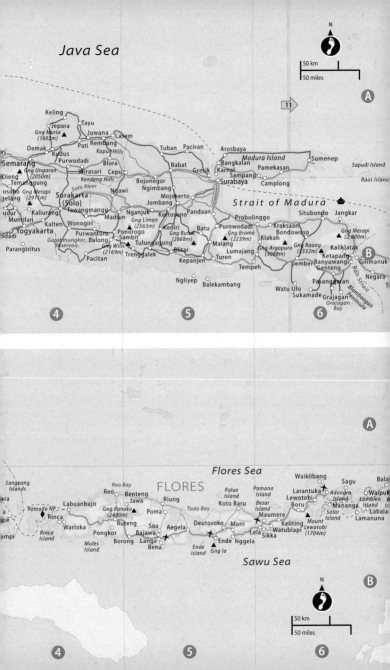

Index

Map symbols

□ Capital city
○ Other city, town
⁓ International border
⁓ Regional border
⊖ Customs
⌒ Contours (approx)
▲ Mountain, volcano
⌣ Mountain pass
⊥⊥⊥ Escarpment
⌣ Glacier
▨ Salt flat
⌣ Rocks
ᵛᵛᵛ Seasonal marshland
▒ Beach, sandbank
⟨⟨⟨ Waterfall
⌁ Reef
═══ Motorway
── Main road
── Minor road
⁓⁓⁓ Track
∷∷∷ Footpath
── Railway
⊣■ Railway with station
✈ Airport
🚍 Bus station
Ⓜ Metro station

- - - - Cable car
⊬⊬⊬⊬ Funicular
⛴ Ferry
▦ Pedestrianized street
⊃ ⊂ Tunnel
⟶ One way-street
▥▥▥ Steps
⌣ Bridge
▟▟ Fortified wall
▨ Park, garden, stadium
● Sleeping
🍴 Eating
🍷 Bars & clubs
▨ Building
✠ Sight
⛪ Cathedral, church
⛩ Chinese temple
🛕 Hindu temple
⚘ Meru
🕌 Mosque
⛩ Stupa
✡ Synagogue
ℹ Tourist office
🏛 Museum
✉ Post office
Ⓟ Police

Ⓢ Bank
@ Internet
♪ Telephone
🛒 Market
✚ Medical services
Ⓟ Parking
⛽ Petrol
⛳ Golf
∴ Archaeological site
♦ National park, wildlife reserve
❊ Viewing point
▲ Campsite
⌂ Refuge, lodge
🏰 Castle, fort
⚓ Diving
🌴 Deciduous, coniferous, palm trees
⌂ Hide
🍇 Vineyard, winery
⚗ Distillery
⚓ Shipwreck
⚔ Historic battlefield
Ⓐ Detail map
Ⓐ Related map

Brinchang and around

In recent years Brinchang, 7 km beyond Tanah Rata, on the far side of the golf course, has grown fast and new hotels have sprung up, mainly catering for Malaysian Chinese and Singaporean package tourists. The **Sam Poh Buddhist Temple**, perched high on a hill just outside Brinchang, is a colourful sight, with its monumental double gates and dragons. The inner chamber with its six red-tiled pillars holds a vast golden effigy of a Buddha.

From the market area in town, the first road on the right leads to **Kea Farm**, www.kea farm.com with its neatly terraced hillsides. From here, fruit and vegetables associated with more temperate climates, such as cabbages, cauliflowers, carrots, tomatoes, strawberries and passion fruit, are taken by truck to the supermarkets of KL and Singapore. There is a farm shop and restaurant at the turning on the main road.

The **Rose Garden** is 2 km further up the mountain. To get there, take the first left turn after the butterfly farm, on Jalan Gunung Brinchang, a very picturesque narrow road. A few kilometres further on is a turning for the **Sungai Palas tea plantation** ⓘ *www.boh.com.my, Tue-Sun 0900-1630, free guided tours*. The visitor centre has a video about tea cultivation and a shop, as well as a charming terrace where you can enjoy tea and scones and dramatic views across the steeply terraced tea plantations.

From the junction with Jalan Gunung Brinchang, a road continues 13 km into the mountains to the **Blue Valley Tea Estate**. At the village of Trinkap, a right turn leads to a large rose-growing area, **Rose Valley** ⓘ *daily 0800-1800, RM3*, which boasts 450 varieties of rose including the thornless rose, the green rose and the elusive black rose.

Ipoh and around ●❷❸❹❺ ►► pp619-629. Colour map 8, C1.

Malaysia's third city, Ipoh, is situated in the Kinta Valley famous for its tin ore production. Few tourists spend long here; most are en route to Penang, KL or Pulau Pangkor. Those who do stay rarely regret it: there are excellent Chinese restaurants (a speciality is the rice noodle dish, *sar hor fun*, which literally means 'melts in your mouth'), Buddhist temples and examples of Straits Chinese architecture. There are also some fine colonial buildings housing notable sights such as the Perak Darul Ridzuan Museum, which provides an interesting insight into Ipoh's history. The city is surrounded by imposing limestone outcrops. These jungle-topped hills, with their precipitous white cliffs, are riddled with passages and caves, many of which have been made into temples. Within easy reach of the city is the Sam Poh Tong, the largest cave temple in the area, and Perak Tong, one of the largest Chinese temples in Malaysia.

Close to Ipoh are the Royal town of Kuala Kangsar, the ancient town of Taiping with its strong Chinatown, Lumut, a holiday destination on the coast and the pleasant island of Pulau Pangkor with good beaches and coral.

Ins and outs

Getting there and around Ipoh is around 200 km north of KL. The airport is 15 km south of town; daily direct flights with KL and international connections with Medan in Sumatra. From the train station on the edge of town there are connections with Butterworth and KL as well as south to Singapore and north to Hat Yai in Thailand. Ipoh is on the main north-south highway and there are regular connections with anywhere of any size on the Peninsula. The long-distance bus terminal is several kilometres north of town and requires a taxi or bus ride to reach. Shared taxis run to KL, Butterworth, Taiping, Alor Star and Tapah. The grid layout of the town's streets makes it easy to navigate.

Tourist information There are three tourist offices, none of which is particularly helpful. **Ipoh City Council Tourist Office** ① *Jl Abdul Adil, Mon-Thu 0800-1245, 1400-1615, Fri 0800-1230, 1400-1615, Sat 0800-1245.* **Perak Information Centre** ① *Pejabat Setiausaha Kerajaan, Jl Panglima Bukit Gantang Wahab, T05-253 1957, Mon-Thu 0800-1245, 1400-1615, Fri 0800-1215, 1445-1615, Sat 0800-1245.* **Tourist Information** ① *Casuarina Hotel, 18 Jl Gopeng, T05-253 2008.* Also see www.perak.gov.my.

Sights

The Kinta River, spanned by the Hugh Low Bridge, separates the old and new parts of town. The **Old Town** is known for its old Chinese and British colonial architecture, particularly on Jalan Sultan Yusuf, Jalan Leech and Jalan Treacher. Prominent landmarks include the **Birch Memorial**, a clocktower erected in memory of the first British resident of Perak, JWW Birch. The four panels decorating the base of the tower depict the development of civilization. The Moorish-style **railway station** (off Jalan Kelab), was built in 1917 and is known as the 'Taj Mahal' of Ipoh. The **Station Hotel** is a colonial classic.

Heading north out of town past **St Michael's School**, on Jalan Panglima Bukit Gantang Wahab, after about 500 m on the right, is an elegant white colonial building housing the **Perak Darul Ridzuan Museum** ① *Sat-Thu 0900-1700, free.* The building, more than 100 years old, once the home of Malay dignitaries of Kinta, now holds a collection showing the history of Ipoh, and mining and forestry within the state.

Around Ipoh

At Gunung Rapatm, 5 km south of Ipoh is **Sam Poh Tong** ① *0730-1800, take Kampar bus No 66,* the largest of the cave temples in the area, with Buddha statues among the stalactites and stalagmites. The temple was founded 100 years ago by a monk who lived and meditated in the cave for 20 years and it has been inhabited by monks ever since. The only break was during the Japanese occupation when the cave was turned into a Japanese ammunition and fuel dump.

The ornately decorated **Perak Tong** ① *6.5 km north of Ipoh on Jl Kuala Kangsar, 0900-1600, take Kuala Kangsar bus or city bus No 3,* is one of the largest Chinese temples in Malaysia. Built in 1926 by a Buddhist priest from China, the temple houses more than 40 Buddha statues and traditional Chinese-style murals depicting legends. It is visited by thousands of pilgrims every year. A path beyond the altar leads into the cave's interior and up a brick stairway to an opening 100 m above ground with a view of the surrounding countryside. Another climb leads to a painting of Kuan Yin, Goddess of Mercy, who looks out from the face of the limestone cliff. A 15-m-high reinforced concrete statue of the Buddha stands in the compound.

A 30-minute drive south of Ipoh, **Kellie's Castle** ① *0830-1930, RM0.50,* is the eccentric edifice of Scotsman William Kellie Smith, a late-19th-century rubber tycoon. The fanciful Moorish-style mansion was never completed as Smith died during its construction (rumour has it, after inhaling the smoke of a poisoned cigar). During the Second World War the grounds were used by the Japanese as an execution area; locals say it is haunted.

Kuala Kangsar → *Colour map 8, C1.*

Halfway between Ipoh and Taiping is the royal riverside town Kuala Kangsar. It is a pleasant place to stop off, with plenty of atmosphere. The first monument you come to is the **Ubudiah Mosque** (1917), one of the most beautiful mosques in the country with its golden domes and elegant minarets. Overlooking the mosque is the residence of the

Perak royal family, **Istana Iskandariah** (1930). It is a massive marble structure with a series of towers, topped by golden onion domes set among trees and rolling lawns. The former yellow palace, **Istana Kenangan**, is open to the public and houses the **Museum di Raja (Perak Royal Museum)** ① *T05-776 5500, 0900-1730, closed Fri lunch for prayers, free,* which exhibits royal regalia. It is a fine example of Malay architecture. Kuala Kangsar is famed for as the site of Malaysia's where the first rubber trees in Malaysia were grown; the last remaining tree is marked with a plaque. Across the road is the attractive red-roofed building of the **Malay College**, where novelist Anthony Burgess once worked. Considered the Eton of Malaysia, the school was built in 1905 for the children of the royal family.

Taiping → *Colour map 8, C1.*

With a backdrop of the Bintang Mountains, Taiping is one of the oldest towns in Malaysia. Around 1840, Chinese immigrants started mining tin in the area and it is the only big Malaysian town with a Chinese name. The town is busy and friendly, with a close-knit, community atmosphere. There is more colonial-era architecture here than in many of Malaysia's towns; there are some fine examples on Jalan Kota, Jalan Main and Jalan Station.

In 1890 the **Lake Garden** was set up on the site of an abandoned tin mine. It is very lush due to the high rainfall and is the pride of the town. Covering 66 ha, the park lies at the foot of **Bukit Larut** (Maxwell Hill), and has a zoo at its southern end. Built in 1883, the lovely colonial **Perak Museum** ① *Jl Taming Sari (Main Rd), opposite the prison, Sun-Thu 0900-1700, Fri 0900-1215, 1445-1700, free,* is the oldest in Malaysia, dating from 1883. It contains a collection of ancient weapons, aboriginal implements, stuffed animals and archaeological finds.

Maxwell Hill ① *12 km east of the Lake Garden, T05-807 7243,* is a highlight of a visit to Taiping. Most people climb the hill, whether on foot or by Land Rover, as a day excursion. At an elevation of 1034 m it was once a tea plantation and now a small resort.

Lumut → *Colour map 8, C1.*

Lumut is primarily a base for the Royal Malaysian Navy and is also a transit point for Pulau Pangkor. There is a **tourist office** ① *Jl Sultan Idris Shah, opposite the jetty, T05-683 4057, Mon-Fri 0900-1700, Sat 0900-1345.* The town is at its zenith during the Pesta Laut, a sea festival, which takes place every August at nearby the popular beach spot of **Teluk Batik**, 7 km south (taxi from Lumut RM20).

Pulau Pangkor → *Colour map 8, C1.*

① *Accessible by air from KL. Regular half hour departures by boat from Lumut. Taxis and minibuses provide transport on the island. It is also possible to hire motorbikes and bicycles.*

Just 7 km across the Straits from Lumut is Pangkor, one of the most easily accessible islands in Malaysia. Once used as a leper colony, the island was settled by Chinese families in the 1950s, who built a vibrant cottage industry producing dried and salted fish. Now, it's home to some laid-back resorts and great seafood restaurants as well which are virtually deserted during the week but packed with holidaying locals at weekends. While some of the beaches are a bit grubby, it's possible to hire a motorbike and laze on some fine secluded sands. The island is small enough to walk round in one day and the interior consists of pristine jungle.

In the south of the island are ruins of a Dutch fort, **Kota Belanda**, built by the Dutch East India Company in 1680 to protect the rich tin traders from Malay pirates. **Pangkor village** is also attractive; its main street lined with stores selling dried fish. Some of the coffee houses along the street still have their original marble-topped tables and Straits wooden chairs.

Pulau Penang ⌂🍴🎨❄☎⛰🏛☎📞 » pp619-629. Colour map 8, B1.

Penang – or, more properly, Pulau Pinang – is the northern gateway to Malaysia and is the country's oldest British settlement. It has been sold to generations of tourists as 'the Pearl of the Orient', but in shape Penang looks more like a frog than a pearl. Although the island is best known as a beach resort, it is also a cultural melting pot with Chinese, Malay and Indian influences. Georgetown has the largest collection of pre-war houses in all Southeast Asia.

In Malay, *pinang* is the word for the areca nut palm, an essential ingredient of betel nut. The palm was incorporated into the state crest in the days of the Straits Settlements during the 19th century. Today Pulau Pinang is translated as 'betel-nut island'.

① Penang

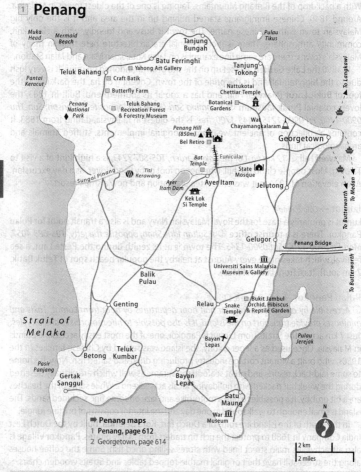

➡ Penang maps
1 Penang, page 612
2 Georgetown, page 614

The first British settlement

In the late 18th century, Penang was ruled by the Sultan of Kedah and suffered repeated invasions by the Thais from the north and Bugis pirates from the sea. When Captain Francis Light arrived in 1786, aboard a ship of a British trading company, he was looking for a trading base on the north shore of the Strait of Melaka. Light struck a deal with the sultan: he promised to provide military protection in exchange for using Penang as a port. A township grew up around the camp by the harbour and soon became the first British settlement on the Malay Peninsula. Light

declared Penang a free port and Georgetown became the capital of the newly established Straits Settlements. But the glory was short-lived. Following Raffles's founding of Singapore in 1819, Georgetown was quickly eclipsed by the upstart at the southern tip of the Peninsula and by the 1830s had been reduced to a colonial backwater. From an architectural perspective, this proved a saving grace; unlike Singapore, Penang suffered little damage in the Second World War and retains many of its original colonial buildings and rich cultural heritage.

Ins and outs

Getting there Beyan Lepas airport, T04-643 4411, is 20 km south of Georgetown and receives flights from KL, JB and Langkawi as well international destinations. Taxis to town operate on a coupon system (30 minutes, RM25). The island is linked with the mainland via the 13-km Penang Bridge (one-way toll to the mainland RM7). There are direct bus links with KL and a host of Peninsula towns, as well as services to Thailand and Singapore. Trains run as far as Butterworth (see page 616) from where ferries make regular crossings, or local taxis make the run across the bridge to the island. Georgetown also has ferry links with Belawan (Sumatra) and Langkawi and from there on to Thailand. ▸▸ *See Transport, page 626.*

Getting around A free shuttle runs to tourist destinations in Georgetown Monday-Friday 0700-1900, Saturday 0700-1400, every 12 minutes; stops are marked with red circular signs enclosing a number. There are plenty of city buses, taxis and trishaws in town. It is possible to hire cars, motorbikes and bicycles to explore the island.

Orientation The capital, **Georgetown**, is on the northeast point of the island, nearest the mainland. The 13 km Penang Bridge, linking the island to Butterworth, is halfway down the east coast. **Batu Ferringhi**, on the north coast, is Penang's most famous beach with a strip of luxury hotels. There are secluded coves with good beaches on the northwest tip of the island. The west is a mixture of jungle-covered hills, rubber plantations and a few fishing kampongs. There are more beaches and fishing villages on the south coast. A short, steep mountain range forms a central spine, including **Penang Hill**, at 850 m above sea level. Street names in Georgetown are confusing as they are known by both their Malay and English names.

Tourist information Penang Tourist Centre ① *Penang Port Commission Building, opposite Fort Cornwallis, T04-262 0202, www.tourismpenang.com.my, Mon-Fri 0900-1800, Sat 0800-1300, closed 1st and 3rd Sat.* Tourism Malaysia **Northern Regional Office** ① *10 Jl Tun Syed Sheh Barakbah, T04-262 0066.* One of the best places is the **Tourist Information Centre** ① *KOMTAR Tower, Jl Penang, T04-261 4461; also at Batu Ferringhi, and the airport, T04-643 0501, Mon-Sat 1000-1800.* The free monthly *Penang Tourist Newspaper* is useful for event information.

Georgetown

Georgetown is one of Malaysia's most appealing cities and has largely retained its rich cultural heritage. These days, the population is predominantly Chinese and the streets are atmospheric with rickshaws, shophouses, temples and colonial buildings. It's a popular stop for backpackers, with plenty of budget accommodation, cheap restaurants and lively nightlife, particularly around Love Lane (officially called Lorong Cinta). The original four streets of Georgetown – Beach (now known as Lebuh Pantai), Lebuh Light, Jalan Masjid Kapitan Kling (previously Lebuh Pitt) and Lebuh Chulia – still form the main thoroughfares. The town was named after King George IV as it was acquired on his birthday; most Malaysians know the town by its nickname, Tanjung.

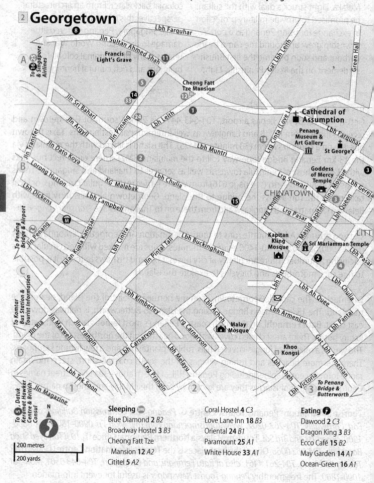

Georgetown

Sleeping 🛏
Blue Diamond **2** *B2*
Broadway Hostel **3** *B3*
Cheong Fatt Tze
  Mansion **12** *A2*
Cititel **5** *A2*

Coral Hostel **4** *C3*
Love Lane Inn **18** *B3*
Oriental **24** *B1*
Paramount **25** *A1*
White House **33** *A1*

Eating 🍴
Dawood **2** *C3*
Dragon King **3** *B3*
Ecco Café **15** *B2*
May Garden **14** *A1*
Ocean-Green **16** *A1*

On the north tip of the island, **Fort Cornwallis** ① *0830-1830, RM3*, marks the site where the British fleet, under Captain Francis Light, first arrived on 16 July 1786. Only its outer walls remain but the amphitheatre hosts concerts and shows. Just opposite the fort, the **Penang Clocktower** was built to commemorate Queen Victoria's Diamond Jubilee. The tower is 60-ft high: one foot for each year of her reign. **Lebuh Pantai** has several interesting buildings including the **ABN-AMRO Arts Centre** ① *No 9, Mon-Sat 1000-1800, free*. It has a stage for gamelan recitals and an art gallery with great photo exhibitions. Recommended.

In the heart of Chinatown, near the cathedral, the **Penang Museum and Art Gallery** ① *corner of Lebuh Light and Lebuh Farquhar, T04-263 1942, Sat-Thu 0900-1700, RM1*, has a fine collection of photographs, maps and historical records charting the growth of Penang from the days of Francis Light. Next to the museum, **St George's Church** ① *Lebuh Farquhar*, was the first Anglican church in Southeast Asia, designed by Captain Robert Smith and built by convict labour in 1817.

➡ **Penang maps**
1 Penang, page 612
2 Georgetown, page 614

The **Goddess of Mercy Temple (Kuan Yin Teng)** ① *Jl Kapitan Kling Mosque/Lorong Steward*, was built at in the 1800s by early Chinese immigrants. Kuan Yin is associated with peace, fortune and fertility. Shops sell lanterns, provisions for the afterlife (such as paper Mercedes cars), incense and figurines.

Georgetown also has significant Indian and Muslim populations. The Hindu **Sri Mahamariamman Temple**, Lebuh Queen/Lebuh Chulia, dates to 1883 and is intricately decorated with deities and mythical animals. The surrounding area is packed with money changers, jewellery shops, tea stalls and banana-leaf restaurants. the Indo-Moorish **Kapitan Kling Mosque** was built by the first Indian Muslim settlers around 1800.

Heading south, on Jalan Acheh the lavishly decorated **Khoo Kongsi** ① *Mon-Fri 0900-1700, Sat 0900-1300, RM5*, is one of the most interesting sights in Georgetown. A *kongsi* is a Chinese clan house, which doubles as a temple and a meeting place. It contains some fine art and sculpture.

West of the cathedral, **Cheong Fatt Tze Mansion** ① *14 Lebuh Leith, T04-262 0006, www.cheongfatttzemansion.com, RM12*, is the Chinese equivalent of a stately home and one of only three surviving mansions in this style; the others are in Manila and Medan (Sumatra). It is possible to stay in one of the 16 decadent bedrooms.

Sea Palace **17** *A2*
Thirty Two **8** *A1*

George's at Sunway
Hotel **5** *D1*
Leith St **1** *B2*

Bars & clubs 🍸
Garage **11** *A2*

Around the island

From Georgetown, the round-island trip is a 70-km circuit. It is recommended as a day trip as there is little accommodation outside Georgetown apart from the north coast beaches. It's possible to hire a car or motorbike, or take a tour. ▸▸ See Activities and tours, page 625.

The majority of visitors to Penang head straight to **Batu Ferringhi**, the island's main beach. Once, a nirvana for Western hippies it has been transformed into an upmarket resort with scores of luxury hotels. Most holidaymakers stick to their hotel swimming pools because the sea is polluted and can be affected by jellyfish. Hotels offer abundant activities, especially watersports. There are also many excellent restaurants, hawker stalls and handicraft shops.

At the western end of the beach is the small fishing kampong of **Teluk Bahang** where the Malabar fishermen used to live. It has been dramatically changed by the **Penang Mutiara Beach Resort**. Beyond Teluk Bahang, around **Muka Head**, the coast is broken into a series of small coves separated by rocky headlands with secluded beaches. Trails lead over the headland from the fishing kampong. One trail goes along the coast past to the Muka Head **lighthouse** (1½hours); another leads over the headland to **Pantai Keracut** (two hours).

In the centre of the island, a **funicular railway** ① every 30 mins 0630-2330, climbs 850 m up **Penang Hill** ① bus No 130 or 101 to Ayer Itam Station, then shuttle bus No 8 to the railway. Most buses from Stand 3 go to Penang Hill. Completed in 1899, it was Malaysia's first colonial hill station. There are good views from the top, as well as pretty gardens, a temple, mosque and some restaurants. A well-marked 8-km path leads down to the Moon Gate at the **Botanical Gardens** (about an hour's walk) from between the post office and the police station; a steep but delightful descent. The hill supports the last path of tropical rainforest on Penang and is of considerable natural value.

South of Ayer Itam, **Kek Lok Si Temple** ①0900-1800, free, donation to climb the 30-m tower, bus No 101 or 130, followed by a 5-min walk, sprawls for 12 ha and can be seen from some distance away. It took Burmese, Chinese and Thai artisans, who were shipped in especially, two decades to build it. The seven-tier pagoda, or **Ban Po**, combines Chinese design with Thai-Buddhist and Burmese, and is covered with thousands of gilded statues.

Other sights of possible interest include the **Snake Temple** ① 12 km south of Georgetown, T04-643 7273, 0700-1900, RM1, bus No 66 or 80, built in 1850. Snakes were kept in the temple as they were believed to be the disciples of the deity Chor Soo Kong, to whom the temple is dedicated. The number of snakes in the temple varies from day to day – there are usually more around during festivals. The incense smoke keeps them in a drugged stupor, and most of them have had their fangs extracted.

On the west side of the island is **Penang National Park** ① entrance through Telok Bahang at the end of Batu Ferringhi Rd, bus No 93 to Telok Bahang; either walk from here or take a boat from the fishing jetty; longer fare stages cost anything up to RM1.5; as the island buses are infrequent, check departure times at each place to avoid being stranded, which has well-marked trails into the jungle and to the bays further round. After the Pantai Acheh junction, and on up a twisting, forested section of road, there is a waterfall with a pleasant pool, suitable for swimming, just off the road (20th milestone), called **Titi Kerawang**.

Butterworth → Colour map 8, B1. Phone code: 04

This industrial and harbour town and base for the Royal Australian Air Force was billeted here under the terms of the Five Powers Pact. It is the main port for ferries to Penang and most tourists head straight for the island; Butterworth is not a recommended stopping point but there are a couple of hotels, should you get stuck.

Alor Star is the capital of Kedah State on the road north to the Thai border. It is the home town of former Prime Minister Dr Mahathir Mohamad and is the commercial centre for northwest Malaysia. Its name, a corruption of Alor Setar, means 'grove of setar trees'. Kedah is now Malaysia's most important rice-growing state; together with neighbouring Perlis, it produces 44% of the country's rice, and is known as *jelapang padi* (rice-barn country).

Nearby is the Bujang Valley Historical Park, where remains of an ancient Hindu kingdom lie. Kuala Perlis is a small fishing port and the jumping-off point for Pulau Langkawi.

Ins and outs

Alor Star's airport is 10 km north of town and has regular flights to/from KL with MAS and **Air Asia**. Trains connect with KL and Singapore and north to the border with Thailand and Hat Tai. Alor Star is also on the main North-South highway and there are bus connections with major towns. The long-distance bus terminal is several kilometres outside town. For Kuala Kedah and the ferry to Langkawi, catch bus No 106 from the local bus station.

Taxis can be chartered for out-of-town trips from the stand on Jalan Langgar in the town centre. The local bus station is on Jalan Stesyen, close to the train station.

For information, the **Kedah State Tourist Office** ① *2nd floor, State Secretariat Building, Jl Sultan Badlisah, Alor Star, T04-733 3302*, has a limited selection of brochures.

Sights

Alor Star has some interesting buildings, most of which are clustered round the central Padang Besar (Jalan Pekan Melayu/Jalan Raja). The most interesting is the **State Mosque** (1912), designed by state architect James Gorman. Almost directly opposite is the Thai-inspired **Balai Besar** (audience hall), built in 1898 and still used by the Sultan of Kedah on ceremonial occasions; it houses the royal throne. Close to the mosque is the state art gallery, **Balai Seni Negeri** ① *Sat-Thu 1000-1800, Fri 1000-1200 and 1430-1800*, which contains historical paintings and antiques, Malay handicrafts and colonial collections.

The **Pekan Rabu** (Wednesday market) offers a wide selection of local handicrafts and traditional food. It does not cater for tourists and is good place to see everyday Malay life.

Bujang Valley Historical Park

① *To get there, change buses at Bedong; it is easier to take a taxi from Alor Star.*

Near the small town of **Sungai Petani**, to the southeast of Kedah Peak, is this site of some of Malaysia's most exciting archaeological discoveries. It is thought to be the site of the capital of the fifth-century Hindu kingdom of Langkas. While the remains are a far cry from those of Cambodia's Angkor Wat, they are of enormous historical significance.

There is a reconstruction of the most significant temple unearthed so far, **Candi Bukit Batu Pahat** ① *Mon-Thu 0900-1600, Fri 1445-1600, Sat-Sun 0900-1215*. Eight sanctuaries have been restored and a museum displays statues and other finds.

Kuala Perlis → *Colour map 8, A1.*

This small fishing port, in the far north of the Peninsula, (the capital of the state of Perlis, the smallest in Malaysia) at the delta of the Sungai Perlis is mainly a jumping-off point for Pulau Langkawi and Phuket (in Thailand). It is noted for its local fast food, *laksa*, and there are foodstalls by the jetty. There is a night market every Tuesday.

The Langkawi group is an archipelago of 99 islands around 30 km off the west coast of Peninsular Malaysia. Pulau Langkawi itself, by far the largest of the group, is a mountainous, palm-fringed island with scattered fishing kampongs, paddy fields and sandy coves. It has seen significant development in recent years and is home to some of Malaysia's most upmarket resorts. Other islands are nothing more than deserted limestone outcrops rearing out of the turquoise sea, cloaked in jungle, and ringed by coral.

The main settlement of locals is in the dusty town of Kuah. There are plenty of top-end resorts, while Pantai Cenang and Tengah also have a smattering of cheaper guesthouses. It's a popular place for those wanting to renew their Thai or Malaysian visas.

Ins and outs

Getting there and around Langkawi's **airport** ① *20 km from Kuah, T04-955 1311*, has connections with KL, JB, KK, Kuching and Penang. There are also flights direct from London and Singapore. Ferries from Kuala Perlis leave roughly every hour to Langkawi and there are four daily departures from Penang by sea. Taxis run throughout the island (prices are fixed according to distance). Cars, motorcycles and bicycles are available for hire. Boats are also available to explore the neighbouring islands. ⟩⟩ *See Transport, page 628.*

Tourist information **Langkawi Tourist Information Centre** ① *Jl Pesiaran Putra, Kuah, T04-966 7789, daily 0900-1700*. The magazine, *Senses of Langkawi*, has ideas of things to do and where to eat. Also useful are www.langkawi-online.com and www.best-of-langkawi.com.

Sights

The main town, **Kuah**, is strung out along the seafront and is the landing point for ferries from Satun (Thailand), Kuala Perlis, Kuala Kedah and Penang. The jetty is 2 km from Kuah itself. The town is growing fast and developers have reclaimed land along the shoreline to cope with the expansion. The old part of Kuah has several restaurants, a few grotty hotels, banks, plenty of coffee shops and a string of duty-free shops, which do a roaring trade in cheap liquor, cigarettes and electronics. There is also an attractive mosque.

Southwest of Kuah, past beautiful paddy fields and coconut groves, are the two main beaches, Pantai Cenang and Pantai Tengah. **Pantai Cenang** is 2 km long, with a range of accommodation. It's a good place for watersports and **Langkawi Underwater World** ① *T04-955 6100, www.langkawigeopark.com.my/underwater_world.htm, daily 1000-1800, RM28*, one of Asia's largest aquariums. Just north of Pantai Cenang the **Muzium Laman Padi** (rice museum garden) ① *T04-955 4312, www.langkawigeopark.com.my/laman_padi.htm, 1000-1800, free*, explains the stages of rice farming and has a rooftop rice garden and restaurant.

Most of the new beach chalet development is along the 3 km stretch of coast from Pantai Cenang to **Pantai Tengah**, at the far southern end around a small promontory. Pantai Tengah is less developed and quieter but not as nice as Pantai Cenang.

The road west leads past the airport to **Pantai Kok**, on the magnificent **Burau Bay**. Once unspoilt, it is now spotted with upmarket resorts and a fancy marina. *Anna and the King* was filmed here; the set can be visited daily 1000-1900, RM3.50.

There are several isolated beaches along the bay, accessible by boat from either Pantai Kok itself, Pantai Cenang (12 km away) or Kampong Kuala Teriang, a small fishing village en route. On the west headland, the **Telaga Tujuh** waterfalls, are not as impressive as they used to be thanks to a pipeline running next to the falls to the **Berjaya Langkawi Beach Resort**.

For Sleeping and Eating price codes,
see inside the front cover.

⊜ Sleeping

Cameron Highlands *p607, map p608*
Book in advance for public holidays or school holidays (Apr, Aug, Dec). Prices rise by 30-50% at this time. The cheapest option if in a group is to share a bungalow. Most bungalows have gardens, log fires and are out of town.

Ringlet *p607*
A-B Lakehouse, a few kilometres from Ringlet, T05-495 6152, www.lakehouse-cameron.com. Tudor-style country. 18 rooms with antique furnishings, 4-poster beds and en suite bathrooms, fantastic views over the lake. Restaurant, bar and lounge have an English country pub feel. A great place to stay.

Tanah Rata *p608*
LL Smokehouse, T05-491 1215, www.the smokehouse.com.my/ch.htm. Modelled on its namesake in the UK, it preserves the 'ye olde English' ethos of old-time resident Colonel Stanley Foster. First-class rooms, restaurant and even a red British telephone box in the garden.
E Hillview Inn, 17 Jl Mentigi, T05-491 2915, hillview_inn@hotmail.com. Charming house, rooms have balcony. TV, internet, laundry, beautiful garden and restaurant. Very peaceful.
F-G Father's Guest House, Jl Gereja, T05-491 2484, www.geocities.com/ fathersplace. Tranquil setting in colonial-era building. Popular with beautiful views, friendly atmosphere, communal area. Cable TV, DVDs, tours, internet. Dorms available (**E**). Good café. Free pick-up from bus station. Recommended.
F-G Twin Pines, 2 Jl Mentigi, T05-491 2169, twinpinech@hotmail.com. Popular guesthouse a short walk from the bus station. Small, clean rooms and dorm. Pleasant leafy garden, internet, TV, friendly. Good value. Bus tickets and tours booked here, good information.

Brinchang and around *p609*
C-D Rainbow, Lot 25, T05-491 4628. Corner hotel with 36 good-value comfortable rooms all with TV and minibar. Good views on one side. Recommended, but no restaurant.
E Kowloon, 34-35 Jl Besar, T05-491 1366. Above a popular Chinese restaurant, nice rooms with shower, good value for money.
D-F Pines and Roses, T05-491 2203, F491 2203. Good value family rooms or dorms, TV and water heater, basic furnishings, clean.

Ipoh *p609*
C-E Grandview, 36 Jl Horley, T05-243 1488. A/c rooms with TV. Lacking in character but the clean and tasteful furnishings and friendly, efficient service. Good value.
C-E Majestic Station, Jl Panglima Bukit Gantang Wahab, T05-255 5605, www.majesticstationhotel.com. A/c, restaurant, 100 rooms. Good range of facilities, great atmosphere, well run. Beautiful location in the heart of the old town. Recommended.
E-F Ritz Kowloon, 92-96 Jl Yang Kalsom, T05-254 7778. Chinese run with a/c, TV, video, safe, tasteful rooms. Very helpful staff.
F Shanghai, 85 Jl Mustapha al-Bakri. Fan only, shower, restaurant, clean and central. Needs modernizing but a good budget option.

Kuala Kangsar *p610*
C-D Rest House (Rumah Rehat Kuala Kangsar), Bukit Candan, T05-776 5872. Pleasant location inside the gates to the palace road, old colonial mansion, huge rooms with a/c, bathroom and hot water, some rooms face the river (fabulous views), friendly, helpful.
E-F Double Lion, 74 Jl Kasa, 300 m from the bus station, T05-776 8010. Some a/c, pleasant enough, large rooms, some overlook the river.

Taiping *p611*
C-D Legend Inn, 2 Jl Long Jaafar, T05-806 0000, www.legendinn.com. Hotel block with 88 rooms, bath, TV, video channel, coffee house, plushest place in town, well-equipped.

E New Champagne, 17 Jl Lim Sweeaqun, T05-806 5060, www.newchampagne hotel.com. Opposite Cathay Cinema. Friendly, helpful staff, pleasant and clean.

E-F Rumah Rehat Baru, 1 Jl Sultan Mansor, Taman Tasek, T05-807 2044. Restaurant, a little out of town, the new block is hardly attractive but rooms are large, with bathrooms, overlooks the Lake Garden and is good value.

Lumut *p611*

C-D Lumut Country Resort, 331 Jl Titi Panjang, T05-683 5109. A hotel with 44 a/c rooms, swimming pool, tennis courts, hand-printed batik bed covers and wooden floors. Disco, function room. One of the best deals in town.

E Harbour View, Lot 13 and 14, Jl Titi Panjang, T05-683 7888. Small, quiet hotel on main road along seafront, a/c, TV, fridge, bathroom. Good value.

F ERA, opposite bus station, T013-505 4991, sykna@hotmail.com. 6-bed dorms and big clean doubles, shared bathrooms, kitchen. Friendly family atmosphere, lots of information.

Pulau Pangkor *p611*

Hotels offer discounts during the week but increase 50% during holidays. Many budget places are at Teluk Nipah on the west coast.

LL Pangkor Laut Resort, T800-9899 9999, www.pangkorlautresort.com. Malaysia's top resort. Idyllic with magnificently set chalets over the sea (linked by wooden walkways) or on the jungled hillside. Wildlife is abundant and the jungle treks are excellent. Highly recommended if you can afford it.

C-D Coral View Beach Resort, Pasir Bogak, T05-685 2190, www.coralviewresort.com. Cute chalets on hillside surrounded by trees; very tranquil and from the backpacker crowd. restaurant, good views, motorbike hire.

E-F Vikry Resort, Pasir Bogak, T05-685 4258. 10 a/c chalets in spacious grounds. The Indian restaurant is excellent. Friendly staff.

F Joe Fisherman Village, Teluk Nipah, T05-685 2389. Popular budget place with A-frame chalets and 2 mattresses on the floor, bicycles for hire, meals available.

Georgetown *p614, map p614*

Most upmarket hotels are around Jl Penang. Cheaper hotels are on Lebuhs Chulia/Leith.

L-B Cheong Fatt Tze Mansion, 14 Leith St, T04-262 0006, www.cheongfatttzemansion. com. Fully restored 19th-century mansion with elegant themed rooms and period furniture.

C-D Oriental, 105 Jl Penang, T04-263 4211, www.oriental.com.my. A/c, restaurant, big rooms and good value, welcoming staff, well located with good views from upper floors.

F White House, 72 Jl Penang, T04-263 2385. Fan and a/c rooms. Lovely staff, clean bathrooms with hot water, excellent value.

F-G Coral Hostel, 99-101 King St, T04-264 4909. Friendly with simple rooms or dorms close to Little India. Well set up for travellers with TV lounge, motorbike and bicycle rental, cheap internet and discounted ferry tickets.

F-G Love Lane Inn, 54 Love Lane, T016-419 8409, ocean008@hotmail.com. Backpacker favourite. Dorms or private rooms, shared cold water bathroom. Very popular.

Batu Ferringhi

Budget options are clustered by the sea next to the turn-off by the **Grand Plaza Parkroyal**.

LL-AL Rasa Sayang, T04-888 8888, www.shangri-la.com. A/c, restaurants, pool. Probably the most popular on the beach strip, Minangkabau-style, horse-shoe design around a pool and garden. Sophisticated, welcoming.

F-G Ah Beng, 54c Batu Ferringhi, right on the beach, T04-881 1036. A/c, clean, rooms with a/c, fan. Friendly, family run.

F-G Baba's, 52 Batu Ferringhi, T04-881 1686, babaguesthouse2000@yahoo.com. Clean, homely and relaxed. Good information. Also owns **ET Budget Guest House**, www.geocities.com/etguesthouse, at No 47.

F-G Shalini's, 56 Batu Ferringhi, T04-881 1859, ahlooi@pc.jaring.my. Lovely little house with balcony overlooking the sea. Clean and homely.

Alor Star *p617*

C-D Seri Malaysia, Mukim Alor Malai, Daerah Kota Setar, Jl Stadium, T04-730 8738, www.seri malaysia.com.my. Clean, well located.

E Regent, 1536 Jl Sultan Badlishah, T04-731 1900. All 25 rooms with a/c, great value. Cable TV, bathrooms and bright, friendly.
F-G Lim Kung, 36A Jl Langgar, T04-722459. Fan only, good value.

Bujang Valley *p617*
C-D Sungai Petani Inn, Jl Kolam Air, Sungai Petani, T04-421 3411. The plushest in town.
C-F Duta, 7 Jl Petri. Best of the budget hotels.

Kuala Perlis *p617*
C-D Seaview, T04-985 2171. Across from the taxi rank. Plain rooms and a coffee house.

Pulau Langkawi *p618*
The island is busy Nov-Feb. Hotels in Kuah tend to be poor value – best to head to the beach.
A-D Asia, 3A-4A Jl Persiaran Putra, Kuah, T04-966 6216. A/c, reasonable place, 15 mins' walk from jetty, some dorm beds. Clean and quiet.

Pantai Cenang
Plenty of hotels and chalets; some are cramped a little too closely together. Despite the development, it is a picturesque beach.
LL-AL Bon Ton, T04-955 1688, www.bonton resort.com.my. 100-year-old Malay houses with modern facilities. Pool, jacuzzi, fantastic fusion restaurant. Romantic setting. Unbeatable atmosphere. Recommended. (See also Spas and therapies in the colour section.)
C-D AB Motel, T04-955 5278, www.geo cities.com/abmotel. By far the most highly recommended mid-range option. Clean rooms with fan or a/c, and showers. Island hopping tours. Restaurant and internet.
F Gecko Guesthouse, T019-428 3801, up a lane on the other side of the main road to the beach. Well-decorated simple rooms with wooden floors. Good bar area, relaxed atmosphere, movies.

Pantai Tengah
A-B Sunset Beach Resort, T/F04-955 1751, www.sunvillage.com.my. Beautiful setting – romantic chalets with Balinese furniture and frangipani flowers in the gardens. Stunning.

F-G Zackry, right at the south end of Pantai Tengah, T04-955 7595, www.langkawi networks.com. Great budget option. Basic rooms, dorms available. All clean and tiled. Just across the road from the beach. Quiet location, friendly. Free bicycle hire.

Pantai Kok and Burau Bay
L-AL Berjaya Langkawi Beach Resort, Burau Bay, T04-959 1888, www.berjaya resorts.com.my. Malaysian-style chalets in tropical rainforest, some on stilts over water, some on jungled hillside. Very comfortably furnished with classical furniture. Excellent facilities, white sand beach, beach restaurant.
A-B Mutiara Burau Bay, Jl Teluk Burau, T04-959 1061, www.mutiarahotels.com. A/c, restaurant, at the far end of Pantai Kok. A fun hotel, good for families with a swimming pool and forest or beach horse riding. Excellent café.

🍴 Eating

Ringlet *p607*
🍴 **Lakehouse**, traditional English food, typical Sun lunch fare and cream teas.

Tanah Rata *p608*
🍴 **Smokehouse**, favourites include beef Wellington, roast beef, Yorkshire pudding, steak and kidney pie and cream teas.
🍴 **Gayatri**, 25 Jl Besar. Claypot and Hainan chicken rice and great tandoori. Excellent breakfast *rotis and murtabak, tables outside.*
🍴 **Suria**, 66A Jl Perisan Camellia 3. Open 24 hrs. Excellent South Indian food served on a banana leaf, vegetarian options, friendly.
🍴 **T Café**, 1F, 4 Jl Besar, T019-5722 8833. Cosy travellers' café with Chinese and Malay dishes as well as Western snacks and cakes, scones and pies. Very friendly and good atmosphere.

Brinchang and around *p609*
🍴 **Ferns**, Rosa Passadena Hotel. Western and oriental, good-value buffet.
🍴 **Parkland**, Parkland Hotel. Grill restaurant with steaks, breakfast menu.

¶ **Brinchang**, below hotel of same name on Jl Besar. Popular for its steamboat, good selection of vegetable dishes.
¶ **Kowloon**, Jl Besar. Busy restaurant, lemon chicken and steamboat are popular.

Ipoh p609

Ipoh is known for its Chinese food, especially Ipoh chicken rice and kway teow. The pomelo and the seedless guava are grown in Perak, and the state is known for its groundnuts.
¶¶¶ **Royal Casuarina Coffee House**, and **Il Ritrove**, 18 Jl Gopeng. Italian restaurant specializing in nouvelle cuisine.
¶ **Restuncle House**, 13 Jl Tun Sanbatham. Super-cheap Malay dishes in a Bob Marley-inspired café, also tables on the street facing the Padang. beautifully presented. Recommended.
¶ **Shal's Curry House**, 4 Jl Dato Maharaja Lela. A/c, excellent South Indian food and good vegetarian dishes.

Kuala Kangsar p610

Many restaurants only open at lunchtime. The smartest restaurant is at the **Hotel Seri Kangsar**. In front of here is an Indian restaurant open until late. The market has foodstalls and there's a bakery beside the **Double Lion Hotel**.

Taiping p611

¶¶ **Nagaria Steak House**, 61 Jl Pasar. Dark interior, popular for beer drinking.
¶ **Kedai Kopi Sentosa**, Jl Kelab Cina. Good Teow Chiew noodles.
¶ **Kum Loong**, 45-47 Jl Kota. Good dim sum. Great place to experience local bustle.

Lumut p611

¶¶ **Ocean Seafood**, 115 Jl Tit Panjang. A/c, specializes in Chinese and seafood.
¶ **Kedai Makan Sin Pinamhui (Green House)**, 95 Jl Titi Panjang. Closed Tue. Good Malay.
¶ **Nasi Kandar**, 46 Jl Sultan Idris Shah. Friendly and clean, excellent vegetarian rice and roti.

Pulau Pangkor p611

Most hotels and chalets have their own restaurants. Seafood is always on the menu

¶¶¶ **Pangkor Laut Resort**, T05-699 1100, reservations T03-2145 9000, www.pangkor lautresort.com. 3 top-quality restaurants serving seafood, steamboats or Western fare.
¶¶ **Coco**, Pasir Bogak. Outdoor seafood restaurant and local dishes.
¶ **Vikry Resort**. Excellent home-cooked Indian dishes on banana leaves.

Georgetown p614, map p614

Specialities include *assam laksa* (a hot-and-sour fish soup), *nasi kandar* (curry), *mee yoke* (prawns in chilli-noodle soup) and *inche kabin* (chicken marinated in spices and fried). Penang is known for Nyonya cuisine (see page 583).
¶¶¶-¶¶ **Thirty Two**, 32 Jl Sultan Ahmad Shah, T04-262 2232. Chinese-owned 1920s mansion. Beautifully maintained. Restaurant has a bar/lounge with live jazz, and a terrace by the water. Asian fusion cuisine. Friendly, sophisticated.
¶¶ **Ecco Café**, Love Lane near junction with Lebuh Chulia. Atmospheric bar/Italian café crammed with bizarre objects. Relaxed and friendly. Penang's best Italian food.
¶ **Dragon King**, 99 Lebuh Bishop. Family-run, probably the best Nyonya food in Malaysia, specializes in fish-head curry, satay, *otak-otak* (fish marinated in lime and wrapped in banana leaf), *curry kapitan* (chicken cooked in coconut milk) and *kiam chye boey* (a meat casserole).
¶ **Kassim Mustafa**, 12 Lebuh Chulia. Coffee shop with a handful of dishes, specialities are *nasi dalcha* (rice cooked with ghee and cinnamon), *ayam negro* and mutton *kurma*. Good *roti bom* and *teh tarik*. Great breakfast.
¶ **May Garden**, 70 Penang Rd (next to **Towne House**). Good seafood restaurant with a tank full of fish and shellfish to choose from. The speciality is frogs' legs, with chilli and ginger.
¶ **Rainforest Restaurant**, 300 Chulia St. Popular with travellers, nachos, steak, pizza, apple crumble Freshly baked bread.

Foodstalls Penang's hawker stalls are famous and particularly atmospheric in the evenings. Recommended places include: **Datuk Keramat Hawker Centre**, junction of Anson and Perak roads, one of the venues for the roving night market (check with tourist centre, T04-261 6663); **Padang Kota Lama/Jl Tun Syed Sheh Barakbah** (Esplanade); **Pesiaran Gurney Seawall** (Gurney Drive), Malay, Chinese and Indian.

Batu Ferringhi and Teluk Bahang

Most big hotels have excellent restaurants.
♦♦♦ **House of Four Seasons**, Penang Mutiara Beach Resort, Jl Teluk Bahang. Good old-fashioned opulence with an interesting menu, Cantonese and Szechuan dishes.
♦♦ **The Catch**, Jl Teluk Bahang. Malay, Chinese, Thai and international seafood dishes, fish-tanks for fresh fish, prawns, crabs, lobster, pleasant setting, one of the best.
♦ **End of the World**, end of Teluk Bahang beach. Huge quantities of fresh seafood, superb chilli crabs and great value lobster (RM25 each), pleasant setting on beach.
♦ **Hollywood**, Tanjung Bungah, Batu Ferringhi. Great views over the beach, serves *inche kabin* chicken stews and a good selection of seafood.
♦ **Papa Din's Bamboo**, 124-B Batu Ferringhi (turn left after police station, 200 m up the Kampong Rd). Home-cooked Malay fish curries.

Butterworth *p616*

Most hotels are 20 mins' walk from the bus terminal, so a taxi ride is advisable.
B **Berlin**, 4802 Jl Bagan Luar, T04-332 1701. A/c, TV. The best option. Restaurant nextdoor.

Alor Star *p617*

♦ **Bunga Tanjong**, Jl Seberang. Indian Muslim food, seafood curries.
♦ **Kway Teow Jonid**, by police station. Fried *kway teow*, washed down with *teh tarik*.
♦ **Rose**, Jl Sultan Badishah. Local café serving good *roti* and *nasi*. Recommended.

Langkawi *p618*

Langkawi's speciality is *mee gulong* – fried noodles cooked with shredded prawns, slices of beef, chicken, carrots, cauliflower rolled into a pancake and served with a potato gravy. There is lots of Thai influence. The roadside foodstalls down from the **Langkasuka Hotel** in Padang Matsirat are highly recommended.

Kuah

♦♦ **Sari Village**, Kompleks Pasar Lama, T04-966 751. On stilts over the sea, with a vast selection of seafood. Beautifully designed with good views. Pakistani-influenced cuisine. Specialities include vegetable curry and fish tandoori.
♦ **Mai**, 131 Langkawi Mall, T04-966 0255. Stylish Thai and Malay food. Set lunch RM10. Mai-blend fruit shake recommended.

Pantai Cenang

♦♦♦-♦♦ **Casa del Mar**, and the **Beach Garden** next door, offer international fare, beautifully prepared. The latter is right on the beach.
♦♦ **Nam**, inside the **Bon Ton Resort** just north of Pantai Cenang. Beautiful restaurant overlooking a lake serving funky fusion food. Try the rock lobster and baked snapper on mango rice. Highly recommended.
♦♦ **Red Tomato Garden Café**. Great place for breakfast or a pizza. At night it gets very cosy with fairy lights. Very friendly.
♦♦ **Sunvillage** and **Matahari Malay**. Both in exquisite surroundings. Extensive menus of traditionally prepared dishes.

Pantai Tengah

♦♦♦ **Unkaizan**, T04-955 4118. Great views from the balcony from this upmarket Japanese joint. Expensive but recommended.
♦♦ **Tang Lung Seafood**, T04-955 8818. Chinese seafood garden, pretty at night with red lanterns. Shuttle service from major hotels.

Pantai Kok

♦♦♦ **Oriental Pearl**, Berjaya Langkawi Beach Resort, Burau Bay. Upmarket but simple Chinese, ocean views, good steamboat.

⚫ Bars and clubs

Tanah Rata *p608*

The **Lakehouse** and **Smokehouse** hotel bars are also popular venues for their country pub atmosphere and air of exclusivity.
Kavy Hotel, the bar under this hotel has a pool table and is a good place for a beer.

Strawberry Park Resort. The only nightlife as such takes place here where there is the only disco in town, karaoke, and a bar.

Georgetown *p614, map p614*
Most of the big hotels have nightclubs. Expect to pay cover charges if you are not a guest.
Chillout Club, Gurney Hotel, 18 Persiaran Gurney, T04-370 7000. Good dance club with R&B and house music. Popular.
The Garage, 2 Penang Rd (opposite E&O Hotel), T04-263 6868. Open 1100-0300. There are several bars and clubs inside this restored art deco garage including **Slippery Senoritas**, a tapas and salsa bar with live South American music and performing bar staff. Recommended.
George's, Sunway Hotel, 33 New Lane. Quintessentially English, live music.
Leith St, Lebuh Leith (next to Waldorf Hotel). Pleasant 150-year-old building with original features, pitchers of Carlsberg, light snacks.

Langkawi *p618*
Pantai Cenang now has a few standalone bars, but they tend to close by 0100. The main places are **Go Slow Café**, right on the beach and the **Irish Bar**, opposite Underwater World. Mutiara Burau Bay has the award-winning **Seashell's**, which is a fun pub and restaurant with dancing on the beach.

☸ Festivals

Georgetown *p614, map p614*
Feb/Mar Chap Goh Meh, celebrated on the 15th night of the 1st month of the Chinese lunar calendar; girls throw oranges into the sea for their suitors to catch.
May/Jun Dragon Boat 'Tuen Ng' Festival near Penang Bridge. Teams from around the region and beyond compete. The **Floral Festival** at the Botanic Gardens sees city parades by Malays, Chinese and Indians.
Sep Lantern Festival, a parade with lanterns.
Oct/Nov Deepavali Open House, festivities in Little India.

○ Shopping

Georgetown *p614, map p614*
The main areas are Jl Penang, Jl Burmah and Lebuh Campbell. There is a moveable night market – ask the tourist office for locations.
Antiques An export licence is required for non-imported goods. Shops are concentrated on Jl Penang. There are also antique shops along Rope Walk (Jl Pintal Tali). Most stock antiques from Thailand, Indonesia, Sabah and Sarawak, as well local bargains. **Oriental Arts Co**, 3f Penang Rd, is a well-established with a fine collection. **Penang Antique House**, 27 Jl Patani, sells Peranakan artefacts – porcelain, rosewood with mother-of-pearl inlay.
Batik Maphilindo Baru, 217 Penang Rd, has an excellent range of batiks and sarongs.
Handicrafts Jl Penang is a good place to start. Also try: **Arts and Culture Information Centre**, T04-264 2273. **See Koon Hoe**, 315 Lebuh Chulia, sells Chinese opera masks, jade seals and paper umbrellas. **The Garage**, 2 Penang Rd (opposite E&O Hotel), is a bright orange art deco restored garage with gift and souvenir stalls. **Mah Jong Factory**, Love Lane, sells high-quality Mah Jong sets.

Batu Ferringhi and Teluk Bahang
Handicrafts Craft Batik, opposite the Grandplaza ParkRoyal, sells batik cloth by metre and as ready-made garments. **Yahong Art Gallery**, 58d Batu Ferringhi Rd, T04-881 1251, has batik paintings by the Teng family, considered the father of Malaysian batik. Free entry, excellent quality.

Langkawi *p618*
Duty free Although Langkawi enjoys duty free status there is not much reason to come here for the shopping. Duty free shops line the main street in Kuah and the jetty.
Handicrafts Many shops in Kuah sell textiles. **Batik Jawa Store**, 58 Pekan Pokok Asam, the best-stocked. **Flint Stones Handicraft**, Jl Pandak Mayah, good Asian handicrafts. **Sunshine Handicraft**, Jl Pandak Mayah, range of *songket* products and sarongs.

⚑ Activities and tours

Georgetown *p614, map p614*

Snorkelling and diving Pulau Payar is usually accessed from Langkawi but trips also run from Penang. **East Marine Holidays**, 5 Lengkok Nun, Penang (for the office), T04-226 3022, www.eastmarine.com.my, runs dive trips (RM320) and snorkelling trips (RM220), including the return ferry and buffet lunch.

Tour operators The 3 main tours offered by companies are: the city tour; the Penang Hill and temple tour; and the round-the-island tour. All cost RM45-85 with 2 departures a day, 0900 and 1400. Most of the budget travel agents are along Lebuh Chulia. Several agencies around the Swettenham Pier.
Everrise Tours & Travel, Lot 323, 2nd floor, Wisma Central, 202 Jl n, T04-226 4329.
Georgetown Tourist Service, Jl Imigresen, T04-229 5788. City island tours. **MS Star Travel Agencies**, 475 Lebuh Chulia, T04-262 2906.
MSL Travel, Ming Court Inn Lobby, Jl Macalister, T04-227 2655 or 340 Lebuh Chulia, T04-261 6154. Student and youth travel bureau. **Renae Agency**, 2 Penang Port Commission Complex, T04-262 2369. **Tour and Incentive Travel**, Suite 7B, 7th floor Menara BHL, Jl Sultan Ahmad Shah, T04-227 4522.

Batu Ferringhi and Teluk Bahang
Simple on-the-beach foot reflexology place opposite **Baba's**. Nice setting for a foot massage. Health clubs – such as the **Do-Club** in the Mar Vista Resort, Batu Ferringhi – in all major hotels offer massage.

⊖ Transport

Tanah Rata *p608*
Those who suffer from travel sickness might want to take anti-nausea medication before setting out on the mountain road.
Bus It is best to book in advance for all buses. The bus station is open 0730-1800. **Kurnia Bistari** has 5 express buses which run between KL's Puduraya terminal and the Cameron

Highlands, 0900-1530 (5 hrs). Most other buses for the Cameron Highlands leave from **Tapah**, 67 km from Tanah Rata. There are connections at least every 2 hrs 0730-1730 with **Ringlet**, **Brinchang** and **Tanah Rata**. Tickets for the return journey can be booked at travel agents or at the bus station in Tanah Rata. From **Tapah** there are express buses to **KL** every 2 hrs 1020-1815. There are 3 express buses to **Ipoh** and onto **Georgetown**, Penang, at 0800, 0900 and 1500 (RM19.50). For the east, a minibus runs from Tanah Rata to Gua Musang for connections onto **Kota Bharu** and **Kuantan** (RM68) leaving Mon, Wed, Fri, 0700.
Car hire **Ravi**, Rainbow Garden Centre (between The Smokehouse and Tanah Rata), T05-491782. Remember to sound your horn at bends and beware of the lorries hurtling along.
Taxi Taxis can be chartered for individual journeys or by the hour, or grab a seat in a shared taxi between Tanah Rata and Brinchang. Taxi and local bus station (T05-491 1485) on either side of the *Shell* station in Tanah Rata. To order a taxi, T05-491 1234.
Train The nearest station is **Tapah**, 67 km from Tanah Rata. There are 2 connections daily with **Ipoh** and onto **Butterworth** and **Hat Yai** in Thailand leaving at 1107 and 2343 and 2 south to **KL** leaving at 0315 and 0403.

Brinchang and around *p609*
Bus Buses run between Tanah Rata, Brinchang and Tapah, or take a taxi (RM4).
Taxi Taxis are available for local travel and can be chartered for about RM15 per hr.

Ipoh *p609*
Air Sultan Azlan Shah Airport, T05-312 2459, 15 km south of town, RM10 taxi ride.
  Airline offices MAS, Lot 108 Bangunan Seri Kinta, Jl Sultan Idris Shah, T05-241 4155.
Bus Ipoh is on the main south-north road and is well connected. The bus terminal is on Medan Kidd, a short taxi from town. Buses to **Taiping**, **Lumut** and **Kuala Kangsar** leave from the local bus terminal opposite. Regular connections with **Butterworth**, **KL** (3 hrs), **Alor Star**, **Kuantan**, **Johor Bahru**, **Kangar**, **Kuala**

Perlis, **Lumut** (1 hr 45 mins, every 30 mins, 0730-1930, RM4.50) and **Tapah** (90 mins). Also services to **Kota Bharu** via Grik/Gerik. An express bus company is at 2 Jl Bendahara, T05-535367. Daily service to **Singapore**, **Johor Bahru**, **KL**, **Butterworth**, **Penang**, **Lumut**, **Alor Star** and **Kuala Kangsar**.

Car hire Avis, at the airport, T05-206586. Hertz, Royal Casuarina Hotel, 18 Jl Gopeng, T05-250 5533, and at airport, T05-312 7109. **Taxi** Nam Taxi Company, 15 Jl Raja Mus Aziz, T05-241 2189. **Radiocab**, T05-254 0241. Shared taxis leave from beside the bus station for **KL**, **Butterworth**, **Taiping**, **Alor Star** and **Tapah**. Connections with **Hat Yai** in Thailand. **Train** Ipoh is on the main north-south line. 2 daily connections north with **Butterworth** and **Hat Yai**; 2 daily south to **KL**, T05-254 0481.

Kuala Kangsar *p610*

Bus The station is on Jl Raja Bendahara. Regular connections with **Ipoh**, **Butterworth**, **KL**, **Lumut**, **Taiping** and **Kota Bharu**.
Taxi The only local transport. Shared taxis congregate by the bus station and run to **Butterworth**, **KL**, **Ipoh** and **Taiping** when full.
Train The station is out of town to the northeast, on Jl Sultan Idris. Trains on the KL-Butterworth route stop here.

Taiping *p611*

Bus The main long-distance bus station is 7 km out of town; take a bus or taxi. Regular connections with **Butterworth**, **Ipoh** and **KL**. Also a morning bus to **Kuantan** on the east coast. For other connections, change at Ipoh. Local buses for **Ipoh** and **Kuala Kangsar** from the central bus station at Jl Masjid/Jl Iskandar.
Train The station is on the west side of town. There are twice daily connections with **Ipoh**, **KL** and **Butterworth**.

Lumut *p611*

Bus The bus station is in the centre of town, a few mins' walk from the jetty. Buses to **Ipoh** (every 30 mins, 1 hr 45 mins), **KL** and **Butterworth**. Less regular connections with **Melaka**. Buses also run to **Singapore**.

Ferry Pan Silver Ferry has regular crossings, at least every 30 mins 0700-2100 from Lumut Jetty to Pangkor village on **Pangkor Island**, RM5 one way. Crossings every 2 hrs 0845-1830 to **Pangkor Island Beach Resort**.
Taxi Services to **Ipoh**, **KL** and **Butterworth**.

Pulau Pangkor *p611*

Air The airport, T05-685 4516, on the north of the island is used by Berjaya Air's 48-seater Dash-7s. Flights to/from **KL** take 50 mins. Leaves KL at 1030, returns 1130 on Mon, Wed, Fri, Sat, Sun, RM225 one way, RM450 return.
Boat Ferries leave from **Lumut** jetty (lots of touts). Connections every 30 mins to Pangkor Jetty (RM5 one way, 30 mins from Lumut 0700-2100; from Pangkor 0640-2100), also regular connections with **Pangkor Island Beach Resort**, jetty close to Golden Sands (RM6 one way). There are inter-island ferries or it is possible to hire fishing boats.
Bus/taxi There is a fleet of pink minibus taxis from Pangkor village to other parts of the island. Prices are fixed.

Georgetown *p614, map p614*

Air Bayan Lepas Airport, T04-643 4411. Taxi to the airport (30 mins) RM25. Regular connections with **Johor Bahru**, **KL** and **Langkawi**. The daily Langkawi flight takes 30 mins (leaving Penang 1215). International connections on **MAS**, most via KL except for direct London to Georgetown, return is via KL. Regular direct connections to **Singapore**, **Bangkok** and **Medan** (Sumatra).

   Airline offices Air Asia, KOMTAR, T04-261 5642; **Cathay Pacific**, AIA Building, Lebuh Farquhar, T04-226 0411; **Emirates**, T04-263 1100; **MAS**, KOMTAR, T04-262 0011 or at the airport, T04-643 0811; **Singapore Airlines**, Wisma Penang Gardens, 42 Jl Sultan Ahmad Shah, T04-226 3201; **Thai International**, Wisma Central, 202 Jl Macalister, T04-226 6000. **United Airlines**, T04-263 6020.
Boat Passenger and car ferries from Pengkalan Raja Tun Uda, T04-331 5780. Ferry service between Georgetown and **Butterworth** runs every 20 mins 0600-2400,

RM1 return. **Selasa Express Ferry Company** has an office by the Penang Clocktower, next to Penang Tourist Office, T04-262 5630. **Sejahtera** and **Fast Ferry Ventures** operate boats between Georgetown and **Langkawi**, 2 departures from each company a day at 0900 and 1430 (3 hrs), RM35 one way, RM60 return. Tickets from travel agents in town. Boats leave from Swettenham Pier. You can take a motorbike or bicycle aboard.

To Indonesia Several ferry companies including **Fast Ferry Ventures** operate a service between Penang and Belawan (to port of **Medan**, Sumatra), from Swettenham Pier. Usually 2 daily at 0800 and 1430, RM90 one way, RM160 return, journey time 4½ hrs. The Sat ferry is often full; book ahead. Tickets from most guesthouses and travel agents. Obtain a visa for Indonesia before you go.

Bus City buses leave from Lebuh Victoria near the Butterworth ferry terminal and serve Georgetown and surrounding areas. Buses around the island leave from Pengkalan Weld (Weld Quay) – next to the ferry terminal; all stop at KOMTAR. Many companies have recently gone bust; check with tourist office or get a copy of the *Penang Tourist* Newspaper.

Long distance The bus terminal is beside the ferry terminal at Butterworth. Booking offices along Lebuh Chulia and inside KOMTAR. Some coaches operate from Pengkalan Weld direct to major towns on the Peninsula (see Butterworth, page 616). **Masa Mara Travel**, 54/4 Jl Burmah, is an agent for direct express buses from Penang to **Kota Bharu** and **KL** (5 hrs). Minibus companies organize pick-ups from your hotel, to **Hat Yai**, for connections north to Thailand. There are also regular bus connections to **Bangkok**, **Phuket** and **Surat Thani**. Some hotels (eg **New Asia** and **Cathay**) organize minibuses to Thailand. Overnight bus to **Singapore**.

Car hire Penang to KL is 4½ hrs. There is a one-way RM7 toll to drive across the bridge to the mainland. Many companies also have offices at the airport. **Budget**, 28 Jl Penang, T04-643 6025. **Hawk Rent-a-car**, T04-881 3886. **Hertz**, 38 Lebuh Farquhar, T04-263

5914. **New Bob Rent-a-Car**, 7/F Gottlieb Rd, T04-229 1111. **Orix**, City Bayview Hotel, 25A Lebuh Farquhar, T1800-881555.

Taxi Long-distance taxis to all destinations on the Peninsula operate from the depot beside the Butterworth ferry on Pengkalan Weld. Taxi stands on Jl Dr Lim Chwee Leong, Pengkalan Weld and Jl Magazine. No meters; agree price before setting off; short distances in the city RM5-7. To the airport costs RM25. **Radio taxis**, T04-890 9918 (at ferry terminal). **CT Radio Taxi Service**, T04-229 9467. Taxis to Thailand: overnight to **Hat Yai**; **Surat Thani** for Koh Samui, **Krabi** for Phuket.

Train The nearest station is by Butterworth ferry terminal, T04-261 0290. Book in advance for onward rail journeys at the station or ferry terminal, Pengkalan Weld, Georgetown. From Butterworth: 2 daily to **Alor Star**, **Taiping**, **Ipoh**, **KL** (6 hrs) and **JB**. See Butterworth, below.

Trishaw Bicycle rickshaws carry 2 people are one of the most practical ways to explore Georgetown. RM1 per half mile or RM15 per hour; agree on the route and price first.

Around the Island *p616*

Bus Blue bus No 93 goes to Batu Ferringhi/ Teluk Bahang from Pengkalan Weld (Weld Quay) or KOMTAR in **Georgetown**, every 30 mins, RM2, 30-40 mins.

Taxi Stands on Batu Ferringhi (opposite **Golden Sands Hotel**). Some taxis operate on commission; call in advance to check rates. From airport to Batu Ferringhi, 40 mins, RM45.

Butterworth *p616*

Butterworth is the main transport hub for Penang, and buses/trains on the east coast.

Bus The bus station is next to the ferry terminal. There are regular connections with many Peninsula towns. Buses leave at least every hour for **Kuala Kedah** (for the Langkawi ferry). There are also buses to **Keroh**, on the border with Thailand, from where it is possible to get Thai taxis to **Betong**.

Ferry Ferries for pedestrians and cars and leave for **Georgetown** every 15-20 mins. The 20-min trip costs RM1, the return trip is free.

Border essentials: Malaysia–Thailand

The North–South Highway runs to the Thai border at **Bukit Kayu Hitam**, from where it is a short walk to the bus and taxi stop for connections to the **Sadao** (Thailand), a few kilometres on, and Hat Yai. This is the easiest way to crosst eh border. Most buses leave from Penang/Butterworth for Bangkok and the Kra Isthmus. There are 2 direct daily buses from Alor Star to Hat Yai (via Changlun and Bukit Kayu Hitam). These leave from the small station on Jl Sultan Badlishah, north of the town centre. Alternatively travel to **Padang Besar** (from Kangar in Perlis), where the railway line crosses the border. From here buses and trains run to Hat Yai.

Taxi From next to the ferry terminal. If you take a taxi to Penang you must pay the taxi fare plus the toll for the bridge (RM7).

Train The station is beside the Penang ferry terminal. There are 2 daily connections with **Alor Star, Taiping, Ipoh, KL** and **JB** and trains to **Bangkok**, (19 hrs) and **Singapore** (14 hrs).

Alor Star *p617*

Air The airport is 10 km north of town. Daily connections with **KL** on **MAS**, 180 Kompleks Alor Star, Lebuhraya Darulaman, T04-71 1 106 and **Air Asia**, office at the airport.

Bus Main bus terminal is 2 km north of centre, off Jl Bakar Bata; most long-distance buses leave from here. Destinations include **KL** (every 2 hrs, RM26), **Melaka, Ipoh, JB** (0830, RM47), **Kota Bharu, Kuantan** and **Kuala Terengganu**. Local southbound buses, including to **Butterworth** and **Kuala Kedah** (for **Langkawi**), leave from the central bus station in front of the railway station on Jl Stesyen, as well as the express bus station. Local buses also leave from the station by the taxi stop, off Jl Langgar; long-distance connections eastwards with **Kota Bharu** leave from here; 2 daily (0900, 2100, RM23.60).

To Singapore There are bus connections from the long-distance terminal, or Express Bus Station, 1 km north of town. A shuttle bus also goes here, from Jl Langar in the centre.

Taxi From the stand just south of Jl Langgar, near the town centre, to **Penang, Kuala Kedah** (for **Langkawi**) and **Kangar** (**Perlis**).

Train The station is off Jl Langgar. There are 2 trains a day (1851 and 2119) to **KL** and **Butterworth**. There is an express train from to **Hat Yai** daily at 1617. The slower **Ekspres Langkawi** train leaves for **Hat Yai** at 0815.

Kuala Perlis *p617*

Bus/taxi From the ferry terminal. Regular connections with **Butterworth**, to **Alor Star**, **KL** (every hour 0900-2200), **Kota Bharu** (2 daily, 0800 and 1945, RM26) and **Pedang Besar** (for connections with Thailand, see below). High-speed ferry: departs Kuala Perlis jetty every hour 0800-2000 to **Pulau Langkawi**, 45 mins, RM12. Last ferry to Kuala Perlis leaves at 2000.

Langkawi *p618*

Air The airport is 20 km from Kuah, 8 km from Pentai Cenang. Taxi to Kuah RM12; buy a coupon in the airport. Daily connections with **JB, KL**, and **Penang** on **MAS. Air Asia** flies between Langkawi and **KL. MAS** and **Silk Air** operate frequent connections with **Singapore. MAS** also has a twice-weekly service to **London**. Direct flights from **Hong Kong**.

Airline offices MAS, Langkawi Fair Mall, Persiaran Putra, T04-746 3000; **Silk Air**, c/o **MAS**, T04-292 3122; **Air Asia**, T04-202 7777.

Boat It is worth hiring a boat if you can get a group together, RM150 per day. Many beach hotels also run boat trips to the islands. Ferries to Langkawi leave from **Kuala Perlis** (14 mins, RM12) and **Kuala Kedah** (1½ hrs, RM15). Timetables subject to seasonal change (fewer boats Apr-Sep). Boats run to **Kuala Perlis** every hour 0800-1900, RM12. To **Kuala Kedah** every hour 0730- 1900, RM15. To **Penang**, 3-4 departures daily, RM45.Leaving Langkawi, there are ticket agents at the ferry. Connections with **KL** are easiest from Kuala Kedah. If heading east to **Kota Bharu** take a ferry to Kuala Perlis. **Qudrat Bistari Agency**, sells tickets, at counter 9 at the Kuah jetty.

To Thailand Langkawi Ferry Services and **Labuan Express** to **Satun** (Thailand), RM20, 1 hr, 4-5 daily 0930-1600.

Bus There are no local buses. It is a 6-hr journey from KL to Kuala Kedah; from there, catch the boat to Langkawi.

Car hire Mayflower Acme, Pelangi Beach Resort, Pantai Cenang, T04-911 001. **Tomo Express**, 14 Jl Pandak Maya 4, Pekan Kuah, T04-966 9252. Expect to pay RM80 per day.

Taxi Fares around the island are fixed. From the jetty to **Kuah** is RM4, to **Pantai Cenang** RM16, to **Datai Bay**, RM25.

● Directory

Tanah Rata *p608*
Banks All banks are on Jl Besar. It is also possible to change money at CS Travel & Tours. **Internet** Almost all hotels and hostels have internet. **Medical facilities** Hospital: opposite gardens at north end of town, on Jl Besar, T05-491 1966. **Police** T05-491 1222, opposite gardens at north end of town.

Brinchang and around *p609*
Banks Public Bank, next to Garden Lodge. **Internet** Next to the Fong Lum, 2nd floor. **Police** Central square. **Post** Opposite the Petronas petrol station at north end of town.

Ipoh *p609*
Banks Several on Jl Sultan Idris Shah and Jl Yang Kalsom; in the new town many banks on Jl Sultan Yussuf. **Internet** Infoweb Station, Jl Dato Onn Jaafar, near Jl Sultan Idris Shah. **Post** Next to the train station, Jl Panglima Bukit Gantang Wahab.

Taiping *p611*
Banks Many banks at crossroads of Jl Kota and Jl Sultan Abdullah. **Poly Travels**, 53 Jl Mesjid and **Fulham Tours**, 25 Jl Kelab Cina, have foreign exchange facilities. **Internet** Discover de Internet, 3 Jl Panggong Wayang, RM2.50 per hr. Helm Computer Technology Centre, Jl Kota. **Post** Jl Barrack.

Georgetown *p614, map p614*
Banks Most banks are in or around the GPO area and Lebuh Pantai. Money changers are here too, and on Jl Masjid Kapitan Keling and Lebuh Pantai, close to the Immigration office. **Consulates** Indonesia, 467 Jl Burmah, T04-227 5141; **Thailand**, 1 Jl Ayer Raja, T04-226 8029 (visas in 2 days); **UK**, Birch House, 73 Jl Datuk Keramat, T04-262 5333. **Immigration** Corner of Lebuh Light and Lebuh Pantai, T04-261 5122. **Internet** Several along Lebuh Chulia, RM3 per hr. **The Global Net**, 94 Love Lane, also sells cut-price ferry tickets to Medan (Sumatra) and Langkawi. **Post** Lebuh Pitt, efficient poste restante, also has a parcel-wrapping service. **Medical services** General Hospital (government), Jl Residensi, T04-229 3333; **Lam Wah Ee Hospital** (private), 141 Jl Batu Lancang, T04-657 1888. **Telephone** Telecoms office (international), Jl Burmah.

Alor Star *p617*
Banks Bank Bumiputra, Jl Tunku Ibrahim; **Chartered Bank, Overseas Union Bank** and **UMBC** are on Jl Raja. **Internet** Plaza shopping centre at end of Jl Tunku Ibrahim. **Post** GPO, Jl Langgar, opposite police station.

Langkawi *p618*
Banks Just off the main street in Kuah. Money changers at the ferry terminal offer poor rates. **Noorul Ameen**, 2nd floor, 15 Jl Pandak Mayah, opposite taxi stand, offers the best rates. Money changers at Pantai Cenang and Pantai Tengah. **Customs** T04-966 6227. **Immigration** T04-969 4005. **Internet** Several including **Langkawi Online**, Langkawi Plaza. **Post** At jetty end of main road.

Southern Peninsula

Melaka is one of the Malaysian tourism industry's trump cards, thanks to its Portuguese, Dutch and British colonial history, its rich Peranakan (Straits Chinese) cultural heritage and its picturesque hinterland of rural Malay kampongs. The route south from Melaka is a pleasant but unremarkable drive through plantation country to Johor Bahru (JB), on the southernmost tip of the Peninsula.

It is a short hop across the causeway from JB to Singapore, and Malaysia's east coast islands and resorts are within easy reach. One of the most famous of these is Pulau Tioman, a large volcanic outcrop on the east coast with perfect strips of sandy beaches, good diving and snorkelling, forest trails, mountain hikes and, for the most part, a laid-back atmosphere. ▶▶ *For listings, see pages 637-643.*

Melaka and around ⊜⊙⊘⊙⚠⊜⊙ ▶▶ *pp637-643. Colour map 8, E2.*

Thanks to its strategic location on the strait that bears its name, Melaka was a rich, cosmopolitan port long before it fell victim to successive colonial invasions. Its wealth and influence are now a thing of the past, and the city's colourful history is itself a major money spinner for Malaysia's tourism industry. With its striking Dutch colonial core and bustling Chinatown, housing the oldest Chinese temple in Malaysia, there's plenty to keep visitors occupied.

Ins and outs

Getting there Express buses ply the KL-Melaka (150 km) and Singapore-Melaka (250 km) routes. From KL airport, take a bus via Nilai to Seremban and from there board a coach direct to Melaka. The modern bus station is a few kilometres out of town on Jalan Tun Razak. Taxis are notorious for ripping off tourists as drivers refuse to use their meters. From the bus station to the centre of town should cost RM12-15. Guesthouse touts often hassle new arrivals but can be helpful for finding budget accommodation. There are daily ferry connections with Dumai in Sumatra. ▶▶ *See Transport, page 641.*

Getting around While Melaka is a largish town it is still possible to enjoy many of the sights on foot; bicycles are also available for hire from some of the guesthouses and shops in town. There is a town bus service; the No 17 bus runs from the bus station to historical Melaka and on to the Portuguese area. Taxis are plentiful. Colourful trishaws are not part of Melaka's public transport system; they survive by providing a service to tourists.

The **Jerak Warisan Heritage Trail** starts at the tourist office on Jalan Kota, near the quayside and covers all the major cultural sights of interest. The route crosses the bridge, to the Baba Nyonya Heritage Museum, takes in some temples on Jonker Street and then heads back across the bridge to Stadthuys, St Paul's Church, St Paul's Hill and the Porta de Santiago Independence Monument. For a handout on the trail, ask at the tourist office.

There are boat tours down the river through the original port area and past some of the old Dutch houses, see Activities and tours, page 640. The river is a little pungent, but the 16th-century sanitation adds to the realism.

Tourist information Tourism Malaysia ⓘ *Jl Kota (opposite Christ Church), T06-281 4803, Sat-Thu 0845-1700, Fri 0845-1215, 1445-1700.* There is also a tourist information desk at **Ayer Keroh** ⓘ *T06-312 5811, www.melaka.gov.my.*

Sights

Melaka's main sights of interest are on the eastern side of the river around Town Square (also known as Dutch Square). Behind the square St Paul's Hill rises above the town. On the other side of the river, Chinatown is lined with shophouses and antique shops. Jalan Hang Jebat (Jonker Walk) is closed off at weekends for the night market, which bustles with activity. Stalls are set up in front of shop houses, selling everything from toys to wooden clogs, while hawkers with pushcarts gather to sell delicious street food.

Town Square

The Dutch colonial architecture in town square is the most striking feature of the riverfront. The most prominent of these is the imposing **Stadthuys** (1660), said to be the oldest-surviving Dutch building in the East. Once the residence of Dutch governors, the building now houses a good **history museum** ① *Sat-Thu 0900-1730, Fri 0900-1245 and 1445-1800, RM5*. Just opposite Stadthuys, **Christ Church** ① *Thu-Tue, (1741-1753)* is Malaysia's oldest Protestant church. The red bricks were shipped out from Zeeland in

Melaka

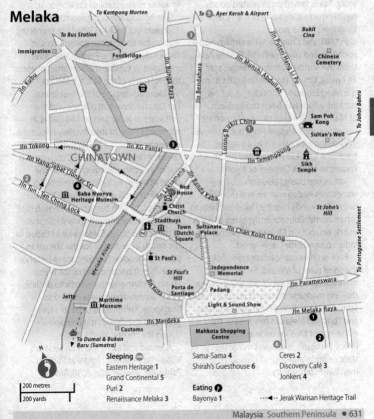

Sleeping 🛏️	Sama-Sama **4**	Ceres **2**
Eastern Heritage **1**	Shirah's Guesthouse **6**	Discovery Café **3**
Grand Continental **5**		Jonkers **4**
Puri **2**	Eating 🍴	
Renaissance Melaka **3**	Bayonya **1**	---◄--- Jerak Warisan Heritage Trail

A brief history of Melaka

Melaka was founded at the end of the 14th century by a fugitive Hindu prince from Sumatra called Parameswara. Parameswara recognized the fishing kampong's strategic potential: it was sheltered from the monsoons by the island of Sumatra and perfectly located for merchants to take advantage of the trade winds. What's more, because the strait's deep-water channel lay close to the Malayan coast, Melaka had command over the ships passing through it. The settlement became wealthy by trading spices and textiles with Indonesia and India. Taxes levied on imported goods rapidly made it into one of the richest kingdoms in the world.

In 1405, the Chinese, who already had a sophisticated trade network linking Asia, India the Middle East and Europe, sent an envoy, Cheng Ho, bearing gifts from the Ming Emperor (including a yellow parasol, which has been the emblem of Malay royalty ever since). They offered to help protect Melaka from the Siamese in exchange for using it as a supply base. The Chinese that settled became known as Straits Chinese or Nyonya.

Indian merchants also arrived. They sometimes had to wait several months before the winds changed to allow them to return home. Consequently, many of them put down roots in Melaka and permanent Indian communities developed.

Ever keen to consolidate trade links, the third ruler of Melaka, Sri Maharaja, married the daughter of the sultan of the thriving maritime state of Sumudra-Pasai, Sumatra. In so doing, he embraced Islam and "hitched Melaka's fortunes to the rising star of Muslim trading fraternity" (Mary Turnbull). Islam was made the state religion and spread through the merchant community.

For three centuries Melaka was at the fulcrum of the Asian trade route and was known as the emporium of the east. Foreign merchants traded in textiles, silk, spices, porcelain, gold, pepper, camphor, sandalwood and tin. By the 16th century, tales of luxury and prosperity attracted the Portuguese, who came in search of trading opportunities, with the aim of breaking the Arab merchants' stranglehold on trade between Europe and Asia. Alfonso d'Albuquerque stormed and conquered the city in 1511, with 18 ships and 1400 men. The sultan fled to Johor to re-establish his kingdom.

The Portuguese occupiers stayed for 130 years but back in Lisbon the monarchy was on the decline, the government in serious debt and the Portuguese never managed to subdue the Sumatran pirates, the real rulers of the Strait of Melaka.

Taking advantage of this weakness, the Dutch entered an alliance with the Sultanate of Johor and, in 1641, after a six-month siege of the city, they forced the surrender of the last Portuguese governor. Over the next 150 years, the Dutch carried out an extensive building programme, some of these, including the red building of Stadhuys, still stand on Dutch Square.

By the late 18th century the English East India Company decided it wanted a share of the action. In 1829, Melaka was ceded to the British in exchange for the Sumatran port of Bencoolen (see Singapore history, page 765). It became part of the British Straits Settlements but went into decline as the administration was moved to Singapore. This proved to be its saving grace and it suffered little damage during the Second World War.

A Sound and Light Show on Melaka's history is presented nightly at Padang Pahlawan, Bandar Hilir, 2030, RM10.

Holland and the floor is still studded with Dutch tombstones. The original pews are intact – as are its ceiling beams, each hewn from a single tree trunk more than 15 m long.

St Paul's Hill

Behind the gate at Stadthuys, a path leads up the hill to the ruins of **St Paul's Church** (1521), built on the site of the last Melakan sultan's *istana*. From 1567-1596 the church was used as a fortress by the Portuguese, but it was badly damaged during the Dutch siege in 1641. There are good views of the city and the ruins now host buskers and souvenir sellers.

Head down the hill the other side of the hill and you reach the **Porta de Santiago**, the remains of the great Portuguese fort **A Famosa**, said to have been built in four months flat under Admiral Alfonso d'Albuquerque's supervision in 1511. The fort sprawled across the whole hill and housed the entire Portuguese administration but it was virtually flattened by the British in 1806-1808 when they occupied Melaka during the Napoleonic Wars.

A wooden replica of Sultan Mansur Shah's 15th-century *istana* is below St Paul's. The **Sultanate Palace (Istana Ke Sultanan)** ⓘ *daily 0900-1730, RM2*, was painstakingly reconstructed in 1985 using traditional techniques and materials. The magnificent palace was destroyed by fire after being struck by lightning the year after Mansur's accession.

Once the social centre of British colonial Melaka, the **Independence Memorial** ⓘ *Sat-Thu 0900-1800, Fri 0900-1200 and 1500-1800, free*, now houses an extensive timeline exhibition covering Malaysia's journey to independence.

East bank

The **Maritime Museum** ⓘ *on the riverbank, 200 m from the river boat embarkation point, Sat-Thu daily 0900-1730, 1215-1445, RM2*, is housed in a full-scale reconstruction of the Portuguese trading vessel *Flor de la Mar* – thought to be the richest ship ever lost. This is one of the best museums in Melaka, given its history of sea trade. It has a collection of models of foreign ships that docked at Melaka during its maritime supremacy from the 14th century to the Portuguese era.

Chinatown

From Dutch Square, a concrete bridge leads to the picturesque **Jalan Tun Tan Cheng Lock**. It is lined with the Straits Chinese community's ancestral homes and is Melaka's Millionaires' Row. Many of the houses have intricately carved doors that were often specially built by immigrant craftsmen from China. Today tour buses exacerbate the local traffic problem, which clogs the narrow one-way street, but many of its Peranakan mansions are still lived in by the same families that built them in the 19th century.

One of the most opulent of these houses has been converted into the **Baba Nyonya Heritage Museum** ⓘ *48-50 Jl Tun Tan Cheng Lock, T06-283 1273, daily 1000-1230 and 1400-1630, RM8*. It is in a well-preserved traditional Peranakan town house, built in 1896 by millionaire rubber planter Chan Cheng Siew. The house contains family heirlooms and antiques, including Nyonya porcelain and blackwood furniture with marble or mother-of-pearl inlay, and silverware. Tours run regularly throughout the day.

West bank

On the west bank is **Kampong Morten**, a village of traditional Melakan houses. It is named after a man who built Melaka's wet market and donated the land to the Malays. The main attraction here is Kassim Mahmood's handcrafted house.

North Melaka

In 1460 when Sultan Mansur Shah married Li Poh, a Ming princess, she took up residence on Melaka's highest hill, **Bukit Cina**, which became the Chinese quarter. It is now the largest traditional Chinese burial ground outside China, containing more than 12,000 graves, some of which date back to the Ming Dynasty.

At the foot of the hill is an old Chinese temple called **Sam Poh Kong**, dedicated to the famous Chinese seafarer, Admiral Cheng Ho. It was originally built to cater for those whose relatives were buried on Bukit Cina. This temple has a peaceful and relaxed atmosphere and is interesting to explore.

Portuguese Settlement

① *3 km east of town, take a No 17 bus from outside the Equatorial Hotel.*

Ujong Pasir has been a Portuguese settlement for nearly five centuries. Unlike the Dutch and British colonial regimes, the Portuguese garrison was encouraged to integrate and inter-marry with the Malays. The process of integration was so successful that when the Dutch, after capturing the city in 1641, offered Portuguese settlers a choice between amnesty and deportation to their nearest colony, many chose to stay. In the 1920s they were allotted a small area of swampland and the settlement visible today was built, its street named after Portuguese heroes largely unrecognized in Malaysia. The main square, built only in 1985, is a concrete replica of a square in Lisbon – and is visibly ersatz. Today these Portuguese Malaysians number around 4500 (20,000 in the whole country).

Johor Bahru ⊜❶❷⊜❶ ›› pp637-643. Colour map 8, F3.

→ *Phone code: 07.*

Modern Johor Bahru – more commonly called JB – is not a pretty town. It lies on the southernmost tip of the Peninsula and is the gateway to Malaysia from Singapore. JB is short on tourist attractions but has for many years served either as a tacky red-light reprieve for Singaporeans and/or as a large retail outlet. There is little reason to stay here, most travellers pass through on their way from or to Singapore.

If you are in town, it's worth visiting the **Istana Besar**. Built by Sultan Abu Bakar in 1866, it is a slice of Victorian England set in beautiful gardens, overlooking the strait and now houses the **Royal Abu Bakar Museum** ① *Jl Tun Dr Ismail, T07-223 0555, Sat-Thu 0900-1700, US$7.* In the north wing is the throne room and museum containing a superb collection of royal treasures, including gruesome hunting trophies such as hollow elephant feet and an array of tusks and skulls, as well as Chinese and Japanese ceramics.

Ins and outs

Senai airport ① *20 km from town, www.senaiairport.com,* has connections with KL, several destinations in Indonesia, and Bangkok. A shuttle bus runs into town. There is a regular bus service between Singapore and KL. The KL–Singapore railway line runs through JB. There is a **FerryLink** service between Changi Point in Singapore and Tanjung Belungkor, in the eastern corner of Johor state. This has the advantage of avoiding the congested causeway across the border. Car hire in JB is cheaper than in Singapore. Cheap taxis (meters not an option) provide the main form of transport. ›› *See Transport, page 641.*

There are two tourist offices at 2 Jalan Air Molek: **JOTIC** ① *T07-224 9960, www.johor tourism.com.my, Mon-Fri 0800-1630, Sat 0800-1230,* and the **Tourism Malaysia Information Centre** ① *T07-222 3591, www.tourismmalaysia.com.my.*

There are a total of 64 islands in the volcanic Seribuat archipelago, off Malaysia's east coast. Many are inaccessible and uninhabited. The most popular is Tioman, made famous by the Hollywood movie *South Pacific*, which has scores of resorts, simple beach huts and dive operators. It is also possible to island hop to bask on deserted beaches or snorkel in coves.

Pulau Tioman ➤ *Phone code: 07*

Tioman, 56 km off Mersing, is the largest island in the archipelago at 20 km by 12 km. The interior is dominated by several jagged peaks and is densely forested, while coast is fringed by white sand beaches and traditional fishing kampongs. Despite development, many of these kampongs have retained their scruffy charm and are still very laid back. Thankfully, as yet, there are no nightclubs or fast food restaurants and the tourist shops are very low key.

Pulau Tioman

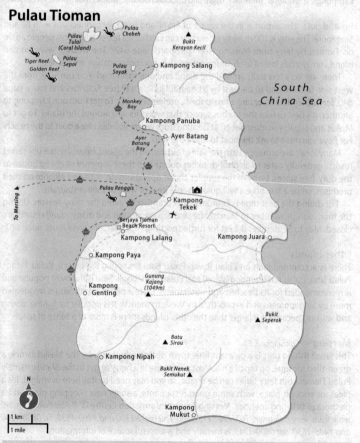

Pulau Chebeh

Pulau Tulai (Coral Island)

Tiger Reef
Golden Reef

Pulau Sepoi

Pulau Soyak

Kampong Salang

Bukit Kerayon Kecil

South China Sea

Monkey Bay

Kampong Panuba

Ayer Batang Bay

Ayer Batang

Pulau Renggis

To Mersing

Kampong Tekek

Berjaya Tioman Beach Resort

Kampong Lalang

Kampong Juara

Kampong Paya

Gunung Kajang (1049m) ▲

Kampong Genting

Bukit Seperok ▲

Batu Sirau ▲

Kampong Nipah

Bukit Nenek Semukut ▲

N

1 km
1 mile

Kampong Mukut

Most of the island's inhabitants live on the west side of the island. The main village, **Tekek**, is where most passengers arrive and has most of the island's facilities including shops, a post office, police post, clinic, money changes and an immigration office. Most of the accommodation is a five- to 10-minute walk south of the jetty, but much of it is run down. The beach is rocky at low tide at **Ayer Batang** (also known as ABC) and the sandy area quite small. There are a couple of mini markets for supplies and souvenirs, a small beach bar and internet. **Kampong Salang** is the northernmost development on the island and is set in a sheltered cove with a beautiful beach. The beach is more rowdy than Ayer Batang, with concrete development and more of a party scene, popular with backpackers. The island is virtually uninhabited on the southeast and southwest sides, with the kampongs of **Nipah** and **Mukut** just starting to open up to tourism. The only place to stay on the east of the island is **Juara**, which has a beautiful long white beach and good breakers (no good for snorkelling). Being on the seaward side, Juara has a different atmosphere from the west coast kampongs; it is quieter, friendlier, more laid back and bucolic, thanks mainly to its seclusion.

Ins and outs The airport is in the centre of Tekek and has daily connections with KL and Singapore. The jetty is 100 m away where you can catch a sea taxi or ferry. Most people arrive on Tioman by ferry from Mersing (see Transport, page 642). The website www.tioman island.com.my has lots of useful information about accommodation and ferries.

There are very few trails around the island and one main road. You can walk from the west side of the island to the east by a beautiful jungle trail (see Activities and tours, page 640, for further details) or hire a taxi in town, preferably 4WD. To get from one kampong to another, it's best to take the sea bus service that works its way around the island. To get to Mukut and Nipah you must get off at Genting from where you can hire a boat to the beach. For Paya you need to ask the boat to make the stop.

Many locals are unhappy with the sale of alcohol on the island. However, the upmarket resorts generally cater to alcohol-drinking guests and there is plenty of cheap booze at the duty-free stores. Many of the simpler chalet operations do not allow alcohol on their premises, while a few others will quietly serve beer or wine at their restaurant.

For **diving** the best time is February to September to avoid the rainy season. During the monsoon (November to March), the seas are very rough and many island resorts are closed. May to September is best for turtle spotting. ▸▸ *See Activities and tours, page 640.*

Other islands

There is accommodation on Pulau Rawa, Pulau Babi Besar (Big Pig Island), Pulau Tinggi, Pulau Sibu, Pulau Aur (Bamboo Island) and Pulau Pemanggil. **Sibu** is the most popular and is recommended for its beaches and watersports. Once a pirate haunt, Sibu is frequented more by Singaporeans and expats than by Western tourists. It is popular for fishing, diving and walking because it is larger than the other islands there is more of a sense of space.

Mersing → *Colour map 8, E3.*

This small fishing port is a pleasant little town distinguished only by the Masjid Jamek, a green-tiled mosque, on top of a hill. Most people are in a hurry to get to the islands, namely Pulau Tioman, but ferry times can be erratic, so you may need to stay here overnight. It's a pleasant enough place, with some good restaurants, a shiny new shopping plaza and a plethora of ticketing agencies. **Mersing Tourist Information Centre** ⓘ *Jl Abu Bakar, 5 mins' walk from Jerry into town, T07-799 5212, Mon-Thu 0800-1300 and 1400-1630, Fri 0800-1200 and 1445-1630, Sat 0800-1245*, is friendly and is a useful source of information.

● Southern Peninsula listings

For Sleeping and Eating price codes, see inside the front cover.

● Sleeping

Melaka *p630, map p631*

There are lots of upmarket hotels around Tanjung Kling; good budget options can be found around Taman Melaka Raya.

LL Renaissance Melaka, Jl Bendahara, T06-284 8888, www.marriott.com. 24 storeys high, it is the tallest building in the town. With 300 rooms, all of which are spacious and elegantly appointed with Malaccan wood furniture, a/c, mini-fridge, TV, in-house video and grand views either over the town or to the sea. Also coffee shop, restaurants, fitness centre, pool on the 9th floor.

C-D Grand Continental, 20 Jl Tun Sri Lanang, T06-284 0088, www.ghihotels.com. 150 a/c rooms, restaurant, large rooms, good service, buffet for all meals, pool, breakfast included. Good value.

C-D Puri, 118 Jl Tun Tan Cheng Lock, T06-282 5588, www.hotelpuri.com. Beautiful hotel in a restored Peranakan house, with a Chinese garden café and a lobby with a piano and spiral staircase. Rooms are clean and tastefully furnished; several have balconies. Wi-Fi. Breakfast included.

E-G Sama-Sama, 26 Jl Tukang Besi (Blacksmith's St), T012-305 1980, www.sama-sama-guesthouse.com. Laid-back option in the heart of Chinatown in a 300-year-old shophouse. Dorms (RM10), doubles and singles around a courtyard with hammocks. Melaka's budget choice with character. Popular, book ahead.

E-G Shirah's Guest House, 207 Taman Melaka Raya, T06-286 1041, shirahgh@tim.net.my. Owner Din is super friendly and organizes trips and barbecues. Rooms are clean and simply furnished with a nice touches like 4-poster beds in some rooms. Internet, bikes for hire and kitchen. Din is a great source of information on Melaka.

F-G Eastern Heritage, 8 Jl Bukit China, T06-283 3026, www.eastern-heritagel.com. Great old Chinese building with carved wood and gold inlay, spacious rooms on 2nd floor, dorm on 3rd floor, small dipping pool on 1st floor, batik lessons, good location. Extremely popular, with an authentic feel.

Johor Bahru *p634*

JB's top hotels cater for businesspeople and have all the 5-star facilities. Most budget travellers don't stop in JB so there really isn't much choice, except for short-stay hotels.

E Causeway Inn, 6 Jl Meldrum, T07-224 8811. A/c, clean, quiet, well-run, smart hotel that does not overcharge. TV, excellent bathroom. Ask for a room with views.

E Top, 12 Jl Meldrum, T07-224 4755. Much better value than most. Large rooms with huge beds. Very good bathrooms.

Pulau Tioman *p635, map p635*

Most accommodation on the island is simple with home-cooked meals. Sandflies can be a problem so take mosquito coils. Expect to pay more for mosquito nets and electricity. Inevitably, beachfront chalets cost more. Due to stiff competition, many prices are negotiable. For more luxurious resorts, check their websites in advance for specials deals; you can find some real bargains, especially in low season.

A-E Babura Sea View, Kampong Tekek, south end of the beach T07-419 1139. The 23 rooms are clean and well maintained; the best are in the newish block on the beachfront. Some a/c, restaurant. Good Chinese restaurant, and **Tioman Reef Divers**, a PADI/NAUI dive shop.

C-D Bamboo Hill Chalets, Ayer Batang, T07-419 1339, www.geocities.com/bamboosu. The flashiest place on the beach tucked into the hills on the northern edge. Beautiful huts with wooden floors and plenty of space. Hot-water showers, fridge, kettle, sofas and balconies facing the sea. There's internet here and a small library of books. Recommended.

C-D Salang Sayang (formally Zaids Place), Kampong Salang, T/F09-419 5019, T013-720 6439, www.salangsayangresort.com. Popular choice, with good management. Some rooms have sea view, others face onto a little garden, more expensive rooms have a/c, and the Honeymoon Suite has a hot shower. Moneychanger, shop, library, good restaurant.

C-F Nazri's, Ayer Batang, T07-419 1329, www.nazris place.com. The most southerly of the guesthouses in Ayer Batang. There's a newish concrete block with more upmarket (for this beach) tiled rooms with a/c. Some rooms in rows with a running veranda (5 with a sea view) and some simple A-frames at the back of the plot, among the mango trees. Spartan but clean rooms, restaurant on seafront, friendly management, good discounts available during low season.

E Nazri II, Ayer Batang, www.nazrisplace.com. Decent, clean and not too cramped rooms with wooden floors and sea views. A raised restaurant provides a spectacular view of the bay. Laundry service, jet skiing, fishing and snorkelling available.

E-F ABC Bungalows, Ayer Batang, T07-419 1154. Very popular place to stay at northern end of the stretch, with some good snorkelling just off the beach. Small A-frames, attractive rather intimate little plot with family atmosphere, good cheap food, hammocks, volleyball, friendly service.

F Tekek Inn, T07-419 1576. This is perhaps the best of the cheaper places to stay. It is on the beach, rooms are OK with attached showers, the management is suitably relaxed and there are snorkels and canoes for hire. No restaurant, just a drinks station.

F-G Lagoon and Riverview Place, Kampong Juara, T09-419 3168 (Riverview), T09-419 3153 (Lagoon), www.riverview-tioman.com. The cheapest yet most scenic places to stay between an aquamarine mangrove swamp and the Sungai Baru River at the northern edge of the bay. Simple chalets right on the beach. Also serves some of the best seafood.

F-G Paradise Point, Kampong Juara, 1 of only 3 places to stay on the northern side of the beach. Simple rooms, attached showers, the chalets closest to the beach get the breeze, a quiet place with a relaxed atmosphere. Restaurant with extensive menu.

Other islands *p636*

A-B Sea Gypsy Village Resort, Pulau Sibu, T07-222 8642, www.siburesort.com. Restaurant, chalets and bungalows. Friendly. The company also work with a Dugong conservation project.

E-F O & H Kampong Huts, Pulau Sibu, c/o 9 Tourist Information Centre, Jl Abu Bakar, Mersing, T07-799 3124. Good restaurant, chalets, some with attached bathrooms, clean and friendly, trekking and snorkelling.

Mersing *p636*

C-D Mersing Inn, 38 Jl Ismail, T07-799 1919. Discounts of 10% on weekdays, clean and bright, a/c, TV, all rooms en suite. Very helpful.

E Kali's Guesthouse, 12E Kampong Sri Lalang, T0 7-799 3613. Friendly and relaxed, longhouse dorms, A-frames and bungalows, *atap*-roofed bar and Italian restaurant by the beach. Take a bus towards Endau. Recommended.

E-F Embassy, 2 Jl Ismail, T07-799 3545. Some a/c, restaurant, very well-kept hotel and scrupulously clean.

F Omar Backpackers' Hostel, Jl Abu Bakar (opposite post office), T07-799 5096. Clean, well kept and a relaxed. Very basic rooms (2 doubles and 1 dorm). Island tours RM70. Excellent information.

● Eating

Melaka *p630, map p631*

Jonkers, 17 Jl Hang Jebat. Old Nyonya house, with restaurant in the old ancestral hall. Good atmosphere and excellent food – Nyonya and international, good-value set menu. Closes 1600.

Ole Sayang, 1988199 Taman Melaka Raya, T06-283 1966. All the favourites, such as chicken *pongteh* (in sweet and sour spicy sauce).

Bayonya, 164 Taman Malaka Raya. Excellent Peranakan cuisine. Owned by a real enthusiast who provides a culture lesson with your meal.

Ceres, 256-257 Jl Melaka Raya. A heaven for veggies and health freaks. Tasty Chinese and Western cuisine made from beancurd in its various guises, alfalfa sprouts and vegetables.
Coconut House, 128 Heeren St. Closed Thu. Excellent woodfire pizzas, fruit juices, beers, coffees and cakes served in a townhouse that doubles as an art gallery, bookshop and art-house cinema. Friendly.
Discovery Café, 3 Jl Bunga Raya. A little haven for backpackers. A small friendly café and bar just along from the tourist office. With games, internet and a library of travel guides.
Nancy's Kitchen, 15 Jl Hang Lekir, in the **Old China Cafe**. Excellent, authentic Nyonya food classics such as chicken candlenut curry.

Foodstalls
Particularly recommended are: **Glutton's Corner**, Jl Merdeka/ Jl Taman. **Prince Satay Celup**, at No 16. **Jl Bunga Raya**, stalls (next to Rex Cinema), seafood. **Jl Semabok** (after Bukit Cina on road to JB), Malay-run fish-head curry stall, a local favourite. **Klebang Beach**, off Jl Klebang Besar, Tanjung Kling – several *ikan panggang* (grilled fish) specialists.

Johor Bahru *p634*
Meisan, **Mutiara** hotel, JL Dato Sulaiman, Century Garden. Superb but expensive Sichuan restaurant, spicy specialities.
Newsroom Café, Puteri Pacific hotel, Jl Abdullah Ibrahim, T07-219 9999. Reasonably priced local and continental dishes.
Seasons Café, branches in City Square and Plaza Pelangi. Café serving Western snacks and breads and Asian rice dishes.

Foodstalls
JB is known for its seafood. The night market on **Jl Wong Ah Fook** is a great place to sample the full array of stall dishes. **Tepian Tebrau**, Jl Skudaí, has good satay and grilled fish. **Pantai Lido** is a well-known hawker centre.

Pulau Tioman *p635, map p635*
Most restaurants are small family-run kitchens attached to beach huts. All provide Western

staples such as omelettes and French toast, as well as Malay dishes. On the whole, the food is of a high standard. Seafood is good and fresh: superb barbecued barracuda, squid, stingray and other fish.

Mersing *p636*
Golden Dragon Restaurant, 2 Jl Ismail. Big Chinese seafood menu, reasonably priced, chilli crabs, drunken prawns, wild boar and *kang-kong belacan*. Excellent banana/ pineapple pancakes for breakfast.
Sin Nam Kee Seafood, 387 Jl Jemaluang, 1 km out of town on Kota Tinggi road. Huge seafood menu and reckoned by locals to be the best restaurant in Mersing. Occasional karaoke nights can be noisy.

O Shopping

Melaka *p630, map p631*
Antiques Melaka is well known for its antique shops, which mainly sell European and Chinese items. **Jl Hang Jebat** (formerly Jonker St) is the best place, selling everything from shadow puppets to Melakan furniture inlaid with mother-of-pearl. **Malacca Woodwork**, 312c Klebang Besar, T06-315 4468. Specialist in authentic reproduction antique furniture including camphor wood chests.
Handicrafts Crystal D'beaute, 18 Medan Portugis. **Dulukala**, Jl Laksamana. A varied collection including prints and batiks.
Karyaneka centres at 1 Jl Laksamana and Mini Malaysia Complex, Ayer Keroh.
Paintings Jonker Art Collection, 76 Jl Hang Jebat, T06-283 6578. A small shop selling prints by local artists, in particular the work of Titi Kwok, son of the well-known Macau-based artist Kwok Se and owner of the **Cheng Hoon Art Gallery** situated a couple of streets away on Jl Tokong. He is often in the shop selling his own beautiful Chinese-style ink paintings. Recommended.
Orang Utan House, 59 Lorong Hang Jebat. Paintings by local artist Charles Cham.

▲ Activities and tours

Melaka *p630, map p631*

Boat tours of Melaka's docks, godowns, old Dutch trading houses, wharves and seafront markets run from the quay close to the Tourism Malaysia office (typically RM10 for 45 mins). Guides are informative, pointing out settlements and wildlife. There are views of the giant lizards on the banks – and plenty of rubbish floating downstream. Boats leave when full and usually there is a departure every hour 1000-1400, depending on the tides. Tickets can be bought from the tourist office (45 mins, RM8). For bookings, T06-286 5468.

Pulau Tioman *p635, map p635*
Boat trips

Boats leave from Kampong Tekek to Pulau Tulai (Coral Island) Turtle Island, to a waterfall at Mukut or an around-island trip. All boats must be full otherwise prices increase. Trips can also be arranged to other nearby islands.

Diving

There are dive shops based in most of the kampongs. Tioman's coral reefs are mainly on the western side of the island, although sadly large areas have been killed off due to damage by fishing boats, the crown-of-thorns starfish, pollution and coral 'harvesting'.

There are still some magnificent coral beds within easy reach of the island. **Pulau Renggis**, just off the Berjaya Tioman Beach Resort, is the most easily accessible dive from the shore, and is a good place for new divers. For more adventurous dives, the islands off the northwest coast offer more of a challenge. There is cave diving off **Pulau Chebeh** (up to 25 m) and varied marine life off the cliff-like rocks of the **Golden Reef** (depths up to 20 m) and nearby **Tiger Reef** (for 9-24 m dives). Off the northeastern tip of the island is **Magicienne Rock** (20-24 m dives), where bigger fish can be seen. Off the southwestern coast is **Bahara Rock** (20 m), considered one of the best spots on the island. Many divers rate the experience

of swimming through gigantic gorgonian sea fans as one of their scuba highlights.

Hiking

The **cross-island trail**, from the mosque in Kampong Tekek to Kampong Juara, on the east coast, is a 2- to 3-hr hike (4 km), which is quite steep in places. It is a great walk but for those planning to stay at Juara, it is a tough climb with a full pack. The trail winds its way through the jungle via a waterfall and an enchanting upland plateau with massive trees such as strangler figs. It is not unusual to see squirrels, monkeys, monitor lizards, shrews and tropical insects. From Tekek, follow the path past the airport and then turn inland towards the mosque. From Juara, the trail begins opposite the pier. Guides are available but the trail is well marked and can be done without one.

There are also many easier jungle and coastal walks along the west coast: south from Tekek, past the resort to kampongs **Paya** and **Genting** and north to **Salang**.

Mersing *p636*

Boats for fishing trips can be chartered by groups of 12 or more from the jetty. Owners may be reluctant to take the long journey out to the far offshore islands.

Tour operators

Competition is intense at peak season and tourists can be hassled for custom. Prices tend to be similar, but it's best to use licensed agents (usually displayed on the door). Many agents are located in the R&R Plaza on Jl Tun Dr Ismail, next to the river. They also promote package deals to specific chalet resorts; sometimes they are good value, but buying a boat ticket puts you under no obligation to stay at a particular place. Recommended agents include: **Dee Travel & Tours**, T07-799 2344, 8 Jl Abu Bakar; **Golden Mal Tours**, 9 Jl Sulaiman, T07-799 1463; **Island Connection Travel & Tours**, 2 Jl Jemaluang, T07-799 2535; **Kebina**, Jl Abu Bakar, T/F07-799 5118; **Omar's**, opposite the post office, T07-799 5096.

⊖ Transport

Melaka p630, map p631

Air Airport is at Batu Berendam, 9 km out of town. **Merpati Airways** runs a 4-weekly flight to **Pekan Baru** (Indonesia). **Pelangi Airways**, T06-317 4685, runs flights on Tue, Thu, Fri and Sun. Indonesian visas should be obtained in advance from the embassy in KL (see page 606).

Boat Express ferries to **Dumai** (Sumatra), leave daily from the public jetty on Melaka River, 2 hrs. Tickets from travel agents. Try **Atlas Travel Service**, Jl Hang Jebat, T06-282 0315. Service leaves Melaka at 0900 and at 1500, one-way RM 80; return RM 150. Ferries also leave for **Bukan Baru** (Sumatra) from the public jetty on Tue, Thu and Sat, 6½ hrs (RM120) at 0950. Tourists need to get an Indonesian visa in advance.

Bus It's less than RM1 round town on local buses. Long-distance buses leave from the terminal on Jl Tun Razak. Regular connections with **KL**, **Seremban**, **Ipoh**, **Butterworth**, **Lumut** (Pulau Pangkor), **Kuantan**, **Kuala Terengganu**, **Kota Bharu**, **Johor Bahru** and **Singapore** (direct, 4 hrs).

Car hire Avis, 124 Jl Bendahara, T06-284 6710; **Hawk**, T06-283 7878; **Sintat**, Renaissance Melaka Hotel, Jl Bendahara, T06-284 8888; **Thrifty**, G-5 Pasar Pelancong, Jl Tun Sri Lanang, T06-284 9471.

Taxi Taxi drivers in Melaka refuse to use their meters. Bargain hard. When directing a taxi be careful not to confuse street names with general district areas; use the former whenever possible. There are taxi ranks outside major hotels and shopping centres. From 0100-0600 there is a 50% surcharge.

There is a taxi station at the long-distance bus station on Jl Tun Razak. Vehicles leave for **KL**, **Seremban**, **Penang**, **Mersing** and **Johor Bahru**. Passengers for Singapore must change taxis at the long-distance terminal in JB.

Johor Bahru p634

Air MAS and Air Asia fly into Senai, JB's airport, 20 km north of the city. Transport to town: buses at least every hour and taxis.

Regular connections with **KL**, **Kota Bharu**, **Kota Kinabalu**, **Kuching**, **Miri** and **Penang**. Air Asia also has direct flights to **Bangkok** and **Jakarta**.

Airline offices MAS, Plaza Pelangi, Menara Pelangi, Jl Kuning, Taman Pelangi, T07-334 1003, 2 km from town centre. **Air Asia**, JOTIC, 2 Jl Ayer Molek, T07-222 4760.

Boat JB's ferry terminal to the east of the causeway operates ferry services to **Tanjung Belungkor**, in the east of Johor state. Bumboats leave from various points along Johor's ragged coastline for **Singapore**; most go to **Changi Point** (Changi Village), on the northeast of the island, where there is an immigration and customs post. The boats run 0700-1600 and depart when full (12 passengers). There is a passenger ferry from Tanjung Belungkor (JB) to **Changi** Ferry Terminal 3 times a day, T06-5323 6088. JB's ferry terminal east of the causeway has connections with **Batam** (Indonesia).

Bus Local buses leave from the main bus terminal on Jl Wong Ah Fook.

The Larkin bus terminal is 4 km north of town. Book tickets at agents opposite railway station on Jl Tun Abdul Razak or it's cheaper at the station itself. Regular connections with **Melaka**, **KL** (RM12.50), **Lumut**, **Ipoh** (RM40), **Butterworth** (RM45), **Mersing** (RM12), **Kuantan** and **Alor Star** (RM45).

Car hire It is much cheaper to hire a car in JB than in Singapore but check if you are allowed to drive into Singapore. **Avis**, Tropical Inn Hotel, 15 Jl Gereja, T07-224 4824; **Budget**, Suite 216, 2nd floor, Orchid Plaza, T07-224 3951; **Calio**, Tropical Inn, Jl Gereja, T07-223 3325; **Halaju Selatan**, 4M-1 Larkin Complex, Jl Larkin; **Hertz**, Room 646, Puteri Pacific Hotel, Jl Salim, T07-223 7520; **National**, 50-B ground floor Bangunan Felda, Jl Sengget, T07-223 0503; **Sintat**, 2nd floor, KOMTAR, Jl Wong Ah Fook, T07-222 7110; **Thrifty**, Holiday Inn, Jl Dato Sulaiman, T07-333 2313.

Taxi The main long-distance taxi station is attached to the Larkin bus terminal 4 km north of town. Taxis from here to destinations including **KL**, **Melaka**, **Mersing** and **Kuantan**.

Border essentials: Malaysia–Singapore

The main border crossing is via the 11-km causeway linking Johor Bahru with Woodlands in the north of Singapore Island. The border crossing is efficent and there is plenty of public transport on both sides. The causeway gets particularly jammed during rush hour and public holidays, so allow plenty of time. There are Malaysian and Singapore immigration desks in the Singapore railway station, so for those wanting to avoid delays on the causeway, this is a quick way to cross the border. There are also ferry connections between Singapore and Tanjung Belungkor in the east of Johor state.

Leaving Malaysia Malaysian taxis leave, when full, for Singapore from the taxi rank on the 1st floor of the car park near KOMTAR on Jl Wong Ah Fook and go to the JB taxi rank on Rochor Canal Rd in Singapore. Drivers provide immigration forms and take care of formalities, making this a painless way of crossing. Touts also hang around JB's taxi rank offering the trip to Singapore in a private car. They will take you directly to your address in Singapore, although their geography of the island is not always expert. This is also a fairly cost-effective way to travel and is reliable. For bus transport, see below.

Leaving Sinagpore From Singapore there are 3 bus services. The non-a/c SBS No 170 runs every 15 mins from Singapore's Ban San Terminal between Queen St and Rochor Canal Rd. Tickets cost RM2 from JB, or S$2 (twice as much) from Singapore. The more frequent a/c Johor Singapore Express leaves from Ban San. Both end up at JB Larkin terminal. The yellow Causeway Link bus runs between Kranji MRT station in Singapore and the Larkin terminal. It takes 20 mins from the border to the MRT station. All buses require you to get off twice – for the Malay border point and its Singaporean counterpart. Take all luggage with you since the bus does not wait; you take the next bus to come along; each bus has its own stop after exiting immigration. Keep your ticket or you will have to buy a new one. Also have a pen handy to fill in immigration forms as they are not provided. If you plan on staying in JB, you don't need to board the bus again after passing Malay immigration. Just walk out of immigration, through the underpass and you're in town. The streets here have lots of budget hotels, or you can catch a taxi. There's little point in going to Larkin bus terminal unless taking a bus out of JB.

Train The station is on Jl Campbell, near the causeway, off Jl Tun Abdul Razak. Regular connections with **KL** and destinations on the west coast, see www.ktmb.com.my for details.

Pulau Tioman p635, map p635

Air Berjaya Air flies from **Singapore** and **KL** daily. Baggage allowance 10 kg. A bus from the **Berjaya Tioman Resort** meets each arrival and transports guests to the hotel. Alternatively, walk to the pier and catch one of the sea buses or ferries to the other beaches.

Airline offices Berjaya Air runs from Berjaya Resort, T07-419 1309, www.berjaya-air.com. Single fares from Tioman to KL or Singapore are around RM250.

Boat Fast boats run between Tioman and **Mersing** every 1-2 hrs (2 hrs, RM45 one way) and there are 1-2 slow boats a day (more than 3 hrs, slow boat, RM35). During the monsoon (Nov-Feb) departures can be erratic; boats may not run if there are insufficient passengers and the sea can get rough. All boats land on the west coast of Tioman and call at the main kampongs so make sure you let the boatman know where you want to disembark.

Beaches and kampongs are connected by an erratic sea bus service, which runs every hour or so 0800-1600. The early morning sea bus goes right round the island; otherwise it is necessary to charter a boat to get to the waterfalls (on the south coast) and Kampong Juara. Sea bus fares (per person, children half price) from Kampong Tekek to **Kampong Ayer Batang**, RM10, **Panuba**, RM12, **Salang**, RM20, **Lalang**, RM10, **Juara**, RM50. The east coast is accessible by taxi, around RM35 per person, by (slow) boat or by the jungle trail.

Mersing p636

Boat The jetty is a 5-min walk from the long distance bus stop. Most ticket offices are by the jetty but tickets to the islands are also sold from booths near the bus stop. The boat to the islands can be extremely rough during the monsoon season; boats will sometimes leave Mersing in the late afternoon, at high tide, but rough seas can delay the voyage considerably. During peak monsoon all ferry services are cancelled and the ferry companies move to the west coast to find work there. It is advisable only to travel during daylight hours.

There are several companies offering speedboats (RM45, just under 2 hrs) and slow boats (RM35, 3 hrs plus). They stop at **Genting**, **Tekek**, **Ayer Batang**, and **Salang**, and you must tell the boat workers where you want to get off in advance.

Bus The local bus station is on Jl Sulaiman opposite the **Country Hotel**.

Long distance buses leave from 2 locations. Those not originating in Mersing leave from the roundabout by the Shell station and those that start from Mersing leave from Jl Abu Bakar, from the car park next to the Plaza R&R. Tickets can be bought from Plaza R&R or from tour agents in town. Regular connections with **KL** (RM23), **Johor Bahru** (RM8), **Kuantan**, **Cherating** (RM22), **Terengganu** (RM26), **Ipoh** (change in KL, RM35), **Singapore** (RM11) and **Kota Bharu** (RM29).

Taxi Taxis leave from Jl Sulaiman opposite the **Country Hotel**, next to the local bus station; **KL**, **JB** (RM100) (for Singapore, change at JB), **Melaka**, **Kuala Terengganu** and **Kuantan** (RM100-120).

❶ Directory

Melaka p630, map p631

Banks Bumiputra, Jl Kota; HSBC, Jl Kota. Several banks on Jl Hang Tuah near bus station and Jl Munshi Abdullah. **Post** General Post Office, T06-283 3844, just off Jl Kota next to Christ Church. **Immigration** Bangunan Persekutuan, Jl Hang Tuah, T06-282 4958 (for visa extensions). **Internet** Several, easy to find and cheap. RM3 per hr. **Internet café**, beside the Youth Museum; Red House, 16 Jl Laksamana. **Medical services** Straits Hospital, 37 Jl Parameswara, T06-282 2344. **Police** Jl Kota, T06-282 2222. **Tourist Police**, Jl Kota, T06-285 4114 (near the Tourism Malaysia office).

Johor Bahru p634

Banks Bumiputra, HSBC and United Asia are on Bukit Timbalan. Several money changers in the big shopping centres and on/around Jl Ibrahim/Jl Meldrum. **Immigration** 1st floor, Block B, Wisma Persekutuan, Jl Air Molek, T07-224 4253. **Internet** There are some internet cafés opposite City Square shopping plaza on Jl Wong Ah Fook. There's also internet on the 2nd floor of Larkin Bus Station. **Medical services** Sultanah Aminah General Hospital, Jl Skudai. **Post** Jl Tun Dr Ismail.

Mersing p636

Banks Maybank, Jl Ismail; UMBC, Jl Ismail, no exchange on Sat. Money changer on Jl Abu Bakar and Giamso Safari, 23 Jl Abu Bakar also changes TCs. **Internet** Mersing EasyNet Café, Jl Dato Mohd Ali (just off the roundabout). open 1000-2300. **Medical services** Doctors: Klinik Grace, 48 Jl Abu Bakar, T07-799 2399. **Post** Jl Abu Bakar.

East Coast Peninsula

It might just be on the other side of the Peninsula, but Malaysia's east coast could as well be on a different planet than the populous, hectic and industrialized west coast. Its coastline, made up of the states of Johor, Pahang, Terengganu and Kelantan, is lined with coconut palms, dotted with sleepy fishing kampongs and interspersed with rubber and oil palm plantations, paddy fields, beaches and mangroves. The string of islands stretching all along the coast offers a mix of lazy getaways from the acclaimed snorkelling and diving sites to parties and barbecues on the beach. For an insight into Malay traditions and artistry, Kota Bharu in the north stages events from kite flying to drumming sessions, while Kuala Terengganu is a souvenir hunting ground with fine silverware and handicraft markets.

If you plan on visiting any of the beaches or islands on the east coast, and especially if you're hoping to dive, the best time to visit is between February and September to avoid the rainy season. During the winter monsoon (November to February), the seas are very rough and many island resorts are closed and boat operators pack up business. Between May and September is the best time for turtle spotting. ▶▶ *For listings, see pages 653-660.*

Kuantan and around ⊜❼▲⊜❻⊙ ▶▶ *pp653-660. Colour map 8, C3.*

→ *Population 280,000.*

The modern capital of the state of Pahang is a bustling, largely Chinese, town at the mouth of the Kuantan River. Kuantan is the main transport and business hub for the east coast; most visitors spend at least a night here as a base to explore the mystical lake of Tasek Chini. The 300-km stretch of coast between Kuantan and Kota Bharu is comprised of long beaches and fishing kampongs and the occasional natural gas processing plant and oil refinery.

Plenty of tourists pass through Kuantan, but not many seem to stay long. The main sight, and well worth seeing, is the **Sultan Ahmad Shah** mosque (Masjid Negeri). Freshly decorated in blue, green and white, with a cool marbled interior, the mosque can be seen across town. It has blue and yellow stained-glass windows and the morning sun projects their coloured patterns on the interior walls. Kuantan has several streets of old shophouses that date from the 1920s. Most of the oldest buildings are on **Jalan Mahkota**.

Ins and outs

Kuantan's airport is 20 km from town and has flights to/from KL. There are bus connections with towns along the east coast as well as with key destinations on the west, including KL. Taxis travel to Kuala Terengganu, KL and Mersing. ▶▶ *See Transport, page 658.*

Visitors can contact the **Padang Tourist Information Centre** ① *Jl Mahkota, T09-516 1007, www.pahangtourism.com.my, Mon-Sat 0800-1730.*

Tasek Chini → *Colour map 8, D3.*

① *Getting there is not easy on public transport. A taxi should cost RM80 and take 1½ hrs.*

Tasek Chini is an amalgam of freshwater lakes, whose fingers reach deep into the surrounding forested hills, 100 km southwest of Kuantan. The lake and the adjoining mountain are sacred to the Malays; legend has it that Lake Chini is the home of a huge white crocodile. The Jakun people proto-Malay aboriginals, who live around Tasek Chini, believe a *naga* (serpent), personifying the spirit of the lake, inhabits and guards its depths. It's a pleasant place to visit, particularly between June and September when the lake is carpeted with red and white lotus flowers.

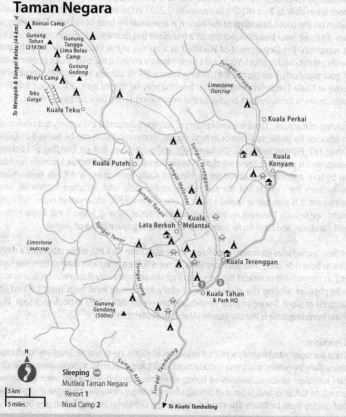
Taman Negara is Malaysia's largest and most popular national park, with excellent opportunities for trekking and wildlife spotting. Covering 434,000 ha of mountainous jungle, it includes Gunung Tahan, the highest mountain on the Peninsula (2187 m). This area was left untouched by successive ice ages and has been covered in jungle for 130 million years, making it older than the rainforests in the Congo or Amazon basins. Vegetation ranges from riverine species and lowland forest to cloud and moss forest at higher elevations and on to a strange subalpine environment rich in strange pitcher plants close to the summit of Gunung Tahan. More than 250 species of bird have been recorded in Taman Negara, and mammals resident in the park include wild ox (gaur), sambar, barking deer, tapir, civet cat, wild boar and even the occasional tiger and elephant herd. However, the more exotic mammals rarely put in an appearance, especially in areas closer to Kuala Tahan.

Taman Negara is open year-round but if you intend to visit during the monsoon (October to January), check the weather and river levels in advance.

Taman Negara

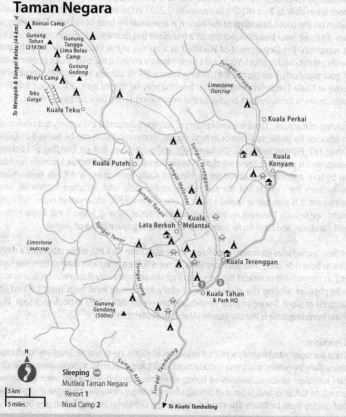

Sleeping
Mutiara Taman Negara Resort 1
Nusa Camp 2

Trekking equipment

A good pair of walking boots is essential even for short excursions, as well as a thick pair of socks and long (loose) trousers. Leeches are common after rain; spraying clothes and boots with insect repellent and wearing leech socks helps. When crossing rivers, hiking sandles or cheap rubber deck shoes help to keep your balance on the slippery rocks. Those undertaking higher altitude treks, such as the Gunung Tahan trail, will need a good fleece, raingear and a sleeping bag. A good torch is essential for those going to hides, as is a water bottle. A raincover and waterproof bags are useful. Equipment can be hired from the shop at Park HQ.

Ins and outs

Getting there Taman Negara is 250 km northeast of KL and can be reached by bus, boat and by train from many different directions. Various companies run tours, but it is quite possible to visit independently. The nearest town is Jerantut; a local bus (RM6) runs two to three times daily to **Park HQ** ① *office open 0800-2200*, in the sleepy riverside village of Kuala Tahan on the south boundary of the park. It is accessible by boat from Kuala Tembeling, a two- to three-hour beautiful journey (or a mundane bus journey). All visitors must check in at reception. The **Department of Wildlife** has a bureau at the Kuala Tembeling jetty and issues permits and licences. You need a permit before entering the park (bring photocopies of your passport). Park permit RM1; fishing licence RM10; camera licence RM5. Those who arrive at Kuala Tembeling jetty without booking may be turned away if boats are full. The website www.tamannegara.org has useful information. ▶▶ *See Transport, page 658.*

Staying in the park There is usually plenty of accommodation for all budgets, but book well in advance for public holidays or in high season. Accommodation can be booked at Kuala Tahan HQ. **Fishing lodges (C-D)** have beds and mattresses, but no bedding or cooking equipment is provided. There are **chalets** in various villages around the park, usually booked up by tour agencies. **Visitor lodges** for hides at Kuala Terengganu and Kuala Kenyam are away from the crowds but are surprisingly comfortable with attached bathrooms and restaurant. It is possible to spend a night in one of the wildlife **observation hides**, RM5 per night (see below). These are raised up among the trees at Tabang, Belau, Yong, Cegar Anjing and Kumbang and have no facilities other than sleeping space and a pit latrine.

Hides Some hides (*bumbun*) are a five-minute walk from Park HQ, while others are a day's trek or boat ride away. You are more likely to see wildlife at the hides further from the Park HQ, as the number of visitors has begun to frighten animals away. Rats, monitor lizards and wild pigs are among the animals not so easily frightened: food bags must be tied up securely at night. During popular periods and on weekends it is best to book your spot. The main breeding time is the dry season (March to September).

Trekking

Trails are signposted from Park HQ; full details on all routes are available. Tours are conducted twice daily by guides and these include night walks and cave treks. Independent day walks can be taken to caves, swimming holes, waterfalls, along rivers (again with swimming areas), to salt-licks and hides and through forest. Longer multi-day treks are also possible but guides must be taken. The most demanding is climbing Gunung Tahan (see below).

Gunung Tahan There are three approaches to climbing the mountain (2187 m), none should be under-estimated, especially during bad weather. A maximum of 48 hikers are allowed on the trail at any one time, so it's best to book in advance. The first route is an eight- to nine-day tough trek from Park HQ at Kuala Tahan. The second route takes seven days, following the same route from Kuala Tahan to the summit before descending on the northwest side of the mountain and exiting the park at Sungai Relau. From this point, a park pick-up can be arranged (if booked in advance) and you can be dropped off at the western Park HQ near Merapoh. From Merapoh it's possible to continue your journey by train to the north or south. The third and shortest route (four to five days) involves climbing the peak on a return trek from the Merapoh and the park entrance at Sungai Relau.

Other activities

The **canopy walk** ① *30-min walk from Park HQ, Sat-Thu 1100-1500 and Fri 0900-1200, RM5*, is worth a visit in order to take in jungle life at close proximity. The walkway is suspended about 30 m above the forest floor and stretches for over 400 m. Also popular are **fishing**, and **boat trips**. ▶▶ *See Activities and tours, page 657.*

Jerantut → *Colour map 8, C2.*

This is the nearest town to Kuala Tembeling and the most popular entry point into Taman Negara, some 16 km away and RM15 by taxi. For those travelling to the park on public transport it may be necessary to spend a night here and there is a range of accommodation on offer, plus backpacker-friendly tour agencies.

Kenong Rimba National Park ●▲● ▶▶ *pp653-660. Colour map 8, C2.*

Not far from Taman Negara, Kenong Rimba Park is home to the Batik Orang Asli tribe. The park, which includes the Kenong River valley and encompasses some 120 sq km, is the home of the Batik Orang Asli tribe, who are shifting cultivators. There is a network of Asli trails around the park and several caves and waterfalls. There are two campsites along the river and chalets. The park is a good alternative to Taman Negara. Though it may not have the same variety of animal life (especially large mammals), it is less touristy and cheaper. A useful website is www.endemicguides.com, which outlines some of the park's climbing, trekking and caving options. Treks from two to six days are possible in Kenong Rimba.

Ins and outs

This park is 1½ hours east of Kuala Lipis by boat down the Jelai River to Kampong Kuala Kenong and is managed by **Kuala Lipis District Forest Office** ① *Government Office Complex, Kuala Lipis, T09-312 3745.* Both a guide and permit are needed before you will be allowed into the park. For tours and treks to Kenong Rimba, see Kuala Lipis Activities and tours, page 657. Entrance to the park is from Batu Sembilan jetty (20 minutes) or an hour's boat ride from the jetty in Kuala Lipis.

Kuala Lipis → *Colour map 8, C2.*

Kuala Lipis is a pleasant and relaxed town on the Jelai and Lipis rivers. Unlike most of Malaysia's towns, there has been very little development and many colonial buildings still survive. In the late 19th century it grew to prominence as a gold mining town and, for a short period, was the area's administrative capital. Today it's a good base from which to trek to Kenong Rimba and is not without charm.

The giant leatherback turtle

The giant leatherback turtle is so-called for its leathery carapace (shell). It is the biggest sea turtle and one of the biggest reptiles in the world. The largest grow to 3 m in length and can weigh up to 700 kg. They spend most of their lives in the mid-Pacific Ocean and return to Rantau Abang each year to lay their eggs (one of just five main breeding sites in the world). Up to 10,000 turtles used to visit the beach but their numbers are seriously diminishing. Eggs are poached for their supposed aphrodisiac qualities and the shell is fashioned into combs and cigarette boxes. The Fisheries Department collects up to 50,000 eggs each season for controlled hatching. Once released, many are picked off by predators, such as gulls and fish, and few reach adulthood. Drift-net fishing and pollution add to the problem. As a result, these beautiful creatures are now an endangered species.

Kampong Cherating and around ●❸❼●❺ ▶▶ pp653-660. Colour map 8, C3.

A quiet seaside village, set among coconut palms, a short walk from the beach, Kampong Cherating has become a haven for those who want to sample kampong life or just hang out in a simple chalet-style budget resort. Over the years it has become more upmarket. There is a large beach, better for windsurfing than swimming, and a couple of beautiful hidden coves tucked into the rocky headland. It is possible to hire boats to paddle through the mangroves of the Cherating River, to the south side of the kampong, where there is a good variety of birdlife as well as monkeys, monitor lizards and otters. Demonstrations of silat, the Malay martial art, can be arranged in the village, as well as top-spinning, kite-flying and batik-printing. The best beach nearby is **Kemasik**, 28 km north. However, the real highlight of the area is **Rantau Abang** (see below), the nesting site for five different species of turtle.

Ins and outs

The nearest airport is Kuantan (see page 644), a 40-minute drive. The bus stop is on the main road around 500 m from the kampong itself. There are connections with Singapore, KL and destinations on the east coast. ▶▶ See Transport, page 659.

Badgerlines Information Services ① 20 m down on left from lane leading from main road bridge, 0900-1700 and 2000-2200, is a good source of information. Also useful is Cherating Travel Post, which offers travel tickets, car and bike hire, internet and tours.

Rantau Abang → Colour map 8, C3.

This strung-out beachside settlement owes its existence to turtles. Every year between May and September, five different species of turtle (Penyuin Malay) come to lay their eggs, including the endangered giant leatherbacks. During the peak egg-laying season (August), the beach gets very crowded. Some areas have restricted access for conservation purposes and a small admission charge is levied. Turtle-watching is free along the stretch around the **Turtle Information Centre** ① 13th Mile Jl Dungun, opposite the big Plaza R&R, T09-844 1533, open Jun-Aug and Sep-Apr, which has an excellent exhibition and film presentation about turtles, focusing on the giant leatherback. The Fisheries Department runs three hatcheries to protect the eggs from predators and egg hunters; these can be visited.

There is a ban on flash photography and unruly behaviour is punishable by a RM1000 fine or six months' imprisonment. Camp fires, excessive noise and littering are illegal.

Kuala Terengganu and around 🏨🍴🛍️▲🏦🎭 ▶▶ pp653-660. Colour map 8, B3.

The royal capital of Terengganu state was a small fishing port (the state accounts for about a quarter of all Malaysia's fishermen) until oil and gas money started pumping into development projects in the 1980s. The town has long been a centre for arts and crafts, and is known for its kain songket, batik, brass and silverware. The focal point of the town is the central market, **Pasar Besar Kedai Payang** ⓘ *Jl Sultan Zainal Abidin, 0700-1800*, particularly in the early morning, when the fishing fleet comes in. The town's colourful history is revealed in the Chinese shophouses and temple, in the **Zainal Abdin Mosque** ⓘ *Jl Masjid*, and the ceremonial house of **Istana Maziah**, once home to the Terengganu royal family. The **State Museum**, ⓘ *5 km southwest of Terengganu in Losong, at the end of Jl Losong Feri, facing Pulau Sekati, Sat-Thu 0900-1700, RM5, 15 mins by bus*, is one of the largest in the country. It exhibits rare Islamic porcelain, silver jewellery, musical instruments and weaponry, including a fine selection of *parangs* and *krises*. Around Terengganu numerous kampongs specialize in handicrafts (see Shopping, page 656).

Ins and outs
The airport is 18 km from town; taxi RM15 into town. Buses connect with major destinations across the country. There are plenty of local taxis. ▶▶ *See Transport, page 659*.

For information contact **Tourism Malaysia** ⓘ *5th floor, Menara Yayasan Islam Terengganu, Jl Sultan Omar, T09-622 1433*. **State Tourist Information Centre (TIC)** ⓘ *Jl Sultan Zainal Abidin, near Istana Meziah on the jetty, T09-622 1891, Sat-Thu 0900-1700*. The website www.terengganutourism.com has further information.

Kuala Terengganu

Sleeping 🛏️
Awi's Yellow House 1
Qurata Riverside 13
Seri Malaysia 10

Eating 🍴
Ping Anchorage
Travellers' Café 5

Marang → *Colour map 8, B3.*

ⓘ *From the main road, follow signs to LKIM Komplex from the north end of the bridge.*

This is a colourful Malay fishing kampong at the mouth of the Marang River, although it has been buffeted by the vagaries of the tourist industry over the last couple of decades. Despite development, it is still a lovely village, with its shallow lagoon full of fishing boats. The best beach is opposite Pulau Kapas at Kampong Ru Muda. It was the centre of a mini-gold-rush in 1988 when gold was found 6 km up the road at Rusila. On the road north of Marang there are a number of batik workshops, all of which welcome visitors.

Pulau Kapas → *Colour map 8, B3.*

Pulau Kapas is 6 km (20 minutes) off the coast, with some good beaches and a very low-key laid-back atmosphere. Those wanting a quiet beach holiday should avoid weekends and public holidays when it is packed. The coral here has been degraded somewhat and there is much better snorkelling at **Pulau Raja**, just off Kapas, which has been declared a marine park. All the guesthouses organize snorkelling and the **Kapas Garden Resort** also has scuba equipment. There is a new resort on the privately owned **Pulau Gemia** (Gem Island), just under 1 km from Kapas. Many hotels can also organize a boat trip to the island.

Redang archipelago ●● ⤴ *pp653-660. Colour map 8, B3.*

The Redang archipelago is a marine park consisting of nine islands 27 km off the coast of Merang. It has some of Malaysia's best reefs, making it one of the most desirable locations for divers. In the months after the monsoon, visibility increases to at least 20 m but during the monsoon the island is usually inaccessible. Line-fishing is permitted and squid fishing, using bright lights, is popular between June and September; the fishermen use a special hook called a candat sotong. The lamps light the surrounding waters, attracting the squid.

The biggest and best-known is **Pulau Redang**, but **Pulau Lang Tengah** is also catching up. **Pulau Bidong** was the base for a Vietnamese refugee camp in the 1970s and 1980s and as many as 40,000 were once crammed on this island. The boat people have long gone now, and most of the camp's buildings have rotted away. Tour agencies in Kuala Terengganu offer day-trips to the island, where there are few memorials to the refugees and some good snorkelling. The only islands with accommodation are Pulau Redang and Pulau Lang Tengah.

Ins and outs

Getting there There is a daily flight to Pulau Redang from KL. Boats leave from Merang twice daily. Most people travelling to the islands are on all-inclusive package deals. ⤴ *See Transport, page 659.*

Tourist information The independently run website, www.redang.org, offers excellent information and reviews of places and diving on Pulau Redang and Lang Tengah. Tourist information from Tourism Malaysia in Kuala Terengganu. Two dives with equipment costs around RM130 on the island, which is fairly reasonable considering the excellent location.

Merang → *Colour map 8, B3.*

Merang (not to be confused with Marang) is a small fishing kampong with a long white sandy beach and a number of resort-style places to stay. It is also the departure point for the many offshore islands.

Perhentian Islands ⓘⓘ▲ⓘⓘ ➤ pp653-660. Colour map 8, B2/3.

The beautiful Perhentian Islands are just over 20 km off the coast and separated by a narrow sound with a strong current. Despite development in recent years, with more hotels, restaurants, bars, diving outfits and noise, the Perhentians remain a paradise, with excellent diving and snorkelling, magnificent white-sand beaches and some of the best places for swimming on the east coast.

Of the two islands, **Perhentian Besar** (big island) is generally more popular with families as it houses slightly more upmarket resorts, although huts on the beach are also available. **Perhentian Kecil** (small) is simpler and attracts a younger crowd of party-going backpackers. There is a fishing village and a turtle hatchery in the middle of Long Beach (Pasir Panjang) on Perhentian Kecil.

Ins and outs

It is important to get to the islands as early as possible due to high demand for accommodation. Boats leave throughout the day from Kuala Besut, which is connected to other towns by regular buses. There are boats between the two islands. ➤ See Transport, page 659.

Kuala Besut → Colour map 8, B2.

This small fishing village provides a transit link to the Perhentians and has one main place to stay. Business has expanded to cater for those tourists passing through and good food can be found at a series of small restaurants along the waterfront. Kuala Besut has lots of travel agents that sell boat and bus tickets and book accommodation on the island. Taxis however seem to favour dropping you off at **Pelangi Travel & Tours**.

Kota Bharu and around ⓘⓘⓘ▲ⓘⓘ ➤ pp653-660. Colour map 8, A2.

Kota Bharu is the royal capital of Kelantan, 'the land of lightning', and is situated near the mouth of the Kelantan River. It is one of the country's Malay strongholds, despite its proximity to the Thai border. This was reinforced during the latest general elections when the opposition PAS (Malaysia's Islamic Party) once again managed to secure KB and Kelantan (the only PAS state in the country). While some people react against the state government's support for an Islamic interpretation of public (and private) morals, Kota Bharu is one of Malaysia's more culturally interesting and colourful towns with eclectic museums, mosques, grandiose royal palaces, an unmissable wet market, and an impressive cultural zone.

Kelantan is also renowned for its crafts – silverware, weaving and metalworking – were partly the result of the state's close relations with the Siamese kingdom of Ayutthaya in the 17th century. The *makyung*, a traditional Malay court dance, is still performed in Kelantan and *wayang kulit* (shadow puppet plays) still provide entertainment on special occasions in the kampongs.

Ins and outs

Getting there and around KB's airport is 8 km from town. There are direct links on MAS with KL, and with KL and JB on **Air Asia**. The train station is 6 km out of town at Wakaf Bharu. The line runs south to KL and Singapore. There are three bus terminals but most express buses depart from the most central. Buses run to most towns, including to Rantau Panjang and Pengkalan Kubor on the Thai border. Taxis have replaced trishaws as the most popular form of local transport. There is also a city bus service. ➤ See Transport, page 660.

Tourist information The **Tourist Information Centre** ① *Jl Sultan Ibrahim, T09-748 5534, Sat-Thu 0800-1300 and 1400-1700*, is helpful and has a good map of the town. It will arrange taxis and ferries to the islands, as well as booking accommodation on the islands.

Safety Since 2004, southern Thailand has been plagued by separatist violence that has killed more than 2500 people. The most severely affected Thai states are still Narathiwat (adjoins Kelantan), Patani and Yala. Check www.britishembassy.gov.uk for the latest information.

Sights

The heart of Kota Bharu is the **central market** ① *off Jl Temenggong, daily 0900-2000*, which is one of the most vibrant and colourful wet markets in the country. It is housed in an octagonal concrete complex painted green with a glass roof. Nearby is the **Istana Jahar** ① *0830-1645, RM3*, constructed in 1889 by Sultan Mohammed IV and now the 'centre for royal customs'. It exemplifies the skilled craftsmanship of the Kelantanese woodcarvers in

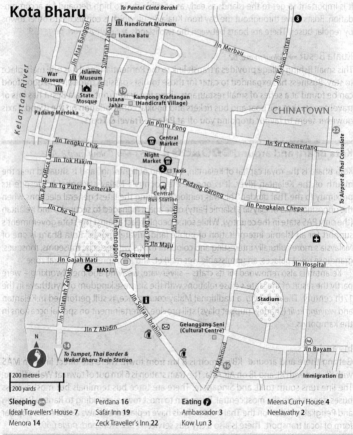

Kota Bharu

Sleeping
Ideal Travellers' House 7
Menora 14
Perdana 16
Safar Inn 19
Zeck Traveller's Inn 22

Eating
Ambassador 3
Kow Lun 3
Meena Curry House 4
Neelavathy 2

its intricately carved beams and panels. The **Kampong Kraftangan** (Handicraft Village) aims to give visitors a taste of Kelantan's arts and crafts all under one roof. The large enclosure, in which merbuk birds (doves) sing in their bamboo cages, contains four wooden buildings built in traditional Malay style. The **Handicraft Museum** ① *Sat-Thu 1000-1800, RM1*, contains traditional Kelantanese crafts and customs. There is also a batik workshop. Opposite, is the **Istana Batu**, the sky-blue Stone Palace, which was built in 1939 and was one of the first concrete buildings in the state and contains many royal possessions.

A little north of the commercial centre is a magnificent two-storey green-and-white mansion with traditional Islamic latticework carving on eaves, which houses the **Islamic Museum** ① *Jl Merdeka, Sat-Thu 0830-1645, donation*. The building is more noteworthy than its contents. Nextdoor, the **War Museum** ① *0830-1645, RM2*, offers an informative account of the Second World War in Southeast Asia. Beginning with Pearl Harbor, it tells the story of the Japanese invasion of Kelantan in 1941 and the subsequent conquest of Malaya.

The **Gelanggang Seni** ① *Jl Mahmud, opposite stadium*, is rather touristy but a good place to see cultural demonstrations. These include: *silat* (Malay self-defence); Kelantan drums, made from hollowed-out logs; top-spinning; *wayang kulit* (shadow-puppets); and kite-flying with the famous paper-and-bamboo *wau bulan* – or Kelantan moon-kites. The latter has been a Kelantanese sport for centuries; the aim is to fly your kite the highest and to defend your kite by being as aggressive as possible towards other competitors' kites. Kite-flying was a favourite hobby in the heyday of the Melaka sultanate in the 15th century.

◉ East Coast Peninsula listings

For Sleeping and Eating price codes, see inside the front cover.

● Sleeping

Kuantan *p644*
Lots of cheap Chinese hotels on Jl Teluk Sisek and Jl Besar. Also several in the **C-E** range.
C-D Classic, 7 Bangunan LKNP, Jl Besar, T09-555 4599. Extremely clean, big rooms with a/c and spacious bathrooms, good value.
E Orchid 11 Jl Merdeka, T09-555 5570. Family-run, very clean, rooms are large with attached bathrooms. Friendly, helpful owners, a/c.
F-G Tong Nam Ah, 98 Jl Besar, T09-514 4204. Convenient for bus station and hawker stalls. Basic rooms with fan and basin.

Tasek Chini *p644*
C-E Rajan Jones Guest House, 30 mins' walk from Lake Chini Resort. The cheapest place but very basic, no running water or electricity, tours and treks arranged. Rate includes meals.
E-G Lake Chini Resort, T09-477 8000, www.lakechini.com. 10 chalets, 10-bed dorm

and camping. Simple restaurant. Excellent fishing, visits to local Orang Asli communities.

Taman Negara National Park
p645, map p645
LL-E Mutiara Taman Negara Resort, Kampong Kuala Tahan, T09-266 2200, www.mutiarahotels.com. Book in advance. From 8-bed dorms to chalets and bungalows, some self-catering. Also runs a lodge in Kuala Terengganu with chalets and a restaurant.
C-D Teresek Hill View, T09-266 3065. Dorms, basic chalets and more sophisticated bungalows with attached bathrooms.
F-G Nusa Camp, 15 mins upriver from Park HQ, T09-266 2369. Dorms, bungalows and tents for hire, restaurant. Trips organized. Take one of the longboats from Park HQ (shuttle boat every 2 hrs); direct daily service from Kuala Tembeling at 0900 and 1400.
Camping Mutiara Taman Negara Resort, see above, has a large garden with facilities (RM1) and rents out tents, as do tourist agencies at Kuala Tahan. Check quality. See map, page 645, for camping locations.

Jerantut p647

C-G Sri Emas, T09-266 4499. Some rooms a/c, shower, excellent information, free transport from bus/train station. Trips organized to the park, dorms, luggage store, internet, restaurant.
E-F Jerantut Guesthouse, T09-266 6200. Some rooms have a/c and bathroom, restaurant, popular, daily trips to the park.

Kuala Lipis p647

E Persona Rimba Resort Kenong, Kuala Lipis, T09-312 5032. Simple huts. Tours organized.
F Kuala Lipis (aka Appu's Guesthouse), 63 Jl Besar, T09-312 3142. Near train station. Dorms and doubles. Some a/c, shared bathrooms, excellent tours and information.
F-G Gin Loke, 64 Jl Besar, T09-312 1388. Simple rooms, shared facilities, treks in Kenong Rimba.

Kampong Cherating p648

E Tanjung Inn, turn right at bottom of lane down main road, T09-581 9081. A charming place with attractive family bungalows and budget chalets, restaurant, landscaped grounds, good restaurant, excellent breakfasts.
F Matahari Chalets, on the southernmost lane from main road. Attractive bungalows with spacious veranda, some with fridge. Pleasant.
F-G Moon, T09-581 9186 (northernmost resort on loop off main road). Attractive rustic chalets with fan and bathroom in spacious grounds, excellent bar and restaurant, chalets and longhouse, more tranquil than the beach.

Rantau Abang p648

C-F Ismail's, T09-844 1054. Good restaurant, beachside set-up.
E-F Dahimah's, 1 km south of visitor centre, T09-845 2483. Restaurant, clean rooms in Malay wooden chalets. Some a/c.

Kuala Terengganu p649, map p649

Cheaper hotels are mainly at the jetty end of Jl Sultan Ismail and on Jl Banggol.
C-D Seri Malaysia, Lot 1640, Jl Hiliran, T03-2161 8223, www.serimalaysia.com.my. A/c, good restaurant, well-run, a/c, TV, minibar, light airy rooms overlooking the river.

E Qurata Riverside, 7 km south, Lot 175K Kuala Ibai, T09-617 5500. Small, friendly hotel, individual wooden chalets on stilts near the river, designed to resemble a Malay village. Comfortable rooms, a/c or fan, TV and shower room. At low tide it is possible to walk across the river mouth to nearby sand beach.
G Awi's Yellow House, Pulau Duyung Besar, T09-624 5046, rohanilongvet@hotmail.com. Built on stilts over the river, very popular. Dorm and atap-roofed huts, some with balconies, pleasant with cool breezes, kitchen. Take a boat from Jl Bandar, or a taxi from KT via the new Sultan Mahmud bridge.

Marang p650

Also some hotels at Kampong Rhu Muda, 2 km before the bridge over the Marang River.
C-F Angullia Beach House, 12¼ milestone, Kampong Rhu Muda, T09-618 1322, Some a/c, good set meals, extremely friendly, family-run chalet resort on lovely sheltered stretch of beach, leafy, well-kept grounds and very clean chalets.
E-F Green Mango Inn, A-71 Bandar Marang, T01-9946 9409. Fan, basic A-frame chalets or doubles. Excellent atmosphere, good views, small garden, and sitting area with games.
E-G Mare Nostrum Holiday Resort, Kampong Rhu Muda, T09-6182417. A/c, restaurant, clean and hospitable, boat trips, pleasant, well-kept compound with chalets.

Pulau Kapas p650

A-C Duta Puri, T09-624 6090. The most upmarket. Charming chalets with dark wood furniture and batiks. All rooms have TV, minibar and wooden floors.
F-G The Lighthouse, T019-215 3558. Owner Din is a real character. The best budget place. All rooms are in an atmospheric longhouse. Very mellow. Lots of beach games, barbecues and the **Tropical Hut** bar.

Redang archipelago p650

Resorts on Redang offer competitive package deals – check with **Tourism Malaysia** in Kuala Terengganu (see page 649). A typical 2-day/

2-night trip costs RM300 per person including food, camping and snorkelling equipment.

Merang *p650*
E Stingray Beach Chalet, T01-9327 8855. Right on the beach, fan, bathroom, immaculately run and offers a dive service.
F Kembara Resort, 474 Pantai Peranginan Merang, 21010 Setiu, T09-623 8771. On a beautiful palm-fringed beach south of the jetty, garden, 8 bungalows and rooms with bathroom and fan. Dorms. Kitchen.

Perhentian Islands *p651*
Perhentian Besar
The majority of accommodation is on the west coast or in the secluded bay of Telok Dalam.
A-B Tuna Bay Island Resort, T09-697 9779, www.tunabay.com.my. Pretty wooden chalets and a lovely open-air restaurant. Dive centre, internet and travel agency. Excellent packages if booked through their website.
A-E Flora Bay Chalet, Telok Dalam, T09-691 1666, www.florabayresort.com. From swanky chalets to A-frames. PADI 5-star dive centre.
C-E Mama's, T019-984 0232, www.mamas chalet.com. Fan, shower. Chalets for families or couples. Daily snorkelling trips.
C-F Abdul's, T09-697 7058. Decent chalets on the beach, fan and shower, with popular restaurant. Good local reputation.
E Coco Hut Chalets, T09-697 7988, www.coco huttravel.com. Decent restaurant, A-frames, including some new ones with showers.
E-F Perhentian Paradise Resort, T010-981 0930. Family rooms or doubles. Good location set slightly back from the beach.
G Camping. RM5 at **Perhentian Island Resort**; camping is not permitted on the beach. Restaurant and dive shop floors go for RM10.

Perhentian Kecil
The 2 most popular places to stay are Long Beach (good for parties and snorkelling); or Coral Bay (cheaper and quieter). There is a 10-min forest walk between them.
C-F Mohsin, T010-333 8897, mohsinchalets@ yahoo.com. Blue-roofed huts on a hill, great

views from the restaurant. Attached bathrooms and 24-hr electricity. Also a 20-bed dorm.
E-F Panorama, T09-697 7542. Attractive chalets with attached bathrooms, fans and mosquito nets set in nice garden. Good value, dinner included in room rate, excellent restaurant. Helpful staff, tours, internet.
F Fatimah's/Aur Beach, T09-697 7694. Simple wooden chalets with bathroom inside. Very friendly staff. Best budget option.

Kuala Besut *p651*
E-F Nan's Guest House, T09-697 4892, near the jetty. A/c or fan, rooms have TV and attached bathrooms. Recommended.

Kota Bharu *p651*, map *p652*
Plenty of budget options and homestays.
A-B Perdana, Jl Mahmud, T09-748 5000. A/c, restaurant, pool, tennis and squash courts, bowling alley, best in town, central, baby-sitting, sauna, massage. Travel agent on site.
C-D Safar Inn, Jl Hilir Kota, T09-747 8000, F747 9000. A hotel with 31 rooms, a/c, TV, carefully furnished rooms with wall-to-wall carpets. Good location, in the heart of town.
F Ideal Travellers' House, 5504a Jl Padang Garong, T09-744 2246, idealtrahouse@ hotmail.com. Quiet, friendly, pleasant veranda, rooms and dorm. Family-run, popular, help with onward travel, free pick-up.
F-G Menora, Wisma Chua Tong Boon, 1st floor, Jl Sultanah Zainab, T09-748 1669. Well kept, TV, powerful showers, dorm.
F-G Zeck Traveller's Inn, 7088-G Jl Sri Cemerlang, T09-747 3423, ztraveller_lnn@ hotmail.com. Some rooms with private shower, dorms, veranda, free pick-up from bus station, one of the most popular places to stay.

🍴 Eating

Kuantan *p644*
Malay cafés and foodstalls along the river bank, behind the long-distance bus station.
🍴 **Tjantek Art Bistro**, 46 Jl Besar (opposite Classic Hotel). A funky art-cum-coffee shop

also serving pasta, steaks, seafood, teas and juices. There's an art gallery on the 1st floor.
† Cantina, 16 Lorong Tun Ismail 1 (off Jl Bukit Ubi). Smart a/c restaurant with waiters in batik *bajus*, Indonesian seafood and curries.
† Sri Patani, 79 Bangunan Udarulaman, Jl Tun Ismail. Excellent Malay/South Thai food.
† Zul Satay, junction of Jl Teluk Sisek and Jl Beserah. Upmarket satay joint.

Kampong Cherating *p648*
††† Sunrise Seafood, one of the newish restaurants on main road, pleasant terrace set back from road, Western and local dishes.
† Cherating Inn, unusually good roti and Cherating Inn Pancakes (made with coconut).
† Deadly Nightshade (**Moon** chalet resort). Mainly Western menu, great atmosphere.
† Intan, along from the Cherating Bayview. A Malay seafood restaurant with local touches.
† Restoran Duyong, T09-581 9578 (inside the **Duyong Beach Resort**). Lovely setting on raised wooden terrace at edge of beach, lobster and prawns sold by weight.
† Seaside Seafood, opposite **Cherating Cottages**, on the beach. Good Chinese/Malay seafood. Fish grilled on banana leaves. One of the most popular. Recommended.

Kuala Terengganu *p649, map p649*
Nasi dagang is a local speciality of glutinous rice, served with *gulai ikan tongkol* (tuna with tamarind and coconut gravy).
† Golden Dragon, 198 Jl Bandar. Good pork, interesting vegetable dishes.
† One-Two-Six, 102 Jl Kampong Tiong 2 (off Jl Sultan Ismail). Big open-air restaurant with hawker stalls, good seafood menu, special: fire chicken wings.
† Ping Anchorage Travellers' Café, Jl Dato'Isaac. Friendly, pleasant, good breakfasts. Guest book has objective comments on nearby islands, resorts and tours.

Foodstalls
Gerai Makanan (foodstalls) opposite the bus station, Malay; **Jalan Batu Buruk**, near the Cultural Centre, excellent Malay food and

seafood. Recommended. **Kampong Tiong** (off Jl Bandar), excellent hawker centre with Malay and Indian food, 0800-late.

Perhentian Islands *p651*
Most chalets have attached restaurants, particularly popular are **Coral View Island Resort**, **Coco Hut Chalets** and **Tuna Bay**. On Long Beach, **Panorama's** is particularly good. **Shake Shack** is a nice place for breakfast inland along the path towards Coral Bay. Lots of seafood BBQs, although avoid eating shark. Some restaurants discreetly offer beer or spirits.

Kota Bharu *p651, map p652*
Alcohol is only available in certain Chinese coffee shops, notably along Jl Kebun Sultan. The Kelantan speciality is *ayam percik* -- roast chicken, marinated in spices and served with a coconut-milk gravy. *Nasi tumpang* is a typical breakfast; banana-leaf funnel of rice layers with prawn and fish curries and salad.
††† Ambassador, 7003 Jl Kebun Sultan. Big Chinese coffee shop, Chinese dishes including pork satay, beer available.
††† Kow Lun, 7005 and 7006 Jl Kebun Sultan. Good lively Chinese coffee shop.
††† Malaysia, 2527 Jl Kebun Sultan. Chinese cuisine, speciality: steamboat.
† Meena Curry House, 3377 Jl Gajah Mati. Indian curry house, banana leaf restaurant.
† Neelavathy, Jl Tengku Maharani (behind **Kencana Inn**). South Indian banana-leaf curries.
† Qing Liang, Jl Zainal Abidin. Excellent Chinese vegetarian, also Malay and Western.

O Shopping

Kuala Terengganu *p649, map p649*
Batik Some of the best batik in Malaysia can be found in the central market (Pasar Besar Kedai Payang). There are a number of small craft and batik factories in Kampong Ladang, the area around Jl Sultan Zainal Abidin.
Handicrafts The Central Market is touristy, but offers a range of textiles and brassware. Surrounding kampongs practise silverwork,

batik printing, *songket* weaving and *wau* kite building. 7 km south of Kuala Terengganu are the excellent Cendering handicraft centres (take Marang-bound buses from Jl Syed Hussin). Worth visiting are: **Kraftangan Malaysia**, **Nor Arfa Batik Factory**, and the **Sutera Semai** silk factory.

Marang *p650*

Handicrafts The market in Marang has a craft market upstairs and there are several handicraft shops along the main street. **Balai Ukiran Terengganu** (Terengganu Wood carving Centre), Kampong Rhu Rendang, near Marang, master-carver Abdul Malek Ariffin runs the east coast's best-known woodcarving workshop, making a wide range of intricately carved furniture from cengal wood, carved with traditional floral geometric and Islamic calligraphic patterns. Shipping arranged.

Kota Bharu *p651, map p652*

Batik Astaka Fesyer, 782K (3rd floor). Recommended; Bazaar Buluh Kubu, Jl Tengku Petra Semerak, across the road from Central Market, has scores of batik boutiques.
Handicrafts The Central Market is cheapest. There are numerous handicraft stalls, silver-workers, kite-makers and woodcarvers along the road north to Pantai Cinta Berahi. At Kampong Penambang, on this road, just outside KB, there is a batik and songket centre.
Silverware On Jl Sultanah Zainab (near the bridge across the Kelantan River), before junction with Jl Hamzah, there are shops selling Kelantan silver, including **KB Permai**. The **Kampong Kraftangan** (Handicraft Village) contains a huge range of batik sarongs and ready-mades, silverware, songket, basketry and various Kelantanese knick-knacks.

▲ Activities and tours

Kuantan *p644*

Kuantan River Cruise, bookings at Jabatan Perhubungan Awam, Majlis Perbandaran Kuantan, Jl Tanah Putih, T09-512 1555,

amjpa2@mpk.gov.my. 1-2 hr crusies from the jetty at IBU Pejabat MPK, taking in mangrove swamps and jungle surrounding the Kuantan River. Boats leave at 1100 and 1430.

Taman Negara National Park *p645, map p645*

Boat trips From Park HQ to the Lata Berkoh rapids on Sungai Tahan, RM 80 for 4 people. Although expensive, this is an enchanting way to see the park.
Fishing The best months are Feb-Mar and Jul-Aug. There are game fishing lodges at Kuala Terengganu and Kuala Kenyam. The rivers Tahan, Kenyam and the more remote Sepia (tributaries of the Tembeling) are reckoned to be the best waters. There are more than 200 species of fish including the *kelasa* – a renowned sport fish. A permit costs RM10, rods are available for hire.
Tour operators See also Jerantut, below.
Mutiara Taman Negara Resort, see page 653. The park's only luxury resort. 3 days, 2 nights for RM400 including 2 treks. Also runs a shuttle from KL to Kuala Temberling jetty.

Jerantut *p647*
Tour operators
Han Travel, 1A Bandar Baru, Kuala Tembeling, T/F09-266 2899, www.taman-negara.com. Boat and bus transfers from KL, Kota Bharu and the Cameron Highlands and into the park, hotel bookings plus tour packages. Fairly standard prices and saves a lot of hassle.
NKS Hotel & Travel, Hotel Sri Emas, T09-260 1777, www.taman-negara.com. Aimed at budget travellers. Bus and boat transfers, package tours, 4 days, 3 nights for RM380. Tours include boat trips, camping, trekking, stayat Orang Asli village and cave exploring.

Kuala Lipis *p647*
Tour operators
Mr Appu Annandaraja of **Kuala Lipis Hotel** runs highly recommended 4-day treks in and out of Kenong Rimba. Trips are also run by: **Gin Loke Hotel**, 64 Jl Besar; and **Tuah Travel & Tours**, 12 Jl Lipis, T09-312144.

Kuala Terengganu *p649, map p649*
Ping Anchorage Travel & Tours, 77A Jl
Sultan Sulaiman, T09-626 2020, www.ping
anchorage.com.my. A very well-organized
and efficient tour service (islands, jungle
trekking, Kenyir Lake), offering seemingly
everything. **Turtleliner**, Jl Sultan Masjid
Abidin, T09-623 7000, services include flight
booking and confirmation, tours. Helpful staff.

Marang *p650*
Half-day river tours and fishing, snorkelling and
jungle trips are organized by **MGH (Marang
Guest House**, chalets **B-C**), little office by the
small jetty, daily 0900-1700, T09-618 1976,
www.marangguesthouse.com.

Pulau Kapas *p650*
The resorts run diving, snorkelling and
fishing trips, and kayaks can be hired. Several
companies run boats (fast boat, RM25 return,
20 mins, 0930-1700). Zack at the **Suria Link
Boat Service** is very helpful and his office is a
good place to buy boat tickets (T01-9983
9454). **MGH** is also recommended.

Perhentian Islands *p651*
The coral off the Perhentian islands is some of
the best on the east coast. Most guesthouses
arrange snorkelling trips and rent equipment.
RM30-40 for a half day. RM10 to hire gear on
the beach. Ubiquitous dive shops (PADI) on
both islands run courses for all levels. **Turtle
Bay Divers** and **Spice Divers** on Kecil are
recommended. If snorkelling off Long Beach,
head for the patch near Moonlight.

Kota Bharu *p651, map p652*
KTIC (Kelantan State Tourist Information
Centre) organizes river and jungle-safari trips,
staying in kampongs and learning local crafts.
It also organizes 3-day 'Kampong Experience'
tours with full board and lodging provided by
host families (such as potters, fishermen,
batik-makers, kite-makers, silversmiths,
top-makers and shadow puppet-makers. Cost
from RM285 (all in); minimum 2 people. It
also runs short Kelantanese cooking courses.

⊖ Transport

Kuantan *p644*
Air Sultan Ahmad Shah Airport is 20 km
south of town. Regular connections with
KL (MAS only). Taxis to town (RM20).
    Airline offices MAS, Wisma
Bolasepak Pahang, Jl Gambut, T09-538 4291.
Bus Local bus station is on Jl Besar/Jl Abdul
Rahman. Regular buses to **Cherating**.
    The long-distance bus station is on Jl
Stadium; companies have offices on 2nd
floor. Regular connections with **KL** (RM17,
2½ hrs), **Mersing, JB, Singapore, Melaka,
Penang, Kuala Terengganu, Kota Bharu**
and **Jerantut** for Taman Negara.
Car hire Budget, 59 Jl Haji Abdul Aziz,
T09- 512 6370. **Hertz**, Samudra River View
Hotel, Jl Besar, T09-512 2688.
Taxi Jl Besar, next to local bus station. **KL,
Mersing** (RM140 for 4) and **Kuala Terengganu**.

Taman Negara National Park
p645, map p645
Bus and boat Most visitors get a bus or taxi
to **Kuala Tembeling** jetty via Jerantut. There
are regular connections from **KL** via Kuantan.
Guesthouses and tour operators in KL arrange
tickets – **NKS Travel** shuttle bus leaves from
Petaling Street in KL's Chinatown (0730, RM30
one way, 3 hrs). The **Mutiara Taman Negara
Resort**'s bus leaves outside the Hotel Istana in
KL (0800, RM35). Both buses connect with a
boat to the park. If you want to take a public
bus, departures are from Pekeling bus station
in **KL** (access via Titiwangsa LRT and Monorail
station). You will need to catch the first bus to
make the boat connection to the park in time,
or you will have to stay in Jerantut overnight.
    At Kuala Tembeling there are boats to the
Park HQ at **Kuala Tahan**, 2½ hrs, RM25 one
way. Boats leave at 0900 and 1400.
    Nusa Camp also operates a boat service
from Kuala Tembeling to their own resort.
Bus It is now possible to go by road all the
way to Kuala Tahan from **Jerantut**. A public
bus runs around 3 times a day to and from
Jerantut bus station, RM6 one way.

Jerantut *p647*
Bus/taxi The bus and taxi station is in town centre. Regular connections from **KL**'s Pekeliling terminal. Taxis direct to Jerantut from KL leave from the Puduraya bus terminal. From the east coast, there 3 daily buses from **Kuantan** (0830, 1300 and 1500); also taxis.

Kuala Lipis *p647*
Bus Buses to **KL** Pekeliling bus terminal every 1½ hrs 0830-2030. Daily connections with **Kota Bharu** and **Kuantan**.
Train There are 2 daily trains to Kuala Lipis from **KL** at 1815 and 1955. From Singaopre the mail train leaves at 0935 and 1857. From **Kota Bharu** (from Wakaf Bharu station, 6 km outside) there are trains at 1719, 1819, and 1919. There are connections with **Jerantut**.

Kampong Cherating *p648*
Air Kuantan Airport is 45 mins' drive away.
Bus Regular buses from Kuantan (Kemaman bus). Bus stops both ends of the kampong. Buses to **Rantau Abang**, **Kuala Terengganu**, **Marang**, **Kota Bharu**, **KL** and **Singapore**.

Kuala Terengganu *p649, map p649*
Air Sultan Mahmud airport 18 km north-west of town, T09-666 4204. Regular flights to **KL** with **MAS**, 13 Jl Sultan Omar, T09-622 1415.
Bus Kuala Terengganu has 2 bus stations. The express, long-distance bus terminal is on Jl Sultan Zainal Abidain Medan Selera, on the northern edge of the city centre. Connections to **KL**, 7 hrs, **JB**, 9 hrs, **Kota Bharu**, **Kuantan**, **Rantau Abang**, **Mersing**, **Singapore**, **Melaka**, **Butterworth**, 9 hrs and **Alor Star** leave from the long-distance terminal. Local buses leave from the MPKT station on Jl Syed Hussin run to **Merang**, **Marang** and **Kuala Besut**.
Taxi Next to the bus station on Jl Masjid and from the waterfront. Destinations include **Kota Bharu**, **Rantau Abang**, **Marang**, **Kuantan**, **KL**, **JB** and **Penang**. Taxi, T09-621 581.

Marang *p650*
Bus Bus stop on the main road up the hill. Tickets bought from the kiosk on Jl Tg Sulong

Musa (sometimes closed so book in advance). Buses to **Kuala Terengganu** every 90 mins. If stuck without a ticket go to Kuala the express bus station (taxi RM15). Taxis wait by the jetty.

Redang archipelago *p650*
Air There is a small air strip on Pulau Redang operated by **Berjaya Air**, www.berjaya-air.com, which flies a 48-seater Dash 7 from **KL** at 1140. The return flight leaves 1310. RM250 one way.
Boat From Merang or the jetty in Kuala Terangganu (**Berjaya** customers only, 2 departures, at 1000 and 1500). It is possible to charter private boats from Merang, RM40 per person one way. Package deals include transport, see www.redang.org.

Merang *p650*
Bus 2 buses a day to/from **Kuala Terengganu** (RM2.50). Minibus connections from **Kuala Terengganu**, from Jl Masjid.
Taxi A/c taxi to **Kuala Terengganu** RM20-30.

Perhentian Islands *p651*
Boat All boats are booked through travel agents in Kuala Besut. More boats leave in the morning, so get there early. Fast boats for 8-10 people (RM60 return) run to/from **Kuala Besut** every hour 0700-1600, 30 mins. Slow boats (RM40 return) leave Kuala Besut at 1000 and 1500, 1 hr, and return at 0800 and 1200. Be wary of the boat trip during the Dec-Feb monsoon season; seas can be rough and boats are ill-equipped. Travel between the islands is by water taxi (fixed rates). A trip between Long Beach and the opposite beach is RM20.

Kuala Besut *p651*
Bus Main express buses go from the station at Jerteh, 20 mins by taxi. From **Kuala Terengganu** (Jl Masjid): Kota Bharu-bound bus to Jerteh, then on to Kuala Besut (regular connections). To **KL**: **Mahligia Express** bus company, T09-690 3699 leaves 0830 and 2030. Buses from KL leave around a similar time.
Taxi Kuala Terengganu (RM48); **Merang Jetty** (RM35, for Redang), **Kota Bharu** (RM25). Taxis to **Jerteh** (RM10).

Border essentials: Malaysia–Thailand

The Thai border is at the Malaysian town of **Rantau Panjang**; the Thai town is **Sungai Golok**. Bus No 29 for Rantau Panjang leaves hourly from the bus station off Jl Hilir Pasar (1½ hrs). From here it is a 1-km walk across the border to Sungai Golok's train/bus stations for connections to Hat Yai, Surat Thani (for Koh Samui) and Bangkok. Trishaws and taxis wait. A quieter, more interesting route into Thailand is via **Pengkalan Kubor** to **Ta Ba** (Tak Bai). Bus Nos 27, 27a and 43 go to Pengkalan Kubor. There is a small car ferry across the river.

Kota Bharu *p651, map p652*
Air The airport is 8 km from town; RM12 per taxi. Regular connections with **KL** and **JB**. Taxi into town RM10 per person, or bus No 9.
Air Asia and **MAS** offices at the airport.
Bus City buses and long-distance express buses leave from the Central Bus Station, Jl Hilir Pasar. Regular connections with most towns, especially on the east coast.
Car hire **Avis**, Hotel Perdana, Jl Sultan Mahmud, T09-748 4457, **South China Sea**, airport, T09-774 4288. **Pacific**, T09-744 7610.
Taxi Taxi station next to the Central Bus Station, Jl Hilir Pasar; many destinations, including **Thailand** (see box) and **Singapore**.
Train Wakaf Bharu station is 6 km out of town. Bus 19 or 27. Several daily connections with **Singapore** and **KL** via **Gua Musang**, **Kuala Lipis**, and **Jerantut**. The train is slow but the scenery is beautiful. Trains to KL leave 1719 and 1819 (journey approx 11 hrs). The train to Singapore leaves at 1919 (approx 14 hrs).

❶ Directory

Kuantan *p644*
Banks Jl Mahkota and Jl Besar, between post office and bus station. **Immigration** Wisma Persekutuan, Jl Gambut, T09-514 2155. **Medical services** Hospital, Jl Mat Kilau.

Taman Negara National Park
p645, map p645
Mutiara Taman Negara Resort has an expensive mini-market (selling goods for trekking and camping); a clinic (daily 0800-1615, 24 hrs for emergencies); a post office, laundry and library.

Kampong Cherating *p648*
Banks Nearest bank is at Kemaman, 12 km north. **Internet** Cherating Travel Post (next to **Mimis**); **Cherating Library** and **Cyber Café** ('Capacity.com'), closed Wed.

Kuala Terengganu *p649, map p649*
Banks Several on Jl Sultan Ismail. Few money changers. **Internet** Golden Wood Internet Café, 59 Jl Tok Lam. **Medical services** Hospital, Jl Peranginan (off Jl Sultan Mahmud), T09-623 3333. **Post** GPO, Jl Sultan Zainal Abidin. **Telephone** Telekom, Jl Sultan Ismail.

Perhentian Islands *p651*
Banks No banks or ATMs and few hotels accept credit cards. Most guesthouses will change money. Dive centres accept credit cards and some will let you have cash.
Internet Upmarket resorts have internet RM12 for 30 mins. Also try **Panorama**, Long Beach. **Perhentian Pro-Diver**, Coral Bay.

Kota Bharu *p651, map p652*
Banks Money changers in main shopping area. **Embassies and consulates** Royal Thai Consulate, Jl Pengkalan Chepa, T09-744 0867 (open Mon-Thu and Sat 0900-1200, 1330-1530). **Immigration** 3rd floor, Federal Bldg, Jl Bayam, T09-748 2120. **Medical services** Hospital, Jl Hospital, T09-748 5533. **Post** Jl Sultan Ibrahim.

Sarawak

Sarawak, the 'land of the hornbill', is the largest state in Malaysia, covering nearly 125,000 sq km in northwest Borneo with a population of just over two million. Sarawak has a swampy coastal plain, a hinterland of undulating foothills and an interior of steep-sided jungle-covered mountains. The lowlands and plains are dissected by a network of broad rivers that are the main arteries of communication and where the majority of the population is settled.

In the mid-19th century, Charles Darwin described Sarawak as "one great wild, untidy, luxuriant hothouse, made by nature for herself". Sarawak is Malaysia's great natural storehouse, where little more than half a century ago great swathes of forest were largely unexplored and where tribal groups, collectively known as the Dayaks, would venture downriver from the heartlands of the state to exchange forest products of hornbill ivory and precious woods.

Today the Dayaks have been incorporated into the mainstream and the market economy has infiltrated the lives of the majority of the population. But much remains unchanged. The forests, although much reduced by a rapacious logging industry, are still some of the most species-rich on the globe. More than two-thirds of Sarawak's land area, roughly equivalent to that of England and Scotland combined, is still covered in jungle, although this is diminishing. ▶▶ *For listings, see pages 675-687.*

Kuching and around ⊕⊙⊕⊙⊙⊖⊙⊙ ▶▶ *pp675-687. Colour map 9, C1.*

Due to Kuching's relative isolation and the fact that it was not bombed during the Second World War, Sarawak's state capital has retained much of its 19th-century dignity and charm, despite the increasing number of modern high-rise buildings. Chinese shophouses still line many of the narrow streets. Kuching is a great starting point and there are many sights within its compact centre, including the Sarawak Museum and the Petra Jaya State Mosque.

Within easy reach is the Semenggoh Orang-Utan Sanctuary and the national parks of Gunung Gading and Kubah. North of Kuching is the Damai Peninsula, featuring the worthwhile Sarawak Cultural Village, and Bako National Park on the Muara Tebas Peninsula.

Ins and outs

Getting there The airport is 10 km south of Kuching, T082-457373. There are daily flights from KL and other Malaysian destinations. International connections are limited to Bandar Seri Begawan (Brunei), Singapore and Perth. From the airport, take the green **Sarawak Transport Co** bus No 12A (RM1) to Lebuh Jawa street, 45 minutes. Buses depart every 50 minutes 0710-2000. Fixed-price taxi RM17.50; buy a coupon from the counter in arrivals.

There is a bus service from Brunei, via Miri. Express boats connect Kuching with Sibu and Sarikei. ▶▶ *See Transport, page 683.*

Getting around The city centre can be negotiated on foot. Sampans (small flat-bottomed wooden boats) operate as river taxis and take passengers across to Fort Margherita and the Astana on the north shore. City buses provide a cheap and fairly efficient service. Taxis are found outside the larger hotels and at designated taxi stands. There are several car hire firms.

Best time to visit Kuching is hot and humid year-round. The rainy season is November to February, but heavy downpours can happen at any time. May and June are the months for **Gawai Dayak Harvest Festival** (see page 585), a time of feasting and celebration. The **Rainforest Music Festival** is held every July at the Sarawak Cultural Village (see page 665).

Tourist information **Sarawak Tourism Board** ⓘ *Jl Tun Abang Haji Openg, T082-410944, www.sarawaktourism.com, Mon-Fri 0800-1800, Sat 0800-1500*, is housed in the beautiful Old Courthouse Complex. It has a good stock of maps and information on buses, travel agents and itineraries. There is a smaller branch on the waterfront by the main bazaar, T082-240620, and at Kuching International Airport, T082-450944. **Tourism Malaysia** ⓘ *Bangunan Rugayah, Jl Song Thian Cheok, T082-246575*, is also helpful and well-informed.

National parks information To book accommodation for Bako, Gunung Gading and Kubah, contact the **National Parks and Wildlife Booking Office** ⓘ *Old Courthouse, Jl Tun Abang Hj Openg, T082-410944, www.forestry.sarawak.gov.my.*

Sarawak Museum
ⓘ *Jl Tun Haji Openg, daily 0900-1700, free. Library and shop attached; proceeds go to charity.*
Kuching's biggest attraction is this internationally renowned museum, housed in two sections, connected by a footbridge. The museum was opened in 1891, with the 'new'

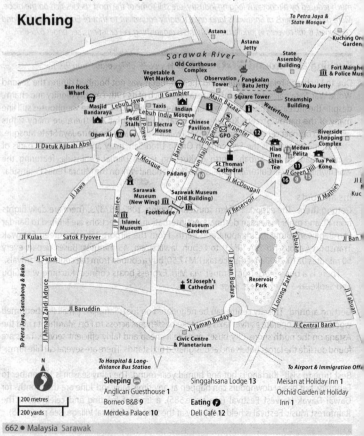

Kuching

Sleeping
Anglican Guesthouse 1
Borneo B&B 9
Merdeka Palace 10
Singgahsana Lodge 13

Eating
Deli Café 12

Meisan at Holiday Inn 1
Orchid Garden at Holiday Inn 1

wing built in 1983. The museum has a strong ethnographic section, although some of its displays have been superseded by the **Sarawak Cultural Village** (see page 665). The old museum's ethnographic section includes a full-scale model of an Iban longhouse, a reproduction of a Penan hut and a selection of Kayan and Kenyah woodcarvings. There is also an impressive collection of Iban war totems (*kenyalang*) and carved Melanau sickness images (*blum*) used in healing ceremonies. The museum's collection of traditional daggers (*kris*) is the best in Malaysia. Chinese and Islamic ceramics include 17th- to 20th-century jars, which are treasured heirlooms in Sarawak. The new Tun Abdul Razak ethnological and historical collection includes prehistoric artefacts from the Niah Caves, Asia's most important archaeological site (see page 671). If planning to visit Niah's Painted Cave, obtain a permit from the curator here, free of charge.

Not far from the Sarawak Museum, the **Islamic Museum** ① *Jl P Ramlee, Sat-Thu 0900-1700, free,* is housed in an elegant, single-storey colonial edifice and is devoted to Islamic artefacts from all the ASEAN countries. The collection includes manuscripts, costumes, jewellery, weaponry, furniture, coinage, textiles and ceramics.

Waterfront

The waterfront has been transformed into a landscaped esplanade through restoration and a land reclamation project. It is a popular meeting place, with foodstalls, restaurants and entertainment facilities including an open-air theatre. There is a restored Chinese pavilion, an observation tower, a tea terrace and musical fountains, as well as a number of modern sculptures. During the day, the waterfront offers excellent views of Fort Margherita and the Malay kampongs that line the north bank of the river. At night, the area comes alive as Kuching's growing middle class make their way down here to stroll and relax.

A good way to see the Sarawak River is to take a **cruise** ① *RM35, 90 mins.* Buy tickets from tourist agencies or at the waterfront booths along the esplanade. Or hire a sampan for around RM30 per hour.

Fort Margherita and the Astana

① *Take a sampan across the river from the Pangkalan Batu jetty next to Square Tower on the Waterfront, RM0.30 one way.*

The **Astana** (palace), was built in 1870 for the White Rajah, Charles Brook. It was originally three colonial-style bungalows, with wooden shingle roofs. Brook is said to have cultivated betel nut in a small plantation behind the Astana, so that he could offer

Perfect Vegetarian Food Centre **11**
Permata Food Centre **2**
See Good **6**

Serapi at Holiday Inn **1**
The Junk **16**

fresh betel nut to visiting Dayak chiefs. Today, it's the official residence of the governor of Sarawak and is only open to the public on Hari Raya Puasa, to mark the end of Ramadan.

A kilometre east of the Astana, **Fort Margherita** is now the **Police Museum** ① *Jl Sapi, Tue-Sun 1000-1800, free*. It was also built by Rajah Charles Brooke in 1879. It commanded the river approach to Kuching and was used as a lookout post to protect against pirates. The fort became a museum in 1971 and is a lot more interesting than it sounds, with a large collection of armour, weaponry, and a reconstructed opium den.

The **Malay kampongs** along the river next to Fort Margherita have beautiful examples of traditional and modern Malay architecture. Behind the fort, the **Kuching Orchid Garden** ① *T082-446688, Tue-Sun 1000-1800, free*, has more than 100 species of orchids.

Petra Jaya

The new **State Mosque** is situated north of the river at Petra Jaya and was completed in 1968. It stands on the site of an older mosque dating from the mid-19th century and boasts an interior of Italian marble. Kuching's architectural heritage did not end with the White Rajahs; many of the town's modern buildings are based on local styles. The **Bapak Malaysia** building is named after the country's first prime minister and houses government offices; the **State Legislative Assembly** next door, is based on the Minangkabau style. Kuching's latest building is the ostentatious **Masjid Jamek**. Also in Petra Jaya, like a space launch overlooking the road to Damai Peninsula, is the **Cat Museum** ① *daily 0900-1700, free, Petra Jaya Transport No 2B or 6*, which houses everything you ever wanted to know about cats.

Around Kuching ● ↠ *pp675-687. Colour map 9, C1.*

Semenggoh Orang-Utan Sanctuary

① *32 km from Kuching, daily 0800-1245, 1400-1615, RM3. Take Sarawak Transport Co bus No 6 from Ban Hock Wharf, Jawa Street or opposite the post office on Jl Tun Haji Openg (RM2). Buses leave hourly. Last bus to Kuching 1600. Taxi RM30 one way, or RM70 for the taxi driver to wait.*

Semenggoh became the first forest reserve in Sarawak when the 800 ha of jungle were set aside by Rajah Vyner Brooke in 1920. They were turned into a wildlife rehabilitation centre for monkeys, orang-utans, honey bears and hornbills. All were either orphaned as a result of logging or were confiscated, having been kept illegally as pets. The aim has been to reintroduce as many of the animals as possible to their natural habitat. In late 1998 many of the functions which previously attracted visitors to Semenggoh were transferred to the Matang Wildlife Centre (see page 665). However, there are a few trails around the park including a plankwalk and a botanical research centre, dedicated to jungle plants with medicinal applications and orang-utans still visit the centre for food handouts.

Gunung Gading National Park

① *T082-735714, RM10, 5 mins' drive from Lundu; tax RM5. From Kuching take STC (Green) Bus Numbers 3A, 6, 8G, 12A to Lundu from the Express Bus stop opposite the post office.*

This park covers 4104 ha either side of Sungai Lundu, 65 km northwest of Kuching. There are some marked trails, the shortest of which takes about two hours and leads to a series of waterfalls on the Sungai Lundu. Gunung Gading (906 m) and Gunung Perigi summit treks take seven to eight hours; it is possible to camp at the summit. The **rafflesia**, the world's largest flower (see box, page 692), is found here but if you're keen to see one in bloom, phone the Park HQ first, since it has a very short flowering period.

Kubah National Park

ⓘ *RM10, information from National Parks and Wildlife Booking Office in Kuching, see page 662. Take Matang Transport Company bus No 11 that departs from outside the Saujana car park (first bus 0630, last return bus at 1640). Ask to be dropped off at the Park HQ. Travel agents arrange tours.*
This is a mainly sandstone, siltstone and shale area, 20 km west of Kuching, covering some 2230 ha with three mountains: **Gunung Serapi**, **Gunung Selang** and **Gunung Sendok**. There are at least seven waterfalls and bathing pools. Flora include mixed dipterocarp and *kerangas* (heath) forest; the park is also rich in palms (93 species) and wild orchids. Wildlife includes bearded pig, mouse deer, hornbills and numerous species of amphibians and reptiles. Unfortunately for visitors here, Kubah's wildlife tends to stay hidden; it's not really a park for 'wildlife encounters'.

The **Matang Wildlife Centre** ⓘ *T082-225012; animal feeding times: orang-utans, daily 0900 and 1500; hornbills, daily 0830 and 1500; sambar deer, daily 0900 and 1500; crocodiles, 1430 Sun only*, houses endangered wildlife in spacious enclosures, which are purposefully placed in the rainforest. The key attraction are the orang-utans, which are rehabilitated for release back into the wild. There is an information centre and education programmes. The centre has also established a series of trails. To get there, take the bus to Kubah National Park but ask to be dropped at the turning for the Polytechnic and wait for a lift. Alternatively take a taxi from Kuching, RM35 one way.

Damai Peninsula ⊙⊗▲⊖ ›› *pp675-687. Colour map 9, C1.*

The peninsula, 35 km north of Kuching, is located at the west mouth of the Santubong River and extends northwards as far as Mount Santubong, a majestic peak of 810 m. Its attractions include the Sarawak Cultural Village, trekking up Mount Santubong, sandy beaches, a golf course, adventure camp and three resorts which are particularly good value off season when promotional rates are available.

Sarawak Cultural Village

ⓘ *35 km north of Kuching, T082-846411, www.scv.com.sg, daily 0900-1730, RM60, price includes cultural show at 1130-1215 and 1630-1715. Regular bus service from Holiday Inn in Kuching in RM10 each way, 0730-2200; last bus back from Damai is at 2100.*
The Sarawak Cultural Village was the brainchild of the **Sarawak Development Corporation** that built Sarawak's 'living museum' at a cost of RM9½ million to promote and preserve Sarawak's cultural heritage, opening it in 1990. With increasing numbers of young tribal people being tempted from their longhouses into the modern sectors of the economy, many of Sarawak's traditional crafts have begun to die out. The Cultural Village set out to teach the old arts and crafts to new generations. For the State Development Corporation, the concept had the added appeal of creating a money-spinning 'Instant Sarawak' for the benefit of tourists lacking the time or inclination to head into the jungle. While it is rather contrived, the Cultural Village has been a great success and contains some superb examples of traditional architecture including a number of full-scale longhouses. It should be on the sightseeing agenda of every visitor to Kuching, if only to provide an introduction to the cultural traditions of all the main ethnic groups in Sarawak.

The Cultural Village is also the venue for the fabulous annual **Rainforest Music Festival** ⓘ *www.rainforestmusic-borneo.com*, which takes place sometime between June and August. There are food stalls and jamming sessions are held in the different sections, culminating in a great evening show.

Bako National Park ◉◑ ↠ *pp675-687. Colour map 9, C1.*

Bako is situated on the beautiful Muara Tebas Peninsula, a former river delta that has been thrust above sea level. Its sandstone cliffs, which are patterned and streaked with iron deposits, have been eroded to produce a dramatic coastline with secluded coves and beaches and rocky headlands. Millions of years of erosion by the sea has resulted in the formation of wave-cut platforms, honeycomb weathering, solution pans, arches and sea stacks. Bako's most distinctive feature is the westernmost headland – Tanjung Sapi – a 100-m-high sandstone plateau, which is unique in Borneo. Established in 1957, Bako was Sarawak's first national park. It is very small (2742 ha) but it has an exceptional variety of flora and guaranteed wildlife spotting, including the rare probocsis monkey. Its beaches and accessible trails make it a wonderful place to relax for a few days.

Ins and outs

Getting there and around Bako lies 37 km north of Kuching, an hour's bus journey (RM2) from Petra Jaya terminal. Take the orange bus No 6 that leaves every hour from just below Electra House on Lebuh Market to Kampong Bako, from where boats run to the park. There are also minibuses from Lebuh Market, RM3. The last buses returning to Kuching depart around 1800. From Kampong Bako, boats run to the Park HQ at Sungai Assam (30 minutes, RM47 per boat each way for up to five people). It is also possible to hire boats to take you around the park: speed boats (for up to six) charge a negotiable rate, usually around RM300 per day; good for exploring the park's beaches and the island of Pulau Lakei.

Tourist information Before leaving Kuching, obtain a permit from the **National Parks and Wildlife Booking Office** ① *c/o Sarawak Tourism Complex, Kuching, T082-248088, daily 0800-1245 (Fri 0800-1100) and 1400-1615, RM10.* On arrival visitors must register at the Park HQ. The information centre has displays on geology, flora and fauna. Bako can be visited on a day trip although this gives almost no opportunity to explore the parks trails – an overnight or two night, three days would be preferable.

Treks

There is a good range of well-marked trails throughout the park; a map is available from Park HQ. The shortest trek is the steep climb up **Tanjung Sapi**, overlooking Telok Assam, with good views of Gunung Santubong, on the opposite peninsula, across Tanjung Sipang, to the west. The 3½-km trek to **Tajor Waterfall** is among the most popular, with varied terrain (including some steep climbs), spectacular views and a chance of a refreshing swim at the waterfall. A few metres further on you reach a secluded beach.

The longest trek is to **Telok Limau**; a five- to seven-hour walk through varied terrain. You can arrange with Park HQ for a boat to bring you back (around RM200). There are plank walkways with shelters at intervals to provide quiet watching spots, particularly required for viewing the proboscis monkey in the early morning or at low tide.

Beaches

There are seven beaches around the park, but some are rather inaccessible, with steep paths down to the cliffs. The best swimming beach is at **Telok Pandan Kecil**, about 1½ hours' walk, northeast of Park HQ. It is also possible to swim at **Telok Assam** and **Telok Paku**. It is not advisable to swim in March and April because of jellyfish. In the monsoon season, November to February, the sea can be rough.

Previously called Simmanggang, Bandar Sri Aman lies on the Batang Lupar, a three- to four-hour journey from Kuching, and is the administrative capital of the Second Division. The river is famous for its tidal bore; several times a year, a wall of water rushes upstream wreaking havoc with boats and divides into several tributaries: the Skrang River is one of these. It is possible to spend the night in longhouse homestays on the river. The Batang Ai National Park is home to hornbills, orang-utans and gibbons.

The major sight in Bandar is the defensive **Fort Alice** (1864). Most tourists do not stop in Bandar but pass through on day trips from Kuching to visit traditional Iban longhouses sited along the Skrang River. The route to Bandar goes through pepper plantations and many 'new' villages. During communist guerrilla activity in the 1960s (see page 729), whole settlements were uprooted in this area and placed in guarded camps.

Ins and outs
Bandar Sri Aman is accessible from Kuching and Sibu by bus. To reach Skrang long-houses, buses and then chartered boats must be arranged. There is one hotel in Batang Ai National Park. It arranges transport for its guests. Trips to longhouses and the national park can be organized through **Borneo Adventure Travel Company**, see page 682.

Skrang longhouses
The Skrang River was one of the first areas settled by Iban immigrants in the 16th to 18th centuries. The slash-and-burn agriculturalists originally came from the Kapual River basin in Kalimantan. They later joined forces with Malay chiefs in the coastal areas and terrorized the Borneo coasts; the first Europeans to encounter these pirates called them Sea Dayaks. The Ibans took many heads; blackened skulls hang in some of the Skrang longhouses. In 1849 more than 800 Iban pirates were massacred by Rajah James Brooke's forces in the notorious Battle of Beting Marau. Four years later the Sultan of Brunei agreed to cede these troublesome districts to Brooke; they became the Second Division of Sarawak.

There are many traditional Iban longhouses along the Skrang River, although those closer to **Pias** and **Lamanak** (the embarkation points on the Skrang) tend to be very touristy. **Long Mujang**, the first Iban longhouse, is an hour upriver. Pias and Lamanak are within five hours' drive of Kuching. Two-hour jungle treks are also available. ➤➤ See box, page 669.

Batang Ai and Batang Ai National Park → Colour map 9, C2.
The Batang Ai River, a tributary of the Batang Lupar, was dammed in 1985 to form Sarawak's first hydroelectric plant; it provides 60% of Sarawak's electricity supply. The area was slowly flooded over a period of six months to give animals and wildlife a chance to escape, but it has affected 29 longhouses, 10 of which are now completely submerged. The rehousing of the longhouse community has been the topic of fierce controversial debate. The communities were moved into modern longhouses and given work opportunities in local palmeries, but many have returned to settle on the banks of the reservoir.

The **Batang Ai National Park**, 250 km from Kuching and two hours from the jetty by boat, covers an area of over 24,040 ha. It protects the much-endangered orang-utan and is home to a wide variety of other wildlife, including hornbills and gibbons. There are no facilities but walking trails have been created, one of which takes in an ancient burial ground. Trips to the longhouses and to Batang Ai National Park are organized by the **Borneo Adventure Travel Company**. ➤➤ See Activities and tours, page 682.

The third largest town in Sarawak, Sibu is sited at the confluence of the Rejang and the Igan rivers 60 km from the sea. It is the starting point for trips up the Rejang to Kapit and Belaga. The Rejang is an important thoroughfare and Malaysia's longest river at 563 km. Tours to upriver longhouses can be organized from Sibu or more cheaply from Kapit and Belaga.

To go upriver beyond Kapit it is necessary to get a permit, which is valid for travel up the Rejang as far as Belaga. For trips beyond Belaga another permit must be obtained there; however, these trips tend to be expensive and less safe. ⟫ *See Activities and tours, page 682.*

Sibu → *Colour map 9, C2.*

This old trading port has a couple of big hotels and a smart esplanade, but it doesn't hold much appeal for travellers. If you're in town, it's worth visiting the seven-storey **pagoda**, adjacent to **Tua Pek Kong Temple**; there are good views over the town from the top. Ask if the entertaining and informative caretaker Tan Teck Chiang can show you around.

Ins and outs The airport, T084-307755, is 25 km from Sibu and receives flights from KL, Kuching and KK. A taxi into town costs RM28; buy a coupon at the airport. Or take Lanang Bus No 3A, which leaves every two hours 0630-1600. The long-distance bus station is 3 km out of town. Take a taxi, RM10, or a Lorong Road bus (no number) or Sungei Merah bus No 12 or 17 to the local bus station near the ferry terminal. There are daily connections with Bintulu and Miri, and Kuching via Sarikei. Boats for Kuching and Sarikei dock at two wharves close to the town centre. ⟫ *See Transport, page 684.*

The **Visitor Information Centre** ⓘ *ground floor, 32 Jl Tukang Besi (around the corner from the Methodist Church), T084-340980, www.sarawaktourism.com, Mon-Fri 0800-1700, Sat 0800-1250, closed 1st and 3rd Sat of the month,* can advise on trips to Kapit and Belaga.

Kapit → *Colour map 9, C3. Population: 100,000.*

Kapit is the capital of Sarawak's Seventh Division, through which flows the **Rejang River** and its main tributaries. It is the last big town on the Rejang and styles itself as the gateway to 'the heart of Borneo', after Redmond O'Hanlon's *Into the Heart of Borneo*, which describes his adventure up the Batang Baleh in the 1980s. It is a trading centre for the tribespeople upriver and has grown enormously in recent years with the expansion of the logging industry upstream. Most visitors simply use the town as a pit stop before continuing their adventures into the interior to explore the upper Rejang and its tributaries, where there are many Iban and Orang Ulu longhouses. One of the most beautiful and accessible longhouses is **Rumah Seligi**, about 30 minutes' drive from Kapit.

The town's main sight is **Fort Sylvia**, built of *belian* by Rajah Charles Brooke in 1880 to stop the belligerent Iban headhunters from attacking Kenyah and Kayan settlements upstream. It is now occupied by the **Kapit Museum** ⓘ *Mon-Fri 0900-1200, 1400-1600, Sat and Sun 0900-1200,* which has displays on Rejang tribes including reconstructions of Iban and Orang Ulu longhouses, *salong* (burial hut), totem pole and a mural painted by local tribespeople. There are also displays on the natural history of the upper Rejang and modern industries such as mining, logging and tourism.

Kapit has a particularly colourful daily **market** in the centre of town. Tribeswomen bring in fruit, vegetables and animals to sell; it is normal to see everything from turtles, frogs, birds and catfish to monkeys, wild boar and even pangolin and pythons. Note that some of the species you will see are endangered and their illegal trade should not be encouraged.

Visiting a longhouse

There are more than 1500 longhouses in Sarawak, usually located along the big rivers and their tributaries such as the Skrang, the Rejang and the Baram. Some longhouses are accessible by road and many are within an hour's longboat ride from town. The further away a longhouse is, the more traditional it is likely to be.

The average longhouse has 20-25 'doors' (although there can be as many as 60). Each represents one family. The word 'long' in a settlement's name – such as Long Terawan – means 'confluence' and does not refer to length. Behind each door is a *bilik* (apartment), which includes the family living room and a loft, where paddy and tools are stored. In traditional longhouses, the living rooms are simple atap-roofed, bamboo-floored rooms; in modern longhouses the living rooms are commonly furnished with sofas, lino floors, a TV and an en suite bathroom. At the front of the *bilik* is the *dapur*, where the cooking takes place. All *biliks* face out onto the *ruai* (gallery), which is the focus of communal life. Attached to the *ruai* there is usually a *tanju* (open veranda) running the full length of the house – where rice and other agricultural products are dried. Long ladders – notched hardwood trunks – lead up to the *tanju*; they can get very slippery.

The most important ground rule is not to visit a longhouse without an invitation. People who arrive unannounced may get an embarrassingly frosty reception. Upriver, particularly at Kapit, on the Rejang, such 'invitations' are not hard to come by; it is good to ensure your host actually comes from the longhouse you are being invited to. The best time to visit Iban longhouses is during the Gawai harvest festival at the beginning of June (see page 585), when communities throw an open house and everyone is invited to join the festivities.

On arrival, visitors should pay an immediate courtesy call on the headman (the *tuai rumah* in Iban longhouses). It is normal to bring him gifts; those staying overnight should offer the headman RM10-20 per person. The money is kept in a central fund and saved for use by the whole community during festivals. Small gifts such as beer, coffee, biscuits, whisky, batik and food (especially rice or chicken) go down well. It is best to arrive at a longhouse during late afternoon after people have returned from the fields. Visitors who have time to stay the night generally have a much more enjoyable experience than those who pay fleeting visits; they can share the evening meal and have time to talk and drink.

If you go beyond the limits of the express boats, it is necessary to charter a longboat. Petrol costs RM2-4 a litre. Guides charge approx RM40-80 a day and sometimes it is necessary to hire a boatman or frontman as well. Permits are required for most upriver areas; these can be obtained at the residents' or district office in the nearest town.

Rules for visiting a longhouse:

- Do not visit without an invitation.
- Take off your shoes when entering.
- Accept food and drink with both hands. If you do not want to eat or drink, touch the brim of the glass/plate and then touch your lips as a symbolic gesture. Sit cross-legged when eating.
- When washing in the river, women should wear a sarong and men, shorts.
- Ask permission to take photos. It's not unusual to be asked for a small fee.
- Do not enter a longhouse during *pantang*, a period of misfortune usually following a death. There is normally a white (leaf) flag hanging outside.
- Bow your head when walking past people older than you.

Ins and outs Maps of the Kapit Division are available from the **Land Survey Department** ① *Jl Beletik on Jl Airport*. Permits for upriver trips are available from the **government administration centre** ① *Resident Office, Kapit Division, 96800 Kapit*, which is outside town near the airport. Take a local bus heading 'downstream' from the town centre, RM2.

Longhouses between Kapit and Belaga on the upper Rejang river are accessible by express boats, but these travel a limited distance on the Balleh River (2½ hours). To go further upriver it is necessary to take a tour or organize your own guides and boatmen. Tourists going up the Balleh River or Upper Rejang must sign a form saying they understand they are travelling at their own risk.

Belaga → *Colour map 9, B3.*

This is the archetypal sleepy little town on the banks of the Rejang; most people while away the time in coffee shops. There are always interesting visitors in town, from itinerant wild honey collectors from Kalimantan to Orang Ulu who have brought their jungle produce downriver to the Belaga bazaar or those who are heading to the metropolis of Kapit for medical treatment. Belaga serves as a small government administration centre for the more remote parts of the Seventh Division as it is the last settlement of any size up the Rejang. It's also a major centre for the illegal logging business, with many locals having been paid off handsomely to say nothing negative regarding the huge scale logging operations close to the Kalimantan border (note the large number of 4WDs and expensive cars).

Belaga is also a good place to arrange visits to the Kayan and Kenyah longhouses on the Linnau River. There is a very pretty **Malay kampong** (Kampong Bharu) along the esplanade downriver from the Belaga Bazaar. The Kejaman burial pole on display outside the Sarawak Museum in Kuching was brought from the Belaga area in 1902. The **District Office** (for upriver permits) is on the far side of the basketball courts.

Many of the longhouses around Belaga are quite modern, although several of the Kenyah and Kayan settlements have beautifully carved wooden *salongs* (tombstones) nearby. All the longhouses beyond Belaga are Orang Ulu tribal groups. Even longhouses that seem to be very remote (such as **Long Busang**) are now connected by logging roads from Kapit, only four hours' drive away. To get well off the beaten track, into Penan country, it is possible to organize treks from Belaga towards the Kalimantan border, staying in longhouses en route. Officially you need a permit, but local guides and boat owners operate with the minimum of paperwork; ask in Belaga hotels and coffee shops.

North coast ○○○▲○○ ➤ *pp675-687.*

The north coast of Sarawak is fairly remote, with Bintulu, Miri and Marudi being the only significant towns. Close to Bintulu is Similajau National Park where green turtles lay their eggs. Niah National Park boasts famous limestone caves and is home to jungle birds and primates. Miri is the launch pad for river trips into the interior and Marudi is an upriver trading post and the start of a cross-border trek. Bintulu is accessible by air, boat and bus. Miri is accessible by air and bus and Marudi by air and boat.

Bintulu → *Colour map 9, B3.*

On the Kemena River, Bintulu is in the heart of Melinau country and was a fishing and farming centre until the largest natural gas reserve in Malaysia was discovered offshore in the late 1970s, making Bintulu a boom town overnight. The town has a modern Moorish-style mosque called the **Masjid Assyakirin** and a colourful Chinese temple called **Tua Pek Kong**.

Few tourists stay long in Bintulu, despite it being the jumping-off point for the Similajau National Park and the Niah Caves. The **longhouses** on the Kemena River are accessible but tend not to be as interesting as those further up the Rejang and Baram rivers. However, the Penan and Kayan tribes are very hospitable.

For information contact **Sarawak Forestry Department** ① *www.sarawak.forestry.gov.my* or **National Parks Booking Office** ① *T086-331117, ext 50.*

Similajau National Park → *Colour map 9, B3.*

Lying 20 km northeast of Bintulu, Similajau is a coastal park with sandy beaches, broken by rocky headlands and backed by primary rainforest. It is Sarawak's most unusually shaped national park being more than 32 km long and only 1½ km wide. **Pasir Mas** (Golden Sands) is a beautiful 3½-km-long stretch of coarse beach, to the north of the Likau River, where green turtles come ashore to lay their eggs between July and September. A few kilometres from the Park HQ at **Kuala Likau** is a small coral reef, known as **Batu Mandi**. The area is renowned for birdwatching and there are a number of trails. Bintulu is not on the main tourist route and consequently the park is very quiet, except at weekends.

Permits are available from the **Bintulu Development Authority**. The information centre ① *T086-332011*, is at Park HQ, at the mouth of Sungai Likau, across the river from the park. A boat is needed to cross the 5 m of crocodile-infested river.

Niah National Park → *Colour map 9, B3.*

Niah's famous caves, tucked into a limestone massif called Gunung Subis (394 m), made world headlines in 1958, when they were confirmed as the most important archaeological site in Asia. A 37,000-year-old human skull was discovered under 2.4 m of guano (bat droppings) and prompted a radical reappraisal of popular theories about where modern man's ancestors had sprung from. The park is one of the most popular tourist attractions in Sarawak receiving more than 15,000 visitors every year.

The **Great Cave** is one of the largest caves in the world and a total of 166 burial sites have now been excavated, 36 of which are Mesolithic (up to 20,000 years ago). The **Painted Cave** contains the only prehistoric wall paintings in Borneo. Most of the drawings are of dancing human figures and boats, thought to be associated with a death ritual. In AD 700 there is thought to have been a flourishing community based in the caves, trading hornbill ivory and birds' nests with the Chinese in exchange for porcelain and beads.

The park primarily comprises alluvial or peat swamp and mixed dipterocarp forest. Long-tailed macaques, hornbills, squirrels, flying lizards and crocodiles have all been recorded in the park. There are also bat hawks, which provide an impressive spectacle when they home in on one of the millions of bats that pour out of the caves at dusk.

Ins and outs The nearest town is Batu Niah. There are regular bus connections with Miri (just under two hours), Bintulu (two hours) and Sibu. From Batu Niah it is around 3 km to the Park HQ. Either walk through the forest (45 minutes), or take a longboat or taxi. There are well-marked trails to the caves from Park HQ. ▶▶ *See Transport, page 385.*

The **Park Information Centre** has displays on birds' nests and flora and fauna. The caves are open daily 0800-1630, RM10. Guides available (RM35 for groups of up to 20). Permits to the Painted Cave can be obtained, free of charge, from the curator's office at the Sarawak Museum, see page 663. Longboats can be hired from Park HQ for upriver trips. Bring a powerful torch for the caves. Walking boots are advisable during the wet season as the plank walk can get very slippery. Wear long trousers and take insect repellent.

Miri and the Baram River → Colour map 9, B3.

Miri is the starting point for adventurous trips upriver to Marudi, Bario and the Kelabit Highlands, as well as the incomparable Gunung Mulu National Park. The capital of Sarawak's Fourth Division is a busy, prosperous town with a new waterfront development and marina. More than half the population is Chinese. Juxtaposed against Miri's modern boom-town image is **Tamu Muhibba**, the 24-hour native jungle produce market, where the Orang Ulu come to sell their produce (see Shopping, page 681). A walk around the market provides an illuminating lesson in jungle nutrition, with impromptu stalls selling all manner of tropical foods and handicrafts. **Taman Bulatan** is a scenic, centrally located park with foodstalls and boats for hire on the manmade lake.

Ins and outs The airport is 8 km west of town; taxi coupon RM14. The **Tourist Information Centre** ⓘ *Jl Malay (next to bus station), T085-434181, www.sarawaktourism.com, Mon-Fri 0800-1800, Sat 0800-1600 (closed 1st and 3rd Sat of each month), Sun 0900-1500*, makes bookings for national parks. If travelling to Bario (see page 674), apply for a permit at the Residents' Office ⓘ *Jl Kwantung, T085-433202/03*, with a passport photocopy. The permit then needs to be stamped at the police station. You can also contact the **National Parks and Wildlife Office** ⓘ *Jl Puchong, T085-432277 (closed 1st and 3rd Sat).* ▸▸ *See Activities and tours, page 683.*

Lambir Hills National Park → Colour map 9, B3.

ⓘ *19 km south of Miri, Park HQ is close to the Miri-Niah road, T085-491030, RM10; take Bintulu or Bakong bus from Park Hotel in Miri (RM3, 40 mins) or go by taxi (RM40, 30 mins).* Consisting of a chain of sandstone hills bounded by rugged cliffs, just visible from town, the park's main attractions are the beautiful waterfalls. *Kerangas* (heath forest) covers the higher ridges while the lowland areas are mixed dipterocarp forest. Bornean gibbons, bearded pigs, barking deer and more than 100 species of bird have been recorded in the park. There are tree towers for birdwatching and several trails that lead to enticing pools for swimming. The park attracts hordes of day trippers from Miri at weekends. It's possible to stay overnight, see Sleeping, page 678.

Marudi → Colour map 9, B3.

Four major tribal groups – Iban, Kelabit, Kayan and Penan – come to Marudi to do business with Chinese, Indian and Malay merchants. Marudi is the furthest upriver trading post on the Baram and services all the longhouses in the Tutoh, Tinjar and Baram river basins. Most tourists only stop long enough in Marudi to down a cold drink before catching the next express boat upriver; as the trip to Mulu National Park can now be done in a day, not many have to spend the night here. Because it is a major trading post, however, there are a lot of hotels, and the standards are reasonably good.

The town's main sight, **Fort Hose** was built in 1901 and is named after the last of the Rajah's residents, the anthropologist, geographer and natural historian Dr Charles Hose. Also of note is the intricately carved **Thaw Peh Kong Chinese Temple** (near the express boat jetty). The temple was shipped from China and erected in the early 1900s.

The **Marudi Kampong Teraja log walk** is normally done from the Brunei end, as the return trek, across the Sarawak/Brunei border, takes a full day. It is, however, possible to reach an Iban longhouse inside Brunei without going the whole distance to Kampong Teraja. The longhouse is on the Sungai Ridan, about 2½ hours down the jungle trail. The trail starts 3 km from Marudi, on the airport road. There is no customs post at the border, but trekkers are advised to take their passports in the unlikely event of being stopped by police.

The impressive peak of Gunung Mulu is the centrepiece of the eponymous national park. The luscious jungle, with its dramatic peaks and deep gorges, offers spectacular trekking, while underneath is the biggest limestone cave system in the world. The cooler climes of the Kelabit Highlands provide good walking opportunities around Bario. Limbang is frontier country and the start of a cross-border trek.

Gunung Mulu National Park → *Colour map 9, B4.*

Tucked in behind Brunei, this 529 sq km park set deep in the rainforest, Mulu is a huge hollow mountain range, with incredible caves and karst formations, covered in 180-million-year-old primary jungle. The park has an astonishing biological diversity due to its great changes in topography, from 50 m above sea level near Park HQ to the summit of Gunung Mulu (2377 m). More than 3500 species of plants recorded in the park, including highly specialized orchids, pitcher plants and the unusual 'One Leaf' plant, which only grows on limestone. As well as visiting the caves, there are excellent opportunities for trekking, the most popular being the **Pinnacles**, and **Gunung Mulu**, Sarawak's second highest mountain.

Ins and outs Most people arrive by air from Miri, Marudi or Limbang; the quickest and cheapest option. There is an airstrip 2 km downriver from Park HQ, from where longboats and minibuses operate. The other option is a 10-hour river trip from Miri. To get there in one day, take an early bus to Kuala Baram, then travel upriver to Marudi where a second boat takes you to Long Terawan. At Long Terawan you must hire a longboat to bring you to the park. It can work out cheaper to visit as part of a tour. ➠ *See Transport, page 686.*

Park entry costs RM10. There is a basic store at the Park HQ and a small shop just outside the park boundary, at Long Pala. All visitors must have a guide (RM 20 per day, extra RM10 per night); arranged from Park HQ or booked in advance from the parks office in Miri (see page 681). The cost for trekking guides depends on the distance covered and number of people in the group. Guides are very well informed about flora and fauna, geology and tribal customs. There is a variety of accommodation in the park (see page 678). It is best to avoid school and public holidays. For information, see www.mulupark.com.

The caves

Only four of the 25 caves that have so far been explored are open to the public. From Park HQ it is an hour's trek along a plank walk to **Deer Cave** has the world's biggest cave mouth and the biggest cave passage, which is 2.2 km long and up to 220 m high. The cave plays host to a number of bat species including the naked, wrinkle-lipped and horseshoe varieties. Hundreds of thousands of these bats pour out of the cave at dusk. The east entrance opens onto the **Garden of Eden** – a luxuriant patch of jungle, where the cave roof has collapsed and light has penetrated, attracting birds, insects and monkeys. Nearby, **Lang's Cave** contains beautiful curtain stalactites and intricate coral-like helictites.

Clearwater Cave can be reached by a 30-minute longboat ride from Park HQ. The cave system is 107 km long and is linked to the **Cave of the Winds**, to the south. Clearwater is named after the jungle pool at the foot of the steps leading up to the cave mouth, where the longboats moor. On the cave walls are coral-like helictites and dramatic photokarsts – tiny needles of rock, all pointing towards the light. These are formed in much the same way as the Pinnacles, by vegetation, in this case algae, eating into and eroding the softer rock, leaving sharp points of harder rock which 'grow' at 0.5 mm a year.

Trekking

A sleeping bag is essential; other important equipment includes good insect repellent, wet weather gear and a powerful torch. Guide fees: Mulu summit trips, around RM1000 for a group of five (four days, three nights); Melinau Gorge and Pinnacles; minimum RM400 for five people (three days, two nights). Ornithological guides cost an additional RM10 a day. Porters can be hired: 10 kg costs RM30 per day, RM1 per extra kilo. Mulu summit, minimum RM90; Melinau Gorge (Camp 5), minimum RM65. It is usual to tip guides and porters.

The Pinnacles The Pinnacles are a forest of sharp limestone needles three-quarters of the way up Gunung Api. Some of the pinnacles rise above the treetops to heights of 45 m. It is a very steep climb all the way and a maximum time of three to four hours is allowed to reach the Pinnacles (1200 m); otherwise you must return. It is not possible to reach the summit of Gunung Api from the Pinnacles. There is no source of water en route. Climbers should wear gloves, long-sleeved shirts, trousers and strong boots to protect against razor-sharp rocks.

Gunung Mulu From the trail towards the summit there are magnificent views of Gunung Benarat, the Melinau Gorge and Gunung Api. The final haul to the summit is steep; there are fixed ropes. Around the summit area, the *Nepenthes muluensis* pitcher plant is common – it is endemic to Mulu. Bring your own food and a gas stove. A sleeping bag and waterproofs are also necessary and spare clothes, wrapped in a plastic bag, are a good idea.

Treks from Camp 5 There are a number of treks using Camp 5 as a base. Camp 5 is located in the **Melinau Gorge** on the Melinau River, about four to six hours upstream from the Park HQ. Visitors are advised to plan their itinerary carefully and take enough food with them. There is a basic shelter that can house about 30 people. River water should be boiled before drinking. For a three-day trip, a longboat will cost about RM400. It takes two to three hours from Park HQ to Kuala Berar; it is then a two- to three-hour trek (8 km) to Camp 5. From the camp it is possible to trek up the gorge as well as to the Pinnacles on Gunung Api.

Bario and the Kelabit Highlands → *Colour map 9, B4.*

The sleepy settlement of Bario (Bareo) lies in the Kelabit Highlands, a plateau 1000 m above sea level close to the Kalimantan border in Indonesia. The undulating Bario valley is surrounded by mountains and fed by countless small streams that in turn feed into a maze of irrigation canals. Bario is only accessible by air or via a seven-day trek from Marudi. For information, see www.kelabit.net. The best time to visit is March to October.

Treks around Bario Because of the rugged terrain surrounding the plateau, the area mainly attracts serious mountaineers. However, there are many trails to the longhouses around the plateau. Treks can be organized through travel agents in Miri, see page 683. Guides can also be hired in Bario and surrounding longhouses for RM30-40 per day. It is best to go through the Penghulu, Ngiap Ayu, the Kelabit chief, who visits the longhouses once a month. Visitors should bring sleeping bags and camping equipment. There are no banks or money changers in Bario and provisions should be brought from Miri or Marudi.

Several of the surrounding mountains can be climbed from Bario, but they are, without exception, difficult climbs. Even on walks just around the Bario area, guides are essential as trails are poorly marked. The lower 'female' peak of **Bukit Batu Lawi** can be climbed without rock-climbing equipment, but the sheer sided 'male' peak is more technical. **Gunung Murudi** (2423 m) is the highest mountain in Sarawak; it is a very tough climb.

Limbang → *Colour map 9, B4.*

Limbang is the finger of Sarawak territory which splits Brunei in two. It is the administrative centre for the Fifth Division and was ceded to the Brooke government by the Sultan of Brunei in 1890. The Trusan Valley, to the east of the wedge of Brunei, had been ceded to Sarawak in 1884. Very few tourists reach Limbang or Lawas but they are good stopping-off points for more adventurous routes to **Sabah** and **Brunei**. To contact the **Residents' Office** ⓘ *T085-21960*.

Limbang's **Old Fort** was built in 1897 and was used as the administrative centre. During the Brooke era half the ground floor was used as a jail. It is now a centre of religious instruction. Limbang is famous for its **Pasar Tamu** every Friday, where jungle and native produce is sold. There is also an attractive small museum, **Muzium Wilayah** ⓘ *400 m south along Jl Kubu, Tue-Sun 0900-1800*, with a collection of ethnic artefacts.

To get to **Gunung Mulu National Park** (see page 673), take a car south to Medamit; from there hire a longboat upriver to Mulu Madang, an Iban longhouse (three hours, depending on water level). Alternatively, go further upriver to Kuala Terikan (six to seven hours when the water's low, four hours when it's high) where there is a simple zinc-roofed camp. From there take a longboat one hour up the Terikan River to Lubang China, which is the start of a two-hour trek along a well-used trail to Camp 5. There is a park rangers' camp about 20 minutes out of Kuala Terikan where it is possible to obtain permits and arrange for a guide to meet you at Camp 5. The longboats are cheaper to hire in the wet season.

Lawas → *Colour map 9, B4.*

Lawas District was ceded to Sarawak in 1905. The Limbang River, which cuts through the town, is the main transport route. It is possible to travel from Miri to Bandar Seri Begawan (Brunei) by road, then on to Limbang and Lawas. From Lawas there are direct buses to Kota Kinabalu in Sabah.

◉ Sarawak listings

For Sleeping and Eating price codes, see inside the front cover.

◔ Sleeping

Kuching *p661, map p662*
Room prices are often negotiable and many hotels offer special deals. There is a good choice of international-standard hotels. For full listings see www.sarawaktourism.com.

The choice at the lower end of the market is limited. Most of the cheaper hotels are concentrated around **Jl Green Hill**, near Tua Pek Kong temple. Some newer, mid-range places have sprung around **Jl Ban Hock**.

For an alternative to the usual hotels and guesthouses, try a homestay, organized by **Borneo Inbound Tours**, 98 Main Bazaar,

T082-711152. These include fishing villages near Kuching and up-country communities.
L-B Merdeka Palace, Jl Tun Haji Openg, T082-258000, www.merdekapalace.com. Central and great value. Pool and health club. The 214 rooms have minibar, satellite TV and broadband. 6 bars and restaurants onsite.
E Singgahsana Lodge, 1 Jl Temple, T082-429277, www.singgahsana.com. Specifically designed for travellers, this superb guesthouse has a fun, vibrant interior, great, super-clean showers, internet and a rooftop bar. Dorms available. Central, excellent value. Sister company to the **Artrageously Ramsayong** art gallery (see page 681). Recommended.
E-G Borneo Bed & Breakfast, 2/F, 3 Jl Green Hill, T082-231200, borneobedbreakfast@yahoo.com. 16 rooms, doubles, triples and dorms, all with shared bathroom. Laundry,

information about upriver tours and culture. Downstairs is the atmospheric Iban-owned **Ruaikitai Tribal Café**; see page 681.
F-G Anglican Guesthouse, back of St Thomas' Cathedral (path from Jl Carpenter), T082-414027. Old building set in beautiful gardens on top of the hill, spacious, pleasantly furnished rooms with basic facilities, fans. Family rooms have sitting room and attached bathroom. Book in advance.

Gunung Gading National Park *p664*
A-G National park accommodation. Bookings taken through the **National Parks and Wildlife Booking Office**, Kuching, T082-248088. Available are 2- and 3-bedroom chalets and a hostel (RM15 per person).

Kubah National Park *p665*
A-G National park accommodation. Book through the **National Parks and Wildlife Booking Office** in Visitor Information Centre, Old Courthouse, Kuching, T082-248088. There are chalets, an 8-room hostel and 5 huge bungalows at the Park HQ with full kitchen facilities, 4 beds (2 rooms), a/c, hot water, TV and veranda. Bring your own food.

Damai Peninsula *p665*
There are 2 main resorts on Damai Baech in the **LL-AL** price range. They **Holiday Inn Resort Damai Beach**, www.ichotels group.com, and the **Santubong Kuching Resort**, www.santubongkuchingresort.com. The latter is popular with golfers.
A-D Permai Rainforest Resort, Pantai Damai Santubong, T082-846487, www.permairain forest.com. This eco-resort is set on 18-ha of tropical rainforest including its own beach. Accommodation is in a/c tree houses or log cabins at the foot of Mt Santubong. Camping available. Outward bound facilities, popular with school groups. Restaurant on site.

Bako National Park *p666*
All bookings to be made at the **National Parks and Wildlife Booking Office**, Kuching, T082-248088 (see page 662). **Hostels** have

mattresses, kerosene stoves and cutlery; **lodges** have electricity and fridges. Both have fans. Accommodation is always booked up, so reserve several days before you want to go. **Lodge**, RM157 per house, RM105 per room. **Hostel**, RM55 per room, RM15.75 per person.
Unless you are intending to trek to the other side of the park, it is not worth camping as monkeys steal anything left lying around. In addition, any rain turns the campsite into a swimming pool. If you go to the beaches on the northeast peninsula, tents can be hired for RM8 (sleeps 4); campsite RM5.

Bandar Sri Aman and around *p667*
C-D Bukit Saban Resort, www.sedc tourism.com/hotel_saban.html, on the rarely visited Paku River, 4½ hrs from Kuching, T082-477145 (Kuching), T083-648949 (resort). 50 rooms in longhouse style with traditional sago palm thatch, restaurant, a/c, TV, hot water.
C-D Champion, 1248 Main Bazaar, T082-320140. A small but central establishment.

Skrang longhouses *p667*
All longhouses along the Skrang River are controlled by the **Ministry of Tourism**, www.tourism.gov.my, so rates are fixed (RM40 including meals). Resthouses can accommodate 20-40; mattresses and mosquito nets are provided in a communal sleeping area. Basic conditions, flush toilet, shower, phone and a clinic nearby. If the stay is 3 days/2 nights, it's possible to camp in the jungle for the2nd night before returning by boat to the longhouse.

Batang Ai and Batang Ai National Park *p667*
Apart from the Hilton, there is not much else. Tour companies provide accommodation in longhouses deeper within the park.
A-B Hilton International Batang Ai Longhouse Resort, T083-584388, www.hilton.com. On the eastern shore of the lake, the resort is made up of 11 longhouses, built of local *belian* (ironwood) to traditional designs. Despite its lakeside location there are no views, except from the walkways. All

100 rooms all have a/c, fan, TV, shower room, minibar. Pool and restaurant. The hotel arranges transport from Kuching.

Sibu *p668*

Cheaper hotels tend to be around the night market in Chinatown but there is also a selection within walking distance of the jetty.

A-B Premier, Jl Kampong Nyabor, T084-323222, www.premierh.com.my. Good restaurant and café with Wi-Fi, clean rooms with a/c, TV, own bath, some with river view. Helpful staff, discounts often available.

A-B Tanahmas, Jl Kampong Nyabor, T084-333188, www.tanahmas.com.my. Modern and well-appointed, a/c, superb restaurant, pool.

E-F Eden Inn, 1 Jl Lanang, T084-337277. Opposite Catholic church. Massive rooms in a big solid building. TV and a/c. Excellent value.

Kapit *p668*

Both are within walking distance of the wharf.

C-D Greenland Inn, 463 Jl Teo Chow Beng, T084-796388. A/c, well-maintained small hotel with good rooms. Although overpriced, it's easily the smartest hotel in town.

F Ark Hill Inn, near Town Square, T084-796168. A/c, bathroom, friendly, clean rooms. On the river, great views from some rooms.

Longhouses

F Rumah Tuan Lepong Balleh, 1 hr from Kapit; take a minibus from Sibu and ask for **Selvat and Friends Traditional Hostel and Longhouse**. RM30 inclusive of meals, generator until 2300, basic.

Belaga *p670*

E-F Belaga Hotel, 14 Belaga Bazaar, T086-461244. Some a/c, restaurant, no hot water, friendly proprietor, good coffee shop, in-house video. Best option.

F Belaga Budget Hotel, 4 Belaga Bazaar (upstairs from **MAS** office), T086-461512. 4 rooms, fan or a/c. Restaurant and internet.

F Sing Soon Huat, 26-27 New Bazaar, T086-461413. Smart, friendly, nice living area with TV and movies. A good choice.

Bintulu *p670*

C-D Plaza, Jl Abang Galau, T086-335111. Smart hotel and excellent value compared with other hotels in Sarawak. A/c, restaurant, pool. Very popular, so worth booking.

E Kemena, 78 Jl Keppel, T086-331533. A/c, refurbished and on a quiet street, good quality rooms with TV, fridge.

E National, 2nd floor, 5 Jl Temple, T086-337222. A/c, clean and well kept.

Similajau National Park *p671*

Contact Similajau National Park, T086-391284.

A-G National park accommodation, 2 chalets, 2 hostels and a 'mega' hostel – with 27 4-bed rooms. The latter has attractive hardwood decor. It can get block booked. 24-hr electricity. The canteen at Park HQ serves basic food and there are picnic shelters.

Niah National Park *p671*

Accommodation should be booked 2-3 days in advance through **Niah National Park**, T085-737454 or **National Parks Booking Office**, T085-434184, www.forestry.sarawak.gov.my.

All options have 24-hr electricity and treated water. **Hostels** have 4-bed rooms, private bathrooms, electric fans, fridges and sitting area. No cooking facilities but kettle and crockery available. RM42 per room, RM15.75 per bed. **Family chalet**, similar to hostel but with cooker and a/c, 2 rooms with 4 beds in each, RM157.50 per chalet. **VIP Resthouse**, RM236.25 per room, a/c, TV, hi-fi. Tents can be hired from Park HQ (RM8) or from the site (RM5).

There are a few accommodation options in Batu Niah (4 km from HQ).

E Niah Caves Inn, T085-737333. A/c, shower, spacious, fully carpeted rooms.

E Park View Hotel, T085-737023. Comfortable rooms with TV, a/c, bath but no shower. Discounts often available.

F Niah Caves, T085-737726. Some a/c, shared facilities, 6 rooms (singles, doubles and triples). Basic, but light and clean, next to river.

Miri and the Baram River p672

Most people going to Mulu spend a night in Miri. Mid-range hotels offer discounts of 30-40% and are based around Jl Yu Seng Selatan. Bottom end hotels are pretty rough.

A-D Parkcity Everly, Jl Temenggong Datuk Oyong Lawai, 2 km from town, T085-440288, www.vhhotels.com. Modern hotel by the river. Popular with families at weekends (check for discounts). 168 a/c rooms with TV, bathroom, minibar, balcony. Sunsets over sea, palm-lined free-form pool with swim-up bar, jacuzzi, sauna.

E-F Pacific Orient Hotel, 49 Jl Brooke, T085-413333, pohotel@streamyx.com. Spacious rooms with attached bath, basic breakfast included, Wi-Fi. A bargain.

F Fairland Inn, Jl Raja, T085-413981. A favourite among travellers, this place offers tiny dark rooms above a karaoke bar. It has a veneer of cleanliness, the place seems safe and the owner is used to travellers.

Lambir Hills National Park p682

Book through **National Parks Booking Office**, T085-434184, www.forestry.sarawak.gov.my.

A-E 1 unit with 2 rooms and 3 beds; 4 units with 2 rooms and 2 beds, RM100 per room or RM150 per house; a/c chalet, 2 rooms with 3 beds, RM50 per room or RM75 per house.

Marudi p672

A-E Grand, Lot 350 Backlane, T085-755711. Good hotel close to jetty, restaurant, 30 clean rooms with cable TV, a/c. Information on trips.

C-D Mount Mulu Hotel, Lot 80 and Lot 90, Marudi Town District, T085-756671. A/c, discounts make this place excellent value.

E Victoria, Lot 961-963 Jl Merdeka, T085-756067. All 21 rooms have cable TV.

F Mayland, 347 Mayland Building, T085-755106. A/c, 41 rooms, slightly run down but a good range of rooms.

Gunung Mulu National Park p673

Park chalets must be booked in advance at the **National Parks and Wildlife Office Forest Department** in Miri or Kuching or through **Borsarmulu Park Management**, T085-424561,

www.mulupark.com. Booking fee is RM20 per party. Confirm 5 days before visit. The **Royal Mulu Resort**, www.royalmuluresort.com, is a 20-min (RM5) boat ride from Park HQ. It is a comfortable place to stay but has sparked resentment among local tribespeople.

C-G Park HQ has various options. **Long-houses (C-D)** have bathroom, a/c, and 4 single beds, or a twin share. For 4 people sharing, it works out at RM30 each. **Rainforest Rooms (E)** sleep up to 4 and have fans and attached bathroom, at just over RM20 per person. The **hostel (F-G)** has 18 dorm beds, fan and shared toilet for RM18 per person. At Camp 5 is an **open-air hostel (F-G)** with sleeping mats and shared bathrooms. **G camping** is only allowed at Park HQ (RM5). Bring your own sleeping bag. There are shelters on the summit trail.

F Melinau Canteen, T085-657884. One of several hostels outside the park, about 5 mins' walk downstream from the Park HQ on the other bank of the river. Dorm beds.

Bario and the Kelabit Highlands p674

F De Plateau Lodge. Pretty wooden house, offering forest guides at RM65 per day.

F JR Lodge (Barview Lodge), T085-791038. Well set up for travellers, airport transfer, restaurant, electricity, board games, motorbike/4WD/bike rental and trekking. Rooms are simple but cheery.

F Tarawe. Well-run and a good source of information. Most visitors camp.

Limbang p675

Many hotels double as brothels.

C-E Metro, Lot 781, Jl Bangkita, T085-211133. Less than 30 small but clean rooms, all with a/c, TV, fridge, good quality beds.

Lawas p675

A-D Country Park Hotel, Lot 235, Jl Trusan, T085-85522. A/c, restaurant.

E Lawas Federal, 8 Jl Masjid Baru, T085-85115. A/c, restaurant.

F Hup Guan Lodging House, T085-85362. Some a/c, can be noisy but rooms are clean and spacious, reasonable value.

❻ Eating

Kuching *p661, map p662*
Local dishes worth looking out for include *umai* – a spicy salad of raw marinated fish with limes and shallots. Other Sarawakian ingredients are *midin* and *paku* – jungle fern shoots. Kuching offers excellent seafood. There are several cheap Indian Muslim restaurants along Lebuh India. At **Kampong Buntal**, 25 km north of Kuching, are several seafood restaurants on stilts over the sea.
♦♦♦ Serapi, Holiday Inn, Jl Tunku Abdul Rahman. Specializes in North Indian tandoori, good vegetable dishes, excellent selection of grills and seafood, imported steak, elegant.
♦♦ The Junk, 80 Jl Wayang, T082-259450. Closed Tue. Intimate restaurant filled with antiques like old cash registers and lit by lanterns. Serves pasta, steaks and other Western and Asian dishes.
♦♦ Orchid Garden, Holiday Inn, Jl Tunku Abdul Rahman. Good breakfast and evening buffets, international and local cuisine.
♦♦ See Good, Jl Bukit Mata Kuching, behind MAS office. Closed 4th and 18th of every month. Extensive range of seafood. Strong-flavoured sauces, lots of herbs, extensive and exotic menu, unlimited free bananas.
♦ Meisan, Holiday Inn, Jl Tunku Abdul Rahman. Dim sum, set lunch; Sun all-you-can-eat special, also Szechuan cuisine.
♦ Perfect Vegetarian Food Centre, Jl Green Hill. Excellent canteen serving Malay and Chinese food and Western breakfasts. Fantastic noodle in pumpkin sauce dish. Recommended.

Coffee shops

There are several Malay/Indian coffee shops on Lebuh India. Many Chinese coffee shops serve excellent *laksa* (breakfast) of curried coconut milk with a side plate of *sambal belacan* (chillied prawn paste).
Deli Café, 88 Main Bazaar, T082-232788. Atmospheric Western-style café, good coffee. Try the excellent carrot cake. Free internet.
Fook Hoi, Jl Padungan. Old-fashioned, famous for its *sio bee* and *ha kau* (pork dumpling).

Foodstalls

There are great open-air informal places along the waterfront selling everything from kebabs to *ais cream goreng* (fried ice cream) that begin early evening. Most foodstalls are clustered at the **Hilton** end of the promenade selling Malay dishes and fruit juices (no alcohol). There are beautiful views of the river, accompanied by popular Malay love songs. Some of the best food centres are in the suburbs; a taxi is essential.
Permata Food Centre, behind **MAS** office. A purpose-built alternative to the central market, bird singing contests (mainly red-whiskered bulbuls and white-rumped sharmas) every Sun morning, excellent range of fresh seafood.
Rex Cinema Hawker Centre, Jl Wayang/ Jl Temple, down an alleyway. Good satay.

Bako National Park *p666*
The canteen is open 0700-2100. It serves local food at reasonable prices and sells tinned foods and drinks. There is a good seafood restaurant near the jetty.

Bandar Sri Aman and around *p667*
♦ Alison Café & Restaurant, 4 Jl Council. Chinese cuisine.
♦ Chuan Hong, 1 Jl Council. Chinese coffee shop, also serves Muslim food.
♦ Melody, 432 Jl Hospital. Chinese and Muslim food.

Sibu *p668*
♦ Blue Splendour, 1st floor, 60-62 Jl Kampong Nyabor (opposite Premier Hotel). Recommended by locals.
♦ Esplanade Seafood & Café, Rejang Esplanade. Best in town. Great alfresco dining, with tables facing the river. Open evenings only when the place is strung with red lanterns. Excellent Chinese and Western dishes.
♦ Peppers Café, Tanahmas Hotel, Jl Kampong Nyabor. Western and local food, curries particularly recommended, popular.
♦ Sheraton, Delta Estate (out of town). Malay (and some Chinese), fish-head curries recommended by locals.

Kapit *p668*

There are foodstalls at the top end of the road opposite the market (dead-end road; brightly painted on the outside). There's a good satay stall on Jl Hospital, next to the lily pond.

Orchard Inn, Jl Teo Chow Beng, T084-796325. The most upmarket restaurant in Kapit, food well presented but no better than the coffee shops, disco 2200-0100.

99, Jl Pedral. Fresh air. Local and Chinese food.

Jade Garden, Jl Pedral. Local and Chinese food, smart.

MI, Jl Pedral. Malay Muslim food.

S'ng Ee Ho, next to **Metox** supermarket. Happy to cook anything you ask for.

Ung Tong Bakery, opposite the market. Bakery and café, good continental-style breakfasts – big selection of rolls and good coffee, fresh bread baked twice daily.

Belaga *p670*

Several small, cheap coffee shops along Belaga Bazaar and Main Bazaar.

Bintulu *p670*

Umai, raw fish pickled with lime or the fruit of wild palms (*assam*) and mixed with salted vegetables, onions and chillies, is a Melanau speciality. Bintulu is famed for its *belacan* – prawn paste – and in the local dialect, prawns are *urang*, not *udang*.

Marco Polo, on the waterfront on edge of town. The pepper steak is recommended.

Fook Lu Shou, Plaza Hotel, Jl Abang Galau. Seafood and Chinese cuisine, including birds' nest soup, boiled in rock sugar.

Kemena Coffee House, Western, Malay and Chinese, open 24 hrs.

Pantai Ria, near Tanjong Batu, seafood foodstalls, evenings only. Recommended.

Niah National Park *p671*

The **Guano Collectors' Cooperative** shop by the plankwalk sells food and cold drinks and camera film. There is a basic **shop/restaurant** just outside the park gates. The park **canteen** serves good local food and Western breakfast, 0700-2300, BBQ sites.

Miri and the Baram River *p672*

Siamese Secrets, Jl Merbau, just before it meets Jl Brooke. Excellent steaks and lamb shank, plenty of firey Thai curries. Popular with locals and tourists for meals or drinks.

Apollo, Lot 394 Jl Yu Seng Selatan (close to **Gloria Hotel**). Good seafood, very popular.

Dave's Deli, **Imperial Mall**, ground floor. Self service, great for a quick hot lunch.

Ming Café, Jl North Yu Seng, opposite the Mega Hotel, T085-422797, mingcafe@gmail.com. Large café on the corner, Chinese, Indian, Malay and Western dishes. Popular. The coffee's pretty bad though.

Nyonya's Family Café, 21 Jl Brooke, T085-429727. Closed Sun. Cheap Nyonya fare in a traditional-style coffee house, Sarawak noodles. Busy at lunchtimes. Recommended.

Marudi *p672*

There are several coffee shops in town.

Rose Garden, opposite **Alisan Hotel**. A/c coffee shop serving mainly Chinese dishes.

Gunung Mulu National Park *p673*

The small store at Park HQ sells basic supplies, and there are stoves and cooking utensils available. The park canteen has a limited menu. As an alternative, cross the suspension bridge and walk along the road to the first house on the left; down the bank from here is the **Mulu Canteen**, which fronts onto the river (no sign on the road). Also **Melinau Canteen**, just downriver from the Park HQ. There is a small shop with basic supplies at Long Pala.

Limbang *p675*

Tong Lok. A/c Chinese restaurant next to **National Inn**, gruesome pink tablecloths and fluorescent lighting, but good Chinese food.

Hai Hong, 1 block south of **Maggie's**. Simple coffee shop – good for breakfast with fried egg and chips on the menu.

Maggie's Café on the riverside near **National Inn**. Chinese coffee shop, pleasant location, tables outside next to river in the evening. Braziers set up in evening for good grilled fish on banana leaf. Recommended.

● Bars and clubs

Kuching p661, map p662

Clubs and discos usually have a cover charge including a drink. Most places have happy hours and 2-for-1 offers. Bars close 0100-0200. Most bars are on **Bukit Mata** off Jl Pandungan and along **Jl Borneo** next to the **Hilton**. **Monsoon**, Riverside Complex, Jl Tunku Abdul Rahman, with a balcony over the river. Good mix of locals and tourists. **Ruaikitai Tribal Café and Restaurant**, 3 Jl Green Hill, underneath **Borneo B&B**. Iban local Peter Jaban runs this cool café/bar. Good decor, rockin' music and tasty food make this a good evening venue. There's sometimes a free welcome *tuak* (fiery local stuff) for patrons. Peter also runs tours to longhouses in the region.
Tropical Pub & Bar, Jl Abell. The place to go for a lively local disco. Malaysian music.

❀ Festivals and events

Damai Peninsula p665

Jul Rainforest Music festival, Sarawak Cultural Village, www.rainforestmusic-borneo.com. Indigenous tribal and international artists unite in the jungle for 3-days of music celebration.

Limbang p675

May The movable **Buffalo Racing Festival** marks the end of the harvesting season.

○ Shopping

Kuching p661, map p662

When it comes to choice, Kuching is the best place in Malaysia to buy tribal handicrafts, textiles and artefacts, but they are not cheap. In some of the smaller coastal and upriver towns, you may find a better bargain. If buying several items, find a shop that sells the lot, as good discounts can be negotiated. Shop around. The best-stocked handicraft and antique shops in the big hotels but they

are also the most expensive. Shops close Sun. It is illegal to export any antiquity without a licence from the curator of the Sarawak Museum. An antiquity is defined as any object made before 1850. Most things sold as antiquities are not; some very convincing weathering and ageing processes are used.

Antiques, art and handicrafts

Most handicraft and antique shops are along **Main Bazaar**, **Lebuh Temple** and **Lebuh Wayang**. There is a **Sun market** on Jl Satok, southwest of town, with a few handicraft stalls. There are rows of pottery stalls along **Jl Penrissen**, take a bus (No 3, 3A, 9A or 9B) or taxi to Ng Hua Seng Pottery bus stop.
Artrageously Ramsay Ong, 94 Main Bazaar, T082-424346, www.artrageouslyasia.com. Art gallery of Sarawak artiste extraordinaire **Ramsay Ong** who made fame with his tree bark works. Now showing an eclectic collection of contemporary Malaysian art. Recommended.

Belaga p670

Chop Teck Hua, Belaga Bazaar. An intriguing selection of tribal jewellery, old coins, beads, feathers, woodcarvings, blowpipes, parangs, tattoo boards and other curios buried under cobwebs and gecko droppings at the back of the shop.

Miri and the Baram River p672

The **jungle market** is in a building with pointed roofs, opposite the **Park Hotel** on the roundabout at Jalan Malay and Jalan Padang. Colourful characters sell all manner of items including cucumbers that look like mangoes, mangoes that look like turnips, huge crimson durians, tiny loofah sponges, sackfuls of fragrant Bario rice, every shape, size and hue of banana, *tuak* (rice wine) in old Heineken bottles and a menagerie of jungle fauna – including mouse deer, falcons, pangolins and the apparently delicious long-snouted *tupai* (jungle squirrel). There are handicrafts and a selection of dried and fresh seafood: fish and *bubok* (tiny prawns) and buckets boiling with catfish or stacked with turtles.

▲ Activities and tours

Kuching *p661, map p662*

Most tour companies offer city tours as well as trips around Sarawak to **Semenggoh**, **Bako**, **Niah**, **Lambir Hills**, **Miri**, **Mulu** and **Bario**. There are competitively priced packages to longhouses (mostly up the Skrang River, see page 667). It is cheaper and easier to take organized tours to Mulu, but arrange these in Miri (see page 681) as they are much more expensive if arranged from Kuching.

Borneo Adventure, No 55 Main Bazaar, T082-245175, www.borneoadventure.com. Known for its environmentally friendly ethos. Offers tours all over Sarawak. Recommended.

Borneo Inbound Tours & Travel, 98 Main Bazaar, T082-237287. The only agency currently organizing scuba-diving around Kuching. Also homestay programmes.

Borneo Interland Travel, 63 Main Bazaar, T082-413595, www.bitravel.com.my. Licensed to sell bus and boat tickets.

Ruaikitai Tribal Café and Restaurant, see page 681. Peter Jaban runs rough 'n' ready but interesting longhouse trips.

Damai Peninsula *p665*

Permai Rainforest Resort, see page 665, offers outdoor pursuits, canoe hire, snorkelling trips to islands and to see turtles. Nearby is the **Damai Cross-Country Track**, a purpose-built mountain bike track; bikes hired at hotels.

Bandar Sri Aman and around *p667*

Many staff in the resort are locals and discreet enquiries may get you a trip to a longhouse and/or Batang Ai National Park for considerably less money than the tour companies charge.

Borneo Adventure Travel Company, 55 Main Bazaar, Kuching, T082-410569, www.borneo adventure.com, and at the **Hilton** in Batang Ai.

Sibu *p668*

Most companies run city tours plus tours of longhouses, Mulu National Park and Niah Caves. It is cheaper to organize upriver trips from Kapit or Belaga than from Sibu.

Sazhong Trading & Travel, 4 Jl Central, T084-336017, www.geocities.com/sazhong. Budget stays for groups in a longhouse in Kapit and beyond. Recommended.

Kapit *p668*

Recommended is local expert **Joshua Muda**, T084-796600, joshuamuda@hotmail.com, who can be found in the **New Rejang Inn**. He arranges sensitive and authentic longhouse trips. Hotels also run trips, or ask at the police station. Some guides in Kapit overcharge for very unsatisfactory tours.

Belaga *p670*

The **Belaga Hotel** will contact guides for upriver trips and the district office can recommend experienced guides. In this part of Sarawak, guides are expensive (up to RM80 a day), because there are not enough tourists to justify full-time work. It is necessary to hire experienced boatmen too, because of the numerous rapids. Recommended guides include: **Andreas Bato**, T019-3722972, niestabato@yahoo.com, an Orang Ulu guide with perfect English; **Hamdani Louis**, T086-461039, hamdani@hotmail.com; **John Belakirk**, T086-461512, johneddie1@hotmail.com.

Much of Belaga's tourism business is under the control of **Councillor Daniel Levoh**, No 34, Lot 1051, Jl Bato Luhat, New Bazaar, H/P 013-8486351, T086-461176, daniellevoh@hotmail.com. He is good at the arranging and bureaucracy side but falls short with the guiding itself.

Prices for longhouse trips upriver vary according to distance and the water level, but are similar to those in Kapit. English is not widely spoken upriver so basic Bahasa comes in handy.

Bintulu *p670*

Deluxe Travel, 30 Jl Law Gek Soon, T086-331293; **Hunda Travel Services**, 8 Jl Somerville, T086-331339; **Similajau Travel and Tours**, Plaza Hotel, Jl Abang Galau offers tours around the city, Niah caves, longhouses and Similajau National Park.

Miri and the Baram River *p672*
Most tour companies offer trips to **Mulu National Park** (see below). From Mulu it is possible to trek to **Bario** and **Mt Murud** as well as to **Limbang**. Costs vary considerably according to the size of the group. An 8-day tour of **Ulu Baram longhouses** cost RM1800 for 1 person and RM1200 per person in a group of 10. For those who want to visit remote longhouses, tour companies present by far the best option. Tour fees cover 'gifts' and all payments to longhouse headmen for food, accommodation and entertainment. **Borneo Mainland**, Jl Merpati, T085-433511; **JJ Tour Travel**, Lot 231, Jl Maju Taman, Jade Centre, T085-418690, ticketing agents; **KKM Travel & Tours**, 236 Jl Maju, T085-417899; **Limbang Travel Service**, 1G Park Arcade (near Park Hotel), T085-413228, efficient ticket service. **Seridan Mulu/Tropical Dives**, Lot 273, ground floor, Brighton Centre, Jl Temenggong Datuk Oyong Lawai, T085-415582, info@seridanmulu.com. Tailor-made trips, and dive operator. Superb knowledge of Miri's diving possibilities.
Tropical Adventure Tours and Travel, ground floor, **Mega Hotel**, Lot 907, Jl Merbau, T085-419337, www.asiabudgetholidays.com. Professional and experienced. Tailor-made trips in Malaysia and Indonesia. Excellent knowledge of remote corners. Recommended.

Gunung Mulu National Park *p673*
Visitors are recommended to go through one of the Miri-based travel agents (see above); it is usually cheaper than trying to go independently. Most itineraries include the caves, pinnacles and summits. Guides can advise on longer, more ambitious treks. The average cost of a Mulu package (per person) is RM350-400 (4 days/3 nights) or RM500 (6 days/5 nights), all accommodation, food, travel and guide costs included.

Limbang *p675*
Sitt Travel, T085-420567. Specializes in treks in this area and the ticketing agent for Miri tour operators.

⊖ Transport

Kuching *p661, map p662*
Air For transport from the airport, see page 661. Regular connections with **KL** (8-10 flights daily), **Kota Kinabalu** (**KK**) and **Brunei**. **Air Asia**, www.airasia.com, flies between KL, KK and Kuching; book online for the best rates. **MAS** has flights to **Singapore**, **Perth**, **Pontianak** (Indonesia) and – via KK – to **Hong Kong**, **Taipei**, **Manila**, **Seoul** and **Tokyo**.

Airline offices **Air Asia**, Wisma Ho Ho Lim, 291 Jl Abell, T082-283222. **MAS**, Lot 215, Jl Song Thian Cheok, T082-246622. **Royal Brunei**, 1st floor, Rugayah Building, Jl Song Thian Cheok, T082-243344. **Sin Hwa Travel Service**, 8 Lebuh Temple, T082-246688.
Boat Express boats leave from the Sin Kheng Hong Wharf, 6 km out of town (taxi RM8). Tickets are only for sale at 2 places in town: **Borneo Interland**, 63 Main Bazaar, T082-413595, and **Lim Magazine bookshop**, 19 Ban Hock Lane, T082-410076. Otherwise turn up at the ferry 30 mins before departure to get a ticket. 2 daily departures for **Sibu** via Sarakei at 0830 and 1230 (4 hrs, RM30).
Bus There are 2 local companies: blue and white **Chin Lian Long** buses serve the city and its suburbs. Major bus stops are at Jl Mosque and opposite the post office. The green and yellow **Sarawak Transport Company (STC)** buses leave from Lebuh Jawa, next to Ban Hock Wharf. **STC** buses operate on regional routes; bus 12A (RM1) airport service runs every 40 mins 0630-1915.

Long-distance buses depart from the **Regional Express Bus Terminal** on Jl Penrissen at Mile 3.5 (taxi RM10). You either have to buy tickets at the bus station itself, or from **Borneo Interland**, 63 Main Bazaar, T082-413595, closed Sun. Buses to **Sibu** (7 hrs, RM40, 0645-2200) **Bintulu** (RM60) and **Miri** (15 hrs, RM80, 0100-2100).

There are several departures daily from Kuching via Miri and Kuala Belait to **Bandar Seri Begawan** (Brunei) RM130. **Car hire** Many offices also at the airport. **Golden System Car Rental & Tours**,

58-1B, 1st floor, Block G, Pearl Commercial Centre, Jl Tun Razak, T082-333609, www.goldencr.com.my. Also offers 4WDs. Free pick-up and delivery in the Kuching area.

Taxi Taxis congregate at the taxi stand on Jl Market, or outside the big hotels; they do not use meters so agree a price before setting off. 24-hr radio taxi service T082-480000. Short distances around town should cost RM5-8.

Damai Peninsula *p665*

Bus There are shuttle buses from the **Holiday Inn** in **Kuching** (RM10 each way, 40 mins, first bus at 0730 from Kuching, last return bus at 2200) or take public bus No 2B, operated by **Petra Jaya Transport** (yellow buses with black and red stripes) to **Santubong** for RM3.30 from the market on Jl Gambier. Tour companies offer packages including transport, entry to Sarawak Cultural Village and lunch.

Taxi From **Kuching** costs RM35.

Bandar Sri Aman and around *p667*

Bus Regular connections with **Kuching**, RM15 (135 km) and **Sibu** (via Sarikei).

Skrang longhouses *p667*

Bus Buses No 14 and 19 to **Pias** and bus No 9 to **Lemanak**. Self-drive car rental (return) or minibus (8-10 people, return) from **Kuching** to **Entaban**. From these points it is necessary to charter a boat to reach the longhouses. Many of the Kuching-based tour agencies offer 1- to 2-day trips to Skrang and Lemanak river longhouses (see page 657). Unless you are already part of a small group, these tours work out cheaper because of the boat costs.

Sibu *p668*

Air Airport 25 km north of town. Regular connections with **Kuching** (RM86, 10 a day), **Bintulu** (RM78, 4 a day), **Miri** (RM126, 4 a day), **Belaga** (RM49, 1 flight only on Wed and Sat), **KK** (RM194, 3 flights a day) and **KL** (MAS, daily, RM334; **Air Asia**, RM100).

Airline offices Air Asia, Jl Kai Peng. MAS, 61 Jl Tunku Osman, T084-326166.

Boat All boats leave from the wharf; buy

tickets at the jetty. There are 2 express boats daily Sibu–**Kuching**. Sejahtera Pertama (T084-321424) boats leave at 0730. **Ekspress Bahagia** (T084-319228) leave at 1130. These boats stop off at **Sarekei**. There are regular express boats to **Kapit**, 2-3 hrs; in the rainy season they continue to **Belaga**, 5-6 hrs. If travelling from Sibu through Kapit to Belaga, take an early morning boat (first boat at 0530), which connects all the way through. The last boat departs at 1300. In the dry season passengers change onto smaller launches to get to Belaga (see below).

Bus Local buses leave from Jl Khoo Peng Loong. Long-distance buses leave from the new terminal at Jl Pahlawan (taxi RM10, or local bus No 12 or No 17). There are 3 main bus companies: **Biaramas Express**, **Borneo Highway Express** and **Suria Express** which all have routes from Sibu to **Bintulu** (hourly 0630-0100, RM20, 3-4 hrs), **Miri** (RM40, 6-7 hrs) and **Kuching**. If possible, buy tickets the day before departure from ticket offices by the jetty or from the bus station. Early morning buses to Bintulu connect with buses to **Batu Niah** (see Bintulu Bus, page 685). There are also 10 daily connections with **Kuching** (8 hrs, RM40) via Sarikei (2 hrs, RM8), 0700-2400.

Kapit *p668*

Boat All 3 wharves are close together. Regular connections with **Sibu**, 0500-1500, 2-3 hrs. Express boats to **Belaga** (RM25); in dry season large express boats cannot go upriver, but speed boats cost RM60-100 per person.

Belaga *p670*

Air Connections on Wed and Sat to **Bintulu** (RM40). The airport can be reached by boat (RM8, 30 mins). Contact **Hasbee Enterprise** (near the jetty), 4 Belaga Bazaar, T086-461240, for flights and airport transfer. **MAS**, c/o Lau Chun Kiat, Main Bazaar.

Boat/bus In the wet season, there is a daily boat from **Kapit** early in the morning, RM25-30, 5 hrs. In the dry season speedboats from Kapit cost from RM60. When the river is very low the only option is to fly or drive.

To **Tabau** and on to **Bintulu**: it is possible to hire a boat from Belaga to Kestima Kem (logging camp) near Rumah Lahanan Laseh (RM260 for 2-3 people); from there logging trucks go to Tabau, but they leave irregularly (3 hrs, dry season only). There are regular express boats from Tabau to Bintulu (RM12). Obtain permission from the Residents' Office and police station in Belaga to take this route.
Car Belaga is relatively isolated and overland links are poor. During the dry season it is possible to travel by 4WD to **Bintulu**, but it costs RM400 for 5 people and takes 5 hrs. The Bakun–Bintulu road is surfaced almost the whole way. The **Belaga Hotel** can help with a 4WD or try Peter Ho at **Soon Soon Café**, T086-461085. He has a car that leaves Belaga for Bintulu at 0800, and back to Belaga at 1500. Watch out for drunk drivers and logging trucks.

Bintulu p670
Air The airport is in the centre of town. Regular connections with **Kuching**, **Miri** and **Sibu**. Also to **Kota Kinabalu** and twice weekly to **Belaga**. MAS, Jl Masjid, T086-331554.
Boat Enquire at the wharf for times and prices. Regular connections with **Tabau**, 2½-3 hrs, last boat at 1400 (RM18). Connections with **Belaga**, via logging road, see above; much cheaper than going from Sibu.
Bus The local bus terminal is in the town centre. The long-distance **Medan Jaya** station is 10 mins by taxi (RM8). Regular connections with **Miri** (RM18), **Sarikei** (RM32), **Batu Niah** (RM10) and **Sibu** (RM16). The main bus company is **Syarikat Bas Suria**, T086-334914.

Similajau National Park p671
Boat/bus There is no regular bus service. Take a taxi, 30 mins, RM 40 Bintulu– Similajau trip, RM 60 for a return trip. Bintulu taxi station, T086-332009. Boats are available from the wharf or arrange through **Similajau Travel and Tours** in Bintulu (see Tour operators, page 682).

Niah National Park p671
From Batu Niah (near the market) to Park HQ at Pangkalan Lubang, Niah National Park by boat (RM10 per person or RM2 if more than 5 people) or 45 mins' walk.
Bus Every 2 hrs for a connection with **Miri** (RM10), 2 hrs; 6 buses a day to **Bintulu** and **Sibu** via Bintulu to **Batu Niah**.
Taxi From **Miri** to Park HQ, will only leave when there are 4 passengers. From **Bintulu** to Batu Niah (RM30). RM10 to Park HQ; however, the riverboat is far more scenic.

Miri and the Baram River p672
Air Airport information, T085-615433. Bus Nos 30 and 28 go hourly to the airport. Ask the driver to drop you off outside the airport, otherwise you will be dropped off on the highway, requiring a 10-min trek to the terminal. Regular connections on **MAS** with **Kuching** (5 daily, RM164), **Sibu**, **Marudi** (RM29), **Bario** (1 daily at 0930, usually full, book ahead), **Bintulu** (RM70), **Limbang**, **Mulu** (RM58, 2 daily) and **Labuan**. Also connections with **KK** (3 daily, RM118). Both MAS (239 Halaman Kabor, T085-414144) and **Air Asia** (T085-438022) have 3 flights daily to **KL**. There are no flights between Miri and Brunei. You need to fly first to Kuching or KK.

MAS Rural Air Service operates Twin Otters to a number of airfields across Sarawak including Miri-Bario (for the **Kelabit Highlands**), Miri-Mulu (for **Gunung Mulu**) and Sibu-Kapit-Belaga (for **Rejang River**). The service can be unreliable in bad weather.
Bus The new bus terminal at Pujuk Padang Kerbau, Jl Padang, is 4 km from town; taxi RM10. Or take bus No 33 from the tourist centre. Regular connections with **Batu Niah**, 2-3 hrs, **Bintulu**, 4 hrs, **Sibu**, 7 hrs, and **Kuching**, 13 hrs. Tickets booths by **Park Hotel**. For services to **Brunei**, see box, page 686.

Regular connections with **Kuala Baram** and the express boat to **Marudi**. Taxis to Kuala Baram, either private or shared. Express boats upriver to **Marudi** from Kuala Baram, 3 hrs. Roughly 1 boat every hour 0715-1430.
Car hire Avis, Permaisuri Rd, T085-430222; Lee Brothers, 17 River Rd, T085-410606; Mega, Sungai Krokop, T085-431885, RM120-150 daily.
Taxi Call T085-432277.

Border essentials: Sarawak–Brunei

The main border crossing is from **Kuala Baram** in Sarawak to **Kuala Belait** in Brunei. Buses leave several times daily to Kuala Belait from Miri's central bus station near the Park Hotel and Tourist Information Centre, 2 hrs, RM13, via Sungai Tujuh checkpoint, with connections to the capital, Bandar Seri Begawan. These buses are run by the Miri Belait Transport Co. From the checkpoint change buses at Kuala Belait for **Seria** (B$1, 1 hr) and on to **Bandar Seri Begawan** (B$6, 1-2 hrs). The last bus from Seria leaves at 1520 so catch a morning bus from Miri (0700, 1000) to make the connection. It takes at least 5 hrs to reach Bandar Seri Begawan. If travelling by car, take the ferry across the Belait River (10 mins); check that it is running before crossing the border.

Marudi p672

Air The airport is 5 km from town. Connections with **Miri** (RM29), **Bario** and Sibu.
Boat These leave opposite the Chinese temple. To **Kuala Baram**, 8 daily 0700-1500 (RM18); to **Tutoh**, for longboats to Long Terawan, 1 boat at 1100 (RM22 express boat or RM32 speed boat); **Long Lama**, for longboats to **Bario**, 1 boat every hour 0730-1400. From Long Terawan the journey takes up to 2 hrs (RM45 per person in group of 5). To **Kuala Baram** take Bus No 1 (RM2.50, 1st bus 0530) or a shared taxi (RM22).

Gunung Mulu National Park p673

Within the park, longboats can be chartered from Park HQ (max 10 per boat). Total costs can be more than RM100. How far these boats get upriver depends on the water level as they may have to be hauled over rapids.
Air The airstrip is just downriver from Park HQ. Currently 2 flights per day from **Miri** (20 mins), **Marudi** and **Limbang**. Flights costs only marginally more than taking the bus/boat from Miri and is infinitely faster.
Bus/taxi/boat Bus or taxi from **Miri** to **Marudi** express boat jetty near **Kuala Baram** at mouth of the Baram River (see page 685). Regular express boats from **Kuala Baram** to **Marudi**, 3 hrs (RM18) 0700-1500. One express boat per day (1100) from Marudi to **Long Terawan** on the Tutoh River (tributary of the Baram), via **Long Apoh**. In the dry season express boats cannot go upriver and stop at

Long Panai, from there longboats continue to Long Terawan (RM20). Longboats leave Long Terawan for **Mulu Park HQ**: this used to be regular and cheap; now that most people travel by air, longboats are less frequent and may need to be privately chartered. Mulu Park HQ is 1½ hrs up the Melinau River (a tributary of the Tutoh), RM45. For a group of 9-10 it's cheaper to charter a boat (RM250 one way). The first jetty on the Melinau River is **Long Pala**, where most tour companies have accommodation. Park HQ is another 15 mins upriver. Longboats returning to Long Terawan leave Park HQ at dawn, calling at jetties en route.

Bario and the Kelabit Highlands p674

Air The only access to Bario is by air on **MAS**. The airstrip is very small and flights are often cancelled due to mist. Book in advance. There is 1 flight a day on **MAS** from **Miri** at 0930. There is also 1 connection a day via **Marudi**.
Foot 7-day trek from **Marudi** to Bario, sleeping in longhouses; organize through a Miri travel agent (see page 683).

Limbang p675

Air The airport is 5 km from town and taxis ferry passengers in. Daily connections with **Miri, Mulu** and **Lawas**, weekly flights to **Labuan** and twice-weekly flights to **KK**.
Boat Regular connections with **Lawas**, early in the morning (2 hrs, RM15). There is also an early morning express departure to **Labuan**.

Regular boat connections with **Bandar Seri Begawan**, Brunei (30 mins, RM15).

Lawas *p675*
Air Connections with **Miri**, **Limbang**, **Kuching**, **Labuan** and **KK**.
Boat Regular connections to **Limbang**, 2 hrs. Daily morning boat departures for **Brunei**.
Bus Connections with **Merapok** on the Sabah border (RM5). From here there are connections to **Beaufort** in Sabah. Twice-daily connections with **KK**, 4 hrs (RM20).

❶ Directory

Kuching *p661, map p662*
Banks All major banks here. Money changers in shopping complexes give better rates for cash. ATMs are everywhere. **Embassies and consulates** Australian Honorary Consul, T082-233350; British Honorary Representative, T012-322 0011; French Honorary Consul, Telong Usan Hotel, T082-415588; Indonesian Consulate, 111 Jl Tun Haji Openg, T082-241734; New Zealand Honorary Consul, T082-482177. **Immigration** 1st floor, Bangunan Sultan Iskandar (Federal Complex) Jl Simpang Tiga, T082-245661. **Internet** There are several; RM4 per hr. **Medical services** Hospitals and clinics: Abdul Rahman Yakub, T082-440055, private hospital with good reputation; Doctor's Clinic, Main Bazaar, opposite Chinese History Museum, said to be excellent (RM20 for consultation); Normah Medical Centre, across the river on Jl Tun Datuk Patinggi Hj; Sarawak General Hospital, Jl Tan Sri Ong Kee Hui, off Jl Tun Haji Openg, T082-257555; Timberland Medical Centre, Rock Rd, T082-234991. Recommended. **Police** Tourist Police T082-241222, opposite Padang Merdeka. **Post** General Post Office, Jl Tun Haji Openg, Mon-Sat 0800-1800, Sun 1000-1300. Operates a poste restante service. **Telephone** International calls can be made from most public cardphones. Major hotels all have cardphones in their lobbies.

Sibu *p668*
Banks Standard Chartered, Jl Cross. HSBC, 17 Jl Wong Nai Siong Hock Hua, Jl Pulau. Cash can also be exchanged at good rates at goldsmiths. **Internet** PCShop, Sarawak House Complex, ground floor. Fast connection. **Police** Jl Kampong Nyabor, T084-322222. **Post** General Post Office, Jl Kampong Nyabor. **Residents' Office** T084-321963.

Kapit *p668*
Banks There are 2 banks that will accept TCs, one in the New Bazaar and the other on Jl Airport, but it's easier to change money in Sibu.

Belaga *p670*
Internet Hasbee Enterprises, 4 Belaga Bazaar (RM6 per hr), 0700-1900. Painfully slow connection. **Post** In the District Office.

Bintulu *p670*
Banks Bank Bumiputra and Bank Utama on Jl Somerville; Standard Chartered, Jl Keppel. **Post** GPO (Pos Laju) far side of the airport near the Residents' Office, 2 km from centre.

Miri and the Baram River *p672*
Banks All major banks here. **Immigration** Pajabat Imigresen, 2nd floor Tingkat 2&3, Yu Lan Plaza, T085-442118. New office in huge skyscraper at Jl Brooke/Jl Raja. For an extension to your entry stamp or visa. Up to 3 months for RM1. **Internet** Cyberworld, 1st floor Wisma Pelita Tunku (RM3 per hr); Cyber Corner, Wisma Pelita Tunku (RM3 per hr); Planet Café, Bintang Plaza (RM4 per hr). **Medical services** Hospital, opposite Ferry Point, T085-420033. **Police** Police Station, Jl Kingsway, T085-432533. **Post** General Post Office, just off Jl Gartak. **Telephone** Telecom Office, Jl Gartak, daily 0730-2200.

Marudi *p672*
Banks There are 2 local banks with foreign exchange facilities. **Police** Police station, Airport Rd. **Post** Post Office, Airport Rd.

Sabah

Sabah may not have the colourful history of neighbouring Sarawak, but there is a great deal to entice the visitor. It is the second largest Malaysian state after Sarawak, covering 72,500 sq km, making it about the size of Ireland. Occupying the northeast corner of Borneo, it is shaped like a dog's head, the jaws reaching out in the Sulu and Celebes seas, and the back of the head facing onto the South China Sea.

The highlights of Sabah are natural and cultural, from caves, reefs, forests and mountains to tribal peoples. The Gunung Kinabalu National Park is named after Sabah's (and Malaysia's) highest peak and is one of the state's most visited destinations. Also popular is the Sepilok Orang-Utan Sanctuary outside Sandakan. Marine sights include the Turtle Islands National Park and Sipadan Island, one of Asia's finest dive sites. While Sabah's indigenous tribes were not cherished as they were in Sarawak by the White Rajahs, areas around towns such as Kudat, Tenom, Keningau and Kota Belud still provide memorable insights into the peoples of the region. ▶▶ For listings, see pages 702-714.

Kota Kinabalu ●🚉🚗🚻⊗☉▲🏖🚌🍴 ▶▶ pp702-714. Colour map 9, A4/5.

KK is most people's introduction to Sabah for the simple reason that it is the only town with extensive air links to other parts of the country. KK is a modern state capital with little dating back more than 50 years. Highlights include the State Museum and the town's markets. The city is strung out along the coast, with jungle-clad hills as a backdrop. Two-thirds of the town is built on land reclaimed from the shallow Gaya Bay and at spring tides it is possible to walk across to Gaya Island. Jalan Pantai, or Beach Road, is now in the centre of town.

Ins and outs

Getting there KK's airport is 6 km south of town, T088-238555. There is a bus stop five minutes' walk from the airport, RM1 to the city centre. Taxis cost around RM13.50; buy coupons in from the booths outside the arrivals hall. There is a limited railway service with trains to Beaufort and Tenom and an extensive network of bus, minibus and taxi links to destinations in Sabah. Ferries arrive throughout the day from Labuan. Getting from Brunei overland takes around five hours plus two ferry crossings at Temburong and Terusan (in Brunei), or a 45-minute flight. ▶▶ *See Transport, page 711.*

Getting around City buses and minibuses provide a service around town and to nearby destinations. Red taxis are unmetered, dark blue taxis metered. There are lots of car hire firms.

Best time to visit Sabah's equatorial climate means that temperatures rarely exceed 32°C or fall below 21°C, making it fairly pleasant all year. October to March is the rainy season, which spoils plans for the beach and makes trekking unpleasant and slippery. For spotting turtles, your best chance is between May and September. **Sabah Fest**, a big carnival of dancing, music and cow races, takes place in May, when the Kadazun/Dusun celebrate their harvest festival. ▶▶ *See Festivals and events, page 585.*

Tourist information Sabah Tourism Board ⓘ *51 Jl Gaya, T088-212121, www.sabah tourism.com, Mon-Fri 0800-1700, Sat 0800-1400,* is well stocked with leaflets and information and has helpful staff. Also try **Tourism Malaysia** ⓘ *ground floor, Uni Asia Building, 1 Jl Sagunting, T088-211732, mtpbki@tourism.gov.my.* A great tourist website for Sabah is www.sabahtravelguide.com. ▶▶ *See Activities and tours, page 709.*

Parks offices All accommodation and trekking at **Mount Kinabalu** and **Poring Hot Springs** is organized through the private company, Sutera Sanctuary Lodges ⓘ *ground floor, Wisma Sabah, KK, T088-243629, www.suterasanctuarylodges.com, Mon-Fri 0900-1830, Sat 0900-1630, Sun 0900-1500.* It's best to book before you go.

For **Danum Valley** and **Maliau Basin**, contact Yayasan Sabah Group (Sabah Foundation) ⓘ *T088-326300, www.borneo forestheritage.org.my.* Borneo Nature Tours ⓘ *Block D, Lot 10, ground floor, Sadong Jaya Complex, T088-267637, www.brl.com.my,* is connected to the Sabah Foundation and deals with the majority of tourism-related activity in Danum Valley and Maliau Basin and are perhaps the easiest first point of contact. You can also contact Sabah Parks ⓘ *Lot 3, Block K, Sinsuran Complex, T088-211881, www.sabahparks.org.my.*

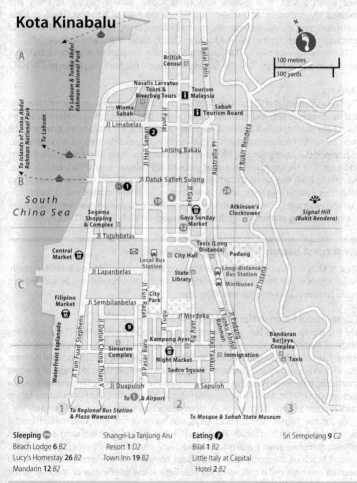

Kota Kinabalu

Sleeping 🛏
Beach Lodge **6** *B2*
Lucy's Homestay **26** *B2*
Mandarin **12** *B2*

Shangri-La Tanjung Aru
Resort **1** *D2*
Town Inn **19** *B2*

Eating 🍴
Bilal **1** *B2*
Little Italy at Capital
Hotel **2** *B2*

Sri Sempelang **9** *C2*

Sights

Only three buildings remain of the old town after it was obliterated by bombs in the Second World War: the old **General Post Office** on Jalan Gaya, **Atkinson's Clocktower** (built in 1905 and named after Jesselton's first district officer) and the old red-roofed **Lands and Surveys building**. The renovated post office now houses the **Sabah Tourism Board**. For a good view of the town and offshore islands, walk to the top of **Signal Hill**, just east of the centre.

Perched on a small hill overlooking the mosque, the purpose-built **Sabah State Museum** ① *Jl Mat Salleh/Bukit Istana Lama, www.mzm.sabah.gov.my, Sat-Thu 0900-1700, RM5, minibuses stop near Wisma Kewangan on the KK–Tanjung Aru road and near Queen Elizabeth Hospital on the KK–Penampang road*, is designed like a Rungus longhouse and well worth a visit. It is divided into ethnography, natural history, ceramics and archaeology, including an excellent display on the uses of bamboo. There is tribal metalwork, pottery, musical instruments and basketry, as well as a collection of skulls and artefacts from Sabah tribes like the Kadazan/Dusun, Bajau, Murut and Rungus.

The nearest decent beach is **Tanjung Aru**, 5 km south. It is popular at weekends and has a good open-air food court. Take the Tanjung Aru (beach) bus from the station by City Hall.

Markets

The **Gaya street market** ① *Sun from 0800*, sells a vast range of goods from jungle produce and handicrafts to pots and pans. The market almost opposite the main minibus station on Jalan Tun Fuad Stephens is known as the **Filipino market** (Pasar Kraftangan) as most of the stalls are run by Filipino immigrants. Filipino and local handicrafts are sold in the hundreds of cramped stalls along winding alleyways strung with low-slung curtains of shells, baskets and bags. The Filipino market is a good place to buy cultured pearls (RM5 each) and has everything from fake gems to camagong-wood salad bowls and traditional Indonesian medicines. Further into town, on the waterfront, is the **central market** selling mainly fish, fruit and vegetables. The daily fishing catch is unloaded on the wharf near the market. There is a lively **evening market** selling cheap T-shirts and jewellery in front of the City Park.

West coast islands ⬛🔵🔴🔺🔵🔵 ⟫ pp702-714.

West of KK is the Tunku Abdul Rahman Park, a reef and coral marine park. Further south, Pulau Tiga National Park is a forest reserve where the pied hornbill can be spotted and Pulau Labuan is a tax-free haven off the coast.

Tunku Abdul Rahman National Park → Colour map 9, A4.

The five islands in Gaya Bay, which make up Tunku Abdul Rahman Park (TAR), lie 3-8 km offshore. Named after Malaysia's first prime minister, the islands are part of the Crocker Range formation, but as sea levels rose after the last ice age, they became isolated from the massif. Sandy beaches and coral reefs fringe all the islands in the park; some of the best snorkelling is between Pulau Gaya and Pulau Sapi. The coral reefs are teeming with exotica such as butterfly fish, Moorish idols, parrot fish, bat fish, razor fish, lion fish and stone fish, in stark contrast to areas that have been depth-charged by Gaya's dynamite fishermen.

By far the largest island, **Pulau Gaya**, has some of the only undisturbed coastal dipterocarp forest left in Sabah. There are 20 km of marked trails including a plank walk across a mangrove swamp and many beautiful little secluded bays. Police Bay is a popular, shaded beach on the north shore. **Pulau Sapi**, popular with weekenders, also has good beaches and trails and is connected to Pulau Gaya at low tide by a sandbar. Closer to the mainland, **Pulau Mamutik** is the smallest island but has a well-preserved reef off the northeast tip. **Pulau Manukan** is probably the best island, but is heavily frequented by day trippers. It has most of the accommodation and facilities and a particularly good beach. The best reefs are off **Pulau Sulug**, which is further away and less developed, making it popular with divers.

Ins and outs The islands can be visited year round. Boats leave from KK's main ferry terminal, 10 minutes' walk north of the town. Park HQ is on Pulau Manukan; there are ranger stations on Gaya, Sapi and Mamutik. Accommodation can be booked through **Sutera Sanctuary Lodges**, see page 689. Camping is possible on Sapi and Mamutik.

Pulau Tiga National Park → *Colour map 9, A4.*
This park is 48 km south of KK. Declared a forest reserve in 1933, the 15,864-ha park is made up of three islands: Pulau Tiga, Kalampunian Damit and Kalampunian Besar. **Pulau Tiga** achieved notoriety as the location for the reality TV series *Survivor*, chosen for its unspoilt natural landscape. Formed by mud volcanoes, the bubbling mud pools across the island are an interesting bathing experience. The pristine dipterocarp forests contain species not found on other west coast islands, such as a poisonous amphibious sea snake (*Laticauda colubrina*). Rare birds such as the pied hornbill and the megapode are found here, as well as flying foxes and monitor lizards. There is excellent coral growth mid-channel and plenty of smaller marine life and fish making this a colourful spot for diving. The small offshore house reef is good, with lots of anemones, clown fish plus the occasional turtle.

Ins and outs Boats from Kuala Penyu take 30 minutes and leave at 1000 and 1500 (from KK take a bus to Beaufort then minibus to Kuala Penyu, 144 km, two hours). Alternatively charter a boat direct from KK; contact **Sipadan Dive Centre** ① *T088-240584, www.pulau-tiga.com*, who run the island's resort, or **Sabah Parks Office**. Speedboats cost RM350 for 10 people. Park HQ is on the south side of Tiga. The best time to visit is February-April, when the seas are calmer.

Pulau Labuan → *Colour map 9, A4.*
Eight kilometres off the coast of Sabah, Labuan was originally part of the Sultanate of Brunei and most travellers use it as a stopover between the two. With its deep-water harbour, it was of strategic importance for the British, who used the previously uninhabited island as a base for operations against piracy. The Sultan of Brunei ceded Labuan to Britain in 1846 under the governance of Rajah James Brooke, and two years later it became a Crown Colony. The island was also used as a penal colony and played a major role during the Second World War. In 1984 Labuan was declared a tax-free haven – or 'International offshore financial centre' – and hence this small tropical island with just 80,000-odd inhabitants has a plethora of banks and investment companies. For the casual visitor – rather than someone wanting to salt away their million – it offers the attraction of being clean and compact, with good hotels, lots of duty-free shopping, a golf course, sport fishing and diving.

Ins and outs The airport is 5 km from town and has connections with KK, Miri, Kuching and KL (MAS and **Air Asia** have daily flights to/from KL). There are regular speedboats from KK and several daily boat connections with Lawas and Limbang (Sarawak) and Sipitang. There's also a regular ferry service with Brunei. Once on the island, there is a reasonable island bus network, a few car hire firms and a small number of taxis. **Tourist Information Office** ① *Lot 4260, Jl Dewan/Jl Berjaya, T087-423445*. See also www.labuantourism.com.my.

Rafflesia: the world's largest flower

The rafflesia (*Rafflesia arnoldi*), named after Stamford Raffles, the founder of modern Singapore, is the largest flower in the world. The Swedish naturalist Eric Mjoberg wrote in 1930 on seeing the flower: "The whole phenomenon seems so amazing, so unfamiliar, so fantastic, that we are tempted to explain: such flowers cannot be real!"

Stamford Raffles, who discovered the flower for Western science 100 years earlier during his first sojourn at Bengkulu on the west coast of Sumatra, noted that it was "a full yard across, weighs 15 pounds, and contains in the nectary no less than eight pints [of nectar]...". The problem is that the rafflesia does not flower for very long – only for a couple of weeks, usually between August and December. At other times of the year there is usually nothing to see. The plant is in fact parasitic, so appropriately its scent is more akin to rotting meat than any perfume. Its natural habitat is moist, shaded areas.

South of Kota Kinabalu ☺❶❷❸❹ ▶▶ pp702-714.

Travelling south from KK, the route winds its way up across the Crocker Range and over the Sinsuran Pass at 1649 m. There are dramatic views down over Kota Kinabalu and the islands, and glimpses of Mount Kinabalu to the northeast. Scattered farming communities grow hill rice, pineapples, bananas, mushrooms and other vegetables that are sold at roadside stalls. After descending from the hills the road enters the sprawling flood plain of Tambunan, which is a magnificent patchwork of greens in season. Continuing south the road passes through the logging town of Keningau and on to Tenom, the last stop on Borneo's only commercial railway. The train snakes its way down the west coast from KK and inland through the beautiful Padas Gorge. The Padas River is the best place to go whitewater rafting in Sabah. Few towns are worth staying in for long on this route but it is a scenic journey.

Rafflesia Forest Reserve → Colour map 9, A5.
The reserve covers an area of 356 ha of Tambunan district that has been set aside to conserve this remarkable flower (see box above). The **information centre** ① *on the roadside, 59 km from KK, T087-774691, Mon-Fri 0845-1245 and 1400-1700, Sat and Sun 0800-1700*, has a comprehensive and attractive display on the rafflesia and its habitat and information on flowers in bloom. If trail maps are temporarily unavailable, ask the ranger to point out the sites where blooms can be seen on the large relief model of the forest reserve at the back of the information centre. The blooming period of the flower is very short so, to avoid disappointment, it's worth phoning the centre first.

Tambunan → Colour map 9, A5. Population: 28,000.
Tambunan (Valley of the Bamboo), so-called as there are at least 12 varieties of bamboo to be found here, is a small, agricultural town about 80 km from KK. Set at an altitude of 650-900 m, it enjoys a spring-like climate for much of the year. The area is largely Kadazan/Dusun, Sabah's largest ethnic group, and it explodes into life each May during the harvest festival when copious quantities of *lihing*, the famed local rice wine, are consumed and *Bobolians* (high priestesses) still conduct various rituals. There is a *lihing* brewery inside the **Tambunan Village Resort Centre** (see Sleeping, page 703) where you can see it being made.

Tenom → *Colour map 9, A4. Population 46,000.*

Situated on the banks of the Sungei Lapas, Tenom is a hilly inland town, with a predominantly Chinese population. It was the administrative centre under the Chartered Company in the early 1900s, but most of the modern town was built during the Japanese occupation in the Second World War. It is in the heart of Murut country, but don't expect to see longhouses and Murut in traditional costume – many now live in modernized bamboo homes. The **Murut Cultural Centre** ① *10 km out of town*, displays basketry, cloth and has an example of the famous *lansaran* dancing trampoline; a wooden platform sprung with bamboo which can support 10 Murut doing a jig. There is also a trampoline at the village of **Kembong**, 25 km south of Tenom.

Tenom is the final stop on the **Sabah State Railway (SSR)**, www.sabah.gov.my/railway, (formerly the **North Borneo Railway**), which runs from Tanjung Aru near KK and dates back to 1905. The most spectacular part of the 134-km journey is from Tenom to Beaufort.

Beaufort → *Colour map 9, A4.*

The unexciting but quaint town of Beaufort has riverside houses built on stilts to escape the constant flooding of the Padas River. It is a stop on the Sabah State railway, but most visitors use it as a base for whitewater rafting.

Sipitang and towards the border → *Colour map 9, A4.*

Located on the coast, Sipitang is a sleepy town with little to offer the traveller apart from a supermarket and a few hotels (see page 704). Sipitang is south of Beaufort and the closest town to the Sarawak border. It is possible to take minibuses from Beaufort to Sipitang and on to Sindumin, where you can connect with buses bound for Lawas in Sarawak by walking across the border to Merapok. There is an immigration checkpoint here and month-long permits are given for visitors to Sarawak.

North of Kota Kinabalu ●❶❸❸❺❻ » *pp702-714.*

From KK, the road heads north to the sleepy Bajau town of Kota Belud, which wakes up on Sunday for its colourful *tamu* (market). Near the northernmost tip of the state is Kudat, the former state capital. The region north of KK is more interesting with Gunung Kinabalu always in sight. From Kota Belud, the mountain looks completely different. It is possible to see its tail, sweeping away to the east, and its western flanks, which rise out of the rolling coastal lowlands.

Kota Belud → *Colour map 9, A5.*

This busy little town is in a beautiful location, nestling in the foothills of Mount Kinabalu on the banks of the Tempasuk River, but is of little interest to tourists except for its market. The area is famous for its Bajau horsemen who wear jewelled costumes, carry spears and ride bareback on ceremonial occasions.

The town bursts into life each Sunday when Sabah's largest *tamu* (market) takes place behind the mosque, starting at 0600. A mix of people – Bajau, Kadazan/Dusun, Rungus, Chinese, Indian and Malay – come to sell their goods and it is a social occasion as much as a market. Aside from the wide variety of food and fresh produce on sale, there is a weekly water buffalo auction at the entrance. Visitors are strongly recommended to get there early, but don't expect to find souvenirs at these markets. The *tamu besar* (big market) held in November has cultural performances and handicrafts on sale.

Kudat → Colour map 9, A5.

The town of Kudat is situated on an inlet of Marudu Bay on the northern tip of Sabah, 160 km from KK. The local people here are the Rungus, members of the Kadazan tribe. Rungus have clung to their traditions more than other Sabahan tribes and some still live in longhouses, dotted around the peninsula. Kudat became the first administrative capital of Sabah in 1881 when it was no more than a handful of atap houses built out into the sea on stilts, surrounded by coconut groves. Today it is a busy town dominated by Chinese and Filipino traders (legal and illegal) and prostitutes. Seafood is also a staple element in the diet and fishing is an important industry. The market is on Mondays.

Beaches There are some beautiful unspoilt white sand beaches north of town; the best known is **Bak-Bak**, 11 km north of Kudat, signposted off the Kota Belud-Kudat road. This beach, however, can get crowded at weekends. To get there take a minibus or a taxi.

Sikuati, 23 km west of Kudat on the northwest side of the Kudat Peninsula, has a good beach. Every Sunday (0800) the Rungus come to the market in this village. Local handicrafts are sold. You can get there by minibus.

Longhouses The **Longhouse Experience** allows visitors to observe and take part in the activities. Rungu longhouses are built in a distinctive style with outward-leaning walls. There are two Baranggaxo longhouses with 10 units. During the day, the longhouse corridor is busy with women at work stringing elaborate beadworks and weaving baskets and traditional cloth. Longhouse meals are homegrown; fish and seafood come from nearby fishing villages, drinks are young coconuts and local rice wine. Evening festivities consist of the playing of gongs with dancers dressed in traditional costume. See box, page 669, for advice on visiting longhouses; for details, contact **Sabah Tourism**, T088-212121, www.sabahtourism.com.

Gunung Kinabalu National Park ◐❶❷❸❹ ⤖ pp702-714. Colour map 9, A5.

Gunung Kinabalu is the pride of Sabah, the focal point of the national park and probably the most magnificent sight in Borneo. At 4101 m, it is the highest mountain Southeast Asia and the park was declared a World Heritage Site by UNESCO in 2000 – a first for Malaysia. Although Gunung Kinabalu has foothills, its dramatic rockfaces, with cloud swirling around them, loom starkly out of the jungle. The view from the top is unsurpassed and on a clear day you can see the shadow of the mountain in the South China Sea, more than 50 km away. Even if you're not planning on climbing Gunung Kinabalu itself, it's well worth spending a few days exploring the park, one of the most biodiverse areas in Borneo.

Ins and outs

Getting there The nearest town is Ranau, 19 km south of the park. Buses and minibuses to Sandakan and Ranau (two hours) will drop you at the turn-off to the park, about 100 m from Park HQ. A fixed-price taxi from the long-distance bus station in KK costs RM60.

Park HQ The park is run by **Sutera Sanctuary Lodges** ⓘ *Wisma Sabah, KK, T088-243629, www.suterasanctuarylodges.com, Mon-Fri 0900-1830, Sat 0900-1630, Sun 0900-1500*. All accommodation and restaurants are within 15 minutes' walk of the main compound. There is a shop selling books, snacks and basic equipment next to Park HQ. Films are shown in the mini-theatre, while naturalists give escorted trail walks (check times at reception). The museum has displays on local flora and fauna, such as beetles and foot-long stick insects.

Permits and guides It costs RM100 per person to climb Gunung Kinabalu; a RM15 entry fee must be paid on arrival and compulsory insurance costs RM7. Hiring a guide is mandatory: RM70 for the main trail; porters costs RM60. Guides and porters should be reserved in advance. There is a briefing at Park HQ every evening. On the morning of your climb, go to Park HQ and a guide will be assigned to you. An organized tour costs around RM500 per person, however it's possible to do the trek independently for as little as RM250 each, if in a group. Most people stay at Park HQ the night before their climb. If staying elsewhere, be sure to arrive at Park HQ before 0900 to be sure of finding a guide. A colour pamphlet, *Mount Kinabalu/A Guide to the Summit Trail* describes the park's wildlife and the trail itself.

There is a daily guided trail walk at 1100 from the park reception. This is a gentle walk with a knowledgeable guide, although the group tends to be large. Most treks are well used and are easy walks, but the **Liwagu Trail** is a good three- to four-hour trek up to where it joins the summit trail and is very steep and slippery in places. For enthusiasts interested in alternative routes to the summit, John Briggs's *Mountains of Malaysia* provides a detailed guide to the climb.

Equipment A thick jacket is recommended, or at the very least a light waterproof to beat the wind chill on the summit. If it's raining, carry a dry sweater and socks in your backpack and change just before you get to the peak – the damp chill is worse than the cold while waiting for the sun to rise. Walking boots are recommended, but many people climb the mountain in trainers. Essential items include a hat, torch, toilet paper, water bottle, plasters, headache pills and suntan lotion. Sleeping bags are provided free of charge in the **Laban Rata Resthouse**. The resthouse has hot water showers. Some rooms are heated, cheaper ones leave you to freeze.

You can hire jackets from Laban Rata but book ahead. There are small shops at Park HQ and Laban Rata that sell gloves, hats, raincoats, torches and food for the climb (cheaper if you stock up in KK). Lockers are available, RM1 per item, at Park HQ.

Best time to visit The average rainfall is 400 cm a year, with an average temperature of 20°C at Park HQ but at Panar Laban it can drop below freezing at night. With the wind chill factor on the summit, it feels very cold. The best time to climb Gunung Kinabalu is in the dry season (March and April) when the views are clearest. The worst time is usually November to December during the monsoon, although wet periods can occur at any time of year. Avoid weekends, school and public holidays if possible.

Climbing Gunung Kinabalu

The climb to the summit requires no special skills, however it should not be undertaken lightly. It can be extremely cold on the top and altitude sickness is a problem. Changes in the weather can be sudden and dramatic and people have perished. Some points of the trail are steep and require adequate footware. Keep to the trails and stick with your group.

A minibus takes groups from Park HQ to the power station at 1829 m where the trail starts (RM5 per person). The climb to the summit and back should take two days: four to six hours from Park HQ at 1585 m to the Panar Laban Huts at 3550 m (including the well-equipped **Laban Rata Resthouse**) on the first day. It is three hours to the summit for dawn on the second day, returning to the Panar Laban for breakfast before descending to Park HQ for around 1200. Most climbers reach Panar Laban (or the other huts) in the early afternoon in order to rest up before a 0300 start the next morning to reach the summit by sunrise.

Much of the track is made up of rough, uneven steps, which can feel unrelenting in places. There are several shelters along the way with toilets and rest stops. The second part of the trail – 3 km long – is more demanding technically, but the trail is well laid out with resting points every 500 m; take it slowly as altitude sickness can kick in towards the summit. Ladders, handrails and ropes are provided for the steeper parts (essential in the wet, as the granite slabs can be very slippery). The final 1 km has no hand rails or ropes but is less steep. The first two hours after dawn are the most likely to be cloud free, affording truly magnificent views out over the plains and the South China Sea.

Mesilau Nature Resort

This rainforest resort nestles at the foot of Mount Kinabalu at 2000 m. The main attractions are the cool climate and the superb views. It is possible to scale the peaks of the mountain using the resort as a base, providing an alternative route to Low's Peak. Alternatively, there are a number of walks to be made around the reserve in this secluded location.

Poring Hot Springs → Colour map 9, A5.

ⓘ *Minibuses leave Park HQ at 0900, 1300, 1600; alternatively, flag down a bus/minibus to Ranau on the main and take a taxi from there to Poring. If you've paid the entrance fee to the national park keep your ticket for entrance to the springs. There is an information centre and restaurant. Avoid weekends and public holidays as it gets very busy.*

Poring lies 43 km from Gunung Kinabalu Park HQ and is part of the national park. The **hot sulphur baths** ⓘ *RM15 per hr, sulphur bath and jacuzzi, RM20 per hr*, were installed during the Japanese occupation of the Second World War for the jungle-weary Japanese troops. There are individual concrete pools that can fit two people, with taps for hot- and cold-spring mineral water. However, many visitors complain that the water is lukewarm. Set in a beautiful garden of hibiscus and other tropical flowers, trees and thousands of butterflies, the springs are a fantastic antidote to tiredness after a tough climb up Gunung Kinabalu.

The **jungle canopy walk** ⓘ *daily 0900-1600, RM5*, is a rope walkway 35 m above the ground, which provides a monkey's-eye view of the jungle. The **Kipungit Falls** are only about 10 minutes' walk; the **Langanan Waterfall** trail takes 90 minutes one way, is uphill, but worth it. There is another hard, 90-minute trail to **Bat Cave** (inhabited by vast numbers of bats). The **Butterfly Farm** ⓘ *Tue-Sun 0900-1600, RM5*, is very educational.

Ranau → Colour map 9, A5.

The small town of Ranau is 20 km from the park, on a plateau surrounding the Kinabalu massif – one of the richest farming areas in Sabah. It's a fairly unremarkable place, but has good transport connections with KK and Sandakan, and a couple of accommodation options in case you get stuck.

Sandakan and the east coast ◯◯▲◯◯◯ ›› pp702-714.

From Ranau it is possible to reach Sandakan by road. Several key sights are within reach easy reach: the Turtle Islands National Park, 40 km north in the Sulu Sea, Sepilok Orang-Utan Rehabilitation Centre and the Kinabatangan Basin, to the southeast. From Sandakan, the route continues south to the wilds the Danum Valley and on to Semporna, the jumping off point for Pulau Sipadan.

Sandakan → Colour map 9, A6.

Sandakan is at the neck of a bay on the northeast coast of Sabah and looks out to the Sulu Sea. It is a post-war town, much of it rebuilt on reclaimed land, and is Malaysia's biggest fishing port. Sandakan is often dubbed 'mini Hong Kong' because of its Cantonese influence; its occupants are well-heeled and the town sustains many prosperous businesses, despite being rather scruffy as a whole. It is now also home to a large Filipino community, mostly traders from Mindanao and the Sulu Islands. Manila still officially claims Sabah in its entirety – Sandakan is only 28 km from Philippines' territorial waters.

In the centre of town is the riotous **daily fish market**, which is the biggest and best in Sabah. The best time to visit is at 0600 when the boats unload their catch. The **Central Market** along the waterfront sells fruit, vegetables, sarongs, seashells, spices and sticky rice cakes. The **Sandakan Heritage Trail** is a 90-minute loop that takes in the town's historical highlights including a good lookout point. The tourist office has trail maps.

Ins and outs The airport is 10 km north of town and has daily connections with KK and other main towns in Sabah. Minibuses run from the airport to the station at the southern end of Jalan Pelabuhan. The long-distance bus terminal is 5 km to the west of town and has connections with KK, Tawau, Ranau, Lahad Datu and Semporna. Sandakan is not a large town and it is easy enough to explore the central area on foot. ▸▸ *See Transport, page 713.*

The privately run **Tourist Information Centre** ① *by the municipal council building opposite Lebuh Empat, T089-22975, Mon-Fri 0800-1230 and 1330-1630, Sat 0800-1230*, offers enthusiastic and impartial advice.

Sandakan Bay

Turtle Islands National Park

Located 40 km north of Sandakan, the Turtle Islands are at the south entrance to Labuk Bay. The park is separated from the Philippine island of Bakkungan Kecil by a narrow stretch of water. These eight tiny islands in the Sulu Sea are among the most important turtle-breeding spots in Asia. The turtle sanctuary is made up of three islands (**Pulau Selingan**, **Pulau Bakkungan Kecil** and **Pulau Gulisan**) and encompasses the surrounding coral reefs, covering 1700 ha. On Pulau Bakkungan Kecil there is a small mud volcano.

The islands are famous for their green turtles (*Chelonia mydas*), which make up 80% of the turtles in the park, and hawksbill turtles (*Eretmochelys imbricata*), known as *sisik*. Most green turtles lay their eggs on Pulau Selingan. Hawksbills prefer to nest on Pulau Gulisan. Both species come ashore, year-round, to lay their eggs, although the peak season is July to October. The turtles should be watched from a distance to avoid upsetting the nesting process. There are hatcheries on all three islands and most nights a batch is released into the sea. They are released at different points on the island to protect them from predators: only about 1% survive.

Borneo's endangered forests

Borneo's virgin forests are some of the most biodiverse habitats on Earth, with 15,000 species of flowering plants, 3000 species of tree, 286 species of terrestrial mammals, 420 species of bird and an undocumented number of invertebrates.

As late as the 19th century up to 95% of Borneo was forested, but due to rapacious logging, the jungle is fast disappearing. Since the mid-1980s there has been a mounting international campaign against deforestation as vast areas of jungle have been cleared to make way for large-scale palm oil plantations. A pillar of Malaysia's economy, palm oil is now found in 10% of products on supermarket shelves across the world, including bread, chocolate, crisps and lipstick. The plantations cause irreparable damage to the land as rainforest is cleared and burned and peatlands are drained. This not only threatens wildlife but has caused the displacement of many indigenous people. The government recognizes that the environment is a hot political issue and is climbing aboard the bandwagon. Tourism is now Malaysia's third biggest source of income and promoting itself as an eco-destination has become a top priority.

Ins and outs The driest months and the calmest seas are March-July. The egg-laying season is July-October. Visitors can stay overnight on Pulau Selingan. The number of visitors is restricted to 50 per night. The park is managed by **Sabah Parks** ① *9th floor, Wisma Khoo, Lebuh Tiga, T089-273453, park entry RM10*. Accommodation must be booked through **Crystal Quest** in Sandakan (see page 710). This is booked up weeks, sometimes months, in advance.

Sepilok Orang-Utan Sanctuary and Rehabilitation Centre → *Colour map 9, A6.*

Sepilok, a reserve of 43 sq km of lowland primary rainforest and mangrove, was set up in 1964 to protect the orang-utan (*Pongo pygmaeus*) from extinction. It is the first and largest of only four orang-utan sanctuaries in the world, attracting 40,000 visitors a year. Logging has seriously threatened Sabah's population of wild orang-utan, as has their capture for zoos and as pets. The orang-utan lives on the islands of Borneo and Sumatra and there are estimated to be as few as 10,000 in the wild.

The sanctuary trains orphaned or captured orang-utans to fend for themselves before being released back into the wild. After an initial period of quarantine at Sepilok, newly arrived orang-utans are taught survival skills by rangers. As they acclimatize, they are moved deeper into the forest and encouraged to forage for themselves. Before release they are given microchip collars so they can be tracked over a distance of up to 150 km. A popular time to see the orang-utans is at feeding times, when they swing along ropes to the platforms.

The **Mangrove Forest Trail** takes two to three hours one way and passes pristine lowland rainforest, a boardwalk into a mangrove forest, water holes and a wildlife track. The **Information Centre**, next to the Park HQ, runs a nature education exhibition with replicas of jungle mammals and videos. On the road in to Sepilok, the **Rainforest Interpretation Centre** ① *Mon-Thu 0815-1215, 1400-1600, Fri 0815-1135, 1400-1600, Sat 0815-1215, free*, has information on tropical rainforests and the need for conservation.

Ins and outs There are several buses a day from Sandakan. The park is open 0900-1630, RM30. If you want to do the walks, arrive at the centre in the morning so you can get a permit. The pass is valid all day so you can see both feeds if you arrive early. Feeding times: Platform A, 1000 and 1500. The morning feed is packed with tour groups; the afternoon feed is quieter.

Birds' nest soup

The Chinese have had a taste for birds' nests for over 1000 years, and the business of collecting them is a lucrative and hazardous profession. Considered a delicacy for their aphrodisiac properties, nests sell for up to US$500 per kg, making them one of the most expensive foods in the world.

The nests are built by the male swiftlets using a glutinous substance produced by the salivary glands, which is regurgitated in long threads; the saliva sets like cement producing a rounded cup that sticks to the cave wall. Once collected, the nests are soaked in water for about three hours and, when softened, feathers and dirt are laboriously removed with tweezers.

There are two annual harvesting periods (February-April and July-September). Anyone caught collecting out of season faces a fine of RM20,000 or a year in jail. Collecting nests from hundreds of feet above the ground is dangerous business and each year there are fatal accidents. Before each harvesting period a chicken or goat is sacrificed to appease the cave spirit.

Gomantong Caves → *Colour map 9, A6.*

ⓘ *Daily 0800-1600, RM30. Park HQ has an information centre and café. Good walking shoes are essential, and a torch. The bats can be seen exiting from the caves 1800-1830; ask permission from Gomantong Wildlife Department, T011-817529, at the information centre.*
The Gomantong Caves are 32 km south of Sandakan Bay, between the road to Sukau and the Kinabatangan River, or 110 km overland on the Sandakan-Sukau road. Located in the 3924 ha Gomantong Forest Reserve, they form the largest cave system in Sabah.

Several chambers can be visited. The main cave, with a ceiling soaring up to 90 m, is a five-minute walk from the registration centre and picnic area. Between 200,000 and 300,000 bats of two different species are thought to live in the caves; at sunset they swarm out to feed. There are also an estimated one million swiftlets that swarm into the cave to roost at sunset; their nests are collected for birds' nest soup (see box, above). Birdlife around the caves is rich, with crested serpent eagles, kingfishers, Asian fairy bluebirds and leafbirds often sighted. Large groups of richly coloured butterflies are also often seen drinking from pools along the track leading from the forest into the caves.

Sungai Kinabatangan and Sukau → *Colour map 9, A6.*

ⓘ *Due to the lack of public transport to the village of Sukau, the only way to visit is with a tour; all tours must be booked in KK, page 709, or Sandakan, page 710.*
At 560 km, this river is Sabah's longest. Much of the lower basin is gazetted under the **Kinabatangan Wildlife Sanctuary** and meanders through a flood plain, creating numerous oxbow lakes and an ideal environment for some of Borneo's best wildlife. The area has remained relatively unscathed by logging because much of the land is permanently waterlogged and the forest contains only a small number of commercially valuable trees.

A boat ride can offer spectacular sightings of birds and mammals, including orang-utans and proboscis monkeys. The latter are best viewed in the late afternoon, when they converge on treetops by the river banks. Sumatran rhinoceros have also been spotted as well as herds of wild elephant, crocodiles, tree snakes, civet cats, and several other types of monkey. The birdlife is particularly good and includes several species of hornbill. At night you can get close to the sleeping birds and they look very colourful. The best way to experience the area is to stay in one of the lodges by the river. ▸▸ *See Sleeping, page 705.*

Tabin Wildlife Reserve → *Colour map 9, A6.*

ⓘ *Contact via Intra Travel Service, Office No 5, Airport Terminal 2, Old Airport Rd, KK, T088-261558, www.tabinwildlife.com.my.*

Tabin is one of Sabah's largest and most important wildlife reserves and one of the last refuges of the critically endangered Sumatran rhino. Since the opening of **Tabin Jungle Resort**, one hour's drive from Lahad Datu, it's also one of the easiest and most comfortable to visit. The reserve is close to a large mud-volcano – favoured as a mineral lick by mammals. There are several huge bubbling mud volcanoes an easy trek from the resort.

Since the reserve consists of large areas of previously logged and now recovering forest and also due to its considerable size, covering 120,500 ha, it's particularly good for observing Bornean mammals. Pygmy elephants, wild pigs, civets and macaques are often seen on evening safaris close to palm oil plantations; otters make their homes in the river below the jungle resort; and by staking out the mud volcano for a night even a close encounter is possible with a sun bear.

Danum Valley Conservation Area → *Colour map 9, A6.*

ⓘ *Tourists are allowed to visit only through the Borneo Rainforest Lodge, see page 705.*

Danum Valley's 438 sq km of virgin jungle is the largest expanse of undisturbed lowland dipterocarp forest in Sabah. Due to its size and remoteness, Danum Valley is home to some of Sabah's rarest animals and plants. Sumatran rhinoceros have been recorded, as have elephant, clouded leopards, orang-utans, proboscis monkeys, crimson langur, pig-tailed macaques, sambar deer, bearded pigs, Western tarsier, sun bears and 275 species of bird including hornbills, rufous picolet, flowerpeckers and kingfishers. The dipterocarp forest is some of the oldest, tallest and most diverse in the world, with 200 species of tree per ha. Features include a canopy walkway, a heart-stoppingly springy platform 107 m long and 27 m above the ground, an ancient Dusun burial site, waterfalls and a self-guided trail.

Semporna and the islands ●●▲●●● » *pp702-714. Colour map 9, B6.*

Semporna is a small fishing Bajau town at the end of the peninsula and is the main departure point for Sipadan Island, which has achieved legendary status for divers and snorkellers. It has a lively and very photogenic market, spilling out onto piers over the water, and is known for its seafood. There are scores of small traditional fishing boats, many with outriggers and square sails. A regatta is held in March. The town is built on an old coral reef, said to be 35,000 years old, which was exposed by the uplift of the seabed. Many illegal Filipino immigrants pass through Semporna, which gives the place a different feel from other Malay towns. In the shallow channels off Semporna there are fishing villages built on stilts.

Sipadan Island Marine Reserve → *Colour map 9, B6.*

The islands off Semporna stand along the edge of the continental shelf, which drops away to a depth of 200 m. The reefs surrounding these islands have around 70 genera of coral, placing them, in terms of their diversity, on a par with Australia's Great Barrier Reef. More than 200 species of fish have also been recorded in these waters.

Ever since Jacques Cousteau 'discovered' Sipadan in 1989 it has become a shangri-la for serious divers and is regularly voted one of the top dive destinations in the world. But Sipadan Island is not just for scuba divers: it is a magnificent, tiny tropical island with pristine beaches and crystal-clear water that can be enjoyed by even the most amateur of snorkellers.

Ins and outs The islands' tourist facilities are run by a handful of tour companies (see Activities and tours, page 709). In 2004, resort facilities on Sipadan were closed to protect the environment; although dive boats can still visit the island. Tourists can stay on Mabul, Kapalai and Mataking. The best diving season is from mid-February to mid-December when visibility is greater (20-60 m). Most of the dives involve drift diving; the night diving is spectacular.

Pulau Sipadan Sipadan is the only oceanic island in Malaysia; it is not attached to the continental shelf and stands on a limestone and coral stalk, rising 600 m from the bed of the Celebes Sea. The limestone pinnacle mushrooms out near the surface, but a few metres offshore drops off in a sheer underwater cliff to the seabed. The reef comes right into the island's small pier, allowing snorkellers to swim along the edge of the coral cliff, while remaining close to the coral-sand beach. The tiny island has a cool, forested interior and it is common to see flying foxes and monitor lizards.

Sipadan is known for its underwater overhangs and caverns, funnels and ledges, all covered in coral. Turtle Cave acquired its fame due to the large numbers of turtles encountered in its depths – some of these turtles had become disorientated and died in the caves. The island's geography and location focus nutrient-rich upwellings towards the island and, in areas such as the South Point and Barracuda Point, large pelagic (open sea) species such as hammerheads and grey reef sharks can be spotted. The area is abundant with green turtles, which come ashore to lay their eggs in August and September.

Mabul Island Located between Semporna and Sipadan, Mabul is considerably larger than Sipadan and is partly home to Bajau fishermen who live in traditional palm-thatched houses. In contrast to Sipadan's untouched forest, the island is predominantly planted with coconut trees. It has already become known as the world's best muck diving, so called because of the silt-filled waters and poor visibility (usually around 12 m). The island is surrounded by gentle sloping reefs with depths from 3-35 m and a wall housing numerous species of hard corals. Since the closure of Sipadan's luxury resorts, several companies have moved their accommodation to Mabul, only 20 minutes away by fast boat. Affordable backpacker accommodation is also available. A return boat trip from Semporna costs from US$12.

Mataking and Kapalai Mataking has only been open as a dive resort for a few years but is set to increase in popularity. There are about 30 good dive sites around the island including various shallow reefs (ideal for beginners), a sea fan garden, a 100-m crevice called Alice Channel that runs to Pulau Sipadan and Sweet Lips rock, a good night diving spot.

Kapalai is a sandbar on top of Ligitan Reefs between Sipadan and Mabul and is good for shallow dives or snorkelling. It has a dive resort on stilts connected by wooden walkways.

Tawau ⬤🅕🅘🅒🅞 ▸▸ pp702-714. Colour map 9, B6.

Tawau is a timber port in Sabah's southeastern corner. It is a busy commercial centre and transport hub and the main entry point of Indonesian workers into Sabah. A great contrast to the newly built hotel and business area, the waterfront has plenty of colourful markets and foodstalls and some picturesque views across the bay, including to Kalimantan.

Tawau centre has been cleaned up and has a few decent hotels and restaurants and it has daily air connections to KL. With the development of a new road cutting across the south of Sabah towards KK nearing completion (passing just to the south of Maliau Basin), Tawau is set to receive more foreign visitors.

Now that the Sandakan area has been almost completely logged, Tawau has taken over as the main logging centre on the east coast. The forest is disappearing fast but there are some reforestation programmes. Tawau is surrounded by plantations and smallholdings of rubber, copra, cocoa and palm oil. The local soils are volcanic and very fertile and palm oil has recently taken over from cocoa as the predominant crop. KL is now an established research centre for palm oil where there are studies on using palm oil as a fuel.

Maliau Basin → Colour map 9, B5.

ⓘ www.borneoforestheritage.org.my. You need to obtain permission in advance. Entry permits (RM50) are sold at the Shell Maliau Basin Reception and Information Building.

In the rugged forest-clad hills in Sabah's heart lies an area known as Sabah's Lost World. Covering 390 sq km, the Maliau Basin is one of the state's last areas of primary rainforest largely unaffected by agriculture or large-scale logging. It has remained undisturbed partly due to the difficulty of access and the geography of the basin. From the air, it looks like a vast meteor crater, measuring up to 25 km in diameter and surrounded by steep cliffs up to 1700 m in height. Maliau has only recently opened its doors to the public and a state-of-the-art visitor centre was completed in 2007. A major logging road cutting across the south of Sabah, from Tawau to Keningau and the west coast, is close to completion as a major paved highway. This will improve access to the zone, but will also increase threats to wildlife.

A network of trails linking a series of comfortable but basic scientific camps provides some of the best, and toughest, trekking in northern Borneo. The treks pass numerous spectacular waterfalls, including the famous multi-tiered Maliau Falls and Takob Akob Falls, over 38 m high. If you're lucky with the weather you should get some panoramic views of the conservation area from the ridge tops.

It's a long drive back to Tawau or Semporna; however, the roads are improving all the time. Make sure you budget for trekking costs, including the entry fee, food of RM80 per day (if you arrange it through the park), accommodation and guide fees. Porters are also available. Each trip has to be individually organized to match trekkers' needs.

◉ Sabah listings

For Sleeping and Eating price codes, see inside the front cover.

🛏 Sleeping

Homestays can be organized through **Nature Heritage Travel and Tours**, ground floor, Wisma Sabah, T088-318747, nhtt@nature-heritage.com.

Kota Kinabalu p688, map p689
Many of the top resorts are out of town, but there are plenty of options in KK itself.
L-AL Shangri-La Tanjung Aru Resort, T088-225800, www.shangri-la.com. A/c, 500 rooms, pool, one of the best hotels in Sabah,

along with its sister hotel, the **Rasa Ria**. Tanjung Aru is a public beach, frequented by kiteflyers, swimmers, joggers and loves. The hotel is popular with honeymooners.
C-D Mandarin, 138 Jl Gaya, T088-225222. A/c, restaurant, marble floors, well-fitted rooms, excellent location, friendly, 6th-floor rooms with good view, deluxe and super-deluxe particularly spacious.
E Town Inn, 31-33 Jl Pantai, T088-225823. A/c, 24 rooms, clean, central location, superb facilities, good value.
E-G Beach Lodge, 46 Jl Pantai, T088-213888, beach_lodge@hotmail.com. Cute little guesthouse with friendly laid-back staff. Only a handful of doubles with shared hot water

showers, so book a week in advance. Also a few 8-bed dorms. Breakfast included, and free airport pick-up. Lots of tour information and small breakfast/lounge area. Very clean.

F-G Lucy's Homestay (Backpacker Lodge), Australia Pl, 25 Lorong Dewan, T088-261495, www.welcome.to/backpackerkk. Friendly, clean dorms and doubles, good breakfast. In a quiet location near Signal Hill, this is one of the best and most relaxed of the backpackers. Tour information, library and kitchen. Book in advance. Great place to meet other travellers.

Tunku Abdul Rahman Park *p690*
Rooms are discounted during the week.
A-B Gayana Island EcoResort, ground floor, Wisma Sabah, Jl Tun Razak, Pulau Gaya, T088-245158, www.gayana-ecoresort.com. Set on the east coast of the island, 44 a/c chalets, good service but slightly rundown, restaurant, private beach, reef rehabilitation research centre. Watersports, jungle trekking and yachting. Some reports of dirty water around the resort from the shanty town.
A-D Chalets, Pulau Manukan, contact **Sutera Sanctuary Lodges**, ground floor, Wisma Sabah, T088-243629, www.suterasanctuary lodges.com, for bookings on Manukan. Pool, restaurant and sports facilities.

Camping
It's possible to camp on any island. Obtain permission from the Sabah Parks Office, Lot 3, Block K, Sinsuran Complex, KK, T088-211881, www.sabahparks.com. The island gets packed with tourists during the day, but if you camp you can enjoy a near-deserted island after 1700 when the rabble departs.

Pulau Tiga National Park *p691*
A-E Pulau Tiga Resort, T088-240584, www.pulau-tiga.com. Chalets with a/c, superior rooms with kingsize beds and budget triples in a longhouse. The resort organizes diving, watersports, treks and trips to nearby islands. Games room, **Survivor Bar** and restaurant. Many packages include meals, excellent value.

There is also a **hostel** that can hold up to 32 people. Book in advance through the **Sabah Parks Office** in KK; there is also an attached canteen. It is possible to camp here.

Pulau Labuan *p691*
Plenty of choice, but little at budget level.
A-B Tiara Labuan, Jl Tanjung Batu, west coast, T087-414300. A 5-min taxi ride from town. Beautiful hotel and apartments built onto Adnan Kashoggi's former mansion, large lotus pond and pool with jacuzzi. It has an Italian feel with terracotta tiles and pink stone. Opulent lounge including an Arab section with low sofas and water pipes. A/c, TV, minibar, electric hob, sink and living room.
C-D Global, Jl OKK Awang Besar (near market), T087-425201. Best value in town, minibar, a/c, TV, video, free shuttle to ferry and airport.
E Victoria, Jl Tun Mustapha, T087-218511. One of the oldest hotels in Labuan, pink exterior with stucco-decorated lobby, 46 en suite rooms, a/c.

Tambunan *p692*
E Tambunan Village Resort Centre (TVRC), signposted off main road, T088-77407. Chalets and a 'longhouse' dorm made of split bamboo. Restaurant and motel. There are some retreat centres about 10 mins' walk away.
E-F Gunung Emas Highlands Resort, Km 52 (7 km from the **Rafflesia Reserve**). Dorms, basic treehouses, a fresh climate and good views. Mini zoo and restaurant. Take the Rabunan or the Keningau minibus and then bus from Tambunan.

Tenom *p693*
Orchid Hotel and **Sri Jaya Hotel** are both within walking distance of the bus stop.
L-C Perkasa, top of the hill above town, T087-735811. Large, modern hotel with superb views. Attractive, spacious rooms, a/c, en suite bathroom, TV. Restaurant. Staff are friendly and helpful in arranging sightseeing.
E Orchid, Block K, Jl Tun Mustapha, T087-737600, excelng@tm.net.my. Small but friendly with clean, well-maintained rooms.

E-F Sri Perdana, Lot 71, Jl Tun Mustapha, T087-734001. Good-value standard rooms.
F-G Rumah Rehat Lagud Sebren (Orchid Research Station Resthouse), 5 km from the agricultural park, a/c. Take a minibus from the main road. If driving, take the road over the railway tracks by the station.

Beaufort *p693*
Poor selection of hotels, all a bit overpriced.
E Beaufort, Lot 19-20, Lochung Park, T087-211911. Central, a/c, 25 rooms.
F Mandarin Inn, Lot 38, Jl Beaufort Jaya, T087-212800. A/c rooms and garners better reviews than the **Beaufort**.

Sipitang *p693*
C-E Asanol, T087-821506. Good-value rooms with bathrooms.
C-E Shangsan, T088-821800. Comfortable rooms with a/c and TV. Ubiquitous coffee shop in the same street.

Kota Belud *p693*
E-F Impian Siu Motel, Kg Sempirai, Jl Kuala Abai, T088-976617. Reasonable, 10 rooms.

Homestay
Living with a family is an excellent and affordable way for travellers to learn the language and gain an in-depth knowledge of the culture. Activities include buffalo riding, jungle trekking, river swimming, cultural dancing, visits to local *tamus*, padi planting. Contact **Nature Heritage Travel and Tours**, ground floor, Wisma Sabah, KK, T088-318747, nhtt@nature-heritage.com, or **Taginambur Homestay**, T088-423993, hopfans@tm.net.my.

Kudat *p694*
E Greenland, Lot 9/10, Block E, Sedco Shophouse (new town), T088-613211. A/c, standard rooms, shared bath.
E Kinabalu, Kudat Old Town, Jl Melor, T088-613888. A/c, clean, average value.
F Southern, Kudat Old Town, T088-613133. 10 rooms, but quite cheap and reasonable value compared with others in this category.

Gunung Kinabalu Park *p694*
The park is managed by **Sutera Sanctuary Lodges**, all accommodation to be booked in advance through: Wisma Sabah, KK, T088-243629, www.suterasanctuarylodges.com.

Park HQ
Each cabin has a fireplace, kitchen, shower, gas cooker and fridge. Electricity and firewood provided. Most expensive is the **Rajah Lodge**, sleeping 6 (RM1500 for the whole lodge). **Kinabalu Lodge**, 8 people, RM540 per night. **Nepenthes Lodge**, 4 people, RM380 per night. **Twin-bedded cabins**, 2 people, RM135 per night, great views. **4-person chalets**, RM300 per night. Unheated **dorms** with shared bathroom, RM46 per bed.

Gunung Kinabalu
Laban Rata Resthouse, 54 rooms (extra space made with mattresses on the floor), a good-quality though pricey canteen, hot water showers, electricity, bedding provided. Heated deluxe rooms at RM300 or RM180 per room, heated dorms for RM69 per bed, while chilly unheated dorms are RM46 per bed.

Close to Park HQ
A-B Haleluyah Retreat Centre, Jl Linouh, Km 61, Tuaran-Ranau Hwy, T088-423993, kandiu@tm.net.my. Set at 1500 m amidst natural jungle, 15 mins' walk from Park HQ, it is isolated but clean, friendly and relaxing. Cooking and washing facilities, camping area. Canteen, dorm beds also available.
A-G Rina Ria Lodge, Batu 36, Jl Tinompok, Ranau, T088-889282. 1 km from the park, rooms have attached kitchen and bathroom, armchairs and beautiful views. Also dorms.
E Mountain View Motel, 5 km east of the park, Ranau-Tamparuli Hwy, T088-875389, bbmtkinabalu@hotmail.com. Breakfast included, hot water, restaurant, laundry, tours, climbing gear available for hire.
F-G Mountain Resthouse and Restaurant, T088-771109. Just outside the park, 4-person dorms that are cheaper, newer, cleaner and warmer than in the park. Spectacular views.

Mesilau Nature Resort *p696*
LL-E Mesilau Nature Resort, managed by
Sutera Sanctuary Lodges, T088-871733,
www.suterasanctuarylodges.com. Tasteful
wooden chalets housing up to 6 (RM520 per
room). Also dorms (RM46 per bed). Laundry,
gift shop. Close to the golf club.

Poring Hot Springs *p696*
Booking recommended. Camping RM6.
Serindit hostel, 24-person dorms, RM12;
Tempua Lodge, 4 people, RM92 per chalet;
Enggang Lodge, 6 people, RM115 per night;
Rajawali Lodge, 6 people, RM380 per night.

Sandakan *p696*
C-D City View, Lot 1, Block 23, 3rd Av, T089-
271122. Restaurant, rooms have bath and
shower, TV, fridge, a/c. For a little more
money, this is a considerable step up.
F Mayfair, 24 Jl Pryer, T089-219855. A/c,
shower, TV and lots of DVDs. Transport to the
airport and Sepilok. Decor leaves something to
be desired but friendly and central, views of
the market and sea, good value. Book ahead.
F Uncle Tan's, Mile 16, Jl Gum Gum (5 km
beyond Sepilok junction), T089-531639,
www.uncletan.com. A simple B&B usually
catering for those heading for **Uncle Tan's
Wildlife Adventure Camp** in Kinabatangan
(see below). Very cheap but noisy. Popular.

Turtle Islands National Park *p697*
The number of visitors is restricted. 3 chalets
(one with 2 doubles, 2 with 6 doubles) on
Pulau Selingan (RM255-370 per person).
Book through **Crystal Quest**, page 710. Tour
agencies can also organize trips to the island.

Sepilok Orang-Utan Sanctuary *p698*
**C-F Sepilok Jungle Resort (and Wildlife
Lodge)**, Km 22 Labuk Rd, 100 m behind the
government resthouse, T089-533031,
www.borneo-online.com.my/sjungleresort.
Pleasant resort on the edge of the forest: the
Wildlife Lodge has 6-bed dorms RM20 per
bed, and doubles with private bathroom and
a/c. More luxurious wood-panelled rooms

with TV, a/c are in the **Jungle Resort** next
door. Pleasant restaurant, great setting, clean,
comfortable, boats for fishing available,
campsite. Also own **Bilit Adventure Camp**,
on the Kinabatangan River. Recommended.
C-F Sepilok Resthouse, Mile 14 Labuk Rd,
T089-534900. Wooden house next to the
orang-utan sanctuary. Government-owned,
now privately run. Big rooms, with bathtub
and balcony. Clean dorms for RM20 per bed.
E Sepilok B&B, Jl Sepilok, Mile 14, PO Box 155,
T089-532288. Breakfast included. 1 km from
the sanctuary. Not bad value but no hot water.

Sungai Kinabatangan *p699*
Most tour companies put their guests up in
Sukau or in camps along the river. See also
Sepilok Jungle Resort, above.
A-B Sukau Rainforest Lodge, Borneo
Eco-Tours, T088-234009, www.borneo
ecotours.com. Accessible by boat from Sukau,
eco-friendly accommodation in traditional
Malaysian-style chalets on stilts. All 20 rooms
with solar-powered fans, twin beds, mosquito
netting, and attached bathroom with hot
water. Open dining area (good restaurant),
garden and sundeck overlooking the
rainforest. Friendly, efficient. Recommended.
F-G Uncle Tan Wildlife Adventures, Mile 16,
Jl Gum Gum, T089-531639, www.uncletan.com.
A long-established budget option. Simple
3-sided huts with a floor mattress, mosquito
net and shared cold water bucket showers.
A 3-day, 2-night package including transport,
river cruises (including night cruise), jungle
treks and meals costs RM240. Deservedly
popular, so book ahead.

Danum Valley Conservation Area *p700*
If you get permission to stay at the centre,
the **Sabah Foundation** has dorms for
RM45 per night, or RM80 for a single room.
L-AL Borneo Rainforest Lodge,
www.borneo rainforestlodge.com. One of
the finest tourism developments in Sabah.
18 bungalows in a magnificent setting by the
river, built on stilts from *belian* (ironwood) in
traditional Kadazan design with connecting

walkways. 28 rooms with bathroom and balcony, good restaurant, jacuzzi. A great way to experience primary rainforest in comfort. Price includes meals and jungle trips.

Semporna *p700*

E Lee's Resthouse and Café, Pekau Baru, T/F089-784491. Some rooms are windowless but clean and fresh with attached bath. Good value but noisy location.

E Sipadan Inn, Block D, Lot No19-24, seafront, T089-782766. Sparkling new hotel. Great location and friendly staff. Small but light and bright rooms, with a/c, TV and bathroom.

E-F Dragon Inn, Jl (next to the jetty), T089-781088, www.dragoninnfloating.com.my. Built on stilts over the sea, a novel setting and great value. A/c, restaurant. Family rooms, en suite doubles, hot water, a/c, TV. Longhouse dorm beds RM15. Discount with voucher from **Uncle Chang's dive shop** at the entrance.

Mabul Island *p700*

With the closure of all Sipadan resorts Mabul Island is a convenient place to stay. For all-inclusive upmarket options try **Mabul Water Bungalows** (www.mabulwater bungalows.com), **Sipadan Mabul Resort**, www.sipadan-mabul.com.my), and **Sipadan Water Village**, www.sipadan-village.com.my.

A-B Borneo Divers Mabul Resort, T088-222226, www.borneo divers.info. Small office by entrance to **Dragon Inn** in Semporna. One of the few mid-range places, prices include food. Swimming pool. Not particularly stylish, but decent value facing the beach and the **Seaventures** platform. All diving facilities.

A-B Seaventures Dive Resort, run by Sea Ventures Dives, T088-261669, www.sea venturesdives.com. Just offshore, this refurbished oil rig is a true diver's spot. Boat dives to Sipadan and other islands and is locally famous for its excellent muck diving and macrolife. Good value and an exciting location.

F pp The Longhouse (book through **Scuba Junkie**, Semporna), price includes food if diving with **Scuba Junkie**. Very basic but superb value. Interesting location in Bajau village house. RM40 each way for transfer to the island if you're not diving.

F pp Uncle Chang's, book through **Uncle Chang's dive shop**, see **Dragon Inn**, Semporna. A good backpacker option in the Bajau village on the far side of the island. Rates include food. Many years of experience.

Mataking and Kapalai *p700*

LL Mataking Island Reef Dive Resort, T/F088-318022, www.mataking.com. Also has a counter in Semporna at the jetty on Jl Kastam. 45 mins by boat from Semporna, the resort has a/c chalets and deluxe rooms, with sea view and balcony. Facilities include a spa, satellite TV, internet, bar and restaurant.

L-AL Sipadan-Kapalai Dive Resort, T089-765200, www.sipadan-kapalai.com. This resort straddles Kapalai's sandbank on stilts. Modelled as a water village, the resort has 40 twin-sharing wooden chalets, with attached bathrooms, balconies and amazing sea views all round, linked by a network of wooden platforms. Dive centre, internet access.

Tawau *p701*

Hotels here are not great value for money. Avoid the cheaper lodging houses around Jl Stephen Tan, Jl Chester and Jl Cole Adams.

A-B Belmont Marco Polo, Jl Abaca/Jl Clinic, T089-777988. A/c, restaurant, best hotel in Tawau although pricier than the competition.

C-D Millennium, 561 Jl Bakau, T089-771155. A/c, spacious rooms. Very acceptable.

E Loong, Jl Abaca, T089-765308. A/c, fully carpeted, clean and light.

E Pan Sabah, Jl Stephen Tan, behind local minibus station, T089-762488. A/c, TV, attached bathrooms, clean rooms and very good value compared to others in town.

Maliau Basin *p702*

F-G pp Maliau Basin camps. Basic dorms, beds must be booked in advance through, www.borneoforestheritage.org.my. Camps have 20-40 beds, apart from Camel Trophy Camp with only 8 places available.

❷ Eating

Kota Kinabalu *p688, map p689*
The new waterfront has a range of restaurants with outdoor seating facing the South China Sea. Seafood is seasonally prone to toxic red tide. Locals will know when it's prevalent. Avoid all shellfish if there's any suspicion.

⟦⟧ Little Italy, ground floor, **Hotel Capital**, 23 Jl Haji Saman, T088-232231. Award-winning pizza and pasta place with Italian chef.

⟦⟧ Sri Melaka, 9 Jl Laiman Diki, Kampong Ayer (Sedco Complex). Popular with the fashionable KK set, great Malay and Nyonya food.

⟦ Bilal, Block B, Lot 1 Segama Complex. Indian Muslim, rotis, chapatis, curries.

⟦ Golf Field Seafood, 0858 Jl Ranca-Ranca. Better known by taxi drivers as **Ahban's Place**. Excellent marine cuisine, local favourite.

⟦ Sri Sempelang, Sinsuran 2 (on the corner with Jl Pasar Baru). Great Malay canteen with enormous fruit juices and tables outside.

Foodstalls

Sedco Square, Kampong Ayer, large square filled with stalls, great atmosphere in the evenings, ubiquitous *ikan panggang* and satay. Night market on **Jl Tugu**, on the Waterfront at the **Sinsuran Food Centre** and at the **Merdeka Foodstall Centre**, Wisma Merdeka.

Tunku Abdul Rahman Park *p690*
Excellent restaurant on Pulau Manukan. Pulau Mamutik and Pulau Sapi each have a small shop with expensive food and drink and Sapi has some hawker-style meals. For Pulau Sulug, Sapi and Mamutik take all the water you need: there is no drinkable water supply here.

Pulau Labuan *p691*
Several basic places to be found along Jl Merdeka and Jl OKK Awang Besar.
⟦⟧ Emperor Chinese, Sheraton Labuan. Top-class Chinese, Cantonese specialities, fresh seafood, dim sum.
⟦⟧ Pulau Labuan, Lot 27-28, Jl Muhibbah. Smart a/c interior with chandeliers. Fish sold by weight; good tiger prawns.

⟦⟧ Wong Kee, Lot 5 and 6, Jl Kemuning. Large, brightly lit restaurant with a/c, good steamboat.

⟦ New Sung Hwa Seafood, Jl Ujong Pasir, PCK Building. Amongst the best-value seafood restaurants in Malaysia, chilli prawns, superb grilled stingray steak, no menu.

Tenom *p693*
⟦ Sapong, Perkasa Hotel. Local and Western.
⟦ Y&L (Young & Lovely) Food & Entertainment, Jl Sapong (2 km out of town). Noisy but easily the best in Tenom. Mainly Chinese food: freshwater fish (steamed *sun hok*, also known as *ikan hantu*) and venison; washed down with the local version of *air limau* (or *kitchai*), which comes with dried plums. Recommended.
⟦ Yong Lee. Coffee shop serving cheap Chinese fare in town centre.

Beaufort *p693*
⟦ Beaufort Bakery, behind **Beaufort Hotel**, 'freshness with every bite'.
⟦ Jin Jin Restaurant, also behind **Beaufort Hotel**, Chinese, popular with locals.

Kota Belud *p693*
Several Indian coffee shops on main square.
⟦ Bismillah Restoran, 35 Jl Keruak (main square), excellent *roti telur*.
⟦ Indonesia Restoran, next to the car park behind the **Kota Belud Hotel**.

Gunung Kinabalu Park *p694*
The restaurants are rather spread out, requiring a walk between buffet and bed. These both open at 0600 for climbers to stock up on high-carb breakfasts. **⟦⟧ Liwagu** restaurant and **⟦ Balsam Cafeteria**.

Mesilau Nature Resort *p696*
⟦⟧ Kedamaian provides the 3 main meals.
⟦ Malaxi Café has a stunning veranda offering great views of the mountain.

Poring Hot Springs *p696*
⟦ Restaurant, quite good Chinese and Malay food at the springs and stalls outside the park.

Sandakan *p696*

Sandakan is renowned for its cheap and delicious seafood. Try the restaurants at the top of Trig (Trigonometry) Hill.

♕ Golden Palace, Trig Hill (2 km from town). Fresh seafood, specializes in drunken prawns, crab and lobster, and steamboats. Transport back to Sandakan provided if no taxis available.

♕ Pesah Putih Baru, on the coast, nearly at the end of Sandakan Bay, 5 km from the port. Great views of Sandakan and good food.

♕ XO Steak House, Lot 16, Hsiang Garden Estate (opposite **Hsiang Garden Hotel**), Mile 1.5, Jl Leila. Lobster and tiger prawns, good choice of fresh fish and steaks. BBQ on Fri.

♖ Fat Cat, 206 Wisma Sandakan, 18 Jl Haji Saman. Several branches, good for breakfast.

♖ Penang Curry House, 15 Jl Dua. Fabulous Indian food for rock-bottom prices. Friendly service. Try *dosa masala*.

♖ Perwira, Hotel Ramai, Jl Leila. Malay and Indonesian food, good value.

Semporna *p700*

♖ Anjung Paghalian, next to police station near bridge to jetty. Simple outdoor place with good cheap seafood and giant iced avocado juices.

♖ Pearl City Restaurant, attached to **Dragon Inn**. Pile house with good seafood; verify prices before ordering. Great setting.

♖ Seafest Restaurant, next to the **Seafest Inn**. Malay food predominantly with some excellent fish dishes. Good standard for very reasonable prices.

Tawau *p701*

Foodstalls along the seafront.

♖ Asnur, 325B, Block 41, Fajar Complex. Thai and Malay, large choice.

♖ Dragon Court, 1st floor, Lot 15, Block 37 Jl Haji Karim. Chinese, popular, lots of seafood.

♖ Venice Coffee House, Marco Polo Hotel, Jl Abaca/Jl Clinic. Hawker centre for late-night eating, Malay and Chinese.

♖ Yun Lo, Jl Abaca (below the **Hotel Loong**). Good Malay and Chinese. A popular spot with locals, good atmosphere. Recommended.

🍷 Bars and clubs

Kota Kinabalu *p688, map p689*

Many popular bars are along the **Waterfront**. Bars and restaurants, all with outdoor seating, are strung along **Beach St**, between Jl Pantai and Jl Gaya. Karaoke is very popular; found in Damai, Foh Sang and KK centre.

BB Café, Beach St. Closes 0300. Rough-and-ready, with cheap beer and pool table.

Beach Club, at the end of the Waterfront. Popular late-night club with a big dance floor, DJ. Quite funky for KK.

Café Upperstar, Segama Complex (opposite **Hotel Hyatt**). Jugs of Long Island iced tea.

Shennanigan's, Hyatt Hotel, Jl Datuk Salleh Sulong, is the smartest disco in town.

✴ Festivals and events

Kota Kinabalu *p688, map p689*

May **Magavau**, a post-harvest celebration, is carried out at Hongkod Koisaan (cultural centre), Mile 4.5, Jl Penampang. To get there, take a green and white bus from the MPKK Building, next to the state library.

Kota Belud *p693*

Nov The annual **Tamu Besar** includes a parade and equestrian games by the Bajau horsemen, a very colourful event. Contact Sabah Tourism for more information.

Gunung Kinabalu Park *p694*

Oct The **Kinabalu Climbathon** sees runners reach the summit and back in under 3 hrs.

🛍 Shopping

Kota Kinabalu *p688, map p689*

Antiques Good antiques shop at bottom of Chun Eng Bldg on Jl Tun Razak, and a couple on Jl Gaya. **Merdeka Complex** and **Wisma Wawasan 2020** hold a number of antiques shops. You need an export licence from Sabah State Museum to export rare antiques.

Handicrafts Mainly baskets, mats, tribal clothing, beadwork and pottery. **Api Tours**, Lot 49, Bandaran Berjaya, has a small selection. **Borneo Handicraft**, 1st floor, Wisma Merdeka, local pottery and material made up into clothes. **Elegance Souvenir**, 1st floor, Wisma Merdeka, lots of beads of local interest. **Kampong Ayer Night Market**, mainly Filipino handicrafts. **Sabah Handicraft Centre**, Lot 49 Bandaran Berjaya, good selection (also at the museum and airport).

Pulau Labuan *p691*
Duty free If you plan to take duty-free goods into Sabah or Sarawak, you have to stay on Labuan for a minimum of 72 hrs. **Labuan Duty Free**, Bangunan Terminal, Jl Merdeka. Claims to be the cheapest duty free in the world. **Monegain**, can undercut most other outlets on the island due to the volume of merchandise it turns over.
Handicrafts Behind Jl Merdeka and before the fish market, there are tin-roofed shacks housing a Filipino handicrafts and textile market and an interesting wet market.

▲ Activities and tours

Kota Kinabalu *p688, map p689*
Tours that are widely available include: **Kota Belud** *tamu* (Sunday market), **Gunung Kinabalu Park** (including Poring Hot Springs), **Sepilok Orang-Utan Rehabilitation Centre**, train trips to **Tenom** through the Padas Gorge and tours of **Tunku Abdul Rahman National Park**. Several companies specialize in diving.

Diving
Do not believe dive shops if they tell you that you must book through their offices in KK – it's often cheaper to book through local offices in the area where you want to dive. One exception to this rule is Sipadan island. Only limited numbers of divers are allowed to dive in the area per day due to conservation concerns. To obtain permits in advance, contact Sipadan tour operators, page 710.

Horse riding
Kindawan Riding Centre, 21 km south of KK at Kinarut, T088-225525, www.kindawan.com. Run by an Australian. 2-hr rides through villages and paddy fields or along the beach. The surroundings are stunning and the horses are well kept. RM50 for 1 hr. Transport from KK.

Tour operators
The Sabah Tourism Board has a full list of tour agents, also see www.sabahtourism.com.
Api Tours, No 13 Jl Punai Dekut, Mile 5, Jl Tuaran, PO Box 12851, T088-424156, www.jaring.my/apitours. Interesting tours such as stays in longhouses. Recommended.
Borneo Divers, ground floor, Wisma Sabag, T088-222227, www.borneodivers.info. Exotic scuba-diving trips all over Borneo including Sipadan, accommodation on Mamutik Island (Tunku Abdul Rahman).
Borneo Eco Tours, Lot 1, Pusat Perindustrian, Kolombong Jaya, 88450, T088-438300, www.borneoecotours.com. Environmentally aware tours. Their **Sukau Rainforest Lodge** on the Kinabatangan River is recommended.
Borneo Nature Tours, Block D, Lot 10, Sadong Jaya Complex, T088-267637, www.borneo naturetours.com. Official agent for the Danum Valley (including **Borneo Rainforest Lodge**), see page 700.
Borneo Ultimate, ground floor, Wisma Sabah, www.borneoultimate.com. Adventure tours including whitewater rafting, mountain biking, jungle trekking, and sea kayaking.
Borneo Wildlife Adventures, Lot F, 1st floor, GPO building, T088-213668, www.borneo-wildlife.com. Specializing in nature tours, wildlife and cultural activities.
Diethelm Borneo Expeditions, Suite 303, 2nd floor, EON-CMG Life Building, 1 Jl Sagunting, T088-222271, dbex@tm.net.my.
Discovery Tours, ground floor, Wisma Sabah, Jl Haji Saman, T088-221244, www.info sabah.com.my/discovery. Recommended.
Intra Travel Service, 1st floor, Tanjung Aru Plaza, Jl Mat Salleh, T088-261558, enquiry@ tabinwildlife.com.my. Best place for trips in the excellent Tabin Wildlife reserve, see page 700.

KK Tours & Travel, Lot 32-1, Block F, Lintas Square, Jl Lintas, T088-238480, www.kktours.com. Good operator, tours include golfing, island hopping and helicopter rides.

Nasalis Larvatus Tours, Lot 226, 2nd floor, Wisma Sabah, Jl Tun Abdul Razak, T088-230 534, www.nasalislarvatustours.com. For **Nature Lodge Kinabatangan**, excellent lodge 1 hr upriver from Sukau. Activities include kayaking, nature walks, trips to local oxbow lake. 2-3 nights advised. Great wildlife viewing.

Riverbug/Traverse Tours, Lot 227-229, 2nd floor, Wisma Sabah, Jl Tun Fuad Stephen, T088-260501, www.traversetours.com. Rafting trips on the Padas (grade III-IV). Good guides, transport and equipment, post-river BBQ. The Kiulu (grades II-III) is picturesque with smaller rapids. Also trekking, biking and camping tours.

Scuba Paradise, Lot G28, Jl Tun Razak Wisma Sabah, T088-266695, www.scubaparadiseborneo.com.my. Reliable dive operator offering courses and fun dives in Tunku Abdul Rahman National Park and Sipadan/Mabul islands.

Sipadan Dive Centre, 11th floor, Wisma Merdeka, Jl Tun Razak, T088-240584, www.sipadandivers.com. Experienced tour outfit, running dives and courses at Sipadan and Tunku Abdul Rahman Park. They also own the new **Proboscis Lodge** at Sukau.

Whitewater rafting
Papar River (grades I, II and IV), Kadamaian River (grades II-III). Usually requires a minimum of 3 people. Main operators include **Api Tours, Diethelm Borneo Expeditions, Traverse Tours/ Riverbug** and **Discovery Tours** (see above).

Pulau Labuan *p691*
Diving Average visibility 12 m. The water is cooler Nov-Feb, when visibility is not as good. Snorkel, mask and fins can be rented at the KK jetty or on Sapi and Manukan.
Borneo Divers, 1 Jl Wawasan, **Waterfront Labuan Financial Hotel**, T087-415867, www.borneodivers.info. 2-day packages diving on shipwrecks for certified scuba divers. Each wreck costs about RM100.

Sandakan *p696*
Crystal Quest, Sabah Park Jetty, Jl Buli Sim Sim, T089-212711, cquest@tm.net.my. The only company running accommodation on Pulau Selingan, Turtle Islands National Park.
SI Tours, 1st floor, Wisma Khoo Siak Chiew, T089-213501, www.sitours.com.my. Well-established company running tours to Gomantong Caves, Kinabatangan and Turtle Islands National Park. Recommended.

Turtle Islands National Park *p697*
The average cost of a 1-night tour including accommodation and boat transfer is RM360 or more. Trips needs to be flexible; bad weather can mess up itineraries. Most visitors book well in advance through **Crystal Quest**, above.

Sungai Kinabatangan *p699*
Tour operators transport guests to the lodge or camp as part of the package. **Uncle Tan's** takes you from B&Bs just outside Sandakan (buses from KK and Lahad Datu stop outside). Book trips through tour operators in Sandakan or KK.

Sipadan Island Marine Reserve *p700*
Dive centres offer PADI courses and arrange permits, equipment (RM75-100 per day), food and accommodation. Walk-in rates are cheaper.
Borneo Divers, Rooms 401-412, 4th floor, Wisma Sabah, KK, T088-222226, bdivers@po.jaring.my. Trips from KK to Sipadan with accommodation on Mabul. 3-day package with 10 dives costs around RM1200.
Pulau Sipadan Resort, 484, Block P, Bandar Sabindo, Tawau, T089-765200, www.sipadan-resort.com. Dive tours, food, lodging and dive courses, snorkelling equipment. It has accommodation on Pulau Kapalai.
Sipadan Dive Centre, A1103, 11th floor, Wisma Merdeka, Jl Tun Razak, KK, T088-240584, sipadan@po.jaring.my. Packages cost US$740 (5 days/4 nights). Recommended.
Uncle Chang's, Semporna, T089-781002. Everything for the budget traveller including bus tickets, shuttle service to the airport, dive trips to Sipadan. 3 boat dives including all equipment hire and lunch for RM270.

○ Transport

Kota Kinabalu *p688, map p689*

Air Air is the most widely used form of transport between the major towns (eg **Sandakan** and **Tawau**), and it's cheap. Regular connections with **KL**. There are also connections from KK with **Bintulu**, **Johor Bahru**, **Kuching**, **Labuan**, **Miri** and **Sibu**. International connections are with **Singapore**, **Brunei**, **Hong Kong**, **Philippines**, **South Korea**, **Japan** and in **China**. Air Asia now have cheap fares between KK and **Bangkok**.

Airline offices Air Asia, Jl Gaya, T088-438222, www.airasia.com. **British Airways**, Jl Haji Saman, T088-428057. **Cathay Pacific**, Kompleks Kowasa, 49 Jl Karamunsing, T088-428733. **Dragonair**, T088-254733. **Garuda Airways**, Wisma Sabah. **MAS**, Karamunsing Kompleks (off Jl Tunku Abdul Rahman), Jl Kemajuan, T088-213555, also at the airport. **Philippine Airlines**, Karamunsing Kompleks, Jl Kemajuan, T088-239600. **Qantas**, T088-216998. **Royal Brunei Airlines**, Kompleks Kowasa, T088-242193, **Sabah Air**, KK Airport, T088-256733. **Singapore Airlines**, Kompleks Kowasa, T088-255 444. **Thai Airways**, T088-232896, Kompleks Kowasa.

Boat There is a ferry service between KK and **Labuan** every day 0800-1500, 2 hrs (RM31 one way). Ferries to **Serasa Muara** (Brunei) from the Labuan jetty 0830-1630, 1hr (RM24).

Bus There is no central bus station in KK. A temporary local bus station is now in front of the post office and next to the city park. Buses further afield but still in the KK region leave from next to Plaza Wawasan, while long-distance buses wait in the scruffy car park at the base of Signal Hill. Buses are cheaper than minibuses but not as regular or efficient.

There are lots of bus companies and touts. All prices should be the same. It's advisable to buy your ticket the day before. The time on the ticket is a rough guide only. Get there 10 mins before to guarantee your seat, but you may have to wait until the bus is full. Buses to **Tenom** (0800, 1200, 1600, RM16), **Keningau** (7 daily, RM12.15), **Beaufort** (more than 10 every day, RM7); **Tawau** (0730, 0800, RM45), **Sandakan** (0730, 0930, 1300, 2000, RM29.25), **Semporna** (0730, RM45).

Minibus/taxi Minibuses have their destinations on the windscreen, most rides in town are less than RM1 and leave when full. You can get off wherever you like.

Taxis and minibuses bound north for **Kota Belud** and **Kudat** and those going south to **Beaufort** and **Tenom** leave from Bandar Berjaya opposite the Padang and clocktower. Taxis and minibuses going west to **Kinabalu National Park**, **Ranau** and **Sandakan** leave from Jl Tunku Abdul Rahman, next to the Padang and opposite the State Library. Tampuruli, 2 km east of Tuaran, serves as a terminus for minibuses heading to **Kinabalu National Park**. Minibuses leave when full and those for long-distance destinations leave in the early morning. Long-distance taxis also leave when full from in front of the clocktower on Jl Tunku Abdul Rahman. Minibus services from KK to **Tuaran**, 45 mins, **Kota Belud** 2 hrs, **Kudat** 4-5 hrs, **Beaufort** 2-3 hrs, **Tenom** 4 hrs, **Kinabalu National Park** 1½ hrs, **Ranau** 2 hrs, **Sandakan** 8-10 hrs.

Car hire Not all roads in the interior are paved and 4WD is advisable for some journeys. Car hire is expensive (RM30-80 per hr) and rates increase outside a 50-km radius of KK. All vehicles have to be returned to KK, although local car hire is usually available. Drivers must be aged 22-60 and have an international driving licence. **Adaras Rent-a-Car**, Lot G03, ground floor, Wisma Sabah, T088-2166671. **Hertz**, Level 1, Lot 39, Kota Kinabalu airport, T088-317740. **Kinabalu Rent-a-Car**, Lot 3.61, 3rd floor, Karamunsing Kompleks, T088-232602, www.kinabalurac.com.

Taxi There are taxi stands outside most of the bigger hotels and outside the General Post Office, the Segama complex, the Sinsuran complex, next to the DPKK building, the Milemewah supermarket, the Capitol cinema and in front of the clocktower (for taxis to **Ranau**, **Keningau** and **Kudat**). Approximate fares from town: RM10 to **Tanjung Aru Resort**,

RM10 to **Sabah Foundation**, RM8 to the museum, RM14 to the airport.

Train The station is 5 km out of town in Tanjung Aru. There is only 1 train line in Sabah, and rolling stock dates from the colonial era. Diesel trains run 3 times daily to **Beaufort**, 2 hrs, and on to **Tenom**, a further 3 hrs. Departure times are subject to change, T088-254611. There is also a steam train that operates along this same line. For transport from the railway station to town, long-distance buses stop near the station.

Tunku Abdul Rahman Park *p690*
Boat Boats leave from the main jetty 10 mins' walk north of town. Small boats carry 6 people and run to any of the islands when full (RM15 per person fixed price), but everyone needs to agree a destination and a return time. Extra RM10 if you want to return the next day. There's a regular service for **Gayana** every 2 hrs 0800-2300, RM10 return, 38 km. If you want to visit more than 1 island, a boat needs to be chartered, RM280 for a 3-island tour or RM360 for a 5-island tour, taking 12 passengers. It's possible to negotiate trips with lcal fishermen.

Pulau Labuan *p691*
Air The airport is 5 km from town. Regular connections with **KK**, **KL**, **Kuching** and **Miri**. Air Asia, T087-416117. MAS, T087-412263.
Boat From Bangunan Terminal Feri Penumpang next to the duty-free shop on Jl Merdeka. Tickets are sold at arrival points at the ferry terminal, but can be bought in town at **Duta Muhibbah Agency**, T087-413827. 2 connections a day with **Menumbok** (RM10, the nearest mainland point) by speedboat (30 mins) or car ferry. It's a 2-hr bus ride from here to **KK**. Currently there are 7 boats a day to **KK**, 2½ hrs, RM31, 0830-1500. There are 2 daily boats to **Limbang** (Sarawak) at 1230 and 1400, 1½ hrs, RM20; and one to **Lawas** (Sarawak), at 1230, 1½ hrs, RM20.
Bus Local buses around the island leave from Jl Bunga Raya. Minibuses abound.
To Brunei On weekends and public holidays in Brunei the ferries are packed. You can reserve tickets to Brunei at: **Victoria Agency House**, T087-412332 (next to the Federal Hotel in Wisma Kee Chia); **Borneo Leisure Travel**, opposite Standard Chartered, T087-410251. 7 boats daily to **Serasa Muara** (Brunei) 0830-1630, 1½ hrs, RM24.
Taxi Taxis can be found at the airport and hotels, but are impossible to get after 1900.

Tambunan *p692*
Buses marked Tambunan go from the long-distance bus station at the bottom of Signal Hill in KK (1½ hrs). Taxi to **KK** RM100.

Tenom *p693*
Minibus Minibuses leave from town centre on Jl Padas. Regular connections with **KK**, 4 hrs.
Taxi To **KK** costs RM200; shared taxis cost a fraction of the price from Jl Padas (main street).
Train The journey through the **Padas River** gorge is particularly spectacular. Leaves 4 times a day and takes about 3 hrs to **Beaufort**.

Beaufort *p693*
Minibus Minibuses meet the train, otherwise they leave from centre of town. To **KK**, 2 hrs.
Train The KK–Tenom line passes through Beaufort: **Tenom**, 2½ hrs, **KK**, 3 hrs.

Sipitang *p693*
Minibuses and taxis can be found along the waterfront. The jetty for ferries to **Labuan** (daily) is a 10-min walk from the centre.

Kota Belud *p693*
Minibus From main square. Regular connections with **KK**, **Kudat** and **Ranau**.

Kudat *p694*
Air Connections with **KK** and **Sandakan**.
Minibus Minibuses leave from Jl Lo Thien Hock. Regular connections with **KK**, 4 hrs.

Gunung Kinabalu Park *p694*
Bus Buses heading to **Sandakan** and **Ranau** will drop you at the turn-off to the park.
Minibus Regular connections from **KK** to **Ranau**, ask to be dropped at the park, 2 hrs.

Return minibus (roughly every hour) must be waved down from the main road. **Taxi** RM60 fixed price, taxi from long-distance bus station in **KK**.

Poring Hot Springs *p696*
Minibuses can be shared from **Ranau** for RM5. Buses between **KK** and **Sandakan** stop in on Jl Kibarambang. Taxis are also available.

Ranau *p696*
Minibus Minibuses leave from the market place. Regular connections to **Park HQ**, **KK** and **Sandakan** (4 hrs).

Sandakan *p696*
Air The airport is 10 km north of town centre (RM15 by taxi). Early morning flights from **KK** to Sandakan allow breathtaking close-up views of Mt Kinabalu as the sun rises. Connections with **Kudat** and **Tawau** (RM87). Also flights to **KL** with **MAS** (ground floor, Sabah Bldg, Jl Pelabuhan, T089-273966) and **Air Asia** (Jl Dua). **Boat** There's a ferry service to **Zamboanga** in the **Philippines**. The journey takes 8 hrs and leaves twice a week (suite RM250-350). **Bus/minibus** Local minibuses from the bus stop between the Esso and Shell stations on Jl Pryer.

Long-distance buses leave from the bus station at Mile 2.5. Most buses and minibus leave when full. Regular connections with most towns including **KK**, 8 hrs (RM29.25) and **Ranau**, 4 hrs. Buses run 0715-1100. After this you will have to take a minibus to **Tawau** (RM28.05, 6 hrs) every 30 mins 0630-1100. **Semporna** (RM30), departure 0800.

Turtle Islands National Park *p697*
Boat Daily speedboat at 0930, returning 1900, RM100, 40 km northeast of Sandakan at Sabah Parks Jetty. Tour operators have their own boats and the fee is included with the package price, so times will vary.

Sepilok Orang-Utan Sanctuary *p698*
Bus 8 daily public buses from **Sandakan**, from the central minibus terminal in front of

Nak Hotel. Ask for the Sepilok Batu 14 line. From the airport, the most convenient way to reach Sepilok is by taxi. Sepilok is 1.9 km from the main road. A taxi should cost around RM25 into Sandakan. You can charter a car for RM30 into Sandakan from **Sepilok Jungle Resort**.

Gomantong Caves *p699*
It is easiest to visit the caves on a tour, see Sandakan above. They are accessible by an old logging road, which can be reached by bus from the main Sandakan-Sukau Rd. The timing of the bus is inconvenient for those wishing to visit the caves. Alternatively take a taxi (around RM150 from Sandakan). It is a good idea to visit the caves on the way to Sukau, where you can stay overnight.

Danum Valley Conservation Area *p700*
From Lahad Datu, turn left along the logging road at Km 15 on the Lahad Datu-Tawau road to Taliwas and then left again to field centre, 85 km west of Lahad Datu. **Borneo Rainforest Lodge** is 97 km (not an easy trip); it provides a transfer service (2 hrs from Lahad Datu); phone the lodge for details.

Semporna *p700*
Bus/minibus Minibus station in front of USNO HQ. Regular connections with **Tawau** (RM5, 1½ hrs). Most departures are in the morning. Minibus to **Tawau airport**. One daily bus to **KK** (1930, RM48, 10 hrs).

Mataking and Kapalai *p701*
Air/sea Flight to Tawau, minibus, taxi or resort van to Semporna (1½ hrs), from where speed boats depart for the islands (30-60 mins). Boats to the islands are taken either with dive companies or as a transfer to a resort. Lots of boats leave daily but generally only in the morning between 0700-1000 for day trips.

Tawau *p701*
Air The airport is 2 km from town centre. Regular connections with **KK** and **Sandakan**.

Air Asia and MAS both run daily flights between Tawau and KL.

Airline offices Air Asia at the airport. MAS, Lot 1A, Wisma SASCO, Fajar Complex, T089-765533. **Merdeka Travel**, 41 Jl Dunlop, T089-772534/1, booking agents for **Bouraq** (Indonesian airline). **Merpati**, 47A Jl Dunlop, 1st floor, next to Borneo Divers, T089-752323. **Sabah Air**, Tawau airport, T089-774005.
Bus Station on Jl Wing Lock (west end of town). Minibus station on Jl Dunlop (centre of town). Direct service from Tawau to **Kota Kinabalu** leaving at 2000 to arrive 0500 in KK.

It's possible to drive from **Sapulut** (south of **Keningau**) across the interior to Tawau on logging roads (4WD vehicle is required).

❶ Directory

Kota Kinabalu p688, map p689
Banks There are money changers in main shopping complexes: **HSBC**, 56 Jl Gaya; **Maybank**, Jl Kemajuan/Jl Pantai; **Sabah Bank**, Wisma Tun Fuad Stephens, Jl Tuaran; **Standard Chartered**, 20 Jl Haji Saman.
Embassies and consulates British Consul, Hong Kong Bank Building, 56 Jl Gaya; **Indonesian Consulate**, Jl Karamunsing, T088-428100; **Immigration** 4th floor, Government Building, Jl Haji Yaakub, visas can be renewed at this office. **Internet** Web access is easily available and cheap. Some places offer free Wi-Fi for customers with their own laptops. Local internet cafés are often noisy and crammed with games-playing locals. **Post** General Post Office, Jl Tun Razak, Segama Quarter (poste restante facilities). **Telephone** Telekom, Block C, Kompleks Kuwaus, Jl Tunku Abdul Rahma. International and local calls, fax service.

Pulau Labuan p691
Banks HSBC, Jl Merdeka; **Standard Chartered**, Jl Tanjung Kubang (next to Victoria Hotel); **Syarikat K Abdul Kader**, money changer. **Post** General Post Office Jl Merdeka.

Beaufort p693
Banks HSBC and Standard Chartered in centre of town. **Post** General Post Office & Telekom, next to Hong Kong Bank.

Kota Belud p693
Banks Bank Pertanian, Jl Kudat; **Public Bank Berhad**, Jl Kota Kinabalu; **Sabah Finance**, Jl Ranau.

Kudat p694
Banks Standard Chartered Bank, Jl Lo Thien Hock.

Sandakan p696
Banks Most are situated on Lebuh Tiga and Jl Pelabuhan. **HSBC**, Lebuh Tiga/Jl Pelabuhan; **Standard Chartered**, Jl Pelabuhan. **Immigration** Federal Bldg, Jl Leila. **Internet** Sandakan Cybercafé, 2nd floor, Wisma Sandakan; also in Centre Point mall. **Parks office** Sabah Parks Office, Room 906, 9th floor, Wisma Khoo, Lebuh Tiga, T089-273453. Bookings for Turtle Islands National Park. **Post** General Post Office, Jl Leila, to the west of town; parcel post off Lebuh Tiga. **Telephone** Telecom Office, 6th floor, Wisma Khoo Siak Chiew, Jl Buli Sim-Sim.

Semporna p700
Internet Cyber Planet (opposite Damai), 1st floor, 0800-2200, RM3 per hr; **Zanna Computer**, next to Maybank, 1st floor; @DCCN opposite bus station, RM2 per hr (often closed). **Post** General Post Office next to minibus station.

Tawau p701
Banks Bumiputra, Jl Nusantor, on seafront; HSBC, 210 Jl Utara, opposite the padang; **Standard Chartered**, 518 Jl Habib Husein (behind HSBC); **exchange kiosk** at wharf. **Embassies and consulates** Indonesian Consulate, Jl Apas, Mile 1.5. **Immigration office** Jl Stephen. **Post** Post Office off Jl Nusantor, behind the fish market.

Background

Peninsular Malaysia history

Pre-colonial Malaya

With the arrival of successive waves of Malay immigrants about five millennia ago, the earliest settlers – the Orang Asli aboriginals – moved into the interior. The Malays established agricultural settlements on the coastal lowlands and in riverine areas and from very early on were in contact with foreign traders, thanks to the peninsula's strategic location on the sea route between India and China. Although the original tribal inhabitants of Malaya were displaced inland, they were not entirely isolated from the coastal peoples. Trade relations in which 'upriver' tribal groups exchanged forest products for commodities like salt and metal implements with 'downstream' Malays, were widespread. Malay culture on the Peninsula reflected these contacts, embracing Indian cultural traditions, Hinduism among them. In the late 14th century, the centre of power shifted from Sumatra's Srivijayan Empire across the Strait to Melaka. In 1430, the third ruler of Melaka embraced Islam and became the first sultan; the city quickly grew into a flourishing trading port. By the early 1500s it was the most important entrepôt in the region and its fame brought it to the attention of the Portuguese who, in 1511, ushered in the colonial epoch. They sacked the town and sent the sultan fleeing to Johor, where a new sultanate was established. But because of internal rivalries and continued conflict with the powerful trading sultanate of Aceh in north Sumatra as well as the Portuguese, Johor never gained the prominence of Melaka, and was forced to alternate its capital between Johor and the Riau archipelago.

The colonials arrive

The Portuguese were the first of three European colonial powers to arrive on the Malay peninsula. They were followed by the Dutch, who took Melaka in 1641 (see page 637 for a history of Melaka). When Holland was occupied by Napoleon's troops at the end of the 18th century, Britain filled the vacuum and the British colonial era began.

During the 17th century, the Dutch came into frequent conflict with the Bugis, the fearsome master-seafarers who the Dutch had displaced from their original homeland in South Sulawesi. In 1784, in league with the Minangkabau of West Sumatra, the Bugis nearly succeeded in storming Melaka and were only stymied by the arrival of Dutch warships. The Bugis eventually established the Sultanate of Selangor on the west coast of the Peninsula and, in the south, exerted increasing influence on the Johor-Riau sultans until they had reduced them to puppet-rulers. By then however, offshoots of the Johor royal family had established the sultanates of Pahang and Perak. The Minangkabau-dominated states between Melaka and Selangor formed a confederacy of nine states, or Negeri Sembilan. To the northeast, the states of Kelantan and Terengganu came under Siamese influence.

British Malaya emerges

The British occupied Dutch colonies during the Napoleonic Wars, including the Dutch East Indies (now Indonesia), following France's invasion of the Netherlands in 1794. Dutch King William of Orange, who fled to London, instructed Dutch governors overseas to end their rivalry with the British and to permit the entry of British troops to their colonies in a bid to keep the French out. Historian William R Roff writes: "From being an Indian power interested primarily ... in the free passage of trade through the Malacca

Straits and beyond to China, the East India Company suddenly found itself possessor not merely of a proposed naval station on Penang island but of numerous other territorial dominions and responsibilities."

The British had their own colonial designs, having already established a foothold on Penang where Captain Francis Light had set up a trading post in 1786. The Anglo-Dutch Treaty of London signed in 1824 effectively divided maritime Southeast Asia into British and Dutch spheres of influence. Britain retained Penang, Melaka (which it swapped for the Sumatran port of Bengkulu) and Singapore – which had been founded by Stamford Raffles in 1819 – and these formed the Straits Settlements. The Dutch regained control of their colonial territories in the Indonesian archipelago. Britain promised to stay out of Sumatra and the Dutch promised not to meddle in the affairs of the peninsula, thus separating two parts of the Malay world whose histories had been intertwined for centuries.

The British did very little to interfere with the Malay sultanates and chiefdoms on the peninsula, but the Straits Settlements grew in importance – particularly Singapore, which soon superceded Penang, which in turn had eclipsed Melaka. Chinese immigrants arrived in all three ports and from there expanded into tin mining, which rapidly emerged as the main source of wealth on the peninsula. The extent of the tin rush in the mid-19th century is exemplified in the town of Larut in northwestern Perak. Around 25,000 Chinese speculators arrived in Larut between 1848 and 1872. The Chinese fought over the rights to mine the most lucrative deposits and organized into secret societies and kongsis, which by the 1860s were engaged in open warfare. At the same time, the Malay rulers in the states on the Peninsula were busily taxing the tin traders while in the Straits Settlements, British investors in the mining industry put increasing pressure on the Colonial Office to intervene in order to stabilize the situation. In late 1873 Britain decided it could not rule the increasingly lawless and anarchic states by remote control any longer and the western-central states were declared a British protectorate. In his account of British intervention, William R Roff quotes a Malay proverb: "Once the needle is in, the thread is sure to follow".

In 1874, the Treaty of Pangkor established the residential system whereby British officers were posted to key districts; it became their job to determine all administrative and policy matters other than those governing Islam and Malay custom. This immediately provoked resentment and sparked uprisings in Perak, Selangor and Negeri Sembilan, as well as a Malay revolt in 1875. The revolts were put down and the system was institutionalized: in 1876 these three states plus Pahang became the Federated Malay States. By 1909 the north states of Kedah, Perlis, Kelantan and Terengganu – which previously came under Siamese suzerainty – finally agreed to accept British advisers and became known as the Unfederated Malay States. Johor remained independent until 1914. The British system of government relied on the political power of the sultans and the Malay aristocracy: residents conferred with the rulers of each state and employed the aristocrats as civil servants. Local headmen (known as penghulu) were used as administrators in rural areas.

Meanwhile, the British continued to encourage the immigration of Chinese, who formed a majority of the population in Perak and Selangor by the early 1920s. Apart from the wealthy traders based in the Straits Settlements, the Chinese immigrants were organized (and exploited) by their secret societies, which provided welfare services, organized work gangs and ran local government. In 1889 the societies were officially banned and while this broke their hold on political power, they simply re-emerged as a criminal underworld. In the Federated Malay States, there was an eight-fold population increase to 1.7 million between 1891 and 1931. Even by 1891 the proportion of Malays had declined to a fraction over a third of the population, with the Chinese making up

41.5% and Indians – imported as indentured labourers by the British – comprising 22%. To the south, Johor, which in the late 1800s was not even a member of the federation, had a similar ethnic balance.

For the most part, the Malay population remained in the countryside and were only gradually drawn into the modern economy. But by the 1920s Malay nationalism was on the rise, partly prompted by the Islamic reform movement and partly by intellectuals in secular circles who looked to the creation of a Greater Malaysia (or Greater Indonesia), under the influence of left-wing Indonesian nationalists. These Malay nationalists were as critical of the Malay élite as they were of the British colonialists. The élite itself was becoming increasingly outspoken for different reasons – it felt threatened by the growing demands of Straits-born Chinese and second-generation Indians for equal rights.

The first semi-political nationalist movement was the Kesatuan Melayu Singapura (Singapore Malay Union), formed in 1926. The Union found early support in the Straits Settlements where Malays were outnumbered and there was no sultan. They gradually spread across the peninsula and held a pan-Malayan conference in 1939. These associations were the forerunners of the post-war Malay nationalist movement. In the run-up to the Second World War the left wing split off to form the Kesatuan Melayu Muda – the Union of Young Malays, which was strongly anti-British and whose leaders were arrested by the colonial authorities in 1940. The Chinese were more interested in business than politics and any political interests were focused on China. The middle class supported the Chinese nationalist Kuomintang (KMT), although it was eventually banned by the British, as was becoming an obvious focus of anti-colonial sentiment. The KMT allowed communists to join the movement until 1927, but in 1930 they split off to form the Malayan Communist Party (MCP) which drew its support from the working class.

Japanese occupation

Under cover of darkness on the night of 8 December 1941, the Japanese army invaded Malaya, landing in South Thailand and pushing into Kedah, and at Kota Bharu in Kelantan. The invasion, which took place an hour before the attack on Pearl Harbor, took the Allies in Malaya and 'Fortress' Singapore completely by surprise. The Japanese forces had air, land and sea superiority and quickly overwhelmed the Commonwealth troops on the peninsula. Militarily, it was a brilliant campaign, made speedier by the fact that the Japanese troops stole bicycles in every town they took, thus making it possible for them to outpace all Allied estimates of their likely rate of advance.

By 28 December they had taken Ipoh and all of northern Malaya. Kuantan fell on the 31st, the Japanese having sunk the British warships *Prince of Wales* and *Repulse*, and Kuala Lumpur on 11 January 1942. They advanced down the east coast, centre and west coast simultaneously and by the end of the month had taken Johor Bahru and were massed across the strait from Singapore. By 15 February they had forced the capitulation of the Allies in Singapore. This was a crushing blow, and, according to Malaysian historian Zainal Abidin bin Abudul Wahid, "the speed with which the Japanese managed to achieve victory, however temporary that might have been, shattered the image of the British, and generally the 'whiteman', as a superior people". Right up until the beginning of the Second World War, the British had managed to placate the aristocratic leaders of the Malay community and the wealthy Chinese merchants and there was little real threat to the status quo. The Japanese defeat of the British changed all that by altering the balance between conservatism and change. Because Britain had failed so miserably to defend Malaya, its credentials as a protector were irrevocably tarnished.

For administrative purposes, the Japanese linked the Peninsula with Sumatra as part of the Greater East Asia Co-Prosperity Sphere. All British officials were interned and the legislative and municipal councils swept aside. But because the Japanese had lost their command of the seas by the end of 1942, nothing could be imported and there was a shortage of food supplies. The 'banana' currency introduced by the Japanese became worthless as inflation soared. Japan merely regarded Malaya as a source of raw materials, yet the rubber and tin industries stagnated and nothing was done to develop the economy.

After initially severing sultans' pensions and reducing their powers, the Japanese realized that their co-operation was necessary if the Malay bureaucracy was to be put to work for the occupation government. The Indians were treated well since they were seen as a key to fighting the British colonial regime in India, but Malaya's Chinese were not trusted. The Japanese, however, came to recognize the importance of the Chinese community in oiling the wheels of the economy. The Chinese Dalforce militia (set up by the Allies as the Japanese advanced southwards) joined the communists and other minor underground dissident groups in forming the Malayan People's Anti-Japanese Army. British army officers and arms were parachuted into the jungle to support the guerrillas. It was during this period that the Malayan Communist Party (MCP) broadened its membership and appeal, under the guise of a nationwide anti-Japanese alliance.

The brutality of the Japanese regime eased with time; as the war began to go against them, they increasingly courted the different communities, giving them more say in the run of things in an effort to undermine any return to colonial rule. But the Japanese's favourable treatment of Malays and their general mistrust of the Chinese did not foster good race relations between the two. A Malay paramilitary police force was put to work to root out Chinese who were anti-Japanese, which exacerbated inter-communal hostility. The Japanese never offered Malaya independence but allowed Malay nationalist sentiments to develop in an effort to deflect attention from the fact they had ceded the North Malay states of Kedah, Perlis, Kelantan and Terengganu to Thailand.

The British return

During the war the British drew up secret plans for a revised administrative structure in Malaya. The plan was to create a Malayan Union by combining the federated and unfederated states as well as Melaka and Penang, leaving Singapore as a crown colony. Plans were also drawn up to buy North Borneo from the Chartered Company and to replace the anachronous White Rajahs of Sarawak with a view to eventually grouping all the territories together as a federation. As soon as the Japanese surrendered in September 1945, the plan was put into action. Historian Mary Turnbull noted that "Malaya was unique [among Western colonies] because the returning British were initially welcomed with enthusiasm and were themselves unwilling to put the clock back. But they were soon overwhelmed by the reaction against their schemes for streamlining the administration and assimilating the different immigrant communities."

A unitary state was formed on the Peninsula and everyone regardless of race or origin who called Malaya 'home' was accorded equal status. But the resentment caused by British high-handedness was the catalyst which triggered the foundation of the United Malays National Organization (UMNO) which provided a focus for opposition to the colonial regime and, following independence, formed the ruling party. Opposition to UMNO, led by the Malay ruling class, forced the British to withdraw the Union proposal. The sultans refused to attend the installation of the governor and the Malays boycotted advisory councils. Mary Turnbull noted that the Malayan Union scheme was "conceived as a civil servant's dream but was born to be a politician's nightmare". Malay opposition prompted negotiations with Malay leaders which hammered out the basis of a Federation of Malaya which was established in February 1948. It was essentially the same as the Union in structure, except that it recognized the sovereignty of the sultans in the 11 states and the so-called 'special position' of the Malays as the indigenous people of Malaya. The federation had a strong central government (headed by a High Commissioner) and a federal executive council.

In this federal system, introduced in 1948, non-Malays could only become Malaysian citizens if they had been resident in Malaya for a minimum of 15 out of the previous 25 years, were prepared to sign a declaration of permanent settlement and were able to speak either Malay or English. This meant only three million of Malaya's five million population qualified as citizens, of whom 78% were Malay, 12% Chinese and 7% Indian. Historian Mary Turnbull said that while the British believed they had achieved their objective of common citizenship (even on more restricted terms), they had, in reality "accepted UMNO's concept of a Malay nation into which immigrant groups would have to be integrated, and many difficulties were to develop from this premise".

The rise of Communism

The Chinese and Indian communities were not consulted in these Anglo-Malay negotiations and ethnic and religious tensions between the three main communities were running high, unleashing the forces of racialism that had been lying dormant for years. Because their part in the political process had been ignored, many more Chinese began to identify with the Malaysian Communist Party (MCP), which was still legal. It was not until the communist victory in China in 1949 that the Chinese began to think of Malaya as home. During the war the MCP had gained legitimacy and prestige as a patriotic resistance movement. The MCP's de facto military wing, the MPAJA, had left arms dumps in the jungle, but the communist leadership was split as to whether negotiation or confrontation was the way forward. Then in 1947 the MCP suffered what many considered to be a disastrous blow: its Vietnamese-born secretary-general, Lai Teck, absconded with all the party's funds having worked as a double agent for both the Japanese and the British. He was suspected of having betrayed the entire MCP central committee to the Japanese in 1942. The new 26-year-old MCP leader, former schoolmaster Chin Peng, immediately abandoned Lai's soft approach.

In June 1948 he opted for armed rebellion and the **Malayan Communist Emergency** commenced with the murder of three European planters. According to John Gullick, the historian and former member of the Malayan civil service, it was called an 'Emergency' because the Malayan economy was covered by the London insurance market for everything other than war. Premiums covered loss of stock, property and equipment through riot and civil commotion, but not through civil war, so the misnomer continued throughout the 12-year insurrection. Others say it got its name from the Emergency Regulations that were passed in June 1948, designed to deny food supplies and weapons to the communists.

The Emergency was characterized by indiscriminate armed communist raids on economic targets – often rubber estates and tin mines – and violent ambushes that were aimed at loosening and undermining central government control. Chinese 'squatters' in areas fringing the jungle (many of whom had fled from the cities during the Japanese occupation) provided an information and supply network for the communists. In 1950 the British administration moved these people into 500 'New Villages', where they could be controlled and protected. This policy, known as 'The Briggs Plan' after the Director of Operations, Lieutenant-General Sir Harold Briggs, was later adopted (rather less successfully) by the Americans in South Vietnam.

In much the same way as they had been caught unprepared by the Japanese invasion in 1941, the British were taken by surprise and in the first few years the MCP (whose guerrillas were labelled 'CTs' – or Communist Terrorists) gained the upper hand. In 1951 British morale all but crumbled when the High Commissioner, Sir Henry Gurney, was ambushed and assassinated on the road to Fraser's Hill (see page 637). His successor, General Sir Gerald Templer, took the initiative, however, with his campaign to 'win the hearts and minds of the people'. Templer's biographer, John Cloake, gave him Japanese General Tomoyuki Yamashita's old sobriquet 'Tiger of Malaya', and there is little doubt that his tough policies won the war. In his book *Emergency Years*, former mine-manager Leonard Rayner says the chain-smoking Templer "exuded nervous energy like an overcharged human battery". Within two years the communists were on the retreat. They had also begun to lose popular support due to the climate of fear they introduced, although the Emergency did not officially end until 1960. Historians believe the communist rebellion failed because it was too slow to take advantage of the economic hardships in the immediate aftermath of the Second World War and because it was almost exclusively Chinese. It also only really appealed to the Chinese working class and alienated and shunned the Chinese merchant community and Straits-born Chinese.

The road to Merdeka

The British had countered the MCP's claim to be a multi-racial nationalist movement by accelerating moves towards Malayan independence, which Britain promised, once the Emergency was over. The only nationalist party with any political credibility was UMNO. Its founder, Dato' Onn bin Jaafar wanted to allow non-Malays to become members, and when his proposal was rejected he resigned to form the Independence of Malaya Party. The brother of the Sultan of Kedah, Tunku Abdul Rahman, took over as head of UMNO and to counter Onn's new party he made an electoral pact with the Malayan Chinese Association (MCA) and the Malayan Indian Congress (MIC). With the MCP out of the picture the Chinese community hesitantly grouped itself around the MCA. The Alliance (which trounced Onn's party in the election) is still in place today, in the form of the ruling Barisan Nasional (National Front). After sweeping the polls in 1955, the Alliance called immediately for *merdeka*, or independence, which the British guaranteed within two years.

With independence promised by non-violent means, Tunku Abdul Rahman offered an amnesty to the communists. Together with Singapore's Chief Minister, David Marshall and Straits-Chinese leader Tan Cheng Lock, he met Chin Peng in 1956. But they failed to reach agreement and the MCP fled through the jungle into the mountains in southern Thailand around Betong. While the Emergency was declared 'over' in 1960, the MCP only finally agreed to lay down its arms in 1989, in a peace agreement brokered by Thailand. The party had been riven by factionalism and its membership had dwindled to under 1000. In 1991, the legendary Chin Peng struck a deal with the Malaysian government allowing former guerrillas to return home. Historian Mary Turnbull wrote: "When Malaya attained independence in 1957 it was a prosperous country with stable political institutions, a sound administrative system and a good infrastructure of education and communications – a country with excellent resources and a thriving economy based on export agriculture and mining". Under the new constitution, a king was to be chosen from one of the nine sultans, and the monarchy was to be rotated every five years. A two-tier parliament was set up, with a Dewan Rakyat (People's House) of elected representatives and a Dewan Negara (Senate) to represent the state assemblies. Each of the 11 states had its own elected government and a sultan or governor.

Politicians in Singapore made it clear that they also wanted to be part of an independent Malaya, but in Kuala Lumpur, UMNO leaders were opposed to a merger because the island had a Chinese majority (a straight merger would have resulted in a small Chinese majority in Malaya.) Increasing nationalist militancy in Singapore was of particular concern to UMNO and the radical wing of the People's Action Party, which was swept to power with Lee Kuan Yew at its head in 1959, was dominated by communists. Fearing the emergence of 'a second Cuba' on Malaysia's doorstep, Tunku Abdul Rahman proposed that Singapore join a greater Malaysian Federation, in which a racial balance would be maintained by the inclusion of Sarawak, Brunei and British North Borneo (Sabah). Britain supported the move, as did all the states involved. Kuala Lumpur was particularly keen on Brunei joining the Federation on two scores: it had Malays and oil. But at the eleventh hour, Brunei's Sultan Omar backed out, mistrustful of Kuala Lumpur's designs on his sultanate's oil revenues and unhappy at the prospect of becoming another sultan in Malaya's collection of nine monarchs.

Prime Minister Tunku Abdul Rahman was disheartened, but the Malaysia Agreement was signed in July 1963 with Singapore, Sarawak and Sabah. Without Brunei, there was a small Chinese majority in the new Malaysia. The Tunku did not have time to dwell on racial arithmetic, however, because almost immediately the new federation was plunged into an undeclared war with Indonesia – which became known as Konfrontasi, or Confrontation (see page 728) – due to President Sukarno's objection to the participation of Sabah and Sarawak. Indonesian saboteurs were landed on the Peninsula and in Singapore and there were Indonesian military incursions along the borders of Sabah and Sarawak with Kalimantan. Konfrontasi was finally ended in 1966 after Sukarno fell from power. But relations with Singapore – which had been granted a greater measure of autonomy than other states – were far from smooth. Communal riots in Singapore in 1964 and Lee Kuan Yew's efforts to forge a nation-wide opposition alliance which called for 'a democratic Malaysian Malaysia' further opened the rift with Kuala Lumpur. Feeling unnerved by calls for racial equality while the Malays did not form a majority of the population, Tunku Abdul Rahman expelled Singapore from the federation in August 1965 against Lee Kuan Yew's wishes.

Racial politics in the 1960s

The expulsion of Singapore did not solve the racial problem on the peninsula, however. As the Malay and Chinese communities felt threatened by each other – one wielded political power, the other economic power – racial tensions built up. Resentment focused on the enforcement of Malay as the medium of instruction in all schools and as the national language and on the privileged educational and employment opportunities afforded to Malays. The tensions finally exploded on 13 May 1969, in the wake of the general election.

The UMNO-led Alliance faced opposition from the Democratic Action Party (DAP) which was built from the ashes of Lee Kuan Yew's People's Action Party. The DAP was a radical Chinese-dominated party and called for racial equality. Also in opposition was Gerakan (the People's Movement), supported by Chinese and Indians, and the Pan-Malayan Islamic Party, which was exclusively Malay and very conservative. In the election, the opposition parties – which were not in alliance – deprived the Alliance of the two-thirds parliamentary majority required to amend the constitution unimpeded. Gerakan and DAP celebrations provoked counter-demonstrations from Malays and in the ensuing mayhem hundreds were killed in Kuala Lumpur.

The government suspended the constitution for over a year and declared a State of Emergency. A new national ideology was drawn up – the controversial New Economic Policy, which was an ambitious experiment in social and economic engineering aimed at ironing out discrepancies between ethnic communities. The Rukunegara, a written national ideology aimed at fostering nation-building, was introduced in August 1970. It demanded loyalty to the king and the constitution, respect for Islam and observance of the law and morally acceptable behaviour. All discussion of the Malays' 'special position' was banned as was discussion about the national language and the sovereignty of the sultans. In the words of historian John Gullick, "Tunku Abdul Rahman, whose anguish at the disaster had impeded his ability to deal with it effectively," resigned the following month and handed over to Tun Abdul Razak. Tun Razak was an able administrator, but lacked the dynamism of his predecessor. He did, however, unify UMNO and patched up the old Alliance, breathing new life into the coalition by incorporating every political party except the DAP and one or two other small parties into the newly named Barisan Nasional (BN), or National Front. In 1974 the Barisan won a landslide majority.

Tun Razak shifted Malaysia's foreign policy from a pro-Western stance to non-alignment and established diplomatic relations with both Moscow and Beijing. Yet within Malaysia communist paranoia was rife: as Indochina fell to communists in the mid-1970s, many Malaysians became increasingly convinced that Malaysia was just another 'domino' waiting to topple. There were even several arrests of prominent Malays (including two newspaper editors and five top UMNO politicians). But when Chin Peng's revolutionaries joined forces with secessionist Muslims in South Thailand, the Thai and Malaysian governments launched a joint clean-out operation in the jungle along the frontier. By the late 1970s the North Kalimantan Communist Party had been beaten into virtual submission too. In 1976 Tun Razak died and was succeeded by his brother-in-law, Dato' Hussein Onn (the son of Umno's founding father). He inherited an economy that was in good shape, thanks to strong commodity prices, and in the general election of 1978 the BN won another comfortable parliamentary majority. Three years later he handed over to Dr Mahathir Mohamad.

Modern politics

On the face of it, Malaysia's political landscape is remarkably unchanging. Abdullah Ahmad Badawi, who succeeded Dr Mahathir Mohamad in October 2003, and won a landslide victory in elections in 2004 heads the Barisan Nasional (BN), or National Front coalition. (Mahathir had ruled for 22 years as Asia's longest-serving elected leader.) Since the first general election was held back in 1959 the largest number of parliamentary seats won by an opposition party has been 27 – by the PAS in 1999. In the latest election in 2004, the ruling coalition expanded their mandate by winning 198 out of the 219 parliamentary seats and 452 out of the 505 state seats. It won control of 11 of the 12 state governments. The opposition secured only 20 parliamentary seats and lost control of Terengganu state and kept control of Kelantan by a wafer-thin margin. The ruling coalition are very much in control and have been over all 11 general elections held since 1959.

With the rapid expansion of Malaysia's economy, and notwithstanding the recession associated with the Asian economic crisis of 1997-1999 and a global slump in 2001-2002, there has emerged a substantial nouveau riche middle class. There has, in turn, been the expectation in some quarters that a more open political system might evolve as prosperous, and increasingly well educated, people demand more of a political say. But the government does not readily tolerate dissent and during the premiership of Dr Mahathir power had, in fact, become increasingly concentrated in the hands of the government. Many Malaysians hoped that Badawi, who was seen as the 'nice guy' in Malaysian politics, would open up the arena. Opinions are divided as to whether or not this was actually the case. One sign of Badawi's potential was the release of Anwar Ibrahim (see below) who had been jailed on corruption and sodomy charges six years previously.

Anwar Ibrahim: Malaysia's trial of the century

It may have become commonplace in Malaysia for opposition politicians, free-thinking jurists, environmentalists and other assorted annoyances to be hounded, arrested, tried and jailed, but not mainstream Malay politicians. It is this which rocked Malaysia's political establishment when Anwar Ibrahim, former deputy prime minister and Mahathir's successor in waiting, was arrested in late 1998. Anwar was sacked by Mahathir on 2 September 1998. This was preceded by a series of murky allegations impugning Anwar's morals. In particular, there were whispers that he was bisexual. Not only is this beyond the pale in a largely Muslim country like Malaysia, but homosexuality remains a crime. Anwar's supporters saw this whispering campaign as politically motivated and the result of a widening gulf between Mahathir and his deputy over how to manage the economy.

A few days after he was sacked, Anwar was arrested and charged with five counts of sodomy and five charges of abuse of power. But before his second appearance in court Anwar appeared with bruised arms and a black eye, and accused the police of beating him. Mahathir seemed to imply that the injuries were self-inflicted. Anwar's treatment at the hands of the police as well as the crude and one-sided coverage in the government-controlled press angered many Malaysians. They did not believe the charges, and as the trial continued they became less and less credible. Nonetheless, on 14 April 1999, Anwar was convicted of corruption with a jail sentence for six years and convicted of sodomy and sentenced to nine years in jail. Anwar appealed against both convictions. In 2002, he lost his final appeal against the corruption charges in the federal court. In September 2004, a federal court of three judges overturned the sodomy conviction at 2 to 1 because of inconsistencies in the prosection's evidence. As Anwar had already served the six years for corruption, he was freed. Shortly after he was freed Anwar tried to have the corruption conviction lifted, but he failed in his appeal. The court found Anwar fairly convicted on those charges. Because his conviction was not lifted, Anwar cannot return to politics until April 2008. Directly after Anwar was freed he flew to Germany for back treatment. He alleged the injuries came from abuse during his arrest and jail time. Prime Minister Badawi cautioned overseas leaders not to visit Anwar.

The immediate aftermath of the Anwar affair brought demonstrators onto the streets of Kuala Lumpur, created demands for *reformasi* and led to the creation of a new opposition party, the Justice Party (Keadilan), led by Anwar's wife Wan Azizah.

Whether the court had exerted its independence or the order for his release came from above, Anwar's freedom would have been unthinkable under Mahathir.

General elections

The 2004 general election was the first one since 1981 not contested by Mahathir who had tearfully resigned and handed over to his deputy Abdullah Ahmad Badawi in October 2003. The sacking and imprisonment on allegedly trumped up charges of Anwar Ibrahim was not an issue. The public had forgotten him despite efforts by the opposition to revive his case. Also Badawi's face was on the election posters, and it was Mahathir who was associated with Anwar's treatment.

Most observers agree that BN's landslide victory came because it played the Islamic fundamentalism card. Many of Malaysia's Muslims follow a moderate form of the religion and do not support the idea of an Islamic state. The Islamist PAS wanted to ban rock concerts, make dress more conservative and separate sexes on beaches and even supermarkets. Moreover, the media is under government control; the BN easily dominated newspapers and TV.

Prime Minister Mr Badawi called an election in March 2008, a year ahead of schedule, but suffered the worst result in decades, winning only a simple majority. Critics point to the fact that Anwar Ibrahim – barred from re-entering political office until April 2008 – was unable to stand at the elections. If he plans to run in the future, Anwar will have to wait up to five years before another general election is called.

Money, politics and corruption

The entrenched position of UMNO and the BN has, in the eyes of the government's critics, allowed money politics and political patronage to flourish. It is argued that the use of political power to dispense favours and make money has become endemic, so much so that it is accepted as just another part of the political landscape.

Badawi has made stamping out corruption one of his main aims and although it is early days, observers note the prime minister has gone some way to achieving them. He has strengthened a number of anti-corruption agencies and arrested some Mahathir-era cronies. However, critics comment that the pace of change is too slow.

Many suggested that Mahathir worsened the corruption problem. They blamed his style and his emphasis on wealth creation. Chandra Muzaffar, a political scientist at the Science University of Malaysia in Penang argued that "He's created a culture that places undue emphasis on wealth accumulation for its own sake. The new heroes are all corporate barons".

Racial relations in the New Malaysia

Since the race riots of 1969, relations between Malaysia's Malay and Chinese populations have dominated political affairs. Now that Malaysia is fast attaining economic maturity a debate is beginning to emerge about whether it is time to consign racial politics, and racial quotas, to the dust heap. Former Prime Minister Mahathir's Vision 2020, which sets out a path to developed country status by 2020, significantly talks of a 'Malaysian race working in full and equal partnership'. There is no mention here of 'bumiputras' and 'Chinese Malaysians', but of a single Malaysian identity which transcends race.

In late 2007 Malaysia saw its biggest street demonstrations in years, when the ethnic Indian community gathered in protest about the affirmative-action policy favouring ethnic Malays. They argued that the Malay-dominated ruling coalition government discriminated against minority groups, denying them basic opportunities in education and business.

Foreign relations

In foreign affairs Malaysia follows a non-aligned stance and is fiercely anti-communist. This, however, has not stopped its enthusiastic investment in Indochina and Myanmar (Burma). Malaysia is a leading light in the Association of Southeast Asian Nations (ASEAN).

Malaysia's most delicate relations are with neighbouring Singapore, a country with which it is connected by history and also by water pipelines and a causeway. Until it was ejected in 1965, Singapore was part of the Malaysian Federation and Singapore's status as a largely Chinese city state makes for an uneasy relationship with Malay-dominated Malaysia. In 1997 sensitivities were made all too clear when a spat threatened to escalate into a major diplomatic conflict. The cause? A dispute over whether Johor Bahru was a safe place or not.

Sarawak background

History

Sarawak earned its place in the archaeological textbooks when a 37,000-year-old human skull belonging to a boy of about 15 was unearthed in the Niah Caves in 1958, predating the earliest relics found on the Malay Peninsula by about 30,000 years. The caves were continuously inhabited for tens of thousands of years and many shards of palaeolithic and neolithic pottery, tools and jewellery as well as carved burial boats have been excavated at the site. There are also prehistoric cave paintings. In the first millennium AD, the Niah Caves were home to a prosperous community, which traded birds' nests, hornbill ivory, bezoar stones, rhinoceros horns and other jungle produce with Chinese traders in exchange for porcelain and beads.

Some of Sarawak's tribes may be descended from these cave people, although others, notably the Iban shifting cultivators, migrated from Kalimantan's Kapuas River valley from the 16th to 19th centuries. Malay Orang Laut, sea people, migrated to Sarawak's coasts and made a living from fishing, trading and piracy. At the height of Sumatra's Srivijayan Empire in the 11th and 12th centuries, many Sumatran Malays migrated to north Borneo. Chinese traders were active along the Sarawak coast from as early as the seventh century: Chinese coins and Han pottery have been discovered at the mouth of the Sarawak River.

From the 14th century right up to the 20th century, Sarawak's history was inextricably intertwined with that of the neighbouring Sultanate of Brunei, which, until the arrival of the White Rajahs of Sarawak, held sway over the coastal areas of north Borneo. For a more detailed account of how Sarawak's White Rajahs came to whittle away the sultan's territory and expand into the vacuum of his receding empire, see Robert Payne's *The White Rajahs of Sarawak*.

Enter James Brooke

As the Sultanate of Brunei began to decline around the beginning of the 18th century, the Malays of coastal Sarawak attempted to break free from their tributary overlord. They claimed an independent ancestry from Brunei and exercised firm control over the Dayak tribes inland and upriver. But in the early 19th century Brunei started to reassert its power over them, dispatching Pangiran Mahkota from the Brunei court in 1827 to govern Sarawak and supervise the mining of high-grade antimony ore, which was exported to Singapore to be used in medicine and as an alloy. The name 'Sarawak' comes from the Malay word serawak, meaning 'antimony'.

Mahkota founded Kuching, but relations with the local Malays became strained and Mahkota's problems were compounded by the marauding Ibans of the Saribas and Skrang rivers who raided coastal communities. In 1836 the local Malay chiefs, led by Datu Patinggi Ali, rebelled against Governor Mahkota, prompting the Sultan of Brunei to send his uncle, Rajah Muda Hashim to suppress the uprising. But Hashim failed to quell the disturbances and the situation deteriorated when the rebels approached the Sultan of Sambas, now in northwest Kalimantan, for help from the Dutch. Then, in 1839, James Brooke sailed up the Sarawak River to Kuching.

Hashim was desperate to regain control and Brooke, in the knowledge that the British would support any action that countered the threat of Dutch influence, struck a deal with him. He pressed Hashim to grant him the governorship of Sarawak in exchange for suppressing the rebellion, which he duly did. In 1842 Brooke became Rajah of Sarawak. Pangiran Mahkota – the now disenfranchised former governor of Sarawak – formed an alliance with an Iban pirate chief on the Skrang River, while another Brunei prince, Pangiran Usop, joined Illanun pirates. Malaysian historian J Kathirithamby-Wells wrote: "… piracy and politics became irrevocably linked and Brooke's battle against his political opponents became advertised as a morally justified war against the pirate communities of the coast."

The suppression of piracy in the 19th century became a full-time job for the Sarawak and Brunei rulers, although the court of Brunei was well known to have derived a large chunk of its income from piracy. Rajah James Brooke believed that as long as pirates were free to pillage the coast, commerce wouldn't grow and his kingdom would never develop; ridding Sarawak's estuaries of pirates – both Iban (Sea Dayaks) and Illanun – became an act of political survival. In *The White Rajahs of Sarawak*, Robert Payne wrote: "Nearly every day people came to Kuching with tales about the pirates: how they had landed in a small creek, made their way to a village, looted everything in sight, murdered everyone they could lay their hands on, and then vanished as swiftly as they came. The Sultan of Brunei was begging for help against them."

Anti-piracy missions afforded James Brooke an excuse to extend his kingdom, as he worked his way up the coasts, 'pacifying' the Sea Dayak pirates. Brooke declared war on them and with the help of Royal Naval Captain Henry Keppel (of latter-day Singapore's Keppel Shipyard fame), he led a number of punitive raids against the Iban Sea Dayaks in 1833, 1834 and 1849. "The assaults", wrote DJM Tate in *Rajah Brooke's Borneo*, "largely achieved their purpose and were applauded in the Straits, but the appalling loss of life incurred upset many drawing room humanitarians in Britain." There were an estimated 25,000 pirates living along the North Borneo coast when Brooke became Rajah. He led many expeditions against them, culminating in his notorious battle against the Saribas pirate fleet in 1849.

In that incident, Brooke ambushed and killed hundreds of Saribas Dayaks at Batang Maru. The barbarity of the ambush (which was reported in the *Illustrated London News*) outraged public opinion in Britain and in Singapore; a commission in Singapore acquitted Brooke, but badly damaged his prestige. In the British parliament, he was cast as a 'mad despot' who had to be prevented from committing further massacres. But the action led the Sultan of Brunei to grant him the Saribas and Skrang districts (now Sarawak's Second Division) in 1853, marking the beginning of the Brooke dynasty's relentless expansionist drive. Eight years later, James Brooke persuaded the sultan to give him what became Sarawak's Third Division, after he drove out the Illanun pirates who disrupted the sago trade from Mukah and Oya, around Bintulu.

In 1857, James Brooke ran into more trouble. Chinese Hakka goldminers, who had been in Bau (further up the Sarawak River) longer than he had been in Kuching, had grown resentful of his attempts to stamp out the opium trade and their secret societies. They attacked Kuching, set the Malay kampongs ablaze and killed several European officials; Brooke escaped by swimming across the river from his astana. His nephew, Charles, led a group of Skrang Dayaks in pursuit of the Hakka invaders, who fled across the border into Dutch Borneo; about 1000 were killed by the Ibans on the way; 2500 survived. Robert Payne writes: "The fighting lasted for more than a month. From time to time Dayaks would return with strings of heads, which they cleaned and smoked over slow fires, especially happy when they could do this in full view of the Chinese in the bazaars who sometimes recognized people they had known." Payne says Brooke was plagued by guilt over how he handled the Chinese rebellion, for so many deaths could not easily be explained away. Neither James nor Charles ever fully trusted the Chinese again, although the Teochew, Cantonese and Hokkien merchants in Kuching never caused them any trouble.

The second generation: Rajah Charles Brooke

Charles Johnson (who changed his name to Brooke after his elder brother, Brooke Johnson, had been disinherited by James for insubordination) became the second Rajah of Sarawak in 1863. He ruled for nearly 50 years. Charles did not have James Brooke's forceful personality, and was much more reclusive – probably as a result of working in remote jungle outposts for 10 years in government service. Robert Payne noted that "in James Brooke there was something of the knight errant at the mercy of his dream. Charles was the pure professional, a stern soldier who thought dreaming was the occupation of fools. There was no nonsense about him." Despite this he engendered great loyalty in his administrators, who worked hard for little reward.

Charles maintained his uncle's consultative system of government and formed a Council Negeri, or national council, of his top government officials, Malay leaders and tribal headmen, which met every few years to hammer out policy changes. His frugal financial management meant that by 1877 Sarawak was no longer in debt and the economy gradually expanded. But it was not wealthy, however, and had few natural resources; its soils proved unsuitable for agriculture. In the 1880s, Charles's faith in the Chinese community was sufficiently restored to allow Chinese immigration, and the government subsidized the new settlers. By using 'friendly' downriver Dayak groups to subdue belligerent tribes upriver, Charles managed to pacify the interior by 1880.

When Charles took over from his ailing uncle in 1863 he proved to be even more of an expansionist. In 1868 he tried to take control of the Baram River valley, but London did not approve secession of the territory until 1882, when it became the Fourth Division. In 1884, Charles acquired the Trusan Valley from the Sultan of Brunei, and in 1890, he annexed Limbang ending a six-year rebellion by local chiefs against the sultan. The two territories were united to form the Fifth Division, after which Sarawak completely surrounded Brunei. In 1905, the British North Borneo Chartered Company gave up the Lawas Valley to Sarawak too. "By 1890," writes Robert Payne, "Charles was ruling over a country as large as England and Scotland with the help of about 20 European officers." When the First World War broke out in 1914, Charles was in England and he ruled Sarawak from Cirencester.

The third generation: Charles Vyner Brooke

In 1916, at the age of 86, Charles handed power to his eldest son, Charles Vyner Brooke, and he died the following year. Vyner was 42 when he became Rajah and had already served his father's government for nearly 20 years. "Vyner was a man of peace, who took no delight in bloodshed and ruled with humanity and compassion," wrote Robert Payne. He was a delegator by nature, and under him the old paternalistic style of government gave way to a more professional bureaucracy. On the centenary of the Brooke administration in September 1941, Vyner promulgated a written constitution, and renounced his autocratic powers in favour of working in cooperation with a Supreme Council. This was opposed by his nephew and heir, Anthony Brooke, who saw it as a move to undermine his succession. To protest against this, and his uncle's decision to appoint a mentally deranged Muslim Englishman as his Chief Secretary, Anthony left for Singapore. The Rajah dismissed him from the service in September 1941. Three months later the Japanese Imperial Army invaded; Vyner Brooke was in Australia at the time, and his younger brother, Bertram, was ill in London.

Japanese troops took Kuching on Christmas Day 1941 having captured the Miri oilfield a few days earlier. European administrators were interned and many later died. A Kuching-born Chinese, Albert Kwok, led an armed resistance against the Japanese in neighbouring British North Borneo (Sabah), but in Sarawak there was no organized guerrilla movement. Iban tribespeople instilled fear into the occupying forces, however, by roaming the jungle taking Japanese heads, which were proudly added to much older longhouse head galleries. Despite the Brooke regime's century-long effort to stamp out headhunting, the practice was encouraged by Tom Harrisson who parachuted into the Kelabit Highlands towards the end of the Second World War and put together an irregular army of upriver tribesmen to fight the Japanese. He offered them 'ten-bob-a-nob' for Japanese heads. Australian forces liberated Kuching on 11 September 1945 and Sarawak was placed under Australian military administration for seven months.

After the war, the Colonial Office in London decided the time had come to bring Sarawak into the modern era, replacing the anachronistic White Rajahs, introducing an education system and building a rudimentary infrastructure. The Brookes had become an embarrassment to the British government as they continued to squabble among themselves. Anthony Brooke desperately wanted to claim what he felt was his, while the Colonial Office wanted Sarawak to become a crown colony or revert to Malay rule. No one was sure whether Sarawak wanted the Brookes back or not.

The end of empire

In February 1946 the ageing Vyner shocked his brother Bertram and his nephew Anthony, the Rajah Muda (or heir apparent), by issuing a proclamation urging the people of Sarawak to accept the King of England as their ruler. In doing so he effectively handed the country over to Britain. Vyner thought the continued existence of Sarawak as the private domain of the Brooke family an anachronism; but Anthony thought it a betrayal. The British government sent a commission to Sarawak to ascertain what the people wanted. In May 1946, the Council Negeri agreed – by a 19-16 majority – to transfer power to Britain, provoking protests and demonstrations and resulting in the assassination of the British governor by a Malay in Sibu in 1949. He and three other anti-cessionists were sentenced to death. Two years later, Anthony Brooke, who remained deeply resentful about the demise of the Brooke Dynasty, abandoned his claim and urged his supporters to end their campaign.

As a British colony, Sarawak's economy expanded and oil and timber production increased, which funded the much-needed expansion of education and health services. As with British North Borneo (Sabah), Britain was keen to give Sarawak political independence and, following Malaysian independence in 1957, saw the best means to this end as being through the proposal of Malaysian Prime Minister Tunku Abdul Rahman. The prime minister suggested the formation of a federation to include Singapore, Sarawak, Sabah and Brunei as well as the peninsula. In the end, Brunei opted out, Singapore left after two years, but Sarawak and Sabah joined the federation, having accepted the recommendations of the British government. Indonesia's President Sukarno denounced the move, claiming it was all part of a neo-colonialist conspiracy. He declared a policy of confrontation – **Konfrontasi**. A United Nations commission which was sent to ensure that the people of Sabah and Sarawak wanted to be part of Malaysia reported that Indonesia's objections were unfounded.

Skulls in the longhouse

Although headhunting has been largely stamped out in Borneo, there is still the odd reported case once every few years. But until the early 20th century, head-hunting was commonplace among many Dayak tribes, particularly among the Iban.

Following a headhunting trip, the freshly taken heads were skinned, placed in rattan nets and smoked over a fire, or sometimes boiled. The skulls were then hung from the rafters of the longhouse and they possessed the most powerful form of magic.

The skulls were considered trophies of manhood, symbols of bravery and they testified to the unity of a longhouse. Festivals (*gawai*) were held to appease the spirits of the skulls. Once placated, the heads were believed to bring great blessing – they could ward off evil spirits, save villages from epidemics, produce rain and increase the yield

of rice harvests. Heads that were insulted or ignored were capable of wreaking havoc in the form of bad dreams, plagues, floods and fires. To keep the spirits of the skulls happy, they would be offered food and cigarettes and made to feel welcome. The magical powers of a skull faded with time, so fresh heads were always in demand. Tribes without heads were seen as spiritually weak.

Today, Dayak men no longer have to take heads to gain respect. They are, however, expected to go on long journeys (the equivalent of the Australian aborigines' Walkabout). The unspoken rule is that they should come back with plenty of good stories, and, these days, as most *bejalai* expeditions translate into stints at timber camps or on oil rigs, they are expected to come home bearing video recorders, TVs and motorbikes.

Communists had been active in Sarawak since the 1930s. The *Konfrontasi* afforded the Sarawak Communist Organization (SCO) Jakarta's support against the Malaysian government. The SCO joined forces with the North Kalimantan Communist Party (NKCP) and were trained and equipped by Indonesia's President Sukarno. But following Jakarta's brutal suppression of the Indonesian communists, the Partai Komunis Indonesia (PKI), in the wake of the attempted coup in 1965, Sarawak's communists fled back across the Indonesian border, along with their Kalimantan comrades. There they continued to wage guerrilla war against the Malaysian government throughout the 1970s. The Sarawak state government offered amnesties to guerrillas wanting to come out of hiding. In 1973 the NKCP leader surrendered along with 482 other guerrillas. A handful remained in the jungle, most of them in the hills around Kuching. The last surrendered in 1990.

Politics and modern Sarawak

In 1957 Kuala Lumpur was keen to have Sarawak and Sabah in the Federation of Malaysia and offered the two states a degree of autonomy, allowing their local governments control over state finances, agriculture and forestry. Sarawak's racial mix was reflected in its chaotic state politics. The Ibans dominated the Sarawak National Party (SNAP), which provided the first chief minister, Datuk Stephen Kalong Ningkan. He raised a storm over Kuala Lumpur's introduction of Bahasa Malaysia in schools and complained bitterly about the federal government's policy of filling the Sarawakian civil service with Malays from the peninsula. An 'us' and 'them' mentality developed: in Sarawak, the Malay word

Tribes of Borneo

Borneo has one of the most varied human social groups in the world. Today, a third of the population is made up of indigenous tribespeople, incorporating 30 Dayak sub-ethnic groups and more than 50 different languages. Some groups are made up of just 30-100 individuals and are threatened with extinction. The colonists converted many of the tribes to Christianity or Islam. However, now it is globalism in the form of logging and large-scale plantations that threatens their traditional way of life.

The **Iban** are traditionally outgoing and welcoming to visitors. The women are skilled weavers; even today a girl is not considered eligible until she has proven her skills at the loom. During the harvest festival in June, visitors are welcome to drink copious amounts of *tuak* (rice wine) and dance through the night. The Iban remain in closely bonded family groups and are a classless society. They have an easy-going attitude to love and sex. Free love is the general rule but once married, the Iban divorce rate is low and they are expected to be monogamous.

The **Kelabit**, who live in the highlands at the source of the Baram River, are closely related to the Murut. They are skilled hill-rice farmers. The hill climate also allows them to cultivate vegetables. Kelabit parties are famed as boisterous occasions, and large quantities of *borak* (rice beer) are consumed. They are regarded as among the most hospitable tribes.

The **Kenyah** and **Kayan** are closely related groups now living mainly in Sarawak and Kalimantan. They were the traditional rivals of the Iban and were notorious for their warlike ways. They have a completely different language to other Dayak groups (which have ancient Malayo-Polynesian roots) and are class conscious, with a well-defined social hierarchy.

Traditionally their society was composed of aristocrats, nobles, commoners and slaves (who were snatched during raids on other tribes). They are much more introverted than the Ibans but renowned for their parties: to test the strength of a new friendship, visitors are given *borak* (rice beer) then have their faces covered in soot before being thrown in the river. Their artwork is made from wood, antlers, metal and beads. They use wooden statues and masks to scare evil spirits from their homes.

The **Kadazan** (also known as Dusuns), live in Sabah and East Kalimantan. They traditionally traded their agricultural produce at large markets called *tamus*. They used to be animists and were said to live in great fear of evil spirits. The job of communicating with the spirits of the dead, the *tombiivo*, was done by priestesses, called *bobohizan*. The big cultural event is the harvest festival in May. The ceremony, known as the *Magavau* ritual, is officiated by a high priestess (elderly women in black costumes and colourful headgear with feathers and beads). The ceremony ends with offerings to the *Bambaazon* (rice spirit) followed by sports such as wrestling and buffalo racing.

The **Murut** ('hill people') live in the southwest of Sabah and North Sarawak. In remote jungle areas they retain a traditional longhouse way of life, but many Murut have opted for detached kampong-style houses. The Murut staples are rice and tapioca; they are known for their weaving and basketry and have a penchant for drinking *tapai*. They are also enthusiastic dancers and devised the *lansaran*, a sprung dance floor like a trampoline. Formally animists, the Murut were the last tribe in Sabah to give up headhunting, a practice stopped by the British North Borneo Chartered Company.

semenanjung (peninsula) was used to label the newcomers. To many, *semenanjung* was Malaysia, Sarawak was Sarawak.

In 1966 the federal government ousted the SNAP, and a new Muslim-dominated government led by the Sarawak Alliance took over in Kuching. But there was still strong political opposition to federal encroachment. Throughout the 1970s, as in Sabah, Sarawak's strongly Muslim government drew the state closer and closer to the peninsula: it supported *Rukunegara* – the policy of Islamization – and promoted the use of Bahasa Malaysia. Muslims make up less than one-third of the population of Sarawak. The Malays, Melanaus and Chinese communities grew rich from the timber industry; the Ibans and the Orang Ulu (the upriver tribespeople) saw little in the way of development. They did not reap the benefits of the expansion of education and social services, they were unable to get public sector jobs and, to make matters worse, logging firms were encroaching on their native lands and threatening their traditional lifestyles.

It has only been in more recent years that the tribespeoples' political voice has been heard at all. In 1983, Iban members of SNAP – which was a part of former Prime Minister Dr Mahathir Mohamad's ruling Barisan Nasional (National Front) coalition – split to form the Party Bansa Dayak Sarawak (PBDS), which, although it initially remained in the coalition, became more outspoken on native affairs. At about the same time, international outrage was sparked over the exploitation of Sarawak's tribespeople by politicians and businessmen involved in the logging industry. The plight of the Penan hunter-gatherers came to world attention due to their blockades of logging roads and the resulting publicity highlighted the rampant corruption and greed that characterized modern Sarawak's political economy.

The National Front remain firmly in control in Sarawak. But unlike neighbouring Sabah, Sarawak's politicians are not dominated by the centre. The chief minister of Sarawak is Taib Mahmud, a Melanau, and his Parti Pesaka Bumiputra Bersatu is a member of the UMNO-dominated (United Malays National Organisation) National Front. But in Sarawak itself UMNO wields little power.

The ruling National Front easily won the 1999 election in Sarawak, successfully playing on voters' local concerns and grievances. The problem for the opposition is that local people think it is the state legislature that can help, not the federal parliament in KL, which seems distant and ineffective. So UMNO does not have a presence and it is the Parti Pesaka Bumiputra Bersatu which represents Sarawak in the National Front.

The challenge of getting the voters out in the most remote areas of the country was clearly shown in Long Lidom. There it cost the government RM65,000 to provide a helicopter to poll just seven Punan Busang in a longhouse on the Upper Kajang, close to the border with Indonesia. Datuk Omar of the Election Commission said that mounting the general election in Sarawak, with its 28 parliamentary seats, was a "logistical nightmare". Along with a small air force of helicopters, the Commission used 1032 long boats, 15 speed boats and 3054 land cruisers. The Commission's workforce numbered a cool 13,788 workers in a state with a population of just two million.

Today there are many in Sarawak as well as in Sabah who wish their governments had opted out of the Federation, as did Brunei. Sarawak is of great economic importance to Malaysia, thanks to its oil, gas and timber. The state now accounts for more than one-third of Malaysia's petroleum production (worth more than US$800 million per year) and more than half of its natural gas. As with neighbouring Sabah however, 95% of Sarawak's oil and gas revenues go directly into federal coffers.

Sabah background

The name Sabah is probably from the Arabic *Zir-e Bad* (the land below the wind). Appropriately, as the state lies just south of the typhoon belt. Officially, the territory has only been called Sabah since 1963, when it joined the Malay federation, but the name appears to have been in use long before that. When Baron Gustav Von Overbeck was awarded the cession rights to North Borneo by the Sultan of Brunei in 1877, one of the titles conferred on him was Maharajah of Sabah. In the *Handbook of British North Borneo*, published in 1890, it says: "In Darvel Bay there are the remnants of a tribe which seems to have been much more plentiful in bygone days – the Sabahans". From the founding of the Chartered Company until 1963, Sabah was British North Borneo.

Sabah has a population of just over 2½ million plus a good number of illegal immigrants on top of that. Sabah's inhabitants can be divided into four main groups: the Kadazan Dusun, the Bajau, the Chinese and the Murut, as well as a small Malay population. These groups are subdivided into several different tribes (see page 730).

History

Prehistoric stone tools have been found in eastern Sabah, suggesting that people were living in limestone caves in the Madai area 17,000-20,000 years ago. The caves were periodically settled from then on; pottery dating from the late neolithic period has been found, and by the early years of the first millennium AD, Madai's inhabitants were making iron spears and decorated pottery. The Madai and Baturong caves were lived in continuously until about the 16th century and several carved stone coffins and burial jars have been discovered in the jungle caves, one of which is exhibited in the Sabah State Museum. The caves were also known for their birds' nests; Chinese traders were buying the nests from Borneo as far back as AD 700. In addition, they exported camphor wood, pepper and other forest products to Imperial China.

There are very few archaeological records indicating Sabah's early history, although there is documentary evidence of links between a long-lost kingdom, based in the area of the Kinabatangan River, and the Sultanate of Brunei, whose suzerainty was once most of North Borneo. By the early 18th century, Brunei's power had begun to wane in the face of European expansionism. To counter the economic decline, it is thought the sultan increased taxation, which led to civil unrest. In 1704 the Sultan of Brunei had to ask the Sultan of Sulu's help in putting down a rebellion in Sabah and, in return, the Sultan of Sulu received most of what is now Sabah.

The would-be White Rajahs of Sabah

It was not until 1846 that the British entered into a treaty with the Sultan of Brunei and took possession of the island of Labuan, in part to counter the growing influence of the Rajah of Sarawak, James Brooke. The British were also wary of the Americans; the US Navy signed a trade treaty with the Sultan of Brunei in 1845 and in 1860 Claude Lee Moses was appointed American consul-general in Brunei Town. However, he was only interested in making a personal fortune and quickly persuaded the sultan to cede him land in Sabah. He sold these rights to two Hong Kong-based American businessmen who formed the American Trading Company of Borneo. They styled themselves as rajahs and set up a base at Kimanis, just south of Papar. It was a disaster. One of them died of malaria, the Chinese labourers they imported from Hong Kong began to starve and the settlement was abandoned in 1866. The idea of a trading colony on the North Borneo coast interested the Austrian consul in Hong Kong, Baron Gustav von Overbeck, who, in turn, sold the concept to Alfred Dent, a wealthy English businessman also based in Hong Kong. With Dent's money, Overbeck bought the Americans' cession from the Sultan of Brunei and extended the territory to cover most of modern-day Sabah. The deal was clinched on 29 December 1877, and Overbeck agreed to pay the sultan 15,000 Straits dollars a year. A few days later Overbeck discovered that the entire area had already been ceded to the Sultan of Sulu 173 years earlier, so he immediately sailed to Sulu and offered the sultan an annual payment of 5000 Straits dollars for the territory. On his return, he dropped three Englishmen off along the coast to set up trading posts; one of them was William Pryer, who founded Sandakan. Three years later, Queen Victoria granted Dent a royal charter and, to the chagrin of the Dutch, the Spanish and the Americans, the British North Borneo Company was formed. London insisted that it was to be a British-only enterprise however, and Overbeck was forced to sell out. The first managing director of the company was the Scottish adventurer and former gunrunner William C Cowie. He was in charge of the day-to-day operations of the territory, while the British government supplied a governor.

The new chartered company, with its headquarters in the City of London, was given sovereignty over Sabah and a free hand to develop it. The British administrators soon began to collect taxes from local people and quickly clashed with members of the Brunei nobility. John Whitehead, a British administrator, wrote: "I must say, it seemed rather hard on these people that they should be allowed to surrender up their goods and chattels to swell even indirectly the revenue of the company". The administration levied poll tax, boat tax, land tax, fishing tax, rice tax, *tapai* (rice wine) tax and a 10% tax on proceeds from the sale of birds' nests. Resentment against these taxes sparked the six-year Mat Salleh rebellion and the Rundum Rebellion, which peaked in 1915, during which hundreds of Muruts were killed by the British.

Relations were not helped by colonial attitudes towards the local Malays and tribal people. One particularly arrogant district officer, Charles Bruce, wrote: "The mind of the average native is equivalent to that of a child of four. So long as one remembers that the native is essentially a child and treats him accordingly he is really tractable." Most recruits to the chartered company administration were fresh-faced graduates from British universities, mainly Oxford and Cambridge. For much of the time there were only 40-50 officials running the country. Besides the government officials, there were planters and businessmen: tobacco, rubber and timber became the most important exports. There were also Anglican and Roman Catholic missionaries. British North Borneo was never much of a money-spinner – the economy suffered whenever commodity prices slumped – but it mostly managed to pay for itself until the Second World War.

The Japanese interregnum

Sabah became part of Dai Nippon, or Greater Japan, on New Year's Day 1942, when the Japanese took Labuan. On the mainland, the Japanese Imperial Army and Kempetai (military police) were faced with the might of the North Borneo Armed Constabulary, about 650 men. Jesselton (Kota Kinabalu) was occupied on 9 January and Sandakan 10 days later. All Europeans were interned and when Singapore fell in 1942, 2740 prisoners of war were moved to Sandakan, most of whom were Australian, where they were forced to build an airstrip. On its completion, the POWs were ordered to march to Ranau, 240 km through the jungle. This became known as the Borneo Death March and only six men survived.

The Japanese were hated in Sabah and the Chinese mounted a resistance movement which was led by the Kuching-born Albert Kwok Hing Nam. He also recruited Bajaus and Sulus to join his guerrilla force which launched the Double Tenth Rebellion (the attacks took place on 10 October 1943). The guerrillas took Tuaran, Jesselton and Kota Belud, killing many Japanese and sending others fleeing into the jungle. But the following day the Japanese bombed the towns and troops quickly retook them and captured the rebels. A mass execution followed in which 175 rebels were decapitated. On 10 June 1945 Australian forces landed at Labuan, under the command of American General MacArthur. Allied planes bombed the main towns and virtually obliterated Jesselton and Sandakan. Sabah was liberated on 9 September and thousands of the remaining 21,000 Japanese troops were killed in retaliation, many by Muruts.

A British military administration governed Sabah in the aftermath of the war and the cash-strapped chartered company sold the territory to the British crown for £1.4 million in 1946. The new crown colony was modelled on the chartered company's administration and rebuilt the main towns and war-shattered infrastructure. In May 1961, following Malaysian independence, Prime Minister Tunku Abdul Rahman proposed the formation of a federation incorporating Malaya (ie Peninsular Malaysia), Singapore, Brunei, Sabah and Sarawak. Later that same year, Tun Fuad Stephens, a timber magnate and newspaper publisher formed Sabah's first-ever political party, the United National Kadazan Organization (UNKO). Two other parties were founded soon afterwards: the Sabah Chinese Association and the United Sabah National Organization (USNO). The British were keen to leave the colony and the Sabahan parties debated the pros and cons of joining the proposed federation. Elections were held in late 1962 in which a UNKO-USNO alliance (the Sabah Alliance) swept to power and the following August Sabah became an independent country ... for 16 days. Like Singapore and Sarawak, Sabah opted to join the federation to the indignation of the Philippines and Indonesia who both had claims on the territory. Jakarta's objections resulted in the *Konfrontasi*, an undeclared war with Malaysia that was not settled until 1966.

Modern Sabah

Politics

Sabah's political scene has always been lively and never more so than in 1994 when the then Malaysian prime minister, Doctor Mahathir Mohamad, pulled off what commentators described as a democratic coup d'état. With great political dexterity, he out-manoeuvered his rebellious rivals and managed to dislodge the opposition state government, despite the fact that it had just won a state election.

Following Sabah's first state election in 1967, the Sabah Alliance ruled until 1975 when the newly formed multi-racial party, Berjaya, swept the polls. Berjaya had been set up with the financial backing of the United Malays National Organization (UMNO), the mainstay of the ruling Barisan Nasional (National Front) coalition on the Peninsula. Over the following decade that corrupt administration crumbled and in 1985 the opposition Sabah United Party (PBS), led by the Christian Kadazan Datuk Joseph Pairin Kitingan, won a landslide victory and became the only state government in Malaysia that did not belong to the UMNO-led coalition. It became an obvious embarrassment to then Prime Minister Doctor Mahathir Mohamad to have a rebel Christian state in his predominantly Muslim federation. Nonetheless, the PBS eventually joined Barisan Nasional, believing its partnership in the coalition would help iron things out. It did not.

When the PBS came to power, the federal government and Sabahan opposition parties openly courted Filipino and Indonesian immigrants in the state, almost all of whom are Muslim, and secured identity cards for many of them, enabling them to vote. Doctor Mahathir has made no secret of his preference for a Muslim government in Sabah. Nothing, however, was able to dislodge the PBS, which was resoundingly returned to power in 1990. The federal government had long been suspicious of Sabahan politicians, particularly following the PBS's defection from Doctor Mahathir's coalition in the run-up to the 1990 general election, a move which bolstered the opposition alliance. Doctor Mahathir described this as "a stab in the back", and referred to Sabah as "a thorn in the flesh of the Malaysian federation". But in the event, the prime minister won the national election convincingly without PBS help, prompting fears of political retaliation. Those fears proved justified in the wake of the election.

Sabah paid heavily for its 'disloyalty'; prominent Sabahans were arrested as secessionist conspirators under Malaysia's Internal Security Act, which provides for indefinite detention without trial. Among them was Jeffrey Kitingan, brother of the chief minister and head of the Yayasan Sabah, or Sabah Foundation. At the same time, Joseph Pairin Kitingan was charged with corruption. The feeling in Sabah was that the men were bearing the brunt of Doctor Mahathir's personal political vendetta.

As the political feud worsened, the federal government added to the fray by failing to promote Sabah to foreign investors. As investment money dried up, so did federal development funds; big road and housing projects were left unfinished for years. Many in Sabah felt their state was being short-changed by the federal government. The political instability had a detrimental effect on the state economy and the business community felt that continued feuding would be economic lunacy. Politicians in the Christian-led PBS, however, continued to claim that Sabah wasn't getting its fair share of Malaysia's economic boom. They said that the agreement which enshrined a measure of autonomy for Sabah when it joined the Malaysian federation had been eroded.

The main bone of contention was the state's oil revenues, worth around US$852 million a year, of which 95% disappeared into federal coffers. There were many other causes of dissatisfaction, too, and as the list of grievances grew longer, the state government exploited them to the full. By 1994, anti-federal feelings were running high. The PBS continued to promote the idea of 'Sabah for Sabahans', a defiant slogan in a country where the federal government was working to centralize power. Because Doctor Mahathir likes to be in control, the idea of granting greater autonomy to a distant, opposition-held state was not on his agenda. A showdown was inevitable.

It began in January 1994. As Datuk Pairin's corruption trial drew to a close, he dissolved the state assembly, paving the way for fresh elections. He did this to cover the eventuality of his being disqualified from office through a 'guilty' verdict: he wanted to have his own team in place to take over from him. He was convicted of corruption but the fine imposed on him was just under the disqualifying threshold and, to the prime minister's fury, he led the PBS into the election. Doctor Mahathir put his newly appointed deputy, Anwar Ibrahim, in charge of the National Front alliance campaign.

Datuk Pairin won the election, but by a much narrower margin than before. He alleged vote buying and ballot rigging. He accused Doctor Mahathir's allies of whipping up the issue of religion. He spoke of financial inducements being offered to Sabah's Muslim voters, some of whom are Malay, but most of whom are Bajau tribespeople and Filipino immigrants. His swearing-in ceremony was delayed for 36 hours; the governor said he was sick; Datuk Parin said his political enemies were trying to woo defectors from the ranks of the PBS to overturn his small majority. He was proved right.

Three weeks later, he was forced to resign; his fractious party had virtually collapsed and a stream of defections robbed him of his majority. Datuk Parin's protestations that his assemblymen had been bribed to switch sides were ignored. The local leader of Doctor Mahathir's ruling party, Tan Sri Sakaran Dandai, was swiftly sworn in as the new chief minister.

In the 1995 general election the PBS did remarkably well, holding onto eight seats and defeating a number of Front candidates who had defected from the PBS the previous year. Sabah was one area, along with the east coast state of Kelantan, which resisted the Mahathir/BN electoral steamroller.

The March 1999 state elections pitted UMNO against Pairin's PBS. Again the issues were local autonomy, vote rigging, the role of national politics and political parties in state elections, and money. A new element was the role that Anwar Ibrahim's trial might play in the campaign but otherwise it was old wine in old bottles.

The outcome was a convincing win for Mahathir and the ruling National Front who gathered 31 of the 48 state assembly seats – three more than the prime minister forecast. Mahathir once again used the lure of development funds from KL to convince local Sabahans where their best interests might lie. "We are not being unfair" Mahathir said. "We are more than fair, but we cannot be generous to the opposition. We can be generous to a National Front government in Sabah. That I can promise."

But, worryingly for the National Front, the opposition Parti Bersatu Sabah (PBS) still managed to garner the great bulk of the Kadazan vote and in so doing won 17 seats. As in Sarawak, the election, in the end, was more about local politics than about the economic crisis and the Anwar trial.

However, in the 2004 state and federal elections, the PBS rejoined the National Front and, faced only with the disunity of opposition parties, the BN-PBS coalition won resounding victories in both polls. A legitimate alternative to KL's ruling steamroller has all but died. The BN gave itself half the seats, one third to non-Malays, and distributed the rest between Chinese representatives. The message is that Sabahans accept dominance by the Malay minority from KL in return for money and development. The next elections are due in 2009.

Singapore

Contents

At a glance

⊖ **Getting around** Very efficient public transport system of buses, trains and taxis.

⊙ **Time required** 2-4 days.

☼ **Weather** Hot throughout the year. Sticky in Nov before the monsoon. Hottest in Jul-Aug. Wettest Nov-Jan.

⊗ **When not to go** There is no bad time to visit.

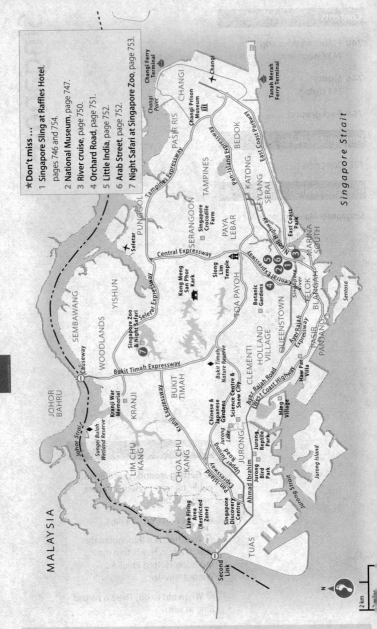

★Don't miss ...
1 Singapore Sling at Raffles Hotel, pages 746 and 754.
2 National Museum, page 747.
3 River cruise, page 750.
4 Orchard Road, page 751.
5 Little India, page 752.
6 Arab Street, page 752.
7 Night Safari at Singapore Zoo, page 753.

MALAYSIA

JOHOR BAHRU

Singapore Strait

To some, Singapore has all the ambience of a supermarket checkout lane and has even been described as a Californian resort town run by Mormons. It has frequently been dubbed sterile and dull and for those who fail to venture beyond the plazas that line Orchard Road, or spend their 3½ days on coach trips to the ersatz cultural extravaganzas, this is not surprising. But there is a cultural and architectural heritage in Singapore beyond the one that the government tries so hard to manufacture. Despite its brash consumerism and toy-town mentality, Singapore is certainly not without its charm.

Singapore is difficult to fathom, especially from afar, but beneath its slick veneer of westernized modernity, many argue that its heart and soul are Asian. Behind the computers, hi-tech industries, marble, steel and smoked-glass tower blocks, highways and shopping centres is a society ingrained with conservative Confucian values.

For those stopping over in Singapore for just a few days, there are several key sights that should not be missed. Many who visit, however, consider that it is far more important to enjoy the food. The island has an unparalleled variety of restaurants to suit every palate and wallet. Hawker centres in particular are a highly recommended part of the Singapore epicurean experience – they are inexpensive, and many are open into the early hours.

Planning your trip

Getting there

Air **Changi Airport** ① *on the eastern tip of the island, 20 km from downtown, www.changi. airport.com.sg*, is Southeast Asia's busiest airport and most long-haul airlines fly here. It is also a hub for budget Asian airlines. **Tiger Airways**, www.tigerairways.com, has some great deals around Southeast Asia and Australia. **Malaysia Airlines**, www.malaysiaairlines.com, though not usually as cheap, has good connections with Sabah, Sarawak and Brunei. **Air Asia**, www.airasia.com, flies from Singapore to Bangkok. Many of the cheapest fares are available exclusively on the internet. If you want to work out connections with specific cities, the Changi website has a useful flight planning facility. ►► *See Transport, page 760.*

Changi is regularly voted the world's leading airport: it takes only 20 minutes from touchdown to baggage claim. Facilities include free Wi-Fi, boutique shops and a rooftop swimming pool. Car hire desks, open 0700-2300, are in the Terminal 2 arrivals hall. Most hotels offer an airport pick-up service. Bus No 36 loops along Orchard Road passing many of the major hotels including the YMCA (0600-2300, less than S$2). An airport shuttle runs every 15 minutes 0600-1800, S$7 (booking counter in arrivals) to destinations within the CBD. If you are in a group of three or more and your hotel is not covered by the door-to-door service, it is probably cheaper to take a taxi. The airport is connected to the MRT underground line. Trains to the centre of Singapore run every 12 minutes 0530-2320, S$1.70, journey time 30 minutes. Taxis queue up outside the arrival halls; they are metered but there is an airport surcharge of S$3 (S$5 on Friday, Saturday and Sunday and after 1700). A trip to the centre of town should cost about S$20 including the surcharge. After midnight fares increase by 50%. ►► *For airport tax, see page 744.*

Rail **Tanjong Pagar Railway Station** ① *south of the city centre, Keppel Rd, T62213390*, is the last stop for the Malaysian railway system, **Keretapi Tanah Melayu** (KTM), www.ktmb.com.my (see page 579). There are two main lines connecting Singapore and Malaysia: one down the west coast from Kuala Lumpur, and another line which runs from Kota Bharu on the northeast coast and down through the centre of Peninsular Malaysia. From the train station, bus No 10 travels up Robinson Road, past Collyer Quay to Empress Place and the Nicoll Highway; bus No 100 goes up Robinson, Fullerton and Beach roads; bus No 30 travels west; bus No 84 goes to Harbour Front; and bus Nos 97 and 131 travel through the centre of town and then up Serangoon Road and through Little India. ►► *See Transport, page 760.*

Road There are two bridges connecting Singapore with mainland Malaysia. Most traffic uses the 11-km causeway in the north of Singapore Island, which links Woodlands with Johor Bahru. The Tuas 'Second Link' in western Singapore can only be used if you have your own transport.

There are services to Singapore from a number of towns in Malaysia, and from Bangkok or Hat Yai in Thailand. Long-distance buses arrive at the **Lavender Street Terminal** at the junction of Lavender Street and Kallang Bahru, while tour group buses (including those from Thailand) arrive outside the **Golden Mile Tower** on Beach Road. ►► *For details of crossing the border from Malaysia to Singapore, see box, page 761.*

Local buses run every 10 minutes between Johor Bahru's Larkin Bus Terminal and Singapore. The service pauses at the Woodlands immigration point for customs formalities before arriving at Singapore's **Ban San Terminal** at the northern end of Queen Street (at the junction with Arab Street) or Kranji MRT station. The journey takes one hour, RM2.

Rather than taking a bus, it is possible to take a long-distance taxi from Malaysia to Singapore. However, this usually requires a change of vehicle in Johor Bahru. (In other words, it is necessary to take a taxi from, say, Melaka, Kuantan, KL or Butterworth to JB, and then another taxi on to Singapore.) From JB there are scores of taxis to the Rochor Road terminus (S$6 per person, but if you need a full cab, S$24).

Sea Singapore is the world's busiest port. Passenger liners arrive from Australia, Europe, USA, India and Hong Kong. Ships either dock at the Singapore Cruise Centre at HarbourFront (formerly the World Trade Centre) or in the main harbour. The main companies are **Star Cruises**, www.starcruises.com, **Orient Lines**, www.orientlines.com, and **Silversea Cruises**, www.silversea.com. A timetable is published daily in the *Shipping Times* (a section of the *Business Times*).

It is possible to enter Singapore from **Malaysia** by bumboat from Johor Bahru, Tanjung Pengileh or Tanjung Surat in southern Johor to Changi Point, on the northeast tip of Singapore, which is a good way of beating the bottleneck at the causeway. Boats run 0700-1600 and leave when full. There is also a passenger ferry from Tanjung Belungkor, east of Johor Bahru, to Changi Ferry Terminal. The ferry runs three times daily (0815, 1530 and 1845) and takes 30 minutes. From the ferry terminal take a taxi to the centre, or bus No 2 from Changi Village.

There are no direct passenger ferries from the main ports of **Indonesia** to Singapore. However, it is possible to travel via the islands of Batam (45 minutes) or Bintan (1½ hours) in Indonesia's Riau Archipelago. PELNI ferries have services from Belawan port in Medan (Sumatra) and Tanjung Priok port in Jakarta (Java). ▶▶ *See Transport, page 762.*

Getting around

Singapore's public transport system is cheap and easy to use. There is a comprehensive **bus** network, with convenient and regular services (make sure you have the correct money as bus drivers don't give change from notes). The **Mass Rapid Transit** (MRT) underground railway is quick and efficient. An **Ez-link card**, www.ezlink.com.sg, S$15 (S$3 travel deposit, S$7 travel value, S$5 non-refundable card deposit) is available from MRT stations and TransitLink ticket offices (see www.transitlink.com.sg for locations). It can be used on buses and the MRT and is worth buying if you plan to use public transport extensively.

Taxis are relatively cheap and the fastest and easiest way to get around the island in comfort (all taxis are metered and air conditioned). They are plentiful but only be hailed at specified points; there are stands outside most main shopping centres and hotels. Don't try to flag down a taxi at night in busy places – even at taxi ranks; you will have to call them by phone. **Trishaws** have all but left the Singapore street scene. A few genuine articles can be found in the depths of Geylang or Chinatown, but most cater only for tourists and charge accordingly. Agree a price before climbing in and expect to pay about S$30 for a 45-minute ride. **Ferries** to the southern islands, such as Sentosa, Kusu and St John's, leave from HarbourFront (formerly the World Trade Centre) or hire a sampan from Jardine Steps on Keppel Road or Clifford Pier. Bumboats (motorized sampans) for the northern islands go from Changi Point or Punggol Point.

Maps and guides A useful guide to Singapore's transport system is the pocket-sized *TransitLink Guide* (S$3.50), listing all bus and MRT routes and stops, available at news outlets, bookshops, MRT stations and hotels. A plethora of city maps are available free from **Singapore Tourism Board (STB)** offices and many hotels. The best street map to Singapore is the *Periplus Map*, available at bookshops. Other useful maps are the *Secret Map of Singapore*, *Secret Food Map of Singapore* and the *Singapore Street Directory*.

Tourist information

The best source of information is the **Singapore Visitor Centre** ① *Tourism Court, 1 Orchard Spring Lane, junction of Orchard and Cairnhill roads, T1800-736 2000 (24-hr and toll-free in Singapore), www.visitsingapore.com, daily 0930-2230, nearest MRT: Orchard.* There are other offices at Liang Court Shopping Centre, Changi Airport, **The Galleria** (Suntec City Mall) and the **InnCrowd Backpackers Hostel** (see page 755). The free *Visitor's Guide to Singapore* has good maps and listings information.

Sleeping → *For hotel price codes, see inside the front cover.*

Rooms are more expensive than elsewhere in the region (S$250-650), but they are run to a very high standard and discounts are often available. Budget hotels are scarce and fill up fast due to limited availability. Popular places may be fully booked two weeks in advance. Some backpackers have quite a shock when they are forced spend their first night in a mid-range hotel. Dorm beds can be found for S$15 and a room for S$40. Taxes of 10% (government) plus 5% (goods) plus 1% (services) are added to bills in all but the cheapest hotels.

Eating → *For restaurant price codes, see inside the front cover.*

Eating is the national pastime in Singapore and is a refined art. Fish-head curry is perhaps the national dish, but you can sample 10 Chinese cuisines, North and South Indian, Malay and Nonya (Straits Chinese) food, plus Indonesian, Vietnamese, Thai, Japanese, Korean, European, Russian, Mexican and Polynesian. Do not be put off by characterless, brightly lit restaurants; the food can be superb. Eating spots range from high-rise revolving restaurants to neon-lit pavement seafood extravaganzas. A delicious dinner can cost as little as S$3 or more than S$100 and the two may be just yards away from each other. For serious epicureans *Singapore's Best Restaurants* (S$10.30) and the *Secret Food Map* (S$5) are available at bookstores. Another worthwhile guide is *Good Food, 500 Great Eating Places near the MRT Station*.

Freshly squeezed fruit juices are widely available at hawker centres and in restaurants. Fresh lime juice is served in most restaurants, and is a perfect complement to the banana-leaf curry, tandoori and dosai. The Malay favourite is *bandung* (a sickly sweet, bright pink concoction of rose essence and condensed milk). Chinese thirst quenchers include soya bean milk or chrysanthemum tea. Tiger and Anchor beers are the local brews, but still fairly expensive (S$8 a bottle in hawker centres; S$10 a glass in bars). The Singapore Sling is the island's best known cocktail. It was invented in the Raffles Hotel in 1915 and contains a blend of gin, cherry brandy, sugar, lemon juice and angostura bitters.

Festivals and events

Singapore's cultural diversity gives Singaporeans the excuse to celebrate plenty of festivals. The Singapore Tourist Board produces a brochure every year on festivals, with their precise dates, or check the STB's website, www.visitsingapore.com.

Shopping

Singapore is a shopper's paradise but it is not the bargain basement place it was. Department stores are fixed price, but most smaller outfits – even those in smart shopping complexes – can often be talked into giving discounts of around 20-30%. Singapore has all the latest electronic gadgetry and probably as wide a choice as you will find anywhere. It also has a big selection of antiques (although they tend to be overpriced), arts and crafts, jewellery, silks and batiks. For branded goods, Singapore is still marginally cheaper than most other places, but for Asian-produced products it is no longer the cheapest place in the region. ▶▶ *See Shopping, page 760.*

Essentials A-Z

Accidents and emergencies
Police T999. **Ambulance/Fire brigade** T995.

Children
Singapore is one of the most child-friendly cities in Asia. It is safe and clean, with world-class medical facilities and there are lots of things for children to do. There are also stacks of places to eat, drink and snack, a very efficient transport system and lots of a/c refuges to cool off. Attractions include: the Big Splash; Sentosa; Haw Par Villa; Jurong Bird Park; the Science Centre; the Singapore Discovery Centre; the superb Singapore Zoological Gardens and Night Safari. See also www.travelforkids.com.

Customs and duty free
Singapore is a duty-free port. The allowance is 1 litre of liquor, 1 litre of wine and 1 litre of beer or stout provided you are not arriving from Malaysia, from where there is no duty-free allowance. Note that there is no duty-free allowance for tobacco.

Visitors can claim back their 7% Goods and Services Tax (GST) from shops displaying the 'Tax Free for Tourists' sign when they spend S$100 or more. Ask for a Global Refund Cheque when you pay and this is then presented at customs on leaving the country, when visitors are reimbursed minus a handling fee. It is also possible to claim by post; the refund is paid either by bank cheque or to a credit card account. The **Singapore Tourism Board** publishes a brochure, *Tax refund for Visitors to Singapore.*

The Singapore government has banned the importation and sale of chewing gum. Chewing tobacco, pornographic material and seditious literature are also prohibited.

Disabled travellers
Singapore is the most wheelchair-friendly city in Southeast Asia. *Access Singapore* is a guidebook especially for physically impaired visitors. An online version is at www.dpa.org.sg/access/contents.htm.

Drugs
Narcotics are strictly forbidden and trafficking is a capital offence, which is rigorously enforced. Singapore has the highest execution rate per head of population in the world. Passengers arriving from Malaysia by rail may have to march, single-file, past sniffer dogs.

Electricity
220-240 volts, 50 cycle AC; most hotels can supply adapters.

Gay and lesbian travellers
Singapore is a conservative place and while it is not illegal to be gay the law criminalizes the homosexual act. Despite this, the government appears to be actively courting the pink dollar and there are plenty of openly gay and lesbian bars and clubs around town, a bloom of gay saunas and big gay events such as the Nation Party in the summer, gay and lesbian film festivals and lots of gay-themed theatre. The best website for events is www.fridae.com. Also check out www.plu.sg, which has lots of information on homosexuality in Singapore.

Health
The water in Singapore is clean and safe to drink straight from the tap. Singapore's medical facilities are among the best in the world. See page 763, for a listing of medical facilities or see the *Yellow Pages* for all public and private hospitals. Most big hotels have their own doctor on 24-hr call.

Cholera and yellow fever **vaccinations** are required if coming from endemic areas within the previous 6 days. There is no malaria risk, but there are sometimes outbreaks of dengue fever.

Internet
Singapore is one of the most wired and internet savvy places in the world, so there are loads of internet cafés. Many cafés and hotels offer free Wi-Fi. It's often worth the price of a coffee.

Language

Mandarin is the national language, although English or rather 'Singlish' is spoken by most people. Singlish is a musical variant of English, which despite sharing 98% of its vocabulary with the Queen's tongue sounds remarkably different. For some entertaining examples see www.geocities.com/tokyo/4883/singlish.html. Or log on to the satirical website www.talkingcock.com and follow the links to the Coxford Singlish Dictionary.

Media

The press is privately owned and legally free, but is carefully monitored and controlled. The *Straits Times*, www.straitstimes.com, has been likened to Beijing's *People's Daily* for the degree to which it is a mouthpiece of the government. Other English language dailies are the *Sunday Times*, which is the best for foreign news; the *Business Times* (www.business times.com.sg); and the *Electric New Paper* (newpaper.asia1.com.sg), Singapore's very own tabloid. The Today (www.today online.com) is a freebie, available Mon-Sat.

There are a number of English-language TV stations, there are also local Chinese, Indian and Malay language stations. For an overview, see www.mediacorpradio.sg.

Money → *US$1=S$1.37, £1=S$2.69, RM1=S$0.42 (Aug 2008)*.

Currency Local currency is dollars and cents. Bank notes are available in denominations of S$2, 5, 10, 20, 50, 100, 500, 1000 and 10,000. Coins are in 1, 5, 10, 20 and 50 cent and 1 dollar denominations. Brunei currency is interchangeable with Singapore currency.

Exchange It is possible to change money at banks, licensed money changers and hotels. Money changers often give the best rates. There is no black market. ATMs are ubiquitous and many allow you to draw cash on Visa or MasterCard. Most of Singapore's hotels, shops, restaurants and banks accept the major international credit cards. If you lose your card: American Express, T68801111; MasterCard, T800-110 0113; Visa, T800-448 1250.

Cost of travelling Singapore is an expensive city compared to its neighbours in Southeast Asia. Hotel rooms are pricey and fine dining and alcohol will burn a hole in your pocket, no-frills food (which is still great) and transport are relatively cheap. You can feast at a hawker stall for around S$5 (although this is still twice the price of an equivalent slap-up meal in Malaysia).

Opening hours

Most shops in the tourist area open 1030-2100. Sun is a normal working day around Orchard and Scotts rds. Bank opening hours are Mon-Fri 0930-1500, Sat 0930-1130. Post offices open Mon-Fri 0900-2100, Sat 0900-1800 and Sun 0900-1600.

Post

The main post office is the Singapore Post Centre at No 8, 10 Eunos Rd (take Paya Lebar MRT). There are 1300 postal outlets, including one at the airport. Local postal charges start at 26¢ (20 g). International postal charges are 50¢ (postcard), S$1.10 (letter, 20 g). For the latest charges see www.singpost.com.sg. Post offices sell sturdy cartons, called Postpacs, for sending parcels abroad. **Air Asia** and **Jetstar Asia** flights can be booked and paid for at 20 post offices. There is a S$5 handling fee.

Safety

Singapore is probably the safest big city in Southeast Asia. Women travelling alone need have few worries. It is wise, however, to take the normal precautions and not wander in lonely places after dark.

Smoking

Smoking is discouraged and prohibited by law in most public places. First offenders can be fined up to S$1000. Many hotels provide non-smoking floors.

Tax

Airport tax This is payable on departure – S$21 for all flights to all countries (but many tickets already include it). Transit passengers staying less than 24 hrs do not have to pay. A PSC (Passenger Service Charge) coupon can be purchased at most hotels, travel agencies and airline offices in town before departure, which saves time at the airport.

GST The 7% Goods and Sales tax is refundable at the airport for goods over US$100 (see Customs and duty free, page 743).

Telephone → *Country code +65.*
Directory enquiries is T103. In public payphones the minimum charge is 10¢ for 3 mins. Card phones are widespread – cards can be bought in all post offices as well as in supermarkets and newsagents, and come in units of S$5, S$10, S$20 and S$50. International calls can be made from most public phones. **International Phone Home Cards** are available at all post offices and come in units of S$10 and S$20. The most widely available card is Singtel's Worldcard. Credit card phones are also available. IDD calls made from hotels are free of any surcharge.

Singapore has 3 mobile phone networks (GSM and UMTS), and 3 mobile phone providers (SingTel, M1 and Starhub). Access codes are: SingTel, 001; for M1, 002; and Starhub, 008. Pre-paid SIM cards can be bought from money changers, 7-Elevens, and many other stores, starting at S$15.

Time
8 hrs ahead of GMT.

Tipping
Tipping is virtually nonexistent and any attempt will be met with a bewildered stare. Most hotels and restaurants add 10% service charge and 5% government tax to bills. In general, only tip for special personal services.

Tourist information
The **Singapore Tourism Board** operates a Touristline number, T1800-736 2000 (24-hr toll-free information number with automated information in English, Mandarin, Japanese and German), T+65-67362000 if calling from overseas, or visit www.visitsingapore.com.

Useful websites
www.aseansec.org Lots of government statistics, information and acronyms.
www.asiatravel.com/singapore.html Useful for hotel reservations, weather reports, the latest travel information and exchange rates, and also has a map detailing sights.
www.singaporeexpats.com A portal geared at expats. Property for rent, entertainment listings, jobs and more.
www.straitstimes.com The website of Singapore's strait-laced English daily. To make the most of the site you must register; US$15 for 1 month. For more English-language newspaper websites, see page 744.
www.visitorsguide.com.sg Tourist information and business contacts.

Visas and immigration
Visitors must have a passport valid for at least 6 months, a confirmed onward ticket, sufficient funds to support themselves and, where applicable, a visa. For the latest visa information check http://app.ica.gov.sg.

No visa is required for citizens of the Commonwealth, USA or Western Europe. On arrival in Singapore by air, citizens of these countries are granted a 1-month visitor permit. Tourists entering Singapore via the causeway from Johor Bahru in Malaysia or by sea are allowed to stay for 14 days. Nationals of most other countries (except India, China and the Commonwealth of Independent States) may stop over in Singapore for up to 14 days without a visa. Keep the stub of your immigration card until you leave.

Visas can be extended for up to 3 months either online (at the website above) or visit the **Visitor Services Centre**, 4th floor, ICA building 10 Kallang Rd, next to Lavender MRT, T63916100, Mon-Fri 0800-1700, Sat 0800-1300. Application takes around a day and costs S$40. It can be just as easy to nip across the causeway to Johor Bahru and then re-enter Singapore on a 2-week permit.

Weights and measures
The metric system is used.

Sights

→ *Colour map 8, F3.*

Singapore is a city state with a land area of just under 650 sq km and, as public transport is impeccably quick and efficient, nowhere is off the beaten track. Situated to the north of the Singapore River, the colonial core is bordered to the northeast by Rochor Road and Rochor Canal Road, to the northwest by Selegie Road and Canning Hill and to the southeast by the sea. The area is small enough to explore on foot – just. To walk from the Singapore Art Museum in the far northwest corner of this area to the mouth of the Singapore River shouldn't take more than 30 minutes. You may want to take a cab to get over to Fort Canning Park if it is a particularly hot and humid day. The river itself is lined with restaurants, bars and leafy walkways. For fun day trips head north of the city for Jurong Bird Park, the zoo, the night safari and Japanese gardens. Going south, Sentosa Island is linked to the mainland by a cable car and offers beaches, an oceanarium, a fun park and a trapeze.

Colonial core

The **Padang** ('playing field' in Malay) is at the centre of the colonial area. Many of the great events in Singapore's short history have been played out within sight or sound of the Padang. It was close to here that Stamford Raffles first set foot on the island on the morning of 28 January 1819, where the Japanese surrendered to Lord Louis Mountbatten on 12 September 1945 and where Lee Kuan Yew, the first prime minister of the city state, declared the country independent in 1959.

Flanking the Padang are the houses of justice and government: the domed **Supreme Court** (formerly the Hotel de l'Europe) and the City Hall. The neoclassical **City Hall** was built with Indian convict labour for a trifling S$2 million and was finished in 1929. Hearings usually start at 1000 and the public are allowed to sit at the back and hear cases in session; you can enter via the lower entrance at the front.

The revamped **Raffles Hotel** – with its 875 designer-uniformed staff (a ratio of two staff to every guest) and over 100 suites (each fitted with Persian carpets), eight restaurants, a culinary academy, five bars, playhouse and custom-built, leather-upholstered cabs – is the jewel in the crown of Singapore's tourist industry. In true Singapore style, it manages to boast a 5000-sq-m shopping arcade and there's even a **museum** ① *daily 1000-1900, free*, of rafflesian memorabilia on the third floor. Raffles Hotel's original (but restored) billiard table still stands in the Billiard Room. The **Palm Court** is still there and so is the **Tiffin Room**, which still serves tiffin (a snack/lunch). See also Sleeping, page 754.

West of Raffles Hotel is **Fort Canning Park**, which, over the last few years, has evolved into something a little more ambitious than just a park. The **Battle Box** ① *daily 1000-1800, last admission 1700, S$8, nearest MRT: Dhoby Ghaut*, opened in 1997, is a museum contained within the bunker where General Percival directed the unsuccessful campaign against the invading Japanese in 1942. Visitors are first shown a 15-minute video recounting the events that led up to the capture of Singapore. They are then led into the Malaya Command headquarters – the Battle Box – where the events of the final historic day, 15 February 1942, are re-enacted. You're given earphones and then taken from the radio room to the cipher rooms and the command room, before the bunker where Percival gathered his senior commanders for their final, fateful, meeting. It is very well done with a good commentary and film. The bunker is also air conditioned, a big plus after the hot walk up.

Above the Battle Box are the **ruins of Fort Canning**; the Gothic gateway, derelict guardhouse and earthworks are all that remain of a fort which once covered 3 ha. There are now some 40 modern sculptures here. Below the sculpture garden to the south is the renovated **Fort Canning Centre** (built 1926), which is the home venue of **Theatre Works** and the **Singapore Dance Theatre**. In front of Fort Canning Centre is an old Christian cemetery – **Fort Green** – where the first settlers, including the architect George Coleman, are buried. Towards the Picnic terrace and a series of steps (which are very slippery after rain) that descend towards Hill Street there's a small Archaeological Dig Exhibition that details the site in which many 14th-century artefacts have been found. These provide some of the oldest clues to Singapore's early history and many of these pieces are now displayed at the newly opened National Museum of Singapore (see below).

Below Canning Hill, on Clemenceau Avenue, is the Hindu **Chettiar Temple**, also known as the **Sri Thandayuthapani Temple**. The original temple on this site was built in the 19th century by wealthy Chettiar Indians (a money lending caste). It has been superseded by a modern version, finished in 1984, and is dedicated to Lord Subramaniam (also known as Lord Muruga). The ceiling has 48 painted glass panels, angled to reflect sunset and sunrise. Its *gopuram*, the five-tiered entrance, aisles, columns and hall all sport rich sculptures depicting Hindu deities, carved by sculptors trained in Madras. This Hindu temple is the richest in Singapore – some argue, in all of Southeast Asia. It is here that the spectacular Kavadi procession of the Thaipusam Festival culminates (see Malaysia, page 585).

The **National Museum of Singapore** ⓘ *93 Stamford Rd, T6332 3659, www.national museum.sg, daily 1000-1800 (History Gallery), 1000-2100 (Living Galleries), S$10, children S$5, free 1800-2100 (Living Galleries only), nearest MRT: Dhoby Ghaut,* is one of Asia's finest museums and shouldn't be missed. The beautiful colonial structure, originally built in 1887, has reopened to the public after several years of painstaking restoration. The museum sits handsomely at the meeting point of Orchard Road, Bencoolen Street and Fort Canning Park. It provides an insight into a city that is a fusion of a fascinating, surprisingly brutal history and state-of-the-art technology and both of these aspects are beautifully encapsulated in this hi-tech renovation. At the Stamford Road entrance beneath the elegant glass dome, visitors are given an audiovisual guide. In the History Gallery, Singapore's past is covered from its 14th-century beginnings through the colonial years, the dark times of the Second World War, to Independence and life as commercial superpower. What makes this so effective is its seamless multimedia execution, combining dramatic recreations of events, historical footage, memoirs and interviews with well-presented artefacts. Allow three to four hours to do the museum justice. Upstairs in the Living Galleries are displays of Singapore's 'living' culture, with exhibitions that explore Singapore through its food, photography and fashion. Singaporean and world cinema screenings are also held. Downstairs are an array of shops and mouthwatering, if pricey, eateries.

Singapore River and the City

The mouth of the river is marked by the bizarre symbol of Singapore – the grotesque **Merlion statue**, which is half lion, half mermaid. The financial heart of the city is just south of here; tall towers cast shadows on streets which on weekdays are a frenzy of bankers and office workers. The most pleasant area is by the river, which offers peaceful walks and has pockets of restaurants and bars making it a lively place at night. The Merlion is best viewed from the Padang side of the river. It is inspired by the two ancient (Sanskrit) names for the island: *Singa Pura* meaning 'lion city', and *Temasek* meaning 'sea-town'.

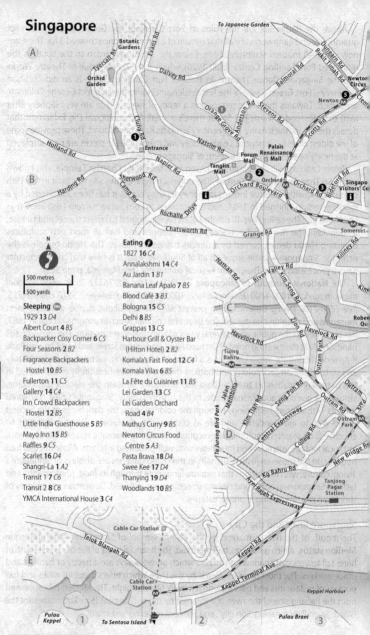

Singapore

To Japanese Garden

Botanic
Gardens

Orchid
Garden

Entrance

Palais
Renaissance
Mall

Forum
Mall

Tanglin
Mall

Orchard Boulevard

Newton
Circus

Singapore
Visitors Ce

N

500 metres

500 yards

Sleeping

1929 **13** D4
Albert Court **4** B5
Backpacker Cosy Corner **6** C5
Four Seasons **2** B2
Fragrance Backpackers
  Hostel **10** B5
Fullerton **11** C5
Gallery **14** C4
Inn Crowd Backpackers
  Hostel **12** B5
Little India Guesthouse **5** B5
Mayo Inn **15** B5
Raffles **9** C5
Scarlet **16** D4
Shangri-La **1** A2
Transit 1 **7** C6
Transit 2 **8** C6
YMCA International House **3** C4

Eating

1827 **16** C4
Annalakshmi **14** C4
Au Jardin **1** B1
Banana Leaf Apalo **7** B5
Blood Café **3** B3
Bologna **15** C5
Delhi **8** B5
Grappas **13** C5
Harbour Grill & Oyster Bar
  (Hilton Hotel) **2** B2
Komala's Fast Food **12** C4
Komala Vilas **6** B5
La Fête du Cuisinier **11** B5
Lei Garden **13** C5
Lei Garden Orchard
  Road **4** B4
Muthu's Curry **9** B5
Newton Circus Food
  Centre **5** A3
Pasta Brava **18** D4
Swee Kee **17** D4
Thanying **19** D4
Woodlands **10** B5

Cable Car Station

Cable Car
Station

Pulau
Keppel

To Sentosa Island

Keppel Harbour

Pulau Brani

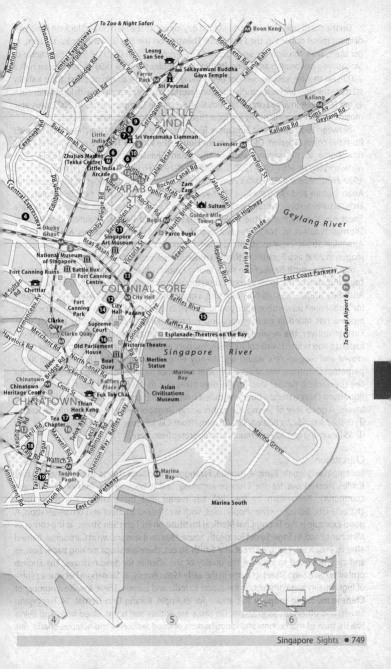

On the north side of the river on Marina Bay, opposite the Merlion and looking like a pair of giant metal durians, is the **Esplanade-Theatres on the Bay** ① *www.esplanade.com, to get there, walk through the underground CityLink Mall (from City Hall MRT)*, the centre of Singapore's performing arts scene. Within the complex there's a 1800-seater concert hall, a 2000-seat theatre, various outdoor performing spaces and a shopping plaza. After a shaky start the theatres are increasingly attracting world class performances, with luminaries such as Ian McKellen in *King Lear* by the Royal Shakespeare Company (RSC) in 2007, plus epic musicals and resurgent, newly hip local theatre adding to the diverse line-up.

Between High Street and Singapore River there are a number of architectural legacies from the colonial period: **Old Parliament House**, the **Victoria Theatre** and Empress Place, now home to the second wing of the **Asian Civilisations Museum** ① *T6332 2982, www.acm.org.sg, Mon 1300-1900, Tue-Sun 0900-1900, Fri until 2100, S$5, Fri free admission 1900-2100, nearest MRT: Raffles Place*. As its name suggests, the focus of the museum is Asian culture and civilization – 5000 years of it. The 10 galleries explore religion, art, architecture, textiles, writing and ceramics from China to West Asia. In front of Victoria Theatre is the original **statue of Sir Thomas Stamford Raffles**, sculpted in bronze by Thomas Woolner in 1887. The first branch of the **Asian Civilisations Museum** is on Armenian Street, close to Stamford Road, but is closed for renovation and scheduled to reopen in 2008 as a Peranakan-themed museum. See www.acm.org.sg for details.

Along the south bank of the river, facing Empress Place, is **Boat Quay**; commercially speaking, one of the most successful restoration projects of the Urban Redevelopment Authority (URA). The strip now provides a great choice of drinking holes and restaurants for Singapore's upwardly mobile young, as well as expats and tourists, although the area's hipness has faded in recent years and is predominantly patronized by tourists only. Further upriver, the newly fashionable **Clarke Quay** has also been renovated at great expense and is lined with colourful shops, bars and restaurants attracting a large expat crowd and Singapore's young and trendy elite. At night Clarke Quay is lit up like a perpetual Christmas tree shaded by giant rainproof mushrooms – worth seeing just for the spectacle. A further stop up the river takes you to the forest of plush hotels around Robertson Quay – trendy, but more quieter, relaxed and popular with wine bar and bistro lovers. A good way of seeing the sights along Singapore River is on a **bumboat cruise** ① *0900-2300, S$12, children S$6, 30 mins*, from Clarke Quay or Boat Quay. A **river taxi** ① *S$1 morning and S$3 afternoon*, also operates from here.

Chinatown

Encompassing Smith, Temple, Pagoda, Terengganu and Sago streets, this was the area that Raffles marked out for the Chinese *kampong* and it became the hub of the Chinese community. Renovation by the URA has meant that these streets still retain their characteristic baroque-style shophouses, with weathered shutters and ornamentation. A good example is the **Thong Chai Medical Institute** on Eu Tong Sen Street, at the corner of Merchant Road. In **Sago Street** (or 'death house alley' as it was known in Cantonese, named after its hospices), **Temple Street** and **Smith Street**, there are shops making paper houses and cars, designed to improve the quality of the afterlife for dead relatives. The English probably gave Sago Street its name in the early 19th century, as Singapore became a centre of high-quality sago production for export to India and Europe. There are also a number of **Chinese medicine shops** in this area – for example, Kwang Onn Herbal, 14 Trengganu Street, and others on Sago Street. On show are antlers and horns, dried frogs and flying lizards, trays of mushrooms and fungi, baskets of dried seahorses and octopus, sharks' fins and ginseng. For anyone looking for a full range of Chinese products – from silk camisoles to herbal medicines, beaded bags and Chinese tea – a good bet is to visit the **Yue Hwa Chinese Emporium** on the corner of Eu Tong Sen and Upper Cross streets.

As if to illustrate Singapore's reputation as a cultural and religious melting pot, the Hindu **Sri Mariamman Temple** is situated nearby at 244 South Bridge Road. It's dedicated to Sri Mariamman, a manifestation of Siva's wife Parvati. The temple is the site of the annual Thimithi Festival, held in late October or early November.

At 48 Pagoda Street is the **Chinatown Heritage Centre** ① *T6325 2878, www.china townheritage.com.sg, daily 0900-1800, S$9.80, children S$6.30,* which is well worth a visit. The centre evocatively captures the lives of early Chinese settlers with mock-ups of boats, coffeehouses, opium dens and squalid housing through the ages, including kitchens, bedrooms and even a prostitute's boudoir.

Telok Ayer Street is full of shophouses and fascinating temples of different religions and was once one of the most important streets in Singapore. The city's oldest Chinese temple, the Taoist **Thian Hock Keng Temple**, or Temple of Heavenly Happiness, is a gem (notwithstanding the naff fibreglass wishing well in one corner). A little way north of Thian Hock Keng is another much smaller Chinese temple, the **Fuk Tak Chi Temple** ① *76 Telok Ayer St, daily 1000-2200, free,* one of the oldest of Singapore's temples, restored in 1998 and now a museum. It's a little oasis of calm amidst the frenetic life of the city and holds a limited display of exhibits, including Peranakan jewellery, Chinese stone inscriptions, a model of a Chinese junk and an excellent diorama of Telok Ayer Street as it must have been in the mid-1850s.

One of Chinatown's more interesting places is the **Tea Chapter** ① *9 Neil Rd, T6226 1175, www.tea-chapter.com.sg, daily 1100-2300,* where visitors are introduced to the intricacies of tea tasting in elegant surroundings. You will be invited to remove your shoes and can sit in one of their special rooms or upstairs on the floor. It's a distinctly soothing experience.

Orchard Road and Botanic Gardens

Orchard Road is a long curl of air-conditioned malls, the spine of modern-day Singapore and home to its national pastime: shopping. This glass-fronted materialism is nicely juxtaposed at its western edge with the Botanic Gardens, an elegant park planted with rubber trees and hundreds of orchids. There are 3 MRT stations on, or close to, Orchard Road: Dhoby Ghaut, at the eastern end, Somerset, on Somerset Road, and Orchard station, which is at the intersection of Orchard Road and Scotts Road. To walk Orchard Road from end to end is quite a slog – from Dhoby Ghaut to the northwestern end of Orchard Road past Scotts Road is around 2½ km.

At the western end of Orchard Road, on Cluny Road, not far from Tanglin, are the **Botanic Gardens** ① *T6471 7361, www.sbg.org.sg, daily 0500-2400, free, many buses run past the Botanic Gardens including Nos 7, 77, 105, 106, 123 and 174 (alight at the junction of Cluny and Napier roads, next to Gleneagles Hospital).* The gardens contain almost 500,000 species of plants and trees from around the world in its 47 ha of landscaped parkland, primary jungle, lawns and lakes. Every morning and evening the park fills with joggers and tai chi fanatics. During the day, wedding parties pose for pictures among the foliage. The bandstand in the is used for live music performances at weekends. A map is available from the Ranger's office.

The Botanic Gardens also house the **National Orchid Garden** ① *www.sbg.org.sg, daily 0830-1900, last ticket sales at 1800, S$5, under-12s free,* where 700 species and 2100 hybrids of Singapore's favourite flower are lovingly cultivated. It is billed as the 'Largest Orchid Showcase in the World'. The closest entrance to the Botanic Gardens for the Orchid Garden is on Tyersall Avenue.

Little India

The city's South Asian community has its roots in the grid of streets branching off Serangoon Road. Spruced-up handicraft shops aimed at tourists are packed into the Little India Arcade opposite the more gritty wet market of the Tekka Centre. The best Indian restaurants lie along Race Course Road, while a bit of exploring will unearth theatres, a Bengali temple and a hand-operated spice mill. **Dunlop Street** links the main arteries of Serangoon Road and Jalan Besar; it's the heart of backpacker land, with plenty of cheap bars and a few hostels melding with the Indian bustle. **Little India MRT station** on the Northeast line has an exit that opens onto the Tekka Centre market.

The lively **Zhujiao** (or Tekka Centre) **Market**, on the corner of Buffalo and Serangoon roads, is an entertaining spot. Spices can be ground to your own requirements. Upstairs is a maze of shops and stalls; the wet market is beyond the hawker centre, west along Buffalo Road. Opposite the market on Serangoon Road is **Little India Arcade**, another Urban Redevelopment Authority (URA) project. These handicraft shops are a great place for Indian knick-knacks: leather sandals, bags, spices, incense, saris and textiles. There is also a food court. The closely packed shops in the surrounding network of streets house astrologers, tailors, spice merchants, jewellers and shops selling Bollywood DVDs and Hindi CDs. Walking up Serangoon Road, take a right at Cuff Road to see Little India's last **spice mill** ① *closed 1300-1400*, in a blue and yellow shophouse. It's hard to miss the chugging of the mill, let alone the rich smells of the spices.

The **Sri Veeramaka Liamman Temple** ① *Serangoon Rd, closed 1230-1600*, is dedicated to Kali, the ferocious incarnation of Siva's wife. You should walk clockwise around the temple hall and, for good luck, an odd number of times. The principal black image of Kali in the temple hall is flanked by her sons, Ganesha and Murugan.

Further up Serangoon Road is another Indian temple, **Sri Perumal** ① *daily 0630-1200, 1800-2100*, with its high *gopuram* sculptured with five manifestations of Vishnu. For the best experience, visit during the two-day festival of **Thaipusam** – usually held in January– celebrating the birthday of Murugan, one of Kali's sons.

Further north is the **Buddhist Sakayamuni Buddha Gaya Temple** (Temple of One Thousand Lights) ① *366 Race Course Rd, daily 0730-1645; remove shoes before entering*. Across the road is the Chinese Mahayana Buddhist **Leong San See Temple** (Dragon Mountain Temple) with its carved entrance (where you don't have to remove your shoes).

Arab Street

The smallest of Singapore's ethnic quarters, Arab Street is a pedestrianized tourist market strip with shops hawking all manner of Middle Eastern and Islamic goods: prayer rugs, Egyptian perfume bottles, baskets, rattan, silk, velvets and jewellery. There are also great Middle Eastern canteens and the imposing golden-domed **Sultan Mosque** ① *North Bridge Rd, 0900-1300, 1400-1600*, which attracts thousands of the faithful every Friday. Remember to dress modestly. In the maze of side streets around the Sultan Mosque, there is a colourful jumble of Malay, Indonesian and Middle Eastern merchandise. Excellent selections of batik (sold in sarong lengths of just over 2 m) jostle for space with silk and Indian textiles (especially along Arab Street), wickerware, jewellery, perfumes and religious paraphernalia. **Bugis Street** is southwest of Arab Street, opposite **Bugis Street MRT station**. It is packed with stalls selling cheap T-shirts and handicrafts, like a street market you might see in Thailand or Malaysia, but something that seems out of place in modern Singapore. The street has been recreated from a road that was demolished for the MRT in the mid-1980s.

Jurong Bird Park

ⓘ *Jl Ahmad Ibrahim, T6265 0022, www.birdpark.com.sg. Daily 0900-1800, S$18, S$9 3-12 year olds; a S$45 ticket (S$22.50 for 3-12 year olds) gives entry to Jurong Bird Park, Singapore Zoo and the Night Safari. Take the MRT westbound to Boon Lay then SBS bus No 194 or 251 from Boon Lay MRT interchange.*

This park is a beautifully kept 20-ha haven for more than 8000 birds of 600 species from all over the world, including a large collection of Southeast Asian birds. Highlights include the world's largest collection of Southeast Asian hornbills and South American toucans and an entertaining air-conditioned penguin corner, complete with snow. Another main attraction is one of the largest walk-in aviaries in the world, with a 30-m-high man-made waterfall and 1500 birds. There are bird shows throughout the day (the birds of prey show, at 1000 and 1600, is particularly good). There is a panorail service (S$4, children S$2) round the park for those who find the heat too much.

Singapore Zoo and Night Safari

ⓘ *80 Mandai Lake Rd, T6269 3411, www.zoo.com.sg, www.nightsafari.com.sg. Zoo: daily 0830-1800, S$16.50, children (3-12) S$8.50; tram ride S$5, children S$2.50. Night Safari: 1930-2400, S$22, children S$11; with tram ride S$32, children S$16. For the all-in-one ticket, see Jurong Bird Park, above; combined Zoo and Night Safari ticket, S$30, children S$15. Take the MRT to Ang Mo Kio and then bus No 138 from the station. A taxi from the city will cost S$15-20 and takes 30 mins.*

These zoological gardens have one of the world's few open zoos – with moats replacing bars – making it also one of the most attractive ones, with animals in environments vaguely reminiscent of their habitats. It contains 332 species of animals (about 3000 actual animals), some of them rare, like Komodo dragons and the golden lion tamarin, as well as many endangered species from Asia, such as the Sumatran tiger and the clouded leopard. The pygmy hippos are relative newcomers; they live in glass-fronted enclosures (as do the polar bears), so visitors can watch their underwater exploits. Animals are sponsored by companies; Tiger beer, for example, sponsors the tigers and Qantas the kangaroos. There are animal shows throughout the day carrying a strong ecological message: elephants (1130 and 1530) and sea lions (1430, extra show at 1700 at weekends). Animal feeding times are provided upon arrival. There are tram tours for those too weary to walk, with recorded commentaries, and several restaurants. Overall, it is a well-managed and informative zoo and well worth the trip out here.

The unique night safari next to the zoo has been cunningly converted into a series of habitats, populated with wildlife from the Indo-Malayan, Indian, Himalayan and African zoological regions. The park supports 1200 animals belonging to 110 species, including the tiger, Indian lion, great Indian rhinoceros, fishing cat, Malayan tapir, Asian elephant, bongo, striped hyena, Cape buffalo and giraffe. Visitors can either hop on a tram to be taken on a 40-minute guided safari through the jungle, walk along three short trails at their own pace or do both. The whole affair is extremely well conceived and managed, with cultural performances and opportunities to meet and sometimes touch animals, such as pythons. There is also a 'creatures of the night show', which on busy nights may be overbooked, so it's worth arriving early. The experience is rewardingly authentic and children especially have a great time. Bear in mind that the combined zoo and night safari tickets, although offering good value, don't include the additional night safari tram ride, which most visitors consider to be a night safari highlight.

◉ Singapore listings

Hotel prices

LL over US$200	**L** US$151-200	**AL** US$101-150
A US$66-100	**B** US$46-65	**C** US$31-45
D US$21-30	**E** US$12-20	**F** US$7-11
G US$6 and under		

Restaurant prices

¶¶¶ over US$12	¶¶ US$6-12	¶ under US$6

◉ Sleeping

Many of the excellent international class hotels are concentrated in the main shopping and business areas, including Orchard Rd and Scotts Rd, and near Raffles City and the Marina complexes. Most budget accommodation is to be found in the Little India and Arab St areas. There are a couple of options near the airport:
A Ambassador Transit Hotel Terminal 1, Level 3 Changi Airport Terminal 1, T6542 5538, www.airport-hotel.com.sg. Short-stay rate quoted (6 hrs). A good place to take a break if you are stuck at Changi for an extended period and no need to clear immigration. It also provides a 'freshen-up' service including showers, sauna and gym.
A Ambassador Transit Hotel Terminal 2, departure/transit lounge south, Changi Airport Terminal 2, T6542 8122, www.airport-hotel.com.sg. Excellent hotel on the airport property, short-stay rate quoted (6 hrs). Booking recommended.

Colonial core *p746, map p748*
LL Raffles, 1 Beach Rd, T6337 1886, www.raffleshotel.com. Singapore's most renowned hotel and a famous landmark, see also page 746 and Spas and therapies in the colour section. There are 9 restaurants, 5 bars and 70 shops. The 103 suites have been immaculately refurbished, with wooden floors, high ceilings, stylish colonial furniture and plenty of space. Bathrooms are the ultimate in luxury and the other facilities are excellent – a peaceful roof-top pool with jacuzzis and a small gym, both 24 hr. Very exclusive. Highly recommended.

LL-L The Gallery, 76 Robertson Quay, T6849 8686, www.galleryhotel.com.sg. Marketed as the 'first hip hotel in Singapore', this Philip Starck-styled hotel provides 222 minimalist rooms, in 3 ultra-modern blocks. Brightly coloured cushions provide some light relief from the austerity in the standard rooms (with showers only). Free internet. 'Smart wired rooms' have their lighting and a/c controlled with sensors, offering features like guiding lights to the bathroom at night. The 5th-floor pool is different, with glass on all sides. A funky choice. The hotel has chillout lounges and bars including the popular **M Studio** club.

Chinatown *p750, map p748*
LL Fullerton, 1 Fullerton Sq, T6733 8388, www.fullertonhotel.com. Great position at the head of the Singapore River, this is Singapore's 5-star newcomer. It has 399 rooms in Phillipe Starck style, very functional and well equipped. The restaurants are excellent: the **Chinese Jade**; international **Town Club**; and seafood **Post Bar**. The infinity pool is stunning with views over the Singapore River.
LL-L The Scarlet, 33 Erskine Rd, T6511 3333, www.thescarlethotel.com. Super swish boutique hotel of dark red fabrics and jet-black marble, this hotel resembles a luxury cross between *Pirates of the Caribbean* and *Dracula*. Helpful staff and a lovely colonial building make for a pricey but memorable base camp in Singapore. Good for a romantic weekend.
AL 1929, 50 Keong Saik Rd, T6347 1929, www.hotel1929.com. Another of Singapore's funky new boutique hotels. The owners have used their own retro and designer furniture for this quirkily restored shophouse. The 32 rooms are small, but so chic that size doesn't matter. There's no pool or gym, but a small jacuzzi, free internet and in-room safes. Recommended.

Orchard Road and Botanic Gardens *p751, map p748*
LL Four Seasons, 190 Orchard Blvd, T6734 1110, www.fourseasons.com/singapore.

Hard to beat, this intimate hotel of 254 rooms (and more than 300 staff) provides exceptional personal service. Rooms are elegantly decorated in traditional European style, with feather pillows, writing desk, multi-disc player and spacious bathrooms. The hotel has a unique Asian art collection, with attractive artwork in all rooms. 2 pools, the only a/c tennis courts in Singapore, a golf simulator and a well-equipped health and fitness centre. Restaurants include Cantonese and contemporary American cuisine, with lunchtime buffet. Although mainly a business hotel, children are well catered for. Recommended.

LL Shangri-La, 22 Orange Grove Rd, T6737 3644, www.shangri-la.com. One of Singapore's finest hotels, set in a beautifully maintained, spacious landscaped garden. There are more than 700 rooms, stylishly refurbished; those in the refined and relaxed Valley Wing are superior and the service is exceptional. Excellent leisure facilities include a spacious pool area with greenery and waterfalls, jacuzzi, indoor pool, good gym, squash and tennis courts, and a 3-hole pitch and putt golf course. Possibly the best conference facilities in town. 3 good restaurants. Winner of Singapore Tourism Board's award for best hotel year after year. Recommended.

AL 81, 41 Bencoolen St, T6336 8181, www.hotel81.com.sg. Conveniently placed minimalist mid-range hotel. Rooms have TV, bath, phone and minibar. Part of a Singapore-wide hotel chain that provides comfortable, well furnished rooms with the minimum of extras at reasonable rates.

AL Bencoolen, 47 Bencoolen St, T6336 0822, www.hotelbencoolen.com. Popular mid-range choice with good bathrooms and breakfast included. There's a small rooftop pool and chillout area on the 1st floor.

AL-A YMCA International House, 1 Orchard Rd, T6336 6000, www.ymca.org.sg. Facilities are well above the usual YMCA standards, a/c, restaurant, rooftop pool, squash, badminton, billiards and fitness centre. Very clean and efficient and in an unbeatable position, at the head of Orchard Rd and next to the newly refurbished National Museum. Rooms are minimalist but clean, spacious and light. Good coffee shop, but the constant religious soundtrack can be a bit much. Not cheap, but good value for the location. Recommended.

Little India *p752, map p748*

L Albert Court, 180 Albert St, T6339 3939, www.albertcourt.com.sg. An unusually designed hotel (a mixture of Western and Peranakan), lying behind a courtyard of renovated shophouses. This is an intimate place built to high specifications, with attractive extras. Ask for a room with big windows. Right next to a good range of restaurants in Albert Court. Recommended.

L Perek Hotel, 12 Perek Rd, T6299 7733, www.peraklodge.net. Recently refurbished, this early 19th-century building has a friendly secure vibe and good location, down a side street in the heart of Little India. Rooms are small but cosy, with the lighter and brighter rooms on the 1st floor; polished wooden floors, comfortable beds, electronic safes in the rooms, plus Wi-Fi add to the appeal. 2 family suites/apartments in the attic.

A The InnCrowd Backpackers Hostel, 73 Dunlop St, T6296 9169, www.the-inn crowd.com. State-of-the-art backpackers' hostel, colourful and welcoming with internet, kitchen, communal lounge with TV and plenty of DVDs, breakfast included and a bar next door. Dorms (**C-E**) are basic but clean with good showers. Note that rooms are often booked weeks in advance.

A-C Mayo Inn, 9A Jl Besar, T6295 6631. Clean and very cheap en suite rooms with TV, a/c and easygoing staff. Good budget option, but smelly carpets in rooms.

B-C Little India Guesthouse, 3 Veerasamy Rd, T6294 2866, www.singapore-guesthouse.com. Some a/c, no en suites, but spotless male/female showers and fairly clean rooms. No food, but plenty on the street. Great spot in the heart of Little India in an attractive salmon-pink shophouse. Recommended.

C-E Fragrance Backpackers Hostel,
63 Dunlop St, T6295 6888, www.fragrance
backpackers.com.sg. Dorms only, clean
and efficient, even a little sterile. Common
room, internet and laundry. Cheap,
good location.

Arab Street p752, map p748

B-E Backpacker Cosy Corner, 2/F, 490 North
Bridge Rd, T6224 6859, www.cozycorner
guest.com. Guesthouse above restaurants on
North Bridge Rd, just south of Liang Seah St.
This place is a good backpacker choice with
clean, simple rooms and dorms with shared
bathrooms only. Free internet and breakfast.

🍴 Eating

The best places to eat are **Chinatown**,
Little India and **Arab St**. The last couple
of years has seen a burgeoning of restaurants
along **Club St**; all are upmarket eateries,
catering for city business people. Restaurants
overlooking the river at **Boat Quay** (bargains
sometimes available), **Clarke Quay** and
Robertson Quay are hugely popular, for
the river breeze and views. Go for a casual
stroll along the river bank to find your
perfect spot.

For North Indian cuisine, the best
option is to the southern end of **Race
Course Rd**, with several good restaurants,
including the famous **Muthu's Curry**,
see page 757. Some of the best vegetarian
restaurants – South Indian particularly –
are found on the other side of **Serangoon
Rd**, along Upper Dickson Rd. **Arab St** is
the best area for Muslim food of all
descriptions – Malay, Indonesian,
Indian or Arabic. Try **New Bugis St** for
simple open-air fare and jugs of cold beer.

Chinese meals are eaten with chopsticks
and Malays and Indians traditionally eat with
their right hands. It is just as acceptable,
however, to eat with spoons and forks.
In Malay and Indian company, do not
use the left hand for eating.

Colonial core p746, map p748

🍴🍴🍴 1827 Thai, Old Parliament House,
1 Parliament Lane, T6337 1871, www.1827
thai.com.sg. Elegant Thai restaurant on the
ground floor of the beautifully renovated
Parliament House. Great ambience.

🍴🍴🍴 Annalakshmi, 02-10 **Excelsior Hotel and
Shopping Centre**, 5 Coleman St, T6339 9993.
North and South Indian vegetarian cuisine.
Staffed by women volunteers, profits go to
the Kalamandhir Indian cultural group. The
health drinks are excellent, especially *mango
tharang* (mango juice, honey and ginger)
and *Annalakshmi special* (fruit juices, yoghurt,
honey and ginger). The restaurant, which
sprawls out onto the veranda overlooking the
tennis courts, closes at 2130. Recommended.
🍴🍴🍴 Grappas, CHIJMES, gallery floor,
30 Victoria St, T6334 9928. Large Italian
restaurant in this trendy courtyard.
Extensive menu, with mostly pasta and
risotto dishes as well as some meat entrées;
booking advisable. Recommended.
🍴🍴🍴 Lei Garden, Gallery floor, CHIJMES, 30
Victoria St, T6339 3822. A menu which is
said to comprise 2000 dishes. Outstanding
Cantonese food: silver codfish, emperor's
chicken and such regulars as dim sum and
Peking duck. Dignitaries, royalty and film
stars dine here. Tasteful decor and a 2-tier
aquarium displaying the day's offerings.
Despite seating for 250, you need to book in
advance. Worth every penny. Recommended.
🍴🍴🍴 Raffles Grill, Raffles Hotel, 1 Beach Rd,
T6412 1185. Excellent French cuisine in an
elegant colonial setting, with silver plate
settings, chandeliers and reproduction
Chippendale furniture.
🍴🍴🍴 Ristorante Bologna, **Marina Mandarin
Hotel**, 6 Raffles Blvd, Marina Sq, T6845 1113.
Award-winning Italian restaurant. Specialities
include *spaghetti alla marinara* and baked
pigeon. Diners lounge amidst sophisticated
decor whilst wandering minstrels strum.
🍴 Komala's Fast Food, Upper Dickson Rd.
South Indian delicacies including *thalis*,
masala dosas and *iddlis* are served in a very
popular a/c restaurant. Recommended.

Chinatown p750, map p748

Thanying, Amara Hotel, T6227 7856. The best Thai food in town with an extensive menu and superb food (the 15 female chefs are all said to have trained in the royal household in Bangkok). Booking necessary. Recommended.

Pasta Brava, 11 Craig Rd, Tanjong Pagar. Tastiest Italian in town in an equally tasty shophouse conversion; fairly expensive, but good choice of genuine Italian fare. Recommended.

Swee Kee, 12 Ann Siang Rd, T6222 8926. This Chinese restaurant is locally renowned as owner Tang Kwong Swee – known to his friends as 'Fish-head' – has run the same place for 60 years (although the location has changed). Recommended are the deep-fried chicken, Hainanese style, fish-head noodle soup and prawns in magi sauce. Very popular.

Orchard Road and Botanic Gardens p751, map p748

Au Jardin, EJH Corner House, Singapore Botanic Gardens Visitors' Centre, 1 Cluny Rd, T6466 8812. In the former garden director's black and white bungalow, with only 12 tables, this French restaurant is elegant and sophisticated, with a menu that is changed weekly. Booking essential.

Blu, Shangri-La Hotel, 22 Orange Grove Rd, T6213 4598. On the 24th floor, **Blu** provides stunning views, great service and excellent Californian food. Recommended.

Harbour Grill and Oyster Bar, Hilton Hotel, 581 Orchard Rd, T6730 3393. Contemporary surroundings with nautical theme, serving international food. Delicacies include caviar and smoked salmon; monthly guest chef. Impeccable service.

Blood Café, 290 Orchard Rd, Paragon, T6735 6765. Funky café with style and fashion magazines to browse. Relaxing place, with an inventive menu featuring couscous, roasted vegetables and chunky sandwiches. Hip and healthy. Good veggie choices. **ProjectShock BloodBrothers** clothes shop on the 2nd floor. Recommended.

Lei Garden, Orchard Shopping Centre, 321 Orchard Rd, T6734 3988, and **Orchard Plaza**, 150 Orchard Rd, T6738 2448. The famous Cantonese restaurant (see page 756). Book in advance. Recommended.

Little India p752, map p748

La Fête du Cuisinier, 161 Middle Rd, T6333 0917, on the corner of Waterloo St and Middle Rd. A surprising location for one of the more sophisticated restaurants in town. Exquisite French Creole cuisine – a lavish menu of foie gras, oysters and crab (and that's only the starters). Attractive setting, elaborate French decor in Marie Antoinette style.

Banana Leaf Apolo, 56-58 Race Course Rd. North Indian food, a popular fish-head curry spot, a/c and more sophisticated than the name might imply, although the food is still served on banana leaves. Recommended.

Delhi, Race Course Rd. North Indian food including chicken tikka, various tandooris, as well as creamy Kashmiri concoctions. Popular and award-winning restaurant.

Khansama, 166 Serangoon Rd, T6299 0300. Good Asian cuisine, pleasant a/c spot upstairs and a free Bollywood classic thrown in.

Komala Vilas, 76-78 Serangoon Rd, T6293 6980, and 12 Buffalo Rd. South Indian *thalis* and *masala dosas*. Bustling café with a little more room upstairs. Recommended.

Muthu's Curry, corner of Rotan Lane and Race Course Rd, T6293 7029. North Indian food, seen by connoisseurs to be among the best banana leaf restaurants in town; Muthu's fish-head curries are famous. Recommended.

Madras Woodlands, 102 Serangoon Rd and slightly more upmarket (alcoholic drinks sold) at 22 Belilios Lane. Good vegetarian Indian food, very clean, but staff can be a little abrupt.

Arab Street p752, map p748

Zam Zam Restaurant, junction of Arab St and North Bridge Rd. Muslim Malay-Indian dishes served in busy and chaotic coffee shop. Very popular and recommended. Spicy meats, chargrilled seafood, creamy curries.

Elsewhere

††† Long Beach Seafood, 31 Marina Park, Marina South, T6323 2222. One of Singapore's most famous seafood restaurants, specializing in pepper and chilli crabs, drunken prawns and baby squid cooked in honey.

Hawker centres and food courts

Food courts are the modern, a/c, sanitized version of Singapore's old hawker centres. Hawker centres are found beneath HDB blocks and in some specially allocated areas in the city; food courts are usually in the basement of shopping plazas. You claim a table, then graze your way down rows of Malay, Chinese and Indian stalls. You don't need to eat from the stall you're sitting next to.

There's a good outdoor food court where Bain and Victoria streets merge, next to the **Allson Hotel**. It's mostly Chinese stalls, but there are also fries, burgers, and, on the healthy side, fabulous fresh juices served by the cranky old couple furthest from the road.
Kopitian Food Hall, corner of Bras Basah Rd and Bencoolen St. Bang in the centre and popular with locals and travellers, this place has everything from modern pig's organ soup to fresh juices and vegetarian curry. A bit personality free, but a/c and good for a breather.
Lau Pa Sat Festival Market (formerly the **Telok Ayer Food Centre**), Raffles Quay end of Shenton Way in the old Victorian market. Good range of food: Chinese, Indian, Nyonya, Korean, Penang, ice creams and fruit drinks. Best in the evening when Boon Tat St is closed off and satay stalls serve cheap, tasty sticks of chicken, beef, mutton or prawns washed down with jugs of Tiger beer.
Lavender Food Square, Lavender Rd, north of Little India. One of the best hawker centres in town.
Newton Circus, Scotts Rd, north of Orchard Rd. Despite threats of closure by the government, this huge food centre of over 100 stalls is still surviving and dishing up some of the best food of its kind. Open later than others so very popular with tourists.

Zhujiao or **Kandang Kerbau (KK) Food Centre**, corner of Buffalo and Serangoon roads. Wide range of dishes, and the best place for Indian Muslim food: curries, rotis, dosa and *murtabak* are hard to beat (buy beer from the Chinese stalls on the other side).

Cafés and bakeries

For young and hip Singaporeans, coffee culture has replaced food court fare. Western-style coffee shops such as **Starbucks**, **The Coffee Bean & Tealeaf** and **The Coffee Connoisseur** are everywhere. Most offer free Wi-Fi. Traditional Singaporean coffee shops or *kopi tiam* are in the older part of the city, usually in old Chinese shophouses. They serve breakfast, lunch and dinner, as well as beer, at only slightly higher prices than hawker centres.
Zhong Guo Hua Tuo Guan, 52 Queen St (name above the teahouse is in Chinese characters), just by the Albert and Waterloo streets roadside market. A traditional Chinese teahouse with several outlets, including this atmospheric one. It sells Hua Tuo's ancient recipes, helpful for 'relieving of heatiness' and 'inhibiting the growth of tumor cells,' amongst other things. Very friendly proprietress will introduce you to wild ginseng and *showfrog* or *longan* (a fruit like a lychee) herbal jelly, and tell you why you will feel better – that's if you can get any of the concoctions down!

❶ Bars and clubs

Singapore *p746, map p748*
There are lots of bars on **Boat** and **Clarke** quays; those at the former are wilder and less packaged, although the last few years has seen a slight deterioration in quality as locals have moved on and tourists have become the dominant clientele. One of the more dramatic changes over the past couple of years is the development along the riverfront westwards. Both **Robertson's Walk** and The Quayside are slowly filling up with shops and restaurants, and the nearby

Mohammed Sultan Rd has become an extremely popular watering hole; the entire street is lined with bars and clubs. The west side is a row of restored shophouses, whilst the east is a modern high-rise block.

There are several quiet bars on **Duxton Hill**, Chinatown, in a pleasant area of restored shophouses – a retreat from the hustle and bustle of Boat Quay or the city. **Duxton Rd** and **Tanjong Pagar Rd** also have a dozen or so bars in restored shophouses.

Peranakan Place just off Hollywood Rd is home to a string of funky New York-style bars carved out of restored shophouses. At S$15 a pint, these places are not cheap, but they are very stylish, albeit for poseurs.

There are several options in the famous **Raffles Hotel**, see page 746, including the **Bar and Billiard Room**, which is lavishly furnished with teak tables, oriental carpets and 2 original billiard tables. **The Long Bar**, home of the Singapore Sling (see the bottom of this page), is now on 2 levels and extremely popular with tourists and locals; gratuitous, tiny, dancing mechanical *punkah-wallahs* sway out of sync to the cover band. The **Writers' Bar**, just off the main lobby, is named in honour of the likes of Somerset Maugham, Rudyard Kipling, Joseph Conrad, Noel Coward and Herman Hesse, who are said either to have wined, dined or stayed at the hotel. Bookcases and mementos in the bar indicate that other literary luminaries from James A Michener to Noel Barber and the great Arthur Hailey also have sipped Tigers at the bar here.

The Pump Room and **Cuba Libre** are trendy bars down at Clarke Quay, but for something truly different you might want to try the **Forbidden City** and **BarCoCoon**, 3A Merchant's Court, Clarke Quay, for a club combination of alcohol, stone warriors and imperial China. The Singapore of the future.

Note The bar and club scene changes fast in Singapore – if you're serious about what's hot and what's not, check local papers, *Time Out Singapore* magazine, or just ask around for the latest tips on the local gigs and DJs. **Singapore Tourism Board** also provides a free *Where to Eat and Party* guide or check www.visitsingapore.com.
The Dubliner, Winsland Conservation House, 165 Penang Rd, T6735 2220. Irish pub set inside a beautifully restored colonial house. Very friendly, good hearty Irish food as well as the compulsory pints of Guinness and Kilkenny. Recommended.
eM Studio, 1 Nanson Rd at **Gallery Hotel** now replaces the old classic **Liquid Room**. Open Wed-Sat, with Phunky Fridays and Suave Saturdays, both of which get pretty busy.
eM By the River is a chilled bar downstairs.
Harry's Bar, 28 Boat Quay. Large bar with seating outside overlooking the river, popular with City boys, pricey food, jazz band.
New Asia Bar, the Equinox Complex, 71st/72nd floors, **Swissôtel The Stamford**. A truly breathtaking vista over the city – some say on a very clear day to Sumatra – in this cutting edge bar/disco. Worth it for the view alone, but good beats and reasonable drinks make this a hit. Several upmarket restaurants in the same complex.
Number 5, 5 Emerald Hill. Happy hours Mon-Sat 1200-2100, Sun 1700-2100. At the top of the pedestrianized section of Emerald Hill, retro-chic restored shophouse bar and restaurant (upstairs), popular with young expats and Chuppies (Chinese yuppies), great music. Recommended.
Prince of Wales, 101 Dunlop St, Little India. Cheap 'n' cheerful no-frills boozer – popular with backpackers.
Trader Vics, 5th floor, **New Otani Hotel**, River Valley Rd. Hawaii 5-0 decor and Chin-Ho's favourite cocktails – try a few goblets of Tikki Puka Puka for something violently different.
Velvet Underground, 17 Jiak Kim St (off Kim Seng Rd), next door to **Zouk** and under the same management. Small nightclub, Tue-Sat 2100-0300, cover S$25, free for women on Wed nights. Recommended. Often has gay or lesbian parties.
Zouk, 17 Jiak Kim St, opposite the **Concorde Hotel**. Huge quirky club, with a fun design. Described as *the* place for hard clubbing.

O Shopping

Singapore *p746, map p748*
Probably the best area for window shopping is around **Scotts Rd** and **Orchard Rd**, where many of the big complexes and department stores are located. This area comes alive after dark and most shops stay open late. The towering **Raffles City Complex**, **Parco** at Bugis Junction, **Suntec City** and **Marina Sq** are the other main shopping centres. Serangoon Rd (or **Little India**), **Arab St** and **Chinatown** offer a more exotic shopping experience with a range of 'ethnic' merchandise.

Antiques Singapore's antique shops stock everything from opium beds, planters' chairs, gramophones, brass fans, porcelain, jade, Peranakan marble-top tables and 17th-century maps, to smuggled Burmese Buddhas, Sulawesian spirit statues and Dayak masks. There are few restrictions on bringing antiques into Singapore or exporting them. Many of the top antique shops are in the Tanglin Shopping Centre, Orchard Rd. The *Guide to Buying Antiques, Arts and Crafts in Singapore* by Anne Jones is recommended.

Batik and silk Malaysian and Indonesian batiks are sold by the metre or in sarong lengths. Arab St and Serangoon Rd are the best areas for batik and silk lengths; big department stores usually have batik ready-mades. Ready-made Chinese silk garments can be found all over Singapore in Chinese emporia. If you want silk without the hassle, at reasonable prices, big department stores (such as **Tang's** on Orchard Rd) have good selections. **China Silk House** designers come up with new collections every month. If you're travelling widely in Southeast Asia, Bangkok remains an excellent location for clothing bargains, with tailored silk garments available at a fraction of Singapore prices.

Electronic goods Singapore has all the latest electronic equipment, hot from Japan at duty-free prices. Prices are still cheaper than in Europe, but can vary enormously. Check that items come with an international guarantee. The centres for electronic goods

are Sim Lim Tower (corner of Jalan Besar, Little India) and Sim Lim Square (corner of Rochor Canal Road, south of Little India). Although be warned you need to know exactly what you want otherwise you will come away with something that may only half meet your requirements. The Japanese **Best Denki** stores are in most of the shopping centres or Singapore's **Harvey Norman** stores also offer a wide variety of electronic goods in a more conventional manner still at competitive prices.

Wet markets The most accessible market of interest is the Zhujiao (formerly KK) Market, on the corner of Bukit Timah and Serangoon roads, at the southern end of Little India. It is a hive of activity and sells everything from flowers to fish and meat to spices, and every conceivable vegetable and fruit. There's also a good hawker centre here. An excellent Sunday market is on Seng Poh Road, Tiong Bahru, between Tiong Bahru and Outram Park MRT stations, which is worth taking in if you go to see the singing birds. A good place to buy orchids is the small Holland Village wet market; it is much cheaper than the more touristy flower shops downtown and will pack them for shipment.

O Transport

Singapore *p746, map p748*
Air
For details of **Changi International Airport**, see page 740. Malaysia's budget airline, **Air Asia**, flies between Singapore and **Bangkok**, and has cheap deals from **Johor Bahru** just across the causeway from Singapore with most major cities in Malaysia. For long-haul flights from Singapore, it is usually cheaper to take a bus or train to Kuala Lumpur in Malaysia and buy onward flights there.

Chartered express coaches ply between Singapore and **JB airport**; they leave Singapore from the **Novotel Orchid Inn** on Dunearn Rd, but are reserved for **MAS** passengers only, S$12. The courier ensures

Border essentials: Singapore–Malaysia

Buses and trains run direct from Singapore to many Malaysian towns, or you can take one of the frequent buses to Johor Bahru and find onward transport from there. The main border crossing is across the Woodlands causeway (see page 740). To get there, the non-air conditioned SBS No 170 runs every 15 mins from Singapore's Ban San Terminal, between Queen St and Rochor Canal Rd. Tickets cost S\$2. The **Johor Singapore Express** is air conditioned and is slightly more frequent and also leaves from Ban San. The yellow **Causeway Link** bus with a smiley face runs between Kranji MRT station in Singapore and the Larkin terminal. It only takes 20 mins from the border to the MRT station. All 3 buses require you to get off twice – for the Malay border point and its Singaporean counterpart. You have to take all your luggage with you since the bus does not wait for you. You wait for the next bus to come along; each bus has its own stop after exiting immigration. Keep your ticket or you will have to buy a new one. Also have a pen handy to fill in immigration forms as they are not provided. See also Malaysia, page 642.

express clearance of Malaysian customs and immigration. Details from **MAS** office in Singapore: 190 Clemenceau Av, T06-336 6777.

Likewise, for those wishing to fly to destinations in **Indonesia**, it is cheaper to take the ferry to the Indonesian island of Batam (see page 762) and then catch a domestic flight from there. However, for most people the saving in fares will probably not outweigh the additional hassle.

Flights from Singapore to **Pulau Tioman** off Malaysia's east coast leave from **Seletar Airport** – a military airport in the north of Singapore island. Although the authorities do not allow photographs on the tarmac, checking in is very relaxed and informal – very different from the rather brusque efficiency of Changi. There are no public buses to Seletar so most people take taxis and as at Changi there is a S\$3 surcharge. When a scheduled flight is arriving from Tioman the airline usually calls so that the required number of taxis are waiting.

Bus

Local SBS (Singapore Bus Service), T1800-225 5663, www.sbstransit.com.sg, is efficient, convenient and cheap. Fares range from 60¢ (non a/c) to S\$1.90. Buses run daily

with a Nite Owl service operating after 2400. **SMRT** buses, www.smrtbuses.com.sg, have fares from 60¢ S\$1.80. It runs a NightRider service. Make sure you have the correct money; bus drivers don't give you change from notes.

The sightseeing **Singapore Explorer** trolley, T6339 6833, www.singaporeexplorer .com.sg, travels between Orchard Rd, the river, Chinatown, Raffles Hotel, Boat Quay, Clarke Quay and Suntec City. Some hotels sell tickets – S\$9, children S\$7 – or buy from the driver for unlimited rides all day.

To Malaysia See box, above, for transport to **Johor Bahru**. There are direct bus connections with many Malaysian towns including **Kuala Lumpur** (S\$23), **Melaka** (S\$18), **Butterworth** (S\$36), **Mersing** (S\$30), **Kuantan** (S\$50), **Ipoh** (S\$31) and **Genting** (S\$30). From Singapore it is cheaper to buy a ticket from the Malaysian buses on Lavender Rd (for KL, Mersing, and Melaka). **Golden Mile** buses are more expensive as they are organized by tour agencies. **Transnasional** (for KL, Genting, Terengganu, and Mersing) has a booking office at Lavender Rd, or T64163948 or T62947034.

Note that long-distance buses tend to leave in the late afternoon. It is best to book tickets a few days ahead of departure, especially if intending to travel over a holiday period. Long-distance bus companies are: **Singapore-Johor Bahru Express**, T06-292 8149; **Kuala Lumpur-Singapore Express**, T06-292 8254; **Malacca-Singapore Express**, T06-293 5915.

To Thailand As well as buses to destinations in Malaysia, there are also direct long-distance services to **Bangkok** and **Hat Yai** in Thailand. These obviously route their journeys through Malaysia. Services to Thailand leave from outside the Golden Mile Tower on Beach Rd and cost S$41 to Hat Yai and S$70 to Bangkok. There are scores of agents selling tickets close to the station. Note that if you are travelling from Singapore to Bangkok, it is cheaper to buy a ticket to Hat Yai and then pay for the rest of the journey in Thai baht. Cheaper still would be to catch a bus to Johor Bahru in Malaysia, take a bus from JB to Hat Yai and then a 3rd from Hat Yai to Bangkok.

Car
Car hire in Singapore is relatively expensive at S$60-350 per day and not really worth it since parking is expensive (coupons can be bought in shops and daily licence booths). If travelling to Malaysia, it is cheaper to hire a car in Johor Bahru.

Driving is on the left, the speed limit 50 kph (80 kph on expressways) and wearing a seat belt is compulsory. Remember that to drive into the restricted zone a licence must be purchased (S$3). Car hire desks are in Terminal 2 arrivals hall, open 0700-2300. **Avis**, T6542 8855; **Hertz**, T6542 5300.

Ferry
For local ferries, see page 741.
To Malaysia Boats to Malaysia leave from **Changi Ferry Terminal**, in the east of Singapore Island. To get to the terminal, take bus No 2 to Changi Village and then a taxi. A passenger-only ferry runs to **Tanjung**

Belungkor, east of Johor Bahru in Malaysia. Most people use this service to get to the beach resort of **Desaru**. Passengers S$16 (S$22 return); journey time 30 mins. Ferry times are Fri-Sun 0715, 1000, 1700 and 2000; Mon-Thu 1000, 1700 and 2000 Singapore to Tanjung Belungkur; and 0815, 1530 and 1845 Tanjung Belungkor to Singapore. Contact **Cruise Ferries**, T06-546 8518, for reservations.

Also from **Changi Ferry Terminal**, bumboats run to **Johor Bahru** (S$5), **Tanjung Pengileh** or **Tanjung Surat** (S$6) in southern Johor. This is a good way of beating the bottleneck at the causeway. Boats run 0700-1600 and depart as soon as they have 12 passengers.

To Indonesia There are regular high-speed ferry connections between Singapore and Indonesia's Riau islands of **Batam** (Sekupang and Batu Ampar) and **Bintan** (Tanjung Pinang and Loban). Return fares to Batam (around S$27, 45 mins), ferries leave from the **Singapore Cruise Centre**, T06-513 2200, www.singaporecruise.com, at HarbourFront, south of town, just a short walk from the HarbourFront MRT. Ferries to Bintan leave from **Tanah Merah ferry terminal** (East Coast), and cost S$34 return (1½ hrs). From the Riau islands it is possible to travel by boat to Sumatra or by air to many other destinations in Indonesia (cheaper than flying direct from Singapore).

Ferry operators have offices in the on the 2nd floor of the HarbourFront Tower. **Penguin Ferries**, T06-271 4866, and **Bintan Resort Ferries**, T06-542 4369, run to Bintan. Passengers should arrive at the terminal 1 hr before departure if they do not already have a booked ticket.

Mass Rapid Transit (MRT)
Singapore has one of the most user-friendly, technologically advanced light railway systems in the world. Trains run 0600-2400, every 2½-8 mins (depending on the time of day). Fare stages are posted in stations, and tickets dispensed, with change, from the

vending machines. Fares range from 80¢ to S$1.80. See www.smrt.com.sg for a map and more on tickets and timetables.

Taxi

Singapore's taxis provide excellent value for money and are definitely the best way to get around. All are metered, a/c and accept credit or debit cards. They can be hailed anywhere but it's best to go to a taxi stand or about 50 m from traffic lights. There are stands outside most main shopping centres and hotels. Drivers are impeccably polite and will even round down fares to the nearest dollar. Unlike most of the rest of Asia, language is not a barrier to communication. Taxis displaying red destination labels on their dashboards are going home and are only required to take passengers in the direction they are going. For taxi services ring: **City Cab**, T6552 2222; **Comfort**, T6552 1111; **SMRT**, T6555 8888.

Train

To Malaysia There are 2 main lines connecting Singapore and Malaysia: one up the west coast to **Kuala Lumpur** and another line which goes through the centre of Peninsular Malaysia and on to Kota Bharu on the northeast coast. 3 fully air-conditioned express trains make the trip daily between Singapore and **KL**, 6½ hrs (S$34-68, and S$19 for 3rd class seat), departing at 0830, 1525 and 2205. The overnight sleeper arrives in KL at 0625. There is no through train to the north, you will need to change in KL. It is possible to take a train (for S$2.90) to **Johor Bahru** – just across the border in Malaysia – and then catch a (much cheaper) connection further north, but it requires a wait. Trains are clean and efficient and overnight trains have cabins in first class, sleeping berths in second class, and restaurants. The service to **Kota Bharu** takes 13 hrs (S$41-51 and S$33 for 3rd class seat). It leaves daily at 2000.

Singaporean exit formalities are done at Woodlands and then continue for 30 mins, before clearing Malaysian immigration and customs at Tanjong Pagar.

❶ Directory

Singapore p746, map p748
Embassies and consulates Australia (High Commission), 25 Napier Rd, T6836 4100, www.australia.org.sg. **Austria**, 600 North Bridge Rd, T6396 6350. **Belgium**, 8 Shenton Way, 1401 Temasek Tower, T6220 7677. **Canada (High Commission)**, 1 George St, T6854 5900. **Denmark**, 1301 United Sq, 101 Thomson Rd, T6355 5010. **France**, 101-103 Cluny Park Rd, T6880 7800. **Germany**, 1200 Singapore Land Tower, 50 Raffles Place, T6533 6002. **Israel**, 24 Stevens Close, T6834 9200. **Italy**, 101 Thomson Rd, No 27-02 United Sq, T6250 6022. **Japan**, 16 Nassim Rd, T6235 8855. **Malaysia (High Commission)**, 30 Hill St, T6235 0111. **Netherlands**, 1301 Liat Towers, 541 Orchard Rd, T6737 1155. **New Zealand (High Commission)**, 391A Orchard Rd, T6235 9966. **Norway**, 1401 Hong Leong Bldg, 16 Raffles Quay, T6220 7122. **South Africa** (High Commission), 15th floor, Odeon Towers, 331 North Bridge Rd, T6339 3319. **Spain**, 3900 Suntec Tower One, 7 Temasek Blvd, T6732 9788. **Sweden**, 111 Somerset Rd, T6415 9720. **Thailand**, 370 Orchard Rd, T6737 2644. **UK (High Commission)**, 100 Tanglin Rd, T6424 4200. **USA**, 27 Napier Rd, T6476 9100.
Medical services Alexandra, 378 Alexandra Rd, T6475 5222. **East Shore**, 321 Joo Chiat Pl, T6344 7588. **Gleneagles**, 6A Napier Rd, T6473 7222. **Mt Alvernia**, 820 Thomson Rd, T253 4818. **Mt Elizabeth**, 3 Mount Elizabeth, T6737 2666. **National University**, 5 Lower Kent Ridge Rd, T6779 5555. **Raffles Hospital**, 585 North Bridge Rd, T6311 1111, www.raffles hospital.com. Not cheap, but has excellent reputation for international medical services. **Singapore General**, Outram Rd, T6222 3322. **Traveller's Health and Vaccination Clinic**, Tan Tock Seng Hospital Medical Centre, Level 1, 11 Jl Tan Tock Seng, T6357 2222, www.ttsh.com.sg. **Telephone** There are no area codes in Singapore; all standard numbers have 8 digits. Dial T020, plus the area code (minus the initial zero) to call a city or town in Malaysia.

Background

What is perhaps unusual is the ease with which Singaporeans have come to terms with their history. The psychology of decolonization, so evident elsewhere, seems not to have afflicted the average Singaporean. Perhaps this is because all the population are the sons and daughters of relatively recent immigrants; perhaps because of the self-evident social and economic achievements of the country; or perhaps it is because there is general acceptance that the colonial experience was beneficial. Unlike other countries, after independence there was no rush to rename streets after resistance fighters and nationalist figures. Empress Place, Connaught Drive, Alexander Road, Clive Street and Dalhousie Pier remain with the names that the British gave them.

Early records

Although Singapore has probably been inhabited for the past two millennia, there are few early records. In the third century, Chinese sailors mention *Pu-luo-chung,* 'the island at the end of the peninsula', and historians speculate that this may have been Singapore. Even its name, *Singapura,* from the Sanskrit for 'Lion City', is unexplained – other than by the legendary account in the *Sejara Melayu* (Malay Annals). It was originally called Temasek – or 'Sea Town' – and may have been a small seaport in the days of the Sumatran Srivijayan Empire. Following Srivijaya's decline in the late 13th century, however, Singapore emerged from the shadows to become, for a short while, a locally important trading centre in its own right.

Marco Polo, the Venetian adventurer, visited Sumatra in the late 1200s and referred to *Chiamassie,* which he says was a 'very large and noble city'. Historians believe this was probably Temasek. According to the 16th-century *Sejara Melayu,* Temasek was a thriving entrepôt by the 14th century, when it changed its name to Singapura. Whatever prosperity it may have had did not last. In the late 1300s it was destroyed by invading Siamese and Javanese, for Singapura fell in the middle ground between the expanding Ayutthaya (Siamese) and Majapahit (Javanese) empires. The ruler – called Parameswara, who was said to be a fugitive prince from Palembang in Sumatra – fled to Melaka, where he founded the powerful Malay sultanate in the 1390s. Following Parameswara's hasty departure, Singapura was abandoned except for a few *Orang Laut* ('Sea People'), who made a living from fishing and piracy. While trade flourished elsewhere in the region, the port, which today is the busiest in the world, was a jungled backwater, and it remained that way for four centuries.

Raffles steps ashore

In the early 1800s, the British East India Company occupied Dutch colonies in the east, to prevent them falling into French hands: Napoleon had occupied Holland and the Dutch East India Company had gone bankrupt. In January 1819, Sir Thomas Stamford Raffles arrived in Singapore with the hope that he could set up a trading post at the mouth of the Singapore River. He was relieved to hear that the Dutch had never been there and promptly struck a deal with the resident *temenggong* (Malay chief) of the Riau-Johor Empire. To seal this agreement, he had to obtain official approval from the Sultan of Riau-Johor.

Due to a succession squabble following the previous sultan's death in 1812, there were two claimants, one on Pulau Lingga (far to the south), who was recognized by the Dutch, and one on Pulau Bintan. Realizing that the Dutch would bar the Lingga sultan from sanctioning his settlement on Singapore, Raffles approached the other one, flattering him, offering him money and pronouncing him Sultan of Johor. He agreed to pay Sultan Hussein Mohammad Shah 5,000 Spanish dollars a year in rent and a further 3000 Spanish dollars to the temenggon. The Union Jack was officially raised over Singapore on 6 February 1819, and Raffles set sail again the next day – having been there less than a week – leaving in charge the former Resident of Melaka, Colonel William Farquhar. It was this act of Raffles' that led to him being accorded the title 'Founder of Singapore'. Yet some historians would give the title to another great, although lesser known, British colonialist, Sir John Crawfurd. Ernest Chew, Professor of History at the National University of Singapore, argues that all Raffles secured in his negotiations was permission to establish a trading post. It was not until Crawfurd became the second Resident of Singapore in 1824 that Britain acquired the island by treaty.

The Treaty of London

The Dutch were enraged by Raffles' bold initiative and the British government was embarrassed. But after a protracted diplomatic frisson, the Treaty of London was finally signed in 1824 and the Dutch withdrew their objection to the British presence on Singapore in exchange for the British withdrawal from Bencoolen (Benkulu) in Sumatra, where Raffles had served as governor. Seven years later, the trading post was tied with Penang (which had been in British hands since 1786) and Melaka (which the Dutch had swapped with Bencoolen). They became known as the Straits Settlements and attracted traders and settlers from all over Southeast Asia, and the world.

Raffles' vision

Although Sir Thomas Stamford Raffles spent little time in Singapore, his vision for the city can still be seen today: "Our object is not territory but trade; a great commercial emporium and a fulcrum whence we may extend our influence politically as circumstances may hereafter require". Each time Raffles departed, he left strict instructions on the layout of the growing city; stipulating, for example, that the streets should be arranged on a grid structure wherever possible. Houses were to have a uniform front and "a verandah open at all times as a continued and covered passage on each side of the street" (the so-called 'five-foot ways') – stipulations that resulted in the unique character of Singapore. During his second visit in 1819, he divided the town into distinct districts, or *kampongs*. Raffles firmly believed that the different ethnic groups should be segregated. The Europeans were to live in the Beach Road area between Stamford canal and Arab Street, the Chinese were to live south of the river (in fact, Chinatown was divided into three separate areas for the different dialect groups), and the Temenggong and the 600-odd Malays were to live along the upper reaches of the river. To the northeast of the European enclave, Kampong Glam housed Sultan Hussein and his Arab followers. The land on the north side of the river was set aside for government buildings. A mere six months after Raffles had landed, more than 5000 people had settled around the mouth of the river. Much of the area to the south was mangrove swamps, but that was reclaimed and settled too.

European merchants soon realized that the beach was inappropriate as a landing area because of the swell. In agreement with Farquhar, they started to unload from the north bank of the river. When Raffles returned for his third and final visit in October 1822, he was horrified by the chaos of the town. He fell out with Farquhar and had him replaced by John Crawfurd.

From fishing village to international port

Within four years of its founding, Singapore had overshadowed Penang in importance and had grown from a fishing village to an international trading port. Thanks to its strategic location, it expanded quickly as an entrepôt, assuming the role Melaka had held in earlier centuries. But by 1833 the British East India Company had lost its China trade monopoly, and consequently its interest in the other Straits Settlements started to wane. Whilst Penang and Melaka declined, however, Singapore boomed. When the Dutch lifted trade restrictions in the 1840s, this boosted Singapore's economy again. New trade channels opened up with the Brooke government in Sarawak and with Thailand. The volume of trade increased fourfold between 1824 and 1868. However, due to the lack of restrictions and regulation, Singapore descended into a state of commercial anarchy, and in 1857 the merchants, who were dissatisfied with the administration, petitioned for Singapore to come under direct British rule.

Ten years later, the Colonial Office in London reluctantly made Singapore a crown colony. Then, in 1869, the Suez Canal opened, which meant that the Strait of Melaka was an even more obvious route for east-west shipping traffic than the Sunda Strait, which was controlled by the Dutch. Five years after that, Britain signed the first of its protection treaties with the Malay sultans on the peninsula. The governor of Singapore immediately became the most senior authority for the Straits Settlements Colony, the Federated Malay States and the British protectorates of Sarawak, Brunei and North Borneo. In one stroke, Singapore had become the political capital of a small empire within an empire. As Malaysia's plantation economy grew (with the introduction of rubber in the late 19th century) and as its tin-mining industry expanded rapidly, Singapore emerged as the expanding territory's financing and administrative centre and export outlet. By then Singapore had become the uncontested commercial and transport centre of Southeast Asia. Between 1873 and 1913 there was an eightfold increase in Singapore's trade. Joseph Conrad dubbed it "the thoroughfare to the East".

The Japanese invasion

The First World War gave Singapore a measure of strategic significance and by 1938 the colony was bristling with guns; it became known as Fortress Singapore. Unfortunately, the impregnable Fortress Singapore had anticipated that any attack would be from the sea and all its big guns were facing seawards. The Japanese entered through the back door. Japan attacked Malaya in December 1941 and, having landed on the northeast coast, they took the entire peninsula in a lightning campaign, arriving in Johor Bahru at the end of January 1942.

The Japanese invasion of Singapore was planned by General Tomoyuki Yamashita and was co-ordinated from the Sultan Ibrahim tower in Johor Bahru, which afforded a commanding view over the strait and north Singapore. Yamashita became known as the 'Tiger of Malaya' for the speed with which the Japanese Army overran the peninsula. The northeast coast of Singapore was heavily protected, but the northwest was vulnerable and this is where the Japanese found their opening. On 13 February 1942, the Japanese captured Kent Ridge and Alexandra Barracks on Alexandra Road. They entered the hospital, where they bayoneted the wounded and executed doctors, surgeons and nurses. The Allies and the local people were left in little doubt as to what was in store.

With their water supplies from the peninsula cut off by the Japanese, and facing an epidemic because of thousands of rotting corpses, British Lieutenant-General Arthur Percival was forced to surrender in the Ford Motor Company boardroom on Bukit Timah

Road, at 1950 on 15 February 1942. The fall of Singapore, which was a crushing humiliation for the British, left 140,000 Australian, British and Indian troops killed, wounded or captured. Japan had taken the island in one week.

Following the defeat, there were accusations that Sir Winston Churchill had 'abandoned' Singapore and let it fall to the Japanese when reinforcements were diverted elsewhere. The motivation for this, it has been suggested, was to get America to join the war. It is significant that Churchill never pressed for an inquiry into the fall of Singapore – the historian Peter Elphick suggests that Churchill was worried that he would emerge as the prime factor behind the capitulation. Apart from Churchill's supposed involvement in the surrender, there were other manifold reasons why Singapore fell. There is little doubt that the defence of Singapore itself, and Malaya more widely, was poorly handled. There was a widespread lack of appreciation of the martial skills of the Japanese. The forces defending Singapore lacked sufficient air cover and were poorly equipped, and training and morale were poor. The massive surrender certainly stands in stark contrast to Churchill's orders issued to General Wavell on 10 February: "There must at this stage be no thought of saving the troops or sparing the population. The honour of the British Empire and of the British Army is at stake."

The occupation

The Japanese ran a brutal regime and their occupation was characterized by terror, starvation and misery. They renamed Singapore *Syonan* – meaning 'light of the south'. The intention was to retain Syonan as a permanent colony, and turn it into a military base and centre in its 'Greater East Asia Co-Prosperity Sphere'. During the war, Singapore became the base of the collaborationist Indian National Army and the Indian Independence League.

In the fortnight that followed the surrender, the Japanese required all Chinese males aged 18-50 to register. 'Undesirables' were herded into trucks and taken for interrogation and torture by the Kempetai military police to the old YMCA building on Stamford Road, or were summarily bayoneted and shot. The purge was known as *sook ching* – or 'the purification campaign'. Thousands were killed (Singapore says 50,000, Japan says 6000), and most of the executions took place on Changi Beach and Sentosa. The sand on Changi Beach is said to have turned red from the blood.

Allied prisoners-of-war were herded into prison camps, the conditions of which are vividly described in James Clavell's book *King Rat*; the author was himself a Changi POW. Many of the Allied troops who were not dispatched to work on the Burma railway or sent to Sandakan in North Borneo, where 2400 people died, were imprisoned in Selarang Barracks on the northeast side of the island.

After Hiroshima and Nagasaki

Following the dropping of atomic bombs on Hiroshima and Nagasaki, the Japanese surrendered on 12 September 1945. The Japanese ffith and 18th Divisions, which had spearheaded the invasion of Singapore and had carried out civilian massacres, were from the towns of Hiroshima and Nagasaki respectively. Lord Louis Mountbatten, who took the surrender, described it as the greatest day of his life.

In the wake of the war, the Japanese partially atoned for their 'blood debt' by extending 'gifts' and 'special loans' to Singapore, totalling some US$50 million. But Japanese war crimes were neither forgiven nor forgotten. Older Singaporeans noted with dismay and concern how Japan had rewritten its historical textbooks to gloss over its wartime atrocities, and many Singaporeans harbour a deep-seated mistrust of the Japanese. Among the most outspoken of them is former Prime Minister Lee Kuan Yew. This mistrust remains, despite former Japanese Prime Minister Toshiki Kaifu's public apology in 1991 for what his countrymen had done 50 years before.

After the war

Following a few months under a British military administration, Singapore became a crown colony and was separated from the other Straits Settlements of Penang, Melaka and Labuan. The Malay sultanates on the peninsula were brought into the Malayan Union. The British decision to keep Singapore separate from the Malayan Union sparked protests on the island and resulted in the founding of its first political party, the Malayan Democratic Union (MDU), which wanted Singapore to be integrated into a socialist union. The Malayan Union was very unpopular on the mainland too and the British replaced it with the Federation of Malaya in 1948. Singapore was excluded again because Malaya's emergent Malay leaders did not want to upset the peninsula's already delicate ethnic balance by incorporating predominantly Chinese Singapore.

In the same year, elections were held for Singapore's legislative council. The MDU, which had been heavily infiltrated by communists, boycotted the election, allowing the Singapore Progressive Party (SPP) – dominated by an English-educated élite – to win a majority. The council was irrelevant to the majority of the population, however, and did nothing to combat poverty and unemployment and little to promote social services. When the Communist Emergency broke out on the peninsula later the same year, the Malayan Communist Party of Malaya (CPM) was banned in Singapore and the MDU disbanded.

Lee Kuan Yew ('Harry Lee' to the British and Americans) returned from study in England in 1950. In 1954, as his political aspirations hardened, he let it be known that he wished to be called Lee Kuan Yew. Ten years later, the British foreign secretary George Brown is still alleged to have remarked to him: "Harry, you're the best bloody Englishman east of Suez".

Political awakening

In 1955 a new constitution was introduced, which aimed to jolt the island's apathetic electorate into political life. Two new parties were formed to contest the election – the Labour Front under lawyer David Marshall (descended from an Iraqi Jewish family) and the People's Action Party (PAP), headed by Lee Kuan Yew. These two parties routed the conservative SPP and Marshall formed a minority government. His tenure as Chief Minister was marked by violence and by tempestuous exchanges in the Legislative Assembly with Lee. Marshall resigned in 1956, after failing to negotiate self-government for Singapore by his self-imposed deadline. His deputy, Lim Yew Hock (who later became a Muslim), took over as chief minister and more communist-instigated violence followed.

The rise of the PAP

The influence of the PAP grew rapidly, in league with the communists and radical union leaders, and through the Chinese-language schools and trade unions. For the anti-communist Lee, it was a Machiavellian alliance of convenience. He mouthed various anti-colonial slogans, but the British, at least, seemed to realize he was playing a long, and cunning, game. The communists came to dominate the PAP central committee and managed to sideline Lee before their leaders were arrested by Marshall's government. At the same time, Singapore's administration was rapidly localized: the four main languages

(Malay, Chinese, Tamil and English) were given parity within the education system and locals took over the civil service. In 1957, as Malaya secured independence from the British, Singapore negotiated terms for full self-government. In 1959 the PAP swept the polls, winning a clear majority, and Lee became prime minister, a post he was to hold for more than three decades.

The PAP government began a programme of rapid industrialization and social reform. Singapore also moved closer to Malaysia, which Lee considered a vital move in order to guarantee free access to the Malaysian market and provide military security in the run-up to its own independence. But the PAP leaders were split over the wisdom of this move, and the extreme left wing, which had come to the forefront again, was becoming more vociferous in its opposition. Malaysia, for its part, felt threatened by Singapore's large Chinese population and by its increasingly communist-orientated government. Tunku Abdul Rahman, independent Malaysia's first prime minister, voiced concerns that an independent Singapore could become 'a second Cuba', a communist state on Malaysia's doorstep. Instead of letting the situation deteriorate, however, Tunku Abdul Rahman cleverly proposed Singapore's inclusion in the Federation of Malaysia.

The Federation of Malaysia and independence
Rahman hoped the racial equilibrium of the federation would be balanced by the inclusion of Sarawak, Brunei and North Borneo. Lee liked the idea, but the radical left wing of the PAP were vehemently opposed to it, having no desire to see Singapore absorbed by a Malay-dominated, anti-communist regime, and in July 1961 they tried to topple Lee's government. Their bid narrowly failed and resulted in the left-wing dissenters breaking away to form the Barisan Sosialis (BS), or Socialist Front. Despite opposition to the merger, a referendum showed that a majority of Singapore's population supported it. In February 1963, in 'Operation Coldstore', more than 100 communist and pro-communist politicians, trades unionists and student leaders were arrested, including half the BS Central Executive Committee.

On 31 August 1963, Singapore joined the Federation of Malaysia. The following month, Singapore declared unilateral independence from Britain. The PAP also won another victory in an election and secured a comfortable majority. Almost immediately, however, the new Federation ran into trouble due to Indonesian objections, and Jakarta launched its *Konfrontasi* – or Confrontation. Indonesian saboteurs infiltrated Singapore and began a bombing spree which severely damaged Singapore's trade. In mid-1964, Singapore was wracked by communal riots which caused great concern in Kuala Lumpur, and Lee and Tunku Abdul Rahman clashed over what they considered undue interference in each others' internal affairs. Tensions rose still further when the PAP contested Malaysia's general election in 1964, and Lee attempted to unite all Malaysian opposition parties under the PAP banner. While the PAP won only one of the 10 seats, it petrified many Malay politicians on the mainland. Finally, on 9 August 1965, Kuala Lumpur forced Singapore to agree to pull out of the Federation, and it became an independent state against the wishes of the government. At a press conference announcing Singapore's expulsion from the Federation, Lee Kuan Yew wept.

As a footnote to Singapore's expulsion from the Federation, in June 1996 Lee Kuan Yew suggested that the island republic might rejoin the Federation should certain conditions be met – like no racial favouritism. Few other politicians, either in Singapore or Malaysia, took the proposal seriously.

Modern Singapore

Singapore still believes in extended families, filial piety, discipline and respect, but above all, it believes in the Asian work ethic. The man who has instilled and preserved these values is former Prime Minister Lee Kuan Yew. But to some – and it should be added that most of these are non-Singaporeans – his far-sighted vision has transformed this clockwork island into a regimented city state. In this view of things, modern, automated Singapore has spawned a generation of angst-ridden, over-programmed people, who have given their country the reputation of being the most crushingly dull in Asia.

But now, all has changed. The architect of modern Singapore has allowed a new generation of Singaporeans to step up to the drawing board. That Lee Kuan Yew's own son, Lee Hsien Loong, took office in 2004 as part of a handover of power without elections, may give the impression that what goes round, comes round.

Politics

In 1965, the newly independent Republic of Singapore committed itself to non-communist, multi-racial, democratic socialist government, and secured Malaysian co-operation in trade and defence. The new government faced what most observers considered impossible: forging a viable economy in a densely populated micro-state with no natural resources. At first, Singapore hoped for re-admission to the Malaysian Federation, but as Lee surprised everyone by presiding over one of the fastest-growing economies in the world, the republic soon realized that striking out alone was the best approach. Within a few years, independent Singapore was being hailed as an 'economic miracle'. Nonetheless, the government had to work hard to forge a sense of nationhood. As most Singaporeans were still more interested in wealth creation than in politics, the government became increasingly paternalistic, declaring that it knew what was best for the people and, because most people agreed, few raised any objections.

Singapore's foreign policy has been built around regional co-operation. It was a founder member in 1967 of the Association of Southeast Asian Nations (ASEAN) and has also been a leading light in the wider Asia-Pacific Economic Cooperation (APEC) grouping. Friendly international relations are considered of paramount importance for a state that relies so heavily on foreign trade and which, in terms of size and population, is a minnow among giants. Although Singapore continued to trade with the former communist states of Eastern Europe and the Soviet Union throughout the period of the Cold War, Lee had a great fear and loathing of Communism. At home, 'communists' became bogeymen; 'hard-core' subversives were imprisoned without trial, under emergency legislation enshrined in the Internal Security Act, a legacy of the British colonial administration.

Singapore's political stability since independence, which has helped attract foreign investors to the island, has been tempered by the government's tendency to stifle criticism. The media are state-owned and are so pro-government that they have become rigidly self-censoring. Foreign publications are summarily banned or their circulation restricted if they are deemed to be meddling in (ie critical of) Singapore's internal affairs. Probably because the People's Action Party (PAP) have been so successful at bringing about economic success, no major political opposition has emerged. Politicians who have stood out against PAP's autocratic style of government have been effectively silenced as the government sets about undermining their credibility in the eyes of the electorate. For 13 years, between 1968 and 1981, PAP held every single seat in parliament. In 2001 the general election saw less than a third of the constituency seats contested, making losing an impossibility for PAP. (This in a country where, if you're eligible to vote, voting is compulsory.) The 2006 elections saw more than half of the constituency seats contested (a first); PAP won 82 out of 84, taking 60% of the popular vote. Opposition won an impressive 30% of the vote and a high proportion of votes cast – 8% – were declared void.

The PAP – losing its way or regaining the initiative?

Perhaps a sign that the PAP was in danger of losing its way came with the country's first presidential election of August 1993, which was billed as a PAP stitch-up. Virtually all observers predicted that the result would be a foregone conclusion. In the event, the favoured candidate, former deputy prime minister Ong Teng Cheong (Lee Kuan Yew, despite much speculation, decided not to stand) did win, but he managed to attract less than 60% of the vote, against more than 40% won by his virtually unknown challenger, a former government accountant, Chua Kim Yeoh. As he did not actively campaign, analysts attributed his sudden popularity not to genuine support but to a protest against the PAP, which had barred two opposition candidates from standing.

Singapore's most recent general election was held in 2006 and some commentators were predicting a further erosion of PAP support, as the republic's increasingly sophisticated electorate bristled at the restrictions placed upon them. Despite increased votes cast for opposition, however, PAP has obviously retained its appeal for the majority of voters.

Lee's succession

As Lee Kuan Yew came to be regarded as one of the region's 'elder statesmen', questions were raised over his succession. The PAP's old guard gradually made way for young blood, but Lee clung on until November 1990. Three months after Singapore's extravagant 25th anniversary, he finally handed over to his first deputy prime minister Goh Chok Tong. Lee, though, remained PAP's chairman. Subsequently a new post was created especially for him; Lee is now the 'Cabinet's Official Mentor'.

When Lee senior stepped down in late 1990, a new era began. Goh promised to usher in a more open, 'people-oriented', consensus-style of government. Among his first acts was the creation of a new Ministry for the Arts, and to underscore his faith in Singapore's maturity, he permitted the showing of porn films, which proved very popular. He also began encouraging a more free press (particularly with regard to foreign publications), as well as releasing long-term political prisoners and allowing ageing exiles to return home. But relaxation in government attitudes should not be regarded as a shift to Western-style liberalism. Indeed, analysts perceived a slight hardening of attitude as Goh's premiership wore on.

Lee Hsien Loong

Although Singapore has been run as a meritocracy since independence, Goh was widely assumed to be a seat-warmer for Lee Kuan Yew's eldest son, Brigadier-General Lee Hsien Loong. Lee Hsien, like his father, got a first at Cambridge, returned to Singapore, joined the army as a platoon commander and within eight years was a Brigadier-General in charge of the Joint Operations Planning Directorate. During that period he obtained a Master's degree at Harvard and then in 1984, at the age of 32, was elected to parliament. The following year he became a cabinet minister and head of the Ministry of Trade and Industry. At 38, he became deputy prime minister and then head of the critical Monetary Authority of Singapore. He celebrated his 54th birthday in 2006.

But Lee Hsien's life has not been one of an inexorable rise to the top. In 1982 his first wife died (he has since remarried). And in 1992 it was revealed that Lee had been diagnosed with lymphoma (in 1997 he was given a clean bill of health).

Since coming to power Lee Hsien has introduced a number of policies, some more popular than others. Diplomatic relations with China have improved, with progress in areas such as tourism and trade, and the establishment of an ASEAN-China Free Trade Agreement on the cards.

In 2005 Lee Hsien introduced the five-day week, abolishing the half working day on Saturday, and in 2006 PAP distributed a S$2.6 billion budget surplus termed the 'Progress Package'. This was given as cash to a huge number of eligible people and led to Lee Hsien being accused by critics and opposition of vote buying, as a general election was just around the corner.

Birth incentives have also been increased. Due to the historically low birth rate (1.26 children per mother, compared with 5.8 in the 1960s), Singapore now finds itself offering incentives to families that have more than two children; an ironic position when you consider that just a few decades ago the government was strongly encouraging sterilization after the second child.

A kinder and more sensitive Singapore?

There have been signs that Singapore is easing up a bit politically. In the bars and taxis of the Republic, people are a lot more critical than the local media might lead one to believe. Taxi drivers cheerfully give visitors a quick run-down of life in Singapore, including the frequent hangings at dawn at Changi Prison. One joke doing the rounds shows the ability of Singaporeans to laugh at themselves: An American remarks to a Somali, a Ukrainian and a Singaporean that food seems to cost a lot of money in the city state, and asks their opinion of this state of affairs. The Somali replies "What's food?", the Ukrainian demands "What's money?", and the Singaporean quietly asks "What's an opinion?".

Literary satire also now has a place on Singapore's bookshelves. The Psychological Defence Division (sounds Brave New World-esque!) of the Ministry of Communications and Information published a book called *Sing Singapore*. The largely inane songs in this official publication were to be taught in schools and transmitted on television and radio. *We are Singapore* gives a flavour of the lyrics: *"This is my country, This is my flag, This is my future, This is my life, This is my family, These are my friends, We are Singapore, Singaporeans, Singapore our homeland, It's here that we belong"*.

A few years later, however, the *Not the Singapore Song Book* appeared to cock a paradonic snook at the original by borrowing some of the tunes and putting them to new lyrics. It represents popular resistance Singapore-style. *Count! Mummies of Singapore* pokes fun at Singapore's family planning policy: *"We have the ova in our bodies, We can conceive, We can conceive. We have a role for Singapore, We must receive, We must receive"*. Then there is the *SDU March*, *"Hey girl! Why aren't you married yet! You girl! A man's not hard to get! Now's the time for you to choose your mate! Don't delay! Do not procrastinate!"*. Other subversive songs include *Babies keep formin' in my bed* (sung to *Raindrops keep falling on my head*), *Three cees* (condominium, credit card and car), and *Gold card blues*. Singapore's political culture does not permit overt expressions of dissent, so Singaporeans have to find alternative avenues for opposition. *The Not the Singapore Song Book* is just one of many forms of covert popular resistance.

To people from countries with long histories and a well-established sense of nationhood, *Sing Singapore* may seem rather crass. But Singapore's leaders have always been worried that a country which did not exist 50 years ago could be just as quickly and easily snuffed out. This is why the country's leaders got so agitated when a survey showed that only six out of 50 young Singaporeans knew that their country had once been part of the Malaysian Federation. This is why the National Heritage Board is so enthusiastically conserving historic sites and why Singapore's history is taking such a prominent place in exhibitions.

All that said, Singapore still holds the dubious honour of having the highest death penalty rate per capita in the world (according to Amnesty International). Singapore continues to use the death penalty for a number of offences, including non-violent drug-related crimes, drawing criticism from human rights organizations and foreign governments. In 2005, for example, the Australian drug trafficker Nguyen Tuong Van was executed despite a diplomatic backlash from Australia.

Defence

Singapore spends more than S$9 billion a year on defence – over 30% of government expenditure. It promotes the idea of 'total defence', meaning that everyone plays some role in protecting the country, economically and militarily. Regular emergency exercises are conducted involving the civilian population, which is designed to instill preparedness. This policy is probably influenced by memories of Singapore's inglorious surrender to the Japanese in February 1942. Men have to serve a compulsory two-year period as Full Time National Servicemen in the Defence Forces, followed by annual training exercises of at least six days for reservists until they are 40 or 50 years old, depending on their rank. Being a predominantly Chinese state in the middle of the Malay world, Singapore feels very vulnerable, and government ministers have expressed fears, despite Singapore's good relations with its Malaysian and Indonesian neighbours. The armed forces are known to be trained by Israelis. Singapore is also the biggest arms manufacturer in the region and is an entrepôt for the arms trade. Ian Buruma, in his book *God's Dust: A Modern Asian Journey* (1989), writes of his fear in Singapore of simply being engulfed: "Singapore was an accident of history, like a bunny that popped out of the magician's hat by mistake. One sleight of hand and the bunny could vanish as swiftly as it appeared."

Singapore and its neighbours

Singapore is a member of the 10-member Association of Southeast Asian Nations (ASEAN) and enjoys generally good relations with its neighbours. However, there have been times of friction, particularly during the mid-1960s when Singapore left the Malaysian Federation and had a diplomatic spat with President Sukarno of Indonesia. As a minute city state with a population less that 2% of Indonesia's, Singapore's leaders have always been acutely aware of the need to build and maintain good relations with its regional neighbours.

Even so, Singapore has not always managed to avoid offending its larger neighbours. This particularly applies to Malaysia, a country with which it shares a common colonial history, but from which it is divided in so many other ways. Malaysia's majority are Malay and Muslim; Singapore's are Chinese. Malaysia has a national policy of positive discrimination in favour of ethnic Malays; Singapore is a meritocracy. Malaysia is still a developing country; Singapore's standard of living is among the highest in the world. This makes for a fierce competitiveness between the two countries, which disguises a lingering bitterness that some commentators trace back to Singapore's ejection from the Malaysian Federation in the mid-1960s. Malaysia is quick to take offence at anything that smacks of Singaporean superiority.

Between 1996 and 1998, relations between Malaysia and Singapore sunk to their lowest level for some years. In June 1996, Lee Kuan Yew offered the thought that Singapore could, conceivably, merge once more with Malaysia. Two months later, Goh Chok Tong seemed to use this as a threat when he warned that if Singapore slipped up, "we will have no option but to ask Malaysia to take us back". The Malaysian government took this as a slight. In their view, the prime minister was threatening the electorate with the possibility that they might be absorbed into Malaysia. In March 1997, Senior Minister Lee Kuan Yew suggested that the Malaysian state of Johor Bahru was "notorious for shootings, muggings and car-jackings" (this was in relation to opposition politician Tang Liang Hong's decision to flee there from Singapore). The Malaysian press and some sections of the government reacted with outrage. Singapore's *Straits Times* then compounded Lee's insensitivity by publishing an article listing recent crimes in Johor – which Malaysians saw as a crass attempt to justify his comments. Just as this spat had run its course, the Asian crisis created further tensions. Malaysia felt Singapore was not doing enough to help the poor economy of its neighbour across the Strait of Johor.

Today, relations are stable, several outstanding disputes notwithstanding. Singapore and Malaysia are members of the Five Power Defence Arrangements, and undertake military exercises together in order to strengthen the ties between their armed forces. Both countries export to each other, with Malaysia supplying much of Singapore's drinking water (another source of tension, as Malaysia is signatory to a historical treaty guaranteeing Singapore's right to buy water from them at what is now below the market rate). Many Malaysians also work in Singapore.

Singapore in the 21st century

Singapore's political system fits no neat category. It is both democratic and authoritarian; although it is tempting to characterize Singapore as a totalitarian state, it is not. Whether the People's Action Party will be able to continue to dominate Singapore's political landscape, as it has done throughout the period since independence, is a key question. There are certainly challenges which the PAP will have to confront. To begin with, social differentiation is making it harder for the PAP to please almost all the people almost all of the time. People's interests are diverging as Singapore's affluence grows. Second, there is the question of whether the PAP, in creating a 'thinking society' necessary for economic success, is not also creating a society that will be more politically creative and combative. Third, and related, there is the question of whether the population will continue to accept such a low level of public debate and the continued ban on public street demonstrations.

Contents

Footprint features

Border crossings

Thailand–Cambodia, *page 881*
Thailand–Laos, *page 908*
Thailand–Malaysia, *page 967*

At a glance

◉ **Getting around** For long-distance travel, take Thailand's excellent sleeper trains.

◉ **Time required** Beach bums should be sated in 2 weeks. Those who want more might need to use their full 30-day entry permit.

◐ **Weather** Andaman Sea monsoon is May-Oct; Gulf of Thailand is Nov-Apr.

✖ **When not to go** During Apr and May the heat can be unbearable.

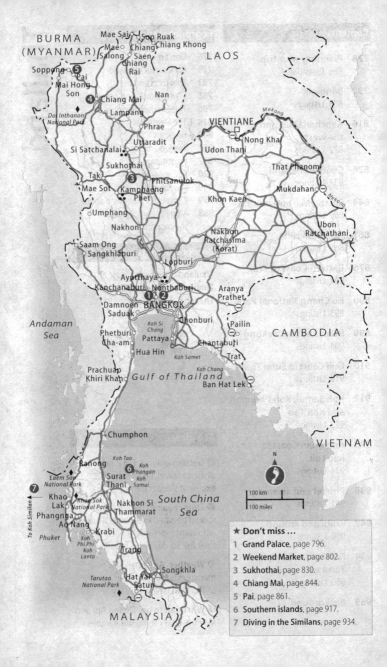

★ **Don't miss ...**

1 **Grand Palace**, page 796.

2 **Weekend Market**, page 802.

3 **Sukhothai**, page 830.

4 **Chiang Mai**, page 844.

5 **Pai**, page 861.

6 **Southern islands**, page 917.

7 **Diving in the Similans**, page 934.

It doesn't take much to shatter an illusion. Take a ride to the city from Bangkok's airport along the vast, elevated highway and you'll understand why. The promise of soothing seas, ancient temples and wafting incense is replaced with an ocean of concrete, ultra-modern skyscrapers and thick exhaust fumes. For many visitors, Bangkok, and its 12 million inhabitants, are too much – "we wanted monks and white sand and elephants", they probably wail. What they get is one of the most invigorating and modern cities on earth, an intense, overwhelming human hive that revels in its dynamism. Yet, if you take the time, you can find calm moments: the waft of jasmine as you walk through a back *soi*; an evening spent watching the city lights reflected in the Chao Phraya River; a visit to the sanctity of one of Bangkok's stunning temples. Always remember that, whatever your expectations, you are going to be dumbfounded. The Kingdom of Thailand is a proud and independent place that burns fiercely with the white heat of modernity while revering the links to its exotic past. Ancient Siam, authentic street food and gorgeous silks sit side by side with massive industry, a thick fug of traffic jams, fast food and seminal hi-tech. Get used to the idea that Thailand is rapidly becoming a highly advanced 21st-century society and you can then enjoy its other countless attractions with a hint of realism.

Why not start with the weird and wonderful? Grab a mouthful of cooked bugs from a street vendor or watch *katoey* (transexual) kickboxing. If you prefer misty vistas shrouding antique temples, then make for Sukhothai and Isaan. Or head for the 2600 km of coastline – the tourist fleshpots at Pattaya and Phuket or the isolated, verdant islands such as Koh Tarutao and the dive mecca of Koh Similan. There are national parks, too, hosting wild animals, deep jungles and fierce rivers, while the gentle mountainous north is home to an absorbing multi-ethnic society.

Planning your trip

Getting there

Air

Most visitors arrive in Thailand through Bangkok's Suvarnabhumi International (see below). Chiang Mai in the north and Phuket in the south also have international airports. More than 35 airlines and charter companies fly to Bangkok. THAI is the national carrier. Fares are 50% higher during high season.

From Europe The approximate flight time from London to Bangkok (non-stop) is 12 hours. From London Heathrow, airlines offering non-stop flights include Qantas, British Airways, THAI and Eva Air. You can easily connect to Thailand from the UK via most other European capitals.

From the USA and Canada THAI have started a non-stop flight from New York to Bangkok: flight time 16 hours. Otherwise, the approximate flight time from Los Angeles to Bangkok is 21 hours. There are one-stop flights from Los Angeles on THAI and two-stops on Delta; one-stop flights from San Francisco on Northwest and United and two-stops on Delta; and one-stop flights from Vancouver on Canadian.

From Australasia There are flights from Sydney and Melbourne (approximately nine hours) daily with Qantas and THAI. There are flights from Perth with THAI and Qantas. From Auckland, Air New Zealand, THAI and British Airways fly to Bangkok.

From Asia THAI, Air India and Indian Airlines, Royal Nepal Airlines and THAI fly from Kathmandu. It is also possible to fly to Chiang Mai and Phuket from many international destinations. There has been a massive proliferation of budget airlines in Southeast Asia with Bangkok becoming one of the primary hubs. The situation is changing rapidly with carriers going in and out of business and routes/frequencies fluctuating – check www.asiaoz.com/thailand_airlines.html for a full up-to-date list of budget air connections. The main players are Air Asia (www.airasia.com) and Bangkok Airways (www.bangkokair.com).

Airport information Suvarnabhumi airport, to the east of the city, which opened in September 2006, has been beset with problems and numerous allegations of corruption. In 2007, due to a mixture of runway cracks and lack of working facilities at Suvarnabhumi, the old airport, 25 km to the north of the city, Don Muang was forced to re-open. See Bangkok pages 792 and 108 for further details. For information on transport from the airport into Bangkok, see page 792.

Discount flight agents
UK
STA Travel, 33 Bedford St, Covent Garden, London WC2E 9ED, T0871-468 0612, www.statravel.co.uk. Specialists in low-cost student flights, tours, IDs and insurance.

Trailfinders, 194 Kensington High St, London, W8 7RG, T020-7938 3939, www.trailfinders.co.uk.

Packing for Thailand

Almost everything is available in Thailand's towns and cities – often at a lower price than in the West. Even apparently remote areas will have shops that stock most things that a traveller might require from toiletries and batteries to pharmaceuticals. Although beware that clothes and shoes may not be available in large sizies. Laundrettes are available everywhere and are cheap and quick.

Checklist Appropriate clothing (see Local customs and laws, page 784); bumbag; earplugs; first-aid kit; hiking boots (if visiting any of the national parks); insect repellent and/or electric mosquito mats, coils; international driving licence; money belt; passports (valid for at least six months); photocopies of essential documents; short wave radio; spare passport photographs; sun hat; sun protection; sunglasses; Swiss Army knife; torch; umbrella; wet wipes; zip-lock bags.

When travelling to out-of-the-way places, carry toilet paper, and if you intend to stay in budget accommodation take cotton sheet sleeping bag; padlock (for hotel room and pack); student card; toilet paper; towel; travel wash.

North America

Air Brokers International, 323 Geary St, Suite 411, San Francisco, CA 94102, T01-800-883 3273, www.airbrokers.com. Consolidator and specialist on RTW and Circle Pacific tickets.
Discount Airfares Worldwide On-Line, www.etn.nl/discount.htm. A hub of consolidator and discount agent links.
International Travel Network/Airlines of the Web, www.itn.net/airlines. Online air travel information and reservations.
STA Travel, 920 Westwood Blvd, Los Angeles, CA 90024, T1-310-824 1574, www.statravel.com.

Travel CUTS, T1-866-246 9762, www.travelcuts.com. Student discount fares, IDs and other travel services.
Travelocity, www.travelocity.com. Online consolidator.

Australia and New Zealand

Flight Centres, 82 Elizabeth St, Sydney, T09-235 3522; 205 Queen St, Auckland, T09-309 6171.
STA Travel, T1300-360960, www.statravel.com.au; 855 George St, Sydney, and 240 Flinders St, Melbourne. In NZ: www.statravel.co.nz, 187 Queen St, Auckland, T09-309 0458.
Travel.com.au, 80 Clarence St, Sydney, T02-1300 130 482, www.travel.com.au.

Road and sea

There are land crossings with Malaysia (see boxes on page 628 and page 660), Cambodia (see box, page 881), Laos (see box, page 908) and Burma. The Burma crossing is the trickiest with the visa and border situation changing constantly.

There are frequent **passenger ferries** from Pak Bara, near Satun, in southern Thailand to Perlis and Langkawi Island, both in Malaysia (see pages 628-629).

Train

Regular services link Singapore and Bangkok, via Kuala Lumpur, Butterworth and the major southern Thai towns. Express air-conditioned trains take two days from Singapore, 34 hours from Kuala Lumpur, 24 hours from Butterworth. All tickets should be booked in advance at Bangkok's Hualamphong station (see page 780).

Getting around

Air

The budget airline boom has finally arrived in Thailand with carriers now offering cheap flights all over the country. **Air Asia, Bangkok Airways,** and **Nok Air** are the present major players in this market. **Thai Airways (THAI)** is the national flag carrier and flies to several destinations in Thailand.

Rail

The State Railway of Thailand, www.railway.co.th/english, is efficient, clean and comfortable – it is safer than bus travel but can take longer. Travelling third class is often the cheapest way to travel long distance. First and second class are more expensive than the bus but infinitely more comfortable. Express and rapid trains are faster as they make fewer stops; there is a surcharge for the service. Excellent and very popular sleeper services cover all the main routes. Reservations for sleepers should be made in advance (up to 60 days ahead) at Bangkok's **Hualamphong station** ① *T02-223 3762/224 7788, the Advance Booking Office is open daily 0700-0400*. It is advisable to book the bottom bunk, as lights are bright on top (in second-class compartments) and the ride more uncomfortable.

Road

Bus Private and state-run buses leave Bangkok for every town in Thailand; it is an extensive network and a cheap way to travel. There are small stop-in-every-town local buses or the faster long-distance buses. The best overnight VIP buses come with only 24 seats and are a good way to cover long distances in comfort. If you're travelling on an overnight, air-conditioned bus bring a light sweater and some earplugs – both the volume of the entertainment system and air-conditioning system are likely to be turned up full blast. The **local buses** are slower and cramped but worthwhile for those wishing to sample local life.

Private tour buses Many tour companies operate bus services in Thailand; travel agents in Bangkok will supply information. These buses are seldom more comfortable than the state buses but are usually more expensive.

Car hire Driving is on the left-hand side of the road. Increasing numbers of people are hiring their own cars and internationally respected car hire firms (such as **Hertz** and **Avis**) are expanding their operations. Roads and service stations are generally excellent.

A few points should be kept in mind. If involved in an accident (and they occur with great frequency), you – as a foreigner – are likely to be found the guilty party and expected to meet the costs. Ensure the cost of hire includes insurance cover. Many local residents recommend that should foreigners be involved in an accident, they should not stop but drive on to the nearest police station – if possible, of course.

The average cost of hiring a car from a reputable firm is ฿1000-2000 per day, ฿6000-10,000 per week, or ฿20,000-30,000 per month. Some rentals automatically include insurance; for others it must be specifically requested and a surcharge is added. An international driver's licence, or a UK, US, French, German, Australian, New Zealand, Singapore or Hong Kong licence is required.

Motorbike hire This is mostly confined to holiday resorts. ฿150-300 per day is usual for a 100-150cc machine. Often licences do not have to be shown and insurance will not be available. Off the main roads and in quieter areas it can be an enjoyable and cheap way to

Train routes and times (samples)

Route	Time
Bangkok to:	
Ayutthaya	1½ hrs
Chiang Mai	11-13 hrs
Hua Hin	4 hrs
Kanchanaburi	2½ hrs
Korat	5 hrs
Nong Khai	11 hrs
Phitsanulok	5-6 hrs
Surat Thani	11 hrs
Trang	15 hrs

To view full details, visit www.railway.co.th/english.

Bus routes and times (samples)

Route	Time
Bangkok north to:	
Ayutthaya	1½ hrs
Sukhothai	7 hrs
Mae Sot	9 hrs
Chiang Mai	9¾ hrs
Chiang Rai	12 hrs
Korat	4½ hrs
Udon Thani	9 hrs
Bangkok south to:	
Hua Hin	3 hrs
Surat Thani	11 hrs
Phuket	13 hrs
Krabi	12 hrs
Pattaya	3 hrs
Trat	5½ hrs
Phuket to:	
Surat Thani	5 hrs
Trang	5 hrs
Chiang Mai to:	
Sukhothai	5 hrs

see the country. Riding with shorts and flip-flops is dangerous; always wear shoes. Borrow a helmet if possible and expect anything larger than you to ignore your presence on the road. Be extremely wary. Thousands of Thais are killed in motorcycle accidents each year and large numbers of tourists also suffer injuries.

Motorbike taxi These are becoming increasingly popular, and are the cheapest, quickest and most dangerous way to get from A to B. They are usually used for short rides down sois or to better local transport points. Riders wear coloured vests (sometimes numbered) and tend to congregate at key intersections or outside shopping centres for example. Agree a price before boarding – expect to pay ₿10 upwards for a short soi hop.

Tuk-tuks Pedal or motorized machines. Fares should be bargained and agreed before setting off. In Bangkok, and most other towns, these vehicles are a motorized, gas-powered scooter.

Songthaew ('two rows') These pick-up trucks are fitted with two benches and can be found in many upcountry towns. They normally run fixed routes, with set fares, but can often be hired and used as a taxi service (agree a price before setting out). To let the driver know you want to stop, press the electric buzzers or tap the side of the vehicle with a coin.

Taxi Standard air-conditioned taxis are found in very few Thai towns with the majority in the capital. In Bangkok all taxis have meters.

Sea
There are numerous boats to and from the Gulf Coast Islands of Koh Samui, Koh Phangan and Koh Tao. Principal services run from Chumphon to Koh Tao and from Surat Thani and the port of Don Sak to Koh Samui

and then on to Koh Phangan. Fast ferries, slow boats and night boats run services daily. On the Andaman Coast there are services to and from Phuket, Koh Phi Phi, Krabi, Koh Lanta, the islands off Trang and from Ban Pak Bara and Koh Tarutao National Park.

Sleeping → *For hotel price codes, see inside the front cover.*

It should be noted that many hotels will have a range of rooms, some with air conditioning (a/c) and attached bathroom facilities, others with just a fan and shared facilities. Prices within the same establishment can therefore vary a great deal. A service charge of 10% and government tax of 7% will usually be added to the bill in the more expensive hotels.

During the off-season, hotels and guesthouses in tourist destinations may halve their room rates so it is always worthwhile bargaining or asking whether there is a special price.

Fans are the norm in most guesthouses although, again, to cash in on the buying power of backpackers with more disposable income, more and more offer a/c rooms as well. Check that mosquito nets are provided.

Security is a problem, particularly in beach resorts where flimsy bungalows offer easy access to thieves. Keep valuables with the office for safekeeping (although there are regular cases of people losing valuables that have been left in 'safekeeping') or on your person when you go out.

Eating → *For restaurant price codes, see inside the front cover.*

Thai food is an intermingling of Tai, Chinese and, to a lesser extent, Indian cuisines. This helps to explain why restaurants produce dishes that must be some of the (spicy) hottest in the world, as well as others which are rather bland. Remarkably, considering how ubiquitous it is in Thai cooking, the chilli pepper is a New World fruit and was not introduced into Thailand until the late 16th century (along with the pineapple and papaya).

A meal usually consists (along with the rice) of a soup like *tom yam kung* (prawn soup), *kaeng* (a curry) and *krueng kieng* (a number of side dishes). Generally, Thai food is chilli-hot, and aromatic herbs and grasses (like lemongrass, coriander, tamarind and ginger) are used to give a distinctive flavour. *Nam pla* (fish sauce made from fermented fish) and *nam prik* (*nam pla*, chillies, garlic, sugar, shrimps and lime juice) are two condiments that are taken with almost all meals. *Nam pla* is made from steeping fish, usually anchovies, in brine for long periods and then bottling the liquor produced. Isaan food, from the Northeast of Thailand, is very popular. Most of the labourers, prostitutes and service staff come from Isaan – particularly in Bangkok – and you won't have to go far to find a rickety street stall selling sticky rice, aromatic *kai yang* (grilled chicken) and fiery *som tam* (papaya salad).

To sample Thai food it is best to go in a group to a restaurant and order a range of dishes. To eat alone is regarded as slightly strange. However, there are a number of 'one-dish' meals like fried rice and *phat thai* (fried noodles) and restaurants will also usually provide *raat khao* ('over rice') which is a dish like a curry served on a bed of rice for a single person.

Strict non-fish-eating **vegetarians** and **vegans** are in for a tough time. Nearly every cooked meal you will eat in Thailand will be liberally doused in *nam pla* or cooked with shrimp paste. There is a network of Taoist restaurants offering more strict veggie fare throughout the country – look out for yellow flags with red Chinese lettering. Also asking for '*mai sai nam pla*' – 'no nam pla' – when ordering might keep the fish sauce out of harms reach.

It is possible to get a tasty and nutritious meal almost anywhere – and at any time – in Thailand. Thais eat out a great deal, so most towns have a range of places. The more

Thai food and fruit

Most dishes can be ordered with *mu* (pork), *nua* (beef), *kai* (chicken), *plaa* (fish), *kung* (prawn), *pet* (duck) or *gai* (egg); just add the word for what you want. If you don't like it spicy ask for "*pet nit noi.*"

Soups (gaeng chud)
Tom yam kung – hot and sour prawn soup
Khao tom – rice soup
Kwaytio – noodle soup

Rice-based dishes
Khao pat – fried rice
Khao gaeng – curry and rice
Khao man kai – rice with chicken

Noodle-based dishes
Khao soi – a form of Kwaytio with egg noodles in a curry broth
Phat thai – Thai fried noodles
Mee krop – Thai crisp-fried noodles

Curries (gaeng)
Gaeng phet – hot chicken/beef curry
Gaeng khiaw waan – green curry
Gaeng phanaeng – red curry

Meat dishes
Larb – chopped (once raw, now more frequently cooked) meat with herbs and spices
Kai/nua phat prik – fried chicken/beef with chillies

Kai tort – Thai fried chicken
Kai tua – chicken in peanut sauce

Seafood
Plaa too tort – Thai fried fish
Haw mok – steamed fish curry
Plaa nerng – steamed fish
Plaa pao – grilled fish

Salads (yam)
Yam nua – Thai beef salad
Som tam – green papaya salad with tomatoes, chillies, garlic, chopped dried shrimps and lemon (can be extremely hot)

Fruits
Khanun – jackfruit (January-June)
Kluay – banana (year round)
Makham wan – tamarind (December-February)
Malakho – papaya (year round)
Manaaw – lime (year round)
Maprao – coconut (year round)
Mamuang – mango (March-June)
Ngo – rambutan (May-September)
Sapparot – pineapple (April-June, December-January)
Som – orange (year round)
Som o – pomelo (August-November)
Taeng mo – watermelon (October-March)
Thurian – durian (May-August)

---

sophisticated restaurants are usually air conditioned and sometimes attached to a hotel. In addition to these more upmarket restaurants are a whole range of places from **noodle shops** to **curry houses** and **seafood restaurants**. Many small restaurants have no menus. But often the speciality of the house will be clear – roasted, honeyed ducks hanging in the window, crab and fish laid out on crushed ice outside. Towards the bottom of the scale are **stalls and food carts**. These tend to congregate at particular places in town – often in the evening, from dusk – although they can be found just about anywhere: outside the local provincial offices, along a cul-de-sac, or under a conveniently placed shady tree. Stall holders will tend to specialize in either noodles, rice dishes, fruit drinks, sweets and so on. Hot meals are usually prepared to order.

Drink

Water in smaller restaurants can be risky, so many people recommend that visitors drink bottled water or hot tea. Many hotels provide bottles of water gratis in their rooms.

Major brands of spirits are served in most hotels and bars, although not always off the tourist path. The most popular spirit among Thais is Mekhong – local cane whisky – which can be drunk straight or with mixers such as Coca-Cola.

Beer drinking is spreading fast. The most popular local beer is Singha beer brewed by Boon Rawd. Singha, Chaing and Heineken are the three most popular beers in Thailand.

Festivals and events

Festivals where the month only is listed are movable. A booklet of holidays and festivals is available from most TAT offices. For movable festivals, check the TAT's website, www.tourismthailand.org. Regional and local festivals are noted in appropriate sections.

1 Jan New Year's Day (public holiday).

Late Jan/early Feb Chinese New Year (movable) is celebrated by Thailand's large Chinese population.

Feb Magha Puja (movable, full moon: public holiday) is a Buddhist holy day and celebrates the occasion when the Buddha's disciples miraculously gathered together to hear him preach.

6 Apr Chakri Day (public holiday) commemorates the founding of the present Chakri Dynasty.

Apr Songkran (movable: public holiday) marks the beginning of the Buddhist New Year. It is a 3- to 5-day celebration with parades, dancing and folk entertainment. The famous water-throwing practice was originally an act of homage to ancestors and family elders. Young people pay respect by pouring scented water over the elders heads. This uninhibited water-throwing continues for all 3 days.

1 May Labour Day (public holiday).

5 May Coronation Day (public holiday) commemorates the present King Bhumibol's crowning in 1950.

May Visakha Puja (full moon: public holiday), holiest of all Buddhist days, it marks the Buddha's birth, enlightenment and death. Candlelit processions are held at most temples.

12 Aug Queen's Birthday (public holiday).

Nov Loi Krathong (full moon) comes at the end of the rainy season and honours the goddess of water. A *krathong* is a model boat made to contain a candle, incense and flowers. The little boats are pushed out onto canals, lakes and rivers.

5 Dec King's Birthday (public holiday). Flags and portraits of the king are erected all over Bangkok, especially down Rachdamnern Av and around the Grand Palace.

10 Dec Constitution Day (public holiday).

31 Dec New Year's Eve (public holiday).

Local customs and laws

Thais are generally understanding of the foibles of *farangs* (foreigners) and will forgive most indiscretions. However, there are a number of 'dos and don'ts' that are worth observing:

Cool and hot hearts Among Thais, the personal characteristic of *jai yen* is very highly regarded; literally, this means to have a 'cool heart'. It embodies calmness, having an even temper and not displaying emotion. Although foreigners generally receive special dispensation, and are not expected to conform to Thai customs (all farang are thought to have *jai rawn* or 'hot hearts'), it is important to keep calm in any disagreement – losing one's temper leads to loss of face and loss of respect.

Clothing In towns and at religious sights, it is courteous to avoid wearing shorts and sleeveless tops. Visitors who are inappropriately dressed may not be allowed into temples.

Greeting people Traditionally, Thais greet one another with a *wai* – the equivalent of a handshake. In a *wai*, hands are held together as if in prayer, and the higher the *wai*, the more respectful the greeting.

Heads and feet Try to not openly point your feet at anyone – feet are viewed as spiritually the lowest part of the body. At the same time, never touch anyone's (even a child's) head, which is the holiest as well as the highest part.

The monarchy Never criticize any member of the royal family or the institution itself – *lèse majesté* remains an offence carrying a sentence of up to 15 years in prison.

Monastery (wat) and monk etiquette Remove shoes on entering any monastery building, do not climb over Buddha images or have your picture taken in front of one, and when sitting in a bot or viharn ensure that your feet are not pointing towards a Buddha image. Wear modest clothing – women should not expose their shoulders or wear dresses that are too short (see Clothing, above). Ideally, they should be calf length although knee-length dresses or skirts are usually acceptable. Women should never touch a monk, hand anything directly to a monk or venture into the monks' quarters. They should also avoid climbing chedis (stupas). As in any other place of worship, visitors should not disturb the peace of a wat.

Sanuk A quality of *sanuk*, which can be roughly translated as 'fun' or *joie de vivre*, is important to Thais. Activities are undertaken because they are *sanuk*, others avoided because they are *mai sanuk* ('not fun'). Perhaps it is because of this apparent love of life that so many visitors returning from Thailand remark on how Thais always appear happy and smiling.

Shopping

Bangkok and Chiang Mai are the shopping 'centres' of Thailand. Many people now prefer Chiang Mai, as the shops are concentrated in a smaller area and there is a good range of quality products, especially handicrafts.

Between shopkeepers competition is fierce. Do not be cajoled into buying something before having a chance to price it elsewhere – Thais can be very persuasive. Also, watch out for guarantees of authenticity – fake antiques abound, and even professionals find it difficult to tell a 1990 Khmer sculpture from a 10th-century one.

Bargaining This is common, except in the large department stores – although they may give a discount on expensive items of jewellery or furniture – and on items like soap, books and most necessities. Expect to pay anything from 25-75% less than the asking price, depending on the bargainer's skill and the shopkeeper's mood. Bargaining is viewed as a game, so enter into it with good humour.

Tricksters Rip-off artists, fraudsters, less-than-honest salesmen – call them what you will – are likely to be far more of a problem than simple theft. People may well approach you in the street offering incredible one-off bargains – be wary in all such cases. Favourite 'bargains' are precious stones, whose authenticity is 'demonstrated' before your very eyes.

Essentials A-Z

Accident and emergency
Police: T191, T123. **Tourist Police** T1699.
Fire: T199. **Ambulance**: T02-2551134-6.
Tourist Assistance Centre: Rachdamnern
Nok Av, Bangkok, T02-2825051. Calling one
of the emergency numbers will not usually
be very productive as few operators speak
English. It is better to call the Tourist Police
or have a hotel employee or other
English-speaking Thai telephone for you.
For more intractable problems contact
your embassy or consulate.

Customs and duty free
Prohibited items include: all narcotics; obscene
literature, pornography; fire arms (except with
a permit from the Police Department or local
registration office); and some species of plants
and animals (for more information contact the
Royal Forestry Department, Phahonyothin
Road, Bangkok, T02-579 2776).

Disabled travellers
Disabled travellers will find Thailand a challenge.
Buses and taxis are not designed for disabled
access and there are relatively few hotels and
restaurants that are disabled-friendly. This is
not to suggest that travel in Thailand is
impossible for the disabled. On the plus side,
you will find Thais to be extremely helpful. The
Global Access – Disabled Travel Network
website, www.globalaccessnews.com, is
useful and **www.access-able.com** has a
specific section for travel in Thailand.

Drugs
Note that foreigners on buses may be searched
for drugs. Sentences for possession of illegal
drugs vary from a fine or 1 year's imprisonment
for marijuana up to life imprisonment or
execution for possession or smuggling of
heroin. The death penalty is usually commuted.

Electricity
220 volts (50 cycles). Most first- and tourist-
class hotels have outlets for shavers and hair
dryers. Adaptors are recommended,
as almost all sockets are 2-pronged.

Embassies and consulates
A useful resource is www.thaiembassy.org.
Australia 131 Macquarie St, Level 8,
Sydney 2000, T02-9241 2542.
Canada 180 Island Park Dr, Ottawa,
Ontario, K1Y 0A2, T613-722 4444.
Germany Lepsiusstrasse 64-66, 12163
Berlin, T030-794810.
New Zealand 2 Cook St, Karori,
PO Box 17226, Wellington, T04-476 8616.
Sweden Floragatan 3, 26220, Stockholm
100 40, T08-791 7340.
UK 29-30 Queens Gate, London, SW7 5JB,
T020-7589 2944.
USA 1024 Wisconsin Av, NW, Suite 401,
Washington, DC 20007, T202-944 3600.

Gay and lesbian travellers
On the surface, Thailand is incredibly tolerant
of homosexuals and lesbians. In Bangkok
and other major cities there's an openness
that can make even San Francisco look tame.
It is for this reason that Thailand's gay scene
has flourished and, more particularly, has
grown in line with international tourism.
However, overt public displays of affection
are still frowned upon. Attitudes in the more
traditional rural areas, particularly the Muslim
regions, are far more conservative than in
the cities. By exercising a degree of cultural
sensitivity any visit should be hassle free.

Health
Medical services are listed in the Directory
section of the relevant areas. There is an
obvious difference in health risks between
the business traveller who tends to stay in
international-class hotels in the large cities
and the backpacker trekking through the
rural areas. There are no hard-and-fast rules
to follow; you will often have to make your
own judgement on the healthiness or
otherwise of your surroundings.

See your doctor or travel clinic at least 6 weeks before your departure for general advice on travel risks, malaria and vaccinations. Make sure you have travel insurance, get a dental check (especially if you are going to be away for more than a month), know your own blood group and if you suffer a long-term condition such as diabetes or epilepsy make sure someone knows or that you have a Medic Alert bracelet/ necklace with this information on it.

Courses or boosters are usually advised for diphtheria, tetanus, poliomyelitis and hepatitis A. **Vaccinations** are sometimes advised for typhoid, tuberculosis, rabies, Japanese B encephalitis and hepatitis B. A yellow fever certificate is required by visitors over 9 months of age who are entering from an infected area.

Health risks

Malaria is common in certain areas, particularly in the jungle. Check with your doctor or travel clinic for the most up-to-date advice on malaria prophylaxis. Malaria can cause death within 24 hrs. It can start as something just resembling an attack of flu. You may feel tired, lethargic, headachy, feverish; or more seriously, develop fits, followed by coma and then death. Have a low index of suspicion because it is very easy to write off vague symptoms, which may actually be malaria. If you have a temperature, go to a doctor as soon as you can and ask for a malaria test. On your return home if you suffer any of these symptoms, get tested as soon as possible, even if any previous test proved negative, the test could save your life.

The most serious viral disease is **dengue fever**, which is hard to protect against as the mosquitoes bite throughout the day as well as at night. Bacterial diseases include **tuberculosis** (TB) and some causes of the more common traveller's **diarrhoea**.

Check with your doctor on the status of avian flu before you go. At the time of writing, Thailand was clear of **bird flu**.

Take good heed of advice regarding protecting yourself against the sun. Overexposure can lead to **sunburn** and, in the longer term, skin cancers and premature skin aging. Avoid exposure to the sun by covering exposed skin, wearing a hat and staying out of the sun if possible, particularly between late morning and early afternoon. Apply a high-factor sunscreen and also make sure it screens against UVB. A further danger in tropical climates is heat exhaustion or more seriously heatstroke. This can be avoided by good hydration, which means drinking water past the point of simply quenching thirst. Also when first exposed to tropical heat take time to acclimatize by avoiding strenuous activity in the middle of the day. If you cannot avoid heavy exercise it is also a good idea to increase salt intake.

If you plan to **dive** make sure that you are fit do so. The **British Sub-Aqua Club** (**BSAC**), Telford's Quay, South Pier Rd, Ellesmere Port, Cheshire CH65 4FL, UK, T01513-506200, www.bsac.com, can put you in touch with doctors who will carry out medical examinations. Check that any dive company you use is reputable and has appropriate certification from BSAC or **Professional Association of Diving Instructors (PADI)**, Unit 7, St Philips Central, Albert Rd, St Philips, Bristol, BS2 OTD, T0117-300 7234, www.padi.com.

Useful websites

www.btha.org British Travel Health Association (UK). This is the official website of an organization of travel health professionals.
www.cdc.gov US Government site that gives excellent advice on travel health and details of disease outbreaks.
www.fitfortravel.scot.nhs.uk A-Z of vaccine/health advice for each country.
www.fco.gov.uk Foreign and Commonwealth Office (UK).
www.nathnac.org National Travel Health Network and Centre (UK).
www.who.int The WHO Blue Book lists the diseases of the world.

Useful words and phrases

Yes/no *chái/mâi chái*
or *krúp (kâ)/mâi krúp (kâ)*
Thank you *kòrp-kOOn*
No thank you *Mâi ao kòrp-kOOn*
Hello, good morning, goodbye *sa-wùt dee krúp(kâ)*
What is your name? My name is...
Koon chêu a-rai krúp (kâ)? Pom chêu...

Excuse me, sorry! *kor-tôht krúp(kâ)*
Can/do you speak English? *KOON pôot pah-sah ung-grìt*
a little, a bit *nít-nòy*
Where's the ...? *yòo têe-nai ...*
How much is ...? *tâo-rài ...*
Pardon? *a-rai ná?*
I don't understand *pom (chún) mâi kao jái*

Insurance

Always take out travel insurance before you set off and read the small print carefully. Check that the policy covers the activities you intend or may end up doing – for instance if you don't have a motorcycle licence and are involved in an accident you may not be covered. **STA Travel** and other reputable student travel organizations offer good-value policies. Young travellers from North America can try the **International Student Insurance Service (ISIS)**, which is available through **STA Travel**, T1-800-781 4040, www.sta-travel.com. Other recommended US companies: **Travel Guard**, T1-800-826 1300, www.noel group.com; **Access America**, T1-800-284 8300; **Travel Insurance Services**, T1-800-937 1387; and **Travel Assistance International**, T1-800-821 2828. Older travellers should note that some companies will not cover people over 65 years old, or may charge higher premiums. The best policies for older travellers (UK) are offered by **Age Concern**, T0845-601 2234.

Internet

Apart from a few remote islands Thailand has an excellent internet network. Tourist areas tend to have numerous internet shops offering a connection for between ฿30-90 per hr. Some guesthouses and hotels have free Wi-Fi.

Language

English is reasonably widely spoken and is taught to all school children. Off the tourist trail, making yourself understood becomes more difficult.

The Thai language is tonal and, strictly speaking, monosyllabic. There are 5 tones: high, low, rising, falling and mid-tone. These are used to distinguish between words that would otherwise be identical. Not surprisingly, many visitors find it hard to hear the different tones, and it is difficult to make much progress during a short visit.

It is still worth trying to learn a few words, even if your visit to Thailand is short.

Media

The 2 major English-language daily papers – the *Bangkok Post* (www.bangkokpost.net) and *The Nation* (www.nationgroup.com) provide good international news and are Thailand's best-known broadsheets.

Money → US$1=฿33.51; €1=฿53.26; £1=฿67 (Aug 2008).

The unit of Thai currency is the **baht** (฿), which is divided into 100 satang. Notes in circulation include ฿20 (green), ฿50 (blue), ฿100 (red), ฿500 (purple) and ฿1000 (orange and grey). Coins include 25 satang and 50 satang, and ฿1, ฿2, ฿5, and ฿10. The 2 smaller coins are disappearing from circulation and the 25 satang coin, equivalent to the princely sum of US$0.003, is rarely found. The colloquial term for 25 satang is saleng.

Exchange

Banks or money changers give better rates than hotels. The exchange booths at Bangkok airport have some of the best rates. There is a charge of ฿23 per cheque when changing traveller's cheques (TCs) so, if using them, it's cheaper to have large denominations.

Credit and debit cards
These are increasingly used in Thailand and just about every town of any size will have a bank with an ATM. Visa and MasterCard are the most widely taken credit cards, and cash cards with the Cirrus logo can also be used to withdraw cash at many banks. Because Thailand has embraced the ATM with such exuberance, many foreign visitors no longer bother with TCs or cash and rely entirely on plastic. Even so, a small stash of US dollars cash can come in handy in a sticky situation.

Opening hours
Banks Mon-Fri 0830-1530.
Exchange services Mon-Sun 0830-2200 in Bangkok, Pattaya, Phuket and Chiang Mai (in other towns hours are usually shorter).
Government offices Mon-Fri 0830-1200, 1300-1630.
Tourist offices Daily 0830-1630.
Shops Daily 0830-1700, larger shops: 1000-1900 or 2100.

Police
The tourist police are specially trained to deal with foreigners. **Tourist police**, Bangkok, T02-2815051 or T02-221 6206. Open daily 0800-2400.

Safety
In general, Thailand is a safe country to visit. Most visitors to Thailand will experience no physical threat whatsoever. However, there have been some widely publicized murders of foreign tourists in recent years and the country does have a very high murder rate. It is best to avoid any situation where violence can occur – what would be a simple punch-up or pushing bout in the West can quickly escalate in Thailand to extreme violence. Also getting drunk with Thais can be a risky business – Westerners visiting the country for short periods won't be versed in the intricacies of Thai social interaction and may commit

unwitting and terrible faux pas. A general rule of thumb if confronted with a situation is to appear conciliatory and offer a way for the other party to back out gracefully.

Robbery is also a threat; it ranges from pick-pocketing to the drugging (and robbing) of bus and train passengers. Watchfulness and simple common sense should be employed. Women travelling alone should be careful. (See also Women travellers, page 791.) Always lock hotel rooms and place valuables in a safe deposit if available (or if not, take them with you).

If you encounter problems contact the tourist police (see Police) rather than the ordinary police.

Insurgency and security in border areas
The UK Foreign and Commonwealth office (www.fco.gov.uk/travel) advises against all but essential travel to the 4 provinces of **Yala**, **Pattani**, **Narathiwat** and **Songkhla**. The US State Department (www.travel.state.gov) does the same and includes **Hat Yai** town in its warning. These areas are the main home of Thailand's Muslim minority and have been the home of a major uprising that escalated considerably in 2004. Also see page 959 and Background page 987.

Traffic
Perhaps the greatest danger is from the traffic – especially if you are attempting to drive yourself. More foreign visitors are killed or injured in traffic accidents than in any other way. Thai drivers have a 'devil may care' attitude towards the highway code, and there are many quite horrific accidents. Be very careful crossing the road – just because there is a pedestrian crossing, do not expect drivers to stop. Be particularly wary when driving or riding a motorcycle (see page 780).

Telephone → Country code 66.
There is direct dialling to most countries available throughout Thailand. Calls from call boxes cost ฿1.

Mobiles

Mobiles are common. Coverage is good except in some border areas. A Thai mobile number is also very easy for a visitor to acquire. **AIS** and **Happy D Prompt** sim cards and top-ups are available throughout the country, cost ฿200 with domestic call charges from ฿3 per min and international calls from ฿8 per min. You will need a valid ID when you buy either. They represent a very good deal and are much cheaper than either phone boxes or hotels. You will need an unlocked phone to use a Thai sim – cheap, unlocked second-hand phones are available throughout Thailand from about ฿700. Using a Thai sim card is highly recommended if you are staying for any period of time in Thailand.

Time

7 hrs ahead of GMT.

Tipping

Tipping is generally unnecessary. However, a 10% service charge is now expected on room, food and drinks bills in the smarter hotels as well as a tip for any personal service. Increasingly, the more expensive restaurants add a 10% service charge; others expect a small tip.

Tourist information
Tourist offices abroad

Australia, Suite 2002, 2nd floor, 56 Pitt St, Sydney, NSW 2000, T09-247-7549, info@Thailand.net.au.
UK, 49 Albermarle St, London WIX 3FE, T020-499 7679, info@tat-uk.demon.co.uk.
USA, 611 North Larchmont Blvd, Los Angeles, CA 90004, T461-9814, tatla@ix.netcom.com.

Tourist offices in Thailand

The **Tourist Authority of Thailand (TAT)** publishes a good range of glossy brochures that provide an idea of what there is, where to go and what it looks like. The main office is at 1600 New Phetburi Rd, Makkasan, Ratchathewi, T02-250 5500, www.tourism thailand.org; also at 4 Rachdamnern Nok Av (intersection with Chakrapatdipong Rd),

Mon-Fri 0830-1630; in addition there are 2 counters at Suvarnabhumi Airport, in the Arrivals halls of Terminals 1 and 2, T02-504 2701, daily 0800-2400. Local offices are found in most major tourist destinations in the country and their addresses are listed in the appropriate sections.

Useful websites

www.tourismthailand.org A useful first stop and generally well regarded.
www.fco.gov.uk/travel/ The UK Foreign and Commonwealth Office's travel warning section.
www.travel.state.gov/travel_warnings.html The US State Department updates travel advisories on its Travel Warnings & Consular Information Sheets. It also has a hotline for American travellers, T202-647-5225.
www.asiasociety.org Homepage of the Asia Society with papers, reports and speeches as well as nearly 1000 links to what they consider to be the best educational, political and cultural sites on the web.
www.bangkokpost.net Homepage for the *Bangkok Post* including back issues and main stories of the day.
www.bangkokrecorder.com Instant access to the hipper side of Thai life from current events, comment, chat and lifestyle features to the best of Bangkok clubbing.
www.thaifolk.com Good site for Thai culture from folk songs and handicrafts through to festivals like Loi Kratong and Thai myths and legends. Information posted in both English and Thai – although the Thai version of the site is better.

Tour operators
In the UK

Exodus Travels, 9 Weir Rd, London, T020-950 0039/020-8673 0859, www.exodus.co.uk. Small group travel for walking and trekking holidays, adventure tours and more.
Magic of the Orient, 14 Frederick Pl, Bristol, BS8 1AS, T0117-311 6050, www.magicofthe

orient.com. Specializes in tailor-made holidays to the region. Established in 1989 the company's philosophy is to deliver first-class service from knowledgeable staff at good value.

Trans Indus, 75 St Mary's Rd and the Old Fire Station, Ealing, London, W5 5RW, T020-8566 2729, www.transindus.co.uk. Tours to Thailand and other Southeast Asian countries.

Travelmood, 214 Edgware Rd, London, W2 1DH; 1 Brunswick Court, Bridge St, Leeds, LS2 7QU; 16 Reform St, Dundee, DD1 1RG, T0871-226 6151, www.travelmood.com. 21 years' experience as a top travel specialist offering tailor-made trips to the Far East and adventure and activity travel in Asia.

In North America

Global Spectrum, 3907 Laro Court, Fairfax, VA 22031, USA, T1800-419 4446, www.globalspectrumtravel.com.

Nine Dragons Travel & Tours, 1476 Orange Grove Rd, Charleston, SC 29407, T1317-281 3895, www.nine-dragons.com. Guided and individually customized tours.

Visas and immigration

For the latest information on visas and tourist visa exemptions see the consular information section of the **Thai Ministry of Foreign Affairs** website, www.mfa.go.th. The immigration office is at **Immigration Bureau**, Soi Suan Plu, Thanon Sathorn Tai, Bangkok 10120, T02-287 3101. Open Mon-Fri 0830-1630, closed Sat, Sun and official holidays (tourists only).

Visas on arrival

For tourists from 20 countries (basically all Western countries, plus some Arabic and other Asian states – see www.mfa.go.th) it is possible to have a special 30-day entry permit issued on arrival. These permits are not strictly visas and differ from 'visa on arrival' service signposted at the airports. Applicants must also have an outbound (return) ticket and

possess funds to meet living expenses of ฿20,000 per person or ฿40,000 per family. Before 2006 it was possible to make unlimited border crossings in order to gain repeated entry for 30 days as a tourist – now visitors are not allowed to stay more than 90 days every 6 months using this method. If you intend to stay in Thailand for a lengthy period over 30 days you'd be best advised to get a 2-month visa before travel.

Tourist visas

These are valid for 60 days from date of entry and must be obtained from a Thai embassy before arrival in Thailand.

Visa extensions

These are obtainable from the Immigration Bureau (see above) for ฿1900. Applicants must bring 2 photocopies of their passport ID page and the page on which their tourist visa is stamped, together with 3 passport photographs. It is also advisable to dress neatly. Visas are issued by all Thai embassies and consulates. The length of time a visa is extended varies according to the office and the official.

Women travellers

Compared with neighbouring East and South Asia, women in Southeast Asia enjoy relative equality of opportunity. This is not to suggest that there is complete equality between the sexes. Buddhism, for example – at least as it is practised in Thailand – accords women a lower position and it is notable how few women there are in positions of political power.

The implications of this for women travellers, and especially solo women travellers, is that they may face some difficulties not encountered by men. Women should make sure that rooms are secure at night and if travelling in remote regions, should try to team up with other travellers.

Bangkok

Ins and outs → *Phone numbers marked with a prefix 'B' mean that they are Bangkok numbers.*

Getting there

Air **Suvarnabhumi International Airport** (pronounced su-wan-na-poom) opened in September 2006 and is around 25 km southeast of the city. Currently, the airport is only accessible by road but construction of a 28-km overhead city rail link between downtown Bangkok and the airport is underway. All facilities at the airport are 24 hours, so you'll have no problem exchanging money, getting something to eat or taking a taxi or other transport into the city at any time. Due to many problems at Suvarnabhumi, the old airport at **Don Muang**, about 25 km north of the city centre, was re-opened in 2007 for a few domestic routes – if you have a connecting flight make sure you know which airport it is departing to/from. It is worth considering Don Muang as your primary choice for domestic routes as there will be fewer queues, it's easier to transit and connections to the city are just as good. There is a shortage of gates at Suvarnabhumi and you can often find your domestic flight stuck miles down the runway followed by a 10-minute bus journey to reach the terminal and a lengthy wait for luggage. ▶▶ *For details of airline offices with flights from Suvarnabhumi International Airport, see page 813.*

From both airports to the city centre It can take well over an hour to get to Central Bangkok from both airports, depending on the time of day and the state of the traffic. Taking the expressway cuts the journey time significantly and outside of rush-hour the transit time should be 35-45 minutes. The airport website, www.bangkokairportonline.com, offers excellent up-to-date information on transport services.

An air-conditioned **airport bus service** operates every 15 minutes (0500-2400), ฿150 to Silom Road (service A1), Khaosan Road (service A2), Wireless/Sukhumvit Road (service A3) and Hua Lumphong train station (service A4). Each service stops at between 12 and 20 popular tourist destinations and hotels. The airport offers full details at the stop located outside the Arrivals area on the pavement. Some of the more popular stops on each line are: **Silom service (A1)**: Pratunam, Central World Plaza, Lumpini Park, Sala Daeng, Patpong, Sofitel Silom. **Khaosan service (A2)**: Pratuman, Amari Watergate Hotel, Asia Hotel, Royal Princess Hotel, Democracy Monument, Phra Artit, Khaosan Road. **Wireless Road service (A3)**: BTS (Skytrain) On Nuts, BTS Thonglor, Rex Hotel, Emporium Shopping Centre Sukhumvit 24, Novotel Sukhumvit, Westin Hotel, Amari Boulevard, Majestic Grande, Central Silom and Nana. **Hua Lumphong service (A4)**: Victory Monument, BTS On Nut, Asia Hotel Ratchathewi, Siam Centre, MBK/National Stadium, Hua Lumphong train station. Many visitors will see the ฿150 as money well spent (although note that for three or four passengers in a taxi it is as cheap or cheaper). However, there will still be a hardened few who will opt for the regular bus service. This is just as slow as it ever was, 1½ to three hours (depending on time of day), prices for air-conditioned buses linking the airport to the city are now a flat rate of ฿35.

The official **taxi** booking service is in the arrivals hall. Official airport limousines have green plates, public taxis have yellow plates; a white plate means the vehicle is not registered as a taxi. There are three sets of taxi/limousine services. First, **airport limos** (before exiting from the restricted area), next airport taxis (before exiting from the terminal building), and finally, a public taxi counter (outside, on the slipway). The latter are the cheapest. Note that airport flunkies sometimes try to direct passengers to the more expensive 'limousine' service: walk through the barriers to the public taxi desk. If taking a metered taxi, the coupon from the booking desk will quote no fare so ensure that the meter is turned on and keep hold of your coupon – some taxi drivers try to pocket it – as it details the obligations of taxi drivers. A public taxi to downtown should cost roughly ฿300. Note that tolls on the expressways are paid on top of the fare on the meter and should be no more than ฿40 per toll. There is a ฿50 airport surcharge on top of the meter cost. Don't be surprised if your driver decides to feign that he does not know where to go: it's all part of being new in town. Some regular airport visitors recommend going up to the departures floor and flagging down a taxi that has just dropped passengers off. Doing it this way will save you around ฿50 and possibly a long wait in a taxi queue.

From Don Muang the same taxi services and charges exist. If you're flying with THAI from Don Muang they operate a City Air Terminal opposite Lad Prao metro station with free buses to and from Don Muang (0400-2000, every 20 minutes). You can also check in here, three hours before your flight leaves. From the airport, these buses depart from just outside the terminal – ask staff. There are other bus services for non-Thai customers.

Getting between the new and old airports, while a pain, is relatively easy: there are regular airport buses and taxis won't cost the earth (฿250-300). To avoid this transfer make sure that if you are on a connecting schedule you don't have to change airports (you can reach all the same destinations from Suvarnabhumi as you can from Don Muang).

Getting around

Bangkok has the unenviable reputation of having some of the worst traffic in the world. The **Skytrain** – an elevated railway – along with the newer **Metro** have made things a lot easier for those areas of the city they cover. Plentiful **buses** travel to all city sights and offer the cheapest way to get around. A **taxi** or **tuk-tuk** ride within the centre should cost ฿50-100. All taxis now have meters. Tuk-tuk numbers are dwindling and the negotiated fares often work out more expensive than a taxi. Walking can be tough in the heat and fumes, although there are some parts of the city where this can be the best way to get around. For an alternative to the smog of Bangkok's streets, hop onboard one of the express **river taxis**, which ply the Chao Phraya River and the network of *khlongs* (canals).

Orientation

Begin in the bejewelled beauty of the **Old City**. The charming **Golden Mount** is a short hop to the east, while to the south are the bewildering alleyways and gaudy temples of Bangkok's frenetic **Chinatown**. Head west over the Chao Phraya River to the magnificent spire of **Wat Arun** and the **khlongs of Thonburi**. To the north are the broad, leafy avenues of **Dusit**, the home of the Thai parliament and the King's residence. Carry on east and south and you'll reach modern Bangkok. A multitude of mini-boutiques forms **Siam Square** and the Thai centre of youth fashion; **Silom** and **Sukhumvit roads** are vibrant runs of shopping centres, restaurants and hotels, while the **Chatuchak Weekend Market** (known to locals as JJ), in the northern suburbs, is one of Asia's greatest markets.

Tourist information

Tourist Authority of Thailand (TAT) ① *main office at 1600 New Phetburi Rd, Makkasan, Ratchathewi, T02-250 5500, www.tourismthailand.org; also at 4 Rachdamnern Nok Av (intersection with Chakrapatdipong Rd), Mon-Fri 0830-1630; 2 counters at Suvarnabhumi Airport, in the arrivals halls of Terminals 1 and 2, T02-504 2701, daily 0800-2400.* The two main offices are very helpful and provide a great deal of information for independent travellers – certainly worth a visit. For information, phone T1672 between 0800 and 2200 for the English-speaking **TAT Call Centre**. A number of good, informative, English-language magazines provide listings of what to do and where to go in Bangkok: *BK Magazine* is a free weekly publication with good listings for clubs, restaurants and live acts. See also www.khao-san-road.com. ▸▸ *For listings, see pages 803-815.*

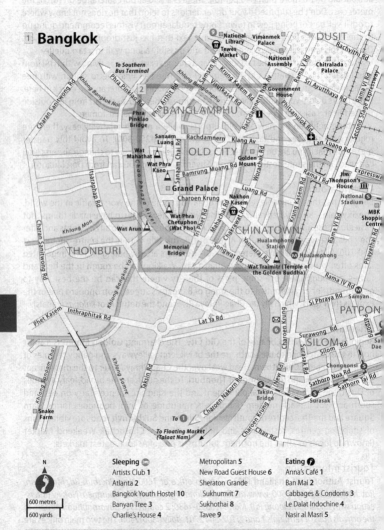

Bangkok

Sleeping
Artists Club **1**
Atlanta **2**
Bangkok Youth Hostel **10**
Banyan Tree **3**
Charlie's House **4**

Metropolitan **5**
New Road Guest House **6**
Sheraton Grande
  Sukhumvit **7**
Sukhothai **8**
Tavee **9**

Eating
Anna's Café **1**
Ban Mai **2**
Cabbages & Condoms **3**
Le Dalat Indochine **4**
Nasir al Masri **5**

Background

The official name for Thailand's capital city is Krungthep-phramaha-nakhonbawon-rathanakosin-mahinthara-yutthayaa-mahadilok-phiphobnobpharaat-raatchathaani-buriir omudomsantisuk. It is not hard to see why Thais prefer the shortened version, Krungthep, or the 'City of Angels'. The name used by the rest of the world – Bangkok – is derived from 17th-century Western maps, which referred to the city as *Bancok*, the 'village of the wild plum'. This name was only superseded by Krungthep in 1782, and so the Western name has deeper historical roots.

In 1767, Ayutthaya, then the capital of Siam, fell to the marauding Burmese for the second time and it was imperative that the remnants of the court and army find a more defensible site for a new capital. Taksin, the Lord of Tak, chose Thonburi, on the western banks of the Chao Phraya, far from the Burmese. In three years, Taksin had established a kingdom and crowned himself king. His reign was short-lived; the pressure of thwarting the Burmese over three arduous years caused him to go mad and in 1782 he was forced to abdicate. General Phraya Chakri was recalled from Cambodia and invited to accept the throne. This marked the beginning of the present Chakri Dynasty. In 1782, Chakri moved his capital across the river to Bangkok anticipating trouble from King Bodawpaya who had seized the throne of Burma.

Bangkok is built on unstable land, much of it below sea level, and floods used to regularly afflict the capital. The most serious were in 1983 when 450 sq km of the city was submerged. Like Venice, Bangkok is sinking by over 10 cm a year in some areas.

Old City and around

Filled with palaces and temples, the Old City is the ancient heart of Bangkok. These days it is the premium destination for the Thai capital's visitors and controversial plans are afoot to change it into a 'tourist zone'. This would strip the area of the usual chaotic charm that typifies Bangkok, moving out the remaining poor people who live in the area and creating an ersatz, gentrified feel.

➡ **Bangkok maps**
1 Bangkok, page 794
2 Bangkok Old City, page 797

Thaniya Garden **6**
Zanotti **7**

Bars & clubs 🍸
Bed Supper Club **8**
Cheap Charlie's **9**

Jools **10**
Narcissus **11**
Noriega's **12**
Q **13**
Tapas **14**

The Emerald Buddha

Wat Phra Kaeo was specifically built to house the Emerald Buddha, the most venerated Buddha image in Thailand. It is carved from green jade (the emerald in the name referring only to its colour) and is a mere 75 cm high, seated in an attitude of meditation.

The image is believed to have been found in 1434 in Chiang Rai, and stylistically belongs to the Late Chiang Saen or Chiang Mai schools. Since then, it has been moved on a number of occasions: to Lampang, Chiang Mai and Laos (both Luang Prabang and Vientiane). It stayed in Vientiane for 214 years before being recaptured by the Thai army in 1778 and placed in Wat Phra Kaeo on 22 March 1784.

The image wears seasonal costumes of gold and jewellery; one each for the hot, cool and the rainy seasons. The changing ceremony takes place three times a year in the presence of the King of Thailand.

Buddha images are often thought to have personalities and the Phra Kaeo is no exception. It is said that such is the antipathy between the Pra Bang image in Luang Prabang (Laos, see page 485) and the Phra Kaeo that the images can never reside in the same town.

Wat Phra Chetuphon (Wat Pho)

ⓘ *Entrance on the south side of the monastery, www.watpho.com; daily 0900-1700, ฿50.*

Wat Phra Chetuphon, or Wat Pho, is the largest and most famous temple in Bangkok. The 'Temple of the Reclining Buddha' was built in 1781 and houses one of the largest reclining Buddhas in the country. The soles of the Buddha's feet are decorated with mother-of-pearl, displaying the 108 auspicious signs of the Buddha. The bustling grounds of the wat contains more than 1000 bronze images, mostly rescued from the ruins of Ayutthaya and Sukhothai, while the bot houses the ashes of Rama I. The bot is enclosed by two galleries that house 394 seated bronze Buddha images. Around the exterior base of the bot are marble reliefs telling the story of the abduction and recovery of Ram's wife Seeda from the second section of the *Ramakien*, as adapted in the Thai poem, 'The Maxims of King Ruang'.

One of Wat Pho's biggest attractions is its role as a respected centre of **traditional Thai massage**. Thousands of tourists, powerful Thai politicians, businessmen and military officers come here to escape the tensions of modern life. The Burmese destroyed most medical texts when they sacked Ayutthaya in 1776 but, in 1832, to help preserve the ancient medical art, Rama III had what was known about Thai massage inscribed onto a series of stones, which were then set into the walls of Wat Pho.

▸▸ *See Activities and tours, page 812.*

Wat Phra Kaeo and Grand Palace

ⓘ *Main entrance is the Viseschaisri Gate, Na Phralan Rd, T02-222 0094, www.palaces.thai.net. Admission to the Grand Palace complex ฿500 (ticket office open daily 0830-1130, 1300-1530 except Buddhist holidays when Wat Phra Kaeo is free but the rest of the palace is closed) includes a free guidebook to the palace (with plan), admission to the Coin Pavilion and to the Vimanmek Palace in the Dusit area (see page 801). No photography allowed inside the bot. All labels in Thai. Free guided tours in English throughout the day; personal audio guides in several languages, ฿100 (2 hrs). No shorts, short skirts, sleeveless shirts, flip-flops or sandals; plastic shoes and trousers are available for hire near the entrance.*

The Grand Palace is situated on the banks of the Chao Phraya River and is the most spectacular – some say 'gaudy' – collection of buildings in Bangkok. The complex, which began life in 1782, covers an area of over 1.5 sq km and the architectural plan is almost identical to that of the Royal Palace in the former capital of Ayutthaya.

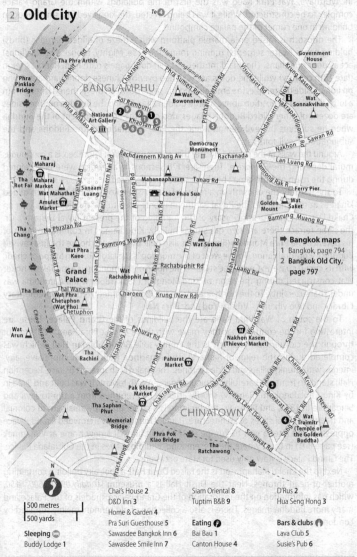

To 4

Khlong Banglamphu

Government House

Tha Phra Arthit

Phra Sumen Rd

Krung Kasem Rd

Phra Arthit Rd

Chakrapong Rd

Prachathipathai Rd

Visutkaset Rd

Nok Av

BANGLAMPHU

Wat Sonnakviharn

Phra Pinklao Bridge

Phra Pinklao Rd

Sol Rambutti

Wat Bowonniwet

Rachdamnoen

Chakrapatdipong Rd

National Art Gallery

Khaosan Rd

Nakhon Sawan Rd

Tha Maharaj

Rachdamnern Klang Av

Democracy Monument

Rachanada

Lan Luang Rd

Tha Rot Fai

Maharaj Market

Rachdamnern Nai Rd

Mahanapharam

Tanao Rd

Damrong Rak R

Ferry Pier

Wat Mahathat

Na Phrathat Rd

Chao Phaa Sua

Golden Mount

Wat Saket

Amulet Market

Sanaam Luang

Bamrung Muang Rd

Tha Chang

Na Phralan Rd

Khlong

Atsadang Rd

Bamrung Muang Rd

Fuang Nakon Rd

Ti Thong Rd

Wat Suthat

➡ Bangkok maps

Wat Phra Kaeo

Rachabuphit Rd

Mahachai Rd

1 Bangkok, page 794

Grand Palace

Sanaam Chai Rd

Wat Rachabophit

Ti Luang Rd

2 Bangkok Old City, page 797

Tha Tien

Thai Wang Rd

Charoen Krung (New Rd)

Wat Phra Chetuphon (Wat Pho) Chetuphon

Rachini Rd

Atsadang Rd

Pahurat Rd

Wat Arun

Chao Phraya River

Tri Phet Rd

Nakhon Kasem (Thieves' Market)

Worachak Rd

Charoen Krung (New Rd)

Sua Pa Rd

Tha Rachini

Pahurat Market

Chakrawat Rd

Yaowarat Rd

Song Sawat Rd

Pak Khlong Market

Chakraphet Rd

Sampeng Lane (Soi Wanit)

Ratchawong Rd

Tha Saphan Phut

CHINATOWN

Wat Traimitr (Temple of the Golden Buddha)

Memorial Bridge

Phra Pok Klao Bridge

Prachadipok Rd

Songwat Rd

Tha Ratchawong

N

500 metres
500 yards

The buildings of greatest interest are clustered around **Wat Phra Kaeo**, or the **Temple of the Emerald Buddha** (see page 796). The glittering brilliance of sunlight bouncing off the coloured-glass mosaic exterior of Wat Phra Kaeo creates an awe-inspiring initial impression for visitors to the Grand Palace. Built by Rama I in imitation of the royal chapel in Ayutthaya, Wat Phra Kaeo was the first of the buildings within the Grand Palace complex to be constructed. While it was being erected, the king lived in a small wooden building in one corner of the palace compound.

The **ubosoth** is raised on a marble platform with a frieze of gilded garudas (birds) holding nagas (water serpents) running round the base. Mighty, bronze *singhas* (lions) act as door guardians. The inlaid mother-of-pearl door panels date from Rama I's reign (late 18th century) while the doors are watched over by Chinese door guardians riding on lions. Inside the temple, the Emerald Buddha peers down on the gathered throng from a lofty, illuminated position above a large golden altar. Facing the Buddha on three sides are dozens of other gilded Buddha images, depicting the enlightenment of the Buddha when he subdues the evil demon Mara, the final temptation of the Buddha and the subjugation of evil spirits.

Around the walls of the shaded **cloister** that encompasses Wat Phra Kaeo, is a continuous mural depicting the *Ramakien*. There are 178 sections in all, which were first painted during the reign of King Rama I but have since been restored.

To the north of the ubosoth on a raised platform is the **Royal Pantheon**, with gilded kinarees at the entrance. The Royal Pantheon is only open to the public once a year on Chakri Day, 6 April (the anniversary of the founding of the present Royal Dynasty). On the same terrace there are two gilt stupas built by King Rama I in commemoration of his parents. The **Phra Mondop** (library) was also built by Rama I to house the first revised Buddhist scriptural canon. To the west of the mondop is the large **Golden Stupa** or chedi, with its circular base, in Ceylonese style. To the north of the mondop is a model of Angkor Wat constructed during the reign of King Mongkut (1851-1868) when Cambodia was under Thai suzerainty. To the north again from the Royal Pantheon is the **Supplementary Library** and two viharns – **Viharn Yod** and **Phra Nak**.

To the south of Wat Phra Kaeo are the buildings of the **Grand Palace**. These are interesting for the contrast that they make with those of Wat Phra Kaeo. Walking out through the cloisters, on your left is the French-style **Boromabiman Hall**, which was completed during the reign of Rama VI. The **Amarinda Hall** has an impressive, airy interior, with chunky pillars and gilded thrones. The **Chakri Mahaprasart** (Palace Reception Hall) stands in front of a carefully manicured garden with topiary. It was built and lived in by King Chulalongkorn (Rama V) shortly after he had returned from a trip to Java and Singapore in 1876, and it shows: the building is a rather unhappy amalgam of colonial and traditional Thai styles of architecture. Rama V found the overcrowded Grand Palace oppressive and after a visit to Europe in 1897 built himself a new home at Vimanmek (see page 801) in Dusit where the present King, Bhumibol, lives in the Chitralada Palace. The Grand Palace is now only used for state occasions.

Next to the Chakri Mahaprasart is the raised **Dusit Hall**, a cool, airy building containing mother-of-pearl thrones. Near the Dusit Hall is a **museum** ⓘ *daily 0900-1600, ฿50*, which has information on the restoration of the Grand Palace, models of the Palace and many more Buddha images. There is also a collection of old cannon, mainly supplied by London foundries.

Sanaam Luang and around

To the north of the Grand Palace, across Na Phralan Road, lies the large open space of the Pramane Ground (the Royal Cremation Ground), better known as Sanaam Luang. This area was originally used for the cremation of kings, queens and important princes. It is the place in Bangkok to eat charcoal-grilled dried squid and have your fortune told by the *mor duu* (seeing doctors), who sit in the shade of the tamarind trees along the inner ring of the southern footpath. Each *mor duu* has a 'James Bond case' – a black briefcase – and having your fortune told costs around ฿30-60, or ฿100 for a full consultation.

North along Na Phrathat Road, on the river side of Sanaam Luang is **Wat Mahathat** (the Temple of the Great Relic) ① *daily 0900-1700*, a temple famous as a meditation centre; walk under the archway marked 'Naradhip Centre for Research in Social Sciences' to reach the wat. At No 24 Maharaj Road a narrow *soi* (lane) leads down towards the river and a large daily **market** selling exotic herbal cures, amulets, clothes and food. At weekends, the market spills out onto the surrounding streets (particularly Phra Chan Road) and amulet sellers line the pavement, their magical and holy talismen carefully displayed.

Banglamphu

Northeast of the National Art Gallery is the district of Banglamphu and the legendary **Khaosan Road**, backpacker haunt and epicentre of Bangkok's travellers' culture.

Golden Mount and around

This area, to the east of the Old City, is where ancient Bangkok begins to give way to the modern thrust of the bewildering 21st-century city. Apart from the Golden Mount there's little reason to hang around here but with the area's history of demonstrations and cries for democracy, it beats a defining pulse in the hearts of most Thais. The Golden Mount itself (also known as the Royal Mount) is an impressive artificial hill nearly 80 m high. The climb to the top is exhausting but worth it for the fabulous views of Bangkok.

Chinatown

South of the Old City, Chinatown covers the area from Charoen Krung (or New Road) down to the river. Few other places in Bangkok match Chinatown for atmosphere. The warren of alleys, lanes and tiny streets are cut through with an industrious hive of shops, temples and restaurants. Weird food, neatly arranged mountains of mechanical parts, gaudy temple architecture, gold, flowers and a constant frenetic bustle will lead to many hours of happy wandering. This is an area to explore on foot, getting lost in the many nooks and crannies.

Nakhon Kasem (Thieves' Market)

Nakhon Kasem, strictly speaking Woeng Nakhon Kasem (Thieves' Market), lies between Charoen Krung and Yaowarat Road, to the east of the khlong that runs parallel to Mahachai Road. Its boundaries are marked by archways. As its name suggests, this market used to be the centre for the fencing of stolen goods. It is not quite as colourful today but there remain a number of second-hand and antique shops, such as the **Good Luck Antique Shop**, which are worth a browse. Among other things, musical instruments, brass ornaments, antique (and not so antique) coffee grinders are all on sale here.

Wat Traimitr (Temple of the Golden Buddha)

ⓘ *Traimitr Rd, Chinatown; daily 0900-1700, β20.*

The most celebrated example of the goldsmith's art in Thailand sits within Wat Traimitr (Temple of the Golden Buddha). The Golden Buddha is housed in a small, rather gaudy and unimpressive room. Although the leaflet offered to visitors says the 3-m-high, 700-year-old image is 'unrivalled in beauty', be prepared for disappointment; it's featureless. What makes it special, drawing large numbers of visitors each day, is that it is made of 5½ tonnes of solid gold. Apparently, when the East Asiatic Company was extending the port of Bangkok, they came across a huge stucco Buddha image, which they obtained permission to move. However, during the move in 1957, it fell from the crane and the stucco cracked to reveal a solid gold image. During the Ayutthayan period it was the custom to cover valuable Buddha images in plaster to protect them from the Burmese and this example had stayed that way for several centuries.

Thonburi and the khlongs

Thonburi is Bangkok's little-known alter ego. Few people cross the Chao Phraya to see this side of the city and, if they do it is usually only to catch a glimpse from the seat of a speeding *hang yaaw* (long-tailed boat) and then climb the steps of **Wat Arun**. But Thonburi, during the reign of King Taksin, was once the capital of ancient Siam. King Rama I believed the other side of the river – present-day Bangkok – could be more easily defended from the Burmese and so, in 1782, he switched riverbanks.

Exploring the khlongs

One of the most enjoyable ways to see Bangkok is by boat – and particularly by the fast and noisy *hang yaaws*, powerful, lean machines that roar around the river and the khlongs at breakneck speed. There are innumerable tours around the khlongs of Thonburi taking in a number of sights, which include the floating market, snake farm and Wat Arun. Boats go from the various piers located along the east bank of the Chao Phraya River. The route skirts past laden rice-barges, squatter communities on public land and houses over-hanging the canals. On private tours the first stop is usually the **Floating Market** (Talaat Nam). This is now an artificial, ersatz gathering that exists purely for the tourist industry. The nearest functioning floating market is at Damnoen Saduak (see page 802). ▸▸ *See Activities and tours, page 812, and Transport, page 108.*

Wat Arun

ⓘ *Daily 0830-1730, β20. Water-taxi from Tha Tien pier (at the end of Thai Wang Rd near Wat Pho) or from Tha Chang (at the end of Na Phralan near Wat Phra Kaeo).*

Facing Wat Pho across the Chao Phraya River is the famous Wat Arun (Temple of the Dawn). The wat stands 81 m high, making it the highest *prang* (tower) in Thailand. It was built in the early 19th century on the site of Wat Chaeng, the Royal Palace complex when Thonburi was briefly the capital of Thailand. Wat Chaeng housed the Emerald Buddha before the image was transferred to Bangkok and it is said that King Taksin vowed to restore the wat after passing it one dawn. The prang is completely covered with fragments of Chinese porcelain and includes some delicate gold and black lacquered doors. The temple is really meant to be viewed from across the river; its scale and beauty can only be appreciated from a distance. The best view of Wat Arun is in the evening from the Bangkok side of the river when the sun sets behind the prang.

Dusit area

The present home of the Thai royal family and the administration is located north of Banglamphu in an area of wide, tree-lined boulevards, more in keeping with a European city. It is grand but lacks the bustling atmosphere found in the rest of Bangkok.

Vimanmek Palace

ⓘ *Just off Rachvithi Rd, to the north of the National Assembly, T02-2811569, www.palaces. thai.net. Daily 0900-1600 (last tickets at 1500), ฿100, ฿20 for children, admission by guided tour only (1 hr). Tickets to the Grand Palace include entrance to Vimanmek Palace. Dance shows 1030, 1400. No shorts or short skirts; sarongs available for hire (฿100, refundable).*

The Vimanmek Palace is the largest golden teakwood mansion in the world, but don't expect to see huge expanses of polished wood – the building is almost entirely painted. It was built by Rama V in 1901 who was clearly taken with Western style. It looks like a large Victorian hunting lodge and is filled with china, silver and paintings from all over the world (as well as some gruesome hunting trophies).

East of the Old City

Siam Square

A 10-minute walk east along Rama I Road is the biggest and busiest modern shopping area in the city, centred on a maze of tiny boutiques and a covered market known as Siam Square. Head to this area if you want to be at the apex of Thai youth culture and the biggest spread of shopping opportunities in the city. Whether you visit the hi-tech market at Panthip Plaza, the host of upmarket stores at one of Southeast Asia's largest malls, Siam Paragon and neighbour Siam Discovery, pure silk at Jim Thompson's House or the warren of tiny boutiques, you should leave with a big hole in your bank account. Thronged with young people, Siam Square plays host to Bangkok's burgeoning youth culture; cutting-edge contemporary and experimental fashions, Thai-style fast food and dozens of urban stylists keep the kids entertained. On the corner of Rama 1 and Phayathai Road is MBK, Bangkok's largest indoor shopping area. Crammed with bargains and outlets of every description, this is one of the Thai capital's most popular shopping spots.

Jim Thompson's House

ⓘ *Soi Kasemsan Song (2), opposite the National Stadium, Rama I Rd, www.jimthompson.com. Mon-Sat 0900-1630, ฿100, children ฿50 (profits to charity). Shoes must be removed before entering; walking barefoot around the house adds to the appreciation of the cool teak floorboards. Compulsory guided tours around the house and no photography allowed.*

Jim Thompson's House is an assemblage of traditional teak northern Thai houses, some more than 200 years old, transported here and reassembled. Jim Thompson arrived in Bangkok as an intelligence officer attached to the United States' OSS (Office of Strategic Services) and then made his name by reinvigorating the Thai silk industry after the Second World War. He disappeared mysteriously in the Malaysian jungle on 27 March 1967 but his silk industry continues to thrive. Jim Thompson chose this site for his house partly because a collection of silk weavers lived nearby on Khlong Saensaep. The house contains an eclectic collection of antiques from Thailand and China, with work displayed as though it was still his home. There is a little café attached to the museum as well as a shop.

Silom and Patpong

Hi-tech, high-rise and clad in concrete and glass, Silom, south of Siam Square, is at the centre of booming Bangkok. Banks, international business and many media companies are based in this area, as is the heart of Bangkok's gay community. Stylish, tacky and sweaty, head down the length of Silom for a full slice of contemporary Bangkok life.

The seedier side of Bangkok life has sadly always been a crowd-puller to the Western tourist. Most people flock to the red-light district of **Patpong**, which runs along two lanes (Patpong 1 and 2) linking Silom to Surawong. These streets were transformed from a row of 'tea houses' (brothels serving local clients) into a high-tech lane of go-go bars in 1969 when an American entrepreneur made a major investment. Patpong 1 is the larger and more active of the streets, with a famous market running down the middle at night, and is largely recognized as the eponymous home of Bangkok's notorious girly shows, complete with acrobatic vaginas. Patpong 2 supports cocktail bars, pharmacies and clinics for STDs, as well as a few go-go bars. There are also restaurants and bars here. Patpong is home to a night market infamous for its line in copied designer handbags.

Sukhumvit Road

With the Skytrain running its length, Sukhumvit Road, east of Siam Square and Silom, has developed into Bangkok's most vibrant strip. Shopping centres, girly bars, some of the city's best hotels and awesome places to eat have been joined by futuristic nightclubs. The grid of sois that run off the main drag are home to a variety of different communities including Arab, African and Korean, as well as throngs of Westerners.

Around Bangkok

Damnoen Saduak floating market

ⓘ *109 km west of Bangkok, 1½ hrs by bus No 79 from the Southern bus terminal in Thonburi (T02-435 5031 for booking) every 40 mins from 0600 (฿a/c 80); ask the conductor to drop you at Thanarat Bridge in Damnoen Saduak, then either walk down the lane (1.5 km) that leads to the market or take a river taxi for ฿10, or a minibus, ฿2. Tour companies also visit here.*
Damnoen Saduak floating market in Ratchaburi Province is (almost) the real thing. Sadly, it is becoming increasingly like the Floating Market in Thonburi (see page 800), although it does still function as a legitimate market. Aim to get to Damnoen Saduak as early as possible, as the market winds down after 0900, leaving only trinket stalls. There are a number of floating markets in the maze of khlongs – Ton Khem, Hia Kui and Khun Phithak – and it is best to hire a *hang yaaw* to explore them (about ฿300 per hour; agree the price before setting out).

Chatuchak Weekend Market

ⓘ *Just off Phahonyothin Rd. Take a Skytrain to Mo Chit station or Chatuchak Park and Kampaeng Phet Metro stations. Officially open Sat-Sun from 0800-1800 (although some shops open at about 0700, some at about 0900), it's best to go early in the day or after 1500.*
Chatuchak is a huge conglomeration of 15,000 stallholders spread over an area of 14 ha selling virtually everything under the sun. There are antique stalls, basket stalls, textile sellers, carvers and painters along with the usual array of fishmongers, vegetable hawkers, butchers and candlestick makers. Beware of pickpockets. The head office and information centre can be found opposite Gate 1 off Kampaengphet Road. The clock tower serves as a good reference point should visitors become disoriented.

Hotel prices
LL over US$200   L US$151-200   AL US$101-150
A US$66-100   B US$46-65   C US$31-45
D US$21-30   E US$12-20   F US$7-11
G US$6 and under

Restaurant prices
♦♦♦ over US$12   ♦♦ US$6-12   ♦ under US$6

⊙ Sleeping

From humble backstreet digs to opulent extravagance, Bangkok has an incredibly diverse range of hotels, guesthouses and serviced apartments. The best bargains are often to be had in the luxury sector; you'll find some of the best hotels in the world here, many offer their rooms at knock-down prices.

Old City and around
p795, maps p794 and p797

The guesthouses of **Khaosan** are cheapish but far more expensive than what you'll find in other parts of the country. Note that rooms facing on to Khaosan Rd tend to be very noisy; the sois off the main road, such as Soi Chana Songkhran or Soi Rambutri, are often quieter.

Sri Ayutthaya, north of Banglamphu, is emerging as an 'alternative' area for budget travellers. It is a central location, with restaurants and foodstalls nearby, but does not suffer the overcrowding and sheer pandemonium of Khaosan Rd.

A Buddy Lodge, 265 Khaosan Rd, T02-629 4477, www.buddylodge.com. One of the more upmarket options around the Khaosan Rd area and one of the first to use the now ubiquitous term 'boutique', Buddy Lodge actually deserves the title with rooms featuring relatively plush modern interiors and chic fittings as well as home comforts like a fridge and TV. There is also a Japanese restaurant, a coffee shop and a pool.

A Phranakorn Nornlen Hotel, 46 Thewet soi 1, T02-628 8188, www.phranakorn-norn len.com. A little gem of an independent hotel with incredible attention to detail. Airy

Thai-style rooms with artistic design are as homely as an artfully crafted doll's house. Wooden shutters, a garden café, beautiful rooftop views and an intimate, relaxed atmosphere. The small team of amicable staff include an informative 'City Guide' who can help with bookings, etc. Daily cookery classes and other creative pursuits. Recommended.

C-E D&D Inn, 68-70 Khaosan Rd, T02-629 0526, www.khaaosanby.com. Large, purpose-built hotel with lift, neat if slightly soulless a/c rooms, and hot showers. The small swimming pool and bar on the roof offers a fine view. Very centrally located.

C-E Sawasdee Bangkok Inn, 126/2 Khaosan Rd, T02-2801251. Good value, clean, fair-sized rooms with wooden floors and some with a/c. A vibrant, popular bar, and friendly staff. Free safety deposit and left luggage.

D Lamphu House, 75 Soi Rambutri, T02-629 5861, www.lamphuhouse.com. Undoubtedly one of the best budget options on offer. Situated down a very quiet soi. Clean, modern, very pleasantly decorated rooms with a/c and very comfy beds, the superior rooms have a large balcony and are the best value. Great restaurant downstairs and an extremely professional spa on the roof terrace. Highly recommended

D-F Siam Oriental, 190 Khaosan Rd, T02-629 0312, siam_oriental@hotmail.com. Fine, clean rooms (some a/c), smart tiled corridors and very friendly staff. Internet facilities downstairs, along with a popular restaurant. Safety box.

D-G Tavee, 83 Sri Ayutthaya Rd, Soi 14, T02-2825983. Restaurant, a quiet, relaxed, and respectable place with a small garden and a number of fish tanks. Friendly management – a world away from the chaos of Khaosan Rd. The Tavee family keep the rooms and shared bathrooms immaculately clean and are a good source of information for travellers. Dorms are also available for ฿80 per night. This place has been operating since 1985 and has managed to maintain a very high standard.

E Shambara, 138 Khaosan Rd, T02-282 7968, www.shambarabangkok.com. 9 rooms ranging from fan to a/c, singles to twins. Individually designed with lots of characters. A lot of thought has gone into making these rooms comfortable. Restaurant and tours. Good value.

E Tuptim Bed and Breakfast, 82 Rambutri, T02-6291 53536, info@tuptimb-b.com. Recommended budget option some rooms with a/c and en suite shower, but even the shared facilities are exceptionally clean, breakfast included. Very friendly staff.

E-F Chai's House, 49/4-8 Chao Fa Soi Rongmai, T02-281 4901. The last house down Soi Rambutri, so away from the competition. Some a/c, friendly atmosphere. Rooms are in traditional Thai-style. They vary in size but are clean and the a/c rooms are good value. Balconies and orchid-filled restaurant make it a quiet and relaxing place. Recommended.

E-F Home and Garden, 16 Samphraya Rd (Samsen 3), T02-280 1475. Away from the main concentration of guesthouses, down a quiet soi (although the roosters tend to ensure an early start for light sleepers). This small house in a delightful leafy compound has a homely atmosphere. The rooms are a fair size with large windows, some face onto a balcony. Friendly owner, excellent value.

E-F Orchid House, Rambutri St, T02-280 2619. Fan and a/c rooms with shower. Cosy, clean and safe with pretty interior touches in the rooms and communal areas. The ground-floor terrace restaurant is a nice quiet spot for reading or people watching. Internet café and travel agent. Recommended.

E-F Pra Suri Guesthouse, 85/1 Soi Pra Suri (off Dinso Rd), 5 mins east of Khaosan Rd not far from the Democracy Monument, T/F02-280 1428. Fan, restaurant, own bathrooms (no hot water), clean, spacious and quiet, very friendly and helpful family-run travellers' guesthouse with all the services to match.

E-F Sawasdee Smile Inn, 35 Soi Rongmai, T02-629321. Restaurant and 24-hr bar, so ask for a room at the back if you want an early night. Rooms are clean and simple, all with cable TV. Free safety boxes available.

F-G Bangkok Youth Hostel, 25/2 Phitsanulok Rd (off Samsen Rd), T02-282 0950. North of the Khaosan Rd, away from the bustle, the dorm beds are great value (฿120) being newly furnished and with a/c. Other rooms are clean and basic but still a bargain for those who don't mind a few hardships. If you don't have a valid YHA membership card, it will cost an extra ฿50 per night.

Thonburi and the khlongs *p800, map p794*
C-E The Artists Club, 61 Soi Tiem Boon Yang, T02-862 0056. Run by an artist, this is a guesthouse/studio/gallery buried deep in the khlongs with clean rooms, some with a/c. It makes a genuine alternative with concerts, drawing lessons and other cultural endeavours.

East of the Old City *p801, map p794*
In all Bangkok, the **Silom** area most resembles a Western city, with its international banks,

skyscrapers, first-class hotels, shopping malls, pizza parlours and pubs. It is also home to one of the world's best-known red-light districts – **Patpong**.

Sukhumvit is now one of Bangkok's premier centres of accommodation and is a great place for restaurants and nightlife with several good bars and clubs. This is also a good area for shopping for furniture: antique and reproduction.

Soi Ngam Duphli to the east is much the smaller of Bangkok's 2 main centres of guesthouse accommodation. This area has seen better days but still makes a viable alternative for budget travellers. **LL Metropolitan**, 27 South Sathorn Rd, T02-625 3333, www.metropolitan.como.bz. From its funky members/guest-only bar through to the beautiful, contemporary designer rooms

and the awesome restaurants (**Glow** and **Cy'an**) this is one of Bangkok's hippest hotels.
LL-L Sheraton Grande Sukhumvit, 250 Sukhumvit, T02-649 8888, www.luxury collection.com/bangkok. Superbly managed business and leisure hotel. Service, food and facilities are impeccable. The rooftop garden is an exotic delight and the spa offers some of the best massage in town. The **Rossini** and **Basil** restaurants are also top class. Great location and, if you can afford it, the best place to stay on Sukhumvit.
LL-L Sukhothai, 13/3 South Sathorn Rd, T02-287 0222, www.sukhothai.com. A competitor for the **Metropolitan**'s crown as the sleekest, chicest place to sleep in the city. Stunning, modern oriental interiors set in landscaped gardens complete with decadent pool area. Recommended.
L Banyan Tree, 21/100 South Sathorn Rd, T02-679 1200, www.banyantree.com. Glittering sumptuous surrounds immediately relax the soul here. Famous for its divine luxury spa and literally breathtaking roof-top **Moon Bar**, all rooms are suites with a good location and set back from busy Sathorn Rd.
A-B Smart Suites, 43/17 Sukhumvit 11, T02-254 6544, www.smartsuites11.com. A boutique hotel with in-house tailoring.
A-E New Road Guest House, 1216/1 Charoen Krung Rd, T02-237 1094. This Danish-owned place provides a range of accommodation from decent budget rooms to hammocks on the roof. A restaurant serves inexpensive Thai dishes and there's a free fruit buffet breakfast. A bar provides a pool table and darts and there's a small outdoor sitting area.
B-D Atlanta, 78 Sukhumvit Soi 2, T02-252 1650, www.theatlantahotel.bizland.com. Basic a/c or fan-cooled rooms. A good large pool and children's pool. Good restaurant. Prides itself on its literary, peaceful atmosphere. Appears to be the cheapest and is certainly the most appealing hotel in the area at this price, particularly suited for families, writers and dreamers, 24-hr email available.

B-D Charlie's House, Soi Saphan Khu, T02-679 8330, www.charlieshousethailand. com. Helpful owners create a friendly atmosphere and the rooms are carpeted and very clean. This is probably the best of the budget bunch. There is a restaurant and coffee corner with good food at reasonable prices. Recommended.
D-E Sam's Lodge, 28-28/1, 2nd floor, Sukhumvit 19, T02-253 2993, www.samslodge. com. Budget accommodation with modern facilities and roof terrace, close to the skytrain.

❶ Eating

Bangkok is one of the greatest food cities on earth. You could spend a lifetime finding the best places to eat in this city that seems totally obsessed with its tastebuds. Many restaurants, especially Thai ones, close early (2200-2230). Street food can be found across the city and a rice or noodle dish will cost ฿25-40 instead of a minimum of ฿50 in the restaurants. Some of the best can be found on the roads between **Silom** and **Surawong Rd**, **Soi Suanphlu** off South Sathorn Rd, down **Soi Somkid**, next to Ploenchit Rd, or opposite on **Soi Tonson**.

Old City and around
p795, maps p794 and p797
Travellers' food such as banana pancakes and muesli is available in the guesthouse/travellers' hotel areas. However, the Thai food sold along Khaosan Rd is some of the worst and least authentic in town, watered down to suit the tastebuds of unadventurous backpackers.
🍴 **D'Rus**, Khaosan Rd. Open 0700-2400. A typical big-screen sports and sofas Khaosan place, but the Thai/Western food is decent and cheap and the coffee is freshly brewed.
🍴 **Bai Bau**, 146 Rambutri St. Tasty Thai food in a quiet corner; best bet for a relaxed authentic meal in a friendly environment. Good value.

Chinatown *p628, map p797*
The street food in Chinatown is some of the best in Thailand. You'll find everything from

fresh lobster through to what can only be described as grilled pig's face. It's very cheap; look for the more popular places and dive in.

¶¶¶ Hua Seng Hong Restaurant, 371-372 Yaowarat Rd, T02-222635. The grimy exterior belies the fantastic restaurant within. Dim sum, noodles, duck and grilled pork are awesome. Perfect spot. Highly recommended.

¶ The Canton House, 530 Yaowarat Rd, T02-221 3335. Hugely popular dimsum canteen set on the main drag. The prices – ฿15 – for a plate of dim sum are legendary and this has to be one of the best-value places to eat in town. The food is OK but nothing exceptional while the frenetic, friendly atmosphere is 100% Chinatown. Recommended.

East of the Old City *p801, map p794*

¶¶¶ Anna's Café, 118 Silom Soi Sala Daeng, T02-632 0619. Daily 1100-2200. Great Thai-fusion restaurant in a villa off Silom Rd named after Anna of *King & I* fame. Some classic Thai dishes like *larb*, *nua yaang* and *som tam* along with fusion dishes and Western desserts such as apple crumble and banoffee pie.

¶¶¶ Cy'an, Metropolitan Hotel, 27 South Sathorn Rd, T02-625 3333, www.metro politan.como.bz. With a menu concocted by one of Asia's leading chefs, Amanda Gale, Cy'an is a scintillating dining experience the like of which is not matched in the entire Thai capital. This is international cuisine of the highest order: the almond-fed Serrano ham and Japanese *wagyu* beef are highlights in a stunning menu. Strangely ignored by wealthy Thais, this is a restaurant at the cutting edge of Bangkok eating, miles ahead of the competition.

¶¶¶ Glow, Metropolitan Hotel, 27 South Sathorn Rd, T02-625 3333, www.metropoli tan.como.bz. An organic lunch bar. Feast on spirulina noodles and tuna sashimi, all washed down with fresh beetroot and ginger juice.

¶¶¶ Rang Mahal, Rembrandt Hotel, Sukhumvit Soi 18, T02-261 7107. Some of the finest Indian food in town, award-winning and very popular with the Indian community. Spectacular views from the rooftop position, sophisticated, elegant and expensive.

¶¶¶ Thaniya Garden Restaurant, Thaniya Plaza, 3rd floor, Room 333-335, 52 Silom Rd, T02-231 2201. Mon-Sat 1100-2200. Excellent Thai food and enormous portions.

¶¶¶ Zanotti, Sala Daeng, Soi 2 (off Silom Rd), T02-636 0002. Daily for lunch and dinner. Extremely popular, sophisticated Italian restaurant serving authentic Italian cuisine, including wonderful breads, salads, pizzas, risotto and exceptional pasta.

¶¶¶ Nasir al-Masri, 4-6 Sukhumvit Soi Nana Nua, T02-253 5582. Reputedly the best Arabic food in Bangkok, falafel, tabouleh, hummus, frequented by lots of Arabs who come for a taste of home.

¶¶-¶ Le Dalat Indochine, 47/1 Sukhumvit Soi 23, T02-661 7967. Daily for lunch and dinner. Reputed to serve the best Vietnamese food in Bangkok. Not only is the food good, but the ambience is satisfying too.

¶ Ban Mai, 121 Sukhumvit Soi 22, Sub-Soi 2. Thai food served amongst Thai-style decorations in an attractive house with a friendly atmosphere. Good value.

¶ Cabbages and Condoms, Sukhumvit Soi 12 (around 400 m down the soi). Population and Community Development Association (PDA) Thai restaurant, so all proceeds go to this charity. Eat rice in the Condom Room, drink in the Vasectomy Room. Good *tom yam khung* and honey-roast chicken, curries all rather similar, good value. Attractive courtyard area.

🅞 Bars and clubs

The city has some fantastic nightlife – everything from pubs through to über-trendy clubs. You can listen to decent jazz and blues or get into the latest overseas DJs. Groovy Map's *Bangkok by Night* (฿120) includes information on bars and dance clubs, the city's gay scene, as well as music venues and drinking spots. Check the Bangkok listing magazines for the latest information on who's spinning and what's opening.

Old City and around
p795, maps p794 and p797

Brick Bar at Buddy Lodge, 365 Khaosan Rd, T02-629 4477. An upmarket and pleasant venue overlooking Khaosan Rd, competitive prices and a mixed crowd of travellers and young locals looking to test their English. Great live bands at night, open all day.

Cinnamon Bar. 106 Rambuttri Rd, T02-629 4075. Look for the water feature from the main road. Chic modern interior using glass and steel. Bar and club, the cocktails do the trick.

Gazebo, 44 Chakrapong Rd, T02-629 0705. Popular with both Thais and farangs. The open-air terrace is home to reasonable live bands, the indoor area plays more up-beat dance music. Reported to stay open till 0600.

Lava Club, 249 Khaosan Rd, T02-281 6565, daily 2000-0100. Playing the ubiquitous Bangkok sounds of hip-hop and house, this large cavernous venue resembles a heavy metal club, decked out in black with red lava running down the walls and floors.

Saxophone, 3/8 Victory Monument, Phayathai Rd, Golden Mount. Daily 1800-0300. Series of alternating house bands, including jazz, blues, ska and soul. Another place with a long-standing – and deserved – reputation for delivering the music goods.

Silk Bar, 129-131 Khaosan Rd. T02-281 9981. The wide decked terrace is a great place to sit and people watch. Live DJs in the evenings.

Susie's Pub, turn right between **Lava Club** and **Lek GH**. Open 2000-0200. This is the place for an alternative Thai experience of clubbing down Khaosan, as it's always absolutely heaving, more with locals than travellers. Top decibel thumping local tunes and all sorts of flashing neon outside announce its presence, but while it might be easy to find, it's not always such a simple thing to get in, as there's a seething mass of bodies to negotiate from relatively early on right up until closing.

East of the Old City *p801, map p794*
The greatest concentration of bars in this area are to be found in the 'red-light' districts of Patpong and in the back sois off Sukhumvit Rd.

Bamboo Bar, **Oriental Hotel**, 48 Oriental Av, T02-236 0400. Sun-Thu 1100-0100, Fri-Sat 1100-0200. One of the best jazz venues in Bangkok, classy and cosy with good food and pricey drinks – but worth it if you like your jazz and can take the hit.

Bed Supper Club, 26 Sukhumvit Soi 11, T02-651 3537, www.bedsupperclub.com. Daily 2000-0200. A futuristic white pod, filled with funky beats, awesome cocktails, superb food, gorgeous designer furniture and hordes of Bangkok's beautiful people.

Cheap Charlie's, 1 Sukhumvit Soi 11. Open 1500 until very late. Very popular with expats, backpackers and locals. Lively, cheap and unpretentious open-air bar in kitsch faux-tropical surrounds.

Jools Bar, 21/3 Nana Tai, Sukhumvit Soi 4. Daily 0900-0100. A favourite watering hole for Brits. Serves classic English food.

Narcissus, 112 Sukhumvit Soi 23, T02-258 2549. Daily 2100-0200. The classy, art deco **Narcissus** was awarded Metro's Best Night-club award in 2001. The music here is trance, house and techno and the clientele are office types trying to hold on to their youth.

Noriega's Bar, 106/108 Soi 4, Silom Rd, T02-233 2814. Daily 1800-0200. Words like minimalist and Zen spring to mind in this relatively quiet watering hole on an otherwise bustling strip. Live acts on Sat, Sun and Mon nights help cater for the guys, gays and gals this place targets with its promise of booze, broads, bites and blues.

Q Bar, 34 Sukhumvit Soi 11, T02-252 3274, www.qbarbangkok.com. Housed in a modern building, it is the reincarnation of photographer David Jacobson's bar of the same name in Ho Chi Minh City. Good beats, great drinks menu and sophisticated layout.

Santika, 253/11 Sukhumvit 63, T02-711 5886, www.santika.com. Live bands and DJs play at this impressively designed venue. More popular with Thais than tourists.

Tapas, 114/17 Silom Soi 4, T02-234 4737. A very popular, sophisticated bar with contagious beats and atmosphere. Attracts a friendly mix of expats and locals. The bar upstairs caters for the dancing crowds at the weekends with live drumming sessions and guest DJs.

Gay and lesbian bars and clubs
The hub of Bangkok's gay scene can be found among the clubs, bars and restaurants on Silom, Sois 2 and 4. If it's your first time in Thailand, **Utopia Tours**, www.utopia-tours.com, are specialists in organizing gay travel, including tours of Bangkok. Its website also contains a huge number of listings, contacts and insights for gay and lesbian travellers.
Balcony, 86-8 Silom Soi 4. Daily 1700-0200. Cute bar where you can hang out on the terraces watching the action below.
DJ Station, Silom Soi 2, www.dj-station.com. Daily 2200-0200, ฿100 admission. This is the busiest and largest club on a busy soi. 3 floors of pumping beats and flamboyant disco. Essential and recommended.
The Expresso, 8/6-8 Silom Soi 2. Daily 2200-0200. Good place to relax, with subdued lights and a lounge atmosphere.
Freeman, Silom Soi 2. Worth seeking out to find one of Bangkok's funniest **katoey** cabarets; it's mostly in Thai but the visual references leave little to the imagination. There's a dance floor on the top floor but it's a little dark and seedy.

⦿ Entertainment

Bangkok *p792, maps p794 and p797*
Cinema
Remember to stand for the National Anthem, which is played before every performance.

Bangkok cinemas are on the whole hi-tech, ultra luxurious and a great escape from the heat of the city. Prices can range from ฿100 to ฿500 for incredibly sumptuous reclining VIP seats, complete with pillows and blankets. Details of showings from English-language newspapers and www. movieseer.com. There are 2 excellent international film festivals held every year and Bangkok is a popular location for many Asian filmmakers.

Easily accessible cinemas with English soundtracks include **Siam Paragon Cineplex**, Rama I Rd, T02-515555; **EGV**, 6th floor, Siam Discovery Centre (Siam Tower), Rama I Rd (opposite Siam Sq), T02-812 9999; **SFX Emporium**, Sukhumvit Soi 24, T02-260 9333; and **SFX Mahboonkrong** (MBK shopping centre), T02-2609333, Bangkok's only independent art house cinema is **House**, www.houserama.com, T02-641 5177.

Thai Boxing (Muay Thai)
Thai boxing, www.muaythaionline.org, is both a sport and a means of self-defence and was first developed during the Ayutthaya period, 1351-1767. It differs from Western boxing in that contestants are allowed to use almost any part of their body. There are 2 main boxing stadiums in Bangkok:
Lumpini, Rama 1V Rd, near Lumpini Park, T02-251 4303. Boxing nights are Tue and Fri (1700-2000) and Sat (2030-2400); tickets cost up to and over ฿1500 for a ringside seat; cheaper seats cost about ฿500-800.
Rachdamnern Stadium, Rachdamnern Rd (near TAT office), T02-281 4205. Boxing nights are Mon, Wed and Sun (1800-2230) and Sat (1700 and 2230), seats from ฿500-1500.

⦿ Festivals and events

Bangkok *p792, maps p794 and p797*
Mar-Apr International Kite Festival is held at Sanaam Luang when kite fighting and demonstrations by kite-flyers take place.
Apr Songkran, the beginning of the Buddhist New Year, is marked by excessive and exuberant water-throwing. The Khaosan Rd and Patpong/Silom are the places to head to/avoid depending on your chaos tolerance levels.

⦿ Shopping

Bangkok *p792, maps p794 and p797*
From flowers and fruit sold at energetic all-night markets through to original and fake

Louis Vuitton, Bangkok has the lot. Most street stalls will try and fleece you, so be prepared to shop around and bargain hard. Some arcades target the wealthier shopper and are dominated by brand-name goods and designer wear. Department stores tend to be fixed price.

Sukhumvit Rd and the sois to the north are lined with shops and stalls, especially around the **Ambassador** and **Landmark** hotels. Many tailors and made-to-measure shoe shops are to be found in this area. Higher up on Sukhumvit Rd particularly around Soi 49 are various antique and furnishing shops.

Antiques
Jim Thompson's, Surawong Rd, www.jim thomspon.com. A range of antiques, wooden artefacts, furnishings and carpets.
L'Arcadia, 12/2 Sukhumvit Soi 23. Burmese antiques, beds, ceramics, doors, good quality and prices are fair.

Clothes and tailoring
Bangkok's tailors are skilled at copying anything, either from fashion magazines or from a piece of your own clothing. Always request at least 2 fittings, ask to see a finished garment and inspect it for stitching quality, ask for a price in writing and pay as small a deposit as possible. Tailors are concentrated along Silom, Sukhumvit and Ploenchit roads and on Gaysorn Sq.

Cheap designer wear with meaningless slogans and a surfeit of labels is available just about everywhere, and especially in tourist areas like Patpong and Sukhumvit. Note that the less you pay, generally, the more likely that the dyes will run, shirts will downsize after washing, and buttons will eject themselves at will.
Ambassador & Smart Fashion, 28-28/1 Sukhumvit 19, T02-253 2993, www.ambassadorfashion.com. Bespoke tailors. Free pick-up available from your hotel.
Fly Now, 2nd floor, Gaysorn Plaza, Ploenchit Rd. Directional but wearable designs blending Thai-style femininity and flair with current Western influences. As seen at London Fashion Week.
Kai Boutique, 187/1 Bangkok Cable Building, Thanon Rachdamri, www.kai boutique.com. This building is worth visiting for those interested in what the best designers in Thailand are doing. One of Bangkok's longest-standing high-fashion outlets.

Handicrafts
Cocoon, 3rd floor, Gaysorn Plaza. Thai objects have been transformed by altering the design slightly and using bright colours. Great for unusual and fun gifts.

Jewellery
Thailand has become the world's largest gem-cutting centre and it is an excellent place to buy both gems and jewellery. The best buy of the native precious stones is the sapphire. Modern jewellery is well designed and of a high quality. Always insist on a certificate of authenticity and a receipt.
Ban Mo, on Pahurat Rd, north of Memorial Bridge, is the centre of the gem business although there are shops in all the tourist areas particularly on Silom Rd near the intersection with Surasak Rd, eg **Rama Gems** 987 Silom Rd. **Uthai Gems**, 28/7 Soi Ruam Rudi, off Ploenchit Rd, just east of Witthayu Rd, is recommended, as is **P Jewellery** (Chantaburi), 9/292 Ramindra Rd, Anusawaree Bangkhan, T02-5221857.

For Western designs, **Living Extra** and **Yves Joaillier** are to be found on the 3rd floor of the Charn Issara Tower, 942 Rama IV Rd. **Jewellery Trade Centre** (aka Galleria Plaza), next door to the **Holiday Inn Crowne Plaza** on the corner of Silom Rd and Surasak Rd, contains a number of gem dealers and jewellery shops on the ground floor. **Tabtim Dreams** at Unit 109, is a good place to buy loose gems.

Markets
The markets in Bangkok are an excellent place to browse, take photographs and pick up bargains.

Khaosan Rd Market, close to Banglamphu Market, is geared to the needs and desires of the foreign tourist: counterfeit CDs, DVDs, designer clothing, rucksacks, leather goods, jewellery, souvenirs and so on.

Nakhon Kasem, known as the **Thieves' Market**, in the heart of Chinatown (see page 799) houses a number of 'antique' shops selling brassware, old electric fans and woodcarvings (tough bargaining is needed and don't expect everything to be genuine).

Pahurat Indian Market, a small slice of India in Thailand, with mounds of sarongs, batiks, buttons and bows.

Pak Khlong Market is a wholesale market selling fresh produce, orchids and cut flowers and is situated near the Memorial Bridge on Tri Phet Rd. An exciting place to visit at night.

Patpong Market, arranged down the middle of Patpong Rd, linking Silom and Surawong roads, geared to tourists. Bargain hard.

Tewes Market, near the National Library, is a photographer's dream; a daily market, selling flowers and plants.

Weekend Market is the largest and is at Chatuchak Park (see page 802).

Shopping malls

The Emporium, on Sukhumvit Soi 24. Daily 1000-2200 (directly accessible from BTS Phrom Phong Station) is an enormous place with many clothes outlets as well as record and book shops, designer shops and more.

Mah Boonkhrong Centre (MBK) on the corner of Phayathai and Rama 1, is long established and downmarket and packed full of bargains with countless small shops/stalls.

Peninsula Plaza, between the **Hyatt Erawan** and **Regent** hotels, is considered one of the smarter shopping plazas in Bangkok.

Siam Discovery Centre (Siam Tower), 6 storeys of high-end fashion across the road from Siam Sq. All the top designers, both Thai and international, have a presence here.

Siam Paragon, Rama 1 Rd, next to Siam Centre, www.siamparagon.co.th. The latest addition and the undisputed holder of the title of most ostentatious shopping experience in town. This multi-billion-baht project houses exclusive and high-end retail, dining and entertainment opportunities beyond the dreams even the most die-hard shopaholic. Its endless designer wares from couture to cars could bust the budget of a billionaire.

Siam Square, at the intersection of Phayathai and Rama I roads. For trendy Western clothing, bags, belts, jewellery and some antique shops.

Silk

Silk varies greatly in quality. Generally, the heavier the weight the more expensive the fabric. 1-ply is the lightest and cheapest (about ฿200 per m), 4-ply the heaviest and most expensive (about ฿300-400 per m). Silk also comes in 3 grades: Grade 1 is the finest and smoothest. There is also 'hard' and 'soft' silk, soft being more expensive. There are a number of specialist silk shops at the top of Surawong Rd (near Rama IV) and a shops along the bottom half of Silom Rd (towards Charoen Krung) and in the Siam Centre on Rama I Rd.

Anita Thai Silk, 294/4-5 Silom Rd, slightly more expensive than some, but the extensive range makes it worth a visit.

Cabbages and Condoms, Sukhumvit Soi 12 and Raja Siam, Sukhumvit Soi 23. Village-made silks.

Jagtar, 37 Sukhumvit Soi 11. Has some lovely silk curtain fabrics as well as cushion covers in unusual shades and other accessories made from silk. Originality means prices are high.

Jim Thompson's, top of Surawong Rd, www.jimthompson.com. Daily 0900-2100. Famous silk shop that's expensive, but has the best selection.

▲ Activities and tours

Bangkok p792, maps p794 and p797

Boat tours

Either book a tour at your hotel or go to one of the piers and organize your own trip. The most frequented piers are located between the **Oriental Hotel** and the Grand Palace, or under Taksin Bridge (which marks the end of the Skytrain line). The pier just to the south of the **Royal Orchid Sheraton Hotel** is recommended. Organizing your own trip gives greater freedom to stop and start when the mood takes you. It is best to go in the morning (0700).

City tours

Bangkok has innumerable tour companies that can take visitors virtually anywhere. If there is not a tour to fit your bill – most run the same range of tours – many companies will produce a customized one for you, for a price. Most top hotels have their own tour desk and it is probably easiest to book there (arrange to be picked up from your hotel as part of the deal). Prices per person are about ฿400-800 for a half day, ฿1000-2000 for a full day (including lunch).

Cookery courses

Blue Elephant, 233 Thanon Sathorn Tai, Bangrak, www.blueelephant.com. T02-673 9353. One of the most famous cooking schools with an innovative menu and beautiful, impeccably equipped surrounds in the former Thai-Chinese Chamber of Commerce. A 1-day course is ฿2800.

May Kaidee, 111 Tanao Rd, www.may kaidee.com. T02-281 7137. A vegetarian restaurant with its own veggie cooking school. At ฿1200 for 10 dishes it's also one of the best budget options.

Massage

Wat Pho, T02-221 2974, www.watpho.com (see page 796). The centre is located at the back of the wat, on the opposite side from the entrance. For details, the school offers body massage with or without herbs and foot massage. The service is available from 0800-1700 and costs from ฿250 for a 30-min body massage to ฿350 for a 1-hr body massage with herbal compress. A foot massage is ฿250 for 45 mins. For Westerners wishing to learn the art of traditional Thai massage, special 30-hr courses can be taken for ฿8500, stretching over either 15 days (2 hrs per day) or 10 days (3 hrs per day). There is also a foot massage course at ฿6500, 30 hrs over 5 or 10 days.

Tour operators

Asian Trails Ltd, 9th floor, SG Tower, 161/1 Soi Mahadlek, Luang 3, Rajdamri Rd, T02-626 2000, www.asiantrails.info. Southeast Asia specialist.
Bangkok Tourist Bureau, 17/1 Phra Arthit Rd, under Phra Pinklao Bridge, T02-225 7612, www.bangkoktourist.com, daily 0900-1900. Offers every imaginable tour of Bangkok by river, bike and even bus. Knowledgeable and reliable. Their white booths are found in popular tourist areas and are easy to spot.
Real Asia, T02-712 9301, www.realasia.net. Cycling and walking tours around the city's 'greenbelt' including the less-explored rural riverside areas of Bang Kra Jao and Phra Padaeng.

⊖ Transport

Bangkok *p792, maps p794 and p797*
Air
For airport information, see page 593.
Airline offices Air France, Vorawat Building, 20th floor, 849 Silom Rd, T02-635 1199. **Alitalia**, SSP Tower 3, 15th floor, Unit 15A, 88 Silom Rd, T02-634 1800. **American Airlines**, 518/5 Ploenchit Rd, T02-251 1393. **Bangkok Airways**, Queen Sirikit National Convention Center, New Rajdapisek Rd, Klongtoey, T02-229 3456, www.bangkok air.com. **British Airways**, 14th floor, Abdulrahim Place, 990 Rama 1V Rd, T02-636 1747. **Canadian Airlines**, 6th floor, Maneeya Building, 518/5 Ploenchit Rd, T02-251 4521.

Cathay Pacific, 11th floor, Ploenchit Tower, 898 Ploenchit Rd, T02-263 0606. **Continental Airlines**, CP Tower, 313 Silom Rd, T02-231 0113. **Delta Airlines**, 7th floor, Patpong Building, Surawong Rd, T02-237 6838. **Eva Airways**, Green Tower, 2nd floor, 425 Rama IV Rd, opposite Esso Head Office. **Finnair** 6th floor, Vorawat Building, 849 Silom Rd, T02-635 1234. **Gulf Air**, 12th floor, Maneeya Building, 518 Ploenchit Rd, T02-254 7931. **KLM**, 19th floor, Thai Wah Tower 11, 21/133-134 South Sathorn Rd, T02-679 1100. **Lufthansa**, 18th floor, Q-House (Asoke), Sukhumvit Rd Soi 21, T02-264 2400. **Qantas**, 14th floor, Abdulrahim Place, 990 Rama IV Rd, T02-636 1747. **SAS**, 8th floor, Glas Haus I, Sukhumvit Rd Soi 25, T02-260 0444. **Singapore Airlines**, 12th floor, Silom Centre, 2 Silom Rd, T02-236 5295/6. **Swiss**, 21st floor Abdulrahim Place, 990 Rama 1V Rd, T02-636 2160. **THAI**, 485 Silom Rd, T02-234 3100 and 89 Vibhavadi-Rangsit Rd, T02-513 0121. **Vietnam Airlines**, 7th floor, Ploenchit Centre, 1202 Sukhumvit 2 Rd, T02-656 9056.

Boat
Water taxi This is the cheapest way to travel on the river. There are 3 types. The **Chao Phraya Express River Taxi** (*rua duan*) runs between Nonthaburi in the north and Rajburana (Big C) in the south. Fares are calculated by zone and range from ฿10-14 for the daily **Standard Express Boat** and ฿12-32 for the **Special Express Boat**. At peak hours boats leave every 10 mins, off-peak about 15-25 mins. **Standard Express Boats** operate daily 0600-1840, and **Special Express Boats**, Mon-Fri 0600-0900, 1200-1900 (see above). The journey from one end of the route to the other takes 75 mins. **Special Express Boats**, flying either a red/orange or a yellow pennant, do not stop at all piers; boats without a flag are the **Standard Express Boats** and stop at all piers. Also, boats will only stop if passengers wish to board or alight, so make your destination known. Be warned that Thais trying to sell boat tours will tell you Express Boats are not

running and will try to extort grossly inflated prices. Walk away and find the correct pier!

Ferries also ply back and forth across the river, between Bangkok and Thonburi.

Khlong or long-tailed boats (*hang yaaw*) can be rented for ฿200 per hr, or more if you feel like splashing out in more ways than one. A good map, *Rivers and Khlongs*, is available from the TAT office.

Bus

This is the cheapest way to get around town although more people have their belongings stolen on city buses than almost anywhere else so beware of pickpockets. There is quite a range of buses, including a/c and non-a/c, micro and expressway. All buses run from 0500-2300, apart from the limited all-night bus service which run from 2300-0500. A routes map is indispensable. Good maps are available from bookshops as well as hotels and travel agents or tour companies. Major bus stops have maps of routes in English. Also see the **BMTA (Bangkok Mass Transit Authority)** website, www.bmta.co.th, for detailed information on all bus routes and tourist destinations in English and Thai. Prices cost from ฿8.50-30.

For bus routes and times, see page 781. There are 3 main bus stations in Bangkok.

Northern bus terminal (or Mo Chit Mai – New Mo Chit – aka Mo Chit 2), is at the western side of Chatuchak Park on Kamphaeng Phet 2 Rd, T02-936 3659. It serves all destinations in the north and north-east as well as towns in the central plains.

Southern bus terminal is on Phra Pinklao Rd, T02-4347192, near the intersection with Route 338. Buses for the west (eg **Kanchanaburi**) and the south leave from here. A/c buses to the south and west leave from the terminal on Charan Santiwong Rd, near Bangkok Noi Train Station in Thonburi, T02-435 1199.

Eastern bus terminal, Sukhumvit Rd (Soi Ekamai), between Soi 40 and Soi 42, T02-391 2504, serves **Pattaya** and other

destinations in the eastern region. Buses leave for most major destinations throughout the day, and often well into the night. There are overnight buses on the longer routes – **Chiang Mai**, **Hat Yai**, **Chiang Rai**, **Phuket**, **Ubon Ratchathani**.

In addition to the government-operated buses, there are many private companies that run **'tour' buses** to most of the major tourist destinations. Tickets bought through travel agents will normally be for these private tour buses which leave from offices all over the city as well as from the public bus terminals. Shop around as prices may vary. Note that although passengers may be picked up from their hotel/guesthouse – therefore saving on the ride (and inconvenience) of getting out to the bus terminal – the private buses are generally more expensive, less reliable and less safe. Many pick up passengers at Khaosan Rd and are notoriously cramped and differ considerably from the 'luxury VIP seating' promised on purchase.

Metro (MRT) and Skytrain (BTS)

The new **Metro**, www.bangkokmetro.co.th, loops through 18 stations and also intersects with the Skytrain. The entire network is a/c, the comfortable trains run regularly and stations are well-lit and airy. There is a lack of integration with the Skytrain – separate tickets are needed and interchanges are awkward and badly planned. At present, fares for the Metro are cheap, ฿15-39.

The **Skytrain**, T02-617 7300, www.bts.co.th, runs on an elevated track through the most developed parts of the city – it is quite a ride, veering between the skyscrapers. Trains run 0600-2400, every 3-5 mins during peak periods and every 10-15 mins out of the rush hour. Fares are ฿15 for 1 stop, ฿40 for the whole route. Multi-trip tickets can also be purchased, which makes things slightly cheaper. The extension over the river to Thonburi is now complete but nobody seems to know when services will begin – hopefully by early 2009.

Taxi

Taxis are usually metered (they must have a/c to register) – look for the 'Taxi Meter' illuminated sign on the roof. Check that the meter is 'zeroed' before setting off. Fares are ฿35 for the first 2 km, ฿4.50 per km up to 12 km, and ฿5 per km thereafter. Most trips in the city should cost ฿40-100. If the travel speed is less than 6 kph – always a distinct possibility in the traffic-choked capital – a surcharge of ฿1.25 per min is automatically added. Passengers also pay the tolls for using the expressway. Taxi drivers sometimes refuse to use the meter despite the fact that they are required to do so by law. Tipping, though not expected, is much appreciated. It is usual to round fares up to the nearest ฿5. To call a taxi **Siam Taxis** T1661 or **Radio Taxi** T1681, they charge ฿20 plus the fare on the meter. Note – fares are due to increase slightly by the end of 2008 but rates are not yet fixed.

Motorcycle taxi These are used to run up and down the long sois that extend out of the main thoroughfares. Riders wear numbered vests and tend to congregate at the end of the busiest sois. The short-hop fare is about ฿10 and there is usually a price list (in Thai) at the gathering point. Some riders will take you on longer journeys across town and fares will then need to be negotiated – expect to pay ฿25-100, dependent on your negotiating skills.

Tuk-tuk Best for short journeys, they are uncomfortable and, being open to the elements, you are likely to be asphyxiated by car fumes. Bargaining is essential and the fare should be negotiated before boarding, though most drivers try to rip tourists off and taking a metered taxi will be less hassle and cheaper. Expect to pay ฿30-100 for a short hop across town.

❶ Directory

Bangkok *p792, maps p794 and p797*
Banks There are countless exchange booths in all the tourist areas open 7 days a week, mostly 0800-1530, some 0800-2100. Rates vary only marginally between banks, although if changing a large sum, it is worth shopping around. ATMs abound in Bangkok and most can be used with credit cards and bank cards. Open 24 hrs a day. **Embassies and consulates Australia**, 37 South Sathorn Rd, T02-287 2680. **Cambodia**, 185 Rachdamri Rd, T02-254 6630. **Canada**, 15th floor Abdulrahim Pl, 990 Rama IV Rd, T02-636 0541. **Laos**, 502/1-3 Soi Ramk- hamhaeng 39, T02-539 6667. **New Zealand**, 93 Wireless Rd, T02-2542530. **South Africa**, 6th floor, Park Place, 231 Soi Sarasin, Rachdamri Rd, T02-253 8473. **UK**, 1031 Wireless Rd, T02-253 0191/9. **USA**, 95 Wireless Rd, T02-205 4000. **Vietnam**, 83/1 Wireless Rd, T02-251 7202, 2 photos, same-day visas available for ฿2700.
Immigration Sathorn Tai Soi Suanphlu, Silom, T02-287 3101. **Internet** Hi-speed access away from the tourist areas will cost from ฿10 per hr; along Khaosan and Sukhumvit prices are ฿30-60 per hr. **Medical services Bangkok Adventist Hospital**, 430 Phitsanu lok Rd, Dusit, T02-281 1422/ 2821100. Efficient vaccination service and 24-hr emergency unit. **Bangkok General Hospital**, New Phetburi Soi 47, T02-318 0066.
Police Tourist police 24-hr hotline T1155, 4 Rachadamnoen Nol Av, Dusit. **Post** Central GPO (Praysani Klang): 1160 Charoen Krung, opposite Ramada Hotel. Mon-Fri 0800-2000, Sat, Sun and holidays 0800-1300.

Kanchanaburi and the west

The wonderful forests, hills and melange of different peoples of this western tract of Thailand are overshadowed by a terrible history – during the Second World War thousands of prisoners of war and local labourers died at the hands of their Japanese captors building a railway line through almost impassable terrain. This piece of history was made famous in David Lean's 1957 Oscar-winning epic, The Bridge on the River Kwai. Today, the bridge, sited at the town of Kanchanaburi, and the war museums and memorials associated with it, has helped turn the region into a tourist mecca. Most come not only to visit the famous bridge but also to relax by Kanchanaburi's elegant Kwai Noi River.

Venture north towards the Burmese border and you'll reach the evocatively named Three Pagodas Pass (Saam Ong), lakeside Sangkhlaburi and an ethnically diverse area of Karen, Mon, Burmese, Indian and Chinese. » *For listings, see pages 822-825.*

Kanchanaburi ⊙⊙⊙⊙⊙⊙⊙⊙ » *pp822-825. Colour map 3, C3.*

Famous for *The* Bridge on the River Kwai, Kanchanaburi is surrounded by a vast area of great natural beauty making it a good base to visit national parks, sail down the Kwai River or travel to one of a number of waterfalls and caves. Over the years, with the languid river providing a charming backdrop, the town has become one of Thailand's biggest tourist destinations for foreigners and Thais alike. The main run of Kanchanaburi's backpacker hang-outs, internet cafés and insipid food available along Mae Nam Kwai Road is reminiscent of Khao San in Bangkok – there's very little local flavour left here. Head out of the backpacker ghetto and large parts of the rest of the town are filled with markets, shophouses and memorials to the dead of the Second World War. It was from here that the Japanese set Allied prisoners of war to work on the construction of the notorious 'death railway', linking Thailand with Burma during the Second World War (see box, page 818). Transport links are good with regular connections by train and bus to Bangkok. The journey from Bangkok takes around 2½ hours by train while any of the numerous buses take two hours. Unfortunately, there are no direct bus connections with Ayutthaya – you can get there by connecting with a slow local service at Suphanburi. This is something local tour operators in Kanchanaburi have taken advantage of, cramming rickety minibuses with backpackers willing to pay inflated prices; you're better advised to travel via Bangkok. Bicycles, motorbikes and jeeps can all be hired in Kanchanaburi and offer the most flexible way to explore the surrounding countryside. Alternatively, tuk-tuks provide short-distance trips around town while rafts and long-tailed boats are available for charter on the river.

To get to the **TAT office** ① *Saengchuto Rd, T034-511200*, walk south, towards Bangkok, from the market and bus station. Most tour operators offer similar excursions: jungle trekking, elephant rides, bamboo rafting, visits to Hellfire Pass and various waterfalls. In Bangkok, virtually every hotel or tour office will be able to offer a day tour (or longer) to Kanchanaburi and surrounding sights.

Kanchanaburi was established in the 1830s, although the ruins of Muang Singh (see page 820) to the west date from the Khmer period. On entering the town (called Muang Kan by most locals), visitors may notice the fish-shaped street signs. Many of the sights in Kanchanaburi are linked to the Second World War, not least the **JEATH War Museum** ① *Wisuttharangsi Rd, by the river, daily 0830-1800, ฿30 (no photographs)*, whose name denotes the countries involved – Japan, England, America, Australia, Thailand and Holland. The museum, which holds an interesting and harrowing display of prisoners working

Kanchanaburi

To Bridge over the River Kwai, Muang Singh Historical
Park, Sai Yok National Park, Sangkhlaburi & Saam Ong

To Death Railway & Hellfire Pass

Sleeping
Apple's Guesthouse 1
Chitanun 4
Inchantree 2
Morning Guesthouse 6
Ploy River Kwai Resort 7
Rainbow Lodge 10
River Kwai Bridge Resort 5
Tamarind 3
VL 19

To ① ⑤ ⑦ &
Bridge (1km)

Saengchuto Rd

Mae Nam Kwai Rd

Rt 323

Water Tower

War Cemetery

So Rong Heeb Oi Rd

Ban Nue Rd

Kwai Yai River

Motorbike Hire

Thetsaban Bamrung Rd

Kratai Thong Rd

Saengchuto Rd

Night Foodstalls

Uthong Rd

To Suphanburi

To Erawan
& Bo Phloi

Bovon Rd

Bus Station

Baak Phraek Rd

Restaurant & Night Foodstalls

Song Kwai Rd

Prasit Rd

Khumuang Rd

Lak Muang Rd

Motorbike Taxis

A/C Bus Stop

Lak Muang

Governor's House

Town Gate

Kamphaeng Muang Rd

Rt 323

To Post Office & Bangkok

JEATH War Museum

Wisuttharangsi Rd

Mae Klong River

Chungkai War Cemetery

Kwai Noi River

Chukkadon Pier

To Wat Tham Kao Poon

200 metres
200 yards

N

The Death Railway

The River Kwai will be forever associated with a small bridge and a bloody railway.

For the Japanese high command during the Second World War, the logic of building a rail link between Siam and Burma was clear – it would cut almost 2000 km off the sea journey from Japan to Rangoon making it easier to supply their fast-expanding empire. The problem was that the Japanese lacked the labour to construct the line through some of the wettest and most inhospitable land in the region. They estimated that it would take five to six years to finish. The solution to their dilemma was simple: employ some of the 300,000 POWs who were being unproductively incarcerated in Singapore.

Work began in June 1942. More than 3,000,000 cu m of rock were shifted, 15 km of bridges built and 415 km of track laid. The workforce, at its peak, numbered 61,000 Allied POWs and an estimated 250,000 Asians. Work was hard: "We started work the day after we arrived, carrying huge baulks of timber. It was the heaviest work I have ever known; the Japs drove us on and by nightfall I was so tired and sore that I could not eat my dinner and just crawled on to the bed and fell asleep. The next day was spent carrying stretchers of earth, also heavy work and incredibly monotonous. The hours were 0830 to 1930 with an hour for lunch."

The Japanese, but particularly the Korean overseers, adopted a harsh code of discipline – face slapping, blows with rifle butts, standing erect for hours on end, and solitary confinement for weeks in small mud and bamboo cells. By 1943, after years of torturous work combined with poor diet, most of the men were in an appalling state.

on the railway, was established in 1977 by the monks of Wat Chanasongkhram. The *Kanchanaburi War Cemetery (Don Rak) i Saengchuto Rd, 1.5 km out of town, daily 0800-1700 (or you can always look over the gates), is immaculately maintained by the Commonwealth Cemeteries Commission. Some 6982 Allied servicemen are buried here, most of whom died as prisoners of war whilst they built the Burma railway. To get there, walk, hire a bicycle (฿20 a day) or take a saamlor. Situated 2 km south of town, the Chungkai (UK) War Cemetery is small, peaceful and well kept, with the graves of 1750 prisoners of war. To get there, take a boat from in front of the town gates, or go by tuk-tuk or bicycle.*

Around Kanchanaburi ▲▶ *pp822-825.*

Bridge over the River Kwai

Situated 3-4 km north of the town just off Saengchuto Road, the Bridge over the River Kwai (pronounced 'kway' in Thai) is architecturally unexciting and is of purely historical interest. To reach here take a tuk-tuk, hire a bicycle, catch a songthaew or board the train, which travels from the town's station to the bridge. The central span was destroyed by Allied bombing towards the end of the war, and has been rebuilt in a different style. Visitors can walk over the bridge, visit the **Second World War Museum and Art Gallery** ① *daily 0900-1630, ฿30*, or browse in the many souvenir stalls. The museum is an odd affair with displays relating to the bridge and the prisoners of war who worked and died here, along with a collection of Thai weaponry and amulets, and some astonishingly bad portraits of Thai kings.

In Colonel Toosey's report of October 1945, he wrote: "On one occasion a party of 60, mostly stretcher cases, were dumped off a train in a paddy field some two miles from the Camp in the pouring rain at 0300 hours. As a typical example I can remember one man who was so thin that he could be lifted easily in one arm. His hair was growing down his back and was full of maggots; his clothing consisted of a ragged pair of shorts soaked with dysentery excreta; he was lousy and covered with flies all the time. He was so weak that he was unable to lift his head to brush away the flies which were clustered on his eyes and on the sore places of his body. I forced the Japanese Staff to come and look at these parties, which could be smelt for some hundreds of yards, but with the exception of the Camp Comdt they showed no signs of sympathy, and sometimes merely laughed."

(Quoted in Peter Davies, *The Man behind the Bridge*, 1991:116).

The railway was finished in late 1943, the line from Nong Pladuk being linked with that from Burma on 17 October. For the POWs it was not the end, however; even after the Japanese capitulated on 10 August 1945, the men had to wait for some while before they were liberated. During this period of limbo, Allied officers were worried most about venereal disease, and Colonel Toosey radioed to Delhi for 10,000 condoms to be dropped by air – an incredible thought given the physical condition of the former POWs. In all, 16,000 Allied prioners lost their lives and Kanchanaburi contains the graves of 7000 of the victims in two war cemeteries. Less well known are the 75,000 Asian forced labourers who also died constructing the railway. Their sufferings are not celebrated.

Death Railway and Hellfire Pass

① *No admission fee, but donations are requested (most visitors leave ฿100); 2 trains leave Kanchanaburi daily at 1045 and 1637, with return trains at 0525 and 1300, approximately 2 hrs. From the Nam Tok station, it is another 14 km to the Hellfire Pass and Museum, for which you need a songthaew (฿400 return, 20 mins one way).*

Only 130 km of the Death Railway remain, passing through what is known as Hellfire Pass to reach the small town of Nam Tok. From Kanchanaburi to Nam Tok the railway sweeps through a tranche of dramatic scenery stopping at the ancient Khmer site of Muang Singh en route (see below). The name of the pass was bestowed by one of the prisoners of war who, looking down on his comrades working below at night by the glow of numerous open fires, remarked that the sight was like 'the jaws of hell'. Australian Rod Beattie, with the support of the Australian government, has developed the pass as a memorial, cutting a path through to the pass and building a museum. Clear, well-written wall panels surrounded by photographs, along with some reproduction objects, provide a very moving account of the cutting of the pass.

Wat Tham Kao Poon

A few kilometres west of town is Wat Tham Kao Poon – hire a bicycle or tuk-tuk to get here. This is a rather gaudy temple with caves attached. Follow the arrows through the cave system where you'll find a large Buddha image at the bottom, as well as *kutis* (cells) in which monks can meditate. Intrepid explorers will find they emerge at the back of the hill. Early in 1996 this cave wat was the site of the murder of British tourist, Johanne Masheder (the cave where the murder took place is permanently closed), by a drug-addicted Thai monk.

Muang Singh Historical Park → *Colour map 3, C2.*

ⓘ *Daily 0800-1700, ฿4. Take the train to Thakilen station from where it is about a 1.5-km walk.*

The Khmer ruins found 45 km west of Kanchanaburi at Muang Singh Historical Park is an ancient Khmer town, situated on the banks of the Kwai Noi River. Built of deep red laterite, Muang Singh reached its apogee during the 12th-13th centuries when it flourished as a trading post linking Siam with the Indian Ocean. The city represents an artistic and strategic outlier of the great Cambodian Empire, and it is mentioned in inscriptions from the reign of the Khmer King Jayavarman VII.

Erawan National Park → *Colour map 3, C2.*

ⓘ *Open 0600-1800, ฿400 entrance fee to the park, regular buses depart every 50 mins from 0800 onwards from Kanchanaburi (1½-2 hrs, a26). The last bus back to Kanchanaburi leaves Erawan at 1600. There are also plenty of places to eat Thai food next to the bus stop.*

One of the most famous parks in Thailand, the Erawan National Park is home to a series of waterfalls, caves and wildlife sanctuaries. The best time to visit the falls is during the rainy season. It is a 35-minute walk from the bus station to the first of the seven falls.

Without doubt this is an area of great natural beauty, situated 65 km north of Kanchanaburi, covering 550 sq km and containing the impressive Erawan Falls. Split into seven levels, the first is popular with swimmers and picnickers. Level three is very beautiful, and level seven is well worth the steep climb with refreshing pools awaiting any intrepid trekker who makes the precarious climb up. The impressive **Phrathat Caves**, with huge and stupendous stalactites and stalagmites, are located about 10 km northwest of headquarters, a good hike or easy drive. Arguably the most striking waterfalls are those at **Huay Khamin**, some 108 km northwest of town. The falls are awkward to reach independently but tour companies will provide arranged trips. The **Thung Yai** and **Huai Kha Khaeng wildlife sanctuaries**, where the falls are based, were once threatened by a proposed dam that would have destroyed rare stands of riverine tropical forest that exist here. Public pressure ensured that the plans were shelved.

◗ *If you want to make like the locals it is considered the done thing to combine Isaan food, such as* som tam *(spicy papaya salad),* kai yang *(grilled chicken)* khao niaow *(sticky rice) with* nam tok *(waterfall).*

Sangkhlaburi and Saam Ong (Three Pagodas Pass) ●❼▲●❶
↠ *pp822-825. Colour map 3, B1/2.*

The route to Sangkhlaburi, or 'Sangkhla', and Saam Ong (Three Pagodas Pass) from Kanchanaburi, a total of some 240 km, follows the valley of the Kwai. The scenery soon becomes increasingly rugged with the road passing through remnant forests and expanses of deep red tropical soils before beginning to wind through a series of steep hills. Just before Sangkhlaburi the road skirts the reservoir; a strange landscape of submerged (now dead) trees and what appear to be raft-houses. This upland area is also home to several different ethnic groups: Karen, Mon and Burmese. Numerous buses and minibuses ply this route from Kanchanaburi to Sangkhlaburi – you'll have to change to a songthaew in the latter to reach Saam Ong.

Visitors to Sangkhlaburi will be greeted by a massive gold-painted reclining Buddha followed by a collection of other enormous golden Buddha statues. This ostentatious display reveals little of the lethargic town down below. Situated on the edge of the huge Khan Laem Reservoir, which was created in 1983 with the damming of three rivers,

Sangkhlaburi is a great place to while away the hours in peaceful surroundings. The town is also a centre for wood and drugs smuggling. There's a remarkably diverse population of Karen, Mon, Burmese, Indians and Chinese. The morning market here provides a range of textiles and various Burmese goods. A 400-m wooden bridge across the lake, leads to an atmospheric Mon village (Waeng Kha).There are also stunning views of the surrounding hills from the bridge. The 8000 inhabitants are mainly displaced Burmese who cannot get a Thai passport and can only work around Sangkhla. From 1948 onwards refugees have fled Burma for the relative safety of Thailand. Most of them will never be allowed a visa or resident's permit. In 1983 the old town of Sangkhlaburi was flooded by the dam and these refugees were again left with no homes or land. The abbot of the flooded Wat Sam Prasop, the spires of which can be seen – so it is said – protruding above the lake waters during the dry season, was able to acquire land for a new wat and helped 500 households to re-establish themselves. These people are not wanted by the Thai government and there have been several raids by the army to round up Mon people without identity cards. Over the years they have been protected by the monks living here, but there is no guarantee this will continue and their existence in Thailand is uncertain to say the least.

Saam Ong (Three Pagodas Pass)

There's a distinct finality in reaching Saam Ong, pressed up tight to the Burmese border. But this is an unexciting spot with a tacky market in a makeshift shelter, which sells a few Burmese goods (teak, umghi, seed pearls) and a lot of Chinese imports (the 'gems' here will be fake). The pagodas, wrapped in red, saffron and white cloth, are tiny and truly unremarkable. This was the traditional invasion route for Burmese soldiers during the Ayutthayan period and even today the border between Burma and Thailand (open 0600-1800), is periodically closed due to political conflict. It is therefore well worth checking the situation at the border before arrival. From here visitors can pay a US$10 immigration fee to enter Burma and the village of **Payathonzu** (meaning Three Pagodas), although you won't get a Thai entry or exit stamp. Motorbike taxis can transport you to the market area of Payathonzu (฿25 from the songthaew drop-off point), which is more market than village. On the border lie the remains of the Burmese/Thai/Japanese railway. The market here is marginally more interesting than at Saam Ong, with a range of handicrafts, jewellery, jade, amulets, Burmese blankets, and an alarming amount of teak furniture. There is also a handful of Thai restaurants and noodle stalls and an Indian-run bakery.

Beyond the village, there is another border post, beyond which visitors are forbidden to go. Note that it is illegal to cross the border anywhere other than at a checkpoint. Similarly, do not go beyond Payathonzu without permission of the Burmese army.

Control of this area has vacillated between the Burmese army and Mon and Karen rebels. At present it is firmly in the hands of the Burmese authorities. If you're undecided about visiting Burma due to its human rights' record then check the facts on Amnesty International's website (www.amnesty.org).

*For Sleeping and Eating price codes,
see inside the front cover.*

● Sleeping

Kanchanaburi *p816, map p817*

B-C River Kwai Bridge Resort, River Kwai Rd, T034-514522, www.riverkwaibridge resort.com. Well-appointed bungalows and rooms all with hot water, a/c, TV, located in fine gardens beside the river in a quiet part of town near the bridge. A good choice.

D Inchantree, T034-624914, www.inchan treeresort.com. Tucked away in a tiny back road just past the River Kwai Bridge, this is a serene place with sleek, well-designed, contemporary Thai-style rooms. There's a natural swimming pool, nice terrace with views over to the bridge and a good restaurant. All rooms have a/c, TV and huge beds – a bargain for the rate. Highly recommended.

D-E Ploy River Kwai Resort, Mae Nam Kwai Rd, T034-515804, www.ploygh.com. Nice, contemporary-design guesthouse in good central location next to the river. Rooms have outdoor showers. Friendly. Excellent value and comes complete with soothing terrace. Free bus/train station pick-up. Recommended.

D-E Rainbow Lodge, 48/5 Soi Rong Heeb Oil, T034-518683, www.seethailand.com. Friendly place with good, split-level mini bungalows and large a/c VIP rooms, all en suite. Good river views and best of the bunch in this part of town. Recommended.

D-F Chitanun Guesthouse, 47/3 Mae Nam Kwai Rd, T034-624785. Great little guesthouse on the opposite side of Mae Nam Rd from the river. Without a riverside location you get more for your baht and the well-designed and managed rooms offering a mix of fan and a/c and hot/cold water are good value. Friendly, quiet and nice gardens. They will also soon be opening the **Chitanun Mansion** on the main Bangkok road. Recommended.

D-G Tamarind Guesthouse, 29/1 Mae Nam Kwai Rd, T034-518790. Probably the best value on the riverfront – you can get a spotless a/c river-view room with balcony for under ฿500 here. There's plenty of terraces and other spaces to lose yourself in and a decent little bar. Owners are friendly and reasonably professional. They also have raft rooms. Recommended.

E-F Apple's Guesthouse, 293 Mae Nam Kwai Rd, T034-512017, www.applenoi-kancha nauri.com. An extremely good guesthouse, with very clean, comfortable mattresses and private showers, run by a very friendly female couple. This is one of the few locally owned businesses on this stretch and the owners also speak excellent English. The very good restaurant (see Eating, below) serves up awesome Thai food. Also offer free pick-up from bus/train station. Some of the touts might tell you it is closed – ignore them. Recommended.

E-G Morning Guesthouse, 337 Mae Nam Kwai Rd, T081-634 3507 (mob). Run by a very friendly woman, Dao, this collection of self-made bungalows down the end of a remote soi, has a vibe all of its own. Rooms have the usual mixed facilities but have enough pretty details to make them feel more homely.

F VL, 18/11 Saengchuto Rd, T034-513546. Some a/c, small restaurant, 3-storey block. Quiet, cool, spacious and secluded rooms (with bathrooms) set back from the busy road. Tasteful decor and breakfast is served in an attractive shady area.

Sangkhlaburi *p820*

B-D Pornpailin Riverside, T034-595322, www.ppailin.com. Nice location, friendly staff. Mostly geared to Thai weekenders. The cheaper rooms are a bit dark while the more expensive ones are huge airy affairs with large balconies overlooking the lake. Restaurant.

E-G Burmese Inn, 52/3 Tambon Nong Loo, T034-595146, www.sangkhlaburi.com. The cheaper rooms are very basic, the more expensive are en suite and a/c. Decent restaurant and friendly atmosphere. Boat and motorbikes available for hire. Tours can also be booked from here.

E-G P Guesthouse, 81/1 Tambon Nong Loo, T034-595061, www.pguesthouse.com. Little stone bungalows with an attractive position overlooking the lake. Good restaurant (with honesty system). It's well set up for travellers, helpful owner will organize tours and trekking (see Tour operators, below). They also rent canoes (฿100 per hr). Recommended.

Saam Ong (Three Pagodas Pass) p821

D-F Three Pagodas Resort, 1.5 km before pass on right-hand side, T034-590098. Reasonably attractive wooden bungalows in a peaceful setting, with restaurant.

🍴 Eating

Kanchanaburi p816, map p817

🍴 **The Brew House**, outstanding value for money. Tasty Thai food and cheap beer served at this friendly wood-and-thatch open-air establishment.

🍴 **Jolly Frogs Restaurant**, 28 Mae Nam Kwai Rd. A wide range of Western and Thai grub with plenty of tourist information plastered on the walls.

🍴 **Krathom Thais Restaurant**, 293 Mai Nam Kwai Rd, **Apple's Guesthouse**. Excellent Thai food – the banana flower fritters and grilled pork salad are delicious. Very friendly English-speaking staff. They also run a very good cookery school and cater for vegetarians. The owners have plans to open a restaurant on the other side of the river a couple of miles upstream. Highly recommended.

🍴 **Prasopsuk Restaurant**, 677 Saengchuto Rd. A large, clean restaurant serving a wide range of dishes. Good cheap Thai food. Attached to the hotel of the same name. Recommended.

🍴 **Sugar Canes Restaurant**, 22 Soi Pakistan, Mae Nam Kwai Rd. Although the menu is limited, this restaurant has a beautiful view of the river.

Numerous stalls set up along the river in the afternoon and evening – the best spot is by Song Kwai Rd – and there is also an excellent night market with a wide range of food available in the vicinity of the bus station. Recommended.

Sangkhlaburi p820

There are many inexpensive restaurants around the Central Market, some serving good Burmese food. In the high season (Nov-Feb) there are also a few places open along Tambon Nong Loo serving up some Western and Thai food.

🍴 **Baan Unrak**, Tambon Nong Loo. This small coffee shop, open all year, serves vegetarian food, fresh coffee and a variety of freshly baked cakes and cookies. It is mostly staffed by Burmese refugees and is a sustainable project run by a nearby orphanage. Recommended.

🍸 Bars and clubs

Kanchanaburi p816, map p817

4Nines, Saengchuto Rd, opposite **River Kwai Hotel**. Open 1600-2400. This small bar is good for British meat pies, whisky and rock 'n' roll, though it can be a little bit seedy.

Brew House, Mae Nam Kwai Rd (Soi India Corner, near the King Naresuan statue), good-value beer in a place run by a UK-educated Thai.

RK Cowboy Bar, just in front of the **River Kwai Hotel**. Hosts live Thai music, serves up beer by the gallon and barbequed meat by the plateful.

Resort Bar, Mae Nam Kwai Rd, just along from the main run of guesthouses. Great place to relax. Set in a huge, old villa and gardens you'll find cheesy live music, good snacks and a big range of drinks. Popular with stylish, younger Thais, this place has a cool, lounge vibe. Recommended. Open 1100-0100.

✷ Festivals and events

Kanchanaburi *p816, map p817*
Nov/Dec River Kwai Bridge Week
(movable). The festival starts with an evening
ceremony conducted by dozens of monks
followed by a procession from the city Pillar
Shrine to the bridge. There's also a very
realistic re-enactment of the destruction of
bridge by the Allies in 1945. Other events
include longboat races, exhibitions, steam
train rides and cultural shows.

✪ Shopping

Kanchanaburi *p816, map p817*
Baak Phraek Rd is a pleasant shopping street.
Blue sapphires, onyx and topaz are all mined
at Bo Phloi, 50 km from Kanchanaburi. Good
prices for them at shops near the bridge or
in the market area of town.

▲ Activities and tours

Around Kanchanaburi *p816, map p817*
Tours and tour operators
AS Mixed Travel, T034-514958, www.apple
noi-kanchanaburi.com. Run by the same
people who own **Apple's Guesthouse**, they
offer a variety of great little tours, some trekking
trips, flight reservations, bus and train tickets.
Complete one-stop shop. Recommended.
Good Times Travel Service, T034-624441,
good_times_travel@hotmail.com, is also
recommended.
State Railways of Thailand offers an all-day
tour from Bangkok to Kanchanaburi on
weekends and holidays leaving Thonburi
station at 0615, stopping at Nakhon Pathom,
the River Kwai Bridge, arriving at Nam Tok at
1130. A minibus connects Khao Pang/Sai Yok
Noi waterfall and the train leaves Nam Tok at
1430, arriving in Kanchanaburi at 1605 for a
brief stop, and finally Bangkok at 1930. State
Railways also offers other tours, with overnight stays, rafting and fishing. Contact the

Railway Advance Book Office, Hualamphong Station in Bangkok, T02-225 6964,
or **Kanchanaburi Train Station**, T034-
511285. Advance booking recommended.

Sangkhlaburi *p820*
Tour operators
P Guesthouse and **Burmese Inn** both
organize trips around Sangkhlaburi. They
include visits to Karen village by boat, a
2-hr elephant ride through the jungle,
swimming and bamboo whitewater rafting.

✇ Transport

Kanchanaburi *p816, map p817*
Bicycle
A good way to get around town and out to
the bridge. Reliable bikes at ฿30-40 per day
can be hired from **Green Bamboo** on the
Mae Nam Kwai Rd, or ask at guesthouses.

Boat
Noisy, long-tailed boats roar up and down
the river; tickets available at guesthouses.
A more peaceful option is to hire canoes.
Safarino, on the Mae Nam Kwai Rd, hires
out canoes for ฿280 per 3 hrs.

Bus
Beware of overpriced songthaews from the
bus station to guesthouse area (should cost
฿60). Non-a/c buses leave from the station in
the market area, behind Saengchuto Rd. A/c
buses leave from the corner of Saengchuto Rd,
opposite Lak Muang Rd. Regular connections
with **Bangkok**'s Southern bus terminal (a/c
bus No 81), 2 hrs, or non-a/c bus, 3-4 hrs. Also
connections with **Nakhon Pathom** (1½ hrs,
฿15) from where there are buses to the floating
market at Damnoen Saduak (see page 802).

Motorbike and scooter
Yankee, Mae Nam Kwai Rd, hires out motorbikes and scooters from ฿150 per day. As
well as the usual 125cc step-throughs they
also have 200cc chopper-style Phantoms.

Train

The station is 2 km northwest of town on Saengchuto Rd, not far from the cemetery, T034-511285. Regular connections with **Nakhon Pathom** and on to Hualampong Station. Weekends and holidays, special service (see Tours and tour operators, above). It is possible to take a local train between Kanchanaburi and **Nam Tok**, getting off along the way. There is a left-luggage office at the station.

Sangkhlaburi *p820*
Bus

Regular connections on non-a/c bus with **Kanchanaburi** (5-6 hrs, ฿90). A/c minibuses run 3 times a day (3½ hrs, ฿130).

Motorbike and scooter

Baan Unrak (see Eating, above) and **P Guesthouse** can help arrange motorbike hire – from ฿250 per day.

Saam Ong (Three Pagodas Pass) *p821*
Songthaew

Songthaews leave every 40 mins from the bus station in Sangkhlaburi, 30 mins (฿30). The last one back to Sangkhlaburi leaves at about 1630; check on arrival.

❶ Directory

Kanchanaburi *p816, map p817*

Banks There are a number near the bus station, most with ATMs. **Bangkok**, 2 Uthong Rd. **Thai Farmers**, 160/80-2 Saengchuto Rd. **Thai Military**, 160/34 Saengchuto Rd. **Internet** There are several along Mae Nam Kwai Rd. **Medical services** Hospital Saengchuto Rd, close to Saengchuto Soi 20. **Laundry** A few of these line Mae Nam Kwai Rd – expect to pay ฿15-20 a kilo. **Police** Corner of Saengchuto and Lak Muang roads. **Post office** Corner of Lak Muang Rd and Baak Phraek Rd (not far from Sathani Rot Fai Rd) – some distance out of town towards Bangkok.

Sangkhlaburi *p820*

Banks Siam Commercial Bank offers exchange services but no ATM. **Internet** Baan Unrak (see Eating, above) run adjoining internet café. **Medical services** Hospital and malaria centre in town. **Post office** Opposite 7-Eleven store.

Central Thailand

For many people the flat open plain that protrudes 400 km north of Bangkok is the cradle of Thai civilization. From here, centred on the ancient capital of Ayutthaya, sprang the once great Siamese empire that so enthralled visitors and historians. Further north, and pre-dating Ayutthaya, sits a remarkable cluster of citadels and ruins. The fulcrum of these antiquities are the remains of the proud city of Sukhothai – itself once an important capital of a dynamic empire. The nearby town of Phitsanalok is still home to one of Thailand's most important and engaging temples – Wat Phra Sri Ratana Mahathat, the 'Big Temple'. Heading west from here takes you to the hills and forests of Mae Sot and Umphang in the heart of Thailand's remote Burmese border regions. ▸▸ *For listings, see pages 837-843.*

Ayutthaya

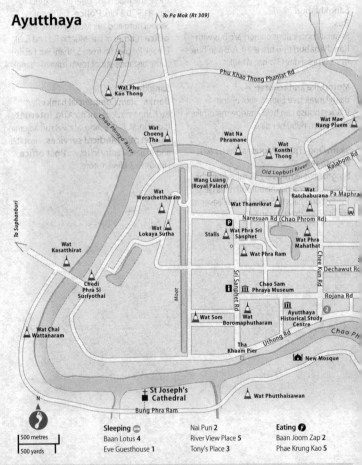

To Pa Mok (Rt 309)

Phu Khao Thong Phanlat Rd

Wat Phu Kao Thong

Chao Phraya River

Wat Choeng Tha

Wat Na Phramane

Wat Mae Nang Pluem

Old Lopburi River

Kalahom Rd

Wang Luang (Royal Palace)

Wat Worachettharam

Wat Thamrikrat

Wat Konthi Thong

Wat Ratchaburana

Pa Maphra

Naresuan Rd (Chao Phrom Rd)

Wat Lokaya Sutha

Stalls

Wat Phra Sri Sanphet

Wat Phra Mahathat

Wat Phra Ram

Chee Kun Rd

Dechawut Rd

To Suphanburi

Wat Kasatthirat

Chedi Phra Si Suriyothai

Moat

Sri Sanphet Rd

Chao Sam Phraya Museum

Rojana Rd

Wat Som

Wat Boromaphutharam

Ayutthaya Historical Study Centre

Chao Ph

Tha Khaam Pier

Uthong Rd

Wat Chai Wattanaram

New Mosque

St Joseph's Cathedral

Bung Phra Ram

Wat Phutthaisawan

N

500 metres
500 yards

Sleeping 🛏
Baan Lotus 4
Eve Guesthouse 1

Nai Pun 2
River View Place 5
Tony's Place 3

Eating 🍴
Baan Joom Zap 2
Phae Krung Kao 5

Ayutthaya ⊖🏧🏪🌺🏛🍴 ⇢ pp 837-843. Colour map 3, C4.

The venerable capital of the Kingdom of Siam, Ayutthaya, had a population of 150,000 during its heyday and was at the epicentre of an empire that controlled more than 500,000 sq km. These days a large portion of the city is a bustling modern Thai conurbation with little to remind the visitor of its halcyon days. Yet, if you head west into the old city of Ayutthaya, it opens up into a series of broad open spaces, littered with atmospheric ruins. Arrive when the setting sun illuminates the deep red-brick ruins and it is not hard to imagine the grandeur of this place that so amazed early European visitors. Here is a stunning complex of palaces, shrines, monasteries and chedis.

Elephant Kraal ⬛
Lopburi River
Pasak River
Night Market Ⓜ
Ⓜ Pier
Chandra assem Palace ✉
Chao Phrom Market 🏛
Wat Pradu Songtham ⛩
Wat Kuti Tao ⛩
Wat Samanakot ⛩
To Wat Maheyong ➡
To Wat Ayutthaya
Pasak River
Uthong Rd
Markin Rd
Rojana Rd
Pridi Damrong Bridge
To Uthong & Bangkok (Rt 309)
RT 309
Wat Suwan Dararam 🏛
Phom Phet Fortress 🏛
Wat Phanan Choeng 🏛
Wat Yai Chai Mongkol ⛩
To Bang Pa-In

Tea & Coffee House 1

Bars & clubs 🎵
Jazz Bar 4
WoGun-T 3

Ins and outs

Most people get here by bus from Bangkok's Northern bus terminal – an easy 1½-hour ride – or by train (1½ hours). Another option is to arrive by boat – three hours from Tha Tien pier in Bangkok. The wats are spread over a considerable area; the town is flat so bicycles are a good option. Long-tailed boats also transport people around the perimeter of the town. There is a **TAT office** ① *Si Sanphet Rd, next to Chao Sam Phraya Museum (temporary office), T035-246076*. For those with an interest in ruins or Thai history, there is more than enough here to occupy a couple of days.

Background

"In 712, a Year of the Tiger, second of the decade, on Friday, the sixth day of the waxing moon of the fifth month, at three nalika and nine bat after the break of dawn, the capital city of Ayutthaya was first established." In translation this is widely accepted to mean Friday 4 March 1351, at about 0900. Ayutthaya's name derives from 'Ayodhya', the sacred town in the Indian epic, the *Ramayana*. It became one of the most prosperous kingdoms in the Southeast Asian region, which stretched from Angkor (Cambodia) in the east, to Pegu (Burma) in the west. The city is situated on an island at the confluence of three rivers: the Chao Phraya, Pasak and Lopburi. Ayutthaya's strong defensive position proved to be valuable as it was attacked by the Burmese on no less than 24 occasions. In the 16th century, the Burmese briefly managed to seize and occupy Ayutthaya, but it wasn't long before the hero-king, Naresuan (1590-1605), recaptured the city and led his country back to independence. Under King Narai (1656-1688), Ayutthaya became a rich, cosmopolitan trading post. Merchants came to the city from Portugal, Spain, Holland, China, Arabia, Persia, Malaya, India and Japan. The city was strongly fortified, with ramparts 20 m high and 5 m thick, and was protected on all sides by waterways. In 1767 the kingdom was again invaded, by the Burmese, who, at the 24th attempt, were finally successful in vanquishing the defenders. The city was sacked and its defences destroyed, but, unable to consolidate their position, the Burmese left for home, reducing the city to ruins. The population was reduced from one million to 10,000 and Ayutthaya never recovered from this final attack.

Sights

① *It's possible to visit many of the abandoned but now restored temples; almost all are open from 0800-1700 with an entry fee of ฿30-50.*

In the town centre, **Wat Ratchaburana** ① *Naresuan Rd*, was built by King Boromraja II in 1424 on the cremation site of his two brothers (princes Ai and Yo), who were killed while contesting the throne. Some of the most important treasures found in Ayutthaya were discovered here: bronze Buddha images, precious stones and golden royal regalia.

Across from Wat Ratchaburana sits the Monastery of the Great Relic, **Wat Phra Mahathat**. It was founded in 1384, making it one of the oldest in the city. The largest of all Ayutthaya's monasteries, it was built to house holy relics of the Buddha. When the Fine Arts Department excavated the site in 1956, it found a number of gold Buddha images as well as relics of the Buddha inside a gold casket, now exhibited in the National Museum, Bangkok.

Further south, the **Ayutthaya Historical Study Centre** ① *Rojana Rd, Wed-Fri 0900-1630, Sat-Sun 0900-1700, ฿100*, recreates Ayutthaya life with some excellent models. The nearby **Chao Sam Phraya Museum** ① *Wed-Sun 0900-1200, 1300-1600 (except public holidays) ฿30*, is home to many of Ayutthaya's relics, in particular the Mongkol Buddha.

Wat Phra Sri Sanphet was sited within the extensive grounds of Wang Luang (the Royal Palace) and is the equivalent of Wat Phra Kaeo in Bangkok. Three restored Ceylonese-style chedis dominate the compound. They contain the ashes of King Boromtrailokant (1448-1488) and his two sons (who were also kings of Ayutthaya). There are no prangs here; the three central chedis are surrounded by alternate smaller chedis and viharns. Remains of walls and leaning pillars give an impression of the vastness of the wat.

Travel back past Wang Luang to the main road, turn east and after 250 m the road crosses the Old Lopburi River. From the bridge you'll see **Wat Na Phramane**, which dates from 1503 and is one of the most complete examples of Ayutthayan architecture. A treaty to end one of the many wars with Burma was signed here in 1549. More than two centuries later, in 1767, the Burmese used the position to attack the city and it is said that the King of Burma suffered a mortal blow from a backfiring cannon. Perhaps because of this, the Burmese – unusually – left the wat intact. It fell into disrepair and was not restored until 1838. The lovely Ayutthayan bot contains an impressive crowned bronze Buddha image.

Southeast of the town is **Wat Yai Chai Mongkol**, or simply Wat Yai (Big Wat), built by King Ramathibodi I in 1357. The imposing 72-m-high chedi was built in the Ceylonese style (now with a rather alarming tilt) to celebrate the victory of King Naresuan over the Prince of Burma in 1592, in single-handed elephant combat. The viharn contains a massive reclining Buddha image that is unusual as its eyes are open.

Northeast of the city, on the banks of the Old Lopburi River, are the only remaining **elephant kraals** in Thailand. The kraals were built in the reign of King Maha Chakrapat in 1580 to capture wild elephants. The kraals are square-shaped enclosures with double walls. The last round-up of wild elephants occurred in May 1903 during King Chulalongkorn's reign. The kraal has been extensively restored and is rather clinical as a result.

The extensive **waterways of Ayutthaya** (more than 50 km of them) are a pleasant way to see some of the less accessible sights. Long-tailed boats can be taken from the landing pier opposite Chandra Kasem Palace, in the northeast corner of the town. During the dry season, it is not possible to circle the entire island; the Old Lopburi River becomes unnavigable. The usual route runs south down the Pasak River and round as far as Wat Chai Wattanaram on the Chao Phraya River.

Lopburi ☺🅐🅑🅒 ➤ pp 837-843. Colour map 3, C4.

Another 50 km north of Ayutthaya is the historical city of Lopburi with its famous palace, museum, monasteries and prangs. The old part of town that houses these sights is also teeming with Lopburi's famous monkeys clambering from one telegraph pole to another, who laze around the temples – particularly Sam Phra Karn – feast on the offerings left by worshippers, and grasp playfully at the hair of unwitting tourists. They have a penchant for stealing sunglasses or spectacles so don't try and feed them as you are likely to provoke a monkey riot. Getting to Lopburi is relatively easy with good bus and train connections to Bangkok, Ayutthaya and towns to the north.

Background

Lopburi has been seemingly caught between competing powers for more than 1000 years. The town became a major centre during the Dvaravati period (sixth-11th century). In AD 950 Lopburi fell to the expanding Khmers who made it a provincial capital. By the 14th century, Khmer influence had waned and the Thais reclaimed Lopburi. However, it fell into obscurity during the 16th century until King Narai (1656-1688) restored the city. With Narai's death in Lopburi, the town entered another period of obscurity but was again restored to glory during Rama IV's reign.

Sights

The **Narai Ratchaniwet Palace** ① Wed-Sun 0830-1200, 1300-1630, ฿30, represents the historical heart of Lopburi, encased by massive walls and bordered to the west by the Lopburi River. King Narai declared Lopburi his second capital in the 17th century and, between 1665 and 1677, built his palace here. The outer courtyard, now in ruins, contained the 'functional' buildings including storage warehouses and stables. In the middle courtyard are various pavilions for hosting visiting dignitaries – one of them has been turned into a Farmer's Museum displaying traditional central plains farming technology. The inner courtyard contains the ruins of King Narai's own residence, the Suttha Sawan Pavilion, where he died on 11 July 1688.

North of Vichayen Road, next to the railway line, is **Wat Phra Prang Sam Yod** (Wat of Three Prangs), a laterite and sandstone Khmer shrine. The temple is also home to a large troupe of cute, vicious monkeys who are best left well alone. It's also here where the locals hold, in late November, an annual feast to honour the monkeys. A giant monkey food-fight is the result – thousands of Thais turn out to watch.

West along Vichayen Road is the Khmer **Prang Khaek**. Built in the late eighth century it was restored in the 17th century, but today lies in ruins.

Further along Vichayen Road are the remains of **Vichayen House** ⓘ ฿30, better known as Constantine Phaulcon's House, after a Greek adventurer and influential adviser to King Narai who was executed by Thai courtiers. The house, European in style, was constructed for Chevalier de Chaumont, the first French ambassador to Thailand who lived here in 1685.

Roughly 24 km south of the old city is **Wat Phra Buddhabat** – catch a Saraburi bus, tell the driver where you want to get off and it's a 1-km walk to the shrine. This wat is founded on the site of the most renowned Buddha footprint in the country. The ornate tile-encrusted mondop, built to cover the footprint, was constructed during Rama I's reign. The footprint itself, which is a natural impression made in the limestone rock (depending on one's beliefs), was first discovered in the reign of King Song Tham (1610-1628).

Sukhothai and around ⊖⊘⊕⊕⊗⊠⊖⊕ ▸▸ pp 837-843. Colour map 3, A3.

The modern conurbation of Sukhothai reveals little of Thailand's ancient capital. Head west about 12 km, keeping an eye on the surrounding landscape, and the ruined brick foundations of ancient religious structures appear in the rice fields, interspersed between wooden shop-houses until the road pierces the ramparts of Old Sukhothai. Officially, the Old City is a national historical park covering 640 ha, which opened in 1988 after a total of 192 wats were restored. The metal lamp posts, concrete-lined ponds and horrible hedgerows of the central area evince overbearing sterility. Head out beyond the city walls and you'll discover dozens of crumbling wats, Buddhas and chedis among the surrounding woodlands.

Ins and outs

You can fly here from Bangkok daily, although most people arrive by bus. There are regular connections with Bangkok as well as other major towns in the north and central plains. There are also two buses a day from Bangkok's northern Mo Chit bus terminal direct to Old Sukhothai. Most people come to Sukhothai to see the ruins of the former capital. Regular buses (every 10 minutes) and songthaews ply the route between old and new cities and it is also easy to hire a motorcycle. The ruins themselves are spread over a considerable area – there are plenty of places to rent bicycles in the Old City. If you want to stay amid ancient surroundings there is some excellent accommodation in the Old City but choice is limited. Staying here gives you a chance to explore the atmospheric outer ruins in the fresh early-morning mist. There's more accommodation available in the new town, a pleasant enough spot to stay while exploring the glories of Old Sukhothai.

Background

If you ask a Thai about the history of Sukhothai, he or she will say that King Intradit ('Glorious Sun-King') founded the Sukhothai Kingdom in 1240, after driving off the Khmers following a single-handed elephant duel with the Khmer commander. King Intradit then founded Wat Mahathat, the geographical and symbolic heart of the new kingdom. Revisionist historians and archaeologists reject this view, regarding it as myth-making on a grand scale. Like Angkor Wat in Cambodia, until comparatively recently Sukhothai was a 'lost city in the jungle'. It was only in 1833 that the future King Mongkut discovered the famous Inscription No 1 and not until 1895 that the French scholar Lucien Fournereau published an incomplete description of the site. The key date, though, is 1907 when crown Prince Maha Vajiravudh made an eight-day visit to Sukhothai. It was his account that laid the foundations for the

Sukhothai 'myth': a proud, glorious and civilized past for a country that was on the verge of being submerged by an alien culture. Sukhothai became the first capital of Siam and the following 200 years (until the early 15th century) are considered the pinnacle of Thai civilization. There were nine kings during the Sukhothai Dynasty, the most famous being Ramkhamhaeng, whose reign is believed to have been 1275-1317. He was the first ruler to leave accounts of the state inscribed in stone (now displayed in the National Museum in Bangkok). These provide a wealth of information on conquests, taxation and political philosophy. Ramkhamhaeng created the Thai script, derived om Mon and Khmer, and the Inscription No 1 of 1292 is regarded by many as the first work of Thai literature.

At its peak Ramkhamhaeng's kingdom encompassed much of present-day Thailand, south down the Malay Peninsula and west into Lower Burma, though the northern kingdom of Lanna Thai, Lopburi and the Khorat Plateau were still controlled by the waning Khmer Empire. Ramkhamhaeng was an absolute monarch, but one who governed his people with justice and magnanimity. If anyone wanted to lodge a complaint, he or she would ring a bell at the gate and the king would grant them an audience. King Ramkhamhaeng was responsible for the introduction of Theravada Buddhism, when he brought Ceylonese monks to his kingdom – partly intended to displace the influence of the Khmers. He displayed considerable diplomatic powers and cultivated good relations with his northern neighbours in order to form an alliance against the Khmers.

Sukhothai Old City

To Kilns & Si Satchanalai

Phra Pai Luang

Sri Chum

Pa Mued

Khao Phrabat Noi

Saphan Hin

San Luang Gate

Aranyik

San Luang Gate & Bicycle Hire

Chang Lom

To Sukhothai New City & Phitsanulok

Chang Rob

Charod with thong Rd

Rt 12

Chedi Ngam

Si Thon

Tuk

Oa Gate

Shrine to Saan Bu Phaa Dam

Trapang Thong Lang

Mangkon

Rt 12

Ho Devalai

Pa Mamuang

Main Entrance

Chedi Soong

Phra Yuen

Namo Gate

Khao Phrabat Yai

Khao Luang

Tham Hip

Ton Chan

Higher ground, partially forested

Chetuphon

Chedi Si Hong

Si Pichit Kirati Kalayaram

N

500 metres
500 yards

Sleeping
Old City Guesthouse 1
Orchid Hibiscus 5

Eating
Coffee Cup 1

Old City
Kamphanghek Gate a
Ramkhamhaeng Museum b
Wat Mahathat c
Royal Palace d
San Da Pa Deng e

Wat Trapang Ngoen f
Wat Trapang Thong g
Wat Sra Sri h
King Ramkhamhaeng's statue j
Wat Sri Sawai k

The Sukhothai period saw a flowering not just of ceramic arts, but of art in general. The Buddha images are regarded as the most beautiful and original to have ever been created in Thailand, with the walking Buddha image being the first free-standing Buddha the country produced. King Ramkhamhaeng's son, Lo Thai (1327-1346), was an ineffectual leader, overshadowed even in death by his father, and much of the territory gained by the previous reign was lost. By the sixth reign of the Sukhothai Dynasty, the kingdom was in decline, and by the seventh, Sukhothai paid homage to Ayutthaya. In 1438 Ayutthaya officially incorporated Sukhothai into its realm; the first Thai kingdom had succumbed to its younger and more vigorous neighbour.

Old City

① *The park is open daily 0600-1800. A new entrance has also been created about 250 m from its original location towards Namo Gate. It is divided into 5 zones, each with an admission charge: ฿40 for the central section, and ฿30 for each of the north, south, east and west sections. If you intend to visit all the zones, then it makes sense to purchase the so-called 'Total' ticket which costs ฿150. There are additional charges: ฿50 per car, ฿10 per bike, ฿20 per motorcycle. If you want to explore the outer ruins, such as Wat Chetuphon and Wat Saphan Hin no ticket is needed and entrance is free.*

The Old City is 1800 m long and 1400 m wide and was originally encompassed by triple earthen ramparts and two moats, pierced by four gates. Within the city there are 21 historical sites; outside the walls are another 70 or so places of historical interest. At one time the city may have been home to as many as 300,000 people, with an efficient tunnel system to bring water from the mountains and a network of roads.

Sited just inside the **Kamphanghek Gate (a)** is the **Ramkhamhaeng National Museum** ① *T055-612167, daily 0900-1600, ฿30 or with Total ticket, see above.* The museum contains a copy of some wonderful Buddha images, along with explanatory information. It also houses a range of household goods giving an indication of the sophistication of Sukhothai society.

The centre of the Sukhothai Kingdom was **Wat Mahathat (c)** and the Royal Palace – the earliest example in Thailand. This was both the religious and the political centre of the kingdom and is usually regarded as the first truly 'Sukhothai' monument. It is said to have been rebuilt in the 1340s to house the hair and neckbone relics of the Buddha that had been brought back from Ceylon. Some original Buddha images still sit among the ruins. Particularly unusual are the two monumental standing Buddhas, in an attitude of forgiveness, on either side of the central sanctuary, enclosed by brick walls, with their heads protruding over the top.

Little remains of the original **Royal Palace (d)**. It was here that King Mongkut, while he was still the Crown Prince, found the famous Inscription No 1 of King Ramkhamhaeng, the Manangsilabat stone throne, and the stone inscription of King Lithai in 1833. All three objects – which became talismens for the Thai people – were carted off to Bangkok. To the north of Wat Mahathat is **San Da Pa Deng (e)**, the oldest existing structure from the Sukhothai era. It is a small Khmer laterite prang built during the first half of the 12th century.

Wat Trapang Ngoen (f) – Temple of the Silver Pond – contains a large lotus-bud chedi, similar to that at Wat Mahathat. **Wat Trapang Thong (g)** sits on an island, after which the monastery is named. It is approached along a rickety bridge. Particularly fine are the stucco reliefs that show the Buddha descending from the Tavatimsa Heaven with the attendant Brahma on his left and Indra on his right.

Wat Sra Sri (h), to the north of Wat Trapang Ngoen, is a popular photo-spot, as the bot is reflected in a pond. A Ceylonese-style chedi dominates the complex, which also contains a fine, large, seated Buddha image enclosed by columns. To the east of here is **King Ramkhamhaeng's statue (j)**, seated on a copy of the stone throne (the Phra Thaen Manang Silabat) that was found on the site of the Royal Palace and which is now in the Wat Phra Kaeo Museum in Bangkok.

To the southwest of Wat Mahathat is **Wat Sri Sawai (k)**, enclosed within laterite walls. It was built during the time that Sukhothai was under Khmer domination. The prang is in the three-tower style, with the largest central prang (rather badly restored) being 20 m tall. The stucco decoration was added to the towers in the 15th century, as were their upper brick portions.

Outside the Old City

To get a better idea of what Sukhothai was like before it became a historical park and was cleared of undergrowth, it's worth visiting some of the outlying ruins, some of which still sit in the forest. Try cycling to these wats during the morning when it is cooler as they are far apart. Alternatively, hire a tuk-tuk.

Take the northwest gate out of the city to visit the impressive **Wat Sri Chum**. A large mondop with a narrow vaulted entrance encloses an enormous brick and stucco seated Buddha image. The temple was probably built during the seventh reign of the Sukhothai Kingdom (mid-14th century) and is said to have caused a Burmese army to flee in terror, such is the power of its withering gaze. The large Buddha seems almost suffocated by the surrounding walls, which must have been added at a later stage. There is a stairway in the mondop that leads up to a space behind the head of the image (closed since 1988). The image here is said to have talked on a number of occasions – although the back stairs provide a useful hiding place for someone to play a practical joke.

East of Wat Sri Chum is **Wat Phra Pai Luang**, the Monastery of the Great Wind, interesting for the remains of three laterite prangs. Built during the reign of King Jayavarman VII (a Khmer king who ruled from 1181-1217), it dates from the Khmer period that preceded the rise of Sukhothai. Its Khmer inspiration is evident in the square base and indented tiers. To the east of the prang is a later stupa and a ruined mondop with the remains of large stucco Buddha images. In total, Wat Phra Pai Luang contains over 30 stupas of assorted styles.

Take the northwest road 3 km beyond the city walls where a large, standing Buddha image is located at the top of an ancient staircase. Sited at the top of a hill amid languorous woodlands **Wat Saphan Hin** has one of the most beautiful locations in Sukhothai. Many Thais still come here, offering prayers and incense. It is also a perfect spot to watch a tropical sunrise, though you'll need to get up early if you want to reach here in time.

On the north side of Route 12 is **Wat Mangkon**, the Dragon Monastery. A relatively large complex, the bot, surrounded by large leaf-shaped boundary stones, has an unusual slate-tiled brick base. To the west of the bot is the base of a pavilion or sala, and to the north the remains of a Ceylonese-style bell-shaped phra chedi. **Wat Phra Yuen** is around 200 m from Wat Mangkon and 1500 m from the city walls, just to the south of Route 12. The remains of a bot can be identified by the *bai sema* (boundary stones) that surround it and a mondop houses a large standing Buddha image.

There are also a series of monasteries to the south and east of the city. The most impressive is **Wat Chetuphon**, one of Sukhothai's more important monasteries. Archaeologists and art historians suspect that the monastery was renovated and expanded on a number of occasions, so how much of the structure is Sukhothai, is a source of conjecture.

Si Satchanalai → *Colour map 3, A3.*

ⓘ *Admission ฿40, ฿50 for a car, ฿30 for a motorbike and ฿10 for a bicycle. See Sukhothai Old City, page 832, for details on the 'Total' ticket, which provides entry to Si Sat and Sukhothai.*

About 50 km to the north of Sukhothai, nestling languidly on the west bank of the Yom River, sit the vast ruins of Si Satchanalai. It makes a fascinating side trip from Sukhothai with examples of Ceylonese-style bell-shaped chedis, Khmer prangs and Sukhothai-era buildings. During the fourth reign of Sukhothai, Si Sat became the seat of the king's son and the two cities were linked by a 50-km-long road, the Phra Ruang Highway. Bounded by a moat 10 m wide and by thick town walls, during its heyday it was the equal of Sukhothai in splendour, and probably superior in terms of its defences. Protected by rapids, swamp and mountains, not to mention a triple moat filled with barbed spikes, Si Sat must have seemed immensely daunting to any prospective attacker. There is no modern town here; the whole area has become a 'historical park'. Buses link 'Si Sat' with new Sukhothai while the compact ruins can be toured either on foot or by bicycle. The Si Satchanalai Historical Park Information Centre is just outside Ram Narong Gate, to the southeast. There's not much information here, just a scale model and map of the park and a few books for sale.

Kamphaeng Phet → *Colour map 3, B3.*

ⓘ *The ancient city sites are open daily 0800-1630 – the ticket office is next to Wat Phra Kaeo; ฿40 to visit both the area within the ancient city walls and the forested area to the north, known as Aranyik. It is possible to walk within the city walls, but vehicles are useful for the Aranyik area, for which the following charges are levied: ฿10 for a bike, ฿20 for a motorbike, ฿30 for a tuk-tuk and ฿50 for a car. It's possible to walk around the site though you can charter a tuk-tuk for roughly ฿150 for 1 hr.*

Head 50 km south from Sukhothai and you'll reach Kamphaeng Phet. Here it is possible to wander through the ruined monasteries and forts, many overgrown with verdant trees, without meeting a single person. The town was originally built by King Lithai in the 14th century as a garrison to protect and consolidate the power of the Sukhothai Kingdom (Kampheng Phet translates as 'Diamond Wall'). Modern **Kamphaeng Phet** is sleepy and easygoing with a proportion of its older, wooden, shuttered and tiled buildings still surviving. Buses link Kamphaeng Phet with Bangkok, Sukhothai and destinations north and south. There's a badly run **Tourist Information Office** ⓘ *Kamphaeng Phet Local Handicraft Centre, Thesa Rd (near Soi 13), which should open 0800-2000,* and a **Tourist Information Centre** next to Wat Phra Kaeo.

The massive 6-m-high defensive walls still stand – earthen ramparts topped with laterite – beyond which is a moat to further deter attackers. Within the walls, encompassing an area of 2.5 km by 500 m, lie two old wats, Wat Phra Kaeo and Wat Phrathat, as well as the **Provincial Museum** ⓘ *Wed-Sun 0900-1600, ฿30.* From the museum, walk west to **Wat Phrathat**, the Monastery of the Great Relic. Not much remains except a chedi and a well-weathered seated Buddha (of laterite) sitting in the viharn. Immediately north, **Wat Phra Kaeo** was probably the largest and most important wat in Kamphaeng Phet.

Most of the more interesting ruins lie outside the ramparts, to the north of town. **Wat Phra Non** which, like many of the structures here, dates from the 15th to the 16th century. There are also the remains of monks quarters, wells and washing areas. North from here, there is the slightly better-preserved **Wat Phra Si Iriyaboth**, locally known as Wat Yuen or the Monastery of the Standing Buddha. This wat derives its name from the large Buddha images that were to be found in the mondop. Near to Wat Phra Si Iriyaboth is **Wat Singh** – just behind here is **Wat Chang Rob** (the Shrine of the Elephants), probably the most impressive structure outside the city walls. This consists of a huge Ceylonese-style laterite chedi with its base surrounded by 68 elephants. Only one row of elephants, on the south side, is preserved.

Phitsanulok → *Colour map 3, A3.*

Phitsanulok, attractively positioned on the banks of the River Nan 50 km to the east of Sukhothai, is home to one of the most striking and important Buddhist shrines in Thailand: Wat Phra Sri Ratana Mahathat (Wat Yai). The city was also the birthplace of one of Thailand's great heroes: King Naresuan the Great of Ayutthaya (reigned 1590-1605) and for a short period during the reign of King Boromtrailokant of Ayutthaya (1448-1488), Phitsanulok was actually the capital of Siam. These days this friendly, bustling city is non-descript with most of its old wooden buildings destroyed in a disastrous fire in the 1960s. Phitsanulok is also an important transport hub, linking the central plains with the north and northeast and it is a convenient base from which to visit nearby Sukhothai and Si Satchanalai. The bus terminal is not central, but bus No 10 travels between the local bus station and the terminal every 10 minutes (and takes 30 minutes). The journey from Bangkok takes five to six hours. It is possible to fly, with plenty of daily connections to Bangkok and also with other northern towns.

Phitsanulok is a good walking city with the main site of interest, Wat Yai, being in the northern part of town while an evening stroll along the river allows you to take in the night market at full swing. The helpful and informative **TAT office** ⓘ *209/7-8 Surasi Shopping Centre, Boromtrailokant Rd, T055-252742, tatphs@loxinfo.co.th; daily 0830-1630*, stocks good maps of the town and surrounding area.

One of the most venerated temples in Thailand, **Wat Phra Sri Ratana Mahathat** ⓘ *daily 0800-1700, donation of ฿50*, recommended, is no museum-like leftover but a thriving place of worship. The Monastery of the Great Relic, known as **Wat Yai**, 'Big Wat' was built in the reign of King Lithai (1347-1368) of Sukhothai, in 1357. The viharn contains one of the most highly regarded and venerated Buddha images in Thailand – the **Phra Buddha Chinaraj**. Through the centuries, successive Thai kings have come to Phitsanulok to pay homage to the bronze image and to make offerings of gifts. The Buddha is a superlative example of late Sukhothai style and is said to have wept tears of blood when the city was captured by the Ayutthayan army in the early 14th century. The three-tiered viharn was built during the Ayutthaya period with the low sweeping roofs accentuating the massive gilded bronze Buddha image seated at the end of the nave. The entrance is through inlaid mother-of-pearl doors, made in 1756 in the reign of King Boromkot. Also in the wat compound is the **Buddha Chinnarat National Museum**, with a small collection of Sukhothai Buddhas and assorted ceramics. Wat Yai is a very popular site for Thai tourists/Buddhists. Most buy offerings of lotuses and incense from a stall at the gate. There's also a large antique, food and trinket market next door to the compound plus rows of lottery ticket sellers; the trick is you gain favour by supplicating yourself to the Buddha and then get lucky.

Mae Sot has a reputation for bandits and smuggling, though the town authorities are eager to build on its burgeoning reputation as a trekking centre. From Mae Sot it's possible to cross the Moei River for a day trip into the Burmese town of Myawadi. There are plentiful buses linking Mae Sot with Bangkok, Sukhothai and Chiang Mai.

The town lies 5 km from the Burmese border, near the end of Route 105, which swoops its way through hills and forest to Mae Sot and the Moei River Valley. The town has developed into an important trading centre and just about every ethnic group can be seen wandering the streets: Thais, Chinese, Burmans, Karen, Hmong and other mountain peoples. Over the last few years the Burmese army have made intermittent incursions into Thailand near Mae Sot pursuing Karen rebels. There have also been several assassinations of high-profile anti-Burmese rebels – Mae Sot's reputation as a slightly 'dangerous' frontier town is still well deserved.

Wat Moni Phraison, on Intharakit Road, has an unusual chedi in which a golden central spire is surrounded by numerous smaller chedis. Many of Mae Sot's older wooden shophouses are still standing and there is a busy morning market between Prasat Withi and Intharakit roads. Mae Sot offers some of the best trekking in northern and western Thailand and most trips incorporate visits to caves, waterfalls, and mountain villages. The Burmese border lies 5 km west of Mae Sot just over the Friendship Bridge. Regular blue songthaews to the Moei River and the Burmese border leave from the west end of Prasat Withi Road. You can cross the border for a US$10 fee, though are restricted to the nearby town – remember all money goes straight to the Burmese Military government.

Umphang → Colour map 3, B2.

The 164 km of road that traces the route of the Burmese border south from Mae Sot to Umphang is one of the most dramatic in the country with vast, jaw-dropping views across into the Burmese hills. To get here you'll need to take a songthaew from Mae Sot. Along this route are also several Karen refugee communities akin to vast holding pens.

Although an organized trek is the best way to see and experience Umphang's beauty (see page 841, or arrange a trek through one of the Umphang guesthouses), it is possible to explore the area on one's own. Umphang town is not much more than an oversized village and the majority of its population are Karen. Another reason to visit Umphang is to see the **Thi Lo Su waterfall** – widely recognized as the most beautiful in the country. Set on a massive limestone escarpment in the middle of the jungle, the 500-m-wide fall drops almost 250 m through a series of pools. It's difficult to reach the waterfall and you'll probably need to hire a car or songthaew from Umphang as it's a 45-km journey along dirt tracks requiring a 3-km walk at the end to reach the falls.

☻ Central Thailand listings

For Sleeping and Eating price codes,
see inside the front cover.

☻ Sleeping

Ayutthaya *p827, map p826*
C River View Place Hotel, T035-241444, www.riverviewplace.com. Originally designed as a condominium, the well-appointed rooms are massive, all with balconies and kitchenettes. Most come with views over the river to Wat Phanan Choeng and beyond. Nice terrace, swimming pool, reasonable food and good quiet location make this the best hotel in the old city, though service, while friendly, is soporific at best. Recommended.
E Eve Guesthouse, 11/19 Moo 2, Tambon Morrattanachai, T081-294 3293 (mob). Very cute and well-maintained guesthouse set in a purpose-built brick cottage. Located on a quiet back soi this place is also sited in a small garden. Rooms are mix of a/c and fan, hot water and cold. Recommended.
E-F Baan Lotus, Pa-Maphrao Rd, T035-251 988. This wonderful, crumbling old school-house, complete with massive gardens and huge lotus pond, despite becoming more and more run down is still one of the most interesting places to stay in Ayutthaya. Run by the engaging English-speaking Khun Kosoom – a retired female medical scientist – the rooms are large and en suite, some fan, some a/c. Often full, you will probably need to book to get in here. Recommended.
E-G Tony's Place, 12/18 Soi 8 Nareasuan Rd, T035-252578. A generic, well-run, backpacker hang-out with all the facilities you'd expect – watered-down Thai food, internet, tours. The rooms, some a/c, are fine and location is good.

Lopburi *p829*
B-D Lopburi Inn, Phahonyothin Rd, T036-411625, F036-412010. There's a slightly overpowering monkey theme employed in this hotel's decor and it is also a long way out of town. Nevertheless, it's the smartest in the

area with good facilities including a gym and a large pool.
F-G Nett, 17/1-2 Rachdamnern Soi 2, T036-411738. Clean, central and quiet, with attached shower rooms. The best of the cheaper hotels.

Sukhothai and around *p830, map p831*
New City
Beware The tuk-tuk drivers at the bus station who are on commission with certain guesthouses/hotels may refuse to take you or try and charge exorbitant rates (it should cost ฿30-40). Call your guesthouse if in doubt – many offer a free pick-up.
C-F Sukhothai Lotus Village, 170 Rachthani Rd, T055-621484, www.lotus-village.com. The large, leafy compound is scattered with several ponds, has a number of attractive teak houses and several spotless bungalows, some with a/c. Tastefully decorated, clean, peaceful, and managed by an informative Thai/French couple. It also serves tasty Western breakfasts of toast, yoghurt, fresh juice and fresh coffee. Beds are very hard. Highly recommended.
D-F Sukhothai Guesthouse, 68 Vichien Chamnong Rd, T055-610453, www.thai.net/ sukhothaiguesthouse. A well-maintained establishment, with attractive teak balconies. Some a/c rooms, hot water showers, restaurant. Friendly and informative owners. Also runs informal cookery classes and offers a range of tours, free bikes, free pick-up at the bus station and internet. Highly recommended.
E-F Ban Thai, 38 Prawert Nakhon Rd, T055-610163, www.geocities.com/guesthouse_ banthai. Overlooking the Yom River, an assortment of clean, well-kept rustic bungalows and rooms in a large natural-style house. Excellent en suite bungalows and small rooms and clean shared toilets. The friendly English-speaking management offers lots of free maps to surrounding area, recycle as much plastic and paper as possible and offers delightful bicycle tours through surrounding villages – from ฿150.

E-F No 4, 140/4 Soi Maerampan Jarodwitheethong Rd, T055-610165, no.4guesthouse@thaimail.com. Very friendly English-speaking lady owner rents out spotless bamboo bungalows, tucked into a small compound in a wonderfully secluded location. Well kept, cute en suite rooms. Excellent Thai food in the restaurant. She also runs cookery classes. Tours organized from here. Good value. Highly recommended.

Old City *p832*

C-E Orchid Hibiscus, T/F055-633284, orchid_hibiscus_guest_house@hotmail.com. Run by the engaging Paolo – an Italian from Rome – and his Thai wife, Pinthong, this is one the nicest guesthouses in Thailand. Rates may be a little high for the average backpacker but the gorgeous en suite, a/c bungalows, swimming pool, gardens, tropical birds and wonderful breakfasts – beware of the highly addictive coconut pudding smothered in fresh, wild honey – certainly make it excellent value. Paolo is a font of local knowledge and knows the outer temples so well he can even tell you the best spots for sunrise and sunset. Highly recommended.

D-G Old City Guesthouse, 28/7 Charodvithithong Rd, in front of the National Museum, north of the entrance to the park, T055-697515. Offers a range of rooms from tiny to enormous, from fan and shared bathroom to en suite, a/c and cable TV, all spotless. Friendly management. Outstanding value and highly recommended.

Si Satchanalai *p834*

B Wang Yom Resort, off Route 101 to Sawankhalok, T055-611179. It has over priced, tatty bungalows. Attached restaurant serves Thai food (🍴).

Camping

You can rent tents (฿80) at the main gate into the park – there's a small campsite in

a nice spot overlooking the river, a toilet/shower block and 24-hr security.

Kamphaeng Phet *p834*

C-D Phet Hotel, 189 Bumrungraj Rd, T055-712810, phethtl@phethotel.com. The most comfortable hotel in town. A/c, small pool (open to non-residents), restaurant serves Thai and international food, snooker club. Good value for money with breakfast included.

E-F Three J Guesthouse, 79 Rachavitee Rd, T055-720384, charin.sri@chaiyo.com. Chintzy, clean bungalows, some a/c, some fan. The cutesy decor might leave you feeling dizzy but this is one of the friendliest places in town. Recommended.

Phitsanulok *p835*

B-D Rajapruk, 99/9 Phra Ong Dam Rd, T055-258788, F055-251395. A/c, restaurant, inviting pool. Comfortable and clean with helpful and friendly staff. Recommended.

F-G Youth Hostel, 38 Sanambin Rd, T055-242060. Southeast of the railway, slightly out of town. This has become the travellers' hang-out, so it is very popular. Relaxing atmosphere in an attractive wooden building. Large, clean rooms with some a/c and some style. Helpful owner, dorm beds available, breakfast included, bicycles for rent. Outdoor sitting area for relaxing with bamboo hammocks. The best option in town for those on a budget. Recommended.

Mae Sot and the Burmese border *p836*

C-D Mae Sot Hill, 100 Asia Rd, T055-532601, F055-532600. Facilities, including a pool, snooker room, gym, bar and decent lakeside restaurant are excellent, though the rooms are a bit worn. The management do the best they can with what they have.

E-F Baan Thai Guesthouse, 740/1 Intharakit Rd, T08-1366 5882, banthai_mth@hotmail.com. An oasis of sorts, consists of one large and some smaller teak buildings nestled in a lush garden. Rooms are large, attractive and clean. A/c, fan, daily laundry and Wi-Fi available. Book in advance as this guesthouse quickly fills up. Highly recommended.

Umphang *p836*
D-G Garden Huts, 106 Palata Rd, T055-561 093. Cute bamboo and wood bungalows some with beds on raised platforms and some with Western toilets. More expensive rooms have a river view and a small sitting area. The complex is set in a pretty location on the banks of the river. Very friendly management with a little English. Recommended.
E-G Tu Ka Su, Palata Rd, T/F055-561295, T08-1825 8238 (mob). Attractive setting, wood and bamboo en suite bungalows. Very clean and pleasant atmosphere. Bicycles for rent (฿200 per day). Recommended.

❶ Eating

Ayutthaya *p827, map p826*
There is a night market with cheap foodstalls in the parking area in front of Chandra Kasem Palace. The covered Chao Phrom Market is also an excellent place for cheap food.
¶ **Baan Joom Zap** (Thai signage only), Uthong Rd. Riverside restaurant, set back from the road and in between **Bannkunpra** and **Old Place** guesthouses. Daily 1000-2200. This great Thai restaurant specializes in excellent Isaan food – it even offers a deep-fried *somtam* (spicy papaya salad) – and Thai-style herbal soups with sea food and glass noodles.
¶ **Nai Pun**, corner of Chee Kun and Uthong roads, is a friendly little Thai restaurant with a homely atmosphere and a/c should the heat be getting to you. The fantastic green curry is a must.
¶ **Phae Krung Kao**, 4 Uthong Rd. Floating restaurant to the south of Pridi Damrong bridge, excellent Chao Phraya river fish – try the *plaa chon* and the tasty deep-fried snake head (a fish!) with chillies.
¶ **The Tea and Coffee house** next door to **Moon Café** offers a fine array of hot

beverages and good Western and Thai breakfasts. Recommended.

Lopburi *p829*
Lopburi has a good selection of Chinese-Thai restaurants, especially along Na Phrakan Rd and Sorasak Rd. The market between Rachdamnern Rd and Rue de France provides the usual range of stall foods, as do the stalls along Sorasak Rd.

Sukhothai and around *p830, map p831*
New City
Night market (*talaat to rung*), on Ramkhamhaeng Rd, off Nikhon Kasem Rd, opposite the cinema, for good stalls. Open 1800-0600. Other stalls open up at about the same time along the walls of Wat Rachthani.
¶ **Dream Café**, Singhawat Rd, near **Sawat-dipong Hotel**. Thai and international dishes in cool interior, with a great collection of bric-a-brac, good for breakfasts.

Old City *p832*
There's a collection of good Thai eateries in the compound just outside the new main entrance and, during the evening, dozens of stalls spring up along the main road selling everything from spicy papaya salad to freshly roasted chicken.
¶ **The Coffee Cup**, opposite the National Museum. A small, friendly café with drinks, snacks and internet facilities.

Si Satchanalai *p834*
Several busloads of tourists arrive each day at Si Sat and most of them eat at the run of overpriced, though decent enough, Thai restaurants on the same stretch of road as the **Wang Yom Resort**. By the main gate (next door to the campsite) is a whole heave of cheap Thai stalls selling the usual fried rice, noodles, ice cream and drinks.

Kamphaeng Phet *p834*
In the evening the best selection of food-stalls can be found at the night bazaar on **Thesa Rd**.

Kitti and **Khrua Wibun**, 101 and 102 Thesa Rd (near Thesa Soi 2). Excellent Thai restaurants serving *khao muu daeng* (red pork and rice), *khao man kai* (chicken and rice) and most simple rice and noodle dishes. Recommended.

Phitsanulok *p835*
Several houseboat restaurants are to be found along Buddha Bucha Rd, near Naresuan Bridge.
Poon Sri, Phaya Lithai Rd. A great little Thai restaurant where you can get a good meal for ฿50 a head. Recommended.
Tiparot, 9 Soi Lue Thai Rd. In the heart of town, authentic and delicious Chinese food.

Mae Sot and the Burmese border *p836*
Aiya Restaurant. 533 Intarakhiri Rd T089-706 2329. Arguably the best Burmese restaurant in town, Aiya cooks up beautifully tasting food. Highly recommended.
Borderline Tea-Shop, 674/14 Intarakhiri Rd, T05-554 6584, www.borderline collective.org. Everything from the presentation of the dishes to the taste of the food impresses. For breakfast, try the flatbread with chickpeas or the ginger salad. Portions are generous and the coffee fresh and strong. Highly recommended.
Casa Mia, Don Kuaw Rd, T08-7204 4701. Home-cooked authentic Italian food, Burmese and Thai dishes, and Western desserts such as brownies and pumpkin pies, all delivered to you by friendly Charlie. Recommended.

Umphang *p836*
Dot.com, Palata Rd, near the bridge. Daily 0800-2400. The friendly English-speaking owner, Pradit, serves up decent breakfasts, drinks and some Thai food. Wi-Fi (฿30 per hr). Recommended.

Bars and clubs

Ayutthaya *p827, map p826*
Jazz Bar, Naresuan Rd, opposite **Tony's Place**. Lively, friendly bar offering good atmosphere and some decent sounds. Open 1400-late.

Wo Gun-T, small bar in a well-maintained shack next to Baan Lotus on Pa Maphrao Rd. Snacks, massive selection of non-alcoholic and alcoholic cocktails. Also the only place in town serving ice-cold Heineken on draft.

Sukhothai and around *p830, map p831*
New City
Chopper Beer Bar, Charodwithithong Rd, about 20 m after the bridge, on the left.

Festivals and events

Ayutthaya *p827, map p826*
Nov **Loi Krathong**, festival of lights (see page 784).

Sukhothai and around *p830, map p831*
Oct/Nov Loi Krathong Sukhothai is reputed to be the 'home' of this most beautiful of Thai festivals. It is said that one of the king's mistresses carved the first krathong from a piece of fruit and floated it down the river to her king. Today, the festival symbolizes the floating away of the previous year's sins, although traditionally it was linked to the gift of water.

Shopping

Mae Sot and the Burmese border *p836*
Handicrafts
Borderline (see Eating, above) sells everything from passport-holders, book-covers and shoulder-bags to scarves and traditional Karen and Burmese clothes. All profits go back to marginalized Burmese ethnic groups who make them.
WEAVE, Intharakit Rd, www.weave-women.org. A women's collective selling hand-woven handicrafts made by women fleeing civil strife and economic hardships in Burma.

▲ Activities and tours

Sukhothai and around *p830, map p831*
Many hotels and guesthouses arrange
tours to the Old City, Kamphaeng Phet
and Si Satchanalai. Expect to pay ฿300
for a tour to the Old City and ฿500 for
Si Satchanalai.

Phitsanulok *p835*
Able Group Company Ltd, 55/45 Sri
Thammatripidok Rd, T055-243851, F055-
242206. Runs sightseeing and trekking
tours and rents out cars.
Piti Tour and Phitsanulok Tour Centre,
55/45 Surasri Trade Centre, 43/11 Boromtrailokant Rd, T055-242206. Organizes
city tours and tours to Sukhothai and
Si Satchanalai by private car.

Mae Sot and the Burmese border *p836*
Borderline Tea-Shop (see Eating, above)
offers a 1-day Burmese, Shan, and Karen
cooking course. From ฿450 per person.
Drop in to the café or visit the website
for details.
Mae Sot Conservation Tour, 415/11
Intrarakhiri Rd, T055-532818, premat@
ksc15.th.com. Runs educational and soft
adventure tours for families and the elderly.
Mae Sot Travel Centre (aka **SP Tours**),
14/21 Asia Rd, T055-531409, F532279.
The main office is out of town, but they
can be contacted at the **Mae Sot Hill** and
the **Siam Hotel**.

Umphang *p836*
Most of the tour companies are on Palata Rd.
Be aware that only a handful of outfits have
English-speaking guides. These more
advanced operations include: **The Eco-
tourist Center**, T055-561063, F055-561065;
Boonchay Camping Tour, 360 M1 Tambol,
T055-561020; **BL Tours**, T055-561021,
F055-561322. Tours are also organized by
guesthouses (see Sleeping, above)

⊖ Transport

Ayutthaya *p827, map p826*
Bicycle and motorbike
Kan Kitti Travel, next to the Jazz Bar on Soi
Naresuan. Offers reliable bikes (฿30 for 24 hrs)
and motorbikes (฿250 for 24 hrs) for hire.
They can also organize train and bus tickets.

Boat
Long-tailed boats can be hired at the jetty
opposite the Chandra Kasem Palace in the
northeast corner of town. Expect to pay ฿250
for 1 hr (boats can take 10 people). From
Bangkok, see **Bangkok Tours**, page 812.
From Tha Tien pier in Bangkok daily at 1000.

Bus
The station is on Naresuan Rd. Regular a/c
and non-a/c connections with **Bangkok**'s
Northern bus terminal (1½ hrs) and stops
north. Some buses travelling from the north
will stop on the highway on the outskirts of
town – tuk-tuks and songthaews should take
you into the centre from here.

Songthaew and tuk-tuk
A tuk-tuk around town costs ฿50-60. For a
songthaew from the train station into town
expect to pay ฿7. They run about the old
town for a flat fare of ฿7. They can also be
chartered for about ฿300 per day.

Train
The station is just off Rojana Rd, across the
Pasak River. Connections with **Bangkok** and
north to **Chiang Mai** (12 hrs). The easiest way
to get from the station to the old city is to
take the small track facing the station down
to the river; from the jetty here ferries cross
over to the other side every 5 mins or so (฿2).

Lopburi *p829*
Bus
The bus station for all buses is in the new town,
2 km from the old town. Regular connections
with **Bangkok** (2-3 hrs), **Ayutthaya**,
Kanchanaburi and destinations north.

Train
Regular connections with **Bangkok** (2¾ hrs), **Ayutthaya** (1 hr) and destinations to the north.

Sukhothai and around p830, map p831
Air
Sukhothai Airport, T055-647224. Bangkok Airways, www.bangkokair.com, provides daily connections with **Bangkok** and **Chiang Mai**.

Bicycle/motorbike hire
Bikes in the new town, ฿50 per day from many guesthouses. There are several places in the old town where a bike costs ฿20 a day. Motorbikes are ฿250-300 per day from many guesthouses.

Bus
For regular connections with **Bangkok** (7 hrs), **Phitsanulok** (1 hr), **Chiang Mai** (6 hrs) and **Lampang** (5 hrs), the station is about 2 km west of town on the bypass road. There are 2 direct buses a day from the Old City to Bangkok's Northern terminal – at 0900 and 2100, ฿256. You can buy tickets from the **Coffee Cup** (see Eating, above). The Chiang Mai bus from the New City also goes through the Old City and you can wait on the main road outside the old entrance and flag one down. Buses for other parts of the kingdom leave from offices at assorted points. For Mae Sot, buses leave from Ban Muang Rd; for **Si Satchanalai** from the corner of Raj Uthit and Charodwithi-thong roads.

Si Satchanalai p834
Bus
Regular connections 0600-1800 with **Sukhothai** from Raj Uthit Rd, 54 km, 1 hr. Ask to be dropped off at the Muang Kao (Old City). For **Chaliang**, get off at the pink archway on Route 101, 2 km before Route 1201, which leads to a suspension foot-bridge crossing the Yom River to Chaliang.

Kamphaeng Phet p834
Bus
Terminal is 2 km from the bridge, some way out of town. There are regular connections with **Bangkok**, **Phitsanulok** and other destinations.

Phitsanulok p835
Air
The airport is just out of town on Sanambin Rd, T055-258029. THAI has multiple daily connections with **Bangkok**.

Bus
Terminal on the road east to Lom Sak (Route 12), 2 km out of town, T055-242430. If the bus travels through town en route to the bus terminal, ask the driver to let you off at the more convenient train station. Bus No 7 leaves the local bus station for the bus terminal every 10 mins (30-min journey). Regular connections with **Bangkok** (5-6 hrs), **Kamphaeng Phet** (2 hrs), **Udon Thani**, **Sukhothai** (every 30 mins), **Pattaya**, **Mae Sot** (5 hrs), **Chiang Mai** (5-6 hrs), **Korat** (6 hrs) and **Chiang Rai** (6-7 hrs).

Train
Swiss chalet-style station, with steam locomotive parked outside. Regular connections with **Bangkok** (6 hrs), **Ayutthaya** (5 hrs) and **Chiang Mai** (6-7 hrs). For those travelling straight on to Sukhothai, take a tuk-tuk the 4 km to the bus station.

Mae Sot and the Burmese border p836
Bus
All buses now depart from the newly built bus terminal on the outskirts of town from where there are a/c and non-a/c bus connections with **Bangkok**'s Northern bus terminal (8-10 hrs) and other destinations. Songthaews for **Umphang** leave every hour from about 0700-1400 (5 hrs).

Motorbike hire
Prasat Withi Rd (close to the **Bangkok Bank**), ฿160 per day.

Umphang *p836*
Several songthaews a day connect Umphang with **Mae Sot**. The first leaves Mae Sot around 0700, the last at about 1400 (4-5 hrs, ฿200). For the return journey they leave Umphang for Mae Sot at 0700, 0800, 0900, 1300, 1400 and 1500.

❶ Directory

Ayutthaya *p827, map p826*
Banks Most of the banks are either on Uthong Rd or Naresuan Rd (Chao Phrom Rd) and change TCs and have ATMs. **Thai Military**, Chao Phrom Rd. **Thai Farmers**, Chao Phrom Rd. **Internet** Log On, sited on Makham Rang Rd, offers fast connection on new machines for ฿15 per hr – it's the best place in town by a mile though a little walk from the main backpacker area.
Police Tourist Police, across the street from TAT office, Si Sanphet Rd, T035-242352.
Post office Uthong Rd (south from the Chandra Kasem Palace).

Lopburi *p829*
Banks Krung Thai, 74 Vichayen Rd. **Thai Military**, corner of Sorasak and Rachdamnern roads. **Post office** On road to Singburi, not far from Prang Sam Yod.

Sukhothai and around *p830, map p831*
Banks Bangkok, 49 Singhawat Rd. Bangkok Bank of Commerce, 15 Singhawat Rd. **Thai Farmers**, 134 Charoen Withi Rd. There is also a currency exchange booth by the Ramkhamhaeng Museum in the Old City – open daily 0830-1200. **Internet** A number of cafés have opened up in both the Old City and Sukhothai; some guesthouses provide internet services. **Medical services** Sukhothai Hospital, Charodwith-ithong Rd, T055-611782, about 4 km out of town on the road towards the Old City.

Police Nikhon Kasem Rd, T055-611010.
Post office Nikhon Kasem Rd. Also sub post office and telephone service in the Old City.

Kamphaeng Phet *p834*
Banks Thai Farmers, 233 Charoensuk Rd, and **Bangkok Bank** both have ATMs.
Internet There are an increasing number of internet cafés in town, mainly situated on Thesa Rd. **Post office** Corner of Thesa Rd and Thesa Soi 3. Also has fax and overseas telephone facilities.

Phitsanulok *p835*
Banks Bangkok, 35 Naresuan Rd. **Krung Thai**, 31/1 Naresuan Rd. **Thai Farmers**, 144/1 Boromtrailokant Rd, TCs and ATM.
Internet A couple of places just over the Aekathossarot Bridge. More internet cafés are opening. **Medical services** Hospital Sithamtripidok Rd, T055-258812.
Police Tourist Police Boromtrailokant Rd, next to TAT office, T055-251179. **Post office and telephone centre** Buddha Bucha Rd.

Mae Sot and the Burmese border *p836*
Banks Siam Commercial, 544/1-5 Intharakit Rd. **Thai Farmers**, 84/9 Prasat Withi Rd. Bangkok Bank, Prasat Withi Rd.
Internet A few internet cafés have opened up at the western ends of Prasat Withi Rd and Intharakit Rd. **Police** Tourist Police on Intharakit Rd (next to No 4 Guesthouse), T055-533523. **Post office** Intharakit Rd (opposite DK Hotel). The main post office is also on Intharakit Rd, but past the **No 4 Guesthouse** about 1 km out of town on the road to the Moei River.

Umphang *p836*
Banks No banks in Umphang – make sure you bring plenty of money. **Internet and telephone** Dot.com on Palata Rd.

Chiang Mai and around

→ *Colour map 2, C2.*

The North begins with an easing of the dusty, overwhelming heat of the plains. Limestone hills, draped with calming verdant forest, roads and rivers twisting into endless switchbacks. This region wasn't incorporated into the Thai nation until the beginning of the 20th century. For centuries local lords held sway over shifting principalities, the most significant being centred on Chiang Mai. A thriving, dynamic and increasingly sophisticated city, the old dusty charm of Chiang Mai is now becoming a distant memory. Yet some of this still lingers in the back streets of the old city or in the nooks and crannies of any one of its numerous venerable and ancient temples. Immensely popular with travellers, the city is also the perfect base for exploration of the forests, hills and peoples of the North. There's a good range of accommodation, some decent food and shopping while the city is one of the most important transport hubs in the country. There are also scores of trekking and other companies offering everything from whitewater rafting to elephant treks. Travel beyond its environs and you'll find Thailand's biggest mountain at Doi Intathon and its most beautiful temple, Wat Phra That Lampang Luang, in Lampang.

▸▸ *For listings, see pages 851-860.*

Ins and outs

The quickest way of getting to Chiang Mai is by air. Several airlines offer multiple flights from Bangkok and also links to some other provincial centres. There are several trains a day to and from Bangkok (12 hours) including the splendid sleeper service. Scores of buses arrive from all over Thailand – from super-luxury VIP buses through to the bone-shaking ordinary variety. Much of the central part of the city can be easily covered on foot. Converted pick-ups – operate as the main mode of public transport, ferrying people around for a fixed fare of between ฿15-20 per person. Just flag one down and pay them at the end – they vary their routes but they'll normally take you anywhere in central Chiang Mai for this price. If you go out of the central area expect to pay more. There are also tuk-tuks, some taxis, and a number of car, motorbike and bicycle hire companies. The very helpful and informative TAT ① office, *105/1 Chiang Mai-Lamphun Rd, T053-248 604, F053-248605, www.tatchiangmai.org, daily 0830-1630,* stocks a good range of maps and leaflets, including information on guesthouses and guidelines for trekking.

Background

In around 1290 King Mengrai annexed the last of the Mon kingdoms at Lamphun and moved his capital from Chiang Rai to a site on the banks of the Ping River called Nopburi Sri Nakawan Ping Chiang Mai. It is said he chose the site after seeing a big mouse accompanied by four smaller mice scurry down a hole beneath a holy Bodhi tree. He made this site the heart of his Lanna kingdom – today it is known more simply as Chiang Mai.

After consolidating power in Chiang Mai, King Mengrai, a great patron of Theravada Buddhism, brought monks from Ceylon to unify his northern state and up until the 15th century, Chiang Mai flourished. As this century ended, relations with up-and-coming Ayutthaya became strained and the two kingdoms engaged in a series of wars.

While Chiang Mai and Ayutthaya were busy fighting, the Burmese eventually captured the city of Chiang Mai in 1556. King Bayinnaung, who had unified Burma, took Chiang Mai after a three-day battle and the city remained a Burmese regency for 220 years. There was constant conflict during these years and by the time the Burmese succeeded in overthrowing Ayutthaya in 1767, the city of Chiang Mai was decimated and depopulated. In 1775, General Taksin united the kingdom of Thailand and a semi-autonomous prince of the Lampang Dynasty was appointed to rule the north. Chiang Mai lost its semi-independence in 1938 and came under direct rule from Bangkok.

Today, Chiang Mai is the second-largest city in Thailand, with a population of roughly 500,000; a thriving commercial centre as well as a favourite tourist destination. Its attractions to the visitor are obvious: the city has a rich and colourful history, still evident in the architecture of the city that includes over 300 wats; it is manageable and still relatively 'user friendly' (unlike Bangkok); it has perhaps the greatest concentration of handicraft industries in the country; and it is also an excellent base from which to go trekking and visit the famous hilltribe villages in the surrounding highlands.

Sights

Chiang Mai is centred on a square moat and defensive wall built during the 19th century. The four corner bastions are reasonably preserved and are a useful reference point when roaming the city. Situated in the northeast of the walled town, **Wat Chiang Man** is on Rachpakinai Road within a peaceful compound. The wat is the oldest in the city and was built by King Mengrai soon after he had chosen the site for his new capital in 1296. It is said that he resided here while waiting for his new city to be constructed and also spent the last years of his life at the monastery. The gold-topped chedi Chang Lom is supported by rows of elephants, similar to those of the two chedis of the same name at Si Satchanalai and Sukhothai. Two ancient Buddha images are contained behind bars within the viharn, the crystal Buddha, Phra Sae Tang Tamani (standing 10 cm high) and Phra Sila (literally, 'Stone Buddha'), believed to have originated in India or Ceylon about 2500 years ago.

To the northeast of Wat Chiang Man, just outside the city walls, is the unique Burmese Shan, **Wat Pa Pao**, which was founded more than 400 years ago by a Shan monk. A narrow soi leads off the busy road through an archway and into the wat's peaceful and rather ramshackle compound.

Wat Phra Singh (Temple of the Lion Buddha) is situated in the west quarter of the old city and was founded in 1345. It contains a number of beautiful buildings decorated with fine woodcarving. Towards the back of the compound is the intimate Lai Kham Viharn, which houses the venerated Phra Buddha Singh image.

On Phra Pokklao Road, to the east of Wat Phra Singh, is the 500-year-old ruined chedi or **Wat Chedi Luang**. It's a charming place to wander around, set in a sizeable compound with huge trees at the boundaries. Judging by the remains, it must have once been an impressive monument.

Outside the moated walls of the old city, **Wat Suan Dok** lies to the west on Suthep Road. Originally built in 1371 but subsequently restored and enlarged, the wat contains the ashes of Chiang Mai's royal family, housed in many white, variously shaped, mini-chedis. Much of the monastery was erected during the reign of King Kawila (1782-1813).

Wat Umong (take a songthaew along Suthep Rd and ask to be let off at the turning for Wat Umong; it is about a 1-km walk from here) was founded in 1371 by King Ku Na (1355-1385) who promoted the establishment of a new, ascetic school of forest-dwelling monks. In 1369 he brought a leading Sukhothai monk to Chiang Mai – the Venerable Sumana – and built Wat Umong for him and his followers. Although the wat is at the edge of the city, set in areas of woodland, it feels much more distant.

The **Chiang Mai Contemporary Art Museum** ① *corner of Nimmahaemin and Suthep roads, T053-933833, Tue-Sun 0930-1700, ฿50*, is set in a large modern structure and

Chiang Mai

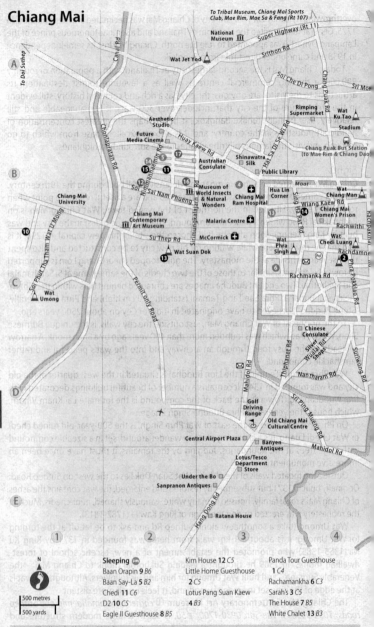

To Tribal Museum, Chiang Mai Sports
Club, Mae Rim, Mae Sa & Fang (Rt 107)

National Museum

Super Highway (Rt 11)

Srithon Rd

Wat Jet Yod

Canal Rd

Soi Che Di Pong

Chang Puak Rd

Sri Mo

A

To Doi Suthep

Rimping Supermarket

Wat Ku Tao

Ha Sa Di Se Wi Rd

Chang Puak Bus Station
(to Mae Rim & Chiang Dao)

Stadium

Aesthetic Studio

Huay Kaew Rd

Future Media Cinema

Shinawatra Silk

Australian Consulate

Public Library

Nimmanhaemin Rd

Chonlapratan Rd

B

17

15 11

16

Museum of World Insects & Natural Wonders

Chiang Mai Ram Hospital

Hua Lin Corner

Wat Chiang Man

Moat

Sing Ha Rat Rd

Wat Chiang Man

Wiang Kaew Rd

Chiang Mai University

12

Soi Sai Nam Phueng

Chiang Mai Contemporary Art Museum

Malaria Centre

Chiang Mai Women's Prison

Rachwithi

Rachadamne

Wat Chedi Luang

Su Thep Rd

McCormick

Wat Phra Singh

Pha Pokklao Rd

2

Peunit only Road

13

Wat Suan Dok

Rachadamne

C

10

Soi Phut Tha Tham Wat U Mong

Wat Umong

Rachmanka Rd

6

Pol

Chinese Consulate

Thiphanet Rd

Silver & Wuala Shops

Sungwong Rd

Nantharam Rd

D

Golf Driving Range

Mahidol Rd

Old Chiang Mai Cultural Centre

Sri Ping Mueng Rd

Central Airport Plaza

Banyen Antiques

Mahidol Rd

Lotus/Tesco Department Store

Under the Bo

Sanpranon Antiques

Hang Dong Rd

E

Ratana House

N

500 metres
500 yards

Sleeping	Kim House **12** *C5*	Panda Tour Guesthouse
Baan Orapin **9** *B6*	Little Home Guesthouse	**1** *C4*
Baan Say-La **5** *B2*	**2** *C5*	Rachamankha **6** *C3*
Chedi **11** *C6*	Lotus Pang Suan Kaew	Sarah's **3** *C5*
D2 **10** *C5*	**4** *B3*	The House **7** *B5*
Eagle II Guesthouse **8** *B5*		White Chalet **13** *B3*

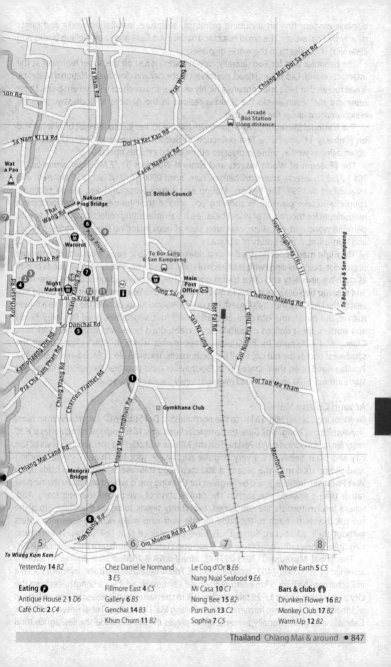

Yesterday 14 *B2*	Chez Daniel le Normand 3 *E5*	Le Coq d'Or 8 *E6*	Whole Earth 5 *C5*
		Nang Nual Seafood 9 *E6*	
Eating 🍴	Fillmore East 4 *C5*	Mi Casa 10 *C1*	**Bars & clubs** 🍸
Antique House 2 1 *D6*	Gallery 6 *B5*	Nong Bee 15 *B2*	Drunken Flower 16 *B2*
Café Chic 2 *C4*	Genchai 14 *B3*	Pun Pun 13 *C2*	Monkey Club 17 *B2*
	Khun Churn 11 *B2*	Sophia 7 *C5*	Warm Up 12 *B2*

displays modern fine art including paintings, sculpture, installation works and prints mostly by Thai artists. The small but chic attached **Art Café** and shop (selling books and ceramics) is classier than the works displayed.

The beautiful **Wat Jet Yod** (literally, 'seven spires') is just off the 'super highway' at the intersection with Ladda Land Road, northwest of the city and close to the National Museum. It was founded in 1453 and contains a highly unusual square chedi with seven spires. These represent the seven weeks the Buddha resided in the gardens at Bodhgaya, after his enlightenment under the Bodhi tree.

The **National Museum** ① *Wed-Sun 0900-1600, ฿30*, lies just to the east of Wat Jet Yod on Highway 11 and has a fine collection of Buddha images and Sawankhalok china downstairs, as well as some impressive ethnological exhibits upstairs.

The **Museum of World Insects and Natural Wonders** ① *72 Nimmanhaemin Soi 13 T053-211891, insects_museum@hotmail.com, open 0900-1630, ฿100, ฿50 children*, was established in 1999. The owners, Manop and Rampa Rattanarithikul, are an eccentric couple who take pleasure in showing you around their house, which has become a mausoleum for thousands of insect beasties. It's an interesting collection of shells, fossils, petrified wood and, of course, case after case of bugs including beetles, moths, roaches and butterflies. A true oddity of a place.

The **night market** dominates the west side of Chang Klang Road. It consists of a number of purpose-built buildings with hundreds of stalls, selling a huge array of tribal goods as well as clothing, jewellery and other tourist goodies (see Shopping, page 855). Near the river, and running two or three streets in from the river, is the **Warorot Market** (on Chiang Mai east of the Old City), the city's largest. It starts on Praisani Road, close to the river, as a flower market, but transforms into a mixed market with fruit, vegetables, dried fish, pigs' heads and trotters, great dollops of buffalo flesh, crabs, dried beans and deep-fried pork skin. Chiang Mai is famous for its Sunday street market which in effect closes down the southwest part of the old city to all but pedestrians. The wats along Rachdamern and Phra Pokklao Road open their space up to foodhawkers and massage therapists. The market starts around 1700 and runs until midnight every Sunday of the year.

Around Chiang Mai

Overlooking Chiang Mai, 16 km to the northwest, is **Doi Suthep** ① *songthaew from Mani Noparat Rd, by Chang Puak Gate; the temple is closed after 1630 and now also charges a ฿30 entry fee (to foreigners only)*. Perched on the hillside and offering spectacular views of the city and plain below, it's a very popular pilgrimage spot for Thais. A steep, winding road climbs 1000 m to the base of a 300-step *naga* staircase, which in turn leads up to **Wat Phrathat**. Initially, you'd be forgiven for thinking you'd arrived at a tacky theme park rather than a revered site, such is the proliferation of overpriced souvenir stalls. And, where foreign tourists are concerned, everybody seems to be on the make, from the tuk-tuk drivers through to the surly temple staff who make sure no foreigner enters without their ฿30 ticket. Some Thais have complained that Doi Suthep is becoming degraded by the influence of tourism. If you don't fancy the climb take the cable car (฿20).

The **Tribal Museum** ① *T053-221933, Mon-Fri 0900-1600; a slide and video show is screened at 1000 and 1400*, attached to the **Tribal Research Institute**, overlooks a lake in Rachamankha Park, 5 km north of town off Chotana Road. Take a songthaew from the city ฿50. It takes about 15-20 minutes to walk to the museum. It houses the fine collection of tribal pieces that were formerly held at Chiang Mai University's Tribal Research Centre. Carefully and professionally presented, the pieces on show include textiles, agricultural

Hilltribes

A visit to a hilltribe village is one of the main reasons why people travel to the north of Thailand. The hilltribe population (Chao Khao in Thai – literally 'Mountain People') numbers about 800,000, or a little over 1% of the total population.

These 800,000 people are far from homogenous: each hilltribe (there are nine recognized by the government), has a different language, dress, religion, artistic heritage and culture. They meet their subsistence needs in different ways and often occupy different ecological niches. In some respects they are as far removed from one another as they are from the lowland Thais.

As their name suggests, the hilltribes occupy the highland areas that fringe the northern region, with the largest populations in the provinces of Chiang Mai (143,000), Chiang Rai (98,000), Mae Hong Son (83,000) and Tak (69,000). These figures are a few years old, but the relative balance between the provinces has not changed significantly. Although this guide follows the tradition of using the term 'hilltribe' to describe these diverse peoples, it is in many regards an unfortunate one. They are not tribes in the anthropological sense, derived as it is from the study of the peoples of Africa. For trekking, see pages 857 and 858.

implements, musical instruments, jewellery and weapons. The museum is particularly worth visiting for those intending to go trekking.

Wiang Kum Kam is a ruined city, 5 km south of Chiang Mai, which was established by the Mon in the 12th or 13th centuries and abandoned in the 18th century. Accessible by bicycle, motorbike or tuk-tuk, take Route 106 south and the ruins are signposted off to the right about 5 km from Chiang Mai – but only in Thai – from where it is another 2 km. Look out for a ruined chedi on the right and ask along the way for confirmation. Today, archaeologists are beginning to uncover a site of about 9 sq km that contains the remains of at least 20 wats. The most complete monument is Wat Chang Kham, which has a marvellous bronze *naga* outside. In front of the wat is the spirit chamber of Chiang Mai's founder, King Mengrai. Nearby are the ruins of Wat Noi and two dilapidated chedis. Perhaps the most impressive single structure is the renovated chedi at Wat Chedi Liam. This takes the form of a stepped pyramid – a unique Mon architectural style of which there are only a handful of examples in Thailand.

Doi Inthanon National Park → Colour map 1, C2.

① Daily 0600-1800, ฿200, ฿100 children, ฿30 car, ฿10 motorbike; best time to visit: just after the end of the rainy season, in late Oct or Nov; by Jan and Feb the air becomes hazy, not least because of forest fires. Buses, minibuses and songthaews for Hang Dong and Chom Thong leave from around the Chiang Mai Gate. From Hang Dong there are songthaews to Doi Inthanon.

Doi Inthanon is Thailand's highest peak, at 2595 m. The park covers 482 sq km and is one of the most visited in Thailand. The winding route to the top is stunning, with terraced rice fields, cultivated valleys and a few hilltribe villages. Although the drive is dramatic, the park's flora and fauna can only really be appreciated by taking one of the hiking trails off the main road. Once the habitat of bears and tigers, the wildlife has been severely depleted through overhunting, though it is still possible to see flying squirrel, red-toothed shrew, Chinese pangolin and Pere David's vole. Several thousand Hmong and Karen people live in the national park, cultivating the slopes. There are a number of waterfalls on the slopes: the

Mae Klang Falls (near the Km 8 marker and not far from the visitor centre), **Wachiratan Falls** (26 km down from the summit and near the Km 21 marker, restaurant here) and **Siriphum Falls** (3-4 km off the road near the Km 31 marker and not far from the park headquarters), as well as the large **Borichinda Cave** (a 2-km hike off the main road near the visitor centre at the Km 9 marker). The **Mae Ya Falls** in the south of the park are the most spectacular, plunging more than 250 m (they lie 15 km from park headquarters and are accessible from Chom Thong town). Ask for details at the visitor centre.

Lampang ⬤❶❷❸❹❺ ➤ pp 852-860. Colour map 1, C3.

An atmospheric provincial capital complete with horse-drawn carriages, soothing riverside hang-outs and the sumptuous temple of Wat Phra That Lampang Luang, Lampang makes a great day or overnight trip from Chiang Mai. There's some decent accommodation and a chance to indulge in a leisurely lunch at one of the great riverside restaurants. Regular buses and trains will bring you here from Chiang Mai (two hours) and destinations further south. The **tourist office** ① *Boonyawat Rd, in the front of the police station, 1st floor, T054-218823*, has good maps and brochures.

Established in the seventh-century Dvaravati period, Lampang prospered as a trading centre, with a wealth of ornate and well-endowed wats. It was re-built in the 19th century as a fortified *wiang* (a walled city) and became an important centre for the teak industry with British loggers making it one of their key centres.

Wat Phra That Lampang Luang ➤ Colour map 3, A2.

① *Daily 0900-1200, 1300-1700, donation, there are foodstalls across the road from the wat. Take a songthaew to Ko Kha and then a motorbike taxi the last 2.5 km to the wat. Alternatively, charter a songthaew from Lampang.*

One of finest temples in Thailand, is easily the best reason to come to Lampang. The monastery stands on a slight hill, surrounded by a brick wall – all that remains of the original fortressed city that was sited here more than 1000 years ago. While the buildings have been restored on a number of occasions over the years, it remains beautifully complete and authentic. Approached by a staircase flanked by guardian lions and *nagas*, visitors enter through an archway of intricate 15th-century stone carving. The large, open central viharn, **Viharn Luang**, houses a *ku* – a brick, stucco and gilded pyramid peculiar to northern wats – containing a Buddha image (dating from 1563), a collection of thrones and some wall paintings. The building, with its intricate woodcarving and fine pattern work on the pillars and ceiling, is dazzling.

Behind the viharn is the principal **chedi**, 45 m high it contains three relics of the Buddha: a hair and the ashes of the Buddha's right forehead and neck bone. The **Buddha Viharn** to the left of the chedi is thought to date from the 13th century and was restored in 1802. Immediately behind this viharn is a small, raised building housing a **footprint of the Buddha** (only men are permitted) and a camera obscura; at certain times of day (from late morning through to early afternoon) the sun's rays pass through a small hole in the building's wall, projecting an inverted image of the chedi onto a sheet.

Thai Elephant Conservation Centre ➤ Colour map 1, C2.

① *www.thaielephant.com. Take an early morning bus towards Chiang Mai; get off at the Km 37 marker (ask the bus driver to let you off at the Conservation Centre). From the road it is a 1.8-km walk by road or take a short cut through the forest. It is possible to stay at the camp.*

Many of the places that offer chances to interact with elephants are poorly run, treating their charges with contempt. Not so this excellent centre that lies 33 km northwest of Lampang near Thung Kwian, on the road to Chiang Mai (Highway 11). Here elephants are trained for forest work, others are released back into the wild, there are elephant musicians, elephant artists and elephant dung paper. There's even an elephant hospital and rescue centre and a small restaurant and souvenir shop. The ECC also runs English-language *mahout* training courses – contact them directly for details.

◉ Chiang Mai and around listings

For Sleeping and Eating price codes,
see inside the front cover.

◉ Sleeping

Chiang Mai *p844, map p846*
Old City
Within the old city walls and the moat is the greatest concentration of guesthouses, plus a couple of small(ish) mid-range places.
LL-AL Rachamankha, 9 Phra Singh Rd, T053-904114, www.rachamankha.com. This oasis of calm is an inspired boutique hotel with a designer's eye for detail, all built using traditional techniques. The a/c rooms can be a bit small and dark but are filled with sumptuous antiques. Service is definitely a bit ropey for the price range. Also has pool, decent library (free internet) and restaurant.
B-C White Chalet, 9/1 Arak Rd, T053-326188, www.chiangmaiwhitechalet.com. As the name suggests, this newly built guesthouse is all in white, from the chairs in the lobby to the covers on the beds. Fresh-looking standard-sized rooms, all with double-bed, flat-screen TV, en suite and a/c. Earplugs are recommended as the busy (night and day) Arak Rd runs straight past it.
D-E Eagle II Guesthouse, 26 Rachwithi Rd, Soi 2, T053-210620, www.eaglehouse.com. Dorms for ฿60. Run by an Irish woman and her Thai husband. Friendly staff, rooms are clean but a little worn with a/c and some attached bathrooms. Excellent food (it is possible to take cookery courses here). Also organizes treks. Attractive area to sit, efficient and friendly set up. Recommended.

E Panda Tour Guesthouse, 130/1 Rachamanka Rd, T053-206420. This friendly, family-run business of over 12 years' standing is a gem of a place. The usual stable-like block has meticulously clean, well-equipped rooms with fans, tiled floors and whitewashed walls. Buzzing little restaurant with exceptional food. Also runs one of the best tour companies in Chiang Mai, with long-standing guides whose knowledge of the surrounding area is phenomenal. Recommended.

East of the Old City
LL-AL The Chedi, 123 Charoen Prathet Rd, T053-253333, www.ghmhotels.com. Stunningly designed property built around the restored 1920s British Consulate – itself a historical treat – has been created here by the river. The rooms are minimalist, with huge tubs and plasma screens while the lobby is spacious and the tones relaxed. Pool, sundeck and great food complete the picture. Expensive but almost certainly the best hotel in town. Highly recommended.
L-A D2, 100 Chang Klang Rd, T053-999 999. www.d2hotels.com. Owned by the **Dusit Thani** chain the D2 attempts to create a designer hotel in the heart of Chiang Mai. However, it doesn't quite pull it off. The rooms, while nicely designed, are small and the over-branded orange-everything is off-putting. The food is great and the location, right in the heart of the night market, can't be beaten.
A-C Baan Orapin, 150 Charoenrat Rd, T053-243677, www.baanorapin.com. It is easy to see why this is one of the most popular places in Chiang Mai. A run of well-maintained bungalows surround a central

teak house, all set in quiet gardens on a road on the east side of the Ping River. The owner speaks great English and is friendly, though can sometimes be hard to find – best to email (see website) or call ahead as **Orapin** is often booked solid. Highly recommended.

C-D Kim House, 62 Charoen Prathet Rd, T/F053-282441. Small hotel in a leafy compound down a secluded soi, with clean rooms (some a/c) and hot showers. Friendly, welcoming atmosphere. Recommended.

D Little Home Guesthouse, 1/1 Kotchasan Soi 3, T/F053-206939. Not a little guesthouse at all, but a large place more like a small hotel. Don't be put off; it is peaceful, down a quiet soi within a leafy compound. The rooms are clean and well maintained and the manage- ment has insisted on no TV, videos or music – professionally run and popular, with cheaper package tours. Recommended.

D Sarah's, 20 Tha Phae Soi 4, T053-208271, www.sarahguesthouse.com. Run by an English woman married to a Thai. 12 basic but clean rooms, with attached bathrooms and shared hot water showers. Trekking, tour services and cookery courses available. This well-established guesthouse in the heart of the guesthouse area remains very popular. Recommended.

West of the Old City

With **Nimmanhaemin** now firmly established as Chiang Mai's artist quarter, a few excellent guesthouses have sprung up. There are also a number of large hotels on **Huay Kaew Rd**.

L-A LotusPang Suan Kaew Hotel, 99/4 Huay Kaew Rd, T053-224333, F053-224493. This massive hotel is ugly from the outside but makes up for it with competitive rates and large, luxurious rooms. A/c, restaurants, pool and gym. Recommended.

A-C Bungalows, Km 31 outstation on the route up the mountain. To book, T02-579 0529 or write to the Superintendent, Doi Inthanon National Park, Chom Thong District, Chiang Mai 50160. Advance reservation recommended as this is a very popular park. The bungalows, sleeping 4-30 people, have been built in the traditional style and the

location is fantastic. The resort organizes treks, teaches about medicinal plants, introduces visitors to Karen dance, etc.

C-D Yesterday, 24 Nimmanhaemin Rd, T053-213809, www.yesterday.co.th. Opened by the friendly and laid-back owners of **Baan Say-La**, this beautiful teak house boasts 28 individually designed rooms complete with a/c, en suite, TV and 2 small houses, as well as free Wi-Fi, airport transfer and a small garden. Recommended.

D-E Baan Say-La, 4-4/1 Nimmanhaemin Rd, Soi 5, T053-894229, baansayla@gmail.com. This cute guesthouse in an old colonial-style house is one of the bargains of Chiang Mai. The tasteful rooms are well designed – some have balconies while everyone has access to the cool air on the roof terrace. Friendly vibe stems from the half-Thai, half-Spanish owner Rodney. Its location right in the heart of hip Nimmanhaemin means that you can escape most of the other tourists. Only drawback is noisy nightclub next door – so bring your earplugs. Recommended.

Lampang p850

A Lampang Wiengthong Hotel, 138/109 Phahonyothin Rd, T054-225801, F054-225803. A/c, restaurant, pool, 250 rooms in this, the smartest and largest of Lampang's hotels, and easily the most luxurious place to stay in town.

D-E Riverside Guesthouse, 286 Talad Kao Rd, T054-227005, www.theriverside lampang.com. Beautiful rooms individually decorated by the friendly Italian owner, housed in an old teak building on the river. Room types include dorm beds, family-sized room and suites. Fan and a/c rooms available, most are en suite. Restaurant overlooking the Wang River. Highly recommended.

❶ Eating

Chiang Mai p844, map p846
Old City

¶¶¶ **The House**, 199 Moon Muang Rd, T053-419011. Set in a funky 1930s colonial house, this is an attempt to serve upmarket international cuisine. It largely succeeds though it is a bit hit and miss. Cute bar. Open 1200-2400.

Café Chic, 105/5 Phra Pokklao Rd, T053-814651. A great little place serving a limited menu of Thai and Western food, its strength lies in its great range of cakes, coffees and teas. A small shop here sells a range of products, artfully displayed and probably overpriced. Thu-Tue 1000-2000. Recommended.

Genchai, 54/1 Sing Ha Rat Rd. Excellent and very popular Isaan and Thai restaurant mostly frequented by locals. Good for sticky rice, grilled catfish and chicken. English menu. Recommended.

East of the Old City

Chez Daniel Le Normand, 255/18 Mahidol Rd, near Ormuang Superhighway, T053-204600. Normandy-style food – home-made charcuterie, wide choice of French wine, French music in the background.

Le Coq d'Or, 68/1 Koh Klang Rd, T053-282024. A long-established international restaurant, set in a pleasant house. Over-zealous waiters anticipate your every need. High standard of cuisine (including mouth-watering steaks), choice of wines.

The Restaurant, The Chedi, 123 Charoen Prathet Rd, T053-253333, www.ghmhotels.com. You'll find great traditional northern Thai specialities and innovative Pacific Rim cuisine complemented by an extensive wine list served in what was once the British Consulate – it also serves afternoon tea. Expensive but recommended.

Antique House 1, 71 Charoen Prathet Rd (next to the **Diamond Riverside Hotel**). Well-prepared Thai and Chinese food in wonderful garden with antiques and an old teak house, built in 1870s (and listed as a National Heritage Site), very nice candlelit ambience, tasty but small servings and rather slow service, live music. Busy road can be intrusive. Open 1100-2400.

The Fillmore East, 15/7 Loi Kroa Rd. Super Angus beef, imported from the US, served up to DVD 'concerts'. Excellent burgers, kebabs

and salads. A popular house dish is the home-made mashed potato. Pool table, friendly staff, happy customers. Recommended.

The Gallery, 25-29 Charoenrat Rd, T053-248601. Quiet and refined Thai restaurant on the River Ping, in a century-old traditional Thai house, superb food, highly recommended for a special night out, art gallery attached, either sit in a leafy veranda (under an ancient makiang tree) overlooking the river, or inside. Particularly recommended are the fish dishes, including steamed sea bass with lime and deep-fried *plaa chon*.

Whole Earth, 88 Sri Donchai Rd. Indian food served in a traditional Thai house in a lovely garden, very civilized, with unobtrusive live Thai classical music. Open 1100-2200. Recommended.

Nang Nual Seafood, 27/1-2-5 Koh Klang Rd. On the east bank of the Ping River, just south of **Westin Hotel**. Serves Chinese and international food, popular with tour groups.

Sophia, Charoen Prathet Soi 1 (down narrow soi between the night market and the river road). Cheap and very popular Muslim restaurant, this soi also usually supports a number of stalls, serving Malay/Muslim dishes from roti to mutton curry.

West of the Old City

Mi Casa, 60/2 Moo 14 Soi Wat Padaeng, Suthep Rd, T053-810088, www.micasachiangmai.com. Mediterranean food served in a beautiful homely setting. A good selection of tapas, wine, and vegetarian dishes makes this restaurant a favourite with the hip Thai crowd.

Khun Churn, 136/28 Nimmanhaemin Rd. Soi 15. Beautiful Thai vegetarian food in a nice, relaxed setting. All-you-can-eat lunch buffet. Recommended.

Nong Bee, 28 Nimmanhaemin Rd. Home-cooked authentic Burmese and Shan food such as fermented tea-leaves salad and tomato-fried rice. Excellent value for money. Open all day.

Pun Pun, Wat Suan Dok, Suthep Rd, www.punpunthailand.org, located in the grounds of Wat Suan Dok. This Thai vegetarian restaurant serves organic food made with ingredients bought from nearby cooperative farms. Beautiful setting, popular with monks and the local expat crowd. Highly recommended.

Foodstalls

Anusarn Market, southeast of night market. Stalls mostly at night, but also some throughout the day, cheap (₿10-15 single-dish meals), lively and fun. Recommended. **Chang Klang Rd** has stalls selling delicious pancakes, ₿3-7. **Somphet Market**, Moon Muang Rd, is good for takeaway curries, fresh fish, meat and fruit. North of **Chang Phuak Gate**, outside the moat, is another congregation of good foodstalls. **Warorot Market**, north of Chang Klang and Tha Phae roads, is a great place for foodstalls at night.

Lampang *p850*

For a cheap meal, try one of the Thai pavement cafés along Ropwiang Rd between the clock tower and the **Lampang Guesthouse**. ¶¶ **Terrace Restaurant**, Tipchang Rd. Reasonable food in open-air wooden house overlooking the river; a great place for a drink and/or a meal.

¶ **Riverside** (Baan Rim Nam), 328 Tipchang Rd. Wooden house overlooking the river, attractive ambience, reasonable Thai and international food. Recommended.

⊕ Bars and clubs

Chiang Mai *p844, map p846*

Chiang Mai has a reasonable bar scene but is fairly subdued compared to Bangkok – there is the usual run of go-go bars along Loi Kroa Rd. **Drunken Flower**, Soi 17 Nimmanhaemin Rd, T053-212081. Alternative politics, art and music mingle in this ramshackle though engaging bar-cum-restaurant. **Early Times**, Kotchasan Rd. Open air with live heavy metal music. **Monkey Club**, 7 Nimmanhaemin Rd., Soi 9, T053-226997. Open 1730-1400. Dance club,

restaurant and bar with a live Thai cover band, very popular with CMU students. Crowded, hot and loud.

North Gate Jazz Bar, Sriphum Rd, next to Khan-Asa. Enjoy nightly jazz performances whilst sipping wine or cocktails in this popular bar.

Rasta Café, off Rachpakinai Rd, near the intersection with Rachwithi Rd. Hang-out of choice for the toking traveller set. Lots of Bob Marley and interesting garden but hardly original.

Riverside Bar and Restaurant, 9-11 Charoenrat Rd. Assorted music from blues to Thai rock; owner is a big Beatles fan. **Warm-Up Café**, 40 Nimmanhaemin Rd, T053 -306253. Open from 1800-0100. Popular club, bar and restaurant, attracting a young crowd of trendy Thai students and expats. Live music and DJ.

Lampang *p850*

Relax, Tipchang Rd (next to **Riverside Restaurant**). Modern-style bar overlooking the river. Cold beer and more, open-air veranda.

❷ Entertainment

Chiang Mai *p844, map p846*
Cinema

Airport Plaza, Hwy 1141 (on the way to the airport), 4th floor, T053-283939. Big cinema complex, showing American blockbusters and the latest Thai movies. Discounts on Tue. **Chiang Mai Contemporary Art Museum** (see page 845), free foreign independent movies on Sat evenings.

Muay Thai (Thai boxing)

Kawila Boxing Stadium, near Nawarat Bridge. Matches start at 2000 every Fri night. For ₿400 you'll see 10 matches between both foreign and Thai boxers, as well as plenty of rowdy locals placing illegal bets (betting is outlawed in Thailand). Tickets can be purchased at the stadium or from travel agents in town.

⊛ Festivals and events

Chiang Mai *p844, map p846*
Feb Flower Festival on the 1st Fri, Sat
and Sun of the month. This great festival is
centred on the inner moat road, at the
southwest corner of the Old City. Small
displays of flowers and plants arranged by
schools, colleges and professional gardeners
and garden shops from across the north.
The highlight is a parade of floral floats
along with the requisite beauty contest.
13-16 Apr Songkran, traditional Thai New
Year (public holiday) celebrated with more
enthusiasm in Chiang Mai than elsewhere.
Boisterous water-throwing, particularly
directed at farangs; expect to be soaked
to the skin for the entire 4 days.
Mid-Nov Loi Krathong, a popular
Buddhist holiday when boats (*krathong*)
filled with flowers and lit candles are floated
down the river. Fireworks at night, and small
hot-air balloons are launched into the sky.
Dec Nimmanhaemin Arts Festival. For the
1st week of the month, pleasant Soi 1 is
closed to traffic and given over to the best
of Chiang Mai's designers in what is rapidly
becoming northern Thailand's premium
arts festival.

O Shopping

Chiang Mai *p844, map p846*
Chiang Mai is a shoppers' paradise. It
provides many of the treasures of Bangkok,
in a compact area. The **night market**,
with its array of handicrafts, antique shops
and fake designer shirts, continues to pack
the tourists in night after night. A quieter,
less frequented spot, is the group of
sophisticated shops, cafés and bars, that
have opened up on Nimmanhaemin Rd,
mostly patronized by trendy Thai students
and the expat crowd. Soi 1 and Soi 4 in
particular (where Nimman Promenade
is located) feature small design boutiques,
galleries and coffee shops.

Antiques and lacquerware
Gong Dee, Soi 1, Nimmaneheimen Rd.
T053-225032, www.gongdeegallery.com.
Beautiful lacquerware and handicrafts
famous for the gold leafs decorating most
products. Occasionally hosts exhibitions
by local artists. Recommended.
Sanpranon Antiques, west side of Hang
Dong Rd, about 4 km from Airport Plaza. Set
off the road in a traditional Thai house, it's a
huge place well worth a visit just to rummage
about. There's an overwhelming amount of
stock (from lacquerware to ceramics to
woodcarvings), much of which is clearly
not antique, but it's fun to nose.

Art galleries
Chiang Mai is generously sprinkled with
some of the best modern art being made in
Southeast Asia today. Read the local papers,
such as *Chiang Mai City Life* (www.chiangmai
news.com) and check out the sois around
Nimmanheimin and Charoenrat Rd for news
about exhibitions and small new galleries
seemingly opening and closing at a whim.
Art Space on 7, Sirimankalajarn Rd, Soi 7,
artspacecm@gmail.com. The ground floor
of the Artspace building houses regular
exhibitions whilst the upper floors hosts art
drawing classes, music classes and school
holiday workshops.
La Luna, 190 Charoenrat Rd, eastern side of
the Ping River, www.lalunagallery.com. One
of a growing number of contemporary art
galleries opening up in Chiang Mai. This airy,
open-plan space houses abstract works and
photography from throughout Southeast
Asia. They also sell a range of high-quality
gifts and prints.
Suvannabhumi Art Gallery, 116, Chareonrat
Rd, T081-031 5309, suvmarmar@gmail.com,
www.suvburma-art.com. A high-calibre
modern art gallery featuring the work of
prominent artists from Burma. Visiting this
transplanted gallery space, you benefit from
not only the owner's excellent taste, but also
her deep connections with the Burmese arts
scene. Not to be missed.

Bookshops
Gecko Books has just opened up its 3rd branch on 2 Rachamanka Rd. The other 2 are near Thae Pae Gate on 2/6 Chang Moi Kao Rd, and at 2 Thae Pae Gate Rd. Big selection of new and used books in English, Dutch, German, French, Swedish, Danish and Norwegian.
Suriwong Book Centre, 54/1-5 Sri Donchai Rd. Most extensive collection of books in English on Thailand in Chiang Mai.

Ceramics and terracotta
Baan Celadon, 7 Moo 3, Chiangmai-Sankamphaeng Rd, T053-338288, F053-338 940. A good range of ceramics for sale from simple everyday bowls to elaborate vases.
Ban Phor Liang Muen, 36 Phra Pokklao Rd. Huge range of terracotta plaques, murals, statues, pots at in outdoor display garden.

Handicrafts
Chiang Mai is the centre for hilltribe handicrafts. There is a bewildering array of goods, much of which is of poor quality (**Tha Phae Rd** seems to specialize in a poorer range of products). Bargain for everything. The **night market** on Chang Klang Rd has a lot on offer but better pieces can be found at the more exclusive shops on **Loi Kroa Rd**.
Chakhriya, 14/7 Nimman Promenade, Nimmanhaemin Rd, T08-1952 5773 (mob). Small and cosy boutique selling everything for the home.
Thai Tribal Crafts, 208 Bumrungrat Rd, near McCormick Hospital – run by Karen and Lahu church organizations on a non-profit basis. Good selection, quality and prices.

Night markets
Situated on the west and east sides of Chang Klang Rd, Chiang Mai's multiple night markets are now a major tourist attraction. Most stalls and shops open at about 1800 and close around 2300.
Huay Kaew Rd night market, north of Nimmanhaemin Rd, caters mainly to students and offers cheap clothes, shoes, accessories, and food. Daily 1800-2300.

Wualai Rd, south of the moat, turns into a walking street on Sat nights. Here you can find everything from cheap clothing and home-made jewellery to art, make-up and kitchenware. Popular with locals. Open 1700-2300.

▲ Activities and tours

Chiang Mai *p844, map p846*
Cookery classes
Chiang Mai Thai Cookery School, book through 47/2 Moon Muang Rd, (opposite Tha Phae Gate). T053-206388, www.thai cookeryschool.com. One of the best. Runs a variety of courses from ฿990 for a day.
You Sabai Home, Baan Thai Project, Mae Teang, T086-096 6439, www.yousabai.com/index.html. Run by lovely Yao and her husband, both fluent English-speakers, they offer 4-day organic vegetarian cooking courses, run out from their farm in You Sabai. Stay in simple earthen huts, participate in breakfast yoga or just enjoy the stunning scenery around their farm. Recommended. Phone for prices.

Swimming
700 Stadium, Canal Rd. For serious swimmers, try the Olympic-size pool within this sports complex, built to accommodate the 1997 ASEAN games. Open 0900-1800, ฿50. **Lotus Hotel** has a big rooftop pool open to the public ฿70, open 0900-2100.

Therapies and massage
There are umpteen places in town offering massage. They tend to charge around the same amount (฿200 per hr). Note that many masseuses seem to have had rudimentary training and the massage rooms consist of mattresses laid on the floors of upper rooms.

In an unusual rehabilitation initiative, **Chiang Mai's women's jail**, sited on Ratchawithi Rd in the middle of the old city, has opened a spa (+66-1-706 1041) staffed entirely by female prisoners. Here, the

Trekking around Chiang Mai

There are scores of trekking companies in Chiang Mai and hundreds of places selling trekking tours. Competition is stiff and most companies provide roughly the same assortment of treks, ranging from one night to over a week. Not many places actually organize the trek themselves and it is rare to meet the guide, or other people in the group, before leaving for the trek. The quality of the guide rather than the organizing company usually makes the trip successful or not and the happiest trekkers are often those who have done their homework and found a company with long-term, permanent staff who they can meet beforehand. For further information, see Trekking companies and Tour operators, page 858.

Like many other areas of tourism, trekking is suffering from its own success. Companies organizing treks are finding it increasingly difficult to present their products as authentic get-away-from-it-all adventures when there is such a high probability of bumping into another group of tourists. As numbers increase so travellers are demanding more authenticity in their trekking experiences. The answer is to avoid the environs of Chiang Mai and trek in less-pressured areas like Mae Hong Son, Nan and Pai. Many trek operators – like those along Moon Muang Rd – are advertising special non-tourist routes, although these so-called special routes are virtually indistinguishable from established routes. Some companies even claim to offer a money-back guarantee should they come into contact with other trekkers.

The TAT office distributes a list of recommended trekking operators and a leaflet on what to look out for when choosing your trip. The Tribal Research Institute (see page 848), provides information on the various hilltribes, maps of the trekking areas, and a library of books on these fascinating people. You can also download a useful pdf file from their website, www.chmai.com/tribal/content.html.

Remember to take protection against mosquitoes; long trousers and long-sleeved shirts are essential for the night-time.

When choosing a guide for the trip, ensure that he or she can speak the hilltribe dialect as well as good English (or French, German, etc). Guides must hold a 'Professional Guide Licence'. Treks must be registered with the Tourist Police; to do this the guide must supply the Tourist Police with a photocopy of the identity page of your passport and your date of entry stamp. You can check on a company's reputation by contacting the police department. Beware of leaving valuables in guesthouses in Chiang Mai; however reliable the owner may appear, it is always safer to deposit valuables such as passport, jewellery and money in a bank (banks on Tha Phae Road have safety deposits and charge about ฿200 per month).

paying public can get body and foot massages, herbal steam and a variety of beauty treatments. Almost all of the money goes directly to the masseuse, helping them to get ready for when they are released.

Oasis Spa, 102 Sirimangkalajan Rd, T053-815000. Luxurious day spa, offering different treatment packages varying from 1½ -4 hrs. Massages, aromatherapy, and herbal scrubs and steams are all on offer in one of the private Lanna-style bungalows.

Tao Garden Health Resort, 274 Moo 7, Luang Nua Doi Saket, T053-495596, www.tao-garden.com. Situated 30 mins outside of Chiang Mai, Tao Garden is an expensive alcohol- and smoke-free retreat. Treatments begin with a Chinese medical check-up, after which you can access many different types of massages, detox methods and aromatherapies, such as holistic dental treatment, inner smile meditation, colonic therapy and a blood-cleaner zapper.

Wat Umong, a couple of kilometres west of the city centre, otherwise known as the Forest Temple, is a popular place at weekends for locals to get a traditional Thai massage. Cheap at ฿99 for 1 hr, and very, very good.

Trekking companies

Many of the companies are concentrated on Tha Phae, Chaiyaphum, Moon Muang and Kotchasan roads. Standards change so rapidly that recommending companies is a dangerous business, but the safest bet is to find somewhere with permanent, long-term staff. Two such outfits are: **Chiang Mai Garden Guesthouse**, 82-86 Rachamanka Rd, T053-278881, and **Panda Tour Guesthouse**, 130/1 Rachmanka Rd, T053-206420, www.pandatour.com.

Prices for treks are highly variable with 2-day trips costing somewhere between ฿1600-1800; 3-day treks ฿1700-2000 and 4-day treks ฿2000-2400. Be aware that the better trips usually cost more, either because they're more off the beaten track and therefore further away, or because the company is paying for one of the better guides, who are worth their weight in gold. If you find a trek for a price that seems too good to be true, it probably is, and will end up being a waste of both money and time.

Tours and tour operators

A range of day tours run from Chiang Mai. Prices vary between companies so make sure you know exactly what is included in the price; some travellers have complained of hidden costs such as road tolls, tips for guides, entrance fees, etc. It is advisable to shop around to secure the best deal. Most tour operators are concentrated around Tha Phae Gate, Chang Klang and Moon Muang (in the vicinity of Tha Phae Gate), so this process is not as time consuming as it may seem. Most operators will also book air, train and bus tickets out of Chiang Mai. The TAT recommends that services should only be bought from companies that register with the Tourist Business and Guide Registration Office. It provides a list of all such companies. As noted in the trekking section, we have decided not to list or recommend companies because standards vary between tours (and guides) with individual outfits, and because these standards can change rapidly. Word of mouth is the best guarantee. Exceptions are:

Chiang Mai Green Tour and Trekking, 29-31 Chiang Mai-Lamphun Rd, A Muang, Chiang Mai 50000, cmgreent@chiangmai.a-net.net.th. A notable operator, which tries to provide eco-friendly and culturally sensitive tours. However, it also runs motorbike treks, which can hardly be described as eco-friendly.

Click and Travel Ltd, www.clickandtravel online.com. A young 'Soft Adventure Company' specializing in bicycle tours.

North Pearl Travel, 332/334 Tha Phae Rd, T/F053-232976.

Many of the larger tour companies and travel agents will also arrange visas and tours to Burma, Cambodia, Laos and Vietnam.

⊖ Transport

Chiang Mai *p844, map p846*
Air

Airport information: T053-270222, www.chiangmaiairportonline.com. The airport is 3 km southwest of town. Chiang Mai airport is now a very busy and important international hub. The situation with the different airlines in Thailand is also very fluid with budget operators appearing for a short period and then going bust. Most of Thailand's budget airlines operate a web-only service for bookings. At the time of writing numerous airlines – THAI, Air Asia, SGA, Nok, PB and Bangkok Airways – connect Chiang Mai with various domestic and regional destinations, including Bangkok, Phuket, Mae Hong Son, Kuala Lumpur, Sukhothai, Pai. Air Mandalay fly to Mandalay and Rangoon (Burma), Silk and Tiger Air fly to Singapore, China Airlines fly to Taipei (Taiwan), HK Express fly to Hong Kong, Bangkok Airways fly to Chang Rung (Burma), Luang Prabang and Vientiane (Laos). THAI also fly to Kunming (China), Chittagong (Bangladesh), Frankfurt (Germany) and Tokyo (Japan).

   Airline offices Air Mandalay (Skybird Tour), 92/3 Sri Donchai Rd, T053-818049. Bangkok Airways, Chiang Mai International Airport, T053-922258, F053-281520.

   Transport to town Taxis to town cost ฿90 (fixed price from the taxi booking counter). THAI operates a shuttle bus service between the airport and its office in town (but you can get off anywhere in town), ฿40.

Bicycle
Available from Chang Phuak Gate, southern end of Moon Muang Rd, ฿50 per day, or on Nakhon Ping Bridge, plus some guesthouses. Bike & Bite, 23/1 Sri Phum Rd, T053-418534. A deposit or your passport will probably be required. Bikes should be locked up and always tie your bag to the basket.

Bus
The long-distance bus station is at the Chiang Mai Arcade, on the corner of the super-highway and Kaew Nawarat Rd, northeast of town, T053-242664. Tuk-tuks and sii-lors wait at the station to take passengers into town. There is an information desk within the main terminal building, with information on all departure times and prices. The tourist police also have a desk here. Regular connections with Bangkok's Northern bus terminal (9-12 hrs), Phitsanulok (6 hrs), Sukhothai

(5 hrs), Chiang Rai (3-4 hrs), Mae Sariang (4-5 hrs), Mae Hong Son (8-9 hrs), Pai (4 hrs), Nan (6 hrs) and other northern towns. Buses to closer destinations (such as Mae Rim, Phrao, Chiang Dao, Fang, Tha Ton and Lamphun) go from Chotana Rd, north of Chang Puak Gate.

Car/jeep hire
Rates start at ฿800-1800 per day, ฿6000 per week. Many guesthouses will arrange rental or there are outfits along Chaiyaphum and Moon Muang roads. National and Avis are slightly more expensive, but are more reliable. North Wheels, 127/2 Moon Muang Rd, T053-216189, www.northwheels.com. Some of the cars have seen better days, but rates are competitive here and they are a local operator who have been established for at least a decade.

Motorbike
The wearing of helmets in Chiang Mai city is compulsory (but you wouldn't know it), and you are also supposed to have a valid motor-bike license. If not wearing a helmet or lacking the right licence, you might be asked to pay ฿200 or more if stopped by the traffic police.

   Hire along Chaiyuphum and Moon Muang roads and at many guesthouses. Rates start at around ฿150-200 for a Honda Dream and rise up to ฿1200 for a chopper or sports bike. Insurance is not available for small motorbikes and most policies only protect you from 50% of the repair costs. POP, 51 Kotchasan Rd, T053-276014, charges ฿250 for 24 hrs.

Songthaews/tuk-tuks
Red songthaews are the most common means of transport around town. Travelling on regular routes costs ฿15-20. Tuk-tuks charge a minimum ฿40 per trip, ฿60-100 for longer journeys.

Train
The station is in the east of the town, on Charoen Muang Rd, across the Ping River.

Ticket office open 0500-2100. Train information, T053-244795; reservations T053-242094. Regular connections with **Bangkok** and towns along the route (11-15 hrs). There is both daytime and sleeper services – booking is required for both.

Transport to town Frequent songthaews and tuk-tuks, or take city bus No 1, 3 or 6, which stop outside the station.

Lampang p850
Bus
The bus station is on Route 1, just east of the railway line (15-min walk from town centre). Regular connections with **Bangkok** (9 hrs), **Chiang Mai** (2 hrs) and other destinations north and south.

Horse-drawn carriages
A tour around town costs ฿80-120. They generally take 2 routes, the cheaper one takes about 20 mins, the more expensive 45 mins or ฿120 per hr.

Train
The station is on the west side of town, at the end of Surain Rd. Regular connections with **Bangkok** (12 hrs) and **Chiang Mai** (2 hrs).

❶ Directory

Chiang Mai p844, map p846
Banks There are several banks on Tha Phae Rd and plenty of exchange services along Chang Klang and Tha Phae roads. Many exchange booths open daily 0800-2000. **Consulates** Australia, 165 Sirimungklajarn Rd, T053-213473, F053-219726. **French Honorary Consulate**, 138 Charoen Prathet Rd, T053-281466,

F053-215719. **Sweden**, Green Valley, Mae Rim, T053-298632. **UK**,198 Bumrungrat Rd, T053-263015, F203408. **USA**, 387 Vichayanon Rd, T053-252629, F053-252633.
Emergencies Fire Emergency: T199. **Immigration**: Fang Rd, 300 m before the entrance to the airport, T053-277510. Mon-Fri 0830-1200, 1300-1630. **Police**: corner of Phra Singh and Jhaban roads. **Police Emergency**: T191. **Tourist Police**: in the same building as the TAT office on the Chiang Mai-Lamphon Rd, T053-248974, at the Arcade Bus Station, the night market and at the airport. **Internet** There are dozens of internet places all around town, ฿1-2 per min in tourist areas. **Medical services Hospitals**: Chiang Mai's medical services have a good reputation. The most popular expat hospital is **Ram**, where there is 24-hr service available and good English-speaking doctors. **Chiang Mai Ram Hospital**, Boonruangrit Rd, T053-224851/224881. **McCormick Hospital**, Kaew Nawarat Rd, T053-241010, **Malaria Centre**, Boonruangrit Rd, north of Suan Dok Gate. Outpatient fees around ฿100-140, emergency fees are not exorbitant either. **Dentist**: Dr Pramote's Clinic, 206 Vichayanon Rd, T053-234453. **Ram Hospital** also has a good dental clinic. **Post office** General Post Office, Charoen Muang Rd (west of the railway station), telegram counter open daily 24 hrs, T053-241056. Chiang Mai's other main post office is the **Mae Ping Post Office** on Praisani Rd, near the Nawarat Bridge.

Lampang p850
Banks Siam Commercial, Chatchai Rd. **Thai Farmers**, 284/8 Chatchai Rd. **Thai Military**, 173-75 Chatchai Rd. **Post office** Surain Rd (opposite the railway station).

Northern Hills

Some of the most spectacular scenery in Thailand lies to the west of Chiang Mai, where the Tenasserim range divides Burma from Thailand. Travelling northwest the road reaches the popular backpacker and trekking town of Pai. From Pai to Soppong is more stunning scenery, then onto the hill town of Mae Hong Son, a centre for trekking and home to fine Burmese-style wats.

Directly north of Chiang Mai is the important city of Chiang Rai – once the capital of the ancient Lanna Kingdom. Not much remains of the original walled city but Chiang Rai is a friendly place with superb facilities and excellent transport links to the rest of the far north.

Mae Sai, 61 km directly north of Chiang Rai, is Thailand's most northerly town and a busy border trading post with Burma. Head east from here and you'll reach the infamous Golden Triangle, the meeting point of Laos, Thailand and Burma. This was once a lawless area filled with smugglers and drug lords but these days it's home to the trashy tourist village of Sop Ruak and the compelling Opium Museum. Downstream, on the banks of the Mekong River, is the small outpost of Chiang Khong – a crossing point into Laos. >> *For listings, see pages 868-875.*

Pai and Soppong → *Colour map 1, C1/2.*

The road from Chiang Mai winds its way through scintillating landscapes and thick forest until the view unfolds into a broad valley. In the middle, encircled by handsome, high ridges, sits Pai. Over the last 25 years this small mountain village has transformed itself into one of Northern Thailand's most popular destinations. Transport links are pretty good – an airstrip has opened just to the north of town with a couple of daily flights to Chiang Mai while there are several buses a day linking Pai to Chiang Mai and Mae Hong Son.

These days, with its organic eateries and reggae bars, Pai could be considered a travellers' oasis. Even hip young city dwellers from Bangkok are slowly catching onto the area's beauty, facilities, hot springs and ethnic diversity. But in January 2008 Pai's idyllic charms were somewhat shattered by the shooting of two Canadian backpackers by a drunk, off-duty policeman. Pai's tourist trade appears robust enough to survive such events – there's excellent trekking, some great food and a good range of accommodation. Don't come here thinking you're going to get an authentic slice of Thai life. This is a generic, contrived Khaosan Road-style experience, though in very pleasant surroundings. Apart from a few average markets there's little to do in Pai except laze about. If you head a few kilometres east you'll arrive at Pai's famous **hot springs**. The hot sulphurous water bubbles up through a system of streams; bring a towel and jump in. In the vicinity there are **Lisu**, **Shan**, **Red Lahu** and **Kuomintang-Chinese villages**.

Soppong, or **Phang Ma Pha**, is a small way station between Pai and Mae Hong Son that is slowly metamorphosing into an alternative to Pai – a few great guesthouses offer a decent array of trekking services. Regular buses ply the route between Mae Hong Son and Pai. The main 'sight' hereabouts is **Lod Cave (Tham Lod)** ① *about 10 km from town, daily 0800-1700*. The cave is a small part of what is presumed to be one of the largest cave systems in northern Thailand. Guides hire out their services to take visitors through the cave. In the nearby village you'll find **Cave Lodge**, one of northern Thailand's longest-running and best guesthouses (see Sleeping page 868).

Mae Hong Son → *Colour map 1, C1.*

Mae Hong Son lies in a forested valley, surrounded by soaring verdant hills and just about lives up to its claim to being the 'Switzerland of Thailand'. The road from Pai is continuous switchback, cutting through spectacular scenery and passing by the diverse ethnicities that populate the area. There are regular flights to/from Chiang Mai and the bus station provides connections with Chiang Mai and Bangkok. An excellent centre for trekking, Mae Hong Son Province is about as far removed from 'Thailand' as you are likely to get, with only an estimated 2% of the population ethnic Thais. The great majority belong to one of the various hilltribes: mostly Karen, but also Lisu, Hmong and Lahu. Historically, Mae Hong Son has always been caught between the competing powers of Burma and Siam/Thailand. For much of recent history the area has been under the (loose) control of various Burmese kingdoms. The influence of Burmese culture is also clearly reflected in the architecture of the town's many monasteries.

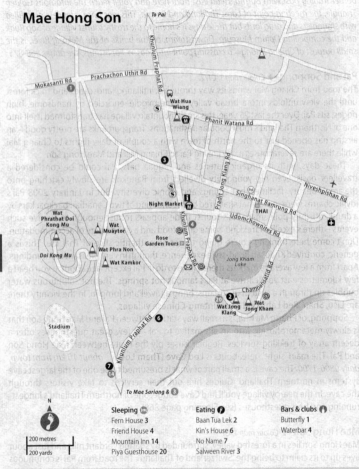

Mae Hong Son

To Pai

Mokasanti Rd

Prachachon Uthit Rd

Khunlum Praphat Rd

Wat Hua Wiang

Phanit Watana Rd

Pradit Jong Klang Rd

Night Market

Singhanat Bamrung Rd

Niveshpishan Rd

THAI

Wat Phrathat Doi Kong Mu

Wat Muaytor

Udomchownnires Rd

Khunlum Praphat Rd

Doi Kong Mu

Rose Garden Tours

Wat Phra Non

Jong Kham Lake

Wat Kamkor

Chambanaatd Rd

Wat Jong Klang

Wat Jong Kham

Stadium

Khunlum Praphat Rd

To Mae Sariang &

Sleeping 🛏
Fern House 3
Friend House 4
Mountain Inn 14
Piya Guesthouse 20

Eating 🍴
Baan Tua Lek 2
Kin's House 6
No Name 7
Salween River 3

Bars & clubs 🍸
Butterfly 1
Waterbar 4

Most postcards of the town picture the lake, with **Wat Jong Klang**, a Burmese wat, in the background. Wat Jong Klang started life as a rest pavilion for monks on pilgrimage, with a wat being built by the Shans living in the area between 1867 and 1871. **Doi Kong Mu**, the hill overlooking the town, provides superb views of the valley and is home to the Burmese-style **Wat Phrathat Doi Kong Mu**, constructed by the first king of Mae Hong Son in the mid19th century.

Chiang Rai → *Colour map 1, B/C3.*

Given the ancient roots of Chiang Rai, the capital of Thailand's most northerly province, there's little here in the way of historical interest, with modern shophouse architecture predominating. What Chiang Rai lacks in sights it makes up for with a dose of rootsy, friendly charm and some great accommodation. It also makes a perfect base for trekking and to visit the towns further to the north. Chiang Rai's airport is 8 km north of the city. There are daily connections with Bangkok and Chiang Mai. The bus station is in the centre of town with regular connections to Bangkok, Chiang Mai, and with other assorted destinations.

Chiang Rai is a sprawling town and, while walking is fine in the morning and evening, during the day many locals choose to travel by tuk-tuk or songthaew. Most of the area's attractions lie in the surrounding countryside, and there are ample vehicle hire shops offering bicycles, cars, motorbikes and jeeps. The well-run **TAT office** ① *448/16 Singhaklai Rd (near the river, opposite Wat Phra Singh), T053-744674, F053-717434* provides useful town maps and information on trekking and accommodation.

Chiang Rai was founded in 1268 by King Mengrai and the city became one of the key *muang* (city states), within the Lanna Kingdom's sphere of control. Today, Chiang Rai has ambitious plans for the future. Lying close to what has been termed the 'Golden Rectangle', linking Thailand with Laos, Myanmar and southern China, the city's politicians and businessmen hope to cash in on the opening up of the latter three countries.

The city's finest monastery, at the north end of Trairat Road, is the 13th-century **Wat Phra Kaeo**. Local legend recounts that the stupa was struck by lightning to reveal the famous Emerald Buddha or Phra Kaeo, now in residence in Bangkok's Temple of the Emerald Buddha (see page 796).

Above Wat Phra Kaeo, perched at the top of a small hill, is **Wat Ngam Muang**, unremarkable save for the views it offers of the city and surrounding countryside. **Wat Phra Singh** (1385), in the north of town on Singhaklai Road, is an important teaching monastery. South of Wat Phra Singh is **Wat Mung Muang**, notable largely for its corpulent image of the Buddha that projects above the monastery walls. The area around Wat Mung Muang supports a daily **market** and, in the mornings from 0600 or so, vegetable hawkers set up along the monastery walls. Building on the success of Chiang Mai's night bazaar or market, Chiang Rai opened its own **night bazaar** off Phahonyothin Road a few years back. It has since expanded and in many ways it is a nicer place to browse than the Chiang Mai night bazaar. It is less frenetic, friendlier, and there is live music and open-air restaurants.

About 10 km south towards Chiang Mai stands one of the north's newest and most popular temples, **Wat Rong Khun** ① *Mon-Fri 0800-1730, Sat and Sun 0800-1800, free.* Crafted by a local artist, this temple looks as though it has been frosted white by a freezing Arctic storm – the entire construction is built in concrete, inlaid with mirrors and then whitewashed. Some might think the result is daring beauty; others could come to the conclusion it is kitsch trash dressed up as art. The masses seem to love the place as, at weekends, queues of camera-phone-wielding Thais eagerly take snaps of this

Chiang Rai

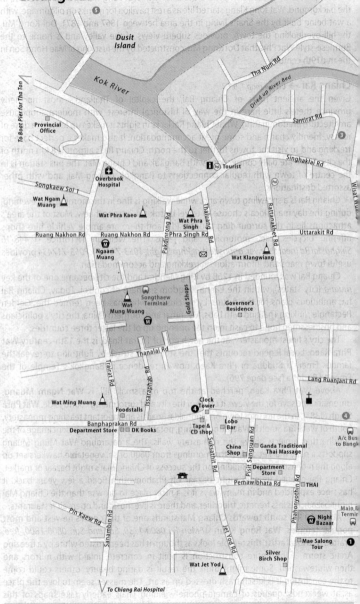

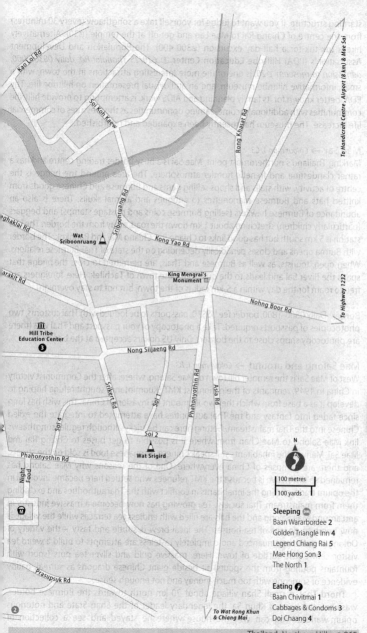

To Handicraft Centre, Airport (8 km) & Mae Sai

Kao Loi Rd

Soi Koh Kaew

Rong Khasat Rd

Sriboonruang Rd

Wat Sriboonruang

Kong Yao Rd

ghaklai Rd

King Mengrai's Monument

arakit Rd

Nohng Boor Rd

To Highway 1232

Hill Tribe Education Center ❸

Nong Siijaeng Rd

Srikert Rd

Phahonyothin Rd

Asia Rd

Soi 1

Soi 4

Soi 2

Phahonyothin Rd

Wat Srigird

Night Food

Prasupsuk Rd

To Wat Rong Khun & Chiang Mai

N

100 metres
100 yards

startling structure. If you want to judge for yourself take a songthaew (every 30 minutes) from the centre of Chiang Rai to Mae Lao and get off at the temple (β30). Alternatively hire a tuk-tuk for a half-day excursion (β300-400). The Population and Development Association's (PDA) **Hilltribe Education Center** ① *620/25 Thanalai Rd, daily 0830-2000; admission to museum β20,* is one of the more interesting attractions in the town, with a small, informative hilltribe museum, and an audiovisual presentation on hilltribe life. The PDA, better known for its family planning and AIDS work, is attempting to provide hilltribe communities with additional income-earning opportunities as the pressures of commercial life increase. The museum has recently been expanded and refurbished.

Mae Sai → *Colour map 1, C3.*
Marking Thailand's northernmost point, Mae Sai is a busy border trading centre and has a rather clandestine and frenetic frontier atmosphere. The area around the bridge is the centre of activity, with stalls and shops selling gems and Burmese and Chinese goods from knitted hats and Burmese marionettes to antiques and animal skulls. There is also an abundance of Burmese hawkers (selling Burmese coins and postage stamps) and beggars (particularly children) stretching about 1 km down the road, away from the border. The bus station is 5 km south but has good links to Chiang Rai, Chiang Mai and Bangkok. The border with Burma opens and closes periodically depending on the state of Thai-Burmese relations. When open, tourists, as well as Burmese and Thais, are permitted to cross the bridge that spans the River Sai and leads to the quiet Burmese town of **Tachilek**. Here, foreigners are free to roam for the day within a 5-km radius of the town, but not to stay overnight.

Border *Daily 0800-1800, border fee US$10, passports to be lodged with Thai customs, two photocopies of passports required.* Take a photocopy of your passport and Thai visa (there are photocopy shops close to the border). Only US dollars accepted at the border.

Mae Salong and around → *Colour map 1, B3.*
West of Mae Sai is the remoter hill town of Mae Salong, where, after the Communist victory in China in 1949, remnants of the nationalist KMT (Kuomintang) sought refuge hoping to develop it as a base from which they would mount an invasion of China. This wish has long since faded into fantasy and the Thai authorities have attempted to integrate the exiled Chinese into the Thai mainstream. Getting here can be tricky although regular songthaews link Mae Salong to Mae Chan from where it is possible to get buses to Chiang Rai and Mae Sai. Many of the inhabitants still speak Chinese, Yunnanese food is sold on the streets, and there are glimpses of China everywhere. One of the reasons why Mae Salong has remained so distinctive is because the KMT refugees who settled here became involved in the opium trade, putting the inhabitants in conflict with the Thai authorities and excluding them from mainstream Thai society. Tea growing has now become a massive industry in and around Mae Salong and the hills are filled with endless tea terraces while the village is now home to dozens of tea-houses. The local brew is subtle and tasty – the variety of Oolong is good. Less nuanced and completely tasteless are attempts to build a weird tea visitor centre just outside of town. Here, massive gold and silver tea pots (soon with fountains pouring from the spouts) sit beside giant Chinese dragons as surreal, gaudy evidence of someone with too much money and not enough sense.

Thord Thai, a small Shan village about 20 km north towards the Burmese border, was once the base of Khun Sa, the legendary leader of the Shan State and notorious opium warlord. You can visit the house where he stayed and see a collection of photographs and other artefacts connected to the man. You'll have to rent a motorbike or arrange your own transport to get here.

Golden Triangle and Sop Ruak → *Colour map 1, B3.*

The mythical Golden Triangle, where Burma, Laos and Thailand meet, has largely forged its reputation on the basis of a somewhat unwarranted association with drugs, intrigue and violence. These days the rather dull village of Sop Ruak has become a busy tourist spot. To get here you'll need to take a songthaew from Mai Sai, a short hop to the west. There is next to nothing to do or see in Sop Ruak, unless rows of tacky stalls hold any fascination, although a succession of maps and marble constructions inform visitors time and again that they are at the Golden Triangle. For those searching for something to elevate their experience, the **Opium Museum** ① *daily 0700-1800, ฿20*, is located just outside town opposite the gate to the Anantara Hotel. It charts the rise of the international opium trade – largely put in place by 19th-century British businessmen with the backing of the British government – and the contemporary effects of the narcotics trade.

Chiang Saen → *Colour map 1, B3.*

Roughly 11 km downstream is Chiang Saen – an ancient walled citadel capital on the banks of the Mekong River. There are regular bus/songthaew connections with Chiang Rai, Mae Sai and Chaing Khong from here as well as several boat services up and down the Mekong. It is a charming, atmospheric one-street market town that is home to numerous monuments and a small branch of the **National Museum** ① *Wed-Sun 0900-1200, 1300-1600, ฿10*, which contains various Buddha images and other artefacts unearthed in the area, as well as a small display of hilltribe handicrafts including clothing and musical instruments. West of Chian Saen, just outside the city ramparts, is the beautiful **Wat Pa Sak** ① *฿30*, or 'Forest of Teak Wat' – so-called because of a wall of 300 teak trees, planted around the wat when it was founded. The monastery was founded in 1295 during the reign of Ramkhamhaeng of Sukhothai and actually predates the town. There are few tourist facilities in Chiang Saen – most people visit on a day trip from Mae Sai or Chiang Rai.

Chiang Khong → *Colour map 1, B3.*

For such a small town Chiang Khong has had a relatively high profile in Thai history. In the 1260s, King Mengrai extended control over the area and Chiang Khong became one of the Lanna Thai Kingdom's major principalities. Later, the town was captured by the Burmese. This border settlement is growing in popularity and becoming increasingly orientated towards tourism, due mainly to the opening of a border crossing into Laos, just the other side of the river. Boats from the town of Huay Xai, the Laos settlement on the opposite side, travel down river to the ancient Laos city of **Luang Prabang**. Chiang Khong does have a relaxed atmosphere making it an attractive spot to unwind. Buses link Chiang Khong to Chiang Rai, Chiang Mai and Bangkok while boats can take you across to Laos or up river to Chiang Saen.

Wat Luang, in the centre of town, dates from the 13th century. An engraved plaque maintains that two hairs of the Buddha were interred in the chedi in AD 704 – a date that would seem to owe more to poor maths or over-optimism than to historical veracity. Like Nong Khai and the other towns that line the Mekong in the northeastern region, the rare (and delicious) *pla buk* catfish is caught here. It is sometimes possible to watch the fishermen catching a giant catfish on the riverbank to the south of town.

For Sleeping and Eating price codes,
see inside the front cover.

Sleeping

Pai *p861*

A-B Phu Pai Art Resort, about 5 km north of town, T053-065111, www.phupai.com. Beautiful resort in a gorgeous location. Lots of nice trimmings – rooms are huge, with all the modern facilities you'd expect; service is a bit patchy, though it's still good value.

D Blue Lagoon, on main road in centre of town, T053-699824. Well-run place. Swimming pool, clean, decent rooms, excellent disabled facilities.

F-G Shan Guesthouse, 4 Wiangtai Rd, T053-699162. Located on the edge of town in a rather exposed position (but with great views), bungalows set in quiet location around a pond, with a Burmese pagoda-esque restaurant in the middle. Bungalows are raised off the ground and made of wood with 'leaf' roofs, good balconies.

G Golden Huts, T053-699949. Very quiet, beautiful out of the way location on the riverbank. Quiet and relaxing atmosphere, French owner provides a friendly service. Small but adequate restaurant with good food and great views. Recommended.

Soppong *p861*

B-E Little Eden, on main road, T053-617053, www.littleeden-guesthouse.com. Cute place with a wide selection of bungalows and even a river-view house. Rooms are fresh and well kept, there's some nice gardens and a cute swimming pool. A/c, hot-water and en suite available. Recommended.

B-E Soppong River Inn, 500 m from village centre towards Mae Hong Son, T053-617107, www.soppong.com. Has a range of great huts, some with verandas overlooking a small gorge. Also offers trekking service, massage and fresh coffee. Friendly and recommended.

E-G Cave Lodge, T053-617203, www.cave lodge.com. Set up 24 years ago, Cave Lodge is a labour of love for its Aussie owner, John Spies. A cluster of small bungalows cling to a steep rock face that leads down to a small glade and stream. Facilities are basic – you are off the beaten track here – but there is everything from en suite rooms with hot water through to dorms; they even have a home-made sauna! Excellent Western, Thai and local cuisine available. John knows the nearby cave systems, trekking routes and different ethnic groups intimately. Cave Lodge attracts a real cross-section of travellers and is one of the best guesthouses in the country. Pick-up from Soppong can be arranged for a fee; otherwise take a motorcycle taxi from Soppong (roughly ฿200-300) or walk the 6 km. Recommended.

Mae Hong Son *p861, map p862*

A-D Mountain Inn, 112 Khunlum Praphat Rd, T053-611802, www.mhsmountain inn.com. A/c, well-thought-out rooms surround an atmospheric garden. Friendly management and also serves good food (see Eating, below). Recommended.

B Fern House, 2 km from Hwy 108 at the turn off for Ban Nua Hum Mae Sakut Village (5 km from town), T053-611374, ferngroup @softhome.net. Wooden bungalows built on rice paddies, Shan style. Simple yet comfortable and tasteful. Set in lovely grounds, friendly and helpful staff; an eco-friendly place, with good walks from here.

E Piya Guesthouse, 1 Soi 3 Khunlum Praphat Rd, T053-611260. In a garden setting, 14 clean rooms next to the lake, all with a/c and TV. Some with double beds, and others twin-bedded. The manager is extremely friendly and all the bungalows have been recently refurbished. Recommended.

F-G Friend House, 21 Pradit Jong Kham Rd, T053-620119. Set back from the road, 10 rooms in this teak house are very clean with solid wooden floors, the shared showers are even cleaner, upstairs rooms have a view of the lake, well managed and carefully maintained, small café downstairs for breakfast, laundry service. Recommended.

Chiang Rai *p863, map p864*
L-AL The Legend Chiang Rai, 124/15 Kohloy Rd, T053-910400, www.thelegend-chiangrai.com. A boutique hotel on the banks of the Mae Kok River.

C Golden Triangle Inn, 590 Phahonyothin Rd, T053-711339, F053-713963. This great little hotel on a tree-filled plot of land has clean and stylish rooms with hot water. Good treks, friendly atmosphere, breakfast included in room rate. Recommended.

D-E The North Hotel, small soi between market and night bazaar, T053-719873, www.thenorth.co.th. Funky little hotel with library, roof terrace, bar and restaurant. One of the coolest places to stay in town. Rooms with a/c, TV and en suite. Owner is friendly and speaks English. Recommended.

E Baan Wararbordee, 59/1 Moo 18, Sanpanard Rd, T053-754888. Sweet little guest-house tucked away on a quiet soi. Very friendly, helpful owner, free coffee, tea and internet. Rooms on the upper floors are better lit – all come with colour TV, en suite, hot water and a/c. There's a garden as well. Recommended.

E-F Mae Hong Son, 126 Singhaklai Rd, T053-715367. Run by Hans, a Dutchman, this friendly guesthouse is situated at the end of a very quiet soi. The traditional wooden house has clean rooms with shared bathrooms, also available are some newer, more expensive rooms with attached bathrooms but no a/c. Treks (recommended, with a great guide), jeep and motorbike hire, good source of information, peaceful, tasty food, good value. Recommended.

Mae Sai *p866*
E Yeesun Hotel, 816/13 Sawlongchong Rd, T053-733455. Decent small hotel aimed mainly at Thais but still a good deal and one of the best of the bunch. Rooms are a/c with hot showers and cable TV. Recommended.

E-F Monkey Island, Sawlongchong Rd, T053-734060. British-owned, riverside guest-house serving food and providing lots of other facilities to travellers. Rooms are OK but characterless. Bar and internet/Wi-Fi available.

Mae Salong and around *p866*
L-E Mae Salong Flower Hills Resort, T053-765496, www.maesalongflower hills.com. This large resort looks out of place with its over-coiffured lawns and gardens but it actually offers surprisingly good value and a friendly welcome. The rooms and bungalows are cast over a steep hillside with spectacular views and all are a/c, en suite and have cable TV. There's even a pool. Recommended.

D-E Mae Salong Farmstay, T084-611 5608, www.maesalongfarmstay.com. A collection of fine bungalows at the end of a dusty track just before you enter town from the north (the owner will collect you from town). Each is en suite and comes with a/c, though luxury increases as you pay more. There's also restaurant and bar – there's free Wi-Fi. The giant teapots are in walking distance and the owners very friendly. Recommended.

E-F Little Home Guesthouse, next to Sinsane, T053-765389, www.maesalong littlehome.com. One of the friendliest and best-run small guesthouses in this part of the north, Little Home's owner, Somboon – an ex child soldier with the KMT – and his family really go out of their way to be hospitable. There are basic, spotless rooms in the teak house at the front and a couple of bungalows for rent at the back. They also serve food, drinks and have internet access. Highly recommended.

Golden Triangle and Sop Ruak *p867*
LL-AL Anantara Golden Triangle, 1 km north of Sop Ruak, T053-784084, F053-784 090. Pool, 'traditional' architecture taken to the limit, good service, wonderful evening views, very well run, good facilities and relatively peaceful. Also runs an excellent Elephant Camp in conjunction with the Elephant Conservation Centre (see page 850).

E Bamboo Hut Guesthouse, a couple of kilometres downstream (south) from Sop Ruak and about 6 km north of Chiang Saen.

Chiang Saen p867
B-D Chiang Saen River Hill Hotel, Phahonyothin Soi 2 (just inside the southern city walls), T053-650826, chiangsaen@ hotmail.com. A/c, restaurant. Best hotel in town with 60 rooms and 4 storeys. Nothing flash, but friendly management and comfortable rooms with attached showers (very clean), minibar and TV.

Chiang Khong p867
C-D Ruan Thai Sophaphan Resort, Tambon Wiang Rd, T053-791023. Wooden house with big clean rooms with own bathroom and hot water. Upstairs rooms are better – downstairs is a little dark. There's a large veranda and restaurant. Also bungalows for 2-4 people, river views, friendly, self-service drinks, price negotiable out of season. Recommended.
D-F Bamboo Riverside, Sai Khlang Rd, T053-791621. Balconies on riverbank, clean, hot showers, friendly owners with good English and full of information. Generally higher standard of huts to the rest of the places in this category. Restaurant serves great Mexican food and freshly baked bread.
E-F Green Tree Guesthouse, Sai Khlang Rd. Friendly owner with exceptional English. Pleasant yet basic rooms with shared hot-water showers. Nice shady restaurant. Lots of information and tours available. Recommended.

🍴 Eating

Pai p861
🍴 **Amido Pizza**, Ratdamrong Rd. Awesome pizza, pasta and lasagne made with love. Just over bridge on the way to the hot springs.
🍴 **Baan Ben Jarong**, edge of town, on the way to Chiang Mai. High-class Thai cuisine – exceptional and one of the best places to eat in the area. Highly recommended.

🍴 **Own Home Restaurant**, Ratdamrong Rd. Some Thai dishes, along with travellers' fare including tortillas, banana porridge, shakes, pizzas, moussaka and sandwiches.

Soppong p861
There are the usual noodle stalls on the main road, which should keep most peoples' hunger in check. For something more upmarket, most of the guesthouses serve reasonable food. The best place to eat locally is at the **Cave Lodge**, 6 km away (see Sleeping, above).

Mae Hong Son p861, map p862
🍴 **Baan Tua Lek**, Chamnansatid Rd, across from Jung Klang Temple, T053-620688. Small coffee-bar with cosy atmosphere, friendly staff and free Wi-Fi. A popular hangout for foreigners and Thais alike. Sells coffee, smoothies and tea as well as home-made sandwiches and cookies. Recommended.
🍴 **Kin's House**, 89 Khunlum Praphat Rd (past **Fern Restaurant**). Selection of traditional and local Thai cuisine and Western food. Nice decor, café/bar atmosphere.
🍴 **Restaurant** (no name), next to **Mountain Inn**. Sells a range of very authentic hilltribe dishes that are extremely popular with locals.
🍴 **Salween River Restaurant**, 3 Singhanat Bamrung Rd, T053-612050. British, Burmese, Shan and Thai dishes available. Generous portions, home-made bread and strong drinks. Sells books and maps, has free Wi-Fi and plenty of information about treks and homestays.

Chiang Rai p863, map p864
In the evenings, the night bazaar off Phahonyothin Rd is good for foodstalls; you can choose from spring rolls, wonton, pancakes, kebabs, noodles, rice dishes, even deep-fried beetles and grubs – and then sit at a table and listen to live music. Great atmosphere.
🍴🍴 **Ratanakosin**, T053-740012. Comes highly recommended for quality of food and atmospheric decor. Faces onto night bazaar, so you can feel part of the action, and dine from the upstairs balcony, whilst watching the Thai dancing down in the bazaar, open 1600-2400.

¶-¶ Baan Chivitmai, opposite the bus station. A perfect spot to gather your thoughts, chomp on a yummy cake and sup on a decent coffee before setting off around town – a little pricey. It is run by a Swedish Christian charity.

¶-¶ Doi Chaang, see map. An outlet for a local community-controlled coffee-growing project that is well worth supporting if only for the fact that they serve a great cup of the brown, roasted stuff. Decent cakes as well.

¶ Cabbages and Condoms, 620/25 Thanalai Rd (attached to the **Hilltribe Museum**). Run by the PDA, a non-governmental organization, all proceeds go to charity. Good northern food and free condoms.

¶ Golden Triangle Café (at **Golden Triangle Inn**), 590 Phahonyothin Rd. Serves international food. Recommended.

Mae Sai p866

¶¶ Daw Restaurant, back down Sawlongchong Rd towards the market from **Monkey Island**, past **Bamboo Guesthouse**. Serves up delicious Thai grub. Highly recommended. There's also a great noodle place right next to Bamboo as well (¶).

¶¶ Monkey Island, see Sleeping. Does some pretty good Western food and the English breakfasts are worth a go.

Mae Salong and around p866

A good place to eat Yunnanese food.

¶¶ Sweet Mae Salong, see map. A new café that serves up probably the best chocolate brownie in the whole country. The friendly owners speak great English and there is free internet for customers. They also sell a range of Thai/Western food and damn, fine coffee. Recommended.

¶ Little Home guesthouse, see Sleeping. Serves up some great noodle and Thai dishes.

¶ Salima Restaurant, 300 m past **Little Home Guesthouse**, is a great Muslim restaurant and is probably the best place to eat in town. The owners are very friendly, speak almost no English and are slightly eccentric. Memorable and recommended.

Chiang Saen p867

There are a number of cheap *kwaytio* stalls along the riverbank and on Phahonyothin Rd.

¶ Riverside, close to the **Chiang Saen Guesthouse** which is on Rimkhong Rd. Probably the best restaurant in town.

Chiang Khong p867

¶¶ Nong Kwan, Sai Khlang Rd. Serves great Thai food at reasonable prices. The chicken and cashew dishes are recommended.

¶¶ Ruan Thai Sophaphan Resort, see Sleeping, above. Worth considering as it's very comfortable with wicker chairs, cold beer, a great view and good food.

Bars and clubs

Pai p861

Be Bop, Rangsiyanon Rd. Live music most nights, extremely popular with travellers. Great atmosphere, serves most Western spirits.

Reggae Bar, Rangsiyanon Rd. If you like sitting around a fire playing bongos and comparing how little money you spent on your gap-year travels, this is the place for you.

Mae Hong Son p861, map p862

Butterfly, at the crossroads on the way to **Mae Kong Son Guesthouse**, the best bar in town. A swanky Thai lounging bar with karaoke, big 1970s-style kitsch chairs, live music and open as long as you care to drink.

Waterbar, across from the Kasikorn Bank on Khunlum Praphat Rd. Seeming slightly out of place in the small town of Mae Hong Son, this modern-looking bar is complete with faux-designer sofas, flatscreen TV and waitresses in tiny plastic outfits.

Chiang Rai p863, map p864

There's now a burgeoning bar scene in Chiang Rai – many can be found in and around Phahonyothin Rd, near the crossroads with Banphaprakan Rd.

Easy House Bar and Restaurant, Permavi-phat Rd (opposite **Wangcome Hotel**), cocktails, beers, live music, self-consciously hip.
Lobo Bar, a lively place down a narrow private soi off Phahonyothin Rd, near the clock tower.

Chiang Khong p867
If you're looking for a place for an evening drink, most of the riverside restaurants are worth contemplating. For dedicated bars try either the **Bam-Boo bar** (which has the added advantage of a free pool) or **999 Bar**. Both are popular.

▲ Activities and tours

Pai and Soppong p861
Rafting
Thai Adventure Rafting, just past the bus station. Pai, T053-699111, www.activethailand. com/rafting. The oldest whitewater rafting company in Thailand. It runs unforgettable, professional 2-day expeditions down the Pai River and beyond. Avoid **Pai Adventure Rafting** who are a poor copy of the real thing.

Therapies
Opposite the **Rim Pai Cottages**, 68 Rachdamrong Rd, Pai. Excellent massage (฿100-150 per hr), friendly people. Also available at other places including the **Foundation of Shivaga Kommapaj**.

Tour operators
Many of the guesthouses run treks and there are plenty of companies offering a choice of treks and rafting trips.
Pai Elephant Camp Tours, 5/3 Rangsiyanon Rd, Pai, T053-699286. One of several companies offering elephant rides. A professional set-up, the owner treats her animals with respect. The camp is out of town towards the hot springs. Recommended – you can even swim with the elephants in the river or ride bare-back.

Mae Hong Son p861, map p862
Therapies
Ban Thai Massage and Spa, 28 Singhanat-bamroong Rd, Pai, T053-620441, banthai_spa@ yahoo.com. Great service, friendly staff and an amazing massage that is particularly welcome for those just back from strenuous treks or after long bus journeys. Highly recommended.

Tours operators
From Pai there are assorted day tours to such sights as Pha Sua Waterfall, Pang Tong Summer Palace, the KMT village of Mae Aw, Tham Plaa (Fish Cave) and Tham Nam Lot (Water Cave). A number of companies also advertise trips to the 'long-necked' Padaung, which involves a bumpy 1-hr trip to their 2 villages. Many people deplore this type of tourism. Most guesthouses will organize treks ranging from trips down the Salween River to the Burmese border to Mae Sot, elephant treks and rafting on the Pai River. Recommended tour operators include **Friend Tour** at Friend Guesthouse, Pai, T053-620119, for trekking, bamboo rafting, elephant rides, boat trips; **Rose Garden Tours**, 86/4 Khunlum Prapaht Rd, Pai, T053-611577 and **Sunflower Tours**, Sunflower Café, eco-conscious birdwatching and nature treks.

Chiang Rai p863, map p864
Therapies
Ganda Traditional Thai Massage, 869/ 59-63 Pisit Sangsuan Rd, is recommended.
Mue Thong Thai Massage, Inn Come Hotel, 172/6 Ratbamrung Rd, T053-717850.
Yogi massage and sauna centre, at the **Royal Princess Hotel**, is the most luxurious place for a Thai Massage. (฿900 for 2-hr massage and 30-min sauna).

Tours and trekking
Before embarking on a trek, it is worthwhile visiting the **Hilltribe Education Center**. Tribes in the area include Karen, Lisu, Lahu and Akha. Day tours to visit hilltribe villages Sop Ruak and the Golden Triangle, Mae Sai,

Mae Salong and Chiang Saen are organized by most of the tour/trekking companies listed below. Motorcycle tours are becoming increasingly popular, and many guesthouses provide rental services and information on routes to take for a day's excursion.

The TAT office produces a list of companies with average prices and other useful advice.

Golden Triangle Tours, 590 Phahonyothin Rd, T053-711339 (attached to the **Golden Triangle Hotel**). Recommended.

Mae Salong Tour, 882/4 Phahonyothin Rd, T053-712515. Treks come recommended, also organizes river cruises on the Mekong that include Laos, China and Thailand.

PDA, 620/25 Thanalai Rd, T053-719167, F053-718869. Primarily a charity, working to improve the lot of the hilltribes, but they also have a trekking 'arm', guides tend to be more knowledgeable of hilltribe ways. Note that all profits from treks are ploughed back into the PDA's charity work. Treks also introduce clients to the PDA's community development projects, advance notice is recommended.

Chiang Khong p867
Tour operators
There are a growing number of tour companies in Chiang Khong. **Ann Tour**, 6/1 Sai Klang Rd, T/F053-791218, is recommended.

At the time of writing, advance visas are still necessary for entry into Laos from Chiang Khong. Get advice before you travel. Most people opt for a 30-day visa that can be purchased from most guesthouses, ฿1200.

⊖ Transport

Pai p861
Air
There's a small airstrip just to the north of Pai. **SGA** (one of Thailand's smallest airlines) run twice-daily flights in tiny 12-seater Cessnas between Pai and **Chiang Mai**. Tickets are available via their website, www.sga.co.th, or call their Pai (T053-698207) or Chiang Mai (T053-280444) offices.

Bus
The bus stop is on Chai Songkhram Rd, near the centre of town. 4 buses run to **Mae Hong Son** daily (3 hrs) and 4 to **Chiang Mai** (4 hrs) for ฿80. A songthaew is also available and provides a slightly quicker (3 hrs), if more uncomfortable, journey to Chiang Mai.

Motorbike
Hire ฿150-250 per day from several guesthouses and shops in town. Pick of the bunch is next door to **Thai Adventure Rafting** with gearless scooters through to dirt bikes; it also offers daily insurance.

Soppong p861
Bus
6-7 buses each day (1 a/c) in each direction – west to **Mae Hong Son** (2 hrs), east to **Pai** (1 hr) and **Chiang Mai** (5 hrs).

Motorbike/scooter
Hire from shop close to the bus stop, though most guesthouses can arrange hire.

Mae Hong Son p861, map p862
Air
The airport is to the north of town on Niveshpishan Rd. Regular daily connections on **Nok Air** with **Chiang Mai** (35 mins), but be aware that between the months of Mar and Apr, the burning of the hillsides might delay or altogether cancel flight services.

Bus
Station on Khunlum Praphat Rd, a short walk from town and most guesthouses. There are 2 routes from **Chiang Mai**: the northern, more gruelling route via Pai, or the route from the south, via Mae Sariang. Buses leave through town in both directions (in total, 7 a day each way, most non-a/c, the first via **Pai** at 0700. Overnight connections with **Bangkok**, 12½ hrs.

Motorbike/jeep
Many places hire out jeeps, motorbikes and scooters. Prices for motorbikes/scooters

from ฿150-180 per day (there are a couple of places at the southern end of Khunlum Praphat Rd), jeeps about ฿800-1000 per day.

Chiang Rai *p863, map p864*
Air
The international airport is 8 km north of the city, just off the main Chiang Rai–Mae Sai Hwy. **THAI** and **Air Asia** provide regular connections with **Chiang Mai** (40 mins) and **Bangkok** (1 hr 25 mins).
   Airline offices THAI, 870 Phahonyothin Rd, T053-711179.

Bus
Central bus station is just off Phahonyothin Rd, T053-711224. Regular connections with **Mae Sai**, **Chiang Mai**, **Chiang Khong** plus **Phitasnulok**, **Sukhothai**, **Bangkok** and destinations in the northeast.

Car and jeep
Hire from one of the many tour operators in town or try the **Mae Hong Son Guesthouse**.

Motorbike
Costs ฿150-200 per day, from most guesthouses and tour companies.
ST Motorcycle, near the clock tower, offers one of the best motorcycle rental services in Northern Thailand. While they rent the usual step-throughs, they also have a fleet of well-maintained 250 to 600cc off-road bikes. In addition they are probably the only place in the north that will allow you – with a large deposit – to ride the bikes into Laos and Burma. The owner, Khun Seksit, is friendly and straight-talking. Highly recommended.

Mae Sai *p866*
Bus
The main bus station is 5 km out of town, off the road to Mae Chan and Chiang Rai. Song-thaews and motorcycle taxis take passengers from town to the terminal. Regular connections with **Bangkok Chiang Mai** and **Chiang Rai**.

Songthaew
Connections with **Chiang Saen**, **Sop Ruak** and the Golden Triangle, every 30-40 mins. Songthaews leave from Phahonyothin Rd, near the centre of town. Songthaews for **Mae Chan** and **Chiang Rai** also leave from town, saving a journey out to the bus terminal.

Mae Salong and around *p866*
To get to and from Chiang Rai, take the Mae Sai-bound bus and get off at Mae Chan. From here there are about 6 songthaews a day, 0600-1400 (1½ hrs). Reverse the trip to get back to Chiang Rai. From Mae Salong to Tha Thon there are 5 songthaews a day (2 hrs), starting at 0730 and finishing at 1530. Little Home guesthouse has the full timetable.

Golden Triangle and Sop Ruak *p867*
Boat
From the pier in Sop Ruak, for trips to **Chiang Saen** and on to **Chiang Khong**.

Songthaew
Regular connections with **Mae Sai** (40 mins) and **Chiang Saen** (10 mins, ฿10). Just flag one down on the road – they run through Sop Ruak about every 40 mins.

Chiang Saen *p867*
Boat
Long-tailed boats can be hired from the riverbank at the end of Phahonyothin Rd.

Bus
Regular connections with **Chiang Rai** (1 hr 20 mins), **Mae Sai** (1 hr) and **Chiang Khong** (2 hrs).

Chiang Khong *p867*
Boat
These can be chartered to make the journey to/from **Chiang Saen**.
   Transport to Laos It is possible for foreigners to cross into Laos from Chiang Khong. Long-tailed boats ferry passengers across the Mekong to Ban Houei Xai. The pier and Thai immigration are 1 km north of town.

Bus

Hourly connections with **Chiang Rai** (3 hrs).
A/c and non-a/c connections with **Bangkok**
and **Chiang Mai**. A/c buses leave from the
office on the main road near Wat Phra Kaew.
Non-a/c buses depart from the bus station,
just over the Huai Sob Som on the south
edge of town.

Songthaew

Regular connections with **Chiang Saen** –
they can be flagged down as they make
their way north through Chiang Khong.

❶ Directory

Pai *p861*

Banks **Krung Thai Bank**, Rangsiyanon Rd
(the largest building in town and hard to
miss). Mon-Fri 0830-1530 (in theory).
Internet Many internet cafés, mainly
concentrated along Chi Songkhram Rd.
Post office Khetkelang Rd. **Medical
services** Pai Hospital, Chai Songkhram Rd
(about 500 m from the town centre).

Soppong *p861*

Banks The nearest bank with exchange
facilities is 1 hr away in Pai.

Mae Hong Son *p861, map p862*

Banks Bank of Ayodhya, 61 Khunlum
Praphat Rd. **Thai Farmers**, 78 Khunlum
Praphat Rd. **Thai Military Bank**, Khunlum
Praphat (at intersection with Panit Wattana
Rd). **Bangkok**, Khunlum Praphat Rd (0830-
1900). **Medical services** Clinic, Khunlum
Praphat Rd. **Hospital**, at the eastern end
of Singhanat Bamrung Rd. **Internet**
Sunflower Café, Mae Hong Son Computer,
80 Khunlum Praphat Rd. **Police** Tourist
Police, 1 Rachathampitak Rd, T053-611812
(claim 24 hrs service). **Post office** Southern
end of town, corner of Khunlum Praphat Rd
and Soi 3, Mon-Fri 0830-1630, Sat and Sun
0900-1200.

Chiang Rai *p863, map p864*

Banks Profusion of exchange booths and
banks on Thanalai and Phahonyothin roads.
Many are open 7 days a week and often into
the evening. **Internet** An abundance
of internet cafés in the area around the
Wangcome Hotel, about ฿30 per hr.
Medical services Hospitals: Overbrook,
opposite Chat House, Trairat Rd, T053-711
366. **Provincial**, on Sanambin Rd. **Chiang Rai
Hospital**, Sathorn Payabarn Rd, T053-711403/
711119. **Police** Tourist Police, Singhaklai Rd
(below the TAT office, opposite Wat Phra
Singh), T053-717779, and a booth at the
night market. Or in an emergency call T1155
(24 hrs). **Police Station,** Rattanakhat Rd,
T053-711444. **Post office** On Uttarakit Rd
at the northern end of Suksathit Rd.

Mae Sai *p866*

Banks A number with money-changing
facilities, some open daily 0830-1700. **Bangkok
Metropolitan Bank**, Phahonyothin Rd. **Krung
Thai**, Phahonyothin Rd. **Thai Farmers**, 122/1
Phahonyothin Rd. **Internet** Internet access
can be found next door to the **Wang Thong
Hotel**. **Post office** Phahonyothin Rd (2 km
from bridge towards Mae Chan).

Mae Salong and around *p866*

Banks A couple with ATMs in the village.
Internet At both the **Little Home Guesthouse** and at the **Sweet Mae Salong Café**.

Golden Triangle and Sop Ruak *p867*

Banks In Sop Ruak there are 2 money
changers by the Opium Museum, a **Thai
Farmers Bank** and a small branch of the **Siam
Commercial Bank**. Open daily 0900-1600.

Chiang Khong *p867*

Banks Siam Commercial, Sai Khlang Rd,
opposite the district office, has a currency
exchange service. **Thai Farmers**, 416 Sai
Khlang Rd. **Internet** There are several
places with internet access at the northern
end of Sai Khlang Rd. **Post office** On
main road next to the army post.

Eastern Coast to Trat

Head down the coast east from Bangkok and you'll find trashy gaudiness, gorgeous beaches, remote forested islands, gem markets and oddball idiosyncrasy. Enigmatic Koh Si Chang is home to weird abandoned palaces, sacred Chinese temples and platoons of monkeys. The notorious fleshpots of Pattaya may recommend little to travellers eager to experience local culture, but this place is still distinctively Thai – right the way down to the katoey (transsexual or 'ladyboy') cabarets. Koh Samet with its beautiful beaches has transformed into an overpriced getaway for wealthy Bangkok students but you can still get away from it all if you pick your spot and moment. Further south, Chantaburi and Trat can provide engaging stop-offs on the way to this coastline's biggest draw – the island of Koh Chang (see page 890).
▶▶ *For listings, see pages 882-889.*

Koh Si Chang ◯◯◯◯◯ ▶▶ *pp 882-889. Colour map 5, A4.*

The nearest island getaway to Bangkok, Koh Si Chang has thankfully never made it onto most people's travel itineraries. Getting here is relatively easy – take a half-hourly bus from Bangkok's Eastern Terminal next to Ekkamai Skytrain station to the town of Si Racha, where hourly boats run to Si Chang daily 0700-1900. You'll be greeted on arrival by a host of huge tuk-tuks – it costs ฿50-100 to get to the island though most accommodation is within walking distance. There are also a couple of places renting bicycles/motorbikes in the town. One of the best sources of information on Koh Si Chang is the excellent www.ko-sichang.com.

Koh Si Chang is one of those places that had a moment in the spotlight – King Rama V built a palace here – and then history moved on. It does make for an entertaining, idiosyncratic short break and is a popular spot for weekenders from the capital. At the northern edge of the town, set up on a hill overlooking the town, the **Chaw Por Khaw Yai Chinese temple** is an odd assortment of decorated shrines and caves. There are great views of the island and this is a very important temple for Thailand's Chinese community. On the east coast – you might see monkeys here – are the ruins of **Rama V's palace**. Abandoned in 1893 when the French took control of the island during a confrontation with the Thais, not much remains though what does has a peculiarly eerie quality. The island also has a number of beaches with reasonable swimming and snorkelling. The quietest beach with the best coral and swimming is **Tham Phang** on the western side of the island.

Pattaya ◯◯◯◯◯▲◯◯ ▶▶ *pp 882-889. Colour map 5, A4.*

Brash, brazen and completely over the top, whatever you feel about Pattaya, it will certainly leave an impression.

Getting here from Bangkok is straightforward – almost all tour companies offer minibuses and private cars and there are plentiful buses from Bangkok's Eastern bus terminal. Most Bangkok taxis will take you here for an agreed fare or on the meter (between ฿1500-2000). There are even a few trains, though the journey time of almost five hours puts off most travellers. In Pattaya itself local transport is abundant with songthaews running regularly between all the tourist centres and scores of people hiring out bikes, motorbikes and jeeps. For tourist information try the helpful **TAT office** ① *382/1 Beach Rd, Pattaya, T038-428750.* There are also several free tourist magazines and maps available in the town.

Prostitution

For many foreigners Thailand is synonymous with prostitution and sex tourism. That prostitution is big business cannot be denied: estimates put the numbers of women employed in the industry at between 120,000 and two million, and the number of brothels at 60,000.

Although the growth of prostitution is usually associated with the arrival of large numbers of GIs on 'Rest & Recreation' during the Vietnam War, and after that with the growth of sex tourism, it is an ancient industry here. In the 1680s, for example, an official was granted a licence to run the prostitution monopoly in Ayutthaya, using 600 women who had been captured and enslaved.

The scale of the prostitution industry in Thailand indicates that the police turn a blind eye and at the same time, no doubt, gain financial reward. There is a brothel or 'tea house' in every town, no matter how small. One survey recorded that 95% of all men over 21 had slept with a prostitute. Some people maintain that the subordinate role of women in Buddhism means that there is less stigma attached to becoming a prostitute. In some villages, having a daughter who has 'gone south', as it is euphemistically termed, is viewed as a good thing. Asia Watch believes there is "clear evidence of direct official involvement in every stage of the trafficking process". There are also women working in the trade from Yunnan (South China), Laos and Cambodia.

Prime Minister Chuan Leekpai tried to clean up the prostitution business and put some new laws on the books: it is now, for example, illegal for men to have sex with girls aged under 18 years old, and parents selling their children will also face prosecution. The problem for the government is that prostitution is so ingrained into the Thai way of life that combating commercial sex work requires a national change of attitude.

Pattaya began to metamorphose from its sleepy fishing-village origins when the US navy set up at nearby Sattahip (40 km further down the coast). As the war in Vietnam escalated, so the influx of GIs on 'R & R' grew and Pattaya responded enthusiastically. Given these origins, it is hardly surprising that Pattaya's stock in trade is sex tourism and at any one time, about 4000 girls are touting for work around the many bars and restaurants.

The official line on Pattaya is that it is going out of its way to promote itself as a 'family' resort. This emphasis on wholesome family fun is hard to reconcile with reality. The busiest and noisiest area is at the southern end of town along what is now known as 'Walking Street.' It's here you'll find the highest concentration of bars, brothels, pole-dancers, ladyboys, drunken sex-pats, street robberies and bad food. Many people find this aspect of Pattaya repugnant. However, there is no pretence here – either on the part of the hosts or their guests.

Jomtien Beach offers a different face of Pattaya. Some gaudier elements still hold sway closer to Pattaya Bay but the further south you head the more presentable it becomes. Cute, mid-range, boutique hotels appear, each with their own laid-back bar and restaurant. At the far end – the beach here is about 4 km long – it becomes decidedly tranquil. If you have time in take a trip up the 240-m **Pattaya Park Tower** ① *T038-251201, ฿200*, sited on the Jomtien headland – it provides spectacular views.

Pattaya is also popular with watersports lovers: there is sailing, parasailing, windsurfing, ski-boating, snorkelling, deep-sea fishing and some excellent scuba-diving schools.

Around Pattaya

Trips out of town include the **Siriporn Orchid Farm** ① *235/14 Moo 5, Tambon Nong Prue, T038-429013, daily 0800-1700; Mini Siam, T038-421628, daily 0700-2200*, a cultural and historical park where 80 of Thailand's most famous 'sights' – including Wat Phra Kaeo and the Bridge over the River Kwai – are recreated at a scale of 1:25. The park lies 3 km north of Pattaya Beach, on the Sukhumvit highway (Route 3) at the Km 143 marker and the **Nong Nooch Tropical Garden** ① *T038-429321, daily 0900-1800, ฿20*, is a 200-ha park containing immaculate gardens with lakes (and boating), an orchid farm, family zoo, Thai handicraft demonstrations and a thrice-daily (1015, 1500 and 1545) 'cultural spectacular' with Thai dancing, Thai boxing and an elephant show. In 2000 a British tourist was gored and killed by an enraged elephant. Most people arrive on a tour. The garden is 15 minutes from Pattaya town, 3 km off the main road, at the Km 163 marker.

The island of **Koh Larn**, a short hop from the main Pattaya pier (boats depart at 0930 and 1130, returning at 1600, 45 minutes, ฿250), offers a decent respite from the intense pace of Pattaya. There is a place to stay here (see Sleeping, page 883) and there's some decent snorkelling and scuba diving.

Koh Samet ☺☻▲☺☺ ▸▸ *pp 882-889. Colour map 5, A4.*

A 6-km-long, lozenge-shaped island sited in a national park, rimmed with stunning beaches and lapped by azure seas, Koh Samet is just a short boat trip from the mainland. Over the years is has transformed from the perfect Bangkok getaway into a noisy spot for weekending Thai students. It still can be a charming spot but if you desire quiet moments to absorb the stunning sunrises/sets then arrive mid-week – at that time accommodation is cheaper as well.

To get there take a bus to Ban Phe from Bangkok's Eastern bus station (three hours), and then one of the regular boats for another 40 minutes or so (฿50 each). All visitors also pay an entrance fee of ฿200 for foreign adults to get into the national park. Many visitors arrive at the main Na Dan Pier in the northeast of the island though some bungalow operators will run boats straight onto the beaches – check beforehand.

Samet is one of the driest places in Thailand (1350 mm rain per year) and a good place to pitch up during the rainy season. Between May and October there can be strong winds and rough seas, while heavy rains can be a problem between July and September. During this period rates are cut and the island is less crowded.

These days, much like other popular destinations in Thailand, Koh Samet has evolved into a badly planned place with terrible damage being done to the local environment and unsightly resorts and karaoke bars lining the beach. What's even stranger to outsiders is that Samet's superb beaches are all part of a national park and should be protected. The park rangers who man the entrance points to the island seem more content squeezing cash out of visitors than actually doing their jobs and Samet seems well on its way to eco-meltdown.

Around the island

It is possible to explore Koh Samet on foot though take plenty of water – the beach walk from end to end is a good adventure. There is now a Koh Samet taxi union operating a fleet of green songthaews on the island. Their fares – both for rental of the entire vehicle and for one person in a shared vehicle – are posted on a notice board at the main pier (see Transport, page 888). They normally travel when full, though do operate to a rough timetable as well). Tracks are negotiable by motorbike, which are available for about ฿300-400 a day.

Koh Samet

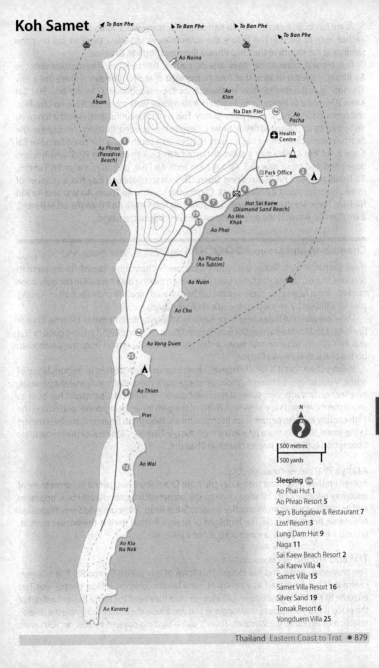

To Ban Phe
To Ban Phe
To Ban Phe
To Ban Phe

Ao Noina

Ao Kham

Ao Klon

Na Dan Pier

Ao Pacha

Health Centre

Ao Phrao
(Paradise Beach)

Park Office

Hat Sai Kaew
(Diamond Sand Beach)

Ao Hin
Khok

Ao Phai

Ao Phutsa
(Ao Tubtim)

Ao Nuan

Ao Cho

Ao Vong Duen

Ao Thian

Pier

Ao Wai

Ao Kiu
Na Nok

Ao Karang

N

500 metres
500 yards

Sleeping
Ao Phai Hut **1**
Ao Phrao Resort **5**
Jep's Bungalow & Restaurant **7**
Lost Resort **3**
Lung Dam Hut **9**
Naga **11**
Sai Kaew Beach Resort **2**
Sai Kaew Villa **4**
Samet Villa **15**
Samet Villa Resort **16**
Silver Sand **19**
Tonsak Resort **6**
Vongduern Villa **25**

There has been a settlement on Koh Samet for many years; junks from China used to anchor here to be checked before the authorities would allow them to sail over the sandbar at the mouth of the Chao Phraya River and north to Bangkok.

The biggest draw these days are, of course, the beaches. The northernmost is **Ao Klong**, a stretch of sand that runs to the west of the Na Dan pier – there are a few 'floating' guesthouses/seafood restaurants built on wooden stilts in the bay. **Hat Sai Kaew** (Diamond or White-Sand Beach) is a 10-minute walk southeast from Na Dan Pier, and remains the most popular place to stay. This is still a beautiful spot, even if it has been disfigured by uncontrolled development. Despite the crowded, bustling atmosphere, the beach remains clean and it has a sandy bottom. Just south along the coast from Hat Sai Kaew is **Ao Hin Khok** while a short distance further south still is **Ao Phai**, which is less developed and more peaceful. About 2 km from Ao Phai, past the smaller **Ao Tubtim**, **Ao Nuan** and **Ao Cho**, is **Ao Vong Duen**. This crescent-shaped bay has a number of more upmarket resort developments. Continuing south is **Ao Thian**, **Ao Wai** and **Ao Kiu Na Nok**. These are the most peaceful locations on Koh Samet. **Ao Phrao** (Paradise Beach), 2 km from Sai Kaew, is the only beach on the west side of the island.

Chantaburi and around ⊖🐟🌐🌐🌐🌑 ▶▶ pp 882-889. Colour map 5, A4.

Head east from Koh Samet and you'll soon reach Chantaburi, famed for its trade in precious stones. Unless you fancy your chances on picking up a bargain in the gemstone market – most farang fair badly against the hard-nosed sapphire and ruby traders – many pass Chantaburi by en route to the island of Koh Chang.

There are plentiful buses here from Bangkok's Eastern bus terminal at Ekkamai (four or five hours) and links to Rayong (for Ban Phe) and Korat (see page 899). Links are good to Trat and Koh Chang while several buses a day travel in each direction from the Cambodian border crossing at Aranya Prathet.

Muang Chan – as it is locally known – is an unusual town with its large population of ethnic Vietnamese, a strong Catholic presence, well-preserved traditional shophouses, excellent restaurants, and some of the finest durian in Thailand. Chantaburi has built its wealth on rubies and sapphires with many of the gem mines being developed during the 19th century by Shan people from Burma, who are thought to be among the best miners in the world. While in town take in the French-style Catholic Cathedral of the Immaculate Conception (1880), the largest church in Thailand.

Aranya Prathet → Colour map 3, C5.

Aranya Prathet, a bit more than a day trip from Chantaburi, has gained some measure of notoriety because of its location close to the border with Cambodia (see box, opposite) and its growing use as an alternative route to **Siem Reap**. The journey to Siem Reap takes around six hours by truck. The highlight of Aranya Prathet itself is the **border market**, around 7 km from town (a moto costs around ฿40-50).

Trat and around → Colour map 5, A5.

The provincial capital and the closest Thai town of any size to Cambodia, Trat is a gem centre that has flourished as a centre of cross-border commerce. Most people visit Trat en route to Koh Chang, not staying any longer than they need to catch a bus or boat out of the place. If you do decide to stay longer in Trat you'll have the chance to sample the diverse selection of excellent guesthouses. There's also a bustling covered market on Sukhumvit

Border essentials: Thailand–Cambodia

It is now possible to cross into Cambodia from several points along Thailand's eastern border. Visas can be obtained at each crossing for US$20 or ฿1000 – you'll need one recent photo. Be aware that some border posts insist on being paid in baht others in US dollars, so take both. These border crossings are also in constant flux, and opening times and other details can change at short notice; for the most recent information check locally. The following are the most useful entry points:

Aranya Prathet

This remains the most popular border crossing with good bus and train connections to Bangkok. It is the best entry point if you want to visit Siem Reap and the ruins at Angkor Wat. Be advised that the road on the Cambodia side of the border is often in an appalling state and journey times to Siem Reap can be lengthy. The border is open daily 0800-2000. Sometimes tourists are asked for an International Vaccination Certificate; this is a means by which local immigration officers boost their income (if you don't have a certificate they demand US$5). The certificate is not legally required; if the border guards insist ask for a receipt and the name of the commanding officer – this usually dissuades them. A tuk-tuk from Aranya Prather train or bus station to the border (7 km from town) should cost around ฿60-80.

Ban Hat Lek

South of Trat and just past the town of Khlong Yai, this is the best entry point if you want to visit Sihanoukville and the southern Cambodian town of Kampot. The border is open 0800-2000. Minibuses (฿100) and songthaews (฿40) run from Trat direct to Hat Lek (1 hr). After crossing the border at Hat Lek you'll arrive on the Cambodian island of Koh Kong. From there a daily boat (departs 0800 – you may need to spend the night on Koh Kong) will take you direct to Sihanoukville (3-4 hrs). The alternatives are minibuses and taxis that depart when full (6 hrs).

Pailin

Open 0900-1700, this is the best crossing if you want to reach Battambang – it could also be used as an alternative route to Siem Reap. Take a Khorat-bound bus from Chantaburi to the small town of Pong Nam Ron (1 hr, ฿30). Just by the turning to the border is a small market – songthaews from here to the border should cost ฿60 (30 mins). Shared taxis await in Pailin to take you to Battambang (4 hrs).

Road offering a good selection of food and drink stalls. On the same road, north of the shopping mall, there is a busy night market. **Wat Buppharam** (Wat Plai Klong), dates from the late Ayutthaya period and is notable for its wooden viharn – it is 2 km west of town.

With Bangkok Airways flying into the nearby airport, Trat is now the official gateway to nearby Koh Chang for the mass tourism market. Buses run from Bangkok's Eastern bus station several times a day and there are also connections to Pattaya and Chantaburi.

A great source of local information is the **Tratosphere bookshop** ① *23 Rimklong Soi*, where the French- and English-speaking owner is exceptionally helpful and knowledgeable about everything to do with Trat, Koh Chang and the surrounding islands.

South of Trat is **Khlong Yai**, the southernmost town on this eastern arm of Thailand and an important fishing port. Take a songthaew from the back of the municipal market (β25) or shared taxi from the front of the market (β35 each). The journey there is worthwhile for the dramatic scenery with the mountains of Cambodia rising to the east and the sea to the west. There are several Cambodian markets and the seafood is excellent. The border crossing at Hat Lek (see page 881) is a short journey south of Khlong Yai.

There's a **TAT office** ① *T039-597255, Mon-Fri 0830-1630*, by the pier in Laem Ngop. This sleepy fishing village – in fact the district capital – has a long pier lined with boats, along with good seafood and a relaxed atmosphere. As Koh Chang becomes Thailand's next island beach resort to hit the big time, expect things to get busier; at present there's a handful of guesthouses and a few waterside restaurants.

⊚ Eastern Coast to Trat listings

*For Sleeping and Eating price codes,
see inside the front cover.*

⊜ Sleeping

Koh Si Chang *p876*
B-D Rim Talay, 250 m north of entrance to Rama V Palace, T038-216116. Mix of rooms and eccentric bungalow/barge affairs (sleeping up to 7 people) that come complete with sea-views. All rooms have TV, a/c and are en suite – the cheapest ones have cold water only.
C House of Dreams, back road 200 m before Pan and David's restaurant (see Eating, below), T084-348 8317. This is a 2-bedroom homestay (the larger one has a balcony and bathtub while both have en suite facilities, TV and a/c) in a brand-new property. Excellent views across the sea to the mainland, friendly English-speaking owners make this one of the nicest spots to stay on the island. Recommended though book ahead.
C-D Sichang View Resort, west coast of island, T038-216210. Great location set along the Khao Khaad cliffs in a remote corner of the island. Nice gardens make great spot for sundowners – huge rooms are well kept with en suite facilities, a/c and TVs. Good food.
C-E Sripitsanu Bungalows, Hat Tham, T038-216024. New management who speak little English are settling into this bungalow operation that is built into the cliff-face overlooking the sea. Range of rooms and bungalows available not far from Hat Tham.

Pattaya *p876*
The high season is Nov-Mar – prices are lower outside this time.

Pattaya Beach and Naklua
LL-A Amari Orchid Resort, 240 Moo 5 Beach Rd, North Pattaya, T038-428161, www.amari.com. A/c, restaurants, Olympic-sized pool, tennis, mini-golf, watersports. 230-room hotel on a tranquil, 4-ha plot of lush gardens at the northern end of the beach, away from most of the bars and discos.
LL-A Woodlands Resort, 164/1 Pattaya Naklua Rd, T038-421707, www.woodland-resort.com. On the edge of Pattaya and Naklua. Has tried to recreate a colonial lodge-type atmosphere. Quiet, leafy and airy with pool and landscaped gardens.
L-A Dusit Resort, 240/2 Beach Rd (north end), T038-425611, www.dusit.com. Excellent hotel with 474 rooms, good service and all facilities. Health club, tennis, squash courts, children's pools, table tennis and a games room, watersports, shopping arcade, disco.
C-E AA Pattaya, 182 Beach Rd, Naklua, T038-420894, F038-429057. In the midst of bar-land, attractive 4th-floor pool, well-equipped rooms. Recommended.
D Garden Lodge, 170 Moo 5 Naklua Rd, T038-429109, www.gardenlodgpattaya. com. A/c, pool, bungalow rooms looking onto gardens, quiet and excellent value. Recommended.

D-E Diana Inn, 216/6-9 Pattaya 2 Rd, between Sois 11 and 12, Naklua, T038-429 675, www.dianapattaya.co.th. A/c, restaurant, pool, on busy road but rooms have good facilities for price, modern, well run, friendly and popular. Recommended.

F Right Spot Inn, 583 Beach Rd, South Pattaya, T038-429629. Clean and quiet with an excellent restaurant.

Jomtien

LL-L Sugar Hut, 391/18 Thaphraya Rd, T038-251686, F038-251689. A/c, restaurant, 2 pools, overgrown gardens with rabbits and peacocks. Thai-style bungalows not on the beach, but very attractive grounds. Recommended.

LL-AL Sheraton Pattaya Resort, 437 Phra Tamnak Rd, T038-259888, www.sheraton. com/pattaya. Superb luxury resort in a great breezy location perched up on the cliffs, which only adds to the stunning rooms and bungalows. Possibly the best luxury resort in town. Fantastic spa, bar and restaurants. Recommended.

LL-A Birds and Bees Resort, 366/11 Moo 12 Phra Tamnak Rd, T038-250556, www.cabbages andcondoms.co.th. Run by the **Cabbages and Condoms** the AIDs awareness organization that has a restaurant in Bangkok (see page 807). A charming and wonderful resort with pool, gardens, children's play area and awesome cliff-top location – a path leads to a secluded beach. It is irreverent with subversive flourishes (check the paths to Communism and Capitalism that both end up in the same place – by a pond filled with frantic, hungry fish that are called 'Greedy Politicians'). It is slightly pricey, though cheaper in low season. The suites offer best value with balcony jacuzzis and sea views. Highly recommended.

L-B Sarita Chalet ad Spa, 279/373 Jomtien Beach Rd, T038-233952, www.sarita chalet.com. Relaxed, professional small hotel in nice part of Jomtien. Stylish rooms, all en suite, with a/c and TV. There's a small pool and spa. Some rooms face the beach. Often booked out. Breakfast included. Recommended.

B-C Jomtien Twelve, 240/13 Moo 12, Jomtien Beach Rd, T038-756865, www.jomtien twelve.com. Brand new, great little hotel right on the beach road in a very quiet part of Jomtien – perfect for a short weekend break. All rooms are well designed with nice touches and an eye for the aesthetic with en suite facilities, full cable TV and a/c. The ones at the front have decent-sized beach-facing balconies. Breakfast included. Best deal on this stretch of beach. Recommended.

Koh Larn

E Koh Larn Resort, Pattaya office at 183 Soi Post Office, T08-1996 3942 (mob). Decent bungalows set alongside a nice beach. Price includes the boat fare and transfer to the bungalows. Watch out for annoying jet-skiers.

Koh Samet p878, map p879

Koh Samet now offers some of the worst value, most overpriced accommodation in Thailand. You'll find accommodation on every beach – we've listed the best.

Hat Sai Kaew

L-AL Sai Kaew Beach Resort, www.kohsametsaikaew.com. Wide range of neat bungalows, some facing onto the beach. It also has a set of beautiful, deluxe bungalows, in a tranquil spot just over the headland. All a/c, cable TV.

L-A Tonsak Resort, T038-644314, www.tonsak.com. Very friendly and well-run resort though the rooms are pretty average – all a/c, en suite and with TVs – and are somewhat overpriced.

A-D Saikaew Villa, T038-644144, www.saikaew.com. Some decent, simple wooden rooms set back from the beach and a few nicer bungalows on offer here. Cheaper ones come with cold water and fan. Tourist-fatigued owners and not a bad deal, but still overpriced.

Ao Hin Khok

AL-E Jep's Bungalow and Restaurant, T038-644112, www.jepbungalow.com.

Good-value rooms, the restaurant has a large range of tasty dishes. Often booked out. Recommended.

D-E Lost Resort, T038-644041, www.thelost resort.net. Set by the road just behind the beach this is one of Samet's only proper guesthouses. Friendly English owner but the rooms – some with a/c and hot water – look a bit tired. Probably best budget option.

D-E Naga, T08-9939 9063 (mob). English-run and friendly, offers home-baked cakes, bread and pastries. The only post office on Koh Samet is located here. Basic huts, some with fans, all have shared, if rather smelly, bathrooms. Naga is also a popular nightspot.

Ao Phai

B-E Ao Phai Hut, T038-644278. Some a/c, friendly, clean operation, wooden huts higher up behind the tree line, mosquitoes prevalent. This place has a library and organizes minibuses to Pattaya.

C-E Samet Villa, T038-644094, F038-644093. This clean and friendly Swiss-run establishment offers some of the best-value accommodation on Samet, all rooms have fans and attached bathrooms. It organizes a number of trips and excursions to neighbouring islands and rents out snorkelling equipment. Recommended.

C-F Silver Sand, T08-1996 5720 (mob). Good-value bungalows, popular restaurant (0930-2200) offering a wide range of dishes, large selection of recent videos, discos at weekends.

Ao Vong Duen

AL-C Vongduern Villa, T038-644260, www.vongduernvilla.com. One of the better-run places on the island. Homely little cabins are spread out through the trees and face onto the quieter end of this busy beach. The more expensive ones come with DVD players, all have hot water, TVs and a/c. Good food and friendly service as well. Recommended.

Ao Thian (Candlelight Beach)

E-F Lung Dam Hut, T038-651810. Basic wooden and bamboo huts with grass roofs

or try their treehouse just a few feet from the sea, only some huts have fans, some have own bath.

Ao Wai

A-E Samet Villa Resort, bookable through the boat **Phra Aphai** at Ban Phe, T08-1321 1284 (mob). The only accommodation on this beach – good bungalows but quite expensive. The location is peaceful and attractive, but lacks places to sit with sea views.

Ao Phrao

LL-AL Ao Phrao Resort and Le Vimarn, T02-438 9771, www.kohsamet aoprao.com and www.kohsametlevimarn. com. Both run by the same company, offer excellent luxurious and expensive accommodation. **Ao Phrao** has a family atmosphere while **Le Vimarn** is more stylish and comes complete with an excellent spa. Both resorts run their own boat service from Ban Phe, where they have an office.

Chantaburi and around *p880*

A-B Maneechan River Resort and Sport Club, 110 Moo 11 Plubpla Rd, T039-343 777, www.maneechanresort.com. Very good hotel with a wide range of amenities including mod cons and decent sports facilities. Excellent pool, tasty Thai food and free Wi-Fi. Recommended.

B-E Eastern, 899 Tha Chalaep Rd, T039-323220. Pool, all rooms have a/c, TV and bath tub. Larger rooms have fridges and are almost twice the price, smaller rooms are good value.

Trat and around *p880*

F Basar, 87 Thana Charoen Rd T039-523 247. Beautifully restored teak house, with a modern funky touch. All rooms have bathroom and mosquito net. There's a small restaurant on the ground floor. Recommended.

F-G Ban Jai Dee, Chaimongkon Rd. T039-520678. The best of the bunch, very friendly English-speaking owners. Rooms have fan, shared bathrooms. Recommended.

F-G NP Guesthouse, 1-3 Soi Luang Aet, Lak Muang Rd, T039-512564. Clean, friendly, well-run, converted shophouse, with a bright little restaurant, shared bathroom, hot showers, dorm beds, internet facilities. Recommended.

❶ Eating

Koh Si Chang *p876*

♥♥-♥ **Pan and David**, 167 Asdang Rd, 200 m before Rama V Palace, next to Marine Police T038-216 075. Mon-Fri 1100-2130, Sat and holidays 0830-2000, Sun 0830-2030. Reservations recommended at the weekends. Fantastic place to eat run by long-term Si Chang residents. Pan cooks up superb steaks, Isaan grub and fresh seafood. David is an American ex-pat who can tell you pretty much anything you need to know about Si Chang. They also run the very informative www.ko-si chang.com website. Highly recommended.

♥ **Lek Naa Wang** and **Noi**, beside the road to the palace, a 10-min walk out of town. Famed for serving up the island's best seafood places.

Pattaya *p876*

♥♥♥ **Empress**, Dusit Resort. Large Chinese restaurant overlooking Pattaya Bay. Good dim sum lunches.

♥♥♥ **La Gritta**, Beach Rd. Some people maintain this restaurant serves the best Italian in town. Pizzas, pasta dishes and seafood specialities.

♥♥♥ **Mex**, at **Sheraton**, see Sleeping. Mon-Sat 1830-2230. This is an excellent restaurant and quite possibly one of the best hotel diners in the country. Playful blends of tastes, textures and aromas – from Asia and beyond – are accompanied by an eye for the finest and freshest ingredients available. Pricey but this is somewhere really worth the splurge.

♥♥♥ **Peppermill**, 16 Beach Rd, near Soi Post Office. First-class French food.

♥♥♥ **Ruen Thai**, Pattaya 2 Rd, opposite Soi Post Office. Very good Thai food and not excessively overpriced. Recommended.

♥♥♥-♥♥ **Jomtien Twelve**, see Sleeping. Good spot to stop for coffee, breakfast, lunch and dinner. Cocktails and beer.

♥♥ **Kiss**, Pattaya 2 Rd, between sois 11 and 12, next to **Diana Inn**. Good range of Western and Thai food at low prices. An excellent place to watch the world go by.

Koh Samet *p878, map p879*

Just about all the resorts and guesthouses on Koh Samet provide the usual Thai dishes and travellers' food. The following places have a particular reputation for their food.

♥♥♥ **Hoi Pim**, opposite the main pier. A/c restaurant providing another good pit stop and some decent Western food.

♥♥♥ **Joe Restaurant**, Hat Sai Kaew on the beach. Food and service are passable but the layout with a nice low terrace is sweet. Good hang-out spot.

♥♥♥ **Miss You**, just before the main entrance into the park at the north end of the island. Serves Samet's best coffee and great ice cream sundaes.

♥♥♥ **Naga**, Ao Hin Khok, see Sleeping, above. Home-baked cakes, bread and pastries, and a popular nightspot.

♥♥♥ **Nuan Kitchen**, Ao Nuan, see Sleeping, above. Very good food.

♥♥♥ **The Pier**, opposite the main pier. New coffee shop that does a mean cappuccino. Good pit stop when you're catching the ferry.

♥♥♥ **Vong Duern Resort**, Ao Wong Duan, see Sleeping, above. A vast range of Thai and Western dishes.

♥ **Excellent foodstall**, between Le Vimarn and Ao Phrao Resort – set up by the resort owners mainly to feed their own staff, sells a variety of excellent Thai and Isaan dishes in a breezy beach-side location. Recommended.

Chantaburi and around *p880*

♥♥ **Luongtoy's**, Sukhaphiban Rd. Relaxed and friendly riverside restaurant with a great range of Thai food. Traditional music in the evenings on Tue, Thu and Fri. Open 1200-2200.

¶¶ Meun-ban ('Homely' restaurant), Saritdet Rd, next to the bus terminal. Probably the best low-budget restaurant in town offering a multitude of Thai dishes (including a huge vegetarian selection and ice creams), at very low prices. The owners speak good English and are a helpful source of local information. It is also in an ideal location if you arrive tired and hungry after a long bus journey and need some refreshment. Recommended.

Trat and around *p880*
The municipal market has a good range of stalls to choose from.
¶¶ Cool Corner, 21-23 Than Charoen Rd. Serves excellent coffee, cake, Thai and veggie food. Recommended.
¶ Isaan shophouse restaurant, Than Charoen Rd, next door to Ban Jai Dee. If your tastebuds are crying out for *som tam*, *larb moo* and sticky rice this is an excellent choice.
¶ Pier 112, 132 Thanachareon Road. Laid-back restaurant and bar set in large garden area. Good range of Western and Thai food, including vegetarian. Serves cocktails.
¶ Vegetarian restaurant, tucked away down Soi Tat Mai – take the first Soi on the left after Ban Jai Dee. Serves delicious and incredibly cheap Thai veggie food. Just point at the dish you want.

① Bars and clubs

Pattaya *p876*
Latitude Lounge, at **Sheraton**, see Sleeping. Get away from the flotsam and jetsam of the Beach Rd and head to this very relaxed, cool, bar-cum-lounge. Beautifully designed and breezy location mean you can spend all evening here supping cocktails while the contemporary sounds add to the ambience.
Jomtien Boathouse, 380/5-6 Jomtien Beach Rd. T038-756143, www.jomtienboathouse. com. You'll find a highly entertaining Elvis Impersonator performing twice a week (call for details) at this well-run Jomtien bar. Also have a giant screen for sports.

② Entertainment

Pattaya *p876*
Mostly performed by members of Pattaya's legendary katoey (transexual) population, a night at the cabaret is essential. The biggest and best are **Alcazar** and **Tiffany's**, both found on the northern end of Pattaya 2 Rd. Shows at Tiffany's are daily at 1900, 2030 and 2200, T038-429642 for reservations – prices starts at ฿255-400. (There's also a gun range in the basement at Tiffany's – from ฿200 – should you want to arm yourself after the show.)

③ Shopping

Pattaya *p876*
There are hundreds of stalls and shops on Pattaya 2 Rd selling jewellery, fashion, handicrafts, leather goods, silk, and a good selection of shopping plazas where most Western goods can be purchased.

Chantaburi and around *p880*
Si Chan Rd, or **'Gem Street'**, has the best selection of jewellery shops and gem stores. However, you are unlikely to pick up a bargain. On Fri, Sat and Sun a gem street market operates along Krachang Lane. Chantaburi is regarded as one of the centres of fine rattan work in Thailand. Available from numerous shops in town.

④ Activities and tours

Pattaya *p876*
In addition to the watersports listed in more detail below, the following are on offer: badminton, bowling, bungee jumping, fishing, fitness, golf, go-karting, helicopter rides, jet-skiing, motor racing, paintball, parasailing, horse riding, sailing, shooting, snooker, speedboat hire, squash, swimming, tennis, waterskiing and windsurfing.

Diving and snorkelling

A lot of work has been done to revitalize Pattaya's diving – dynamite fishing has been outlawed and coral beds protected. Marine life, after years of degrading, is slowly returning to normal with stunning coral, sea turtles, rays and angelfish all making an appearance. There are even a couple of wrecks within easy reach as well as some great dive schools. This makes Pattaya an excellent place to learn to dive.
Seafari, Soi 12, opposite Lek Hotel, T038-429060, www.seafari.co.th. 5-star PADI resort. Recommended. A PADI Open Water course costs ฿14,000, including all equipment (except course manuals), dives and boat fees. Certified divers can do a day's diving (all equipment, 2 dives, boat fees, lunch and soft drinks) to the nearby islands and wrecks for ฿3200.

Other operators include **Aquanauts**, 437/17 Soi Yodsak, T038-361724, www.aquanautsdive.com; **Dave's Divers Den**, Pattaya-Naklua Rd, T038-420411 (NAUI); and **Mermaid's Dive School**, Soi Mermaid, Jomtien Beach, T038-232219.

Game fishing

There are several game-fishing operators in Pattaya. Commonly caught fish include shark, king mackerel, garoupa and marlin.
The Fisherman's Club, Soi Yodsak (Soi 6). Takes groups of 4-10 anglers and offer 3 different packages (including an overnight trip).
Martin Henniker, at Jenny's Hotel Soi Pattayaland 1. Recommended.

Tours

There are countless tours organized by travel agents in town: the standard long-distance trips are to Koh Samet, the sapphire mines near Chantaburi, Ayutthaya, Bangkok, the floating market, Kanchanaburi and the River Kwai Bridge (2 days). Prices for day tours (meal included) range from ฿600-1200.

Koh Samet *p878, map p879*

The major beaches offer sailing, windsurfing, snorkelling, waterskiing and jet-skiing – many of the bungalows display notices requesting visitors not to hire jetskis because they are dangerous to swimmers, damage the coral, and disrupt the peace. Some of the jet-ski operators are notorious rip-off artists and the whole activity is best avoided. You can also scuba dive here but the diving isn't great and you'd be better saving your money to dive in other parts of the country. Ao Vong Duen has the best watersports. The best snorkelling is to be found at Ao Wai, Ao Kiu Na Nok and Ao Phrao. **Samet Villa**, at Ao Phai (see Sleeping), runs an adventure tour to Koh Mun Nok, Koh Mun Klang and Koh Mun Nai for ฿500 per person, trips to Thalu and Kuti for 300, and trips around the island for ฿200 per person.

⊙ Transport

Koh Si Chang *p876*
Boat
Regular daytime hourly ferry service from Jermjomphon Rd, Soi 14 in Si Racha, 0700-1900 (40 mins, ฿30).

Tuk-tuks
There are a number of massive motorized tuk-tuks on the island – a tour of all the sights should be no more than ฿200.

Pattaya *p876*
Air
There is an airport at U-Tapao, south of Pattaya. Service is gradually expanding with daily connections on **Bangkok Airways** to Koh Samui,1 hr.
Airline offices Bangkok Airways, 75/8 Moo 9, Pattaya 2nd Rd, T038-412382. **THAI**, T038-602192.

Bicycle/motorbike/jeep/car hire
Along Beach Rd (bargaining required), ฿100 per day or 20 per hr, jeeps ฿500-700 per day

(jeeps are rarely insured), motorbikes from ฿150 per day. **Avis** at Dusit Resort (T038-425611) and the Royal Cliff Beach Resort (T038-250421).

Bus

A/c buses stop at the a/c bus terminal on North Pattaya Rd, near to the intersection with Sukhumvit Rd. Regular connections with Bangkok's Eastern bus terminal, next to Ekamai Skytrain station. There are bus connections direct with Suvarnabhumi Airport. The main terminal (non-a/c) for buses to other Eastern region destinations is in Jomtien, near the intersection of Beach and Chaiyapruk roads. If staying in Pattaya City, it is possible to stand on the Sukhumvit Rd and wave down a bus. Tour buses to the north (Chiang Mai, etc) leave from the station on Sukhumvit Rd, near the intersection with Central Pattaya Rd. Nearby, buses also leave for Ubon and Nong Khai.

Songthaew

Songthaews are in abundance along Beach Rd (for travelling south) and on Pattaya 2 Rd (for travelling north), ฿5 for short trips around Pattaya Bay (although it is not uncommon for visitors to be charged ฿10), ฿10 between Naklua and Pattaya Beach, ฿20 to Jomtien. To avoid being charged more than the standard fare, present the driver with the correct fare – do not try to negotiate the price, as the driver will expect you to hire the vehicle as a taxi.

Train

The station is off the Sukhumvit Hwy, 200 m north of the intersection with Central Pattaya Rd. The Bangkok–Pattaya train leaves at 0700, and the Pattaya–Bangkok at 1330.

Koh Samet p878, map p879

As Koh Samet is only 6 km long and 3 km wide it is possible to walk everywhere.

Boat

To **Na Dan** from Ban Phe Pier throughout the day (30-40 mins, ฿50) – most are now forced to stick to a rough timetable with the last boat leaving at 1700. Also many boats to various beaches from Nuanthip Pier and Seree Ban Phe Pier, which lie just to the west of the main pier. Most of these boats are run by bungalow operators and they tend to cost ฿40-50. It may be difficult to find out which boat is going where; boat operators try hard to get visitors to stay at certain bungalows. It is best not to agree to stay anywhere until arrival on the island whereupon claims of cleanliness and luxury can be checked out. Travel agents on Khaosan Rd, Bangkok, also arrange packages to Samet but quality may be dubious.

Bus

Regular connections from Bangkok's Eastern bus terminal to Ban Phe, the departure point for the boat to Koh Samet. It is also possible to catch a bus to Rayong and then a connecting songthaew to Ban Phe. There is also a daily bus from Ban Phe to Koh Chang ฿250 with tickets on sale at several places on Samet.

Motorbike hire

Motorbikes can be hired all over the island – ฿300-400 per day.

Songthaew

These are the main form of public transport. Rates are posted on a board at the main pier. To **Hat Sai Kaew** from the main pier its ฿10 per person in a shared vehicle and ฿100 to hire the whole thing; to **Ao Vong Duen** it's ฿30/250 and to **Ao Kiu** at the end of the island it's ฿60/550. Don't negotiate – just pay the guy the set rate at the end of your journey.

Chantaburi and around p880

Regular connections with Bangkok's Eastern bus terminal. Also buses from Pattaya. If coming from Koh Samet get a boat to Ban Phe, songthaew to Rayong (฿20) and then a bus to Chantaburi – buses leave every hour, the journey takes 2 hrs. There are less regular bus connections with destinations in the northeast including Korat. There are roughly 8 buses a day from Chantaburi (3 hrs) to Aranya Prathet.

Trat and around *p880*
Air
Bangkok Airways, www.bangkokair.com, runs twice daily flights in each direction from **Bangkok** to Trat, fares start at about ฿2200.

Boat
Boats leave for **Koh Mak** from Klom Long Chumporn pier at 0930, 1000, 1400 and 1600, ฿450, 1hr. Speedboats for **Koh Kood** leave from Dankao pier at 0800, 0830 and 0900, Laem Sok pier 1300 and Coral beach at 1400. All cost ฿550 and take approximately 1½ hrs. A slow boat leaves from the Dankao pier at 1000, ฿300, 5hrs.

Bus
A new bus station has been built a couple of kilometres northeast of the town past the post office (฿40 by songthaew). Regular connections with **Bangkok**'s Eastern bus terminal (฿250, 5 hrs) Pattaya (3 ½ hrs), and **Chantaburi** (1 hr 40 mins).

Songthaew
To Laem Ngop from outside the municipal market, opposite KFC, on Sukhumvit Rd, ฿40). To Dankao pier, ฿100 (charter, not per person). There are also regular connections to Khlong Yai, ฿60.

❶ Directory

Koh Si Chang *p876*
Banks Thai Farmers, 9-9/1-2 Coast Rd. There's an ATM here. **Internet** Couple of places down near the pier.

Pattaya *p876*
Banks There are countless exchange facilities both on the beach road and on the sois running east-west, many stay open until 2200. Internet connections are easy to find. **Medical services** Pattaya **International Clinic**, Soi 4, Beach Rd, T038-428374. **Pattaya Memorial Hospital**, 328/1 Central Pattaya Rd, T038-429422, 24-hr service. There are plenty of drug stores on South Pattaya Rd. **Police** Tourist police, T038-429371, or T1699 for 24-hr service. **Sea rescue** Beach Rd, next to the TAT office, T038-433752.

Koh Samet *p878, map p879*
Banks The island has no banks but a couple of ATMs near Hat Sai Kaew and one at Ao Vong Duen. For the best rates, change money on the mainland. Many bungalows and travel agents also offer money-changing but take a 5% fee. **Medical services** Koh Samet Health Centre, a small public health unit, is situated on the road south from Na Dan to Hat Sai Kaew. **Post office** Situated inside Naga Bungalows (see Sleeping) – Mon-Fri 0830-1500, Sat 0830-1200. **Telephone and internet** Many places offer international calls for about ฿30 per min while internet charges should be ฿2 per min. **Miss You** coffee shop by the National Park office at Hat Sai Kaew has new machines and a fast connection.

Chantaburi and around *p880*
Banks Thai Farmers, 103 Sirong Muang Rd. Bangkok, 50 Tha Chalaep Rd. **Post office** Intersection of Amphawan and Si Chan roads.

Trat and around *p880*
Banks On Sukhumvit Rd. **Post office** Tha Reua Jang Rd on northeast side of town.

Koh Chang National Park

Koh Chang, Thailand's second-largest island, is part of a national marine park that includes 50-odd islands and islets covering 650 sq km. Despite the 'protection' that its national park status should offer, Koh Chang is developing rapidly, with resorts and bungalows springing up along its shores. It is Thailand's last tropical island idyll – at least of any size – to be developed and it supports excellent beaches, sea, coral and diving. There are treks, waterfalls, rivers and pools, villages, mangroves, three peaks of over 700 m, and a rich variety of wildlife.

The outlying islands in the national park have developed at a much slower rate than Koh Chang, though the likes of Koh Kood are now figuring in the plans of many travellers.
▶▶ For listings, see pages 893-898.

Koh Chang ◉❷❶▲❸❺ ▶▶ *pp893 -898. Colour map 5, C1.*

As you set sail from the mainland across the glittering seas, Koh Chang (Elephant Island), covered in thick, verdant forest and with a vivid, sweeping skyline, rises up to meet you. This 40-km-long and 16-km-wide island is teeming with wildlife, rustic appeal and wonderful beaches that have long attracted the more adventurous traveller.

Things are changing. Koh Chang has now been earmarked as Thailand's next big destination. Hotel chains and tour operators are moving in and the beaches are now almost entirely colonized by Thai and European package tourists. It's not all upmarket; odious 'monkey schools' (where monkey's are forced to perform degrading tricks) and that definitive marker of tourist saturation, the 'girlie bar', have now made their home on Koh Chang. Any recent visitor has to work harder to find the best parts of the island.

Elephant Island also forms the fulcrum of the Koh Chang National Park – an archipelago of dozens of smaller islands that stretch to the south. Many of these are also being taken over by mass tourism/backpackers and the recently pristine environment is suffering. If you do visit these outlying islands be very aware of your impact – some of them are overwhelmed with mountains of plastic water bottles and other detritus.

Ins and outs

With regular flights to nearby Trat (see page 889), Koh Chang is getting easier to reach. From Bangkok catch a bus from the Eastern bus terminal to Trat. From Trat there are regular songthaews to Laem Ngop and the other ferry points. During the high season (November to May) boats leave every hour from Laem Ngop for Koh Chang. But during the low season departures are much more intermittent. Koh Chang's best beaches are on the western side of the island – **Hat Sai Kaew** (White Sand) and **Hat Khlong Phrao** – and, on the southern coast – **Hat Bang Bao**. These can be reached either by jeep taxi from Ao Sapparot (price ranging from ฿50-100, depending upon destination and whether you manage to fill up the taxi) or by boat from Laem Ngop. There is a paved road up the east coast and down the west coast as far south as Bang Bao. (If you need to travel later in the day there are lots of pick-up trucks that you can catch a lift with. However, it is still not possible to travel between Bang Boa and Salak Phet. In addition to songthaews there are also motorbikes (around ฿200 per day) and mountain bikes for hire. For walkers, there is a path crossing the middle of the island from Ban Khlong Phrao to Than Ma Yom but it is a strenuous day-long hike and locals recommend taking a guide. There are several places claiming to be official tourist information offices on the island – all are agents trying to get you to buy day trips.

The best time to visit is November to May, when visibility is at its best. This is also the best time to visit from the weather point of view. Koh Chang is a wet island with an annual rainfall of over 3000 mm (the wettest month is August). Mosquitoes (carrying malaria) and sandflies are a problem on Koh Chang and surrounding islands, so repellent and anti-malarials are essential. Take a net if camping.

Koh Chang is now well on its way to being another 'international resort island' similar to Phuket. All of the outer islands have now experienced some sort of development with numerous luxury resorts appearing where before there might have been just the occasional cluster of bamboo bungalows. Some of the islands are very small, so it does raise the question of where the resorts get their water supply from and how long the demands of five-star resort guests can be satisfied.

Koh Chang

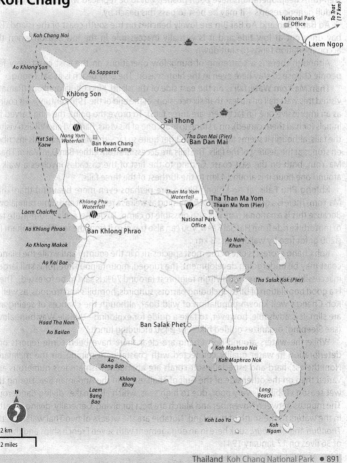

Around the island

Khlong Son, near the northern tip, is the island's largest settlement on the island. Even so, there's not much here: a health clinic, a few small noodle shops, a monastery, post office and school. Further south on the western side is **Hat Sai Kaew** (White Sand Beach). **Hat Khlong Phrao**, 5 km south of Hat Sai Kaew, and 2 km long, is spread out each side of the mouth of the Khlong Phrao canal and is a beautiful beach but the water tends to be very shallow. At **Ao Khlong Makok** there is almost no beach at high tide and just a couple of bungalow operations that are virtually deserted in the low season. **Ao Kai Bae** is the southernmost beach on the west coast. It is beautiful but swimming is tricky as the water is very shallow and covered with rocks and dead coral.

Haad Tha Nam (Lonely Beach) is an attractive stretch of coastline and much more quiet and relaxed than the more accessible northern stretches. However, most of the well-run, cheap operations have been pushed out to be replaced with awful bungalows or dull generic resorts – it may be best to pass this beach by.

Ao Bang Bao and **Ao Bai Bin** are lovely beaches on the south coast of the island. The bay dries out at low tide and it is virtually inaccessible in the low season when the accommodation tends to shut down.

Although there is a scattering of bungalow operations on the east coast, very few people choose to stay here even in the high season. The only beach is at **Sai Thong**.

Than Ma Yom Waterfall is on the east side of the island. King Chulalongkorn (Rama V) visited this waterfall on no less than six occasions at the end of the 19th century, so it counts as an impressive one (in fact there are three falls). To prove the point, the king carved his initials (or had them carved), on a stone to mark one of his visits. Rama VI and VII also visited the falls, although it seems that they didn't get quite so far – they left their initials inscribed on stones at the nearest of the falls. The falls are accessible from either Ban Dan Mai or Thaan Ma Yom, both on the east coast. Getting to the first of the cascades involves a walk of around one hour; it is around 4 km to the furthest of the three falls.

Khlong Phu Falls, at Ao Khlong Phrao, are perhaps even more beautiful than Than Ma Yom. There is a good pool here for swimming as well as a restaurant and some bungalows. Because this is a national park it is also possible to camp. To get here, it's a 10-minute taxi or motorbike ride from Hat Sai Kaew; you can also travel to it from the road by elephant for ฿200 or for free by walking just 3 km.

Koh Chang's forest is one of the most species-rich in the country and while the island's coast may be undergoing development, the rugged, mountainous interior is still largely inaccessible and covered with virgin rainforest (around 70% is said to be forested). There is a good population of birds, including parrots, sunbirds, hornbills and trogons, as well as Koh Chang's well-known population of wild boar, although the chances of seeing any are slim. It is advisable, however, to take a guide for exploring – Jungle Way bungalows (see Sleeping) organizes guided hikes for ฿450 including lunch.

While the waters around Koh Chang are clear there have been some reports of a deterioration in water quality connected with coastal gem mining on the mainland. Nonetheless, hard and especially soft corals are abundant. Fish are less numerous and varied than on the other side of the Gulf of Thailand or in the Andaman Sea. During the wet season visibility is very poor, due to high seas, which also makes diving dangerous. The months between November and March are best for diving. Generally, diving is better in the waters to the south of the island. Notable are the wrecks of two Thai warships, the *Thonburi* and *Chonburi*, sunk here in an engagement with seven French ships and the loss of 36 lives on 17 January 1941.

Outlying islands

On many of the other islands within the national park a fair amount of land, particularly around the coast, has been cleared for agriculture – mostly coconut plantations.

Koh Kood, the next largest island after Koh Chang, has lovely beaches, especially on the west side, and a number of small fishing villages linked by dirt roads. So far it has managed to escape the ravages of development; there aren't any 7-Elevens, banks or girly bars, making this an ideal place to escape and relax. There is an impressive waterfall and the coral is also said to be good. During high season, speedboats (฿550, 1½ hours) leave daily, 0800, 0830 and 0900, from Dankao pier in Trat, you should tell the driver where you are staying so you are dropped off at the correct pier on the island. A slow boat (฿300, five hours) also from Dankao pier leaves at 1000. Songthaews leave from opposite KFC in Trat to the pier, ฿100 per songthaew, not per person. Additional speedboats leave from Laem Sok pier, 1300 and Coral Beach, 1400, both ฿550. A good source of information is www.kohkood.com.

Koh Mak, the third largest island in the archipelago, is privately owned by a few wealthy local families and a little over half of the island has been cleared for coconut plantations. But there is still a reasonable area of forest and the coral is also good. The best beach is on the northwest shore. It is said that many of the prime pieces of shorefront have been sold to Bangkok-based developers, so it remains to be seen what happens to Koh Mak. Boats leave daily, 0930, 1000, 1400, 1600 (฿450), from Klom long Chumporn pier in Laem Ngop for Koh Mak during the high season; departures may be suspended during the low season.

Koh Kham, a tiny island, is well known for its swallows' nests and turtle eggs, as well as good coral and rock formations for divers. Boats leave from Laem Ngop (3½ hours, ฿150).

Koh Ngam, two hours from Laem Ngop by boat, is a very small island with lush vegetation and beautiful beaches. It has two upmarket resorts.

Koh Whai has two resorts but these are better value than those at Koh Ngam. There's a daily ferry from Laem Ngop at 0800, returning at 1500 (฿130).

Many of the more sophisticated bungalow operations on Koh Chang organize day trips to **Koh Lao Ya**, **Koh Phrao**, **Koh Khlum**, **Koh Kra Dad** (which has exceptionally beautiful beaches and lush vegetation) and **Koh Rayang Nok** during the high season, when the seas are calmer, the visibility greater and there is generally more demand. In the low season few boats go to these islands and most of the accommodation closes down.

◉ Koh Chang National Park listings

*For Sleeping and Eating price codes,
see inside the front cover.*

● Sleeping

Koh Chang *p890, map p891*
The backpacker heaven that was once very evident on Koh Chang with endless runs of cheap bungalows is slowly being replaced by generic 4- and 5-star upmarket operators. There are still a few cheaper options left, especially when you head further south away from White Sand Beach, though their lifespan

may be limited. If you're staying in a basic bamboo hut be careful with valuables. Rapid development means the list below may date very quickly. The best source of information is at the **Tratosphere** bookshop in Trat see page 881. Prices rise in Dec and Jan. Some accommodation closes during the low season.

Ao Khlong Son
LL-AL Aiyapura Resort & Spa, T039-555 111, www.aiyapura.com. Luxury and very expensive development of huge villas built into the hillside and nicely shaded with trees. Good views. The villas are well furnished but

not particularly elegant. Pool and all the other facilities you'd expect for the price.
E-F Jungle Way, about 2 km from the coastal road into the interior (there's a big sign in Khlong Son pointing the way), T089-247 3161. www.jungleway.com. Simple bungalows in pretty jungle location, next to bubbling stream. Run by an English/Thai couple. Yoga and reiki courses available. Closed Jun-Sep.

Hat Sai Kaew (White Sand Beach)

The most-developed stretch on the island with lots of mid-range resorts, shops, bars and burgeoning sex tourism.
L-A Koh Chang Kacha Resort, 88-89 Moo 4, T039-551223, www.kohchangkacha.com. Exceptionally well-designed villas and bungalows set in a luscious garden with a beautiful pool. Deluxe villas have huge bath. Friendly management. Recommended.
AL-A Mac Bungalow, T08-1864 6463 (mob). A very popular centrally located resort with some hotel rooms available in addition to the bungalows. Possibly overpriced. The restaurant is probably the best on the beach and has fantastic barbecues and breakfasts.
AL-C KC Grande Resort, 1/2 Moo 4. T081-331010, www.kcresortkohchang.com. Clean huts arranged along the seafront in a very good location, quiet but not too secluded. Friendly restaurant and staff.
C Plaloma Cliff Resort, 11/2 Moo 4, T039-551119. www.plalomacliff.com. German/Swiss-run operation on the southern tip of the bay, some bungalows with a sea view. No beach, but the restaurant is very good, small library.
B White Sand Beach Resort, further up the beach from Rock Sand, T086-310 5553 (mob), www.whitesandbeachresort.net. On the quietest, least developed stretch of White Sands Beach. Nicely designed bungalows all with a/c, fridge, TV and most have great sea views.
D-F Apple Bungalow, T039-551228. Slightly smarter huts than other places in this price category. Great huts for the price and location.
E Tonsai Home, next to **Palm Garden Hotel**, T089-895 7229 (mob). Tastefully designed wooden bungalows with fan, mosquito net

and bathroom. Set back from the road in a small garden. 2 mins' walk from the beach. Best of the cheap options. Great restaurant. Highly recommended.

Hat Khlong Phrao

LL-AL Aanna Resort & Spa, Klong Praow, 19/2 Moo 4, T09-551539, www.aanaresort.com. Set back quite a distance from the beach. The most interesting style of accommodation at this luxury resort and spa, are the villa rooms. Built on stilts, the individual huts are connected by elevated wooden walkways. All rooms have a/c, TV, DVD player and fridge. There are 2 pools and a restaurant that overlooks the river. A boat transfers guests to the beach.
LL-AL Amari Emerald Cove, T039-552000, T02-255 2588 (reservations), www.amari.com. The island's first 5-star resort has wonderful rooms, great restaurants (the best veggie selection on the island) and all the amenities you'd expect. The layout, though, is very dull – a uniform arc of rooms facing onto the pool.
A-C Boutique Resort and Spa, T02-325 0927, www.boutiqueresortandhealthspa.com. Brilliant pixie-like huts with beautiful interiors. A health spa is attached where you can fine-tune your yoga positions.
B Royal Coconut Resort, T08-1781 7078 (mob), www.koh-chang/theroyalcoconut resort/index.htm. Newly built hotel with a/c, friendly staff and fantastic views down the beach, lovely individual floating dining areas.
B-E KP Huts, 51 Moo 4, T084-099 5100. Amongst coconut palms, these wood cabins are basic but clean. There's a range of options from fan with bathroom outside to a/c huts on stilts right on the beach with huge balconies.
E-F Tiger Huts, 13/16 Moo 1, T084-109 9660. Although these bamboo huts, some with bathroom, have seen better days and could be cleaner, the peaceful location, right on the beach, can't be faulted. There is also a restaurant serving reasonable Thai and Western food.

Ao Kai Bae

LL-A Sea View Resort, 10/2 Moo 4. T081-830 7529. www.seaviewkohchang.com.

Very comfortable bungalows set on a steep hill in a landscaped garden.

A Siam Bay Resort, southern end of beach, T081-859 5529, www.siambayresort.in.th. Spacious modern bungalows with TV, a/c and sea view. Secluded spot at the foot of jungle-covered cliffs. Swimming pool and restaurant.

A-E Warapura Resort, T081-824 4177. Swish and very modern, the sea-view bungalows have a lounge area, equipped with a flat-screen TV and a huge balcony right on the water's edge. At the time of writing, cheaper fan cottages are being built a little way back from the sea. There's no sandy beach here; that's a 10-min walk away. Recommended.

D-E Kachapura, 40/20 Moo 1, T086-050 0754, www.kachapura.com. These new, beautifully designed bungalows set in a landscaped garden are incredible value. A/c or fan they come with roofless bathrooms. The beach is a 5-min walk. For the price, highly recommended.

E Paradise Cottage, 104/1 Moo 1, T039-558121, y_yinggg@hotmail.com. Laid-back vibe, with plenty of chill-out areas. These new bungalows (fan only) are basic but well designed and have been built using natural materials. On a rocky part of the beach. Internet, bar and restaurant. Recommended.

Bai Lan Bay

D-E Bai Lan Hut, T087-028 0796, info@bailanhuts.com. Basic bamboo huts available with either fan or a/c, both with bathroom. Although the beach is rocky here, it's very peaceful. Restaurant serves Thai and Western food.

D-E Rock Inn, 4/7 Moo 1, T039-558126, gerhard@rockinn-kohchang.com. These huts, with bathroom and fan are set in a nice garden about 5 mins' walk from a sandy beach. They are all individually designed and have lots of character. There is a restaurant serving quality Thai and Western food. Long-term rates available.

E-F Bailan Family Bungalows, T089-051 2701, www.bailanfamilybungalow.com. Typical basic bamboo huts on a gentle slope that leads to the beach. Fan and a/c rooms. Restaurant serves Thai and European food.

Ao Bang Bao and Ao Bai Bin

LL-AL Nirvana, 12/4 Moo 1, T039-558061-4, www.nirvanakohchang.com. On a secluded part of the beach. Large, well-appointed rooms with somewhat chunky furniture. Fresh-water and salt-water swimming pools. Recommended for its peaceful location.

A Bang Bao Sea Hut, 28 Moo 1, T081-285 0570. Stunning location at the end of the pier, these spacious wooden huts on stilts over the water. A/c, TV, fridge and a balcony. Prices include breakfast. Recommended.

C-D Buddha View, 28 Moo 1 T039-558157. Nicely decorated log-cabin-style rooms at the end of the pier, some en suite, others with shared bathroom, all with a/c.

Outlying islands *p893*
Koh Kood

Most backpacker options are found on and around the peaceful sandy **Ao Klong Chao**.

C-D Mangrove Bungalows, further along the road from Mark House. About a 5-min walk behind the beach, these clean a/c and fan bungalows overlook the mangroves of the Klong Jao River. This is a serene spot. The restaurant serves good Thai and Western food and the price includes breakfast. There are kayaks for rent so you can explore the river.

C-D Mark House Bungalows, 43/4 Moo 2, T086-133 0402, www.markhousebungalow.com. These comfortable and clean wooden bungalows, fan and a/c, are a 5-min walk from the beach. Set in a small garden.

C-E Happy Days Guesthouse & Restaurant, next to the post office, 1 min walk from beach, T087-144 5945, kaikohkood@yahoo.com. Spotlessly clean rooms, all with bathroom, fan and a/c. 2 family bungalows available. Extremely helpful and knowledgeable owners speak English, Thai and German. Motorbikes for hire (β300). Highly recommended.

D-F Baan Klong Jao Homestay, next to Mark House Bungalows, T087-0750943. Clean and homely a/c and fan rooms, with shared bathroom. This is a traditional Thai teak house on stilts overlooking the river. The Thai food in the restaurant is recommended.

F Seaview Bungalows, 43/5 Moo 2, T087-908 3593. Cheap, cheerful and clean huts with fan and bathroom (most have squat toilet) Garden setting, 2 mins from the beach. Friendly staff. There's an excellent shop selling fresh fruit and veg. The restaurant is recommended.

Ao Ngam Kho

B Hindard Resort, 162 Moo 2, T039-521359, www.hindardresort.com. Bright, airy wooden huts on a small rise with stunning sea views. Fan and a/c. The beach is a 2-min walk through a landscaped garden. Maybe overpriced.

E Ngamkho Resort, next to **Hin Dat Resort**. T08-1825 7076. www.kohkood-ngamkho.com. Beautiful huts made of natural materials on a gentle slope leading to the beach. All bungalows have a mosquito net, hammock, bathroom and fan. For the price these are exceptional value. Highly recommended.

Ao Bang Bao

B Koh Kood Resort & Spa, 45 Moo 5, T01-829 7751, www.kohkoodresortandspa.com. Spacious wooden bungalows in a tropical garden that leads to a secluded beach. All the bungalows have lots of natural light, mosquito nets, a/c and a huge bathroom.

Laem Khlang Chao

L-C Away Resorts, 43/8 Moo 2, T02-696 8239, www.awayresorts.com. Well-designed bunga lows with TV, a/c and hot water. The safari-style tents are the most interesting option, with 25 sq m and en suite hot-water bathrooms. Great views across the bay. The beach is either a 10-min walk or a 1-min transfer by kayak. Professional, friendly and helpful management. Excellent and very reasonably priced restaurant. Recommended.

Koh Mak

AL-A Ban Laem Chan, T08-1914 2593 (mob). 7 wooden cottages with seaview, attached bathrooms and 'club house'.

D-E TK Hut Bungalow, T087-134 8435. Affordable clean bungalows in a decent location. Free Wi-Fi and pick-up from the pier.

Koh Kham

B-D Koh Kham Resort, T081-303 1229, www.kohkhamisland.com. Average bunga-low operation with en suite fan rooms in nice enough location. They offer packages that include transfers from Trat and food. Overpriced.

Koh Ngam

B-C Royal Paradise Koh-Ngam Resort. Simple bungalows on stilts arranged in a row. Pricey; you're paying for the location. Restaurant.

Koh Whai

C-E Koh Wai Pakarang, T08-4113 8946 (mob), www.kohwaipakarang.com. Only open Oct-May. Your standard basic bungalow on offer here in beachside location. Rooms come with fan, a/c options, all en suite. There are also some rooms in a concrete block.

● Eating

Koh Chang p890, map p891
Hat Sai Kaew (White Sand Beach)
₸₸₸-₸₸ Texas Steak House. Tasty steaks in pleasant surroundings, sea views from the balcony, just!

₸₸ 15 Palms. A wide range of delicious Thai and Western food.

₸₸ India Hut, next to the post office on the main road. Authentic Indian food.

₸₸ Mac Bungalows. A must for barbecues.

₸₸ Thor's Palace. Excellent restaurant where you sit on the floor at low, lamp-lit tables, good Thai curries, very friendly management and popular, library.

₸₸-₸ Tapas Bar, next to **Koh Chang Lagoon Resort**. Funky beach-front bar serving pizza and baguettes.

₸₸-₸ Tonsai Restaurant, opposite **Sangtawan Bungalows**. This 2nd-floor restaurant is built around a 'Tonsai' tree and is a magical place to enjoy lunch, dinner or cocktails. Friendly staff, delicious Thai food. Highly recommended.

₸ A Biento Coffee, main road, opposite **Kacha Spa and Resort**. Coffee and sandwiches in a/c café, offering respite from the heat.

Hat Khlong Prao

†¹-† Crust Bakery, 19/5 Moo 4. Bakery, deli, restaurant and bar. Fantastic range of gourmet food: truffles, Bavarian beer, Bavarian bread, salami … the list goes on. Try the baguettes.

Bai Lan Bay

† Rock Inn, 4/7 Moo 7. The Western food is recommended.

† Sundown Terrace. Superb location overlooking the bay. Reasonable Thai food.

Outlying islands *p893*
Koh Kood

†† Away Restaurant, 43/8 Moo 2. Delicious Thai and Western food. Cocktails and fresh coffee are also available. Restaurant overlooks the bay.

† Baan Klong Jao Homestay. Baan Klong Jao. Serves tasty spicy Thai food. Remember to order your food not spicy if you can't handle the chillies!

† Mangrove. Excellent Thai food dished up on the bank of the River Klong Jao.

† Sunset Restaurant and Bar. Good range of Thai and Western food. Cocktails. They occasionally have beach BBQs.

⦿ Bars and clubs

Koh Chang *p890, map p891*
Dolphin Divers Bar, Klong Prao. Opposite the turning for **Chok Dee Bungalows**. Small open bamboo huts serve drinks at bargain prices. Happy Hour 1800-2000 – buy 1 get 1 free.

Sabay Bar, Hat Sai Kaew, just next to the **Sabay Resort**, is a night-time location where you can either relax on cushions on the beach or dance the night away inside.

White Sands Cat Bar, Hat Sai Kaew, opposite **Best Garden Resort** is a friendly little well-stocked bar and an excellent source of information as well as a good place to hire motorbikes.

▲ Activities and tours

Koh Chang *p890, map p891*
For diving, the best spots are off the islands south of Koh Chang.

Diving Dolphin Divers, T087-028 1627, www.dolphinkohchang.com. This Swiss-owned outfit has its main office on Khlong Phrao and offers all PADI courses from Open Water through to Instructor. It runs dive trips (2 dives) around the Koh Chang archipelago.

Elephant Trekking Ban Kwan Chang elephant camp, near Khlong Son, was set up to look after elephants that were no longer working in northern Thailand. To fund the project it runs elephant treks ranging from ฿500-900. The price includes transport, food and drink, and a trek.

Tree Top Adventure Park, Ao Bai Lan, T084-310 7600. Obstacle course in the jungle, test your skill and daring by walking along platforms suspended from trees. Costs ฿700. (฿100 cheaper for Thais).

Outlying islands *p893*
Koh Kood

Away Resorts, the only place on the island with PADI-certified diving instructors. Call T08-4466 5554 for more information.

Koh Kood Happy Days Info Centre rent snorkelling equipment (฿150 per day), kayaks and motorbikes (฿300 per day).

⊖ Transport

Koh Chang *p890, map p891*
With regular departures from both the Eastern and Northern bus terminals it is now easy to reach Koh Chang in a day from Bangkok. To avoid having to charter a taxi once you arrive on Koh Chang, you should leave no later than 1100. (Beware of **Sea Horse**, who reputedly run minibuses to Laem Ngop and allegedly drive deliberately slowly to miss the last ferry so that they get to choose where you stay – and take a commission.)

To get to Koh Chang, take a bus to Trat then a songthaew to Laem Ngop and then a boat to the island. When leaving the island it is advisable to get immediately into a songthaew to Trat (if that is where you want to go) rather than hanging around – if you miss the one that meets the boat you may have to wait hrs for the next one or have to charter one.

Bicycle
Some of the guesthouses have mountain bikes for hire (around ฿100 per day).

Boat
Boats leave daily for the various beaches from one of the 3 piers in Laem Ngop hourly between 0600 and 1900. This service is reduced to every 2 hrs in the wet season. The ferry costs about ฿100 one-way or ฿160 return and takes an hour; on arrival share taxis wait to take passengers to different beaches. It costs about ฿100 to travel to the south of the island in a shared taxi. The main pier is right at the end of the road from Trat, before you fall into the sea.

Car ferry
Car ferries leave from Koh Chang Centrepoint Pier, northwest of Laem Ngop, 12 times daily.

Motorbike
Hire from many of the guesthouses – it can be a much cheaper option if you intend to travelling around the island; ฿200 for 24 hrs.

Taxi
There are no cars, but there are motorbike and jeep taxis. These are pretty expensive (about ฿20-40 per 5 km). The usual rule of not getting into an empty one without checking the price first applies of course. The high prices date back to the days when the roads were poor and the machines had a very short lifespan but there is really no excuse for it now that the roads have been improved.

Outlying islands p893
Koh Kood
Boat Daily departures from Sapannamlook to Dankao pier 1100, ฿350.

Speedboats depart first for Koh Mak (฿300) and then Trat, Laem Sok pier (฿550) at 1000 and 1300 daily in high season. The price to Laem Sok includes transfer to the town centre or bus station. Additional speedboats, also ฿550, depart at 0900 for Coral beach and Dankao pier at 1300. Speedboat to Koh Chang departs 0900, via Koh Mak ฿400, direct ฿900.

Motorbike Motorbikes can be hired from several guesthouses including **Happy Days Guesthouse** (฿300 a day), although it isn't recommended that you learn how to ride a bike here.

ⓒ Directory

Koh Chang p890, map p891
Banks Koh Chang now has several ATMs located at Hat Sai Kaew and Khlong Phrao – there is also a Siam Bank branch at Khlong Phrao – opposite Boutique Resort offering an exchange service 1000-1800. **Internet, post and telephone** There are now dozens of phone boxes and internet cafés throughout the island and a post office at the southern end of Sai Kaew beach. **Medical services Bangkok Hospital**, White Sand Beach, T039-551555. For more serious injuries patients are transferred to Laem Ngop. **Police** There are 6 police officers permanently at the station in Khlong Son. Thefts should be reported immediately.

Outlying islands p893
Koh Kood
Medical services Hospital can be contacted on T086-836 4177. Have English-speaking staff. **Post office and shop** Next to **Happy Days Guesthouse**.

Isaan and the Mekong

When compared with the rest of Thailand, there's something very different about travelling in Isaan. For a start there's almost no tourist fatigue, people are friendlier and prices lower. Then comes the food – the earthy, zesty flavours of Isaan food, as exemplified by the famous som tam (spicy papaya salad), larb moo (spicy ground pork) and khao niaow (sticky rice), are some of the most popular in Thailand. The Isaan dialect has far more in common with Laos and for hundreds of years the region was ruled by the Khmers who built a series of extraordinary temples. Isaan people tend to be shorter and darker than the Thais of the Central Plains – a fact the whiter, taller elite of Bangkok never let them forget – Isaan people are often the butt of many Thai jokes. But for Thai aficionados Isaan is one of the most popular places to visit. In many ways Isaan is the soul of Thailand – hardworking, super-friendly, joyous and a bit wild. A journey along the banks of the Mekong, a day spent at the Khmer temple of Phnom Rung or just the opportunity to engage with some affable Isaan folk is unlikely to be forgotten. *For listings, see pages 904-909.*

Nakhon Ratchasima (Korat) and around ●●▲●●● pp904-909.
Colour map 3, C5.

Most visitors to the northeast only travel as far as Nakhon Ratchasima, more commonly known as Korat, the largest city in the northeast and an important provincial capital. The city has made huge strides to become a pleasant place to visit and there are nice shady parks and promenades circling the city moat. Korat is also a handy base for visiting the magnificent Khmer monuments of Phimai and Phnom Rung and the very popular Khao Yai National Park, just to the south of the city.

Ins and outs
Korat's airport is 5 km south of town with daily connections to Bangkok. There are three bus terminals serving Korat and other destinations around the country. The railway station is west of the town centre and provides links with Bangkok and other destinations in the northeast. A city bus system is provided by a plentiful supply of fixed route songthaews (฿8 per person) while tuk-tuks provide personal transportation. A **tourist information office** ① *2102-2104 Mittraphap Rd, T044-213666, daily 0830-1630*, is a little way out of town. Good town maps are available, along with other information on the rest of Isaan.

Sights
Korat was established when the older settlements of Sema and Khorakpura were merged under King Narai in the 17th century. The older part of the town lies to the west, while the newer section is within the moat, to the east. The remains of the town walls, and the moat that still embraces the city, date from the eighth to 10th centuries. In the centre of town, by the Chumphon Gate, you'll find the Thao Suranari Shrine – a bronze monument erected in 1934 to commemorate the revered wife of a provincial governor, popularly known as Khunying Mo, who in 1826 saved the town from an invading Lao army. In late March and early April a 10-day-long festival honours this heroine. The **night market** ① *Manat Rd, between Chumphon and Mahatthai roads, daily from 1800*, has lots of food-stalls, as well as some clothes and handicraft stalls. The **general market** ① *Suranari Rd*, is opposite Wat Sakae.

Around Nakhon Ratchasima

The **Khao Yai National Park** ⓘ *south of Korat, ฿200, ฿100 for children, ฿30 for a car,* has a tourist office and visitor centre, which provide maps and organize guides. The best time to see wildlife is weekday mornings and late afternoons – at weekends the park is busy. There are a few buses a day from Korat to the nearby town of Pak Chong; from here songthaews will take visitors to the park's northern entrance. This fine park covers an area of 2168 sq km, encompassing the limestone Dangrek mountain range, a large area of rainforest, waterfalls and a surprisingly wide selection of wildlife such as Asiatic black bear, Javan mongoose and gibbons, although recent reports have indicated a distinct lack of wildlife. The 50 km of trails are extensive and well marked. **Kong Kaeo Waterfall** is a short walk from the visitor centre and 6 km east is the **Haew Suwat Waterfall** (three to four hours' walk).

A small, ancient town to the north of Korat, **Phimai**, sited on the Mun River, is a charming place that is home to an alluring Khmer temple ruin and a pretty good museum. There are regular bus services to and from Korat, and Phimai town is small enough to walk around. Dating from the reign of the Cambodian King Jayavarman VII (1181-1201), Phimai was built at the western edge of his Khmer Kingdom. The **original complex** ⓘ *daily 0730-1800, ฿40,* houses the central prang, which at the time of construction was a major departure for Khmer architecture and probably became the model for the famous towers at Angkor. Another unusual feature of Phimai is the predominance of carved Buddhist motifs. As Phimai predates Angkor, there is speculation that it served as the prototype for Angkor Wat. The **Phimai open-air museum** ⓘ *0900-1600, ฿60,* on the edge of the town, just before the bridge, displays carved lintels and statues found in the area.

Phnom Rung ⓘ *daily 0730-1800, ฿40, about 100 km east of Korat,* is the finest Khmer temple in Thailand and was built in sandstone and laterite over a period of 200 years between the 10th and early 13th centuries. It stands majestically at the top of Rainbow Hill, an inactive volcano overlooking the Thai-Cambodian border. To get here is tricky –

Nong Khai

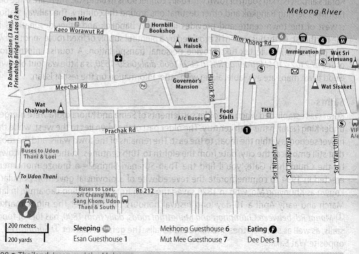

| 200 metres / 200 yards | **Sleeping** 🛏 Esan Guesthouse 1 | Mekhong Guesthouse 6 Mut Mee Guesthouse 7 | **Eating** 🍴 Dee Dees 1 |

take a Surin-bound bus from Korat and get off at Ban Tako where motorcycle taxis wait at the bus stop and charge ₱250 for a round trip. The best way to visit Phnom Rung is to go on a tour. One of Phnom Rung's most striking features is the monumental staircase which is reached via a five-headed naga bridge. The detail is superb: crowned heads studded with jewels, carefully carved scales and backbones and magnificent rearing bodies. The **Prasat Phnom Rung** (central Hindu sanctuary) was probably built between 1050 and 1150 by the Khmer King Suryavarman II. The outstanding stone carvings on the central prang illustrate scenes from the Hindu epics, the Ramayana and the Mahabharata. The quality of this carving is regarded by some as being the finest of the Angkor period.

North to Nong Khai and the Mekong 🚌🚐🛺🚆✈️🚕 ⏩ *pp904-909.*

The journey north from Korat heads through the hot, flat central plains of Isaan and on to the burgeoning cities of **Khon Kaen** and Udon Thani – both well served by good transport links with numerous bus, train and flights linking to Bangkok and other parts of Thailand.

At present few visitors stop at sleepy **Udon Thani** just south of the busy Laos border, preferring to carry on to the frontier town of Nong Khai. If you do find yourself in Udon, don't forget to check out **Precha market** ⓘ *daily 1800 to 2200ish*, in a huge area just to the west of the railway station. Endless runs of stalls sell awesome Isaan and Thai food – everything from sweet, sticky cakes through to the market's speciality: salted, barbecued fish.

Udon also makes a good base to visit **Ban Chiang** ⓘ *Wed-Sun 0830-1700, ₱20*, one of the most important archaeological sites in Southeast Asia. Buses run direct to the village from the bus stand opposite the Thai-Isaan market on Udon Dutsadee Road every hour from 0600, though the last one back leaves Ban Chiang at 1400 (₱20). Organized excavations only really commenced during the 1970s when a site spanning a time period of over 5000 years was revealed. Perhaps the greatest discovery is the **bronzeware** that has been dated to 3600 BC, thus pre-dating bronzeware found in the Middle East by 500 years. Check out the excellent **museum** where the Ban Chiang story is retold.

The last stop before the Friendship Bridge and communist Laos, **Nong Khai** is a charming laid-back riverside town: the sort of place where jaded travellers get 'stuck' for several days. With good access to Laos and its capital Vientiane, the town has become increasingly popular – it's also, with French-style colonial architecture, one of the most attractive in the region. Situated at the end of Route 2, the Friendship Highway, visitors to Laos cross the Mekong by road-bridge; visas are available on arrival. The bus station is on the east side of town and there are connections with Bangkok and destinations in the northeast. There's also a train station with a nightly sleeper service to Bangkok. Tuk-tuks provide the main means of local

Hadda **4**
Nem Nuang Deng **3**

transport; the town is strung out along the river, so it is quite a hike getting from one end to the other. Some guesthouses hire out bicycles and motorbikes. Nong Khai's riverfront has now been redeveloped into a 'promenade' and it makes for quite a pleasant stroll with the setting sun as a backdrop. The riverside market is now almost fully covered – most of the goods on sale in the market are imported from China and not particularly good quality. The influence of the French in Indochina is clearly reflected in the architecture along Meechai Road – the most impressive building is the 1920s French colonial style Governor's Mansion. It's now disused but there are plans to open it to the public. Notable among the wats are **Wat Pho Chai** – with its venerated solid gold-headed Buddha (the body is bronze), looted from Vientiane by Rama I – and **Phrathat Nong Khai**, better known as **Phrathat Klang Nam** (Phrathat in the Middle of the River), which is only visible during the dry season when it emerges from the muddy river and is promptly bedecked with pennants. To see it, walk east along Meechai Road for about 2 km from town, and turn left down Soi Paa Phrao 3.

One of the most bizarre sights in the region is found just outside Nong Khai at **Sala Kaew Ku** ① *daily 0830-1800, ฿20*. To get here cycle from town or take a tuk-tuk (including one hour's wait, should cost ฿120). Home to bizarre giant sculptures too weird to miss, Sala Kaew Ku was established in the late 1970s by a Laotian artist named Luang Poo Boun Leua Sourirat, who died in 1996 at the age of 72. Luang Poo saw himself as part holy man, part artist and part sage. Reflecting Luang Poo's beliefs, the wat promotes a strange mixture of Buddhism and Hinduism and is dominated by a vast array of strange brick and cement statues. Enter the surreal domed temple, climb to the top floor and you'll find Luang Poo's mausoleum. At the back, surrounded by a kitsch horde of plastic flowers and fairy lights, lies the shrouded corpse of Luang Poo, his mummified head sticking out of orange sheets.

If you head east along the Mekong from Nong Khai you'll find the sleepy riverside town of **Chiang Khan**. There's little to do here except laze about in the pleasant surroundings – favourite travellers' past-times. Transport connections are tricky – you'll probably need to go first to Loei and change to a local bus there.

Head south from the Mekong and you'll find the frontier settlement of **Loei**. Packed with dusty streets and seedy-looking shophouses, most visitors arrive here to sample the remarkable scenery of the area, particularly at the **Phu Kradung National Park** ① *82 km south of Loei, Sep-May 0700-1400 (closed Jun-Aug), ฿200*. There are regular buses linking Loei with Udon, Khon Kaen and Bangkok. The park station has an information centre, restaurants and porters. Buses from Loei to Phu Kradung town take 1½ hours (the Khon Kaen bus, every 30 minutes); from here there are motorcycles, songthaews and tuk-tuks.

Southern Mekong to Ubon Ratchatani ⊙❶❸▲❺ ›› pp904-909.

Follow the curve of the Mekong south and you'll reach **Nakhon Phanom**. There's little to do here except admire the view of the majestic river as it sweeps past the distant mountains of Laos. Like Nong Khai, there are several striking French colonial buildings scattered along the riverfront. Most people only visit Nakhon Phanom en route to **Wat That Phanom** – the northeast's most revered religious shrine – which is 50 km to the south. This impressive temple, set in the small town of **That Phanom**, is dominated by a 52-m white-and-gold Lao-style chedi. During festivals and religious holidays, the wat is seething with people making offerings of flowers and incense. Upstream from town, on Mondays and Thursdays from around 0800 until 1200, an interesting Lao **market** is held.

Regular buses link both Nakhon Phanom and That Phanom to Bangkok, Udon and other places in Isaan.

Head into the far southeastern corner of Isaan and you'll find one of the region's most important cities – **Ubon Ratchathani**. Administrative capital and transport hub, it is a friendly stop-off point while investigating the more impressive sights of this far-flung corner of Thailand. With the border crossing fully open at Chongmek this also now forms an important land route into Laos – there are regular bus connections between Ubon and the Laos city of Pakxe – you'll need a visa before travel. There are plentiful transport links to Ubon with regular flights from Bangkok, excellent bus connections to destinations throughout the country and sleeper trains to and from the capital. There are lots of tuk-tuks to get you about town and a **TAT office** ① *264/1 Khuan Thani Rd (facing the Srikamol Hotel), T045-243770, daily 0830-1630*. In Ubon there is a good archaeological, historical and cultural **museum** ① *Khuan Thani Rd, Wed-Sun 0900-1600, ฿30*. Erected in 1918 as a palace for King Vajiravudh (Rama VI), the collection includes prehistoric and Khmer artefacts, local textiles and musical instruments.

About 100 km west of Ubon is **Surin** – regular buses link the town to other places in Isaan and Bangkok – famous for its annual Elephant Round-up staged by the Suay people, who have a unique relationship with these huge beasts. Held in the third week of November, 40,000 people come to watch the Suay practise their skills with at least 200 elephants. The **Surin Museum** ① *Chitbamrung Rd, Wed-Sun*, displays many of the accessories used by the Suay to capture wild elephants, including the magical talismans that are worn to protect men from injury. **Ban Tha Klang** is a Suay settlement, 58 km north of Surin, near the town of Tha Tum. There's an hourly bus from Surin (two hours). It is sometimes possible to see training in progress here, particularly in the weeks just prior to the round-up when the villagers are intensively preparing for the festival.

An hour's bus ride northwest from Ubon is **Yasothon**, which hosts a yearly skyrocket festival. Some of these mammoth fireworks weigh hundreds of kilos and are suitably blessed by Buddhist monks before being fired into the heavens.

Elsewhere, **Phra Viharn** ① *daily 0800-1530, ฿100*, a hop south of Ubon – one of the most spectacular Khmer temples ever built – nestles invitingly just across the Cambodian border. The hardest thing is getting here and you should take your passport along in case officials at the border checkpoint want to see it. Catch a bus towards Kantharalak, halfway along Route 221 to the site, getting off at Phum Saron. From here it is necessary to hitch or take a motorcycle taxi. There are occasional songthaews travelling the road, but they don't always go the whole way. Alternatively, hire a motorbike or car. There is a ฿100 crossing fee.

The 'Holy Monastery' of **Prasat Khao Phra Viharn**, known in Cambodian as **Preah Vihear**, is perched on a 500-m-high escarpment. It is a magnificent Khmer sanctuary, in one of the most spectacular positions of any monument in Southeast Asia and lies close to a hotly disputed section of the Cambodian border – you'd be wise to check the fluid state of this dispute before travel. The temple is orientated north-south along the escarpment, with a sheer drop on one side of 500 m to the Cambodian jungle below. In total, the walkways, courtyards and gates stretch 850 m along the escarpment, climbing 120 m in the process. In places the stairs are cut from the rock itself; elsewhere, they have been assembled from rock quarried and then carted to the site. In total, there are five *gopuras*, numbered I to V from the sanctuary outwards. Multiple *nagas*, *kalas* and *kirtamukhas* decorate these gateways and the balustrades, pediments and pillars that link them. When Prasat Phra Viharn was built is not certain. Much seems to be linked to King Suryavarman I (1002-1050) but there are also inscriptions from the reign of King Suryavarman II (1113-1150).

For Sleeping and Eating price codes,
see inside the front cover.

⊜ **Sleeping**

Nakhon Ratchasima (Korat)
and around *p899*

B-C Sima Thani Hotel, 2112/2 Mittraphap Rd,
T044-213100, www.simathani.co.th. On the
western edge of town next to the TAT office.
Complex of restaurants, with pool, health club,
gift shops and over 130 a/c rooms. A little worn
around the edges but good value.

C-D Srivichai, 9-11 Buarong Rd, T044-241
284. Some a/c, breakfast and drinks available,
friendly place with pleasant rooms and a
good central location. Recommended.

E-F San Sabai, 335 Suranaree Rd, T081-
547 3066. This small hotel/guesthouse is
a real find amongst the bustle of Korat city
centre. The owner, a kindly English-speaking
Thai woman called Tim, has created the
best place by far to stay in Korat. There are
spotless budget fan rooms (all with colour
TV!), some with balconies; the newer, massive
a/c rooms have wooden floors and are nicely
decorated. Every room is en suite with hot
water as well. There's a small café/bar and
even a courtyard to relax in. Food is available
to guests and there are plans for Wi-Fi as
well. Excellent value, great location and
highly recommended.

Around Nakhon Ratchasima *p900*
Khao Yai National Park

B Juldis Khao Yai Resort, Thannarat Rd,
Km17 (15-25 mins north of the northern gate
to the park), T044-2352414. Resort-style
hotel, with both bungalows and larger blocks.
A/c, restaurant, pool, tennis courts and golf.

D-E National Park Lodges, T044-7223579.
(book at the National Park Accommodation
Office, T044-5614292-3). Price includes bedding
and bath facilities. Accommodation ranges
from dormitories to individual bungalows.
Booking highly recommended at weekends.

Phimai

E Phimai Hotel, 305/1-2 Haruethairome Rd,
T044-471306, www.korat.in.th/phimaihotel/
index.htm. Some a/c, comfortable but plain
rooms. Front rooms are noisy, but it's good
value and has worthwhile tourist information.

E Phimai Inn, 33/1 Bypass Rd, about 2 km
west of the town, T044-287228. Easily the
best accommodation in Phimai. All the rooms
are excellent value in this medium-sized,
modern hotel, with TV, shower, a/c and hot
water. There is a very nice, large swimming
pool, pretty gardens, good restaurant and
cheap internet facilities. Highly recommended.

North to Nong Khai and the Mekong
p901, map p900
Khon Kaen

C-D Bussarakam, 68 Phimphasut Rd,
T043-333666, bussarakamhotel@yahoo.com.
This decent, friendly, new mid-range hotel,
has agreeable en suite, a/c rooms. There's a
tasty Chinese/Thai restaurant, it's in a good
central location and they provide free Wi-Fi
in the lobby. Recommended.

G Saen Samran Hotel, 555-59 Klang Muang
Rd, T043-239611. Cheap and cheerful. Very
low prices and good value. The rooms are
clean and basic, complete with a private, cold
(though refreshing) shower/toilet – the ones
upstairs at the back are the quietest and have
the best light. Best low-budget option.

Udon Thani

D-E City Lodge, 83/14-15 Wattananuwong
Rd, T081-049 4816. Good location near the
railway station. Lots of ex-pats with their girl-
friends stay here but it is still a well-run,
decent hotel. All rooms are en suite with a/c
and colour TV. The Western food is pretty
good (see Eating) and the price includes
breakfast and free Wi-Fi. Recommended.

D-F Charoensri Palace, 60 Pho Sri Rd, T042-
242611, F042-222601. A/c, clean, spacious
rooms with fridge and TV. Although a little
dated, a good-value option. Recommended.

Nong Khai

E Mekong Guesthouse, 519 Rim Khong, T042-412320, naga_tour@hotmail.com. Clean, cute wooden rooms, on the river with a good veranda for sundowners and info. Restaurant next door and internet café attached (฿30 per hr). But noisy from the road.

D-F Mut Mee Guesthouse, 1111/4 Kaeo Worawut Rd, F042-460717, mutmee@nk. ksc.co.th. Restaurant, large rooms and bungalows, nice garden by the river, very friendly English/Thai management, good source of information on Laos, bikes for rent, widely regarded as the best place in town. The rooms are well maintained and mostly en suite. Recommended.

F-G Esan, 538 Soi Srikunmuang. Meechai Rd, T042-412008. Cute little guesthouse set in a quiet soi near the river. The owner, Den, is very friendly and the clean, stylish cheaper rooms (fan and shared facilities) set in an authentic teak villa are probably the best bargain in town. They also have a small selection of rooms with a/c, TV and private bathrooms. Recommended.

Loei

C-E Royal Inn, off Chumsai Rd, T042-830 178. Plush renovation of average buildings, large comfortable rooms, all amenities. A good-value option but the rooms at the front can be noisy.

F-G Friendship Guesthouse, 257/41 Soi Buncharoen Rd, T042-832408, north of wat, 200 m left off main road. Large rooms, shared facilities and huts on riverside.

Chiang Khan

F-G Chiang Khan, 282 Chai Khong Rd, T042-821691, pimchiang@hotmail.com. Opposite end of town from the Loei bus stop, very clean and attractive rooms, with friendly management. Pretty riverside position and excellent cheap restaurant.

F-G Poonsawat, 251/2 Chai Khong Rd, Soi 9, T042-821114. Attractive wooden hotel, clean rooms, friendly management, shared

bathrooms, small book collection to help while away the hours. Recommended.

Southern Mekong to Ubon Ratchatani *p902*

Nakhon Phanom

There is no decent accommodation in That Phanom and this is the best place to base yourself if you want to visit the temple.

B-D Nakhon Phanom River View, 9 Nakhon Phanom–That Phanom Rd, T042-522333, www.northeast-hotel.com. A/c, restaurant, pool, fitness centre. Good food, friendly atmosphere and standard rooms with balconies facing directly onto the Mekong make this the best place in Nakhon Phanom.

F-G Windsor Hotel, 272 Bamrungmuang Rd, T042-511946. Good rooms, some a/c, some fan, all clean, well presented and en suite. Recommended.

Ubon Ratchatani

B-D Tohsang Hotel, 251 Palochai Rd, T045-245531, www.tohsang.com. Good rooms in an interesting location. They aspire to be a contemporary boutique hotel but don't quite pull it off. Decent food.

D-F Montana Hotel, 179/1 Uparat Rd, T045-261752. A/c, 40 comfortable rooms and friendly staff, central location close to town square, room rate includes breakfast. Very popular. Recommended.

D-F Si Isaan 1 and 2, 62 Rachabut Rd, T045-754204, service@sriisanhotel.com. Some a/c, open airy and clean hotel with very friendly management. Rooms have tea- and coffee-making facilities and room service at very reasonable prices. A delightful place to stay, free transport to train and bus stations.

Surin

E Maneerote, 11/1 Soi Poytango, Krungsi-Nai Rd, T044-539477, www.maneerote hotel.com. Nice clean rooms in sparkling, new block. All have a/c and balconies and are en suite. Recommended.

G Pirom-Arees House, 55, 326 Soi Arunee, T044-513234. Cute guesthouse set down a rural soi about 1.5 km out of town (a tuk-tuk costs ฿50-60). The owners, Pirom and Aree, are very friendly. Basic small rooms, larger rooms have good views. Shared facilities, some nice areas to lounge in and gardens make this a great spot to relax. Recommended.

Yasathon

E-F Yod Nakhon, 143 Uthairamrit Rd, T045-711481, F045-711476. Some a/c, featureless but comfortable enough, a/c rooms have TV but no hot water. Coffee shop.

❶ Eating

Nakhon Ratchasima (Korat) and around p899

Cabbages and Condoms, Suebsiri Rd. Good mix of Thai food (see page 807), profits go to promote sexual health. Prices are little high, though your conscience will also get fed.

Dok Som Restaurant, 130-142 Chumphon Rd. Pleasant restaurant with covered terrace area, Thai and Western food. Recommended.

Veterans of Foreign Wars Café, **Siri Hotel**, 167-8 Phoklang Rd. Restaurants serving a range of Western dishes along with simple Thai food, a good place for breakfast.

Around Nakhon Ratchasima p900
Khao Yai National Park

The best place to eat in Pak Chong is at the **night market**, which begins around 1700.

Phimai

Steak House, on main road. Excellent little steakhouse serving up very cheap and hearty meals. Recommended.

North to Nong Khai and the Mekong
p901, map p900
Khon Kaen

Kham Hom, Na Muang Rd. Open 1000-2300. Good Thai food served up in this Isaan entertainment joint popular with the locals.

Vietnamese. A small local eatery next to the **Saen Samran Hotel**. Good selection of Vietnamese and Thai grub.

Udon Thani

City Lodge (see Sleeping). Great British breakfasts, they even have good sausages and HP sauce, and a mean roast. Some stonking desserts: the apple crumble with cream is great. Recommended.

Rabeang Pochana, 53 Saphakit Janya Rd, T042-241515 (beside the lake). Locals continue to recommend this restaurant as the best in town. Highly recommended.

Nong Khai

Nem Nuang Deng, Soi Thepbanterng opposite **Thasadej Café**, near the river. Open 1000-2200. Serves good Vietnamese food including delicious Vietnamese-style spring rolls. Eat in or take away. Recommended.

Dee Dees, Prachak Rd. One of the most popular places in town with the locals and deservedly so. Huge array of Thai and Isaan food served up in this large, spotless roadside diner. Recommended.

Hadda, Rim Khong Rd, between the immigration office and the market, T042-411543. Wide-ranging menu including a selection of fish dishes. Fantastic setting with river views and very popular with locals. Recommended.

Loei

Nang Nuan, 68 Sathorn Chiang Khan Rd. Attractive, well-run outdoor restaurant with *nua yaang* speciality – cook-it-yourself barbecue. Recommended.

Southern Mekong to Ubon Ratchatani p902
Nakhon Phanom

Golden Giant Catfish, Sunthorn Vichit Rd, serves *pla buk*, the famed giant Mekong catfish, in a variety of guises. Recommended.

Ubon Ratchatani

Ponthip, Suriyat Rd, corner of soi 16. Open 0800-1800. This is allegedly the best grilled chicken and *som tam* place in town and is often packed. There's a nice veranda-style section upstairs and the friendly owner speaks some English. Recommended.

† Som Chai, Palochai Rd (you can't miss the 2 giant concrete chickens outside). Open 0900-1900. Excellent grilled chicken, spicy salads and catfish curries in this large, popular, down-to-earth establishment. Recommended.

Surin
† Cocaa, Soi Thetsabarn 2 Rd. Open 1000-2300. Thai and Chinese dishes, excellent seafood.

❀ Festivals and events

Southern Mekong to Ubon Ratchatani *p902*
Jan/Feb (full moon) Phra That Phanom Chedi Homage-paying Fair, the northeast's largest temple fair.
May Bun bang fai (skyrocket festival), Yasathon.
Nov (3rd week) Elephant Round-up in Surin. Contact the TAT in Bangkok for details.

▲ Activities and tours

Nakhon Ratchasima (Korat) and around *p899*
For tour operators try **Hill Top Tour**, 516/4 Friendship Rd, Pak Chong, T044-311671 and **Prayurakit**, 40-44 Suranari Rd, T044-252114.

North to Nong Khai and the Mekong *p901, map p900*
Plenty of bog-standard tour operators can be found in Nong Khai along Meechai or Prachak roads – **Rapport Travel Services** has a good reputation. Nong Khai is also home to the **Open Mind**, 1039/3 Kaeworawut Rd, who run non-profit programmes for volunteer workers in several eco, fairtrade tourism projects in Thailand and Laos. As well as working in the local community you are expected to pay a fee (€350 per month) to cover rent and food. This is so that the projects are financed without the intrusion of big business or government sponsorship.

Southern Mekong to Ubon Ratchatani *p902*
In Ubon Ratchatani, good tour operators include **Chongmek Travellers**, Srikamol Hotel, 26 Ubonsak Rd, T045-255804 and **Takerng Tour**, 425 Phromathep Rd, T045-25577.

◉ Transport

Nakhon Ratchasima (Korat) and around *p899*
Air The airport is 5 km south of town on Route 304. Daily connections with **Bangkok** (30 mins).
Bus A/c buses for **Bangkok** on Mittraphap Rd. Connections with Bangkok's Northeastern bus terminal (4-5 hrs). There are 2 more long-distance bus terminals: Terminal 2, 2 km northwest of town on Route 2 serves most eastern and northeastern destinations; Terminal 1, off Burin Rd, closer to the centre of town, serves the rest of the country.
Train The station is on Mukamontri Rd, in the west of town (T044-242044). Connections with **Bangkok** and with **Ubon** and **Nong Khai**.

Around Nakhon Ratchasima *p900*
Khao Yai National Park
Bus 4 buses leave Korat for **Pak Chong** in the morning (₿20), or it is possible to catch a Bangkok-bound bus and get off in Pak Chong.

North to Nong Khai and the Mekong *p901, map p900*
Khon Kaen
Air The airport is 6 km from town. Several flights a day to **Bangkok**.
Bus The vast non-a/c bus station is on Prachasamoson Rd; a/c buses leave from the terminal just off Klang Muang Rd. Regular connections with **Bangkok** and all Thailand.
Train Station is in southwest quarter of town. Regular connections with **Bangkok** other stops en route north to Nong Khai.

Udon Thani
Air The airport is 2 km south out of town – regular flights to Bangkok.

Border essentials: Thailand–Laos

If you want the convenience of a through bus connection to Laos you will need a visa before travel. You can pick up visas from the Laos Embassy in Bangkok and the consulate in Khon Kaen – the price is US$30 (you'll need a couple of photos and leave a day for processing of visa). If you want to get your visa at the border you can still travel via Isaan though you will often have to cobble together local tuk-tuks, taxis and buses to make this work; a viable option. A visa on arrival costs US$35 or ฿1750 so you're better off paying in dollars.

Friendship Bridge

At Tambon Meechai, 2 km from Nong Khai, the Friendship Bridge offers a road link across the Mekong to Vientiane. The bridge is open daily 0600-2200. Visas are available upon entry to Laos for US$35, a passport photo is required. To get to the Friendship Bridge, take a tuk-tuk to the last bus stop before the bridge and from there catch a bus to Thai immigration. There are direct bus connections from Udon Thani and Nong Khai to Vientiane.

Chongmek and Mukdahan

You can also take a bus from Ubon Ratchathani to Pakse via Chongmek, and the new bridge at Mukdahan will undoubtedly lead to more services being introduced.

Bus Udon has 2 main bus stations – the main one is about 2 km from the centre along Pho Sri Rd. Buses leave here for **Chiang Mai** and **Chiang Rai** in the north, **Nakhon Phanom** and **Nong Khai** in the northeast, **Phitsanulok**, and **Bangkok**.
Train The station is off Lang Sathanirot-fai Rd. Connections with **Bangkok** and **Nong Khai**.

Nong Khai

Bus The terminal is on the east side of town on Praserm Rd, off Prachak Rd. Regular connections with **Bangkok** and other north-eastern towns. There are direct buses to Vientiane (see box, above, for Laos visa details). VIP buses for Bangkok leave from 745 Prachak Rd. A/c buses from the corner of Haisok and Prachak roads.
Train Station 3 km from town, west on Kaeo Worawut Rd. Regular connections with **Bangkok**'s Hualamphong station (11 hrs). The sleeper service gets busy; book ahead.

Loei

Bus Bus terminal on Maliwan Rd, 1 km south of town with regular connections to all major destinations. For **Chiang Khan** and other stops along the Mekong, buses leave from the junction of Maliwan and Ruanchai roads.

Southern Mekong to Ubon Ratchatani *p902*
Nakhon Phanom
Bus The station for local buses and songthaews is near the market, opposite the Nakhon Phanom Hotel. There is another bus terminal 2 km southwest of town. Buses to **That Phanom** come back into town at the southern clock tower and then head south. Connections with **Nong Khai** and **Sakhon Nakhon**. Tour buses running south to **Ubon** leave every 2 hrs during the day from near the Windsor Hotel (4½ hrs). Songthaews to **That Phanom** leave from the local bus station.

That Phanom
Bus No bus terminal as such. Buses stop on Chaiyangkun Rd (the main Route 212, north

to Nakhon Phanom and south to Ubon).
Regular connections with **Nakhon Phanom**,
Mukdahan, **Sakhon Nakhon**, **Udon Thani**
and **Ubon Ratchatani**. **Bangkok** buses leave
from the southern end of Chayangkun Rd.

Ubon Ratchatani
Air Airport on the north side of town. Regular
daily connections with **Bangkok** (1 hr).
Bus The station for a/c buses is at the back
of the market on Chayangkun Rd, south of
the Pathumrat Hotel. Regular connections
from here to pretty much anywhere. 4 direct
connections a day from Ubon to Pakxe in
Laos. You will need your visa before travel.
Train The station is south of the river in
Warin Chamrap. Town buses Nos 2 and 6 run
into town. Regular connections with
Bangkok and all stations in between.

Surin
Bus The station is off Chitbamrung Rd. A/c
and non-a/c connections with **Bangkok**.
Train The station is at the north end of
Tanasarn Rd, with a statue of 3 elephants
outside. Connections with **Bangkok** and **Ubon**.

ⓘ Directory

**Nakhon Ratchasima (Korat)
and around** *p899*
Banks Mittraphap and Chumphon roads.
Medical services Maharaj Hospital, near
the bus station on Suranari Rd, T044-254
990. **Post office** The main office is on
Assadang Rd, between Prachak and Manat
roads; there's also a more convenient branch
at 48 Jomsurangyaat Rd. **Police** Sanpasit
Rd, T044-242010. **Tourist Police**, 2102-
2104 Mittraphap Rd (on the western edge
of town), T044-213333.

North to Nong Khai and the Mekong
p901, map p900
Khon Kaen
Banks Krung Thai, 457-461 Sri Chand Rd.
Siam Commercial, 491 Sri Chand Rd.
Medical services Hospital: Sri Chand Rd,
T043-236005. **Police** Klang Muang Rd,
T043-211162 (near post office). **Post
office** Klang Muang Rd, T043-221147.

Udon Thani
Banks Krung Thai, 216 Mak Khaeng Rd.
Thai Farmers, 236 Pho Sri Rd. **Medical
services** Pho Niyom Rd, T042-222572.
Police Sri Suk Rd, T042-222285. **Post
office** Wattana Nuwong Rd (near the
Provincial Governor's Office).

Nong Khai
Banks Bangkok, 374 Sisaket Rd. Krung Thai,
102 Meechai Rd. **Thai Farmers**, 929 Meechai
Rd. **Internet** Hornbill Bookshop, Kaeworawut Rd. **Embassies/consulates** Closest
Lao consulate is in Khon Kaen, although travel
agents in Nong Khai will also arrange visas,
for a fee, 439 Aphibarn Bancha Rd. **Internet**
Windsor Hotel. **Medical services**
Sunthorn Vichit Rd, T042-511422. **Post
office** Sunthorn Vichit Rd (northern end).

Ubon Ratchatani
Banks Bangkok, 88 Chayangkun Rd. Thai
Farmers Bank, 356/9 Phromathep Rd.
Thai Military, 130 Chayangkun Rd. Siam
Commercial, Chayangkun Rd. All have
ATMs. **Medical services** Rom Kao
Hospital, Upparat Rd (close to the Mun
River), is said to be the best in the city.
Police Tourist Police: Corner of Srinarong
and Upparat Roads, T045-243770. **Post
office** Corner of Srinarong and Luang Rd.

Surin
Banks Thai Farmers, 353 Tanasarn Rd.
Post office Corner of Tanasarn and
Thetsabarn 1 Rds.

Gulf Coast to Surat Thani

The first notable place heading south from Bangkok is the historic town of Phetburi, home to several Ayutthayan-era temples – it can be visited as a day trip from the capital. Another 70 km south is Hua Hin, one of Thailand's premier beach resorts and the destination of choice for generations of Thai royalty. This resort town manages to maintain a lot more character than its bigger rivals, with a virtually intact waterfront of old wooden fishing houses. Close by is Cha-am, a smaller seaside resort mostly frequented by blue-collar Thais looking for some good grilled pork, sun and sea. Further south is the pleasant resort of Prachuap Khiri Khan, with the stunning beach of Ao Manao, and the long, less-developed coast down to Chumphon. Chumpon offers attractions such as kitesurfing and diving but is mainly the launch pad to the island of Koh Tao. Surat Thani, a proud and friendly town, is home to regular ferries and boats to Koh Samui and Koh Phangan. ▸▸ *For listings, see pages 912-916.*

Phetburi → *Colour map 5, A3.*

Phetburi's initial wealth and influence was based upon the coastal salt pans found in the vicinity, and which Thai chronicles record as being exploited as early as the 12th century. It became particularly important during the Ayutthaya period (14th century) and, because the town wasn't sacked by the Burmese, its fine examples of Ayutthayan art and architecture are in good condition. Today, Phetburi is famous for its paid assassins who usually carry out their work with pistols from the backs of motorcycles – don't worry, they don't target tourists. There are regular bus and train connections with Bangkok and towns further south.

Situated in the centre of town on Damnoenkasem Road, **Wat Phra Sri Ratana Mahathat** can be seen from a distance. It is dominated by five much-restored, Khmer-style white prangs, probably dating from the Ayutthaya period (14th century). At the western edge of the city is **Phra Nakhon Khiri**, popularly known as **Khao Wang** (Palace on the Mountain), built in 1858 during the reign of Rama IV. Watch out for the monkeys on the hill – it's best not to feed them as they can become very aggressive.

Cha-am → *Colour map 5, A3.*

Cha-am is reputed to have been a stopping place for King Naresuan's troops when they were travelling south. Today Cha-am is a beach resort with some excellent hotels and a sizeable building programme of new hotels and condominiums for wealthy Bangkokians. Transport is provided by regular buses that link to Hua Hin and Bangkok. The beach is a classic stretch of golden sand, filled with beach umbrellas and inner-tube renters. The northern end of the beach is much quieter, with a line of trees providing cooling shade.

Hua Hin → *Colour map 5, A3.*

Thailand's first beach resort, Hua Hin, has had an almost continuous royal connection since the late 19th century. In 1868, King Mongkut journeyed to Hua Hin to observe a total eclipse of the sun. In 1910, Prince Chakrabongse, brother of Rama VI, visited Hua Hin on a hunting trip and was so enchanted by the area that he built himself a villa. These days Hua Hin is a thriving resort town that, in places, has managed to retain some of its charm – particularly the waterfront. The suburbs are filled with holiday villas, while most of the high-end hotels are several kilometres to the north of the town. These luxury places are some of the best in Thailand, if not the world, and are a big draw for many visitors. Transport links are excellent and there is also a good network of local public transport: songthaews run along fixed routes, there are taxis, tuks-tuks, bicycles and motorbikes. There is a **tourist office**

ⓘ 114 Phetkasem Rd, T032-532433, Mon-Fri 0830-2000 (closed 1200-1300). As Hua Hin is billed as a beach resort people come here expecting a beautiful tropical beach, but that isn't quite the case. Many of the nicest stretches of sand are in front of hotels (don't forget that all beaches in Thailand are public). The famous Railway Hotel was built in 1923 by a Thai prince, Purachatra, who headed the State Railways of Thailand. It was renovated and substantially expanded in 1986 and is now an excellent five-star hotel (see Sleeping).

Prachuap Khiri Khan → Colour map 5, A3.

This is a small and peaceful resort with a long walled seafront. The town is more popular with Thais than with farangs and has a reputation for good seafood. Trains from Bangkok stop in the town while buses will drop you off a few kilometres away on the highway. At the northern end of town is **Khao Chong Krachok** where an exhausting 20-minute climb – past armies of aggressive, preening monkeys – is rewarded with fine views. **Ao Manao**, 5 km south of town, is one of best beaches on this stretch of coast. A gently sloping slice of sand is fringed by refreshing woodlands and framed by distant islands. Ao Manao is situated in the middle of a military base and development is strictly controlled; you'll find good, cheap Thai food and other facilities. To get there, take a motorbike taxi or tuk-tuk (฿30).

Chumphon → Colour map 5, B2.

Chumphon is considered the 'gateway to the south'. Trains from Bangkok and further south arrive in town while the bus station, with links to Phuket and the Andaman Coast, is 15 km away. You can get boats to Koh Tao from here. There isn't much to see in the town itself, but there are good beaches and islands nearby. The waters off the coast also provide excellent diving opportunities, with dive sites around the islands of **Koh Ngam Noi** (parcelled

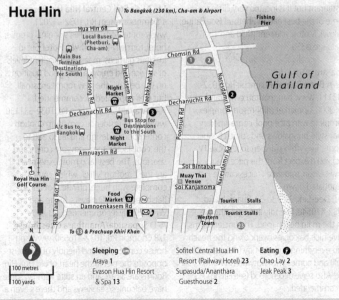

Hua Hin

To Bangkok (230 km), Cha-am & Airport

Fishing Pier

Hua Hin 68 Rd

Local Buses (Phetburi, Cha-am)

Main Bus Terminal (Destinations for South)

Chomsin Rd

Gulf of Thailand

Srasong Rd

Phetkasem Rd

Neebkhaehat Rd

Naresdamri Rd

Night Market

Dechanuchit Rd

A/c Bus to Bangkok

Dechanuchit Rd

Bus Stop for Destinations to the South

Night Market

Poonsuk Rd

Amnuaysin Rd

Riab Tang Rot Fai Rd

Royal Hua Hin Golf Course

Soi Bintabat

Muay Thai Venue

Soi Kanjanoma

Naresdamri Rd

Food Market

Damnoenkasem Rd

Tourist Stalls

Tourist Stalls

Western Tours

N

To ⑬ & Prachuap Khiri Khan

100 metres
100 yards

Sleeping 🛏
Araya 1
Evason Hua Hin Resort & Spa 13

Sofitel Central Hua Hin Resort (Railway Hotel) 23
Supasuda/Ananthara Guesthouse 2

Eating 🍴
Chao Lay 2
Jeak Peak 3

Thailan

out to concessionaires) and **Koh Ngam Yai. Hat Thung Wua Laen**, 18 km north of Chumphon, is a beautiful beach that turns into something of a mecca for kite-surfers from November to January. To get to the beach, take a songthaew (∅20) from the market in Chumphon.

Surat Thani → *Colour map 5, C2.*

Surat Thani, or 'City of the Good People', has an interesting riverfront worth a visit and some fabulously stocked markets, its main purpose is as a transportation hub. It has an airport with several daily flights to Bangkok while buses and trains provide regular links to Bangkok and most other southern destinations. Boats also connect Surat Thani with Koh Samui, Koh Phangan and Koh Tao. The tourist office, **TAT** ⓘ *5 Talat Mai Rd, T077-288817, daily 0830-1200, 1300-1630,* southwest of the town, is a good source of information. Boats can be hired for trips on the river (∅200 for up to six people). The better journey is upstream.

◉ Gulf Coast to Surat Thani listings

For Sleeping and Eating price codes,
see inside the front cover.

● Sleeping

Phetburi *p910*
D-F Phetkasem, 86/1 Phetkasem Rd, T032-425581. Best-value place to stay in this category. 30 clean rooms, some with a/c. Friendly management. There is no restaurant but it is located very close to some of the best eats in Phetburi (see Eating, below). Motorcycle rent ∅250 and Thai massage ∅350.

Cha-am *p910*
LL-A Bann Pantai, Ruamchit Rd, T032-433111, www.bannpantai.com. Brand new for 2008, upmarket mini-resort complex, complete with nice pool, contemporary Thai-style bungalows and some cheaper rooms. Everything (a/c, en suite, cable TV, etc) you'd expect from this price range. Low-season, mid-week prices can be negotiated down.
C-E Dee-Lek, 225/30-33, Ruamchit Rd, T032-470548. Friendly little guesthouse on the main beach road. The pricier rooms have nice balconies overlooking the beach and everything is clean, tidy (maybe a little dull) and comes with hotwater, TV and a/c. Also serve decent food (see Eating). Recommended.

Hua Hin *p910, map p911*
LL-AL Evason Hua Hin Resort and Spa, 9 Paknampran Beach, Prachuap Khiri Khan, T032-618200, www.six-senses.com. About 20 km south of Hua Hin (not far from Pranburi) is this stylish resort, set in spacious grounds with a beautiful pool. The groundbreaking **Earth Spa** – conical naturally cooled mud huts – provides the last word in pampering. Good value in low season. Recommended.
LL-AL Sofitel Central Hua Hin Resort, 1 Damnoenkasem Rd, T032-512021, www.sofitel.com. Hua Hin's original premier hotel, formerly the **Railway Hotel**. Set in luscious gardens, maintains excellent levels of service and enjoys a very good position on the beach – the new rooms are small but well appointed. Recommended.
A-C Araya, 15/1 Chomsin Rd, T032-531130, www.araya-residence.com. With enough contemporary design and art to add to the 'cool' factor, the rooms are comfy and spacious. The best (and most expensive) are the 2 rooftop 'villas', which come complete with huge, private roof terrace, flatscreen TV, DVD players, fridge and free Wi-Fi. Highly recommended.
A-D Supasuda/Ananthara Guesthouse, 1/8 Chomsin Rd, T032-516650, www.spg house.com. Stylish and friendly guesthouse opposite the pier in the heart of old Hua Hin. Rooms are all a/c and en suite with TV, some have balconies/sea views and there's even a

private terrace on the roof. There's also a relaxing lounge bar on the ground floor. Recommended.

Prachuap Khiri Khan p911
D Fah Chom Klun, Ao Manao beach front, T032-661088. This military-run establishment is the only accommodation next to the Ao Manao beach and is often booked out. Rooms are basic and spotlessly clean – all en suite, some have sea views. Recommended though reservations are essential.
D-E Hadthong, 21 Susuek Rd, T032-601050, www.hadthong.com. Comfortable rooms (but small bathrooms in the standard rooms) overlooking the sea with great views. The pool also enjoys views of the bay. It is good value and the best hotel in town. The restaurant serves good Thai food and a reasonable breakfast.

Chumphon p911
B-E Chuan Phun Lodge, 54/3 Moo 8, Thung Wua Laen Beach, T077-560120/230. New, with nice en suite rooms; the ones at the front have sea-facing balconies. Good value.
B-E Chumphon Gardens, 66/1 Tha Tapao Rd, T077-506888. New hotel in central location, set back a little from the road, so quiet. The cheaper rooms are excellent value – clean, with TV, en suite. Recommended.

Surat Thani p912
E Phongkaew Hotel, 126/3 Talat Mai Rd, T077-223410. Small, tidy rooms, complete a/c, hot water, free Wi-Fi and full cable TV package make this one of the best deals in town. Friendly and in a good location near the TAT office. Recommended.

● Eating

Phetburi p910
Phetburi is well known for its desserts including *khanom mo kaeng* – a hard custard made of mung bean, egg, coconut and sugar, baked over an open fire.

❦ Rabieng Restaurant Guesthouse, Damnoenkasem Rd, 0830-0100. Attractively furnished riverside restaurant, serving a good range of Thai and Western food. The spicy squid salad is particularly good. Breakfasts are small and overpriced. Recommended.

Cha-am p910
On the road into town from the highway you'll find dozens of places selling excellent grilled pork and Isaan-style food.
❦❦ Dee Lek, sited in the guesthouse of the same name (see Sleeping). This is a friendly beachside café/restaurant selling decent Thai/Euro food.
❦ Moo Hang Nai Wang, almost opposite the KS golf sign on the road in from the highway. This small shack, with Thai signage only, is arguably the best purveyor of authentic Isaan food on this stretch. Succulent grilled pork and chicken come with superlative, spicy papaya salad and filling sticky rice.

Hua Hin p910, map p911
❦❦ Chao Lay, 15 Naresdamri Rd, T032-513436, Daily 1000-2200. This place, with its blue-and-white checked cloths on a stilted building jutting out into the sea, is hugely popular with Thais. It has 2 decks and is a great for watching the sunset. Fruits of the sea including steamed squid, huge seabass, rock lobster and prawns, are served up with military precision.
❦ Jeak Peak, corner of Naebkhaehat and Dechanuchit roads. This is one of Hua Hin's most famous noodle shops. Renowned for its seafood noodles and pork satay, it has been in the same location for 63 years and has lots of olde worlde charm. It's often packed but the queues are worth it. Recommended.

Prachuap Khiri Khan p911
❦❦-❦ Panphochana, in the centre of town, 2 doors down from the **Hadthong Hotel**, T032-611195. Open 1000-2200. Welcoming, English-speaking owner, offers a vast range of seafood, pork and chicken. Breakfasts also served. Interior and outdoor dining possible with great views of the bay.

Chumphon *p911*
¶ **Lanna Han Isaan**, set near the railway tracks. Delicious, cheap Isaan food that is very popular with locals. The food here is very spicy so ask for *pet nit noi* (a little spicy).

Surat Thani *p912*
There's a good **night market** on Na Muang Rd, and a plentiful supply of fruit and *khanom* stalls along the waterfront.
¶ **Lucky**, 452/84-85 Talat Mai Rd, T077-270 3267. Open 0900-2200. Lots of fried fish – snapper, mullet and butterfish – served up in the airy dining room with its faux-ranch ambience. Friendly, English-speaking staff.

▲▲ Activities and tours

Hua Hin *p910, map p911*
Golf
There are 5 championship golf courses close to Hua Hin the most famous being the **Royal Hua Hin Golf Course**, behind the railway station, T032-512475. Designed in 1924 by a Scottish engineer working on the Royal Siamese Railway, it is the oldest in Thailand. Open to the public daily 0530-1930.

Muay Thai (Thai boxing)
Muay Thai Boxing Garden, 8/1 Th Phunsuk, T032-515269. Every Tue and Sat, 2100, ฿300 plus free drink.

Therapies
Six Senses Earth Spa, at the **Evason**. Awesome treatments – everything from reiki to basic Swedish massage – are available at this award-winning spa. Prices are high (฿2500-6000) but this is one of the most approachable and luxurious spas in Hua Hin. Recommended.

Tour operators
Tour operators are concentrated on Damnoenkasem and Phetkasem roads.
Western Tours, 1 Damnoenkasem Rd, T032-533303, www.westerntours

huahin.com. Daily tours, **THAI** agent, transport tickets. Kayaking, elephant riding and golf tours organized.

Chumphon *p911*
Diving
Easy Divers, Ta Taphao Rd, T077-570085, www.chumphoneasydivers.com. Takes divers to sites around the 41 islands off Chumphon.

Kite surfing
The beach at Chumphon is fast becoming one of the premium kitesurfing locations in the country – **Kite Thailand**, T08-1090 3730, T08-9970 1797 (mob), www.kitethailand.com.

Tour operators
Fame Tour and Service, 118/20-21 Saladaeng Rd, T077-571077, www.chumphon-kohtao.com, open 0430-2400. Tours, boat tickets (taxi to pier included), visa extension, internet, motorbike and car rental, restaurant, taxi, shower (free, ฿20 if towel required) and guesthouse.

Surat Thani *p912*
Tour operators
Phantip Travel, 293/6-8 Talat Mai Rd, T077-272230. A well-regarded and helpful agency dealing with boats, buses, trains and planes. Recommended.

⊖ Transport

Phetburi *p910*
Bus Regular a/c connections with **Bangkok** (1½ hrs), **Hua Hin** (2¼ hrs, ฿35) and other southern destinations, between 0600-1800. These buses leave from the town centre.

Train The station is 1.5 km northwest of town, T032-425211. Regular connections with **Bangkok**, **Hua Hin**, **Surat Thani** and southern destinations.

Cha-am p910

Bus Cha-am is 25 km north of Hua Hin. There are regular connections with **Bangkok**, **Phetburi**, **Hua Hin** and southern destinations. A/c buses from Bangkok drop you right on the beach but other buses from Phetburi or Hua Hin stop on the Phetkasem – motorbike taxis take you from here to the beach.

Hua Hin p910, map p911

Air Hua Hin's **Bofai Airport**, T032-520343. SGA flies to **Bangkok** in a 12-seat Cessna. SGA, T032-522300, www.sga.aero.

Bus There are 3 bus stations: a/c bus station to BKK is on Srasong Rd, next to the Chatchai market, T032-511654; a/c buses to the south leave from the main terminal and from opposite the Bangkok bus terminal on Srasong Rd, T08-1108 5319 (mob); local buses to **Phetburi** and **Cha-am** leave from Srasong Rd between streets 70 and 72 off Phetkasem Rd.

Train The station is on Damnoenkasem Rd, T032-511073/1690. Regular connections with **Bangkok** and points further south.

Prachuap Khiri Khan p911

Bus Buses no longer come into town. They pull over on the highway where you will need to get a motorbike or tuk-tuk into town. To **Bangkok** and also destinations south including **Chumphon**.

Train The station, T032-611175, on the west of town, has connections with **Bangkok** (5 hrs), **Hua Hin** and destinations south.

Chumphon p911

Boat **Koh Tao** can be reached by boat from 2 piers, one 10 km southeast of the town, the other 30 km away at Thung Makham Noi. Tickets for these boats can be bought at all the travel agents in town.

Lomprayah speed ferry uses the Thung Makham Noi Pier and offers the quickest connection to Koh Tao. **Songserm** offers a slower service that leaves from the

nearest pier and carries on to Samui and Phangan. A night boat sails several times a week.

Bus The terminal is 15 km outside of town, ฿200 per person in taxi to get there. There are regular a/c connections to **Bangkok** and **Phuket**. Minivans to **Surat Thani** leave from Krom Louang Rd, next to the **7-Eleven** shop.

Train The station is at the west end of Krom Luang Chumphon Rd. Regular connections with **Bangkok** and all stops south.

Surat Thani p912

Air The airport is 28 km south of town on Phetkasem Rd, T077-253500. **THAI**, 3/27-28 Karunrat Rd, T075-273710; **Air Asia**, www.airasia.com – all fly daily to Bangkok.

Boat **Seatran Ferry**, Bandon Rd, T077-275060/251555, www.seatranferry.com. Office hours 0500-1800. Buses leave Surat Thani for Don Sak (the port) every hour 0530-1730. Boats leave Don Sak hourly 0600-1900 for **Koh Samui**. Contact **Phantip Travel**, see Tour operators, above, for tickets. The train from Bangkok that arrives at Phun Phin is met by **Phantip Travel** for the 0900 ferry. Airport transfer with Samui boat ticket, ฿280. **Seatran** ferries also go to Koh Phangan.

Night boats leave from the pier behind the **Seatran** office.

Bus The 2 central bus stations in Surat Thani are within easy walking distance of one another – **Talat Kaset Nung** is for local buses and buses to Phun Phin (train station) and **Talat Kaset Song** for longer-distance journeys to destinations in the south such as Phuket, Krabi, and Trang. Regular a/c connections with **Bangkok** depart from a third out-of-town terminal, T077-200031.

Train The station is at Phun Phin, T077-311213, 14 km west of Surat Thani.

Local buses go to town stopping at the **Talat Kaset Nung** (1) terminal. Connections with **Bangkok**, Trang and south to the Malaysian border. Trains out of Phun Phin are often full; advance booking can be made at **Phantip Travel**, see Tour operators, above. Buses meet the train for the transfer to the ferry terminals.

O Directory

Phetburi *p910*
Banks Siam Commercial Bank, Damnoen-kasem Rd, changes cash/TCs, and has an ATM.

Cha-am *p910*
Banks There are several banks on either side of Phetkasem Rd where the buses pull up. **Post office** The main post office is on the Narathip Rd, close to the bus station and Phetkasem Hwy. Overseas calls can be made from here. There is also a small post office on Ruamchit Rd.

Hua Hin *p910, map p911*
Banks There are dozens of banks, ATMs and currency exchange booths all over

town. **Internet** A number of small internet cafés have opened up around town. **Medical services** Medihouse Pharmacy, Naresdamri Rd, daily 0930-2300. **Police** Damnoenkasem Rd, T032-515995. **Post office** 21 Damnoenkasem Rd.

Prachuap Khiri Khan *p911*
Banks Bangkok Bank, corner of Sarathip/Salashiep and Maitri Ngam roads, 1 block west of the **Hadthong Hotel**, has an ATM. **Internet** Beside Hadthong Hotel, ฿30 per hr.

Chumphon *p911*
Banks Thai Farmers Bank, Saladaeng Rd. **Post office** Paramin Manda Rd about 1 km out of town on the left-hand side. **Telephone** Paramin Manda Rd. For overseas calls go slightly further than the post office, on the right.

Surat Thani *p912*
Banks Several banks with ATMs on Na Muang and Chonkasem roads. **Internet** There are about 4 internet shops on Chonkasem Rd. **Medical services** Taksin Hospital, Talat Mai Rd, heading south towards Nakhon, T077-273239.

Koh Samui, Koh Phangan and Koh Tao

Over the last decade tourism on Koh Samui has exploded and the palm-studded tropical island has made the transition from backpackers' haven to sophisticated beach resort. Unlike Phuket, it still caters for the budget traveller with a variety of bungalows scattered around its shores. Its popularity is certainly deserved as it boasts some beautiful bays with sandy beaches hemmed by coconut palms seducing many a traveller in search of a paradise beach. The two most popular beaches are Lamai and Chaweng, both on the east side of the island. They are the longest uninterrupted beaches on the island, with good swimming and busy nightlife – Mae Nam and Bophut, on the north shore, are a little more laid-back. ⏵⏵ *For listings, see pages 922-932.*

Koh Samui → *Colour map 5, C3.*

The largest in an archipelago of 80 islands, many of which are inhabited, many of Koh Samui's original inhabitants were not Thai, but Chinese from Hainan who settled on the

Koh Samui

Sleeping 🛌
Anantara 1
Bill Resort 2
Chalee Villa 3
Emerald Cove 8
Lamai Coconut Resort 4

Lucky Mother 5
Maenam Resort 6
Oasis Bungalows 17
Palace 7
Red House 9
Shady Resort 10

Shambala 12
Spa Resort 13
Sunbeam 14
Tradewinds 15
Wiesenthal Resort 11
World Resort 16

island 150 to 200 years ago. Today, about 60,000 people live on Koh Samui but the number of annual visitors is many times this figure. Most visitors get here by plane – the airport, in the northeast, is privately owned by Bangkok Airways who offer daily connections with Bangkok, Phuket and Pattaya. Most budget travellers arrive by ferry from Surat Thani or from Chumphon via Koh Tao. Songthaews run around the north and east of the island during daylight hours and can be flagged down anywhere. There are scores of places renting out motorbikes and jeeps.

Note The accident rate on Koh Samui is horrifically high – anyone renting a motorbike should be extremely cautious, not drink and ride and ALWAYS wear a helmet.

The first foreign tourists began stepping ashore on Samui in the mid-1960s. At that time there were no hotels, electricity (except generator-supplied), telephones or surfaced roads, just an over-abundance of coconuts. This is still evident because, apart from tourism, the mainstay of the economy is coconuts; two million are exported to Bangkok each month.

The island's main attractions are its wonderful beaches; most people head straight to one, and remain there until they leave. **Nathon** is Koh Samui's capital and is where the ferry docks. It is a town geared to tourists, with travel agents, exchange booths, clothes stalls, bars and restaurants. The **TAT office** ① *370 Moo 3, T077-420720, daily 0830-1630*, is helpful.

The north coast is home to some on the island's most popular beaches. **Bang Po** (Ban Poh) is a secluded beach, good for swimming. **Mae Nam** is a serene beach with lots of coconut palms and fringed with coral reefs to tempt swimmers and snorkellers. **Bophut** is one of the few places on the island where there are still traditional wooden Hainanese Samui houses. The small **Big Buddha (Bang Ruk)** bay has become increasingly popular with travellers although the beach is quiet and palm fringed. **Choeng Mon**, at the northeast of the island, is, arguably, the prettiest beach on the north coast with a crescent of extremely fine white sand.

The east coast of Koh Samui is home to the biggest and busiest beaches. **Central Chaweng** is an attractive sweep of sand with lovely water for swimming and is lined with resorts, bungalows, restaurants and bars. **Lamai**, at 5 km long, is Koh Samui's 'second' beach and has a large assortment of accommodation. The beach is nice but rocky and, during the early months of the year, the sea can be wild and suitable only for competent swimmers. The small, often stony, beaches that line the south coast from **Ban Hua Thanon** west to **Thong Krut** are quieter and less developed with only a handful of hotels and bungalows, although there are some beautiful little coves here. Ban Hua Thanon itself is an attractive rambling village with wooden shophouses and the only Muslim community on Koh Samui. Like the south coast, the western coastline is undeveloped with secluded coves and beautiful sunsets. **Phangka**, near the southwest tip of the island, has good snorkelling in the quiet waters of a small bay. **Thong Yang**, further north, is an isolated beach, relatively untouched by frantic development.

Koh Phangan → *Colour map 5, A3.*

Koh Phangan is the gulf's party island. World renowned for the full moon party, it attracts thousands of young people looking for the night of their life on the sands at Hat Rin. The beaches that rim the island are attractive enough and apart from Hat Rin are relatively uncrowded. The water is good for snorkelling, particularly during the dry season when clarity is at its best. Fishing and coconut production remain mainstays of the economy – although tourism is now by far the largest single industry.

Koh Phangan offers natural sights such as waterfalls, forests, coral and viewpoints but little of historical or cultural interest. Sometimes the best way to explore the island is on foot, following tracks that link the villages and beaches. There is no airport on the island so everyone arrives by boat. There are daily ferries from Surat Thani on the mainland and also from Koh Samui and Koh Tao. Songthaews run on most of the main roads – the more inaccessible beaches are best reached by long-tailed boat. Motorbikes and mountain bikes are also available for hire. There is no official tourist information on the island, but www.kohphangan.com and www.phangan.info are both useful sources.

The main town of Koh Phangan is the port of **Thong Sala** (pronounced Tong-sala) where most boats from Koh Samui, Surat Thani and Koh Tao dock. Thong Sala has banks, ATMs, telephone, internet access, travel agents, a small supermarket, dive shops, motor-bike hire and a second-hand bookstore. **Phaeng Waterfall** is to be found in the interior of the island, about 4.5 km from Thong Sala and 2 km from the village of **Maduawan**. This and other waterfalls can be reached on foot and the highest point is **Khao Ra** (627 m). The stretch of beach from **Ao Bang Charu** to **Ao Hinsong Kon** is unpopular with visitors due to its proximity to Thong Sala and as a result accommodation is good value. The beach

Koh Phangan

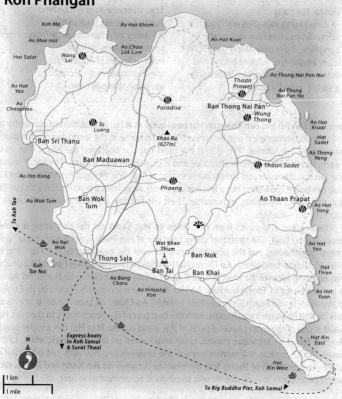

Full moon parties

The Full Moon Parties, which have been going since 1989, are now accompanied by Half and Black Moon Parties, Saturday Night Parties and Pre-Full Moon parties.

On Full Moon night, if you aren't planning to party till dawn, it's advisable to stay on Hat Rin West or elsewhere, unless you feel you can sleep to the boom of the bass from the beach. Up to 10,000 people turn up on Hat Rin East every month to dance to the music, watch the jugglers, fire eaters and fireworks displays and drink themselves into oblivion. Even the dogs take part as partygoers paint their pooches in psychedelic paint.

Tips for the party
→ Don't bring valuables with you; if a safety deposit box is an option at your bungalow, leave everything there. Don't leave anything of value in bungalows that are easily broken into. Reportedly it's a big night for burglars.

→ Do not eat or drink anything that is offered by strangers.
→ Wear shoes. The beach gets littered with broken glass and some people suffer serious injury from this.
→ If you lose your brain and your way (and a lot of people do) carry the business (name) card of your bungalow to show sober folk once you've left the party.
→ Don't take drugs. It's not worth the risk. At almost every party plainclothes policemen take a number of westerners down to the jail from where they will only be released on bail if they can pay the fine; otherwise they will be held for five to six weeks prior to trial.

Further information can be found on the following websites: www.fullmoon.phangan.info; www.halfmoonfestival.com; and www.kohphangan.com.

---

between **Ban Tai** and **Ban Khai** may not be as good as at Hat Rin but this is made up for by cheaper accommodation and less noise. Hat Rin is home to the world-famous full moon parties (see box, above). This is also the most popular beach on the island. The 'east' beach, **Hat Rin Nok**, is more attractive and is cleaned every morning. The 'west' beach, **Hat Rin Nai**, is smaller and almost non-existent at high tide. At night the noise on Hat Rin Nok can be overpowering but a few minutes' walk away from the action towards Hat Rin Nai, the music, incredibly, is inaudible. Theft has become a real problem in the area – protect your valuables.

The beaches and coves from **Hat Thien to Hat Sadet** on the east coast are only accessible by boat. The stretch of stony coastline at Hat Thien is not a bad choice, with cheap guesthouses and the possibility to walk over the headland to Hat Yuan and its beautiful white-sand beach. **Ao Thong Nai Pan Noi** and **Ao Thong Nai Pan Yai** is a double bay boasting some of the most beautiful, quiet, white-sand beaches on the island. About 5 km northwest of Thong Nai Pan, **Ao Hat Kuat**, more commonly known by its English translation 'Bottle Beach', is even more isolated. **Ao Chao Lok Lum** is a deep, sheltered bay on Koh Phangan's north coast, with the best part of the beach being to the east. **Hat Salat** is one of the most peaceful parts of the island and **Ao Mae Hat** has a super beach. **Ao Hat Yao** is an attractive curved, clean beach sited on the west coast while, to the south, **Ao Chaophao** is a relatively quiet and undeveloped bay with just a handful of places to stay. North of Thong Sala the beaches between **Ao Hin Kong** and **Ao Nai Wok** aren't particularly striking but there is some good accommodation here.

Koh Tao → *Colour map 5, A3.*

A boat hop from Phangan is Koh Tao, the smallest of the three famous Gulf of Thailand islands. It is a big dive and snorkelling centre with plenty of shallow coral beds and tropical fish. The waters – especially in the south and east – are stunning, a marbling of turquoise blue, sapphire, emerald and seaweed green. For non-divers this small island offers a surprisingly high number of independent upmarket resorts, with the added bonus of quiet beaches.

Over the last few years Koh Tao has transformed itself from unknown destination to one of the most popular places to learn to dive on the planet. The accessibility of interesting marine life at depths available to beginners, the fairly gentle currents and the low costs have all contributed to this popularity. The presence of giant manta rays and whale sharks means that more experienced divers will also find something of interest here. There are regular boats here from Chumphon, Surat Thani, Koh Samui and Koh Phangan.

There's only one surfaced road on Koh Tao, which runs from the north end of Sai Ri to Chalok Ban Kao. Motorbike taxis and pick-ups are the main form of local transport and the island is great for walking. Long-tailed boats can be chartered to reach more remote beaches. For **tourist information** try www.kohtao.com or the free quarterly *Koh Tao Info* magazine, www.kohtaoinfo.tv.

These days the number of rooms for tourists outnumbers the Thai residents on the island. Most people come here for the diving and lazy beach life. The harbour is at the island's main village of **Ban Mae Hat**. On both sides of the harbour there are small beaches with a few resorts. To the north of Ban Mae Hat on the west coast, is the white-sand curved beach of **Hat Sai Ri**. Stretching to around 2 km, it is the longest beach on the island and has the widest range of accommodation and nightlife.

Off the northwest coast of Koh Tao is **Koh Nang Yuan**. Once a detention centre for political prisoners, this privately owned island consists of three peaks and three connecting sandbars, a mini-archipelago. **Lomprayah** runs boats here.

Continuing south, the remote bay of **Ao Ta Not** has a good beach while **Ao Chalok Ban Kao** is home to a gently shelving beach and a good range of accommodation. **Hat Sai Nuan** is a quiet, isolated bay, only accessible by long-tailed boat. There are just a handful of places to stay and a relaxed atmosphere. It is arguably the best spot on the island.

Koh Tao

Koh Nang Yuan

Ao Mamuang (Mango Bay)

Ao Kluai Tuen

Khao Hat Sai Re

Ao Hin Wong

To Chumphon

Hat Sai Ri

Ao Mao

Laem Thian

Ban Mae Hat

Jansom Bay

Ao Ta Not

To Thong Sala (Koh Phangan & Koh Samui)

Hat Sai Nuan

Lang Khaai Bay

Ao Chun Chua

Ao Leuk

Ao Chalok Ban Kao

Ao Thian Ok

Hat Sai Daeng

N

Hat Taa Toh Yai

Laem Tato

1 km
1 miles

For Sleeping and Eating price codes,
see inside the front cover.

● Sleeping

Koh Samui *p917, map p917*
Prices tend to soar Jul-Aug and Dec-Apr but
are a bargain off season.

Nathon
D-E Palace Hotel, on the seafront road,
T077-421079. A/c, 33 clean, adequate and
well-maintained rooms with hot water.

Bang Po
D-E Sunbeam, T077-420600. Secluded
bungalows, quiet location, clean, friendly,
private beach.

Mae Nam
A-C Maenam Resort, 1/3 Moo 4, T077-247
287, www.maenamresort.com. Alpinesque
bungalows with little balconies, wicker
furniture, wardrobes, desk and a/c in luscious
gardens. Some have wonderful positions set
on the gently sloping beach with shallow
waters. Popular with young families. Friendly
management. Recommended.
B-E Shady Resort, T077-425392, Offers
20 bungalows on a yellow-sand beach
bordered by bowing coconut palms. Rooms
are nice, white and bright with desks and
fridges. A/c bungalows with gardens are the
most expensive. Friendly and good value.

Bophut Village
A-B The Red House, T077-425686,
www.design-visio.com. A delightful place with
4 boudoirs with balconies that are elegantly
furnished with Chinese textiles in deep reds
and attractive furniture. The 4-poster beds
look over the sea. The downstairs is a shoe
emporium. Friendly and recommended.
C-E Oasis Bungalows, opposite **Starfish &
Coffee**, T077-425143. The alleyway beside
the restaurant opens onto a beautiful garden

with 6 bungalows ranging from concrete fan
huts to larger, newer wooden bungalows. All
have TV and hot-water showers. Good value.

Bophut Beach
LL Anantara, 101/3 Bophut, T077-428300,
www.anantara.com. With resorts and spas
throughout Thailand, Anantara's well-
designed Samui resort is chic and comfortable
with a luxurious yet traditional feel.
AL-B World Resort, 175/Moo 1, T077-
425355, www.samuiworldresort.com. Fan
and a/c, spacious wood-panelled bungalows.
There is a large pool and a beach restaurant
that serves Thai and Western food.
D-E Chalee Villa, western tip of the beach,
T078-857884. This is a blast from the past
with simple Thai-style beach bungalows spread
leisurely along the shore a few metres from
the waves. Basic, but clean and comfortable
with friendly staff and a relaxed ambience –
the best of the strip's budget accommodation.

Big Buddha
A-C Secret Garden, 22/1 Moo 4, T077-
245255, www.secretgarden.co.th. The cheaper
rooms are in a converted building, the others
are concrete bungalows. All rooms in this small
resort have a/c, TV, fridge and hot water. Clean
and comfortable. Friendly British owner.
D-E Shambala, 23/2 Moo 4, T077-425330,
www.samui-shambala.com. A well-kept
bohemian beach resort with 14 pretty, bright,
blue, fan bungalows in a sweet garden with
flourishing bougainvillea. A good choice if
you're looking for a serene, budget option and
relaxed atmosphere. There's a great chill-out
area with books and games and a detailed
information board. Run by friendly and
helpful Brits Julz and Jessica. Recommended.

Samrong Bay
LL Sila Evason Hideaway, T077-245678,
www.sixsenses.com. Infamous ultra-chic
and exclusive resort and spa with cool, calm
and minimalist lines. 66 hidden villas with

rectangular private pools and luxury sun-decks. There are 2 restaurants, a gym, shop and **Six Senses Spa** (1000-2200). The massage rooms overlook the sea. Recommended.

Choeng Mon

L-A The White House, centre of the beach, 59/3 Moo 5, T077-245315, www.hotelthewhite house.com. Set in a delightful shady tropical garden, this is a small collection of large white houses with Thai details. Recommended.
C Choeng Mon Guesthouse, centre of the beach, www.choengmonburi.com. 20 rooms right on the beach that offer a cheap alternative on this attractive bay. No pool.

Chaweng

AL Tradewinds, 17/14 Moo 3, T077-230602, www.tradewinds-samui.com. An appealing resort as the excellent bungalows are set out in an attractive part of the beach. As a result of its size, it is an intimate place and is peaceful at night. There is a beachside bar and restaurant.
AL-A Corto Maltese, 119/3 Moo 2, T077-230041, www.corto-samui.com. Interestingly designed small resort, next to the beach, far removed from the generic hotel room design. The bright blue huts have colourful and playfully sculptured interiors, which are very comfortable, with a/c, fridge and TV as standard. Recommended.
B-E Lucky Mother, northern end, T077-230 931. Friendly, clean, excellent food, some private bathrooms. Several different types of accommodation on offer.

Lamai

LL-B Spa Resort, T077-230855, www.spa samui.com. As far as holistic health resorts go, this is excellent: the services provided are good value, the staff welcoming and restaurant award winning. The cheaper bungalows with attached bathrooms are excellent value.
L-C Bill Resort, T077-424403, www.bill resort.com. A fabulously quirky and stylish retreat with excellent standards of service

and accommodation on an attractive and fairly secluded beach. Recommended.
C-D Lamai Coconut Resort, 124/4 Moo 3, T077-232169. With 33 immaculate bunga-lows close to the beach, this resort has some of Lamai's best-value rooms. With shiny wooden floors, linen, fridges, elegant furniture and large windows, the bungalows feel rather luxurious despite the modest fan room rate. Recommended.

Thong Krut

E-F Emerald Cove, 62 Moo 4 Taling Ngam, Phanga Beach, T077-334100. Although isolated and poorly signposted, this attractive spot on the southwest corner of the island is worth seeking out. 10 en suite bungalows, with the more expensive rooms featuring a rock-lined bathroom, TV, fridge, kitchen sink and oddly dated decor despite being newly built. Recommended.

West coast

AL-B Wiesenthal Resort, 227 Moo 3 Taling Ngam, T077-235165, www.sawadee.com/ hotel/samui/wiesenthal/wisnthal@samart.co.th. Standing out among its competitors on the west of the island, this German-owned business is clean, excellent value and sits directly on an attractive beach with great views out to sea. The spotless octagonal a/c rooms have TVs and fridges. Recommended.

Koh Phangan *p918, map p919*

During the high season (Dec-Feb, Jul-Sep), prices are 50% higher; bargain if bungalows seem empty. Over full moon most places insist on a 7-night stay at inflated prices. Don't turn up expecting to find a room in Hat Rin.

Thong Sala

C-D Phangan Centrepoint, 26/6 Moo 1. T077-377232. Right in the centre of town, upmarket spacious hotel-style a/c rooms.

Bang Charu and Ao Hinsong Kon

F Liberty Bungalows, T077-238171. This is a nice compound of 10 bungalows with bamboo furnishings and hammocks set amid bougainvillea and cactus. Rooms are clean and comfortable with attached shower rooms.

Ban Tai to Ban Khai
B-F Phangnan Rainbow, 25/3 Moo 4, T077-238236. Very comfortable fan rooms with high-quality furnishings. The cheapest bungalows have a shared bathroom. Location and size determines the price, some have a sea view. Recommended.
E-F Lee Garden Resort Ban Khai, T077-238150, lees_garden@yahoo.com. A scattering of bungalows set in a garden next to the beach with balconies and hammocks in a quiet location.

Hat Rin Nok (East)
L-B Palita Lodge, T801-375170, www.koh phanganlodge.com. The management have moved upmarket with the construction of 10 immaculate suites with rock bath tubs that fill from a fountain and rain showers. Breakfast is included.
B-D Sea Garden Resort & Spa, 137 Moo 6, T077-375281, www.seagarden_resort.com. Bungalows and a/c rooms in a 2 storey building, peaceful garden setting across the road from the beach. Cheapest rooms are fan only, whilst the deluxe rooms have bathtub and stereo. Good value for the area.

Hat Rin Nai (West)
L-A Phangan Buri Resort & Spa, T077-375481, www.phanganburiresort.net. A more expensive resort away from the crowds with a lovely beachfront pool. Bungalows are attractively furnished. Non-guests can use the pool for ฿100.
C-F Black & White, 110/2 Moo 6, T077-375187. There are over 60 rooms at this resort ranging from fan bungalows to a/c rooms in a modern building. Very close to sunset beach.

Leela Beach
D-F Lighthouse Bungalows, T077-375075, www.lighthousebungalows.com. This great

place is a 20-min walk from Hat Rin on the western side of the headland. It is reached by a long wooden causeway around the rocks to the bungalows of various sizes and prices. The sunsets are fantastic. Recommended.

Hat Thien to Hat Sadet
AL-F The Sanctuary, Hat Yuan, T08-1271 3614 (mob), www.thesanctuary-kpg.com. Renowned for its post- and pre-party 'detox and retox' programmes. Accommodation ranges from dorms to palatial open-plan hilltop houses.
E-F Horizon Boxing Camp, between Ao Hat Yuan and Ao Hat Thien, T072-778570, www.horizonmuaythai.com. Basic thatched huts with outside toilets and some more expensive en suite options, overlooking the beach. The impressive boxing gym and ring sets it apart from competitors.

Ao Thong Nai Pan Yai
F Dolphin Bungalows, Bar & Restaurant, Southern end of the beach. Enjoys almost legendary status amongst guests that keep returning year after year. Spectacularly and lovingly landscaped jungle-garden houses the wooden fan bungalows, which are all en suite with hammocks on the balcony. Highly recommended.
F White Sand, T077-445123. At the southern end of the beach, this is one of the beach's best budget options. Serves some of the best Thai food on the beach. Recommended.

Ao Hat Kuat (Bottle Beach)
E Smile, T077-445155. Blue-roofed bungalows set up amongst the boulders reached by little stone paths and rooms with jungle views are particularly peaceful. Recommended.

Ao Chao Lok Lum
B-F Fanta Bungalows, 113/1 Moo 7, T077-374132. Clean, well-kept wooden bungalows, some are right on the beach. All have bathroom inside and mosquito net. There's a large a/c bungalow on the beach too. Good deal for the location.

D-F Wattana Resort, T077-374022. The larger rooms have balconies on 2 sides with hammocks and mosquito screens. The cheaper rooms are large, but basic, with mosquito nets.

Hat Salat and Ao Mae Hat

B-F Wang Sai Resort, Ao Mae Hat, T077-374238. In a beautiful setting behind a stream close to the sandbar, the attractive bungalows, some perched on boulders, are clean and well maintained, although few have sea views.

E-F Island View Cabana, Ao Mae Hat, T077-374172. One of the oldest places on the island, set in a wide part of the beach where a sandbar stretches out to Koh Ma, providing good snorkelling. Simple huts, some have attached shower rooms with Western toilets.

Ao Hat Yao

B-E Sandy Bay, T077-349119. A good selection of smart spacious a/c and traditional fan bungalows on the beach. All are kept clean and have large verandas with hammocks or varnished wood furniture. Recommended.

Ao Chaophao

AL-B Sunset Cove Sea & Forest Boutique Resort, 78/11 Moo 8, T077-349211, www.thaisunsetcove.com. All rooms have a/c and are furnished to a very high standard, with comfy duvets on the beds and open bathrooms. The cottages have a separate lounge area and wooden bathtubs. Infinity pool and jacuzzi.

B-D Seaflower, T077-349090. Prices vary with distance from the beach. Run by a Canadian-Thai couple, well-laid out wooden bungalows, with high-peaked thatched roofs set in a mature, shady garden. Recommended.

Ao Hin Kong to Ao Nai Wok

B Moo 6, Moo 6 Hinkong Beach, T077-238 520. Absolutely stunning villas with kitchen, lounge area and bathroom. Finished to an extremely high standard with a/c, cable TV and hot water showers. Recommended.

D-F Cookies, Ao Plaay Laem, T077-377 499, cookies_bungalow@hotmail.com.

30 attractive bamboo bungalows, set in a green garden with a small splash pool. Some have shared bathroom, some have a/c and DVD players. Recommended.

Koh Tao *p921, map p921*

Despite the rapid rate of bungalow construction it remains difficult for non-divers to find empty, cheap accommodation during the high season. If diving, you should head straight for the dive shops where they will find you a place to stay in affiliated accommodation.

Ban Mae Hat

LL-A Charm Churee Villa and Spa, Jansom Bay, T077-456393, www.charmchuree villa.com. An expensive and stylishly upmarket resort. Bungalows on stilts are perched on the hillside, amongst coconut trees, with wonderful sea views from the balconies. Recommended.

A-D Crystal Dive Resort, just left of the pier on the beach, T077-456106, www.crystal dive.com. Awarded the PADI Gold Palm 5-star qualification for its excellent facilities. A range of rooms and bungalows are available with good rates for divers.

Hat Sai Ri

L-A Koh Tao Coral Grand Resort, T077-456431, www.kohtaocoral.com. Large, dusty pink cabins with wooden floors, TVs, fridges. Dive centre attached, www.coral granddivers.com. Recommended.

AL-E Ban's Diving Resort, T077-456466, www.amazingkohtao.com. This resort offers everything from gorgeous a/c luxury rooms with silk furnishings and large balconies to plain fan rooms around the pool for divers. Recommended.

C-E In Touch Resort, T077-456514. Very funky resort with an equally cool beach-front restaurant. Brightly coloured individual huts have lots of character. The cheapest huts are wooden bungalows with open-air bathrooms. Recommended.

C-F Blue Wind Bakery and Resort, T077-456116, bluewind_wa@yahoo.com. A small, friendly and attractive place with excellent-value fan and a/c rooms and a charming beach restaurant. Pretty wood bungalows nestled in a beautiful mature garden. Recommended.

Nangyuan Island
LL-B Nangyuan Island Dive Resort, Koh Nang Yuan, T077-456088, www.nangyuan.com. The only bungalow complex on this beautiful trio of islands has a/c rooms. PADI dive courses and diving trips arranged. Facilities and atmosphere are excellent but it's a little overpriced.

Ao Ta Not
C-E Diamond Resort, 40/7 Aow Tanote, T077-456591. The cheaper rooms are excellent value; they have cold-water showers but are very comfortable and spacious with plenty of windows. Homely feel. Fan only. Next to a very quiet beach.
E-F Mountain Reef Resort, T077-456697/9. At the southern end of the bay. A family-run resort that takes guests out fishing for their dinner. Larger rooms are more expensive – go for the ones overlooking the beach which get great sunrise views.

Ao Chalok Ban Kao
B-E- Bhora Bhora, T077-456044, www.bhorabhora.com. 21 spacious rooms in wood or concrete with nice bamboo beds and mosquito screens on the windows. Recommended.
C-D View Point Resort, T077-456444, www.viewpoint.com. The large bamboo-and-thatch rooms in Balinese-style are clean, attractive and quiet with gorgeous views. The cheapest have shared showers. Good bargains for divers. Fairly secluded. Recommended.

Hat Sai Nuan
A-G Sai Thong Resort and Spa, T077-456476. A rather special and secluded spot, well worth taking the trip off the beaten track for. Accommodation ranges from hillside huts to beach-front bungalows. Relaxed restaurant with cushions, hammocks, a garden and small private beach. Recommended.

C-F Tao Thong Villa, T077-456078. On the headland so sea views on both sides. Simple wood and bamboo huts with large verandas. Excellent location.

🍴 Eating

Koh Samui *p917, map p917*
Nathon
🍴 **Sunset**, 175/3 Moo 3, T077-421244. Open 1000-2200. South end of town overlooking the sea. Great Thai food, especially fish dishes.
🍴-🍴 **Coffee Island**, T077-423153. Open 0600-2400. Open-fronted café right opposite the pier with good Colombian, Brazilian and Ethiopian coffee and a full range of cakes as well as steaks, shakes, curry and seafood.

Mae Nam
Angela's Bakery, 64/29 Moo 1, opposite the police station on the main road, T077-427396. Open 0800-1800. Sandwiches, bagels, cakes and pretzels, and has a deli offering cheeses and cold meat. Popular with foreigners.

Bophut
🍴🍴-🍴🍴 **La Sirene**, 65/1 Moo 1, T077-425301. Open 1000-2300. A delightful little restaurant run by a friendly Frenchman. The seafood is fresh and locally caught and displayed outside the restaurant, the coffee is excellent too. French and Thai food offered. Recommended.
🍴🍴 **Starfish & Coffee**, 51/7 Moo 1, T077-427201. Open 1100-0100. Another lovely setting for a meal or a quick drink on the outside terrace in this big airy building. Plenty of seafood and international cuisine in the maroon-themed restaurant with wrought-iron and leopard-print decor.

Big Buddha
🍴🍴-🍴 **BBC (Big Buddha Café)**, 202 Moo 5, right next to the wat, T08-1788 9051 (mob). Open 0900-2300. High-quality Thai and international food, reasonably priced in this island-style open-plan layout; an enjoyable place to sit and watch the sunset.

Elephant & Castle. Upholds the English tradition. Excellent choice. Open 0900-0200.

Choeng Mon
Honey Seafood Restaurant and Bar, at the most easterly tip of the beach. Great seafood. Recommended.
O Soleil, towards the western end. Best value for local specialities.

Chaweng
Poppies, T077-422419. An excellent Thai and international restaurant, one of the best on the beach. Live classical guitar accompaniment on Tue, Thu and Fri and a Thai night on Sat. Booking recommended.
The Islander, near soi Green Mango, T077-230836. For anyone missing English dishes, this place provides 'full monty' breakfasts and Sunday roast with all the trimmings.
Sojeng Kitchen, 155/9 Chaweng Beach, T08-1892 2841 (mob). Open 1000-2200, opposite **My Friend Travel Agency**, offering tasty food at excellent prices.

Lamai
Will Wait Bakery, T077-042 4263. Delicious pastries, croissants and pizzas. A popular breakfast joint.
The Spa, Spa Resort. An award-winning restaurant that serves a range of attractively presented vegetarian and Thai food, as well as detoxing/healthy specialities and great seafood. Well-priced menu, friendly service and a relaxed ambience. Recommended.

Ban Hua Thanon
There are 2 restaurants here. Try **Hua Thanan** for seafood or **Aow Thai**, T077-418348, for northeastern Thai food.

Koh Phangan *p918, map p919*
Many people eat at their bungalows, which often serve excellent, cheap seafood.

Thong Sala
Absolute Island, T077-349109. A cliff-top restaurant with gorgeous views and a romantic ambience serving up great Thai food and seafood.
Phantip Food Market. Just before the 7-Eleven on the main road to the pier. Reasonable examples of Thai street food.

Hat Rin
Nic's Restaurant & Bar, Moo 5, T08-70073769, www.nics-restaurant.com. Open 1700 until late. A welcome stylish addition to the area, serving delicious but very reasonably priced tapas, pasta, pizza and Thai food. Chill-out areas and a big screen showing major sporting events. Highly recommended.
The Rock. Run by **Paradise Bungalows**, The Rock has unbeatable views of the beach, and dishes out exquisite seafood, an unusual range of bar snacks including the ever-popular garlic bread and salads. Recommended.

Koh Tao *p921, map p921*
Ban Mae Hat
Café del Sol, Mae Hat Sq, T077-456578. Open 0800-2300. Great place for breakfast, also serves sandwiches, bruschetta and coffee. For dinner the French/Italian chef prepares salmon or steak and other international cuisine.
Puk's Thai Kitchen, Mae Hat Sq, T077-456685. Open 0800-late. Serves Thai but also does a full English breakfast.

Hat Sai Ri
Papa's Tapas, opposite **Siam Scuba Dive Center**, Sai Ri village, T077-456298. Open 1900-late. A sophisticated addition to the island and Thailand's only absinthe bar. Sample wonderfully concocted Asian fusion tapas with attention to detail. Recommended.
Thipwimarn Restaurant, on the northwest headland, T077-456409. Open 0700-2200. This has become one of the more popular spots for fashionable dining due to the stunning views over Sai Ri bay and excellent Thai and seafood. Free pick-up.
Coffee Boat, on the main road just before the main drag down to the beach in Sai Ri village, T077-456178. A cheap and cheerful

authentic Thai diner and bakery. Ample portions of tasty, hot Thai food. Cakes made to order.

Ao Ta Not
¶¶ **Poseidon**, T077-456735. Open 0730-2200. A popular restaurant serving fried fish, a good range of vegetarian dishes and unusual milkshakes – including cookie vanilla flavour and prune lassies.

Ao Chalok Ban Kao
¶¶ **New Heaven**, rather a climb, at the top of the hill, T077-456462. Evenings only. A bit pricey but good food and fantastic views over the gorgeous Thian Og Bay.
¶¶ **Sunshine Dive School**. Has a BBQ evening buffet every night with baked potatoes, garlic bread, calamari, kebabs, salad and some rice dishes.
¶ **Viewpoint Restaurant**, beyond the **Bubble Dive Resort** at the eastern end of the beach, T077-456777. Open 0700-2200. Wide menu of Thai and some Western food. Also perched above the sea it enjoys great views.

❶ Bars and clubs

Koh Samui *p917, map p917*
Bophut
Billabong Surf Club, 79/2 Moo 1, T077-430144. A full-on sports bar with TVs and sports pictures plastering the wall and a small balcony for drinking.
The Tropicana, T077-425304. With large fish tanks built into the walls, this unusual venue for an evening drink can make for a refreshing change from the popular sports bars.

Chaweng
Most of the bars are at the northern end of the strip, which is also home to a variety of go-go bars.
Dew Drop Huts tends to draw a young crowd and puts on beach parties during high season.
Green Mango, on the main road. A rather jaunty venue with Western DJs playing

garage and house music. Also host to live Thai bands performing Western pop and rock.

Lamai
Bauhaus is a large, popular venue consisting of a pub, restaurant and discotheque. Shows mainstream Western movies during the day and early evening and hosts live bands.

Koh Phangan *p918, map p919*
Hat Rin
At full moon, every store, bar and restaurant turns itself into a bar selling plastic buckets stuffed with spirits and mixers. The 3 best and loudest clubs on Hat Rin Beach East are **Vinyl Club**, **Zoom Bar** and the **Drop in Club**, www.dropinclub.com, which play upbeat dance music – and not just on full moon nights.
Backyard Club, Hat Rin West. Infamous for its full moon after-parties, which start at 1100 the morning after with the best of the DJs.

Koh Tao *p921, map p921*
Ban Mae Hat
Whitening, on the road to the **Sensi Paradise Resort**. The staple diver's after-hours spot with a pleasant bar on the beach and decent menu. Fri night parties.
Dragon Bar, Pier Rd. Wooden tables spill onto the street from this relatively new bar playing different music every night: indie, 1980s, hip hop, jazz and alternative rock. Look out for flyers.

Hat Sai Ri
Pure, south Sai Ri beach. The hippest place in town stylishly scattered with big red bean bags. Open every night until 0200 but watch out for the popular party nights.

❷ Entertainment

Koh Samui *p917, map p917*
Chaweng
Star Club, 200/11 Chaweng Rd, T077-414218. Puts on a pretty hilarious katoey

(transsexual) show with audience participation, a lot of feathers and make-up at 2230 nightly. Beers are ฿100. No admission charge, customers must buy drinks. Recommended.
Chaweng Stadium, T077-413504, free transfers, a good place to see Muay Thai (Thai boxing), 8 fights from 2100.

Lamai
In the stadium at the north end (and several others around the island) is Buffalo fighting. Far tamer than it sounds, animals are rarely injured in the 'fights' and it's more a show of tradition than a fierce face-off. Ask at your hotel for date of the next event.

▲ Activities and tours

Koh Samui *p917, map p917*
Cookery course
Blue Banana, 2 Moo 4, Big Buddha Beach, T077-245080. Classes with 'Toy'.

Diving
Bo Phut Diving School, next to **Eden Bungalows**, Bophut, T077-425496, www. bophut diving.com. Also offers snorkelling.
Captain Caveman, at the **Shambala Resort**, Big Buddha, and on Chaweng Beach Rd, T08-6282 2983 (mob), www.samuireef.com. Office hours 1000-2100, closed Sun morning. A 5-star PADI dive centre. Prides itself on small classes. Snorkelling trips to Ang Thong Marine National Park, ฿3750, to Koh Tao and Nangyuan and Mango Bay, ฿2500.
Big Blue Diving, South Chaweng Beach Rd, Chaweng, T077-422617, www.bigbluediving samui.com. Popular Swedish dive centre.

Spas and therapies
Samui Dharma Healing Centre, 63 Moo Tee 1, Ao Santi Beach, near Nathon, T077-234170, www.dharmahealingintl.com. Runs alternative health programmes to inspire and rejuvenate. 7- to 21-day fasting courses are directed according to Dharma Buddhist principles in alternative health:

fasting, colonic irrigation, yoga, reflexology, iridology and many other therapies. Accommodation is available.
Thalasso Spa, **Samui Peninsula Spa & Resort**, T077-428100, www.samuipeninsula.com. Professional treatments in attractive rooms; mud treatments are the speciality.

Tour operators
One Hundred Degrees East, 23/2 Moo 4, Big Buddha, T08-6282 2983 (mob), www.100 degreeseast.com. Charter trips run by Ivan Douglas who runs Captain Caveman. Private charters. A direct charter from Samui to Tao is ฿18,000.
My Friend Travel Agency, 14/62-64 Mo 2, Chaweng Beach Rd, Chaweng, T077-413364. Open 1000-2300. Run by a friendly and helpful woman called Amporn who speaks English.

Koh Phangan *p918, map p919*
Diving
Chaloklum Diving, Chao Lok Lum Village, T077-374025, www.chaloklum-diving.com. One of the longest-standing operations on the island with an excellent reputation. Its small-group policy guarantees personal attention.
Crystal Dive, in Hat Rin T077-375535, www.crystaldive.com. This booking branch of the respected dive resort in Koh Tao is run by **Backpackers Information Centre**.

Tour operators and travel agents
Thong Sala Centre, 44/13 Thong Sala Pier, T077-238984, jamareei@hotmail.com. Run by twin sisters for the last 25 years. Can organize boat, train, plane tickets and offer sound travel advice. Trustworthy.
Backpackers, Hat Rin, T077-375535, www.backpackersthailand.com. An invaluable source of information and the only TAT-registered independent travel agent on the island. Good website.

Therapies
Chakra, Hat Rin, off the main drag leading up from the pier, T077-375401, www.chakrayoga.com. Open until 2400.

Good traditional body, face and foot Thai massages, reiki, reflexology and acupressure treatments.

Monte Vista Retreat Centre, Thong Sala T077-238951, www.montevistathailand.com. The latest addition to the island's holistic health scene and already winning rave reviews.

Wat Pho Herbal Sauna, close to Ban Tai beach on the southwest coast. This traditional herbal sauna is run on donations and uses traditional methods and ingredients.

Koh Tao *p921, map p921*
Diving

Diving is popular year round on Koh Tao. It is said to be the cheapest place in Thailand to learn to dive. There's a **decompression chamber** in Ban Mae Hat – T077-456664. A PADI Open Water course costs roughly ฿9000 and a fun dive for qualified divers is around ฿1800. Remember that you shouldn't compromise on safety when diving – plenty of accidents occur on Koh Tao due to poor equipment, too many divers per instructor and diving while intoxicated. Check the reputation of the school, the equipment and ratios of students to instructors before handing over your cash. Recommended dive schools include:

Big Blue, Ban Mae Hat, T077-456050, or Hat Sai Ri, T077-456179, www.bigbluediving.com.
Buddha View Dive Resort, Chalok Ban Kao, T077-456074, www.buddhaview-diving.com.
Crystal Dive Resort, Ban Mae Hat and Sai Ri, T077-456107, www.crystaldive.com.
Easy Divers, Ban Mae Hat, T077-456010, www.thaidive.com.
Siam Scuba Dive Center, Sai Ri village, T077-456628, www.scubadive.com.

Therapies

Jamahkiri Spa & Resort, Ao Thian Ok, T077-456400. Open 1000-2200. Free pick-ups available. Indulge in 1 of the reasonably priced packages available at this spa in grounds overlooking the sea. Steam sauna and a variety of massages are available. Recommended.

◎ Transport

Koh Samui *p917, map p917*
Air

The airport is in the northeast of the island, T077-428500 and is owned by **Bangkok Airways**. There are multiple daily connections with **Bangkok** and regular flights to **Phuket**, **U-Tapao** (Pattaya).

Airline offices Bangkok Airways is at the southern end of Chaweng, T077-422513.

Transport to town or the beach is by a/c minibus to Bophut, Mae Nam, Chaweng, Choeng Mon, Lamai and Big Buddha. There's also a limousine service at domestic arrivals, T077-245598, samuiaccom@hotmail.com. (Minivan ฿150 to Chaweng, ฿300 to Lamai, ฿150-300 to the north coast).

Boat

There are numerous daily boat options. Schedules, journey times and prices change according to the season. Tickets from travel agents will cost more but include scheduling advice and transfers. See Transport sections for **Surat Thani** (page 912), **Koh Phangan** and **Koh Tao** (below) for boat services to Koh Samui.

Lomprayah, main road, Mae Nam, on the corner of the road to the Baan Fah Resort, office Mon-Sat 0800-1700, telephone lines daily T077-427765, www.lomprayah.com. Daily service departing from Wat Na Phra Lam pier to **Koh Phangan**, **Koh Tao** and **Chumporn** (฿900). They also sell combined bus tickets to Hua Hin and Bangkok. Price includes transfer to pier.

Songserm Travel, seafront road, Nathon, T077-420157, office hours 0800-1800. Runs express passenger boats daily. These boats leave from the southern pier in Nathon to **Surat Thani**, **Koh Phangan** and **Koh Tao**. Seatran (office on pier, daily 0500-1700, T077-426001-2) operates hourly boats to **Surat Thani** from the main northerly pier in Nathon.

The slow overnight boat to Surat Thani leaves Nathon at 2100, arriving in **Don Sak** at around 0300/0400.

Bus/train
Buses and trains from **Bangkok** to **Surat Thani** are easy to link to ferry services to and from Koh Samui – speak to a local travel agent or for more details see Transport: Surat Thani, page 915.

Car/motorbike hire
It's cheaper to hire from the town of Nathon than on the beaches. Motorbikes cost ฿150-200 per day, and around ฿250 for an automatic. Helmets must be provided. The fine for not wearing one is ฿200-500. Jeep/car hire from ฿800-1000 per day including insurance.

Motorbike taxi
Available all over the island. They wait in clusters wearing coloured cloth jackets. You'll need to haggle the fares, though a rough benchmark is **Nathon-Chaweng**, ฿150-180.

Songthaew
The most common form of transport, Songthaews circulate between the island's northern and eastern beaches during daylight hours. Their final destination is usually written on the front of the vehicle and they stop anywhere when flagged down (prices start at ฿50 per person but are often inflated and some haggling may be required). Occasional night-time songthaews run from 1830 and charge double. From Nathon, songthaews travel in a clockwise direction to Chaweng and anti-clockwise to Lamai.

Taxi
Expensive yellow meter taxis cruise the island all day though they are scarce after 0100 but any bar or hotel owner will know one. The taxis do not use their meters and on average a fare from **Nathon** to **Chaweng** is ฿500.

Koh Phangan p918, map p919
Boat
Long-tailed boats take passengers to and from Hat Rin, Ao Thong Nai Pan, Ao Hat Yao and Ao Hat Kuat to Thong Sala and Ban Khai piers. Most boats dock at the pier at Thong

Sala, although there's a ferry, the *Haad Rin Queen*, T077-375113, from **Big Buddha** pier on Samui going straight to Hat Rin. From **Thong Sala to Koh Samui**: With Songsern (T077-377704) to Nathon pier, Mae Nam beach with Lomprayah (T077-238411), Big Buddha pier with Seatran (T077-238679). **Speed Boat Line** to **Bophut**, **Koh Samui**, To Koh Tao from Thong Sala with **Seatran**, **Lomprayah** and **Songsern**. To **Surat Thani** from Thong Sala with **Songserm**, **Raja Ferry**, prices include bus ticket to bus and train stations. The **night boat** leaves Koh Phangan for **Surat Thani** at 2200 (although times can vary, so it's worth checking in good time), 6 hrs. To **Chumphon** with **Lomprayah**.

Motorbike hire
In Thong Sala and the more popular beaches. Some guesthouses hire from ฿200 per day.

Songthaew
Songthaews run from the pier to any of the bays served by road. A trip to **Hat Rin** from Thong Sala is ฿80-100. At Hat Rin songthaews wait close to the **Drop in Club Resort**.

Koh Tao p921, map p921
Boat
There are boats of various speeds and sizes going to and from Koh Tao. Connections are with **Chumphon** (see page 915), and Koh Samui, via Koh Phangan.

To **Chumphon** with **Lomprayah**, T077-456176; with **Songserm**, T077-456274, (with **Seatran** T077-456907, 1000, 1600, 2 hrs, ฿550; with **Ko Jaroen**, T08-1797 0276 (mob), the nightboat at 2200, 5 hrs. To **Koh Samui** and **Koh Phangan** with **Lomprayah**; with **Songserm**, T077-456274; with **Seatran**, T077-456907 and to **Surat Thani** with **Songserm**.

Motorbike hire
Unless you are an experienced dirt bike rider this is not really an advisable form of transport. **Lederhosenbikes**, Ban Mae Hat, T08-1752 8994 (mob), www.cycling-koh-tao.com. Rents bikes from ฿200/day.

Taxi

Taxis and motorbike taxis wait at the end of Mae Hat pier. Sharing taxis makes sense as the cost is per journey, not per person. From Mae Hat to Ao Ta Not costs ฿200-300 with a minimum of 4 in the car.

● Directory

Koh Samui *p917, maps p917*

Banks Countless exchanges and ATMs scattered all over the island. **Immigration** Immigration office, on main road next to the police station, Nathon, T077-421069, Mon-Fri 0830-1200 and 1300-1630. Visas can be extended here. **Internet** There are internet cafés in all the beach resorts, ฿1 per min, and most travel agencies. **Medical services** 24-hr emergency clinic and the **Samui International Hospital**, Chaweng, T077-422 272, www.sih.co.th (also has a dental clinic). It's best to take injured people to the hospital; the ambulance service can be slow. A reasonable level of English is spoken. **Bandon International Hospital**, Bophut, T077-245 236, www.bandonhospital.com. **Police** Tourist police, 3 km south of Nathon, T077-4212815, open 24 hrs, past turning to Hin Lad Waterfall. **Emergency**, T1169; **police**, T191. **Post office** Nathon Post Office, to the north of the pier, Mon-Fri 0830-1630, Sat-Sun 0830-1200. **Lamai Post Office**, south end of the main road.

Koh Phangan *p918, map p919*

Banks There are banks with ATMs on the main road in Thong Sala. There are many ATMs in Hat Rin and plenty of foreign exchange outlets. **Internet** There are now plenty of internet cafés, all vying for business and charging ฿2 per min. **Medical services** Bandon International Hospital, in Hat Rin, T077-375471, is a 24-hr private clinic with English-speaking staff. **Police** Tourist Police, T077-421281. **Post office** Hat Rin, close to pier, Mon-Fri 0830-1640, Sat 0900-1200.

Koh Tao *p921, map p921*

Banks There is an exchange office just east of the pier in Ban Mae Hat, run by the **Krung Thai Bank**, daily 0900-1600. **Siam City Bank**, Pier Rd, Ban Mae Hat, east of the pier on the left with ATM, exchange and TCs changed, Mon-Fri 0830-1630. There are also a couple of ATMs between Ban Mae Hat and Sai Ri and in Chalok. **Internet** There are numerous internet cafés in Ban Mae Hat and Sai Ri and Chalok, ฿2/min everywhere. **Medical services** Badalaveda Diving Medicine Centre, Sai Ri, T077-456664. **Koh Tao Physician Clinic**, Sai Ri T077-456037/ 081-737 5444, daily 0800-1900. **Koh Tao Health Centre**, Mae Hat, T077-456007. **Post office** Thongnual Rd, Mae Hat, straight up from the pier and turn left, Mon-Fri 0830-1630.

Andaman Coast to Khao Lak

The southern run to the Andaman Coast reveals a wild, untouched landscape with waterfalls, lush rainforest and dense mountains, all home to fantastical species like the largest flower in the world and insects the size of a man's hand. Ranong is the site of famous hot springs and, like Mae Sot, with its proximity to Burma fosters a border diaspora as Burmese workers – many illegal – hasten across, desperately searching for work. Nearby is Laem Son National Park – home to a plethora of gorgeous islands. The rest of the Andaman Coast comprises great long sandy bays with the occasional peninsula or rocky headland. Inland is the stunning Khao Sok National Park and further down the shoreline is the resort town of Khao Lak. The proximity to the Similan and Surin islands makes this entire run of coast an ideal stopover for divers. **▸▸** *For listings, see page 934-937.*

Ranong → *Colour map 5, C2.*

Surrounded by forested mountains, Ranong is a scenic place to stay for a day or two. It's a small and unpretentious provincial capital and an important administrative centre. It's possible to fly from Bangkok and regular buses also head down from the capital – travellers can also link by bus to Chumphon where both the Gulf ferries and southern railway stops.

The excellent geo-thermal mineral water springs (65°C) are found at **Wat Tapotharam** ⓘ *2 km east of the town and behind the Jansom Thara Hotel, free.* These municipal hot springs are a charming spot, where the area's varied population gathers to enjoy the ever-hot water. To get there, walk or take a songthaew along Route 2; ask for '*bor nam rawn*' (hot water well). The Port of Ranong lies 3 km from town. Each morning the dock seethes with activity as Thai and Burmese fishing boats unload their catches. Boats can be hired at a pontoon next to the dock to explore the port and cross to Burma (approximately ฿400). Border officials can be touchy so carry your passport.

Laem Son National Park → *Colour map 5, C1.*

There are a number of notable beaches and islands near Ranong, many within the limits of the Laem Son National Park. The water here is warm and a pleasure to swim in, especially around the reefs, though visibility isn't great. Travel agents can organize day trips or taxi boats run from Ranong out to Koh Chang and Koh Phayam a few times a day in high season and once a day May to October. The islands hide some wonderful secluded white-sand beaches and have good birdlife (there are around 138 bird species in the park).

Unlike the larger Koh Chang on Thailand's east coast, Ranong's tiny **Koh Chang** is best known for its distinctly laid-back ambience. The beaches here are mediocre at best and the island also hibernates from June to mid-October when the monsoon rains lash down.

Only on **Koh Phayam** would there be both full moon parties – albeit low-key ones – and a Miss Cashew Nut Beauty Competition (held during the Cashew Nut Festival). Good spots are the long and curving white-sand beaches at Ao Yai 'Sunset Bay' or Ao Khao Kwai 'Buffalo Bay'. There is also a tiny fishing village on the east coast of the island and a sea gypsy settlement to the west.

Khao Sok National Park → *Colour map 5, C1.*

ⓘ *www.khaosok.com, entry ฿400.*

Khao Sok National Park has limestone karst mountains (the tallest reaches more than 900 m), low mountains covered with evergreen forest, streams and waterfalls and a large reservoir and dam. The impressive scenery alone would be a good enough reason to visit, but Khao Sok also has an exceptionally large number of mammals, birds, reptiles and other fauna. The list of 48 confirmed species of mammals include: wild elephants, tigers, barking deer, bears, gibbons and cloud leopards. If you visit between December and February, the world's largest flower, the **rafflesia Kerri Meijer**, is in bloom. Buses from Takua Pa – which is linked to Khao Lak, Ranong and Phuket – stop at the park entrance. Most visitors arrive with any one of numerous tour companies which operate from most southern destinations. At the centre of the park is the **Rachabrapah Reservoir** – the best location for animal spotting.

Khao Lak → Colour map 5, C1.

A few years ago, before the infamous 2004 Tsunami that killed 5000 here and before the construction boom that followed it, Khao Lak was a quintessential sleepy beach town.

These days endless generic resorts, some illegally pouring concrete onto the beach, are destroying one of Thailand's nicest spots. Buses from Phuket, Phnaganga, Ranong and Bangkok stop in Khao Lak. The town itself is little more than a facsimile of every other dull resort town in Thailand serving up bad Thai and Western food and endless tourist trinkets. There are a few plus points – you should still be able to find some space on one of Khao Lak's long beaches. Given its proximity to the Koh Similans, Khao Lak is now becoming something of a dive mecca and there are a few excellent dive operators based here.

Koh Similan

The Similan Islands, 80 km northwest of Phuket and 65 km west of Khao Lak are some of the most beautiful, unspoilt tropical idylls in Southeast Asia. Boats head here from both Ranong and Phuket – many dive operators also offer 'live-aboard' overnight boat trips. The best time to visit is December to April as the west monsoon makes the islands virtually inaccessible during the rest of the year; be warned that transport away from the islands is unpredictable. At the end of March and beginning of April underwater visibility is not good, but this is the best time to see manta rays and whale sharks.

The water surrounding the archipelago supports a wealth of marine life and is considered one of the best diving locations in the world, as well as a good place for anglers. **Koh Miang**, named after the king's daughter, houses the park office and some dormitory and camping accommodation.

◉ Andaman Coast to Khao Lak listings

For Sleeping and Eating price codes,
see inside the front cover.

⬤ Sleeping

Ranong p933

AL-A Jansom Hot Spa Hotel 2/10 Petkasem Rd, 077-811510-3, www.jansomhotspa.com. In places this is a slightly shabby spa hotel – the rooms, pool and a huge jacuzzi all supplied by the hot-springs. Remains a good deal with bathtubs, linen, fridge and TV.

D-F Rim Than Resort, Chon Rau Rd, T077-833792. A little out of town, just past the hot springs on the road up to Ranong Canyon, this small eccentric family-run resort offers a range of simple, clean fan and a/c bungalows set in a pretty garden with balconies right over the river. Recommended.
F Bangsan (TV Bar), 281 Ruangrat Rd, T077-811240. Super-cheap, very basic rooms with fan above the trendiest cocktail bar in town. Hip with the young Thai and backpacker crowd.

Laem Son National Park p933
Koh Chang

Many guesthouses shut down during the monsoon season so you do need to check.

E-F Cashew Resort, T077-820116. The granddaddy of the resorts and the largest with a variety of bungalows, pool table, travel services, credit card facilities, money exchange and attached yoga school. The resort has its own boat for fishing and trawling.

E-F Lae Tawan, T077-820179. Tucked away in a slightly-out-of-the-way spot this cosy little place is one of the few open all year round. Thai restaurant. Recommended.

G Sunset, T077-820171. This small family-run operation has clean, airy bungalows and a friendly atmosphere. It shares its boat with **Cashew Resort**.

Koh Phayam

C-G Bamboo Bungalows, www.bamboo-bungalows.com, T077-820012. A beachside idyll and probably the most popular place on Ao Yai – booking is recommended during high season – although it is one of the few operations open year round. Bungalows range from new luxurious wooden villas with sprung mattresses, sofas, marble floors, sliding balcony doors and woven gables, through to pretty A-frame shell-covered bungalows. The excellent restaurant with huge portions and home-baked bread attracts visitors from neighbouring bungalows.

D-F Hornbill Hut, T077-825543, hornbill_hut@yahoo.com. Fantastically friendly family-run place with a great reputation and several styles of basic bamboo bungalows with concrete bathrooms set among the trees, along with a few excellent-value concrete villas with high ceilings and windows that allow the sea breeze to whistle through. Recommended.

E-F Vijit Bungalows, T077-834082, www.kohpayam-vijit.com. Another of the island's original operations, this place is popular and renowned for its laid-back ambience.

Khao Sok National Park p933

A-D Art's Riverview Lodge, T08-64703234, artsriverviewlodge@yahoo.co.uk. Art's is long-running, stylish and popular so book ahead. Its 30 rooms include substantial lodges with balconies overlooking the river, solid furniture and many rooms have a spare bedroom and small dining room. There is no hot water. The restaurant is beside the river near a swimming hole with a rope providing endless entertainment. Impertinent monkeys congregate at sunset to be fed bananas by residents.

C Khao Sok Green Valley Resort, T077-395145. Run by the friendly Eit, this is a great little resort with 8 spotless bungalows, all with hot water and a/c. Recommended.

E-F Nung House, T077-395147, nunghouse 2002@hotmail.com. Popular with back-packers, Nung's 12 spacious and comfortable bungalows are good value, starting at just ฿150, and its restaurant is the place to meet trekking companions.

Takua Pa

C-F Extra Hotel, just behind the Esso garage next to the town's main road, across the river from the bus station, T076-421026. If visitors are forced to spend a night in Takua Pa, this is the best option. Take a room in the new block.

Khao Lak p934

LL-L Le Meridien Khao Lak Beach and Spa Resort, 9/9 Moo 1, Khuk Kak beach, T076-427500, www.starwoodhotels.com. Huge, well-managed resort beside a beautiful stretch of sand about 8 km north of Khao Lak town. Superb kids' facilities and range of accommodation from standard rooms through to stunning villas. Recommended.

A-D Khao Lak Palm Hill Resort and Spa, 4/135 Moo 7, Khuk Kak, T076-485138, www.khaolakpalmhill.com. Friendly, well-run small resort set on a back soi a 5 min walk from the beach, The rooms are spacious, cool affairs all backing out onto a large swimming pool. Recommended.

C-D Motive Cottage, 21/16 Moo 5, Khuk Kak, T076-486820, www.motivecottage resort.com. Elegant minimalist rooms, each with their own little balcony and surrounding a bijou pool make this an uplifting place to stay. All rooms a/c and with en suite facilities. Short walk to beach. Recommended.

D-F Father and Son Bungalow, T076-48527. The friendly Nom family are planning to add to their 10 fan bungalows spread around a charming, shaded garden where the road is barely audible. The more expensive en suite rooms are good value at ฿500.

Koh Similan p934

E-F Reservations for the National Park accommodation can be made at the **Similan National Park Office**, Thai Muang, or at Tap Lamu Pier, T076-411914.

🍴 Eating

Ranong p933

The markets on **Ruangrat Rd** offer excellent roast pork and duck.

🍴-🍴 **Somboon Restaurant**, opposite the Jansom Thara Hotel. Delicious Thai and Chinese seafood.

🍴 **D&D coffee**, Ruangrat Rd. Where Ranong's café society congregates to discuss the day's issues, eat delicious Thai dishes over rice and sample a wide selection of good coffees.

Laem Son National Park p933
Koh Phayam

Most guesthouses have cheap restaurants.

🍴 **Middle Village**, on the road to Ao Yai. Renowned for its excellent Isaan (north-eastern Thai) dishes and rowdy karaoke nights.

🍴 **Oscar's Bar**, also in the village, turn right from the pier. Run by the infamously affable Englishman Richard, a self-proclaimed food buff who serves great Western and Thai dishes.

Khao Lak p934

🍴🍴-🍴🍴 **Pizzeria**, main road, next to Siam Commercial Bank, T076-485271. Open

1200-2300. Passable pizzas, pasta and other Italian dishes.

🍴🍴 **Discovery Cafe**, main road near Nang Thong Beach, T08-1425 6236. Open 0930-2400, tasty cheeseburgers on offer here along with some good Thai food.

🍴🍴 **Sun Star Siam**, 26/27 Moo 7, Khuk Kak, T076-485637. Friendly, homely Thai/Swiss-run place serving up excellent Thai food.

🔺 Activities and tours

Ranong p933
Diving

A-One-Diving, www.a-one-diving.com, T077-832984. Has branches at 256 Ruangrat Rd as well as a dive school on Koh Phayam (opposite the pier). Organizes trips all over the Andaman Sea including the Similans, Surin and Burma.

Tour operators

Pon's Place Travel Agency, T077-823344, by the new market on Ruangrat Rd, run by the affable Mr Pon who is an excellent source of information on the islands and areas surrounding Ranong and can help with tours, travel information, guesthouse/ hotel bookings and car and bike rental.

Khao Lak p934
Diving

Diving operations, including live-aboard boats, day trips and courses, are still widely available from various operators. Dive sites along the coast, include the Similan Islands, Koh Surin and Richelieu Rock.

Khao Lak Scuba Adventures, 13/47 Moo 7, Khuk Kak, T076-485602, www.khaolakscuba adventures.com. Well-run 5-Star PADI dive resort located in central Khao Lak offering all the usual PADI courses and live-aboard trip.

Sea Dragon, 9/1 Moo 7, T Khuk Kak, T076-420420, www.seadragondivecenter.com, is a well-established operation organizing day trips or liveaboards. Teaches PADI dive courses.

Tour operators
Khao Lak Oasis Tour, T076-485501/ T08-7271 4326 (just down the road from Khao Lak Scuba Adventures). One of the best and most affordable tour operators in Khao Lak. Private cars, minibus tickets, train and flight reservations and packages for Khao Sok can all be arranged here. Recommended.

Koh Similan *p934*
Hotels and tour operators organize boat and dive trips and most dive companies in Phuket offer tours to the Similan Islands.

⊜ Transport

Ranong *p933*
Air
There is an airport 20 km south of town; in summer 2008 budget airline **Air Asia** (www.airasia.com) were flying once a day in both directions between Ranong and **Bangkok**.

Bus
The road journey from the north is arduous – 8 hrs at least; the last half of which is through mountains. Consider taking the train from Bangkok to **Chumphon** and the bus from there. The bus terminal is on the edge of town, Hwy 4, near the **Jansom Thara Hotel**. However, the buses stop in town on Ruangrat Rd before the terminal. Songthaew number 2 passes the terminal. Regular a/c and non-a/c connections with **Bangkok Chumphon**, **Surat Thani** and **Phuket**.

Khao Sok National Park *p933*
Bus If visiting the park independently, take a local bus from **Takua Pa** to Phun Phin near Surat Thani town, or vice versa, and ask the driver to stop at the Khao Sok National Park (*oo-tayaan-haeng-chart-khao-sok*). When you arrive at the stop there will usually be a number of bungalow operators waiting

to whisk you off to their establishment; it's quite a hike to some bungalows.

Khao Lak *p934*
Bus Many buses now travel on a new road that bypasses Khao Lak and goes straight to Phangnga town, and then on to Phuket. Check that your bus passes through Khao Lak/Takua Pa/Ranong if you want to get off here. Different bus companies have different routes. There are some a/c and non-a/c connections with the Southern terminal in **Bangkok**.

Koh Similan *p934*
Boat Vessels depart from **Thap Lamu** pier, near Khao Lak, to the Similans, 40 km offshore. Boats also leave from Ao Chalong and Patong Beach, **Phuket Songserm Travel**, T076-222570. Getting to and from Similan independently can be very tricky indeed and you might be best advised to travel with a tour operator.

⊙ Directory

Ranong *p933*
Banks On Tha Muang Rd there are branches of **Bank of Ayudya**, **Siam Commercial Bank**, **Thai Farmers Bank** and **Thai Military Bank**, all with ATMs and/or exchange facilities. **Medical services Hospital**, at the junction of Permphon Rd and Kamlungsab Rd. **Post office** Chon Rao Rd, near the junction with Dap Khadi Rd. There is a regional branch of the Tourist Police on Petkasem Rd.

Khao Lak *p934*
All the usual facilities are now back online in Khao Lak. **Banks** There are plenty of exchange booths and ATMs on the main road. **Post office** There's a post office next to the police station a little way north of town on the main road.

Phuket and around

Known as 'the Pearl of Thailand' because of its shape, Phuket lies on the west coast of the Kra Isthmus in the warm Andaman Sea and is connected to the mainland by the 700-m-long Sarasin causeway. It is a fully developed resort island with hundreds of hotels including some that are world renowned. There is still tropical rainforest to be found on Phuket at Khao Phrao Thaeo National Park. Nearby Phangnga Bay, with limestone rocks towering out of the sea, is best known as the beautiful location for the 1974 James Bond movie The Man with the Golden Gun. *It's also home to the islands of Koh Yao's Noi and Yai.* ▶ *For listings, see pages 941-946.*

Phuket ⊜⚫⚙⚫⚙▲⚫⚫ ▶ *pp 941-946. Colour map 7, A1.*

Ins and outs

Phuket was first 'discovered' by Arab and Indian navigators around the end of the ninth century, although it is rumoured that the island appears on charts as early as the first century. The first Europeans (Dutch pearl traders) arrived in the 16th century. These days travellers arrive mainly by numerous flights at Phuket International Airport in the north of the island. There are international connections and multiple daily connections with Bangkok, Koh Samui and Chiang Mai. The main bus terminal is in Phuket City and there are regular connections with Bangkok (14 hours) as well as destinations in the south. It is possible to take a train to Phun Phin near Surat Thani and then catch a connecting bus.

Songthaews run from Phuket City to all the beaches at regular intervals from 0600-1800 for ฿20. There are numerous places to hire cars/jeeps, motorbikes and tuk-tuks. Local buses stop around 1800. Metered taxis aren't allowed to pick up passengers from anywhere in Phuket except at the airport or unless they are booked privately.

The **TAT office** ⓘ *73-75 Phuket Rd, T076-212213, tathkt@phuket.ksc.co.th, daily 0830-1630*, is good for specific local questions. Two good sources of free information are *Phuket Holiday Guide*, and *Phuket Gazette*, www.phuketgazette.net.

Background

Much of Phuket's considerable wealth was derived from tin and the island was dubbed 'Junk Ceylon' in the mid-16th century – a name thought to have been bestowed on the island by early European visitors. Phuket Town became so wealthy that paved roads and cars appeared around 1910. Now, tourism is the big earner, with rubber, coconut and fisheries also contributing to the island's wealth.

Sights

Treated largely as a stopover by divers en route to the Similan or Surin islands and beach junkies headed further up the coast, Phuket City is now anxious to revamp its image and pull in a more sophisticated crowd. So, in addition to its Sino-Portuguese architectural heritage, which is reminiscent of Georgetown in Malaysian Penang – a leftover of the wealthy Chinese tin barons of the 19th century – there is a burgeoning arts and literary scene and even a foreign film festival once a year. A particularly notable example of one of Phuket's finer older buildings is the **Government House**, which stood in as the 'American Embassy' in Phnom Penh in the classic film – *The Killing Fields*. Preservation orders have been placed on all buildings in Old Phuket. Among the finer ones are the **Chartered Bank**

Phuket Island

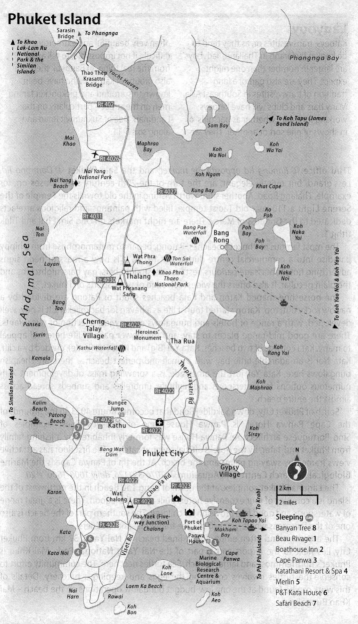

To Khao Lak-Lam Ru National Park & the Similan Islands

Sarasin Bridge

To Phangnga

Phangnga Bay

Thao Thep Krasattri Bridge

Yacht Haven

Rt 402

Mai Khao

Som Bay

To Koh Tapu (James Bond Island)

Koh Wa Noi

Koh Wa Yai

Maphrao Bay

Rt 4026

Nai Yang National Park

Nai Yang Beach

Koh Ngam

Khat Cape

Kung Bay

Ao Poh

Poh Bay

Koh Naka Yai

Rt 4031

Bang Pae Waterfall

Bang Rong

Poh Bay

Nai Ton

Layan

Wat Phra Thong

Ton Sai Waterfall

Koh Naka Noi

Andaman Sea

Rt 4030

Thalang

Khao Phra Thaeo National Park

Wat Phranang Sang

Bang Tao

Pansea

Surin

Cherng Talay Village

Rt 4025

Heroines' Monument

Tha Rua

To Koh Yao Noi & Koh Yao Yai

Kamala

Kathu Waterfall

Koh Rang Yai

To Similan Islands

Bungee Jump

Rt 4022

Koh Maphrao

Kalim Beach

Patong Beach

Rt 4029

Kathu

Rt 4022

Koh Siray

Bang Wat Dam

Phuket City

Gypsy Village

Karon

Rt 4022

Chao Fa Rd

Rt 4023

To Krabi

Kata

Wat Chalong

Rt 4021

Haa-Yaek (Five-way Junction) Chalong

Koh Tapao Yai

Kata Noi

Rt 4028

Viset Rd

Port of Phuket

Panwa House

Makham Bay

Cape Panwa

To Phi Phi Islands

Nai Harn

Rawai

Koh Lone

Marine Biological Research Centre & Aquarium

Koh Aeo

Laem Ka Beach

Koh Bon

N

2 km
2 miles

Sleeping

Banyan Tree **8**
Beau Rivage **1**
Boathouse Inn **2**
Cape Panwa **3**
Katathani Resort & Spa **4**
Merlin **5**
P&T Kata House **6**
Safari Beach **7**

Thailand Phuket and around ● 939

Ladyboys

Katoeys, transvestites or, as they tend to be known by farang in Thailand, 'ladyboys', are larger in number than one might expect. They are also part of a long tradition of transvestites in Southeast Asia. Many bars and clubs will have katoeys working for them, whether as bar 'girls' or in shows of one sort or another. They are often very beautiful and extraordinarily difficult, if not impossible, to tell apart from the real thing. In Bangkok there are also groups of katoeys who have been known to surround and pickpocket farang men on the street – particularly on the Landmark side of Sukhumvit Road and along sois 5-11.

THAI office ① *Ranong Rd opposite the market*, and the **Sala Phuket** ① *Damrong Rd*. Less grand, but quietly elegant, are the turn-of-the-20th-century **shophouses** on, for example, Thalang Road. Another sight worth visiting in the old town is the **Temple of the Serene Light** a 110-year-old Taoist temple, filled with paintings and religious artefacts dedicated to the Goddess of Mercy. There are **night markets** on Ong Sim Phai and Tilok Uthit 1.

The most famous of Phuket's beaches, Patong, began to metamorphose from a hippy paradise into a commercial centre during the 1970s. It is now a mass of neon signs advertising hotels, massage parlours, restaurants, straight bars, gay bars, nightclubs and the plain peculiar. It also offers the widest selection of watersports on Phuket.

The horseshoe-shaped Karon and Kata beaches south of Patong are divided by a narrow rocky outcrop. **Karon** started tourist life as a haven for backpackers. It is now well developed, with a range of hotels and bungalows and a wide selection of restaurants. There are good mid-range places to stay, and the slower pace of life here will appeal to many. Kata consists of two beaches: **Kata Yai** (Big) and **Kata Noi** (Little), divided by a cliff. Kata Noi is an adorable little bay with a small and perfect beach – there are cheapish bungalows here. Kata Yai, just the other side, is a sprawling mass of development with numerous options for watersports and nightlife; umbrellas and sunbeds spread across almost the entire beach.

South of Phuket City, down Sakdidej Road that becomes Route 4023, in the grounds of the **Cape Panwa Hotel**, is **Panwa House**, one of Phuket's finest examples of Sino-Portuguese architecture. Panwa House was formerly inhabited by a fishing family from Phuket and, later, by the hotel's official coconut catcher. The first floor has attractive views framed by swaying palms and the beach. At the tip of Panwa Cape is the **Marine Biological Research Centre and Aquarium** ① *T076-391126, daily 1000-1600, ฿20*.

The **Laguna Phuket** complex, at the north of **Bang Tao Beach** in the northwest of the island is a complex of four expensive hotels built around a lagoon. There is a great range of watersports and good free provision for children. The southern part of the beach is also one of the few areas where you will still see traditional boat builders.

The attractive and often empty forest-lined beach of **Nai Yang**, 37 km from Phuket City, lies next to the airport and is part of the **Nai Yang National Park**. **Mai Khao** is Phuket's northernmost and largest beach. Sea turtles nest here. The community effort to conserve the turtles involves collecting the eggs and keeping a hatchery. Details of this work can be found at the one low-budget bungalow operations on the beach – **Mai Khao Bungalows**.

Phangnga Bay ⬤❼⛰❶❻ ⤏ pp 941-946. Colour map 7, A1.

The poor relation to its neighbouring tourist hotspots of Phuket and Krabi, Phangnga Town is often overlooked by visitors. Its relaxed, authentic Thai feel, dramatic setting and interesting daytrips make it an excellent place to pass a few days. The only way here is by bus with regular connections to Bangkok, Phuket and Krabi. Songthaews are the main form of transport around town and to surrounding villages. If you want urban sophistication and multiple culinary options, then Phangnga may disappoint – this is a non-tourist Thai experience. Due to the limestone geology, there are a number of caves in the vicinity. The most memorable are at **Wat Thomtharpan Amphoe Muang**, the so-called 'Heaven and Hell Caves' and **Tham Phung Chang** both just outside town. The **Phangnga Bay National Park** ① *entrance fee ฿200*, is a few kilometres south of town. To get there take a songthaew. Excellent-value boat tours of Phangnga Bay can be booked from one of the travel agents in town. The standard tour winds through mangrove swamps past striking limestone cliffs and onto weird caves and Sea Gypsy townships.

There are also two islands in the bay that offer accommodation and other facilities – **Koh Yao Noi** and **Koh Yao Yai**. Consistently untouched by tourism. There's a strong Muslim and Sea Gypsy community and the locals prefer outsiders to dress modestly and not to drink alcohol outside resorts or restaurants. Koh Yao Noi has only very few restaurants and shops. Koh Yao Yai, the larger of the two islands, has better beaches for swimming but fewer places to stay. The main attraction is the peace and quiet.

◉ Phuket and around listings

For Sleeping and Eating price codes, see inside the front cover.

⬤ Sleeping

Phuket *p938, map p939*
Low season (Jun-Oct) rates can be half high season price. Rates quoted are peak season.

Phuket City
A The Taste Phuket, 16, 18 Rassada Rd, T076-222812, www.thetastephuket.com. Decent hotel in a converted shophouse on the upmarket side of Phuket City accommodation. Rooms come with hot-water rain shower, a/c, cable TV and large double bed. The expensive rooms have massive TVs, DVD players and gardens. Recommended.
C-D Raya Thai Cuisine, 48 Deebuk Rd, T076-218155. This 70-year-old Macao-style house has 5 simple rooms. Quirky in the nicest possible way, rooms are simply furnished and decorated. Friendly owners

full of tales about Old Phuket. The food is also good here. Recommended.
E Forty-three, 43 Thalang Rd, T076-258127. This tucked-away gem has 4 room types; snazziest with private gardens or balconies, as well as outdoor showers. Definitely worth a look if you're in Phuket City on a budget.

Patong Beach
LL-L Merlin, 44 Moo 4, Thaweewong Rd, T076-340037-41, www.merlinphuket.com/patongmerlin/index.html. A/c, restaurant, 3 sculptured pools and a children's pool, large 4-storey hotel, attractively laid out with well-designed, spacious rooms. Recommended.
LL-AL Safari Beach, 136 Thaweewong Rd, T076-341171, www.safaribeachhotel.com. A/c rooms only, restaurant attached. Small hotel set around pool in leafy compound just north of Soi Bangla. The location is sought after as it is on the beach and the standard rooms are spacious. Recommended.
C-D Beau Rivage, 77/15-17 Rat Uthit Rd, T076-340725. Some a/c, large rooms – some

suites – with clean bathrooms, spacious and good value although, like the other hotels on Rat Uthit Rd, it is some way from the beach.

Karon and Kata beaches

LL Boathouse Inn, T076-330015, www.boat house.net. Southern end of Kata Beach, a/c, pool. This establishment, also known as **Mom Tri's Boathouse**, is clearly a labour of love. Its creator, Mom Tri Devakul, is an architect and artist, and there's an art gallery supporting local Phuket artists. The villa also has a salt-water pool and a professional health spa. Recommended.

LL Katathani Resort and Spa, 14 Kata Noi Rd, T076-330124-26, www.katathani.com. Stunning location in this quiet cove. All rooms have seafront balcony and there are even louvered panels in the bathroom that can be opened if you want to gaze at the sea from your bath. Recommended.

E-F P&T Kata House 104/1 Koktanod Rd, T076-284203. One of several guesthouses at the southern end of Kata Beach set back from the shore, past a 7-Eleven, offering some of the island's cheapest rooms outside Phuket City. The rooms are clean with fresh linen and many overlook a garden. There is no hot water but a/c rooms are available. Recommended.

Cape Panwa

LL-AL Cape Panwa, T076-391123, 27 Moo 8, Sakdidej Rd, www.capepanwa.com. Beautifully secluded, a variety of accommodation including bungalows. There are Italian and Thai fusion restaurants and an excellent cocktail bar. Good breakfast buffet. While you may never wish to leave the hotel, there is also a shuttle service into Phuket Old Town. Recommended.

Bang Tao Beach

L Banyan Tree, T076-324374, www.banyan tree.com. Spa pool villas with private pool, jacuzzi, sunken baths, outdoor showers and beds sheathed in silk that 'float' over lily ponds. The spa itself is similarly spectacular.

A-C Bangtao Lagoon Bungalow, 72/3 Moo 3, Tambon Cherng Talay, T076-324260.

Some a/c, small pool, a bungalow develop-ment in a comparatively isolated position. Chalets range from simple fan bungalows to 'deluxe' a/c affairs, the latter are small and featureless. Clean, family cottages also available.

Nai Yang

LL-D Nai Yang Beach Resort, T076-328300, www.phuket.com/naiyangbeach. Well-built bungalows with good facilities and simple decor. Some a/c. Set in large grounds with plenty of trees for shade. Friendly staff. A bit pricey at the upper end but excellent value at the lower end. Right next to the **Pearl Village** and a hop over the road to the beach. **C Garden Cottage**, 53/1 Moo 1, T076-327293, gardencot@yahoo.com. 2 mins from the airport and walking distance from the beach, charm-ing cottage-style bungalows, friendly owners willing to show you the island. Excellent value with a masseur and attractive restaurant and communal areas. Recommended.

Mai Khao

A-E Mai Khao Beach Bungalows, T081-538 0781 1233 (mob), www.mai-khao-beach.com. Quite a find for Phuket. Tucked away in a grassy clearing shaded by large casuarina trees and shrubs right on the beach. There are smaller bamboo and palm-roof huts with shared bathrooms and larger en suite concrete and wood rooms. You can pitch a tent for ฿150. The owners set up a regular campfire to chat at during the night. It's a good idea to contact the bungalow in advance to organize transport with their help. Recommended.

Phangnga Bay *p941*
Phangnga Town

B-D Phangnga Inn, 2/2 Soi Lohakit, Petkasem Rd, T076-411963. A beautiful family house converted into a cosy hotel with a range of contrasting, immaculately clean en suite rooms. It is off the main road, and clearly marked by a purple sign. Recommended.

D-F Phangnga Guest House, 99/1 Petkasem Rd, T076-411358. Excellent value fan and a/c, fastidiously clean small rooms, sparkling café downstairs. Cantankerous staff who grow on you. Recommended.

Koh Yao Yai
LL-L The Paradise Koh Yao Boutique Beach Resort and Spa, 24 Moo 4, T08-1892 4878/9 (mob), www.theparadise.biz. 48 superior studios, 16 deluxe studios and 6 pool villas on the beach in the north of Koh Yao Noi. Has its own passenger transfer boats and you can even get here by seaplane.
C-E Thiwson Bungalows, 58/2 Moo 4, Ko Yao Yai Rd, T08-1956 7582 (mob). Sweet, clean rooms in the usual bamboo-and-wood style, with bedside lights and Western toilets. Restaurant, deck chairs on the verandas and a pleasant garden overlooking one of the nicest beaches on the island. Recommended.

Koh Yao Noi
LL Six Senses Hideaway, 56 Moo 5, T076-418500, www.sixsenses.com. Set amid trees – you hardly notice they're there at all – are 56 luxurious wooden villas, all complete with private pool, sunken tubs and sala. Everything is done in natural fabrics and materials, with only a hint of concrete. Six Senses donate a percentage of revenue to carefully selected local projects. Eating here is unforgettable; they have an in-house deli stocking the best cheeses and charcuterie you'll find anywhere in Thailand. Prices are high but you get a lot for your money. Highly recommended.
C-E Sabai Corner Bungalows, T076-597 497, 08-1892 1827 (mob), www.sabaicorner bungalows.com. 10 romantic bungalows set among cashew and coconut trees with magnificent views over Pasai Beach. Attached toilets. A popular option, often full so ring ahead.
D-E Coconut Corner Bungalows, T076-597134. A handful of bungalows, all basic but charming, with attached toilets. The attached restaurant serves excellent food; eating with the family is often the norm. Recommended.

❶ Eating

Phuket *p938, map p939*
Phuket City
The best place to browse for street food is around the market on **Ranong Rd**.
♦♦♦ Raya Thai Cuisine, 48 Deebuk Rd, T076-218155. This restaurant is in a 70-year-old Macao-style house with a garden. It has a guesthouse (see Sleeping, above) and is well preserved with original fittings. It serves Thai dishes and local specialities; try the spicy *nam bu bai cha plu* (crab curry with local herbs served with Chinese rice noodles).
♦ Kow-Tom-Hua-Pla (Boiled Fish Rice) opposite **Caramba Bar** on Phuket Rd past Thalang Rd. Popular with locals, this simple noodle café (open 1700-2400) serves an eclectic mix of noodles. Recommended.
♦ Nong Jote Café, 16 Yaowarat Rd. This 100-plus-year-old building looks like a café in Lisbon with high ceilings and, along one side, ceiling-to-floor antique glassed cabinets in teak. Excellent southern Thai food. Try the spicy *yum tour plu*. Recommended.

Patong Beach
♦♦♦ White Box, 247/5 Prabaramee Rd, Patong, Kathu, T076-346271, www.whitebox restaurant.com. A simple concept: it's white and it looks like a large box. The setting is ideal, far enough away from the madness of Patong, but with decent views over Patong Bay. Good Mediterranean and Thai food.
♦ Woody's Sandwich Shoppe, Aroonsom Plaza, T076-290468, www.khunwoody.com. Woody's Shoppe, run by local computer guru Woody Leonhard, is something of an institution in Phuket. For about ฿100 to ฿150, you can get a sandwich that puts Subway to shame. Woody also offers free Wi-Fi access.

Karon and Kata beaches
♦♦♦ JaoJong Seafood, 4/2 Patak Rd, KataNoi, T076-330136. Unpretentious sea-shanty feel to this spacious open-fronted seafood restaurant. Good selection of freshly caught seafood and well executed. Recommended.

Ψ Swiss Bakery, Kata beach, Bougainvillea Terrace House, 117.1 Patak Rd, T076-33139. 0800-2400. Open-air terrace, Swiss delicacies here include Bouguionne and Tartaren Hut. Also do burgers and sandwiches from ฿120.

Cape Panwa

ΨΨΨ-Ψ Panwa House, Cape Panwa, on the beach. Everything is here for the perfect meal: indoor and outdoor dining, excellent service and deliciously executed dishes. Try their lobster with shavings of caramelized shallot, palm sugar and tamarind. Recommended.

Bang Tao

ΨΨΨ Lotus Restaurant, Banyan Tree Beach, Moo 4, Cherng Talay, T081-797 3110, T076-362625-6. Slightly expensive, but the food is good and the vibe next to the sea is unbeatable.

Nai Yang

ΨΨ Nai Yang Seafood, Nai Yang beach. One of several charming spots next to the empty beach, all of which serve excellent seafood.

Mai Khao

ΨΨΨ Rivet Grill, Indigo Pearl Resort, Mai Khao, www.indigo-pearl.com/dining-rivetgrill.html. Expensive but serves the best steaks in Phuket and probably the whole of Southern Thailand. Countless touches reflect the overall tin mining theme at the resort.

Phangnga Bay *p941*

ΨΨ-Ψ Ivy's House, 38 Petkasem Rd, next door to a dental clinic. A tiny European-style café with a gas-fired oven for pizza, Italian wines and liquors and decent pastries. Good source of information. Recommended.

Ψ Ran Ja Jang, Soi Bamrungrat. Superb seafood soup with egg and Tom Yee sauce, tiger prawns and squid. Recommended.

On **Koh Yao Noi** and **Koh Yao Yai** most people eat at the restaurant attached to their bungalows, although **Tha Khao Seafood** is right next to the pier. On Koh Yao Yai, try the *pla ching chang* (dried anchovy paste), which is used with rice and noodles.

Bars and clubs

Phuket *p938, map p939*
Phuket's club scene has experienced a resurgence and is attracting the attention of DJs and promoters who have previously favoured Pha-ngan and Samui islands.

Phuket City

9Richter, Rassada Rd. Despite the strange name, this is a great place to hang out because very few foreigners make it inside. Stays open until about 0100 with the usual Thai songs sung by live bands and a DJ who isn't afraid to rupture eardrums with bizarre techno music.

Kor Tor Mor, Chana Charoen Rd, near Nimit Circle, T076-232285. Large Thai club that gets ludicrously busy on Fri and Sat. Get there early or else you may be turned away. Buy a bottle of whiskey, drink, kick back, dance and enjoy.

Patong Beach

Banana, T076-340306. Bustling club on the beach road, this is a firm favourite with the locals and tourists. It doesn't stay open very late and the drinks are reasonably priced. Expect to hear a range of rock music, hip hop and pop.

Club Lime, T085-798 1850, 085-798 8511, www.clublime.info. Along the beach road is one of the few clubs in Phuket with a decent music policy. Past guest DJs include Jo Mills and Barry Ashworth. The music ranges from electro and house to tribal and techno. Expect to pay a cover charge of up to ฿300 with one or two drinks included.

Karon and Kata Beaches

Ratri Jazztaurant, Kata Hill, T076-333538, www.ratrijazztaurant.com. The perfect spot for a romantic dinner for two or just kicking back for a few drinks while enjoying the splendid view. As the name suggests, this place is all about jazz. It isn't the cheapest spot around, but it can't be beaten in terms of setting and ambience.

⊛ Festivals and events

Phuket p938, map p939

Oct (movable) **Chinese Vegetarian Festival**, *Ngan Kin Jeh*, lasts 9 days and marks the beginning of Taoist lent. This must be one of the star attractions of a visit to Phuket.

▲ Activities and tours

Phuket p938, map p939

Canoeing

John Gray's Sea Canoe Thailand, 124 Soi 1 Yaowarat Rd, T076-254505/6, www.johngray-seacanoe.com. John Gray has had over 20 years' experience and is the man for day trips and overnights with the advantage being the limited number of guests in the combo long-tail and kayak expeditions.

Diving

Most diving companies are to be found along Patong Beach Rd, on Kata and Karon beaches, at Ao Chalong and in Phuket City. Over 25 dive centres offer a range of courses (introductory to advanced), day trips and liveaboard. For those with experience there are tours ranging from single day, 2-dive outings to local dive spots to 1-week expeditions to offshore islands such as the Similan and Surin. **Santana**, 222 Thanon Sawatdirak Rd, Patong Beach, T076-294220, www.santanaphuket. com. A prestigious 5-star PADI instructor training centre. This operation has 25 years experience. It does liveaboards to the Similan Islands, Surin and Hin Daeng. Courses in English, German and Thai. It has even named dive sites such as Elephant Head.
Scuba Cats, 94 Thaweewong Rd, Patong Beach, T076-293120, www.scubacats.com. Also a 5-star PADI Instructor Development Centre offering liveaboards to the Similan Islands, Koh Bon, Koh Tachai and Richelieu Rock as well as fun dives around Phuket. Phuket's first **National Geographic Dive Centre**, it is also a **Go-Eco** operator and is involved in marine clean-up.

Muay Thai (Thai boxing)

Tiger Muay Thai and MMA Training Camp, 7/6 Moo 5 Soi Tad-ied, Chalong, T076-367071, www.tigermuaythai.com. One of Phuket's most famous camps. Anyone is invited to attend for serious training. Walk-ins welcome.
Bangla Boxing Stadium, T086-940 5463, T089-724 1581, 198/4 Rat-u-thit 200 Pee Rd, Patong, www.banglamuaythai.com/bangla_stadium. Php. A decent place to watch a fight.

Phangnga Bay p941

Tour operators

The 3 main tour companies in town – **Sayan**, **Kean**, T076-430619, and **MT Tours** – run similar tours that are worthwhile and good value.

◎ Transport

Phuket p938, map p939

Air

The airport is to the north of the island, 30 km from Phuket City. For flight reservations call T076-327230-7. Regular cheap connections with **Air Asia**, **Nok Air**, **THAI** to **Bangkok** and **Chiang Mai**. **Bangkok Airways** also runs daily connections with **Koh Samui**. A mixture of buses, taxis and limos take you into town.
 Airline offices Bangkok Airways, 158/2-3 Yaowarat Rd, T076-225033.
THAI, 78/1 Ranong Rd, T076-211195.

Boat

During the high season (Nov-May) there are 3 ferries a day to and from **Koh Phi Phi** leaving from Rassada Pier on Phuket's east coast. Tourist offices sell tickets and can confirm boat times, which vary through the season.
 There are many boats to **Koh Yao Yai**, with vessels leaving from Laem Hin Pier Tien Sin Pier and Rassada Port. 5 boats a day from Phuket to **Koh Yao Noi** leave Bang Rong Pier.

Bus

The station is on Phangnga Rd in Phuket City, T076-211480. It's cheaper to buy tickets here than through travel agents. The information desk usually has a timetable and fare list with details of all departures and of local transport. Regular a/c and non-a/c connections with **Bangkok**'s Southern bus terminal (14 hrs). Regular connections with **Trang**, **Surat Thani**, **Phangnga**, **Takua Pa** (for Khao Sok), **Ranong** and **Krabi**.

Motorbike
From ฿200-350 per day. In Kata Noi Beach, a reliable agent is **Boy's Shop Travel and Tour**, 4/12 Moo2, T076-284062/ 01-891 1910. Tours, car rental, international tickets and hotels

Motorbike taxi and tuk-tuk
Men (and women) with red vests will whisk passengers almost anywhere for a minimum of about ฿40. The motorbike taxis congregate at intersections. Avoid tuk-tuks if possible. They are overpriced and uncomfortable. From Patong to Phuket City, or vice versa, will cost you about ฿450. Travel within Phuket City shouldn't be more than about ฿100.

Songthaew
For Patong, Kamala, Surin, Makham Bay, Nai Yang, Kata, Karon, Nai Harn, Rawai, Thalang and Chalong buses leave every 30 mins, 0600-1800 from the market on Ranong Rd in Phuket City. Fares range from ฿20-25 to whatever the ticket collector thinks he can get away with.

Train
There is no rail service to Phuket. Some visitors take the train to **Phun Phin**, outside Surat Thani, then a bus on to Phuket (6 hrs).

Phangnga Bay *p941*
Bus
The bus station is on Petkasem Rd, near the town centre. Regular connections with Bangkok (VIP at night) **Phuket**, **Krabi**, **Ranong**, **Takua Pa (for Khao Sok)** and **Trang**.

Songthaew
Cramped but rather extraordinary teak songthaews with unpadded seats constantly ply the main road, ฿5.

Koh Yao Noi and Koh Yao Yai
Boat
From Koh Yao Yai to **Phuket** (to Laem Hin Pier, Tien Sin Pier, Rassada Port, and Bang Rong). From both Koh Yao Yai and Koh Yao Noi to **Krabi** and **Phangnga** usually from around 0700. Times vary; check in advance.

ⒹDirectory

Phuket *p938, map p939*
Phuket City
Banks Branches of all major banks on Rasada, Phuket, Phangnga and Thepkrasatri roads, all with ATMs and currency exchange. **Immigration office** South Phuket Rd (close to Saphan Hin). Ask for the boxing stadium; the office is next door, T076-212108. **Internet** Many hotels and guesthouses offer internet at varying prices. **Medical services** Bangkok Hospital Phuket, 2/1 Hongyok utis Rd, T076-254421, www.phuket hospital.com. World-class treatment and facilities. **Vachira Hospital Phuket**, Yaowarat Rd, T076-212150, www.vachiraphuket.go.th. Not far from Bangkok Hospital. **Police** Tourist Police T076-219878 (until 1630). **Emergency**, T1699, or T076-212046 to reach the police. **Post office** Montri Rd (corner of Thalang Rd). **Telephone** 122/2 Phangnga Rd, open 24 hrs.

Patong Beach
Banks Banks and currency exchange booths are concentrated on Patong Beach Rd (Thaweewong Rd). **Medical services** Kathu Hospital on Rat Uthit Rd. **Police** Tourist Police, Patong Beach Rd. **Kathu Police Station**, T076-342719, 076-342721. **Post office** Patong Beach Rd (beachfront road), near Soi Permpong Pattana (aka Soi Post Office).

Phangnga Bay *p941*
Banks ATMs on Petkasem Rd. **Internet** Kean tour company (at the bus station); Petkasem Rd toward Thung Jadee School. **Post office** Petkasem Rd, 2 km from centre on main road coming from Phuket.

Krabi and around

→ *Colour map 7, A2.*

The provincial town of Krabi provides visitors to southern Thailand with an important hub of transport and facilities. There are beaches nearby at Rai Leh and the resorts of Ao Nang while the town itself a perfect place to either prepare for, or recuperate from, island-hopping. From here travellers can connect with buses and planes and easily reach the popular islands of Koh Lanta and Koh Phi Phi – the latter, while firmly in the grip of mass tourism, is still one of the most beautiful islands in the country. Back in Krabi town you can stock up on bread – it has excellent bakeries – fetch your newspapers and get a decent café latte before heading back to the nature reserve for some more hammock swinging. ➤➤ *For listings, see pages 950-953.*

Krabi Town ⊕⊙⊘⊘⊛⊜⊙ ➤➤ *pp 950-953. Colour map 7, A2.*

Since the mid to late 1980s tourism in Krabi has boomed. It wasn't always like that – in the early 1970s communist bandits operated roadblocks along the only surfaced road in the area – Highway 4. Only those motorists who knew an ever-changing password would be allowed to travel. Travellers today don't have to suffer such travails as Krabi has excellent transport connections. The airport, 15 km from town, offers daily flights to and from Bangkok and there are boats to Koh Phi Phi and Koh Lanta. Buses not only provide regular services to Bangkok but also link to the southern railway at Surat Thani's Phun Phin station. Songthaews are the main form of local transport, and motorbikes are widely available for hire. There's a small **TAT office** ① *Uttarakit Rd, across from Kasikorn Bank, daily 0830-1630.* Krabi town is exceptionally well served with well-priced cafés and restaurants, catering for both tourists and locals and good quirky bars. There is a **night market** close to the Chao Fah Pier that's full of food stalls frequented mainly by locals. Wat Tham Sua – the Tiger Cave temple – is 8 km northeast of town, hire a motorbike or get a tour operator to bring you out here. It's home to dozens of *kutis* (monastic cells) set into the limestone cliff.

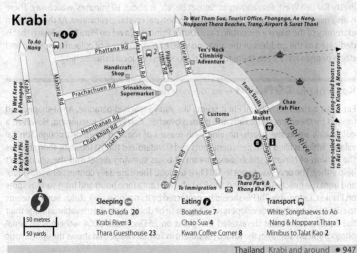

Krabi

Sleeping ⊕	Eating ⊙	Transport ⊟
Ban Chaofa 20	Boathouse 7	White Songthaews to Ao
Krabi River 3	Chao Sua 4	Nang & Nopparat Thara 1
Thara Guesthouse 23	Kwan Coffee Corner 8	Minibus to Talat Kao 2

Tiger Cave is so called because a large tiger apparently lived there leaving his pawprints as proof – some visitors find this claim dubious as the pawprints are not at all paw-like. Take the 1237 steps up to the top of a 600-m-high karst peak for fantastic views. Mangroves line the river opposite Krabi town. This is a protected area and it is worth visiting for the birds, monitor lizards and macaques. Long-tailed boats can be hired for a trip into the mangroves at the Chao Fah Pier (rates are negotiable and depend on the time of year, length of time and number of passengers).

Ao Nang ◎◎◉◐▲◎◐ » pp 950-953. Colour map 7, A2.

A resort town 15 km to the west of Krabi town, the beach at Ao Nang is neither sweeping nor glorious – one end is filled with kayaks and long-tailed boats for transporting tourists to Rai Leh and other beaches. Songthaews will take you to and from Krabi town. The town itself is a generic collection of souvenir shops, small resorts and bad restaurants. There are pleasant features in spite of all this – the beach front is lined with coconut palms and mango trees with limestone walls at one end and lovely views of the islands on the horizon. Ao Nang is also good at providing facilities including diving, windsurfing, fishing and tours. But it is really the surrounding beaches, coves, caves and grottoes that make the place bearable, particularly at **Hat Nopparat Thara**, about 3 km northwest of Ao Nang, a deliciously long stretch of soft, pale beige sand covered in tiny seashells and backed by paperbark forests.

Rai Leh ◎▲◎ » pp 950-953.

Located on Phra Nang peninsula to the south of Ao Nang, there are no roads to Rai Leh lending it a secret-hideaway ambience. The place consists mainly of **Rai Leh West** and **Rai Leh East**. Over the last few years Rai Leh has become something of a mecca for rock climbers. This is partly because limestone is porous so that the water cuts into it and makes the natural grips ideal for climbers. The best beach is on the west side – a truly picture-postcard affair. Rai Leh East also acts as a pier for taxi boats to and from Krabi. Pretty Rai Leh West, also known as 'Sunset Beach', is about 10 minutes' walk away. There is also good snorkelling and swimming in archetypal crystal-clear water. At the southern extremity of the bay is a mountain cave (**Outer Princess Cave**) on Phra Nang Beach that is dedicated to the goddess of the area and where an abundance of colourful wooden and stone penises have been there to bribe the goddess by local fishermen.

Koh Phi Phi ◎◎◉◐▲◎◐ » pp 950-953. Colour map 7, A2.

For most arrivals on Koh Phi Phi it seems like you've reached paradise. Anvil-shaped and fringed by sheer limestone cliffs and golden beaches, Koh Phi Phi is stunning. However, a quick walk along the beach, heaving with masses of roasting flesh, or through Ton Sai village, which is filled with persistent touts and standardized tourist facilities, soon shatters the illusion of Nirvana; the endless stream of boats spewing diesel into the sea doesn't help either. The only way to get to Phi Phi is by boat. There are daily connections with Krabi and from the beaches of Ao Nang and Rai Leh, Koh Lanta (one hour) and from various spots on Phuket. Ostensibly Phi Phi should be protected by its national park status but this seems to cut little ice with the developers who appear to be doing more irretrievable damage than the Asian tsunami that devastated the island on 26 December 2004 – there is an aerial photograph on display in the **Amico** restaurant in Ton Sai village that shows the apocalyptic

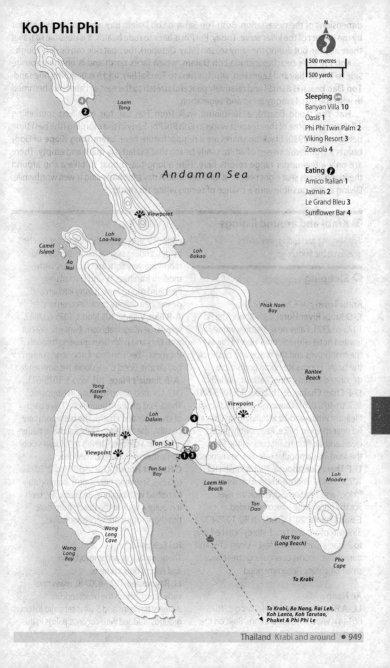

Koh Phi Phi

N

500 metres
500 yards

Andaman Sea

Laem Tong

Viewpoint

Loh Laa-Naa

Camel Island

Ao Nui

Loh Bakao

Phak Nam Bay

Rantee Beach

Yong Kasem Bay

Loh Dalam

Viewpoint

Viewpoint

Viewpoint

Ton Sai

Ton Sai Bay

Laem Hin Beach

Loh Moodee

Ton Dao

Wang Long Cave

Wang Long Bay

Hat Yao (Long Beach)

Pho Cape

To Krabi

To Krabi, Ao Nang, Rai Leh, Koh Lanta, Koh Tarutao, Phuket & Phi Phi Le

Sleeping
Banyan Villa **10**
Oasis **1**
Phi Phi Twin Palm **2**
Viking Resort **3**
Zeavola **4**

Eating
Amico Italian **1**
Jasmin **2**
Le Grand Bleu **3**
Sunflower Bar **4**

dimensions of the devastation. Both Ton Sai and Loh Dalem Bay were almost wiped out by the impact of the killer wave. Today, Phi Phi is back to rude health. It is possible to travel there all year, but during the rainy season (May-October), the boat ride can be very rough.

Koh Phi Phi's beaches include **Loh Dalam**, which faces north and is on the opposite side to Ton Sai Bay and **Laem Hin**, which is next to Ton Sai Bay, and has beautiful fine sand. **Ton Dao** beach is a small and relatively peaceful stretch to the east of Laem Hin, hemmed in with the usual craggy rocks and vegetation.

Hat Yao (Long Beach), a 30-minute walk from Ton Sai, has excellent snorkelling offshore and some of the cleanest water in Koh Phi Phi. Early in the morning (the best time being before 0930) black-tip sharks are a regular fixture here. **Laem Tong (Cape of God)** boasts a wonderful sweep of white sandy beach that's relatively quiet and empty. There are only a few upper range resorts here. Hire a long-tailed boat to take a trip around the island. Boats seat eight people, ฿1000 per boat. A day trip snorkelling is well worthwhile. Diving is also possible with a chance of seeing white-tip sharks.

◉ Krabi and around listings

For Sleeping and Eating price codes, see inside the front cover.

● Sleeping

Krabi Town *p947, map p947*
C-D Krabi River Hotel, 73/1 Khongkha Rd, T075-612321. Fairly new, 5-storey white-fronted hotel with splendid view of the river, the mangroves and the hustle and bustle of the boats. Rooms are bright and simply decorated if uninspiring. Recommended.
D-F Chan Chalay, 55 Uttarakit Rd, T075-620 952/01-978 8081, chanchalay@hotmail.com. Pleasant white-and-blue building on Uttarakit Rd near the post office. Reasonably priced, clean and airy rooms set back a little from the road. Has a popular café. Recommended.
D-F Thara Guesthouse, 79/3 Kongkha Rd, T075-630499. Bright and airy rooms with fridges and TVs. Some overlook the river. For the price range – recommended.
E Ban Chaofa, 20/1 Chao Fah Rd, T075-630 359. Mix of a/c and fan, 2-storey hotel edging to 2-star. Japanese/Ikea feel – clean, chic and minimalist. Rooms overlooking street have small balconies. Recommended.

Ao Nang *p948*
LL-A Royal Nakara, 155/4-7 Moo 3, T075-661441, www.royalnakara.com. Built on the

edge of a steep drop, the rooms are reached by descending several flights of stairs. All rooms are very light and spacious, with modern furniture, TV and DVD player. Premium rooms have pantry kitchen and dining area. Infinity pool. Recommended.
A-B Blue Village, 105 Moo 3, T075-637887. www.bluevillagekrabi.com. Fantastic lay-out with huts and palm trees growing through the roofs – beds on floor futon-style, sunken bathrooms. Good cheap food. Recommended.
A-B Jinnie's Place, 101 Moo 3, T075-621 042. Located down the road in Nopparat Thara. Red brick a/c bungalows have bags of character and charm. The bathrooms are possibly the largest in Krabi and have baths and even a garden. There's a children's pool and a main pool. Recommended.
C Harvest House, 420/18-19 Moo 2, T075-695256. Spanking new rooms, comfortably furnished with balcony, a/c, cable TV, bath. It is quite a walk to the beach from here but these rooms are very good value.

Rai Leh *p948*
There is a lack of accommodation and eating options here.
LL Rayavadee, T075-620740, www.raya vadee.com. Set on the headland. 98, 2-storey pavilions and 5 villas set amid luscious grounds studded with coconut palms in this

luxurious, isolated getaway. Price includes airport transfer. Recommended.

LL-B Railei Beach Club, T08-1464 4338 (mob), www.raileibeachclub.com. West Rai Leh. Traditional Thai-style houses have been sold as holiday homes. Their owners let them when they are not in residence. Kitchens and bathrooms but no a/c.

A-C Rai Leh Viewpoint Resort and Spa, T075-621686-7, www.viewpointresort66.com. Large upgraded resort. Friendly, well run, and clean. Good restaurant, mini-mart, internet and pool. Some of the best bungalows.

Koh Phi Phi *p948, map p949*

Accommodation on Phi Phi is expensive.
LL Zeavola, Laem Tong, T075-627000, www.zeavola.com. Some of the beautifully furnished wooden suites have outside showers and bathrooms with coloured ceramic sinks. Outside living areas with chairs and minibars although the mosquitoes can be horrific. Excellent spa.
LL-C Viking Resort, T075-819398, www.pp vikingresort.com. These huts have been individually designed with Balinese influences. Most sit on the cliff-side with sea views, all have bags of character. Very quiet and secluded sandy beach. Recommended.
A Banyan Villa, Ton Sai, T075-611233. Right in the centre of Ton Sai though its large gardens and pool create a secluded feel. Well run, though nothing too exciting, each room is en suite, with a/c and TV.
C-D Phi Phi Twin Palm, T075-601285, Loh Dalum Bay. Simple bamboo huts, with fan, very near to the beach. More expensive ones have bathroom inside. Friendly smiling staff.
D Oasis, Phi Phi Don, after Gypsy Village. All 12 rooms in this wooden building have fan and en suite with hot water. Friendly management.

❶ Eating

Krabi Town *p947, map p947*
₩ Chao Sua, on Maharaj Rd (the sign, with a leopard on it, is in Thai). Considered by many locals to be one of the best restaurants in Krabi. Serves excellent Thai food.
₩-₩ The Boathouse, Soi Hutangkonn. A restaurant in a real wooden boat set in a garden with a fake moat around it. Perfectly executed main courses, like steamed bass with plum sauce. Recommended.
₩-₩ Europa Café, 1/9 Soi Ruamjit Rd, T075-620407. A favourite with locals and expats. Serves tasty northern European food. Possibly the best Western breakfast in town.
₩ Kwan Coffee Corner, Khongkha Rd, T075-611706, kwan_café_kbi@hotmail.com. Delicious fresh coffee and cheap and tasty Thai food, good breakfasts of fruit and muesli. A good place to acclimatize to Krabi, has chatty owners. **Kwan** has become so much of an institution that they have their own T-shirts for sale. Recommended.

Ao Nang *p948*
₩₩₩ The Roof Restaurant, Ao Nang. Attractive building with a flower-filled dining room and setting although not on the beach. Good extensive menu, which offers organic steak as well as Thai dishes. Expensive, but worth it.
₩ Azzurra, Beach Front Rd, ao Nang. Can become rather dusty during the drier months of Jan-Mar. Good, unpredictable Italian fare with decent ingredients.

Koh Phi Phi *p948, map p949*
₩₩₩ Le Grand Bleu, Ton Sai. French and Thai run restaurant near the pier. Excellent wine list and seafood make this one of the best places to eat on the island.
₩₩₩-₩₩ Amico Italian Restaurant, Ton Sai, T08-1894 0876 (mob). Great little pizza and pasta place near the pier. Perfect pit stop if you're jumping on the ferry. Friendly with good, efficient service.
₩-₩ Jasmin, Laem Tong beach. A tiny little Thai eatery next to the sea gypsy village. Tak (translates as grasshopper), the owner, is a friendly character who serves up excellent Thai food. The seafood is great and the beachside tables romantic. Highly recommended.

Bars and clubs

Krabi Town *p947, map p947*
Kwan Fang Live Music, Sudmongkol Rd, next to **Mixer Pub**. Country and western bands.
Mixer Pub, 100 Sudmongkol Rd. Pulls in a solid local crowd. At **Mixer** they prepare your poison all night with your choice of mixer.

Ao Nang *p948*
Full Moon Bar, formerly the **Full Moon House**. Tried and trusted and right in the centre of Ao Nang.
The Lost Pirate Bar, Beachfront Rd, down from La Luna. Slightly more adventurous crowd – good information about parties.

Koh Phi Phi *p948, map p949*
Carlito's Bar, east from Ton Sai Bay. Became a hub for volunteers and humanitarian aid groups as well as residents after the tsunami. Well worth visiting.
Sunflower Bar, at The end of Loh Dalum Bay. This bar, made from flotsam and other debris, is a good place to chill out and enjoy a few cocktails. BBQ and live music.

Activities and tours

Krabi Town *p947, map p947*
Canoeing
Europa Café, T075-620407, see Eating, above. Offers a mangrove/canoeing tour with an English-speaking guide.

Tour operators
Concentrated on Uttarakit and Ruen-Ruedee roads and close to the Chao Fah Pier.
Krabi Somporn Travel and Service, 72 Khongkha Rd, opposite the old pier, T08-1895 7873 (mob). This is run by Mrs Tree. She is friendly and doesn't overcharge.

Ao Nang *p948*
Canoeing
Sea Canoe, T075-212252, www.seacanoe. net. Provides small-scale sea canoeing trips

(self-paddle), exploring the overhanging cliffs and caves, and the rocky coastline of Phra Nang, Rai Leh and nearby islands.

Diving
Ao Nang Divers (PADI certification) at Krabi Seaview Resort.

Shooting
Ao Nang Shooting Range, 99/9 Moo 2, Ao Nang Rd, Ao Nang, T075-695555. Fire shotguns, Berettas, semi-automatics and Magnums at this well-run shooting range. Prices start at around ฿890 for a full clip.

Tour operators
AP Travel, Beachfront Rd, T075-637642. Offer a range of tours to various temples and short 'jungle tours' – very helpful and friendly though not terribly exciting.

Rai Leh *p948*
Rock climbing
Tex's Rock Climbing Adventure, Rai Leh Beach, www.molon.de/galleries/thailand/krabi/climbing. Mr 'Tex' is a bit of a local hero who also runs a children's overnight adventure camp just outside town for orphans and street children.

Koh Phi Phi *p948, map p949*
Diving
There are around 15 dive shops operating on Koh Phi Phi. Most charge the same.
Phi Phi Scuba Diving, main street in Ton Sai, T075-612665, www.phiphi-scuba.com.
SSI (Scuba School International), offers a 5-day certificate course. Alternatively, book up with one of the dive centres on Phuket.

Rock climbing
KE Hang Out, main street down from the pier at Ton Sai Bay. Experienced climbers who have been there for 7 years. Offer courses and trips.

Tour operators
The North Star Travel. 125/101 Moo 7, T075-601279, northpole_nts@hotmail.com.

Very helpful and friendly tourist information and booking centre – boat tickets can be bought here. Good English. Recommended.

Transport

Krabi Town p947, map p947

Air

The international airport is 17 km northeast of the town on Hwy 4, T075-636546. Served by THAI, Air Asia, Tiger and Singapore Airlines. Vast bulk of flights go to Bangkok.

Boat

The monsoon season affects timetables as does the low season. There is a new pier outside of Krabi town called Chao Fah Pier that services Koh Lanta and Koh Phi Phi. The boat runs to Koh Lanta from mid-Oct to mid-May. During the rest of the year a minibus runs to Koh Lanta – contact a tour operator for details. There are also boats from Krabi to Koh Yao Yai and Koh Yao Noi though times change – ask at the TAT office for details.

Bus

The station is 5 km out of town – red songthaews regularly run between the bus station and town, ฿15. Motorcycle taxis also wait to ferry bus passengers into town. Numerous connections with Bangkok, Phuket, Phangnga, Surat Thani, and Trang.

Songthaew

Songthaews drive through town, stopping at various places such as Phattana Rd, in front of Travel & Tour for Ao Nang. They also run to the bus station at Talaat Kao, 5 km from town.

Ao Nang p948

Boat

Regular long-tailed boats to Rai Leh during high season (Oct-May), from the beach opposite Sea Canoe, 15 mins, approx ฿100. The Ao Nang Princess links Ao Nang with Rai Leh and Koh Phi Phi daily during high season. Arrange a ticket through your guesthouse.

Songthaew

Regular white songthaew connections with Krabi (30 mins, ฿40) leave from the eastern end of the beach road, opposite Sea Canoe. The service runs regularly 0600-1800.

Rai Leh p948

Boat

Long tails link Rai Leh with Krabi and Ao Nang. The Ao Nang Princess links Phi Phi, Ao Nang and Rai Leh during the high season.

Koh Phi Phi p948, map p949

Boat

Services can vary according to the season. Phi Phi lies between Krabi and Phuket and can be reached from both. Daily services to Krabi, Ao Nang and Rai Leh. There are also boat connections with Koh Lanta and Phuket.

Directory

Krabi Town p947, map p947

Banks Branches of all major banks with ATMs. **Immigration office** Uttarakit Rd, a little way up from the post office on the same side of the road. You can get visa extensions here. **Internet** Lots of services available around the town, especially on Uttarakit Rd, Chao Fah Rd and around Hollywood. **Post office** Uttarakit Rd (halfway up the hill, not far from the Customs Pier).

Ao Nang p948

Banks Mobile exchange booths along Ao Nang beachfront and a more permanent place opposite the Phra Nang Inn, run by the Siam City Bank. **Internet** At most guesthouses and hotels. **Tourist police** Near the Ao Nang Bay Resort and Spa and another general police box near the Phra Nang Inn.

Koh Phi Phi p948, map p949

Banks Money can be exchanged but for poor rates. Best to change money on the mainland. There are ATMs. **Post office** Letters can be posted in the village.

Koh Lanta, Trang and Tarutao

Quieter beaches and remoter, more authentic touches greet the visitor who heads into this part of Thailand. While the island of Koh Lanta is home to upmarket resorts and tourist trinkets it is still an engaging place to absorb miles of beaches and gorgeous sunsets. Trang is a friendly rootsy place whose charms grow on anyone who gives it a chance – it is also the gateway to the deep south of the country. The highlight of the south is the remote Tarutao National Park, home to dozens of beautiful, magical islands that are the source of myth and tales of pirates. Unfortunately, due to rough seas Tarutao is only accessible from October to April. Off-limits all year, at least for the moment, are the southern provinces running along the Malaysian border – Muslim insurgents are active here and we don't recommend travel to this region (see box, page 959). ▸▸ *For listings, see pages 960-968.*

Koh Lanta ⊜❼▲❺❻ ▸▸ *pp 960-968. Colour map 7, A2.*

The story of Koh Lanta can be applied to most of the popular islands in Thailand: transformed in a generation from comatose tropical idyll without telephones, electricity or roads into a thrusting parade of generic resorts, all eager to separate visitors from their cash. But that's not the whole story – there are still great beaches and cheap backpacker bungalows, perfect places to lose yourself for weeks. Regular boats arrive daily from Krabi and, during the high season (November to March), from Phi Phi. Both stop at the village of Sala Dan, sited at the northern end of the island – this is also where most of the minibuses from Krabi and Trang stop. During the long wet season (May to October), things on Koh Lanta grind to a halt and many places close. Songthaews are the main form of public transport around the island, though they are few and far between. Motorbikes and mountain bikes are available for hire and there is a smattering of overpriced tuk-tuks in Sala Dan. Koh Lanta is packed with bungalows and resorts. Some of these set-ups are replete with internet, mini-marts, souvenir shops, spas, restaurants, pools and bars so that guests need never leave.

Sala Dan is most arrivees' introduction to Koh Lanta and is geared to emptying the pockets of tourists as quickly as possible. It provides numerous overpriced facilities such as banks, ATMs, internet, bars and restaurants. Koh Lanta's other main town, Ban Koh Lanta, the official 'capital,' is on the eastern coast and rarely visited by tourists. It's a cute ensemble of original old wooden shophouse/fishing houses and Thai-Chinese ambience, and there are homely bed and breakfasts and galleries here. There are no beaches but there are excellent restaurants offering authentic local dishes – something almost impossible to find elsewhere.

Ao Khlong Dao, which starts on the edge of Sala Dan, was one of the first bays to open to tourism in Koh Lanta. While it is a lovely bay with soft sand, development here has been rapid and unplanned. The bay is now heavily developed with most resorts encroaching onto the beach.

Ao Phra-Ae, also known as Long Beach, is a lovely beach to stroll on with soft white sand. This beach is catering increasingly to retirees and families, particularly the Scandinavians, although there are still remnants of its earlier days as a backpacker haven. Hat Khlong Khoang is advertised by some as the 'most beautiful beach on Lanta'. But the beach is fairly steep down to the sea and the sand not as fine as that at Long Beach. There are a handful of establishments with real character and charm. Ao Khlong Nin is a bit of a mixed

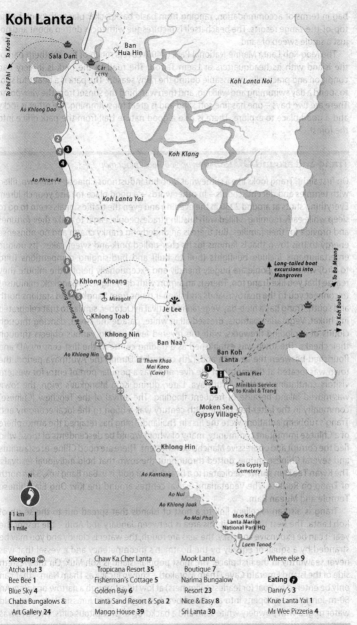

Koh Lanta

To Krabi

To Phi Phi

Sala Dan

Car Ferry

Ban Hua Hin

Koh Lanta Noi

Ao Khlong Dao

Koh Klang

Ao Phrae-Ae

Koh Lanta Yai

Long-tailed boat excursions into Mangroves

To Ba Muang

Khlong Khoang

To Koh Bubu

Minigolf

Je Lee

Khlong Toab

Khlong Nin

Ban Naa

Ao Khlong Nin

Tham Khao Mai Kaeo (Cave)

Ban Koh Lanta

Lanta Pier

Minibus Service to Krabi & Trang

Moken Sea Gypsy Village

Khlong Hin

Ao Kantiang

Sea Gypsy Cemetery

Ao Nui

Ao Khlong Jaak

Ao Mai Phai

Moo Koh Lanta Marine National Park HQ

Laem Tanod

N

1 km

1 mile

Sleeping
Atcha Hut **3**
Bee Bee **1**
Blue Sky **4**
Chaba Bungalows & Art Gallery **24**

Chaw Ka Cher Lanta Tropicana Resort **35**
Fisherman's Cottage **5**
Golden Bay **6**
Lanta Sand Resort & Spa **2**
Mango House **39**

Mook Lanta Boutique **7**
Narima Bungalow Resort **23**
Nice & Easy **8**
Sri Lanta **30**

Where else **9**

Eating
Danny's **3**
Krue Lanta Yai **1**
Mr Wee Pizzeria **4**

bag in terms of accommodation, ranging from basic backpacker places through to the top-of-the-range resorts. The beach itself is picturesque with rocks dotted about and not just a single sweep of sand.

The Moo Koh Lanta Marine National Park (฿400) covers much of the southern part of the island with its headquarters at Laem Tanod. The road to the park is in very bad condition and practically impassable during the rainy season. The park is a beautiful spot to spend a day swimming and walking, and then watching the sunset from the viewpoint. There are two bays – one has fine soft sand and is great for swimming, the other is rocky and a good place to explore. There is also a good nature trail from the park office into the forest.

Trang and around ⊜❼▲⊖❶ ➤➤ *pp 960-968. Colour map 7, A3.*

On first sight, Trang looks like a somewhat drab but industrious Chinese-Thai town, filled with temples and decent schools – in other words – a good place to raise your children. Everything shuts at around 2230 in the evening and even the traffic signals seem to go to sleep while early morning is filled with bustling tradespeople, eager to make their fortunes and provide for their families. But there is an underlying cranky charm and no-nonsense energy to this town that is famous for its char-grilled pork and sweet cakes. Its unique entertainments include bullfights (bull to bull) and bird-singing competitions (bird to bird) while the people are hugely friendly and exceptionally helpful the minute they realize that you like Trang too. There is an airport with daily flights to Bangkok, minibuses to connect you to the nearby islands and sleeper trains from Bangkok and stations north and south. Trang has a nine-day Vegetarian Festival in October, similar to that celebrated in Phuket. Vegetarian patriots, dressed all in white, parade the street, dancing through clouds of exploding fireworks, with the revered few shoving various objects through their cheeks. The town was established as a trading centre in the first century AD and flourished between the seventh and 12th centuries. During the Ayutthaya period, the town was located at the mouth of the river and was a popular port of entry for western visitors continuing north to Ayutthaya. Later, during King Mongkut's reign, the town was moved inland because of frequent flooding. The arrival of the Teochew (Chinese) community in the latter half of the 19th century was a boon to the local economy and Trang's rubber plantations were the first in Thailand. Trang has retained the atmosphere of a Chinese immigrant community, many of whom would be descendents of those who fled the corrupt and oppressive Manchu government. There are good Chinese restaurants and several Chinese shrines dotted throughout the town that hold individual festivals. The **Kwan Tee Hun shrine**, dedicated to a bearded war god, is in Ban Bang Rok, 3 km north of Trang on Route 4. The Vegetarian Festival centres around the **Kiw Ong Eia Chinese Temple** and **Muean Ram**.

Trang is also an excellent link to a host of islands that spread out to the south of Koh Lanta. The best time to visit this area is between January and April – the rest of the year it can be expensive and risky: the seas are rough, the water is cloudy and you may be stranded by a squall or equally by the boatmen's incompetency and a vessel that was never seaworthy in the first place. The most popular island is Koh Muk. On the western side of the island **Emerald Cave** (Tham Morakot) – known locally as Tham Nam – that can only be entered by boat (or fearless swimmers) at low tide, through a narrow opening. An 80-m-long passage opens into an inland beach straight out of Jurassic Park – emerald water ringed with powdery white sand and a backdrop of precipitous cliffs. The cave was only discovered during a helicopter survey not very long ago and is thought to have been a pirates' lair. Unfortunately, groups of Southeast Asian tourists – combine swimming into the cave with positive reinforcement songs shouted in unison – 'we can do this' and 'we will succeed, onward, onward' – destroying the mystique. The only way around the group scene is to hire a long-tail boat privately. The rest of the west coast has white-sand beaches and high cliffs while the east coast is also rimmed by stunning stretches of sand.

Tarutao National Park 😊👤🔺😊🌀 ➤ pp 960-968. Colour map 7, B2/3.

ⓘ *There are no ATMs or banks on any of the islands; bring adequate funds with you.*
While some say that Tarutao is merely a mispronunciation of the Malay words ta lo trao, meaning 'plenty of bay', when first spying this ominous humped island rising out of the sea, it is far easier to believe a second interpretation. That is, that Tarutao comes from the Malay word for old, mysterious and primitive. Resonating with a murky history of pirates, prisoners and ancient curses, the island waters, located in the remotest corner of the southern Andaman sea, still have reasonable coral, and provide some of the best dive sites in Thailand – particularly around the stone arch on Koh Khai. Adang Island has magnificent coral reefs. These are part of Thailand's best-preserved marine park, where turtles, leopard sharks, whales and dolphins can be spotted. Getting to Tarutao National Park requires some planning. For much of the year, it is not advisable to take a boat to these beautiful islands. Ferries run from October to June, but speedboats or privately hired long-tailed boats can be chartered at other times of year. If you are based on Koh Lipe or Koh Bulon-Leh, then hiring private long-tails to other islands is advised as you will otherwise be facing a roundabout route from Ban Pak Bara adding hours to your journey. Rented bicycles provide an adequate means of traversing Tarutao's main road, which is a gruelling route of steep curves occupied at times by cobras and pythons sunning themselves. Inland, half of Koh Tarutao is dense dark rainforest with only a single 12-km road cutting through the length of the island and scant paths leading into a potentially lethal jungle filled with poisonous snakes and volatile beasts like the wild boar. Created in 1974, the marine national park comprises 51 islands – the main ones being Tarutao, Adang, Rawi, Lipe, Klang, Dong and Lek. Tarutao Park itself is divided into two main sections– the Tarutao archipelago and the Adang-Rawi archipelago.

November to April are the best months; the coolest are November and December. The park is officially closed from the end of May to 15 October, but it is still possible to get there. Services run providing the weather is alright. Koh Bulon-Leh is accessible year round, although most resorts are closed for six months of the year so it is wise to ring ahead. The entrance fee to Tarutao is ฿400 for adults, ฿200 for children under 14. This charge is not enforced on the other islands although the ferry to Koh Lipe costs a fairly steep ฿550. The **national park headquarters** ⓘ *close to the ferry port at Pak Bara, T074-781285*, provides information and books accommodation on Tarutao and Adang (messages are radioed to the islands). There can be a shortage in high season. Camping spaces are usually available. On Koh Tarutao and Koh Adang the accommodation is Forestry Department (ie government) run; Koh Lipe and Koh Bulon-Leh are the only islands where the private sector has a presence, meaning the resorts are better and activities more varied.

Koh Tarutao boasts the remains of the prison that held around 10,000 criminals and political prisoners, some of whom became pirates during the Second World War to stave off starvation. Island rumour also has it that somewhere on Koh Tarutao a tonne of gold dust looted from a French ship still remains buried along with the murdered pirates that attacked the unfortunate vessel. It is now believed that the political prisoners received the best of the treatment on Koh Tarutao where the general criminals may even have served them. Certainly the two groups did not mix, with the criminals held in the eastern part at the present-day Taloh Wow Cove and the political prisoners detained at Udang Cove in the southern tip. But all suffered during the Second World War when the island was completely cut off – along with essential food supplies. In cahoots with the guards, prisoners took to ambushing passing ships, originally for food and then for anything of value. This only came to an end in 1947 when the British, who had retaken Malaya, sent in the Royal Navy to quell the pirates. Afterwards, the island was left in total isolation.

Tarutao is the largest of the islands in the Tarutao Archipelago with a mountainous spine running north-south down the centre of the island, with its highest point reaching 708 m. The main beaches are **Ao Moh Lai**, **Hin Ngam**, **Ao Phante**, **Ao Chak** and **Ao Sone**, mostly on the west side of the island, which has long sweeps of sand punctuated by headlands and mangrove. Ao Sone is notorious as the beach where a lone pirate killed a camping tourist in the 1980s, this eerie strip has quite a physical presence, unlike any of the other beaches along the west coast. **Tae Bu cliff**, just behind the park headquarters on Ao Phante, has good sunset views. You climb up an imaginative route that includes a path cut into the hill, rickety wooden plank steps and extraordinary rock formations, all the while hearing the sound of monkeys, mouse deer, hornbills and perhaps wild boar. The prison at Ao Talo U-Dang, in the south, was established in 1939 and was once used for Thailand's political prisoners. The other main camp, at Ao Talo Wao on the east side of the island, was used for high-security criminals.

Coconut plantations still exist on Tarutao but the forests have barely been touched, providing a habitat for flying lizards, wild cats, lemur, wild boar, macaques, mouse deer and

Tarutao National Park

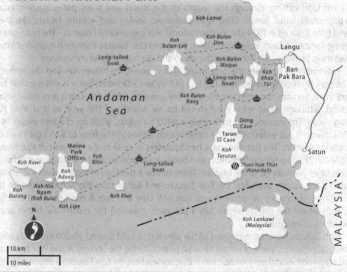

Terrorism in the deep south

Along with Narathiwat, Songkhla, Pattani and Yala, Satun province was a hotbed for Islamic insurgents during the 1970s and 1980s until a government amnesty saw 20,000 fighters handing in their arms in 1987. Then, in December 2001, it all began again with hit-and-run attacks on police, military outposts, schools and commercial sites.

The Australian government, following the Bali bombings, warned its citizens to exercise particular vigilance in Satun province and overland travel to the Malaysian border. The UK Foreign Office advises against all but essential travel to the four southern provinces. Among the risks are kidnapping from resorts and piracy in the Straits of Malacca.

Much of the violence has been blamed on Thaksin Shinawatra's hair-brained attempts to stamp out the separatist movement by rounding up suspected militants (but on the basis of unsound intelligence), thus creating a wave of resentment in the region. The military leaders who deposed the oligarch-turned-politician in late 2006 have made overtures to the separatists, apologising for Thaksin's policies, with mixed success.

Much of the tension in Satun province and throughout the deep south can be traced back to the late 1890s when these provinces – once part of Muslim and animist Malaysia – were Siamised, their names translated to Thai and the people reclassified as Malay-Thais. Satun was formerly called Setol. But the south also claims that, because it is not fully Thai, it is punished with low funding and poor schools and has become a dumping ground for corrupt and inept military and government officials. Certainly, banditry is rife throughout the southern provinces.

The Bahasa-speaking inhabitants certainly see themselves as more Malaysian than Thai and this is evident in the excellent cuisine, which is not as hot as Thai food but is spicier with quieter, more layered curries and a subtler sweetness. And the restaurant owners may often tell you that the ingredients are all Malaysian.

The far south also has spectacular national parks – including Tarutao with its tremendous marine life and awe-inspiring scenery.

---

feral cows, believed to have bred when the prisoners were taken from the island. Crocodiles once inhabited Khlong Phante and there is a large cave on the Choraka (crocodile) water system known as **Crocodile Cave** (bring a torch). The best way to see wildlife is to walk down the 12-km road during the dry season when animals come out in search of water. While the waters around Tarutao are home to four species of turtle (the Pacific Ridleys, green, hawksbill and leatherback), whales and dolphins are also occasionally seen; the sea is clearer further west in the waters of the Adang-Rawi archipelago.

Koh Bulon-Leh, the second main island in the Tarutao archipelago, is just north of the main island. Although it has developed into a beach resort it is only in the past 50 years or so that Koh Bulon-Leh has had year-round residents: a Muslim population of around 50. The reason for this is down to the superstition of the Moken fisherpeople who believed the island was cursed and that everyone who lived there met an untimely death. This kept the island uninhabited until after the Second World War; since then it was discovered that the high mortality rate was due to tuberculosis. The lifestyle here is exceedingly laid-back and, in the more expensive resorts, boho-chic.

Adang and Rawi lie 43 km west of Tarutao and are the main islands in the archipelago of the same name. They offer a stark contrast to Tarutao. While Tarutao is composed of limestone and sandstone, the rugged hills of Adang and Rawi are granite. Adang's highest mountain rises to 703 m while Rawi's is 463 m in height. Koh Adang is almost entirely forested and there is a trail that leads up to the summit, Chado Cliff, for good views over Koh Lipe and the Andaman Sea. There are also a handful of trails through the dense vegetation; to spot the shy inhabitants – including a variety of squirrels, mouse deer and wild pigs – it is best to wait half an hour or so in silence. The main beaches on Adang are Khai, Laem Son, Ao Lo Lae Lae and Lo Lipa, and Sai Khao on Rawi. Koh Lipe, the main destination in this archipelago, is still a tropical idyll occupied by Chao Le Sea Gypsies although the main beach – Pattaya – is now fairly densely populated by tourist bungalows and resorts. It is a beautiful island that attracts many returnees, mainly because of the laid-back and gentle populace, excellent snorkelling in some of the clearest waters in the Andaman Sea, blindingly white sand beaches and terrific seafood. The Chao Le have also managed to keep their culture and language and hold a traditional ceremony called *pla juk* twice a year. For this, a miniature boat is built out of *rakam* and *teenped* wood by the villagers. Once the boat is completed, offerings are placed in it, and the Chao Le dance until dawn and then launch the boat out to sea, loaded with the village's communal bad luck.

◉ Koh Lanta, Trang and Tarutao listings

For Sleeping and Eating price codes, see inside the front cover.

● Sleeping

Koh Lanta *p954, map p955*
Most bungalows offer free pick-ups from the pier at Sala Dan. There is considerable variation between high-season (roughly, Nov-May) and low-season (Jun-Oct) rates.

Ban Koh Lanta
A-B Mango House, middle of the main street, T075-697181, www.kolanta.net/southernlanta resort.htm. Nicely restored old wooden house overlooking the sea. Was once, allegedly, a government-run opium den. Rooms are nicely decorated and some have views. No a/c, shared facilities throughout. The owners also have a number of villas and houses for rent (**A-C**). One of the most original places to stay on the island and a massive departure from the clichéd resorts aimed at package tourists or dull-as-dishwater bamboo huts that are the preserve of the unadventurous backpacker. Highly recommended.

Ao Khlong Dao
LL-AL Lanta Sand Resort and Spa, Ao Khlong Dao edging to Ao Phra-Ae, T075-684633, www.lantasand.com. Spacious rooms, amazing bathroom with glass wall so that the monkeys can peer in while you are taking a bath. Good service, fine food. Recommended.
AL-B Golden Bay, 22 Moo 3, T075-684 161, www.goldenbaylanta.com. There are 3 styles of room all with TV, fridge, a/c and hot water. Hotel room ambience. Friendly, helpful owners and an easy place to get to. Awesome restaurant serving some of the best Thai and Isaan food on the beach.
A-E Chaba Bungalows & Art Gallery, 20 Moo 3, Khlong Dao beach, T075-684 118, www.krabidir.com/chababungalows. Walk along Khlong Dao beach and you'll eventually come across a series of strange, brightly coloured, amorphous shapes. The rooms and bungalows are not that inspired but it is very friendly. The art gallery holds various exhibitions differing in quality. Good food. Recommended.

Ao Phra-Ae

AL-A Chaw Ka Cher Lanta Tropicana Resort, 352 Moo 2, T08-1895 9718 (mob), www.lantatropicanaresort.com. Set on a hill just off the main road at the far southern end of Ao Phra-Ae this is a very friendly and beautifully set out resort. The gorgeous bungalows have open-air bathrooms. Pool, excellent restaurant, free internet, huge library. 500 m from the beach; owners supply bicycles to get you there. Recommended.

AL-E Mook Lanta, 343 Moo 2, T075-684638, www.mooklanta.com. Both the bungalows and rooms have been built with considerable attention to detail. All rooms, even fan, come with hot water and Wi-Fi access. Beautifully designed with nice finishes such as silk throws, mood lighting and curtains. The management go out of their way to be helpful. Highly recommended.

B Last Horizon Resort, 175 Moo 2, Baan Phu Klom Beach, www.lantalanta.com/last_horizon_resort/index.html. 25 nicely designed stone bungalows in a coconut grove with attached showers, 24-hr electricity, restaurant and beach bar. Friendly management. Recommended.

D-E Blue Sky Resort & Restaurant, 238 Moo 3, T075-684871, www.krabidir.com/blueskylanta. Bamboo huts, very clean and surprisingly spacious. Super friendly staff. Recommended for its beach front location.

Hat Khlong Khoang

B Nice and Easy, 315 Moo 2, T075-667105. It's easy to spot this resort as the owner's art deco house, come spaceship, fronts onto the beach. The a/c bungalows resemble Swiss cottages inside, very quaint. There is a small pool and the staff are friendly.

B-E Where Else Resort, next to **Bee Bee**, T075-667173. Bags of character and well designed bamboo bungalows half hidden in the jungle garden – all have bathrooms, mosquito screens and hammocks on the balcony. The ones at the back are a little cramped together. Recommended.

D Fisherman's Cottage, 190 Moo 2, Klong Khong Beach, T08-1476 1529 (mob), www.krabidir.com/fishermanscottage. Collection of 11 bungalows, all with sea views, decorated with style. Staff are very family friendly – so is the beach, a safe place to swim. Recommended.

E-G Bee Bee, www.kuh.cx/beebee, T081-537 9932. A village-like set-up of unusual-looking bamboo bungalows set just back from the beach in a coconut plantation. Some with 2 levels and all with bamboo bathrooms. Charming and different. Closed during the low season. Recommended.

Ao Khlong Nin

AL Sri Lanta, T075-662688, www.srilanta.com. Spacious, well-designed bamboo-and-wood bungalows with a/c (but sadly no mosquito screening or ceiling fans) and hot showers. Beautiful spot with access to a sandy beach. Recommended.

AL-B Narima Bungalow Resort, 98 Moo 5, Klong Nin, T075-662668, www.narima-lanta.com. Large bungalows with wooden floors overlooking a quiet part of beach. Good Thai food. Pool, exercise bicycle, DVDs, CDs and a mini-library. Recommended.

E Atcha Hut, 70 Moo 6, T08-9470 4607. www.atchahut.com. Good bungalows, with an arty vibe, though the party atmosphere might be a little too much for those seeking tranquillity. Beach front bar and yoga classes.

Trang and around p956

A-D Wattana Park, 315/7 Huay Yod Rd, T075-216216. A little way out from the town centre on the road in from Krabi. A modern hotel with good rooms and friendly service – probably the best value business-class hotel in Trang. Does not have a pool. Recommended.

E My Friend, 25/17 Sathani Rd, T075-255447, www.myfriend-trang.com. All rooms in this clean, well-run guesthouse are en suite with TV and a/c. Convenient location near the station – they'll let you check-in early, if they have availability, good news for those arriving on the sleeper train from Bangkok. Internet, lots of local information, staff are helpful and friendly, though don't speak much English. Free tea and filter coffee.

E-G Yannawa Bed and Breakfast, 94 Visetkul Rd, T075-216617. Clean, comfortable rooms in a shophouse. Good price and helpful staff. The rooms at the top are not so dark but avoid the noisy street front. The single rooms are the best value. Recommended at this price.

Koh Muk

The majority of the accommodation here shuts 6 months of the year due to navigational difficulties and drought.

B-E Rubber Tree Bungalows, T075-215972, www.mookrubbertree.com. Up a long wooden staircase cut into the hill are these marvellous, family-run bungalows. Attached toilet and bathroom. Set in a working rubber tree plantation so you may be woken early in the morning by the lanterns of the rubber tree tappers. You are welcome to observe them at work. The attached restaurant has easily the best food on the island – cooked by a northern Thai native. Let her choose what to cook if you can't decide. This is a magical place to have an evening drink with dozens of twinkling lights providing a dreamy backdrop. Recommended.

F-G Mookies. Down the lane/dirt path towards the sea gypsy village (there is only one path on from **Rubber Tree**). Cross over a wooden bridge and follow the disco music to **Mookie's Bar**, T08-7275 6533 (mob). This is a completely eccentric set-up. Rooms are large with spring mattresses and 24-hr electricity with light and fan inside. While the toilet and shower are shared, they are kept clean to military standards. Open all year round. The shower outside also has hot water. Highly recommended.

Tarutao National Park *p957, map p958*
Ban Pak Bara

E Best House Resort, T074-783058/783568. Close to the pier, 10 a/c and clean bungalows with comfortable beds, friendly owners and a good restaurant. Recommended.

Koh Tarutao

Book through the National Park office in Bangkok, T02-579052, or the Pak Bara office, T074-783485. Accommodation is in the north and west of Tarutao. There are 3 choices: multi-occupancy bungalows that can accommodate families or groups, longhouses and tents. The 3 main beaches – **Ao Pante**, **Ao Molae** and **Ao Sone** all offer some or all of these types, with Ao Pante, the one closest to the pier and where the park warden offices are, offering the most selection. The rooms may also have shared outside toilets. The bungalows are sparsely furnished wooden structures, set along the side of the road against the cliffs. Tents are on the beach with a public shower and toilet. Check your tent for size and condition. If you intend to stay for more than 2 nights it's best to buy a tent from the mainland; it will pay for itself and be clean, in good condition and odour-free. The treatment given to tent visitors varies. Hired tent cost ฿100-200; own tent ฿60. Best spots for camping are on Ao Jak and Ao Sone. You can also camp on the beach close to the national park bungalows (฿30 per night per person, as in other Thai national parks).

Ban Molae, Ao Molae. ฿1000. 4-person bungalows that are more upmarket. 2 rooms and 2 toilets.

Ban Nangnoi, Ao Pante. ฿650. 6-person bungalow. 2 rooms and 2 toilets.

Ban Tabang, Ao Pante. ฿1200. 4-person bungalow with 2 rooms and 2 toilets.

Ban Taboon, Ao Pante. ฿1000. 4-person bungalow. 2 rooms and 1 toilet.

Samed Dang Long House, Ao Pante. ฿500. 4 people per room. Toilet outside.

Samed Kaw Long House, Ao Pante. ฿500. 4 people per room. Toilet outside.

Koh Bulon-Leh

C-D Pansand Resort, T08-1397 0802 (mob), or **First Andaman Travel** (Trang), T075-218035. Well-maintained and welcoming bungalows with attached bathrooms and dormitories. The views are good, and the garden pleasant. Watersports, camping, snorkelling and boat trips. Has an evening internet service. Set in from main beach but this is a plus as it makes it feel more exclusive. Recommended. Closed Jul-Sep.

D Chaolae Food and Bungalows. Run by a Chao Le family. 8 raised brick and bamboo bungalows – all adorable – set up hill further on from **Bulon Viewpoint Resort**. It has sunken bathrooms with squat toilet and shower but no fans. Plenty of personal touches. Restaurant with shell mobiles and lined with cacti and brightly hued flowers in pots. You can choose your fish from the daily catch for beautiful cooking with herbs and spices. Excellent reports from guests. Recommended.

E Bulon Le Resort, T08-1897 9084 (mob). Well positioned where the boats dock overlooking a beautiful beach. A wide range of bungalows from nice, spacious, almost colonial options to the more basic, single rooms with spotless shared bathrooms. All in good shape and run by friendly and helpful management. Electricity 1800-0200. Good restaurant and the island's best breakfast. Recommended.

E Panka Bay Resort, T074-711982/783097. Up the hill and down on the Panka Bay side of the island, this is the only resort here. There are 21 bungalows at this Muslim Malay/Thai family-run establishment. They are arranged along the beach and in tiers up a hill with handmade stone and sand steps built by the family. The beach is not great as it has a rocky shore, but you can walk to the other beach in 20 mins and see some amazing bird and lizard life on the way. Excellent service – they offer a free pick up from the **Bulon-Le Resort**. Another perk is electricity until 0500. Huge restaurant with superb Thai-Malay fusion food. Recommended.

Koh Adang and Koh Rawi
Accommodation is all on the southern swathe of Adang island, with longhouses offering **B-D** rates, where some rooms accommodate sometimes up to 10 people.

Tents are available on Adang: big ฿200, small ฿100, own tent ฿60 at Laem Son. There is a simple restaurant. The island essentially closes down during the rainy season.

The bungalows here differ in terms of the perks offered (eg hot showers).
Laem Son, ฿400. 4 people per bungalow. Big tents (8-10 people), ฿300, medium/middle tents (3-5 people), ฿300, small tents (2 people), ฿150.
Rawi Long House, ฿400. 4 people per room. Toilet outside.

Koh Lipe
A-E Varin Resort, Pattaya Beach, T074-728 080/081-598 2225. The most upmarket spot on the beach, these 109 exceptionally clean bungalows, suites and villas are set in an attractive, if fairly cramped and regimental layout facing each other. Still, it offers the highest standard of accommodation on Lipe with new luxury villas opened early 2007. The operation is run by a Muslim Thai/Malay family. The restaurant is a little characterless but service is excellent and attentive. Recommended.

C-E Mountain Resort, bay to west of Sunlight Beach, T074-728131, www.mt-resort.com. One of Lipe's best resorts with spacious grounds and corrugated-roofed bamboo bungalows. The rooms have 24-hr electricity, large verandas and basic tiled bathrooms. The large romantic wooden restaurant is set on a shaded cliff high above idyllic views over the sandbanks with great sea breeze. Steep steps down the cliff lead to a gorgeous shallow beach and the **Karma** beach bar. Fan and a/c rooms. Recommended.

D-F Andaman Resort, Sunlight Beach, T074-728017. A mix of 40 concrete, log and bamboo bungalows generously spaced along a pristine quiet beach and well-shaded by trees. The best rooms are the white-and-blue concrete row on the beach near the restaurant, although they lack some of the other huts' character. Clean, quiet, bright rooms popular with families. Owned by a Chao Le-Chinese-Thai family. Recommended.

E Pooh's, Sunlight Beach, T074-722220. Has 6 clean fan bungalows set in Pooh's excellent, friendly, family-run complex of bar, internet, restaurant, travel agency and dive shop. Nice enough bungalows but they are not on the beach. Breakfast and 10 mins on the internet are included. Convenient for early morning coffee and everything else at this one-stop operation run by the affable Mr Pooh ('crab' in English). Guests get a discount at the dive shop. Recommended.

E-F Porn Bungalows, Sunset Beach, T08-9464 5765 (mob). A Chao-Le run operation headed by Mr Gradtai (Rabbit). Fairly self-contained resort with simple woven bamboo huts on a beautiful beach; incredibly popular with return visitors – especially families with small children. The staff can take time to warm to newcomers but it's worth the work. The restaurant is a bit overpriced but the menu of the nearby **Flour Power** bakery is an excellent alternative (see Eating, below).

🍴 Eating

Koh Lanta p954, map p955
All the guesthouses and hotels provide restaurants with similar menus.

Ban Koh Lanta Yai
ψψψ-ψ **Mango Bar & Bistro**, below **Mango House** guesthouse. Decent Thai and Western food for sale in this great little hangout spot. Bar serves cocktails and various whiskies.
ψψ **Krue Lanta Yai Restaurant**, at the end of 'town', T075-697062. Hours variable. A restaurant on the pier along a walkway filled with plants. Good selection of fresh seafood nicely prepared. Recommended.

Ao Khlong Dao
ψψψ-ψ **Chaba Bungalows & Art Gallery**, 20 Moo 3, Khlong Dao beach, T075-684118. Good Mexican-, Thai- and Mediterranean-inspired food in this funky restaurant.

ψψψ-ψ **Golden Bay Cottage**, 22 Moo 3, T075-684161. Beachside restaurant in the bungalow operation of the same name (see Sleeping, above). Excellent Thai and Isaan food on sale here. They also BBQ a fresh catch of seafood daily and offer discounts in low season. Reasonably priced in comparison to other places.
ψψ **Danny's**, southern end of Khlong Dao beach. Huge menu of seafood, Thai and international, Sun evening Thai buffets are very popular.

Ao Phra-Ae
ψψ-ψ **Mr Wee Pizzeria**, near the **Ozone Bar**. Good oven pizza in an open-air beachfront restaurant. Fire shows and cheap drinks too.

Trang and around p956
Trang's BBQ pork is delicious and one of the town's few claims to national fame. It is made from a traditional recipe brought here by the town's immigrant Chinese community and is usually served with rice. It's the speciality of several Chinese restaurants and can also be bought from street vendors, usually only available from 0900-1500ish.
ψψ **Koh Chai Pla Phrao**, Rusda Rd. Look for a bright yellow sign (Thai only) and a big open-plan eatery for one of the most popular places in Trang. Don't be fooled by the cheap plastic furniture, the Thai food here is awesome. House speciality is grilled fish – so fresh it will be staring back at you – or steamed fish with a mood-altering chilli-and-lime sauce. Highly recommended.
ψ **BBQ Pork Shophouse**, corner of a small soi on Kantang Rd. This tiny Chinese place is often packed to the rafters with families queuing for either takeaway or a table. Only really sells one dish – BBQ pork smothered in a sweet gravy with leafy green vegetables on rice. You can also get chicken satay if you ask nicely. Highly recommended.
ψ **Ko Rak**, also called **Somrak**, 158-160 Kantang Rd. Friendly shophouse-style eatery surrounded by a throng of stalls that sell tender duck and pork rice and noodles.

The family who runs this packed place is originally from the Chinese island of Hainan and first came to Trang over 70 years ago. Full of bustle and good grub. Recommended.

¶ **Meeting Point Restaurant and Internet Café**, right along from the railway station. This does a good breakfast, decent coffees in an airy café with tiled ceramic floor and wooden benches. Recommended.

Koh Muk

¶ **Mookies Bar** does spare ribs, hamburgers and grilled chicken but you need to order ahead of time so he can get the supplies from the mainland.

Tarutao National Park p957, map p958
Koh Tarutao

Just one Thai restaurant with coupon system for paying for food: purchase your coupons at the table next to the restaurant, and return any not used for a cash refund.

Koh Bulon-Leh

¶ **Orchid**, near **Ban Sulaida Bungalows**. A good, cheap restaurant.

Koh Lipe

¶¶¶ **Pooh's**, T074-722220, on the path between **Chao Le Resort** and Pattaya Beach. Usually the busiest place, offering music, a good bar and tasty meals in a well-decorated, relaxed airy setting. The bakery also serves up typically delicious goods.

¶¶ **Daya**, west end of Pattaya Beach. One of the best places for barbecued fish thanks to an exquisite marinade.

¶ **Banana Tree Restaurant**, in the village (take a left at **Forra Dive Centre**). An off-beach setting with shady floor seating under the trees. A popular spot with an extensive Thai menu, it shows movies in the evenings.

¶ **Flour Power Bakery**, Sunset Beach, behind **Sabye Sports**. It has expanded its seating area along with its repertoire to include a mouth-watering selection of Thai and Western dishes, such as lemon chicken, as well as its staple fruit pies, brownies, fresh

bread and cinnamon rolls. The vegetarian selection is good and all meals are served with fresh bread or baked potatoes and salad.

▲▲ Activities and tours

Koh Lanta p954, map p955
Cookery classes
Time for Lime, T075-684590/08-947 45171 (mob), www.timeforlime.net. Contact Junie Kovacs. Learn Thai cookery on the beach.

Diving
Blue Planet Divers, 3 Moo 1, T075-684165; **Lanta Discovery Divers**, Long Beach Resort, T075-684035/08-1797 2703 (mob); **Scool Divers**, T075-684654. See also Tour operators, below.

Tour operators
The following are well run and friendly, and can offer motorcycle rental, and boat and bus tickets: **Makaira Tour Centre**, 18 Moo 1 Sala Dan; **Amour Travel and Tour**, Khlong Dao beachfront, T075-684897.

For long-tailed boat trips from Ban Koh Lanta including fishing and camping tours, contact **Sun Fishing and Island Tours**, main waterfront Rd, Lanta Old town, T087- 8916619, www.lantalongtail.com.

Trang and around p956
Bull fighting
Fights between bulls take place at random, depending on whether the farmers have a suitable bull. The only way to find out if they are taking place is to ask around. But be warned – this is a very much a local entertainment and you might get some curious looks when you ask, particularly if you are a woman. The fights are usually held during the week and only in the day-time. They occur in a field off Trang-Pattalung Rd near the **Praya Ratsadanupradit Monument**. The best way to get there is by tuk-tuk that takes about 20 mins from the railway station. They are always packed with

an excitable betting crowd screaming with dismay or joy and there are plenty of stalls about selling drinks and foods including noodles and fruit. Dusty and hot but exciting.

Diving
Rainbow Divers, in **Koh Ngai Resort**, T075-206962. www.rainbow-diver.com. Run by a German couple, they offer PADI courses and excursions, mid-Nov until the end of Apr.

Tour operators
Choa Mai Tour Ltd, 15 Satanee Rd, contact Jongkoolnee Usaha, T075-216380. Reliable and trustworthy, they go out of their way to help, can make hotel reservations, offer tourist information, airport reservations and a/c bus/van, and tours. Good level of English spoken. www.chaomai-tour-trang.com. Recommended.
PJ Guesthouse, 25/12 Sathani Rd, also run an excellent and well-informed travel service that is as much about you getting to experience local life as making money. They can set you up with private cars and also English-speaking tuk-tuk drivers who organize Trang tours (from ฿200 per hr) showing you all the nooks and crannies of this vibrant town. Recommended.

Tarutao National Park *p957, map p958*
Ban Pak Bara
Tarutao Travel, T074-781284/781360, in La-Ngu town (on the way to Pak Bara Pier).
Udom Tour, Pak Bara, just before the port, T08-1897 4765 (mob).

Koh Lipe
Dang's Tours, a stone's throw from **Pooh's** on the way to **Chao Ley Resort** is just one of the outfits that arranges all day snorkelling tours for around ฿1000 each for 6 people.
Forra Dive Centre, near Chao Ley Resort.
Jack's Tours, on the beach at Koh Lipe.
Lotus Dive (Pooh's), **Ocean Pro Divers** near Leepay Resort.

Sabye Sports, T08-94645884, T/F074-734 104, info@sabye-divers.com. The island's first scuba diving and sports centre, next to **Porn Bungalows**, offers diving and rents canoes (฿500 per day) and snorkelling equipment (฿200 per day).
Starfish Scuba, T074-728089, www.starfish scuba.com, next to the Leepay Resort on Pattaya Beach. Also offers diving courses.

⊖ Transport

Koh Lanta *p954, map p955*
Boat
There are daily departures to **Phi Phi**, **Phuket** and **Krabi** – schedules do vary according to the season.

Minibus
There are hourly minibuses from Sala Dan to **Krabi** town and the airport and Trang until 1500. Some may pick up along the length of the island.

Motorbikes
One of the best ways to see the island though roads can be rutted and steep – drive safely and wear a helmet. From ฿200 – available from many guesthouses or tour operators.

Songthaews
Songthaews run sporadically along the main road – can be pricey so check for prices before you get on.

Trang and around *p956*
Air
The airport is 7 km from town. Daily flights at 1020 and 1145, with **Nok air**, T075- 212-229, www.nokair.com. Fares start at ฿1800. Minivan to town centre ฿100 per person.

Boat
For **Koh Muk** take a boat from Kuantungku pier. Minibuses leave every 30 mins from the minibus station (฿100 approx).

Border essentials: Thailand–Malaysia

Satun
Ferries leave from Satun and dock at 1 of 2 places, depending on the tide. If the tide is sufficiently high, boats leave from the jetty at the end of Samanta Prasit Road. At low water boats dock at Tammalang Pier, south of Satun. Songthaews run to the pier from Buriwanit Road. There are daily connections with Langkawi and Kuala Perlis. Tickets can be purchased in advance from **Charan Tour** – 19/6 Satunthani Road, T074-711453/081-957 3908. There is 1 boat a day from Tammalang Pier in Satun to the islands (Tarutao and Lipe Oct-Apr). Overnight buses connect Satun to **Bangkok** (15 hrs) and leave from Sarit Phuminaraot Rd. There are also regular connections with **Trang**.

Buses and minibuses
For **Koh Lanta** minibuses leave from outside **KK Travel**, opposite the train station, every hr from 0930 until 1630 and are by far the easiest way to get to the island as they drop you off at your resort so you avoid the touts at Sala Dan.

Buses for **Bangkok** leave from the bus station on Ploenpitak Rd. There are also buses for **Phuket**, **Ban Pak Bura** (for Tarutao) from here. Check with local tour operators for through buses to Malaysia and Singapore.

Motorbike
PJ Guesthouse can arrange hire from ฿250 per day.

Train
The sleeper train is one of the most popular ways to get to Trang from Bangkok with 2 daily departures in both directions – the station is in the centre of town.

Tarutao National Park *p957, map p958*
Ban Pak Bara
Boat Ferries leave from Pak Bara, T074-783 010. Call for departure times and prices. To see all the islands, the ฿900 return ticket allows stops at **Tarutao**, **Lipe**, **Adang** and **Bulon**. Boats to **Koh Tarutao** (docking at Ao Phante Malaka on the island's west coast) at 1030 and 1330 from Nov-May (1½ hrs, ฿300 return) and then on to **Koh Lipe** and **Koh Adang** (3 hrs, ฿900 return).

Speedboats also leave for **Tarutao**, **Lipe** and **Adang** during the season at 0900 and 1300. The ferry stops at Tarutao (฿400 one way) and then continues for ฿1300 return.

The daily boat to **Koh Bulon-Leh** leaves at 1400 (1½ hrs, ฿500 return).

It is often too rough between May and Oct for ferries to operate, and the park is officially closed in any case. However, boats can be chartered throughout the year (฿1500 plus). Long-tailed boat charters from Pak Bara to **Koh Bulon-Leh** cost ฿700-1000 per boat.

Bus There are regular buses to **Trang** and to **Satun**, 60 km south.

Koh Tarutao
Boat Koh Tarutao lies off the coast 30 km south of Pak Bara; Koh Adang, Rawi and Lipe are another 40 km out into the Andaman Sea, while Koh Bulon-Leh is 20 km due west of Pak Bara.

Beware of travelling to any of these islands during bad weather; it is dangerous and a number of boats have foundered.

The boat to **Pak Bara** departs at 0900 and 1300. To **Koh Lipe**, 2½-3½ hrs. Transfer from ferry to long-tailed boat to Koh Lipe and Koh Adang, ฿30. Boats can also be chartered from Tarutao. To **Satun** from Tarutao at 1700.

Koh Lipe
Boat Return ferry to **Koh Tarutao** at 0900.

Koh Bulon-Leh

Boat From Bulon-Leh to **Koh Tarutao** and **Ban Pak Bara**, the boats leave at 0900 and 1200. Boats travel on from Koh Bulon-Leh to **Koh Adang** and **Koh Lipe** at 1430.

ⓘ Directory

Koh Lanta *p954, map p955*
Banks Siam City Bank Exchange, Sala Dan. ATMs are common place. **Medical services** Health centre, Sala Dan. **Police** Sala Dan. **Post office** Lanta Pier.

Trang *p956*
Banks Banks are clustered along Phraram VI Rd. **Internet** Plenty of internet locations along Phraram VI Rd and also one a

My Friend guesthouse. **Post office** Jermpanya Rd.

Tarutao National Park *p957, map p958*
Banks No ATMs or banks. On Koh Lipe a few places may exchange cash or advance on credit cards – expect a heavy commission of 5%-10%. Bring plenty of cash with you. **Internet** The school on Koh Lipe runs a cyber-café with all profits helping them buy and maintain equipment. **Medical services** The park office on Koh Tarutao may be able to offer some basic help though nothing official. On Koh Lipe there is a small health clinic staffed by a nurse next to the school. **Telephone** Both major Thai mobile networks – DTAC and AIS – are available on Tarutao and Lipe.

Background

Today, the population of Thailand is made up of Tai-speaking peoples. It has long been thought that the Tai migrated from southern China about 2000 years ago, filtering down the valleys and along the river courses that cut north-south down the country. These migrants settled in the valleys of north Thailand, on the Khorat Plateau, and in parts of the lower Chao Phraya basin. Even at this early date there was a clear division between hill and lowland people. The lowland Tai mastered the art of wet rice cultivation, supporting large populations and enabling powerful states and impressive civilizations to evolve. In the highlands, people worked with the forest, living in small itinerant groups, eking out a living through shifting cultivation or hunting and gathering. In exchange for metal implements, salt and pottery, the hill peoples traded natural forest products: honey, resins such as *lac*, wild animal skins, ivory and herbs. Even today, lowland 'civilized' Thais view the forest (*pa*) as a wild place (*thuan*), inhabited by spirits and hill peoples. This is reflected in the words used to denote 'civilized' lowland Thais – *Khon Muang*, People of the Town – and 'barbaric' upland people – *Khon Pa*, People of the Forest.

Mon, Srivijayan and Khmer influences

Before the Tais emerged as the dominant force in the 13th century, Thailand was dominated by **Mon** and **Khmer peoples**. The Mon were a people and a civilization centred on the western edge of the central plains. They established the enigmatic kingdom of Dvaravati, see below, of which very little is known, to the extent that the location of its capital is far from certain. From the small collection of inscriptions and statues scholars do know, however, that the kingdom was Buddhist and extended eastwards towards Cambodia, northwards towards Chiang Mai, and westwards into Burma. The Khmer were the people, and (usually) a kingdom, centred on present-day Cambodia with their capital at Angkor. They controlled large areas of Thailand (particularly the northeast) and Laos (the south) as well as Cambodia.

Prior to the 13th century the people of the **Srivijayan Kingdom** also extended their influence across Thailand. This was a Hindu-Buddhist kingdom that had its capital near present-day Palembang (Sumatra) and that built its wealth on controlling the trade through the Straits of Melaka between China and India/Middle East. Because of the monsoon winds (northeast/southwest) boats powered by sail had to 'winter' in island Southeast Asia, waiting for the winds to change before they could continue their journeys. Srivijaya, for which we have little solid evidence, is thought to have been one of the most – if not the most – powerful maritime kingdom in the region.

Dvaravati

The Mon Kingdom of Dvaravati was centred close to Bangkok, with cities at modern-day Uthong and Nakhon Pathom and was an artistic and political outlier of the Mon Empire of Burma. Dvaravati relics have also been found in the north and northeast, along what are presumed to have been the trade routes between Burma east to Cambodia, north to Chiang Mai and northeast to the Khorat Plateau and Laos. The Dvaravati Kingdom lasted from the sixth to the 11th centuries; only the tiny Mon kingdom of Haripunjaya, with its capital at Lamphun in the north, managed to survive annexation by the powerful Khmer Empire and remained independent until the 13th century. Unfortunately, virtually nothing of the architecture of the Dvaravati period remains. Buildings were constructed of laterite blocks, faced with stucco (a mixture of sand and lime) and, apparently, bound together with vegetable glue. In Thailand, only the stupa of Wat Kukut outside Lamphun shows Dvaravati architecture (it was last rebuilt in 1218428). Dvaravati sculpture is much better represented and the National Gallery in Bangkok has some fine examples. The sculptors of the period drew their inspiration from India's late-Gupta cave temples, rendering human form almost supernaturally.

Srivijaya

The powerful Srivijayan Empire, with its capital at Palembang in Sumatra, extended its control over south Thailand from the seventh to the 13th centuries. Inscriptions and sculptures dating from the Srivijayan period have been found near the modern Thai towns of Chaiya and Sating Phra in Surat Thani, and Songkhla provinces. They reveal an eclectic mixture of Indian, Javanese, Mon and Khmer artistic influences, and incorporate both Hindu and Mahayana Buddhist iconography. Probably the best examples of what little remains of Srivijayan architecture in Thailand are Phra Boromthat and a sanctuary at Wat Kaeo, both in Chaiya.

The Khmer

Of all the external empires to impinge on Thailand before the rise of the Tai, the most influential was the Khmer. Thailand lay on the fringes of the Angkorian Kingdom, but nonetheless many Thai towns are Khmer in origin: That Phanom, Sakhon Nakhon and Phimai in the northeast; Lopburi, Suphanburi and Ratburi in the lower central plain; and Phitsanulok, Sawankhalok and Sukhothai in the upper central plain.

The peak of the Khmer period in Thailand lasted from the 11th to the 13th centuries, corresponding with the flowering of the Angkorian period in Cambodia. However, antiquities have been found that date back as far as the seventh and eighth century AD. The period of Khmer inspiration is referred to as 'Lopburi', after the Central Thai town of the same name that was a Khmer stronghold. The most impressive architectural remains are to be found in the northeastern region: Phimai, not far from Nakhon Ratchasima (Korat), Muang Tham and Phnom Rung, both south of Buriram (see page 899). As Cambodia's treasures are still relatively expensive and hard to get to, these 'temple cities' are a substitute, giving some idea of the economic power and artistic brilliance of the Khmer period. There are also many lesser Khmer ruins scattered over the northeastern region, many barely researched, and these offer worthwhile forays for those with a real interest in Thailand's historical and archaeological past.

The Tai

The Tai did not begin to exert their dominance over modern Thailand until the 12th and 13th centuries when the Khmer Empire had begun to decline. By then they had taken control of Lamphun in the north, founded Chiang Mai, established the Sukhothai Kingdom in the Yom River valley, and gained control of the southern peninsula. From the 13th century onwards, the history of Thailand becomes a history of the Tai people.

An important unit of organization among the Tai was the *muang*. Today, *muang* is usually translated as 'town'. But it means much more than this, and to an extent defies translation. The muang was a unit of control, and denoted those people who came under the sway of a *chao* or lord. In a region where people were scarce but land was abundant, the key to power was to control manpower, and thereby to turn forest into riceland. At the beginning of the 13th century, some Tai lords began to extend their control over neighbouring *muang*, forging kingdoms of considerable power.

Chiang Mai or Lanna Thai

In northern Thailand, various Tai chiefs began to expand at the expense of the Mon. The most powerful of these men was **King Mengrai**, born in October 1239 at Chiang Saen, a fortified town on the Mekong. It is said that Mengrai, concerned that the constant warring and squabbling between the lords of the north was harming the population, took it upon himself to unite the region under one king. That, inevitably, was himself. Entranced by the legendary wealth of Haripunjaya, Mengrai spent almost a decade hatching a plot to capture this powerful prize. He sent one of his scribes – Ai Fa – to ingratiate himself with the king of Haripunjaya, and having done this encouraged the scribe to sow seeds of discontent. By 1280, the king of Haripunjaya was alienated from his court and people, and in 1281, Mengrai attacked with a huge army and took the city without great trouble. Mengrai then set about uniting his expansive new kingdom. This was helped to a significant degree by the propagation of Ceylonese Theravada Buddhism, which transcended tribal affiliations and helped to create a new identity of northern Thai. The *Lanna* ('Million rice fields') Thai Kingdom created by Mengrai was to remain the dominant power in the north until the mid-16th century, and was not truly incorporated into the Thai state until the 19th century.

In 1296, Mengrai built a new capital that he named Chiang Mai – or 'New Town' (see page 844). The art of this era is called Chiang Saen and dates from the 11th century. It is still in evidence throughout the north – in Chiang Saen, Chiang Mai, Lamphun and Lampang – and shows strong stylistic links with Indian schools of art.

Sukhothai

South of Chiang Mai, at the point where the rivers of the north spill out onto the wide and fertile central plains, a second Thai Kingdom was evolving during the 13th century: the Sukhothai Kingdom. Sri Indraditya was the first known king of Sukhothai, in the 1240s when it was a small kingdom, and it remained a weak local power until the reign of its most famous king, **Ramkhamhaeng** (c1279-1298) or 'Rama the Brave', who gained his name – so it is said – after defeating an enemy general in single-handed elephant combat at the age of 19. When Ramkhamhaeng ascended to the throne in 1275, Sukhothai was a relatively small kingdom occupying part of the upper central plain. When he died in 1298, extensive swathes of land came under the king of Sukhothai's control, and only King Mengrai of Lanna and King Ngam Muang of Phayao could be regarded as his equals. In his first few years as king, Ramkhamhaeng had incorporated the area around Sukhothai into his mandala alongside Sawankhalok, Uttaradit, Kamphaeng Phet and Tak. But King Ramkhamhaeng is remembered as much for his artistic achievements as for his raw power. Under Khmer tutelage, he is said to have devised the Thai writing system and also made a number of administrative reforms. The inscription No 1 from his reign, composed in 1292, is regarded as the first work of Thai literature, and contains the famous lines:

"In the time of King Ramkhamhaeng, this land of Sukhothai is thriving. In the water there are fish, in the fields there is rice. The lord of the realm does not levy toll on his subjects for travelling the roads; they lead their cattle to trade or ride their horses to sell; whoever wants to trade in elephants does so; whoever wants to trade in horses, does so;

whoever wants to trade in silver and gold, does so. When any commoner or man of rank dies, his estate – his elephants, wives, children, granaries, rice, retainers and groves of areca and betel – is left in its entirety to his son ... When [the king] sees someone's rice he does not covet it, when he sees someone's wealth he does not get angry ... He has hung a bell in the opening of the gate over there: if any commoner in the land has a grievance which sickens his belly and gripes his heart, and which he wants to make known to his ruler and lord, it is easy; he goes and strikes the bell which the king has hung there; King Ramkhamhaeng, the ruler of the kingdom, hears the call; he goes and questions the man, examines the case, and decides it justly for him. So the people of this *muang* of Sukhotai praise him."

Every Thai schoolchild is taught to memorize the opening lines of the inscription, ones that seemingly just about every book on Thailand also repeats: *Nai naam mii plaa, nai naa mii khao*: "in the water there are fish, in the fields there is rice".

Although the kingdom of Sukhothai owed a significant cultural and artistic debt to the Khmers, by the 13th century the Tais of Sukhotai were beginning to explore and develop their own interpretations of politics, art and life. The kingdom promoted Theravada Buddhism, sponsoring missionary monks to spread the word. In 1298, Ramkhamhaeng died and was succeeded by his son Lo Thai. His father's empire began to wane and by 1321 Sukhothai had declined in influence and become a small principality among many competing states. For many Thais today, the Sukhothai period – which lasted a mere 200 years – represents the apogee, the finest flowering of Thai brilliance. A visit to the ruins of Sukhothai or its sister city of Si Satchanalai reinforces this (see pages 830and 834).

Ayutthaya

From the mid-14th century
In the middle of the 14th century, Sukhothai's influence began to be challenged by another Thai kingdom, Ayutthaya. Located over 300 km south on the Chao Phraya River, Ayutthaya was the successor to the Mon Kingdom of Lavo (Lopburi). It seems that from the 11th century, Tais began to settle in the area and were peacefully incorporated into the Mon state, where they gradually gained influence. Finally, in 1351, a Tai lord took control of the area and founded a new capital at the confluence of the Pa Sak, Lopburi and Chao Phraya rivers. He called the city Ayutthaya – after the sacred town of Ayodhya in the Hindu epic, the Ramayana. This kingdom would subsequently be known as Siam. From 1351, Ayutthaya began to extend its power south as far as Nakhon Si Thammarat, and east to Cambodia, raiding Angkor in the late 14th century and taking the city in 1432. The palace at Angkor was looted by the Thai forces and the Khmers abandoned their capital, fleeing eastwards towards present-day Phnom Penh. Although Sukhothai and Ayutthaya initially vied with one another for supremacy, Ayutthaya eventually proved the more powerful. In 1438, King Boromraja II placed his seven-year-old son, Ramesuan (later to become King Boromtrailokant), on the throne, signalling the end of Sukhothai as an independent power.

During the Ayutthayan period, the basis of Thai common law was introduced by King Ramathibodi (1351-1369), who drew upon the Indian legal Code of Manu, while the powerful King Boromtrailokant (1448-1488) centralized the administration of his huge kingdom and introduced various other civil, economic and military reforms. Perhaps the most important was the *sakdi naa* system, in which an individual's social position was related to the size of his landholdings. The heir apparent controlled 16,000 ha, the highest official 1600 ha, and the lowest commoner 4 ha. A code of conduct for royalty was also introduced, with punishments again linked to position: princes of high rank who had violated the law were to be bound by gold fetters, those of lower rank by silver. The execution of a member of the royal family was, it has been said, carried out by placing them in a sack and either beating them to death with scented sandalwood clubs or having them trampled by white elephants. Even kicking a palace door would, in theory, lead to the amputation of the offending foot.

By King Boromtrailokant's reign, Ayutthaya had extended its control over 500,000 sq km, and the capital had a population of 150,000. Although the art of Ayutthaya is not as 'pure' as that of Sukhothai, the city impressed 16th- and 17th-century European visitors. The German surgeon Christopher Fryke remarked that "there is not a finer city in all India". Perhaps it was the tiger and elephant fights that excited the Europeans so much. The elephants (regarded as noble and representing the state) were expected to win by tossing the tiger (regarded as wild and representing disorder) repeatedly into the air. The fact that the tigers were often tied to a stake or attacked by several elephants at once must have lengthened the odds against them. (In Vietnam it was reported that tigers sometimes had their claws removed and jaws sewn together.) Despite the undoubted might of Ayutthaya and the absolute power that lay within each monarch's grasp, kings were not, in the main, able to name their successors. Blood was not an effective guarantee to kingship – and a strong competitor could easily usurp a rival, even though he might – on paper – have a better claim to the throne. As a result, the history of Ayutthaya is peppered with court intrigues, bloody succession struggles and rival claims.

16th-18th centuries (Burmese invasion)

During this period, the fortunes of the Ayutthayan Kingdom were bound up with those of Burma. Over a 220-year period, the Burmese invaded on no less than six occasions. The first time was in 1548 when the Burmese king of Pegu, Tabengshweti, encircled the capital. King Mahachakrapat only survived the ensuing battle when one of his wives drove her elephant in front of an approaching warrior. Elephants figured heavily in war and diplomacy during the Ayutthayan period: Tabengshweti justified his invasion by pointing out that he had no white elephants, the holiest of beasts (the Buddha's last reincarnation before his enlightenment was as a white elephant). The Ayutthayan king meanwhile had a whole stable of them, and was not willing to part with even one. Although this attack failed, in 1569, King Bayinnaung mounted another invasion and plundered the city, making Ayutthaya a vassal state. When the Burmese withdrew to Pegu, they left a ravaged countryside devoid of people, and large areas of riceland returned to scrub and forest. But a mere 15 years later, Prince Naresuan re-established Thai sovereignty, and began to lay the foundations for a new golden age in which Ayutthaya would be more powerful and prosperous than ever before.

17th century (commercial and diplomatic expansion)

The 17th century saw a period of intense commercial contact with the Dutch, English and French. In 1608, Ayutthaya sent a diplomatic mission to the Netherlands and in 1664 a trading treaty was concluded with the Dutch. Even as early as the 17th century, Thailand had a flourishing prostitution industry. In the 1680s an official was given a monopoly of prostitution in the capital; he used 600 women to generate considerable state revenues. The kings of Ayutthaya also made considerable use of foreigners as advisers and ministers at the court. The most influential such family was founded by two Persian brothers, who arrived at the beginning of the 17th century. However, the best known was the Greek adventurer Constantine Phaulcon, who began his life in the East as a mere cabin boy with the East India Company and rose to become one of King Narai's (1656-1688) closest advisers and one of the kingdom's most influential officials before being executed in 1688. He was implicated in a plot with the French against King Narai and his execution heralded 100 years of relative isolation as the Thais became wary of, and avoided close relations with, the West.

18th century (Ayutthaya's zenith)

The height of Ayutthaya's power and glory is often associated with the reign of King Boromkot (literally, 'the King in the urn [awaiting cremation]', as he was the last sovereign to be honoured in this way). Boromkot ruled from 1733 to 1758 and he fulfilled many of the imagined pre-requisites of a great king: he promoted Buddhism and ruled effectively over a vast territory. But, in retrospect, signs of imperial senility were beginning to materialize even as Ayutthaya's glory was approaching its zenith. In particular, King Boromkot's sons began to exert their ambitions. Prince Senaphithak, the eldest, went so far as to have some of the king's officials flogged; in retaliation, one of the officials revealed that the prince had been having an affair with one of Boromkot's three queens. He admitted to the liaison and was flogged to death, along with his lover.

The feud with Burma was renewed in 1760 when the Burmese King Alaungpaya invaded Thailand. His attack was repulsed after one of the siege guns exploded, seriously injuring the Burmese king. He died soon afterwards during the arduous march back to Pegu. Three years later his successor, King Hsinbyushin, raised a vast army and took Chiang Mai, Lamphun and Luang Prabang (Laos). By 1765, the Burmese were ready to mount a second assault on Ayutthaya. Armies approached from the north and west and at the beginning of 1766 met up outside the city, from where they laid siege to the capital. King Suriyamarin offered to surrender, but King Hsinbyushin would hear nothing of it. The city fell after a year, in 1767. David Wyatt, in *Thailand: A short history*, wrote: "The Burmese wrought awful desolation. They raped, pillaged and plundered and led tens of thousands of captives away to Burma. They put the torch to everything flammable and even hacked at images of the Buddha for the gold with which they were coated. King Suriyamarin is said to have fled the city in a small boat and starved to death 10 days later."

The city was too damaged to be renovated for a second time, and the focus of the Thai state moved southwards once again – to Thonburi, and from there to Bangkok.

Bangkok and the Rattanakosin period

After the sacking of Ayutthaya, **General Taksin** moved the capital 74 km south to Thonburi, on the other bank of the Chao Pharaya River from modern day Bangkok. Taksin's original name was Sin. Proving himself an adept administrator, he was appointed Lord of Tak (a city in the upper central plain), or Phraya Tak. Hence his name Tak-sin. From Thonburi, Taksin successfully fought Burmese invasions, until the stress caused his mental health to deteriorate to the extent that he was forced to abdicate in 1782. A European visitor wrote in a letter that, "He [Taksin] passed all his time in prayer, fasting, and meditation, in order by these means to be able to fly through the air." He became madder by the month and on 6 April 1782 a group of rebels marched on Thonburi, captured the king and asked one of Taksin's generals, Chao Phya Chakri, to assume the throne. The day that Chao Phya Chakri became King Ramathobodi, 6 April, remains a public holiday in Thailand – Chakri Day – and marks the beginning of the current Chakri Dynasty. Worried about the continuing Burmese threat, Rama I (as Chao Phya Chakri is known) moved his capital to the opposite, and safer, bank of the Chao Phraya River, founded Bangkok and began the process of consolidating his kingdom. By the end of the century, the Burmese threat had dissipated, and the Siamese were once again in a position to lead the Tai world.

19th century (Rama II's reign)

During Rama II's reign (1809-1824), a new threat emerged to replace the Burmese: that of the Europeans. In 1821, the English *East India Company* sent John Crawfurd as an envoy to Siam to open up trading relations. Although the king and his court remained unreservedly opposed to unfettered trade, Crawfurd's visit served to impress upon those more prescient Siamese where the challenges of the 19th century would lie.

Rama II's death and succession illustrates the dangers inherent in having a claim to the throne of Siam, even in the 19th century. The court chronicles record that in 1824 Prince Mongkut (the second son of Rama II) was ordained as a monk because the death of a royal elephant indicated it was an 'ill-omened time'. Historians believe that Rama II, realizing his death was imminent, wished to protect the young prince by bundling him off to a monastery, where the robes of a monk might protect him from court intrigues.

Rama III was the son of Rama II by a junior wife. When King Rama II died he was chosen by the accession council over Mongkut because the latter was in the monkhood. Rama III's reign (1824-1851) saw an invasion by an army led by the Lao King Anou. In 1827, Anou took Nakhon Ratchasima on the edge of the central plain and was within striking distance of Bangkok before being defeated. After their victory, the Siamese marched on Vientiane, plundering the city and subjugating the surrounding countryside. In 1829, King Anou himself was captured and transported to Bangkok, where he was displayed to the public in a cage. Anou died shortly after this humiliation – some say of shame, others say of self-administered poison. Before he died he is said to have laid a curse on the Chakri dynasty, swearing that never again would a Chakri king set foot on Lao soil. None has, and when the present King Bhumibol attended the opening of the Thai-Lao Friendship bridge over the Mekong in 1994, he did so from a sand bar in the middle of the river.

There were also ructions at the court in Bangkok: in 1848 Prince Rakrannaret (a distant relative of Rama III's) was found guilty of bribery and corruption and, just for good measure, homosexuality and treason as well. Rama III had him beaten to death with sandalwood clubs, in time-honoured Thai fashion.

The 19th century was a dangerous time for Siam. Southeast Asia was being methodically divided between Britain, France and Holland as they scrambled for colonial territories. The same fate might have befallen Siam, had it not been blessed with two brilliant kings: **King Mongkut (Rama IV – 1851-1868)** and **King Chulalongkorn (Rama V – 1868-1910)**.

King Mongkut (the second son of Rama II) was a brilliant scholar. He learnt English and Latin and when he sat his oral Pali examination, he performed brilliantly. Indeed, his 27 years in a monastery allowed him to study the religious texts to such depth that he concluded that all Siamese ordinations were invalid. He established a new sect based upon the stricter Mon teachings, an order that became known as the *Thammayutika* or 'Ordering Adhering to the Dharma'. To distinguish themselves from those 'fallen' monks who made up most of the Sangha, they wore their robes with both of their shoulders covered. Mongkut derisively called the main Thai order – the *Mahanikai* – the 'Order of Long-standing Habit'.

But Mongkut was not an other-worldly monk with scholarly inclinations. He was a rational, pragmatic man who well appreciated the economic and military might of the Europeans. He recognized that if his kingdom was to survive he would have to acquiesce to the colonial powers, rather than try to resist them. He did not accede to the throne until he was 47, and it is said that during his monastic studies he came to realize that if China, the Middle Kingdom, had to bow to Western pressure, then he would have to do the same.

He set about modernizing his country, along with the support of other modern-thinking princes. He established a modern ship-building industry, trained his troops in European methods and studied Western medicine. Most importantly, in 1855, he signed the **Bowring Treaty** with Britain, giving British merchants access to the Siamese market, and setting in train a process of agricultural commercialization and the clearing of the vast central plains for rice cultivation. As David Wyatt wrote: "At the stroke of a pen, old Siam faced the thrust of a surging economic and political power with which they were unprepared to contend or compete." Mongkut's meeting with Sir John Bowring illustrates the lengths to which he went to meet the West on its own terms: he received the British envoy and offered him port and cigars from his own hand, an unheard of action in Thai circles.

It would seem that King Mongkut and **Sir John Bowring** were men of like mind. Both were scholars who believed in the power of rational argument. Bowring was a close friend of the philosophers Jeremy Bentham and John Stuart Mill, and he wrote a number of articles for the *Westminster Review*. He was a radical reformer, in favour of free trade and prison reform and bitterly opposed to slavery. He was a member of the House of Commons for six years, governor of Hong Kong, and Her Majesty's Consul in Canton (China). He was a remarkable man, just as Mongkut was a remarkable man, and his achievements during a long 80-year life were enough to satisfy a dozen ambitious men. It seems that Bowring used a mixture of veiled military force and rational argument to encourage Mongkut to sign the Bowring Treaty, perhaps the single most important treaty in Thailand's history. Bowring's account of his visit, the two volume *The kingdom and people of Siam*, published in 1857, is a remarkably perceptive work, especially given the brevity of Bowring's visit to Siam. As David Wyatt wrote in a reprint of the work (Oxford University Press, 1977), the book is undoubtedly "the finest account of Thailand at the middle of the 19th century, when it stood on the threshold of revolutionary change".

Unfortunately, in the West, Mongkut is not known for the skilful diplomacy that kept at bay expansionist nations considerably more powerful than his own, but for his characterization in the film *The King and I* (in which he is played by Yul Brynner). Poorly adapted from Anna Leonowens' own distorted accounts of her period as governess in the Siamese court, both the book and the film offend the Thai people. According to contemporary accounts, Mrs Leonowens was a bad-tempered lady obviously given to flights of fantasy. She never became a trusted confidant of King Mongkut, who scarcely needed her limited skills, and there is certainly no evidence to indicate that he was attracted to her sexually.

King Mongkut died on 1 October 1868 and was succeeded by his 15-year-old son **Chulalongkorn**. However, for the next decade a regent controlled affairs of state, and it was not until 1873, when Chulalongkorn was crowned for a second time, that he could begin to mould the country according to his own vision. The young king quickly showed himself to be a reformer like his father – for in essence Mongkut had only just begun the process of modernization. Chulalongkorn set about updating the monarchy by establishing ministries and ending the practice of prostration. He also accelerated the process of economic development by constructing roads, railways, schools and hospitals. The opium trade was regulated, court procedures streamlined and slavery finally completely abolished in 1905. Although a number of princes were sent abroad to study – Prince Rajebuidirekrit went to Oxford – Chulalongkorn had to also rely on foreign advisors to help him undertake these reforms. In total he employed 549 foreigners – the largest number being British, but also Dutch, Germans, French and Belgians. Chulalongkorn even held fancy dress parties at New Year and visited Europe twice. These visits included trips to the poor East End of London and showed Chulalongkorn that for all the power of Britain and France, they were still unable to raise the living standards of a large part of the population much above subsistence levels.

These reforms were not introduced without difficulty. The *Hua Boran* – or 'The Ancients' – as the king derogatorily called them, strongly resisted the changes and in late December 1874 Prince Wichaichan attempted to take the royal palace and usurp the king. The plot was thwarted at the last possible moment, but it impressed upon Chulalongkorn that reform could only come slowly. Realizing he had run ahead of many of his subjects in his zeal for change, he reversed some of his earlier reforms, and toned-down others. Nevertheless, Siam remained on the path of modernization – albeit progressing at a rather slower pace. As during Mongkut's reign, Chulalongkorn also managed to keep the colonial powers at bay. Although the king himself played a large part in placating the Europeans by skilful diplomacy and by presenting an image of urbane sophistication, he was helped in this respect by a brilliant minister of foreign affairs, his son, Prince Devawongse (1858-1923), who controlled Siam's foreign relations for 38 years. Devawongse looked into European systems of government with the aim of reforming Siam's administration and even attended the celebrations marking Queen Victoria's 50 years on the throne of Great Britain in 1887. During his time controlling Siam's foreign affairs, a new administrative system and a new system of ministries was introduced to extend Bangkok's power to the outer provinces.

The fundamental weakness of the Siamese state, in the face of the European powers, was illustrated in the dispute with France over Laos. Despite attempts by Prince Devawongse to manufacture a compromise, the French forced Siam to cede Laos to France in 1893 and to pay compensation – even though they had little claim to the territory. (The land on the far banks of the Mekong came under Thai suzerainty. The French annexed Laos on some rather dubious evidence that Vietnam – which they controlled – claimed suzerainty over Laos.) As it is said, power grows out of the barrel of a gun, and Chulalongkorn could not compete with France in military might. After this humiliating climb-down, the king essentially retired from public life, broken in spirit and health. In 1909, the British chipped away at more of Siam's territory, gaining rights of suzerainty over the Malay states of Kelantan, Terengganu, Kedah and Perlis. In total, Siam relinquished nearly 500,000 sq km of territory to maintain the integrity of the core of the kingdom. King Chulalongkorn died on 24 October 1910, sending the whole nation into deep and genuine mourning.

20th century
The kings that were to follow Mongkut and Chulalongkorn could not have been expected to have had such illustrious, brilliant reigns. Absolute kingship was becoming increasingly incompatible with the demands of the modern world, and the kings of Thailand were resisting the inevitable. Rama VI, **King Vajiravudh** (1910-1925), second son of Chulalongkorn, was educated at Oxford and Sandhurst Military Academy and seemed

well prepared for kingship. However, he squandered much of the wealth built up by Chulalongkorn and ruled in a rather heavy-handed, uncoordinated style. He did try to inculcate a sense of 'nation' with his slogan 'nation, religion, king', but seemed more interested in Western theatre and literature than in guiding Siam through a difficult period in its history. He died at the age of only 44, leaving an empty treasury.

Like his older brother, **King Prajadhipok** (Rama VII – 1925-1935), was educated in Europe: at Eton, the Woolwich Military Academy and at the École Supérieure de Guerre in France. But he never expected to become king and was thrust onto the throne at a time of great strain. Certainly, he was more careful with the resources that his treasury had to offer, but could do little to prevent the country being seriously affected by the Great Depression of the 1930s. The price of rice, the country's principal export, declined by two-thirds and over the same two-year period (1930-1932) land values in Bangkok fell by 80%. The economy was in crisis and the government appeared to have no idea how to cope. In February 1932, King Prajadhipok told a group of military officers:

"The financial war is a very hard one indeed. Even experts contradict one another until they become hoarse. Each offers a different suggestion. I myself know nothing at all about finances, and all I can do is listen to the opinions of others and choose the best. I have never experienced such a hardship; therefore if I have made a mistake I really deserve to be excused by the officials and people of Siam."

The people, both the peasantry and the middle class, were dissatisfied by the course of events and with their declining economic position. But neither group was sufficiently united to mount a threat to the king and his government. Nevertheless, Prajadhipok was worried: there was a prophesy linked to Rama I's younger sister Princess Narinthewi, which predicted that the Chakri Dynasty would survive for 150 years and end on 6 April 1932.

The Revolution of 1932
The date itself passed without incident, but just 12 weeks later on 24 June a clique of soldiers and civilians staged a **coup d'état**, while the king was holidaying at the seaside resort of Hua Hin. This episode is often called the Revolution of 1932, but it was not in any sense a revolution involving a large rump of the people. It was orchestrated by a small élite, essentially for the élite. The king accepted the terms offered to him, and wrote:

"I have received the letter in which you invite me to return to Bangkok as a constitutional monarch. For the sake of peace; and in order to save useless bloodshed; to avoid confusion and loss to the country; and, more, because I have already considered making this change myself, I am willing to cooperate in the establishment of a constitution under which I am willing to serve."

Reign of Prince Ananda Mahidol
However, King Prajadhipok had great difficulty adapting to his lesser role and, falling out with the military, he abdicated in favour of his young nephew, Prince Ananda Mahidol, in 1935. The prince at the time was only 10 years old, and at school in Switzerland, so the newly created National Assembly appointed two princes to act as regents. From this point, until after the Second World War, the monarchy was only partially operative. Ananda was out of the country for most of the time, and the civilian government took centre stage. Ananda was not to physically reoccupy the throne until December 1945 and just six months later he was found dead in bed, a bullet through his head. The circumstances behind his death have never been satisfactorily explained and it remains a subject on which Thais are not openly permitted to speculate.

Phibun Songkhram and Pridi Panomyong

While the monarchy receded from view, the civilian government was going through the intrigues and power struggles that were to become such a feature of the future politics of the country. The two key men at this time were the army officer Phibun Songkhram and the left-wing idealist lawyer Pridi Panomyong. Between them they managed to dominate Thai politics until 1957.

When **Prime Minister Pridi Panomyong** tried to introduce a socialist economic programme in 1933, pushing for the state control of the means of production, he was forced into exile in Europe. This is often seen as the beginning of the tradition of authoritarian, right-wing rule in Thailand, although to be fair, Pridi's vision of economic and political reform was poorly thought through and rather romantic. Nonetheless, with Pridi in Paris – at least for a while – it gave the more conservative elements in the government the chance to promulgate an anti-communist law, and thereby to usher in a period of ultra-nationalism. Anti-Chinese propaganda became more shrill, with some government positions being reserved for ethnic Tais. In 1938 the populist writer Luang Wichit compared the Chinese in Siam with the Jews in Germany, and thought that Hitler's policies might be worth considering for his own country.

This shift in policy can be linked to the influence of one man: Luang Phibun Songkhram. Born of humble parents in 1897, he worked his way up through the army ranks and then into politics. He became Prime Minister in 1938 and his enduring influence makes him the most significant figure in 20th century Thai politics. Under his direction, Siam became more militaristic, xenophobic, as well as 'religiously' nationalistic, avidly pursuing the reconversion of Siamese Christians back to Buddhism. As if to underline these developments, in 1939 Siam adopted a new name: Thailand. Phibun justified this change on the grounds that it would indicate that the country was controlled by Thais and not by the Chinese or any other group.

Second World War

During the Second World War, Phibun Songkhram sided with the Japanese who he felt sure would win. He saw the war as an opportunity to take back some of the territories lost to the French (particularly) and the British. In 1940, Thai forces invaded Laos and Western Cambodia. A year later, the Japanese used the kingdom as a launching pad for their assaults on the British in Malaya and Burma. Thailand had little choice but to declare war on the Allies and to agree a military alliance with Japan in December 1941. As allies of the Japanese, Phibun's ambassadors were instructed to declare war on Britain and the United States. However, the ambassador in Washington, Seni Pramoj, refused to deliver the declaration (he considered it illegal) and Thailand never formally declared war on the United States. In Thailand itself, Pridi, who had returned as regent to the young monarch King Ananda, helped to organize the Thai resistance – the Free Thai Movement. They received help from the US Office of Strategic Services (OSS) and the British Force 136, and also from many Thais. As the tide of the war turned in favour of the Allies, so Prime Minister Phibun was forced to resign. He spent a short time in gaol in Japan, but was allowed to return to Thailand in 1947.

Post-war Thailand

After the war, Seni Pramoj, Thailand's ambassador in the USA, became Prime Minister. He was soon followed by Pridi Panomyong as Prime Minister, who had gathered a good deal of support due to the role he played during the conflict. However, in 1946 King Ananda was mysteriously found shot dead in his royal apartments and Pridi was implicated in a plot. He was forced to resign, so enabling Phibun to become Prime Minister once again – a post he kept until 1957. Phibun's fervent anti-Communism quickly gained support in the USA, who contributed generous amounts of aid as the country became a front-line state in the battle against the 'red tide' that seemed to be engulfing Asia. Phibun's closest brush with death occurred in June 1951. He was leading a ceremony on board a dredge, the *Manhattan*, when he was taken prisoner during a military coup and transferred to the Thai navy flagship *Sri Ayutthaya*. The airforce and army stayed loyal to Phibun, and planes bombed the ship. As it sank, the Prime Minister was able to swim to safety. The attempted coup resulted in 1200 dead – mostly civilians. For the navy, it has meant that ever since it has been treated as the junior member of the armed forces, receiving far less resources than the army and airforce.

Prime Minister Phibun Songkhram was deposed following a coup d'état in 1957 and was replaced by **General Sarit Thanarat**. General Sarit established the National Economic Development Board (now the National Economic and Social Development Board) and introduced Thailand's first five-year national development plan in 1961. He was a tough and uncompromising leader, and following his death in 1963 was replaced by another General – **Thanom Kitticachorn**. With the war in Indochina escalating, Thanom allowed US planes to be based in Thailand, from where they flew bombing sorties over the Lao panhandle and Vietnam. In 1969 a general election was held, which Thanom won, but as the political situation in Thailand deteriorated, so Prime Minister Thanom declared martial law. However, unlike his predecessors Sarit and Phibun, Thanom could not count on the loyalty of all elements within the armed forces, and although he tried to take the strongman – or *nak laeng* – approach, his administration always had a certain frailty about it. In addition, historian David Wyatt argues that developments in Thai society – particularly an emergent middle-class and an increasingly combative body of students – made controlling the country from the centre rather harder than it had been over the previous decades.

The October Revolution

It was Thailand's students who precipitated probably the single most tumultuous event since the Revolution of 1932. The student body felt that Thanom had back-tracked and restricted the evolution of a more open political system in the country. In June 1973 they began to demonstrate against the government, printing highly critical pamphlets and calling for the resignation of Thanom. A series of demonstrations, often centred on Sanaam Luang near the radical Thammasat University and the Grand Palace, brought crowds of up to 500,000 onto the streets. During the demonstrations, Thanom lost the support of the army: the Commander-in-Chief, General Krit Sivara, was unwilling to send his troops out to quell the disturbances, while Thanom, apparently, was quite willing to kill thousands if necessary. With the army unwilling to confront the students, and with the king – crucially – also apparently siding with Thanom's army opponents, he was forced to resign from the premiership and fled the country.

David Wyatt wrote of the **October revolution**: "In many important respects, the events of October 1973 deserved far more the name *revolution* than either the events of 1932 or the authoritarian program of Sarit. They brought about an end to one-man, authoritarian rule; and if they did not bring an end to the military role in politics, then they at least signalled a new consciousness of the necessity of sharing political power more widely than had ever been the case in the past."

The October revolution ushered in a period of turbulent democratic government in Thailand, the first such period in the country's history. It was an exciting time: radical scholars could openly speak and publish, students could challenge the establishment, labour unions could organize and demonstrate, and leftist politicians could make their views known. But it was also a period of political instability. While there had been just five prime ministers between 1948 and 1973, the three years following 1973 saw the rapid coming and going of another four: Sanya Dharmasakti, Seni Pramoj, Kukrit Pramoj and Seni Pramoj. This instability was reinforced by the feeling among the middle classes that the students were pushing things too far. The fall of Vietnam, Cambodia and Laos to Communism left many Thais wondering whether they would be the next 'domino' to topple. This gave an opening for rightist groups to garner support, and anti-Communist organizations like the Red Gaurs and the Village Scouts gained in influence and began, with the support and connivance of the police, to harass and sometimes to murder left-wingers. "Violence, vituperation, and incivility" – as Wyatt wrote – "were now a part of public life as they never had been before in Thailand."

Thammaset University Massacre

This was the background that led the army to feel impelled to step in once again. However, the trigger for the appalling events of October 1976 was the return of former Prime Minister Thanom from exile, who joined the sangha and became a monk. Installed in a Bangkok monastery, Thanom was visited by members of the royal family. The students took this as royal recognition of a man who had led the country into violence and to the edge of civil war. Demonstrations broke out in Bangkok. This time, though, the students were not able to face down the forces of the Right. Newspapers printed pictures apparently showing the Crown Prince being burnt in effigy by students at Thammasat, and right-wing groups, along with the police and the army, advanced on the university on 6 October. Details of the hours that followed are hazy. However, it seems clear that an orgy of killing ensued. With the situation rapidly deteriorating, the army stepped in and imposed martial law. Tanin Kraivixien was installed as Prime Minister, to be replaced the following year by Kriangsak Chomanan.

In 1996, on the 20th anniversary of the massacre, newspapers in Thailand were filled with the reminiscences of those from both sides who were involved. Such was the coverage of the event – far more detailed and honest than anything at the time – that it was almost as if the Thai nation were engaged in a collective catharsis, cauterizing the wounds of 20 years earlier. Yet in a way the debate over the massacre said as much about the present as the past. Kasian Tejapira, one of the student leaders involved, and by 1996 a university lecturer, suggested that the anniversary was an opportunity "to redefine the meaning of Thai identity – one that is anti-elitist and not conservative; one that was put down at Thammasat 20 years ago". The former student activists are now in positions of power and influence. Some are wealthy businessmen, others university lecturers, while more still are involved in politics. Most seem to have retained their commitment to building a more just society. It must be depressing for them to find the students of today more interested in fashions and consumer goods than in social justice. In a way that – in microcosm – is the problem with Thailand's political culture: too much money and too few ethics.

The 1976 massacre was a shot in the arm for the **Communist Party of Thailand (CPT)**. Left-wing intellectuals and many students, feeling that they could no longer influence events through the political system, fled to the jungle and joined the CPT. The victories of the Communists in neighbouring Indochina also reinforced the sense that ultimately the

CPT would emerge victorious. By the late 1970s the ranks of the party had swelled to around 14,000 armed guerrillas, who controlled large areas of the northeast, north and south. However, with the ascendancy of Prem Tinsulanond to the premiership in 1980 and a rapidly changing global political environment, the CPT fragmented and quickly lost support. Its leaders were divided between support for China and the Cambodian Khmer Rouge on the one hand, and the Soviet Union and Vietnam on the other. When the government announced an amnesty in 1980, many of the students who had fled into the forests and hills following the riots of 1973 returned to mainstream politics, exhausted and disenchanted with revolutionary life. In true Thai style, they were largely forgiven and re-integrated into society. But those who died on Sanaam Luang and in the streets leading off it have never been acknowledged, and in many cases their parents were never informed that they had been killed. Nor were they allowed to collect their children's bodies. As the Thai historian Thongchai Winichakul lamented on the 20th anniversary of the massacre in 1996, this showed the extent to which Thai society still valued national stability over individual rights: "Life is more significant than the nation."

Prem Tinsulanond presided over the most stable period in Thai politics since the end of the Second World War. He finally resigned in 1988, and by then Thailand – or so most people thought – was beginning to outgrow the habit of military intervention in civilian politics. Chatichai Choonhaven replaced Prem after general elections in 1988, by which time the country was felt to be more stable and economically prosperous than at any time in recent memory. During his reign, the present King Bhumibol has played a crucial role in maintaining social stability, while the political system has been in turmoil. He is highly revered by his subjects, and has considerable power to change the course of events. There are essentially two views on the role of the king in contemporary Thailand. The general view is that he has influence far beyond that which his constitutional position permits, but that he is careful not to over exercise that power. The king, in short, is his own man and acts in the best interests of the Thai people. The alternative view is that after his coronation, influential courtiers and generals tried to diminish the power of the king by making him a semi-divine figurehead and surrounding him in protocol. The king became a tool used by right-wing dictators and the army to justify their authoritarian ways. (For further background on the king, see the box on page 988.)

From massacre to crisis: 1991-1997

The widely held belief that the Thai political system had come of age proved ill-founded. In February 1991, with the Prime Minister daring to challenge the armed forces, General Suchinda Kraprayoon staged a bloodless coup d'état and ousted the democratically elected government of Chatichai Choonhavan. The last decade of the 20th century was a pretty eventful one for Thailand. At the end of the year, egged on by two generals-turned-politicians – Chamlong Srimuang and Chaovalit Yongchaiyut – 100,000 people gathered in Bangkok to protest against a Suchinda and military-imposed constitution. Elections in March 1992 produced no clear winner and General Suchinda tearfully agreed to become premier – something he had previously promised he would not do. Chamlong Srimuang took this as his cue to call his supporters onto the streets and announced he was going on hunger strike. Tens of thousands of people gathered around the Parliament buildings and Sanaam Luang, near the Grand Palace. Suchinda buckled under this weight of public outrage and appeared to agree to their demands. But Suchinda then went back on his word, and in response tens of thousands of demonstrators returned to the streets of Bangkok. Suchinda called in the army and scores of people were killed.

Three days after the confrontation between the army and the demonstrators, **King Bhumibol** ordered both Suchinda and opposition leader Chamlong – who had to be released from gaol for the meeting – to his palace. There, television cameras were waiting to witness Suchinda's public humiliation. He and Chamlong prostrated themselves on the floor while the king lectured them, asking rhetorically: "What is the use of victory when the winner stands on wreckage?" Immediately afterwards, the army and the demonstrators withdrew from the streets. On Friday, Suchinda offered his resignation to the king, and on Saturday, less than one week after the killing began, Suchinda Kraprayoon fled the country. Suchinda accepted responsibility for the deaths.

After the riots of May 1992, and General Suchinda's humiliating climb-down, Anand Panyarachun was appointed interim prime minister. New elections were set for September, which the Democrat Party won. **Chuan Leekpai** was appointed 1992's fourth prime minister. Chuan, a mild-mannered Southerner from a poor background, gained his law degree while living as a novice monk in a monastery. Never one for flashiness and quick fixes, Chuan became known as Chuan Chuengcha – or 'Chuan the slowmover'. He may have been slow but his government lasted more than 2½ years, making it the longest serving elected government in Thai history, before he was forced to resign over a land scandal.

The Chart Thai Party, led by **Banharn Silpa-Archa**, won the largest number of seats – and formed a coalition government of seven parties. Bangkok's intelligentsia were horrified. Like Chuan, Banharn came from a poor background and was a self-made man. But in almost all other respects, Banharn and Chuan could not have been more different. Banharn's Chart Thai was associated with the military junta and was viewed as corrupt. As British political scientist Duncan McCargo explained: "There's no movement for [true] democracy. There's nothing but the money, and the results [of the election] bear that out." Two Chart Thai candidates in the elections were even accused of involvement in the narcotics trade. Thanong Wongwan was indicted in California with drug trafficking, where he was reportedly known as 'Thai Tony', and the party's deputy leader Vatana Asavahame had a visa request turned down by the US authorities on similar grounds. Banharn was even accused of plagiarism in his Master's thesis, which is said to bear a striking similarity to a paper by his academic advisor – who Banharn appointed to his cabinet.

While the press may have hated Banharn – *The Nation* stated that "the only way for 1996 to be a good year is for the Banharn government to go" – he survived because he was an arch populist politician. He used to step from his limousine and order local officials to mend roads, provide electricity, or improve health services. Here was a man getting things done, sweeping away red tape, and putting the interests of ordinary people first. But while Banharn might have been able to ignore the press, he couldn't ignore the king. In late summer 1995, Banharn's government found itself explicitly criticized by the palace when the king highlighted government failures to address Bangkok's infrastructural mess and its shortcomings in dealing with serious flooding. Ministers, the king said, only "talk, talk, talk and argue, argue, argue". Taking the king's cue, the great and the good including businessmen, influential civil servants, four former Bank of Thailand governors, opposition politicians (of course), even his own daughter, demanded that he step down. On 21 September 1996 Banharn announced his resignation. The king dissolved parliament.

The elections of 17 November 1996 were close, with **Chaovalit Yongchaiyudh's** New Aspirations Party (NAP) just managing to win the largest number of seats, and after the usual bickering he managed to stitch together a six-party coalition. Chaovalit, a canny 64-year-old former army commander-in-chief, never completely managed to hide his ambition to become premier. He was an old-style patronage politician who depended on his links with the army and on handing out lucrative concessions to his supporters.

The mid-1990s were a watershed in contemporary Thai history. On 18 July 1995 the Princess Mother (the king's mother) died. After the king she was probably the most revered person in the country. Born a commoner and trained as a nurse, she married a prince. Their two sons, Mahidol and Bhumipol, unexpectedly became kings (Mahidol for only a short time before his tragic death). Her funeral in 1996 was a grandiose affair. That year also saw the 50th anniversary of King Bhumibol's accession to the throne and the country threw a massive party. The celebrations were as much a mark of Thailand's coming of age as of the king's golden jubilee and no expense was spared. Both events – the Princess Mother's funeral and the king's jubilee – were, for those so inclined, omens. The night before the funeral there was an unseasonable rainstorm; and during the procession of royal boats on the Chao Phraya it also poured. The king's boat was washed off course and had to be rescued. As it turned out, 1996 was the last year when money was no object.

Modern Thailand

Bust, boom and bust

As Thailand entered the 21st century and the third millennium, the country was also, rather shakily, recovering from the deepest contraction of the economy since the 1930s. Until July 1997, everything was hunky-dory in Thailand. Or that, at least, is what the World Bank and most business people and pundits thought. The kingdom's economy was expanding at close to double-digit rates and the country was being showered with strings of congratulatory epithets. It was a 'miracle' economy, an Asian 'tiger' or 'dragon' ready to pounce on an unsuspecting world. Thailand was the 'Cinderella' of Southeast Asia – a beautiful woman long disguised beneath shabby clothes – and academics and journalists were turning out books with glowing titles like *Thailand's Boom* (1996), *Thailand's Turn: Profile of a New Dragon* (1992) and *Thailand's Macro-economic Miracle* (1996). Wealth was growing, poverty falling and Bangkok was chock-full of designer shops, meeting the consumer needs of a growing – and increasingly hedonistic – middle-class.

Of course even in the heady days of double-digit economic growth there were those who questioned the direction and rapidity of the country's development, and the social, economic and environmental tensions and conflicts that arose. By the mid-1990s Bangkok was overstretched, its transport system on the verge of collapse and the air barely fit to breath. While a few breezed from boutique to club in their air-conditioned Mercedes, around one million people were living in slum conditions in the capital. Deforestation had become so rampant, and so uncontrolled, that the government felt impelled to impose a nationwide logging ban in 1989. Even the kingdom's national parks were being systematically poached and encroached. In the poor northeastern region, incomes had stagnated, causing social tensions to become more acute and millions to migrate to the capital each dry season in a desperate search for work. In some villages in the north, meanwhile, AIDS had already spread to the extent that scarcely a household was not touched by the epidemic.

Most of these problems, though, were viewed by many analysts as side effects of healthy economic growth – problems to be managed through prudent planning and not reasons to doubt the wisdom of the country's broader development strategy.

Economic crisis

Then everything went horribly wrong. The local currency, the baht, went into freefall, the stock market crashed, unemployment more than doubled, and the economy contracted. Bankrupt business people, the *nouveau pauvre*, cashed in their Mercedes, and wives were put on strict spending diets. Almost overnight, apparently prescient commentators who had remained strangely silent during the years of growth were offering their own interpretations of Thailand's fall from economic grace. A distinct whiff of schadenfreude filled the air. Epithet writers went back to their computers and came up with titles like the 'Asian contagion', the 'Asian mirage', 'Frozen miracles' and 'Tigers lose their grip'. In Thailand itself, locals began to talk of the *Thaitanic* as it sank faster than the doomed liner.

The financial crisis of July 1997 quickly became a much wider economic crisis. The failure of the economy was, in turn, interpreted as a failure of government. Prime Minister Chaovalit Yongchaiyut tried to sound convincing in the face of a collapsing currency and a contracting economy, but he resigned before the year was out. Chuan Leekpai, his successor, manfully struggled to put things to rights but after little more than two years at the helm was trounced in a general election in early 2001 by telecoms billionaire Thaksin Shinawatra. Perhaps most importantly in the long term, while Thailand was on the economic ropes, Parliament approved a radically new constitution aimed at cleaning up the country's notoriously corrupt political system.

In the 1970s some scholars suggested that the country could be encapsulated by reference to the 'four Rs': rice, rivers, religion and royalty. Today, computer parts, jewellery and garments all exceed rice in terms of export value. Highways have replaced rivers as arteries of communication and religion has become so commercialized that Thais have coined a word to describe it: *Buddhapanich*. Only the king has stood head and shoulders above the fray, the one thread of continuity in a country changing and re-inventing itself with bewildering speed.

'Traditional' Thai life is becoming the stuff of history as modernity engulfs people and places. But just as the recent past becomes sepia-tinted, so the future becomes less compelling. The country's green movement has long lamented the environmental costs of economic growth, and sociologists have highlighted the wasted youth, the drug culture and the underclass as evidence of the corrosive social effects of modernization. Tourism has brought its own problems as popular islands creak under the pressure of growing numbers of visitors. Some educated Thais blame tourists for the explosion of the sex industry and the proliferation of AIDS. Where Thailand is headed as it continues its roller-coaster ride is as much a mystery as a challenge.

Politics during an economic crisis: 1997-2000

Chaovalit was, in a sense, unlucky to take over the reins of government when he did. Economic conditions were a cause for concern in the country in late 1996, but no one – scholar or pundit – predicted the economic meltdown that was just a few months away. He appointed the well-respected Amnuay Virawan as Finance Minister. But the collapse of the baht, the Bangkok stock market, the property and finance sectors, and a haemorrhaging loss of domestic and international confidence created conditions that were impossible to manage. Even so, his performance was hardly memorable. As *The Economist* tartly put it, "he dithered when decisions were needed, bumbled when clear words might have helped, and smiled benignly while the economy got worse". The central bank spent a staggering US$10bn trying to defend the baht's peg to the US dollar, and interest rates were raised to 1300% for offshore borrowers in an ultimately futile attempt to keep the speculators at bay. The baht was allowed to float on 2 July, ending 13 years during which it had been pegged to the US dollar. Two cabinet reshuffles during August did little to stem the criticism of Chaovalit and his administration, and there was talk of military intervention – though the army commander-in-chief quickly distanced himself from any such suggestion. In September, Chaovalit used his promised support for a vote on a new constitution (see below) to defeat a no-confidence motion. Even so, the end of Chaovalit's administration was in sight. On 7 November, Chaovalit resigned as Prime Minister after less than a year in power.

Following Chaovalit's resignation, **Chuan Leekpai**, leader of the Democrat Party, stitched together a new seven-party, 208-person coalition and became Prime Minister for the second time. Given talk of military intervention a few months earlier, it was a relief to many that Thailand had achieved a peaceful change of government. The key question, however, was whether Chuan could do any better than Chaovalit, particularly given the mixed make-up of his coalition government. Chuan and his finance minister, Tarrin Nimmanahaeminda – the year's fourth – vigorously implemented the International Monetary Fund's (IMF) rescue package and even managed to negotiate a slight loosening of the terms of the package.

The economic crisis enabled a coterie of young, reform-minded politicians to gain high office – like urbane, US-educated foreign minister Surin Pitsuwan. Fed up with coups and corruption, and backed by an assertive middle-class, these politicians were committed to change. As Chuan's special assistant, Bunaraj Smutharaks, explained to journalist Michael Vatikiotis, "If we don't seize this opportunity to instigate change, the future generations will see this [economic] crisis as a lost opportunity." (*Far Eastern Economic Review*, 30.6.98)

Under Chuan's leadership, Thailand became a role model for the IMF and foreign investors applauded the government's attempts to put things in order. The difficulty that Chuan faced throughout his second stint as premier was that the economy didn't bounce back after Thailand had taken the IMF's unpalatable medicine. Many foreign commentators praised Chuan's efforts seeing him as honest and pragmatic. But domestic commentators tended to depict him as bumbling and ineffectual, toadying to the IMF while Thailand's poor were squeezed by multilateral organizations and Thai companies were sold to foreign interests at 'fire sale' prices.

Thaksin Shinawatra takes over

The beginning of January 2001 saw the election of **Thaksin Shinawatra** and the Thai Rak Thai party, in a landslide victory over Chuan Leekpai and the Democrats. Thaksin won for two reasons: first, he made grand promises and second, his opponent, Chuan, was stuck with the charge that he had sold the country out to the IMF and foreign business interests. A good dose of populism won the day. But his victory was remarkable in one telling respect: for the first time in Thai political history a party won (almost) a majority of seats in the lower House of Representatives. While Thaksin decided to form a coalition he had no need to do this. And a few months after the election a minor party – Seritham – with 14 MPs merged with Thai Rak Thai to give Thaksin an absolute majority. Here was a man with an unprecedented mandate to rule.

Thaksin won the election by promising the world – or at least rather more than the dour Chuan could manage. Fed up with three-and-a-half years of belt tightening, the electorate grabbed at Thaksin's pledges of grants of one million baht (US$23,200) to each of Thailand's 70,000 villages, a debt moratorium for poorer farmers, cheap medical care, and more. But Thaksin was more than a populist prime minister; he brought to Thai politics a business sense honed while managing one of the country's most successful companies. Rather than handing out bottles of fish sauce and ฿100 notes to poor farmers in a crass attempt to buy their support, he employed pollsters and consultants to judge the mood of the electorate. And he delivered on his promises: the debt moratorium was introduced in July 2001 and in October 2001 health care became available to all Thais at a standard rate of ฿30 per visit.

There are those, however, who feared that Thaksin was too powerful. Like Italian Prime Minister Silvio Berlusconi, he not only headed the country, but also the country's largest and most influential media group. He had little time for the checks and balances of the new constitution – designed to prevent Thailand reverting to its old political ways – and when his family's company purchased the only remaining private television station, iTV, journalists and commentators critical of his ways were promptly sacked.

Liberal authoritarian

As his first term progressed Thaksin revealed an increasingly alarming authoritarian side. With an economic boom slowly re-establishing itself, a whole set of social problems had to be evaporated. To this end, in 2003, a war against drugs was declared. This wasn't a poster campaign nor an attempt to stop smuggling. It involved the wholesale extra-judicial murder of thousands of suspected drug dealers, drug addicts and anyone else the police didn't really like that much. Some commentators felt that the notoriously corrupt Thai police were just getting rid of their competition, others that this form of social cleansing was the only way to control the nefarious criminals who ran the illegal drug trade. Organizations such as Amnesty condemned the deaths – many victims were shot in the back or executed with a single headshot while restrained – though the international community, to its shame, was largely silent.

The year 2003 also marked the invasion of Iraq with Thailand taking its place as the tenth largest member in the coalition of the willing. This was a bold step for a country not known for foreign adventure. The troops, all of whom were used in civil activities, left in 2004, just in time for the beginning of an **insurgency in the south of Thailand** that is slowly coming to dominate the nation's politics.

The Muslim south has long felt apart from the mainstream of Thai society. With another period of economic prosperity in place – something that hardly touched the Muslims of the south – a series of demonstrations, killings and bombings took place. However, it wasn't until October 2004 that an event occurred that gave this insurrection a sense of urgency.

After a violent demonstration outside a government building in the small town of Tak Bai, hundreds of Muslim demonstrators were arrested. Beaten and shackled, they were then loaded into army trucks like human logs, stacked one on top of another, four or five deep. More than 80 died of suffocation. A wave of violence followed with Buddhist monks and teachers becoming targets and explosions a regular occurrence.

Thaksin's response to the situation was surreal. He ordered school children around Thailand to make origami cranes – the bird is a symbol of peace and goodwill in Asian cultures. Millions were loaded onto planes and dropped onto the Islamic communities of the south. The bizarre rationale was that the tiny paper birds would show the Muslims that the rest of the country cared about them. The insurgency gathered pace, draconian emergency rule was declared – suspending many judicial and constitutional rights – and by September 2005 the death toll had reached 1000.

King Bhumibol and the monarchy

Although Thailand has been a constitutional monarchy since the Revolution of 1932, King Bhumibol Adulyadej and the Royal Family have an influence that far exceeds their formal constitutional powers. It seems that the leaders of the Revolution shied away from emasculating the monarchy, and decided to keep the king at the centre of the Thai social and political universe. Nonetheless, the only truly active king since 1932 has been the present one, King Bhumibol, who acceded to the throne in 1945 and in 2005 celebrated 60 years as Sovereign.

King Bhumibol Adulyadej has virtually single-handedly resurrected the Thai monarchy. After returning from his studies abroad to become king he entered the monkhood, and since then has continuously demonstrated his concern for the welfare of his people. The king has largely managed to maintain his independence from the hurly-burly of Thai politics. When he has intervened, he has done so with great effect. In October 1973, after the riots at Thammasat University, he requested that Prime Minister Thanom, along with his henchmen Praphat and Narong, leave the country to stem the tide of civil disorder. They obeyed. In a repeat of the events of 1973, in May 1992 the king called Prime Minister General Suchinda Kraprayoon to his palace where, recorded on television, he was publicly – though not overtly – humiliated for ordering the army to quell demonstrations against his premiership. Three days later, Suchinda had resigned and left the country.

The undoubted love and respect that virtually all Thais hold for their king raises the question of the future and whether the monarchy can remain a stabilizing force. The suitability of his eldest son Crown Prince Vajiralongkorn has been questioned, while his eldest daughter Crown Princess Sirindhorn is respected and loved almost as much as the king himself. Thais worried about the succession are comforted by a legend that the Chakri Dynasty would only have nine monarchs: King Bhumibol is the ninth.

Visitors should avoid any open criticism of the Royal Family: *lèse majesté* is still an offence in Thailand, punishable by up to 15 years in prison In cinemas, the national anthem is played before the film and the audience – including foreigners – are expected to stand. In towns in the countryside, at 0800 every morning, the national anthem is relayed over PA systems, and pedestrians are again expected to stop what they are doing and stand to attention.

Second term

The December 2004 tsunami overshadowed many of the events in the south. Thaksin's handling of this disaster was seen, at least initially, to be efficient and statesmanlike. An election was called soon after in February 2005 and with the economy in a full-scale boom and free face-whitening cream for female voters, Thaksin's TRT won a landslide.

Yet Thaksin's style of rule, popular with the impoverished masses but not with the middle classes and Bangkok élite, soon began to divide Thailand. Early in 2006, and fuelled by an alleged tax-avoidance scam by the Shinawatra family who'd just sold their large telecoms company into foreign hands, a series of demonstrations aimed at Thaksin's ruling party began to turn into a serious movement. Alongside this, Thaksin was accused by certain parts of the media of not showing sufficient respect to the king and even of *lèse majesté* – a serious offence in Thailand.

With demonstrations now becoming massive affairs – up to 200,000 people – and with deadlock on the streets, Thaksin, desperate to re-assert his authority, called a snap election pencilled in for April 2006. His opponents, led by the Democrat Party, realizing they could never beat Thaksin at the ballot box, decided to withdraw all their candidates, effectively boycotting the election. This led to a constitutional crisis that eventually caused the annulment of the ensuing Thaksin landslide. A period of stalemate ensued, only resolved after a series of negotiations when Thaksin agreed to take on the role of caretaker PM and stand down by October 2006 when new elections would be called.

September 2006 changed everything. On the morning of 19 September (UK time) the BBC's news website began reporting that PM Thaksin – then in New York at a UN conference – had declared a state of emergency. By the afternoon the BBC were reporting that tanks were on the streets and Thaksin's government had been replaced by an army council – a full scale military coup had taken place.

If you walked around the streets of the capital a few days later you'd be forgiven for wondering whether anything had happened at all. In a move designed to win over the masses, a national holiday was declared and by the end of the first week locals were delivering flowers and food to the army. A typically Thai sense of surreal fun descended on the capital and tourists posed with the tanks for photo ops. The coup had seemed to unite the nation: peace prevailed.

Within a few weeks a new PM, General Surayud Chulanont, was installed and the hard-fought-for, though ultimately flawed, 1997 constitution was shredded. New elections and a new constitution were mooted for later in 2007 and a civilian cabinet was put in place. With Thaksin skulking in China and the country united behind the king, a feeling of optimism grew. It didn't last long. After the civilian unity cabinet made a series of poor judgements regarding foreign investment, which lead to a mini stock market crash, and several bombs exploded in Bangkok on New Year's Eve, killing nine people, authority seemed to be draining from the new regime.

By mid-2007, in an effort to appear to be taking matters in hand, the junta got the process to draft Thailand's new constitution well underway. The final draft revealed a shift of power back from parliament and the elected executive to the elites, bureaucracy and the military. A senate filled with 50% appointees was to be created and broad security powers designed to override the constitution were to be placed on the statute books. The upshot was that Thailand's drift towards the globalising neo-liberalism of the Thaksin years was over.

To cement this, Thaksin's Thai Rak Thai party was officially broken up with many senior members, including ex-PM Thaksin banned from re-entering politics for 5 years or more. Warrants were also issued for Thaksin's arrest. In response to this, and in an effort to keep his name in the headlines, Thaksin made the surreal choice of buying Manchester City FC – a senior English Premier League football team. It proved a good tactic with Thaksin's supporters now seen wearing Manchester City team shirts on the streets of Bangkok.

In August 2007 a referendum on the new constitution was held. The coup leaders allowed security personnel to be involved in the yes campaign and banned any campaign for a no vote. Even with these draconian measures in place 40% still voted against the new constitution that came into law in late 2007.

A general election was called for 23 December 2007 with the favourites being the newly formed People's Power Party built on the remains of Thaksin's TRT. In the weeks before the election the PPP's leader, Samak Sundaravej, a fierce right-winger with links to the Thammasat Massacre of 1975 and a supporter of the 1992 military crackdown on pro-democracy activists, made it very clear that he was Thaksin's proxy and nominee. The PPP won a majority and formed a new government with Samak as PM.

With a friendly government in place Thaksin returned to the country in February 2008 to much fanfare. Upon landing at Bangkok's airport he was formerly charged with a variety of offences but immediately released. However, it wasn't all plain sailing for the ex-PM. By June proceedings against him were in full swing, with assets and passport seized by the courts.

It also didn't take long for problems to emerge for PM Samak – with the People's Alliance for Democracy holding massive demonstrations on the streets of Bangkok, Samak provoked much condemnation when he called for these demonstrators to be met with force – something that failed to materialise. On 18 June the Democrat Party tried to bring about a vote of no-confidence against Samak. This move ultimately failed but by 10 July the wheels began to fall off his government. After initially supporting Cambodia's right to have the 900-year-old Preah Vihear temple declared a UN World Heritage site, the PPP's Foreign Secretary was forced to resign. Other senior PPP officials, with corruption allegations hanging over them, followed and by late-July 2008, as Cambodian and Thai troops faced off at the site of the Preah Vihear temple, Thailand, once again, seemed to be teetering on the brink of constitutional and political crisis.

Contents

Footprint features

Border crossings

Vietnam–Laos, *pages 1033 and 1055*
Vietnam–Cambodia, *page 1116*

At a glance

○ **Getting around** Open Tour Bus, rail, plane and boat.

● **Time required** 2-6 weeks.

☼ **Weather** Dec-Mar is best.

✖ **When not to go** Monsoon season in the Mekong is Sep-Nov. Central region can suffer tropical storms May-Nov. Around Tet transport and hotels are booked up.

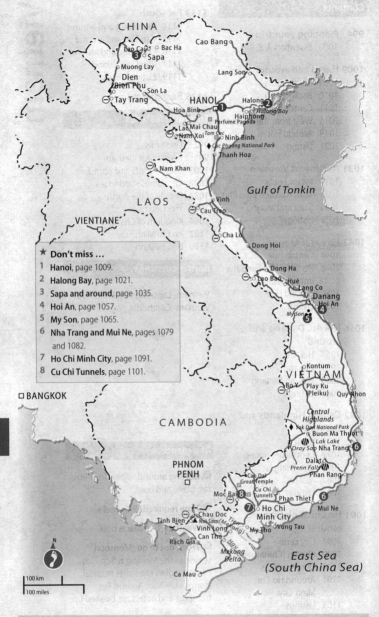

CHINA

Cao Bang

Lao Cai Bac Ha
3 Sapa
Muong Lay
Dien
Bien Phu
Tay Trang Son La
Lang Son

HANOI 1 Halong 2
Hoa Binh Halong Bay
Haiphong
Perfume Pagoda
Lac Mai Chau
Nam Xoi Tam Coc
Ninh Binh
Cuc Phuong National Park
Thanh Hoa

Nam Khan

Gulf of Tonkin

LAOS

Vinh
Cau Treo

VIENTIANE

Cha Lo

Dong Hoi

Dong Ha
Lao Bao Hué
Lang Co
Danang
Hoi An 4
My Son 5

Kontum

VIETNAM

Bo Y Play Ku
(Pleiku) Quy Nhon

Central
Highlands
Yok Don National Park
Buon Ma Thuot
Lak Lake
Dray Sap Nha Trang 6

□ BANGKOK

CAMBODIA

Dalat
Prenn Falls
Phan Rang

PHNOM
PENH

Cao Dai
Great Temple
Moc Bai Cu Chi
8 Tunnels Phan Thiet
7 Ho Chi 6
Chau Doc Minh City Mui Ne
Tinh Bien Nui Sam (Mt Sam)
Vinh Long My Tho Vung Tau
Can Tho

N

Rach Gia

Mekong
Delta

100 km
100 miles

Ca Mau

East Sea
(South China Sea)

In modern-day Vietnam one thing in particular stands out. It is, quite simply, the remarkable speed at which the country is developing and the extraordinary ambitions its leaders are planning to achieve. Vietnam now hovers in an enigmatic and paradoxical time zone, somewhere between the late Industrial Revolution and the post-industrial age. High school children in Ho Chi Minh City vie for the trendiest motorbikes, mobile phones and trainers, while children in the Northern Highlands are happy with a pair of sandals. Youngsters in the Mekong Delta have email accounts yet 10 years ago they didn't have a telephone. And while staff in call centres gossip about the latest fashions, their parents harvest rice by hand. Vietnam has experienced war and bloody revolution in the past 100 years. But the revolution it is now undergoing is peaceful and prosperous. Vast strides in economic development are apace with the government hoping to be crowned a middle income country by 2020. It is, in part, these changes that make Vietnam the absorbing and gripping place that it is.

War? Yes, Vietnam survived several, in fact, over the last century. The Vietnamese people have seen much water flow under the bridge since the war ended but the government will not let it drop. Even now, 30 years on, new war memorials are being erected. It is as if legitimacy of the government somehow depends on having won the war resulting in an odd mixture of war legacy in modern Vietnam. Heroic communist monuments and war memorabilia abound in museums but the Vietnamese people have set their sights firmly on the future. There is no looking back, no nostalgia for the past. And this explains the lack of fuss every time an old building is flattened. Forget yesterday, look to tomorrow.

Planning your trip

Getting there

Air

Vietnam is relatively isolated in comparison to Bangkok, Hong Kong and Singapore. Most major airlines have direct flights from Europe, North America and Australasia to these hubs. Ho Chi Minh City, and to a lesser extent Hanoi, is pretty well connected with other Southeast Asian countries which remain the source of most foreign visitors. Connections have also increased in the last few years with the rise of budget airlines. Prices vary according to the high (November to April, July to August) and low season. International departure taxes are now included in the airline ticket price.

Flights from Europe There are direct flights to Vietnam from Paris with **Vietnam Airlines/Air France**. These code-shared flights take 12 hours. **Vietnam Airlines** has an office in the UK at Flighthouse, Fernhill Road, Horley, Surrey RH6 9SY, T0871-2229233, www.vietnamairlines. uk.com, or flights can be booked online. There are also direct **Vietnam Airlines** flights from Moscow. Flights from London and other European hubs go via Bangkok, Singapore, Kuala Lumpur or Hong Kong. From London to Vietnam takes 16 to18 hours, depending on the length of stopover. It is also possible to fly into Hanoi and depart from Ho Chi Minh City.

Flights from the USA and Canada There are flights to Vietnam from several major US hubs but these are very expensive. By far the best option is to fly via **Bangkok**, **Taipei** or **Hong Kong** and from there to Vietnam. The approximate flight time from Los Angeles to **Bangkok** is 21 hours. **United** flies from San Francisco and from LA via Tokyo and from Chicago via Hong Kong to Vietnam. **Thai** (www.thaiair.com), **Delta** (www.delta.com), **Northwest** (www.nwa.com), **United** (www.united.com) and **Air Canada** (www.aircanada.com) fly to Bangkok from a number of US and Canadian cities. **Eva Airlines** (www.evaair.com) has good deals via Taiwan.

Flights from Australia and New Zealand There are direct flights to Vietnam from Adelaide, Melbourne, Sydney, Perth, Auckland and Wellington with **Cathay Pacific** (www.cathaypacific.com), **Malaysia Airlines** (www.malaysianairlines.com), **Singapore Airlines** (www.singaporeair.com) and **Thai** (www.thaiair.com). **Qantas** (www.qantas.com) flies from Sydney, Adelaide and Melbourne to Ho Chi Minh City.

Budget airlines from Australia include **Jetstar** (www.jetstar.com) from Sydney to Ho Chi Minh City. From Sydney the flights to Vietnam take eight hours and 45 minutes direct.

Boat

There are no normal sea crossings into Vietnam although an increasing number of cruise liners sail into Vietnamese waters. The only other international connection by boat is the Mekong River crossing with Phnom Penh to Chau Doc. A new service is due to start running between Ha Tien in the Mekong Delta to Kep in Cambodia.

Rail

Vietnam's only international rail connection is with China. There are connections with Beijing via Nanning to Hanoi, crossing at Lang Son. The lines are slow and the distances are great.

Packing for Vietnam

While not yet on a par with Bangkok there is far more available now in Vietnam than a couple of years ago. Bottled water is widely available and there is no need to bring water filters unless trekking in remote areas. Good books are scarce, so bring plenty. Hotels, even the cheaper ones, usually provide mosquito nets so you shouldn't need to bring your own.

The following are also useful: passport photos; small first-aid kit; torch; penknife; photocopies of passport and visa (and entry permit, issued on arrival); insect repellent; strong padlock for locking bags in hotel rooms and while travelling; and money belt. For clothes, pack long-sleeved shirts, long trousers and socks to prevent mosquitoes from biting in the evening. Warm clothing is necessary for upland areas in winter. Women might consider wearing dresses rather than jeans when travelling, for easier access to squat toilets. You don't need to pack waterproofs or an umbrella for the wet season, as these are ubiquitous and cheap in Vietnam.

Road

Cambodia There is a road crossing at Moc Bai on Highway 1 connecting Phnom Penh in Cambodia with Ho Chi Minh City via Tay Ninh Province. Further south there is a second crossing to Phnom Penh via Chau Doc at Vinh Xuong in the Mekong Delta by boat, and another road crossing into Cambodia at Tinh Bien, approximately 22 km south of Chau Doc. Right at the very south of the country, you can cross at Xà Xía and Khanh Binh.

China There are three land crossings between China and Vietnam: at Lao Cai, Dong Dang and Mong Cai. There is no train across the border at Lao Cai at the moment. The train from Hanoi does cross at Dong Dang. The Mong Cai crossing is by road. If you enter Vietnam by land your visa must specify the exact road crossing.

Laos There is a popular road crossing open at Lao Bao, north of Hué (Quang Tri Province), which enables travel through to Savannakhet in Laos. In the north there is a crossing at Tay Trang near Dien Bien Phu (Dien Bien Phy Province). Closer to Hanoi are the crossings at Nam Can (Nghe An Province) and Cau Treo (Ha Tinh Province) accessible from Vinh. You can also cross close to Kontum at Bo-Y (Kontum Province).

Getting around

Air

Vietnam Airlines flies from Hanoi or Ho Chi Minh City to Dien Bien Phu, Hué, Danang, Nha Trang, Dalat, Buon Ma Thuot, Play Ku, Rach Gia and Phu Quoc. They also fly to Phnom Penh, Siem Reap and Bangkok. From Hanoi they fly to Luang Prabang. There are two other domestic carriers, **Pacific Airlines** (www.pacificairlines.com.vn) and **Vasco Airlines**.

Rail

The Vietnamese rail network extends from Hanoi to Ho Chi Minh City. **Vietnam Railways** (www.vr.com.vn) runs the 2600-km rail network. With overnight stays at hotels along the way to see the sights, a rail sight-seeing tour from Hanoi to Ho Chi Minh City should take a minimum of 10 days but you would need to buy tickets for each separate journey.

The difference in price between first and second class is small and it is worth paying the extra. There are three seating classes and four sleeping classes, including hard and soft seats and hard and soft sleepers; some are air-conditioned, others are not. The kitchen on the Hanoi-Ho Chi Minh City service serves soups and simple, but adequate, rice dishes (it is a good idea to take additional food and drink on long journeys though). First-class long-distance tickets include the price of meals. Six trains leave Hanoi for Ho Chi Minh City daily and vice versa. The express trains (**Reunification Express**) take between 29-39 hours. Most ticket offices have some staff who speak English. Queues can be long and sometimes confusing and some offices keep unusual hours. If you are short of time and short on patience it may well pay to get a tour operator to book your ticket for a small fee. All sleepers should be booked three days in advance.

River
The **Victoria** hotel chain (www.victoriahotels-asia.com) runs a Mekong Delta service for its guests. There are also services from Chau Doc to Phnom Penh, see page 1116. Ferries operate between Ho Chi Minh City and Vung Tau; Rach Gia and Phu Quoc; Haiphong and Cat Ba Island; and Halong Bay and Mong Cai.

Road
Open Tour Buses, see below, are very useful and cheap for bridging important towns. Train travel is exciting and overnight journeys are a good way of covering long distances. Many travellers opt to take a tour to reach remote areas.

Bus Roads in Vietnam are notoriously dangerous. Since Highway 1 is so dangerous and public transport buses are poor and slow, most travellers opt for the cheap and regular **Open Tour Bus** (private minibus or coach) that covers the length of the country. Almost every Vietnamese tour operator/travellers' café listed in this guide will run a minibus service or act as an agent. The ticket is a flexible, one-way ticket from Ho Chi Minh City to Hanoi and vice versa. The buses run daily from their own offices and include the following stops: Ho Chi Minh City, Mui Ne, Nha Trang, Dalat, Hoi An, Hué, Ninh Binh and Hanoi. They will also stop off at tourist destinations along the way such as Lang Co, Hai Van Pass, Marble Mountains and Po Klong Garai. You may join at any leg of the journey, paying for one trip or several as you go. The Hanoi to Hué and vice versa is an overnight trip but although you might save on a night's accommodation you are unlikely to get much sleep. Note that bus listings in this chapter refer to Open Tours Buses unless otherwise stated.

If you do opt for public buses note that most bus stations are on the outskirts of town; in bigger centres there may be several stations. Long-distance buses invariably leave very early in the morning (0400-0500). Buses are the cheapest form of transport, although sometimes foreigners find they are being asked two or three times the correct price. Prices are normally prominently displayed at bus stations. Less comfortable but quicker are the minibus services (some air-conditioned) which ply the more popular routes. These are usually grossly over laden and driven by maniacs.

Car hire Self-drive car hire is not available in Vietnam. It is, however, possible to hire cars with drivers and this is a good way of getting to more remote areas with a group of people. Cars with drivers can be hired for around US$50-70 per day. All cars are modern and air-conditioned. Car hire prices increase by 50% or more during Tet. A standard, air-conditioned modern car including the driver, fuel, road fees and food and accommodation for the driver in and around Hanoi and the north would cost around US$250 for one week. For travelling the length of the country the cost could escalate to around US$1200 for a week including fuel, driver and food and accommodation for the driver or a discount may be offered for a one-way service where a company has multiple branches throughout the country.

Motorbike and bicycle hire Most towns are small enough for bicycles to be an attractive option but if taking in a sweep of the surrounding countryside (touring around the Central Highlands, for example) then a motorbike will mean you can see more. Motorbikes can be rented easily and are an excellent way of getting off the beaten track. You do not need a driver's licence or proof of motorbike training to hire a motorbike in Vietnam. It is only compulsory for motorcyclists riding on highways to wear helmets. Take time to familiarize yourself with road conditions and ride slowly.

Bicycles can be rented by the day in the cities and are useful for getting out into the countryside. Hotels often have bicycles for hire and there is usually someone willing to lend their machine for a small charge (US$1-2 per day). Many travellers' cafés rent out bicycles and motorbikes too, the latter for around US$6 a day. Motorbikes are hired out with helmets and bicycles with locks. Always park your bicycle or motorbike in a guarded parking place (*gui xe*). Ask for a ticket. The 2000d this costs is worth every dong, even if you are just popping in to the post office to post a letter.

Motorbike taxi and cyclo Motorcycle taxis, known as *honda ôm* or *xe ôm* are ubiquitous and cheap. You will find them on most street corners, outside hotels or in the street. With their uniform baseball caps and dangling cigarette, *xe ôm* drivers are readily recognizable. If they see you before you see them, they will shout 'moto' to get your attention. In the north and upland areas the Honda is replaced with the Minsk. The shortest hop would be at least 5000d. Always bargain though.

Cyclos are bicycle trishaws. Cyclo drivers charge double that of a *xe ôm*. A number of streets in the centres of Ho Chi Minh City and Hanoi are one-way or out of bounds to cyclos, necessitating lengthy detours which add to the time and cost. Do not take a cyclo after dark unless the driver is well known to you or you know the route. It is a wonderful way to get around the Old Quarter of Hanoi, though, and for those with plenty of time on their hands it is not so hazardous in smaller towns.

Taxi Taxis ply the streets of Hanoi and Ho Chi Minh City and other large towns and cities. They are cheap, around 12,000d per kilometre, and the drivers are better English speakers than cyclo drivers. See page 1008 for an explanation of Vietnamese addresses. Always keep a selection of small denomination notes with you so that when the taxi stops you can round up the fare to the nearest small denomination. At night use the better known taxi companies rather than the unlicensed cars that often gather around popular nightspots.

Sleeping → *For hotel price codes, see inside the front cover.*

Accommodation ranges from luxury suites in international five-star hotels and spa resorts to small, family hotels (mini hotels) and homestays with local people in the Mekong Delta and with the ethnic minorities in the Central Highlands and northwest Vietnam. During peak seasons – especially December to March and particularly during busy holidays such as Tet, Christmas, New Year's Eve and around Easter – booking is essential. Expect staff to speak English in all top hotels. Do not expect it in cheaper hotels or in more remote places, although most places employ someone with a smattering of a foreign language.

Private, mini hotels are worth seeking out as, being family-run, guests can expect quite good service. Mid-range and tourist hotels may provide a decent breakfast which is often included in the price. Many luxury and first-class hotels charge extra for breakfast and, on top of this, also charge VAT and service charge. There are some world-class beach resorts in Nha Trang, Mui Ne, Hoi An and Danang. In the northern uplands, in places like Sapa and Mai Chau, it is possible to stay in an ethnic minority house. Bathrooms are basic and will consist of a cold shower and a natural toilet. To stay in a homestay, you must book through a tour operator or through the local tourist office; you cannot just turn up. Homestays are also possible on farms and in orchards in the Mekong Delta. Here, guests sleep on camp beds and share a Western bathroom with hot and cold water. National parks offer everything from air-conditioned bungalows to shared dormitory rooms to campsites where, sometimes, it is possible to hire tents. Visitors may spend a romantic night on a boat in Halong Bay or on the Mekong Delta. Boats range from the fairly luxurious to the basic. Most people book through tour operators. The Vietnam Hostelling International Association (www.hihostels.com) has been established, operating hostels on Cat Ba Island and in Hanoi, Hoi An and Sapa.

You will have to leave your passport at hotel reception desks for the duration of your stay. It will be released to you temporarily for bank purposes or buying an air ticket. Credit cards are widely accepted but there is often a 2-4% fee for paying in this manner.

Camping in Vietnam is limited mainly because the authorities insist on foreign visitors sleeping in registered accommodation. There are no campsites but visitors bringing tents may be able to pitch them around Sapa or on Cat Ba Island and surrounding islands. Some guesthouses in Mui Ne and other seaside places have tents.

Eating and drinking → *For restaurant price codes, see inside the front cover.*

Vietnam offers outstanding Vietnamese, French and international cuisine in restaurants that range from first class to humble foodstalls. At either the quality will be, in the main, exceptional. The accent is on local, seasonal and fresh produce and the rich pickings from the sea, along Vietnam's 2000-km coastline will always make it far inland too. You will find more hearty stews in the remote north and more salad dishes along the coast. All restaurants offer a variety of cuisine from the regions and some specialize in certain types of food – Hué cuisine, Cha Ca Hanoi etc. *Pho* (pronounced *fer*), noodle soup, is utterly delicious.

All Vietnamese food is dipped, whether in fish sauce, soya sauce, chilli sauce, peanut sauce or pungent prawn sauce (*mam tom* – avoid if possible) before eating. As each course is served so a new set of dips will accompany it. Follow the guidance of your waiter or Vietnamese friends to pair the right dip with the right dish.

Locally produced fresh beer is called *bia hoi*. Bar customers have a choice of Tiger, Heineken, Carlsberg, San Miguel, 333, Saigon Beer or Huda. Rice and fruit wines are produced and consumed in large quantities in upland areas, particularly in the north of Vietnam. The Chinese believe that snake wines increase their virility and as such are normally found in areas of high Chinese concentration. Soft drinks and bottled still and sparkling mineral water are widely available. Tea and coffee is widely available. Coffee is drunk with condensed milk.

Local customs and laws

Vietnam is remarkably relaxed and easy going with regard to conventions. The people, especially in small towns and rural areas, can be pretty old-fashioned, but it is difficult to cause offence unwittingly. The main complaint Vietnamese have of foreigners is their fondness for dirty and torn clothing. Backpackers come in for particularly severe criticism and the term *tay ba lo* (literally Western backpacker) is a contemptuous one reflecting the low priority many budget travellers seem to allocate to personal hygiene and the antiquity and inadequacy of their shorts and vests.

Shoes should be removed before entering temples and before going into people's houses. Modesty should be preserved and excessive displays of bare flesh are not considered good form, particularly in temples and private houses. Shorts are fine for the beach and travellers' cafés but not for smart restaurants.

Public displays of affection are likely to draw wide attention, not much of it favourable. But walking hand in hand is now accepted as a common, if slightly eccentric, Western habit. Hand shaking among men is the standard greeting (often with both hands for added cordiality) and although Vietnamese women will consent to the process, it is often clear that they would prefer not to. The head is held by some to be sacred and people would rather you didn't pat them on it, but the Vietnamese do not have the hang-ups the Thais have about someone's feet being higher than their head. In short, the Vietnamese are pragmatic and tolerant, and only the most unfeeling behaviour is likely to trouble them.

Festivals and events

Festivals are timed according to the Vietnamese lunar calendar. To help you work out on which day these events fall, see the following website, which converts the Gregorian calendar to the lunar calendar: www.mandarintools.com/calconv_old.html.

Late Jan-Mar (public holiday, movable) **Tet** The traditional new year and Vietnam's biggest celebration. It is the time to forgive and forget and to pay off debts. It is also everyone's birthday – everyone adds a year to their age at Tet. Great attention is paid to the preparations for Tet, because it is believed that the 1st week of the new year dictates the fortunes for the rest of the year. The 1st visitor to the house on New Year's morning should be an influential, lucky and happy person, so families take care to arrange a suitable caller.
3 Feb Founding anniversary of the Communist Party of Vietnam (public holiday).
Mar (movable) **Hai Ba Trung Day** Celebrates the Trung sisters who led a revolt against the Chinese in AD 41.
Apr Thanh Minh (New Year of the Dead or Feast of the Pure Light). People are supposed to walk outdoors to evoke the

spirit of the dead. Family shrines and tombs are traditionally cleaned and decorated.
30 Apr Liberation Day of South Vietnam and HCMC (public holiday).
May (movable) **Celebration of the birth, death and enlightenment of Buddha**.
1 May Labour Day (public holiday).
19 May Anniversary of the birth of Ho Chi Minh (government holiday). The majority of state institutions will be shut on this day but businesses in the private sector remain open.
Aug (movable) **Trung Nguyen** (Wandering Souls Day). One of the most important festivals. During this time, prayers can absolve the sins of the dead who leave hell and return hungry and naked, to their relatives. The Wandering Souls are those with no homes to go to. Celebrations in Buddhist temples and homes.
Sep (movable) **Tet Trung Thi** (Mid-Autumn Festival). This festival is particularly celebrated

by children. In the evening families prepare food including sticky rice, fruit and chicken to be placed on the ancestral altars. Moon cakes (egg, green beans and lotus seed) are baked, lanterns are made and painted, and children parade through towns with music and lanterns. It is particularly popular in Hanoi and toy shops in the Old Quarter decorate shops with lanterns and masks.

2 Sep National Day (public holiday).
3 Sep President Ho Chi Minh's Anniversary (public holiday).
Nov (movable) **Confucius' Birthday**.

Shopping

Vietnam is increasingly a good destination for shopping. A wide range of designer clothing, silk goods, high quality handicrafts, ceramics and lacquerware are available at excellent value. The main shopping centres are Hanoi, Ho Chi Minh City and Hoi An. Hoi An is the best place to get clothes made. The majority of shops and markets are open from early in the morning to late at night every day and do not close for lunch. Shops and markets will accept US dollars and Vietnamese dong and most shops accept credit cards.

Export of wood or antiques is banned and anything antique or antique-looking will be seized at customs. In order to avoid this happening you will need to get an export licence from the **Customs Department** ① *162 Nguyen Van Cu St, Hanoi, T04-8265260*. Do not buy any marine turtle products.

Lacquerware is plentiful and cheap. Ethnic products, fabrics, wickerware and jewellery is best bought (and cheapest) in the uplands but plenty is available in the two main cities. Junk collectors will have a field day in Ho Chi Minh City and Hanoi; many trinkets were left behind by the French, Americans and Russians, including old cameras, watches, cigarette lighters (most Zippos are fake), 1960s Coca-Cola signs and 1930s Pernod ashtrays.

Essentials A-Z

Accident and emergency
Contact the relevant emergency service and your embassy. Make sure you obtain police/medical records in order to file insurance claims. If you need to report a crime visit your local police station and take a local with you who speaks English. Ambulance T115, Fire T114, Police T113.

Children
Vietnam Airlines offers under 12s a reduced fare. The railways allow children under 5 to travel free and charge 50% of the adult fare for those aged 5-10. The Open Tour Bus tickets and tours are likewise free for children under 2 but those aged 2-6 pay 75% of the adult price.

Customs and duty free
Duty-free allowance is 400 cigarettes, 50 cigars or 100 g of tobacco, 1.5 litres of spirits, plus items for personal use. You cannot import pornography, anti-government literature, photographs or movies nor culturally unsuitable children's toys.

Disabled travellers
Some of the more upmarket hotels have a few designated rooms for the disabled. For those with walking difficulties many of the better hotels have lifts. Wheelchair access is improving with more shopping centres, hotels and restaurants providing ramps for easy access. People sensitive to noise will find Vietnam, at times, almost intolerable.

RADAR, 12 City Forum, 250 City Rd, London, EC1V 8AF, T0207-2503222, www.radar.org.uk.
SATH, 347 Fifth Avenue, Suite 605, New York City, NY 10016, T0212-4477284, www.sath.org.

Drugs

Drugs are common and cheap and the use of hard drugs by Vietnamese is a rapidly growing problem. Attitudes towards users are incredibly lax and the worst that will happen is that certain bars and nightclubs may be closed for a few weeks. In such an atmosphere of easy availability and tolerance, many visitors may be tempted to indulge, and to excess, but beware that the end result can be disastrous. Attitudes to traffickers are harsh, although the death penalty is usually reserved for Vietnamese and other Asians, whose governments are less likely to kick up a fuss.

Electricity

Voltage 110. Sockets are round 2-pin. Sometimes they are 2 flat pin. A number of top hotels now use UK 3 square-pin sockets.

Embassies and consulates

Australia, 6 Timbarra Cres, O'Malley Canberra, ACT 2606, T+61-2-6286 6059/2.
Cambodia, 436 Monivong, Phnom Penh, T+855-23-364741.
Canada, 470 Wilbrod St, Ottawa, Ontario, K1N 6M8, T+1-613-236 0772.
France, 62-66 R Boileau-75016, Paris, T+33-1-4414 6447.
Laos, That Luang Rd, Vientiane, T+856-21-413409; 118 Si-Sa-Vang-Vong Moung Khanthabouli, Savannakhet, T+856-41-212418.
South Africa, 87 Brooks St, Brooklyn, Pretoria, T+27-12-362 8119.
Thailand, 83/1 Wireless Rd, Lumpini, Pathumwan, Bangkok 10330, T+66-2-251 5838.
UK, 12-14 Victoria Rd, London W8 5RD, T+44-(0)207 937 1912.
USA, 1233, 20th St, NW Suite 400 Washington DC, 20036, T+1-202-861 0737.

Gay and lesbian

The Vietnamese are tolerant of homosexuality. There are no legal restraints for 2 people of the same sex co-habitating in the same room be they Vietnamese or non-Vietnamese. There are several bars in central HCMC popular with gays. Cruising in dark streets is not advised. An Asian online resource for gays and lesbians which includes a list of scams and warnings in Vietnam as well as gay-friendly bars in Hanoi and HCMC is www.utopia-asia.com.

Health

See your doctor or travel clinic at least 6 weeks before your departure for general advice on travel risks, malaria and vaccinations. Make sure you have travel insurance, get a dental check (especially if you are going to be away for more than a month), know your own blood group and if you suffer a long-term condition such as diabetes or epilepsy make sure someone knows or that you have a Medic Alert bracelet/necklace with this information on it, www.medicalert.co.uk.

The following **vaccinations** are usually advised before travel: BCG, diphtheria, hepatitis A, polio, tetanus and typhoid. The following are sometimes advised: hepatitis B, Japanese B encephalitis and rabies. A yellow fever vaccination certificate is required if coming from areas with risk of transmission.

Health risks

Malaria exists in rural areas in Vietnam. However, there is no risk in Hanoi, Ho Chi Minh City, Danang, Nha Trang, the Red River Delta and the coastal plains north of Nha Trang.

The choice of malaria prophylaxis will need to be something other than chloroquine for most people, since there is such a high level of resistance to it. Always check with your doctor or travel clinic for the most up-to-date advice.

Malaria can cause death within 24 hrs. It can start as something just resembling an attack of flu. You may feel tired, lethargic, headachy, feverish; or more seriously, develop fits, followed by coma and then death. Have a low index of suspicion because it is very easy to write off vague symptoms, which may actually be malaria. If you have a temperature, go to a doctor as soon as you can and ask for a malaria test. On your return home if you suffer any of these symptoms, get tested as soon as possible, even if any previous test proved negative, the test could save your life.

The most serious viral disease is **dengue fever**, which is hard to protect against as the mosquitoes bite throughout the day as well as at night. Bacterial diseases include **tuberculosis** (TB) and some causes of the more common traveller's **diarrhoea**. Each year there is the possibility that **avian flu** or **SARS** might rear their ugly heads. Check the news reports. If there is a problem in an area you are due to visit you may be advised to have an ordinary flu shot or to seek expert advice. Vietnam has the second highest fatalities from Avian influenza (46 deaths out of a population of 84 million). Consult the WHO wesbite www.who.int, for further information and heed local advice on the ground. There are high rates of HIV in the region, especially among sex workers.

Medical services

Medical services are listed in the Directory section of relevant areas. Western hospitals exist in Hanoi and Ho Chi Minh City.
Columbia Asia (Saigon International Clinic), 8 Alexander de Rhodes St, HCMC, T08-8238455 (T08-8238888, 24-hr emergency), www.columbiaasia.com. International doctors offering a full range of services.
International SOS, Central Building, 31 Hai Ba Trung St, Hanoi, T04-934066, www.internationalsos.com/countries/Vietnam. Open 24 hrs for emergencies, routine and medical evacuation. Dental service too.

Useful websites
www.btha.org British Travel Health Association (UK). This is the official website of an organization of travel health professionals.
www.cdc.gov US Government site which gives excellent advice on travel health and details of disease outbreaks.
www.fitfortravel.scot.nhs.uk A-Z of vaccine/health advice for each country.
www.who.int The WHO Blue Book lists the diseases of the world.

Insurance
Always take out travel insurance before you set off and read the small print carefully. Check that the policy covers the activities you intend or may end up doing. Also check exactly what your medical cover includes, eg ambulance, helicopter rescue or emergency flights back home. Also check the payment protocol. You may have to cough up first before the insurance company reimburses you. It is always best to dig out all the receipts for expensive personal effects like jewellery or cameras. Take photos of these items and note down all serial numbers. You are advised to shop around. **STA Travel** and other reputable student travel organisations offer good value policies. Young travellers from North America can try the **International Student Insurance Service (ISIS)**, which is available through **STA Travel**, T01-800-777 0112, www.sta-travel.com. Other recommended travel insurance companies in North America include: **Travel Guard**, www.noelgroup.com; **Access America**, www.accessamerica.com; **Travel Insurance Services**, www.travel insure.com; and **Travel Assistance International**, www.travelassistance.com. Older travellers should note that some companies will not cover people over 65 years old, or may charge higher premiums. The best policies for older travellers (UK) are offered by **Age Concern**, www.ageconcern.org.uk.

Internet
Although emailing is now usually easy enough in Vietnam, access to the internet

Useful words and phrases

Hello/goodbye	*Xin chào/tam biệt*	Tomorrow	*Ngày mai*
Thank you	*Càm ơn*	Where is the …?	*Ở đâu …?*
Yes/no	*Vâng/Không*	Is it far ?	*Có xa không ?*
Today	*Hôm nay*	How much is it?	*Giá bao nhiêu?*
Yesterday	*Hôm qua*	It's too expensive	*Mắc quá*

from within Vietnam is restricted as the authorities battle vainly to firewall Vietnam-related topics. Access has greatly improved with broadband available in many places in Hanoi and HCMC and there are internet cafés in nearly every town. Rates are 3000-30,000d per hr.

Language

You are likely to find a smattering of English wherever there are tourist services but outside tourist centres communication can be a problem for those who have no knowledge of Vietnamese. Furthermore, the Vietnamese language is not easy to learn. For example, pronunciation presents enormous difficulties as it is tonal. On the plus side, Vietnamese is written in a Roman alphabet making life much easier: place and street names are instantly recognizable. French is still spoken and often very well by the more elderly and educated.

In HCMC, language courses of several months duration are offered by the **Department of Vietnamese Studies and Vietnamese Language for Foreigners**, 12 Dinh Tien Hoang St, District 1, T8-8225009.

Media

Unlike western newspapers, Vietnamese papers are less interested in what has happened (that is to say, news), preferring instead to report on what will happen or what should happen, featuring stories such as 'Party vows to advance ethical lifestyles' and 'Output of fertilizer to grow 200%'. The English language daily *Vietnam News* is widely available. Inside the back page is

an excellent 'What's on' section. *The Guide*, a monthly magazine on leisure and tourism produced by the *Vietnam Economic Times*, can be found in tourist centres. Good hotels will have cable TV that features a full range of options.

Money → *US$1 = 16,575, £1= 32,396 €1 = 25,659 (Aug 2008).*

The unit of currency is the **dong**. Under law, shops should only accept dong but in practice this is not enforced and dollars are accepted almost everywhere. If possible, however, try to pay for everything in dong as prices are usually lower and in more remote areas people may be unaware of the latest exchange rate. Also, to ordinary Vietnamese, 15,000d is a lot of money, while US$1 means nothing. **ATMs** are plentiful in HCMC and Hanoi and can also be found in other major tourist centres, but it is a good idea to travel with US$ cash as a backup. Banks in the main centres will change other major currencies including UK pound sterling, Hong Kong dollar, Thai baht, Swiss franc, Euros, Australian dollars, Singapore dollars and Canadian dollars. **Credit cards** are increasingly accepted, particularly Visa, MasterCard, Amex and JCB. Large hotels, expensive restaurants and medical centres invariably take them but beware of a surcharge of 2.5-4.5%. Most hotels will not add a surcharge onto your bill if paying by credit card. Traveller's cheques are best denominated in US$ and can only be cashed in banks in the major towns. Commission of 2-4% is payable if cashing into dollars but not if you are converting them direct to dong.

Cost of travelling

On a budget expect to pay around US$6-12 per night for accommodation and about the same each day for food. A good mid-range hotel will cost US$12-30. There are comfort and cost levels anywhere from here up to US$200 per night. For travelling many use the Open Tour Buses as they are inexpensive and, by Vietnamese standards, 'safe'. Slightly more expensive are trains followed by planes.

Opening hours

Banks Mon-Fri 0800-1600. Many close 1100-1300 or 1130-1330.
Offices Mon-Fri 0730-1130, 1330-1630.
Restaurants, **cafés**, **bars** Daily from 0700 or 0800 although some open earlier. Bars are meant to close at 2400 by law.
Shops Daily 0800-2000. Some open for another hour or 2, especially in tourist centres.

Police and the law

If you are robbed in Vietnam, report the incident to the police (for your insurance claim). Otherwise, the police are of no use whatsoever. They will do little or nothing (apart from log the crime on an incident sheet which you will need for your insurance claim). Vietnam is not the best place to come into conflict with the law. Avoid getting arrested. If you are arrested, however, ask for consular assistance immediately and English-speaking staff.

Involvement in politics, possession of political material, business activities that have not been licensed by appropriate authorities, or non-sanctioned religious activities can result in detention. Sponsors of small, informal religious gatherings such as bible-study groups in hotel rooms, as well as distributors of religious materials, have been detained, fined and expelled. (Source: US State Department.) The army are extremely sensitive about their military buildings and become exceptionally irate if you take a photo. There are signs to this effect outside all military installations, of which there are hundreds.

Post

Postal services are pretty good. Post offices open daily 0700-2100; smaller ones close for lunch. Outgoing packages are opened and checked by the censor.

Safety

Useful points of contact for up-to-date safety information include: the US State Department's travel advisories: **Travel Warnings & Consular Information Sheets**, www.travel.state.gov/travel_ warnings.html; and the UK Foreign and Commonwealth Office's travel warning section, www.fco.gov.uk/travel.

Do not take any valuables on to the streets of HCMC as bag and jewellery snatching is a common and serious problem. Thieves work in teams, often with beggar women carrying babies as a decoy. Beware of people who obstruct your path (pushing a bicycle across the pavement is a common ruse); your pockets are being emptied from behind. Young men on fast motorbikes also cruise the central streets of HCMC waiting to pounce on unwary victims. The situation in other cities is not as bad but take care in Nha Trang and Hanoi. Never go by cyclo in a strange part of town after dark.

Lone women travellers have fewer problems than in many other Asian countries. The most common form of harassment usually consists of comic and harmless displays of macho behaviour.

Unexploded ordnance is still a threat in some areas. It is best not to stray too far from the beaten track and don't unearth bits of suspicious metal.

Single western men will be targeted by prostitutes on street corners, in tourist bars and those cruising on motorbikes.

Student travellers

There are discounts available on some **Vietnam Airlines** routes and the train. Discount travel is provided to those under 22 and over 60. Anyone in full-time education is entitled to an **International Student Identity Card** (www.isic.org). These are issued by student travel offices and travel agencies and offer special rates on all forms of transport and other concessions and services. They sometimes permit free admission to museums and sights, at other times a discount on the admission.

Telephone → *Country code +84.*
To make a domestic call dial 0 + area code + phone number. Note that all numbers in this chapter include the 0 and the area code. Most shops or cafés will let you call a local number for 2000d: look for the blue sign *'dien thoai cong cong'* (meaning public telephone). All post offices provide international telephone services. The cost of calls has greatly reduced but some post offices and hotels still insist on charging for a minimum of 3 mins. You start paying for an overseas call from the moment you ring even if the call is not answered. By dialling 171 or 178 followed by 0 or 00 to make an international call, it is approximately 30% cheaper. Vietnam's IDD is 0084; directory enquires 1080; operator-assisted domestic long-distance calls 103; international directory enquiries 143; Yellow pages 1081. Numbers beginning with 091 or 090 are mobile numbers.

Time
7 hrs ahead of GMT.

Tipping
Vietnamese do not normally tip if eating in small family restaurants but may tip extravagantly in expensive bars. Foreigners normally leave the small change. Big hotels and some restaurants add 5-10% service charge and the government tax of 10% to the bill. Taxis are rounded up to the nearest 5000d, hotel porters 20,000d.

Tourist information
The national tourist office is **Vietnam National Administration of Tourism** (www.vietnamtourism.com), whose role is to promote Vietnam as a tourist destination. Visitors to their offices can get some information and maps but are more likely to be offered tours. There are exceptions eg **Saigontourist** (www.saigon-tourist.com). Good tourist information is available from tour operators in the main tourist centres.

Tour operators
For countrywide tour operators, refer to the Activities and tours listings in each area.

In the UK
Adventure Company, Cross & Pillory House, Cross & Pillory Lane, Alton, Hampshire GU34 1HL, T0845-450 5316, www.adventurecompany.co.uk.
Audley Travel, New Mill, New Mill Lane, Whitney, Oxfordshire OX29 9SX, T01993-838100, www.audleytravel.com.
Explore, Nelson House, 55 Victoria Rd, Farnborough, Hants GU14 7PA, T0870-333 4002, www.explore.co.uk.
Guerba Adventure & Discovery Holidays, Wessex House, 40 Station Rd, Westbury, Wiltshire BA13 3JN, T01373-826611, www.guerba.co.uk.
Regent Holidays, Fromsgate House, Rupert St, Bristol BS1 2QJ, T0845-277 3317, www.regent-holidays.co.uk.
Silk Steps, Odyssey Lodge, Holy Well Rd, Edington, Bridgwater, Somerset TA7 9JH, T01278-722460, www.silksteps.co.uk.
Steppes Travel, 51 Castle St, Cirencester, Glos GL7 1QD, T01285-880980, www.steppestravel.co.uk.
Symbiosis Expedition Planning, Holly House, Whilton, Daventry, Northants, NN11 2NN, T0845-123 2844, www.symbiosis-travel.com.
Trans Indus, Northumberland House, 11 The Pavement, Popes Lane, London W5 4NG, T020-8566 2729, www.transindus.co.uk. Tailor-made holidays and group tours.
Travel Indochina, 2nd floor, Chester House, George St, Oxford OX1 2AY, T01865-268940, www.travelindochina.co.uk. Small group journeys and tailor-made holidays.

Travelmood, 214 Edgware Rd, London W2 1DH; 1 Brunswick Court, Leeds LS2 7QU; 16 Reform St, Dundee, DD1 1RG, T0800-298 9815, www.travelmoodadventures.com.
Trips Worldwide, 14 Frederick Pl, Clifton, Bristol BS8 1AS, T0117-311 4400, www.tripsworldwide.co.uk.
Visit Asia (Tennyson Travel), 30-32 Fulham High St, London SW6 3LQ, T020-7736 4347, www.visitasia.co.uk. Tours throughout Asia.

In North America
Adventure Center, 1311 63rd St, Suite 200, Emeryville, CA, T+1-800-227 8747, www.adventurecenter.com.
Global Spectrum, 3907 Laro Court, Fairfax, VA 22031, T+1-800-419 4446, www.globalspectrumtravel.com.
Hidden Treasure Tours, 509 Lincoln Blvd, Long Beach, NY 11561, T01-87-7761 7276 (USA toll free), www.hiddentreasuretours.com.
Journeys, 107 April Drive, Suite 3, Ann Arbor MI 46103, T+1-800-255 8735 (USA toll free), www.journeys-intl.com.
Myths & Mountains, 976 Tree Court, Incline Village, Nevada 89451, T1-800-670 6984, www.mythsandmountains.com. Organizes travel to all 3 countries.
Nine Dragons Travel & Tours, 1476 Orange Grove Rd, Charleston, SC 29407, T+1-317-281 3895, www.nine-dragons.com.

In Australia and New Zealand
Intrepid Travel, 360 Bourke St, Melbourne, Victoria 3000, T+61-03-8602 0500, www.intrepidtravel.com.au.
Travel Indochina, Level 10, HCF House, 403 George St, Sydney, NSW 2000, T+61-1300-138755 (toll free), www.travelindochina.com.au. Small group journeys and tailor-made holidays.

In Vietnam
Asia Pacific Travel, 14 Cua Bac St, Ba Dinh District, Hanoi, T+84-4-756 8868, www.asiapacifictravel.com.vn. Offers affordable, small group adventure trips and a wide choice of tours.

Asian Trails Ltd, 21 Nguyen Trung Ngan St, Hanoi, T-84-8-910 2871, www.asiantrails.info.
Asiatica Travel, 1A Trang Tien, Hanoi, T+84-4-933 1702, www.asiatica-travel.com. Specialist in adventure travel and customized tours.
Buffalo tours, 94 Ma May St, Hanoi, T+84-8-828 0702 (HCMC, T8-827 9169), www.buffalotours.com. Adventure and trekking tours.

Visas and immigration
Valid passports with visas issued by a Vietnamese embassy are required by all visitors. Visas are normally valid only for arrival by air at Hanoi and HCMC. Those wishing to enter or leave Vietnam by land must specify the border crossing when applying. It is possible to alter the point of departure at immigration offices in Hanoi and HCMC.

The standard tourist visa is valid for 1 month for 1 entry only. Tourist visas cost £38 (US$75) and generally take 5 days to process. Express visas cost £55 (2 days). Citizens of Sweden, Norway, Denmark and Finland may visit, visa free, for not more than 15 days.

Multiple entry visas
If you are planning on staying for a while or making a side trip to Laos or Cambodia with the intention of coming back to Vietnam then a 1-month multiple entry visa, £70 (US$139) will make life much simpler.

Visa extensions
Visa regulations are ever changing: usually it is possible to extend visas within Vietnam. Travel agencies and hotels will probably add their own mark-up but for many people it is worth paying to avoid the difficulty of making 1 or 2 journeys to an embassy. Visas can be extended for 1 month for US$15-30. Depending on where you are it will take between 1 day and a week. A visa valid for 1 month can only be extended for 1 month.

Weights and measures
Metric.

Vietnamese addresses

Odd numbers usually run consecutively on one side of the street, evens on the other; bis after a number, as in 16 bis Hai Ba Trung Street, means there are two houses with the same number and ter after the number means there are three houses with the same number. Large buildings with a single street number are usually subdivided 21A, 21B, etc; some buildings may be further subdivided 21C1, 21C2, and so on. An oblique (/ – sec or tren in Vietnamese) in a number, as in 23/16

Dinh Tien Hoang Street, means the address is to be found in a small side street (hem) – in this case running off Dinh Tien Hoang by the side of no 23: the house in question will probably be signed 23/16 rather than just 16. Usually, but by no means always, a hem will be quieter than the main street. Q stands for quận (district); this points you in the right general direction and is important in locating your destination as a long street may run through several quan.

Working in Vietnam

Officially, anyone working in Vietnam should have a business visa and a work permit. In practice there does seem to be a relatively relaxed attitude to foreigners working for short periods. Those with specific skills, notably IT and English language teaching, will not find it hard to get work. In Hanoi and HCMC there are hundreds of language schools keen to engage native speakers and the best ones pay quite well to those with the relevant qualifications.

Voluntary work is available but best organized in advance through volunteer agencies such as **Voluntary Service Overseas** (www.vso.org.uk) and the **Australian Volunteers International** (www.osb.org.au). There are few NGOs in Vietnam compared with Thailand and Cambodia. The first port of call for further information should be the **NGO Resource Centre**, La Thanh Hotel, 218 Doi Can, Hanoi, T4-8328570, www.ngocentre.org.vn.

Hanoi and around

→ *Colour map 2, B2/3.*

Hanoi is a small city of broad tree-lined boulevards, lakes, parks, weathered colonial buildings, elegant squares and some of the newest office blocks and hotels in Southeast Asia. It lies nearly 100 km from the sea on a bend in the Red River and from this geographical feature the city derives its name – Hanoi – meaning 'within a river bend'.

Hanoi is the capital of the world's 14th most populous country, but, in an age of urban sprawl, the city remains small and compact, historic and charming. Much of its charm lies not so much in the official 'sights' but in the unofficial and informal: the traffic zooming around the broad streets or the cyclos taking a mellow pedal through the Old Quarter, small shops packed with traders' goods or stacks of silk for visitors, skewered poultry on pavement stalls, mobile flower stalls piled on the backs of bikes, the bustle of pedestrians, the ubiquitous tinkle of the ice cream man's bicycle, and the political posters, now raised to an art form, dotted around the city.

At the heart of the city is Hoan Kiem Lake and the famous Sunbeam Bridge. The Old Quarter (36 Streets and Guilds) area, north of the lake, is bustling with commerce, its ancient buildings crumbling from the weight of history and activity. The French Quarter, which still largely consists of French buildings, is south of the lake. Here you'll find the Opera House and the grandest hotels, shops and offices.

Accessible on a tour from the city, the primates at Cuc Phuong National Park and the waters of Halong Bay make this area one of the most visited in Vietnam. ⟩⟩ *For listings see pages 1021-1030.*

Ins and outs

Getting there

Air **Noi Bai Airport** (HAN) is 35 km from Hanoi, a 45-minute to one-hour drive, and is the hub for international and domestic flights. There is a tourist information desk with scant information (daily 0700-1700) and an airport information desk (daily 0600-2300).

The official **Airport Taxi**, T04-873 3333, charges a fixed price of US$7.50 to the city centre. The airport minibus service (every 30 minutes, daily 0900-2000, US$2), terminates opposite the **Vietnam Airlines** office, Quang Trung Street, T04-825 0872. Return buses leave the Vietnam Airlines office at regular intervals from 0500-1800.

Bus Open Tour Buses leave and depart from tour operator offices in the city for destinations in the south, including Hué, Hoi An, Dalat, Nha Trang, Mui Ne and Ho Chi Minh City.

Train The train station is a short taxi ride (40,000-65,000d) from the Old Quarter, north of Hoan Kiem Lake. There are regular trains to Ho Chi Minh City, and all points on the route south, as well as to Lao Cai (for Sapa) in the north. ⟩⟩ *See Transport, page 1029.*

Getting around

At the heart of the city is Hoan Kiem Lake. The majority of visitors make straight for the Old Quarter (36 Streets and Guilds) area north of the lake, which is densely packed and bustling with commerce. The French Quarter, which still largely consists of French buildings, is south of the lake. Here you'll find the Opera House and the grandest hotels, shops and offices. A large block of the city west of Hoan Kiem Lake (Ba Dinh District) represents the heart of the government and the civil and military administration of Vietnam. To the north of the city is the West Lake, Tay Ho District, fringed with the suburban homes of the new middle class.

Hanoi is getting more frenetic by the minute but, thanks to the city's elegant, tree-lined boulevards, walking and cycling can still be delightful. If you like the idea of being pedalled around town, then a cyclo is the answer but be prepared for some concentrated haggling. There are also motorbike taxis (*xe ôm*), and self-drive motorbikes for hire as well as a fleet of metered taxis. Local buses have also improved.

Best time to visit

For much of the year Hanoi's weather is decidedly non-tropical. It benefits from glorious Europe-like springs and autumns, when temperatures are warm but not too hot and not too cold. From May until early November Hanoi is fearfully hot and steamy. You cannot take a step without breaking into a sweat. The winter months from November to February can be chilly and Hanoians wrap themselves up well in warm coats, woolly hats, gloves and scarves. Most museums are closed on Mondays.

Tourist information

The new privately run **Tourist Information Center** ① *7 Dinh Tien Hoang St, T04-926 3366, www.vntourists.com, daily 0800-2200*, at the northern end of the lake, is proving useful. It provides information and maps and will book hotels and transport tickets at no extra cost; also currency exchange and ATM. **Hanoi Administration of Tourism** ① *3 Le Lai St, T04-824 7652*. Useful information is also available from the multitude of tour operators in the city.

▶▶ *See Activities and tours, page 1027.*

Background

The origins of Hanoi as a great city lie with a temple orphan, Ly Cong Uan. Ly rose through the ranks of the palace guards to become their commander and in 1010, four years after the death of the previous King Le Hoan, was enthroned, marking the beginning of the 200-year Ly Dynasty. On becoming king, Ly Cong Uan moved his capital from Hoa Lu to Dai La, which he renamed **Thang Long** (Soaring Dragon). Thang Long is present-day Hanoi.

During the period of French expansion into Indochina, the Red River was proposed as an alternative trade route to that of the Mekong. The French attacked and captured the citadel of Hanoi under the dubious pretext that the Vietnamese were about to attack. Recognizing that if a small expeditionary force could be so successful, then there would be little chance against a full-strength army, Emperor Tu Duc acceded to French demands. At the time that the French took control of Annam, Hanoi could still be characterized more as a collection of villages than a city. From 1882 onwards, Hanoi, along with the port city of Haiphong, became the focus of French activity in the north. Hanoi was made the capital of the new colony of Annam and the French laid out a 2 sq km residential and business district, constructing mansions, villas and public buildings incorporating both French and Asian architectural styles. At the end of the Second World War, with the French battling to keep Ho Chi Minh and his forces at bay, Hanoi became little more than a service centre. After the French withdrew in 1954, Ho Chi Minh concentrated on building up Vietnam and in particular Hanoi's industrial base.

Although Ho Chi Minh City has attracted the lion's share of Vietnam's foreign inward investment, Hanoi, as the capital, also receives a large amount. But whereas Ho Chi Minh City's investment tends to be in industry, Hanoi has received a great deal of attention from property developers, notably in the hotel and office sectors.

Hoan Kiem Lake

Hoan Kiem Lake, or Ho Guom (Lake of the Restored Sword) as it is more commonly referred to in Hanoi, is named after an incident that occurred during the 15th century. Emperor Le Thai To (1428-1433), following a momentous victory against an army of invading Ming Chinese, was sailing on the Lake when a golden turtle appeared from the depths to take back the charmed sword which had secured the victory and restore it to the Lake from whence it came. Like the sword in the stone of British Arthurian legend, Le Thai To's sword assures the Vietnamese of divine intervention in time of national crisis and the story is graphically portrayed in water puppet theatres across the country. There is a modest and rather dilapidated tower (the **Tortoise Tower**) commemorating the event on an islet in the southern part of the lake. In fact, the lake does contain large turtles, believed to be a variety of Asian soft-shell tortoise; one captured in 1968 was reputed to have weighed 250 kg.

Located on a small island on the lake, the **Ngoc Son Temple** ① *daily 0730-1800, 3000d*, was constructed in the early 19th century on the foundations of the old Khanh Thuy Palace, which had been built in 1739. The temple is dedicated to Van Xuong, the God of Literature, although the 13th-century hero Tran Hung Dao, the martial arts genius Quan Vu and the physician La To are also worshipped here. The island is linked to the shore by a red, arched wooden bridge, **The Huc (Sunbeam) Bridge**, constructed in 1875.

The park that surrounds the shore is used by the residents of the city every morning for jogging and t'ai chi (Chinese shadow boxing) and is regarded by locals as one of the city's beauty spots.

Old Quarter and 36 Streets

Stretching north from the Lake is the Old Quarter (36 Streets and Guilds or 36 Pho Phuong), the most beautiful area of the city. The narrow streets are each named after the products that are (or were) sold there (**Basket Street**, **Paper Street**, **Silk Street**, etc) and create an intricate web of activity and colour. By the 15th century there were 36 short lanes here, each specializing in a particular trade and representing one of the 36 guilds. Among them were the **Phuong Hang Dao (Dyers' Guild Street)**, and the **Phuong Hang Bac (Silversmiths' Street)**. Some of the area's past is still in evidence: at the south end of **Hang Dau Street**, for example, is a mass of stalls selling nothing but shoes, while Tin Street is still home to a community of pot and pan menders (and sellers). Generally, however, the crafts and trades have given way to new activities – karaoke bars and tourist shops – but it is remarkable the extent to which the streets still specialize in the production and sale of just one type of merchandise.

The dwellings in this area are known as *nha ong* (**tube houses**); they have narrow shop fronts, sometimes only 3 m wide, but can stretch back from the road for up to 50 m. In the countryside the dimensions of houses were calculated on the basis of the owner's own physical dimensions; in urban areas the tube houses evolved so that each house could have an, albeit very small, area of shop frontage facing onto the main street, its width determined by the social class of the owner. The houses tend to be interspersed by courtyards or 'wells' to permit light into the house and allow some space for outside activities like washing and gardening. The structures were built of bricks 'cemented' together with sugar-cane juice. The older houses tend to be lower; commoners were not permitted to build higher than the Emperor's own residence. Other regulations prohibited attic windows looking down on the street; this was to prevent assassination

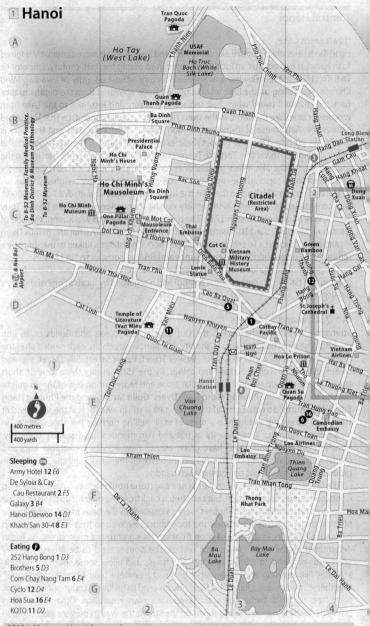

1 Hanoi

Tran Quoc Pagoda

Ho Tay (West Lake)

Thanh Nien

USAF Memorial

Ho Truc Bach (White Silk Lake)

Pho Duc Chinh

Yen Phu

Quan Thanh Pagoda

Quan Thanh

Hang Than

Phan Dinh Phung

Ba Dinh Square

Long Bien

Presidential Palace

Hang Dau Station

Gam Cau

Hang Khoai

Ho Chi Minh's House

To B-52 Museum, Family Medical Practice, Ba Dinh District & Museum of Ethnology

Ngoc Ha

Hung Vuong

Bac Son

Hoang Dieu

Nguyen Tri Phuong

Ly Nam De

Cua Dong

Dong Xuan

Luong Van Can

Hang Gai

Ho Chi Minh's Mausoleum

Ho Chi Minh Museum

Ba Dinh Square

Citadel (Restricted Area)

Cha Ca

One Pillar Pagoda

Mausoleum Entrance

Chua Mot Cot

Thai Embassy

Green Bamboo

To B-52 Museum

Ong Ich Khiem

Doi Can

Le Hong Phong

Cot Co

Duong Thanh

Ly Quoc Su

Hang Trong

Vietnam Military History Museum

Hang Bong

St Joseph's Cathedral

Nha Chung

To Sa & Noi Bai Airport

Kim Ma

Nguyen Thai Hoc

Tran Phu

Cao Ba Quat

Nguyen Khuyen

Lenin Statue

Dien Bien Phu

Cathay Pacific

Trang Thi

Chung

Vietnam Airlines

Hai Ba Trung

Cat Linh

Temple of Literature (Van Mieu Pagoda)

Van Mieu

Quoc Tu Giam

Ton Duc Thang

Nam Ngu

Hoa Lo Prison

Phan Boi Chau

Ly Thuong Kiet

Hanoi Station

Van Chuong Lake

Le Duan

Tran Quy Cap

Quan Su Pagoda

Ly Thuong

Tran Hung Dao

Cambodian Embassy

Kham Thien

Tran Quoc Toan

Lao Airlines

Nguyen Du

Lao Embassy

Le Duan

Thien Quang Lake

Quang Trung

Tran Nhan Tong

De La Thanh

Thong Nhat Park

Hoa Ma

Ba Trieu

Ba Mau Lake

Bay Mau Lake

Le Dai Hanh

N ↓

400 metres
400 yards

Sleeping 🛏

Army Hotel **12** *E6*
De Syloia & Cay
  Cau Restaurant **2** *F5*
Galaxy **3** *B4*
Hanoi Daewoo **14** *D1*
Khach San 30-4 **8** *E3*

Eating 🍴

252 Hang Bong **1** *D3*
Brothers **5** *D3*
Com Chay Nang Tam **6** *E4*
Cyclo **12** *D4*
Hoa Sua **16** *E4*
KOTO **11** *D2*

➡ **Hanoi maps**
1 Hanoi, page 1012
2 Hanoi centre, page 1014

and to stop people from looking down on a passing king. As far as colour and decoration were concerned, purple and gold were strictly for royal use only, as was the decorative use of the dragon.

By the early 20th century, traditional tube houses were being replaced with buildings inspired by French architecture. Many fine buildings from this era remain and are best appreciated by standing back and looking upwards. Shutters, cornices, columns and wrought-iron balconies and balustrades are common decorative features. An ornate façade sometimes conceals a pitched roof behind. There are some good examples on **Nguyen Sieu Street**. On Ma May Street, the shophouse at **No 87** ⓘ *daily 0800-1200, 1300-1700, 5000d, guide included*, is a wonderfully preserved example of an original Hanoi building.

Further north is the large and varied **Dong Xuan Market**, on Dong Xuan Street. This covered market was destroyed in a fire in 1994. It has since been rebuilt and now specializes in clothes and household goods.

St Joseph's Cathedral
To the west of Hoan Kiem Lake, in a little square stands the twin-towered neo-Gothic Saint Joseph's Cathedral. Built in 1886, the cathedral is important as one of the very first colonial-era buildings in Hanoi finished, as it was, soon after the Treaty of Tientsin which gave France control over Vietnam. Some fine stained-glass windows remain.

Opera House
ⓘ *Not open to the public except during public performances. See the billboards outside or visit the box office for details.*
To the south and east of Hoan Kiem Lake is the proud-looking French-era Opera House. It was built between 1901 and 1911 by François Lagisquet and is one of the finest French colonial buildings in Hanoi. Some 35,000 bamboo piles were sunk into the mud of the Red River to provide foundations for the lofty edifice. The exterior is a mass of

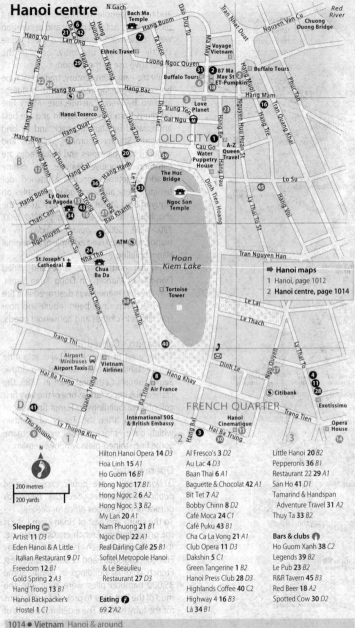

Hanoi centre

N Gach
Bach Ma Temple
Hang Buom
Red River
Chuong Duong Bridge
N Gach
Hang Vai
Lan Ong
Hang Duong
Ta Hien
Dao Duy Tu
Ma May
Tran Nhat Duat
Nguyen Van Cu
Ethnic Travel
Luong Ngoc Quyen
Voyage Vietnam
Thuoc Bac
H Hoang
Hang Can
Hang Bac
Buffalo Tours
87 Ma May St ET-Pumpkin
Buffalo Tours
Phuc Tan
Hang Bo
Hang Thiec
Hang Non
Hanoi Toserco
Luong Van Can
Dinh Liet
Trung Yen
Gai Ngu
Love Planet
A-Z Queen Travel
Hang Mam
Hang Tre
Tran Quang Khai
Hang Gai
Hang Manh
Hang Gai
OLD CITY
Cau Go Water Puppetry House
Lo Su
Hang Hanh
The Huc Bridge
Ngoc Son Temple
Dinh Tien Hoang
Ly Thai To
Hang Voi
Ly Quoc Su Pagoda
Chan Cam
Ngo Huyen
ATM
Ngoc Son Temple
Hoan Kiem Lake
Tran Nguyen Han
Ly Quoc Su
Nha Tho
Chua Ba Da
St Joseph's Cathedral
Tortoise Tower
Le Lai
Le Thach
Le Thai To
Trang Thi
Airport Minibuses
Airport Taxis
Vietnam Airlines
Hang Khay
Dinh Le
Ngo Quyen
Ly Thai To
Hai Ba Trung
Air France
FRENCH QUARTER
Citibank
Exotissimo
International SOS & British Embassy
Ba Trieu
Hang Bai
Hanoi Cinematique
Trang Tien
Opera House
Tho Nhuom
Ly Thuong Kiet
Hai Ba Trung

Hanoi maps
1 Hanoi, page 1012
2 Hanoi centre, page 1014

N
200 metres
200 yards

Sleeping
Artist **11** D3
Eden Hanoi & A Little
 Italian Restaurant **9** D1
Freedom **12** B1
Gold Spring **2** A3
Hang Trong **13** B1
Hanoi Backpacker's
 Hostel **1** C1

Hilton Hanoi Opera **14** D3
Hoa Linh **15** A1
Ho Guom **16** B1
Hong Ngoc **17** B1
Hong Ngoc 2 **6** A2
Hong Ngoc 3 **3** B2
My Lan **20** A1
Nam Phuong **21** B1
Ngoc Diep **22** A1
Real Darling Café **25** B1
Sofitel Metropole Hanoi
 & Le Beaulieu
 Restaurant **27** D3

Eating
69 **2** A2

Al Fresco's **3** D2
Au Lac **4** D3
Baan Thai **6** A1
Baguette & Chocolat **42** A1
Bit Tet **7** A2
Bobby Chinn **8** D2
Café Moca **24** C1
Café Puku **43** B1
Cha Ca La Vong **21** A1
Club Opera **11** D3
Dakshin **5** C1
Green Tangerine **1** B2
Hanoi Press Club **28** D3
Highlands Coffee **40** C2
Highway 4 **16** B3
Lá **34** B1

Little Hanoi **20** B2
Pepperonis **36** B1
Restaurant 22 **29** A1
San Ho **41** D1
Tamarind & Handspan
 Adventure Travel **31** A2
Thuy Ta **33** B2

Bars & clubs
Ho Guom Xanh **38** C2
Legends **39** B2
Le Pub **23** B2
R&R Tavern **45** B3
Red Beer **18** A2
Spotted Cow **30** D2

shutters, wrought-iron work, little balconies and a tiled frieze. The top balustrade is capped with griffins. Inside, there are dozens of little boxes and fine decoration evocative of the French era. Having suffered years of neglect, the Opera House was eventually lavishly restored, opening in time for the Francophone Summit held in 1997. The restoration cost US$14 million, a colossal sum to spend on the reappointment of a colonial edifice.

Museum of Vietnamese History

ⓘ *1 Trang Tien St, Tue-Sun 0800-1130, 1330-1630; 15,000d.*

The history museum (**Bao Tang Lich Su**) is housed in a splendid building, completed in 1931. It was built as the home of the École Française d'Extrême-Orient, a distinguished archaeological, historical and ethnological research institute, by Ernest Hébrard. The collection spans Vietnamese history from the Neolithic period to the 20th century of Ho Chi Minh and is arranged in chronological order.

Galleries on the first floor lead from the Neolithic (Bac Son) represented by stone tools and jewellery to the Bronze Age (Dong Son) with some finely engraved ceremonial bronze drums, symbolizing wealth and power. Wooden stakes that were used to impale invading Chinese forces in 1288 were found in 1976 at the cross of the Chanh River and Bach Dang River – a photo of some remaining in the river bed is interesting and a giant oil painting depicting the famous battle is hypnotically fascinating. The giant turtle, a symbol of longevity, supports a vast stela which praises the achievements of Le Loi (reigned 1428-1433), founder of the Le Dynasty who harnessed nationalist sentiment and repelled the war-hungry Chinese. A replica of the oldest Buddha Amitabha statue dominates the far end of the first floor. Amitabha is the Buddha of Infinite Light and the original dates from 1057 and was from Phat Tich Pagoda in Bac Ninh Province. Opposite the statue the oldest minted coins in Vietnam are displayed. They date from AD 968 and were minted by the Dinh Dynasty. A collection of outsized paper currency from the French colonial days is also interesting. These date from 1875 when the French established the Bank of Indochina. The second floor begins with the 15th century to the present day; Champa is represented by some well-preserved stone carvings of apsaras, mythical dancing girls and a head of Garuda, found at Quang Nam. There are relics such as 18th-century, unusually shaped, bronze pagoda gongs and urns of successive royal dynasties from Le to Nguyen. Unfortunately, some of the pieces are reproductions, including a number of the stelae.

Hoa Lo Prison

ⓘ *1 Hoa Lo, Tue-Sun 0800-1130, 1330-1630, 5000d which includes a useful pamphlet; 10,000d for a larger one.*

Hoa Lo Prison (Maison Centrale), better known as the **Hanoi Hilton**, is the prison where US POWs were incarcerated during the Vietnamese War. Up until 1969, prisoners were also tortured here. Two US Air Force officers, Charles Tanner and Ross Terry, rather than face torture, concocted a story about two other members of their squadron who had been court-martialled for refusing to fly missions against the north. Thrilled with this piece of propaganda, visiting Japanese Communists were told the story and it filtered back to the US. Unfortunately for Tanner and Terry, they had called their imaginary pilots Clark Kent and Ben Casey (both TV heroes). When the Vietnamese realized they had been made fools of, the two prisoners were again tortured. The final prisoners of war were not released until 1973, some having been held in the north since 1964. At the end of 1992, a US mission was shown around the prison where 2000 inmates had been housed in squalid conditions.

Despite pleas from war veterans and party members, the site was sold to a Singapore-Vietnamese joint venture and is now a hotel and shopping complex, **Hanoi Towers**. As part of the deal the developers had to leave a portion of the prison for use as a museum. There are recreations of conditions under colonial rule when the French incarcerated patriotic Vietnamese from 1896: by 1953 they were holding 2000 prisoners in a space designed for 500. Less prominence is given to the role of the prison for holding American pilots, but Douglas 'Pete' Peterson, the first post-war American Ambassador to Vietnam (1997-2001), who was one such occupant (imprisoned 1966-1973), has his mug-shot on the wall, as does John McCain (imprisoned 1967-1973), now a US presidential candidate.

West from the Citadel

Vietnam Military History Museum

ⓘ *28 Dien Bien Phu St, Tue-Thu, Sat and Sun 0800-1130, 1300-1630; 5000d, camera use, 20,000d. ATM and Highlands Coffee Café on site.*

Tanks, planes and artillery fill the courtyard of the Army Museum (Bao Tang Quan Doi). Symbolically, an untouched Mig-21 stands at the museum entrance while wreckage of B-52s, F1-11s and Q2Cs is piled up at the back. The museum illustrates battles and episodes in Vietnam's fight for independence, from the struggles with China through to the resistance to the French and the Battle of Dien Bien Phu (illustrated by a good model). Inevitably, of course, there are lots of photographs and exhibits of the American war and although much is self-evident, unfortunately a lot of the explanations are in Vietnamese only.

In the precincts of the museum is the **Cot Co**, a flag tower, raised up on three platforms. Built in 1812, it is the only substantial part of the original **citadel** still standing. There are good views over Hanoi from the top. The walls of the citadel were destroyed by the French between 1894 and 1897, presumably as they symbolized the power of the Vietnamese emperors. The French were highly conscious of the projection of might, power and authority through large structures, which helps explain their own remarkable architectural legacy. Other remaining parts of the citadel are in the hands of the Vietnamese army and out of bounds to visitors. Across the road from the museum's front entrance is a **statue of Lenin**.

Ho Chi Minh's Mausoleum and Ba Dinh Square

ⓘ *1 Apr-1 Oct Tue-Thu 0730-1100, 1400-1600, Fri 0730-1100, Sat and Sun 0730-1100, 1400-1630; 30 Nov-31 Mar Tue-Thu 0800-1100, 1330-1600, Fri 0800-1100, Sat and Sun 0800-1100, 1330-1630; closed Oct and Nov for conservation. Before entering the mausoleum, visitors must leave possessions at the office (Ban To Chuc) on Huong Vuong, just south of and a few mins' walk from the Mausoleum. Visitors must be respectful: dress neatly, walk solemnly, do not talk and do not take anything in that could be construed as a weapon, for example a penknife.*

The Vietnamese have made the mausoleum housing Ho Chi Minh's body a holy place of pilgrimage and visitors march in file to see Ho's embalmed corpse inside the mausoleum (Lang Chu Tich Ho Chi Minh). The embalming and eternal display of Ho Chi Minh's body was contrary to Ho's own wishes: he wanted to be cremated and his ashes placed in three urns to be positioned atop three unmarked hills in the north, centre and south of the country. He once wrote that "cremation is not only good from the point of view of hygiene, but it also saves farmland". The embalming of Ho's body was undertaken by the chief Soviet embalmer, Dr Sergei Debrov, who also pickled such Communist luminaries as Klenient

Gottwald (President of Czechoslovakia), Georgi Dimitrov (Prime Minister of Bulgaria) and Forbes Burnham (President of Guyana). Debrov was flown to Hanoi from Moscow as Ho lay dying, bringing with him two transport planes packed with air conditioners (to keep the corpse cool) and other equipment. To escape US bombing, the team moved Ho to a cave, taking a full year to complete the embalming process. Russian scientists still check-up on their handiwork, servicing Ho's body regularly. Their embalming methods and the fluids they use are still a closely guarded secret. In an interview, Debrov noted with pleasure the poor state of China's Chairman Mao's body, which was embalmed without Soviet help.

The mausoleum, built between 1973 and 1975, is a massive, square and forbidding structure and must be among the best constructed, maintained and air-conditioned buildings in Vietnam. Opened in 1975, it is a modelled closely on Lenin's Mausoleum in Moscow. Ho lies with a guard at each corner of his bier and visitors march past in file to see his body.

In front of Ho Chi Minh's Mausoleum is **Ba Dinh Square** where Ho read out the Vietnamese Declaration of Independence on 2 September 1945. Following Ho's declaration, 2 September became Vietnam's National Day. Coincidentally, 2 September was also the date on which Ho died in 1969, although his death was not officially announced until 3 September in order not to mar people's enjoyment of National Day in the beleaguered north of the country.

Ho Chi Minh's house and the Presidential Palace

ⓘ *1 Bach Thao St, T04-0804 4529, summer Tue-Thu, Sat and Sun 0730-1100, 1400-1600, Fri 0730-1100; winter Tue-Thu, Sat and Sun 0800-1100, 1330-1600, Fri 0800-1100; 5000d. The Presidential Palace is not open to the public.*

From the mausoleum, visitors are directed to Ho Chi Minh's house built in the compound of the former Presidential Palace. The palace, now a party guesthouse, was the residence of the Governors-General of French Indochina and was built between 1900 and 1908. In 1954, when North Vietnam's struggle for independence was finally achieved, Ho Chi Minh declined to live in the palace, saying that it belonged to the people. Instead, he stayed in what is said to have been an electrician's house in the same compound. He lived here from 1954 to 1958, before moving to a new stilt house built on the other side of the small lake (Ho Chi Minh's 'Fish Farm', swarming with massive and well-fed carp). The house was designed by Ho and an architect, Nguyen Van Ninh. This modest house made of rare hardwoods is airy and personal and immaculately kept. Ho conducted meetings under the house, which is raised up on wooden pillars, and slept and worked above from May 1958 to August 1969. Behind the house is Ho's bomb shelter and, behind that, the hut where he died in 1969.

One Pillar Pagoda and Ho Chi Minh Museum

Close by is the **Chua Mot Cot** (One Pillar Pagoda), one of the few structures remaining from the original foundation of the city. It was built in 1049 by Emperor Ly Thai Tong, although the shrine has since been rebuilt on several occasions, most recently in 1955 after the French destroyed it, before withdrawing from the country. The emperor built the pagoda in a fit of religious passion after he dreamt that he saw the goddess Quan Am (Vietnam's equivalent of the Chinese goddess Kuan-yin, sitting on a lotus and holding a young boy, whom she handed to the Emperor. On the advice of counsellors who interpreted the dream, the Emperor built a little lotus-shaped temple in the centre of a water-lily pond and shortly afterwards his queen gave birth to a son. As the name suggests, it is supported on a single (concrete) pillar with a brick and stone staircase running up one side. The pagoda symbolizes the 'pure' lotus sprouting from the sea of sorrow. Original in design, with dragons running along the apex of the elegantly-curved tiled roof, the temple is one of the most revered monuments in Vietnam.

Overshadowing the One Pillar Pagoda is the **Ho Chi Minh Museum** ① *19 Ngoc Ha St, T04-846 3752, Tue-Thu and Sat 0800-1130, 1400-1600, Fri 0800-1130, 10,000d, 40,000d for guide*, opened in 1990 in celebration of the centenary of Ho's birth. Contained in a large and impressive modern building, it is the best arranged and most innovative museum in Vietnam. The displays trace Ho's life and work from his early wanderings around the world to his death and final victory over the south.

Temple of Literature
① *Entrance on Quoc Tu Giam St, T04-845 2917, open daily summer 0730-1730, winter daily 0730-1700; 5000d, 45-min tour in French or English 50,000d, 3000d for brochure. ATM inside.*
The temple of literature (Van Mieu Pagoda) is the largest and, probably, the most important, temple complex in Hanoi. It was founded in 1070 by Emperor Ly Thanh Tong, dedicated to Confucius who had a substantial following in Vietnam, and modelled, so it is said, on a temple in Shantung, China, the birthplace of the sage. Some researchers while acknowledging the date of the foundation, challenge the view that it was built as a Confucian institution pointing to the ascendancy of Buddhism during the Ly Dynasty. Confucian principles and teaching rapidly replaced Buddhism, however and Van Mieu subsequently became the intellectual and spiritual centre of the kingdom as a cult of literature and education spread amongst the court, the mandarins and then among the common people. At one time there were said to be 20,000 schools teaching the Confucian classics in northern Vietnam alone.

The temple and its compound are arranged north-south; visitors enter at the southern end from Quoc Tu Giam Street. On the pavement two pavilions house stelae bearing the inscription *ha ma* (climb down from your horse), a nice reminder that even the most elevated dignitaries had to proceed on foot. The main **Cong Van Mieu Mon** (Van Mieu Gate) is adorned with 15th-century dragons. Traditionally, the large central gate was opened only on ceremonial occasions. The path leads through the Cong Dai Trung to a second courtyard and the **Van Khue Gac Pavilion**, which was built in 1805 and dedicated to the Constellation of Literature. The roof is tiled according to the yin-yang principle.

Beyond lies the **Courtyard of the Stelae** at the centre of which is the rectangular pond or Cieng Thien Quang (**Well of Heavenly Clarity**). More important are the stelae themselves, on which are recorded the names of 1306 successful examination scholars (*tien si*). Of the 82 stelae that survive (30 are missing), the oldest dates back to 1442 and the most recent to 1779. Each stela is carried on the back of a tortoise, symbol of strength and longevity. The stelae are arranged in no order but three chronological categories can be identified. Fourteen date from the 15th and 16th centuries; they are the smallest and embellished with floral motifs and yin-yang symbols but not dragons (a royal emblem). Twenty-five stelae are from the 17th century and ornamented with dragons (by now permitted), pairs of phoenix and other creatures mythical or real. The remaining 43 stelae are of 18th-century origin; they are the largest and decorated with two stylized dragons, some merging with flame clouds.

Passing the examination was not easy: in 1733, out of some 3000 entrants only eight passed the doctoral examination (*Thai Hoc Sinh*) and became Mandarins, a task that took 35 days. This tradition was begun in 1484, on the instruction of Emperor Le Thanh Tong, and continued through to 1878, during which time 116 examinations were held.

The Temple of Literature was not used only for examinations, however: food was also distributed from here to the poor and infirm, 500 g of rice at a time. In 1880, the French Consul Monsieur de Kergaradec recorded that 22,000 impoverished people came to receive this meagre handout.

Continuing north, the **Dai Thanh Mon** (Great Success Gate) leads on to a courtyard flanked by two buildings which date from 1954, the originals having been destroyed in 1947. These buildings were reserved for 72 disciples of Confucius. Facing is the **Dai Bai Duong** (Great House of Ceremonies) which was built in the 19th century but in the earlier style of the Le Dynasty. The carved wooden friezes with their dragons, phoenix, lotus flowers, fruits, clouds and yin-yang discs are all symbolically charged, depicting the order of the universe and by implication reflecting the god-given hierarchical nature of human society, each in his place. It is not surprising that the Communist government has hitherto had reservations about preserving a temple extolling such heretical doctrine. Inside is an altar on which sit statues of Confucius and his closest disciples. Adjoining is the **Dai Thanh Sanctuary** (Great Success Sanctuary), which also contains a statue of Confucius.

B-52 Museum
ⓘ *157 Doi Can St, free.*

The remains of downed B-52s have been hawked around Hanoi over many years but seem to have found a final resting place at the **Bao Tang Chien Tang B-52** (B-52 Museum). This curious place is not really a museum but this doesn't matter because what everyone wants to do is to walk over the wings and tail of a shattered B-52, and the B-52 in question lies scattered around the yard. As visitors to Vietnamese museums will come to expect, any enemy objects are heaped up as junk while the Vietnamese pieces are painted, cared for and carefully signed with the names of whichever heroic unit fought in them. There are anti-aircraft guns, the devastating SAMs that wreaked so much havoc on the US Air Force and a Mig-21. Curiously the signs omit to mention the fact that all this hardware was made in Russia.

Vietnam Museum of Ethnology
ⓘ *Nguyen Van Huyen Rd, some distance west of the city centre in Cau Giay District, T04-756 2193, Tue-Sun 0830-1730, 20,000d, photography 50,000d, tour guide 50,000d. Take a taxi or catch the No 14 minibus from Dinh Tien Hoang St, north of Hoan Kiem Lake, to the Nghia Tan stop; turn right and walk down Hoang Quoc Viet St for 1 block, before turning right at the Petrolimex station down Nguyen Van Huyen; the museum is on the left.*

The collection here of some 25,000 artefacts, 15,000 photographs and documentaries of practices and rituals is excellent and, more to the point, is attractively and informatively presented with labels in Vietnamese, English and French. It displays the material culture (textiles, musical instruments, jewellery, tools, baskets and the like) of the majority Kinh people as well as Vietnam's 53 other designated minority peoples. While much is historical, the museum is also attempting to build up its contemporary collection. There is a shop attached to the museum and ethnic minorities' homes have been recreated in the grounds.

Around Hanoi ⊛▲▸ *pp1021-1030. Colour map 2, B2-4.*

There are a number of worthwhile day and overnight trips from Hanoi: the Perfume Pagoda lies to the southwest; Tam Coc and Cuc Phuong National Park are some three hours south, while Halong Bay, best visited on an overnight trip, is three hours to the east.

Perfume Pagoda → *Colour map 2, B2.*

ⓘ *A tour from Hanoi costs about US$30 and includes the return boat trip along the Yen River.*
The Perfume Pagoda (Chua Huong or Chua Huong Tich) is 60 km southwest of Hanoi. A sampan takes visitors along the Yen River, a diverting 4-km ride through a flooded landscape to the Mountain of the Perfume Traces. From here it is a 3-km hike up the mountain to the cool, dark cave where the Perfume Pagoda is located. The stone statue of Quan Am in the principal pagoda was carved in 1793 after Tay Son rebels had stolen and melted down its bronze predecessor to make cannon balls. Dedicated to Quan Am, it is one of a number of shrines and towers built amongst limestone caves and is regarded as one of the most beautiful spots in Vietnam. Emperor Le Thanh Tong (1460-1497) described it as *"Nam Thien de nhat dong"* or "foremost cave under the Vietnamese sky". It is a popular pilgrimage spot, particularly during the festival months of March and April.

Tam Coc → *Colour map 2, B3.*

ⓘ *The turning to Tam Coc is 4 km south of Ninh Binh on Hwy 1. US$2 plus US$1.50 per person for the boat ride. Can easily be reached from Hanoi on a day trip, either as part of an organized tour or by hiring a car and driver. Take plenty of sun cream and a hat.*
An area of enchanting natural beauty, Tam Coc means literally 'three caves'. Those who have seen the film *Indochine*, some of which was shot here, will be familiar with the nature of the beehive-type scenery created by limestone towers, similar to those of Halong Bay. The highlight of this excursion is an enchanting boat ride up the little Ngo Dong River through the eponymous three caves. The exact form varies from wet to dry season; when flooded, the channel disappears and one or two of the caves may be drowned; in the dry season, the shallow river meanders between fields of golden rice. Women punt pitch-and-resin tubs that look like elongated coracles through the tunnels. It is a leisurely experience and a chance to observe at close quarters the extraordinary method of rowing with the feet. The villagers have a rota to decide whose turn it is to row and, to supplement their fee, will try and sell visitors embroidered tablecloths. Enterprising photographers snap you setting off from the bank and will surprise you 1 km upstream with copies of your cheesy grin already printed. On a busy day the scene from above is like a two-way, nose-to-tail procession of water boatmen, so to enjoy Tam Coc at its best, visit in the morning.

Cuc Phuong National Park → *Colour map 2, B2.*

ⓘ *Nho Quan district, 120 km south of Hanoi and 45 km west of Ninh Binh, T030-848006, www.cuc phuongtourism.com; 40,000d. Can be visited as a day trip from Hanoi, either on an organized tour (a sensible option for lone travellers or pairs) or by hiring a car with driver or a motorbike.*
Located in an area of deeply-cut limestone and reaching elevations of up to 800 m, this park is covered by 22,000 ha of humid tropical montagne forest. It is home to an estimated 2000 species of flora, including the giant parashorea, cinamomum and sandoricum trees. Wildlife, however, has been much depleted by hunting, so that only 117 mammal, 307 bird species and 110 reptiles and amphibians are thought to remain. April and May sees fat grubs and pupae metamorphosing into swarms of beautiful butterflies that mantle the forest in fantastic shades of greens and yellows. The government has resettled a number of the park's 30,000 Muong minority people but Muong villages do still exist and can be visited. The **Endangered Primate Rescue Centre** ⓘ *www.primatecenter.org, daily 0900-1100, 1330-1600, limited entrance every 30 mins, 10,000d,* is a big draw in the park, with more than 30 cages, four houses and two semi-wild enclosures for the 130 animals in breeding programmes.

Halong Bay → *Colour map 2, B4.*

ⓘ *Most boats depart from Halong City, 110 km east of Hanoi. Http://halongbay. halong.net.vn, has comprehensive information on the area, including transport details. US$1 admission for each cave and attraction. You need 4-5 hrs to see the bay properly but an overnight stay aboard a boat is enjoyable. The majority of people visit on an all-inclusive tour with tourist cafés or tour operators from Hanoi (see page 1027). It can be stormy in Jun-Aug; Jul and Aug are also the wettest months; winter is cool and dry; rain is possible at all times of year.*

Halong means 'descending dragon'. An enormous beast is said to have careered into the sea at this point, cutting the fantastic bay from the rocks as it thrashed its way into the depths. Vietnamese poets, including the 'Poet King' Le Thanh Tong, have traditionally extolled the beauty of this romantic area, with its rugged islands that protrude from a sea dotted with sailing junks. Artists, too, have drawn inspiration from the crooked islands, seeing the forms of monks and gods in the rock faces, and dragon's lairs and fairy lakes in the depths of the caves. Another myth says that the islands are dragons sent by the gods to impede the progress of an invasion flotilla. The area was the location of two famous sea battles in the 10th and 13th centuries and is now a UNESCO World Heritage Site.

Geologically, the tower-karst scenery of Halong Bay is the product of millions of years of chemical action and river erosion working on the limestone to produce a pitted landscape. At the end of the last ice age, when the glaciers melted, the sea level rose and inundated the area turning hills into islands. The islands of the bay are divided by a broad channel: to the east are the smaller outcrops of Bai Tu Long, while to the west are the larger islands with caves and secluded beaches. Rocks can be treacherously slippery, so sensible footwear is advised. Many of the caves are a disappointment, with harrying vendors, mounds of litter and disfiguring graffiti. Among the more spectacular, however, are **Hang Hanh**, which extends for 2 km. Tour guides will point out fantastic stalagmites and stalactites which, with imagination, become heroes, demons and animals. **Hang Luon** is another flooded cave, which leads to the hollow core of a doughnut-shaped island. It can be swum or navigated by coracle. **Hang Dau Go** is the cave in which Tran Hung Dao stored his wooden stakes prior to studding them in the bed of the Bach Dang River in 1288 to destroy the boats of invading Mongol hordes. **Hang Thien Cung** is a hanging cave, a short 50-m haul above sea level, with dripping stalactites, stumpy stalagmites and solid rock pillars.

◉ Hanoi and around listings

Hotel prices
LL over US$200   L US$151-200   AL US$101-150
A US$66-100   B US$46-65   C US$31-45
D US$21-30   E US$12-20   F US$7-11
G US$6 and under

Restaurant prices
††† over US$12   †† US$6-12   † under US$6

● Sleeping

Old Quarter buildings are tightly packed and have small rooms, sometimes without windows. Hotels in this area offer the best value for money.

Central Hanoi *p1011, maps p1012 and p1014*
LL-AL Hanoi Daewoo, 360 Kim Ma St, T04-831 5000, www.hanoi-daewoo.com. A giant hotel with an adjoining apartment complex and office tower. The hotel is one of Vietnam's most plush with luxuriously decorated rooms, a large pool, shops and 4 restaurants. The **Edo** is considered as serving some of the finest Japanese food in town.
L-A De Syloia, 17A Tran Hung Dao St, T04-824 5346, www.desyloia.com. An attractive and friendly small boutique, business hotel south of the lake. 33 rooms and suites, a business centre and gym in

good central location. The popular **Cay Cau** restaurant specializes in Vietnamese dishes and the daily set-lunch is excellent value.

L-A Ho Guom, 76 Hang Trong St, T04-824 3565, hoguomtjc@hn.vnn.vn. Very near the lake and set back from the road in a quiet courtyard with a nice position. All rooms are furnished in Hué imperial style and are fully equipped. Staff are friendly and helpful. This hotel is upgrading to 4 stars and prices were not available at the time of going to press.

A Army Hotel, 33C Pham Ngu Lao St, T04-825 2896, armyhotel@fpt.vn. Owned and run by the Army, this is a surprisingly pleasant and attractive hotel. Set around a decent-sized swimming pool, it is quiet and comfortable. Has 69 a/c rooms and a restaurant.

A Galaxy, 1 Phan Dinh Phung St, T04-828 2888, www.tctgroup.com.vn. Well-run 3-star business hotel (built in 1918) with 50 carpeted rooms and full accessories including the all-important bedside reading lights which too many expensive hotels forget.

A Hong Ngoc, 30-34 Hang Manh St, T04-828 5053, hongngochotel@hn.vnn.vn. This is a real find. A small, family-run hotel, with comfortable rooms and huge bathrooms with baths. It is spotlessly clean through-out and run by cheerful and helpful staff. Breakfast included. There are 2 other Hong Ngoc's in the Old Quarter: **Hong Ngoc 2**, 99 Ma May St, T04-8283631, hongngochotel@ hn.vnn.vn, and **Hong Ngoc 3** (see below).

A-D Eden Hanoi, 78 Tho Nhuom St, T04-942 3273, www.edenhanoihotel.com. Good location but small rooms; worth paying more for the suites. Popular and handy for **A Little Italian** restaurant.

C-D Gold Spring Hotel, 22 Nguyen Huu Huan St, T04-926 3057, www.goldenspring hotel.com.vn. On the edge of the Old Quarter. 22 fine rooms that are attractively decorated. Breakfast and free internet included.

C-D Hang Trong, 56 Hang Trong St, T04-825 1346, thiencotravelvn@yahoo.com. A/c and hot water (showers only), a few unusual and quite decent rooms set back from the road,

either on a corridor or in a courtyard. The ones that don't overlook the courtyard are dark and airless. Very convenient for every part of town. Internet and booking office for **Sinh Café** tours.

C-D Hong Ngoc 3, 39 Hang Bac St, T04-926 0322, hongngochotel@hn.vnn.vn. Some staff here are exceptionally helpful, others are not. A mixed bag. Rooms are clean and comfortable with TVs, a/c and baths. It's in a great central location and surprisingly quiet. You may want to pass on the breakfast.

C-F Freedom, 57 Hang Trong St, T04-826 7119, freedomhotel@hn.vnn.vn. Not far from Hoan Kiem lake and the cathedral. 11 spacious rooms with desks. Some have baths; those without have small bathrooms. Friendly family.

C-F Hoa Linh, 35 Hang Bo St, T04-824 3887, hoalinhhotel@hn.vnn.vn. Right in the centre of the Old Quarter, this hotel has lovely bedrooms decked out in the dark wood of Hué imperial style. The larger, more expensive rooms have a double and a single bed and a balcony. It is worth paying extra for a view of the decoration on the crumbling buildings opposite. Bathrooms are basic with plastic showers and no curtains. Breakfast included.

C-G Hanoi Backpacker's Hostel, 48 Ngo Huyen St, T04-828 5372 (last minute reserv-ations 1800 1552 toll free), www.hanoiback packershostel.com. Dorm rooms and double suites in a house that belonged to the Brazilian ambassador. A friendly and busy place with plenty of opportunities to meet other travellers and gather advice. Breakfast, internet, tea and coffee, and luggage store is included. Don't miss the BBQs on the roof terrace and the Sun sessions.

D-F Artist Hotel, 22A Hai Ba Trung St, T04-824 4433, artist_hotel@yahoo.com. This small hotel is set above the pleasant and quiet courtyard of the **Hanoi Cinematique**. Some of the rooms, all with a/c, are a little dark but the price is great for such a central and unusual location.

D-F Nam Phuong, 16 Bao Khanh St, T04-825 8030, www.ktscom@vnn.vn. Pleasant position near Hoan Kiem Lake,

9 a/c rooms with good soundproofing. Rooms at the back are cheaper. Breakfast and free internet included.

D-G Khach San 30-4, 115 Tran Hung Dao St, T04-942 0807. Opposite railway station with cheap and good-value rooms; cheaper fan rooms have shared bathroom facilities.

D-G Real Darling Café, 33 Hang Quat St, T04-826 9386, darling_cafe@hotmail.com. Travellers' café which has 16 rooms, a/c and a 6 bed dorm with fan for US$3 per person. Friendly.

E-G My Lan, 70 Hang Bo St, T04-824 5510, hotelmylan@yahoo.com. Go through the dentist's surgery where an elderly French-speaking doctor has 10 rooms to rent, a/c or fans. Rather tightly packed but light and breezy; also 1 nice rooftop apartment with kitchen and terrace, US$400 a month. Recommended.

E-G Ngoc Diep, 83 Thuoc Bac St, through the Chinese pharmacy, T04-825 0020, thugiangguesthouse@yahoo.com. Cheaper rooms all have fan; more expensive rooms a/c. All rooms have hot water and TV, and free internet; breakfast can be included. Bus station and railway station pick up. Popular and friendly, long-stay discounts available.

🍴 Eating

Hanoi has Western-style coffee bars, restaurants and watering holes that stand up well to comparison with their equivalents in Europe. It also has a good number of excellent Vietnamese restaurants.

Note Dog (thit chó or thit cay) is an esteemed delicacy in the north but is mostly served in shacks on the edge of town – so you are unlikely to order it inadvertently.

Central Hanoi p1011, maps p1012 and p1014

🍴 Hanoi Press Club, 59A Ly Thai To St, Hoan Kiern District, T04-340888, www.hanoi-pressclub.com. There are 3 good food outlets in this stylish complex directly behind the **Sofitel Metropole Hotel: The Restaurant**

has remained consistently one of the most popular dining experiences in Hanoi. The food is imaginative and superb and there's a fine wine list. The service is faultless. This is a memorable dining experience. In the same building is **The Deli**, T04-825 5337; keep its delivery menu by the telephone for pizza, pasta, salads, sandwiches; or fill up in the canteen area with fat stuffed sandwiches and cakes. **The Library Bar** stocks a good range for cigars and whiskies.

🍴 Le Beaulieu, 15 Ngo Quyen St (in the **Metropole Hotel**), T04-826 6919. A good French and international restaurant open for breakfast, lunch and dinner; last orders 2200. Its Sun brunch buffet is regarded as one of the best in Asia. A great selection of French seafood, oysters, prawns, cold and roast meats and cheese. All for US$35.

🍴-🍴 Bobby Chinn, 1 Ba Trieu St, T04-934 8577, www.bobbychinn.com. One of Hanoi's better known and more expensive fusion restaurants blending Western and Asian ingredients and flavours; it has an award-winning wine list. It is stylish, with hanging rosebuds dropped from the ceiling but the sparkle and warmth has gone. The popular bar has been moved from the centre of the restaurant to the side leaving a lacklustre air.

🍴-🍴 Club Opera, 59 Ly Thai To St, T04-824 6950, clubopera@fpt.vn, daily 1100-1400 and 1730-2230. A small, cosy restaurant with an extensive Vietnamese menu in the attractive setting of a restored French villa. The menu is varied, the tables are beautifully laid and the food is appealingly presented.

🍴-🍴 San Ho, 58 Ly Thuong Kiet St, T04-934 9184, ando@hn.vnn.vn, daily 1100-1400, 1700-2200. Live piano music 1900-2100. Vietnamese food. This is Hanoi's most popular seafood restaurant which offers a series of set menus for US$15, US$20 and US$37.

🍴 Al Fresco's, 23L Hai Ba Trung St, T04-826 7782. A popular Australian grill bar serving ribs, steak, pasta, pizza and fantastic salads. Giant portions, lively atmosphere, a memorable experience. Recommended.

Hoa Sua, 28A Ha Hoi St (off Tran Hung Dao St), T04-942 4448, www.hoasuaschool.com, daily1100-2200. French training restaurant for disadvantaged youngsters, where visitors eat excellently prepared French and Vietnamese cuisine in an attractive and secluded courtyard setting. Reasonably cheap and popular. Cooking classes now available.

Pepperonis, 31 Bao Khanh St, T04-928 7030, Mon-Sat 1130-1330. A popular pizza and pasta place right in the heart of a busy bar/restaurant area. Cheap and cheerful. A great all-you-can-eat lunch.

69 Restaurant Bar, 69 Ma May St, T04-926 1720, daily 0700-2300. The restaurant is up a steep flight of wooden stairs in a restored 19th-century house in the Old Quarter, with 2 tables on the tiny shuttered balcony. Plenty of Vietnamese and seafood dishes, including Hong Kong duck (chargrilled and stuffed with 5 spices, ginger, onion and garlic) and sunburnt beef: beef strips deep fried in 5 spice butter. Special mulled wine is offered on cold nights.

Baan Thai, 3B Cha Ca St, T04-828 8588, daily 1030-1400, 1630-2200. Authentic Thai fare that has received good reviews.

Brothers, 26 Nguyen Thai Hoc St, T04-733 3866, daily 1100-1400, 1830-2200. Set in a restored villa, part of the pleasure of dining here is the sumptuous surroundings. An extensive menu of delicious Vietnamese food forms the buffet lunches and dinner. Lunch is remarkable value at US$6 and one of the best deals in the country. Visitors may be inclined to try the **Brothers** restaurant in Hoi An which, like this one, is part of the Khai Silk empire.

Cay Cau, De Syloia Hotel, 17A Tran Hung Dao St, T04-933 1010. Good Vietnamese fare at reasonable prices in this popular place. Daily set lunch at 130,000d is good value.

Cyclo, 38 Duong Thanh St, T04-828 6844. Nicely furnished restaurant (diners sit in converted cyclos) with garden bar. Vietnamese and French dishes on offer.

Dakshin, 94 Hang Trong St, T04-928 6872, daily 1000-1430, 1800-2230. This upstairs Indian vegetarian restaurant is

popular and well worth a visit. Elegant with rattan furniture and nicely attired waitresses, it specializes in southern Indian *dosas*, pancakes served with different sauces. The menu provides a useful glossary of the many unusual dishes served. All come on stainless-steel platters lined with a banana leaf. Prices are reasonable, just a couple of US dollars for a light *dosa* and less for starters.

Green Tangerine, 48 Hang Be St, T04-825 1286, greentangerine@vnn.vn. This is a gorgeous French restaurant with a lovely spiral staircase, wafting fans, tasselled curtain cords, abundant glassware and a gleaming black sidecar on display. The US$7.50 set lunch menu with 2 courses is excellent value. Try boneless frogs legs, candid duck leg or anything from the sumptuous dessert list.

Highway 4, 5 Hang Tre St, T04-926 0639, daily 0900-0200. A second branch is open at 54 Mai Hac De St. This restaurant specializes in ethnic minority dishes from North Vietnam. The fruit and rice wines – available in many flavours – are the highlight of this place. On the upper 2 floors guests sit cross-legged on cushions; downstairs there's conventional dining. There's plenty to eat – ostrich, fried scorpions, bull's penis steamed with Chinese herbs. Quite a remarkable experience.

Au Lac, 57 Ly Thai To St, T04-825 7807, daily 0700-2300. Nice café in the garden of a French villa. Breakfasts, sandwiches, pizzas, soups and pastas are available. The green papaya salad with grilled beef and sesame seeds is recommended as are the sautéed oysters with turmeric and lemon grass.

Bit Tet (Beefsteak), 51 Hang Buom St, T04-825 1211, daily 1700-2100. If asked to name the most authentic Vietnamese diner in town it would be hard not to include this on the list. The soups and steak frites are simply superb; it's rough and ready and you'll share your table as, at around US$2-3 per head, it is understandably crowded. (Walk to the end of the alley and turn right for the dining room.)

Café Moca, 14-16 Nha Tho, T04-825 6334, daily 0700-2400. This open space has big windows, wafting fans and marble-topped tables. Cinnamon-flavoured cappuccino, smoked salmon and Bengali specials. It's a favourite for coffee on rainy afternoons.

Cha Ca La Vong, 14 Cha Ca St, T04-825 3929, daily 1100-2100. Serves one dish only, the eponymous *cha ca Hanoi*, fried fish fillets in mild spice and herbs served with noodles. It's delicious and popular with both visitors and locals, although expensive at 70,000d for the meal.

Com Chay Nang Tam, 79A Tran Hung Dao St, T04-942 4140, daily 1100-1400, 1700-2200. This popular little a/c vegetarian restaurant is down an alley off Tran Hung Dao St and serves excellent and inexpensive 'Buddhist' dishes in a small, family-style dining room.

Lá, 25 Ly Quoc Su St, T04-928 8933. This restaurant serves up marvellous Vietnamese and international food. Try the fillet of salmon with passion fruit and sauvignon blanc glaze or the lamb shank braised in orange, sweet capiscum and espresso. Do not leave Hanoi without sampling the sherry fool. For those in the know these are the people who used to run **Café Thyme** on Lo Su St.

Little Hanoi, 21 Hang Gai St, T04-828 8333, daily 0730-2300. An all-day restaurant/café serving outstanding sandwiches. The cappuccinos, home-made yoghurt with honey and the apple pie are also top class.

Restaurant 22, 22 Hang Can St, T04-826 7160, daily 1200-2100. Good menu, popular and tasty Vietnamese food, succulent duck. At just a couple of dollars per main course it represents excellent value for money.

Tamarind, 80 Ma May St, T04-926 0580, tamarind_café@yahoo.com. A whole new standard in travel café food. Comfortable café at the front and smart restaurant behind in the **Handspan Adventure Travel** office. Lengthy vegetarian selection, delicious juices and the recommended Thai glass noodle salad.

West of the Citadel *p1016, map p1012*
KOTO, 59 Van Mieu St, T04-747 0337, www.koto.com.au, Mon 0730-1800, Tue-Sun

0730-2230. A training restaurant for under-privileged young people. Next to the Temple of Literature, pop in for lunch after a morning's sightseeing. The food is international, filling and delicious. Upstairs is the new **Temple Bar** with Wi-Fi. Recommended.

Cafés

252 Hang Bong, actually in what is now Cua Nam St. Pastries, yoghurt and crème caramel, very popular for breakfast.
Baguette and Chocolat, 11 Cha Ca St, T04-923 1500, daily 0700-2200. Part of the Hoa Sua restaurant training school for under-privileged youngsters. This is really nothing more than a café-cum-bakery but meals are available. Good for breakfast.
Café Puku, upstairs 60 Hang Trong St, T04-928 5244. Funky arty hang-out with tiny stalls on a balcony or inside on the blue and orange sofas or at big tables. An unobtrusive hideaway. Daily specials and a variety of snacks.
Highlands Coffee, southwest corner of Hoan Kiem Lake. Under the trees overlooking the lake. Great place for a coffee or a cold drink.
Thuy Ta, 1 Le Thai To St, T04-828 8148. Nice setting on the northwest corner of Hoan Kiem Lake and a popular meeting place for Vietnamese and travellers. Snacks, ice creams and drinks served.

Bars and clubs

Hanoi *p1011, maps p1012 and p1014*
The Bao Khanh and Hang Hanh area is packed with bars. It's very lively all day and evening but, like most places in Hanoi, shuts down around 2400.
Apocalypse Now, 2 Pho Dong Tac, daily 2000-0200. Like its HCMC counterpart this is popular with a wide cross-section of society. Music, pool and dancing. However, it has moved from its central location to way out of town making it a less obvious nightstop.
Ho Guom Xanh, 32 Le Thai To St, T04-828 8806, daily 1600-2400. From outside it's impossible to imagine the colourful and

operatic stage shows this nightclub puts on nightly. It's loud, packed and popular with a mainly local crowd but a real visual treat. Drinks are fairly expensive for what is a predominantly Vietnamese menu.

Legends, 1-5 Dinh Tien Hoang St, T04-936 0345, www.legendsbeer.com.vn, daily 0800-2300. One of Hanoi's popular micro-breweries. The German *helles bier* (light) and particularly the *dunkels bier*(dark) are strong and tasty. This café bar has views over Hoan Kiem Lake. An extensive food menu too and good for snacks and ice cream.

Le Pub, 25 Hang Be St, T04-926 2104, www.lepub.org. Drink well or plump for the all-day breakfast or gorge yourself on comfort food – burgers, pizzas, nachos and chicken nuggets. This place has outdoor seating on one of the Old Quarter's busiest streets and is an increasingly popular place to hang out.

Mao's Red Lounge, 7 Ha Tien St, T04-926 3104. The beers are 15,000d in this all-red cubby hole on a tiny street. Don't miss the hilarious photomontage of Prince Charles with a mop of ginger hair.

R & R Tavern, 47 Lo Su St, T04-934 4109, daily 0730-2400; live music Thu, Fri and Sat evenings. A popular and lively bar with a great selection of bar food. Noticeboards and leaflets; good for picking up information.

Red Beer, 97 Ma May St, T04-826 0247, daily 1000-2300. This microbrewery serves outstanding Belgian brews, 28,000d for 650ml glass.

Spotted Cow, 23C Hai Ba Trung St, T04-824 1028, 1130-0300. Cheerful and lively pub decorated in Friesian cows. Happy hour until 1800, food until 2400. The Hash House Harriers bus leaves from here on Sun.

✺ Entertainment

Hanoi *p1011, maps p1012 and p1014*
Dance and theatre
Opera House, T04-933 0113, nthavinh@hn.vn.vn, box office daily 0800-1700. Housed in an impressive French-era building at the east end of Trang Tien St (see page 1013). A variety of Vietnamese and Western concerts, operas and plays are staged. Schedule in *Vietnam News* or from the box office.

Water puppet theatre
Water Puppetry House, 57 Dinh Tien Hoang St, www.thanglongwaterpuppet.org, box office daily 0830-1200, 1530-2000. Fabulous shows with exciting live music and beautiful comedy: the technical virtuosity of the puppeteers is astonishing. Performances Mon-Sat 1715, 1830 and 2000, additional matinee Sun 0930. Admission 40,000d (1st class), 20,000d (2nd class); children 10,000d and 5000d. This is not to be missed.

✸ Festivals and events

Around Hanoi *p1019*
Perfume Pagoda Festival From 6th day of the 1st lunar month to end of 3rd lunar month (15th-20th day of 2nd lunar month is the main period). This festival focuses on the worship of the Goddess of Mercy (Quan Am). Thousands flock to this famous pilgrimage site during the festival period. Worshippers take part in dragon dances and a royal barge sails on the river.

◎ Shopping

Hanoi *p1011, maps p1012 and p1014*
The city is a shopper's paradise with cheap silk and expert tailors, handicrafts and antiques and some good designer shops. Hang Gai St is well geared to the souvenir hunter and stocks an excellent range of clothes, fabrics and lacquerware.

Art and antiques
Shops along Hang Khay and Trang Tien streets, on the south edge of Hoan Kiem Lake, sell silver ornaments, porcelain, jewellery and carvings. Not everything is either antique or silver; bargain hard.

Art shops abound near Hoan Kiem Lake, especially on Trang Tien St and on Dinh Tien Hoang St at the northeast corner.

Apricot Gallery, 40B Hang Bong St, T04-828 8965, www.apricot-artvietnam.com. High prices but spectacular exhibits.

Dien Dam Gallery, 4B Dinh Liet St and 60 Hang Hom St, T04-825 9881, www.dien dam-gallery.com. Beautiful photographs.

Hanoi Gallery, 17 Nha Chung St,T04-928 7943, propaganda_175@yahoo.com. This is a great find: hundreds of propaganda posters for sale. Original posters cost US$200 upwards; US$8 for a rice paper copy. Some of the reproductions aren't faithful to the colours of the originals, choose carefully.

Clothes, fashions, silk and accessories

The greatest concentration is in the Hoan Kiem Lake area particularly on Nha Tho, Nha Chung, Hang Trong and Hang Gai.

Co, 18 Nha Tho, T04-289925, conhatho@yahoo.com, daily 0830-1900. Clothes shop with a very narrow entrance. Some unusual prints, the craftsmanship is recommended.

Ipa Nima, 34 Han Thuyen St, T04-933 4000, www.ipa-nima.com. Enter the glittering and sparkling world of Ipa Nima. Shiny shoes, bags, clothes and jewellery boxes. Hong Kong designer Christina Yu is the creative force behind the label.

Song, 27 Nha Tho, T04-928 8733, www.asia songdesign.com, daily 0900-2000. The Song shop is run by friendly staff and has beautiful designer clothes, accessories and homeware but its floor space is much smaller than the HCMC store (see page 1110).

Tina Sparkle, 17 Nha Tho St, T04-928 7616, tinasparkle@ipa-nima.com, daily 0900-2000. Funky boutique that sells bags in an array of designs, from tropical prints to big sequinned flowers. Also, sequinned shoes by Christina Yu. Occasional sales will save you 50%.

Handicrafts

Chi Vang, 17 Trang Tien, T04-936 0027, chivang@fpt.vn. Exquisitely embroidered cloths, babies' bed linen and clothing,

cushion covers, tablecloths and unusual-shaped cushions. All the goods displayed are embroidered by hand.

Mosaique, 22 Nha Tho St, T04-928 6181, mosaique@fpt.vn, daily 0830-2000. Embroidered tablerunners, lamps and stands, silk flowers, silk curtains, metal ball lamps, and lotus flower-shaped lamps.

▲ Activities and tours

Hanoi *p1011, maps p1012 and p1014*
Tour operators
The most popular option for travellers are the budget cafés, which offer reasonably priced tours and an opportunity to meet fellow travellers. Operators match their rivals' prices and itineraries closely and many operate a clearing system to consolidate passenger numbers to more profitable levels. Many Hanoi tour operators run tours to **Halong Bay** (see page 1021). Some also offer kayaking trips.

A-Z Queen Travel, 49 Hang Be St, T04-926 2734, www.azqueencafe.com. A well-connected organization capable of handling tailor-made as well as standard tours for individuals or small groups, visas.

Buffalo Tours Vietnam, 94 Ma May St, T04-8280702, www.buffalotours.com. Well-established and well-regarded organization. It has its own boat for Halong Bay trips and offers tours around the north as well as day trips around Hanoi. Staff are friendly and the guides are informative and knowledgeable.

Diethelm Travel, HCO Building, Suite 1701, 44B Ly Thuong Kiet St, T04-934 4844. A well-known and long-established tour operator.

Discovery Indochina, 63A Cua Bac St, T04-716 4132, www.discoveryindochina.com. Private and customized tours throughout Vietnam, Cambodia and Laos.

Ethnic Travel, 35 Hang Giay St, T04-926 1951, www.ethnictravel.com. A 1-man show but, to judge by the comments of satisfied customers, it is well worth investigating. The owner, Mr Khanh, runs individual tours to Bai Tu Long Bay (next to Halong Bay) and to Ninh Binh.

Offers homestays and always tries to show travellers the 'real' Vietnam.

ET-Pumpkin, 89 Ma May St, T04-926 0739, www.et-pumpkin.com. Very professional in attitude, offering a good selection of travel services, particularly for visitors to the northwest. Now offering motorbike tours of the north. Good place for jeep hire.

Exotissimo, 26 Tran Nhat Duat St, T04-828 2150, www.exotissimo.com. Specializes in more upmarket tours, nationwide service.

Green Bamboo, 2A Duong Thanh St, T04-828 6504, www.greenbambootravel.com. Another well-established leader in the budget market, organizes tours of Halong Bay and Sapa.

Haivenu Tours, 12 Nguyen Trung Truc St, Ba Dinh, T04-927 2917, www.haivenu-vietnam.com. Tailor-made tours.

Handspan Adventure Travel, 78-80 Ma May St, T04-926 2828, www.handspan.com. Reputable business specializing in adventure tours, trekking in the north, mountain biking and kayaking in Halong Bay. Has its own junk.

Hanoi Toserco, 18 Luong Van Can St, T04-828 7552, www.tosercohanoi.com. It runs an efficient Open Tour service.

Kangaroo Café, 18 Pho Bao Khanh St, T04-828 9931, www.kangaroocafe.com. Since 1994, Griswald's Vietnamese Vacations and Kangaroo Café in Hanoi have specialized in genuine small group and tailor-made tours for singles, couples and families.

Love Planet, 25 Hang Bac St, T04-828 4864, www.loveplanettravel.com. Individual and small group tours; organizes visas. Helpful and patient service. Good book exchange.

Luxury Travel Co, Ltd, 35 Hong Phic St, T04-927 4120, www.luxurytravelvietnam.com. Luxury tours to Vietnam, Cambodia and Laos.

Real Darling Café, 33 Hang Quat St, T04-826 9386, darling_café@hotmail.com. Long-established and efficient. Concentrates on tours of the north and has a visa service.

Sinh Café, 52 Luong Ngoc Quyen St, T04-926 1568. The only official branch of **Sinh** in Hanoi. It is only listed here so you know it is the official office. It is not recommended. There are dozens of far

superior and efficient tour operators more deserving of your patronage.

Topas, 52 To Ngoc Van St, Tay Ho, T04-715 1005, www.topasvietnam.com. Good and well-run tour operator.

Trekking Travel, 108 Hang Bac St, T04-926 0572, www.trekkingtravel.com.vn. Small group tours to Halong Bay and Sapa, and 1-day tours around Hanoi.

Vietnam Indochine, 5-118/239/71 Nguyen Van Cu St, T04-872 2319, www.vietnam holidays.biz. Range of trips in Vietnam.

Voyage Vietnam Co, Mototours Asia, 1-2 Luong Ngoc Quyen St, T04-926 2616, www.voyagevietnam.net. Well-organized, reliable and good fun motorbiking, trekking and kayaking tours, especially of the north. Super-friendly and knowledgeable Tuan will take professional bikers to China, Laos and the Golden Triangle. 4WD car hire also available. The only company permitted to import your bike into Vietnam and to organize trips from Vietnam through to China and Tibet.

⊖ Transport

Hanoi *p1011, maps p1012 and p1014*
Air
Hanoi receives an increasing number of international and domestic connections. See page 994, for further details.

Airline offices Air France, 1 Ba Trieu St, T04-825 3484. **Cathay Pacific**, 49 Hai Ba Trung St, T04-826 7298. **Lao Airlines**, 40 Quang Trung St, T04-942 5362. **Malaysian Airlines**, 49 Hai Ba Trung St, T04-826 8820. **Pacific Airlines**, 36 Dien Bien Phu St, Ba Dinh District, T04-733 9999. **Singapore Airlines**, 17 Ngo Quyen St, T04-826 8888. **Thai**, 44B Ly Thuong Kiet St, T04-826 7921. **Vietnam Airlines**, 1 Quang Trung St, T04-832 0320.

Bicycle
The most popular form of local transport and is an excellent way to get around the city. Bikes can be hired from the little shops at 29-33 Ta Hien St and from most tourist cafés and hotels; expect to pay about US$2 per day.

Bus
Tour operators run Open Tour Buses from offices in the Old Quarter to major tourist destinations in the south. See Getting around, page 995.

Cyclo
Cyclos are ubiquitous especially in the Old Quarter. A trip from the railway station to Hoan Kiem Lake should cost no more than 15,000d. The same trip on a *xe ôm* would be 10,000d.

Motorbike

Hiring a motorbike is a good way of getting to some of the more remote places. Tourist cafés and hotels rent machines for US$5-40 per day. Note that hire shops insist on keeping the renter's passport, so it can be hard to rent other than at your hotel.

Taxi and private car

There are plenty of metered taxis in Hanoi, the following companies are recommended: **Airport Taxi**, T04-873 3333; **City Taxi**, T04-822 2222; **Hanoi Taxi**, T04-853 5353; **Mai Linh Taxi**, T04-822 2666. Private cars with drivers can be chartered from most hotels and from many tour operators, see page 1027.

Train

The **central station** (*Ga Hanoi*) is at 120 Le Duan St (a 10-min taxi ride from the centre of town), T04-747 0666. For trains to **HCMC** and the south, enter the station from Le Duan St. For trains to **Lao Cai** (for Sapa) enter the station from Tran Quy Cap St. There are regular daily connections with **HCMC**; advance booking required.

Overnight trains from Hanoi to **Lao Cai**, 8½-10 hrs, from where a fleet of minibuses ferries passengers on to **Sapa**. The train carriages are run by different companies. The very popular **Victoria Express**, with dining carriage, is for Victoria Hotel guests only, and departs Hanoi Sun-Fri at 2155, arriving 0630 the following morning. The dining carriage is only available Mon, Wed and Fri. The return trip departs from Lao Cai on Tue 1845 (LC2) arriving 0400, on Thu and Sat at 0915 (LC4) arriving 1955, and on Sun at 1930 (LC6) arriving 0415. Prices vary. **Royal Train**, T04-824 5222, leaves Hanoi daily at 2115 (SP1) arriving at 1535. **Tulico** carriages, T04-828 7806, leave 2040 (LC5), arriving at Lao Cai at 0455. This service returns on the LC6 at 1930 Sun arriving 0415. **Ratraco** (part of Vietnam Railways), 2F Vietnam Railtour Building, 95-97 Le Duan St, T04-942 2889, ratraco@hn.vnn.vn, has berths on several trains.

⊙ Directory

Hanoi *p1011, maps p1012 and p1014*
Banks Commission is charged on cashing TCs into US$ but not into dong. It is better to withdraw dong from the bank and pay for everything in dong. Most hotels will change dollars, often at quite fair rates. ATMs are found in most large hotels and in some post offices. **ANZ Bank**, 14 Le Thai To St, T04-825 8190, Mon-Fri 0830-1600. Provides full banking services including cash advances on credit cards, 2% commission on TCs, 24-hr ATMs. **Citibank**, 17 Ngo Quyen St, T04-825 1950. Cashes TCs into dong. **Incombank**, 37 Hang Bo St, T04-825 4276. Dollar TCs can be changed here. Deals with Amex, Visa, MasterCard and Citicorp. **Vietcombank**, 198 Tran Quang Khai St, T04-824 3108. 2% commission if converted to dollars cash.
Embassies and consulates Australia, 8 Dao Tan St, T04-831 7755. **Cambodia**, 71 Tran Hung Dao St, T04-9427646. **Canada**, 31 Hung Vuong St, T04-823 5500. **Laos**, 22 Tran Binh Trong St, T04-942 4576. **Thailand**, 63-65 Hoang Dieu St, T04-823 5092. **UK**, Central Building, 31 Hai Ba Trung St, T04-936 0500. **USA**, 7 Lang Ha St, T04-772 1500.
Medical services Family Medical Practice Hanoi, Van Phuc Compound, 298 I Kim Ma Rd, Ba Dinh, T04-843 0748, 24 hr emergency (T09-040 1919), www.vietnammedicalpractice.com. 24-hr medical service, dental care. **Hospital Bach Mai**, Giai Phong St, T04-869 3731. English-speaking doctors. Dental service. **International SOS**, Central Building, 31 Hai Ba Trung St, T04-934 0555, www.internationalsos.com/countries/Vietnam/. 24-hr, emergencies and medical evacuation. Dental service too.
Immigration Immigration Dept, 40A Hang Bai St, T04-826 6200. **Internet** Internet access is cheap and easy. The cheapest rates are about 3000d per hr, the most expensive are 200-300d/min. **Post office** GPO, 75 Dinh Tien Hoang St. International telephone service also available at the PO at 66-68 Trang Tien St; 66 Luong Van Can St and at the PO on Le Duan next to the train station. **DHL**, at the GPO.

Northwest Vietnam

The north is a mountainous region punctuated by limestone peaks and luscious valleys of terraced paddy fields, tea plantations, stilt houses and water hyacinth-quilted rivers. Large cones and towers, some with vertical walls and overhangs, rise dramatically from the flat alluvial plains. This landscape, dotted with bamboo thickets, is one of the most evocative in Vietnam; its hazy images seem to linger deep in the collective Vietnamese psyche and perhaps symbolize a sort of primaeval Garden of Eden.

Sapa, in the far northwest, is a former French hill station, home of the Hmong and set in a stunning valley, carpeted with Alpine flowers. It is a popular centre for trekking. Scattered around are market towns and villages populated by Vietnam's ethnic minorities such as the Black Hmong, Red Dao, Flower Hmong, Phu La, Dao Tuyen, La Chi and Tay – the latter being Vietnam's largest ethnic minority.

Nor is the region without wider significance; the course of world history was altered at Dien Bien Phu in May 1954 when the Vietnamese defeated the French. In 2004 a vast bronze statue commemorating the victory was erected; it towers over the town. Closer to Hanoi is Hoa Binh where villages of the Muong and Dao can be seen and the beautiful Mai Chau Valley, home to the Black and White Thai whose attractive houses nestle amid the verdant paddies of the hills.
▶▶ For listings, see pages 1038-1041.

Ins and outs

Getting there and around
There are three points of entry for the northwest circuit: to the south **Hoa Binh** (reached by road); to the north **Lao Cai/Sapa** (reached by road or preferably by train) and, bang in the middle, **Dien Bien Phu** reached by road or by plane. Which option you pick will depend upon how much time you have available and how much flexibility you require.

Expect overland journeys to be slow and sometimes arduous in this mountainous region but the discomfort is more than compensated for by the majesty of the landscapes. The road south of Dien Bien Phu has been significantly upgraded over recent years but the route north to Sapa is still poor and a 4WD is recommended. Jeeps with driver can be hired from some tour operators in Hanoi (see page 1027) for the five- or six-day round trip for US$330-370. A good and slightly cheaper option is to leave the jeep in Sapa (about US$275) and catch the overnight train back to Hanoi from Lao Cai. For those willing to pay more, Japanese land cruisers offer higher levels of comfort.

Another option is to do the whole thing by motorbike. The rugged terrain and relatively quiet roads make this quite a popular choice for many people. It has the particular advantage of allowing countless side trips and providing access to really remote and untouched areas. It is not advised to attempt the whole circuit using public transport as this would involve fairly intolerable levels of discomfort and a frustrating lack of flexibility. ▶▶ See Transport, page 1041.

Best time to visit
The region is wet from May to September. This makes travel quite unpleasant. Owing to the altitude of much of the area winter can be quite cool, especially around Sapa, so make sure you go well prepared.

The road from Hanoi to Dien Bien Phu winds its way for 420 km into the Annamite Mountains that mark the frontier with Laos. The round trip from Hanoi and back via Dien Bien Phu and Sapa is about 1200 km and offers, perhaps, the most spectacular scenery anywhere in Vietnam. Opportunities to experience the lives, customs and costumes of some of Vietnam's ethnic minorities abound. The loop can be taken in a clockwise or anti-clockwise direction; the advantage of following the clock is the opportunity to recover from the rigours of the journey in the tranquil setting of Sapa.

Highway 6, which has been thoroughly rebuilt along almost the entire route from Hanoi to Son La, leads southwest out of Hanoi to Hoa Binh. Setting off in the early morning (this is a journey of dawn starts and early nights), the important arterial function of this road to Hanoi can be clearly seen: ducks, chickens, pigs, bamboo and charcoal all pour in – the energy and building materials of the capital – much of it transported by bicycle. Beyond the city limits, the fields are highly productive, with market gardens and intensive rice production.

Hoa Binh → Colour map 2, B2.
Hoa Binh, on the banks of the Da (Black) River, marks the southern limit of the interior highlands and is 75 km from Hanoi, a journey of about 2½ hours. Major excavation sites of the Hoabinhian prehistoric civilization (10,000 BC) were found in the province, which is its main claim to international fame.

Bao Tang Tinh Hoa Binh (Hoa Binh Province Museum) ① *daily 0800-1030, 1400-1700, 10,000d*, contains items of archaeological, historical and ethnographical importance. Relics of the First Indochina War, including a French amphibious landing craft, remain from the bitterly fought campaign of 1951-1952 which saw Viet Minh forces dislodge the French.

Muong and **Dao minority villages** are accessible from Hoa Binh. **Xom Mo** is 8 km from Hoa Binh and is a village of the Muong minority. There are around 10 stilt houses, where overnight stays are possible (contact **Hoa Binh Tourism**, T018-854374, www.hoahbin tourism.com), and there are nearby caves to visit. **Duong** and **Phu** are villages of the Dao Tien (Money Dao), located 25 km up river. Boat hire (US$25) is available from **Hoa Binh Tourism**. A permit is required for an overnight stay.

Mai Chau and Lac → Colour map 2, B2.
After leaving Hoa Binh, Highway 6 heads in a south-southwest direction as far as the Chu River. Thereafter it climbs through spectacular mountain scenery before descending into the beautiful Mai Chau Valley. During the first half of this journey, the turtle-shaped roofs of the Muong houses predominate but, after passing Man Duc, the road enters the territory of the Thai, northwest Vietnam's most prolific ethnic minority, heralding a subtle change in the style of stilted-house architecture. This region is dominated by Black Thai communities (a sub-ethnic group of the Thai) but White Thai also live in the area.

The growing number of foreign and domestic tourists visiting the area in recent years has had a significant impact on the economy of Mai Chau and the lifestyles of its inhabitants. Some foreign visitors complain that the valley offers a manicured hill-tribe village experience to the less adventurous tourist who wants to sample the quaint lifestyle of the ethnic people without too much discomfort. There may be some truth in this allegation, yet there is another side to the coin. Since the region first opened its doors to foreign tourists in 1993, the **Mai Chau People's Committee** has attempted to control the effect of tourism on the valley. **Lac** (WhiteThai village) is the official tourist village to

Border essentials: Vietnam–Laos

Tay Trang

The Lao border is only 34 km from Dien Bien Phu, at Tay Trang. This border crossing has only recently been opened to foreign tourists. A Laos visa is not available at the border and must be bought in Hanoi or at the Lao embassy.

Transport There's a bus to the border crossing at Tay Trang to Muang Khua (Laos) every other day leaving at 0500.

---

which tour groups are led and, although it is possible to visit and even stay in the others, the committee hopes that by 'sacrificing' one village to tourism, the impact on other communities will be limited. Income generated from tourism by the villagers of Lac has brought about a significant enhancement to the lifestyles of people throughout the entire valley, enabling many villagers to tile their roofs and purchase consumer products such as television sets, refrigerators and motorbikes.

Lac is easily accessible from the main road from the direction of Hoa Binh. Take the track to the right, immediately before the red-roofed **People's Committee Guesthouse**. This leads directly into the village. You can borrow or rent a bicycle from your hosts and wobble across narrow bunds to the neighbouring hamlets, enjoying the ducks, buffalos, children and lush rice fields as you go – a delightful experience.

About 5 km south of Mai Chau on Route 15A is the Naon River on which, in the dry season, a boat can be taken to visit a number of large and impressive grottoes. Others can be reached on foot. If you wish to visit them, ask your hosts or at the **People's Committee Guesthouse** for details, see page 1038.

Dien Bien Phu → Colour map 1, B6.

ⓘ *The airport is 2 km north of town. The battlefield sites, most of which lie to the west of the Nam Yum River, are a bit spread out and best visited by car or by motorbike. Since the majority of visitors arrive in Dien Bien Phu using their own transport, this is not normally a problem.*

Dien Bien Phu lies in the Muong Thanh valley, a region where, even today, ethnic Vietnamese still represent less than one-third of the total population. For such a remote and apparently insignificant little town to have earned itself such an important place in the history books is a considerable achievement. And yet, the Battle of Dien Bien Phu in 1954 was a turning point in colonial history. It was the last calamitous battle between the French and the forces of Ho Chi Minh's Viet Minh and was waged from March to May 1954. The French, who under Vichy rule had accepted the authority of the Japanese during the Second World War, attempted to regain control after the Japanese had surrendered. Ho, following his Declaration of Independence on 2 September 1945, thought otherwise, heralding nearly a decade of war before the French finally gave up the fight after their catastrophic defeat here. It marked the end of French involvement in Indochina and heralded the collapse of its colonial empire. Had the Americans, who shunned French appeals for help, taken more careful note of what happened at Dien Bien Phu they might have avoided their own calamitous involvement in Vietnamese affairs just a decade later.

General de Castries' bunker ⓘ *daily 0700-1100, 1330-1700, 5000d*, has been rebuilt on the sight of the battlefield and eight of the 10 French tanks are scattered over the valley, along with US-made artillery pieces. East of the river, **Hill A1** ⓘ *daily 0700-1800*, known as Eliane 2

People of the north

Ethnic groups belonging to the Sino-Tibetan language family such as the Hmong and Dao, or the Ha Nhi and Phula of the Tibeto-Burman language group are relatively recent arrivals. Migrating south from China only within the past 250-300 years, these people have lived almost exclusively on the upper mountain slopes, practising slash-and-burn agriculture and posing little threat to their more numerous lowland-dwelling neighbours, notably the Thai.

Thus was established the pattern of human and political settlement that would persist in North Vietnam for more than 1000 years right down to the colonial period – a centralized Viet state based in the Red River Delta area, with powerful Thai vassal lordships dominating the Northwest. Occupying lands located in some cases almost equidistant from Hanoi, Luang Prabang and Kunming, the Thai, Lao, Lu and Tay lords were obliged during the pre-colonial period to pay tribute to the royal courts of Nam Viet, Lang Xang (Laos) and China, though in times of upheaval they could – and frequently did – play one power off against the other for their own political gain. Considerable effort was thus required by successive Viet kings in Thang Long (Hanoi) and later in Hué to

ensure that their writ and their writ alone ruled in the far north. To this end there was ultimately no substitute for the occasional display of military force, but the enormous cost of mounting a campaign into the northern mountains obliged most Viet kings simply to endorse the prevailing balance of power there by investing the most powerful local lords as their local government mandarins, resorting to arms only when separatist tendencies became too strong. Such was the political situation inherited by the French colonial government following its conquest of Indochina in the latter half of the 19th century. Its subsequent policy towards the ethnic minority chieftains of North Vietnam was to mirror that of the Vietnamese monarchy whose authority it assumed; through-out the colonial period responsibility for colonial administration at both local and provincial level was placed in the hands of seigneurial families of the dominant local ethnicity, a policy which culminated during the 1940s in the establishment of a series of ethnic minority 'autonomous zones' ruled over by the most powerful seigneurial families.

to the French, was the scene of the fiercest fighting. Remains of the conflict include a bunker, the bison (tank) known as Gazelle, a war memorial dedicated to the Vietnamese who died on the hill and, around at the back, the entrance to a tunnel dug by coal miners from Hon Gai. Their tunnel ran for several hundred metres to beneath French positions and was filled with 1000 kg of high explosives. It was detonated at 2300 on 6 May 1954 as a signal for the final assault. The huge crater is still there. Opposite the hill, the renovated **Nha Trung Bay Thang Lich Su Dien Bien Phu** (Historic Victory Exhibition Museum) ① *daily 0700-1100, 1330-1800, 5000d*, has a good collection of assorted Chinese, American and French weapons and artillery in its grounds. Inside are photographs and other memorabilia, together with a large illuminated model of the valley illustrating the course of the campaign and an accompanying video. While every last piece of Vietnamese junk is carefully catalogued, displayed and described, French relics are heaped into tangled piles. The **Revolutionary Heroes' Cemetery** ① *opposite the Exhibition Museum next to Hill*

A1, *daily 0700-1100, 1330-1800*, contains the graves of 15,000 Vietnamese soldiers killed during the course of the Dien Bien Phu campaign. At the north end of town, the **Tuong Dai Chien Dien Bien Phu** (Victory monument) ① *entrance next to the TV station on 6 Pho Muong Thanh; look for the tower and large pond*, erected on D1 at a cost of US$2.27 million, is the largest monument in Vietnam. The 120-tonne bronze sculpture depicts three Vietnamese soldiers standing on top of de Castries' bunker. It was commissioned to mark the 50th anniversary of the Vietnamese victory over the French.

Sapa and around ○○●●○▲●○ ▸▸ *pp1038-1041. Colour map 2, A1.*

Despite the countless thousands of tourists who have poured in every year for the past decade, Sapa retains great charm. Its beauty derives from two things: the impressive natural setting high on a valley side, with Fan Si Pan, Vietnam's tallest mountain either clearly visible or brooding in the mist; and the clamour and colour of the ethnic minorities selling jewellery and clothes. Distinctly oriental but un-Vietnamese in manner and appearance are the Hmong, Dao and other groups who come to Sapa to trade. Interestingly, the Hmong (normally so reticent) have been the first to seize the commercial opportunities presented

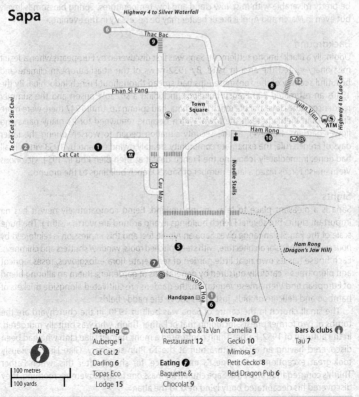

Sapa

Highway 4 to Silver Waterfall

Thac Bac

Phan Si Pang

Town Square

To Cat Cat & Sin Chai

Highway 4 to Lao Cai

Xuan Vien

Cat Cat

Ham Rong

Cau May

Noodle Stalls

Ham Rong (Dragon's Jaw Hill)

Muong Hoa

Handspan

To Topas Tours & ⑮

N

100 metres
100 yards

Sleeping ○
Auberge **1**
Cat Cat **2**
Darling **6**
Topas Eco
Lodge **15**
Victoria Sapa & Ta Van
Restaurant **12**

Eating ○
Baguette &
Chocolat **9**

Camellia **1**
Gecko **10**
Mimosa **5**
Petit Gecko **8**
Red Dragon Pub **6**

Bars & clubs ○
Tau **7**

by tourism. Saturday night is always a big occasion for Black Hmong and Red Dao teenagers in the Sapa area, as youngsters from miles around come to the so-called 'Love Market' to find a partner. The market proved so popular with tourists that the teenagers now arrange their trysts and liaisons in private. Sapa's regular market is at its busiest and best on Sunday mornings, when most tourists scoot off to Bac Ha (see page 1038).

Ins and outs

Getting there and around Travel to Sapa is either by road on the northwest circuit or by overnight train from Hanoi, via Lao Cai. A fleet of minibuses ferries passengers from Lao Cai railway station to Sapa. Sapa is small enough to walk around easily. From Sapa there are a great many walks and treks to outlying villages. ▸▸ *See Transport, pages 1030 and 1041.*

Best time to visit At 1650 m Sapa enjoys warm days and cool evenings in the summer but gets very cold in winter. Snow falls, on average, every couple of years and settles on the surrounding peaks of the Hoang Lien Son Mountains. Rain and cloud can occur at any time of year but the wettest months are May to September with nearly 1000 mm of rain in July and August alone, the busiest months for Vietnamese tourists. December and January can be pretty miserable with mist, low cloud and low temperatures. Spring blossom is lovely but even in March and April a fire or heater may be necessary in the evening.

Background

Originally a Black Hmong settlement, Sapa was first discovered by Europeans when a Jesuit missionary visited the area in 1918. By 1932 news of the quasi-European climate and beautiful scenery of the Tonkinese Alps had spread throughout French Indochina. By the 1940s an estimated 300 French buildings, including a sizeable prison and the summer residence of the Governor of French Indochina, had sprung up. Until 1947 there were more French than Vietnamese in the town, which became renowned for its many parks and flower gardens. However, as the security situation began to worsen during the latter days of French rule, the expatriate community steadily dwindled, and by 1953 virtually all had gone. Immediately following the French defeat at Dien Bien Phu in 1954, victorious Vietnamese forces razed a large number of Sapa's French buildings to the ground.

Sights

Sapa is a pleasant place to relax in and unwind. Being comparatively new it has no important sights but several French buildings in and around are worth visiting. The huge scale of the Fan Si Pan range gives Sapa an Alpine feel and this impression is reinforced by *haut savoie* vernacular architecture, with steep pitched roofs, window shutters and chimneys. Each house has its own neat little garden of temperate flora – foxgloves, roses, apricot and plum trees – carefully nurtured by generations of gardeners. But in an alluring blend of European and Vietnamese vegetation, the gardens are cultivated alongside thickets of bamboo and delicate orchids, just yards above the paddy fields.

The small **church** in the centre of Sapa was built in 1930. In the churchyard are the tombs of two former priests, including that of Father Thinh, who was brutally murdered. In the autumn of 1952, Father Thinh confronted a monk named Giao Linh who had been discovered having an affair with a nun at the Ta Phin seminary. Giao Linh obviously took great exception to the priest's interference, for shortly after this, when Father Thinh's congregation arrived at Sapa church for mass one foggy November morning, they discovered his decapitated body lying next to the altar.

Trekking rules

Tourists wanting to trek around Sapa are no longer allowed to go it alone. Visitors must now have a touring card, sightseeing ticket and a licensed tour guide to trek six permitted routes in the area, although it is possible to trek to Cat Cat, Sin Chai and the silver waterfall without a guide and permit. Additional routes may be added in the future. Ticket checkpoints have been set up at starting points. Tour guides who violate these new rules will have their licences withdrawn and tourists who do so will be disciplined, according to the

People's Committee of Sapa District. The following are permitted routes from Sapa:

- Round trip to Cat Cat and Sin Chai
- Round trip to Cat Cat, Y Linh Ho, Lao Chai and Ta Van
- Round trip to Lao Chai, Ta Van, Ban Ho, Thanh Phu and Nam Cang
- Round trip to Lao Chai, Ta Van, Su Pan and Thanh Kim
- Round trip to Ta Phin, Mong Sen and Takco
- Ascent of Mount Fan Si Pan

Ham Rong (Dragon's Jaw Hill) ① *daily 0600-1800, 30,000d, free for children under 5*, offers excellent views of the town. The path winds its way through a number of interesting limestone outcrops and miniature grottoes as it nears the summit. Traditional dance performances take place here. ▸▸ *See Entertainment, page 1041.*

Around Sapa → *Colour map 2, A1.*

Trekking to the villages around Sapa is a highlight of this region. It is a chance to observe rural life led in reasonable prosperity. Wet rice forms the staple income, weaving for the tourist market puts a bit of meat on the table. Here, nature is kind: there is rich soil and no shortage of water. It's clear how the landscape has been engineered to suit man's needs: the terracing is on an awesome scale (in places more than 100 steps), the result of centuries of labour to convert steep slopes into level fields which can be flooded to grow rice. Technologically, and in no sense pejoratively, the villages might be described as belonging to a bamboo age: bamboo trunks carry water huge distances from spring to village; water flows across barriers and tracks in bamboo aqueducts; mechanical rice huskers made of bamboo are driven by water requiring no human effort; houses are held up with bamboo; bottoms are parked on bamboo chairs; and tobacco and other substances are inhaled through bamboo pipes. In late 2004, regulations were brought in, which mean that trekking without a licensed guide is no longer possible, see Trekking regulations, see page 1037.

The track heading west from Sapa through the market area offers either a short 5-km round-trip walk to the Black Hmong village of **Cat Cat** (accessible without a guide) or a longer 10-km round-trip walk to **Sin Chai** (Black Hmong). Both options take in some beautiful scenery; foreigners must pay 15,000d to use the track. The path to Cat Cat leads off to the left of the Sin Chai track after about 1 km, following the line of pylons down through the rice paddies to Cat Cat village; beyond the village over the river bridge you can visit the **cascade waterfall** (from which the village takes its name) and an old French hydro-electric power station that still produces electricity. Sin Chai village is 4 km northwest of here. Walking to **Lau Chai village** (Black Hmong) and **Ta Van village** (Zay or Giay) with a licensed guide is a longer round trip of 20 km taking in minority villages and beautiful scenery. **Mount Fan Si Pan**, at a height of 3143 m, is Vietnam's highest mountain and is a three-day trek from Sapa. It lies on a bearing of 240° from Sapa;

9 km as the crow flies but 14 km by track. The route involves dropping to 1200 m and crossing a rickety bamboo bridge before ascending.

North of Sapa is an abandoned **French seminary**, where the names of the bishop who consecrated it and the presiding Governor of Indochina can be seen engraved on stones at the west end. Built in 1942 and under the ecclesiastical jurisdiction of the Parish of Sapa, the building was destroyed 10 years later by militant Vietnamese hostile to the intentions of the order. Beyond the seminary, the path descends into a valley of beautifully sculpted rice terraces and past Black Hmong settlements, with their shy and retiring inhabitants, to **Ta Phin**, a Red Dao village.

Bac Ha, located to the northeast of Sapa, is really only notable for one thing and that is its Sunday morning market. Hundreds of local minority people flock in from the surrounding districts to shop and socialize, while tourists from all corners of the earth pour in to watch them do it. The market draws in the Flower Hmong, Phu La, Dao Tuyen, La Chi and Tay, and is a riot of colour and fun. While the women trade and gossip, the men consume vast quantities of rice wine; by late morning they can no longer walk so are heaved onto donkeys by their wives and led home. If you have your own transport arrive early; if you haven't, nearly all the hotels and all the tour operators in Sapa organize trips.
▶▶ See Activities and tours, page 1041.

◉ Northwest Vietnam listings

For Sleeping and Eating price codes,
see inside the front cover.

◉ Sleeping

Hoa Binh *p1032*
C-D Hoa Binh 1, 54 Phuong Lam, T018-852 051. On Hwy 6 out of Hoa Binh towards Mai Chau. Clean rooms with a/c and TV; some rooms built in minority style. There's also an ethnic minority dining experience complete with rice drunk through bamboo straws. Gift shop stocks local produce.
C-D Hoa Binh 2, 160 An Duong Vuong, T018-852001. Has the same facilities as its sister hotel but no restaurant.

Mai Chau and Lac *p1032*
L-AL Mai Chau Lodge, a short walk southwest of Lac village, T018-868959, www.maichaulodge.com. Owned by **Buffalo Tours** and staffed by locals, there are 16 rooms with modern facilities. The lodge has 2 restaurants, a bar, swimming pool, sauna and jacuzzi. Bicycling and trekking tours are offered. The price includes a 2-day 1-night trip with accommodation, tours and other services.

D-F Ethnic Houses, Lac Village. Trips to homestays must be booked by tour operators, usually in Hanoi. In Mai Chau, visitors can spend the night in a White Thai ethnic house on stilts. Mat, pillow, duvet, mosquito net, communal washing facilities and sometimes fan provided. Particularly recommended as the hospitality and easy manner of the people is a highlight of many visitors' stay in Vietnam. Food and local rice wine provided. Avoid the large houses in the centre if possible. **Guesthouse No 6**, T018-867168, is popular, with plentiful food and rice wine. The owner fought the French at Dien Bien Phu. Minimal English is spoken.

Dien Bien Phu *p1033*
C-D May Hong, Tran Dang Ninh, T023-826 300. Opposite Vietnam Airlines booking office. Standard rooms with a/c and hot water.
C-E Muong Thanh Hotel, 25 Him Lam-TP, T023-810043. Breakfast included with the more expensive rooms. 62 standard rooms with TV, a/c, minibar and fan. Internet service, swimming pool (10,000d for non-guests), karaoke, Thai massage and free airport transfer. Souvenir shop and bikes for rent.

E-G Brewery, 62 Muong Thanh 10 St (Hoang Van Thai St), T023-824635. Beyond Hill A1 at the east end of town. 10 rooms, basic and clean, with fan or a/c, no restaurant but, as the name suggests, plenty of beer. A *bia hoi* next to the gate offers fresh cool beer at 1500d a glass.

Sapa *p1035, map p1035*

A host of guesthouses has sprung up to cater for Sapa's rejuvenation and the appeal of the town has, perhaps, been a little compromised by the new structures. Prices tend to rise Jun-Oct to coincide with northern hemisphere university holidays and at weekends. Hoteliers are accustomed to bargaining; healthy competition ensures fare rates in Sapa.

L-AL Topas Eco Lodge, Than Kimh, Lao Cai, 18 km from Sapa, T020-872404, www.topas-eco-lodge.com. Vietnam's first eco-lodge is perched on a plateau overlooking the Hoang Vien Valley. Palm-thatched bungalows, each with its own bathroom and porch, run on solar power, enjoy fantastic views over the valley. Trekking, horse riding, mountain biking and handicraft workshops are organized daily for guests and are included in the full-board price. Free transport from Sapa; discounts available.

L-A Victoria Sapa, T020-871522, www.victoria hotels-asia.com. With 77 rooms, this hotel is easily the best in town. Comfortable, with well-appointed rooms, it is a lovely place in which to relax and enjoy the peace. In winter there are warming open fires in the bar and dining rooms. The food is very good and the set buffets are excellent value. The Health Centre offers everything from the traditional massage to reflexology. The centre, pool, tennis courts and sauna are open to non-guests. Packages are available.

C-F Darling, Thac Bac St, T020-871349, www.tulico-sapa.com.vn. It's a short walk from town to this secluded building but for those seeking peace it's worth every step. Simple and clean with a warm welcome, stunning views and a colourful garden. There are 45 rooms, most with fabulous views. The top terrace bedroom has the best view in all of Sapa. Swimming pool, gym and pool table.

D-F Auberge, Muong Hoa St, T020-871243, www.sapanowadays.com. Mr Dang Trung, the French-speaking owner, shows guests his wonderful informal garden with pride: sweet peas, honeysuckle, snap dragons, foxgloves, roses and irises – all familiar to visitors from temperate climes – grow alongside sub-Alpine flora and a fantastic collection of orchids. The rooms are simply furnished but clean and boast baths and log fires in winter. There's a restaurant on the lovely terrace.

D-G Cat Cat, Cat Cat St, through the market, T020-871387, www.catcathotel.com. The guesthouse has expanded up the hillside, with new terraces and bungalows with balconies all with views down the valley. Friendly and popular, its 40 rooms span the price range but all represent good value for money. Some enjoy the best views in Sapa. The hotel has a good restaurant and, like most others, arranges tours and provides useful information.

Around Sapa *p1037*

It is possible to spend the night in one of the ethnic houses in the Sapa district. However, in line with the trekking rules (see page 1037), homestays must be organized through reputable tour operators and are only permitted in the following villages: **Ta Van Giay**, **Ban Den**, **Muong Bo**, **Ta Phin Commune Central Area**, **Sa Xeng Cultural Village** and **Sin Chai**, as well as at **Topas Eco Lodge**. The Black Hmong villages are probably the best bet, though facilities are considerably more basic than in the Muong and Thai stilted houses of Hoa Binh and Mai Chau and travellers will need to bring their own bedding materials and mosquito net. A contribution of around 30,000d should be made (or more if dinner is included).

🍴 Eating

Hoa Binh *p1032*

🍴 **Thanh Toi**, 22a Cu Chinh Lan, T018-853951. Local specialities, including wild boar and stir-fried aubergine.

Mai Chau and Lac p1032

Most people will eat with their hosts. Mai Chau town itself has a couple of simple *com pho* places near the market. The rice wine in Mai Chau is excellent, particularly when mixed with local honey.

Dien Bien Phu p1033

¶ **Lien Tuoi**, 27 Muong Thanh 8 St, next to the Vietnamese cemetery and Hill A1, T023-824919, daily 0700-2200. Delicious local fare in a family-run restaurant.
¶ **Muong Thanh Hotel Restaurant**, 25 Him Lam-TP, T023-810043, daily 0600-2200. Breakfasts, plenty of Vietnamese dishes and a few pasta dishes. Also duck, boar, pork, frog, curry, seafood and some tofu dishes.

Sapa p1035, map p1035

There are rice and noodle stalls in the market and along the path by the church.
¶¶¶ **Ta Van**, in **Victoria Sapa**, see Sleeping, T020-871522. The food is very good, served in the large dining room with an open fire, and the set buffets are excellent value.
¶¶-¶ **The Gecko**, T020-871504, daily 0730-2230. Attractive with dining room and tables on its front terrace. Good French and Vietnamese food. Pizzas go from US$5; main courses around US$6. Delicious with the restaurant's home-made bread. The daily set lunch at US$11 is good value. Opposite is the **Petit Gecko** offering snacks and takeaway sandwiches. It's cosier than its big brother and serves the best hot chocolate in town.
¶ **Baguette & Chocolat**, Thac Bac St, T020-871766, www.hoasuaschool.com, daily 0700-2100. The ground floor of the guesthouse comprises a stylish restaurant and café, with small boulangerie attached; lovely home-made cakes for exhausted trekkers go down a treat. Picnic kits from 32,000d are a useful and welcome service.
¶ **Camellia**, Cat Cat St, just through market on the right, T020-871455. Big menu, delicious food, rice and fruit wine. The grilled deer is good, the **Camellia** salad is spicy and excellent, and the apple wine warm and strong.

¶ **Mimosa**, up a small path off Cay Mau St, T020-871377, daily 0700-2300. A small, slightly chaotic, family-run restaurant. Sit cosy indoors or in the fresh air on a small terrace. A long menu of good Western and Asian dishes. Very popular and service is incredibly slow when busy. Pizzas, pastas and burgers as well as boar, deer, pork and vegetarian dishes.
¶ **Red Dragon Pub**, 21 Muong Hoa St, T020-872085, reddragonpub@hn.vnn.vn, daily 0750-2300 (food until 2230). Done out like an English tearoom with mock Tudor beams and red and white checked table-cloths. Tea, cornflakes, and a mean shepherd's pie. Pub upstairs. Fantastic views of the valley.

Bars and clubs

Sapa p1035, map p1035

Red Dragon Pub, see Eating. The balcony is perfect for a sunset drink.
Tau Bar, 42 Cau May St, beneath the Tau Hotel, T0912-927756, funkybarsapa@yahoo.com, daily 1500-late. It must have the longest bar made of a single tree trunk in the world and worth a beer just to see it. Minimalist, with white walls, stools, darts board and pool table. Range of beers and spirits.

Entertainment

Hoa Binh p1032

Hoa Binh Ethnic Minority Culture Troupe, **Hoa Binh 1 Hotel**. 1-hr shows featuring dance and music of the Muong, Thai, Hmong and Dao.

Mai Chau and Lac p1032

Mai Chau Ethnic Minority Dance Troupe. Thai dancing culminating in the communal drinking of sweet, sticky rice wine through straws from a large pot. This troupe performs most nights in Lac in one of the large stilt houses. Admission is included for people on tours; otherwise give a small contribution.

Sapa *p1035, map p1035*
Ethnic minority dancing, Dragon's Jaw Hill, daily at 0930 and 1500, 10,000d. Also at the **Bamboo Hotel**, 2030-2200; free as long as you buy drinks at **Victoria Sapa** Sat at 2030.

O Shopping

Mai Chau and Lac *p1032*
Mai Chau is probably the best place for handicrafts in the northwest. Villagers sell woven goods and fabrics and are dependent on them for a living. There are also paintings and wicker baskets, pots, traps and pouches.

Sapa *p1035, map p1035*
Sapa is good for ethnic clothes but it is not possible to buy walking shoes, rucksacks, coats, jackets or mountaineering equipment. **Wild Orchid**, 3 shops on Cau May St, T020-871665. Beautiful wall hangings and clothes.

▲ Activities and tours

Hoa Binh *p1032*
Hoa Binh Tourism, next to **Hoa Binh 1**, T018-854374, www.hoabinhtourism.com. Can arrange boat hire as well as visits to minority villages, trekking and transport.

Mai Chau and Lac *p1032*
Hanoi tour operators run overnight tours to the area.

Sapa *p1035, map p1035*
Victoria Sapa. Massage and other treatments are available in the hotel treatment centre, US$19. The pool area is being renovated to accommodate a better spa.

Tour operators
Handspan, 8 Cau May St, T020-872110, www.handspan.com. Diverse range of tours in the vicinity of Sapa, including a range of treks, mountain bike excursions, homestays and jeep expeditions.

Topas, 24 Muong Hoa St, T020-871331, www.topas-adventure-vietnam.com. A Danish and Vietnamese operator offering treks from fairly leisurely 1-day walks to an arduous 4-day assault on Mount Fan Si Pan. Also organizes bicycling tours, horse riding and family tours. Well-run operation, with an office in Hanoi.

○ Transport

Dien Bien Phu *p1033*
For overland transport, see page 1031.
Air The airport (T023-824416) is 2 km north of town, off Hwy 12. Flights to and from **Hanoi** with **Vietnam Airlines**, office inside Airport Hotel, daily 0700-1100, 1330-1630.

Sapa *p1035, map p1035*
Train For train details, see Hanoi Transport, page 1030. Passengers alighting at Lao Cai will either be met by their hotel or there is a desk selling minibus tickets to Sapa. Tour operators in Hanoi can also book your ticket for you for a small fee. It is often less hassle than organizing it yourself and, if you are in a hurry, it's a great time saver.

○ Directory

Dien Bien Phu *p1033*
Banks Vietcombank and Nong Nghiep Bank. **Internet** Muong Thanh Hotel, 25 Him Lam-T.

Sapa *p1035, map p1035*
Banks Agribank, 1 Pho Cau May St, T020-871206, Mon-Fri and Sat morning. Changes many currencies, as will most hotels, but at poor rates. Also changes US dollar and euro TCs. **BIDV**, Ngu Chi Son St, T020-872569, opposite the lake, has a visa ATM and will change cash and TCs. **Internet** Many of the better hotels have email and allow customers to use it. Internet café opposite the Delta Restaurant. **Post office** There are 2 where international phone calls can be made. The main post office offers internet.

Hué and around

→ *Colour map 4, B4.*

Hué, a gracious imperial city that housed generations of the country's most powerful emperors, was built on the banks of the Huong Giang (Perfume River), 100 km south of the 17th parallel. The river is named after a scented shrub which is supposed to grow at its source.

In many respects, Hué epitomizes the best of Vietnam and, in a country that is rapidly disappearing under concrete, it represents a link to a past where people live in old buildings and don't lock their doors. Whether it is because of the royal heritage or the city's Buddhist tradition, the people of Hué are the gentlest in the country. They speak good English and drive their motorbikes more carefully than anyone else.

Just south of the city are the last resting places of many Vietnamese emperors. A number of war relics in the Demilitarized Zone (DMZ) can be easily visited from Hué. ▶▶ *For listings, see pages 1051-1055.*

Ins and outs

Getting there Hué's Phu Bai airport is a 25-minute drive from the city. There are daily connections with Hanoi and Ho Chi Minh City. **Vietnam Airlines** runs a bus service in to town which costs 30,000d; a taxi costs 125,000d. The railway station is more central. The trains tend to fill up, so advance booking is recommended, especially for sleepers.
▶▶ *See Transport, page 1054.*

Getting around For the city itself, walking is an option, interspersed, perhaps, with the odd cyclo journey. However, most guesthouses hire out bicycles and this is a very pleasant and slightly more flexible way of exploring Hué and some of the surrounding countryside. A motorbike makes it possible to visit many more sights in a day. Cyclos are pleasant for visiting the more central attractions. *Xe ôm* are a speedier way to see the temples.

Getting to and around the **Imperial Tombs** is easiest by motorbike or car as they are spread over a large area. Most hotels and cafés organize tours either by minibus, bike or by boat. Sailing up the Perfume River is the most peaceful way to travel but only a few of the tombs can be reached by boat so *xe ôm* wait at the riverbank to take passengers on to the tombs. All the tombs are accessible by bicycle but you'll need to set out early. It is also possible to go on the back of a motorbike taxi. Further details are given for each tomb.
▶▶ *See Activities and tours, page 1054.*

Best time to visit Hué has a reputation for bad weather. Rainfall of 2770 mm has been recorded in a single month. The rainy season runs from September to January and rainfall is particularly heavy between September and November; the best time to visit is therefore between February and August. However, even in the 'dry' season an umbrella is handy. Temperatures in Hué can also be pretty cool in winter, compared with Danang, Nha Trang and other places to the south, as cold air tends to get bottled here, trapped by mountains to the south. For several months each year neither fans nor air-conditioning are required.

Background

Hué was the capital of Vietnam during the Nguyen Dynasty, which ruled Vietnam between 1802 and 1945. For the first time in Vietnamese history a single court controlled the land from Yunnan (southern China) southwards to the Gulf of Siam. To link the north and south (more than 1500 km), the Nguyen emperors built and maintained the Mandarin Road (Quan Lo), interspersed with relay stations. Even in 1802, when it was not yet complete, it took couriers just 13 days to travel between Hué and Ho Chi Minh City, and five days between Hué and Hanoi. If they arrived more than two days late, couriers

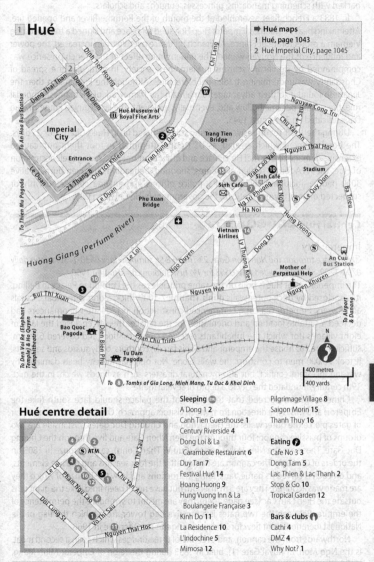

Hué

⇒ **Hué maps**
1 Hué, page 1043
2 Hué Imperial City, page 1045

Hué centre detail

Sleeping
A Dong 1 2
Canh Tien Guesthouse 1
Century Riverside 4
Dong Loi & La
  Carambole Restaurant 6
Duy Tan 7
Festival Hué 14
Hoang Huong 9
Hung Vuong Inn & La
  Boulangerie Française 3
Kinh Do 11
La Residence 10
L'Indochine 5
Mimosa 12

Pilgrimage Village 8
Saigon Morin 15
Thanh Thuy 16

Eating
Cafe No 3 3
Dong Tam 5
Lac Thien & Lac Thanh 2
Stop & Go 10
Tropical Garden 12

Bars & clubs
Cathi 4
DMZ 4
Why Not? 1

were punished with a flogging. There cannot have been a better road in Southeast Asia nor a more effective incentive system.

Although the Confucian bureaucracy and some of the dynasty's technical achievements may have been remarkable, there was continued discontent and uprisings. Court was packed with scheming mandarins, princesses, eunuchs and scholars.

In 1883 a French fleet assembled at the mouth of the Perfume River and opened fire. After taking heavy casualties, Emperor Hiep Hoa sued for peace and signed a treaty making Vietnam a protectorate of France. As French influence over Vietnam increased, the power and influence of the Nguyen waned. The undermining effect of the French presence was compounded by significant schisms in Vietnamese society. In particular, the spread of Christianity was undermining traditional hierarchies. Although the French and then the Japanese found it to their advantage to maintain the framework of Vietnamese imperial rule, the system became hollow and, eventually, irrelevant. The last Nguyen Emperor, Bao Dai, abdicated on 30 August 1945.

During the 1968 Tet offensive, Viet Cong soldiers holed up in Hué's Citadel for 25 days. The bombardment which ensued, as US troops attempted to root them out, caused extensive damage to the Thai Hoa Palace and other monuments. During their occupation of Hué, the NVA forces settled old scores, shooting, beheading and even burning alive 3000 people, including civil servants, police officers and anyone connected with, or suspected of being sympathetic to, the government in Ho Chi Minh City.

Central Hué ⬤🄰🄱🄵🄶🄾🄰🄴🄶🄲 ➤ *pp1051-1055.*

Imperial City

ⓘ *Entrance through the Ngo Mon Gate, 23 Thang 8 St, summer daily 0630-1730, winter daily 0700-1700; 55,000d. Guided tour US$3 for 1½ hrs; Guiding can last until 1900.*

The Imperial City at Hué is built on the same principles as the Forbidden Palace in Beijing. It is enclosed by thick outer walls (**Kinh Thanh**), 7-10 m thick, along with moats, canals and towers. Emperor Gia Long commenced construction in 1804 after geomancers had decreed a suitable location and orientation for the palace. The site enclosed the land of eight villages (for which the inhabitants received compensation) and covered 6 sq km, sufficient area to house the emperor and all his family, courtiers, bodyguards and servants. It took 20,000 men to construct the walls alone. Not only has the city been damaged by war and incessant conflict, but also by natural disasters such as floods which, in the mid-19th century, inundated the city to a depth of several metres.

Chinese custom decreed that the 'front' of the palace should face south (like the Emperor) and this is the direction from which visitors approach. Over the outer moat, a pair of gates pierce the outer walls: the **Hien Nhon** and **Chuong Duc** gates. Just inside are two groups of massive cannon; four through the Hien Nhon Gate and five through the Chuong Duc Gate. These are the Nine Holy Cannon (**Cuu Vi Than Cong**), cast in bronze in 1803 on the orders of Gia Long. The cannon are named after the four seasons and the five elements, and on each is carved its name, rank, firing instructions and how the bronze of which they are made was acquired. They are 5 m in length but have never been fired. Like the giant urns outside the Hien Lam Cac (see page 1046), they are meant to symbolize the permanence of the empire. Between the two gates is a massive **flag tower**, from which the flag of the National Liberation Front flew for 24 days during the Tet Offensive in 1968.

Northwards from the cannon, and over one of three bridges which span a second moat, is the **Ngo Mon**, or Royal Gate (1), built in 1833 during the reign of Emperor Minh Mang.

(The ticket office is just to the right.) The gate, remodelled on a number of occasions since its original construction, is surmounted by a pavilion from where the emperor would view palace ceremonies. Of the five entrances, the central Ngo Mon was only opened for the emperor to pass through. UNESCO has thrown itself into the restoration of Ngo Mon with vigour and the newly finished pavilion atop the gate now gleams and glints in the sun; those who consider it garish can console themselves with the thought that this is how it might have appeared in Minh Mang's time.

North from the Ngo Mon is the **Golden Water Bridge** (2) – again reserved solely for the emperor's use – between two tanks (3), lined with laterite blocks. This leads to the **Dai Trieu Nghi** (Great Rites Courtyard, 4), on the north side of which is the **Thai Hoa Palace** (Palace of Supreme Harmony), constructed by Gia Long in 1805 and used for his coronation in 1806. From here, sitting on his throne raised up on a dais, the emperor would receive ministers,

② Hué Imperial City

➡ Hué maps
1 Hué, page 1043
2 Hué Imperial City, page 1045

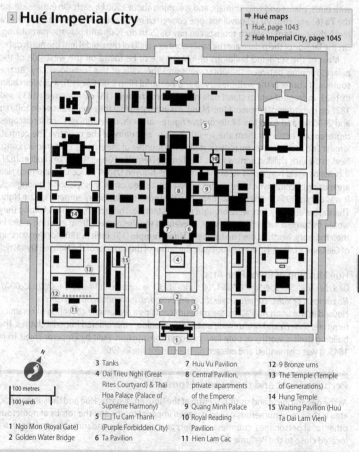

100 metres
100 yards

1 Ngo Mon (Royal Gate)
2 Golden Water Bridge
3 Tanks
4 Dai Trieu Nghi (Great Rites Courtyard) & Thai Hoa Palace (Palace of Supreme Harmony)
5 ☐ Tu Cam Thanh (Purple Forbidden City)
6 Ta Pavilion
7 Huu Vu Pavilion
8 Central Pavilion, private apartments of the Emperor
9 Quang Minh Palace
10 Royal Reading Pavilion
11 Hien Lam Cac
12 9 Bronze urns
13 Thé Temple (Temple of Generations)
14 Hung Temple
15 Waiting Pavilion (Huu Ta Dai Lam Vien)

foreign emissaries, mandarins and military officers during formal ceremonial occasions. In front of the palace are 18 stone stelae, which stipulate the arrangement of the nine mandarinate ranks on the Great Rites Courtyard: the upper level was for ministers, mandarins and officers of the upper grade; the lower for those of lower grades. Civil servants would stand on the left and the military on the right. Only royal princes were allowed to stand in the palace itself, which is perhaps the best-preserved building in the Imperial City complex. Its columns, tiled floor and ceiling have all been restored.

North of the Palace of Supreme Harmony is the **Tu Cam Thanh** (Purple Forbidden City **5**), reserved for the use of the emperor and his family, and surrounded by walls, 1 m thick, to form a city within a city. Tragically, the Forbidden City was virtually destroyed during the 1968 Tet offensive. The two **Mandarin Palaces** and the **Royal Reading Pavilion (10)** are all that survive. The Royal Reading Pavilion has been rebuilt but, needless to say, has no books.

At the far side of Thai Hoa Palace are two enormous **bronze urns** (Vac Dong) decorated with birds, plants and wild animals, and weighing about 1500 kg each. On either side are the **Ta (6)** and **Huu Vu (7)** pavilions, one converted into a souvenir art shop, the other a mock throne room in which tourists can pay US$5 to dress up and play the part of king. On the far side of the palace are the outer northern walls of the citadel and the north gate.

Most of the surviving buildings of interest are to be found on the west side of the palace, running between the outer walls and the walls of the Forbidden City. At the southwest corner is the well-preserved and beautiful **Hien Lam Cac (12)**, a pavilion built in 1821, in front of which stand nine massive **bronze urns (13)** cast between 1835 and 1837 on the orders of Emperor Minh Mang. It is estimated that they weigh between 1500 kg and 2600 kg, and each has 17 decorative figures, animals, rivers, flowers and landscapes representing between them the wealth, beauty and unity of the country. The central, largest and most ornate urn is dedicated to the founder of the empire, Emperor Gia Long. Next to the urns walking northwards is **Thé Temple** (Temple of Generations, **14**). Built in 1821, it contains altars honouring 10 of the kings of the Nguyen Dynasty (Duc Duc and Hiep Hoa are missing) behind which are meant to be kept a selection of their personal belongings. It was only in 1954 that the stelae depicting the three Revolutionary emperors, Ham Nghi, Thanh Thai and Duy Tan, were brought into the temple. The French, perhaps fearing they would become a focus of discontent, prevented the Vietnamese from erecting altars in their memory. North of the Thé Temple is **Hung Temple (15)**, built in 1804 for the worship of Gia Long's father, Nguyen Phuc Luan, the father of the founder of the Nguyen Dynasty.

Hué Museum of Royal Fine Arts
① *3 Le Truc St, Tue-Sun 0700-1700, until 1730 in summer (14 Apr-14 Oct); 35,000d. No cameras or video cameras; over shoes are provided; information in English.*
Housed in the Long An Palace, the museum contains a reasonable collection of ceramics, furniture, screens and bronzeware and some stunning, embroidered imperial clothes. The building itself is worthy of note for its elegant construction. Built by Emperor Thieu Tri in 1845, it was dismantled and erected on the present site in 1909.

Perfume River and the imperial tombs

As the geographical and spiritual centre of the Nguyen Dynasty, Hué and the surrounding area is the site of numerous pagodas, seven imperial tombs and the tombs of numerous other royal personages, countless courtiers and successful mandarins. Many of these are located close to the Perfume River.

Each of the tombs follows the same stylistic formula, although they also reflect the individual tastes of the emperor in question. The tombs were built during the lifetime of each emperor, who took a great interest in their design and construction; they were, after all, meant to ensure his comfort in the next life. Each mausoleum, variously arranged, has five design elements: a courtyard with statues of elephants, horses and military and civil mandarins (usually approached through a park of rare trees); a stela pavilion (with an engraved eulogy composed by the king's son and heir); a Temple of the Soul's Tablets; a pleasure pavilion, and a grave. Geomancers decreed that they should also have a stream and a mountainous screen in front. The tombs faithfully copy Chinese prototypes, although most art historians claim that they fall short in terms of execution.

Thien Mu Pagoda → Colour map 4, B4.

ⓘ *Easy 4-km bicycle (or cyclo) ride from the city, following the north bank of the river upstream.*

Thien Mu Pagoda (the Elderly Goddess Pagoda), also known as the Thien Mau Tu Pagoda, and locally as the **Linh Mu Pagoda** (the name used on most local maps), is the finest in Hué and beautifully sited on the north bank of the Perfume River. It was built in 1601 by Nguyen Hoang, the governor of Hué, after an old woman appeared to him and said that the site had supernatural significance and should be marked by the construction of a pagoda. The monastery is the oldest in Hué, and the seven-storey **Phuoc Duyen** (Happiness and Grace Tower), built later by Emperor Thieu Tri in 1844, is 21 m high, with each storey containing an altar to a different Buddha. The summit of the tower is crowned with a water pitcher to catch the rain, water representing the source of happiness. Arranged around the tower are four smaller buildings one of which contains the **Great Bell**, cast in 1710 under the orders of the Nguyen Lord, Nguyen Phuc Chu, and weighing 2200 kg. Beneath another of the surrounding pavilions is a monstrous **marble turtle** on which is a stela, carved in 1715 and 2.6 m high, recounting the development of Buddhism in Hué. Beyond the tower, the entrance to the pagoda is through a triple gateway patrolled by six carved and vividly painted guardians, two on each gate. The roof of the sanctuary itself is decorated with jataka stories (birth stories of the Buddha). At the front of the sanctuary is a laughing Buddha in brass. Behind that are an assortment of gilded Buddhas and a crescent-shaped gong, cast in 1677 by Jean de la Croix. Thich Quang Duc, the first monk to commit suicide through self immolation, came from this pagoda (see page 1097); the grey Austin in which he made the journey to his death in Ho Chi Minh City is still kept here in a garage in the temple garden.

Tomb of Emperor Gia Long → Colour map 4, B4.

ⓘ *South of town on a tributary of the Perfume River, daily 0630-1730; 55,000d for the upkeep of the tomb. Get there by bicycle or motorbike.*

The Tomb of Emperor Gia Long is the most distant from Hué and is rarely visited. Overgrown with venerable mango trees and devoid of tourists, touts and ticket sellers, it is the most atmospheric of all the tombs. And, given the historical changes that were to be wrought by the dynasty Gia Long founded, this is arguably the most significant tomb in Hué.

Nguyen Anh, or Gia Long as he was crowned in 1802, came to power with French support. His reign was despotic: when his European advisers suggested that encouragement of industry would lead to the betterment of his poorer subjects, Gia Long replied that he preferred them poor. In fact, the poor were virtual slaves during his reign: the price for one healthy young buffalo was one healthy young girl. It's not surprising, then, that a study by a Vietnamese scholar estimated that there were 105 peasant uprisings between 1802 and

1820 alone. The Vietnamese have never forgiven Gia Long for his despotism nor for the fact that he gave the French a foothold in Vietnam; they still say of him that "*cong ran can ga nha*" (he carried home the snake that killed the chicken).

To reach Gia Long's tomb, take Dien Bien Phu Street out of town. After a couple of kilometres turn right at the T-junction facing pine-shrouded Dan Nam Giao Temple and take the first left onto Minh Mang. Continue past the sign marking your departure from Hué and take the right-hand branch of the fork in the road. After a short distance the road joins the riverbank and heads for some 2 km towards the new Hué bypass (Highway 1) across the river. Follow the riverbank directly underneath this bridge and continue straight on as the road begins to deteriorate. A few metres beyond the Ben Do 1 km milestone is a red sign to 'Gia Long Tomb'. Down a steep path a sampan waits to ferry passengers across this tributary of the Perfume River (bargain but expect to pay US$2-3 return); on the far side, follow the track upstream for about 1 km. Turn right by a café with two billiard tables and then, almost immediately, turn left. Keep on this path. Ask for directions along the way.

Gia Long's geomancers did a great job finding this site: with the mountainous screen in front it is a textbook example of a final resting place. Interestingly, although they had first choice of all the possible sites, this is the furthest tomb from the palace: clearly they took their task seriously. Gia Long's mausoleum was built between 1814 and 1820 and, as the first of the dynasty, set the formula for the later tombs. There is a surrounding lotus pond and steps lead up to a courtyard, where the Minh Thanh ancestral temple stands resplendent in red and gold. To the right is a double burial chamber, walled and locked, where Gia Long and his wife are interred (the emperor's tomb is fractionally the taller). The chamber is perfectly lined up with the two huge obelisks on the far side of the lake. Beyond this is a courtyard with five, now headless, mandarins, horses and elephants on each side; steps lead up to the stela eulogizing the emperor's reign, composed, presumably, by his eldest son, Minh Mang, as was the custom. This grey monolith, engraved in Chinese characters, remained miraculously undisturbed during two turbulent centuries.

Tomb of Emperor Minh Mang → *Colour map 4, B4.*

① *12 km south of Hué. Daily 0630-1730; 55,000d. To get there by bicycle or motorbike follow the directions for Gia Long's tomb (page 1048) but cross the Perfume River using the new road bridge; on the far side of the bridge turn left.*

The Tomb of Emperor Minh Mang is possibly the finest of all the imperial tombs. Built between 1841 and 1843, it is sited south of the city. In terms of architectural poise and balance, and richness of decoration, it has no peer in the area. The tomb's layout, along a single central and sacred axis (*Shendao*), is unusual in its symmetry; no other tomb, with the possible exception of Khai Dinh, achieves the same unity of constituent parts, nor draws the eye onwards so easily and pleasantly from one visual element to the next. The tomb was traditionally approached through the **Dai Hong Mon**; today, visitors pass through a side gate into the ceremonial courtyard, which contains an array of statuary. Next is the stela pavilion in which there is a carved eulogy to the emperor composed by his son, Thieu Tri. Continuing downwards through a series of courtyards visitors see, in turn, the **Sung An Temple** dedicated to Minh Mang and his empress; a small garden with flower beds that once formed the Chinese character for 'longevity', and two sets of stone bridges. The first consists of three spans, the central one of which (**Trung Dao Bridge**) was for the sole use of the emperor. The second, single bridge, leads to a short flight of stairs with naga balustrades at the end of which is a locked bronze door (no access). The door leads to the tomb itself which is surrounded by a circular wall.

Tomb of Tu Duc → *Colour map 4, B4.*

ⓘ *7 km south Hué, daily 0630-1730; 55,000d. If you're travelling by boat, a return xe ôm trip from the riverbank is 20,000d.*

The Tomb of Tu Duc was built between 1864 and 1867 in a pine wood. The complex is enclosed by a wall and encompasses a lake, with lotus and water hyacinth. An island on the Lake has a number of replicas of famous temples, built by the king, which are now rather difficult to discern. Tu Doc often came here to relax, and composed poetry and listened to music. The **Xung Khiem Pavilion**, built in 1865, has recently been restored with UNESCO's help and is the most attractive building here.

West of the lake, the tomb complex follows the formula described above: ceremonial square, mourning yard with pavilion and then the tomb itself. To the left of Tu Duc's tomb are the tombs of his Empress, Le Thien Anh, and adopted son, Kien Phuc. Many of the pavilions are crumbling and ramshackle, lending the complex a rather tragic air. This is appropriate since, though he had 104 wives, Tu Duc fathered no sons and was therefore forced to write his own eulogy, a fact which he took as a bad omen. The eulogy itself recounts the sadness in Tu Duc's life. It was shortly after Tu Duc's reign that France gained full control of Vietnam.

Tomb of Khai Dinh

ⓘ *10 km south of Hué, daily 0630-1730; 55,000d. To get there by motorbike or bicycle follow the directions for Gia Long's tomb (page 1048) but turn immediately left past small shops after the new river crossing (Hwy 1) and head straight on, over a small crossroads, parallel to the main road. If you're travelling by boat, a return xe ôm trip from the riverbank is 25,000-30,000d.*

The Tomb of Khai Dinh was built between 1920 and 1932 and is the last mausoleum of the Nguyen Dynasty. By the time Khai Dinh was contemplating the afterlife, brick had given way in popularity to concrete, so the structure is now beginning to deteriorate. Nevertheless, it occupies a fine position on the Chau Mountain facing southwest towards a large white statue of Quan Am, also built by Khai Dinh. The valley, used for the cultivation of cassava and sugar cane, and the pine-covered mountains, make this one of the most beautifully sited and peaceful of the tombs. Indeed, before construction could begin, Khai Dinh had to remove the tombs of Chinese nobles who had already selected the site for its beauty and auspicious orientation. A total of 127 steep steps lead up to the Honour Courtyard with statuary of mandarins, elephants and horses. An octagonal stela pavilion in the centre of the mourning yard contains a stone stela engraved with a eulogy to the emperor. At the top of some more stairs, are the tomb and shrine of Khai Dinh, containing a bronze statue of the emperor sitting on his throne and holding a jade sceptre. The body is interred 9 m below ground level. The interior is richly decorated with ornate and colourful murals (the artist incurred the wrath of the emperor and only just escaped execution), floor tiles, and decorations built up with fragments of porcelain. It is the most elaborate of all the tombs and took 11 years to build. Such was the cost of construction that Khai Dinh had to levy additional taxes to fund the project.

Amphitheatre and Elephant Temple

ⓘ *South bank of the river, about 3 km west of Hué railway station. Free. To get there by bicycle or motorbike turn left up a paved track opposite 203 Bui Thi Xuan St; the track for the Elephant Temple runs in front of the amphitheatre (off to the right).*

The Ho Quyen (Amphitheatre) was built in 1830 by Emperor Minh Mang as a venue for the popular duels between elephants and tigers. This royal sport was in earlier centuries staged on an island in the Perfume River or on the riverbanks themselves but, by 1830, it was considered desirable for the royal party to be able to observe the duels without placing themselves at risk from escaping tigers. The amphitheatre is said to have been last used in 1904. The walls of the amphitheatre are 5 m high and the arena is 44 m in diameter. On the south side, beneath the royal box, is one large gateway (for the elephant) and, to the north, five smaller entrances for the tigers.

Den Voi Re, the Temple of the Elephant Trumpet, dedicated to the call of the fighting elephant, is a few hundred metres away. It is a modest little place and fairly run down, with a large pond in front and two small elephant statues. Presumably this is where elephants were blessed before battle or perhaps where the unsuccessful ones were mourned.

Thanh Toan Covered Bridge
ⓘ *8 km west of Hué.*

The bridge was built in the reign of King Le Hien Tong (1740-1786) by Tran Thi Dao, a childless woman, as an act of charity, hoping that God would bless her with a baby. The structure, with its shelter for the tired and homeless, attracted the interest of several kings who granted the village immunity from a number of taxes. Unfortunately, the original yin-yang tiles have been replaced with ugly green enamelled tube tiles but the bridge is still in good condition. The route to the bridge passes through beautiful countryside. Travel there by bicycle or motorbike in the glow of the late afternoon sun.

Around Hué

The Demilitarized Zone (DMZ) → *Colour map 4, A3/4.*
ⓘ *Most visitors see the sights of the DMZ, including Khe Sanh and the Ho Chi Minh Trail, on a tour. A 1-day tour of all the DMZ sights can be booked from any of Hué's tour operators for around US$10; depart 0600, return 1800-2000.* ▸▸ *See Activities and tours, page 1054.*

The incongruously named Demilitarized Zone (DMZ), scene of some of the fiercest fighting of the Vietnam War, lies along the Ben Hai River and the better-known 17th Parallel. The **Hien Luong Bridge** on the 17th parallel is included in most tours. The DMZ was the creation of the 1954 Geneva Peace Accord, which divided the country into two spheres of influence prior to elections that were never held. Like its counterpart in Germany, the boundary evolved into a national border, separating Communist from Capitalist but, unlike its European equivalent, it was the triumph of Communism that saw its demise.

At **Dong Ha**, to the north of Hué, Highway 9 branches off the main coastal Highway 1 and heads 80 km west to the border with Laos (see below). Along this route is **Khe Sanh** (now called Huong Hoa), the site of one of the most famous battles of the war. The battleground is 3 km from the village. There's also a small **museum** ⓘ *25,000d*, at the former Tacon military base, surrounded by military hardware.

A section of the **Ho Chi Minh Trail** runs close to Khe Sanh. This is another popular but inevitably disappointing sight, given that its whole purpose was to be as inconspicuous as possible and anything you see was designed to be invisible, from the air at least. However, it's worthy of a pilgrimage considering the sacrifice of millions of Vietnamese porters and the role it played in the American defeat (see page 1102).

Tours to the DMZ usually also include the **tunnels of** Vinh Moc ⓘ *13 km off Hwy 1 and 6 km north of Ben Hai River, 25,000d*, which served a similar function to the better known Cu Chi tunnels in the south. They evolved as families in the heavily bombed village dug themselves shelters beneath their houses and then joined up with their neighbours. Later the tunnels developed a more offensive role when Viet Cong soldiers fought from them. Some regard these tunnels as more 'authentic' than the 'touristy' tunnels of Cu Chi.

The **Rock Pile** is a 230-m-high limestone outcrop just south of the DMZ. It served as a US observation post, with troops, ammunition, Budweiser and prostitutes all being helicoptered in. Although it was chosen as an apparently unassailable position, the sheer walls of the Rock Pile were eventually scaled by the Viet Cong.

Hai Van Pass and Lang Co → *Colour map 4, B5.*

Between Hué and Danang a finger of the Truong Son Mountains juts eastwards, extending all the way to the sea: almost as though God were somewhat roguishly trying to divide the country into two equal halves. The mountains act as an important climatic barrier, trapping the cooler, damper air masses to the north and bottling them up over Hué, which accounts for Hué's shocking weather. They also mark an abrupt linguistic divide: the Hué dialect (the language of the royal court) to the north is still the source of bemusement to many southerners. The physical barrier to north-south communication has resulted in some spectacular engineering solutions: the single track and narrow gauge **railway line** closely follows the coastline, sometimes almost hanging over the sea while Highway 1 winds its way equally precariously over the Lang Co lagoon and Hai Van Pass.

The road passes through many pretty, red-tiled villages, compact and surrounded by clumps of bamboo and fruit trees, which provide shade, shelter and sustenance. Windowless jalopies from the French era trundle along picking up passengers and their bundles, while station wagons from the American era provide an inter-village shared taxi service. The idyllic fishing village of **Lang Co** is just off Highway 1, about 65 km south of Hué, and has a number of cheap and good seafood restaurants.

Shortly after crossing the Lang Co lagoon, dotted with coracles and fish traps, the road begins the long haul up to **Hai Van Pass** (Deo Hai Van or 'Pass of the Ocean Clouds'), known to the French as 'Col des Nuages'. The pass is 497 m above the waves and once marked the border between Vietnam and Champa. The pass is peppered with abandoned pillboxes and crowned with an old fort, originally built by the Nguyen Dynasty from Hué and used as a relay station for the pony express on the old Mandarin Road. Subsequently used by the French, it is a pretty shabby affair today, collecting wind-blown litter and sometimes used by the People's Army for a quiet brew-up and a smoke. Looking back to the north, stretching into the haze is the littoral and lagoon of Lang Co; to the south is Danang Bay and Monkey Mountain, and at your feet lies a patch of green paddies which belong to the leper colony, accessible only by boat.

◉ Hué listings

For Sleeping and Eating price codes, see inside the front cover.

● Sleeping

Hué *p1042, map p1043*
Most hotels lie to the south of the Perfume River, although there are a couple to the north in the old Vietnamese part of town. Hué still

suffers from a dearth of quality accommodation but this has improved in recent years and more properties are planned.
LL-AL La Residence Hotel & Spa, 5 Le Loi St, T054-837475, www.la-residence-hue.com. For lovers of art deco, it is an essential place to stay and to visit. Home of the French governor of Annam in the 1920s, it has been beautifully restored with 122 rooms,

a restaurant, lobby bar, spa and swimming pool. The rooms in the original governor's residence are the most stylish, with 4-poster beds and dark wood furnishings; other rooms are extremely comfortable too, with all mod cons. Filling breakfasts and free internet. Highly recommended.

LL-A The Pilgrimage Village, 130 Minh Mang Rd, T054-885461, www.pilgrimage village.com. Beautifully designed rooms in a village setting ranging from honeymoon and pool suites to superior rooms. There are 2 restaurants, a number of bars, a gorgeous spa and 2 pools. Cooking and t'ai chi classes are available. There's a complimentary shuttle service to and from town.

L-AL Saigon Morin, 30 Le Loi St, T054-823 526, www.morinhotel.com.vn. The best hotel in Hué, this is still recognizable as the fine hotel built by the Morin brothers in the 1880s. Arranged around a courtyard with a small pool, the rooms are large and comfortable. All have a/c, satellite TV and hot water. The courtyard is a delightful place to sit in the evening and enjoy a quiet drink.

A Century Riverside, 49 Le Loi St, T054-823 390, www.centuryriversidehue.com. Fabulous river views and comfortable, nicely furnished rooms in this very imposing building. Note that not all rooms have been renovated, so enquire before booking. Vietnamese and Western food is served at the restaurants. There's a pool, tennis courts and a massage service. Used by dozens of tour operators.

A-D Duy Tan, 12 Hung Vuong St, T054-825001, www.duytanhotel.com.vn. Large building in a bustling part of town, with comfortable superior rooms. The standard rooms are spartan but fully equipped.

A-D Festival Hué Hotel, 15 Ly Thuong Kiet St, T054-823071, www.festivalhuehotel.com.vn. The Festival hotel has now renovated all its rooms and is situated just outside the main bustle of downtown activity. There's a very sheltered pool and breakfast is included.

C-F L'Indochine (formerly Dong Duong), 2 Hung Vuong St, T054-823866, indochine-hotel@dng.vnn.vn. Priciest rooms in the old

villa in front with baths in bathrooms; the building behind is sterile and modern and the cheapest rooms (with showers only) are here. The first-class rooms are looking a little worn around the edges. There are 3 restaurants and not much English is spoken.

C-G Dong Loi, 19 Pham Ngu Lao St, T054-822296, www.hoteldongloi.com. Well situated and surrounded by internet cafés, shops and restaurants, this is a bright, breezy, airy and comfortable hotel. All rooms have a/c and hot water and all except the cheapest have a bath. Family-run, friendly and helpful service. The excellent **La Carambole Restaurant** adjoins the hotel.

D-F Kinh Do, 1 Nguyen Thai Hoc St, T054-823566. Architecturally unattractive with 35 smallish rooms but comfortable, in a central location and quiet with friendly staff and 2 restaurants. The price includes breakfast.

D-G A Dong 1, 1 bis Chu Van An St, T054-824148, adongcoltd@dng.vnn.vn. 7 rooms in this friendly hotel, with a/c, fridge and bath; also has an attractive upstairs terrace. There's also an **A Dong 2** on Doi Cung St.

The little *hem* (alley) opposite the **Century Riverside** has some really nice rooms in comfortable and cheerful guesthouses – easily the best-value accommodation in Hué. Recommended are:

D-G Canh Tien Guesthouse, 9/66 Le Loi St, T054-822772, http://canhtienhotel.chez. tiscali.fr. 12 rooms with fan or a/c. Cheaper rooms have fans; the most expensive have a balcony. Welcoming family.

D-G Mimosa, 66/10 (10 Kiet 66) Le Loi St, T054-828068. French is spoken when the owner is here. 8 rooms, with a/c, hot water and bath that are quiet, simple and clean. Rooms with fan are cheaper.

E-G Hoang Huong, 66/2 (2 Kiet 66) Le Loi St, T054-828509. Some a/c or cheaper rooms with fan; friendly and helpful family guesthouse. Cheap dormitories and bicycles and motos rented.

E-G Hung Vuong Inn, 20 Hung Vuong St, T054-821068, truongdung2000@yahoo.com. Above **La Boulangerie**. There are 9 double and twin rooms above the shop that are all spotlessly clean. Rooms have a TV and minibar and baths; some have a balcony. It is quieter on the back side of the building. **E-G Thanh Thuy**, 66/4 (4 Kiet 66) Le Loi St, T054-824585, thanhthuy66@dng.vnn.vn. Small, peaceful, clean and friendly family-run guesthouse. 4 rooms, with a/c and hot water. Car hire at good rates (around US$25/day).

🍴 Eating

Hué cuisine is excellent; delicately flavoured and painstakingly prepared. Hué dishes are robust, notably the famed *bun bo Hué* – round white noodles in soup, with slices of beef, laced with chilli oil of exquisite piquancy. Restaurants for locals tend to close early; get there before 2000. Traveller cafés and restaurants keep serving till about 2200.

Hué p1042, map p1043

¶¶ **La Carambole**, 19 Pham Ngu Lao St, T054-810491, la_carambole@hotmail.com, daily 0700-2300. One of the most popular restaurants in town and deservedly so. It is incredibly busy especially for dinner when the imperial-style dinner is recommended.
¶¶ **Saigon Morin**, see Sleeping. Excellent buffets for US$12 in a garden setting with a range of specialty Hué cuisine. While you dine, be entertained by Royal Music performers.
¶¶-¶ **The Tropical Garden Restaurant**, 27 Chu Van An St, T054-8471431, tropicalgarden@vnn.vn. Dine alfresco in a small leafy garden, just a short walk from the Perfume River. Beef soup with starfruit and mackerel baked in pineapple.
¶ **Café No 3**, 3 Le Loi St, T054-824514. Near the railway station, a cheap and popular café serving standard Vietnamese, Western and vegetarian food. A useful source of information and with bikes for rent.
¶ **Dong Tam**, 7/66 (7 Kiet 66) Le Loi St, T054-828403. Tucked away in the little *hem* opposite **Century Riverside**, this is Hué's vegetarian restaurant. Sit in a pleasant and quiet yard

while choosing from the very reasonably priced menu. Its credentials are reflected in its popularity with the city's monkish population.
¶ **La Boulangerie Française**, 20 Hung Vuong St, T054-821068, daily 0700-2030. There's a large range of Western and Vietnamese food served up by very friendly staff. Proceeds from the bakery go to help Vietnamese orphans via a French charity (AEVN-France).
¶ **Lac Thien**, 6 Dinh Tien Hoang St, T054-527348, and ¶ **Lac Thanh**, 6A Dinh Tien Hoang St, T054-524674. Arguably Hué's most famous restaurants, run by schismatic branches of the same deaf-mute family in adjacent buildings. You go to one or the other: under no circumstances should clients patronize both establishments. **Lac Thien** serves excellent dishes from a diverse and inexpensive menu, and the family is riotous and entertaining, but service has been known to be slack.
¶ **Stop and Go**, 18 Ben Nghe St, T054-827051, stopandgocafe@yahoo.com. Next door to **Ben Nghe Guesthouse**. Run by the Mr Do. Specialities include rice pancakes and the Hué version of spring rolls, excellent and cheap.
¶ **Y Thao Garden**, 3 Thach Han St, T054-523 018, ythaogarden@gmail.com. Eating here is an extraordinary experience. The set menu of 8 courses is a culinary adventure with some amazing animals-from-food sculpture. The old house is delightful. Recommended.

🍸 Bars and clubs

Hué p1042, map p1043

Cathi, 64 Le Lo Sti, T054-831210. A friendly place offering lots of titbits with drinks. Coloured lanterns, tree trunks to sit on inside for drinks, and a garden. Large drinks list including cocktails and teas, and a small menu of meat, noodles and rice.
DMZ Bar, 60 Le Loi St, T054-823414, www.dmz-bar.com, daily 0900-0200. Hué's first bar, with pool table, cold beer and spirits at affordable prices. Good place to meet people and pick up tourist information.

Why Not?, 21 Vo Thi Sau St. Slightly arty café bar, with a decent selection of food and drink.

🎭 Entertainment

Hué *p1042, map p1043*
Rent a **dragon boat** and sail up the Perfume River with private singers and musicians; tour offices and major hotels will arrange groups.

See a **Royal Court performance** in the Imperial City's theatre or listen to performers during the **Saigon Morin**'s evening buffet.

🛍 Shopping

Hué *p1042, map p1043*
Shops around the **Century Riverside Hotel**, for example Le Loi and Pham Ngu Lao streets, sell ceramics, silk and clothes. The *non bai tho* or poem hats are also available. These are a unique Hué form of the standard conical hat (*non lá*), made from bamboo and palm leaves, with love poetry, songs, proverbs or simply a design stencilled on to them. The decoration is only visible if the hat is held up to the light and viewed from the inside.

No Vietnamese visitor would leave Hué without having previously stocked up on *me xung*, a sugary, peanut and toffee confection coated in sesame seeds.

▲ Activities and tours

Hué *p1042, map p1043*
Tour operators
Almost every travellers' café acts as an agent for a tour operator and will take bookings. Bus and boat tours to the **Imperial Tombs** are organized by tour operators and hotels. Local tour operators charge round US$6 per person to visit Thien Mu Pagoda, Hon Chien Temple, Tu Duc, Minh Mang and Khai Dinh's Tombs, 0800, returning 1530.

There are also day tours to some of the sights of the Vietnam War, US$10 for 9 sights,

including **Vinh Moc** tunnels and museum, the **Ho Chi Minh Trail** and **Khe Sanh**, 0600, return 1800-2000. Those wishing to travel overland to Laos can arrange to be dropped off in Khe Sanh and pay less.
Lienhoang, 12 Nguyen Thien Ke St, T054-823 507/091-414 7378 (mob), tienbicycles@gmail.com. Mr Tien runs recommended cycling tours around the country, including one to the DMZ, US$12 a day including bike, support car, guide, accommodation and entrance fees.
Stop and Go Café, 18 Ben Nghe St, T054-827 051/090-512 6767 (mob), stopandgocafe@yahoo.com. Known for its tours of the DMZ (all-day tour, US$16 on a motorbike, US$60 in a car) which are led by ARVN veterans. Highly recommended.
Sinh Café, 7 Nguyen Tri Phuong St, T054-848 626, and at 12 Hung Vuong St, T054-845 0222, www.sinhcafevn.com. Competitively priced tours and money changing facilities.

🚌 Transport

Hué *p1042, map p1043*
Air
There are flights to **Hanoi** and **HCMC**. **Phu Bai Airport** is a 25-min drive south of Hué.
Airline offices Vietnam Airlines, 23 Nguyen Van Cu St, 0715-1115, 1330-1630.

Bicycle and motorbike
Bikes and motorbikes (US$6 per day) can be hired from hotels, guesthouses and cafés.

Boat
Boats can be hired through tour agents and from any berth on the south bank of the river, east of Trang Tien Bridge or through travel cafés. Good for either a gentle cruise, or an attractive way of getting to some of the temples and mausoleums, around US$5-10 depends on time and if singers are employed. If you travel by boat you may have to pay a moto driver to take you to the tomb as they are often 1 km or so from the riverbank.

Border essentials: Vietnam–Laos

Lao Bao

The Vietnamese border post is 3 km beyond Lao Bao village at the western end of Highway 9; Lao immigration is 500 m west at Dansavanh. Once in Laos, Route 9 heads west over the Annamite Mountains to Xepon (45 km) and on to Savannakhet (236 km from the border). We have received reports of long delays at this border crossing, particularly entering Vietnam, as paperwork is scrutinized and bags are checked and double-checked. Don't be surprised if formalities take 1 hr – and keep smiling! Expect to pay 'overtime fees' on the Lao side if you come through on a Sat or Sun or after 1600 on a weekday. Lao immigration can issue 30-day tourist visas for US$30-42. You can also get a Lao visa in advance from the Lao consulate in Danang (12 Tran Qui Cap St, T0511-821208, 0800-1100, 1400-1600); it takes 24 hrs to process. The closest Vietnamese consulate is in Savannakhet; see page 531 for visa application details and opening hours.

Transport There are buses from Hué direct to Savannakhet or buses to Khe Sanh where there are connections to Lao Bao. There are also buses direct to the border from Le Duan St in Dong Ha, 1-1½ hrs. *Xe ôm* from Khe Sanh to the border costs US$3, or from Lao Bao village to the border, US$1. There are daily departures for the Lao town of Savannakhet from Dansavanh. Buses also depart from Xepon (45 km west of the border) to Savannakhet daily 0800, 30,000 kip. Those crossing into Vietnam from Laos may be able to get a ride with the DMZ tour bus from Khe Sanh back to Hué (see page 1050) in the late afternoon. Otherwise, there are Vietnam-bound buses from Savannakhet (see page 531) and numerous songthaews to the border from the market in Xepon, 45 km, 1 hr, 20,000 kip but you'll need to get there by 0700 to ensure a space.

Accommodation Mountain, Lao Bao village. A simple, clean and friendly guesthouse.

Bus

The An Cuu station, 43 Hung Vuong St serves destinations south of Hué. The An Hoa station up at the northwest corner of the citadel serves destinations north of **Hué**. Tourist buses to **Savannakhet**, Laos, via Lao Bao, leave at 0600, US$15. Buses to **Vientiane** leave at 1730, US$18. Book with tour operators.

Cyclo and xe ôm

Cyclos and *xe ôm* are available everywhere.

Taxi

Hué Taxi, T054-833333; **Mai Linh Taxi**, T054-898989.

Train

Hué Railway Station, 2 Bui Thi Xuan, west end of Le Loi St, T054-830666, booking office open daily 0700-2200. It serves all stations south to **HCMC** and north to **Hanoi**. Advance booking, especially for sleepers, is essential. The 4-hr journey to **Danang** is recommended.

⑥ Directory

Hué *p1042, maps p1043*
Banks Incombank, 2A Le Quy Don St, daily 0700-1130, 1330-1700, closed Thu afternoon. Has a Visa and MasterCard ATM. **Vietcom Bank**, 78 Hung Vuong St, daily 0700-2200. Visa ATM to the left of **La Résidence** hotel. **Internet** Most hotels and guesthouses listed here offer internet. **Medical services** Hué General Hospital, 16 Le Loi St, T054-822325. **Post office and telephone** 8 Hoang Hoa Tham St; 91 Tran Hung Dao, daily 0630-2130.

Hoi An, Danang and around

The city of Danang has no real charm and no sense of permanence but few cities in the world have such spectacular beaches on their doorstep, let alone three UNESCO World Heritage Sites – Hué, Hoi An and My Son – within a short drive. The ancient town of Hoi An (formerly Faifo) lies on the banks of the Thu Bon River. During its heyday 200 years ago, when trade with China and Japan flourished, it was a prosperous little port. Much of the merchants' wealth was spent on family chapels and Chinese clan houses which remain little altered today. The city of Hoi An is currently experiencing a revival: the river may be too shallow for shipping but it is perfect for tourist boats; the silk merchants may not export any produce but that's because everything they make leaves town on the backs of satisfied customers. ▸▸ *For listings, see pages 1066-1071.*

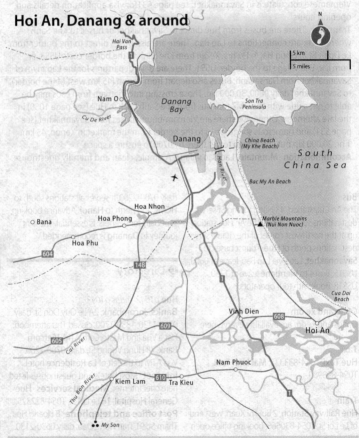

Hoi An, Danang & around

Hoi An's tranquil riverside setting, its diminutive scale, friendly people and its shops and galleries have made it one of the most popular destinations in Vietnam for tourists. There is much of historical interest in the town, plus a nearby beach and plenty of superb, inexpensive restaurants. That said, Hoi An's historic character is being slowly submerged by the rising tide of tourism. Although physically intact, virtually every one of its fine historic buildings either markets some aspect of its own heritage or touts in some other way for the tourist dollar; increasingly it is coming to resemble the 'Vietnam' pavilion in a Disney theme park. Nevertheless, visitors to Hoi An are charmed by the gentleness of the people and the sedate pace of life.

Most of Hoi An's more attractive buildings and assembly halls (*hoi quan*) are found either on, or just off, Tran Phu Street, which stretches west to east from the Japanese Covered Bridge to the market, running parallel to the river.

Ins and outs

Getting there and around There are direct minibus connections with Ho Chi Minh City, Hanoi, Hué and Nha Trang. The quickest way of getting from Hanoi or Ho Chi Minh City is by flying to Danang airport (see page 1061) and then getting a taxi direct to Hoi An (40 minutes, US$12-15). The town itself is compact, quite busy and best explored on foot, although guesthouses also hire out bicycles. ▸▸ *See Transport, page 1071.*

Best time to visit On the 14th day of the lunar month the town converts itself into a Chinese lantern fest and locals dress in traditional costume. The old town is pedestrianized for the night and poetry and music are performed in the streets.

Tourist information Entrance to most historic buildings is by sightseeing ticket, 75,000d, on sale at **Hoi An Tourist Office** ① *12 Phan Chu Trinh St, T0510-861276, and at 1 Nguyen Truong To St, T0510-861327, www.hoianoldtown.vn, open 0630-1800,* which has English-speaking staff and can arrange car and minibus hire as well as sightseeing guides. Sights in Hoi An are open September to March 0700-1730 and April to August 0630-1800. The sightseeing ticket is segregated into five categories of different sights, allowing visitors admission to one of each. It is valid for three days. If you want to see additional sights and have used up your tokens for that particular category you must buy additional tickets; 10,000d tokens for additional sights are no longer available. At least a full day is needed to see the town properly.

Background

Hoi An is divided into five quarters, or 'bangs', each of which would traditionally have had its own pagoda and supported one Chinese clan group. The Chinese, along with some Japanese, settled here in the 16th century and controlled trade between the islands of Southeast Asia, East Asia (China and Japan) and India. Portuguese and Dutch vessels also docked at the port. Chinese vessels tended to visit Hoi An during the spring, returning to China in the summer. By the end of the 19th century the Thu Bon River had started to silt up and Hoi An was gradually eclipsed by Danang as the most important port of the area.

Japanese Covered Bridge (Cau Nhat Ban)

ⓘ *Tran Phu St, 1 'other' token; keep your ticket to get back across the bridge.*

The Japanese Covered Bridge – also known as the Pagoda Bridge and the Faraway People's Bridge – is Hoi An's most famous landmark and was built in the 16th century. Its popular name reflects a long-standing belief that it was built by the Japanese, although no documentary evidence exists to support this. One of its other names, the Faraway People's Bridge, is said to have been coined because vessels from far away would moor close to the bridge. On its north side there is a pagoda, Japanese in style, for the protection of sailors, while at each end of the bridge are statues of two dogs (at the west end) and two monkeys (at the east end). It is said that the bridge was begun in the year of the monkey and finished

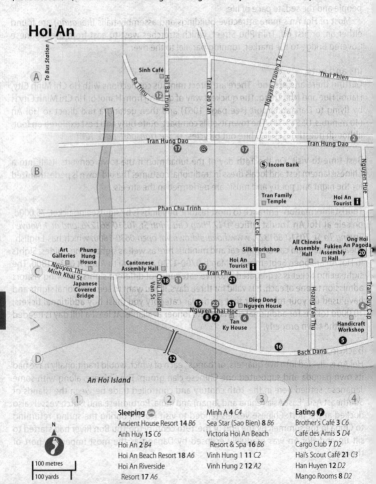

Hoi An

Sleeping 🛏

Ancient House Resort **14** *B6*
Anh Huy **15** *C6*
Hoi An **2** *B4*
Hoi An Beach Resort **18** *A6*
Hoi An Riverside
  Resort **17** *A6*
Minh A **4** *C4*
Sea Star (Sao Bien) **8** *B6*
Victoria Hoi An Beach
  Resort & Spa **16** *B6*
Vinh Hung 1 **11** *C2*
Vinh Hung 2 **12** *A2*

Eating 🍴

Brother's Café **3** *C6*
Café des Amis **5** *D4*
Cargo Club **7** *D2*
Hai's Scout Café **21** *C3*
Han Huyen **12** *D2*
Mango Rooms **8** *D2*

in the year of the dog, although some scholars have pointed out that this would mean a two-year period of construction, an inordinately long time for such a small bridge. They maintain, instead, that the two animals represent points of the compass, WSW (monkey) and NW (dog). Father Benigne Vachet, a missionary who lived in Hoi An between 1673 and 1683, notes in his memoirs that the bridge was the haunt of beggars and fortune tellers hoping to benefit from the stream of people crossing over it.

Bach Dang Street and the French quarter

Just south of the Covered Bridge is Bach Dang Street, which runs along the bank of the Thu Bon River, where there are boats, activity and often a cooling breeze, before looping round to the Hoi An Market. Further on, the small but interesting French quarter around Phan Boi Chau Street is worth taking time over; it's not on the regular 'tourist circuit' and requires no entry fee but the colonnaded fronts here are particularly attractive. As in all historical quarters of Vietnamese towns, visitors should raise their gaze above street level to appreciate the architectural detail of upper floors, which is more likely to have survived, and less likely to be covered up.

Assembly Halls (Hoi Quan)

Chinese traders in Hoi An (like elsewhere in Southeast Asia) established self-governing dialect associations or clan houses which owned their own schools, cemeteries, hospitals and temples. The clan houses (*hoi quan*) may be dedicated to a god or an individual and may contain a temple, although they are not themselves temples. There are five *hoi quan* in Hoi An, four for use by people of specific ethnicities – Fukien, Cantonese, Hainan, Chaozhou – and the fifth for use by any visiting Chinese sailors or merchants.

Strolling east from the Covered Bridge down Tran Phu Street all the assembly halls can be seen. Merchants from Guangdong would meet at the **Quang Dong Hoi Quan** (Cantonese Assembly Hall) ① *176 Tran Phu St, 1 'assembly hall' token*. This assembly hall is dedicated to Quan Cong, a Han Chinese general and dates from 1786. The hall, with its fine embroidered hangings, is in a cool, tree-filled compound and is a good place to rest.

Next is the **All Chinese Assembly Hall** (Ngu Bang Hoi Quan) ⓘ *64 Tran Phu St, free*, sometimes referred to as **Chua Ba** (Goddess Temple). Unusually for an assembly hall, it was a mutual aid society open to any Chinese trader or seaman, regardless of dialect or region of origin. The assembly hall would help shipwrecked or ill sailors and also performed the burial rites of merchants with no relatives in Hoi An. Built in 1773 as a meeting place for all five groups (the four listed above plus Hakka) and also for those with no clan house of their own, today it accommodates a Chinese School, Truong Le Nghia, where children of the diaspora learn the language of their forebears.

The **Phuc Kien Hoi Quan** (Fukien Assembly Hall) ⓘ *46 Tran Phu St, 1 'assembly hall' token*, was founded around 1690 and served Hoi An's largest Chinese ethnic group, those from Fukien. It is an intimate building within a large compound and is dedicated to Thien Hau, goddess of the sea and protector of sailors. She is the central figure on the main altar, clothed in gilded robes, who, together with her assistants, can hear the cries of distress of drowning sailors. Immediately on the right on entering the temple is a mural depicting Thien Hau rescuing a sinking vessel. Behind the main altar is a second sanctuary which houses the image of Van Thien whose blessings pregnant women invoke on the lives of their unborn children.

Further east, the **Hai Nam Hoi Quan** (Hainan Assembly Hall) ⓘ *10 Tran Phu St, free*, has a more colourful history. It was founded in 1883 in memory of more than 100 sailors and passengers who were killed when three ships were plundered by an admiral in Emperor Tu Duc's navy. In his defence the admiral claimed that the victims were pirates; some sources maintain he even had the ships painted black to strengthen his case.

Exquisite wood carving is the highlight of the **Chaozhou (Trieu Chau) Assembly Hall** ⓘ *362 Nguyen Duy Hieu St, 1 'assembly hall' token*. The altar and its panels depict images from the sea and women from the Beijing court, which were presumably intended to console homesick traders.

Merchants' houses and temples

Tan Ky House ⓘ *101 Nguyen Thai Hoc St, 1 'old house' token*, dates from the late 18th century. The Tan Ky family had originally arrived in Hoi An from China 200 years earlier and the house reflects not only the prosperity the family had acquired in the intervening years but also the architecture of their Japanese and Vietnamese neighbours, whose styles had presumably influenced the aesthetic taste and appreciation of the younger family members.

At the junction of Le Loi and Phan Chu Trinh streets, the **Tran Family Temple** ⓘ *1 'old house' token*, has survived for 15 generations (although the current generation has no son, which means the lineage has been broken). The building exemplifies Hoi An's construction methods and the harmonious fusion of Chinese and Japanese styles. It is roofed with heavy yin and yang tiling, which requires strong roof beams; these are held up by a triple-beamed support in the Japanese style (also seen on the roof of the covered bridge). Some beams have Chinese-inspired ornately carved dragons. The outer doors are Japanese, the inner are Chinese. On a central altar rest small wooden boxes which contain the photograph or likeness of the deceased together with biographical details. Beyond, at the back of the house, is a small, raised Chinese herb, spice and flower garden with a row of bonsai trees. As at all Hoi An's family houses, guests are received warmly and courteously and served lotus tea and dried coconut.

Diep Dong Nguyen House ⓘ *80 Nguyen Thai Hoc St*, with two Chinese lanterns hanging outside, was once a Chinese dispensary. The owner is friendly, hospitable and not commercially minded. He takes visitors into his house and shows them everything with pride and smiles.

Just west of the Japanese Bridge is **Phung Hung House** ⓘ *4 Nguyen Thi Minh Khai St, 1 'old house' token.* Built over 200 years ago it has been in the same family for eight generations. The house, which can be visited, is constructed of 80 columns of ironwood on marble pedestals. During the floods of 1964, Phung Hung House became home to 160 locals who camped upstairs for three days as the water rose to a height of 2.5 m.

Ong Hoi An Pagoda and around
At the east end of Tran Phu Street, at No 24, close to the intersection with Nguyen Hue Street, is the **Ong Hoi An Pagoda** ⓘ *1 'other' token.* This temple is in fact two interlinked pagodas built back-to-back: Chua Quan Cong, and behind that Chua Quan Am. Their date of construction is not known, although both certainly existed in 1653. In 1824 Emperor Minh Mang made a donation of 300 luong (1 luong being equivalent to 1½ oz of silver) for the support of the pagodas. They are dedicated to Quan Cong and Quan Am respectively.

Virtually opposite the Ong Hoi An Pagoda is **Hoi An Market** (Cho Hoi An). The market extends down to the river and then along the river road (Bach Dang Street, see page 1059). At the Tran Phu Street end it is a covered market selling mostly dry goods. Numerous cloth merchants and seamstresses will produce made-to-measure shirts in a few hours but not all to the same standard. On the riverside is the local **fish market**, which comes alive at 0500-0600 as boats arrive with the night's catch.

Cua Dai Beach
ⓘ *4 km east of Hoi An. You must leave your bicycle (5000d) or moto (1000d) just before Cua Dai beach in a car park.*
A very white sand beach with a few areas of shelter, Cua Dai Beach is a pleasant 20-minute bicycle ride or one-hour walk from Hoi An. Head east down Tran Hung Dao Street or, for a quieter route, set off down Nguyen Duy Hieu Street, which peters out into a walking and cycling path. This is a lovely route past paddy fields and ponds; nothing is signed but those with a good sense of direction will make their way back to the main road a kilometre or so before Cua Dai and those with a poor sense of direction can come to no harm. Behind the beach are a handful of hotels where food and refreshments can be bought.

Danang ⊕⊘▲⊕⊖ ▸▸ pp1066-1071. Colour map 4, B5.

Danang, Vietnam's third-largest port and a trading centre of growing importance, is situated on a peninsula of land at the point where the Han River flows into the South China Sea. It was first known as Cua Han (Mouth of the Han River) and renamed Tourane (a rough transliteration of Cua Han) by the French. It later acquired the title, Thai Phien, and finally Danang. An important port from French times, Danang gained world renown when two US Marine battalions landed here in March 1965 to secure the airfield. They were the first of a great many more US military personnel who would land on the beaches and airfields of South Vietnam.

Ins and outs
Getting there Flights from Bangkok, Hanoi, Ho Chi Minh City, Buon Ma Thuot, Dalat, Pleiku and Nha Trang arrive at Danang airport on the edge of the city; a taxi into town costs US$3 and takes five to 10 minutes. Danang is on the north-south railway line linking

Hanoi and Ho Chi Minh City. Regular bus and minibus connections link Danang with all major cities in the south as far as Ho Chi Minh City, and in the north as far as Hanoi. There are also daily buses from Danang to the Lao town of Savannakhet on the Mekong via the border at Lao Bao (see page 1055). Visas are available from the Lao consulate in Danang.
➤ See Transport, page 1071.

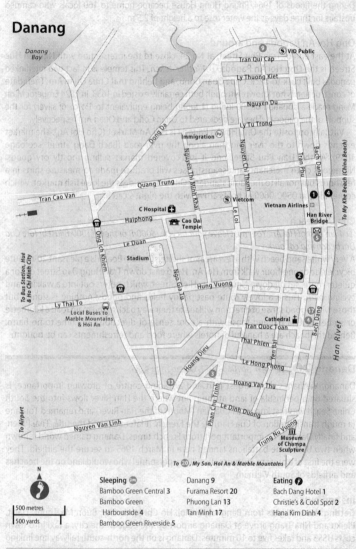

Danang

Sleeping 🛌
Bamboo Green Central **3**
Bamboo Green
Harbourside **4**
Bamboo Green Riverside **5**

Danang **9**
Furama Resort **20**
Phuong Lan **13**
Tan Minh **17**

Eating 🍴
Bach Dang Hotel **1**
Christie's & Cool Spot **2**
Hana Kim Dinh **4**

Getting around Danang is a sizeable town, rather too large to explore on foot, but there is abundant public transport, including cyclos, taxis and *Honda ôm*. Bicycles and motorbikes are available for hire from most hotels and guesthouses.

Tourist information An Phu Tourist ① *20 Dong Da St, T0511-3818366*, can help with information. You can also ask tour operators.

Museum of Champa Sculpture

① *Intersection of Trung Nu Vuong and Bach Dang streets, daily 0700-1700; 30,000d. The museum booklet (US$9) has been written as an art history, not as a guide to the collection, and is of little help. However, there are now books on Champa art which extensively catalogue the exhibits, US$8. Labels are in English.*

The museum (Bao Tang Dieu Khac Champa Da Nang) contains the largest display of Cham art anywhere in the world and testifies to a lively, creative and long-lasting civilization. Each room is dedicated to work from a different part of the Champa kingdom and, since different parts of Champa flowered artistically at different times from the fourth to the 14th centuries, the rooms reveal the evolution of Cham art and the prevailing outside influences, from Cambodia to Java.

Many pieces from **My Son** (page 1065) illustrate the Hindu trinity: Brahma the Creator, Vishnu the Preserver and Siva the Destroyer. An altar is inscribed with scenes from the wedding story of Sita and Rama, taken from the *Ramayana*, the Hindu epic. Ganesh, the elephant-headed son of Siva, was a much-loved god and is also well represented here.

At the end of the ninth century **Dong Duong** replaced My Son as the centre of Cham art. At this time Buddhism became the dominant religion of court, although it never fully replaced Hinduism. The Dong Duong room is illustrated with scenes from the life of Buddha. Faces from this period become less stylistic and more human and the bodies of the figures are more graceful and flowing.

The subsequent period of Cham art is known as the late **Tra Kieu** style. In this section there are *apsaras* (celestial dancing maidens), whose fluid and animated forms are exquisitely captured in stone. Thereafter Cham sculpture went into artistic decline.

The **Thap Mam** style (late 11th to early 14th century) sees a range of mythical beasts whose range and style is unknown elsewhere in Southeast Asia. Also in this room is a pedestal surrounded by 28 breast motifs. It is believed they represent Uroha, the mythical mother of the Indrapura nation (incorporating My Son, Tra Kieu, Dong Duong), but the meaning of the pedestal and others like it is unknown.

China Beach (My Khe Beach) → *Colour map 4, B5.*

① *With the opening of the new River Han Bridge, My Khe Beach is just a short ride from the centre of Danang by bicycle or motorbike (15-20 mins). Turn right just after the bridge, then take the first big turning on the left into Nguyen Cong Tru St; the beach is right at the end.*

Despite being only 20 minutes from Danang centre, **China Beach** is an 'undiscovered' and undeveloped asset, with the potential to transform Danang into the Río de Janeiro of Asia. It has miles and miles of fine white sand, clean water and a glorious setting: the hills of Monkey Mountain to the north and the Marble Mountains clearly visible to the south. There is a merciful absence of vendors, no litter and a number of excellent seafood restaurants. At times, though, there is a dangerous cross-current and undertow.

As an R&R retreat during the Vietnam War, the white sand and surf made My Khe popular with American soldiers, who named it China Beach. It became a fabled resort

Kingdom of Champa

The powerful kingdom of Champa was one of the most glorious in ancient Southeast Asia. Chinese texts suggest that in AD 192 a group of tribes, probably of Indonesian descent, formed a union known as Lin-Yi, later to become Champa. The first Champa capital, Tra Kieu (fourth to 10th centuries), was about 30 km from Danang, but the kingdom's territories extended far afield and other major sites included Dong Duong (eighth to 10th centuries), Po Nagar, Thap Mam and Cha Ban. Tra Kieu, My Son (page 1065) and Dong Duong were the three most important centres of the kingdom.

The polytheistic religion of Champa was a fusion of Buddhism, Sivaism, local elements and, later, Islam, and was expressed in an abundance of religious (and secular) sculptures and monuments. The kingdom reached its apogee in the 10th and 11th centuries but, unlike the Khmers, Champa never had the opportunity to create a capital city matching the magnificence of Angkor. For long periods the Cham were compelled to pay tribute to the Chinese and, after that, they were dominated in turn by the Javanese, Annamese (the Vietnamese) and then the Khmers. The Cham kingdom was finally eradicated in 1471, although there are still an estimated 90,000 Cham living in central Vietnam (mostly Brahmanists and Muslims). Given this turbulent history, it is perhaps surprising that the Cham found any opportunity for artistic endeavours. It should perhaps be added that since the demise of the kingdom, the number of Cham sculptures has increased enormously as forgers have carved more of these beautiful images.

celebrated in rock songs. Since 1975, however, it has been called T20 Beach, after the military code used by the North Vietnamese Army. Today the whole area including the hotels still belongs to the Vietnamese Army.

Two kilometres south of China Beach and 8 km from the centre of Danang is **Bac My An Beach**, next to the **Furama Resort**. This is a clean and attractive beach with some seafood stalls. Most visitors here go direct to the resort from the airport.

Around Danang

Marble Mountains (Nui Non Nuoc) → *Colour map 4, B5.*
① *12 km from Danang, 20 km from Hoi An. Many visitors stop off at Marble Mountain en route to Hoi An; catch the red-and-white bus towards Hoi An from Danang's local bus station (opposite 350 Hung Vuong St), 25 mins, or take a xe ôm.*

The Marble Mountains overlook the city of Danang and its airfield, about 12 km to the west of town. The name was given to these five peaks by the Nguyen Emperor Minh Mang on his visit in 1825, although they are in fact limestone crags with marble outcrops. They are also known as the mountains of the five elements (fire, water, soil, wood and metal). An important religious spot for the Cham, the peaks became havens for Communist guerrillas during the war, owing to their commanding view over Danang airbase. From here, a force with sufficient firepower could control much of what went on below, and the guerrillas harried the Americans incessantly. The views from the mountain, overlooking Danang Bay, are impressive. On the Marble Mountains are a number of important sites, often associated with caves and grottoes formed by chemical action on the limestone.

Of the mountains, the most visited is Thuy Son. There are several grottos and cave pagodas in the mountain, which are marked by steps cut into the rock. The **Tam Thai Pagoda**, reached by a staircase cut into the mountain, is on the site of a much older Cham place of worship. Constructed in 1825 by Minh Mang, and subsequently rebuilt, the central statue is of the Buddha Sakyamuni (the historic Buddha) flanked by the Bodhisattva Quan Am (a future Buddha and the Goddess of Mercy) and a statue of Van Thu (symbolizing wisdom). At the rear of the grotto is another cave, the **Huyen Khong Cave**. Originally a place of animist worship, it later became a site for Buddhist pilgrimage. The entrance is protected by four door guardians. The high ceiling of the cave is pierced by five holes through which the sun filters and, in the hour before midday, illuminates the central statue of the Buddha Sakyamuni. In the cave are various natural rock formations which, according to the young cave guides look like storks, elephants, an arm, a fish and a face.

A few hundred metres to the south on the right is a track leading to **Chua Quan The Am**, which has its own grotto, complete with stalactites, stalagmites and pillars.

My Son → *Colour map 4, B5.*

ⓘ *60 km south of Danang via Tra Kieu or 45-km west of Hoi An via Nam Phuoc. From the ticket office (6 km beyond the village of Kiem Lam) it's a 2 km jeep ride (included in the ticket price) and a short walk to My Son. Daily 00630-1630, 60,000d. Tour operators in Hoi An and Danang offer tours. It is not clear how thoroughly the area has been de-mined so do not stray too far from the road and path. Take a hat, sun cream and water.*

My Son, with its detailed carved masonry, was the spiritual centre of the Cham empire (see page 1064). Declared a World Heritage Site by UNESCO in 1999, it is one of Vietnam's most ancient monuments. Weather, jungle and years of strife have wrought their worst on My Son. But, arguably, the jungle under which My Son remained hidden to the outside world provided it with its best protection, for more has been destroyed in the past 40 years than the previous 400. Today, far from anywhere, My Son is a tranquil archaeological treasure. Not many visitors have time to make an excursion to see it which makes it all the more appealing to those that do. The thin red bricks of the towers and temples have been beautifully carved and the craftsmanship of many centuries still remains abundantly visible today. The trees and creepers have been pushed back but My Son remains cloaked in green; shoots and saplings sprout up everywhere and one senses that were its custodians to turn their backs for even a short time My Son would be quickly reclaimed by nature.

My Son consists of more than 70 monuments spread over a large area. It was rediscovered and investigated by French archaeologists of the École Française d'Extrême-Orient in 1898. Their excavations revealed a site that had been settled from the early eighth to the 15th centuries, the longest uninterrupted period of development of any monument in Southeast Asia. Its maximum population is unknown but it seems to have had a holy or spiritual function rather than being the seat of power and was, very probably, a burial place of its god kings. Unfortunately, My Son was a Viet Cong field headquarters, located within one of the US 'free fire' zones during the Vietnam War. The finest sanctuary in the complex was demolished by US sappers and temple groups A, E and H were badly damaged. Groups B and C have largely retained their temples but many statues, altars and linga have been removed to the Museum of Champa Sculpture in Danang (see page 1063). Currently Group C is being restored by UNESCO; the F building is covered in cobwebs and propped up by scaffolding.

It is important to see My Son in the broader context of Indian influence on Southeast Asia, not just in terms of architecture but also in terms of spiritual and political development around the region. Falling as it did so strongly under Chinese influence, it is all the more remarkable to find such compelling evidence of Indian culture and iconography in Vietnam. Indeed this was one of the criteria cited by UNESCO as justification for My Son's World Heritage listing.

Angkor in Cambodia, with which My Son is broadly contemporaneous, is the most famous example of a temple complex founded by a Hindu or Sivaist god king (*deva-raja*). The Hindu cult of *deva-raja* was developed by the kings of Angkor and later employed by Cham kings to bolster their authority but, because Cham kings were far less wealthy and powerful than the god kings of Angkor, the monuments are correspondingly smaller and more personal. One of the great joys of Cham sculpture and building is its unique feel, its graceful lines and unmistakable form.

The characteristic Cham architectural structure is the tower, built to reflect the divinity of the king: tall and rectangular, with four porticoes, each of which is 'blind' except for that on the west face. Originally built of wood (not surprisingly, none remains), they were later made of brick, of which the earliest (seventh century) are located at My Son. The bricks are exactly laid and held together with a form of vegetable cement, probably the resin of the day tree. Sandstone is sometimes used for plinths and lintels but, overwhelmingly, brick is the medium of construction. It is thought that on completion, each tower was surrounded by wood and fired over several days in what amounted to a vast outdoor kiln. The red bricks at My Son have worn amazingly well and are intricately carved with Hindu, Sivaist and Buddhist images and ornaments. Sivaist influence at My Son is unmissable, with Siva often represented, as in other Cham relics throughout Vietnam, by the linga or phallus.

⏺ Hoi An, Danang and around listings

For Sleeping and Eating price codes, see inside the front cover.

⏺ Sleeping

Hoi An *p1057, map p1058*
LL-AL Victoria Hoi An Beach Resort & Spa, Cua Dai Beach, T0510-927040, www.victoriahotels-asia.com. A charming resort right on the beach with 105 beautifully furnished rooms facing the sea or the river. There is a large pool, the **L'Annam Restaurant** (which serves very tasty but expensive dishes), a couple of bars, a kids' club, BBQ beach parties, live music and dancing, a host of watersports and all with charming service. Free shuttle bus runs between the hotel and the town.
L-AL Hoi An Beach Resort, 1 Cua Dai Beach Rd, Cua Dai Beach, T0510-927011, www.hoiantourist.com. A quiet, attractively designed resort with its own stretch of private beach just across the road. Its rooms are

simply designed and spacious with large bathrooms; some enjoy little terraces or balconies overlooking the river. A good choice for some peace and quiet but with a free shuttle service to town. **Rainbow Divers**, T09-4224102 (mob), www.divevietnam.com, is on site.
L-AL Hoi An Riverside Resort, 175 Cua Dai Rd, Cua Dai Beach, T0510-864800, www.hoianriverresort.com. A short, 5 min cycle ride from the beach and a 15-min pedal from town, this hotel faces the Thu Bon River. There is a pool set in landscaped gardens with hammocks. Standard rooms have balconies and all rooms have showers. **Song Do** restaurant is the best place to be at sunset
A Ancient House Resort, 377 Cua Dai St, T0510-923377, www.ancienthouseresort.com. This is a beautiful, small hotel set around a garden. There is a pool, shop, billiards, free shuttle to town and beach, free bicycle service and a restaurant. Behind the hotel is a traditional Ancient House. Breakfast is included.

A Hoi An, 10 Tran Hung Dao St, T0510-861 445, www.hoiantourist.com. An attractive colonial building set well back from the road in spacious grounds with attractively furnished, comfortable rooms with all mod cons and en suite bathrooms with baths. Has a pool and new Zen spa and beauty salon. Discounts offered in Hoi An's summer low season. Staff are welcoming and there are a host of activities from Chinese lantern making to trips to local villages, see page 508.

A Vinh Hung 1, 143 Tran Phu St, T0510-861621, www.vinhhungresort.com. An attractive old building, decorated with dark wood in Chinese style. It is halving its room capacity and upgrading the 6 remaining.

C-D Vinh Hung 2, Ba Trieu St, T0510-863717, www.vinhhungresort.com. A sister hotel with 40 rooms, a short walk away, built in traditional style, with a pool and all mod cons but lacking the atmosphere of the original.

C-F Sea Star (Sao Bien), 489 Cua Dai St, on the road to the beach, T0510-861589. A privately run hotel. Rooms with a/c and hot water. Travel services, bicycle, motorbike and car hire on offer. Efficient and popular but possibly a little complacent.

D-E Anh Huy Hotel, 30 Phan Boi Chau St, T0510-862116, www.anhuyhotel.com. Opposite **Brother's Café**, with courtyards that create a breeze and shutters that keep the noise out. Spacious rooms are beautifully decorated in Japanese style and the staff are very friendly. Breakfast and free internet.

E-G Minh A, 2 Nguyen Thai Hoc St, T0510-861368. This is a very special little place. An old family house with just 5 guestrooms that are all different. Guests are made to feel part of the family. Communal bathrooms have hot water and fan. Next to the market in a busy part of town. Very welcoming, and recommended.

Danang p1061, map p1062

LL-AL Furama Resort, 68 Ho Xuan Huong St, Bac My An Beach, 8 km from Danang, T0511-384 7888, www.furamavietnam.com. 198 rooms and suites beautifully designed and furnished. It has 2 pools, 1 of which is an infinity pool overlooking the private beach. All its facilities are first class. Watersports, diving, mountain biking, tennis and a health centre offering a number of massages and treatments. Operates a free and very useful shuttle to and from the town, Marble Mountains and Hoi An. Surprisingly the price does not include breakfast.

A-D Bamboo Green, there are 3 hotels in this chain: **Bamboo Green Central**, 158 Phan Chu Trinh St, T0511-382 2996, **Bamboo Green Harbourside** (a somewhat tenuous claim), 177 Tran Phu St, T0511-382 2722; and **Bamboo Green Riverside**, 68 Bach Dang St, T0511-3832591. All share the bamboogreen@dng.vnn.vn email address. All are well-run, well-equipped, comfortable, business-type hotels with efficient staff and in central locations offering excellent value for money. **Riverside** has a particularly attractive outlook.

C-D Danang, 50 Bach Dong St, T0511-382 3649, bdhotel@dng.vnn.vn. Large and centrally located hotel. Rooms rather cramped for the price; some with river views; cheaper rooms in an older building at the back. All rooms have satellite TV and baths. There's quite a good restaurant on site.

D-F Phuong Lan, 178 Hoang Dieu St, T0511-382 0373. Rooms with a/c, satellite TV, and hot water. It's good value (after some bargaining), free airport pick-up and motorbikes for rent.

D-F Tan Minh, 142 Bach Dang St, T0511-382 7456. On the riverfront, a small, well-kept hotel, friendly staff speak good English.

China Beach (My Khe Beach) p1063

A-D Tourane, My Khe Beach, T0511-393 2666, touranehotel@dng.vnn.vn. A 'resort-style' hotel with accommodation in decent villa-type blocks. A/c and hot water.

C-F My Khe Beach, 241 Nguyen Van Thoai St, My Khe Beach, T0511-383 6125. Accommodation here is in rather austere-looking blocks set among the sea pines. All with a/c and hot water, price includes breakfast. **Conroy's Bar** is on the ground-floor of the block nearest the sea.

🍴 Eating

Hoi An *p1057, map p1058*

A Hoi An speciality is *cao lau*, a noodle soup with slices of pork and croutons, traditionally made with water from one particular well. The quality of food in Hoi An, especially the fish, is outstanding and the value for money is not matched by any other town in Vietnam. Bach Dang St is particularly pleasant in the evening, when tables and chairs are set up almost the whole way along the river.

₹₹₹-₹₹ Brother's Café, 27 Phan Boi Chau St, T0510-914150, www.brothercafehoian.com.vn. It is excellent news that these little cloistered French houses should have been put to such good use and renovated in such exquisite taste. The house and garden leading down to the river are beautifully restored. The menu is strong on Vietnamese specialities, especially seafood, and at US$12 the daily set menu still offers good value in such charming surroundings.

₹₹-₹ Café des Amis, 52 Bach Dang St, near the river, T0510-861616. The set menu of fish/seafood or vegetarian dishes changes daily and is widely acclaimed and excellent value. The owner, Mr Nguyen Manh Kim, spends several months a year cooking in Europe. Highly recommended.

₹₹-₹ Mango Rooms, 111 Nguyen Thai Hoc St, T0510-910839, www.mangorooms.com. A very welcome addition to Hoi An and the superior cooking makes a repeat visit a must. Enjoy slices of baguette layered with shrimp mousse served with a mango coconut curry or the delicious ginger and garlic-marinated shrimps wrapped in tender slices of beef and pan-fried with wild spicy butter and soy-garlic sauce; the seared tuna steak with mango salsa is outstanding. Complimentary tapas-style offerings such as tapioca crisps are a welcome touch. Highly recommended.

₹₹ Nhu Y (aka Mermaid), 2 Tran Phu St, T0510-861527, www.hoianhospitality.com. Miss Vy turns out all the local specialities as well as some of her own. The 5-course set dinner is particularly recommended.

₹₹ Tam Tam Café, 110 Nguyen Thai Hoc St, T0510-862212, tamtamha@dng.vnn.vn. A great little café in a renovated tea house. Cocktails, draft beer, music, book exchange, plus attached restaurant serving French and Italian cuisine. A relaxing place for a drink, espresso or meal.

₹₹ Thanh, 76 Bach Dang St, T0510-861 366. A charming old house overlooking the river, recognizable by its Chinese style and flowering *hoa cat dang* creepers; the shrimp is excellent. Friendly service.

₹₹ Vinh Hung, 147B Tran Phu St, T0510-862203 (See Sleeping). Another attractive building with Chinese lanterns and traditional furniture. An excellent range of seafood dishes and Vietnamese specials at fair prices.

₹ Cargo Club, 107-109 Nguyen Thai Hoc St, T0510-910489. This extremely popular venue serves up filling Vietnamese and Western fodder including club sandwiches, Vietnamese salads and overpriced fajitas. The service is quicker downstairs than up on the balcony overlooking the river. The patisserie, groaning with cakes and chocolate is the best thing.

₹ Hai's Scout Café, 111 Tan Phu St/98 Nguyen Thai Hoc St, T0510-863210, www.visit hoian.com. The central area of this back-to-back café has a photographic exhibition of the WWF's invaluable work in the threatened environment around Hoi An. It offers good food in a relaxing courtyard or attractive café setting. Cookery courses can be arranged.

₹ Han Huyen. This former floating restaurant has been moved to 35 Nguyen Phuc Chu St, to make way for a bridge construction, T510-861462. Serves excellent seafood.

₹ Yellow River, 38 Tran Phu St, T0510-861053. Good Hoi An family eatery, the fried wanton is recommended. French is spoken.

Danang *p1061, map p1062*

Seafood is good here and Danang has its own beers, Da Nang 'Export' and Song Han. There are a number of cafés and restaurants along Bach Dang St, overlooking the river.

₹₹ Hana Kim Dinh, 7 Bach Dang St. This is a restaurant on a small pier shaped like a boat,

opposite the **Bach Dang Hotel**. Western and Vietnamese menus; mainly seafood served.
¶-¶ Christie's and **Cool Spot**, 112 Tran Phu St, T0511-824040, ccdng@dng.vnn.vn. The old premises were demolished in the construction of the River Han Bridge, the new location is 1 block in from the river and has merged forces with the **Cool Spot** bar. Frequented by expats from Danang and outlying provinces, it has a small bar downstairs and a restaurant upstairs. Cold beer, Western and Japanese food and tasty home-made pizzas.
¶ Bach Dang Hotel, 50 Bach Dang St. Informal restaurant, with glimpses of river and decent food.

China Beach (My Khe Beach) *p1063*
The many restaurants here are virtually in-distinguishable and it is impossible to single any one out for special mention. They all have excellent fish, prawn, crab, clams and cuttlefish, grilled, fried or steamed. 2 people can eat well for US$7-10 including local beers.

❶ Bars and clubs

Hoi An *p1057, map p1058*
Champa, 75 Nguyen Thai Hoc St, T0510-861159. This is a rambling place with pool tables and an upstairs cultural show in the evenings. Downstairs hits from the 1960s and 1970s predominate.
Sa Long, 102 Nguyen Thai Hoc St, T0913-684401, daily 1100-late. Formerly the **Lounge Bar**, this is one of the more popular places in town to hang at the bar or blend into the sofas. The mojitos go down too easily.
Tam Tam Café, 110 Nguyen Thai Hoc St. Mainly a café/restaurant but also has a good bar and a pool table. An attractive place to sit.
Treat's, 158 Tran Phu St, T0510-861125, open till late. One of Hoi An's few bars and a very well-run one. 2 pool tables, airy, attractive style: popular happy hour and attractive balcony. Also at 69 and 93 Tran Hung Dao St which are very popular at night.

❻ Entertainment

Hoi An *p1057, map p1058*
Hoi An Handicraft Workshop, 9 Nguyen Thai Hoc St, T0510-910216, www.hoianhandicraft.com. Traditional music performances Tue-Sun at 1015 and 1515, with the Vietnamese monochord and dancers. At the back there is a potter's wheel, straw mat making, embroiderers, conical hat makers, wood carvers and iron ornament makers.

❺ Shopping

Hoi An *p1057, map p1058*
Hoi An is a shopper's paradise. **Tran Phu** and **Le Loi** are the main shopping streets. 2 items stand out, paintings and clothes.

Accessories and handicrafts
Hoi An is the place to buy handbags and purses and attractive Chinese silk lanterns, indeed anything that can be made from silk, including scarves and shoes. **41 Le Loi Street** is a silk workshop where the whole process from silkworm to woven fabric can be seen and fabrics purchased, daily 0745-2200. There is also chinaware available, mainly modern, some reproduction and a few antiques.
53a Le Loi, 53a Le Loi, T091-409 7344 (mob). A handbag and shoe shop with lots of choice. Have your bag made here but not your shoes.
Reaching Out, Hoa-nhap Handicrafts, 103 Nguyen Thai Hoc, T0510-910168, Tue-Sun 0730-1930. Fair trade shop selling arts and crafts, cards and notebooks, textiles and silk sleeping bags all made by disabled artisans living in Hoi An. Profits support the disabled community.

Art
Vietnamese artists have been inspired by Hoi An's old buildings and a Hoi An school of art has developed. Countless galleries sell original works of art but the more serious galleries are to be found in a cluster on Nguyen Thi Minh Khai St, west of the Japanese Bridge.

Tailors

Hoi An is famed for its tailors – there are now reckoned to be more than 140 in town – who will knock up silk or cotton clothing in 24 hrs. The quality of the stitching varies from shop to shop, so see some samples first, and the range of fabrics is limited, so many people bring their own. A man's suit can cost anywhere from US$30-295 and a woman's from US$50-395, depending on fabric and quality of workmanship. Thai silk costs more than Vietnamese silk and Hoi An silk is quite coarse.

Visitors talk of the rapid speed at which shops can produce the goods but bear in mind that, if every visitor to Hoi An wants something made in 12-24 hrs, this puts enormous strain on staff. Quite apart from the workers having to stay up all night, the quality of the finished garment could suffer. So, if you are in Hoi An for a few days, give yourself time to accommodate 2nd or 3rd fittings which may be necessary.

Lan Ha, 1A Hai Ba Trung St, T0510-910706, leco50@hotmail.com, daily 0900-2200. This shop unit is recommended because of the speed of service, the quality of the goods, the excellent prices and the fact that, unlike many other tailors in town, 2nd, 3rd or even 4th fittings are usually not required.

Yaly, 47 Nguyen Thai Hoc St, T0510-910474, yalyshop@dng.vnn.vn, daily 0700-2030. Professional staff, very good, quality results across a range of clothing, including shoes. Women's blouses are around US$20 and dresses US$30-80. There are now 4 branches of **Yaly** in town but this is the original.

▲ Activities and tours

Hoi An p1057, map p1058
Boat rides
Boat rides are available on the Thu Bon River. Local boatwomen charge US$1 or so per hr.

Cookery classes
Red Bridge Cooking School, run out of the **Hai Scout Café**, 98 Nguyen Thai Hoc St,

T0510-863210. Visit the market to be shown local produce, then take a 20-min boat ride to the cooking school where you're shown the herb garden. Next, you watch the chefs make a number of dishes such as warm squid salad served in ½ a pineapple and grilled aubergine stuffed with vegetables. Move inside and you get to make your own fresh spring rolls and learn Vietnamese food carving, which is a lot harder than it looks. US$15. (**Red Bridge Cooking School**, Thon 4, Cam Thanh, T0510-933222, www.visithoian. com. Operates all year, 0815-1330. The restaurant is open to the public Fri, Sat, Sun).

Tour operators
An Phu Tourist, 141 Tran Phu St, T0510-861 447, www.anphutouristhoian.com. Several offices in town, offering a wide range of tour services and reliable Open Tour Buses.

Hoi An Travel, Hotel Hoi An, 6 Tran Hung Dao St, and at Hoi An Beach Resort, T0510-910400, www.hoiantravel.com, 0630-2200. Offers a variety of tours including some unusual ones: a visit to a vegetable village, fishing at Thanh Ha pottery village, and visiting the Cham Islands. Can also arrange trips to Savannakhet and Pakse, Laos and from Bangkok to Hoi An, Danang and Hué and returning to Laos and Thailand.

Sinh Café, 18B Hai Ba Trung St, T0510-863 948, www.sinhcafevn.com, daily 0630-2200. Branch of the chain offering tours, transport, reservations and internet use. Its Open Tour bus departs and arrives at the Phuong Nam Hotel, to the north of the office, off Hai Ba Trung St. My Son tour, US$3; with return boat trip via Kim Bong carpentry village, US$5.

Son My Son Tours, 17/2 Tran Hung Dao St, T0510-861121, mysontour@dng.vnn.vn. Cheap minibus tickets to Hué, Nha Trang and HCMC, car and motorbike hire, useful advice.

Trekking Company-Mr Tung, 1 Hai Ba Trung, T0510-14218, trekkingtravel_hoian@ yahoo.com.vn. This small operation but does a good job booking bus tickets and arranging tours to My Son, etc. Tours to My Son US$2 by bus, US$3 by boat; taxi and minivan to

Da Nang US$8-12; bus to Hanoi US$14;
to Nha Trang US$16. Recommended.

Danang *p1061, map p1062*
Therapies
**Tamarind Spa, Victoria Hoi An Beach
Resort & Spa**, Cua Dai Beach, T0510-927040,
www.victoriahotels-asia.com, 0900-2100.
A lovely, friendly spa centre with a wide range
of treatments from body wraps to facials. The
foot reflexology treatment is especially good.

⊖ Transport

Hoi An *p1057, map p1058*
Bicycle and motorbike
Hotels have 2WD and 4WD vehicles for hire.
Bicycle hire, 10,000d per day, motorbike
US$4-8 per day.

Bus
The bus station is 1 km west of the centre of
town on Ly Thuong Kiet St. There are regular
connections from **Danang**'s bus station, from
0530 until 1800, 1 hr, 20,000d. Open Tour
Buses go north to **Hanoi** and South to **HCMC**.
Book through local tour operators (see above).

Danang *p1061, map p1062*
Air
The airport is 2.5 km southwest of the city.
There are daily connections with **Bangkok,
Phnom Penh, Siem Reap, Singapore, Hong
Kong, Paris, Tokyo, Vientiane, Nha Trang,
Hanoi, HCMC** and **Pleiku**. There are plans
to expand the airport. A taxi from Danang
airport to Hoi An will cost about US$15 or
less (bargain hard), 40 mins.
   Airline offices Vietnam Airlines
Booking Office, 35 Tran Phu St, T0511-382
1130. **Pacific Airlines**, 35 Nguyen Van Linh
St, Hai Chau District, T0511-3583583.

Bicycle
Bicycles are available from many hotels.
Some cafés and hotels also rent motorbikes
for US$5-7 per day.

Taxi
Airport Taxi, T0511-3825555. **Dana Taxi**,
T0511-3815815.

Train
Danang Railway Station, 122 Haiphong St,
2 km west of town, T0511-3750666. Express
trains to and from **Hanoi**, **HCMC** and **Hué**.

❶ Directory

Hoi An *p1057, map p1058*
Banks Hoi An Bank, 4 Hoang Dieu St.
Accepts most major currencies, US dollar
withdrawal from credit/debit card, no
commission for cashing Amex TCs, daily
0730-1900. **Hoi An Incombank**, 9 Le
Loi St, offers identical services and an ATM.
Internet Widely available in cafés and
hotels. **Nguyen Tan Hieu**, 89 Tran Hung
Dao St. **Medical services** 4 Tran Hung Dao
St, T0510-864566, daily 0700-2200. **Tram y
Te Pharmacy**, 72 Nguyen Thai Hoc St. **Post
office** 5 Tran Hung Dao St, T0510-861480.
Has Poste Restante, inter- national telephone,
fax service and ATM.

Danang *p1061, map p1062*
Banks VID Public Bank, 2 Tran Phu St.
Vietcombank, 104 Le Loi St. Will change
most major currencies, cash and TCs.
Internet There are numerous internet
cafés all over town. **Medical services**
C Hospital, 74 Haiphong St, T0511-3821480.
Post office 60 Bach Dang St, corner of
Bach Dang and Le Duan streets. Telex, fax
and telephone facilities.

Central Highlands and the coast

The Central Highlands consist of the Truong Son Mountain Range and its immediate environs. The mountain range is commonly referred to as the backbone of Vietnam and borders Laos and Cambodia to the west. The highlands provide flowers and vegetables to the southern lowlands and have several tea and coffee plantations that supply the whole of Vietnam. Tourism is an additional source of revenue. Most highlanders belong to one of 26 indigenous groups and, beyond the main towns of Dalat, Buon Ma Thuot, Play Ku (Pleiku) and Kontum, their way of life remains unchanged.

East of the highlands, on the coast, Nha Trang is a seaside resort with diving, boat tours and spas to entice foreign visitors. Further south, Mui Ne has golden sands and the best kitesurfing in Vietnam. ▸▸ For listings, see pages 1083-1090.

Ins and outs
In terms of climate, the best time to visit this region is from December to April. However, as there are many different indigenous groups within its borders, there are festivals in the region all year round.

Background
The Central Highlands have long been associated with Vietnam's hilltribes. Under the French, the colonial administration deterred ethnic Vietnamese from settling here but missionaries were active among the minorities of the region, although with uneven success. Bishop Cuenot (page 1078) dispatched two missionaries to Buon Ma Thuot, where they received a hostile reception from the M'nong, however in Kontum, among the Ba-na, they found more receptive souls for their evangelizing. Today many of the ethnic minorities in the Central Highlands are Roman Catholic, although some (such as the Ede) are Protestant.

At the same time French businesses were hard at work establishing plantations to supply the home market. Rubber and coffee were the staple crops. The greatest difficulty they faced was recruiting sufficient labour. Men and women of the ethnic minorities were happy in their villages drinking rice wine and cultivating their own small plots. They were poor but content and saw no reason to accept the hard labour and slave wages of the plantation owners. Norman Lewis travelled in the Central Highlands and describes the situation well in his book, *A Dragon Apparent*.

Since 1984 there has been a bit of a free-for-all and a scramble for land in the highlands. Ethnic Vietnamese have encroached on minority land and planted it with coffee, pepper and fruit trees. As an indicator of progress, Vietnam is now the second-largest producer of coffee in the world, although it produces cheaper robusta rather than arabica coffee. The way of life of the minorities is disappearing with the forests: there are no trees from which to build traditional stilt houses nor shady forests in which to live and hunt.

Dalat ●❼⊘⚫▲⊖● ▸▸ pp1083-1090. Colour map 6, A5.

Dalat is situated on a plateau in the Central Highlands, at an altitude of almost 1500 m. The town itself, a former French hill station, is centred on a Lake – Xuan Huong – amidst rolling countryside. To the north are the five volcanic peaks of **Langbian Mountain**, rising to 2400 m. The ascent is recommended for stunning views and abundant birdlife. In the vicinity of Dalat are lakes, forests, waterfalls, and an abundance of orchids, roses and other temperate flora. Dalat is the honeymoon capital of southern Vietnam and there is a quaint belief that unless you go on honeymoon to Dalat you are not really married at all.

Ins and outs

Getting there and around There are daily direct flights to Dalat from Ho Chi Minh City and Hanoi. Open Tour Buses pass through Dalat heading to Nha Trang, Mui Ne and Ho Chi Minh City and innumerable local buses plough the inter-provincial routes between Dalat, Play Ku, Kontum, Ho Chi Minh City, Nha Trang, Buon Ma Thuot, Phan Thiet and Phan Rang. Alternatively it is possible to hire a car and driver. Taxis and *xe ôm* are available around town and the cool climate means that it is very pleasant to reach outlying attractions by bicycle. In fact a day spent travelling can be more enjoyable than the sights themselves.
▶▶ *See Transport, page 1089.*

Tourist information **Dalat Travel Bureau** ① *www.dalattourist.com*, is the state-run travel company for Lam Dong Province. There are also a number of tour operators in town.
▶▶ *See Activities and tours, page 1087.*

Background

Dr Alexandre Yersin, a protégé of Luis Pasteur, founded Dalat in 1893. He stumbled across Dalat as he was trying to find somewhere cool to escape from the sweltering summer heat of the coast and lowlands. The lush alpine scenery of Dalat impressed the French and it soon became the second city in the south after Saigon. In the summer months the government and bureaucrats moved lock, stock and barrel to Dalat where it was cooler. There are still plenty of original French-style villas in the town, many of which have been converted into hotels. The last Emperor of Vietnam Bao Dai also lived here.

Dalat soon took on the appearance of Paris in the mountains. A golf course was made and a luxurious hotel was built. In both the Second World War and the American War, high-ranking officials of the opposing armies would while away a pleasant couple of days playing golf against each other before having to return to the battlefields. Of all the highland cities, Dalat was the least affected by the American War. The main reason being that, at the time, the only way to Dalat was via the Prenn pass. There was a small heliport at Cam Ly and also a radio-listening station on Langbian Mountain but nothing else of note.

Xuan Huong Lake and the centre

Xuan Huong Lake was created as the Grand Lake in 1919, after a small dam was constructed on the Cam Ly River, and renamed in 1954. It is a popular exercise area for the local inhabitants, many of whom walk around the lake first thing in the morning, stopping every so often to perform t'ai chi exercises. At the northeast end of the Lake is the **Dalat Flower Garden** ① *0700-1800, 8000d.* Established in 1966, it supports a modest range of temperate and tropical plants including orchids (of which Dalat is renowned throughout Vietnam), roses, camellias, lilies and hydrangeas.

Dalat Cathedral ① *Mass is held twice a day Mon-Sat, and 5 times on Sun,* is a single-tiered cathedral, visible from the lake. It is referred to locally as the 'Chicken Cathedral' because of the chicken-shaped wind dial at the top of the turret. Construction began in 1931, although the building was not completed until the Japanese 'occupation' in the 1940s. The stained-glass windows, with their vivid colours and use of pure, clean lines, were crafted in France by Louis Balmet, the same man who made the windows in Nha Trang and Danang cathedrals, between 1934 and 1940. Sadly, most have not survived the ravages of time.

At the end of Nguyen Thi Minh Khai Street, **Dalat Market (Cho Dalat)** sells an array of exotic fruits and vegetables: plums, strawberries, carrots, potatoes, loganberries, cherries, apples, onions and avocados. The forbidding appearance of the market is masked by the riot of colourful flowers also on sale, including gladioli, irises, roses, chrysanthemums and marigolds.

Tran Hung Dao Street

Many of the large **colonial villas**, almost universally washed in pastel yellow, are 1930s and 1940s vintage. Some have curved walls, railings and are almost nautical in inspiration; others are reminiscent of houses in Provence. Many of the larger villas can be found along **Tran Hung Dao Street**, although many have fallen into a very sorry state of repair. Perhaps the largest and most impressive house on Tran Hung Dao is the former residence of the

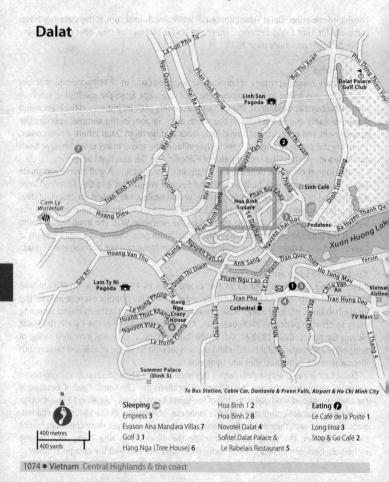

Dalat

Sleeping
Empress **3**
Evason Ana Mandara Villas **7**
Golf **3 1**
Hang Nga (Tree House) **6**

Hoa Binh 1 **2**
Hoa Binh 2 **8**
Novotel Dalat **4**
Sofitel Dalat Palace &
Le Rabelais Restaurant **5**

Eating
Le Café de la Poste **1**
Long Hoa **3**
Stop & Go Café **2**

To Bus Station, Cable Car, Dantanla & Prenn Falls, Airport & Ho Chi Minh City

Governor General at No12. It occupies a magnificent position set among mountain pines, overlooking the town. The villa, now the **Hotel Dinh 2**, is 1930s in style, with large airy rooms and uncomfortable furniture.

Summer Palace (Dinh 3)
ⓘ *Le Hong Phong St, about 2 km from the town centre, daily 0700-1700, 5000d; visitors have to wear covers on their shoes to protect the wooden floors.*

Vietnam's last emperor, Bao Dai, chose Dalat for his Summer Palace, built between 1933 and 1938 on a hill with views on every side, it is art deco in style, both inside and out, and rather modest for a palace. The stark interior contains little to indicate that this was the home of an emperor, especially since almost all of Bao Dai's personal belongings have been removed. The impressive dining room contains an etched-glass map of Vietnam, while the study has Bao Dai's desk, books, a few personal ornaments and, notably, photographs of the royal family, who were exiled permanently to France in 1954. One of the photos shows Bao Dai's son, the prince Bao Long, in full military dress uniform. He was a distinguished and gallant soldier who died during the war. Of all the members of the royal family, he is the only one that is regarded with respect by the government. He is considered to be a good, patriotic Vietnamese who fought for his country. The emperor's bedroom, balcony and bathroom are also open to the public, as is the family drawing room. The gardens are colourful and well maintained.

Lam Ty Ni Pagoda and around
Lam Ty Ni Pagoda, off Le Hong Phong St, is unremarkable save for the charming monk, Vien Thuc, who has lived here since 1968. He has created a garden, almost Japanese in inspiration, around the pagoda, known as the Divine Calmness Bamboo Garden. Vien Thuc is a scholar, poet, artist, philosopher, mystic, divine and entrepreneur but is best known for his paintings of which, by his own reckoning, there are more than 100,000. Wandering through the maze of rustic huts and shacks tacked on to the back of the temple you will see countless hanging sheets bearing his simple but distinctive calligraphy and philosophy: "Living in the present how beautiful this very moment is", "Zen painting destroys millennium

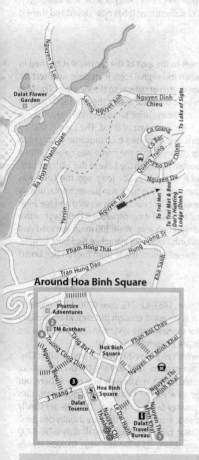

Around Hoa Binh Square

sorrows", and so on. Vien Thuc's work is widely known and has been exhibited in Paris, New York and the Netherlands, as well as on the internet.

The slightly wacky theme is maintained at the nearby **Hang Nga Guest House and Art Gallery (Crazy House)** ① *3 Huynh Thuc Khang, T063-22070; art gallery daily 0700-1700, 8000d,* where Doctor Hang Viet Nga has, over a period of many years, built up a hotel in organic fashion. Rooms and gardens resemble scenes from the pages of a fairy storybook; guests sleep inside mushrooms, trees and giraffes, and sip tea under giant cobwebs. It is not a particularly comfortable place to stay and the number of visitors limits privacy but it is well worth visiting. ▶ *See Sleeping, page 1083.*

Bao Dai's hunting lodge (Dinh 1)
Emperor Bao Dai also had a hunting lodge that used to be a museum. East of the town centre, Dinh 1 sported 1930s furniture, antique telephone switchboards, and although it was not sumptuous, nevertheless had a feel of authenticity. It has now closed and there is talk of it reopening as a casino.

Railway to Trai Mat Village
Dalat Railway Station, off Quang Trung Street to the east of the centre, was opened in 1938 and is the last station in Vietnam to retain its original French art deco architecture and coloured-glass windows. In 1991, a 7-km stretch of railway to the village of **Trai Mat** was reopened and every day a small Russian-built diesel car makes the journey ① *daily at 0630, 0805, 0940, 1115, 1405, 1545, US$5 return, 30 mins, minimum 6 people.* The journey to Trai Mat takes you near the **Lake of Sighs**, 5 km northeast of Dalat. The Lake is said by some to be named after the sighs of the girls being courted by handsome young men from the military academy in Dalat. Another theory is that the name was coined after a young Vietnamese maiden, Mai Nuong, drowned herself in the Lake in the 18th century, believing that her lover, Hoang Tung, had rejected her. Not long ago the Lake was surrounded by thick forest but today it is a thin wood. The track also passes immaculately tended vegetable gardens; no space on the valley floors or sides is wasted and the high intensity agriculture is a marvellous sight. Trai Mat itself is a prosperous K'Ho village with a market selling piles of produce from the surrounding area. Walk 300 m up the road and take a narrow lane to the left to reach Chua Linh Phuoc, an attractive Buddhist temple, notable for its huge Buddha and mosaic-adorned pillars, made from broken rice bowls and fragments of beer bottle.

Waterfalls around Dalat
Cam Ly Waterfall ① *2 km from the centre of town, T063-824145, daily 0700-1700, 6000d,* is the closest waterfall to Dalat town centre. It is pleasant enough but should be avoided during the dry season, as it is the overflow for the sewerage system in Dalat. The falls are not particularly noteworthy but the gardens are peaceful and serene.

More cascades can be found south of town off Highway 20 towards Ho Chi Minh City. The first of these is **Datanla Falls** ① *5 km out of town, T063-831804, 0700-1700; 5000d.* A path leads steeply downwards into a forested ravine; it is an easy hike to get there, but tiring on the return journey. However, the new Alpine Coaster, a toboggan on rails ① *T063-831804, 35,000d return* makes the journey faster and easier. The falls are hardly spectacular but few people come here, except at weekends, so they are usually peaceful. Not far from the falls is the terminus of the **Dalat cable car (Càp Treo)** ① *daily 0730-1700 but may be closed May-Nov if the wind is too strong, 35,000d one way, 50,000d return,* which starts from the top of Prenn Pass, about 100 m from the bus station. The journey from top to bottom takes about 15 minutes and gives a different perspective of the Dalat area.

Prenn Falls, next to Highway 20, 12 km south of Dalat, were dedicated to Queen Sirikit of Thailand when she visited in 1959. The area has recently undergone a large renovation and is cleaner and better equipped than it used to be. The falls are not that good but there is a rope bridge that can be crossed and pleasant views of the surrounding area. About 20 km north of Bao Loc on the Bao Loc Plateau are the **Dambri Falls** ① *Hwy 20, 120 km from Dalat, Jul-Nov only; get a xe ôm from Bao Loc or take a tour.* These are considered the most impressive falls in southern Vietnam and are worth an excursion for those who have time.

Central provinces ⬤⬤ ➤➤ *pp1083-1090.*

Ins and outs
Getting there and around There are direct flights from Ho Chi Minh City and Danang to Buon Ma Thuot and Play Ku. Local buses plough the inter-provincial routes between Dalat, Play Ku, Kontum, Ho Chi Minh City, Nha Trang, Buon Ma Thuot, Phan Thiet and Phan Rang. Alternatively, hire a car and driver. ➤➤ *See Transport, page 1089.*

Buon Ma Thuot ➤ *Colour map 6, A5.*
Buon Ma Thuot, the provincial capital of Daklak Province, is located at the junction of Highway 14 and Highway 26. Until the 1950s big game hunting was Buon Ma Thuot's main claim to fame but now the town has surpassed its illustrious and renowned neighbour of Dalat to be the main centre for tea and coffee production. With the rise of the Trung Nguyen coffee empire, Buon Ma Thuot has changed from a sleepy backwater to a thriving modern city. The government also instigated a resettlement programme here, taking land from the ethnic minority groups to give to Vietnamese settlers. The Ede did not take kindly to having their land encroached upon by outsiders; tensions reached their peak in late 2001 and early 2002, when there was widespread rioting in Buon Ma Thuot. Today, the best Ede village to visit is **Buon Tur**, southwest of Buon Ma Thuot, off Highway 14. Apart from the odd TV aerial, life has changed little in this community of 20 stilt houses and, despite the efforts of the government to stop it, Ede is still taught in school. **Daklak Tourist Office** ① *3 Phan Chu Trinh St (within the grounds of Thang Loi Hotel), T050-852108, www.daklaktourist.com,* provides useful information about the province and has knowledgeable, English-speaking staff.

Dray Sap waterfalls ➤ *Colour map 6, A5.*
① *2 km off Hwy 14 towards Ho Chi Minh City, 20 km from Buon Ma Thuot, daily 0700-1700; 6000-8000d.*
The waterfalls consist of several different cascades all next to each other. The 100-m-wide torrent is particularly stunning in the wet season when the spray justifies the name 'waterfall of smoke'. There are two paths to choose from: one down by the river and the other on the high ground. Note, though, that access may occasionally be limited in the wet season, if the paths are too treacherous to use.

Lak Lake ➤ *Colour map 6, A5.*
The serene Lak Lake is about 50 km southeast of Buon Ma Thuot and can be explored by dugout. It is an attraction in its own right but is all the more compelling on account of

the surrounding **Mnong villages**. Early morning mists hang above the calm waters and mingle with the columns of woodsmoke rising from the longhouses. The Mnong number about 50,000 and are matriarchal. They have been famed as elephant catchers for hundreds of years, although the elephants are now used for tourist rides rather than in their traditional role for dragging logs from the forest. In order to watch the elephants taking their evening wallow in the cool waters and to appreciate the tranquillity of sunrise over the lake, stay overnight at a Mnong village, **Buon Juin**. An evening supping with your hosts, sharing rice wine and sleeping in the simplicity of a Mnong longhouse is an ideal introduction to these genial people. ►► *See Sleeping, page 1084.*

Yok Don National Park → *Colour map 6, A4.*

ⓘ *40 km northwest of Buon Ma Thuot, T050-783049, yokdonecotourism@vnn.vn. Tour guide section Mr Hung 090-5197501 (mob), daily 0700-2200. Tours range from elephant riding (US$20 for 2 per hr; US$45 for 3hrs) to elephant trekking (US$190 for 2 for 3 days) to animal spotting by night (US$70). While there is a bridge under construction travellers must pay to cross the river on a pull boat, US$4 per group. Accommodation is available.*

This 115,000 ha wildlife reserve is home to 250 species of birds and at least 63 species of mammals, 17 of which are on the worldwide endangered list. It is believed that several rare white elephants survive here. The best chance of spotting wildlife is on an overnight guided hike or elephant safari. Within the park boundaries are also 17 different ethnic tribes.

Play Ku (Pleiku) and around → *Colour map 4, C5.*

Nearly 200 km north of Buon Ma Thuot, Play Ku is located in a valley at the bottom of a local mountain and is visible from 12 km away. It is a modern, thriving, bustling town, surrounded by rubber, pepper, coffee and tea plantations. There was fierce fighting here during the American War and, as a result, the town itself has little to offer the tourist but nearby are several Jarai villages that are worth a visit. Contact **Gia Lia Tourist** ⓘ *215 Hung Vuong St (in Hung Vuong Hotel), T059-874571, www.gialiatourist.com, daily 0730-1100, 1330-1630,* for information and, for the sake of preserving the traditional way of life, only visit those villages where foreigners no longer need a licence.

Plei Fun is about 16 km north of Play Ku and is the village **Gia Lai Tourist** will take you to if you book a tour through them. The local villagers have wised up to tourism and may try and charge you 30,000d to see their graveyard, in which tiled or wooden roofs shelter the worldly possessions of the deceased: bottles, bowls and even the odd bicycle. Traditional Jarai carved hardwood statues guard the graves. Push on to **Plei Mun**, another 5 km down the road and left 2 km down a dirt road, for some even finer examples. There is also a traditional wooden *rong* house here but it has a corrugated iron roof.

Kontum → *Colour map 4, C5.*

Kontum is a small, sleepy market town, 44 km north of Play Ku on Highway 14. There are a couple of notable sights that make a side trip to Kontum worthwhile, plus scores of Ba-na villages in the vicinity that can be reached by motorbike and on foot. Contact **Kontum Tourist Office** ⓘ *2 Phan Dinh Phung St (on the ground floor of the Dakbla Hotel 1), T060-861626, www.kontumtourism.com, daily 0700-1100, 1300-1700,* for details about tours and further information.

The French Bishop and missionary Stephano Theodore Cuenot founded Kontum in the mid 1800s and succeeded in converting many of the local tribespeople to Christianity.

He was arrested on Emperor Tu Duc's orders but died in Binh Dinh prison on 14 November 1861, a day before the beheading instructions arrived. He was beatified in 1909. Cuenot and other French priests and missionaries slain by Emperor Tu Duc are commemorated by a plaque set into the altar of **Tan Huong Church** ① *92 Nguyen Hue St (if the church is shut ask in the office adjacent and they will gladly open it)*. The whitewashed façade has an interesting depiction of St George and the dragon. It is not immediately evident that the church is built on stilts, but crouch down and look under one of the little arches that run along the side and the stilts, joists and floorboards are clear. Many of the windows are original but, unfortunately, the roof is a modern replacement, although the original style of fish-scale tiling can still be seen in the tower. The interior of the church is exquisite, with dark wooden columns and a fine vaulted ceiling made of wattle and daub.

Further east (1 km) on the same street is the superb **Wooden Church**. Built by the French with Ba-na labour in 1913, it remains largely unaltered, with the original wooden frame and wooden doors. Inside, the blue walls combine with the dark-brown polished wood to produce a very serene effect. Unfortunately the windows are modern tinted glass and rather crude. In the grounds to the right stands a *rong* house and a statue of Cuenot, the first Catholic bishop of East Cochin China diocese.

Nha Trang ☺⊘⊘▲⊜⊙ ➤ *pp1084-1090. Colour map 6, A6.*

Nha Trang is Vietnam's only real seaside town, with a long, golden beach. The centuries-old fishing settlement nestles in the protective embrace of the surrounding hills and islands at the mouth of the Cai Estuary. The light here has a beautifully radiant quality and the air is clear: colours are vivid, particularly the blues of the sea, sky and fishing boats moored on the river. The name Nha Trang is thought to be derived from the Cham word *yakram*, meaning bamboo river. Certainly, the surrounding area was a focal point of the Cham Kingdom (see page 1064), with some of the country's best-preserved Cham towers located nearby.

Nha Trang's clear waters and offshore islands won wide acclaim in the 1960s and its current prosperity is based firmly on tourism. Word has spread and Nha Trang's days as an undiscovered treasure are over. The town is now a firmly established favourite of Vietnamese as well as foreign visitors. There is a permanent relaxed holiday atmosphere, the streets are not crowded and the motorbikes cruise at a leisurely pace. There are, in reality, two Nha Trangs: popular Nha Trang, which is a sleepy, sedate seaside town consisting of a long, palm and casuarina-fringed beach and one or two streets running parallel to it, and commercial Nha Trang to the north of Yersin Street, which is a bustling city with an attractive array of Chinese shophouses.

Ins and outs

Getting there The airport is 34 km from Nha Trang at Cam Ranh. There are daily flights to Hanoi and Ho Chi Minh City and regular flights to Danang. The town is on the main north-south railway line, with trains to Ho Chi Minh City, Hanoi and stops between. The main bus terminal is west of the town centre. Note that inter-provincial buses do not go into Nha Trang but drop off on Highway 1 which bypasses the town. *Xe ôms* take passengers into town. ➤ *See Transport, page 1089.*

Getting around Nha Trang is just about negotiable on foot but there are also bicycles and motorbikes for hire everywhere and the usual cyclos.

Tourist information **Khanh Hoa Tourism** ① *1 Tran Hung Dao St, T058-526753, www.nhatrangtourist.com.vn, daily 0700-1130, 1330-1700*, is the official tour office and can arrange visa extensions, car and boat hire and tours of the area. It's also Vietnam Airlines booking office.

Nha Trang

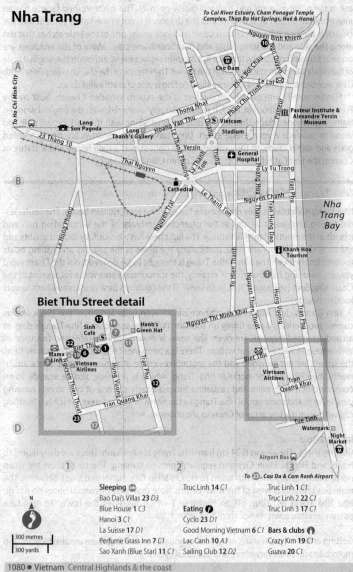

To Cai River Estuary, Cham Ponagar Temple Complex, Thap Ba Hot Springs, Hué & Hanoi

Nguyen Binh Khiem

Cho Dam

Pasteur Institute & Alexandre Yersin Museum

Long Son Pagoda

Long Thanh's Gallery

Vietcom

Stadium

General Hospital

Cathedral

Nha Trang Bay

Khanh Hoa Tourism

Biet Thu Street detail

Sinh Café

Hanh's Green Hat

Mama Linh

Biet Thu

Vietnam Airlines

Vietnam Airlines

Waterpark

Night Market

Airport Bus

To Ho Chi Minh City

23 Thang 10

Thai Nguyen

2 Thang 4

Thong Nhat

Hoang Van Thu

Le Thanh Phuong

Yersin

Nguyen Thai

Le Thanh Ton

Phan Boi Chau

Phan Chu Trinh

Quang Trung

Ngo Quyen

Le Loi

Pasteur

Hoang Hoa Than

Ly Tu Trong

Nguyen Chanh

Tran Phu

Tran Hung Dao

Hung Vuong

To Hien Thanh

Khanh Thanh

Nguyen Thien Thuat

Nguyen Thi Minh Khai

Hung Vuong

Tran Phu

Biet Thu

Tran Quang Khai

Tue Tinh

To ②③, Cau Da & Cam Ranh Airport

N

| 300 metres |
| 300 yards |

Sleeping 🛌
Bao Dai's Villas *23 D3*
Blue House *1 C3*
Hanoi *3 C1*
La Suisse *17 D1*
Perfume Grass Inn *7 C1*
Sao Xanh (Blue Star) *11 C1*

Truc Linh *14 C1*

Eating 🍴
Cyclo *23 D1*
Good Morning Vietnam *6 C1*
Lac Canh *10 A3*
Sailing Club *12 D2*

Truc Linh *1 C1*
Truc Linh 2 *22 C1*
Truc Linh 3 *17 C1*

Bars & clubs 🍸
Crazy Kim *19 C1*
Guava *20 C1*

Sights

Known as Thap Ba, the temple complex of **Cham Ponagar** ① *follow 2 Thang 4 St north out of town; Cham Ponagar is just over Xom Bong bridge, daily 0600-1800, 5000d,* is on a hill just outside the city. Originally the complex consisted of eight towers, four of which remain. Their stylistic differences indicate they were built at different times between the seventh and 12th centuries. The largest (23 m high) was built in AD 817 and contains a statue of Lady Thien Y-ana, also known as Ponagar (the beautiful wife of Prince Bac Hai), as well as a fine and very large linga. She taught the people of the area weaving and new agricultural techniques, and they built the tower in her honour. The other towers are dedicated to gods: the central tower to Cri Cambhu (which has become a fertility temple for childless couples); the northwest tower to Sandhaka (wood cutter and foster-father to Lady Thien Y-ana); and the south tower to Ganeca (Lady Thien Y-ana's daughter). The best time to visit the towers is in the afternoon, after 1600.

En route to the towers, the road crosses the **Cai River estuary**, where you'll see Nha Trang's elegant fleet of blue fishing boats, decorated with red trim and painted eyes for spotting the fish. The boats have coracles (*cái thúng*) for getting to and from the shore and mechanical fish traps, which take the form of nets supported by long arms; the arms are hinged to a platform on stilts and are raised and lowered by wires connected to a capstan which is turned, sometimes by hand but more commonly by foot.

The best known pagoda in Nha Trang is the **Long Son Pagoda** ① *23 Thang 10 St*, built in 1963. Inside the sanctuary is an unusual image of the Buddha, backlit with natural light. Murals depicting the jataka stories (birth stories of the Buddha) decorate the upper walls. To the right of the sanctuary, stairs lead up to a 9-m-high white Buddha, perched on a hill top, from where there are fine views. The pagoda commemorates those monks and nuns who died demonstrating against the Diem government, in particular those who, through their self-immolation, brought the despotic nature of the Diem regime and its human rights abuses to the attention of the American public. Before reaching the white pagoda, take a left on the stairs. Through an arch behind the pagoda you'll see a 14-m long reclining Buddha. Commissioned in 2003, it is an impressive sight.

The **Alexandre Yersin Museum** ① *8 Tran Phu St, T058-829540, Mon-Fri 0800-1100, 1400-1630, Sat 0800-1100, 26,000d,* is contained within the colonnaded **Pasteur Institute** founded by the great scientist's protégé, Dr Alexandre Yersin. Swiss-born Yersin first arrived in Vietnam in 1891 and spent much of the rest of his life in Nha Trang. He was responsible for identifying the bacillus which causes the plague. The museum contains the lab equipment used by Yersin, his library and stereoscope through which visitors can see in 3-D the black-and-white slides, including shots taken by Yersin on his visits to the highlands. The museum's curator is helpful, friendly, and fluent in French and English.

The **Cho Dam** (central market) close to Nguyen Hong Son Street is a good place to wander and browse and is quite well-stocked with useful items. In the vicinity of the market, along **Phan Boi Chau Street** for example, are some bustling streets with old colonial-style shuttered houses.

Long Thanh is one of Vietnam's most distinguished photographers and has a **gallery** ① *126 Hoang Van Thu St, near the railway station, T058-824875, lvntrang50@hotmail.com,* in his native Nha Trang. Long Thanh works only in black and white and has won a series of international awards and recognition for his depictions of Cham children and of wistful old men and women, who have witnessed generations of change in a single lifetime. Many of his famous pictures were taken in and around Nha Trang. Long Thanh speaks English and welcomes visitors to his gallery.

Thap Ba Hot Springs

① 2 km beyond Cham Ponagar, not far from the Cai River, T058-835335, www.thapbahot spring.com, around US$3 per adult although charges vary.

A soak in mineral water or a mud bath is a relaxing and refreshing experience. Baths and pools of differing sizes are available for individuals, couples and groups. The water is 40°C and is rich in sodium silicate chloride. Steam baths and massages are available.

Islands around Nha Trang

① The islands are reached on boat trips from Cau Da pier. Departures 0900. Around US$5 including a seafood lunch and snorkelling equipment; cold beers cost extra. Boat charters also available. Visitors must now pay a Nha Trang sightseeing fee.

The **islands** off Nha Trang are sometimes known as the **Salangane** islands after the sea swallows that nest here. The sea swallow (*yen*) produces the highly prized bird's nest from which the famous soup is made.

There's an uninspiring aquarium on **Mieu Island** but no other sights. The islands (including **Hon Mun**, **Hon Tam** and **Hon Mot**) are usually a bit of an anti-climax for, as so often in Vietnam, to travel is to better than to arrive; it's often a case of lovely boat trip, disappointing beach. The best part is anchoring offshore and jumping into the cool water while your skipper prepares a sumptuous feast and chills some beers. The best known boat trips to the islands are run by **Hanh's Green Hat** and **Mama Linh**
➤➤ *See Activities and tours, page 1088.*

Mui Ne ⊖⊜⚲⚙▲⊜⚙ ➤➤
pp1085-1090. Colour map 6, B5.

Further down the coast and east of the small fishing town of **Phan Thiet** is Mui Ne, a 20-km sweep of golden sand where Vietnam's finest coastal resorts can be found. Watersports are available here as well as one of the country's most attractive golf courses.
➤➤ *See Activities and tours, page 1088.*

Ins and outs

Getting there Open Tour Buses nearly all divert to Mui Ne and drop off/pick up from just about every hotel along the beach. It is also possible and quicker to hire a car; from Ho Chi Minh City it will cost about US$75. ➤➤ *See Transport, page 1090.*

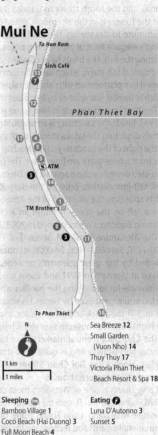

Mui Ne

To Hon Rom
Sinh Café

Phan Thiet Bay

ATM

TM Brother's

To Phan Thiet

N

1 km
1 miles

Sleeping ⊜
Bamboo Village 1
Coco Beach (Hai Duong) 3
Full Moon Beach 4
Hiep Hoa 5
Mui Ne Resort 13
Sailing Club 11

Sea Breeze 12
Small Garden
(Vuon Nho) 14
Thuy Thuy 17
Victoria Phan Thiet
Beach Resort & Spa 18

Eating ⊖
Luna D'Autonno 3
Sunset 5

Bars & clubs ⚙
Guava 8
Pogo 7

Best time to visit The weather is best in the dry season, November to May. Mui Ne is most popular with overseas visitors in the Christmas to Easter period when prices at the some of the better hotels rise by 20% or more. From December to March, Mui Ne loses much of its beach to the sea.

Sights

Mui Ne (Cape Ne) is the name of the famous sandy cape and the small fishing village that lies at its end. Mui Ne's two claims to fame are its *nuoc mam* (fish sauce) and its **beaches**, where it's possible to play a host of watersports, including kitesurfing for which it is justly famous. The cape is dominated by some impressive **sand dunes**, which are quite red in parts due to the underlying geology.

Around the village, visitors may notice a strong smell of rotting fish. This is the unfortunate but inevitable by-product of fish sauce fermenting in wooden barrels. The process takes a year but to Vietnamese palates it is worth every day. The *nuoc mam* of Phan Thiet is made from anchovies and is highly regarded but not as reverentially as that from the southern island of Phu Quoc.

◉ Central Highlands and the coast listings

For Sleeping and Eating price codes, see inside the front cover.

◉ Sleeping

Dalat *p1072, map p1074*

LL-AL Evason Ana Mandara Villas & Six Senses Spa at Dalat, Le Lai St, T063-555888, www.sixsenses.com. Restored French villas are perched on a hillside, surrounded by fruit farms. Each villa has a couple of bedrooms, a sitting room and dining room; guests have dedicated butlers. A number of pools are scattered about the hotel complex. There is also a central villa that houses a French bistro and wine bar. The **Six Senses Spa** experience has been created in one of the villas with river and mountain views, outdoor pools and hot tubs.

A Empress Hotel, 5 Nguyen Thai Hoc St, T063-833888, empressdl@hcm.vnn.vn. This is a particularly attractive hotel in a lovely position overlooking the lake. All rooms are arranged around a small courtyard which traps the sun and is a great place for breakfast or to pen a postcard. The rooms are large with very comfortable beds and the more expensive ones have luxurious bathrooms

so try to get a room upgrade. Attentive and courteous staff. A great value hotel with the best view of Xuan Huong Lake.

A Golf 3 Hotel, 4 Nguyen Thi Minh Khai St, T063-826042, golf3.dalat@vinagolf.vn. Smart, centrally located hotel with comfortable rooms; cheaper rooms have showers only. It has a good range of facilities, including bar, restaurant, massage, nightclub and karaoke. The location by Dalat market is excellent. One drawback though is that because it is so near to the market the rooms facing the street are noisy. Breakfast is included.

C-G Hang Nga (Tree House), 3 Huynh Thuc Khang St, T063-822070. If you fancy a fantasy night in a mushroom, a tree or a giraffe then this is the place for you. It is an architectural meander through curves, twists and bizarre rooms and ornamentation. The guesthouse was designed by Hang Nga, whose father, Truong Chinh, formed the triumvirate of power following the death of Ho Chi Minh. Prices are reasonable but the rooms tend to be visited by curious tourists and the furniture is sturdily made and not too comfortable.

E-G Hoa Binh 1 (Peace Hotel 1), 64 Truong Cong Dinh St, T063-822787, peace12@hcm.vnn.vn. One of the better low-cost places with 16 rooms in a good location, including 5 at the back around a small yard, quiet but not much view. Rooms at the front have a view but can be a bit noisy. The rooms have TV, fan and mosquito nets. A friendly place with an all-day café.

E-G Hoa Binh 2 (Peace Hotel 2), 67 Truong Cong Dinh St, T063-822982, peace12@ hcm.vnn.vn. Almost opposite its sister hotel, this is rather an attractive 1930s building. It's clean and some rooms have small balconies.

Buon Ma Thuot *p1077*

C-D Thang Loi Hotel, 1 Phan Chu Trinh St, T050-857615, www.daklaktourist.com.vn. In a central location, opposite the victory monument. The rooms are large and come with en suite facilities. The staff speak good English. Food in the restaurant is fresh, well presented, good value and plentiful. ATM.

E-G Duy Hoang Hotel, 30 Ly Thuong Kiet St, T050-858020. Spacious, well-furnished rooms with en suite facilities and a/c. Cheaper rooms have fan and shared bathrooms. Staff are efficient and friendly and have a reasonable grasp of English. Excellent value for money.

Lak Lake *p1077*

It costs US$5 to stay in a Mnong long-house at Buon Jun; contact **Daklak Tourist** for arrangements.

Play Ku *p1078*

D-F Ialy Hotel, 89 Hung Vuong St, T059-824843, ialyhotel@dng.vnn.vn. Excellent location opposite the main post office. Reasonable sized, good value rooms with en suite facilities, a/c and satellite TV. Staff are friendly enough but no English is spoken. The restaurant on the 1st floor is only open for breakfast. ATM in the lobby.

Kontum *p1078*

D-F Dakbla 1 Hotel, 2 Phan Dinh Phung St, T060-863333. Set amid attractive grounds, this hotel has a small restaurant and jetty on the riverbank. Staff are friendly and helpful and have a basic understanding of English and French. Rooms have minibars, satellite TV, a/c, hot water and en suite bathrooms. The restaurant provides good food at a reasonable price.

Nha Trang *p1079, map p1080*

LL Evason Hideaway & Six Senses Spa at Ana Mandara, Ninh Vinh Bay; 30 km north of Nha Trang, T058-728222, www.evasonhide aways.com. Beach Villas, Rock Villas and Hilltop Villas are laid out in the full dramatic curve of Ninh Van Bay. You can't get more exceptionally luxurious than this; the Rock Villas are perched on rocks at the tip of the bay with bathrooms overlooking the sea and fronted by small infinity pools. The resort is large; from the Rock Villas to the main restaurant is an enormous hike. Beach Villas are more centrally located. While your days away in the herb garden, **Six Senses Spa**, library or bar and be attended by your personal butler. It's highly romantic, very secluded and very expensive; the food is exceptional. The resort is 1 hr ahead of real time which is far too confusing.

L-AL Whale Island Resort, off Nha Trang, T058-840501, www.whaleislandresort.com. This is a great place in which to relax amid the aquamarine waters of the South China Sea. Bungalows right on this island beach, 2½ hrs north of Nha Trang. The price includes full board and return transfers to Nha Trang and gets cheaper the longer you stay. Activities include diving, windsurfing, canoeing and catamaran sailing and there's plenty of wildlife to observe.

A-E Bao Dai's Villas, Tran Phu St (just before Cau Da village), T058-590147, http://vn realty.com/nt/baodai/index.html. Several villas of former Emperor Bao Dai, with magnificent views over the harbour and outlying islands, sited on a small promontory, with large elegant a/c rooms. There are an additional 40 rooms in assorted buildings that lack the scale and elegance, not surprisingly, of the emperor's own quarters. Overrun with sightseers during holiday periods.

C-G Perfume Grass Inn (Que Thao), 4A Biet Thu St, T058-524286, www.perfume-grass. com. Well-run and friendly family hotel with

21 rooms. Restaurant and internet service. Good value for money. Book in advance.

D-F La Suisse Hotel, 34 Tran Quang Khai St, T058-524353, www.lasuissehotel.com. Excellent new hotel with 24 rooms on 5 floors, nicely built, and offering excellent value for money. The best rooms (VIP) are large and have attractive balconies with sea view. All rooms have baths. Breakfast included.

D-G Sao Xanh (Blue Star), 1B Biet Thu St, T058-525447, quangc@dng.vnn.vn. Another popular, clean and friendly family-run hotel. 23 rooms, free coffee and bananas, more expensive rooms have breakfast included. Near the beach and in a popular area.

E-G Blue House, 12/8 Hung Vuong St, T058-522505, ngothaovy1983@yahoo.com. vn. Down a little alley in a quiet setting. 14 a/c and fan rooms in a small, neat blue building. Friendly and excellent value for money.

E-G Hanoi, 31C Biet Thu St, T058-525127, hanoihotel-nt@yahoo.com. Set in a quiet cul-de-sac at the end of the road, this small 12-room hotel has a/c and fan rooms. Breakfast costs US$2 extra, helpful.

E-G Truc Linh, 27B Hung Vuong St, T058-522201. Best known for its restaurant, this guesthouse is popular with budget travellers. It's moved from across the street. The 15 rooms have a/c, hot water, TV and minibar and some have a sea view. Try to opt for a room with external windows.

Mui Ne p1082, map p1082

L-AL Coco Beach (Hai Duong), T062-847 1113, www.cocobeach.net. Coco Beach was the first resort on Mui Ne and remains among the best. Not luxurious but friendly and impeccably kept. Wooden bungalows and 2-bedroom 'villas' facing the beach in a beautiful setting with a lovely pool. Price includes a decent buffet breakfast. There are 2 restaurants: the French **Champa** (Tue-Sun 1500-2300 only) and **Paradise Beach Club** (open all day).

L-AL Victoria Phan Thiet Beach Resort & Spa, T062-813000, www.victoriahotels-asia.com. Part of the French-run Victoria Group, the resort has 59 upgraded thatch-roof bungalows with outdoor rain showers and 3 villas, built in country-house style in an attractive landscaped setting. It is well equipped with restaurants, several bars, an attractive pool and a spa.

L-A Bamboo Village, T062-847007, www.bamboovillageresortvn.com. Attractive, simple, hexagonal bamboo huts peppered around a lovely shady spot at the top of the beach. More expensive rooms have a/c and hot-water showers. An excellent restaurant and attractive swimming pool.

L-A Sailing Club, T062-847440, www.sailing clubvietnam.com. This is a stunning resort, designed in the most charming style with bungalows and rooms that are simple and cool and surrounded by dense vegetation. Its pool has been extended and the bathrooms for the superior rooms enlarged. It has an excellent restaurant and bar. A good buffet breakfast is included.

A Full Moon Beach, T062-847008, www.windsurf-vietnam.com. Visitors are assured of a friendly reception by the French and Vietnamese couple who own and run the place. Some rooms are spacious, others a little cramped, some brick, some bamboo. The most attractive rooms have a sea view. There is a good restaurant.

A-F Small Garden (Vuon Nho), T062-874 012, nguyengrimm@yahoo.com. Run by a Vietnamese family, it consists of simple and cheap bamboo hut accommodation near the road and new, small, a/c concrete bungalows nearer the beach. Although lacking in amenities it is in a good part of the beach with plenty of cafés and restaurants nearby.

C-D Miu Ne Resort (Sinh Café), T062-847 542, www.sinhcafevn.com. Large and new hotel that has cleverly packed the narrow site with 48 rooms and brick-built bungalows. It has a nice pool, bar and restaurant.

C-D Sea Breeze, T062-847373, www.muine seabreeze.com. This far north the beach is getting a bit narrow and the road is a little close to some of the rooms for comfort.

Although they are slightly pricier, insist on a sea-view room of which there are 2 categories. Well kept, clean and comfortable. Breakfast included. Motorbikes and bicycles for rent.

C-D Thuy Thuy, T062-847357, T091-816 0637 (mob), thuythuyresort2000@yahoo.com. 7 pleasant a/c bungalows with TV run by the friendly Elaine. Newer bungalows are a bit more expensive but the originals are perfectly comfortable. Set on the 'wrong' side of the road (eg away from the beach) this is nevertheless a rather charming and nicely run little place, highly praised by guests. Attractive pool.

C-F Hiep Hoa, T062-847262, T091-812 4149 (mob), hiephoatourism@yahoo.com. Attractive and simple little place with 25 a/c rooms. It's quiet, clean and with its own stretch of beach. Popular and should be booked in advance. Its rate are excellent value for Mui Ne; they go down in the low season.

⊘ Eating

Dalat p1072, map p1074
In the evening, street stalls line Nguyen Thi Minh Khai St, leading to Dalat market, which is itself the ideal place to buy picnic provisions. Lakeside cafés and restaurants may look attractive but they serve indifferent food.

⊮-⊮ Empress Restaurant, Empress hotel. Open all day and specializing in Chinese fare but with a good selection of Vietnamese and Western dishes. Ideal breakfast setting, al fresco around the fountain in the courtyard.

⊮-⊮ Le Café de la Poste, 12 Tran Phu St. Adjacent to the **Sofitel** and under the same management. International comfort food at near-Western prices in an airy and cool building. The 3-course lunch menu is great value. A pool table dominates the café. Upstairs is a Vietnamese restaurant.

⊮ Hoa Binh 1, 67 Truong Cong Dinh St. An all-day eatery serving standard backpacker fare: fried noodles, vegetarian dishes and pancakes at low prices.

⊮ Long Hoa, 6 3 Thang 2, T063-822934. In the best traditions of French family restaurants, this place has delicious food with fish, meat, venison and super breakfasts. Popular with Dalat's expats and visitors. The chicken soup and beefsteak are particularly recommended and sample Madame's home-made strawberry wine. Service is erratic.

⊮ Stop and Go Café, 2A Ly Tu Trong St, T063-828458. A café and art gallery run by the local poet, Mr Duy Viet. Sit inside or on the terrace as he bustles around rustling up breakfast, pulling out volumes of visitors' books and his own collected works. The garden is an overrun wilderness.

Nha Trang p1079, map p1080

A local speciality is nem nuong, grilled pork wrapped in rice paper with salad leaves and bun, fresh rice noodles. The French bread in Nha Trang is also excellent. On the beach near **Nha Trang Waterpark** is a night market, where stalls serve freshly cooked fish and barbecued meat.

⊮-⊮ Good Morning Vietnam, 19B Biet Thu St, T058-815071, daily 1000-2300. Popular Italian restaurant, part of a small chain to be found in major tourist centres.

⊮-⊮ Sailing Club, 72-74 Tran Phu St, T058-524628, sailingnt@dng.vnn.vn, daily 0700-2300. Although best known as a bar, this busy and attractive beachfront area also includes several restaurants: Japanese, Italian and global cuisine. None is cheap but all serve good food and represent decent value.

⊮ Cyclo, 130 Nguyen Thien Thuat St, T058-524208, khuongthuy@hotmail.com, daily 0700-2400. Outstanding little family-run restaurant that has moved to new premises a few doors away. Italian and Vietnamese dishes. Real attention to detail in the cooking.

⊮ Lac Canh, 44 Nguyen Binh Khiem St, T058-821391. Specializes in beef, squid and prawns, which you barbecue at your table. Also excellent fish and a special dish of eel mixed with vermicelli. Smoky atmosphere and can be hard to get a table. Highly recommended.

Truc Linh, 11 Biet Thu St, T058-526742. Deservedly popular with sensible prices. Good fruit shake and *op la* (fried eggs). There's also **Truc Linh 2**, at 21 Biet Thu St, T058-521089, and **Truc Linh 3**, at 80 Hung Vuong St, T058-525259. Nos 2 and 3 are recommended as the best.

Mui Ne *p1082, map p1082*
Of the hotel restaurants the Sailing Club, Bamboo Village and Coco Beach stand out, see Sleeping, page 1085.
Luna D'Autonno, T062-847591. One of the best Italian restaurants in the country. Inspired menu that goes way beyond the standard pizzas and pasta with daily fish specials and BBQs. Huge portions, good wine list.
Sunset, T062-847605. Good Vietnamese food, especially fish. Efficient service and excellent value.

◑ Bars and clubs

Nha Trang *p1079, map p1080*
Crazy Kim, 19 Biet Thu St, T058-816072, open until late. A busy, lively bar in the heart of a popular part of town. Pool, table tennis, food.
Guava, 17 Biet Thu St, T058-524140, daily 1100-2400. Striking orange front. Stylish relaxing café, cocktail bar and lounge bar with garden. Good music and bar games.
Sailing Club, 74-76 Tran Phu St, T058-524 628, open until late. Lively bar, especially on Sat nights when locals and visitors enjoy pool, cold beer, dancing and music.

Mui Ne *p1082, map p1082*
Pogo Beach Bar, www.thepogobar.com. Just down from **Sinh Café** with cocktails, movies, beer and local and international food.
Guava. Like its namesake in Nha Trang this is a large funky place in which to lounge or drink at the bar. Atmospherically candlelit at night. International food is served.

◯ Shopping

Dalat *p1072, map p1074*
Dalat has a well-deserved reputation for producing not only beautiful flowers but also some of the best handmade silk paintings in Vietnam.

▲▲ Activities and tours

Dalat *p1072, map p1074*
Golf
Dalat Palace Golf Course, 1 Phu Dong Thien Vuong St, T063-823507, www.vietnam golfresorts.com. Originally built for Emperor Bao Dai in 1922, it was rebuilt in 1994 and is now an 18-hole championship golf course. Rated by some as the finest in Vietnam and one of the best in the region. Green fees US$90, include caddie fee.

Tour operators
Dalat Toserco, No7, 3 Thang 2 St, T063-822 125. Budget transport and a good selection of tours. Slightly more expensive than **Sinh Café** and **TM Brothers**.
Dalat Travel Bureau, 1 Nguyen Thi Minh Khai, T063-510104, www.dalattourist.com.vn. The state-run travel company for Lam Dong Province. Tours include: city, trekking, canyoning, rock climbing, exploring and biking; the majority of these tours cost US$10 per person.
Phattire Adventures, 73 Truong Cong Dinh St, T063-829422, www.phattireadventures. com. Canyoning, from US$24; rock climbing, US$30; mountain biking, from US$32; trekking from US$17; kayaking, US$27.
Sinh Café, 4a Bui Thi Xuan, T063-822663, www.sinhcafevn.com. Part of the nationwide **Sinh Café** chain. Primarily provides cheap travel to HCMC and Nha Trang. Also arranges local tours.
TM Brothers, 58 Truong Cong Dinh St, T063-828383, tmbrother_dalat@yahoo.com. Similar to **Sinh Café** in that they provide budget tours and transportation. Has a

wide range of tours including to Yok Don National Park. Central Highlands tours range from US$45-100 per person. Motorbike rental US$4-6/day.

Buon Ma Thuot *p1077*
Tour operators
Vietnam Highland Travel, 24 Ly Thuong Kiet, T050-855009, www.vietnamhighland travel.com.vn. Offer adventure packages, including elephant trekking and homestays.

Nha Trang *p1079, map p1080*
Diving
Dry season only (Jan-May).
Rainbow Divers, 90A Hung Vuong St, T058-524351, T090-878 1756 (mob), www.divevietnam.com. A full range of training and courses, including the National Geographic dive courses. Good reports regarding equipment and focus on safety. Qualified instructors speak a variety of European languages.

    The Evason Hideaway also offers diving packages.

Fishing
Boats and equipment can be hired from Cau Da Pier; contact **Khanh Hoa Tourism**, 1 Tran Hung Dao St, T058-526753, www.nhatrangtourist.com.vn, for details.

Therapies
Six Senses Spa, Ana Mandara Resort, www.six senses.com. Japanese and Vichy showers, hot tubs and massages in beautiful surroundings. Programmes for vitality, stress-management and meditation that include tailored spa treatments. 5-day lifestyle packages are US$990 not including accommodation.

Tour operators
The following tour operators arrange trips to **Buon Ma Thuot** and the **Central Highlands**.
Hanh's Green Hat, 2C Biet Thu St, T058-526 494, biendaotour@yahoo.com. Boat trips (US$5 including lunch and pick-up from hotel, excluding entrance fees and

snorkelling fees). Also other local tours, car, motorbike and bicycle hire.
Mama Linh, 23C Biet Thu St, T058-522844, www.mamalinhvn@yahoo.com. Standard boat trips for US$6 and minibus tickets to Hoi An, Phan Thiet, HCMC and Dalat.
Sinh Café, 10 Biet Thu St, T058-524329, www.sinhcafevn.com. Offers tours and Open Bus Tour tickets. **Sinh Café** buses arrive and depart from here.

Watersports
The **Ana Mandara Resort** offers windsurfing, parasailing, hobiecats and fishing.

Mui Ne *p1082, map p1082*
Golf
Ocean Dunes Golf Club, 1 Ton Duc Thang St, T062-823366, www.vietnamgolfresorts.com. Phan Thiet's 18-hole golf course, designed by Nick Faldo, is highly regarded. Fully equipped club house with bar and restaurant. Green fee US$90 Mon-Fri, weekends and holidays US$100 including caddie fees.

Therapies
Lotus Day Spa, Sailing Club, T062-847440, www.sailingclubvietnam.com. Massage treatments are available in special cabins in the grounds.

Tour operators
Sinh Café, 144 Nguyen Dinh Chieu, T062-847 542, muine@sinhcafevn.com. Good for Open Tour tickets and local tours.
TM Brother's, with several outlets, T062-847 359, T098-407 4507 (mob). Local tours and Open Tour Bus service.

Watersports
Windsurfing, kitesurfing and other watersports are popular in Mui Ne. The wind is normally brisk and the sight of the kitesurfers zooming around on the waves is great for those of us too cowardly to try. Equipment and training is offered by a couple of resorts.

Airwaves, T090-330 8313 (mob), www.air
waveskitesurfing.com, has stations at the
Sailing Club, Sea Horse Resort and Bon
Bien Resort. There are also 2 Airwaves
shops in town. Prices vary according
to lessons and equipment needed.
Kitesurfing lesson, US$100; windsurf
lesson including equipment, US$20/hr;
surf lesson, US$16/hr.

Jibe's Beach Club, T062-847405, T091-316
2005 (mob), www.windsurf-vietnam.com,
part of and close to **Full Moon Beach Resort**.
Equipment is available for purchase or for hire
by the hour, day or week. A 5-hr kitesurfing
lesson is US$200; 5-hr windsurfing lesson,
US$170; surfboard hire, US$5; kayaking,
US$5/hr per person. Instruction available
in 9 languages.

⊖ Transport

Dalat *p1072, map p1074*
Air
See page 1073. **Vietnam Airlines**, No 2 and
No 40 Ho Tuong Mau St, T/F063-833499,
open daily 0730-1130, 1330-1630, closes
30 mins earlier at weekends.

Bus
Open Tour Buses operate daily trips to **HCMC**,
7hrs, **Nha Trang**, 6 hrs, and **Mui Ne**, 6 hrs.

Car
It is possible to hire cars and taxis. Many
tour operators have cars for hire and
there are numerous taxis to choose from.

Central provinces *p1077*
Air
Vietnam Airlines has offices at Buon
Ma Thuot (T050-954442) and Play Ku
(T059-823058) airports and at 129 Ba
Trieu St in Kontum, T060-862282.

Bus
Regular local buses link provincial
centres throughout the region.

Car
Cars with drivers are available for hire; contact
the provincial tourist offices or your hotel.
Play Ku to **Buon Ma Thuot**, 3½ hrs, US$50.

Nha Trang *p1079, map p1080*
Air
See page 1079. Some hotels offer free bus
rides to town. The airport bus costs 70,000d
from the airport and 25,000d from Nha
Trang, 34 km. Taxis wait at the bus station
to transport passengers to hotels. A taxi
from the airport to town costs 200,000d.
  Vietnam Airlines, 91 Nguyen Thien
Thuat St, T058-826768.

Bicycle and motorbike
Bicycles can be hired from almost every hotel
and every café for around 20,000d per day
for a bicycle. Motorbikes can be hired from
hotels and cafés for around 64,000d per day.

Bus
The long-distance bus station is out of town
at 23 Thang 10 St and has connections with
**HCMC, Phan Rang, Danang, Quy Nhon,
Buon Ma Thuot, Dalat, Hué** and **Vinh**.
Open Tour Buses arrive at and depart
from their relevant operator's café (see
Tour operators, above).

Taxi
Mai Linh, T058-910910.

Train
There are regular train connections with stops
to and from **Hanoi** and **HCMC**. The station is
at 17 Thai Nguyen St, T058-820666.
  5 Star Express, 15B Thai Nguyen St,
T058-562 1868, www.5starexpress.com.vn.
This new and comfortable train departs
Nha Trang at 1455, arriving in HCMC at
2318. There's also a day train leaving at
0500, arriving 1810, US$56. There are a
variety of carriages, and tickets are priced
according to the class; tickets range from
US$10 one way for the entire route up to
US$150. Highly recommended.

Mui Ne p1082, map p1082
Bus
A local bus plies the route from Phan Thiet bus station to **Mui Ne**, as do taxis. **Sinh Café** and **TM Brother's** Open Tour Buses drop off and pick up from all resorts on **Mui Ne**.

ⓘ Directory

Dalat p1072, map p1074
Banks BIDV, 42 Hoa Binh Sq. **Incombank**, 46-48 Hoa Binh Sq, Mon-Fri 0700-1000, 1300-1600, Sat until 1100. It has a bureau de change, an ATM and also cashes TCs. **Internet** Internet cafés galore along Nguyen Chi Thanh St, heading from Hoa Binh Sq to Xuan Huong Lake. **Medical services** 4 Pham Ngoc Thach St, T063-822 154. Well-equipped hospital. Doctors speak English and French. **Post office and telephone** 14 Tran Phu St, opposite Novotel Hotel. Offers internet and IDD.

Nha Trang p1079, map p1080
Banks **Vietcombank**, 17 Quang Trung St. Will change most major currencies, cash, TCs (2% commission), and arrange cash advances on some credit cards. There's a **Vietcombank** exchange bureau at 8A Biet Thu St. **Internet** Internet cafés all over town, particularly in Biet Thu St and Hong Vuong St. **Medical services** General Hospital, 19 Yersin St, T058-822168. **Post office** GPO, 2 Le Loi St; Biet Thu St, near Nguyen Thien Thuat St.

Mui Ne p1082, map p1082
Banks No banks but a couple of ATMs; the **Saigon Mui Ne Resort** has one and there is one in front of the **Ocean Star Resort** that is next to the Sailing Club. **Internet** There are a few internet cafés, particularly the tour cafés, some of which offer free service to customers and almost all hotels offer internet access to their guests. Prices are quite high. **Medical services** Polyclinic, next to **Swiss Resort**, T062-84749, 091-821 0504 (mob), open daily 1130-1330, 1730-2100

Ho Chi Minh City and around

→ Colour map 6, B3 and B4.

Ho Chi Minh City is a manic, capitalistic hothouse, clogged with traffic, bustling with energy and enlivened by top restaurants, shops and bars. Its streets are evidence of a vibrant historical past with pagodas and temples and a bustling Chinatown. During the 1960s and early 1970s, Saigon, the Pearl of the Orient, boomed and flourished under the American occupation. In more recent times it was the seat of the South Vietnam government until the events that led to the country's reunification.

Today, Ho Chi Minh City is dedicated to commerce and hedonistic pleasures. Officially renamed in 1975, it remains to most the bi-syllabic, familiar 'Saigon'. It is the largest city in Vietnam and still growing at a prodigious rate. It is also the nation's foremost commercial and industrial centre, a place of remorseless, relentless activity and expanding urban sprawl. For the visitor, Ho Chi Minh City is a fantastic place to shop, eat and drink, while admiring its historical past and enjoying its energetic present.

The city is surrounded by fascinating historical sites to the north and by the liquid fingers of the river delta to its south. The Mekong region is a veritable Garden of Eden, stuffed full of bountiful fruit trees, decorated in pink bougainvillea and carpeted with brilliant green rice paddies. Waterways are as busy as highways, with fishing boats chug chug chugging their way along the brown river. Elsewhere in the south, historical, cultural, religious and pleasurable treasures abound: the Viet Cong tunnels at Cu Chi, the fantastical Cao Dai temple at Tay Ninh and dazzling white, remote beaches at Phu Quoc. ▸▸ *For listings, see pages 1103-1112.*

Ins and outs

Getting there **Tan Son Nhat airport** (SGN), T08-848 5383/0832 0320, is 30 minutes from the centre. By taxi the cost is about US$5-7. Taxi drivers may try and demand a flat fee in US dollars but you should insist on using the meter, which is the law, and pay in dong. On the right of the international terminal is the domestic terminal.

Open Tour Buses generally depart and leave from offices in the Pham Ngu Lao district. There is also a daily bus service from Ho Chi Minh City to Phnom Penh (Cambodia). The railway station is northwest of the city centre. There are regular daily connections to/from Hanoi and all stops on the line north. ▸▸ *See Transport, page 1111.*

Getting around Ho Chi Minh City has abundant transport. Metered taxis, motorcycle taxis and cyclos vie for business. Those who prefer some level of independence opt to hire (or even buy) a bicycle or motorbike. There are now so many motorbikes on the streets of Ho Chi Minh City that intersections seem lethally confused. Miraculously, the riders miss each other (most of the time), while pedestrians safely make their way through waves of machines. Take an organized tour to reach sights outside the city.

Orientation Virtually all of Ho Chi Minh City lies to the west of the Saigon River. Most visitors to Ho Chi Minh City head straight for hotels in Districts 1 or 3. Many will arrive on buses in De Tham or Pham Ngu Lao streets, the backpacker area, in District 1, not far from the city centre. Many of the sights are also in District 1 (also still known as Saigon). Cholon or Chinatown (District 5) is a mile west of the centre. All the sights of Central Ho Chi Minh City can be reached on foot or cyclo in no more than 30 minutes from the major hotels on Nguyen Hue, Dong Khoi and Ton Duc Thang streets.

Background

Before the 15th century, Ho Chi Minh City was a small village surrounded by a wilderness of forest and swamp. Through the years it was ostensibly incorporated into the Funan and then the Khmer empires but it's unlikely that these kingdoms had any lasting influence on the community. In fact, the Khmers, who called the region *Prei Nokor*, used it for hunting. By 1623 the town had become an important commercial centre and, in the mid-17th century, it became the residence of the so-called Vice-King of Cambodia. In 1698, the Viets managed to extend their control to the far south and Saigon was finally brought under Vietnamese control. By 1790, the city had a population of 50,000 and Emperor Gia Long made it his place of residence until Hué was selected as the capital of the Nguyen Dynasty.

In the middle of the 19th century, the French began to challenge Vietnamese authority in the south. Between 1859 and 1862, in response to Nguyen persecution of the Catholics in Vietnam, the French attacked and captured Saigon. The Treaty of Saigon in 1862 ratified the conquest and created the new French colony of Cochin China. Saigon was

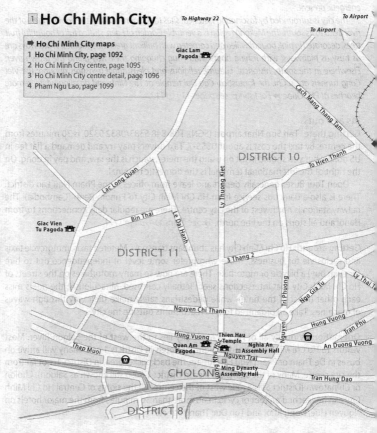

1 Ho Chi Minh City

To Highway 22
To Airport
To Airport

Giac Lam Pagoda

Cach Mang Thang Tam

DISTRICT 10

To Hien Thanh

Lac Long Quan

Ly Thuong Kiet

Bin Thai

Le Dai Hanh

Giac Vien Tu Pagoda

DISTRICT 11

3 Thang 2

Tri Phuong

Ngo Gia Tu

Ly Thai To

Nguyen Chi Thanh

Hung Vuong

Tran Phu

Thap Muoi

Hung Vuong   Thien Hau Temple

Quan Am Pagoda   Nghia An Assembly Hall

Nguyen Trai

An Duong Vuong

CHOLON   Ming Dynasty Assembly Hall

Tran Hung Dao

DISTRICT 8

developed in French style, with wide, tree-lined boulevards, street-side cafés, elegant French architecture, boutiques and the smell of baking baguettes.

During the course of the Vietnam War, as refugees spilled in from a devastated countryside, the population of Saigon almost doubled from 2.4 million in 1965 to around 4.5 million by 1975. With reunification in 1976, the new Communist authorities pursued a policy of depopulation, believing that the city had become too large and parasitic, preying on the surrounding countryside.

The population of Ho Chi Minh City today is officially seven million and rising fast as the rural poor are lured by tales of streets paved with gold. Vietnam's economic reforms are most in evidence in Ho Chi Minh City, where average annual incomes, at US$1800, are more than double the national average. It is also here that the country's largest population (around 380,000) of Hoa (ethnic Chinese) is to be found. Once persecuted for their economic success, they still have the greatest economic influence and acumen. Under the current regime, best described as crony capitalism, the city is once more being rebuilt.

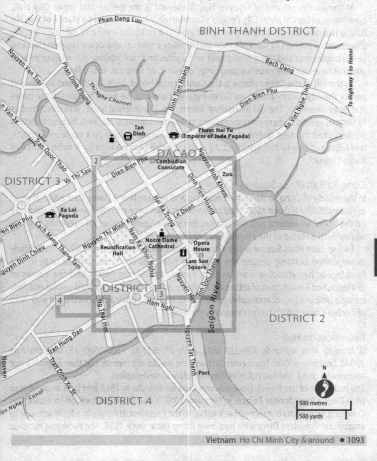

City centre

The centre of Ho Chi Minh City is, in many respects, the most interesting. A saunter down **Dong Khoi Street**, the old rue Catinat, can still give an impression of life in a more elegant and less frenzied era. Much remains on a small and personal scale and within a 100 yard radius of Dong Khoi or Thai Van Lung streets there are dozens of cafés, restaurants and boutiques.

Around Lam Son Square

Lam Son Square is the centre of Ho Chi Minh City. The **Rex Hotel**, a pre-Liberation favourite with US officers, stands at the intersection of Le Loi and Nguyen Hue boulevards. This was the scene of the daily 'Five O'clock Follies' where the military briefed an increasingly sceptical press corps during the Vietnam War. A short distance northeast of the Rex, is the once impressive, French-era **Opera House**, once home to the National Assembly. When it is open, it provides a varied programme of events.

At the northwest end of Nguyen Hue Boulevard is the yellow and white **City Hall**, now home to Ho Chi Minh City People's Committee, which overlooks a **statue of Bac Ho** (Uncle Ho) offering comfort, or perhaps advice, to a child. On weekend evenings literally thousands of young city men, women and families cruise up and down Nguyen Hue and Le Loi boulevards and Dong Khoi street on bicycles and motorbikes; this whirl of people and machines is known as *chay long rong*, 'cruising', or *song voi*, 'living fast'.

To the left of the Opera House is the **Continental Hotel**, built in 1880 and an integral part of the city's history. Graham Greene stayed here and the hotel features in the novel *The Quiet American*. The old journalists' haunt, the 'Continental Shelf', was described as "a famous veranda where correspondents, spies, speculators, traffickers, intellectuals and soldiers used to meet during the war to glean information and pick up secret reports, half false, half true or half disclosed. All of this is more than enough for it to be known as Radio Catinat".

Cong Xa Pari (Paris Square)

In the middle of Cong Xa Pari is the imposing and austere **Notre Dame Cathedral** ① *open to visitors 0800-1100 and 1500-1600 on weekdays*, built between 1877 and 1880, allegedly on the site of an ancient pagoda. The red-brick, twin-spired cathedral overlooks a grassy square with a statue of the Virgin Mary holding an orb.

Facing onto Paris Square is the **General Post Office**, built in the 1880s, a particularly distinguished building despite the veneer of junk that has been slapped onto it. The front façade has attractive cornices with French and Khmer motifs and the names of distinguished French men of letters and science. Inside, the high, vaulted ceiling and fans create a deliciously cool atmosphere in which to scribble a postcard. Note the old wall-map of Cochin-China, which has miraculously survived.

Reunification Hall

① *Nam Ky Khoi Nghia St, T08-822 3652, daily 0730-1100, 1300-1600; 15,000d, children 2000d, brochure 5000d. Tours every 10 mins; the guides are friendly but their English is not always very good. The hall is sometimes closed for state occasions.*

The residence of the French governor was built on this site in 1868 and later became Ngo Dinh Diem's **Presidential Palace**. In February 1962, a pair of planes took off to attack Viet Cong emplacements but turned back to bomb the Presidential Palace in a futile attempt to assassinate President Diem who had been living there since 1954. The president escaped with his family to the cellar but the palace had to be demolished and replaced with a new building, now renamed Reunification Hall, or the **Thong Nhat Conference Hall**. One of the two pilots, Nguyen Thanh Trung, is now a Vice President of Vietnam Airlines and still flies government officials around to keep his pilot's licence current.

② **Ho Chi Minh City centre**

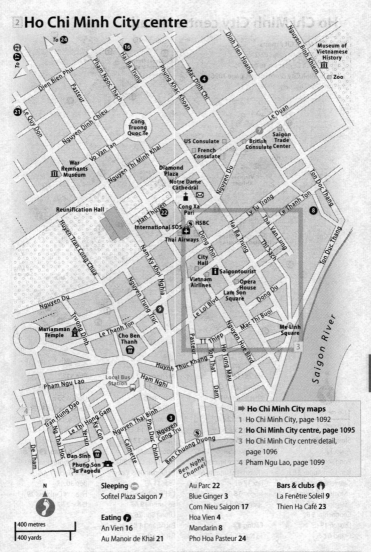

N

400 metres
400 yards

Sleeping 🛏
Sofitel Plaza Saigon **7**

Eating 🍴
An Vien **16**
Au Manoir de Khai **21**

Au Parc **22**
Blue Ginger **3**
Com Nieu Saigon **17**
Hoa Vien **4**
Mandarin **8**
Pho Hoa Pasteur **24**

Bars & clubs 🍸
La Fenêtre Soleil **9**
Thien Ha Café **23**

➡ **Ho Chi Minh City maps**
1 Ho Chi Minh City, page 1092
2 **Ho Chi Minh City centre, page 1095**
3 Ho Chi Minh City centre detail, page 1096
4 Pham Ngu Lao, page 1099

One of the most memorable photographs taken during the war was of a North Vietnamese Army (NVA) tank crashing through the gates of the Palace on 30 April 1975, symbolizing the end of South Vietnam and its government. A similar tank is now displayed in the forecourt. The President of South Vietnam, General Duong Van Minh, along with his

▣ Ho Chi Minh City centre detail

➡ Ho Chi Minh City maps
1 Ho Chi Minh City, page 1092
2 Ho Chi Minh City centre, page 1095
3 **Ho Chi Minh City centre detail, page 1096**
4 Pham Ngu Lao, page 1099

N
100 metres
100 yards

Sleeping 🛌
Asian 1 *B2*
Bong Sen 2 *B2*
Bong Sen Annex 3 *B3*
Caravelle, Restaurant
  Nineteen & Saigon
  Siagon Bar 4 *B2*
Continental 5 *B2*
Duxton 19 *C2*
Grand 6 *C3*

Ho Sen 14 *B3*
Huong Sen 7 *C2*
Khach San 69 8 *B3*
Majestic 10 *C3*
Mogambo 22 *A3*
Orchid 13 *A3*
Palace 15 *C2*
Park Hyatt Saigon 11 *B2*
Renaissance Riverside &
  Kabin Restaurant 16 *C3*
Rex 17 *B1*
Saigon 18 *B3*
Spring 20 *A2*

Eating 🍽
13 Ngo Duc Ke 1 *C3*

Al Fresco's 57 *B3*
Ashoka 4 *A3*
Augustin 5 *B2*
Bi Bi 6 *A3*
Cay Xoai 12 *A2*
Chao Thai 13 *A3*
Hoang Yen 17 *C3*
Huong Lai 18 *A1*
Kem Bach Dang 20 *C1*
La Camargue & Vasco
  Bar 11 *A3*
La Fourchette 21 *C3*
Le Jardin 19 *A2*
Luong Son 26 *A2*
Pacharan 14 *B3*
Pacific 50 *A3*

Pho 51 *C3*
Pomodoro 58 *B3*
Qucina 55 *B2*
Saigon India 37 *C2*
Temple Club 42 *C1*
Underground 44 *C3*

Bars & clubs 🍸
Apocalypse Now 3 *B3*
Blue Gecko 7 *A2*
Bop 30 *A3*
Heart of Darkness 29 *A3*
Q Bar 2 *B2*

entire cabinet, was arrested in the palace shortly afterwards but the hall has been preserved as it was found in 1975. In the Vice President's Guest Room is a lacquered painting of the Temple of Literature in Hanoi, while the Presenting of Credentials Room contains a fine 40-piece lacquer work showing diplomats presenting their credentials during the Le Dynasty (15th century). In the basement, there are operations rooms, military maps, radios and other official paraphernalia.

War Remnants Museum

ⓘ 28 Vo Van Tan St, District 3, T08-930 6325. Mon-Fri and public holidays 0730-1100, 1330-1715; 10,000d.

All the horrors of the Vietnam War from the Vietnamese perspective are piled from floor to ceiling in this museum. The courtyard is stacked with tanks, bombs, planes and helicopters, while the museum, arranged in rooms around the courtyard, record man's inhumanity to man, with displays of deformed foetuses alongside photographs of atrocities and of military action. The exhibits cover the Son My (My Lai) massacre on 16 March 1968, the effects of napalm and phosphorous, and the after-effects of Agent Orange defoliation. Many of the pictures are horrific.

One of the most interesting rooms is dedicated to war photographers and their pictures. It is a requiem to those who died pursuing their craft and, unusually, depicts the military struggle from both sides. The war, as captured through the lens, is an Heironymous Bosch-like hell of mangled metal, suffocating mud and injured limbs. The wall-to-wall images include shots from Robert Capa's last roll of film (before the famous photographer stood on a land mine on 25 May 1954 and died); *Life* magazine's first colour coverage of the conflict, and quotes from those that perished, including a memorable one from Georgette Louise Meyer, aka Dickey Chapelle, who described the thrill of being on the "bayonet border" of the world. Understandably, there is no record of North Vietnamese atrocities carried out on US and South Vietnamese troops.

Xa Loi Pagoda

ⓘ 89 Ba Huyen Thanh Quan St, daily 0630-1100, 1430-1700.

The Xa Loi Pagoda is not far from the War Remnants Museum and is surrounded by foodstalls. Built in 1956, the pagoda contains a multi-storeyed tower, which is particularly revered, as it houses a relic of the Buddha. The main sanctuary contains a large, bronze-gilded Buddha in an attitude of meditation. Around the walls are a series of silk paintings depicting the previous lives of the Buddha (with an explanation of each life to the right of the entrance into the sanctuary). The pagoda is historically, rather than artistically, important as it became a focus of dissent against the Diem regime in 1963 when several monks committed suicide through self-immolation.

Le Duan Street

Le Duan Street was the former corridor of power with Ngo Dinh Diem's Palace at one end, the zoo at the other and the former embassies of the three major powers, France, the US and the UK, in between. Nearest the Reunification Hall is the compound of the **French Consulate**. A block away is the **former US Embassy**. After diplomatic ties were resumed in 1995, the Americans lost little time in demolishing the 1960s embassy, which held so many bad memories. The US Consulate General now stands on this site. A **memorial** outside, on the corner of Mac Dinh Chi Street, records the attack by Viet Cong special forces during the Tet Offensive of 1968 and the final victory in 1975. On the other side of the road, a little further northeast at 25 Le Duan, is the **former British Embassy**, erected in the late 1950s, now the British Consulate General and British Council.

Museum of Vietnamese History

ⓘ *2 Nguyen Binh Khiem St, T08-8298146, daily 0800-1100, 1330-1630; 5000d. No photography. Water puppet shows held daily at 0900, 1000, 1400, 1500 and 1600, 15 mins; US$2.*

The history museum (Bao Tang Lich Su Viet Nam) occupies an elegant 1928 building with a pagoda-based design. The collection spans a wide range of artefacts from the prehistoric (300,000 years ago) and the Dong Son periods (3500 BC to AD 100), right through to the birth of the Vietnamese Communist Party in 1930. Particularly impressive are the Cham sculptures, of which the standing bronze Buddha, showing Indian stylistic influence, is probably the finest. There is also a delicately carved Devi (goddess) dating from the 10th century, as well as the head of Siva (Hindu destroyer and creator) and Ganesh (elephant-headed son of Siva and Parvati) both dating from the eighth to the ninth century.

Representative pieces from the Chen-la, Funan, Khmer, Oc-eo and Han Chinese periods are also on display, along with items from the various Vietnamese dynasties and some ethnic minority artefacts. Other highlights include the wooden stakes planted in the Bach Dang riverbed to repel the war ships of the Mongol Yuan in the 13th century; a beautiful Phoenix head from the Tran Dynasty (13th to 14th century) and a Hgor (big drum) of the Jorai people, made from the skin of two elephants.

Ben Thanh Market (Cho Ben Thanh)

A large, covered central market, Ben Thanh Market faces a statue of Tran Nguyen Han at a large and chaotic roundabout, known as the Ben Thanh gyratory system. Ben Thanh is well stocked with clothes, household goods, a good choice of souvenirs, lacquerware, embroidery and so on, as well as some terrific lines in food, including cold meats, fresh and dried fruits. It is not cheap (most local people window-shop here and purchase elsewhere) but the quality is high and the selection probably without equal. Outside the north gate (*cua Bac*) on Le Thanh Ton Street are some particularly tempting displays of fresh fruit (the oranges and apples are imported) and beautiful cut flowers. The **Ben Thanh Night Market** has flourished since 2003; starting at dusk and continuing until after midnight, it offers clothes and cheap jewellery and an abundance of food stalls.

Phung Son Tu Pagoda and Dan Sinh market

On Nguyen Cong Tru Street is **Phung Son Tu Pagoda**, a small temple built just after the Second World War by Fukien Chinese; its most notable features are the wonderful painted entrance doors with their fearsome armed warriors. Incense spirals hang in the open well of the pagoda, which is dedicated to Ong Bon, the Guardian of Happiness and Virtue.

Close to the pagoda, on the same street, is the **War Surplus Market (Dan Sinh)**. Merchandise on sale includes dog tags and military clothing and equipment (not all of it authentic). The market is popular with Western visitors looking for mementoes of their visit, so bargain particularly hard.

Pham Ngu Lao

Most backpackers arriving overland in Ho Chi Minh City are dropped off in this bustling district, a 10 to 15-minute walk from downtown. There are countless hotels, guesthouses and rooms to rent and the area is peppered with restaurants, cafés, bars, email services, tour agencies and money changers, all fiercely competitive.

Cholon (Chinatown)

Cholon (*Cho lon* or 'big market' or Chinatown), which encompasses District 5 to the southwest of the city centre, is inhabited predominantly by Vietnamese of Chinese origin. Since 1975, the authorities have alienated many Chinese, causing hundreds of thousands to leave the country. (Between 1977 and 1982, 709,570 refugees were recorded by the UNHCR as having fled Vietnam.) In making their escape many have died, either through drowning – as their perilously small and overladen craft foundered – or at the hands of pirates in the South China Sea. By the late 1980s, the flow of boat people was being driven by economic rather than by political forces: there was little chance of making good in a country as poor, and in an economy as moribund, as that of Vietnam. Even with this exodus of Chinese out of the country, there is still a large population of Chinese Vietnamese living in Cholon, an area which, to the casual visitor, appears to be the most populated, noisiest and, in general, the most vigorous part of Ho Chi Minh City, if not of Vietnam. It is here that entrepreneurial talent and private funds are concentrated; both resources that the government are keen to mobilize in their attempts to reinvigorate the economy.

Cholon is worth visiting not only for the bustle and activity, but also because the temples and assembly halls found here are the finest in Ho Chi Minh City. As with any town in Southeast Asia boasting a sizeable Chinese population, the early settlers established meeting rooms which offered social, cultural and spiritual support to members of a dialect group. These assembly halls (*hoi quan*) are most common in Hoi An and Cholon. Temples within the buildings attract Vietnamese as well as Chinese worshippers and, today, the halls serve little of their former purpose.

Assembly halls and temples

Nghia An Assembly Hall ① *678 Nguyen Trai St*, has a magnificent, carved, gold-painted wooden boat hanging over the entrance. To the left, on entering the temple, is a larger

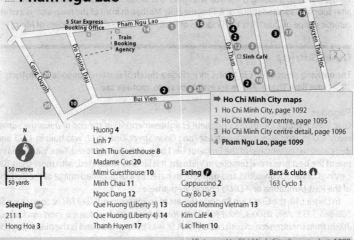

④ **Pham Ngu Lao**

➡ **Ho Chi Minh City maps**
1 Ho Chi Minh City, page 1092
2 Ho Chi Minh City centre, page 1095
3 Ho Chi Minh City centre detail, page 1096
4 **Pham Ngu Lao, page 1099**

N

50 metres
50 yards

Sleeping 🛏
211 **1**
Hong Hoa **3**
Huong **4**
Linh **7**
Linh Thu Guesthouse **8**
Madame Cuc **20**
Mimi Guesthouse **10**
Minh Chau **11**
Ngoc Dang **12**
Que Huong (Liberty 3) **13**
Que Huong (Liberty 4) **14**
Thanh Huyen **17**

Eating 🍴
Cappuccino **2**
Cay Bo De **3**
Good Morning Vietnam **13**
Kim Café **4**
Lac Thien **10**

Bars & clubs 🍸
163 Cyclo **1**

than life representation of Quan Cong's horse and groom. At the main altar are three figures in glass cases: the central red-faced figure with a green cloak is Quan Cong himself; to the left and right are his trusty companions, General Chau Xuong (very fierce) and the mandarin Quan Binh respectively. On leaving the temple, note the fine gold figures of guardians on the inside of the door panels.

Thien Hau Temple ① *710 and 802 Nguyen Trai St,* is one of the largest in the city. Constructed in the early 19th century, it is Chinese in inspiration and is dedicated to the worship of both the Buddha and the Goddess Thien Hau (goddess of the sea and the protector of sailors). Thien Hau was born in China and, as a girl, saved her father from drowning but not her brother. Thien Hau's festival is marked here on the 23rd day of the third lunar month. Inside, the principal altar supports the gilded form of Thien Hau, with a boat to one side. Silk paintings depicting religious scenes decorate the walls. By far the most interesting part of the pagoda is the roof, which can be best seen from the small open courtyard. It is one of the finest and most richly ornamented in Vietnam, with a high-relief frieze depicting episodes from the Legends of the Three Kingdoms. In the post-1975 era, many would-be refugees prayed here for safe deliverance before casting themselves adrift on the South China Sea. A number of those who survived the perilous voyage sent offerings to the merciful goddess and the temple has been well maintained since. Look up on leaving to see, over the front door, a picture of a boiling sea peppered with sinking boats. A benign Thien An looks down mercifully from a cloud.

Dinh Minh Huong Gia Thanh (Ming Dynasty Assembly Hall) ① *380 Tran Hung Dao St,* was built by the Cantonese community, which arrived in Ho Chi Minh City via Hoi An in the 18th century. The assembly hall was built in 1789 to the dedication and worship of the Ming Dynasty, although the building today dates largely from an extensive renovation carried out in 1960s. In the main hall there are three altars, which following imperial tradition: the central altar is dedicated to the royal family (Ming Dynasty in this case); the right-hand altar to two mandarin officers (military), and the left-hand altar to two mandarin officers (civil).

Quan Am Pagoda ① *12 Lao Tu St, just off Luong Nhu Hoc St,* is thought to be one of the oldest in the city. Its roof supports four sets of impressive mosaic-encrusted figures, while inside, the main building is fronted with gold and lacquer panels of guardian spirits. The altar supports a seated statue of A-Pho, the Holy Mother. In front of the main altar is a white ceramic statue of Quan Am, the Goddess of Purity and Motherhood (Goddess of Mercy).

Outer districts

The outlying areas of Ho Chi Minh City include a clutch of scattered pagodas in districts 3, 10, 11 and Binh Thanh. All are accessible by cyclo, moto or taxi.

Pagodas
Giac Vien Pagoda (Buddha's Complete Enlightenment) ① *at the end of a narrow, rather seedy 400-m-long alley running off Lac Long Quan Street, District 11,* was built in 1771 and dedicated to the worship of the Emperor Gia Long. Although restored, Giac Vien remains one of the best preserved temples in Vietnam. It is lavishly decorated, with more than 100 carvings of various divinities and spirits, dominated by a large gilded image of the Buddha of the Past (Amitabha or *A Di Da Phat* in Vietnamese).

In District 10, the **Giac Lam Pagoda** (Forest of Enlightenment) ① *118 Lac Long Quan St, T08-865 3933, daily 0500-1200, 1400-2100, through an arch and down a short track about 300 m from the intersection with Le Dai Hanh St,* was built in 1744 and is the oldest pagoda in Ho Chi Minh City. There is a sacred Bodhi tree in the temple courtyard and the pagoda is set among fruit trees and vegetable plots. The interior of Giac Lam feels, initially, like a rather cluttered private house. In one section, there are rows of funerary tablets with pictures of the deceased. The main altar is particularly impressive, with layers of Buddhas, dominated by the gilded form of the Buddha of the Past. Note the 49-Buddha oil lamp with little scraps of paper tucked in to it. On these scraps are the names of the mourned. Behind the main temple in the section with the funerary tablets is a bust of Ho Chi Minh. At the very back of the pagoda is a hall with murals showing scenes of torture from hell. Each sin is punished in a very specific and appropriate way. An unusual feature is the use of blue and white porcelain plates to decorate the roof and some of the small towers in the garden facing the pagoda. These towers are the burial places of former head monks.

Phuoc Hai Tu (Emperor of Jade Pagoda) ① *73 Mai Thi Luu St, off Dien Bien Phu St, daily 0700-1800* can be found, nestling behind low pink walls, just before the Thi Nghe Channel. The Emperor of Jade is the supreme god of the Taoists, although this temple, built in 1900, contains a wide range of other deities. These include the archangel Michael of the Buddhists, a Sakyamuni (historic) Buddha, statues of the two generals who tamed the Green Dragon (representing the east) and the White Dragon (representing the west) to the left and right of the first altar respectively and Quan Am. The Hall of Ten Hells in the left-hand sanctuary has reliefs depicting the 1000 tortures of hell.

Around Ho Chi Minh City

The Cu Chi Tunnels are the most popular day trip, followed closely by an excursion to the Mekong Delta, especially My Tho. ▶▶ *See Activities and tours, page 1110.*

Cu Chi Tunnels → *Colour map 6, B3.*
① *About 40 km northwest of Ho Chi Minh City, daily 0700-1700, 70,000d. Most visitors reach Cu Chi on a tour or charter a car and include a visit to Tay Ninh.*

Begun by the Viet Minh in 1948, these tunnels were later expanded by the Viet Cong and used for storage and refuge. Between 1960 and 1970, 200 km of tunnels were built, containing sleeping quarters, hospitals and schools. The original tunnels were only 80 cm high and the width of the tunnel entry at ground level was 22 cm by 30 cm. The tunnels are too narrow for most Westerners, but a short section of the 250 km of tunnels has been especially widened to allow tourists to share the experience.

Cu Chi was one of the most fervently Communist districts around Ho Chi Minh City and the tunnels were used as the base from which the VC mounted the operations of the Tet Offensive in 1968. When the Americans first discovered this underground network on their doorstep (Dong Du GI base was nearby) they would simply pump CS gas down the tunnel openings and then set explosives. They also pumped river water in and used German Shepherd dogs to smell out air holes, although the VC smothered the holes in garlic to deter the dogs. Around 40,000 VC were killed in the tunnels in 10 years but, later, realizing the tunnels might also yield valuable intelligence, the Americans sent volunteer 'tunnel rats' into the earth to capture prisoners.

Cu Chi district initially was a free-fire zone and was assaulted using the full battery of ecological warfare. Defoliants were sprayed and 20-tonne Rome Ploughs carved up the area in the search for tunnels. It was said that even a crow flying over Cu Chi district had to carry its own lunch. Later it was carpet bombed: 50,000 tonnes were dropped on the area in 10 years evidenced by the B-52 bomb craters.

Ho Chi Minh Trail

The Ho Chi Minh Trail was used by the North Vietnamese Army to ferry equipment from the North to the South via Laos. The road, or more accurately roads (there were between eight and 10 routes to reduce "choke points") were camouflaged in places, allowing the NVA to get supplies to their comrades in the South through the heaviest bombing by US planes. Even the USA's use of defoliants such as Agent Orange only marginally stemmed the flow. Neil Sheehan, in his book *A Bright Shining Lie*, estimates that at no time were more than one third of the supply trucks destroyed and, by marching through the most dangerous sections, the forces themselves suffered a loss rate of only 10-20%.

The Ho Chi Minh Trail was built and kept operational by 300,000 full-time workers and by another 200,000 part-time North Vietnamese peasants. Initially, supplies were carried along the trail on bicycles; later, as supplies of trucks from China and the Soviet Union became more plentiful, they were carried by motorized transport. By the end of the conflict the Trail comprised 15,360 km of all-weather and secondary roads. One Hero of the People's Army is said, during the course of the war, to have carried and pushed 55 tonnes of supplies a distance of 41,025 km – roughly the circumference of the world.

The Ho Chi Minh Trail represents perhaps the best example of how, through revolutionary fervour, ingenuity and weight of people (not of arms), the Viet Cong were able to vanquish the might of the US. But American pilots did exact a terrible toll through the years. Again, Sheehan writes: "Driving a truck year in, year out with 20-25% to perhaps 30% odds of mortality was not a military occupation conducive to retirement on pension."

The cemetery for those who died on the trail covers 16 ha and contains 10,306 named headstones; many more died unnamed and unrecovered.

At **Cu Chi 1** (Ben Dinh) ① *70,000d*, visitors are shown a somewhat antique but interesting film of the tunnels during the war, before being taken into the tunnels themselves and seeing some of the rooms and the booby traps the GIs encountered. You will also be invited to a firing range to try your hand with ancient AK47s at a buck a bang. **Cu Chi 2** (Ben Duoc), has a temple, built in 1993, devoted to the memory of the dead and visited by those whose relatives are still 'missing'. The sculpture behind the temple is of a massive tear cradled in the hands of a mother.

Cao Dai Great Temple → *Colour map 6, B3.*

① *Tay Ninh, 64 km beyond Cu Chi town (96 km northwest of Ho Chi Minh City). It can be visited on a day trip from the city and can easily be combined with a visit to the Cu Chi tunnels. Ceremonies 1 hr long, daily 0600, 1200, 1800 and 2400; visitors should not wander in and out during services but can watch from the balcony. At other times keep to the side aisles and do not enter the central portion of the nave. Photography is allowed. Shoes must be removed.*

The Cao Dai religion was founded on Phu Quoc Island (page 1118) in 1920, when civil servant Ngo Van Chieu communed with the spirit world and made contact with the Supreme Being. The idiosyncratic, twin-towered Cao Dai Great Temple, the 'cathedral' of the religion, was built from 1933 to 1955 and is European in inspiration but with distinct Oriental features. On the façade are figures of Cao Dai saints in high relief and, at the entrance to the cathedral, there is a painting depicting writer Victor Hugo flanked by the Vietnamese poet Nguyen Binh Khiem and the Chinese nationalist Sun Yat Sen.

The temple provokes strong reactions: Novelist Graham Greene in *The Quiet American* called it "The Walt Disney Fantasia of the East". Monsieur Ferry, an acquaintance of travel writer Norman Lewis, described the cathedral in even more outlandish terms, saying it "looked like a fantasy from the brain of Disney, and all the faiths of the Orient had been ransacked to create the pompous ritual...". Lewis himself was clearly unimpressed with the structure and the religion, writing in *A Dragon Apparent* that this "cathedral must be the most outrageously vulgar building ever to have been erected with serious intent".

After removing shoes and hats, women enter the cathedral through a door to the left, men to the right, and they then proceed down their respective aisles towards the altar, usually accompanied by a Cao Dai priest dressed in white with a black turban. During services they don red, blue and yellow robes signifying Confucianism, Taoism and Buddhism respectively. Two rows of pink pillars entwined with green, horned dragons line the nave, leading up to the main altar which supports a large globe on which is painted a single staring eye: the divine, all-seeing eye. Above the altar is the Cao Dai pantheon: at the top in the centre is Sakyamuni Buddha; next to him, on the left, is Lao Tzu, master of Taoism; left of Lao Tzu is Quan Am, Goddess of Mercy, sitting on a lotus blossom; on the other side of the Buddha statue is Confucius; right of the sage is the red-faced Chinese God of War, Quan Cong; below Sakyamuni Buddha is the poet and leader of the Chinese saints, Li Ti Pei; below him is Jesus, and, below Christ, is Jiang Zhia, master of Geniism.

◉ Ho Chi Minh City and around listings

For Sleeping and Eating price codes,
see inside the front cover.

● Sleeping

City centre *p1094, maps p1095 and p1096*
LL Caravelle, 19-23 Lam Son Square, T08-823 4999, www.caravellehotel.com. Central and one of HCMC's top hotels. Comfortable with well-trained and friendly staff. **Restaurant Nineteen** serves a fantastic buffet lunch and dinner with free flow of fine French wine included (see Eating), and **Saigon Saigon**, the rooftop bar, draws the crowds until the early hours of the morning (see Bars and clubs). Also has a suite of boutique shops and ATM.
LL-AL Majestic, 1 Dong Khoi St, T08-829 5517, www.majesticsaigon.com. Built in 1925, this riverside hotel has character and charm and has been tastefully restored and recently expanded. More expensive and large rooms have superb views over the river; from the new bar on the top floor there are magnificent views of the riverfront, especially at night.

L-AL Continental, 132-134, Dong Khoi St, T08-829 9201, www.continental-saigon.com. Built in 1880 and renovated in 1989, this is an integral part of the city's history (see page 1094). It has an air of faded colonial splendour and its large but dated rooms need upgrading. The hotel boasts a couple of restaurants, a business centre, fitness room and a pool. Probably in an attempt to stamp out the theft of souvenirs, you can purchase every item in the room.
L-AL Duxton, 63 Nguyen Hue Blvd, T08-822 2999, www.duxton.com. A very attractively appointed and well finished hotel, popular with Japanese visitors. It has 198 finely decorated rooms, a health club, pool and a restaurant.
L-AL Grand, 8 Dong Khoi St, T08-823 0163, www.grandhotel.vn. A 1930s building, extensively renovated but, happily, the stained glass and marble staircase have largely survived the process. A huge, modern featureless wing has been added. Good value hotel with a very reasonably priced

restaurant. **Saigontourist** is to upgrade this hotel to 5 stars in 2009.

L-AL Renaissance Riverside, 8-15 Ton Duc Thang St, T08-822 0033, www.marriott.com. Despite its 21 floors and 349 rooms and suites this is, in style and feel, almost a boutique hotel. Very well run, comfortable and popular with its customers. It also boasts Vietnam's highest atrium. It has several excellent restaurants, including **Kabin** Chinese restaurant, and an attractive pool.

L-AL Rex, 141 Nguyen Hue Blvd, T08-829 2185, www.rexhotelvietnam.com. An historically important hotel with unusual interior decor and an expansion underway. Superior rooms have small baths and are interior facing. Deluxe rooms are double the size but those on the main road are noisy. The **Mimosa Club** has a pool, rooftop tennis court, fitness centre and beauty salon. It has the famous rooftop terrace bar, popular with journalists and upmarket tour groups.

A Bong Sen, 117-123 Dong Khoi St, T08-829 1516, www.hotelbongsen.com. Operated by **Saigontourist**. Well-run and upgraded in a perfect location in the heart of the shopping district. Good value for the location but standard rooms are very small. Larger superior rooms are only slightly more expensive and have baths. Few rooms have views. There is a restaurant and the **Green Leaf** café.

A Bong Sen Hotel Annex, 61-63 Hai Ba Trung St, T08-823 5818, www.hotelbong sen.com. Sister hotel of the **Bong Sen**, this is a well-managed hotel with standard a/c rooms and a restaurant.

A Huong Sen, 66-70 Dong Khoi St, T08-829 1415, huongsen@hcm.vnn.vn. This central hotel is popular with tour groups and good value on this street. A rooftop bar on the 7th floor is a nice place for a beer.

A Palace, 56-66 Nguyen Hue Blvd, T08-829 2860, www.palacesaigon.com. **Saigon-tourist**-run hotel with some decent-sized rooms. It's very central with a restaurant and small rooftop pool.

A Saigon, 45-47 Dong Du St, T08-8299734, saigonhotel@hcm.vnn.vn. Opposite the

mosque in a good central location. Some rooms a bit dark and small, but it's popular and clean. Prices have risen which makes it not quite such good value.

A-D Asian, 146-150 Dong Khoi St, T08-829 6979, asianhotel@hcm.fpt.vn. Rooms with a/c and satellite TV are a little small. There's a restaurant and breakfast is included. The location is central.

A-D Ho Sen, 4B-4C Thi Sach St, T08-8232281, www.hosenhotel.com.vn. This bland looking hotel in a very central location is a good find. Rooms are surprisingly very quiet, fairly spacious and comfortable with TVs. Staff are friendly and helpful and will store luggage.

A-D Spring, 44-46 Le Thanh Ton St, T08-829 7362, springhotel@hcm.vnn.vn. Central, comfortable with charming and helpful staff. Book well in advance if you want to stay in this well-run family hotel that is excellent value; breakfast included. Recommended.

C-D Mogambo, 20Bis Thi Sach St, T08-825 1311, mogambo@saigonnet.vn. A/c, satellite TV, a few good and fairly priced rooms above this popular American-run diner.

C-D Orchid, 29A Thai Van Lung St, T08-823 1809. In a good, central spot, surrounded by restaurants and bars, worth taking a look at. Rooms have a/c and satellite TV.

D-F Khach San 69, 69 Hai Ba Trung St, T08-829 1513, 69hotel@saigonnet.vn. Central location with clean a/c rooms that back onto HCMC's Indian mosque.

Pham Ngu Lao p1098, map p1099
Shared rooms can be had for as little as US$4-5 per night and dormitory rooms for less but facilities and comfort levels at the bottom end are very basic.

A Que Huong (Liberty 4), 265 Pham Ngu Lao St, T08-836 5822, www.libertyhotel saigon.com. Formerly **Hoang Vu**, a perfectly comfortable hotel. It has had to moderate its prices which means it is now possibly fair value but priced way too high for this area. Breakfast is included.

A Que Huong (Liberty 3), 187 Pham Ngu Lao St, T08-836 9522, www.libertyhotel

saigon.com. Less popular with travellers than previously as there is now more choice; cheapest rooms are on the upper floors, rather noisy.

C-D Huong, 40/19 Bui Vien St, T08-836 9158. Rooms with a/c, hot water, private bathrooms.

C-F 211, 211-213 Pham Ngu Lao St, T08-836 7353, hotelduy@hotmail.com. Some a/c, clean, rooftop terrace and rooms in 3 price categories.

C-G Ngoc Dang, 254 De Tham St, T08-837 1896, www.ngocdanghotel.com. Clean, friendly and pleasant; some a/c and fan rooms.

D-F Hong Hoa, 185/28 Pham Ngu Lao St, T08-836 1915, www.honghoavn.com. A well-run family hotel with 9 rooms, all a/c, hot water and private bathroom. Downstairs has free email terminals and a supermarket.

D-F Linh Thu Guesthouse, 72 Bui Vien St, T08-836 8421, linhthu72@saigonnet.vn. Fan rooms with bathroom and some more expensive a/c rooms too.

D-F Thanh Huyen, 175/1 Pham Ngu Lao St, T08-8370 760. Above a small eatery and off the main drag, 3 clean and quiet rooms (1 a/c, 2 fan).

D-G Linh, 40/10 Bui Vien St, T/F8-836 9641, linh.hb@hcm.vnn.vn. Well-priced, clean, friendly, family-run hotel with a/c and hot water. Attracts some long-stay guests.

D-G Hotel Madam Cuc, 64 Bui Vien St, T08-836 5073, 127 Cong Quynh St, T08-836 8761, and 184 Cong Quynh St, T08-8361679, www.madamcuchotels.com. The reception staff at No 64 could be a lot friendlier. Rooms are quite small but the US$20 room is the bargain of the place.

D-G Mimi Guesthouse, 40/5 Bui Vien St, T08-836 9645, mimihotel405@yahoo.fr. 6 rooms with private bathroom, a/c, fan rooms and hot water. Motorbikes, bicycles and the internet.

D-G Minh Chau, 75 Bui Vien St, T08-836 7588. Price includes breakfast, some a/c, hot water and private bathrooms. Spotlessly clean and run by 2 sisters. It has been recommended by lone women travellers.

❶ Eating

HCMC has a rich culinary tradition and, as home to people from most of the world's imagined corners, its cooking is diverse. Do not overlook street-side stalls, staples consist of pho (noodle soup), bánh xeo (savoury pancakes), cha giò (spring rolls) and banh mi pate (baguettes stuffed with pâté and salad) all usually fresh and very cheap.

City centre p1094, maps p1095 and p1096

¶¶¶ **Au Manoir de Khai**, 251 Dien Bien Phu St, District 3, T08-930 3394, daily 1100-2200. Au Manoir is Khai's (of Khaisilk fame) French restaurant. As one would expect, it scores well in the design and style departments. The villa is nicely restored and the garden is beautiful. Food is lavishly presented.

¶¶¶ **An Vien**, 178A Hai Ba Trung St, T08-824 3877, daily 1000-2300. Excellent and intimate restaurant that serves the most fragrant rice in Vietnam. Attentive service and rich decor. The banh xeo and crispy fried squid are recommended.

¶¶¶ **Bi Bi**, 8A/8D2 Thai Van Lung St, T08-829 5783, Mon-Sat 1000-2300, Sun 1700-2300. Ideal for long lunches. A relaxed, brightly decorated and informal restaurant, popular with diplomats and bankers, serving excellent French food. Most highly recommended is the superb Chateaubriand (for 2) and the tiger shrimp with parsley and cognac. The set-menu lunch of 3 courses plus coffee is good value.

¶¶¶ **Kabin**, Renaissance Riverside Hotel, T08-8220033. One of the city's best Chinese restaurants; it sometimes features visiting chefs from China.

¶¶¶ **La Fourchette**, 9 Ngo Duc Ke St, T08-829 8143, daily 1200-1430, 1830-2230. Truly excellent and authentic French bistro offering a warm welcome, well-prepared dishes and generous portions of tender local steak. Booking advised. Recommended.

¶¶¶ **Mandarin**, 11A Ngo Van Nam St, T08-822 9783, daily 1130-1400, 1730-2300. One of the finest restaurants in HCMC serving up a culinary mix of exquisite flavours from across the country amid elegant decor including stunning, richly coloured silk tablecloths. The food is delicious but it's not very Vietnamese and the service is a little over the top.

Qucina, 7 Lam Son Sq, T08-824 6325, Mon-Sat 1800-2300. Smart and stylish Italian restaurant in the basement of the Opera House. The sophisticated menu includes grilled tuna in black butter and rolled chocolate cake with vanilla cream – enough to satisfy any gourmet.

La Camargue, 16 Cao Ba Quat St, corner of Thi Sach St, T08-824 3148, daily 1800-2300. One of HCMC's longest-standing restaurants and bars, and remains one of the most successful and popular places in town. Large French villa with a lovely upstairs open-air terrace restaurant. Consistently excellent food from an international menu with a strong French bias. Downstairs is a relaxing garden area and the ever popular **Vasco** nightclub (see Bars and clubs).

Pacharan, 97 Hai Ba Trung St, T08-825 6024, daily 1100-late. A hit from the beginning, this Spanish restaurant is nearly full every night with happy and satisfied customers. The open-air rooftop bar that overlooks the Opera House is a winner when there's a cool breeze blowing through the terrace. Fans of Spanish fare will love the (expensive) Iberian cured ham from rare, semi-wild, acorn-fed black-footed pigs as well as staples such as anchovies, olives, mushrooms and prawns; all the tapas are beautifully presented.

Restaurant Nineteen, Caravelle Hotel, Lam Son Sq, T08-823 4999, daily 1130-1430, 1745-2200. Japanese sushi, Chinese dim sum, seafood, cheeses and puddings galore. The food is stacked up so luxuriously and abundantly, it is like a gastro-cinematic experience. Weekends are especially extravagant with tender roast beef. The free wine makes it tremendous value for money.

Temple Club, 29 Ton That Thiep St, T08-829 9244, daily 1100-1400, 1830-2230. Beautifully furnished club and restaurant

open to non-members. French-colonial style and tasty Vietnamese dishes. Excellent value. The restaurant is popular so it's wise to book.

Augustin, 10 Nguyen Thiep St, T08-829 2941, Mon-Sat 1100-1400, 1800-2230. Fairly priced and some of the best, unstuffy French cooking in HCMC; tables pretty closely packed, congenial atmosphere. Excellent onion soup, baked clams and rack of lamb.

Blue Ginger (Saigon Times Club), 37 Nam Ky Khoi Nghia St, T08-829 8676, daily 0700-1430, 1700-2200. A gorgeous restaurant that offers a feast of Vietnamese food for diners with more than 100 dishes on the menu. Dine indoors in the cellar-like restaurant or outdoors in a small courtyard. Charming staff offer courteous and discrete service.

Cay Xoai (Mango), Thi Sach St, open all day. Offers a wide range of fish and crustacea. It is rightly famous for its delicious crab in tamarind sauce. All very tasty and it remains very good value for money.

Hoa Vien, 28 bis Mac Dinh Chi St, T08-829 0585, daily 0900-2400. A vast Czech bierkeller boasting Ho Chi Minh City's first micro-brewery. Freshly brewed dark and light beer available by the litre or in smaller measures. Grilled mackerel, pork and sausages are very useful for soaking up the alcohol.

Le Jardin, 31 Thai Van Lung St, T08-825 8465, daily 1100-1400, 1700-2130. Excellent French café, part of the **French Cultural Institute**. Eat inside or in the shady garden, good food, fairly priced.

Pomodoro, 79 Hai Ba Trung St, T08-823 8957, daily 1000-1400, 1830-2200. This is an excellent Italian restaurant. Authentic dishes, well prepared. Good service.

Saigon India, first floor, 73 Mac Thi Buoi St, T08-824 5671, daily 1115-1430, 1730-2230. Proving to be a very popular Indian restaurant it has a wide range of dishes from the north and south with tandoori dishes and plenty of vegetarian options. Delicious garlic naan bread.

Underground, 69 Dong Khoi St, T08-829 9079, daily 1000-24000. Instantly recognizable by its London Underground symbol, this bar in its stygian gloom is an unlikely place to find some of HCMC's best food. The menu spans the full Mediterranean-Mexico spectrum and is superb. Portions are gigantic and prices are reasonable. Lunchtime specials are excellent value. There's often a shortage of tables. This is a popular venue for watching televised sporting events, particularly rugby.

†† -† Al Fresco's, 27 Dong Du St, T08-822 7317, daily 0830-1400, 1830-2300. A huge success from its first day. Australian run. Specializes in ribs, steak, pizzas, hamburgers and Mexican dishes which are all excellent and highly popular. Book or be prepared to wait. Delivery available.

†† -† Ashoka, 17A/10 Le Thanh Ton St, T08-823 1372, daily 1100-1400, 1700-2230. Delicious food from an extensive menu. The set lunch lists 11 options with a further, 19 curry dishes. Highlights are the mutton shami kebab, prawn vindaloo and kadhai fish – barbecued chunks of fresh fish cooked in kadhai (a traditional Indian-style wok with Peshwari ground spices and sautéd with onion and tomatoes). Those with a sweet tooth should try the bizarre Coke with ice cream for pudding.

†† -† Chao Thai, 16 Thai Van Lung St, T08-824 1457, daily 1100-1400, 1730-2230. Considered the best Thai restaurant in town. Attractive setting and attentive service.

†† -† Huong Lai, 38 Ly Tu Trong St, T08-822 6814, daily 1200-1400, 1800-2115. An interesting little place, behind the City Hall, operated rather successfully by former street children. Try sautéed shrimp with coconut sauce. The set lunch menu of 6 dishes is good value. The young staff are eager to please.

† 13 Ngo Duc Ke, 13 Ngo Duc Ke St, T08-823 9314, daily 0600-2230. Fresh, well cooked, honest Vietnamese fare. Chicken in lemon grass (no skin, no bone) is a great favourite and bo luc lac melts in the mouth. Popular with locals, expats and travellers.

† Au Parc, 23 Han Thuyen St, T08-829 2772, daily 0700-2100. Facing on to the park in front of the old Presidential Palace, this attractive café serves snacks and light meals including sandwiches, salads, juices and drinks. Also does a good Sun brunch 1100-1530. Delivery available.

† Com Nieu Saigon, 6C Tu Xuong St, District 3, T08-9326388, daily 1000-2200. Best known for the theatrics which accompany the serving of the speciality baked rice: one waiter smashes the earthenware pot before tossing the contents across the room to his nimble-fingered colleague standing by your table. Deserves attention for its excellent food and selection of soups.

† Hoang Yen, 5-7 Ngo Duc Ke St, T08-823 1101, daily 1000-2200. Plain setting and decor but absolutely fabulous Vietnamese dishes, as the throngs of local lunchtime customers testify. Soups and chicken dishes are ravishing.

† Kem Bach Dang, 26-28 Le Loi Blvd. On opposite corners of Pasteur St. A very popular café serving fruit juice, shakes and ice cream. Try the coconut ice cream (kem dua) served in a coconut.

† Luong Son (aka Bo Tuong Xeo), 31 Ly Tu Trong St, T08-825 1330, daily 0900-2200. Noisy, smoky, chaotic and usually packed, this large canteen specializes in bo tung xeo (sliced beef barbecued at the table served with mustard sauce). The beef, barbecued squid and other delicacies are truly superb. Also the place to sample unusual dishes such as scorpion, porcupine, fried cricket and cockerel's testicles. Recommended.

† Pacific, 15A Le Thanh Ton St. Central and excellent bia hoi which is packed with locals and visitors every night. The beer is served in a pint glass as soon as you arrive and is ridiculously cheap. Also a decent range of simple dishes: venison, beef, squid and chips, barbecued goat and hot pot with snakehead fish. Amiable and welcoming waiters.

† Pho, 37 Dong Khoi St, T08-829 6415, daily 0700-2400. This is a new Japanese-run pho shop. A bowl of pho is cheap but drinks are (by comparison) a bit expensive. Attractively and eccentrically furnished with heavy wooden tables and chairs and an interesting collection of pictures and ornaments.

† Pho Hoa Pasteur, 260C Pasteur St, daily 0600-2400. Probably the best known pho restaurants and packed with customers. The *pho*, which is good, and costs more than average comes in 10 options. Chinese bread and wedding cake (*banh xu xe*) provide the only alternative in this specialist restaurant.

Foodstalls

Just north of the centre on the south side of Tan Dinh market **Anh Thu**, 49 Dinh Cong Trang St (and numerous other stalls nearby) serve excellent *cha gio, banh xeo, bi cuon* and other Vietnamese street food.

Also head north of the market to the foodstalls on Hia Ba Trung St. Everyone has their favourite but nos **362-376** and no **381** (Hong Phat) are particularly good. All charge just over US$2 for steamed chicken and rice (*com gà hap*) with soup.

Pham Ngu Lao *p1098, map p1099*
Pham Ngu Lao, the backpacker area, is chock-a-block with low-cost restaurants many of which are just as good as the more expensive places elsewhere. All restaurants here are geared to the habits and tastes of Westerners.

♥♥♥ **Good Morning Vietnam**, 197 De Tham St, T08-837 1894, daily 0900-2400. Italian owned and serving authentic Italian flavours. Good but not cheap. The pizzas are delicious and salads are good.

♥ **Cappuccino**, 258 and 222 De Tham St, T08-837 1467, daily 0800-2300. A good range of well-prepared Italian food at sensible prices. Very good lasagne and zabaglione. Also at 86 Bui Vien St, T08-8989706.

♥ **Cay Bo De** (Original Bodhi Tree), 175/4 Pham Ngu Lao St, T08-837 1910, daily 0800-2200. HCMC's most popular vegetarian eatery. Excellent food at amazing prices. Mexican pancake, vegetable curry, rice in coconut and braised mushrooms are classics.

♥ **Kim Café**, 268 De Tham St, T08-836 8122, open all day. Wide range of food, popular with travellers and expats. The breakfast must rate among the best value in the country.

♥ **Lac Thien**, 28/25 Bui Vien St, T08-837 1621, daily 0800-2300. Vietnamese food. Outpost of the well-known Lac Thien in Hué and run by the same family. *Banh xeo* (savoury pancake) is a major feature on the menu.

⊙ Bars and clubs

Some of these bars sometimes succeed in staying open until 0200 or 0300 but at other times the police shut them down at 2400. Those in the Pham Ngu Lao area tend to be busy later at night and tend to stay open longer than those in the centre.

Ho Chi Minh City *p1091, maps p1092, p1095, p1096 and p1099*
163 Cyclo Bar, 163 Pham Ngu Lao St, T08-920 1567, daily 0700-2400. Clean, civilized and a welcome addition to this neighbourhood. There's an open bar downstairs; upstairs has a/c and live music from 2000 nightly. Inexpensive drinks and light meals.
Apocalypse Now, 2C Thi Sach St, free admission for Westerners. This legendary venue remains one of the most popular and successful bars and clubs in HCMC. Draws a very wide cross section of punters of all ages and nationalities. Quite a large outside area at the back where conversation is possible.
Blue Gecko 31 Ly Tu Trong St, T08-824 3483. This bar has been adopted by HCMC's Australian community so expect cold beer and Australian flags above the pool table.
Bop, 8a1/d1 Thai Van Lung, T08-825 1901, daily 1630-2400. HCMC's first jazz club. Top cocktails and good live tunes daily.
Heart of Darkness, 17B Le Thanh Ton St, T08-823 1080, daily 1700-2400 (often until later), ladies get free gin from 1900-2100. Off-shoot of the famous Phnom Penh bar. Khmer in style with Cambodian-style decor.
La Fenêtre Soleil, 2nd floor, 135 Le Thanh Ton St (entrance at 125 Nam Ky Khoi Nghia), T08-822 5209, Mon-Sat café 0900-1900 bar 1900-2400. Don't be put off by the slightly

grimy side entrance; climb up into the boho-Indochine world of this gorgeous café/bar, artfully cluttered with antiques, lamps, comfy sofas and home-made cakes, muffins, smoothies and other delights. The high-energy drinks of mint, passion fruit, and ginger juice are lovely. Highly recommended.

Q Bar, 7 Lam Son Square, T08-823 3479, daily 1800-late. Haunt of a wide cross-section of HCMC society: the sophisticated, intelligent, witty, rich, handsome, cute, curvaceous, camp, glittering and famous are all to be found here. Striking decor and design, with Caravaggio-esque murals.

Rex Hotel Bar, 14 Nguyen Hue Blvd. The open-air rooftop bar that is the height of bad taste, with giant animal statues, strange fish tanks, song birds and topiary. Come for the good views, cooling breeze, snacks – and for a link with history (page 1094).

Saigon Saigon, 10th floor, **Caravelle Hotel**, 19 Lam Son Sq, T08-824 3999. Breezy and cool, with large comfortable chairs and superb views by day and night. Excellent cocktails but not cheap.

Underground, 69 Dong Khoi St, T08-829 9079. Screens football, rugby, F1 racing and other sporting events. As the evening wears on, tables are packed away and the space fills with drinkers and dancers.

Vasco, La Camargue restaurant (see Eating), 16 Cao Ba Quat St, T08-824 3148. A great spot any evening but only gets busy after 2200 Fri and Sat when a live band plays. Very popular with younger expats.

Evening cafés
Vietnamese tend to prefer non-alcoholic drinks. Young romantic couples sit in virtual darkness listening to Vietnamese love songs, all too often played at a deafening volume, while sipping coffee. These cafés are an agreeable way of relaxing after dinner in a more typically Vietnamese setting. **Thien Ha Café** at 25A Tu Xuong, District 3, which features piano and violin duets, is a prime and popular example.

🎭 Entertainment

Ho Chi Minh City p1091, maps p1092, p1095, p1096 and p1099

Cinema
French Cultural Institute (Idecaf), 31 Thai Van Lung, T08-829 5451. Shows French films.
Diamond Plaza, 34 Le Duan St. The cinema on the 13th floor of this shopping centre screens English-language films.

🛍 Shopping

Ho Chi Minh City p1091, maps p1092, p1095, p1096 and p1099

Antiques
Most antique shops are on Dong Khoi, Mac Thi Buoi and Ngo Duc Ke streets but for less touristy stuff visitors would be advised to browse the shops along Le Cong Trieu St. It runs between Nam Ky Khoi Nghia and Pho Duc Chinh streets just south of Ben Thanh market. Among the bric-à-brac are some interesting items of furniture, statuary and ceramics. Bargaining essential.
Lac Long, 143 Le Thanh Ton St, T08-829 3373, daily 0800-1900. Mr Long sometimes has some unusual items for sale even if there is nothing of interest on display.

Art, crafts and home accessories
Ancient/Apricot, 50-52 Mac Thi Buoi St, T08-822 7962, www.apricot-artvietnam.com. Specializes in famous artists; high prices.
Dogma, 29A Dong Khoi St, www.dogma. vietnam.com. Sells propaganda posters, funky T-shirts and postcards.
Gaya, 39 Ton That Thiep, T08-914 3769, www.gayavietnam.com. A 3-storey shop with heavenly items. The 1st floor has embroidered tablecloths, ceramics and screens. The 2nd floor has silk designer clothes by Romyda Keth.
Hanoi Gallery, 43 Le Loi Blvd, T098-203 8803 (mob). Like its counterpart in Hanoi it sells original or reproduction propaganda posters.
Lotus Gallery, 55 Dong Khoi St, T08-829 2695. Another expensive gallery at the top

end of the market. Many are members of the Vietnam Fine Arts Association and many have exhibited around the world.
Mosaique, 98 Mac Thi Buoi, T08-823 4634, daily 0900-2100. Like its sister store in Hanoi, this boutique is a home accessories parlour.
Nguyen Freres, 2 Dong Khoi St, T08-823 9459, www.nguyenfreres.com. An absolute Aladdin's cave. Don't miss this – even if it's just to potter among the collectable items.
Saigon Kitsch, Ton That Thiep St, daily 0900-2000, www.saigonkitsch.com. Communist kitsch ranging from big propaganda art posters to place mats and mugs.

Clothing and silk
Many female visitors head straight for Dong Khoi St for Vietnamese silk and traditional dresses (*ao dai*). Also check out Ben Thanh market in Binh Thanh District.
Khai Silk, 107 Dong Khoi, T08-829 1146. Part of Mr Khai's growing empire. Beautifully made, quality silks in a range of products.
Song, 76D Le Thanh Ton, T08-824 6986, daily 0900-2000, www.valeriegregorim ckenzie.com. A beautiful clothes emporium. Lovely, flowing summer dresses from designer Valerie Gregori McKenzie plus other stylish and unique pieces and accessories.

Department stores
Tax Department Store (Russian market), corner of Le Loi and Nguyen Hue streets. The widest range of shopping under one roof in HCMC: CDs, DVDs (all pirate, of course) and a good selection of footwear, coats and shirts.

▲▲ Activities and tours

Ho Chi Minh City *p1091, maps p1092, p1095, p1096 and p1099*
Tour operators
Asian Trails, 5th floor, 21 Nguyen Trung Ngan St, District 1, T08-910 2871, www.asian trails.info. Southeast Asia specialist.

Buffalo Tours, Suite 502, Jardine House, 58 Dong Khoi St, District 1, T08-827 9170 (1-800-1583), www.buffalotours.com. Organizes general tours, a Cu Chi cycling trip with good bikes, overland trips to Dalat and trips to Can Tho.
Cuu Long Tourist, 97A Nguyen Cu Trinh St, District 1, T08-920 0339, cuulongtourist@ hcm.vnn.vn. Branch of Vinh Long provincial tourist authority. Tours to the Mekong Delta.
Delta Adventure Tours, 267 De Tham St, T08-920 2112, www.deltaadventure tours.com. Slow and express bus and boat tours through the Mekong Delta to Phnom Penh, Cambodia at very good prices.
Exotissimo, Saigon Finance Center, 9 Dinh Tien Hoang St, T08-825 1723, www.exotissimo. com. An efficient agency that can handle all the travel needs of visitors to Vietnam.
Handspan Adventure Travel, F7, Titan Building, 18A Nam Quoc Cang, T08-925 7605, www.handspan.com. Reputable and well-organized. Specializes in adventure tours.
Kim Café, 270 De Tham St, District 1, T08-920 5552, www.kimtravel.com. Organizes minibuses to Nha Trang, Dalat, etc, and tours of the Mekong from US$7. A good source of information.
Luxury Travel Co, Ltd, Suite 404, Eden Mall, 4 Le Loi St, T08-824 3408, www.luxurytravel vietnam.com. Offers luxury travel to Vietnam, Cambodia and Laos.
Sinh Café, 246-248 De Tham St, District 1, T08-836 7338, www.sinhcafevn.com. Tours are generally good value and the open ticket is excellent value. For many people, especially budget travellers, **Sinh Café** is the first port of call. Tours to the Mekong Delta and Cambodia are organized from US$26.
TM Brother's Café, 228 De Tham St, T08-837 7764 and 4 Do Quang Dau St, T08-837 8394, tmbrothers_saigon@yahoo. com. Genuine version is a reliable Open Tour Bus operator. Runs trips to the Mekong Delta and Cambodia.
Vidotour, 145 Nam Ky Khoi Nghia St, District 1, T08-933 0457, www.vidotour travel.com. One of the most efficient organizers of group travel in the country.

Around Ho Chi Minh City *p1101*

Swimming
Saigon Water Park, Go Dua Bridge, Kha Van Can St, Thu Duc District, T08-897 0456, Mon-Fri 0900-1700, Sat and Sun 0900-2000, 70,000d for adults, 30,000d for children. A Western-style water park, 10 km outside HCMC. It has a variety of water slides of varying degrees of excitement and a child's pool on a 5-ha site. To get there jump in a taxi, 70,000d, or catch a bus from Ben Thanh market.

Some hotels may also allow non-residents to use their pool for a fee.

⊖ Transport

Ho Chi Minh City *p1091, maps p1092, p1095, p1096 and p1099*

Air
See page 1091.

Airline offices **Air France**, 130 Dong Khoi St, T08-829 0981, www.air france.com. **Bangkok Airways**, Unit 103, Saigon Trade Center, 37 Ton Duc Thang St, T08-910 4490, www.bangkokair.com. **Cathay Pacific**, 115 Nguyen Hue Blvd, T08-822 3203, www.cathay pacific.com. **Emirates Airlines**, 170-172 Nam Ky Khoi Nghia, District 3, T08- 930 2939, www.emirates.com. **Eva Air**, 19-25 Nguyen Hue Blvd, T08-821 7151, www.evaair. com. **Lao Airlines**, 93 Pasteur St, T08-823 4789. **Lufthansa**, 19-25 Nguyen Hue Blvd, T08-829 8529, www.lufthansa.com. **Pacific Airlines**, 177 Vo Thi Sau St, District 3, T08-932 5979. **Qantas**, Saigon Trade Center, unit 102, first floor, 37 Ton Duc Thang St, T08-910 5373, www.qantas.com.au. **Siem Reap Airways International**, 132-134 Dong Khoi St, T08-823 9288. **Thai Airways**, 65 Nguyen Du St, T08-829 2810, www.thaiair.com. **United Airlines**, ground floor, 17 Le Duan, T08-823 4755. **Vietnam Airlines**, 116 Nguyen Hue Blvd, T08-832 0320, www.vietnamairlines.com.

Bicycle
Bikes and motorbikes can be hired from some of the cheaper hotels and cafés, especially in Pham Ngu Lao St. They should always be parked in the roped-off compounds (*gui xe*), found all over town; they will be looked after for a small fee (500d by day, 1000d after dark, 2000d for motorbikes; always get a ticket).

Bus
All city buses start from or stop by the Ben Thanh bus station opposite Ben Thanh Market, District 1, T08-8217182. A free map of all bus routes can also be obtained here. The buses are green or yellow and run at intervals of 10-20 mins depending on the time of day; during rush hours they are jammed with passengers and can run late. There are bus stops every 500 m. Tickets cost 2000d per person.

Open Tour Buses leave from company offices in the centre, including **Sinh Café** in Pham Ngu Lao.

Cyclo
Cyclos are a peaceful way to get around the city. They can be hired for approximately US$2-3 per hr or to reach a specific destination. Some drivers speak English. Some visitors complain that cyclo drivers in HCMC have an annoying habit of 'forgetting' the agreed price, however, the drivers will argue that cyclos are being banned from more and more streets in the centre of HCMC, which means that journeys are often longer and more expensive than expected.

Motorcycle taxi
Honda om or *xe ôm* are the quickest way to get around town and are cheaper than cyclos; just agree a price and hop on the back. *Xe ôm* drivers can be recognized by their baseball caps and their tendency to chain smoke; they hang around on most street corners.

Taxi
All taxis are metered. **Airport** (white or blue), T08-844 6666. **Mai Linh Taxi** (green and white, but note that the Deluxe version is more expensive), T08-827 7979. **Saigontourist**, T08-846 4646. **Vinasun** (white), T08-827 2727. **Vinataxi** (yellow), T08-811 1111.

Train

Thong Nhat Railway Station, 1 Nguyen Thong St, Ward 9, District 3, T08-562 1683, is 2 km from the centre of the city. There is now also a **Train Booking Agency**, 275c Pham Ngu Lao St, T08-836 7640, daily 0730-1130, 1330-1630, which saves a journey out to the station. Daily connections with **Hanoi** and all points north. Express trains take between 36 hrs and 40 hrs to reach Hanoi; hard and soft berths are available. Sleepers should be booked in advance. The **5 Star Express**, 297 Pham Ngu Lao St, T08-920 6868, www.5starexpress.com.vn, is a new, very comfortable and enjoyable train. 5 Star Express leaves HCMC at 0615 for Nha Trang stopping off at Muong Man (for Phan Thiet/Mui Ne) and arriving in **Nha Trang** at 1333. There are a variety of carriages and tickets are priced accordingly; tickets range from US$10 one way for the entire route up to US$150. Buoyed by success, the company has already introduced a night train to Nha Trang leaving 2020 arriving 0620, US$56. Highly recommended.

⊙ Directory

Ho Chi Minh City *p1091, maps p1092, p1095, p1096 and p1099*

Banks There are now dozens of ATMs in shops, hotels and banks. Remember to take your passport if cashing TCs and withdrawing money from a bank. **ANZ Bank**, 11 Me Linh Sq, T08-823 2218, a 2% commission charged on cashing TCs into US$ or VND, ATM. **HSBC, Hong Kong and Shanghai Bank**, 235 Dong Khoi St, T08-829 2288, provides all financial services, 2% commission on TCs, ATM.

Vietcombank, 8 Nguyen Hue Blvd (opposite the Rex Hotel). **Embassies and consulates Australia**, Landmark Building, 5B Ton Duc Thang St, T08-829 6035. **Cambodia**, 41 Phung Khac Khoan St, T08-8292751. **Canada**, Metropole Building, 235 Dong Khoi St, T08-8279899. **Laos**, 9B Pasteur St, T08-829 7667. **New Zealand**, Room 909, Metropole Building, 235 Dong Khoi St, T08-822 6907. **Thailand**, 77 Tran Quoc Thao St, District 3, T08-932 7637. **UK**, 25 Le Duan St, T08-829 8433. **USA**, 4 Le Duan St, T08-82 29433. **Immigration** Immigration Office, 254 Nguyen Trai St, T08-832 2300. For visa extensions and to change visas to specify overland travel to Cambodia via Moc Bai (see page 1116) or for overland travel to Laos or China. **Internet** There are numerous internet cafés in all parts of town.

Laundry There are several places that will do your laundry around Pham Ngu Lao St. **Medical services** Columbia Asia (Saigon International Clinic), 8 Alexander de Rhodes St, T08-823 8888; international doctors. **Family Medical Practice HCMC**, Diamond Plaza, 34 Le Duan St, T08-822 7848, www.vietnam medicalpractice.com, well-equipped practice, 24-hr emergency service and an evacuation service; Australian and European doctors. Also provides a useful major and minor disease outbreak service on its website. **International SOS**, 55 Nguyen Du St, T08-829 8424, Comprehensive 24-hr medical and dental service and medical evacuation. **Post office and telephone** The **GPO** is at 2 Cong Xa Paris (facing the cathedral), daily 0630-2100. Telex, telegram and international telephone services available.

Far south

At its verdant best the Mekong Delta is a riot of greens: pale rice seedlings deepen in shade as they sprout ever taller; palm trees and orchards make up an unbroken horizon of foliage. But at its muddy worst the paddy fields ooze with slime and sticky clay; grey skies, hostile clouds and incessant rain make daily life a misery and the murky rising waters, the source of all the natural wealth of the delta, also cause hundreds of fatalities.

Boat trips along canals and down rivers are the highlights of this region, as is a visit to Phu Quoc – Vietnam's largest island. Lying off the southwest coast, Phu Quoc remains largely undeveloped with beautiful sandy beaches along much of its coastline and forested hills inland. ⬥ *For listings, see pages 1119-1124.*

Ins and outs

Getting there and around There are several highways throughout the Mekong Delta linking the major towns. Highway 1 from Ho Chi Minh City goes to My Tho, Vinh Long and Can Tho and Highway 91 links Can Tho, Long Xuyen and Chau Doc. Beyond these towns, however, roads are narrow and pot-holed and travel is generally slow. Ferry crossings make travel more laborious still. The easiest way to explore the region is to take a tour from Ho Chi Minh City to Can Tho, My Tho or Chau Doc. There are also flights to Can Tho and, if money is no object, the Victoria hotel group runs boats from Ho Chi Minh City to Can Tho and Chau Doc. ⬥ *See Transport, page 1122; for transport to Phu Quoc Island, see page 1123.*

Best time to visit December to May is when the Mekong Delta is at its best. During the monsoon, from June to November, the weather is poor, with constant background drizzle, interrupted by bursts of torrential rain. In October flooding may interrupt movement particularly in remote areas and around Chau Doc and Dong Thap Province.

Background

The Mekong River enters Vietnam in two branches known traditionally as the Mekong (to the north) and the Bassac but now called the Tien and the Hau respectively. Over the 200 km journey to the sea they divide to form nine mouths, the so-called 'Nine Dragons' or Cuu Long of the delta. In response to the rains of the southwest monsoon, river levels in the delta begin to rise in June, usually reaching a peak in October and falling to normal in December. This seasonal pattern is ideal for growing rice, around which the whole way of life of the delta has evolved. Even prior to the creation of French Cochin China in the 19th century, rice was being transported from here to Hué, the imperial capital.

The region has had a restless history. Conflict between Cambodians and Vietnamese for ownership of the wide plains resulted in ultimate Viet supremacy (although important Khmer relics remain). From 1705 onwards Vietnamese emperors began building canals to improve navigation in the delta. This task was taken up enthusiastically by the French in order to open up new areas to rice cultivation and export. By the 1930s the population of the delta had reached 4.5 million with 2,200,000 ha of land under rice cultivation. The Mekong Delta, along with the Irrawaddy (Burma) and Chao Phraya (Thailand) became one of the great rice-exporting areas of Southeast Asia, shipping over 1.2 million tonnes annually. During the French and American wars, the Mekong Delta produced many of the most fervent fighters for independence.

Today, the Mekong Delta remains Vietnam's rice bowl. The delta covers 67,000 sq km, of which about half is cultivated. Rice yields are in fact generally lower than in the north but the huge area under cultivation and the larger size of farms means that both individual households and the region produce a surplus for export. In the Mekong Delta there is nearly three times as much rice land per person as there is in the north.

My Tho ☺❼▲☺☻ ➤➤ pp1119-1124. Colour map 6, B3.

My Tho is an important riverside market town on the banks of the Tien River, a tributary of the Mekong. The town has had a turbulent history: it was Khmer until the 17th century, when the advancing Vietnamese took control of the surrounding area. In the 18th century Thai forces annexed the territory, before being driven out in 1784. Finally, the French gained control in 1862. This historical melting pot is reflected in **Vinh Trang Pagoda** ① 60 Nguyen Trung Truc St, daily 0900-1200, 1400-1700 (best to go by bicycle or cyclo), which was built in 1849 and displays a mixture of architectural styles – Chinese, Vietnamese and colonial. The façade is almost fairytale in inspiration and the entrance to the temple is through an ornate porcelain-encrusted gate.

Ins and outs
From Ho Chi Minh City to My Tho the main route is Highway 1. The majority of travellers join an inclusive tour or catch an Open Tour Bus, which allows greater flexibility.
➤➤ See Transport, page 1122.

Tien River islands
① The best way of getting to the islands is to take a tour. Hiring a private boat is not recommended due to the lack of insurance, the communication difficulties and lack of explanations. Prices vary according to the number of people. ➤➤ See Activities and tours, page 1122.
There are four islands in the Tien River between My Tho and Ben Tre: Dragon, Tortoise, Phoenix and Unicorn. Immediately opposite My Tho is **Tan Long** (Dragon Island), noted for its longan cultivation. Honey tea is made on the islands from the longan flower, with a splash of kumquat juice to balance the flavour. There are many other fruits to sample here, as well as rice whisky. It is also pleasant to wander along the island's narrow paths.

The Island of the Coconut Monk, also known as **Con Phung** (Phoenix Island), is about 3 km from My Tho. The 'Coconut Monk' established a retreat on this island shortly after the end of the Second World War where he developed a new 'religion', a fusion of Buddhism and Christianity. He is said to have meditated for three years on a stone slab, eating nothing but coconuts. Persecuted by both the South Vietnamese government and by the Communists, the monastery on the island has since fallen into disuse.

On **Con Qui** (Tortoise Island) there is an abundance of dragon fruit, banana and papaya. Here visitors are treated to singing accompanied by a guitar and Vietnamese monochord.

Vinh Long and around ☺❼▲☺☻ ➤➤ pp1119-1124. Colour map 6, B3.

Vinh Long is a rather ramshackle riverside town on the banks of the Co Chien River. It was one of the focal points in the spread of Christianity in the Mekong Delta and there is a cathedral and Roman Catholic seminary in town as well as a Cao Dai church. The main reason for visiting Vinh Long is to spend a night at a homestay on the lovely and tranquil island of An Binh.

Ins and outs

Tourist information Cuu Long Tourist ⓘ *No 1, 1 Thang 5 St, T070-823616, www.cuulong tourist.net, daily 0700-1700*, is one of the friendlier and more helpful of the state-run companies and runs tours and homestays. Ask for Mr Phu; he is helpful and has a good understanding of English and French.

Around Vinh Long

The river trips taking in the islands and orchards around Vinh Long are as charming as any in the delta but can be expensive. Officially, **Cuu Long Tourist** has a monopoly on excursions by foreigners. Local boatmen are prepared to risk a fine and take tourists for one-tenth of the amount. **Binh Hoa Phuoc Island** makes a pleasant side trip (see also Sleeping, page 1119) or you could spend a morning visiting the floating market at **Cai Be**, about 10 km from Vinh Long. It's not quite as spectacular as the floating markets around Can Tho (see page 1116) but nevertheless makes for a diverting trip.

An Binh Island is just a 10-minute ferry ride from Phan Boi Chau Street and represents a great example of a delta landscape, stuffed with fruit-bearing trees and flowers. It is a large island that is further sliced into smaller islands by ribbons of small canals. Sights include the ancient **Tien Chau Pagoda** and a *nuoc mam* (fish sauce factory). Travel is by sampan or walking down the winding paths that link the communities. If you choose to stay on the island, you will be given tea and fruit at a traditional house, see ricecakes and popcorn being made, and visit a brick factory, where terracotta pots are made and then fired in pyramid-shaped kilns.

Can Tho and around ●●▲●● ›› *pp1119-1124. Colour map 6, C3.*

Can Tho is a large and rapidly growing commercial town situated in the heart of the Mekong Delta. Lying chiefly on the west bank of the Can Tho River, it is the largest city in the delta and also the most welcoming and agreeable. It is the launch pad for trips to some of the region's floating markets. A small settlement was established at Can Tho at the end of the 18th century, although the town did not prosper until the French took control of the delta a century later and rice production for export began to take off. Despite the city's rapid recent growth there are still strong vestiges of French influence apparent in the broad boulevards, as well as many elegant buildings. Can Tho was also an important US base.

Ins and outs

Getting there and around Virtually all visitors arrive by road. With the My Thuan Bridge (near Vinh Long) there is now only one ferry crossing between Ho Chi Minh City and Can Tho, so journey times have fallen. Most of Can Tho can be explored on foot but the floating markets are best visited by boat. ›› *See Transport, page 1122.*

Sights

Hai Ba Trung Street, alongside the river, is the heart of the town, where, at dusk, families stroll in the park in their Sunday best. There is also a bustling **market** here, along the bank of the river. Opposite the park, at number 34, is **Chua Ong Pagoda**, dating from 1894 and built by Chinese from Guangzhou. Unusually for a Chinese temple it is not free standing but part of a terrace of buildings. The right-hand side of the pagoda is dedicated to the Goddess of Fortune, while the left-hand side belongs to General Ma Tien, who, to judge from his unsmiling statue, is fierce and warlike and not to be trifled with.

Border essentials: Vietnam–Cambodia

Chau Doc and Moc Bai

The river crossing is on the Mekong at Chau Doc and the land crossing is at Moc Bai, close to Tay Ninh in Vietnam.

Transport Daily morning boat departures from Chau Doc through the crossing at Vinh Xuong can be arranged through tour operators in Chau Doc, 9 hrs, US$6-15. A quicker option is the fast boat offered by Victoria Hotels & Resorts, www.victoria hotels-asia.com, but it is open to hotel guests only, leaving Chau Doc at 0700, 5 hrs, US$50, minimum 2 people. The return leaves at 1330. There is also an uncomfortable 10-hour public bus ride from Chau Doc to Phnom Penh via Moc Bai. Sinh Café, 248 De Tham St, Ho Chi Minh City, T08-836 9420, www.sinhcafevn.com, runs a 2-day tour through the Mekong Delta from Ho Chi Minh City to Phnom Penh by land, US$21. To travel direct from Ho Chi Minh City to Moc Bai takes about 3 hrs, and from Moc Bai to Phnom Penh a further 6 hrs, with one ferry crossing.

Note If you intend to enter Cambodia from Vietnam you will need to obtain a visa in advance (available from the Immigration Office in Ho Chi Minh City, page 1112).

Floating markets

ⓘ *Busiest at around 0600-0900. Sampans are available to rent in Hai Ba Trung St. Expect to pay about 30,000d per hr for 2 people. Set off as early as possible to beat the tour boats.*

The river markets near Can Tho are colourful and bustling confusions of boats, goods, vendors, customers, and tourists. From their boats the market traders attach samples of their wares to bamboo poles, which they hold out to attract customers. Up to seven vegetables can be seen dangling from the staffs – wintermelon, pumpkin, spring onions, giant parsnips, grapefruit, garlic, mango, onions and Vietnamese plums – and the boats are usually piled high with more produce. Housewives paddle their sampans from boat to boat and barter, haggle, and gossip; small sampans are the best means of transport here as they can negotiate the narrowest canals to take the shopper (or the visitor) into the heart of the area. It is recommended to take at least a five-hour round trip in order to see the landscape at a leisurely pace.

Chau Doc and around ●❼●● ⟩⟩ pp1119-1124. Colour map 6, B2.

Chau Doc was once an attractive, bustling riverside town on the west bank of the Hau or Bassac River, bordering Cambodia. It is still a bustling market town but no longer so appealing, since it has become an important trading and marketing centre for the surrounding agricultural communities. One of its biggest attractions, however, is the nearby **Nui Sam** (Sam Mountain), which is dotted with pagodas and tombs, and from whose summit superb views of the plains below can be enjoyed.

Ins and outs

Getting there Chau Doc is an increasingly important border crossing into Cambodia. There are connections by boat with Phnom Penh as well as by road. There are tours to Chau Doc from Ho Chi Minh City. It is also possible (but expensive) to arrive by boat from Can Tho or Ho Chi Minh City (private charter only or with the Victoria Hotel group boat).

Getting around Chau Doc itself is easily small enough to explore on foot and Nui Sam, the nearby sacred mountain, can be reached by motorbike. ▸▸ *See Transport, page 1122.*

Best time to visit Nui Sam is one of the holiest sites in southern Vietnam and, as such, has vast numbers of pilgrims visiting it on auspicious days. From a climatic viewpoint, the best time to visit is between December and April.

Background
Until the mid-18th century Chau Doc was part of Cambodia: it was given to the Nguyen lord, Nguyen Phuc Khoat, after he had helped to put down an insurrection in the area. The area still supports a large Khmer population, as well as the largest Cham settlement in the delta. Cambodia's influence can be seen in the tendency for women to wear the *kramar*, Cambodia's characteristic chequered scarf, instead of the *non lá* conical hat, and in the people's darker skin, indicating Khmer blood.

Nui Sam (Sam Mountain) → *Colour map 6, B2.*
Nui Sam, 5 km southwest of Chau Doc, is one of the holiest sites in southern Vietnam. Rising from the flood plain, it is a favourite spot for Vietnamese tourists who throng here, especially at festival time. The mountain, really a barren, rock-strewn hill, can be seen at the end of the continuation of Nguyen Van Thoai Street. It is literally honeycombed with tombs, sanctuaries and temples. It is possible to walk or drive right up the hill for good views of the surrounding countryside and from the summit it is easy to appreciate that this is some of the most fertile land in Vietnam.

The **Tay An Pagoda**, at the foot of the hill, facing the road, represents an eclectic mixture of styles – Chinese, Islamic, perhaps even Italian – and contains a bewildering display of more than 200 statues. A short distance on from the pagoda, to the right, past shops and stalls, is the **Chua Xu**. It is rather a featureless building, though highly revered by the Vietnamese and honours the holy Lady Xu, whose statue is enshrined in the new multi-roofed pagoda. From the 23rd to the 25th of the fourth lunar month the holy lady is commemorated, during which time, hundreds of Vietnamese flock to see her being washed and reclothed. Lady Xu is a major pilgrimage for traders and business from Ho Chi Minh City and the south, all hoping that sales will soar and profits leap during this auspicious time.

On the other side of the road is the tomb of **Thoai Ngoc Hau** (1761-1829); an enormous head of the man graces the entranceway. Thoai is a local hero having played a role in the resistance against the French but is known more for his engineering feats in canal building and draining swamps.

Hang Pagoda is a 200-year-old temple situated halfway up Nui Sam. In the first level of the temple are some vivid cartoon drawings of the tortures of hell. The second level is built at the mouth of a cave, which, last century, was home to a woman named Thich Gieu Thien. Her likeness and tomb can be seen in the first pagoda. Fed up with her lazy and abusive husband she left her home in Cholon and came to live in this cave, as an ascetic supposedly waited on by two snakes.

Phu Quoc Island ⊜⊘▲⊕ℂ ▸▸ *pp1119-1124. Colour map 6, B/C1.*

Lying off the southwest coast of the country, Phu Quoc is Vietnam's largest island. It remains largely undeveloped, with beautiful sandy beaches along much of its coastline and forested hills inland. Most of the beaches benefit from crystal clear waters, making them perfect for swimming. The island's remoteness and lack of infrastructure means that tourism here is still in its infancy, and, although new resorts are planned, the pace of development is slow. After the rigours of sightseeing, Phu Quoc is well worth a visit for a few days' relaxation in southern Vietnam.

Ins and outs

Getting there and around You can get to Phu Quoc by plane from Ho Chi Minh City and most hotels will provide a free pick-up service from the airport if accommodation is booked in advance. There is also a high-speed boat service to the island from Rach Gia. There are only two asphalt roads on the island from Duong Dong to An Thoi and from Duong Dong to Ham Ninh. Hiring a motorbike is cheap and convenient but makes for dusty and very hot travelling; limited signposting can make some places pretty hard to find without local assistance. There are also plenty of motorbike taxis available, as well as cars with drivers at fairly reasonable prices; ask at hotels.
▸▸ *See Transport, page 1122.*

Around the island

Vietnamese fish sauce (nuoc mam) is produced on Phu Quoc. You'll see dozens of fish laid out to dry on land and on trestle tables, destined for the fish sauce factory at **Duong Dong**, the main town on the island. Here, 95 massive wooden barrels act as vats, each containing fish and salt weighing in at 14 tonnes and ringing in the till at US$5000 a barrel. If the sauce is made in concrete vats, the taste is lost and so the sauce is cheaper.

The island is also a centre for South Sea pearls, with 10,000 collected offshore each year. At the **Phu Quoc Pearl Gallery** ① *10 km south of Duong Dong, daily 0800-1800*, a video demonstrates the farming operation, the tasting of pearl meat and pearl-making is illustrated in the gallery. South of the pearl farm, on the coast road, are two **whale dedication temples**. Whales have long been worshipped in Vietnam. Ever since the days of the Champa, the whale has been credited with saving the lives of drowning fishermen. The Cham believed that Cha-Aih-Va, a powerful god, could assume the form of a whale in order to rescue those in need. Emperor Gia Long is said to have been rescued by a whale when his boat sank. After he ascended to the throne, Gia Long awarded the whale the title 'Nam Hai Cu Toc Ngoc Lam Thuong Dang Than' – Superior God of the Southern Sea. Coastal inhabitants always

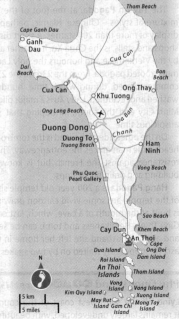

Phu Quoc Island

Thom Beach
Cape Ganh Dau
Ganh Dau
Cua Can
Dai Beach
Bon Beach
Cua Can
Ong Thay
Khu Tuong
Ong Lang Beach
Da Ban
Duong Dong
Chanh
Duong To
Truong Beach
Ham Ninh
Vong Beach
Phu Quoc Pearl Gallery
Sao Beach
Cay Dun
Khem Beach
An Thoi
Dua Island
Cape
Ong Doi
Dam Island
Roi Island
An Thoi Islands
Thom Island
N
Vong Island
Vang Island
Kim Quy Island
Xuong Island
May Rut Island
Mong Tay Island
Gam Chi Island
5 km
5 miles

try to help whales in difficulty and cut them free of their nets. If a whale should die, a full funeral is arranged.

Inland, the **Da Ban** and **Chanh** streams and waterfalls are not very dramatic in the dry season but still provide a relaxing place to swim and walk in the forests.

The stunning, dazzling-white sands of **Sao Beach**, on the southeast coast, are worth visiting by motorbike but finding the beach can be difficult, as it is not well signposted, so you made need your resort or a tour operator to help you. One of the biggest draws are the boat trips around the **An Thoi islands**, which are scattered off the southern coast and offer opportunities for swimming, snorkelling and fishing.

◉ Far south listings

For Sleeping and Eating price codes,
see inside the front cover.

● Sleeping

My Tho *p1114*

C-D Chuong Duong, No 10, 30 Thang 4 St, T073-870875, www.chuongduonghotel.com. This large hotel occupies a prime riverside location. By far the best hotel in town and very good value. All the rooms overlook the river and have en suite facilities, satellite TV and minibar. The restaurant provides good food and some tables enjoy river views.
E-G Cong Doan, No 61, 30 Thang 4 St, T073-874324, congdoantourist@hcm.vnn.vn. Clean hotel with 5 fan rooms that are cheaper than the 18 with a/c. Good views and location for the boat trips. Recommended.

Vinh Long and around *p1114*

A Mekong Homestays, An Binh Island, Vinh Long. Organized by **Cuu Long Tourist**, page 1115. Accommodation is basic, with camp beds, shared bathrooms and mosquito nets, and a home-cooked dinner of the fruits of the delta. Evening entertainment consists of chatting with the owner. The price includes a boat trip around the island, transfers from Vinh Long, local guide, 1 dinner and 1 breakfast.
C-D Cuu Long (B), No 1, 1 Thang 5 St, T070-823616, www.cuulongtourist.net. Set back from the river and conveniently opposite the quay where boats leave for An Binh Island. 34 a/c rooms; price includes breakfast (over the road at the **Phuy Thuong Restaurant**).

D-F Nam Phuong, 11 Le Loi St, T070-822226, phuong-mai9v9@yahoo.com. Comfortable rooms with a/c and hot water; clean and cheap and very friendly.

Can Tho *p1115*

L-AL Victoria Can Tho Resort, Cai Khe Ward, T071-810111, www.victoriahotelsasia.com. This is one of the most beautiful hotels in Vietnam. With its riverside garden location, combined with an harmonious interior, breezy, open reception area and emphasis on comfort and plenty of genuine period features, it inspires relaxation. The centre-piece is the gorgeous, flood-lit pool, flanked by the lobby bar and restaurant. Rooms are elegantly decorated. Other facilities include a tennis court and therapies in divine massage cabins. The hotel offers a complimentary shuttle bus to the town centre. The boat shuttle may be up and running again by the time this book goes to press.
L-A Golf Hotel, 2 Hai Ba Trung St, T071-812 210, www.vinagolf.vn. Newest and tallest hotel in town. The staff are friendly, knowledgeable and multilingual. The rooms are well equipped with a/c, satellite TV, en suite facilities, decent-sized bath, well stocked minibar, electronic safe in the room. The restaurants provide fine dining and the views from the **Windy Restaurant** (8th floor) are superb. ATM on site.
C-D Saigon Can Tho, 55 Phan Dinh Phung St, T071-825831, sgcthotel@hmc.vnn.vn. A/c, comfortable, good value central business hotel in the competent hands

of **Saigontourist**. The staff are friendly and helpful. Rooms are well-equipped with a/c, satellite TV, en suite facilities, minibar. There's a currency exchange, free internet for guests, sauna and breakfast included.

D-F Tay Ho, 42 Hai Ba Trung St, T071-823 392, kstayho-ct@hcm.vnn.vn. This lovely place has a variety of rooms and a great public balcony that can be enjoyed by those paying for back rooms. Some rooms have baths and others share bathrooms and are cheaper. The staff are friendly.

D-G Hau Giang B, 27 Chau Van Liem St, T071-821950. A/c rooms with hot water, TV and fridge. Used by backpacker groups from HCMC, good value. Virtually no English spoken.

Chau Doc *p1116*

L-AL Victoria Chau Doc, 32 Le Loi St, T076-865010, www.victoriahotelsasia.com. This old, cream building with its riverfront pool is the perfect location in which to relax. All rooms are attractively decorated. The hotel group runs a speedboat to Phnom Penh.

C-D Ben Da Sam Mountain Resort, Hwy 91, T076-861745. This resort consists of 4 hotels, a restaurant and bar. The staff speak good English. The place to stay for a bit of luxury. Sam Mountain is 5 mins' walk away.

D-F Thuan Loi, 18 Tran Hung Dao St, T076-866134. A/c and good river views, clean and friendly, restaurant.

E-G My Loc, 51B Nguyen Van Thoai St, T076-866455. Some rooms with a/c, TV and fridge and others with fan and homestay showers. It's a friendly place in a quiet area.

G Mekong Guesthouse, Duong Len Tao Ngo, Nui Sam, T076-861870, mekongguest house@yahoo.com. This small place on the lower slopes of the mountain is a basic guesthouse and a good base for walking in the area. All rooms have fan, mosquito nets, blankets and homestay shower; some have a/c. The 2 dorms share a bathroom. Food is served all day and breakfast is less than US$1. Hammocks, DVDs, book exchange, internet access and bicycle hire make this an excellent value budget option.

Phu Quoc Island *p1117, map p1118*
During peak periods, such as Christmas and Tet, it is advisable to book accommodation well in advance, otherwise accommodation is easily obtained on arrival at the airport. Representatives from different resorts meet most flights, providing free transfers and touting for business. Most of the resorts lie along the west coast to the south of Duong Dong and are within a few km of the airport. Others are on On Lang Beach and in An Thoi.

A Saigon Phu Quoc Resort, 1 Trang Hung Dao St, Duong Dong, T077-846999, www.vietnamphuquoc.com. This resort, overlooking the sea, has a very attractive swimming pool surrounded by bungalows of varying prices and is set on a hillside garden. An enviable list of facilities includes a reasonably priced restaurant, internet, motorbikes for rent, fishing, tennis, massage, snorkelling, horse riding and bicycling.

A-D Mango Bay Resort, Ong Lang Beach, T090-338 2207 (mob), www.mangobay phuquoc.com. A small and exclusive environ- mentally friendly private resort located on the beach close to pepper farms. Bungalows are made from rammed earth and come with fans and coconut doorknobs and are kitted out with bamboo furniture and tiled floors. The 5 rooms share a wonderful, large communal veranda, some have outdoor bathrooms. The resort has information on birds and fish, a swimming pool and the restaurant provides a mixture of Vietnamese and Western food at very reasonable prices.

A-D Tropicana Resort, Duong Dong, T077-847127, www.tropicanaphuquoc.com. High- quality wooden bungalows and rooms next to the beach with a lovely pool. Prices vary according to the facilities required, although the beachfront balconied bungalows are overpriced. The resort has one of the best restaurants, a well-stocked bar and internet.

C-F Kim Hoa Resort, Duong Dong, T077-384 7039, http://vnrealty.com/pq/kimhoa/ index.html. This small resort offers typical wooden bungalows on a clean strip of sand in front of the resort. Bungalows have

1 double and 1 single bed and either have fan or a/c. The rooms which aren't on the beach have small bathrooms and are basic.
D-F Thang Loi, Ong Lang Beach, T077-398 5002, www.phuquoc.de. A rustic hotel with wooden bungalows set in a remote coconut plantation on Ong Lang beach for those who want complete peace and quiet. Good bar and restaurant with friendly German owners. Bungalows are basically furnished with bamboo, fans and mosquito nets; some have hot water. There is a library, music and great food including *wiener schnitzel*. A newly built jetty juts out into the sea, a short walk from the bungalows.

❶ Eating

My Tho *p1114*
A speciality of the area is *hu tieu my tho* – a spicy soup of vermicelli, sliced pork, dried shrimps and fresh herbs. At night, noodle stalls spring up on the pavement on Le Loi St at the junction with Le Dai Han St.
¶ Banh Xeo 46, 11 Trung Trac St. Serves *bánh xèo*, savoury pancakes filled with bean-sprouts, mushrooms and prawns; delicious.
¶ Hu Tien 44, 44 Nam Ky Khoi Nghia St, daily 0500-1200. Specializes in *hu tien my tho*. At 8000d for a good-sized bowl filled to top.

Vinh Long and around *p1114*
There are a few restaurants along 1 Thang 5 St, just beyond **Cuu Long Hotel (A)**.
¶ Nem Nuong, 12 1 Thang 5 St, open all day. Sells grilled meat with noodles.
¶ Phuong Thuy Restaurant, No 1, 1 Thang 5 St, T070-824786, daily 0600-2100. A 'stilt' restaurant on the river with Vietnamese and Western dishes and welcoming service. Cuttlefish and shrimp feature strongly.

Can Tho *p1115*
Hai Ba Trung St by the river offers a good range of excellent and very well-priced little restaurants; the riverside setting is an attractive one.

¶¶-¶ Victoria Can Tho Spices (see Sleeping). Excellent location on the riverbank where it's possible to dine al fresco or inside the elegant restaurant. The food is delicious and the service is excellent.
¶ Mekong, 38 Hai Ba Trung St. Perfectly good little place near the river in this popular restaurant strip. Serves decent Vietnamese fare at reasonable prices.
¶ Nam Bo, 50 Hai Ba Trung St, T071-823908. Delightful French house on the corner of a street. Its balcony seating area overlooks the market clutter and riverside promenade. Tasty Vietnamese and French dishes. The set menu is US$6. Small café downstairs. Recommended.
¶ Phuong Nam, 48 Hai Ba Trung St, T071-812 077. Similar to the next door Nam Bo, good food, less stylish, a popular travellers' haunt and reasonable prices.

Chau Doc *p1116*
¶¶¶-¶¶ La Bassac, in **Victoria Chau Doc**. The extravagant French and Vietnamese menus at this riverside restaurant include rack of lamb coated in Mekong herbs, sweet potato puree and pork wine reduction or spaghetti with flambéed shrimps in vodka paprika sauce.
¶ Bay Bong, 22 Thung Dang Le St, T076-867 271. Specializes in hot pots and soups and also offers a good choice of fresh fish. The staff are friendly.
¶ Lam Hung Ky, 71 Chi Lang St. Excellent freshly prepared and cooked food.

Phu Quoc Island *p1117, map p1118*
¶¶-¶ Tropicana Resort. This is one of the best restaurants on the island where a sun-drenched terrace and well-stocked bar allows luxuriant al fresco dining overlooking the sea. Enjoy succulent squid stir-fried with lemon grass, braised shrimps in coconut juice, Italian spaghettis or a range from the set menus.
¶ My Lan, Sao Beach, T077-844447, dungmyt@yahoo.com, daily 0600-2100. On a gorgeous beach. Tables are under little thatched roofs. Sit back and enjoy a beer with the fresh seafood dishes. Recommended.

▲ Activities and tours

My Tho p1114
You can hire boats to take you to visit the islands. Once there, walk or cycle.

Tour operators
Chuong Duong Tourist, next to the hotel, T073-870876, cdhoteltravel@vnn.vn. **Tien Giang Tourist**, 63 Trung Trac St, Ward 1, T073-872105, www.tiengiangtourist.com. Dockside location is at No 8, 30 Thang 4 St, T073-873184. Boat trips to the islands cost US$16 for 1-3 people (2½ hrs). Also dinner with traditional music on the Mekong US$28.

Vinh Long and around p1114
Tour operators
Cuu Long Tourist, No 1, 1 Thang 5 St, T070-823616, www.cuulongtourist.net. Trips to An Binh Island – a highlight of the area – include a visit to the small floating market of Cai Be. A tour of the area including homestay, dinner and breakfast costs US$67. A day trip to Cai Be passing the floating market, US$25; from HCMC, the tour costs US$120.

Can Tho p1115
Boat trips
Trans Mekong, 97/10 Ngo Quyen, P An Cu, T071-829540, www.transmekong.com. Operates the *Bassac*, a converted 24-m wooden rice barge which can sleep 12 passengers in 6, a/c cabins with private bathrooms. *Bassac II*, catering for 24 guests has been newly launched.

Swimming
The **Victoria Can Tho**, has a pool open to the public for a fee.

Therapies
The **Annam Pavilion**, Victoria Can Tho, see Sleeping, has several beautiful massage cabins right on the riverfront offering a host of treatments. Open to non-guests and recommended.

Tour operators
Can Tho Tourist, 20 Hai Ba Trung St, T071-821852, www.canthotourist.com.vn. It's quite expensive and organizes tours in powerful boats; not the best way to see the delta. The staff are helpful and knowledgeable. Tours include trips to Cai Rang, Phong Dien and Phung Hiep floating markets, to Soc Trang, city tours, canal tours, cycle tours, trekking tours and homestays that involve working with farmers in the fields.

Phu Quoc Island p1117, map p1118
Diving
Rainbow Divers, T091-340 0964 (mob), www.divevietnam.com, operates out of the Rainbow Bar between the Saigon Phu Quoc resort and the Kim Hoa resort.

Tour operators
Discovery Tour, Tran Hung Dao St, Duong Dong, T077-846587, daily 0700-1800. Run by the friendly Mr Loi. **Tony's Tours**, T091-319 7334 (mob), tonyphuquoc@yahoo.com. Tony knows Phu Quoc extremely well and speaks fluent English. He would be able to organize almost anything: island tours, snorkelling and deep-sea fishing excursions, car and motorbike rental and hotel and transport reservations.

◉ Transport

My Tho p1114
As in all Mekong Delta towns local travel to visit the orchards, islands and remoter places is often by boat. On land there are *xe ôms* and the *xe lôi*, the local equivalent of the cyclo; a trailer towed by a bicycle or a motorbike.

There are ferries to **Chau Doc** and **Vinh Long**. Enquire locally about departure times and prices as they vary.

Can Tho p1115
Air
Vietnam Airlines, 66 Chau Van Liem St. The airport is about 3 km from the centre

of Can Tho and is currently being upgraded to international status. There are no flights at present.

Boat
Victoria Hotels & Resorts, 2nd floor, 101 Tran Hung Dao St, District 1, HC MC, T08-837 3031, www.victoriahotels-asia.com, runs boats from Can Tho to **Chau Doc**, 1330, 3 hrs, US$35 per person, minimum 2 people. The same journey by chartered boat, US$300. Also by request to **HCMC**,1100, 5 hrs, US$55 per person, minimum 5 people; chartered boat, US$550.

The Can Tho ferry is 24 hrs and highly efficient, with not much waiting, 15,000d per car and 2000d per moto, 20 mins. A bridge is being built to Can Tho and is expected to be finished in 2010. **Vinashin**, T071-820527, www.cawaco.com.vn, operates a high-speed boat on Thu from 2 Hai Ba Trung St (the Ninh Kieu jetty) at 0700 to **Phnom Penh** (US$45) returning Sun at 0700 (US$35). The boat also stops at **Chau Doc** (US$10), 2 hrs from **Can Tho**, and **Long Xuyen** (US$5), 1½ hrs from **Can Tho**.

There is a boat to **Ca Mau** at 0700, 0800, 0900, US$7. Ask at **Can Tho Tourist** for details. To **Con Dao** on Fri, 0700, 3¾ hrs, US$44 return.

Car
Cars with drivers can be hired from the larger hotels.

Taxi
Mai Linh Taxi, T071-822266.

Chau Doc *p1116*
Boat
Daily ferries along the Vinh Te canal to **Ha Tien**, 10 hrs, US$5, take food and water. There are daily departures to Phnom Penh. A couple of tour operators in town organize boat tickets, see page 1116 for further information.

Phu Quoc Island *p1117, map p1118*
Air
Vietnam Airlines fly to **Ho Chi Minh City**.

Boat
There are 3 express boat services from **Rach Gia** on the mainland to Phu Quoc: **Hai Au**, 16 Trang Hung Dao, Duong Dong, T077-398 1000. 160,000d adults on the top floor of the boat, 130,000d ground floor, children ½ price. Leaves for Rach Gia daily 1330, arriving at 1535. **Superdong**, Duong Dong, T077-846180. Leaves for Rach Gia at 1300, arriving 1535; adults 130,000d, children 70,000d. **Trameco**, Khu Pho 1, Duong Dong, T077-980666, leaves for Rach Gia at 0830, 2 hrs 10 mins; adults 130,000d, children 70,000d.

Car and bicycle
Cars and bicycles can be rented from resorts such as the **Tropicana** and **Saigon Phu Quoc**.

Motorbike
Can be rented from most resorts for about US$7-8 per day.

● Directory

My Tho *p1114*
Bank BIDV, 5 Le Van Duyet St. Offers a bureau de change service. **Internet** The post office and **Choung Dong** hotel are the best places. **Post office** No 59, 30 Thang 4 St. Also has facilities for international telephone calls, 0600-2100.

Vinh Long and around *p1114*
Banks Nong Nghiep Bank (Agribank), 28 Hung Dao Vuong St. Visa ATM next to the Cuu Long B hotel. **Internet** The post office and Cuu Long (B) hotel offer internet access and there are a couple of email places on Ly Thuong Kiet St. **Post office** 12c Hoang Thai Hieu St, T070-825888, daily 0600-2100.

Can Tho *p1115*
Banks Nong Nghiep Bank, 3 Phan Dinh
Phung St. **Vietcombank**, 7 Hoa Binh Blvd,
T071-820445. Bureau de change service.
Internet No Gia, 71 Vo Van Tan St, and
several others on the same street.
Alternatively, the big hotels have email
facilities. **Post office** 2 Hoa Binh Blvd,
T071-827280. It offers internet access,
171 calling (cheap long-distance and
international calls).

Chau Doc *p1116*
Banks Nong Nghiep Bank, 51B Ton Duc
Thang St. **Vietcombank**, 1 Hung Vuong St.
Internet In the post office and also in
Victoria Chau Doc Hotel.

Medical services Located opposite the
Victoria Chau Doc Hotel. **Post office**
73 Le Loi St, daily 0600-2100, internet access
(0600-2100 only), 171 service and fax service.

Phu Quoc Island *p1117, map p1118*
Banks It is best to bring enough money with
you to Phu Quoc. Some resorts will exchange
TCs as will the banks in Duong Dong but rates
are worse than on the mainland. **Phu Quoc
Bank**, Duong Dong, cashes TCs. **Vietcom
Bank**, daily 0700-1100, 1300-1700, has Visa
and MasterCard ATM. **Medical services**
The hospital is in Khu Pho, 1 Duong Dong,
T077-848075. **Post office** Phu Quoc Post
Office, Khu Pho 2, Duong Dong, daily
0645-2030, internet access.

Background

Vietnam prehistory

The earliest record of humans in Vietnam is from an archaeological site on Do Mountain, in the northern Thanh Hoa Province. The remains discovered here have been dated to the Lower Palaeolithic (early Stone Age). So far, all early human remains have been unearthed in North Vietnam, invariably in association with limestone cliff dwellings. Unusually, tools are made of basalt rather than flint, the more common material found at similar sites in other parts of the world.

Archaeological excavations have shown that between 5000 and 3000 BC, two important Mesolithic cultures occupied North Vietnam: these are referred to as the **Hoa Binh** and **Bac Son** cultures after the principal excavation sites in Tonkin. Refined stone implements and distinctive hand axes with polished edges (known as Bacsonian axes) are characteristic of the two cultures. These early inhabitants of Vietnam were probably small, dark-skinned and of Melanesian or Austronesian stock.

There are 2000 years of recorded Vietnamese history and another 2000 years of legend. The Vietnamese people trace their origins back to 15 tribal groups known as the **Lac Viet** who settled in what is now North Vietnam at the beginning of the Bronze Age. Here they established an agrarian kingdom known as Van-lang that seems to have vanished during the third century BC.

A problem with early **French archaeological studies** in Vietnam was that most of the scholars were either Sinologists or Indologists. In consequence, they looked to Vietnam as a receptacle of Chinese or Indian cultural influences and spent little time uncovering those aspects of culture, art and life that were indigenous in origin and inspiration. The French archaeologist Bezacier for example, expressed the generally held view that 'Vietnamese' history only began in the seventh century AD. Such sites as Hoa Binh, Dong Son and Oc-Eo, which pre-date the seventh century, were regarded as essentially Chinese or Indonesian, their only 'Vietnamese-ness' being their location. This perspective was more often than not based on faulty and slapdash scholarship, and reflected the prevailing view that Southeast Asian art was basically derivative.

Pre-colonial history

The beginning of Vietnamese recorded history coincides with the start of **Chinese cultural hegemony** over the north, in the second century BC. The Chinese dominated Vietnam for more than 1000 years until the 10th century AD and the cultural legacy is still very much in evidence, making Vietnam distinctive in Southeast Asia. Even after the 10th century, and despite breaking away from Chinese political domination, Vietnam was still overshadowed and greatly influenced by its illustrious neighbour to the north. Nonetheless, the fact that Vietnam could shrug off 1000 years of Chinese subjugation and emerge with a distinct cultural heritage and language says a lot for Vietnam's strength of national identity.

Ly Dynasty

The Ly Dynasty (1009-1225) was the first independent Vietnamese dynasty. Its capital, Thang Long, was at the site of present day Hanoi and the dynasty based its system of government and social relations closely upon the Chinese Confucianist model.

The Vietnamese owe a considerable debt to the Chinese – mainly in the spheres of government, philosophy and the arts – but they have always been determined to maintain their independence. Vietnamese Confucianist scholars were unsparing in their criticism of Chinese imperialism. Continuous Chinese invasions, all ultimately futile, served to cement an enmity between the two countries, which is still in evidence today – despite their having normalized diplomatic relations in October 1991.

The first Ly emperor, and one of Vietnam's great kings, was Ly Cong Uan who was born in AD 974. He is usually known by his posthumous title, **Ly Thai To**, and reigned for 19 years from 1009-28. Ly Cong Uan was raised and educated by monks and acceded to the throne when, as the commander of the palace guard in Hoa Lu (the capital of Vietnam before Thang Long or Hanoi) and with the support of his great patron, the monk Van Hanh, he managed to gain the support of the Buddhist establishment and many local lords. During his reign, he enjoyed a reputation not just as a great soldier, but also as a devout man who paid attention to the interests and well-being of his people. He also seemed, if the contemporary records are to be believed, to have been remarkably sensitive to those he ruled. He tried to re-establish the harmony between ruler and ruled which had suffered during the previous years and he even sent his son to live outside the walls of the palace so that he could gain a taste of ordinary life and an understanding of ordinary people. As he approached death he is said to have increasingly retired from everyday life, preparing himself for the everlasting.

Ly Cong Uan was succeeded by his son, Ly Phat Ma, who is better known as **Ly Thai Tong** (reigned 1028-1054). Ly Phat Ma had been prepared for kingship since birth and he proved to be an excellent ruler during his long reign. It is hard to generalize about this period in Vietnamese history because Ly Phat Ma adapted his pattern of rule no less than six times during his reign. Early on he challenged the establishment, contending for example that good governance was not merely a consequence of following best practice (which the logic of bureaucratic Confucianism would maintain) but depended upon the qualities of the man at the helm. Later he was more of an establishment figure, holding much greater store by the institutions of kingship. Perhaps his greatest military success was the mounting of a campaign to defeat the Cham in 1044 from which he returned with shiploads of plunder. His greatest artistic legacy was the construction of the One Pillar Pagoda or Chua Mot Cot in Hanoi (see page 1017).

Ly Phat Ma was succeeded by his son, Ly Nhat Ton, posthumously known as **Ly Thanh Tong** (reigned 1054-1072). History is not as kind about Ly Thanh Tong as it is about his two forebears. Nonetheless he did challenge the might of the Chinese along Vietnam's northern borders – largely successfully – and like his father also mounted a campaign against Champa (see page 1129) in 1069. Indeed his expedition against the Cham mirrored his father's in most respects and, like his father, he won. Records indicate that he spent a great deal of time trying to father a son. At last, a son was born to a concubine of common blood in 1066 and named Ly Can Duc.

Ly Can Duc was proclaimed emperor in 1072 when he was only six years old and, surprisingly, remained king until he died in 1127. During the early years of his reign the kingdom faced a succession of crises, largely due to the fact that his young age meant that there was no paramount leader. His death marks the end of the Ly Dynasty for he left no heir and the crown passed to the maternal clan of his nephew. There followed a period of instability and it was not until 1225 that a new dynasty – the Tran Dynasty – managed to subdue the various competing cliques and bring a semblance of order to the country.

Tran Dynasty

Scholars do not know a great deal about the four generations of kings of the Tran Dynasty. It seems that they established the habit of marrying within the clan, and each king took queens who were either their cousins or, in one case, a half-sister. Such a long period of intermarriage, one imagines, would have had some far-reaching genetic consequences, although ironically the collapse of the dynasty seems to have been brought about after one foolish king decided to marry outside the Tran clan. The great achievement of the Tran Dynasty was to resist the expansionist tendencies of the Mongol forces who conquered China in the 1250s and then set their sights on Vietnam. In 1284 a huge Mongol-Yuan force, consisting of no fewer than four armies, massed on the border to crush the Vietnamese. Fortunately the Tran were blessed with a group of brave and resourceful princes, the most notable of whom was Tran Quoc Tuan, better known – and now immortalized in street names in just about every Vietnamese town – as **Tran Hung Dao**. Although the invading forces captured Thang Long (Hanoi) they never managed to defeat the Vietnamese in a decisive battle and in the end the forces of the Tran Dynasty were victorious.

Le Dynasty and the emergence of Vietnam

Le Loi

During its struggle with the Cham, nascent Dai Viet had to contend with the weight of Ming Chinese oppression from the north, often in concert with their Cham allies. Despite 1000 years of Chinese domination and centuries of internal dynastic squabbles the Viet retained a strong sense of national identity and were quick to respond to charismatic leadership. As so often in Vietnam's history one man was able to harness nationalistic sentiment and mould the country's discontent into a powerful fighting force: in 1426 it was Le Loi. Together with the brilliant tactician **Nguyen Trai**, Le Loi led a campaign to remove the Chinese from Vietnamese soil. Combining surprise, guerrilla tactics and Nguyen Trai's innovative and famous propaganda, designed to convince defending Ming of the futility of their position, the Viet won a resounding victory which led to the enlightened and artistically distinguished Le period. Le Loi's legendary victory lives on in popular form and is celebrated in the tale of the restored sword in water puppet performances across the country. Following his victory against the Ming he claimed the throne in 1428 and reigned until his death five years later.

Le Thanh Ton

With Le Loi's death the Le Dynasty worked its way through a succession of young kings who seemed to hold the throne barely long enough to warm the cushions before they were murdered. It was not until 1460 that a king of substance was to accede: Le Thanh Ton (reigned 1460-1497). His reign was a period of great scholarship and artistic accomplishment. He established the system of rule that was to guide successive Vietnamese emperors for 500 years. He also mounted a series of military campaigns, some as far as Laos to the west.

Le expansion

The expansion of the Vietnamese state, under the Le, south from its heartland in the Tonkin Delta, followed the decline of the Cham Kingdom at the end of the 15th century. By the early 18th century the Cham were extinct as an identifiable political and military force and the Vietnamese advanced still further south into the Khmer-controlled territories of the Mekong Delta. This geographical over-extension and the sheer logistical impracticability of ruling from distant Hanoi, disseminating edicts and collecting taxes, led to the disintegration of the – ever tenuous – imperial rule. The old adage 'The edicts of the emperor stop at the village gate' was particularly apt more than 1000 km from the capital. Noble families, locally dominant, challenged the emperor's authority and the Le Dynasty gradually dissolved into internecine strife and regional fiefdoms, namely Trinh in the north and Nguyen in the south, a pattern that was to reassert itself 300 years later. But although on paper the Vietnamese – now consisting of two dynastic houses, Trinh and Nguyen – appeared powerful, the people were mired in poverty.

There were numerous peasant rebellions in this period, of which the most serious was the **Tay Son rebellion** of 1771. One of the three Tay Son brothers, Nguyen Hue, proclaimed himself **Emperor Quang Trung** in 1788, only to die four years later.

The death of Quang Trung paved the way for the establishment of the **Nguyen Dynasty** (the last Vietnamese dynasty) in 1802 when Emperor Gia Long ascended to the throne in Hué. Despite the fact that this period heralded the arrival of the French, it is regarded as a golden period in Vietnamese history. During the Nguyen Dynasty, Vietnam was unified as a single state and Hué emerged as the heart of the kingdom.

History of the non-Viet civilizations

Any history of Vietnam must include the non-Vietnamese peoples and civilizations. The central and southern parts of Vietnam have only relatively recently been dominated by the Viets. Before that, these lands were in the hands of people of Indian or Khmer origins.

Funan (AD 100-600)

According to Chinese sources, Funan was a Hindu kingdom founded in the first century AD with its capital, Vyadhapura, close to the Mekong River near the border with Cambodia. A local legend records that Kaundinya, a great Indian Brahmin, acting on a dream, sailed to the coast of Vietnam carrying with him a bow and arrow. When he arrived, Kaundinya shot the arrow and where it landed he established the capital of Funan. Following this act, Kaundinya married the princess Soma, daughter of the local King of the Nagas (giant water serpents). The legend symbolizes the union between Indian and local cultural traditions – the naga representing indigenous fertility rites and customs, and the arrow, the potency of the Hindu religion.

Oc-Eo

Funan built its wealth and power on its strategic location on the sea route between China and the islands to the south. Maritime technology at the time forced seafarers travelling between China and island Southeast Asia and India to stop and wait for the winds to change before they could continue on their way. This sometimes meant a stay of up to five months. The large port city of Oc-Eo offered a safe harbour for merchant vessels and the revenues generated enabled the kings of the empire to expand rice cultivation, dominate a host of surrounding vassal states as far away as the Malay coast and South Burma, and build a series of impressive temples, cities and irrigation works. Although the Chinese chronicler K'ang T'ai records that the Funanese were barbarians – "ugly, black, and frizzy-haired" – it is clear from Chinese court annals that they were artistically and technologically accomplished. It is recorded for example that one Chinese emperor was so impressed by the skill of some visiting musicians in AD 263 that he ordered the establishment of an institute of Funanese music.

Funan reached the peak of its powers in the fourth century and went into decline during the fifth century AD when improving maritime technology made Oc-Eo redundant as a haven for sailing vessels. No longer did merchants hug the coastline; ships were now large enough, and navigation skills sophisticated enough, to make the journey from South China to the Malacca Strait without landfall. By the mid-sixth century, Funan, having suffered from a drawn-out leadership crisis, was severely weakened. Neighbouring competing powers took advantage of this crisis, absorbing previously Funan-controlled lands. Irrigation works fell into disrepair as state control weakened and peasants left the fields to seek more productive lands elsewhere. The Cham ultimately conquered Funan, having lost both the economic wealth and the religious legitimacy on which its power had been based.

What is interesting about Funan is the degree to which it provided a model for future states in Southeast Asia. Funan's wealth was built on its links with the sea, and with its ability to exploit maritime trade. The later rulers of Champa, Langkasuka (Malaya), Srivijaya (Sumatra) and Malacca (Malaya) repeated this formula.

Champa (AD 200–1720)

In South Vietnam, where the dynastic lords achieved hegemony only in the 18th century, the kingdom of Champa – or Lin-yi as the Chinese called it – was the most significant power. The kingdom evolved in the second century AD and was focused on the narrow ribbon of lowland that runs north-south down the Annamite coast with its various capitals near the present-day city of Danang. Chinese sources record that in AD 192 a local official, Kiu-lien, rejected Chinese authority and established an independent kingdom. From then on, Champa's history was one of conflict with its neighbour; when Imperial China was powerful, Champa was subservient and sent ambassadors and tributes in homage to the Chinese court; when it was weak, the rulers of Champa extended their own influence and ignored the Chinese.

The difficulty for scholars is to decide whether Champa had a single identity or whether it consisted of numerous mini-powers with no dominant centre. The accepted wisdom at the moment is that Champa was more diffuse than previously thought and that only rarely during its history is it possible to talk of Champa in singular terms. The endless shifting of the capital of Champa is taken to reflect the shifting centres of power that characterized this kingdom'.

Like Funan, Champa built its power on its position on the maritime trading route through Southeast Asia. During the fourth century, as Champa expanded into formerly Funan-controlled lands, they came under the influence of the Indian cultural traditions of the Funanese. These were enthusiastically embraced by Champa's rulers who tacked the suffix '-varman' onto their names (for example Bhadravarman) and adopted the Hindu-Buddhist cosmology. Though a powerful trading kingdom, Champa was geographically poorly endowed. The coastal strip between the Annamite highlands to the west, and the sea to the east, is narrow and the potential for extensive rice cultivation limited. This may explain why the Champa Empire was never more than a moderate power: it was unable to produce the agricultural surplus necessary to support an extensive court and army, and therefore could not compete with either the Khmers to the south nor with the Viets to the north. But the Cham were able to carve out a niche for themselves between the two, and to many art historians, their art and architecture represent the finest that Vietnam has ever produced (see pages 1063 and 1065). Remains are to be found on the central Vietnamese coast from Quang Tri in the north, to Ham Tan 800 km to the south.

Ho Chi Minh: 'He who enlightens'

Ho Chi Minh, one of a number of pseudonyms Ho adopted during his life, was born Nguyen Sinh Cung, or possibly Nguyen Van Thanh (Ho did not keep a diary during much of his life, so parts of his life are still a mystery); in Nghe An Province near Vinh on the 19 May 1890, and came from a poor scholar-gentry family. In the village, the family was aristocratic; beyond it they were little more than peasants. His father, though not a revolutionary, was a dissenter and rather than go to Hué to serve the French, he chose to work as a village school teacher. Ho must have been influenced by his father's implacable animosity towards the French, although Ho's early years are obscure. He went to Quoc Hoc College in Hué and then worked for a while as a teacher in Phan Thiet, a fishing village in South Annam.

In 1911, under the name Nguyen Tat Thanh, he travelled to Saigon and left the country as a messboy on the French ship *Amiral Latouche-Tréville*. He is said to have used the name 'Ba' so that he would not shame his family by accepting such lowly work. This marked the beginning of three years of travel during which he visited France, England, America (where the skyscrapers of Manhattan both amazed and appalled him) and North Africa. Seeing the colonialists on their own turf and reading such revolutionary literature as the French Communist Party newspaper *L'Humanité*, he was converted to Communism. In Paris he mixed with leftists, wrote pamphlets and attended meetings of the French Socialist Party. He also took odd jobs: for a while he worked at the Carlton Hotel in London and became an assistant pastry chef under the legendary French chef Georges Escoffier.

An even more unlikely story emerges from Gavin Young's *A Wavering Grace*. In the book he recounts an interview he conducted with Mae West in 1968 shortly after he had returned from reporting the Tet offensive. On hearing of Vietnam, Mae West innocently said that she "used to know someone *very*, very important there ... His name was Ho ... Ho ... Ho something". At the time she was staying at the Carlton while starring in a London show, *Sex*. She confided to Young: "There was this waiter, cook, I don't know what he was. I know he had the slinkiest eyes though. We met in the corridor. We – well ..." Young writes that "Her voice trailed off in a husky sigh ..."

Gradually Ho became an even more committed Communist, contributing articles to radical newspapers and working his way into the web of Communist and leftist groups. At the same time he remained, curiously, a French cultural chauvinist, complaining

For over 1000 years the Cham resisted the Chinese and the Vietnamese. But by the time Marco Polo wrote of the Cham, their power and prestige were much reduced. After 1285, when invading Mongol hordes were repelled by the valiant Viets, Champa and Dai Viet enjoyed an uneasy peace maintained by the liberal flow of royal princesses south across the Col des Nuages (Hai Van Pass) in exchange for territory. During the peaceful reign of Che A-nan a Franciscan priest, Odoric of Pordenone, reported of Champa "'tis a very fine country, having a great store of victuals and of all good things". Of particular interest, he refers to the practice of suti, writing "When a man dies in this country, they burn his wife with him, for they say that she should live with him in the other world also". Clearly, some of the ancient Indian traditions continued.

for example about the intrusion of English words like *le manager* and *le challenger* (referring to boxing contests) into the French language. He even urged the French prime minister to ban foreign words from the French press. In 1923 he left France for Moscow and was trained as a Communist activist – effectively a spy. From there, Ho travelled to Canton where he was instrumental in forming the Vietnamese Communist movement. This culminated in the creation of the Indochina Communist Party in 1930. His movements during these years are scantily documented: he became a Buddhist monk in Siam (Thailand), was arrested in Hong Kong for subversive activities and received a six month sentence, travelled to China several times, and in 1940 even returned to Vietnam for a short period – his first visit for nearly 30 years. Despite his absence from the country, the French had already recognized the threat that he posed and sentenced him to death in absentia in 1930. He did not adopt the pseudonym by which he is now best known – Ho Chi Minh – until the early 1940s.

Ho was a consummate politician and, despite his revolutionary fervour, a great realist. He was also a charming man, and during his stay in France between June and October 1946 he made a great number of friends. Robert Shaplen in his book *The Lost Revolution* (1965) talks of his "wit, his oriental courtesy, his savoir-faire ... above all his seeming sincerity and simplicity". He talked with farmers and fishermen and debated with priests; he impressed people wherever he travelled. He died in Hanoi at his house in the former governor's residence in 1969 (see page 1017).

Since the demise of Communism in the former Soviet Union, the Vietnamese leadership have been concerned that secrets about Ho's life might be gleaned from old comintern files in Moscow by nosy journalists. To thwart such an eventuality, they have, reportedly, sent a senior historian to scour the archives. To date, Ho's image remains largely untarnished – making him an exception amongst the tawdry league of former Communist leaders. But a Moscow-based reporter has unearthed evidence implying Ho was married, challenging the official hagiography that paints Ho as a celibate who committed his entire life to the revolution. It takes a brave Vietnamese to challenge established 'fact'. In 1991, when the popular Vietnamese *Youth* or *Tuoi Tre* newspaper dared to suggest that Ho had married Tang Tuyet Minh in China in 1926, the editor was summarily dismissed from her post.

Champa saw a late flowering under King Binasuos who led numerous successful campaigns against the Viet, culminating in the sack of Hanoi in 1371. Subsequently, the treachery of a low-ranking officer led to Binasuos' death in 1390 and the military eclipse of the Cham by the Vietnamese. The demographic and economic superiority of the Viet coupled with their gradual drift south contributed most to the waning of the Cham Kingdom, but finally, in 1471 the Cham suffered a terrible defeat at the hands of the Vietnamese. Some 60,000 of their soldiers were killed and another 36,000 captured and carried into captivity, including the King and 50 members of the royal family. The kingdom shrank to a small territory in the vicinity of Nhà Trang that survived until 1720 when surviving members of the royal family and many subjects fled to Cambodia to escape from the advancing Vietnamese.

Colonial period

One of the key motivating factors that encouraged the **French** to undermine the authority of the Vietnamese emperors was their treatment of Roman Catholics. Jesuits had been in the country from as early as the 17th century – one of them, Alexandre-de-Rhodes, converted the Vietnamese writing system from Chinese characters to Romanized script – but persecution of Roman Catholics began only in the 1830s. Emperor Minh Mang issued an imperial edict outlawing the dissemination of Christianity as a heterodox creed in 1825. The first European priest to be executed was François Isidore Gagelin who was strangled by six soldiers as he knelt on a scaffold in Hué in 1833. Three days later, having been told that Christians believe they will come to life again, Minh Mang had the body exhumed to confirm the man's death. In 1840 Minh Mang actually read the Old Testament in Chinese translation, declaring it to be 'absurd'.

Yet, Christianity continued to spread as Buddhism declined and there was a continual stream of priests willing to risk their lives proselytizing. In addition, the economy was in disarray and natural disasters common. Poor Vietnamese saw Christianity as a way to break the shackles of their feudal existence. Fearing a peasants' revolt, the Emperor ordered the execution of 25 European priests, 300 Vietnamese priests, and 30,000 Vietnamese Catholics between 1848 and 1860. Provoked by these killings, the French attacked and took Saigon in 1859. In 1862 **Emperor Tu Duc** signed a treaty ceding the three southern provinces to the French, thereby creating the colony of **Cochin China**. This treaty of 1862 effectively paved the way for the eventual seizure by the French of the whole kingdom. The French, through weight of arms, also forced the Emperor to end the persecution of Christians in his kingdom. In retrospect, although many Christians did die cruelly, the degree of persecution was not on the scale of similar episodes elsewhere: Minh Mang's successors Thieu Tri (1841-1847) and Tu Duc (1847-1883), though both fervently anti-Christian, appreciated French military strength and the fact that they were searching for pretexts to intervene.

The **French conquest of the north** was motivated by a desire to control trade and the route to what were presumed to be the vast riches of China. In 1883 and 1884, the French forced the Emperor to sign treaties making Vietnam a French protectorate. In August 1883 for example, just after Tu Duc's death, a French fleet appeared off Hué to force concessions. François Harmand, a native affairs official on board one of the ships, threatened the Vietnamese by stating: "Imagine all that is terrible and it will still be less than reality ... the word 'Vietnam' will be erased from history." The emperor called on China for assistance and demanded that provinces resist French rule; but the imperial bidding proved ineffective, and in 1885 the **Treaty of Tientsin** recognized the French protectorates of Tonkin (North Vietnam) and Annam (Central Vietnam), to add to that of Cochin China (South Vietnam).

Resistance to the French: the prelude to revolution

Like other European powers in Southeast Asia, the French managed to achieve military victory with ease, but they failed to stifle Vietnamese nationalism. After 1900, as Chinese translations of the works of Rousseau, Voltaire and social Darwinists such as Herbert Spence began to find their way into the hands of the Vietnamese intelligentsia, so resistance grew. Foremost among these early nationalists were Phan Boi Chau (1867-1940) and Phan Chau Trinh (1871-1926) who wrote tracts calling for the expulsion of the French. But these men and others such as Prince Cuong De (1882-1951) were traditional nationalists, their beliefs rooted in Confucianism rather than revolutionary Marxism. Their efforts and perspectives were essentially in the tradition of the nationalists who had resisted Chinese domination.

Quoc Dan Dang (**VNQDD**), founded at the end of 1927, was the first nationalist party, while the first significant Communist group was the **Indochina Communist Party (ICP)** established by **Ho Chi Minh** in 1930 (see box, page 1130). Both the VNQDD and the ICP organized resistance to the French and there were numerous strikes and uprisings, particularly during the harsh years of the Great Depression. The Japanese 'occupation' from August 1940 (Vichy France permitted the Japanese full access to military facilities in exchange for allowing continued French administrative control) saw the creation of the **Viet Minh** to fight for the liberation of Vietnam from Japanese and French control.

Vietnam wars

First Indochina War (1945-1954)

The Vietnam War started in September 1945 in the south of the country and in 1946 in the north. These years marked the onset of fighting **between the Viet Minh and the French** and the period is usually referred to as the First Indochina War. The Communists, who had organized against the Japanese, proclaimed the creation of the **Democratic Republic of Vietnam** (DRV) on 2 September 1945 when Ho Chi Minh read out the Vietnamese **Declaration of Independence** in Hanoi's Ba Dinh Square. The US was favourably disposed towards the Viet Minh and Ho. Operatives of the OSS (the wartime precursor to the CIA) met Ho and supported his efforts during the war and afterwards Roosevelt's inclination was to prevent France claiming their colony back. Only Winston Churchill's persuasion changed his mind.

The French, although they had always insisted that Vietnam be returned to French rule, were in no position to force the issue. Instead, in the south, it was British troops (mainly Gurkhas) who helped the small force of French against the Viet Minh. Incredibly, the British also ordered the Japanese, who had only just capitulated, to help fight the Vietnamese. When 35,000 French reinforcements arrived, the issue in the south – at least superficially – was all but settled, with Ca Mau at the southern extremity of the country falling on 21 October. From that point, the war in the south became an underground battle of attrition, with the north providing support to their southern comrades.

In the north, the Viet Minh had to deal with 180,000 rampaging Nationalist Chinese troops, while preparing for the imminent arrival of a French force. Unable to confront both at the same time, and deciding that the French were probably the lesser of two evils, Ho Chi Minh decided to negotiate. To make the DRV government more acceptable to the French, Ho proceeded cautiously, only nationalizing a few strategic industries, bringing moderates into the government, and actually dissolving the Indochina Communist Party (at least on paper) in November 1945. But in the same month Ho also said: "The French colonialists should know that the Vietnamese people do not wish to spill blood, that it loves peace. But if it must sacrifice millions of combatants, lead a resistance for long years to defend the independence of the country, and preserve its children from slavery, it will do so. It is certain the resistance will win."

Chinese withdrawal

In February 1946, the French and Chinese signed a treaty leading to the withdrawal of Chinese forces and shortly afterwards Ho concluded a treaty with French President de Gaulle's special emissary to Vietnam, Jean Sainteny, in which Vietnam was acknowledged as a 'free' (the Vietnamese word *doc lap* being translated as free, but not yet independent) state that was within the French Union and the Indochinese Federation.

It is interesting to note that in negotiating with the French, Ho was going against most of his supporters who argued for confrontation. But Ho, ever a pragmatist, believed at this stage that the Viet Minh were ill-trained and poorly armed and he appreciated the need for time to consolidate their position. The episode that is usually highlighted as the flashpoint that led to the resumption of hostilities was the French government's decision to open a customs house in Haiphong at the end of 1946. The Viet Minh forces resisted and the rest, as they say, is history. It seems that during the course of 1946 Ho changed his view of the best path to independence. Initially he asked: "Why should we sacrifice 50 or 100,000 men when we can achieve independence within five years through negotiation?" although he later came to the conclusion that it was necessary to fight for independence. The customs house episode might, therefore, be viewed as merely an excuse. The French claimed that 5000 Vietnamese were killed in the ensuing bombardment, versus five Frenchmen; the Vietnamese put the toll at 20,000.

In a pattern that was to become characteristic of the entire 25-year conflict, while the French controlled the cities, the Viet Minh were dominant in the countryside. By the end of 1949, with the success of the Chinese Revolution and the establishment of the Democratic People's Republic of Korea (North Korea) in 1948, the US began to offer support to the French in an attempt to stem the 'Red Tide' that seemed to be sweeping across Asia. At this early stage, the odds appeared stacked against the Viet Minh, but Ho was confident that time was on their side. As he remarked to Sainteny "If we have to fight, we will fight. You can kill 10 of my men for every one I kill of yours but even at those odds, I will win and you will lose". It also became increasingly clear that the French were not committed to negotiating a route to independence. A secret French report prepared in 1948 was obtained and published by the Viet Minh in which the High Commissioner, Monsieur Bollaert, wrote: "It is my impression that we must make a concession to Vietnam of the term, independence; but I am convinced that this word need never be interpreted in any light other than that of a religious verbalism."

Dien Bien Phu (1954) and the Geneva Agreement

The decisive battle of the First Indochina War was at Dien Bien Phu in the hills of the northwest, close to the border with Laos. At the end of 1953 the French, with American support, parachuted 16,000 men into the area in an attempt to protect Laos from Viet Minh incursions and to tempt them into open battle. The French in fact found themselves trapped, surrounded by Viet Minh and overlooked by artillery. There was some suggestion that the US might become involved, and even use tactical nuclear weapons, but this was not to be. In May 1954 the French surrendered – the most humiliating of French colonial defeats – effectively marking the end of the French presence in Indochina. In July 1954, in Geneva, the French and Vietnamese agreed to divide the country along the 17th parallel, so creating two states – the Communists occupying the north and the non-Communists occupying the south. The border was kept open for 300 days and over that period about 900,000 – mostly Roman Catholic – Vietnamese travelled south. At the same time nearly 90,000 Viet Minh troops along with 43,000 civilians went north, although many Viet Minh remained in the south to continue the fight there.

Second Indochina War (1954-1975)

The Vietnam War, but particularly the American part of that war, is probably the most minutely studied, reported, analysed and recorded in history. Yet, as with all wars, there are still large grey areas and continuing disagreement over important episodes.

Most crucially, there is the question of whether the US might have won had their forces been given a free hand and were not forced, as some would have it, to fight with one hand tied behind their backs. This remains the view among many members of the US military.

Ngo Dinh Diem

At the time of the partition of Vietnam along the 17th parallel, the government in the south was chaotic and the Communists could be fairly confident that in a short time their sympathizers would be victorious. This situation was to change with the rise of Ngo Dinh Diem. Born in Hué in 1901 to a Roman Catholic Confucian family, Diem wished to become a priest. He graduated at the top of his class from the French School of Administration and at the age of 32 was appointed to the post of minister of the interior at the court of Emperor Bao Dai. Here, according to the political scientist William Turley, "he worked with uncommon industry and integrity" only to resign in exasperation at court intrigues and French interference. He withdrew from political activity during the First Indochina War and in 1946 Ho Chi Minh offered him a post in the DRV government – an offer he declined.

In July 1954 Diem returned from his self-imposed exile at the Maryknoll Seminary in New Jersey to become Premier of South Vietnam. It is usually alleged that the US administration was behind his rise to power, although this has yet to be proved. He held two rigged elections (in October 1955, 450,000 registered voters cast 605,025 votes) that gave some legitimacy to his administration in American eyes. He proceeded to suppress all opposition in the country. His brutal brother, Ngo Dinh Nhu, was appointed to head the security forces and terrorized much of Vietnamese society.

During the period of Diem's premiership, opposition to his rule, particularly in the countryside, increased. This was because the military's campaign against the Viet Minh targeted – both directly and indirectly – many innocent peasants. At the same time, the nepotism and corruption that was endemic within the administration also turned many people into Viet Minh sympathizers. That said, Diem's campaign was successful in undermining the strength of the Communist Party in the south. While there were perhaps 50,000-60,000 party members in 1954, this figure had declined through widespread arrests and intimidation to only 5000 by 1959.

The erosion of the Party in the south gradually led, from 1959, to the north changing its strategy towards one of more overt military confrontation. The same year also saw the establishment of Group 559 which was charged with the task of setting up what was to become the Ho Chi Minh Trail, along which supplies and troops were moved from the north to the south (see page 1102). But, even at this stage, the Party's forces in the south were kept from open confrontation and many of its leaders were hoping for victory without having to resort to open warfare. There was no call for a 'People's War' and armed resistance was left largely to guerrillas belonging to the Cao Dai and Hoa Hao (Buddhist millenarian) sects. The establishment of the National Liberation Front of Vietnam in 1960 was an important political and organizational development towards creating a credible alternative to Diem – although it did not hold its first congress until 1962.

Escalation of the armed conflict (1959-1963)

Viet Cong

The armed conflict began to intensify from the beginning of 1961 when all the armed forces under the Communists' control were unified under the banner of the **People's**

Liberation Armed Forces (PLAF). By this time the Americans were already using the term Viet Cong (or VC) to refer to Communist troops. They reasoned that the victory at Dien Bien Phu had conferred almost heroic status on the name Viet Minh. American psychological warfare specialists therefore invented the term Viet Cong, an abbreviation of *Viet-nam Cong-san* (or Vietnamese Communists) and persuaded the media in Saigon to begin substituting it for Viet Minh from 1956.

The election of **John F Kennedy** to the White House in January 1961 coincided with the Communists' decision to widen the war in the south. In the same year Kennedy dispatched 400 special forces troops and 100 special military advisers to Vietnam, in flagrant contravention of the Geneva Agreement. With the cold war getting colder, and Soviet Premier Nikita Khrushchev confirming his support for wars of 'national liberation', Kennedy could not back down and by the end of 1962 there were 11,000 US personnel in South Vietnam. At the same time the NLF had around 23,000 troops at its disposal. Kennedy was still saying that: "In the final analysis, it's their war and they're the ones who have to win or lose it". But just months after the Bay of Pigs debacle in Cuba, Washington set out on the path that was ultimately to lead to America's first large-scale military defeat.

The bungling and incompetence of the forces of the south, the interference that US advisers and troops had to face, the misreading of the situation by US military commanders, and the skill – both military and political – of the Communists, are most vividly recounted in Neil Sheehan's massive book, *A Bright Shining Lie*. The conflict quickly escalated from 1959. The north infiltrated about 44,000 men and women into the south between then and 1964, while the number recruited in the south was between 60,000 and 100,000. In August 1959, the first consignment of arms was carried down the **Ho Chi Minh Trail** into South Vietnam. Meanwhile, Kennedy began supporting, arming and training the Army of the Republic of Vietnam (ARVN). The US however, shied away from any large-scale, direct confrontation between its forces and the Viet Cong.

An important element in Diem's military strategy at this time was the establishment of **strategic hamlets**, better known simply as 'hamleting'. This strategy was modelled on British anti-guerrilla warfare during Malaya's Communist insurgency, and aimed to deny the Communists any bases of support in the countryside while at the same time making it more difficult for Communists to infiltrate the villages and 'propagandize' there. The villages which were ringed by barbed wire were labelled 'concentration camps' by the Communists, and the often brutal, forced relocation that peasants had to endure probably turned even more of them into Communist sympathizers. Of the 7000-8000 villages sealed in this way, only a fifth could ever have been considered watertight.

In January 1963 at **Ap Bac**, not far from the town of My Tho, the Communists scored their first significant victory in the south. Facing 2000 well-armed ARVN troops, a force of just 300-400 PLAF inflicted heavy casualties and downed five helicopters. After this defeat, many American advisers drew the conclusion that if the Communists were to be defeated, it could not be left to the ARVN alone – US troops would have to become directly involved.

In mid-1963 a Buddhist monk from Hué committed suicide by dousing his body with petrol and setting it alight. This was the first of a number of **self-immolations**, suggesting that even in the early days the Diem regime was not only losing the military war but also the 'hearts and minds' war. He responded with characteristic heavy handedness by ransacking suspect pagodas. On 2 December 1963, Diem and his brother Nhu were both assassinated during an army coup.

American war in Vietnam

The US decision to enter the war has been the subject of considerable disagreement. Until recently, the received wisdom was that the US administration had already taken the decision, and manufactured events to justify their later actions. However, the recent publication of numerous State Department, Presidential, CIA, Defence Department and National Security Council files – all dating from 1964 – has shed new light on events leading up to American intervention (these files are contained in the United States Government Printing Office's 1108 page-long *Vietnam 1964*).

In Roger Warner's *Back Fire* (1995), which deals largely with the CIA's secret war in Laos, he recounts a story of a war game commissioned by the Pentagon and played by the Rand Corporation in 1962. They were asked to play a week-long game simulating a 10-year conflict in Vietnam. At the end of the week, having committed 500,000 men, the US forces were bogged down, there was student unrest and the American population had lost confidence in their leaders and in the conduct of the war. When the game was played a year later but, on the insistence of the US Air Force, with much heavier aerial bombing, the conclusions were much the same. If only, if only …

By all accounts, **Lyndon Johnson** was a reluctant warrior. In the 1964 presidential campaign he repeatedly said: "We don't want our American boys to do the fighting for Asian boys". This was not just for public consumption. The files show that LBJ always doubted the wisdom of intervention. But he also believed that John F Kennedy had made a solemn pledge to help the South Vietnamese people, a pledge that he was morally obliged to keep. In most respects, LBJ was completely in agreement with Congress, together with sections of the American public, who were disquietened by events in South Vietnam. The Buddhist monk's self-immolation, broadcast on prime-time news, did not help matters.

It has usually been argued that the executive manufactured the **Gulf of Tonkin Incident** to force Congress and the public to approve an escalation of America's role in the conflict. It was reported that two American destroyers, the *USS Maddox* and *USS C Turner Joy*, were attacked without provocation in international waters on the 2 August 1964 by North Vietnamese patrol craft. The US responded by bombing shore installations while presenting the Gulf of Tonkin Resolution to an outraged Congress for approval. Only two Congressmen voted against the resolution and President Johnson's poll rating jumped from 42% to 72%. In reality, the *USS Maddox* had been involved in electronic intelligence gathering while supporting clandestine raids by South Vietnamese mercenaries – well inside North Vietnamese territorial waters. This deception only became apparent in 1971 when the **Pentagon papers**, documenting the circumstances behind the incident, were leaked to the *New York Times* (the Pentagon papers were commissioned by Defense Secretary McNamara in June 1967 and written by 36 Indochina experts).

But these events are not sufficient to argue that the incident was manufactured to allow LBJ to start an undeclared war against North Vietnam. On 4 August, Secretary of State Dean Rusk told the American representative at the United Nations that: "In no sense is this destroyer a pretext to make a big thing out of a little thing". Even as late as the end of 1964, the President was unconvinced by arguments that the US should become more deeply involved. On 31 August, McGeorge Bundy wrote in a memorandum to Johnson: "A still more drastic possibility which no one is discussing is the use of substantial US armed forces in operation against the Viet Cong. I myself believe that before we let this country go we should have a hard look at this grim alternative, and I do not at all think that it is a repetition of Korea."

But events overtook President Johnson, and by 1965 the US was firmly embarked on the road to defeat. In March 1965, he ordered the beginning of the air war against the north perhaps acting on Air Force General Curtis Le May's observation that "we are swatting flies when we should be going after the manure pile". **Operation Rolling Thunder**, the most intense bombing campaign any country had yet experienced, began in March 1965 and ran through to October 1968. In 3½ years, twice the tonnage of bombs was dropped on Vietnam (and Laos) as during the entire Second World War. During its peak in 1967, 12,000 sorties were being flown each month – a total of 108,000 were flown throughout 1967. North Vietnam claimed that 4000 out of its 5788 villages were hit. Most terrifying were the B-52s that dropped their bombs from such an altitude (17,000 m) that the attack could not even be heard until the bombs hit their targets. Each aircraft carried 20 tonnes of bombs. By the end of the American war in 1973, 14 million tonnes of all types of munitions had been used in Indochina, an explosive force representing 700 times that of the atomic bomb dropped on Hiroshima. As General Curtis Le May explained on 25 November 1965 – "We should bomb them back into the Stone Age". In the same month that Rolling Thunder commenced, marines landed at Danang to defend its airbase, and by June 1965 there were 74,000 US troops in Vietnam. Despite President Johnson's reluctance to commit the US to the conflict, events forced his hand. He realized that the undisciplined South Vietnamese could not prevent a Communist victory. Adhering to the domino theory, and with his own and the US's reputation at stake, he had no choice. As Johnson is said to have remarked to his press secretary Bill Moyers: "I feel like a hitchhiker caught in a hail storm on a Texas highway. I can't win. I can't hide. And I can't make it stop."

Dispersal of the North's industry

In response to the bombing campaign, industry in the north was decentralized and dispersed to rural areas. Each province was envisaged as a self-sufficient production unit. In order to protect the population in the north, they too were relocated to the countryside. By the end of 1967 Hanoi's population was a mere 250,000 essential citizens – about a quarter of the pre-war figure. The same was true of other urban centres. What the primary US objective was in mounting the air war remains unclear. In part, it was designed to destroy the north's industrial base and its ability to wage war; to dampen the people's will to fight; to sow seeds of discontent; to force the leadership in the north to the negotiating table; and perhaps to punish those in the north for supporting their government. By October 1968 the US realized the bombing was having little effect and they called a halt. The legacy of Operation Rolling Thunder, though, would live on. Turley wrote: "... The bombing had destroyed virtually all industrial, transportation and communications facilities built since 1954, blotted out 10 to 15 years' potential economic growth, flattened three major cities and 12 of 29 province capitals, and triggered a decline in per capita agricultural output".

However, it was not just the bombing campaign that was undermining the north's industrial and agricultural base. Socialist policies in the countryside were labelling small land owners as 'landlords' – in effect, traitors to the revolutionary cause – thus alienating many farmers. In the cities, industrial policies were no less short-sighted. Though Ho's policies in the battlefield were driven by hard-headed pragmatism, in the field of economic development they were informed – tragically – by revolutionary fervour.

William Westmoreland, the general appointed to command the American effort, aimed to use the superior firepower and mobility of the US to 'search and destroy' PAVN forces. North Vietnamese bases in the south were to be identified using modern technology, jungle hideouts revealed by dumping chemical defoliants and then attacked with shells, bombs and by helicopter-borne troops. In 'free-fire zones' the army and air force were permitted to use whatever level of firepower they felt necessary to dislodge the enemy. 'Body counts' became the measure of success and collateral damage – or civilian casualties – was a cost that just had to be borne. As one field commander famously explained: 'We had to destroy the town to save it'. By 1968 the US had more than 500,000 troops in Vietnam, while **South Korean, Australian, New Zealand, Filipino** and **Thai** forces contributed another 90,000. The ARVN officially had 1.5 million men under arms (100,000 or more of these were 'flower' or phantom soldiers, the pay for whom was pocketed by officers in an increasingly corrupt ARVN). Ranged against this vastly superior force were perhaps 400,000 PAVN and National Liberation Front forces.

1964-1968: who was winning?

The leadership in the north tried to allay serious anxieties about their ability to defeat the American-backed south by emphasizing human over physical and material resources. **Desertions** from the ARVN were very high – there were 113,000 from the army in 1965 alone (200,000 in 1975) – and the PAVN did record a number of significant victories. The Communists also had to deal with large numbers of desertions – 28,000 men in 1969. By 1967 world opinion, and even American public opinion, appeared to be swinging against the war. Within the US, **anti-war demonstrations** and 'teach-ins' were spreading, officials were losing confidence in the ability of the US to win the war, and the president's approval rating was sinking fast.

But although the Communists may have been winning the psychological and public opinion wars, they were increasingly hard-pressed to maintain this advantage on the ground. Continual American strikes against their bases, and the social and economic dislocations in the countryside, were making it more difficult for the Communists to recruit supporters. At the same time, the fight against a vastly better equipped enemy was also taking its toll in sheer exhaustion. Despite what is now widely regarded as a generally misguided US military strategy in Vietnam, there were notable US successes (for example, the Phoenix Programme, see page 1141). American GIs were always sceptical about the 'pacification' programmes that aimed to win the 'hearts and minds' war. GIs were fond of saying, 'If you've got them by the balls, their hearts and minds will follow'. At times, the US military and politicians appeared to view the average Vietnamese as inferior to the average American. This latent racism was reflected in General Westmoreland's remark that Vietnamese "don't think about death the way we do" and in the use by most US servicemen of the derogatory name "gook" to refer to Vietnamese.

At the same time as the Americans were trying to win 'hearts and minds', the Vietnamese were also busy indoctrinating their men and women, and the population in the 'occupied' south. In Bao Ninh's moving *The Sorrow of War* (1994), the main character, Kien, who fights with a scout unit describes the indoctrination that accompanied the soldiers from their barracks to the field: "Politics continuously. Politics in the morning, politics in the afternoon, politics again in the evening. 'We won, the enemy lost. The enemy will surely lose. The north had a good harvest, a bumper harvest. The people will rise up and welcome you. Those who don't just lack awareness. The world is divided into three camps.' More politics."

By 1967, the war had entered a period of military (though not political) stalemate. As Robert McNamara writes in his book *In Retrospect: the Tragedy and Lessons of Vietnam*, it was at this stage that he came to believe that Vietnam was "a problem with no solution". In retrospect, he argues that the US should have withdrawn in late 1963, and certainly by late 1967. Massive quantities of US arms and money were preventing the Communists from making much headway in urban areas, while American and ARVN forces were ineffective in the countryside – although incessant bombing and ground assaults wreaked massive destruction. A black market of epic proportions developed in Saigon, as millions of dollars of assistance went astray. American journalist Stanley Karnow once remarked to a US official that "we could probably buy off the Vietcong at US$500 a head". The official replied that they had already calculated the costs, but came to "US$2500 a head".

Tet Offensive, 1968: the beginning of the end

By mid-1967, the Communist leadership in the north felt it was time for a further escalation of the war in the south to regain the initiative. They began to lay the groundwork for what was to become known as the Tet (or New Year) Offensive – perhaps the single most important series of battles during the American War in Vietnam. During the early morning of 1 February 1968, shortly after noisy celebrations had welcomed in the New Year, 84,000 Communist troops simultaneously attacked targets in 105 urban centres. Utterly surprising the US and South Vietnamese, the Tet Offensive had begun.

Preparations for the offensive had been laid over many months. Arms, ammunition and guerrillas were smuggled and infiltrated into urban areas and detailed planning was undertaken. Central to the strategy was a 'sideshow' at Khe Sanh. By mounting an attack on the marine outpost at **Khe Sanh**, the Communists successfully convinced the American and Vietnamese commanders that another Dien Bien Phu was underway. General Westmoreland moved 50,000 US troops away from the cities and suburbs to prevent any such humiliating repetition of the French defeat. But Khe Sanh was just a diversion, a feint designed to draw attention away from the cities. In this the Communists were successful; for days after the Tet offensive, Westmoreland and the South Vietnamese President Thieu thought Khe Sanh to be the real objective and the attacks in the cities the decoy.

The most interesting aspect of the Tet Offensive was that although it was a strategic victory for the Communists, it was also a considerable tactical defeat. They may have occupied the US embassy in Saigon for a few hours but, except in Hué, Communist forces were quickly repulsed by US and ARVN troops. The government in the south did not collapse nor did the ARVN. Cripplingly high casualties were inflicted on the Communists – cadres at all echelons were killed – morale was undermined and it became clear that the cities would not rise up spontaneously to support the Communists. Tet, in effect, put paid to the VC as an effective fighting force. The fight was now increasingly taken up by the North Vietnamese Army (NVA). This was to have profound effects on the government of South Vietnam after reunification in 1975; southern Communists and what remained of the political wing of the VC – the government in waiting – were entirely overlooked as northern Communists were given all the positions of political power, a process that continues. This caused intense bitterness at the time and also explains the continued mistrust of many southerners for Hanoi. Walt Rostow wrote in 1995 that "Tet was an utter military and political defeat for the Communists in Vietnam", but adding "yet a political disaster in the United States". But this was not to matter; Westmoreland's request for more troops was turned down and US public support for the war slumped still further as they heard reported that the US embassy itself had been 'over-run'. Those who for years had been claiming it was only a matter of time before the Communists were defeated seemed to be contradicted by the scale and intensity of the offensive. Even President Johnson was stunned by the VC's successes for he too had believed the US propaganda. As it turned out the VC incursion was by a 20-man unit from Sapper Battalion C-10 who were all killed in the action.

Their mission was not to take the embassy but to 'make a psychological gesture'. In that regard at least, the mission must have exceeded the leadership's wildest expectations.

The **Phoenix Programme**, established in the wake of the Tet Offensive, aimed to destroy the Communists' political infrastructure in the Mekong Delta. Named after the Vietnamese mythical bird the Phung Hoang, which could fly anywhere, the programme sent CIA-recruited and trained Counter Terror Teams – in effect assassination units – into the countryside. The teams were ordered to try and capture Communist cadres; invariably they fired first and asked questions later. By 1971, it was estimated that the programme had led to the capture of 28,000 members of the VCI (Viet Cong Infrastructure), the death of 20,000 and the defection of a further 17,000. By the early 1970s the countryside in the Mekong Delta was more peaceful than it had been for years; towns that were previously strongholds of the Viet Cong had reverted to the control of the local authorities. Critics have questioned what proportion of those killed, captured and sometimes tortured were Communist cadres, but even Communist documents admit that it seriously undermined their support network in the area. In these terms, the Phoenix Programme was a great success.

The costs

The Tet Offensive concentrated American minds. The costs of the war by that time had been vast. The US budget deficit had risen to 3% of Gross National Product by 1968, inflation was accelerating, and thousands of young men had been killed for a cause that, to many, was becoming less clear by the month. Before the end of the year President Johnson had ended the bombing campaign. Negotiations began in Paris in 1969 to try and secure an honourable settlement for the US. Although the last American combat troops were not to leave until March 1973, the Tet Offensive marked the beginning of the end. It was from that date the Johnson administration began to search seriously for a way out of the conflict. The illegal bombing of Cambodia in 1969 and the resumption of the bombing of the north in 1972 (the most intensive of the entire conflict) were only flurries of action on the way to an inevitable US withdrawal.

Paris Agreement (1972)

US Secretary of State **Henry Kissinger** records the afternoon of 8 October 1972, a Sunday, as the moment when he realized that the Communists were willing to agree a peace treaty. There was a great deal to discuss, particularly whether the treaty would offer the prospect of peaceful reunification, or the continued existence of two states: a Communist north, and non-Communist south. Both sides tried to force the issue: the US mounted further attacks and at the same time strengthened and expanded the ARVN. They also tried to play the 'Madman Nixon' card, arguing that **President Richard Nixon** was such a vehement anti-Communist that he might well resort to the ultimate deterrent, the nuclear bomb. It is true that the PAVN was losing men through desertion and had failed to recover its losses in the Tet Offensive. Bao Ninh in his book *The Sorrow of War* about Kinh, a scout with the PAVN, wrote: "The life of the B3 Infantrymen after the Paris Agreement was a series of long suffering days, followed by months of retreating and months of counter-attacking, withdrawal, then counter-attack. Victory after victory, withdrawal after withdrawal. The path of war seemed endless, desperate, and leading nowhere."

But the Communist leadership knew well that the Americans were committed to withdrawal – the only question was when, so they felt that time was on their side. By 1972, US troops in the south had declined to 95,000, the bulk of whom were support troops.

The north gambled on a massive attack to defeat the ARVN and moved 200,000 men towards the demilitarized zone that marked the border between north and south. On 30 March the PAVN crossed into the south and quickly overran large sections of Quang Tri province. Simultaneous attacks were mounted in the west highlands, at Tay Ninh and in the Mekong Delta. For a while it looked as if the south would fall altogether. The US responded by mounting a succession of intense bombing raids that eventually forced the PAVN to retreat. The spring offensive may have failed, but like Tet, it was strategically important, for it demonstrated that without US support the ARVN was unlikely to be able to withstand a Communist attack.

Both sides, by late 1972, were ready to compromise. Against the wishes of South Vietnam's President Nguyen Van Thieu, the US signed a treaty on 27 January 1973, the ceasefire going into effect on the same day. Before the signing, Nixon ordered the bombing of the north – the so-called Christmas Campaign. It lasted 11 days from 18 December (Christmas Day was a holiday) and was the most intensive of the war. With the ceasefire and President Thieu, however shaky, both in place, the US was finally able to back out of its nightmare and the last combat troops left in March 1973.

Final Phase (1973-1975)

The Paris Accord settled nothing; it simply provided a means by which the Americans could withdraw from Vietnam. It was never going to resolve the deep-seated differences between the two regimes and with only a brief lull, the war continued, this time without US troops. Thieu's government was probably in terminal decline even before the peace treaty was signed. Though ARVN forces were at their largest ever and, on paper, considerably stronger than the PAVN, many men were weakly committed to the cause of the south. Corruption was endemic, business was in recession, and political dissent was on the increase. The North's Central Committee formally decided to abandon the Paris Accord in October 1973; by the beginning of 1975 they were ready for the final offensive. It took only until April for the Communists to achieve total victory. ARVN troops deserted in their thousands, and the only serious resistance was offered at Xuan Loc, less than 100 km from Saigon. President Thieu resigned on 27 April. ARVN generals, along with their men, were attempting to flee as the PAVN advanced on Saigon. The end was quick: at 1045 on 30 April a T-54 tank (number 843) crashed its way through the gates of the Presidential Palace, symbolizing the end of the Second Indochina War. For the US, the aftermath of the war would lead to years of soul searching; for Vietnam, to stagnation and isolation. A senior State Department figure, George Ball, reflected afterwards that the war was "probably the greatest single error made by America in its history".

Legacy of the Vietnam War

The Vietnam War (or 'American War' to the Vietnamese) is such an enduring feature of the West's experience of the country that many visitors look out for legacies of the conflict. There is no shortage of physically deformed and crippled Vietnamese. Many men were badly injured during the war, but large numbers also received their injuries while serving in Cambodia (1979-1989). It is tempting to associate deformed children with the enduring effects of the pesticide **Agent Orange** (1.7 million tonnes had been used by 1973), although this has yet to be proven scientifically; American studies claim that there is no significant difference in congenital malformation. One thing is certain: Agent Orange is detectable today only in tiny isolated spots, often near former military bases.

Bomb damage

Bomb damage is most obvious from the air: well over five million tonnes of bombs were dropped on the country (north and south) and there are said to be 20 million bomb craters – the sort of statistic people like to recount, but no one can legitimately verify. Many craters have yet to be filled in and paddy fields are still pockmarked. Some farmers have used these holes in the ground to farm fish and to use as small reservoirs to irrigate vegetable plots. War scrap was one of the country's most valuable exports. The cities in the north are surprisingly devoid of obvious signs of the bombing campaigns; Hanoi remains remarkably intact. In Hué the Citadel and the Forbidden Palace were extensively damaged during the Tet offensive in 1968 although much has now been rebuilt.

Psychological effect of the war

The Vietnamese Communist Party leadership still seem to be preoccupied by the conflict and school children are routinely shown war museums and Ho Chi Minh memorials. But despite the continuing propaganda offensive, people harbour surprisingly little animosity towards America or the West. Indeed, of all westerners, it is often Americans who are most warmly welcomed, particularly in the south.

But it must be remembered that about 60% of Vietnam's population has been born since the US left in 1973, so have no memory of the American occupation. Probably the least visible but most lasting of all the effects of the war is in the number of elderly widowed women and the number of middle aged women who never married.

The deeper source of antagonism is the continuing divide between the north and south. It was to be expected that the forces of the north would exact their revenge on their foes in the south and many were relieved that the predicted bloodbath didn't materialize. But few would have thought that this revenge would be so long lasting. The 250,000 southern dead are not mourned or honoured, or even acknowledged. Former soldiers are denied jobs and the government doesn't recognize the need for national reconciliation.

This is the multiple legacy of the War on Vietnam and the Vietnamese. The legacy on the US and Americans is more widely appreciated. The key question that still occupies the minds of many, though, is, was it worth it? Economic historian Walt Rostow, ex-Singaporean prime minister Lee Kuan Yew and others would probably answer 'yes'. If the US had not intervened, Communism would have spread farther in Southeast Asia; more dominoes, in their view, would have fallen. In 1973, when the US withdrawal was agreed, Lee Kuan Yew observed that the countries of Southeast Asia were much more resilient and resistant to Communism than they had been, say, at the time of the Tet offensive in 1968. The US presence in Vietnam allowed them to reach this state of affairs. Yet Robert McNamara in his book *In Retrospect: the Tragedy and Lessons of Vietnam*, wrote:

"Although we sought to do the right thing – and believed we were doing the right thing – in my judgment, hindsight proves us wrong. We both overestimated the effects of South Vietnam's loss on the security of the West and failed to adhere to the fundamental principle that, in the final analysis, if the South Vietnamese were to be saved, they had to win the war themselves."

After the war

The Socialist Republic of Vietnam (SRV) was born from the ashes of the Vietnam War on 2 July 1976 when former North and South Vietnam were reunified. Hanoi was proclaimed as the capital of the new country. But few Vietnamese would have guessed that their emergent country would be cast by the US in the mould of a pariah state for almost 18 years. First President George Bush I, and then his successor Bill Clinton, eased the US trade embargo bit by bit in a dance of appeasement and procrastination, as they tried to comfort American business clamouring for a slice of the Vietnamese pie, while also trying to stay on the right side of the vociferous lobby in the US demanding more action on the MIA issue. Appropriately, the embargo, which was first imposed on the former North in May 1964, and then nationwide in 1975, was finally lifted a few days before the celebrations of Tet, Vietnamese New Year, on 4 February 1994.

On the morning of 30 April 1975, just before 1100, a T-54 tank crashed through the gates of the Presidential Palace in Saigon, symbolically marking the end of the Vietnam War. Twenty years later, the same tank – number 843 – became a symbol of the past as parades and celebrations, and a good deal of soul searching, marked the anniversary of the end of the War. To many Vietnamese, in retrospect, 1975 was more a beginning than an end: it was the beginning of a collective struggle to come to terms with the war, to build a nation, to reinvigorate the economy and to excise the ghosts of the past. Two decades after the armies of the South laid down their arms and the last US servicemen and officials frantically fled by helicopter to carriers waiting in the South China Sea, the Vietnamese government is still trying, as they put it, to get people to recognize that 'Vietnam is a country, not a war'. A further 20 years from now, it may seem that only in 1995 did the war truly end.

Re-education camps

The newly formed Vietnam government ordered thousands of people to report for re-education camps in 1975. Those intended were ARVN members, ex-South Vietnam government members and those that had collaborated with the South regime including priests, artists, teachers and doctors. It was seen as a means of revenge and a way of indoctrinating the 'unbelievers' with Communist propaganda. It was reported in the Indochina Newsletter in 1982 that some 80 camps existed with an estimated 100,000 still languishing in them seven years after the war ended. Detainees were initially told that they would be detained for between three days and one month. Those that were sent to the camp were forced to undertake physical labour and survived on very little food and without basic medical facilities all the while undergoing Communist indoctrination.

Boat people

Many Vietnamese also fled, first illegally and then legally through the Orderly Departure Programme. The peak period of the crisis spanned the years 1976-1979, with 270,882 leaving the country in 1979 alone. The flow of refugees slowed during 1980 and 1981 to about 50,000 and until 1988 averaged about 10,000 each year. But in the late 1980s the numbers picked up once again, with most sailing for Hong Kong and leaving from the north. It seems that whereas the majority of those sailing in the first phase (1976-1981) were political refugees, the second phase of the exodus was driven by economic pressures. With more than 40,000 refugees in camps in Hong Kong, the Hong Kong authorities began to forcibly repatriate those screened as economic migrants at the end of 1989. Such was the international outcry as critics highlighted fears of persecution that the programme was suspended. In May 1992, an agreement was reached between the British and the Vietnamese governments to repatriate the 55,700 boat people living in camps in Hong Kong and the orderly return programme was quietly restarted.

Ironically, the evidence is that those repatriated are doing very well – better than those who never left the shores of Vietnam. With the European Community and the UN offering assistance to returnees, they have set up businesses, enrolled on training courses and become embroiled in Vietnam's thrust for economic growth.

Invasion of Cambodia

In April 1975, the Khmer Rouge took power in Cambodia. Border clashes with Vietnam erupted just a month after the Phnom Penh regime change but matters came to a head in 1977 when the Khmer Rouge accused Vietnam of seeking to incorporate Kampuchea into an Indochinese Federation. Hanoi's determination to oust Pol Pot only really became apparent on Christmas Day 1978, when 120,000 Vietnamese troops invaded. By 7 January they had installed a puppet government that proclaimed the foundation of the **People's Republic of Kampuchea (PRK)**: Heng Samrin, a former member of the Khmer Rouge, was appointed president. The Vietnamese compared their invasion to the liberation of Uganda from Idi Amin – but for the rest of the world it was an unwelcome Christmas present. The new government was accorded scant recognition abroad, while the toppled government of Democratic Kampuchea retained the country's seat at the United Nations.

But the country's 'liberation' by Vietnam did not end the misery; in 1979 nearly half of Cambodia's population was in transit, either searching for their former homes or fleeing across the Thai border into refugee camps. The country reverted to a state of outright war again, for the Vietnamese were not greatly loved in Cambodia – especially by the Khmer Rouge. American political scientist Wayne Bert wrote: "The Vietnamese had long seen a special role for themselves in uniting and leading a greater Indochina Communist movement and the Cambodian Communists had seen with clarity that such a role for the Vietnamese could only be at the expense of their independence and prestige."

Under the Lon Nol and Khmer Rouge regimes, Vietnamese living in Cambodia were expelled or exterminated. Resentment had built up over the years Hanoi – exacerbated by the apparent ingratitude of the Khmer Rouge for Vietnamese assistance in fighting Lon Nol's US-supported Khmer Republic in the early 1970s. As relations between the Khmer Rouge and the Vietnamese deteriorated, the Communist superpowers, China and the Soviet Union, polarized too – the former siding with Khmer Rouge and the latter with Hanoi.

The Vietnamese invasion had the full backing of Moscow, while the Chinese and Americans began their support for the anti-Vietnamese rebels.

Following the Vietnamese invasion, three main anti-Hanoi factions were formed. In June 1982 they banded together in an unholy alliance of convenience to fight the PRK and called themselves the **Coalition Government of Democratic Kampuchea (CGDK)**, which was immediately recognised by the UN. The three factions of the CGDK were: The Communist Khmer Rouge whose field forces had recovered to at least 18,000 by the late 1980s. Supplied with weapons by China, they were concentrated in the Cardamom Mountains in the southwest and were also in control of some of the refugee camps along the Thai border. The National United Front for an Independent Neutral Peaceful and Co-operative Cambodia (Funcinpec) – known by most people as the **Armée National Sihanoukiste (ANS)**. It was headed by Prince Sihanouk – although he spent most of his time exiled in Beijing; the group had fewer than 15,000 well-equipped troops – most of whom took orders from Khmer Rouge commanders. The anti-Communist **Khmer People's National Liberation Front (KPNLF)**, headed by Son Sann, a former prime minister under Sihanouk. Its 5000 troops were reportedly ill-disciplined in comparison with the Khmer Rouge and the ANS.

The three CGDK factions were ranged against the 70,000 troops loyal to the government of President Heng Samrin and Prime Minister Hun Sen (previously a Khmer Rouge cadre) they were backed by Vietnamese forces until September 1989.

In the late 1980s the Association of Southeast Asian Nations (ASEAN) – for which the Cambodian conflict had almost become its raison d'être – began steps to bring the warring factions together over the negotiating table. ASEAN countries were united in wanting the Vietnamese out of Cambodia. After Mikhail Gorbachev had come to power in the Soviet Union, Moscow's support for the Vietnamese presence in Cambodia gradually evaporated. Gorbachev began leaning on Vietnam as early as 1987, to withdraw its troops. Despite saying their presence in Cambodia was 'irreversible', Vietnam completed its withdrawal in September 1989, ending nearly 11 years of Hanoi's direct military involvement. The withdrawal led to an immediate upsurge in political and military activity, as forces of the exiled CGDK put increased pressure on the now weakened Phnom Penh regime to begin a round of power-sharing negotiations.

Border incursions with China

In February 1979 the Chinese marched into the far north of Vietnam justifying the invasion because of Vietnam's invasion of Cambodia, its treatment of Chinese in Vietnam, the ownership of the Paracel and Spratley Islands in the East Sea (South China Sea) also claimed by China and a stand against Soviet expansion into Asia (Hanoi was strongly allied with the then USSR). They withdrew a month later following heavy casualties although both sides have claimed to be victorious. Vietnamese military hardware was far superior to the Chinese and their casualties were estimated to be between 20,000 and 60,000; Vietnamese casualties were around 15,000. In 1987 fighting again erupted on the Sino-Vietnamese border resulting in high casualties.

Modern Vietnam

Politics

The **Vietnamese Communist Party (VCP)** was established in Hong Kong in 1930 by Ho Chi Minh and arguably has been more successful than any other such party in Asia in mobilizing and maintaining support. While others have fallen, the VCP has managed to stay firmly in control. To enable them to get their message to a wider audience, the Communist Party of Vietnam have launched their own website, www.cpv.org.vn.

Vietnam is a one party state. In addition to the Communist Party the posts of president and prime minister were created when the constitution was revised in 1992. The president is head of state and the prime minister is head of the cabinet of ministries (including three deputies and 26 ministries), all nominated by the National Assembly. The current president is Nguyen Minh Triet and the current prime minister is Nguyen Tan Dung. Although the National Assembly is the highest instrument of state it can still be directed by the Communist Party. The vast majority of National Assembly members are also party members. Elections for the National Assembly are held every five years. The Communist Party is run by a politburo of 14 members. The head is the general secretary, currently Nong Duch Manh. The politburo, last elected in 2006 at the Tenth Party Congress, meets every five years and sets policy directions of the Party and the government. In addition, there is a Central Committee made up of 160 members, who are also elected at the Party Congress.

In 1986, at the Sixth Party Congress, the VCP launched its economic reform programme known as *doi moi*, which was a momentous step in ideological terms. However, although the programme has done much to free up the economy, the party has ensured that it retains ultimate political power. Marxism-Leninism and Ho Chi Minh thought are still taught to Vietnamese school children and even so-called 'reformers' in the leadership are not permitted to diverge from the party line. In this sense, while economic reforms have made considerable progress – particularly in the south – there is a very definite sense that the limits of political reform have been reached, at least for the time being.

From the late 1990s to the first years of the new millennium there have been a number of arrests and trials of dissidents charged with what might appear to be fairly innocuous crimes (see The future of Communism in Vietnam, page 1150) and, although the economic reforms enacted since the mid-1980s are still in place, the party resolutely rejects any moves towards greater political pluralism.

Looking at the process of political succession in Vietnam and the impression is not one of a country led by young men and women with innovative ideas. Each year commentators consider the possibility of an infusion of new blood and reformist ideas but the Party Congress normally delivers more of the same: dyed-in-the-wool party followers who are more likely to maintain the status quo than challenge it along with just one or two reformers. The Asian economic crisis did, if anything, further slow down the pace of change. To conservative party members, the Asian crisis – and the political instability that it caused – were taken as warnings of what can happen if you reform too far and too fast. The latest change of faces in the leadership occurred during the Ninth Party Congress in April 2001.

For many westerners there is something strange about a leadership calling for economic reform and liberalization while, at the same time, refusing any degree of political pluralism. How long the VCP can maintain this charade, along with China, while other Communist governments have long since fallen, is a key question. Despite the reforms, the leadership is still divided over the road ahead. But the fact that debate is continuing, sometimes openly, suggests that there is disagreement over the necessity for political reform and the degree of economic reform that should be encouraged. One small chink in the armour is the proposed bill to allow referenda. The draft report indicates that referenda would be held on the principles of universality, equality, directness and secret ballot but that the subject of referenda would be decided by the party.

In the country as a whole there is virtually no political debate at all, certainly not in the open. There are two reasons for this apparently curious state of affairs. First there is a genuine fear of discussing something that is absolutely taboo. The police have a wide network of informers who report back on a regular basis and no one wants to accumulate black marks that make it difficult to get the local police reference required for a university place, passport or even a job. Second, and more importantly, is the booming economy. Since the 1990s, economic growth in Vietnam has been unprecedented. As every politician knows, the one thing that keeps people happy is rising income. Hence with not much to complain about most Vietnamese people are content with their political status quo.

Nevertheless it would be foolish to think that everyone was happy. That political tensions are bubbling somewhere beneath the surface of Vietnamese society became clear in 1997 with serious disturbances in the poor coastal northern province of Thai Binh, 80 km southeast of Hanoi. In May, 3000 local farmers began to stage protests in the provincial capital, complaining of corruption and excessive taxation. There were reports of rioting and some deaths – strenuously denied, at least at first, by officials. However, a lengthy report appeared in the army newspaper *Quan Doi Nhan Dan* in September detailing moral decline and corruption in the Party in the province. For people in Thai Binh, and many others living in rural areas, the reforms of the 1980s and 1990s have brought little benefit. People living in Ho Chi Minh City may tout mobile phones and drive cars and motorbikes, but in much of the rest of the country average monthly incomes are around US$50. The Party's greatest fear is that ordinary people might lose confidence in the leadership and in the system. The fact that many of those who demonstrated in Thai Binh were, apparently, war veterans didn't help either. Nor can the leadership have failed to remember that Thai Binh was at the centre of peasant disturbances against the French. A few months later riots broke out in prosperous and staunchly Roman Catholic Dong Nai, just north of Ho Chi Minh City. The catalyst to these disturbances was the seizure of church land by a corrupt Chairman of the People's Committee. The mob razed the Chairman's house and stoned the fire brigade. Clearly, pent up frustrations were seething beneath the surface for Highway 1 had to be closed for several days while the unrest continued. While the Dong Nai troubles went wholly unreported in Vietnam, a *Voice of Vietnam* broadcast admitted to them and went on to catalogue a list of previous civil disturbances, none of which was known to the outside world; it appears the purpose was to advise Western journalists that this was just another little local difficulty and not the beginning of the end of Communist rule. But reports of disturbances continue to filter out of Vietnam. At the beginning of 2001 thousands of ethnic minorities rioted in the Central Highland provinces of Gia Lai and Dac Lac and the army had to be called in to re-impose order. All foreigners were banned from the Central Highlands.

Again in April 2004 violence between ethnic minorities and the government flared in the Central Highlands, resulting in 'unknown numbers of dead and injured and reports of people missing' according to Amnesty International. Once more the cause was religious freedom and land rights although the government persists in its implausible conspiracy theory about 'outside forces' and extremists in the US wanting to destabilize it; a pretext, some fear, for the use of the jackboot and the imprisonment of trouble makers. To its shame (not that they are aware of such a concept) the Cambodian government simply hands refugees – many of who are asylum seekers in the strictest meaning – straight back to the Vietnamese forces. Much of the border area is a no-go zone in both countries, neither country allowing representatives of UNHCR anywhere near.

HRW reports than more than 350 ethnic minority people from the Central Highlands have been jailed, charged under Vietnam's Penal Code.

In more recent years, others have been prepared to voice their views. In 2006 Bloc 8406, a pro-democracy group named after its founding date of 8 April 2006, was set up. Catholic priest Father Nguyen Van Ly, editor of the underground online magazine *Free Speech* and a founding member of Bloc 8406, was sentenced to eight years in jail for anti-government activity. Four others were also sentenced with him. His trial can be seen on You Tube, including images of him having his mouth covered up and being bundled out of the courtroom. In March 2007 Nguyen Van Dai and Le Thi Cong Nhan, two human rights lawyers, were arrested on the grounds of distributing material "dangerous to the State" and were sentenced to four and five years in prison respectively.

As well as Bloc 8406, other pro-democracy movements include the US-based Viet Tan Party, www.viettan.org, with offices also in Australia, France, Japan, and the People's Democratic Party, among others.

International relations

In terms of international relations, Vietnam's relationship with the countries of the Association of Southeast Asian Nations (ASEAN) have warmed markedly since the dark days of the early and mid-1980s and in mid-1995 Vietnam became the association's seventh – and first Communist – member. The delicious irony of Vietnam joining ASEAN was that it was becoming part of an organization established to counteract the threat of Communist Vietnam itself – although everyone was too polite to point this out. No longer is there a deep schism between the capitalist and Communist countries of the region, either in terms of ideology or management. The main potential flashpoint concerns China. The enmity and suspicion which underlies the relationship between the world's last two real Communist powers stretches back over 2000 years. Indeed, one of the great attractions to Vietnam of joining ASEAN was the bulwark that it created against a potentially aggressive and actually economically ascendant China.

China and Vietnam, along with Malaysia, Taiwan, Brunei and the Philippines, all claim part (or all) of the South China Sea's Spratly Islands. These tiny islands, many no more than coral atolls, would have caused scarcely an international relations ripple were it not for the fact that they are thought to sit above huge oil reserves. Whoever can prove rights to the islands lays claim to this undersea wealth. Although the parties are committed to settling the dispute without resort to force, most experts see the Spratly Islands as the key potential flashpoint in Southeast Asia – and one in which Vietnam is seen to be a central player. The Paracel Islands further north are similarly disputed by Vietnam and China.

Rapprochement with the US   One of the keys to a lasting economic recovery was a normalization of relations with the US. From 1975 until early 1994 the US made it largely illegal for any American or American company to have business relations with Vietnam. The US, with the support of Japan and other Western nations, also blackballed attempts by Vietnam to gain membership to the IMF, World Bank and Asian Development Bank, thus cutting off access to the largest source of cheap credit. In the past, it has been the former Soviet Union and the countries of the Eastern Bloc that have filled the gap, providing billions of dollars of aid (US$6 billion 1986-1990), training and technical expertise. But in 1990 the Soviet Union halved its assistance to Vietnam, making it imperative that the government improve relations with the West and particularly the US.

In April 1991 the US opened an official office in Hanoi to assist in the search for Missing in Action (MIAs), the first such move since the end of the war, and in December 1992 allowed US companies to sign contracts to be implemented after the US trade embargo had been lifted. In 1992, both Australia and Japan lifted their embargoes on aid to Vietnam and the US also eased restrictions on humanitarian assistance. Support for a full normalization of relations was provided by French President Mitterand during his visit in February 1993, the first by a Western leader since the end of the war. He said that the US veto on IMF and World Bank assistance had "no reason for being there", and applauded Vietnam's economic reforms. He also pointed out to his hosts that respect for human rights was now a universal obligation, which did not go down quite so well. Nonetheless he saw his visit as marking the end of one chapter and the beginning of another.

This inexorable process towards normalization continued with the full lifting of the trade embargo on 4 February 1994 when President Bill Clinton announced the normalization of trade relations. Finally, on 11 July 1995 Bill Clinton declared the full normalization of relations between the two countries and a month later Secretary of State Warren Christopher opened the new American embassy in Hanoi.

Even though the embargo is now a thing of the past, there are still the families of over 2000 American servicemen listed as Missing in Action who continue to hope that the remains of their loved ones might, some day, make their way back to the US. (The fact there are still an estimated 300,000 Vietnamese MIAs is, of course, of scant interest to the American media.) It was this, among other legacies of the war, which made progress towards a full normalization of diplomatic and commercial relations such a drawn-out business.

The normalization of trade relations between the two countries was agreed in a meeting between Vietnamese and US officials in July 1999 and marked the culmination of three years' discussions. But conservatives in the politburo prevented the agreement being signed into law worried, apparently, about the social and economic side effects of such reform. This did not happen until 28 November 2001 when Vietnam's National Assembly finally ratified the treaty. It has led to a substantial increase in bilateral trade. In 2003 the USA imported US$4.5 billion worth of Vietnamese goods, roughly four times more than it exported to Vietnam. And not only goods: by 2004 the US Consulate General in Ho Chi Minh City handled more applications for American visas than any other US mission in the world.

Recent progress More good news came for Vietnam when it became the 150th member of the World Trade Organization in January 2007. The immediate effect was the lifting of import quotas from foreign countries thereby favouring Vietnamese exporters. Full benefits are expected to be realised when Vietnam gains full market economy status in 12 years' time. In June President Nguyen Minh Triet became the first president of Vietnam to visit the US. He met with George W Bush in Washington to discuss relations between the two countries; trade between the two former enemies now racks up US$9 billion a year. And, in October 2007 to round off a promising year, Vietnam was elected to the UN Security Council from 1 January 2008 as a non-permanent member for two years.

The future of Communism in Vietnam

In his book *Vietnam at the Crossroads*, BBC World Service commentator Michael Williams asks the question: "Does Communism have a future in Vietnam?" He answers that "the short answer must be no, if one means by Communism the classical Leninist doctrines and central planning". Instead some bastard form of Communism has been in the process of evolving. As Williams adds: "Even party leaders no longer appear able to distinguish between Communism and Capitalism".

There is certainly **political opposition** and disenchantment in Vietnam. At present this is unfocused and dispersed. Poor people in the countryside, especially in the north, resent the economic gains in the cities, particularly those of the south (see the section on serious disturbances, page 1147, in Thai Binh). But this rump of latent discontent has little in common with those intellectual and middle class Vietnamese itching for more political freedom or those motivated entrepreneurs pressing for accelerated economic reforms or those Buddhist monks and Christians demanding freedom of worship and respect for human rights. Unless and until this loose broth of opposition groups coalesces, it is hard to see a coherent opposition movement evolving.

Nonetheless, each year a small number of brave, foolhardy or committed individuals challenge the authorities. Most are then arrested, tried, and imprisoned for various loosely defined crimes including anti-government activity (see page 1148). There is always the possibility that cataclysmic, and unpredictable, political change will occur.

The tensions between reform and control are constantly evident. A **press law** which came into effect in mid-1993 prohibits the publication of works "hostile to the socialist homeland, divulging state or [Communist] party secrets, falsifying history or denying the gains of the revolution". The Party's attempts to control the flow of information have extended to the internet. In 1997 a National Internet Control Board was established and all internet and email usage is strictly monitored. The authorities attempt to firewall topics relating to Vietnam in a hopeless attempt to censor incoming information.

Contents

Footnotes

Index → *Entries in bold refer to maps*

Advertisers' index

Credits

Footprint credits

Editorial team: Felicity Laughton,
Nicola Gibbs, Sara Chare, Ria Gane,
Jenny Haddington
Map editor: Sarah Sorensen
Colour section: Alan Murphy,
Kassia Gawronski

Managing Director: Andy Riddle
Publisher: Patrick Dawson
Cartography: Robert Lunn, Kevin Feeney,
Emma Bryers
Cover design: Robert Lunn
Design: Mytton Williams
Sales and marketing: Zoë Jackson,
Hannah Bonnell
Advertising sales manager: Renu Sibal
Finance and administration:
Elizabeth Taylor

Photography credits

Front cover: Scenic rice fields, Pujung,
Ubud, Bali_age fotostock/SuperStock
Back cover: Vietnam Hoi An, woman
riding on a bicycle, Serge Kozak/Alamy
Diving section: Beth and Shaun Tierney

Manufactured in India by Nutech
Photolithographers, Delhi

Pulp from sustainable forests

Footprint feedback

We try as hard as we can to make each
Footprint guide as up to date as possible
but, of course, things always change. If you
want to let us know about your experiences –
good, bad or ugly – then don't delay, go to
www.footprintbooks.com and send in
your comments.

Publishing information

Footprint Southeast Asia
1st edition
© Footprint Handbooks Ltd
September 2008

ISBN: 978 1 906098 24 7
CIP DATA: A catalogue record for this book
is available from the British Library

® Footprint Handbooks and the Footprint
mark are a registered trademark of Footprint
Handbooks Ltd

Published by Footprint
6 Riverside Court
Lower Bristol Road
Bath BA2 3DZ, UK
T +44 (0)1225 469141
F +44 (0)1225 469461
discover@footprintbooks.com
www.footprintbooks.com

Distributed in the USA by Globe Pequot Press,
Guilford, Connecticut

Acknowledgements

Firstly, grateful thanks to Joshua Eliot and Jane Bickersteth for the enormous amount of work they put in to compiling the core of this book, which builds on many years of research.

Thanks too to every reader who writes in with feedback for future editions, whether to alert of downward turns in terms of service, to set us straight about false promises, to celebrate new heroes in hospitality or to champion new corners of beauty – be they beach, temple or jungle. We read every word – please keep them coming.

In addition to the two main authors, Paul Dixon and Andrew Spooner, Footprint would like to thank **Beth and Shaun Tierney** for supplying all the text and images for the colour diving section, **Jock O Tailan**, who updated the Laos text, and the other authors who contributed to this book:

Claire Boobbyer Claire is a freelance writer, editor and photographer. She first visited Vietnam in 2004 when she fell in love with the food, the fabrics and the beauty of the country. She is the author of *Footprint Vietnam* and has contributed to *Footprint Thailand*. She has previously hopped to the other side of the globe and is author of *Footprint Guatemala* and co-author of *Footprint Belize, Guatemala and Southern Mexico*. Her photography has appeared in Footprint guides to Asia, Latin America and Cuba, as well as several other publications.

Steve Frankham All his life Steve has possessed an unending passion to explore the world's wild places, its wildlife and its people. He started in Mexico in 1999 and a year of volunteering, making a fool of himself and travelling in Central and South America led to the icy teeth of the Peruvian Andes and the sweat-inducing vast Amazon paradise of the Manu Biosphere Reserve. A year working with Manu's Yine tribe on an ecotourism project led to his first Footprint contract in the Bolivian Amazon. Steve has since worked in the Americas, Africa and Asia – sometimes against his better judgement!

Trails of Asia

Journey through lost kingdoms and
hidden history of Asia
and let Asian Trails be your guide!

Choose Asian Trails, the specialists in Asia.
We will organise your holiday, hotels, flights and tours to the region's
most fascinating and undiscovered tourist destinations.
Contact us for our brochure or log into
www.asiantrails.info or www.asiantrails.net or www.asiantrails.com or www.asiantrails.travel

CAMBODIA
Asian Trails Ltd. (Phnom Penh Office)
No. 22, Street 294, Sangkat Boeng Keng Kong I, Khan Chamkarmorn,
P.O. Box 621, Phnom Penh, Cambodia
Tel: (855 23) 216 555, Fax: (855 23) 216 591, E-mail: res@asiantrails.com.kh

CHINA
Asian Trails China
Rm 1001, Scitech Tower No.22 Jianguomenwai Avenue, Beijing 100004, P.R. China
Tel: (86 10) 6515 9259 & 9279 Fax: (86 10) 6515 9293
E-mail: kris.vangoethem@asiantrailschina.com

INDONESIA
P.T. Asian Trails Indonesia
Jl. By Pass Ngurah Rai No. 260, Sanur, Denpasar 80228, Bali, Indonesia
Tel: (62 361) 285 771, Fax: (62 361) 281 515, E-mail: info@asiantrailsbali.com

LAO P.D.R.
Asian Trails Laos (AT Lao Co., Ltd.)
P.O. Box 5422, Unit 10, Ban Khounta Thong, Sikhottabong District, Vientiane, Lao P.D.R.
Tel: (856 21) 263 936, Fax: (856 21) 262 956, E-mail: vte@asiantrails.laopdr.com

MALAYSIA
Asian Trails (M) Sdn. Bhd.
11-2-B Jalan Manau off Jalan Kg. Attap 50460 Kuala Lumpur, Malaysia
Tel: (60 3) 2274 9488, Fax: (60 3) 2274 9588, E-mail: res@asiantrails.com.my

MYANMAR
Asian Trails Tour Ltd.
73 Pyay Road, Dagon Township, Yangon, Myanmar
Tel: (95 1) 211 212, 223 262, Fax: (95 1) 211 670, E-mail: res@asiantrails.com.mm

THAILAND
Asian Trails Ltd. (Bangkok Office)
9th Floor, SG Tower, 161/1 Soi Mahadlek Luang 3, Rajdamri Road
Lumpini, Pathumwan, Bangkok 10330, Thailand
Tel: (66 2) 626 2000, Fax: (66 2) 651 8111, E-mail: res@asiantrails.org

VIETNAM
Asian Trails Co., Ltd.
5th Floor, 21 Nguyen Trung Ngan Street, District 1, Ho Chi Minh City, Vietnam
Tel: (84 8) 910 2871, Fax: (84 8) 910 2874
E-mail: asiantrails@hcm.vnn.vn